Complete Solutions Guide

PRECALCULUS

FIFTH EDITION

Larson/Hostetler

Dianna L. Zook
Indiana University—
Purdue University at
Fort Wayne, Indiana

Laurel Technical Services

Mike Jones

HOUGHTON MIFFLIN COMPANY   **Boston   New York**

Editor-in-Chief: Jack Shira
Managing Editor: Cathy Cantin
Development Manager: Maureen Ross
Associate Editor: Laura Wheel
Assistant Editor: Carolyn Johnson
Supervising Editor: Karen Carter
Project Editor: Patty Bergin
Art Supervisor: Gary Crespo
Marketing Manager: Michael Busnach
Senior Manufacturing Coordinator: Sally Culler
Composition and Art: Meridian Creative Group

Printed in the United States of America

ISBN: 0-618-07273-X

123456789-CRS-04 03 02 01 00

CONTENTS

PART I

CHAPTER P
Prerequisites

CHAPTER P
Prerequisites

Section P.1   Real Numbers

■ You should know the following sets.

(a) The set of real numbers includes the rational numbers and the irrational numbers.

(b) The set of rational numbers includes all real numbers that can be written as the ratio p/q of two integers, where $q \neq 0$.

(c) The set of irrational numbers includes all real numbers which are not rational.

(d) The set of integers: $\{\ldots, -3, -2, -1, 0, 1, 2, 3, \ldots\}$

(e) The set of whole numbers: $\{0, 1, 2, 3, 4, \ldots\}$

(f) The set of natural numbers: $\{1, 2, 3, 4, \ldots\}$

■ The real number line is used to represent the real numbers.

■ Know the inequality symbols.

(a) $a < b$ means a is less than b.   (b) $a \leq b$ means a is less than or equal to b.

(c) $a > b$ means a is greater than b.   (d) $a \geq b$ means a is greater than or equal to b.

■ You should know that
$$|a| = \begin{cases} a, \text{ if } a \geq 0 \\ -a, \text{ if } a < 0. \end{cases}$$

■ Know the properties of absolute value.

(a) $|a| \geq 0$ (b) $|-a| = |a|$ (c) $|ab| = |a|\,|b|$ (d) $\left|\dfrac{a}{b}\right| = \dfrac{|a|}{|b|}, b \neq 0$

■ The distance between a and b on the real line is $d(a, b) = |b - a| = |a - b|$.

■ You should be able to identify the terms in an algebraic expression.

■ You should know and be able to use the basic rules of algebra.

■ Commutative Property

(a) Addition: $a + b = b + a$ (b) Multiplication: $a \cdot b = b \cdot a$

■ Associative Property

(a) Addition: $(a + b) + c = a + (b + c)$ (b) Multiplication: $(ab)c = a(bc)$

■ Identity Property

(a) Addition: 0 is the identity; $a + 0 = 0 + a = a$.   (b) Multiplication: 1 is the identity; $a \cdot 1 = 1 \cdot a = a$.

■ Inverse Property

(a) Addition: $-a$ is the additive inverse of a; $a + (-a) = -a + a = 0$.

(b) Multiplication: $1/a$ is the multiplicative inverse of a, $a \neq 0$; $a(1/a) = (1/a)a = 1$.

■ Distributive Property

(a) $a(b + c) = ab + ac$ (b) $(a + b)c = ac + bc$

—CONTINUED—

■ Properties of Negation

(a) $(-1)a = -a$

(b) $-(-a) = a$

(c) $(-a)b = a(-b) = -ab$

(d) $(-a)(-b) = ab$

(e) $-(a + b) = (-a) + (-b) = -a - b$

■ Properties of Equality

(a) If $a = b$, then $a + c = b + c$.

(b) If $a = b$, then $ac = bc$.

(c) If $a + c = b + c$, then $a = b$.

(d) If $ac = bc$ and $c \neq 0$, then $a = b$.

■ Properties of Zero

(a) $a \pm 0 = a$

(b) $a \cdot 0 = 0$

(c) $0 \div a = 0/a = 0, a \neq 0$

(d) $a/0$ is undefined.

(e) If $ab = 0$, then $a = 0$ or $b = 0$.

■ Properties of Fractions $(b \neq 0, d \neq 0)$

(a) Equivalent Fractions: $a/b = c/d$ if and only if $ad = bc$.

(b) Rule of Signs: $-a/b = a/-b = -(a/b)$ and $-a/-b = a/b$

(c) Equivalent Fractions: $a/b = ac/bc, c \neq 0$

(d) Addition and Subtraction

1. Like Denominators: $(a/b) \pm (c/b) = (a \pm c)/b$

2. Unlike Denominators: $(a/b) \pm (c/d) = (ad \pm bc)/bd$

(e) Multiplication: $(a/b) \cdot (c/d) = (ac)/(bd)$

(f) Division: $(a/b) \div (c/d) = (a/b) \cdot (d/c) = (ad)/(bc)$ if $c \neq 0$.

Solutions to Odd-Numbered Exercises

1. $-9, -\frac{7}{2}, 5, \frac{2}{3}, \sqrt{2}, 0, 1, -4, 2, -11$

(a) Natural numbers: $5, 1, 2$

(b) Integers: $-9, 5, 0, 1, -4, 2, -11$

(c) Rational numbers: $-9, -\frac{7}{2}, 5, \frac{2}{3}, 0, 1, -4, 2, -11$

(d) Irrational numbers: $\sqrt{2}$

3. $2.01, 0.666 \ldots, -13, 0.010110111 \ldots, 1, -6$

(a) Natural numbers: 1

(b) Integers: $-13, 1, -6$

(c) Rational numbers: $2.01, 0.666 \ldots, -13, 1, -6$

(d) Irrational numbers: $0.010110111 \ldots$

5. $-\pi, -\frac{1}{3}, \frac{6}{3}, \frac{1}{2}\sqrt{2}, -7.5, -1, 8, -22$

(a) Natural numbers: $\frac{6}{3}$ (since it equals 2), 8

(b) Integers: $\frac{6}{3}, -1, 8, -22$

(c) Rational numbers: $-\frac{1}{3}, \frac{6}{3}, -7.5, -1, 8, -22$

(d) Irrational numbers: $-\pi, \frac{1}{2}\sqrt{2}$

7. $\frac{5}{8} = 0.625$

9. $\frac{41}{333} = 0.\overline{123}$

11. $4.1 = \frac{41}{10}$

13. $10.\overline{2} = \frac{92}{9}$

15. $-2.01\overline{2} = -\frac{1811}{900}$

17. $-1 < 2.5$

19. $-4 > -8$

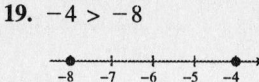

21. $\frac{3}{2} < 7$

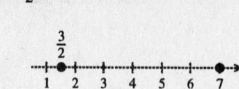

23. $\frac{5}{6} > \frac{2}{3}$

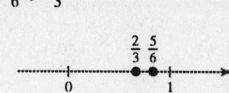

25. The inequality $x \le 5$ denotes the set of all real numbers less than or equal to 5. The interval is unbounded.

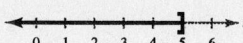

27. The inequality $x < 0$ denotes the set of all negative real numbers. The interval is unbounded.

29. The inequality $x \ge 4$ denotes the set of all real numbers greater than or equal to 4. The interval is unbounded.

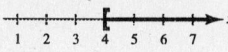

31. The inequality $-2 < x < 2$ denotes the set of all real numbers greater than -2 and less than 2. The interval is bounded.

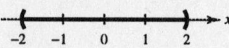

33. The inequality $-1 \le x < 0$ denotes the set of all negative real numbers greater than or equal to -1. The interval is bounded.

35. $\frac{127}{90} \approx 1.41111, \frac{584}{413} \approx 1.41404, \frac{7071}{5000} = 1.41420, \sqrt{2} \approx 1.41421, \frac{47}{33} \approx 1.42424$

37. $-2 < x \le 4$

39. $y \ge 0$

41. $10 \le t \le 22$

43. $W > 65$

45. This interval consists of all real numbers greater than or equal to zero, but less than 8.

47. This interval consists of all real numbers greater than -6.

49. $|-10| = -(-10) = 10$

51. If $x \le 3$, then $|3 - x| = 3 - x$
If $x > 3$, then $|3 - x| = -(3 - x) = -3 + x = x - 3$

53. $|-1| - |-2| = 1 - 2 = -1$

55. $\frac{-5}{|-5|} = \frac{-5}{-(-5)} = \frac{-5}{5} = -1$

57. If $x < -2$, then $x + 2$ is negative.
Thus $\frac{|x + 2|}{x + 2} = \frac{-(x + 2)}{x + 2} = -1$

59. $|-3| > -|-3|$ since $3 > -3$.

61. $-5 = -|5|$ since $-5 = -5$.

63. $-|-2| = -|2|$ since $-2 = -2$.

65. $d(-1, 3) = |3 - (-1)| = |3 + 1| = 4$

67. $d(126, 75) = |75 - 126| = 51$

69. $d\left(-\frac{5}{2}, 0\right) = \left|0 - \left(-\frac{5}{2}\right)\right| = \frac{5}{2}$

71. $d\left(\frac{16}{5}, \frac{112}{75}\right) = \left|\frac{112}{75} - \frac{16}{5}\right| = \frac{128}{75}$

73. (a) Since $A > 0$, $-A < 0$. The expression is negative.

(b) Since $B < A$, $B - A < 0$. The expression is negative.

75. $d(18, 7) = |7 - 18| = 11$ miles

77. $d(23°, 60°) = |60° - 23°| = 37°$

79. $d(x, 5) = |x - 5|$ and $d(x, 5) \leq 3$, thus $|x - 5| \leq 3$.

81. $d(y, 0) = |y - 0| = |y|$ and $d(y, 0) \geq 6$, thus $|y| \geq 6$.

83.
Budgeted Expense, b	Actual Expense, a	$|a - b|$	0.05b
$112,700	$113,356	$656	$5635

The actual expense difference is greater than $500 (but is less than 5% of the budget) so the actual expense does not pass the test.

85.
Budgeted Expense, b	Actual Expense, a	$|a - b|$	0.05b
$37,640	$37,335	$305	$1882

Since $305 < $500 and $305 < $1882, the actual expense passes the "budget variance test."

87. Receipts = $92.5 billion; $|\text{Receipts} - \text{Outlay}| = |92.5 - 92.2| = \$0.3$ billion surplus

89. Receipts = $1032.0 billion; $|\text{Receipts} - \text{Outlay}| = |1032.0 - 1253.2| = \$221.2$ billion deficit

91. $7x + 4$

Terms: $7x, 4$

Coefficient: 7

93. $\sqrt{3}x^2 - 8x - 11$

Terms: $\sqrt{3}x^2, -8x, -11$

Coefficients: $\sqrt{3}, -8$

95. $4x^3 + \dfrac{x}{2} - 5$

Terms: $4x^3, \dfrac{x}{2}, -5$

Coefficients: $4, \dfrac{1}{2}$

97. $4x - 6$

(a) $4(-1) - 6 = -4 - 6 = -10$

(b) $4(0) - 6 = 0 - 6 = -6$

99. $x^2 - 3x + 4$

(a) $(-2)^2 - 3(-2) + 4 = 4 + 6 + 4 = 14$

(b) $(2)^2 - 3(2) + 4 = 4 - 6 + 4 = 2$

101. $\dfrac{x + 1}{x - 1}$

(a) $\dfrac{1 + 1}{1 - 1} = \dfrac{2}{0}$

Division by zero is undefined

(b) $\dfrac{-1 + 1}{-1 - 1} = \dfrac{0}{-2} = 0$

103. $x + 9 = 9 + x$

Commutative Property of Addition

105. $\dfrac{1}{(h + 6)}(h + 6) = 1, h \neq -6$

Multiplicative Inverse Property

107. $2(x + 3) = 2x + 6$

Distributive Property

109. $1 \cdot (1 + x) = 1 + x$

Multiplicative Identity Property

111. $x(3y) = (x \cdot 3)y$ Associative Property of Multiplication

$= (3x)y$ Commutative Property of Multiplication

113. $\dfrac{3}{16} + \dfrac{5}{16} = \dfrac{8}{16} = \dfrac{1}{2}$

115. $\dfrac{5}{8} - \dfrac{5}{12} + \dfrac{1}{6} = \dfrac{15}{24} - \dfrac{10}{24} + \dfrac{4}{24} = \dfrac{9}{24} = \dfrac{3}{8}$

117. $12 \div \dfrac{1}{4} = 12 \cdot \dfrac{4}{1} = 12 \cdot 4 = 48$

119. $\dfrac{2x}{3} - \dfrac{x}{4} = \dfrac{8x}{12} - \dfrac{3x}{12} = \dfrac{5x}{12}$

121. $-3 + \dfrac{3}{7} \approx -2.57$

123. $\dfrac{11.46 - 5.37}{3.91} \approx 1.56$

125. (a)

n	1	0.5	0.01	0.0001	0.000001
5/n	5	10	500	50,000	5,000,000

(b) The value of $\dfrac{5}{n}$ approaches infinity as n approaches 0.

127. (a) $|u + v| \neq |u| + |v|$ if u is positive and v is negative or vice versa.

(b) $|u + v| \leq |u| + |v|$

They are equal when u and v have the same sign. If they differ in sign, $|u + v|$ is less than $|u| + |v|$.

129. The only even prime number is 2, because its factors are itself and 1.

131. False. The denominators cannot be added when adding fractions.

133. Yes, if a is a negative number, then $-a$ is positive. Thus, $|a| = -a$ if a is negative.

Section P.2   Exponents and Radicals

- ■ You should know the properties of exponents.

    (a) $a^1 = a$

    (b) $a^0 = 1, a \neq 0$

    (c) $a^m a^n = a^{m+n}$

    (d) $a^m/a^n = a^{m-n}, a \neq 0$

    (e) $a^{-n} = 1/a^n, a \neq 0$

    (f) $(a^m)^n = a^{mn}$

    (g) $(ab)^n = a^n b^n$

    (h) $(a/b)^n = a^n/b^n, b \neq 0$

    (i) $(a/b)^{-n} = (b/a)^n, a \neq 0, b \neq 0$

    (j) $|a^2| = |a|^2 = a^2$

- ■ You should be able to write numbers in scientific notation, $c \times 10^n$, where $1 \leq c < 10$ and n is an integer.

- ■ You should be able to use your calculator to evaluate expressions involving exponents.

- ■ You should know the properties of radicals.

    (a) $\sqrt[n]{a^m} = \left(\sqrt[n]{a}\right)^m, a > 0$

    (b) $\sqrt[n]{a} \cdot \sqrt[n]{b} = \sqrt[n]{ab}$

    (c) $\dfrac{\sqrt[n]{a}}{\sqrt[n]{b}} = \sqrt[n]{\dfrac{a}{b}}, b \neq 0$

    (d) $\sqrt[m]{\sqrt[n]{a}} = \sqrt[mn]{a}$

    (e) $\left(\sqrt[n]{a}\right)^n = a$

    (f) For n even, $\sqrt[n]{a^n} = |a|$.
    For n odd, $\sqrt[n]{a^n} = a$.

    (g) $a^{1/n} = \sqrt[n]{a}$

    (h) $a^{m/n} = \left(\sqrt[n]{a}\right)^m = \sqrt[n]{a^m}, a \geq 0$

- ■ You should be able to simplify radicals.

    (a) All possible factors have been removed from the radical sign.

    (b) All fractions have radical-free denominators.

    (c) The index for the radical has been reduced as far as possible.

- ■ You should be able to use your calculator to evaluate radicals.

Solutions to Odd-Numbered Exercises

1. $8^5 = (8)(8)(8)(8)(8)$

3. $-0.4^6 = -(0.4 \times 0.4 \times 0.4 \times 0.4 \times 0.4 \times 0.4)$

5. $(4.9)(4.9)(4.9)(4.9)(4.9)(4.9) = 4.9^6$

7. $(-10)(-10)(-10)(-10)(-10) = (-10)^5$

9. (a) $3^2 \cdot 3 = 3^3 = 27$

(b) $3 \cdot 3^3 = 3^4 = 81$

11. (a) $(3^3)^2 = 3^6 = 729$

(b) $-3^2 = -9$

13. (a) $\dfrac{3 \cdot 4^{-4}}{3^{-4} \cdot 4^{-1}} = 3^{1-(-4)} \cdot 4^{-4-(-1)} = 3^5 \cdot 4^{-3} = \dfrac{3^5}{4^3} = \dfrac{243}{64}$

(b) $32(-2)^{-5} = \dfrac{32}{(-2)^5} = \dfrac{32}{-32} = -1$

15. (a) $2^{-1} + 3^{-1} = \frac{1}{2} + \frac{1}{3} = \frac{3}{6} + \frac{2}{6} = \frac{5}{6}$

(b) $(2^{-1})^{-2} = 2^{(-1)(-2)} = 2^2 = 4$

17. $(-4)^3(5^2) = (-64)(25) = -1600$

19. $\dfrac{3^6}{7^3} = \dfrac{729}{343} \approx 2.125$

21. When $x = 2$, $-3x^3 = -3(2)^3 = -24$.

23. When $x = 10$, $6x^0 = 6(10)^0 = 6(1) = 6$

25. When $x = -3$, $2x^3 = 2(-3)^3 = 2(-27) = -54$

27. When $x = -\frac{1}{2}$, $4x^2 = 4\left(-\frac{1}{2}\right)^2 = 4\left(\frac{1}{4}\right) = 1$

29. (a) $(-5z)^3 = (-5)^3 z^3 = -125z^3$

(b) $5x^4(x^2) = 5x^{4+2} = 5x^6$

31. (a) $6y^2(2y^4)^2 = 6y^2 2^2 y^8 = 6 \cdot 4y^{2+8} = 24y^{10}$

(b) $\dfrac{3x^5}{x^3} = 3x^{5-3} = 3x^2$

33. (a) $\dfrac{7x^2}{x^3} = 7x^{2-3} = 7x^{-1} = \dfrac{7}{x}$

(b) $\dfrac{12(x + y)^3}{9(x + y)} = \dfrac{4}{3}(x + y)^{3-1} = \dfrac{4}{3}(x + y)^2$

35. (a) $(x + 5)^0 = 1,\ x \neq -5$

(b) $(2x^2)^{-2} = \dfrac{1}{(2x^2)^2} = \dfrac{1}{4x^4}$

37. (a) $(-2x^2)^3(4x^3)^{-1} = \dfrac{-8x^6}{4x^3} = -2x^3$

(b) $\left(\dfrac{x}{10}\right)^{-1} = \dfrac{10}{x}$

39. (a) $(4a^{-2}b^3)^{-3} = 4^{-3}a^6 b^{-9} = \dfrac{a^6}{4^3 b^9} = \dfrac{a^6}{64b^9}$

(b) $\left(\dfrac{5x^2}{y^{-2}}\right)^{-4} = (5x^2 y^2)^{-4} = \dfrac{1}{(5x^2 y^2)^4} = \dfrac{1}{625x^8 y^8}$

41. (a) $3^n \cdot 3^{2n} = 3^{n+2n} = 3^{3n}$

(b) $\left(\dfrac{a^{-2}}{b^{-2}}\right)\left(\dfrac{b}{a}\right)^3 = \left(\dfrac{b^2}{a^2}\right)\left(\dfrac{b^3}{a^3}\right) = \dfrac{b^5}{a^5}$

Radical Form	*Rational Exponent Form*
43. $\sqrt{9} = 3$ Given	$9^{1/2} = 3$ Answer
45. $\sqrt[5]{32} = 2$ Answer	$32^{1/5} = 2$ Given
47. $\sqrt{196} = 14$ Answer	$196^{1/2} = 14$ Given
49. $\sqrt[3]{-216} = -6$ Given	$(-216)^{1/3} = -6$ Answer
51. $\sqrt[3]{27^2} = \left(\sqrt[3]{27}\right)^2 = 9$ Answer	$27^{2/3} = 9$ Given
53. $\sqrt[4]{81^3} = 27$ Given	$81^{3/4} = 27$ Answer

55. (a) $\sqrt{9} = 3$

(b) $\sqrt[3]{8} = 2$

57. (a) $-\sqrt[3]{-27} = -(-3) = 3$

(b) $\dfrac{4}{\sqrt{64}} = \dfrac{4}{8} = \dfrac{1}{2}$

59. (a) $\left(\sqrt[3]{-125}\right)^3 = -125$

(b) $27^{1/3} = \sqrt[3]{27} = 3$

61. (a) $32^{-3/5} = \dfrac{1}{32^{3/5}} = \dfrac{1}{\left(\sqrt[5]{32}\right)^3} = \dfrac{1}{(2)^3} = \dfrac{1}{8}$

(b) $\left(\dfrac{16}{81}\right)^{-3/4} = \left(\dfrac{81}{16}\right)^{3/4} = \left(\sqrt[4]{\dfrac{81}{16}}\right)^3 = \left(\dfrac{3}{2}\right)^3 = \dfrac{27}{8}$

63. (a) $\left(-\dfrac{1}{64}\right)^{-1/3} = (-64)^{1/3} = \sqrt[3]{-64} = -4$

(b) $\left(\dfrac{1}{\sqrt{32}}\right)^{-2/5} = \left(\sqrt{32}\right)^{2/5} = \sqrt[5]{\left(\sqrt{32}\right)^2} = \sqrt[5]{32} = 2$

65. (a) $\sqrt{57} \approx 7.550$

(b) $\sqrt[5]{-27^3} = (-27)^{3/5} \approx -7.225$

67. (a) $(1.2^{-2})\sqrt{75} + 3\sqrt{8} \approx 14.499$

(b) $\dfrac{-3 + \sqrt{21}}{3} \approx 0.528$

69. (a) $(-12.4)^{-1.8} \approx -0.011$

(b) $\left(5\sqrt{3}\right)^{-2.5} \approx 0.005$

71. (a) $\sqrt{8} = \sqrt{4 \cdot 2} = \sqrt{4}\sqrt{2} = 2\sqrt{2}$

(b) $\sqrt[3]{24} = \sqrt[3]{8 \cdot 3} = \sqrt[3]{8}\sqrt[3]{3} = 2\sqrt[3]{3}$

73. (a) $\sqrt{72x^3} = \sqrt{36x^2 \cdot 2x} = 6x\sqrt{2x}$

(b) $\sqrt{\dfrac{18^2}{z^3}} = \dfrac{\sqrt{18^2}}{\sqrt{z^2 \cdot z}} = \dfrac{18}{z\sqrt{z}}$

75. (a) $\sqrt[3]{16x^5} = \sqrt[3]{8x^3 \cdot 2x^2} = 2x\sqrt[3]{2x^2}$

(b) $\sqrt{75x^2y^{-4}} = \sqrt{\dfrac{75x^2}{y^4}} = \dfrac{\sqrt{25x^2 \cdot 3}}{\sqrt{y^4}} = \dfrac{5|x|\sqrt{3}}{y^2}$

77. $5^{4/3} \cdot 5^{8/3} = 5^{12/3} = 5^4 = 625$

79. $\dfrac{(2x^2)^{3/2}}{2^{1/2}x^4} = \dfrac{2^{3/2}(x^2)^{3/2}}{2^{1/2}x^4} = \dfrac{2^{3/2}x^3}{2^{1/2}x^4} = 2^{3/2-1/2}x^{3-4} = 2^1 x^{-1} = \dfrac{2}{x}$

81. $\dfrac{x^{-3} \cdot x^{1/2}}{x^{3/2} \cdot x^{-1}} = \dfrac{x^{1/2} \cdot x^1}{x^{3/2} \cdot x^3} = x^{1/2+1-3/2-3} = x^{-3} = \dfrac{1}{x^3}, x > 0$

83. (a) $\dfrac{1}{\sqrt{3}} = \dfrac{1}{\sqrt{3}} \cdot \dfrac{\sqrt{3}}{\sqrt{3}} = \dfrac{\sqrt{3}}{3}$

(b) $\dfrac{8}{\sqrt[3]{2}} = \dfrac{8}{\sqrt[3]{2}} \cdot \dfrac{\sqrt[3]{4}}{\sqrt[3]{4}} = \dfrac{8\sqrt[3]{4}}{2} = 4\sqrt[3]{4}$

85. (a) $\dfrac{2x}{5 - \sqrt{3}} = \dfrac{2x}{5 - \sqrt{3}} \cdot \dfrac{5 + \sqrt{3}}{5 + \sqrt{3}} = \dfrac{2x(5 + \sqrt{3})}{25 - 3} = \dfrac{2x(5 + \sqrt{3})}{22} = \dfrac{x(5 + \sqrt{3})}{11}$

(b) $\dfrac{3}{\sqrt{5} + \sqrt{6}} = \dfrac{3}{\sqrt{5} + \sqrt{6}} \cdot \dfrac{\sqrt{5} - \sqrt{6}}{\sqrt{5} - \sqrt{6}} = \dfrac{3(\sqrt{5} - \sqrt{6})}{5 - 6} = \dfrac{3(\sqrt{5} - \sqrt{6})}{-1} = -3(\sqrt{5} - \sqrt{6}) = 3(\sqrt{6} - \sqrt{5})$

87. (a) $\dfrac{\sqrt{8}}{2} = \dfrac{\sqrt{4 \cdot 2}}{2} = \dfrac{2\sqrt{2}}{2} = \dfrac{\sqrt{2}}{1} \cdot \dfrac{\sqrt{2}}{\sqrt{2}} = \dfrac{2}{\sqrt{2}}$

(b) $\sqrt[3]{\dfrac{9}{25}} = \dfrac{\sqrt[3]{9}}{\sqrt[3]{25}} \cdot \dfrac{\sqrt[3]{3}}{\sqrt[3]{3}} = \dfrac{\sqrt[3]{27}}{\sqrt[3]{75}} = \dfrac{3}{\sqrt[3]{75}}$

89. (a) $\dfrac{\sqrt{5} + \sqrt{3}}{3} = \dfrac{\sqrt{5} + \sqrt{3}}{3} \cdot \dfrac{\sqrt{5} - \sqrt{3}}{\sqrt{5} - \sqrt{3}} = \dfrac{5 - 3}{3(\sqrt{5} - \sqrt{3})} = \dfrac{2}{3(\sqrt{5} - \sqrt{3})}$

(b) $\dfrac{\sqrt{7} - 3}{4} = \dfrac{\sqrt{7} - 3}{4} \cdot \dfrac{\sqrt{7} + 3}{\sqrt{7} + 3} = \dfrac{7 - 9}{4(\sqrt{7} + 3)} = \dfrac{-2}{4(\sqrt{7} + 3)} = -\dfrac{1}{2(\sqrt{7} + 3)}$

91. (a) $\sqrt[4]{3^2} = 3^{2/4} = 3^{1/2} = \sqrt{3}$

(b) $\sqrt[6]{(x + 1)^4} = (x + 1)^{4/6} = (x + 1)^{2/3} = \sqrt[3]{(x + 1)^2}$

93. (a) $\sqrt{\sqrt{32}} = (32^{1/2})^{1/2} = 32^{1/4} = \sqrt[4]{32} = \sqrt[4]{16 \cdot 2} = 2\sqrt[4]{2}$

(b) $\sqrt{\sqrt[4]{2x}} = ((2x)^{1/4})^{1/2} = (2x)^{1/8} = \sqrt[8]{2x}$

95. (a) $2\sqrt{50} + 12\sqrt{8} = 2\sqrt{25 \cdot 2} + 12\sqrt{4 \cdot 2} = 2(5\sqrt{2}) + 12(2\sqrt{2}) = 10\sqrt{2} + 24\sqrt{2} = 34\sqrt{2}$

(b) $10\sqrt{32} - 6\sqrt{18} = 10\sqrt{16 \cdot 2} - 6\sqrt{9 \cdot 2} = 10(4\sqrt{2}) - 6(3\sqrt{2}) = 40\sqrt{2} - 18\sqrt{2} = 22\sqrt{2}$

97. (a) $5\sqrt{x} - 3\sqrt{x} = 2\sqrt{x}$

(b) $-2\sqrt{9y} + 10\sqrt{y} = -2(3\sqrt{y}) + 10\sqrt{y} = -6\sqrt{y} + 10\sqrt{y} = 4\sqrt{y}$

99. (a) $3\sqrt{x + 1} + 10\sqrt{x + 1} = 13\sqrt{x + 1}$

(b) $7\sqrt{80x} - 2\sqrt{125x} = 7\sqrt{16 \cdot 5x} - 2\sqrt{25 \cdot 5x} = 7(4\sqrt{5x}) - 2(5\sqrt{5x}) = 28\sqrt{5x} - 10\sqrt{5x} = 18\sqrt{5x}$

101. $\sqrt{5} + \sqrt{3} \approx 3.968$ and $\sqrt{5 + 3} = \sqrt{8} \approx 2.828$
Thus, $\sqrt{5} + \sqrt{3} > \sqrt{5 + 3}$.

103. $\sqrt{3^2 + 2^2} = \sqrt{9 + 4} = \sqrt{13} \approx 3.606$
Thus, $5 > \sqrt{3^2 + 2^2}$.

105. $57,300,000 = 5.73 \times 10^7$ square miles

107. $0.0000899 = 8.99 \times 10^{-5}$ gram per cubic centimeter

109. $6.048 \times 10^8 = 604,800,000$ servings

111. $1.602 \times 10^{-19} = 0.0000000000000000001602$ coulomb

113. (a) $\sqrt{25 \times 10^8} = 5 \times 10^4 = 50,000$

(b) $\sqrt[3]{8 \times 10^{15}} = 2 \times 10^5 = 200,000$

115. (a) $750\left(1 + \dfrac{0.11}{365}\right)^{800} \approx 954.448$

(b) $\dfrac{67,000,000 + 93,000,000}{0.0052} = 30,769,230,769.2 \approx 3.077 \times 10^{10}$

117. (a) $\sqrt{4.5 \times 10^9} \approx 67,082.039$

(b) $\sqrt[3]{6.3 \times 10^4} \approx 39.791$

119. When any positive integer is squared, the units digit is 0, 1, 4, 5, 6, or 9. Therefore, $\sqrt{5233}$ is not an integer.

121. $T = 2\pi\sqrt{\dfrac{2}{32}} = 2\pi\sqrt{\dfrac{1}{16}} = 2\pi\left(\dfrac{1}{4}\right) = \dfrac{\pi}{2} \approx 1.57$ seconds

123. $t = 0.03[12^{5/2} - (12 - 7)^{5/2}] = 0.03[12^{5/2} - 5^{5/2}] \approx 13.29$ seconds

125. $r = 1 - \left(\dfrac{3225}{12,000}\right)^{1/4} \approx 0.280$ or 28%

127. True. When dividing variables, you subtract exponents.

129. $1 = \dfrac{a^m}{a^m} = a^{m-m} = a^0, a \neq 0$

131. No. A number written in scientific notation has the form $c \times 10^n$, where $1 \leq c < 10$ and n is an integer. In true scientific notation, the number 52.7×10^5 is 5.27×10^6.

Section P.3 Polynomials and Factoring

- Given a polynomial in x, $a_n x^n + a_{n-1} x^{n-1} + \ldots + a_1 x + a_0$, where $a_n \neq 0$, and n is a nonnegative integer, you should be able to identify the following.

  (a) Degree: n

  (b) Terms: $a_n x^n, a_{n-1} x^{n-1}, \ldots, a_1 x, a_0$

  (c) Coefficients: $a_n, a_{n-1}, \ldots, a_1, a_0$

  (d) Leading coefficient: a_n

  (e) Constant term: a

- You should be able to add and subtract polynomials.

- You should be able to multiply polynomials by the Distributive Properties.

- You should be able to multiply two binomials by the FOIL Method.

- You should know the special binomial products.

  (a) $(u + v)(u - v) = u^2 - v^2$

  (b) $(u \pm v)^2 = u^2 \pm 2uv + v^2$

  (c) $(u \pm v)^3 = u^3 \pm 3u^2 v + 3uv^2 \pm v^3$

- You should be able to factor out all common factors, the first step in factoring.

- You should be able to factor the following special polynomial forms.

  (a) $u^2 - v^2 = (u + v)(u - v)$

  (b) $u^2 \pm 2uv + v^2 = (u \pm v)^2$

  (c) $u^3 \pm v^3 = (u \pm v)(u^2 \mp uv + v^2)$

- You should be able to factor by grouping.

- You should be able to factor some trinomials by grouping.

Solutions to Odd-Numbered Exercises

1. (d) 12 is a polynomial of degree zero.

3. (b) $1 - 2x^3 = -2x^3 + 1$ is a binomial with leading coefficient -2.

5. (f) $\frac{2}{3} x^4 + x^2 + 10$ is a trinomial with leading coefficient $\frac{2}{3}$.

7. Answers will vary. One possible third-degree polynomial with leading coefficient -2 is:

   $-2x^3 + 4x^2 - 3x + 20$

9. Answers will vary. One possible fourth-degree polynomial with a negative leading coefficient is:

   $-15x^4 + 1$

11. Standard form: $2x + 3$

Degree: 1

Leading coefficient: 2

13. Standard form: $-4x^5 + 6x^4 - x + 1$

Degree: 5

Leading coefficient: -4

15. Standard form: $x^2y^3 + 4x^3y - 3xy^2$

Degree: 5 (add the exponents on x and y)

Leading coefficient: 1

17. $2x - 3x^3 + 8$ *is* a polynomial.

Standard form: $-3x^3 + 2x + 8$

19. $\dfrac{3x + 4}{x} = 3 + \dfrac{4}{x}$ is *not* a polynomial.

21. $y^2 - y^4 + y^3$ *is* a polynomial.

Standard form: $-y^4 + y^3 + y^2$

23. $(2x^2 + 1) - (x^2 - 2x + 1) = 2x^2 + 1 - x^2 + 2x - 1$
$$= x^2 + 2x$$

25. $(15x^2 - 6) - (-8.3x^3 - 14.7x^2 - 17) = 15x^2 - 6 + 8.3x^3 + 14.7x^2 + 17$
$$= 8.3x^3 + (15x^2 + 14.7x^2) + (-6 + 17)$$
$$= 8.3x^3 + 29.7x^2 + 11$$

27. $5z - [3z - (10z + 8)] = 5z - (3z - 10z - 8)$
$$= 5z - 3z + 10z + 8$$
$$= (5z - 3z + 10z) + 8$$
$$= 12z + 8$$

29. $3x(x^2 - 2x + 1) = 3x(x^2) + 3x(-2x) + 3x(1)$
$$= 3x^3 - 6x^2 + 3x$$

31. $-5z(3z - 1) = -5z(3z) + (-5z)(-1)$
$$= -15z^2 + 5z$$

33. $(1 - x^3)(4x) = 1(4x) - x^3(4x)$
$$= 4x - 4x^4$$
$$= -4x^4 + 4x$$

35. $(2.5x^2 + 3)(3x) = (2.5x^2)(3x) + (3)(3x)$
$$= 7.5x^3 + 9x$$

37. $-4x\left(\tfrac{1}{8}x + 3\right) = (-4x)\left(\tfrac{1}{8}x\right) + (-4x)(3)$
$$= -\tfrac{1}{2}x^2 - 12x$$

39. $(x + 3)(x + 4) = x^2 + 4x + 3x + 12$ FOIL
$$= x^2 + 7x + 12$$

41. $(3x - 5)(2x + 1) = 6x^2 + 3x - 10x - 5$ FOIL
$$= 6x^2 - 7x - 5$$

43. $(2x + 3)^2 = (2x)^2 + 2(2x)(3) + 3^2$
$$= 4x^2 + 12x + 9$$

45. $(2x - 5y)^2 = 4x^2 - 2(5y)(2x) + 25y^2$
$$= 4x^2 - 20xy + 25y^2$$

47. $(x + 10)(x - 10) = x^2 - 100$

49. $(x + 2y)(x - 2y) = x^2 - (2y)^2 = x^2 - 4y^2$

51. $[(m - 3) + n][(m - 3) - n] = (m - 3)^2 - n^2$
$$= m^2 - 6m + 9 - n^2$$
$$= m^2 - n^2 - 6m + 9$$

53. $[(x - 3) + y]^2 = (x - 3)^2 + 2y(x - 3) + y^2$
$$= x^2 - 6x + 9 + 2xy - 6y + y^2$$
$$= x^2 + 2xy + y^2 - 6x - 6y + 9$$

55. $(2r^2 - 5)(2r^2 + 5) = (2r)^2 - 5^2 = 4r^4 - 25$

57. $(x + 1)^3 = x^3 + 3x^2(1) + 3x(1^2) + 1^3$
$$= x^3 + 3x^2 + 3x + 1$$

59. $(2x - y)^3 = (2x)^3 - 3(2x)^2 y + 3(2x)y^2 - y^3$
$$= 8x^3 - 12x^2 y + 6xy^2 - y^3$$

61. $\left(\frac{1}{2}x - 3\right)^2 = \left(\frac{1}{2}x\right)^2 - 2\left(\frac{1}{2}x\right)(3) + (3)^2 = \frac{1}{4}x^2 - 3x + 9$

63. $\left(\frac{1}{3}x - 2\right)\left(\frac{1}{3}x + 2\right) = \left(\frac{1}{3}x\right)^2 - (2)^2 = \frac{1}{9}x^2 - 4$

65. $(1.2x + 3)^2 = (1.2x)^2 + 2(1.2x)(3) + (3)^2$
$$= 1.44x^2 + 7.2x + 9$$

67. $(1.5x - 4)(1.5x + 4) = (1.5x)^2 - (4)^2$
$$= 2.25x^2 - 16$$

69. $5x(x + 1) - 3x(x + 1) = 2x(x + 1)$
$$= 2x^2 + 2x$$

71. $(u + 2)(u - 2)(u^2 + 4) = (u^2 - 4)(u^2 + 4)$
$$= u^4 - 16$$

73. $\left(\sqrt{x} + \sqrt{y}\right)\left(\sqrt{x} - \sqrt{y}\right) = \left(\sqrt{x}\right)^2 - \left(\sqrt{y}\right)^2 = x - y$

75. $\left(x - \sqrt{5}\right)^2 = x^2 - 2(x)\left(\sqrt{5}\right) + \left(\sqrt{5}\right)^2$
$$= x^2 - 2\sqrt{5}x + 5$$

77. $(x^3 + 2x^2 + x + 2) = (x + 2)(x^2 + 1)$ **is completely factored.**

79. $x^3 + x^2 - 7x - 7 = (x^2 - 7)(x + 1)$ can be factored further into $\left(x + \sqrt{7}\right)\left(x - \sqrt{7}\right)(x + 1)$.

81. $3x + 6 = 3(x + 2)$

83. $2x^3 - 6x = 2x(x^2 - 3)$

85. $x(x - 1) + 6(x - 1) = (x - 1)(x + 6)$

87. $(x + 3)^2 - 4(x + 3) = (x + 3)[(x + 3) - 4]$
$$= (x + 3)(x - 1)$$

89. $\frac{1}{2}x^3 + 2x^2 - 5x = \frac{1}{2}x^3 + \frac{4}{2}x^2 - \frac{10}{2}x$
$$= \frac{1}{2}x(x^2 + 4x - 10)$$

91. $\frac{2}{3}x(x - 3) - 4(x - 3) = \frac{2}{3}x(x - 3) - \frac{12}{3}(x - 3)$
$$= \frac{2}{3}(x - 3)(x - 6)$$

93. $16y^2 - 9 = (4y + 3)(4y - 3)$

95. $16x^2 - \frac{1}{9} = (4x)^2 - \left(\frac{1}{3}\right)^2$
$$= \left(4x + \frac{1}{3}\right)\left(4x - \frac{1}{3}\right)$$

97. $(x - 1)^2 - 4 = [(x - 1) + 2][(x - 1) - 2]$
$$= (x + 1)(x - 3)$$

99. $9u^2 - 4v^2 = (3u)^2 - (2v)^2$
$$= (3u + 2v)(3u - 2v)$$

101. $x^2 - 4x + 4 = x^2 - 2(2)x + 2^2 = (x - 2)^2$

103. $36y^2 - 108y + 81 = (6y)^2 - 2(6y)(9) + (9)^2 = (6y - 9)^2$
OR:
$9(4y^2 - 12y + 9) = 9(2y - 3)^2$

105. $9u^2 + 24uv + 16v^2 = (3u)^2 + 2(3u)(4v) + (4v)^2$
$\qquad = (3u + 4v)^2$

107. $x^2 - \frac{4}{3}x + \frac{4}{9} = x^2 - 2(x)\left(\frac{2}{3}\right) + \left(\frac{2}{3}\right)^2$
$\qquad = \left(x - \frac{2}{3}\right)^2$

109. $x^2 + x - 2 = (x + 2)(x - 1)$

111. $s^2 - 5s + 6 = (s - 3)(s - 2)$

113. $20 - y - y^2 = (5 + y)(4 - y)$ or $-(y + 5)(y - 4)$

115. $3x^2 - 5x + 2 = (3x - 2)(x - 1)$

117. $5x^2 + 26x + 5 = (5x + 1)(x + 5)$

119. $-9z^2 + 3z + 2 = -(9z^2 - 3z - 2)$
$\qquad = -(3z - 2)(3z + 1)$

121. $x^3 - 8 = x^3 - 2^3 = (x - 2)(x^2 + 2x + 4)$

123. $y^3 + 64 = y^3 + 4^3 = (y + 4)(y^2 - 4y + 16)$

125. $8t^3 - 1 = (2t)^3 - 1^3 = (2t - 1)(4t^2 + 2t + 1)$

127. $u^3 + 27v^3 = u^3 + (3v)^3$
$\qquad = (u + 3v)(u^2 - 3uv + 9v^2)$

129. $x^3 - x^2 + 2x - 2 = x^2(x - 1) + 2(x - 1)$
$\qquad = (x - 1)(x^2 + 2)$

131. $2x^3 - x^2 - 6x + 3 = x^2(2x - 1) - 3(2x - 1)$
$\qquad = (2x - 1)(x^2 - 3)$

133. $6x^3 - 2x + 3x^2 - 1 = 2x(3x^2 - 1) + 1(3x^2 - 1)$
$\qquad = (3x^2 - 1)(2x + 1)$

135. $a \cdot c = (3)(8) = 24.$ Rewrite the middle term,
$10x = 6x + 4x,$ since $(6)(4) = 24$ and $6 + 4 = 10.$
$3x^2 + 10x + 8 = 3x^2 + 6x + 4x + 8$
$\qquad = 3x(x + 2) + 4(x + 2)$
$\qquad = (x + 2)(3x + 4)$

137. $a \cdot c = (15)(2) = 30.$ Rewrite the middle term,
$-11x = -6x - 5x,$ since $(-6)(-5) = 30$ and $(-6) + (-5) = -11.$
$15x^2 - 11x + 2 = 15x^2 - 6x - 5x + 2$
$\qquad = 3x(5x - 2) - 1(5x - 2)$
$\qquad = (5x - 2)(3x - 1)$
$\qquad = (3x - 1)(5x - 2)$

139. $6x^2 - 54 = 6(x^2 - 9)$
$\qquad = 6(x + 3)(x - 3)$

141. $x^3 - 4x^2 = x^2(x - 4)$

143. $2x^2 + 4x - 2x^3 = -2x(-x - 2 + x^2)$
$\qquad = -2x(x^2 - x - 2)$
$\qquad = -2x(x + 1)(x - 2)$

145. $3x^3 + x^2 + 15x + 5 = x^2(3x + 1) + 5(3x + 1)$
$\qquad = (3x + 1)(x^2 + 5)$

147. $\frac{1}{81}x^2 + \frac{2}{9}x - 8 = \frac{1}{81}x^2 + \frac{18}{81}x - \frac{648}{8}$
$\qquad = \frac{1}{81}(x^2 + 18x - 648)$
$\qquad = \frac{1}{81}(x + 36)(x - 18)$

149. $x^4 - 4x^3 + x^2 - 4x = x(x^3 - 4x^2 + x - 4)$
$$= x[x^2(x - 4) + (x - 4)]$$
$$= x(x - 4)(x^2 + 1)$$

151. $(x^2 + 1)^2 - 4x^2 = [(x^2 + 1) + 2x][(x^2 + 1) - 2x]$
$$= (x^2 + 2x + 1)(x^2 - 2x + 1)$$
$$= (x + 1)^2(x - 1)^2$$

153. $2t^3 - 16 = 2(t^3 - 8) = 2(t - 2)(t^2 + 2t + 4)$

155. $4x(2x - 1) + (2x - 1)^2 = (2x - 1)[4x + (2x - 1)]$
$$= (2x - 1)(6x - 1)$$

157. $7(3x + 2)^2(1 - x)^2 + (3x + 2)(1 - x)^3 = (3x + 2)(1 - x)^2[7(3x + 2) + (1 - x)]$
$$= (3x + 2)(1 - x)^2[21x + 14 + 1 - x]$$
$$= (3x + 2)(1 - x)^2(20x + 15)$$
$$= (3x + 2)(1 - x)^2(5)(4x + 3)$$
$$= 5(1 - x)^2(3x + 2)(4x + 3)$$

159. $3(x - 2)^2(x + 1)^4 + (x - 2)^3(4)(x + 1)^3 = (x - 2)^2(x + 1)^3[3(x + 1) + (x - 2)(4)]$
$$= (x - 2)^2(x + 1)^3[3x + 3 + 4x - 8]$$
$$= (x - 2)^2(x + 1)^3(7x - 5)$$

161. For $x^2 + bx - 15$ to be factorable, b must equal $m + n$ where $mn = -15$.

Factors of -15	Sum of factors
$(15)(-1)$	$15 + (-1) = 14$
$(-15)(1)$	$-15 + 1 = -14$
$(3)(-5)$	$3 + (-5) = -2$
$(-3)(5)$	$-3 + 5 = 2$

The possible b values are $14, -14, -2,$ or 2.

163. For $x^2 + bx - 12$ to be factorable, b must be equal $m + n$ where $mn = -12$.

Factors of -12	Sum of factors
$(-1)(12)$	$-1 + 12 = 11$
$(1)(-12)$	$1 + (-12) = -11$
$(-2)(6)$	$-2 + 6 = 4$
$(2)(-6)$	$2 + (-6) = -4$
$(-3)(4)$	$(-3) + 4 = 1$
$(3)(-4)$	$3 + (-4) = -1$

The possible b values are $11, -11, 4, -4, 1,$ or -1.

165. For $2x^2 + 5x + c$ to be factorable, the factors of $2c$ must add up to 5.

Possible c values	$2c$	Factors of $2c$ that add up to 5
2	4	$(1)(4) = 4$ and $1 + 4 = 5$
3	6	$(2)(3) = 6$ and $2 + 3 = 5$
-3	-6	$(6)(-1) = -6$ and $6 + (-1) = 5$
-7	-14	$(7)(-2) = -14$ and $7 + (-2) = 5$
-12	-24	$(8)(-3) = -24$ and $8 + (-3) = 5$

These are a few possible c values. There are *many* correct answers.

If $c = 2 : 2x^2 + 5x + 2 = (2x + 1)(x + 2)$

If $c = 3 : 2x^2 + 5x + 3 = (2x + 3)(x + 1)$

If $c = -3 : 2x^2 + 5x - 3 = (2x - 1)(x + 3)$

If $c = -7 : 2x^2 + 5x - 7 = (2x + 7)(x - 1)$

If $c = -12: 2x^2 + 5x - 12 = (2x - 3)(x + 4)$

167. For $3x^2 - x + c$ to be factorable, the factors of $3c$ must add up to -1.

Possible c values	$3c$	Factors of $3c$ that add up to -1
-2	-6	$(-3)(2) = -6$ and $(-3) + 2 = -1$
-4	-12	$(-4)(3) = -12$ and $(-4) + 3 = -1$
-10	-30	$(-6)(5) = -30$ and $(-6) + 5 = -1$
-30	-90	$(-10)(9) = -90$ and $(-10) + 9 = -1$
-44	-132	$(-12)(11) = -132$ and $(-12) + 11 = -1$

These are a few possible c values. There are *many* correct answers.

If $c = -2: 3x^2 - x - 2 = (3x + 2)(x - 1)$

If $c = -4: 3x^2 - x - 4 = (3x - 4)(x + 1)$

If $c = -10: 3x^2 - x - 10 = (3x + 5)(x - 2)$

If $c = -30: 3x^2 - x - 30 = (3x - 10)(x + 3)$

If $c = -44: 3x^2 - x - 44 = (3x + 11)(x - 4)$

169. Profit = Revenue − Cost

$P(x) = 95x - (73x + 25,000) = 22x - 25,000$

When $x = 5000$, $P(5000) = 22(5000) - 25,000 = \$85,000$

171. (a) $500(1 + r)^2 = 500(r + 1)^2 = 500(r^2 + 2r + 1)$

$$= 500r^2 + 1000r + 500$$

(b)

r	$2\frac{1}{2}\%$	3%	4%	$4\frac{1}{2}\%$	5%
$500(1 + r)^2$	\$525.31	\$530.45	\$540.80	\$546.01	\$551.25

(c) As r increases, the amount increases.

173. $V = \text{length} \times \text{width} \times \text{height}$

$$= (26 - 2x)(18 - 2x)x$$

$$= 2(13 - x)2(9 - x)x$$

$$= 4x(13 - x)(9 - x), \ 0 < x < 9$$

When $x = 1$: $V = 4(1)(12)(8) = 384 \text{ cm}^3$.

When $x = 2$: $V = 4(2)(11)(7) = 616 \text{ cm}^3$.

When $x = 3$: $V = 4(3)(10)(6) = 720 \text{ cm}^3$.

175. (a) Area of shaded region $=$ Area of rectangle $-$ Area of triangle

$$A = (4x - 2)(3x) - \tfrac{1}{2}(4x - 2)(3x)$$

$$= \tfrac{1}{2}(4x - 2)(3x)$$

$$= (2x - 1)(3x)$$

$$= 6x^2 - 3x$$

(b) Area of shaded region $=$ Area of larger triangle $-$ Area of smaller triangle

$$A = \tfrac{1}{2}(10x)(10x) - \tfrac{1}{2}(4x)(4x)$$

$$= 50x^2 - 8x^2$$

$$= 42x^2$$

177. $A = \text{length} \times \text{width}$

$$= (18 + 2x)(14 + x)$$

$$= 252 + 18x + 28x + 2x^2$$

$$= 2x^2 + 46x + 252$$

179. $3x^2 + 7x + 2 = (3x + 1)(x + 2)$

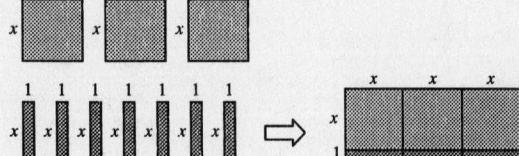

181. $A = \pi(r + 2)^2 - \pi r^2$

$= \pi[(r + 2)^2 - r^2]$

$= \pi[r^2 + 4r + 4 - r^2]$

$= \pi(4r + 4)$

$= 4\pi(r + 1)$

183. $A = 8(18) - 4x^2$

$= 4(36 - x^2)$

$= 4(6 - x)(6 + x)$

185. (a) $V = \pi R^2 h - \pi r^2 h$

$= \pi h(R^2 - r^2)$

$= \pi h(R - r)(R + r)$

(b) The average radius is $\dfrac{R + r}{2}$.

The thickness of the shell is $R - r$.

$V = \pi h(R - r)(R + r) = 2\pi\left(\dfrac{R + r}{2}\right)(R - r)h$

187. False. $(4x^2 + 1)(3x + 1) = 12x^3 + 4x^2 + 3x + 1$
which is a third-degree polynomial.

189. True. $a^2 - b^2 = (a + b)(a - b)$

191. If $P(x)$ is a polynomial of degree m and $Q(x)$ is a polynomial of degree n,
then the degree of $P(x)Q(x)$ is $m + n$.

193. $(x + y)^2 \neq x^2 + y^2$

Let $x = 3$ and $y = 4$.

$(3 + 4)^2 = (7)^2 = 49$

$3^2 + 4^2 = 9 + 16 = 25$ $\Bigg\rangle$ Not Equal

If either x or y is zero, then $(x + y)^2$ would equal $x^2 + y^2$.

195. $x^{2n} - y^{2n} = (x^n)^2 - (y^n)^2 = (x^n + y^n)(x^n - y^n)$

197. $x^{3n} - y^{2n}$ does not factor.

Section P.4 Rational Expressions

■ You should be able to find the domain of a rational expression.

■ You should know that a rational expression is the quotient of two polynomials.

■ You should be able to simplify rational expressions by reducing them to lowest terms. This may involve factoring both the numerator and the denominator.

■ You should be able to add, subtract, multiply, and divide rational expressions.

■ You should be able to simplify complex fractions.

■ You should be able to simplify expressions with negative or fraction exponents.

Solutions to Odd-Numbered Exercises

1. The domain of the polynomial $3x^2 - 4x + 7$ is the set of all real numbers.

3. The domain of the polynomial $4x^3 + 3$, $x \geq 0$ is the set of non-negative real numbers, since the polynomial is restricted to that set.

5. The domain of $\dfrac{1}{x - 2}$ is the set of all real numbers x such that $x \neq 2$.

7. The domain of $\sqrt{x + 1}$ is the set of all real numbers x such that $x \geq -1$.

9. $\dfrac{5}{2x} = \dfrac{5(3x)}{(2x)(3x)} = \dfrac{5(3x)}{6x^2}$, $x \neq 0$

   The missing factor is $3x$, $x \neq 0$.

11. $\dfrac{x + 1}{x} = \dfrac{(x + 1)(x - 2)}{x(x - 2)}$, $x \neq 2$

    The missing factor is $x - 2$, $x \neq 2$.

13. $\dfrac{3x}{x - 3} = \dfrac{3x(x)}{(x - 3)(x)} = \dfrac{3x^2}{x^2 - 3x}$, $x \neq 0$

    The missing factor is x, $x \neq 0$.

15. $\dfrac{15x^2}{10x} = \dfrac{5x(3x)}{5x(2)} = \dfrac{3x}{2}$, $x \neq 0$

17. $\dfrac{3xy}{xy + x} = \dfrac{x(3y)}{x(y + 1)} = \dfrac{3y}{y + 1}$, $x \neq 0$

19. $\dfrac{4y - 8y^2}{10y - 5} = \dfrac{-4y(2y - 1)}{5(2y - 1)} = -\dfrac{4y}{5}$, $y \neq \dfrac{1}{2}$

21. $\dfrac{x - 5}{10 - 2x} = \dfrac{x - 5}{-2(x - 5)} = -\dfrac{1}{2}$, $x \neq 5$

23. $\dfrac{y^2 - 16}{y + 4} = \dfrac{(y + 4)(y - 4)}{y + 4} = y - 4$, $y \neq -4$

25. $\dfrac{x^3 + 5x^2 + 6x}{x^2 - 4} = \dfrac{x(x + 2)(x + 3)}{(x + 2)(x - 2)} = \dfrac{x(x + 3)}{x - 2}$, $x \neq -2$

27. $\dfrac{y^2 - 7y + 12}{y^2 + 3y - 18} = \dfrac{(y - 3)(y - 4)}{(y + 6)(y - 3)} = \dfrac{y - 4}{y + 6}$, $y \neq 3$

29. $\dfrac{2 - x + 2x^2 - x^3}{x^2 - 4} = \dfrac{(2 - x) + x^2(2 - x)}{(x + 2)(x - 2)} = \dfrac{(2 - x)(1 + x^2)}{(x + 2)(x - 2)} = \dfrac{-(x - 2)(x^2 + 1)}{(x + 2)(x - 2)} = -\dfrac{x^2 + 1}{x + 2}$, $x \neq 2$

31. $\dfrac{z^3 - 8}{z^2 + 2z + 4} = \dfrac{(z - 2)(z^2 + 2z + 4)}{z^2 + 2z + 4} = z - 2$

33.

x	0	1	2	3	4	5	6
$\dfrac{x^2 - 2x - 3}{x - 3}$	1	2	3	Undef.	5	6	7
$x + 1$	1	2	3	4	5	6	7

The expressions are equivalent except at $x = 3$.

35. $\dfrac{5x^3}{2x^3 + 4} = \dfrac{5x^3}{2(x^3 + 2)}$. There are no common factors so this expression cannot be simplified.

    In this case factors of terms were incorrectly cancelled.

37. $\dfrac{\pi r^2}{(2r)^2} = \dfrac{\pi r^2}{4r^2} = \dfrac{\pi}{4}, \quad r \neq 0$

39. $\dfrac{5}{x - 1} \cdot \dfrac{x - 1}{25(x - 2)} = \dfrac{1}{5(x - 2)}, \quad x \neq 1$

41. $\dfrac{(x + 5)(x - 3)}{x + 2} \cdot \dfrac{1}{(x + 5)(x + 2)} = \dfrac{x - 3}{(x + 2)^2}, \quad x \neq -5$

43. $\dfrac{r}{r - 1} \cdot \dfrac{r^2 - 1}{r^2} = \dfrac{r(r + 1)(r - 1)}{r^2(r - 1)} = \dfrac{r + 1}{r}, \quad r \neq 1$

45. $\dfrac{t^2 - t - 6}{t^2 + 6t + 9} \cdot \dfrac{t + 3}{t^2 - 4} = \dfrac{(t - 3)(t + 2)(t + 3)}{(t + 3)^2(t + 2)(t - 2)} = \dfrac{t - 3}{(t + 3)(t - 2)}, \quad t \neq -2$

47. $\dfrac{x^2 + xy - 2y^2}{x^3 + x^2y} \cdot \dfrac{x}{x^2 + 3xy + 2y^2} = \dfrac{(x + 2y)(x - y)}{x^2(x + y)} \cdot \dfrac{x}{(x + 2y)(x + y)} = \dfrac{x - y}{x(x + y)^2}, \quad x \neq -2y$

49. $\dfrac{3(x + y)}{4} \div \dfrac{x + y}{2} = \dfrac{3(x + y)}{4} \cdot \dfrac{2}{x + y} = \dfrac{3}{2}, \quad x \neq -y$

51. $\dfrac{x^2 + 16}{5x + 20} \div \dfrac{x + 4}{5x^2 - 20} = \dfrac{x^2 + 16}{5x + 20} \cdot \dfrac{5x^2 - 20}{x + 4} = \dfrac{x^2 + 16}{5(x + 4)} \cdot \dfrac{5(x^2 - 4)}{x + 4} = \dfrac{(x^2 + 16)(x + 2)(x - 2)}{(x + 4)^2}$

53. $\dfrac{x^2 - 36}{x} \div \dfrac{x^3 - 6x^2}{x^2 + x} = \dfrac{x^2 - 36}{x} \cdot \dfrac{x^2 + x}{x^3 - 6x^2} = \dfrac{(x + 6)(x - 6)}{x} \cdot \dfrac{x(x + 1)}{x^2(x - 6)} = \dfrac{(x + 6)(x + 1)}{x^2}, \quad x \neq 6$

55. $\dfrac{5}{x - 1} + \dfrac{x}{x - 1} = \dfrac{5 + x}{x - 1} = \dfrac{x + 5}{x - 1}$

57. $6 - \dfrac{5}{x + 3} = \dfrac{6(x + 3)}{(x + 3)} - \dfrac{5}{x + 3} = \dfrac{6(x + 3) - 5}{x + 3} = \dfrac{6x + 18 - 5}{x + 3} = \dfrac{6x + 13}{x + 3}$

59. $\dfrac{3}{x - 2} + \dfrac{5}{2 - x} = \dfrac{3}{x - 2} - \dfrac{5}{x - 2} = -\dfrac{2}{x - 2}$

61. $\dfrac{2}{x^2 - 4} - \dfrac{1}{x^2 - 3x + 2} = \dfrac{2}{(x + 2)(x - 2)} - \dfrac{1}{(x - 1)(x - 2)}$

$\qquad = \dfrac{2(x - 1) - (x + 2)}{(x + 2)(x - 2)(x - 1)} = \dfrac{2x - 2 - x - 2}{(x + 2)(x - 2)(x - 1)} = \dfrac{x - 4}{(x + 2)(x - 2)(x - 1)}$

63. $\dfrac{1}{x^2 - x - 2} - \dfrac{x}{x^2 - 5x + 6} = \dfrac{1}{(x - 2)(x + 1)} - \dfrac{x}{(x - 2)(x - 3)}$

$\qquad = \dfrac{(x - 3) - x(x + 1)}{(x + 1)(x - 2)(x - 3)} = \dfrac{x - 3 - x^2 - x}{(x + 1)(x - 2)(x - 3)}$

$\qquad = \dfrac{-x^2 - 3}{(x + 1)(x - 2)(x - 3)} = -\dfrac{x^2 + 3}{(x + 1)(x - 2)(x - 3)}$

65. $-\dfrac{1}{x} + \dfrac{2}{x^2 + 1} + \dfrac{1}{x^3 + x} = \dfrac{-(x^2 + 1)}{x(x^2 + 1)} + \dfrac{2x}{x(x^2 + 1)} + \dfrac{1}{x(x^2 + 1)}$

$\qquad = \dfrac{-x^2 - 1 + 2x + 1}{x(x^2 + 1)} = \dfrac{-x^2 + 2x}{x(x^2 + 1)} = \dfrac{-x(x - 2)}{x(x^2 + 1)}$

$\qquad = -\dfrac{x - 2}{x^2 + 1} = \dfrac{2 - x}{x^2 + 1}, \quad x \neq 0$

67. $x^5 - 2x^{-2} = x^{-2}(x^7 - 2) = \dfrac{x^7 - 2}{x^2}$

69. $3x^{3/2} - 2x^{-1/2} = x^{-1/2}(3x^2 - 2) = \dfrac{3x^2 - 2}{x^{1/2}}$

71. $x^2(x^2 + 1)^{-5} - (x^2 + 1)^{-4} = (x^2 + 1)^{-5}\big[x^2 - (x^2 + 1)\big] = -\dfrac{1}{(x^2 + 1)^5}$

73. $2x^2(x - 1)^{1/2} - 5(x - 1)^{-1/2} = (x - 1)^{-1/2}\big[2x^2(x - 1)^1 - 5\big] = \dfrac{2x^3 - 2x^2 - 5}{(x - 1)^{1/2}}$

75. $\dfrac{x + 4}{x + 2} - \dfrac{3x - 8}{x + 2} = \dfrac{(x + 4) - (3x - 8)}{x + 2}$

$\qquad\qquad = \dfrac{x + 4 - 3x + 8}{x + 2}$

$\qquad\qquad = \dfrac{-2x + 12}{x + 2}$

$\qquad\qquad = \dfrac{-2(x - 6)}{x + 2}$

77. $\dfrac{\left(\dfrac{x}{2} - 1\right)}{(x - 2)} = \dfrac{\left(\dfrac{x}{2} - \dfrac{2}{2}\right)}{\left(\dfrac{x - 2}{1}\right)}$

$\qquad = \dfrac{x - 2}{2} \cdot \dfrac{1}{x - 2}$

$\qquad = \dfrac{1}{2}, \quad x \neq 2$

The error was incorrect subtraction in the numerator.

79. $\dfrac{\left[\dfrac{x^2}{(x + 1)^2}\right]}{\left[\dfrac{x}{(x + 1)^3}\right]} = \dfrac{x^2}{(x + 1)^2} \cdot \dfrac{(x + 1)^3}{x} = x(x + 1), \quad x \neq -1, 0$

81. $\dfrac{\left(\dfrac{1}{x} - \dfrac{1}{x + 1}\right)}{\left(\dfrac{1}{x + 1}\right)} = \dfrac{\dfrac{(x + 1) - x}{x(x + 1)}}{\dfrac{1}{x + 1}} = \dfrac{1}{x(x + 1)} \cdot \dfrac{x + 1}{1} = \dfrac{1}{x}, \quad x \neq -1$

83. $\dfrac{\left(\dfrac{x + 3}{x - 3}\right)^2}{\left(\dfrac{1}{x + 3} + \dfrac{1}{x - 3}\right)} = \dfrac{\dfrac{(x + 3)^2}{(x - 3)^2}}{\dfrac{(x - 3) + (x + 3)}{(x + 3)(x - 3)}} = \dfrac{(x + 3)^2}{(x - 3)^2} \cdot \dfrac{(x + 3)(x - 3)}{2x} = \dfrac{(x + 3)^3}{2x(x - 3)}, \quad x \neq -3$

85. $\dfrac{\left[\dfrac{1}{(x + h)^2} - \dfrac{1}{x^2}\right]}{h} = \dfrac{\left[\dfrac{1}{(x + h)^2} - \dfrac{1}{x^2}\right]}{h} \cdot \dfrac{x^2(x + h)^2}{x^2(x + h)^2}$

$\qquad\qquad = \dfrac{x^2 - (x + h)^2}{hx^2(x + h)^2}$

$\qquad\qquad = \dfrac{x^2 - (x^2 + 2xh + h^2)}{hx^2(x + h)^2}$

$\qquad\qquad = \dfrac{-h(2x + h)}{hx^2(x + h)^2}$

$\qquad\qquad = -\dfrac{2x + h}{x^2(x + h)^2}, \quad h \neq 0$

87. $\dfrac{\left(\sqrt{x} - \dfrac{1}{2\sqrt{x}}\right)}{\sqrt{x}} = \dfrac{\left(\sqrt{x} - \dfrac{1}{2\sqrt{x}}\right)}{\sqrt{x}} \cdot \dfrac{2\sqrt{x}}{2\sqrt{x}} = \dfrac{2x - 1}{2x}, \quad x > 0$

89. $\dfrac{3x^{1/3} - x^{-2/3}}{3x^{-2/3}} = \dfrac{3x^{1/3} - x^{-2/3}}{3x^{-2/3}} \cdot \dfrac{x^{2/3}}{x^{2/3}} = \dfrac{3x^1 - x^0}{3x^0} = \dfrac{3x - 1}{3}, \quad x \neq 0$

91. $\dfrac{x(x+1)^{-3/4} - (x+1)^{1/4}}{x^2} = \dfrac{x(x+1)^{-3/4} - (x+1)^{1/4}}{x^2} \cdot \dfrac{(x+1)^{3/4}}{(x+1)^{3/4}}$

$= \dfrac{x(x+1)^0 - (x+1)^1}{x^2(x+1)^{3/4}} = \dfrac{x - x - 1}{x^2(x+1)^{3/4}} = -\dfrac{1}{x^2(x+1)^{3/4}}$

93. $\dfrac{\sqrt{x+2} - \sqrt{x}}{2} = \dfrac{\sqrt{x+2} - \sqrt{x}}{2} \cdot \dfrac{\sqrt{x+2} + \sqrt{x}}{\sqrt{x+2} + \sqrt{x}}$

$= \dfrac{(x+2) - x}{2(\sqrt{x+2} + \sqrt{x})}$

$= \dfrac{2}{2(\sqrt{x+2} + \sqrt{x})}$

$= \dfrac{1}{\sqrt{x+2} + \sqrt{x}}$

95. (a) $\dfrac{1}{16}$ minute

(b) $x\left(\dfrac{1}{16}\right) = \dfrac{x}{16}$ minutes

(c) $\dfrac{60}{16} = \dfrac{15}{4}$ minutes

97. Average $= \dfrac{\left(\dfrac{x}{3} + \dfrac{2x}{5}\right)}{2} = \dfrac{\left(\dfrac{x}{3} + \dfrac{2x}{5}\right)}{2} \cdot \dfrac{15}{15} = \dfrac{5x + 6x}{30} = \dfrac{11x}{30}$

99. (a) $r = \dfrac{\left(\dfrac{24[48(400) - 16,000]}{48}\right)}{\left[16,000 + \dfrac{48(400)}{12}\right]} \approx 0.0909 = 9.09\%$

(b) $r = \dfrac{\left[\dfrac{24(NM - P)}{N}\right]}{\left(P + \dfrac{NM}{12}\right)} = \dfrac{24(NM - P)}{N} \cdot \dfrac{12}{12P + NM}$

$= \dfrac{288(NM - P)}{N(12P + NM)}$

$r = \dfrac{288[48(400) - 16,000]}{48[12(16,000) + 48(400)]} \approx 0.0909 = 9.09\%$

101. $T = 10\left(\dfrac{4t^2 + 16t + 75}{t^2 + 4t + 10}\right)$

(a)

t	0	2	4	6	8	10
T	75°	55.9°	48.3°	45°	43.3°	42.3°

t	12	14	16	18	20	22
T	41.7°	41.3°	41.1°	40.9°	40.7°	40.6°

(b) T is approaching 40°.

103. $\dfrac{x\left(\dfrac{x}{3}\right)}{x(x+3)} = \dfrac{\dfrac{x}{3}}{x+3} \cdot \dfrac{3}{3} = \dfrac{x}{3(x+3)}$

105. $\dfrac{7(x+1)}{6(x+1)(x^2 + 5x)} = \dfrac{7}{6x(x+5)}$

107. False. In order for the simplified expression to be equivalent to the original expression, the domain of the simplified expression needs to be restricted. If n is even, $x \neq -1, 1$. If n is odd, $x \neq 1$.

109. False. The least common denominator of several fractions consists of the product of all *prime factors* in the denominators, with each factor given the highest power of its occurrence in any denominator.

111. $\dfrac{ax - b}{b - ax} = \dfrac{ax - b}{-(ax - b)} = -1$ if $x \neq \dfrac{b}{a}$

It is true as long as $x \neq \dfrac{b}{a}$, so it is *not true* for *all* nonzero real numbers a and b.

Section P.5   Solving Equations

- You should know how to solve linear equations.

  $ax + b = 0$

- An identity is an equation whose solution consists of every real number in its domain.

- To solve an equation you can:

  (a) Add or subtract the same quantity from both sides.

  (b) Multiply or divide both sides by the same nonzero quantity.

- To solve an equation that can be simplified to a linear equation:

  (a) Remove all symbols of grouping and all fractions.

  (b) Combine like terms.

  (c) Solve by algebra.

  (d) Check the answer.

- A "solution" that does not satisfy the original equation is called an extraneous solution.

- You should be able to solve a quadratic equation by factoring, if possible.

- You should be able to solve a quadratic equation of the form $u^2 = d$ by extracting square roots.

- You should be able to solve a quadratic equation by completing the square.

- You should know and be able to use the Quadratic Formula: For $ax^2 + bx + c = 0, a \neq 0$,

$$x = \frac{-b \pm \sqrt{b^2 - 4ac}}{2a}.$$

- You should be able to solve polynomials of higher degree by factoring.

- For equations involving radicals or fractional powers, raise both sides to the same power.

- For equations with fractions, multiply both sides by the least common denominator to clear the fractions.

- For equations involving absolute value, remember that the expression inside the absolute value can be positive or negative.

Solutions to Odd-Numbered Exercises

1. $2(x - 1) = 2x - 2$ is an *identity* by the Distributive Property. It is true for all real values of x.

3. $-6(x - 3) + 5 = -2x + 10$ is *conditional*. There are real values of x for which the equation is not true.

5. $4(x + 1) - 2x = 4x + 4 - 2x = 2x + 4 = 2(x + 2)$

   This is an *identity* by simplification. It is true for all real values of x.

7. $x^2 - 8x + 5 = (x - 4)^2 - 11$ is an *identity* since $(x - 4)^2 - 11 = x^2 - 8x + 16 - 11 = x^2 - 8x + 5$.

9. $3 + \dfrac{1}{x + 1} = \dfrac{4x}{x + 1}$ is *conditional*. There are real values of x for which the equation is not true.

11.
$$x + 11 = 15$$
$$x + 11 - 11 = 15 - 11$$
$$x = 4$$

13.
$$7 - 2x = 25$$
$$7 - 7 - 2x = 25 - 7$$
$$-2x = 18$$
$$\frac{-2x}{-2} = \frac{18}{-2}$$
$$x = -9$$

15.
$$8x - 5 = 3x + 20$$
$$8x - 3x - 5 = 3x - 3x + 20$$
$$5x - 5 = 20$$
$$5x - 5 + 5 = 20 + 5$$
$$5x = 25$$
$$\frac{5x}{5} = \frac{25}{5}$$
$$x = 5$$

17.
$$2(x + 5) - 7 = 3(x - 2)$$
$$2x + 10 - 7 = 3x - 6$$
$$2x + 3 = 3x - 6$$
$$-x = -9$$
$$x = 9$$

19.
$$x - 3(2x + 3) = 8 - 5x$$
$$x - 6x - 9 = 8 - 5x$$
$$-5x - 9 = 8 - 5x$$
$$-5x + 5x - 9 = 8 - 5x + 5x$$
$$-9 \neq 8$$

No solution

21.
$$\frac{5x}{4} + \frac{1}{2} = x - \frac{1}{2}$$
$$4\left(\frac{5x}{4}\right) + 4\left(\frac{1}{2}\right) = 4(x) - 4\left(\frac{1}{2}\right)$$
$$5x + 2 = 4x - 2$$
$$x = -4$$

23.
$$\tfrac{3}{2}(z + 5) - \tfrac{1}{4}(z + 24) = 0$$
$$4\left(\tfrac{3}{2}\right)(z + 5) - 4\left(\tfrac{1}{4}\right)(z + 24) = 4(0)$$
$$6(z + 5) - (z + 24) = 0$$
$$6z + 30 - z - 24 = 0$$
$$5z = -6$$
$$z = -\tfrac{6}{5}$$

25.
$$0.25x + 0.75(10 - x) = 3$$
$$4(0.25x) + 4(0.75)(10 - x) = 4(3)$$
$$x + 3(10 - x) = 12$$
$$x + 30 - 3x = 12$$
$$-2x = -18$$
$$x = 9$$

27.
$$x + 8 = 2(x - 2) - x$$
$$x + 8 = 2x - 4 - x$$
$$x + 8 = x - 4$$
$$8 \neq -4$$

No solution

29.
$$\frac{100 - 4u}{3} = \frac{5u + 6}{4} + 6$$
$$12\left(\frac{100 - 4u}{3}\right) = 12\left(\frac{5u + 6}{4}\right) + 12(6)$$
$$4(100 - 4u) = 3(5u + 6) + 72$$
$$400 - 16u = 15u + 18 + 72$$
$$-31u = -310$$
$$u = 10$$

31. $\dfrac{5x - 4}{5x + 4} = \dfrac{2}{3}$

$3(5x - 4) = 2(5x + 4)$

$15x - 12 = 10x + 8$

$5x = 20$

$x = 4$

33. $10 - \dfrac{13}{x} = 4 + \dfrac{5}{x}$

$\dfrac{10x - 13}{x} = \dfrac{4x + 5}{x}$

$10x - 13 = 4x + 5$

$6x = 18$

$x = 3$

35. $\dfrac{x}{x + 4} + \dfrac{4}{x + 4} + 2 = 0$

$\dfrac{x + 4}{x + 4} + 2 = 0$

$1 + 2 = 0$

$3 \neq 0$

Contradiction : no solution
The variable is divided out.

37. $\dfrac{1}{x} + \dfrac{2}{x - 5} = 0$ Multiply both sides by $x(x - 5)$

$1(x - 5) + 2x = 0$

$3x - 5 = 0$

$3x = 5$

$x = \dfrac{5}{3}$

39. $\dfrac{2}{(x - 4)(x - 2)} = \dfrac{1}{x - 4} + \dfrac{2}{x - 2}$ Multiply both sides by $(x - 4)(x - 2)$.

$2 = 1(x - 2) + 2(x - 4)$

$2 = x - 2 + 2x - 8$

$2 = 3x - 10$

$12 = 3x$

$4 = x$

A check reveals that $x = 4$ is an extraneous solution–it makes the denominator zero. There is no real solution.

41. $\dfrac{1}{x - 3} + \dfrac{1}{x + 3} = \dfrac{10}{x^2 - 9}$

$\dfrac{(x + 3) + (x - 3)}{x^2 - 9} = \dfrac{10}{x^2 - 9}$

$2x = 10$

$x = 5$

43. $\dfrac{3}{x^2 - 3x} + \dfrac{4}{x} = \dfrac{1}{x - 3}$ Multiply both sides by $x(x - 3)$.

$3 + 4(x - 3) = x$

$3 + 4x - 12 = x$

$3x = 9$

$x = 3$

A check reveals that $x = 3$ is an extraneous solution, so there is no solution.

45. $(x + 2)^2 + 5 = (x + 3)^2$

$x^2 + 4x + 4 + 5 = x^2 + 6x + 9$

$4x + 9 = 6x + 9$

$-2x = 0$

$x = 0$

47. $(x + 2)^2 - x^2 = 4(x + 1)$

$x^2 + 4x + 4 - x^2 = 4x + 4$

$4 = 4$

The equation is an identity; every real number is a solution.

49. $2x^2 = 3 - 8x$

General form: $2x^2 + 8x - 3 = 0$

51. $(x - 3)^2 = 3$

$x^2 - 6x + 9 = 3$

General form: $x^2 - 6x + 6 = 0$

53. $\frac{1}{5}(3x^2 - 10) = 18x$

$3x^2 - 10 = 90x$

General form: $3x^2 - 90x - 10 = 0$

55. $6x^2 + 3x = 0$

$3x(2x + 1) = 0$

$3x = 0$ or $2x + 1 = 0$

$x = 0$ or $x = -\frac{1}{2}$

57. $x^2 - 2x - 8 = 0$

$(x - 4)(x + 2) = 0$

$x - 4 = 0$ or $x + 2 = 0$

$x = 4$ or $x = -2$

59. $x^2 + 10x + 25 = 0$

$(x + 5)(x + 5) = 0$

$x + 5 = 0$

$x = -5$

61. $3 + 5x - 2x^2 = 0$

$(3 - x)(1 + 2x) = 0$

$3 - x = 0$ or $1 + 2x = 0$

$x = 3$ or $x = -\frac{1}{2}$

63. $x^2 + 4x = 12$

$x^2 + 4x - 12 = 0$

$(x + 6)(x - 2) = 0$

$x + 6 = 0$ or $x - 2 = 0$

$x = -6$ or $x = 2$

65. $\frac{3}{4}x^2 + 8x + 20 = 0$

$4\left(\frac{3}{4}x^2 + 8x + 20\right) = 4(0)$

$3x^2 + 32x + 80 = 0$

$(3x + 20)(x + 4) = 0$

$3x + 20 = 0$ or $x + 4 = 0$

$x = -\frac{20}{3}$ or $x = -4$

67. $x^2 + 2ax + a^2 = 0$

$(x + a)^2 = 0$

$x + a = 0$

$x = -a$

69. $x^2 = 49$

$x = \pm\sqrt{49}$

$= \pm 7$

$= \pm 7.00$

71. $x^2 = 11$

$x = \pm\sqrt{11}$

$x \approx \pm 3.32$

73. $3x^2 = 81$

$x^2 = 27$

$x = \pm\sqrt{27} = \pm 3\sqrt{3}$

$x \approx \pm 5.20$

75. $(x - 12)^2 = 16$

$x - 12 = \pm\sqrt{16}$

$x = 12 \pm 4$

$x = 16$ or $x = 8$

$x = 16.00$ or $x = 8.00$

77. $(x + 2)^2 = 14$

$\quad x + 2 = \pm\sqrt{14}$

$\quad\quad x = -2 \pm \sqrt{14}$

$\quad\quad x \approx 1.74 \quad \text{or} \quad x \approx -5.74$

79. $(2x - 1)^2 = 18$

$\quad 2x - 1 = \pm\sqrt{18}$

$\quad\quad 2x = 1 \pm 3\sqrt{2}$

$\quad\quad x = \dfrac{1 \pm 3\sqrt{2}}{2}$

$\quad x \approx 2.62 \quad \text{or} \quad x \approx -1.62$

81. $(x - 7)^2 = (x + 3)^2$

$\quad x - 7 = \pm(x + 3)$

$x - 7 = x + 3 \quad \text{or} \quad x - 7 = -x - 3$

$-7 \neq 3 \quad\quad\quad\quad\quad 2x = 4$

No solution $\quad\quad\quad\quad x = 2 = 2.00$

83. $\quad x^2 - 2x = 0$

$x^2 - 2x + 1 = 0 + 1$

$\quad (x - 1)^2 = 1$

$\quad x - 1 = \pm\sqrt{1}$

$\quad\quad x = 1 \pm 1$

$\quad\quad x = 0 \quad \text{or} \quad x = 2$

85. $x^2 + 4x - 32 = 0$

$\quad x^2 + 4x = 32$

$x^2 + 4x + 2^2 = 32 + 2^2$

$\quad (x + 2)^2 = 36$

$\quad x + 2 = \pm\sqrt{36}$

$\quad\quad x = -2 \pm 6$

$\quad\quad x = 4 \quad \text{or} \quad x = -8$

87. $x^2 + 6x + 2 = 0$

$\quad x^2 + 6x = -2$

$x^2 + 6x + 3^2 = -2 + 3^2$

$\quad (x + 3)^2 = 7$

$\quad x + 3 = \pm\sqrt{7}$

$\quad\quad x = -3 \pm \sqrt{7}$

89. $\quad 9x^2 - 18x = -3$

$\quad x^2 - 2x = -\dfrac{1}{3}$

$x^2 - 2x + 1 = -\dfrac{1}{3} + 1$

$\quad (x - 1)^2 = \dfrac{2}{3}$

$\quad x - 1 = \pm\sqrt{\dfrac{2}{3}}$

$\quad\quad x = 1 \pm \sqrt{\dfrac{6}{9}}$

$\quad\quad x = 1 \pm \dfrac{\sqrt{6}}{3}$

91. $\quad 8 + 4x - x^2 = 0$

$\quad -x^2 + 4x + 8 = 0$

$\quad x^2 - 4x - 8 = 0$

$\quad\quad x^2 - 4x = 8$

$x^2 - 4x + 2^2 = 8 + 2^2$

$\quad (x - 2)^2 = 12$

$\quad x - 2 = \pm\sqrt{12}$

$\quad\quad x = 2 \pm 2\sqrt{3}$

93. $2x^2 + x - 1 = 0$

$$x = \frac{-b \pm \sqrt{b^2 - 4ac}}{2a}$$

$$= \frac{-1 \pm \sqrt{1^2 - 4(2)(-1)}}{2(2)}$$

$$= \frac{-1 \pm 3}{4} = \frac{1}{2}, -1$$

95. $16x^2 + 8x - 3 = 0$

$$x = \frac{-b \pm \sqrt{b^2 - 4ac}}{2a}$$

$$= \frac{-8 \pm \sqrt{8^2 - 4(16)(-3)}}{2(16)}$$

$$= \frac{-8 \pm 16}{32} = \frac{1}{4}, -\frac{3}{4}$$

97. $2 + 2x - x^2 = 0$

$$x = \frac{-b \pm \sqrt{b^2 - 4ac}}{2a}$$

$$= \frac{-2 \pm \sqrt{2^2 - 4(-1)(2)}}{2(-1)}$$

$$= \frac{-2 \pm 2\sqrt{3}}{-2} = 1 \pm \sqrt{3}$$

99. $x^2 + 14x + 44 = 0$

$$x = \frac{-b \pm \sqrt{b^2 - 4ac}}{2a}$$

$$= \frac{-14 \pm \sqrt{14^2 - 4(1)(44)}}{2(1)}$$

$$= \frac{-14 \pm 2\sqrt{5}}{2} = -7 \pm \sqrt{5}$$

101. $x^2 + 8x - 4 = 0$

$$x = \frac{-b \pm \sqrt{b^2 - 4ac}}{2a}$$

$$= \frac{-8 \pm \sqrt{8^2 - 4(1)(-4)}}{2(1)}$$

$$= \frac{-8 \pm 4\sqrt{5}}{2}$$

$$= -4 \pm 2\sqrt{5}$$

103.
$$12x - 9x^2 = -3$$
$$-9x^2 + 12x + 3 = 0$$

$$x = \frac{-b \pm \sqrt{b^2 - 4ac}}{2a}$$

$$= \frac{-12 \pm \sqrt{12^2 - 4(-9)(3)}}{2(-9)}$$

$$= \frac{-12 \pm 6\sqrt{7}}{-18} = \frac{2}{3} \pm \frac{\sqrt{7}}{3}$$

105. $9x^2 + 24x + 16 = 0$

$$x = \frac{-b \pm \sqrt{b^2 - 4ac}}{2a}$$

$$= \frac{-24 \pm \sqrt{24^2 - 4(9)(16)}}{2(9)}$$

$$= \frac{-24 \pm 0}{18}$$

$$= -\frac{4}{3}$$

107. $4x^2 + 4x = 7$

$$4x^2 + 4x - 7 = 0$$
$$x = \frac{-b \pm \sqrt{b^2 - 4ac}}{2a}$$

$$= \frac{-4 \pm \sqrt{4^2 - 4(4)(-7)}}{2(4)}$$

$$= \frac{-4 \pm 8\sqrt{2}}{8} = -\frac{1}{2} \pm \sqrt{2}$$

109.
$$28x - 49x^2 = 4$$
$$-49x^2 + 28x - 4 = 0$$

$$x = \frac{-b \pm \sqrt{b^2 - 4ac}}{2a}$$

$$= \frac{-28 \pm \sqrt{28^2 - 4(-49)(-4)}}{2(-49)}$$

$$= \frac{-28 \pm 0}{-98} = \frac{2}{7}$$

111.
$$8t = 5 + 2t^2$$
$$-2t^2 + 8t - 5 = 0$$

$$t = \frac{-b \pm \sqrt{b^2 - 4ac}}{2a}$$

$$= \frac{-8 \pm \sqrt{8^2 - 4(-2)(-5)}}{2(-2)}$$

$$= \frac{-8 \pm 2\sqrt{6}}{-4} = 2 \pm \frac{\sqrt{6}}{2}$$

113.
$$(y - 5)^2 = 2y$$
$$y^2 - 12y + 25 = 0$$
$$x = \frac{-b \pm \sqrt{b^2 - 4ac}}{2a}$$
$$= \frac{-(-12) \pm \sqrt{(-12)^2 - 4(1)(25)}}{2(1)}$$
$$= \frac{12 \pm 2\sqrt{11}}{2} = 6 \pm \sqrt{11}$$

115. $\frac{1}{2}x^2 + \frac{3}{8}x = 2$
$$4x^2 + 3x = 16$$
$$4x^2 + 3x - 16 = 0$$
$$x = \frac{-b \pm \sqrt{b^2 - 4ac}}{2a}$$
$$= \frac{-3 \pm \sqrt{3^2 - 4(4)(-16)}}{2(4)}$$
$$= \frac{-3 \pm \sqrt{265}}{8} = -\frac{3}{8} \pm \frac{\sqrt{265}}{8}$$

117. $5.1x^2 - 1.7x - 3.2 = 0$
$$x = \frac{1.7 \pm \sqrt{(-1.7)^2 - 4(5.1)(-3.2)}}{2(5.1)}$$
$$x \approx 0.976, \, -0.643$$

119. $-0.067x^2 - 0.852x + 1.277 = 0$
$$x = \frac{-(-0.852) \pm \sqrt{(-0.852)^2 - 4(-0.067)(1.277)}}{2(-0.067)}$$
$$x \approx -14.071, \, 1.355$$

121. $422x^2 - 506x - 347 = 0$
$$x = \frac{506 \pm \sqrt{(-506)^2 - 4(422)(-347)}}{2(422)}$$
$$x \approx 1.687, \, -0.488$$

123. $12.67x^2 + 31.55x + 8.09 = 0$
$$x = \frac{-31.55 \pm \sqrt{(31.55)^2 - 4(12.67)(8.09)}}{2(12.67)}$$
$$x \approx -2.200, \, -0.290$$

125. $x^2 - 2x - 1 = 0$
$$x^2 - 2x = 1$$
$$x^2 - 2x + 1^2 = 1 + 1^2$$
$$(x - 1)^2 = 2$$
$$x - 1 = \pm\sqrt{2}$$
$$x = 1 \pm \sqrt{2}$$

127. $(x + 3)^2 = 81$
$$x + 3 = \pm 9$$
$$x + 3 = 9 \quad \text{or} \quad x + 3 = -9$$
$$x = 6 \quad \text{or} \qquad x = -12$$

129. $x^2 - x - \frac{11}{4} = 0$ Complete the Square
$$x^2 - x = \frac{11}{4}$$
$$x^2 - x + \left(\frac{1}{2}\right)^2 = \frac{11}{4} + \left(\frac{1}{2}\right)^2$$
$$\left(x - \frac{1}{2}\right)^2 = \frac{12}{4}$$
$$x - \frac{1}{2} = \pm\sqrt{\frac{12}{4}}$$
$$x = \frac{1}{2} \pm \sqrt{3}$$

131. $(x + 1)^2 = x^2$ Extract Square Roots
$$x^2 = (x + 1)^2$$
$$x = \pm(x + 1)$$
For $x = +(x + 1)$:
$$0 \neq 1 \quad \text{No solution}$$
For $x = -(x + 1)$:
$$2x = -1$$
$$x = -\frac{1}{2}$$

133. $3x + 4 = 2x^2 - 7$ Quadratic Formula

$$0 = 2x^2 - 3x - 11$$

$$x = \frac{-(-3) \pm \sqrt{(-3)^2 - 4(2)(-11)}}{2(2)}$$

$$= \frac{3 \pm \sqrt{97}}{4} = \frac{3}{4} \pm \frac{\sqrt{97}}{4}$$

135. $4x^4 - 18x^2 = 0$

$$2x^2(2x^2 - 9) = 0$$

$$2x^2 = 0 \implies x = 0$$

$$2x^2 - 9 = 0 \implies x = \pm\frac{3\sqrt{2}}{2}$$

137. $x^4 - 81 = 0$

$$(x^2 + 9)(x + 3)(x - 3) = 0$$

$$x^2 + 9 = 0 \implies x = \pm 3i$$

$$x + 3 = 0 \implies x = -3$$

$$x - 3 = 0 \implies x = 3$$

139. $x^3 + 216 = 0$

$$x^3 + 6^3 = 0$$

$$(x + 6)(x^2 - 6x + 36) = 0$$

$$x + 6 = 0 \implies x = -6$$

$$x^2 - 6x + 36 = 0 \implies x = 3 \pm 3\sqrt{3}i$$

(By completing the square)

141. $5x^3 + 30x^2 + 45x = 0$

$$5x(x^2 + 6x + 9) = 0$$

$$5x(x + 3)^2 = 0$$

$$5x = 0 \implies x = 0$$

$$x + 3 = 0 \implies x = -3$$

143. $x^3 - 3x^2 - x + 3 = 0$

$$x^2(x - 3) - (x - 3) = 0$$

$$(x - 3)(x^2 - 1) = 0$$

$$(x - 3)(x + 1)(x - 1) = 0$$

$$x - 3 = 0 \implies x = 3$$

$$x + 1 = 0 \implies x = -1$$

$$x - 1 = 0 \implies x = 1$$

145. $x^4 - x^3 + x - 1 = 0$

$$x^3(x - 1) + (x - 1) = 0$$

$$(x - 1)(x^3 + 1) = 0$$

$$(x - 1)(x + 1)(x^2 - x + 1) = 0$$

$$x - 1 = 0 \implies x = 1$$

$$x + 1 = 0 \implies x = -1$$

$$x^2 - x + 1 = 0 \implies x = \frac{1}{2} \pm \frac{\sqrt{3}}{2}i \quad \text{(By the Quadratic Formula)}$$

147. $x^4 - 4x^2 + 3 = 0$

$$(x^2 - 3)(x^2 - 1) = 0$$

$$\left(x + \sqrt{3}\right)\left(x - \sqrt{3}\right)(x + 1)(x - 1) = 0$$

$$x + \sqrt{3} = 0 \implies x = -\sqrt{3}$$

$$x - \sqrt{3} = 0 \implies x = \sqrt{3}$$

$$x + 1 = 0 \implies x = -1$$

$$x - 1 = 0 \implies x = 1$$

149. $4x^4 - 65x^2 + 16 = 0$

$$(4x^2 - 1)(x^2 - 16) = 0$$

$$(2x + 1)(2x - 1)(x + 4)(x - 4) = 0$$

$$2x + 1 = 0 \implies x = -\tfrac{1}{2}$$

$$2x - 1 = 0 \implies x = \tfrac{1}{2}$$

$$x + 4 = 0 \implies x = -4$$

$$x - 4 = 0 \implies x = 4$$

151.
$$x^6 + 7x^3 - 8 = 0$$
$$(x^3 + 8)(x^3 - 1) = 0$$
$$(x + 2)(x^2 - 2x + 4)(x - 1)(x^2 + x + 1) = 0$$
$$x + 2 = 0 \implies x = -2$$
$$x^2 - 2x + 4 = 0 \implies x = 1 \pm \sqrt{3}i \text{ (By the Quadratic Formula)}$$
$$x - 1 = 0 \implies x = 1$$
$$x^2 + x + 1 = 0 \implies x = -\frac{1}{2} \pm \frac{\sqrt{3}}{2}i \text{ (By the Quadratic Formula)}$$

153. $\sqrt{2x} - 10 = 0$
$$\sqrt{2x} = 10$$
$$2x = 100$$
$$x = 50$$

155. $\sqrt{x - 10} - 4 = 0$
$$\sqrt{x - 10} = 4$$
$$x - 10 = 16$$
$$x = 26$$

157. $\sqrt[3]{2x + 5} + 3 = 0$
$$\sqrt[3]{2x + 5} = -3$$
$$2x + 5 = -27$$
$$2x = -32$$
$$x = -16$$

159. $-\sqrt{26 - 11x} + 4 = x$
$$4 - x = \sqrt{26 - 11x}$$
$$16 - 8x + x^2 = 26 - 11x$$
$$x^2 + 3x - 10 = 0$$
$$(x + 5)(x - 2) = 0$$
$$x + 5 = 0 \implies x = -5$$
$$x - 2 = 0 \implies x = 2$$

161. $\sqrt{x + 1} = \sqrt{3x + 1}$
$$x + 1 = 3x + 1$$
$$-2x = 0$$
$$x = 0$$

163. $(x - 5)^{3/2} = 8$
$$(x - 5)^3 = 8^2$$
$$x - 5 = 8^{2/3}$$
$$x = 5 + 4$$
$$x = 9$$

165. $(x + 3)^{2/3} = 8$
$$(x + 3)^2 = 8^3$$
$$x + 3 = \pm\sqrt{8^3}$$
$$x + 3 = \pm\sqrt{512}$$
$$x = -3 \pm 16\sqrt{2}$$

167. $(x^2 - 5)^{3/2} = 27$
$$x^2 - 5 = 27^{2/3}$$
$$x^2 = 5 + 9$$
$$x^2 = 14$$
$$x = \pm\sqrt{14}$$

169. $3x(x - 1)^{1/2} + 2(x - 1)^{3/2} = 0$
$$(x - 1)^{1/2}[3x + 2(x - 1)] = 0$$
$$(x - 1)^{1/2}(5x - 2) = 0$$
$$(x - 1)^{1/2} = 0 \implies x - 1 = 0 \implies x = 1$$
$$5x - 2 = 0 \implies x = \tfrac{2}{5} \text{ which is extraneous.}$$

171. $\dfrac{20 - x}{x} = x$

$$20 - x = x^2$$

$$0 = x^2 + x - 20$$

$$0 = (x + 5)(x - 4)$$

$$x + 5 = 0 \implies x = -5$$

$$x - 4 = 0 \implies x = 4$$

173. $\dfrac{1}{x} - \dfrac{1}{x + 1} = 3$

$$x(x + 1)\dfrac{1}{x} - x(x + 1)\dfrac{1}{x + 1} = x(x + 1)(3)$$

$$x + 1 - x = 3x(x + 1)$$

$$1 = 3x^2 + 3x$$

$$0 = 3x^2 + 3x - 1; \ a = 3, \ b = 3, \ c = -1$$

$$x = \dfrac{-3 \pm \sqrt{(3)^2 - 4(3)(-1)}}{2(3)} = \dfrac{-3 \pm \sqrt{21}}{6}$$

175. $x = \dfrac{3}{x} + \dfrac{1}{2}$

$$(2x)(x) = (2x)\left(\dfrac{3}{x}\right) + (2x)\left(\dfrac{1}{2}\right)$$

$$2x^2 = 6 + x$$

$$2x^2 - x - 6 = 0$$

$$(2x + 3)(x - 2) = 0$$

$$2x + 3 = 0 \implies x = -\dfrac{3}{2}$$

$$x - 2 = 0 \implies x = 2$$

177. $\dfrac{4}{x + 1} - \dfrac{3}{x + 2} = 1$

$$4(x + 2) - 3(x + 1) = (x + 1)(x + 2), x \neq -2, -1$$

$$4x + 8 - 3x - 3 = x^2 + 3x + 2$$

$$x^2 + 2x - 3 = 0$$

$$(x - 1)(x + 3) = 0$$

$$x - 1 = 0 \implies x = 1$$

$$x + 3 = 0 \implies x = -3$$

179. $|2x - 1| = 5$

$$2x - 1 = 5 \implies x = 3$$

$$-(2x - 1) = 5 \implies x = -2$$

181. $|x| = x^2 + x - 3$

$$x = x^2 + x - 3 \quad \text{OR} \qquad -x = x^2 + x - 3$$

$$x^2 - 3 = 0 \qquad\qquad x^2 + 2x - 3 = 0$$

$$x = \pm\sqrt{3} \qquad\qquad (x - 1)(x + 3) = 0$$

$$x - 1 = 0 \implies x = 1$$

$$x + 3 = 0 \implies x = -3$$

Only $x = \sqrt{3}$, and $x = -3$ are solutions to the original equation. $x = -\sqrt{3}$ and $x = 1$ are extraneous.

183.
$$|x + 1| = x^2 - 5$$

$x + 1 = x^2 - 5$	OR $\quad -(x + 1) = x^2 - 5$
$x^2 - x - 6 = 0$	$-x - 1 = x^2 - 5$
$(x - 3)(x + 2) = 0$	$x^2 + x - 4 = 0$
$x - 3 = 0 \Rightarrow x = 3$	$x = \dfrac{-1 \pm \sqrt{17}}{2}$
$x + 2 = 0 \Rightarrow x = -2$	

Only $x = 3$ and $x = \dfrac{-1 - \sqrt{17}}{2}$ are solutions to the original equation. $x = -2$ and $x = \dfrac{-1 + \sqrt{17}}{2}$ are extraneous.

185.
$$16 = 0.432x - 10.44$$
$$26.44 = 0.432x$$
$$\frac{26.44}{0.432} = x$$
$$x \approx 61.2 \text{ inches}$$

187. $10,000 = 0.32m + 2500$
$$7,500 = 0.32m$$
$$\frac{7,500}{0.32} = m$$
$$m = 23,437.5 \text{ miles}$$

189. (a)
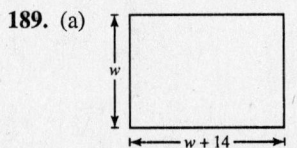

(b) $\quad w(w + 14) = 1632$

$\quad w^2 + 14w - 1632 = 0$

(c) $(w - 34)(w + 48) = 0$

$\quad w = 34 \quad \text{or} \quad w = -48 \text{ Extraneous}$

$\quad l = 34 + 14 = 48$

width: 34 feet

length: 48 feet

191.
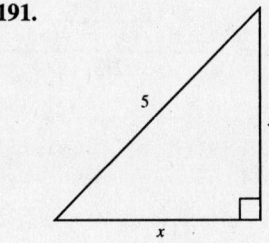

$$x^2 + x^2 = 5^2$$
$$2x^2 = 25$$
$$x^2 = \frac{25}{2}$$
$$x = \sqrt{\frac{25}{2}} = \frac{5}{\sqrt{2}} = \frac{5\sqrt{2}}{2} \approx 3.54 \text{ centimeters}$$

193. Let $r =$ speed of the eastbound plane and $r + 50 =$ speed of the northbound plane. After 3 hours the eastbound plane has traveled $3r$ miles and the northbound plane has traveled $3(r + 50)$ miles.

$$[3r^2] + [3(r + 50)]^2 = 2440^2$$
$$9r^2 + 9(r^2 + 100r + 2500) = 5,953,600$$
$$18r^2 + 900r - 5,931,100 = 0$$

By the Quadratic Formula, $r \approx 550$ (discard the negative value of r as extraneous).

Speed of the eastbound plane: 550 miles per hour

Speed of the northbound plane: 600 miles per hour

195. $x(20 - 0.0002x) = 500,000$

$20x - 0.0002x^2 = 500,000$

$0 = 0.0002x^2 - 20x + 500,000$

By the Quadratic Formula, $x = 50,000$ units.

197. $240 = 75.82 - 2.11x + 43.51\sqrt{x}$

$2.11x - 43.51\sqrt{x} + 164.18 = 0$

Let $u = \sqrt{x}$, then we have

$2.11u^2 - 43.51u + 164.18 = 0$

By the Quadratic Formula, $u \approx 15.6484$ or $u \approx 4.9724$.

Since $5 \le x \le 40$, we discard the larger value of u.

$\sqrt{x} \approx 4.9724$

$x \approx 24.725$ pounds per square inch

199. False. The product must equal **zero** for the Zero Factor Property to be used.

201. The student should have subtracted $15x$ from both sides so that the equation is equal to zero. By factoring out an x, there are **two** solutions.

$x = 0$ or $x = 6$

203. Remove symbols of grouping, combine like terms, reduce fractions.

Add (or subtract) the same quantity to (from) both sides of the equation.

Multiply (or divide) both sides of the equation by the same nonzero quantity.

Interchange the two sides of the equation.

205. (a) $ax^2 + bx = 0,\ a \neq 0, b \neq 0$

$x(ax + b) = 0$

$x = 0$ or $ax + b = 0$

$ax = -b$

$x = -\dfrac{b}{a}$

(b) $ax^2 - ax = 0,\ a \neq 0$

$ax(x - 1) = 0$

$ax = 0$ or $x - 1 = 0$

$x = 0$ $x = 1$

207. Isolate the absolute value by subtracting x from both sides of the equation. The expression inside the absolute value signs can be positive or negative, so two separate equations must be solved.

Section P.6   Solving Inequalities

- You should know the properties of inequalities.

  (a) Transitive: $a < b$ and $b < c$ implies $a < c$.

  (b) Addition: $a < b$ and $c < d$ implies $a + c < b + d$.

  (c) Adding or Subtracting a Constant: $a \pm c < b \pm c$ if $a < b$.

  (d) Multiplying or Dividing a Constant: For $a < b$,

    1. If $c > 0$, then $ac < bc$ and $\dfrac{a}{c} < \dfrac{b}{c}$.

    2. If $c < 0$, then $ac > bc$ and $\dfrac{a}{c} > \dfrac{b}{c}$.

- You should be able to solve absolute value inequalities.

  (a) $|x| < a$ if and only if $-a < x < a$.   (b) $|x| > a$ if and only if $x < -a$ or $x > a$.

- You should be able to solve polynomial inequalities, or rational inequalities.

  (a) Find the critical number.

    1. Values that make the expression zero

    2. Values that make the expression undefined

  (b) Test one value in each interval on the real number line resulting from the critical numbers.

  (c) Determine the solution intervals.

Solutions to Odd-Numbered Exercises

1. Interval: $[-1, 5]$

Inequality: $-1 \le x \le 5$

The interval is bounded.

3. Interval: $(11, \infty)$

Inequality: $11 < x < \infty$

The interval is unbounded.

5. Interval: $(-\infty, -2)$

Inequality: $-\infty < x < -2$

The interval is unbounded.

7. $x < 3$

Matches (b)

9. $-3 < x \le 4$

Matches (d)

11. $|x| < 3 \implies -3 < x < 3$

Matches (e)

13. (a) $x = 3$

$$5(3) - 12 \overset{?}{>} 0$$

$$3 > 0$$

Yes, $x = 3$ is a solution.

(c) $x = \frac{5}{2}$

$$5\left(\tfrac{5}{2}\right) - 12 \overset{?}{>} 0$$

$$\tfrac{1}{2} > 0$$

Yes, $x = \frac{5}{2}$ is a solution.

(b) $x = -3$

$$5(-3) - 12 \overset{?}{>} 0$$

$$-27 \not> 0$$

No, $x = -3$ is not a solution.

(d) $x = \frac{3}{2}$

$$5\left(\tfrac{3}{2}\right) - 12 \overset{?}{>} 0$$

$$-\tfrac{9}{2} \not> 0$$

No, $x = \frac{3}{2}$ is not a solution.

15. (a) $x = 4$

$$0 \overset{?}{<} \frac{4-2}{4} \overset{?}{<} 2$$

$$0 < \frac{1}{2} < 2$$

Yes, $x = 4$ is a solution.

(c) $x = 0$

$$0 \overset{?}{<} \frac{0-2}{4} \overset{?}{<} 2$$

$$0 \not< -\frac{1}{2} < 2$$

No, $x = 0$ is not a solution.

(b) $x = 10$

$$0 \overset{?}{<} \frac{10-2}{4} \overset{?}{<} 2$$

$$0 < 2 \not< 2$$

No, $x = 10$ is not a solution.

(d) $x = \frac{7}{2}$

$$0 \overset{?}{<} \frac{\frac{7}{2}-2}{4} \overset{?}{<} 2$$

$$0 < \frac{3}{8} < 2$$

Yes, $x = \frac{7}{2}$ is a solution.

17. (a) $x = 13$

$$|13 - 10| \overset{?}{\geq} 3$$

$$3 \geq 3$$

Yes, $x = 13$ is a solution.

(c) $x = 14$

$$|14 - 10| \overset{?}{\geq} 3$$

$$4 \geq 3$$

Yes, $x = 14$ is a solution.

(b) $x = -1$

$$|-1 - 10| \overset{?}{\geq} 3$$

$$11 \geq 3$$

Yes, $x = -1$ is a solution.

(d) $x = 9$

$$|9 - 10| \overset{?}{\geq} 3$$

$$1 \not\geq 3$$

No, $x = 9$ is not a solution.

19. $4x < 12$

$$\tfrac{1}{4}(4x) < \tfrac{1}{4}(12)$$

$$x < 3$$

21. $2x > 3$

$$x > \frac{3}{2}$$

23. $x - 5 \geq 7$

$$x \geq 12$$

25. $2x + 7 < 3 + 4x$

$$-2x < -4$$

$$x > 2$$

27. $2x - 1 \geq 1 - 5x$

$$7x \geq 2$$

$$x \geq \frac{2}{7}$$

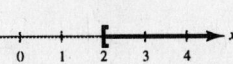

29. $4 - 2x < 3(3 - x)$

$$4 - 2x < 9 - 3x$$

$$x < 5$$

31. $\frac{3}{4}x - 6 \leq x - 7$

$$-\tfrac{1}{4}x \leq -1$$

$$x \geq 4$$

33. $\frac{1}{2}(8x + 1) \geq 3x + \frac{5}{2}$

$$4x + \tfrac{1}{2} \geq 3x + \tfrac{5}{2}$$

$$x \geq 2$$

35. $3.6x + 11 \geq -3.4$

$$3.6x \geq -14.4$$

$$x \geq -4$$

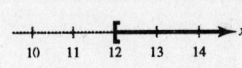

37. $1 < 2x + 3 < 9$

$-2 < 2x < 6$

$-1 < x < 3$

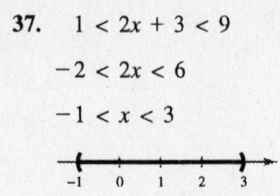

39. $-4 < \dfrac{2x - 3}{3} < 4$

$-12 < 2x - 3 < 12$

$-9 < 2x < 15$

$-\dfrac{9}{2} < x < \dfrac{15}{2}$

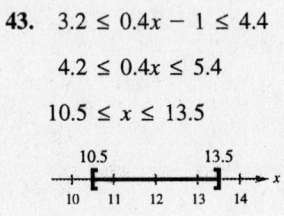

41. $\dfrac{3}{4} > x + 1 > \dfrac{1}{4}$

$-\dfrac{1}{4} > x > -\dfrac{3}{4}$

$-\dfrac{3}{4} < x < -\dfrac{1}{4}$

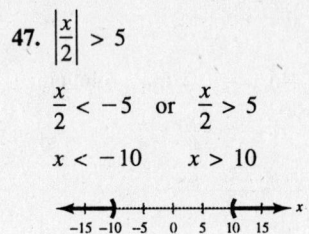

43. $3.2 \le 0.4x - 1 \le 4.4$

$4.2 \le 0.4x \le 5.4$

$10.5 \le x \le 13.5$

45. $|x| < 6$

$-6 < x < 6$

47. $\left|\dfrac{x}{2}\right| > 5$

$\dfrac{x}{2} < -5$ or $\dfrac{x}{2} > 5$

$x < -10$ $x > 10$

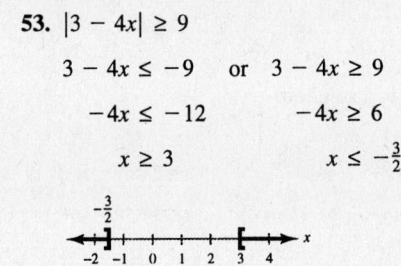

49. $|x - 5| < -1$

No solution. The absolute value of a number cannot be less than a negative number.

51. $|x - 20| \le 6$

$-6 \le x - 20 \le 6$

$14 \le x \le 26$

53. $|3 - 4x| \ge 9$

$3 - 4x \le -9$ or $3 - 4x \ge 9$

$-4x \le -12$ $-4x \ge 6$

$x \ge 3$ $x \le -\dfrac{3}{2}$

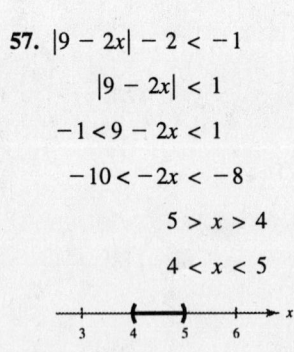

55. $\left|\dfrac{x - 3}{2}\right| \ge 5$

$\dfrac{x - 3}{2} \le -5$ or $\dfrac{x - 3}{2} \ge 5$

$x - 3 \le -10$ $x - 3 \ge 10$

$x \le -7$ $x \ge 13$

57. $|9 - 2x| - 2 < -1$

$|9 - 2x| < 1$

$-1 < 9 - 2x < 1$

$-10 < -2x < -8$

$5 > x > 4$

$4 < x < 5$

59. $2|x + 10| \ge 9$

$|x + 10| \ge \dfrac{9}{2}$

$x + 10 \le -\dfrac{9}{2}$ or $x + 10 \ge \dfrac{9}{2}$

$x \le -\dfrac{29}{2}$ $x \ge -\dfrac{11}{2}$

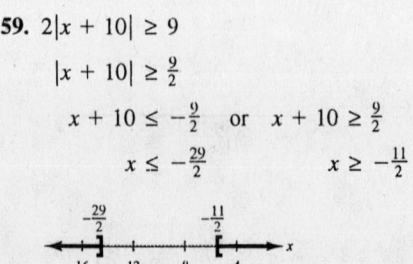

61. $6x > 12$

$x > 2$

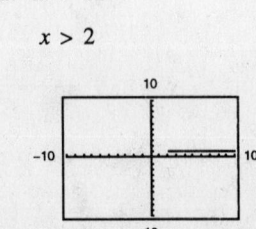

63. $5 - 2x \geq 1$

$-2x \geq -4$

$x \leq 2$

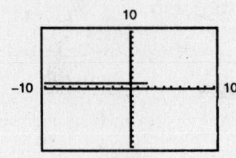

65. $|x - 8| \leq 14$

$-14 \leq x - 8 \leq 14$

$-6 \leq x \leq 22$

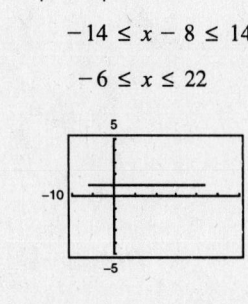

67. $2|x + 7| \geq 13$

$|x + 7| \geq \frac{13}{2}$

$x + 7 \leq -\frac{13}{2}$ or $x + 7 \geq \frac{13}{2}$

$x \leq -\frac{27}{2}$ $x \geq -\frac{1}{2}$

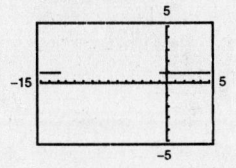

69. $x - 5 \geq 0$

$x \geq 5$

$[5, \infty)$

71. $x + 3 \geq 0$

$x \geq -3$

$[-3, \infty)$

73. $7 - 2x \geq 0$

$-2x \geq -7$

$x \leq \frac{7}{2}$

$\left(-\infty, \frac{7}{2}\right]$

75. $|x - 10| < 8$

All real numbers within 8 units of 10

77. The midpoint of the interval $[-3, 3]$ is 0. The interval represents all real numbers x no more than 3 units from 0.

$|x - 0| \leq 3$

$|x| \leq 3$

79. The graph shows all real numbers at least 3 units from 7.

$|x - 7| \geq 3$

81. All real numbers within 10 units of 12.

$|x - 12| < 10$

83. All real numbers more than 5 units from -3.

$|x - (-3)| > 5$

$|x + 3| > 5$

85. $x^2 - 3 < 0$

(a) $x = 3$

$(3)^2 - 3 \overset{?}{<} 0$

$6 \not< 0$

No, $x = 3$ is not a solution.

(b) $x = 0$

$(0)^2 - 3 \overset{?}{<} 0$

$-3 < 0$

Yes, $x = 0$ is a solution.

(c) $x = \frac{3}{2}$

$\left(\frac{3}{2}\right)^2 - 3 \overset{?}{<} 0$

$-\frac{3}{4} < 0$

Yes, $x = \frac{3}{2}$ is a solution.

(d) $x = -5$

$(-5)^2 - 3 \overset{?}{<} 0$

$22 \not< 0$

No, $x = -5$ is not a solution.

87. $\dfrac{x+2}{x-4} \geq 3$

   (a) $x = 5$

$$\dfrac{5+2}{5-4} \overset{?}{\geq} 3$$

$$7 \geq 3$$

Yes, $x = 5$ is a solution.

   (c) $x = -\dfrac{9}{2}$

$$\dfrac{-\frac{9}{2}+2}{-\frac{9}{2}-4} \overset{?}{\geq} 3$$

$$\dfrac{5}{17} \not\geq 3$$

No, $x = -\dfrac{9}{2}$ is not a solution.

   (b) $x = 4$

$$\dfrac{4+2}{4-4} \overset{?}{\geq} 3$$

$$\dfrac{6}{0} \not\geq 3; \ \dfrac{6}{0} \text{ is undefined}$$

No, $x = 4$ is not a solution.

   (d) $x = \dfrac{9}{2}$

$$\dfrac{\frac{9}{2}+2}{\frac{9}{2}-4} \overset{?}{\geq} 3$$

$$13 \geq 3$$

Yes, $x = \dfrac{9}{2}$ is a solution.

89. $2x^2 - x - 6 = (2x + 3)(x - 2)$

$2x + 3 = 0 \implies x = -\dfrac{3}{2}$

$x - 2 = 0 \implies x = 2$

Critical numbers: $x = -\dfrac{3}{2}, x = 2$

91. $2 + \dfrac{3}{x-5} = \dfrac{2(x-5)+3}{x-5} = \dfrac{2x-7}{x-5}$

$2x - 7 = 0 \implies x = \dfrac{7}{2}$

$x - 5 = 0 \implies x = 5$

Critical numbers: $x = \dfrac{7}{2}, x = 5$

93. $\qquad x^2 \leq 9$

$\qquad x^2 - 9 \leq 0$

$(x + 3)(x - 3) \leq 0$

Critical numbers: $x = \pm 3$

Test intervals: $(-\infty, -3), (-3, 3), (3, \infty)$

Test: Is $(x + 3)(x - 3) \leq 0$?

Interval	x-value	Value of $x^2 - 9$	Conclusion
$(-\infty, -3)$	$x = -4$	$16 - 9 = 7$	Positive
$(-3, 3)$	$x = 0$	$0 - 9 = -9$	Negative
$(3, \infty)$	$x = 4$	$16 - 9 = 7$	Positive

Solution set: $[-3, 3]$

95. $\qquad (x + 2)^2 < 25$

$\qquad x^2 + 4x + 4 < 25$

$\qquad x^2 + 4x - 21 < 0$

$\qquad (x + 7)(x - 3) < 0$

— CONTINUED —

95. **— CONTINUED —**

Critical numbers: $x = -7, x = 3$

Test intervals: $(-\infty, -7), (-7, 3), (3, \infty)$

Test: Is $(x + 7)(x - 3) < 0$?

Interval	x-value	Value of $(x + 7)(x - 3)$	Conclusion
$(-\infty, -7)$	$x = -10$	$(-3)(-13) = 39$	Positive
$(-7, 3)$	$x = 0$	$(7)(-3) = -21$	Negative
$(3, \infty)$	$x = 5$	$(12)(2) = 24$	Positive

Solution set: $(-7, 3)$

97. $x^2 + 4x + 4 \geq 9$

$x^2 + 4x - 5 \geq 0$

$(x + 5)(x - 1) \geq 0$

Critical numbers: $x = -5, x = 1$

Test intervals: $(-\infty, -5), (-5, 1), (1, \infty)$

Test: Is $(x + 5)(x - 1) \geq 0$?

Interval	x-value	Value of $(x + 5)(x - 1)$	Conclusion
$(-\infty, -5)$	$x = -6$	$(-1)(-7) = 7$	Positive
$(-5, 1)$	$x = 0$	$(5)(-1) = -5$	Negative
$(1, \infty)$	$x = 2$	$(7)(1) = 7$	Positive

Solution set: $(-\infty, -5] \cup [1, \infty)$

99. $x^2 + x < 6$

$x^2 + x - 6 < 0$

$(x + 3)(x - 2) < 0$

Critical numbers: $x = -3, x = 2$

Test intervals: $(-\infty, -3), (-3, 2), (2, \infty)$

Test: Is $(x + 3)(x - 2) < 0$?

Interval	x-value	Value of $(x + 3)(x - 2)$	Conclusion
$(-\infty, -3)$	$x = -4$	$(-1)(-6) = 6$	Positive
$(-3, 2)$	$x = 0$	$(3)(-2) = -6$	Negative
$(2, \infty)$	$x = 3$	$(6)(1) = 6$	Positive

Solution set: $(-3, 2)$

101. $x^2 + 2x - 3 < 0$

$(x + 3)(x - 1) < 0$

Critical numbers: $x = -3, x = 1$

Test intervals: $(-\infty, -3), (-3, 1), (1, \infty)$

Test: Is $(x + 3)(x - 1) < 0$?

Interval	x-value	Value of $(x + 3)(x - 1)$	Conclusion
$(-\infty, -3)$	$x = -4$	$(-1)(-5) = 5$	Positive
$(-3, 1)$	$x = 0$	$(3)(-1) = -3$	Negative
$(1, \infty)$	$x = 2$	$(5)(1) = 5$	Positive

Solution set: $(-3, 1)$

103. $x^2 + 8x - 5 \geq 0$

$x^2 + 8x - 5 = 0$ Complete the Square

$x^2 + 8x + 16 = 5 + 16$

$(x + 4)^2 = 21$

$x + 4 = \pm\sqrt{21}$

$x = -4 \pm \sqrt{21}$

Critical Numbers: $x = -4 \pm \sqrt{21}$

Test Intervals: $\left(-\infty, -4 - \sqrt{21}\right), \left(-4 - \sqrt{21}, -4 + \sqrt{21}\right), \left(-4 + \sqrt{21}, \infty\right)$

Test: Is $x^2 + 8x - 5 \geq 0$?

Interval	x-value	Value of $x^2 + 8x - 5$	Conclusion
$\left(-\infty, -4, -\sqrt{21}\right)$	$x = -10$	$100 - 80 - 5 = 15$	Positive
$\left(-4 - \sqrt{21}, -4 + \sqrt{21}\right)$	$x = 0$	$0 + 0 - 5 = -5$	Negative
$\left(-4 + \sqrt{21}, \infty\right)$	$x = 2$	$4 + 16 - 5 = 15$	Positive

Solution set: $\left(-\infty, -4 - \sqrt{21}\right] \cup \left[-4 + \sqrt{21}, \infty\right)$

105. $x^3 - 3x^2 - x + 3 > 0$

$x^2(x - 3) - 1(x - 3) > 0$

$(x^2 - 1)(x - 3) > 0$

$(x + 1)(x - 1)(x - 3) > 0$

Critical Numbers: $x = \pm 1, x = 3$

Test Intervals: $(-\infty, -1), (-1, 1), (1, 3), (3, \infty)$

Test: Is $(x + 1)(x - 1)(x - 3) > 0$?

— CONTINUED —

105. — CONTINUED —

Interval	x-value	Value of $(x + 1)(x - 1)(x - 3)$	Conclusion
$(-\infty, -1)$	$x = -2$	$(-1)(-3)(-5) = -15$	Negative
$(-1, 1)$	$x = 0$	$(1)(-1)(-3) = 3$	Positive
$(1, 3)$	$x = 2$	$(3)(1)(-1) = -3$	Negative
$(3, \infty)$	$x = 4$	$(5)(3)(1) = 15$	Positive

Solution set: $(-1, 1) \cup (3, \infty)$

107. $x^3 - 2x^2 - 9x - 2 \geq -20$

$x^3 - 2x^2 - 9x + 18 \geq 0$

$x^2(x - 2) - 9(x - 2) \geq 0$

$(x - 2)(x^2 - 9) \geq 0$

$(x - 2)(x + 3)(x - 3) \geq 0$

Critical Numbers: $x = 2, x = \pm 3$

Test Intervals: $(-\infty, -3), (-3, 2), (2, 3), (3, \infty)$

Test: Is $(x - 2)(x + 3)(x - 3) \geq 0$?

Interval	x-value	Value of $(x - 2)(x + 3)(x - 3)$	Conclusion
$(-\infty, -3)$	$x = -4$	$(-6)(-1)(-7) = -42$	Negative
$(-3, 2)$	$x = 0$	$(-2)(3)(-3) = 18$	Positive
$(2, 3)$	$x = 2.5$	$(0.5)(5.5)(-0.5) = -1.375$	Negative
$(3, \infty)$	$x = 4$	$(2)(7)(1) = 14$	Positive

Solution set: $[-3, 2] \cup [3, \infty)$

109. $4x^3 - 6x^2 < 0$

$2x^2(2x - 3) < 0$

Critical numbers: $x = 0, x = \frac{3}{2}$

Test intervals: $(-\infty, 0), \left(0, \frac{3}{2}\right), \left(\frac{3}{2}, \infty\right)$

Test: Is $2x^2(2x - 3) < 0$?

By testing an x-value in each test interval in the inequality, we see that the solution set is:

$(-\infty, 0) \cup \left(0, \frac{3}{2}\right)$

111. $x^3 - 4x \geq 0$

$x(x + 2)(x - 2) \geq 0$

Critical numbers: $x = 0, x = \pm 2$

Test intervals: $(-\infty, -2), (-2, 0), (0, 2), (2, \infty)$

Test: Is $x(x + 2)(x - 2) \geq 0$?

By testing an x-value in each test interval in the inequality, we see that the solution set is:

$[-2, 0] \cup [2, \infty)$

113. $(x - 1)^2(x + 2)^3 \geq 0$

Critical numbers: $x = 1, x = -2$

Test intervals: $(-\infty, -2), (-2, 1), (1, \infty)$

Test: Is $(x - 1)^2(x + 3)^3 \geq 0$?

By testing an x-value in each test interval in the inequality, we see that the solution set is: $[-2, \infty)$

115. $\dfrac{1}{x} - x > 0$

$\dfrac{1 - x^2}{x} > 0$

Critical numbers: $x = 0, x = \pm 1$

Test intervals: $(-\infty, -1), (-1, 0), (0, 1), (1, \infty)$

Test: Is $\dfrac{1 - x^2}{x} > 0$?

By testing an x-value in each test interval in the inequality, we see that the solution set is:

$(-\infty, -1) \cup (0, 1)$

117. $\dfrac{x + 6}{x + 1} - 2 < 0$

$\dfrac{x + 6 - 2(x + 1)}{x + 1} < 0$

$\dfrac{4 - x}{x + 1} < 0$

Critical numbers: $x = -1, x = 4$

Test intervals: $(-\infty, -1), (-1, 4), (4, \infty)$

Test: Is $\dfrac{4 - x}{x + 1} < 0$?

By testing an x-value in each test interval in the inequality, we see that the solution set is:

$(-\infty, -1) \cup (4, \infty)$

119. $\dfrac{3x - 5}{x - 5} > 4$

$\dfrac{3x - 5}{x - 5} - 4 > 0$

$\dfrac{3x - 5 - 4(x - 5)}{x - 5} > 0$

$\dfrac{15 - x}{x - 5} > 0$

Critical numbers: $x = 5, x = 15$

Test intervals: $(-\infty, 5), (5, 15), (15, \infty)$

Test: Is $\dfrac{15 - x}{x - 5} > 0$?

By testing an x-value in each test interval in the inequality, we see that the solution set is: $(5, 15)$

121. $\dfrac{4}{x + 5} > \dfrac{1}{2x + 3}$

$\dfrac{4}{x + 5} - \dfrac{1}{2x + 3} > 0$

$\dfrac{4(2x + 3) - (x + 5)}{(x + 5)(2x + 3)} > 0$

$\dfrac{7x + 7}{(x + 5)(2x + 3)} > 0$

Critical numbers: $x = -1, x = -5, x = -\dfrac{3}{2}$

Test intervals: $(-\infty, -5), \left(-5, -\dfrac{3}{2}\right),$

$\left(-\dfrac{3}{2}, -1\right), (-1, \infty)$

Test: Is $\dfrac{7(x + 1)}{(x + 5)(2x + 3)} > 0$?

By testing an x-value in each test interval in the inequality, we see that the solution set is:

$\left(-5, -\dfrac{3}{2}\right) \cup (-1, \infty)$

123.

$$\frac{1}{x-3} \le \frac{9}{4x+3}$$

$$\frac{1}{x-3} - \frac{9}{4x+3} \le 0$$

$$\frac{4x+3-9(x-3)}{(x-3)(4x+3)} \le 0$$

$$\frac{30-5x}{(x-3)(4x+3)} \le 0$$

Critical numbers: $x = 3, x = -\frac{3}{4}, x = 6$

Test intervals: $\left(-\infty, -\frac{3}{4}\right), \left(-\frac{3}{4}, 3\right), (3, 6), (6, \infty)$

Test: Is $\dfrac{5(6-x)}{(x-3)(4x+3)} \le 0$?

By testing an x-value in each test interval in the inequality, we see that the solution set is:

$$\left(-\frac{3}{4}, 3\right) \cup [6, \infty)$$

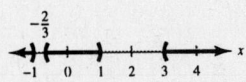

125.

$$\frac{x^2+2x}{x^2-9} \le 0$$

$$\frac{x(x+2)}{(x+3)(x-3)} \le 0$$

Critical numbers: $x = 0, x = -2, x = \pm 3$

Test intervals: $(-\infty, -3), (-3, -2), (-2, 0), (0, 3), (3, \infty)$

Test: Is $\dfrac{x(x+2)}{(x+3)(x-3)} \le 0$?

By testing an x-value in each test interval in the inequality, we see that the solution set is: $(-3, -2] \cup [0, 3)$

127.

$$\frac{5}{x-1} - \frac{2x}{x+1} < 1$$

$$\frac{5}{x-1} - \frac{2x}{x+1} - 1 < 0$$

$$\frac{5(x+1) - 2x(x-1) - (x-1)(x+1)}{(x-1)(x+1)} < 0$$

$$\frac{5x+5 - 2x^2 + 2x - x^2 + 1}{(x-1)(x+1)} < 0$$

$$\frac{-3x^2 + 7x + 6}{(x-1)(x+1)} < 0$$

$$\frac{-(3x+2)(x-3)}{(x-1)(x+1)} < 0$$

Critical Numbers: $x = -\frac{2}{3}, x = 3, x = \pm 1$

Test Intervals: $(-\infty, -1), \left(-1, -\frac{2}{3}\right), \left(-\frac{2}{3}, 1\right), (1, 3), (3, \infty)$

Test: Is $\dfrac{-(3x+2)(x-3)}{(x-1)(x+1)} < 0$?

By testing an x-value in each test interval in the inequality, we see that the solution set is: $(-\infty, -1) \cup \left(-\frac{2}{3}, 1\right) \cup (3, \infty)$

129. $4 - x^2 \geq 0$

$(2 + x)(2 - x) \geq 0$

Critical numbers: $x = \pm 2$

Test intervals: $(-\infty, -2), (-2, 2), (2, \infty)$

Test: Is $4 - x^2 \geq 0$?

By testing an x-value in each test interval in the inequality, we see that the domain is: $[-2, 2]$

131. $x^2 - 7x + 12 \geq 0$

$(x - 3)(x - 4) \geq 0$

Critical numbers: $x = 3, x = 4$

Test intervals: $(-\infty, 3), (3, 4), (4, \infty)$

Test: Is $(x - 3)(x - 4) \geq 0$?

By testing an x-value in each test interval in the inequality, we see that the domain is: $(-\infty, 3] \cup [4, \infty)$

133. $\dfrac{x}{x^2 - 2x - 35} \geq 0$

$\dfrac{x}{(x + 5)(x - 7)} \geq 0$

Critical Numbers: $x = 0, x = -5, x = 7$

Test Intervals: $(-\infty, -5), (-5, 0), (0, 7), (7, \infty)$

Test: Is $\dfrac{x}{(x + 5)(x - 7)} \geq 0$?

By testing an x-value in each test interval in the inequality, we see that the domain is: $(-5, 0] \cup (7, \infty)$

135. $0.4x^2 + 5.26 < 10.2$

$0.4x^2 - 4.94 < 0$

$0.4(x^2 - 12.35) < 0$

Critical numbers: $x \approx \pm 3.51$

Test intervals: $(-\infty, -3.51), (-3.51, 3.51), (3.51, \infty)$

By testing an x-value in each test interval in the inequality, we see that the solution set is: $(-3.51, 3.51)$

137. $-0.5x^2 + 12.5x + 1.6 > 0$

The zeros are $x = \dfrac{-12.5 \pm \sqrt{(12.5)^2 - 4(-0.5)(1.6)}}{2(-0.5)}$.

Critical numbers: $x \approx -0.13, x \approx 25.13$

Test intervals: $(-\infty, -0.13), (-0.13, 25.13),$

$(25.13, \infty)$

By testing x-values in each test interval in the inequality, we see that the solution set is: $(-0.13, 25.13)$

139. $\dfrac{1}{2.3x - 5.2} > 3.4$

$\dfrac{1}{2.3x - 5.2} - 3.4 > 0$

$\dfrac{-7.82x + 18.68}{2.3x - 5.2} > 0$

Critical numbers: $x \approx 2.39, x = 2.26$

Test intervals: $(-\infty, 2.26), (2.26, 2.39), (2.39, \infty)$

By testing x-values in each test interval in the inequality, we see that the solution set is: $(2.26, 2.39)$

141. Company B fee > Company A fee

$150 + 0.25x > 250$

$0.25x > 100$

$x > 400$

If you drive more than 400 miles in a week, the rental fee for Company B is greater than the rental fee for Company A.

143. $1000(1 + r(2)) > 1062.50$

$1 + 2r > 1.0625$

$2r > 0.0625$

$r > 0.03125$

$r > 3.125\% \approx 3.1\%$

145. $\left| \dfrac{h - 68.5}{2.7} \right| \le 1$

$-1 \le \dfrac{h - 68.5}{2.7} \le 1$

$-2.7 \le h - 68.5 \le 2.7$

$65.8 \le h \le 71.2$ inches

147. $2L + 2W = 100 \implies W = 50 - L$

$LW \ge 500$

$L(50 - L) \ge 500$

$-L^2 + 50L - 500 \ge 0$

By the Quadratic Formula we have:

Critical numbers: $L = 25 \pm 5\sqrt{5}$

Test: Is $-L^2 + 50L - 500 \ge 0$?

Solution set: $25 - 5\sqrt{5} \le L \le 25 + 5\sqrt{5}$

13.8 meters $\le L \le 36.2$ meters

149. $1000(1 + r)^2 > 1100$

$(l + r)^2 > 1.1$

$1 + 2r + r^2 - 1.1 > 0$

$r^2 + 2r - 0.1 > 0$

By the Quadratic Formula we have:

Critical Numbers: $r = -1 \pm \sqrt{1.1}$

Since r cannot be negative, $r = -1 + \sqrt{1.1} \approx 0.0488$

$= 4.88\%$

Thus, $r > 4.88\%$

151. $\dfrac{1}{R} = \dfrac{1}{R_1} + \dfrac{1}{2}$

$2R_1 = 2R + RR_1$

$2R_1 = R(2 + R_1)$

$\dfrac{2R_1}{2 + R_1} = R$

Since $R \ge 1$, we have

$\dfrac{2R_1}{2 + R_1} \ge 1$

$\dfrac{2R_1}{2 + R_1} - 1 \ge 0$

$\dfrac{R_1 - 2}{2 + R_1} \ge 0.$

Since $R_1 > 0$, the only critical number is $R_1 = 2$.

The inequality is satisfied when $R_1 \ge 2$ ohms.

153. False. c has to be greater than zero for $ac \le bc$.

155. True. $x^3 - 2x^2 - 11x + 12 = (x - 4)(x + 3)(x - 1)$.

The critical numbers are $x = 4, x = -3,$ and $x = 1$.

The test intervals are $(-\infty, -3), (-3, 1), (1, 4)$ and $(4, \infty)$.

157. $|x - a| \geq 2$

$x - a \leq -2$ or $x - a \geq 2$

$x \leq a - 2$ or $x \geq a + 2$

Matches graph (b)

159. $x^2 + bx + 4 = 0$

To have at least one real solution,

$b^2 - 4(1)(4) \geq 0$

$b^2 - 16 \geq 0$

Critical numbers: $b = \pm 4$

Test intervals: $(-\infty, -4), (-4, 4), (4, \infty)$

Test: Is $b^2 - 16 \geq 0$?

By testing values in each test interval, we see that $b^2 - 16$ is greater than or equal to zero on the intervals $(-\infty, -4] \cup [4, \infty)$.

161. $3x^2 + bx + 10 = 0$

To have at least one real solution,

$b^2 - 4(3)(10) \geq 0$

$b^2 - 120 \geq 0$

Critical numbers: $b = \pm\sqrt{120} = \pm 2\sqrt{30}$

Test intervals: $\left(-\infty, -2\sqrt{30}\right), \left(-2\sqrt{30}, 2\sqrt{30}\right), \left(2\sqrt{30}, \infty\right)$

Test: Is $b^2 - 120 \geq 0$?

By testing values in each test interval, we see that $b^2 - 120$ is greater than or equal to zero on the intervals $\left(-\infty, -2\sqrt{30}\right] \cup \left[2\sqrt{30}, \infty\right)$.

163. If $a > 0$ and $c \leq 0$, then b can be any real number since $b^2 - 4ac$ would always be positive.

If $a > 0$ and $c > 0$, then $b \leq -2\sqrt{ac}$ or $b \geq 2\sqrt{ac}$, as in problems 159 and 161.

165. $(x - a)(x - b)$

(a) The polynomial is zero when $x = a$ or $x = b$.

(b)
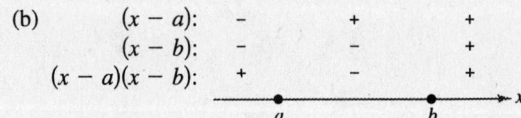

(c) A polynomial changes signs at its zeros.

Section P.7   Errors and the Algebra of Calculus

- You should be able to recognize and avoid the common algebraic errors involving parentheses, fractions, exponents, radicals, and cancellation.

- You should be able to "unsimplify" algebraic expressions by the following methods.

  (a) Unusual Factoring

  (b) Rewriting with Negative Exponents

  (c) Writing a Fraction as a Sum of Terms

  (d) Inserting Factors or Terms

Solutions to Odd-Numbered Exercises

1. $2x - (3y + 4) = 2x - 3y - 4$

Change all signs when distributing the minus sign.

3. $\dfrac{4}{16x - (2x + 1)} = \dfrac{4}{16x - 2x - 1} = \dfrac{4}{14x - 1}$

Change all signs when distributing the minus sign.

5. $(5z)(6z) = 30z^2$

z occurs twice as a factor.

7. $a\left(\dfrac{x}{y}\right) = \dfrac{a}{1} \cdot \dfrac{x}{y} = \dfrac{ax}{y}$

The fraction as a whole is multiplied by a, not the numerator and denominator separately.

9. $\left(\dfrac{x}{y}\right)^3 = \dfrac{x^3}{y^3}$

The exponent applies to the denominator also.

11. $\sqrt{x + 9}$ does not simplify.
Do not apply the radical to the terms.

13. $\dfrac{6x + y}{6x - y}$ does not simplify.

Reduce common factors, not common factors of terms.

15. $\dfrac{1}{x + y^{-1}} = \dfrac{1}{x + (1/y)} \cdot \dfrac{y}{y} = \dfrac{y}{xy + 1}$

The negative exponent is on a term of the denominator, not a factor.

17. $x(2x - 1)^2 = x(4x^2 - 4x + 1)$

Exponents are applied before multiplying.

19. $\sqrt[3]{x^3 + 7x^2} = \sqrt[3]{x^2(x + 7)} = \sqrt[3]{x^2}\sqrt[3]{x + 7}$

Radicals apply to every factor of the radicand.

21. $\dfrac{3}{x} + \dfrac{4}{y} = \dfrac{3}{x} \cdot \dfrac{y}{y} + \dfrac{4}{y} \cdot \dfrac{x}{x} = \dfrac{3y + 4x}{xy}$

To add fractions, they must have a common denominator.

23. $\dfrac{3x + 2}{5} = \dfrac{1}{5}(3x + 2)$

The required factor is $3x + 2$.

25. $\frac{2}{3}x^2 + \frac{1}{3}x + 5 = \frac{2}{3}x^2 + \frac{1}{3}x + \frac{15}{3} = \frac{1}{3}(2x^2 + x + 15)$

The required factor is $2x^2 + x + 15$.

27. $\frac{5}{2}z^2 - \frac{1}{4}z + 2 = \frac{10}{4}z^2 - \frac{1}{4}z + \frac{8}{4} = \frac{1}{4}(10z^2 - z + 8)$

The required factor is $\frac{1}{4}$.

29. $x(1 - 2x^2)^3 = \frac{-4x}{-4}(1 - 2x^2)^3 = \left(-\frac{1}{4}\right)(-4x)(1 - 2x^2)^3$

$= \left(-\frac{1}{4}\right)(1 - 2x^2)^3(-4x)$

The required factor is $-\frac{1}{4}$.

31. $\frac{x + 1}{(x^2 + 2x - 3)^2} = \frac{1}{2} \cdot \frac{2(x + 1)}{(x^2 + 2x - 3)^2}$

$= \left(\frac{1}{2}\right)\left(\frac{1}{(x^2 + 2x - 3)^2}\right)(2x + 2)$

The required factor is $\frac{1}{2}$.

33. $\frac{3}{x} + \frac{5}{2x^2} - \frac{3}{2}x = \frac{6x}{2x^2} + \frac{5}{2x^2} - \frac{3x^3}{2x^2}$

$= \left(\frac{1}{2x^2}\right)(6x + 5 - 3x^3)$

The required factor is $\frac{1}{2x^2}$.

35. $\frac{9x^2}{25} + \frac{16y^2}{49} = \frac{9}{25} \cdot \frac{x^2}{1} + \frac{16}{49} \cdot \frac{y^2}{1}$

$= \frac{1}{25/9} \cdot \frac{x^2}{1} + \frac{1}{49/16} \cdot \frac{y^2}{1}$

$= \frac{x^2}{(25/9)} + \frac{y^2}{(49/16)}$

The required factors are $\frac{25}{9}$ and $\frac{49}{16}$.

37. $\frac{x^2}{1/12} - \frac{y^2}{2/3} = x^2\left(\frac{12}{1}\right) - y^2\left(\frac{3}{2}\right) = \frac{12x^2}{1} - \frac{3y^2}{2}$

The required factors are 1 and 2.

39. $x^{1/3} - 5x^{4/3} = x^{1/3}(1 - 5x^{3/3}) = x^{1/3}(1 - 5x)$

The required factor is $1 - 5x$.

41. $(1 - 3x)^{4/3} - 4x(1 - 3x)^{1/3} = (1 - 3x)^{1/3}[(1 - 3x)^1 - 4x]$

$= (1 - 3x)^{1/3}(1 - 7x)$

The required factor is $1 - 7x$.

43. $\frac{1}{10}(2x + 1)^{5/2} - \frac{1}{6}(2x + 1)^{3/2} = \frac{3}{30}(2x + 1)^{3/2}(2x + 1)^1 - \frac{5}{30}(2x + 1)^{3/2}$

$= \frac{1}{30}(2x + 1)^{3/2}[3(2x + 1) - 5]$

$= \frac{1}{30}(2x + 1)^{3/2}(6x - 2)$

$= \frac{1}{30}(2x + 1)^{3/2}2(3x - 1)$

$= \frac{1}{15}(2x + 1)^{3/2}(3x - 1)$

The required factor is $3x - 1$.

45. $\frac{16 - 5x - x^2}{x} = \frac{16}{x} - \frac{5x}{x} - \frac{x^2}{x} = \frac{16}{x} - 5 - x$

47. $\frac{4x^3 - 7x^2 + 1}{x^{1/3}} = \frac{4x^3}{x^{1/3}} - \frac{7x^2}{x^{1/3}} + \frac{1}{x^{1/3}}$

$= 4x^{3-1/3} - 7x^{2-1/3} + \frac{1}{x^{1/3}}$

$= 4x^{8/3} - 7x^{5/3} + \frac{1}{x^{1/3}}$

49. $\frac{3 - 5x^2 - x^4}{\sqrt{x}} = \frac{3}{\sqrt{x}} - \frac{5x^2}{\sqrt{x}} - \frac{x^4}{\sqrt{x}}$

$= \frac{3}{\sqrt{x}} - 5x^{2-1/2} - x^{4-1/2}$

$= \frac{3}{\sqrt{x}} - 5x^{3/2} - x^{7/2}$

51. $\dfrac{-2(x^2 - 3)^{-3}(2x)(x + 1)^3 - 3(x + 1)^2(x^2 - 3)^{-2}}{[(x + 1)^3]^2} = \dfrac{(x^2 - 3)^{-3}(x + 1)^2[-4x(x + 1) - 3(x^2 - 3)]}{(x + 1)^6}$

$$= \dfrac{-4x^2 - 4x - 3x^2 + 9}{(x^2 - 3)^3(x + 1)^4}$$

$$= \dfrac{-7x^2 - 4x + 9}{(x^2 - 3)^3(x + 1)^4}$$

53. $\dfrac{(6x + 1)^3(27x^2 + 2) - (9x^3 + 2x)(3)(6x + 1)^2(6)}{[(6x + 1)^3]^2} = \dfrac{(6x + 1)^2[(6x + 1)(27x^2 + 2) - 18(9x^3 + 2x)]}{(6x + 1)^6}$

$$= \dfrac{162x^3 + 12x + 27x^2 + 2 - 162x^3 - 36x}{(6x + 1)^4}$$

$$= \dfrac{27x^2 - 24x + 2}{(6x + 1)^4}$$

55. $\dfrac{(x + 2)^{3/4}(x + 3)^{-2/3} - (x + 3)^{1/3}(x + 2)^{-1/4}}{[(x + 2)^{3/4}]^2} = \dfrac{(x + 2)^{-1/4}(x + 3)^{-2/3}[(x + 2) - (x + 3)]}{(x + 2)^{6/4}}$

$$= \dfrac{x + 2 - x - 3}{(x + 2)^{1/4}(x + 3)^{2/3}(x + 2)^{6/4}}$$

$$= -\dfrac{1}{(x + 3)^{2/3}(x + 2)^{7/4}}$$

57. $\dfrac{2(3x - 1)^{1/3} - (2x + 1)\left(\frac{1}{3}\right)(3x - 1)^{-2/3}(3)}{(3x - 1)^{2/3}} = \dfrac{(3x - 1)^{-2/3}[2(3x - 1) - (2x + 1)]}{(3x - 1)^{2/3}}$

$$= \dfrac{6x - 2 - 2x - 1}{(3x - 1)^{2/3}(3x - 1)^{2/3}}$$

$$= \dfrac{4x - 3}{(3x - 1)^{4/3}}$$

59. $\dfrac{1}{(x^2 + 4)^{1/2}} \cdot \dfrac{1}{2}(x^2 + 4)^{-1/2}(2x) = \dfrac{1}{(x^2 + 4)^{1/2}} \cdot \dfrac{1}{(x^2 + 4)^{1/2}} \cdot \dfrac{1}{2}(2x)$

$$= \dfrac{1}{(x^2 + 4)^1}(x)$$

$$= \dfrac{x}{x^2 + 4}$$

61. $(x^2 + 5)^{1/2}\left(\dfrac{3}{2}\right)(3x - 2)^{1/2}(3) + (3x - 2)^{3/2}\left(\dfrac{1}{2}\right)(x^2 + 5)^{-1/2}(2x) = \dfrac{9}{2}(x^2 + 5)^{1/2}(3x - 2)^{1/2} + x(x^2 + 5)^{-1/2}(3x - 2)^{3/2}$

$$= \dfrac{9}{2}(x^2 + 5)^{1/2}(3x - 2)^{1/2} + \dfrac{2}{2}x(x^2 + 5)^{-1/2}(3x - 2)^{3/2}$$

$$= \dfrac{1}{2}(x^2 + 5)^{-1/2}(3x - 2)^{1/2}[9(x^2 + 5)^1 + 2x(3x - 2)^1]$$

$$= \dfrac{1}{2}(x^2 + 5)^{-1/2}(3x - 2)^{1/2}(9x^2 + 45 + 6x^2 - 4x)$$

$$= \dfrac{(3x - 2)^{1/2}(15x^2 - 4x + 45)}{2(x^2 + 5)^{1/2}}$$

63. (a) $y_1 = x^2\left(\frac{1}{3}\right)(x^2 + 1)^{-2/3}(2x) + (x^2 + 1)^{1/3}(2x)$

$= 2x(x^2 + 1)^{-2/3}\left[\frac{x^2}{3} + (x^2 + 1)\right]$

$= 2x(x^2 + 1)^{-2/3}\left[\frac{x^2}{3} + \frac{3(x^2 + 1)}{3}\right]$

$= \frac{2x}{(x^2 + 1)^{2/3}} \cdot \frac{4x^2 + 3}{3}$

$= \frac{2x(4x^2 + 3)}{3(x^2 + 1)^{2/3}}$

$= y_2$

(b)

x	-2	-1	$-\frac{1}{2}$	0	1	2	$\frac{5}{2}$
y_1	-8.7	-2.9	-1.1	0	2.9	8.7	12.5
y_2	-8.7	-2.9	-1.1	0	2.9	8.7	12.5

65. $y_1 = 2x\sqrt{1 - x^2} - \frac{x^3}{\sqrt{1 - x^2}}$ $y_2 = \frac{2 - 3x^2}{\sqrt{1 - x^2}}$

When $x = 0$, $y_1 = 0$.   When $x = 0$, $y_2 = 2$.

Thus, $y_1 \neq y_2$.

$y_1 = \frac{2x\sqrt{1 - x^2}}{1} - \frac{x^3}{\sqrt{1 - x^2}} = \frac{2x\sqrt{1 - x^2}}{1} \cdot \frac{\sqrt{1 - x^2}}{\sqrt{1 - x^2}} - \frac{x^3}{\sqrt{1 - x^2}}$

$= \frac{2x(1 - x^2) - x^3}{\sqrt{1 - x^2}} = \frac{2x - 2x^3 - x^3}{\sqrt{1 - x^2}}$

$= \frac{2x - 3x^3}{\sqrt{1 - x^2}}$

Let $y_2 = \frac{2x - 3x^3}{\sqrt{1 - x^2}}$. Then $y_1 = y_2$.

67. False. Cannot move term-by-term from denominator to numerator.

$\dfrac{1}{x^{-2} + y^{-1}} = \dfrac{1}{\dfrac{1}{x^2} + \dfrac{1}{y}} = \dfrac{1}{\dfrac{y + x^2}{x^2 y}} = \dfrac{x^2 y}{y + x^2}$

69. False. $x^2 - 9$ does not factor into $(\sqrt{x} + 3)(\sqrt{x} - 3)$.

$\dfrac{x^2 - 9}{\sqrt{x} - 3} = \dfrac{(x + 3)(x - 3)}{\sqrt{x} - 3} \cdot \dfrac{\sqrt{x} + 3}{\sqrt{x} + 3}$

$= \dfrac{(x + 3)(x - 3)(\sqrt{x} + 3)}{x - 9}$

71. $(x^n)^{2n} + (x^{2n})^n = x^{2n^2} + x^{2n^2} = 2x^{2n^2}$

There is no error.

73. $\dfrac{x^{2n} \cdot x^{3n}}{x^{3n} + x^2} = \dfrac{x^{2n+3n}}{x^{3n} + x^2} = \dfrac{x^{5n}}{x^{3n} + x^2}$

There is no error.

Section P.8   Graphical Representation of Data

- You should be able to plot points.
- You should know that the distance between (x_1, y_1) and (x_2, y_2) in the plane is

  $d = \sqrt{(x_2 - x_1)^2 + (y_2 - y_1)^2}$.

- You should know that the midpoint of the line segment joining (x_1, y_1) and (x_2, y_2) is

  $\left(\dfrac{x_1 + x_2}{2}, \dfrac{y_1 + y_2}{2}\right)$.

Solutions to Odd-Numbered Exercises

1.

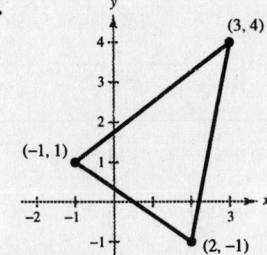

3.

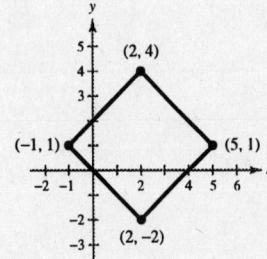

5. A: $(2, 6)$, B: $(-6, -2)$, C: $(4, -4)$, D: $(-3, 2)$

7. $(-3, 4)$

9. $(-5, -5)$

11. $x > 0$ and $y < 0$ in Quadrant IV.

13. $x = -4$ and $y > 0$ in Quadrant II.

15. $y < -5$ in Quadrants III and IV.

17. $(x, -y)$ is in the second Quadrant means that (x, y) is in Quadrant III.

19. (x, y), $xy > 0$ means x and y have the same signs. This occurs in Quadrants I and III.

21. $(-2 + 2, -4 + 5) = (0, 1)$

$(2 + 2, -3 + 5) = (4, 2)$

$(-1 + 2, -1 + 5) = (1, 4)$

23. $(-7 + 4, -2 + 8) = (-3, 6)$

$(-2 + 4, 2 + 8) = (2, 10)$

$(-2 + 4, -4 + 8) = (2, 4)$

$(-7 + 4, -4 + 8) = (-3, 4)$

25.

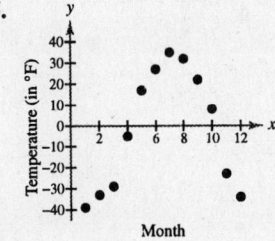

27. The highest price of milk is approximately \$1.65 per gallon. This occurred in 1996.

29. $\left[\dfrac{(1600 - 600)}{600}\right](100) \approx 166.67\%$

31. The minimum wage had the greatest increase in the 1990s.

33. The point $(65, 83)$ represents an entrance exam score of 65.

35. $d = |5 - (-3)| = 8$

37. $d = |2 - (-3)| = 5$

39. (a) The distance between $(0, 2)$ and $(4, 2)$ is 4.

The distance between $(4, 2)$ and $(4, 5)$ is 3.

The distance between $(0, 2)$ and $(4, 5)$ is

$\sqrt{(4 - 0)^2 + (5 - 2)^2} = \sqrt{16 + 9} = \sqrt{25} = 5$.

(b) $4^2 + 3^2 = 16 + 9 = 25 = 5^2$

41. (a) The distance between $(-1, 1)$ and $(9, 1)$ is 10.

The distance between $(9, 1)$ and $(9, 4)$ is 3.

The distance between $(-1, 1)$ and $(9, 4)$ is

$\sqrt{(9 - (-1))^2 + (4 - 1)^2} = \sqrt{100 + 9} = \sqrt{109}$.

(b) $10^2 + 3^2 = 109 = \left(\sqrt{109}\right)^2$

43. (a)

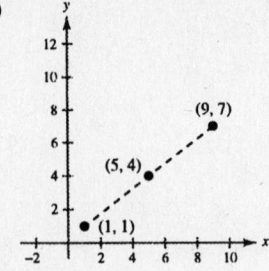

(b) $d = \sqrt{(9-1)^2 + (7-1)^2}$

$= \sqrt{64 + 36} = 10$

(c) $\left(\dfrac{9+1}{2}, \dfrac{7+1}{2}\right) = (5, 4)$

45. (a)

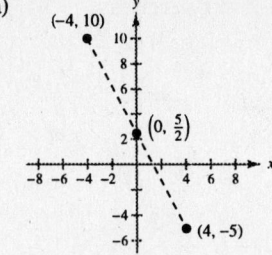

(b) $d = \sqrt{(4+4)^2 + (-5-10)^2}$

$= \sqrt{64 + 225} = 17$

(c) $\left(\dfrac{4-4}{2}, \dfrac{-5+10}{2}\right) = \left(0, \dfrac{5}{2}\right)$

47. (a)

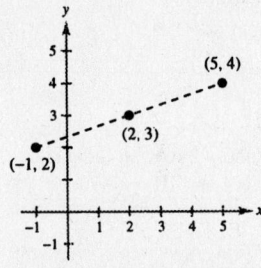

(b) $d = \sqrt{(5+1)^2 + (4-2)^2}$

$= \sqrt{36 + 4} = 2\sqrt{10}$

(c) $\left(\dfrac{-1+5}{2}, \dfrac{2+4}{2}\right) = (2, 3)$

49. (a)

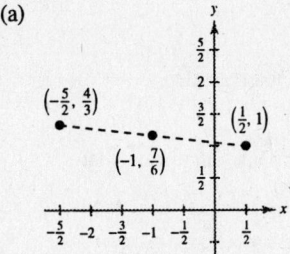

(b) $d = \sqrt{\left(\dfrac{1}{2} + \dfrac{5}{2}\right)^2 + \left(1 - \dfrac{4}{3}\right)^2}$

$d = \sqrt{9 + \dfrac{1}{9}} = \dfrac{\sqrt{82}}{3}$

(c) $\left(\dfrac{-\frac{5}{2} + \frac{1}{2}}{2}, \dfrac{\frac{4}{3} + 1}{2}\right) = \left(-1, \dfrac{7}{6}\right)$

51. (a)

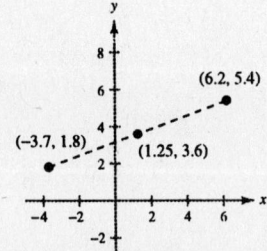

(b) $d = \sqrt{(6.2 + 3.7)^2 + (5.4 - 1.8)^2}$

$= \sqrt{98.01 + 12.96}$

$= \sqrt{110.97}$

(c) $\left(\dfrac{6.2 - 3.7}{2}, \dfrac{5.4 + 1.8}{2}\right) = (1.25, 3.6)$

53. (a)

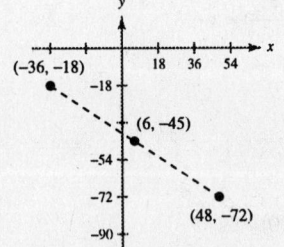

(b) $d = \sqrt{(48 + 36)^2 + (-72 + 18)^2}$

$= \sqrt{7056 + 2916}$

$= \sqrt{9972} = 6\sqrt{277}$

(c) $\left(\dfrac{-36 + 48}{2}, \dfrac{-18 - 72}{2}\right) = (6, -45)$

55. $\left(\dfrac{1996 + 2000}{2}, \dfrac{\$520{,}000 + \$740{,}000}{2}\right) = (1998, \$630{,}000)$

In 1998 the sales were \$630,000.

57. $d_1 = \sqrt{(4 - 2)^2 + (0 - 1)^2} = \sqrt{5}$

$d_2 = \sqrt{(4 + 1)^2 + (0 + 5)^2} = \sqrt{50}$

$d_3 = \sqrt{(2 + 1)^2 + (1 + 5)^2} = \sqrt{45}$

$\left(\sqrt{5}\right)^2 + \left(\sqrt{45}\right)^2 = \left(\sqrt{50}\right)^2$

59. $d_1 = \sqrt{(0 - 2)^2 + (9 - 5)^2} = \sqrt{4 + 16} = \sqrt{20} = 2\sqrt{5}$

$d_2 = \sqrt{(-2 - 0)^2 + (0 - 9)^2} = \sqrt{4 + 81} = \sqrt{85}$

$d_3 = \sqrt{(0 - (-2))^2 + (-4 - 0)^2} = \sqrt{4 + 16} = \sqrt{20} = 2\sqrt{5}$

$d_4 = \sqrt{(0 - 2)^2 + (-4 - 5)^2} = \sqrt{4 + 81} = \sqrt{85}$

Opposite sides have equal lengths of $2\sqrt{5}$ and $\sqrt{85}$.

61. Since $x_m = \dfrac{x_1 + x_2}{2}$ and $y_m = \dfrac{y_1 + y_2}{2}$ we have:

$$2x_m = x_1 + x_2 \qquad\qquad 2y_m = y_1 + y_2$$

$$2x_m - x_1 = x_2 \qquad\qquad 2y_m - y_1 = y_2$$

Thus, $(x_2, y_2) = (2x_m - x_1, 2y_m - y_1)$.

63. The midpoint of the given line segment is $\left(\dfrac{x_1 + x_2}{2}, \dfrac{y_1 + y_2}{2}\right)$.

The midpoint between (x_1, y_1) and $\left(\dfrac{x_1 + x_2}{2}, \dfrac{y_1 + y_2}{2}\right)$ is $\left(\dfrac{x_1 + \frac{x_1 + x_2}{2}}{2}, \dfrac{y_1 + \frac{y_1 + y_2}{2}}{2}\right) = \left(\dfrac{3x_1 + x_2}{4}, \dfrac{3y_1 + y_2}{4}\right)$.

The midpoint between $\left(\dfrac{x_1 + x_2}{2}, \dfrac{y_1 + y_2}{2}\right)$ and (x_2, y_2) is $\left(\dfrac{\frac{x_1 + x_2}{2} + x_2}{2}, \dfrac{\frac{y_1 + y_2}{2} + y_2}{2}\right) = \left(\dfrac{x_1 + 3x_2}{4}, \dfrac{y_1 + 3y_2}{4}\right)$.

Thus, the three points are

$$\left(\dfrac{3x_1 + x_2}{4}, \dfrac{3y_1 + y_2}{4}\right), \left(\dfrac{x_1 + x_2}{2}, \dfrac{y_1 + y_2}{2}\right), \text{ and } \left(\dfrac{x_1 + 3x_2}{4}, \dfrac{y_1 + 3y_2}{4}\right).$$

65. $d = \sqrt{(45 - 10)^2 + (40 - 15)^2} = \sqrt{35^2 + 25^2} = \sqrt{1850} = 5\sqrt{74} \approx 43$ yards

67.

(a) The point is reflected through the y-axis.

(b) The point is reflected through the x-axis.

(c) The point is reflected through the origin.

69. (1996, 696.5), (1998, 1308.7)

The midpoint is $\left(\dfrac{1996 + 1998}{2}, \dfrac{696.5 + 1308.7}{2}\right) = (1997, 1002.6)$

Annual sales in 1997 were approximately \$1002.6 million.

71. False, you would have to use the Midpoint Formula 15 times.

73. On the x-axis, $y = 0$

On the y-axis, $x = 0$

75. Use the Midpoint Formula to prove the diagonals of the parallelogram bisect each other.

$$\left(\frac{b + a}{2}, \frac{c + 0}{2}\right) = \left(\frac{a + b}{2}, \frac{c}{2}\right)$$

$$\left(\frac{a + b + 0}{2}, \frac{c + 0}{2}\right) = \left(\frac{a + b}{2}, \frac{c}{2}\right)$$

77. Since (x_0, y_0) lies in Quadrant II, $(-2x_0, y_0)$ must lie in Quadrant I. Matches (c)

79. Since (x_0, y_0) lies in Quadrant II, $(-x_0, -y_0)$ must lie in Quadrant IV. Matches (a)

Review Exercises for Chapter P

Solutions to Odd-Numbered Exercises

1. $\{11, -14, -\frac{8}{9}, \frac{5}{2}, \sqrt{6}, 0.4\}$

   (a) Natural numbers: 11

   (b) Integers: 11, −14

   (c) Rational numbers: $11, -14, -\frac{8}{9}, \frac{5}{2}, 0.4$

   (d) Irrational numbers: $\sqrt{6}$

3. (a) $\frac{5}{6} = 0.8\overline{3}$

   (b) $\frac{7}{8} = 0.875$

   $\frac{5}{6} < \frac{7}{8}$

5. $x \le 7$

The set consists of all real numbers less than or equal to 7.

7. $d(-92, 63) = |63 - (-92)| = 155$

9. $d(23.7°, -0.9°) = |-0.9° - 23.7°| = 24.6°$ F change.

11. $|0.017| = 0.017$

13. $-5|14 - 21| = -5(7) = -35$

15. $\dfrac{x}{x - 3}$

   (a) $x = -3$: $\dfrac{-3}{-3 - 3} = \dfrac{-3}{-6} = \dfrac{1}{2}$

   (b) $x = 3$: $\dfrac{3}{3 - 3} = \dfrac{3}{0}$ which is undefined.

       You cannot divide by zero.

17. $\dfrac{|-10|}{-10} = \dfrac{10}{-10} = -1$

19. $(16 - 8) \div 4 = 8 \div 4 = 2$

21. $-4[16 - 3(7 - 10)] = -4[16 - 3(-3)] = -4[16 + 9]$
$$= -4[25] = -100$$

23. (a) $(x + y^{-1})^{-1} = \left(x + \dfrac{1}{y}\right)^{-1}$

$$= \left(\dfrac{xy + 1}{y}\right)^{-1}$$

$$= \dfrac{y}{xy + 1}$$

   (b) $\left(\dfrac{x^{-3}}{y}\right)\left(\dfrac{x}{y}\right)^{-1} = \left(\dfrac{1}{x^3 y}\right)\left(\dfrac{y}{x}\right)$

$$= \dfrac{1}{x^4}$$

$$= x^{-4}$$

25. $0.3048 = 3.048 \times 10^{-1}$

27. $\sqrt[4]{32^4} = 32$

29. $\dfrac{\sqrt[3]{24u^4}}{\sqrt[3]{3u}} = \sqrt[3]{\dfrac{24u^4}{3u}} = \sqrt[3]{8u^3} = 2u, \; u \neq 0$

31. (a) $\sqrt{8x^3} + \sqrt{2x} = \sqrt{(2x)^2 2x} + \sqrt{2x} = 2x\sqrt{2x} + \sqrt{2x} = (2x + 1)\sqrt{2x}$

   (b) $\sqrt{18x^5} - \sqrt{8x^3} = \sqrt{(3x^2)^2 2x} - \sqrt{(2x)^2 2x} = 3x^2\sqrt{2x} - 2x\sqrt{2x}$
   $$= (3x^2 - 2x)\sqrt{2x}$$

33. $\dfrac{\sqrt{x} - 1}{2} = \dfrac{\sqrt{x} - 1}{2} \cdot \dfrac{\sqrt{x} + 1}{\sqrt{x} + 1} = \dfrac{x - 1}{2(\sqrt{x} + 1)}$

35. $(64)^{-2/3} = \dfrac{1}{\sqrt[3]{64^2}} = \dfrac{1}{\left(\sqrt[3]{64}\right)^2} = \dfrac{1}{(4)^2} = \dfrac{1}{16}$

37. $(x - 1)^{1/3}(x - 1)^{-1/4} = (x - 1)^{(1/3) + (-1/4)} = (x - 1)^{(4/12) - (3/12)} = (x - 1)^{1/12}$

39. Radical form: $\sqrt[4]{16} = 2$,
   Rational exponent form: $16^{1/4} = 2$

41. Standard form: $-5x^5 + 3x^3 + x - 4$

43. Standard form: $-7x^2 + 12x + 6$

45. $8y - [2y^2 - (3y - 8)] = 8y - 2y^2 + (3y - 8)$
   $$= -2y^2 + 11y - 8$$

47. $\left(x - \dfrac{1}{x}\right)(x + 2) = x^2 + 2x - 1 - \dfrac{2}{x}$

49. $(6x + 5)(6x - 5) = (6x)^2 - (5)^2 = 36x^2 - 25$

51. $(x - 4)^3 = x^3 - 3x^2(4) + 3x(4)^2 - (4)^3$
   $$= x^3 - 12x^2 + 48x - 64$$

53. $x^3 - x = x(x^2 - 1) = x(x + 1)(x - 1)$

55. $25x^2 - 49 = (5x)^2 - 7^2 = (5x + 7)(5x - 7)$

57. $x^3 - 64 = x^3 - 4^3 = (x - 4)(x^2 + 4x + 16)$

59. $2x^2 + 21x + 10 = (2x + 1)(x + 10)$

61. $x^3 - x^2 + 2x - 2 = x^2(x - 1) + 2(x - 1)$
   $$= (x - 1)(x^2 + 2)$$

63. The domain of $\dfrac{1}{x + 6}$ is the set of all real numbers except $x \neq -6$.

65. $\dfrac{x^2 - 64}{5(3x + 24)} = \dfrac{(x + 8)(x - 8)}{5 \cdot 3(x + 8)} = \dfrac{x - 8}{15}, \; x \neq -8$

67. $\dfrac{x^2 - 4}{x^4 - 2x^2 - 8} \cdot \dfrac{x^2 + 2}{x^2} = \dfrac{(x^2 - 4)(x^2 + 2)}{(x^2 - 4)(x^2 + 2)x^2} = \dfrac{1}{x^2}, \; x \neq \pm 2$

69. $2x + \dfrac{3}{2(x - 4)} = \dfrac{2x}{1} + \dfrac{3}{2(x - 4)} = \dfrac{2x(2)(x - 4) + 3}{2(x - 4)}$
   $$= \dfrac{4x^2 - 16x + 3}{2(x - 4)}$$

71. $\dfrac{1}{x-1} + \dfrac{1-x}{x^2+x+1} = \dfrac{(x^2+x+1)+(1-x)(x-1)}{(x-1)(x^2+x+1)}$

$= \dfrac{x^2+x+1-x^2+2x-1}{(x-1)(x^2+x+1)}$

$= \dfrac{3x}{(x-1)(x^2+x+1)}$

$= \dfrac{3x}{x^3-1}$

73. $\dfrac{\left[\dfrac{3a}{\dfrac{a^2}{x}-1}\right]}{\left(\dfrac{a}{x}-1\right)} = \dfrac{\dfrac{3ax}{a^2-x}}{\dfrac{a-x}{x}}$

$= \dfrac{3ax}{a^2-x} \cdot \dfrac{x}{a-x}$

$= \dfrac{3ax^2}{(a^2-x)(a-x)}$

75. $6-(x-2)^2 = 6-(x^2-4x+4)$

$= 2+4x-x^2$

The equation is an indentity.

77. $-x^3+x(7-x)+3 = -x^3-x^2+7x+3$

$x(-x^2-x)+7(x+1)-4 = -x^3-x^2+7x+3$

The equation is an indentity.

79. $3x-2(x+5) = 10$

$3x-2x-10 = 10$

$x = 20$

81. $4(x+3)-3 = 2(4-3x)-4$

$4x+12-3 = 8-6x-4$

$4x+9 = -6x+4$

$10x = -5$

$x = -\dfrac{1}{2}$

83. Let x = the number of liters of pure antifreeze.

30% of $(10-x)$ + 100% of x = 50% of 10

$0.30(10-x)+1.00x = 0.50(10)$

$3-0.30x+1.00x = 5$

$0.70x = 2$

$x = \dfrac{2}{0.70} = \dfrac{20}{7} = 2\dfrac{6}{7}$ liters

85. $2x^2-x-28 = 0$

$(2x+7)(x-4) = 0$

$2x+7 = 0 \quad \text{or} \quad x-4 = 0$

$x = -\dfrac{7}{2} \quad \text{or} \qquad x = 4$

87. $16x^2 = 25$

$x^2 = \dfrac{25}{16}$

$x = \pm\sqrt{\dfrac{25}{16}} = \pm\dfrac{5}{4}$

89. $(x-8)^2 = 15$

$x-8 = \pm\sqrt{15}$

$x = 8 \pm \sqrt{15}$

91. $x^2+6x-3 = 0$

$a = 1, \quad b = 6, \quad c = -3$

$x = \dfrac{-6 \pm \sqrt{6^2-4(1)(-3)}}{2(1)}$

$= \dfrac{-6 \pm \sqrt{48}}{2} = -3 \pm 2\sqrt{3}$

93. $-20-3x+3x^2 = 0$

$3x^2-3x-20 = 0$

$a = 3, b = -3, c = -20$

$x = \dfrac{-(-3) \pm \sqrt{(-3)^2-4(3)(-20)}}{2(3)}$

$= \dfrac{3 \pm \sqrt{249}}{6} = \dfrac{1}{2} \pm \dfrac{\sqrt{249}}{6}$

95. $4x^3 - 6x^2 = 0$

$x^2(4x - 6) = 0$

$x^2 = 0 \Rightarrow x = 0$

$4x - 6 = 0 \Rightarrow x = \frac{3}{2}$

97. $9x^4 + 27x^3 - 4x^2 - 12x = 0$

$9x^3(x + 3) - 4x(x + 3) = 0$

$(9x^3 - 4x)(x + 3) = 0$

$x(9x^2 - 4)(x + 3) = 0$

$x(3x + 2)(3x - 2)(x + 3) = 0$

$x = 0$

$3x + 2 = 0 \Rightarrow x = -\frac{2}{3}$

$3x - 2 = 0 \Rightarrow x = \frac{2}{3}$

$x + 3 = 0 \Rightarrow x = -3$

99. $\sqrt{x - 2} - 8 = 0$

$\sqrt{x - 2} = 8$

$x - 2 = 64$

$x = 66$

101. $\sqrt{3x - 2} = 4 - x$

$3x - 2 = (4 - x)^2$

$3x - 2 = 16 - 8x + x^2$

$0 = 18 - 11x + x^2$

$0 = (x - 9)(x - 2)$

$0 = x - 9 \Rightarrow x = 9$, extraneous

$0 = x - 2 \Rightarrow x = 2$

103. $(x + 2)^{3/4} = 27$

$x + 2 = 27^{4/3}$

$x + 2 = 81$

$x = 79$

105. $8x^2(x^2 - 4)^{1/3} + (x^2 - 4)^{4/3} = 0$

$(x^2 - 4)^{1/3}[8x^2 + x^2 - 4] = 0$

$(x^2 - 4)^{1/3}(9x^2 - 4) = 0$

$(x - 2)^{1/3}(x + 2)^{1/3}(3x - 2)(3x + 2) = 0$

$x - 2 = 0 \Rightarrow x = 2$

$x + 2 = 0 \Rightarrow x = -2$

$3x - 2 = 0 \Rightarrow x = \frac{2}{3}$

$3x + 2 = 0 \Rightarrow x = -\frac{2}{3}$

107. $|2x + 3| = 7$

$2x + 3 = 7$ or $2x + 3 = -7$

$2x = 4$ or $2x = -10$

$x = 2$ $x = -5$

109. $|x^2 - 6| = x$

$x^2 - 6 = x$ or $-(x^2 - 6) = x$

$x^2 - x - 6 = 0$ $x^2 + x - 6 = 0$

$(x - 3)(x + 2) = 0$ $(x + 3)(x - 2) = 0$

$x - 3 = 0 \Rightarrow x = 3$ $x - 2 = 0 \Rightarrow x = 2$

$x + 2 = 0 \Rightarrow x = -2$, extraneous $x + 3 = 0 \Rightarrow x = -3$, extraneous

111. $6x - 17 > 0$

    (a) $x = 3$

        $6(3) - 17 \overset{?}{>} 0$

               $1 > 0$

        Yes, $x = 3$ is a solution.

    (b) $x = -4$

        $6(-4) - 17 \overset{?}{>} 0$

            $-41 \not> 0$

        No, $x = -4$ is not a solution.

    (c) $x = 2.9$

        $6(2.9) - 17 \overset{?}{>} 0$

            $0.4 > 0$

        Yes, $x = 2.9$ is a solution.

    (d) $x = 1$

        $6(1) - 17 \overset{?}{>} 0$

           $-11 \not> 0$

        No $x = 1$ is not a solution.

113. $9x - 8 \leq 7x + 16$

        $2x \leq 24$

        $x \leq 12$

    $(-\infty, 12]$

115. $4(5 - 2x) \leq \frac{1}{2}(8 - x)$

    $20 - 8x \leq 4 - \frac{1}{2}x$

    $-\frac{15}{2}x \leq -16$

        $x \geq \frac{32}{15}$

  $\left[\frac{32}{15}, \infty\right)$

117. $-19 < 3x - 17 \leq 34$

    $-2 < 3x \leq 51$

    $-\frac{2}{3} < x \leq 17$

    $\left(-\frac{2}{3}, 17\right]$

119. $|x| \leq 4$

    $-4 \leq x \leq 4$

    $[-4, 4]$

121. $|x - 3| > 4$

    $x - 3 > 4$ or $x - 3 < -4$

        $x > 7$ $x < -1$

    $(-\infty, -1) \cup (7, \infty)$

123. $R > C$

    $125.33x > 92x + 1200$

    $33.33x > 1200$

        $x > \dfrac{1200}{33.33} \approx 36$ units

125. $x^2 - 6x - 27 < 0$

    $(x + 3)(x - 9) < 0$

    Critical numbers: $x = -3, x = 9$

    Test intervals: $(-\infty, -3), (-3, 9), (9, \infty)$

    Test: Is $(x + 3)(x - 9) < 0$?

    Solution set: $(-3, 9)$

127. $6x^2 + 5x < 4$

$6x^2 + 5x - 4 < 0$

$(3x + 4)(2x - 1) < 0$

Critical numbers: $x = -\dfrac{4}{3}, x = \dfrac{1}{2}$

Test intervals: $\left(-\infty, -\dfrac{4}{3}\right), \left(-\dfrac{4}{3}, \dfrac{1}{2}\right), \left(\dfrac{1}{2}, \infty\right)$

Test: Is $(3x + 4)(2x - 1) < 0$?

Solution set: $\left(-\dfrac{4}{3}, \dfrac{1}{2}\right)$

129. $\dfrac{2}{x + 1} \leq \dfrac{3}{x - 1}$

$\dfrac{2(x - 1) - 3(x + 1)}{(x + 1)(x - 1)} \leq 0$

$\dfrac{2x - 2 - 3x - 3}{(x + 1)(x - 1)} \leq 0$

$\dfrac{-(x + 5)}{(x + 1)(x - 1)} \leq 0$

Critical numbers: $x = -5, x = \pm 1$

Test intervals: $(-\infty, -5), (-5, -1), (-1, 1), (1, \infty)$

Test: Is $\dfrac{-(x + 5)}{(x + 1)(x - 1)} \leq 0$?

Solution set: $[-5, -1) \cup (1, \infty)$

131. $\dfrac{x^2 + 7x + 12}{x} \geq 0$

$\dfrac{(x + 4)(x + 3)}{x} \geq 0$

Critical numbers: $x = -4, x = -3, x = 0$

Test intervals: $(-\infty, -4), (-4, -3), (-3, 0), (0, \infty)$

Test: Is $\dfrac{(x + 4)(x + 3)}{x} \geq 0$?

Solution set: $[-4, -3] \cup (0, \infty)$

133. $5000(1 + r)^2 > 5500$

$(1 + r)^2 > 1.1$

$1 + r > 1.0488$

$r > 0.0488$

$r > 4.9\%$

135. The multiplication in the parentheses comes first.

$10(4 \cdot 7) = 10(28) = 280$

137. The exponent must be applied to the entire quantity inside parentheses.

$(2x)^4 = 2^4 x^4 = 16x^4$

139. To raise a power to a power, the exponents must be multiplied.

$(3^4)^4 = 3^{4 \cdot 4} = 3^{16}$

141. Add the quantities in the parentheses first before squaring.

$(5 + 8)^2 = (13)^2 = 169 \neq 5^2 + 8^2$

143. $\dfrac{2}{3}x^4 - \dfrac{3}{8}x^3 + \dfrac{5}{6}x^2 = \dfrac{16}{24}x^4 - \dfrac{9}{24}x^3 + \dfrac{20}{24}x^2$

$= \dfrac{1}{24}x^2(16x^2 - 9x + 20)$

The missing factor is $16x^2 - 9x + 20$.

145. $2x(x^2 - 3)^{1/3} - 5(x^2 - 3)^{4/3} = (x^2 - 3)^{1/3}[2x - 5(x^2 - 3)]$

$= (x^2 - 3)^{1/3}(-5x^2 + 2x + 15)$

The missing factor is $-5x^2 + 2x + 15$.

147. $x(x + 2)^{-1/2} + (x + 2)^{1/2} = (x + 2)^{-1/2}[x + (x + 2)^1]$

$= \dfrac{1}{(x + 2)^{1/2}}(2x + 2)$

$= \dfrac{2(x + 1)}{(x + 2)^{1/2}}$

149. $\dfrac{x^2 - 4x + 2}{x} = \dfrac{x^2}{x} - \dfrac{4x}{x} + \dfrac{2}{x} = x - 4 + 2x^{-1}$

151. $\dfrac{2x^3 - 4x^2 + 3}{\sqrt{x}} = \dfrac{2x^3}{x^{1/2}} - \dfrac{4x^2}{x^{1/2}} + \dfrac{3}{x^{1/2}}$

$\qquad\qquad\qquad = 2x^{5/2} - 4x^{3/2} + 3x^{-1/2}$

153.

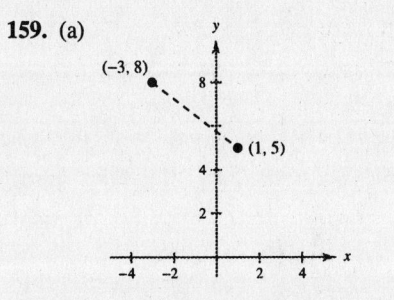

$d_1 = \sqrt{(13-5)^2 + (11-22)^2} = \sqrt{64+121} = \sqrt{185}$

$d_2 = \sqrt{(2-13)^2 + (3-11)^2} = \sqrt{121+64} = \sqrt{185}$

$d_3 = \sqrt{(2-5)^2 + (3-22)^2} = \sqrt{9+361} = \sqrt{370}$

$d_1{}^2 + d_2{}^2 = 185 + 185 = 370 = d_3{}^2$

Thus, the triangle is a right triangle.

155. $x > 0$ and $y = -2$ in Quadrant IV.

157. $(-x, y)$ is in the third Quadrant means that (x, y) is in Quadrant IV

159. (a)

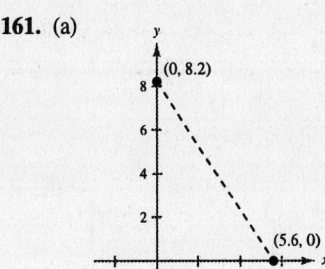

(b) $d = \sqrt{(-3-1)^2 + (8-5)^2} = \sqrt{16+9} = 5$

161. (a)

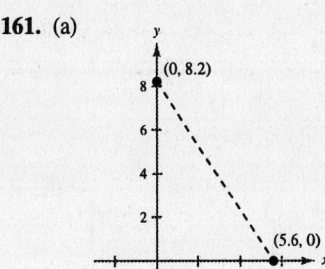

(b) $d = \sqrt{(5.6-0)^2 + (0-8.2)^2}$

$\qquad = \sqrt{31.36 + 67.24} = \sqrt{98.6} \approx 9.9$

163. (a)

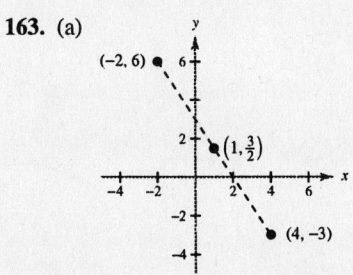

(b) Midpoint: $\left(\dfrac{-2+4}{2}, \dfrac{6+(-3)}{2}\right) = \left(1, \dfrac{3}{2}\right)$

165. (a)

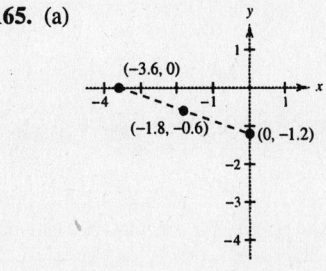

(b) Midpoint: $\left(\dfrac{0+(-3.6)}{2}, \dfrac{-1.2+0}{2}\right) = (-1.8, -0.6)$

167. Change in apparent temperature: $150°\,\text{F} - 70°\,\text{F} = 80°\,\text{F}$

169. False. There is also a cross-product term when a binomial sum is squared.

$(x + a)^2 = (x + a)(x + a) = x^2 + 2ax + a^2$

171. True. If a quadratic equation cannot be factored, then the Quadratic Formula can be used to solve the equation.

173. (a) Since there are three solutions, the equation is not linear nor is it quadratic.
Neither

(b) Since there is only one solution, the equation could have been either linear
or quadratic. Both

(c) Since there are two solutions, the equation is not linear but could be quadratic.
Quadratic

(d) Since there are four solutions, the equation is not linear nor is it quadratic.
Neither

175. $\sqrt{5u} + \sqrt{3u} \neq 2\sqrt{2u}$

Radicals cannot be added unless both the index
and the radicand are the same.

177. Answers will vary.

Chapter P   Practice Test

1. Evaluate $\dfrac{|-42| - 20}{15 - |-4|}$.

2. Simplify $\dfrac{x}{z} - \dfrac{z}{y}$.

3. The distance between x and 7 is no more than 4. Use absolute value notation to describe this expression.

4. Evaluate $10(-x)^3$ for $x = 5$.

5. Simplify $(-4x^3)(-2x^{-5})\left(\frac{1}{16}x\right)$.

6. Change 0.0000412 to scientific notation.

7. Evaluate $125^{2/3}$.

8. Simplify $\sqrt[4]{64x^7y^9}$.

9. Rationalize the denominator and simplify $\dfrac{6}{\sqrt{12}}$.

10. Simplify $3\sqrt{80} - 7\sqrt{500}$.

11. Simplify $(8x^4 - 9x^2 + 2x - 1) - (3x^3 + 5x + 4)$.

12. Multiply $(x - 3)(x^2 + x - 7)$.

13. Multiply $[(x - 2) - y]^2$.

14. Factor $16x^4 - 1$.

15. Factor $6x^2 + 5x - 4$.

16. Factor $x^3 - 64$.

17. Combine and simplify $-\dfrac{3}{x} + \dfrac{x}{x^2 + 2}$.

18. Combine and simplify $\dfrac{x - 3}{4x} \div \dfrac{x^2 - 9}{x^2}$.

19. Simplify $\dfrac{1 - \dfrac{1}{x}}{1 - \dfrac{1}{1 - \dfrac{1}{x}}}$.

20. (a) Plot the points $(-3, 7)$ and $(5, -1)$,

    (b) find the distance between the points, and

    (c) find the midpoint of the line segment joining the points.

21. Solve $x^2 - 2x - 35 = 0$

    (a) by factoring.

    (b) by completing the square.

    (c) by the Quadratic Formula.

22. Solve $x^5 - 5x^3 + 4x = 0$ by factoring.

23. Solve $x = 2\sqrt{x + 3}$.

24. Solve $x^2 - 16 \le 0$.

25. Solve $\left|\dfrac{4 - x}{3}\right| > 2$.

CHAPTER 1
Functions and Their Graphs

C H A P T E R   1
Functions and Their Graphs

Section 1.1   Graphs of Equations

■ You should be able to use the point-plotting method of graphing.

■ You should be able to find x- and y-intercepts.

  (a) To find the x-intercepts, let $y = 0$ and solve for x.

  (b) To find the y-intercepts, let $x = 0$ and solve for y.

■ You should be able to test for symmetry.

  (a) To test for x-axis symmetry, replace y with $-y$.

  (b) To test for y-axis symmetry, replace x with $-x$.

  (c) To test for origin symmetry, replace x with $-x$ and y with $-y$.

■ You should know the standard equation of a circle with center (h, k) and radius r:

  $$(x - h)^2 + (y - k)^2 = r^2$$

Solutions to Odd-Numbered Exercises

1. $y = \sqrt{x + 4}$

  (a) $(0, 2)$: $2 \overset{?}{=} \sqrt{0 + 4}$

  $2 = 2$

  Yes, the point *is* on the graph.

  (b) $(5, 3)$: $3 \overset{?}{=} \sqrt{5 + 4}$

  $3 = \sqrt{9}$

  Yes, the point *is* on the graph.

3. $y = 4 - |x - 2|$

  (a) $(1, 5)$: $5 \overset{?}{=} 4 - |1 - 2|$

  $5 \neq 4 - 1$

  No, the point is *not* on the graph.

  (b) $(6, 0)$: $0 \overset{?}{=} 4 - |6 - 2|$

  $0 = 4 - 4$

  Yes, the point *is* on the graph.

5. $y = -2x + 5$

x	-1	0	1	2	$\frac{5}{2}$
y	7	5	3	1	0

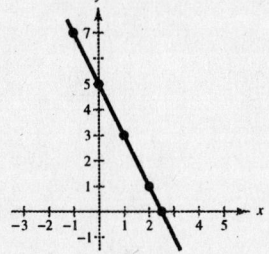

7. $y = x^2 - 3x$

x	-1	0	1	2	3
y	4	0	-2	-2	0

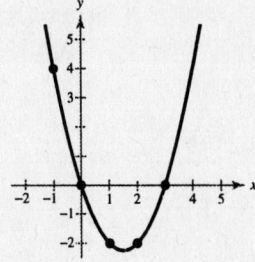

65

9. $x^2 - y = 0$

$(-x)^2 - y = 0 \implies x^2 - y = 0 \implies$ *y*-axis symmetry

$x^2 - (-y) = 0 \implies x^2 + y = 0 \implies$ No *x*-axis symmetry

$(-x)^2 - (-y) = 0 \implies x^2 + y = 0 \implies$ No origin symmetry

11. $y = x^3$

$y = (-x)^3 \implies y = -x^3 \implies$ No *y*-axis symmetry

$-y = x^3 \implies y = -x^3 \implies$ No *x*-axis symmetry

$-y = (-x)^3 \implies -y = -x^3 \implies y = x^3 \implies$ Origin symmetry

13. $y = \dfrac{x}{x^2 + 1}$

$y = \dfrac{-x}{(-x)^2 + 1} \implies y = \dfrac{-x}{x^2 + 1} \implies$ No *y*-axis symmetry

$-y = \dfrac{x}{x^2 + 1} \implies y = \dfrac{-x}{x^2 + 1} \implies$ No *x*-axis symmetry

$-y = \dfrac{-x}{(-x)^2 + 1} \implies -y = \dfrac{-x}{x^2 + 1} \implies y = \dfrac{x}{x^2 + 1} \implies$ Origin symmetry

15. $xy^2 + 10 = 0$

$(-x)y^2 + 10 = 0 \implies -xy^2 + 10 = 0 \implies$ No *y*-axis symmetry

$x(-y)^2 + 10 = 0 \implies xy^2 + 10 = 0 \implies$ *x*-axis symmetry

$(-x)(-y)^2 + 10 = 0 \implies -xy^2 + 10 = 0 \implies$ No origin symmetry

17. *y*-axis symmetry

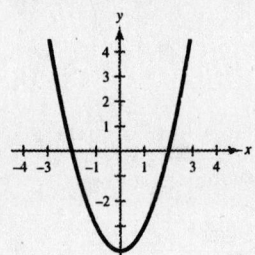

19. Origin symmetry

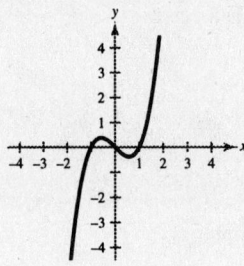

21. $y = 1 - x$ has intercepts $(1, 0)$ and $(0, 1)$. Matches graph (c).

23. $y = x^3 - x + 1$ has a *y*-intercept of $(0, 1)$ and the points $(1, 1)$ and $(-2, -5)$ are on the graph. Matches graph (b).

25. $y = 16 - 4x^2$

x-intercepts: $0 = 16 - 4x^2$

$4x^2 = 16$

$x^2 = 4$

$x = \pm 2$

$(-2, 0), (2, 0)$

y-intercept: $y = 16 - 4(0)^2 = 16$

$(0, 16)$

27. $y = 2x^3 - 5x^2$

x-intercepts: $0 = 2x^3 - 5x^2$

$0 = x^2(2x - 5)$

$x = 0 \quad \text{or} \quad x = \tfrac{5}{2}$

$(0, 0), \left(\tfrac{5}{2}, 0\right)$

y-intercept: $y = 2(0)^3 - 5(0)^2$

$= 0$

$(0, 0)$

29. $y = -3x + 1$

x-intercept: $\left(\frac{1}{3}, 0\right)$

y-intercept: $(0, 1)$

No symmetry

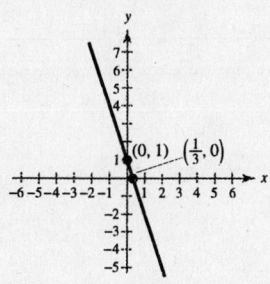

31. $y = x^2 - 2x$

Intercepts: $(0, 0), (2, 0)$

No symmetry

x	-1	0	1	2	3
y	3	0	-1	0	3

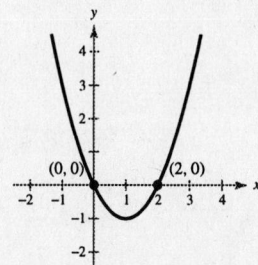

33. $y = x^3 + 3$

Intercepts: $(0, 3), \left(\sqrt[3]{-3}, 0\right)$

No symmetry

x	-2	-1	0	1	2
y	-5	2	3	4	11

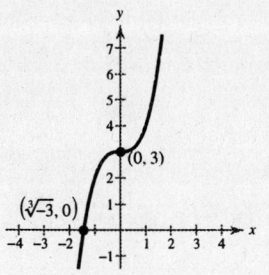

35. $y = \sqrt{x - 3}$

Domain: $[3, \infty)$

Intercept: $(3, 0)$

No symmetry

x	3	4	7	12
y	0	1	2	3

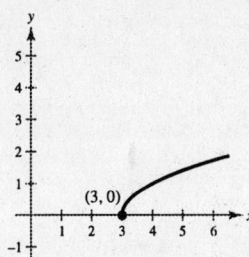

37. $y = |x - 6|$

Intercepts: $(0, 6), (6, 0)$

No symmetry

x	-2	0	2	4	6	8	10
y	8	6	4	2	0	2	4

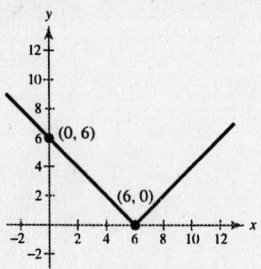

39. $x = y^2 - 1$

Intercepts: $(0, -1), (0, 1), (-1, 0)$

x-axis symmetry

x	-1	0	3
y	0	± 1	± 2

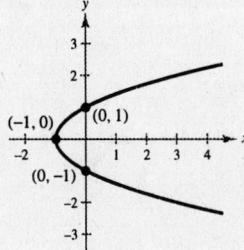

41. $y = 3 - \frac{1}{2}x$

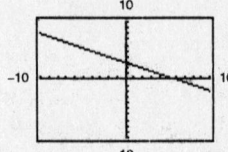

Intercepts: $(6, 0), (0, 3)$

43. $y = x^2 - 4x + 3$

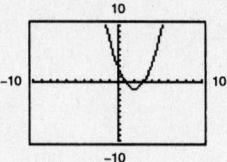

Intercepts: $(3, 0), (1, 0), (0, 3)$

45. $y = \dfrac{2x}{x - 1}$

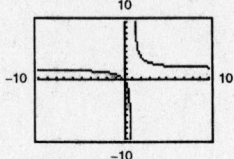

Intercept: $(0, 0)$

47. $y = \sqrt[3]{x}$

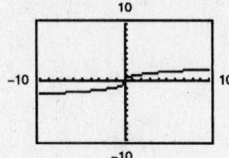

Intercept: $(0, 0)$

49. $y = x\sqrt{x + 6}$

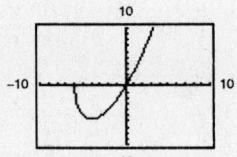

Intercepts: $(0, 0), (-6, 0)$

51. $y = |x + 3|$

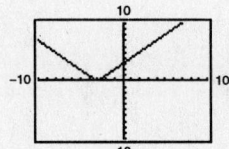

Intercepts: $(-3, 0), (0, 3)$

53. Center: $(0, 0)$; radius: 4

Standard form: $(x - 0)^2 + (y - 0)^2 = 4^2$

$$x^2 + y^2 = 16$$

55. Center: $(2, -1)$; radius: 4

Standard form: $(x - 2)^2 + (y - (-1))^2 = 4^2$

$$(x - 2)^2 + (y + 1)^2 = 16$$

57. Center: $(-1, 2)$; solution point: $(0, 0)$

$(x - (-1))^2 + (y - 2)^2 = r^2$

$(0 + 1)^2 + (0 - 2)^2 = r^2 \Longrightarrow 5 = r^2$

Standard form: $(x + 1)^2 + (y - 2)^2 = 5$

59. Endpoints of a diameter: $(0, 0), (6, 8)$

Center: $\left(\dfrac{0 + 6}{2}, \dfrac{0 + 8}{2}\right) = (3, 4)$

$(x - 3)^2 + (y - 4)^2 = r^2$

$(0 - 3)^2 + (0 - 4)^2 = r^2 \Longrightarrow 25 = r^2$

Standard form: $(x - 3)^2 + (y - 4)^2 = 25$

61. $x^2 + y^2 = 25$

Center: $(0, 0)$

Radius: 5

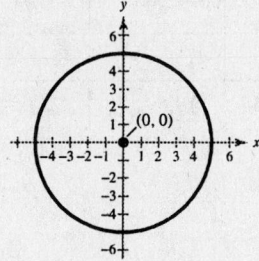

63. $(x - 1)^2 + (y + 3)^2 = 9$

Center: $(1, -3)$

Radius: 3

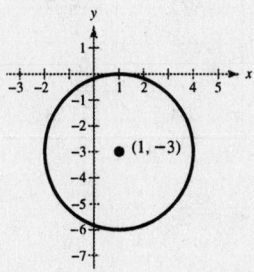

65. $\left(x - \frac{1}{2}\right)^2 + \left(y - \frac{1}{2}\right)^2 = \frac{9}{4}$

Center: $\left(\frac{1}{2}, \frac{1}{2}\right)$

Radius: $\frac{3}{2}$

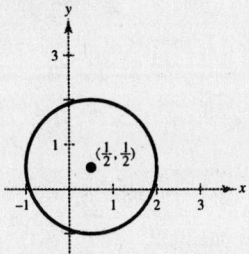

67. $y_1 = 4 + \sqrt{25 - x^2}$

$y_2 = 4 - \sqrt{25 - x^2}$

The graph represents a circle.

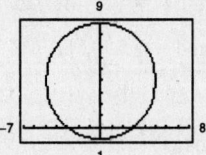

69. $y = 225{,}000 - 20{,}000t, \ 0 \leq t \leq 8$

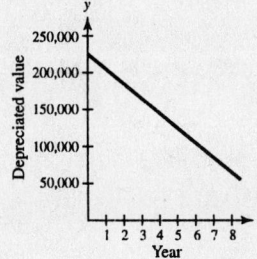

71. (a)

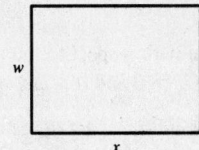

(b) $2x + 2w = 12 \Rightarrow w = 6 - x$

$A = x \cdot w = x(6 - x)$

(c)

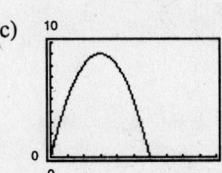

(d) The area is maximum when $x = 3$ and $w = 6 - 3 = 3$.

$x = 3$ meters

$w = 3$ meters

73. (a) and (b)

Year	1950	1960	1970	1980	1990	1994	1997	1998
Per Capita Debt	$1688	$1572	$1807	$3981	$12,848	$15,750	$20,063	$20,513
t	0	10	20	30	40	44	47	48
y	$1837.433	$1204.583	$1763.133	$4851.083	$11,806.433	$15,971.157	$19,692.78	$21,054.377

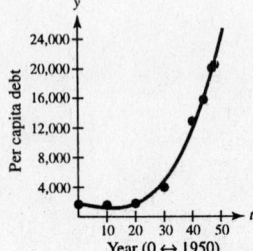

(c) for the year 2002, $t = 52$ and $y \approx \$27,141.725$

for the year 2004, $t = 54$ and $y \approx \$30,588.707$

75. $y = \dfrac{10,770}{50^2} - 0.37 \approx 3.9$ ohms

77. True. All linear equations of the form $y = mx + b$, which excludes vertical lines, cross the y-axis one time.

79. $y = ax^2 + bx^3$

(a) If the graph is symmetric with respect to the y-axis, then you can replace x with $-x$ and the result is an equivalent equation. This happens when $b = 0$ and a is any real number.

(b) If the graph is symmetric with respect to the origin, then you can replace x with $-x$ and y with $-y$ and the result is an equivalent equation. This happens when $a = 0$ and b is any real number.

81. False. $\dfrac{1}{3 \cdot 4^{-1}} = \dfrac{1}{\dfrac{3}{4}} = \dfrac{4}{3} \neq 3 \cdot 4$

83. $9x^5 + 4x^3 - 7$

Terms: $9x^5, 4x^3, -7$

85. $\sqrt{18x} - \sqrt{2x} = 3\sqrt{2x} - \sqrt{2x} = 2\sqrt{2x}$

87. $\dfrac{70}{\sqrt{7x}} = \dfrac{70}{\sqrt{7x}} \cdot \dfrac{\sqrt{7x}}{\sqrt{7x}} = \dfrac{70\sqrt{7x}}{7x} = \dfrac{10\sqrt{7x}}{x}$

89. $\sqrt[6]{t^2} = t^{2/6} = |t|^{1/3} = \sqrt[3]{|t|}$

Section 1.2   Linear Equations in Two Variables

You should know the following important facts about lines.

■ The graph of $y = mx + b$ is a straight line. It is called a linear equation in two variables.

■ The slope of the line through (x_1, y_1) and (x_2, y_2) is

$$m = \frac{y_2 - y_1}{x_2 - x_1} = \frac{\text{change in } y}{\text{change in } x} = \frac{\text{rise}}{\text{run}}.$$

■ (a) If $m > 0$, the line rises from left to right.

   (b) If $m = 0$, the line is horizontal.

   (c) If $m < 0$, the line falls from left to right.

   (d) If m is undefined, the line is vertical.

■ Equations of Lines

   (a) Slope-Intercept: $y = mx + b$

   (b) Point-Slope: $y - y_1 = m(x - x_1)$

   (c) Two-Point: $y - y_1 = \dfrac{y_2 - y_1}{x_2 - x_1}(x - x_1)$

   (d) General: $Ax + By + C = 0$

   (e) Vertical: $x = a$

   (f) Horizontal: $y = b$

■ Given two distinct nonvertical lines

   $L_1: y = m_1x + b_1$ and $L_2: y = m_2x + b_2$

   (a) L_1 is parallel to L_2 if and only if $m_1 = m_2$ and $b_1 \neq b_2$.

   (b) L_1 is perpendicular to L_2 if and only if $m_1 = -1/m_2$.

Solutions to Odd-Numbered Exercises

1. (a) $m = \frac{2}{3}$. Since the slope is positive, the line rises. Matches L_2.

   (b) m is undefined. The line is vertical. Matches L_3.

   (c) $m = -2$. The line falls. Matches L_1.

3.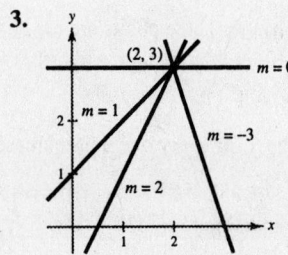

5. Two points on the line: $(0, 0)$ and $(5, 8)$

$\text{Slope} = \dfrac{\text{rise}}{\text{run}} = \dfrac{8}{5}$

7. Two points on the line: $(0, 3)$ and $(1, 3)$

$\text{Slope} = \dfrac{\text{rise}}{\text{run}} = \dfrac{0}{1} = 0$

9. Two points on the line: $(0, 8)$ and $(2, 0)$

$\text{Slope} = \dfrac{\text{rise}}{\text{run}} = \dfrac{-8}{2} = -4$

11.

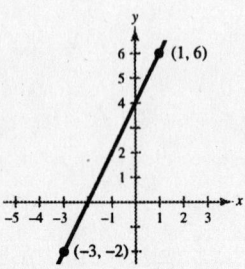

$m = \dfrac{6 - (-2)}{1 - (-3)} = \dfrac{8}{4} = 2$

13.

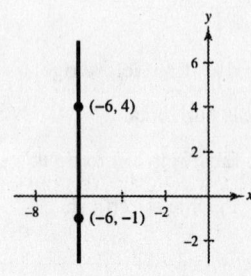

$m = \dfrac{4 - (-1)}{-6 - (-6)} = \dfrac{5}{0}$

m is undefined

15.

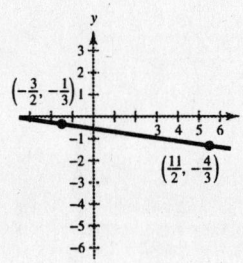

$m = \dfrac{-\dfrac{1}{3} - \left(-\dfrac{4}{3}\right)}{-\dfrac{3}{2} - \dfrac{11}{2}} = -\dfrac{1}{7}$

17.

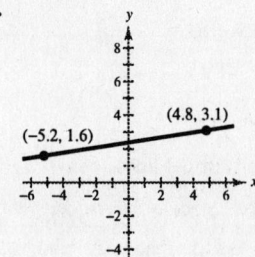

$m = \dfrac{1.6 - 3.1}{-5.2 - 4.8} = \dfrac{-1.5}{-10}$

$= 0.15$

19. Point: $(2, 1)$ Slope: $m = 0$

Since $m = 0$, y does not change. Three points are $(0, 1)$, $(3, 1)$, and $(-1, 1)$.

21. Point: $(5, -6)$ Slope: $m = 1$

Since $m = 1$, y increases by 1 for every one unit increase in x. Three points are $(6, -5)$, $(7, -4)$, and $(8, -3)$.

23. Point: $(-8, 1)$ Slope is undefined

Since m is undefined, x does not change. Three points are $(-8, 0)$, $(-8, 2)$, and $(-8, 3)$.

25. Point: $(-5, 4)$ Slope: $m = 2$

Since $m = 2 = \frac{2}{1}$, y increases by 2 for every one unit increase in x.
Three additional points are $(-4, 6)$, $(-3, 8)$, and $(-2, 10)$.

27. Point: $(7, -2)$ Slope: $m = \frac{1}{2}$

Since $m = \frac{1}{2}$, y increases by 1 unit for every two unit increase in x.
Three additional points are $(9, -1)$, $(11, 0)$, and $(13, 1)$.

29. Slope of L_1: $m = \dfrac{9 + 1}{5 - 0} = 2$

Slope of L_2: $m = \dfrac{1 - 3}{4 - 0} = -\dfrac{1}{2}$

L_1 and L_2 are perpendicular.

31. Slope of L_1: $m = \dfrac{0 - 6}{-6 - 3} = \dfrac{2}{3}$

Slope of L_2: $m = \dfrac{\frac{7}{3} + 1}{5 - 0} = \dfrac{2}{3}$

L_1 and L_2 are parallel.

33. (a) $m = 135$. The sales are increasing 135 units per year.

(b) $m = 0$. There is no change in sales.

(c) $m = -40$. The sales are decreasing 40 units per year.

35. (a) The greatest increase (largest positive slope) was from 1990 to 1991 and from 1996 to 1997.
The greatest decrease (largest negative slope) was from 1997 to 1998.

(b) $(1, 0.98)$ and $(11, 1.35)$

$$m = \frac{1.35 - 0.98}{11 - 1} = \frac{0.37}{10} = 0.037$$

(c) On average, the earnings per share increased by $0.037 per year over this 10 year period.

37. (a) and (b)

x	300	600	900	1200	1500	1800	2100
y	-25	-50	-75	-100	-125	-150	-175

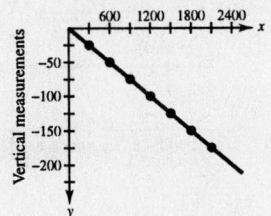

Horizontal measurements

(c) $m = \dfrac{-50 - (-25)}{600 - 300} = \dfrac{-25}{300} = -\dfrac{1}{12}$

$y - (-50) = -\dfrac{1}{12}(x - 600)$

$y + 50 = -\dfrac{1}{12}x + 50$

$y = -\dfrac{1}{12}x$

(d) Since $m = -\frac{1}{12}$, for every 12 horizontal measurements
the vertical measurement decreases by 1.

(e) $\dfrac{1}{12} \approx 0.083 = 8.3\%$ grade

39. $\dfrac{\text{rise}}{\text{run}} = \dfrac{3}{4} = \dfrac{x}{\frac{1}{2}(32)}$

$\dfrac{3}{4} = \dfrac{x}{16}$

$4x = 48$

$x = 12$

The maximum height in the attic is 12 feet.

41. $y = x - 10$

Slope: $m = 1$

y-intercept: $(0, -10)$

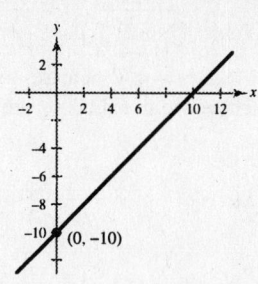

43. $3y + 5 = 0$

$3y = -5$

$y = -\dfrac{5}{3}$

Slope: $m = 0$

y-intercept: $\left(0, -\dfrac{5}{3}\right)$

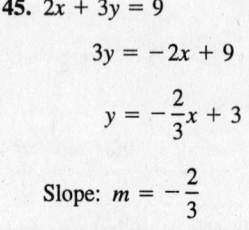

45. $2x + 3y = 9$

$3y = -2x + 9$

$y = -\dfrac{2}{3}x + 3$

Slope: $m = -\dfrac{2}{3}$

y-intercept: $(0, 3)$

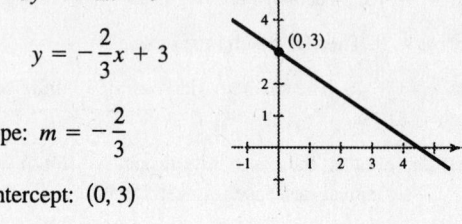

47. $m = -1, (0, 10)$

$y - 10 = -1(x - 0)$

$y - 10 = -x$

$y = -x + 10$

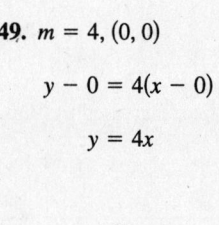

49. $m = 4, (0, 0)$

$y - 0 = 4(x - 0)$

$y = 4x$

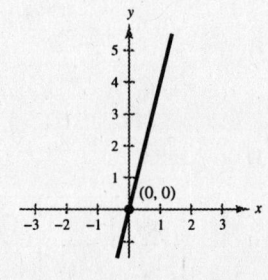

51. $m = \frac{3}{4}, (-2, -5)$

$y + 5 = \frac{3}{4}(x + 2)$

$4y + 20 = 3x + 6$

$4y = 3x - 14$

$y = \frac{3}{4}x - \frac{7}{2}$

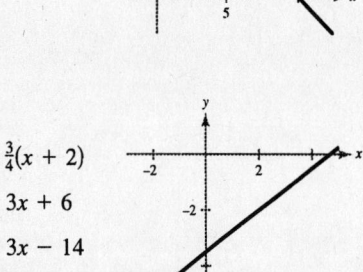

53. $m = 0, (-10, 4)$

$y - 4 = 0(x + 10)$

$y - 4 = 0$

$y = 4$

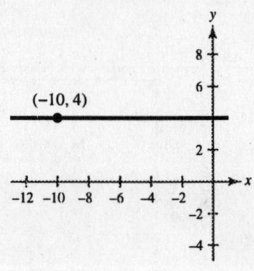

55. $m = -3, \left(-\dfrac{1}{2}, \dfrac{3}{2}\right)$

$y - \dfrac{3}{2} = -3\left(x + \dfrac{1}{2}\right)$

$y - \dfrac{3}{2} = -3x - \dfrac{3}{2}$

$y = -3x$

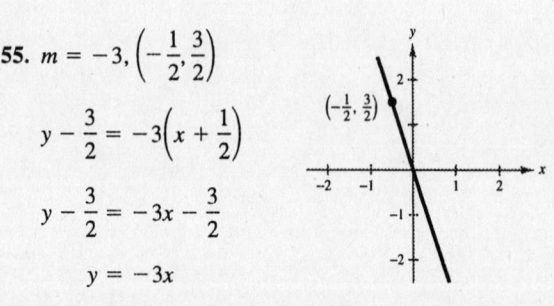

57. $m = -\frac{5}{2}, (2.3, -8.5)$

$y - (-8.5) = -\frac{5}{2}(x - 2.3)$

$y + 8.5 = -2.5x + 5.75$

$y = -2.5x - 2.75$

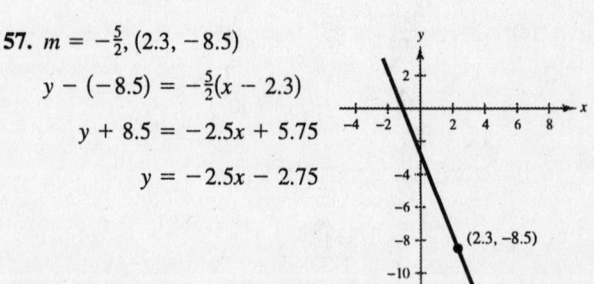

59. $(4, 3), (-4, -4)$

$$y - 3 = \frac{-4 - 3}{-4 - 4}(x - 4)$$

$$y - 3 = \frac{7}{8}(x - 4)$$

$$y - 3 = \frac{7}{8}x - \frac{7}{2}$$

$$y = \frac{7}{8}x - \frac{1}{2}$$

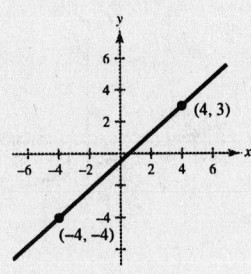

61. $(-1, 4), (6, 4)$

$$y - 4 = \frac{4 - 4}{6 - (-1)}(x + 1)$$

$$y - 4 = 0(x + 1)$$

$$y - 4 = 0$$

$$y = 4$$

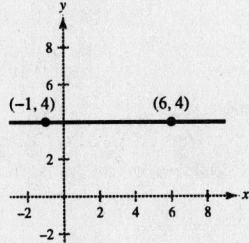

63. $(1, 1), \left(6, -\frac{2}{3}\right)$

$$y - 1 = \frac{-\frac{2}{3} - 1}{6 - 1}(x - 1)$$

$$y - 1 = -\frac{1}{3}(x - 1)$$

$$y - 1 = -\frac{1}{3}x + \frac{1}{3}$$

$$y = -\frac{1}{3}x + \frac{4}{3}$$

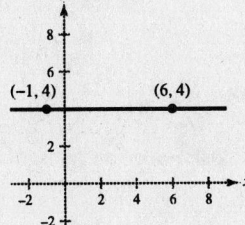

65. $\left(\frac{3}{4}, \frac{3}{2}\right), \left(-\frac{4}{3}, \frac{7}{4}\right)$

$$y - \frac{3}{2} = \frac{\frac{7}{4} - \frac{3}{2}}{-\frac{4}{3} - \frac{3}{4}}\left(x - \frac{3}{4}\right)$$

$$y - \frac{3}{2} = \frac{\frac{1}{4}}{-\frac{25}{12}}\left(x - \frac{3}{4}\right)$$

$$y - \frac{3}{2} = -\frac{3}{25}\left(x - \frac{3}{4}\right)$$

$$y - \frac{3}{2} = -\frac{3}{25}x + \frac{9}{100}$$

$$y = -\frac{3}{25}x + \frac{159}{100}$$

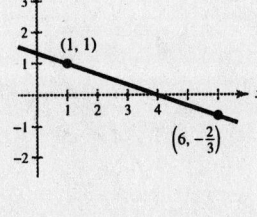

67. $(-8, 0.6), (2, -2.4)$

$$y - 0.6 = \frac{-2.4 - 0.6}{2 - (-8)}(x + 8)$$

$$y - 0.6 = -\frac{3}{10}(x + 8)$$

$$10y - 6 = -3(x + 8)$$

$$10y - 6 = -3x - 24$$

$$10y = -3x - 18$$

$$y = -\frac{3}{10}x - \frac{9}{5} \quad \text{or} \quad y = -0.3x - 1.8$$

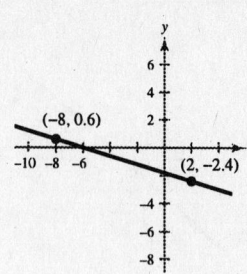

69. $(-3, 0), (0, 4)$

$$\frac{x}{-3} + \frac{y}{4} = 1$$

$$(-12)\frac{x}{-3} + (-12)\frac{y}{4} = (-12) \cdot 1$$

$$4x - 3y + 12 = 0$$

71. $\left(\frac{2}{3}, 0\right), (0, -2)$

$$\frac{x}{\frac{2}{3}} + \frac{y}{-2} = 1$$

$$\frac{3x}{2} - \frac{y}{2} = 1$$

$$3x - y - 2 = 0$$

73. $(d, 0), (0, d), (-3, 4)$

$$\frac{x}{d} + \frac{y}{d} = 1$$

$$x + y = d$$

$$-3 + 4 = d$$

$$1 = d$$

$$x + y = 1$$

$$x + y - 1 = 0$$

75. $x + y = 7$

$$y = -x + 7$$

Slope: $m = -1$

(a) $m = -1, (-3, 2)$

$$y - 2 = -1(x + 3)$$

$$y - 2 = -x - 3$$

$$y = -x - 1$$

(b) $m = 1, (-3, 2)$

$$y - 2 = 1(x + 3)$$

$$y = x + 5$$

77. $5x + 3y = 0$

$$3y = -5x$$

$$y = -\frac{5}{3}x$$

Slope: $m = -\frac{5}{3}$

(a) $m = -\frac{5}{3}, \left(\frac{7}{8}, \frac{3}{4}\right)$

$$y - \frac{3}{4} = -\frac{5}{3}\left(x - \frac{7}{8}\right)$$

$$24y - 18 = -40\left(x - \frac{7}{8}\right)$$

$$24y - 18 = -40x + 35$$

$$24y = -40x + 53$$

$$y = -\frac{5}{3}x + \frac{53}{24}$$

(b) $m = \frac{3}{5}, \left(\frac{7}{8}, \frac{3}{4}\right)$

$$y - \frac{3}{4} = \frac{3}{5}\left(x - \frac{7}{8}\right)$$

$$40y - 30 = 24\left(x - \frac{7}{8}\right)$$

$$40y - 30 = 24x - 21$$

$$40y = 24x + 9$$

$$y = \frac{3}{5}x + \frac{9}{40}$$

79. $x = 4$

m is undefined.

(a) $(2, 5)$, m is undefined.

$$x = 2$$

(b) $(2, 5)$, $m = 0$

$$y = 5$$

81. $6x + 2y = 9$

$$2y = -6x + 9$$

$$y = -3x + \frac{9}{2}$$

Slope: $m = -3$

(a) $(-3.9, -1.4)$, $m = -3$

$$y - (-1.4) = -3(x - (-3.9))$$

$$y + 1.4 = -3x - 11.7$$

$$y = -3x - 13.1$$

(b) $(-3.9, -1.4)$, $m = \frac{1}{3}$

$$y - (-1.4) = \frac{1}{3}(x - (-3.9))$$

$$y + 1.4 = \frac{1}{3}x + 1.3$$

$$y = \frac{1}{3}x - 0.1$$

83. (a) $y = \frac{2}{3}x$ (b) $y = -\frac{3}{2}x$ (c) $y = \frac{2}{3}x + 2$

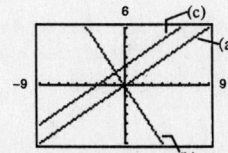

(a) is parallel to (c). (b) is perpendicular to (a) and (c).

85. (a) $y = x - 8$ (b) $y = x + 1$ (c) $y = -x + 3$

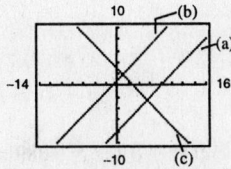

(a) is parallel to (b). (c) is perpendicular to (a) and (b).

87. $(1, 156)$, $m = 4.50$

$$V - 156 = 4.50(t - 1)$$

$$V - 156 = 4.50t - 4.50$$

$$V = 4.5t + 151.5$$

89. The y-intercept is 8.5 and the slope is 2, which represents the increase in hourly wage per unit produced. Matches graph (c).

91. The y-intercepts is 750 and the slope is -100, which represents the decrease in the value of the word processor each year. Matches graph (d).

93. Set the distance between $(6, 5)$ and (x, y) equal to the distance between $(1, -8)$ and (x, y).

$$\sqrt{(x - 6)^2 + (y - 5)^2} = \sqrt{(x - 1)^2 + (y - (-8))^2}$$

$$(x - 6)^2 + (y - 5)^2 = (x - 1)^2 + (y + 8)^2$$

$$x^2 - 12x + 36 + y^2 - 10y + 25 = x^2 - 2x + 1 + y^2 + 16y + 64$$

$$x^2 + y^2 - 12x - 10y + 61 = x^2 + y^2 - 2x + 16y + 65$$

$$-12x - 10y + 61 = -2x + 16y + 65$$

$$-10x - 26y - 4 = 0$$

$$-2(5x + 13y + 2) = 0$$

$$5x + 13y + 2 = 0$$

$$13y = -5x - 2$$

$$y = -\tfrac{5}{13}x - \tfrac{2}{13}$$

95. Set the distance between $\left(-\tfrac{1}{2}, -4\right)$ and (x, y) equal to the distance between $\left(\tfrac{7}{2}, \tfrac{5}{4}\right)$ and (x, y).

$$\sqrt{\left(x - \left(-\tfrac{1}{2}\right)\right)^2 + (y - (-4))^2} = \sqrt{\left(x - \tfrac{7}{2}\right)^2 + \left(y - \tfrac{5}{4}\right)^2}$$

$$\left(x + \tfrac{1}{2}\right)^2 + (y + 4)^2 = \left(x - \tfrac{7}{2}\right)^2 + \left(y - \tfrac{5}{4}\right)^2$$

$$x^2 + x + \tfrac{1}{4} + y^2 + 8y + 16 = x^2 - 7x + \tfrac{49}{4} + y^2 - \tfrac{5}{2}y + \tfrac{25}{16}$$

$$x^2 + y^2 + x + 8y + \tfrac{65}{4} = x^2 + y^2 - 7x - \tfrac{5}{2}y + \tfrac{221}{16}$$

$$x + 8y + \tfrac{65}{4} = -7x - \tfrac{5}{2}y + \tfrac{221}{16}$$

$$8x + \tfrac{21}{2}y + \tfrac{39}{16} = 0$$

$$128x + 168y + 39 = 0$$

$$168y = -128x - 39$$

$$y = -\tfrac{16}{21}x - \tfrac{13}{56}$$

97. $t = 0$ represents 1996

$(0, 3927)$ and $(1, 3981)$

$$m = \frac{3981 - 3927}{1 - 0} = 54$$

$N = 54t + 3927$

$t = 3$ represents 1999: $N = 54(3) + 3927 = 4089$ stores.

$t = 4$ represents 2000: $N = 54(4) + 3927 = 4143$ stores.

99. $F = \frac{9}{5}C + 32$

$F = 0°;\qquad 0 = \frac{9}{5}C + 32\qquad\qquad C = -10°;\; F = \frac{9}{5}(-10) + 32$

$\qquad\qquad\quad -32 = \frac{9}{5}C\qquad\qquad\qquad\qquad F = -18 + 32$

$\qquad\qquad\quad -17.8 \approx C\qquad\qquad\qquad\qquad\; F = 14$

$C = 10°;\; F = \frac{9}{5}(10) + 32\qquad F = 68°;\; 68 = \frac{9}{5}C + 32$

$\qquad\qquad F = 18 + 32\qquad\qquad\qquad\quad 36 = \frac{9}{5}C$

$\qquad\qquad F = 50\qquad\qquad\qquad\qquad\quad 20 = C$

$F = 90°;\qquad 90 = \frac{9}{5}C + 32\qquad C = 177°;\; F = \frac{9}{5}(177) + 32$

$\qquad\qquad\quad 58 = \frac{9}{5}C\qquad\qquad\qquad\qquad F = 318.6 + 32$

$\qquad\qquad\quad 32.2 \approx C\qquad\qquad\qquad\qquad F = 350.6$

C	$-17.8°$	$-10°$	$10°$	$20°$	$32.2°$	$177°$
F	$0°$	$14°$	$50°$	$68°$	$90°$	$350.6°$

101. Let $t = 0$ represent 1998.

$(0, 2546)$ and $(2, 2702)$

$m = \dfrac{2702 - 2546}{2 - 0} = 78$

$N = 78t + 2546$

$t = 6$ represents 2004: $N = 78(6) + 2546 = 3014$ students.

103. $(0, 25{,}000)$ and $(10, 2000)$

$m = \dfrac{2000 - 25000}{10 - 0} = -2300$

$V = -2300t + 25{,}000, \quad 0 \le t \le 10$

105. $W = 0.75x + 11.50$

107. $(580, 50)$ and $(625, 47)$

(a) $m = \dfrac{47 - 50}{625 - 580} = \dfrac{-3}{45} = -\dfrac{1}{15}$

$\qquad x - 50 = -\dfrac{1}{15}(p - 580)$

$\qquad x - 50 = -\dfrac{1}{15}p + \dfrac{116}{3}$

$\qquad\qquad x = -\dfrac{1}{15}p + \dfrac{266}{3}$

(b) $x = -\dfrac{1}{15}(655) + \dfrac{266}{3} = 45$ units

(c) $x = -\dfrac{1}{15}(595) + \dfrac{266}{3} = 49$ units

109. $W = 0.07S + 2500$

111. Let x = amount invested in the $2\frac{1}{2}\%$ fund and z = amount invested in the 4% fund.

(a) $x + z = 12{,}000 \Rightarrow z = 12{,}000 - x$ in the 4% fund.

(b) $y = 0.025x + 0.04(12000 - x)$

$\qquad = 0.025x + 480 - 0.04x$

$\qquad = -0.015x + 480$

(c)

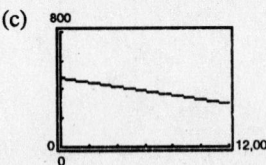

(d) As the amount invested at the lower interest rate increases, the annual interest decreases.

113.

x	18	10	19	16	13	15
y	87	55	96	79	76	82

(a) and (b)

(c) Answers will vary. One approximation is $y = 4x + 19$.

(d) Answers will vary, depending on the equation found in part (c).

$\qquad y = 4(17) + 19 = 87$

(e) If 4 points are added to each y-value, then each point would move up 4 units on the graph, and the y-intercept in the equation would increase by 4.

115. $(-8, 2)$ and $(-1, 4): m_1 = \dfrac{4 - 2}{-1 - (-8)} = \dfrac{2}{7}$

$(0, -4)$ and $(-7, 7): m_2 = \dfrac{7 - (-4)}{-7 - 0} = \dfrac{11}{-7}$

False, the lines are not parallel.

117. On a vertical line, all the points have the same x-value, so when you evaluate $m = \dfrac{y_2 - y_1}{x_2 - x_1}$, you would have a zero in the denominator, and division by zero is undefined.

119. Since $|-4| > \left|\frac{5}{2}\right|$, the steeper line is the one with a slope of -4.
The slope with the greatest magnitude corresponds to the steepest line.

121. Any pair of distinct points on a line can be used to calculate the slope of the line.
The rate of change remains constant on a straight line.

123. $y = 8 - 3x$ is a linear equation with slope $m = -3$. Matches graph (d).

125. $y = \frac{1}{2}x^2 + 2x + 1$ is a quadratic equation. Its graph is a parabola.
Matches graph (a).

127. $-7(3 - x) = 14(x - 1)$

$\quad -21 + 7x = 14x - 14$

$\quad\quad\quad -7x = 7$

$\quad\quad\quad\quad x = -1$

129. $2x^2 - 21x + 49 = 0$

$\quad (2x - 7)(x - 7) = 0$

$\quad 2x - 7 = 0 \quad$ or $\quad x - 7 = 0$

$\quad\quad x = \frac{7}{2} \quad$ or $\quad\quad x = 7$

131. $\sqrt{x - 9} + 15 = 0$

$\quad\quad \sqrt{x - 9} = -15$

No Real Solution

The square root of $x - 9$ cannot be negative.

Section 1.3   Functions

- Given a set or an equation, you should be able to determine if it represents a function.
- Given a function, you should be able to do the following.
    - (a) Find the domain and range.
    - (b) Evaluate it at specific values.
- You should be able to use function notation.

Solutions to Odd-Numbered Exercises

1. Yes, the relationship is a function. Each domain value is matched with only one range value.

3. No, the relationship is not a function. The domain values are each matched with three range values.

5. Yes, it does represent a function. Each input value is matched with only one output value.

7. No, it does not represent a function. The input values of 10 and 7 are each matched with two output values.

9. (a) Each element of A is matched with exactly one element of B, so it does represent a function.

   (b) The element 1 in A is matched with two elements, -2 and 1 of B, so it does not represent a function.

   (c) Each element of A is matched with exactly one element of B, so it does represent a function.

   (d) The element 2 in A is not matched with an element of B, so it does not represent a function.

11. Each is a function. For each year there corresponds one and only one circulation.

13. $x^2 + y^2 = 4 \implies y = \pm\sqrt{4 - x^2}$

No, y *is not* a function of x.

15. $x^2 + y = 4 \implies y = 4 - x^2$

Yes, y *is* a function of x.

17. $2x + 3y = 4 \implies y = \frac{1}{3}(4 - 2x)$

Yes, y *is* a function of x.

19. $y^2 = x^2 - 1 \implies y = \pm\sqrt{x^2 - 1}$

No, y *is not* a function of x.

21. $y = |4 - x|$

Yes, y *is* a function of x.

23. $f(s) = \dfrac{1}{s + 1}$

(a) $f(4) = \dfrac{1}{(4) + 1}$

(b) $f(0) = \dfrac{1}{(0) + 1}$

(c) $f(4x) = \dfrac{1}{(4x) + 1}$

(d) $f(x + c) = \dfrac{1}{(x + c) + 1}$

25. $f(x) = 2x - 3$

(a) $f(1) = 2(1) - 3 = -1$

(b) $f(-3) = 2(-3) - 3 = -9$

(c) $f(x - 1) = 2(x - 1) - 3 = 2x - 5$

27. $V(r) = \frac{4}{3}\pi r^3$

(a) $V(3) = \frac{4}{3}\pi(3)^3 = \frac{4}{3}\pi(27) = 36\pi$

(b) $V\!\left(\frac{3}{2}\right) = \frac{4}{3}\pi\!\left(\frac{3}{2}\right)^3 = \frac{4}{3}\pi\!\left(\frac{27}{8}\right) = \frac{9}{2}\pi$

(c) $V(2r) = \frac{4}{3}\pi(2r)^3 = \frac{4}{3}\pi(8r^3) = \frac{32}{3}\pi r^3$

29. $f(y) = 3 - \sqrt{y}$

(a) $f(4) = 3 - \sqrt{4} = 1$

(b) $f(0.25) = 3 - \sqrt{0.25} = 2.5$

(c) $f(4x^2) = 3 - \sqrt{4x^2} = 3 - 2|x|$

31. $q(x) = \dfrac{1}{x^2 - 9}$

(a) $q(0) = \dfrac{1}{0^2 - 9} = -\dfrac{1}{9}$

(b) $q(3) = \dfrac{1}{3^2 - 9}$ is undefined.

(c) $q(y + 3) = \dfrac{1}{(y + 3)^2 - 9} = \dfrac{1}{y^2 + 6y}$

33. $f(x) = \dfrac{|x|}{x}$

(a) $f(2) = \dfrac{|2|}{2} = 1$

(b) $f(-2) = \dfrac{|-2|}{-2} = -1$

(c) $f(x - 1) = \dfrac{|x - 1|}{x - 1}$

35. $f(x) = \begin{cases} 2x + 1, & x < 0 \\ 2x + 2, & x \geq 0 \end{cases}$

(a) $f(-1) = 2(-1) + 1 = -1$

(b) $f(0) = 2(0) + 2 = 2$

(c) $f(2) = 2(2) + 2 = 6$

37. $f(x) = x^2 - 3$

x	-2	-1	0	1	2
$f(x)$	1	-2	-3	-2	1

39. $h(t) = \frac{1}{2}|t + 3|$

t	-5	-4	-3	-2	-1
$h(t)$	1	$\frac{1}{2}$	0	$\frac{1}{2}$	1

41. $f(x) = \begin{cases} -\frac{1}{2}x + 4, & x \leq 0 \\ (x - 2)^2, & x > 0 \end{cases}$

x	-2	-1	0	1	2
$f(x)$	5	$\frac{9}{2}$	4	1	0

43. $15 - 3x = 0$

$\qquad 3x = 15$

$\qquad x = 5$

45. $\dfrac{3x - 4}{5} = 0$

$3x - 4 = 0$

$x = \dfrac{4}{3}$

47. $x^2 - 9 = 0$

$x^2 = 9$

$x = \pm 3$

49. $\qquad x^3 - x = 0$

$\qquad x(x^2 - 1) = 0$

$x(x + 1)(x - 1) = 0$

$x = 0,\ x = -1, \text{or } x = 1$

51. $\qquad f(x) = g(x)$

$\qquad x^2 = x + 2$

$\qquad x^2 - x - 2 = 0$

$(x + 1)(x - 2) = 0$

$x = -1 \ \text{ or } \ x = 2$

53. $\qquad f(x) = g(x)$

$\sqrt{3x} + 1 = x + 1$

$\qquad \sqrt{3x} = x$

$\qquad 3x = x^2$

$\qquad 0 = x^2 - 3x$

$\qquad 0 = x(x - 3)$

$x = 0 \ \text{ or } \ x = 3$

55. $f(x) = 5x^2 + 2x - 1$

Since $f(x)$ is a polynomial, the domain is all real numbers x.

57. $h(t) = \dfrac{4}{t}$

Domain: All real numbers except $t = 0$

59. $g(y) = \sqrt{y - 10}$

Domain: $y - 10 \geq 0$

$\qquad\qquad y \geq 10$

61. $f(x) = \sqrt[4]{1 - x^2}$

Domain: $1 - x^2 \geq 0$

$\qquad -x^2 \geq -1$

$\qquad x^2 \leq 1$

$\qquad x^2 - 1 \leq 0$

Critical Numbers: $x = \pm 1$

Test Intervals: $(-\infty, -1), (-1, 1), (1, \infty)$

Test: Is $x^2 - 1 \leq 0$?

Solution: $[-1, 1]$ or $-1 \leq x \leq 1$

63. $g(x) = \dfrac{1}{x} - \dfrac{1}{x + 2}$

Domain: All real numbers except $x = 0,\ x = -2$

65. $f(s) = \dfrac{\sqrt{s - 1}}{s - 4}$

Domain: $s - 1 \geq 0 \Longrightarrow s \geq 1$ and $s \neq 4$

The domain consists of all real numbers s, such that $s \geq 1$ and $s \neq 4$.

67. $f(x) = \dfrac{\sqrt[3]{x - 4}}{x}$

The domain is all real numbers except $x = 0$.

69. $f(x) = x^2$

$\{(-2, 4), (-1, 1), (0, 0), (1, 1), (2, 4)\}$

71. $f(x) = \sqrt{x + 2}$

$\{(-2, 0), (-1, 1), (0, \sqrt{2}), (1, \sqrt{3}), (2, 2)\}$

73. By plotting the points, we have a parabola, so $g(x) = cx^2$. Since $(-4, -32)$ is on the graph, we have $-32 = c(-4)^2 \implies c = -2$. Thus, $g(x) = -2x^2$.

75. Since the function is undefined at 0, we have $r(x) = c/x$. Since $(-4, -8)$ is on the graph, we have $-8 = c/-4 \implies c = 32$. Thus, $r(x) = 32/x$.

77.
$$f(x) = x^2 - x + 1$$
$$f(2 + h) = (2 + h)^2 - (2 + h) + 1$$
$$= 4 + 4h + h^2 - 2 - h + 1$$
$$= h^2 + 3h + 3$$
$$f(2) = (2)^2 - 2 + 1 = 3$$
$$f(2 + h) - f(2) = h^2 + 3h$$
$$\frac{f(2 + h) - f(2)}{h} = \frac{h^2 + 3h}{h} = h + 3, \ h \neq 0$$

79. $f(x) = x^3$
$$f(x + c) = (x + c)^3 = x^3 + 3x^2c + 3xc^2 + c^3$$
$$\frac{f(x + c) - f(x)}{c} = \frac{(x^3 + 3x^2c + 3xc^2 + c^3) - x^3}{c}$$
$$= \frac{c(3x^2 + 3xc + c^2)}{c}$$
$$= 3x^2 + 3xc + c^2, \ c \neq 0$$

81. $g(x) = 3x - 1$
$$\frac{g(x) - g(3)}{x - 3} = \frac{(3x - 1) - 8}{x - 3} = \frac{3x - 9}{x - 3} = \frac{3(x - 3)}{x - 3} = 3, \ x \neq 3$$

83. $f(x) = \sqrt{5x}$
$$\frac{f(x) - f(5)}{x - 5} = \frac{\sqrt{5x} - 5}{x - 5}$$

85. $A = s^2$ and $P = 4s \implies \dfrac{P}{4} = s$
$$A = \left(\frac{P}{4}\right)^2 = \frac{P^2}{16}$$

87.

$$8^2 + \left(\frac{b}{2}\right)^2 = s^2$$
$$\frac{b^2}{4} = s^2 - 64$$
$$b^2 = 4(s^2 - 64)$$
$$b = 2\sqrt{s^2 - 64}$$

Thus, $A = \dfrac{1}{2}bh$

$$= \frac{1}{2}\left(2\sqrt{s^2 - 64}\right)(8)$$

$$= 8\sqrt{s^2 - 64} \text{ square inches.}$$

89. (a)

Height, x	Width	Volume, V
1	$24 - 2(1)$	$1[24 - 2(1)]^2 = 484$
2	$24 - 2(2)$	$2[24 - 2(2)]^2 = 800$
3	$24 - 2(3)$	$3[24 - 2(3)]^2 = 972$
4	$24 - 2(4)$	$4[24 - 2(4)]^2 = 1024$
5	$24 - 2(5)$	$5[24 - 2(5)]^2 = 980$
6	$24 - 2(6)$	$6[24 - 2(6)]^2 = 864$

The volume is maximum when $x = 4$.

(b)

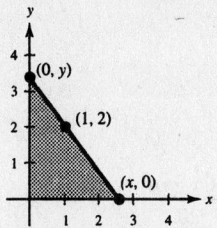

V is a function of x.

(c) $V = x(24 - 2x)^2$

Domain: $0 < x < 12$

91. $A = \dfrac{1}{2}bh = \dfrac{1}{2}xy$

Since $(0, y)$, $(2, 1)$, and $(x, 0)$ all lie on the same line, the slopes between any pair are equal.

$$\frac{1 - y}{2 - 0} = \frac{0 - 1}{x - 2}$$

$$\frac{1 - y}{2} = \frac{-1}{x - 2}$$

$$y = \frac{2}{x - 2} + 1$$

$$y = \frac{x}{x - 2}$$

Therefore,

$$A = \frac{1}{2}x\left(\frac{x}{x - 2}\right) = \frac{x^2}{2(x - 2)}.$$

The domain of A includes x-values such that $x^2/[2(x - 2)] > 0$.
Using methods of Section 1.8 we find that the domain is $x > 2$.

93. $p(t) = \begin{cases} 17.27 + 1.036t, & -6 \le t \le 11 \\ -4.807 + 2.882t - 0.011t^2, & 12 \le t \le 17 \end{cases}$

where $t = 0$ represents 1980

1978: $t = -2$ and $p(-2) = 17.27 + 1.036(-2)$

$= 15.198$ thousand dollars

$= \$15{,}198$

1988: $t = 8$ and $p(8) = 17.27 + 1.036(8)$

$= 25.558$ thousand dollars

$= \$25{,}558$

1993: $t = 13$ and $p(13) = -4.807 + 2.882(13) - 0.011(13)^2$

$= 30.8$ thousand dollars

$= \$30{,}800$

1997: $t = 17$ and $p(17) = -4.807 + 2.882(17) - 0.011(17)^2$

$= 41.008$ thousand dollars

$= \$41{,}008$

95. (a) Cost = variable costs + fixed costs

$C = 12.30x + 98{,}000$

(b) Revenue = price per unit × number of units

$R = 17.98x$

(c) Profit = Revenue − Cost

$P = 17.98x - (12.30x + 98{,}000)$

$P = 5.68x - 98{,}000$

97. (a) $R = n(\text{rate}) = n[8.00 - 0.05(n - 80)], \ n \ge 80$

$R = 12.00n - 0.05n^2 = 12n - \dfrac{n^2}{20} = \dfrac{240n - n^2}{20}, \ n \ge 80$

(b)

n	90	100	110	120	130	140	150
$R(n)$	\$675	\$700	\$715	\$720	\$715	\$700	\$675

The revenue is maximum when 120 people take the trip.

99. (a)

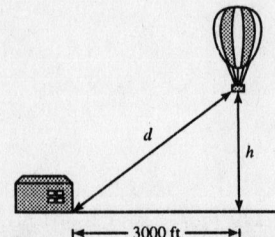

d

h

3000 ft

(b) $(3000)^2 + h^2 = d^2$

$h = \sqrt{d^2 - (3000)^2}$

Domain: $d \ge 3000$

(since both $d \ge 0$ and $d^2 - (3000)^2 \ge 0$)

101. $y = -\frac{1}{10}x^2 + 3x + 6$

$y(30) = -\frac{1}{10}(30)^2 + 3(30) + 6 = 6$ feet

If the child holds a glove at a height of 5 feet, then the ball *will* be over the child's head since it will be at a height of 6 feet.

103. True, the set represents a function. Each *x*-value corresponds to one *y*-value.

105. The domain is the set of inputs of the function, and the range is the set of outputs.

107. $\dfrac{t}{3} + \dfrac{t}{5} = 1$

$15\left(\dfrac{t}{3} + \dfrac{t}{5}\right) = 15(1)$

$5t + 3t = 15$

$8t = 15$

$t = \dfrac{15}{8}$

109. $\dfrac{3}{x(x+1)} - \dfrac{4}{x} = \dfrac{1}{x+1}$

$x(x+1)\left[\dfrac{3}{x(x+1)} - \dfrac{4}{x}\right] = x(x+1)\left(\dfrac{1}{x+1}\right)$

$3 - 4(x+1) = x$

$3 - 4x - 4 = x$

$-1 = 5x$

$-\dfrac{1}{5} = x$

111. $(-2, -5)$ and $(4, -1)$

$m = \dfrac{-1 - (-5)}{4 - (-2)} = \dfrac{4}{6} = \dfrac{2}{3}$

$y - (-5) = \dfrac{2}{3}(x - (-2))$

$y + 5 = \dfrac{2}{3}x + \dfrac{4}{3}$

$3y + 15 = 2x + 4$

$2x - 3y - 11 = 0$

113. $(-6, 5)$ and $(3, -5)$

$m = \dfrac{-5 - 5}{3 - (-6)} = -\dfrac{10}{9}$

$y - 5 = -\dfrac{10}{9}(x - (-6))$

$9y - 45 = -10x - 60$

$10x + 9y + 15 = 0$

Section 1.4   Analyzing Graphs of Functions

- ■ You should be able to determine the domain and range of a function from its graph.

- ■ You should be able to use the vertical line test for functions.

- ■ You should be able to find the zeros of a function.

- ■ You should be able to determine when a function is constant, increasing, or decreasing.

- ■ You should be able to approximate relative minimums and relative maximums from the graph of a function.

- ■ You should know that *f* is

  (a) odd if $f(-x) = -f(x)$.

  (b) even if $f(-x) = f(x)$.

Solutions to Odd-Numbered Exercises

1. $f(x) = \frac{2}{3}x - 4$

Domain: All real numbers

Range: All real numbers

3. $f(x) = 1 - x^2$

Domain: All real numbers

Range: $(-\infty, 1]$

5. $f(x) = \sqrt{x^2 - 1}$

Domain: $(-\infty, -1] \cup [1, \infty)$

Range: $[0, \infty)$

7. $h(x) = \sqrt{16 - x^2}$

Domain: $[-4, 4]$

Range: $[0, 4]$

9. $y = \frac{1}{2}x^2$

A vertical line intersects the graph just once, so y is a function of x.

11. $x - y^2 = 1 \implies y = \pm\sqrt{x - 1}$

y is not a function of x.
Some vertical lines cross the graph twice.

13. $x^2 = 2xy - 1$

A vertical line intersects the graph just once, so y is a function of x.

15. $\quad 2x^2 - 7x - 30 = 0$

$\quad (2x + 5)(x - 6) = 0$

$\quad 2x + 5 = 0 \quad$ or $\quad x - 6 = 0$

$\qquad x = -\frac{5}{2} \quad$ or $\qquad x = 6$

17. $\dfrac{x}{9x^2 - 4} = 0$

$\qquad x = 0$

19. $\quad \frac{1}{2}x^3 - x = 0$

$\qquad x^3 - 2x = 2(0)$

$\quad x(x^2 - 2) = 0$

$\quad x = 0 \quad$ or $\quad x^2 - 2 = 0$

$\qquad\qquad\qquad x^2 = 2$

$\qquad\qquad\qquad x = \pm\sqrt{2}$

21. $\qquad 4x^3 - 24x^2 - x + 6 = 0$

$\qquad 4x^2(x - 6) - 1(x - 6) = 0$

$\qquad\qquad (x - 6)(4x^2 - 1) = 0$

$\qquad (x - 6)(2x + 1)(2x - 1) = 0$

$\qquad x - 6 = 0, \quad 2x + 1 = 0, \quad 2x - 1 = 0$

$\qquad x = 6, \qquad x = -\frac{1}{2}, \qquad x = \frac{1}{2}$

23. $\quad 3 + \dfrac{5}{x} = 0$

$\quad 3x + 5 = 0$

$\qquad x = -\dfrac{5}{3}$

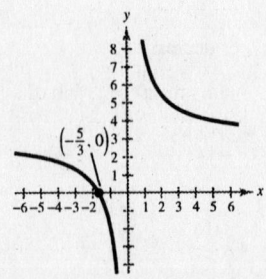

25. $\quad \sqrt{2x + 11} = 0$

$\qquad 2x + 11 = 0$

$\qquad\qquad x = -\frac{11}{2}$

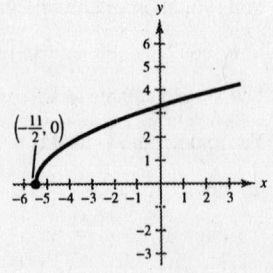

27. $\dfrac{3x-1}{x-6} = 0$

$3x - 1 = 0$

$x = \dfrac{1}{3}$

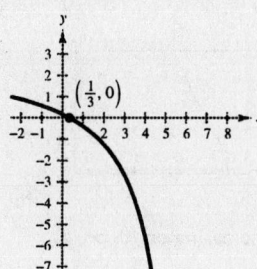

29. $f(x) = \frac{3}{2}x$

(a) f is increasing on $(-\infty, \infty)$.

(b) Since $f(-x) = -f(x)$, f is odd.

31. $f(x) = x^3 - 3x^2 + 2$

(a) f is increasing on $(-\infty, 0)$ and $(2, \infty)$.

f is decreasing on $(0, 2)$.

(b) $f(-x) \neq -f(x)$

$f(-x) \neq f(x)$

f is neither odd nor even.

33. $f(x) = 3$

(a)

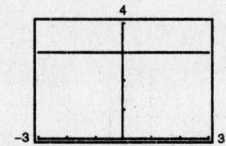

Constant on $(-\infty, \infty)$

(b)

x	-2	-1	0	1	2
$f(x)$	3	3	3	3	3

35. $f(x) = 5 - 3x$

(a)

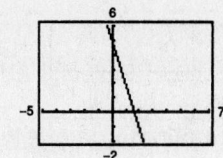

Decreasing on $(-\infty, \infty)$

(b)

x	-2	-1	0	1	2
$f(x)$	11	8	5	2	-1

37. $g(s) = \dfrac{s^2}{4}$

(a)

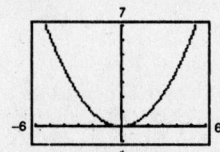

Decreasing on $(-\infty, 0)$

Increasing on $(0, \infty)$

(b)

s	-4	-2	0	2	4
$g(s)$	4	1	0	1	4

39. $f(t) = -t^4$

(a)

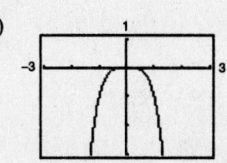

Increasing on $(-\infty, 0)$

Decreasing on $(0, \infty)$

(b)

t	-2	-1	0	1	2
$f(t)$	-16	-1	0	-1	-16

41. $f(x) = \sqrt{1 - x}$

(a)

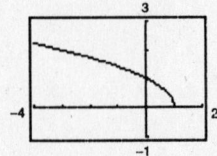

Decreasing on $(-\infty, 1)$

(b)

x	-3	-2	-1	0	1
$f(x)$	2	$\sqrt{3}$	$\sqrt{2}$	1	0

43. $f(x) = x^{3/2}$

(a)

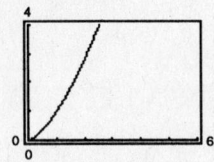

Increasing on $(0, \infty)$

(b)

x	0	1	2	3	4
$f(x)$	0	1	2.82	5.2	8

45. $g(t) = \sqrt[3]{t - 1}$

(a)

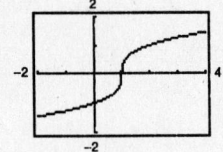

Increasing on $(-\infty, \infty)$

(b)

t	-2	-1	0	1	2
$g(t)$	-1.44	-1.26	-1	0	1

47. $f(x) = |x + 2|$

(a)

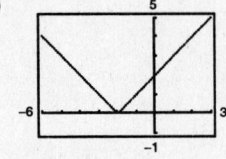

Decreasing on $(-\infty, -2)$

Increasing on $(-2, \infty)$

(b)

x	-6	-4	-2	0	2
$f(x)$	4	2	0	2	4

49. $f(x) = \begin{cases} x + 3, & x \le 0 \\ 3, & 0 < x < 2 \\ 2x - 1, & x > 2 \end{cases}$

(a)

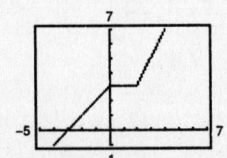

Increasing on $(-\infty, 0)$ and $(2, \infty)$

Constant on $(0, 2)$

(b)

x	-2	-1	0	1	2	3	4
$f(x)$	1	2	3	3	3	5	7

51. $f(x) = (x - 4)(x + 2)$

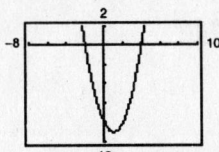

Relative Minimum at $(1, -9)$

53. $f(x) = x(x - 2)(x + 3)$

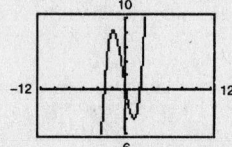

Relative Minimum at $(1.12, -4.06)$

Relative Maximum at $(-1.79, 8.21)$

55. $f(x) = 2x^3 - 5x^2 - 4x - 1$

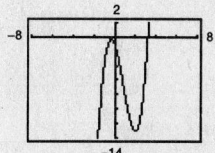

Relative Minimum at $(2, -13)$

Relative Maximum at $(-0.33, -0.30)$

57. $f(x) = 2x - 1$

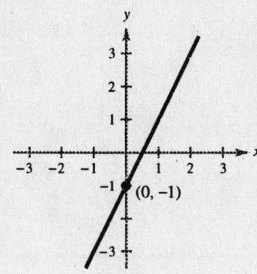

59. $f(x) = -x - \frac{3}{4}$

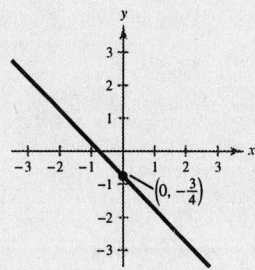

61. $f(x) = -\frac{1}{6}x - \frac{5}{2}$

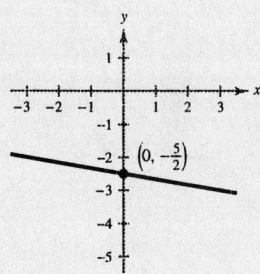

63. $f(x) = 2.5x - 1.8$

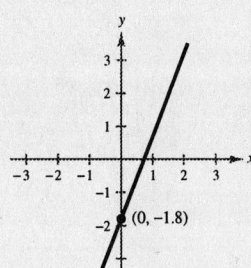

65. $f(1) = 4, f(0) = 6$

$(1, 4)$ and $(0, 6)$

$m = \dfrac{6 - 4}{0 - 1} = -2$

$y - 6 = -2(x - 0)$

$y = -2x + 6$

$f(x) = -2x + 6$

67. $f(5) = -4, f(-2) = 17$

$(5, -4)$ and $(-2, 17)$

$m = \dfrac{17 - (-4)}{-2 - 5} = \dfrac{21}{-7} = -3$

$y - (-4) = -3(x - 5)$

$y + 4 = -3x + 15$

$y = -3x + 11$

$f(x) = -3x + 11$

69. $f(-5) = -5$, $f(5) = -1$

$(-5, -5)$ and $(5, -1)$

$m = \dfrac{-1 - (-5)}{5 - (-5)} = \dfrac{4}{10} = \dfrac{2}{5}$

$y - (-5) = \dfrac{2}{5}(x - (-5))$

$y + 5 = \dfrac{2}{5}x + 2$

$y = \dfrac{2}{5}x - 3$

$f(x) = \dfrac{2}{5}x - 3$

71. $f\left(\dfrac{1}{2}\right) = -6$, $f(4) = -3$

$\left(\dfrac{1}{2}, -6\right)$ and $(4, -3)$

$m = \dfrac{-3 - (-6)}{4 - \dfrac{1}{2}} = \dfrac{3}{7/2} = \dfrac{6}{7}$

$y - (-3) = \dfrac{6}{7}(x - 4)$

$y + 3 = \dfrac{6}{7}x - \dfrac{24}{7}$

$y = \dfrac{6}{7}x - \dfrac{45}{7}$

$f(x) = \dfrac{6}{7}x - \dfrac{45}{7}$

73. Vertical shift 2 units downward.

$f(x) = [\![x]\!] - 2$

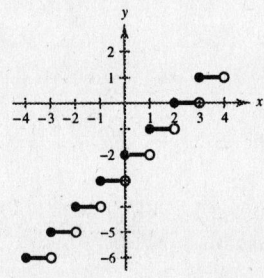

75. $f(x) = \begin{cases} 2x + 3, & x < 0 \\ 3 - x, & x \geq 0 \end{cases}$

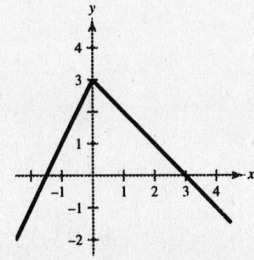

77. $f(x) = \begin{cases} x^2 + 5, & x \leq 1 \\ -x^2 + 4x + 3, & x > 1 \end{cases}$

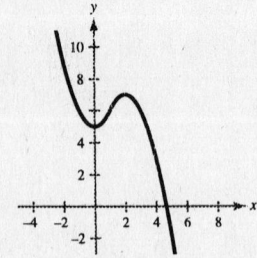

79. $f(x) = 4 - x$

$f(x) \geq 0$ on $(-\infty, 4]$.

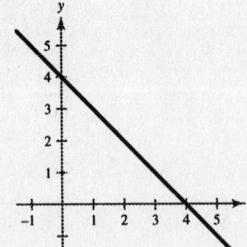

81. $f(x) = x^2 - 9$

$f(x) \geq 0$ on $(-\infty, -3]$ and $[3, \infty)$.

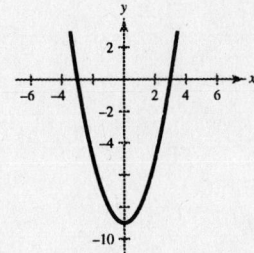

83. $f(x) = 1 - x^4$

$f(x) \geq 0$ on $[-1, 1]$.

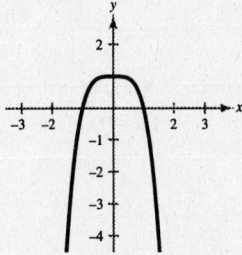

85. $f(x) = x^2 + 1$

$f(x) \geq 0$ on $(-\infty, \infty)$.

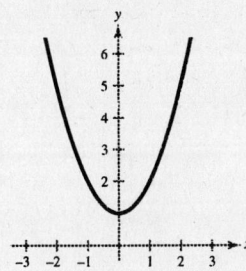

87. $f(x) = -5$, $f(x) < 0$ for all x.

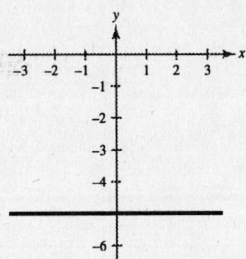

89. $f(x) = \begin{cases} 1 - 2x^2, & x \leq -2 \\ -x + 8, & x > -2 \end{cases}$

$f(x) \geq 0$ on $(-2, 8]$

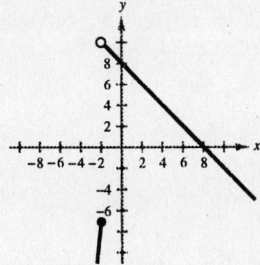

91. $s(x) = 2\left(\frac{1}{4}x - \left[\!\left[\frac{1}{4}x\right]\!\right]\right)$

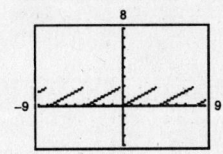

Domain: $(-\infty, \infty)$

Range: $[0, 2)$

Sawtooth pattern

93. $f(x) = x^6 - 2x^2 + 3$

$f(-x) = (-x)^6 - 2(-x)^2 + 3$

$\quad\quad = x^6 - 2x^2 + 3$

$\quad\quad = f(x)$

f is even.

95. $g(x) = x^3 - 5x$

$g(-x) = (-x)^3 - 5(-x)$

$\quad\quad = -x^3 + 5x$

$\quad\quad = -g(x)$

g is odd.

97. $f(t) = t^2 + 2t - 3$

$f(-t) = (-t)^2 + 2(-t) - 3$

$= t^2 - 2t - 3$

$\neq f(t), \neq -f(t)$

f is neither even nor odd.

99. $\left(-\frac{3}{2}, 4\right)$

(a) If f is even, another point is $\left(\frac{3}{2}, 4\right)$.

(b) If f is odd, another point is $\left(\frac{3}{2}, -4\right)$.

101. $(4, 9)$

(a) If f is even, another point is $(-4, 9)$

(b) If f is odd, another point is $(-4, -9)$

103. (a) $C_2(t) = 1.05 - 0.38[\![-(t - 1)]\!]$ is the appropriate model since the cost does not increase until after the next minute of conversation has started.

(b)

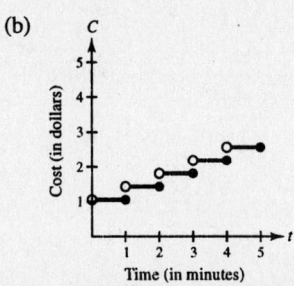

$C = 1.05 - 0.38[\![-17.75]\!] = \$7.89$

105. $L = -0.294x^2 + 97.744x - 664.875, 20 \leq x \leq 90$

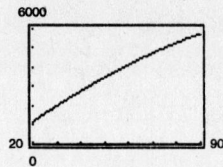

$L = 2000$ when $x \approx 29.9645 \approx 30$ watts

107. $h = \text{top} - \text{bottom}$

$= 3 - (4x - x^2)$

$= 3 - 4x + x^2$

109. $h = \text{top} - \text{bottom}$

$= 2 - \sqrt[3]{x}$

111. $L = \text{right} - \text{left}$

$= 2 - \sqrt[3]{2y}$

113. $L = \text{right} - \text{left}$

$= \frac{2}{y} - 0$

$= \frac{2}{y}$

115.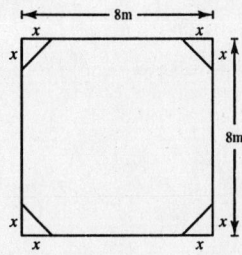

(a) $A = (8)(8) - 4\left(\frac{1}{2}\right)(x)(x)$

   $= 64 - 2x^2$

   Domain: $0 \le x \le 4$

(b)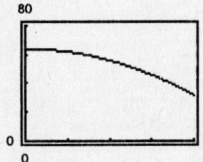

   Range: $32 \le A \le 64$

(c) When $x = 4$, the resulting figure is a square.

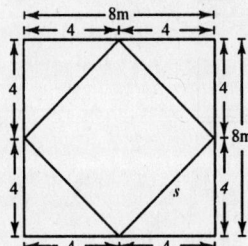

By the Pythagorean Theorem, $4^2 + 4^2 = s^2 \implies s = \sqrt{32} = 4\sqrt{2}$ meters.

117.

Interval	Intake Pipe	Drainpipe 1	Drainpipe 2
$[0, 5]$	Open	Closed	Closed
$[5, 10]$	Open	Open	Closed
$[10, 20]$	Closed	Closed	Closed
$[20, 30]$	Closed	Closed	Open
$[30, 40]$	Open	Open	Open
$[40, 45]$	Open	Closed	Open
$[45, 50]$	Open	Open	Open
$[50, 60]$	Open	Open	Closed

119. False. A piecewise-defined function is a function that is defined by two or more equations over a specified domain. That domain may or may not include x- and y-intercepts.

121. $f(x) = a_{2n}x^{2n} + a_{2n-2}x^{2n-2} + \cdots + a_2x^2 + a_0$

$f(-x) = a_{2n}(-x)^{2n} + a_{2n-2}(-x)^{2n-2} + \cdots + a_2(-x)^2 + a_0$

$\qquad = a_{2n}x^{2n} + a_{2n-2}x^{2n-2} + \cdots + a_2x^2 + a_0$

$\qquad = f(x)$

Therefore, $f(x)$ is even.

123.   Yes, the graph in Exercise 11 does represent x as a function of y.
Each y-value corresponds to only one x-value.

125.   (a) $y = x$ $\qquad\qquad\qquad$ (b) $y = x^2$ $\qquad\qquad\qquad$ (c) $y = x^3$

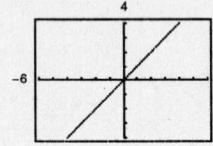 $\qquad$ 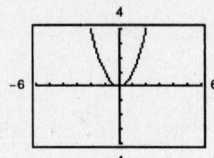 $\qquad$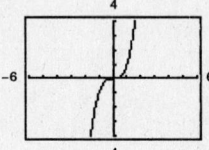

(d) $y = x^4$ $\qquad\qquad\qquad$ (e) $y = x^5$ $\qquad\qquad\qquad$ (f) $y = x^6$

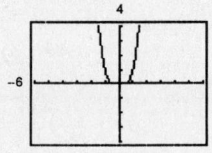 $\qquad$ 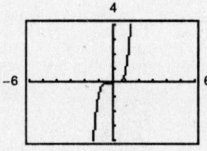 $\qquad$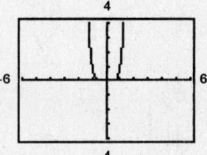

All the graphs pass through the origin. The graphs of the odd powers of x are symmetric with respect to
the origin and the graphs of the even powers are symmetric with respect to the y-axis. As the powers increase,
the graphs become flatter in the interval $-1 < x < 1$.

127. $x^2 - 10x = 0$ $\qquad\qquad\qquad\qquad\qquad$ **129.** $x^3 - x = 0$

$x(x - 10) = 0$ $\qquad\qquad\qquad\qquad\qquad\qquad\quad$ $x(x^2 - 1) = 0$

$x = 0 \quad\text{or}\quad x = 10$ $\qquad\qquad\qquad\qquad\quad$ $x = 0 \quad\text{or}\quad x^2 - 1 = 0$

$\qquad\qquad\qquad\qquad\qquad\qquad\qquad\qquad\qquad\qquad x^2 = 1$

$\qquad\qquad\qquad\qquad\qquad\qquad\qquad\qquad\qquad\quad x = \pm 1$

131. $f(x) = 5x - 8$

(a) $f(9) = 5(9) - 8 = 37$

(b) $f(-4) = 5(-4) - 8 = -28$

(c) $f(x - 7) = 5(x - 7) - 8 = 5x - 35 - 8 = 5x - 43$

133. $f(x) = \sqrt{x - 12} - 9$

(a) $f(12) = \sqrt{12 - 12} - 9 = 0 - 9 = -9$

(b) $f(40) = \sqrt{40 - 12} - 9 = \sqrt{28} - 9 = 2\sqrt{7} - 9$

(c) $f(-\sqrt{36}) = \sqrt{-\sqrt{36} - 12} - 9 = \sqrt{-6 - 12} - 9 = \sqrt{-18} - 9$

$\qquad\qquad\qquad\qquad\qquad\qquad\qquad\qquad = 3\sqrt{2}i - 9$

$\qquad\qquad\qquad\qquad\qquad\qquad\qquad\qquad = -9 + 3\sqrt{2}i$

135. $f(x) = x^2 - 2x + 9$

$f(3 + h) = (3 + h)^2 - 2(3 + h) + 9$

$= 9 + 6h + h^2 - 6 - 2h + 9$

$= h^2 + 4h + 12$

$f(3) = 3^2 - 2(3) + 9 = 12$

$$\frac{f(3 + h) - f(3)}{h} = \frac{(h^2 - 4h + 12) - (12)}{h}$$

$$= \frac{h^2 + 4h}{h}$$

$$= \frac{h(h + 4)}{h}$$

$$= h + 4, h \neq 0$$

Section 1.5   Shifting, Reflecting, and Stretching Graphs

■   You should know the basic types of transformations.

Let $y = f(x)$ and let c be a positive real number.

1. $h(x) = f(x) + c$ Vertical shift c units upward

2. $h(x) = f(x) - c$ Vertical shift c units downward

3. $h(x) = f(x - c)$ Horizontal shift c units to the right

4. $h(x) = f(x + c)$ Horizontal shift c units to the left

5. $h(x) = -f(x)$ Reflection in the x-axis

6. $h(x) = f(-x)$ Reflection in the y-axis

7. $h(x) = cf(x), c > 1$ Vertical stretch

8. $h(x) = cf(x), 0 < c < 1$ Vertical shrink

Solutions to Odd-Numbered Exercises

1. (a) $f(x) = x^3 + c$

  $c = -2 : f(x) = x^3 - 2$ Vertical shift 2 units downward

  $c = 0 : f(x) = x^3$ Basic cubic function

  $c = 2 : f(x) = x^3 + 2$ Vertical shift 2 units upward

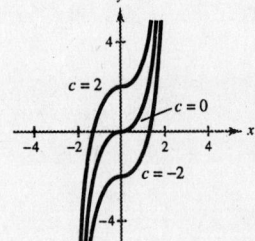

—CONTINUED—

1. **—CONTINUED—**

(b) $f(x) = (x - c)^3$

$c = -2 : f(x) = (x + 2)^3$ Horizontal shift 2 units to the left

$c = 0 : f(x) = x^3$ Basic cubic function

$c = 2 : f(x) = (x - 2)^3$ Horizontal shift 2 units to the right

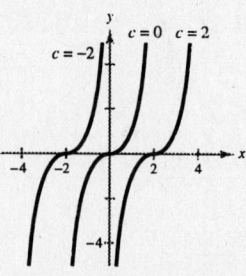

3. (a) $f(x) = \sqrt{x} + c$ Vertical shifts

$c = -3 : f(x) = \sqrt{x} - 3$ 3 units downward

$c = -1 : f(x) = \sqrt{x} - 1$ 1 unit downward

$c = 1 : f(x) = \sqrt{x} + 1$ 1 unit upward

$c = 3 : f(x) = \sqrt{x} + 3$ 3 units upward

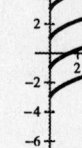

(b) $f(x) = \sqrt{x - c}$ Horizontal shifts

$c = -3 : f(x) = \sqrt{x + 3}$ 3 units to the left

$c = -1 : f(x) = \sqrt{x + 1}$ 1 unit to the left

$c = 1 : f(x) = \sqrt{x - 1}$ 1 unit to the right

$c = 3 : f(x) = \sqrt{x - 3}$ 3 units to the right

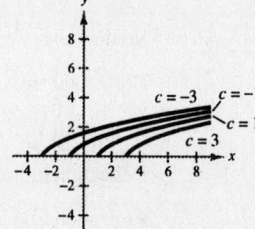

(c) $f(x) = \sqrt{x - 3} + c$ Horizontal shift 3 units to the right and a vertical shift

$c = -3 : f(x) = \sqrt{x - 3} - 3$ 3 units downward

$c = -1 : f(x) = \sqrt{x - 3} - 1$ 1 unit downward

$c = 1 : f(x) = \sqrt{x - 3} + 1$ 1 unit upward

$c = 3 : f(x) = \sqrt{x - 3} + 3$ 3 units upward

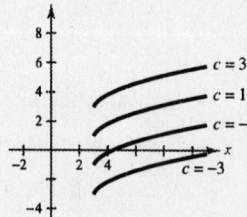

5. (a) $y = f(x) + 2$

Vertical shift 2 units upward.

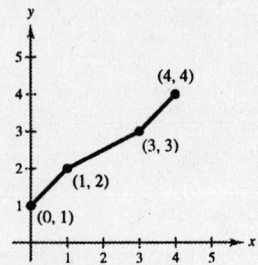

(b) $y = f(x - 2)$

Horizontal shift 2 units to the right.

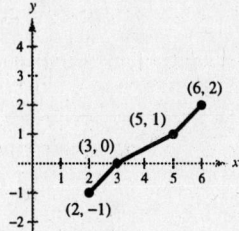

(c) $y = 2f(x)$

Vertical stretch by a factor of 2.

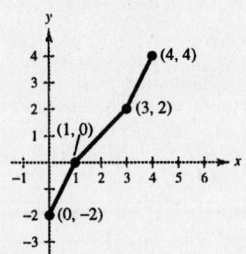

(d) $y = -f(x)$

Reflection in the *x*-axis.

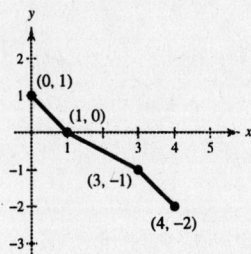

(e) $y = f(x + 3)$

Horizontal shift 3 units to the left.

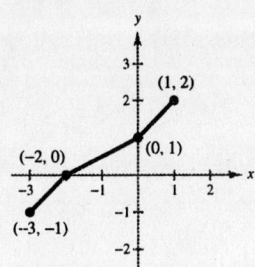

(f) $y = f(-x)$

Reflection in the *y*-axis.

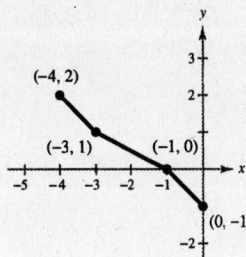

7. (a) $y = f(x) - 1$

Vertical shift 1 unit downward.

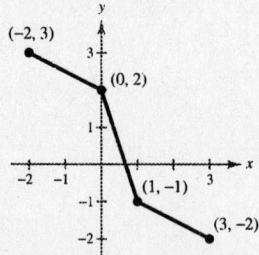

(c) $y = f(-x)$

Reflection about the y-axis.

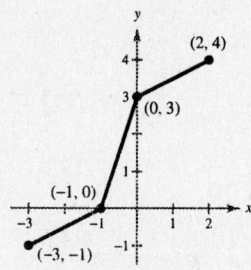

(e) $y = -f(x - 2)$

Reflection about the x-axis and a
horizontal shift 2 units to the right.

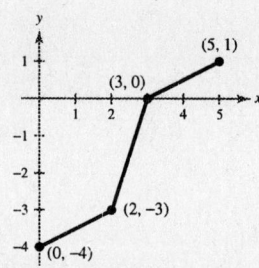

(b) $y = f(x - 1)$

Horizontal shift 1 unit to the right.

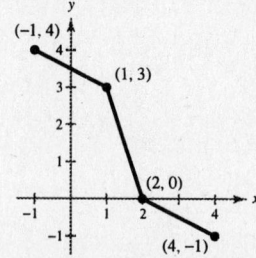

(d) $y = f(x + 1)$

Horizontal shift 1 unit to the left.

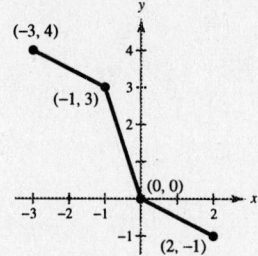

(f) $y = \frac{1}{2} f(x)$

Vertical shrink by a factor of $\frac{1}{2}$.

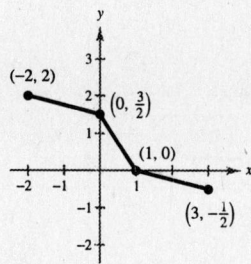

9. (a) Vertical shift 1 unit downward.

$$f(x) = x^2 - 1$$

(b) Reflection about the x-axis, horizontal shift
1 unit to the left, and a vertical shift 1 unit upward.

$$f(x) = -(x + 1)^2 + 1$$

(c) Reflection about the x-axis, horizontal shift
2 units to the right, and a vertical shift 6 units upward.

$$f(x) = -(x - 2)^2 + 6$$

(d) Horizontal shift 5 units to the right and a
vertical shift 3 units downward.

$$f(x) = (x - 5)^2 - 3$$

11. (a) Vertical shift 5 units upward.

$$f(x) = |x| + 5$$

(b) Reflection in the x-axis and a horizontal shift
3 units to the left.

$$f(x) = -|x + 3|$$

(c) Horizontal shift 2 units to the right and a
vertical shift 4 units downward.

$$f(x) = |x - 2| - 4$$

(d) Reflection in the x-axis, horizontal shift 6 units
to the right, and a vertical shift 1 unit downward.

$$f(x) = -|x - 6| - 1$$

13. Common function: $f(x) = x^3$

Horizontal shift 2 units to the right: $y = (x - 2)^3$

15. Common function: $f(x) = x^2$

Reflection in the x-axis: $y = -x^2$

17. Common function: $f(x) = \sqrt{x}$

Reflection in the x-axis and a vertical shift 1 unit upward: $y = -\sqrt{x} + 1$

19. $f(x) = 12 - x^2$

Common function: $g(x) = x^2$

Reflection in the x-axis and a vertical shift 12 units upward.

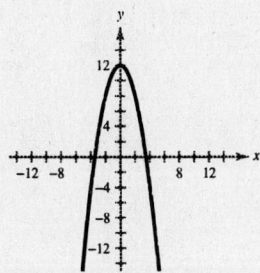

21. $f(x) = x^3 + 7$

Common function: $g(x) = x^3$

Vertical shift 7 units upward.

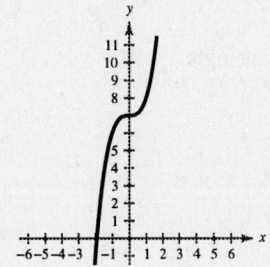

23. $f(x) = 2 - (x + 5)^2$

Common function: $g(x) = x^2$

Reflection in the x-axis, horizontal shift 5 units to the left, and a vertical shift 2 units upward.

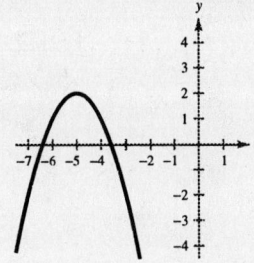

25. $f(x) = (x - 1)^3 + 2$

Common function: $g(x) = x^3$

Horizontal shift 1 unit to the right and a vertical shift 2 units upward.

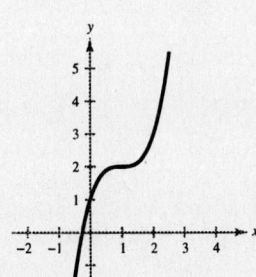

27. $f(x) = -|x| - 2$

Common function: $g(x) = |x|$

Reflection in the x-axis and a vertical shift 2 units downward.

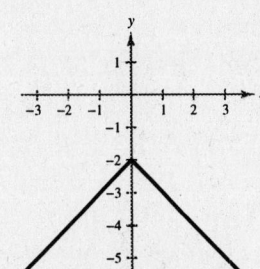

29. $f(x) = -|x + 4| + 8$

Common function: $g(x) = |x|$

Reflection in the x-axis, horizontal shift 4 units
to the left, and a vertical shift 8 units upward.

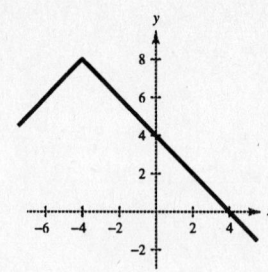

31. $f(x) = \sqrt{x - 9}$

Common function: $g(x) = \sqrt{x}$

Horizontal shift 9 units to the right.

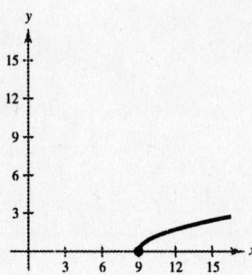

33. $f(x) = \sqrt{7 - x} - 2$ or $f(x) = \sqrt{-(x - 7)} - 2$

Reflection in the y-axis, horizontal shift 7 units
to the right, and a vertical shift 2 units downward.

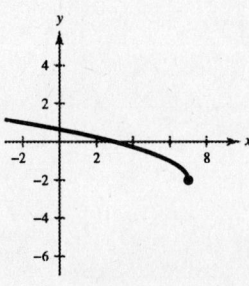

35. $f(x) = x^2$ moved 2 units to the right and 8 units down.

$g(x) = (x - 2)^2 - 8$

37. $f(x) = x^3$ moved 13 units to the right.

$g(x) = (x - 13)^3$

39. $f(x) = |x|$ moved 10 units up and reflected
about the x-axis.

$g(x) = -(|x| + 10) = -|x| - 10$

41. $f(x) = \sqrt{x}$ moved 6 units to the left and reflected
in both the x and y axes.

$g(x) = -\sqrt{-x + 6}$

43. $f(x) = x^2$

(a) Reflection in the x-axis and a vertical stretch
by a factor of 3.

$g(x) = -3x^2$

(b) Vertical shift 3 units upward and a vertical stretch
by a factor of 4.

$g(x) = 4x^2 + 3$

45. $f(x) = |x|$

(a) Reflection in the x-axis and a vertical shrink
by a factor of $\frac{1}{2}$.

$g(x) = -\frac{1}{2}|x|$

(b) Vertical stretch by a factor of 3 and a vertical shift
3 units downward.

$g(x) = 3|x| - 3$

47. Common function: $f(x) = x^3$

Vertical stretch by a factor of $\frac{3}{2}$: $g(x) = \frac{3}{2}x^3$

49. Common function: $f(x) = x^2$

Reflection in the x-axis and a vertical shrink
by a factor of $\frac{1}{2}$: $g(x) = -\frac{1}{2}x^2$

51. Common function: $f(x) = \sqrt{x}$

Reflection in the y-axis and a vertical shrink
by a factor or $\frac{1}{2}$: $g(x) = \frac{1}{2}\sqrt{-x}$

53. Common function: $f(x) = x^3$

Reflection in the x-axis, horizontal shift
2 units to the right and a vertical shift
2 units upward: $g(x) = -(x - 2)^3 + 2$

55. Common function: $f(x) = \sqrt{x}$

Reflection in the x-axis and a vertical shift 3 units
downward: $g(x) = -\sqrt{x} - 3$

57. (a) $g(x) = f(x) + 2$

Vertical shift 2 unit upward.

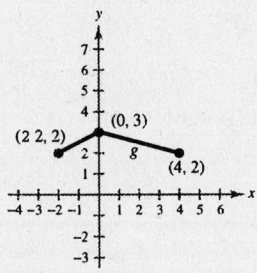

(b) $g(x) = f(x) - 1$

Vertical shift 1 unit downward.

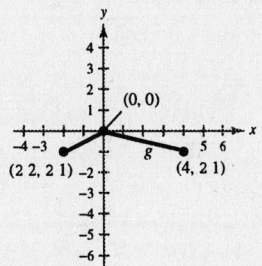

(c) $g(x) = f(-x)$

Reflection in the y-axis.

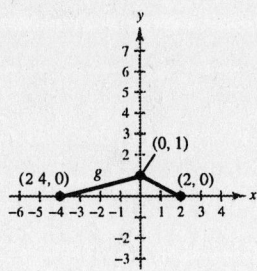

(d) $g(x) = -2f(x)$

Reflection in the x-axis and a
vertical stretch by a factor of 2.

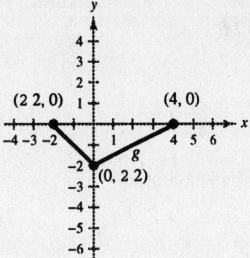

59. $F = f(t) = 20.46 + 0.04t^2$

(a) Common function: $f(x) = x^2$
Vertical shrink by a factor of 0.04 and
a vertical shift of 20.46 units.

(b) This represents a horizontal shift 10 units
to the left, so
$g(t) = f(t + 10) = 20.46 + 0.04(t + 10)^2$.

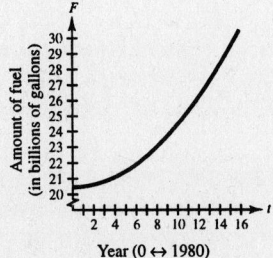

61. True, since $|x| = |-x|$, the graphs of $f(x) = |x| + 6$ and $f(x) = |-x| + 6$ are identical.

63. (a) The profits were only $\frac{3}{4}$ as large as expected: $g(t) = \frac{3}{4}f(t)$

(b) The profits were \$10,000 greater than predicted: $g(t) = f(t) + 10{,}000$

(c) There was a 2-year delay: $g(t) = f(t - 2)$

65. $y = f(x + 2) - 1$

Horizontal shift 2 units to the left and a vertical shift 1 unit downward.

$(0, 1) \rightarrow (0 - 2, 1 - 1) = (-2, 0)$

$(1, 2) \rightarrow (1 - 2, 2 - 1) = (-1, 1)$

$(2, 3) \rightarrow (2 - 2, 3 - 1) = (0, 2)$

67. $\dfrac{4}{x} + \dfrac{4}{1 - x} = \dfrac{4(1 - x) + 4x}{x(1 - x)} = \dfrac{4 - 4x + 4x}{x(1 - x)} = \dfrac{4}{x(1 - x)}$

69. $\dfrac{3}{x - 1} - \dfrac{2}{x(x - 1)} = \dfrac{3x - 2}{x(x - 1)}$

71. $(x - 4)\left(\dfrac{1}{\sqrt{x^2 - 4}}\right) = \dfrac{x - 4}{\sqrt{x^2 - 4}} = \dfrac{(x - 4)\sqrt{x^2 - 4}}{x^2 - 4}$

73. $(x^2 - 9) \div \left(\dfrac{x + 3}{5}\right) = \dfrac{(x + 3)(x - 3)}{1} \cdot \dfrac{5}{x + 3}$

$= 5(x - 3), x \neq -3$

75. $f(x) = x^2 - 6x + 11$

(a) $f(-3) = (-3)^2 - 6(-3) + 11 = 38$

(b) $f\left(-\frac{1}{2}\right) = \left(-\frac{1}{2}\right)^2 - 6\left(-\frac{1}{2}\right) + 11 = \frac{1}{4} + 3 + 11 = \frac{57}{4}$

(c) $f(x - 3) = (x - 3)^2 - 6(x - 3) + 11 = x^2 - 6x + 9 - 6x + 18 + 11$

$= x^2 - 12x + 38$

77. $f(x) = \dfrac{2}{11 - x}$

Domain: All real numbers except $x = 11$

79. $f(x) = \sqrt{81 - x^2}$

$81 - x^2 \geq 0$

$(9 + x)(9 - x) \geq 0$

Critical Numbers: $x = \pm 9$

Test Intervals: $(-\infty, -9), (-9, 9), (9, \infty)$

Test: Is $81 - x^2 \geq 0$?

Solution: $[-9, 9]$

Domain of $f(x)$: $-9 \leq x \leq 9$

Section 1.6   Combinations of Functions

■ Given two functions, f and g, you should be able to form the following functions (if defined):

1. Sum: $(f + g)(x) = f(x) + g(x)$

2. Difference: $(f - g)(x) = f(x) - g(x)$

3. Product: $(fg)(x) = f(x)g(x)$

4. Quotient: $(f/g)(x) = f(x)/g(x), g(x) \neq 0$

5. Composition of f with g: $(f \circ g)(x) = f(g(x))$

6. Composition of g with f: $(g \circ f)(x) = g(f(x))$

Solutions to Odd-Numbered Exercises

1.

x	0	1	2	3
f	2	3	1	2
g	-1	0	$\frac{1}{2}$	0
$f + g$	1	3	$\frac{3}{2}$	2

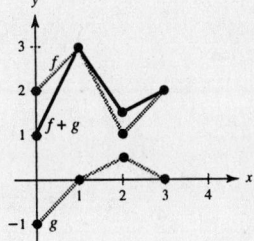

3.

x	-2	0	1	2	4
f	2	0	1	2	4
g	4	2	1	0	2
$f + g$	6	2	2	2	6

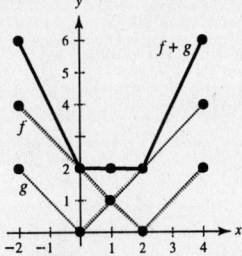

5. $f(x) = x + 2, g(x) = x - 2$

(a) $(f + g)(x) = f(x) + g(x) = (x + 2) + (x - 2) = 2x$

(b) $(f - g)(x) = f(x) - g(x) = (x + 2) - (x - 2) = 4$

(c) $(fg)(x) = f(x) \cdot g(x) = (x + 2)(x - 2) = x^2 - 4$

(d) $\left(\dfrac{f}{g}\right)(x) = \dfrac{f(x)}{g(x)} = \dfrac{x + 2}{x - 2}$

Domain: all real numbers except $x = 2$

7. $f(x) = x^2, g(x) = 2 - x$

$(f + g)(x) = f(x) + g(x) = x^2 + (2 - x) = x^2 - x + 2$

$(f - g)(x) = f(x) - g(x) = x^2 - (2 - x) = x^2 + x - 2$

$(fg)(x) = f(x) \cdot g(x) = x^2(2 - x) = 2x^2 - x^3$

$\left(\dfrac{f}{g}\right)(x) = \dfrac{f(x)}{g(x)} = \dfrac{x^2}{2 - x}$,   Domain: all real numbers except $x = 2$

9. $f(x) = x^2 + 6, g(x) = \sqrt{1 - x}$

$(f + g)(x) = f(x) + g(x) = (x^2 + 6) + \sqrt{1 - x}$

$(f - g)(x) = f(x) - g(x) = (x^2 + 6) - \sqrt{1 - x}$

$(fg)(x) = f(x) \cdot g(x) = (x^2 + 6)\sqrt{1 - x}$

$\left(\dfrac{f}{g}\right)(x) = \dfrac{f(x)}{g(x)} = \dfrac{x^2 + 6}{\sqrt{1 - x}}, \quad$ Domain: $x < 1$

11. $f(x) = \dfrac{1}{x}, g(x) = \dfrac{1}{x^2}$

$(f + g)(x) = f(x) + g(x) = \dfrac{1}{x} + \dfrac{1}{x^2} = \dfrac{x + 1}{x^2}$

$(f - g)(x) = f(x) - g(x) = \dfrac{1}{x} - \dfrac{1}{x^2} = \dfrac{x - 1}{x^2}$

$(fg)(x) = f(x) \cdot g(x) = \dfrac{1}{x}\left(\dfrac{1}{x^2}\right) = \dfrac{1}{x^3}$

$\left(\dfrac{f}{g}\right)(x) = \dfrac{f(x)}{g(x)} = \dfrac{1/x}{1/x^2} = \dfrac{x^2}{x} = x, \; x \neq 0$

For Exercises 13–24, $f(x) = x^2 + 1$ and $g(x) = x - 4$

13. $(f + g)(2) = f(2) + g(2) = (2^2 + 1) + (2 - 4) = 3$

15. $(f - g)(0) = f(0) - g(0) = (0^2 + 1) - (0 - 4) = 5$

17. $(f - g)(3t) = f(3t) - g(3t) = [(3t)^2 + 1] - (3t - 4)$

$\qquad\qquad\qquad = 9t^2 - 3t + 5$

19. $(fg)(6) = f(6)g(6) = (6^2 + 1)(6 - 4) = 74$

21. $\left(\dfrac{f}{g}\right)(5) = \dfrac{f(5)}{g(5)} = \dfrac{5^2 + 1}{5 - 4} = 26$

23. $\left(\dfrac{f}{g}\right)(-1) - g(3) = \dfrac{f(-1)}{g(-1)} - g(3)$

$\qquad\qquad\qquad = \dfrac{(-1)^2 + 1}{-1 - 4} - (3 - 4)$

$\qquad\qquad\qquad = -\dfrac{2}{5} + 1 = \dfrac{3}{5}$

25. $f(x) = \frac{1}{2}x, g(x) = x - 1, (f + g)(x) = \frac{3}{2}x - 1$

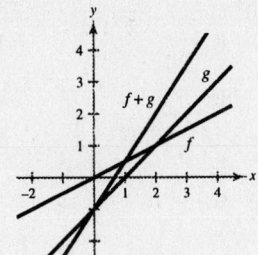

27. $f(x) = x^2, g(x) = -2x, (f + g)(x) = x^2 - 2x$

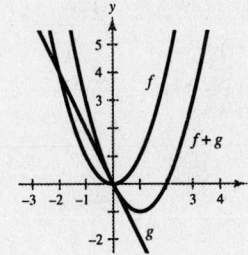

29. $f(x) = 3x, g(x) = -\dfrac{x^3}{10}, (f + g)(x) = 3x - \dfrac{x^3}{10}$

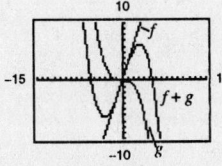

For $0 \le x \le 2$, $f(x)$ contributes most to the magnitude.
For $x > 6$, $g(x)$ contributes most to the magnitude.

31. $T(x) = R(x) + B(x) = \frac{3}{4}x + \frac{1}{15}x^2$

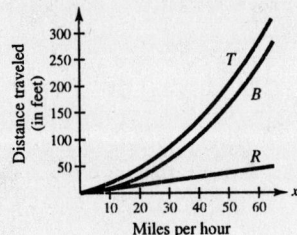

33.

Year	1990	1991	1992	1993	1994	1995	1996
y_1	144.4	151.6	159.5	163.6	164.8	166.7	171.2
y_2	238.6	259.4	282.5	303.3	315.6	326.9	337.3
y_3	21.8	24.0	25.1	27.3	29.6	31.7	32.4

$y_1 = -0.59x^2 + 7.66x + 144.90$

$y_2 = 16.58x + 245.06$

$y_3 = 1.85x + 21.88$

35. (a) T is a function of t since for each time t there corresponds one and only one temperature T.

(b) $T(4) = 60°$

$T(15) = 72°$

(c) $H(t) = T(t - 1)$; All the temperature changes would be one hour later.

(d) $H(t) = T(t) - 1$; The temperature would be decreased by one degree.

37. $f(x) = x^2, g(x) = x - 1$

(a) $(f \circ g)(x) = f(g(x)) = f(x - 1) = (x - 1)^2$

(b) $(g \circ f)(x) = g(f(x)) = g(x^2) = x^2 - 1$

(c) $(f \circ f)(x) = f(f(x)) = f(x^2) = (x^2)^2 = x^4$

39. $f(x) = 3x + 5, g(x) = 5 - x$

(a) $(f \circ g)(x) = f(g(x)) = f(5 - x) = 3(5 - x) + 5 = 20 - 3x$

(b) $(g \circ f)(x) = g(f(x)) = g(3x + 5) = 5 - (3x + 5) = -3x$

(c) $(f \circ f)(x) = f(f(x)) = f(3x + 5) = 3(3x + 5) + 5 = 9x + 20$

41. $f(x) = \sqrt{x + 4}$ Domain: $x \geq -4$

$g(x) = x^2$ Domain: all real numbers

(a) $(f \circ g)(x) = f(g(x)) = f(x^2) = \sqrt{x^2 + 4}$

   Domain: all real numbers

(b) $(g \circ f)(x) = g(f(x)) = g(\sqrt{x + 4}) = (\sqrt{x + 4})^2 = x + 4$

   Domain: $x \geq -4$

43. $f(x) = \frac{1}{3}x - 3$ Domain: all real numbers

$g(x) = 3x + 1$ Domain: all real numbers

(a) $(f \circ g)(x) = f(g(x)) = f(3x + 1) = \frac{1}{3}(3x + 1) - 3 = x - \frac{8}{3}$ Domain: all real numbers

(b) $(g \circ f)(x) = g(f(x)) = g(\frac{1}{3}x - 3) = 3(\frac{1}{3}x - 3) + 1 = x - 8$ Domain: all real numbers

45. $f(x) = x^4$ Domain: all real numbers

$g(x) = x^4$ Domain: all real numbers

(a) and (b) $(f \circ g)(x) = (g \circ f)(x) = (x^4)^4 = x^{16}$

   Domain: all real numbers

47. $f(x) = |x|$ Domain: all real numbers

$g(x) = x + 6$ Domain: all real numbers

(a) $(f \circ g)(x) = f(g(x)) = f(x + 6) = |x + 6|$ Domain: all real numbers

(b) $(g \circ f)(x) = g(f(x)) = g(|x|) = |x| + 6$ Domain: all real numbers

49. $f(x) = \frac{1}{x}$ Domain: all real numbers except $x = 0$

$g(x) = x + 3$ Domain: all real numbers

(a) $(f \circ g)(x) = f(g(x)) = f(x + 3) = \frac{1}{x + 3}$

   Domain: all real numbers except $x = -3$

(b) $(g \circ f)(x) = g(f(x)) = g\left(\frac{1}{x}\right) = \frac{1}{x} + 3$

   Domain: all real numbers except $x = 0$

51. (a) $(f + g)(3) = f(3) + g(3) = 2 + 1 = 3$

(b) $\left(\dfrac{f}{g}\right)(2) = \dfrac{f(2)}{g(2)} = \dfrac{0}{2} = 0$

53. (a) $(f \circ g)(2) = f(g(2)) = f(2) = 0$

(b) $(g \circ f)(2) = g(f(2)) = g(0) = 4$

55. Let $f(x) = x^2$ and $g(x) = 2x + 1$, then $(f \circ g)(x) = h(x)$. This is not a unique solution.

For example, if $f(x) = (x + 1)^2$ and $g(x) = 2x$, then $(f \circ g)(x) = h(x)$ as well.

57. Let $f(x) = \sqrt[3]{x}$ and $g(x) = x^2 - 4$, then $(f \circ g)(x) = h(x)$.

This answer is not unique. Other possibilities may be:

$f(x) = \sqrt[3]{x - 4}$ and $g(x) = x^2$

or $f(x) = \sqrt[3]{-x}$ and $g(x) = 4 - x^2$

or $f(x) = \sqrt[9]{x}$ and $g(x) = (4 - x^2)^3$

59. Let $f(x) = 1/x$ and $g(x) = x + 2$, then $(f \circ g)(x) = h(x)$. This is not a unique solution.

Other possibilities may be:

$$f(x) = \dfrac{1}{x + 2} \text{ and } g(x) = x$$

$$\text{or } f(x) = \dfrac{1}{x + 1} \text{ and } g(x) = x + 1$$

$$\text{or } f(x) = \dfrac{1}{x^2 + 2} \text{ and } g(x) = \sqrt{x}$$

61. Let $f(x) = \dfrac{x + 3}{4 + x}$ and $g(x) = -x^2$, then $(f \circ g)(x) = h(x)$. This answer is not unique.

Other possibilities may be:

$$f(x) = \dfrac{x + 1}{x + 2} \text{ and } g(x) = -x^2 + 2$$

$$\text{or } f(x) = x^2 \text{ and } g(x) = \sqrt{\dfrac{-x^2 + 3}{4 - x^2}}$$

$$\text{or } f(x) = \sqrt{x} \text{ and } g(x) = \left(\dfrac{-x^2 + 3}{4 - x^2}\right)^2$$

63. (a) $r(x) = \dfrac{x}{2}$

(b) $A(r) = \pi r^2$

(c) $(A \circ r)(x) = A(r(x)) = A\left(\dfrac{x}{2}\right) = \pi\left(\dfrac{x}{2}\right)^2$

$(A \circ r)(x)$ represents the area of the circular base of the tank on the square foundation with side length x.

65. $(C \circ x)(t) = C(x(t))$

$= 60(50t) + 750$

$= 3000t + 750$

$(C \circ x)(t)$ represents the cost after t production hours.

67. True. The range of g must be a subset of the domain of f for $(f \circ g)(x)$ to be defined. Since $(f \circ g)(x) = f(g(x))$ and since $g(x)$ represents the range of g, then f is being evaluated with values from g's range.

69. Let $f(x)$ and $g(x)$ be two odd functions and define $h(x) = f(x)g(x)$. Then

$$h(-x) = f(-x)g(-x)$$
$$= [-f(x)][-g(x)] \quad \text{Since } f \text{ and } g \text{ are odd}$$
$$= f(x)g(x)$$
$$= h(x)$$

Thus, $h(x)$ is even.

Let $f(x)$ and $g(x)$ be two even functions and define $h(x) = f(x)g(x)$. Then

$$h(-x) = f(-x)g(-x)$$
$$= f(x)g(x) \quad \text{Since } f \text{ and } g \text{ are even}$$
$$= h(x)$$

Thus, $h(x)$ is even.

71. $f(x) = 3x - 4$

$$\frac{f(x+h) - f(x)}{h} = \frac{[3(x+h) - 4] - (3x - 4)}{h}$$
$$= \frac{3x + 3h - 4 - 3x + 4}{h}$$
$$= \frac{3h}{h}$$
$$= 3$$

73. $f(x) = \dfrac{4}{x}$

$$\frac{f(x+h) - f(x)}{h} = \frac{\dfrac{4}{x+h} - \dfrac{4}{x}}{h} = \frac{\dfrac{4x - 4(x+h)}{x(x+h)}}{\dfrac{h}{1}}$$
$$= \frac{4x - 4x - 4h}{x(x+h)} \cdot \frac{1}{h}$$
$$= \frac{-4h}{x(x+h)} \cdot \frac{1}{h}$$
$$= \frac{-4}{x(x+h)}$$

75. Point: $(2, -4)$ Slope: $m = 3$

$$y - (-4) = 3(x - 2)$$
$$y + 4 = 3x - 6$$
$$3x - y - 10 = 0$$

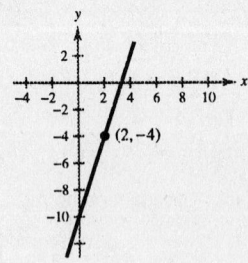

77. Point: $(8, -1)$ Slope: $m = -\frac{3}{2}$

$$y - (-1) = -\tfrac{3}{2}(x - 8)$$
$$y + 1 = -\tfrac{3}{2}x + 12$$
$$2y + 2 = -3x + 24$$
$$3x + 2y - 22 = 0$$

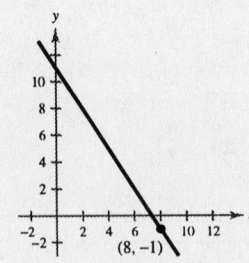

Section 1.7   Inverse Functions

- Two functions f and g are inverses of each other if $f(g(x)) = x$ for every x in the domain of g and $g(f(x)) = x$ for every x in the domain of f.

- A function f has an inverse function if and only if no **horizontal** line crosses the graph of f at more than one point.

- Be able to find the inverse of a function, if it exists.

  1. Use the Horizontal Line Test to see if f^{-1} exists.

  2. Replace $f(x)$ with y.

  3. Interchange x and y and solve for y.

  4. Replace y with $f^{-1}(x)$.

Solutions to Odd-Numbered Exercises

1. The inverse is a line through $(-1, 0)$.

Matches graph (c).

3. The inverse is half a parabola starting at $(1, 0)$.

Matches graph (a).

5. $f^{-1}(x) = \dfrac{x}{6} = \dfrac{1}{6}x$

$f(f^{-1}(x)) = f\left(\dfrac{x}{6}\right) = 6\left(\dfrac{x}{6}\right) = x$

$f^{-1}(f(x)) = f^{-1}(6x) = \dfrac{6x}{6} = x$

7. $f^{-1}(x) = x - 9$

$f(f^{-1}(x)) = f(x - 9) = (x - 9) + 9 = x$

$f^{-1}(f(x)) = f^{-1}(x + 9) = (x + 9) - 9 = x$

9. $f^{-1}(x) = \dfrac{x - 1}{3}$

$f(f^{-1}(x)) = f\left(\dfrac{x - 1}{3}\right) = 3\left(\dfrac{x - 1}{3}\right) + 1 = x$

$f^{-1}(f(x)) = f^{-1}(3x + 1) = \dfrac{(3x + 1) - 1}{3} = x$

11. $f^{-1}(x) = x^3$

$f(f^{-1}(x)) = f(x^3) = \sqrt[3]{x^3} = x$

$f^{-1}(f(x)) = f^{-1}(\sqrt[3]{x}) = (\sqrt[3]{x})^3 = x$

13. (a) $f(g(x)) = f\left(\dfrac{x}{2}\right) = 2\left(\dfrac{x}{2}\right) = x$

$g(f(x)) = g(2x) = \dfrac{2x}{2} = x$

(b)

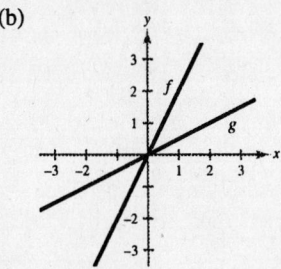

15. (a) $f(g(x)) = f\left(\dfrac{x - 1}{5}\right) = 5\left(\dfrac{x - 1}{5}\right) + 1 = x$

(a) $g(f(x)) = g(5x + 1) = \dfrac{(5x + 1) - 1}{5} = x$

(b)

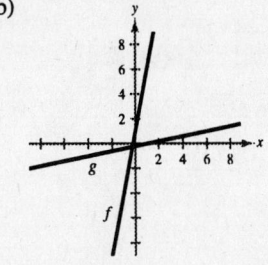

17. (a) $f(g(x)) = f\left(\sqrt[3]{x}\right) = \left(\sqrt[3]{x}\right)^3 = x$

$g(f(x)) = g(x^3) = \sqrt[3]{x^3} = x$

(b)

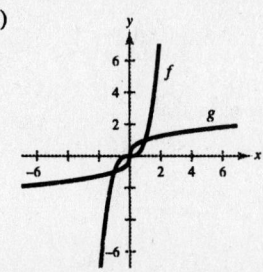

19. (a) $f(g(x)) = f(x^2 + 4), \; x \geq 0$

$\qquad = \sqrt{(x^2 + 4) - 4} = x$

$g(f(x)) = g\left(\sqrt{x - 4}\right)$

$\qquad = \left(\sqrt{x - 4}\right)^2 + 4 = x$

(b)

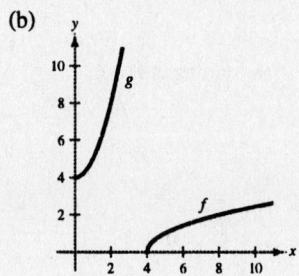

21. (a) $f(g(x)) = f\left(\sqrt{9 - x}\right), \; x \leq 9$

$\qquad = 9 - \left(\sqrt{9 - x}\right)^2 = x$

$g(f(x)) = g(9 - x^2), \; x \geq 0$

$\qquad = \sqrt{9 - (9 - x^2)} = x$

(b)

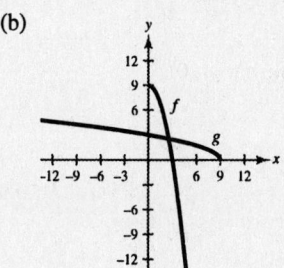

23. (a) $f(g(x)) = f\left(-\dfrac{5x + 1}{x - 1}\right)$

$= \dfrac{\left(-\dfrac{5x + 1}{x - 1} - 1\right)}{\left(-\dfrac{5x + 1}{x - 1} + 5\right)} \cdot \dfrac{x - 1}{x - 1}$

$= \dfrac{-(5x + 1) - (x - 1)}{-(5x + 1) + 5(x - 1)}$

$= \dfrac{-6x}{-6}$

$= x$

$g(f(x)) = g\left(\dfrac{x - 1}{x + 5}\right)$

$= -\dfrac{\left[5\left(\dfrac{x - 1}{x + 5}\right) + 1\right]}{\left[\dfrac{x - 1}{x + 5} - 1\right]} \cdot \dfrac{x + 5}{x + 5}$

$= -\dfrac{5(x - 1) + (x + 5)}{(x - 1) - (x + 5)}$

$= -\dfrac{6x}{-6}$

$= x$

(b)

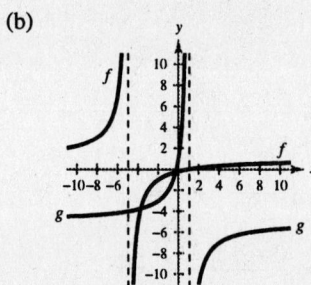

25. No, $\{(-2, -1), (1, 0), (2, 1), (1, 2), (-2, 3), (-6, 4)\}$ does not represent a function.
-2 and 1 are paired with two different values.

27.

x	-2	0	2	4	6	8
$f^{-1}(x)$	-2	-1	0	1	2	3

29. Since no horizontal line crosses the graph of f at more than one point, f **has** an inverse.

31. Since some horizontal lines cross the graph of f twice, f does **not** have an inverse.

33. $g(x) = \dfrac{4 - x}{6}$

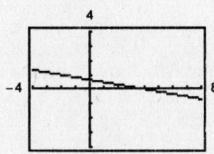

g passes the horizontal line test, so g **has** an inverse.

35. $h(x) = |x + 4| - |x - 4|$

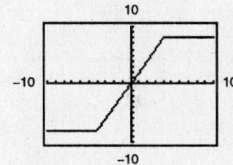

h does not pass the horizontal line test, so h does **not** have an inverse.

37. $f(x) = -2x\sqrt{16 - x^2}$

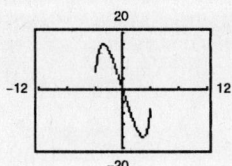

f does not pass the horizontal line test, so f does **not** have an inverse.

39. $f(x) = 2x - 3$

$y = 2x - 3$

$x = 2y - 3$

$y = \dfrac{x + 3}{2}$

$f^{-1}(x) = \dfrac{x + 3}{2}$

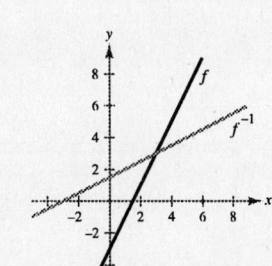

41. $f(x) = x^5 - 2$

$y = x^5 - 2$

$x = y^5 - 2$

$y = \sqrt[5]{x + 2}$

$f^{-1}(x) = \sqrt[5]{x + 2}$

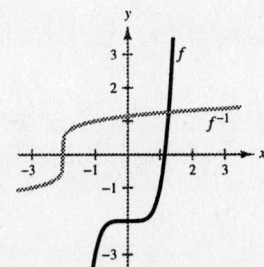

43. $f(x) = \sqrt{x}$

$y = \sqrt{x}$

$x = \sqrt{y}$

$y = x^2$

$f^{-1}(x) = x^2, \ x \geq 0$

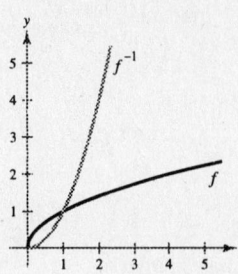

45. $f(x) = \sqrt{4 - x^2}, \ 0 \leq x \leq 2$

$y = \sqrt{4 - x^2}$

$x = \sqrt{4 - y^2}$

$f^{-1}(x) = \sqrt{4 - x^2}, \ 0 \leq x \leq 2$

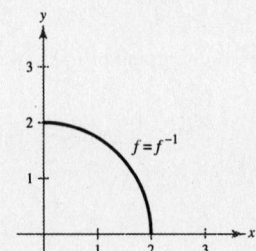

47. $f(x) = \dfrac{4}{x}$

$y = \dfrac{4}{x}$

$x = \dfrac{4}{y}$

$xy = 4$

$y = \dfrac{4}{x}$

$f^{-1}(x) = \dfrac{4}{x}$

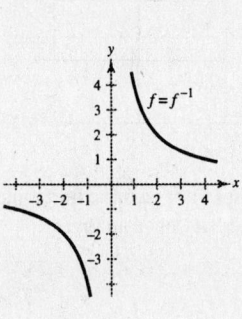

49. $f(x) = \dfrac{x + 1}{x - 2}$

$y = \dfrac{x + 1}{x - 2}$

$x = \dfrac{y + 1}{y - 2}$

$x(y - 2) = y + 1$

$xy - 2x = y + 1$

$xy - y = 2x + 1$

$y(x - 1) = 2x + 1$

$y = \dfrac{2x + 1}{x - 1}$

$f^{-1}(x) = \dfrac{2x + 1}{x - 1}$

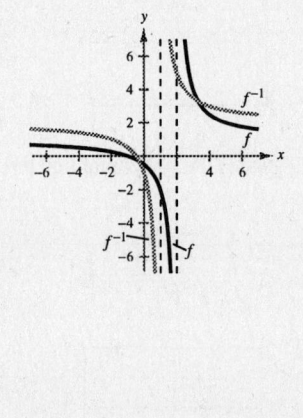

51. $f(x) = \sqrt[3]{x - 1}$

$y = \sqrt[3]{x - 1}$

$x = \sqrt[3]{y - 1}$

$x^3 = y - 1$

$y = x^3 + 1$

$f^{-1}(x) = x^3 + 1$

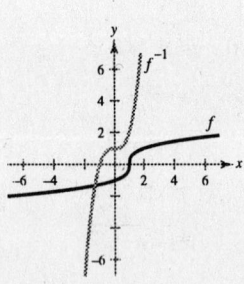

53. $f(x) = \dfrac{6x + 4}{4x + 5}$

$$y = \dfrac{6x + 4}{4x + 5}$$

$$x = \dfrac{6y + 4}{4y + 5}$$

$$x(4y + 5) = 6y + 4$$

$$4xy + 5x = 6y + 4$$

$$4xy - 6y = -5x + 4$$

$$y(4x - 6) = -5x + 4$$

$$y = \dfrac{-5x + 4}{4x - 6}$$

$$f^{-1}(x) = \dfrac{-5x + 4}{4x - 6} = \dfrac{5x - 4}{6 - 4x}$$

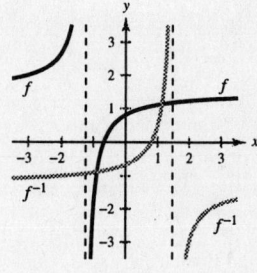

55. $f(x) = x^4$

$$y = x^4$$

$$x = y^4$$

$$y = \pm\sqrt[4]{x}$$

This does not represent y as a function of x.
f does not have an inverse.

57. $g(x) = \dfrac{x}{8}$

$$y = \dfrac{x}{8}$$

$$x = \dfrac{y}{8}$$

$$y = 8x$$

This is a function of x, so g has an inverse.
$g^{-1}(x) = 8x$

59. $p(x) = -4$

$$y = -4$$

Since $y = -4$ for all x, the graph is a horizontal line and fails the horizontal line test. p does not have an inverse.

61. $f(x) = (x + 3)^2, \; x \geq -3 \; \Rightarrow \; y \geq 0$

$$y = (x + 3)^2, \; x \geq -3, \; y \geq 0$$

$$x = (y + 3)^2, \; y \geq -3, \; x \geq 0$$

$$\sqrt{x} = y + 3, \; y \geq -3, \; x \geq 0$$

$$y = \sqrt{x} - 3, \; x \geq 0, \; y \geq -3$$

This is a function of x, so f has an inverse.

$f^{-1}(x) = \sqrt{x} - 3, \; x \geq 0$

63. $f(x) = \begin{cases} x + 3, & x < 0 \\ 6 - x, & x \geq 0 \end{cases}$

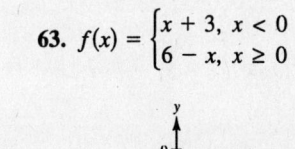

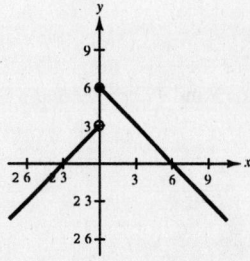

The graph fails the horizontal line test, so $f(x)$ does not have an inverse.

65. $h(x) = \dfrac{1}{x}$

$$y = \dfrac{1}{x}$$

$$xy = 1$$

$$y = \dfrac{1}{x}$$

This is a function of x, so h has an inverse.

$$h^{-1}(x) = \dfrac{1}{x}$$

67. $f(x) = \sqrt{2x + 3} \implies x \geq -\dfrac{3}{2}, \ y \geq 0$

$$y = \sqrt{2x + 3}, \ x \geq -\dfrac{3}{2}, \ y \geq 0$$

$$x = \sqrt{2y + 3}, \ y \geq -\dfrac{3}{2}, \ x \geq 0$$

$$x^2 = 2y + 3, \ x \geq 0, \ y \geq -\dfrac{3}{2}$$

$$y = \dfrac{x^2 - 3}{2}, \ x \geq 0, \ y \geq -\dfrac{3}{2}$$

This is a function of x, so f has an inverse.

$$f^{-1}(x) = \dfrac{x^2 - 3}{2}, \ x \geq 0$$

In Exercises 69, 71, and 73, $f(x) = \frac{1}{8}x - 3$, $f^{-1}(x) = 8(x + 3)$, $g(x) = x^3$, $g^{-1}(x) = \sqrt[3]{x}$.

69. $(f^{-1} \circ g^{-1})(1) = f^{-1}(g^{-1}(1)) = f^{-1}(\sqrt[3]{1}) = 8(\sqrt[3]{1} + 3) = 32$

71. $(f^{-1} \circ f^{-1})(6) = f^{-1}(f^{-1}(6)) = f^{-1}(8[6 + 3]) = 8[8(6 + 3) + 3] = 600$

73. $\quad (f \circ g)(x) = f(g(x)) = f(x^3) = \frac{1}{8}x^3 - 3$

$$y = \tfrac{1}{8}x^3 - 3$$

$$x = \tfrac{1}{8}y^3 - 3$$

$$x + 3 = \tfrac{1}{8}y^3$$

$$8(x + 3) = y^3$$

$$\sqrt[3]{8(x + 3)} = y$$

$$(f \circ g)^{-1}(x) = 2\sqrt[3]{x + 3}$$

In Exercises 75 and 77, $f(x) = x + 4$, $f^{-1}(x) = x - 4$, $g(x) = 2x - 5$, $g^{-1}(x) = \dfrac{x + 5}{2}$.

75. $(g^{-1} \circ f^{-1})(x) = g^{-1}(f^{-1}(x)) = g^{-1}(x - 4) = \dfrac{(x - 4) + 5}{2} = \dfrac{x + 1}{2}$

77. $(f \circ g)(x) = f(g(x)) = f(2x - 5) = (2x - 5) + 4 = 2x - 1$

$$(f \circ g)^{-1}(x) = \dfrac{x + 1}{2}$$

Note: Comparing Exercises 75 and 77, we see that $(f \circ g)^{-1}(x) = (g^{-1} \circ f^{-1})(x)$.

79. (a)
$$y = 8 + 0.75x$$
$$x = 8 + 0.75y$$
$$x - 8 = 0.75y$$
$$\frac{x - 8}{0.75} = y$$
$$f^{-1}(x) = \frac{x - 8}{0.75}$$

(b) x = hourly wage

y = number of units produced

(c) $y = \dfrac{22.25 - 8}{0.75} = 19$ units

81. (a)
$$y = 0.03x^2 + 245.50, \ 0 < x < 100$$
$$x = 0.03y^2 + 245.50$$
$$x - 245.50 = 0.03y^2$$
$$\frac{x - 245.50}{0.03} = y^2$$
$$\sqrt{\frac{x - 245.50}{0.03}} = y, \ 245.50 < x < 545.50$$
$$f^{-1}(x) = \sqrt{\frac{x - 245.50}{0.03}}$$

x = temperature in degrees Fahrenheit

y = percent load for a diesel engine

(b)

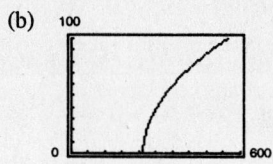

(c)
$$0.03x^2 + 245.50 < 500$$
$$0.03x^2 < 254.50$$
$$x^2 < 92.11$$
$$x < 92.11$$

Thus, $0 < x < 90.46$.

83. No, since both 1994 and 1998 would be paired with the same y-value, the inverse would not exist. It would not pass the Horizontal Line Test.

85. (a) Yes, f^{-1} exists. It would represent the year for a given per capita consumption of regular soft drinks.

(b) $f^{-1}(39.8) = 5$ which represents 1995.

87. True. If $f(x) = x - 6$ and $f^{-1}(x) = x + 6$, then the y-intercept of f is $(0, -6)$ and the x-intercept of f^{-1} is $(-6, 0)$.

89. False. Some examples:

$$f(x) = f^{-1}(x) = x$$

$$f(x) = f^{-1}(x) = \frac{1}{x}$$

$$f(x) = f^{-1}(x) = \sqrt{4 - x^2}, \quad 0 \le x \le 2$$

91.

x	$f(x)$
-2	-5
-1	-2
1	2
3	3

x	$f^{-1}(x)$
-5	-2
-2	-1
2	1
3	3

93.

x	$f(x)$
-4	3
-2	4
0	0
3	-1

The graph does not pass the Horizontal Line Test, so $f^{-1}(x)$ does not exist.

95. $x^2 = 64$

$$x = \pm\sqrt{64} = \pm 8$$

97. $4x^2 - 12x + 9 = 0$

$$(2x - 3)^2 = 0$$

$$2x - 3 = 0$$

$$x = \tfrac{3}{2}$$

99. $x^2 - 6x + 4 = 0$ Complete the Square

$$x^2 - 6x = -4$$

$$x^2 - 6x + 9 = -4 + 9$$

$$(x - 3)^2 = 5$$

$$x - 3 = \pm\sqrt{5}$$

$$x = 3 \pm \sqrt{5}$$

101. $50 + 5x = 3x^2$

$$0 = 3x^2 - 5x - 50$$

$$0 = (3x + 10)(x - 5)$$

$$3x + 10 = 0 \implies x = -\tfrac{10}{3}$$

$$x - 5 = 0 \implies x = 5$$

103. $f(x) = \sqrt[3]{x + 4}$

Domain: all real numbers

105. $g(x) = \dfrac{2}{x^2 - 4x} = \dfrac{2}{x(x - 4)}$

Domain: all real numbers except $x = 0$ and $x = 4$

107. Let $2n$ = first positive even integer. Then $2n + 2$ = next positive even integer.

$$2n(2n + 2) = 288$$

$$4n^2 + 4n - 288 = 0$$

$$4(n^2 + n - 72) = 0$$

$$4(n + 9)(n - 8) = 0$$

$n + 9 = 0 \implies n = -9$ Not a solution since the

$n - 8 = 0 \implies n = 8$ integers are positive.

Thus, $2n = 16$ and $2n + 2 = 18$.

Section 1.8   Mathematical Modeling

You should know the following the following terms and formulas.

- ■ Direct Variation (varies directly, directly proportional)

    (a) $y = kx$

    (b) $y = kx^n$ (as nth power)

- ■ Inverse Variation (varies inversely, inversely proportional)

    (a) $y = k/x$

    (b) $y = k/(x^n)$ (as nth power)

- ■ Joint Variation (varies jointly, jointly proportional)

    (a) $z = kxy$

    (b) $z = kx^n y^m$ (as nth power of x and mth power of y)

- ■ k is called the constant of proportionality.

- ■ Least Squares Regression Line $y = ax + b$. Use your calculator or computer to enter the data points and to find the "best-fitting" linear model.

Solutions to Odd-Numbered Exercises

1. $y = 125,151.5 + 1495.68t,\ 0 \le t \le 7$

Year	1990	1991	1992	1993	1994	1995	1996	1997
Actual Number (in thousands)	125,840	126,346	128,105	129,200	131,056	132,304	133,943	136,297
Model	125,152	126,647	128,143	129,639	131,134	132,630	134,126	135,621

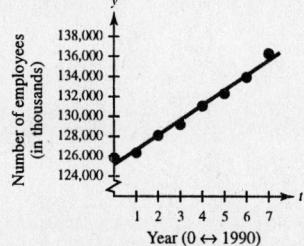

The model is a "good fit" for the actual data.

3. The graph appears to represent $y = 4/x$, so y varies inversely as x.

5. $k = 1$

x	2	4	6	8	10
$y = kx^2$	4	16	36	64	100

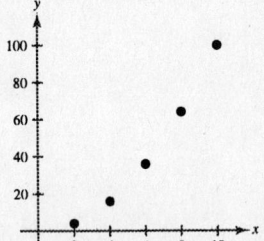

7. $k = \frac{1}{2}$

x	2	4	6	8	10
$y = kx^2$	2	8	18	32	50

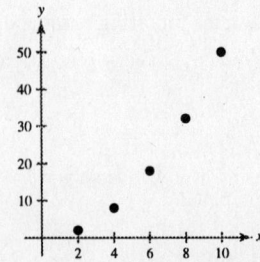

9. $k = 2$

x	2	4	6	8	10
$y = \dfrac{k}{x^2}$	$\dfrac{1}{2}$	$\dfrac{1}{8}$	$\dfrac{1}{18}$	$\dfrac{1}{32}$	$\dfrac{1}{50}$

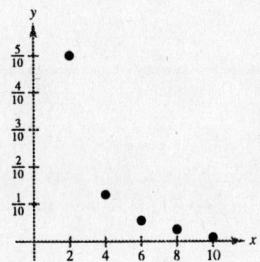

11. $k = 10$

x	2	4	6	8	10
$y = \dfrac{k}{x^2}$	$\dfrac{5}{2}$	$\dfrac{5}{8}$	$\dfrac{5}{18}$	$\dfrac{5}{32}$	$\dfrac{1}{10}$

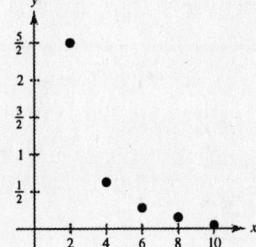

13. The chart represents the equation $y = \dfrac{5}{x}$.

15. $y = kx$

$-7 = k(10)$

$-\frac{7}{10} = k$

$y = -\frac{7}{10}x$

This equation checks with the other points given in the chart.

17. $y = kx$

$12 = k(5)$

$\frac{12}{5} = k$

$y = \frac{12}{5}x$

19. $y = kx$

$2050 = k(10)$

$205 = k$

$y = 205x$

21. $I = kP$

$87.50 = k(2500)$

$0.035 = k$

$I = 0.035P$

23. $y = kx$

$33 = k(13)$

$\frac{33}{13} = k$

$y = \frac{33}{13}x$

Inches	5	10	20	25	30
Centimeters	12.7	25.4	50.8	63.5	76.2

25. $y = kx$

$5520 = k(150{,}000)$

$0.0368 = k$

$y = 0.0368x$

$y = 0.0368(200{,}000) = \$7360$

27. $d = kF$

$0.15 = k(265)$

$\frac{3}{5300} = k$

$d = \frac{3}{5300}F$

(a) $d = \frac{3}{5300}(90) \approx 0.05$ meter

(b) $0.1 = \frac{3}{5300}F$

$\frac{530}{3} = F$

$F = 176\frac{2}{3}$ newtons

29. $d = kF$

$1.9 = k(25) \implies k = 0.076$

$d = 0.076F$

When the distance compressed is 3 inches, we have

$3 = 0.076F$

$F \approx 39.47.$

No child over 39.47 pounds should use the toy.

31. $A = kr^2$

33. $y = \dfrac{k}{x^2}$

35. $F = \dfrac{kg}{r^2}$

37. $P = \dfrac{k}{V}$

39. $F = \dfrac{km_1 m_2}{r^2}$

41. $A = \frac{1}{2}bh$

The area of a triangle is jointly proportional to its base and height.

43. $V = \dfrac{4}{3}\pi r^3$

The volume of a sphere varies directly as the cube of its radius.

45. $r = \dfrac{d}{t}$

Average speed is directly proportional to the distance and inversely proportional to the time.

47. $A = kr^2$

$9\pi = k(3)^2$

$\pi = k$

$A = \pi r^2$

49. $y = \dfrac{k}{x}$

$7 = \dfrac{k}{4}$

$28 = k$

$y = \dfrac{28}{x}$

51. $F = krs^3$

$4158 = k(11)(3)^3$

$k = 14$

$F = 14rs^3$

53. $z = \dfrac{kx^2}{y}$

$6 = \dfrac{k(6)^2}{4}$

$\dfrac{24}{36} = k$

$\dfrac{2}{3} = k$

$z = \dfrac{\frac{2}{3}x^2}{y} = \dfrac{2x^2}{3y}$

55. $d = kv^2$

$0.02 = k\left(\dfrac{1}{4}\right)^2$

$k = 0.32$

$d = 0.32v^2$

$0.12 = 0.32v^2$

$v^2 = \dfrac{0.12}{0.32} = \dfrac{3}{8}$

$v = \dfrac{\sqrt{3}}{2\sqrt{2}} = \dfrac{\sqrt{6}}{4} \approx 0.61$ mi/hr

57. $r = \dfrac{kl}{A}, \; A = \pi r^2 = \dfrac{\pi d^2}{4}$

$r = \dfrac{4kl}{\pi d^2}$

$66.17 = \dfrac{4(1000)k}{\pi\left(\dfrac{0.0126}{12}\right)^2}$

$k \approx 5.73 \times 10^{-8}$

$r = \dfrac{4(5.73 \times 10^{-8})l}{\pi\left(\dfrac{0.0126}{12}\right)^2}$

$33.5 = \dfrac{4(5.73 \times 10^{-8})l}{\pi\left(\dfrac{0.0126}{12}\right)^2}$

$\dfrac{33.5\pi\left(\dfrac{0.0126}{12}\right)^2}{4(5.73 \times 10^{-8})} = l$

$l \approx 506$ feet

59. $s = kt^2$

$144 = k(3)^2$

$16 = k$

$s = 16t^2$

$s = 16(5)^2 = 400$ feet

61. $P = kA = k(\pi r^2) = k\pi\left(\dfrac{d}{2}\right)^2$

$8.78 = k\pi\left(\dfrac{9}{2}\right)^2$

$\dfrac{4(8.78)}{81\pi} = k$

$k \approx 0.138$

However, we do not obtain $11.78 when $d = 12$ inches.

$P = 0.138\pi\left(\dfrac{12}{2}\right)^2 \approx \$15.61$

Instead, $k = \dfrac{11.78}{36\pi} \approx 0.104$.

For the 15-inch pizza, we have $k = \dfrac{4(14.18)}{225\pi} \approx 0.080$.

The price is not directly proportional to the surface area. The best buy is the 15-inch pizza.

63. $v = \dfrac{k}{A}$

(a) $v = \dfrac{k}{0.75A} = \dfrac{4}{3}\left(\dfrac{k}{A}\right)$

The velocity is increased by one-third.

(b) $v = \dfrac{k}{\left(1 + \frac{1}{3}\right)A} = \dfrac{k}{\frac{4}{3}A} = \dfrac{3}{4}\left(\dfrac{k}{A}\right)$

The velocity is decreased by one-fourth.

65. (a)

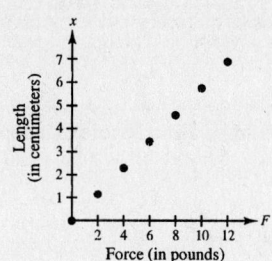

(b) It appears to fit Hooke's Law.

$k \approx \dfrac{6.9}{12} = 0.575$

(c) $x = kF$

$9 = 0.575F$

$F \approx 15.7$ pounds

67. $y = \dfrac{262.76}{x^{2.12}}$

(a)

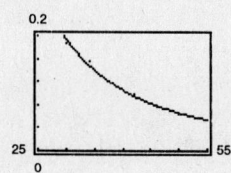

(b) $y = \dfrac{262.76}{(25)^{2.12}} \approx 0.2857$ microwatts per square centimeter

69. (a) $y = 127.4t + 218.4$, $t \geq 0$

(b)

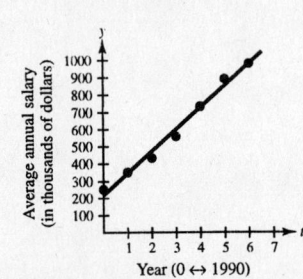

(c) 1997: $y = 127.4(7) + 218.4 \approx \$1110$ thousand

1998: $y = 127.4(8) + 218.4 \approx \$1238$ thousand

1999: $y = 127.4(9) + 218.4 \approx \$1365$ thousand

71. (a) $y = 489.58t + 5628.4$, $t \geq 0$

(b)

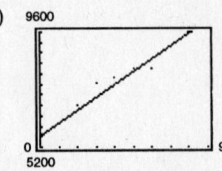

(c) 1999: $y = 489.58(9) + 5628.4 \approx \$10{,}035$ million

(d) Answers will vary.

73. (a) $y = -0.0186x + 689$

(b)

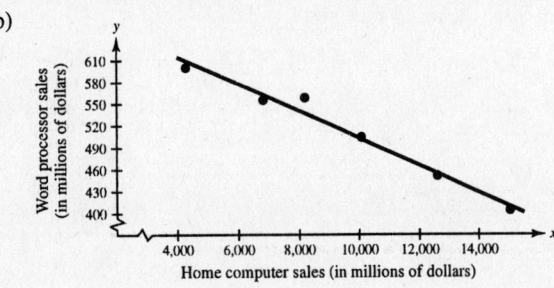

(c) $y = -0.0186(18000) + 689 \approx \$354$ million

75. False. E is jointly proportional (not "directly proportional") to the mass of an object and the square of its velocity.

77. The points do not follow a linear pattern. A linear model would be a poor approximation. A quadratic model would be better.

79. The data shown could be represented by a linear model which would be a good approximation.

81.

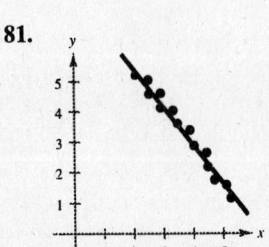

The line appears to pass through $(2, 5.5)$ and $(6, 0.5)$, so its equation is

$$y = -\tfrac{5}{4}x + 8.$$

83.

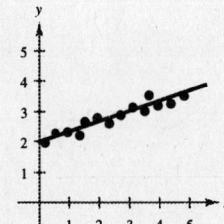

The line appears to pass through $(0, 2)$ and $(3, 3)$ so its equation is

$$y = \tfrac{1}{3}x + 2.$$

85.
$$(x - 5)^2 \geq 1$$
$$x^2 - 10x + 25 - 1 \geq 0$$
$$x^2 - 10x + 24 \geq 0$$
$$(x - 4)(x - 6) \geq 0$$

Critical Numbers: $x = 4, x = 6$

Test Intervals: $(-\infty, 4), (4, 6), (6, \infty)$

Test: Is $(x - 4)(x - 6) \geq 0$?

Solution: $x \leq 4, x \geq 6$

87. $6x^3 - 30x^2 > 0$
$$6x^2(x - 5) > 0$$

Critical Numbers: $x = 0, x = 5$

Test Intervals: $(-\infty, 0), (0, 5), (5, \infty)$

Test: Is $6x^2(x - 5) > 0$?

Solution: $x > 5$

89. $f(x) = \dfrac{x^2 + 5}{x - 3}$

(a) $f(0) = \dfrac{0^2 + 5}{0 - 3} = -\dfrac{5}{3}$

(b) $f(-3) = \dfrac{(-3)^2 + 5}{-3 - 3} = \dfrac{14}{-6} = -\dfrac{7}{3}$

(c) $f(4) = \dfrac{4^2 + 5}{4 - 3} = 21$

91. $f(x) = -10x^2 - x - 1$

Since f is a polynomial, the domain is all real numbers.

93. $f(x) = \dfrac{x - 1}{x + 7}$

The domain is all real numbers except $x = -7$.

Review Exercises for Chapter 1

Solutions to Odd-Numbered Exercises

1. $y = 3x - 5$

x	-2	-1	0	1	2
y	-11	-8	-5	-2	1

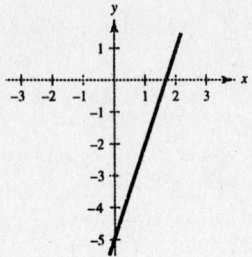

3. $y = x^2 - 3x$

x	-1	0	1	2	3	4
y	4	0	-2	-2	0	4

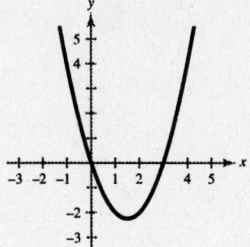

5. $y = 2x - 9$

x-intercept: $0 = 2x - 9 \implies x = \frac{9}{2}$

$\left(\frac{9}{2}, 0\right)$ is the x-intercept

y-intercept: $y = 2(0) - 9 = -9$

$(0, -9)$ is the y-intercept

7. $y = (x + 1)^2$

x-intercept: $0 = (x + 1)^2 \implies x = -1$

$(-1, 0)$ is the x-intercept

y-intercept: $y = (0 + 1)^2 = 1$

$(0, 1)$ is the y-intercept

9. $y = 5 - x^2$

Intercepts: $\left(\pm\sqrt{5}, 0\right), (0, 5)$

y-axis symmetry

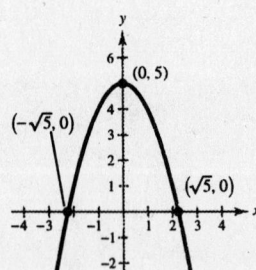

11. $y = \sqrt{x + 5}$

Domain: $[-5, \infty)$

Intercepts: $(-5, 0), \left(0, \sqrt{5}\right)$

No axis or origin symmetry

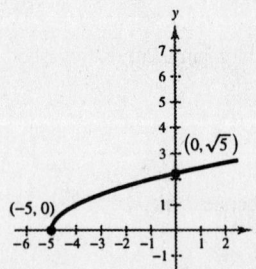

13. $x^2 + y^2 = 25$

Center: $(0, 0)$

Radius: 5

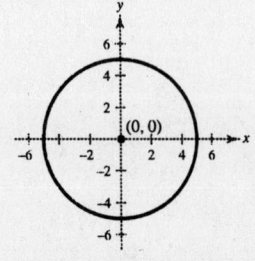

15. $(x + 2)^2 + y^2 = 16$

$(x - (-2))^2 + (y - 0)^2 = 4^2$

Center: $(-2, 0)$

Radius: 4

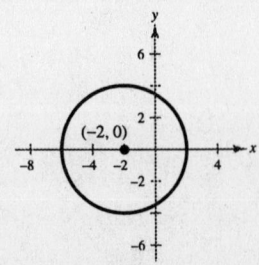

17. Endpoints of a diameter: $(0, 0)$ and $(4, -6)$

Center: $\left(\dfrac{0 + 4}{2}, \dfrac{0 + (-6)}{2}\right) = (2, -3)$

Radius: $r = \sqrt{(2 - 0)^2 + (-3 - 0)^2} = \sqrt{4 + 9} = \sqrt{13}$

Standard form: $(x - 2)^2 + (y - (-3))^2 = \left(\sqrt{13}\right)^2$

$$(x - 2)^2 + (y + 3)^2 = 13$$

19. $y = 0.073t + 0.644$

t	0	2	4	6	8
y	0.644	0.790	0.936	1.082	1.228

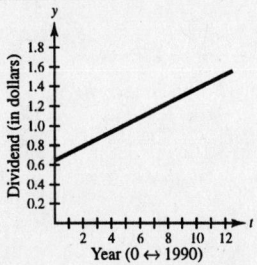

The dividend share will be \$1.50 when t is between 11 and 12, which corresponds to the year 2001.

21. $y = 6$

Horizontal line

y-intercept: $(0, 6)$

Slope: $m = 0$

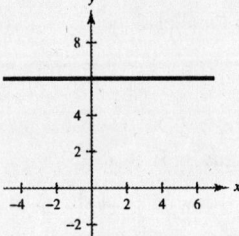

23. $y = 3x + 13$

y-intercept: $(0, 13)$

Slope: $m = 3 = \dfrac{3}{1}$

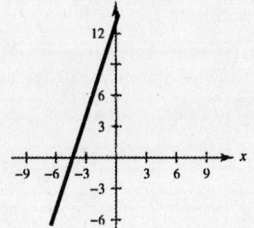

25. (a) $m = \frac{3}{2} > 0 \implies$ The line rises. Matches L_2.

 (b) $m = 0 \implies$ The line is horizontal. Matches L_3.

 (c) $m = -3 < 0 \implies$ The line falls. Matches L_1.

 (d) $m = -\frac{1}{5} < 0 \implies$ The line gradually falls. Matches L_4.

27. $(-1, 8), (6, 5)$

$$m = \frac{5 - 8}{6 - (-1)} = \frac{-3}{7}$$

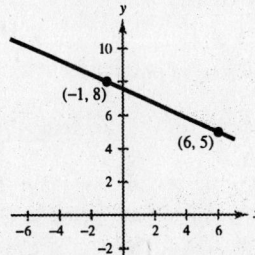

29. $(-3, 2), (8, 2)$

$$m = \frac{2 - 2}{-3 - 8} = \frac{0}{-11} = 0$$

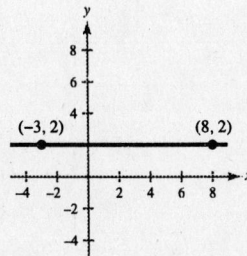

31. $(2, 5), (-2, -1)$

$$m = \frac{-1 - 5}{-2 - 2} = \frac{-6}{-4} = \frac{3}{2}$$

$$y - 5 = \frac{3}{2}(x - 2)$$

$$y - 5 = \frac{3}{2}x - 3$$

$$y = \frac{3}{2}x + 2$$

$$2y = 3x + 4$$

$$3x - 2y + 4 = 0$$

33. $(11, -2), (6, -1)$

$$m = \frac{-1 - (-2)}{6 - 11} = -\frac{1}{5}$$

$$y - (-2) = -\frac{1}{5}(x - 11)$$

$$y + 2 = -\frac{1}{5}x + \frac{11}{5}$$

$$y = -\frac{1}{5}x + \frac{1}{5}$$

$$5y = -x + 1$$

$$x + 5y - 1 = 0$$

35. Point: $(-2, 6)$

Slope: $m = 0$

$$y - 6 = 0(x - (-2))$$

$$y - 6 = 0$$

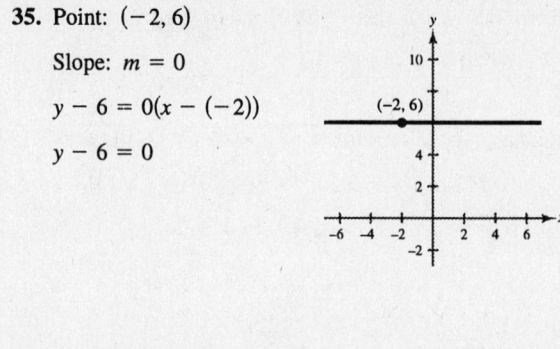

37. Point: $(-8, 5)$

Slope: Undefined

$$x = -8$$

$$x + 8 = 0$$

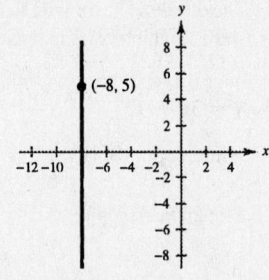

39. $(-8, 3), 2x + 3y = 5$

$$3y = 5 - 2x$$

$$y = \frac{5}{3} - \frac{2}{3}x$$

(a) Parallel slope: $m = -\frac{2}{3}$

$$y - 3 = -\frac{2}{3}(x + 8)$$

$$3y - 9 = -2x - 16$$

$$2x + 3y + 7 = 0$$

(b) Perpendicular slope: $m = \frac{3}{2}$

$$y - 3 = \frac{3}{2}(x - (-8))$$

$$2y - 6 = 3x + 24$$

$$0 = 3x - 2y + 30$$

41. $(0, 72.95), m = 5.15$

$$y - 72.95 = 5.15(x - 0)$$

$$y - 72.95 = 5.15x$$

$$y = 5.15x + 72.95$$

43. $2x - y - 3 = 0$

$$2x - 3 = y$$

Yes, the equation represents y as a function of x.

45. $|y| = x + 2$ corresponds to $y = x + 2$ or $-y = x + 2$.
y is not a function of x. Each x-value corresponds to two y-values.

47. $g(x) = x^{4/3}$

(a) $g(8) = 8^{4/3} = 2^4 = 16$

(b) $g(t + 1) = (t + 1)^{4/3}$

(c) $\dfrac{g(8) - g(1)}{8 - 1} = \dfrac{16 - 1}{7} = \dfrac{15}{7}$

(d) $g(-x) = (-x)^{4/3} = x^{4/3}$

49. $f(x) = 3x + 4$

Domain: All real numbers

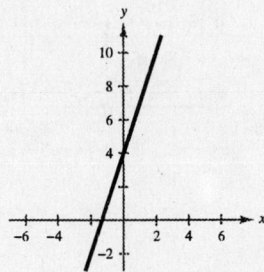

51. $f(t) = |t + 1|$

Domain: All real numbers

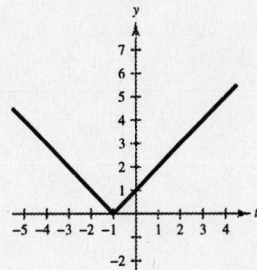

53. (a) $f(x) = 0.40(50 - x) + 1.00x$

$\qquad = 0.4(50 - x) + x$

$\qquad = 20 + 0.6x$

(b) Domain: $0 \leq x \leq 50$

Range: When $x = 0$; $f(0) = 20$

When $x = 50$; $f(50) = 50$

$20 \leq y \leq 50$

(c) $20 + 0.6x = 0.5(50)$

$20 + 0.6x = 25$

$0.6x = 5$

$x = \dfrac{5}{0.6} = \dfrac{50}{6} = 8\dfrac{1}{3}$ liters

55. $y = -\frac{3}{5}x^3 - 2x + 1$

The graph passes the Vertical Line Test.
y **is** a function of x.

57. $x = -|4 - y|$

The graph fails the Vertical Line Test. Some vertical lines cross the graph twice. y is **not** a function of x.

59. $\qquad f(x) = 5x^2 + 4x - 1$

$5x^2 + 4x - 1 = 0$

$(5x - 1)(x + 1) = 0$

$5x - 1 = 0 \implies x = \frac{1}{5}$

$x + 1 = 0 \implies x = -1$

61. $\qquad f(x) = x^3 - x^2 - 25x + 25$

$x^3 - x^2 - 25x + 25 = 0$

$x^2(x - 1) - 25(x - 1) = 0$

$(x^2 - 25)(x - 1) = 0$

$(x + 5)(x - 5)(x - 1) = 0$

$x + 5 = 0 \implies x = -5$

$x - 5 = 0 \implies x = 5$

$x - 1 = 0 \implies x = 1$

63. $f(x) = (x^2 - 4)^2$

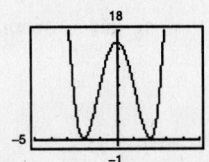

Increasing on $(-2, 0)$ and $(2, \infty)$

Decreasing on $(-\infty, -2)$ and $(0, 2)$

65. $g(x) = \sqrt[3]{x(x+3)^2}$

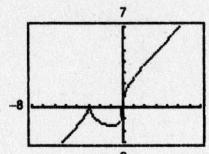

Increasing on $(-\infty, -3)$ and $(-1, \infty)$

Decreasing on $(-3, -1)$

67. $f(0) = -5$, $f(4) = -8$

$$m = \frac{-8 - (-5)}{4 - 0} = -\frac{3}{4}$$

$$y - (-5) = -\frac{3}{4}(x - 0)$$

$$y = -\frac{3}{4}x - 5$$

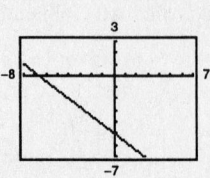

69. $f(3.3) = 5.6$, $f(-4.7) = -1.4$

$$m = \frac{-1.4 - 5.6}{-4.7 - 3.3} = \frac{-7}{-8} = \frac{7}{8}$$

$$y - 5.6 = \frac{7}{8}(x - 3.3)$$

$$y - \frac{56}{10} = \frac{7}{8}\left(x - \frac{33}{10}\right)$$

$$y = \frac{7}{8}x - \frac{231}{80} + \frac{56}{10} \cdot \frac{8}{8}$$

$$y = \frac{7}{8}x + \frac{217}{80}$$

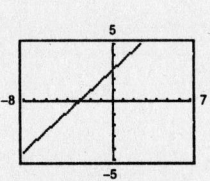

71. $f(x) = \begin{cases} x^2 - 2, & x < -2 \\ 5, & -2 \le x \le 0 \\ 8x - 5, & x > 0 \end{cases}$

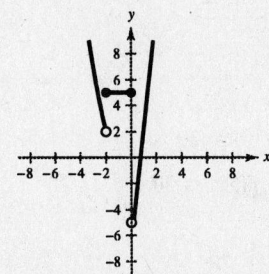

73. $f(x) = x^4 - 20x^2$

$f(-x) = (-x)^4 - 20(-x)^2$

$= x^4 - 20x^2$

$= f(x)$

The function is even.

75. $f(x) = \sqrt[5]{6x^2}$

$f(-x) = \sqrt[5]{6(-x)^2}$

$= \sqrt[5]{6x^2}$

The function is even.

77. Common Function: $f(x) = x^2$

Transformation: Reflection in the x-axis and a horizontal shift 3 units to the left.

$h(x) = -(x + 3)^2$

79. $f(x) = \sqrt{x}$

$h(x) = \sqrt{x - 7}$

Transformation: Horizontal shift 7 units to the right.

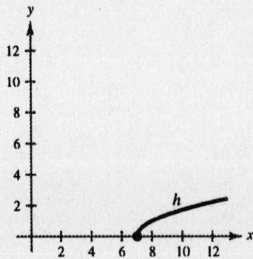

81. $f(x) = x^2$

$h(x) = -(x + 3)^2 + 1$

Transformation: Reflection in the *x*-axis, horizontal shift 3 units to the left, and a vertical shift 1 unit upward.

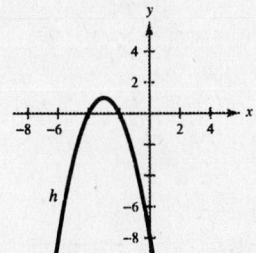

83. $f(x) = x^3$

$h(x) = -\frac{1}{3}x^3$

Transformation: Reflection in the *x*-axis and a vertical shrink by a factor of 1/3.

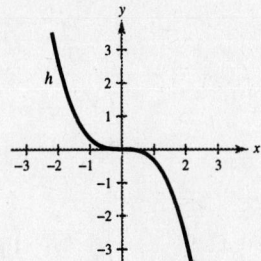

For Exercises 85 and 87, let $f(x) = 3 - 2x$, $g(x) = \sqrt{x}$, and $h(x) = 3x^2 + 2$.

85. $\left(\dfrac{f}{h}\right)(0) = \dfrac{f(0)}{h(0)} = \dfrac{3 - 2(0)}{3(0)^2 + 2} = \dfrac{3}{2}$

87. $(g \circ f)(-2) = g(f(-2)) = g(3 - 2(-2)) = g(7) = \sqrt{7}$

89. $\quad y_1 \approx 0.8x^2 + 3.33x + 24.23$

$\quad y_2 \approx -0.43x^2 + 18.14x + 62.89$

$y_1 + y_2 \approx 0.37x^2 + 21.47x + 87.12$

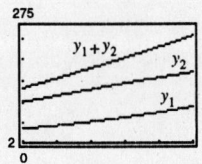

When $x = 12$; $y_1 + y_2 = \$398.04$ billion

91. $\quad f(x) = \frac{1}{12}x$

$\quad f^{-1}(x) = 12x$

$\quad f(f^{-1}(x)) = \frac{1}{12}(12x) = x$

$\quad f^{-1}(f(x)) = 12\left(\frac{1}{12}x\right) = x$

93. $\quad f(x) = x + 5$

$\quad f^{-1}(x) = x - 5$

$\quad f(f^{-1}(x)) = (x - 5) + 5 = x$

$\quad f^{-1}(f(x)) = (x + 5) - 5 = x$

95. $f(x) = -\frac{1}{4}x^2 - 3$

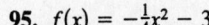

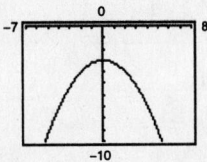

$f(x)$ does not pass the Horizontal Line Test, so $f(x)$ does **not** have an inverse.

97. $f(x) = -|x + 2| + |7 - x|$

$f(x)$ does not pass the Horizontal Line Test, so $f(x)$ does **not** have an inverse.

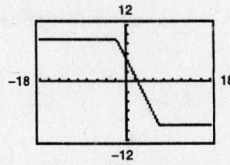

99. $f(x) = 5x - 7$

(a)
$$y = 5x - 7$$
$$x = 5y - 7$$
$$x + 7 = 5y$$
$$\frac{x + 7}{5} = y$$
$$f^{-1}(x) = \frac{x + 7}{5}$$

(b)

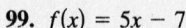

(c) $f^{-1}(f(x)) = \dfrac{(5x - 7) + 7}{5}$

$$= \frac{5x}{5} = x$$

$$f(f^{-1}(x)) = 5\left(\frac{x + 7}{5}\right) - 7$$

$$= x + 7 - 7 = x$$

101. $f(x) = x^3 + 2$

(a)
$$y = x^3 + 2$$
$$x = y^3 + 2$$
$$x - 2 = y^3$$
$$\sqrt[3]{x - 2} = y$$
$$f^{-1}(x) = \sqrt[3]{x - 2}$$

(b)

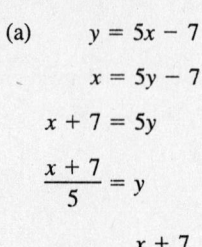

(c) $f^{-1}(f(x)) = \sqrt[3]{(x^3 + 2) - 2}$

$$= \sqrt[3]{x^3} = x$$

$$f(f^{-1}(x)) = \left(\sqrt[3]{x - 2}\right)^3 + 2$$

$$= x - 2 + 2$$

103. $f(x) = |x - 2| = \begin{cases} x - 2, & x \geq 2 \\ -(x - 2), & x < 2 \end{cases}$

$f(x)$ is increasing on $[2, \infty)$ or $x \geq 2$ so we will restrict the domain to this interval.

$$f(x) = |x - 2| = x - 2, x \geq 2 \text{ and } y \geq 0$$

$f^{-1}(x) = x + 2, x \geq 0$ [Note: The domain of f^{-1} is the range of f.]

105. 2.5 miles = 4 kilometers $\Rightarrow$ 1 mile $= \dfrac{4}{2.5} = 1.6$ kilometers

$$y = 1.6x$$

Miles, x	2	5	10	12
Kilometers, $1.6x$	3.2	8	16	19.2

107. $F = ks^2$

If s is doubled; $F = k(2s)^2 = 4ks^2$.

The force is changed by a factor of 4.

109. $F = cx\sqrt{y}$

$$6 = c(9)\sqrt{4}$$
$$6 = 18c$$
$$\frac{1}{3} = c$$
$$F = \frac{1}{3}x\sqrt{y}$$

111. False. The graph is reflected in the x-axis, shifted 9 units to the left, then shifted 13 units down.

113. A function from a set A to a set B is a relation that assigns to each element x in set A exactly one element y in the set B.

115. If $y = kx$, then the y-intercept is $(0, 0)$.

Chapter 1   Practice Test

1. Graph $y = \sqrt{7 - x}$

2. Find the domain $y = \sqrt{25 - x^2}$

3. Write the standard equation of the circle with center $(-3, 5)$ and radius 6.

4. Find the equation of the line through $(2, 4)$ and $(3, -1)$.

5. Find the equation of the line with slope $m = 4/3$ and y-intercept $b = -3$.

6. Find the equation of the line through $(4, 1)$ perpendicular to the line $2x + 3y = 0$.

7. If it costs a company \$32 to produce 5 units of a product and \$44 to produce 9 units, how much does it cost to produce 20 units? (Assume that the cost function is linear.)

8. Given $f(x) = x^2 - 2x + 1$, find $f(x - 3)$.

9. Given $f(x) = 4x - 11$, find $\dfrac{f(x) - f(3)}{x - 3}$

10. Find the domain and range of $f(x) = \sqrt{36 - x^2}$.

11. Which equations determine y as a function of x?

    (a) $6x - 5y + 4 = 0$

    (b) $x^2 + y^2 = 9$

    (c) $y^3 = x^2 + 6$

12. Sketch the graph of $f(x) = x^2 - 5$.

13. Sketch the graph of $f(x) = |x + 3|$.

14. Sketch the graph of $f(x) = \begin{cases} 2x + 1 & \text{if } x \geq 0, \\ x^2 - x & \text{if } x < 0. \end{cases}$

15. Use the graph of $f(x) = |x|$ to graph the following:

    (a) $f(x + 2)$

    (b) $-f(x) + 2$

16. Given $f(x) = 3x + 7$ and $g(x) = 2x^2 - 5$, find the following:

(a) $(g - f)(x)$

(b) $(fg)(x)$

17. Given $f(x) = x^2 - 2x + 16$ and $g(x) = 2x + 3$, find $f(g(x))$.

18. Given $f(x) = x^3 + 7$, find $f^{-1}(x)$.

19. Which of the following functions have inverses?

(a) $f(x) = |x - 6|$

(b) $f(x) = ax + b, \ a \neq 0$

(c) $f(x) = x^3 - 19$

20. Given $f(x) = \sqrt{\dfrac{3 - x}{x}}$, $0 < x \leq 3$, find $f^{-1}(x)$.

Exercises 21–23, true or false?

21. $y = 3x + 7$ and $y = \frac{1}{3}x - 4$ are perpendicular.

22. $(f \circ g)^{-1} = g^{-1} \circ f^{-1}$

23. If a function has an inverse, then it must pass both the vertical line test and the horizontal line test.

24. If z varies directly as the cube of x and inversely as the square root of y, and $z = -1$ when $x = -1$ and $y = 25$, find z in terms of x and y.

25. Use your calculator to find the least square regression line for the data.

x	-2	-1	0	1	2	3
y	1	2.4	3	3.1	4	4.7

CHAPTER 2
Polynomial and Rational Functions

CHAPTER 2
Polynomial Functions

Section 2.1   Quadratic and Rational Functions

You should know the following facts about parabolas.

- $f(x) = ax^2 + bx + c$, $a \neq 0$, is a quadratic function, and its graph is a parabola.

- If $a > 0$, the parabola opens upward and the vertex is the point with the minimum y-value.
  If $a < 0$, the parabola opens downward and the vertex is the point with the maximum y-value.

- The vertex is $(-b/2a, f(-b/2a))$.

- To find the x-intercepts (if any), solve
  $$ax^2 + bx + c = 0.$$

- The standard form of the equation of a parabola is
  $$f(x) = a(x - h)^2 + k$$
  where $a \neq 0$.

  (a) The vertex is (h, k).

  (b) The axis is the vertical line $x = h$.

Solutions to Odd-Numbered Exercises

1. $f(x) = (x - 2)^2$ opens upward and has vertex $(2, 0)$. Matches graph (g).

3. $f(x) = x^2 - 2$ opens upward and has vertex $(0, -2)$. Matches graph (b).

5. $f(x) = 4 - (x - 2)^2 = -(x - 2)^2 + 4$ opens downward and has vertex $(2, 4)$. Matches graph (f).

7. $f(x) = -(x - 3)^2 - 2$ opens downward and has vertex $(3, -2)$. Matches graph (e).

9. (a) $y = \frac{1}{2}x^2$

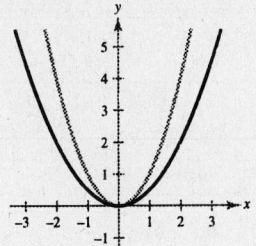

Vertical shrink

(b) $y = -\frac{1}{8}x^2$

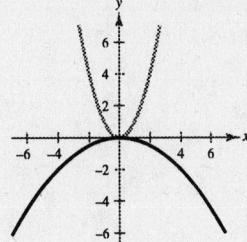

Vertical shrink and reflection in the *x*-axis

(c) $y = \frac{3}{2}x^2$

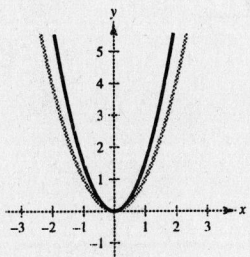

Vertical stretch

(d) $y = -3x^2$

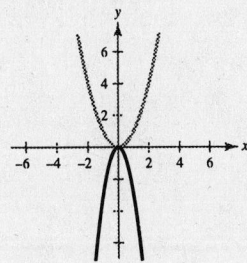

Vertical stretch and reflection in the *x*-axis

11. (a) $y = (x - 1)^2$

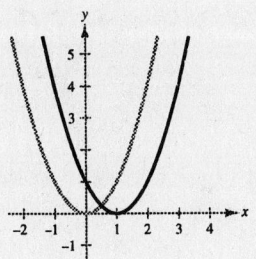

Horizontal translation one unit to the right

(b) $y = (x + 1)^2$

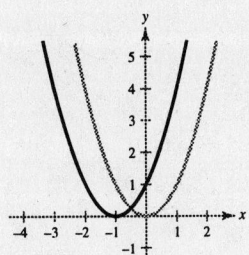

Horizontal translation one unit to the left

(c) $y = (x - 3)^2$

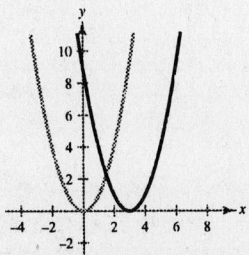

Horizontal translation three units to the right

(d) $y = (x + 3)^2$

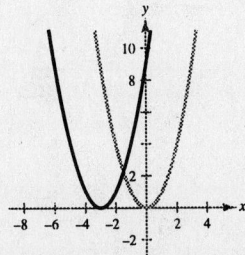

Horizontal translation three units to the left

13. $f(x) = x^2 - 5$

Vertex: $(0, -5)$

Find x-intercepts:

$$x^2 - 5 = 0$$
$$x^2 = 5$$
$$x = \pm\sqrt{5}$$

x-intercepts: $\left(-\sqrt{5}, 0\right), \left(\sqrt{5}, 0\right)$

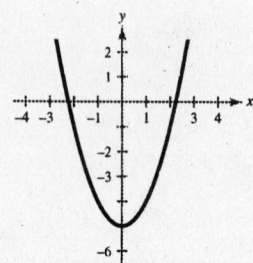

15. $f(x) = \frac{1}{2}x^2 - 4 = \frac{1}{2}(x - 0)^2 - 4$

Vertex: $(0, -4)$

Find x-intercepts.

$$\frac{1}{2}x^2 - 4 = 0$$
$$x^2 = 8$$
$$x = \pm\sqrt{8} = \pm2\sqrt{2}$$

x-intercepts: $\left(-2\sqrt{2}, 0\right), \left(2\sqrt{2}, 0\right)$

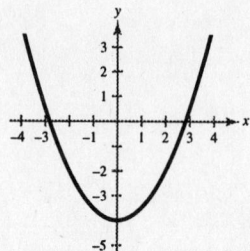

17. $f(x) = (x + 5)^2 - 6$

Vertex: $(-5, -6)$

Find x-intercepts:

$$(x + 5)^2 - 6 = 0$$
$$(x + 5)^2 = 6$$
$$x + 5 = \pm\sqrt{6}$$
$$x = -5 \pm \sqrt{6}$$

x-intercepts: $\left(-5 - \sqrt{6}, 0\right), \left(-5 + \sqrt{6}, 0\right)$

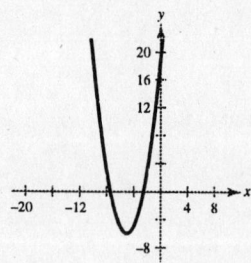

19. $h(x) = x^2 - 8x + 16 = (x - 4)^2$

Vertex: $(4, 0)$

x-intercept: $(4, 0)$

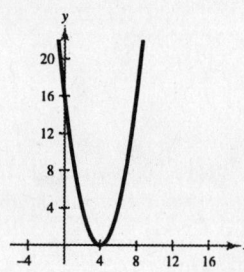

21. $f(x) = x^2 - x + \frac{5}{4}$

$\quad = \left(x^2 - x + \frac{1}{4}\right) - \frac{1}{4} + \frac{5}{4}$

$\quad = \left(x - \frac{1}{2}\right)^2 + 1$

Vertex: $\left(\frac{1}{2}, 1\right)$

Find x-intercepts:

$$x^2 - x + \frac{5}{4} = 0$$
$$x = \frac{1 \pm \sqrt{1 - 5}}{2}$$

Not a real number $\Longrightarrow$ No x-intercepts

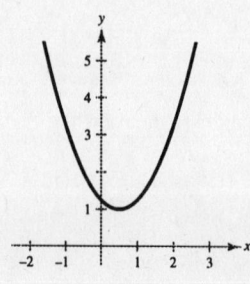

23. $f(x) = -x^2 + 2x + 5$

$\quad = -(x^2 - 2x + 1) - (-1) + 5$

$\quad = -(x - 1)^2 + 6$

Vertex: $(1, 6)$

Find x-intercepts:

$\quad -x^2 + 2x + 5 = 0$

$\quad x^2 - 2x - 5 = 0$

$\quad\quad x = \dfrac{2 \pm \sqrt{4 + 20}}{2}$

$\quad\quad\quad = 1 \pm \sqrt{6}$

x-intercepts: $\left(1 - \sqrt{6}, 0\right), \left(1 + \sqrt{6}, 0\right)$

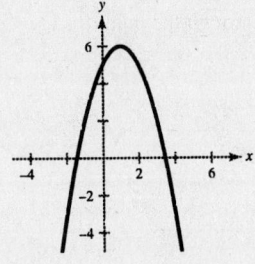

25. $h(x) = 4x^2 - 4x + 21$

$\quad = 4\left(x^2 - x + \frac{1}{4}\right) - 4\left(\frac{1}{4}\right) + 21$

$\quad = 4\left(x - \frac{1}{2}\right)^2 + 20$

Vertex: $\left(\frac{1}{2}, 20\right)$

Find x-intercepts:

$\quad 4x^2 - 4x + 21 = 0$

$\quad\quad x = \dfrac{4 \pm \sqrt{16 - 336}}{2(4)}$

Not a real number $\Rightarrow$ No x-intercepts

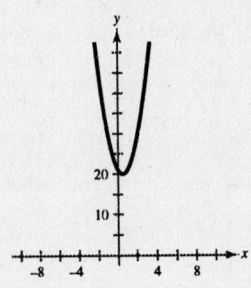

27. $f(x) = \frac{1}{4}x^2 - 2x - 12$

$\quad = \frac{1}{4}(x^2 - 8x + 16) - \frac{1}{4}(16) - 12$

$\quad = \frac{1}{4}(x - 4)^2 - 16$

Vertex: $(4, -16)$

Find x-intercepts:

$\quad \frac{1}{4}x^2 - 2x - 12 = 0$

$\quad x^2 - 8x - 48 = 0$

$\quad (x + 4)(x - 12) = 0$

$\quad x = -4 \quad \text{or} \quad x = 12$

x-intercepts: $(-4, 0), (12, 0)$

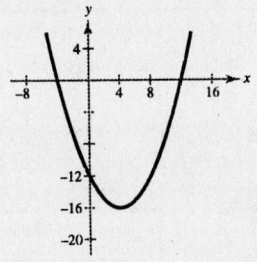

29. $f(x) = -(x^2 + 2x - 3) = -(x + 1)^2 + 4$

Vertex: $(-1, 4)$

x-intercepts: $(-3, 0), (1, 0)$

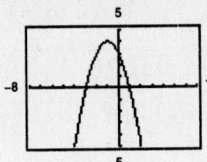

31. $g(x) = x^2 + 8x + 11 = (x + 4)^2 - 5$

Vertex: $(-4, -5)$

x-intercepts: $\left(-4 \pm \sqrt{5}, 0\right)$

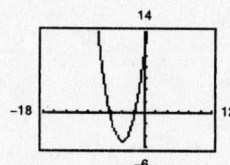

33. $f(x) = 2x^2 - 16x + 31$

$= 2(x - 4)^2 - 1$

Vertex: $(4, -1)$

x-intercepts: $\left(4 \pm \frac{1}{2}\sqrt{2}, 0\right)$

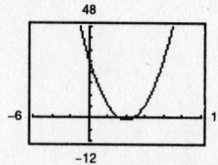

35. $g(x) = \frac{1}{2}(x^2 + 4x - 2) = \frac{1}{2}(x + 2)^2 - 3$

Vertex: $(-2, -3)$

x-intercepts: $\left(-2 \pm \sqrt{6}, 0\right)$

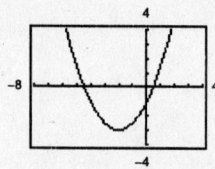

37. $(1, 0)$ is the vertex.

$y = a(x - 1)^2 + 0 = a(x - 1)^2$

Since the graph passes through the point $(0, 1)$, we have:

$1 = a(0 - 1)^2$

$1 = a$

$y = 1(x - 1)^2 = (x - 1)^2$

39. $(-1, 4)$ is the vertex.

$y = a(x + 1)^2 + 4$

Since the graph passes through the point $(1, 0)$, we have:

$0 = a(1 + 1)^2 + 4$

$-4 = 4a$

$-1 = a$

$y = -1(x + 1)^2 + 4 = -(x + 1)^2 + 4$

41. $(-2, 2)$ is the vertex.

$y = a(x + 2)^2 + 2$

Since the graph passes through the point $(-1, 0)$, we have:

$0 = a(-1 + 2)^2 + 2$

$-2 = a$

$y = -2(x + 2)^2 + 2$

43. $(-2, 5)$ is the vertex.

$f(x) = a(x + 2)^2 + 5$

Since the graph passes through the point $(0, 9)$, we have:

$9 = a(0 + 2)^2 + 5$

$4 = 4a$

$1 = a$

$f(x) = 1(x + 2)^2 + 5 = (x + 2)^2 + 5$

45. $(3, 4)$ is the vertex.

$f(x) = a(x - 3)^2 + 4$

Since the graph passes through the point $(1, 2)$, we have:

$2 = a(1 - 3)^2 + 4$

$-2 = 4a$

$-\frac{1}{2} = a$

$f(x) = -\frac{1}{2}(x - 3)^2 + 4$

47. $(5, 12)$ is the vertex.

$$f(x) = a(x - 5)^2 + 12$$

Since the graph passes through the point $(7, 15)$, we have:

$$15 = a(7 - 5)^2 + 12$$

$$3 = 4a \implies a = \tfrac{3}{4}$$

$$f(x) = \tfrac{3}{4}(x - 5)^2 + 12$$

49. $\left(-\tfrac{1}{4}, \tfrac{3}{2}\right)$ is the vertex.

$$f(x) = a\left(x + \tfrac{1}{4}\right)^2 + \tfrac{3}{2}$$

Since the graph passes through the point $(-2, 0)$, we have:

$$0 = a\left(-2 + \tfrac{1}{4}\right)^2 + \tfrac{3}{2}$$

$$-\tfrac{3}{2} = \tfrac{49}{16}a \implies a = -\tfrac{24}{49}$$

$$f(x) = -\tfrac{24}{49}\left(x + \tfrac{1}{4}\right)^2 + \tfrac{3}{2}$$

51. $\left(-\tfrac{5}{2}, 0\right)$ is the vertex.

$$f(x) = a\left(x + \tfrac{5}{2}\right)^2$$

Since the graph passes through the point $\left(-\tfrac{7}{2}, -\tfrac{16}{3}\right)$, we have:

$$-\tfrac{16}{3} = a\left(-\tfrac{7}{2} + \tfrac{5}{2}\right)^2$$

$$-\tfrac{16}{3} = a$$

$$f(x) = -\tfrac{16}{3}\left(x + \tfrac{5}{2}\right)^2$$

53. $y = x^2 - 16$ $\qquad\qquad$ $0 = x^2 - 16$

x-intercepts: $(\pm 4, 0)$ $\qquad$ $x^2 = 16$

$\qquad\qquad\qquad\qquad\qquad$ $x = \pm 4$

The x-intercepts and the solutions of the equation are the same.

55. $y = x^2 - 4x - 5$ $\qquad\qquad$ $0 = x^2 - 4x - 5$

x-intercepts: $(5, 0), (-1, 0)$ $\quad$ $0 = (x - 5)(x + 1)$

$\qquad\qquad\qquad\qquad\qquad$ $x = 5$ or $x = -1$

The x-intercepts and the solutions of the equation are the same.

57. $f(x) = x^2 - 4x$ $\qquad$ $0 = x^2 - 4x$

$\qquad\qquad\qquad\qquad\qquad$ $0 = x(x - 4)$

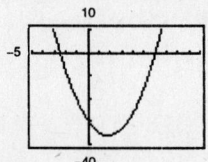

$\qquad\qquad\qquad\qquad\qquad$ $x = 0$ or $x = 4$

x-intercepts: $(0, 0), (4, 0)$

59. $f(x) = x^2 - 9x + 18$ $\qquad$ $0 = x^2 - 9x + 18$

$\qquad\qquad\qquad\qquad\qquad\qquad$ $0 = (x - 3)(x - 6)$

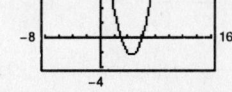

$\qquad\qquad\qquad\qquad\qquad\qquad$ $x = 3$ or $x = 6$

x-intercepts: $(3, 0), (6, 0)$

61. $f(x) = 2x^2 - 7x - 30$ $\quad$ $0 = 2x^2 - 7x - 30$

$\qquad\qquad\qquad\qquad\qquad\qquad$ $0 = (2x + 5)(x - 6)$

$\qquad\qquad\qquad\qquad\qquad\qquad$ $x = -\tfrac{5}{2}$ or $x = 6$

x-intercepts: $\left(-\tfrac{5}{2}, 0\right), (6, 0)$

63. $f(x) = -\tfrac{1}{2}(x^2 - 6x - 7)$ $\quad$ $0 = -\tfrac{1}{2}(x^2 - 6x - 7)$

$\qquad\qquad\qquad\qquad\qquad\qquad\qquad$ $0 = x^2 - 6x - 7$

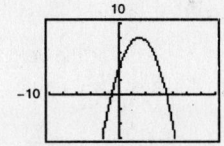

$\qquad\qquad\qquad\qquad\qquad\qquad\qquad$ $0 = (x + 1)(x - 7)$

$\qquad\qquad\qquad\qquad\qquad\qquad\qquad$ $x = -1$ or $x = 7$

x-intercepts: $(-1, 0), (7, 0)$

65. $f(x) = [x - (-1)](x - 3)$ opens upward

   $= (x + 1)(x - 3)$

   $= x^2 - 2x - 3$

   $g(x) = -[x - (-1)](x - 3)$ opens downward

   $= -(x + 1)(x - 3)$

   $= -(x^2 - 2x - 3)$

   $= -x^2 + 2x + 3$

Note: $f(x) = a(x + 1)(x - 3)$ has x-intercepts $(-1, 0)$ and $(3, 0)$ for all real numbers $a \neq 0$.

67. $f(x) = (x - 0)(x - 10)$ opens upward

   $= x^2 - 10x$

   $g(x) = -(x - 0)(x - 10)$ opens downward

   $= -x^2 + 10x$

Note: $f(x) = a(x - 0)(x - 10) = ax(x - 10)$ has x-intercepts $(0, 0)$ and $(10, 0)$ for all real numbers $a \neq 0$.

69. $f(x) = [x - (-3)][x - (-\frac{1}{2})](2)$ opens upward

   $= (x + 3)(x + \frac{1}{2})(2)$

   $= (x + 3)(2x + 1)$

   $= 2x^2 + 7x + 3$

   $g(x) = -(2x^2 + 7x + 3)$ opens downward

   $= -2x^2 - 7x - 3$

Note: $f(x) = a(x + 3)(2x + 1)$ has x-intercepts $(-3, 0)$ and $\left(-\frac{1}{2}, 0\right)$ for all real numbers $a \neq 0$.

71. Let $x =$ the first number and $y =$ the second number. Then the sum is

$$x + y = 110 \implies y = 110 - x.$$

The product is $P(x) = xy = x(110 - x) = 110x - x^2$.

   $P(x) = -x^2 + 110x$

   $= -(x^2 - 110x + 3025 - 3025)$

   $= -[(x - 55)^2 - 3025]$

   $= -(x - 55)^2 + 3025$

The maximum value of the product occurs at the vertex of $P(x)$ and is 3025. This happens when $x = y = 55$.

73. Let $x =$ the first number and $y =$ the second number. Then the sum is

$$x + 2y = 24 \implies y = \frac{24 - x}{2}.$$

The product is $P(x) = xy = x\left(\frac{24 - x}{2}\right)$.

$$P(x) = \frac{1}{2}(-x^2 + 24x)$$

$$= -\frac{1}{2}(x^2 - 24x + 144 - 144)$$

$$= -\frac{1}{2}[(x - 12)^2 - 144] = -\frac{1}{2}(x - 12)^2 + 72$$

The maximum value of the product occurs at the vertex of $P(x)$ and is 72. This happens when $x = 12$ and $y = (24 - 12)/2 = 6$. Thus, the numbers are 12 and 6.

75.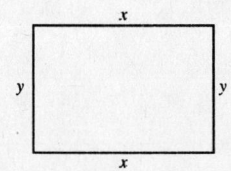

$2x + 2y = 100$

$y = 50 - x$

(a) $A(x) = xy = x(50 - x)$

Domain: $0 < x < 50$

(b)

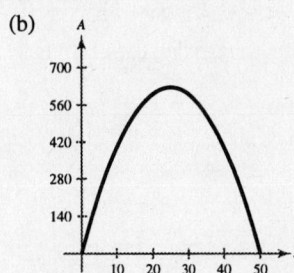

(c) The area is maximum (625 square feet) when $x = y = 25$. The rectangle has dimensions 25 ft × 25 ft.

77. (a) $4x + 3y = 200 \implies y = \frac{1}{3}(200 - 4x)$

x	y	Area
2	$\frac{1}{3}[200 - 4(2)]$	$2xy = (2)(2)(\frac{1}{3})[200 - 4(2)] = 256$
4	$\frac{1}{3}[200 - 4(4)]$	$2xy = (2)(4)(\frac{1}{3})[200 - 4(4)] \approx 491$
6	$\frac{1}{3}[200 - 4(6)]$	$2xy = (2)(6)(\frac{1}{3})[200 - 4(6)] = 704$
8	$\frac{1}{3}[200 - 4(8)]$	$2xy = (2)(8)(\frac{1}{3})[200 - 4(8)] = 896$
10	$\frac{1}{3}[200 - 4(10)]$	$2xy = (2)(10)(\frac{1}{3})[200 - 4(10)] \approx 1067$
12	$\frac{1}{3}[200 - 4(12)]$	$2xy = (2)(12)(\frac{1}{3})[200 - 4(12)] = 1216$

(b)

x	y	Area
20	$\frac{1}{3}[200 - 4(20)]$	$2xy = (2)(20)(\frac{1}{3})[200 - 4(20)] = 1600$
22	$\frac{1}{3}[200 - 4(22)]$	$2xy = (2)(22)(\frac{1}{3})[200 - 4(22)] \approx 1643$
24	$\frac{1}{3}[200 - 4(24)]$	$2xy = (2)(24)(\frac{1}{3})[200 - 4(24)] = 1664$
26	$\frac{1}{3}[200 - 4(26)]$	$2xy = (2)(26)(\frac{1}{3})[200 - 4(26)] = 1664$
28	$\frac{1}{3}[200 - 4(28)]$	$2xy = (2)(28)(\frac{1}{3})[200 - 4(28)] \approx 1643$
30	$\frac{1}{3}[200 - 4(30)]$	$2xy = (2)(30)(\frac{1}{3})[200 - 4(30)] = 1600$

(c) $A = 2xy = 2x\left(\dfrac{200 - 4x}{3}\right) = \dfrac{2x(4)(50 - x)}{3}$

$\qquad = \dfrac{8x(50 - x)}{3}$

(d)

This area is maximum when $x = 25$ feet and $y = \frac{100}{3} = 33\frac{1}{3}$ feet.

(e) $A = \frac{8}{3}x(50 - x)$

$\qquad = -\frac{8}{3}(x^2 - 50x)$

$\qquad = -\frac{8}{3}(x^2 - 50x + 625 - 625)$

$\qquad = -\frac{8}{3}[(x - 25)^2 - 625]$

$\qquad = -\frac{8}{3}(x - 25)^2 + \frac{5000}{3}$

The maximum area occurs at the vertex and is 5000/3 square feet. This happens when $x = 25$ feet and $y = (200 - 4(25))/3 = 100/3$ feet. The dimensions are $2x = 50$ feet by $33\frac{1}{3}$ feet.

79. $R = 900x - 0.1x^2 = -0.1x^2 + 900x$

The vertex occurs at $x = -\dfrac{b}{2a} = -\dfrac{900}{2(-0.1)} = 4500$. The revenue is maximum when $x = 4500$ units.

81. $C = 800 - 10x + 0.25x^2 = 0.25x^2 - 10x + 800$

The vertex occurs at $x = -\dfrac{b}{2a} = -\dfrac{-10}{2(0.25)} = 20$. The cost is minimum when $x = 20$ fixtures.

83. $P = 0.0002x^2 + 140x - 250,000$

The vertex occurs at $x = -\dfrac{b}{2a} = -\dfrac{140}{2(-0.0002)} = 350,000.$

The profit is maximum when $x = 350,000$ units.

85. $y = -\dfrac{1}{12}x^2 + 2x + 4$

(a) When $x = 0$, $y = 4$ feet.

(b) The vertex occurs at $x = -\dfrac{b}{2a} = -\dfrac{2}{2\left(-\frac{1}{12}\right)} = 12$. The maximum height is

$y = -\dfrac{1}{12}(12)^2 + 2(12) + 4 = 16$ feet.

(c) When the ball strikes the ground, $y = 0$.

$$0 = -\frac{1}{12}x^2 + 2x + 4$$

$$0 = x^2 - 24x - 48 \qquad\qquad \text{Multiply both sides by } -12.$$

$$x = \frac{-(-24) \pm \sqrt{(-24)^2 - 4(1)(-48)}}{2(1)}$$

$$= \frac{24 \pm \sqrt{768}}{2} = \frac{24 \pm 16\sqrt{3}}{2} = 12 \pm 8\sqrt{3}$$

Using the positive value for x, we have $x = 12 + 8\sqrt{3} \approx 25.86$ feet.

87. $y = -\dfrac{4}{9}x^2 + \dfrac{24}{9}x + 12$

The vertex occurs at $-\dfrac{b}{2a} = \dfrac{-24/9}{2(-4/9)} = 3.$

The maximum height is $y(3) = -\dfrac{4}{9}(3)^2 + \dfrac{24}{9}(3) + 12 = 16$ feet.

89. (a)

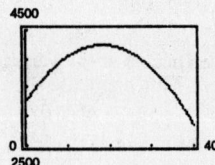

(b) Vertex $\approx (18, 4242)$

The vertex occurs when $y \approx 4242$ which is the maximum average annual consumption. The warnings may not have had an immediate effect, but over time they and other findings about the health risks of cigarettes have had an effect.

(c) $C(10) = 4038.29$

Annually: $\dfrac{116,530,000(4038.29)}{48,500,000} \approx 9703$ cigarettes

Daily: $\dfrac{9703}{366} \approx 27$ cigarettes

(1960 was a leap year.)

91. (a) and (c)

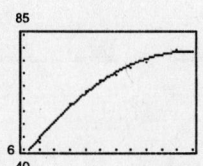

(b) $y = -0.35t^2 + 11.8t - 21$

(d) No, the model decreases and and eventually becomes negative.

93. True. The vertex of $f(x)$ is $\left(-\frac{5}{4}, \frac{53}{4}\right)$ and the vertex of $g(x)$ is $\left(-\frac{5}{4}, -\frac{71}{4}\right)$.

95. Conditions (a) and (d) are preferable because profits would be increasing.

97. If $f(x) = ax^2 + bx + c$ has two real zeros, then by the Quadratic Formula they are

$$x = \frac{-b \pm \sqrt{b^2 - 4ac}}{2a}.$$

The average of the zeros of f is

$$\frac{\dfrac{-b - \sqrt{b^2 - 4ac}}{2a} + \dfrac{-b + \sqrt{b^2 - 4ac}}{2a}}{2} = \frac{\dfrac{-2b}{2a}}{2} = -\frac{b}{2a}.$$

This is the x-coordinate of the vertex of the graph.

99. $(-4, 3)$ and $(2, 1)$

$$m = \frac{1 - 3}{2 - (-4)} = \frac{-2}{6} = -\frac{1}{3}$$

$$y - 1 = -\frac{1}{3}(x - 2)$$

$$y - 1 = -\frac{1}{3}x + \frac{2}{3}$$

$$y = -\frac{1}{3}x + \frac{5}{3}$$

101. $4x + 5y = 10 \implies y = -\frac{4}{5}x + 2$ and $m = -\frac{4}{5}$

The slope of the perpendicular line through $(0, 3)$ is $m = \frac{5}{4}$ and the y-intercept is $b = 3$.

$$y = \frac{5}{4}x + 3$$

For Exercises 103, 105, and 107, let $f(x) = 14x - 3$, and $g(x) = 8x^2$.

103. $(f + g)(-3) = f(-3) + g(-3) = [14(-3) - 3] + 8(-3)^2 = 27$

105. $(fg)\left(-\frac{4}{7}\right) = f\left(-\frac{4}{7}\right)g\left(-\frac{4}{7}\right) = \left[14\left(-\frac{4}{7}\right) - 3\right]\left[8\left(-\frac{4}{7}\right)^2\right] = (-11)\left(\frac{128}{49}\right) = -\frac{1408}{49}$

107. $(f \circ g)(-1) = f(g(-1)) = f(8) = 14(8) - 3 = 109$

Section 2.2   Polynomial Functions of Higher Degree

You should know the following basic principles about polynomials.

- $f(x) = a_n x^n + a_{n-1} x^{n-1} + \cdots + a_2 x^2 + a_1 x + a_0$ is a polynomial function of degree n.
- If f is of odd degree and
  - (a) $a_n > 0$, then
    1. $f(x) \to \infty$ as $x \to \infty$.
    2. $f(x) \to -\infty$ as $x \to -\infty$.
  - (b) $a_n < 0$, then
    1. $f(x) \to -\infty$ as $x \to \infty$.
    2. $f(x) \to \infty$ as $x \to -\infty$.
- If f is of even degree and
  - (a) $a_n > 0$, then
    1. $f(x) \to \infty$ as $x \to \infty$.
    2. $f(x) \to \infty$ as $x \to -\infty$.
  - (b) $a_n < 0$, then
    1. $f(x) \to -\infty$ as $x \to \infty$.
    2. $f(x) \to -\infty$ as $x \to -\infty$.
- The following are equivalent for a polynomial function.
  - (a) $x = a$ is a zero of a function.
  - (b) $x = a$ is a solution of the polynomial equation $f(x) = 0$.
  - (c) $(x - a)$ is a factor of the polynomial.
  - (d) $(a, 0)$ is an x-intercept of the graph of f.
- A polynomial of degree n has at most n distinct zeros and at most $n - 1$ turning points.
- If f is a polynomial function such that $a < b$ and $f(a) \neq f(b)$, then f takes on every value between $f(a)$ and $f(b)$ in the interval $[a, b]$.
- If you can find a value where a polynomial is positive and another value where it is negative, then there is at least one real zero between the values.

Solutions to Odd-Numbered Exercises

1. $f(x) = -2x + 3$ is a line with y-intercept $(0, 3)$. Matches graph (c).

3. $f(x) = -2x^2 - 5x$ is a parabola with x-intercepts $(0, 0)$ and $\left(-\frac{5}{2}, 0\right)$ and opens downward. Matches graph (h).

5. $f(x) = -\frac{1}{4}x^4 + 3x^2$ has intercepts $(0, 0)$ and $\left(\pm 2\sqrt{3}, 0\right)$. Matches graph (a).

7. $f(x) = x^4 + 2x^3$ has intercepts $(0, 0)$ and $(-2, 0)$. Matches graph (d).

9. $y = x^3$

(a) $f(x) = (x - 2)^3$

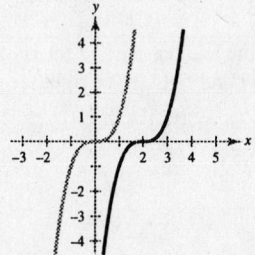

Horizontal shift two units to the right

(b) $f(x) = x^3 - 2$

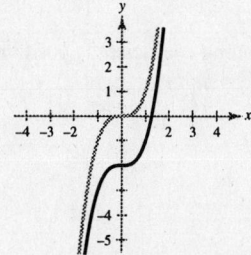

Vertical shift two units downward

(c) $f(x) = -\frac{1}{2}x^3$

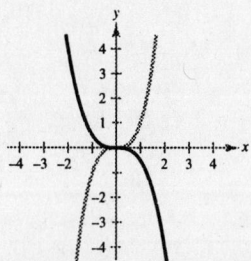

Reflection in the x-axis and a vertical shrink

(d) $f(x) = (x - 2)^3 - 2$

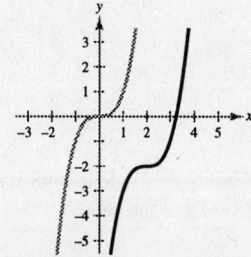

Horizontal shift two units to the right and a vertical shift two units downward

11. $y = x^4$

(a) $f(x) = (x + 3)^4$

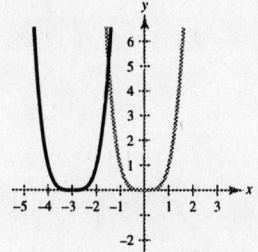

Horizontal shift three units to the left

(b) $f(x) = x^4 - 3$

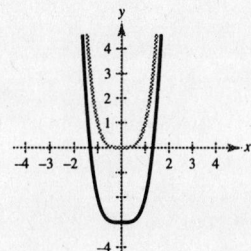

Vertical shift three units downward

(c) $f(x) = 4 - x^4$

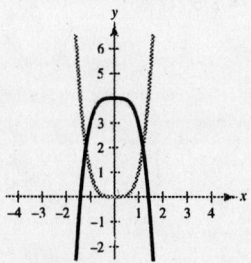

Reflection in the x-axis and then a vertical shift four units upward

(d) $f(x) = \frac{1}{2}(x - 1)^4$

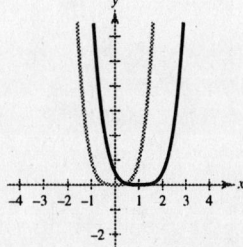

Horizontal shift one unit to the right and a vertical shrink

13. $f(x) = \frac{1}{3}x^3 + 5x$

Degree: 3

Leading coefficient: $\frac{1}{3}$

The degree is odd and the leading coefficient is positive. The graph falls to the left and rises to the right.

15. $g(x) = 5 - \frac{7}{2}x - 3x^2$

Degree: 2

Leading coefficient: -3

The degree is even and the leading coefficient is negative. The graph falls to the left and falls to the right.

17. $f(x) = -2.1x^5 + 4x^3 - 2$

Degree: 5

Leading coefficient: -2.1

The degree is odd and the leading coefficient is negative. The graph rises to the left and falls to the right.

19. $f(x) = 6 - 2x + 4x^2 - 5x^3$

Degree: 3

Leading coefficient: -5

The degree is odd and the leading coefficient is negative. The graph rises to the left and falls to the right.

21. $h(t) = -\frac{2}{3}(t^2 - 5t + 3)$

Degree: 2

Leading coefficient: $-\frac{2}{3}$

The degree is even and the leading coefficient is negative. The graph falls to the left and falls to the right.

23. $f(x) = 3x^3 - 9x + 1$; $g(x) = 3x^3$

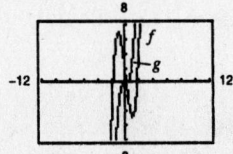

25. $f(x) = -(x^4 - 4x^3 + 16x)$; $g(x) = -x^4$

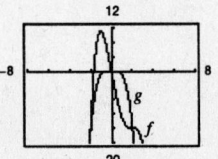

27. $f(x) = x^2 - 25$

$0 = (x + 5)(x - 5)$

$x = \pm 5$

29. $h(t) = t^2 - 6t + 9$

$0 = (t - 3)^2$

$t = 3$

31. $f(x) = \frac{1}{3}x^2 + \frac{1}{3}x - \frac{2}{3}$

$0 = \frac{1}{3}(x + 2)(x - 1)$

$x = -2, 1$

33. $f(x) = 3x^2 - 12x + 3$

$0 = 3(x^2 - 4x + 1)$

$x = \dfrac{4 \pm \sqrt{16 - 4}}{2} = 2 \pm \sqrt{3}$

35. $f(t) = t^3 - 4t^2 + 4t$

$0 = t(t - 2)^2$

$t = 0, 2$

37. $g(t) = \frac{1}{2}t^4 - \frac{1}{2}$

$0 = \frac{1}{2}(t + 1)(t - 1)(t^2 + 1)$

$t = \pm 1$

39. $g(t) = t^5 - 6t^3 + 9t$

$0 = t(t^2 - 3)^2$

$0 = t(t + \sqrt{3})^2(t - \sqrt{3})^2$

$t = 0, \pm\sqrt{3}$

41. $f(x) = 5x^4 + 15x^2 + 10$

$0 = 5(x^4 + 3x^2 + 2)$

$0 = 5(x^2 + 2)(x^2 + 1)$

No real zeros

43. $y = 4x^3 - 20x^2 + 25x$

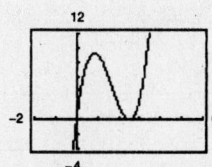

x-intercepts: $(0, 0), \left(\frac{5}{2}, 0\right)$

$0 = 4x^3 - 20x^2 + 25x$

$0 = x(2x - 5)^2$

$x = 0 \text{ or } x = \frac{5}{2}$

The solutions are the same as the x-coordinates of the x-intercepts.

45. $y = x^5 - 5x^3 + 4x$

x-intercepts: $(0, 0), (\pm 1, 0), (\pm 2, 0)$

$0 = x^5 - 5x^3 + 4x$

$0 = x(x^2 - 1)(x^2 - 4)$

$0 = x(x + 1)(x - 1)(x + 2)(x - 2)$

$x = 0, \pm 1, \pm 2$

The solutions are the same as the x-coordinates of the x-intercepts.

47. $f(x) = (x - 0)(x - 10)$

$f(x) = x^2 - 10x$

Note: $f(x) = a(x - 0)(x - 10) = ax(x - 10)$
has zeros 0 and 10 for all real numbers $a \neq 0$.

49. $f(x) = (x - 2)(x - (-6))$

$= (x - 2)(x + 6)$

$= x^2 + 4x - 12$

Note: $f(x) = a(x - 2)(x + 6)$ has zeros 2 and -6
for all real numbers $a \neq 0$.

51. $f(x) = (x - 0)(x - (-2))(x - (-3))$

$= x(x + 2)(x + 3)$

$= x^3 + 5x^2 + 6x$

Note: $f(x) = ax(x + 2)(x + 3)$ has zeros
$0, -2, -3$ for all real numbers $a \neq 0$.

53. $f(x) = (x - 4)(x + 3)(x - 3)(x - 0)$

$= (x - 4)(x^2 - 9)x$

$= x^4 - 4x^3 - 9x^2 + 36x$

Note: $f(x) = a(x^4 - 4x^3 - 9x^2 + 36x)$ has these
zeros for all real numbers $a \neq 0$.

55. $f(x) = \left[x - \left(1 + \sqrt{3}\right)\right]\left[x - \left(1 - \sqrt{3}\right)\right]$

$= \left[(x - 1) - \sqrt{3}\right]\left[(x - 1) + \sqrt{3}\right]$

$= (x - 1)^2 - \left(\sqrt{3}\right)^2$

$= x^2 - 2x + 1 - 3$

$= x^2 - 2x - 2$

Note: $f(x) = a(x^2 - 2x - 2)$ has these zeros for all real numbers $a \neq 0$.

57. $f(x) = (x - (-2))(x - (-2)) = (x + 2)^2 = x^2 + 4x + 4$

Note: $f(x) = a(x^2 + 4x + 4), a \neq 0$, has degree 2 and zero $x = -2$.

59. $f(x) = (x - (-3))(x - 0)(x - 1) = x(x + 3)(x - 1) = x^3 + 2x^2 - 3x$

Note: $f(x) = a(x^3 + 2x^2 - 3x), a \neq 0$, has degree 3 and zeros $x = -3, 0, 1$.

61. $f(x) = (x - 0)(x - \sqrt{3})(x - (-\sqrt{3}))$

$= x(x - \sqrt{3})(x + \sqrt{3})$

$= x^3 - 3x$

Note: $f(x) = a(x^3 - 3x)$, $a \neq 0$, has degree 3 and zeros $x = 0, \sqrt{3}, -\sqrt{3}$.

63. $f(x) = (x - (-5))^2(x - 1)(x - 2) = x^4 + 7x^3 - 3x^2 - 55x + 50$

or $f(x) = (x - (-5))(x - 1)^2(x - 2) = x^4 + x^3 - 15x^2 + 23x - 10$

or $f(x) = (x - (-5))(x - 1)(x - 2)^2 = x^4 - 17x^2 + 36x - 20$

Note: Any nonzero scalar multiple of these functions would also have degree 4 and zeros $x = -5, 1, 2$.

65. $f(x) = x^4(x + 4) = x^5 + 4x^4$

or $f(x) = x^3(x + 4)^2 = x^5 + 8x^4 + 16x^3$

or $f(x) = x^2(x + 4)^3 = x^5 + 12x^4 + 48x^3 + 64x^2$

or $f(x) = x(x + 4)^4 = x^5 + 16x^4 + 96x^3 + 256x^2 + 256x$

Note: Any nonzero scalar multiple of these functions would also have degree 5 and zeros $x = 0$ and -4.

67. $f(x) = x^3 - 9x = x(x^2 - 9) = x(x + 3)(x - 3)$

(a) Falls to the left

Rises to the right

(b) Zeros: $0, -3, 3$

(c)

x	-3	-2	-1	0	1	2	3
$f(x)$	0	10	8	0	-8	-10	0

(d)

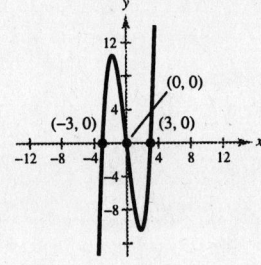

69. $f(t) = \frac{1}{4}(t^2 - 2t + 15) = \frac{1}{4}(t - 1)^2 + \frac{7}{2}$

(a) Rises to the left

Rises to the right

(b) No real zero (no x-intercepts)

(c)

t	-1	0	1	2	3
$f(t)$	4.5	3.75	3.5	3.75	4.5

(d) The graph is a parabola with vertex $\left(1, \frac{7}{2}\right)$.

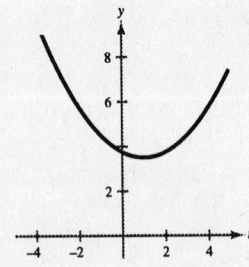

71. $f(x) = x^3 - 3x^2 = x^2(x - 3)$

(a) Falls to the left

Rises to the right

(b) Zeros: 0 and 3

(c)

x	-1	0	1	2	3
$f(x)$	-4	0	-2	-4	0

(d)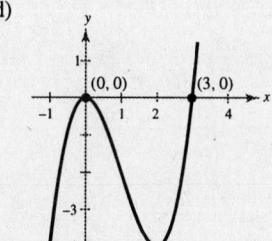

73. $f(x) = 3x^3 - 15x^2 + 18x = 3x(x - 2)(x - 3)$

(a) Falls to the left

Rises to the right

(b) Zeros: 0, 2, 3

(c)

x	0	1	2	2.5	3	3.5
$f(x)$	0	6	0	-1.875	0	7.875

(d)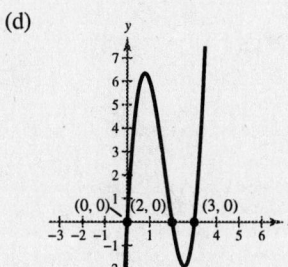

75. $f(x) = -5x^2 - x^3 = -x^2(5 + x)$

(a) Rises to the left

Falls to the right

(b) Zeros: 0, -5

(c)

x	-5	-4	-3	-2	-1	0	1
$f(x)$	0	-16	-18	-12	-4	0	-6

(d)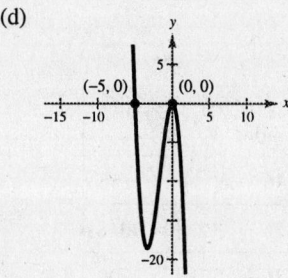

77. $f(x) = x^2(x - 4)$

(a) Falls to the left

Rises to the right

(b) Zeros: 0, 4

(c)

x	-1	0	1	2	3	4	5
$f(x)$	-5	0	-3	-8	-9	0	25

(d)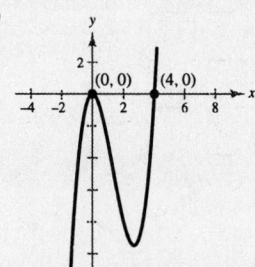

79. $g(t) = -\frac{1}{4}(t - 2)^2(t + 2)^2$

(a) Falls to the left

Falls to the right

(b) Zeros: 2 and -2

(c)

t	-3	-2	-1	0	1	2	3
$g(t)$	$-\frac{25}{4}$	0	$-\frac{9}{4}$	-4	$-\frac{9}{4}$	0	$-\frac{25}{4}$

(d)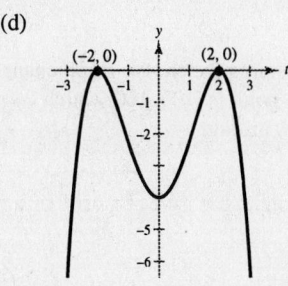

81. $f(x) = x^3 - 4x = x(x + 2)(x - 2)$

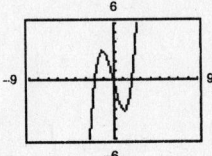

Zeros: $0, -2, 2$ all of multiplicity 1

83. $g(x) = \frac{1}{5}(x + 1)^2(x - 3)(2x - 9)$

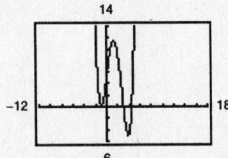

Zeros: -1 of multiplicity 2, 3 of multiplicity 1, and $\frac{9}{2}$ of multiplicity 1

85. $f(x) = x^3 - 3x^2 + 3$

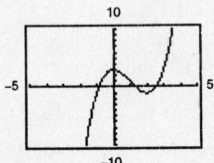

The function has three zeros. They are in the intervals $(-1, 0)$, $(1, 2)$ and $(2, 3)$.

87. $g(x) = 3x^4 + 4x^3 - 3$

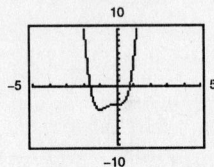

The function has two zeros. They are in the intervals $(-2, -1)$ and $(0, 1)$.

89. (a) and (b)

Box Height	Box Width	Box Volume, V
1	$36 - 2(1)$	$1[36 - 2(1)]^2 = 1156$
2	$36 - 2(2)$	$2[36 - 2(2)]^2 = 2048$
3	$36 - 2(3)$	$3[36 - 2(3)]^2 = 2700$
4	$36 - 2(4)$	$4[36 - 2(4)]^2 = 3136$
5	$36 - 2(5)$	$5[36 - 2(5)]^2 = 3380$
6	$36 - 2(6)$	$6[36 - 2(6)]^2 = 3456$
7	$36 - 2(7)$	$7[36 - 2(7)]^2 = 3388$

Volume is maximum at 3456 cubic inches when the height is 6 inches and the length and width are each 24 inches. So the dimensions are $6 \times 24 \times 24$ inches.

(c) Volume = length × width × height

height = x

length = width = $36 - 2x$

Thus, $V(x) = (36 - 2x)(36 - 2x)(x) = x(36 - 2x)^2$

Domain: $0 < x < 18$

(d)

The maximum point on the graph occurs at $x = 6$. This agrees with the maximum found in part (b).

91. $R = \frac{1}{100,000}(-x^3 + 600x^2)$

The point of diminishing returns (where the graph changes from curving upward to curving downward) occurs when $x = 200$. The point is $(200, 160)$ which corresponds to spending \$2,000,000 on advertising to obtain a revenue of \$160 million.

93. False. A fifth degree polynomial can have at most four turning points.

95. (a) Degree: 3

Leading coefficient: Positive

(b) Degree: 2

Leading coefficient: Positive

(c) Degree: 4

Leading coefficient: Positive

(d) Degree: 5

Leading coefficient: Positive

97. (a) $y_1 = -\frac{1}{3}(x - 2)^5 + 1$ is decreasing.

$y_2 = \frac{3}{5}(x + 2)^5 - 3$ is increasing.

(c) $H(x) = x^5 - 3x^3 + 2x + 1$

Since $H(x)$ is not always increasing or always decreasing, $H(x) \neq a(x - h)^5 + k$.

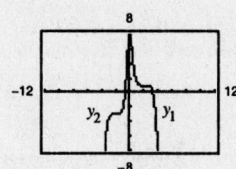

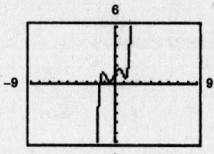

(b) The graph is either always increasing or always decreasing.

The behavior is determined by a.

If $a > 0$, $g(x)$ will always be increasing.

If $a < 0$, $g(x)$ will always be decreasing.

99. $3x^2 - 22x - 16 = 0$

$(3x + 2)(x - 8) = 0$

$3x + 2 = 0 \quad \text{or} \quad x - 8 = 0$

$x = -\frac{2}{3} \quad \text{or} \quad x = 8$

101. $x^2 + 24x + 144 = 0$

$(x + 12)^2 = 0$

$x + 12 = 0$

$x = -12$

103. $x^2 - 8x + 2 = 0$

$x^2 - 8x = -2$

$x^2 - 8x + 16 = -2 + 16$

$(x - 4)^2 = 14$

$x - 4 = \pm\sqrt{14}$

$x = 4 \pm \sqrt{14}$

105. $3x^2 + 4x - 9 = 0$

$x^2 + \frac{4}{3}x - 3 = 0$

$x^2 + \frac{4}{3}x = 3$

$x^2 + \frac{4}{3}x + \frac{4}{9} = 3 + \frac{4}{9}$

$\left(x + \frac{2}{3}\right)^2 = \frac{31}{9}$

$x + \frac{2}{3} = \pm\sqrt{\frac{31}{9}}$

$x = -\frac{2}{3} \pm \frac{\sqrt{31}}{3}$

$x = \frac{-2 \pm \sqrt{31}}{3}$

107. $6x^3 - 61x^2 + 10x = x(6x^2 - 61x + 10)$

$\qquad\qquad\qquad\ = x(6x - 1)(x - 10)$

109. $y^3 + 216 = y^3 + 6^3$

$\qquad\qquad\quad = (y + 6)(y^2 - 6y + 36)$

Section 2.3   Polynomial and Synthetic Division

You should know the following basic techniques and principles of polynomial division.

- The Division Algorithm (Long Division of Polynomials)
- Synthetic Division
- $f(k)$ is equal to the remainder of $f(x)$ divided by $(x - k)$.
- $f(k) = 0$ if and only if $(x - k)$ is a factor of $f(x)$.

Solutions to Odd-Numbered Exercises

1. $y_1 = \dfrac{4x}{x - 1}$ and $y_2 = 4 + \dfrac{4}{x - 1}$

$$
\begin{array}{r}
4 \\
x - 1 \overline{)\, 4x + 0} \\
\underline{4x - 4} \\
4
\end{array}
$$

Thus, $\dfrac{4x}{x - 1} = 4 + \dfrac{4}{x - 1}$ and $y_1 = y_2$.

3. $y_1 = \dfrac{x^2}{x + 2}$ and $y_2 = x - 2 + \dfrac{4}{x + 2}$

$$
\begin{array}{r}
x - 2 \\
x + 2 \overline{)\, x^2 + 0x + 0} \\
\underline{x^2 + 2x} \\
-2x + 0 \\
\underline{-2x - 4} \\
4
\end{array}
$$

Thus, $\dfrac{x^2}{x + 2} = x - 2 + \dfrac{4}{x + 2}$ and $y_1 = y_2$.

5. $y_1 = \dfrac{x^5 - 3x^3}{x^2 + 1}$ and $y_2 = x^3 - 4x + \dfrac{4x}{x^2 + 1}$

$$
\begin{array}{r}
x^3 - 4x \\
x^2 + 0x + 1 \overline{)\, x^5 + 0x^4 - 3x^3 + 0x^2 + 0x + 0} \\
\underline{x^5 + 0x^4 + \ x^3} \\
-4x^3 + 0x^2 + 0x \\
\underline{-4x^3 + 0x^2 - 4x} \\
4x + 0
\end{array}
$$

Thus, $\dfrac{x^5 - 3x^3}{x^2 + 1} = x^3 - 4x + \dfrac{4x}{x^2 + 1}$ and $y_1 = y_2$.

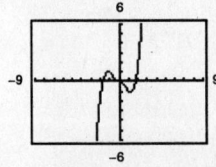

7.
$$
\begin{array}{r}
2x + 4 \\
x + 3 \overline{)\, 2x^2 + 10x + 12} \\
\underline{2x^2 + \ 6x} \\
4x + 12 \\
\underline{4x + 12} \\
0
\end{array}
$$

$$\frac{2x^2 + 10x + 12}{x + 3} = 2x + 4$$

9.
$$
\begin{array}{r}
x^2 - \ 3x + 1 \\
4x + 5 \overline{)\, 4x^3 - \ 7x^2 - 11x + 5} \\
\underline{4x^3 + \ 5x^2} \\
-12x^2 - 11x \\
\underline{-12x^2 - 15x} \\
4x + 5 \\
\underline{4x + 5} \\
0
\end{array}
$$

$$\frac{4x^3 - 7x^2 - 11x + 5}{4x + 5} = x^2 - 3x + 1$$

11.
$$
\begin{array}{r}
x^3 + 3x^2 \quad\ - 1 \\
x + 2 \overline{\smash{\big)}\ x^4 + 5x^3 + 6x^2 - x - 2} \\
\underline{x^4 + 2x^3} \\
3x^3 + 6x^2 \\
\underline{3x^3 + 6x^2} \\
- x - 2 \\
\underline{- x - 2} \\
0
\end{array}
$$

$$\frac{x^4 + 5x^3 + 6x^2 - x - 2}{x + 2} = x^3 + 3x^2 - 1$$

13.
$$
\begin{array}{r}
7 \\
x + 2 \overline{\smash{\big)}\ 7x + 3} \\
\underline{7x + 14} \\
- 11
\end{array}
$$

$$\frac{7x + 3}{x + 2} = 7 - \frac{11}{x + 2}$$

15.
$$
\begin{array}{r}
3x + 5 \\
2x^2 + 0x + 1 \overline{\smash{\big)}\ 6x^3 + 10x^2 + \ x + 8} \\
\underline{6x^3 + \ 0x^2 + 3x} \\
10x^2 - 2x + 8 \\
\underline{10x^2 + 0x + 5} \\
- 2x + 3
\end{array}
$$

$$\frac{6x^3 + 10x^2 + x + 8}{2x^2 + 1} = 3x + 5 + \frac{-2x + 3}{2x^2 + 1} = 3x + 5 - \frac{2x - 3}{2x^2 + 1}$$

17.
$$
\begin{array}{r}
x^2 + 2x + \ 4 \\
x^2 - 2x + 3 \overline{\smash{\big)}\ x^4 + 0x^3 + 3x^2 + 0x + \ 1} \\
\underline{x^4 - 2x^3 + 3x^2} \\
2x^3 + 0x^2 + 0x \\
\underline{2x^3 - 4x^2 + 6x} \\
4x^2 - 6x + \ 1 \\
\underline{4x^2 - 8x + 12} \\
2x - 11
\end{array}
$$
$\Rightarrow$ $\dfrac{x^4 + 3x^2 + 1}{x^2 - 2x + 3} = x^2 + 2x + 4 + \dfrac{2x - 11}{x^2 - 2x + 3}$

19.
$$
\begin{array}{r}
x + 3 \\
x^3 - 3x^2 + 3x - 1 \overline{\smash{\big)}\ x^4 + 0x^3 + 0x^2 + 0x + 0} \\
\underline{x^4 - 3x^3 + 3x^2 - \ x} \\
3x^3 - 3x^2 + \ x + 0 \\
\underline{3x^3 - 9x^2 + 9x - 3} \\
6x^2 - 8x + 3
\end{array}
$$

$$\frac{x^4}{(x - 1)^3} = x + 3 + \frac{6x^2 - 8x + 3}{(x - 1)^3}$$

21.
$$
\begin{array}{r|rrrr}
5 & 3 & -17 & 15 & -25 \\
  &   & 15 & -10 & 25 \\
\hline
  & 3 & -2 & 5 & 0
\end{array}
$$

$$\frac{3x^3 - 17x^2 + 15x - 25}{x - 5} = 3x^2 - 2x + 5$$

23.
$$
\begin{array}{r|rrrr}
-2 & 4 & 8 & -9 & -18 \\
   &   & -8 & 0 & 18 \\
\hline
   & 4 & 0 & -9 & 0
\end{array}
$$

$$\frac{4x^3 + 8x^2 - 9x - 18}{x + 2} = 4x^2 - 9$$

25.

$$-10 \,\big|\begin{array}{cccc} -1 & 0 & 75 & -250 \\ & 10 & -100 & 250 \\ \hline -1 & 10 & -25 & 0 \end{array}$$

$$\frac{-x^3 + 75x - 250}{x + 10} = -x^2 + 10x - 25$$

27.

$$4 \,\big|\begin{array}{cccc} 5 & -6 & 0 & 8 \\ & 20 & 56 & 224 \\ \hline 5 & 14 & 56 & 232 \end{array}$$

$$\frac{5x^3 - 6x^2 + 8}{x - 4} = 5x^2 + 14x + 56 + \frac{232}{x - 4}$$

29.

$$6 \,\big|\begin{array}{ccccc} 10 & -50 & 0 & 0 & -800 \\ & 60 & 60 & 360 & 2160 \\ \hline 10 & 10 & 60 & 360 & 1360 \end{array}$$

$$\frac{10x^4 - 50x^3 - 800}{x - 6} = 10x^3 + 10x^2 + 60x + 360 + \frac{1360}{x - 6}$$

31.

$$-8 \,\big|\begin{array}{cccc} 1 & 0 & 0 & 512 \\ & -8 & 64 & -512 \\ \hline 1 & -8 & 64 & 0 \end{array}$$

$$\frac{x^3 + 512}{x + 8} = x^2 - 8x + 64$$

33.

$$2 \,\big|\begin{array}{ccccc} -3 & 0 & 0 & 0 & 0 \\ & -6 & -12 & -24 & -48 \\ \hline -3 & -6 & -12 & -24 & -48 \end{array}$$

$$\frac{-3x^4}{x - 2} = -3x^3 - 6x^2 - 12x - 24 - \frac{48}{x - 2}$$

35.

$$6 \,\big|\begin{array}{ccccc} -1 & 0 & 0 & 180 & 0 \\ & -6 & -36 & -216 & -216 \\ \hline -1 & -6 & -36 & -36 & -216 \end{array}$$

$$\frac{180x - x^4}{x - 6} = -x^3 - 6x^2 - 36x - 36 - \frac{216}{x - 6}$$

37.

$$-\tfrac{1}{2} \,\big|\begin{array}{cccc} 4 & 16 & -23 & -15 \\ & -2 & -7 & 15 \\ \hline 4 & 14 & -30 & 0 \end{array}$$

$$\frac{4x^3 + 16x^2 - 23x - 15}{x + \frac{1}{2}} = 4x^2 + 14x - 30$$

39. $f(x) = x^3 - x^2 - 14x + 11, \; k = 4$

$$4 \,\big|\begin{array}{cccc} 1 & -1 & -14 & 11 \\ & 4 & 12 & -8 \\ \hline 1 & 3 & -2 & 3 \end{array}$$

$$f(x) = (x - 4)(x^2 + 3x - 2) + 3$$
$$f(4) = 4^3 - 4^2 - 14(4) + 11 = 3$$

41. $f(x) = 15x^4 + 10x^3 - 6x^2 + 14, \; k = -\tfrac{2}{3}$

$$-\tfrac{2}{3} \,\big|\begin{array}{ccccc} 15 & 10 & -6 & 0 & 14 \\ & -10 & 0 & 4 & -\frac{8}{3} \\ \hline 15 & 0 & -6 & 4 & \frac{34}{3} \end{array}$$

$$f(x) = \left(x + \tfrac{2}{3}\right)(15x^3 - 6x + 4) + \tfrac{34}{3}$$
$$f\left(-\tfrac{2}{3}\right) = 15\left(-\tfrac{2}{3}\right)^4 + 10\left(-\tfrac{2}{3}\right)^3 - 6\left(-\tfrac{2}{3}\right)^2 + 14 = \tfrac{34}{3}$$

43. $f(x) = x^3 + 3x^2 - 2x - 14, \; k = \sqrt{2}$

$$\sqrt{2} \,\big|\begin{array}{cccc} 1 & 3 & -2 & -14 \\ & \sqrt{2} & 2 + 3\sqrt{2} & 6 \\ \hline 1 & 3 + \sqrt{2} & 3\sqrt{2} & -8 \end{array}$$

$$f(x) = \left(x - \sqrt{2}\right)\left[x^2 + \left(3 + \sqrt{2}\right)x + 3\sqrt{2}\right] - 8$$
$$f\left(\sqrt{2}\right) = \left(\sqrt{2}\right)^3 + 3\left(\sqrt{2}\right)^2 - 2\sqrt{2} - 14 = -8$$

45. $f(x) = -4x^3 + 6x^2 + 12x + 4, \; k = 1 - \sqrt{3}$

$$1 - \sqrt{3} \,\big|\begin{array}{cccc} -4 & 6 & 12 & 4 \\ & -4 + 4\sqrt{3} & -10 + 2\sqrt{3} & -4 \\ \hline -4 & 2 + 4\sqrt{3} & 2 + 2\sqrt{3} & 0 \end{array}$$

$$f(x) = \left[x - \left(1 - \sqrt{3}\right)\right]\left[-4x^2 + \left(2 + 4\sqrt{3}\right)x + \left(2 + 2\sqrt{3}\right)\right]$$
$$f\left(1 - \sqrt{3}\right) = -4\left(1 - \sqrt{3}\right)^3 + 6\left(1 - \sqrt{3}\right)^2 + 12\left(1 - \sqrt{3}\right) + 4 = 0$$

47. $f(x) = 4x^3 - 13x + 10$

(a)
$$1 \,\big|\; \begin{array}{cccc} 4 & 0 & -13 & 10 \\ & 4 & 4 & -9 \\ \hline 4 & 4 & -9 & \underline{1} = f(1) \end{array}$$

(b)
$$-2 \,\big|\; \begin{array}{cccc} 4 & 0 & -13 & 10 \\ & -8 & 16 & -6 \\ \hline 4 & -8 & 3 & \underline{4} = f(-2) \end{array}$$

(c)
$$\tfrac{1}{2} \,\big|\; \begin{array}{cccc} 4 & 0 & -13 & 10 \\ & 2 & 1 & -6 \\ \hline 4 & 2 & -12 & \underline{4} = f\!\left(\tfrac{1}{2}\right) \end{array}$$

(d)
$$8 \,\big|\; \begin{array}{cccc} 4 & 0 & -13 & 10 \\ & 32 & 256 & 1944 \\ \hline 4 & 32 & 243 & \underline{1954} = f(8) \end{array}$$

49. $h(x) = 3x^3 + 5x^2 - 10x + 1$

(a)
$$3 \,\big|\; \begin{array}{cccc} 3 & 5 & -10 & 1 \\ & 9 & 42 & 96 \\ \hline 3 & 14 & 32 & \underline{97} = h(3) \end{array}$$

(b)
$$\tfrac{1}{3} \,\big|\; \begin{array}{cccc} 3 & 5 & -10 & 1 \\ & 1 & 2 & -\tfrac{8}{3} \\ \hline 3 & 6 & -8 & \underline{-\tfrac{5}{3}} = h\!\left(\tfrac{1}{3}\right) \end{array}$$

(c)
$$-2 \,\big|\; \begin{array}{cccc} 3 & 5 & -10 & 1 \\ & -6 & 2 & 16 \\ \hline 3 & -1 & -8 & \underline{17} = h(-2) \end{array}$$

(d)
$$-5 \,\big|\; \begin{array}{cccc} 3 & 5 & -10 & 1 \\ & -15 & 50 & -200 \\ \hline 3 & -10 & 40 & \underline{-199} = h(-5) \end{array}$$

51.
$$2 \,\big|\; \begin{array}{cccc} 1 & 0 & -7 & 6 \\ & 2 & 4 & -6 \\ \hline 1 & 2 & -3 & 0 \end{array}$$

$$x^3 - 7x + 6 = (x - 2)(x^2 + 2x - 3)$$
$$= (x - 2)(x + 3)(x - 1)$$

Zeros: $2, -3, 1$

53.
$$\tfrac{1}{2} \,\big|\; \begin{array}{cccc} 2 & -15 & 27 & -10 \\ & 1 & -7 & 10 \\ \hline 2 & -14 & 20 & 0 \end{array}$$

$$2x^3 - 15x^2 + 27x - 10$$
$$= \left(x - \tfrac{1}{2}\right)(2x^2 - 14x + 20)$$
$$= (2x - 1)(x - 2)(x - 5)$$

Zeros: $\tfrac{1}{2}, 2, 5$

55.
$$\sqrt{3} \,\big|\; \begin{array}{cccc} 1 & 2 & -3 & -6 \\ & \sqrt{3} & 3 + 2\sqrt{3} & 6 \\ \hline 1 & 2 + \sqrt{3} & 2\sqrt{3} & 0 \end{array}$$

$$-\sqrt{3} \,\big|\; \begin{array}{ccc} 1 & 2 + \sqrt{3} & 2\sqrt{3} \\ & -\sqrt{3} & -2\sqrt{3} \\ \hline 1 & 2 & 0 \end{array}$$

$$x^3 + 2x^2 - 3x - 6 = \left(x - \sqrt{3}\right)\left(x + \sqrt{3}\right)(x + 2)$$

Zeros: $\pm\sqrt{3}, -2$

57.
$$1 + \sqrt{3} \,\big|\; \begin{array}{cccc} 1 & -3 & 0 & 2 \\ & 1 + \sqrt{3} & 1 - \sqrt{3} & -2 \\ \hline 1 & -2 + \sqrt{3} & 1 - \sqrt{3} & 0 \end{array}$$

$$1 - \sqrt{3} \,\big|\; \begin{array}{ccc} 1 & -2 + \sqrt{3} & 1 - \sqrt{3} \\ & 1 - \sqrt{3} & -1 + \sqrt{3} \\ \hline 1 & -1 & 0 \end{array}$$

$$x^3 - 3x^2 + 2 = \left[x - \left(1 + \sqrt{3}\right)\right]\left[x - \left(1 - \sqrt{3}\right)\right](x - 1)$$
$$= (x - 1)\left(x - 1 - \sqrt{3}\right)\left(x - 1 + \sqrt{3}\right)$$

Zeros: $1, 1 \pm \sqrt{3}$

59. $f(x) = 2x^3 + x^2 - 5x + 2$; Factors: $(x + 2), (x - 1)$

(a)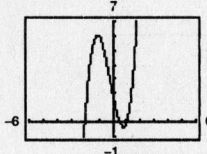

$$
\begin{array}{r|rrrr}
-2 & 2 & 1 & -5 & 2 \\
   &   & -4 & 6 & -2 \\
\hline
   & 2 & -3 & 1 & 0
\end{array}
$$

$$
\begin{array}{r|rrr}
1 & 2 & -3 & 1 \\
  &   & 2 & -1 \\
\hline
  & 2 & -1 & 0
\end{array}
$$

Both are factors of $f(x)$ since the remainders are zero.

(b) The remaining factor of $f(x)$ is $(2x - 1)$.

(c) $f(x) = (2x - 1)(x + 2)(x - 1)$

(d) Zeros: $\frac{1}{2}, -2, 1$

(e)

61. $f(x) = x^4 - 4x^3 - 15x^2 + 58x - 40$; Factors: $(x - 5), (x + 4)$

(a)

$$
\begin{array}{r|rrrrr}
5 & 1 & -4 & -15 & 58 & -40 \\
  &   & 5 & 5 & -50 & 40 \\
\hline
  & 1 & 1 & -10 & 8 & 0
\end{array}
$$

$$
\begin{array}{r|rrrr}
-4 & 1 & 1 & -10 & 8 \\
   &   & -4 & 12 & -8 \\
\hline
   & 1 & -3 & 2 & 0
\end{array}
$$

Both are factors of $f(x)$ since the remainders are zero.

(b) $x^2 - 3x + 2 = (x - 1)(x - 2)$

The remaining factors are $(x - 1)$ and $(x - 2)$.

(c) $f(x) = (x - 1)(x - 2)(x - 5)(x + 4)$

(d) Zeros: $1, 2, 5, -4$

(e)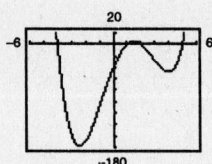

63. $f(x) = 6x^3 + 41x^2 - 9x - 14$; Factors: $(2x + 1), (3x - 2)$

(a)
$$-\tfrac{1}{2} \begin{array}{|rrrr} 6 & 41 & -9 & -14 \\ & -3 & -19 & 14 \\ \hline 6 & 38 & -28 & 0 \end{array}$$

$$\tfrac{2}{3} \begin{array}{|rrr} 6 & 38 & -28 \\ & 4 & 28 \\ \hline 6 & 42 & 0 \end{array}$$

Both are factors since the remainders are zero.

(b) $6x + 42 = 6(x + 7)$

This shows that $\dfrac{f(x)}{\left(x + \tfrac{1}{2}\right)\left(x - \tfrac{2}{3}\right)} = 6(x + 7)$, so $\dfrac{f(x)}{(2x + 1)(3x - 2)} = x + 7$.

The remaining factor is $(x + 7)$.

(c) $f(x) = (x + 7)(2x + 1)(3x - 2)$

(d) Zeros: $-7, -\tfrac{1}{2}, \tfrac{2}{3}$

(e)

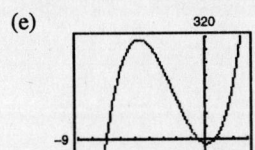

65. $f(x) = 2x^3 - x^2 - 10x + 5$; Factors: $(2x - 1), \left(x + \sqrt{5}\right)$

(a)
$$\tfrac{1}{2} \begin{array}{|rrrr} 2 & -1 & -10 & 5 \\ & 1 & 0 & -5 \\ \hline 2 & 0 & -10 & 0 \end{array}$$

$$-\sqrt{5} \begin{array}{|rrr} 2 & 0 & -10 \\ & -2\sqrt{5} & 10 \\ \hline 2 & -2\sqrt{5} & 0 \end{array}$$

Both are factors since the remainders are zero.

(b) $2x - 2\sqrt{5} = 2\left(x - \sqrt{5}\right)$

This shows that $\dfrac{f(x)}{\left(x - \tfrac{1}{2}\right)\left(x + \sqrt{5}\right)} = 2\left(x - \sqrt{5}\right)$, so $\dfrac{f(x)}{(2x - 1)\left(x + \sqrt{5}\right)} = x - \sqrt{5}$.

The remaining factor is $\left(x - \sqrt{5}\right)$.

(c) $f(x) = \left(x + \sqrt{5}\right)\left(x - \sqrt{5}\right)(2x - 1)$

(d) Zeros: $-\sqrt{5}, \sqrt{5}, \tfrac{1}{2}$

(e)

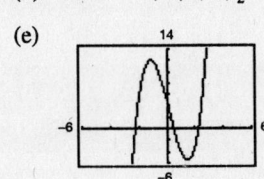

67. $f(x) = x^3 - 2x^2 - 5x + 10$

(a) The zeros of f are 2 and $\approx \pm 2.236$.

(b)
$$
\begin{array}{r|rrrr}
2 & 1 & -2 & -5 & 10 \\
  &   & 2 & 0 & -10 \\
\hline
  & 1 & 0 & -5 & 0
\end{array}
$$

$f(x) = (x - 2)(x^2 - 5)$

$\quad = (x - 2)(x - \sqrt{5})(x + \sqrt{5})$

69. $h(t) = t^3 - 2t^2 - 7t + 2$

(a) The zeros of h are 2, ≈ 3.732, ≈ 0.268.

(b)
$$
\begin{array}{r|rrrr}
-2 & 1 & -2 & -7 & 2 \\
   &   & -2 & 8 & -2 \\
\hline
   & 1 & -4 & 1 & 0
\end{array}
$$

$h(t) = (t + 2)(t^2 - 4t + 1)$

By the Quadratic Formula, the zeros of

$\quad t^2 - 4t + 1$ are $2 \pm \sqrt{3}$.

Thus, $h(t) = (t + 2)\left[t - \left(2 + \sqrt{3}\right)\right]\left[t - \left(2 - \sqrt{3}\right)\right]$.

71.
$$
\begin{array}{r|rrrr}
\frac{3}{2} & 4 & -8 & 1 & 3 \\
            &   & 6 & -3 & -3 \\
\hline
            & 4 & -2 & -2 & 0
\end{array}
$$

$\dfrac{4x^3 - 8x^2 + x + 3}{x - \frac{3}{2}} = 4x^2 - 2x - 2$

Thus, $\dfrac{4x^3 - 8x^2 + x + 3}{2x - 3} = 2x^2 - x - 1, x \neq \dfrac{3}{2}$

73.
$$
\begin{array}{r|rrrr}
-1 & 1 & 3 & -1 & -3 \\
   &   & -1 & -2 & 3 \\
\hline
   & 1 & 2 & -3 & 0
\end{array}
$$

$\dfrac{x^3 + 3x^2 - x - 3}{x + 1} = x^2 + 2x - 3, x \neq -1$

75. Note that $x^2 + 3x + 2 = (x + 1)(x + 2)$.

$$
\begin{array}{r|rrrrr}
-1 & 1 & 6 & 11 & 6 & 0 \\
   &   & -1 & -5 & -6 & 0 \\
\hline
   & 1 & 5 & 6 & 0 & 0
\end{array}
$$

$$
\begin{array}{r|rrrr}
-2 & 1 & 5 & 6 & 0 \\
   &   & -2 & -6 & 0 \\
\hline
   & 1 & 3 & 0 & 0
\end{array}
$$

$\dfrac{x^4 + 6x^3 + 11x^2 + 6x}{(x + 1)(x + 2)} = x^2 + 3x, x \neq -2, -1$

77.

t	-2	-1	0	1	2	3	4	5	6	7
R	13.86	15.21	16.78	18.10	19.08	19.39	21.62	23.07	24.41	26.48

(a)

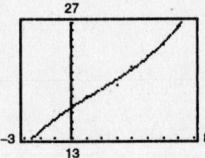

(b) $y = 0.01326x^3 - 0.06765x^2 + 1.23061x + 16.67697 \approx 0.01326t^3 - 0.0677t^2 + 1.231t + 16.68$

(c)

t	-2	-1	0	1	2	3	4	5	6	7
R	13.84	15.37	16.68	17.85	18.97	20.12	21.37	22.80	24.49	26.52

The values predicted by the model are close to the actual data.

(d)

$$
\begin{array}{r|rrrr}
12 & 0.01326 & -0.06765 & 1.23061 & 16.67697 \\
   &   & 0.15912 & 1.09764 & 27.93900 \\
\hline
   & 0.01326 & 0.09147 & 2.32825 & 44.61597
\end{array}
$$

For $t = 12$, the model predicts a monthly rate of about \$44.62.

No, the model is not accurate in predicting future cable rates because the model will approach infinity quickly.

79. False. If $(7x + 4)$ is a factor of f, then $-\frac{4}{7}$ is a root of f.

81.

$$
\begin{array}{r}
x^{2n} + 6x^n + 9 \\
x^n + 3 \overline{) x^{3n} + 9x^{2n} + 27x^n + 27} \\
\underline{x^{3n} + 3x^{2n}} \\
6x^{2n} + 27x^n \\
\underline{6x^{2n} + 18x^n} \\
9x^n + 27 \\
\underline{9x^n + 27} \\
0
\end{array}
$$

$$\frac{x^{3n} + 9x^{2n} + 27x^n + 27}{x^n + 3} = x^{2n} + 6x^n + 9$$

83. A divisor divides evenly into a dividend if the remainder is zero.

85.

$$
\begin{array}{r|rrrr}
5 & 1 & 4 & -3 & c \\
  &   & 5 & 45 & 210 \\
\hline
  & 1 & 9 & 42 & c + 210
\end{array}
$$

For $c + 210$ to equal zero, c must equal -210.

87. $f(x) = (x + 3)^2(x - 3)(x + 1)^3$

The remainder when $k = -3$ is zero since $(x + 3)$ is a factor of $f(x)$.

89. $f(x) = (x - k)q(x) + r$

  (a) $k = 2$, $r = 5$, $q(x) = $ any quadratic $ax^2 + bx + c$ where $a > 0$.

    One example: $f(x) = (x - 2)x^2 + 5 = x^3 - 2x^2 + 5$

  (b) $k = -3$, $r = 1$, $q(x) = $ any quadratic $ax^2 + bx + c$ where $a < 0$.

    One example: $f(x) = (x + 3)(-x^2) + 1 = -x^3 - 3x^2 + 1$

91. $16x^2 - 21 = 0$

$$16x^2 = 21$$

$$x^2 = \frac{21}{16}$$

$$x = \pm\sqrt{\frac{21}{16}}$$

$$x = \pm\frac{\sqrt{21}}{4}$$

93. $8x^2 - 22x + 15 = 0$

$$(4x - 5)(2x - 3) = 0$$

$$4x - 5 = 0 \quad \text{or} \quad 2x - 3 = 0$$

$$x = \tfrac{5}{4} \quad \text{or} \quad x = \tfrac{3}{2}$$

95. $x^2 + 3x - 3 = 0$

$$x = \frac{-3 \pm \sqrt{3^2 - 4(1)(-3)}}{2(1)} = \frac{-3 \pm \sqrt{21}}{2}$$

97. $f(x) = (x - (-6))(x - 1)$

$$= (x + 6)(x - 1)$$

$$= x^2 + 5x - 6$$

Note: Any nonzero scalar multiple of $f(x)$ would also have these zeros.

99. $f(x) = (x - 1)[x - (-2)][x - (2 + \sqrt{3})][x - (2 - \sqrt{3})]$

$$= (x - 1)(x + 2)[(x - 2) - \sqrt{3}][(x - 2) + \sqrt{3}]$$

$$= (x^2 + x - 2)[(x - 2)^2 - (\sqrt{3})^2]$$

$$= (x^2 + x - 2)(x^2 - 4x + 1)$$

$$= x^4 - 3x^3 - 5x^2 + 9x - 2$$

Note: Any nonzero scalar multiple of $f(x)$ would also have these zeros.

Section 2.4   Complex Numbers

- Standard form: $a + bi$.

  If $b = 0$, then $a + bi$ is a real number.

  If $a = 0$ and $b \neq 0$, then $a + bi$ is a pure imaginary number.

- Equality of Complex Numbers: $a + bi = c + di$ if and only if $a = c$ and $b = d$

- Operations on complex numbers

  (a) Addition: $(a + bi) + (c + di) = (a + c) + (b + d)i$

  (b) Subtraction: $(a + bi) - (c + di) = (a - c) + (b - d)i$

  (c) Multiplication: $(a + bi)(c + di) = (ac - bd) + (ad + bc)i$

  (d) Division: $\dfrac{a + bi}{c + di} = \dfrac{a + bi}{c + di} \cdot \dfrac{c - di}{c - di} = \dfrac{ac + bd}{c^2 + d^2} + \dfrac{bc - ad}{c^2 + d^2}i$

- The complex conjugate of $a + bi$ is $a - bi$:

  $(a + bi)(a - bi) = a^2 + b^2$

- The additive inverse of $a + bi$ is $-a - bi$.

- The multiplicative inverse of $a + bi$ is

  $\dfrac{a - bi}{a^2 + b^2}$.

- $\sqrt{-a} = \sqrt{a}\,i$ for $a > 0$.

Solutions to Odd-Numbered Exercises

1. $a + bi = -10 + 6i$

$a = -10$

$b = 6$

3. $(a - 1) + (b + 3)i = 5 + 8i$

$a - 1 = 5 \implies a = 6$

$b + 3 = 8 \implies b = 5$

5. $4 + \sqrt{-9} = 4 + 3i$

7. $2 - \sqrt{-27} = 2 - \sqrt{27}\,i = 2 - 3\sqrt{3}\,i$

9. $\sqrt{-75} = \sqrt{75}\,i = 5\sqrt{3}\,i$

11. $8 = 8 + 0i = 8$

13. $-6i + i^2 = -6i - 1 = -1 - 6i$

15. $\sqrt{-0.09} = \sqrt{0.09}\,i = 0.3i$

17. $(5 + i) + (6 - 2i) = 11 - i$

19. $(8 - i) - (4 - i) = 8 - i - 4 + i = 4$

21. $\left(-2 + \sqrt{-8}\right) + \left(5 - \sqrt{-50}\right) = -2 + 2\sqrt{2}\,i + 5 - 5\sqrt{2}\,i = 3 - 3\sqrt{2}\,i$

23. $13i - (14 - 7i) = 13i - 14 + 7i = -14 + 20i$

25. $-\left(\frac{3}{2} + \frac{5}{2}i\right) + \left(\frac{5}{3} + \frac{11}{3}i\right) = -\frac{3}{2} - \frac{5}{2}i + \frac{5}{3} + \frac{11}{3}i$

$\qquad = -\frac{9}{6} - \frac{15}{6}i + \frac{10}{6} + \frac{22}{6}i$

$\qquad = \frac{1}{6} + \frac{7}{6}i$

27. $\sqrt{-6} \cdot \sqrt{-2} = \left(\sqrt{6}\,i\right)\left(\sqrt{2}\,i\right) = \sqrt{12}\,i^2 = \left(2\sqrt{3}\right)(-1)$

$\qquad = -2\sqrt{3}$

29. $\left(\sqrt{-10}\right)^2 = \left(\sqrt{10}\,i\right)^2 = 10i^2 = -10$

31. $(1 + i)(3 - 2i) = 3 - 2i + 3i - 2i^2 = 3 + i + 2 = 5 + i$

33. $6i(5 - 2i) = 30i - 12i^2 = 30i + 12 = 12 + 30i$

35. $\left(\sqrt{14} + \sqrt{10}\,i\right)\left(\sqrt{14} - \sqrt{10}\,i\right) = 14 - 10i^2 = 14 + 10 = 24$

37. $(4 + 5i)^2 = 16 + 40i + 25i^2$

$\qquad = 16 + 40i - 25$

$\qquad = -9 + 40i$

39. $(2 + 3i)^2 + (2 - 3i)^2 = 4 + 12i + 9i^2 + 4 - 12i + 9i^2$

$\qquad = 4 + 12i - 9 + 4 - 12i - 9$

$\qquad = -10$

41. The complex conjugate of $6 + 3i$ is $6 - 3i$.

$(6 + 3i)(6 - 3i) = 36 - (3i)^2 = 36 + 9 = 45$

43. The complex conjugate of $-1 - \sqrt{5}\,i$ is $-1 + \sqrt{5}\,i$.

$\left(-1 - \sqrt{5}\,i\right)\left(-1 + \sqrt{5}\,i\right) = (-1)^2 - \left(\sqrt{5}\,i\right)^2$

$\qquad = 1 + 5 = 6$

45. The complex conjugate of $\sqrt{-20} = 2\sqrt{5}\,i$ is $-2\sqrt{5}\,i$.

$\left(2\sqrt{5}\,i\right)\left(-2\sqrt{5}\,i\right) = -20i^2 = 20$

47. The complex conjugate of $\sqrt{8}$ is $\sqrt{8}$.

$\left(\sqrt{8}\right)\left(\sqrt{8}\right) = 8$

49. $\dfrac{5}{i} = \dfrac{5}{i} \cdot \dfrac{-i}{-i} = \dfrac{-5i}{1} = -5i$

51. $\dfrac{2}{4 - 5i} = \dfrac{2}{4 - 5i} \cdot \dfrac{4 + 5i}{4 + 5i} = \dfrac{2(4 + 5i)}{16 + 25} = \dfrac{8 + 10i}{41} = \dfrac{8}{41} + \dfrac{10}{41}i$

53. $\dfrac{3+i}{3-i} = \dfrac{3+i}{3-i} \cdot \dfrac{3+i}{3+i}$

$\qquad = \dfrac{9+6i+i^2}{9+1}$

$\qquad = \dfrac{8+6i}{10}$

$\qquad = \dfrac{4}{5} + \dfrac{3}{5}i$

55. $\dfrac{6-5i}{i} = \dfrac{6-5i}{i} \cdot \dfrac{-i}{-i}$

$\qquad = \dfrac{-6i+5i^2}{1}$

$\qquad = -5 - 6i$

57. $\dfrac{3i}{(4-5i)^2} = \dfrac{3i}{16-40i+25i^2} = \dfrac{3i}{-9-40i} \cdot \dfrac{-9+40i}{-9+40i}$

$\qquad = \dfrac{-27i+120i^2}{81+1600} = \dfrac{-120-27i}{1681}$

$\qquad = -\dfrac{120}{1681} - \dfrac{27}{1681}i$

59. $\dfrac{2}{1+i} - \dfrac{3}{1-i} = \dfrac{2(1-i)-3(1+i)}{(1+i)(1-i)}$

$\qquad = \dfrac{2-2i-3-3i}{1+1}$

$\qquad = \dfrac{-1-5i}{2}$

$\qquad = -\dfrac{1}{2} - \dfrac{5}{2}i$

61. $\dfrac{i}{3-2i} + \dfrac{2i}{3+8i} = \dfrac{i(3+8i)+2i(3-2i)}{(3-2i)(3+8i)}$

$\qquad = \dfrac{3i+8i^2+6i-4i^2}{9+24i-6i-16i^2}$

$\qquad = \dfrac{4i^2+9i}{9+18i+16}$

$\qquad = \dfrac{-4+9i}{25+18i} \cdot \dfrac{25-18i}{25-18i}$

$\qquad = \dfrac{-100+72i+225i-162i^2}{625+324}$

$\qquad = \dfrac{-100+297i+162}{949}$

$\qquad = \dfrac{62+297i}{949}$

$\qquad = \dfrac{62}{949} + \dfrac{297}{949}i$

63. $x^2 - 2x + 2 = 0;\; a = 1,\; b = -2,\; c = 2$

$\quad x = \dfrac{-(-2) \pm \sqrt{(-2)^2 - 4(1)(2)}}{2(1)}$

$\qquad = \dfrac{2 \pm \sqrt{-4}}{2}$

$\qquad = \dfrac{2 \pm 2i}{2}$

$\qquad = 1 \pm i$

65. $4x^2 + 16x + 17 = 0;\; a = 4,\; b = 16,\; c = 17$

$\quad x = \dfrac{-16 \pm \sqrt{(16)^2 - 4(4)(17)}}{2(4)} = \dfrac{-16 \pm \sqrt{-16}}{8} = \dfrac{-16 \pm 4i}{8} = -2 \pm \dfrac{1}{2}i$

67. $4x^2 + 16x + 15 = 0;\; a = 4,\; b = 16,\; c = 15$

$\quad x = \dfrac{-16 \pm \sqrt{(16)^2 - 4(4)(15)}}{2(4)} = \dfrac{-16 \pm \sqrt{16}}{8} = \dfrac{-16 \pm 4}{8}$

$\quad x = -\dfrac{12}{8} = -\dfrac{3}{2} \quad$ or $\quad x = -\dfrac{20}{8} = -\dfrac{5}{2}$

69. $\frac{3}{2}x^2 - 6x + 9 = 0$ Multiply both sides by 2.

$3x^2 - 12x + 18 = 0$

$x = \dfrac{-(-12) \pm \sqrt{(-12)^2 - 4(3)(18)}}{2(3)} = \dfrac{12 \pm \sqrt{-72}}{6} = \dfrac{12 \pm 6\sqrt{2}i}{6} = 2 \pm \sqrt{2}i$

71. $1.4x^2 - 2x - 10 = 0$ Multiply both sides by 5.

$7x^2 - 10x - 50 = 0$

$x = \dfrac{-(-10) \pm \sqrt{(-10)^2 - 4(7)(-50)}}{2(7)} = \dfrac{10 \pm \sqrt{1500}}{14} = \dfrac{10 \pm 10\sqrt{15}}{14} = \dfrac{5 \pm 5\sqrt{15}}{7} = \dfrac{5}{7} \pm \dfrac{5\sqrt{15}}{7}$

73. (a) $i^{40} = i^4 \cdot i^4 \cdot i^4 \cdot i^4 \cdot i^4 \cdot i^4 \cdot i^4 \cdot i^4 \cdot i^4 \cdot i^4$

$\qquad = 1 \cdot 1 \cdot 1 \cdot 1 \cdot 1 \cdot 1 \cdot 1 \cdot 1 \cdot 1 \cdot 1$

$\qquad = 1$

(b) $i^{25} = i^4 \cdot i^4 \cdot i^4 \cdot i^4 \cdot i^4 \cdot i^4 \cdot i$

$\qquad = 1 \cdot 1 \cdot 1 \cdot 1 \cdot 1 \cdot 1 \cdot i$

$\qquad = i$

(c) $i^{50} = i^{25} \cdot i^{25} = i \cdot i = i^2 = -1$

(d) $i^{67} = i^{50} \cdot i^{17} = -1 \cdot i^4 \cdot i^4 \cdot i^4 \cdot i^4 \cdot i = -i$

75. $4i^2 - 2i^3 = -4 + 2i$

77. $(-i)^3 = (-1)(i^3) = (-1)(-i) = i$

79. $\left(\sqrt{-2}\right)^6 = \left(\sqrt{2}i\right)^6 = 8i^6 = 8i^4i^2 = -8$

81. $\dfrac{1}{(2i)^3} = \dfrac{1}{8i^3} = \dfrac{1}{-8i} \cdot \dfrac{8i}{8i} = \dfrac{8i}{-64i^2} = \dfrac{1}{8}i$

83. (a) $2^4 = 16,$

(b) $(-2)^4 = 16$

(c) $(2i)^4 = 2^4i^4 = 16(1) = 16$

(d) $(-2i)^4 = (-2)^4i^4 = 16(1) = 16$

85. False, if $b = 0$ then $a + bi = a - bi = a$. That is, if the complex number is real, the number equals its conjugate.

87. False.

$i^{44} + i^{150} - i^{74} - i^{109} + i^{61} = (i^4)^{11} + (i^4)^{37}(i^2) - (i^4)^{18}(i^2) - (i^4)^{27}(i) + (i^4)^{15}(i)$

$\qquad\qquad = (1)^{11} + (1)^{37}(-1) - (1)^{18}(-1) - (1)^{27}(i) + (1)^{15}(i)$

$\qquad\qquad = 1 + (-1) + 1 - i + i = 1$

89. $(a_1 + b_1i)(a_2 + b_2i) = a_1a_2 + a_1b_2i + a_2b_1i + b_1b_2i^2$

$\qquad\qquad = (a_1a_2 - b_1b_2) + (a_1b_2 + a_2b_1)i$

The conjugate of this product is $(a_1a_2 - b_1b_2) - (a_1b_2 + a_2b_1)i$.

The product of the conjugates is:

$(a_1 - b_1i)(a_2 - b_2i) = a_1a_2 - a_1b_2i - a_2b_1i + b_1b_2i$

$\qquad\qquad = (a_1a_2 - b_1b_2) - (a_1b_2 + a_2b_1)i$

Thus, the conjugate of the product of two complex numbers is the product of their conjugates.

91. $(4 + 3x) + (8 - 6x - x^2) = -x^2 - 3x + 12$

93. $\left(3x - \frac{1}{2}\right)(x + 4) = 3x^2 + 12x - \frac{1}{2}x - 2 = 3x^2 + \frac{23}{2}x - 2$

Section 2.5   Zeros of Polynomial Functions

- ■ You should know that if f is a polynomial of degree $n > 0$, then f has at least one zero in the complex number system.
- ■ You should know the Rational Zero Test.
- ■ You should know shortcuts for the Rational Zero Test. Possible rational zeros $= \dfrac{\text{factors of constant term}}{\text{factors of leading coefficients}}$
  - (a) Use a graphing or programmable calculator.
  - (b) Sketch a graph.
  - (c) After finding a root, use synthetic division to reduce the degree of the polynomial.
- ■ You should know that if $a + bi$ is a complex zero of a polynomial f, with real coefficients, then $a - bi$ is also a complex zero of f.
- ■ You should know the difference between a factor that is irreducible over the rationals (such as $x^2 - 7$) and a factor that is irreducible over the reals (such as $x^2 + 9$).
- ■ You should know Descartes's Rule of Signs.
  - (a) The number of positive real zeros of f is either equal to the number of variations of sign of f or is less than that number by an even integer.
  - (b) The number of negative real zeros of f is either equal to the number of variations in sign of $f(-x)$ or is less than that number by an even integer.
  - (c) When there is only one variation in sign, there is exactly one positive (or negative) real zero.
- ■ You should be able to observe the last row obtained from synthetic division in order to determine upper or lower bounds.
  - (a) If the test value is positive and all of the entries in the last row are positive or zero, then the test value is an upper bound.
  - (b) If the test value is negative and the entries in the last row alternate from positive to negative, then the test value is a lower bound. (Zero entries count as positive or negative.)

Solutions to Odd-Numbered Exercises

1. $f(x) = x(x - 6)^2 = x(x - 6)(x - 6)$

The three zeros are: $x = 0, x = 6, x = 6$.

3. $g(x) = (x - 2)(x + 4)^3 = (x - 2)(x + 4)(x + 4)(x + 4)$

The four zeros are: $x = 2, x = -4, x = -4, x = -4$.

5. $f(x) = (x + 6)(x + i)(x - i)$

The three zeros are: $x = -6, x = -i, x = i$.

7. $f(x) = x^3 + 3x^2 - x - 3$

Possible rational zeros: $\pm 1, \pm 3$

Zeros shown on graph: $-3, -1, 1$

9. $f(x) = 2x^4 - 17x^3 + 35x^2 + 9x - 45$

Possible rational zeros: $\pm 1, \pm 3, \pm 5, \pm 9, \pm 15, \pm 45, \pm\frac{1}{2}, \pm\frac{3}{2}, \pm\frac{5}{2}, \pm\frac{9}{2}, \pm\frac{15}{2}, \pm\frac{45}{2}$

Zeros shown on graph: $-1, \frac{3}{2}, 3, 5$

11. $f(x) = x^3 - 6x^2 + 11x - 6$

Possible rational zeros: $\pm 1, \pm 2, \pm 3, \pm 6$

$$
\begin{array}{r|rrrr}
1 & 1 & -6 & 11 & -6 \\
  &   & 1 & -5 & 6 \\
\hline
  & 1 & -5 & 6 & 0
\end{array}
$$

$x^3 - 6x^2 + 11x - 6 = (x - 1)(x^2 - 5x + 6) = (x - 1)(x - 2)(x - 3)$

Thus, the real zeros are 1, 2, and 3.

13. $g(x) = x^3 - 4x^2 - x + 4 = x^2(x - 4) - 1(x - 4) = (x - 4)(x^2 - 1)$

$\qquad = (x - 4)(x - 1)(x + 1)$

Thus, the zeros of $g(x)$ are 4 and ± 1.

15. $h(t) = t^3 + 12t^2 + 21t + 10$

Possible rational zeros: $\pm 1, \pm 2, \pm 5, \pm 10$

$$
\begin{array}{r|rrrr}
-1 & 1 & 12 & 21 & 10 \\
   &   & -1 & -11 & -10 \\
\hline
   & 1 & 11 & 10 & 0
\end{array}
$$

$t^3 + 12t^2 + 21t + 10 = (t + 1)(t^2 + 11t + 10)$

$\qquad\qquad\qquad\qquad = (t + 1)(t + 1)(t + 10)$

$\qquad\qquad\qquad\qquad = (t + 1)^2(t + 10)$

Thus, the zeros are -1 and -10.

17. $C(x) = 2x^3 + 3x^2 - 1$

Possible rational zeros: $\pm 1, \pm \frac{1}{2}$

$$
\begin{array}{r|rrrr}
-1 & 2 & 3 & 0 & -1 \\
   &   & -2 & -1 & 1 \\
\hline
   & 2 & 1 & -1 & 0
\end{array}
$$

$2x^3 + 3x^2 - 1 = (x + 1)(2x^2 + x - 1)$

$\qquad\qquad\quad = (x + 1)(x + 1)(2x - 1)$

$\qquad\qquad\quad = (x + 1)^2(2x - 1)$

Thus, the zeros are -1 and $\frac{1}{2}$.

19. $f(x) = 9x^4 - 9x^3 - 58x^2 + 4x + 24$

Possible rational zeros: $\pm 1, \pm 2, \pm 3, \pm 4, \pm 6, \pm 8, \pm 12, \pm 24, \pm \frac{1}{3}, \pm \frac{2}{3},$
$\pm \frac{4}{3}, \pm \frac{8}{3}, \pm \frac{1}{9}, \pm \frac{2}{9}, \pm \frac{4}{9}, \pm \frac{8}{9}$

$$
\begin{array}{r|rrrrr}
-2 & 9 & -9 & -58 & 4 & 24 \\
   &   & -18 & 54 & 8 & -24 \\
\hline
   & 9 & -27 & -4 & 12 & 0
\end{array}
$$

$$
\begin{array}{r|rrrr}
3 & 9 & -27 & -4 & 12 \\
  &   & 27 & 0 & -12 \\
\hline
  & 9 & 0 & -4 & 0
\end{array}
$$

$9x^4 - 9x^3 - 58x^2 + 4x - 24 = (x + 2)(x - 3)(9x^2 - 4)$

$\qquad\qquad\qquad\qquad\qquad = (x + 2)(x - 3)(3x - 2)(3x + 2)$

Thus, the zeros are $-2, 3,$ and $\pm \frac{2}{3}$.

21. $z^4 - z^3 - 2z - 4 = 0$

Possible rational zeros: $\pm 1,\ \pm 2,\ \pm 4$

$$
\begin{array}{r|rrrrr}
-1 & 1 & -1 & 0 & -2 & -4 \\
   &   & -1 & 2 & -2 & 4 \\
\hline
   & 1 & -2 & 2 & -4 & 0
\end{array}
$$

$$
\begin{array}{r|rrrr}
2 & 1 & -2 & 2 & -4 \\
  &   & 2 & 0 & 4 \\
\hline
  & 1 & 0 & 2 & 0
\end{array}
$$

$z^4 - z^3 - 2z - 4 = (x + 1)(x - 2)(x^2 + 2)$

The only real zeros are -1 and 2.

23. $2y^4 + 7y^3 - 26y^2 + 23y - 6 = 0$

Possible rational zeros: $\pm 1,\ \pm 2,\ \pm 3,\ \pm 6,\ \pm\frac{1}{2},\ \pm\frac{3}{2}$

$$
\begin{array}{r|rrrrr}
1 & 2 & 7 & -26 & 23 & -6 \\
  &   & 2 & 9 & -17 & 6 \\
\hline
  & 2 & 9 & -17 & 6 & 0
\end{array}
$$

$$
\begin{array}{r|rrrr}
-6 & 2 & 9 & -17 & 6 \\
   &   & -12 & 18 & -6 \\
\hline
   & 2 & -3 & 1 & 0
\end{array}
$$

$$
\begin{aligned}
2y^4 + 7y^3 - 26y^2 + 23y - 6 &= (y - 1)(y + 6)(2y^2 - 3y + 1) \\
&= (y - 1)(y + 6)(2y - 1)(y - 1) \\
&= (y - 1)^2(y + 6)(2y - 1)
\end{aligned}
$$

The only real zeros are $1,\ -6,$ and $\frac{1}{2}$.

25. $f(x) = x^3 + x^2 - 4x - 4$

(a) Possible rational zeros: $\pm 1,\ \pm 2,\ \pm 4$

(b)

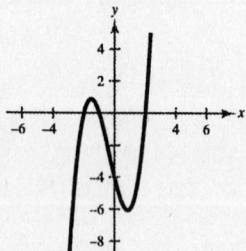

(c) The zeros are: $-2,\ -1,\ 2$

27. $f(x) = -4x^3 + 15x^2 - 8x - 3$

(a) Possible rational zeros: $\pm 1,\ \pm 3,\ \pm\frac{1}{2},\ \pm\frac{3}{2},\ \pm\frac{1}{4},\ \pm\frac{3}{4}$

(b)

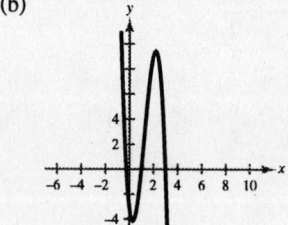

(c) The zeros are: $-\frac{1}{4},\ 1,\ 3$

29. $f(x) = -2x^4 + 13x^3 - 21x^2 + 2x + 8$

(a) Possible rational zeros: $\pm 1,\ \pm 2,\ \pm 4,\ \pm 8,\ \pm\frac{1}{2}$

(b)

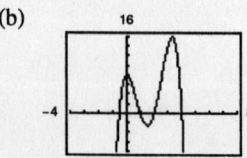

(c) The zeros are: $-\frac{1}{2},\ 1,\ 2,\ 4$

31. $f(x) = 32x^3 - 52x^2 + 17x + 3$

(a) Possible rational zeros: $\pm 1,\ \pm 3,\ \pm\frac{1}{2},\ \pm\frac{3}{2},\ \pm\frac{1}{4},\ \pm\frac{3}{4},\ \pm\frac{1}{8},\ \pm\frac{3}{8},\ \pm\frac{1}{16},\ \pm\frac{3}{16},\ \pm\frac{1}{32},\ \pm\frac{3}{32}$

(b)

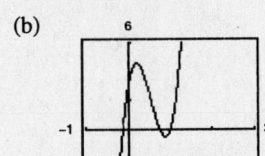

(c) The zeros are: $-\frac{1}{8},\ \frac{3}{4},\ 1$

33. $f(x) = x^4 - 3x^2 + 2$

(a) From the calculator we have

$x = \pm 1$ and $x \approx \pm 1.414.$

(b)

$$\begin{array}{r|rrrrr}
1 & 1 & 0 & -3 & 0 & 2 \\
  &   & 1 & 1 & -2 & -2 \\
\hline
  & 1 & 1 & -2 & -2 & 0
\end{array}$$

$$\begin{array}{r|rrrr}
-1 & 1 & 1 & -2 & -2 \\
   &   & -1 & 0 & 2 \\
\hline
   & 1 & 0 & -2 & 0
\end{array}$$

$f(x) = (x - 1)(x + 1)(x^2 - 2)$

$\quad\ = (x - 1)(x + 1)(x - \sqrt{2})(x + \sqrt{2})$

The exact roots are $x = \pm 1,\ \pm\sqrt{2}.$

35. $h(x) = x^5 - 7x^4 + 10x^3 + 14x^2 - 24x$

(a) $h(x) = x(x^4 - 7x^3 + 10x^2 + 14x - 24)$

From the calculator we have

$x = 0,\ 3,\ 4$ and $x \approx \pm 1.414.$

(b)

$$\begin{array}{r|rrrrr}
3 & 1 & -7 & 10 & 14 & -24 \\
  &   & 3 & -12 & -6 & 24 \\
\hline
  & 1 & -4 & -2 & 8 & 0
\end{array}$$

$$\begin{array}{r|rrrr}
4 & 1 & -4 & -2 & 8 \\
  &   & 4 & 0 & -8 \\
\hline
  & 1 & 0 & -2 & 0
\end{array}$$

$f(x) = x(x - 3)(x - 4)(x^2 - 2)$

$\quad\ = x(x - 3)(x - 4)(x - \sqrt{2})(x + \sqrt{2})$

The exact roots are $x = 0,\ 3,\ 4,\ \pm\sqrt{2}.$

37. $f(x) = (x - 1)(x - 5i)(x + 5i)$

$\quad\ = (x - 1)(x^2 + 25)$

$\quad\ = x^3 - x^2 + 25x - 25$

Note: $f(x) = a(x^3 - x^2 + 25x - 25).$
where a is any nonzero real number, has the zeros 1 and $\pm 5i$.

39. $f(x) = (x - 6)[x - (-5 + 2i)][x - (-5 - 2i)]$

$\quad\ = (x - 6)[(x + 5) - 2i][(x + 5) + 2i]$

$\quad\ = (x - 6)[(x + 5)^2 - (2i)^2]$

$\quad\ = (x - 6)(x^2 + 10x + 25 + 4)$

$\quad\ = (x - 6)(x^2 + 10x + 29)$

$\quad\ = x^3 + 4x^2 - 31x - 174$

Note: $f(x) = a(x^3 + 4x^2 - 31x - 174)$, where a is any nonzero real number, has the zeros 6, and $-5 \pm 2i$.

41. If $3 + \sqrt{2}i$ is a zero, so is its conjugate, $3 - \sqrt{2}i$.

$f(x) = (3x - 2)(x + 1)[x - (3 + \sqrt{2}i)][x - (3 - \sqrt{2}i)]$

$\quad\ = (3x - 2)(x + 1)[(x - 3) - \sqrt{2}i][(x - 3) + \sqrt{2}i]$

$\quad\ = (3x^2 + x - 2)[(x - 3)^2 - (\sqrt{2}i)^2]$

$\quad\ = (3x^2 + x - 2)(x^2 - 6x + 9 + 2)$

$\quad\ = (3x^2 + x - 2)(x^2 - 6x + 11)$

$\quad\ = 3x^4 - 17x^3 + 25x^2 + 23x - 22$

Note: $f(x) = a(3x^4 - 17x^3 + 25x^2 + 23x - 22)$, where a is any nonzero real number, has the zeros $\frac{2}{3},\ -1,$ and $3 \pm \sqrt{2}i$.

43. $f(x) = x^4 + 6x^2 - 27$

(a) $f(x) = (x^2 + 9)(x^2 - 3)$

(b) $f(x) = (x^2 + 9)(x + \sqrt{3})(x - \sqrt{3})$

(c) $f(x) = (x + 3i)(x - 3i)(x + \sqrt{3})(x - \sqrt{3})$

45.

$$
\begin{array}{r}
x^2 - 2x + 3 \\
x^2 - 2x - 2 \overline{\smash{)}\, x^4 - 4x^3 + 5x^2 - 2x - 6} \\
\underline{x^4 - 2x^3 - 2x^2} \\
-2x^3 + 7x^2 - 2x \\
\underline{-2x^3 + 4x^2 + 4x} \\
3x^2 - 6x - 6 \\
\underline{3x^2 - 6x - 6} \\
0
\end{array}
$$

$f(x) = (x^2 - 2x - 2)(x^2 - 2x + 3)$

(a) $f(x) = (x^2 - 2x - 2)(x^2 - 2x + 3)$

(b) $f(x) = (x - 1 + \sqrt{3})(x - 1 - \sqrt{3})(x^2 - 2x + 3)$

(c) $f(x) = (x - 1 + \sqrt{3})(x - 1 - \sqrt{3})(x - 1 + \sqrt{2}\,i)(x - 1 - \sqrt{2}\,i)$

Note: Use the Quadratic Formula for (b) and (c).

47. $f(x) = 2x^3 + 3x^2 + 50x + 75$

Since $5i$ is a zero, so is $-5i$.

$$
\begin{array}{r|rrrr}
5i & 2 & 3 & 50 & 75 \\
 & & 10i & -50 + 15i & -75 \\
\hline
 & 2 & 3 + 10i & 15i & 0
\end{array}
$$

$$
\begin{array}{r|rrr}
-5i & 2 & 3 + 10i & 15i \\
 & & -10i & -15i \\
\hline
 & 2 & 3 & 0
\end{array}
$$

The zero of $2x + 3$ is $x = -\frac{3}{2}$.

The zeros of $f(x)$ are $x = -\frac{3}{2}$ and $x = \pm 5i$.

<u>Alternate Solution</u>

Since $x = \pm 5i$ are zeros of $f(x)$, $(x + 5i)(x - 5i) = x^2 + 25$ is a factor of $f(x)$.
By long division we have:

$$
\begin{array}{r}
2x + 3 \\
x^2 + 0x + 25 \overline{\smash{)}\, 2x^3 + 3x^2 + 50x + 75} \\
\underline{2x^3 + 0x^2 + 50x} \\
3x^2 + 0x + 75 \\
\underline{3x^2 + 0x + 75} \\
0
\end{array}
$$

Thus, $f(x) = (x^2 + 25)(2x + 3)$ and the zeros of f are $x = \pm 5i$ and $x = -\frac{3}{2}$.

49. $f(x) = 2x^4 - x^3 + 7x^2 - 4x - 4$

Since $2i$ is a zero, so is $-2i$.

$$
\begin{array}{r|rrrrr}
2i & 2 & -1 & 7 & -4 & -4 \\
   &   & 4i & -8-2i & 4-2i & 4 \\
\hline
   & 2 & -1+4i & -1-2i & -2i & 0
\end{array}
$$

$$
\begin{array}{r|rrrr}
-2i & 2 & -1+4i & -1-2i & -2i \\
    &   & -4i & 2i & 2i \\
\hline
    & 2 & -1 & -1 & 0
\end{array}
$$

The zeros of $2x^2 - x - 1 = (2x + 1)(x - 1)$ are $x = -\frac{1}{2}$ and $x = 1$.

The zeros of $f(x)$ are $x = \pm 2i$, $x = -\frac{1}{2}$, and $x = 1$.

<u>Alternate Solution</u>

Since $x = \pm 2i$ are zeros of $f(x)$, $(x + 2i)(x - 2i) = x^2 + 4$ is a factor of $f(x)$.
By long division we have:

$$
\begin{array}{r}
2x^2 - x - 1 \\
x^2 + 0x + 4 \overline{)2x^4 - x^3 + 7x^2 - 4x - 4} \\
\underline{2x^4 + 0x^3 + 8x^2} \\
-x^3 - x^2 - 4x \\
\underline{-x^3 + 0x^2 - 4x} \\
-x^2 + 0x - 4 \\
\underline{-x^2 + 0x - 4} \\
0
\end{array}
$$

Thus, $f(x) = (x^2 + 4)(2x^2 - x - 1)$

$$= (x + 2i)(x - 2i)(2x + 1)(x - 1)$$

and the zeros of $f(x)$ are $x = \pm 2i$, $x = -\frac{1}{2}$, and $x = 1$.

51. $g(x) = 4x^3 + 23x^2 + 34x - 10$

Since $-3 + i$ is a zero, so is $-3 - i$.

$$
\begin{array}{r|rrrr}
-3+i & 4 & 23 & 34 & -10 \\
     &   & -12+4i & -37-i & 10 \\
\hline
     & 4 & 11+4i & -3-i & 0
\end{array}
$$

$$
\begin{array}{r|rrr}
-3-i & 4 & 11+4i & -3-i \\
     &   & -12-4i & 3+i \\
\hline
     & 4 & -1 & 0
\end{array}
$$

The zero of $4x - 1$ is $x = \frac{1}{4}$. The zeros of $g(x)$ are $x = -3 \pm i$ and $x = \frac{1}{4}$.

<u>Alternate Solution</u>

Since $-3 \pm i$ are zeros of $g(x)$,
$$[x - (-3 + i)][x - (-3 - i)] = [(x + 3) - i][(x + 3) + i]$$
$$= (x + 3)^2 - i^2$$
$$= x^2 + 6x + 10$$
is a factor of $g(x)$. By long division we have:

$$
\begin{array}{r}
4x - 1 \\
x^2 + 6x + 10 \overline{)4x^3 + 23x^2 + 34x - 10} \\
\underline{4x^3 + 24x^2 + 40x} \\
-x^2 - 6x - 10 \\
\underline{-x^2 - 6x - 10} \\
0
\end{array}
$$

Thus, $g(x) = (x^2 + 6x + 10)(4x - 1)$ and the zeros of $g(x)$ are $x = -3 \pm i$ and $x = \frac{1}{4}$.

53. Since $-3 + \sqrt{2}\, i$ is a zero, so is $-3 - \sqrt{2}\, i$, and

$$\left[x - \left(-3 + \sqrt{2}\, i\right)\right]\left[x - \left(-3 - \sqrt{2}\, i\right)\right]$$
$$= \left[(x + 3) - \sqrt{2}\, i\right]\left[(x + 3) + \sqrt{2}\, i\right]$$
$$= (x + 3)^2 - \left(\sqrt{2}\, i\right)^2$$
$$= x^2 + 6x + 11$$

is a factor of $f(x)$. By long division, we have:

$$
\begin{array}{r}
x^2 - 3x + 2 \\
x^2 + 6x + 11\,\overline{\smash{\big)}\,x^4 + 3x^3 - 5x^2 - 21x + 22} \\
\underline{x^4 + 6x^3 + 11x^2} \\
-3x^3 - 16x^2 - 21x \\
\underline{-3x^3 - 18x^2 - 33x} \\
2x^2 + 12x + 22 \\
\underline{2x^2 + 12x + 22} \\
0
\end{array}
$$

Thus, $f(x) = (x^2 + 6x + 11)(x^2 - 3x + 2)$

$$= (x^2 + 6x + 11)(x - 1)(x - 2)$$

and the zeros of f are $x = -3 \pm \sqrt{2}\, i, x = 1$, and $x = 2$.

57. $h(x) = x^2 - 4x + 1$

h has no rational zeros.

By the Quadratic Formula, the zeros are $x = \dfrac{4 \pm \sqrt{16 - 4}}{2} = 2 \pm \sqrt{3}$.

$$h(x) = \left[x - \left(2 + \sqrt{3}\right)\right]\left[x - \left(2 - \sqrt{3}\right)\right] = \left(x - 2 - \sqrt{3}\right)\left(x - 2 + \sqrt{3}\right)$$

59. $f(x) = x^4 - 81$

$$= (x^2 - 9)(x^2 + 9)$$
$$= (x + 3)(x - 3)(x + 3i)(x - 3i)$$

The zeros of $f(x)$ are $x = \pm 3$ and $x = \pm 3i$.

61. $f(z) = z^2 - 2z + 2$

f has no rational zeros.

By the Quadratic Formula, the zeros are $z = \dfrac{2 \pm \sqrt{4 - 8}}{2} = 1 \pm i$.

$$f(z) = \left[z - (1 + i)\right]\left[z - (1 - i)\right] = (z - 1 - i)(z - 1 + i)$$

55. $f(x) = x^2 + 25$

$$= (x + 5i)(x - 5i)$$

The zeros of $f(x)$ are $x = \pm 5i$.

63. $g(x) = x^3 - 6x^2 + 13x - 10$

Possible rational zeros: $\pm 1, \pm 2, \pm 5, \pm 10$

$$
\begin{array}{r|rrrr}
2 & 1 & -6 & 13 & -10 \\
  &   & 2 & -8 & 10 \\
\hline
  & 1 & -4 & 5 & 0
\end{array}
$$

By the Quadratic Formula, the zeros of

$x^2 - 4x + 5$ are $x = \dfrac{4 \pm \sqrt{16 - 20}}{2} = 2 \pm i.$

The zeros of $g(x)$ are $x = 2$ and $x = 2 \pm i.$

$g(x) = (x - 2)[x - (2 + i)][x - (2 - i)]$

$\quad = (x - 2)(x - 2 - i)(x - 2 + i)$

65. $h(x) = x^3 - x + 6$

Possible rational zeros: $\pm 1, \pm 2, \pm 3, \pm 6$

$$
\begin{array}{r|rrrr}
-2 & 1 & 0 & -1 & 6 \\
   &   & -2 & 4 & -6 \\
\hline
   & 1 & -2 & 3 & 0
\end{array}
$$

By the Quadratic Formula, the zeros of $x^2 - 2x + 3$ are

$x = \dfrac{2 \pm \sqrt{4 - 12}}{2} = 1 \pm \sqrt{2}\, i.$

The zeros of $h(x)$ are $x = -2$ and $x = 1 \pm \sqrt{2}\, i.$

$h(x) = [x - (-2)]\left[x - \left(1 + \sqrt{2}\, i\right)\right]\left[x - \left(1 - \sqrt{2}\, i\right)\right]$

$\quad = (x + 2)\left(x - 1 - \sqrt{2}\, i\right)\left(x - 1 + \sqrt{2}\, i\right)$

67. $f(x) = 5x^3 - 9x^2 + 28x + 6$

Possible rational zeros: $\pm 1, \pm 2, \pm 3, \pm 6, \pm \frac{1}{5}, \pm \frac{2}{5}, \pm \frac{3}{5}, \pm \frac{6}{5}$

$$
\begin{array}{r|rrrr}
-\frac{1}{5} & 5 & -9 & 28 & 6 \\
   &   & -1 & 2 & -6 \\
\hline
   & 5 & -10 & 30 & 0
\end{array}
$$

By the Quadratic Formula, the zeros of $5x^2 - 10x + 30 = 5(x^2 - 2x + 6)$ are

$x = \dfrac{2 \pm \sqrt{4 - 24}}{2} = 1 \pm \sqrt{5}\, i.$

The zeros of $f(x)$ are $x = -\frac{1}{5}$ and $x = 1 \pm \sqrt{5}\, i.$

$f(x) = \left[x - \left(-\frac{1}{5}\right)\right](5)\left[x - \left(1 + \sqrt{5}\, i\right)\right]\left[x - \left(1 - \sqrt{5}\, i\right)\right]$

$\quad = (5x + 1)\left(x - 1 - \sqrt{5}\, i\right)\left(x - 1 + \sqrt{5}\, i\right)$

69. $g(x) = x^4 - 4x^3 + 8x^2 - 16x + 16$

Possible rational zeros: $\pm 1, \pm 2, \pm 4, \pm 8, \pm 16$

$$
\begin{array}{r|rrrrr}
2 & 1 & -4 & 8 & -16 & 16 \\
  &   & 2 & -4 & 8 & -16 \\
\hline
  & 1 & -2 & 4 & -8 & 0
\end{array}
$$

$$
\begin{array}{r|rrrr}
2 & 1 & -2 & 4 & -8 \\
  &   & 2 & 0 & 8 \\
\hline
  & 1 & 0 & 4 & 0
\end{array}
$$

$g(x) = (x - 2)(x - 2)(x^2 + 4) = (x - 2)^2(x + 2i)(x - 2i)$

The zeros of $g(x)$ are 2 and $\pm 2i.$

71. $f(x) = x^4 + 10x^2 + 9$

$\quad = (x^2 + 1)(x^2 + 9)$

$\quad = (x + i)(x - i)(x + 3i)(x - 3i)$

The zeros of $f(x)$ are $x = \pm i$ and $x = \pm 3i.$

73. $f(x) = x^3 + 24x^2 + 214x + 740$

Possible rational zeros: $\pm 1, \pm 2, \pm 4, \pm 5, \pm 10, \pm 20, \pm 37, \pm 74, \pm 148, \pm 185, \pm 370, \pm 740$

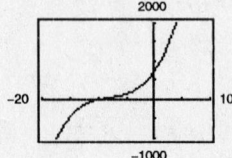

Based on the graph, try $x = -10$.

$$
\begin{array}{r|rrrr}
-10 & 1 & 24 & 214 & 740 \\
    &   & -10 & -140 & -740 \\
\hline
    & 1 & 14 & 74 & 0
\end{array}
$$

By the Quadratic Formula, the zeros of $x^2 + 14x + 74$ are
$$x = \frac{-14 \pm \sqrt{196 - 296}}{2} = -7 \pm 5i.$$

The zeros of $f(x)$ are $x = -10$ and $x = -7 \pm 5i$.

75. $f(x) = 16x^3 - 20x^2 - 4x + 15$

Possible rational zeros: $\pm 1, \pm 3, \pm 5, \pm 15, \pm \frac{1}{2}, \pm \frac{3}{2}, \pm \frac{5}{2}, \pm \frac{15}{2}, \pm \frac{1}{4}, \pm \frac{3}{4}$
$\pm \frac{5}{4}, \pm \frac{15}{4}, \pm \frac{1}{8}, \pm \frac{3}{8}, \pm \frac{5}{8}, \pm \frac{15}{8}, \pm \frac{1}{16}, \pm \frac{3}{16}, \pm \frac{5}{16}, \pm \frac{15}{16}$

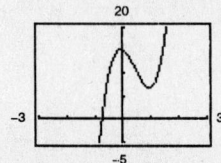

Based on the graph, try $x = -\frac{3}{4}$.

$$
\begin{array}{r|rrrr}
-\frac{3}{4} & 16 & -20 & -4 & 15 \\
             &   & -12 & 24 & -15 \\
\hline
             & 16 & -32 & 20 & 0
\end{array}
$$

By the Quadratic Formula, the zeros of $16x^2 - 32x + 20 = 4(4x^2 - 8x + 5)$ are
$$x = \frac{8 \pm \sqrt{64 - 80}}{8} = 1 \pm \frac{1}{2}i.$$

The zeros of $f(x)$ are $x = -\frac{3}{4}$ and $x = 1 \pm \frac{1}{2}i$.

77. $f(x) = 2x^4 + 5x^3 + 4x^2 + 5x + 2$

Possible rational zeros: $\pm 1, \pm 2, \pm\frac{1}{2}$

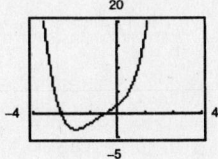

Based on the graph, try $x = -2$ and $x = -\frac{1}{2}$.

$$
\begin{array}{r|rrrrr}
-2 & 2 & 5 & 4 & 5 & 2 \\
   &   & -4 & -2 & -4 & -2 \\
\hline
   & 2 & 1 & 2 & 1 & 0 \\
\end{array}
$$

$$
\begin{array}{r|rrrr}
-\frac{1}{2} & 2 & 1 & 2 & 1 \\
            &   & -1 & 0 & -1 \\
\hline
            & 2 & 0 & 2 & 0 \\
\end{array}
$$

The zeros of $2x^2 + 2 = 2(x^2 + 1)$ are $x = \pm i$.

The zeros of $f(x)$ are $x = -2$, $x = -\frac{1}{2}$, and $x = \pm i$.

79. $g(x) = 5x^5 + 10x = 5x(x^4 + 2)$

Let $f(x) = x^4 + 2$.

Sign variations: 0, positive zeros: 0

$f(-x) = x^4 + 2$

Sign variations: 0, negative zeros: 0

81. $h(x) = 3x^4 + 2x^2 + 1$

Sign variations: 0, positive zeros: 0

$h(-x) = 3x^4 + 2x^2 + 1$

Sign variations: 0, negative zeros: 0

83. $g(x) = 2x^3 - 3x^2 - 3$

Sign variations: 1, positive zeros: 1

$g(-x) = -2x^3 - 3x^2 - 3$

Sign variations: 0, negative zeros: 0

85. $f(x) = -5x^3 + x^2 - x + 5$

Sign variations: 3, positive zeros: 3 or 1

$f(-x) = 5x^3 + x^2 + x + 5$

Sign variations: 0, negative zeros: 0

87. $f(x) = x^4 - 4x^3 + 15$

(a)
$$
\begin{array}{r|rrrrr}
4 & 1 & -4 & 0 & 0 & 15 \\
  &   & 4 & 0 & 0 & 0 \\
\hline
  & 1 & 0 & 0 & 0 & 15 \\
\end{array}
$$

4 is an upper bound.

(b)
$$
\begin{array}{r|rrrrr}
-1 & 1 & -4 & 0 & 0 & 15 \\
   &   & -1 & 5 & -5 & 5 \\
\hline
   & 1 & -5 & 5 & -5 & 20 \\
\end{array}
$$

-1 is a lower bound.

89. $f(x) = x^4 - 4x^3 + 16x - 16$

(a)
$$
\begin{array}{r|rrrrr}
5 & 1 & -4 & 0 & 16 & -16 \\
  &   & 5 & 5 & 25 & 205 \\
\hline
  & 1 & 1 & 5 & 41 & 189 \\
\end{array}
$$

5 is an upper bound.

(b)
$$
\begin{array}{r|rrrrr}
-3 & 1 & -4 & 0 & 16 & -16 \\
   &   & -3 & 21 & -63 & 141 \\
\hline
   & 1 & -7 & 21 & -47 & 125 \\
\end{array}
$$

-3 is a lower bound.

91. $f(x) = 4x^3 - 3x - 1$

Possible rational zeros: $\pm 1, \pm\frac{1}{2}, \pm\frac{1}{4}$

$$
\begin{array}{r|rrrr}
1 & 4 & 0 & -3 & -1 \\
  &   & 4 & 4 & 1 \\
\hline
  & 4 & 4 & 1 & 0 \\
\end{array}
$$

$4x^3 - 3x - 1 = (x - 1)(4x^2 + 4x + 1) = (x - 1)(2x + 1)^2$

Thus, the zeros are 1 and $-\frac{1}{2}$.

93. $f(y) = 4y^3 + 3y^2 + 8y + 6$

Possible rational zeros: $\pm 1, \ \pm 2, \ \pm 3, \ \pm 6, \ \pm \frac{1}{2}, \ \pm \frac{3}{2}, \ \pm \frac{1}{4}, \ \pm \frac{3}{4}$

$$
\begin{array}{r|rrrr}
-\frac{3}{4} & 4 & 3 & 8 & 6 \\
& & -3 & 0 & -6 \\
\hline
& 4 & 0 & 8 & 0
\end{array}
$$

$4y^3 + 3y^2 + 8y + 6 = \left(y + \frac{3}{4}\right)(4y^2 + 8) = \left(y + \frac{3}{4}\right)4(y^2 + 2) = (4y + 3)(y^2 + 2)$

Thus, the only real zero is $-\frac{3}{4}$.

95. $P(x) = x^4 - \frac{25}{4}x^2 + 9$

$\quad = \frac{1}{4}(4x^4 - 25x^2 + 36)$

$\quad = \frac{1}{4}(4x^2 - 9)(x^2 - 4)$

$\quad = \frac{1}{4}(2x + 3)(2x - 3)(x + 2)(x - 2)$

The zeros are $\pm \frac{3}{2}$ and ± 2.

97. $f(x) = x^3 - \frac{1}{4}x^2 - x + \frac{1}{4}$

$\quad = \frac{1}{4}(4x^3 - x^2 - 4x + 1)$

$\quad = \frac{1}{4}[x^2(4x - 1) - 1(4x - 1)]$

$\quad = \frac{1}{4}(4x - 1)(x^2 - 1)$

$\quad = \frac{1}{4}(4x - 1)(x + 1)(x - 1)$

The zeros are $\frac{1}{4}$ and ± 1.

99. $f(x) = x^3 - 1 = (x - 1)(x^2 + x + 1)$

Rational zeros: 1 $(x = 1)$

Irrational zeros: 0

Matches (d).

101. $f(x) = x^3 - x = x(x + 1)(x - 1)$

Rational zeros: 3 $(x = 0, \pm 1)$

Irrational zeros: 0

Matches (b).

103. Zeros: $-2, \frac{1}{2}, 3$

$f(x) = -(x + 2)(2x - 1)(x - 3)$

$\quad = -2x^3 + 3x^2 + 11x - 6$

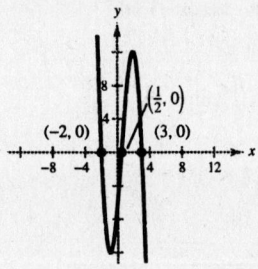

Any nonzero scalar multiple of f would have the same three zeros.

Let $g(x) = af(x), \ a > 0$.

There are infinitely many possible functions for f.

105. Interval: $(-\infty, -2), \ (-2, 1), \ (1, 4), \ (4, \infty)$

Value of $f(x)$: Positive Negative Negative Positive

(a) Zeros of $f(x)$: $x = -2, \ x = 1, \ x = 4$.

(b) The graph touches the x-axis at $x = 1$.

(c) The least possible degree of the function is 4 because there are at least four real zeros (1 is repeated) and a function can have at most the number of real zeros equal to the degree of the function. The degree cannot be odd by the definition of multiplicity.

(d) The leading coefficient of f is positive. From the information in the table, you can conclude that the graph will eventually rise to the left and to the right.

(e) $f(x) = (x + 2)(x - 1)^2(x - 4)$

$\quad = x^4 - 4x^3 - 3x^2 + 14x - 8$

(Any nonzero multiple of $f(x)$ is also a solution.)

(f)

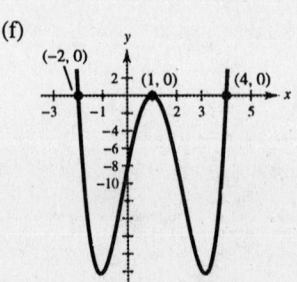

107. (a)

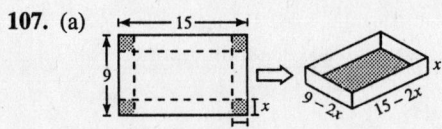

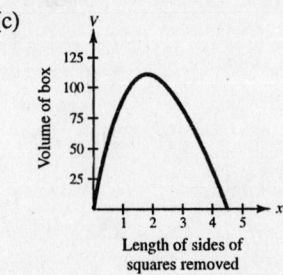

(b) $V = l \cdot w \cdot h = (15 - 2x)(9 - 2x)x$

$= x(9 - 2x)(15 - 2x)$

Since length, width, and height must be positive, we have $0 < x < \frac{9}{2}$ for the domain.

(c)

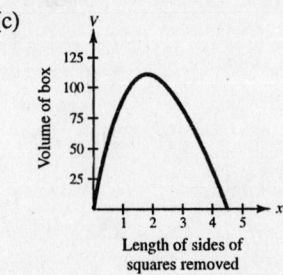

Volume of box

125
100
75
50
25

1   2   3   4   5

Length of sides of
squares removed

The volume is maximum when $x \approx 1.82$.

The dimensions are: length $\approx 15 - 2(1.82) = 11.36$

width $\approx 9 - 2(1.82) = 5.36$

height $= x \approx 1.82$

$1.82 \text{ cm} \times 5.36 \text{ cm} \times 11.36 \text{ cm}$

(d) $56 = x(9 - 2x)(15 - 2x)$

$56 = 135x - 48x^2 + 4x^3$

$0 = 4x^3 - 48x^2 + 135x - 56$

The zeros of this polynomial are $\frac{1}{2}, \frac{7}{2}$, and 8. x cannot equal 8 since it is not in the domain of V. [The length cannot equal -1 and the width cannot equal -7. The product of $(8)(-1)(-7) = 56$ so it showed up as an extraneous solution.]

109.

$$P = -76x^3 + 4830x^2 - 320{,}000, \; 0 \le x \le 60$$

$$2{,}500{,}000 = -76x^3 + 4830x^2 - 320{,}000$$

$$76x^3 - 4830x^2 + 2{,}820{,}000 = 0$$

The zeros of this equation are $x \approx 46.1$, $x \approx 38.4$, and $x \approx -21.0$. Since $0 \le x \le 60$, we disregard $x \approx -21.0$. The smaller remaining solution is $x \approx 38.4$. The advertising amount is $384,000.

111. $C = 100\left(\dfrac{200}{x^2} + \dfrac{x}{x + 30}\right), \; 1 \le x$

C is minimum when $3x^3 - 40x^2 - 2400x - 36000 = 0$.

The only real zero is $x \approx 40$.

113. $h = -16t^2 + 48t, \; 0 \le t \le 3$

$= -16(t^2 - 3t)$

$= -16\left(t^2 - 3t + \frac{9}{4} - \frac{9}{4}\right)$

$= -16\left[\left(t - \frac{3}{2}\right)^2 - \frac{9}{4}\right]$

$= -16\left(t - \frac{3}{2}\right)^2 + 36$

The maximum height that the baseball reaches is 36 feet when $t = 1.5$ seconds.
No, it is not possible for the ball to reach a height of 64 feet.

<u>Alternate Solution</u>

Let $h = 64$ and solve for t.

$$64 = -16t^2 + 48t$$

$$16t^2 - 48t + 64 = 0$$

$$16(t^2 - 3t + 4) = 0$$

$$t^2 - 3t + 4 = 0$$

$$t = \frac{3 \pm \sqrt{9 - 16}}{2} = \frac{3 \pm \sqrt{7}\,i}{2}$$

No, it is not possible since solving this equation yields only imaginary roots.

115. False. The most nonreal complex zeros it can have is two and the Linear Factorization Theorem guarantees that there are 3 linear factors, so one zero must be real.

117. $g(x) = -f(x)$. This function would have the same zeros as $f(x)$ so r_1, r_2, and r_3 are also zeros of $g(x)$.

119. $g(x) = f(x - 5)$. The graph of $g(x)$ is a horizontal shift of the graph of $f(x)$ five units to the right so the zeros of $g(x)$ are $5 + r_1$, $5 + r_2$, and $5 + r_3$.

121. $g(x) = 3 + f(x)$. Since $g(x)$ is a vertical shift of the graph of $f(x)$, the zeros of $g(x)$ cannot be determined.

123. $f(x) = x^4 - 4x^2 + k$

$$x^2 = \frac{-(-4) \pm \sqrt{(-4)^2 - 4(1)(k)}}{2(1)} = \frac{4 \pm 2\sqrt{4 - k}}{2} = 2 \pm \sqrt{4 - k}$$

$$x = \pm\sqrt{2 \pm \sqrt{4 - k}}$$

(a) For there to be four distinct real roots, both $4 - k$ and $2 \pm \sqrt{4 - k}$ must be positive.
This occurs when $0 < k < 4$.. Thus, some possible k-values are $k = 1$, $k = 2$, $k = 3$, $k = \frac{1}{2}$, $k = \sqrt{2}$, etc.

(b) For there to be two real roots, each of multiplicity 2, $4 - k$ must equal zero. Thus, $k = 4$.

(c) For there to be two real zeros and two complex zeros, $2 + \sqrt{4 - k}$ must be positive and $2 - \sqrt{4 - k}$ must be negative.
This occurs when $k < 0$. Thus, some possible k-values are $k = -1$, $k = -2$, $k = -\frac{1}{2}$, etc.

(d) For there to be four complex zeros, $2 \pm \sqrt{4 - k}$ must be nonreal. This occurs when $k > 4$.
Some possible k-values are $k = 5$, $k = 6$, $k = 7.4$, etc.

125. (a) $f(x) = \left(x - \sqrt{b}i\right)\left(x + \sqrt{b}i\right) = x^2 + b$

(b) $f(x) = [x - (a + bi)][x - (a - bi)]$

$= [(x - a) - bi][(x - a) + bi]$

$= (x - a)^2 - (bi)^2$

$= x^2 - 2ax + a^2 + b^2$

127. $(-3 + 6i) - (8 - 3i) = -3 + 6i - 8 + 3i = -11 + 9i$

129. $(6 - 2i)(1 + 7i) = 6 + 42i - 2i - 14i^2 = 20 + 40i$

131. $\dfrac{1 + i}{1 - i} = \dfrac{1 + i}{1 - i} \cdot \dfrac{1 + i}{1 + i} = \dfrac{1 + 2i + i^2}{1 + 1} = \dfrac{2i}{2} = i$

133. $g(x) = f(x - 2)$

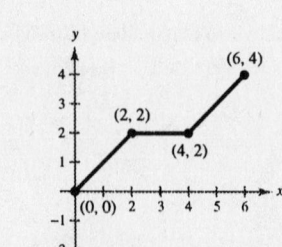

Horizontal shift two units to the right

135. $g(x) = 2f(x)$

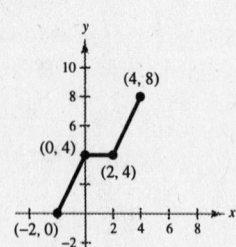

Vertical stretch

137. $g(x) = f(2x)$

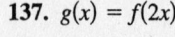
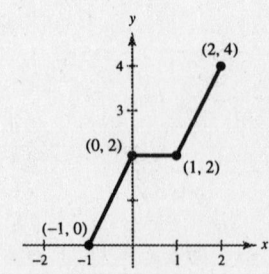

Horizontal shrink

Section 2.6   Rational Functions

■ You should know the following basic facts about rational functions.

(a) A function of the form $f(x) = N(x)/D(x)$, $D(x) \neq 0$, where $N(x)$ and $D(x)$ are polynomials, is called a rational function.

(b) The domain of a rational function is the set of all real numbers except those which make the denominator zero.

(c) If $f(x) = N(x)/D(x)$ is in reduced form, and a is a value such that $D(a) = 0$, then the line $x = a$ is a vertical asymptote of the graph of f. $f(x) \to \infty$ or $f(x) \to -\infty$ as $x \to a$.

(d) The line $y = b$ is a horizontal asymptote of the graph of f if $f(x) \to b$ as $x \to \infty$ or $x \to -\infty$.

(e) Let $f(x) = \dfrac{N(x)}{D(x)} = \dfrac{a_n x^n + a_{n-1} x^{n-1} + \cdots + a_1 x + a_0}{b_m x^m + b_{m-1} x^{m-1} + \cdots + b_1 x + b_0}$ where $N(x)$ and $D(x)$ have no common factors.

1. If $n < m$, then the x-axis $(y = 0)$ is a horizontal asymptote.

2. If $n = m$, then $y = \dfrac{a_n}{b_m}$ is a horizontal asymptote.

3. If $n > m$, then there are no horizontal asymptotes.

■ You should be able to graph $f(x) = \dfrac{N(x)}{D(x)}$ where $N(x)$ and $D(x)$ are polynomials with no common factors.

(a) Find the x-and y-intercepts.

(b) Find any vertical or horizontal asymptotes.

(c) Plot additional points.

(d) If the degree of the numerator is one more than the degree of the denominator, use long division to find the slant asymptote.

Solutions to Odd-Numbered Exercises

1. $f(x) = \dfrac{1}{x - 1}$

(a)

x	$f(x)$	x	$f(x)$	x	$f(x)$
0.5	-2	1.5	2	5	0.25
0.9	-10	1.1	10	10	$0.\overline{1}$
0.99	-100	1.01	100	100	$0.\overline{01}$
0.999	-1000	1.001	1000	1000	$0.\overline{001}$

(b) The zero of the denominator is $x = 1$, so $x = 1$ is a vertical asymptote. The degree of the numerator is less than the degree of the denominator so the x-axis, or $y = 0$, is a horizontal asymptote.

(c) The domain is all real numbers except $x = 1$.

3. $f(x) = \dfrac{4x}{|x-1|}$

(a)

x	$f(x)$
0.5	4
0.9	36
0.99	396
0.999	3996

x	$f(x)$
1.5	12
1.1	44
1.01	404
1.001	4004

x	$f(x)$
5	5
10	$4.\overline{44}$
100	$4.\overline{04}$
1000	$4.\overline{004}$

(b) The zero of the denominator is $x = 1$, so $x = 1$ is a vertical asymptote. Since $f(x) \rightarrow 4$ as $x \rightarrow \infty$ and $f(x) \rightarrow -4$ as $x \rightarrow -\infty$, both $y = 4$ and $y = -4$ are horizontal asymptotes.

(c) The domain is all real numbers except $x = 1$.

5. $f(x) = \dfrac{3x^2}{x^2 - 1}$

(a)

x	$f(x)$
0.5	-1
0.9	-12.79
0.99	-147.8
0.999	-1498

x	$f(x)$
1.5	5.4
1.1	17.29
1.01	152.3
1.001	1502

x	$f(x)$
5	3.125
10	$3.\overline{03}$
100	$3.\overline{0003}$
1000	3

(b) The zeros of the denominator are $x = \pm 1$ so both $x = 1$ and $x = -1$ are vertical asymptotes. Since the degree of the numerator equals the degree of the denominator, $y = \frac{3}{1} = 3$ is a horizontal asymptote.

(c) The domain is all real numbers except $x = \pm 1$.

7. $f(x) = \dfrac{1}{x^2}$

Domain: all real numbers except $x = 0$

Vertical asymptote: $x = 0$

Horizontal asymptote: $y = 0$

[Degree of $N(x) <$ degree of $D(x)$]

9. $f(x) = \dfrac{2 + x}{2 - x} = \dfrac{x + 2}{-x + 2}$

Domain: all real numbers except $x = 2$

Vertical asymptote: $x = 2$

Horizontal asymptote: $y = -1$

[Degree of $N(x) =$ degree of $D(x)$]

11. $f(x) = \dfrac{x^3}{x^2 - 1}$

Domain: all real numbers except $x = \pm 1$

Vertical asymptotes: $x = \pm 1$

Horizontal asymptote: None

[Degree of $N(x) >$ degree of $D(x)$]

13. $f(x) = \dfrac{3x^2 + 1}{x^2 + x + 9}$

Domain: All real numbers. The denominator has no real zeros. [Try the Quadratic Formula on the denominator.]

Vertical asymptote: None

Horizontal asymptote: $y = 3$

[Degree of $N(x) =$ degree of $D(x)$]

15. $f(x) = \dfrac{2}{x + 3}$

Vertical asymptote: $y = -3$

Matches graph (d).

17. $f(x) = \dfrac{3x + 1}{x}$

Horizontal asymptote: $y = 3$

Matches graph (f).

19. $f(x) = \dfrac{x - 1}{x - 4}$

Vertical asymptote: $x = 4$

Horizontal asymptote: $y = 1$

Matches graph (e).

21. $g(x) - \dfrac{x^2 - 1}{x + 1} = \dfrac{(x - 1)(x + 1)}{x + 1}$

The only zero of $g(x)$ is $x = 1$.

$x = -1$ makes $g(x)$ undefined.

23. $f(x) = 1 - \dfrac{3}{x - 3}$

$$1 - \dfrac{3}{x - 3} = 0$$

$$1 = \dfrac{3}{x - 3}$$

$$x - 3 = 3$$

$$x = 6 \text{ is a zero of } f(x).$$

25. $f(x) = \dfrac{1}{x + 2}$

(a) y-intercept: $\left(0, \tfrac{1}{2}\right)$

(b) Vertical asymptote: $x = -2$
Horizontal asymptote: $y = 0$

(c) No origin or axis symmetry

(d)

x	-4	-3	-1	0	1
y	$-\tfrac{1}{2}$	-1	1	$\tfrac{1}{2}$	$\tfrac{1}{3}$

(e)

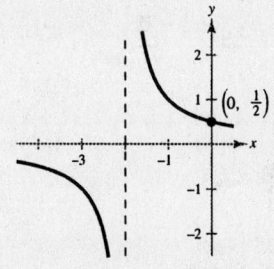

27. $h(x) = \dfrac{-1}{x + 2}$

(a) y-intercept: $\left(0, -\tfrac{1}{2}\right)$

(b) Vertical asymptote: $x = -2$

Horizontal asymptote: $y = 0$

(c) No origin or axis symmetry

(d)

x	-4	-3	-1	0
y	$-\tfrac{1}{2}$	1	-1	$\tfrac{1}{2}$

(e)

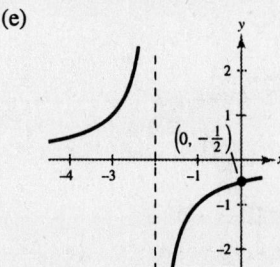

Note: This is the graph of $f(x) = \dfrac{1}{x + 2}$

(Exercise 25) reflected about the x-axis.

29. $C(x) = \dfrac{5 + 2x}{1 + x} = \dfrac{2x + 5}{x + 1}$

(a) x-intercept: $\left(-\frac{5}{2}, 0\right)$

y-intercept: $(0, 5)$

(b) Vertical asymptote: $x = -1$

Horizontal asymptote: $y = 2$

(c) No origin or axis symmetry

(d)

x	-4	-3	-2	0	1	2
$C(x)$	1	$\frac{1}{2}$	-1	5	$\frac{7}{2}$	3

(e)

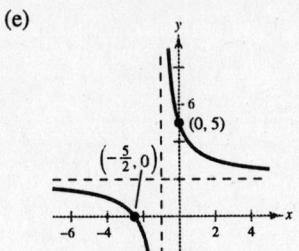

31. $g(x) = \dfrac{1}{x + 2} + 2 = \dfrac{2x + 5}{x + 2}$

(a) x-intercept: $\left(-\frac{5}{2}, 0\right)$

y-intercept: $\left(0, \frac{5}{2}\right)$

(b) Vertical asymptote: $x = -2$

Horizontal asymptote: $y = 2$

(c) No origin or axis symmetry

(d)

x	-4	-3	-1	0	1
y	$\frac{3}{2}$	1	3	$\frac{5}{2}$	$\frac{7}{3}$

(e)

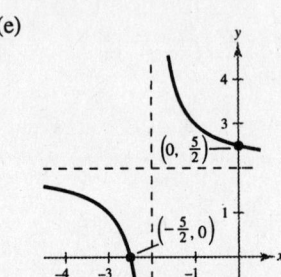

Note: This is the graph of $f(x) = \dfrac{1}{x + 2}$
(Exercise 25) shifted upward two units.

33. $f(x) = \dfrac{x^2}{x^2 + 9}$

(a) Intercept: $(0, 0)$

(b) Horizontal asymptote: $y = 1$

(c) y-axis symmetry

(d)

x	± 1	± 2	± 3
y	$\frac{1}{10}$	$\frac{4}{13}$	$\frac{1}{2}$

(e)

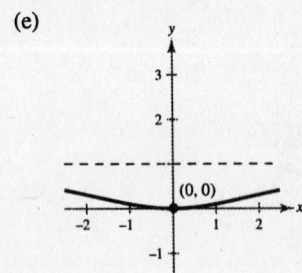

35. $h(x) = \dfrac{x^2}{x^2 - 9}$

(a) Intercept: $(0, 0)$

(b) Vertical asymptotes: $x = \pm 3$

Horizontal asymptote: $y = 1$

(c) y-axis symmetry

(d)

x	± 5	± 4	± 2	± 1	0
y	$\frac{25}{16}$	$\frac{16}{7}$	$-\frac{4}{5}$	$-\frac{1}{8}$	0

(e)

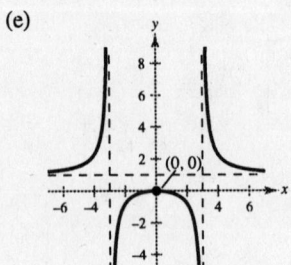

37. $g(s) = \dfrac{s}{s^2 + 1}$

(a) Intercept: $(0, 0)$

(b) Horizontal asymptote: $y = 0$

(c) Origin symmetry

(d)

s	-2	-1	0	1	2
$g(s)$	$-\frac{2}{5}$	$-\frac{1}{2}$	0	$\frac{1}{2}$	$\frac{2}{5}$

(e)

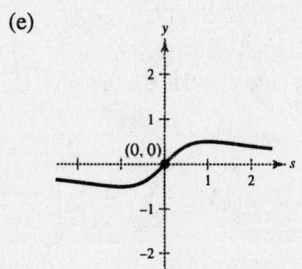

39. $g(x) = \dfrac{4(x + 1)}{x(x - 4)}$

(a) Intercept: $(-1, 0)$

(b) Vertical asymptotes: $x = 0$ and $x = 4$

Horizontal asymptote: $y = 0$

(c) No origin or axis symmetry

(d)

x	-2	-1	1	2	3	5	6
y	$-\frac{1}{3}$	0	$-\frac{8}{3}$	-3	$-\frac{16}{3}$	$\frac{24}{5}$	$\frac{7}{3}$

(e)

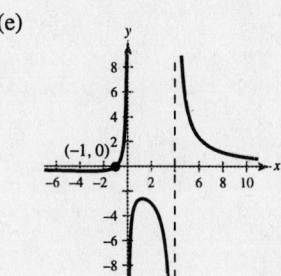

41. $f(x) = \dfrac{3x}{x^2 - x - 2} = \dfrac{3x}{(x + 1)(x - 2)}$

(a) Intercept: $(0, 0)$

(b) Vertical asymptotes: $x = -1$ and $x = 2$

Horizontal asymptote: $y = 0$

(c) No origin or axis symmetry

(d)

x	-3	0	1	3	4
y	$-\frac{9}{10}$	0	$-\frac{3}{2}$	$\frac{9}{4}$	$\frac{6}{5}$

(e)

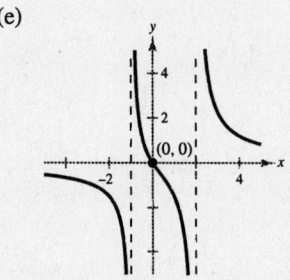

43. $f(x) = \dfrac{6x}{x^2 - 5x - 14} = \dfrac{6x}{(x + 2)(x - 7)}$

(a) Intercept: $(0, 0)$

(b) Vertical asymptotes: $x = -2$, and $x = 7$

Horizontal asymptotes: $y = 0$

(c) No origin or axis symmetry

(d)

x	-6	-4	0	2	4	6	8	10
$f(x)$	$-\frac{9}{13}$	$-\frac{12}{11}$	0	$-\frac{3}{5}$	$-\frac{4}{3}$	$-\frac{9}{2}$	$\frac{24}{5}$	$\frac{5}{3}$

(e)

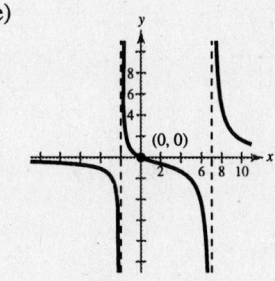

45. $f(x) = \dfrac{x^2 - 1}{x + 1}$, $g(x) = x - 1$

(a) Domain of f: all real numbers except -1

   Domain of g: all real numbers

(b) Because $(x + 1)$ is a factor of both the numerator and the denominator of f, $x = -1$ is not a vertical asymptote. f has no vertical asymptotes.

(c)

x	-3	-2	-1.5	-1	-0.5	0	1
$f(x)$	-4	-3	-2.5	Undef.	-1.5	-1	0
$g(x)$	-4	-3	-2.5	-2	-1.5	-1	0

(d)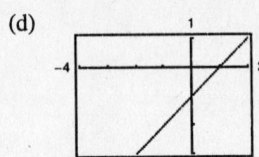

(e) Because there are only a finite number of pixels, the utility may not attempt to evaluate the function where it does not exist.

47. $f(x) = \dfrac{x - 2}{x^2 - 2x}$, $g(x) = \dfrac{1}{x}$

(a) Domain of f: all real numbers except 0 and 2

   Domain of g: all real numbers except 0

(b) Because $(x - 2)$ is a factor of both the numerator and the denominator of f, $x = 2$ is not a vertical asymptote. The only vertical asymptote of f is $x = 0$.

(c)

x	-0.5	0	0.5	1	1.5	2	3
$f(x)$	-2	Undef.	2	1	$\frac{2}{3}$	Undef.	$\frac{1}{3}$
$g(x)$	-2	Undef.	2	1	$\frac{2}{3}$	$\frac{1}{2}$	$\frac{1}{3}$

(d)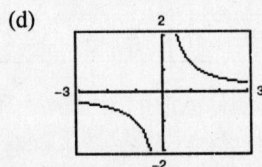

(e) Because there are only a finite number of pixels, the utility may not attempt to evaluate the function where it does not exist.

49. $h(t) = \dfrac{4}{t^2 + 1}$

Domain: all real numbers

Horizontal asymptote: $y = 0$

y-axis symmetry

t	± 2	± 1	0
$h(t)$	$\frac{4}{5}$	2	4

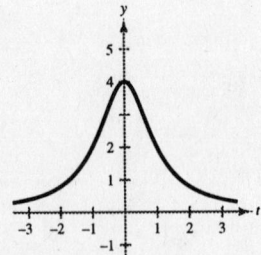

51. $f(t) = \dfrac{2t^2}{t^2 - 4}$

Domain: all real numbers except ± 2,

Vertical asymptotes: $t = \pm 2$

Horizontal asymptote: $y = 2$

y-axis symmetry

t	± 4	± 3	± 1	0
$f(t)$	$\frac{8}{3}$	$\frac{18}{5}$	$-\frac{2}{3}$	0

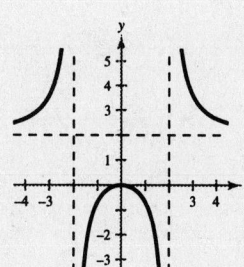

53. $f(x) = \dfrac{20x}{x^2 + 1} - \dfrac{1}{x} = \dfrac{19x^2 - 1}{x(x^2 + 1)}$

Domain: all real numbers except 0,

Vertical asymptote: $x = 0$

Horizontal asymptote: $y = 0$

Origin symmetry

x	-2	-1	1	2
y	$-\frac{15}{2}$	-9	9	$\frac{15}{2}$

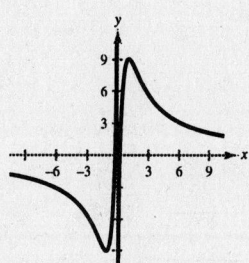

55. $f(x) = \dfrac{2x^2 + 1}{x} = 2x + \dfrac{1}{x}$

(a) No intercepts

(b) Vertical asymptote: $x = 0$
Slant asymptote: $y = 2x$

(c) Origin symmetry

(d)

x	-4	-2	2	4	6
$f(x)$	$-\frac{33}{4}$	$-\frac{9}{2}$	$\frac{9}{2}$	$\frac{33}{4}$	$\frac{73}{6}$

(e)

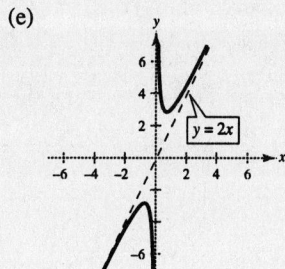

57. $g(x) = \dfrac{x^2 + 1}{x} = x + \dfrac{1}{x}$

(a) No intercepts

(b) Vertical asymptote: $x = 0$
Slant asymptote: $y = x$

(c) Origin symmetry

(d)

x	-4	-2	2	4	6
$g(x)$	$-\frac{17}{4}$	$-\frac{5}{2}$	$\frac{5}{2}$	$\frac{17}{4}$	$\frac{37}{6}$

(e)

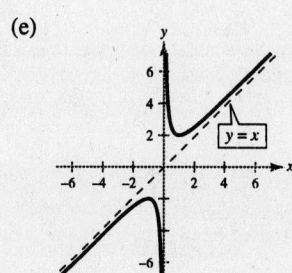

59. $f(x) = \dfrac{x^3}{x^2 - 1} = x + \dfrac{x}{x^2 - 1}$

(a) Intercept: $(0, 0)$

(b) Vertical asymptotes: $x = \pm 1$
Slant asymptote: $y = x$

(c) Origin symmetry

(d)

x	-4	-2	0	2	4
$f(x)$	$-\frac{64}{15}$	$-\frac{8}{3}$	0	$\frac{8}{3}$	$\frac{64}{15}$

(e)

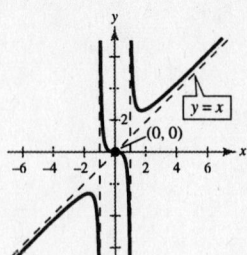

61. $f(x) = \dfrac{x^2 - x + 1}{x - 1} = x + \dfrac{1}{x - 1}$

(a) y-intercept: $(0, -1)$

(b) Vertical asymptote: $x = 1$
Slant asymptote: $y = x$

(c) No axis or origin symmetry

(d)

x	-4	-2	0	2	4
$f(x)$	$-\frac{21}{5}$	$-\frac{7}{3}$	-1	3	$\frac{13}{3}$

(e)

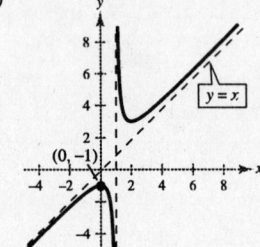

63. $f(x) = \dfrac{x^2 + 5x + 8}{x + 3} = x + 2 + \dfrac{2}{x + 3}$

Domain: all real numbers except -3

y-intercept: $\left(0, \frac{8}{3}\right)$

Vertical asymptote: $x = -3$

Slant asymptote: $y = x + 2$

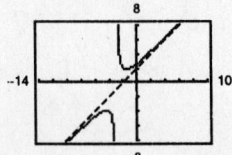

65. $g(x) = \dfrac{1 + 3x^2 - x^3}{x^2} = \dfrac{1}{x^2} + 3 - x = -x + 3 + \dfrac{1}{x^2}$

Domain: all real numbers except 0

Vertical asymptote: $x = 0$

Slant asymptote: $y = -x + 3$

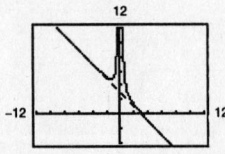

67. (a) x-intercept: $(-1, 0)$

(b) $\quad 0 = \dfrac{x + 1}{x - 3}$

$\quad 0 = x + 1$

$\quad -1 = x$

69. (a) x-intercepts: $(\pm 1, 0)$

(b) $\quad 0 = \dfrac{1}{x} - x$

$\quad x = \dfrac{1}{x}$

$\quad x^2 = 1$

$\quad x = \pm 1$

71. $C = \dfrac{255p}{100 - p}$, $0 \le p < 100$

    (a) $C(10) = \dfrac{255(10)}{100 - 10} \approx 28.33$ million dollars

    (b) $C(40) = \dfrac{255(40)}{100 - 40} = 170$ million dollars

    (c) $C(75) = \dfrac{255(75)}{100 - 75} = 765$ million dollars

    (d) $C \rightarrow \infty$ as $x \rightarrow 100$. No, it would not be possible to remove 100% of the pollutants.

73. $N = \dfrac{20(5 + 3t)}{1 + 0.04t}$, $0 \le t$

    (a) $N(5) \approx 333$ deer

        $N(10) = 500$ deer

        $N(25) = 800$ deer

    (b) The herd is limited by the horizontal asymptote: $N = \dfrac{60}{0.04} = 1500$ deer

75.

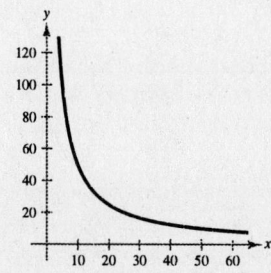

    (a) $xy = 500$

        $y = \dfrac{500}{x}$

    (b) Domain: $x > 0$ or $(0, \infty)$

    (c) When $x = 30$ m, $y = \dfrac{500}{30} = 16\dfrac{2}{3}$ m.

77. $C = \dfrac{3t^2 + t}{t^3 + 50}$, $0 > t$

    (a) Since the degree of $N(x) <$ degree of $D(x)$, the horizontal asymptote is $C = 0$. The chemical will eventually dissipate.

    (b)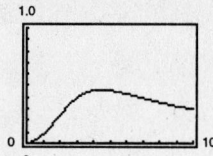

        C is maximum when $t \approx 4.5$ hours

79. False. Polynomials do not have vertical asymptotes.

81. Vertical asymptotes: $x = -2, x = 1$

The denominator is zero when $x = -2$ and $x = 1$, so $(x + 2)$ and $(x - 1)$ are factors of the denominator.

One possibility: $f(x) = \dfrac{1}{(x + 2)(x - 1)} = \dfrac{1}{x^2 + x - 2}$
(Answers may vary).

83. Vertical asymptotes: None

Horizontal asymptote: $y = 2$

Since there are no vertical asymptotes, the denominator is never zero (if it is reduced),

and since there is a horizontal asymptote, the degree of the numerator equals the

degree of the denominator. Also, $\dfrac{a_n}{b_n} = 2$.

One possibility: $f(x) = \dfrac{2x^2}{x^2 + 1}$ (Answers may vary).

85. Domain: All real numbers

One possibility: $f(x) = \dfrac{1}{x^2 + 2}$

Domain: All real numbers except $x = 20$.

One possibility: $f(x) = \dfrac{1}{x - 20}$

(Answers are not unique).

87. Vertical asymptote: $x = 2$

Slant asymptote: $y = x + 1$

Zero of the function: $x = -2$

Let $f(x) = \underbrace{x + 1}_{\substack{\text{Slant} \\ \text{asymptote}}} + \underbrace{\dfrac{k}{x - 2}}_{\substack{\text{Vertical} \\ \text{asymptote}}}$

Since $f(-2) = 0$, we have $-2 + 1 + \dfrac{k}{-2 - 2} = 0$

$$-1 - \dfrac{k}{4} = 0$$

$$-\dfrac{k}{4} = 1$$

$$k = -4$$

Thus, $f(x) = x + 1 - \dfrac{4}{x - 2}$

$$= \dfrac{(x + 1)(x - 2) - 4}{x - 2}$$

$$= \dfrac{x^2 - x - 6}{x - 2}$$

89. $g(x) = \dfrac{x^2 + x - 2}{x - 1} = \dfrac{(x + 2)(x - 1)}{x - 1}$

Since $N(x)/D(x)$ is not reduced, and $x - 1$ is a factor of both $N(x)$ and $D(x)$, $x = 1$ is **not** a vertical asymptote.

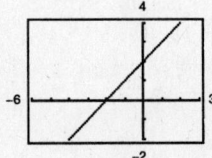

91. $3x^2 + 23x - 36 = (3x - 4)(x + 9)$

93 $x^3 + 6x^2 - 2x - 12 = x^2(x + 6) - 2(x + 6)$

$$= (x + 6)(x^2 - 2)$$

$$= (x + 6)(x + \sqrt{2})(x - \sqrt{2})$$

95. $5 - 2x > 5(x + 1)$

$5 - 2x > 5x + 5$

$-7x > 0$

$x < 0$

97. $\frac{1}{2}|2x + 3| \geq 5$

$|2x + 3| \geq 10$

$2x + 3 \leq -10$ or $2x + 3 \geq 10$

$2x \leq -13$ $\qquad$ $2x \geq 7$

$x \leq -\frac{13}{2}$ $\qquad$ $x \geq \frac{7}{2}$

Section 2.7   Partial Fractions

■   You should know how to decompose a rational function $\dfrac{N(x)}{D(x)}$ into partial fractions.

(a) If the fraction is improper, divide to obtain

$$\frac{N(x)}{D(x)} = p(x) + \frac{N_1(x)}{D(x)}$$

where $p(x)$ is a polynomial.

(b) Factor the denominator completely into linear and irreducible (over the reals) quadratic factors.

(c) For each factor of the form $(px + q)^m$, the partial fraction decomposition includes the terms

$$\frac{A_1}{(px + q)} + \frac{A_2}{(px + q)^2} + \cdots + \frac{A_m}{(px + q)^m}.$$

(d) For each factor of the form $(ax^2 + bx + c)^n$, the partial fraction decomposition includes the terms

$$\frac{B_1x + C_1}{ax^2 + bx + c} + \frac{B_2x + C_2}{(ax^2 + bx + c)^2} + \cdots + \frac{B_nx + C_n}{(ax^2 + bx + c)^n}.$$

■   You should know how to determine the values of the constants in the numerators.

(a) Set $\dfrac{N_1(x)}{D(x)} = $ partial fraction decomposition.

(b) Multiply both sides by $D(x)$ to obtain the basic equation.

(c) For distinct linear factors, substitute the zeros of the distinct linear factors into the basic equation.

(d) For repeated linear factors, use the coefficients found in part (c) to rewrite the basic equation. Then use other values of x to solve for the remaining coefficients.

(e) For quadratic factors, expand the basic equation, collect like terms, and then equate the coefficients of like terms.

Solutions to Odd-Numbered Exercises

1. $\dfrac{3x - 1}{x(x - 4)} = \dfrac{A}{x} + \dfrac{B}{x - 4}$

Matches (b).

3. $\dfrac{3x - 1}{x(x^2 + 4)} = \dfrac{A}{x} + \dfrac{Bx + C}{x^2 + 4}$

Matches (d)

5. $\dfrac{7}{x^2 - 14x} = \dfrac{7}{x(x - 14)} = \dfrac{A}{x} + \dfrac{B}{x - 14}$

7. $\dfrac{12}{x^3 - 10x^2} = \dfrac{12}{x^2(x - 10)} = \dfrac{A}{x} + \dfrac{B}{x^2} + \dfrac{C}{x - 10}$

9. $\dfrac{4x^2 + 3}{(x - 5)^3} = \dfrac{A}{x - 5} + \dfrac{B}{(x - 5)^2} + \dfrac{C}{(x - 5)^3}$

11. $\dfrac{2x - 3}{x^3 + 10x} = \dfrac{2x - 3}{x(x^2 + 10)} = \dfrac{A}{x} + \dfrac{Bx + C}{x^2 + 10}$

13. $\dfrac{x - 1}{x(x^2 + 1)^2} = \dfrac{A}{x} + \dfrac{Bx + C}{x^2 + 1} + \dfrac{Dx + E}{(x^2 + 1)^2}$

15. $\dfrac{1}{x^2 - 1} = \dfrac{A}{x + 1} + \dfrac{B}{x - 1}$

   $1 = A(x - 1) + B(x + 1)$

   Let $x = -1$: $1 = -2A \implies A = -\dfrac{1}{2}$

   Let $x = 1$: $1 = 2B \implies B = \dfrac{1}{2}$

   $\dfrac{1}{x^2 - 1} = \dfrac{\frac{1}{2}}{x - 1} - \dfrac{\frac{1}{2}}{x + 1} = \dfrac{1}{2}\left(\dfrac{1}{x - 1} - \dfrac{1}{x + 1}\right)$

17. $\dfrac{1}{x^2 + x} = \dfrac{A}{x} + \dfrac{B}{x + 1}$

   $1 = A(x + 1) + Bx$

   Let $x = 0$: $1 = A$

   Let $x = -1$: $1 = -B \implies B = -1$

   $\dfrac{1}{x^2 + x} = \dfrac{1}{x} - \dfrac{1}{x + 1}$

19. $\dfrac{1}{2x^2 + x} = \dfrac{A}{2x + 1} + \dfrac{B}{x}$

   $1 = Ax + B(2x + 1)$

   Let $x = -\dfrac{1}{2}$: $1 = -\dfrac{1}{2}A \implies A = -2$

   Let $x = 0$: $1 = B$

   $\dfrac{1}{2x^2 + x} = \dfrac{1}{x} - \dfrac{2}{2x + 1}$

21. $\dfrac{3}{x^2 + x - 2} = \dfrac{A}{x - 1} + \dfrac{B}{x + 2}$

   $3 = A(x + 2) + B(x - 1)$

   Let $x = 1$: $3 = 3A \implies A = 1$

   Let $x = -2$: $3 = -3B \implies B = -1$

   $\dfrac{3}{x^2 + x - 2} = \dfrac{1}{x - 1} - \dfrac{1}{x + 2}$

23. $\dfrac{x^2 + 12x + 12}{x^3 - 4x} = \dfrac{A}{x} + \dfrac{B}{x + 2} + \dfrac{C}{x - 2}$

   $x^2 + 12x + 12 = A(x + 2)(x - 2) + Bx(x - 2) + Cx(x + 2)$

   Let $x = 0$: $12 = -4A \implies A = -3$

   Let $x = -2$: $-8 = 8B \implies B = -1$

   Let $x = 2$: $40 = 8C \implies C = 5$

   $\dfrac{x^2 + 12x + 12}{x^3 - 4x} = -\dfrac{3}{x} - \dfrac{1}{x + 2} + \dfrac{5}{x - 2}$

25. $\dfrac{4x^2 + 2x - 1}{x^2(x + 1)} = \dfrac{A}{x} + \dfrac{B}{x^2} + \dfrac{C}{x + 1}$

$4x^2 + 2x - 1 = Ax(x + 1) + B(x + 1) + Cx^2$

Let $x = 0$: $-1 = B$

Let $x = -1$: $1 = C$

Let $x = 1$: $\quad 5 = 2A + 2B + C$

$\qquad\qquad 5 = 2A - 2 + 1$

$\qquad\qquad 6 = 2A$

$\qquad\qquad 3 = A$

$\dfrac{4x^2 + 2x - 1}{x^2(x + 1)} = \dfrac{3}{x} - \dfrac{1}{x^2} + \dfrac{1}{x + 1}$

27. $\dfrac{3x}{(x - 3)^2} = \dfrac{A}{x - 3} + \dfrac{B}{(x - 3)^2}$

$3x = A(x - 3) + B$

Let $\quad x = 3$: $9 = B$

Let $\quad x = 0$: $0 = -3A + B$

$\qquad\qquad\quad 0 = -3A + 9$

$\qquad\qquad\quad 3 = A$

$\dfrac{3x}{(x - 3)^2} = \dfrac{3}{x - 3} + \dfrac{9}{(x - 3)^2}$

29. $\dfrac{x^2 - 1}{x(x^2 + 1)} = \dfrac{A}{x} + \dfrac{Bx + C}{x^2 + 1}$

$x^2 - 1 = A(x^2 + 1) + (Bx + C)x$

$\qquad\quad = Ax^2 + A + Bx^2 + Cx$

$\qquad\quad = (A + B)x^2 + Cx + A$

Equating coefficients of like terms gives

$1 = A + B, 0 = C,$ and $-1 = A.$

Therefore, $A = -1, B = 2,$ and $C = 0.$

$\dfrac{x^2 - 1}{x(x^2 + 1)} = -\dfrac{1}{x} + \dfrac{2x}{x^2 + 1}$

31. $\dfrac{x}{x^3 - x^2 - 2x + 2} = \dfrac{x}{(x - 1)(x^2 - 2)} = \dfrac{A}{x - 1} + \dfrac{Bx + C}{x^2 - 2}$

$x = A(x^2 - 2) + (Bx + C)(x - 1)$

$\quad = Ax^2 - 2A + Bx^2 - Bx + Cx - C$

$\quad = (A + B)x^2 + (C - B)x - (2A + C)$

Equating coefficients of like terms gives

$0 = A + B, 1 = C - B,$ and $0 = 2A + C.$

Therefore, $A = -1, B = 1,$ and $C = 2.$

$\dfrac{x}{x^3 - x^2 - 2x + 2} = \dfrac{-1}{x - 1} + \dfrac{x + 2}{x^2 - 2}$

33. $\dfrac{x^2}{x^4 - 2x^2 - 8} = \dfrac{x^2}{(x^2 - 4)(x^2 + 2)} = \dfrac{x^2}{(x + 2)(x - 2)(x^2 + 2)}$

$$= \frac{A}{x + 2} + \frac{B}{x - 2} + \frac{Cx + D}{x^2 + 2}$$

$$x^2 = A(x - 2)(x^2 + 2) + B(x + 2)(x^2 + 2) + (Cx + D)(x + 2)(x - 2)$$

$$= A(x^3 - 2x^2 + 2x - 4) + B(x^3 + 2x^2 + 2x + 4) + (Cx + D)(x^2 - 4)$$

$$= Ax^3 - 2Ax^2 + 2Ax - 4A + Bx^3 + 2Bx^2 + 2Bx + 4B + Cx^3 + Dx^2 - 4Cx - 4D$$

$$= (A + B + C)x^3 + (-2A + 2B + D)x^2 + (2A + 2B - 4C)x + (-4A + 4B - 4D)$$

Equating coefficients of like terms gives

$0 = A + B + C, 1 = -2A + 2B + D, 0 = 2A + 2B - 4C$, and $0 = -4A + 4B - 4D$

Using the first and third equation, we have $A + B + C = 0$ and $A + B - 2C = 0$;
by subtraction, $C = 0$.

Using the second and fourth equation, we have

$-2A + 2B + D = 1$ and $-2A + 2B - 2D = 0$; by subtraction, $3D = 1$,
so $D = \frac{1}{3}$. Substituting 0 for C and $\frac{1}{3}$ for D in the first and second equations, we have

$A + B = 0$ and $-2A + 2B = \frac{2}{3}$, so $A = -\frac{1}{6}$ and $B = \frac{1}{6}$.

$$\frac{x^2}{x^4 - 2x^2 - 8} = \frac{-\frac{1}{6}}{x + 2} + \frac{\frac{1}{6}}{x - 2} + \frac{\frac{1}{3}}{x^2 + 2}$$

$$= \frac{1}{3(x^2 + 2)} - \frac{1}{6(x + 2)} + \frac{1}{6(x - 2)}$$

35. $\dfrac{x}{16x^4 - 1} = \dfrac{x}{(4x^2 - 1)(4x^2 + 1)} = \dfrac{x}{(2x + 1)(2x - 1)(4x^2 + 1)}$

$$= \frac{A}{2x + 1} + \frac{B}{2x - 1} + \frac{Cx + D}{4x^2 + 1}$$

$$x = A(2x - 1)(4x^2 + 1) + B(2x + 1)(4x^2 + 1) + (Cx + D)(2x + 1)(2x - 1)$$

$$= A(8x^3 - 4x^2 + 2x - 1) + B(8x^3 + 4x^2 + 2x + 1) + (Cx + D)(4x^2 - 1)$$

$$= 8Ax^3 - 4Ax^2 + 2Ax - A + 8Bx^3 + 4Bx^2 + 2Bx + B + 4Cx^3 + 4Dx^2 - Cx - D$$

$$= (8A + 8B + 4C)x^3 + (-4A + 4B + 4D)x^2 + (2A + 2B - C)x + (-A + B - D)$$

Equating coefficients of like terms gives $0 = 8A + 8B + 4C, 0 = -4A + 4B + 4D, 1 = 2A + 2B - C$,
and $0 = -A + B - D$.

Using the first and third equations, we have $2A + 2B + C = 0$ and $2A + 2B - C = 1$;
by subtraction, $2C = -1$, so $C = -\frac{1}{2}$.

Using the second and fourth equations, we have $-A + B + D = 0$ and $-A + B - D = 0$;
by subtraction $2D = 0$, so $D = 0$.

Substituting $-\frac{1}{2}$ for C and 0 for D in the first and second equations,
we have $8A + 8B = 2$ and $-4A + 4B = 0$, so $A = \frac{1}{8}$ and $B = \frac{1}{8}$.

$$\frac{x}{16x^4 - 1} = \frac{\frac{1}{8}}{2x + 1} + \frac{\frac{1}{8}}{2x - 1} + \frac{\left(-\frac{1}{2}\right)x}{4x^2 + 1}$$

$$= \frac{1}{8(2x + 1)} + \frac{1}{8(2x - 1)} - \frac{x}{2(4x^2 + 1)}$$

37. $\dfrac{x^2 + 5}{(x + 1)(x^2 - 2x + 3)} = \dfrac{A}{x + 1} + \dfrac{Bx + C}{x^2 - 2x + 3}$

$$x^2 + 5 = A(x^2 - 2x + 3) + (Bx + C)(x + 1)$$
$$= Ax^2 - 2Ax + 3A + Bx^2 + Bx + Cx + C$$
$$= (A + B)x^2 + (-2A + B + C)x + (3A + C)$$

Equating coefficients of like terms gives

$1 = A + B, 0 = -2A + B + C,$ and $5 = 3A + C.$

Subtracting both sides of the second equation from the first gives $1 = 3A - C$; combining this with the third equation gives $A = 1$ and $C = 2$. Since $A + B = 1$, we also have $B = 0$.

$$\dfrac{x^2 + 5}{(x + 1)(x^2 - 2x + 3)} = \dfrac{1}{x + 1} + \dfrac{2}{x^2 - 2x + 3}$$

39. $\dfrac{x^2 - x}{x^2 + x + 1} = 1 + \dfrac{-2x - 1}{x^2 + x + 1} = 1 - \dfrac{2x + 1}{x^2 + x + 1}$

41. $\dfrac{2x^3 - x^2 + x + 5}{x^2 + 3x + 2} = 2x - 7 + \dfrac{18x + 19}{(x + 1)(x + 2)}$

$\dfrac{18x + 19}{(x + 1)(x + 2)} = \dfrac{A}{x + 1} + \dfrac{B}{x + 2}$

$18x + 19 = A(x + 2) + B(x + 1)$

Let $x = -1$: $1 = A$

Let $x = -2$: $-17 = -B \implies B = 17$

$\dfrac{2x^3 - x^2 + x + 5}{x^2 + 3x + 2} = 2x - 7 + \dfrac{1}{x + 1} + \dfrac{17}{x + 2}$

43. $\dfrac{x^4}{(x - 1)^3} = \dfrac{x^4}{x^3 - 3x^2 + 3x - 1} = x + 3 + \dfrac{6x^2 - 8x + 3}{(x - 1)^3}$

$\dfrac{6x^2 - 8x + 3}{(x - 1)^3} = \dfrac{A}{x - 1} + \dfrac{B}{(x - 1)^2} + \dfrac{C}{(x - 1)^3}$

$6x^2 - 8x + 3 = A(x - 1)^2 + B(x - 1) + C$

Let $x = 1$: $1 = C$

Let $x = 0$: $3 = A - B + 1$ $\quad\rbrace\quad A - B = 2$

Let $x = 2$: $11 = A + B + 1$ $\quad\rbrace\quad A + B = 10$

So, $A = 6$ and $B = 4$.

$\dfrac{x^4}{(x - 1)^3} = x + 3 + \dfrac{6}{x - 1} + \dfrac{4}{(x - 1)^2} + \dfrac{1}{(x - 1)^3}$

45. $\dfrac{5-x}{2x^2+x-1} = \dfrac{A}{2x-1} + \dfrac{B}{x+1}$

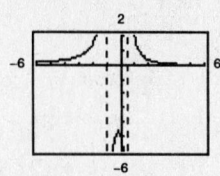

$$-x+5 = A(x+1) + B(2x-1)$$

Let $x = \dfrac{1}{2}$: $\dfrac{9}{2} = \dfrac{3}{2}A \implies A = 3$

Let $x = -1$: $6 = -3B \implies B = -2$

$$\dfrac{5-x}{2x^2+x-1} = \dfrac{3}{2x-1} - \dfrac{2}{x+1}$$

47. $\dfrac{x-1}{x^3+x^2} = \dfrac{A}{x} + \dfrac{B}{x^2} + \dfrac{C}{x+1}$

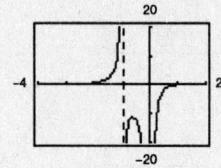

$$x-1 = Ax(x+1) + B(x+1) + Cx^2$$

Let $x = -1$: $-2 = C$

Let $x = 0$: $-1 = B$

Let $x = 1$: $0 = 2A + 2B + C$

$$0 = 2A - 2 - 2$$

$$2 = A$$

$$\dfrac{x-1}{x^3+x^2} = \dfrac{2}{x} - \dfrac{1}{x^2} - \dfrac{2}{x+1}$$

49. $\dfrac{x^2+x+2}{(x^2+2)^2} = \dfrac{Ax+B}{x^2+2} + \dfrac{Cx+D}{(x^2+2)^2}$

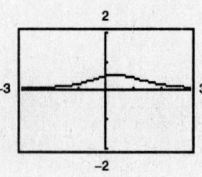

$$x^2+x+2 = (Ax+B)(x^2+2) + Cx + D$$

$$x^2+x+2 = Ax^3 + Bx^2 + (2A+C)x + (2B+D)$$

Equating coefficients of like powers:

$$0 = A$$

$$1 = B$$

$$1 = 2A + C \implies C = 1$$

$$2 = 2B + D \implies D = 0$$

$$\dfrac{x^2+x+2}{(x^2+2)^2} = \dfrac{1}{x^2+2} + \dfrac{x}{(x^2+2)^2}$$

51. $\dfrac{2x^3 - 4x^2 - 15x + 5}{x^2 - 2x - 8} = 2x + \dfrac{x+5}{(x+2)(x-4)}$

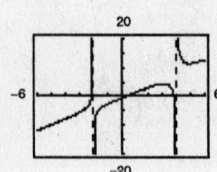

$$\dfrac{x+5}{(x+2)(x-4)} = \dfrac{A}{x+2} + \dfrac{B}{x-4}$$

$$x+5 = A(x-4) + B(x+2)$$

Let $x = -2$: $3 = -6A \implies A = -\dfrac{1}{2}$

Let $x = 4$: $9 = 6B \implies B = \dfrac{3}{2}$

$$\dfrac{2x^3 - 4x^2 - 15x + 5}{x^2 - 2x - 8} = 2x + \dfrac{1}{2}\left(\dfrac{3}{x-4} - \dfrac{1}{x+2}\right)$$

53. $\dfrac{x-12}{x(x-4)} = \dfrac{A}{x} + \dfrac{B}{x-4}$

$x - 12 = A(x - 4) + Bx$

Let $x = 0$: $-12 = -4A \implies A = 3$

Let $x = 4$: $-8 = 4B \implies B = -2$

$\dfrac{x-12}{x(x-4)} = \dfrac{3}{x} - \dfrac{2}{x-4}$

$y = \dfrac{x-12}{x(x-4)}$ 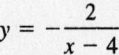 $y = \dfrac{3}{x}$ $y = -\dfrac{2}{x-4}$

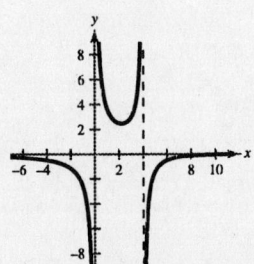 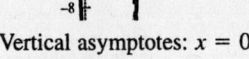 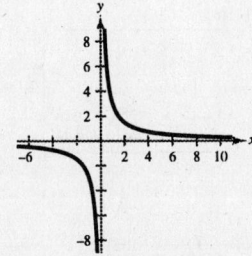 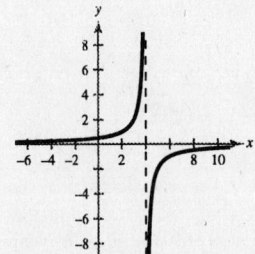

Vertical asymptotes: $x = 0$ Vertical asymptote: $x = 0$ Vertical asymptote: $x = 4$
and $x = 4$

The combination of the vertical asymptotes of the terms of the decomposition are
the same as the vertical asymptotes of the rational function.

55. $\dfrac{2(4x-3)}{x^2-9} = \dfrac{A}{x-3} + \dfrac{B}{x+3}$

$2(4x - 3) = A(x + 3) + B(x - 3)$

Let $x = 3$: $18 = 6A \implies A = 3$

Let $x = -3$: $-30 = -6B \implies B = 5$

$\dfrac{2(4x-3)}{x^2-9} = \dfrac{3}{x-3} + \dfrac{5}{x+3}$

$y = \dfrac{2(4x-3)}{x^2-9}$ $y = \dfrac{3}{x-3}$ $y = \dfrac{5}{x+3}$

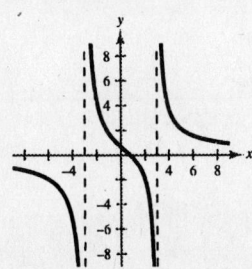 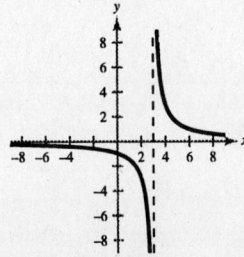 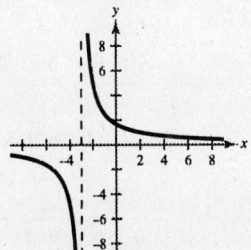

Vertical asymptotes: $x = \pm 3$ Vertical asymptote: $x = 3$ Vertical asymptote: $x = -3$

The combination of the vertical asymptotes of the terms of the decomposition are
the same as the vertical asymptotes of the rational function.

57. (a) $\dfrac{2000(4 - 3x)}{(11 - 7x)(7 - 4x)} = \dfrac{A}{11 - 7x} + \dfrac{B}{7 - 4x}, \ 0 < x \le 1$

$$2000(4 - 3x) = A(7 - 4x) + B(11 - 7x)$$

Let $x = \dfrac{11}{7}$: $\ -\dfrac{10{,}000}{7} = \dfrac{5}{7}A \ \Rightarrow \ A = -2000$

Let $x = \dfrac{7}{4}$: $\ -2500 = -\dfrac{5}{4}B \ \Rightarrow \ B = 2000$

$$\dfrac{2000(4 - 3x)}{(11 - 7x)(7 - 4x)} = \dfrac{-2000}{11 - 7x} + \dfrac{2000}{7 - 4x} = \dfrac{2000}{7 - 4x} - \dfrac{2000}{11 - 7x}, \ 0 < x \le 1$$

(b) $y_{max} = \left| \dfrac{2000}{7 - 4x} \right|$

$\quad\ y_{min} = \left| \dfrac{2000}{11 - 7x} \right|$

59. False. The expression is an improper rational expression, so you must first divide before applying partial fraction decomposition.

61. $\dfrac{1}{x(x + a)} = \dfrac{A}{x} + \dfrac{B}{x + a}, \ a$ is a constant.

$$1 = A(x + a) + Bx$$

Let $x = 0$: $1 = aA \ \Rightarrow \ A = \dfrac{1}{a}$

Let $x = -a$: $1 = -aB \ \Rightarrow \ B = -\dfrac{1}{a}$

$$\dfrac{1}{x(x + a)} = \dfrac{1}{a}\left(\dfrac{1}{x} - \dfrac{1}{x + a} \right)$$

63. $\dfrac{1}{(x + 1)(a - x)} = \dfrac{A}{x + 1} + \dfrac{B}{a - x}, \ a$ is a positive integer.

$$1 = A(a - x) + B(x + 1)$$

Let $x = -1$: $1 = A(a + 1) \ \Rightarrow \ A = \dfrac{1}{a + 1}$

Let $x = a$: $1 = B(a + 1) \ \Rightarrow \ B = \dfrac{1}{a + 1}$

$$\dfrac{1}{(x + 1)(a - x)} = \dfrac{1}{a + 1}\left(\dfrac{1}{x + 1} + \dfrac{1}{a - x} \right)$$

65. $f(x) = 6 - x$

Intercepts: $(0, 6)$ and $(6, 0)$

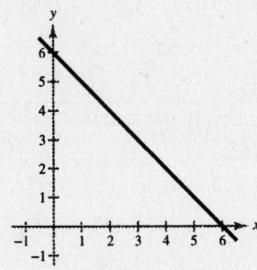

67. $f(x) = \frac{1}{4}x^2 + 1$

Vertex: $(0, 1)$

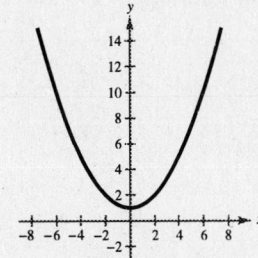

69. $f(x) = 2x^2 - 9x - 5 = (2x + 1)(x - 5)$

   $= 2\left(x - \frac{9}{4}\right)^2 - \frac{121}{8}$

Vertex: $\left(\frac{9}{4}, -\frac{121}{8}\right)$

x-intercepts: $\left(-\frac{1}{2}, 0\right), (5, 0)$

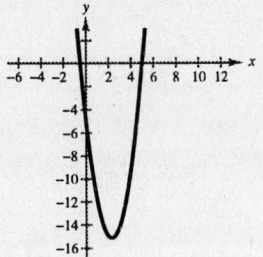

71. $f(x) = \frac{1}{2}x^3 - 1$

Intercepts: $(0, -1), \left(\sqrt[3]{2}, 0\right)$

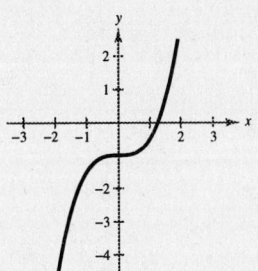

73. $f(x) = \dfrac{1 - 4x}{x} = \dfrac{-4x + 1}{x}$

x-intercept: $\left(\frac{1}{4}, 0\right)$

Vertical asymptote: $x = 0$

Horizontal asymptote: $y = -4$

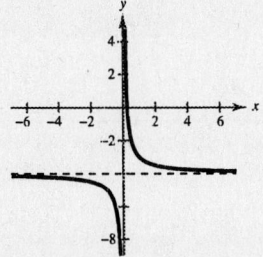

75. $f(x) = \dfrac{3x - 1}{x^2 + 4x - 12} = \dfrac{3x - 1}{(x + 6)(x - 2)}$

x-intercept: $\left(\frac{1}{3}, 0\right)$

Vertical asymptotes: $x = -6$ and $x = 2$

Horizontal asymptote: $y = 0$

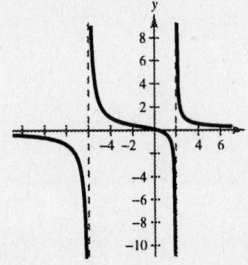

77. $f(x) = \dfrac{2x - 3}{x^2 - 16}$

x-intercept: $\left(\frac{3}{2}, 0\right)$

Vertical asymptotes: $x = -4$ and $x = 4$

Horizontal asymptote: $y = 0$

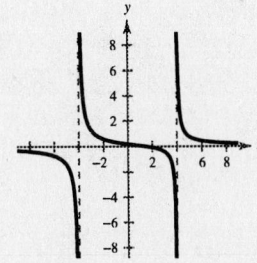

Review Exercises for Chapter 2

Solutions to Odd-Numbered Exercises

1. (a) $y = 2x^2$
Vertical stretch

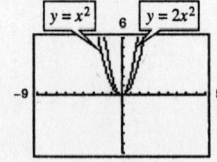

(b) $y = -2x^2$
Vertical stretch and a reflection in the x-axis

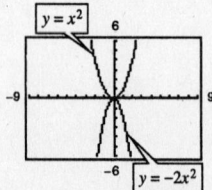

(c) $y = x^2 + 2$
Vertical shift two units upward

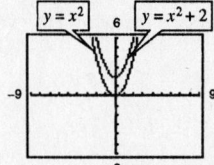

(d) $y = (x + 2)^2$
Horizontal shift two units to the left

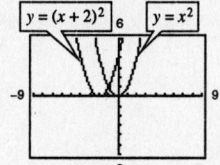

3. Vertex: $(4, 1)$ $\Rightarrow$ $f(x) = a(x - 4)^2 + 1$

Point: $(2, -1)$ $\Rightarrow$ $-1 = a(2 - 4)^2 + 1$

$-2 = 4a$

$-\frac{1}{2} = a$

Thus, $f(x) = -\frac{1}{2}(x - 4)^2 + 1$.

5. Vertex: $(1, -4)$ $\Rightarrow$ $f(x) = a(x - 1)^2 - 4$

Point: $(2, -3)$ $\Rightarrow$ $-3 = a(2 - 1)^2 - 4$

$1 = a$

Thus, $f(x) = (x - 1)^2 - 4$.

7. $g(x) = x^2 - 2x$

$= x^2 - 2x + 1 - 1$

$= (x - 1)^2 - 1$

Vertex: $(1, -1)$

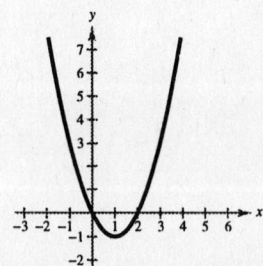

9. $f(x) = x^2 + 8x + 10$

$= x^2 + 8x + 16 - 16 + 10$

$= (x + 4)^2 - 6$

Vertex: $(-4, -6)$

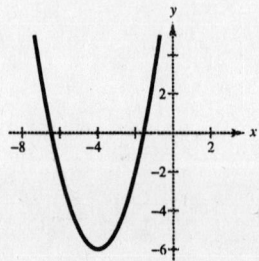

11. $f(t) = -2t^2 + 4t + 1$

$\qquad = -2(t^2 - 2t + 1 - 1) + 1$

$\qquad = -2[(t-1)^2 - 1] + 1$

$\qquad = -2(t-1)^2 + 3$

Vertex: $(1, 3)$

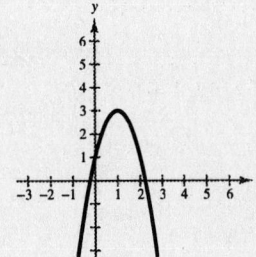

13. $h(x) = 4x^2 + 4x + 13$

$\qquad = 4(x^2 + x) + 13$

$\qquad = 4\left(x^2 + x + \frac{1}{4} - \frac{1}{4}\right) + 13$

$\qquad = 4\left(x^2 + x + \frac{1}{4}\right) - 1 + 13$

$\qquad = 4\left(x + \frac{1}{2}\right)^2 + 12$

Vertex: $\left(-\frac{1}{2}, 12\right)$

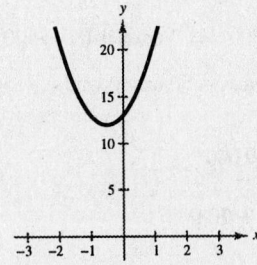

15. $h(x) = x^2 + 5x - 4$

$\qquad = x^2 + 5x + \frac{25}{4} - \frac{25}{4} - 4$

$\qquad = \left(x + \frac{5}{2}\right)^2 - \frac{25}{4} - \frac{16}{4}$

$\qquad = \left(x + \frac{5}{2}\right)^2 - \frac{41}{4}$

Vertex: $\left(-\frac{5}{2}, -\frac{41}{4}\right)$.

17. $f(x) = \frac{1}{3}(x^2 + 5x - 4)$

$\qquad = \frac{1}{3}\left(x^2 + 5x + \frac{25}{4} - \frac{25}{4} - 4\right)$

$\qquad = \frac{1}{3}\left[\left(x + \frac{5}{2}\right)^2 - \frac{41}{4}\right]$

$\qquad = \frac{1}{3}\left(x + \frac{5}{2}\right)^2 - \frac{41}{12}$

Vertex: $\left(-\frac{5}{2}, -\frac{41}{12}\right)$

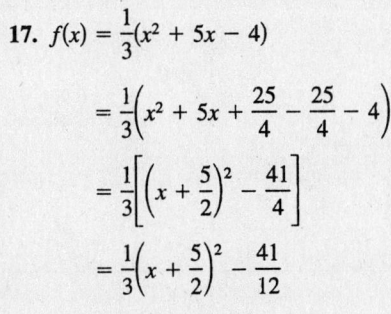

19. (a)

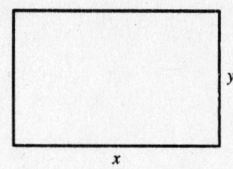

(b) $2x + 2y = 200$

$$y = \frac{200 - 2x}{2}$$

$$y = 100 - x$$

$$A = xy = x(100 - x)$$

$$= 100x - x^2$$

(c) $A = -x^2 + 100x$

$$= -(x^2 - 100x)$$

$$= -(x^2 - 100x + 2500 - 2500)$$

$$= -[(x - 50)^2 - 2500]$$

$$= -(x - 50)^2 + 2500 \implies \text{Vertex is } (50, 2500)$$

Area is maximum when $x = 50$ meters and $y = 50$ meters.

21. $C = 0.055x^2 - 120x + 20{,}000$

$$= 0.055\left(x^2 - \frac{24{,}000}{11}x\right) + 20{,}000$$

$$= 0.055\left(x^2 - \frac{24{,}000}{11}x + \frac{144{,}000{,}000}{121}\right)$$

$$-0.055\left(\frac{144{,}000{,}000}{121}\right) + 20{,}000 \approx \left(x - \frac{12{,}000}{11}\right)^2 - 45{,}454.55$$

C is minimum when $x = \dfrac{12{,}000}{11} \approx 1091$ units

23. $y = x^3$, $f(x) = -(x - 4)^3$

$f(x)$ is a reflection in the x-axis and a horizontal shift 4 units to the right of the graph of $y = x^3$.

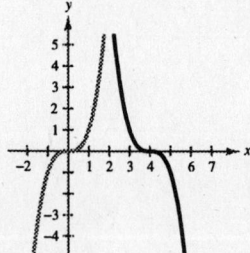

25. $y = x^4$, $f(x) = 2 - x^4$

$f(x)$ is a reflection in the x-axis and a vertical shift 2 units upward of the graph of $y = x^4$.

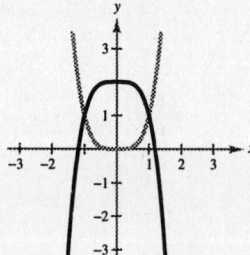

27. $y = x^5$, $f(x) = (x - 3)^5$

$f(x)$ is a horizontal shift 3 units to the right of the graph of $y = x^5$.

29. $f(x) = -x^2 + 6x + 9$

The degree is even and the leading coefficient is negative. The graph falls to the left and falls to the right.

31. $f(x) = \frac{3}{4}(x^4 + 3x^2 + 2)$

The degree is even and the leading coefficient is positive.
The graph rises to the left and rises to the right.

33. $f(x) = 2x^2 + 11x - 21 = 2\left(x + \frac{11}{4}\right)^2 - \frac{289}{8}$

Vertex: $(-2.75, -36.125)$

Zeros: $2x^2 + 11x - 21 = 0$

$$(2x - 3)(x + 7) = 0$$

$$2x - 3 = 0 \implies x = \frac{3}{2}$$

$$x + 7 = 0 \implies x = -7$$

The graph rises to the left and rises to the right.

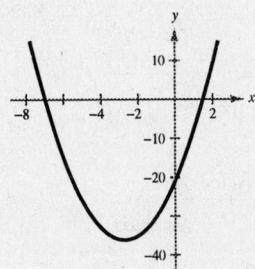

35. $f(t) = t^3 - 3t = t(t^2 - 3)$

Zeros: $x = 0, \pm\sqrt{3}$

The graph rises to the right and falls to the left.

x	-2	-1	0	1	2
y	-2	2	0	-2	2

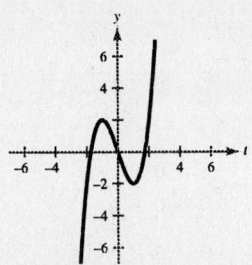

37. $f(x) = -12x^3 + 20x^2 = -4x^2(3x - 5)$

Zeros: $x = 0, \frac{5}{3}$

The graph rises to the left and falls to the right.

x	-2	-1	0	1	2
y	176	32	0	8	-16

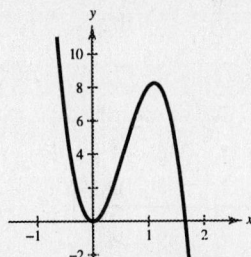

39. $f(x) = 3x^3 - x^2 + 3$

$f(-1) = -1 < 0$

$f(0) = 3 > 0$

$f(x)$ has a zero in the interval $(-1, 0)$.

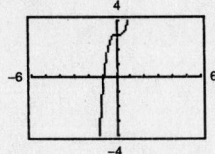

41. $f(x) = x^4 - 5x - 1$

$f(-1) = 5 > 0$

$f(0) = -1 < 0$

$f(1) = -5 < 0$

$f(2) = 5 > 0$

$f(x)$ has zeros in the intervals $(-1, 0)$ and $(1, 2)$.

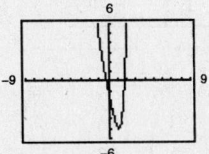

43.

$$
\begin{array}{r}
8x + 5 \\
3x - 2\overline{)24x^2 - x - 8} \\
\underline{24x^2 - 16x} \\
15x - 8 \\
\underline{15x - 10} \\
2
\end{array}
$$

Thus, $\dfrac{24x^2 - x - 8}{3x - 2} = 8x + 5 + \dfrac{2}{3x - 2}$.

45.

$$
\begin{array}{r}
5x + 2 \\
x^2 - 3x + 1\overline{)5x^3 - 13x^2 - x + 2} \\
\underline{5x^3 - 15x^2 + 5x} \\
2x^2 - 6x + 2 \\
\underline{2x^2 - 6x + 2} \\
0
\end{array}
$$

Thus, $\dfrac{5x^3 - 13x^2 - x + 2}{x^2 - 3x + 1} = 5x + 2$.

47.

$$
\begin{array}{r}
x^2 - 3x + 2 \\
x^2 + 0x + 2\overline{)x^4 - 3x^3 + 4x^2 - 6x + 3} \\
\underline{x^4 + 0x^3 + 2x^2} \\
-3x^3 + 2x^2 - 6x \\
\underline{-3x^3 + 0x^2 - 6x} \\
2x^2 + 0x + 3 \\
\underline{2x^2 + 0x + 4} \\
-1
\end{array}
$$

Thus,
$$\frac{x^4 - 3x^3 + 4x^2 - 6x + 3}{x^2 + 2} = x^2 - 3x + 2 - \frac{1}{x^2 + 2}.$$

49. $\dfrac{2}{3}\Big|\begin{array}{ccccc} 6 & -4 & -27 & 18 & 0 \\ & 4 & 0 & -18 & 0 \\ \hline 6 & 0 & -27 & 0 & 0 \end{array}$

Thus, $\dfrac{6x^4 - 4x^3 - 27x^2 + 18x}{x - \frac{2}{3}} = 6x^3 - 27x$

51. $4\Big|\begin{array}{cccc} 2 & -19 & 38 & 24 \\ & 8 & -44 & -24 \\ \hline 2 & -11 & -6 & 0 \end{array}$

Thus, $\dfrac{2x^3 - 19x^2 + 38x + 24}{x - 4} = 2x^2 - 11x - 6$

53. $f(x) = 20x^4 + 9x^3 - 14x^2 - 3x$

(a) $-1\Big|\begin{array}{ccccc} 20 & 9 & -14 & -3 & 0 \\ & -20 & 11 & 3 & 0 \\ \hline 20 & -11 & -3 & 0 & 0 \end{array}$

Yes, $x = -1$ is a zero of f.

(b) $\dfrac{3}{4}\Big|\begin{array}{ccccc} 20 & 9 & -14 & -3 & 0 \\ & 15 & 18 & 3 & 0 \\ \hline 20 & 24 & 4 & 0 & 0 \end{array}$

Yes, $x = \dfrac{3}{4}$ is a zero of f.

(c) $0\Big|\begin{array}{ccccc} 20 & 9 & -14 & -3 & 0 \\ & 0 & 0 & 0 & 0 \\ \hline 20 & 9 & -14 & -3 & 0 \end{array}$

Yes, $x = 0$ is a zero of f.

(d) $1\Big|\begin{array}{ccccc} 20 & 9 & -14 & -3 & 0 \\ & 20 & 29 & 15 & 12 \\ \hline 20 & 29 & 15 & 12 & 12 \end{array}$

No, $x = 1$ is not a zero of f.

55. $f(x) = x^4 + 10x^3 - 24x^2 + 20x + 44$

(a) $-3\Big|\begin{array}{ccccc} 1 & 10 & -24 & 20 & 44 \\ & -3 & -21 & 135 & -465 \\ \hline 1 & 7 & -45 & 155 & -421 \end{array}$

Thus, $f(-3) = -421$

(b) $-1\Big|\begin{array}{ccccc} 1 & 10 & -24 & 20 & 44 \\ & -1 & -9 & 33 & -53 \\ \hline 1 & 9 & -33 & 53 & -9 \end{array}$

Thus, $f(-1) = -9$

57. $f(x) = x^3 + 4x^2 - 25x - 28$

(a)
$$
\begin{array}{r}
x^2 + 8x + 7 \\
x - 4 \overline{\smash{)}\, x^3 + 4x^2 - 25x - 28} \\
\underline{x^3 - 4x^2} \\
8x^2 - 25x \\
\underline{8x^2 - 32x} \\
7x - 28 \\
\underline{7x - 28} \\
0
\end{array}
$$

Since the remainder is 0, $(x - 4)$ is a factor of $f(x)$.

(b) $f(x) = (x - 4)(x^2 + 8x + 7)$

$\qquad = (x - 4)(x + 7)(x + 1)$

The remaining factors of $f(x)$ are $(x + 7)$ and $(x + 1)$.

(c) $f(x) = (x + 7)(x + 1)(x - 4)$

(d) The zeros of $f(x)$ are: $x = -7, -1, 4$

(e)

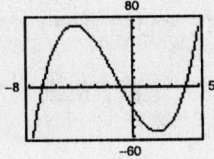

59. $f(x) = x^4 - 4x^3 - 7x^2 + 22x + 24$

(a)
$$
\begin{array}{r|rrrrr}
-2 & 1 & -4 & -7 & 22 & 24 \\
   &   & -2 & 12 & -10 & -24 \\
\hline
   & 1 & -6 & 5 & 12 & 0 \\
3 & 1 & -6 & 5 & 12 \\
  &   & 3 & -9 & -12 \\
\hline
  & 1 & -3 & -4 & 0
\end{array}
$$

Since the remainders are zero, both $(x + 2)$ and $(x - 3)$ are factors of $f(x)$.

(b) $f(x) = (x + 2)(x - 3)(x^2 - 3x - 4)$

$\qquad = (x + 2)(x - 3)(x + 1)(x - 4)$

(c) $f(x) = (x + 1)(x - 4)(x + 2)(x - 3)$

(d) The zeros of $f(x)$ are: $x = -1, 4, -2, 3$

(e)

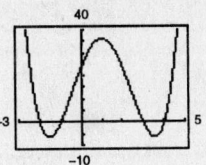

61.

t	0	1	2	3	4	5	6	7
V	671.4	688	695.5	717.1	759.2	807	860.9	912.3

(a) and (b)

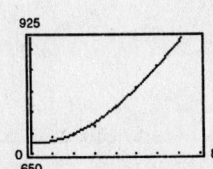

$V = -0.215t^3 + 6.693t^2 - 2.128t + 675.279$

(c)

t	0	1	2	3	4	5	6	7
V	675.3	679.6	696.1	723.3	760.1	805.1	857	914.6

(d) $1175.6 billion

No. According to the model, the value of farm real estate will eventually become negative.

63. $3 - \sqrt{-25} = 3 - 5i$

65. $-5i + i^2 = -5i - 1 = -1 - 5i$

67. $\left(\dfrac{\sqrt{2}}{2} - \dfrac{\sqrt{2}}{2}i\right) - \left(\dfrac{\sqrt{2}}{2} + \dfrac{\sqrt{2}}{2}i\right) = \dfrac{\sqrt{2}}{2} - \dfrac{\sqrt{2}}{2}i - \dfrac{\sqrt{2}}{2} - \dfrac{\sqrt{2}}{2}i = -2\dfrac{\sqrt{2}}{2}i = -\sqrt{2}i$

69. $(1 + 6i)(5 - 2i) = 5 - 2i + 30i - 12i^2 = 17 + 28i$

71. $i(6 + i)(3 - 2i) = i(18 - 12i + 3i - 2i^2) = i(20 - 9i)$
$= 20i - 9i^2 = 9 + 20i$

73. $\dfrac{3 + 2i}{5 + i} = \dfrac{3 + 2i}{5 + i} \cdot \dfrac{5 - i}{5 - i} = \dfrac{15 - 3i + 10i - 2i^2}{25 - i^2}$
$= \dfrac{17 + 7i}{26} = \dfrac{17}{26} + \dfrac{7}{26}i$

75. $\dfrac{1}{2 + i} - \dfrac{5}{1 + 4i} = \dfrac{1 + 4i - 5(2 + i)}{(2 + i)(1 + 4i)} = \dfrac{-9 - i}{-2 + 9i}$
$= \dfrac{9 + i}{2 - 9i} \cdot \dfrac{2 + 9i}{2 + 9i} = \dfrac{18 + 81i + 2i + 9i^2}{4 - 81i^2}$
$= \dfrac{9 + 83i}{85} = \dfrac{9}{85} + \dfrac{83}{85}i$

77. $2 + 8x^2 = 0$
$8x^2 = -2$
$x^2 = -\dfrac{1}{4}$
$x = \pm\sqrt{-\dfrac{1}{4}} = \pm\dfrac{1}{2}i$

79. $6x^2 + 3x + 27 = 0$
$3(2x^2 + x + 9) = 0$
By the Quadratic Formula: $x = \dfrac{-1 \pm \sqrt{-71}}{4}$
$= -\dfrac{1}{4} \pm \dfrac{\sqrt{71}}{4}i$

81. $f(x) = (x - 4)(x + 9)^2$
There are three zeros (one repeating zero at $x = -9$).
The zeros are: $x = 4, -9$

83. $f(x) = x^3 + 6x$
There are three zeros.
$f(x) = x(x^2 + 6) = x(x + \sqrt{6}i)(x - \sqrt{6}i)$
The zeros are: $x = 0, \pm\sqrt{6}i$

85. $f(x) = (x - 8)(x - 5)^2(x - 3 + i)(x - 3 - i)$
There are five zeros (one repeating zero).
The zeros are: $x = 8, 5, 3 \pm i$

87. $f(x) = 3x^4 + 4x^3 - 5x^2 - 8$
Possible rational zeros: $\pm1, \pm2, \pm4, \pm8, \pm\frac{1}{3}, \pm\frac{2}{3}, \pm\frac{4}{3}, \pm\frac{8}{3}$

89. $f(x) = 3x^3 - 20x^2 + 7x + 30$
Possible rational zeros: $\pm1, \pm2, \pm3, \pm5, \pm6, \pm10, \pm15,$
$\pm30, \pm\frac{1}{3}, \pm\frac{2}{3}, \pm\frac{5}{3}, \pm\frac{10}{3}$
$x = -1$ is a zero.

$$
\begin{array}{r|rrrr}
-1 & 3 & -20 & 7 & 30 \\
   &   & -3 & 23 & -30 \\
\hline
   & 3 & -23 & 30 & 0
\end{array}
$$

$f(x) = (x + 1)(3x^2 - 23x + 30)$
$= (x + 1)(3x - 5)(x - 6)$
The zeros of $f(x)$ are: $x = -1, \frac{5}{3}, 6$

91. $f(x) = x^3 + 9x^2 + 24x + 20$
Possible rational zeros: $\pm1, \pm2, \pm4, \pm5, \pm10, \pm20$
$x = -5$ is a zero.

$$
\begin{array}{r|rrrr}
-5 & 1 & 9 & 24 & 20 \\
   &   & -5 & -20 & -20 \\
\hline
   & 1 & 4 & 4 & 0
\end{array}
$$

$f(x) = (x + 5)(x^2 + 4x + 4)$
$= (x + 5)(x + 2)^2$
The zeros of $f(x)$ are: $x = -5, -2$

93. $f(x) = 25x^4 + 25x^3 - 154x^2 - 4x + 24$

Possible rational zeros:

$\pm 1, \pm 2, \pm 3, \pm 4, \pm 6, \pm 8, \pm 12, \pm 24, \pm\frac{1}{5}, \pm\frac{2}{5}, \pm\frac{3}{5}, \pm\frac{4}{5},$

$\pm\frac{6}{5}, \pm\frac{8}{5}, \pm\frac{12}{5}, \pm\frac{24}{5}, \pm\frac{1}{25}, \pm\frac{2}{25}, \pm\frac{3}{25}, \pm\frac{4}{25}, \pm\frac{6}{25}, \pm\frac{8}{25}, \pm\frac{12}{25}, \pm\frac{24}{25}$

$x = 2$ and $x = -3$ are zeros.

$$
\begin{array}{r|rrrrr}
2 & 25 & 25 & -154 & -4 & 24 \\
  &   & 50 & 150 & -8 & -24 \\
\hline
  & 25 & 75 & -4 & -12 & 0 \\
\end{array}
$$

$$
\begin{array}{r|rrrr}
-3 & 25 & 75 & -4 & -12 \\
   &   & -75 & 0 & 12 \\
\hline
   & 25 & 0 & -4 & 0 \\
\end{array}
$$

$f(x) = (x - 2)(x + 3)(25x^2 - 4)$

$\quad = (x - 2)(x + 3)(5x - 2)(5x + 2)$

The zeros of $f(x)$ are: $x = 2, -3, \pm\frac{2}{5}$

95. $f(x) = (x - 2)(x + 3)[x - (1 - 2i)][x - (1 + 2i)]$

$(x^2 + x - 6)[x^2 - x - 2ix - x + 2ix + (1 - 4i^2)]$

$(x^2 + x - 6)(x^2 - 2x + 5)$

$x^4 - x^3 - 3x^2 + 17x - 30$

97. $f(x) = x^4 - 2x^3 - 2x^2 - 2x - 3$

$$
\require{enclose}
\begin{array}{r}
x^2 - 2x - 3 \\
x^2 + 0x + 1 \enclose{longdiv}{x^4 - 2x^3 - 2x^2 - 2x - 3} \\
\underline{x^4 + 0x^3 + x^2} \\
-2x^3 - 3x^2 - 2x \\
\underline{-2x^3 + 0x^2 - 2x} \\
-3x^2 + 0x - 3 \\
\underline{-3x^2 + 0x - 3} \\
0
\end{array}
$$

(a) Rationals: $f(x) = (x^2 + 1)(x^2 - 2x - 3)$

$\qquad\qquad\quad = (x^2 + 1)(x + 1)(x - 3)$

(b) Linear and Quadratic Factors:

$\quad f(x) = (x^2 + 1)(x + 1)(x - 3)$

(c) Completely factored:

$\quad f(x) = (x + i)(x - i)(x + 1)(x - 3)$

99. $f(x) = x^3 - 2x^2 - 14x + 40$

Since $3 - i$ is a zero, so is $3 + i$.

$$
\begin{array}{r|rrrr}
3 - i & 1 & -2 & -14 & 40 \\
      &   & 3 - i & 2 - 4i & -40 \\
\hline
      & 1 & 1 - i & -12 - 4i & 0 \\
\end{array}
$$

$$
\begin{array}{r|rrr}
3 + i & 1 & 1 - i & -12 - 4i \\
      &   & 3 + i & 12 + 4i \\
\hline
      & 1 & 4 & 0 \\
\end{array}
$$

$f(x) = [x - (3 - i)][x - (3 + i)](x + 4)$

The zeros of $f(x)$ are: $x = 3 \pm i, -4$

101. $h(x) = -2x^5 + 4x^3 - 2x^2 + 5$

$h(-x) = 2x^5 - 4x^3 - 2x^2 + 5$

$h(x)$ has three sign changes $\Rightarrow$ One or three positive zeros.

$h(-x)$ has two sign changes $\Rightarrow$ Two or no negative zeros.

103. $f(x) = \dfrac{3x^2}{1 + 3x}$

$1 + 3x \neq 0$

$\quad 3x = -1$

$\quad\ x = -\dfrac{1}{3}$

Domain: all real numbers except $x = -\frac{1}{3}$

105. $f(x) = \dfrac{x^2 - x - 2}{x^2 + 4}$

Domain: all real numbers

107. $f(x) = \dfrac{2x^2 + 5x - 3}{x^2 + 2}$

Vertical asymptote: none

Horizontal asymptote: $y = 2$

109. $g(x) = \dfrac{1}{(x - 3)^2}$

Vertical asymptote: $x = 3$

Horizontal asymptote: $y = 0$

111. $f(x) = \dfrac{4}{x}$

No intercepts

Origin symmetry

Vertical asymptote: $x = 0$

Horizontal asymptote: $y = 0$

x	-3	-2	-1	1	2	3
y	$-\frac{4}{3}$	-2	-4	4	2	$\frac{4}{3}$

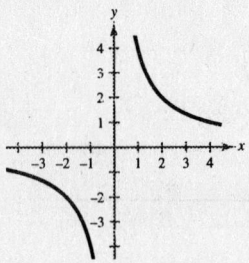

113. $h(x) = \dfrac{x - 3}{x - 2}$

x-intercept: $(3, 0)$

y-intercept: $\left(0, \dfrac{3}{2}\right)$

No axis or origin symmetry

Vertical asymptote: $x = 2$

Horizontal asymptote: $y = 1$

x	-1	0	1	3	4	5
y	$\frac{4}{3}$	$\frac{3}{2}$	2	0	$\frac{1}{2}$	$\frac{2}{3}$

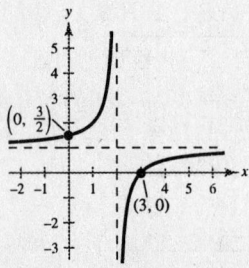

115. $f(x) = \dfrac{2x}{x^2 + 4}$

Intercept: $(0, 0)$

Origin symmetry

Horizontal asymptote: $y = 0$

x	-2	-1	0	1	2
y	$-\frac{1}{2}$	$-\frac{2}{5}$	0	$\frac{2}{5}$	$\frac{1}{2}$

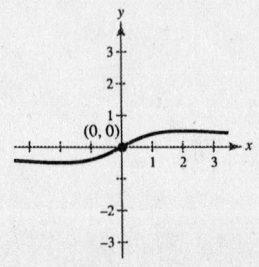

117. $h(x) = \dfrac{4}{(x - 1)^2}$

y-intercept: $(0, 4)$

No axis or origin symmetry

Vertical asymptote: $x = 1$

Horizontal asymptote: $y = 0$

x	-2	-1	0	2	3	4
y	$\frac{4}{9}$	1	4	4	1	$\frac{4}{9}$

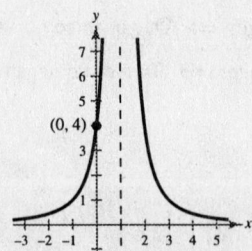

119. $y = \dfrac{2x^2}{x^2 - 4}$

Intercept: $(0, 0)$

y-axis symmetry

Vertical asymptotes: $x = 2, x = -2$

Horizontal asymptote: $y = 2$

x	± 5	± 4	± 3	± 1	0
y	$\frac{50}{21}$	$\frac{8}{3}$	$\frac{18}{5}$	$-\frac{2}{3}$	0

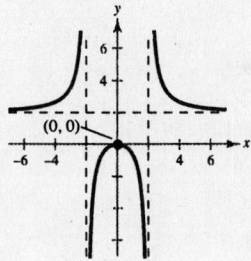

121. $g(x) = \dfrac{-2}{(x + 3)^2}$

y-intercept: $\left(0, -\dfrac{2}{9}\right)$

No axis or origin symmetry

Vertical asymptote: $x = -3$

Horizontal asymptote: $y = 0$

x	-6	-5	-4	-2	-1	0
y	$-\frac{2}{9}$	$-\frac{1}{2}$	-2	-2	$-\frac{1}{2}$	$-\frac{2}{9}$

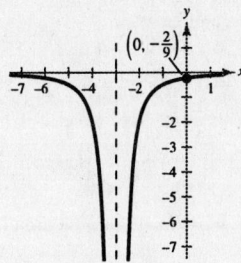

123. $f(x) = \dfrac{x^2 + 1}{x + 1}$

Using long division, $f(x) = \dfrac{x^2 + 1}{x + 1} = x - 1 + \dfrac{2}{x + 1}$

Slant aysmptote: $y = x - 1$

Vertical asymptote: $x = -1$

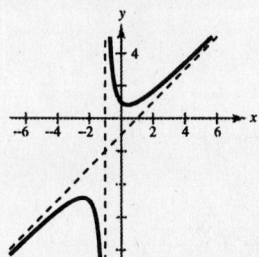

125. $f(x) = \dfrac{x^3}{x^2 - 4}$

Using long division, $f(x) = \dfrac{x^3}{x^2 - 4} = x + \dfrac{4x}{x^2 - 4}$

Slant asymptote: $y = x$

Vertical asymptotes: $x = \pm 2$

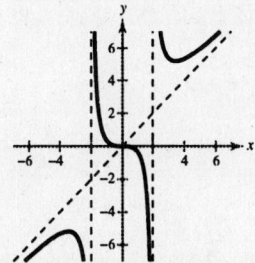

127. $C = \dfrac{528p}{100 - p}, \quad 0 \le p < 100$

(a) When $p = 25$, $C = \dfrac{528(25)}{100 - 25} = \$176$ million.

(b) When $p = 50$, $C = \dfrac{528(50)}{100 - 50} = \$528$ million.

(c) When $p = 75$, $C = \dfrac{528(75)}{100 - 75} = \$1584$ million.

(d) As $p \to 100$, $C \to \infty$.   No, it is not possible.

129. (a)

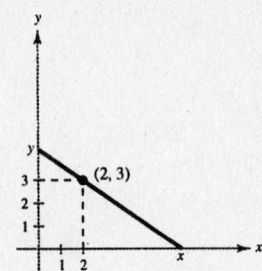

(b) $A = \frac{1}{2}bh$ where $b = x$ and $h = y$.

Slope: $\dfrac{y - 0}{0 - x} = \dfrac{0 - 3}{x - 2}$

$$y = -x\left(\dfrac{-3}{x - 2}\right) = \dfrac{3x}{x - 2}$$

Area: $A = \dfrac{1}{2}xy = \dfrac{1}{2}x\left(\dfrac{3x}{x - 2}\right) = \dfrac{3x^2}{2(x - 2)}, \ x > 2$

(c)

x	2.5	3	3.5	4	4.5
y	18.75	13.50	12.25	12	12.15

The area is minimum when

$$x = 4 \text{ and } y = \dfrac{3(4)}{4 - 2} = 6.$$

(d)

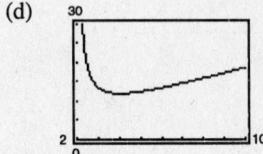

The area is minimum (12)
when $x = 4$ and $y = 6$.

(e) $A = \dfrac{3x^2}{2x - 4} = \dfrac{3}{2}x + 3 + \dfrac{12}{2x - 4} = \dfrac{3}{2}(x + 2) + \dfrac{6}{x - 2}$

The slant asymptote is $y = \frac{3}{2}(x + 2)$. The area increases without bound as x increases.

131. $\dfrac{x - 8}{x^2 - 3x - 28} = \dfrac{x - 8}{(x - 7)(x + 4)} = \dfrac{A}{x - 7} + \dfrac{B}{x + 4}$

133. $\dfrac{x - 2}{x(x^2 + 2)^2} = \dfrac{A}{x} + \dfrac{Bx + C}{x^2 + 2} + \dfrac{Dx + E}{(x^2 + 2)^2}$

135. $\dfrac{-x}{x^2 + 3x + 2} = \dfrac{A}{x + 1} + \dfrac{B}{x + 2}$

$-x = A(x + 2) + B(x + 1)$

Let $x = -1: 1 = A$

Let $x = -2: 2 = -B \implies B = -2$

$\dfrac{-x}{x^2 + 3x + 2} = \dfrac{1}{x + 1} - \dfrac{2}{x + 2}$

137. $\dfrac{9}{x^2 - 9} = \dfrac{A}{x - 3} + \dfrac{B}{x + 3}$

$9 = A(x + 3) + B(x - 3)$

Let $x = 3: 9 = 6A \implies A = \dfrac{3}{2}$

Let $x = -3: 9 = -6B \implies B = -\dfrac{3}{2}$

$\dfrac{9}{x^2 - 9} = \dfrac{1}{2}\left(\dfrac{3}{x - 3} - \dfrac{3}{x + 3}\right)$

139. $\dfrac{4x - 2}{3(x - 1)^2} = \dfrac{A}{x - 1} + \dfrac{B}{(x - 1)^2}$

$\dfrac{4}{3}x - \dfrac{2}{3} = A(x - 1) + B$

Let $x = 1: \dfrac{2}{3} = B$

Let $x = 2: 2 = A + \dfrac{2}{3} \implies A = \dfrac{4}{3}$

$\dfrac{4x - 2}{3(x - 1)^2} = \dfrac{4}{3(x - 1)} + \dfrac{2}{3(x - 1)^2}$

141. $\dfrac{4x^2}{(x - 1)(x^2 + 1)} = \dfrac{A}{x - 1} + \dfrac{Bx + C}{x^2 + 1}$

$4x^2 = A(x^2 + 1) + (Bx + C)(x - 1)$

$= Ax^2 + A + Bx^2 - Bx + Cx - C$

$= (A + B)x^2 + (-B + C)x + (A - C)$

Equating coefficients of like powers:

$4 = A + B, 0 = -B + C$, and $0 = A - C$.

Solving this system yields: $A = 2, B = 2, C = 2$

$\dfrac{4x^2}{(x - 1)(x^2 + 1)} = \dfrac{2}{x - 1} + \dfrac{2x + 2}{x^2 + 1}$

$= 2\left(\dfrac{1}{x - 1} + \dfrac{x + 1}{x^2 + 1}\right)$

143. False. The domain of $f(x) = \dfrac{1}{x^2 + 1}$ is the set of all real numbers.

145. $f(x) = a(x - h)^2 + k$

Since there are no horizontal or vertical shifts, $h = 0$ and $k = 0$.
If a is negative then the graph of $f(x) = x^2$ is reflected in the x-axis
with either a shrink or a stretch (as long as $a \neq 1$).

147. False. For a complex number, $a + bi$, if $a = 0$ or if $b = 0$, then
the square of the complex number is a real number. Otherwise, the
square is not a real number.

Chapter 2   Practice Test

1. Sketch the graph of $f(x) = x^2 - 6x + 5$ and identify the vertex and the intercepts.

2. Find the number of units x that produce a minimum cost C if
$C = 0.01x^2 - 90x + 15,000$.

3. Find the quadratic function that has a maximum at $(1, 7)$ and passes through the point $(2, 5)$.

4. Find two quadratic functions that have x-intercepts $(2, 0)$ and $\left(\frac{4}{3}, 0\right)$.

5. Use the leading coefficient test to determine the right and left end behavior of the graph of the polynomial function $f(x) = -3x^5 + 2x^3 - 17$.

6. Find all the real zeros of $f(x) = x^5 - 5x^3 + 4x$.

7. Find a polynomial function with 0, 3, and -2 as zeros.

8. Sketch $f(x) = x^3 - 12x$.

9. Divide $3x^4 - 7x^2 + 2x - 10$ by $x - 3$ using long division.

10. Divide $x^3 - 11$ by $x^2 + 2x - 1$.

11. Use synthetic division to divide $3x^5 + 13x^4 + 12x - 1$ by $x + 5$.

12. Use synthetic division to find $f(-6)$ given $f(x) = 7x^3 + 40x^2 - 12x + 15$.

13. Find the real zeros of $f(x) = x^3 - 19x - 30$.

14. Find the real zeros of $f(x) = x^4 + x^3 - 8x^2 - 9x - 9$.

15. List all possible rational zeros of the function $f(x) = 6x^3 - 5x^2 + 4x - 15$.

16. Find the rational zeros of the polynomial $f(x) = x^3 - \frac{20}{3}x^2 + 9x - \frac{10}{3}$.

17. Write $f(x) = x^4 + x^3 + 5x - 10$ as a product of linear factors.

18. Find a polynomial with real coefficients that has 2, $3 + i$, and $3 - 2i$ as zeros.

19. Use synthetic division to show that $3i$ is a zero of $f(x) = x^3 + 4x^2 + 9x + 36$.

20. Sketch the graph of $f(x) = \dfrac{x-1}{2x}$ and label all intercepts and asymptotes.

21. Find all the asymptotes of $f(x) = \dfrac{8x^2 - 9}{x^2 + 1}$.

22. Find all the asymptotes of $f(x) = \dfrac{4x^2 - 2x + 7}{x - 1}$.

23. Given $z_1 = 4 - 3i$ and $z_2 = -2 + i$, find the following:

(a) $z_1 - z_2$

(b) $z_1 z_2$

(c) z_1/z_2

For Exercises 24–25, write the partial fraction decomposition for the rational expression.

24. $\dfrac{1 - 2x}{x^2 + x}$

25. $\dfrac{6x - 17}{(x - 3)^2}$

C H A P T E R   3
Exponential and Logarithmic Functions

CHAPTER 3
Exponential and Logarithmic Functions

Section 3.1   Exponential Functions and Their Graphs

Solutions to Odd-Numbered Exercises

■ You should know that a function of the form $f(x) = a^x$, where $a > 0$, $a \neq 1$, is called an exponential function with base a.

■ You should be able to graph exponential functions.

■ You should know formulas for compound interest.

(a) For n compoundings per year: $A = P\left(1 + \dfrac{r}{n}\right)^{nt}$.

(b) For continuous compoundings: $A = Pe^{rt}$.

---

1. $(3.4)^{5.6} \approx 946.852$

3. $(1.005)^{400} \approx 7.352$

5. $5^{-\pi} \approx 0.006$

7. $100^{\sqrt{2}} \approx 673.639$

9. $e^{-3/4} \approx 0.472$

11. $f(x) = 2^x$

Increasing

Asymptote: $y = 0$

Intercept: $(0, 1)$

Matches graph (d).

13. $f(x) = 2^{-x}$

Decreasing

Asymptote: $y = 0$

Intercept: $(0, 1)$

Matches graph (a).

15. $f(x) = 3^x$

$g(x) = 3^{x-4}$

Because $g(x) = f(x - 4)$, the graph of g can be obtained by shifting the graph of f four units to the right.

17. $f(x) = -2^x$

$g(x) = 5 - 2^x$

Because $g(x) = 5 + f(x)$, the graph of g can be obtained by shifting the graph of f five units upward.

19. $f(x) = \left(\frac{3}{5}\right)^x$

$g(x) = -\left(\frac{3}{5}\right)^{x+4}$

Because $g(x) = -f(x + 4)$, the graph of g can be obtained by reflecting the graph of f in the x-axis and shifting f four units to the left.

21. $f(x) = 0.3^x$

$g(x) = -0.3^x + 5$

Because $g(x) = -f(x) + 5$, the graph of g can be obtained by reflecting the graph of f in the x-axis and shifting f five units upward.

23. $f(x) = \left(\frac{1}{2}\right)^x$

x	-2	-1	0	1	2
$f(x)$	4	2	1	0.5	0.25

Asymptote: $y = 0$

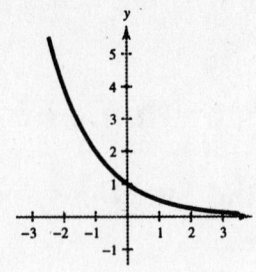

25. $f(x) = \left(\frac{1}{2}\right)^{-x} = 2^x$

x	-2	-1	0	1	2
$f(x)$	0.25	0.5	1	2	4

Asymptote: $y = 0$

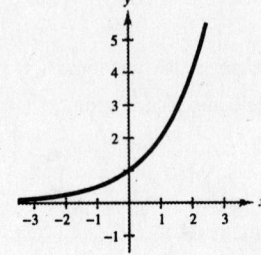

27. $f(x) = 2^{x-1}$

x	-2	-1	0	1	2
$f(x)$	0.125	0.25	0.5	1	2

Asymptote: $y = 0$

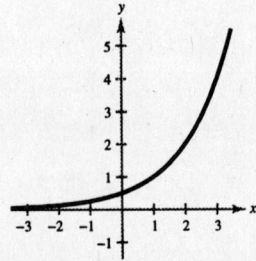

29. $f(x) = e^x$

x	-2	-1	0	1	2
$f(x)$	0.135	0.368	1	2.718	7.389

Asymptote: $y = 0$

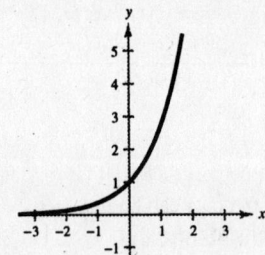

31. $f(x) = 3e^{x+4}$

x	-8	-7	-6	-5	-4
$f(x)$	0.055	0.149	0.406	1.104	3

Asymptote: $y = 0$

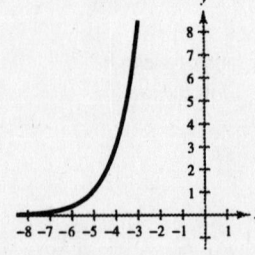

33. $f(x) = 2e^{x-2} + 4$

x	-2	-1	0	1	2
$f(x)$	4.037	4.100	4.271	4.736	6

Asymptote: $y = 4$

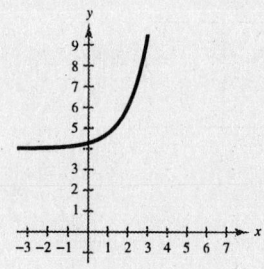

35. $f(x) = 4^{x-3} + 3$

x	-1	0	1	2	3
$f(x)$	3.003	3.016	3.063	3.25	4

Asymptote: $y = 3$

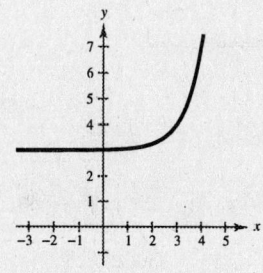

37. $g(x) = 5^x$

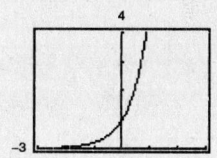

39. $f(x) = \left(\dfrac{1}{5}\right)^x = 5^{-x}$

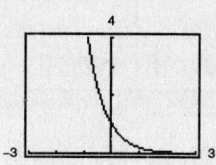

41. $h(x) = 5^{x-2}$

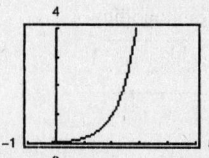

43. $g(x) = 5^{-x} - 3$

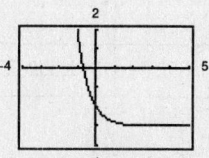

45. $y = 2^{-x^2}$

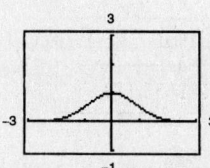

47. $f(x) = 3^{x-2} + 1$

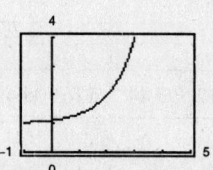

49. $y = 1.08^{-5x}$

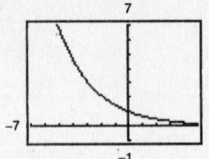

51. $s(t) = 2e^{0.12t}$

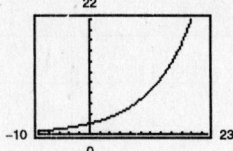

53. $g(x) = 1 + e^{-x}$

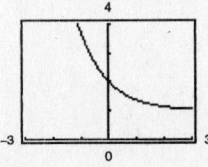

55. $P = \$2500$, $r = 8\%$, $t = 10$ years

Compounded n times per year: $A = P\left(1 + \dfrac{r}{n}\right)^{nt} = 2500\left(1 + \dfrac{0.08}{n}\right)^{10n}$

Compounded continuously: $A = Pe^{rt} = 2500e^{0.08(10)}$

n	1	2	4	12	365	Continuous Compounding
A	\$5397.31	\$5477.81	\$5520.10	\$5549.10	\$5563.36	\$5563.85

57. $P = \$2500$, $r = 8\%$, $t = 20$ years

Compounded n times per year: $A = P\left(1 + \dfrac{r}{n}\right)^{nt} = 2500\left(1 + \dfrac{0.08}{n}\right)^{20n}$

Compounded continuously: $A = Pe^{rt} = 2500e^{0.08(20)}$

n	1	2	4	12	365	Continuous Compounding
A	\$11,652.39	\$12,002.55	\$12,188.60	\$12,317.01	\$12,380.41	\$12,382.58

59. $A = Pe^{rt}$

$A = 12000e^{0.08t}$

t	1	10	20	30	40	50
A	\$12,999.44	\$26,706.49	\$59,436.39	\$132,278.12	\$294,390.36	\$655,177.80

61. $A = Pe^{rt}$

$A = 12000e^{0.065t}$

t	1	10	20	30	40	50
A	\$12,805.91	\$22,986.49	\$44,031.56	\$84,344.25	\$161,564.86	\$309,484.08

63. $A = 25{,}000e^{(0.0875)(25)} \approx \$222{,}822.57$

65. (a) The steeper curve represents the investment earning compound interest, because compound interest earns more than simple interest. With simple interest there is no compounding so the growth is linear.

(b) Compound interest formula: $A = 500\left(1 + \dfrac{0.07}{1}\right)^{(1)t}$

$$= 500(1.07)^t$$

Simple interest formula: $A = Prt + P$

$$= 500(0.07)t + 500$$

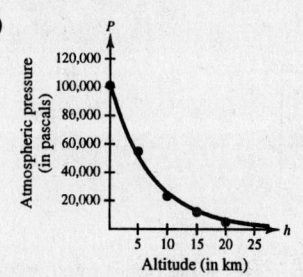

67. $C(10) = 23.95(1.04)^{10} \approx \$35.45$

69. $P(t) = 100e^{0.2197t}$

(a) $P(0) = 100$

(b) $P(5) \approx 300$

(c) $P(10) \approx 900$

71. $Q = 25\left(\frac{1}{2}\right)^{t/1620}$

(a) When $t = 0$, $Q = 25\left(\frac{1}{2}\right)^{0/1620} = 25(1) = 25$ units.

(b) When $t = 1000$, $Q = 25\left(\frac{1}{2}\right)^{1000/1620} \approx 16.30$ units.

(c)

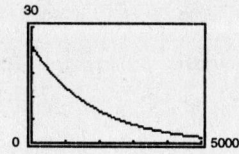

73. $P = 102{,}303e^{-0.137h}$

(a)

(b)

h	0	5	10	15	20
P	102,303	51,570	25,996	13,104	6606

(c) $P(8) \approx 34{,}190$ Pascals

(d) $21{,}000 = 102{,}303e^{-0.137h}$ when $h \approx 11.6$ km

75. True. As $x \to -\infty$, $f(x) \to 0$ but never reaches zero.

77. $f(x) = 3^{x-2}$

$$= 3^x 3^{-2}$$

$$= 3^x\left(\frac{1}{3^2}\right)$$

$$= \frac{1}{9}(3^x)$$

$$= h(x)$$

Thus, $f(x) \neq g(x)$, but $f(x) = h(x)$.

79.

$f(x) = 16(4^{-x})$ and

$$= 4^2(4^{-x})$$

$$= 4^{2-x}$$

$$= \left(\frac{1}{4}\right)^{-(2-x)}$$

$$= \left(\frac{1}{4}\right)^{x-2}$$

$$= g(x)$$

$f(x) = 16(4^{-x})$

$$= 16(2^2)^{-x}$$

$$= 16(2^{-2x})$$

$$= h(x)$$

Thus, $f(x) = g(x) = h(x)$.

81. $y = 3^x$ and $y = 4^x$

x	-2	-1	0	1	2
3^x	$\frac{1}{9}$	$\frac{1}{3}$	1	3	9
4^x	$\frac{1}{16}$	$\frac{1}{4}$	1	4	16

(a) $4^x < 3^x$ when $x < 0$.

(b) $4^x > 3^x$ when $x > 0$.

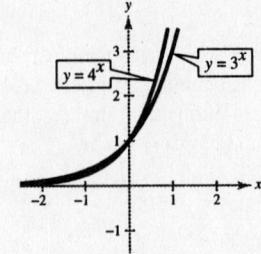

83. (a) $f(x) = \dfrac{8}{1 + e^{-0.5x}}$

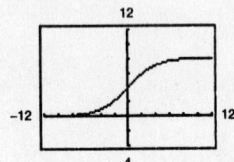

Horizontal asymptotes: $y = 0$ and $y = 8$

(b) $g(x) = \dfrac{8}{1 + e^{-0.5/x}}$

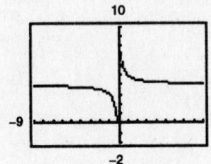

Horizontal asymptote: $y = 4$

Vertical asymptote: $x = 0$

85.

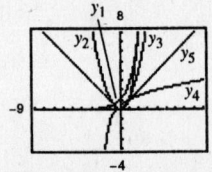

$y_1 = e^x$

$y_2 = x^2$

$y_3 = x^3$

$y_4 = \sqrt{x}$

$y_5 = |x|$

The function that increases at the fastest rate for "large" values of x is $y_1 = e^x$. (Note: One of the intersection points of $y = e^x$ and $y = x^3$ is approximately $(4.536, 93)$ and past this point $e^x > x^3$. This is not shown on the graph above.)

87. It usually implies rapid growth.

89. In Exercise 88 $f(x) = \left[1 + \dfrac{0.5}{x}\right]^x$ appears to approach $g(x) = e^{0.5}$ as x increases without bound. Therefore,

the value of $\left[1 + \dfrac{r}{x}\right]^x$ approaches e^r as x increases without bound.

x	1	10	100	200	500	1100	10,000
$\left[1 + \left(\dfrac{1}{x}\right)\right]^x$	2	2.5937	2.7048	2.7115	2.7156	2.7170	2.718

$e^1 \approx 2.718281828\ldots$

91. Since $\sqrt{2} \approx 1.414$ we know that $1 < \sqrt{2} < 2$.

Thus, $2^1 < 2^{\sqrt{2}} < 2^2$

$2 < 2^{\sqrt{2}} < 4$.

93. $y_4 = 1 + \dfrac{x}{1!} + \dfrac{x^2}{2!} + \dfrac{x^3}{3!} + \dfrac{x^4}{4!}$

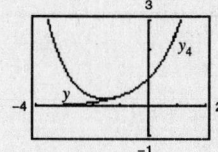

As more terms are added, the polynomial approaches e^x.

$$e^x = 1 + \frac{x}{1!} + \frac{x^2}{2!} + \frac{x^3}{3!} + \frac{x^4}{4!} + \frac{x^5}{5!} + \cdots$$

95. $2x - 7y + 14 = 0$

$\qquad 2x + 14 = 7y$

$\qquad \frac{1}{7}(2x + 14) = y$

97. $x^2 + y^2 = 25$

$\qquad y^2 = 25 - x^2$

$\qquad y = \pm\sqrt{25 - x^2}$

99. $f(x) = \dfrac{2}{9 + x}$

Vertical asymptote: $x = -9$

Horizontal asymptote: $y = 0$

x	-11	-10	-8	-7
$f(x)$	-1	-2	2	1

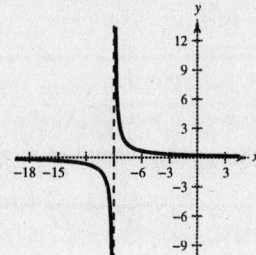

101. $f(x) = \dfrac{6}{x^2 + 5x - 24} = \dfrac{6}{(x + 8)(x - 3)}$

Vertical asymptotes: $x = -8, x = 3$

Horizontal asymptote: $y = 0$

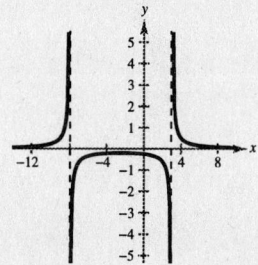

x	-10	-9	-7	-5	-3	-1	0	1	2	4	5
$f(x)$	0.23	0.5	-0.6	-0.25	-0.2	-0.21	-0.25	-0.33	-0.6	0.5	0.23

Section 3.2   Logarithmic Functions and Their Graphs

■ You should know that a function of the form $y = \log_a x$, where $a > 0$, $a \neq 1$, and $x > 0$, is called a logarithm of x to base a.

■ You should be able to convert from logarithmic form to exponential form and vice versa.

$$y = \log_a x \iff a^y = x$$

■ You should know the following properties of logarithms.

(a) $\log_a 1 = 0$ since $a^0 = 1$.

(b) $\log_a a = 1$ since $a^1 = a$.

(c) $\log_a a^x = x$ since $a^x = a^x$.

(d) If $\log_a x = \log_a y$, then $x = y$.

■ You should know the definition of the natural logarithmic function.

$$\log_e x = \ln x, \, x > 0$$

■ You should know the properties of the natural logarithmic function.

(a) $\ln 1 = 0$ since $e^0 = 1$.

(b) $\ln e = 1$ since $e^1 = e$.

(c) $\ln e^x = x$ since $e^x = e^x$.

(d) If $\ln x = \ln y$, then $x = y$.

■ You should be able to graph logarithmic functions.

Solutions to Odd-Numbered Exercises

1. $\log_4 64 = 3 \implies 4^3 = 64$

3. $\log_7 \frac{1}{49} = -2 \implies 7^{-2} = \frac{1}{49}$

5. $\log_{32} 4 = \frac{2}{5} \implies 32^{2/5} = 4$

7. $\ln 1 = 0 \implies e^0 = 1$

9. $5^3 = 125 \implies \log_5 125 = 3$

11. $81^{1/4} = 3 \implies \log_{81} 3 = \frac{1}{4}$

13. $6^{-2} = \frac{1}{36} \implies \log_6 \frac{1}{36} = -2$

15. $e^3 = 20.0855\ldots \implies \ln 20.0855\ldots = 3$

17. $e^0 = 1 \implies \ln 1 = 0$

19. $\log_2 16 = \log_2 2^4 = 4$

21. $\log_{16} 4 = \log_{16} 16^{1/2} = \frac{1}{2}$

23. $\log_7 1 = \log_7 7^0 = 0$

25. $\log_{10} 0.01 = \log_{10} 10^{-2} = -2$

27. $\log_8 32 = \log_8 8^{5/3} = \frac{5}{3}$

29. $\ln e^3 = 3$

31. $\log_a a^2 = 2$

33. $\log_{10} 345 \approx 2.538$

35. $\log_{10} \frac{4}{5} \approx -0.097$

37. $\ln 18.42 \approx 2.913$

39. $3 \ln 0.32 \approx -3.418$

41. $\ln\left(1 + \sqrt{3}\right) \approx 1.005$

43. $\ln \frac{2}{3} \approx -0.405$

45. $f(x) = \log_3 x + 2$

Asymptote: $x = 0$

Point on graph: $(1, 2)$

Matches graph (c).

47. $f(x) = -\log_3(x + 2)$

Asymptote: $x = -2$

Point on graph: $(-1, 0)$

Matches graph (d).

49. $f(x) = \log_3(1 - x)$

Asymptote: $x = 1$

Point on graph: $(0, 0)$

Matches graph (b).

51. $f(x) = \log_4 x$

Domain: $x > 0 \implies$ The domain is $(0, \infty)$.

x-intercept: $(1, 0)$

Vertical asymptote: $x = 0$

$y = \log_4 x \implies 4^y = x$

x	$\frac{1}{4}$	1	4	2
$f(x)$	-1	0	1	$\frac{1}{2}$

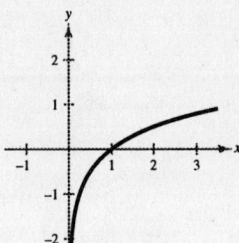

53. $y = -\log_3 x + 2$

Domain: $(0, \infty)$

x-intercept:

$$-\log_3 x + 2 = 0$$
$$2 = \log_3 x$$
$$3^2 = x$$
$$9 = x$$

The x-intercept is $(9, 0)$.

Vertical asymptote: $x = 0$

$y = -\log_3 x + 2$

$\log_3 x = 2 - y \implies 3^{2-y} = x$

x	27	9	3	1	$\frac{1}{3}$
y	-1	0	1	2	3

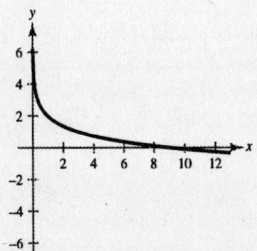

55. $f(x) = -\log_6(x + 2)$

Domain: $x + 2 > 0 \implies x > -2$

The domain is $(-2, \infty)$.

x-intercept:

$$0 = -\log_6(x + 2)$$
$$0 = \log_6(x + 2)$$
$$6^0 = x + 2$$
$$1 = x + 2$$
$$-1 = x$$

The x-intercept is $(-1, 0)$.

Vertical asymptote: $x + 2 = 0 \implies x = -2$

$$y = -\log_6(x + 2)$$
$$-y = \log_6(x + 2)$$
$$6^{-y} - 2 = x$$

x	4	-1	$-1\frac{5}{6}$	$-1\frac{35}{36}$
$f(x)$	-1	0	1	2

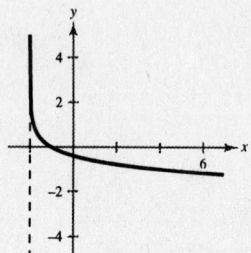

57. $y = \log_{10}\left(\dfrac{x}{5}\right)$

Domain: $\dfrac{x}{5} > 0 \implies x > 0$

The domain is $(0, \infty)$.

x-intercept:

$$\log_{10}\left(\frac{x}{5}\right) = 0$$
$$\frac{x}{5} = 10^0$$
$$\frac{x}{5} = 1 \implies x = 5$$

The x-intercept is $(5, 0)$.

Vertical asymptote: $\dfrac{x}{5} = 0 \implies x = 0$

The vertical asymptote is the y-axis.

x	1	2	3	4	5	6	7
y	-0.70	-0.40	-0.22	-0.10	0	0.08	0.15

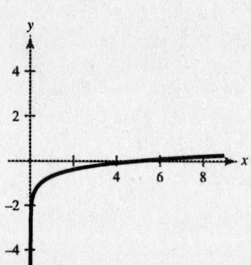

59. $f(x) = \ln(x - 2)$

Domain: $x - 2 > 0 \implies x > 2$

The domain is $(2, \infty)$.

x-intercept:

$$0 = \ln(x - 2)$$
$$e^0 = x - 2$$
$$3 = x$$

The x-intercept is $(3, 0)$.

Vertical asymptote: $x - 2 = 0 \implies x = 2$

x	2.5	3	4	5
$f(x)$	-0.69	0	0.69	1.10

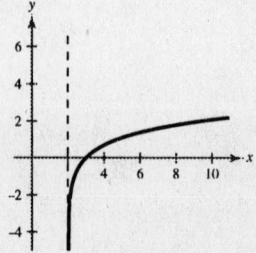

61. $g(x) = \ln(-x)$

Domain: $-x > 0 \implies x < 0$

The domain is $(-\infty, 0)$.

x-intercept:

$$0 = \ln(-x)$$
$$e^0 = -x$$
$$-1 = x$$

The x-intercept is $(-1, 0)$.

Vertical asymptote: $-x = 0 \implies x = 0$

x	-0.5	-1	-2	-3
$g(x)$	-0.69	0	0.69	1.10

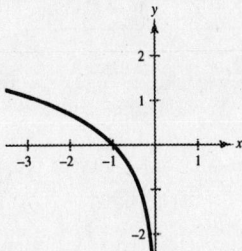

63. $y_1 = \log(x + 1)$

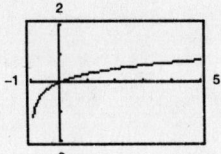

65. $y_1 = \ln(x - 1)$

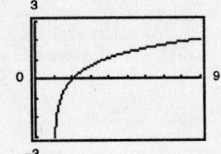

67. $y = \ln x + 2$

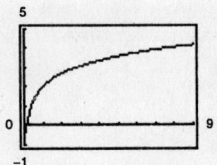

69. $f(t) = 80 - 17\log_{10}(t + 1), \ 0 \le t \le 12$

(a) $f(0) = 80 - 17\log_{10} 1 = 80.0$

(b) $f(4) = 80 - 17\log_{10} 5 \approx 68.1$

(c) $f(10) = 80 - 17\log_{10} 11 \approx 62.3$

71. $t = \dfrac{\ln 2}{r}$

(a)

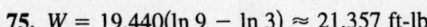

r	0.005	0.01	0.015	0.02	0.025	0.03
t	138.6	69.3	46.2	34.7	27.7	23.1

(b) Answers will vary.

73. $y = 80.4 - 11\ln x$

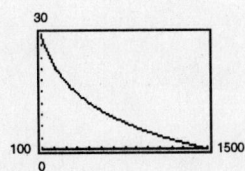

$y(300) = 80.4 - 11\ln 300 \approx 17.66 \ \text{ft}^3/\text{min}$

75. $W = 19{,}440(\ln 9 - \ln 3) \approx 21{,}357$ ft-lb

77. $t = 12.542\ln\left(\dfrac{1100.65}{1100.65 - 1000}\right) \approx 30$ years

79. Total amount $= (1100.65)(12)(30) = \$396{,}234$

Interest $= 396{,}234 - 150{,}000 = \$246{,}234$

81. $f(x) = \dfrac{\ln x}{x}$

(a)

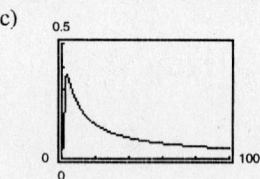

x	1	5	10	10^2	10^4	10^6
$f(x)$	0	0.322	0.230	0.046	0.00092	0.0000138

(b) As $x \to \infty$, $f(x) \to 0$.

(c)

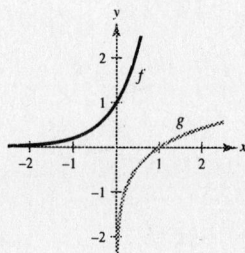

83. True, $\log_3 27 = 3 \implies 3^3 = 27$.

85. $f(x) = 5^x$, $g(x) = \log_5 x$

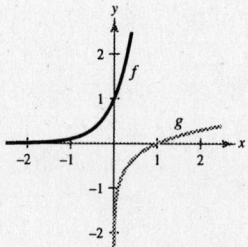

f and g are inverses. Their graphs are reflected about the line $y = x$.

87. $f(x) = 10^x$, $g(x) = \log_{10} x$

f and g are inverses. Their graphs are reflected about the line $y = x$.

89. (a) False. If y were an exponential function of x, then $y = a^x$, but $a^1 = a$, not 0. Because one point is $(1, 0)$, y is not an exponential function of x.

(c) True. $x = a^y$

For $a = 2$, $x = 2^y$.

$y = 0$, $2^0 = 1$

$y = 1$, $2^1 = 2$

$y = 3$, $2^3 = 8$

(b) True. $y = \log_a x$

For $a = 2$, $y = \log_2 x$.

$x = 1$, $\log_2 1 = 0$

$x = 2$, $\log_2 2 = 1$

$x = 8$, $\log_2 8 = 3$

(d) False. If y were a linear function of x, the slope between $(1, 0)$ and $(2, 1)$ and the slope between $(2, 1)$ and $(8, 3)$ would be the same.

However,

$$m_1 = \frac{1 - 0}{2 - 1} = 1 \text{ and } m_2 = \frac{3 - 1}{8 - 2} = \frac{2}{6} = \frac{1}{3}.$$

Therefore, y is not a linear function of x.

91. $y_4 = (x - 1) - \frac{1}{2}(x - 1)^2 + \frac{1}{3}(x - 1)^3 - \frac{1}{4}(x - 1)^4$

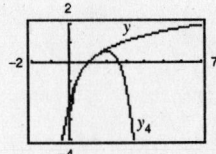

The pattern implies that $\ln x = (x - 1) - \frac{1}{2}(x - 1)^2 + \frac{1}{3}(x - 1)^3 - \frac{1}{4}(x - 1)^4 + \cdots$.

93. $f(x) = |\ln x|$

(a)

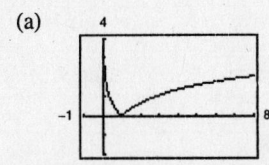

(b) Increasing on $(1, \infty)$

Decreasing on $(0, 1)$

(c) Relative minimum: $(1, 0)$

95. $f(x) = \frac{x}{2} - \ln\frac{x}{4}$

(a)

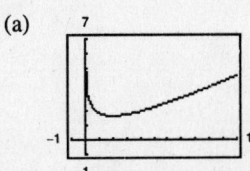

(b) Increasing on $(2, \infty)$

Decreasing on $(0, 2)$

(c) Relative minimum: $\left(2, 1 - \ln\frac{1}{2}\right)$

97. $8n - 3$

99. $83.95 + 37.50t$ Parts and labor

101. $f(x) = \dfrac{4}{-8 - x}$

Vertical asymptote: $x = -8$

Horizontal asymptote: $y = 0$

103. $f(x) = \dfrac{x + 5}{2x^2 + x - 15} = \dfrac{x + 5}{(2x - 5)(x + 3)}$

Vertical asymptotes: $x = \dfrac{5}{2}, x = -3$

Horizontal asymptote: $y = 0$

105. $e^6 \approx 403.429$

107. $e^{-4} \approx 0.018$

Section 3.3   Properties of Logarithms

■   You should know the following properties of logarithms.

(a) $\log_a x = \dfrac{\log_b x}{\log_b a}$ $\log_a x = \dfrac{\log_{10} x}{\log_{10} a}$ $\log_a x = \dfrac{\ln x}{\ln a}$

(b) $\log_a(uv) = \log_a u + \log_a v$ $\ln(uv) = \ln u + \ln v$

(c) $\log_a(u/v) = \log_a u - \log_a v$ $\ln(u/v) = \ln u - \ln v$

(d) $\log_a u^n = n \log_a u$ $\ln u^n = n \ln u$

■   You should be able to rewrite logarithmic expressions using these properties.

Solutions to Odd-Numbered Exercises

1. $\log_3 7 = \dfrac{\log_{10} 7}{\log_{10} 3} = \dfrac{\ln 7}{\ln 3} \approx 1.771$

3. $\log_{1/2} 4 = \dfrac{\log_{10} 4}{\log_{10}(1/2)} = \dfrac{\ln 4}{\ln(1/2)} = -2.000$

5. $\log_9(0.4) = \dfrac{\log_{10} 0.4}{\log_{10} 9} = \dfrac{\ln 0.4}{\ln 9} \approx -0.417$

7. $\log_{15} 1250 = \dfrac{\log_{10} 1250}{\log_{10} 15} = \dfrac{\ln 1250}{\ln 15} \approx 2.633$

9. (a) $\log_5 x = \dfrac{\log_{10} x}{\log_{10} 5}$

   (b) $\log_5 x = \dfrac{\ln x}{\ln 5}$

11. (a) $\log_{\frac{1}{5}} x = \dfrac{\log_{10} x}{\log_{10}\left(\frac{1}{5}\right)}$

   (b) $\log_{\frac{1}{5}} x = \dfrac{\ln x}{\ln\left(\frac{1}{5}\right)}$

13. (a) $\log_x \dfrac{3}{10} = \dfrac{\log_{10}\left(\frac{3}{10}\right)}{\log_{10} x}$

   (b) $\log_x \dfrac{3}{10} = \dfrac{\ln\left(\frac{3}{10}\right)}{\ln x}$

15. (a) $\log_{2.6} x = \dfrac{\log_{10} x}{\log_{10} 2.6}$

   (b) $\log_{2.6} x = \dfrac{\ln x}{\ln 2.6}$

17. $f(x) = \log_2 x = \dfrac{\log_{10} x}{\log_{10} 2} = \dfrac{\ln x}{\ln 2}$

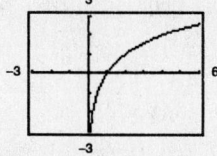

19. $f(x) = \log_{\frac{1}{2}} x = \dfrac{\log_{10} x}{\log_{10}\frac{1}{2}} = \dfrac{\ln x}{\ln\left(\frac{1}{2}\right)}$

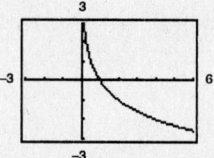

21. $f(x) = \log_{11.8} x = \dfrac{\log_{10} x}{\log_{10} 11.8} = \dfrac{\ln x}{\ln 11.8}$

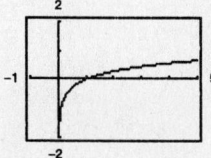

23. $\log_{10} 5x = \log_{10} 5 + \log_{10} x$

25. $\log_{10} \dfrac{5}{x} = \log_{10} 5 - \log_{10} x$

27. $\log_8 x^4 = 4\log_8 x$

29. $\ln \sqrt{z} = \ln z^{1/2} = \frac{1}{2} \ln z$

31. $\ln xyz = \ln x + \ln y + \ln z$

33. $\ln \sqrt{a-1} = \frac{1}{2}\ln(a-1),\, a > 1$

35. $\ln z(z-1)^2 = \ln z + \ln(z-1)^2$
$= \ln z + 2\ln(z-1),\, z > 1$

37. $\ln\sqrt[3]{\dfrac{x}{y}} = \dfrac{1}{3}\ln\dfrac{x}{y}$

$\qquad = \dfrac{1}{3}[\ln x - \ln y]$

$\qquad = \dfrac{1}{3}\ln x - \dfrac{1}{3}\ln y$

39. $\ln\left(\dfrac{x^4\sqrt{y}}{z^5}\right) = \ln x^4\sqrt{y} - \ln z^5$

$\qquad = \ln x^4 + \ln\sqrt{y} - \ln z^5$

$\qquad = 4\ln x + \dfrac{1}{2}\ln y - 5\ln z$

41. $\log_b\left(\dfrac{x^2}{y^2z^3}\right) = \log_b x^2 - \log_b y^2z^3$

$\qquad = \log_b x^2 - [\log_b y^2 + \log_b z^3]$

$\qquad = 2\log_b x - 2\log_b y - 3\log_b z$

43. $\ln x + \ln 3 = \ln 3x$

45. $\log_4 z - \log_4 y = \log_4 \dfrac{z}{y}$

47. $2\log_2(x + 4) = \log_2(x + 4)^2$

49. $\dfrac{1}{4}\log_3 5x = \log_3(5x)^{1/4} = \log_3\sqrt[4]{5x}$

51. $\ln x - 3\ln(x + 1) = \ln x - \ln(x + 1)^3$

$\qquad = \ln\dfrac{x}{(x + 1)^3}$

53. $\ln(x - 2) - \ln(x + 2) = \ln\left(\dfrac{x - 2}{x + 2}\right)$

55. $\ln x - 4[\ln(x + 2) + \ln(x - 2)] = \ln x - 4\ln(x + 2)(x - 2)$

$\qquad = \ln x - 4\ln(x^2 - 4)$

$\qquad = \ln x - \ln(x^2 - 4)^4$

$\qquad = \ln\dfrac{x}{(x^2 - 4)^4}$

57. $\dfrac{1}{3}[2\ln(x + 3) + \ln x - \ln(x^2 - 1)] = \dfrac{1}{3}[\ln(x + 3)^2 + \ln x - \ln(x^2 - 1)]$

$\qquad = \dfrac{1}{3}[\ln x(x + 3)^2 - \ln(x^2 - 1)]$

$\qquad = \dfrac{1}{3}\ln\dfrac{x(x + 3)^2}{x^2 - 1}$

$\qquad = \ln\sqrt[3]{\dfrac{x(x + 3)^2}{x^2 - 1}}$

59. $\dfrac{1}{3}[\ln y + 2\ln(y + 4)] - \ln(y - 1) = \dfrac{1}{3}[\ln y + \ln(y + 4)^2] - \ln(y - 1)$

$\qquad = \dfrac{1}{3}\ln y(y + 4)^2 - \ln(y - 1)$

$\qquad = \ln\sqrt[3]{y(y + 4)^2} - \ln(y - 1)$

$\qquad = \ln\dfrac{\sqrt[3]{y(y + 4)^2}}{y - 1}$

61. $2 \ln 3 - \dfrac{1}{2} \ln(x^2 + 1) = \ln 3^2 - \ln \sqrt{x^2 + 1}$

$$= \ln \dfrac{9}{\sqrt{x^2 + 1}}$$

63. $\log_2 \dfrac{32}{4} = \log_2 32 - \log_2 4 \neq \dfrac{\log_2 32}{\log_2 4}$

The first two expressions are equal by Property 2.

65. $\log_3 9 = 2 \log_3 3 = 2$

67. $\log_4 16^{1.2} = 1.2(\log_4 16) = 1.2 \log_4 4^2 = 1.2(2) = 2.4$

69. $\log_3(-9)$ is undefined. -9 is not in the domain of $\log_3 x$.

71. $\log_5 75 - \log_5 3 = \log_5 \dfrac{75}{3} = \log_5 25 = \log_5 5^2 = 2 \log_5 5 = 2$

73. $\ln e^2 - \ln e^5 = 2 - 5 = -3$

75. $\log_{10} 0$ is undefined. 0 is not in the domain of $\log_{10} x$.

77. $\ln e^{4.5} = 4.5$

79. $\log_4 8 = \dfrac{\log_2 8}{\log_2 4} = \dfrac{\log_2 2^3}{\log_2 2^2} = \dfrac{3}{2}$

81. $\log_5 \dfrac{1}{250} = \log_5 \left(\dfrac{1}{125} \cdot \dfrac{1}{2} \right) = \log_5 \dfrac{1}{125} + \log_5 \dfrac{1}{2}$

$$= \log_5 5^{-3} + \log_5 2^{-1}$$

$$= -3 - \log_5 2$$

83. $\ln(5e^6) = \ln 5 + \ln e^6 = \ln 5 + 6 = 6 + \ln 5$

85. $f(t) = 90 - 15 \log_{10}(t + 1), \ 0 \le t \le 12$

(a) $f(0) = 90$

(b) $f(6) \approx 77$

(c) $f(12) \approx 73$

(d) $\quad 75 = 90 - 15 \log_{10}(t + 1)$

$\quad -15 = -15 \log_{10}(t + 1)$

$\quad\quad 1 = \log_{10}(t + 1)$

$\quad 10^1 = t + 1$

$\quad\quad t = 9$ months

(e) $f(t) = 90 - \log_{10}(t + 1)^{15}$

(f)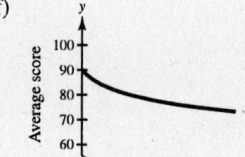

87. $f(x) = \ln x$

False, $f(0) \neq 0$ since 0 is not in the domain of $f(x)$. $f(1) = \ln 1 = 0$

89. False. $f(x) - f(2) = \ln x - \ln 2 = \ln \dfrac{x}{2} \neq \ln(x - 2)$

91. False. $f(u) = 2f(v) \implies \ln u = 2 \ln v \implies \ln u = \ln v^2 \implies u = v^2$

93. Let $x = \log_b u$ and $y = \log_b v$, then $b^x = u$ and $b^y = v$.

$$\dfrac{u}{v} = \dfrac{b^x}{b^y} = b^{x-y}$$

Then $\log_b \left(\dfrac{u}{v} \right) = \log_b(b^{x-y}) = x - y = \log_b u - \log_b v$

95. $f(x) = \log_{10} x$

$g(x) = \dfrac{\ln x}{\ln 10}$

$f(x) = g(x)$

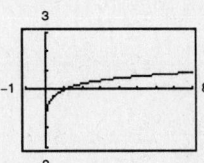

97. $f(x) = \ln \dfrac{x}{2}$, $g(x) = \dfrac{\ln x}{\ln 2}$, $h(x) = \ln x - \ln 2$

$f(x) = h(x)$ by Property 2.

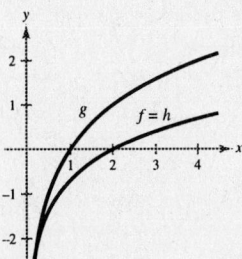

99. $\dfrac{24xy^{-2}}{16x^{-3}y} = \dfrac{24xx^3}{16yy^2} = \dfrac{3x^4}{2y^3}, x \neq 0$

101. $(18x^3y^4)^{-3}(18x^3y^4)^3 = \dfrac{(18x^3y^4)^3}{(18x^3y^4)^3} = 1$ if $x \neq 0, y \neq 0$.

103. $(2.8)^{7.6} \approx 2502.655$

105. $7^{-\pi} \approx 0.002$

107. $\sqrt[4]{350} \approx 4.325$

109. $\log_{10} 26 \approx 1.415$

111. $\ln 10.6 \approx 2.361$

Section 3.4   Exponential and Logarithmic Equations

- To solve an exponential equation, isolate the exponential expression, then take the logarithm of both sides.
  Then solve for the variable.
  1. $\log_a a^x = x$
  2. $\ln e^x = x$
- To solve a logarithmic equation, rewrite it in exponential form. Then solve for the variable.
  1. $a^{\log_a x} = x$
  2. $e^{\ln x} = x$
- If $a > 0$ and $a \neq 1$ we have the following:
  1. $\log_a x = \log_a y \iff x = y$
  2. $a^x = a^y \iff x = y$
- Check for extraneous solutions.

Solutions to Odd-Numbered Exercises

1. $4^{2x-7} = 64$

(a) $x = 5$

$4^{2(5)-7} = 4^3 = 64$

Yes, $x = 5$ is a solution.

(b) $x = 2$

$4^{2(2)-7} = 4^{-3} = \frac{1}{64} \neq 64$

No, $x = 2$ is not a solution.

3. $3e^{x+2} = 75$

   (a) $x = -2 + e^{25}$

      $3e^{(-2+e^{25})+2} = 3e^{e^{25}} \neq 75$

      No, $x = -2 + e^{25}$ is not a solution.

   (b) $x = -2 + \ln 25$

      $3e^{(-2+\ln 25)+2} = 3e^{\ln 25} = 3(25) = 75$

      Yes, $x = -2 + \ln 25$ is a solution.

   (c) $x \approx 1.2189$

      $3e^{1.2189+2} = 3e^{3.2189} \approx 75$

      Yes, $x \approx 1.2189$ is a solution.

5. $\log_4(3x) = 3 \implies 3x = 4^3 \implies 3x = 64$

   (a) $x \approx 20.3560$

      $3(20.3560) = 61.0680 \neq 64$

      No, $x \approx 20.3560$ is not a solution.

   (b) $x = -4$

      $3(-4) = -12 \neq 64$

      No, $x = -4$ is not a solution.

   (c) $x = \frac{64}{3}$

      $3\left(\frac{64}{3}\right) = 64$

      Yes, $x = \frac{64}{3}$ is a solution.

7. $4^x = 16$

   $4^x = 4^2$

   $x = 2$

9. $5^x = 625$

   $5^x = 5^4$

   $x = 4$

11. $7^x = \frac{1}{49}$

   $7^x = 7^{-2}$

   $x = -2$

13. $\left(\frac{1}{2}\right)^x = 32$

   $2^{-x} = 2^5$

   $-x = 5$

   $x = -5$

15. $\left(\frac{3}{4}\right)^x = \frac{27}{64}$

   $\left(\frac{3}{4}\right)^x = \left(\frac{3}{4}\right)^3$

   $x = 3$

17. $3^{x-1} = 27$

   $3^{x-1} = 3^3$

   $x - 1 = 3$

   $x = 4$

19. $\ln x - \ln 2 = 0$

   $\ln x = \ln 2$

   $x = 2$

21. $e^x = 2$

   $\ln e^x = \ln 2$

   $x = \ln 2$

   $x \approx 0.693$

23. $\ln x = -1$

   $e^{\ln x} = e^{-1}$

   $x = e^{-1}$

   $x \approx 0.368$

25. $\log_4 x = 3$

   $4^{\log_4 x} = 4^3$

   $x = 4^3$

   $x = 64$

27. $\log_{10} x - 2 = 0$

   $\log_{10} x = 2$

   $10^{\log_{10} x} = 10^2$

   $x = 10^2$

   $x = 100$

29. $\log_{10} x = -1$

   $10^{\log_{10} x} = 10^{-1}$

   $x = 10^{-1}$

   $x = \frac{1}{10}$

31. $f(x) = g(x)$

   $2^x = 8$

   $2^x = 2^3$

   $x = 3$

   Point of intersection: $(3, 8)$

33. $f(x) = g(x)$

   $\log_3 x = 2$

   $x = 3^2$

   $x = 9$

   Point of intersection: $(9, 2)$

35. $\log_{10} 10^{x^2} = x^2$

37. $8^{\log_8(x-2)} = x - 2$

39. $\ln e^{7x+2} = 7x + 2$

41. $e^{\ln(5x+2)} = 5x + 2$

43. $-1 + \ln e^{2x} = -1 + 2x = 2x - 1$

45. $e^x = 10$

$x = \ln 10 \approx 2.303$

47. $7 - 2e^x = 5$

$-2e^x = -2$

$e^x = 1$

$x = \ln 1 = 0$

49. $e^{3x} = 12$

$3x = \ln 12$

$x = \dfrac{\ln 12}{3} \approx 0.828$

51. $500e^{-x} = 300$

$e^{-x} = \dfrac{3}{5}$

$-x = \ln \dfrac{3}{5}$

$x = -\ln \dfrac{3}{5} = \ln \dfrac{5}{3} \approx 0.511$

53. $e^{2x} - 4e^x - 5 = 0$

$(e^x + 1)(e^x - 5) = 0$

$e^x = -1 \quad$ or $\quad e^x = 5$

(No solution) $\qquad x = \ln 5 \approx 1.609$

55. $20(100 - e^{x/2}) = 500$

$100 - e^{x/2} = 25$

$-e^{x/2} = -75$

$e^{x/2} = 75$

$\dfrac{x}{2} = \ln 75$

$x = 2 \ln 75 \approx 8.635$

57. $10^x = 42$

$x = \log_{10} 42 \approx 1.623$

59. $3^{2x} = 80$

$\ln 3^{2x} = \ln 80$

$2x \ln 3 = \ln 80$

$x = \dfrac{\ln 80}{2 \ln 3} \approx 1.994$

61. $5^{-t/2} = 0.20$

$5^{-t/2} = \dfrac{1}{5}$

$5^{-t/2} = 5^{-1}$

$-\dfrac{t}{2} = -1$

$t = 2$

63. $2^{3-x} = 565$

$\ln 2^{3-x} = \ln 565$

$(3 - x) \ln 2 = \ln 565$

$3 \ln 2 - x \ln 2 = \ln 565$

$-x \ln 2 = \ln 565 - \ln 2^3$

$x \ln 2 = \ln 8 - \ln 565$

$x = \dfrac{\ln 8 - \ln 565}{\ln 2} \approx -6.142$

65. $g(x) = 6e^{1-x} - 25$

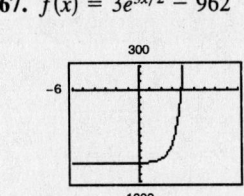

The zero is $x \approx -0.427$.

67. $f(x) = 3e^{3x/2} - 962$

The zero is $x \approx 3.847$.

69. $g(t) = e^{0.09t} - 3$

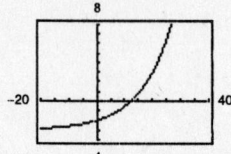

The zero is $x \approx 12.207$.

71. $h(t) = e^{0.125t} - 8$

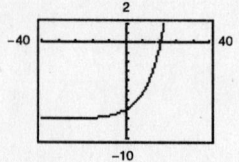

The zero is $x \approx 16.636$.

73.
$$8(10^{3x}) = 12$$
$$10^{3x} = \frac{12}{8}$$
$$\log_{10} 10^{3x} = \log_{10}\left(\frac{3}{2}\right)$$
$$3x = \log_{10}\left(\frac{3}{2}\right)$$
$$x = \frac{1}{3}\log_{10}\left(\frac{3}{2}\right) \approx 0.059$$

75.
$$3(5^{x-1}) = 21$$
$$5^{x-1} = 7$$
$$\ln 5^{x-1} = \ln 7$$
$$(x-1)\ln 5 = \ln 7$$
$$x - 1 = \frac{\ln 7}{\ln 5}$$
$$x = 1 + \frac{\ln 7}{\ln 5} \approx 2.209$$

77.
$$\left(1 + \frac{0.065}{365}\right)^{365t} = 4$$
$$\ln\left(1 + \frac{0.065}{365}\right)^{365t} = \ln 4$$
$$365t \ln\left(1 + \frac{0.065}{365}\right) = \ln 4$$
$$t = \frac{\ln 4}{365 \ln\left(1 + \frac{0.065}{365}\right)} \approx 21.330$$

79.
$$\left(1 + \frac{0.10}{12}\right)^{12t} = 2$$
$$\ln\left(1 + \frac{0.10}{12}\right)^{12t} = \ln 2$$
$$12t \ln\left(1 + \frac{0.10}{12}\right) = \ln 2$$
$$t = \frac{\ln 2}{12 \ln\left(1 + \frac{0.10}{12}\right)} \approx 6.960$$

81.
$$\frac{3000}{2 + e^{2x}} = 2$$
$$3000 = 2(2 + e^{2x})$$
$$1500 = 2 + e^{2x}$$
$$1498 = e^{2x}$$
$$\ln 1498 = 2x$$
$$x = \frac{\ln 1498}{2} \approx 3.656$$

83. $\ln x = -3$
$$x = e^{-3} \approx 0.050$$

85. $\ln 2x = 2.4$
$$2x = e^{2.4}$$
$$x = \frac{e^{2.4}}{2} \approx 5.512$$

87. $3 \ln 5x = 10$

$$\ln 5x = \frac{10}{3}$$

$$5x = e^{10/3}$$

$$x = \frac{e^{10/3}}{5} \approx 5.606$$

89. $\ln \sqrt{x + 2} = 1$

$$\sqrt{x + 2} = e^1$$

$$x + 2 = e^2$$

$$x = e^2 - 2 \approx 5.389$$

91. $\ln(x + 1)^2 = 2$

$$2 \ln|x + 1| = 2$$

$$\ln|x + 1| = 1$$

$$|x + 1| = e^1$$

$$x + 1 = \pm e$$

$$x = \pm e - 1$$

$$x \approx -3.718 \quad \text{or} \quad x \approx 1.718$$

93. $\ln x + \ln(x - 2) = 1$

$$\ln[x(x - 2)] = 1$$

$$x(x - 2) = e^1$$

$$x^2 - 2x - e = 0$$

$$x = \frac{2 \pm \sqrt{4 + 4e}}{2}$$

$$= \frac{2 \pm 2\sqrt{1 + e}}{2}$$

$$= 1 \pm \sqrt{1 + e}$$

The negative value is extraneous. The only solution is

$$x = 1 + \sqrt{1 + e} \approx 2.928.$$

95. $\ln (x + 5) = \ln(x - 1) - \ln(x + 1)$

$$\ln(x + 5) = \ln\left(\frac{x - 1}{x + 1}\right)$$

$$x + 5 = \frac{x - 1}{x + 1}$$

$$(x + 5)(x + 1) = x - 1$$

$$x^2 + 6x + 5 = x - 1$$

$$x^2 + 5x + 6 = 0$$

$$(x + 2)(x + 3) = 0$$

$$x = -2 \quad \text{or} \quad x = -3$$

Both of these solutions are extraneous,
so the equation has no solution.

97. $\log_{10}(z - 3) = 2$

$$10^{\log_{10}(z - 3)} = 10^2$$

$$z - 3 = 10^2$$

$$z = 10^2 + 3 = 103$$

99. $6 \log_3(0.5x) = 11$

$$\log_3(0.5x) = \tfrac{11}{6}$$

$$3^{\log_3(0.5x)} = 3^{11/6}$$

$$0.5x = 3^{11/6}$$

$$x = 2(3^{11/6}) \approx 14.988$$

101. $\log_{10}(x + 4) - \log_{10} x = \log_{10}(x + 2)$

$$\log_{10}\left(\frac{x + 4}{x}\right) = \log_{10}(x + 2)$$

$$\frac{x + 4}{x} = x + 2$$

$$x + 4 = x^2 + 2x$$

$$0 = x^2 + x - 4$$

$$x = \frac{-1 \pm \sqrt{17}}{2} \qquad \text{Quadratic Formula}$$

Choosing the positive value of x (the negative value is extraneous), we have

$$x = \frac{-1 + \sqrt{17}}{2} \approx 1.562.$$

103. $\log_4 x - \log_4(x - 1) = \dfrac{1}{2}$

$$\log_4\left(\frac{x}{x - 1}\right) = \frac{1}{2}$$

$$4^{\log_4\left(\frac{x}{x-1}\right)} = 4^{1/2}$$

$$\frac{x}{x - 1} = 4^{1/2}$$

$$x = 2(x - 1)$$

$$x = 2x - 2$$

$$-x = -2$$

$$x = 2$$

105. $\log_{10} 8x - \log_{10}\left(1 + \sqrt{x}\right) = 2$

$$\log_{10}\frac{8x}{1 + \sqrt{x}} = 2$$

$$\frac{8x}{1 + \sqrt{x}} = 10^2$$

$$8x = 100\left(1 + \sqrt{x}\right)$$

$$2x = 25\left(1 + \sqrt{x}\right)$$

$$2x = 25 + 25\sqrt{x}$$

$$2x - 25 = 25\sqrt{x}$$

$$(2x - 25)^2 = \left(25\sqrt{x}\right)^2$$

$$4x^2 - 100x + 625 = 625x$$

$$4x^2 - 725x + 625 = 0$$

$$x = \frac{725 \pm \sqrt{725^2 - 4(4)(625)}}{2(4)}$$

$$x = \frac{725 \pm \sqrt{515625}}{8}$$

$$x = \frac{25\left(29 \pm 5\sqrt{33}\right)}{8}$$

$$x \approx 0.866 \text{ (extraneous)} \quad \text{or} \quad x \approx 180.384$$

The only solution is $x = \dfrac{25\left(29 + 5\sqrt{33}\right)}{8} \approx 180.384$

107. $y_1 = 7$

$y_2 = 2^x$

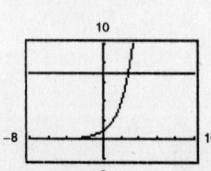

From the graph we have $x \approx 2.807$ when $y = 7$.

The point of intersection is approximately $(2.807, 7)$.

109. $y_1 = 3$

$y_2 = \ln x$

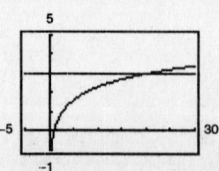

From the graph we have $x \approx 20.806$ when $y = 3$.

The point of intersection is approximately $(20.086, 3)$.

111.
$$A = Pe^{rt}$$
$$2000 = 1000e^{0.085t}$$
$$2 = e^{0.085t}$$
$$\ln 2 = 0.085t$$
$$\frac{\ln 2}{0.085} = t$$
$$t \approx 8.2 \text{ years}$$

113.
$$A = Pe^{rt}$$
$$3000 = 1000e^{0.085t}$$
$$3 = e^{0.085t}$$
$$\ln 3 = 0.085t$$
$$\frac{\ln 3}{0.085} = t$$
$$t \approx 12.9 \text{ years}$$

115. $p = 500 - 0.5(e^{0.004x})$

(a)
$$p = 350$$
$$350 = 500 - 0.5(e^{0.004x})$$
$$300 = e^{0.004x}$$
$$0.004x = \ln 300$$
$$x \approx 1426 \text{ units}$$

(b)
$$p = 300$$
$$300 = 500 - 0.5(e^{0.004x})$$
$$400 = e^{0.004x}$$
$$0.004x = \ln 400$$
$$x \approx 1498 \text{ units}$$

117. $V = 6.7e^{-48.1/t}$, $t \geq 0$

(a)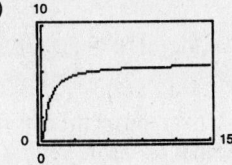

(b) As $t \to \infty$, $V \to 6.7$.

Horizontal asymptote: $V = 6.7$

The yield will approach 6.7 million cubic feet per acre.

(c)
$$1.3 = 6.7e^{-48.1/t}$$
$$\frac{1.3}{6.7} = e^{-48.1/t}$$
$$\ln\left(\frac{13}{67}\right) = \frac{-48.1}{t}$$
$$t = \frac{-48.1}{\ln(13/67)} \approx 29.3 \text{ years}$$

119. (a) From the graph shown in the textbook, we see horizontal asymptotes at $y = 0$ and $y = 100$. These represent the lower and upper percent bounds; the range falls between 0% and 100%.

(b) Males
$$50 = \frac{100}{1 + e^{-0.6114(x-69.71)}}$$
$$1 + e^{-0.6114(x-69.71)} = 2$$
$$e^{-0.6114(x-69.71)} = 1$$
$$-0.6114(x - 69.71) = \ln 1$$
$$-0.6114(x - 69.71) = 0$$
$$x = 69.71 \text{ inches}$$

Females
$$50 = \frac{100}{1 + e^{-0.66607(x-64.51)}}$$
$$1 + e^{-0.66607(x-64.51)} = 2$$
$$e^{-0.66607(x-64.51)} = 1$$
$$-0.66607(x - 64.51) = \ln 1$$
$$-0.66607(x - 64.51) = 0$$
$$x = 64.51 \text{ inches}$$

121. $T = 20[1 + 7(2^{-h})]$

    (a) From the graph in the textbook we see a horizontal asymptote at $T = 20$.
        This represents the room temperature.

    (b) $100 = 20[1 + 7(2^{-h})]$

             $5 = 1 + 7(2^{-h})$

             $4 = 7(2^{-h})$

             $\dfrac{4}{7} = 2^{-h}$

             $\ln\left(\dfrac{4}{7}\right) = \ln 2^{-h}$

             $\ln\left(\dfrac{4}{7}\right) = -h \ln 2$

             $\dfrac{\ln\left(\frac{4}{7}\right)}{-\ln 2} = h$

             $h \approx 0.81$ hour

123. $\log_a(uv) = \log_a u + \log_a v$

    True by Property 1 in Section 5.3.

125. $\log_a(u - v) = \log_a u - \log_a v$

    False.

    $1.95 \approx \log_{10}(100 - 10) \neq \log_{10} 100 - \log_{10} 10 = 1$

127. $A = Pe^{rt}$

    (a) $A = (2P)e^{rt} = 2(Pe^{rt})$ This doubles your money.

    (b) $A = Pe^{(2r)t} = Pe^{rt}e^{rt} = e^{rt}(Pe^{rt})$

    (c) $A = Pe^{r(2t)} = Pe^{rt}e^{rt} = e^{rt}(Pe^{rt})$

    Doubling the interest rate yields the same result as doubling the number of years.

    If $2 > e^{rt}$ (i.e., $rt < \ln 2$), then doubling your investment would yield the most money. If $rt > \ln 2$, then doubling either the interest rate or the number of years would yield more money.

129. No. Doubling time does not depend on the amount of the investment, but depends on the interest rate, r.

    $2P = Pe^{rt}$

      $2 = e^{rt}$

    $\ln 2 = rt$

    $\dfrac{\ln 2}{r} = t$

131. $\sqrt{32} - 2\sqrt{25} = \sqrt{16 \cdot 2} - 2(5)$

                  $= 4\sqrt{2} - 10$

133. $\dfrac{3}{\sqrt{10} - 2} = \dfrac{3}{\sqrt{10} - 2} \cdot \dfrac{\sqrt{10} + 2}{\sqrt{10} + 2}$

             $= \dfrac{3\left(\sqrt{10} + 2\right)}{10 - 4}$

             $= \dfrac{3\left(\sqrt{10} + 2\right)}{6}$

             $= \dfrac{\sqrt{10} + 2}{2}$

             $= \dfrac{1}{2}\sqrt{10} + 1$

135. $t = \dfrac{k}{s^3}$

137. $x = \dfrac{k}{b - 3}$

139. $\log_6 9 = \dfrac{\log_{10} 9}{\log_{10} 6} = \dfrac{\ln 9}{\ln 6} \approx 1.226$

141. $\log_{3/4} 5 = \dfrac{\log_{10} 5}{\log_{10}\left(\dfrac{3}{4}\right)} = \dfrac{\ln 5}{\ln\left(\dfrac{3}{4}\right)} \approx -5.595$

Section 3.5   Exponential and Logarithmic Models

■ You should be able to solve growth and decay problems.

 (a) Exponential growth if $b0$ and $y = ae^{bx}$.

 (b) Exponential decay if $b > 0$ and $y = ae^{-bx}$.

■ You should be able to use the Gaussian model

 $y = ae^{-(x-b)^2/c}$.

■ You should be able to use the logistics growth model

 $y = \dfrac{a}{1 + be^{-rx}}$.

■ You should be able to use the logarithmic models

 $y = a + b \ln x, \; y = a + b \log_{10} x$.

Solutions to Odd-Numbered Exercises

1. $y = 2e^{x/4}$

This is an exponential growth model. Matches graph (c)

3. $y = 6 + \log_{10}(x + 2)$

This is a logarithmic function shifted up 6 units and left 2 units. Matches graph (b)

5. $y = \ln(x + 1)$

This is a logarithmic model. Matches graph (d)

7. Since $A = 1000e^{0.12t}$, the time to double is given by $2000 = 1000e^{0.12t}$ and we have

$2000 = 1000e^{0.12t}$

$2 = e^{0.12t}$

$\ln 2 = \ln e^{0.12t}$

$\ln 2 = 0.12t$

$t = \dfrac{\ln 2}{0.12} \approx 5.78$ years.

Amount after 10 years: $A = 1000e^{1.2} \approx \$3320.12$

9. Since $A = 750e^{rt}$ and $A = 1500$ when $t = 7.75$, we have the following.

$$1500 = 750e^{7.75r}$$

$$2 = e^{7.75r}$$

$$\ln 2 = \ln e^{7.75r}$$

$$\ln 2 = 7.75r$$

$$r = \frac{\ln 2}{7.75} \approx 0.089438 = 8.9438\%$$

Amount after 10 years: $A = 750e^{0.089438(10)} \approx \$1834.37$

11. Since $A = 500e^{rt}$ and $A = \$1505.00$ when $t = 10$, we have the following.

$$1505.00 = 500e^{10r}$$

$$r = \frac{\ln(1505.00/500)}{10} \approx 0.110 = 11.0\%$$

The time to double is given by

$$1000 = 500e^{0.110t}$$

$$t = \frac{\ln 2}{0.110} \approx 6.3 \text{ years.}$$

13. Since $A = Pe^{0.045t}$ and $A = 10,000.00$ when $t = 10$, we have the following.

$$10,000.00 = Pe^{0.045(10)}$$

$$\frac{10,000.00}{e^{0.045(10)}} = P \approx \$6376.28$$

The time to double is given by

$$t = \frac{\ln 2}{0.045} \approx 15.40 \text{ years.}$$

15. $500,000 = P\left(1 + \dfrac{0.075}{12}\right)^{12(20)}$

$$P = \frac{500,000}{\left(1 + \dfrac{0.075}{12}\right)^{12(20)}} = \frac{500,000}{1.00625^{240}} \approx \$112,087.09$$

17. $P = 1000, r = 11\%$

(a) $n = 1$

$$(1 + 0.11)^t = 2$$

$$t \ln 1.11 = \ln 2$$

$$t = \frac{\ln 2}{\ln 1.11} \approx 6.642 \text{ years}$$

(c) $n = 365$

$$\left(1 + \frac{0.11}{365}\right)^{365t} = 2$$

$$365t \ln\left(1 + \frac{0.11}{365}\right) = \ln 2$$

$$t = \frac{\ln 2}{365 \ln\left(1 + \frac{0.11}{365}\right)} \approx 6.302 \text{ years}$$

(b) $n = 12$

$$\left(1 + \frac{0.11}{12}\right)^{12t} = 2$$

$$12t \ln\left(1 + \frac{0.11}{12}\right) = \ln 2$$

$$t = \frac{\ln 2}{12 \ln\left(1 + \frac{0.11}{12}\right)} \approx 6.330 \text{ years}$$

(d) Continuously

$$e^{0.11t} = 2$$

$$0.11t = \ln 2$$

$$t = \frac{\ln 2}{0.11} \approx 6.301 \text{ years}$$

19. $3P = Pe^{rt}$

$3 = e^{rt}$

$\ln 3 = rt$

$\dfrac{\ln 3}{r} = t$

r	2%	4%	6%	8%	10%	12%
$t = \dfrac{\ln 3}{r}$ (years)	54.93	27.47	18.31	13.73	10.99	9.16

21. $3P = P(1 + r)^t$

$3 = (1 + r)^t$

$\ln 3 = \ln(1 + r)^t$

$\ln 3 = t \ln(1 + r)$

$\dfrac{\ln 3}{\ln(1 + r)} = t$

r	2%	4%	6%	8%	10%	12%
$t = \dfrac{\ln 3}{\ln(1 + r)}$ (years)	55.48	18.01	18.85	14.27	11.53	9.69

23. Continuous compounding results in faster growth.

$A = 1 + 0.075[\![t]\!]$ and $A = e^{0.07t}$

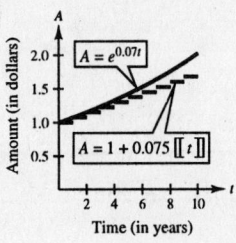

25. $\dfrac{1}{2}C = Ce^{k(1620)}$

$0.5 = e^{k(1620)}$

$\ln 0.5 = \ln e^{k(1620)}$

$\ln 0.5 = k(1620)$

$k = \dfrac{\ln 0.5}{1620}$

Given $C = 10$ grams after 1000, years we have

$y = 10e^{[(\ln 0.5)/1620](1000)}$

≈ 6.52 grams.

27. $\dfrac{1}{2}C = Ce^{k(5730)}$

$0.5 = e^{k(5730)}$

$\ln 0.5 = \ln e^{k(5730)}$

$\ln 0.5 = k(5730)$

$k = \dfrac{\ln 0.5}{5730}$

Given $y = 2$ grams after 1000 years, we have

$2 = Ce^{[(\ln 0.5)/5730](1000)}$

$C \approx 2.26$ grams.

29. $\dfrac{1}{2}C = Ce^{k(24,360)}$

$0.5 = e^{k(24,360)}$

$\ln 0.5 = \ln e^{k(24,360)}$

$\ln 0.5 = k(24,360)$

$k = \dfrac{\ln 0.5}{24,360}$

Given $y = 2.1$ grams after 1000 years, we have

$2.1 = Ce^{[(\ln 0.5)/24,360](1000)}$

$C \approx 2.16$ grams.

31. $y = ae^{bx}$

$1 = ae^{b(0)} \implies 1 = a$

$10 = e^{b(3)}$

$\ln 10 = 3b$

$\dfrac{\ln 10}{3} = b \implies b \approx 0.7675$

Thus, $y = e^{0.7675x}$.

33. $y = ae^{bx}$

$5 = ae^{b(0)} \implies 5 = a$

$1 = 5e^{b(4)}$

$\dfrac{1}{5} = e^{4b}$

$\ln\left(\dfrac{1}{5}\right) = 4b$

$\dfrac{\ln\left(\dfrac{1}{5}\right)}{4} = b \implies b \approx -0.4024$

Thus, $y = 5e^{-0.4024x}$.

35. $$P = 105{,}300e^{0.015t}$$

$$150{,}000 = 105{,}300e^{0.015t}$$

$$\ln \tfrac{1500}{1053} = 0.015t$$

$$t \approx 23.59$$

The population will reach 150,000 during 2023.
[Note: 2000 + 23.59]

37. $P = 2500e^{kt}$

For 1945, use $t = -55$

$$1350 = 2500e^{k(-55)}$$

$$\ln\left(\frac{1350}{2500}\right) = -55k \implies k \approx 0.0112$$

For 2010, use $t = 10$

$$P = 2500e^{0.0112(10)} \approx 2796 \text{ people}$$

39.

Country	1997	2020
Croatia	5.0	4.8
Mali	9.9	20.4
Singapore	3.5	4.3
Sweden	8.9	9.5

(a) Croatia: $\qquad a = 5.0$

$$4.8 = 5.0e^{b(23)}$$

$$\ln\left(\frac{4.8}{5.0}\right) = 23b \implies b \approx -0.0018$$

For 2030, use $t = 33$

$$y = 5.0e^{-0.0018(33)} \approx 4.7 \text{ million}$$

Mali: $\qquad a = 9.9$

$$20.4 = 9.9e^{b(23)}$$

$$\ln\left(\frac{20.4}{9.9}\right) = 23b \implies b \approx 0.0314$$

For 2030, use $t = 33$

$$y = 9.9e^{0.0314(33)} \approx 27.9 \text{ million}$$

Singapore: $\qquad a = 3.5$

$$4.3 = 3.5e^{b(23)}$$

$$\ln\left(\frac{4.3}{3.5}\right) = 23b \implies b \approx 0.0090$$

For 2030, use $t = 33$

$$y = 3.5e^{0.0090(33)} \approx 4.7 \text{ million}$$

Sweden: $\qquad a = 8.9$

$$9.5 = 8.9e^{b(23)}$$

$$\ln\left(\frac{9.5}{8.9}\right) = 23b \implies b \approx 0.0028$$

For 2030, use $t = 33$

$$y = 8.9e^{0.0028(33)} \approx 9.8 \text{ million}$$

(b) The constant b determines the growth rates. The greater the rate of growth, the greater the value of b.

(c) The constant b determines whether the population is increasing ($b > 0$) or decreasing ($b < 0$).

41. $N = 250e^{kt}$

$280 = 250e^{k(10)}$

$1.12 = e^{10k}$

$k = \dfrac{\ln 1.12}{10}$

$N = 250e^{[(\ln 1.12)/10]t}$

$500 = 250e^{[(\ln 1.12)/10]t}$

$2 = e^{[(\ln 1.12)/10]t}$

$\ln 2 = [(\ln 1.12)/10]t$

$t = \dfrac{\ln 2}{(\ln 1.12)/10} \approx 61.16 \text{ hours}$

43. $y = Ce^{kt}$

$\dfrac{1}{2}C = Ce^{5730k}$

$\ln \dfrac{1}{2} = 5730k$

$k = \dfrac{\ln (1/2)}{5730}$

The ancient charcoal has only 15% as much radioactive carbon.

$0.15C = Ce^{[(\ln 0.5)/5730]t}$

$\ln 0.15 = \dfrac{\ln 0.5}{5730}t$

$t = \dfrac{5730 \ln 0.15}{\ln 0.5} \approx 15{,}683 \text{ years}$

45. $(0, 2000), (2, 500)$

(a) $m = \dfrac{500 - 2000}{2 - 0} = -750$

$V = -750t + 2000$

(b) $500 = 2000e^{k(2)}$

$\ln \dfrac{1}{4} = 2k \implies k \approx -0.6931$

$V = 2000e^{-0.6931t}$

(c)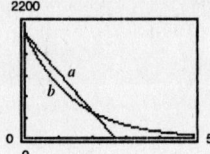

The exponential model depreciates faster in the first 2 years.

(d)

t	1	3
$V = -750t + 2000$	\$1250	$-\$250$
$V = 2000e^{-0.6931t}$	\$1000	\$250

(e) The slope of the linear model means that the computer depreciates \$750 per year.

47. $S = \dfrac{500{,}000}{1 + 0.6e^{kt}}$

(a) $300{,}000 = \dfrac{500{,}000}{1 + 0.6e^{2k}}$

$1 + 0.6e^{2k} = \dfrac{5}{3}$

$0.6e^{2k} = \dfrac{2}{3}$

$e^{2k} = \dfrac{10}{9}$

$2k = \ln\left(\dfrac{10}{9}\right)$

$k = \dfrac{1}{2}\ln\left(\dfrac{10}{9}\right) \approx 0.053$

$S = \dfrac{500{,}000}{1 + 0.6e^{0.053t}}$

(b) When $t = 5$:

$S = \dfrac{500{,}000}{1 + 0.6e^{[0.5\ln(10/9)](5)}} \approx 280{,}771$ units

49. $y = ae^{bt}$

$632{,}000 = 742{,}000e^{b(2)}$

$\dfrac{632}{742} = e^{2b}$

$b = \dfrac{1}{2}\ln\left(\dfrac{632}{742}\right)$

$y = 742{,}000e^{0.5[\ln(632/742)](3)} \approx \$583{,}275$

51. $p(t) = \dfrac{1000}{1 + 9e^{-0.1656t}}$

(a)

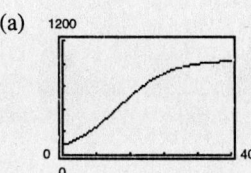

The horizontal asymptotes are $p = 0$ and $p = 1000$. The asymptote with the larger p-value, $p = 1000$, indicates that the population size will approach 1000 as time increases.

(b) $p(5) = \dfrac{1000}{1 + 9e^{-0.1656(5)}} \approx 203$ animals

(c) $500 = \dfrac{1000}{1 + 9e^{-0.1656t}}$

$1 + 9e^{-0.1656t} = 2$

$9e^{-0.1656t} = 1$

$e^{-0.1656t} = \dfrac{1}{9}$

$t = -\dfrac{\ln(1/9)}{0.1656} \approx 13$ months

53. $R = \log_{10}\dfrac{I}{I_0} = \log_{10} I$ since $I_0 = 1$.

(a) $8.6 = \log_{10} I$

$10^{8.6} = I \approx 398{,}107{,}171$

(b) $6.7 = \log_{10} I$

$10^{6.7} = I \approx 5{,}011{,}872$

(c) $7.7 = \log_{10} I$

$10^{7.7} = I \approx 50{,}118{,}723$

55. $\beta(I) = 10 \log_{10} \dfrac{I}{I_0}$ where $I_0 = 10^{-12}$ watt/m^2

(a) $\beta(10^{-9}) = 10 \log_{10} \dfrac{10^{-9}}{10^{-12}} = 10 \log_{10} 10^3 = 30$ decibels

(b) $\beta(10^{-3.5}) = 10 \log_{10} \dfrac{10^{-3.5}}{10^{-12}} = 10 \log_{10} 10^{8.5} = 85$ decibels

(c) $\beta(10^{-3}) = 10 \log_{10} \dfrac{10^{-3}}{10^{-12}} = 10 \log_{10} 10^9 = 90$ decibels

(d) $\beta(10^{-0.5}) = 10 \log_{10} \dfrac{10^{-0.5}}{10^{-12}} = 10 \log_{10} 10^{11.5} = 115$ decibels

57. $\beta = 10 \log_{10} \dfrac{I}{I_0}$

$10^{\beta/10} = \dfrac{I}{I_0}$

$I = I_0 \, 10^{\beta/10}$

% decrease $= \dfrac{I_0 \, 10^{8.8} - I_0 \, 10^{7.2}}{I_0 \, 10^{8.8}} \times 100 \approx 97\%$

59. pH $= -\log_{10}[\text{H}^+] = -\log_{10}[11.3 \times 10^{-6}] \approx 4.95$

61. $3.2 = -\log_{10}[\text{H}^+]$

$10^{-3.2} = [\text{H}^+]$

$[\text{H}^+] \approx 6.3 \times 10^{-4}$ moles per liter

63. $\text{pH} - 1 = -\log_{10}[\text{H}^+]$

$-(\text{pH} - 1) = \log_{10}[\text{H}^+]$

$10^{-(\text{pH}-1)} = [\text{H}^+]$

$10^{-\text{pH}+1} = [\text{H}^+]$

$10^{-\text{pH}} \cdot 10 = [\text{H}^+]$

The hydrogen ion concentration is increased by a factor of 10.

65. $u = 120{,}000 \left[\dfrac{0.075t}{1 - \left(\dfrac{1}{1 + 0.075/12}\right)^{12t}} - 1 \right]$

(a)

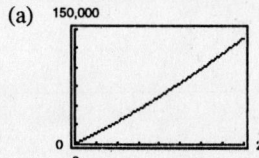

(b) From the graph, $u = \$120{,}000$ when $x \approx 21$ years. It would take approximately 37.6 years to pay \$240,000 in interest. Yes, it is possible to pay twice as much in interest charges as the size of the mortgage. It is especially likely when the interest rates are higher.

67. $t = -2.5 \ln \dfrac{T - 70}{98.6 - 70}$

At 9:00 A.M. we have:

$t = -2.5 \ln \dfrac{85.7 - 70}{98.6 - 70} \approx 1.5$ hours

From this you can conclude that the person died at 7:30 A.M.

69. False. A logistics growth function never has an x-intercept.

71. (a) Logarithmic

(b) Logistic

(c) Exponential (decay)

(d) Linear

(e) None of the above (appears to be a combination of a linear and a quadratic)

(f) Exponential (growth)

73. Answers will vary.

75.
$$\frac{3}{2} \begin{array}{|rrrr} 8 & -36 & 54 & -27 \\ & 12 & -36 & 27 \\ \hline 8 & -24 & 18 & 0 \end{array}$$

Thus, $\dfrac{8x^3 - 36x^2 + 54x - 27}{x - (3/2)} = 8x^2 - 24x + 18.$

77.
$$-5 \begin{array}{|rrrrr} 1 & 0 & 0 & -3 & 1 \\ & -5 & 25 & -125 & 640 \\ \hline 1 & -5 & 25 & -128 & 641 \end{array}$$

Thus, $\dfrac{x^4 - 3x + 1}{x + 5} = x^3 - 5x^2 + 25x - 128 + \dfrac{641}{x + 5}.$

79. $y = -4x - 1$

Line

Slope: $m = -4$

y-intercept: $(0, -1)$

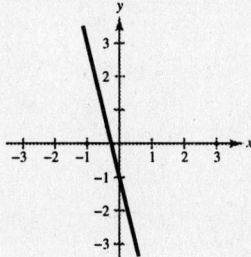

81. $y = 2x^2 - 7x - 30$

$\quad = (2x + 5)(x - 6)$

$\quad = 2\left(x - \frac{7}{4}\right)^2 - \frac{289}{8}$

Parabola

Vertex: $\left(\frac{7}{4}, -\frac{289}{8}\right)$

x-intercepts: $\left(-\frac{5}{2}, 0\right), (6, 0)$

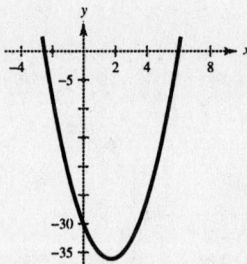

83. $-x^2 - 8y = 0$

$\quad\quad x^2 = -8y$

Parabola

Vertex: $(0, 0)$

Focus: $(0, -2)$

Directrix: $y = 2$

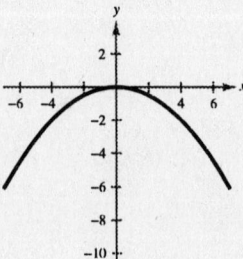

85. $y = \dfrac{x^2}{-x-2} = -x + 2 + \dfrac{4}{-x-2}$

Vertical asymptote: $x = -2$

Slant asymptote: $y = -x + 2$

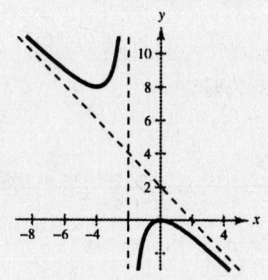

87. $(x - 4)^2 + (y + 7) = 4$

$(x - 4)^2 = -y - 7 + 4$

$(x - 4)^2 = -(y + 3)$

Parabola

Vertex: $(4, -3)$

$P = -\frac{1}{4}$

Focus: $(4, -3.25)$

Directrix: $y = -2.75$

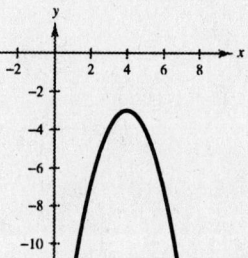

89. $f(x) = -2^{-x-1} - 1$

Horizontal asymptote: $y = -1$

x	-2	-1	0	1	2
$f(x)$	-3	-2	$-\frac{3}{2}$	$-\frac{5}{4}$	$-\frac{9}{8}$

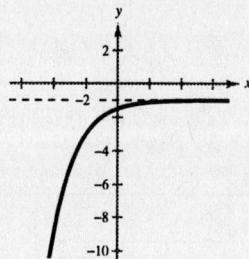

91. $f(x) = -3^x + 4$

Horizontal asymptote: $y = 4$

x	-2	-1	0	1	2
$f(x)$	$3\frac{8}{9}$	$3\frac{2}{3}$	3	1	-5

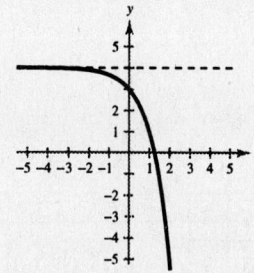

Review Exercises for Chapter 3

Solutions to Odd-Numbered Exercises

1. $(6.1)^{2.4} \approx 76.699$

3. $2^{-0.5\pi} \approx 0.337$

5. $60^{\sqrt{3}} \approx 1201.845$

7. $f(x) = 4^x$

Intercept: $(0, 1)$

Horizontal asymptote: x-axis

Increasing on: $(-\infty, \infty)$

Matches graph (c)

9. $f(x) = -4^x$

Intercept: $(0, -1)$

Horizontal asymptote: x-axis

Decreasing on: $(-\infty, \infty)$

Matches graph (a)

11. $f(x) = 4^{-x} + 4$

Horizontal asymptote: $y = 4$

x	-1	0	1	2	3
$f(x)$	8	5	4.25	4.0625	4.016

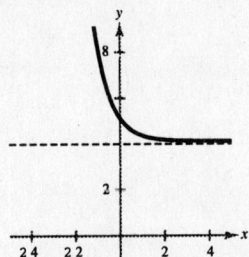

13. $f(x) = -2.65^{x+1}$

Horizontal asymptote: $y = 0$

x	-2	-1	0	1	2
$f(x)$	-0.377	-1	-2.65	-7.023	-18.61

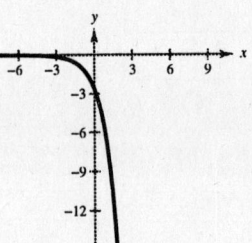

15. $f(x) = 5^{x-2} + 4$

Horizontal asymptote: $y = 4$

x	-1	0	1	2	3
$f(x)$	4.008	4.04	4.2	5	9

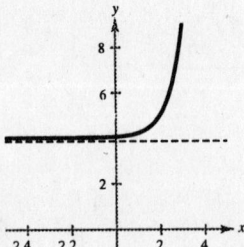

17. $f(x) = \left(\frac{1}{2}\right)^{-x} + 3 = 2^x + 3$

Horizontal asymptote: $y = 3$

x	-2	-1	0	1	2
$f(x)$	3.25	3.5	4	5	7

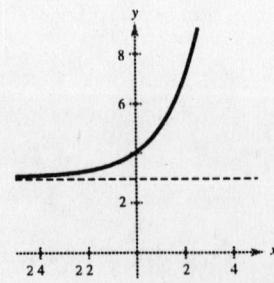

19. $e^8 \approx 2980.958$

21. $e^{-1.7} \approx 0.183$

23. $h(x) = e^{-x/2}$

x	-2	-1	0	1	2
$h(x)$	2.72	1.65	1	0.61	0.37

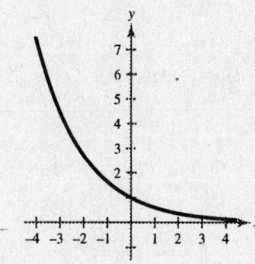

25. $f(x) = e^{x+2}$

x	-3	-2	-1	0	1
$f(x)$	0.37	1	2.72	7.39	20.09

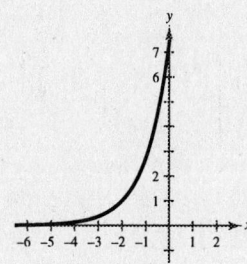

27. $A = 3500\left(1 + \dfrac{0.065}{n}\right)^{10n}$ or $A = 3500e^{(0.065)(10)}$

n	1	2	4	12	365	Continuous Compounding
A	\$6569.98	\$6635.43	\$6669.46	\$6692.64	\$6704.00	\$6704.39

29. $200{,}000 = Pe^{0.08t}$

$$P = \frac{200{,}000}{e^{0.08t}}$$

t	1	10	20	30	40	50
P	\$184,623.27	\$89,865.79	\$40,379.30	\$18,143.59	\$8,152.44	\$3,663.13

31. $F(t) = 1 - e^{-t/3}$

(a) $F\left(\frac{1}{2}\right) \approx 0.154$

(b) $F(2) \approx 0.487$

(c) $F(5) \approx 0.811$

33. (a) $A = 50{,}000e^{(0.0875)(35)} \approx \$1{,}069{,}047.14$

(b) The doubling time is

$$\frac{\ln 2}{0.0875} \approx 7.9 \text{ years.}$$

35. $\quad 4^3 = 64$

$\log_4 64 = 3$

37. $\log_{10} 1000 = \log_{10} 10^3 = 3$

39. $\log_2 \frac{1}{8} = \log_2 2^{-3} = -3$

41. $g(x) = \log_7 x \implies x = 7^y$

Vertical asymptote: $x = 0$

x	$\frac{1}{7}$	1	7	49
$g(x)$	-1	0	1	2

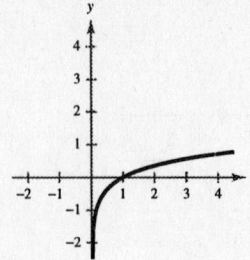

43. $f(x) = \log_{10}\left(\dfrac{x}{3}\right) \implies \dfrac{x}{3} = 10^y \implies x = 3(10^y)$

Vertical asymptote: $x = 0$

x	0.03	0.3	3	30
$f(x)$	-2	-1	0	1

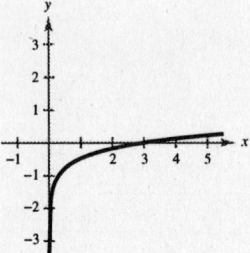

45. $f(x) = 4 - \log_{10}(x + 5)$

Vertical asymptote: $x = -5$

x	-4	-3	-2	-1	0	1
$f(x)$	4	3.70	3.52	3.40	3.30	3.22

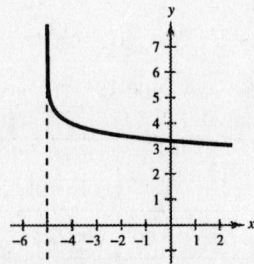

47. $\ln 22.6 \approx 3.118$

49. $\ln e^{-12} = -12$

51. $\ln\left(\sqrt{7} + 5\right) \approx 2.034$

53. $f(x) = \ln x + 3$

Domain: $(0, \infty)$

Vertical asymptote: $x = 0$

x	1	2	3	$\frac{1}{2}$	$\frac{1}{4}$
$f(x)$	3	3.69	4.10	2.31	1.61

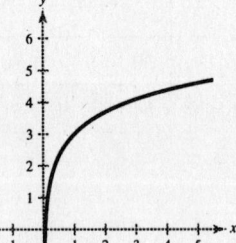

55. $h(x) = \ln(x^2) = 2\ln|x|$

Vertical asymptote: $x = 0$

x	± 0.5	± 1	± 2	± 3	± 4
y	-1.39	0	1.39	2.20	2.77

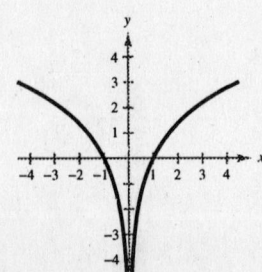

57. $s = 25 - \dfrac{13 \ln(10/12)}{\ln 3} \approx 27.16$ miles

59. $\log_{12} 200 = \dfrac{\log_{10} 200}{\log_{10} 12} \approx 2.132$

$\log_{12} 200 = \dfrac{\ln 200}{\ln 12} \approx 2.132$

61. $\log_3 0.28 = \dfrac{\log_{10} 0.28}{\log_{10} 3} \approx -1.159$

$\log_3 0.28 = \dfrac{\ln 0.28}{\ln 3} \approx -1.159$

63. $-\ln\left(\frac{1}{12}\right) = -[\ln 1 - \ln 12] = -[0 - \ln 12] = \ln 12$

65. $\log_8\left(\dfrac{\sqrt{x}}{y^3}\right) = \log_8 \sqrt{x} - \log_8 y^3 = \dfrac{1}{2}\log_8 x - 3\log_8 y$

67. $\log_5 5x^2 = \log_5 5 + \log_5 x^2$

$\qquad = 1 + 2\log_5|x|$

69. $\log_{10} \dfrac{5\sqrt{y}}{x^2} = \log_{10} 5\sqrt{y} - \log_{10} x^2$

$\qquad = \log_{10} 5 + \log_{10} \sqrt{y} - \log_{10} x^2$

$\qquad = \log_{10} 5 + \dfrac{1}{2}\log_{10} y - 2\log_{10}|x|$

71. $\log_2 5 + \log_2 x = \log_2 5x$

73. $\dfrac{1}{2}\ln|2x - 1| - 2\ln|x + 1| = \ln \sqrt{|2x - 1|} - \ln|x + 1|^2$

$\qquad = \ln \dfrac{\sqrt{|2x - 1|}}{(x + 1)^2}$

75. $t = 50 \log_{10} \dfrac{18,000}{18,000 - h}$

(a) Domain: $0 \le h < 18,000$

(b)
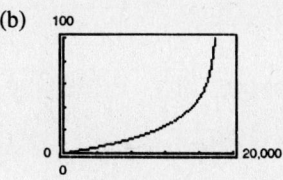

Vertical asymptote: $h = 18,000$

(c) As the plane approaches its absolute ceiling, it climbs at a slower rate, so the time required increases.

(d) $50 \log_{10} \dfrac{18,000}{18,000 - 4000} \approx 5.46$ minutes

77. $3^x = 729$

$3^x = 3^6$

$x = 6$

79. $6^{x-2} = 1296$

$6^{x-2} = 6^4$

$x - 2 = 4$

$x = 6$

81. $\log_x 243 = 5$

$x^5 = 243$

$x^5 = 3^5$

$x = 3$

83. $e^{3x} = 25$

$\ln e^{3x} = \ln 25$

$3x = \ln 25$

$x = \dfrac{\ln 25}{3} \approx 1.073$

85. $14e^{3x+2} = 560$

$e^{3x+2} = 40$

$\ln e^{3x+2} = \ln 40$

$3x + 2 = \ln 40$

$x = \dfrac{(\ln 40) - 2}{3} \approx 0.563$

87. $e^x - 28 = -8$

$e^x = 20$

$x = \ln 20 \approx 2.996$

89. $2(12^x) = 190$

$12^x = 95$

$\ln 12^x = \ln 95$

$x \ln 12 = \ln 95$

$x = \dfrac{\ln 95}{\ln 12} \approx 1.833$

91. $e^{2x} - 6e^x + 8 = 0$

$(e^x - 2)(e^x - 4) = 0$

$e^x = 2 \quad$ or $\quad e^x = 4$

$x = \ln 2 \qquad x = \ln 4$

$x \approx 0.693 \qquad x \approx 1.386$

93. $4^{-0.2x} + x = 0$

Graph $y_1 = 4^{-0.2x} + x$.

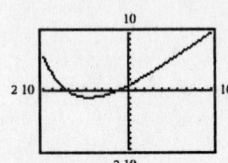

The x-intercepts are at $x \approx -7.04$ and $x \approx -1.53$.

95. $4e^{1.2x} = 9$

Graph $y_1 = 4e^{1.2x}$ and $y_2 = 9$.

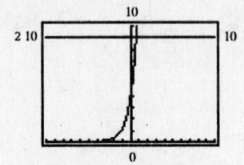

The intersection is at $x \approx 0.68$.

97. $\ln 5x = 7.2$

$5x = e^{7.2}$

$x = \dfrac{e^{7.2}}{5} \approx 267.886$

99. $4 \ln 3x = 15$

$\ln 3x = \dfrac{15}{4}$

$3x = e^{15/4}$

$x = \dfrac{e^{15/4}}{3} \approx 14.174$

101. $\ln \sqrt{x + 8} = 3$

$\frac{1}{2} \ln(x + 8) = 3$

$\ln(x + 8) = 6$

$x + 8 = e^6$

$x = e^6 - 8 \approx 395.429$

103. $\ln x - \ln 5 = 4$

$\ln \dfrac{x}{5} = 4$

$\dfrac{x}{5} = e^4$

$x = 5e^4 \approx 272.991$

105. $\log_{10}(x + 2) - \log_{10} x = \log_{10}(x + 5)$

$\log_{10}\left(\dfrac{x + 2}{x}\right) = \log_{10}(x + 5)$

$\dfrac{x + 2}{x} = x + 5$

$x + 2 = x^2 + 5x$

$0 = x^2 + 4x - 2$

$x = -2 \pm \sqrt{6} \quad$ Quadratic Formula

Only $x = -2 + \sqrt{6} \approx 0.449$ is a valid solution.

107. $\log_{10}(-x - 4) = 2$

$-x - 4 = 10^2$

$-x = 100 + 4$

$x = -104$

109. $6 \log_{10}(x^2 + 1) - x = 0$

Graph

$$y_1 = 6 \log_{10}(x^2 + 1) - x.$$

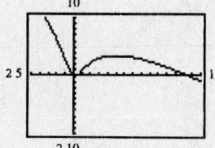

Zoom in to see the behavior near the origin.

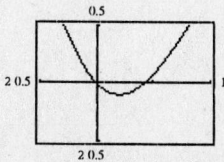

The solutions of the equation occur at the x-intercepts, which are at $x = 0$, $x \approx 0.42$, and $x \approx 13.63$.

111. $x - 2 \log_{10}(x + 4) = 0$

Graph

$$y_1 = x - 2 \log_{10}(x + 4)$$

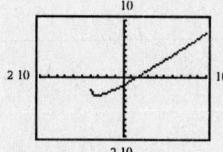

Note that $x = -4$ is a vertical asymptote, but the graph's behavior near $x = -4$ is not visible in most typical viewing windows. Zoom in to see the behavior near $x = -4$.

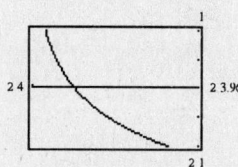

The solutions of the equation occur at the x-intercepts, which are at $x \approx -3.99$ and $x \approx 1.48$.

113. $4(2240) = 2240e^{0.065t}$

$$4 = e^{0.065t}$$

$$\ln 4 = 0.065t$$

$$\frac{\ln 4}{0.065} = t$$

$$t \approx 21.3 \text{ years}$$

115. $y = e^{-2x/3}$

Exponential decay model

Matches graph (e)

117. $y = \ln(x + 3)$

Logarithmic model

Vertical asymptote: $x = -3$

Graph includes $(-2, 0)$

Matches graph (f)

119. $y = 2e^{-(x+4)^2/3}$

Gaussian model

Matches graph (a)

121. $\quad 17000 = 12620e^{0.0118t}$

$$\frac{17000}{12620} = e^{0.0118t}$$

$$\ln\left(\frac{17000}{12620}\right) = 0.0118t$$

$$\frac{\ln\left(\dfrac{17000}{12620}\right)}{0.0118} = t$$

$$t \approx 25.25 \text{ years}$$

This corresponds to the year 2025.

123. (a) $20{,}000 = 10{,}000e^{r(5)}$

$$2 = e^{5r}$$

$$\ln 2 = 5r$$

$$\frac{\ln 2}{5} = r$$

$$r \approx 0.138629 = 13.8629\%$$

(b) $A = 10{,}000e^{0.138629}$

$$\approx \$11{,}486.98$$

125. $\quad y = ae^{bx}$

$$\frac{1}{2} = ae^{b(0)} \implies a = \frac{1}{2}$$

$$5 = \frac{1}{2}e^{b(5)}$$

$$10 = e^{5b}$$

$$\ln 10 = 5b$$

$$\frac{\ln 10}{5} = b$$

$$b \approx 0.4605$$

$$y = \frac{1}{2}e^{0.4605x}$$

127. $N = \dfrac{157}{1 + 5.4e^{-0.12t}}$

(a) When $N = 50$:

$$50 = \frac{157}{1 + 5.4e^{-0.12t}}$$

$$1 + 5.4e^{-0.12t} = \frac{157}{50}$$

$$5.4e^{-0.12t} = \frac{107}{50}$$

$$e^{-0.12t} = \frac{107}{270}$$

$$-0.12t = \ln\frac{107}{270}$$

$$t = \frac{\ln(107/270)}{-0.12} \approx 7.7 \text{ weeks}$$

(b) When $N = 75$:

$$75 = \frac{157}{1 + 5.4e^{-0.12t}}$$

$$1 + 5.4e^{-0.12t} = \frac{157}{75}$$

$$5.4e^{-0.12t} = \frac{82}{75}$$

$$e^{-0.12t} = \frac{82}{405}$$

$$-0.12t = \ln\frac{82}{405}$$

$$t = \frac{\ln(82/405)}{-0.12} \approx 13.3 \text{ weeks}$$

129. $R = \log_{10} I$ since $I_0 = 1$.

(a) $\log_{10} I = 8.4$

$$I = 10^{8.4} \approx 251,188,643$$

(b) $\log_{10} I = 6.85$

$$I = 10^{6.85} \approx 7,079,458$$

(c) $\log_{10} I = 9.1$

$$I = 10^{9.1} \approx 1,258,925,412$$

131. True by properties of exponents.

$$e^{x-1} = e^x \cdot e^{-1} = \frac{e^x}{e}$$

133. False.

$$\ln(x \cdot y) = \ln x + \ln y \neq \ln(x + y)$$

135. False. The domain of $f(x) = \ln x$ is $(0, \infty)$.

Chapter 3   Practice Test

1. Solve for x: $x^{3/5} = 8$.

2. Solve for x: $3^{x-1} = \frac{1}{81}$.

3. Graph $f(x) = 2^{-x}$.

4. Graph $g(x) = e^x + 1$.

5. If \$5000 is invested at 9% interest, find the amount after three years if the interest is compounded

   (a) monthly.   (b) quarterly.   (c) continuously.

6. Write the equation in logarithmic form: $7^{-2} = \frac{1}{49}$.

7. Solve for x: $x - 4 = \log_2 \frac{1}{64}$.

8. Given $\log_b 2 = 0.3562$ and $\log_b 5 = 0.8271$, evaluate $\log_b \sqrt[4]{8/25}$.

9. Write $5 \ln x - \frac{1}{2} \ln y + 6 \ln z$ as a single logarithm.

10. Using your calculator and the change of base formula, evaluate $\log_9 28$.

11. Use your calculator to solve for N: $\log_{10} N = 0.6646$

12. Graph $y = \log_4 x$.

13. Determine the domain of $f(x) = \log_3(x^2 - 9)$.

14. Graph $y = \ln(x - 2)$.

15. True or false: $\dfrac{\ln x}{\ln y} = \ln(x - y)$

16. Solve for x: $5^x = 41$

17. Solve for x: $x - x^2 = \log_5 \frac{1}{25}$

18. Solve for x: $\log_2 x + \log_2(x - 3) = 2$

19. Solve for x: $\dfrac{e^x + e^{-x}}{3} = 4$

20. Six thousand dollars is deposited into a fund at an annual interest rate of 13%. Find the time required for the investment to double if the interest is compounded continuously.

CHAPTER 4
Trigonometry

C H A P T E R   4
Trigonometry

Section 4.1   Radian and Degree Measure

You should know the following basic facts about angles, their measurement, and their applications.

- ■ Types of Angles:
  - (a) Acute: Measure between 0° and 90°.
  - (b) Right: Measure 90°.
  - (c) Obtuse: Measure between 90° and 180°.
  - (d) Straight: Measure 180°.
- ■ α and β are complementary if $\alpha + \beta = 90°$. They are supplementary if $\alpha + \beta = 180°$.
- ■ Two angles in standard position that have the same terminal side are called coterminal angles.
- ■ To convert degrees to radians, use $1° = \pi/180$ radians.
- ■ To convert radians to degrees, use 1 radian $= (180/\pi)°$.
- ■ $1' =$ one minute $= 1/60$ of $1°$.
- ■ $1'' =$ one second $= 1/60$ of $1' = 1/3600$ of $1°$.
- ■ The length of a circular arc is $s = r\theta$ where θ is measured in radians.
- ■ Linear speed $= \dfrac{\text{arc length}}{\text{time}} = \dfrac{s}{t}$
- ■ Angular speed $= \theta/t = s/rt$

Solutions to Odd-Numbered Exercises

1.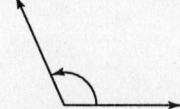

The angle shown is approximately 2 radians.

3.

The angle shown is approximately -3 radians.

5.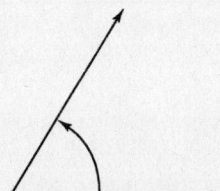

The angle shown is approximately 1 radian.

7. (a) Since $0 < \dfrac{\pi}{5} < \dfrac{\pi}{2}$; $\dfrac{\pi}{5}$ lies in Quadrant I.

    (b) Since $\pi < \dfrac{7\pi}{5} < \dfrac{3\pi}{2}$; $\dfrac{7\pi}{5}$ lies in Quadrant III.

9. (a) Since $-\dfrac{\pi}{2} < -\dfrac{\pi}{12} < 0$; $-\dfrac{\pi}{12}$ lies in Quadrant IV.

    (b) Since $-\dfrac{3\pi}{2} < -\dfrac{11\pi}{9} < -\pi$; $-\dfrac{11\pi}{9}$ lies in Quadrant II.

11. (a) Since $\pi < 3.5 < \dfrac{3\pi}{2}$; 3.5 lies in Quadrant III.

(b) Since $\dfrac{\pi}{2} < 2.25 < \pi$; 2.25 lies in Quadrant II.

13. (a)

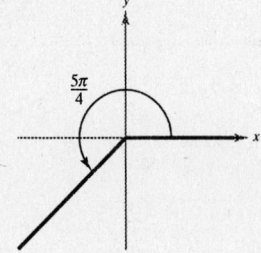

(b)

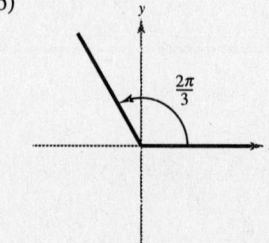

15. (a)

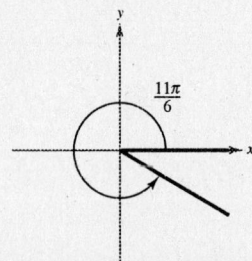

(b)

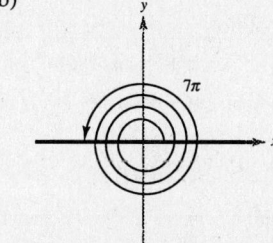

17. (a) Coterminal angles for $\dfrac{\pi}{6}$

$$\frac{\pi}{6} + 2\pi = \frac{13\pi}{6}$$

$$\frac{\pi}{6} - 2\pi = -\frac{11\pi}{6}$$

(b) Coterminal angles for $\dfrac{5\pi}{6}$

$$\frac{5\pi}{6} + 2\pi = \frac{17\pi}{6}$$

$$\frac{5\pi}{6} - 2\pi = -\frac{7\pi}{6}$$

19. (a) Coterminal angles for $\dfrac{2\pi}{3}$

$$\frac{2\pi}{3} + 2\pi = \frac{8\pi}{3}$$

$$\frac{2\pi}{3} - 2\pi = -\frac{4\pi}{3}$$

(b) Coterminal angles for $\dfrac{\pi}{12}$

$$\frac{\pi}{12} + 2\pi = \frac{25\pi}{12}$$

$$\frac{\pi}{12} - 2\pi = -\frac{23\pi}{12}$$

21. (a) Complement: $\dfrac{\pi}{2} - \dfrac{\pi}{3} = \dfrac{\pi}{6}$

Supplement: $\pi - \dfrac{\pi}{3} = \dfrac{2\pi}{3}$

(b) Complement: Not possible; $\dfrac{3\pi}{4}$ is greater than $\dfrac{\pi}{2}$.

Supplement: $\pi - \dfrac{3\pi}{4} = \dfrac{\pi}{4}$

23. (a) Complement: $\dfrac{\pi}{2} - 1 \approx 0.57$

Supplement: $\pi - 1 \approx 2.14$

(b) Complement: Not possible. 2 is greater than $\dfrac{\pi}{2}$.

Supplement: $\pi - 2 \approx 1.14$

25. (a) $30° = 30\left(\dfrac{\pi}{180}\right) = \dfrac{\pi}{6}$

(b) $150° = 150\left(\dfrac{\pi}{180}\right) = \dfrac{5\pi}{6}$

27. (a) $-20° = -20\left(\dfrac{\pi}{180}\right) = -\dfrac{\pi}{9}$

(b) $-240° = -240\left(\dfrac{\pi}{180}\right) = -\dfrac{4\pi}{3}$

29. $115° = 115\left(\dfrac{\pi}{180}\right) \approx 2.007$ radians

31. $-216.35° = -216.35\left(\dfrac{\pi}{180}\right) \approx -3.776$ radians

33. $532° = 532\left(\dfrac{\pi}{180}\right) \approx 9.285$ radians

35. $-0.83° = -0.83\left(\dfrac{\pi}{180}\right) \approx -0.014$ radian

37. (a) $\dfrac{3\pi}{2} = \dfrac{3\pi}{2}\left(\dfrac{180}{\pi}\right)° = 270°$

(b) $\dfrac{7\pi}{6} = \dfrac{7\pi}{6}\left(\dfrac{180}{\pi}\right)° = 210°$

39. (a) $\dfrac{7\pi}{3} = \dfrac{7\pi}{3}\left(\dfrac{180}{\pi}\right)° = 420°$

(b) $-\dfrac{11\pi}{30} = -\dfrac{11\pi}{30}\left(\dfrac{180}{\pi}\right)° = -66°$

41. $\dfrac{\pi}{7} = \dfrac{\pi}{7}\left(\dfrac{180}{\pi}\right)° \approx 25.714°$

43. $\dfrac{15\pi}{8} = \dfrac{15\pi}{8}\left(\dfrac{180}{\pi}\right)° = 337.5°$

45. $-4.2\pi = -4.2\pi\left(\dfrac{180}{\pi}\right)° = -756°$

47. $-2 = -2\left(\dfrac{180}{\pi}\right)° \approx -114.592°$

49.

The angle shown is approximately $210°$.

51.

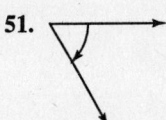

The angle shown is approximately $-60°$.

53.

The angle shown is approximately $165°$.

55. (a) Since $90° < 130° < 180°$; $130°$ lies in Quadrant II.

(b) Since $270° < 285° < 360°$; $285°$ lies in Quadrant IV.

57. (a) Since $-180° < -132°50' < -90°$; $-132° 50'$ lies in Quadrant III.

(b) Since $-360° < -336° < -270°$; $-336°$ lies in Quadrant I.

59. (a)

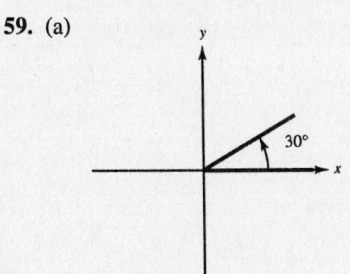

(b)

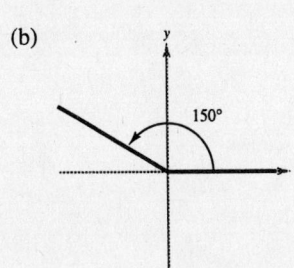

61. (a)

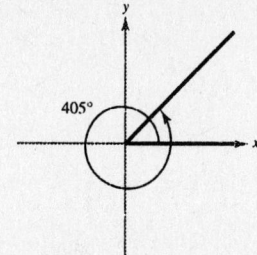

(b)

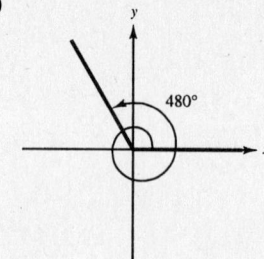

63. (a) Coterminal angles for 45°

$45° + 360° = 405°$

$45° - 360° = -315°$

(b) Coterminal angles for $-36°$

$-36° + 360° = 324°$

$-36° - 360° = -396°$

65. (a) Coterminal angles for 240°

$240° + 360° = 600°$

$240° - 360° = -120°$

(b) Coterminal angles for $-180°$

$-180° + 360° = 180°$

$-180° - 360° = -540°$

67. (a) Complement: $90° - 18° = 72°$

Supplement: $180° - 18° = 162°$

(b) Complement: Not possible; 115° is greater than 90°.

Supplement: $180° - 115° = 65°$

69. (a) Complement: $90° - 79° = 11°$

Supplement: $180° - 79° = 101°$

(b) Complement: Not possible. 150° is greater than 90°.

Supplement: $180° - 150° = 30°$

71. (a) $54° \, 45' = 54° + \left(\frac{45}{60}\right)° = 54.75°$

(b) $-128° \, 30' = -128° - \left(\frac{30}{60}\right)° = -128.5°$

73. (a) $85° \, 18' \, 30'' = \left(85 + \frac{18}{60} + \frac{30}{3600}\right)° \approx 85.308°$

(b) $330° \, 25'' = \left(330 + \frac{25}{3600}\right)° \approx 330.007°$

75. (a) $240.6° = 240° + 0.6(60)' = 240° \, 36'$

(b) $-145.8° = -[145° + 0.8(60')] = -145° \, 48'$

77. (a) $2.5° = 2° \, 30'$

(b) $-3.58° = -3° \, 30' \, 48''$

79. $s = r\theta$

$6 = 5\theta$

$\theta = \frac{6}{5}$ radians

81. $s = r\theta$

$32 = 7\theta$

$\theta = \frac{32}{7} = 4\frac{4}{7}$ radians

83. $s = r\theta$

$6 = 27\theta$

$\theta = \frac{6}{27} = \frac{2}{9}$ radian

85. $s = r\theta$

$25 = 14.5\theta$

$\theta = \frac{25}{14.5} = \frac{50}{29}$ radians

87. $s = r\theta, \ \theta$ in radians

$s = 15(180)\left(\frac{\pi}{180}\right) = 15\pi$ inches

≈ 47.12 inches

89. $s = r\theta, \ \theta$ in radians

$s = 3(1) = 3$ meters

91. $\theta = 41° \ 15' \ 42'' - 32° \ 47' \ 9'' = 8° \ 28' \ 33'' \approx 8.47583° \approx 0.14793$ radian

$s = r\theta = 4000(0.14793) \approx 591.72$ miles

93. $\theta = 42° \ 7' \ 15'' - 25° \ 46' \ 37'' = 16° \ 20' \ 38'' \approx 0.285255$ radian

$s = r\theta = 4000(0.285255) \approx 1141.02$ miles

95. $\theta = \dfrac{s}{r} = \dfrac{400}{6378} \approx 0.063$ radian $\approx 3.59°$

97. $\theta = \dfrac{s}{r} = \dfrac{2.5}{6} = \dfrac{25}{60} = \dfrac{5}{12}$ radian

99. (a) 65 miles per hour $= \dfrac{65(5280)}{60} = 5720$ feet per minute

The circumference of the tire is $C = 2.5\pi$ feet.

The number of revolutions per minute is $r = \dfrac{5720}{2.5\pi} \approx 728.3$ rev/min.

(b) The angular speed is $\dfrac{\theta}{t}$.

$\theta = \dfrac{5720}{2.5\pi}(2\pi) = 4576$ radians

Angular speed $= \dfrac{4576 \text{ radians}}{1 \text{ minute}} = 4576$ rad/min

101. Circumference: $C = 2\pi(1.68) = 3.36\pi$ inches

360 rev/min $= 6$ rev/sec

Linear speed: $(3.36\pi)(6) = 20.16\pi$ inches/sec

103. False. A measurement of 4π radians corresponds to two complete revolutions from the initial to the terminal side of an angle.

105. (a) An angle is in standard position if its vertex is at the origin and its initial side is on the positive x-axis.

(b) A negative angle is generated by a clockwise rotation of the terminal side.

(c) Two angles in standard position with the same terminal sides are coterminal.

(d) An obtuse angle measures between $90°$ and $180°$.

107. 1 Radian $= \left(\dfrac{180}{\pi}\right)° \approx 57.3°$, so one radian is much larger than one degree.

109. The area of a circle is $A = \pi r^2 \implies \pi = \dfrac{A}{r^2}$.

The circumference of a circle is $C = 2\pi r$.

$C = 2\left(\dfrac{A}{r^2}\right)r$

$C = \dfrac{2A}{r}$

$\dfrac{Cr}{2} = A$

For a sector, $C = s = r\theta$

Thus, $A = \dfrac{(r\theta)r}{2} = \dfrac{1}{2}\theta r^2$ for a sector.

111. $f(x) = x^5 - 4$

Vertical shift 4 units downward

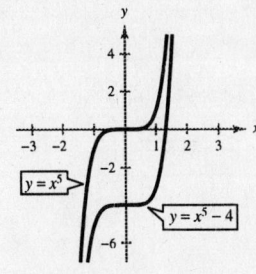

113. $f(x) = -(x + 3)^5$

Reflection in the x-axis and a horizontal shift
3 units to the left.

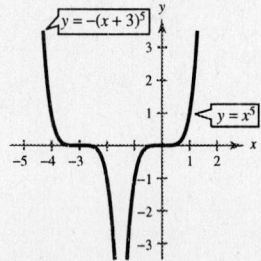

115. $f(x) = 6^x - 2$

Vertical shift of the graph of $y = 6^x$ two units
downward. Horizontal asymptote: $y = -2$

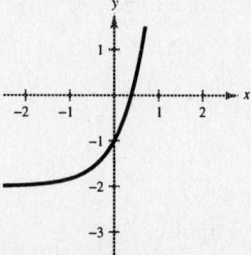

117. $f(x) = 6^{x+1}$

Horizontal shift of the graph of $y = 6^x$
one unit to the left. Horizontal asymptote: $y = 0$

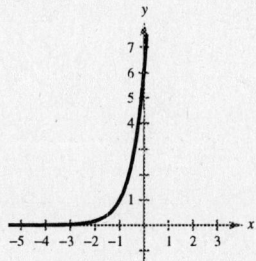

119. $f(x) = \log_4 x + 5$

Vertical shift of the graph of $y = \log_4 x$
5 units upward. Vertical asymptote: $x = 0$

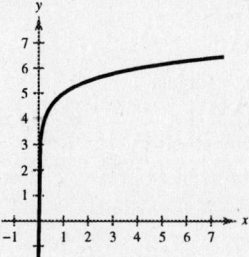

121. $f(x) = \log_4 (x + 5)$

Horizontal shift of the graph of $y = \log_4 x$
5 units to the left. Vertical asymptote: $x = -5$

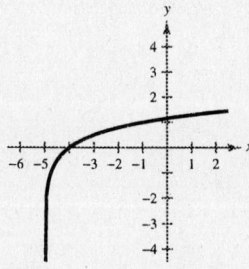

123. $f(x) = -\log_4(x + 5)$

Reflection in the x-axis and a horizontal shift of the
graph of $y = \log_4 x$ 5 units to the left.
Vertical asymptote: $x = -5$

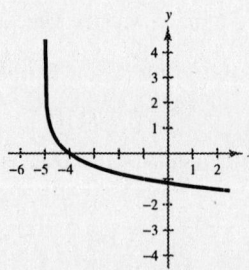

125. $\dfrac{2}{\sqrt{3}} = \dfrac{2}{\sqrt{3}} \cdot \dfrac{\sqrt{3}}{\sqrt{3}} = \dfrac{2\sqrt{3}}{3}$

127. $\dfrac{5\sqrt{5}}{2\sqrt{10}} = \dfrac{5}{2}\sqrt{\dfrac{5}{10}} = \dfrac{5}{2}\sqrt{\dfrac{1}{2}} = \dfrac{5}{2\sqrt{2}} \cdot \dfrac{\sqrt{2}}{\sqrt{2}} = \dfrac{5\sqrt{2}}{4}$

129. $\sqrt{18^2 + 12^2} = \sqrt{324 + 144} = \sqrt{468}$
$$= \sqrt{36 \cdot 13} = 6\sqrt{13}$$

131. $\sqrt{17^2 - 9^2} = \sqrt{289 - 81} = \sqrt{208}$
$$= \sqrt{16 \cdot 13} = 4\sqrt{13}$$

Section 4.2 Trigonometric Functions: The Unit Circle

■ You should know the definition of the trigonometric functions in terms of the unit circle. Let t be a real number and (x, y) the point on the unit circle corresponding to t.

$$\sin t = y \qquad\qquad \csc t = \frac{1}{y}, \quad y \neq 0$$

$$\cos t = x \qquad\qquad \sec t = \frac{1}{x}, \quad x \neq 0$$

$$\tan t = \frac{y}{x}, \quad x \neq 0 \qquad\qquad \cot t = \frac{x}{y}, \quad y \neq 0$$

■ The cosine and secant functions are even.

$$\cos(-t) = \cos t \qquad\qquad \sec(-t) = \sec t$$

■ The other four trigonometric functions are odd.

$$\sin(-t) = -\sin t \qquad\qquad \csc(-t) = -\csc t$$

$$\tan(-t) = -\tan t \qquad\qquad \cot(-t) = -\cot t$$

■ Be able to evaluate the trigonometric functions with a calculator.

Solutions to Odd-Numbered Exercises

1. $x = -\dfrac{8}{17}, \quad y = \dfrac{15}{17}$

$$\sin t = y = \frac{15}{17} \qquad\qquad \csc t = \frac{1}{y} = \frac{17}{15}$$

$$\cos t = x = -\frac{8}{17} \qquad\qquad \sec t = \frac{1}{x} = -\frac{17}{8}$$

$$\tan t = \frac{y}{x} = -\frac{15}{8} \qquad\qquad \cot t = \frac{x}{y} = -\frac{8}{15}$$

3. $x = \dfrac{12}{13}, \quad y = -\dfrac{5}{13}$

$$\sin t = y = -\frac{5}{13} \qquad\qquad \csc t = \frac{1}{y} = -\frac{13}{5}$$

$$\cos t = x = \frac{12}{13} \qquad\qquad \sec t = \frac{1}{x} = \frac{13}{12}$$

$$\tan t = \frac{y}{x} = -\frac{5}{12} \qquad\qquad \cot t = \frac{x}{y} = -\frac{12}{5}$$

5. $t = \dfrac{\pi}{4}$ corresponds to $\left(\dfrac{\sqrt{2}}{2}, \dfrac{\sqrt{2}}{2}\right)$.

7. $t = \dfrac{7\pi}{6}$ corresponds to $\left(-\dfrac{\sqrt{3}}{2}, -\dfrac{1}{2}\right)$.

9. $t = \dfrac{4\pi}{3}$ corresponds to $\left(-\dfrac{1}{2}, -\dfrac{\sqrt{3}}{2}\right)$.

11. $t = \dfrac{3\pi}{2}$ corresponds to $(0, -1)$.

13. $t = \dfrac{\pi}{4}$ corresponds to $\left(\dfrac{\sqrt{2}}{2}, \dfrac{\sqrt{2}}{2}\right)$.

$$\sin t = y = \frac{\sqrt{2}}{2}$$

$$\cos t = x = \frac{\sqrt{2}}{2}$$

$$\tan t = \frac{y}{x} = 1$$

15. $t = -\dfrac{\pi}{6}$ corresponds to $\left(\dfrac{\sqrt{3}}{2}, -\dfrac{1}{2}\right)$.

$$\sin t = y = -\frac{1}{2}$$

$$\cos t = x = \frac{\sqrt{3}}{2}$$

$$\tan t = \frac{y}{x} = -\frac{1}{\sqrt{3}} = -\frac{\sqrt{3}}{3}$$

17. $t = -\dfrac{7\pi}{4}$ corresponds to $\left(\dfrac{\sqrt{2}}{2}, \dfrac{\sqrt{2}}{2}\right)$.

$$\sin t = y = \dfrac{\sqrt{2}}{2}$$

$$\cos t = x = \dfrac{\sqrt{2}}{2}$$

$$\tan t = \dfrac{y}{x} = 1$$

19. $t = \dfrac{11\pi}{6}$ corresponds to $\left(\dfrac{\sqrt{3}}{2}, -\dfrac{1}{2}\right)$.

$$\sin t = y = -\dfrac{1}{2}$$

$$\cos t = x = \dfrac{\sqrt{3}}{2}$$

$$\tan t = \dfrac{y}{x} = -\dfrac{1}{\sqrt{3}} = -\dfrac{\sqrt{3}}{3}$$

21. $t = -\dfrac{3\pi}{2}$ corresponds to $(0, 1)$.

$$\sin t = y = 1$$
$$\cos t = x = 0$$

$$\tan t = \dfrac{y}{x} \text{ is undefined.}$$

23. $t = \dfrac{3\pi}{4}$ corresponds to $\left(-\dfrac{\sqrt{2}}{2}, \dfrac{\sqrt{2}}{2}\right)$.

$$\sin t = y = \dfrac{\sqrt{2}}{2} \qquad\qquad \csc t = \dfrac{1}{y} = \sqrt{2}$$

$$\cos t = x = -\dfrac{\sqrt{2}}{2} \qquad\qquad \sec t = \dfrac{1}{x} = -\sqrt{2}$$

$$\tan t = \dfrac{y}{x} = -1 \qquad\qquad \cot t = \dfrac{x}{y} = -1$$

25. $t = \dfrac{\pi}{2}$ corresponds to $(0, 1)$.

$$\sin t = y = 1 \qquad\qquad \csc t = \dfrac{1}{y} = 1$$

$$\cos t = x = 0 \qquad\qquad \sec t = \dfrac{1}{x} \text{ is undefined.}$$

$$\tan t = \dfrac{y}{x} \text{ is undefined.} \qquad \cot t = \dfrac{x}{y} = 0$$

27. $t = -\dfrac{\pi}{3}$ corresponds to $\left(\dfrac{1}{2}, -\dfrac{\sqrt{3}}{2}\right)$.

$$\sin t = y = -\dfrac{\sqrt{3}}{2} \qquad\qquad \csc t = \dfrac{1}{y} = -\dfrac{2\sqrt{3}}{3}$$

$$\cos t = x = \dfrac{1}{2} \qquad\qquad \sec t = \dfrac{1}{x} = 2$$

$$\tan t = \dfrac{y}{x} = -\sqrt{3} \qquad\qquad \cot t = \dfrac{x}{y} = -\dfrac{\sqrt{3}}{3}$$

29. $\sin 5\pi = \sin \pi = 0$

31. $\cos \dfrac{8\pi}{3} = \cos \dfrac{2\pi}{3} = -\dfrac{1}{2}$

33. $\cos(-3\pi) = \cos \pi = -1$

35. $\sin\left(-\dfrac{9\pi}{4}\right) = \sin\left(\dfrac{7\pi}{4}\right) = -\dfrac{\sqrt{2}}{2}$

37. $\sin t = \dfrac{1}{3}$

    (a) $\sin(-t) = -\sin t = -\dfrac{1}{3}$

    (b) $\csc(-t) = -\csc t = -3$

39. $\cos(-t) = -\dfrac{1}{5}$

    (a) $\cos t = \cos(-t) = -\dfrac{1}{5}$

    (b) $\sec(-t) = \dfrac{1}{\cos(-t)} = -5$

41. $\sin y = \dfrac{4}{5}$

   (a) $\sin(\pi - t) = \sin t = \dfrac{4}{5}$

   (b) $\sin(t + \pi) = -\sin t = -\dfrac{4}{5}$

43. $\sin \dfrac{\pi}{4} \approx 0.7071$

45. $\csc 1.3 = \dfrac{1}{\sin 1.3} \approx 1.0378$

47. $\cos(-1.7) \approx -0.1288$

49. $\csc 0.8 = \dfrac{1}{\sin 0.8} \approx 1.3940$

51. $\sec 22.8 = \dfrac{1}{\cos 22.8} \approx -1.4486$

53. (a) $\sin 5 \approx -1$

   (b) $\cos 2 \approx -0.4$

55. (a) $\sin t = 0.25$

        $t \approx 0.25$ or 2.89

   (b) $\cos t = -0.25$

        $t \approx 1.82$ or 4.46

57. $\cos 1.5 \approx 0.0707$

    $2 \cos 0.75 \approx 1.4634$

    $\cos 2t \neq 2 \cos t$

59. $y(t) = \dfrac{1}{4} \cos 6t$

   (a) $y(0) = \dfrac{1}{4} \cos 0 = 0.2500$ feet

   (b) $y\left(\dfrac{1}{4}\right) = \dfrac{1}{4} \cos \dfrac{3}{2} \approx 0.0177$ feet

   (c) $y\left(\dfrac{1}{2}\right) = \dfrac{1}{4} \cos 3 \approx -0.2475$ feet

61. False. $\sin(-t) = -\sin t$ means the function is odd, not that the sine of a negative angle is a negative number.

For example: $\sin\left(-\dfrac{3\pi}{2}\right) = -\sin\left(\dfrac{3\pi}{2}\right) = -(-1) = 1.$

Even though the angle is negative, the sine value is positive.

63. (a) The points have y-axis symmetry.

   (b) $\sin t_1 = \sin(\pi - t_1)$ since they have the same y-value.

   (c) $\cos(\pi - t_1) = -\cos t_1$ since the x-values have the opposite signs.

65. $\cos \theta = x = \cos(-\theta)$

   $\sec \theta = \dfrac{1}{x} = \sec(-\theta)$

    $\sin \theta = y$

   $\sin(-\theta) = -y = -\sin \theta$

    $\csc \theta = \dfrac{1}{y}$

   $\csc(-\theta) = -\dfrac{1}{y} = -\csc \theta$

    $\tan \theta = \dfrac{y}{x}$

   $\tan(-\theta) = \dfrac{-y}{x} = -\tan \theta$

    $\cot \theta = \dfrac{x}{y}$

   $\cot(-\theta) = \dfrac{x}{-y} = -\cot \theta$

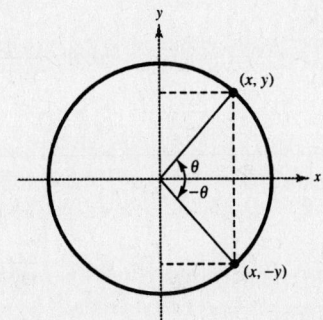

67. $f(t) = \sin t$ and $g(t) = \tan t$

Both f and g are odd functions.

$h(t) = f(t)g(t) = \sin t \tan t$

$h(-t) = \sin(-t)\tan(-t)$

$\qquad = (-\sin t)(-\tan t)$

$\qquad = \sin t \tan t = h(t)$

The function $h(t) = f(t)g(t)$ is even.

69. $f(x) = \frac{1}{4}x^3 + 1$

$\qquad y = \frac{1}{4}x^3 + 1$

$\qquad x = \frac{1}{4}y^3 + 1$

$\qquad x - 1 = \frac{1}{4}y^3$

$\quad 4(x - 1) = y^3$

$\qquad y = \sqrt[3]{4(x - 1)}$

$\quad f^{-1}(x) = \sqrt[3]{4(x - 1)}$

71. $f(x) = \dfrac{2x}{x + 1}, x > -1$

$\qquad y = \dfrac{2x}{x + 1}, x > -1$

$\qquad x = \dfrac{2y}{y + 1}$

$\quad xy + x = 2y$

$\qquad x = 2y - xy$

$\qquad x = y(2 - x)$

$\qquad \dfrac{x}{2 - x} = y, x < 2$

$\quad f^{-1}(x) = \dfrac{x}{2 - x}, x < 2$

Section 4.3   Right Triangle Trigonometry

■ You should know the right triangle definition of trigonometric functions.

(a) $\sin \theta = \dfrac{\text{opp}}{\text{hyp}}$ (b) $\cos \theta = \dfrac{\text{adj}}{\text{hyp}}$ (c) $\tan \theta = \dfrac{\text{opp}}{\text{adj}}$

(d) $\csc \theta = \dfrac{\text{hyp}}{\text{opp}}$ (e) $\sec \theta = \dfrac{\text{hyp}}{\text{adj}}$ (f) $\cot \theta = \dfrac{\text{adj}}{\text{opp}}$

■ You should know the following identities.

(a) $\sin \theta = \dfrac{1}{\csc\theta}$ (b) $\csc \theta = \dfrac{1}{\sin\theta}$ (c) $\cos \theta = \dfrac{1}{\sec\theta}$

(d) $\sec \theta = \dfrac{1}{\cos\theta}$ (e) $\tan \theta = \dfrac{1}{\cot\theta}$ (f) $\cot \theta = \dfrac{1}{\tan\theta}$

(g) $\tan \theta = \dfrac{\sin\theta}{\cos\theta}$ (h) $\cot \theta = \dfrac{\cos\theta}{\sin\theta}$ (i) $\sin^2 \theta + \cos^2 \theta = 1$

(j) $1 + \tan^2 \theta = \sec^2 \theta$ (k) $1 + \cot^2 \theta = \csc^2 \theta$

■ You should know that two acute angles α and β are complementary if $\alpha + \beta = 90°$, and that cofunctions of complementary angles are equal.

■ You should know the trigonometric function values of $30°$, $45°$, and $60°$, or be able to construct triangles from which you can determine them.

Solutions to Odd-Numbered Exercises

1. hyp $= \sqrt{6^2 + 8^2} = \sqrt{36 + 64} = \sqrt{100} = 10$

$$\sin \theta = \frac{\text{opp}}{\text{hyp}} = \frac{6}{10} = \frac{3}{5} \qquad \csc \theta = \frac{\text{hyp}}{\text{opp}} = \frac{10}{6} = \frac{5}{3}$$

$$\cos \theta = \frac{\text{adj}}{\text{hyp}} = \frac{8}{10} = \frac{4}{5} \qquad \sec \theta = \frac{\text{hyp}}{\text{adj}} = \frac{10}{8} = \frac{5}{4}$$

$$\tan \theta = \frac{\text{opp}}{\text{adj}} = \frac{6}{8} = \frac{3}{4} \qquad \cot \theta = \frac{\text{adj}}{\text{opp}} = \frac{8}{6} = \frac{4}{3}$$

3. adj $= \sqrt{41^2 - 9^2} = \sqrt{1681 - 81} = \sqrt{1600} = 40$

$$\sin \theta = \frac{\text{opp}}{\text{hyp}} = \frac{9}{41} \qquad \csc \theta = \frac{\text{hyp}}{\text{opp}} = \frac{41}{9}$$

$$\cos \theta = \frac{\text{adj}}{\text{hyp}} = \frac{40}{41} \qquad \sec \theta = \frac{\text{hyp}}{\text{adj}} = \frac{41}{40}$$

$$\tan \theta = \frac{\text{opp}}{\text{adj}} = \frac{9}{40} \qquad \cot \theta = \frac{\text{adj}}{\text{opp}} = \frac{40}{9}$$

5. adj $= \sqrt{3^2 - 1^2} = \sqrt{8} = 2\sqrt{2}$

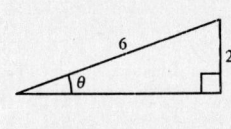

$$\sin \theta = \frac{\text{opp}}{\text{hyp}} = \frac{1}{3} \qquad \csc \theta = \frac{\text{hyp}}{\text{opp}} = 3$$

$$\cos \theta = \frac{\text{adj}}{\text{hyp}} = \frac{2\sqrt{2}}{3} \qquad \sec \theta = \frac{\text{hyp}}{\text{adj}} = \frac{3}{2\sqrt{2}} = \frac{3\sqrt{2}}{4}$$

$$\tan \theta = \frac{\text{opp}}{\text{adj}} = \frac{1}{2\sqrt{2}} = \frac{\sqrt{2}}{4} \qquad \cot \theta = \frac{\text{adj}}{\text{opp}} = 2\sqrt{2}$$

adj $= \sqrt{6^2 - 2^2} = \sqrt{32} = 4\sqrt{2}$

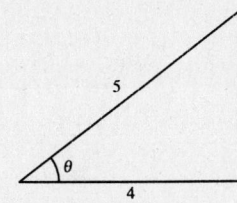

$$\sin \theta = \frac{\text{opp}}{\text{hyp}} = \frac{2}{6} = \frac{1}{3} \qquad \csc \theta = \frac{\text{hyp}}{\text{opp}} = \frac{6}{2} = 3$$

$$\cos \theta = \frac{\text{adj}}{\text{hyp}} = \frac{4\sqrt{2}}{6} = \frac{2\sqrt{2}}{3} \qquad \sec \theta = \frac{\text{hyp}}{\text{adj}} = \frac{6}{4\sqrt{2}} = \frac{3}{2\sqrt{2}} = \frac{3\sqrt{2}}{4}$$

$$\tan \theta = \frac{\text{opp}}{\text{adj}} = \frac{2}{4\sqrt{2}} = \frac{1}{2\sqrt{2}} = \frac{\sqrt{2}}{4} \qquad \cot \theta = \frac{\text{adj}}{\text{opp}} = \frac{4\sqrt{2}}{2} = 2\sqrt{2}$$

The function values are the same since the triangles are similar and the corresponding sides are proportional.

7. opp $= \sqrt{5^2 - 4^2} = 3$

$$\sin \theta = \frac{\text{opp}}{\text{hyp}} = \frac{3}{5} \qquad \csc \theta = \frac{\text{hyp}}{\text{opp}} = \frac{5}{3}$$

$$\cos \theta = \frac{\text{adj}}{\text{hyp}} = \frac{4}{5} \qquad \sec \theta = \frac{\text{hyp}}{\text{adj}} = \frac{5}{4}$$

$$\tan \theta = \frac{\text{opp}}{\text{adj}} = \frac{3}{4} \qquad \cot \theta = \frac{\text{adj}}{\text{opp}} = \frac{4}{3}$$

— CONTINUED —

7. — CONTINUED —

$opp = \sqrt{1.25^2 - 1^2} = 0.75$

$$\sin\theta = \frac{opp}{hyp} = \frac{0.75}{1.25} = \frac{3}{5} \qquad \csc\theta = \frac{hyp}{opp} = \frac{1.25}{0.75} = \frac{5}{3}$$

$$\cos\theta = \frac{adj}{hyp} = \frac{1}{1.25} = \frac{4}{5} \qquad \sec\theta = \frac{hyp}{adj} = \frac{1.25}{1} = \frac{5}{4}$$

$$\tan\theta = \frac{opp}{adj} = \frac{0.75}{1} = \frac{3}{4} \qquad \cot\theta = \frac{adj}{opp} = \frac{1}{0.75} = \frac{4}{3}$$

The function values are the same since the triangles are similar and the corresponding sides are proportional.

9. Given: $\sin\theta = \dfrac{3}{4} = \dfrac{opp}{hyp}$

$3^2 + (adj)^2 = 4^2$

$adj = \sqrt{7}$

$\cos\theta = \dfrac{\sqrt{7}}{4}$

$\tan\theta = \dfrac{3\sqrt{7}}{7}$

$\cot\theta = \dfrac{\sqrt{7}}{3}$

$\sec\theta = \dfrac{4\sqrt{7}}{7}$

$\csc\theta = \dfrac{4}{3}$

11. Given: $\sec\theta = 2 = \dfrac{2}{1} = \dfrac{hyp}{adj}$

$(opp)^2 + 1^2 = 2^2$

$opp = \sqrt{3}$

$\sin\theta = \dfrac{\sqrt{3}}{2}$

$\cos\theta = \dfrac{1}{2}$

$\tan\theta = \sqrt{3}$

$\cot\theta = \dfrac{\sqrt{3}}{3}$

$\csc\theta = \dfrac{2\sqrt{3}}{3}$

13. Given: $\tan\theta = 3 = \dfrac{3}{1} = \dfrac{opp}{adj}$

$3^2 + 1^2 = (hyp)^2$

$hyp = \sqrt{10}$

$\sin\theta = \dfrac{3\sqrt{10}}{10}$

$\cos\theta = \dfrac{\sqrt{10}}{10}$

$\cot\theta = \dfrac{1}{3}$

$\sec\theta = \sqrt{10}$

$\csc\theta = \dfrac{\sqrt{10}}{3}$

15. Given: $\cot\theta = \dfrac{3}{2} = \dfrac{adj}{opp}$

$2^2 + 3^2 = (hyp)^2$

$hyp = \sqrt{13}$

$\sin\theta = \dfrac{2}{\sqrt{13}} = \dfrac{2\sqrt{13}}{13}$

$\cos\theta = \dfrac{3}{\sqrt{13}} = \dfrac{3\sqrt{13}}{13}$

$\tan\theta = \dfrac{2}{3}$

$\csc\theta = \dfrac{\sqrt{13}}{2}$

$\sec\theta = \dfrac{\sqrt{13}}{3}$

17. $\sin 60° = \dfrac{\sqrt{3}}{2}$, $\cos 60° = \dfrac{1}{2}$

(a) $\tan 60° = \dfrac{\sin 60°}{\cos 60°} = \sqrt{3}$

(b) $\sin 30° = \cos 60° = \dfrac{1}{2}$

(c) $\cos 30° = \sin 60° = \dfrac{\sqrt{3}}{2}$

(d) $\cot 60° = \dfrac{\cos 60°}{\sin 60°} = \dfrac{1}{\sqrt{3}} = \dfrac{\sqrt{3}}{3}$

19. $\csc\theta = \dfrac{\sqrt{13}}{2},\ \sec\theta = \dfrac{\sqrt{13}}{3}$

(a) $\sin\theta = \dfrac{1}{\csc\theta} = \dfrac{2}{\sqrt{13}} = \dfrac{2\sqrt{13}}{13}$

(b) $\cos\theta = \dfrac{1}{\sec\theta} = \dfrac{3}{\sqrt{13}} = \dfrac{3\sqrt{13}}{13}$

(c) $\tan\theta = \dfrac{\sin\theta}{\cos\theta} = \dfrac{\frac{2\sqrt{13}}{13}}{\frac{3\sqrt{13}}{13}} = \dfrac{2}{3}$

(d) $\sec(90^\circ - \theta) = \csc\theta = \dfrac{\sqrt{13}}{2}$

21. $\cos\alpha = \dfrac{1}{3}$

(a) $\sec\alpha = \dfrac{1}{\cos\alpha} = 3$

(b) $\sin^2\alpha + \cos^2\alpha = 1$

$\sin^2\alpha + \left(\dfrac{1}{3}\right)^2 = 1$

$\sin^2\alpha = \dfrac{8}{9}$

$\sin\alpha = \dfrac{2\sqrt{2}}{3}$

(c) $\cot\alpha = \dfrac{\cos\alpha}{\sin\alpha} = \dfrac{\frac{1}{3}}{\frac{2\sqrt{2}}{3}} = \dfrac{1}{2\sqrt{2}} = \dfrac{\sqrt{2}}{4}$

(d) $\sin(90^\circ - \alpha) = \cos\alpha = \dfrac{1}{3}$

23. (a) $\cos 60^\circ = \dfrac{1}{2}$

(b) $\csc 30^\circ = 2$

(c) $\tan 60^\circ = \sqrt{3}$

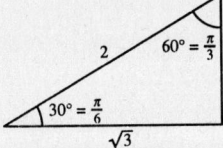

25. (a) $\sin 45^\circ = \dfrac{1}{\sqrt{2}} = \dfrac{\sqrt{2}}{2}$

(b) $\cos 30^\circ = \dfrac{\sqrt{3}}{2}$

(c) $\tan 30^\circ = \dfrac{1}{\sqrt{3}} = \dfrac{\sqrt{3}}{3}$

27. (a) $\sin 10^\circ \approx 0.1736$

(b) $\cos 80^\circ \approx 0.1736$

Note: $\cos 80^\circ = \sin(90^\circ - 80^\circ) = \sin 10^\circ$

29. (a) $\sin 16.35^\circ \approx 0.2815$

(b) $\csc 16.35^\circ = \dfrac{1}{\sin 16.35^\circ} \approx 3.5523$

31. (a) $\sec 42^\circ 12' = \sec 42.2^\circ = \dfrac{1}{\cos 42.2^\circ} \approx 1.3499$

(b) $\csc 48^\circ 7' = \dfrac{1}{\sin\left(48 + \frac{7}{60}\right)^\circ} \approx 1.3432$

33. (a) $\cot 11^\circ 15' = \dfrac{1}{\tan 11.25^\circ} \approx 5.0273$

(b) $\tan 11^\circ 15' = \tan 11.25^\circ \approx 0.1989$

35. (a) $\csc 32^\circ 40' 3'' = \dfrac{1}{\sin 32.6675^\circ} \approx 1.8527$

(b) $\tan 44^\circ 28' 16'' \approx \tan 44.4711^\circ \approx 0.9817$

37. (a) $\sin\theta = \dfrac{1}{2} \implies \theta = 30^\circ = \dfrac{\pi}{6}$

(b) $\csc\theta = 2 \implies \theta = 30^\circ = \dfrac{\pi}{6}$

39. (a) $\sec\theta = 2 \implies \theta = 60^\circ = \dfrac{\pi}{3}$

(b) $\cot\theta = 1 \implies \theta = 45^\circ = \dfrac{\pi}{4}$

41. (a) $\csc \theta = \dfrac{2\sqrt{3}}{3} \implies \theta = 60° = \dfrac{\pi}{3}$

   (b) $\sin \theta = \dfrac{\sqrt{2}}{2} \implies \theta = 45° = \dfrac{\pi}{4}$

43. (a) $\sin \theta = 0.0145 \implies \theta \approx 0.83° \approx 0.015$ radian

   (b) $\sin \theta = 0.4565 \implies \theta \approx 27° \approx 0.474$ radian

45. (a) $\tan \theta = 0.0125 \implies \theta \approx 0.72° \approx 0.012$ radian

   (b) $\tan \theta = 2.3545 \implies \theta \approx 67° \approx 1.169$ radians

47.

$\tan 30° = \dfrac{30}{x}$

$\dfrac{1}{\sqrt{3}} = \dfrac{30}{x}$

$x = 30\sqrt{3}$

49.

$\tan 60° = \dfrac{32}{x}$

$\sqrt{3} = \dfrac{32}{x}$

$\sqrt{3}\, x = 32$

$x = \dfrac{32}{\sqrt{3}} = \dfrac{32\sqrt{3}}{3}$

51. $\tan \theta \cot \theta = \tan \theta \left(\dfrac{1}{\tan \theta} \right) = 1$

53. $\tan \alpha \cos \alpha = \left(\dfrac{\sin \alpha}{\cos \alpha} \right) \cos \alpha = \sin \alpha$

55. $(1 + \cos \theta)(1 - \cos \theta) = 1 - \cos^2 \theta$

$= (\sin^2 \theta + \cos^2 \theta) - \cos^2 \theta$

$= \sin^2 \theta$

57. $(\sec \theta + \tan \theta)(\sec \theta - \tan \theta) = \sec^2 \theta - \tan^2 \theta$

$= (1 + \tan^2 \theta) - \tan^2 \theta$

$= 1$

59. $\dfrac{\sin \theta}{\cos \theta} + \dfrac{\cos \theta}{\sin \theta} = \dfrac{\sin^2 \theta + \cos^2 \theta}{\sin \theta \cos \theta}$

$= \dfrac{1}{\sin \theta \cos \theta}$

$= \dfrac{1}{\sin \theta} \cdot \dfrac{1}{\cos \theta}$

$= \csc \theta \sec \theta$

61. (a)

h, 132, 6, 3

Not drawn to scale

   (b) $\dfrac{6}{3} = \dfrac{h}{135}$

   (c) $2(135) = h$

   $h = 270$ feet

63. (a)

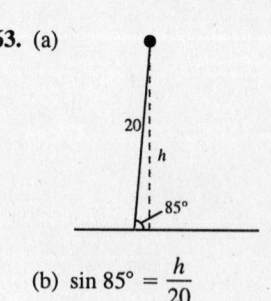

20, h, 85°

   (b) $\sin 85° = \dfrac{h}{20}$

   (c) $h = 20 \sin 85° \approx 19.9$ meters

65. Let $x =$ distance from the boat to the shoreline

$$\tan 4° = \frac{40}{x}$$

$$x = \frac{40}{\tan 4°} \approx 572 \text{ feet}$$

67.

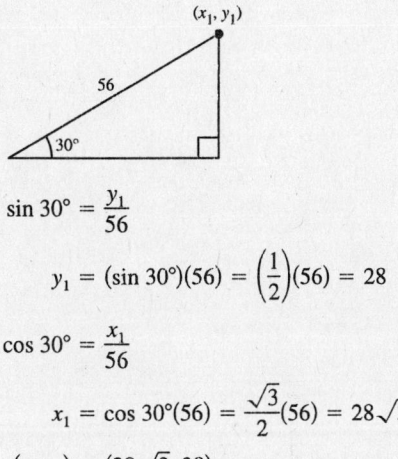

$$\sin 30° = \frac{y_1}{56}$$

$$y_1 = (\sin 30°)(56) = \left(\frac{1}{2}\right)(56) = 28$$

$$\cos 30° = \frac{x_1}{56}$$

$$x_1 = \cos 30°(56) = \frac{\sqrt{3}}{2}(56) = 28\sqrt{3}$$

$$(x_1, y_1) = (28\sqrt{3}, 28)$$

$$\sin 60° = \frac{y_2}{56}$$

$$y_2 = \sin 60°(56) = \left(\frac{\sqrt{3}}{2}\right)(56) = 28\sqrt{3}$$

$$\cos 60° = \frac{x_2}{56}$$

$$x_2 = (\cos 60°)(56) = \left(\frac{1}{2}\right)(56) = 28$$

$$(x_2, y_2) = (28, 28\sqrt{3})$$

69. $x \approx 9.397,\ y \approx 3.420$

$$\sin 20° = \frac{y}{10} \approx 0.34$$

$$\cos 20° = \frac{x}{10} \approx 0.94$$

$$\tan 20° = \frac{y}{x} \approx 0.36$$

$$\cot 20° = \frac{x}{y} \approx 2.75$$

$$\sec 20° = \frac{10}{x} \approx 1.06$$

$$\csc 20° = \frac{10}{y} \approx 2.92$$

71. True, $\csc x = \dfrac{1}{\sin x} \implies \sin 60° \csc 60° = \sin 60°\left(\dfrac{1}{\sin 60°}\right) = 1$

73. False, $\dfrac{\sqrt{2}}{2} + \dfrac{\sqrt{2}}{2} = \sqrt{2} \neq 1$

75. False, $\dfrac{\sin 60°}{\sin 30°} = \dfrac{\cos 30°}{\sin 30°} = \cot 30° \approx 1.7321;\ \sin 2° \approx 0.0349$

77. This is true because the corresponding sides of similar triangles are proportional.

79. (a)

θ	0.1	0.2	0.3	0.4	0.5
$\sin \theta$	0.0998	0.1987	0.2955	0.3894	0.4794

(b) As $\theta \rightarrow 0, \sin \theta \rightarrow 0$

81. $\dfrac{x^2 - 6x}{x^2 + 4x - 12} \cdot \dfrac{x^2 + 12x + 36}{x^2 - 36} = \dfrac{x(x - 6)}{(x + 6)(x - 2)} \cdot \dfrac{(x + 6)(x + 6)}{(x + 6)(x - 6)}$

$\qquad\qquad\qquad\qquad\qquad\qquad = \dfrac{x}{x - 2}, x \neq \pm 6$

83. $\dfrac{3}{x + 2} - \dfrac{2}{x - 2} + \dfrac{x}{x^2 + 4x + 4} = \dfrac{3(x + 2)(x - 2) - 2(x + 2)^2 + x(x - 2)}{(x - 2)(x + 2)^2}$

$\qquad\qquad\qquad\qquad\qquad\qquad = \dfrac{3(x^2 - 4) - 2(x^2 + 4x + 4) + x^2 - 2x}{(x - 2)(x + 2)^2}$

$\qquad\qquad\qquad\qquad\qquad\qquad = \dfrac{2x^2 - 10x - 20}{(x - 2)(x + 2)^2} = \dfrac{2(x^2 - 5x - 10)}{(x - 2)(x + 2)^2}$

85. $\dfrac{4}{x - 4} = \dfrac{12x}{24 - x}$

$\quad 4(24 - x) = 12x(x - 4)$

$\quad 96 - 4x = 12x^2 - 48x$

$\qquad\quad 0 = 12x^2 - 44x - 96$

$\qquad\quad 0 = 4(3x^2 - 11x - 24)$

$\quad x = \dfrac{-(-11) \pm \sqrt{(-11)^2 - 4(3)(-24)}}{2(3)}$

$\qquad = \dfrac{11 \pm \sqrt{409}}{6}$

87. $\dfrac{2}{x + 3} + \dfrac{4}{x - 2} = \dfrac{12}{x^2 + x - 6}$

$\quad 2(x - 2) + 4(x + 3) = 12$

$\qquad 2x - 4 + 4x + 12 = 12$

$\qquad\qquad\qquad 6x + 8 = 12$

$\qquad\qquad\qquad\quad 6x = 4$

$\qquad\qquad\qquad\quad x = \dfrac{2}{3}$

Section 4.4   Trigonometric Functions of Any Angle

- Know the Definitions of Trigonometric Functions of Any Angle.

  If θ is in standard position, (x, y) a point on the terminal side and $r = \sqrt{x^2 + y^2} \neq 0$, then

  $$\sin \theta = \frac{y}{r} \qquad\qquad \csc \theta = \frac{r}{y},\ y \neq 0$$

  $$\cos \theta = \frac{x}{r} \qquad\qquad \sec \theta = \frac{r}{x},\ x \neq 0$$

  $$\tan \theta = \frac{y}{x},\ x \neq 0 \qquad \cot \theta = \frac{x}{y},\ y \neq 0$$

- You should know the signs of the trigonometric functions in each quadrant.

- You should know the trigonometric function values of the quadrant angles 0, $\dfrac{\pi}{2}$, π, and $\dfrac{3\pi}{2}$.

- You should be able to find reference angles.

- You should be able to evaluate trigonometric functions of any angle. (Use reference angles.)

- You should know that the period of sine and cosine is 2π.

Solutions to Odd-Numbered Exercises

1. (a) $(x, y) = (4, 3)$

$r = \sqrt{16 + 9} = 5$

$$\sin \theta = \frac{y}{r} = \frac{3}{5} \qquad\qquad \csc \theta = \frac{r}{y} = \frac{5}{3}$$

$$\cos \theta = \frac{x}{r} = \frac{4}{5} \qquad\qquad \sec \theta = \frac{r}{x} = \frac{5}{4}$$

$$\tan \theta = \frac{y}{x} = \frac{3}{4} \qquad\qquad \cot \theta = \frac{x}{y} = \frac{4}{3}$$

(b) $(x, y) = (8, -15)$

$r = \sqrt{64 + 225} = 17$

$$\sin \theta = \frac{y}{r} = -\frac{15}{17} \qquad \csc \theta = \frac{r}{y} = -\frac{17}{15}$$

$$\cos \theta = \frac{x}{r} = \frac{8}{17} \qquad\qquad \sec \theta = \frac{r}{x} = \frac{17}{8}$$

$$\tan \theta = \frac{y}{x} = -\frac{15}{8} \qquad\quad \cot \theta = \frac{x}{y} = -\frac{8}{15}$$

3. (a) $(x, y) = \left(-\sqrt{3}, -1\right)$

$r = \sqrt{3 + 1} = 2$

$$\sin \theta = \frac{y}{r} = -\frac{1}{2} \qquad\qquad \csc \theta = \frac{r}{y} = -2$$

$$\cos \theta = \frac{x}{r} = -\frac{\sqrt{3}}{2} \qquad\quad \sec \theta = \frac{r}{x} = -\frac{2\sqrt{3}}{3}$$

$$\tan \theta = \frac{y}{x} = \frac{\sqrt{3}}{3} \qquad\qquad \cot \theta = \frac{x}{y} = \sqrt{3}$$

(b) $(x, y) = (-4, 1)$

$r = \sqrt{16 + 1} = \sqrt{17}$

$$\sin \theta = \frac{y}{r} = \frac{\sqrt{17}}{17} \qquad\quad \csc \theta = \frac{r}{y} = \sqrt{17}$$

$$\cos \theta = \frac{x}{r} = -\frac{4\sqrt{17}}{17} \qquad \sec \theta = \frac{r}{x} = -\frac{\sqrt{17}}{4}$$

$$\tan \theta = \frac{y}{x} = -\frac{1}{4} \qquad\qquad \cot \theta = \frac{x}{y} = -4$$

5. $(x, y) = (7, 24)$

$r = \sqrt{49 + 576} = 25$

$\sin \theta = \dfrac{y}{r} = \dfrac{24}{25}$ $\qquad$ $\csc \theta = \dfrac{r}{y} = \dfrac{25}{24}$

$\cos \theta = \dfrac{x}{r} = \dfrac{7}{25}$ $\qquad$ $\sec \theta = \dfrac{r}{x} = \dfrac{25}{7}$

$\tan \theta = \dfrac{y}{x} = \dfrac{24}{7}$ $\qquad$ $\cot \theta = \dfrac{x}{y} = \dfrac{7}{24}$

7. $(x, y) = (-4, 10)$

$r = \sqrt{16 + 100} = 2\sqrt{29}$

$\sin \theta = \dfrac{y}{r} = \dfrac{5\sqrt{29}}{29}$ $\qquad$ $\csc \theta = \dfrac{r}{y} = \dfrac{\sqrt{29}}{5}$

$\cos \theta = \dfrac{x}{r} = -\dfrac{2\sqrt{29}}{29}$ $\qquad$ $\sec \theta = \dfrac{r}{x} = -\dfrac{\sqrt{29}}{2}$

$\tan \theta = \dfrac{y}{x} = -\dfrac{5}{2}$ $\qquad$ $\cot \theta = \dfrac{x}{y} = -\dfrac{2}{5}$

9. $(x, y) = (-3.5, 6.8)$

$r = \sqrt{12.25 + 46.24} \approx 7.65$

$\sin \theta = \dfrac{y}{r} = \dfrac{6.8}{7.65} \approx 0.9$ $\qquad$ $\csc \theta = \dfrac{r}{y} = \dfrac{7.65}{6.8} \approx 1.1$

$\cos \theta = \dfrac{x}{r} = -\dfrac{3.5}{7.65} \approx -0.5$ $\qquad$ $\sec \theta = \dfrac{r}{x} = -\dfrac{7.65}{3.5} \approx -2.2$

$\tan \theta = \dfrac{y}{x} = -\dfrac{6.8}{3.5} \approx -1.9$ $\qquad$ $\cot \theta = \dfrac{x}{y} = -\dfrac{3.5}{6.8} \approx -0.5$

11. $\sin \theta < 0 \Longrightarrow \theta$ lies in Quadrant III or in Quadrant IV.

$\cos \theta < 0 \Longrightarrow \theta$ lies in Quadrant II or in Quadrant III.

$\sin \theta < 0 \ and \cos \theta < 0 \Longrightarrow \theta$ lies in Quadrant III.

13. $\sin \theta > 0 \Longrightarrow \theta$ lies in Quadrant I or in Quadrant II.

$\tan \theta < 0 \Longrightarrow \theta$ lies in Quadrant II or in Quadrant IV.

$\sin \theta > 0 \ and \tan \theta < 0 \Longrightarrow \theta$ lies in Quadrant II.

15. $\sin \theta = \dfrac{y}{r} = \dfrac{3}{5} \Longrightarrow x^2 = 25 - 9 = 16$

θ in Quadrant II $\Longrightarrow x = -4$

$\sin \theta = \dfrac{y}{r} = \dfrac{3}{5}$ $\qquad$ $\csc \theta = \dfrac{r}{y} = \dfrac{5}{3}$

$\cos \theta = \dfrac{x}{r} = -\dfrac{4}{5}$ $\qquad$ $\sec \theta = \dfrac{r}{x} = -\dfrac{5}{4}$

$\tan \theta = \dfrac{y}{x} = -\dfrac{3}{4}$ $\qquad$ $\cot \theta = \dfrac{x}{y} = -\dfrac{4}{3}$

17. $\tan \theta = \dfrac{y}{x} = \dfrac{-15}{8}$

$\sin \theta < 0$ and $\tan \theta < 0 \Longrightarrow \theta$ is in Quadrant IV $\Longrightarrow$
$y < 0$ and $x > 0$.

$x = 8, y = -15, r = 17$

$\sin \theta = \dfrac{y}{r} = -\dfrac{15}{17}$ $\qquad$ $\csc \theta = \dfrac{r}{y} = -\dfrac{17}{15}$

$\cos \theta = \dfrac{x}{r} = \dfrac{8}{17}$ $\qquad$ $\sec \theta = \dfrac{r}{x} = \dfrac{17}{8}$

$\tan \theta = \dfrac{y}{x} = -\dfrac{15}{8}$ $\qquad$ $\cot \theta = \dfrac{x}{y} = -\dfrac{8}{15}$

19. $\cot \theta = \dfrac{x}{y} = -\dfrac{3}{1} = \dfrac{3}{-1}$

$\cos \theta > 0 \Longrightarrow \theta$ is in Quadrant IV $\Longrightarrow x$ is positive;
$x = 3, y = -1, r = \sqrt{10}$

$\sin \theta = \dfrac{y}{r} = -\dfrac{\sqrt{10}}{10}$ $\qquad$ $\csc \theta = \dfrac{r}{y} = -\sqrt{10}$

$\cos \theta = \dfrac{x}{r} = \dfrac{3\sqrt{10}}{10}$ $\qquad$ $\sec \theta = \dfrac{r}{x} = \dfrac{\sqrt{10}}{3}$

$\tan \theta = \dfrac{y}{x} = -\dfrac{1}{3}$ $\qquad$ $\cot \theta = \dfrac{x}{y} = -3$

21. $\sec \theta = \dfrac{r}{x} = \dfrac{2}{-1} \Longrightarrow y^2 = 4 - 1 = 3$

$\sin \theta > 0 \Longrightarrow \theta$ is in Quadrant II $\Longrightarrow y = \sqrt{3}$

$\sin \theta = \dfrac{y}{r} = \dfrac{\sqrt{3}}{2}$ $\qquad$ $\csc \theta = \dfrac{r}{y} = \dfrac{2\sqrt{3}}{3}$

$\cos \theta = \dfrac{x}{r} = -\dfrac{1}{2}$ $\qquad$ $\sec \theta = \dfrac{r}{x} = -2$

$\tan \theta = \dfrac{y}{x} = -\sqrt{3}$ $\qquad$ $\cot \theta = \dfrac{x}{y} = -\dfrac{\sqrt{3}}{3}$

23. $\cot \theta$ is undefined, $\dfrac{\pi}{2} \le \theta \le \dfrac{3\pi}{2} \Longrightarrow y = 0 \Longrightarrow \theta = \pi$

$\sin \pi = 0$ $\qquad$ $\csc \pi$ is undefined

$\cos \pi = -1$ $\qquad$ $\sec \pi = -1$

$\tan \pi = 0$ $\qquad$ $\cot \pi$ is undefined

25. To find a point on the terminal side of θ, use any point on the line $y = -x$ that lies in Quadrant II. $(-1, 1)$ is one such point.

$x = -1, y = 1, r = \sqrt{2}$

$\sin \theta = \dfrac{1}{\sqrt{2}} = \dfrac{\sqrt{2}}{2}$ $\qquad$ $\csc \theta = \sqrt{2}$

$\cos \theta = -\dfrac{1}{\sqrt{2}} = -\dfrac{\sqrt{2}}{2}$ $\qquad$ $\sec \theta = -\sqrt{2}$

$\tan \theta = -1$ $\qquad$ $\cot \theta = -1$

27. To find a point on the terminal side of θ, use any point on the line $y = 2x$ that lies in Quadrant III. $(-1, -2)$ is one such point.

$x = -1, y = -2, r = \sqrt{5}$

$\sin \theta = -\dfrac{2}{\sqrt{5}} = -\dfrac{2\sqrt{5}}{5}$ $\qquad$ $\csc \theta = \dfrac{\sqrt{5}}{-2} = -\dfrac{\sqrt{5}}{2}$

$\cos \theta = -\dfrac{1}{\sqrt{5}} = -\dfrac{\sqrt{5}}{5}$ $\qquad$ $\sec \theta = \dfrac{\sqrt{5}}{-1} = -\sqrt{5}$

$\tan \theta = \dfrac{-2}{-1} = 2$ $\qquad$ $\cot \theta = \dfrac{-1}{-2} = \dfrac{1}{2}$

29. $(x, y) = (-1, 0), r = 1$

$\cos \pi = \dfrac{x}{r} = \dfrac{-1}{1} = -1$

31. $(x, y) = (-1, 0), r = 1$

$\sec \pi = \dfrac{r}{x} = \dfrac{1}{-1} = -1$

33. $(x, y) = (0, 1), r = 1$

$\tan \dfrac{\pi}{2} = \dfrac{y}{x} = \dfrac{1}{0}$ undefined.

35. $(x, y) = (0, 1)$

$\cot \dfrac{\pi}{2} = \dfrac{x}{y} = \dfrac{0}{1} = 0$

37. $\theta = 203°$

$\theta' = 203° - 180° = 23°$

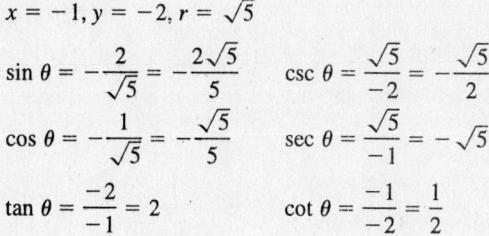

39. $\theta = -245°$

$360° - 245° = 115°$ (coterminal angle)

$\theta' = 180° - 115° = 65°$

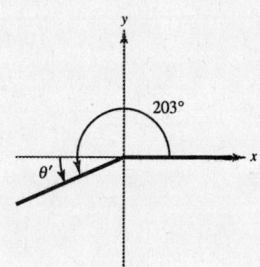

41. $\theta = \dfrac{2\pi}{3}$

$\theta' = \pi - \dfrac{2\pi}{3} = \dfrac{\pi}{3}$

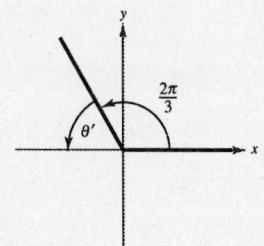

43. $\theta = 3.5$

$\theta' = 3.5 - \pi$

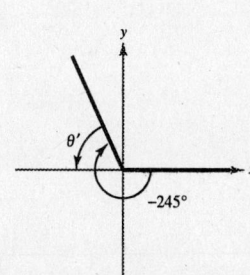

45. $\theta' = 45°$, Quadrant III

$$\sin 225° = -\sin 45° = -\frac{\sqrt{2}}{2}$$

$$\cos 225° = -\cos 45° = -\frac{\sqrt{2}}{2}$$

$$\tan 225° = \tan 45° = 1$$

47. $\theta' = 30°$, Quadrant I

$$\sin 750° = \sin 30° = \frac{1}{2}$$

$$\cos 750° = \cos 30° = \frac{\sqrt{3}}{2}$$

$$\tan 750° = \tan 30° = \frac{\sqrt{3}}{3}$$

49. $\theta' = 30°$, Quadrant III

$$\sin(-150°) = -\sin 30° = -\frac{1}{2}$$

$$\cos(-150°) = -\cos 30° = -\frac{\sqrt{3}}{2}$$

$$\tan(-150°) = \tan 30° = \frac{\sqrt{3}}{3}$$

51. $\theta' = \frac{\pi}{3}$, Quadrant III

$$\sin\frac{4\pi}{3} = -\sin\frac{\pi}{3} = -\frac{\sqrt{3}}{2}$$

$$\cos\frac{4\pi}{3} = -\cos\frac{\pi}{3} = -\frac{1}{2}$$

$$\tan\frac{4\pi}{3} = \tan\frac{\pi}{3} = \sqrt{3}$$

53. $\theta' = \frac{\pi}{6}$, Quadrant IV

$$\sin\left(-\frac{\pi}{6}\right) = -\sin\frac{\pi}{6} = -\frac{1}{2}$$

$$\cos\left(-\frac{\pi}{6}\right) = \cos\frac{\pi}{6} = \frac{\sqrt{3}}{2}$$

$$\tan\left(-\frac{\pi}{6}\right) = -\tan\frac{\pi}{6} = -\frac{\sqrt{3}}{3}$$

55. $\theta' = \frac{\pi}{4}$, Quadrant II

$$\sin\frac{11\pi}{4} = \sin\frac{\pi}{4} = \frac{\sqrt{2}}{2}$$

$$\cos\frac{11\pi}{4} = -\cos\frac{\pi}{4} = -\frac{\sqrt{2}}{2}$$

$$\tan\frac{11\pi}{4} = -\tan\frac{\pi}{4} = -1$$

57. $\theta' = \frac{\pi}{2}$

$$\sin\left(-\frac{3\pi}{2}\right) = \sin\frac{\pi}{2} = 1$$

$$\cos\left(-\frac{3\pi}{2}\right) = \cos\frac{\pi}{2} = 0$$

$$\tan\left(-\frac{3\pi}{2}\right) = \tan\frac{\pi}{2} \text{ which is undefined}$$

59. $\sin 10° \approx 0.1736$

61. $\cos(-110°) \approx -0.3420$

63. $\tan 4.5 \approx 4.6373$

65. $\tan\frac{\pi}{9} \approx 0.3640$

67. $\sin(-0.65) \approx -0.6052$

69. (a) $\sin \theta = \dfrac{1}{2} \implies$ reference angle is 30° or $\dfrac{\pi}{6}$ and θ is in Quadrant I or Quadrant II.

Values in degrees: 30°, 150°

Values in radians: $\dfrac{\pi}{6}, \dfrac{5\pi}{6}$

(b) $\sin \theta = -\dfrac{1}{2} \implies$ reference angle is 30° or $\dfrac{\pi}{6}$ and θ is in Quadrant III or Quadrant IV.

Values in degrees: 210°, 330°

Values in radians: $\dfrac{7\pi}{6}, \dfrac{11\pi}{6}$

71. (a) $\csc \theta = \dfrac{2\sqrt{3}}{3} \implies$ reference angle is 60° or $\dfrac{\pi}{3}$ and θ is in Quadrant I or Quadrant II.

Values in degrees: 60°, 120°

Values in radians: $\dfrac{\pi}{3}, \dfrac{2\pi}{3}$

(b) $\cot \theta = -1 \implies$ reference angle is 45° or $\dfrac{\pi}{4}$ and θ is in Quadrant II or Quadrant IV.

Values in degrees: 135°, 315°

Values in radians: $\dfrac{3\pi}{4}, \dfrac{7\pi}{4}$

73. (a) $\tan \theta = 1 \implies$ reference angle is 45° or $\dfrac{\pi}{4}$ and θ is in Quadrant I or Quadrant III.

Values in degrees: 45°, 225°

Values in radians: $\dfrac{\pi}{4}, \dfrac{5\pi}{4}$

(b) $\cot \theta = -\sqrt{3} \implies$ reference angle is 30° or $\dfrac{\pi}{6}$ and θ is in Quadrant II or Quadrant IV.

Values in degrees: 150°, 330°

Values in radians: $\dfrac{5\pi}{6}, \dfrac{11\pi}{6}$

75. $\sin \theta = 0.8191$

Quadrant I: $\theta = \sin^{-1} 0.8191 \approx 54.99°$

Quadrant II: $\theta = 180° - \sin^{-1} 0.8191 \approx 125.01°$

77. $\cos \theta = -0.4367 \implies \theta' \approx 64.11°$

Quadrant II: $\theta \approx 180° - 64.11° = 115.89°$

Quadrant III: $\theta \approx 180° + 64.11° = 244.11°$

79. $\cos \theta = 0.9848 \implies \theta' \approx 0.175$

Quadrant I: $\theta = \cos^{-1}(0.9848) \approx 0.175$

Quadrant IV: $\theta = 2\pi - \theta' \approx 6.109$

81. $\tan \theta = 1.192 \implies \theta' \approx 0.873$

Quadrant I: $\theta = \tan^{-1} 1.192 \approx 0.873$

Quadrant III: $\theta = \pi + \theta' \approx 4.014$

83. $\sec \theta = -2.6667 \Rightarrow \theta' = \cos^{-1}\left(\dfrac{1}{2.6667}\right) \approx 1.1864$

Quadrant II: $\theta = \pi - 1.1864 \approx 1.955$

Quadrant III: $\theta = \pi + 1.1864 \approx 4.328$

85. $\sin \theta = -\dfrac{3}{5}$

$\sin^2 \theta + \cos^2 \theta = 1$

$\cos^2 \theta = 1 - \sin^2 \theta$

$\cos^2 \theta = 1 - \left(-\dfrac{3}{5}\right)^2$

$\cos^2 \theta = 1 - \dfrac{9}{25}$

$\cos^2 \theta = \dfrac{16}{25}$

$\cos \theta > 0$ in Quadrant IV.

$\cos \theta = \dfrac{4}{5}$

87. $\tan \theta = \dfrac{3}{2}$

$\sec^2 \theta = 1 + \tan^2 \theta$

$\sec^2 \theta = 1 + \left(\dfrac{3}{2}\right)^2$

$\sec^2 \theta = 1 + \dfrac{9}{4}$

$\sec^2 \theta = \dfrac{13}{4}$

$\sec \theta < 0$ in Quadrant III.

$\sec \theta = -\dfrac{\sqrt{13}}{2}$

89. $\cos \theta = \dfrac{5}{8}$

$\cos \theta = \dfrac{1}{\sec \theta} \Rightarrow \sec \theta = \dfrac{1}{\cos \theta}$

$\sec \theta = \dfrac{1}{\frac{5}{8}} = \dfrac{8}{5}$

91. (a) $t = 1$

$T = 45 - 23 \cos\left[\dfrac{2\pi}{365}(1 - 32)\right] \approx 25.2°\,\text{F}$

(b) $t = 185$

$T = 45 - 23 \cos\left[\dfrac{2\pi}{365}(185 - 32)\right] \approx 65.1°\,\text{F}$

(c) $t = 291$

$T = 45 - 23 \cos\left[\dfrac{2\pi}{365}(291 - 32)\right] \approx 50.8°\,\text{F}$

93. $y(t) = 2 \cos 6t$

(a) $y(0) = 2 \cos 0 = 2$ centimeters

(b) $y\left(\frac{1}{4}\right) = 2 \cos\left(\frac{3}{2}\right) \approx 0.14$ centimeter

(c) $y\left(\frac{1}{2}\right) = 2 \cos 3 \approx -1.98$ centimeters

95. $I = 5e^{-2t} \sin t$

$I(0.7) = 5e^{-1.4} \sin 0.7 \approx 0.79$

97. False. In each of the four quadrants, the sign of the secant function and the cosine function will be the same since they are reciprocals of each other.

99. As θ increases from $0°$ to $90°$, x decreases from 12 cm to 0 cm and y increases from 0 cm to 12 cm.

Therefore, $\sin \theta = \dfrac{y}{12}$ increases from 0 to 1 and $\cos \theta = \dfrac{x}{12}$ decreases from 1 to 0. Thus,

$\tan \theta = \dfrac{y}{x}$ increases without bound, and when $\theta = 90°$ the tangent is undefined.

101. First, determine a positive coterminal angle. Then determine the trigonometric function of the reference angle and prefix the appropriate sign.

103. $y = 3^{x+1} + 2$

Intercept: $(0, 5)$

Horizontal asymptote: $y = 2$

Domain: All real numbers

Range: $y > 2$

x	-2	-1	0	1
y	$2\frac{1}{3}$	3	5	11

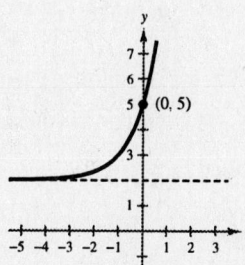

105. $y = 3^{(x+1)/2}$

Intercept: $(0, \sqrt{3})$

Horizontal asymptote: $y = 0$

Domain: All real numbers

Range: $y > 0$

x	-2	-1	0	1
y	$1/\sqrt{3}$	1	$\sqrt{3}$	3

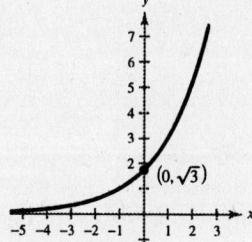

107. $y = \ln x^4 = 4 \ln|x|$

Intercepts: $(\pm 1, 0)$

Vertical asymptote: $x = 0$

Domain: All real numbers except $x = 0$.

Range: All real numbers

x	± 6	± 4	± 2	± 1	0
y	7.17	5.55	2.77	0	$-\infty$

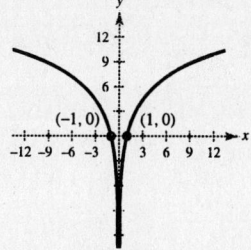

109. $y = \log_{10}(-3x)$

Intercept: $\left(-\frac{1}{3}, 0\right)$

Vertical asymptote: $x = 0$

Domain: $x < 0$

Range: All real numbers

x	-4	-3	-2	-1	-0.1
y	1.08	0.95	0.78	0.48	-0.52

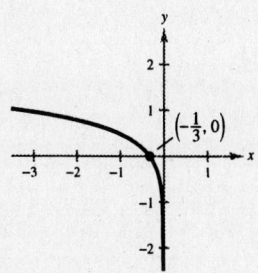

Section 4.5   Graphs of Sine and Cosine Functions

- You should be able to graph $y = a\sin(bx - c)$ and $y = a\cos(bx - c)$. (Assume $b > 0$)
- Amplitude: $|a|$
- Period: $\dfrac{2\pi}{|b|}$
- Shift: Solve $bx - c = 0$ and $bx - c = 2\pi$.
- Key Increments: $\dfrac{1}{4}$ (period)

Solutions to Odd-Numbered Exercises

1. $y = 3\sin 2x$

Period: $\dfrac{2\pi}{2} = \pi$

Amplitude: $|3| = 3$

3. $y = \dfrac{5}{2}\cos\dfrac{x}{2}$

Period: $\dfrac{2\pi}{\frac{1}{2}} = 4\pi$

Amplitude: $\left|\dfrac{5}{2}\right| = \dfrac{5}{2}$

5. $y = \dfrac{1}{2}\sin\dfrac{\pi x}{3}$

Period: $\dfrac{2\pi}{\frac{\pi}{3}} = 6$

Amplitude: $\left|\dfrac{1}{2}\right| = \dfrac{1}{2}$

7. $y = -2 \sin x$

Period: $\dfrac{2\pi}{1} = 2\pi$

Amplitude: $|-2| = 2$

9. $y = 3 \sin 10x$

Period: $\dfrac{2\pi}{10} = \dfrac{\pi}{5}$

Amplitude: $|3| = 3$

11. $y = \dfrac{1}{2} \cos \dfrac{2\pi}{3}$

Period: $\dfrac{2\pi}{\frac{2}{3}} = 3\pi$

Amplitude: $\left|\dfrac{1}{2}\right| = \dfrac{1}{2}$

13. $y = \dfrac{1}{4} \sin 2\pi x$

Period: $\dfrac{2\pi}{2\pi} = 1$

Amplitude: $\left|\dfrac{1}{4}\right| = \dfrac{1}{4}$

15. $f(x) = \sin x$

$g(x) = \sin(x - \pi)$

The graph of g is a horizontal shift to the right π units of the graph of f (a phase shift).

17. $f(x) = \cos 2x$

$g(x) = -\cos 2x$

The graph of g is a reflection in the x-axis of the graph of f.

19. $f(x) = \cos x$

$g(x) = \cos 2x$

The period of f is twice that of g.

21. $f(x) = \sin 2x$

$f(x) = 3 + \sin 2x$

The graph of g is a vertical shift 3 units upward of the graph of f.

23. The graph of g has twice the amplitude as the graph of f. The period is the same.

25. The graph of g is a horizontal shift π units to the right of the graph of f.

27. $f(x) = -2 \sin x$

Period: 2π

Amplitude: 2

$g(x) = 4 \sin x$

Period: 2π

Amplitude: 4

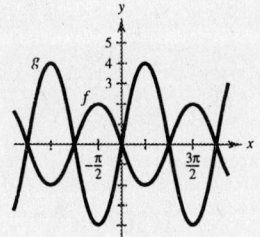

29. $f(x) = \cos x$

Period: 2π

Amplitude: 1

$g(x) = 1 + \cos x$

is a vertical shift of the graph of $f(x)$ one unit upward.

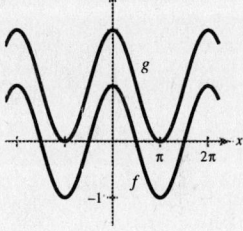

31. $f(x) = -\dfrac{1}{2} \sin \dfrac{x}{2}$

Period: 4π

Amplitude: $\dfrac{1}{2}$

$g(x) = 3 - \dfrac{1}{2} \sin \dfrac{x}{2}$ is the graph of $f(x)$ shifted vertically three units upward.

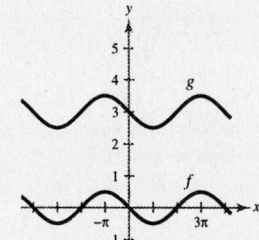

33. $f(x) = 2 \cos x$

Period: 2π

Amplitude: 2

$g(x) = 2 \cos(x + \pi)$ is the graph of $f(x)$ shifted π units to the left.

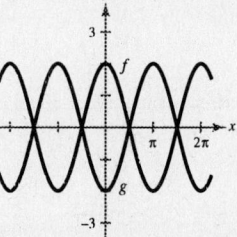

35. $y = -2 \sin 6x$; $a = -2$, $b = 6$, $c = 0$

Period: $\dfrac{2\pi}{6} = \dfrac{\pi}{3}$

Amplitude: $|-2| = 2$

Key points: $(0, 0), \left(\dfrac{\pi}{12}, -2\right), \left(\dfrac{\pi}{6}, 0\right), \left(\dfrac{\pi}{4}, 2\right), \left(\dfrac{\pi}{3}, 0\right)$

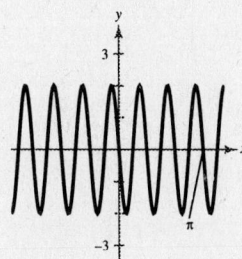

37. $y = \cos 2\pi x$

Period: $\dfrac{2\pi}{2\pi} = 1$

Amplitude: 1

Key points: $(0, 1), \left(\dfrac{1}{4}, 0\right), \left(\dfrac{1}{2}, -1\right), \left(\dfrac{3}{4}, 0\right)$

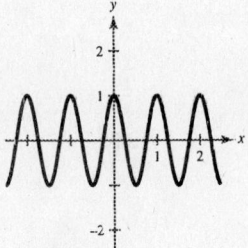

39. $y = -\sin \dfrac{2\pi x}{3}$; $a = -1, b = \dfrac{2\pi}{3}, c = 0$

Period: $\dfrac{2\pi}{\dfrac{2\pi}{3}} = 3$

Amplitude: 1

Key points: $(0, 0), \left(\dfrac{3}{4}, -1\right), \left(\dfrac{3}{2}, 0\right), \left(\dfrac{9}{4}, 1\right), (3, 0)$

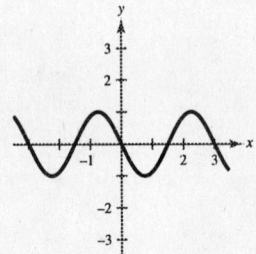

41. $y = \sin\left(x - \dfrac{\pi}{4}\right)$; $a = 1, b = 1, c = \dfrac{\pi}{4}$

Period: 2π

Amplitude: 1

Shift: Set $x - \dfrac{\pi}{4} = 0$ and $x - \dfrac{\pi}{4} = 2\pi$

$x = \dfrac{\pi}{4}$ $x = \dfrac{9\pi}{4}$

Key points: $\left(\dfrac{\pi}{4}, 0\right), \left(\dfrac{3\pi}{4}, 1\right), \left(\dfrac{5\pi}{4}, 0\right), \left(\dfrac{7\pi}{4}, -1\right), \left(\dfrac{9\pi}{4}, 0\right)$

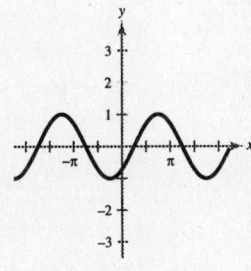

43. $y = 3\cos(x + \pi)$

Period: 2π

Amplitude: 3

Shift: Set $x + \pi = 0$ and $x + \pi = 2\pi$

$x = -\pi$ $x = \pi$

Key points: $(-\pi, 3), \left(-\dfrac{\pi}{2}, 0\right), (0, -3), \left(\dfrac{\pi}{2}, 0\right), (\pi, 3)$

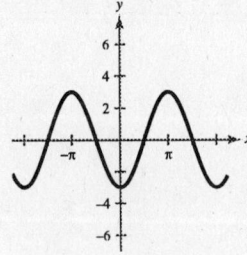

45. $y = 2 - \sin \dfrac{2\pi x}{3}$

Vertical shift 2 units upward
of the graph in Exercise 39.

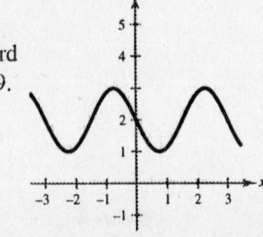

47. $y = 2 + \dfrac{1}{10}\cos 60\pi x$

Period: $\dfrac{2\pi}{60\pi} = \dfrac{1}{30}$

Amplitude: $\dfrac{1}{10}$

Vertical shift 2 units
upward

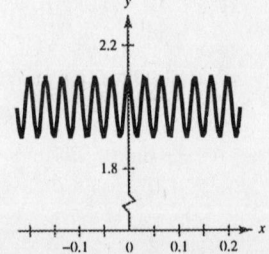

Key points:

$(0, 2.1), \left(\dfrac{1}{120}, 2\right), \left(\dfrac{1}{60}, 1.9\right), \left(\dfrac{1}{40}, 2\right), \left(\dfrac{1}{30}, 2.1\right)$

49. $y = 3\cos(x + \pi) - 3$

Vertical shift 3 units downward of the graph in Exercise 43.

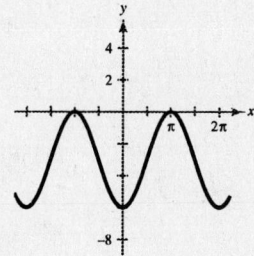

51. $y = \dfrac{2}{3}\cos\left(\dfrac{x}{2} - \dfrac{\pi}{4}\right);\ a = \dfrac{2}{3},\ b = \dfrac{1}{2},\ c = \dfrac{\pi}{4}$

Period: 4π

Amplitude: $\dfrac{2}{3}$

Shift: $\dfrac{x}{2} - \dfrac{\pi}{4} = 0$ and $\dfrac{x}{2} - \dfrac{\pi}{4} = 2\pi$

$\qquad x = \dfrac{\pi}{2} \qquad\qquad x = \dfrac{9\pi}{2}$

Key points: $\left(\dfrac{\pi}{2}, \dfrac{2}{3}\right),\ \left(\dfrac{3\pi}{2}, 0\right),\ \left(\dfrac{5\pi}{2}, \dfrac{-2}{3}\right),\ \left(\dfrac{7\pi}{2}, 0\right),\ \left(\dfrac{9\pi}{2}, \dfrac{2}{3}\right)$

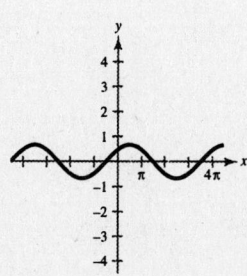

53. $y = -2\sin(4x + \pi)$

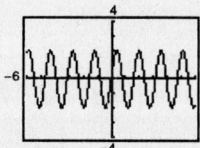

55. $y = \cos\left(2\pi x - \dfrac{\pi}{2}\right) + 1$

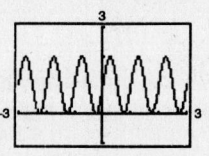

57. $y = 5\sin(\pi - 2x) + 10$

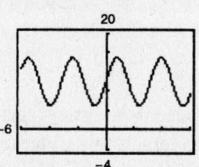

59. $y = -0.1\sin\left(\dfrac{\pi x}{10} + \pi\right)$

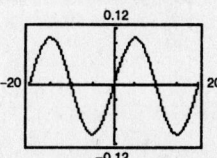

61. $f(x) = a\cos x + d$

Amplitude: $\frac{1}{2}[3 - (-1)] = 2 \implies a = 2$

Vertical shift 1 unit upward of $g(x) = 2\cos x \implies d = 1$.
Thus, $f(x) = 2\cos x + 1$.

63. $f(x) = a\cos x + d$

Amplitude: $\frac{1}{2}[8 - 0] = 4$

Since $f(x)$ is the graph of $g(x) = 4\cos x$ reflected in the x-axis and shifted vertically 4 units upward, we have $a = -4$ and $d = 4$. Thus, $f(x) = -4\cos x + 4$.

65. $y = a\sin(bx - c)$

Amplitude: $|a| = |3|$ Since the graph is reflected in the x-axis, we have $a = -3$.

Period: $\dfrac{2\pi}{b} = \pi \implies b = 2$

Phase shift: $c = 0$

Thus, $y = -3\sin 2x$.

67. $y = a\sin(bx - c)$

Amplitude: $a = 2$

Period: $2\pi \implies b = 1$

Phase shift: $bx - c = 0$ when $x = -\dfrac{\pi}{4}$

$(1)\left(\dfrac{-\pi}{4}\right) - c = 0 \implies c = -\dfrac{\pi}{4}$

Thus, $y = 2\sin\left(x + \dfrac{\pi}{4}\right)$.

69. $y_1 = \sin x$

$y_2 = -\dfrac{1}{2}$

In the interval $[-2\pi, 2\pi]$, $\sin x = -\dfrac{1}{2}$ when

$x = -\dfrac{5\pi}{6}, \ -\dfrac{\pi}{6}, \ \dfrac{7\pi}{6}, \ \dfrac{11\pi}{6}$.

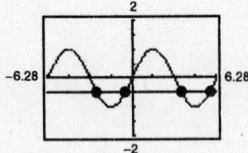

71. $y_1 = \cos x$

$y_2 = \dfrac{\sqrt{2}}{2}$

In the interval $[-2\pi, 2\pi]$, $\cos x = \dfrac{\sqrt{2}}{2}$

when $x = \pm\dfrac{\pi}{4}, \ \pm\dfrac{7\pi}{4}$.

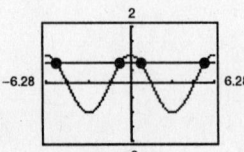

73. $y = 0.85 \sin \dfrac{\pi t}{3}$

(a) Time for one cycle five one period $= \dfrac{2\pi}{\dfrac{\pi}{3}} = 6$ sec

(b) Cycles per min $= \dfrac{60}{6} = 10$ cycles per min

(c) Amplitude: 0.85

Period: 6

Key points: $(0, 0)$, $\left(\dfrac{3}{2}, 0.85\right)$, $(3, 0)$, $\left(\dfrac{9}{2}, -0.85\right)$, $(6, 0)$

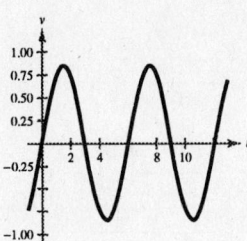

75. $y = 0.001 \sin 880\pi t$

(a) Period: $\dfrac{2\pi}{880\pi} = \dfrac{1}{440}$ seconds

(b) $f = \dfrac{1}{p} = 440$ cycles per second

77. (a) $C(t) = 56.35 + 27.35 \sin\left(\dfrac{\pi t}{6} + 4.19\right)$

(b)

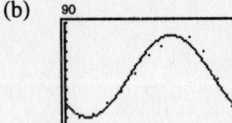

The model is a good fit for most months.

(c)

The model is a good fit.

(d) Use the constant term of each model to estimate the average annual temperature.

Honolulu: 84.40°

Chicago: 56.35°

(e) Each model has a period of 12. This corresponds to the 12 months in a year.

(f) Chicago has a greater variability in temperatures during the year. The amplitude of each model indicates this variability.

79. $S = 74.50 + 43.75 \sin \dfrac{\pi t}{6}$

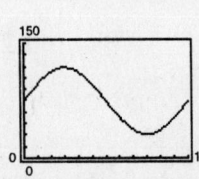

81. (a) and (c)

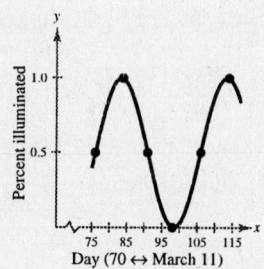

Day (70 ↔ March 11)

(d) For May 8, 2005, use $x = 128$

$y(128) \approx 0$

(b) Vertical shift: $\dfrac{1}{2} \Rightarrow d = \dfrac{1}{2}$

Amplitude: $\dfrac{1}{2} \Rightarrow a = \dfrac{1}{2}$

Period: $30 \Rightarrow \dfrac{2\pi}{b} = 30 \Rightarrow b = \dfrac{\pi}{15}$

Horizontal shift: $76 \Rightarrow \dfrac{\pi}{15}(76) + c = c \Rightarrow c = -\dfrac{76\pi}{15}$

$y = \dfrac{1}{2} + \dfrac{1}{2}\sin\left(\dfrac{\pi}{15}x - \dfrac{76\pi}{15}\right)$

$= \dfrac{1}{2} + \dfrac{1}{2}\sin\dfrac{\pi}{15}(x - 76)$

The model is a good fit.

83. False. $y = \dfrac{1}{2}\cos 2x$ has an amplitude that is **half** that of $y = \cos x$. For $y = a\cos bx$, the amplitude is $|a|$.

85. $y = 2 + \sin x$

$y = 3.5 + \sin x$

$y = -2 + \sin x$

Each value of d produces a vertical shift of $y = \sin x$ upward (or downward) by d units.

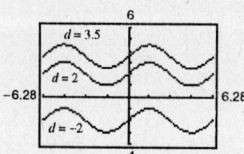

87. $y = \sin(x - 1)$

$y = \sin(x - 3)$

$y = \sin(x - (-2)) = \sin(x + 2)$

Each value of c produces a horizontal shift of $y = \sin x$ to the left (or right) by c units.

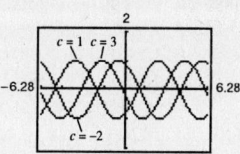

89. $f(x) = \sin x, \; g(x) = -\cos\left(x + \dfrac{\pi}{2}\right)$

x	0	$\dfrac{\pi}{2}$	π	$\dfrac{3\pi}{2}$	2π
$\sin x$	0	1	0	-1	0
$-\cos\left(x - \dfrac{\pi}{2}\right)$	0	1	0	-1	0

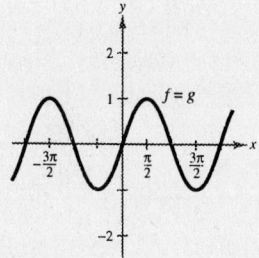

Conjecture: $\sin x = -\cos\left(x + \dfrac{\pi}{2}\right)$

91. $f(x) = \cos x, \; g(x) = -\cos(x - \pi)$

x	0	$\dfrac{\pi}{2}$	π	$\dfrac{3\pi}{2}$	2π
$\cos x$	1	0	-1	0	1
$-\cos(x - \pi)$	1	0	-1	0	1

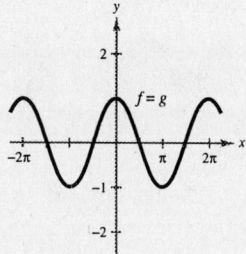

Conjecture: $\cos x = -\cos(x - \pi)$

93. (a) $\sin\dfrac{1}{2} \approx \dfrac{1}{2} - \dfrac{\left(\frac{1}{2}\right)^3}{3!} + \dfrac{\left(\frac{1}{2}\right)^5}{5!} \approx 0.4794$

$\sin\dfrac{1}{2} \approx 0.4794$ (by calculator)

(b) $\sin 1 \approx 1 - \dfrac{1}{3!} + \dfrac{1}{5!} \approx 0.8417$

$\sin 1 \approx 0.8415$ (by calculator)

(c) $\sin\dfrac{\pi}{6} \approx 1 - \dfrac{\left(\frac{\pi}{6}\right)^3}{3!} + \dfrac{\left(\frac{\pi}{6}\right)^5}{5!} \approx 0.5000$

$\sin\dfrac{\pi}{6} = 0.5$ (by calculator)

(d) $\cos(-0.5) \approx 1 - \dfrac{(-0.5)^2}{2!} + \dfrac{(-0.5)^4}{4!} \approx 0.8776$

$\cos(-0.5) \approx 0.8776$ (by calculator)

(e) $\cos 1 \approx 1 - \dfrac{1}{2!} + \dfrac{1}{4!} \approx 0.5417$

$\cos 1 \approx 0.5403$ (by calculator)

(f) $\cos\dfrac{\pi}{4} \approx 1 - \dfrac{\left(\frac{\pi}{4}\right)^2}{2!} + \dfrac{\left(\frac{\pi}{4}\right)^4}{4!} = 0.7074$

$\cos\dfrac{\pi}{4} \approx 0.7071$ (by calculator)

The error in the approximation is not the same in each case. The error appears to increase as x moves farther away from 0.

95. $f(x)$ is even $\Rightarrow f(-x) = f(x)$

$g(x)$ is odd $\Rightarrow g(-x) = -g(x)$

(a) $h(x) = [f(x)]^2$

$h(-x) = [f(-x)]^2$

$= [f(x)]^2$

$= h(x) \Rightarrow h(x)$ is even

(b) $h(x) = [g(x)]^2$

$h(-x) = [g(-x)]^2$

$= [-g(x)]^2$

$= [g(x)]^2$

$= h(x) \Rightarrow h(x)$ is even

97. $\log_2[x^2(x-3)] = \log_2 x^2 + \log_2(x-3)$

$= 2\log_2 x + \log_2(x-3)$

99. $\ln\sqrt{\dfrac{z}{z^2+1}} = \dfrac{1}{2}\ln\left(\dfrac{z}{z^2+1}\right) = \dfrac{1}{2}\left[\ln z - \ln(z^2+1)\right]$

$= \dfrac{1}{2}\ln z - \dfrac{1}{2}\ln(z^2+1)$

101. $2\log_2 x + \log_2(xy) = \log_2 x^2 + \log_2(xy)$

$= \log_2 x^2(xy)$

$= \log_2 x^3 y$

103. $\dfrac{1}{2}(\ln 2x - 2\ln x) + 3\ln x = \dfrac{1}{2}(\ln 2x - \ln x^2) + \ln x^3$

$= \dfrac{1}{2}\left(\ln\dfrac{2x}{x^2}\right) + \ln x^3$

$= \ln\sqrt{\dfrac{2x}{x^2}} + \ln x^3$

$= \ln\left(x^3\sqrt{\dfrac{2x}{x^2}}\right)$

Section 4.6   Graphs of Other Trigonometric Functions

■ You should be able to graph

$y = a \tan (bx - c)$ $\qquad$ $y = a \cot (bx - c)$

$y = a \sec (bx - c)$ $\qquad$ $y = a \csc (bx - c)$

■ When graphing $y = a \sec (bx - c)$ or $y = a \csc (bx - c)$ you should first graph $y = a \cos (bx - c)$ or $y = a \sin (bx - c)$ because

(a) The x-intercepts of sine and cosine are the vertical asymptotes of cosecant and secant.

(b) The maximums of sine and cosine are the local minimums of cosecant and secant.

(c) The minimums of sine and cosine are the local maximums of cosecant and secant.

■ You should be able to graph using a damping factor.

Solutions to Odd-Numbered Exercises

1. $y = \sec 2x$

Period: $\dfrac{2\pi}{2} = \pi$

Matches graph (e).

3. $y = \dfrac{1}{2} \cot \pi x$

Period: $\dfrac{\pi}{\pi} = 1$

Matches graph (a).

5. $y = -\csc x$

Period: 2π

Matches graph (d).

7. $y = \dfrac{1}{3} \tan x$

Period: π

Two consecutive
asymptotes:

$x = -\dfrac{\pi}{2}$ and $x = \dfrac{\pi}{2}$

x	$-\dfrac{\pi}{4}$	0	$\dfrac{\pi}{4}$
y	$-\dfrac{1}{3}$	0	$\dfrac{1}{3}$

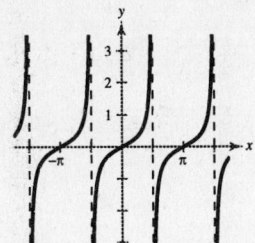

9. $y = \tan 3x$

Period: $\dfrac{\pi}{3}$

Two consecutive
asymptotes:

$3x = -\dfrac{\pi}{2} \implies x = -\dfrac{\pi}{6}$

$3x - \dfrac{\pi}{2} \implies x = \dfrac{\pi}{6}$

x	$-\dfrac{\pi}{12}$	0	$\dfrac{\pi}{12}$
y	-1	0	1

11. $y = -\dfrac{1}{2} \sec x$

Graph $y = -\dfrac{1}{2} \cos x$ first.

Period: 2π

One cycle: 0 to 2π

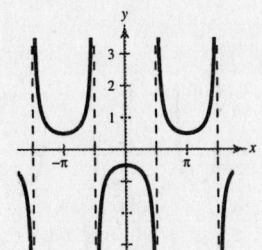

13. $y = \csc \pi x$

Graph $y = \sin \pi x$ first.

Period: $\dfrac{2\pi}{\pi} = 2$

One cycle: 0 to 2

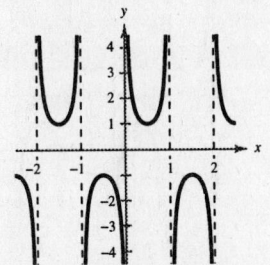

15. $y = \sec \pi x - 1$

Graph $y = \cos \pi x$ first

Period: $\dfrac{2\pi}{\pi} = 2$

One cycle: 0 to 2

Vertical shift 1 unit downward.

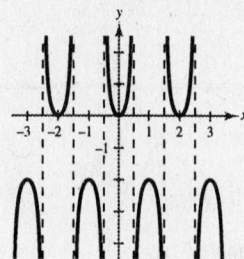

17. $y = \csc \dfrac{x}{2}$

Graph $y = \sin \dfrac{x}{2}$ first.

Period: $\dfrac{2\pi}{\frac{1}{2}} = 4\pi$

One cycle: 0 to 4π

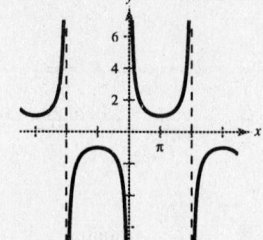

19. $y = \cot \dfrac{x}{2}$

Period: $\dfrac{\pi}{\frac{1}{2}} = 2\pi$

x	$\dfrac{\pi}{2}$	π	$\dfrac{3\pi}{2}$
y	1	0	-1

Two consecutive asymptotes: $\dfrac{x}{2} = 0 \Rightarrow x = 0$

$\dfrac{x}{2} = \pi \Rightarrow x = 2\pi$

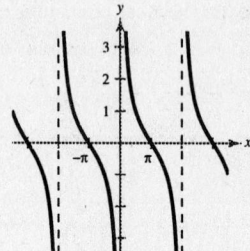

21. $y = \dfrac{1}{2} \sec 2x$

Graph $y = \dfrac{1}{2} \cos 2x$ first.

Period: $\dfrac{2\pi}{2} = \pi$

One cycle: 0 to π

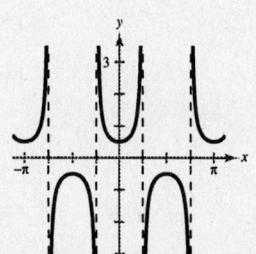
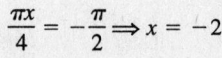

23. $y = \tan \dfrac{\pi x}{4}$

Period: $\dfrac{\pi}{\frac{\pi}{4}} = 4$

Two consecutive asymptotes:

$\dfrac{\pi x}{4} = -\dfrac{\pi}{2} \Rightarrow x = -2$

$\dfrac{\pi x}{4} = \dfrac{\pi}{2} \Rightarrow x = 2$

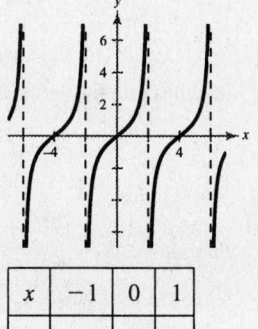

x	-1	0	1
y	-1	0	1

25. $y = \csc (\pi - x)$

Graph $y = \sin(\pi - x)$ first.

Period: 2π

Shift: Set $\pi - x = 0$ and $\pi - x = 2\pi$

$\qquad\qquad x = \pi \qquad\qquad x = -\pi$

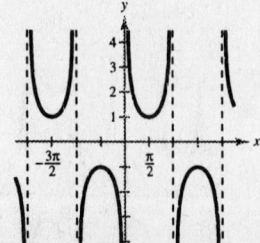

27. $y = \dfrac{1}{4} \csc\left(x + \dfrac{\pi}{4}\right)$

Graph $y = \dfrac{1}{4} \sin\left(x + \dfrac{\pi}{4}\right)$ first.

Period: 2π

Shift: Set $x + \dfrac{\pi}{4} = 0$ and $x + \dfrac{\pi}{4} = 2\pi$

$\qquad\qquad x = -\dfrac{\pi}{4} \quad$ to $\quad x = \dfrac{7\pi}{4}$

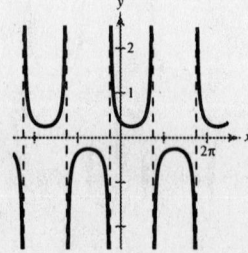

29. $y = \tan \dfrac{x}{3}$

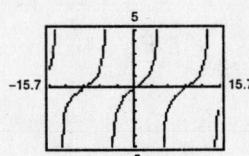

31. $y = -2 \sec 4x$

$= \dfrac{-2}{\cos 4x}$

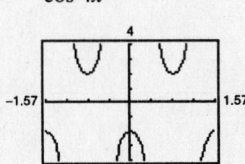

33. $y = \tan\left(x - \dfrac{\pi}{4}\right)$

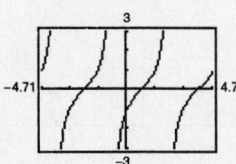

35. $y = \dfrac{1}{4} \cot\left(x - \dfrac{\pi}{2}\right)$

$= \dfrac{1}{4 \tan\left(x - \dfrac{\pi}{2}\right)}$

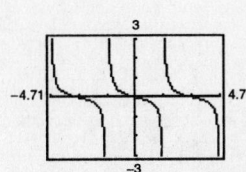

37. $y = 0.1 \tan\left(\dfrac{\pi x}{4} + \dfrac{\pi}{4}\right)$

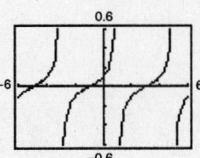

39. $\tan x = 1$

$x = -\dfrac{7\pi}{4}, -\dfrac{3\pi}{4}, \dfrac{\pi}{4}, \dfrac{5\pi}{4}$

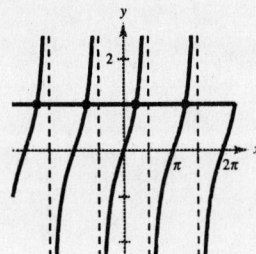

41. $\cot x = -\dfrac{\sqrt{3}}{3}$

$x = -\dfrac{4\pi}{3}, -\dfrac{\pi}{3}, \dfrac{2\pi}{3}, \dfrac{5\pi}{3}$

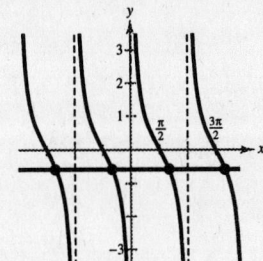

43. $\sec x = -2$

$x = \pm\dfrac{2\pi}{3}, \pm\dfrac{4\pi}{3}$

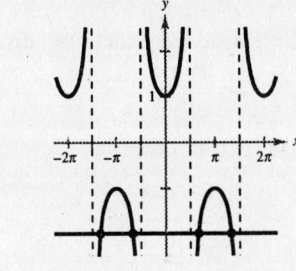

45. $\csc x = \sqrt{2}$

$x = -\dfrac{7\pi}{4}, -\dfrac{5\pi}{4}, \dfrac{\pi}{4}, \dfrac{3\pi}{4}$

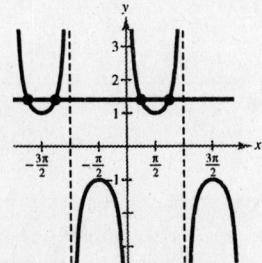

47. The graph of $f(x) = \sec x$ has y-axis symmetry. Thus, the function is even.

49. $f(x) = 2 \sin x$

$g(x) = \dfrac{1}{2} \csc x$

(a)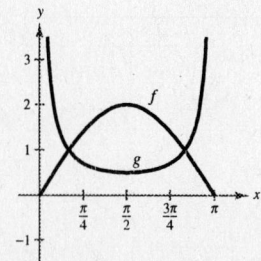

(b) $f > g$ on the interval, $\dfrac{\pi}{6} < x < \dfrac{5\pi}{6}$

(c) As $x \to \pi$, $f(x) = 2 \sin x \to 0$ and

$g(x) = \dfrac{1}{2} \csc x \to \pm\infty$ since $g(x)$ is the reciprocal of $f(x)$.

51. $y_1 = \sin x \csc x$ and $y_2 = 1$

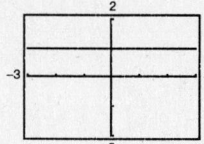

$\sin x \csc x = \sin x \left(\dfrac{1}{\sin x} \right) = 1, \sin x \neq 0$

The expressions are equivalent except when $\sin x = 0$ and y_1 is undefined.

53. $y_1 = \dfrac{\cos x}{\sin x}$ and $y_2 = \cot x = \dfrac{1}{\tan x}$

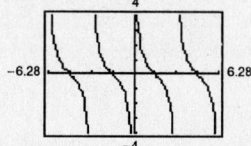

$\cot x = \dfrac{\cos x}{\sin x}$

The expressions are equivalent.

55. $f(x) = |x \cos x|$

As $x \to 0$, $f(x) \to 0$.

Matches graph (d).

57. $g(x) = |x| \sin x$

As $x \to 0$, $g(x) \to 0$.

Matches graph (b).

59. $f(x) = \sin x + \cos\left(x + \dfrac{\pi}{2}\right)$, $g(x) = 0$

$f(x) = g(x)$ The graph is the line $y = 0$.

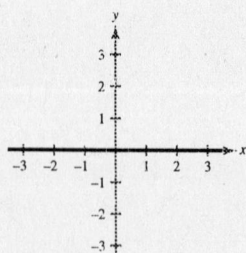

61. $f(x) = \sin^2 x$, $g(x) = \dfrac{1}{2}(1 - \cos 2x)$

$f(x) = g(x)$

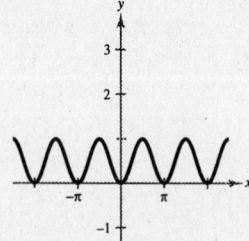

63. $f(x) = 2^{-x/4} \cos \pi x$

$-2^{-x/4} \leq f(x) \leq 2^{-2x/4}$

The damping factor is $y = 2^{-x/4}$.

As $x \to \infty, f(x) \to 0$

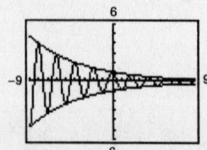

65. $g(x) = e^{-x^2/2} \sin x$

$-e^{-x^2/2} \leq g(x) \leq e^{-x^2/2}$

The damping factor is $y = e^{-x^2/2}$.

As $x \to \infty, g(x) \to 0$

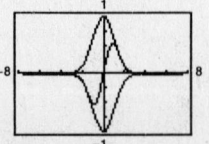

67. $y = \dfrac{6}{x} + \cos x, \; x > 0$

As $x \to 0, \; y \to \infty$.

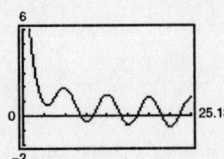

69. $g(x) = \dfrac{\sin x}{x}$

As $x \to 0, \; g(x) \to 1$.

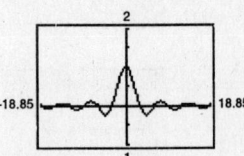

71. $f(x) = \sin \dfrac{1}{x}$

As $x \to 0, f(x)$ oscillates between -1 and 1.

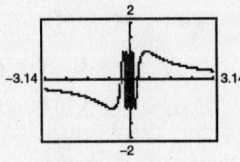

73. $\tan x = \dfrac{7}{d}$

$d = \dfrac{7}{\tan x} = 7 \cot x$

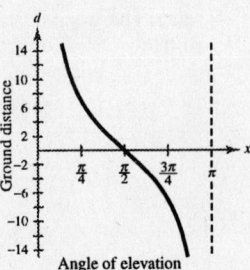

75. $S = 74 + 3x + 40 \sin \dfrac{\pi t}{6}$

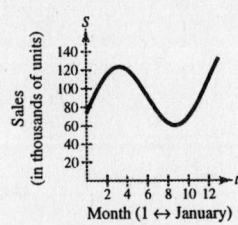

77. $H(t) = 54.33 - 20.38 \cos \dfrac{\pi t}{6} - 15.69 \sin \dfrac{\pi t}{6}$

$L(t) = 39.36 - 15.70 \cos \dfrac{\pi t}{6} - 14.16 \sin \dfrac{\pi t}{6}$

(a) Period of $\cos \dfrac{\pi t}{6}$: $\dfrac{2\pi}{\frac{\pi}{6}} = 12$

   Period of $\sin \dfrac{\pi t}{6}$: $\dfrac{2\pi}{\frac{\pi}{6}} = 12$

   Period of $H(t)$: 12

   Period of $L(t)$: 12

(b) From the graph, it appears that the greatest difference between high and low temperatures occurs in summer. The smallest difference occurs in winter.

(c) The highest high and low temperatures appear to occur around the middle of July, roughly one month after the time when the sun is northernmost in the sky.

79. True. Since $y = \csc x = \dfrac{1}{\sin x}$, for a given value of x, the y-coordinate of $\csc x$ is the reciprocal of the y-coordinate of $\sin x$.

81. As $x \to \dfrac{\pi}{2}$ from the left, $f(x) = \tan x \to \infty$.

As $x \to \dfrac{\pi}{2}$ from the right, $f(x) = \tan x \to -\infty$.

83. $f(x) = x - \cos x$

(a)

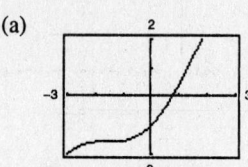

The zero between 0 and 1 appears to occur at $x \approx 0.739$.

(b) $x_n = \cos(x_{n-1})$

$x_0 = 1$

$x_1 = \cos 1 \approx 0.5403$

$x_2 = \cos 0.5403 \approx 0.8576$

$x_3 = \cos 0.8576 \approx 0.6543$

$x_4 = \cos 0.6543 \approx 0.7935$

$x_5 = \cos 0.7935 \approx 0.7014$

$x_6 = \cos 0.7014 \approx 0.7640$

$x_7 = \cos 0.7640 \approx 0.7221$

$x_8 = \cos 0.7221 \approx 0.7504$

$x_9 = \cos 0.7504 \approx 0.7314$

$\vdots$

This sequence appears to be approaching the zero of f: $x \approx 0.739$.

85. $y_1 = \sec x$

$$y_2 = 1 + \frac{x^2}{2!} + \frac{5x^4}{4!}$$

The approximation appears to coincide on the interval $-1.1 \le x \le 1.1$.

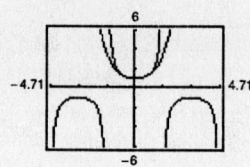

87. $e^{2x} = 54$

$2x = \ln 54$

$$x = \frac{\ln 54}{2} \approx 1.994$$

89. $\dfrac{300}{1 + e^{-x}} = 100$

$\dfrac{300}{100} = 1 + e^{-x}$

$3 = 1 + e^{-x}$

$2 = e^{-x}$

$\ln 2 = -x$

$x = -\ln 2 \approx -0.693$

91. $\ln(3x - 2) = 73$

$3x - 2 = e^{73}$

$3x = 2 + e^{73}$

$x = \dfrac{2 + e^{73}}{3}$

$\approx 1.684 \times 10^{31}$

93. $\ln(x^2 + 1) = 3.2$

$x^2 + 1 = e^{3.2}$

$x^2 = e^{3.2} - 1$

$x = \pm\sqrt{e^{3.2} - 1} \approx \pm 4.851$

95. $\log_8 x + \log_8(x - 1) = \dfrac{1}{3}$

$\log_8[x(x - 1)] = \dfrac{1}{3}$

$x(x - 1) = 8^{1/3}$

$x^2 - x = 2$

$x^2 - x - 2 = 0$

$(x - 2)(x + 1) = 0$

$x = 2, -1$

$x = -1$ is extraneous (not in the domain of $\log_8 x$) so only $x = 2$ is a solution.

Section 4.7 Inverse Trigonometric Functions

■ You should know the definitions, domains, and ranges of $y = \arcsin x$, $y = \arccos x$, and $y = \arctan x$.

Function	Domain	Range
$y = \arcsin x \implies x = \sin y$	$-1 \le x \le 1$	$-\dfrac{\pi}{2} \le y \le \dfrac{\pi}{2}$
$y = \arccos x \implies x = \cos y$	$-1 \le x \le 1$	$0 \le y \le \pi$
$y = \arctan x \implies x = \tan y$	$-\infty < x < \infty$	$-\dfrac{\pi}{2} < x < \dfrac{\pi}{2}$

■ You should know the inverse properties of the inverse trigonometric functions.

$$\sin(\arcsin x) = x \quad \text{and} \quad \arcsin(\sin y) = y, \ -\frac{\pi}{2} \le y \le \frac{\pi}{2}$$

$$\cos(\arccos x) = x \quad \text{and} \quad \arccos(\cos y) = y, \ 0 \le y \le \pi$$

$$\tan(\arctan x) = x \quad \text{and} \quad \arctan(\tan y) = y, \ -\frac{\pi}{2} < y < \frac{\pi}{2}$$

■ You should be able to use the triangle technique to convert trigonometric functions of inverse trigonometric functions into algebraic expressions.

Solutions to Odd-Numbered Exercises

1. $y = \arcsin \dfrac{1}{2} \implies \sin y = \dfrac{1}{2}$ for

$$-\frac{\pi}{2} \le y \le \frac{\pi}{2} \implies y = \frac{\pi}{6}$$

3. $y = \arccos \dfrac{1}{2} \implies \cos y = \dfrac{1}{2}$ for

$$0 \le y \le \pi \implies y = \frac{\pi}{3}$$

5. $y = \arctan \dfrac{\sqrt{3}}{3} \implies \tan y = \dfrac{\sqrt{3}}{3}$ for

$$-\frac{\pi}{2} < y < \frac{\pi}{2} \implies y = \frac{\pi}{6}$$

7. $y = \arccos\left(-\dfrac{\sqrt{3}}{2}\right) \implies \cos y = -\dfrac{\sqrt{3}}{2}$ for

$$0 \le y \le \pi \implies y = \frac{5\pi}{6}$$

9. $y = \arctan\left(-\sqrt{3}\right) \implies \tan y = -\sqrt{3}$ for

$$-\frac{\pi}{2} < y < \frac{\pi}{2} \implies y = -\frac{\pi}{3}$$

11. $y = \arccos\left(-\dfrac{1}{2}\right) \implies \cos y = -\dfrac{1}{2}$ for

$$0 \le y \le \pi \implies y = \frac{2\pi}{3}$$

13. $y = \arcsin \dfrac{\sqrt{3}}{2} \implies \sin y = \dfrac{\sqrt{3}}{2}$ for

$$-\frac{\pi}{2} \le y \le \frac{\pi}{2} \implies y = \frac{\pi}{3}$$

15. $y = \arctan 0 \implies \tan y = 0$ for $-\dfrac{\pi}{2} < y < \dfrac{\pi}{2} \implies y = 0$

17. $\arccos 0.28 = \cos^{-1} 0.28 \approx 1.29$

19. $\arcsin(-0.75) = \sin^{-1}(-0.75) \approx -0.85$

21. $\arctan(-3) = \tan^{-1}(-3) \approx -1.25$

23. $\arcsin 0.31 = \sin^{-1} 0.31 \approx 0.32$

25. $\arccos(-0.41) = \cos^{-1}(-0.41) \approx 1.99$

27. $\arctan 0.92 = \tan^{-1} 0.92 \approx 0.74$

29. $\arcsin\left(\dfrac{3}{4}\right) = \sin^{-1}(0.75) \approx 0.85$

31. $\arctan\left(\dfrac{7}{2}\right) = \tan^{-1}(3.5) \approx 1.29$

33. This is the graph of $y = \arctan x$. The coordinates are $\left(-\sqrt{3}, -\dfrac{\pi}{3}\right), \left(-\dfrac{\sqrt{3}}{3}, -\dfrac{\pi}{6}\right)$, and $\left(1, \dfrac{\pi}{4}\right)$.

35. $f(x) = \tan x$ and $g(x) = \arctan x$

Graph $y_1 = \tan x$

Graph $y_2 = \tan^{-1} x$

Graph $y_3 = x$

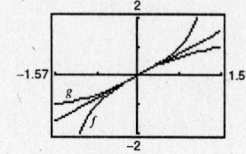

37. $\tan\theta = \dfrac{x}{4}$

$\theta = \arctan\dfrac{x}{4}$

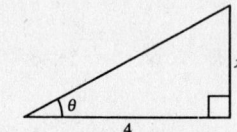

39. $\sin\theta = \dfrac{x + 2}{5}$

$\theta = \arcsin\left(\dfrac{x + 2}{5}\right)$

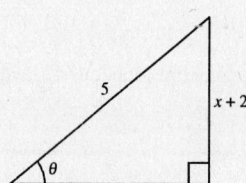

41. $\cos\theta = \dfrac{x + 3}{2x}$

$\theta = \arccos\left(\dfrac{x + 3}{2x}\right)$

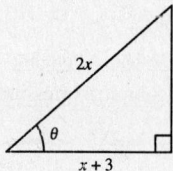

43. $\sin(\arcsin 0.3) = 0.3$

45. $\cos[\arccos(-0.1)] = -0.1$

47. $\arcsin(\sin 3\pi) = \arcsin(0) = 0$

Note: 3π is not in the range of the arcsine function.

49. Let $y = \arctan\dfrac{3}{4}$. Then,

$\tan y = \dfrac{3}{4}$, $0 < y < \dfrac{\pi}{2}$

and $\sin y = \dfrac{3}{5}$.

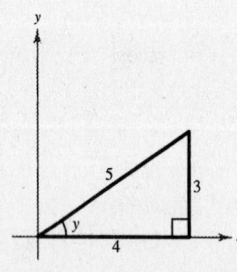

51. Let $y = \arctan 2$. Then,

$\tan y = 2 = \dfrac{2}{1}$, $0 < y < \dfrac{\pi}{2}$

and $\cos y = \dfrac{1}{\sqrt{5}} = \dfrac{\sqrt{5}}{5}$.

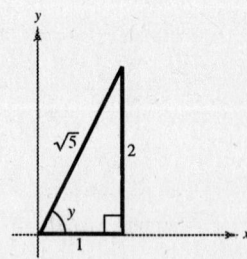

53. Let $y = \arcsin\dfrac{5}{13}$. Then,

$\sin y = \dfrac{5}{13}$, $0 < y < \dfrac{\pi}{2}$

and $\cos y = \dfrac{12}{13}$.

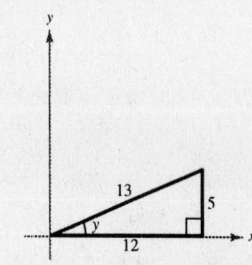

55. Let $y = \arctan\left(-\dfrac{3}{5}\right)$. Then,

$\tan y = -\dfrac{3}{5}$, $-\dfrac{\pi}{2} < y < 0$

and $\sec y = \dfrac{\sqrt{34}}{5}$.

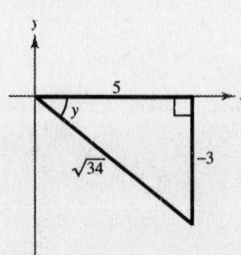

57. Let $y = \arccos\left(-\dfrac{2}{3}\right)$. Then,

$\cos y = -\dfrac{2}{3}, \dfrac{\pi}{2} < y < \pi$

and $\sin y = \dfrac{\sqrt{5}}{3}$.

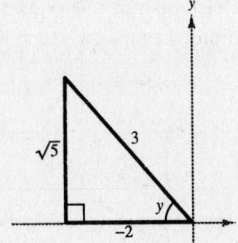

59. Let $y = \arctan x$. Then,

$\tan y = x = \dfrac{x}{1}$

and $\cot y = \dfrac{1}{x}$.

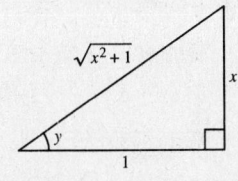

61. Let $y = \arcsin(2x)$. Then,

$\sin y = 2x = \dfrac{2x}{1}$

and $\cos y = \sqrt{1 - 4x^2}$.

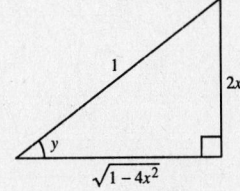

63. Let $y = \arccos x$. Then,

$\cos y = x = \dfrac{x}{1}$

and $\sin y = \sqrt{1 - x^2}$.

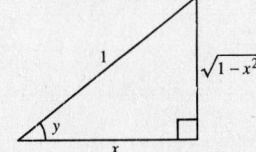

65. Let $y = \arccos\left(\dfrac{x}{3}\right)$. Then,

$\cos y = \dfrac{x}{3}$

and $\tan y = \dfrac{\sqrt{9 - x^2}}{x}$.

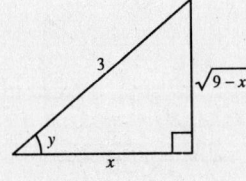

67. Let $y = \arctan \dfrac{x}{\sqrt{2}}$. Then,

$\tan y = \dfrac{x}{\sqrt{2}}$

and $\csc y = \dfrac{\sqrt{x^2 + 2}}{x}$.

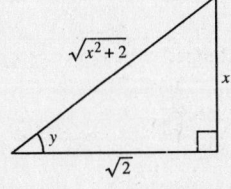

69. $f(x) = \sin(\arctan 2x)$, $g(x) = \dfrac{2x}{\sqrt{1 - 4x^2}}$

Let $y = \arctan 2x$. Then,

$\tan y = 2x = \dfrac{2x}{1}$

and $\sin y = \dfrac{2x}{\sqrt{1 + 4x^2}}$.

$g(x) = \dfrac{2x}{\sqrt{1 + 4x^2}} = f(x)$

The graph has horizontal asymptotes at $y = \pm 1$.

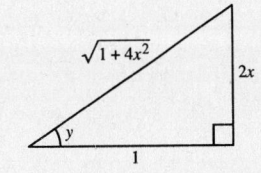

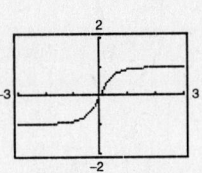

71. Let $y = \arctan \dfrac{9}{x}$. Then,

$\tan y = \dfrac{9}{x}$ and $\sin y = \dfrac{9}{\sqrt{x^2 + 81}}, x > 0; \dfrac{-9}{\sqrt{x^2 + 81}}, x < 0$

Thus, $\arcsin y = \dfrac{9}{\sqrt{x^2 + 81}}, x > 0$; $\arcsin y = \dfrac{-9}{\sqrt{x^2 + 81}}, x < 0$

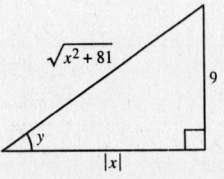

73. Let $y = \arccos \dfrac{3}{\sqrt{x^2 - 2x + 10}}$. Then,

$\cos y = \dfrac{3}{\sqrt{x^2 - 2x + 10}} = \dfrac{3}{\sqrt{(x - 1)^2 + 9}}$

and $\sin y = \dfrac{|x - 1|}{\sqrt{(x - 1)^2 + 9}}$.

Thus, $\arcsin y = \dfrac{|x - 1|}{\sqrt{(x - 1)^2 + 9}} = \arcsin \dfrac{|x - 1|}{\sqrt{x^2 - 2x + 10}}$.

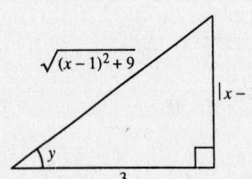

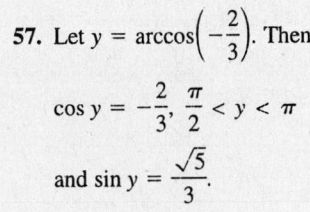

75. $y = 2 \arccos x$

Domain: $-1 \le x \le 1$

Range: $0 \le y \le 2\pi$

Vertical stretch of $f(x) = \arccos x$

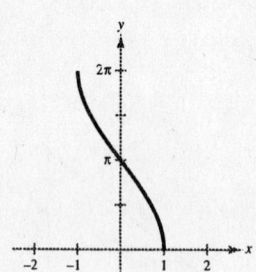

77. The graph of $f(x) = \arcsin(x - 1)$ is a horizontal translation of the graph of $y = \arcsin x$ by one unit.

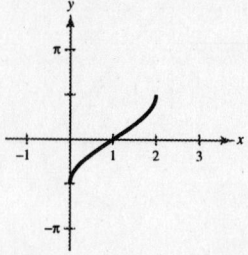

79. $f(x) = \arctan 2x$

Domain: all real numbers

Range: $-\dfrac{\pi}{2} < y < \dfrac{\pi}{2}$

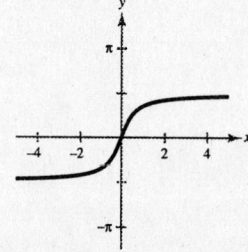

81. $h(v) = \tan(\arccos v) = \dfrac{\sqrt{1 - v^2}}{v}$

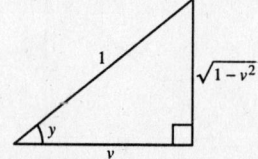

Domain: $-1 \le v \le 1, v \ne 0$

Range: all real numbers

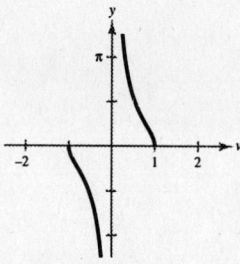

83. $f(x) = 2 \arccos (2x)$

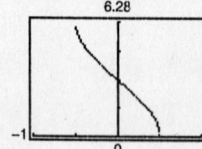

85. $f(x) = \arctan (2x - 3)$

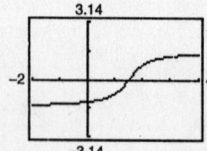

87. $f(x) = \pi - \arcsin\left(\dfrac{2}{3}\right) \approx 2.412$

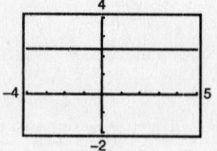

89. $f(t) = 3 \cos 2t + 3 \sin 2t = \sqrt{3^2 + 3^2} \sin\left(3t + \arctan \dfrac{3}{3}\right)$

$\qquad = 3\sqrt{2} \sin(3t + \arctan 1)$

$\qquad = 3\sqrt{2} \sin\left(3t + \dfrac{\pi}{4}\right)$

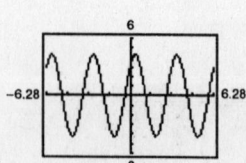

The graphs are the same.

91. (a) $\sin\theta = \dfrac{5}{s}$

$\theta = \arcsin\dfrac{5}{s}$

(b) $s = 40$: $\theta = \arcsin\dfrac{5}{40} \approx 0.13$

$s = 20$: $\theta = \arcsin\dfrac{5}{20} \approx 0.25$

93. $\beta = \arctan\dfrac{3x}{x^2 + 4}$

(a)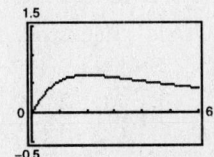

(b) β is maximum when $x = 2$.

(c) The graph has a horizontal asymptote at $\beta = 0$. As x increases, β decreases.

95. (a) $\tan\theta = \dfrac{x}{20}$

$\theta = \arctan\dfrac{x}{20}$

(b) $x = 5$: $\theta = \arctan\dfrac{5}{20} \approx 0.24$

$x = 12$: $\theta = \arctan\dfrac{12}{20} \approx 0.54$

97. False; $\arctan 1 = \dfrac{\pi}{4}$. $\dfrac{5\pi}{4}$ is not in the range of the arctangent function.

99. $y = \text{arccot } x$ if and only if $\cot y = x$.

Domain: $-\infty < x < \infty$

Range: $0 < x < \pi$

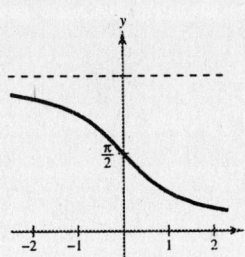

101. $y = \text{arccsc } x$ if and only if $\csc y = x$.

Domain: $(-\infty, -1] \cup [1, \infty)$

Range: $\left[-\dfrac{\pi}{2}, 0\right) \cup \left(0, \dfrac{\pi}{2}\right]$

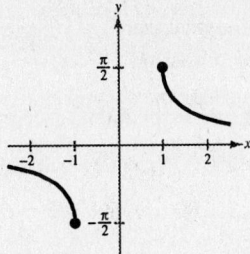

103. $f(x) = \sqrt{x}$

$g(x) = 6 \arctan x$

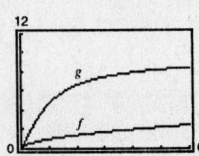

As x increases to infinity, g approaches 3π, but f has no maximum. Using the solve feature of the graphing utility, you find $a \approx 87.54$.

105. Let $y = \arcsin(-x)$. Then,

$\sin y = -x$

$-\sin y = x$

$\sin(-y) = x$

$-y = \arcsin x$

$y = -\arcsin x$.

Therefore, $\arcsin(-x) = -\arcsin x$.

107. $y = \pi - \arccos x$

$\cos y = \cos(\pi - \arccos x)$

$\cos y = \cos \pi \cos(\arccos x) + \sin \pi \sin(\arccos x)$

$\cos y = -x$

$\quad y = \arccos(-x)$

Therefore, $\arccos(-x) = \pi - \arccos x$

109. Let $\alpha = \arcsin x$ and $\beta = \arccos x$, then

$\sin \alpha = x$ and $\cos \beta = x$. Thus, $\sin \alpha = \cos \beta$ which implies that α and β are complementary angles and we have

$$\alpha + \beta = \frac{\pi}{2}$$

$$\arcsin x + \arccos x = \frac{\pi}{2}.$$

111. $\sin \theta = \dfrac{3}{4} = \dfrac{\text{opp}}{\text{hyp}}$

$(\text{adj})^2 + (3)^2 = (4)^2$

$(\text{adj})^2 + 9 = 16$

$(\text{adj})^2 = 7$

$\text{adj} = \sqrt{7}$

113. $\cos \theta = \dfrac{5}{6} = \dfrac{\text{adj}}{\text{hyp}}$

$(\text{opp})^2 + (5)^2 = (6)^2$

$(\text{opp})^2 + 25 = 36$

$(\text{opp})^2 = 11$

$\text{opp} = \sqrt{11}$

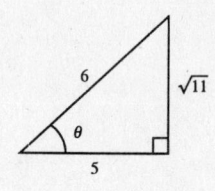

115. $(8.2)^{3.4} \approx 1279.284$

117. $(1.1)^{50} \approx 117.391$

119. Let $x =$ the number of people presently in the group.

Each person's share is now $\dfrac{250,000}{x}$.   If two more join

the group, each person's share would then be $\dfrac{250,000}{x + 2}$.

$$\begin{array}{c} \text{Share per person with} \\ \text{two more people} \end{array} = \begin{array}{c} \text{Original share} \\ \text{per person} \end{array} - 6250$$

$$\frac{250,000}{x + 2} = \frac{250,000}{x} - 6250$$

$$250,000x = 250,000(x + 2) - 6250x(x + 2)$$

$$250,000x = 250,000x + 500,000 - 6250x^2 - 12500x$$

$$6250x^2 + 12500x - 500,000 = 0$$

$$6250(x^2 + 2x - 80) = 0$$

$$6250(x + 10)(x - 8) = 0$$

$$x = -10 \quad \text{or} \quad x = 8$$

$x = -10$ is not possible.

There were 8 people in the original group.

Section 4.8   Applications and Models

- ■ You should be able to solve right triangles.
- ■ You should be able to solve right triangle applications.
- ■ You should be able to solve applications of simple harmonic motion.

Solutions to Odd-Numbered Exercises

1. Given: $A = 20°$, $b = 10$

$\tan A = \dfrac{a}{b} \implies a = b \tan A = 10 \tan 20° \approx 3.64$

$\cos A = \dfrac{b}{c} \implies c = \dfrac{b}{\cos A} = \dfrac{10}{\cos 20°} \approx 10.64$

$B = 90° - 20° = 70°$

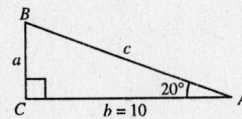

3. Given: $B = 71°$, $b = 24$

$\tan B = \dfrac{b}{a} \implies a = \dfrac{b}{\tan B} = \dfrac{24}{\tan 71°} \approx 8.26$

$\sin B = \dfrac{b}{c} \implies c = \dfrac{b}{\sin B} = \dfrac{24}{\sin 71°} \approx 25.38$

$A = 90° - 71° = 19°$

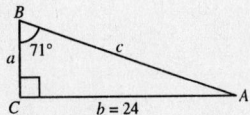

5. Given: $a = 6$, $b = 10$

$c^2 = a^2 + b^2 \implies c = \sqrt{36 + 100}$

$\qquad\qquad\qquad = 2\sqrt{34} \approx 11.66$

$\tan A = \dfrac{a}{b} = \dfrac{6}{10} \implies A = \arctan \dfrac{3}{5} \approx 30.96°$

$B = 90° - 30.96° = 59.04°$

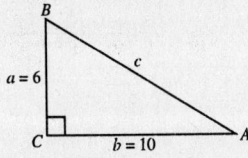

7. $b = 16$, $c = 52$

$a = \sqrt{52^2 - 16^2}$

$\quad = \sqrt{2448} = 12\sqrt{17} \approx 49.48$

$\cos A = \dfrac{16}{52}$

$\qquad A = \arccos \dfrac{16}{52} \approx 72.08°$

$\qquad B = 90° - 72.08° \approx 17.92°$

9. $A = 12° 15'$, $c = 430.5$

$B = 90° - 12° 15' = 77° 45'$

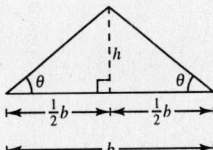

$\sin 12° 15' = \dfrac{a}{430.5}$

$\qquad a = 430.5 \sin 12° 15' \approx 91.34$

$\cos 12° 15' = \dfrac{b}{430.5}$

$\qquad b = 430.5 \cos 12° 15' \approx 420.70$

11. $\tan \theta = \dfrac{h}{\frac{1}{2}b} \implies h = \dfrac{1}{2}b \tan \theta$

$\qquad h = \dfrac{1}{2}(4) \tan 52° \approx 2.56$ inches

13. $\tan \theta = \dfrac{h}{\frac{1}{2}b} \implies h = \dfrac{1}{2}b \tan \theta$

$h = \dfrac{1}{2}(46) \tan 41° \approx 19.99$ inches

15. $\tan 25° = \dfrac{50}{x}$

$x = \dfrac{50}{\tan 25°} \approx 107.2$ feet

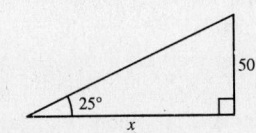

17. $\sin 80° = \dfrac{h}{20}$

$20 \sin 80° = h$

$h \approx 19.7 \text{ feet}$

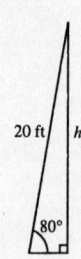

20 ft   h

80°

19. (a)

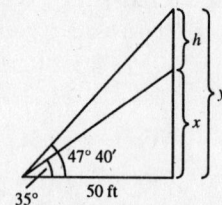

h

y

x

47° 40′

35°   50 ft

(b) Let the height of the church $= x$ and the height of the church and steeple $= y$. Then,

$$\tan 35° = \frac{x}{50} \quad \text{and} \quad \tan 47°40′ = \frac{y}{50}$$

$$x = 50 \tan 35° \text{ and } y = 50 \tan 47°40′$$

$$h = y - x = 50 \left(\tan 47°40′ - \tan 35°\right).$$

(c) $h \approx 19.9 \text{ feet}$

21. $\sin 34° = \dfrac{x}{4000}$

$x = 4000 \sin 34°$

$\approx 2236.8 \text{ feet}$

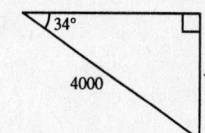

34°

4000

x

23. $\tan \theta = \dfrac{75}{50}$

$\theta = \arctan \dfrac{3}{2} \approx 56.3°$

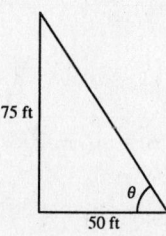

75 ft

θ

50 ft

25. $10{,}900 \text{ feet} = \dfrac{10{,}900}{5280} \text{ miles} \approx 2.0644 \text{ miles}$

$\sin \theta = \dfrac{4000}{4002.0644}$

$\theta = \arcsin \left(\dfrac{4000}{4002.0644}\right)$

$\theta \approx 88.16° \alpha$

4,002.0644 mi

θ

α

4,000 mi

(Not drawn to scale)

27. Since the airplane speed is

$$\left(275 \frac{\text{ft}}{\text{sec}}\right)\left(60 \frac{\text{sec}}{\text{min}}\right) = 16{,}500 \frac{\text{ft}}{\text{min}},$$

after one minute its distance travelled in 16,500 feet.

$\sin 18° = \dfrac{a}{16{,}500}$

$a = 16{,}500 \sin 18°$

$\approx 5099 \text{ ft}$

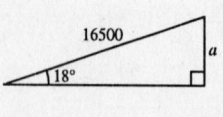

16500

a

18°

29. $\sin 10.5° = \dfrac{x}{4}$

$x = 4 \sin 10.5°$

$\approx 0.73 \text{ mile}$

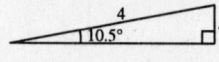

4

10.5°   x

31. The plane has traveled $1.5 (600) = 900$ miles.

$\sin 38° = \dfrac{a}{900} \Rightarrow a \approx 554 \text{ miles north}$

$\cos 38° = \dfrac{b}{900} \Rightarrow b \approx 709 \text{ miles east}$

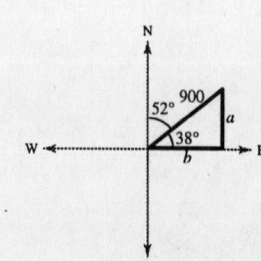

N

900

52°

a

38°

W   b   E

S

33. $\theta = 32°, \ \phi = 68°$

(a) $\alpha = 90° - 32° = 58°$

(b) Bearing from A to C: N 58° E

$$\beta = \theta = 32°$$

$$\gamma = 90° - \phi = 22°$$

$$C = \beta + \gamma = 54°$$

$$\tan C = \frac{d}{50} \implies \tan 54° = \frac{d}{50} \implies d \approx 68.82 \text{ meters}$$

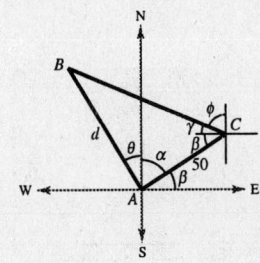

35. $\tan \theta = \frac{45}{30} \implies \theta \approx 56.3°$

Bearing: N 56.3° W

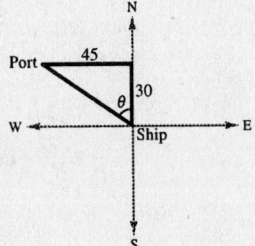

37. $\tan 6.5° = \frac{350}{d} \implies d \approx 3071.91 \text{ ft}$

$$\tan 4° = \frac{350}{D} \implies D \approx 5005.23 \text{ ft}$$

Distance between ships: $D - d \approx 1933.32 \text{ ft}$

39. $\tan 57° = \frac{a}{x} \implies x = a \cot 57°$

$$\tan 16° = \frac{a}{x + \frac{55}{6}}$$

$$\tan 16° = \frac{a}{a \cot 57° + \frac{55}{6}}$$

$$\cot 16° = \frac{a \cot 57° + \frac{55}{6}}{a}$$

$$a \cot 16° - a \cot 57° = \frac{55}{6} \implies a \approx 3.23 \text{ miles}$$

$$\approx 17,054 \text{ ft}$$

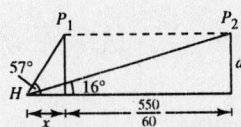

41. L_1: $3x - 2y = 5 \implies y = \frac{3}{2}x - \frac{5}{2} \implies m_1 = \frac{3}{2}$

L_2: $x + y = 1 \implies y = -x + 1 \implies m_2 = -1$

$$\tan \alpha = \left| \frac{-1 - \frac{3}{2}}{1 + (-1)\left(\frac{3}{2}\right)} \right| = \left| \frac{-\frac{5}{2}}{-\frac{1}{2}} \right| = 5$$

$$\alpha = \arctan 5 \approx 78.7°$$

43. The diagonal of the base has a length of $\sqrt{a^2 + a^2} = \sqrt{2}a$.

Now, we have $\tan \theta = \frac{a}{\sqrt{2}a} = \frac{1}{\sqrt{2}}$

$$\theta = \arctan \frac{1}{\sqrt{2}}$$

$$\theta \approx 35.3°.$$

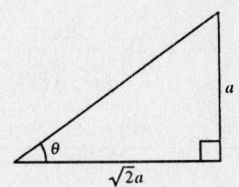

45. $\sin 36° = \frac{d}{25} \implies d \approx 14.69$

Length of side: $2d \approx 29.4 \text{ inches}$

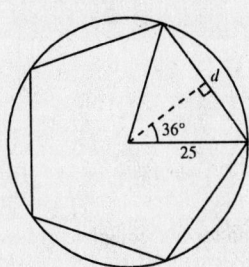

47. $\cos 30° = \dfrac{b}{r}$

$b = r \cos 30°$

$b = \dfrac{\sqrt{3}r}{2}$

$y = 2b = 2\left(\dfrac{\sqrt{3}r}{2}\right) = \sqrt{3}r$

49. $\tan 35° = \dfrac{b}{10}$

$b = 10 \tan 35° \approx 7$

$\cos 35° = \dfrac{10}{a}$

$a = \dfrac{10}{\cos 35°} \approx 12.2$

51. $d = 4 \cos 8\pi t$

(a) Maximum displacement $=$ amplitude $= 4$

(b) Frequency $= \dfrac{\omega}{2\pi} = \dfrac{8\pi}{2\pi}$

$= 4$ cycles per unit of time

(c) $8\pi t = \dfrac{\pi}{2} \implies t = \dfrac{1}{16}$

53. $d = \dfrac{1}{16} \sin 120\pi t$

(a) Maximum displacement $=$ amplitude $= \dfrac{1}{16}$

(b) Frequency $= \dfrac{\omega}{2\pi} = \dfrac{120\pi}{2\pi}$

$= 60$ cycles per unit of time

(c) $120\pi t = \pi \implies t = \dfrac{1}{120}$

55. $d = 0$ when $t = 0$, $a = 4$, Period $= 2$

Use $d = a \sin \omega t$ since $d = 0$ when $t = 0$.

$\dfrac{2\pi}{\omega} = 2 \implies \omega = \pi$

Thus, $d = 4 \sin \pi t$.

57. $d = 3$ when $t = 0$, $a = 3$, Period $= 1.5$

Use $d = a \cos \omega t$ since $d = 3$ when $t = 0$.

$\dfrac{2\pi}{\omega} = 1.5 \implies \omega = \dfrac{4\pi}{3}$

Thus, $d = 3 \cos\left(\dfrac{4\pi}{3}t\right) = 3 \cos\left(\dfrac{4\pi t}{3}\right)$.

59. $d = a \sin \omega t$

Period $= \dfrac{2\pi}{\omega} = \dfrac{1}{\text{frequency}}$

$\dfrac{2\pi}{\omega} = \dfrac{1}{264}$

$\omega = 2\pi(264) = 528\pi$

61. $y = \dfrac{1}{4} \cos 16t, \ t > 0$

(a)

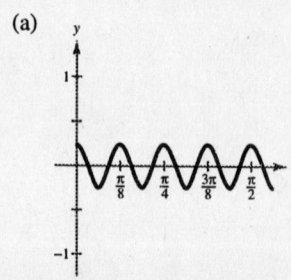

(b) Period: $\dfrac{2\pi}{16} = \dfrac{\pi}{8}$

(c) $\dfrac{1}{4} \cos 16t = 0$ when $16t = \dfrac{\pi}{2} \implies t = \dfrac{\pi}{32}$

63. False. One period is the time for one complete cycle of the motion.

65. (a) & (b)

Base 1	Base 2	Altitude	Area
8	$8 + 16 \cos 10°$	$8 \sin 10°$	22.1
8	$8 + 16 \cos 20°$	$8 \sin 20°$	42.5
8	$8 + 16 \cos 30°$	$8 \sin 30°$	59.7
8	$8 + 16 \cos 40°$	$8 \sin 40°$	72.7
8	$8 + 16 \cos 50°$	$8 \sin 50°$	80.5
8	$8 + 16 \cos 60°$	$8 \sin 60°$	83.1
8	$8 + 16 \cos 70°$	$8 \sin 70°$	80.7

The maximum occurs when $\theta = 60°$ and is approximately 83.1 square feet.

(c) $A(\theta) = [8 + (8 + 16 \cos \theta)]\left[\dfrac{8 \sin \theta}{2}\right]$

$= (16 + 16 \cos \theta)(4 \sin \theta)$

$= 64 (1 + \cos \theta)(\sin \theta)$

(d)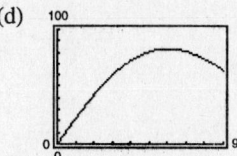

The maximum of 83.1 square feet occurs when $\theta = \dfrac{\pi}{3} = 60°$.

67. (a)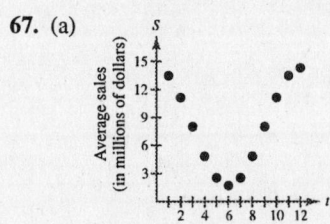

(b) $a = \dfrac{1}{2}(14.3 - 1.7) = 6.3$

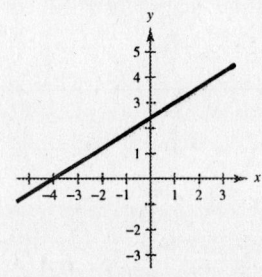

$\dfrac{2\pi}{b} = 12 \implies b = \dfrac{\pi}{6}$

Shift: $d = 14.3 - 6.3 = 8$

$S = d + a \cos bt$

$S = 8 + 6.3 \cos\left(\dfrac{\pi t}{6}\right)$

Note: Another model is $S = 8 + 6.3 \sin\left(\dfrac{\pi t}{6} + \dfrac{\pi}{2}\right)$

The model is a good fit.

(c) Period: $\dfrac{2\pi}{\pi/6} = 12$

This corresponds to the 12 months in a year. Since the sales of outerwear is seasonal this is reasonable.

(d) The amplitude represents the maximum displacement from average sales of 8 million dollars. Sales are greatest in December (cold weather + Christmas) and least in June.

69. $5y - 3x = 12$

$5y = 3x + 12$

$y = \dfrac{3}{5}x + \dfrac{12}{5}$

The graph is a line with $m = \dfrac{3}{5}$ and y-intercept $\left(0, \dfrac{12}{5}\right)$.

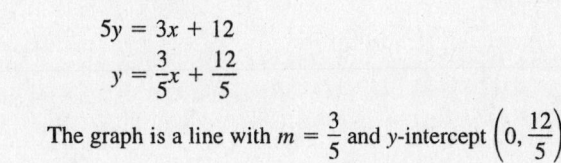

71. $(x + 3)^2 = 5y - 8$

$(x + 3)^2 = 5\left(y - \dfrac{8}{5}\right)$

x	0	-6
y	$\dfrac{17}{5}$	$\dfrac{17}{5}$

Parabola with vertex $\left(-3, \dfrac{8}{5}\right)$

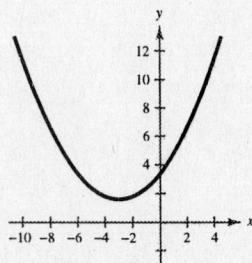

73. $2x^2 + y^2 - 4 = 0$

$$2x^2 + y^2 = 4$$

$$\frac{x^2}{2} + \frac{y^2}{4} = 1$$

Ellipse with center $(0, 0)$

Vertical major axis

$a = 2, b = \sqrt{2}$

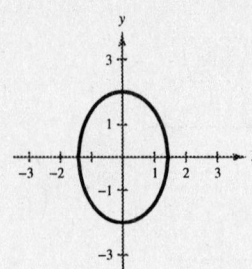

75. $\dfrac{y^2}{4} - \dfrac{(x + 2)^2}{25} - 1 = 0$

$$\frac{y^2}{4} - \frac{(x + 2)^2}{25} = 1$$

Hyperbola with center $(-2, 0)$

Vertical transverse axis $a = 2, \ b = 5$

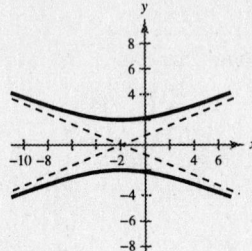

77. $(x - 2)^2 + y^2 = 25$

Circle with center $(2, 0)$ and radius $r = 5$

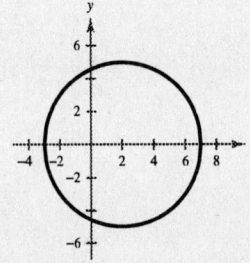

Review Exercises for Chapter 4

Solutions to Odd-Numbered Exercises

1. $\theta \approx 1$ radian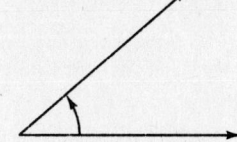

3. $\theta \approx 5$ radians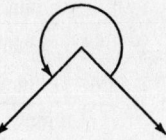

5. $\theta = \dfrac{11\pi}{4}$

Coterminal angles: $\dfrac{11\pi}{4} - 2\pi = \dfrac{3\pi}{4}$

$\dfrac{3\pi}{4} - 2\pi = -\dfrac{5\pi}{4}$

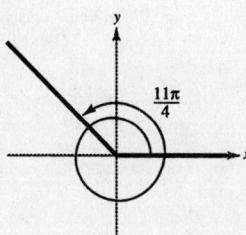

7. $\theta = -\dfrac{4\pi}{3}$

Coterminal angles: $-\dfrac{4\pi}{3} + 2\pi = \dfrac{2\pi}{3}$

$-\dfrac{4\pi}{3} - 2\pi = -\dfrac{10\pi}{3}$

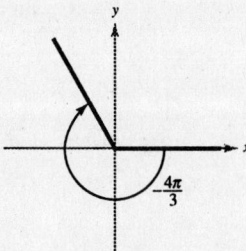

9. $\theta = 70°$

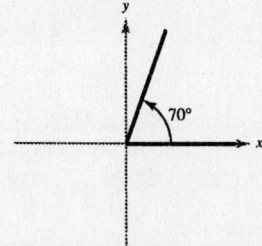

Coterminal angles: $70° + 360° = 430°$

$70° - 360° = -290°$

11. $\theta = -110°$

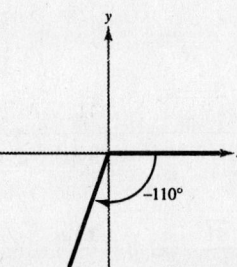

Coterminal angles: $-110° + 360° = 250°$

$-110° - 360° = -470°$

13. $\dfrac{5\pi \, \text{rad}}{7} = \dfrac{5\pi \, \text{rad}}{7} \cdot \dfrac{180°}{\pi \, \text{rad}} \approx 128.57°$

15. $-3.5 \, \text{rad} = -3.5 \, \text{rad} \cdot \dfrac{180°}{\pi \, \text{rad}} \approx -200.54°$

17. $480° = 480° \cdot \dfrac{\pi \, \text{rad}}{180°} = \dfrac{8\pi}{3} \, \text{radians} \approx 8.3776 \, \text{radians}$

19. $-33°45' = -33.75° = -33.75° \cdot \dfrac{\pi \text{ rad}}{180°} = -\dfrac{3\pi}{16} \text{ radian} \approx -0.5890 \text{ radian}$

21. (a) Angular speed $= \dfrac{\left(33\frac{1}{3}\right)(2\pi) \text{ radians}}{1 \text{ minute}}$

$= 66\frac{2}{3}\pi \text{ radians per minute}$

(b) Linear speed $= \dfrac{6\left(66\frac{2}{3}\pi\right) \text{ inches}}{1 \text{ minute}}$

$= 400\pi \text{ inches per minute}$

23. $t = \dfrac{2\pi}{3}$ corresponds to the point $\left(-\dfrac{1}{2}, \dfrac{\sqrt{3}}{2}\right)$.

25. $t = \dfrac{5\pi}{6}$ corresponds to the point $\left(-\dfrac{\sqrt{3}}{2}, \dfrac{1}{2}\right)$.

27. $t = \dfrac{7\pi}{6}$ corresponds to the point $\left(-\dfrac{\sqrt{3}}{2}, -\dfrac{1}{2}\right)$.

$\sin\dfrac{7\pi}{6} = y = -\dfrac{1}{2}$ $\qquad \csc\dfrac{7\pi}{6} = \dfrac{1}{y} = -2$

$\cos\dfrac{7\pi}{6} = x = -\dfrac{\sqrt{3}}{2}$ $\qquad \sec\dfrac{7\pi}{6} = \dfrac{1}{x} = -\dfrac{2\sqrt{3}}{3}$

$\tan\dfrac{7\pi}{6} = \dfrac{y}{x} = \dfrac{1}{\sqrt{3}} = \dfrac{\sqrt{3}}{3}$ $\qquad \cot\dfrac{7\pi}{6} = \dfrac{x}{y} = \sqrt{3}$

29. $t = -\dfrac{2\pi}{3}$ corresponds to the point $\left(-\dfrac{1}{2}, -\dfrac{\sqrt{3}}{2}\right)$.

$\sin\left(-\dfrac{2\pi}{3}\right) = y = -\dfrac{\sqrt{3}}{2}$ $\qquad \csc\left(-\dfrac{2\pi}{3}\right) = \dfrac{1}{y} = -\dfrac{2\sqrt{3}}{3}$

$\cos\left(-\dfrac{2\pi}{3}\right) = x = -\dfrac{1}{2}$ $\qquad \sec\left(-\dfrac{2\pi}{3}\right) = \dfrac{1}{x} = -2$

$\tan\left(-\dfrac{2\pi}{3}\right) = \dfrac{y}{x} = \sqrt{3}$ $\qquad \cot\left(-\dfrac{2\pi}{3}\right) = \dfrac{x}{y} = \dfrac{\sqrt{3}}{3}$

31. $\sin\dfrac{11\pi}{4} = \sin\dfrac{3\pi}{4} = \dfrac{\sqrt{2}}{2}$

33. $\sin\left(-\dfrac{17\pi}{6}\right) = \sin\left(-\dfrac{5\pi}{6}\right) = -\dfrac{1}{2}$

35. $\tan 33 \approx -75.31$

37. $\sec\dfrac{12\pi}{5} = \dfrac{1}{\cos\left(\dfrac{12\pi}{5}\right)} \approx 3.24$

39. $\text{opp} = 4, \text{adj} = 5, \text{hyp} = \sqrt{4^2 + 5^2} = \sqrt{41}$

$\sin\theta = \dfrac{\text{opp}}{\text{hyp}} = \dfrac{4}{\sqrt{41}} = \dfrac{4\sqrt{41}}{41}$ $\qquad \csc\theta = \dfrac{\text{hyp}}{\text{opp}} = \dfrac{\sqrt{41}}{4}$

$\cos\theta = \dfrac{\text{adj}}{\text{hyp}} = \dfrac{5}{\sqrt{41}} = \dfrac{5\sqrt{41}}{41}$ $\qquad \sec\theta = \dfrac{\text{hyp}}{\text{adj}} = \dfrac{\sqrt{41}}{5}$

$\tan\theta = \dfrac{\text{opp}}{\text{adj}} = \dfrac{4}{5}$ $\qquad\qquad \cot\theta = \dfrac{\text{adj}}{\text{opp}} = \dfrac{5}{4}$

41. opp $= 4$, hyp $= 8$, adj $= \sqrt{8^2 - 4^2} = \sqrt{48} = 4\sqrt{3}$

$$\sin \theta = \frac{\text{opp}}{\text{hyp}} = \frac{4}{8} = \frac{1}{2} \qquad \csc \theta = \frac{\text{hyp}}{\text{opp}} = \frac{8}{4} = 2$$

$$\cos \theta = \frac{\text{adj}}{\text{hyp}} = \frac{4\sqrt{3}}{8} = \frac{\sqrt{3}}{2} \qquad \sec \theta = \frac{\text{hyp}}{\text{adj}} = \frac{8}{4\sqrt{3}} = \frac{2\sqrt{3}}{3}$$

$$\tan \theta = \frac{\text{opp}}{\text{adj}} = \frac{4}{4\sqrt{3}} = \frac{\sqrt{3}}{3} \qquad \cot \theta = \frac{\text{adj}}{\text{opp}} = \frac{4\sqrt{3}}{4} = \sqrt{3}$$

43. $\sin \theta = \dfrac{1}{3}$

(a) $\csc \theta = \dfrac{1}{\sin \theta} = 3$

(b) $\sin^2 \theta + \cos^2 \theta = 1$

$$\left(\frac{1}{3}\right)^2 + \cos^2\theta = 1$$

$$\cos^2 \theta = 1 - \frac{1}{9}$$

$$\cos^2 \theta = \frac{8}{9}$$

$$\cos \theta = \sqrt{\frac{8}{9}}$$

$$\cos \theta = \frac{2\sqrt{2}}{3}$$

(c) $\sec \theta = \dfrac{1}{\cos \theta} = \dfrac{3}{2\sqrt{2}} = \dfrac{3\sqrt{2}}{4}$

(d) $\tan \theta = \dfrac{\sin \theta}{\cos \theta} = \dfrac{\frac{1}{3}}{\frac{2\sqrt{2}}{3}} = \dfrac{1}{2\sqrt{2}} = \dfrac{\sqrt{2}}{4}$

45. $\csc \theta = 4$

(a) $\sin \theta = \dfrac{1}{\csc \theta} = \dfrac{1}{4}$

(b) $\sin^2 \theta + \cos^2 \theta = 1$

$$\left(\frac{1}{4}\right)^2 + \cos^2 \theta = 1$$

$$\cos^2 \theta = 1 - \frac{1}{16}$$

$$\cos^2 \theta = \frac{15}{16}$$

$$\cos \theta = \sqrt{\frac{15}{16}}$$

$$\cos \theta = \frac{\sqrt{15}}{4}$$

(c) $\sec \theta = \dfrac{1}{\cos \theta} = \dfrac{4}{\sqrt{15}} = \dfrac{4\sqrt{15}}{15}$

(d) $\tan \theta = \dfrac{\sin \theta}{\cos \theta} = \dfrac{\frac{1}{4}}{\frac{\sqrt{15}}{4}} = \dfrac{1}{\sqrt{15}} = \dfrac{\sqrt{15}}{15}$

47. $\tan 33° \approx 0.65$

49. $\sin 34.2° \approx 0.56$

51. $\cot 15°14' \approx \cot 15.2333° = \dfrac{1}{\tan 15.2333°} \approx 3.67$

53. $\sin 1°10' = \dfrac{x}{3.5}$

$x = 3.5 \sin 1°10' \approx 0.07$ Kilometer

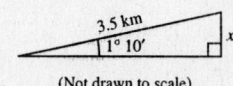

(Not drawn to scale)

55. $x = 12$, $y = 16$, $r = \sqrt{144 + 256} = \sqrt{400} = 20$

$$\sin \theta = \frac{y}{r} = \frac{4}{5} \qquad\qquad \csc \theta = \frac{r}{y} = \frac{5}{4}$$

$$\cos \theta = \frac{x}{r} = \frac{3}{5} \qquad\qquad \sec \theta = \frac{r}{x} = \frac{5}{3}$$

$$\tan \theta = \frac{y}{x} = \frac{4}{3} \qquad\qquad \cot \theta = \frac{x}{y} = \frac{3}{4}$$

57. $x = \frac{2}{3}, y = \frac{5}{2}$

$$r = \sqrt{\left(\frac{2}{3}\right)^2 + \left(\frac{5}{2}\right)^2} = \frac{\sqrt{241}}{6}$$

$$\sin\theta = \frac{y}{r} = \frac{\frac{5}{2}}{\frac{\sqrt{241}}{6}} = \frac{15}{\sqrt{241}} = \frac{15\sqrt{241}}{241} \qquad \csc\theta = \frac{r}{y} = \frac{\frac{\sqrt{241}}{6}}{\frac{5}{2}} = \frac{2\sqrt{241}}{30} = \frac{\sqrt{241}}{15}$$

$$\cos\theta = \frac{x}{r} = \frac{\frac{2}{3}}{\frac{\sqrt{241}}{6}} = \frac{4}{\sqrt{241}} = \frac{4\sqrt{241}}{241} \qquad \sec\theta = \frac{r}{x} = \frac{\frac{\sqrt{241}}{6}}{\frac{2}{3}} = \frac{\sqrt{241}}{4}$$

$$\tan\theta = \frac{y}{x} = \frac{\frac{5}{2}}{\frac{2}{3}} = \frac{15}{4} \qquad \cot\theta = \frac{x}{y} = \frac{\frac{2}{3}}{\frac{5}{2}} = \frac{4}{15}$$

59. $x = -0.5, y = 4.5$

$$r = \sqrt{(-0.5)^2 + 4.5^2} \approx 4.528$$

$$\sin\theta = \frac{y}{r} \approx 1 \qquad\qquad \csc\theta = \frac{r}{y} \approx 1$$

$$\cos\theta = \frac{x}{r} \approx -0.1 \qquad \sec\theta = \frac{r}{x} \approx -9$$

$$\tan\theta = \frac{y}{x} \approx -9 \qquad \cot\theta = \frac{x}{y} \approx -0.1$$

61. $(x, 4x), x > 0$

$x = x, y = 4x$

$$r = \sqrt{x^2 + (4x)^2} = \sqrt{17}\,x$$

$$\sin\theta = \frac{y}{r} = \frac{4x}{\sqrt{17}\,x} = \frac{4\sqrt{17}}{17} \qquad \csc\theta = \frac{r}{y} = \frac{\sqrt{17}\,x}{4x} = \frac{\sqrt{17}}{4}$$

$$\cos\theta = \frac{x}{r} = \frac{x}{\sqrt{17}\,x} = \frac{\sqrt{17}}{17} \qquad \sec\theta = \frac{r}{x} = \frac{\sqrt{17}\,x}{x} = \sqrt{17}$$

$$\tan\theta = \frac{y}{x} = \frac{4x}{x} = 4 \qquad\qquad \cot\theta = \frac{x}{y} = \frac{x}{4x} = \frac{1}{4}$$

63. $\sec\theta = \frac{6}{5}$, $\tan\theta < 0 \implies \theta$ is in Quadrant IV.

$$r = 6, x = 5, y = -\sqrt{36 - 25} = -\sqrt{11}$$

$$\sin\theta = \frac{y}{r} = -\frac{\sqrt{11}}{6} \qquad \csc\theta = -\frac{6\sqrt{11}}{11}$$

$$\cos\theta = \frac{x}{r} = \frac{5}{6} \qquad\qquad \sec\theta = \frac{6}{5}$$

$$\tan\theta = \frac{y}{x} = -\frac{\sqrt{11}}{5} \qquad \cot\theta = -\frac{5\sqrt{11}}{11}$$

65. $\sin \theta = \dfrac{3}{8}$, $\cos \theta < 0 \implies \theta$ is in Quadrant II.

$y = 3, r = 8, x = -\sqrt{55}$

$\sin \theta = \dfrac{y}{r} = \dfrac{3}{8}$ $\csc \theta = \dfrac{8}{3}$

$\cos \theta = \dfrac{x}{r} = -\dfrac{\sqrt{55}}{8}$ $\sec \theta = -\dfrac{8}{\sqrt{55}} = -\dfrac{8\sqrt{55}}{55}$

$\tan \theta = \dfrac{y}{x} = -\dfrac{3}{\sqrt{55}} = -\dfrac{3\sqrt{55}}{55}$ $\cot \theta = -\dfrac{\sqrt{55}}{3}$

67. $\cos \theta = \dfrac{x}{r} = \dfrac{-2}{5} \implies y^2 = 21$

$\sin \theta > 0 \implies \theta$ is in Quadrant II $\implies y = \sqrt{21}$

$\sin \theta = \dfrac{y}{r} = \dfrac{\sqrt{21}}{5}$

$\tan \theta = \dfrac{y}{x} = -\dfrac{\sqrt{21}}{2}$

$\csc \theta = \dfrac{r}{y} = \dfrac{5}{\sqrt{21}} = \dfrac{5\sqrt{21}}{21}$

$\sec \theta = \dfrac{r}{x} = \dfrac{5}{-2} = -\dfrac{5}{2}$

$\cot \theta = \dfrac{x}{y} = \dfrac{-2}{\sqrt{21}} = -\dfrac{2\sqrt{21}}{21}$

69. $\tan \dfrac{\pi}{3} = \sqrt{3}$

71. $\cos \left(-\dfrac{7\pi}{3} \right) = \cos \dfrac{\pi}{3} = \dfrac{1}{2}$

73. $\cos 495° = -\cos 45° = -\dfrac{\sqrt{2}}{2}$

75. $\sin 4 \approx -0.76$

77. $\sin(-3.2) \approx 0.06$

79. $\sin 3\pi = 0$

81. $\sec \dfrac{12\pi}{5} = \dfrac{1}{\cos\left(\dfrac{12\pi}{5}\right)} \approx 3.24$

83. $y = \sin x$

Amplitude: 1

Period: 2π

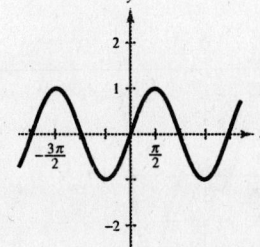

85. $f(x) = 5 \sin \dfrac{2x}{5}$

Amplitude: 5

Period: $\dfrac{2\pi}{\frac{2}{5}} = 5\pi$

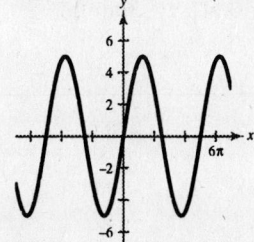

87. $y = 2 + \sin x$

Shift the graph of $y = \sin x$ two units upward.

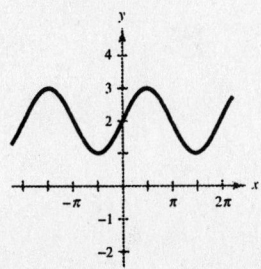

89. $g(t) = \dfrac{5}{2} \sin(t - \pi)$

Amplitude: $\dfrac{5}{2}$

Period: 2π

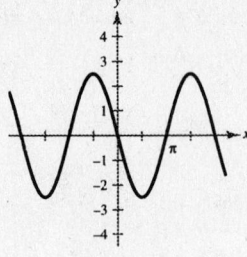

91. $y = a \sin bx$

(a) $a = 2, \dfrac{2\pi}{b} = \dfrac{1}{264} \Rightarrow b = 528\pi$

$y = 2 \sin(528\pi x)$

(b) $f = \dfrac{1}{\frac{1}{264}} = 264$ cycles per second.

93. $f(x) = \tan x$

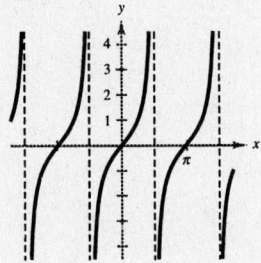

95. $f(x) = \cot x$

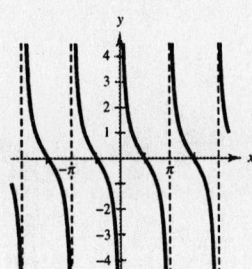

97. $f(x) = \sec x$

Graph $y = \cos x$ first.

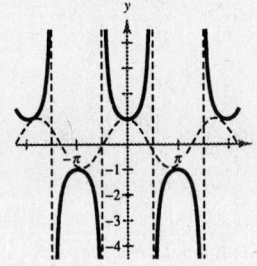

99. $f(x) = \csc x$

Graph $y = \sin x$ first.

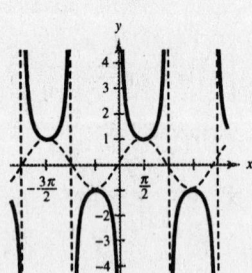

101. $f(x) = x \cos x$

Graph $y = x$ and $y = -x$ first

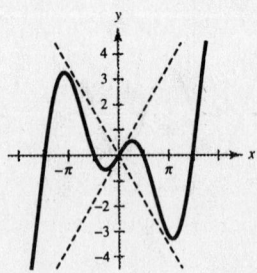

103. $\arcsin\left(-\dfrac{1}{2}\right) = -\arcsin\dfrac{1}{2} = -\dfrac{\pi}{6}$

105. $\arcsin 0.4 \approx 0.41$ radian

107. $\sin^{-1}(-0.44) \approx -0.46$ radian

109. $\arccos \dfrac{\sqrt{3}}{2} = \dfrac{\pi}{6}$

111. $\cos^{-1}(-1) = \pi$

113. $\arccos 0.324 \approx 1.24$ radians

115. $\arctan 0.123 \approx 0.12$ radian

117. $\arctan 5.783 \approx 1.40$ radians

119. $\tan^{-1}(-1.5) \approx -0.98$ radian

121. $\sin(\arcsin 0.72) = 0.72$

123. $\arctan(\tan \pi) = \arctan 0 = 0$

125. $\cos\left(\arctan \dfrac{3}{4}\right) = \dfrac{4}{5}$. Use a right triangle.

Let $\theta = \arctan \dfrac{3}{4}$

then $\tan \theta = \dfrac{3}{4}$

and $\cos \theta = \dfrac{4}{5}$

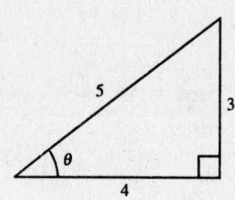

127. $\sec\left(\arctan \dfrac{12}{5}\right) = \dfrac{13}{5}$ Use a right triangle.

Let $\theta = \arctan \dfrac{12}{5}$

then $\tan \theta = \dfrac{12}{5}$

and $\sec \theta = \dfrac{13}{5}$

129. $\tan \theta = \dfrac{70}{30}$

$\theta = \arctan\left(\dfrac{70}{30}\right) \approx 66.8°$

131. $\sin 48° = \dfrac{d_1}{650} \Longrightarrow d_1 \approx 483$

$\cos 25° = \dfrac{d_2}{810} \Longrightarrow d_2 \approx 734$

$\left.\begin{array}{c} \end{array}\right\}$ $d_1 + d_2 = 1217$

$\cos 48° = \dfrac{d_3}{650} \Longrightarrow d_3 \approx 435$

$\sin 25° = \dfrac{d_4}{810} \Longrightarrow d_4 \approx 342$

$\left.\begin{array}{c} \end{array}\right\}$ $d_3 - d_4 \approx 93$

$\tan \theta \approx \dfrac{93}{1217} \Longrightarrow \theta \approx 4.4°$

$\sec 4.4° \approx \dfrac{D}{1217} \Longrightarrow D \approx 1217 \sec 4.4° \approx 1221$

The distance is 1221 miles and the bearing is N 85.6° E.

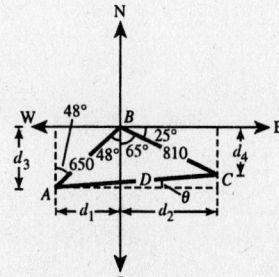

133. False. The sine or cosine functions are often useful for modeling simple harmonic motion.

135. False. For each θ there corresponds exactly one value of y.

137. $y = 3 \sin x$

Amplitude: 3

Period: 2π

Matches graph (d)

139. $y = 2 \sin \pi x$

Amplitude: 2

Period: 2

Matches graph (b)

141. $f(\theta) = \sec \theta$ is undefined at the zeros of $g(\theta) = \cos \theta$ since $\sec \theta = \dfrac{1}{\cos \theta}$.

143. The ranges for the other four trigonometric functions are not bounded. For $y = \tan x$ and $y = \cot x$, the range is $(-\infty, \infty)$. For $y = \sec x$ and $y = \csc x$, the range is $(-\infty, -1] \cup [1, \infty)$

145. (a) $\tan\theta = \dfrac{x}{12}$

$x = 12 \tan \theta$

Area = Area of triangle − Area of sector

$$= \left(\frac{1}{2}bh\right) - \left(\frac{1}{2}r^2\theta\right)$$

$$= \frac{1}{2}(12)(12 \tan \theta) - \frac{1}{2}(12^2)(\theta)$$

$$= 72 \tan\theta - 72\theta$$

$$= 72 (\tan\theta - \theta)$$

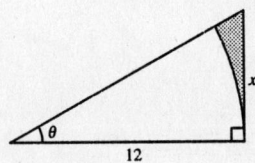

(b)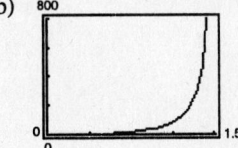

As $\theta \Rightarrow \dfrac{\pi}{2}, A \Rightarrow \infty.$

The area increases without bound as θ approaches $\dfrac{\pi}{2}$.

147. Answers will vary.

Chapter 4   Practice Test

1. Express 350° in radian measure.

2. Express $(5\pi)/9$ in degree measure.

3. Convert 135°14′12″ to decimal form.

4. Convert −22.569° to D°M′S″ form.

5. If $\cos \theta = \frac{2}{3}$, use the trigonometric identities to find $\tan \theta$.

6. Find θ given $\sin \theta = 0.9063$.

7. Solve for x in the figure below.

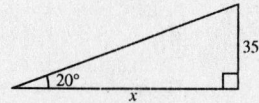

8. Find the magnitude of the reference angle for $\theta = (6\pi)/5$.

9. Evaluate csc 3.92.

10. Find $\sec \theta$ given that θ lies in Quadrant III and $\tan \theta = 6$.

11. Graph $y = 3 \sin \dfrac{x}{2}$.

12. Graph $y = -2 \cos(x - \pi)$.

13. Graph $y = \tan 2x$.

14. Graph $y = -\csc\left(x + \dfrac{\pi}{4}\right)$.

15. Graph $y = 2x + \sin x$, using a graphing calculator.

16. Graph $y = 3x \cos x$, using a graphing calculator.

17. Evaluate arcsin 1.

18. Evaluate arctan (-3).

19. Evaluate $\sin\left(\arccos \dfrac{4}{\sqrt{35}}\right)$.

20. Write an algebraic expression for $\cos\left(\arcsin \dfrac{x}{4}\right)$.

For Exercises 21–23, solve the right triangle.

21. $A = 40°$, $c = 12$

22. $B = 6.84°$, $a = 21.3$

23. $a = 5$, $b = 9$

24. A 20-foot ladder leans against the side of a barn. Find the height of the top of the ladder if the angle of elevation of the ladder is 67°.

25. An observer in a lighthouse 250 feet above sea level spots a ship off the shore. If the angle of depression to the ship is 5°, how far out is the ship?

CHAPTER 5
Analytic Trigonometry

C H A P T E R   5
Analytic Trigonometry

Section 5.1   Using Fundamental Identities

■ You should know the fundamental trigonometric identities.

(a) Reciprocal Identities

$$\sin u = \frac{1}{\csc u} \qquad\qquad \csc u = \frac{1}{\sin u}$$

$$\cos u = \frac{1}{\sec u} \qquad\qquad \sec u = \frac{1}{\cos u}$$

$$\tan u = \frac{1}{\cot u} = \frac{\sin u}{\cos u} \qquad\qquad \cot u = \frac{1}{\tan u} = \frac{\cos u}{\sin u}$$

(b) Pythagorean Identities

$$\sin^2 u + \cos^2 u = 1$$

$$1 + \tan^2 u = \sec^2 u$$

$$1 + \cot^2 u = \csc^2 u$$

(c) Cofunction Identities

$$\sin\left(\frac{\pi}{2} - u\right) = \cos u \qquad\qquad \cos\left(\frac{\pi}{2} - u\right) = \sin u$$

$$\tan\left(\frac{\pi}{2} - u\right) = \cot u \qquad\qquad \cot\left(\frac{\pi}{2} - u\right) = \tan u$$

$$\sec\left(\frac{\pi}{2} - u\right) = \csc u \qquad\qquad \csc\left(\frac{\pi}{2} - u\right) = \sec u$$

(d) Even/Odd Identities

$$\sin(-x) = -\sin x \qquad\qquad \csc(-x) = -\csc x$$

$$\cos(-x) = \cos x \qquad\qquad \sec(-x) = \sec x$$

$$\tan(-x) = -\tan x \qquad\qquad \cot(-x) = -\cot x$$

■ You should be able to use these fundamental identities to find function values.

■ You should be able to convert trigonometric expressions to equivalent forms by using the fundamental identities.

Solutions to Odd-Numbered Exercises

1. $\sin x = \dfrac{\sqrt{3}}{2}$, $\cos x = -\dfrac{1}{2}$ $\implies$ x is in Quadrant II.

$\tan x = \dfrac{\sin x}{\cos x} = \dfrac{\sqrt{3}/2}{-1/2} = -\sqrt{3}$

$\cot x = \dfrac{1}{\tan x} = -\dfrac{1}{\sqrt{3}} = -\dfrac{\sqrt{3}}{3}$

$\sec x = \dfrac{1}{\cos x} = \dfrac{1}{-1/2} = -2$

$\csc x = \dfrac{1}{\sin x} = \dfrac{1}{\sqrt{3}/2} = \dfrac{2}{\sqrt{3}} = \dfrac{2\sqrt{3}}{3}$

3. $\sec \theta = \sqrt{2}$, $\sin \theta = -\dfrac{\sqrt{2}}{2}$ $\implies$ θ is in Quadrant IV.

$\cos \theta = \dfrac{1}{\sec \theta} = \dfrac{1}{\sqrt{2}} = \dfrac{\sqrt{2}}{2}$

$\tan \theta = \dfrac{\sin \theta}{\cos \theta} = \dfrac{-\sqrt{2}/2}{\sqrt{2}/2} = -1$

$\cot \theta = \dfrac{1}{\tan \theta} = -1$

$\csc \theta = \dfrac{1}{\sin \theta} = -\sqrt{2}$

5. $\tan x = \dfrac{5}{12}$, $\sec x = -\dfrac{13}{12}$ $\implies$ x is in

Quadrant III.

$\cos x = \dfrac{1}{\sec x} = -\dfrac{12}{13}$

$\sin x = -\sqrt{1 - \cos^2 x} = -\sqrt{1 - \dfrac{144}{169}} = -\dfrac{5}{13}$

$\cot x = \dfrac{1}{\tan x} = \dfrac{12}{5}$

$\csc x = \dfrac{1}{\sin x} = -\dfrac{13}{5}$

7. $\sec \phi = \dfrac{3}{2}$, $\csc \phi = -\dfrac{3\sqrt{5}}{5}$ $\implies$ ϕ is in Quadrant IV.

$\sin \phi = \dfrac{1}{\csc \phi} = \dfrac{1}{-3\sqrt{5}/5} = -\dfrac{\sqrt{5}}{3}$

$\cos \phi = \dfrac{1}{\sec \phi} = \dfrac{1}{3/2} = \dfrac{2}{3}$

$\tan \phi = \dfrac{\sin \phi}{\cos \phi} = \dfrac{-\sqrt{5}/3}{2/3} = -\dfrac{\sqrt{5}}{2}$

$\cot \phi = \dfrac{1}{\tan \phi} = \dfrac{1}{-\sqrt{5}/2} = -\dfrac{2}{\sqrt{5}} = -\dfrac{2\sqrt{5}}{5}$

9. $\sin(-x) = -\dfrac{1}{3}$ $\implies$ $\sin x = \dfrac{1}{3}$, $\tan x = -\dfrac{\sqrt{2}}{4}$ $\implies$ x is

in Quadrant II.

$\cos x = -\sqrt{1 - \sin^2 x} = -\sqrt{1 - \dfrac{1}{9}} = -\dfrac{2\sqrt{2}}{3}$

$\cot x = \dfrac{1}{\tan x} = \dfrac{1}{-\sqrt{2}/4} = -2\sqrt{2}$

$\sec x = \dfrac{1}{\cos x} = \dfrac{1}{-2\sqrt{2}/3} = -\dfrac{3\sqrt{2}}{4}$

$\csc x = \dfrac{1}{\sin x} = \dfrac{1}{1/3} = 3$

11. $\tan \theta = 2$, $\sin \theta < 0$ $\implies$ θ is in Quadrant III.

$\sec \theta = -\sqrt{\tan^2 \theta + 1} = -\sqrt{4 + 1} = -\sqrt{5}$

$\cos \theta = \dfrac{1}{\sec \theta} = -\dfrac{1}{\sqrt{5}} = -\dfrac{\sqrt{5}}{5}$

$\sin \theta = -\sqrt{1 - \cos^2 \theta}$

$\qquad = -\sqrt{1 - \dfrac{1}{5}} = -\dfrac{2}{\sqrt{5}} = -\dfrac{2\sqrt{5}}{5}$

$\csc \theta = \dfrac{1}{\sin \theta} = -\dfrac{\sqrt{5}}{2}$

$\cot \theta = \dfrac{1}{\tan \theta} = \dfrac{1}{2}$

13. $\sin \theta = -1$, $\cot \theta = 0$ $\implies$ $\theta = \dfrac{3\pi}{2}$

$\cos \theta = \sqrt{1 - \sin^2 \theta} = 0$

$\sec \theta$ is undefined.

$\tan \theta$ is undefined.

$\csc \theta = -1$

15. $\sec x \cos x = \sec x \cdot \dfrac{1}{\sec x} = 1$

The expression is matched with (d).

17. $\cot^2 x - \csc^2 x = \cot^2 x - (1 + \cot^2 x) = -1$

The expression is matched with (b).

19. $\dfrac{\sin(-x)}{\cos(-x)} = \dfrac{-\sin x}{\cos x} = -\tan x$

The expression is matched with (e).

21. $\sin x \sec x = \sin x \cdot \dfrac{1}{\cos x} = \tan x$

The expression is matched with (b).

23. $\sec^4 x - \tan^4 x = (\sec^2 x + \tan^2 x)(\sec^2 x - \tan^2 x)$

$$= (\sec^2 x + \tan^2 x)(1) = \sec^2 x + \tan^2 x$$

The expression is matched with (f).

25. $\dfrac{\sec^2 x - 1}{\sin^2 x} = \dfrac{\tan^2 x}{\sin^2 x} = \dfrac{\sin^2 x}{\cos^2 x} \cdot \dfrac{1}{\sin^2 x} = \sec^2 x$

The expression is matched with (e).

27. $\cot \theta \sec \theta = \dfrac{\cos \theta}{\sin \theta} \cdot \dfrac{1}{\cos \theta} = \dfrac{1}{\sin \theta} = \csc \theta$

29. $\sin \phi (\csc \phi - \sin \phi) = (\sin \phi)\dfrac{1}{\sin \phi} - \sin^2 \phi$

$$= 1 - \sin^2 \phi = \cos^2 \phi$$

31. $\dfrac{\cot x}{\csc x} = \dfrac{\cos x / \sin x}{1 / \sin x}$

$$= \dfrac{\cos x}{\sin x} \cdot \dfrac{\sin x}{1} = \cos x$$

33. $\dfrac{1 - \sin^2 x}{\csc^2 x - 1} = \dfrac{\cos^2 x}{\cot^2 x} = \cos^2 x \tan^2 x = (\cos^2 x)\dfrac{\sin^2}{\cos^2}$

$$= \sin^2 x$$

35. $\sec \alpha \dfrac{\sin \alpha}{\tan \alpha} = \dfrac{1}{\cos \alpha}(\sin \alpha) \cot \alpha$

$$= \dfrac{1}{\cos \alpha}(\sin \alpha)\left(\dfrac{\cos \alpha}{\sin \alpha}\right) = 1$$

37. $\cos\left(\dfrac{\pi}{2} - x\right)\sec x = (\sin x)(\sec x)$

$$= (\sin x)\left(\dfrac{1}{\cos x}\right)$$

$$= \dfrac{\sin x}{\cos x}$$

$$= \tan x$$

39. $\dfrac{\cos^2 y}{1 - \sin y} = \dfrac{1 - \sin^2 y}{1 - \sin y}$

$$= \dfrac{(1 + \sin y)(1 - \sin y)}{1 - \sin y}$$

$$= 1 + \sin y$$

41. $\sin \beta \tan \beta + \cos \beta = (\sin \beta)\dfrac{\sin \beta}{\cos \beta} + \cos \beta$

$$= \dfrac{\sin^2 \beta}{\cos \beta} + \dfrac{\cos^2 \beta}{\cos \beta}$$

$$= \dfrac{\sin^2 \beta + \cos^2 \beta}{\cos \beta}$$

$$= \dfrac{1}{\cos \beta}$$

$$= \sec \beta$$

43. $\cot u \sin u + \tan u \cos u = \dfrac{\cos u}{\sin u}(\sin u) + \dfrac{\sin u}{\cos u}(\cos u)$

$$= \cos u + \sin u$$

45. $\tan^2 x - \tan^2 x \sin^2 x = \tan^2 x(1 - \sin^2 x)$

$$= \tan^2 x \cos^2 x$$

$$= \dfrac{\sin^2 x}{\cos^2 x} \cdot \cos^2 x$$

$$= \sin^2 x$$

47. $\sin^2 x \sec^2 x - \sin^2 x = \sin^2 x(\sec^2 x - 1)$

$$= \sin^2 x \tan^2 x$$

49. $\dfrac{\sec^2 x - 1}{\sec x - 1} = \dfrac{(\sec x + 1)(\sec x - 1)}{\sec x - 1} = \sec x + 1$

51. $\tan^4 x + 2\tan^2 x + 1 = (\tan^2 x + 1)^2$

$$= (\sec^2 x)^2$$

$$= \sec^4 x$$

53. $\sin^4 x - \cos^4 x = (\sin^2 x + \cos^2 x)(\sin^2 x - \cos^2 x)$

$$= (1)(\sin^2 x - \cos^2 x)$$

$$= \sin^2 x - \cos^2 x$$

55. $\csc^3 x - \csc^2 x - \csc x + 1 = \csc^2 x(\csc x - 1) - 1(\csc x - 1)$

$$= (\csc^2 x - 1)(\csc x - 1)$$

$$= \cot^2 x(\csc x - 1)$$

57. $(\sin x + \cos x)^2 = \sin^2 x + 2\sin x \cos x + \cos^2 x$

$$= (\sin^2 x + \cos^2 x) + 2 \sin x \cos x$$

$$= 1 + 2 \sin x \cos x$$

59. $(2 \csc x + 2)(2 \csc x - 2) = 4 \csc^2 x - 4 = 4(\csc^2 x - 1) = 4 \cot^2 x$

61. $\dfrac{1}{1 + \cos x} + \dfrac{1}{1 - \cos x} = \dfrac{1 - \cos x + 1 + \cos x}{(1 + \cos x)(1 - \cos x)}$

$$= \dfrac{2}{1 - \cos^2 x}$$

$$= \dfrac{2}{\sin^2 x}$$

$$= 2 \csc^2 x$$

63. $\dfrac{\cos x}{1 + \sin x} + \dfrac{1 + \sin x}{\cos x} = \dfrac{\cos^2 x + (1 + \sin x)^2}{\cos x(1 + \sin x)} = \dfrac{\cos^2 x + 1 + 2\sin x + \sin^2 x}{\cos x(1 + \sin x)}$

$$= \dfrac{2 + 2\sin x}{\cos x(1 + \sin x)}$$

$$= \dfrac{2(1 + \sin x)}{\cos x(1 + \sin x)}$$

$$= \dfrac{2}{\cos x}$$

$$= 2\sec x$$

65. $\dfrac{\sin^2 y}{1 - \cos y} = \dfrac{1 - \cos^2 y}{1 - \cos y}$

$\qquad = \dfrac{(1 + \cos y)(1 - \cos y)}{1 - \cos y}$

$\qquad = 1 + \cos y$

67. $\dfrac{3}{\sec x - \tan x} \cdot \dfrac{\sec x + \tan x}{\sec x + \tan x} = \dfrac{3(\sec x + \tan x)}{\sec^2 x - \tan^2 x}$

$\qquad = \dfrac{3(\sec x + \tan x)}{1}$

$\qquad = 3(\sec x + \tan x)$

69. $y_1 = \cos\left(\dfrac{\pi}{2} - x\right)$, $y_2 = \sin x$

x	0.2	0.4	0.6	0.8	1.0	1.2	1.4
y_1	0.1987	0.3894	0.5646	0.7174	0.8415	0.9320	0.9855
y_2	0.1987	0.3894	0.5646	0.7174	0.8415	0.9320	0.9855

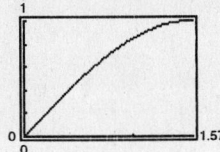

Conclusion: $y_1 = y_2$

71. $y_1 = \dfrac{\cos x}{1 - \sin x}$, $y_2 = \dfrac{1 + \sin x}{\cos x}$

x	0.2	0.4	0.6	0.8	1.0	1.2	1.4
y_1	1.2230	1.5085	1.8958	2.4650	3.4082	5.3319	11.6814
y_2	1.2230	1.5085	1.8958	2.4650	3.4082	5.3319	11.6814

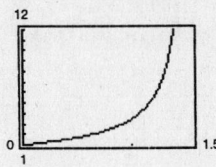

Conclusion: $y_1 = y_2$

73. $y_1 = \cos x \cot x + \sin x = \csc x$

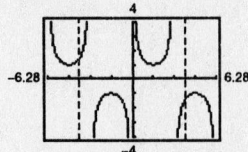

$$\cos x \cot x + \sin x = \cos x\left(\frac{\cos x}{\sin x}\right) + \sin x$$

$$= \frac{\cos^2 x}{\sin x} + \frac{\sin^2 x}{\sin x}$$

$$= \frac{\cos^2 x + \sin^2 x}{\sin x} = \frac{1}{\sin x} = \csc x$$

75. $y_1 = \dfrac{1}{\sin x}\left(\dfrac{1}{\cos x} - \cos x\right) = \tan x$

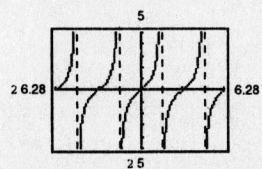

$$\frac{1}{\sin x}\left(\frac{1}{\cos x} - \cos x\right) = \frac{1}{\sin x \cos x} - \frac{\cos x}{\sin x}$$

$$= \frac{1 - \cos^2 x}{\sin x \cos x} = \frac{\sin^2 x}{\sin x \cos x} = \frac{\sin x}{\cos x} = \tan x$$

77. Let $x = 3 \cos \theta$, then

$$\sqrt{9 - x^2} = \sqrt{9 - (3 \cos \theta)^2} = \sqrt{9 - 9 \cos^2 \theta} = \sqrt{9(1 - \cos^2 \theta)}$$

$$= \sqrt{9 \sin^2 \theta} = 3 \sin \theta$$

79. Let $x = 3 \sec \theta$, then

$$\sqrt{x^2 - 9} = \sqrt{(3 \sec \theta)^2 - 9}$$

$$= \sqrt{9 \sec^2 \theta - 9}$$

$$= \sqrt{9\,(\sec^2 \theta - 1)}$$

$$= \sqrt{9 \tan^2 \theta}$$

$$= 3 \tan \theta$$

81. Let $x = 5 \tan \theta$, then

$$\sqrt{x^2 + 25} = \sqrt{(5 \tan \theta)^2 + 25}$$

$$= \sqrt{25 \tan^2 \theta + 25}$$

$$= \sqrt{25(\tan^2 \theta + 1)}$$

$$= \sqrt{25 \sec^2 \theta}$$

$$= 5 \sec \theta$$

83. Let $x = 3 \sin \theta$, then $\sqrt{9 - x^2} = 3$ becomes

$$\sqrt{9 - (3 \sin^2 \theta)^2} = 3$$

$$\sqrt{9 - 9 \sin^2 \theta} = 3$$

$$\sqrt{9(1 - \sin^2 \theta)} = 3$$

$$\sqrt{9 \cos^2 \theta} = 3$$

$$3 \cos \theta = 3$$

$$\cos \theta = 1$$

$$\sin \theta = \sqrt{1 - \cos^2 \theta} = \sqrt{1 - (1)^2} = 0$$

85. Let $x = 2 \cos \theta$, then $\sqrt{16 - 4x^2} = 2\sqrt{2}$ becomes

$$\sqrt{16 - 4(2 \cos \theta)^2} = 2\sqrt{2}$$

$$\sqrt{16 - 16 \cos^2 \theta} = 2\sqrt{2}$$

$$\sqrt{16(1 - \cos^2 \theta)} = 2\sqrt{2}$$

$$\sqrt{16 \sin^2 \theta} = 2\sqrt{2}$$

$$4 \sin \theta = 2\sqrt{2}$$

$$\sin \theta = \frac{\sqrt{2}}{2}$$

$$\cos \theta = \sqrt{1 - \sin^2 \theta} = \sqrt{1 - \frac{1}{2}} = \sqrt{\frac{1}{2}} = \frac{\sqrt{2}}{2}$$

87. $\sin \theta = \sqrt{1 - \cos^2 \theta}$

Let $y_1 = \sin x$ and $y_2 = \sqrt{1 - \cos^2 x}$, $0 \le x \le 2\pi$.

$y_1 = y_2$ for $0 \le x \le \pi$, so we have

$\sin \theta = \sqrt{1 - \cos^2 \theta}$ for $0 \le \theta \le \pi$.

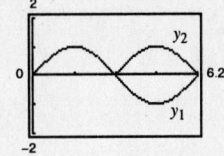

89. $\sec \theta = \sqrt{1 + \tan^2 \theta}$

Let $y_1 = \dfrac{1}{\cos x}$ and $y_2 = \sqrt{1 + \tan^2 x}$, $0 \le x \le 2\pi$.

$y_1 = y_2$ for $0 \le x < \dfrac{\pi}{2}$ and $\dfrac{3\pi}{2} < x \le 2\pi$, so we have

$\sec \theta = \sqrt{1 + \tan^2 \theta}$ for $0 \le \theta < \dfrac{\pi}{2}$ and $\dfrac{3\pi}{2} < \theta \le 2\pi$.

91. $\ln|\cos \theta| - \ln|\sin \theta| = \ln \dfrac{|\cos \theta|}{|\sin \theta|} = \ln|\cot \theta|$

93. $\ln|\cot t| + \ln(1 + \tan^2 t) = \ln\left[|\cot t|(1 + \tan^2 t)\right]$

$$= \ln|\cot t \sec^2 t| = \ln\left|\frac{\cos t}{\sin t} \cdot \frac{1}{\cos^2 t}\right|$$

$$= \ln\left|\frac{1}{\sin t \cos t}\right| = \ln|\csc t \sec t|$$

95. (a) $\csc^2 132° - \cot^2 132° \approx 1.8107 - 0.8107 = 1$

(b) $\csc^2\dfrac{2\pi}{7} - \cot^2\dfrac{2\pi}{7} \approx 1.6360 - 0.6360 = 1$

97. $\cos\left(\dfrac{\pi}{2} - \theta\right) = \sin\theta$

(a) $\theta = 80°$

$\cos(90° - 80°) = \sin 80°$

$0.9848 = 0.9848$

(b) $\theta = 0.8$

$\cos\left(\dfrac{\pi}{2} - 0.8\right) = \sin 0.8$

$0.7174 = 0.7174$

99. $\mu W \cos\theta = W \sin\theta$

$$\mu = \frac{W\sin\theta}{W\cos\theta} = \tan\theta$$

101. False. A cofunction identity can be used to transform a tangent function so that it can be represented by a cotangent function.

103. As $x \to 0^+$,

$\cos x \to 1$ and $\sec x = \dfrac{1}{\cos x} \to 1$.

105. As $x \to \pi^+$,

$\sin x \to 0$ and $\csc x = \dfrac{1}{\sin x} \to -\infty$.

107. The equation is **not** an identity.

$\cot\theta = \pm\sqrt{\csc^2\theta - 1}$

109. The equation is **not** an identity.

$$\frac{1}{5\cos\theta} = \frac{1}{5}\left(\frac{1}{\cos\theta}\right) = \frac{1}{5}\sec\theta \neq 5\sec\theta$$

111. The equation is **not** an identity because the angles may not be the same.

$\sin\theta\csc\phi = \sin\theta\left(\dfrac{1}{\sin\phi}\right) \neq 1$ unless $\theta = \phi$

113. $\cos \theta$

$\sin \theta = \pm \sqrt{1 - \cos^2 \theta}$

$\tan \theta = \dfrac{\sin \theta}{\cos \theta} = \pm \dfrac{\sqrt{1 - \cos^2 \theta}}{\cos \theta}$

$\csc \theta = \dfrac{1}{\sin \theta} = \pm \dfrac{1}{\sqrt{1 - \cos^2 \theta}}$

$\sec \theta = \dfrac{1}{\cos \theta}$

$\cot \theta = \dfrac{1}{\tan \theta} = \pm \dfrac{\cos \theta}{\sqrt{1 - \cos^2 \theta}}$

115. $\sqrt{v}\left(\sqrt{20} - \sqrt{5}\right) = \sqrt{20v} - \sqrt{5v}$

$\qquad = 2\sqrt{5v} - \sqrt{5v}$

$\qquad = \sqrt{5v}$

117. $\dfrac{50x}{\sqrt{30} - 5} = \dfrac{50x}{\sqrt{30} - 5} \cdot \dfrac{\sqrt{30} + 5}{\sqrt{30} + 5} = \dfrac{50x\left(\sqrt{30} + 5\right)}{30 - 25} = \dfrac{50x\left(\sqrt{30} + 5\right)}{5} = 10x\left(\sqrt{30} + 5\right)$

119. $y = 3 \sec(\pi x - \pi)$

Graph $y = 3 \cos(\pi x - \pi)$ first.

Amplitude: $|3| = 3$

Period: $\dfrac{2\pi}{\pi} = 2$

Shift: $\pi x - \pi = 0 \Rightarrow x = 1$ to $\pi x - \pi = 2\pi \Rightarrow x = 3$

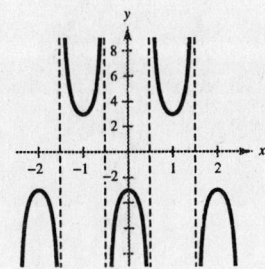

121. $y = \dfrac{1}{4} \sec 2x$

Graph $y = \dfrac{1}{4} \cos 2x$ first.

Amplitude: $\left|\dfrac{1}{4}\right| = \dfrac{1}{4}$

Period: $\dfrac{2\pi}{\pi} = 2$

Shift: $2x = 0 \Rightarrow x = 0$ to $2x = 2\pi \Rightarrow x = \pi$

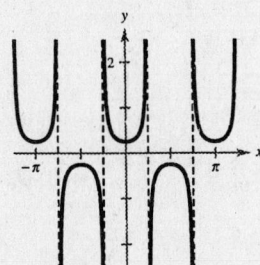

Section 5.2   Verifying Trigonometric Identities

■ You should know the difference between an expression, a conditional equation, and an identity.

■ You should be able to solve trigonometric identities, using the following techniques.

(a) Work with *one* side at a time. Do not "cross" the equal sign.

(b) Use algebraic techniques such as combining fractions, factoring expressions, rationalizing denominators, and squaring binomials.

(c) Use the fundamental identities.

(d) Convert all the terms into sines and cosines.

Solutions to Odd-Numbered Exercises

1. $\sin t \csc t = \sin t \left(\dfrac{1}{\sin t} \right) = 1$

3. $(1 + \sin \alpha)(1 - \sin \alpha) = 1 - \sin^2 \alpha = \cos^2 \alpha$

5. $\cos^2 \beta - \sin^2 \beta = (1 - \sin^2 \beta) - \sin^2 \beta$
$$= 1 - 2 \sin^2 \beta$$

7. $\tan^2 \theta + 4 = (\sec^2 \theta - 1) + 4$
$$= \sec^2 \theta + 3$$

9. $\sin^2 \alpha - \sin^4 \alpha = \sin^2 \alpha (1 - \sin^2 \alpha)$
$$= (1 - \cos^2 \alpha)(\cos^2 \alpha)$$
$$= \cos^2 \alpha - \cos^4 \alpha$$

11. $\dfrac{\csc^2 \theta}{\cot \theta} = \csc^2 \theta \left(\dfrac{1}{\cot \theta} \right) = \csc^2 \theta \tan \theta$

$$= \left(\dfrac{1}{\sin^2 \theta} \right) \left(\dfrac{\sin \theta}{\cos \theta} \right) = \left(\dfrac{1}{\sin \theta} \right) \left(\dfrac{1}{\cos \theta} \right)$$

$$= \csc \theta \sec \theta$$

13. $\dfrac{\cot^2 t}{\csc t} = \dfrac{\cos^2 t}{\sin^2 t} \cdot \sin t$

$$= \dfrac{\cos^2 t}{\sin t}$$

$$= \dfrac{1 - \sin^2 t}{\sin t} = \dfrac{1}{\sin t} - \dfrac{\sin^2 t}{\sin t}$$

$$= \csc t - \sin t$$

15. $\sin^{1/2} x \cos x - \sin^{5/2} x \cos x = \sin^{1/2} x \cos x (1 - \sin^2 x) = \sin^{1/2} x \cos x \cdot \cos^2 x = \cos^3 x \sqrt{\sin x}$

17. $\dfrac{1}{\sec x \tan x} = \cos x \cot x = \cos x \cdot \dfrac{\cos x}{\sin x}$

$$= \dfrac{\cos^2 x}{\sin x}$$

$$= \dfrac{1 - \sin^2 x}{\sin x}$$

$$= \dfrac{1}{\sin x} - \sin x$$

$$= \csc x - \sin x$$

19. $\cot \alpha + \tan \alpha = \dfrac{\cos \alpha}{\sin \alpha} + \dfrac{\sin \alpha}{\cos \alpha}$

$$= \dfrac{\cos^2 \alpha + \sin^2 \alpha}{\sin \alpha \cos \alpha}$$

$$= \dfrac{1}{\sin \alpha \cos \alpha}$$

$$= \dfrac{1}{\sin \alpha} \cdot \dfrac{1}{\cos \alpha}$$

$$= \csc \alpha \sec \alpha$$

21. $\sin x \cos x + \sin^3 x \sec x = \sin x \left[\cos x + \sin^2 x \left(\dfrac{1}{\cos x} \right) \right]$

$$= \sin x \left[\dfrac{\cos^2 x + \sin^2 x}{\cos x} \right]$$

$$= \sin x \left(\dfrac{1}{\cos x} \right)$$

$$= \dfrac{\sin x}{\cos x}$$

$$= \tan x$$

23. $\dfrac{1}{\tan x} + \dfrac{1}{\cot x} = \dfrac{\cot x + \tan x}{\tan x \cot x}$

$$= \dfrac{\cot x + \tan x}{1}$$

$$= \tan x + \cot x$$

25. $\dfrac{\cos \theta \cot \theta}{1 - \sin \theta} - 1 = \dfrac{\cos \theta \cot \theta - (1 - \sin \theta)}{1 - \sin \theta}$

$$= \dfrac{\cos \theta \left(\dfrac{\cos \theta}{\sin \theta} \right) - 1 + \sin \theta}{1 - \sin \theta} \cdot \dfrac{\sin \theta}{\sin \theta}$$

$$= \dfrac{\cos^2 \theta - \sin \theta + \sin^2 \theta}{\sin \theta (1 - \sin \theta)}$$

$$= \dfrac{1 - \sin \theta}{\sin \theta (1 - \sin \theta)}$$

$$= \dfrac{1}{\sin \theta}$$

$$= \csc \theta$$

27. $\dfrac{1}{\sin x + 1} + \dfrac{1}{\csc x + 1} = \dfrac{\csc x + 1 + \sin x + 1}{(\sin x + 1)(\csc x + 1)}$

$$= \dfrac{\sin x + \csc x + 2}{\sin x \csc x + \sin x + \csc x + 1}$$

$$= \dfrac{\sin x + \csc x + 2}{1 + \sin x + \csc x + 1}$$

$$= \dfrac{\sin x + \csc x + 2}{\sin x + \csc x + 2}$$

$$= 1$$

29. $\tan \left(\dfrac{\pi}{2} - \theta \right) \tan \theta = \cot \theta \tan \theta = \left(\dfrac{1}{\tan \theta} \right) \tan \theta = 1$

31. $\dfrac{\csc(-x)}{\sec(-x)} = \dfrac{\dfrac{1}{\sin(-x)}}{\dfrac{1}{\cos(-x)}}$

$$= \dfrac{\cos(-x)}{\sin(-x)}$$

$$= \dfrac{\cos x}{-\sin x}$$

$$= -\cot x$$

33. $\dfrac{\cos(-\theta)}{1 + \sin(-\theta)} = \dfrac{\cos \theta}{1 - \sin \theta} \cdot \dfrac{1 + \sin \theta}{1 + \sin \theta}$

$$= \dfrac{\cos \theta (1 + \sin \theta)}{1 - \sin^2 \theta}$$

$$= \dfrac{\cos \theta (1 + \sin \theta)}{\cos^2 \theta}$$

$$= \dfrac{1 + \sin \theta}{\cos \theta}$$

$$= \dfrac{1}{\cos \theta} + \dfrac{\sin \theta}{\cos \theta}$$

$$= \sec \theta + \tan \theta$$

35. $\dfrac{\sin x \cos y + \cos x \sin y}{\cos x \cos y - \sin x \sin y} = \dfrac{\dfrac{\sin x \cos y}{\cos x \cos y} + \dfrac{\cos x \sin y}{\cos x \cos y}}{\dfrac{\cos x \cos y}{\cos x \cos y} - \dfrac{\sin x \sin y}{\cos x \cos y}} = \dfrac{\tan x + \tan y}{1 - \tan x \tan y}$

37. $\dfrac{\tan x + \cot y}{\tan x \cot y} = \dfrac{\dfrac{1}{\cot x} + \dfrac{1}{\tan y}}{\dfrac{1}{\cot x} \cdot \dfrac{1}{\tan y}} \cdot \dfrac{\cot x \tan y}{\cot x \tan y} = \tan y + \cot x$

39. $\sqrt{\dfrac{1 + \sin \theta}{1 - \sin \theta}} = \sqrt{\dfrac{1 + \sin \theta}{1 - \sin \theta} \cdot \dfrac{1 + \sin \theta}{1 + \sin \theta}}$

$\qquad = \sqrt{\dfrac{(1 + \sin \theta)^2}{1 - \sin^2 \theta}}$

$\qquad = \sqrt{\dfrac{(1 + \sin \theta)^2}{\cos^2 \theta}}$

$\qquad = \dfrac{1 + \sin \theta}{|\cos \theta|}$

41. $\cos^2 \beta + \cos^2\left(\dfrac{\pi}{2} - \beta\right) = \cos^2 \beta + \sin^2 \beta = 1$

43. $\sin t \csc\left(\dfrac{\pi}{2} - t\right) = \sin t \sec t = \sin t\left(\dfrac{1}{\cos t}\right)$

$\qquad = \dfrac{\sin t}{\cos t} = \tan t$

45. $2 \sec^2 x - 2 \sec^2 x \sin^2 x - \sin^2 x - \cos^2 x = 2 \sec^2 x(1 - \sin^2 x) - (\sin^2 x + \cos^2 x)$

$\qquad = 2 \sec^2 x(\cos^2 x) - 1$

$\qquad = 2 \cdot \dfrac{1}{\cos^2 x} \cdot \cos^2 x - 1$

$\qquad = 2 - 1$

$\qquad = 1$

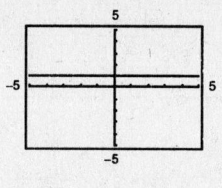

47. $2 + \cos^2 x - 3 \cos^4 x = (1 - \cos^2 x)(2 + 3 \cos^2 x)$

$\qquad = \sin^2 x(2 + 3 \cos^2 x)$

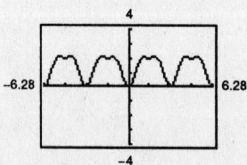

49. $\csc^4 x - 2 \csc^2 x + 1 = (\csc^2 x - 1)^2$

$\qquad = (\cot^2 x)^2 = \cot^4 x$

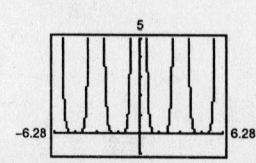

51. $\sec^4 \theta - \tan^4 \theta = (\sec^2 \theta + \tan^2 \theta)(\sec^2 \theta - \tan^2 \theta)$

$\qquad\qquad = (1 + \tan^2 \theta + \tan^2 \theta)(1)$

$\qquad\qquad = 1 + 2 \tan^2 \theta$

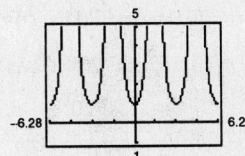

53. $\dfrac{\cos x}{1 + \sin x} = \dfrac{\cos x}{1 + \sin x} \cdot \dfrac{1 - \sin x}{1 - \sin x}$

$\qquad\quad = \dfrac{\cos x(1 - \sin x)}{1 - \sin^2 x}$

$\qquad\quad = \dfrac{\cos x(1 - \sin x)}{\cos^2 x}$

$\qquad\quad = \dfrac{1 - \sin x}{\cos x}$

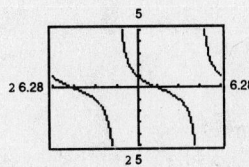

55. $\dfrac{\tan^3 \alpha - 1}{\tan \alpha - 1} = \dfrac{(\tan \alpha - 1)(\tan^2 \alpha + \tan \alpha + 1)}{\tan \alpha - 1} = \tan^2 \alpha + \tan \alpha + 1$

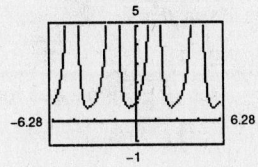

57. $\ln|\tan \theta| = \ln\left|\dfrac{\sin \theta}{\cos \theta}\right|$

$\qquad\quad = \ln\dfrac{|\sin \theta|}{|\cos \theta|}$

$\qquad\quad = \ln|\sin \theta| - \ln|\cos \theta|$

59. $-\ln(1 + \cos \theta) = \ln(1 + \cos \theta)^{-1}$

$\qquad\qquad = \ln\left(\dfrac{1}{1 + \cos \theta} \cdot \dfrac{1 - \cos \theta}{1 - \cos \theta}\right)$

$\qquad\qquad = \ln\dfrac{1 - \cos \theta}{1 - \cos^2 \theta}$

$\qquad\qquad = \ln\dfrac{1 - \cos \theta}{\sin^2 \theta}$

$\qquad\qquad = \ln(1 - \cos \theta) - \ln \sin^2 \theta$

$\qquad\qquad = \ln(1 - \cos \theta) - 2 \ln|\sin \theta|$

61. $\sin^2 25° + \sin^2 65° = \sin^2 25° + \cos^2(90° - 65°) = \sin^2 25° + \cos^2 25° = 1$

63. $\cos^2 20° + \cos^2 52° + \cos^2 38° + \cos^2 70° = \cos^2 20° + \cos^2 52° + \sin^2(90° - 38°) + \sin^2(90° - 70°)$

$$= \cos^2 20° + \cos^2 52° + \sin^2 52° + \sin^2 20°$$

$$= (\cos^2 20° + \sin^2 20°) + (\cos^2 52° + \sin^2 52°)$$

$$= 1 + 1$$

$$= 2$$

65. $\cos x - \csc x \cot x = \cos x - \dfrac{1}{\sin x} \dfrac{\cos x}{\sin x}$

$$= \cos x\left(1 - \dfrac{1}{\sin^2 x}\right)$$

$$= \cos x(1 - \csc^2 x)$$

$$= -\cos x(\csc^2 x - 1)$$

$$= -\cos x \cot^2 x$$

67. True. An identity is an equation that is true for all real values in the domain of the variable.

69. $\tan \theta = \sqrt{\sec^2 \theta - 1}$

True identity: $\tan \theta = \pm \sqrt{\sec^2 \theta - 1}$

$\tan \theta = \sqrt{\sec^2 \theta - 1}$ is not true for $\pi/2 < \theta < \pi$ or $3\pi/2 < \theta < 2\pi$. Thus, the equation is not true for $\theta = 3\pi/4$.

71. $\sqrt{\sin^2 x + \cos^2 x} = \sin x + \cos x$

$\sqrt{\sin^2 x + \cos^2 x} \neq \sin x + \cos x$

The left side is 1 for any x, but the right side is not necessarily 1. The equation is not true for $x = \pi/4$.

73. $\sin\left[\dfrac{(12n + 1)\pi}{6}\right] = \sin\left[\dfrac{1}{6}(12n\pi + \pi)\right]$

$$= \sin\left(2n\pi + \dfrac{\pi}{6}\right)$$

$$= \sin \dfrac{\pi}{6} = \dfrac{1}{2}$$

Thus, $\sin\left[\dfrac{(12n + 1)\pi}{6}\right] = \dfrac{1}{2}$ for all integers n.

75. $(2 - 5i)^2 = (2 - 5i)(2 - 5i)$

$$= 4 - 20i + 25i^2$$

$$= 4 - 20i - 25$$

$$= -21 - 20i$$

77. $(3 + 2i)^3 = (3 + 2i)(3 + 2i)(3 + 2i)$

$$= (9 + 12i + 4i^2)(3 + 2i)$$

$$= (5 + 12i)(3 + 2i)$$

$$= 15 + 10i + 36i + 24i^2$$

$$= -9 + 46i$$

79. $x^2 + 5x + 7 = 0$

$a = 1, b = 5, c = 7$

$$x = \dfrac{-5 \pm \sqrt{5^2 - 4(1)(7)}}{2(1)} = \dfrac{-5 \pm \sqrt{-3}}{2} = \dfrac{-5 \pm \sqrt{3}i}{2}$$

81. $8x^2 - 4x + 3 = 0$

$a = 8, b = -4, c = 3$

$$x = \dfrac{-(-4) \pm \sqrt{(-4)^2 - 4(8)(3)}}{2(8)} = \dfrac{4 \pm \sqrt{-80}}{16}$$

$$= \dfrac{4 \pm 4\sqrt{5}i}{16} = \dfrac{4(1 \pm \sqrt{5}i)}{16} = \dfrac{1 \pm \sqrt{5}i}{4}$$

83. $14x^2 - 10x + 9 = 0$

$a = 14, b = -10, c = 9$

$$x = \dfrac{-(-10) \pm \sqrt{(-10)^2 - 4(14)(9)}}{2(14)} = \dfrac{10 \pm \sqrt{-404}}{28}$$

$$= \dfrac{10 \pm 2\sqrt{101}i}{28} = \dfrac{2(5 \pm \sqrt{101}i)}{28}$$

$$= \dfrac{5 \pm \sqrt{101}i}{14}$$

85. $13x^2 + 5x + 2 = 0$

$a = 13, b = 5, c = 2$

$x = \dfrac{-5 \pm \sqrt{5^2 - 4(13)(2)}}{2(13)} = \dfrac{-5 \pm \sqrt{-79}}{26}$

$\quad = \dfrac{-5 \pm \sqrt{79}i}{26}$

Section 5.3   Solving Trigonometric Equations

- ■ You should be able to identify and solve trigonometric equations.
- ■ A trigonometric equation is a conditional equation. It is true for a specific set of values.
- ■ To solve trigonometric equations, use algebraic techniques such as collecting like terms, taking square roots, factoring, squaring, converting to quadratic form, using formulas, and using inverse functions. Study the examples in this section.

Solutions to Odd-Numbered Exercises

1. $2 \cos x - 1 = 0$

  (a) $2 \cos \dfrac{\pi}{3} - 1 = 2\left(\dfrac{1}{2}\right) - 1 = 0$

  (b) $2 \cos \dfrac{5\pi}{3} - 1 = 2\left(\dfrac{1}{2}\right) - 1 = 0$

3. $3 \tan^2 2x - 1 = 0$

  (a) $3\left[\tan 2\left(\dfrac{\pi}{12}\right)\right]^2 - 1 = 3 \tan^2 \dfrac{\pi}{6} - 1$

$\qquad\qquad\qquad = 3\left(\dfrac{1}{\sqrt{3}}\right)^2 - 1$

$\qquad\qquad\qquad = 0$

  (b) $3\left[\tan 2\left(\dfrac{5\pi}{12}\right)\right]^2 - 1 = 3 \tan^2 \dfrac{5\pi}{6} - 1$

$\qquad\qquad\qquad = 3\left(-\dfrac{1}{\sqrt{3}}\right)^2 - 1$

$\qquad\qquad\qquad = 0$

5. $2 \sin^2 x - \sin x - 1 = 0$

  (a) $2 \sin^2 \dfrac{\pi}{2} - \sin \dfrac{\pi}{2} - 1 = 2(1)^2 - 1 - 1$

$\qquad\qquad\qquad = 0$

  (b) $2 \sin^2 \dfrac{7\pi}{6} - \sin \dfrac{7\pi}{6} - 1 = 2\left(-\dfrac{1}{2}\right)^2 - \left(-\dfrac{1}{2}\right) - 1$

$\qquad\qquad\qquad = \dfrac{1}{2} + \dfrac{1}{2} - 1$

$\qquad\qquad\qquad = 0$

7. $2 \cos x + 1 = 0$

$2 \cos x = -1$

$\cos x = -\dfrac{1}{2}$

$x = \dfrac{2\pi}{3} + 2n\pi$

or $x = \dfrac{4\pi}{3} + 2n\pi$

9. $\sqrt{3} \csc x - 2 = 0$

$\sqrt{3} \csc x = 2$

$\csc x = \dfrac{2}{\sqrt{3}}$

$x = \dfrac{\pi}{3} + 2n\pi$

or $x = \dfrac{2\pi}{3} + 2n\pi$

11. $3 \sec^2 x - 4 = 0$

$\sec^2 x = \dfrac{4}{3}$

$\sec x = \pm\dfrac{2}{\sqrt{3}}$

$x = \dfrac{\pi}{6} + n\pi$

or $x = \dfrac{5\pi}{6} + n\pi$

13. $\sin x(\sin x + 1) = 0$

$\sin x = 0$ or $\sin x = -1$

$x = n\pi$ $\qquad$ $x = \dfrac{3\pi}{2} + 2n\pi$

15. $4 \cos^2 x - 1 = 0$

$\cos^2 x = \dfrac{1}{4}$

$\cos^2 x = \pm\dfrac{1}{2}$

$x = \dfrac{\pi}{3} + n\pi$ or $x = \dfrac{2\pi}{3} + n\pi$

17. $2 \sin^2 2x = 1$

$\sin 2x = \pm\dfrac{1}{\sqrt{2}} = \pm\dfrac{\sqrt{2}}{2}$

$2x = \dfrac{\pi}{4} + 2n\pi,\ 2x = \dfrac{3\pi}{4} + 2n\pi,\ 2x = \dfrac{5\pi}{4} + 2n\pi,\ 2x = \dfrac{7\pi}{4} + 2n\pi.$

Thus, $x = \dfrac{\pi}{8} + n\pi,\ \dfrac{3\pi}{8} + n\pi,\ \dfrac{5\pi}{8} + n\pi,\ \dfrac{7\pi}{8} + n\pi.$

19. $\tan 3x(\tan x - 1) = 0$

$\tan 3x = 0$ or $\tan x - 1 = 0$

$3x = n\pi$ $\qquad$ $\tan x = 1$

$x = \dfrac{n\pi}{3}$ $\qquad$ $x = \dfrac{\pi}{4} + n\pi$

21. $\qquad\cos^3 x = \cos x$

$\cos^3 x - \cos x = 0$

$\cos x(\cos^2 x - 1) = 0$

$\cos x = 0$ $\qquad$ or $\cos^2 x - 1 = 0$

$x = \dfrac{\pi}{2}, \dfrac{3\pi}{2}$ $\qquad\qquad$ $\cos x = \pm 1$

$x = 0,\ \pi$

23. $\qquad 3 \tan^3 x - \tan x = 0$

$\tan x(3 \tan^2 x - 1) = 0$

$\tan x = 0$ or $3 \tan^2 x - 1 = 0$

$x = 0,\ \pi$ $\qquad\qquad$ $\tan x = \pm\dfrac{\sqrt{3}}{3}$

$x = \dfrac{\pi}{6}, \dfrac{5\pi}{6}, \dfrac{7\pi}{6}, \dfrac{11\pi}{6}$

25. $\qquad \sec^2 x - \sec x - 2 = 0$

$(\sec x - 2)(\sec x + 1) = 0$

$\sec x - 2 = 0$ $\qquad$ or $\sec x + 1 = 0$

$\sec x = 2$ $\qquad\qquad$ $\sec x = -1$

$x = \dfrac{\pi}{3}, \dfrac{5\pi}{3}$ $\qquad\qquad$ $x = \pi$

27. $2 \sin x + \csc x = 0$

$$2 \sin x + \frac{1}{\sin x} = 0$$

$$2 \sin^2 x + 1 = 0$$

$$\sin^2 x = -\frac{1}{2} \implies \text{No solution}$$

29. $2 \cos^2 x + \cos x - 1 = 0$

$$(2 \cos x - 1)(\cos x + 1) = 0$$

$$2 \cos x - 1 = 0 \quad \text{or} \quad \cos x + 1 = 0$$

$$\cos x = \frac{1}{2} \qquad\qquad \cos x = -1$$

$$x = \frac{\pi}{3}, \frac{5\pi}{3} \qquad\qquad x = \pi$$

31. $\qquad 2 \sec^2 x + \tan^2 x - 3 = 0$

$$2(\tan^2 x + 1) + \tan^2 x - 3 = 0$$

$$3 \tan^2 x - 1 = 0$$

$$\tan x = \pm\frac{\sqrt{3}}{3}$$

$$x = \frac{\pi}{6}, \frac{5\pi}{6}, \frac{7\pi}{6}, \frac{11\pi}{6}$$

33. $\cos 2x = \frac{1}{2}$

$$2x = \frac{\pi}{3} + 2n\pi \quad \text{or} \quad 2x = \frac{5\pi}{3} + 2n\pi$$

$$x = \frac{\pi}{6} + n\pi \qquad\qquad x = \frac{5\pi}{6} + n\pi$$

35. $\tan 3x = 1$

$$3x = \frac{\pi}{4} + 2n\pi \qquad \text{or} \qquad 3x = \frac{5\pi}{4} + 2n\pi$$

$$x = \frac{\pi}{12} + \frac{2n\pi}{3} \qquad\qquad x = \frac{5\pi}{12} + \frac{2n\pi}{3}$$

These can be combined as $x = \frac{\pi}{12} + \frac{n\pi}{3}$.

37. $\cos\left(\frac{x}{2}\right) = \frac{\sqrt{2}}{2}$

$$\frac{x}{2} = \frac{\pi}{4} + 2n\pi \quad \text{or} \quad \frac{x}{2} = \frac{7\pi}{4} + 2n\pi$$

$$x = \frac{\pi}{2} + 4n\pi \qquad\qquad x = \frac{7\pi}{2} + 4n\pi$$

39. $y = \sin \frac{\pi x}{2} + 1$

From the graph in the textbook we see that the curve has x-intercepts at $x = -1$ and at $x = 3$.

41. $y = \tan^2\left(\frac{\pi x}{6}\right) - 3$

From the graph in the textbook we see that the curve has x-intercepts at $x = \pm 2$.

43. $\qquad 6y^2 - 13y + 6 = 0$

$$(3y - 2)(2y - 3) = 0$$

$$3y - 2 = 0 \quad \text{or} \quad 2y - 3 = 0$$

$$y = \frac{2}{3} \qquad\qquad y = \frac{3}{2}$$

$$6 \cos^2 x - 13 \cos x + 6 = 0$$

$$(3 \cos x - 2)(2 \cos x - 3) = 0$$

$$3 \cos x - 2 = 0 \qquad \text{or} \quad 2 \cos x - 3 = 0$$

$$\cos x = \frac{2}{3} \qquad\qquad\qquad \cos x = \frac{3}{2} \quad \text{(No solution)}$$

$$x \approx 0.8411 + 2n\pi, \, 5.4421 + 2n\pi$$

45. $2\sin x + \cos x = 0$

$$2\sin x = -\cos x$$

$$2 = -\frac{\cos x}{\sin x}$$

$$2 = -\cot x$$

$$-2 = \cot x$$

$$-\frac{1}{2} = \tan x$$

$$x = \arctan\left(-\frac{1}{2}\right)$$

$$x = \pi - \arctan\left(\frac{1}{2}\right) \approx 2.6779$$

$$\text{or } x = 2\pi - \arctan\left(\frac{1}{2}\right) \approx 5.8195$$

Graph $y_1 = 2\sin x + \cos x$

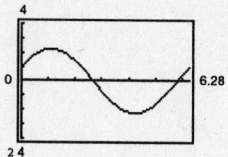

The x-intercepts occur at $x \approx 2.6779$ and $x \approx 5.8195$

47.
$$\frac{1 + \sin x}{\cos x} + \frac{\cos x}{1 + \sin x} = 4$$

$$\frac{(1 + \sin x)^2 + \cos^2 x}{\cos x(1 + \sin x)} = 4$$

$$\frac{1 + 2\sin x + \sin^2 x + \cos^2 x}{\cos x(1 + \sin x)} = 4$$

$$\frac{2 + 2\sin x}{\cos x(1 + \sin x)} = 4$$

$$\frac{2}{\cos x} = 4$$

$$\cos x = \frac{1}{2}$$

$$x = \frac{\pi}{3}, \frac{5\pi}{3}$$

Graph $y_1 = \dfrac{1 + \sin x}{\cos x} + \dfrac{\cos x}{1 + \sin x} - 4.$

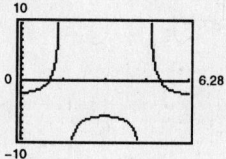

The x-intercepts occur at $x = \dfrac{\pi}{3} \approx 1.0472$ and $x = \dfrac{5\pi}{3} \approx 5.2360.$

49. $x\tan x - 1 = 0$

Graph $y_1 = x\tan x - 1$

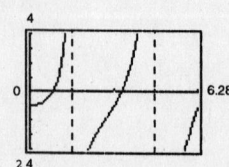

The x-intercepts occur at $x \approx 0.8603$ and $x \approx 3.4256$

51. $\sec^2 x + 0.5\tan x - 1 = 0$

Graph $y_1 = \dfrac{1}{(\cos x)^2} + 0.5\tan x - 1.$

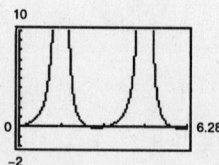

The x-intercepts occur at $x = 0$, $x \approx 2.6779$, $x = \pi \approx 3.1416$, and $x \approx 5.8195$.

53. $2 \tan^2 x + 7 \tan x - 15 = 0$

$(2 \tan x - 3)(\tan x + 5) = 0$

$2 \tan x - 3 = 0$ or $\tan x + 5 = 0$

      $\tan x = 1.5$ $\tan x = -5$

         $x \approx 0.9828, 4.1244$ $x \approx 1.7682, 4.9098$

Graph $y_1 = 2 \tan^2 x + 7 \tan x - 15$.

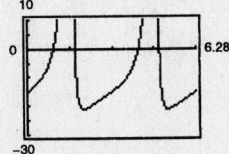

The x-intercepts occur at $x \approx 0.9828$, $x \approx 1.7682$, $x \approx 4.1244$, and $x \approx 4.9098$.

55. $12 \sin^2 x - 13 \sin x + 3 = 0$

$$\sin x = \frac{-(-13) \pm \sqrt{(-13)^2 - 4(12)(3)}}{2(12)}$$

$$= \frac{13 \pm 5}{24}$$

$\sin x = \frac{1}{3}$ or $\sin x = \frac{3}{4}$

   $x \approx 0.3398, 2.8018$ $x \approx 0.8481, 2.2935$

Graph $y_1 = 12 \sin^2 x - 13 \sin x + 3$.

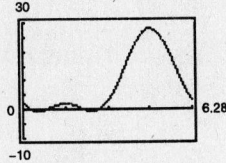

The x-intercepts occur at $x \approx 0.3398$, $x \approx 0.8481$, $x \approx 2.2935$, and $x \approx 2.8018$.

57. $\tan^2 x + 3 \tan x + 1 = 0$

$$\tan x = \frac{-3 \pm \sqrt{3^2 - 4(1)(1)}}{2(1)} = \frac{-3 \pm \sqrt{5}}{2}$$

$\tan x = \dfrac{-3 - \sqrt{5}}{2}$ or $\tan x = \dfrac{-3 + \sqrt{5}}{2}$

   $x \approx 1.9357, 5.0773$ $x \approx 2.7767, 5.9183$

Graph $y_1 = \tan^2 x + 3 \tan x + 1$.

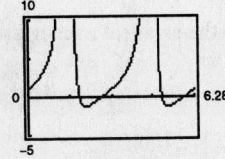

The x-intercepts occur at $x \approx 1.9357$, $x \approx 2.7767$, $x \approx 5.0773$, and $x \approx 5.9183$.

59. $\tan^2 x - 6 \tan x + 5 = 0$

$(\tan x - 1)(\tan x - 5) = 0$

$\tan x - 1 = 0 \quad \text{or} \quad \tan x - 5 = 0$

$\tan x = 1 \qquad\qquad \tan x = 5$

$x = \dfrac{\pi}{4}, \dfrac{5\pi}{4} \qquad\quad x = \arctan 5, \arctan 5 + \pi$

61. $2 \cos^2 x - 5 \cos x + 2 = 0$

$(2 \cos x - 1)(\cos x - 2) = 0$

$2 \cos x - 1 = 0 \qquad \text{or} \quad \cos x - 2 = 0$

$\cos x = \dfrac{1}{2} \qquad\qquad \cos x = 2$

$x = \dfrac{\pi}{3}, \dfrac{5\pi}{3} \qquad\quad x = \arccos 2,$

$2\pi - \arccos 2$

63. (a) $f(x) = \sin x + \cos x$

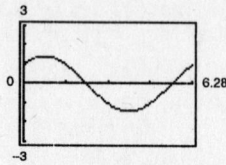

Maximum: $\left(\dfrac{\pi}{4}, \ \sqrt{2} \right)$

Minimum: $\left(\dfrac{5\pi}{4}, \ -\sqrt{2} \right)$

(b) $\cos x - \sin x = 0$

$\cos x = \sin x$

$1 = \dfrac{\sin x}{\cos x}$

$\tan x = 1$

$x = \dfrac{\pi}{4}, \dfrac{5\pi}{4}$

$f\left(\dfrac{\pi}{4} \right) = \sin \dfrac{\pi}{4} + \cos \dfrac{\pi}{4} = \dfrac{\sqrt{2}}{2} + \dfrac{\sqrt{2}}{2} = \sqrt{2}$

$f\left(\dfrac{5\pi}{4} \right) = \sin \dfrac{5\pi}{4} + \cos \dfrac{5\pi}{4} = -\sin \dfrac{\pi}{4} + \left(-\cos \dfrac{\pi}{4} \right) = -\dfrac{\sqrt{2}}{2} - \dfrac{\sqrt{2}}{2} = -\sqrt{2}$

Therefore, the maximum point in the interval $[0, 2\pi)$ is $\left(\pi/4, \ \sqrt{2} \right)$ and the minimum point is $\left(5\pi/4, \ -\sqrt{2} \right)$.

65. $f(x) = \tan \dfrac{\pi x}{4}$

Since $\tan \pi/4 = 1$, $x = 1$ is the smallest nonnegative fixed point.

67. $f(x) = \cos \dfrac{1}{x}$

(a) The domain of $f(x)$ is all real numbers except 0.

(b) The graph has y-axis symmetry and a horizontal asymptote at $y = 1$.

(c) As $x \to 0$, $f(x)$ oscillates between -1 and 1.

(d) There are infinitely many solutions in the interval $[-1, 1]$.

(e) The greatest solution appears to occur at $x \approx 0.6366$.

69.
$$y = \frac{1}{12}(\cos 8t - 3 \sin 8t)$$

$$\frac{1}{12}(\cos 8t - 3 \sin 8t) = 0$$

$$\cos 8t = 3 \sin 8t$$

$$\frac{1}{3} = \tan 8t$$

$$8t \approx 0.32175 + n\pi$$

$$t \approx 0.04 + \frac{n\pi}{8}$$

In the interval $0 \le t \le 1$, $t \approx$ 0.04, 0.43, and 0.83.

71. $S = 74.50 + 43.75 \sin \dfrac{\pi t}{6}$

t	1	2	3	4	5	6	7	8	9	10	11	12
S	96.4	112.4	118.3	112.4	96.4	74.5	52.6	36.6	30.8	36.6	52.6	74.5

Sales exceed 100,000 units during February, March, and April.

73. Range $= 1000$ yards $= 3000$ feet

$v_0 = 1200$ feet per second

$f = \frac{1}{32} v_0^2 \sin 2\theta$

$3000 = \frac{1}{32}(1200)^2 \sin 2\theta$

$\sin 2\theta \approx 0.066667$

$2\theta \approx 3.8°$

$\theta \approx 1.9°$

75. $f(x) = 3 \sin(0.6x - 2)$

(a) Zero: $\sin(0.6x - 2) = 0$

$$0.6x - 2 = 0$$

$$0.6x = 2$$

$$x = \frac{2}{0.6} = \frac{10}{3}$$

(c) $-0.45x^2 + 5.52x - 13.70 = 0$

$$x = \frac{-5.52 \pm \sqrt{(5.52)^2 - 4(-0.45)(-13.70)}}{2(-0.45)}$$

$x \approx 3.46, 8.81$

The zero of g on $[0, 6]$ is 3.46. The zero is close
to the zero $\frac{10}{3} \approx 3.33$ of f.

(b) $g(x) = -0.45x^2 + 5.52x - 13.70$

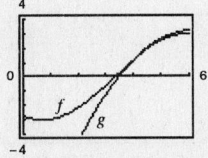

For $3.5 \le x \le 6$ the approximation appears to be good.

77. True. The period of $2 \sin 4t - 1$ is $\dfrac{\pi}{2}$ and the period of $2 \sin t - 1$ is 2π.

In the interval $[0, 2\pi)$ the first equation has four cycles whereas the second
equation has only one cycle, thus the first equation has four times the
x-intercepts (solutions) as the second equation.

79. $y_1 = 2\sin x$

$y_2 = 3x + 1$

From the graph we see that there is only one point of intersection.

81.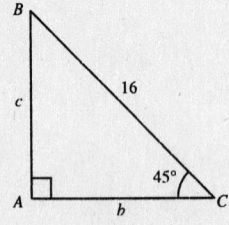

$$B = 90° - 45° = 45°$$

$$\tan 45° = \frac{b}{c} = 1 \implies b = c$$

$$\cos 45° = \frac{b}{16}$$

$$16\left(\frac{\sqrt{2}}{2}\right) = b$$

$$b = 8\sqrt{2} \approx 11.31$$

$$c \approx 11.31$$

83.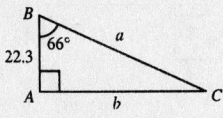

$$C = 90° - 66° = 24°$$

$$\cos 66° = \frac{22.3}{a}$$

$$a\cos 66° = 22.3$$

$$a = \frac{22.3}{\cos 66°} \approx 54.8$$

$$\tan 66° = \frac{b}{22.3}$$

$$b = 22.3\tan 66° \approx 50.1$$

85. $\theta = 390°$, $\theta' = 390° - 360° = 30°$, θ is in Quadrant I.

$$\sin 390° = \sin 30° = \frac{1}{2}$$

$$\cos 390° = \cos 30° = \frac{\sqrt{3}}{2}$$

$$\tan 390° = \tan 30° = \frac{1}{\sqrt{3}} = \frac{\sqrt{3}}{3}$$

87. $\theta = 495°$, $\theta' = 45°$, θ is in Quadrant II.

$$\sin 495° = \sin 45° = \frac{\sqrt{2}}{2}$$

$$\cos 495° = -\cos 45° = -\frac{\sqrt{2}}{2}$$

$$\tan 495° = -\tan 45° = -1$$

89. $\theta = -1845°$, $\theta' = 45°$, θ is in Quadrant IV.

$$\sin(-1845°) = -\sin 45° = -\frac{\sqrt{2}}{2}$$

$$\cos(-1845°) = \cos 45° = \frac{\sqrt{2}}{2}$$

$$\tan(-1845°) = -\tan 45° = -1$$

91.

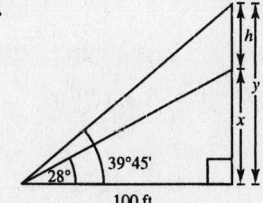

$$h = y - x$$

$$\tan 39.75° = \frac{y}{100}$$

$$100 \tan 39.75° = y$$

$$\tan 28° = \frac{x}{100}$$

$$100 \tan 28° = x$$

$$h = 100 \tan 39.75° - 100 \tan 28°$$

$$h \approx 30 \text{ feet}$$

Section 5.4   Sum and Difference Formulas

■ You should know the sum and difference formulas.

$$\sin(u \pm v) = \sin u \cos v \pm \cos u \sin v$$

$$\cos(u \pm v) = \cos u \cos v \mp \sin u \sin v$$

$$\tan(u \pm v) = \frac{\tan u \pm \tan v}{1 \mp \tan u \tan v}$$

■ You should be able to use these formulas to find the values of the trigonometric functions of angles whose sums or differences are special angles.

■ You should be able to use these formulas to solve trigonometric equations.

Solutions to Odd-Numbered Exercises

1. (a) $\cos\left(\dfrac{\pi}{4} + \dfrac{\pi}{3}\right) = \cos\dfrac{\pi}{4}\cos\dfrac{\pi}{3} - \sin\dfrac{\pi}{4}\sin\dfrac{\pi}{3}$

$$= \frac{\sqrt{2}}{2} \cdot \frac{1}{2} - \frac{\sqrt{2}}{2} \cdot \frac{\sqrt{3}}{2}$$

$$= \frac{\sqrt{2} - \sqrt{6}}{4}$$

(b) $\cos\dfrac{\pi}{4} + \cos\dfrac{\pi}{3} = \dfrac{\sqrt{2}}{2} + \dfrac{1}{2} = \dfrac{\sqrt{2}+1}{2}$

3. (a) $\sin\left(\dfrac{7\pi}{6} - \dfrac{\pi}{3}\right) = \sin\dfrac{5\pi}{6} = \sin\dfrac{\pi}{6} = \dfrac{1}{2}$

(b) $\sin\dfrac{7\pi}{6} - \sin\dfrac{\pi}{3} = -\dfrac{1}{2} - \dfrac{\sqrt{3}}{2} = \dfrac{-1-\sqrt{3}}{2}$

5. (a) $\cos(120° + 45°) = \cos 120° \cos 45° - \sin 120° \sin 45°$

$$= \left(-\frac{1}{2}\right)\left(\frac{\sqrt{2}}{2}\right) - \left(\frac{\sqrt{3}}{2}\right)\left(\frac{\sqrt{2}}{2}\right)$$

$$= \frac{-\sqrt{2} - \sqrt{6}}{4}$$

(b) $\cos 120° + \cos 45° = -\dfrac{1}{2} + \dfrac{\sqrt{2}}{2} = \dfrac{-1+\sqrt{2}}{2}$

7. $\sin 105° = \sin(60° + 45°)$

$\qquad = \sin 60° \cos 45° + \cos 60° \sin 45°$

$\qquad = \dfrac{\sqrt{3}}{2} \cdot \dfrac{\sqrt{2}}{2} + \dfrac{1}{2} \cdot \dfrac{\sqrt{2}}{2}$

$\qquad = \dfrac{\sqrt{2}}{4}\left(\sqrt{3} + 1\right)$

$\cos 105° = \cos(60° + 45°)$

$\qquad = \cos 60° \cos 45° - \sin 60° \sin 45°$

$\qquad = \dfrac{1}{2} \cdot \dfrac{\sqrt{2}}{2} - \dfrac{\sqrt{3}}{2} \cdot \dfrac{\sqrt{2}}{2}$

$\qquad = \dfrac{\sqrt{2}}{4}\left(1 - \sqrt{3}\right)$

$\tan 105° = \tan(60° + 45°)$

$\qquad = \dfrac{\tan 60° + \tan 45°}{1 - \tan 60° \tan 45°}$

$\qquad = \dfrac{\sqrt{3} + 1}{1 - \sqrt{3}} = \dfrac{\sqrt{3} + 1}{1 - \sqrt{3}} \cdot \dfrac{1 + \sqrt{3}}{1 + \sqrt{3}}$

$\qquad = \dfrac{4 + 2\sqrt{3}}{-2} = -2 - \sqrt{3}$

9. $\sin 195° = \sin(225° - 30°)$

$\qquad = \sin 225° \cos 30° - \cos 225° \sin 30°$

$\qquad = -\sin 45° \cos 30° + \cos 45° \sin 30°$

$\qquad = -\dfrac{\sqrt{2}}{2} \cdot \dfrac{\sqrt{3}}{2} + \dfrac{\sqrt{2}}{2} \cdot \dfrac{1}{2}$

$\qquad = \dfrac{\sqrt{2}}{4}\left(1 - \sqrt{3}\right)$

$\cos 195° = \cos(225° - 30°)$

$\qquad = \cos 225° \cos 30° + \sin 225° \sin 30°$

$\qquad = -\cos 45° \cos 30° - \sin 45° \sin 30°$

$\qquad = -\dfrac{\sqrt{2}}{2} \cdot \dfrac{\sqrt{3}}{2} - \dfrac{\sqrt{2}}{2} \cdot \dfrac{1}{2}$

$\qquad = -\dfrac{\sqrt{2}}{4}\left(\sqrt{3} + 1\right)$

$\tan 195° = \tan(225° - 30°)$

$\qquad = \dfrac{\tan 225° - \tan 30°}{1 + \tan 225° \tan 30°}$

$\qquad = \dfrac{\tan 45° - \tan 30°}{1 + \tan 45° \tan 30°}$

$\qquad = \dfrac{1 - \left(\dfrac{\sqrt{3}}{3}\right)}{1 + \left(\dfrac{\sqrt{3}}{3}\right)} = \dfrac{3 - \sqrt{3}}{3 + \sqrt{3}} \cdot \dfrac{3 - \sqrt{3}}{3 - \sqrt{3}}$

$\qquad = \dfrac{12 - 6\sqrt{3}}{6} = 2 - \sqrt{3}$

11. $\sin \dfrac{11\pi}{12} = \sin\left(\dfrac{3\pi}{4} + \dfrac{\pi}{6}\right)$

$\qquad = \sin \dfrac{3\pi}{4} \cos \dfrac{\pi}{6} + \cos \dfrac{3\pi}{4} \sin \dfrac{\pi}{6}$

$\qquad = \dfrac{\sqrt{2}}{2} \cdot \dfrac{\sqrt{3}}{2} + \left(-\dfrac{\sqrt{2}}{2}\right)\dfrac{1}{2}$

$\qquad = \dfrac{\sqrt{2}}{4}\left(\sqrt{3} - 1\right)$

$\cos \dfrac{11\pi}{12} = \cos\left(\dfrac{3\pi}{4} + \dfrac{\pi}{6}\right)$

$\qquad = \cos \dfrac{3\pi}{4} \cos \dfrac{\pi}{6} - \sin \dfrac{3\pi}{4} \sin \dfrac{\pi}{6}$

$\qquad = -\dfrac{\sqrt{2}}{2} \cdot \dfrac{\sqrt{3}}{2} - \dfrac{\sqrt{2}}{2} \cdot \dfrac{1}{2}$

$\qquad = -\dfrac{\sqrt{2}}{4}\left(\sqrt{3} + 1\right)$

$\tan \dfrac{11\pi}{4} = \tan\left(\dfrac{3\pi}{4} + \dfrac{\pi}{6}\right)$

$\qquad = \dfrac{\tan \dfrac{3\pi}{4} + \tan \dfrac{\pi}{6}}{1 - \tan \dfrac{3\pi}{4} \tan \dfrac{\pi}{6}}$

$\qquad = \dfrac{-1 + \dfrac{\sqrt{3}}{3}}{1 - (-1)\dfrac{\sqrt{3}}{3}}$

$\qquad = \dfrac{-3 + \sqrt{3}}{3 + \sqrt{3}} \cdot \dfrac{3 - \sqrt{3}}{3 - \sqrt{3}}$

$\qquad = \dfrac{-12 + 6\sqrt{3}}{6} = -2 + \sqrt{3}$

13. $\sin \dfrac{17\pi}{12} = \sin\left(\dfrac{9\pi}{4} - \dfrac{5\pi}{6}\right)$

$\qquad = \sin\dfrac{9\pi}{4}\cos\dfrac{5\pi}{6} - \cos\dfrac{9\pi}{4}\sin\dfrac{5\pi}{6}$

$\qquad = \dfrac{\sqrt{2}}{2}\left(-\dfrac{\sqrt{3}}{2}\right) - \left(\dfrac{\sqrt{2}}{2}\right)\left(\dfrac{1}{2}\right)$

$\qquad = -\dfrac{\sqrt{2}}{4}\left(\sqrt{3} + 1\right)$

$\cos\dfrac{17\pi}{12} = \cos\left(\dfrac{9\pi}{4} - \dfrac{5\pi}{6}\right)$

$\qquad = \cos\dfrac{9\pi}{4}\cos\dfrac{5\pi}{6} + \sin\dfrac{9\pi}{4}\sin\dfrac{5\pi}{6}$

$\qquad = \dfrac{\sqrt{2}}{2}\left(-\dfrac{\sqrt{3}}{2}\right) + \dfrac{\sqrt{2}}{2}\left(\dfrac{1}{2}\right)$

$\qquad = \dfrac{\sqrt{2}}{4}\left(1 - \sqrt{3}\right)$

$\tan\dfrac{17\pi}{12} = \tan\left(\dfrac{9\pi}{4} - \dfrac{5\pi}{6}\right)$

$\qquad = \dfrac{\tan(9\pi/4) - \tan(5\pi/6)}{1 + \tan(9\pi/4)\tan(5\pi/6)}$

$\qquad = \dfrac{1 - \left(-\sqrt{3}/3\right)}{1 + \left(-\sqrt{3}/3\right)}$

$\qquad = \dfrac{3 + \sqrt{3}}{3 - \sqrt{3}} \cdot \dfrac{3 + \sqrt{3}}{3 + \sqrt{3}}$

$\qquad = \dfrac{12 + 6\sqrt{3}}{6} = 2 + \sqrt{3}$

15. $285° = 225° + 60°$

$\sin 285° = \sin(225° + 60°)$

$\qquad = \sin 225° \cos 60° + \cos 225° \sin 60°$

$\qquad = -\dfrac{\sqrt{2}}{2}\left(\dfrac{1}{2}\right) - \dfrac{\sqrt{2}}{2}\left(\dfrac{\sqrt{3}}{2}\right) = -\dfrac{\sqrt{2}}{4}\left(\sqrt{3} + 1\right)$

$\cos 285° = \cos(225° + 60°)$

$\qquad = \cos 225° \cos 60° - \sin 225° \sin 60°$

$\qquad = -\dfrac{\sqrt{2}}{2}\left(\dfrac{1}{2}\right) - \left(-\dfrac{\sqrt{2}}{2}\right)\left(\dfrac{\sqrt{3}}{2}\right) = \dfrac{\sqrt{2}}{4}\left(\sqrt{3} - 1\right)$

$\tan 285° = \tan(225° + 60°)$

$\qquad = \dfrac{\tan 225° + \tan 60°}{1 - \tan 225° \tan 60°} = \dfrac{1 + \sqrt{3}}{1 - \sqrt{3}} \cdot \dfrac{1 + \sqrt{3}}{1 + \sqrt{3}}$

$\qquad = \dfrac{4 + 2\sqrt{3}}{-2} = -2 - \sqrt{3} = -\left(2 + \sqrt{3}\right)$

17. $-165° = -(120° + 45°)$

$\sin(-165°) = \sin\left[-(120° + 45°)\right]$

$\qquad = -\sin(120° + 45°)$

$\qquad = -\left[\sin 120° \cos 45° + \cos 120° \sin 45°\right]$

$\qquad = -\left[\dfrac{\sqrt{3}}{2} \cdot \dfrac{\sqrt{2}}{2} - \dfrac{1}{2} \cdot \dfrac{\sqrt{2}}{2}\right]$

$\qquad = -\dfrac{\sqrt{2}}{4}\left(\sqrt{3} - 1\right)$

$\cos(-165°) = \cos\left[-(120° + 45°)\right]$

$\qquad = \cos(120° + 45°)$

$\qquad = \cos 120° \cos 45° - \sin 120° \sin 45°$

$\qquad = -\dfrac{1}{2} \cdot \dfrac{\sqrt{2}}{2} - \dfrac{\sqrt{3}}{2} \cdot \dfrac{\sqrt{2}}{2}$

$\qquad = -\dfrac{\sqrt{2}}{4}\left(1 + \sqrt{3}\right)$

$\tan(-165°) = \tan\left[-(120° + 45°)\right]$

$\qquad = -\tan(120° + \tan 45°)$

$\qquad = -\dfrac{\tan 120° + \tan 45°}{1 - \tan 120° \tan 45°}$

$\qquad = -\dfrac{-\sqrt{3} + 1}{1 - (-\sqrt{3})(1)}$

$\qquad = -\dfrac{1 - \sqrt{3}}{1 + \sqrt{3}} \cdot \dfrac{1 - \sqrt{3}}{1 - \sqrt{3}}$

$\qquad = -\dfrac{4 - 2\sqrt{3}}{-2}$

$\qquad = 2 - \sqrt{3}$

19. $\dfrac{13\pi}{12} = \dfrac{3\pi}{4} + \dfrac{\pi}{3}$

$$\sin \dfrac{13\pi}{12} = \sin\left(\dfrac{3\pi}{4} + \dfrac{\pi}{3}\right)$$

$$= \sin \dfrac{3\pi}{4} \cos \dfrac{\pi}{3} + \cos \dfrac{3\pi}{4} \sin \dfrac{\pi}{3}$$

$$= \dfrac{\sqrt{2}}{2} \cdot \dfrac{1}{2} + \left(-\dfrac{\sqrt{2}}{2}\right)\left(\dfrac{\sqrt{3}}{2}\right)$$

$$= \dfrac{\sqrt{2}}{4}\left(1 - \sqrt{3}\right)$$

$$\cos \dfrac{13\pi}{12} = \cos\left(\dfrac{3\pi}{4} + \dfrac{\pi}{3}\right)$$

$$= \cos \dfrac{3\pi}{4} \cos \dfrac{\pi}{3} - \sin \dfrac{3\pi}{4} \sin \dfrac{\pi}{3}$$

$$= -\dfrac{\sqrt{2}}{2} \cdot \dfrac{1}{2} - \dfrac{\sqrt{2}}{2} \cdot \dfrac{\sqrt{3}}{2} = -\dfrac{\sqrt{2}}{4}\left(1 + \sqrt{3}\right)$$

$$\tan \dfrac{13\pi}{12} = \tan\left(\dfrac{3\pi}{4} + \dfrac{\pi}{3}\right)$$

$$= \dfrac{\tan\left(\dfrac{3\pi}{4}\right) + \tan\left(\dfrac{\pi}{3}\right)}{1 - \tan\left(\dfrac{3\pi}{4}\right)\tan\left(\dfrac{\pi}{3}\right)}$$

$$= \dfrac{-1 + \sqrt{3}}{1 - (-1)(\sqrt{3})}$$

$$= -\dfrac{1 - \sqrt{3}}{1 + \sqrt{3}} \cdot \dfrac{1 - \sqrt{3}}{1 - \sqrt{3}}$$

$$= -\dfrac{4 - 2\sqrt{3}}{-2}$$

$$= 2 - \sqrt{3}$$

21. $\qquad -\dfrac{13\pi}{12} = -\left(\dfrac{3\pi}{4} + \dfrac{\pi}{3}\right)$

$$\sin\left[-\left(\dfrac{3\pi}{4} + \dfrac{\pi}{3}\right)\right] = -\sin\left(\dfrac{3\pi}{4} + \dfrac{\pi}{3}\right)$$

$$= -\left[\sin \dfrac{3\pi}{4} \cos \dfrac{\pi}{3} + \cos \dfrac{3\pi}{4} \sin \dfrac{\pi}{3}\right]$$

$$= -\left[\dfrac{\sqrt{2}}{2}\left(\dfrac{1}{2}\right) + \left(-\dfrac{\sqrt{2}}{2}\right)\left(\dfrac{\sqrt{3}}{2}\right)\right]$$

$$= -\dfrac{\sqrt{2}}{4}\left(1 - \sqrt{3}\right) = \dfrac{\sqrt{2}}{4}\left(\sqrt{3} - 1\right)$$

$$\cos\left[-\left(\dfrac{3\pi}{4} + \dfrac{\pi}{3}\right)\right] = \cos\left(\dfrac{3\pi}{4} + \dfrac{\pi}{3}\right)$$

$$= \cos \dfrac{3\pi}{4} \cos \dfrac{\pi}{3} - \sin \dfrac{3\pi}{4} \sin \dfrac{\pi}{3}$$

$$= -\dfrac{\sqrt{2}}{2}\left(\dfrac{1}{2}\right) - \dfrac{\sqrt{2}}{2}\left(\dfrac{\sqrt{3}}{2}\right) = -\dfrac{\sqrt{2}}{4}\left(\sqrt{3} + 1\right)$$

$$\tan\left[-\left(\dfrac{3\pi}{4} + \dfrac{\pi}{3}\right)\right] = -\tan\left(\dfrac{3\pi}{4} + \dfrac{\pi}{3}\right)$$

$$= -\dfrac{\tan\dfrac{3\pi}{4} + \tan\dfrac{\pi}{3}}{1 - \tan\dfrac{3\pi}{4}\tan\dfrac{\pi}{3}} = -\dfrac{-1 + \sqrt{3}}{1 - (-\sqrt{3})}$$

$$= \dfrac{1 - \sqrt{3}}{1 + \sqrt{3}} \cdot \dfrac{1 - \sqrt{3}}{1 - \sqrt{3}} = \dfrac{4 - 2\sqrt{3}}{-2} = -2 + \sqrt{3}$$

23. $\cos 25° \cos 15° - \sin 25° \sin 15° = \cos(25° + 15°) = \cos 40°$

25. $\dfrac{\tan 325° - \tan 86°}{1 + \tan 325° \tan 86°} = \tan(325° - 86°) = \tan 239°$

27. $\sin 3 \cos 1.2 - \cos 3 \sin 1.2 = \sin(3 - 1.2) = \sin 1.8$

29. $\dfrac{\tan 2x + \tan x}{1 - \tan 2x \tan x} = \tan(2x + x) = \tan 3x$

31. $\sin 330° \cos 30° - \cos 330° \sin 30° = \sin(330° - 30°)$
$$= \sin 300°$$
$$= -\frac{\sqrt{3}}{2}$$

33. $\sin \dfrac{\pi}{12} \cos \dfrac{\pi}{4} + \cos \dfrac{\pi}{12} \sin \dfrac{\pi}{4} = \sin\left(\dfrac{\pi}{12} + \dfrac{\pi}{4}\right)$
$$= \sin \frac{\pi}{3}$$
$$= \frac{\sqrt{3}}{2}$$

35. $\dfrac{\tan 25° + \tan 110°}{1 - \tan 25° \tan 110°} = \tan(25° + 110°)$
$$= \tan 135°$$
$$= -1$$

For Exercises 37 – 43, we have:

$\sin u = \frac{5}{13}, \ u$ **in Quadrant II** $\implies \cos u = -\frac{12}{13}, \tan u = -\frac{5}{12}$

$\cos v = -\frac{3}{5}, v$ **in Quadrant II** $\implies \sin v = \frac{4}{5}, \tan v = -\frac{4}{3},$

37. $\sin(u + v) = \sin u \cos v + \cos u \sin v$
$$= \left(\tfrac{5}{13}\right)\left(-\tfrac{3}{5}\right) + \left(-\tfrac{12}{13}\right)\left(\tfrac{4}{5}\right)$$
$$= -\frac{63}{65}$$

39. $\cos(u + v) = \cos u \cos v - \sin u \sin v$
$$= \left(-\tfrac{12}{13}\right)\left(-\tfrac{3}{5}\right) - \left(\tfrac{5}{13}\right)\left(\tfrac{4}{5}\right)$$
$$= \frac{16}{65}$$

41. $\tan(u + v) = \dfrac{\tan u + \tan v}{1 - \tan u \tan v} = \dfrac{-\frac{5}{12} + \left(-\frac{4}{3}\right)}{1 - \left(-\frac{5}{12}\right)\left(-\frac{4}{3}\right)} = \dfrac{-\frac{21}{12}}{1 - \frac{5}{9}}$
$$= \left(-\frac{7}{4}\right)\left(\frac{9}{4}\right) = -\frac{63}{16}$$

43. $\sec(v - u) = \dfrac{1}{\cos(v - u)} = \dfrac{1}{\cos v \cos u + \sin v \sin u}$
$$= \dfrac{1}{\left(-\frac{3}{5}\right)\left(-\frac{12}{13}\right) + \left(\frac{4}{5}\right)\left(\frac{5}{13}\right)} = \dfrac{1}{\left(\frac{36}{65}\right) + \left(\frac{20}{65}\right)} = \dfrac{1}{\frac{56}{65}}$$
$$= \frac{65}{56}$$

For Exercises 45–49, we have:

$\sin u = -\frac{7}{25}$, u in Quadrant III $\implies \cos u = -\frac{24}{25}$, $\tan u = \frac{7}{24}$

$\cos v = -\frac{4}{5}$, v in Quadrant III $\implies \sin v = -\frac{3}{5}$, $\tan v = \frac{3}{4}$

45. $\cos(u + v) = \cos u \cos v - \sin u \sin v$

$$= \left(-\frac{24}{25}\right)\left(-\frac{4}{5}\right) - \left(-\frac{7}{25}\right)\left(-\frac{3}{5}\right)$$

$$= \frac{3}{5}$$

47. $\tan(u - v) = \dfrac{\tan u - \tan v}{1 + \tan u \tan v}$

$$= \frac{\frac{7}{24} - \frac{3}{4}}{1 + \left(\frac{7}{24}\right)\left(\frac{3}{4}\right)} = \frac{-\frac{11}{24}}{\frac{39}{32}} = -\frac{44}{117}$$

49. $\sec(u + v) = \dfrac{1}{\cos(u + v)} = \dfrac{1}{\frac{3}{5}} = \dfrac{5}{3}$

Use Exercise 45 for $\cos(u + v)$.

51. $\sin(\arcsin x + \arccos x) = \sin(\arcsin x)\cos(\arccos x) + \sin(\arccos x)\cos(\arcsin x)$

$$= x \cdot x + \sqrt{1 - x^2} \cdot \sqrt{1 - x^2}$$

$$= x^2 + 1 - x^2$$

$$= 1$$

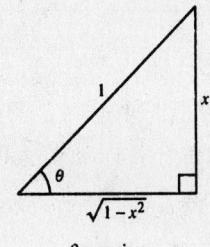

$\theta = \arcsin x$

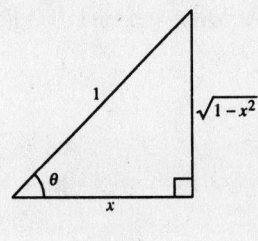

$\theta = \arccos x$

53. $\cos(\arccos x + \arcsin x) = \cos(\arccos x)\cos(\arcsin x) - \sin(\arccos x)\sin(\arcsin x)$

$$= x \cdot \sqrt{1 - x^2} - \sqrt{1 - x^2} \cdot x$$

$$= 0$$

(Use the triangles in Exercise 51.)

55. $\sin(3\pi - x) = \sin 3\pi \cos x - \sin x \cos 3\pi = (0)(\cos x) - (-1)(\sin x) = \sin x$

57. $\sin\left(\dfrac{\pi}{6} + x\right) = \sin\dfrac{\pi}{6}\cos x + \cos\dfrac{\pi}{6}\sin x = \dfrac{1}{2}\left(\cos x + \sqrt{3}\sin x\right)$

59. $\cos(\pi - \theta) + \sin\left(\dfrac{\pi}{2} + \theta\right) = \cos\pi\cos\theta + \sin\pi\sin\theta + \sin\dfrac{\pi}{2}\cos\theta + \cos\dfrac{\pi}{2}\sin\theta$

$$= (-1)(\cos\theta) + (0)(\sin\theta) + (1)(\cos\theta) + (\sin\theta)(0)$$

$$= -\cos\theta + \cos\theta$$

$$= 0$$

61. $\cos(x + y)\cos(x - y) = (\cos x \cos y - \sin x \sin y)(\cos x \cos y + \sin x \sin y)$

$$= \cos^2 x \cos^2 y - \sin^2 x \sin^2 y$$

$$= \cos^2 x(1 - \sin^2 y) - \sin^2 x \sin^2 y$$

$$= \cos^2 x - \cos^2 x \sin^2 y - \sin^2 x \sin^2 y$$

$$= \cos^2 x - \sin^2 y(\cos^2 x + \sin^2 x)$$

$$= \cos^2 x - \sin^2 y$$

63. $\sin(x + y) + \sin(x - y) = \sin x \cos y + \cos x \sin y + \sin x \cos y - \cos x \sin y$

$$= 2 \sin x \cos y$$

65. $\cos\left(\dfrac{3\pi}{2} - x\right) = \cos\dfrac{3\pi}{2}\cos x + \sin\dfrac{3\pi}{2}\sin x$

$$= (0)(\cos x) + (-1)(\sin x)$$

$$= -\sin x$$

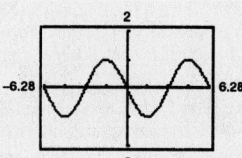

67. $\sin\left(\dfrac{3\pi}{2} - \theta\right) = \sin\dfrac{3\pi}{2}\cos\theta + \cos\dfrac{3\pi}{2}\sin\theta$

$$= (-1)(\cos\theta) + (0)(\sin\theta)$$

$$= -\cos\theta$$

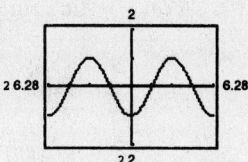

69.
$$\sin\left(x + \frac{\pi}{3}\right) + \sin\left(x - \frac{\pi}{3}\right) = 1$$

$$\sin x \cos\frac{\pi}{3} + \cos x \sin\frac{\pi}{3} + \sin x \cos\frac{\pi}{3} - \cos x \sin\frac{\pi}{3} = 1$$

$$2 \sin x(0.5) = 1$$

$$\sin x = 1$$

$$x = \frac{\pi}{2}$$

71.
$$\cos\left(x + \frac{\pi}{4}\right) - \cos\left(x - \frac{\pi}{4}\right) = 1$$

$$\cos x \cos \frac{\pi}{4} - \sin x \sin \frac{\pi}{4} - \left(\cos x \cos \frac{\pi}{4} + \sin x \sin \frac{\pi}{4}\right) = 1$$

$$-2 \sin x\left(\frac{\sqrt{2}}{2}\right) = 1$$

$$-\sqrt{2} \sin x = 1$$

$$\sin x = -\frac{1}{\sqrt{2}}$$

$$\sin x = -\frac{\sqrt{2}}{2}$$

$$x = \frac{5\pi}{4}, \frac{7\pi}{4}$$

73.   Analytically: $\cos\left(x + \frac{\pi}{4}\right) + \cos\left(x - \frac{\pi}{4}\right) = 1$

$$\cos x \cos \frac{\pi}{4} - \sin x \sin \frac{\pi}{4} + \cos x \cos \frac{\pi}{4} + \sin x \sin \frac{\pi}{4} = 1$$

$$2 \cos x\left(\frac{\sqrt{2}}{2}\right) = 1$$

$$\sqrt{2} \cos x = 1$$

$$\cos x = \frac{1}{\sqrt{2}}$$

$$\cos x = \frac{\sqrt{2}}{2}$$

$$x = \frac{\pi}{4}, \frac{7\pi}{4}$$

Graphically: Graph $y_1 = \cos\left(x + \frac{\pi}{4}\right) + \cos\left(x - \frac{\pi}{4}\right)$ and $y_2 = 1$.

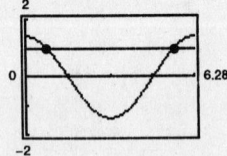

The points of intersection occur at $x = \frac{\pi}{4}$ and $x = \frac{7\pi}{4}$.

75. $y = \frac{1}{3} \sin 2t + \frac{1}{4} \cos 2t$

(a) $a = \frac{1}{3}$, $b = \frac{1}{4}$, $B = 2$

$C = \arctan \frac{b}{a} = \arctan \frac{3}{4} \approx 0.6435$

$y \approx \sqrt{\left(\frac{1}{3}\right)^2 + \left(\frac{1}{4}\right)^2} \sin(2t + 0.6435)$

$= \frac{5}{12} \sin(2t + 0.6435)$

(b) Amplitude: $\frac{5}{12}$ feet

(c) Frequency: $\frac{1}{\text{period}} = \frac{B}{2\pi} = \frac{2}{2\pi} = \frac{1}{\pi}$ cycles per second

77. False. $\sin(u \pm v) = \sin u \cos v \pm \cos u \sin v$.

In Exercises 1–6, parts (a) and (b) are unequal.

79. False. $\cos\left(x - \frac{\pi}{2}\right) = \cos x \cos \frac{\pi}{2} + \sin x \sin \frac{\pi}{2}$

$= (\cos x)(0) + (\sin x)(1)$

$= \sin x$

81. $\cos(n\pi + \theta) = \cos n\pi \cos \theta - \sin n\pi \sin \theta$

$= (-1)^n (\cos \theta) - (0)(\sin \theta)$

$= (-1)^n (\cos \theta)$, where n is an integer.

83. $C = \arctan \frac{b}{a} \implies \sin C = \frac{b}{\sqrt{a^2 + b^2}}$, $\cos C = \frac{a}{\sqrt{a^2 + b^2}}$

$\sqrt{a^2 + b^2} \sin(B\theta + C) = \sqrt{a^2 + b^2}\left(\sin B\theta \cdot \frac{a}{\sqrt{a^2 + b^2}} + \frac{b}{\sqrt{a^2 + b^2}} \cdot \cos \beta\theta\right) = a \sin B\theta + b \cos B\theta$

85. $\sin \theta + \cos \theta$

$a = 1$, $b = 1$, $B = 1$

(a) $C = \arctan \frac{b}{a} = \arctan 1 = \frac{\pi}{4}$

$\sin \theta + \cos \theta = \sqrt{a^2 + b^2} \sin(B\theta + C)$

$= \sqrt{2} \sin\left(\theta + \frac{\pi}{4}\right)$

(b) $C = \arctan \frac{a}{b} = \arctan 1 = \frac{\pi}{4}$

$\sin \theta + \cos \theta = \sqrt{a^2 + b^2} \cos(B\theta - C)$

$= \sqrt{2} \cos\left(\theta - \frac{\pi}{4}\right)$

87. $12 \sin 3\theta + 5 \cos 3\theta$

$a = 12$, $b = 5$, $B = 3$

(a) $C = \arctan \frac{b}{a} = \arctan \frac{5}{12} \approx 0.3948$

$12 \sin 3\theta + 5 \cos 3\theta = \sqrt{a^2 + b^2} \sin(B\theta + C)$

$\approx 13 \sin(3\theta + 0.3948)$

(b) $C = \arctan \frac{a}{b} = \arctan \frac{12}{5} \approx 1.1760$

$12 \sin 3\theta + 5 \cos 3\theta = \sqrt{a^2 + b^2} \cos(B\theta - C)$

$\approx 13 \cos(3\theta - 1.1760)$

89. $C = \arctan \dfrac{b}{a} = \dfrac{\pi}{2} \implies a = 0$

$\sqrt{a^2 + b^2} = 2 \implies b = 2$

$B = 1$

$2 \sin\left(\theta + \dfrac{\pi}{2}\right) = (0)(\sin\theta) + (2)(\cos\theta) = 2\cos\theta$

91.

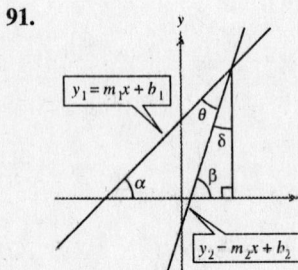

$m_1 = \tan\alpha$ and $m_2 = \tan\beta$

$\beta + \delta = 90° \implies \delta = 90° - \beta$

$\alpha + \theta + \delta = 90° \implies \alpha + \theta + (90° - \beta) = 90° \implies \theta = \beta - \alpha$

Therefore, $\theta = \arctan m_2 - \arctan m_1$

For $y = x$ and $y = \sqrt{3}x$ we have $m_1 = 1$ and $m_2 = \sqrt{3}$

$\theta = \arctan\sqrt{3} - \arctan 1$

$\quad = 60° - 45°$

$\quad = 15°$

93. $\sin^2\left(\theta + \dfrac{\pi}{4}\right) + \sin^2\left(\theta - \dfrac{\pi}{4}\right) = \left[\sin\theta\cos\dfrac{\pi}{4} + \cos\theta\sin\dfrac{\pi}{4}\right]^2 + \left[\sin\theta\cos\dfrac{\pi}{4} - \cos\theta\sin\dfrac{\pi}{4}\right]^2$

$= \left[\dfrac{\sin\theta}{\sqrt{2}} + \dfrac{\cos\theta}{\sqrt{2}}\right]^2 + \left[\dfrac{\sin\theta}{\sqrt{2}} - \dfrac{\cos\theta}{\sqrt{2}}\right]^2$

$= \dfrac{\sin^2\theta}{2} + \sin\theta\cos\theta + \dfrac{\cos^2\theta}{2} + \dfrac{\sin^2\theta}{2} - \sin\theta\cos\theta + \dfrac{\cos^2\theta}{2}$

$= \sin^2\theta + \cos^2\theta$

$= 1$

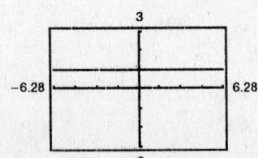

95. To prove the identity for $\sin(u + v)$ we first need to prove the identity for $\cos(u - v)$. Assume $0 < v < u < 2\pi$ and locate u, v, and $u - v$ on the unit circle.

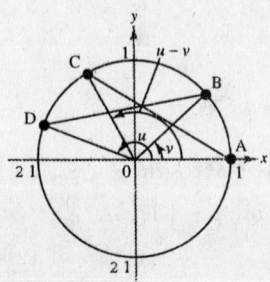

— **CONTINUED** —

95. — CONTINUED —

The coordinates of the points on the circle are:

$A = (1, 0)$, $B = (\cos v, \sin v)$, $C = (\cos(u - v), \sin(u - v))$, and $D = (\cos u, \sin u)$.

Since $\angle DOB = \angle COA$, chords AC and BD are equal. By the distance formula we have:

$$\sqrt{[\cos(u - v) - 1]^2 + [\sin(u - v) - 0]^2} = \sqrt{(\cos u - \cos v)^2 + (\sin u - \sin v)^2}$$

$$\cos^2(u - v) - 2\cos(u - v) + 1 + \sin^2(u - v) = \cos^2 u - 2\cos u \cos v + \cos^2 v + \sin^2 u - 2\sin u \sin v + \sin^2 v$$

$$[\cos^2(u + v) + \sin^2(u - v)] + 1 - 2\cos(u - v) = (\cos^2 u + \sin^2 u) + (\cos^2 v + \sin^2 v) - 2\cos u \cos v - 2\sin u \sin v$$

$$2 - 2\cos(u - v) = 2 - 2\cos u \cos v - 2\sin u \sin v$$

$$-2\cos(u - v) = -2(\cos u \cos v + \sin u \sin v)$$

$$\cos(u - v) = \cos u \cos v + \sin u \sin v$$

Now, to prove the identity for $\sin(u + v)$, use cofunction identities.

$$\sin(u + v) = \cos\left[\frac{\pi}{2} - (u + v)\right] = \cos\left[\left(\frac{\pi}{2} - u\right) - v\right]$$

$$= \cos\left(\frac{\pi}{2} - u\right)\cos v + \sin\left(\frac{\pi}{2} - u\right)\sin v$$

$$= \sin u \cos v + \cos u \sin v$$

97. $f(x) = 5(x - 3)$

$y = 5(x - 3)$

$\dfrac{y}{5} = x - 3$

$\dfrac{y}{5} + 3 = x$

$\dfrac{x}{5} + 3 = y$

$f^{-1}(x) = \dfrac{x + 15}{5}$

$f(f^{-1}(x)) = f\left(\dfrac{x + 15}{5}\right) = 5\left[\dfrac{x + 15}{5} - 3\right]$

$\qquad = 5\left(\dfrac{x + 15}{5}\right) - 5(3)$

$\qquad = x + 15 - 15$

$\qquad = x$

$f^{-1}(f(x)) = f^{-1}(5(x - 3)) = \dfrac{5(x - 3) + 15}{5}$

$\qquad = \dfrac{5x - 15 + 15}{5}$

$\qquad = \dfrac{5x}{5}$

$\qquad = x$

99. $f(x) = x^2 - 8$

f is not one-to-one so f^{-1} does not exist.

101. $\log_3 3^{4x - 3} = 4x - 3$

103. $e^{\ln(6x - 3)} = 6x - 3$

Section 5.5   Multiple–Angle and Product–to–Sum Formulas

■ You should know the following double-angle formulas.

(a) $\sin 2u = 2 \sin u \cos u$

(b) $\cos 2u = \cos^2 u - \sin^2 u$

$\quad\quad = 2 \cos^2 u - 1$

$\quad\quad = 1 - 2 \sin^2 u$

(c) $\tan 2u = \dfrac{2 \tan u}{1 - \tan^2 u}$

■ You should be able to reduce the power of a trigonometric function.

(a) $\sin^2 u = \dfrac{1 - \cos 2u}{2}$

(b) $\cos^2 u = \dfrac{1 + \cos 2u}{2}$

(c) $\tan^2 u = \dfrac{1 - \cos 2u}{1 + \cos 2u}$

■ You should be able to use the half-angle formulas.

(a) $\sin \dfrac{u}{2} = \pm \sqrt{\dfrac{1 - \cos u}{2}}$

(b) $\cos \dfrac{u}{2} = \pm \sqrt{\dfrac{1 + \cos u}{2}}$

(c) $\tan \dfrac{u}{2} = \dfrac{1 - \cos u}{\sin u} = \dfrac{\sin u}{1 + \cos u}$

■ You should be able to use the product-sum formulas.

(a) $\sin u \sin v = \dfrac{1}{2} \left[\cos(u - v) - \cos(u + v) \right]$

(b) $\cos u \cos v = \dfrac{1}{2} \left[\cos(u - v) + \cos(u + v) \right]$

(c) $\sin u \cos v = \dfrac{1}{2} \left[\sin(u + v) + \sin(u - v) \right]$

(d) $\cos u \sin v = \dfrac{1}{2} \left[\sin(u + v) - \sin(u - v) \right]$

■ You should be able to use the sum-product formulas.

(a) $\sin x + \sin y = 2 \sin\left(\dfrac{x + y}{2}\right) \cos\left(\dfrac{x - y}{2}\right)$

(b) $\sin x - \sin y = 2 \cos\left(\dfrac{x + y}{2}\right) \sin\left(\dfrac{x - y}{2}\right)$

(c) $\cos x + \cos y = 2 \cos\left(\dfrac{x + y}{2}\right) \cos\left(\dfrac{x - y}{2}\right)$

(d) $\cos x - \cos y = -2 \sin\left(\dfrac{x + y}{2}\right) \sin\left(\dfrac{x - y}{2}\right)$

Solutions to Odd-Numbered Exercises

Figure for Exercises 1–7

$$\sin \theta = \frac{\sqrt{17}}{17}$$

$$\cos \theta = \frac{4\sqrt{17}}{17}$$

$$\tan \theta = \frac{1}{4}$$

1. $\sin \theta = \dfrac{\sqrt{17}}{17}$

3.
$$\begin{aligned}
\cos 2\theta &= 2 \cos^2 \theta - 1 \\
&= 2\left(\frac{4\sqrt{17}}{17}\right)^2 - 1 \\
&= \frac{32}{17} - 1 \\
&= \frac{15}{17}
\end{aligned}$$

5.
$$\begin{aligned}
\tan 2\theta &= \frac{2 \tan \theta}{1 - \tan^2 \theta} \\
&= \frac{2\left(\frac{1}{4}\right)}{1 - \left(\frac{1}{4}\right)^2} \\
&= \frac{\frac{1}{2}}{1 - \frac{1}{16}} \\
&= \frac{1}{2} \cdot \frac{16}{15} \\
&= \frac{8}{15}
\end{aligned}$$

7.
$$\begin{aligned}
\csc 2\theta &= \frac{1}{\sin 2\theta} \\
&= \frac{1}{2 \sin \theta \cos \theta} \\
&= \frac{1}{2\left(\frac{\sqrt{17}}{17}\right)\left(\frac{4\sqrt{17}}{17}\right)} \\
&= \frac{17}{8}
\end{aligned}$$

9.
$$\begin{aligned}
\sin 2x - \sin x &= 0 \\
2 \sin x \cos x - \sin x &= 0 \\
\sin x(2 \cos x - 1) &= 0
\end{aligned}$$

$$\sin x = 0 \quad \text{or} \quad 2 \cos x - 1 = 0$$

$$x = 0, \pi \qquad \cos x = \frac{1}{2}$$

$$x = \frac{\pi}{3}, \frac{5\pi}{3}$$

$$x = 0, \frac{\pi}{3}, \pi, \frac{5\pi}{3}$$

11.
$$\begin{aligned}
4 \sin x \cos x &= 1 \\
2 \sin 2x &= 1 \\
\sin 2x &= \frac{1}{2}
\end{aligned}$$

$$2x = \frac{\pi}{6} + 2n\pi \quad \text{or} \quad 2x = \frac{5\pi}{6} + 2n\pi$$

$$x = \frac{\pi}{12} + n\pi \qquad x = \frac{5\pi}{12} + n\pi$$

$$x = \frac{\pi}{12}, \frac{13\pi}{12} \qquad x = \frac{5\pi}{12}, \frac{17\pi}{12}$$

13.
$$\cos 2x = \cos x$$
$$\cos^2 x - \sin^2 x = \cos x$$
$$\cos^2 x - (1 - \cos^2 x) - \cos x = 0$$
$$2\cos^2 x - \cos x - 1 = 0$$
$$(2\cos x + 1)(\cos x - 1) = 0$$
$$2\cos x + 1 = 0 \qquad \text{or} \quad \cos x - 1 = 0$$
$$\cos x = -\frac{1}{2} \qquad\qquad \cos x = 1$$
$$x = \frac{2\pi}{3}, \frac{4\pi}{3} \qquad\qquad x = 0$$

15.
$$\tan 2x - \cot x = 0$$
$$\frac{2\tan x}{1 - \tan^2 x} = \cot x$$
$$2\tan x = \cot x(1 - \tan^2 x)$$
$$2\tan x = \cot x - \cot x \tan^2 x$$
$$2\tan x = \cot x - \tan x$$
$$3\tan x = \cot x$$
$$3\tan x - \cot x = 0$$
$$3\tan x - \frac{1}{\tan x} = 0$$
$$\frac{3\tan^2 x - 1}{\tan x} = 0$$
$$\frac{1}{\tan x}(3\tan^2 x - 1) = 0$$
$$\cot x(3\tan^2 x - 1) = 0$$
$$\cot x = 0 \qquad \text{or} \quad 3\tan^2 x - 1 = 0$$
$$x = \frac{\pi}{2}, \frac{3\pi}{2} \qquad\qquad \tan^2 x = \frac{1}{3}$$
$$\tan x = \pm\frac{\sqrt{3}}{3}$$
$$x = \frac{\pi}{6}, \frac{5\pi}{6}, \frac{7\pi}{6}, \frac{11\pi}{6}$$
$$x = \frac{\pi}{6}, \frac{\pi}{2}, \frac{5\pi}{6}, \frac{7\pi}{6}, \frac{3\pi}{2}, \frac{11\pi}{6}$$

17.
$$\sin 4x = -2\sin 2x$$
$$\sin 4x + 2\sin 2x = 0$$
$$2\sin 2x \cos 2x + 2\sin 2x = 0$$
$$2\sin 2x(\cos 2x + 1) = 0$$
$$2\sin 2x = 0 \qquad \text{or} \quad \cos 2x + 1 = 0$$
$$\sin 2x = 0 \qquad\qquad \cos 2x = -1$$
$$2x = n\pi \qquad\qquad 2x = \pi + 2n\pi$$
$$x = \frac{n}{2}\pi \qquad\qquad x = \frac{\pi}{2} + n\pi$$
$$x = 0, \frac{\pi}{2}, \pi, \frac{3\pi}{2} \qquad\qquad x = \frac{\pi}{2}, \frac{3\pi}{2}$$

19. $6\sin x \cos x = 3(2\sin x \cos x)$
$$= 3\sin 2x$$

21. $4 - 8\sin^2 x = 4(1 - 2\sin^2 x)$
$$= 4\cos 2x$$

23. $\sin u = -\dfrac{4}{5}, \ \pi < u < \dfrac{3\pi}{2} \implies \cos u = -\dfrac{3}{5}$

$\sin 2u = 2 \sin u \cos u = 2\left(-\dfrac{4}{5}\right)\left(-\dfrac{3}{5}\right) = \dfrac{24}{25}$

$\cos 2u = \cos^2 u - \sin^2 u = \dfrac{9}{25} - \dfrac{16}{25} = -\dfrac{7}{25}$

$\tan 2u = \dfrac{2 \tan u}{1 - \tan^2 u} = \dfrac{2\left(\frac{4}{3}\right)}{1 - \frac{16}{9}} = \dfrac{8}{3}\left(-\dfrac{9}{7}\right) = -\dfrac{24}{7}$

25. $\tan u = \dfrac{3}{4}, \ 0 < u < \dfrac{\pi}{2} \implies \sin u = \dfrac{3}{5}$ and $\cos u = \dfrac{4}{5}$

$\sin 2u = 2 \sin u \cos u = 2\left(\dfrac{3}{5}\right)\left(\dfrac{4}{5}\right) = \dfrac{24}{25}$

$\cos 2u = \cos^2 u - \sin^2 u = \dfrac{16}{25} - \dfrac{9}{25} = \dfrac{7}{25}$

$\tan 2u = \dfrac{2 \tan u}{1 - \tan^2 u} = \dfrac{2\left(\frac{3}{4}\right)}{1 - \frac{9}{16}} = \dfrac{3}{2}\left(\dfrac{16}{7}\right) = \dfrac{24}{7}$

27. $\sec u = -\dfrac{5}{2}, \ \dfrac{\pi}{2} < u < \pi \implies \sin u = \dfrac{\sqrt{21}}{5}$ and $\cos u = -\dfrac{2}{5}$

$\sin 2u = 2 \sin u \cos u = 2\left(\dfrac{\sqrt{21}}{5}\right)\left(-\dfrac{2}{5}\right) = -\dfrac{4\sqrt{21}}{25}$

$\cos 2u = \cos^2 u - \sin^2 u = \left(-\dfrac{2}{5}\right)^2 - \left(\dfrac{\sqrt{21}}{5}\right)^2 = -\dfrac{17}{25}$

$\tan 2u = \dfrac{2 \tan u}{1 - \tan^2 u} = \dfrac{2\left(-\frac{\sqrt{21}}{2}\right)}{1 - \left(-\frac{\sqrt{21}}{2}\right)^2}$

$= \dfrac{-\sqrt{21}}{1 - \frac{21}{4}} = \dfrac{4\sqrt{21}}{17}$

29. $\cos^4 x = (\cos^2 x)(\cos^2 x) = \left(\dfrac{1 + \cos 2x}{2}\right)\left(\dfrac{1 + \cos 2x}{2}\right) = \dfrac{1 + 2\cos 2x + \cos^2 2x}{4}$

$= \dfrac{1 + 2\cos 2x + \dfrac{1 + \cos 4x}{2}}{4}$

$= \dfrac{2 + 4\cos 2x + 1 + \cos 4x}{8}$

$= \dfrac{3 + 4\cos 2x + \cos 4x}{8}$

$= \dfrac{1}{8}(3 + 4\cos 2x + \cos 4x)$

31. $(\sin^2 x)(\cos^2 x) = \left(\dfrac{1 - \cos 2x}{2}\right)\left(\dfrac{1 + \cos 2x}{2}\right)$

$$= \frac{1 - \cos^2 2x}{4}$$

$$= \frac{1}{4}\left(1 - \frac{1 + \cos 4x}{2}\right)$$

$$= \frac{1}{8}(2 - 1 - \cos 4x)$$

$$= \frac{1}{8}(1 - \cos 4x)$$

33. $\sin^2 x \cos^4 x = \sin^2 x \cos^2 x \cos^2 x = \left(\dfrac{1 - \cos 2x}{2}\right)\left(\dfrac{1 + \cos 2x}{2}\right)\left(\dfrac{1 + \cos 2x}{2}\right)$

$$= \frac{1}{8}(1 - \cos 2x)(1 + \cos 2x)(1 + \cos 2x)$$

$$= \frac{1}{8}(1 - \cos^2 2x)(1 + \cos 2x)$$

$$= \frac{1}{8}(1 + \cos 2x - \cos^2 2x - \cos^3 2x)$$

$$= \frac{1}{8}\left[1 + \cos 2x - \left(\frac{1 + \cos 4x}{2}\right) - \cos 2x\left(\frac{1 + \cos 4x}{2}\right)\right]$$

$$= \frac{1}{16}[2 + 2\cos 2x - 1 - \cos 4x - \cos 2x - \cos 2x \cos 4x]$$

$$= \frac{1}{16}\left[1 + \cos 2x - \cos 4x - \left(\frac{1}{2}\cos 2x + \frac{1}{2}\cos 6x\right)\right]$$

$$= \frac{1}{32}(2 + 2\cos 2x - 2\cos 4x - \cos 2x - \cos 6x)$$

$$= \frac{1}{32}(2 + \cos 2x - 2\cos 4x - \cos 6x)$$

Figure for Exercises 35 – 39

$\sin \theta = \frac{8}{17}$

$\cos \theta = \frac{15}{17}$

35. $\cos \dfrac{\theta}{2} = \sqrt{\dfrac{1 + \cos \theta}{2}} = \sqrt{\dfrac{1 + \frac{15}{17}}{2}} = \sqrt{\dfrac{32}{34}} = \sqrt{\dfrac{16}{17}} = \dfrac{4\sqrt{17}}{17}$

37. $\tan \dfrac{\theta}{2} = \dfrac{\sin \theta}{1 + \cos \theta} = \dfrac{\frac{8}{17}}{1 + \frac{15}{17}} = \dfrac{8}{17} \cdot \dfrac{17}{32} = \dfrac{1}{4}$

39. $\csc \dfrac{\theta}{2} = \dfrac{1}{\sin \frac{\theta}{2}} = \dfrac{1}{\sqrt{\dfrac{(1 - \cos \theta)}{2}}} = \dfrac{1}{\sqrt{\dfrac{1 - \frac{15}{17}}{2}}} = \dfrac{1}{\sqrt{\dfrac{1}{17}}} = \sqrt{17}$

41. $\sin 75° = \sin\left(\frac{1}{2} \cdot 150°\right) = \sqrt{\frac{1 - \cos 150°}{2}} = \sqrt{\frac{1 + \frac{\sqrt{3}}{2}}{2}}$

$\qquad = \frac{1}{2}\sqrt{2 + \sqrt{3}}$

$\cos 75° = \cos\left(\frac{1}{2} \cdot 150°\right) = \sqrt{\frac{1 + \cos 150°}{2}} = \sqrt{\frac{1 - \frac{\sqrt{3}}{2}}{2}}$

$\qquad = \frac{1}{2}\sqrt{2 - \sqrt{3}}$

$\tan 75° = \tan\left(\frac{1}{2} \cdot 150°\right) = \frac{\sin 150°}{1 + \cos 150°} = \frac{\frac{1}{2}}{1 - \frac{\sqrt{3}}{2}}$

$\qquad = \frac{1}{2 - \sqrt{3}} \cdot \frac{2 + \sqrt{3}}{2 + \sqrt{3}} = \frac{2 + \sqrt{3}}{4 - 3} = 2 + \sqrt{3}$

43. $\sin 112° \, 30' = \sin\left(\frac{1}{2} \cdot 225°\right) = \sqrt{\frac{1 - \cos 225°}{2}} = \sqrt{\frac{1 + \frac{\sqrt{2}}{2}}{2}} = \frac{1}{2}\sqrt{2 + \sqrt{2}}$

$\cos 112° \, 30' = \cos\left(\frac{1}{2} \cdot 225°\right) = -\sqrt{\frac{1 + \cos 225°}{2}} = -\sqrt{\frac{1 - \frac{\sqrt{2}}{2}}{2}} = -\frac{1}{2}\sqrt{2 - \sqrt{2}}$

$\tan 112° \, 30' = \tan\left(\frac{1}{2} \cdot 225°\right) = \frac{\sin 225°}{1 + \cos 225°} = \frac{-\frac{\sqrt{2}}{2}}{1 - \frac{\sqrt{2}}{2}} = -1 - \sqrt{2}$

45. $\sin\frac{\pi}{8} = \sin\left[\frac{1}{2}\left(\frac{\pi}{4}\right)\right] = \sqrt{\frac{1 - \cos\frac{\pi}{4}}{2}} = \frac{1}{2}\sqrt{2 - \sqrt{2}}$

$\cos\frac{\pi}{8} = \cos\left[\frac{1}{2}\left(\frac{\pi}{4}\right)\right] = \sqrt{\frac{1 + \cos\frac{\pi}{4}}{2}} = \frac{1}{2}\sqrt{2 + \sqrt{2}}$

$\tan\frac{\pi}{8} = \tan\left[\frac{1}{2}\left(\frac{\pi}{4}\right)\right] = \frac{\sin\frac{\pi}{4}}{1 + \cos\frac{\pi}{4}} = \frac{\frac{\sqrt{2}}{2}}{1 + \frac{\sqrt{2}}{2}} = \sqrt{2} - 1$

47. $\sin\frac{3\pi}{8} = \sin\left(\frac{1}{2} \cdot \frac{3\pi}{4}\right) = \sqrt{\frac{1 - \cos\frac{3\pi}{4}}{2}} = \sqrt{\frac{1 + \frac{\sqrt{2}}{2}}{2}} = \frac{1}{2}\sqrt{2 + \sqrt{2}}$

$\cos\frac{3\pi}{8} = \cos\left(\frac{1}{2} \cdot \frac{3\pi}{4}\right) = \sqrt{\frac{1 + \cos\frac{3\pi}{4}}{2}} = \sqrt{\frac{1 - \frac{\sqrt{2}}{2}}{2}} = \frac{1}{2}\sqrt{2 - \sqrt{2}}$

$\tan\frac{3\pi}{8} = \tan\left(\frac{1}{2} \cdot \frac{3\pi}{4}\right) = \frac{\sin\frac{3\pi}{4}}{1 + \cos\frac{3\pi}{4}} = \frac{\frac{\sqrt{2}}{2}}{1 - \frac{\sqrt{2}}{2}} = \frac{\frac{\sqrt{2}}{2}}{\frac{(2 - \sqrt{2})}{2}} = \frac{\sqrt{2}}{2 - \sqrt{2}} = \sqrt{2} + 1$

49. $\sin u = \dfrac{5}{13}, \dfrac{\pi}{2} < u < \pi \implies \cos u = -\dfrac{12}{13}$

$$\sin\left(\frac{u}{2}\right) = \sqrt{\frac{1 - \cos u}{2}} = \sqrt{\frac{1 + \frac{12}{13}}{2}} = \frac{5\sqrt{26}}{26}$$

$$\cos\left(\frac{u}{2}\right) = \sqrt{\frac{1 + \cos u}{2}} = \sqrt{\frac{1 - \frac{12}{13}}{2}} = \frac{\sqrt{26}}{26}$$

$$\tan\left(\frac{u}{2}\right) = \frac{\sin u}{1 + \cos u} = \frac{\frac{5}{13}}{1 - \frac{12}{13}} = 5$$

51. $\tan u = -\dfrac{5}{8}, \dfrac{3\pi}{2} < u < 2\pi \implies \sin u = -\dfrac{5}{\sqrt{89}}$ and $\cos u = \dfrac{8}{\sqrt{89}}$

$$\sin\left(\frac{u}{2}\right) = \sqrt{\frac{1 - \cos u}{2}} = \sqrt{\frac{1 - \frac{8}{\sqrt{89}}}{2}} \sqrt{\frac{\sqrt{89} - 8}{2\sqrt{89}}} = \sqrt{\frac{89 - 8\sqrt{89}}{178}}$$

$$\cos\left(\frac{u}{2}\right) = -\sqrt{\frac{1 + \cos u}{2}} = -\sqrt{\frac{1 + \frac{8}{\sqrt{89}}}{2}} = -\sqrt{\frac{\sqrt{89} + 8}{2\sqrt{89}}} = -\sqrt{\frac{89 + 8\sqrt{89}}{178}}$$

$$\tan\left(\frac{u}{2}\right) = \frac{1 - \cos u}{\sin u} = \frac{1 - \frac{8}{\sqrt{89}}}{-\frac{5}{\sqrt{89}}} = \frac{8 - \sqrt{89}}{5}$$

53. $\csc u = -\dfrac{5}{3}, \pi < u < \dfrac{3\pi}{2} \implies \sin u = -\dfrac{3}{5}$ and $\cos u = -\dfrac{4}{5}$

$$\sin\left(\frac{u}{2}\right) = \sqrt{\frac{1 - \cos u}{2}} = \sqrt{\frac{1 + \frac{4}{5}}{2}} = \frac{3\sqrt{10}}{10}$$

$$\cos\left(\frac{u}{2}\right) = -\sqrt{\frac{1 + \cos u}{2}} = -\sqrt{\frac{1 - \frac{4}{5}}{2}} = -\frac{\sqrt{10}}{10}$$

$$\tan\left(\frac{u}{2}\right) = \frac{1 - \cos u}{\sin u} = \frac{1 + \frac{4}{5}}{-\frac{3}{5}} = -3$$

55. $\sqrt{\dfrac{1 - \cos 6x}{2}} = |\sin 3x|$

57. $-\sqrt{\dfrac{1 - \cos 8x}{1 + \cos 8x}} = -\dfrac{\sqrt{\dfrac{1 - \cos 8x}{2}}}{\sqrt{\dfrac{1 + \cos 8x}{2}}}$

$$= -\left|\frac{\sin 4x}{\cos 4x}\right|$$

$$= -|\tan 4x|$$

59. $\sin \dfrac{x}{2} + \cos x = 0$

$$\pm \sqrt{\dfrac{1 - \cos x}{2}} = -\cos x$$

$$\dfrac{1 - \cos x}{2} = \cos^2 x$$

$$0 = 2\cos^2 x + \cos x - 1$$

$$= (2\cos x - 1)(\cos x + 1)$$

$$\cos x = \dfrac{1}{2} \quad \text{or} \quad \cos x = -1$$

$$x = \dfrac{\pi}{3}, \dfrac{5\pi}{3} \qquad x = \pi$$

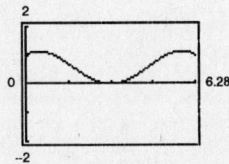

By checking these values in the original equation, we see that $x = \pi/3$ and $x = 5\pi/3$ are extraneous, and $x = \pi$ is the only solution.

61. $\cos \dfrac{x}{2} - \sin x = 0$

$$\pm \sqrt{\dfrac{1 + \cos x}{2}} = \sin x$$

$$\dfrac{1 + \cos x}{2} = \sin^2 x$$

$$1 + \cos x = 2\sin^2 x$$

$$1 + \cos x = 2 - 2\cos^2 x$$

$$2\cos^2 x + \cos x - 1 = 0$$

$$(2\cos x - 1)(\cos x + 1) = 0$$

$$2\cos x - 1 = 0 \quad \text{or} \quad \cos x + 1 = 0$$

$$\cos x = \dfrac{1}{2} \qquad\qquad \cos x = -1$$

$$x = \dfrac{\pi}{3}, \dfrac{5\pi}{3} \qquad\qquad x = \pi$$

$$x = \dfrac{\pi}{3}, \ \pi, \ \dfrac{5\pi}{3}$$

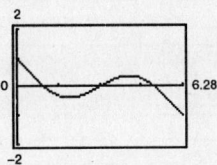

$\pi/3$, π, and $5\pi/3$ are all solutions to the equation.

63. $6 \sin \dfrac{\pi}{4} \cos \dfrac{\pi}{4} = 6 \cdot \dfrac{1}{2}\left[\sin\left(\dfrac{\pi}{4} + \dfrac{\pi}{4}\right) + \sin\left(\dfrac{\pi}{4} - \dfrac{\pi}{4}\right) \right] = 3\left(\sin \dfrac{\pi}{2} + \sin 0 \right)$

65. $\cos 4\theta \sin 6\theta = \dfrac{1}{2}[\sin(4\theta + 6\theta) - \sin(4\theta - 6\theta)] = \dfrac{1}{2}[\sin 10\theta - \sin(-2\theta)]$

$$= \dfrac{1}{2}(\sin 10\theta + \sin 2\theta)$$

67. $5 \cos(-5\beta) \cos 3\beta = 5 \cdot \dfrac{1}{2}[\cos(-5\beta - 3\beta) + \cos(-5\beta + 3\beta)] = \dfrac{5}{2}[\cos(-8\beta) + \cos(-2\beta)]$

$$= \dfrac{5}{2}(\cos 8\beta + \cos 2\beta)$$

69. $\sin(x + y) \sin(x - y) = \dfrac{1}{2}(\cos 2y - \cos 2x)$

71. $\cos(\theta - \pi) \sin(\theta + \pi) = \dfrac{1}{2}(\sin 2\theta + \sin 2\pi)$

73. $10 \cos 75° \cos 15° = 10\left(\dfrac{1}{2}\right)[\cos(75° - 15°) + \cos(75° + 15°)] = 5[\cos 60° + \cos 90°]$

75. $\sin 60° + \sin 30° = 2 \sin\left(\dfrac{60° + 30°}{2}\right) \cos\left(\dfrac{60° - 30°}{2}\right) = 2 \sin 45° \cos 15°$

77. $\cos \dfrac{3\pi}{4} - \cos \dfrac{\pi}{4} = -2 \sin\left(\dfrac{\dfrac{3\pi}{4} + \dfrac{\pi}{4}}{2}\right) \sin\left(\dfrac{\dfrac{3\pi}{4} - \dfrac{\pi}{4}}{2}\right) = -2 \sin \dfrac{\pi}{2} \sin \dfrac{\pi}{4}$

79. $\sin 5\theta - \sin 3\theta = 2\cos\left(\dfrac{5\theta + 3\theta}{2}\right)\sin\left(\dfrac{5\theta - 3\theta}{2}\right) = 2\cos 4\theta \sin\theta$

81. $\cos 6x + \cos 2x = 2\cos\left(\dfrac{6x + 2x}{2}\right)\cos\left(\dfrac{6x - 2x}{2}\right) = 2\cos 4x \cos 2x$

83. $\sin(\alpha + \beta) - \sin(\alpha - \beta) = 2\cos\left(\dfrac{\alpha + \beta + \alpha - \beta}{2}\right)\sin\left(\dfrac{\alpha + \beta - \alpha + \beta}{2}\right) = 2\cos\alpha \sin\beta$

85. $\cos\left(\theta + \dfrac{\pi}{2}\right) - \cos\left(\theta - \dfrac{\pi}{2}\right) = -2\sin\left[\dfrac{\left(\theta + \dfrac{\pi}{2}\right) + \left(\theta - \dfrac{\pi}{2}\right)}{2}\right]\sin\left[\dfrac{\left(\theta + \dfrac{\pi}{2}\right) - \left(\theta - \dfrac{\pi}{2}\right)}{2}\right]$

$$= -2\sin\theta \sin\dfrac{\pi}{2}$$

87.
$$\sin 6x + \sin 2x = 0$$
$$2\sin\left(\dfrac{6x + 2x}{2}\right)\cos\left(\dfrac{6x - 2x}{2}\right) = 0$$
$$2(\sin 4x)\cos 2x = 0$$

$\sin 4x = 0$ or $\cos 2x = 0$

$$4x = n\pi \qquad\qquad 2x = \dfrac{\pi}{2} + n\pi$$

$$x = \dfrac{n\pi}{4} \qquad\qquad x = \dfrac{\pi}{4} + \dfrac{n\pi}{2}$$

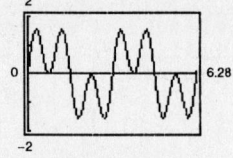

In the interval $[0, 2\pi)$ we have

$$x = 0,\ \dfrac{\pi}{4},\ \dfrac{\pi}{2},\ \dfrac{3\pi}{4},\ \pi,\ \dfrac{5\pi}{4},\ \dfrac{3\pi}{2},\ \dfrac{7\pi}{4}.$$

89. $\dfrac{\cos 2x}{\sin 3x - \sin x} - 1 = 0$

$$\dfrac{\cos 2x}{\sin 3x - \sin x} = 1$$

$$\dfrac{\cos 2x}{2\cos 2x \sin x} = 1$$

$$2\sin x = 1$$

$$\sin x = \dfrac{1}{2}$$

$$x = \dfrac{\pi}{6},\ \dfrac{5\pi}{6}$$

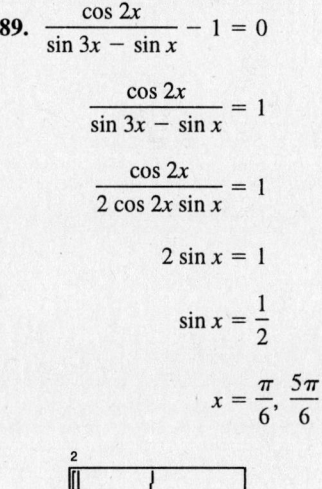

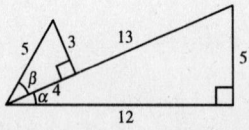

Figure for Exercises 91 and 93

91. $\sin^2\alpha = \left(\dfrac{5}{13}\right)^2 = \dfrac{25}{169}$

$\sin^2\alpha = 1 - \cos^2\alpha = 1 - \left(\dfrac{12}{13}\right)^2$

$$= 1 - \dfrac{144}{169} = \dfrac{25}{169}$$

93. $\sin\alpha \cos\beta = \left(\dfrac{5}{13}\right)\left(\dfrac{4}{5}\right) = \dfrac{4}{13}$

$\sin\alpha \cos\beta = \cos\left(\dfrac{\pi}{2} - \alpha\right)\sin\left(\dfrac{\pi}{2} - \beta\right)$

$$= \left(\dfrac{5}{13}\right)\left(\dfrac{4}{5}\right) = \dfrac{4}{13}$$

95. $\csc 2\theta = \dfrac{1}{\sin 2\theta}$

$\qquad = \dfrac{1}{2\sin\theta\cos\theta}$

$\qquad = \dfrac{1}{\sin\theta} \cdot \dfrac{1}{2\cos\theta}$

$\qquad = \dfrac{\csc\theta}{2\cos\theta}$

97. $\cos^2 2\alpha - \sin^2 2\alpha = \cos\left[2(2\alpha)\right]$

$\qquad\qquad\qquad\quad = \cos 4\alpha$

99. $(\sin x + \cos x)^2 = \sin^2 x + 2\sin x\cos x + \cos^2 x$

$\qquad\qquad\qquad = (\sin^2 x + \cos^2 x) + 2\sin x\cos x$

$\qquad\qquad\qquad = 1 + \sin 2x$

101. $1 + \cos 10y = 1 + \cos^2 5y - \sin^2 5y$

$\qquad\qquad\quad = 1 + \cos^2 5y - (1 - \cos^2 5y)$

$\qquad\qquad\quad = 2\cos^2 5y$

103. $\sec\dfrac{u}{2} = \dfrac{1}{\cos\dfrac{u}{2}}$

$\qquad = \pm\sqrt{\dfrac{2}{1 + \cos u}}$

$\qquad = \pm\sqrt{\dfrac{2\sin u}{\sin u(1 + \cos u)}}$

$\qquad = \pm\sqrt{\dfrac{2\sin u}{\sin u + \sin u\cos u}}$

$\qquad = \pm\sqrt{\dfrac{\dfrac{2\sin u}{\cos u}}{\dfrac{\sin u}{\cos u} + \dfrac{\sin u\cos u}{\cos u}}}$

$\qquad = \pm\sqrt{\dfrac{2\tan u}{\tan u + \sin u}}$

105. $\dfrac{\sin x \pm \sin y}{\cos x + \cos y} = \dfrac{2\sin\left(\dfrac{x \pm y}{2}\right)\cos\left(\dfrac{x \mp y}{2}\right)}{2\cos\left(\dfrac{x + y}{2}\right)\cos\left(\dfrac{x - y}{2}\right)}$

$\qquad\qquad\qquad = \tan\left(\dfrac{x \pm y}{2}\right)$

107. $\dfrac{\cos 4x + \cos 2x}{\sin 4x + \sin 2x} = \dfrac{2\cos\left(\dfrac{4x + 2x}{2}\right)\cos\left(\dfrac{4x - 2x}{2}\right)}{2\sin\left(\dfrac{4x + 2x}{2}\right)\cos\left(\dfrac{4x - 2x}{2}\right)}$

$\qquad\qquad\qquad = \dfrac{2\cos 3x\cos x}{2\sin 3x\cos x}$

$\qquad\qquad\qquad = \cot 3x$

109. $\sin\left(\dfrac{\pi}{6} + x\right) + \sin\left(\dfrac{\pi}{6} - x\right) = 2\sin\dfrac{\pi}{6}\cos x$

$\qquad\qquad\qquad\qquad\qquad = 2 \cdot \dfrac{1}{2}\cos x$

$\qquad\qquad\qquad\qquad\qquad = \cos x$

111. $\cos 3\beta = \cos(2\beta + \beta)$

$\qquad = \cos 2\beta \cos\beta - \sin 2\beta \sin\beta$

$\qquad = (\cos^2\beta - \sin^2\beta)\cos\beta - 2\sin\beta\cos\beta\sin\beta$

$\qquad = \cos^3\beta - \sin^2\beta\cos\beta - 2\sin^2\beta\cos\beta$

$\qquad = \cos^3\beta - 3\sin^2\beta\cos\beta$

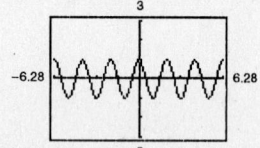

113. $\dfrac{\cos 4x - \cos 2x}{2\sin 3x} = \dfrac{-2\sin\left(\dfrac{4x + 2x}{2}\right)\sin\left(\dfrac{4x - 2x}{2}\right)}{2\sin 3x}$

$\qquad\qquad = \dfrac{-2\sin 3x \sin x}{2\sin 3x}$

$\qquad\qquad = -\sin x$

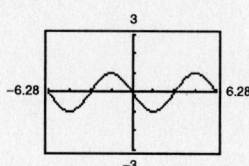

115. $\sin^2 x = \dfrac{1 - \cos 2x}{2} = \dfrac{1}{2} - \dfrac{\cos 2x}{2}$

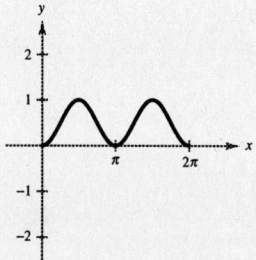

117. $\sin(2\arcsin x) = 2\sin(\arcsin x)\cos(\arcsin x) = 2x\sqrt{1 - x^2}$

119. (a) $\qquad A = \dfrac{1}{2}bh$

$\qquad \cos\dfrac{\theta}{2} = \dfrac{h}{10} \implies h = 10\cos\dfrac{\theta}{2}$

$\qquad \sin\dfrac{\theta}{2} = \dfrac{(1/2)b}{10} \implies \dfrac{1}{2}b = 10\sin\dfrac{\theta}{2}$

$\qquad A = 10\sin\dfrac{\theta}{2}10\cos\dfrac{\theta}{2} \implies A = 100\sin\dfrac{\theta}{2}\cos\dfrac{\theta}{2}$

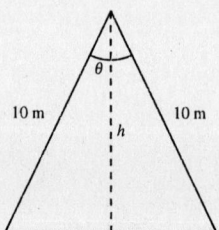

(b) $A = 100\sin\dfrac{\theta}{2}\cos\dfrac{\theta}{2}$

$\quad A = 50\left(2\sin\dfrac{\theta}{2}\cos\dfrac{\theta}{2}\right)$

$\quad A = 50\sin\theta$

When $\theta = \pi/2$, $\sin\theta = 1 \implies$ the area is a maximum.

$A = 50\sin\dfrac{\pi}{2} = 50(1) = 50$ square feet

121. $\sin \dfrac{\theta}{2} = \dfrac{1}{4.5}$

$$\dfrac{\theta}{2} = \arcsin\left(\dfrac{1}{4.5}\right)$$

$$\theta = 2 \arcsin\left(\dfrac{1}{4.5}\right)$$

$$\theta \approx 0.4482$$

123. False. For $u < 0$,

$$\sin 2u = -\sin(-2u)$$

$$= -2\sin(-u)\cos(-u)$$

$$= -2(-\sin u)\cos u$$

$$= 2\sin u \cos u$$

125. (a) $y = 4\sin\dfrac{x}{2} + \cos x$

Maximum: $(\pi, 3)$

(b) $\qquad 2\cos\dfrac{x}{2} - \sin x = 0$

$$2\left(\pm\sqrt{\dfrac{1 + \cos x}{2}}\right) = \sin x$$

$$4\left(\dfrac{1 + \cos x}{2}\right) = \sin^2 x$$

$$2(1 + \cos x) = 1 - \cos^2 x$$

$$\cos^2 x + 2\cos x + 1 = 0$$

$$(\cos x + 1)^2 = 0$$

$$\cos x = -1$$

$$x = \pi$$

127. $f(x) = \sin^4 x + \cos^4 x$

(a) $\sin^4 x + \cos^4 x = (\sin^2 x)^2 + (\cos^2 x)^2$

$$= \left(\dfrac{1 - \cos 2x}{2}\right)^2 + \left(\dfrac{1 + \cos 2x}{2}\right)^2$$

$$= \dfrac{1}{4}[(1 - \cos 2x)^2 + (1 + \cos 2x)^2]$$

$$= \dfrac{1}{4}(1 - 2\cos 2x + \cos^2 2x + 1 + 2\cos 2x + \cos^2 2x)$$

$$= \dfrac{1}{4}(2 + 2\cos^2 2x)$$

$$= \dfrac{1}{4}\left[2 + 2\left(\dfrac{1 + \cos 2(2x)}{2}\right)\right]$$

$$= \dfrac{1}{4}(3 + \cos 4x)$$

(b) $\sin^4 x + \cos^4 x = (\sin^2 x)^2 + \cos^4 x$

$$= (1 - \cos^2 x)^2 + \cos^4 x$$

$$= 1 - 2\cos^2 x + \cos^4 x + \cos^4 x$$

$$= 2\cos^4 x - 2\cos^2 x + 1$$

(c) $\sin^4 x + \cos^4 x = \sin^4 x + 2\sin^2 x \cos^2 x + \cos^4 x - 2\sin^2 x \cos^2 x$

$$= (\sin^2 x + \cos^2 x)^2 - 2\sin^2 x \cos^2 x$$

$$= 1 - 2\sin^2 x \cos^2 x$$

— CONTINUED —

127. — CONTINUED —

(d) $1 - 2 \sin^2 x \cos^2 x = 1 - (2 \sin x \cos x)(\sin x \cos x)$

$$= 1 - (\sin 2x)\left(\frac{1}{2} \sin 2x\right)$$

$$= 1 - \frac{1}{2} \sin^2 2x$$

(e) No, it does not mean that one of you is wrong. There is often more than one way to rewrite a trigonometric expression.

129. Let x = profit for September,
then $x + 0.16x$ = profit for October.

$$x + (x + 0.16x) = 507{,}600$$

$$2.16x = 507{,}600$$

$$x = 235{,}000$$

$$x + 0.16x = 272{,}600$$

Profit for September: $235,000

Profit for October: $272,600

131. Let x = number of gallons of 100% concentrate.

$$0.30(55 - x) + 1.00x = 0.50(55)$$

$$16.50 - 0.30x + x = 27.50$$

$$0.70x = 11$$

$$x \approx 15.7 \text{ gallons}$$

Review Exercises for Chapter 5

Solutions to Odd-Numbered Exercises

1. $\dfrac{1}{\cos x} = \sec x$

3. $\dfrac{1}{\sec x} = \cos x$

5. $\dfrac{\cos x}{\sin x} = \cot x$

7. $\sin x = \dfrac{3}{5},\ \cos x = \dfrac{4}{5}$

$$\tan x = \frac{\sin x}{\cos x} = \frac{\frac{3}{5}}{\frac{4}{5}} = \frac{3}{4}$$

$$\cot x = \frac{1}{\tan x} = \frac{4}{3}$$

$$\sec x = \frac{1}{\cos x} = \frac{5}{4}$$

$$\csc x = \frac{1}{\sin x} = \frac{5}{3}$$

9. $\sin\left(\dfrac{\pi}{2} - x\right) = \dfrac{\sqrt{2}}{2} \Rightarrow \cos x = \dfrac{1}{\sqrt{2}} = \dfrac{\sqrt{2}}{2},\ \sin x = -\dfrac{\sqrt{2}}{2}$

$$\tan x = \frac{\sin x}{\cos x} = \frac{-\dfrac{1}{\sqrt{2}}}{\dfrac{1}{\sqrt{2}}} = -1$$

$$\cot x = \frac{1}{\tan x} = -1$$

$$\sec x = \frac{1}{\cos x} = \sqrt{2}$$

$$\csc x = \frac{1}{\sin x} = -\sqrt{2}$$

11. $\dfrac{1}{\cot^2 x + 1} = \dfrac{1}{\csc^2 x} = \sin^2 x$

13. $\tan^2 x(\csc^2 x - 1) = \tan^2 x(\cot^2 x) = \tan^2 x\left(\dfrac{1}{\tan^2 x}\right) = 1$

15. $\dfrac{\sin\left(\dfrac{\pi}{2} - \theta\right)}{\sin \theta} = \dfrac{\cos \theta}{\sin \theta} = \cot \theta$

17. $\cos^2 x + \cos^2 x \cot^2 x = \cos^2 x(1 + \cot^2 x) = \cos^2 x(\csc^2 x)$

$$= \cos^2 x\left(\frac{1}{\sin^2 x}\right) = \frac{\cos^2 x}{\sin^2 x} = \cot^2 x$$

19. $(\tan x + 1)^2\cos x = (\tan^2 x + 2\tan x + 1)\cos x$

$$= (\sec^2 x + 2\tan x)\cos x$$

$$= \sec^2 x \cos x + 2\left(\frac{\sin x}{\cos x}\right)\cos x = \sec x + 2\sin x$$

21. $\dfrac{1}{\csc\theta + 1} - \dfrac{1}{\csc\theta - 1} = \dfrac{(\csc\theta - 1) - (\csc\theta + 1)}{(\csc\theta + 1)(\csc\theta - 1)}$

$\qquad\qquad\qquad\qquad\qquad = \dfrac{-2}{\csc^2\theta - 1}$

$\qquad\qquad\qquad\qquad\qquad = \dfrac{-2}{\cot^2\theta}$

$\qquad\qquad\qquad\qquad\qquad = -2\tan^2\theta$

23. $\sin^{-1/2} x\cos x = \dfrac{1}{\sqrt{\sin x}}(\cos x) = \dfrac{\sqrt{\sin x}}{\sin x}(\cos x)$

$\qquad\qquad\qquad = \sqrt{\sin x}\left(\dfrac{\cos x}{\sin x}\right) = \sqrt{\sin x}\cot x$

25. $\sec^2 x\cot x - \cot x = \cot x(\sec^2 x - 1) = \cot x\tan^2 x$

$\qquad\qquad\qquad\qquad = \left(\dfrac{1}{\tan x}\right)\tan^2 x = \tan x$

27. $\cot\left(\dfrac{\pi}{2} - x\right) = \tan x$ by the Cofunction Identity

29. $\dfrac{1}{\tan x\csc x\sin x} = \dfrac{1}{(\tan x)\left(\dfrac{1}{\sin x}\right)(\sin x)} = \dfrac{1}{\tan x}$

$\qquad\qquad\qquad\qquad = \cot x$

31. $\cos^3 x\sin^2 x = \cos x\cos^2 x\sin^2 x$

$\qquad\qquad\quad = \cos x(1 - \sin^2 x)\sin^2 x$

$\qquad\qquad\quad = \cos x(\sin^2 x - \sin^4 x)$

$\qquad\qquad\quad = (\sin^2 x - \sin^4 x)\cos x$

33. $4\cos\theta = 1 + 2\cos\theta$

$\qquad 2\cos\theta = 1$

$\qquad \cos\theta = \dfrac{1}{2}$

$\qquad \theta = \dfrac{\pi}{3} + 2n\pi$ or $\dfrac{5\pi}{3} + 2n\pi$

35. $\dfrac{1}{2}\sec x - 1 = 0$

$\qquad \dfrac{1}{2}\sec x = 1$

$\qquad \sec x = 2$

$\qquad \cos x = \dfrac{1}{2}$

$\qquad x = \dfrac{\pi}{3} + 2n\pi$ or $\dfrac{5\pi}{3} + 2n\pi$

37. $4\tan^2 u - 1 = \tan^2 u$

$\qquad 3\tan^2 u - 1 = 0$

$\qquad \tan^2 u = \dfrac{1}{3}$

$\qquad \tan u = \pm\dfrac{1}{\sqrt{3}} = \pm\dfrac{\sqrt{3}}{3}$

$\qquad u = \dfrac{\pi}{6} + n\pi$ or $\dfrac{5\pi}{6} + n\pi$

39. $\qquad 2\sin^2 x - 3\sin x = -1$

$\qquad 2\sin^2 x - 3\sin x + 1 = 0$

$\qquad (2\sin x - 1)(\sin x - 1) = 0$

$\qquad 2\sin x - 1 = 0$ or $\sin x - 1 = 0$

$\qquad\quad \sin x = \dfrac{1}{2}$ $\sin x = 1$

$\qquad\quad x = \dfrac{\pi}{6}, \dfrac{5\pi}{6}$ $x = \dfrac{\pi}{2}$

41. $\qquad \sin^2 x + 2\cos x = 2$

$\qquad 1 - \cos^2 x + 2\cos x = 2$

$\qquad\qquad 0 = \cos^2 x - 2\cos x + 1$

$\qquad\qquad 0 = (\cos x - 1)^2$

$\qquad\quad \cos x - 1 = 0$

$\qquad\qquad \cos x = 1$

$\qquad\qquad\quad x = 0$

43. $\sqrt{3}\tan 3x = 0$

$\qquad \tan 3x = 0$

$\qquad 3x = 0, \pi, 2\pi, 3\pi, 4\pi, 5\pi$

$\qquad x = 0, \dfrac{\pi}{3}, \dfrac{2\pi}{3}, \pi, \dfrac{4\pi}{3}, \dfrac{5\pi}{3}$

45. $3 \csc^2 5x = -4$

$$\csc^2 5x = -\frac{4}{3}$$

$$\csc 5x = \pm \sqrt{-\frac{4}{3}}$$

No real solution

47. $2 \cos^2 x + 3 \cos x = 0$

$$\cos x(2 \cos x + 3) = 0$$

$$\cos x = 0 \quad \text{or} \quad 2 \cos x + 3 = 0$$

$$x = \frac{\pi}{2}, \frac{3\pi}{2} \qquad 2 \cos x = -3$$

$$\cos x = -\frac{3}{2}$$

No solution

49. $\sec^2 x - 6 \tan x + 4 = 0$

$$1 + \tan^2 x + 6 \tan x + 4 = 0$$

$$\tan^2 x + 6 \tan x + 5 = 0$$

$$(\tan x + 5)(\tan x + 1) = 0$$

$$\tan x + 5 = 0 \quad \text{or} \qquad \tan x + 1 = 0$$

$$\tan x = -5 \qquad\qquad \tan x = -1$$

$$x = \arctan(-5) + \pi \qquad x = \frac{3\pi}{4}, \frac{7\pi}{4}$$

$$x = \arctan(-5) + 2\pi$$

51. $\sin(345°) = \sin(300° + 45°)$

$$= \sin 300° \cos 45° + \cos 300° \sin 45°$$

$$= -\frac{\sqrt{3}}{2} \cdot \frac{\sqrt{2}}{2} + \frac{1}{2} \cdot \frac{\sqrt{2}}{2}$$

$$= \frac{\sqrt{2}}{4}\left(-\sqrt{3} + 1\right) = \frac{\sqrt{2}}{4}\left(1 - \sqrt{3}\right)$$

$\cos(345°) = \cos(300° + 45°)$

$$= \cos 300° \cos 45° - \sin 300° \sin 45°$$

$$= \frac{1}{2} \cdot \frac{\sqrt{2}}{2} - \left(-\frac{\sqrt{3}}{2}\right)\frac{\sqrt{2}}{2}$$

$$= \frac{\sqrt{2}}{4}\left(1 + \sqrt{3}\right)$$

$\tan(345°) = \tan(300° + 45°)$

$$= \frac{\tan 300° + \tan 45°}{1 - \tan 300° \tan 45°} = \frac{-\sqrt{3} + 1}{1 + \sqrt{3}(1)} \cdot \frac{1 - \sqrt{3}}{1 - \sqrt{3}}$$

$$= \frac{4 - 2\sqrt{3}}{-2} = -2 + \sqrt{3}$$

53. $\sin\left(\dfrac{19\pi}{12}\right) = \sin\left(\dfrac{11\pi}{6} - \dfrac{\pi}{4}\right)$

$= \sin\dfrac{11\pi}{6}\cos\dfrac{\pi}{4} - \cos\dfrac{11\pi}{6}\sin\dfrac{\pi}{4}$

$= -\dfrac{1}{2}\cdot\dfrac{\sqrt{2}}{2} - \dfrac{\sqrt{3}}{2}\cdot\dfrac{\sqrt{2}}{2}$

$= -\dfrac{\sqrt{2}}{4}\left(1 + \sqrt{3}\right) = -\dfrac{\sqrt{2}}{4}\left(\sqrt{3} + 1\right)$

$\cos\left(\dfrac{19\pi}{12}\right) = \cos\left(\dfrac{11\pi}{6} - \dfrac{\pi}{4}\right)$

$= \cos\dfrac{11\pi}{6}\cos\dfrac{\pi}{4} + \sin\dfrac{11\pi}{6}\sin\dfrac{\pi}{4}$

$= \dfrac{\sqrt{3}}{2}\cdot\dfrac{\sqrt{2}}{2} + \left(-\dfrac{1}{2}\right)\dfrac{\sqrt{2}}{2}$

$= \dfrac{\sqrt{2}}{4}\left(\sqrt{3} - 1\right)$

$\tan\left(\dfrac{19\pi}{12}\right) = \tan\left(\dfrac{11\pi}{6} - \dfrac{\pi}{4}\right)$

$= \dfrac{\tan\dfrac{11\pi}{6} - \tan\dfrac{\pi}{4}}{1 + \tan\dfrac{11\pi}{6}\tan\dfrac{\pi}{4}}$

$= \dfrac{-\dfrac{\sqrt{3}}{3} - 1}{1 + \left(-\dfrac{\sqrt{3}}{3}\right)(1)} = \dfrac{-\sqrt{3} - 3}{3 - \sqrt{3}}\cdot\dfrac{3 + \sqrt{3}}{3 + \sqrt{3}}$

$= \dfrac{-\left(12 + 6\sqrt{3}\right)}{6} = -2 - \sqrt{3}$

55. $\cos 45° \cos 120° - \sin 45° \sin 120° = \cos(45° + 120°) = \cos 165°$

57. $\dfrac{\tan 68° - \tan 115°}{1 + \tan 68° \tan 115°} = \tan(68° - 115°) = \tan(-47°)$

Figures for Exercises 59–63

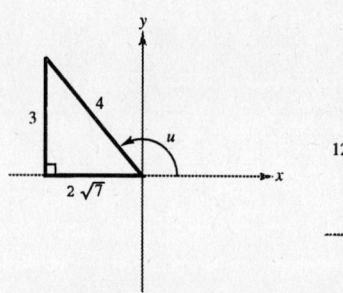
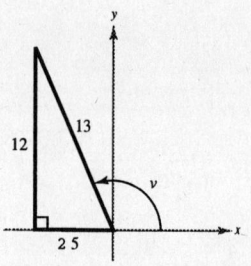

59. $\tan(u + v) = \dfrac{\tan u + \tan v}{1 - \tan u \tan v} = \dfrac{\left(-\dfrac{3}{\sqrt{7}}\right) + \left(-\dfrac{12}{5}\right)}{1 - \left(-\dfrac{3}{\sqrt{7}}\right)\left(-\dfrac{12}{5}\right)}$

$= \dfrac{15 + 12\sqrt{7}}{36 - 5\sqrt{7}}\cdot\dfrac{36 + 5\sqrt{7}}{36 + 5\sqrt{7}} = \dfrac{960 + 507\sqrt{7}}{1121}$

61. $\sin(u - v) = \sin u \cos v - \cos u \sin v$

$= \left(\dfrac{3}{4}\right)\left(-\dfrac{5}{13}\right) - \left(-\dfrac{\sqrt{7}}{4}\right)\left(\dfrac{12}{13}\right)$

$= \dfrac{-15 + 12\sqrt{7}}{52} = \dfrac{12\sqrt{7} - 15}{52}$

63. $\tan(u - v) = \dfrac{\tan u - \tan v}{1 + \tan u \tan v} = \dfrac{\left(-\dfrac{3}{\sqrt{7}}\right) - \left(-\dfrac{12}{5}\right)}{1 + \left(-\dfrac{3}{\sqrt{7}}\right)\left(-\dfrac{12}{5}\right)}$

$= \dfrac{-15 + 12\sqrt{7}}{36 + 5\sqrt{7}}\cdot\dfrac{36 - 5\sqrt{7}}{36 - 5\sqrt{7}} = \dfrac{-960 + 507\sqrt{7}}{1121}$

65.
$$\cos\left(x + \frac{\pi}{6}\right) - \cos\left(x - \frac{\pi}{6}\right) = 1$$

$$\left(\cos x \cos \frac{\pi}{6} - \sin x \sin \frac{\pi}{6}\right) - \left(\cos x \cos \frac{\pi}{6} + \sin x \sin \frac{\pi}{6}\right) = 1$$

$$-2\sin x \sin \frac{\pi}{6} = 1$$

$$-2\sin x\left(\frac{1}{2}\right) = 1$$

$$\sin x = -1$$

$$x = \frac{3\pi}{2}$$

67.
$$\cos\left(x + \frac{3\pi}{4}\right) - \cos\left(x - \frac{3\pi}{4}\right) = 0$$

$$\left(\cos x \cos \frac{3\pi}{4} - \sin x \sin \frac{3\pi}{4}\right) - \left(\cos x \cos \frac{3\pi}{4} + \sin x \sin \frac{3\pi}{4}\right) = 0$$

$$-2\sin x \sin \frac{3\pi}{4} = 0$$

$$-2\sin x\left(\frac{\sqrt{2}}{2}\right) = 0$$

$$-\sqrt{2}\sin x = 0$$

$$\sin x = 0$$

$$x = 0,\ \pi$$

69.
$$\frac{1 - \cos 2x}{1 + \cos 2x} = \frac{1 - (1 - 2\sin^2 x)}{1 + (2\cos x^2 - 1)}$$

$$= \frac{2\sin^2 x}{2\cos^2 x}$$

$$= \tan^2 x$$

71. $\cos u = -\dfrac{2}{\sqrt{5}},\ \dfrac{\pi}{2} < u < \pi \Rightarrow \sin u = \dfrac{1}{\sqrt{5}}$ and $\tan u = -\dfrac{1}{2}$

$$\sin 2u = 2\sin u \cos u = 2\left(\frac{1}{\sqrt{5}}\right)\left(-\frac{2}{\sqrt{5}}\right) = -\frac{4}{5}$$

$$\cos 2u = \cos^2 u - \sin^2 u = \left(-\frac{2}{\sqrt{5}}\right)^2 - \left(\frac{1}{\sqrt{5}}\right)^2 = \frac{3}{5}$$

$$\tan 2u = \frac{2\tan u}{1 - \tan^2 u} = \frac{2\left(-\frac{1}{2}\right)}{1 - \left(-\frac{1}{2}\right)^2} = \frac{-1}{\frac{3}{4}} = -\frac{4}{3}$$

73. $\tan^2 2x = \dfrac{\sin^2 2x}{\cos^2 2x} = \dfrac{\dfrac{1 - \cos 4x}{2}}{\dfrac{1 + \cos 4x}{2}} = \dfrac{1 - \cos 4x}{1 + \cos 4x}$

75. $\sin^2 x \tan^2 x = \sin^2 x \left(\dfrac{\sin^2 x}{\cos^2 x}\right) = \dfrac{\sin^4 x}{\cos^2 x}$

$\qquad = \dfrac{\left(\dfrac{1 - \cos 2x}{2}\right)^2}{\dfrac{1 + \cos 2x}{2}} = \dfrac{\dfrac{1 - 2\cos 2x + \cos^2 2x}{4}}{\dfrac{1 + \cos 2x}{2}}$

$\qquad = \dfrac{1 - 2\cos 2x + \dfrac{1 + \cos 4x}{2}}{2(1 + \cos 2x)}$

$\qquad = \dfrac{2 - 4\cos 2x + 1 + \cos 4x}{4(1 + \cos 2x)}$

$\qquad = \dfrac{3 - 4\cos 2x + \cos 4x}{4(1 + \cos 2x)}$

77. $\sin(-75°) = -\sqrt{\dfrac{1 - \cos 150°}{2}} = -\sqrt{\dfrac{1 - \left(-\dfrac{\sqrt{3}}{2}\right)}{2}} = -\dfrac{\sqrt{2 + \sqrt{3}}}{2}$

$\qquad = -\dfrac{1}{2}\sqrt{2 + \sqrt{3}}$

$\cos(-75°) = \sqrt{\dfrac{1 + \cos 150°}{2}} = \sqrt{\dfrac{1 + \left(-\dfrac{\sqrt{3}}{2}\right)}{2}} = \dfrac{\sqrt{2 - \sqrt{3}}}{2}$

$\qquad = \dfrac{1}{2}\sqrt{2 - \sqrt{3}}$

$\tan(-75°) = -\left(\dfrac{1 - \cos 150°}{\sin 150°}\right) = -\left(\dfrac{1 - \left(-\dfrac{\sqrt{3}}{2}\right)}{\dfrac{1}{2}}\right) = -\left(2 + \sqrt{3}\right)$

$\qquad = -2 - \sqrt{3}$

79. $\sin\left(\dfrac{19\pi}{12}\right) = -\sqrt{\dfrac{1 - \cos\dfrac{19\pi}{6}}{2}} = -\sqrt{\dfrac{1 - \left(-\dfrac{\sqrt{3}}{2}\right)}{2}} = -\dfrac{\sqrt{2 + \sqrt{3}}}{2}$

$\qquad\qquad = -\dfrac{1}{2}\sqrt{2 + \sqrt{3}}$

$\cos\left(\dfrac{19\pi}{12}\right) = \sqrt{\dfrac{1 + \cos\dfrac{19\pi}{6}}{2}} = \sqrt{\dfrac{1 + \left(-\dfrac{\sqrt{3}}{2}\right)}{2}} = \dfrac{\sqrt{2 + \sqrt{3}}}{2}$

$\qquad\qquad = \dfrac{1}{2}\sqrt{2 - \sqrt{3}}$

$\tan\left(\dfrac{19\pi}{12}\right) = \dfrac{1 - \cos\dfrac{19\pi}{6}}{\sin\dfrac{19\pi}{6}} = \dfrac{1 - \left(-\dfrac{\sqrt{3}}{2}\right)}{-\dfrac{1}{2}} = -2 - \sqrt{3}$

81. $-\sqrt{\dfrac{1 + \cos 10x}{2}} = -\left|\cos\dfrac{10x}{2}\right| = -\left|\cos 5x\right|$

83. Volume V of the trough will be the area A of the isosceles triangle times the length l of the trough.

$\qquad V = A \cdot l$

(a) $A = \dfrac{1}{2}bh$

Not to scale

$\qquad \cos\dfrac{\theta}{2} = \dfrac{h}{0.5} \Rightarrow h = 0.5 \cos\dfrac{\theta}{2}$

$\qquad \sin\dfrac{\theta}{2} = \dfrac{\dfrac{b}{2}}{0.5} \Rightarrow \dfrac{b}{2} = 0.5 \sin\dfrac{\theta}{2}$

$\qquad A = 0.5 \sin\dfrac{\theta}{2}\, 0.5 \cos\dfrac{\theta}{2}$

$\qquad\quad = (0.5)^2 \sin\dfrac{\theta}{2} \cos\dfrac{\theta}{2}$

$\qquad\quad = 0.25 \sin\dfrac{\theta}{2} \cos\dfrac{\theta}{2}$ square meters

$\qquad V = (0.25)(4) \sin\dfrac{\theta}{2} \cos\dfrac{\theta}{2}$ cubic meters

$\qquad\quad = \sin\dfrac{\theta}{2} \cos\dfrac{\theta}{2}$ cubic meters

(b) $V = \sin\dfrac{\theta}{2} \cos\dfrac{\theta}{2}$

$\qquad\; = \dfrac{1}{2}\left(2 \sin\dfrac{\theta}{2} \cos\dfrac{\theta}{2}\right)$

$\qquad\; = \dfrac{1}{2} \sin\theta$ cubic meters

$\qquad$ Volume is maximum when $\theta = \dfrac{\pi}{2}$.

85. $6 \sin 15° \sin 45° = 6\left(\dfrac{1}{2}\right)[\cos(15° - 45°) - \cos(15° + 45°)]$

$\qquad\qquad\qquad\quad = 3[\cos(-30°) - \cos 60°]$

$\qquad\qquad\qquad\quad = 3(\cos 30° - \cos 60°)$

87. $4 \sin 3\alpha \cos 2\alpha = 4\left(\dfrac{1}{2}\right)[\sin(3\alpha + 2\alpha) + \sin(3\alpha - 2\alpha)]$

$\qquad\qquad\qquad\quad = 2(\sin 5\alpha + \sin \alpha)$

89. $\cos 3\theta + \cos 2\theta = 2 \cos\left(\dfrac{3\theta + 2\theta}{2}\right) \cos\left(\dfrac{3\theta - 2\theta}{2}\right)$

$$= 2 \cos \frac{5\theta}{2} \cos \frac{\theta}{2}$$

91. $\sin\left(x + \dfrac{\pi}{4}\right) - \sin\left(x - \dfrac{\pi}{4}\right) = 2 \cos\left[\dfrac{\left(x + \dfrac{\pi}{4}\right) + \left(x - \dfrac{\pi}{4}\right)}{2}\right] \sin\left[\dfrac{\left(x + \dfrac{\pi}{4}\right) - \left(x - \dfrac{\pi}{4}\right)}{2}\right]$

$$= 2 \cos x \sin \frac{\pi}{4}$$

93. False. If $\dfrac{\pi}{2} < \theta < \pi$, then $\dfrac{\pi}{4} < \dfrac{\theta}{2} < \dfrac{\pi}{2}$ and $\dfrac{\theta}{2}$ is in Quadrant I. $\cos\dfrac{\theta}{2} > 0$

95. True. $4 \sin(-x)\cos(-x) = 4(-\sin x)\cos x$

$$= -4 \sin x \cos x = -2(2 \sin x \cos x)$$

$$= -2 \sin 2x$$

97. Reciprocal Identities: $\sin \theta = \dfrac{1}{\csc \theta}$ $\csc \theta = \dfrac{1}{\sin \theta}$

$$\cos \theta = \frac{1}{\sec \theta} \qquad \sec \theta = \frac{1}{\cos \theta}$$

$$\tan \theta = \frac{1}{\cot \theta} \qquad \cot \theta = \frac{1}{\tan \theta}$$

Quotient Identities: $\tan \theta = \dfrac{\sin \theta}{\cos \theta}$ $\cot \theta = \dfrac{\cos \theta}{\sin \theta}$

Pythagorean Identities: $\sin^2 \theta + \cos^2 \theta = 1$

$$1 + \tan^2 \theta = \sec^2 \theta$$

$$1 + \cot^2 \theta = \csc^2 \theta$$

99. No. For an equation to be an identity, the equation must be true for all real numbers. $\sin \theta = \frac{1}{2}$ has an infinite number of solutions but is not an identity.

101. The graph of y_1 is a vertical shift of the graph of y_2 one unit upward so $y_1 = y_2 + 1$.

103. $y = \sqrt{x + 3} + 4 \cos x$

Zeros: $x \approx -1.8431, 2.1758, 3.9903, 8.8935, 9.8820$

Chapter 5   Practice Test

1. Find the value of the other five trigonometric functions, given $\tan x = \frac{4}{11}$, $\sec x < 0$.

2. Simplify $\dfrac{\sec^2 x + \csc^2 x}{\csc^2 x(1 + \tan^2 x)}$.

3. Rewrite as a single logarithm and simplify $\ln|\tan \theta| - \ln|\cot \theta|$.

4. True or false:
$$\cos\left(\frac{\pi}{2} - x\right) = \frac{1}{\csc x}$$

5. Factor and simplify: $\sin^4 x + (\sin^2 x) \cos^2 x$

6. Multiply and simplify: $(\csc x + 1)(\csc x - 1)$

7. Rationalize the denominator and simplify:
$$\frac{\cos^2 x}{1 - \sin x}$$

8. Verify:
$$\frac{1 + \cos \theta}{\sin \theta} + \frac{\sin \theta}{1 + \cos \theta} = 2 \csc \theta$$

9. Verify:
$$\tan^4 x + 2 \tan^2 x + 1 = \sec^4 x$$

10. Use the sum or difference formulas to determine:

    (a) $\sin 105°$ (b) $\tan 15°$

11. Simplify: $(\sin 42°) \cos 38° - (\cos 42°) \sin 38°$

12. Verify $\tan\left(\theta + \dfrac{\pi}{4}\right) = \dfrac{1 + \tan \theta}{1 - \tan \theta}$.

13. Write $\sin(\arcsin x - \arccos x)$ as an algebraic expression in x.

14. Use the double-angle formulas to determine:

    (a) $\cos 120°$ (b) $\tan 300°$

15. Use the half-angle formulas to determine:

    (a) $\sin 22.5°$ (d) $\tan \dfrac{\pi}{12}$

16. Given $\sin = 4/5$, θ lies in Quadrant II, find $\cos(\theta/2)$.

17. Use the power-reducing identities to write $(\sin^2 x) \cos^2 x$ in terms of the first power of cosine.

18. Rewrite as a sum: $6(\sin 5\theta) \cos 2\theta$.

19. Rewrite as a product:
$\sin(x + \pi) + \sin(x - \pi)$.

20. Verify $\dfrac{\sin 9x + \sin 5x}{\cos 9x - \cos 5x} = -\cot 2x$.

21. Verify:
$(\cos u) \sin v = \frac{1}{2}[\sin(u + v) - \sin(u - v)]$.

22. Find all solutions in the interval $[0, 2\pi)$:
$4 \sin^2 x = 1$

23. Find all solutions in the interval $[0, 2\pi)$:
$\tan^2 \theta + \left(\sqrt{3} - 1\right) \tan\theta - \sqrt{3} = 0$

24. Find all solutions in the interval $[0, 2\pi)$:
$\sin 2x = \cos x$

25. Use the quadratic formula to find all solutions in the interval $[0, 2\pi)$:
$\tan^2 x - 6 \tan x + 4 = 0$

C H A P T E R 6
Additional Topics in Trigonometry

C H A P T E R 6
Additional Topics in Trigonometry

Section 6.1 Law of Sines
Solutions to Odd-Numbered Exercises

- If ABC is any oblique triangle with sides a, b, and c, then

$$\frac{a}{\sin A} = \frac{b}{\sin B} = \frac{c}{\sin C}.$$

- You should be able to use the Law of Sines to solve an oblique triangle for the remaining three parts, given:

  (a) Two angles and any side (AAS or ASA)

  (b) Two sides and an angle opposite one of them (SSA)

  1. If A is acute and $h = b \sin A$:

     (a) $a < h$, no triangle is possible.

     (b) $a = h$ or $a > b$, one triangle is possible.

     (c) $h < a < b$, two triangles are possible.

  2. If A is obtuse and $h = b \sin A$:

     (a) $a \leq b$, no triangle is possible.

     (b) $a > b$, one triangle is possible.

- The area of any triangle equals one-half the product of the lengths of two sides times the sine of their included angle.

$$A = \tfrac{1}{2}ab \sin C = \tfrac{1}{2}ac \sin B = \tfrac{1}{2}bc \sin A$$

---

1. Given: $A = 30°$, $B = 45°$, $a = 20$

$C = 180° - A - B = 105°$

$b = \dfrac{a}{\sin A}(\sin B) = \dfrac{20 \sin 45°}{\sin 30°} = 20\sqrt{2} \approx 28.28$

$c = \dfrac{a}{\sin A}(\sin C) = \dfrac{20 \sin 105°}{\sin 30°} \approx 38.64$

3. Given: $A = 25°$, $B = 35°$, $a = 3.5$

$C = 180° - A - B = 120°$

$b = \dfrac{a}{\sin A}(\sin B) = \dfrac{3.5}{\sin 25°}(\sin 35°) \approx 4.8$

$c = \dfrac{a}{\sin A}(\sin C) = \dfrac{3.5}{\sin 25°}(\sin 120°) \approx 7.2$

5. Given: $A = 36°$, $a = 8$, $b = 5$

$\sin B = \dfrac{b \sin A}{a} = \dfrac{5 \sin 36°}{8} \approx 0.36737 \implies B \approx 21.55°$

$C = 180° - A - B \approx 180° - 36° - 21.55 = 122.45°$

$c = \dfrac{a}{\sin A}(\sin C) = \dfrac{8}{\sin 36°}(\sin 122.45°) \approx 11.49$

7. Given: $A = 102.4°$, $C = 16.7°$, $a = 21.6$

$B = 180° - A - C = 60.9°$

$b = \dfrac{a}{\sin A}(\sin B) = \dfrac{21.6}{\sin 102.4°}(\sin 60.9°) \approx 19.3$

$c = \dfrac{a}{\sin A}(\sin C) = \dfrac{21.6}{\sin 102.4°}(\sin 16.7°) \approx 6.4$

9. Given: $A = 83° \, 20'$, $C = 54.6°$, $c = 18.1$

$$B = 180° - A - C = 180° - 83° \, 20' - 54° \, 36' = 42° \, 4'$$

$$a = \frac{c}{\sin C}(\sin A) = \frac{18.1}{\sin 54.6°}(\sin 83° \, 20') \approx 22.05$$

$$b = \frac{c}{\sin C}(\sin B) = \frac{18.1}{\sin 54.6°}(\sin 42° \, 4') \approx 14.88$$

11. Given: $B = 15° \, 30'$, $a = 4.5$, $b = 6.8$

$$\sin A = \frac{a \sin B}{b} = \frac{4.5 \sin 15° \, 30'}{6.8} \approx 0.17685 \implies A \approx 10° \, 11'$$

$$C = 180° - A - B \approx 180° - 10° \, 11' - 15° \, 30' = 154° \, 19'$$

$$c = \frac{b}{\sin B}(\sin C) = \frac{6.8}{\sin 15° \, 30'}(\sin 154° \, 19') \approx 11.03$$

13. Given: $C = 145°$, $b = 4$, $c = 14$

$$\sin B = \frac{b \sin C}{c} = \frac{4 \sin 145°}{14} \approx 0.16387 \implies B \approx 9.43°$$

$$A = 180° - B - C \approx 180° - 9.43° - 145° = 25.57°$$

$$a = \frac{c}{\sin C}(\sin A) \approx \frac{14}{\sin 145°}(\sin 25.57°) \approx 10.53$$

15. Given: $A = 110° \, 15'$, $a = 48$, $b = 16$

$$\sin B = \frac{b \sin A}{a} = \frac{16 \sin 110° \, 15'}{48} \approx 0.31273 \implies B \approx 18° \, 13'$$

$$C = 180° - A - B \approx 180° - 110° \, 15' - 18° \, 13' = 51° \, 32'$$

$$c = \frac{a}{\sin A}(\sin C) = \frac{48}{\sin 110° \, 15'}(\sin 51° \, 32') \approx 40.06$$

17. Given: $A = 55°$, $B = 42°$, $c = \frac{3}{4}$

$$C = 180° - A - B = 83°$$

$$a = \frac{c}{\sin C}(\sin A) = \frac{0.75}{\sin 83°}(\sin 55°) \approx 0.62$$

$$b = \frac{c}{\sin C}(\sin B) = \frac{0.75}{\sin 83°}(\sin 42°) \approx 0.51$$

19. Given: $a = 4.5$, $b = 12.8$, $A = 58°$

$$h = 12.8 \sin 58° \approx 10.86$$

Since $a < h$, no triangle is formed.

21. Given: $a = 18, b = 20, A = 76°$

$$h = 20 \sin 76° \approx 19.41$$

Since $a < h$, no triangle is formed.

23. Given: $a = 125$, $b = 200$, $A = 110°$

No triangle is formed because A is obtuse and $a < b$.

25. Given: $a = \dfrac{5}{12}, b = 1\dfrac{3}{8}, A = 22°$

$h = \left(1\dfrac{3}{8}\right)\sin 22° \approx 0.52$

Since $a < h$, no triangle is formed.

27. Given: $A = 36°$, $a = 5$

   (a) One solution if $b \le 5$ or $b = \dfrac{5}{\sin 36°}$

   (b) Two solutions if $5 < b < \dfrac{5}{\sin 36°}$

   (c) No solution if $b > \dfrac{5}{\sin 36°}$

29. Given: $A = 10°$, $a = 10.8$

   (a) One solution if $b \le 10.8$ or $b = \dfrac{10.8}{\sin 10°}$

   (b) Two solutions if $10.8 < b < \dfrac{10.8}{\sin 10°}$

   (c) No solution if $b > \dfrac{10.8}{\sin 10°}$

31. Area $= \frac{1}{2}ab \sin C = \frac{1}{2}(4)(6) \sin 120° \approx 10.4$

33. Area $= \frac{1}{2}bc \sin A = \frac{1}{2}(57)(85) \sin 43° \, 45' \approx 1675.2$

35. Area $= \frac{1}{2}ac \sin B = \frac{1}{2}(105)(64)\sin(72°30') \approx 3204.5$

37. $C = 180° - 23° - 94° = 63°$

$h = \dfrac{35}{\sin 63°}(\sin 23°) \approx 15.3$ meters

39. $\dfrac{\sin(42° - \theta)}{10} = \dfrac{\sin 48°}{17}$

$\sin(42° - \theta) \approx 0.43714$

$42° - \theta \approx 25.9°$

$\theta \approx 16.1°$

41. Given: $c = 100$

$A = 74° - 28° = 46°,$

$B = 180° - 41° - 74° = 65°,$

$C = 180° - 46° - 65° = 69°$

$a = \dfrac{c}{\sin C}(\sin A) = \dfrac{100}{\sin 69°}(\sin 46°) \approx 77$ meters

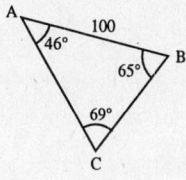

43. (a)

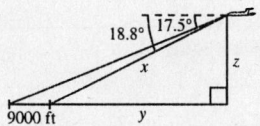

   (b) $\dfrac{x}{\sin 17.5°} = \dfrac{9000}{\sin 1.3°}$

         $x \approx 119{,}289.1261$ feet ≈ 22.6 miles

   (c) $\dfrac{y}{\sin 71.2°} = \dfrac{x}{\sin 90°}$

         $y = x \sin 71.2° \approx 119{,}289.1261 \sin 71.2°$

           $\approx 112{,}924.963$ feet ≈ 21.4 miles

   (d) $z = x \sin 18.8° \approx 119{,}289.1261 \sin 18.8° \approx 38{,}443$ feet

45.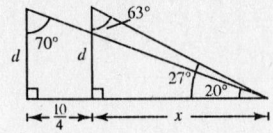

In 15 minutes the boat has traveled

$$(10 \text{ mph})\left(\frac{1}{4} \text{ hr}\right) = \frac{10}{4} \text{ miles}$$

$$\tan 63° = \frac{x}{d} \qquad \Rightarrow d \tan 63° = x$$

$$\tan 70° = \frac{x + (10/4)}{d} \Rightarrow d \tan 70° = x + \frac{10}{4}$$

$$\Rightarrow d \tan 70° - \frac{10}{4} = x$$

$$d \tan 70° - \frac{10}{4} = d \tan 63°$$

$$d \tan 70° - d \tan 63° = \frac{10}{4}$$

$$d(\tan 70° - \tan 63°) = 2.5$$

$$d = \frac{2.5}{\tan 70° - \tan 63°} \approx 3.2 \text{ miles}$$

47. $\alpha = 180 - (\phi + 180 - \theta) = \theta - \phi$

$$\frac{d}{\sin \theta} = \frac{2}{\sin \alpha}$$

$$d = \frac{2 \sin \theta}{\sin(\theta - \phi)}$$

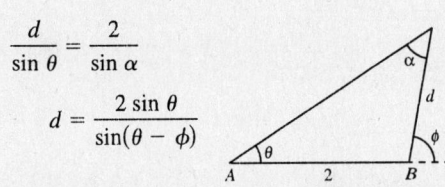

49. False. Two sides and one opposite angle do not necessarily determine a unique triangle.

51. (a) $A = \dfrac{1}{2}(30)(20) \sin\left(\theta + \dfrac{\theta}{2}\right) - \dfrac{1}{2}(8)(20) \sin \dfrac{\theta}{2} - \dfrac{1}{2}(8)(30) \sin \theta$

$$= 300 \sin \frac{3\theta}{2} - 80 \sin \frac{\theta}{2} - 120 \sin \theta$$

$$= 20\left[15 \sin \frac{3\theta}{2} - 4 \sin \frac{\theta}{2} - 6 \sin \theta\right]$$

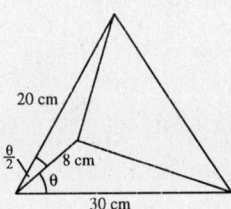

(b)

(c) Domain: $0 \le \theta \le 1.6690$

The domain would increase in length and the area would increase if the 8-centimeter line segment were decreased.

53. $\cos x = \dfrac{1}{5}, \dfrac{3\pi}{2} < x < 2\pi \implies x$ is in Quadrant IV.

$$\sin^2 x + \left(\dfrac{1}{5}\right)^2 = 1$$

$$\sin^2 x = 1 - \dfrac{1}{25}$$

$$\sin^2 x = \dfrac{24}{25}$$

$$\sin x = -\sqrt{\dfrac{24}{25}} = -\dfrac{2\sqrt{6}}{5}$$

$$\tan x = \dfrac{\sin x}{\cos x} = \dfrac{-\dfrac{2\sqrt{6}}{5}}{\dfrac{1}{5}} = -2\sqrt{6}$$

$$\cot x = \dfrac{1}{\tan x} = \dfrac{1}{-2\sqrt{6}} = -\dfrac{\sqrt{6}}{12}$$

$$\sec x = \dfrac{1}{\cos x} = \dfrac{1}{\dfrac{1}{5}} = 5$$

$$\csc x = \dfrac{1}{\sin x} = \dfrac{1}{-\dfrac{2\sqrt{6}}{5}} = -\dfrac{5}{2\sqrt{6}} = -\dfrac{5\sqrt{6}}{12}$$

55. $\tan x = -5, \dfrac{\pi}{2} < x < \pi \implies x$ is in Quadrant II.

$$1 + (-5)^2 = \sec^2 x$$

$$26 = \sec^2 x$$

$$\sec x = -\sqrt{26}$$

$$\cos x = \dfrac{1}{\sec x} = \dfrac{1}{-\sqrt{26}} = -\dfrac{\sqrt{26}}{26}$$

$$\dfrac{\sin x}{\cos x} = \tan x \implies \sin x = \cos x \tan x$$

$$\sin x = \left(-\dfrac{\sqrt{26}}{26}\right)(-5) = \dfrac{5\sqrt{26}}{26}$$

$$\cot x = \dfrac{1}{\tan x} = -\dfrac{1}{5}$$

$$\csc x = \dfrac{1}{\sin x} = \dfrac{1}{\dfrac{5\sqrt{26}}{26}} = \dfrac{26}{5\sqrt{26}} = \dfrac{\sqrt{26}}{5}$$

57. $\tan x \cos x \sec x = \tan x \cos x \dfrac{1}{\cos x} = \tan x$

59. $1 + \cot^2\left(\dfrac{\pi}{2} - x\right) = 1 + \tan^2 x = \sec^2 x$

Section 6.2   Law of Cosines

- If ABC is any oblique triangle with sides a, b, and c, the following equations are valid.

  (a) $a^2 = b^2 + c^2 - 2bc \cos A$ or $\cos A = \dfrac{b^2 + c^2 - a^2}{2bc}$

  (b) $b^2 = a^2 + c^2 - 2ac \cos B$ or $\cos B = \dfrac{a^2 + c^2 - b^2}{2ac}$

  (c) $c^2 = a^2 + b^2 - 2ab \cos C$ or $\cos C = \dfrac{a^2 + b^2 - c^2}{2ab}$

- You should be able to use the Law of Cosines to solve an oblique triangle for the remaining three parts, given:

  (a) Three sides (SSS)

  (b) Two sides and their included angle (SAS)

- Given any triangle with sides of length a, b, and c, the area of the triangle is

  $$\text{Area} = \sqrt{s(s - a)(s - b)(s - c)}, \text{ where } s = \dfrac{a + b + c}{2}.$$ (Heron's Formula)

Solutions to Odd-Numbered Exercises

1. Given: $a = 7, b = 10, c = 15$

$$\cos C = \frac{a^2 + b^2 - c^2}{2ab} = \frac{49 + 100 - 225}{2(7)(10)} \approx -0.5429 \implies C \approx 122.88°$$

$$\sin B = \frac{b \sin C}{c} = \frac{10 \sin 122.88°}{15} \approx 0.5599 \implies B \approx 34.05°$$

$$A \approx 180° - 34.05° - 122.88° \approx 23.07°$$

3. Given: $A = 30°, \ b = 15, \ c = 30$

$$a^2 = b^2 + c^2 - 2bc \cos A$$

$$= 225 + 900 - 2(15)(30) \cos 30° \approx 345.5771$$

$$a \approx 18.6$$

$$\cos B = \frac{a^2 + c^2 - b^2}{2ac} \approx \frac{(18.6)^2 + 900 - 225}{2(18.6)(30)} \approx 0.9148$$

$$B \approx 23.8°$$

$$C \approx 180° - 30° - 23.8° = 126.2°$$

5. $a = 11, b = 14, c = 20$

$$\cos C = \frac{a^2 + b^2 - c^2}{2ab} = \frac{121 + 196 - 400}{2(11)(14)} \approx -0.2695 \implies C \approx 105.63°$$

$$\sin B = \frac{b \sin C}{c} = \frac{14 \sin 105.63°}{20} \approx 0.6741 \implies B \approx 42.39°$$

$$A \approx 180° - 42.39° - 105.63° \approx 31.98°$$

7. Given: $a = 75.4, \ b = 52, \ c = 52$

$$\cos A = \frac{b^2 + c^2 - a^2}{2bc} = \frac{52^2 + 52^2 - 75.4^2}{2(52)(52)} = -0.05125 \implies A \approx 92.94°$$

$$\sin B = \frac{b \sin A}{a} \approx \frac{52(0.9987)}{75.4} \approx 0.68875 \implies B \approx 43.53°$$

$$C = B \approx 43.53°$$

9. Given: $A = 135°, b = 4, c = 9$

$$a^2 = b^2 + c^2 - 2bc \cos A = 16 + 81 - 2(4)(9)\cos 135° \approx 147.9117 \implies a \approx 12.16$$

$$\sin B = \frac{b \sin A}{a} = \frac{4 \sin 135°}{12.16} \approx 0.2326 \implies B \approx 13.45°$$

$$C \approx 180° - 135° - 13.45° \approx 31.55°$$

11. Given: $B = 10° \, 35', a = 40, c = 30$

$$b^2 = a^2 + c^2 - 2ac \cos B = 1600 + 900 - 2(40)(30)\cos 10° \, 35' \approx 140.8268 \implies b \approx 11.9$$

$$\sin C = \frac{c \sin B}{b} = \frac{30 \sin 10° \, 35'}{11.9} \approx 0.4630 \implies C \approx 27.58° \approx 27° \, 35'$$

$$A \approx 180° - 10° \, 35' - 27° \, 35' = 141° \, 50'$$

13. Given: $C = 125° \, 40'$, $a = 32$, $b = 32$

$c^2 = a^2 + b^2 - 2ab \cos C \approx 32^2 + 32^2 - 2(32)(32)(-0.5831) \approx 3242.1 \implies c \approx 56.9$

$A = B \implies 2A = 180° - 125° \, 40' = 54° \, 20' \implies A = B = 27° \, 10'$

15. $C = 43°, a = \dfrac{4}{9}, b = \dfrac{7}{9}$

$c^2 = a^2 + b^2 - 2ab \cos C = \left(\dfrac{4}{9}\right)^2 + \left(\dfrac{7}{9}\right)^2 - 2\left(\dfrac{4}{9}\right)\left(\dfrac{7}{9}\right)\cos 43° \approx 0.2968 \implies c \approx 0.5448$

$\sin A = \dfrac{a \sin C}{c} = \dfrac{(4/9)\sin 43°}{0.5448} \approx 0.5564 \implies A \approx 33.8°$

$B \approx 180° - 43° - 33.8° \approx 103.2°$

17.

$d^2 = 5^2 + 8^2 - 2(5)(8)\cos 45° \approx 32.4315 \implies d \approx 5.69$

$2\phi = 360° - 2(45°) = 270° \implies \phi = 135°$

$c^2 = 5^2 + 8^2 - 2(5)(8)\cos 135° \approx 145.5685 \implies c \approx 12.07$

19.

$\cos \phi = \dfrac{10^2 + 14^2 - 20^2}{2(10)(14)}$

$\phi \approx 111.8°$

$2\theta \approx 360° - 2(111.8°)$

$\theta = 68.2°$

$d^2 = 10^2 + 14^2 - 2(10)(14) \cos 68.2°$

$d \approx 13.86$

21.

$\cos \alpha = \dfrac{(12.5)^2 + (15)^2 - 10^2}{2(12.5)(15)} = 0.75 \implies \alpha \approx 41.41°$

$\cos \beta = \dfrac{10^2 + 15^2 - (12.5)^2}{2(10)(15)} = 0.5625 \implies \beta \approx 55.77°$

$z = 180° - \alpha - \beta = 82.82°$

— CONTINUED —

21. — CONTINUED —

$$u = 180° - z = 97.18°$$

$$b^2 = 12.5^2 + 10^2 - 2(12.5)(10)\cos 97.18° \approx 287.4967 \implies b \approx 16.96$$

$$\cos \gamma = \frac{12.5^2 + 16.96^2 - 10^2}{2(12.5)(16.96)} \approx 0.8111 \implies \gamma \approx 35.80°$$

$$\theta = \alpha + \gamma = 41.41° + 35.80° \approx 77.2°$$

$$2\phi = 360° - 2\theta \implies \phi = \frac{360° - 2(77.2°)}{2} = 102.8°$$

23. $a = 5, b = 7, c = 10 \implies s = \dfrac{a + b + c}{2} = 11$

Area $= \sqrt{s(s - a)(s - b)(s - c)} = \sqrt{11(6)(4)(1)} \approx 16.25$

25. $a = 2.5, b = 10.2, c = 9 \implies s = \dfrac{a + b + c}{2} = 10.85$

Area $= \sqrt{s(s - a)(s - b)(s - c)} = \sqrt{10.85(8.35)(0.65)(1.85)} \approx 10.44$

27. $a = 12.32, b = 8.46, c = 15.05 \implies s = \dfrac{a + b + c}{2} = 17.915$

Area $= \sqrt{s(s - a)(s - b)(s - c)} = \sqrt{17.915(5.595)(9.455)(2.865)} \approx 52.11$

29.

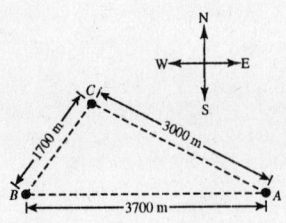

$$\cos B = \frac{1700^2 + 3700^2 - 3000^2}{2(1700)(3700)} \implies B \approx 52.9°$$

Bearing: $90° - 52.9° = $ N $37.1°$ E

$$\cos C = \frac{1700^2 + 3000^2 - 3700^2}{2(1700)(3000)} \implies C \approx 100.2°$$

Bearing: $A = 180° - 52.9° - 100.2° = 26.9° \implies$ S $63.1°$ E

31.

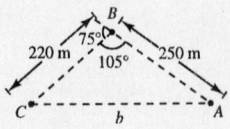

$$b^2 = 220^2 + 250^2 - 2(220)(250)\cos 105° \implies b \approx 373.3 \text{ meters}$$

33.

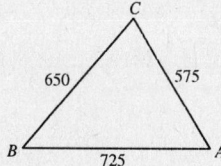

The largest angle is across from the largest side.

$$\cos C = \frac{650^2 + 575^2 - 725^2}{2(650)(575)}$$

$$C \approx 72.3°$$

35. $C = 180° - 53° - 67° = 60°$

$$c^2 = a^2 + b^2 - 2ab \cos C$$

$$= 36^2 + 48^2 - 2(36)(48)(0.5)$$

$$= 1872$$

$$c \approx 43.3 \text{ mi}$$

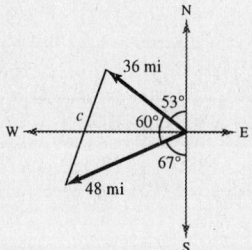

37. (a) $\cos \theta = \dfrac{273^2 + 178^2 - 235^2}{2(273)(178)}$

$$\theta \approx 58.4°$$

Bearing: N 58.4° W

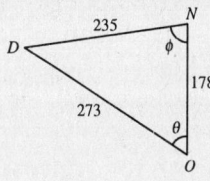

    (b) $\cos \phi = \dfrac{235^2 + 178^2 - 273^2}{2(235)(178)}$

$$\phi \approx 81.5°$$

Bearing: S 81.5° W

39. $d^2 = 60.5^2 + 90^2 - 2(60.5)(90) \cos 45° \approx 4059.8572 \implies d \approx 63.7 \text{ ft}$

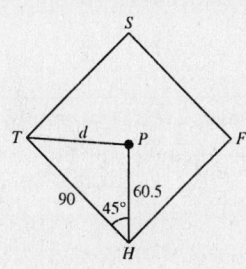

41. $a^2 = 35^2 + 20^2 - 2(35)(20)\cos 42° \implies a \approx 24.2 \text{ miles}$

43. $\overline{RS} = \sqrt{8^2 + 10^2} = \sqrt{164} = 2\sqrt{41} \approx 12.8$ ft

$\overline{PQ} = \frac{1}{2}\sqrt{16^2 + 10^2} = \frac{1}{2}\sqrt{356} = \sqrt{89} \approx 9.4$ ft

$\tan P = \frac{10}{16}$

$\qquad P = \arctan\frac{5}{8} \approx 32.0°$

$\overline{QS} \approx \sqrt{8^2 + 9.4^2 - 2(8)(9.4)\cos 32°} \approx \sqrt{24.81} \approx 5.0$ ft

45. $d^2 = 10^2 + 7^2 - 2(10)(7)\cos\theta$

$\theta = \arccos\left[\dfrac{10^2 + 7^2 - d^2}{2(10)(7)}\right]$

$s = \dfrac{360° - \theta}{360°}(2\pi r) = \dfrac{(360° - \theta)\pi}{45}$

d (inches)	9	10	12	13	14	15	16
θ (degrees)	60.9°	69.5°	88.0°	98.2°	109.6°	122.9°	139.8°
s (inches)	20.88	20.28	18.99	18.28	17.48	16.55	15.37

47. $a = 200, b = 500, c = 600 \Longrightarrow s = \dfrac{200 + 500 + 600}{2} = 650$

Area $= \sqrt{650(450)(150)(50)} \approx 46{,}837.5$ square feet

49. False. The average of the three sides of a triangle is $\dfrac{a + b + c}{3}$, not $\dfrac{a + b + c}{2}$.

51. (a) Working with $\triangle OBC$, we have $\cos\alpha = \dfrac{\frac{a}{2}}{R}$.

This implies that $2R = \dfrac{a}{\cos\alpha}$.

Since we know that

$$\frac{a}{\sin A} = \frac{b}{\sin B} = \frac{c}{\sin C},$$

we can complete the proof by showing that $\cos\alpha = \sin A$. The solution of the system

$A + B + C = 180°$

$\alpha - C + A = \beta$

$\qquad \alpha + \beta = B$

is $\alpha = 90° - A$. Therefore:

$$2R = \frac{a}{\cos\alpha} = \frac{a}{\cos(90° - A)} = \frac{a}{\sin A}.$$

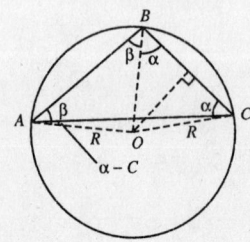

(b) By Heron's Formula, the area of the triangle is

$\qquad$ Area $= \sqrt{s(s - a)(s - b)(s - c)}$.

We can also find the area by dividing the area into six triangles and using the fact that the area is $\frac{1}{2}$ the base times the height. Using the figure as given, we have

Area $= \dfrac{1}{2}xr + \dfrac{1}{2}xr + \dfrac{1}{2}yr + \dfrac{1}{2}yr + \dfrac{1}{2}zr + \dfrac{1}{2}zr$

$\qquad = r(x + y + z)$

$\qquad = rs.$

Therefore: $\quad rs = \sqrt{s(s - a)(s - b)(s - c)} \Longrightarrow$

$$r = \sqrt{\frac{(s - a)(s - b)(s - c)}{s}}.$$

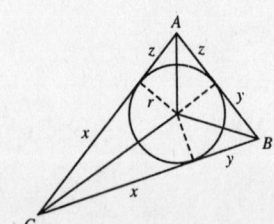

53. Given: $a = 200$ ft, $b = 250$ ft, $c = 325$ ft

$$s = \frac{200 + 250 + 325}{2} \approx 387.5$$

Radius of the inscribed circle: $r = \sqrt{\frac{(s-a)(s-b)(s-c)}{s}} = \sqrt{\frac{(187.5)(137.5)(62.5)}{387.5}} \approx 64.5$ ft

Circumference of an inscribed circle: $C = 2\pi r \approx 2\pi(64.5) \approx 405.3$ ft

55. $\frac{1}{2}bc(1 - \cos A) = \frac{1}{2}bc\left[1 + \frac{a^2 - (b^2 + c^2)}{2bc}\right]$

$= \frac{1}{2}bc\left[\frac{2bc + a^2 - b^2 - c^2}{2bc}\right]$

$= \frac{a^2 - (b^2 - 2bc + c^2)}{4}$

$= \frac{a^2 - (b - c)^2}{4}$

$= \left(\frac{a - (b - c)}{2}\right)\left(\frac{a + (b - c)}{2}\right)$

$= \frac{a - b + c}{2} \cdot \frac{a + b - c}{2}$

57. $\arccos 0 = \dfrac{\pi}{2}$

59. $\arctan(-\sqrt{3}) = -\arctan\sqrt{3} = -\dfrac{\pi}{3}$

61. $\arccos\left(-\dfrac{\sqrt{3}}{2}\right) = \pi - \arccos\dfrac{\sqrt{3}}{2} = \pi - \dfrac{\pi}{6} = \dfrac{5\pi}{6}$

63. Let $u = \arccos 3x$

$\cos u = 3x = \dfrac{3x}{1}$.

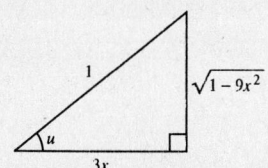

$\tan(\arccos 3x) = \tan u = \dfrac{\sqrt{1 - 9x^2}}{3x}$

65. Let $u = \arcsin\dfrac{x - 1}{2}$

$\sin u = \dfrac{x - 1}{2}$.

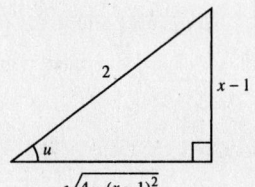

$\cos\left(\arcsin\dfrac{x - 1}{2}\right) = \cos u$

$\phantom{\cos\left(\arcsin\dfrac{x - 1}{2}\right)} = \dfrac{\sqrt{4 - (x - 1)^2}}{2}$

67. $x = 2 \cos \theta, \; -\dfrac{\pi}{2} < \theta < \dfrac{\pi}{2}$

$-\sqrt{2} = \sqrt{4 - x^2}$

$-\sqrt{2} = \sqrt{4 - (2 \cos \theta)^2}$

$-\sqrt{2} = \sqrt{4 - 4 \cos^2 \theta}$

$-\sqrt{2} = \sqrt{4(1 - \cos^2 \theta)}$

$-\sqrt{2} = \sqrt{4 \sin^2 \theta}$

$-\sqrt{2} = 2 \sin \theta$

$-\dfrac{\sqrt{2}}{2} = \sin \theta \;\Rightarrow\; \cos \theta = \dfrac{\sqrt{2}}{2} \;\Rightarrow\; x = 2\!\left(\dfrac{\sqrt{2}}{2}\right) = \sqrt{2}$

$\sec \theta = \dfrac{1}{\cos \theta} = \dfrac{1}{\frac{\sqrt{2}}{2}} = \sqrt{2}$

$\csc \theta = \dfrac{1}{\sin \theta} = \dfrac{1}{-\frac{\sqrt{2}}{2}} = -\sqrt{2}$

69. $x = 6 \tan \theta, \; -\dfrac{\pi}{2} < \theta < \dfrac{\pi}{2}$

$12 = \sqrt{36 + x^2}$

$12 = \sqrt{36 + (6 \tan \theta)^2}$

$12 = \sqrt{36 + 36 \tan^2 \theta}$

$12 = \sqrt{36(1 - \tan^2 \theta)}$

$12 = \sqrt{36 \sec^2 \theta}$

$12 = 6 \sec \theta$

$2 = \sec \theta$

$\cos \theta = \dfrac{1}{2}$

$\sin^2 \theta + \left(\dfrac{1}{2}\right)^2 = 1$

$\sin^2 \theta = 1 - \dfrac{1}{4} = \dfrac{3}{4}$

$\sin \theta = \pm \sqrt{\dfrac{3}{4}} = \pm \dfrac{\sqrt{3}}{2}$

$\csc \theta = \dfrac{1}{\sin \theta} = \dfrac{1}{\pm \frac{\sqrt{3}}{2}} = \pm \dfrac{2}{\sqrt{3}} = \pm \dfrac{2\sqrt{3}}{3}$

Section 6.3   Vectors in the Plane

- A vector **v** is the collection of all directed line segments that are equivalent to a given directed line segment $\overrightarrow{PQ}$.
- You should be able to *geometrically* perform the operations of vector addition and scalar multiplication.
- The component form of the vector with initial point $P = (p_1, p_2)$ and terminal point $Q = (q_1, q_2)$ is

  $\overrightarrow{PQ} = \langle q_1 - p_1, q_2 - p_2 \rangle = \langle v_1, v_2 \rangle = \mathbf{v}.$
- The magnitude of $\mathbf{v} = \langle v_1, v_2 \rangle$ is given by $\|\mathbf{v}\| = \sqrt{v_1^2 + v_2^2}$.
- If $\|\mathbf{v}\| = 1$, **v** is a unit vector.
- You should be able to perform the operations of scalar multiplication and vector addition in component form.

  (a) $\mathbf{u} + \mathbf{v} = \langle u_1 + v_1, u_2 + v_2 \rangle$ (b) $k\mathbf{u} = \langle ku_1, ku_2 \rangle$
- You should know the following properties of vector addition and scalar multiplication.

  (a) $\mathbf{u} + \mathbf{v} = \mathbf{v} + \mathbf{u}$

  (b) $(\mathbf{u} + \mathbf{v}) + \mathbf{w} = \mathbf{u} + (\mathbf{v} + \mathbf{w})$

  (c) $\mathbf{u} + \mathbf{0} = \mathbf{u}$

  (d) $\mathbf{u} + (-\mathbf{u}) = \mathbf{0}$

  (e) $c(d\mathbf{u}) = (cd)\mathbf{u}$

  (f) $(c + d)\mathbf{u} = c\mathbf{u} + d\mathbf{u}$

  (g) $c(\mathbf{u} + \mathbf{v}) = c\mathbf{u} + c\mathbf{v}$

  (h) $1(\mathbf{u}) = \mathbf{u}, \; 0\mathbf{u} = \mathbf{0}$

  (i) $\|c\mathbf{v}\| = |c| \, \|\mathbf{v}\|$

— CONTINUED —

— CONTINUED —

■ A unit vector in the direction of $\mathbf{v}$ is $\mathbf{u} = \dfrac{\mathbf{v}}{\|\mathbf{v}\|}$.

■ The standard unit vectors are $\mathbf{i} = \langle 1, 0 \rangle$ and $\mathbf{j} = \langle 0, 1 \rangle$. $\mathbf{v} = \langle v_1, v_2 \rangle$ can be written as $\mathbf{v} = v_1\mathbf{i} + v_2\mathbf{j}$.

■ A vector $\mathbf{v}$ with magnitude $\|\mathbf{v}\|$ and direction θ can be written as $\mathbf{v} = a\mathbf{i} + b\mathbf{j} = \|\mathbf{v}\|(\cos \theta)\mathbf{i} + \|\mathbf{v}\|(\sin \theta)\mathbf{j}$ where $\tan \theta = b/a$.

Solutions to Odd-Numbered Exercises

1. Initial point: $(0, 0)$

Terminal point: $(3, 2)$

$\mathbf{v} = \langle 3 - 0, 2 - 0 \rangle = \langle 3, 2 \rangle$

$\|\mathbf{v}\| = \sqrt{3^2 + 2^2} = \sqrt{13}$

3. Initial point: $(2, 2)$

Terminal point: $(-1, 4)$

$\mathbf{v} = \langle -1 - 2, 4 - 2 \rangle = \langle -3, 2 \rangle$

$\|\mathbf{v}\| = \sqrt{(-3)^2 + 2^2} = \sqrt{13}$

5. Initial point: $(3, -2)$

Terminal point: $(3, 3)$

$\mathbf{v} = \langle 3 - 3, 3 - (-2) \rangle = \langle 0, 5 \rangle$

$\|\mathbf{v}\| = \sqrt{0^2 + 5^2} = \sqrt{25} = 5$

7. Initial point: $(-1, 5)$

Terminal point: $(15, 12)$

$\mathbf{v} = \langle 15 - (-1), 12 - 5 \rangle = \langle 16, 7 \rangle$

$\|\mathbf{v}\| = \sqrt{16^2 + 7^2} = \sqrt{305}$

9. Initial point: $(-3, -5)$

Terminal point: $(5, 1)$

$\mathbf{v} = \langle 5 - (-3), 1 - (-5) \rangle = \langle 8, 6 \rangle$

$\|\mathbf{v}\| = \sqrt{8^2 + 6^2} = \sqrt{100} = 10$

11. Initial point: $(1, 3)$

Terminal point: $(-8, -9)$

$\mathbf{v} = \langle -8 - 1, -9 - 3 \rangle = \langle -9, -12 \rangle$

$\|\mathbf{v}\| = \sqrt{(-9)^2 + (-12)^2} = \sqrt{225} = 15$

13.

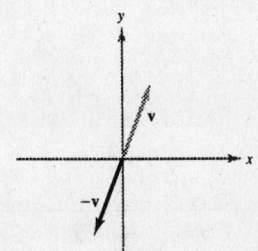

15.

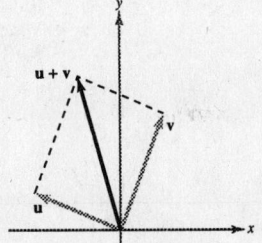

17. $\mathbf{u} + 2\mathbf{v}$

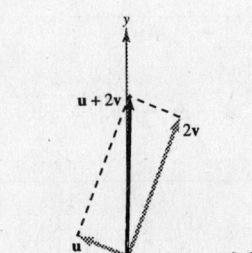

19. $\mathbf{u} = \langle 2, 1 \rangle$, $\mathbf{v} = \langle 1, 3 \rangle$

(a) $\mathbf{u} + \mathbf{v} = \langle 3, 4 \rangle$

(b) $\mathbf{u} - \mathbf{v} = \langle 1, -2 \rangle$

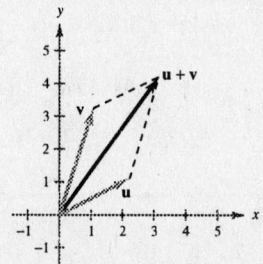

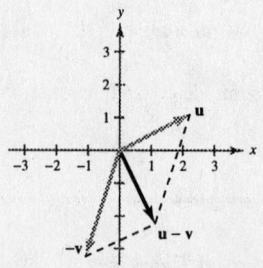

(c) $2\mathbf{u} - 3\mathbf{v} = \langle 4, 2 \rangle - \langle 3, 9 \rangle = \langle 1, -7 \rangle$

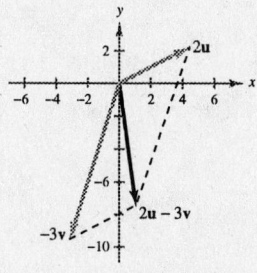

21. $\mathbf{u} = \langle -5, 3 \rangle$, $\mathbf{v} = \langle 0, 0 \rangle$

(a) $\mathbf{u} + \mathbf{v} = \langle -5, 3 \rangle = \mathbf{u}$

(b) $\mathbf{u} - \mathbf{v} = \langle -5, 3 \rangle = \mathbf{u}$

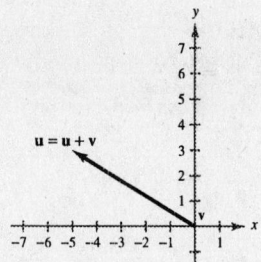

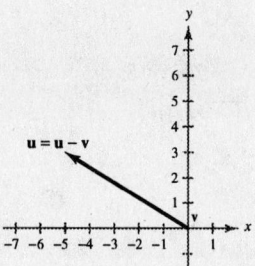

(c) $2\mathbf{u} - 3\mathbf{v} = 2\mathbf{u} = \langle -10, 6 \rangle$

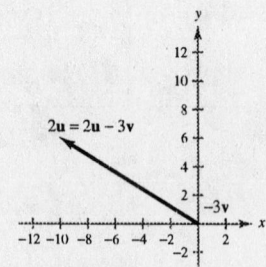

23. $\mathbf{u} = \mathbf{i} + \mathbf{j}, \mathbf{v} = 2\mathbf{i} - 3\mathbf{j}$

(a) $\mathbf{u} + \mathbf{v} = 3\mathbf{i} - 2\mathbf{j}$

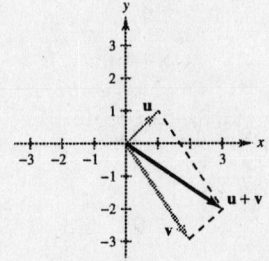

(b) $\mathbf{u} - \mathbf{v} = -\mathbf{i} + 4\mathbf{j}$

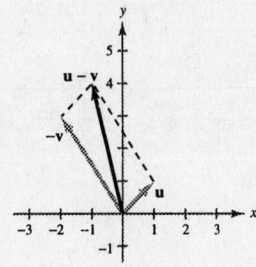

(c) $2\mathbf{u} - 3\mathbf{v} = (2\mathbf{i} + 2\mathbf{j}) - (6\mathbf{i} - 9\mathbf{j}) = -4\mathbf{i} + 11\mathbf{j}$

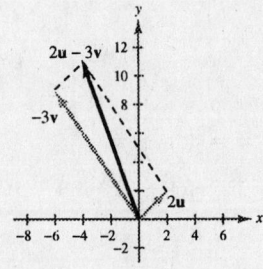

25. $\mathbf{u} = 2\mathbf{i}, \mathbf{v} = \mathbf{j}$

(a) $\mathbf{u} + \mathbf{v} = 2\mathbf{i} + \mathbf{j}$

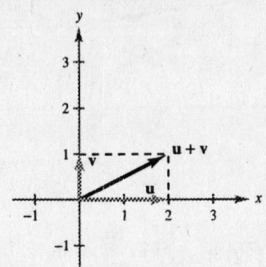

(b) $\mathbf{u} - \mathbf{v} = 2\mathbf{i} - \mathbf{j}$

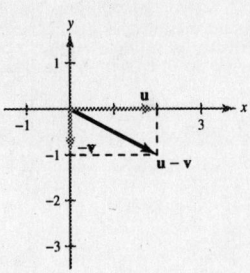

(c) $2\mathbf{u} - 3\mathbf{v} = 4\mathbf{i} - 3\mathbf{j}$

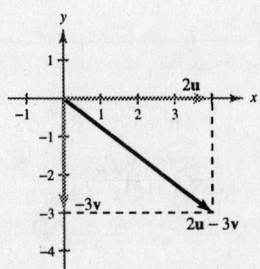

27. $\mathbf{v} = \dfrac{1}{\|\mathbf{u}\|}\mathbf{u} = \dfrac{1}{\sqrt{3^2 + 0^2}}\langle 3, 0\rangle = \dfrac{1}{3}\langle 3, 0\rangle = \langle 1, 0\rangle$

29. $\mathbf{u} = \dfrac{1}{\|\mathbf{v}\|}\mathbf{v} = \dfrac{1}{\sqrt{(-2)^2 + 2^2}}\langle -2, 2\rangle = \dfrac{1}{2\sqrt{2}}\langle -2, 2\rangle$

$$= \left\langle -\dfrac{1}{\sqrt{2}}, \dfrac{1}{\sqrt{2}}\right\rangle$$

31. $\mathbf{u} = \dfrac{1}{\|\mathbf{v}\|}\mathbf{v} = \dfrac{1}{\sqrt{6^2 + (-2)^2}}(6\mathbf{i} - 2\mathbf{j}) = \dfrac{1}{\sqrt{40}}(6\mathbf{i} - 2\mathbf{j})$

$\qquad = \dfrac{1}{2\sqrt{10}}(6\mathbf{i} - 2\mathbf{j}) = \dfrac{3}{\sqrt{10}}\mathbf{i} - \dfrac{1}{\sqrt{10}}\mathbf{j}$

33. $\mathbf{u} = \dfrac{1}{\|\mathbf{w}\|}\mathbf{w} = \dfrac{1}{4}(4\mathbf{j}) = \mathbf{j}$

35. $\mathbf{u} = \dfrac{1}{\|\mathbf{w}\|}\mathbf{w} = \dfrac{1}{\sqrt{1^2 + (-2)^2}}(\mathbf{i} - 2\mathbf{j}) = \dfrac{1}{\sqrt{5}}(\mathbf{i} - 2\mathbf{j})$

$\qquad = \dfrac{1}{\sqrt{5}}\mathbf{i} - \dfrac{2}{\sqrt{5}}\mathbf{j}$

37. $5\left(\dfrac{1}{\|\mathbf{u}\|}\mathbf{u}\right) = 5\left(\dfrac{1}{\sqrt{3^2 + 3^2}}\langle 3, 3 \rangle\right) = \dfrac{5}{3\sqrt{2}}\langle 3, 3 \rangle$

$\qquad = \left\langle \dfrac{5}{\sqrt{2}}, \dfrac{5}{\sqrt{2}} \right\rangle$

39. $9\left(\dfrac{1}{\|\mathbf{u}\|}\mathbf{u}\right) = 9\left(\dfrac{1}{\sqrt{2^2 + 5^2}}\langle 2, 5 \rangle\right) = \dfrac{9}{\sqrt{29}}\langle 2, 5 \rangle$

$\qquad = \left\langle \dfrac{18}{\sqrt{29}}, \dfrac{45}{\sqrt{29}} \right\rangle$

41. $\mathbf{v} = \dfrac{3}{2}\mathbf{u}$

$\qquad = \dfrac{3}{2}(2\mathbf{i} - \mathbf{j})$

$\qquad = 3\mathbf{i} - \dfrac{3}{2}\mathbf{j} = \langle 3, -\dfrac{3}{2} \rangle$

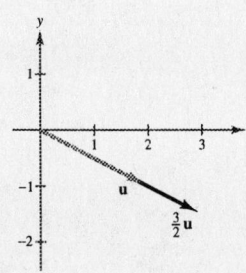

43. $\mathbf{v} = \mathbf{u} + 2\mathbf{w}$

$\qquad = (2\mathbf{i} - \mathbf{j}) + 2(\mathbf{i} + 2\mathbf{j})$

$\qquad = 4\mathbf{i} + 3\mathbf{j} = \langle 4, 3 \rangle$

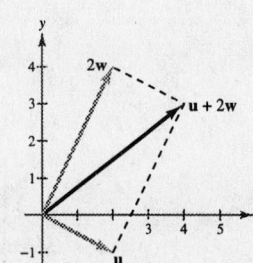

45. $\mathbf{v} = \dfrac{1}{2}(3\mathbf{u} + \mathbf{w})$

$\qquad = \dfrac{1}{2}(6\mathbf{i} - 3\mathbf{j} + \mathbf{i} + 2\mathbf{j})$

$\qquad = \dfrac{7}{2}\mathbf{i} - \dfrac{1}{2}\mathbf{j} = \langle \dfrac{7}{2}, -\dfrac{1}{2} \rangle$

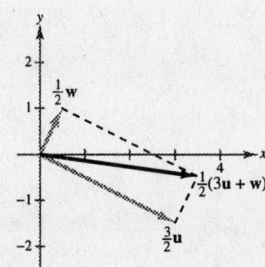

47. $\mathbf{v} = 3(\cos 60°\mathbf{i} + \sin 60°\mathbf{j})$

$\qquad \|\mathbf{v}\| = 3, \ \theta = 60°$

49. $\mathbf{v} = 6\mathbf{i} - 6\mathbf{j}$

$\qquad \|\mathbf{v}\| = \sqrt{6^2 + (-6)^2} = \sqrt{72} = 6\sqrt{2}$

$\qquad \tan \theta = \dfrac{-6}{6} = -1$

$\qquad$ Since $\mathbf{v}$ lies in Quadrant IV, $\theta = 315°$.

51. $\mathbf{v} = \langle 3 \cos 0°, 3 \sin 0° \rangle$

$\qquad = \langle 3, 0 \rangle$

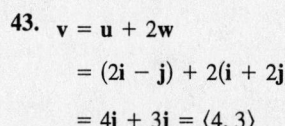

53. $\mathbf{v} = \left\langle \dfrac{7}{2} \cos 150°, \dfrac{7}{2} \sin 150° \right\rangle$

$\qquad = \left\langle -\dfrac{7\sqrt{3}}{4}, \dfrac{7}{4} \right\rangle$

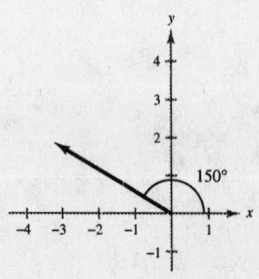

55. $\mathbf{v} = \langle 3\sqrt{2} \cos 150°, 3\sqrt{2} \sin 150° \rangle$

$\qquad = \left\langle -\dfrac{3\sqrt{6}}{2}, \dfrac{3\sqrt{2}}{2} \right\rangle$

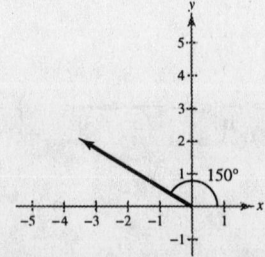

57. $\mathbf{v} = 2\left(\dfrac{1}{\sqrt{1^2 + 3^2}}\right)(\mathbf{i} + 3\mathbf{j})$

$\quad = \dfrac{2}{\sqrt{10}}(\mathbf{i} + 3\mathbf{j})$

$\quad = \dfrac{\sqrt{10}}{5}\mathbf{i} + \dfrac{3\sqrt{10}}{5}\mathbf{j} = \left\langle \dfrac{\sqrt{10}}{5}, \dfrac{3\sqrt{10}}{5} \right\rangle$

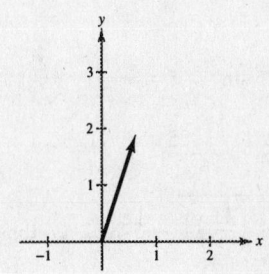

59. $\mathbf{u} = \langle 5\cos 0°, 5\sin 0° \rangle = \langle 5, 0 \rangle$

$\quad \mathbf{v} = \langle 5\cos 90°, 5\sin 90° \rangle = \langle 0, 5 \rangle$

$\quad \mathbf{u} + \mathbf{v} = \langle 5, 5 \rangle$

61. $\mathbf{u} = \langle 20\cos 45°, 20\sin 45° \rangle = \langle 10\sqrt{2}, 10\sqrt{2} \rangle$

$\quad \mathbf{v} = \langle 50\cos 180°, 50\sin 180° \rangle = \langle -50, 0 \rangle$

$\quad \mathbf{u} + \mathbf{v} = \langle 10\sqrt{2} - 50, 10\sqrt{2} \rangle$

63. $\mathbf{v} = \mathbf{i} + \mathbf{j}$

$\quad \mathbf{w} = 2\mathbf{i} - 2\mathbf{j}$

$\quad \mathbf{u} = \mathbf{v} - \mathbf{w} = -\mathbf{i} + 3\mathbf{j}$

$\quad \|\mathbf{v}\| = \sqrt{2}$

$\quad \|\mathbf{w}\| = 2\sqrt{2}$

$\quad \|\mathbf{v} - \mathbf{w}\| = \sqrt{10}$

$\quad \cos\alpha = \dfrac{\|\mathbf{v}\|^2 + \|\mathbf{w}\|^2 - \|\mathbf{v} - \mathbf{w}\|^2}{2\|\mathbf{v}\|\,\|\mathbf{w}\|} = \dfrac{2 + 8 - 10}{2\sqrt{2} \cdot 2\sqrt{2}} = 0$

$\quad \alpha = 90°$

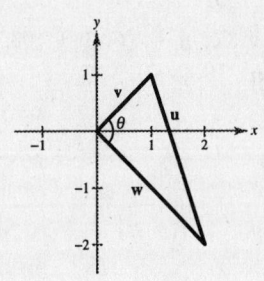

65. $\mathbf{v} = \mathbf{i} + \mathbf{j}$

$\quad \mathbf{w} = 3\mathbf{i} - \mathbf{j}$

$\quad \mathbf{u} = \mathbf{v} - \mathbf{w} = -2\mathbf{i} + 2\mathbf{j}$

$\quad \cos\alpha = \dfrac{\|\mathbf{v}\|^2 + \|\mathbf{w}\|^2 - \|\mathbf{v} - \mathbf{w}\|^2}{2\|\mathbf{v}\|\,\|\mathbf{w}\|} = \dfrac{2 + 10 - 8}{2\sqrt{2}\,\sqrt{10}} \approx 0.4472$

$\quad \alpha = 63.4°$

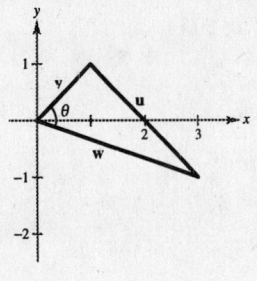

67. Force One: $\mathbf{u} = 45\mathbf{i}$

Force Two: $\mathbf{v} = 60\cos\theta\mathbf{i} + 60\sin\theta\mathbf{j}$

Resultant Force: $\mathbf{u} + \mathbf{v} = (45 + 60\cos\theta)\mathbf{i} + 60\sin\theta\mathbf{j}$

$\|\mathbf{u} + \mathbf{v}\| = \sqrt{(45 + 60\cos\theta)^2 + (60\sin\theta)^2} = 90$

$\qquad\qquad 2025 + 5400\cos\theta + 3600 = 8100$

$\qquad\qquad\qquad 5400\cos\theta = 2475$

$\qquad\qquad\qquad\qquad \cos\theta = \dfrac{2475}{5400} \approx 0.4583$

$\qquad\qquad\qquad\qquad\qquad \theta \approx 62.7°$

69. $\mathbf{u} = 300\mathbf{i}$

$$\mathbf{v} = (125 \cos 45°)\mathbf{i} + (125 \sin 45°)\mathbf{j} = \frac{125}{\sqrt{2}}\mathbf{i} + \frac{125}{\sqrt{2}}\mathbf{j}$$

$$R = \mathbf{u} + \mathbf{v} = \left(300 + \frac{125}{\sqrt{2}}\right)\mathbf{i} + \frac{125}{\sqrt{2}}\mathbf{j}$$

$$\|R\| = \sqrt{\left(300 + \frac{125}{\sqrt{2}}\right)^2 + \left(\frac{125}{\sqrt{2}}\right)^2} \approx 398.32 \text{ newtons}$$

$$\tan \theta = \frac{\dfrac{125}{\sqrt{2}}}{300 + \left(\dfrac{125}{\sqrt{2}}\right)} \implies \theta \approx 12.8°$$

71. $\mathbf{u} = (75 \cos 30°)\mathbf{i} + (75 \sin 30°)\mathbf{j} \approx 64.95\mathbf{i} + 37.5\mathbf{j}$

$\mathbf{v} = (100 \cos 45°)\mathbf{i} + (100 \sin 45°)\mathbf{j} \approx 70.71\mathbf{i} + 70.71\mathbf{j}$

$\mathbf{w} = (125 \cos 120°)\mathbf{i} + (125 \sin 120°)\mathbf{j} \approx -62.5\mathbf{i} + 108.3\mathbf{j}$

$\mathbf{u} + \mathbf{v} + \mathbf{w} \approx 73.16\mathbf{i} + 216.5\mathbf{j}$

$\|\mathbf{u} + \mathbf{v} + \mathbf{w}\| \approx 228.5 \text{ pounds}$

$$\tan \theta \approx \frac{216.5}{73.16} \approx 2.9592$$

$$\theta \approx 71.3°$$

73. Horizontal component of velocity: $70 \cos 35° \approx 57.34$ feet per second

Vertical component of velocity: $70 \sin 35° \approx 40.15$ feet per second

75. Cable $\overrightarrow{AC}$: $\mathbf{u} = \|\mathbf{u}\|(\cos 50°\mathbf{i} - \sin 50°\mathbf{j})$

Cable $\overrightarrow{BC}$: $\mathbf{v} = \|\mathbf{v}\|(\cos 30°\mathbf{i} - \sin 30°\mathbf{j})$

Resultant: $\mathbf{u} + \mathbf{v} = -2000\mathbf{j}$

$\|\mathbf{u}\| \cos 50° - \|\mathbf{v}\| \cos 30° = 0$

$-\|\mathbf{u}\| \sin 50° - \|\mathbf{v}\|\sin 30° = -2000$

Solving this system of equations yields:

$T_{AC} = \|\mathbf{u}\| \approx 1758.8$ pounds

$T_{BC} = \|\mathbf{v}\| \approx 1305.4$ pounds

77. Towline 1: $\mathbf{u} = \|\mathbf{u}\|(\cos 18°\mathbf{i} + \sin 18°\mathbf{j})$

Towline 2: $\mathbf{v} = \|\mathbf{u}\|(\cos 18°\mathbf{i} - \sin 18°\mathbf{j})$

Resultant: $\mathbf{u} + \mathbf{v} = 6000\mathbf{i}$

$\|\mathbf{u}\| \cos 18° + \|\mathbf{u}\| \cos 18° = 6000$

$\|\mathbf{u}\| \approx 3154.4$

Therefore, the tension on each towline is

$\|\mathbf{u}\| \approx 3154.4$ pounds.

79. Airspeed: $\mathbf{u} = (875 \cos 32°)\mathbf{i} - (875 \sin 32°)\mathbf{j}$

Groundspeed: $\mathbf{v} = (800 \cos 40°)\mathbf{i} - (800 \sin 40°)\mathbf{j}$

Wind: $\mathbf{w} = \mathbf{v} - \mathbf{u} = (800 \cos 40° - 875 \cos 32°)\mathbf{i} + (-800 \sin 40° + 875 \sin 32°)\mathbf{j}$

$$\approx -129.2065\mathbf{i} - 50.5507\mathbf{j}$$

Wind speed: $\|\mathbf{w}\| \approx \sqrt{(-129.2065)^2 + (-50.5507)^2}$

$$\approx 138.7 \text{ kilometers per hour}$$

Wind direction: $\tan \theta \approx \dfrac{-50.5507}{-129.2065}$

$$\theta \approx 21.4°$$

$$\text{N } 21.4° \text{ E}$$

81. $W = FD = (100 \cos 50°)(30) = 1928.4$ foot–pounds

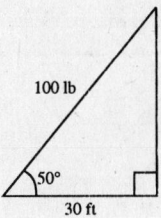

100 lb

50°

30 ft

83. True. See Example 1.

85. False, $a = b = 0$.

87. (a) The angle between them is $0°$.

(b) The angle between them is $180°$.

(c) No. At most it can be equal to the sum when the angle between them is $0°$.

89. Let $\mathbf{v} = (\cos \theta)\mathbf{i} + (\sin \theta)\mathbf{j}$.

$\|\mathbf{v}\| = \sqrt{\cos^2 \theta + \sin^2 \theta} = \sqrt{1} = 1$

Therefore, $\mathbf{v}$ is a unit vector for any value of θ.

91. $\mathbf{u} = \langle 5 - 1, 2 - 6 \rangle = \langle 4, -4 \rangle$

$\mathbf{v} = \langle 9 - 4, 4 - 5 \rangle = \langle 5, -1 \rangle$

$\mathbf{u} - \mathbf{v} = \langle -1, -3 \rangle$ or $\mathbf{v} - \mathbf{u} = \langle 1, 3 \rangle$

93. $\sqrt{x^2 - 64} = \sqrt{(8 \sec \theta)^2 - 64}$

$\qquad = \sqrt{64(\sec^2 \theta - 1)}$

$\qquad = 8\sqrt{\tan^2 \theta}$

$\qquad = 8 \tan \theta$ for $0 < \theta < \dfrac{\pi}{2}$

95. $\sqrt{x^2 + 36} = \sqrt{(6 \tan \theta)^2 + 36}$

$\qquad = \sqrt{36(\tan^2 \theta + 1)}$

$\qquad = 6\sqrt{\sec^2 \theta}$

$\qquad = 6 \sec \theta$ for $0 < \theta < \dfrac{\pi}{2}$

97. $\cos x(\cos x + 1) = 0$

$\cos x = 0$ or $\cos x + 1 = 0$

$x = \dfrac{\pi}{2} + n\pi \qquad \cos x = -1$

$\qquad\qquad\qquad\qquad x = \pi + 2n\pi$

99. $3 \sec x \sin x - 2\sqrt{3} \sin x = 0$

$\sin x(3 \sec x - 2\sqrt{3}) = 0$

$\sin x = 0$ or $3 \sec x - 2\sqrt{3} = 0$

$x = n\pi \qquad\qquad \sec x = \dfrac{2\sqrt{3}}{3}$

$\qquad\qquad\qquad \cos x = \dfrac{3}{2\sqrt{3}} = \dfrac{\sqrt{3}}{2}$

$\qquad\qquad\qquad x = \dfrac{\pi}{6} + 2n\pi$

$\qquad\qquad\qquad x = \dfrac{11\pi}{6} + 2n\pi$

101. $(\sin^2 x - 1)\sin^2 x = 0$

$\sin^2 x - 1 = 0$ or $\sin^2 x = 0$

$\sin^2 x = 1 \qquad \sin x = 0$

$\sin x = \pm 1 \qquad x = n\pi$

$x = \dfrac{\pi}{2} + n\pi$

These solutions can be expressed collectively as $x = \dfrac{n\pi}{2}$.

Section 6.4   Vectors and Dot Products

- Know the definition of the dot product of $\mathbf{u} = \langle u_1, u_2 \rangle$ and $\mathbf{v} = \langle v_1, v_2 \rangle$.

  $\mathbf{u} \cdot \mathbf{v} = u_1 v_1 + u_2 v_2$

- Know the following properties of the dot product:
  1. $\mathbf{u} \cdot \mathbf{v} = \mathbf{v} \cdot \mathbf{u}$
  2. $\mathbf{0} \cdot \mathbf{v} = 0$
  3. $\mathbf{u} \cdot (\mathbf{v} + \mathbf{w}) = \mathbf{u} \cdot \mathbf{v} + \mathbf{u} \cdot \mathbf{w}$
  4. $\mathbf{v} \cdot \mathbf{v} = \|\mathbf{v}\|^2$
  5. $c(\mathbf{u} \cdot \mathbf{v}) = c\mathbf{u} \cdot \mathbf{v} = \mathbf{u} \cdot c\mathbf{v}$

- If θ is the angle between two nonzero vectors $\mathbf{u}$ and $\mathbf{v}$, then

  $$\cos \theta = \frac{\mathbf{u} \cdot \mathbf{v}}{\|\mathbf{u}\| \, \|\mathbf{v}\|}.$$

- The vectors $\mathbf{u}$ and $\mathbf{v}$ are orthogonal if $\mathbf{u} \cdot \mathbf{v} = 0$.

- Know the definition of vector components.

  $\mathbf{u} = \mathbf{w}_1 + \mathbf{w}_2$ where $\mathbf{w}_1$ and $\mathbf{w}_2$ are orthogonal, and $\mathbf{w}_1$ is parallel to $\mathbf{v}$. $\mathbf{w}_1$ is called the projection of $\mathbf{u}$ onto $\mathbf{v}$

  and is denoted by $\mathbf{w}_1 = \text{proj}_\mathbf{v}\mathbf{u} = \left(\dfrac{\mathbf{u} \cdot \mathbf{v}}{\|\mathbf{v}\|^2} \right) \mathbf{v}$. Then we have $\mathbf{w}_2 = \mathbf{u} - \mathbf{w}_1$.

- Know the definition of work.
  1. Projection form: $w = \|\text{proj}_{\overrightarrow{PQ}} \mathbf{F}\| \, \|\overrightarrow{PQ}\|$
  2. Dot product form: $w = \mathbf{F} \cdot \overrightarrow{PQ}$

Solutions to Odd-Numbered Exercises

1. $\mathbf{u} = \langle 6, 1 \rangle$, $\mathbf{v} = \langle -2, 3 \rangle$

$\mathbf{u} \cdot \mathbf{v} = 6(-2) + 1(3) = -9$

3. $\mathbf{u} = 4\mathbf{i} - 2\mathbf{j}$, $\mathbf{v} = \mathbf{i} - \mathbf{j}$

$\mathbf{u} \cdot \mathbf{v} = 4(1) + (-2)(-1) = 6$

5. $\mathbf{u} = \langle 2, 2 \rangle$

$\mathbf{u} \cdot \mathbf{u} = 2(2) + 2(2) = 8$

The result is a scalar.

7. $\mathbf{u} = \langle 2, 2 \rangle$, $\mathbf{v} = \langle -3, 4 \rangle$

$(\mathbf{u} \cdot \mathbf{v})\mathbf{v} = [(2)(-3) + 2(4)]\langle -3, 4 \rangle$

$\qquad = 2\langle -3, 4 \rangle = \langle -6, 8 \rangle$

The result is a vector.

9. $\mathbf{u} = \langle -5, 12 \rangle$

$\|\mathbf{u}\| = \sqrt{\mathbf{u} \cdot \mathbf{u}} = \sqrt{(-5)^2 + 12^2} = 13$

11. $\mathbf{u} = 20\mathbf{i} + 25\mathbf{j}$

$\|\mathbf{u}\| = \sqrt{(20)^2 + (25)^2} = \sqrt{1025} = 5\sqrt{41}$

13. $\mathbf{u} = 6\mathbf{j}$

$\|\mathbf{u}\| = \sqrt{(0)^2 + (6)^2} = \sqrt{36} = 6$

15. $\mathbf{u} = \langle 1, 0 \rangle$, $\mathbf{v} = \langle 0, -2 \rangle$

$$\cos \theta = \frac{\mathbf{u} \cdot \mathbf{v}}{\|\mathbf{u}\| \, \|\mathbf{v}\|} = \frac{0}{(1)(2)} = 0$$

$$\theta = 90°$$

17. $\mathbf{u} = 3\mathbf{i} + 4\mathbf{j}$, $\mathbf{v} = -2\mathbf{j}$

$$\cos \theta = \frac{\mathbf{u} \cdot \mathbf{v}}{\|\mathbf{u}\| \, \|\mathbf{v}\|} = -\frac{8}{(5)(2)}$$

$$\theta = \arccos\left(-\frac{4}{5}\right)$$

$$\theta \approx 143.13°$$

19. $\mathbf{u} = 2\mathbf{i} - \mathbf{j}$, $\mathbf{v} = 6\mathbf{i} + 4\mathbf{j}$

$$\cos \theta = \frac{\mathbf{u} \cdot \mathbf{v}}{\|\mathbf{u}\| \, \|\mathbf{v}\|} = \frac{8}{\sqrt{5}\sqrt{52}} \Rightarrow \theta \approx 60.26°$$

21. $\mathbf{u} = 5\mathbf{i} + 5\mathbf{j}$, $\mathbf{v} = -6\mathbf{i} + 6\mathbf{j}$

$$\cos \theta = \frac{\mathbf{u} \cdot \mathbf{v}}{\|\mathbf{u}\| \, \|\mathbf{v}\|} = 0 \Rightarrow \theta = 90°$$

23. $\mathbf{u} = \left(\cos \dfrac{\pi}{3}\right)\mathbf{i} + \left(\sin \dfrac{\pi}{3}\right)\mathbf{j} = \dfrac{1}{2}\mathbf{i} + \dfrac{\sqrt{3}}{2}\mathbf{j}$

$\mathbf{v} = \left(\cos \dfrac{3\pi}{4}\right)\mathbf{i} + \left(\sin \dfrac{3\pi}{4}\right)\mathbf{j} = -\dfrac{\sqrt{2}}{2}\mathbf{i} + \dfrac{\sqrt{2}}{2}\mathbf{j}$

$\|\mathbf{u}\| = \|\mathbf{v}\| = 1$

$$\cos \theta = \frac{\mathbf{u} \cdot \mathbf{v}}{\|\mathbf{u}\| \, \|\mathbf{v}\|} = \mathbf{u} \cdot \mathbf{v} = \left(\frac{1}{2}\right)\left(-\frac{\sqrt{2}}{2}\right) + \left(\frac{\sqrt{3}}{2}\right)\left(\frac{\sqrt{2}}{2}\right) = \frac{-\sqrt{2} + \sqrt{6}}{4}$$

$$\theta = \arccos\left(\frac{-\sqrt{2} + \sqrt{6}}{4}\right) = 75° = \frac{5\pi}{12}$$

25. $P = (1, 2)$, $Q = (3, 4)$, $R = (2, 5)$

$\overrightarrow{PQ} = \langle 2, 2 \rangle$, $\overrightarrow{PR} = \langle 1, 3 \rangle$, $\overrightarrow{QR} = \langle -1, 1 \rangle$

$$\cos \alpha = \frac{\overrightarrow{PQ} \cdot \overrightarrow{PR}}{\|\overrightarrow{PQ}\| \, \|\overrightarrow{PR}\|} = \frac{8}{(2\sqrt{2})(\sqrt{10})} \Rightarrow \alpha = \arccos \frac{2}{\sqrt{5}} \approx 26.6°$$

$$\cos \beta = \frac{\overrightarrow{PQ} \cdot \overrightarrow{QR}}{\|\overrightarrow{PQ}\| \, \|\overrightarrow{QR}\|} = 0 \Rightarrow \beta = 90°. \quad \text{Thus, } \gamma = 180° - 26.6° - 90° = 63.4°.$$

27. $P = (-3, 0)$, $Q = (2, 2)$, $R = (0, 6)$

$\overrightarrow{QP} = \langle -5, -2 \rangle$, $\overrightarrow{PR} = \langle 3, 6 \rangle$, $\overrightarrow{QR} = \langle -2, 4 \rangle$

$$\cos \alpha = \frac{\overrightarrow{PQ} \cdot \overrightarrow{PR}}{\|\overrightarrow{PQ}\| \, \|\overrightarrow{PR}\|} = \frac{27}{\sqrt{29}\sqrt{45}} \Rightarrow \alpha \approx 41.6°$$

$$\cos \beta = \frac{\overrightarrow{QP} \cdot \overrightarrow{QR}}{\|\overrightarrow{QP}\| \, \|\overrightarrow{PR}\|} = \frac{2}{\sqrt{29}\sqrt{20}} \Rightarrow \beta \approx 85.2°$$

$$\delta = 180° - 41.6° - 85.2° = 53.2°$$

29. $\mathbf{u} \cdot \mathbf{v} = \|\mathbf{u}\| \, \|\mathbf{v}\| \cos \theta$

$$= (4)(10) \cos \frac{2\pi}{3}$$

$$= 40\left(-\frac{1}{2}\right)$$

$$= -20$$

31. $\mathbf{u} \cdot \mathbf{v} = \|\mathbf{u}\| \|\mathbf{v}\| \cos \theta$

$$= (81)(64)\cos \frac{\pi}{4}$$

$$= 5184\left(\frac{\sqrt{2}}{2}\right)$$

$$= 2592\sqrt{2}$$

33. $\mathbf{u} = \langle -12, 30 \rangle$, $\mathbf{v} = \left\langle \frac{1}{2}, -\frac{5}{4} \right\rangle$

$\mathbf{u} = -24\mathbf{v} \implies \mathbf{u}$ and $\mathbf{v}$ are parallel.

35. $\mathbf{u} = \frac{1}{4}(3\mathbf{i} - \mathbf{j})$, $\mathbf{v} = 5\mathbf{i} + 6\mathbf{j}$

$\mathbf{u} \neq k\mathbf{v} \implies$ Not parallel

$\mathbf{u} \cdot \mathbf{v} \neq 0 \implies$ Not orthogonal

Neither

37. $\mathbf{u} = 2\mathbf{i} - 2\mathbf{j}$, $\mathbf{v} = -\mathbf{i} - \mathbf{j}$

$\mathbf{u} \cdot \mathbf{v} = 0 \implies \mathbf{u}$ and $\mathbf{v}$ are orthogonal.

39. $\mathbf{u} = \langle 2, 2 \rangle$, $\mathbf{v} = \langle 6, 1 \rangle$

$$\mathbf{w}_1 = \text{proj}_{\mathbf{v}}\mathbf{u} = \left(\frac{\mathbf{u} \cdot \mathbf{v}}{\|\mathbf{v}\|^2}\right)\mathbf{v} = \frac{14}{37}\mathbf{v} = \frac{14}{37}\langle 6, 1 \rangle$$

$$\mathbf{w}_2 = \mathbf{u} - \mathbf{w}_1 = \langle 2, 2 \rangle - \frac{14}{37}\langle 6, 1 \rangle = \left\langle -\frac{10}{37}, \frac{60}{37} \right\rangle = \frac{10}{37}\langle -1, 6 \rangle$$

41. $\mathbf{u} = \langle 0, 3 \rangle$, $\mathbf{v} = \langle 2, 15 \rangle$

$$\mathbf{w}_1 = \text{proj}_{\mathbf{v}}\mathbf{u} = \left(\frac{\mathbf{u} \cdot \mathbf{v}}{\|\mathbf{v}\|^2}\right)\mathbf{v} = \frac{45}{229}\langle 2, 15 \rangle$$

$$\mathbf{w}_2 = \mathbf{u} - \mathbf{w}_1 = \langle 0, 3 \rangle - \frac{45}{229}\langle 2, 15 \rangle = \left\langle -\frac{90}{229}, \frac{12}{229} \right\rangle = \frac{6}{229}\langle -15, 2 \rangle$$

43. $\mathbf{u} = \langle 3, 5 \rangle$

For $\mathbf{v}$ to be orthogonal to $\mathbf{u}$, $\mathbf{u} \cdot \mathbf{v}$ must equal 0.

Two possibilities: $\langle -5, 3 \rangle$ and $\langle 5, -3 \rangle$

45. $\mathbf{u} = \frac{1}{2}\mathbf{i} - \frac{2}{3}\mathbf{j}$

For $\mathbf{u}$ and $\mathbf{v}$ to be orthogonal, $\mathbf{u} \cdot \mathbf{v}$ must equal 0.

Two possibilities: $\frac{2}{3}\mathbf{i} + \frac{1}{2}\mathbf{j}$ and $-\frac{2}{3}\mathbf{i} - \frac{1}{2}\mathbf{j}$

47. $\mathbf{w} = \| \text{proj}_{\overrightarrow{PQ}} \mathbf{v}\| \|\overrightarrow{PQ}\|$ where $\overrightarrow{PQ} = \langle 4, 7 \rangle$ and $\mathbf{v} = \langle 1, 4 \rangle$.

$$\text{proj}_{\overrightarrow{PQ}} \mathbf{v} = \left(\frac{\mathbf{v} \cdot \overrightarrow{PQ}}{\|\overrightarrow{PQ}\|^2}\right)\overrightarrow{PQ} = \left(\frac{32}{65}\right)\langle 4, 7 \rangle$$

$$\mathbf{w} = \| \text{proj}_{\overrightarrow{PQ}} \mathbf{v}\| \|\overrightarrow{PQ}\| = \left(\frac{32\sqrt{65}}{65}\right)\left(\sqrt{65}\right) = 32$$

49. $\mathbf{u} = \langle 1650, 3200 \rangle$, $\mathbf{v} = \langle 15.25, 10.50 \rangle$

$\mathbf{u} \cdot \mathbf{v} = 1650(15.25) + 3200(10.50) = \$58,762.50$

This gives the total revenue that can be earned by selling all of the units.

51. (a) $\mathbf{F} = -30{,}000\mathbf{j}$ Gravitational force

$\mathbf{v} = (\cos 5°)\mathbf{i} + (\sin 5°)\mathbf{j}$

$\mathbf{w}_1 = \text{proj}_\mathbf{v}\mathbf{F} = \left(\dfrac{\mathbf{F} \cdot \mathbf{v}}{\|\mathbf{v}\|^2}\right)\mathbf{v} = (\mathbf{F} \cdot \mathbf{v})\mathbf{v} \approx -2614.7\mathbf{v}$

The magnitude of this force is 2614.7, therefore a force of 2614.7 pounds is needed to keep the truck from rolling down the hill.

(b) $\mathbf{w}_2 = \mathbf{F} - \mathbf{w}_1 = -30{,}000\mathbf{j} + 2614.7(\cos 5°\mathbf{i} + \sin 5°\mathbf{j})$

$= 2614.7 \cos 5°\mathbf{i} + (2614.7 \sin 5° - 30{,}000)\mathbf{j}$

$\|\mathbf{w}_2\| \approx 29{,}885.8$ pounds

53. $\mathbf{w} = (245)(3) = 735$ Newton-meters

55. $\mathbf{w} = (\cos 30°)(45)(20) \approx 779.4$ foot-pounds

57. False. Work is represented by a scalar.

59. (a) $\mathbf{u} \cdot \mathbf{v} = 0 \implies \mathbf{u}$ and $\mathbf{v}$ are orthogonal and $\theta = \dfrac{\pi}{2}$.

(b) $\mathbf{u} \cdot \mathbf{v} > 0 \implies \cos\theta > 0 \implies 0 \le \theta < \dfrac{\pi}{2}$

(c) $\mathbf{u} \cdot \mathbf{v} < 0 \implies \cos\theta < 0 \implies \dfrac{\pi}{2} < \theta \le \pi$

61. In a rhombus, $\|\mathbf{u}\| = \|\mathbf{v}\|$. The diagonals are $\mathbf{u} + \mathbf{v}$ and $\mathbf{u} - \mathbf{v}$.

$(\mathbf{u} + \mathbf{v}) \cdot (\mathbf{u} - \mathbf{v}) = (\mathbf{u} + \mathbf{v}) \cdot \mathbf{u} - (\mathbf{u} + \mathbf{v}) \cdot \mathbf{v}$

$= \mathbf{u} \cdot \mathbf{u} + \mathbf{v} \cdot \mathbf{u} - \mathbf{u} \cdot \mathbf{v} - \mathbf{v} \cdot \mathbf{v}$

$= \|\mathbf{u}\|^2 - \|\mathbf{v}\|^2 = 0$

Therefore, the diagonals are orthogonal.

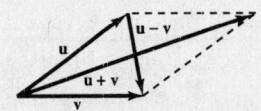

63. (a) Let $\mathbf{v} = \langle v_1, v_2 \rangle$.

$\mathbf{0} \cdot \mathbf{v} = 0(v_1) + 0(v_2) = 0$

(b) Let $\mathbf{u} = \langle u_1, u_2 \rangle$, $\mathbf{v} = \langle v_1, v_2 \rangle$ and $\mathbf{w} = \langle w_1, w_2 \rangle$.

$\mathbf{u} \cdot (\mathbf{v} + \mathbf{w}) = \langle u_1, u_2 \rangle \cdot \langle v_1 + w_1, v_2 + w_2 \rangle$

$= u_1(v_1 + w_1) + u_2(v_2 + w_2)$

$= u_1v_1 + u_1w_1 + u_2v_2 + u_2w_2$

$= (u_1v_1 + u_2v_2) + (u_1w_1 + u_2w_2)$

$= \mathbf{u} \cdot \mathbf{v} + \mathbf{u} \cdot \mathbf{w}$

(c) Let $\mathbf{u} = \langle u_1, u_2 \rangle$ and $\mathbf{v} = \langle v_1, v_2 \rangle$.

$c(\mathbf{u} \cdot \mathbf{v}) = c(u_1v_1 + u_2v_2)$

$= c(u_1v_1) + c(u_2v_2)$

$= u_1(cv_1) + u_2(cv_2)$

$= \mathbf{u} \cdot (c\mathbf{v})$

65. $\sin 2x - \sqrt{3} \sin x = 0$

$2 \sin x \cos x - \sqrt{3} \sin x = 0$

$\sin x(2 \cos x - \sqrt{3}) = 0$

$\sin x = 0$ or $2 \cos x - \sqrt{3} = 0$

$x = 0, \pi$ $\cos x = \dfrac{\sqrt{3}}{2}$

$x = \dfrac{\pi}{6}, \dfrac{11\pi}{6}$

67.
$$2 \tan x = \tan 2x$$

$$2 \tan x = \frac{2 \tan x}{1 - \tan^2 x}$$

$$2 \tan x(1 - \tan^2 x) = 2 \tan x$$

$$2 \tan x(1 - \tan^2 x) - 2 \tan x = 0$$

$$2 \tan x[(1 - \tan^2 x) - 1] = 0$$

$$2 \tan x(-\tan^2 x) = 0$$

$$-2 \tan^3 x = 0$$

$$\tan x = 0$$

$$x = 0, \pi$$

For Exercises 69. and 71.

$\sin u = -\frac{12}{13}, u$ in Quadrant IV $\Rightarrow \cos u = \frac{5}{13}$

$\cos v = \frac{24}{25}, v$ in Quadrant IV $\Rightarrow \sin v = -\frac{7}{25}$

69. $\sin(u - v) = \sin u \cos v - \cos u \sin v$

$\quad = \left(-\frac{12}{13}\right)\left(\frac{24}{25}\right) - \left(\frac{5}{13}\right)\left(-\frac{7}{25}\right)$

$\quad = -\frac{253}{325}$

71. $\cos(v - u) = \cos v \cos u + \sin v \sin u$

$\quad = \left(\frac{24}{25}\right)\left(\frac{5}{13}\right) + \left(-\frac{7}{25}\right)\left(-\frac{12}{13}\right)$

$\quad = \frac{204}{325}$

Section 6.5   Trigonometric Form of a Complex Number

■ You should be able to graphically represent complex numbers and know the following facts about them.

■ The absolute value of the complex number $z = a + bi$ is $|z| = \sqrt{a^2 + b^2}$.

■ The trigonometric form of the complex number $z = a + bi$ is $z = r(\cos \theta + i \sin \theta)$ where

(a) $a = r \cos \theta$

(b) $b = r \sin \theta$

(c) $r = \sqrt{a^2 + b^2}$; r is called the modulus of z.

(d) $\tan \theta = \frac{b}{a}$; θ is called the argument of z.

■ Given $z_1 = r_1(\cos \theta_1 + i \sin \theta_1)$ and $z_2 = r_2(\cos \theta_2 + i \sin \theta_2)$:

(a) $z_1 z_2 = r_1 r_2 [\cos(\theta_1 + \theta_2) + i \sin(\theta_1 + \theta_2)]$

(b) $\dfrac{z_1}{z_2} = \dfrac{r_1}{r_2}[\cos(\theta_1 - \theta_2) + i \sin(\theta_1 - \theta_2)]$, $z_2 \neq 0$

■ You should know DeMoivre's Theorem: If $z = r(\cos \theta + i \sin \theta)$,   then for any positive integer n,

$\quad z^n = r^n(\cos n\theta + i \sin n\theta)$.

■ You should know that for any positive integer n, $z = r(\cos \theta + i \sin \theta)$ has n distinct nth roots given by

$$\sqrt[n]{r}\left[\cos\left(\frac{\theta + 2\pi k}{n}\right) + i \sin\left(\frac{\theta + 2\pi k}{n}\right)\right]$$

where $k = 0, 1, 2, \ldots, n - 1$.

Solutions to Odd-Numbered Exercises

1. $|-7i| = \sqrt{0^2 + (-7)^2}$

$= \sqrt{49} = 7$

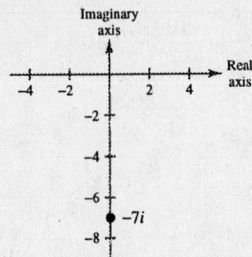

3. $|-4 + 4i| = \sqrt{(-4)^2 + (4)^2}$

$= \sqrt{32} = 4\sqrt{2}$

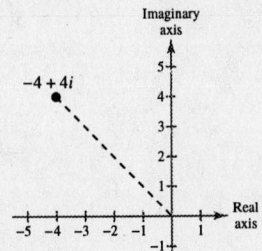

5. $|6 - 7i| = \sqrt{6^2 + (-7)^2}$

$= \sqrt{85}$

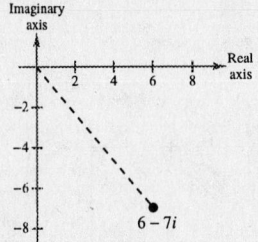

7. $z = 3i$

$r = \sqrt{0^2 + 3^2} = \sqrt{9} = 3$

$\tan \theta = \dfrac{3}{0}$, undefined $\implies \theta = \dfrac{\pi}{2}$

$z = 3\left(\cos \dfrac{\pi}{2} + i \sin \dfrac{\pi}{2}\right)$

9. $z = 3 - i$

$r = \sqrt{(3)^2 + (-1)^2} = \sqrt{10}$

$\tan \theta = -\dfrac{1}{3}$, θ is in Quadrant IV.

$\theta \approx 5.96$ radians

$z \approx \sqrt{10}(\cos 5.96 + i \sin 5.96)$

11. $z = 3 - 3i$

$r = \sqrt{3^2 + (-3)^2} = \sqrt{18} = 3\sqrt{2}$

$\tan \theta = \dfrac{-3}{3} = -1$, θ is in Quadrant IV $\implies \theta = \dfrac{7\pi}{4}$.

$z = 3\sqrt{2}\left(\cos \dfrac{7\pi}{4} + i \sin \dfrac{7\pi}{4}\right)$

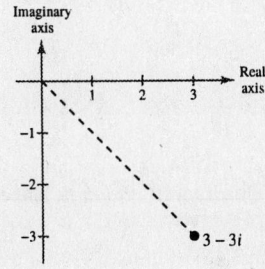

13. $z = \sqrt{3} + i$

$r = \sqrt{\left(\sqrt{3}\right)^2 + 1^2} = \sqrt{4} = 2$

$\tan \theta = \dfrac{1}{\sqrt{3}} = \dfrac{\sqrt{3}}{3} \implies \theta = \dfrac{\pi}{6}$

$z = 2\left(\cos \dfrac{\pi}{6} + i \sin \dfrac{\pi}{6}\right)$

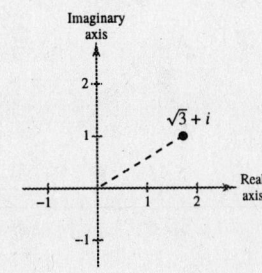

15. $z = -2(1 + \sqrt{3}i)$

$r = \sqrt{(-2)^2 + (-2\sqrt{3})^2} = \sqrt{16} = 4$

$\tan \theta = \dfrac{\sqrt{3}}{1} = \sqrt{3}$, θ is in Quadrant III $\Rightarrow \theta = \dfrac{4\pi}{3}$.

$z = 4\left(\cos\dfrac{4\pi}{3} + i \sin\dfrac{4\pi}{3}\right)$

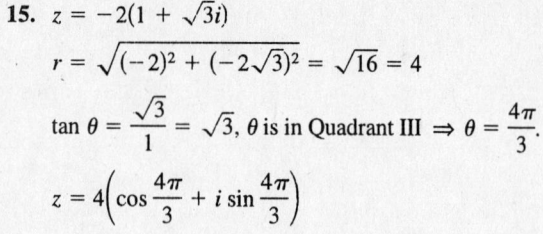
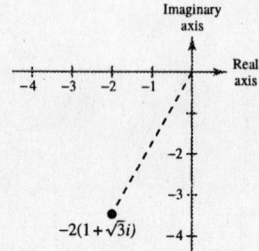

17. $z = -5i$

$r = \sqrt{0^2 + (-5)^2} = \sqrt{25} = 5$

$\tan \theta = \dfrac{-5}{0}$, undefined $\Rightarrow \theta = \dfrac{3\pi}{2}$

$z = 5\left(\cos\dfrac{3\pi}{2} + i \sin\dfrac{3\pi}{2}\right)$

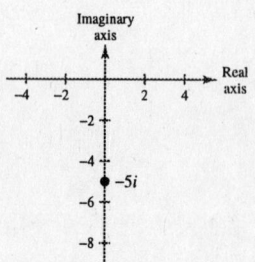

19. $z = -7 + 4i$

$r = \sqrt{(-7)^2 + (4)^2} = \sqrt{65}$

$\tan \theta = \dfrac{4}{-7}$, θ is in Quadrant II $\Rightarrow \theta \approx 2.62$.

$z \approx \sqrt{65}(\cos 2.62 + i \sin 2.62)$

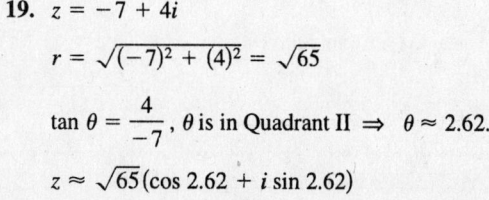
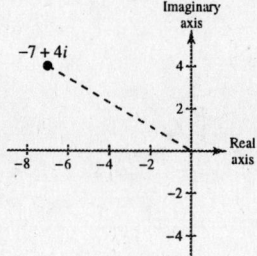

21. $z = 7 + 0i$

$r = \sqrt{(7)^2 + (0)^2} = \sqrt{49} = 7$

$\tan \theta = \dfrac{0}{7} = 0 \Rightarrow \theta = 0$

$z = 7(\cos 0 + i \sin 0)$

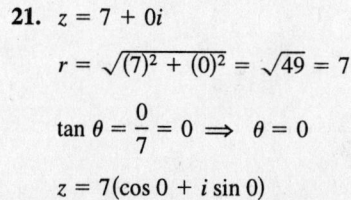
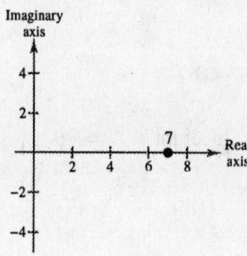

23. $z = 3 + \sqrt{3}i$

$r = \sqrt{(3)^2 + \left(\sqrt{3}\right)^2} = \sqrt{12}$

$\qquad = 2\sqrt{3}$

$\tan \theta = \dfrac{\sqrt{3}}{3} \Rightarrow \theta = \dfrac{\pi}{6}$

$z = 2\sqrt{3}\left(\cos\dfrac{\pi}{6} + i \sin\dfrac{\pi}{6}\right)$

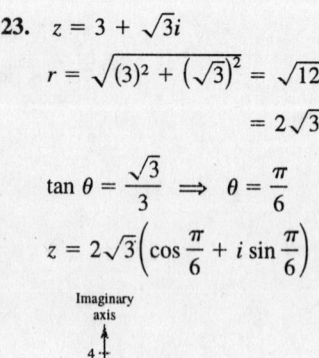
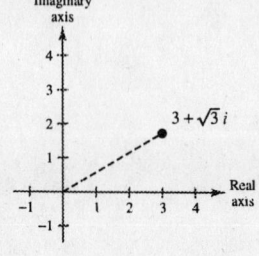

25. $z = -3 - i$

$r = \sqrt{(-3)^2 + (-1)^2} = \sqrt{10}$

$\tan \theta = \dfrac{-1}{-3} = \dfrac{1}{3}$, θ is in Quadrant III $\Rightarrow \theta \approx 3.46$.

$z \approx \sqrt{10}(\cos 3.46 + i \sin 3.46)$

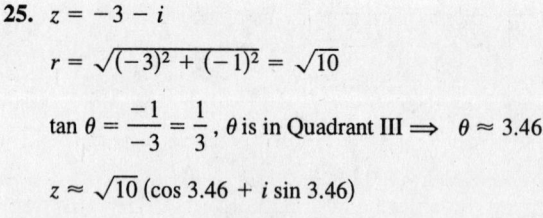
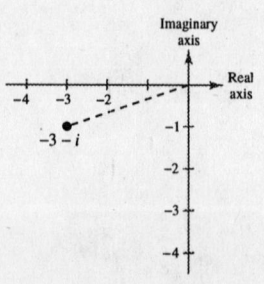

27. $z = 5 + 2i$

$r \approx 5.39$

$\theta \approx 0.38$

$z \approx 5.39(\cos 0.38 + i \sin 0.38)$

29. $z = -3 + i$

$r \approx 3.16$

$\theta \approx 2.82$

$z \approx 3.16(\cos 2.82 + i \sin 2.82)$

31. $z = 3\sqrt{2} - 7i$

$r \approx 8.19$

$\theta \approx 5.26$

$z \approx 8.19(\cos 5.26 + i \sin 5.26)$

33. $z = -8 - 5\sqrt{3}i$

$r \approx 11.79$

$\theta \approx 3.97$

$z \approx 11.79(\cos 3.97 + i \sin 3.97)$

35. $3(\cos 120° + i \sin 120°) = 3\left(-\dfrac{1}{2} + \dfrac{\sqrt{3}}{2}i\right)$

$$= -\dfrac{3}{2} + \dfrac{3\sqrt{3}}{2}i$$

37. $\dfrac{3}{2}(\cos 300° + i \sin 300°) = \dfrac{3}{2}\left[\dfrac{1}{2} + i\left(-\dfrac{\sqrt{3}}{2}\right)\right]$

$$= \dfrac{3}{4} - \dfrac{3\sqrt{3}}{4}i$$

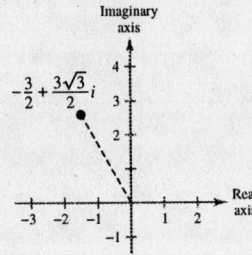

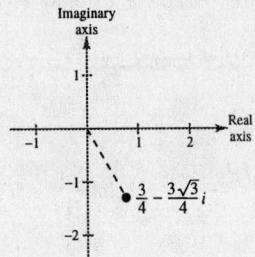

39. $3.75\left(\cos\dfrac{3\pi}{4} + i \sin\dfrac{3\pi}{4}\right) = -\dfrac{15\sqrt{2}}{8} + \dfrac{15\sqrt{2}}{8}i$

41. $8\left(\cos\dfrac{\pi}{2} + i \sin\dfrac{\pi}{2}\right) = 8(0 + i) = 8i$

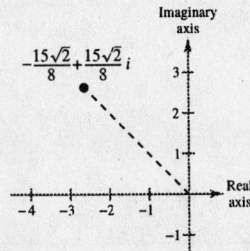

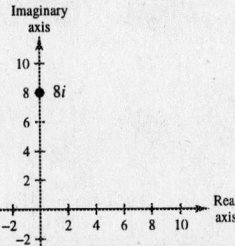

43. $3[\cos(18°45') + i \sin(18°45')] \approx 2.8408 + 0.9643i$

45. $5\left(\cos\dfrac{\pi}{9} + i \sin\dfrac{\pi}{9}\right) \approx 4.70 + 1.71i$

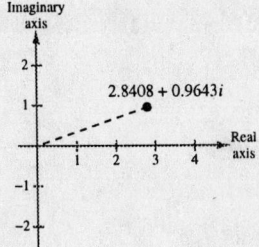

47. $3(\cos 165.5° + i \sin 165.5°) \approx -2.90 + 0.75i$

49. $\left[2\left(\cos\dfrac{\pi}{4} + i\sin\dfrac{\pi}{4}\right)\right]\left[6\left(\cos\dfrac{\pi}{12} + i\sin\dfrac{\pi}{12}\right)\right] = (2)(6)\left[\cos\left(\dfrac{\pi}{4} + \dfrac{\pi}{12}\right) + i\sin\left(\dfrac{\pi}{4} + \dfrac{\pi}{12}\right)\right]$

$$= 12\left(\cos\dfrac{\pi}{3} + i\sin\dfrac{\pi}{3}\right)$$

51. $\left[\tfrac{5}{3}(\cos 140° + i\sin 140°)\right]\left[\tfrac{2}{3}(\cos 60° + i\sin 60°)\right] = \left(\tfrac{5}{3}\right)\left(\tfrac{2}{3}\right)[\cos(140° + 60°) + i\sin(140° + 60°)]$

$$= \tfrac{10}{9}(\cos 200° + i\sin 200°)$$

53. $[0.45(\cos 310° + i\sin 310°)][0.60(\cos 200° + i\sin 200°)] = (0.45)(0.60)[\cos(310° + 200°) + i\sin(310° + 200°)]$

$$= 0.27(\cos 510° + i\sin 510°)$$
$$= 0.27(\cos 150° + i\sin 150°)$$

55. $\dfrac{\cos 50° + i\sin 50°}{\cos 20° + i\sin 20°} = \cos(50° - 20°) + i\sin(50° - 20°)$

$$= \cos 30° + i\sin 30°$$

57. $\dfrac{\cos\dfrac{5\pi}{3} + i\sin\dfrac{5\pi}{3}}{\cos \pi + i\sin \pi} = \cos\left(\dfrac{5\pi}{3} - \pi\right) + i\sin\left(\dfrac{5\pi}{3} - \pi\right) = \cos\left(\dfrac{2\pi}{3}\right) + i\sin\left(\dfrac{2\pi}{3}\right)$

59. $\dfrac{12(\cos 52° + i\sin 52°)}{3(\cos 110° + i\sin 110°)} = 4[\cos(52° - 110°) + i\sin(52° - 110°)]$

$$= 4[\cos(-58°) + i\sin(-58°)]$$

61. (a) $2 + 2i = 2\sqrt{2}\left(\cos\dfrac{\pi}{4} + i\sin\dfrac{\pi}{4}\right)$

$1 - i = \sqrt{2}\left[\cos\left(-\dfrac{\pi}{4}\right) + i\sin\left(-\dfrac{\pi}{4}\right)\right]$

(b) $(2 + 2i)(1 - i) = \left[2\sqrt{2}\left(\cos\dfrac{\pi}{4} + i\sin\dfrac{\pi}{4}\right)\right]\left[\sqrt{2}\left(\cos\left(-\dfrac{\pi}{4}\right) + i\sin\left(-\dfrac{\pi}{4}\right)\right)\right] = 4(\cos 0 + i\sin 0) = 4$

(c) $(2 + 2i)(1 - i) = 2 - 2i + 2i - 2i^2 = 2 + 2 = 4$

63. (a) $-2i = 2\left[\cos\left(-\dfrac{\pi}{2}\right) + i\sin\left(-\dfrac{\pi}{2}\right)\right]$

$1 + i = \sqrt{2}\left(\cos\dfrac{\pi}{4} + i\sin\dfrac{\pi}{4}\right)$

(b) $-2i(1 + i) = 2\left[\cos\left(-\dfrac{\pi}{2}\right) + i\sin\left(-\dfrac{\pi}{2}\right)\right]\left[\sqrt{2}\left(\cos\dfrac{\pi}{4} + i\sin\dfrac{\pi}{4}\right)\right]$

$$= 2\sqrt{2}\left[\cos\left(-\dfrac{\pi}{4}\right) + i\sin\left(-\dfrac{\pi}{4}\right)\right]$$

$$= 2\sqrt{2}\left[\dfrac{1}{\sqrt{2}} - \dfrac{1}{\sqrt{2}}i\right] = 2 - 2i$$

(c) $-2i(1 + i) = -2i - 2i^2 = -2i + 2 = 2 - 2i$

65. (a) $3 + 4i \approx 5(\cos 0.93 + i \sin 0.93)$

$1 - \sqrt{3}i = 2\left(\cos\dfrac{5\pi}{3} + i \sin\dfrac{5\pi}{3}\right)$

(b) $\dfrac{3 + 4i}{1 - \sqrt{3}i} \approx \dfrac{5(\cos 0.93 + i \sin 0.93)}{2\left(\cos\dfrac{5\pi}{3} + i \sin\dfrac{5\pi}{3}\right)}$

$\approx 2.5[\cos(-4.31) + i \sin(-4.31)]$

$\approx -0.982 + 2.299i$

(c) $\dfrac{3 + 4i}{1 - \sqrt{3}i} = \dfrac{3 + 4i}{1 - \sqrt{3}i} \cdot \dfrac{1 + \sqrt{3}i}{1 + \sqrt{3}i}$

$= \dfrac{3 + \left(4 + 3\sqrt{3}\right)i + 4\sqrt{3}i^2}{1 + 3}$

$= \dfrac{3 - 4\sqrt{3}}{4} + \dfrac{4 + 3\sqrt{3}}{4}i$

$\approx -0.982 + 2.299i$

67. (a) $5 = 5(\cos 0 + i \sin 0)$

$2 + 3i \approx \sqrt{13}(\cos 0.98 + i \sin 0.98)$

(b) $\dfrac{5}{2 + 3i} \approx \dfrac{5(\cos 0 + i \sin 0)}{\sqrt{13}(\cos 0.98 + i \sin 0.98)} = \dfrac{5\sqrt{13}}{13}[\cos(-0.98) + i \sin(-0.98)] \approx 0.769 - 1.154i$

(c) $\dfrac{5}{2 + 3i} = \dfrac{5}{2 + 3i} \cdot \dfrac{2 - 3i}{2 - 3i} = \dfrac{10 - 15i}{13} = \dfrac{10}{13} - \dfrac{15}{13}i \approx 0.769 - 1.154i$

69. Let $z = x + iy$ such that:

$|z| = 2 \implies 2 = \sqrt{x^2 + y^2}$

$\implies 4 = x^2 + y^2$: circle with radius of 2

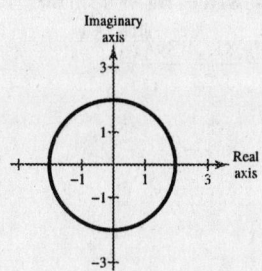

71. Let $\theta = \dfrac{\pi}{6}$.

Let $z = x + iy$ such that:

$\tan\dfrac{\pi}{6} = \dfrac{y}{x}$; line $y = \dfrac{\sqrt{3}}{3}x$

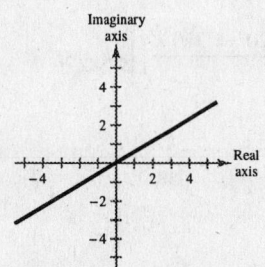

73. $(1 + i)^5 = \left[\sqrt{2}\left(\cos\dfrac{\pi}{4} + i \sin\dfrac{\pi}{4}\right)\right]^5$

$= \left(\sqrt{2}\right)^5\left(\cos\dfrac{5\pi}{4} + i \sin\dfrac{5\pi}{4}\right)$

$= 4\sqrt{2}\left(-\dfrac{\sqrt{2}}{2} - \dfrac{\sqrt{2}}{2}i\right)$

$= -4 - 4i$

75. $(-1 + i)^{10} = \left[\sqrt{2} \left(\cos \frac{3\pi}{4} + i \sin \frac{3\pi}{4} \right) \right]^{10}$

$$= (\sqrt{2})^{10} \left(\cos \frac{30\pi}{4} + i \sin \frac{30\pi}{4} \right)$$

$$= 32 \left[\cos \left(\frac{3\pi}{2} + 6\pi \right) + i \sin \left(\frac{3\pi}{2} + 6\pi \right) \right]$$

$$= 32 \left(\cos \frac{3\pi}{2} + i \sin \frac{3\pi}{2} \right)$$

$$= 32[0 + i(-1)]$$

$$= -32i$$

77. $2(\sqrt{3} + i)^7 = 2 \left[2 \left(\cos \frac{\pi}{6} + i \sin \frac{\pi}{6} \right) \right]^7$

$$= 2 \left[2^7 \left(\cos \frac{7\pi}{6} + i \sin \frac{7\pi}{6} \right) \right]$$

$$= 256 \left(-\frac{\sqrt{3}}{2} - \frac{1}{2}i \right)$$

$$= -128\sqrt{3} - 128i$$

79. $[5(\cos 20° + i \sin 20°)]^3 = 5^3(\cos 60° + i \sin 60°) = \dfrac{125}{2} + \dfrac{125\sqrt{3}}{2}i$

81. $\left(\cos \dfrac{\pi}{4} + i \sin \dfrac{\pi}{4} \right)^{12} = \cos \dfrac{12\pi}{4} + i \sin \dfrac{12\pi}{4}$

$$= \cos 3\pi + i \sin 3\pi$$

$$= -1$$

83. $[5(\cos 3.2 + i \sin 3.2)]^4 = 5^4(\cos 12.8 + i \sin 12.8)$

$$\approx 608.02 + 144.69i$$

85. $(3 - 2i)^5 \approx [3.6056[\cos(-0.588) + i \sin(-0.588)]]^5$

$$\approx (3.6056)^5[\cos(-2.94) + i \sin(-2.94)]$$

$$\approx -597 - 122i$$

87. $[3(\cos 15° + i \sin 15°)]^4 = 81(\cos 60° + i \sin 60°)$

$$= \frac{81}{2} + \frac{8\sqrt{3}}{2}i$$

89. $\left[2 \left(\cos \dfrac{\pi}{10} + i \sin \dfrac{\pi}{10} \right) \right]^5 = 2^5 \left(\cos \dfrac{\pi}{2} + i \sin \dfrac{\pi}{2} \right)$

$$= 32i$$

91. (a) Square roots of $5(\cos 120° + i \sin 120°)$:

$$\sqrt{5} \left[\cos \left(\frac{120° + 360°k}{2} \right) + i \sin \left(\frac{120° + 360°k}{2} \right) \right], \ k = 0, 1$$

$k = 0$: $\sqrt{5}(\cos 60° + i \sin 60°)$

$k = 1$: $\sqrt{5}(\cos 240° + i \sin 240°)$

(c) $\dfrac{\sqrt{5}}{2} + \dfrac{\sqrt{15}}{2}i, \ -\dfrac{\sqrt{5}}{2} - \dfrac{\sqrt{15}}{2}i$

(b)

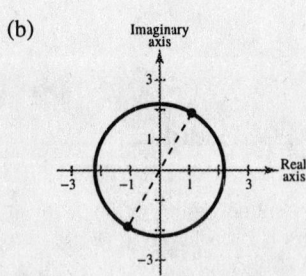

93. (a) Cube roots of $8\left(\cos\dfrac{2\pi}{3} + i\sin\dfrac{2\pi}{3}\right)$:

$$\sqrt[3]{8}\left[\cos\left(\dfrac{\dfrac{2\pi}{3} + 2\pi k}{3}\right) + i\sin\left(\dfrac{\dfrac{2\pi}{3} + 2\pi k}{3}\right)\right], \ k = 0, 1, 2$$

$k = 0$: $2\left(\cos\dfrac{2\pi}{9} + i\sin\dfrac{2\pi}{9}\right)$

$k = 1$: $2\left(\cos\dfrac{8\pi}{9} + i\sin\dfrac{8\pi}{9}\right)$

$k = 2$: $2\left(\cos\dfrac{14\pi}{9} + i\sin\dfrac{14\pi}{9}\right)$

(c) $1.5321 + 1.2856i$

    $-1.8794 + 0.6840i$

    $0.3473 - 1.9696i$

(b)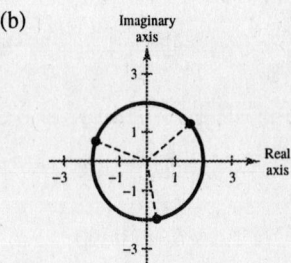

95. (a) Square roots of $-25i = 25\left(\cos\dfrac{3\pi}{2} + i\sin\dfrac{3\pi}{2}\right)$:

$$\sqrt{25}\left[\cos\left(\dfrac{\dfrac{3\pi}{2} + 2k\pi}{2}\right) + i\sin\left(\dfrac{\dfrac{3\pi}{2} + 2k\pi}{2}\right)\right], \ k = 0, 1$$

$k = 0$: $5\left(\cos\dfrac{3\pi}{4} + i\sin\dfrac{3\pi}{4}\right)$

$k = 1$: $5\left(\cos\dfrac{7\pi}{4} + i\sin\dfrac{7\pi}{4}\right)$

(c) $-\dfrac{5\sqrt{2}}{2} + \dfrac{5\sqrt{2}}{2}i, \ \dfrac{5\sqrt{2}}{2} - \dfrac{5\sqrt{2}}{2}i$

(b)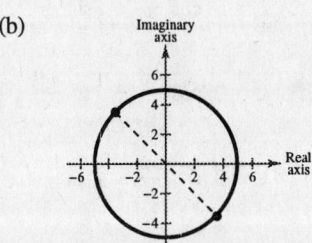

97. (a) Cube roots of $-\dfrac{125}{2}(1 + \sqrt{3}i) = 125\left(\cos\dfrac{4\pi}{3} + i\sin\dfrac{4\pi}{3}\right)$:

$$\sqrt[3]{125}\left[\cos\left(\dfrac{\dfrac{4\pi}{3} + 2k\pi}{3}\right) + i\sin\left(\dfrac{\dfrac{4\pi}{3} + 2k\pi}{3}\right)\right], \ k = 0, 1, 2$$

$k = 0$: $5\left(\cos\dfrac{4\pi}{9} + i\sin\dfrac{4\pi}{9}\right)$

$k = 1$: $5\left(\cos\dfrac{10\pi}{9} + i\sin\dfrac{10\pi}{9}\right)$

$k = 2$: $5\left(\cos\dfrac{16\pi}{9} + i\sin\dfrac{16\pi}{9}\right)$

(c) $0.8682 + 4.924i, \ -4.6984 - 1.710i, \ 3.8302 - 3.214i$

(b)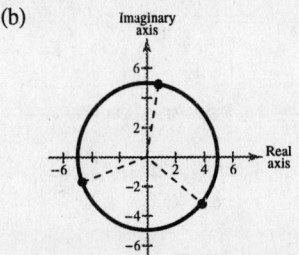

99. (a) Fourth roots of $16 = 16(\cos 0 + i \sin 0)$:

$$\sqrt[4]{16}\left[\cos\frac{0 + 2\pi k}{4} + i \sin\frac{0 + 2\pi k}{4}\right], k = 0, 1, 2, 3$$

$k = 0$: $2(\cos 0 + i \sin 0)$

$k = 1$: $2\left(\cos\dfrac{\pi}{2} + i \sin\dfrac{\pi}{2}\right)$

$k = 2$: $2(\cos \pi + i \sin \pi)$

$k = 3$: $2\left(\cos\dfrac{3\pi}{2} + i \sin\dfrac{3\pi}{2}\right)$

(c) $2, 2i, -2, -2i$

(b)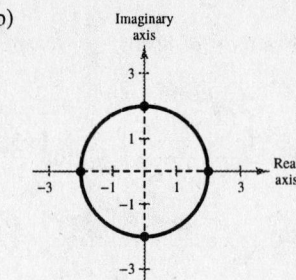

101. (a) Fifth roots of $1 = \cos 0 + i \sin 0$:

$$\cos\left(\frac{2k\pi}{5}\right) + i \sin\left(\frac{2k\pi}{5}\right), k = 0, 1, 2, 3, 4$$

$k = 0$: $\cos 0 + i \sin 0$

$k = 1$: $\cos\dfrac{2\pi}{5} + i \sin\dfrac{2\pi}{5}$

$k = 2$: $\cos\dfrac{4\pi}{5} + i \sin\dfrac{4\pi}{5}$

$k = 3$: $\cos\dfrac{6\pi}{5} + i \sin\dfrac{6\pi}{5}$

$k = 4$: $\cos\dfrac{8\pi}{5} + i \sin\dfrac{8\pi}{5}$

(c) $1, 0.3090 + 0.9511i, -0.8090 + 0.5878i, -0.8090 - 0.5878i, 0.3090 - 0.9511i$

(b)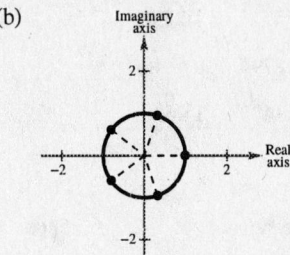

103. (a) Cube roots of $-125 = 125(\cos \pi + i \sin \pi)$:

$$\sqrt[3]{125}\left[\cos\left(\frac{\pi + 2\pi k}{3}\right) + i \sin\left(\frac{\pi + 2\pi k}{3}\right)\right], k = 0, 1, 2$$

$k = 0$: $5\left(\cos\dfrac{\pi}{3} + i \sin\dfrac{\pi}{3}\right)$

$k = 1$: $5(\cos \pi + i \sin \pi)$

$k = 2$: $5\left(\cos\dfrac{5\pi}{3} + i \sin\dfrac{5\pi}{3}\right)$

(b)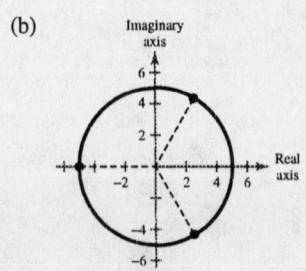

(c) $\dfrac{5}{2} + \dfrac{5\sqrt{3}}{2}i, -5, \dfrac{5}{2} - \dfrac{5\sqrt{3}}{2}i$

105. (a) Fifth roots of $128(-1 + i) = 128\sqrt{2}\left(\cos\dfrac{3\pi}{4} + i \sin\dfrac{3\pi}{4}\right)$:

$$\sqrt[5]{128\sqrt{2}}\left[\cos\left(\dfrac{\dfrac{3\pi}{4} + 2\pi k}{5}\right) + i \sin\left(\dfrac{\dfrac{3\pi}{4} + 2\pi k}{5}\right)\right], \; k = 0, 1, 2, 3, 4$$

$k = 0$: $2\sqrt[5]{4\sqrt{2}}\left(\cos\dfrac{3\pi}{20} + i \sin\dfrac{3\pi}{20}\right)$

$k = 1$: $2\sqrt[5]{4\sqrt{2}}\left(\cos\dfrac{11\pi}{20} + i \sin\dfrac{11\pi}{20}\right)$

$k = 2$: $2\sqrt[5]{4\sqrt{2}}\left(\cos\dfrac{19\pi}{20} + i \sin\dfrac{19\pi}{20}\right)$

$k = 3$: $2\sqrt[5]{4\sqrt{2}}\left(\cos\dfrac{27\pi}{20} + i \sin\dfrac{27\pi}{20}\right)$

$k = 4$: $2\sqrt[5]{4\sqrt{2}}\left(\cos\dfrac{7\pi}{4} + i \sin\dfrac{7\pi}{4}\right)$

(b)

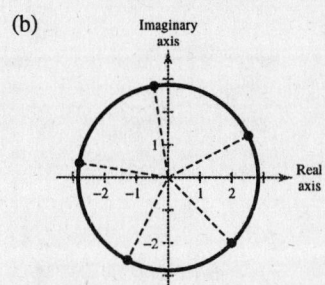

(c) $2.5201 + 1.2841i, \; -0.4425 + 2.7936i, \; -2.7936 + 0.4425i,$
$-1.2841 - 2.5201i, \; 2 - 2i$

107. $x^4 - i = 0$

$x^4 = i$

The solutions are the fourth roots of $i = \cos\dfrac{\pi}{2} + i \sin\dfrac{\pi}{2}$:

$$\sqrt[4]{1}\left[\cos\left(\dfrac{\dfrac{\pi}{2} + 2k\pi}{4}\right) + i \sin\left(\dfrac{\dfrac{\pi}{2} + 2k\pi}{4}\right)\right], \; k = 0, 1, 2, 3$$

$k = 0$: $\cos\dfrac{\pi}{8} + i \sin\dfrac{\pi}{8}$

$k = 1$: $\cos\dfrac{5\pi}{8} + i \sin\dfrac{5\pi}{8}$

$k = 2$: $\cos\dfrac{9\pi}{8} + i \sin\dfrac{9\pi}{8}$

$k = 3$: $\cos\dfrac{13\pi}{8} + i \sin\dfrac{13\pi}{8}$

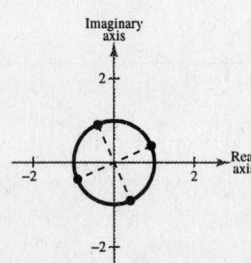

109. $x^5 + 243 = 0$

$$x^5 = -243$$

The solutions are the fifth roots of $-243 = 243(\cos \pi + i \sin \pi)$:

$$\sqrt[5]{243}\left[\cos\left(\frac{\pi + 2k\pi}{5}\right) + i \sin\left(\frac{\pi + 2k\pi}{5}\right)\right], \ k = 0, 1, 2, 3, 4$$

$k = 0: 3\left(\cos\dfrac{\pi}{5} + i \sin\dfrac{\pi}{5}\right)$

$k = 1: 3\left(\cos\dfrac{3\pi}{5} + i \sin\dfrac{3\pi}{5}\right)$

$k = 2: 3(\cos \pi + i \sin \pi) = -3$

$k = 3: 3\left(\cos\dfrac{7\pi}{5} + i \sin\dfrac{7\pi}{5}\right)$

$k = 4: 3\left(\cos\dfrac{9\pi}{5} + i \sin\dfrac{9\pi}{5}\right)$

111. $x^4 + 16i = 0$

$$x^4 = -16i$$

The solutions are the fourth roots of $-16i = 16\left(\cos\dfrac{3\pi}{2} + i \sin\dfrac{3\pi}{2}\right)$:

$$\sqrt[4]{16}\left[\cos\frac{\dfrac{3\pi}{2} + 2\pi k}{4} + i \sin\frac{\dfrac{3\pi}{2} + 2\pi k}{4}\right], k = 0, 1, 2, 3$$

$k = 0: 2\left(\cos\dfrac{3\pi}{8} + i \sin\dfrac{3\pi}{8}\right)$

$k = 1: 2\left(\cos\dfrac{7\pi}{8} + i \sin\dfrac{7\pi}{8}\right)$

$k = 2: 2\left(\cos\dfrac{11\pi}{8} + i \sin\dfrac{11\pi}{8}\right)$

$k = 3: 2\left(\cos\dfrac{15\pi}{8} + i \sin\dfrac{15\pi}{8}\right)$

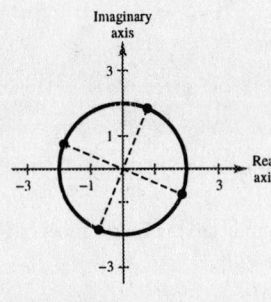

113. $x^3 - (1 - i) = 0$

$$x^3 = 1 - i = \sqrt{2}\left(\cos\frac{7\pi}{4} + i \sin\frac{7\pi}{4}\right)$$

The solutions are the cube roots of $1 - i$:

$$\sqrt[3]{\sqrt{2}}\left[\cos\left(\frac{\dfrac{7\pi}{4} + 2\pi k}{3}\right) + i \sin\left(\frac{\dfrac{7\pi}{4} + 2\pi k}{3}\right)\right], \ k = 0, 1, 2$$

$k = 0: \sqrt[6]{2}\left(\cos\dfrac{7\pi}{12} + i \sin\dfrac{7\pi}{12}\right)$

$k = 1: \sqrt[6]{2}\left(\cos\dfrac{5\pi}{4} + i \sin\dfrac{5\pi}{4}\right)$

$k = 2: \sqrt[6]{2}\left(\cos\dfrac{23\pi}{12} + i \sin\dfrac{23\pi}{12}\right)$

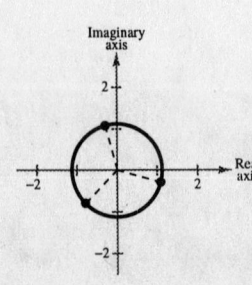

115. True, by the definition of the absolute value of a complex number.

117. True. $z_1 z_2 = r_1 r_2 [\cos(\theta_1 + \theta_2) + i \sin(\theta_1 + \theta_2)]$ and $z_1 z_2 = 0$ if and only if $r_1 = 0$ and/or $r_2 = 0$.

119.
$$\frac{z_1}{z_2} = \frac{r_1(\cos \theta_1 + i \sin \theta_1)}{r_2(\cos \theta_2 + i \sin \theta_2)} \cdot \frac{\cos \theta_2 - i \sin \theta_2}{\cos \theta_2 - i \sin \theta_2}$$

$$= \frac{r_1}{r_2(\cos^2 \theta_2 + \sin^2 \theta_2)} [\cos \theta_1 \cos \theta_2 + \sin \theta_1 \sin \theta_2 + i(\sin \theta_1 \cos \theta_2 - \sin \theta_2 \cos \theta_1)]$$

$$= \frac{r_1}{r_2} [\cos(\theta_1 - \theta_2) + i \sin(\theta_1 - \theta_2)]$$

121. (a)
$$z\bar{z} = [r(\cos \theta + i \sin \theta)][r(\cos(-\theta) + i \sin(-\theta))]$$
$$= r^2[\cos(\theta - \theta) + i \sin(\theta - \theta)]$$
$$= r^2[\cos 0 + i \sin 0]$$
$$= r^2$$

(b)
$$\frac{z}{\bar{z}} = \frac{r(\cos \theta + i \sin\theta)}{r[\cos(-\theta) + i \sin(-\theta)]}$$

$$= \frac{r}{r}[\cos(\theta - (-\theta)) + i \sin(\theta - (-\theta))]$$

$$= \cos 2\theta + i \sin 2\theta$$

123.
$$-\frac{1}{2}(1 + \sqrt{3}i) = -\left(\cos \frac{4\pi}{3} + i \sin \frac{4\pi}{3}\right)$$

$$\left[-\frac{1}{2}(1 + \sqrt{3}i)\right]^6 = \left[-\left(\cos \frac{4\pi}{3} + i \sin \frac{4\pi}{3}\right)\right]^6$$

$$= \cos 8\pi + i \sin 8\pi$$

$$= 1$$

125. (a) $2(\cos 30° + i \sin 30°)$

$2(\cos 150° + i \sin 150°)$

$2(\cos 270° + i \sin 270°)$

(b) These are the cube roots of $8i$.

127. $A = 22°, a = 8$

$B = 90° - A = 68°$

$$\tan 22° = \frac{8}{b} \implies b = \frac{8}{\tan 22°} \approx 19.80$$

$$\sin 22° = \frac{8}{c} \implies c = \frac{8}{\sin 22°} \approx 21.36$$

129. $A = 30°, b = 112.6$

$B = 90° - A = 60°$

$$\tan 30° = \frac{a}{112.6} \implies a = 112.6 \tan 30° \approx 65.01$$

$$\cos 30° = \frac{112.6}{c} \implies c = \frac{112.6}{\cos 30°} \approx 130.02$$

131. $A = 42°15' = 42.25°, c = 11.2$

$B = 90° - A = 47°45'$

$$\sin 42.25° = \frac{a}{11.2} \implies a = 11.2 \sin 42.25° \approx 7.53$$

$$\cos 42.25° = \frac{b}{11.2} \implies b = 11.2 \cos 42.25° \approx 8.29$$

133. $d = 16 \cos \frac{\pi}{4} t$

Maximum displacement: $|16| = 16$

$$16 \cos \frac{\pi}{4} t = 0 \implies \frac{\pi}{4} t = \frac{\pi}{2} \implies t = 2$$

135. $d = \frac{1}{16} \sin \frac{5}{4} \pi t$

Maximum displacement: $\left|\frac{1}{16}\right| = \frac{1}{16}$

$$\frac{1}{16} \sin \frac{5}{4} \pi t = 0 \implies \frac{5}{4} \pi t = 0 \implies t = 0$$

Review Exercises for Chapter 6

Solutions to Odd-Numbered Exercises

1. Given: $A = 35°, B = 71°, a = 8$

$C = 180° - 35° - 71° = 74°$

$b = \dfrac{a \sin B}{\sin A} = \dfrac{8 \sin 71°}{\sin 35°} \approx 13.19$

$c = \dfrac{a \sin C}{\sin A} = \dfrac{8 \sin 74°}{\sin 35°} \approx 13.41$

3. Given: $B = 72°, C = 82°, b = 54$

$A = 180° - 72° - 82° = 26°$

$a = \dfrac{b \sin A}{\sin B} = \dfrac{54 \sin 26°}{\sin 72°} \approx 24.89$

$c = \dfrac{b \sin C}{\sin B} = \dfrac{54 \sin 82°}{\sin 72°} \approx 56.23$

5. Given: $A = 16°, B = 98°, c = 8.4$

$C = 180° - 16° - 98° = 66°$

$a = \dfrac{c \sin A}{\sin C} = \dfrac{8.4 \sin 16°}{\sin 66°} \approx 2.53$

$b = \dfrac{c \sin B}{\sin C} = \dfrac{8.4 \sin 98°}{\sin 66°} \approx 9.11$

7. Given: $A = 24°, C = 48°, b = 27.5$

$B = 180° - 24° - 48° = 108°$

$a = \dfrac{b \sin A}{\sin B} = \dfrac{27.5 \sin 24°}{\sin 108°} \approx 11.76$

$c = \dfrac{b \sin C}{\sin B} = \dfrac{27.5 \sin 48°}{\sin 108°} \approx 21.49$

9. Given: $B = 150°, b = 30, c = 10$

$\sin C = \dfrac{c \sin B}{b} = \dfrac{10 \sin 150°}{30} \approx 0.1667 \Rightarrow C \approx 9.59°$

$A \approx 180° - 150° - 9.59° = 20.41°$

$a = \dfrac{b \sin A}{\sin B} = \dfrac{30 \sin 20.41°}{\sin 150°} \approx 20.92$

11. $A = 75°, a = 51.2, b = 33.7$

$\sin B = \dfrac{b \sin A}{a} = \dfrac{33.7 \sin 75°}{51.2} \approx 0.6358 \Rightarrow B \approx 39.48°$

$C \approx 180° - 75° - 39.48° = 65.52°$

$c = \dfrac{a \sin C}{\sin A} = \dfrac{51.2 \sin 65.52°}{\sin 75°} \approx 48.24$

13. Area $= \dfrac{1}{2}bc \sin A = \dfrac{1}{2}(5)(7)\sin 27° \approx 7.945$

15. Area $= \dfrac{1}{2}ab \sin C = \dfrac{1}{2}(16)(5)\sin 123° \approx 33.547$

17. $\tan 17° = \dfrac{h}{x + 50} \Rightarrow h = (x + 50)\tan 17°$

$\qquad\qquad\qquad h = x \tan 17° + 50 \tan 17°$

$\tan 31° = \dfrac{h}{x} \Rightarrow h = x \tan 31°$

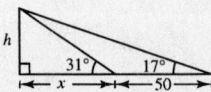

$x \tan 17° + 50 \tan 17° = x \tan 31°$

$50 \tan 17° = x(\tan 31° - \tan 17°)$

$\dfrac{50 \tan 17°}{\tan 31° - \tan 17°} = x$

$x \approx 51.7959$

$h = x \tan 31°$

$\approx 51.7959 \tan 31°$

$\approx 31.1 \text{ meters}$

19.

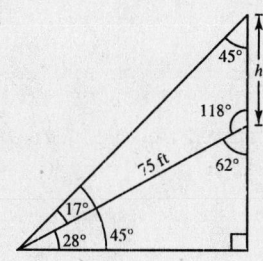

$$\frac{h}{\sin 17°} = \frac{75}{\sin 45°}$$

$$h = \frac{75 \sin 17°}{\sin 45°}$$

$$h \approx 31.01 \text{ feet}$$

21. Given: $a = 80, b = 60, c = 100$

$$\cos C = \frac{a^2 + b^2 - c^2}{2ab} = \frac{6400 + 3600 - 10,000}{2(80)(60)} = 0 \Rightarrow C = 90°$$

$$\sin A = \frac{80}{100} = 0.8 \Rightarrow A \approx 53.13°$$

$$\sin B = \frac{60}{100} = 0.6 \Rightarrow B \approx 36.87°$$

23. Given: $a = 16.4, b = 8.8, c = 12.2$

$$\cos A = \frac{b^2 + c^2 - a^2}{2bc} = \frac{8.8^2 + 12.2^2 - 16.4^2}{2(8.8)(12.2)} \approx -0.1988 \Rightarrow A \approx 101.47°$$

$$\sin B = \frac{b \sin A}{a} \approx \frac{8.8 \sin 101.47°}{16.4} \approx 0.5259 \Rightarrow B \approx 31.73°$$

$$C \approx 180° - 101.47° - 31.73° = 46.80°$$

25. Given: $B = 150°, a = 10, c = 20$

$$b^2 = 10^2 + 20^2 - 2(10)(20)\cos 150° \Rightarrow b \approx 29.09$$

$$\sin A = \frac{a \sin B}{b} \approx \frac{10 \sin 150°}{29.09} \Rightarrow A \approx 9.90°$$

$$C \approx 180° - 150° - 9.90° = 20.10°$$

27. Given: $A = 62°, b = 11.34, c = 19.52$

$$a^2 = 11.34^2 + 19.52^2 - 2(11.34)(19.52)\cos 62° \Rightarrow a \approx 17.37$$

$$\sin B = \frac{b \sin A}{a} \approx \frac{11.34 \sin 62°}{17.37} \Rightarrow B \approx 35.20°$$

$$C \approx 180° - 62° - 35.20° = 82.80°$$

29. $d^2 = 850^2 + 1060^2 - 2(850)(1060)\cos 72°$

$\approx 1,289,251$

$d \approx 1135$ miles

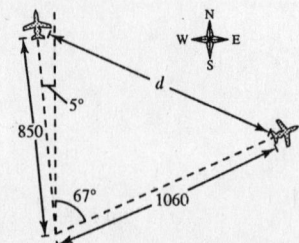

31. $a = 15, b = 8, c = 10$

$s = \dfrac{15 + 8 + 10}{2} = 16.5$

Area $= \sqrt{16.5(1.5)(8.5)(6.5)} \approx 36.979$

33. $a = 38.1, b = 26.7, c = 19.4$

$s = \dfrac{38.1 + 26.7 + 19.4}{2} = 42.1$

Area $= \sqrt{42.1(4)(15.4)(22.7)} \approx 242.630$

35. Initial point: $(3, 4)$

Terminal point: $(-5, -7)$

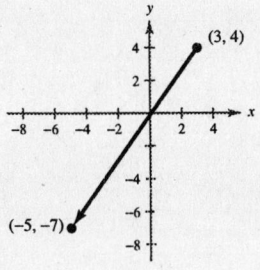

37. Initial point: $(-6, -8)$

Terminal point: $(8, 3)$

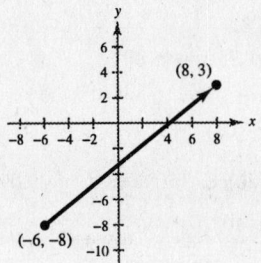

39. Initial point: $(0, 1)$

Terminal point: $\left(6, \frac{7}{2}\right)$

$\mathbf{v} = \left\langle 6 - 0, \frac{7}{2} - 1 \right\rangle = \left\langle 6, \frac{5}{2} \right\rangle$

41. Initial point: $(1, 5)$

Terminal point: $(15, 9)$

$\mathbf{v} = \langle 15 - 1, 9 - 5 \rangle = \langle 14, 4 \rangle$

43. $\|\mathbf{v}\| = \dfrac{1}{2}, \theta = 225°$

$\left\langle \dfrac{1}{2} \cos 225°, \dfrac{1}{2} \sin 225° \right\rangle = \left\langle -\dfrac{\sqrt{2}}{4}, -\dfrac{\sqrt{2}}{4} \right\rangle$

45. $\mathbf{u} = 6\mathbf{i} - 5\mathbf{j}, \quad \mathbf{v} = 10\mathbf{i} + 3\mathbf{j}$

$4\mathbf{u} - 5\mathbf{v} = (24\mathbf{i} - 20\mathbf{j}) - (50\mathbf{i} + 15\mathbf{j}) = -26\mathbf{i} - 35\mathbf{j}$

$= \langle -26, -35 \rangle$

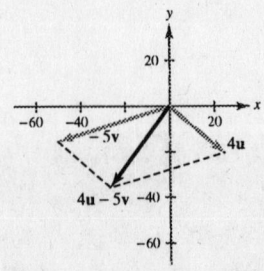

47. $\mathbf{v} = 10\mathbf{i} + 3\mathbf{j}$

$\frac{1}{2}\mathbf{v} = 5\mathbf{i} + \frac{3}{2}\mathbf{j} = \left\langle 5, \frac{3}{2} \right\rangle$

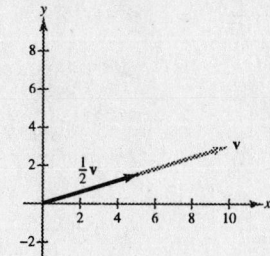

49. $\mathbf{u} = \langle -6, -8 \rangle = -6\mathbf{i} - 8\mathbf{j}$

51. Initial point: $(-2, 7)$

Terminal point: $(5, -9)$

$\mathbf{u} = \langle 5 - (-2), -9 - 7 \rangle = \langle 7, -16 \rangle = 7\mathbf{i} - 16\mathbf{j}$

53. $\mathbf{v} = 4\mathbf{i} - \mathbf{j}$

$\|\mathbf{v}\| = \sqrt{4^2 + (-1)^2} = \sqrt{17}$

$\tan \theta = \frac{-1}{4}$, θ in Quadrant IV $\Rightarrow$ $\theta \approx 346°$

$\mathbf{v} \approx \sqrt{17}(\cos 346° \, \mathbf{i} + \sin 346° \, \mathbf{j})$

55. $\mathbf{v} = 3(\cos 150°\mathbf{i} + \sin 150° \mathbf{j})$

$\|\mathbf{v}\| = 3, \; \theta = 150°$

57. $\mathbf{v} = -4\mathbf{i} + 7\mathbf{j}$

$\|\mathbf{v}\| = \sqrt{(-4)^2 + 7^2} = \sqrt{65}$

$\tan \theta = \frac{7}{-4}$, θ in Quadrant II $\Rightarrow$ $\theta \approx 119.7°$

59. $\mathbf{v} = 8\mathbf{i} - \mathbf{j}$

$\|\mathbf{v}\| = \sqrt{8^2 + (-1)^2} = \sqrt{65}$

$\tan \theta = \frac{-1}{8}$, θ in Quadrant IV $\Rightarrow$ $\theta \approx 352.9°$

61. Rope One: $\mathbf{u} = \|\mathbf{u}\|(\cos 30°\mathbf{i} - \sin 30°\mathbf{j}) = \|\mathbf{u}\|\left(\frac{\sqrt{3}}{2}\mathbf{i} - \frac{1}{2}\mathbf{j} \right)$

Rope Two: $\mathbf{v} = \|\mathbf{u}\|(-\cos 30°\mathbf{i} - \sin 30°\mathbf{j}) = \|\mathbf{u}\|\left(-\frac{\sqrt{3}}{2}\mathbf{i} - \frac{1}{2}\mathbf{j} \right)$

Resultant: $\mathbf{u} + \mathbf{v} = -\|\mathbf{u}\|\mathbf{j} = -180\mathbf{j}$

$\|\mathbf{u}\| = 180$

Therefore, the tension on each rope is $\|\mathbf{u}\| = 180$ lb.

63. $\mathbf{u} = \langle 6, 7 \rangle$

$\mathbf{v} = \langle -3, 9 \rangle$

$\mathbf{u} \cdot \mathbf{v} = 6(-3) + 7(9) = 45$

65. $\mathbf{u} = 3\mathbf{i} + 7\mathbf{j}$

$\mathbf{v} = 11\mathbf{i} - 5\mathbf{j}$

$\mathbf{u} \cdot \mathbf{v} = 3(11) + 7(-5) = -2$

67. $\mathbf{u} = \langle -3, 4 \rangle$

$2\mathbf{u} = \langle -6, 8 \rangle$

$2\mathbf{u} \cdot \mathbf{u} = (-6)(-3) + 8(4) = 50$

The result is a scalar.

69. $\mathbf{u} = \langle -3, 4 \rangle, \mathbf{v} = \langle 2, 1 \rangle$

$\mathbf{u} \cdot \mathbf{v} = (-3)(2) + 4(1) = -2$

$\mathbf{u}(\mathbf{u} \cdot \mathbf{v}) = \mathbf{u}(-2) = -2\mathbf{u} = \langle 6, -8 \rangle$

The result is a vector.

71. $\mathbf{u} = \cos\dfrac{7\pi}{4}\mathbf{i} + \sin\dfrac{7\pi}{4}\mathbf{j} = \left\langle \dfrac{1}{\sqrt{2}}, -\dfrac{1}{\sqrt{2}} \right\rangle$

$\mathbf{v} = \cos\dfrac{5\pi}{6}\mathbf{i} + \sin\dfrac{5\pi}{6}\mathbf{j} = \left\langle -\dfrac{\sqrt{3}}{2}, \dfrac{1}{2} \right\rangle$

$\cos\theta = \dfrac{\mathbf{u}\cdot\mathbf{v}}{\|\mathbf{u}\|\,\|\mathbf{v}\|} = \dfrac{-\sqrt{3}-1}{2\sqrt{2}} \Rightarrow \theta = \dfrac{11\pi}{12}$

73. $\mathbf{u} = \langle 2\sqrt{2}, -4 \rangle, \mathbf{v} = \langle -\sqrt{2}, 1 \rangle$

$\cos\theta = \dfrac{\mathbf{u}\cdot\mathbf{v}}{\|\mathbf{u}\|\,\|\mathbf{v}\|} = \dfrac{-8}{(\sqrt{24})(\sqrt{3})} \Rightarrow \theta \approx 160.5°$

75. $\mathbf{u} = \langle -3, 8 \rangle$

$\mathbf{v} = \langle 8, 3 \rangle$

$\mathbf{u}\cdot\mathbf{v} = -3(8) + 8(3) = 0$

$\mathbf{u}$ and $\mathbf{v}$ are orthogonal.

77. $\mathbf{u} = -\mathbf{i}$

$\mathbf{v} = \mathbf{i} + 2\mathbf{j}$

$\mathbf{u}\cdot\mathbf{v} \neq 0 \Rightarrow$ Not orthogonal

$\mathbf{v} \neq k\mathbf{u} \Rightarrow$ Not parallel

Neither

79. $\mathbf{u} = \langle -4, 3 \rangle, \mathbf{v} = \langle -8, -2 \rangle$

$\mathbf{w}_1 = \text{proj}_\mathbf{v}\mathbf{u} = \left(\dfrac{\mathbf{u}\cdot\mathbf{v}}{\|\mathbf{v}\|^2}\right)\mathbf{v} = \left(\dfrac{26}{68}\right)\langle -8, -2 \rangle$

$\qquad = -\dfrac{13}{17}\langle 4, 1 \rangle$

$\mathbf{w}_2 = \mathbf{u} - \mathbf{w}_1 = \langle -4, 3 \rangle - \left(-\dfrac{13}{17}\right)\langle 4, 1 \rangle$

$\qquad = \dfrac{16}{17}\langle -1, 4 \rangle$

81. $\mathbf{u} = \langle 2, 7 \rangle, \mathbf{v} = \langle 1, -1 \rangle$

$\mathbf{w}_1 = \text{proj}_\mathbf{v}\mathbf{u} = \left(\dfrac{\mathbf{u}\cdot\mathbf{v}}{\|\mathbf{v}\|^2}\right)\mathbf{v} = -\dfrac{5}{2}\langle 1, -1 \rangle$

$\qquad = \dfrac{5}{2}\langle -1, 1 \rangle$

$\mathbf{w}_2 = \mathbf{u} - \mathbf{w}_1 = \langle 2, 7 \rangle - \left(\dfrac{5}{2}\right)\langle -1, 1 \rangle$

$\qquad = \dfrac{9}{2}\langle 1, 1 \rangle$

83. $P = (5, 3), Q = (8, 9) \Rightarrow \overrightarrow{PQ} = \langle 3, 6 \rangle$

$W = \mathbf{F}\cdot\overrightarrow{PQ} = \langle 2, 7 \rangle \cdot \langle 3, 6 \rangle = 48$

85. $|7i| = \sqrt{0^2 + 7^2} = 7$

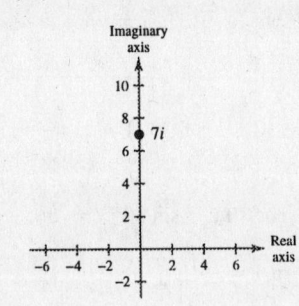

87. $|5 + 3i| = \sqrt{5^2 + 3^2} = \sqrt{34}$

89. $5 - 5i$

$r = \sqrt{5^2 + (-5)^2} = \sqrt{50} = 5\sqrt{2}$

$\tan\theta = \dfrac{-5}{5} = -1 \Rightarrow \theta = \dfrac{7\pi}{4}$ since the

complex number is in Quadrant IV.

$5 - 5i = 5\sqrt{2}\left(\cos\dfrac{7\pi}{4} + i\sin\dfrac{7\pi}{4}\right)$

91. $-3\sqrt{3} + 3i$

$r = \sqrt{(-3\sqrt{3})^2 + 3^2} = \sqrt{36} = 6$

$\tan\theta = \dfrac{3}{-3\sqrt{3}} = -\dfrac{1}{\sqrt{3}} \implies \theta = \dfrac{5\pi}{6}$

since the complex number is in Quadrant II.

$-3\sqrt{3} + 3i = 6\left(\cos\dfrac{5\pi}{6} + i\sin\dfrac{5\pi}{6}\right)$

93. (a) $z_1 = 2\sqrt{3} - 2i = 4\left(\cos\dfrac{11\pi}{6} + i\sin\dfrac{11\pi}{6}\right)$

$z_2 = -10i = 10\left(\cos\dfrac{3\pi}{2} + i\sin\dfrac{3\pi}{2}\right)$

(b) $z_1 z_2 = \left[4\left(\cos\dfrac{11\pi}{6} + i\sin\dfrac{11\pi}{6}\right)\right]\left[10\left(\cos\dfrac{3\pi}{2} + i\sin\dfrac{3\pi}{2}\right)\right]$

$= 40\left(\cos\dfrac{10\pi}{3} + i\sin\dfrac{10\pi}{3}\right)$

$\dfrac{z_1}{z_2} = \dfrac{4\left(\cos\dfrac{11\pi}{6} + i\sin\dfrac{11\pi}{6}\right)}{10\left(\cos\dfrac{3\pi}{2} + i\sin\dfrac{3\pi}{2}\right)}$

$= \dfrac{2}{5}\left(\cos\dfrac{\pi}{3} + i\sin\dfrac{\pi}{3}\right)$

95. $\left[5\left(\cos\dfrac{\pi}{12} + i\sin\dfrac{\pi}{12}\right)\right]^4 = 5^4\left(\cos\dfrac{4\pi}{12} + i\sin\dfrac{4\pi}{12}\right)$

$= 625\left(\cos\dfrac{\pi}{3} + i\sin\dfrac{\pi}{3}\right)$

$= 625\left(\dfrac{1}{2} + \dfrac{\sqrt{3}}{2}i\right)$

$= \dfrac{625}{2} + \dfrac{625\sqrt{3}}{2}i$

97. $(2 + 3i)^6 \approx \left[\sqrt{13}(\cos 56.3° + i\sin 56.3°)\right]^6$

$= 13^3(\cos 337.9° + i\sin 337.9°)$

$\approx 13^3(0.9263 - 0.3769i)$

$\approx 2035 - 828i$

99. (a) The trigonometric form of the three roots shown is:

$4(\cos 60° + i\sin 60°)$

$4(\cos 180° + i\sin 180°)$

$4(\cos 300° + i\sin 300°)$

(b) Since there are three evenly spaced roots on the circle of radius 4, they are cube roots of a complex number of modulus $4^3 = 64$. Cubing them yields -64.

$[4(\cos 60° + i\sin 60°)]^3 = -64$

$[4(\cos 180° + i\sin 180°)]^3 = -64$

$[4(\cos 300° + i\sin 300°)]^3 = -64$

101. Sixth roots of $-729i = 729\left(\cos\dfrac{3\pi}{2} + i\sin\dfrac{3\pi}{2}\right)$:

$$\sqrt[6]{729}\left[\cos\left(\dfrac{\dfrac{3\pi}{2} + 2k\pi}{6}\right) + i\sin\left(\dfrac{\dfrac{3\pi}{2} + 2k\pi}{6}\right)\right], k = 0, 1, 2, 3, 4, 5$$

$k = 0:\ 3\left(\cos\dfrac{\pi}{4} + i\sin\dfrac{\pi}{4}\right)$ $k = 3:\ 3\left(\cos\dfrac{5\pi}{4} + i\sin\dfrac{5\pi}{4}\right)$

$k = 1:\ 3\left(\cos\dfrac{7\pi}{12} + i\sin\dfrac{7\pi}{12}\right)$ $k = 4:\ 3\left(\cos\dfrac{19\pi}{12} + i\sin\dfrac{19\pi}{12}\right)$

$k = 2:\ 3\left(\cos\dfrac{11\pi}{12} + i\sin\dfrac{11\pi}{12}\right)$ $k = 5:\ 3\left(\cos\dfrac{23\pi}{12} + i\sin\dfrac{23\pi}{12}\right)$

103. $x^4 + 81 = 0$

$\quad x^4 = -81$ Solve by finding the fourth roots of -81.

$\quad -81 = 81(\cos\pi + i\sin\pi)$

$$\sqrt[4]{-81} = \sqrt[4]{81}\left[\cos\left(\dfrac{\pi + 2\pi k}{4}\right) + i\sin\left(\dfrac{\pi + 2\pi k}{4}\right)\right], k = 0, 1, 2, 3$$

$k = 0:\ 3\left(\cos\dfrac{\pi}{4} + i\sin\dfrac{\pi}{4}\right) = \dfrac{3\sqrt{2}}{2} + \dfrac{3\sqrt{2}}{2}i$

$k = 1:\ 3\left(\cos\dfrac{3\pi}{4} + i\sin\dfrac{3\pi}{4}\right) = -\dfrac{3\sqrt{2}}{2} + \dfrac{3\sqrt{2}}{2}i$

$k = 2:\ 3\left(\cos\dfrac{5\pi}{4} + i\sin\dfrac{5\pi}{4}\right) = -\dfrac{3\sqrt{2}}{2} - \dfrac{3\sqrt{2}}{2}i$

$k = 3:\ 3\left(\cos\dfrac{7\pi}{4} + i\sin\dfrac{7\pi}{4}\right) = \dfrac{3\sqrt{2}}{2} - \dfrac{3\sqrt{2}}{2}i$

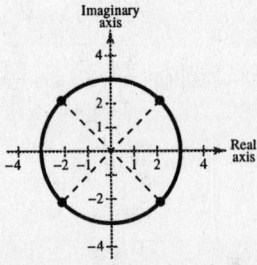

105. $x^3 + 8i = 0$

$\quad x^3 = -8i$ Solve by finding the cube roots of $-8i$.

$\quad -8i = 8\left(\cos\dfrac{3\pi}{2} + i\sin\dfrac{3\pi}{2}\right)$

$$\sqrt[3]{-8i} = \sqrt[3]{8}\left[\cos\left(\dfrac{\dfrac{3\pi}{2} + 2\pi k}{3}\right) + i\sin\left(\dfrac{\dfrac{3\pi}{2} + 2\pi k}{3}\right)\right], k = 0, 1, 2$$

$k = 0:\ 2\left(\cos\dfrac{\pi}{2} + i\sin\dfrac{\pi}{2}\right) = 2i$

$k = 1:\ 2\left(\cos\dfrac{7\pi}{6} + i\sin\dfrac{7\pi}{6}\right) = -\sqrt{3} - i$

$k = 2:\ 2\left(\cos\dfrac{11\pi}{6} + i\sin\dfrac{11\pi}{6}\right) = \sqrt{3} - i$

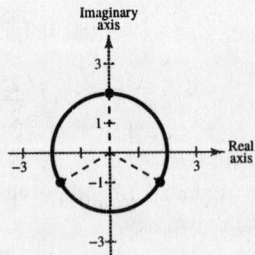

107. True. sin 90° is defined in the Law of Sines.

109. $\dfrac{a}{\sin A} = \dfrac{b}{\sin B} = \dfrac{c}{\sin C}$ or $\dfrac{\sin A}{a} = \dfrac{\sin B}{b} = \dfrac{\sin C}{c}$

111. Since $\cos 90° = 0$, $c^2 = a^2 + b^2 - 2ab \cos 90°$ becomes $c^2 = a^2 + b^2$.

This is the Pythagorean Theorem.

113. A and C appear to have the same magnitude and direction.

115. If $k > 0$, the direction of $k\mathbf{u}$ is the same, and the magnitude is $k\|\mathbf{u}\|$.

If $k < 0$, the direction of $k\mathbf{u}$ is the opposite direction of $\mathbf{u}$ and the magnitude is $|k|\,\|\mathbf{u}\|$.

117. $z_1 = 2(\cos \theta + i \sin \theta)$

$z_2 = 2(\cos(\pi - \theta) + i \sin(\pi - \theta))$

$z_1 z_2 = (2)(2)[\cos(\theta + (\pi - \theta)) + i \sin(\theta + (\pi - \theta))]$

$\qquad = 4(\cos \pi + i \sin \pi)$

$\qquad = -4$

$\dfrac{z_1}{z_2} = \dfrac{2(\cos \theta + i \sin \theta)}{2(\cos(\pi - \theta) + i \sin(\pi - \theta))}$

$\qquad = 1[\cos(\theta - (\pi - \theta)) + i \sin(\theta - (\pi - \theta))]$

$\qquad = \cos(2\theta - \pi) + i \sin(2\theta - \pi)$

$\qquad = \cos 2\theta \cos \pi + \sin 2\theta \sin \pi + i(\sin 2\theta \cos \pi - \cos 2\theta \sin \pi)$

$\qquad = -\cos 2\theta - i \sin 2\theta$

Chapter 6   Practice Test

For Exercises 1 and 2, use the Law of Sines to find the remaining sides and angles of the triangle.

1. $A = 40°$, $B = 12°$, $b = 100$ **2.** $C = 150°$, $a = 5$, $c = 20$

3. Find the area of the triangle: $a = 3$, $b = 6$, $C = 130°$.

4. Determine the number of solutions to the triangle: $a = 10$, $b = 35$, $A = 22.5°$.

For Exercises 5 and 6, use the Law of Cosines to find the remaining sides and angles of the triangle.

5. $a = 49$, $b = 53$, $c = 38$ **6.** $C = 29°$, $a = 100$, $b = 300$

7. Use Heron's Formula to find the area of the triangle: $a = 4.1$, $b = 6.8$, $c = 5.5$.

8. A ship travels 40 miles due east, then adjusts its course 12° southward. After traveling 70 miles in that direction, how far is the ship from its point of departure?

9. $\mathbf{w} = 4\mathbf{u} - 7\mathbf{v}$ where $\mathbf{u} = 3\mathbf{i} + \mathbf{j}$ and $\mathbf{v} = -\mathbf{i} + 2\mathbf{j}$. Find $\mathbf{w}$.

10. Find a unit vector in the direction of $\mathbf{v} = 5\mathbf{i} - 3\mathbf{j}$.

11. Find the dot product and the angle between $\mathbf{u} = 6\mathbf{i} + 5\mathbf{j}$ and $\mathbf{v} = 2\mathbf{i} - 3\mathbf{j}$.

12. $\mathbf{v}$ is a vector of magnitude 4 making an angle of 30° with the positive x-axis. Find $\mathbf{v}$ in component form.

13. Find the projection of $\mathbf{u}$ onto $\mathbf{v}$ given $\mathbf{u} = \langle 3, -1 \rangle$ and $\mathbf{v} = \langle -2, 4 \rangle$.

14. Give the trigonometric form of $z = 5 - 5i$.

15. Give the standard form of $z = 6(\cos 225° + i \sin 225°)$.

16. Multiply $[7(\cos 23° + i \sin 23°)][4(\cos 7° + i \sin 7°)]$.

17. Divide $\dfrac{9\left(\cos \dfrac{5\pi}{4} + i \sin \dfrac{5\pi}{4}\right)}{3(\cos \pi + i \sin \pi)}$.   **18.** Find $(2 + 2i)^8$.

19. Find the cube roots of $8\left(\cos \dfrac{\pi}{3} + i \sin \dfrac{\pi}{3}\right)$.   **20.** Find all the solutions to $x^4 + i = 0$.

CHAPTER 7
Systems of Equations and Inequalities

CHAPTER 7
Systems of Equations and Inequalities

Section 7.1   Solving Systems of Equations

Solutions to Odd-Numbered Exercises

■ You should be able to solve systems of equations by the method of substitution.

   1. Solve one of the equations for one of the variables.

   2. Substitute this expression into the other equation and solve.

   3. Back-substitute into the first equation to find the value of the other variable.

   4. Check your answer in each of the original equations.

■ You should be able to find solutions graphically. (See Example 5 in textbook.)

---

1. $\begin{cases} 4x - y = \ \ 1 \\ 6x + y = -6 \end{cases}$

(a) $4(0) - (-3) \neq 1$

$(0, -3)$ is **not** a solution.

(b) $4(-1) - (-4) \neq 1$

$(-1, -4)$ is **not** a solution.

(c) $4\left(-\frac{3}{2}\right) - (-2) \neq 1$

$\left(-\frac{3}{2}, -2\right)$ is **not** a solution.

(d) $4\left(-\frac{1}{2}\right) - (-3) = \ \ 1$

$6\left(-\frac{1}{2}\right) + (-3) = -6$

$\left(-\frac{1}{2}, -3\right)$ **is** a solution.

3. $\begin{cases} \quad\ \ y = -2e^x \\ 3x - y = \ \ 2 \end{cases}$

(a) $0 \neq -2e^{-2}$

$(-2, 0)$ is **not** a solution.

(b) $\qquad -2 = -2e^0$

$3(0) - (-2) = 2$

$(0, -2)$ **is** a solution.

(c) $-3 \neq -2e^0$

$(0, -3)$ is **not** a solution.

(d) $2 \neq -2e^{-1}$

$(-1, 2)$ is **not** a solution.

5. $\begin{cases} \ \ 2x + y = 6 \qquad \text{Equation 1} \\ -x + y = 0 \qquad \text{Equation 2} \end{cases}$

Solve for y in Equation 1: $y = 6 - 2x$

Substitute for y in Equation 2: $-x + (6 - 2x) = 0$

Solve for x: $-3x + 6 = 0 \implies x = 2$

Back-substitute $x = 2$: $y = 6 - 2(2) = 2$

Solution: $(2, 2)$

7. $\begin{cases} x - y = -4 & \text{Equation 1} \\ x^2 - y = -2 & \text{Equation 2} \end{cases}$

Solve for y in Equation 1: $y = x + 4$

Substitute for y in Equation 2: $x^2 - (x + 4) = -2$

Solve for x: $x^2 - x - 2 = 0 \implies (x + 1)(x - 2) = 0 \implies x = -1, 2$

Back-substitute $x = -1$: $y = -1 + 4 = 3$

Back-substitute $x = 2$: $y = 2 + 4 = 6$

Solutions: $(-1, 3), (2, 6)$

9. $\begin{cases} -2x + y = -5 & \text{Equation 1} \\ x^2 + y^2 = 25 & \text{Equation 2} \end{cases}$

Solve for y in Equation 1: $y = 2x - 5$

Substitute for y in Equation 2: $x^2 + (2x - 5)^2 = 25$

Solve for x: $5x^2 - 20x = 0 \implies 5x(x - 4) = 0 \implies x = 0, 4$

Back-substitute $x = 0$: $y = 2(0) - 5 = -5$

Back-substitute $x = 4$: $y = 2(4) - 5 = 3$

Solutions: $(0, -5), (4, 3)$

11. $\begin{cases} x^2 + y = 0 & \text{Equation 1} \\ x^2 - 4x - y = 0 & \text{Equation 2} \end{cases}$

Solve for y in Equation 1: $y = -x^2$

Substitute for y in Equation 2: $x^2 - 4x - (-x^2) = 0$

Solve for x: $2x^2 - 4x = 0 \implies 2x(x - 2) = 0 \implies x = 0, 2$

Back-substitute $x = 0$: $y = -0^2 = 0$

Back-substitute $x = 2$: $y = -2^2 = -4$

Solutions: $(0, 0), (2, -4)$

13. $\begin{cases} y = x^3 - 3x^2 + 1 & \text{Equation 1} \\ y = x^2 - 3x + 1 & \text{Equation 2} \end{cases}$

Substitute for y in Equation 2.

$$x^3 - 3x^2 + 1 = x^2 - 3x + 1$$

$$x^3 - 4x^2 + 3x = 0$$

$$x(x - 1)(x - 3) = 0 \implies x = 0, 1, 3$$

Back-substitute $x = 0$: $y = 0^3 - 3(0)^2 + 1 = 1$

Back-substitute $x = 1$: $y = 1^3 - 3(1)^2 + 1 = -1$

Back-substitute $x = 3$: $y = 3^3 - 3(3)^2 + 1 = 1$

Solutions: $(0, 1), (1, -1), (3, 1)$

15. $\begin{cases} x - y = 0 & \text{Equation 1} \\ 5x - 3y = 10 & \text{Equation 2} \end{cases}$

Solve for y in Equation 1: $y = x$

Substitute for y in Equation 2: $5x - 3x = 10$

Solve for x: $2x = 10 \implies x = 5$

Back-substitute in Equation 1: $y = x = 5$

Solution: $(5, 5)$

17. $\begin{cases} 2x - y + 2 = 0 & \text{Equation 1} \\ 4x + y - 5 = 0 & \text{Equation 2} \end{cases}$

Solve for y in Equation 1: $y = 2x + 2$

Substitute for y in Equation 2: $4x + (2x + 2) - 5 = 0$

Solve for x: $6x - 3 = 0 \implies x = \frac{1}{2}$

Back-substitute $x = \frac{1}{2}$: $y = 2x + 2 = 2\left(\frac{1}{2}\right) + 2 = 3$

Solution: $\left(\frac{1}{2}, 3\right)$

19. $\begin{cases} 1.5x + 0.8y = 2.3 & \text{Equation 1} \\ 0.3x - 0.2y = 0.1 & \text{Equation 2} \end{cases}$

Multiply the equations by 10.

$\qquad 15x + 8y = 23 \qquad$ Revised Equation 1

$\qquad\ \ 3x - 2y = \ \ 1 \qquad$ Revised Equation 2

Solve for y in revised Equation 2: $y = \frac{3}{2}x - \frac{1}{2}$

Substitute for y in revised Equation 1: $15x + 8\left(\frac{3}{2}x - \frac{1}{2}\right) = 23$

Solve for x: $15x + 12x - 4 = 23 \implies 27x = 27 \implies x = 1$

Back-substitute $x = 1$: $y = \frac{3}{2}(1) - \frac{1}{2} = 1$

Solution: $(1, 1)$

21. $\begin{cases} \frac{1}{5}x + \frac{1}{2}y = \ \ 8 & \text{Equation 1} \\ x + \ \ y = 20 & \text{Equation 2} \end{cases}$

Solve for x in Equation 2: $x = 20 - y$

Substitute for x in Equation 1: $\frac{1}{5}(20 - y) + \frac{1}{2}y = 8$

Solve for y: $4 + \frac{3}{10}y = 8 \implies y = \frac{40}{3}$

Back-substitute $y = \frac{40}{3}$: $x = 20 - y = 20 - \frac{40}{3} = \frac{20}{3}$

Solution: $\left(\frac{20}{3}, \frac{40}{3}\right)$

23. $\begin{cases} 6x + 5y = -3 & \text{Equation 1} \\ -x - \frac{5}{6}y = -7 & \text{Equation 2} \end{cases}$

Solve for x in Equation 2: $x = 7 - \frac{5}{6}y$

Substitute for x in Equation 1: $6\left(7 - \frac{5}{6}y\right) + 5y = -3$

Solve for y: $42 - 5y + 5y = -3 \implies 42 = -3$ (False)

No solution

25. $\begin{cases} x^2 - y = 0 & \text{Equation 1} \\ 2x + y = 0 & \text{Equation 2} \end{cases}$

Solve for y in Equation 2: $y = -2x$

Substitute for y in Equation 1: $x^2 - (-2x) = 0$

Solve for x: $x^2 + 2x = 0 \implies x(x + 2) = 0 \implies x = 0, -2$

Back-substitute $x = 0$: $y = -2(0) = 0$

Back-substitute $x = -2$: $y = -2(-2) = 4$

Solutions: $(0, 0), (-2, 4)$

27. $\begin{cases} x^3 - y = 0 & \text{Equation 1} \\ x - y = 0 & \text{Equation 2} \end{cases}$

Solve for y in Equation 2: $y = x$

Substitute for y in Equation 1: $x^3 - x = 0$

Solve for x: $x(x + 1)(x - 1) = 0 \implies x = 0, \pm 1$

Back-substitute $x = 0$: $y = 0$

Back-substitute $x = 1$: $y = 1$

Back-substitute $x = -1$: $y = -1$

Solutions: $(0, 0), (1, 1), (-1, -1)$

29. $\begin{cases} -x + 2y = 2 \implies y = \dfrac{x + 2}{2} \\ 3x + y = 15 \implies y = -3x + 15 \end{cases}$

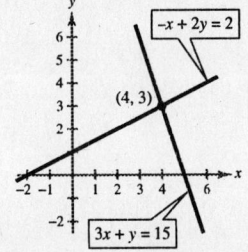

Point of intersection: $(4, 3)$

31. $\begin{cases} x - 3y = -2 \implies y = \dfrac{1}{3}(x + 2) \\ 5x + 3y = 17 \implies y = \dfrac{1}{3}(-5x + 17) \end{cases}$

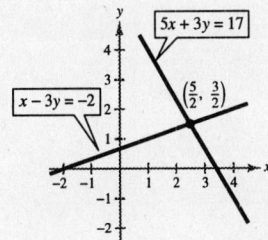

Point of intersection: $\left(\dfrac{5}{2}, \dfrac{3}{2}\right)$

33. $\begin{cases} x + y = 4 \implies y = -x + 4 \\ x^2 + y^2 - 4x = 0 \implies (x - 2)^2 + y^2 = 4 \end{cases}$

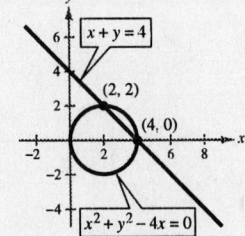

Points of intersection: $(2, 2), (4, 0)$

35. $\begin{cases} x - y + 3 = 0 \implies y = x + 3 \\ y = x^2 - 4x + 7 \implies y = (x - 2)^2 + 3 \end{cases}$

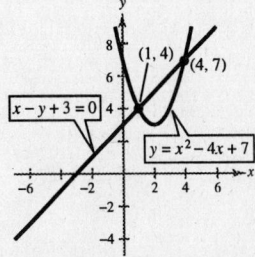

Points of intersection: $(1, 4), (4, 7)$

37. $\begin{cases} 7x + 8y = 24 \implies y = -\dfrac{7}{8}x + 3 \\ x - 8y = 8 \implies y = \dfrac{1}{8}x - 1 \end{cases}$

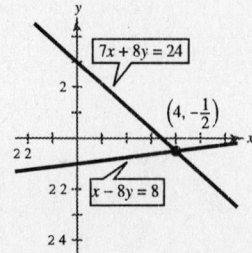

Point of intersection: $\left(4, -\dfrac{1}{2}\right)$

39. $\begin{cases} 3x - 2y = 0 \implies y = \dfrac{3}{2}x \\ x^2 - y^2 = 4 \implies \dfrac{x^2}{4} - \dfrac{y^2}{4} = 1 \end{cases}$

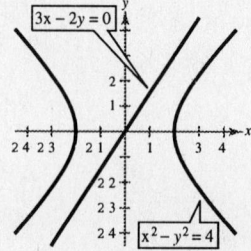

No points of intersection

41. $\begin{cases} x^2 + y^2 = 25 \\ 3x^2 - 16y = 0 \implies y = \dfrac{3}{16}x^2 \end{cases}$

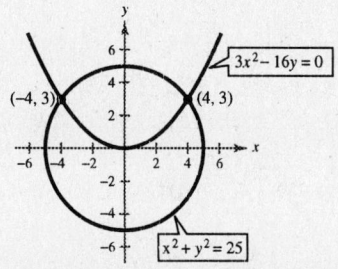

Point of intersection: $(-4, 3)$ and $(4, 3)$.

Algebraically we have:

$$x^2 = 25 - y^2$$
$$y = \frac{3}{16}(25 - y^2)$$
$$16y = 75 - 3y^2$$
$$3y^2 + 16y - 75 = 0$$
$$(3y + 25)(y - 3) = 0$$
$$y = -\frac{25}{3} \quad \text{or} \quad y = 3$$
$$x^2 = -\frac{400}{9} \quad \text{or} \quad x^2 = 16$$

Extraneous solutions: $(-4, 3)$ and $(4, 3)$.

43. $\begin{cases} y = e^x \\ x - y + 1 = 0 \implies y = x + 1 \end{cases}$

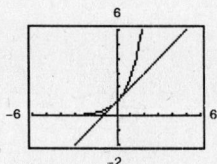

Point of intersection: $(0, 1)$

45. $\begin{cases} x + 2y = 8 \implies y = -\dfrac{1}{2}x + 4 \\ y = \log_2 x \implies y = \dfrac{\ln x}{\ln 2} \end{cases}$

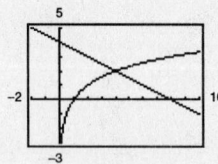

Point of intersection: $(4, 2)$

47. $\begin{cases} y = \sqrt{x} \\ y = x \end{cases}$

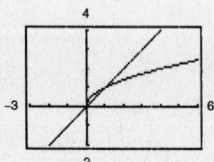

Points of intersection: $(0, 0), (1, 1)$

49. $\begin{cases} x^2 + y^2 = 169 \implies y_1 = \sqrt{169 - x^2} \text{ and } y_2 = -\sqrt{169 - x^2} \\ x^2 - 8y = 104 \implies y_3 = \frac{1}{8}x^2 - 13 \end{cases}$

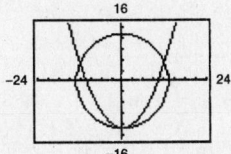

Points of intersection: $(0, -13), (\pm 12, 5)$

51. $\begin{cases} y = 2x & \text{Equation 1} \\ y = x^2 + 1 & \text{Equation 2} \end{cases}$

Substitute for y in Equation 2: $2x = x^2 + 1$

Solve for x: $x^2 - 2x + 1 = (x - 1)^2 = 0 \implies x = 1$

Back-substitute $x = 1$ in Equation 1: $y = 2x = 2$

Solution: $(1, 2)$

53. $\begin{cases} 3x - 7y + 6 = 0 & \text{Equation 1} \\ \quad x^2 - y^2 = 4 & \text{Equation 2} \end{cases}$

Solve for y in Equation 1: $y = \dfrac{3x + 6}{7}$

Substitute for y in Equation 2: $x^2 - \left(\dfrac{3x + 6}{7}\right)^2 = 4$

Solve for x: $x^2 - \left(\dfrac{9x^2 + 36x + 36}{49}\right) = 4$

$$49x^2 - (9x^2 + 36x + 36) = 196$$

$$40x^2 - 36x - 232 = 0$$

$4(10x - 29)(x + 2) = 0 \implies x = \dfrac{29}{10}, -2$

Back-substitute $x = \dfrac{29}{10}$: $y = \dfrac{3x + 6}{7} = \dfrac{3(29/10) + 6}{7} = \dfrac{21}{10}$

Back-substitute $x = -2$: $y = \dfrac{3x + 6}{7} = \dfrac{3(-2) + 6}{7} = 0$

Solutions: $\left(\dfrac{29}{10}, \dfrac{21}{10}\right), (-2, 0)$

55. $\begin{cases} x - 2y = 4 & \text{Equation 1} \\ x^2 - y = 0 & \text{Equation 2} \end{cases}$

Solve for y in Equation 2: $y = x^2$

Substitute for y in Equation 1: $x - 2x^2 = 4$

Solve for x: $0 = 2x^2 - x + 4 \implies x = \dfrac{1 \pm \sqrt{1 - 4(2)(4)}}{2(2)} \implies x = \dfrac{1 \pm \sqrt{-31}}{4}$

The discriminant in the Quadratic Formula is negative.

No real solution

57. $\begin{cases} y - e^{-x} = 1 & \Rightarrow & y = e^{-x} + 1 \\ y - \ln x = 3 & \Rightarrow & y = \ln x + 3 \end{cases}$

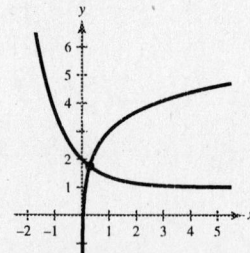

Point of intersection: Approximately $(0.287, 1.75)$

59. $\begin{cases} y = x^4 - 2x^2 + 1 & \text{Equation 1} \\ y = 1 - x^2 & \text{Equation 2} \end{cases}$

Substitute for y in Equation 1: $1 - x^2 = x^4 - 2x^2 + 1$

Solve for x: $x^4 - x^2 = 0 \Rightarrow x^2(x^2 - 1) = 0$

$$\Rightarrow x = 0, \pm 1$$

Back-substitute $x = 0$: $1 - x^2 = 1 - 0^2 = 1$

Back-substitute $x = 1$: $1 - x^2 = 1 - 1^2 = 0$

Back-substitute $x = -1$: $1 - x^2 = 1 - (-1)^2 = 0$

Solutions: $(0, 1)$, $(\pm 1, 0)$

61. $\begin{cases} xy - 1 = 0 & \text{Equation 1} \\ 2x - 4y + 7 = 0 & \text{Equation 2} \end{cases}$

Solve for y in Equation 1: $y = \dfrac{1}{x}$

Substitute for y in Equation 2: $2x - 4\left(\dfrac{1}{x}\right) + 7 = 0$

Solve for x: $2x^2 - 4 + 7x = 0 \Rightarrow (2x - 1)(x + 4) = 0 \Rightarrow x = \dfrac{1}{2}, -4$

Back-substitute $x = \dfrac{1}{2}$: $y = \dfrac{1}{1/2} = 2$

Back-substitute $x = -4$: $y = \dfrac{1}{-4} = -\dfrac{1}{4}$

Solutions: $\left(\dfrac{1}{2}, 2\right), \left(-4, -\dfrac{1}{4}\right)$

63. $C = 8650x + 250{,}000$, $R = 9950x$

$R = C$

$9950x = 8650x + 250{,}000$

$1300x = 250{,}000$

$x \approx 192$ units

65. $C = 5.5\sqrt{x} + 10,000, \ R = 3.29x$

$$R = C$$

$$3.29x = 5.5\sqrt{x} + 10,000$$

$$3.29x - 5.5\sqrt{x} - 10,000 = 0$$

Let $u = \sqrt{x}$.

$$3.29u^2 - 5.5u - 10,000 = 0$$

$$u = \frac{5.5 \pm \sqrt{(-5.5)^2 - 4(3.29)(-10,000)}}{2(3.29)}$$

$$u = \frac{5.5 \pm \sqrt{131,630.25}}{6.58}$$

$$u \approx 55.974, \ -54.302$$

Choosing the positive value for u, we have

$$x = u^2 \implies x = (55.974)^2 \approx 3133 \text{ units.}$$

67. $C = 3.45x + 16,000, \ R = 5.95x$

(a) $\qquad R = C$

$$5.95x = 3.45x + 16,000$$

$$2.50x = 16,000$$

$$x = 6400 \text{ units}$$

(b) $\qquad P = R - C$

$$6000 = 5.95x - (3.45x + 16,000)$$

$$6000 = 2.5x - 16,000$$

$$22,000 = 2.5x$$

$$x = 8800 \text{ units}$$

69. (a) $\begin{cases} x + y = 25,000 \\ 0.06x + 0.085y = 2000 \end{cases}$

(b) $y_1 = 25,000 - x$

$$y_2 = \frac{2000 - 0.06x}{0.085}$$

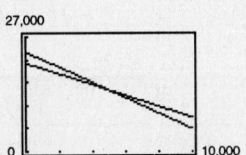

As the amount at 6% increases, the amount at 8.5% decreases. The amount of interest is fixed at $2000.

(c) The point of intersection occurs when $x = 5000$, so the most that can be invested at 6% and still earn $2000 per year in interest is $5000.

71. $0.06x = 0.03x + 350$

$$0.03x = 350$$

$$x \approx \$11,666.67$$

To make the straight commission offer the better offer, you would have to sell more than $11,666.67 per week.

73. $\begin{cases} V = (D - 4)^2, 5 \leq D \leq 40 \\ V = 0.79D^2 - 2D - 4, 5 \leq D \leq 40 \end{cases}$ Doyle Log Rule
Scribner Log Rule

(a)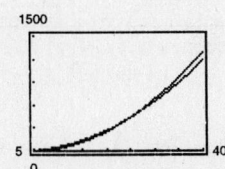

(b) The graphs intersect when $D \approx 24.7$ inches.

(c) For large logs, the Doyle Log Rule gives a greater volume for a given diameter.

75. $2l + 2w = 30 \implies l + w = 15$

$l = w + 3 \implies (w + 3) + w = 15$

$$2w = 12$$

$$w = 6$$

$l = w + 3 = 9$

Dimensions: 6×9 meters

77. $2l + 2w = 42 \implies l + w = 21$

$w = \frac{3}{4}l \implies l + \frac{3}{4}l = 21$

$$\frac{7}{4}l = 21$$

$$l = 12$$

$w = \frac{3}{4}l = 9$

Dimensions: 9×12 inches

79. $2l + 2w = 40 \implies l + w = 20 \implies w = 20 - l$

$lw = 96 \implies l(20 - l) = 96$

$$20l - l^2 = 96$$

$$0 = l^2 - 20l + 96$$

$$0 = (l - 8)(l - 12)$$

$$l = 8 \text{ or } l = 12$$

If $l = 8$, then $w = 12$.

If $l = 12$, then $w = 8$.

Since the length is supposed to be greater than the width, we have
$l = 12$ kilometers and $w = 8$ kilometers. Dimensions: 8×12 kilometers

81. $(3, 43.1), (4, 45.7), (5, 46.6), (6, 47.9)$

(a) Linear model: $f(t) = 1.53t + 38.94$

Quadratic model: $g(t) = -0.325t^2 + 4.455t + 32.765$

(b)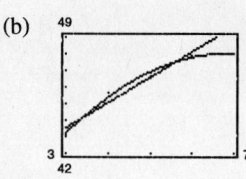

(c) Points of intersection: $(3.382, 44.114), (5.618, 47.536)$

83. False. The system can have at most 4 solutions because a parabola and a circle can intersect at most 4 times.

85. For a linear system the result will be a contradictory equation such as $0 = N$, where N is a nonzero real number. For a nonlinear system there may be an equation with imaginary solutions.

87. $y = x^2$

(a) Line with two points of intersection.

$y = 2x$

$(0, 0)$ and $(2, 4)$

(b) Line with one point of intersection.

$y = 0$

$(0, 0)$

(c) Line with no points of intersection.

$y = x - 2$

89. $(-2, 7), (5, 5)$

$$m = \frac{5 - 7}{5 - (-2)} = -\frac{2}{7}$$

$$y - 7 = -\frac{2}{7}(x - (-2))$$

$$7y - 49 = -2x - 4$$

$$2x + 7y - 45 = 0$$

91. $(6, 3), (10, 3)$

$$m = \frac{3 - 3}{10 - 6} = 0 \implies \text{The line is horizontal.}$$

$$y = 3$$
$$y - 3 = 0$$

93. $\left(\frac{3}{5}, 0\right), (4, 6)$

$$m = \frac{6 - 0}{4 - \frac{3}{5}} = \frac{6}{\frac{17}{5}} = \frac{30}{17}$$

$$y - 6 = \frac{30}{17}(x - 4)$$

$$17y - 102 = 30x - 120$$

$$0 = 30x - 17y - 18$$

$$30x - 17y - 18 = 0$$

95. $f(x) = \dfrac{5}{x - 6}$

Domain: All real numbers except $x = 6$.

Horizontal asymptote: $y = 0$

Vertical asymptote: $x = 6$

97. $f(x) = \dfrac{x^2 + 2}{x^2 - 16}$

Domain: All real numbers except $x = \pm 4$.

Horizontal asymptote: $y = 1$

Vertical asymptotes: $x = \pm 4$

99. $y = -2^{0.5x}$

x	-4	-2	0	2	4
y	$-\frac{1}{4}$	$-\frac{1}{2}$	-1	-2	-4

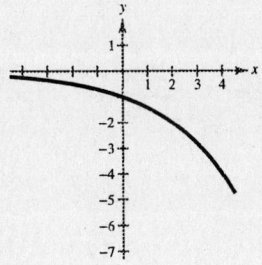

101. $y = 3e^{-x-4}$

x	-6	-4	-2	0	2
y	22.167	3	0.406	0.055	0.007

Section 7.2   Two-Variable Linear Systems

■ You should be able to solve a linear system by the method of elimination.

1. Obtain coefficients for either x or y that differ only in sign. This is done by multiplying all the terms of one or both equations by appropriate constants.

2. Add the equations to eliminate one of the variables and then solve for the remaining variable.

3. Use back-substitution into either original equation and solve for the other variable.

4. Check your answer.

■ You should know that for a system of two linear equations, one of the following is true.

1. There are infinitely many solutions; the lines are identical. The system is consistent.

2. There is no solution; the lines are parallel. The system is inconsistent.

3. There is one solution; the lines intersect at one point. The system is consistent.

Solutions to Odd-Numbered Exercises

1. $\begin{cases} 2x + y = 5 & \text{Equation 1} \\ x - y = 1 & \text{Equation 2} \end{cases}$

   Add to eliminate y: $3x = 6 \implies x = 2$

   Substitute $x = 2$ in Equation 2: $2 - y = 1 \implies y = 1$

   Solution: $(2, 1)$

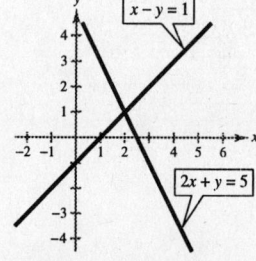

3. $\begin{cases} x + y = 0 & \text{Equation 1} \\ 3x + 2y = 1 & \text{Equation 2} \end{cases}$

   Multiply Equation 1 by -2: $-2x - 2y = 0$

   Add this to Equation 2 to eliminate y: $x = 1$

   Substitute $x = 1$ in Equation 1: $1 + y = 0 \implies y = -1$

   Solution: $(1, -1)$

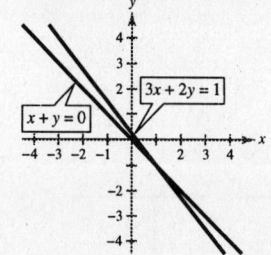

5. $\begin{cases} x - y = 2 & \text{Equation 1} \\ -2x + 2y = 5 & \text{Equation 2} \end{cases}$

   Multiply Equation 1 by 2: $2x - 2y = 4$

   Add this to Equation 2: $0 = 9$

   There are no solutions.

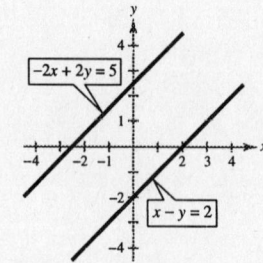

7. $\begin{cases} 3x - 2y = 5 & \text{Equation 1} \\ -6x + 4y = -10 & \text{Equation 2} \end{cases}$

Multiply Equation 1 by 2 and add to Equation 2: $0 = 0$

The equations are dependent. There are infinitely many solutions.

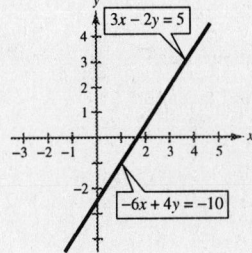

9. $\begin{cases} 9x + 3y = 1 & \text{Equation 1} \\ 3x - 6y = 5 & \text{Equation 2} \end{cases}$

Multiply Equation 2 by (-3): $\quad 9x + 3y = 1$
$$-9x + 18y = -15$$

Add to eliminate x: $21y = -14 \implies y = -\frac{2}{3}$

Substitute $y = -\frac{2}{3}$ in Equation 1: $9x + 3\left(-\frac{2}{3}\right) = 1$
$$x = \frac{1}{3}$$

Solution: $\left(\frac{1}{3}, -\frac{2}{3}\right)$

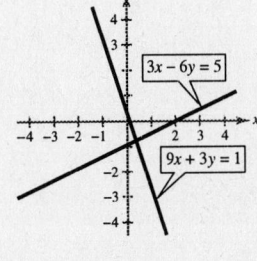

11. $\begin{cases} x + 2y = 4 & \text{Equation 1} \\ x - 2y = 1 & \text{Equation 2} \end{cases}$

Add to eliminate y:

$$2x = 5$$
$$x = \frac{5}{2}$$

Substitute $x = \frac{5}{2}$ in Equation 1:

$$\frac{5}{2} + 2y = 4 \implies y = \frac{3}{4}$$

Solution: $\left(\frac{5}{2}, \frac{3}{4}\right)$

13. $\begin{cases} 2x + 3y = 18 & \text{Equation 1} \\ 5x - y = 11 & \text{Equation 2} \end{cases}$

Multiply Equation 2 by 3: $15x - 3y = 33$

Add this to Equation 1 to eliminate y:

$$17x = 51 \implies x = 3$$

Substitute $x = 3$ in Equation 1:

$$6 + 3y = 18 \implies y = 4$$

Solution: $(3, 4)$

15. $\begin{cases} 3x + 2y = 10 & \text{Equation 1} \\ 2x + 5y = 3 & \text{Equation 2} \end{cases}$

Multiply Equation 1 by 2 and Equation 2 by (-3):

$$\begin{cases} 6x + 4y = 20 \\ -6x - 15y = -9 \end{cases}$$

Add to eliminate x: $-11y = 11 \implies y = -1$

Substitute $y = -1$ in Equation 1:

$$3x - 2 = 10 \implies x = 4$$

Solution: $(4, -1)$

17. $\begin{cases} 5u + 6v = 24 & \text{Equation 1} \\ 3u + 5v = 18 & \text{Equation 2} \end{cases}$

Multiply Equation 1 by 5 and Equation 2 by -6:

$$\begin{cases} 25u + 30v = 120 \\ -18u - 30v = -108 \end{cases}$$

Add to eliminate v: $7u = 12 \implies u = \frac{12}{7}$

Substitute $u = \frac{12}{7}$ in Equation 1:

$$5\left(\frac{12}{7}\right) + 6v = 24 \implies 6v = \frac{108}{7} \implies v = \frac{18}{7}$$

Solution: $\left(\frac{12}{7}, \frac{18}{7}\right)$

19. $\begin{cases} 1.8x + 1.2y = 4 & \text{Equation 1} \\ 9x + 6y = 3 & \text{Equation 2} \end{cases}$

Multiply Equation 1 by 10 and Equation 2 by -2:

$\begin{cases} 18x + 12y = 40 \\ -18x - 12y = -6 \end{cases}$

Add to eliminate x and y: $0 = 34$

Inconsistent

No solution

21. $\begin{cases} \dfrac{x}{4} + \dfrac{y}{6} = 1 & \text{Equation 1} \\ x - y = 3 & \text{Equation 2} \end{cases}$

Multiply Equation 1 by 6: $\dfrac{3}{2}x + y = 6$

Add this to Equation 2 to eliminate y:

$$\frac{5}{2}x = 9 \implies x = \frac{18}{5}$$

Substitute $x = \dfrac{18}{5}$ in Equation 2:

$$\frac{18}{5} - y = 3$$

$$y = \frac{3}{5}$$

Solution: $\left(\dfrac{18}{5}, \dfrac{3}{5} \right)$

23. $\begin{cases} 2.5x - 3y = 1.5 & \text{Equation 1} \\ 2x - 2.4y = 1.2 & \text{Equation 2} \end{cases}$

Multiply Equation 1 by 20 and Equation 2 by -25:

$$50x - 60y = 30$$
$$-50x + 60y = -30$$

Add to eliminate x and y: $0 = 0$

The equations are dependent.

There are infinitely many solutions.

Let $x = a$, then $2.5a - 3y = 1.5 \implies$
$y = \dfrac{2.5a - 1.5}{3} = \dfrac{5}{6}a - \dfrac{1}{2}$.

Solution: $\left(a, \dfrac{5}{6}a - \dfrac{1}{2} \right)$ where a is any real number.

25. $\begin{cases} 0.05x - 0.03y = 0.21 & \text{Equation 1} \\ 0.07x + 0.02y = 0.16 & \text{Equation 2} \end{cases}$

Multiply Equation 1 by 200 and Equation 2 by 300:

$\begin{cases} 10x - 6y = 42 \\ 21x + 6y = 48 \end{cases}$

Add to eliminate y: $31x = 90$

$$x = \frac{90}{31}$$

Substitute $x = \dfrac{90}{31}$ in Equation 2:

$$0.07\left(\frac{90}{31}\right) + 0.02y = 0.16$$

$$y = -\frac{67}{31}$$

Solution: $\left(\dfrac{90}{31}, -\dfrac{67}{31} \right)$

27. $\begin{cases} 4b + 3m = 3 & \text{Equation 1} \\ 3b + 11m = 13 & \text{Equation 2} \end{cases}$

Multiply Equation 1 by 3 and Equation 2 by (-4):

$\begin{cases} 12b + 9m = 9 \\ -12b - 44m = -52 \end{cases}$

Add to eliminate b: $-35m = -43$

$$m = \frac{43}{35}$$

Substitute $m = \dfrac{43}{35}$ in Equation 1:

$$4b + 3\left(\frac{43}{35}\right) = 3 \implies b = -\frac{6}{35}$$

Solution: $\left(-\dfrac{6}{35}, \dfrac{43}{35} \right)$

29. $\begin{cases} \dfrac{x+3}{4} + \dfrac{y-1}{3} = 1 & \text{Equation 1} \\ 2x - y = 12 & \text{Equation 2} \end{cases}$

Multiply Equation 1 by 12 and Equation 2 by 4:

$\begin{cases} 3x + 4y = 7 \\ 8x - 4y = 48 \end{cases}$

Add to eliminate y: $11x = 55 \implies x = 5$

Substitute $x = 5$ into Equation 2:

$$2(5) - y = 12 \implies y = -2$$

Solution: $(5, -2)$

31. $\begin{cases} 2x - 5y = 0 \implies y = \frac{2}{5}x \\ x - y = 3 \implies y = x - 3 \end{cases}$

The system is consistent. There is one solution.

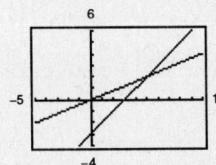

33. $\begin{cases} \frac{3}{5}x - y = 3 \implies y = \frac{3}{5}x - 3 \\ -3x + 5y = 9 \implies y = \frac{3}{5}x + \frac{9}{5} \end{cases}$

The lines are parallel. The system is inconsistent.

There are no solutions.

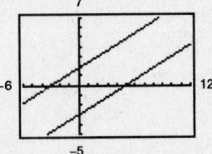

35. $\begin{cases} x + 7y = 2 \implies y = -\frac{1}{7}x + \frac{2}{7} \\ 4x - y = 9 \implies y = 4x - 9 \end{cases}$

The system is consistent.

There is one solution.

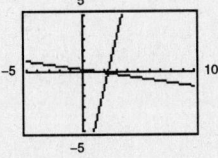

37. $\begin{cases} -x + 7y = 3 \implies y = \frac{1}{7}x + \frac{3}{7} \\ -\frac{1}{7}x + y = 5 \implies y = \frac{1}{7}x + 5 \end{cases}$

The lines are parallel.

The system is inconsistent.

There are no solutions.

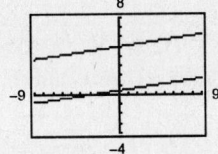

39. $\begin{cases} 8x + 9y = 42 \implies y = -\frac{8}{9}x + \frac{14}{3} \\ 6x - y = 16 \implies y = 6x - 16 \end{cases}$

Solution: $(3, 2)$

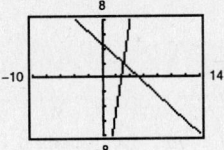

41. $\begin{cases} \frac{3}{2}x - \frac{1}{5}y = 8 \implies y = \frac{15}{2}x - 40 \\ -2x + 3y = 3 \implies y = \frac{2}{3}x + 1 \end{cases}$

Solution: $(6, 5)$

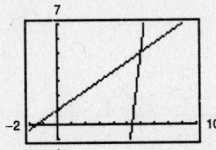

43. $\begin{cases} 0.5x + 2.2y = 9 \implies y = -\frac{5}{22}x + \frac{45}{11} \\ 6x + 0.4y = -22 \implies y = -15x - 55 \end{cases}$

Solution: $(-4, 5)$

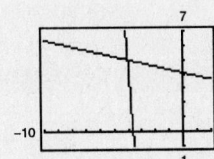

45. $\begin{cases} 7x - 2y = 24 \implies y = \frac{7}{2}x - 12 \\ 5x + 6y = -20 \implies y = -\frac{5}{2}x - \frac{10}{3} \end{cases}$

Solution: $(2, -5)$

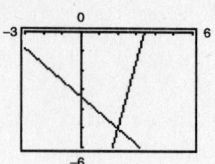

47. $\begin{cases} 3x - 5y = 7 & \text{Equation 1} \\ 2x + y = 9 & \text{Equation 2} \end{cases}$

Multiply Equation 2 by 5:

$\qquad 10x + 5y = 45$

Add this to Equation 1:

$\qquad 13x = 52 \implies x = 4$

Back-substitute $x = 4$ into Equation 2:

$\qquad 2(4) + y = 9 \implies y = 1$

Solution: $(4, 1)$

49. $\begin{cases} y = 2x - 5 & \text{Equation 1} \\ y = 5x - 11 & \text{Equation 2} \end{cases}$

Since both equations are solved for y, set them equal to one another and solve for x.

$\qquad 2x - 5 = 5x - 11$

$\qquad\qquad 6 = 3x$

$\qquad\qquad 2 = x$

Back-substitute $x = 2$ into Equation 1:

$\qquad y = 2(2) - 5 = -1$

Solution: $(2, -1)$

51. $\begin{cases} x - 5y = 21 & \text{Equation 1} \\ 6x + 5y = 21 & \text{Equation 2} \end{cases}$

Add the equations: $7x = 42 \implies x = 6$

Back-substitute $x = 6$ into Equation 1:

$\qquad 6 - 5y = 21 \implies -5y = 15 \implies y = -3$

Solution: $(6, -3)$

53. $\begin{cases} -2x + 8y = 19 & \text{Equation 1} \\ \qquad\quad y = x - 3 & \text{Equation 2} \end{cases}$

Substitute the expression for y from Equation 2 into Equation 1.

$\qquad -2x + 8(x - 3) = 19 \implies -2x + 8x - 24 = 19 \implies 6x = 43 \implies x = \frac{43}{6}$

Back-substitute $x = \frac{43}{6}$ into Equation 2:

$\qquad y = \frac{43}{6} - 3 \implies y = \frac{25}{6}$

Solution: $\left(\frac{43}{6}, \frac{25}{6}\right)$

55. $\quad 50 - 0.5x = 0.125x$

$\qquad\qquad 50 = 0.625x$

$\qquad\qquad\;\, x = 80 \text{ units}$

$\qquad\qquad\;\, p = \$10$

Solution: $(80, 10)$

57. $140 - 0.00002x = 80 + 0.00001x$

$\qquad\qquad 60 = 0.00003x$

$\qquad\qquad\;\; x = 2{,}000{,}000 \text{ units}$

$\qquad\qquad\;\; p = \$100.00$

Solution: $(2{,}000{,}000, 100)$

59. Let $r_1 = $ the air speed of the plane
and $r_2 = $ the wind air speed.

$$3.6(r_1 - r_2) = 1800 \qquad \text{Equation 1}$$
$$3(r_1 + r_2) = 1800 \qquad \text{Equation 2}$$

$$
\begin{aligned}
r_1 - r_2 &= 500 \\
r_1 + r_2 &= 600 \\
2r_1 \quad\;\; &= 1100 \\
r_1 &= 550 \\
550 + r_2 &= 600 \\
r_2 &= 50
\end{aligned}
$$

The air speed of the plane is 550 mph and the speed of the wind is 50 mph.

61. Let $x = $ the number of liters at 20%

Let $y = $ the number of liters at 50%.

(a) $\begin{cases} x + y = 10 \\ 0.2x + 0.5y = 0.3(10) \end{cases}$

(b)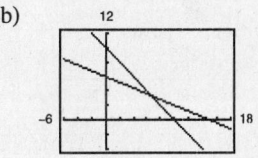

(c)
$$
\begin{array}{ll}
-2 \cdot \text{Equation 1} & -2x - 2y = -20 \\
10 \cdot \text{Equation 2} & 2x + 5y = 30 \\
\hline
& 3y = 10 \\
& y = \frac{10}{3} \\
& x + \frac{10}{3} = 10 \\
& x = \frac{20}{3}
\end{array}
$$

As x increases, y decreases.

(c) In order to obtain the specified concentration of the final mixture, $6\frac{2}{3}$ liters of the 20% solution and $3\frac{1}{3}$ liters of teh 50% solution are required.

63. Let $x = $ amount invested at 7.5%

$y = $ amount invested at 9%

$\begin{cases} x + y = 12{,}000 \qquad \text{Equation 1} \\ 0.075x + 0.09y = 990 \qquad \text{Equation 2} \end{cases}$

Multiply Equation 1 by 9 and Equation 2 by -100.

$$
\begin{cases}
9x + 9y = 108{,}000 \\
-7.5x - 9y = -99{,}000
\end{cases}
$$
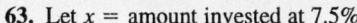
$$
\begin{aligned}
1.5x \quad\;\; &= 9{,}000 \qquad \text{Add the equations} \\
x &= \$6000 \\
y &= \$6000
\end{aligned}
$$

The most that can be invested at 7.5% is $6000.

65. Let $x = $ number of student tickets

$y = $ number of adult tickets

$\begin{cases} x + y = 1435 \qquad \text{Equation 1} \\ 1.50x + 5.00y = 3552.50 \qquad \text{Equation 2} \end{cases}$

Multiply Equation 1 by -1.50

$$
\begin{cases}
-1.50x - 1.50y = -2152.50 \\
1.50x + 5.00y = 3552.50
\end{cases}
$$
$$
\begin{aligned}
3.50y &= 1400.00 \quad \text{Add the equations} \\
y &= 400 \\
x &= 1035
\end{aligned}
$$

Solution: 1035 student tickets and 400 adult tickets were sold.

67. Let x = number of deodorant containers produced by Machine 1

y = number of deodorant containers produced by Machine 2

$x + y = 1764$ Equation 1

$x = 1.8y$ Equation 2

Substitute $1.8y$ for x in Equation 1.

$1.8y + y = 1764 \implies 2.8y = 1764 \implies y = 630$

Back-substitute $y = 630$ into Equation 2.

$x = 1.8(630) \implies x = 1134$

Solution: Machine 1 produces 1134 deodorant containers and Machine 2 produces 630 deodorant containers.

69. $\begin{cases} 5b + 10a = 20.2 \implies -10b - 20a = -40.4 \\ 10b + 30a = 50.1 \implies 10b + 30a = 50.1 \end{cases}$

$\begin{aligned} 10a &= 9.7 \\ a &= 0.97 \\ b &= 2.10 \end{aligned}$

Least squares regression line:

$y = 0.97x + 2.10$

71. $\begin{cases} 7b + 21a = 35.1 \implies -21b - 63a = -105.3 \\ 21b + 91a = 114.2 \implies 21b + 91a = 114.2 \end{cases}$

$\begin{aligned} 28a &= 8.9 \\ a &= \tfrac{89}{280} \\ b &= \tfrac{1137}{280} \end{aligned}$

Least squares regression line:

$y = \tfrac{1}{280}(89x + 1137)$

$y \approx 0.318x + 4.061$

73. $\begin{cases} 4b + 4a = 8 \implies 4b + 4a = 8 \\ 4b + 6a = 4 \implies -4b - 6a = -4 \end{cases}$

$\begin{aligned} -2a &= 4 \\ a &= -2 \\ b &= 4 \end{aligned}$

Least squares regression line: $y = -2x + 4$

75. $(1.00, 450), (1.25, 375), (1.50, 330)$

(a) $\begin{cases} 3b + 3.75a = 1155 \\ 3.75b + 4.8125a = 1413.75 \end{cases}$

By elimination we have $a = -240$ and $b = 685$.

(b) Least squares regression line:

$y = -240x + 685$

(c)

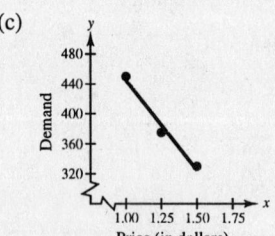

(d) $y = -240(1.40) + 685$

$= 349$ units

77. False. Two lines that coincide have infinitely many points of intersection.

79. True. If there are no points of intersection (solutions) then the lines must be parallel.

81. There are infinitely many systems that have the solution $(8, -2)$. One possible system is:

$$8 - 2 = 6 \Rightarrow x + y = 6$$
$$2(8) - (-2) = 18 \Rightarrow 2x - y = 18$$

83. There are infinitely many systems that have the solution $\left(-\frac{2}{3}, -10\right)$. One possible system is:

$$3\left(-\frac{2}{3}\right) + 3(-10) = -32 \Rightarrow 3x + 3y = -32$$
$$3\left(-\frac{2}{3}\right) + 6(-10) = -62 \Rightarrow 3x + 6y = -62$$

85. $\begin{cases} 21x - 20y = 0 & \text{Equation 1} \\ 13x - 12y = 120 & \text{Equation 2} \end{cases}$

Multiply Equation 2 by $\left(-\frac{5}{3}\right)$: $-\frac{65}{3}x + 20y = -200$

Add this to Equation 1 to eliminate y: $-\frac{2}{3}x = -200 \Rightarrow x = 300$

Back-substitute $x = 300$ in Equation 1: $21(300) - 20y = 0 \Rightarrow y = 315$

Solution: $(300, 315)$

The lines are not parallel. It is necessary to change the scale on the axes to see the point of intersection.

87. Answers will vary.

(a) No solution

$\begin{cases} x + y = 10 \\ x + y = 20 \end{cases}$

(b) Infinite number of solutions

$\begin{cases} x + y = 3 \\ 2x + 2y = 6 \end{cases}$

89. $\begin{cases} 15x + 3y = 6 \Rightarrow & 30x + 6y = 12 \\ -10x + ky = 9 \Rightarrow & \underline{-30x + 3ky = 27} \\ & (6 + 3k)y = 39 \end{cases}$

If $k = -2$, then we would have $0 = 39$ and the system would be inconsistent.

91. $2(x - 3) > -5x + 1$

$2x - 6 > -5x + 1$

$7x > 7$

$x > 1$

93. $-6 \le 3x - 10 < 6$

$4 \le 3x < 16$

$\frac{4}{3} \le x < \frac{16}{3}$

95. $|x + 10| \ge -3$

All real numbers x

97. $3x^2 + 12x > 0$

$3x(x + 4) > 0$

Critical numbers: $x = 0, -4$

Test Intervals: $(-\infty, -4), (-4, 0), (0, \infty)$

Test: Is $3x(x + 4) > 0$?

Solution: $x < -4, x > 0$

99. $\dfrac{3}{x(x^2 - 1)} = \dfrac{3}{x(x + 1)(x - 1)}$

$\qquad\qquad = \dfrac{A}{x} + \dfrac{B}{x + 1} + \dfrac{C}{x - 1}$

$\qquad\quad 3 = A(x + 1)(x - 1) + Bx(x - 1) + Cx(x + 1)$

Let $x = \quad 0$: $3 = -A \implies A = -3$

Let $x = -1$: $3 = 2B \implies B = \dfrac{3}{2}$

Let $x = \quad 1$: $3 = 2C \implies C = \dfrac{3}{2}$

$\dfrac{3}{x(x^2 - 1)} = \dfrac{-3}{x} + \dfrac{3/2}{x + 1} + \dfrac{3/2}{x - 1}$

$\qquad\qquad = \dfrac{1}{2}\left(-\dfrac{6}{x} + \dfrac{3}{x + 1} + \dfrac{3}{x - 1}\right)$

101. $\ln x - 5\ln(x + 3) = \ln x - \ln(x + 3)^5$

$\qquad\qquad\qquad = \ln\left[\dfrac{x}{(x + 3)^5}\right]$

103. $\frac{1}{4}\log_6 3x = \log_6 \sqrt[4]{3x}$

105. $30x - 40y - 33 = 0$

$10x + 20y - 21 = 0 \implies y = -\frac{1}{2}x + \frac{21}{20}$

$30x - 40\left(-\frac{1}{2}x + \frac{21}{20}\right) - 33 = 0$

$\quad 30x + 20x - 42 - 33 = 0$

$\qquad\qquad\qquad 50x = 75$

$\qquad\qquad\qquad\quad x = \frac{3}{2}$

$\qquad\qquad\quad y = -\frac{1}{2}\left(\frac{3}{2}\right) + \frac{21}{20} = \frac{6}{20} = \frac{3}{10}$

Solution: $\left(\frac{3}{2}, \frac{3}{10}\right)$

Section 7.3   Multivariable Linear Systems

■   You should know the operations that lead to equivalent systems of equations:

(a) Interchange any two equations.

(b) Multiply all terms of an equation by a nonzero constant.

(c) Replace an equation by the sum of itself and a constant multiple of any other equation in the system.

■   You should be able to use the method of Gaussian elimination with back-substitution.

Solutions to Odd-Numbered Exercises

1. $\begin{cases} 3x - y + z = 1 \\ 2x \quad - 3z = -14 \\ \quad 5y + 2z = 8 \end{cases}$

(a) $3(2) - (0) + (-3) \neq 1$

$(2, 0, -3)$ is **not** a solution.

(b) $3(-2) - (0) + 8 \neq 1$

$(-2, 0, 8)$ is **not** a solution.

(c) $3(0) - (-1) + 3 \neq 1$

$(0, -1, 3)$ is **not** a solution.

(d) $3(-1) - (0) + 4 = 1$

$2(-1) \quad - 3(4) = -14$

$5(0) + 2(4) = 8$

$(-1, 0, 4)$ **is** a solution.

3. $\begin{cases} 4x + y - z = 0 \\ -8x - 6y + z = -\frac{7}{4} \\ 3x - y = -\frac{9}{4} \end{cases}$

(a) $4\left(\frac{1}{2}\right) + \left(-\frac{3}{4}\right) - \left(-\frac{7}{4}\right) \neq 0$

$\left(\frac{1}{2}, -\frac{3}{4}, -\frac{7}{4}\right)$ is **not** a solution.

(b) $4\left(-\frac{3}{2}\right) + \left(\frac{5}{4}\right) - \left(-\frac{5}{4}\right) \neq 0$

$\left(-\frac{3}{2}, \frac{5}{4}, -\frac{5}{4}\right)$ is **not** a solution.

(c) $4\left(-\frac{1}{2}\right) + \left(\frac{3}{4}\right) - \left(-\frac{5}{4}\right) = 0$

$-8\left(-\frac{1}{2}\right) - 6\left(\frac{3}{4}\right) + \left(-\frac{5}{4}\right) = -\frac{7}{4}$

$3\left(-\frac{1}{2}\right) - \left(\frac{3}{4}\right) = -\frac{9}{4}$

$\left(-\frac{1}{2}, \frac{3}{4}, -\frac{5}{4}\right)$ **is** a solution.

(d) $4\left(-\frac{1}{2}\right) + \left(\frac{1}{6}\right) - \left(-\frac{3}{4}\right) \neq 0$

$\left(-\frac{1}{2}, \frac{1}{6}, -\frac{3}{4}\right)$ is **not** a solution.

5. $\begin{cases} 2x - y + 5z = 24 & \text{Equation 1} \\ y + 2z = 6 & \text{Equation 2} \\ z = 4 & \text{Equation 3} \end{cases}$

Back-substitute $z = 4$ into Equation 2.

$y + 2(4) = 6$

$y = -2$

Back-substitute $y = -2$ and $z = 4$ into Equation 1.

$2x - (-2) + 5(4) = 24$

$2x + 22 = 24$

$x = 1$

Solution: $(1, -2, 4)$

7. $\begin{cases} 2x + y - 3z = 10 & \text{Equation 1} \\ y = 2 & \text{Equation 2} \\ y - z = 4 & \text{Equation 3} \end{cases}$

Back-substitute $y = 2$ into Equation 3.

$2 - z = 4$

$z = -2$

Back-substitute $y = 2$ and $z = -2$ into Equation 1.

$2x + 2 - 3(-2) = 10$

$2x + 8 = 10$

$x = 1$

Solution: $(1, 2, -2)$

9. $\begin{cases} 4x - 2y + z = 8 & \text{Equation 1} \\ 2z = 4 & \text{Equation 2} \\ -y + z = 4 & \text{Equation 3} \end{cases}$

From Equation 2 we have $z = 2$. Back-substitute

$z = 2$ into Equation 3.

$-y + 2 = 4$

$y = -2$

Back-substitute $y = -2$ and $z = 2$ into Equation 1.

$4x - 2(-2) + 2 = 8$

$4x + 6 = 8$

$x = \frac{1}{2}$

Solution: $\left(\frac{1}{2}, -2, 2\right)$

11. $\begin{cases} x - 2y + 3z = 5 & \text{Equation 1} \\ -x + 3y - 5z = 4 & \text{Equation 2} \\ 2x - 3z = 0 & \text{Equation 3} \end{cases}$

Add Equation 1 to Equation 2.

$\begin{cases} x - 2y + 3z = 5 \\ y - 2z = 9 \\ 2x - 3z = 0 \end{cases}$

This is the first step in putting the system in row-echelon form.

13.
$$\begin{cases} x + y + z = 6 & \text{Equation 1} \\ 2x - y + z = 3 & \text{Equation 2} \\ 3x - z = 0 & \text{Equation 3} \end{cases}$$

$$\begin{cases} x + y + z = 6 \\ -3y - z = -9 & -2\text{Eq.1} + \text{Eq.2} \\ -3y - 4z = -18 & -3\text{Eq.1} + \text{Eq.3} \end{cases}$$

$$\begin{cases} x + y + z = 6 \\ -3y - z = -9 \\ -3z = -9 & -\text{Eq.2} + \text{Eq.3} \end{cases}$$

$$\begin{cases} x + y + z = 6 \\ -3y - z = -9 \\ z = 3 & -\frac{1}{3}\text{Eq.3} \end{cases}$$

$-3y - 3 = -9 \Rightarrow y = 2$

$x + 2 + 3 = 6 \Rightarrow x = 1$

Solution: $(1, 2, 3)$

15.
$$\begin{cases} 2x + 2z = 2 \\ 5x + 3y = 4 \\ 3y - 4z = 4 \end{cases}$$

$$\begin{cases} x + z = 1 & \frac{1}{2}\text{Eq.1} \\ 5x + 3y = 4 \\ 3y - 4z = 4 \end{cases}$$

$$\begin{cases} x + z = 1 \\ 3y - 5z = -1 & -5\text{Eq.1} + \text{Eq.2} \\ 3y - 4z = 4 \end{cases}$$

$$\begin{cases} x + z = 1 \\ 3y - 5z = -1 \\ z = 5 & -\text{Eq.2} + \text{Eq.3} \end{cases}$$

$3y - 5(5) = -1 \Rightarrow y = 8$

$x + 5 = 1 \Rightarrow x = -4$

Solution: $(-4, 8, 5)$

17.
$$\begin{cases} 3x + 3y = 9 & \text{Interchange Equations.} \\ 2x - 3z = 10 \\ 6y + 4z = -12 \end{cases}$$

$$\begin{cases} x + y = 3 & \frac{1}{3}\text{Eq.1} \\ 2x - 3z = 10 \\ 6y + 4z = -12 \end{cases}$$

$$\begin{cases} x + y = 3 \\ -2y - 3z = 4 & -2\text{Eq.1} + \text{Eq.2} \\ 6y + 4z = -12 \end{cases}$$

$$\begin{cases} x + y = 3 \\ -2y - 3z = 4 \\ -5z = 0 & 3\text{Eq.2} + \text{Eq.3} \end{cases}$$

$$\begin{cases} x + y = 3 \\ -2y - 3z = 4 \\ z = 0 & -\frac{1}{5}\text{Eq.3} \end{cases}$$

$-2y - 3(0) = 4 \Rightarrow y = -2$

$x - 2 = 3 \Rightarrow x = 5$

Solution: $(5, -2, 0)$

19.
$$\begin{cases} x - 2y + 2z = -9 & \text{Interchange Equations.} \\ 2x + y - z = 7 \\ 3x - y + z = 5 \end{cases}$$

$$\begin{cases} x - 2y + 2z = -9 \\ 5y - 5z = 25 & -2\text{Eq.1} + \text{Eq.2} \\ 5y - 5z = 32 & -3\text{Eq.1} + \text{Eq.3} \end{cases}$$

$$\begin{cases} x - 2y + 2z = -9 \\ 5y - 5z = 25 \\ 0 = 7 & -\text{Eq.2} + \text{Eq.3} \end{cases}$$

Inconsistent, no solution.

21. $\begin{cases} 3x - 5y + 5z = 1 \\ 5x - 2y + 3z = 0 \\ 7x - y + 3z = 0 \end{cases}$

$\begin{cases} 6x - 10y + 10z = 2 \\ 5x - 2y + 3z = 0 \\ 7x - y + 3z = 0 \end{cases}$ 2Eq.1

$\begin{cases} x - 8y + 7z = 2 \\ 5x - 2y + 3z = 0 \\ 7x - y + 3z = 0 \end{cases}$ $-$Eq.2 + Eq.1

$\begin{cases} x - 8y + 7z = 2 \\ 38y - 32z = -10 \\ 55y - 46z = -14 \end{cases}$ -5Eq.1 + Eq.2
-7Eq.1 + Eq.3

$\begin{cases} x - 8y + 7z = 2 \\ 2090y - 1760z = -550 \\ -2090y + 1748z = 532 \end{cases}$ 55Eq.2
-38Eq.3

$\begin{cases} x - 8y + 7z = 2 \\ 2090y - 1760z = -550 \\ -12z = -18 \end{cases}$ Eq.2 + Eq.3

$-12z = -18 \Rightarrow z = \frac{3}{2}$

$38y - 32\left(\frac{3}{2}\right) = -10 \Rightarrow y = 1$

$x - 8(1) + 7\left(\frac{3}{2}\right) = 2 \Rightarrow x = -\frac{1}{2}$

Solution: $\left(-\frac{1}{2}, 1, \frac{3}{2}\right)$

23. $\begin{cases} x + 2y - 7z = -4 \\ 2x + y + z = 13 \\ 3x + 9y - 36z = -33 \end{cases}$

$\begin{cases} x + 2y - 7z = -4 \\ -3y + 15z = 21 \\ 3y - 15z = -21 \end{cases}$ -2Eq.2 + Eq.2
-3Eq.1 + Eq.3

$\begin{cases} x + 2y - 7z = -4 \\ -3y + 15z = 21 \\ 0 = 0 \end{cases}$ Eq.2 + Eq.3

$\begin{cases} x + 2y - 7z = -4 \\ y - 5z = -7 \end{cases}$ $-\frac{1}{3}$Eq.2

$\begin{cases} x + 3z = 10 \\ y - 5z = -7 \end{cases}$ -2Eq.2 + Eq.1

Let $z = a$, then:

$y = 5a - 7$

$x = -3a + 10$

Solution: $(-3a + 10, 5a - 7, a)$

25. $\begin{cases} 3x - 3y + 6z = 6 \\ x + 2y - z = 5 \\ 5x - 8y + 13z = 7 \end{cases}$

$\begin{cases} x - y + 2z = 2 \\ x + 2y - z = 5 \\ 5x - 8y + 13z = 7 \end{cases}$ $\frac{1}{3}$Eq.1

$\begin{cases} x - y + 2z = 2 \\ 3y - 3z = 3 \\ -3y + 3z = -3 \end{cases}$ $-$Eq.1 + Eq.2
-5Eq.1 + Eq.3

$\begin{cases} x - y + 2z = 2 \\ y - z = 1 \\ 0 = 0 \end{cases}$ $\frac{1}{3}$Eq.2
Eq.2 + Eq.3

$\begin{cases} x + z = 3 \\ y - z = 1 \end{cases}$ Eq.2 + Eq.1

Let $z = a$, then:

$y = a + 1$

$x = -a + 3$

Solution: $(-a + 3, a + 1, a)$

27. $\begin{cases} x - 2y + 5z = 2 \\ 4x - z = 0 \end{cases}$

Let $z = a$, then $x = \frac{1}{4}a$.

$\frac{1}{4}a - 2y + 5a = 2$

$a - 8y + 20a = 8$

$-8y = -21a + 8$

$y = \frac{21}{8}a - 1$

Answer: $\left(\frac{1}{4}a, \frac{21}{8}a - 1, a\right)$

To avoid fractions, we could go back and let
$z = 8a$, then $4x - 8a = 0 \Rightarrow x = 2a$.

$2a - 2y + 5(8a) = 2$

$-2y + 42a = 2$

$y = 21a - 1$

Solution: $(2a, 21a - 1, 8a)$

29. $\begin{cases} 2x - 3y + z = -2 \\ -4x + 9y = 7 \end{cases}$

$\begin{cases} 2x - 3y + z = -2 \\ 3y + 2z = 3 \end{cases}$ 2Eq.1 + Eq.2

$\begin{cases} 2x + 3z = 1 \\ 3y + 2z = 3 \end{cases}$ Eq.2 + Eq.1

Let $x = a$, then:

$y = -\frac{2}{3}a + 1$

$x = -\frac{3}{2}a + \frac{1}{2}$

Solution: $\left(-\frac{3}{2}a + \frac{1}{2}, -\frac{2}{3}a + 1, a\right)$

31.
$$\begin{cases} x & + 3w = 4 \\ 2y - z - w = 0 \\ 3y - 2w = 1 \\ 2x - y + 4z = 5 \end{cases}$$

$$\begin{cases} x & + 3w = 4 \\ 2y - z - w = 0 \\ 3y - 2w = 1 \\ -y + 4z - 6w = -3 \end{cases} \quad -2\text{Eq.1} + \text{Eq.4}$$

$$\begin{cases} x & + 3w = 4 \\ y - 4z + 6w = 3 \\ 2y - z - w = 0 \\ 3y - 2w = 1 \end{cases} \quad \begin{array}{l} -\text{Eq.4 and} \\ \text{interchange} \\ \text{the equations.} \end{array}$$

$$\begin{cases} x & + 3w = 4 \\ y - 4z + 6w = 3 \\ 7z - 13w = -6 \\ 12z - 20w = -8 \end{cases} \quad \begin{array}{l} -\text{Eq.2} + \text{Eq.3} \\ -3\text{Eq.2} + \text{Eq.4} \end{array}$$

$$\begin{cases} x & + 3w = 4 \\ y - 4z + 6w = 3 \\ z - 3w = -2 \\ 12z - 20w = -8 \end{cases} \quad -\tfrac{1}{2}\text{Eq.4} + \text{Eq.3}$$

$$\begin{cases} x & + 3w = 4 \\ y - 4z + 6w = 3 \\ z - 3w = -2 \\ 16w = 16 \end{cases} \quad -12\text{Eq.3} + \text{Eq.4}$$

$$16w = 16 \implies w = 1$$
$$z - 3(1) = -2 \implies z = 1$$
$$y - 4(1) + 6(1) = 3 \implies x = 1$$
$$x + 3(1) = 4 \implies x = 1$$

Solution: $(1, 1, 1, 1)$

33.
$$\begin{cases} x & + 4z = 1 \\ x + y + 10z = 10 \\ 2x - y + 2z = -5 \end{cases}$$

$$\begin{cases} x & + 4z = 1 \\ y + 6z = 9 \\ -y - 6z = -7 \end{cases} \quad \begin{array}{l} -\text{Eq.1} + \text{Eq.2} \\ -2\text{Eq.1} + \text{Eq.3} \end{array}$$

$$\begin{cases} x & + 4z = 1 \\ y + 6z = 9 \\ 0 = 2 \end{cases} \quad \text{Eq.2} + \text{Eq.3}$$

No solution, inconsistent

35.
$$\begin{cases} 2x + 3y = 0 \\ 4x + 3y - z = 0 \\ 8x + 3y + 3z = 0 \end{cases}$$

$$\begin{cases} 2x + 3y = 0 \\ -3y - z = 0 \\ -9y + 3z = 0 \end{cases} \quad \begin{array}{l} -2\text{Eq.1} + \text{Eq.2} \\ -4\text{Eq.1} + \text{Eq.3} \end{array}$$

$$\begin{cases} 2x + 3y = 0 \\ -3y - z = 0 \\ 6z = 0 \end{cases} \quad -3\text{Eq.2} + \text{Eq.3}$$

$$6z = 0 \implies z = 0$$
$$-3y - 0 = 0 \implies y = 0$$
$$2x + 3(0) = 0 \implies x = 0$$

Solution: $(0, 0, 0)$

37.
$$\begin{cases} 12x + 5y + z = 0 \\ 23x + 4y - z = 0 \end{cases}$$

$$\begin{cases} 24x + 10y + 2z = 0 \\ 23x + 4y - z = 0 \end{cases} \quad 2\text{Eq.1}$$

$$\begin{cases} x + 6y + 3z = 0 \\ 23x + 4y - z = 0 \end{cases} \quad -\text{Eq.2} + \text{Eq.1}$$

$$\begin{cases} x + 6y + 3z = 0 \\ -134y - 70z = 0 \end{cases} \quad -23\text{Eq.1} + \text{Eq.2}$$

$$\begin{cases} x + 6y + 3z = 0 \\ -67y - 35z = 0 \end{cases} \quad -\tfrac{1}{2}\text{Eq.2}$$

To avoid fractions, let $z = 67a$, then:
$$-67y - 35(67a) = 0$$
$$y = -35a$$
$$x + 6(-35a) + 3(67a) = 0$$
$$x = 9a$$

Solution: $(9a, -35a, 67a)$

39. $y = ax^2 + bx + c$ passing through $(0, 0)$, $(2, -2)$, $(4, 0)$

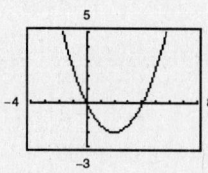

$(0, \quad 0)$: $\quad 0 = \qquad\qquad\quad c$

$(2, -2)$: $-2 = \quad 4a + 2b + c \implies -1 = 2a + b$

$(4, \quad 0)$: $\quad 0 = 16a + 4b + c \implies \quad 0 = 4a + b$

Solution: $a = \frac{1}{2}, b = -2, c = 0$

The equation of the parabola is $y = \frac{1}{2}x^2 - 2x$.

41. $y = ax^2 + bx + c$ passing through $(2, 0)$, $(3, -1)$, $(4, 0)$

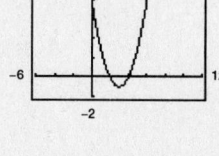

$(2, \quad 0)$: $\quad 0 = 4a + 2b + c$

$(3, -1)$: $-1 = 9a + 3b + c$

$(4, \quad 0)$: $\quad 0 = 16a + 4b + c$

$$\begin{cases} 0 = 4a + 2b + c \\ -1 = 5a + \quad b \qquad -\text{Eq.1} + \text{Eq.2} \\ 0 = 12a + 2b \qquad -\text{Eq.1} + \text{Eq.3} \end{cases}$$

$\quad 0 = 4a + 2b + c$

$-1 = 5a + \quad b$

$\quad 2 = 2a \qquad\qquad -2\text{Eq.2} + 3\text{Eq.}$

Solution: $a = 1, b = -6, c = 8$

The equation of the parabola is $y = x^2 - 6x + 8$.

43. $x^2 + y^2 + Dx + Ey + F = 0$ passing through $(0, 0)$, $(2, 2)$, $(4, 0)$

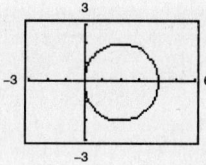

$(0, 0)$: $\qquad\qquad\qquad F = 0$

$(2, 2)$: $\quad 8 + 2D + 2E + F = 0 \implies D + E = -4$

$(4, 0)$: $16 + 4D \qquad + F = 0 \implies D = -4$ and $E = 0$

The equation of the circle is $x^2 + y^2 - 4x = 0$.

To graph, let $y_1 = \sqrt{4x - x^2}$ and $y_2 = -\sqrt{4x - x^2}$.

45. $x^2 + y^2 + Dx + Ey + F = 0$ passing through $(-3, -1)$, $(2, 4)$, $(-6, 8)$

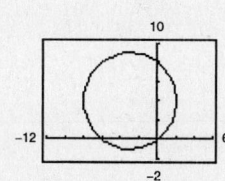

$(-3, -1)$: $\quad 10 - 3D - \quad E + F = 0 \implies \quad 10 = \quad 3D + \quad E - F$

$(\quad 2, \quad 4)$: $\quad 20 + 2D + 4E + F = 0 \implies \quad 20 = -2D - 4E - F$

$(-6, \quad 8)$: $100 - 6D + 8E + F = 0 \implies 100 = \quad 6D - 8E - F$

Solution: $D = 6, E = -8, F = 0$

The equation of the circle is $x^2 + y^2 + 6x - 8y = 0$.

To graph, complete the squares first, then solve for y.

$(x^2 + 6x + 9) + (y^2 - 8y + 16) = 0 + 9 + 16$

$(x + 3)^2 + (y - 4)^2 = 25$

$(y - 4)^2 = 25 - (x + 3)^2$

$y - 4 = \pm\sqrt{25 - (x + 3)^2}$

$y = 4 \pm \sqrt{25 - (x + 3)^2}$

Let $y_1 = 4 + \sqrt{25 - (x + 3)^2}$ and $y_2 = 4 - \sqrt{25 - (x + 3)^2}$.

47. $s = \frac{1}{2}at^2 + v_0t + s_0$

$(1, 128), (2, 80), (3, 0)$

$128 = \frac{1}{2}a + v_0 + s_0 \implies a + 2v_0 + 2s_0 = 256$

$80 = 2a + 2v_0 + s_0 \implies 2a + 2v_0 + s_0 = 80$

$0 = \frac{9}{2}a + 3v_0 + s_0 \implies 9a + 6v_0 + 2s_0 = 0$

Solving this system yields $a = -32$, $v_0 = 0$, $s_0 = 144$.

Thus, $s = \frac{1}{2}(-32)t^2 + (0)t + 144$

$\qquad = -16t^2 + 144$.

49. $s = \frac{1}{2}at^2 + v_0t + s_0$

$(1, 452), (2, 372), (3, 260)$

$452 = \frac{1}{2}a + v_0 + s_0 \implies a + 2v_0 + 2s_0 = 904$

$372 = 2a + 2v_0 + s_0 \implies 2a + 2v_0 + s_0 = 372$

$260 = \frac{9}{2}a + 3v_0 + s_0 \implies 9a + 6v_0 + 2s_0 = 520$

Solving this system yields $a = -32$, $v_0 = -32$, $s_0 = 500$.

Thus, $s = \frac{1}{2}(-32)t^2 + (-32)t + 500$

$\qquad = -16t^2 - 32t + 500$.

51. Let x = number of touchdowns

Let y = number of extra-point kicks

Let z = number of field goals

$$\begin{cases} x + y + z = 20 \\ 6x + y + 3z = 72 \\ \quad\; y - z = 0 \end{cases}$$

$$\begin{cases} x + y + z = 20 \\ \quad -5y - 3z = -48 \qquad -6\text{Eq.1} + \text{Eq.2} \\ \quad\;\; y - z = 0 \end{cases}$$

$$\begin{cases} x + y + z = 20 \\ \quad\;\; y - z = 0 \qquad \text{Interchange Equations} \\ \quad -5y - 3z = -48 \end{cases}$$

$$\begin{cases} x + y + z = 20 \\ \quad\;\; y - z = 0 \\ \quad\quad\;\; -8z = -48 \qquad 5\text{Eq.2} + \text{Eq.3} \end{cases}$$

$-8z = -48 \implies z = 6$

$y - 6 = 0 \implies y = 6$

$x + 6 + 6 = 20 \implies x = 8$

So, 8 touchdowns, 6 extra-point kicks, and 6 field goals were scored.

53. Let x = amount at 8%

Let y = amount at 9%

Let z = amount at 10%

$$\begin{cases} x + y + z = 775,000 \\ 0.08x + 0.09y + 0.10z = 67,500 \\ x = 4z \end{cases}$$

$y + 5z = 775,000 \qquad$ Substitute $4z$ for x in Eq.1 and Eq.2

$0.09y + 0.42z = 67,500$

$z = 75,000$

$y = 775,000 - 5z = 400,000$

$x = 4z = 300,000$

$300,000 was borrowed at 8%

$400,000 was borrowed at 9%

$75,000 was borrowed at 10%

55. Let C = amount in certificates of deposit

Let M = amount in municipal bonds

Let B = amount in blue-chip stocks

Let G = amount in growth or speculative stocks

$$\begin{cases} C + M + B + G = 500,000 \\ 0.10C + 0.08M + 0.12B + 0.13G = 0.10(500,000) \\ B + G = \frac{1}{4}(500,000) \end{cases}$$

This system has infinitely many solutions.

Let $G = s$, then $B = 125,000 - s$

$$M = 125,000 + \tfrac{1}{2}s$$

$$C = 250,000 - \tfrac{1}{2}s$$

One possible solution is to let $s = 50,000$.

Certificates of deposit: $225,000

Municipal bonds: $150,000

Blue-chip stocks: $75,000

Growth or speculative stocks: $50,000

57. Let x = liters of spray X

Let y = liters of spray Y

Let z = liters of spray Z

Chemical A: $\left.\frac{1}{5}x + \frac{1}{2}z = 12\right\}$ $\Rightarrow x = 20, z = 16$

Chemical B: $\left.\frac{2}{5}x + \frac{1}{2}z = 16\right\}$

Chemical C: $\frac{2}{5}x + \ y = 26$ $\Rightarrow y = 18$

20 liters of spray X, 18 liters of spray Y, and 16 liters of spray Z are needed to get the desired mixture.

59.

	Product	
Truck	A	B
Large	6	3
Medium	4	4
Small	0	3

Let x = number of large trucks

Let y = number of medium trucks

Let z = number of small trucks

$$\begin{cases} 6x + 4y \geq 15 \\ 3x + 4y + 3z \geq 16 \end{cases}$$

Possible solutions:

(1) 4 medium trucks

(2) 2 large trucks, 1 medium truck, 2 small trucks

(3) 3 large trucks, 1 medium truck, 1 small truck

(4) 3 large trucks, 3 small trucks

61. $\begin{cases} t_1 - 2t_2 \quad\quad = \ 0 \\ t_1 \quad\quad - 2a = 128 \\ \quad\quad t_2 + \ a = 32 \end{cases}$

$\Rightarrow \quad 2t_2 - 2a = \ \ 128$

$\Rightarrow -2t_2 - 2a = -64$

$$-4a = \ \ 64$$
$$a = -16$$
$$t_2 = \ \ 48$$
$$t_1 = \ \ 96$$

So, $t_1 = 96$ pounds

$t_2 = 48$ pounds

$a = -16$ feet per second squared

63. $\dfrac{1}{x^3 - x} = \dfrac{A}{x} + \dfrac{B}{x - 1} + \dfrac{C}{x + 1}$

$\qquad 1 = A(x + 1)(x - 1) + Bx(x + 1) + Cx(x - 1)$

$\qquad 1 = Ax^2 - A + Bx^2 + Bx + Cx^2 - Cx$

$\qquad 1 = (A + B + C)x^2 + (B - C)x - A$

Let $x = 0$: $1 = -A \Rightarrow A = -1$

Let $x = 1$: $1 = 2B \Rightarrow B = \dfrac{1}{2}$

Let $x = -1$: $1 = 2C \Rightarrow C = \dfrac{1}{2}$

$\dfrac{1}{x^3 - x} = \dfrac{-1}{x} + \dfrac{\frac{1}{2}}{x - 1} + \dfrac{\frac{1}{2}}{x + 1} = \dfrac{1}{2}\left(-\dfrac{2}{x} + \dfrac{1}{x - 1} + \dfrac{1}{x + 1}\right)$

65. $\dfrac{x^2 - 3x - 3}{x(x - 2)(x + 3)} = \dfrac{A}{x} + \dfrac{B}{x - 2} + \dfrac{C}{x + 3}$

$\qquad x^2 - 3x - 3 = A(x - 2)(x + 3) + Bx(x + 3) + Cx(x - 2)$

Let $x = 0$: $-3 = -6A \Rightarrow A = \dfrac{1}{2}$

Let $x = 2$: $-5 = 10B \Rightarrow B = -\dfrac{1}{2}$

Let $x = -3$: $15 = 15C \Rightarrow C = 1$

$\dfrac{x^2 - 3x - 3}{x(x - 2)(x + 3)} = \dfrac{\frac{1}{2}}{x} - \dfrac{\frac{1}{2}}{x - 2} + \dfrac{1}{x + 3} = \dfrac{1}{2}\left(\dfrac{1}{x} - \dfrac{1}{x - 2} + \dfrac{2}{x + 3}\right)$

67. $\begin{cases} 4c \quad + \ 40a = \quad 19 \\ \quad 40b \qquad \quad = -12 \\ 40x \ + 544a = \ 160 \end{cases}$

$\begin{cases} 4c \quad + \ 40a = \quad 19 \\ \quad 40b \qquad \quad = -12 \\ \qquad \quad 144a = -30 \qquad -10\text{Eq.1} + \text{Eq.3} \end{cases}$

$\qquad\qquad 144a = -30 \Rightarrow a = -\dfrac{5}{24}$

$\qquad\qquad 40b = -12 \Rightarrow b = -\dfrac{3}{10}$

$\qquad 4c + 40\left(-\dfrac{5}{24}\right) = \quad 19 \Rightarrow c = \dfrac{41}{6}$

Least squares regression parabola: $y = -\dfrac{5}{24}x^2 - \dfrac{3}{10}x + \dfrac{41}{6}$

69.
$$\begin{cases} 4c + 9b + 29a = 20 \\ 9c + 29b + 99a = 70 \\ 29c + 99b + 353a = 254 \end{cases}$$

$$\begin{cases} 9c + 29b + 99a = 70 \\ 4c + 9b + 29a = 20 \\ 29c + 99b + 353a = 254 \end{cases}$$ Interchange equations.

$$\begin{cases} c + 11b + 41a = 30 \\ -35b - 135a = -100 \\ -220b - 836a = -616 \end{cases}$$ $-2\text{Eq.2} + \text{Eq.1}$
$-4\text{Eq.1} + \text{Eq.2}$
$-29\text{Eq.1} + \text{Eq.3}$

$$\begin{cases} c + 11b + 41a = 30 \\ 1540b + 5940a = 4400 \\ -1540b - 5852a = -4312 \end{cases}$$ -44Eq.2
7Eq.3

$$\begin{cases} c + 11b + 41a = 30 \\ 1540b + 5940a = 4400 \\ 88a = 88 \end{cases}$$ $\text{Eq.2} + \text{Eq.3}$

$$88a = 88 \implies a = 1$$

$$1540b + 5940(1) = 4400 \implies b = -1$$

$$c + 11(-1) + 41(1) = 30 \implies c = 0$$

Least squares regression parabola: $y = x^2 - x$

71. (a) $(30, 55), (40, 105), (50, 188)$

Quadratic model: $y \approx 0.165x^2 - 6.55x + 103$

(b)

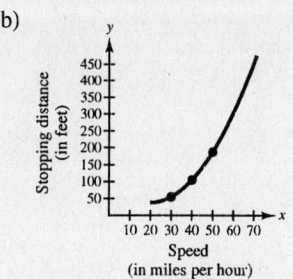

(c) When $x = 70$, $y = 453$ feet.

73.
$$\begin{cases} y + \lambda = 0 \\ x + \lambda = 0 \end{cases} \implies x = y = -\lambda$$
$$x + y - 10 = 0 \implies 2x - 10 = 0$$
$$x = 5$$
$$y = 5$$
$$\lambda = -5$$

75.
$$\begin{cases} 2x - 2x\lambda = 0 \implies 2x(1 - \lambda) = 0 \implies \lambda = 1 \text{ or } x = 0 \\ -2y + \quad \lambda = 0 \\ \quad y - \quad x^2 = 0 \end{cases}$$

If $\lambda = 1$:

$$2y = \lambda \implies y = \frac{1}{2}$$

$$x^2 = y \implies x = \pm\sqrt{\frac{1}{2}} = \pm\frac{\sqrt{2}}{2}$$

If $x = 0$:

$$x^2 = y \implies y = 0$$

$$2y = \lambda \implies \lambda = 0$$

Solution: $x = \pm\dfrac{\sqrt{2}}{2}$ or $x = 0$

$\qquad\qquad y = \dfrac{1}{2} \qquad\qquad y = 0$

$\qquad\qquad \lambda = 1 \qquad\qquad \lambda = 0$

77. False. Equation 2 does not have a leading coefficient of 1.

79. No, they are not equivalent. These are two arithmetic errors. The constant in the second equation should be -11 and the coefficient of z in the third equation should be 2.

81. When using Gaussian elimination to solve a system of linear equations, a system has no solution when there is a row representing a contradictory equation such as $0 = N$, where N is a nonzero real number.

For instance: $x + y = 3$ Equation 1
$\qquad\qquad\qquad -x - y = 3$ Equation 2

$\qquad\qquad\qquad\quad x + y = 0$
$\qquad\qquad\qquad\qquad\quad 0 = 6 \qquad$ Eq.1 + Eq.2

No solution

83. There are an infinite number of linear systems that have $(-5, -2, 1)$ as their solution. One such system is:

$$\begin{cases} x + \ y + \ z = \ -6 \\ -2x - \ y + 3z = \ \ 15 \\ x + 4y - \ z = -14 \end{cases}$$

85. There are an infinite number of linear systems that have $\left(-\frac{3}{2}, 4, -7\right)$ as their solution. One such system is:

$$\begin{cases} 2x - \ y + 3z = -28 \\ -6x + 4y + \ z = \ \ 18 \\ -4x - 2y - 3z = \ \ 19 \end{cases}$$

87. $225 = x(150)$

$\qquad x = 1.5 \text{ or } 150\%$

89. $0.48x = 132$

$\qquad x = 275$

91. $f(x) = -8x^4 + 32x^2$

(a) $-8x^4 + 32x^2 = 0$

$-8x^2(x^2 - 4) = 0$

Zeros: $x = 0, \pm 2$

(b)

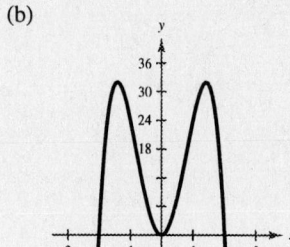

93. $f(x) = 6x^3 - 29x^2 - 6x + 5$

(a) $6x^3 - 29x^2 - 6x + 5 = 0$

$$
\begin{array}{r|rrrr}
5 & 6 & -29 & -6 & 5 \\
  &   & 30 & 5 & -5 \\
\hline
  & 6 & 1 & -1 & 0
\end{array}
$$

$f(x) = (x - 5)(6x^2 + x - 1)$

$\quad = (x - 5)(3x - 1)(2x + 1)$

Zeros: $x = 5, \frac{1}{3}, -\frac{1}{2}$

(b)

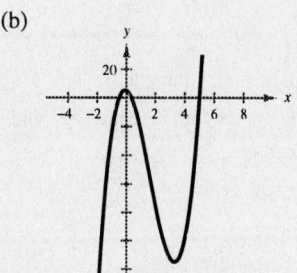

95. $y = \left(\frac{5}{2}\right)^{-x+1} - 4$

Horizontal asymptote: $y = -4$

x	y
-2	11.625
-1	2.25
0	-1.5
1	-3
2	-3.6

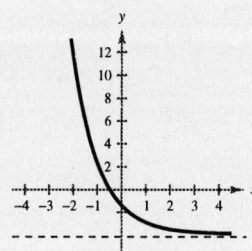

97. $y = 3.5^{-x+2} + 6$

Horizontal asymptote: $y = 6$

x	y
$-\frac{1}{2}$	28.918
0	18.25
$\frac{1}{2}$	12.548
1	9.5
2	7

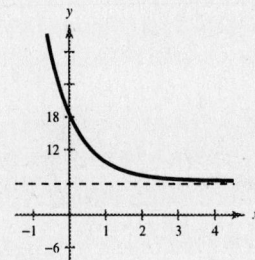

99.
$$\begin{cases} 6x - 5y = 3 & \text{Equation 1} \\ 10x - 12y = 5 & \text{Equation 2} \end{cases}$$

$$\begin{cases} 72x - 60y = 36 & 12\text{Eq.1} \\ -50x + 60y = -25 & -5\text{Eq.2} \end{cases}$$

$$22x = 11$$

$$x = \tfrac{1}{2}$$

$6\left(\tfrac{1}{2}\right) - 5y = 3 \implies y = 0$

Solution: $\left(\tfrac{1}{2}, 0\right)$

Section 7.4   Systems of Inequalities

■ You should be able to sketch the graph of an inequality in two variables.

    (a) Replace the inequality with an equal sign and graph the equation. Use a dashed line for $<$ or $>$, a solid line for $\le$ or $\ge$.

    (b) Test a point in each region formed by the graph. If the point satisfies the inequality, shade the whole region.

■ You should be able to sketch systems of inequalities.

Solutions to Odd-Numbered Exercises

1. $x \ge 2$

Using a solid line, graph the vertical line $x = 2$ and shade to the right of this line.

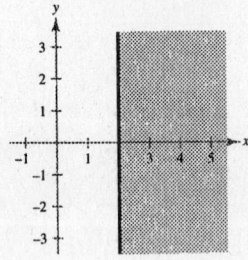

3. $y \ge -1$

Using a solid line, graph the horizontal line $y = -1$ and shade above this line.

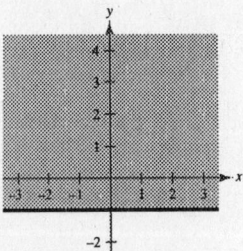

5. $y < 2 - x$

Using a dashed line, graph $y = 2 - x$, and then shade below the line. $\left(\text{Use } (0, 0) \text{ as a test point.}\right)$

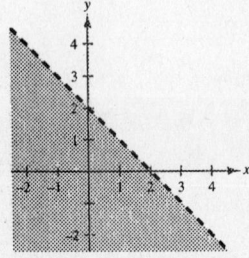

7. $2y - x \ge 4$

Using a solid line, graph $2y - x = 4$, and then shade above the line. $\left(\text{Use } (0, 0) \text{ as a test point.}\right)$

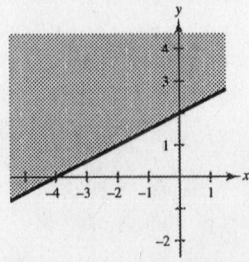

9. $(x + 1)^2 + (y - 2)^2 < 9$

Using a dashed line, sketch the circle
$(x + 1)^2 + (y - 2)^2 = 9$.

Center: $(-1, 2)$

Radius: 3

Test point: $(0, 0)$. Shade the inside of the circle.

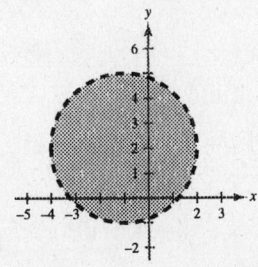

11. $y \leq \dfrac{1}{1 + x^2}$

Using a solid line, graph $y = \dfrac{1}{1 + x^2}$, and then

shade below the curve. $\left(\text{Use } (0, 0) \text{ as a test point.}\right)$

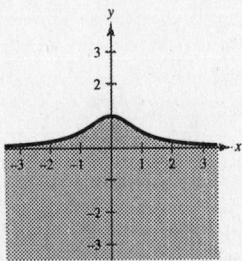

13. $y < \ln x$

Using a dashed line, sketch $y = \ln x$, and then shade
below the curve. (Use $(e, 0)$ as a test point.)

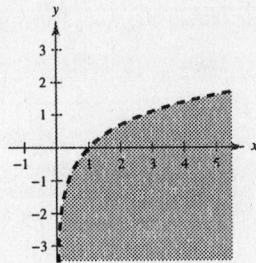

15. $y < 3^{-x-4}$

Using a dashed line, sketch $y = 3^{-x-4}$, and then
shade below the curve. (Use $(0, 0)$ as a test point.)

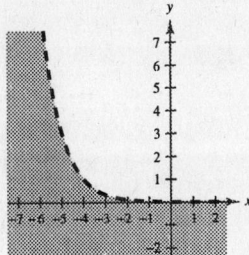

17. $y \geq \dfrac{2}{3}x - 1$

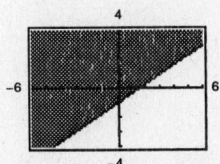

19. $y < -3.8x + 1.1$

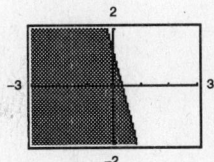

21. $x^2 + 5y - 10 \leq 0$

$$y \leq 2 - \frac{x^2}{5}$$

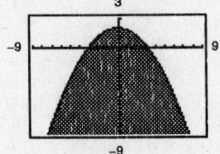

23. $\dfrac{5}{2}y - 3x^2 - 6 \geq 0$

$$y \geq \frac{2}{5}(3x^2 + 6)$$

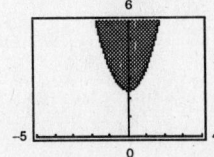

25. The line through $(-4, 0)$ and $(0, 2)$ is

$y = \frac{1}{2}x + 2$. For the shaded region below the

line, we have $y \leq \frac{1}{2}x + 2$.

27. The line through $(0, 2)$ and $(3, 0)$ is $y = -\frac{2}{3}x + 2$.

For the shaded region above the line, we have

$$y \geq -\frac{2}{3}x + 2$$

29. $\begin{cases} x \geq -4 \\ y > -3 \\ y \leq -8x - 3 \end{cases}$

(a) $0 \leq -8(0) - 3$, False

   $(0, 0)$ is **not** a solution.

(b) $-3 > -3$, False

   $(-1, -3)$ is **not** a solution.

(c) $-4 \geq -4$, True

   $0 > -3$, True

   $0 \leq -8(-4) - 3$, True

   $(-4, 0)$ **is** a solution.

(d) $-3 \geq -4$, True

   $11 > -3$, True

   $11 < -8(-3) - 3$, True

   $(-3, 11)$ **is** a solution.

31. $\begin{cases} 3x + y > 1 \\ -y - \frac{1}{2}x^2 \leq -4 \\ -15x + 4y > 0 \end{cases}$

(a) $3(0) + (10) > 1$, True

   $-10 - \frac{1}{2}(0)^2 \leq -4$, True

   $-15(0) + 4(10) > 0$, True

   $(0, 10)$ **is** a solution.

(b) $3(0) + (-1) > 1$, False $\Rightarrow$ $(0, -1)$ is **not** a solution.

(c) $3(2) + (9) > 1$, True

   $-9 - \frac{1}{2}(2)^2 \leq -4$, True

   $-15(2) + 4(9) > 0$, True

   $(2, 9)$ **is** a solution.

(d) $3(-1) + 6 > 1$, True

   $-6 - \frac{1}{2}(-1)^2 \leq -4$, True

   $-15(-1) + 4(6) > 0$, True

   $(-1, 6)$ **is** a solution.

33. $\begin{cases} x + y \leq 1 \\ -x + y \leq 1 \\ y \geq 0 \end{cases}$

First, find the points of intersection of each pair
of equations.

Vertex A	Vertex B	Vertex C
$x + y = 1$	$x + y = 1$	$-x + y = 1$
$-x + y = 1$	$y = 0$	$y = 0$
$(0, 1)$	$(1, 0)$	$(-1, 0)$

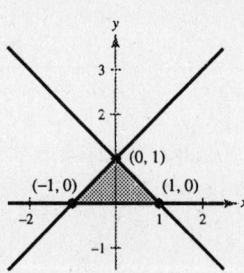

35. $\begin{cases} x^2 + y \leq 5 \\ x \geq -1 \\ y \geq 0 \end{cases}$

First, find the points of intersection of each pair
of equations.

Vertex A	Vertex B	Vertex C
$x^2 + y = 5$	$x^2 + y = 5$	$x = -1$
$x = -1$	$y = 0$	$y = 0$
$(-1, 4)$	$(\pm\sqrt{5}, 0)$	$(-1, 0)$

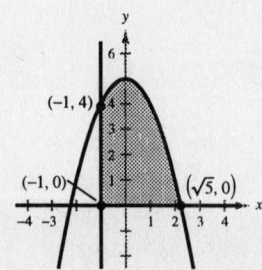

37. $\begin{cases} -3x + 2y < 6 \\ x - 4y > -2 \\ 2x + y < 3 \end{cases}$

First, find the points of intersection of each pair of equations.

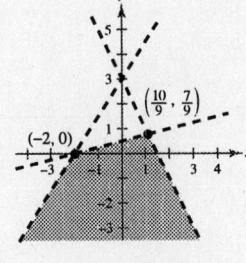

Vertex A	Point B	Vertex C
$-3x + 2y = 6$	$-3x + 2y = 6$	$x - 4y = -2$
$x - 4y = -2$	$2x + y = 3$	$2x + y = 3$
$(-2, 0)$	$(0, 3)$	$\left(\frac{10}{9}, \frac{7}{9}\right)$

Note that B is not a vertex of the solution region.

39. $\begin{cases} 2x + y > 2 \\ 6x + 3y < 2 \end{cases}$

The lines are parallel. There are no points of intersection. There is no region common to both inequalities.

The system has no solution.

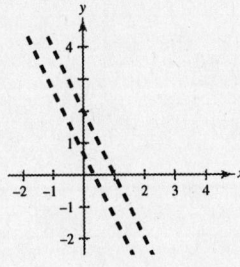

41. $\begin{cases} x > y^2 \\ x < y + 2 \end{cases}$

Points of intersection:

$$y^2 = y + 2$$
$$y^2 - y - 2 = 0$$
$$(y + 1)(y - 2) = 0$$
$$y = -1, 2$$

$(1, -1), (4, 2)$

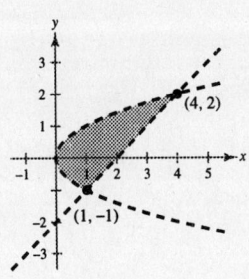

43. $\begin{cases} x^2 + y^2 \le 9 \\ x^2 + y^2 \ge 1 \end{cases}$

There are no points of intersection. The region common to both inequalities is the region between the circles.

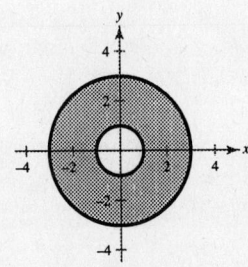

45. $3x + 4 \geq y^2$

$x - y < 0$

Points of intersection:

$x - y = 0 \Rightarrow y = x$

$3y + 4 = y^2$

$0 = y^2 - 3y - 4$

$0 = (y - 4)(y + 1)$

$y = 4$ or $y = -1$

$x = 4 \qquad x = -1$

$(4, 4)$ and $(-1, -1)$

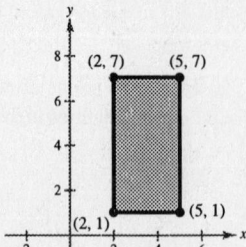

47. $\begin{cases} y \leq \sqrt{3x} + 1 \\ y \geq x^2 + 1 \end{cases}$

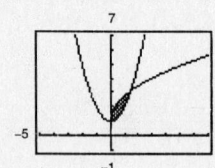

49. $\begin{cases} y < x^3 - 2x + 1 \\ y > -2x \\ x \leq 1 \end{cases}$

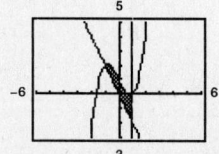

51. $\begin{cases} x^2y \geq 1 \Rightarrow y \geq \dfrac{1}{x^2} \\ 0 < x \leq 4 \\ \qquad y \leq 4 \end{cases}$

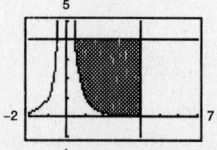

53. $\begin{cases} y \leq 4 - x \\ x \geq 0 \\ y \geq 0 \end{cases}$

55. Line through points $(0, 4)$ and $(4, 0)$: $y = 4 - x$

Line through points $(0, 2)$ and $(8, 0)$: $y = 2 - \frac{1}{4}x$

$\begin{cases} y \geq 4 - x \\ y \geq 2 - \frac{1}{4}x \\ x \geq 0 \\ y \geq 0 \end{cases}$

57. $\begin{cases} x^2 + y^2 \leq 16 \\ \qquad x \geq 0 \\ \qquad y \geq 0 \end{cases}$

59. Rectangular region with vertices at $(2, 1)$, $(5, 1)$, $(5, 7)$, and $(2, 7)$

$\begin{cases} x \geq 2 \\ x \leq 5 \\ y \geq 1 \\ y \leq 7 \end{cases}$

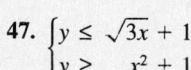

This system may be written as:

$\begin{cases} 2 \leq x \leq 5 \\ 1 \leq y \leq 7 \end{cases}$

61. Triangle with vertices at $(0, 0)$, $(5, 0)$, $(2, 3)$

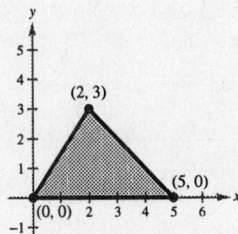

$(0, 0)$, $(5, 0)$ Line: $y = 0$

$(0, 0)$, $(2, 3)$ Line: $y = \frac{3}{2}x$

$(2, 3)$, $(5, 0)$ Line: $y = -x + 5$

$$\begin{cases} y \le \frac{3}{2}x \\ y \le -x + 5 \\ y \ge \quad 0 \end{cases}$$

63.   Demand = Supply

$50 - 0.5x = 0.125x$

$50 = 0.625x$

$80 = x$

$10 = p$

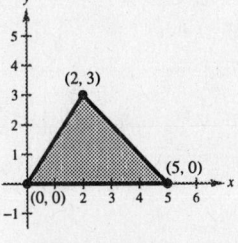

Point of equilibrium: $(80, 10)$

The consumer surplus is the area of the triangular region defined by

$$\begin{cases} p \le 50 - 0.5x \\ p \ge 10 \\ x \ge \quad 0. \end{cases}$$

Consumer surplus $= \frac{1}{2}(\text{base})(\text{height}) = \frac{1}{2}(80)(40) = \$1600$

The producer surplus is the area of the triangular region defined by

$$\begin{cases} p \ge 0.125x \\ p \le 10 \\ x \ge 0. \end{cases}$$

Producer surplus $= \frac{1}{2}(\text{base})(\text{height}) = \frac{1}{2}(80)(10) = \$400$

65.   Demand = Supply

$140 - 0.00002x = 80 + 0.00001x$

$60 = 0.00003x$

$2{,}000{,}000 = x$

$100 = p$

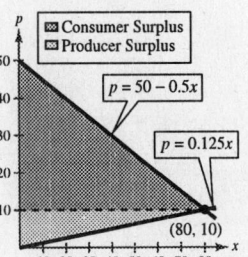

Point of equilibrium: $(2{,}000{,}000, 100)$

The consumer surplus is the area of the triangular region defined by

$$\begin{cases} p \le 140 - 0.00002x \\ p \ge 100 \\ x \ge \quad 0. \end{cases}$$

Consumer surplus $= \frac{1}{2}(\text{base})(\text{height}) = \frac{1}{2}(2{,}000{,}000)(40) = \$40{,}000{,}000$ or \$40 million

The producer surplus is the area of the triangular region defined by

$$\begin{cases} p \ge \quad 80 + 0.00001x \\ p \le 100 \\ x \ge \quad 0. \end{cases}$$

Producer surplus $= \frac{1}{2}(\text{base})(\text{height}) = \frac{1}{2}(2{,}000{,}000)(20) = \$20{,}000{,}000$ or \$20 million

67. x = number of tables

y = number of chairs

$$\begin{cases} x + \frac{3}{2}y \le 12 & \text{Assembly center} \\ \frac{4}{3}x + \frac{3}{2}y \le 15 & \text{Finishing center} \\ \quad x \ge 0 \\ \quad y \ge 0 \end{cases}$$

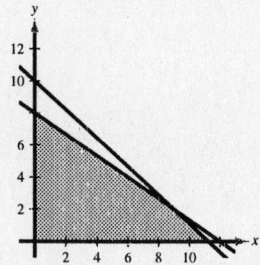

69. x = amount in smaller account

y = amount in larger account

Account constraints:

$$\begin{cases} x + y \le 20{,}000 \\ \quad y \ge 2x \\ \quad x \ge 5{,}000 \\ \quad y \ge 5{,}000 \end{cases}$$

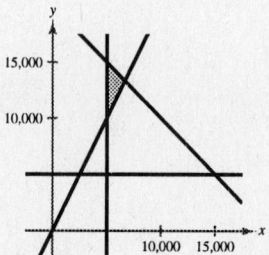

71. x = number of packages of gravel

y = number of bags of stone

$$\begin{cases} 55x + 70y \le 7500 & \text{Weight} \\ \quad x \ge 50 \\ \quad y \ge 40 \end{cases}$$

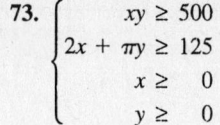

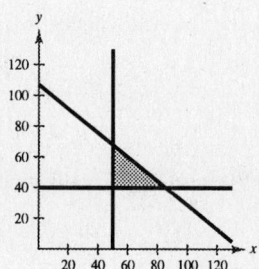

73.
$$\begin{cases} \quad xy \ge 500 & \text{Body = building space} \\ 2x + \pi y \ge 125 & \text{Track (Two semi–circles and two lengths)} \\ \quad x \ge 0 \\ \quad y \ge 0 \end{cases}$$

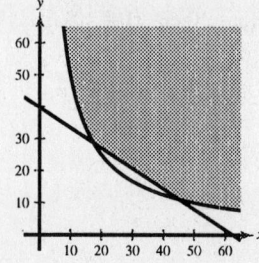

75. False. The graph shows the solution of the system

$$\begin{cases} \quad y < 6 \\ -4x - 9y < 6 \\ 3x + y^2 \ge 2. \end{cases}$$

77. $x^2 + y^2 \le 16 \implies$ region inside the circle

$x + y \le 4 \implies$ region below the line

Matches graph (b).

79. $x^2 + y^2 \ge 16 \implies$ region outside the circle

$x + y \le 4 \implies$ region below the line

Matches graph (a).

81. x = radius of smaller circle

y = radius of larger circle

(a) Constraints on circles: $\pi y^2 - \pi x^2 \geq 10$

$$y > x$$

$$x > 0$$

(b)

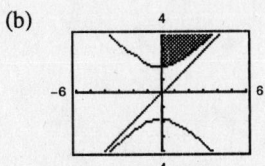

(c) The line is an asymptote to the boundary. The larger the circles, the closer the radii can be and the constraint still be satisfied.

83. The graph is a half-line on the real number line; on the rectangular coordinate system, the graph is a half-plane.

85. $(-8, 0), (3, -1)$

$$m = \frac{-1 - 0}{3 - (-8)} = -\frac{1}{11}$$

$$y - 0 = -\frac{1}{11}(x - (-8))$$

$$y = -\frac{1}{11}x - \frac{8}{11}$$

$$11y = -x - 8$$

$$x + 11y + 8 = 0$$

87. $\left(-\frac{1}{2}, 0\right), \left(\frac{11}{2}, 12\right)$

$$m = \frac{12 - 0}{\frac{11}{2} - \left(\frac{1}{2}\right)} = \frac{12}{6} = 2$$

$$y - 0 = 2\left(x - \left(-\frac{1}{2}\right)\right)$$

$$y = 2x + 1$$

$$2x - y + 1 = 0$$

89. $(-4.1, -3.8), (2.9, 8.2)$

$$m = \frac{8.2 - (-3.8)}{2.9 - (-4.1)} = \frac{12}{7}$$

$$y + 3.8 = \frac{12}{7}(x + 4.1)$$

$$y + 3.8 = \frac{12}{7}x + \frac{246}{35}$$

$$y = \frac{12}{7}x + \frac{113}{35}$$

$$35y = 60x + 113$$

$$60x - 35y + 113 = 0$$

91. $(2.7)^{3.99} \approx 52.619$

93. $1.5^{-3\pi} \approx 0.022$

95. $e^{-11/4} \approx 0.064$

97. $\begin{cases} -x - 2y + 3z = -23 \\ 2x + 6y - z = 17 \\ 5y + z = 8 \end{cases}$

$\begin{cases} x + 2y - 3z = 23 \\ 2x + 6y - z = 17 \\ 5y + z = 8 \end{cases}$ $-$Eq.1

$\begin{cases} x + 2y - 3z = 23 \\ 2y + 5z = -29 \\ 5y + z = 8 \end{cases}$ -2Eq.1 + Eq.2

$\begin{cases} x + 2y - 3z = 23 \\ 5y + z = 8 \\ 2y + 5z = -29 \end{cases}$ Interchange equations.

$\begin{cases} x + 2y - 3z = 33 \\ y - 9z = 66 \\ 2y + 5z = -29 \end{cases}$ -2Eq.3 + Eq.2

$\begin{cases} x + 2y - 3z = 33 \\ y - 9z = 66 \\ 23z = -161 \end{cases}$ -2Eq.2 + Eq.3

$\begin{cases} x + 2y - 3z = 33 \\ y - 9z = 66 \\ z = -7 \end{cases}$ $\frac{1}{23}$Eq.3

$y - 9(-7) = 66 \Rightarrow y = 3$

$x + 2(3) - 3(-7) = 23 \Rightarrow x = -4$

Solution: $(-4, 3, -7)$

Section 7.5   Linear Programming

■ To solve a linear programming problem:
1. Sketch the solution set for the system of constraints.
2. Find the vertices of the region.
3. Test the objective function at each of the vertices.

Solutions to Odd-Numbered Exercises

1. $z = 4x + 3y$

At $(0, 5)$: $z = 4(0) + 3(5) = 15$

At $(0, 0)$: $z = 4(0) + 3(0) = 0$

At $(5, 0)$: $z = 4(5) + 3(0) = 20$

The minimum value is 0 at $(0, 0)$.

The minimum value is 20 at $(5, 0)$.

3. $z = 3x + 8y$

At $(0, 5)$: $z = 3(0) + 8(5) = 40$

At $(0, 0)$: $z = 3(0) + 8(0) = 0$

At $(5, 0)$: $z = 3(5) + 8(0) = 15$

The minimum value is 0 at $(0, 0)$.

The maximum value is 40 at $(0, 5)$.

5. $z = 3x + 2y$

At $(0, 5)$: $z = 3(0) + 2(5) = 10$

At $(4, 0)$: $z = 3(4) + 2(0) = 12$

At $(3, 4)$: $z = 3(3) + 2(4) = 17$

At $(0, 0)$: $z = 3(0) + 2(0) = 0$

The minimum value is 0 at $(0, 0)$.

The maximum value is 17 at $(3, 4)$.

7. $z = 5x + 0.5y$

At $(0, 5)$: $z = 5(0) + \frac{5}{2} = \frac{5}{2}$

At $(4, 0)$: $z = 5(4) + \frac{0}{2} = 20$

At $(3, 4)$: $z = 5(3) + \frac{4}{2} = 17$

At $(0, 0)$: $z = 5(0) + \frac{0}{2} = 0$

The minimum value is 0 at $(0, 0)$.

The maximum value is 20 at $(4, 0)$.

9. $z = 10x + 7y$

At $(0, 45)$: $z = 10(0) + 7(45) = 315$

At $(30, 45)$: $z = 10(30) + 7(45) = 615$

At $(60, 20)$: $z = 10(60) + 7(20) = 740$

At $(60, 0)$: $z = 10(60) + 7(0) = 600$

At $(0, 0)$: $z = 10(0) + 7(0) = 0$

The minimum value is 0 at $(0, 0)$.

The maximum value is 740 at $(60, 20)$.

11. $z = 25x + 30y$

At $(0, 45)$: $z = 25(0) + 30(45) = 1350$

At $(30, 45)$: $z = 25(30) + 30(45) = 2100$

At $(60, 20)$: $z = 25(60) + 30(20) = 2100$

At $(60, 0)$: $z = 25(60) + 30(0) = 1500$

At $(0, 0)$: $z = 25(0) + 30(0) = 0$

The minimum value is 0 at $(0, 0)$.

The maximum value is 2100 at any point along the line segment connecting $(30, 45)$ and $(60, 20)$.

13. $z = 6x + 10y$

At $(0, 2)$: $z = 6(0) + 10(2) = 20$

At $(5, 0)$: $z = 6(5) + 10(0) = 30$

At $(0, 0)$: $z = 6(0) + 10(0) = 0$

The minimum value is 0 at $(0, 0)$.

The maximum value is 30 at $(5, 0)$.

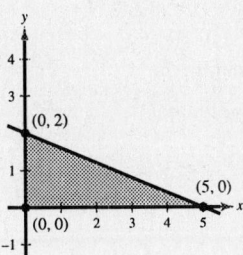

15. $z = 9x + 24y$

At $(0, 2)$: $z = 9(0) + 24(2) = 48$

At $(5, 0)$: $z = 9(5) + 24(0) = 45$

At $(0, 0)$: $z = 9(0) + 24(0) = 0$

The minimum value is 0 at $(0, 0)$.

The maximum value is 48 at $(0, 2)$.

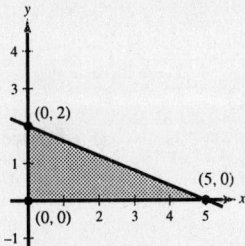

17. $z = 4x + 5y$

At $(10, 0)$: $z = 4(10) + 5(0) = 40$

At $(5, 3)$: $z = 4(5) + 5(3) = 35$

At $(0, 8)$: $z = 4(0) + 5(8) = 40$

The minimum value is 35 at $(5, 3)$.

The region is unbounded. There, is no maximum.

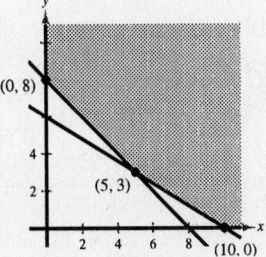

19. $z = 2x + 7y$

At $(10, 0)$: $z = 2(10) + 7(0) = 20$

At $(5, 3)$: $z = 2(5) + 7(3) = 31$

At $(0, 8)$: $z = 2(0) + 7(8) = 56$

The minimum value is 20 at $(10, 0)$.

The region is unbounded. There is no maximum.

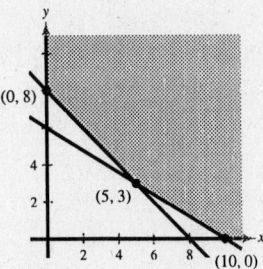

21. $z = 4x + y$

At $(36, 0)$: $z = 4(36) + 0 = 144$

At $(40, 0)$: $z = 4(40) + 0 = 160$

At $(24, 8)$: $z = 4(24) + 8 = 104$

The minimum value is 104 at $(24, 8)$.

The maximum value is 160 at $(40, 0)$.

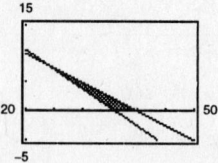

23. $z = x + 4y$

At $(36, 0)$: $z = 36 + 4(0) = 36$

At $(40, 0)$: $z = 40 + 4(0) = 40$

At $(24, 8)$: $z = 24 + 4(8) = 56$

The minimum value is 36 at $(36, 0)$.

The maximum value is 56 at $(24, 8)$.

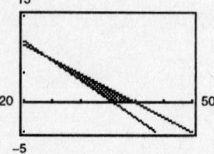

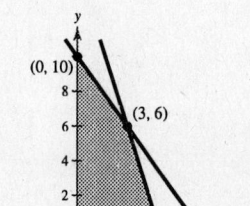

Figure for Exercises 25 and 27

25. $z = 2x + y$

At $(0, 10)$: $z = 2(0) + (10) = 10$

At $(3, 6)$: $z = 2(3) + (6) = 12$

At $(5, 0)$: $z = 2(5) + (0) = 10$

At $(0, 0)$: $z = 2(0) + (0) = 0$

The maximum value is 12 at $(3, 6)$.

27. $z = x + y$

At $(0, 10)$: $z = (0) + (10) = 10$

At $(3, 6)$: $z = (3) + (6) = 9$

At $(5, 0)$: $z = (5) + (0) = 5$

At $(0, 0)$: $z = (0) + (0) = 0$

The maximum value is 10 at $(0, 10)$.

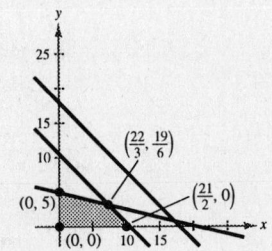

Figure for Exercises 29 and 31

29. $z = x + 5y$

At $(0, 5)$: $z = 0 + 5(5) = 25$

At $\left(\frac{22}{3}, \frac{19}{6}\right)$: $z = \frac{22}{3} + 5\left(\frac{19}{6}\right) = \frac{139}{6}$

At $\left(\frac{21}{2}, 0\right)$: $z = \frac{21}{2} + 5(0) = \frac{21}{2}$

At $(0, 0)$: $z = 0 + 5(0) = 0$

The maximum value is 25 at $(0, 5)$.

31. $z = 4x + 5y$

At $(0, 5)$: $z = 4(0) + 5(5) = 25$

At $\left(\frac{22}{3}, \frac{19}{6}\right)$: $z = 4\left(\frac{22}{3}\right) + 5\left(\frac{19}{6}\right) = \frac{271}{6}$

At $\left(\frac{21}{2}, 0\right)$: $z = 4\left(\frac{21}{2}\right) + 5(0) = 42$

At $(0, 0)$: $z = 4(0) + 5(0) = 0$

The maximum value is $\frac{271}{6}$ at $\left(\frac{22}{3}, \frac{19}{6}\right)$.

33. x = number of Model A

y = number of Model B

Constraints: $2x + 2.5y \le 4000$

$\qquad\qquad\quad 4x + y \le 4800$

$\qquad\qquad\quad x + 0.75y \le 1500$

$\qquad\qquad\qquad\qquad x \ge 0$

$\qquad\qquad\qquad\qquad y \ge 0$

Objective function: $P = 45x + 50y$

Vertices: $(0, 0), (0, 1600), (750, 1000), (1050, 600), (1200, 0)$

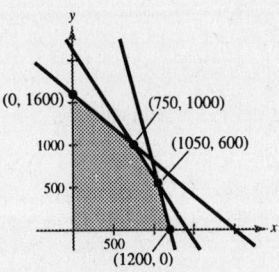

At $(0, 0)$: $\quad P = 45(0) + 50(0) = 0$

At $(0, 1600)$: $\quad P = 45(0) + 50(1600) = 80,000$

At $(750, 1000)$: $P = 45(750) + 50(1000) = 83,750$

At $(1050, 600)$: $P = 45(1050) + 50(600) = 77,250$

At $(1200, 0)$: $\quad P = 45(1200) + 50(0) = 54,000$

The maximum profit of \$83,750 occurs when 750 units of Model A and 1000 units of Model B are produced.

35. x = number of $150 models

y = number of $200 models

Constraints: $150x + 200y \le 40,000$

$\qquad\qquad x + \quad y \le 250$

$\qquad\qquad\qquad x \ge 0$

$\qquad\qquad\qquad y \ge 0$

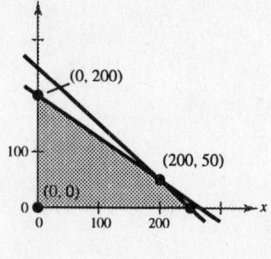

Objective function: $P = 25x + 40y$

Vertices: $(0, 0), (0, 200), (200, 50), (250, 0)$

At $(0, 0)$: $P = 25(0) + 40(0) = 0$

At $(0, 200)$: $P = 25(0) + 40(200) = 8000$

At $(200, 50)$: $P = 25(200) + 40(50) = 7000$

At $(250, 0)$: $P = 25(250) + 40(0) = 6250$

To maximize the profit, the merchant should stock 200 units of the model costing $200 and none of the $150 models. Then the maximum profit would be $8000.

37. x = number of bags of Brand X

y = number of bags of Brand Y

Constraints: $2x + \quad y \ge 12$

$\qquad\qquad 2x + 9y \ge 36$

$\qquad\qquad 2x + 3y \ge 24$

$\qquad\qquad\quad x \ge \quad 0$

$\qquad\qquad\quad y \ge \quad 0$

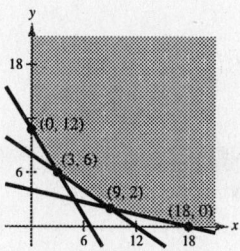

Objective function: $C = 25x + 20y$

Vertices: $(0, 12), (3, 6), (9, 2), (18, 0)$

At $(0, 12)$: $C = 25(0) + 20(12) = 240$

At $(3, 6)$: $C = 25(3) + 20(6) = 195$

At $(9, 2)$: $C = 25(9) + 20(2) = 265$

At $(18, 0)$: $C = 25(18) + 20(0) = 450$

To minimize cost, use three bags of Brand X and six bags of Brand Y for a total cost of $195.

39. x = number of audits

y = number of tax returns

Constraints: $100x + 12.5y \le 800$

$\qquad\qquad 8x + \quad 2y \le 96$

$\qquad\qquad\qquad x \ge \quad 0$

$\qquad\qquad\qquad y \ge \quad 0$

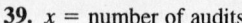

Objective Function: $R = 2000x + 300y$

Vertices: $(0, 0), (0, 48), (4, 32), (8, 0)$

At $(0, 0)$: $R = 2000(0) + 300(0) = 0$

At $(0, 48)$: $R = 2000(0) + 300(48) = 14,400$

At $(4, 32)$: $R = 2000(4) + 300(32) = 17,600$

At $(8, 0)$: $R = 2000(8) + 300(0) = 16,000$

The revenue will be maximum if the firm does 4 audits and 32 tax returns each week. The maximum revenue is $17,600.

41. Objective function: $z = 2.5x + y$

Constraints: $x \geq 0, y \geq 0, 3x + 5y \leq 15, 5x + 2y \leq 10$

At $(0, 0)$: $z = 0$

At $(2, 0)$: $z = 5$

At $\left(\frac{20}{19}, \frac{45}{19}\right)$: $z = \frac{95}{19} = 5$

At $(0, 3)$: $z = 3$

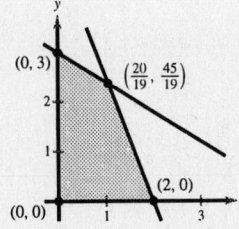

z is maximum at any point on the line segment connecting $(2, 0)$ and $\left(\frac{20}{19}, \frac{45}{19}\right)$.

43. Objective function: $z = -x + 2y$

Constraints: $x \geq 0, y \geq 0, x \leq 10, x + y \leq 7$

At $(0, 0)$: $z = -0 + 2(0) = 0$

At $(0, 7)$: $z = -0 + 2(7) = 14$

At $(7, 0)$: $z = -7 + 2(0) = -7$

The constraint $x \leq 10$ is extraneous.

The maximum value of 14 occurs at $(0, 7)$.

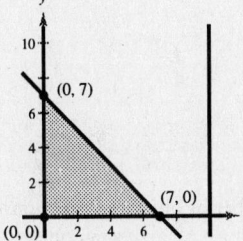

45. Objective function: $z = 3x + 4y$

Constraints: $x \geq 0, y \geq 0, x + y \leq 1, 2x + y \leq 4$

At $(0, 0)$: $z = 3(0) + 4(0) = 0$

At $(0, 1)$: $z = 3(0) + 4(1) = 4$

At $(1, 0)$: $z = 3(1) + 4(0) = 3$

The constraint $2x + y \leq 4$ is extraneous.

The maximum value of 4 occurs at $(0, 1)$.

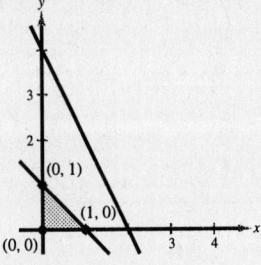

47. True. The objective function has a maximum value at any point on the line segment connecting the two vertices.

49. Constraints: $x \geq 0, y \geq 0, x + 3y \leq 15, 4x + y \leq 16$

Vertex	Value of $z = 3x + ty$
$(0, 0)$	$z = 0$
$(0, 5)$	$z = 5t$
$(3, 4)$	$z = 9 + 4t$
$(4, 0)$	$z = 12$

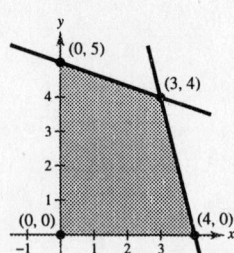

(a) For the maximum value to be at $(0, 5)$, $z = 5t$ must be greater than or equal to $z = 9 + 4t$ and $z = 12$.

$5t \geq 9 + 4t$ and $5t \geq 12$

$t \geq 9$ $\qquad$ $t \geq \frac{12}{5}$

Thus, $t \geq 9$.

(b) For the maximum value to be at $(3, 4)$, $z = 9 + 4t$ must be greater than or equal to $z = 5t$ and $z = 12$.

$9 + 4t \geq 5t$ and $9 + 4t \geq 12$

$9 \geq t$ $\qquad$ $4t \geq 3$

$\qquad\qquad\qquad$ $t \geq \frac{3}{4}$

Thus, $\frac{3}{4} \leq t \leq 9$.

51. There are an infinite number of objective functions that would have a maximum at $(0, 4)$. One such objective function is $z = x + 5y$.

53. There are an infinite number of objective functions that would have a maximum at $(5, 0)$. One such objective function is $z = 4x + y$.

55. $\dfrac{\dfrac{9}{x}}{\left(\dfrac{6}{x} + 2\right)} = \dfrac{\dfrac{9}{x}}{\dfrac{6 + 2x}{x}} = \dfrac{9}{x} \cdot \dfrac{x}{2(3 + x)} = \dfrac{9}{2(3 + x)} = \dfrac{9}{2(x + 3)}, \quad x \neq 0$

57. $\dfrac{\left(\dfrac{4}{x^2 - 9} + \dfrac{2}{x - 2}\right)}{\left(\dfrac{1}{x + 3} + \dfrac{1}{x - 3}\right)} = \dfrac{\dfrac{4(x - 2) + 2(x^2 - 9)}{(x - 2)(x^2 - 9)}}{\dfrac{(x - 3) + (x + 3)}{x^2 - 9}}$

$= \dfrac{2x^2 + 4x - 26}{(x - 2)(x^2 - 9)} \cdot \dfrac{x^2 - 9}{2x}$

$= \dfrac{2(x^2 + 2x - 13)}{(x - 2)(2x)}$

$= \dfrac{x^2 + 2x - 13}{x(x - 2)}, \quad x \neq \pm 3$

59. $e^{2x} + 2e^x - 15 = 0$

$(e^x + 5)(e^x - 3) = 0$

$e^x = -5$ or $e^x = 3$

No real $\qquad$ $x = \ln 3$

solution. $\qquad$ $x \approx 1.099$

61. $8(62 - e^{x/4}) = 192$

$62 - e^{x/4} = 24$

$-e^{x/4} = -38$

$e^{x/4} = 38$

$\dfrac{x}{4} = \ln 38$

$x = 4 \ln 38$

$x \approx 14.550$

63. $7 \ln 3x = 12$

$\ln 3x = \dfrac{12}{7}$

$3x = e^{12/7}$

$x = \dfrac{e^{12/7}}{3}$

$x \approx 1.851$

Review Exercises for Chapter 7

Solutions to Odd-Numbered Exercises

1. $\begin{cases} x^2 - y^2 = 9 \\ x - y = 1 \implies x = y + 1 \end{cases}$

$(y + 1)^2 - y^2 = 9$

$2y + 1 = 9$

$y = 4$

$x = 5$

Solution: $(5, 4)$

3. $\begin{cases} y = 2x^2 \\ y = x^4 - 2x^2 \implies 2x^2 = x^4 - 2x^2 \end{cases}$

$0 = x^4 - 4x^2$

$0 = x^2(x^2 - 4)$

$0 = x^2(x + 2)(x - 2)$

$x = 0, x = -2, x = 2$

$y = 0, y = 8, y = 8$

Solutions: $(0, 0), (-2, 8), (2, 8)$

5. $\begin{cases} 2x - y = 10 \\ x + 5y = -6 \end{cases}$

Point of intersection: $(4, -2)$

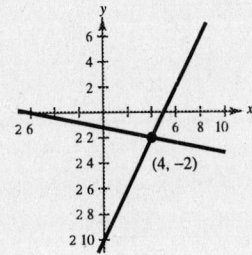

7. $\begin{cases} y = -2e^{-x} \\ 2e^x + y = 0 \implies y = -2e^x \end{cases}$

Point of intersection: $(0, -2)$

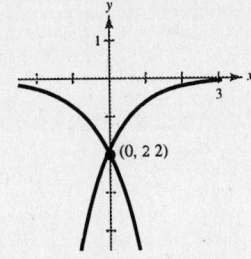

9. $\begin{cases} y = 2x^2 - 4x + 1 \\ y = x^2 - 4x + 3 \end{cases}$

Point of intersection: $(1.41, -0.66), (-1.41, 10.66)$

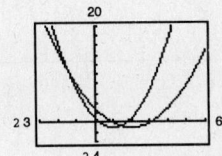

11. $C = 2.15x + 50,000$

$R = 6.95x$

Break-Even: $\quad R = C$

$\quad 6.95x = 2.15x + 50,000$

$\quad 4.80x = 50,000$

$\quad x \approx 10,417$ units

13.
$$2l + 2w = 480$$
$$l = 1.50w$$
$$2(1.50w) + 2w = 480$$
$$5w = 480$$
$$w = 96$$
$$l = 144$$

The dimensions are 96×144 meters.

15. $\begin{cases} 40x + 30y = 24 \\ 20x - 50y = -14 \end{cases} \Rightarrow \begin{aligned} 40x + 30y &= 24 \\ \underline{-40x + 100y} &\underline{= 28} \\ 130y &= 52 \\ y &= \tfrac{2}{5} \end{aligned}$

Back-substitute $y = \tfrac{2}{5}$ in Equation 1.

$40x + 30\left(\tfrac{2}{5}\right) = 24$

$\quad\quad 40x = 12$

$\quad\quad\quad x = \tfrac{3}{10}$

Solution: $\left(\tfrac{3}{10}, \tfrac{2}{5}\right)$

17. $\begin{cases} 12x + 42y = -17 \\ 30x - 18y = 19 \end{cases} \Rightarrow \begin{aligned} 36x + 126y &= -51 \\ \underline{210x + 126y} &\underline{= 133} \\ 246x &= 82 \\ x &= \tfrac{1}{3} \end{aligned}$

Back-substitute $x = \tfrac{1}{3}$ in Equation 1.

$12\left(\tfrac{1}{3}\right) + 42y = -17$

$\quad\quad 42y = -21$

$\quad\quad\quad y = -\tfrac{1}{2}$

Solution: $\left(\tfrac{1}{3}, -\tfrac{1}{2}\right)$

19. $\begin{cases} 7x + 12y = 63 \\ 2x + 3(y + 2) = 21 \end{cases}$

$\begin{cases} 7x + 12y = 63 \\ 2x + 3y = 15 \end{cases} \Rightarrow \begin{aligned} -7x - 12y &= -63 \\ \underline{8x + 12y} &\underline{= 60} \\ x &= -3 \end{aligned}$

Back-substitute $x = -3$ in Equation 1.

$7(-3) + 12y = 63$

$\quad\quad 12y = 84$

$\quad\quad\quad y = 7$

Solution: $(-3, 7)$

21. $\begin{cases} 1.5x + 2.5y = 8.5 \\ 6x + 10y = 24 \end{cases} \Rightarrow \begin{aligned} 3x + 5y &= 17 \\ \underline{-3x - 5y} &\underline{= -12} \\ 0 &= 5 \end{aligned}$

The system is inconsistent. There is no solution.

23. $\begin{cases} \tfrac{1}{5}x = -4 + y \Rightarrow y = \tfrac{1}{5}x + 4 \\ 5y = x \Rightarrow y = \tfrac{1}{5}x \end{cases}$

The system is inconsistent.
The lines are parallel.
No solution.

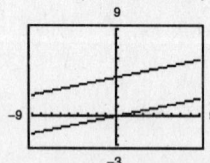

25. $\begin{cases} \tfrac{8}{5}x - y = 3 \Rightarrow y = \tfrac{8}{5}x - 3 \\ -5y + 8x = -2 \Rightarrow y = \tfrac{8}{5}x + \tfrac{2}{5} \end{cases}$

The system is inconsistent.
The lines are parallel.
No solution.

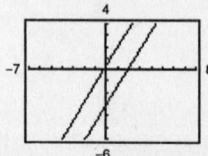

27. x = number of \$9.95 compact discs

y = number of \$14.95 compact discs

$$x + y = 650 \implies y = 650 - x$$

$$9.95x + 14.90y = 7717.50$$

$$9.95x + 14.95(650 - x) = 7717.50$$

$$-5x = -2000$$

$$x = 400$$

$$y = 250$$

Solution: 400 at \$9.95 and 250 at \$14.95

29. $37 - 0.0002x = 22 + 0.00001x$

$$15 = 0.00021x$$

$$x = \frac{500,000}{7}, p = \frac{159}{7}$$

Point of equilibrium: $\left(\dfrac{500,000}{7}, \dfrac{159}{7} \right)$

31. $\begin{cases} x - 4y + 3z = 3 \\ \quad -y + z = -1 \\ \qquad z = -5 \end{cases}$

$$-y + (-5) = -1 \implies y = -4$$

$$x - 4(-4) + 3(-5) = 3 \implies x = 2$$

Solution: $(2, -4, -5)$

33. $\begin{cases} x + 2y + 6z = 4 \\ -3x + 2y - z = -4 \\ 4x + 2z = 16 \end{cases}$

$\begin{cases} x + 2y + 6z = 8 \\ \quad 8y + 17z = 0 \qquad \text{3Eq.1 + Eq.2} \\ \quad -8y - 22z = 4 \qquad \text{−4Eq.1 + Eq.3} \end{cases}$

$\begin{cases} x + 2y + 6z = 4 \\ \quad 8y + 17z = 8 \\ \qquad -5z = 8 \qquad \text{Eq.2 + Eq.3} \end{cases}$

$\begin{cases} x + 2y + 6z = 4 \\ \quad 8y + 17z = 8 \\ \qquad z = -\frac{8}{5} \qquad -\frac{1}{5}\text{Eq.3} \end{cases}$

$$8y + 17\left(-\tfrac{8}{5}\right) = 8 \implies y = \tfrac{22}{5}$$

$$x + 2\left(\tfrac{22}{5}\right) + 6\left(-\tfrac{8}{5}\right) = 4 \implies x = \tfrac{24}{5}$$

Solution: $\left(\tfrac{24}{5}, \tfrac{22}{5}, -\tfrac{8}{5} \right)$

35. $\begin{cases} x - 2y + z = -6 \\ 2x - 3y = -7 \\ -x + 3y - 3z = 11 \end{cases}$

$\begin{cases} x - 2y + z = -6 \\ \quad y - 2z = 5 \qquad -2\text{Eq.1 + Eq.2} \\ \quad y - 2z = 5 \qquad \text{Eq.1 + Eq.3} \end{cases}$

$\begin{cases} x - 2y + z = -6 \\ \quad y - 2z = 5 \\ \qquad 0 = 0 \qquad -\text{Eq.2 + Eq.3} \end{cases}$

Let $z = a$, then:

$$y = 2a + 5$$

$$x - 2(2a + 5) + a = -6$$

$$x - 3a - 10 = -6$$

$$x = 3a + 4$$

Solution: $(3a + 4, 2a + 5, a)$ where a is any real number.

37. $y = ax^2 + bx + c$ through $(0, -5)$, $(1, -2)$, and $(2, 5)$.

$\begin{array}{lll} (0, -5): -5 = \ \ + c \implies & c = -5 \\ (1, -2): -2 = a + b + c \implies & \begin{cases} a + b = 3 \\ 2a + b = 5 \end{cases} \\ (2, \ \ 5): \ \ 5 = 4a + 2b + c \implies \end{array}$

$\begin{cases} 2a + b = 5 \\ -a - b = -3 \end{cases}$

$$a = 2$$

$$b = 1$$

The equation of the parabola is $y = 2x^2 + x - 5$.

39. $x^2 + y^2 + Dx + Ey + F = 0$ through $(-1, -2)$, $(5, -2)$ and $(2, 1)$.

$$
\begin{array}{ll}
(-1,-2)\colon & 5 - D - 2E + F = 0 \Rightarrow \\
(5,-2)\colon & 29 + 5D - 2E + F = 0 \Rightarrow \\
(2,1)\colon & 5 + 2D + 2E + F = 0 \Rightarrow
\end{array}
\left\{
\begin{array}{rcr}
D + 2E - F = & 5 \\
5D - 2E + F = & -29 \\
2D + E + F = & -5
\end{array}
\right.
$$

From the first two equations we have

$$6D = -24$$

$$D = -4.$$

Substituting $D = -4$ into the second and third equations yields:

$$
\begin{array}{rcr}
-20 - 2E + F = -29 \Rightarrow & \\
-8 + E + F = -5 \Rightarrow &
\end{array}
\left|
\begin{array}{rcr}
-2E + F = & -9 \\
-E - F = & -3 \\
\hline
-3E = & -12 \\
E = & 4 \\
F = & -1
\end{array}
\right.
$$

The equation of the circle is $x^2 + y^2 - 4x + 4y - 1 = 0$.

41.
$$
\left\{
\begin{array}{l}
5b + 10a = 17.8 \Rightarrow \\
10b + 30a = 45.7 \Rightarrow
\end{array}
\right.
\left|
\begin{array}{rcr}
-10b - 20a = & -35.6 \\
10b + 30a = & 45.7 \\
\hline
10a = & 10.1 \\
a = & 1.01 \\
b = & 1.54
\end{array}
\right.
$$

Least squares regression line: $y = 1.01x + 1.54$

43.
$$
\left\{
\begin{array}{l}
5x - 12y + 7z = 16 \Rightarrow \\
3x - 7y + 4z = 9 \Rightarrow
\end{array}
\right.
\left|
\begin{array}{rcr}
15x - 36y + 21z = & 48 \\
-15x + 35y - 20z = & -45 \\
\hline
-y + z = & 3
\end{array}
\right.
$$

Let $y = a$

Then $z = a + 3$

and $5x - 12a + 7(a + 3) = 16 \Rightarrow x = a - 1$

Solution: $(a - 1, a, a + 3)$ where a is any real number.

45. From the following chart we obtain our system of equations.

	A	B	C
Mixture X	$\frac{1}{5}$	$\frac{2}{5}$	$\frac{2}{5}$
Mixture Y	0	0	1
Mixture Z	$\frac{1}{3}$	$\frac{1}{3}$	$\frac{1}{3}$
Desired Mixture	$\frac{6}{27}$	$\frac{8}{27}$	$\frac{13}{27}$

$$
\left.
\begin{array}{l}
\frac{1}{5}x + \frac{1}{3}z = \frac{6}{27} \\
\frac{2}{5}x + \frac{1}{3}z = \frac{8}{27}
\end{array}
\right\} x = \frac{10}{27},\ z = \frac{12}{27}
$$

$$\frac{2}{5}x + y + \frac{1}{3}z = \frac{13}{27} \Rightarrow y = \frac{5}{27}$$

To obtain the desired mixture, use 10 gallons of spray X, 5 gallons of spray Y, and 12 gallons of spray Z.

47.
$$
\begin{array}{rcll}
5c + 10a = & 9.1 & \Rightarrow & 10c - 20a = -18.2 \\
10b = & 8.0 & & \\
10c + 34a = & 19.8 & \Rightarrow & 10c - 34a = 19.8 \\
\hline
& & & 14a = 1.6 \\
& & & a \approx 0.114 \\
& & & c = 1.591 \\
& & & b = 0.8
\end{array}
$$

Least squares parabola: $y = 0.114x^2 + 0.800x + 1.591$

49. $3y - x \geq 7$

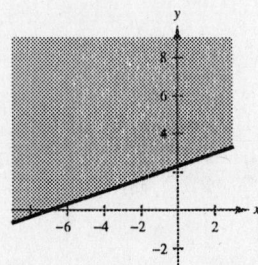

51. $y \leq 2 \ln x - 6$

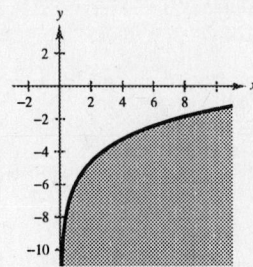

53. $\begin{cases} 2x + 3y \leq 24 \\ 2x + y \leq 16 \\ x \geq 0 \\ y \geq 0 \end{cases}$

Vertices: $(0, 0), (0, 8), (6, 4), (8, 0)$

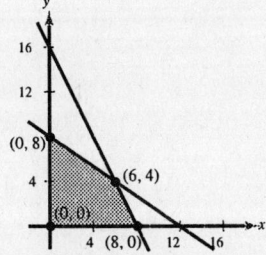

55. $\begin{cases} 2x + y \geq 16 \\ x + 3y \geq 18 \\ 0 \leq x \leq 25 \\ 0 \leq y \leq 25 \end{cases}$

Vertices: $(6, 4), (0, 16), (0, 25), (25, 25), (25, 0), (18, 0)$

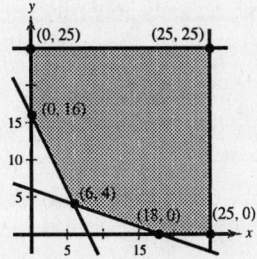

57. $\begin{cases} y \leq 6 - 2x - x^2 \\ y \geq x + 6 \end{cases}$

Vertices: $\quad x + 6 = 6 - 2x - x^2$

$x^2 + 3x = 0$

$x(x + 3) = 0 \implies x = 0, -3$

$(0, 6), (-3, 3)$

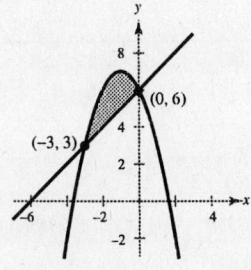

59. $\begin{cases} x^2 + y^2 \leq 9 \implies y^2 \leq 9 - x^2 \\ (x - 3)^2 + y^2 \leq 9 \implies y^2 \leq 9 - (x - 3) \end{cases}$

Vertices: $\qquad 9 - x^2 = 9 - (x - 3)^2$

$(x - 3)^2 - x^2 = 0$

$x^2 - 6x + 9 - x^2 = 0$

$x = \dfrac{3}{2}$

$\left(\dfrac{3}{2}, \pm \dfrac{3\sqrt{3}}{2} \right)$

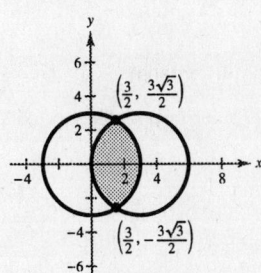

61. x = number of units of Product I

y = number of units of Product II

$$\begin{cases} 20x + 30y \le 24,000 \\ 12x + 8y \le 12,400 \\ x \ge 0 \\ y \ge 0 \end{cases}$$

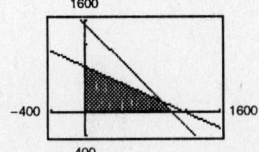

63. $130 - 0.0002x = 30 + 0.0003x$

$$100 = 0.0005x$$

$$x = 200,000 \text{ units}$$

$$p = \$90$$

Point of equilibrium: $(200,000, 90)$

Consumer surplus: $\frac{1}{2}(200,000)(40) = \$4,000,000$

Producer surplus: $\frac{1}{2}(200,000)(60) = \$6,000,000$

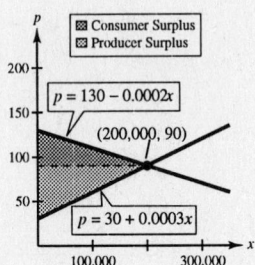

65. Minimize $z = 10x + 7y$ subject to the following constraints:

$$x \ge 0$$

$$y \ge 0$$

$$2x + y \ge 100$$

$$x + y \ge 75$$

At $(0, 100)$: $z = 10(0) + 7(100) = 700$

At $(25, 50)$: $z = 10(25) + 7(50) = 600,$

At $(75, 0)$: $z = 10(75) + 7(0) = 750$

The minimum value is 600 at $(25, 50)$.

67. Maximize $z = 50x + 70y$ subject to the following constraints:

$$x \ge 0$$

$$y \ge 0$$

$$x + 2y \le 1500$$

$$5x + 2y \le 3500$$

At $(0, 0)$: $z = 50(0) + 70(0) = 0$

At $(0, 750)$: $z = 50(0) + 70(750) = 52,500$

At $(500, 500)$: $z = 50(500) + 70(500) = 60,000$

At $(700, 0)$: $z = 50(700) + 70(0) = 35,000$

The maximum value is 60,000 at $(500, 500)$.

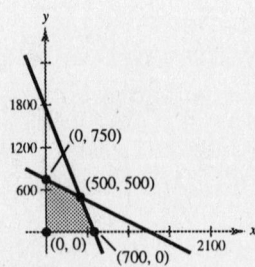

69. x = number of product A.

y = number of product B.

Maximize $P = 18x + 24y$ subject to the following constraints:

$4x + 2y \leq 24$

$x + 2y \leq 9$

$x + y \leq 8$

$x \geq 0$

$y \geq 0$

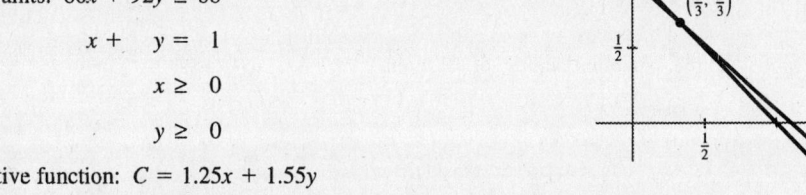

At $(0, 0)$: $P = 18(0) + 24(0) = 0$

At $(6, 0)$: $P = 18(6) + 24(0) = 108$

At $(5, 2)$: $P = 18(5) + 24(2) = 138$

At $\left(0, \frac{9}{2}\right)$: $P = 19(0) + 24\left(\frac{9}{2}\right) = 108$

The maximum profit of $138 occurs when 5 units of product A and 2 units of product B are produced.

71. x = fraction of type A

y = fraction of type B

Constraints: $80x + 92y \geq 88$

$x + y = 1$

$x \geq 0$

$y \geq 0$

Objective function: $C = 1.25x + 1.55y$

Note that the "region" defined by the constraints is actually the line segment connecting $(0, 1)$ and $\left(\frac{1}{3}, \frac{2}{3}\right)$.

At $(0, 1)$: $C = 1.25(0) + 1.55(1) = 1.55$

At $\left(\frac{1}{3}, \frac{2}{3}\right)$: $C = 1.25\left(\frac{1}{3}\right) + 1.55\left(\frac{2}{3}\right) = 1.45$

The minimum cost is $1.45 and occurs with a mixture of $\frac{1}{3}$ gallon of type A and $\frac{2}{3}$ gallon of type B.

73. False. A linear programming problem either has one optional solution or infinitely many optimal solutions. (However, in real-life situations where the variables must have integer values, it is possible to have exactly ten integer-valued solutions.)

75. There are in infinite number of linear systems with the solution $(5, -4)$. One possible system is:

$$\begin{cases} x - y = 9 \\ 3x + y = 11 \end{cases}$$

77. There are an infinite number of linear systems with the solution $\left(-1, \frac{9}{4}\right)$. One possible system is:

$$\begin{cases} -x + 4y = 10 \\ 3x - 8y = -21 \end{cases}$$

79. There are an infinite number of linear systems with the solution $(-3, 5, 6)$.
One possible system is:

$$\begin{cases} x - 2y + z = -7 \\ 2x + y - 4z = -25 \\ -x + 3y - z = 12 \end{cases}$$

81. There are an infinite number of linear systems with the solution $\left(\frac{3}{4}, -2, 8\right)$.
One possible system is:

$$4x + y - z = -7$$
$$8x + 3y + 2z = 16$$
$$4x - 2y + 3z = 31$$

83. For a linear system, the result will be a contradictory equation such as $0 = N$, where N is a nonzero real number. For a nonlinear system, there may be an equation with imaginary roots.

85. There are a finite number of solutions.

(a) If both equations are linear, then the maximum number of solutions to a finite system is *one*.

(b) If one equation is linear and the other is quadratic, then the maximum number of solutions is *two*.

(c) If both equations are quadratic, then the maximum number of solutions is *four*.

Chapter 7   Practice Test

For Exercises 1–3, solve the given system by the method of substitution.

1. $\begin{cases} x + y = 1 \\ 3x - y = 15 \end{cases}$

2. $\begin{cases} x - 3y = -3 \\ x^2 + 6y = 5 \end{cases}$

3. $\begin{cases} x + y + z = 6 \\ 2x - y + 3z = 0 \\ 5x + 2y - z = -3 \end{cases}$

4. Find the two numbers whose sum is 110 and product is 2800.

5. Find the dimensions of a rectangle if its perimeter is 170 feet and its area is 1500 square feet.

For Exercises 6–8, solve the linear system by elimination.

6. $\begin{cases} 2x + 15y = 4 \\ x - 3y = 23 \end{cases}$

7. $\begin{cases} x + y = 2 \\ 38x - 19y = 7 \end{cases}$

8. $\begin{cases} 0.4x + 0.5y = 0.112 \\ 0.3x - 0.7y = -0.131 \end{cases}$

9. Herbert invests $17,000 in two funds that pay 11% and 13% simple interest, respectively. If he receives $2080 in yearly interest, how much is invested in each fund?

10. Find the least squares regression line for the points $(4, 3)$, $(1, 1)$, $(-1, -2)$, and $(-2, -1)$.

For Exercises 11–13, solve the system of equations.

11. $\begin{cases} x + y & = -2 \\ 2x - y + z = 11 \\ \quad\; 4y - 3z = -20 \end{cases}$

12. $\begin{cases} 4x - y + 5z = 4 \\ 2x + y - z = 0 \\ 2x + 4y + 8z = 0 \end{cases}$

13. $\begin{cases} 3x + 2y - z = 5 \\ 6x - y + 5z = 2 \end{cases}$

14. Find the equation of the parabola $y = ax^2 + bx + c$ passing through the points $(0, -1)$, $(1, 4)$ and $(2, 13)$.

15. Find the position equation $s = \frac{1}{2}at^2 + v_0 t + s_0$ given that $s = 12$ feet after 1 second, $s = 5$ feet after 2 seconds, and $s = 4$ after 3 seconds.

16. Graph $x^2 + y^2 \geq 9$.

17. Graph the solution of the system.

$\begin{cases} x + y \leq 6 \\ \quad x \geq 2 \\ \quad y \geq 0 \end{cases}$

18. Derive a set of inequalities to describe the triangle with vertices $(0, 0)$, $(0, 7)$, and $(2, 3)$.

19. Find the maximum value of the objective function, $z = 30z + 26y$, subject to the following constraints.

$\begin{cases} \quad\quad x \geq 0 \\ \quad\quad y \geq 0 \\ 2x + 3y \leq 21 \\ 5x + 3y \leq 30 \end{cases}$

20. Graph the system of inequalities.

$\begin{cases} \quad\quad x^2 + y^2 \leq 4 \\ (x - 2)^2 + y^2 \geq 4 \end{cases}$

C H A P T E R 8
Matrices and Determinants

CHAPTER 8
Matrices and Determinants

Section 8.1   Matrices and Systems of Equations
Solutions to Odd-Numbered Exercises

■ You should be able to use elementary row operations to produce a row–echelon form (or reduced row–echelon form) of a matrix.

1. Interchange two rows.

2. Multiply a row by a nonzero constant.

3. Add a multiple of one row to another row.

■ You should be able to use either Gaussian elimination with back–substitution or Gauss–Jordan elimination to solve a system of linear equations.

---

1. Since the matrix has one row and two columns, its order is 1×2.

3. Since the matrix has three rows and one column, its order is 3×1.

5. Since the matrix has two rows and two columns, its order is 2×2.

7. $\begin{cases} 4x - 3y = -5 \\ -x + 3y = 12 \end{cases}$

$\begin{bmatrix} 4 & -3 & \vdots & -5 \\ -1 & 3 & \vdots & 12 \end{bmatrix}$

9. $\begin{cases} x + 10y - 2z = 2 \\ 5x - 3y + 4z = 0 \\ 2x + y = 6 \end{cases}$

$\begin{bmatrix} 1 & 10 & -2 & \vdots & 2 \\ 5 & -3 & 4 & \vdots & 0 \\ 2 & 1 & 0 & \vdots & 6 \end{bmatrix}$

11. $\begin{cases} 7x - 5y + z = 13 \\ 19x - 8z = 10 \end{cases}$

$\begin{bmatrix} 7 & -5 & 1 & \vdots & 13 \\ 19 & 0 & -8 & \vdots & 10 \end{bmatrix}$

13. $\begin{bmatrix} 1 & 2 & \vdots & 7 \\ 2 & -3 & \vdots & 4 \end{bmatrix}$

$\begin{cases} x + 2y = 7 \\ 2x - 3y = 4 \end{cases}$

15. $\begin{bmatrix} 2 & 0 & 5 & \vdots & -12 \\ 0 & 1 & -2 & \vdots & 7 \\ 6 & 3 & 0 & \vdots & 2 \end{bmatrix}$

$\begin{cases} 2x + 5z = -12 \\ y - 2z = 7 \\ 6x + 3y = 2 \end{cases}$

17. $\begin{bmatrix} 9 & 12 & 3 & 0 & \vdots & 0 \\ -2 & 18 & 5 & 2 & \vdots & 10 \\ 1 & 7 & -8 & 0 & \vdots & -4 \\ 3 & 0 & 2 & 0 & \vdots & -10 \end{bmatrix}$

$\begin{cases} 9x + 12y + 3z = 0 \\ -2x + 18y + 5z + 2w = 10 \\ x + 7y - 8z = -4 \\ 3x + 2z = -10 \end{cases}$

19. $\begin{bmatrix} 1 & 0 & 0 & 0 \\ 0 & 1 & 1 & 5 \\ 0 & 0 & 0 & 0 \end{bmatrix}$

This matrix is in reduced row–echelon form.

21. $\begin{bmatrix} 2 & 0 & 4 & 0 \\ 0 & -1 & 3 & 6 \\ 0 & 0 & 1 & 5 \end{bmatrix}$

The first nonzero entries in rows one and two are not one. The matrix is not in row–echelon form.

23. $\begin{bmatrix} 1 & 4 & 3 \\ 2 & 10 & 5 \end{bmatrix}$

$-2R_1 + R_2 \rightarrow \begin{bmatrix} 1 & 4 & 3 \\ 0 & \boxed{2} & -1 \end{bmatrix}$

25. $\begin{bmatrix} 1 & 1 & 4 & -1 \\ 3 & 8 & 10 & 3 \\ -2 & 1 & 12 & 6 \end{bmatrix}$

$\begin{matrix} -3R_1 + R_2 \rightarrow \\ 2R_1 + R_3 \rightarrow \end{matrix} \begin{bmatrix} 1 & 1 & 4 & -1 \\ 0 & 5 & \boxed{-2} & \boxed{6} \\ 0 & 3 & \boxed{20} & \boxed{4} \end{bmatrix}$

$\tfrac{1}{5}R_2 \rightarrow \begin{bmatrix} 1 & 1 & 4 & -1 \\ 0 & 1 & -\frac{2}{5} & \frac{6}{5} \\ 0 & 3 & \boxed{20} & \boxed{4} \end{bmatrix}$

27. $\begin{bmatrix} -2 & 5 & 1 \\ 3 & -1 & -8 \end{bmatrix} \rightarrow \begin{bmatrix} 13 & 0 & -39 \\ 3 & -1 & -8 \end{bmatrix}$

Add five times Row 2 to Row 1.

29. $\begin{bmatrix} 0 & -1 & -5 & 5 \\ -1 & 3 & -7 & 6 \\ 4 & -5 & 1 & 3 \end{bmatrix} \rightarrow \begin{bmatrix} -1 & 3 & -7 & 6 \\ 0 & -1 & -5 & 5 \\ 0 & 7 & -27 & 27 \end{bmatrix}$

Interchange Row 1 and Row 2. Then add four times the new Row 1 to Row 3.

31. $\begin{bmatrix} 1 & 2 & 3 \\ 2 & -1 & -4 \\ 3 & 1 & -1 \end{bmatrix}$

(a) $\begin{bmatrix} 1 & 2 & 3 \\ 0 & -5 & -10 \\ 3 & 1 & -1 \end{bmatrix}$

(b) $\begin{bmatrix} 1 & 2 & 3 \\ 0 & -5 & -10 \\ 0 & -5 & -10 \end{bmatrix}$

(c) $\begin{bmatrix} 1 & 2 & 3 \\ 0 & -5 & -10 \\ 0 & 0 & 0 \end{bmatrix}$

(d) $\begin{bmatrix} 1 & 2 & 3 \\ 0 & 1 & 2 \\ 0 & 0 & 0 \end{bmatrix}$

(e) $\begin{bmatrix} 1 & 0 & -1 \\ 0 & 1 & 2 \\ 0 & 0 & 0 \end{bmatrix}$ This matrix is in reduced row–echelon form.

33. $\begin{bmatrix} 1 & 1 & 0 & 5 \\ -2 & -1 & 2 & -10 \\ 3 & 6 & 7 & 14 \end{bmatrix}$

$\begin{matrix} 2R_1 + R_2 \rightarrow \\ -3R_1 + R_3 \rightarrow \end{matrix} \begin{bmatrix} 1 & 1 & 0 & 5 \\ 0 & 1 & 2 & 0 \\ 0 & 3 & 7 & -1 \end{bmatrix}$

$-3R_2 + R_3 \rightarrow \begin{bmatrix} 1 & 1 & 0 & 5 \\ 0 & 1 & 2 & 0 \\ 0 & 0 & 1 & -1 \end{bmatrix}$

35. $\begin{bmatrix} 1 & -1 & -1 & 1 \\ 5 & -4 & 1 & 8 \\ -6 & 8 & 18 & 0 \end{bmatrix}$

$\begin{matrix} -5R_1 + R_2 \rightarrow \\ 6R_1 + R_3 \rightarrow \end{matrix} \begin{bmatrix} 1 & -1 & -1 & 1 \\ 0 & 1 & 6 & 3 \\ 0 & 2 & 12 & 6 \end{bmatrix}$

$-2R_2 + R_3 \rightarrow \begin{bmatrix} 1 & -1 & -1 & 1 \\ 0 & 1 & 6 & 3 \\ 0 & 0 & 0 & 0 \end{bmatrix}$

37. Use the reduced row–echelon form feature of a graphing utility.

$$\begin{bmatrix} 3 & 3 & 3 \\ -1 & 0 & -4 \\ 2 & 4 & -2 \end{bmatrix} \Rightarrow \begin{bmatrix} 1 & 0 & 0 \\ 0 & 1 & 0 \\ 0 & 0 & 1 \end{bmatrix}$$

39. Use the reduced row–echelon form feature of a graphing utility.

$$\begin{bmatrix} 1 & 2 & 3 & -5 \\ 1 & 2 & 4 & -9 \\ -2 & -4 & -4 & 3 \\ 4 & 8 & 11 & -14 \end{bmatrix} \Rightarrow \begin{bmatrix} 1 & 2 & 0 & 0 \\ 0 & 0 & 1 & 0 \\ 0 & 0 & 0 & 1 \\ 0 & 0 & 0 & 0 \end{bmatrix}$$

41. Use the reduced row–echelon form feature of a graphing utility.

$$\begin{bmatrix} -3 & 5 & 1 & 12 \\ 1 & -1 & 1 & 4 \end{bmatrix} \Rightarrow \begin{bmatrix} 1 & 0 & 3 & 16 \\ 0 & 1 & 2 & 12 \end{bmatrix}$$

43. $\begin{cases} x - 2y = 4 \\ y = -3 \end{cases}$

$x - 2(-3) = 4$

$x = -2$

Solution: $(-2, -3)$

45. $\begin{cases} x - y + 2z = 4 \\ y - z = 2 \\ z = -2 \end{cases}$

$y - (-2) = 2$

$y = 0$

$x - 0 + 2(-2) = 4$

$x = 8$

Solution: $(8, 0, -2)$

47. $\begin{bmatrix} 1 & 0 & \vdots & 3 \\ 0 & 1 & \vdots & -4 \end{bmatrix}$

$x = 3$

$y = -4$

Solution: $(3, -4)$

49. $\begin{bmatrix} 1 & 0 & 0 & \vdots & -4 \\ 0 & 1 & 0 & \vdots & -10 \\ 0 & 0 & 1 & \vdots & 4 \end{bmatrix}$

$x = -4$

$y = -10$

$z = 4$

Solution: $(-4, -10, 4)$

51. $\begin{cases} x + 2y = 7 \\ 2x + y = 8 \end{cases}$

$$\begin{bmatrix} 1 & 2 & \vdots & 7 \\ 2 & 1 & \vdots & 8 \end{bmatrix}$$

$-2R_1 + R_2 \to \begin{bmatrix} 1 & 2 & \vdots & 7 \\ 0 & -3 & \vdots & -6 \end{bmatrix}$

$-\frac{1}{3}R_2 \to \begin{bmatrix} 1 & 2 & \vdots & 7 \\ 0 & 1 & \vdots & 2 \end{bmatrix}$

$\begin{cases} x + 2y = 7 \\ y = 2 \end{cases}$

$y = 2$

$x + 2(2) = 7 \Rightarrow x = 3$

Solution: $(3, 2)$

53. $\begin{cases} 3x - 2y = -27 \\ x + 3y = 13 \end{cases}$

$$\begin{bmatrix} 3 & -2 & \vdots & -27 \\ 1 & 3 & \vdots & 13 \end{bmatrix}$$

$\begin{matrix} R_1 \\ R_2 \end{matrix} \begin{bmatrix} 1 & 3 & \vdots & 13 \\ 3 & -2 & \vdots & -27 \end{bmatrix}$

$-3R_1 + R_2 \to \begin{bmatrix} 1 & 3 & \vdots & 13 \\ 0 & -11 & \vdots & -66 \end{bmatrix}$

$-\frac{1}{11}R_2 \to \begin{bmatrix} 1 & 3 & \vdots & 13 \\ 0 & 1 & \vdots & 6 \end{bmatrix}$

$\begin{cases} x + 3y = 13 \\ y = 6 \end{cases}$

$y = 6$

$x + 3(6) = 13 \Rightarrow x = -5$

Solution: $(-5, 6)$

55. $\begin{cases} -2x + 6y = -22 \\ x + 2y = -9 \end{cases}$

$$\begin{bmatrix} -2 & 6 & \vdots & -22 \\ 1 & 2 & \vdots & -9 \end{bmatrix}$$

$\begin{matrix} R_1 \\ R_2 \end{matrix}$ $\begin{bmatrix} 1 & 2 & \vdots & -9 \\ -2 & 6 & \vdots & -22 \end{bmatrix}$

$2R_1 + R_2 \rightarrow \begin{bmatrix} 1 & 2 & \vdots & -9 \\ 0 & 10 & \vdots & -40 \end{bmatrix}$

$\frac{1}{10}R_2 \rightarrow \begin{bmatrix} 1 & 2 & \vdots & -9 \\ 0 & 1 & \vdots & -4 \end{bmatrix}$

$\begin{cases} x + 2y = -9 \\ y = -4 \end{cases}$

$y = -4$

$x + 2(-4) = -9 \Rightarrow x = -1$

Solution: $(-1, -4)$

57. $\begin{cases} -x + 2y = 1.5 \\ 2x - 4y = 3.0 \end{cases}$

$$\begin{bmatrix} -1 & 2 & \vdots & 1.5 \\ 2 & -4 & \vdots & 3.0 \end{bmatrix}$$

$2R_1 + R_2 \rightarrow \begin{bmatrix} -1 & 2 & \vdots & 1.5 \\ 0 & 0 & \vdots & 6.0 \end{bmatrix}$

The system is inconsistent and there is no solution.

59. $\begin{cases} x \quad\ - 3z = -2 \\ 3x + y - 2z = 5 \\ 2x + 2y + z = 4 \end{cases}$

$$\begin{bmatrix} 1 & 0 & -3 & \vdots & -2 \\ 3 & 1 & -2 & \vdots & 5 \\ 2 & 2 & 1 & \vdots & 4 \end{bmatrix}$$

$\begin{matrix} -3R_1 + R_2 \rightarrow \\ -2R_1 + R_3 \rightarrow \end{matrix} \begin{bmatrix} 1 & 0 & -3 & \vdots & -2 \\ 0 & 1 & 7 & \vdots & 11 \\ 0 & 2 & 7 & \vdots & 8 \end{bmatrix}$

$-2R_2 + R_3 \rightarrow \begin{bmatrix} 1 & 0 & -3 & \vdots & -2 \\ 0 & 1 & 7 & \vdots & 11 \\ 0 & 0 & -7 & \vdots & -14 \end{bmatrix}$

$-\frac{1}{7}R_3 \rightarrow \begin{bmatrix} 1 & 0 & -3 & \vdots & -2 \\ 0 & 1 & 7 & \vdots & 11 \\ 0 & 0 & 1 & \vdots & 2 \end{bmatrix}$

$\begin{cases} x \ - 3z = -2 \\ y + 7z = 11 \\ z = 2 \end{cases}$

$z = 2$

$y + 7(2) = 11 \Rightarrow y = -3$

$x - 3(2) = -2 \Rightarrow x = 4$

Solution: $(4, -3, 2)$

61. $\begin{cases} -x + y - z = -14 \\ 2x - y + z = 21 \\ 3x + 2y + z = 19 \end{cases}$

$$\begin{bmatrix} -1 & 1 & -1 & \vdots & -14 \\ 2 & -1 & 1 & \vdots & 21 \\ 3 & 2 & 1 & \vdots & 19 \end{bmatrix}$$

$-R_1 \rightarrow \begin{bmatrix} 1 & -1 & 1 & \vdots & 14 \\ 2 & -1 & 1 & \vdots & 21 \\ 3 & 2 & 1 & \vdots & 19 \end{bmatrix}$

$\begin{matrix} -2R_1 + R_2 \rightarrow \\ -3R_1 + R_3 \rightarrow \end{matrix} \begin{bmatrix} 1 & -1 & 1 & \vdots & 14 \\ 0 & 1 & -1 & \vdots & -7 \\ 0 & 5 & -2 & \vdots & -23 \end{bmatrix}$

$-5R_2 + R_3 \rightarrow \begin{bmatrix} 1 & -1 & 1 & \vdots & 14 \\ 0 & 1 & -1 & \vdots & -7 \\ 0 & 0 & 3 & \vdots & 12 \end{bmatrix}$

$\frac{1}{3}R_3 \rightarrow \begin{bmatrix} 1 & -1 & 1 & \vdots & 14 \\ 0 & 1 & -1 & \vdots & -7 \\ 0 & 0 & 1 & \vdots & 4 \end{bmatrix}$

$\begin{cases} x - y + z = 14 \\ y - z = -7 \\ z = 4 \end{cases}$

$z = 4$

$y - 4 = -7 \Rightarrow y = -3$

$x - (-3) + 4 = 14 \Rightarrow x = 7$

Solution: $(7, -3, 4)$

63. $\begin{cases} x + 2y - 3z = -28 \\ 4y + 2z = 0 \\ -x + y - z = -5 \end{cases}$

$$\begin{bmatrix} 1 & 2 & -3 & \vdots & -28 \\ 0 & 4 & 2 & \vdots & 0 \\ -1 & 1 & -1 & \vdots & -5 \end{bmatrix}$$

$\begin{matrix} \frac{1}{4}R_2 \rightarrow \\ R_1 + R_3 \rightarrow \end{matrix} \begin{bmatrix} 1 & 2 & -3 & \vdots & -28 \\ 0 & 1 & \frac{1}{2} & \vdots & 0 \\ 0 & 3 & -4 & \vdots & -33 \end{bmatrix}$

$-3R_2 + R_3 \rightarrow \begin{bmatrix} 1 & 2 & -3 & \vdots & -28 \\ 0 & 1 & \frac{1}{2} & \vdots & 0 \\ 0 & 0 & -\frac{11}{2} & \vdots & -33 \end{bmatrix}$

$-\frac{2}{11}R_3 \rightarrow \begin{bmatrix} 1 & 2 & -3 & \vdots & -28 \\ 0 & 1 & \frac{1}{2} & \vdots & 0 \\ 0 & 0 & 1 & \vdots & 6 \end{bmatrix}$

$\begin{cases} x + 2y - 3z = -28 \\ y + \frac{1}{2}z = 0 \\ z = 6 \end{cases}$

$$z = 6$$

$$y + \tfrac{1}{2}(6) = 0 \implies y = -3$$

$$x + 2(-3) - 3(6) = -28 \implies x = -4$$

Solution: $(-4, -3, 6)$

65. $\begin{cases} x + y - 5z = 3 \\ x - 2z = 1 \\ 2x - y - z = 0 \end{cases}$

$$\begin{bmatrix} 1 & 1 & -5 & \vdots & 3 \\ 1 & 0 & -2 & \vdots & 1 \\ 2 & -1 & -1 & \vdots & 0 \end{bmatrix}$$

$\begin{matrix} -R_1 + R_2 \rightarrow \\ -2R_1 + R_3 \rightarrow \end{matrix} \begin{bmatrix} 1 & 1 & -5 & \vdots & 3 \\ 0 & -1 & 3 & \vdots & -2 \\ 0 & -3 & 9 & \vdots & -6 \end{bmatrix}$

$-R_2 \rightarrow \begin{bmatrix} 1 & 1 & -5 & \vdots & 3 \\ 0 & 1 & -3 & \vdots & 2 \\ 0 & -3 & 9 & \vdots & -6 \end{bmatrix}$

$\begin{matrix} R_2 + R_1 \rightarrow \\ \\ 3R_2 + R_3 \rightarrow \end{matrix} \begin{bmatrix} 1 & 0 & -2 & \vdots & 1 \\ 0 & 1 & -3 & \vdots & 2 \\ 0 & 0 & 0 & \vdots & 0 \end{bmatrix}$

$\begin{cases} x - 2z = 1 \\ y - 3z = 2 \end{cases}$

$$z = a$$

$$y - 3a = 2 \implies y = 3a + 2$$

$$x - 2a = 1 \implies x = 2a + 1$$

Solution: $(2a + 1, 3a + 2, a)$

67. $\begin{cases} x + 2y + z + 2w = 8 \\ 3x + 7y + 6z + 9w = 26 \end{cases}$

$$\begin{bmatrix} 1 & 2 & 1 & 2 & \vdots & 8 \\ 3 & 7 & 6 & 9 & \vdots & 26 \end{bmatrix}$$

$-3R_1 + R_2 \rightarrow \begin{bmatrix} 1 & 2 & 1 & 2 & \vdots & 8 \\ 0 & 1 & 3 & 3 & \vdots & 2 \end{bmatrix}$

$-2R_2 + R_1 \rightarrow \begin{bmatrix} 1 & 0 & -5 & -4 & \vdots & 4 \\ 0 & 1 & 3 & 3 & \vdots & 2 \end{bmatrix}$

$\begin{cases} x - 5z - 4w = 4 \\ y + 3z + 3w = 2 \end{cases}$

$$w = a, z = b$$

$$y + 3b + 3a = 2 \implies y = 2 - 3b - 3a$$

$$x - 5b - 4a = 4 \implies x = 4 + 5b + 4a$$

Solution: $(4 + 5b + 4a, 2 - 3b - 3a, b, a)$,
   where a and b are real numbers.

69. $\begin{cases} -x + y = -22 \\ 3x + 4y = 4 \\ 4x - 8y = 32 \end{cases}$

$$\begin{bmatrix} -1 & 1 & \vdots & -22 \\ 3 & 4 & \vdots & 4 \\ 4 & -8 & \vdots & 32 \end{bmatrix}$$

$-R_1 \rightarrow \begin{bmatrix} 1 & -1 & \vdots & 22 \\ 3 & 4 & \vdots & 4 \\ 4 & -8 & \vdots & 32 \end{bmatrix}$

$\begin{matrix} -3R_1 + R_2 \rightarrow \\ -4R_1 + R_3 \rightarrow \end{matrix} \begin{bmatrix} 1 & -1 & \vdots & 22 \\ 0 & 7 & \vdots & -62 \\ 0 & -4 & \vdots & -56 \end{bmatrix}$

$\begin{matrix} \frac{1}{7}R_2 \rightarrow \\ -\frac{1}{4}R_3 \rightarrow \end{matrix} \begin{bmatrix} 1 & -1 & \vdots & 22 \\ 0 & 1 & \vdots & -\frac{62}{7} \\ 0 & 1 & \vdots & 14 \end{bmatrix}$

$-R_2 + R_3 \rightarrow \begin{bmatrix} 1 & -1 & \vdots & 22 \\ 0 & 1 & \vdots & -\frac{62}{7} \\ 0 & 0 & \vdots & \frac{162}{7} \end{bmatrix}$

The system is inconsistent and there is no solution.

71. Use the reduced row–echelon form feature of a graphing utility.

$$\begin{cases} 3x + 3y + 12z = 6 \\ x + y + 4z = 2 \\ 2x + 5y + 20z = 10 \\ -x + 2y + 8z = 4 \end{cases} \quad \begin{bmatrix} 3 & 3 & 12 & \vdots & 6 \\ 1 & 1 & 4 & \vdots & 2 \\ 2 & 5 & 20 & \vdots & 10 \\ -1 & 2 & 8 & \vdots & 4 \end{bmatrix} \Rightarrow \begin{bmatrix} 1 & 0 & 0 & \vdots & 0 \\ 0 & 1 & 4 & \vdots & 2 \\ 0 & 0 & 0 & \vdots & 0 \\ 0 & 0 & 0 & \vdots & 0 \end{bmatrix}$$

$z = a$
$y = 2 - 4a$
$x = 0$

$$\begin{cases} x = 0 \\ y + 4z = 2 \end{cases}$$

Solution: $(0, 2 - 4a, a)$

73. Use the reduced row–echelon form feature of a graphing utility.

$$\begin{cases} 2x + y - z + 2w = -6 \\ 3x + 4y + w = 1 \\ x + 5y + 2z + 6w = -3 \\ 5x + 2y - z - w = 3 \end{cases} \quad \begin{bmatrix} 2 & 1 & -1 & 2 & \vdots & -6 \\ 3 & 4 & 0 & 1 & \vdots & 1 \\ 1 & 5 & 2 & 6 & \vdots & -3 \\ 5 & 2 & -1 & -1 & \vdots & 3 \end{bmatrix} \Rightarrow \begin{bmatrix} 1 & 0 & 0 & 0 & \vdots & 1 \\ 0 & 1 & 0 & 0 & \vdots & 0 \\ 0 & 0 & 1 & 0 & \vdots & 4 \\ 0 & 0 & 0 & 1 & \vdots & -2 \end{bmatrix}$$

$x = 1$

$y = 0$

$z = 4$

$w = -2$

Solution: $(1, 0, 4, -2)$

75. Use the reduced row–echelon form feature of a graphing utility.

$$\begin{cases} x + y + z + w = 0 \\ 2x + 3y + z - 2w = 0 \\ 3x + 5y + z = 0 \end{cases} \quad \begin{bmatrix} 1 & 1 & 1 & 1 & \vdots & 0 \\ 2 & 3 & 1 & -2 & \vdots & 0 \\ 3 & 5 & 1 & 0 & \vdots & 0 \end{bmatrix} \Rightarrow \begin{bmatrix} 1 & 0 & 2 & 0 & \vdots & 0 \\ 0 & 1 & -1 & 0 & \vdots & 0 \\ 0 & 0 & 0 & 1 & \vdots & 0 \end{bmatrix}$$

$$\begin{cases} x + 2z = 0 \\ y - z = 0 \\ w = 0 \end{cases}$$

Let $z = a$. Then $x = -2a$ and $y = a$.

Solution: $(-2a, a, a, 0)$, where a is a real number.

77. (a) $\begin{cases} x - 2y + z = -6 \\ y - 5z = 16 \\ z = -3 \end{cases}$

$y - 5(-3) = 16$

$y = 1$

$x - 2(1) + (-3) = -6$

$x = -1$

Solution: $(-1, 1, -3)$

(b) $\begin{cases} x + y - 2z = 6 \\ y + 3z = -8 \\ z = -3 \end{cases}$

$y + 3(-3) = -8$

$y = 1$

$x + (1) - 2(-3) = 6$

$x = -1$

Solution: $(-1, 1, -3)$

Both systems yield the same solution, namely $(-1, 1, -3)$.

79. (a) $\begin{cases} x - 4y + 5z = 27 \\ \quad\ y - 7z = -54 \\ \qquad\quad z = 8 \end{cases}$

$$y - 7(8) = -54$$

$$y = 2$$

$$x - 4(2) + 5(8) = 27$$

$$x = -5$$

Solution: $(-5, 2, 8)$

(b) $\begin{cases} x - 6y + \ z = 15 \\ \quad\ y + 5z = 42 \\ \qquad\quad z = 8 \end{cases}$

$$y + 5(8) = 42$$

$$y = 2$$

$$x - 6(2) + (8) = 15$$

$$x = 19$$

Solution: $(19, 2, 8)$

The systems do *not* yield the same solution.

81. $\begin{cases} x + 3y + \ z = 3 \\ x + 5y + 5z = 1 \\ 2x + 6y + 3z = 8 \end{cases}$

$$\begin{bmatrix} 1 & 3 & 1 & \vdots & 3 \\ 1 & 5 & 5 & \vdots & 1 \\ 2 & 6 & 3 & \vdots & 8 \end{bmatrix}$$

$$\begin{matrix} \\ -R_1 + R_2 \rightarrow \\ -2R_1 + R_3 \rightarrow \end{matrix} \begin{bmatrix} 1 & 3 & 1 & \vdots & 3 \\ 0 & 2 & 4 & \vdots & -2 \\ 0 & 0 & 1 & \vdots & 2 \end{bmatrix}$$

$$\begin{matrix} \\ \frac{1}{2}R_2 \rightarrow \\ \ \end{matrix} \begin{bmatrix} 1 & 3 & 1 & \vdots & 3 \\ 0 & 1 & 2 & \vdots & -1 \\ 0 & 0 & 1 & \vdots & 2 \end{bmatrix}$$ This is a matrix in row–echelon form.

$$\begin{bmatrix} 1 & 3 & \frac{3}{2} & \vdots & 4 \\ 0 & 1 & \frac{7}{4} & \vdots & -\frac{3}{2} \\ 0 & 0 & 1 & \vdots & 2 \end{bmatrix}$$ The row—echelon—form feature of a graphing utility yeilds $\therefore$

There are infinitely many matrices in row–echelon form that correspond to the original system of equations. All such matrices will yield the same solution, namely $(16, -5, 2)$.

83. $\dfrac{4x^2}{(x + 1)^2(x - 1)} = \dfrac{A}{x - 1} + \dfrac{B}{x + 1} + \dfrac{C}{(x + 1)^2}$

$$4x^2 = A(x + 1)^2 + B(x + 1)(x - 1) + C(x - 1)$$

Let $x = 1$: $4 = 4A \implies A = 1$

Let $x = -1$: $4 = -2C \implies C = -2$

Let $x = 0$: $0 = A - B - C \implies 0 = 1 - B - (-2) \implies B = 3$

Thus, $\dfrac{4x^2}{(x + 1)^2(x - 1)} = \dfrac{1}{x - 1} + \dfrac{3}{x + 1} - \dfrac{2}{(x + 1)^2}.$

85. x = amount at 9%, y = amount at 10%, z = amount at 12%

$$x + y + z = 500{,}000$$
$$0.09x + 0.10y + 0.12z = 52{,}000$$
$$2.5x - y = 0$$

$$\begin{bmatrix} 1 & 1 & 1 & \vdots & 500{,}000 \\ 0.09 & 0.10 & 0.12 & \vdots & 52{,}000 \\ 2.5 & -1 & 0 & \vdots & 0 \end{bmatrix}$$

$$\begin{matrix} \\ -0.09R_1 + R_2 \rightarrow \\ -2.5R_1 + R_3 \rightarrow \end{matrix} \begin{bmatrix} 1 & 1 & 1 & \vdots & 500{,}000 \\ 0 & 0.10 & 0.03 & \vdots & 7{,}000 \\ 0 & -3.5 & -2.5 & \vdots & -1{,}250{,}000 \end{bmatrix}$$

$$\begin{matrix} \\ 100R_2 \rightarrow \\ 2R_3 \rightarrow \end{matrix} \begin{bmatrix} 1 & 1 & 1 & \vdots & 500{,}000 \\ 0 & 1 & 3 & \vdots & 700{,}000 \\ 0 & -7 & -5 & \vdots & -2{,}500{,}000 \end{bmatrix}$$

$$\begin{matrix} -R_2 + R_1 \rightarrow \\ \\ 7R_2 + R_3 \rightarrow \end{matrix} \begin{bmatrix} 1 & 0 & -2 & \vdots & -200{,}000 \\ 0 & 1 & 3 & \vdots & 700{,}000 \\ 0 & 0 & 16 & \vdots & 2{,}400{,}000 \end{bmatrix}$$

$$\begin{matrix} \\ \\ \tfrac{1}{16}R_3 \rightarrow \end{matrix} \begin{bmatrix} 1 & 0 & -2 & \vdots & -200{,}000 \\ 0 & 1 & 3 & \vdots & 700{,}000 \\ 0 & 0 & 1 & \vdots & 150{,}000 \end{bmatrix}$$

$$\begin{cases} x - 2z = -200{,}000 \\ y + 3z = 700{,}000 \\ z = 150{,}000 \end{cases}$$

$$y + 3(150{,}000) = 700{,}000 \implies y = 250{,}000$$

$$x - 2(150{,}000) = -200{,}000 \implies x = 100{,}000$$

Solution: $(100{,}000, 250{,}000, 150{,}000)$

Answer: \$100,000 at 9%, \$250,000 at 10%, \$150,000 at 12%

87. $f(x) = ax^2 + bx + c$

$$f(1) = a + b + c = 9$$
$$f(2) = 4a + 2b + c = 8$$
$$f(3) = 9a + 3b + c = 5$$

$$\begin{bmatrix} 1 & 1 & 1 & \vdots & 9 \\ 4 & 2 & 1 & \vdots & 8 \\ 9 & 3 & 1 & \vdots & 5 \end{bmatrix}$$

$$\begin{matrix} \\ -4R_1 + R_2 \rightarrow \\ -9R_1 + R_3 \rightarrow \end{matrix} \begin{bmatrix} 1 & 1 & 1 & \vdots & 9 \\ 0 & -2 & -3 & \vdots & -28 \\ 0 & -6 & -8 & \vdots & -76 \end{bmatrix}$$

$$\begin{matrix} \\ -\tfrac{1}{2}R_2 \rightarrow \\ \\ \end{matrix} \begin{bmatrix} 1 & 1 & 1 & \vdots & 9 \\ 0 & 1 & \tfrac{3}{2} & \vdots & 14 \\ 0 & -6 & -8 & \vdots & -76 \end{bmatrix}$$

$$\begin{matrix} \\ \\ -6R_2 + R_3 \rightarrow \end{matrix} \begin{bmatrix} 1 & 1 & 1 & \vdots & 9 \\ 0 & 1 & \tfrac{3}{2} & \vdots & 14 \\ 0 & 0 & 1 & \vdots & 8 \end{bmatrix}$$

$$\begin{cases} a + b + c = 9 \\ b + \tfrac{3}{2}c = 14 \\ c = 8 \end{cases}$$

$$c = 8$$

$$b + \tfrac{3}{2}(8) = 14 \implies b = 2$$

$$a + (2) + (8) = 9 \implies a = -1$$

Equation of parabola: $y = -x^2 + 2x + 8$

89. $(5, 421), (6, 595), (7, 512)$

(a) $f(x) = ax^2 + bx + c$

$f(5) = 25a + 5b + c = 421$

$f(6) = 36a + 6b + c = 595$

$f(7) = 49a + 7b + c = 512$

$$\begin{bmatrix} 25 & 5 & 1 & : & 421 \\ 36 & 6 & 1 & : & 595 \\ 49 & 7 & 1 & : & 512 \end{bmatrix}$$

$$0.04R_1 \rightarrow \begin{bmatrix} 1 & 0.2 & 0.04 & : & 16.84 \\ 36 & 6 & 1 & : & 595 \\ 49 & 7 & 1 & : & 512 \end{bmatrix}$$

$$\begin{matrix} \\ -36R_1 + R_2 \rightarrow \\ -49R_1 + R_2 \rightarrow \end{matrix} \begin{bmatrix} 1 & 0.2 & 0.04 & : & 16.84 \\ 0 & -1.2 & -0.44 & : & -11.24 \\ 0 & -2.8 & -0.96 & : & -313.16 \end{bmatrix}$$

$$\begin{matrix} \\ 5R_2 \rightarrow \\ 2.5R_3 \rightarrow \end{matrix} \begin{bmatrix} 1 & 0.2 & 0.04 & : & 16.84 \\ 0 & -6 & -2.2 & : & -56.2 \\ 0 & 7 & 2.4 & : & 782.9 \end{bmatrix}$$

$$R_3 + R_2 \rightarrow \begin{bmatrix} 1 & 0.2 & 0.04 & : & 16.84 \\ 0 & 1 & 0.2 & : & 726.7 \\ 0 & 7 & 2.4 & : & 782.9 \end{bmatrix}$$

$$\begin{matrix} -0.2R_2 + R_1 \rightarrow \\ \\ -7R_2 + R_3 \rightarrow \end{matrix} \begin{bmatrix} 1 & 0 & 0 & : & -128.5 \\ 0 & 1 & 0.2 & : & 726.7 \\ 0 & 0 & 1 & : & -4304 \end{bmatrix}$$

$$-0.2R_3 + R_2 \rightarrow \begin{bmatrix} 1 & 0 & 0 & : & -128.5 \\ 0 & 1 & 0 & : & 1587.5 \\ 0 & 0 & 1 & : & -4304 \end{bmatrix}$$

$a = -128.5, b = 1587.5, c = -4304$

$y = -128.5x^2 + 1587.5x - 4304.0$

(b)

(c) When $x = 10, y = -1279$. The estimate is not reasonable because it is a negative number.

91. (a) $x_1 + x_2 = 300$

$x_1 + x_3 = 150 + x_4 \implies x_1 + x_3 - x_4 = 150$

$x_2 + 200 = x_3 + x_5 \implies x_2 - x_3 - x_5 = -200$

$x_4 + x_5 = 350$

$$\begin{bmatrix} 1 & 1 & 0 & 0 & 0 & : & 300 \\ 1 & 0 & 1 & -1 & 0 & : & 150 \\ 0 & 1 & -1 & 0 & -1 & : & -200 \\ 0 & 0 & 0 & 1 & 1 & : & 350 \end{bmatrix}$$

$-R_1 + R_2 \rightarrow \begin{bmatrix} 1 & 1 & 0 & 0 & 0 & : & 300 \\ 0 & -1 & 1 & -1 & 0 & : & -150 \\ 0 & 1 & -1 & 0 & -1 & : & -200 \\ 0 & 0 & 0 & 1 & 1 & : & 350 \end{bmatrix}$

$R_2 + R_3 \rightarrow \begin{bmatrix} 1 & 1 & 0 & 0 & 0 & : & 300 \\ 0 & -1 & 1 & -1 & 0 & : & -150 \\ 0 & 0 & 0 & -1 & -1 & : & -350 \\ 0 & 0 & 0 & 1 & 1 & : & 350 \end{bmatrix}$

$\begin{matrix} -R_2 \rightarrow \\ -R_3 \rightarrow \\ R_3 + R_4 \rightarrow \end{matrix} \begin{bmatrix} 1 & 1 & 0 & 0 & 0 & : & 300 \\ 0 & 1 & -1 & 1 & 0 & : & 150 \\ 0 & 0 & 0 & 1 & 1 & : & 350 \\ 0 & 0 & 0 & 0 & 0 & : & 0 \end{bmatrix}$

$\begin{cases} x_1 + x_2 &= 300 \\ x_2 - x_3 + x_4 &= 150 \\ x_4 + x_5 &= 350 \end{cases}$

Let $x_5 = t$.

$x_4 + t = 350 \implies x_4 = 350 - t$

Let $x_3 = s$.

$x_2 - s + (350 - t) = 150 \implies x_2 = -200 + s + t$

$x_1 + (-200 + s + t) = 300 \implies x_1 = 500 - s - t$

Solution: $x_1 = 500 - s - t, x_2 = -200 + s + t, x_3 = s, x_4 = 350 - t, x_5 = t$, where s and t are real numbers.

(b) When $x_2 = 200$ and $x_3 = 50$,

$x_2 = -200 + s + t$

$200 = -200 + 50 + t \implies t = 350$.

$x_1 = 100, x_2 = 200, x_3 = 50, x_4 = 0, x_5 = 350$

(c) When $x_2 = 150$ and $x_3 = 0$,

$x_2 = -200 + s + t$

$150 = -200 + 0 + t \implies t = 350$.

$x_1 = 150, x_2 = 150, x_3 = 0, x_4 = 0, x_5 = 350$

93. False. The rows are in the wrong order. To change this matrix to reduced row–echelon form, interchange Row 1 and Row 4, and interchange Row 2 and Row 3.

95. $z = a$

$y = -4a + 1$

$x = -3a - 2$

One possible system is:

$\begin{cases} x + y + 7z = (-3a - 2) + (-4a + 1) + 7a = -1 \\ x + 2y + 11z = (-3a - 2) + 2(-4a + 1) + 11a = 0 \\ 2x + y + 10z = 2(-3a - 2) + (-4a + 1) + 10a = -3 \end{cases}$

or

$\begin{cases} x + y + 7z = -1 \\ x + 2y + 11z = 0 \\ 2x + y + 10z = -3 \end{cases}$

(Note that the coefficients of x, y, and z have been chosen so that the a–terms cancel.)

97. 1. Interchange two rows.

2. Multiply a row by a nonzero constant.

3. Add a multiple of one row to another row.

99. A matrix in row–echelon form is in reduced row–echelon form if every column that has a leading 1 has zeros in every position above and below its leading 1.

101. $f(x) = \dfrac{4x}{5x^2 + 2}$

Horizontal asymptote: $y = 0$

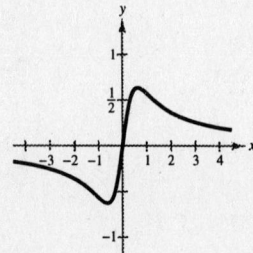

103. $g(x) = 3^{-x+2}$

x	-1	0	1	2	3	4
y	27	9	3	1	$\frac{1}{3}$	$\frac{1}{9}$

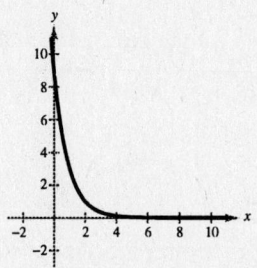

105. $f(x) = 3 + \ln x \implies y - 3 = \ln x \implies e^{y-3} = x$

x	0.05	0.14	0.37	1	2.72
y	0	1	2	3	4

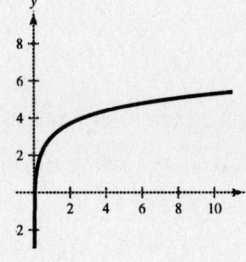

Section 8.2   Operations with Matrices

■ $A = B$ if and only if they have the same order and $a_{ij} = b_{ij}$.

■ You should be able to perform the operations of matrix addition, scalar multiplication, and matrix multiplication.

■ Some properties of matrix addition and scalar multiplication are:

   (a) $A + B = B + A$

   (b) $A + (B + C) = (A + B) + C$

   (c) $(cd)A = c(dA)$

   (d) $1A = A$

   (e) $c(A + B) = cA + cB$

   (f) $(c + d)A = cA + dA$

■ You should remember that $AB \neq BA$ in general.

■ Some properties of matrix multiplication are:

   (a) $A(BC) = (AB)C$

   (b) $A(B + C) = AB + AC$

   (c) $(A + B)C = AC + BC$

   (d) $c(AB) = (cA)B = A(cB)$

■ You should know that I_n, the identity matrix of order n, is an $n \times n$ matrix consisting of 1's on its main diagonal and 0's elsewhere. If A is an $n \times n$ matrix, then $AI_n = I_nA = A$.

Solutions to Odd–Numbered Exercises

1. $x = -4$, $y = 22$

3. $2x + 1 = 5$, $3x = 6$, $3y - 5 = 4$

$x = 2$, $y = 3$

5. (a) $A + B = \begin{bmatrix} 1 & -1 \\ 2 & -1 \end{bmatrix} + \begin{bmatrix} 2 & -1 \\ -1 & 8 \end{bmatrix} = \begin{bmatrix} 1+2 & -1-1 \\ 2-1 & -1+8 \end{bmatrix} = \begin{bmatrix} 3 & -2 \\ 1 & 7 \end{bmatrix}$

(b) $A - B = \begin{bmatrix} 1 & -1 \\ 2 & -1 \end{bmatrix} - \begin{bmatrix} 2 & -1 \\ -1 & 8 \end{bmatrix} = \begin{bmatrix} 1-2 & -1+1 \\ 2+1 & -1-8 \end{bmatrix} = \begin{bmatrix} -1 & 0 \\ 3 & -9 \end{bmatrix}$

(c) $3A = 3\begin{bmatrix} 1 & -1 \\ 2 & -1 \end{bmatrix} = \begin{bmatrix} 3(1) & 3(-1) \\ 3(2) & 3(-1) \end{bmatrix} = \begin{bmatrix} 3 & -3 \\ 6 & -3 \end{bmatrix}$

(d) $3A - 2B = \begin{bmatrix} 3 & -3 \\ 6 & -3 \end{bmatrix} - 2\begin{bmatrix} 2 & -1 \\ -1 & 8 \end{bmatrix} = \begin{bmatrix} 3 & -3 \\ 6 & -3 \end{bmatrix} + \begin{bmatrix} -4 & 2 \\ 2 & -16 \end{bmatrix} = \begin{bmatrix} -1 & -1 \\ 8 & -19 \end{bmatrix}$

7. $A = \begin{bmatrix} 6 & -1 \\ 2 & 4 \\ -3 & 5 \end{bmatrix}$, $B = \begin{bmatrix} 1 & 4 \\ -1 & 5 \\ 1 & 10 \end{bmatrix}$

(a) $A + B = \begin{bmatrix} 7 & 3 \\ 1 & 9 \\ -2 & 15 \end{bmatrix}$

(b) $A - B = \begin{bmatrix} 5 & -5 \\ 3 & -1 \\ -4 & -5 \end{bmatrix}$

(c) $3A = \begin{bmatrix} 18 & -3 \\ 6 & 12 \\ -9 & 15 \end{bmatrix}$

(d) $3A - 2B = \begin{bmatrix} 18 & -3 \\ 6 & 12 \\ -9 & 15 \end{bmatrix} - \begin{bmatrix} 2 & 8 \\ -2 & 10 \\ 2 & 20 \end{bmatrix} = \begin{bmatrix} 16 & -11 \\ 8 & 2 \\ -11 & -5 \end{bmatrix}$

9. $A = \begin{bmatrix} 2 & 2 & -1 & 0 & 1 \\ 1 & 1 & -2 & 0 & -1 \end{bmatrix}$, $B = \begin{bmatrix} 1 & 1 & -1 & 1 & 0 \\ -3 & 4 & 9 & -6 & -7 \end{bmatrix}$

(a) $A + B = \begin{bmatrix} 3 & 3 & -2 & 1 & 1 \\ -2 & 5 & 7 & -6 & -8 \end{bmatrix}$

(b) $A - B = \begin{bmatrix} 1 & 1 & 0 & -1 & 1 \\ 4 & -3 & -11 & 6 & 6 \end{bmatrix}$

(c) $3A = \begin{bmatrix} 6 & 6 & -3 & 0 & 3 \\ 3 & 3 & -6 & 0 & -3 \end{bmatrix}$

(d) $3A - 2B = \begin{bmatrix} 6 & 6 & -3 & 0 & 3 \\ 3 & 3 & -6 & 0 & -3 \end{bmatrix} - \begin{bmatrix} 2 & 2 & -2 & 2 & 0 \\ -6 & 8 & 18 & -12 & -14 \end{bmatrix} = \begin{bmatrix} 4 & 4 & -1 & -2 & 3 \\ 9 & -5 & -24 & 12 & 11 \end{bmatrix}$

11. $A = \begin{bmatrix} 6 & 0 & 3 \\ -1 & -4 & 0 \end{bmatrix}$, $B = \begin{bmatrix} 8 & -1 \\ 4 & -3 \end{bmatrix}$

(a) $A + B$ is not possible. A and B do not have the same order.

(b) $A - B$ is not possible. A and B do not have the same order.

(c) $3A = \begin{bmatrix} 18 & 0 & 9 \\ -3 & -12 & 0 \end{bmatrix}$

(d) $3A - 2B$ is not possible. A and B do not have the same order.

13. $\begin{bmatrix} -5 & 0 \\ 3 & -6 \end{bmatrix} + \begin{bmatrix} 7 & 1 \\ -2 & -1 \end{bmatrix} + \begin{bmatrix} -10 & -8 \\ 14 & 6 \end{bmatrix} = \begin{bmatrix} -5 + 7 + (-10) & 0 + 1 + (-8) \\ 3 + (-2) + 14 & -6 + (-1) + 6 \end{bmatrix} = \begin{bmatrix} -8 & -7 \\ 15 & -1 \end{bmatrix}$

15. $4\left(\begin{bmatrix} -4 & 0 & 1 \\ 0 & 2 & 3 \end{bmatrix} - \begin{bmatrix} 2 & 1 & -2 \\ 3 & -6 & 0 \end{bmatrix} \right) = 4 \begin{bmatrix} -6 & -1 & 3 \\ -3 & 8 & 3 \end{bmatrix} = \begin{bmatrix} -24 & -4 & 12 \\ -12 & 32 & 12 \end{bmatrix}$

17. $-3\left(\begin{bmatrix} 0 & -3 \\ 7 & 2 \end{bmatrix} + \begin{bmatrix} -6 & 3 \\ 8 & 1 \end{bmatrix} \right) - 2\begin{bmatrix} 4 & -4 \\ 7 & -9 \end{bmatrix} = -3\begin{bmatrix} -6 & 0 \\ 15 & 3 \end{bmatrix} - \begin{bmatrix} 8 & -8 \\ 14 & -18 \end{bmatrix} = \begin{bmatrix} 18 & 0 \\ -45 & -9 \end{bmatrix} - \begin{bmatrix} 8 & -8 \\ 14 & -18 \end{bmatrix} = \begin{bmatrix} 10 & 8 \\ -59 & 9 \end{bmatrix}$

19. $\frac{3}{7}\begin{bmatrix} 2 & 5 \\ -1 & -4 \end{bmatrix} + 6\begin{bmatrix} -3 & 0 \\ 2 & 2 \end{bmatrix} \approx \begin{bmatrix} -17.143 & 2.143 \\ 11.571 & 10.286 \end{bmatrix}$

21. $-\begin{bmatrix} 3.211 & 6.829 \\ -1.004 & 4.914 \\ 0.055 & -3.889 \end{bmatrix} - \begin{bmatrix} -1.630 & -3.090 \\ 5.256 & 8.335 \\ -9.768 & 4.251 \end{bmatrix} = \begin{bmatrix} -1.581 & -3.739 \\ -4.252 & -13.249 \\ 9.713 & -0.362 \end{bmatrix}$

23. $X = 3\begin{bmatrix} -2 & -1 \\ 1 & 0 \\ 3 & 4 \end{bmatrix} - 2\begin{bmatrix} 0 & 3 \\ 2 & 0 \\ -4 & -1 \end{bmatrix} = \begin{bmatrix} -6 & -3 \\ 3 & 0 \\ 9 & -12 \end{bmatrix} - \begin{bmatrix} 0 & 6 \\ 4 & 0 \\ -8 & -2 \end{bmatrix} = \begin{bmatrix} -6 & -9 \\ -1 & 0 \\ 17 & -10 \end{bmatrix}$

25. $X = -\frac{3}{2}A + \frac{1}{2}B = -\frac{3}{2}\begin{bmatrix} -2 & -1 \\ 1 & 0 \\ 3 & -4 \end{bmatrix} + \frac{1}{2}\begin{bmatrix} 0 & 3 \\ 2 & 0 \\ -4 & -1 \end{bmatrix} = \begin{bmatrix} 3 & \frac{3}{2} \\ -\frac{3}{2} & 0 \\ -\frac{9}{2} & 6 \end{bmatrix} + \begin{bmatrix} 0 & \frac{3}{2} \\ 1 & 0 \\ -2 & -\frac{1}{2} \end{bmatrix} = \begin{bmatrix} 3 & 3 \\ -\frac{1}{2} & 0 \\ -\frac{13}{2} & \frac{11}{2} \end{bmatrix}$

27. (a) $AB = \begin{bmatrix} 1 & 2 \\ 4 & 2 \end{bmatrix}\begin{bmatrix} 2 & -1 \\ -1 & 8 \end{bmatrix} = \begin{bmatrix} (1)(2) + (2)(-1) & (1)(-1) + (2)(8) \\ (4)(2) + (2)(-1) & (4)(-1) + (2)(8) \end{bmatrix} = \begin{bmatrix} 0 & 15 \\ 6 & 12 \end{bmatrix}$

  (b) $BA = \begin{bmatrix} 2 & -1 \\ -1 & 8 \end{bmatrix}\begin{bmatrix} 1 & 2 \\ 4 & 2 \end{bmatrix} = \begin{bmatrix} (2)(1) + (-1)(4) & (2)(2) + (-1)(2) \\ (-1)(1) + (8)(4) & (-1)(2) + (8)(2) \end{bmatrix} = \begin{bmatrix} -2 & 2 \\ 31 & 14 \end{bmatrix}$

  (c) $A^2 = \begin{bmatrix} 1 & 2 \\ 4 & 2 \end{bmatrix}\begin{bmatrix} 1 & 2 \\ 4 & 2 \end{bmatrix} = \begin{bmatrix} (1)(1) + (2)(4) & (1)(2) + (2)(2) \\ (4)(1) + (2)(4) & (4)(2) + (2)(2) \end{bmatrix} = \begin{bmatrix} 9 & 6 \\ 12 & 12 \end{bmatrix}$

29. (a) $AB = \begin{bmatrix} 3 & -1 \\ 1 & 3 \end{bmatrix}\begin{bmatrix} 1 & -3 \\ 3 & 1 \end{bmatrix} = \begin{bmatrix} (3)(1) + (-1)(3) & (3)(-3) + (-1)(1) \\ (1)(1) + (3)(3) & (1)(-3) + (3)(1) \end{bmatrix} = \begin{bmatrix} 0 & -10 \\ 10 & 0 \end{bmatrix}$

  (b) $BA = \begin{bmatrix} 1 & -3 \\ 3 & 1 \end{bmatrix}\begin{bmatrix} 3 & -1 \\ 1 & 3 \end{bmatrix} = \begin{bmatrix} (1)(3) + (-3)(1) & (1)(-1) + (-3)(3) \\ (3)(3) + (1)(1) & (3)(-1) + (1)(3) \end{bmatrix} = \begin{bmatrix} 0 & -10 \\ 10 & 0 \end{bmatrix}$

  (c) $A^2 = \begin{bmatrix} 3 & -1 \\ 1 & 3 \end{bmatrix}\begin{bmatrix} 3 & -1 \\ 1 & 3 \end{bmatrix} = \begin{bmatrix} (3)(3) + (-1)(1) & (3)(-1) + (-1)(3) \\ (1)(3) + (3)(1) & (1)(-1) + (3)(3) \end{bmatrix} = \begin{bmatrix} 8 & -6 \\ 6 & 8 \end{bmatrix}$

31. (a) $AB = \begin{bmatrix} 7 \\ 8 \\ -1 \end{bmatrix}\begin{bmatrix} 1 & 1 & 2 \end{bmatrix} = \begin{bmatrix} 7(1) & 7(1) & 7(2) \\ 8(1) & 8(1) & 8(2) \\ -1(1) & -1(1) & -1(2) \end{bmatrix} = \begin{bmatrix} 7 & 7 & 14 \\ 8 & 8 & 16 \\ -1 & -1 & -2 \end{bmatrix}$

  (b) $BA = \begin{bmatrix} 1 & 1 & 2 \end{bmatrix}\begin{bmatrix} 7 \\ 8 \\ -1 \end{bmatrix} = [(1)(7) + (1)(8) + (2)(-1)] = [13]$

  (c) A^2 is not possible.

33. A is 3×2 and B is 3×3. AB is not possible.

35. A is 3×3, B is $3 \times 2 \implies AB$ is 3×2.

$\begin{bmatrix} 0 & -1 & 0 \\ 4 & 0 & 2 \\ 8 & -1 & 7 \end{bmatrix}\begin{bmatrix} 2 & 1 \\ -3 & 4 \\ 1 & 6 \end{bmatrix} = \begin{bmatrix} (0)(2) + (-1)(-3) + (0)(1) & (0)(1) + (-1)(4) + (0)(6) \\ (4)(2) + (0)(-3) + (2)(1) & (4)(1) + (0)(4) + (2)(6) \\ (8)(2) + (-1)(-3) + (7)(1) & (8)(1) + (-1)(4) + (7)(6) \end{bmatrix} = \begin{bmatrix} 3 & -4 \\ 10 & 16 \\ 26 & 46 \end{bmatrix}$

37. A is 3×3, B is $3 \times 3 \implies AB$ is 3×3.

$$\begin{bmatrix} 1 & 0 & 0 \\ 0 & 4 & 0 \\ 0 & 0 & -2 \end{bmatrix}\begin{bmatrix} 3 & 0 & 0 \\ 0 & -1 & 0 \\ 0 & 0 & 5 \end{bmatrix} = \begin{bmatrix} (1)(3) + (0)(0) + (0)(0) & (1)(0) + (0)(-1) + (0)(0) & (1)(0) + (0)(0) + (0)(5) \\ (0)(3) + (4)(0) + (0)(0) & (0)(0) + (4)(-1) + (0)(0) & (0)(0) + (4)(0) + (0)(5) \\ (0)(3) + (0)(0) + (-2)(0) & (0)(0) + (0)(-1) + (-2)(0) & (0)(0) + (0)(0) + (-2)(5) \end{bmatrix}$$

$$= \begin{bmatrix} 3 & 0 & 0 \\ 0 & -4 & 0 \\ 0 & 0 & -10 \end{bmatrix}$$

39. A is 3×3, B is $3 \times 3 \implies AB$ is 3×3.

$$\begin{bmatrix} 0 & 0 & 5 \\ 0 & 0 & -3 \\ 0 & 0 & 4 \end{bmatrix}\begin{bmatrix} 6 & -11 & 4 \\ 8 & 16 & 4 \\ 0 & 0 & 0 \end{bmatrix} =$$

$$\begin{bmatrix} (0)(6) + (0)(8) + (5)(0) & (0)(-11) + (0)(16) + (5)(0) & (0)(4) + (0)(4) + (5)(0) \\ (0)(6) + (0)(8) + (-3)(0) & (0)(-11) + (0)(16) + (-3)(0) & (0)(4) + (0)(4) + (-3)(0) \\ (0)(6) + (0)(8) + (4)(0) & (0)(-11) + (0)(16) + (4)(0) & (0)(4) + (0)(4) + (4)(0) \end{bmatrix} = \begin{bmatrix} 0 & 0 & 0 \\ 0 & 0 & 0 \\ 0 & 0 & 0 \end{bmatrix}$$

41. $\begin{bmatrix} 5 & 6 & -3 \\ -2 & 5 & 1 \\ 10 & -5 & 5 \end{bmatrix}\begin{bmatrix} 1 & -1 & 2 \\ 8 & 1 & 4 \\ 4 & -2 & 9 \end{bmatrix} = \begin{bmatrix} 41 & 7 & 7 \\ 42 & 5 & 25 \\ -10 & -25 & 45 \end{bmatrix}$

43. $\begin{bmatrix} -3 & 8 & -6 & 8 \\ -12 & 15 & 9 & 6 \\ 5 & -1 & 1 & 5 \end{bmatrix}\begin{bmatrix} 3 & 1 & 6 \\ 24 & 15 & 14 \\ 16 & 10 & 21 \\ 8 & -4 & 10 \end{bmatrix} = \begin{bmatrix} 151 & 25 & 48 \\ 516 & 279 & 387 \\ 47 & -20 & 87 \end{bmatrix}$

45. A is 2×4 and B is $2 \times 4 \implies AB$ is not possible.

47. $\begin{bmatrix} 3 & 1 \\ 0 & -2 \end{bmatrix}\begin{bmatrix} 1 & 0 \\ -2 & 2 \end{bmatrix}\begin{bmatrix} 1 & 0 \\ 2 & 4 \end{bmatrix} = \begin{bmatrix} 5 & 8 \\ -4 & -16 \end{bmatrix}$

49. $\begin{bmatrix} 0 & 2 & -2 \\ 4 & -1 & 2 \end{bmatrix}\left(\begin{bmatrix} 4 & 0 \\ 0 & -1 \\ -1 & 2 \end{bmatrix} + \begin{bmatrix} -2 & 3 \\ -3 & 5 \\ 0 & -3 \end{bmatrix} \right) = \begin{bmatrix} -4 & 10 \\ 3 & 14 \end{bmatrix}$

51. (a) $\begin{bmatrix} -1 & 1 \\ -2 & 1 \end{bmatrix}\begin{bmatrix} x_1 \\ x_2 \end{bmatrix} = \begin{bmatrix} 4 \\ 0 \end{bmatrix}$

(b)
$$\begin{bmatrix} -1 & 1 & \vdots & 4 \\ -2 & 1 & \vdots & 0 \end{bmatrix}$$

$-R_2 + R_1 \rightarrow \begin{bmatrix} 1 & 0 & \vdots & 4 \\ -2 & 1 & \vdots & 0 \end{bmatrix}$

$2R_1 + R_2 \rightarrow \begin{bmatrix} 1 & 0 & \vdots & 4 \\ 0 & 1 & \vdots & 8 \end{bmatrix}$

$X = \begin{bmatrix} 4 \\ 8 \end{bmatrix}$

53. (a) $\begin{bmatrix} -2 & -3 \\ 6 & 1 \end{bmatrix}\begin{bmatrix} x_1 \\ x_2 \end{bmatrix} = \begin{bmatrix} -4 \\ -36 \end{bmatrix}$

(b)
$$\begin{bmatrix} -2 & -3 & \vdots & -4 \\ 6 & 1 & \vdots & -36 \end{bmatrix}$$

$3R_1 + R_2 \rightarrow \begin{bmatrix} -2 & -3 & \vdots & -4 \\ 0 & -8 & \vdots & -48 \end{bmatrix}$

$\begin{matrix} -\frac{1}{2}R_1 \rightarrow \\ -\frac{1}{8}R_2 \rightarrow \end{matrix} \begin{bmatrix} 1 & \frac{3}{2} & \vdots & 2 \\ 0 & 1 & \vdots & 6 \end{bmatrix}$

$-\frac{3}{2}R_2 + R_1 \rightarrow \begin{bmatrix} 1 & 0 & \vdots & -7 \\ 0 & 1 & \vdots & 6 \end{bmatrix}$

$X = \begin{bmatrix} -7 \\ 6 \end{bmatrix}$

55. (a) $A = \begin{bmatrix} 1 & -2 & 3 \\ -1 & 3 & -1 \\ 2 & -5 & 5 \end{bmatrix}\begin{bmatrix} x_1 \\ x_2 \\ x_3 \end{bmatrix} = \begin{bmatrix} 9 \\ -6 \\ 17 \end{bmatrix}$

(b) $\begin{bmatrix} 1 & -2 & 3 & \vdots & 9 \\ -1 & 3 & -1 & \vdots & -6 \\ 2 & -5 & 5 & \vdots & 17 \end{bmatrix}$

$\begin{matrix} R_1 + R_2 \to \\ -2R_2 + R_3 \to \end{matrix} \begin{bmatrix} 1 & -2 & 3 & \vdots & 9 \\ 0 & 1 & 2 & \vdots & 3 \\ 0 & -1 & -1 & \vdots & -1 \end{bmatrix}$

$\begin{matrix} 2R_2 + R_1 \to \\ \\ R_2 + R_3 \to \end{matrix} \begin{bmatrix} 1 & 0 & 7 & \vdots & 15 \\ 0 & 1 & 2 & \vdots & 3 \\ 0 & 0 & 1 & \vdots & 2 \end{bmatrix}$

$\begin{matrix} -7R_3 + R_1 \to \\ -2R_3 + R_2 \to \end{matrix} \begin{bmatrix} 1 & 0 & 0 & \vdots & 1 \\ 0 & 1 & 0 & \vdots & -1 \\ 0 & 0 & 1 & \vdots & 2 \end{bmatrix}$

$X = \begin{bmatrix} 1 \\ -1 \\ 2 \end{bmatrix}$

57. (a) $\begin{bmatrix} 1 & -5 & 2 \\ -3 & 1 & -1 \\ 0 & -2 & 5 \end{bmatrix}\begin{bmatrix} x_1 \\ x_2 \\ x_3 \end{bmatrix} = \begin{bmatrix} -20 \\ 8 \\ -16 \end{bmatrix}$

(b) $\begin{bmatrix} 1 & -5 & 2 & \vdots & -20 \\ -3 & 1 & -1 & \vdots & 8 \\ 0 & -2 & 5 & \vdots & -16 \end{bmatrix}$

$3R_1 + R_2 \to \begin{bmatrix} 1 & -5 & 2 & \vdots & -20 \\ 0 & -14 & 5 & \vdots & -52 \\ 0 & -2 & 5 & \vdots & -16 \end{bmatrix}$

$-R_3 + R_2 \to \begin{bmatrix} 1 & -5 & 2 & \vdots & -20 \\ 0 & -12 & 0 & \vdots & -36 \\ 0 & -2 & 5 & \vdots & -16 \end{bmatrix}$

$-\frac{1}{12}R_2 \to \begin{bmatrix} 1 & -5 & 2 & \vdots & -20 \\ 0 & 1 & 0 & \vdots & 3 \\ 0 & -2 & 5 & \vdots & -16 \end{bmatrix}$

$\begin{matrix} 5R_2 + R_1 \to \\ \\ 2R_2 + R_3 \to \end{matrix} \begin{bmatrix} 1 & 0 & 2 & \vdots & -5 \\ 0 & 1 & 0 & \vdots & 3 \\ 0 & 0 & 5 & \vdots & -10 \end{bmatrix}$

$\frac{1}{5}R_3 \to \begin{bmatrix} 1 & 0 & 2 & \vdots & -5 \\ 0 & 1 & 0 & \vdots & 3 \\ 0 & 0 & 1 & \vdots & -2 \end{bmatrix}$

$-2R_3 + R_1 \to \begin{bmatrix} 1 & 0 & 0 & \vdots & -1 \\ 0 & 1 & 0 & \vdots & 3 \\ 0 & 0 & 1 & \vdots & -2 \end{bmatrix}$

$X = \begin{bmatrix} -1 \\ 3 \\ -2 \end{bmatrix}$

For 59–67, A is of order 2×3, B is of order 2×3, C is of order 3×2 and D is of order 2×2.

59. $A + 2C$ is not possible. A and C are not of the same order.

61. AB is not possible. The number of columns of A does not equal the number of rows of B.

63. $BC - D$ is possible. The resulting order is 2×2.

65. (CA) is 3×3 so $(CA)D$ is not possible.

67. $D(A - 3B)$ is possible. The resulting order is 2×3.

69. $1.2\begin{bmatrix} 70 & 50 & 25 \\ 35 & 100 & 70 \end{bmatrix} = \begin{bmatrix} 84 & 60 & 30 \\ 42 & 120 & 84 \end{bmatrix}$

71. $BA = \begin{bmatrix} 3.50 & 6.00 \end{bmatrix}\begin{bmatrix} 125 & 100 & 75 \\ 100 & 175 & 125 \end{bmatrix} = \begin{bmatrix} \$1037.50 & \$1400.00 & \$1012.50 \end{bmatrix}$

The entries in the matrix represent the profits for both crops at the three outlets.

73. $ST = \begin{bmatrix} 3 & 2 & 2 & 3 & 0 \\ 0 & 2 & 3 & 4 & 3 \\ 4 & 2 & 1 & 3 & 2 \end{bmatrix} \begin{bmatrix} 840 & 1100 \\ 1200 & 1350 \\ 1450 & 1650 \\ 2650 & 3000 \\ 3050 & 3200 \end{bmatrix} = \begin{bmatrix} \$15,770 & \$18,300 \\ \$26,500 & \$29,250 \\ \$21,260 & \$24,150 \end{bmatrix}$

The entries represent the wholesale and retail inventory values of the inventories at the three outlets.

75. $ST = \begin{bmatrix} 1 & 0.5 & 0.2 \\ 1.6 & 1.0 & 0.2 \\ 2.5 & 2.0 & 0.4 \end{bmatrix} \begin{bmatrix} 12 & 10 \\ 9 & 8 \\ 8 & 7 \end{bmatrix} = \begin{bmatrix} \$18.10 & \$15.40 \\ \$29.80 & \$25.40 \\ \$51.20 & \$43.80 \end{bmatrix}$

This represents the labor cost for each boat size at each plant.

77. True. The sum of two matrices of different orders is undefined.

79. False. $\begin{bmatrix} -2 & 4 \\ -3 & 0 \\ 6 & 1 \end{bmatrix} \begin{bmatrix} 1 & 1 \\ 1 & 1 \end{bmatrix} = \begin{bmatrix} 2 & 2 \\ -3 & -3 \\ 7 & 7 \end{bmatrix}$

81. $AB = \begin{bmatrix} 3 & 3 \\ 4 & 4 \end{bmatrix} \begin{bmatrix} 1 & -1 \\ -1 & 1 \end{bmatrix} = \begin{bmatrix} 0 & 0 \\ 0 & 0 \end{bmatrix}$

$AB = O$ and neither A nor B is O.

83. $A = \begin{bmatrix} 0 & -i \\ i & 0 \end{bmatrix}$

$A^2 = \begin{bmatrix} 0 & -i \\ i & 0 \end{bmatrix} \begin{bmatrix} 0 & -i \\ i & 0 \end{bmatrix} = \begin{bmatrix} (0)(0)+(-i)(i) & (0)(-i)+(-i)(0) \\ (i)(0)+(0)(i) & (i)(-i)+(0)(0) \end{bmatrix} = \begin{bmatrix} 1 & 0 \\ 0 & 1 \end{bmatrix} = I$, the identity matrix.

85. $3x^2 + 20x - 32 = 0$

$(3x - 4)(x + 8) = 0$

$3x - 4 = 0 \quad \text{or} \quad x + 8 = 0$

$x = \frac{4}{3} \qquad\qquad x = -8$

Solutions: $\frac{4}{3}, -8$

87. $4x^3 + 10x^2 - 3x = 0$

$x(4x^2 + 10x - 3) = 0$

$x = 0 \quad \text{or} \quad 4x^2 + 10x - 3 = 0$

$x = \dfrac{-10 \pm \sqrt{10^2 - 4(4)(-3)}}{2(4)} = \dfrac{-10 \pm \sqrt{148}}{8}$

$= \dfrac{-5 \pm \sqrt{37}}{4}$ by the Quadratic Formula

Solutions: $0, \dfrac{-5 \pm \sqrt{37}}{4}$

89. $3x^3 - 12x^2 + 5x - 20 = 0$

$3x^2(x - 4) + 5(x - 4) = 0$

$(x - 4)(3x^2 + 5) = 0$

$x - 4 = 0 \quad \text{or} \quad 3x^2 + 5 = 0$

$x = 4 \qquad\qquad x^2 = -\dfrac{5}{3}$

$x = \pm\sqrt{-\dfrac{5}{3}} = \pm\dfrac{\sqrt{15}}{3}i$

Solutions: $4, \pm\dfrac{\sqrt{15}}{3}i$

91. $\begin{cases} -x + 4y = -9 & \text{Eq. 1} \\ 5x - 8y = 39 & \text{Eq. 2} \end{cases}$

$\begin{array}{ll} -5x + 20y = -45 & \text{5 Eq. 1} \\ \underline{5x - 8y = 39} & \\ 12y = -6 & \text{Add equations.} \\ y = -\frac{1}{2} \end{array}$

$-x + 4\left(-\frac{1}{2}\right) = -9 \Rightarrow x = 7$

Solution: $\left(7, -\frac{1}{2}\right)$

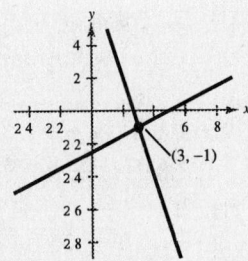

93. $\begin{cases} -x + 2y = -5 & \text{Eq. 1} \\ -3x - y = -8 & \text{Eq. 2} \end{cases}$

$\begin{array}{ll} -x + 2y = -5 & \\ \underline{-6x - 2y = -16} & \text{2 Eq. 2} \\ -7x = -21 & \text{Add equations.} \\ x = 3 \end{array}$

$-3 + 2y = -5 \Rightarrow y = -1$

Solution: $(3, -1)$

Section 8.3   The Inverse of a Square Matrix

■   You should know that the inverse of an $n \times n$ matrix A is the $n \times n$ matrix A^{-1}, if is exists, such that $AA^{-1} = A^{-1}A = I$, where I is the $n \times n$ identity matrix.

■   You should be able to find the inverse, if it exists, of a square matrix.

   (a) Write the $n \times 2n$ matrix that consists of the given matrix A on the left and the $n \times n$ identity matrix I on the right to obtain $[A \;\vdots\; I]$. Note that we separate the matrices A and I by a dotted line. We call this process **adjoining** the matrices A and I.

   (b) If possible, row reduce A to I using elementary row operations of the *entire* matrix $[A \;\vdots\; I]$. The result will be the matrix $[I \;\vdots\; A^{-1}]$. If this is not possible, then A is not invertible.

   (c) Check your work by multiplying to see that $AA^{-1} = I = A^{-1}A$.

■   The inverse of $A = \begin{bmatrix} a & b \\ c & d \end{bmatrix}$ is $A^{-1} = \dfrac{1}{ad - bc}\begin{bmatrix} d & -b \\ -c & a \end{bmatrix}$ if $ad - cb \neq 0$.

■   You should be able to use inverse matrices to solve systems of linear equations.

Solutions to Odd-Numbered Exercises

1. $AB = \begin{bmatrix} 2 & 1 \\ 5 & 3 \end{bmatrix}\begin{bmatrix} 3 & -1 \\ -5 & 2 \end{bmatrix} = \begin{bmatrix} 6 - 5 & -2 + 2 \\ 15 - 15 & -5 + 6 \end{bmatrix} = \begin{bmatrix} 1 & 0 \\ 0 & 1 \end{bmatrix}$

$BA = \begin{bmatrix} 3 & -1 \\ -5 & 2 \end{bmatrix}\begin{bmatrix} 2 & 1 \\ 5 & 3 \end{bmatrix} = \begin{bmatrix} 6 - 5 & 3 - 3 \\ -10 + 10 & -5 + 6 \end{bmatrix} = \begin{bmatrix} 1 & 0 \\ 0 & 1 \end{bmatrix}$

3. $AB = \begin{bmatrix} 1 & 2 \\ 3 & 4 \end{bmatrix}\begin{bmatrix} -2 & 1 \\ \frac{3}{2} & -\frac{1}{2} \end{bmatrix} = \begin{bmatrix} -2 + 3 & 1 - 1 \\ -6 + 6 & 3 - 2 \end{bmatrix} = \begin{bmatrix} 1 & 0 \\ 0 & 1 \end{bmatrix}$

$BA = \begin{bmatrix} -2 & 1 \\ \frac{3}{2} & -\frac{1}{2} \end{bmatrix}\begin{bmatrix} 1 & 2 \\ 3 & 4 \end{bmatrix} = \begin{bmatrix} -2 + 3 & -4 + 4 \\ \frac{3}{2} - \frac{3}{2} & 3 - 2 \end{bmatrix} = \begin{bmatrix} 1 & 0 \\ 0 & 1 \end{bmatrix}$

5. $AB = \begin{bmatrix} 2 & -17 & 11 \\ -1 & 11 & -7 \\ 0 & 3 & -2 \end{bmatrix}\begin{bmatrix} 1 & 1 & 2 \\ 2 & 4 & -3 \\ 3 & 6 & -5 \end{bmatrix} = \begin{bmatrix} 2-17+33 & 2-68+66 & 4+51-55 \\ -1+22-21 & -1+44-42 & -2-33+35 \\ 6-6 & 12-12 & -9+10 \end{bmatrix} = \begin{bmatrix} 1 & 0 & 0 \\ 0 & 1 & 0 \\ 0 & 0 & 1 \end{bmatrix}$

$BA = \begin{bmatrix} 1 & 1 & 2 \\ 2 & 4 & -3 \\ 3 & 6 & -5 \end{bmatrix}\begin{bmatrix} 2 & -17 & 11 \\ -1 & 11 & -7 \\ 0 & 3 & -2 \end{bmatrix} = \begin{bmatrix} 2-1 & -17+11+6 & 11-7-4 \\ 4-4 & -34+44-9 & 22-28+6 \\ 6-6 & -51+66-15 & 33-42+10 \end{bmatrix} = \begin{bmatrix} 1 & 0 & 0 \\ 0 & 1 & 0 \\ 0 & 0 & 1 \end{bmatrix}$

7. $AB = \begin{bmatrix} 2 & 0 & 1 & 1 \\ 3 & 0 & 0 & 1 \\ -1 & 1 & -2 & 1 \\ 4 & -1 & 1 & 0 \end{bmatrix}\begin{bmatrix} -1 & 2 & -1 & -1 \\ -4 & 9 & -5 & -6 \\ 0 & 1 & -1 & -1 \\ 3 & -5 & 3 & 3 \end{bmatrix}$

$= \begin{bmatrix} -2+3 & 4+1-5 & -2-1+3 & -2-1+3 \\ 0 & 6-5 & 0 & 0 \\ 1-4+3 & -2+9-2-5 & 1-5+2+3 & 1-6+2+3 \\ 0 & 8-9+1 & -4+5-1 & -4+6-1 \end{bmatrix} = \begin{bmatrix} 1 & 0 & 0 & 0 \\ 0 & 1 & 0 & 0 \\ 0 & 0 & 1 & 0 \\ 0 & 0 & 0 & 1 \end{bmatrix}$

$BA = \begin{bmatrix} -1 & 2 & -1 & -1 \\ -4 & 9 & -5 & -6 \\ 0 & 1 & -1 & -1 \\ 3 & -5 & 3 & 3 \end{bmatrix}\begin{bmatrix} 2 & 0 & 1 & 1 \\ 3 & 0 & 0 & 1 \\ -1 & 1 & -2 & 1 \\ 4 & -1 & 1 & 0 \end{bmatrix}$

$= \begin{bmatrix} -2+6+1-4 & 0 & -1+2-1 & -1+2-1 \\ -8+27+5-24 & -5+6 & -4+10-6 & -4+9-5 \\ 3+1-4 & 0 & 2-1 & 0 \\ 6-15-3+12 & 0 & 3-6+3 & 3-5+3 \end{bmatrix} = \begin{bmatrix} 1 & 0 & 0 & 0 \\ 0 & 1 & 0 & 0 \\ 0 & 0 & 1 & 0 \\ 0 & 0 & 0 & 1 \end{bmatrix}$

9. $AB = \frac{1}{3}\begin{bmatrix} -2 & 2 & 3 \\ 1 & -1 & 0 \\ 0 & 1 & 4 \end{bmatrix}\begin{bmatrix} -4 & -5 & 3 \\ -4 & -8 & 3 \\ 1 & 2 & 0 \end{bmatrix} = \frac{1}{3}\begin{bmatrix} -8+8+3 & 10-16+6 & -6+6 \\ -4+4 & -5+8 & 3-3 \\ -4+4 & -8+8 & 3 \end{bmatrix}$

$= \frac{1}{3}\begin{bmatrix} 3 & 0 & 0 \\ 0 & 3 & 0 \\ 0 & 0 & 3 \end{bmatrix} = \begin{bmatrix} 1 & 0 & 0 \\ 0 & 1 & 0 \\ 0 & 0 & 1 \end{bmatrix}$

$BA = \frac{1}{3}\begin{bmatrix} -4 & -5 & 3 \\ -4 & -8 & 3 \\ 1 & 2 & 0 \end{bmatrix}\begin{bmatrix} -2 & 2 & 3 \\ 1 & -1 & 0 \\ 0 & 1 & 4 \end{bmatrix} = \frac{1}{3}\begin{bmatrix} 8-5 & -8+5+3 & -12+12 \\ 8-8 & -8+8+3 & -12+12 \\ -2+2 & 2-2 & 3 \end{bmatrix} = \begin{bmatrix} 1 & 0 & 0 \\ 0 & 1 & 0 \\ 0 & 0 & 1 \end{bmatrix}$

11. $[A \;\vdots\; I] = \begin{bmatrix} 2 & 0 & \vdots & 1 & 0 \\ 0 & 3 & \vdots & 0 & 1 \end{bmatrix}$

$\begin{matrix} \frac{1}{2}R_1 \rightarrow \\ \frac{1}{3}R_2 \rightarrow \end{matrix} \begin{bmatrix} 1 & 0 & \vdots & \frac{1}{2} & 0 \\ 0 & 1 & \vdots & 0 & \frac{1}{3} \end{bmatrix} = [I \;\vdots\; A^{-1}]$

$A^{-1} = \begin{bmatrix} \frac{1}{2} & 0 \\ 0 & \frac{1}{3} \end{bmatrix}$

13. $[A \;\vdots\; I] = \begin{bmatrix} 1 & -2 & \vdots & 1 & 0 \\ 2 & -3 & \vdots & 0 & 1 \end{bmatrix}$

$-2R_1 + R_2 \rightarrow \begin{bmatrix} 1 & -2 & \vdots & 1 & 0 \\ 0 & 1 & \vdots & -2 & 1 \end{bmatrix}$

$2R_2 + R_1 \rightarrow \begin{bmatrix} 1 & 0 & \vdots & -3 & 2 \\ 0 & 1 & \vdots & -2 & 1 \end{bmatrix} = [I \;\vdots\; A^{-1}]$

$A^{-1} = \begin{bmatrix} -3 & 2 \\ -2 & 1 \end{bmatrix}$

15. $[A \ \vdots \ I] = \begin{bmatrix} -1 & 1 & \vdots & 1 & 0 \\ -2 & 1 & \vdots & 0 & 1 \end{bmatrix}$

$-R_2 + R_1 \rightarrow \begin{bmatrix} 1 & 0 & \vdots & 1 & -1 \\ -2 & 1 & \vdots & 0 & 1 \end{bmatrix}$

$2R_1 + R_2 \rightarrow \begin{bmatrix} 1 & 0 & \vdots & 1 & -1 \\ 0 & 1 & \vdots & 2 & -1 \end{bmatrix} = [I \ \vdots \ A^{-1}]$

$A^{-1} = \begin{bmatrix} 1 & -1 \\ 2 & -1 \end{bmatrix}$

17. $[A \ \vdots \ I] = \begin{bmatrix} 2 & 4 & \vdots & 1 & 0 \\ 4 & 8 & \vdots & 0 & 1 \end{bmatrix}$

$-2R_1 + R_2 \rightarrow \begin{bmatrix} 2 & 4 & \vdots & 1 & 0 \\ 0 & 0 & \vdots & -2 & 1 \end{bmatrix}$

The two zeros in the second row imply that the inverse does not exist.

19. $A = \begin{bmatrix} 2 & 7 & 1 \\ -3 & -9 & 2 \end{bmatrix}$

A has no inverse because it is not square.

21. $\begin{bmatrix} 1 & 1 & 1 & \vdots & 1 & 0 & 0 \\ 3 & 5 & 4 & \vdots & 0 & 1 & 0 \\ 3 & 6 & 5 & \vdots & 0 & 0 & 1 \end{bmatrix}$

$\begin{matrix} -3R_1 + R_2 \rightarrow \\ -3R_1 + R_3 \rightarrow \end{matrix} \begin{bmatrix} 1 & 1 & 1 & \vdots & 1 & 0 & 0 \\ 0 & 2 & 1 & \vdots & -3 & 1 & 0 \\ 0 & 3 & 2 & \vdots & -3 & 0 & 1 \end{bmatrix}$

$\tfrac{1}{2}R_2 \rightarrow \begin{bmatrix} 1 & 1 & 1 & \vdots & 1 & 0 & 0 \\ 0 & 1 & \tfrac{1}{2} & \vdots & -\tfrac{3}{2} & \tfrac{1}{2} & 0 \\ 0 & 3 & 2 & \vdots & -3 & 0 & 1 \end{bmatrix}$

$\begin{matrix} -R_2 + R_1 \rightarrow \\ \\ -3R_2 + R_3 \rightarrow \end{matrix} \begin{bmatrix} 1 & 0 & \tfrac{1}{2} & \vdots & \tfrac{5}{2} & -\tfrac{1}{2} & 0 \\ 0 & 1 & \tfrac{1}{2} & \vdots & -\tfrac{3}{2} & \tfrac{1}{2} & 0 \\ 0 & 0 & \tfrac{1}{2} & \vdots & \tfrac{3}{2} & -\tfrac{3}{2} & 1 \end{bmatrix}$

$\begin{matrix} -R_3 + R_1 \rightarrow \\ -R_3 + R_2 \rightarrow \\ \end{matrix} \begin{bmatrix} 1 & 0 & 0 & \vdots & 1 & 1 & -1 \\ 0 & 1 & 0 & \vdots & -3 & 2 & -1 \\ 0 & 0 & \tfrac{1}{2} & \vdots & \tfrac{3}{2} & -\tfrac{3}{2} & 1 \end{bmatrix}$

$2R_3 \rightarrow \begin{bmatrix} 1 & 0 & 0 & \vdots & 1 & 1 & -1 \\ 0 & 1 & 0 & \vdots & -3 & 2 & -1 \\ 0 & 0 & 1 & \vdots & 3 & -3 & 2 \end{bmatrix} = [I \ \vdots \ A^{-1}]$

$A^{-1} = \begin{bmatrix} 1 & 1 & -1 \\ -3 & 2 & -1 \\ 3 & -3 & 2 \end{bmatrix}$

23. $[A \;\vdots\; I] = \begin{bmatrix} 1 & 0 & 0 & \vdots & 1 & 0 & 0 \\ 3 & 4 & 0 & \vdots & 0 & 1 & 0 \\ 2 & 5 & 5 & \vdots & 0 & 0 & 1 \end{bmatrix}$

$\begin{matrix} -3R_1 + R_2 \to \\ -2R_1 + R_3 \to \end{matrix} \begin{bmatrix} 1 & 0 & 0 & \vdots & 1 & 0 & 0 \\ 0 & 4 & 0 & \vdots & -3 & 1 & 0 \\ 0 & 5 & 5 & \vdots & -2 & 0 & 1 \end{bmatrix}$

$-\frac{5}{4}R_2 + R_3 \to \begin{bmatrix} 1 & 0 & 0 & \vdots & 1 & 0 & 0 \\ 0 & 4 & 0 & \vdots & -3 & 1 & 0 \\ 0 & 0 & 5 & \vdots & \frac{7}{4} & -\frac{5}{4} & 1 \end{bmatrix}$

$\begin{matrix} \frac{1}{4}R_2 \to \\ \frac{1}{5}R_3 \to \end{matrix} \begin{bmatrix} 1 & 0 & 0 & \vdots & 1 & 0 & 0 \\ 0 & 1 & 0 & \vdots & -\frac{3}{4} & \frac{1}{4} & 0 \\ 0 & 0 & 1 & \vdots & \frac{7}{20} & -\frac{1}{4} & \frac{1}{5} \end{bmatrix} = [I \;\vdots\; A^{-1}]$

$A^{-1} = \begin{bmatrix} 1 & 0 & 0 \\ -\frac{3}{4} & \frac{1}{4} & 0 \\ \frac{7}{20} & -\frac{1}{4} & \frac{1}{5} \end{bmatrix}$

25. $[A \;\vdots\; I] = \begin{bmatrix} -8 & 0 & 0 & 0 & \vdots & 1 & 0 & 0 & 0 \\ 0 & 1 & 0 & 0 & \vdots & 0 & 1 & 0 & 0 \\ 0 & 0 & 4 & 0 & \vdots & 0 & 0 & 1 & 0 \\ 0 & 0 & 0 & -5 & \vdots & 0 & 0 & 0 & 1 \end{bmatrix}$

$\begin{matrix} -\frac{1}{8}R_1 \to \\ \\ \frac{1}{4}R_3 \to \\ -\frac{1}{5}R_4 \to \end{matrix} \begin{bmatrix} 1 & 0 & 0 & 0 & \vdots & -\frac{1}{8} & 0 & 0 & 0 \\ 0 & 1 & 0 & 0 & \vdots & 0 & 1 & 0 & 0 \\ 0 & 0 & 1 & 0 & \vdots & 0 & 0 & \frac{1}{4} & 0 \\ 0 & 0 & 0 & 1 & \vdots & 0 & 0 & 0 & -\frac{1}{5} \end{bmatrix} = [I \;\vdots\; A^{-1}]$

$A^{-1} = \begin{bmatrix} -\frac{1}{8} & 0 & 0 & 0 \\ 0 & 1 & 0 & 0 \\ 0 & 0 & \frac{1}{4} & 0 \\ 0 & 0 & 0 & -\frac{1}{5} \end{bmatrix}$

27. $A = \begin{bmatrix} 1 & 2 & -1 \\ 3 & 7 & -10 \\ -5 & -7 & -15 \end{bmatrix}$

$A^{-1} = \begin{bmatrix} -175 & 37 & -13 \\ 95 & -20 & 7 \\ 14 & -3 & 1 \end{bmatrix}$

29. $A = \begin{bmatrix} 1 & 1 & 2 \\ 3 & 1 & 0 \\ -2 & 0 & 3 \end{bmatrix}$

$A^{-1} = \frac{1}{2} \begin{bmatrix} -3 & 3 & 2 \\ 9 & -7 & -6 \\ -2 & 2 & 2 \end{bmatrix} = \begin{bmatrix} -1.5 & 1.5 & 1 \\ 4.5 & -3.5 & -3 \\ -1 & 1 & 1 \end{bmatrix}$

31. $A = \begin{bmatrix} -\frac{1}{2} & \frac{3}{4} & \frac{1}{4} \\ 1 & 0 & -\frac{3}{2} \\ 0 & -1 & \frac{1}{2} \end{bmatrix}$

$A^{-1} = \begin{bmatrix} -12 & -5 & -9 \\ -4 & -2 & -4 \\ -8 & -4 & -6 \end{bmatrix}$

33. $A = \begin{bmatrix} 0.1 & 0.2 & 0.3 \\ -0.3 & 0.2 & 0.2 \\ 0.5 & 0.4 & 0.4 \end{bmatrix}$

$A^{-1} = \frac{5}{11} \begin{bmatrix} 0 & -4 & 2 \\ -22 & 11 & 11 \\ 22 & -6 & -8 \end{bmatrix} = \begin{bmatrix} 0 & -1.\overline{81} & 0.\overline{90} \\ -10 & 5 & 5 \\ 10 & -2.\overline{72} & -3.\overline{63} \end{bmatrix}$

35. $A = \begin{bmatrix} 1 & 0 & 3 & 0 \\ 0 & 2 & 0 & 4 \\ 1 & 0 & 3 & 0 \\ 0 & 2 & 0 & 4 \end{bmatrix}$

A^{-1} does not exist.

37. $A = \begin{bmatrix} -1 & 0 & 1 & 0 \\ 0 & 2 & 0 & -1 \\ 2 & 0 & -1 & 0 \\ 0 & -1 & 0 & 1 \end{bmatrix}$

$A^{-1} = \begin{bmatrix} 1 & 0 & 1 & 0 \\ 0 & 1 & 0 & 1 \\ 2 & 0 & 1 & 0 \\ 0 & 1 & 0 & 2 \end{bmatrix}$

39. $A = \begin{bmatrix} a & b \\ c & d \end{bmatrix}, A^{-1} = \dfrac{1}{ad - bc} \begin{bmatrix} d & -b \\ -c & a \end{bmatrix}$

$A = \begin{bmatrix} 5 & -2 \\ 2 & 3 \end{bmatrix}$

$ad - bc = (5)(3) - (-2)(2) = 19$

$A^{-1} = \dfrac{1}{19} \begin{bmatrix} 3 & 2 \\ -2 & 5 \end{bmatrix} = \begin{bmatrix} \frac{3}{19} & \frac{2}{19} \\ -\frac{2}{19} & \frac{5}{19} \end{bmatrix}$

41. $A = \begin{bmatrix} -4 & -6 \\ 2 & 3 \end{bmatrix}$

$ad - bc = (-4)(3) - (-2)(-6) = 0$

Since $ad - bc = 0$, A^{-1} does not exist.

43. $A = \begin{bmatrix} \frac{7}{2} & -\frac{3}{4} \\ \frac{1}{5} & \frac{4}{5} \end{bmatrix}$

$ad - bc = \left(\frac{7}{2}\right)\left(\frac{4}{5}\right) - \left(-\frac{3}{4}\right)\left(\frac{1}{5}\right) = \frac{28}{10} + \frac{3}{20} = \frac{59}{20}$

$A^{-1} = \dfrac{1}{\frac{59}{20}} \begin{bmatrix} \frac{4}{5} & \frac{3}{4} \\ -\frac{1}{5} & \frac{7}{2} \end{bmatrix} = \dfrac{20}{59} \begin{bmatrix} \frac{4}{5} & \frac{3}{4} \\ -\frac{1}{5} & \frac{7}{2} \end{bmatrix} = \begin{bmatrix} \frac{16}{59} & \frac{15}{59} \\ -\frac{4}{59} & \frac{70}{59} \end{bmatrix}$

45. $\begin{bmatrix} x \\ y \end{bmatrix} = \begin{bmatrix} -3 & 2 \\ -2 & 1 \end{bmatrix} \begin{bmatrix} 5 \\ 10 \end{bmatrix} = \begin{bmatrix} 5 \\ 0 \end{bmatrix}$

Solution: $(5, 0)$

47. $\begin{bmatrix} x \\ y \end{bmatrix} = \begin{bmatrix} -3 & 2 \\ -2 & 1 \end{bmatrix} \begin{bmatrix} 4 \\ 2 \end{bmatrix} = \begin{bmatrix} -8 \\ -6 \end{bmatrix}$

Solution: $(-8, -6)$

49. $\begin{bmatrix} x \\ y \\ z \end{bmatrix} = \begin{bmatrix} 1 & 1 & -1 \\ -3 & 2 & -1 \\ 3 & -3 & 2 \end{bmatrix} \begin{bmatrix} 0 \\ 5 \\ 2 \end{bmatrix} = \begin{bmatrix} 3 \\ 8 \\ -11 \end{bmatrix}$

Solution: $(3, 8, -11)$

51. $\begin{bmatrix} x_1 \\ x_2 \\ x_3 \\ x_4 \end{bmatrix} = \begin{bmatrix} -24 & 7 & 1 & -2 \\ -10 & 3 & 0 & -1 \\ -29 & 7 & 3 & -2 \\ 12 & -3 & -1 & 1 \end{bmatrix} \begin{bmatrix} 0 \\ 1 \\ -1 \\ 2 \end{bmatrix} = \begin{bmatrix} 2 \\ 1 \\ 0 \\ 0 \end{bmatrix}$

Solution: $(2, 1, 0, 0)$

53. $A = \begin{bmatrix} 3 & 4 \\ 5 & 3 \end{bmatrix}$

$A^{-1} = \dfrac{1}{9 - 20} \begin{bmatrix} 3 & -4 \\ -5 & 3 \end{bmatrix}$

$\begin{bmatrix} x \\ y \end{bmatrix} = -\dfrac{1}{11} \begin{bmatrix} 3 & -4 \\ -5 & 3 \end{bmatrix} \begin{bmatrix} -2 \\ 4 \end{bmatrix} = -\dfrac{1}{11} \begin{bmatrix} -22 \\ 22 \end{bmatrix} = \begin{bmatrix} 2 \\ -2 \end{bmatrix}$

Solution: $(2, -2)$

55.
$$A = \begin{bmatrix} -0.4 & 0.8 \\ 2 & -4 \end{bmatrix}$$

$$A^{-1} = \frac{1}{1.6 - 1.6} \begin{bmatrix} -4 & -0.8 \\ -2 & -0.4 \end{bmatrix}$$

A^{-1} does not exist.

This implies that there is no unique solution; that is, either the system is inconsistent *or* there are infinitely many solutions.

Find the reduced row–echelon form of the matrix corresponding to the system.

$$\begin{bmatrix} -0.4 & 0.8 & \vdots & 1.6 \\ 2 & -4 & \vdots & 5 \end{bmatrix}$$

$$-2.5R_1 \rightarrow \begin{bmatrix} 1 & -2 & \vdots & -4 \\ 2 & -4 & \vdots & 5 \end{bmatrix}$$

$$-2R_1 + R_2 \rightarrow \begin{bmatrix} 1 & -2 & \vdots & -4 \\ 0 & 0 & \vdots & 13 \end{bmatrix}$$

The given system is inconsistent and there is no solution.

59. $A = \begin{bmatrix} -\frac{1}{4} & \frac{3}{8} \\ \frac{3}{2} & \frac{3}{4} \end{bmatrix}$

$$A^{-1} = \frac{1}{-\frac{3}{16} - \frac{9}{16}} \begin{bmatrix} \frac{3}{4} & -\frac{3}{8} \\ -\frac{3}{2} & -\frac{1}{4} \end{bmatrix} = -\frac{4}{3} \begin{bmatrix} \frac{3}{4} & -\frac{3}{8} \\ -\frac{3}{2} & -\frac{1}{4} \end{bmatrix} = \begin{bmatrix} -1 & \frac{1}{2} \\ 2 & \frac{1}{3} \end{bmatrix}$$

$$\begin{bmatrix} x \\ y \end{bmatrix} = \begin{bmatrix} -1 & \frac{1}{2} \\ 2 & \frac{1}{3} \end{bmatrix} \begin{bmatrix} -2 \\ -12 \end{bmatrix} = \begin{bmatrix} -4 \\ -8 \end{bmatrix}$$

Solution: $(-4, -8)$

61. $A = \begin{bmatrix} 4 & -1 & 1 \\ 2 & 2 & 3 \\ 5 & -2 & 6 \end{bmatrix}$

Find A^{-1}.

$$[A : I] = \begin{bmatrix} 4 & -1 & 1 & \vdots & 1 & 0 & 0 \\ 2 & 2 & 3 & \vdots & 0 & 1 & 0 \\ 5 & -2 & 6 & \vdots & 0 & 0 & 1 \end{bmatrix}$$

$$\begin{matrix} R_1 \\ \\ R_3 \end{matrix} \begin{bmatrix} 5 & -2 & 6 & \vdots & 0 & 0 & 1 \\ 2 & 2 & 3 & \vdots & 0 & 1 & 0 \\ 4 & -1 & 1 & \vdots & 1 & 0 & 0 \end{bmatrix}$$

$$-R_3 + R_1 \rightarrow \begin{bmatrix} 1 & -1 & 5 & \vdots & -1 & 0 & 1 \\ 2 & 2 & 3 & \vdots & 0 & 1 & 0 \\ 4 & -1 & 1 & \vdots & 1 & 0 & 0 \end{bmatrix}$$

$$\begin{matrix} -2R_1 + R_2 \rightarrow \\ -4R_1 + R_3 \rightarrow \end{matrix} \begin{bmatrix} 1 & -1 & 5 & \vdots & -1 & 0 & 1 \\ 0 & 4 & -7 & \vdots & 2 & 1 & -2 \\ 0 & 3 & -19 & \vdots & 5 & 0 & -4 \end{bmatrix}$$

$$-R_3 + R_2 \rightarrow \begin{bmatrix} 1 & -1 & 5 & \vdots & -1 & 0 & 1 \\ 0 & 1 & 12 & \vdots & -3 & 1 & 2 \\ 0 & 3 & -19 & \vdots & 5 & 0 & -4 \end{bmatrix}$$

57.
$$A = \begin{bmatrix} 3 & 6 \\ 6 & 14 \end{bmatrix}$$

$$A^{-1} = \frac{1}{42 - 36} \begin{bmatrix} 14 & -6 \\ -6 & 3 \end{bmatrix}$$

$$\begin{bmatrix} x \\ y \end{bmatrix} = \frac{1}{6} \begin{bmatrix} 14 & -6 \\ -6 & 3 \end{bmatrix} \begin{bmatrix} 6 \\ 11 \end{bmatrix} = \frac{1}{6} \begin{bmatrix} 18 \\ -3 \end{bmatrix} = \begin{bmatrix} 3 \\ -\frac{1}{2} \end{bmatrix}$$

Solution: $\left(3, -\frac{1}{2}\right)$

— **CONTINUED** —

61. — CONTINUED —

$$
\begin{matrix} R_2 + R_1 \rightarrow \\ \\ -3R_2 + R_3 \rightarrow \end{matrix}
\begin{bmatrix} 1 & 0 & 17 & \vdots & -4 & 1 & 3 \\ 0 & 1 & 12 & \vdots & -3 & -1 & 2 \\ 0 & 0 & -55 & \vdots & 14 & -3 & -10 \end{bmatrix}
$$

$$
\begin{matrix} \\ \\ -\frac{1}{55}R_3 \rightarrow \end{matrix}
\begin{bmatrix} 1 & 0 & 17 & \vdots & -4 & 1 & 3 \\ 0 & 1 & 12 & \vdots & -3 & -1 & 2 \\ 0 & 0 & 1 & \vdots & -\frac{14}{55} & \frac{3}{55} & \frac{2}{11} \end{bmatrix}
$$

$$
\begin{matrix} -17R_3 + R_1 \rightarrow \\ -12R_3 + R_2 \rightarrow \\ \\ \end{matrix}
\begin{bmatrix} 1 & 0 & 0 & \vdots & \frac{18}{55} & \frac{4}{55} & -\frac{1}{11} \\ 0 & 1 & 0 & \vdots & \frac{3}{55} & \frac{19}{55} & -\frac{2}{11} \\ 0 & 0 & 1 & \vdots & -\frac{14}{55} & \frac{3}{55} & \frac{2}{11} \end{bmatrix} = [I \; \vdots \; A^{-1}]
$$

$$
A^{-1} = \frac{1}{55}\begin{bmatrix} 18 & 4 & -5 \\ 3 & 19 & -10 \\ -14 & 3 & 10 \end{bmatrix}
$$

$$
\begin{bmatrix} x \\ y \\ z \end{bmatrix} = \frac{1}{55}\begin{bmatrix} 18 & 4 & -5 \\ 3 & 19 & -10 \\ -14 & 3 & 10 \end{bmatrix}\begin{bmatrix} -5 \\ 10 \\ 1 \end{bmatrix} = \frac{1}{55}\begin{bmatrix} -55 \\ 165 \\ 110 \end{bmatrix} = \begin{bmatrix} -1 \\ 3 \\ 2 \end{bmatrix}
$$

Solution: $(-1, 3, 2)$

63. $A = \begin{bmatrix} 5 & -3 & 2 \\ 2 & 2 & -3 \\ 1 & -7 & 8 \end{bmatrix}$

A^{-1} does not exist. This implies that there is no unique solution; that is, either the system is inconsistent *or* the system has infinitely many solution. Use a graphing utility to find the reduced row–echelon form of the matrix corresponding to the system.

$$
\begin{bmatrix} 5 & -3 & 2 & \vdots & 2 \\ 2 & 2 & -3 & \vdots & 3 \\ 1 & -7 & 8 & \vdots & -4 \end{bmatrix}
$$

$$
\begin{bmatrix} 1 & 0 & -\frac{5}{16} & \vdots & \frac{13}{16} \\ 0 & 1 & -\frac{19}{16} & \vdots & \frac{11}{16} \\ 0 & 0 & 0 & \vdots & 0 \end{bmatrix}
$$

$$
\begin{cases} x - \frac{5}{16}z = \frac{13}{16} \\ y - \frac{19}{16}z = \frac{11}{6} \end{cases}
$$

Let $z = a$. Then $x = \frac{5}{16}a + \frac{13}{16}$ and $y = \frac{19}{16}a + \frac{11}{16}$.

Solution: $\left(\frac{5}{16}a + \frac{13}{16}, \frac{19}{16}a + \frac{11}{16}, 16a\right)$, where a is a real number.

65. $A = \begin{bmatrix} 2 & 3 & 5 \\ 3 & 5 & 9 \\ 5 & 9 & 17 \end{bmatrix}$

A^{-1} does not exist. This implies that there is no unique solution; that is, either the system is inconsistent *or* the system has infinitely many solution. Use a graphing utility to find the reduced row–echelon form of the matrix corresponding to the system.

$$
\begin{bmatrix} 2 & 3 & 5 & \vdots & 4 \\ 3 & 5 & 9 & \vdots & 7 \\ 5 & 9 & 17 & \vdots & 13 \end{bmatrix}
$$

$$
\begin{bmatrix} 1 & 0 & -2 & \vdots & -1 \\ 0 & 1 & 3 & \vdots & 2 \\ 0 & 0 & 0 & \vdots & 0 \end{bmatrix}
$$

$$
\begin{cases} x - 2z = -1 \\ y + 3z = 2 \end{cases}
$$

Let $z = a$. Then $x = 2a - 1$ and $y = -3a + 2$.

Solution: $(2a - 1, -3a + 2, a)$, where a is a real number.

67. $A = \begin{bmatrix} 7 & -3 & 0 & 2 \\ -2 & 1 & 0 & -1 \\ 4 & 0 & 1 & -2 \\ -1 & 1 & 0 & -1 \end{bmatrix}$

$A^{-1} = \begin{bmatrix} 0 & -1 & 0 & 1 \\ -1 & -5 & 0 & 3 \\ -2 & -4 & 1 & -2 \\ -1 & -4 & 0 & 1 \end{bmatrix}$

$\begin{bmatrix} x \\ y \\ z \\ w \end{bmatrix} = \begin{bmatrix} 0 & -1 & 0 & 1 \\ -1 & -5 & 0 & 3 \\ -2 & -4 & 1 & -2 \\ -1 & -4 & 0 & 1 \end{bmatrix} \begin{bmatrix} 41 \\ -13 \\ 12 \\ -8 \end{bmatrix} = \begin{bmatrix} 5 \\ 0 \\ -2 \\ 3 \end{bmatrix}$

Solution: $(5, 0, -2, 3)$

69. $A = \begin{bmatrix} 1 & 1 & 1 \\ 0.065 & 0.07 & 0.09 \\ 0 & 2 & -1 \end{bmatrix}$

$[A \;\vdots\; I] = \begin{bmatrix} 1 & 1 & 1 & \vdots & 1 & 0 & 0 \\ 0.065 & 0.07 & 0.09 & \vdots & 0 & 1 & 0 \\ 0 & 2 & -1 & \vdots & 0 & 0 & 1 \end{bmatrix}$

$200R_2 \rightarrow \begin{bmatrix} 1 & 1 & 1 & \vdots & 1 & 0 & 0 \\ 13 & 14 & 18 & \vdots & 0 & 200 & 0 \\ 0 & 2 & -1 & \vdots & 0 & 0 & 1 \end{bmatrix}$

$-13R_1 + R_2 \rightarrow \begin{bmatrix} 1 & 1 & 1 & \vdots & 1 & 0 & 0 \\ 0 & 1 & 5 & \vdots & -13 & 200 & 0 \\ 0 & 2 & -1 & \vdots & 0 & 0 & 1 \end{bmatrix}$

$\begin{matrix} -R_2 + R_1 \rightarrow \\ \\ -2R_2 + R_3 \rightarrow \end{matrix} \begin{bmatrix} 1 & 0 & -4 & \vdots & 14 & -200 & 0 \\ 0 & 1 & 5 & \vdots & -13 & 200 & 0 \\ 0 & 0 & -11 & \vdots & 26 & -400 & 1 \end{bmatrix}$

$-\tfrac{1}{11}R_3 \rightarrow \begin{bmatrix} 1 & 0 & -4 & \vdots & 14 & -200 & 0 \\ 0 & 1 & 5 & \vdots & -13 & 200 & 0 \\ 0 & 0 & 1 & \vdots & -\frac{26}{11} & \frac{400}{11} & -\frac{1}{11} \end{bmatrix}$

$\begin{matrix} 4R_3 + R_1 \rightarrow \\ -5R_3 + R_2 \rightarrow \\ \\ \end{matrix} \begin{bmatrix} 1 & 0 & 0 & \vdots & \frac{50}{11} & -\frac{600}{11} & -\frac{4}{11} \\ 0 & 1 & 0 & \vdots & -\frac{13}{11} & \frac{200}{11} & \frac{5}{11} \\ 0 & 0 & 1 & \vdots & -\frac{26}{11} & \frac{400}{11} & -\frac{1}{11} \end{bmatrix} = [I \;\vdots\; A^{-1}]$

$X = A^{-1}B = \tfrac{1}{11} \begin{bmatrix} 50 & -600 & -4 \\ -13 & 200 & 5 \\ -26 & 400 & -1 \end{bmatrix} \begin{bmatrix} 10{,}000 \\ 705 \\ 0 \end{bmatrix} = \begin{bmatrix} 7000 \\ 1000 \\ 2000 \end{bmatrix}$

Answer: $7000 in AAA–rated bonds, $1000 in A–rated bonds, $2000 in B–rated bonds

71. Use the inverse matrix A^{-1} from Exercise 69.

$X = A^{-1}B = \tfrac{1}{11} \begin{bmatrix} 50 & -600 & -4 \\ -13 & 200 & 5 \\ -26 & 400 & -1 \end{bmatrix} \begin{bmatrix} 12{,}000 \\ 835 \\ 0 \end{bmatrix} = \begin{bmatrix} 9000 \\ 1000 \\ 2000 \end{bmatrix}$

Answer: $9000 in AAA–rated bonds, $1000 in A–rated bonds, $2000 in B–rated bonds

73. $A = \begin{bmatrix} 2 & 0 & 4 \\ 0 & 1 & 4 \\ 1 & 1 & -1 \end{bmatrix}$

$[A : I] = \begin{bmatrix} 2 & 0 & 4 & \vdots & 1 & 0 & 0 \\ 0 & 1 & 4 & \vdots & 0 & 1 & 0 \\ 1 & 1 & -1 & \vdots & 0 & 0 & 1 \end{bmatrix}$

$\begin{matrix} R_1 \\ \\ R_3 \end{matrix} \begin{bmatrix} 1 & 1 & -1 & \vdots & 0 & 0 & 1 \\ 0 & 1 & 4 & \vdots & 0 & 1 & 0 \\ 2 & 0 & 4 & \vdots & 1 & 0 & 0 \end{bmatrix}$

$\begin{matrix} \\ \\ -2R_1 + R_3 \rightarrow \end{matrix} \begin{bmatrix} 1 & 1 & -1 & \vdots & 0 & 0 & 1 \\ 0 & 1 & 4 & \vdots & 0 & 1 & 0 \\ 0 & -2 & 6 & \vdots & 1 & 0 & -2 \end{bmatrix}$

$\begin{matrix} -R_2 + R_1 \rightarrow \\ \\ 2R_2 + R_3 \rightarrow \end{matrix} \begin{bmatrix} 1 & 0 & -5 & \vdots & 0 & -1 & 1 \\ 0 & 1 & 4 & \vdots & 0 & 1 & 0 \\ 0 & 0 & 14 & \vdots & 1 & 2 & -2 \end{bmatrix}$

$\begin{matrix} \\ \\ \frac{1}{14}R_3 \rightarrow \end{matrix} \begin{bmatrix} 1 & 0 & -5 & \vdots & 0 & -1 & 1 \\ 0 & 1 & 4 & \vdots & 0 & 1 & 0 \\ 0 & 0 & 1 & \vdots & \frac{1}{14} & \frac{1}{7} & -\frac{1}{7} \end{bmatrix}$

$\begin{matrix} 5R_3 + R_1 \rightarrow \\ -4R_3 + R_2 \rightarrow \\ \\ \end{matrix} \begin{bmatrix} 1 & 0 & 0 & \vdots & \frac{5}{14} & -\frac{2}{7} & \frac{2}{7} \\ 0 & 1 & 0 & \vdots & -\frac{2}{7} & \frac{3}{7} & \frac{4}{7} \\ 0 & 0 & 1 & \vdots & \frac{1}{14} & \frac{1}{7} & -\frac{1}{7} \end{bmatrix} = [I : A^{-1}]$

$A^{-1} = \frac{1}{14}\begin{bmatrix} 5 & -4 & 4 \\ -4 & 6 & 8 \\ 1 & 2 & -2 \end{bmatrix}$

$\begin{bmatrix} I_1 \\ I_2 \\ I_3 \end{bmatrix} = \frac{1}{14}\begin{bmatrix} 5 & -4 & 4 \\ -4 & 6 & 8 \\ 1 & 2 & -2 \end{bmatrix}\begin{bmatrix} 14 \\ 28 \\ 0 \end{bmatrix} = \begin{bmatrix} -3 \\ 8 \\ 5 \end{bmatrix}$

Answer: $I_1 = -3$ amperes, $I_2 = 8$ amperes, $I_3 = 5$ amperes

75. True. If B is the inverse of A, then $AB = I = BA$.

77. True. If A is of order $m \times n$ and B is of order $n \times m$ (where $m \neq n$), the products AB and BA are of different orders and so cannot be equal to each other.

79. The inverse matrix can be calculated once and used for more than one exercise.

81. $3^{x/2} = 315$

$\ln 3^{x/2} = \ln 315$

$\frac{x}{2} \ln 3 = \ln 315$

$x = \frac{2 \ln 315}{\ln 3} \approx 10.47$

83. $\log_2 x - 2 = 4.5$

$\log_2 x = 6.5$

$x = 2^{6.5} \approx 90.51$

85. $-3\begin{bmatrix} -4 & 6 \\ 2 & -8 \\ 1 & 12 \end{bmatrix} = \begin{bmatrix} 12 & -18 \\ -6 & 24 \\ -3 & -36 \end{bmatrix}$

87. $\begin{bmatrix} 2 & 7 \\ -3 & -1 \end{bmatrix} - 4\begin{bmatrix} -1 & 2 \\ 6 & -5 \end{bmatrix} = \begin{bmatrix} 2 & 7 \\ -3 & -1 \end{bmatrix} - \begin{bmatrix} -4 & 8 \\ 24 & -20 \end{bmatrix} = \begin{bmatrix} 6 & -1 \\ -27 & 19 \end{bmatrix}$

Section 8.4   The Determinant of a Square Matrix

■ You should be able to determine the determinant of a matrix of order 2×2 by using the difference of the products of the diagonals.

■ You should be able to use expansion by cofactors to find the determinant of a matrix of order 3×3 or greater.

■ The determinant of a triangular matrix equals the product of the entries on the main diagonal.

Solutions to Odd-Numbered Exercises

1. 5

3. $\begin{vmatrix} 2 & 1 \\ 3 & 4 \end{vmatrix} = 2(4) - 1(3) = 8 - 3 = 5$

5. $\begin{vmatrix} 5 & 2 \\ -6 & 3 \end{vmatrix} = 5(3) - 2(-6) = 15 + 12 = 27$

7. $\begin{vmatrix} -7 & 0 \\ 3 & 0 \end{vmatrix} = -7(0) - 0(3) = 0$

9. $\begin{vmatrix} 2 & 6 \\ 0 & 3 \end{vmatrix} = 2(3) - 6(0) = 6$

11. $\begin{vmatrix} -3 & -2 \\ -6 & -1 \end{vmatrix} = (-3)(-1) - (-2)(-6) = 3 - 12 = -9$

13. $\begin{vmatrix} 9 & 0 \\ 7 & 8 \end{vmatrix} = 9(8) - 0(7) = 72 - 0 = 72$

15. $\begin{vmatrix} -\frac{1}{2} & \frac{1}{3} \\ -6 & \frac{1}{3} \end{vmatrix} = -\frac{1}{2}\left(\frac{1}{3}\right) - \frac{1}{3}(-6) = -\frac{1}{6} + 2 = \frac{11}{6}$

17. $\begin{vmatrix} 0.3 & 0.2 & 0.2 \\ 0.2 & 0.2 & 0.2 \\ -0.4 & 0.4 & 0.3 \end{vmatrix} = -0.002$

19. $\begin{vmatrix} 0.9 & 0.7 & 0 \\ -0.1 & 0.3 & 1.3 \\ -2.2 & 4.2 & 6.1 \end{vmatrix} = -4.842$

21. $\begin{vmatrix} 1 & 4 & -2 \\ 3 & 6 & -6 \\ -2 & 1 & 4 \end{vmatrix} = 0$

23. $\begin{bmatrix} 3 & 4 \\ 2 & -5 \end{bmatrix}$

(a) $M_{11} = -5$ (b) $C_{11} = M_{11} = -5$

   $M_{12} = 2$ $C_{12} = -M_{12} = -2$

   $M_{21} = 4$ $C_{21} = -M_{21} = -4$

   $M_{22} = 3$ $C_{22} = M_{22} = 3$

25. $\begin{bmatrix} 3 & 1 \\ -2 & -4 \end{bmatrix}$

(a) $M_{11} = -4$ (b) $C_{11} = M_{11} = -4$

   $M_{12} = -2$ $C_{12} = -M_{12} = 2$

   $M_{21} = 1$ $C_{21} = -M_{21} = -1$

   $M_{22} = 3$ $C_{22} = M_{22} = 3$

27. $\begin{bmatrix} 4 & 0 & 2 \\ -3 & 2 & 1 \\ 1 & -1 & 1 \end{bmatrix}$

(a) $M_{11} = \begin{vmatrix} 2 & 1 \\ -1 & 1 \end{vmatrix} = 2 - (-1) = 3$

$M_{12} = \begin{vmatrix} -3 & 1 \\ 1 & 1 \end{vmatrix} = -3 - 1 = -4$

$M_{13} = \begin{vmatrix} -3 & 2 \\ 1 & -1 \end{vmatrix} = 3 - 2 = 1$

$M_{21} = \begin{vmatrix} 0 & 2 \\ -1 & 1 \end{vmatrix} = 0 - (-2) = 2$

$M_{22} = \begin{vmatrix} 4 & 2 \\ 1 & 1 \end{vmatrix} = 4 - 2 = 2$

$M_{23} = \begin{vmatrix} 4 & 0 \\ 1 & -1 \end{vmatrix} = -4 - 0 = -4$

$M_{31} = \begin{vmatrix} 0 & 2 \\ 2 & 1 \end{vmatrix} = 0 - 4 = -4$

$M_{32} = \begin{vmatrix} 4 & 2 \\ -3 & 1 \end{vmatrix} = 4 - (-6) = 10$

$M_{33} = \begin{vmatrix} 4 & 0 \\ -3 & 2 \end{vmatrix} = 8 - 0 = 8$

(b) $C_{11} = (-1)^2 M_{11} = 3$

$C_{12} = (-1)^3 M_{12} = 4$

$C_{13} = (-1)^4 M_{13} = 1$

$C_{21} = (-1)^3 M_{21} = -2$

$C_{22} = (-1)^4 M_{22} = 2$

$C_{23} = (-1)^5 M_{23} = 4$

$C_{31} = (-1)^4 M_{31} = -4$

$C_{32} = (-1)^5 M_{32} = -10$

$C_{33} = (-1)^6 M_{33} = 8$

29. $\begin{bmatrix} 3 & -2 & 8 \\ 3 & 2 & -6 \\ -1 & 3 & 6 \end{bmatrix}$

(a) $M_{11} = \begin{vmatrix} 2 & -6 \\ 3 & 6 \end{vmatrix} = 12 + 18 = 30$

$M_{12} = \begin{vmatrix} 3 & -6 \\ -1 & 6 \end{vmatrix} = 18 - 6 = 12$

$M_{13} = \begin{vmatrix} 3 & 2 \\ -1 & 3 \end{vmatrix} = 9 + 2 = 11$

$M_{21} = \begin{vmatrix} -2 & 8 \\ 3 & 6 \end{vmatrix} = -12 - 24 = -36$

$M_{22} = \begin{vmatrix} 3 & 8 \\ -1 & 6 \end{vmatrix} = 18 + 8 = 26$

$M_{23} = \begin{vmatrix} 3 & -2 \\ -1 & 3 \end{vmatrix} = 9 - 2 = 7$

$M_{31} = \begin{vmatrix} -2 & 8 \\ 2 & -6 \end{vmatrix} = 12 - 16 = -4$

$M_{32} = \begin{vmatrix} 3 & 8 \\ 3 & -6 \end{vmatrix} = -18 - 24 = -42$

$M_{33} = \begin{vmatrix} 3 & -2 \\ 3 & 2 \end{vmatrix} = 6 + 6 = 12$

(b) $C_{11} = (-1)^2 M_{11} = 30$

$C_{12} = (-1)^3 M_{12} = -12$

$C_{13} = (-1)^4 M_{13} = 11$

$C_{21} = (-1)^3 M_{21} = 36$

$C_{22} = (-1)^4 M_{22} = 26$

$C_{23} = (-1)^5 M_{23} = -7$

$C_{31} = (-1)^4 M_{31} = -4$

$C_{32} = (-1)^5 M_{32} = 42$

$C_{33} = (-1)^6 M_{33} = 12$

31. (a) $\begin{vmatrix} -3 & 2 & 1 \\ 4 & 5 & 6 \\ 2 & -3 & 1 \end{vmatrix} = -3 \begin{vmatrix} 5 & 6 \\ -3 & 1 \end{vmatrix} - 2 \begin{vmatrix} 4 & 6 \\ 2 & 1 \end{vmatrix} + \begin{vmatrix} 4 & 5 \\ 2 & -3 \end{vmatrix} = -3(23) - 2(-8) - 22 = -75$

(b) $\begin{vmatrix} -3 & 2 & 1 \\ 4 & 5 & 6 \\ 2 & -3 & 1 \end{vmatrix} = -2 \begin{vmatrix} 4 & 6 \\ 2 & 1 \end{vmatrix} + 5 \begin{vmatrix} -3 & 1 \\ 2 & 1 \end{vmatrix} + 3 \begin{vmatrix} -3 & 1 \\ 4 & 6 \end{vmatrix} = -2(-8) + 5(-5) + 3(-22) = -75$

33. (a) $\begin{vmatrix} 5 & 0 & -3 \\ 0 & 12 & 4 \\ 1 & 6 & 3 \end{vmatrix} = 0 \begin{vmatrix} 0 & -3 \\ 6 & 3 \end{vmatrix} + 12 \begin{vmatrix} 5 & -3 \\ 1 & 3 \end{vmatrix} - 4 \begin{vmatrix} 5 & 0 \\ 1 & 6 \end{vmatrix} = 0(18) + 12(18) - 4(30) = 96$

(b) $\begin{vmatrix} 5 & 0 & -3 \\ 0 & 12 & 4 \\ 1 & 6 & 3 \end{vmatrix} = 0 \begin{vmatrix} 0 & 4 \\ 1 & 3 \end{vmatrix} + 12 \begin{vmatrix} 5 & -3 \\ 1 & 3 \end{vmatrix} - 6 \begin{vmatrix} 5 & -3 \\ 0 & 4 \end{vmatrix} = 0(-4) + 12(18) - 6(20) = 96$

35. (a) $\begin{vmatrix} 6 & 0 & -3 & 5 \\ 4 & 13 & 6 & -8 \\ -1 & 0 & 7 & 4 \\ 8 & 6 & 0 & 2 \end{vmatrix} = -4 \begin{vmatrix} 0 & -3 & 5 \\ 0 & 7 & 4 \\ 6 & 0 & 2 \end{vmatrix} + 13 \begin{vmatrix} 6 & -3 & 5 \\ -1 & 7 & 4 \\ 8 & 0 & 2 \end{vmatrix} - 6 \begin{vmatrix} 6 & 0 & 5 \\ -1 & 0 & 4 \\ 8 & 6 & 2 \end{vmatrix} - 8 \begin{vmatrix} 6 & 0 & -3 \\ -1 & 0 & 7 \\ 8 & 6 & 0 \end{vmatrix}$

$= -4(-282) + 13(-298) - 6(-174) - 8(-234) = 170$

(b) $\begin{vmatrix} 6 & 0 & -3 & 5 \\ 4 & 13 & 6 & -8 \\ -1 & 0 & 7 & 4 \\ 8 & 6 & 0 & 2 \end{vmatrix} = 0 \begin{vmatrix} 4 & 6 & -8 \\ -1 & 7 & 4 \\ 8 & 0 & 2 \end{vmatrix} + 13 \begin{vmatrix} 6 & -3 & 5 \\ -1 & 7 & 4 \\ 8 & 0 & 2 \end{vmatrix} + 0 \begin{vmatrix} 6 & -3 & 5 \\ 4 & 6 & -8 \\ 8 & 0 & 2 \end{vmatrix} + 6 \begin{vmatrix} 6 & -3 & 5 \\ 4 & 6 & -8 \\ -1 & 7 & 4 \end{vmatrix}$

$= 0 + 13(-298) + 0 + 6(674) = 170$

37. Expand along Column 1.

$\begin{vmatrix} 2 & -1 & 0 \\ 4 & 2 & 1 \\ 4 & 2 & 1 \end{vmatrix} = 2 \begin{vmatrix} 2 & 1 \\ 2 & 1 \end{vmatrix} - 4 \begin{vmatrix} -1 & 0 \\ 2 & 1 \end{vmatrix} + 4 \begin{vmatrix} -1 & 0 \\ 2 & 1 \end{vmatrix} = 2(0) - 4(-1) + 4(-1) = 0$

39. Expand along Row 2.

$\begin{vmatrix} 6 & 3 & -7 \\ 0 & 0 & 0 \\ 4 & -6 & 3 \end{vmatrix} = 0 \begin{vmatrix} 3 & -7 \\ -6 & 3 \end{vmatrix} - 0 \begin{vmatrix} 6 & -7 \\ 4 & 3 \end{vmatrix} + 0 \begin{vmatrix} 6 & 3 \\ 4 & -6 \end{vmatrix} = 0$

41. $\begin{vmatrix} -1 & 2 & 5 \\ 0 & 3 & 4 \\ 0 & 0 & 3 \end{vmatrix} = (-1)(3)(3) = -9$ (Upper Triangular)

43. Expand along Column 3.

$\begin{vmatrix} 1 & 4 & -2 \\ 3 & 2 & 0 \\ -1 & 4 & 3 \end{vmatrix} = -2 \begin{vmatrix} 3 & 2 \\ -1 & 4 \end{vmatrix} + 3 \begin{vmatrix} 1 & 4 \\ 3 & 2 \end{vmatrix} = -2(14) + 3(-10) = -58$

45. $\begin{vmatrix} 2 & 4 & 6 \\ 0 & 3 & 1 \\ 0 & 0 & -5 \end{vmatrix} = (2)(3)(-5) = -30$ (Upper Triangular)

47. Expand along Column 3.

$\begin{vmatrix} 2 & 6 & 6 & 2 \\ 2 & 7 & 3 & 6 \\ 1 & 5 & 0 & 1 \\ 3 & 7 & 0 & 7 \end{vmatrix} = 6\begin{vmatrix} 2 & 7 & 6 \\ 1 & 5 & 1 \\ 3 & 7 & 7 \end{vmatrix} - 3\begin{vmatrix} 2 & 6 & 2 \\ 1 & 5 & 1 \\ 3 & 7 & 7 \end{vmatrix} = 6(-20) - 3(16) = -168$

49. Expand along Column 1.

$\begin{vmatrix} 5 & 3 & 0 & 6 \\ 4 & 6 & 4 & 12 \\ 0 & 2 & -3 & 4 \\ 0 & 1 & -2 & 2 \end{vmatrix} = 5\begin{vmatrix} 6 & 4 & 12 \\ 2 & -3 & 4 \\ 1 & -2 & 2 \end{vmatrix} - 4\begin{vmatrix} 3 & 0 & 6 \\ 2 & -3 & 4 \\ 1 & -2 & 2 \end{vmatrix} = 5(0) - 4(0) = 0$

51. Expand along Column 2, then along Column 4.

$\begin{vmatrix} 3 & 2 & 4 & -1 & 5 \\ -2 & 0 & 1 & 3 & 2 \\ 1 & 0 & 0 & 4 & 0 \\ 6 & 0 & 2 & -1 & 0 \\ 3 & 0 & 5 & 1 & 0 \end{vmatrix} = -2\begin{vmatrix} -2 & 1 & 3 & 2 \\ 1 & 0 & 4 & 0 \\ 6 & 2 & -1 & 0 \\ 3 & 5 & 1 & 0 \end{vmatrix} = (-2)(-2)\begin{vmatrix} 1 & 0 & 4 \\ 6 & 2 & -1 \\ 3 & 5 & 1 \end{vmatrix} = 4(103) = 412$

53. $\begin{vmatrix} 3 & 8 & -7 \\ 0 & -5 & 4 \\ 8 & 1 & 6 \end{vmatrix} = -126$

55. $\begin{vmatrix} 7 & 0 & -14 \\ -2 & 5 & 4 \\ -6 & 2 & 12 \end{vmatrix} = 0$

57. $\begin{vmatrix} 1 & -1 & 8 & 4 \\ 2 & 6 & 0 & -4 \\ 2 & 0 & 2 & 6 \\ 0 & 2 & 8 & 0 \end{vmatrix} = -336$

59. $\begin{vmatrix} 3 & -2 & 4 & 3 & 1 \\ -1 & 0 & 2 & 1 & 0 \\ 5 & -1 & 0 & 3 & 2 \\ 4 & 7 & -8 & 0 & 0 \\ 1 & 2 & 3 & 0 & 2 \end{vmatrix} = 410$

61. (a) $\begin{vmatrix} -1 & 0 \\ 0 & 3 \end{vmatrix} = -3$

(b) $\begin{vmatrix} 2 & 0 \\ 0 & -1 \end{vmatrix} = -2$

(c) $\begin{bmatrix} -1 & 0 \\ 0 & 3 \end{bmatrix}\begin{bmatrix} 2 & 0 \\ 0 & -1 \end{bmatrix} = \begin{bmatrix} -2 & 0 \\ 0 & -3 \end{bmatrix}$

(d) $\begin{vmatrix} -2 & 0 \\ 0 & -3 \end{vmatrix} = 6$

63. (a) $\begin{vmatrix} 4 & 0 \\ 3 & -2 \end{vmatrix} = -8$

(b) $\begin{vmatrix} -1 & 1 \\ -2 & 2 \end{vmatrix} = 0$

(c) $\begin{bmatrix} 4 & 0 \\ 3 & -2 \end{bmatrix}\begin{bmatrix} -1 & 1 \\ -2 & 2 \end{bmatrix} = \begin{bmatrix} -4 & 4 \\ 1 & -1 \end{bmatrix}$

(d) $\begin{vmatrix} -4 & 4 \\ 1 & -1 \end{vmatrix} = 0$

65. (a) $\begin{vmatrix} 0 & 1 & 2 \\ -3 & -2 & 1 \\ 0 & 4 & 1 \end{vmatrix} = -21$

(b) $\begin{vmatrix} 3 & -2 & 0 \\ 1 & -1 & 2 \\ 3 & 1 & 1 \end{vmatrix} = -19$

(c) $\begin{bmatrix} 0 & 1 & 2 \\ -3 & -2 & 1 \\ 0 & 4 & 1 \end{bmatrix} \begin{bmatrix} 3 & -2 & 0 \\ 1 & -1 & 2 \\ 3 & 1 & 1 \end{bmatrix} = \begin{bmatrix} 7 & 1 & 4 \\ -8 & 9 & -3 \\ 7 & -3 & 9 \end{bmatrix}$

(d) $\begin{vmatrix} 7 & 1 & 4 \\ -8 & 9 & -3 \\ 7 & -3 & 9 \end{vmatrix} = 399$

67. (a) $\begin{vmatrix} -1 & 2 & 1 \\ 1 & 0 & 1 \\ 0 & 1 & 0 \end{vmatrix} = 2$

(b) $\begin{vmatrix} -1 & 0 & 0 \\ 0 & 2 & 0 \\ 0 & 0 & 3 \end{vmatrix} = -6$

(c) $\begin{bmatrix} -1 & 2 & 1 \\ 1 & 0 & 1 \\ 0 & 1 & 0 \end{bmatrix} \begin{bmatrix} -1 & 0 & 0 \\ 0 & 2 & 0 \\ 0 & 0 & 3 \end{bmatrix} = \begin{bmatrix} 1 & 4 & 3 \\ -1 & 0 & 3 \\ 0 & 2 & 0 \end{bmatrix}$

(d) $\begin{vmatrix} 1 & 4 & 3 \\ -1 & 0 & 3 \\ 0 & 2 & 0 \end{vmatrix} = -12$

69. $\begin{vmatrix} w & x \\ y & z \end{vmatrix} = wz - xy$

$-\begin{vmatrix} y & z \\ w & x \end{vmatrix} = -(xy - wz) = wz - xy$

Thus, $\begin{vmatrix} w & x \\ y & z \end{vmatrix} = -\begin{vmatrix} y & z \\ w & x \end{vmatrix}$.

71. $\begin{vmatrix} w & x \\ y & z \end{vmatrix} = wz - xy$

$\begin{vmatrix} w & x + cw \\ y & z + cy \end{vmatrix} = w(z + cy) - y(x + cw) = wz - xy$

Thus, $\begin{vmatrix} w & x \\ y & z \end{vmatrix} = \begin{vmatrix} w & x + cw \\ y & z + cy \end{vmatrix}$.

73. $\begin{vmatrix} 1 & x & x^2 \\ 1 & y & y^2 \\ 1 & z & z^2 \end{vmatrix} = \begin{vmatrix} y & y^2 \\ z & z^2 \end{vmatrix} - \begin{vmatrix} x & x^2 \\ z & z^2 \end{vmatrix} + \begin{vmatrix} x & x^2 \\ y & y^2 \end{vmatrix}$

$= (yz^2 - y^2z) - (xz^2 - x^2z) + (xy^2 - x^2y)$

$= yz^2 - xz^2 - y^2z + x^2z + xy(y - x)$

$= z^2(y - x) - z(y^2 - x^2) + xy(y - x)$

$= z^2(y - x) - z(y - x)(y + x) + xy(y - x)$

$= (y - x)[z^2 - z(y + x) + xy]$

$= (y - x)[z^2 - zy - zx + xy]$

$= (y - x)[z^2 - zx - zy + xy]$

$= (y - x)[z(z - x) - y(z - x)]$

$= (y - x)(z - x)(z - y)$

75. $\begin{vmatrix} x-1 & 2 \\ 3 & x-2 \end{vmatrix} = 0$

$(x-1)(x-2) - 6 = 0$

$x^2 - 3x - 4 = 0$

$(x+1)(x-4) = 0$

$x = -1$ or $x = 4$

77. $\begin{vmatrix} x+3 & 2 \\ 1 & x+2 \end{vmatrix} = 0$

$(x+3)(x+2) - 2 = 0$

$x^2 + 5x + 4 = 0$

$(x+1)(x+4) = 0$

$x = -1$ or $x = -4$

79. $\begin{vmatrix} 4u & -1 \\ -1 & 2v \end{vmatrix} = 8uv - 1$

81. $\begin{vmatrix} e^{2x} & e^{3x} \\ 2e^{2x} & 3e^{3x} \end{vmatrix} = 3e^{5x} - 2e^{5x} = e^{5x}$

83. $\begin{vmatrix} x & \ln x \\ 1 & \dfrac{1}{x} \end{vmatrix} = 1 - \ln x$

85. True. If an entire row is zero, then each cofactor in the expansion is multiplied by zero.

87. Let $A = \begin{bmatrix} 1 & 3 \\ -2 & 4 \end{bmatrix}$ and $B = \begin{bmatrix} -4 & 0 \\ 3 & 5 \end{bmatrix}$.

$|A| = \begin{vmatrix} 1 & 3 \\ -2 & 4 \end{vmatrix} = 10,\ |B| = \begin{vmatrix} -4 & 0 \\ 3 & 5 \end{vmatrix} = -20,\ |A| + |B| = -10$

$A + B = \begin{bmatrix} -3 & 3 \\ 1 & 9 \end{bmatrix},\ |A + B| = \begin{vmatrix} -3 & 3 \\ 1 & 9 \end{vmatrix} = -30$

Thus, $|A + B| \neq |A| + |B|$. Your answer may differ, depending on how you choose A and B.

89. A square matrix is a square array of numbers. The determinant of a square matrix is a real number.

91. $\begin{cases} x + y \le 8 \\ \quad\ x \ge -3 \\ 2x - y < 5 \end{cases}$

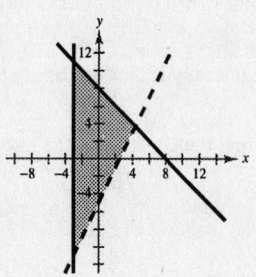

93. $[A \,\vdots\, I] = \begin{bmatrix} -4 & 1 & \vdots & 1 & 0 \\ 8 & -1 & \vdots & 0 & 1 \end{bmatrix}$

$2R_1 + R_2 \rightarrow \begin{bmatrix} -4 & 1 & \vdots & 1 & 0 \\ 0 & 1 & \vdots & 2 & 1 \end{bmatrix}$

$-R_2 + R_1 \rightarrow \begin{bmatrix} -4 & 0 & \vdots & -1 & -1 \\ 0 & 1 & \vdots & 2 & 1 \end{bmatrix}$

$-\tfrac{1}{4}R_1 \rightarrow \begin{bmatrix} 1 & 0 & \vdots & \tfrac{1}{4} & \tfrac{1}{4} \\ 0 & 1 & \vdots & 2 & 1 \end{bmatrix} = [I \,\vdots\, A^{-1}]$

$A^{-1} = \begin{bmatrix} \tfrac{1}{4} & \tfrac{1}{4} \\ 2 & 1 \end{bmatrix}$

95. $[A \,\vdots\, I] = \begin{bmatrix} -7 & 2 & 9 & \vdots & 1 & 0 & 0 \\ 2 & -4 & -6 & \vdots & 0 & 1 & 0 \\ 3 & 5 & 2 & \vdots & 0 & 0 & 1 \end{bmatrix}$

$4R_2 + R_1 \rightarrow \begin{bmatrix} 1 & -14 & -15 & \vdots & 1 & 4 & 0 \\ 2 & -4 & -6 & \vdots & 0 & 1 & 0 \\ 3 & 5 & 2 & \vdots & 0 & 0 & 1 \end{bmatrix}$

$\begin{matrix} -2R_1 + R_2 \rightarrow \\ -3R_1 + R_3 \rightarrow \end{matrix} \begin{bmatrix} 1 & -14 & -15 & \vdots & 1 & 4 & 0 \\ 0 & 24 & 24 & \vdots & -2 & -7 & 0 \\ 0 & 47 & 47 & \vdots & -3 & -12 & 1 \end{bmatrix}$

$-\tfrac{47}{24}R_2 + R_3 \rightarrow \begin{bmatrix} 1 & -14 & -15 & \vdots & 1 & 4 & 0 \\ 0 & 24 & 24 & \vdots & -2 & -7 & 0 \\ 0 & 0 & 0 & \vdots & \tfrac{11}{12} & \tfrac{41}{24} & 1 \end{bmatrix}$

The zeros in Row 3 imply that the inverse does not exist.

97.

$$[A \vdots I] = \begin{bmatrix} -4 & 1 & \vdots & 1 & 0 \\ 8 & -1 & \vdots & 0 & 1 \end{bmatrix}$$

$$2R_1 + R_2 \rightarrow \begin{bmatrix} -4 & 1 & \vdots & 1 & 0 \\ 0 & 1 & \vdots & 2 & 1 \end{bmatrix}$$

$$-R_2 + R_1 \rightarrow \begin{bmatrix} -4 & 0 & \vdots & -1 & -1 \\ 0 & 1 & \vdots & 2 & 1 \end{bmatrix}$$

$$-\tfrac{1}{4}R_1 \rightarrow \begin{bmatrix} 1 & 0 & \vdots & \tfrac{1}{4} & \tfrac{1}{4} \\ 0 & 1 & \vdots & 2 & 1 \end{bmatrix} = [I \vdots A^{-1}]$$

$$A^{-1} = \begin{bmatrix} \tfrac{1}{4} & \tfrac{1}{4} \\ 2 & 1 \end{bmatrix}$$

99.

$$[A \vdots I] = \begin{bmatrix} -7 & 2 & 9 & \vdots & 1 & 0 & 0 \\ 2 & -4 & -6 & \vdots & 0 & 1 & 0 \\ 3 & 5 & 2 & \vdots & 0 & 0 & 1 \end{bmatrix}$$

$$4R_2 + R_1 \rightarrow \begin{bmatrix} 1 & -14 & -15 & \vdots & 1 & 4 & 0 \\ 2 & -4 & -6 & \vdots & 0 & 1 & 0 \\ 3 & 5 & 2 & \vdots & 0 & 0 & 1 \end{bmatrix}$$

$$\begin{matrix} -2R_1 + R_2 \rightarrow \\ -3R_1 + R_3 \rightarrow \end{matrix} \begin{bmatrix} 1 & -14 & -15 & \vdots & 1 & 4 & 0 \\ 0 & 24 & 24 & \vdots & -2 & -7 & 0 \\ 0 & 47 & 47 & \vdots & -3 & -12 & 1 \end{bmatrix}$$

$$-\tfrac{47}{24}R_2 + R_3 \rightarrow \begin{bmatrix} 1 & -14 & -15 & \vdots & 1 & 4 & 0 \\ 0 & 24 & 24 & \vdots & -2 & -7 & 0 \\ 0 & 0 & 0 & \vdots & \tfrac{11}{12} & \tfrac{41}{24} & 1 \end{bmatrix}$$

The zeros in Row 3 imply that the inverse does not exist.

Section 8.5   Applications of Matrices and Determinants

■ You should be able to use Cramer's Rule to solve a system of linear equations.

■ Now you should be able to solve a system of linear equations by substitution, elimination, elementary row operations on an augmented matrix, using the inverse matrix, or Cramer's Rule.

■ You should be able to find the area of a triangle with vertices (x_1, y_1), (x_2, y_2), and (x_3, y_3).

$$\text{Area} = \pm\tfrac{1}{2} \begin{vmatrix} x_1 & y_1 & 1 \\ x_2 & y_2 & 1 \\ x_3 & y_3 & 1 \end{vmatrix}$$

The ± symbol indicates that the appropriate sign should be chosen so that the area is positive.

■ You should be able to test to see if three points, (x_1, y_1), (x_2, y_2), and (x_3, y_3), are collinear.

$$\begin{vmatrix} x_1 & y_1 & 1 \\ x_2 & y_2 & 1 \\ x_3 & y_3 & 1 \end{vmatrix} = 0, \text{ if and only if they are collinear.}$$

■ You should be able to find the equation of the line through (x_1, y_1) and (x_2, y_2) by evaluating.

$$\begin{vmatrix} x & y & 1 \\ x_1 & y_1 & 1 \\ x_2 & y_2 & 1 \end{vmatrix} = 0$$

■ You should be able to encode and decode messages by using an invertible $n \times n$ matrix.

Solutions to Odd-Numbered Exercises

1. $\begin{cases} 3x + 4y = -2 \\ 5x + 3y = 4 \end{cases}$

$x = \dfrac{\begin{vmatrix} -2 & 4 \\ 4 & 3 \end{vmatrix}}{\begin{vmatrix} 3 & 4 \\ 5 & 3 \end{vmatrix}} = \dfrac{-22}{-11} = 2$

$y = \dfrac{\begin{vmatrix} 3 & -2 \\ 5 & 4 \end{vmatrix}}{\begin{vmatrix} 3 & 4 \\ 5 & 3 \end{vmatrix}} = \dfrac{22}{-11} = -2$

Solution: $(2, -2)$

3. $\begin{cases} -0.04 + 0.8y = 1.6 \\ 0.2x + 0.3y = 2.2 \end{cases}$

$x = \dfrac{\begin{vmatrix} 1.6 & 0.8 \\ 2.2 & 0.3 \end{vmatrix}}{\begin{vmatrix} -0.4 & 0.8 \\ 0.2 & 0.3 \end{vmatrix}} = \dfrac{-1.28}{-0.28} = \dfrac{32}{7}$

$y = \dfrac{\begin{vmatrix} -0.4 & 1.6 \\ 0.2 & 2.2 \end{vmatrix}}{\begin{vmatrix} -0.4 & 0.8 \\ 0.2 & 0.3 \end{vmatrix}} = \dfrac{-1.20}{-0.28} = \dfrac{30}{7}$

Solution: $\left(\dfrac{32}{7}, \dfrac{30}{7}\right)$

5. $\begin{cases} 4x - y + z = -5 \\ 2x + 2y + 3z = 10 \\ 5x - 2y + 6z = 1 \end{cases}$ $\quad D = \begin{vmatrix} 4 & -1 & 1 \\ 2 & 2 & 3 \\ 5 & -2 & 6 \end{vmatrix} = 55$

$x = \dfrac{\begin{vmatrix} -5 & -1 & 1 \\ 10 & 2 & 3 \\ 1 & -2 & 6 \end{vmatrix}}{55} = \dfrac{-55}{55} = -1$

$y = \dfrac{\begin{vmatrix} 4 & -5 & 1 \\ 2 & 10 & 3 \\ 5 & 1 & 6 \end{vmatrix}}{55} = \dfrac{165}{55} = 3$

$z = \dfrac{\begin{vmatrix} 4 & -1 & -5 \\ 2 & 2 & 10 \\ 5 & -2 & 1 \end{vmatrix}}{55} = \dfrac{110}{55} = 2$

Solution: $(-1, 3, 2)$

7. $\begin{cases} x + 2y + 3z = -3 \\ -2x + y - z = 6 \\ 3x - 3y + 2z = -11 \end{cases}$ $\quad D = \begin{vmatrix} 1 & 2 & 3 \\ -2 & 1 & -1 \\ 3 & -3 & 2 \end{vmatrix} = 10$

$x = \dfrac{\begin{vmatrix} -3 & 2 & 3 \\ 6 & 1 & -1 \\ -11 & -3 & 2 \end{vmatrix}}{10} = \dfrac{-20}{10} = -2$

$y = \dfrac{\begin{vmatrix} 1 & -3 & 3 \\ -2 & 6 & -1 \\ 3 & -11 & 2 \end{vmatrix}}{10} = \dfrac{10}{10} = 1$

$z = \dfrac{\begin{vmatrix} 1 & 2 & -3 \\ -2 & 1 & 6 \\ 3 & -3 & -11 \end{vmatrix}}{10} = \dfrac{-10}{10} = -1$

Solution: $(-2, 1, -1)$

9. $\begin{cases} 3x + 3y + 5z = 1 \\ 3x + 5y + 9z = 2 \\ 5x + 9y + 17z = 4 \end{cases}$ $\quad D = \begin{vmatrix} 3 & 3 & 5 \\ 3 & 5 & 9 \\ 5 & 9 & 17 \end{vmatrix} = 4$

$x = \dfrac{\begin{vmatrix} 1 & 3 & 5 \\ 2 & 5 & 9 \\ 4 & 9 & 17 \end{vmatrix}}{4} = 0, \quad y = \dfrac{\begin{vmatrix} 3 & 1 & 5 \\ 3 & 2 & 9 \\ 5 & 4 & 17 \end{vmatrix}}{4} = -\dfrac{1}{2}, \quad z = \dfrac{\begin{vmatrix} 3 & 3 & 1 \\ 3 & 5 & 2 \\ 5 & 9 & 4 \end{vmatrix}}{4} = \dfrac{1}{2}$

Solution: $\left(0, -\dfrac{1}{2}, \dfrac{1}{2}\right)$

11. $\begin{cases} 2x + y + 2z = 6 \\ -x + 2y - 3z = 0 \\ 3x + 2y - z = 6 \end{cases}$ $\quad D = \begin{vmatrix} 2 & 1 & 2 \\ -1 & 2 & -3 \\ 3 & 2 & -1 \end{vmatrix} = -18$

$x = \dfrac{\begin{vmatrix} 6 & 1 & 2 \\ 0 & 2 & -3 \\ 6 & 2 & -1 \end{vmatrix}}{-18} = 1, \quad y = \dfrac{\begin{vmatrix} 2 & 6 & 2 \\ -1 & 0 & -3 \\ 3 & 6 & -1 \end{vmatrix}}{-18} = 2, \quad z = \dfrac{\begin{vmatrix} 2 & 1 & 6 \\ -1 & 2 & 0 \\ 3 & 2 & 6 \end{vmatrix}}{-18} = 1$

Solution: $(1, 2, 1)$

13. Vertices: $(0, 0)$, $(3, 1)$, $(1, 5)$

$$\text{Area} = \frac{1}{2}\begin{vmatrix} 0 & 0 & 1 \\ 3 & 1 & 1 \\ 1 & 5 & 1 \end{vmatrix} = \frac{1}{2}\begin{vmatrix} 3 & 1 \\ 1 & 5 \end{vmatrix} = 7 \text{ square units}$$

15. Vertices: $(-2, -3)$, $(2, -3)$, $(0, 4)$

$$\text{Area} = \frac{1}{2}\begin{vmatrix} -2 & -3 & 1 \\ 2 & -3 & 1 \\ 0 & 4 & 1 \end{vmatrix} = \frac{1}{2}\left(-2\begin{vmatrix} -3 & 1 \\ 4 & 1 \end{vmatrix} - 2\begin{vmatrix} -3 & 1 \\ 4 & 1 \end{vmatrix}\right) = \frac{1}{2}(14 + 14) = 14 \text{ square units}$$

17. Vertices: $\left(0, \frac{1}{2}\right)$, $\left(\frac{5}{2}, 0\right)$, $(4, 3)$

$$\text{Area} = \frac{1}{2}\begin{vmatrix} 0 & \frac{1}{2} & 1 \\ \frac{5}{2} & 0 & 1 \\ 4 & 3 & 1 \end{vmatrix} = \frac{1}{2}\left(-\frac{1}{2}\begin{vmatrix} \frac{5}{2} & 1 \\ 4 & 1 \end{vmatrix} + 1\begin{vmatrix} \frac{5}{2} & 0 \\ 4 & 3 \end{vmatrix}\right) = \frac{1}{2}\left(\frac{3}{4} + \frac{15}{2}\right) = \frac{33}{8} \text{ square units}$$

19. Vertices: $(-2, 4)$, $(2, 3)$, $(-1, 5)$

$$\text{Area} = \frac{1}{2}\begin{vmatrix} -2 & 4 & 1 \\ 2 & 3 & 1 \\ -1 & 5 & 1 \end{vmatrix} = \frac{1}{2}\left[\begin{vmatrix} 2 & 3 \\ -1 & 5 \end{vmatrix} - \begin{vmatrix} -2 & 4 \\ -1 & 5 \end{vmatrix} + \begin{vmatrix} -2 & 4 \\ 2 & 3 \end{vmatrix}\right] = \frac{1}{2}(13 + 6 - 14) = \frac{5}{2} \text{ square units}$$

21. Vertices: $(-3, 5)$, $(2, 6)$, $(3, -5)$

$$\text{Area} = -\frac{1}{2}\begin{vmatrix} -3 & 5 & 1 \\ 2 & 6 & 1 \\ 3 & -5 & 1 \end{vmatrix} = -\frac{1}{2}\left[\begin{vmatrix} 2 & 6 \\ 3 & -5 \end{vmatrix} - \begin{vmatrix} -3 & 5 \\ 3 & -5 \end{vmatrix} + \begin{vmatrix} -3 & 5 \\ 2 & 6 \end{vmatrix}\right] = -\frac{1}{2}(-28 + 0 - 28) = 28 \text{ square units}$$

23. $4 = \pm\dfrac{1}{2}\begin{vmatrix} -5 & 1 & 1 \\ 0 & 2 & 1 \\ -2 & x & 1 \end{vmatrix}$

$\pm 8 = -5\begin{vmatrix} 2 & 1 \\ x & 1 \end{vmatrix} - 2\begin{vmatrix} 1 & 1 \\ 2 & 1 \end{vmatrix}$

$\pm 8 = -5(2 - x) - 2(-1)$

$\pm 8 = 5x - 8$

$x = \dfrac{8 \pm 8}{5}$

$x = \dfrac{16}{5}$ or $x = 0$

25. $6 = \pm\dfrac{1}{2}\begin{vmatrix} -2 & -3 & 1 \\ 1 & -1 & 1 \\ -8 & x & 1 \end{vmatrix}$

$\pm 12 = \begin{vmatrix} 1 & -1 \\ -8 & x \end{vmatrix} - \begin{vmatrix} -2 & -3 \\ -8 & x \end{vmatrix} + \begin{vmatrix} -2 & -3 \\ 1 & -1 \end{vmatrix}$

$\pm 12 = (x - 8) - (-2x - 24) + 5$

$\pm 12 = 3x + 21$

$x = \dfrac{-21 \pm 12}{3} = -7 \pm 4$

$x = -3$ or $x = -11$

27. Vertices: $(0, 25)$, $(10, 0)$, $(28, 5)$

$$\text{Area} = \frac{1}{2}\begin{vmatrix} 0 & 25 & 1 \\ 10 & 0 & 1 \\ 28 & 5 & 1 \end{vmatrix} = 250 \text{ square miles}$$

29. Points: $(3, -1)$, $(0, -3)$, $(12, 5)$

$$\begin{vmatrix} 3 & -1 & 1 \\ 0 & -3 & 1 \\ 12 & 5 & 1 \end{vmatrix} = 3\begin{vmatrix} -3 & 1 \\ 5 & 1 \end{vmatrix} + 12\begin{vmatrix} -1 & 1 \\ -3 & 1 \end{vmatrix} = 3(-8) + 12(2) = 0$$

The points are collinear.

31. Points: $\left(2, -\frac{1}{2}\right)$, $(-4, 4)$, $(6, -3)$

$$\begin{vmatrix} 2 & -\frac{1}{2} & 1 \\ -4 & 4 & 1 \\ 6 & -3 & 1 \end{vmatrix} = \begin{vmatrix} -4 & 4 \\ 6 & -3 \end{vmatrix} - \begin{vmatrix} 2 & -\frac{1}{2} \\ 6 & -3 \end{vmatrix} + \begin{vmatrix} 2 & -\frac{1}{2} \\ -4 & 4 \end{vmatrix} = -12 + 3 + 6 = -3 \neq 0$$

The points are not collinear.

33. Points: $(0, 2)$, $(1, 2.4)$, $(-1, 1.6)$

$$\begin{vmatrix} 0 & 2 & 1 \\ 1 & 2.4 & 1 \\ -1 & 1.6 & 1 \end{vmatrix} = -2\begin{vmatrix} 1 & 1 \\ -1 & 1 \end{vmatrix} + \begin{vmatrix} 1 & 2.4 \\ -1 & 1.6 \end{vmatrix} = -2(2) + 4 = 0$$

The points are collinear.

35.

$$\begin{vmatrix} 2 & -5 & 1 \\ 4 & x & 1 \\ 5 & -2 & 1 \end{vmatrix} = 0$$

$$2\begin{vmatrix} x & 1 \\ -2 & 1 \end{vmatrix} + 5\begin{vmatrix} 4 & 1 \\ 5 & 1 \end{vmatrix} + \begin{vmatrix} 4 & x \\ 5 & -2 \end{vmatrix} = 0$$

$$2(x + 2) + 5(-1) + (-8 - 5x) = 0$$

$$-3x - 9 = 0$$

$$x = -3$$

37. Points: $(0, 0)$, $(5, 3)$

Equation: $\begin{vmatrix} x & y & 1 \\ 0 & 0 & 1 \\ 5 & 3 & 1 \end{vmatrix} = -\begin{vmatrix} x & y \\ 5 & 3 \end{vmatrix} = 5y - 3x = 0 \Rightarrow 3x - 5y = 0$

39. Points: $(-4, 3)$, $(2, 1)$

Equation: $\begin{vmatrix} x & y & 1 \\ -4 & 3 & 1 \\ 2 & 1 & 1 \end{vmatrix} = x\begin{vmatrix} 3 & 1 \\ 1 & 1 \end{vmatrix} - y\begin{vmatrix} -4 & 1 \\ 2 & 1 \end{vmatrix} + \begin{vmatrix} -4 & 3 \\ 2 & 1 \end{vmatrix} = 2x + 6y - 10 = 0 \Rightarrow x + 3y - 5 = 0$

41. Points: $\left(-\frac{1}{2}, 3\right)$, $\left(\frac{5}{2}, 1\right)$

Equation: $\begin{vmatrix} x & y & 1 \\ -\frac{1}{2} & 3 & 1 \\ \frac{5}{2} & 1 & 1 \end{vmatrix} = x\begin{vmatrix} 3 & 1 \\ 1 & 1 \end{vmatrix} - y\begin{vmatrix} -\frac{1}{2} & 1 \\ \frac{5}{2} & 1 \end{vmatrix} + \begin{vmatrix} -\frac{1}{2} & 3 \\ \frac{5}{2} & 1 \end{vmatrix} = 2x + 3y - 8 = 0$

43. The uncoded row matrices are the rows of the 7×3 matrix on the left.

$$
\begin{array}{cccc}
T & R & O \\
U & B & L \\
E & & I \\
N & & R \\
I & V & E \\
R & & C \\
I & T & Y
\end{array}
\begin{bmatrix}
20 & 18 & 15 \\
21 & 2 & 12 \\
5 & 0 & 9 \\
14 & 0 & 18 \\
9 & 22 & 5 \\
18 & 0 & 3 \\
9 & 20 & 25
\end{bmatrix}
\begin{bmatrix}
1 & -1 & 0 \\
1 & 0 & -1 \\
-6 & 2 & 3
\end{bmatrix}
=
\begin{bmatrix}
-52 & 10 & 27 \\
-49 & 3 & 34 \\
-49 & 13 & 27 \\
-94 & 22 & 54 \\
1 & 1 & -7 \\
0 & -12 & 9 \\
-121 & 41 & 55
\end{bmatrix}
$$

Solution: $[-52 \; 10 \; 27], [-49 \; 3 \; 34], [-49 \; 13 \; 27], [-94 \; 22 \; 54], [11 \; -7], [0 \; -12 \; 9], [-121 \; 41 \; 55]$

In Exercises 45–47, use the matrix $A = \begin{bmatrix} 1 & 2 & 2 \\ 3 & 7 & 9 \\ -1 & -4 & -7 \end{bmatrix}$.

45. C A L L _ A T _ N O O N

$[3 \quad 1 \quad 12] [12 \quad 0 \quad 1] [20 \quad 0 \quad 14] [15 \quad 15 \quad 14]$

$[3 \quad 1 \quad 12] A = [-6 \; -35 \; -69]$

$[12 \quad 0 \quad 1] A = [11 \quad 20 \quad 17]$

$[20 \quad 0 \quad 14] A = [6 \; -16 \; -58]$

$[15 \quad 15 \quad 14] A = [46 \quad 79 \quad 67]$

Cryptogram: $-6 \; -35 \; -69 \; 11 \; 20 \; 17 \; 6 \; -16 \; -58 \; 46 \; 79 \; 67$

47. H A P P Y _ B I R T H D A Y _

$[8 \quad 1 \quad 16] [16 \quad 25 \quad 0] [2 \quad 9 \quad 18] [20 \quad 8 \quad 4] [1 \quad 25 \quad 0]$

$[8 \quad 1 \quad 16] A = [5 \; -41 \; -87]$

$[16 \quad 25 \quad 0] A = [91 \quad 207 \quad 257]$

$[2 \quad 9 \quad 18] A = [11 \; -5 \; -41]$

$[20 \quad 8 \quad 4] A = [40 \quad 80 \quad 84]$

$[1 \quad 25 \quad 0] A = [76 \quad 177 \quad 227]$

Cryptogram: $-5 \; -41 \; -87 \; 91 \; 207 \; 257 \; 11 \; -5 \; -41 \; 40 \; 80 \; 84 \; 76 \; 177 \; 227$

49. $A^{-1} = \begin{bmatrix} 1 & 2 \\ 3 & 5 \end{bmatrix}^{-1} = \begin{bmatrix} -5 & 2 \\ 3 & -1 \end{bmatrix}$

$$
\begin{bmatrix}
11 & 21 \\
64 & 112 \\
25 & 50 \\
29 & 53 \\
23 & 46 \\
40 & 75 \\
55 & 92
\end{bmatrix}
\begin{bmatrix}
-5 & 2 \\
3 & -1
\end{bmatrix}
=
\begin{bmatrix}
8 & 1 \\
16 & 16 \\
25 & 0 \\
14 & 5 \\
23 & 0 \\
25 & 5 \\
1 & 18
\end{bmatrix}
\begin{array}{cc}
H & A \\
P & P \\
Y & \\
N & E \\
W & \\
Y & E \\
A & R
\end{array}
$$

Message: HAPPY NEW YEAR

51. $A^{-1} = \begin{bmatrix} 1 & -1 & 0 \\ 1 & 0 & -1 \\ -6 & 2 & 3 \end{bmatrix}^{-1} = \begin{bmatrix} -2 & -3 & -1 \\ -3 & -3 & -1 \\ -2 & -4 & -1 \end{bmatrix}$

$\begin{bmatrix} 9 & -1 & -9 \\ 38 & -19 & -19 \\ 28 & -9 & -19 \\ -80 & 25 & 41 \\ -64 & 21 & 31 \\ 9 & -5 & -4 \end{bmatrix} \begin{bmatrix} -2 & -3 & -1 \\ -3 & -3 & -1 \\ -2 & -4 & -1 \end{bmatrix} = \begin{bmatrix} 3 & 12 & 1 \\ 19 & 19 & 0 \\ 9 & 19 & 0 \\ 3 & 1 & 14 \\ 3 & 5 & 12 \\ 5 & 4 & 0 \end{bmatrix} \begin{matrix} C & L & A \\ S & S & \\ I & S & \\ C & A & N \\ C & E & L \\ E & D & \end{matrix}$ Message: CLASS IS CANCELED

53. $A^{-1} = \begin{bmatrix} 1 & 2 & 2 \\ 3 & 7 & 9 \\ -1 & -4 & -7 \end{bmatrix}^{-1} = \begin{bmatrix} -13 & 6 & 4 \\ 12 & -5 & -3 \\ -5 & 2 & 1 \end{bmatrix}$

$\begin{bmatrix} 20 & 17 & -15 \\ -12 & -56 & -104 \\ 1 & -25 & -65 \\ 62 & 143 & 181 \end{bmatrix} \begin{bmatrix} -13 & 6 & 4 \\ 12 & -5 & -3 \\ -5 & 2 & 1 \end{bmatrix} = \begin{bmatrix} 19 & 5 & 14 \\ 4 & 0 & 16 \\ 12 & 1 & 14 \\ 5 & 19 & 0 \end{bmatrix} \begin{matrix} S & E & N \\ D & & P \\ L & A & N \\ E & S & \end{matrix}$ Message: SEND PLANES

55. Let A be the 2×2 matrix needed to decode the message.

$\begin{bmatrix} -18 & -18 \\ 1 & 16 \end{bmatrix} A = \begin{bmatrix} 0 & 18 \\ 15 & 14 \end{bmatrix} \begin{matrix} R \\ O & N \end{matrix}$

$A = \begin{bmatrix} -18 & -18 \\ 1 & 16 \end{bmatrix}^{-1} \begin{bmatrix} 0 & 18 \\ 15 & 14 \end{bmatrix} = \begin{bmatrix} -\frac{8}{135} & -\frac{1}{15} \\ \frac{1}{270} & \frac{1}{15} \end{bmatrix} \begin{bmatrix} 0 & 18 \\ 15 & 14 \end{bmatrix} = \begin{bmatrix} -1 & -2 \\ 1 & 1 \end{bmatrix}$

$\begin{bmatrix} 8 & 21 \\ -15 & -10 \\ -13 & -13 \\ 5 & 10 \\ 5 & 25 \\ 5 & 19 \\ -1 & 6 \\ 20 & 40 \\ -18 & -18 \\ 1 & 16 \end{bmatrix} \begin{bmatrix} -1 & -2 \\ 1 & 1 \end{bmatrix} = \begin{bmatrix} 13 & 5 \\ 5 & 20 \\ 0 & 13 \\ 5 & 0 \\ 20 & 15 \\ 14 & 9 \\ 7 & 8 \\ 20 & 0 \\ 0 & 18 \\ 15 & 14 \end{bmatrix} \begin{matrix} M & E \\ E & T \\ & M \\ E & \\ T & O \\ N & I \\ G & H \\ T & \\ & R \\ O & N \end{matrix}$ Message: MEET ME TONIGHT RON

57. True. If the determinant of the coefficient matrix is zero, the solution of the system would result in division by zero which is undefined.

59. Answers will vary. To solve a system of linear equations you can use graphing, substitution, elimination, elementary row operations on an augmented matrix (Gaussian elimination with back–substitution or Gauss–Jordan elimination), the inverse of a matrix, or Cramer's Rule.

61. $\begin{cases} 3x + 8y = 11 & \text{Eq. 1} \\ -2x + 12y = -16 & \text{Eq. 2} \end{cases}$

$\begin{cases} 9x + 24y = 33 & 3 \text{ Eq. 1} \\ \underline{4x - 24y = 32} & -2 \text{ Eq. 2} \\ 13x \qquad = 65 & \text{Add the equations.} \\ \qquad x = \frac{65}{13} = 5 \end{cases}$

$3(5) + 8y = 11 \implies 8y = -4 \implies y = -\frac{1}{2}$

Solution: $\left(5, -\frac{1}{2}\right)$

63. $\begin{cases} 5x - y - z = 7 \\ -2x + 3y + z = -5 \\ 4x + 10y - 5z = -37 \end{cases}$

$A^{-1} = \begin{bmatrix} 5 & -1 & -1 \\ -2 & 3 & 1 \\ 4 & 10 & -5 \end{bmatrix}^{-1} = \begin{bmatrix} \frac{25}{87} & \frac{5}{29} & -\frac{2}{87} \\ \frac{2}{29} & \frac{7}{29} & \frac{1}{29} \\ \frac{32}{87} & \frac{18}{29} & -\frac{13}{87} \end{bmatrix}$

$\begin{bmatrix} x \\ y \\ z \end{bmatrix} = A^{-1} \begin{bmatrix} 7 \\ -5 \\ -37 \end{bmatrix} = \begin{bmatrix} 2 \\ -2 \\ 5 \end{bmatrix}$

Solution: $(2, -2, 5)$

65. Objective function: $z = 6x + 7y$

Constraints:
$$x \geq 0$$
$$y \geq 0$$
$$4x + 3y \geq 24$$
$$x + 3y \geq 15$$

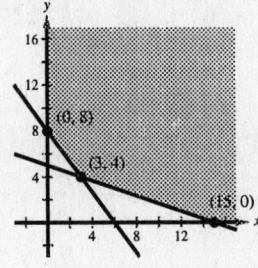

Since the region is unbounded, there is no maximum value of the objective function. To find the minimum value, check the vertices.

At $(0, 8)$: $z = 6(0) + 7(8) = 56$

At $(3, 4)$: $z = 6(3) + 7(4) = 46$

At $(15, 0)$: $z = 6(15) + 7(0) = 90$

The minimum value of 46 occurs at $(3, 4)$.

67. $\begin{vmatrix} 2.4 & -4.7 \\ -1.4 & -3 \end{vmatrix} = 2.4(-3) - (-4.7)(-1.4) = -13.78$

69. $\begin{vmatrix} 1 & 4 & -3 \\ 7 & -1 & 2 \\ 6 & 0 & -5 \end{vmatrix} = 6\begin{vmatrix} 4 & -3 \\ -1 & 2 \end{vmatrix} + 5\begin{vmatrix} 1 & 4 \\ 7 & -1 \end{vmatrix}$

$= 6(8 - 3) + 5(-1 - 28)$

$= -115$

Review Exercises for Chapter 8

1. $\begin{bmatrix} -4 \\ 0 \\ 5 \end{bmatrix}$

Order: 3×1

3. $[3]$

Order: 1×1

5. $\begin{cases} 3x - 10y = 15 \\ 5x + 4y = 22 \end{cases}$

$\begin{bmatrix} 3 & -10 & \vdots & 15 \\ 5 & 4 & \vdots & 22 \end{bmatrix}$

7. $\begin{bmatrix} 5 & 1 & 7 & \vdots & -9 \\ 4 & 2 & 0 & \vdots & 10 \\ 9 & 4 & 2 & \vdots & 3 \end{bmatrix}$ $\begin{cases} 5x + y + 7z = -9 \\ 4x + 2y = 10 \\ 9x + 4y + 2z = 3 \end{cases}$

9.

$\begin{bmatrix} 0 & 1 & 1 \\ 1 & 2 & 3 \\ 2 & 2 & 2 \end{bmatrix}$

$\begin{matrix} R_1 \\ R_2 \end{matrix} \begin{bmatrix} 1 & 2 & 3 \\ 0 & 1 & 1 \\ 2 & 2 & 2 \end{bmatrix}$

$-2R_1 + R_3 \rightarrow \begin{bmatrix} 1 & 2 & 3 \\ 0 & 1 & 1 \\ 0 & -2 & -6 \end{bmatrix}$

$\begin{matrix} -2R_2 + R_1 \rightarrow \\ \\ 2R_2 + R_3 \rightarrow \end{matrix} \begin{bmatrix} 1 & 0 & 1 \\ 0 & 1 & 1 \\ 0 & 0 & -4 \end{bmatrix}$

$-\tfrac{1}{4}R_3 \rightarrow \begin{bmatrix} 1 & 0 & 1 \\ 0 & 1 & 1 \\ 0 & 0 & 1 \end{bmatrix}$

$\begin{matrix} -R_3 + R_1 \rightarrow \\ -R_3 + R_2 \rightarrow \end{matrix} \begin{bmatrix} 1 & 0 & 0 \\ 0 & 1 & 0 \\ 0 & 0 & 1 \end{bmatrix}$

11. $\begin{bmatrix} 1 & 2 & 3 & \vdots & 9 \\ 0 & 1 & -2 & \vdots & 2 \\ 0 & 0 & 0 & \vdots & 0 \end{bmatrix}$

Consistent

Infinitely many solutions

13. $\begin{bmatrix} 1 & 2 & 3 & \vdots & 9 \\ 0 & 1 & -2 & \vdots & 2 \\ 0 & 0 & 1 & \vdots & -3 \end{bmatrix}$

Consistent

One solution

15. $\begin{bmatrix} 5 & 4 & \vdots & 2 \\ -1 & 1 & \vdots & -22 \end{bmatrix}$

$4R_2 + R_1 \rightarrow \begin{bmatrix} 1 & 8 & \vdots & -86 \\ -1 & 1 & \vdots & -22 \end{bmatrix}$

$R_1 + R_2 \rightarrow \begin{bmatrix} 1 & 8 & \vdots & -86 \\ 0 & 9 & \vdots & -108 \end{bmatrix}$

$\tfrac{1}{9}R_2 \rightarrow \begin{bmatrix} 1 & 8 & \vdots & -86 \\ 0 & 1 & \vdots & -12 \end{bmatrix}$

$\begin{cases} x + 8y = -86 \\ y = -12 \end{cases}$

$y = -12$

$x + 8(-12) = -86 \Longrightarrow x = 10$

Solution: $(10, -12)$

17. $\begin{bmatrix} 0.3 & -0.1 & \vdots & -0.13 \\ 0.2 & -0.3 & \vdots & -0.25 \end{bmatrix}$

$\begin{matrix} 10R_1 \rightarrow \\ 10R_2 \rightarrow \end{matrix} \begin{bmatrix} 3 & -1 & \vdots & -1.3 \\ 2 & -3 & \vdots & -2.5 \end{bmatrix}$

$-R_2 + R_1 \rightarrow \begin{bmatrix} 1 & 2 & \vdots & 1.2 \\ 2 & -3 & \vdots & -2.5 \end{bmatrix}$

$-2R_1 + R_2 \rightarrow \begin{bmatrix} 1 & 2 & \vdots & 1.2 \\ 0 & -7 & \vdots & -4.9 \end{bmatrix}$

$-\tfrac{1}{7}R_2 \rightarrow \begin{bmatrix} 1 & 2 & \vdots & 1.2 \\ 0 & 1 & \vdots & 0.7 \end{bmatrix}$

$\begin{cases} x + 2y = 1.2 \\ y = 0.7 \end{cases}$

$y = 0.7$

$x + 2(0.7) = 1.2 \Longrightarrow x = -0.2$

Solution: $(-0.2, 0.7)$

19.
$$\begin{bmatrix} 2 & 3 & 1 & \vdots & 10 \\ 2 & -3 & -3 & \vdots & 22 \\ 4 & -2 & 3 & \vdots & -2 \end{bmatrix}$$

$$\begin{matrix} -R_1 + R_2 \to \\ -2R_1 + R_3 \to \end{matrix} \begin{bmatrix} 2 & 3 & 1 & \vdots & 10 \\ 0 & -6 & -4 & \vdots & 12 \\ 0 & -8 & 1 & \vdots & -22 \end{bmatrix}$$

$$\begin{matrix} \frac{1}{2}R_1 \to \\ -\frac{1}{6}R_2 \to \\ \end{matrix} \begin{bmatrix} 1 & \frac{3}{2} & \frac{1}{2} & \vdots & 5 \\ 0 & 1 & \frac{2}{3} & \vdots & -2 \\ 0 & -8 & 1 & \vdots & -22 \end{bmatrix}$$

$$\begin{matrix} \\ \\ 8R_2 + R_3 \end{matrix} \begin{bmatrix} 1 & \frac{3}{2} & \frac{1}{2} & \vdots & 5 \\ 0 & 1 & \frac{2}{3} & \vdots & -2 \\ 0 & 0 & \frac{19}{3} & \vdots & -38 \end{bmatrix}$$

$$\begin{matrix} \\ \\ \frac{3}{19}R_3 \to \end{matrix} \begin{bmatrix} 1 & \frac{3}{2} & \frac{1}{2} & \vdots & 5 \\ 0 & 1 & \frac{2}{3} & \vdots & -2 \\ 0 & 0 & 1 & \vdots & -6 \end{bmatrix}$$

$z = -6$

$y + \frac{2}{3}(-6) = -2 \Longrightarrow y = 2$

$x + \frac{3}{2}(2) + \frac{1}{2}(-6) = 5 \Longrightarrow x = 5$

Solution: $(5, 2, -6)$

21.
$$\begin{bmatrix} 2 & 1 & 2 & \vdots & 4 \\ 2 & 2 & 0 & \vdots & 5 \\ 2 & -1 & 6 & \vdots & 2 \end{bmatrix}$$

$$\begin{matrix} -R_1 + R_2 \to \\ -R_1 + R_3 \to \end{matrix} \begin{bmatrix} 2 & 1 & 2 & \vdots & 4 \\ 0 & 1 & -2 & \vdots & 1 \\ 0 & -2 & 4 & \vdots & -2 \end{bmatrix}$$

$$\begin{matrix} -R_2 + R_1 \to \\ \\ 2R_2 + R_3 \to \end{matrix} \begin{bmatrix} 2 & 0 & 4 & \vdots & 3 \\ 0 & 1 & -2 & \vdots & 1 \\ 0 & 0 & 0 & \vdots & 0 \end{bmatrix}$$

$$\begin{matrix} \frac{1}{2}R_1 \to \\ \\ \end{matrix} \begin{bmatrix} 1 & 0 & 2 & \vdots & \frac{3}{2} \\ 0 & 1 & -2 & \vdots & 1 \\ 0 & 0 & 0 & \vdots & 0 \end{bmatrix}$$

Let $z = a$, then:

$y - 2a = 1 \implies y = 2a + 1$

$x + 2a = \frac{3}{2} \implies x = -2a + \frac{3}{2}$

Solution: $\left(-2a + \frac{3}{2}, 2a + 1, a\right)$

23.
$$\begin{bmatrix} 2 & 1 & 1 & 0 & \vdots & 6 \\ 0 & -2 & 3 & -1 & \vdots & 9 \\ 3 & 3 & -2 & -2 & \vdots & -11 \\ 1 & 0 & 1 & 3 & \vdots & 14 \end{bmatrix}$$

$$-R_4 + R_1 \begin{bmatrix} 1 & 1 & 0 & -3 & \vdots & -8 \\ 0 & -2 & 3 & -1 & \vdots & 9 \\ 3 & 3 & -2 & -2 & \vdots & -11 \\ 1 & 0 & 1 & 3 & \vdots & 14 \end{bmatrix}$$

$$\begin{matrix} \\ \\ -3R_1 + R_3 \to \\ -R_1 + R_4 \to \end{matrix} \begin{bmatrix} 1 & 1 & 0 & -3 & \vdots & -8 \\ 0 & -2 & 3 & -1 & \vdots & 9 \\ 0 & 0 & -2 & 7 & \vdots & 13 \\ 0 & -1 & 1 & 6 & \vdots & 22 \end{bmatrix}$$

$$\begin{matrix} \\ -3R_4 + R_2 \to \\ \\ \end{matrix} \begin{bmatrix} 1 & 1 & 0 & -3 & \vdots & -8 \\ 0 & 1 & 0 & -19 & \vdots & -57 \\ 0 & 0 & -2 & 7 & \vdots & 13 \\ 0 & -1 & 1 & 6 & \vdots & 22 \end{bmatrix}$$

$$\begin{matrix} \\ \\ \\ R_2 + R_4 \to \end{matrix} \begin{bmatrix} 1 & 1 & 0 & -3 & \vdots & -8 \\ 0 & 1 & 0 & -19 & \vdots & -57 \\ 0 & 0 & -2 & 7 & \vdots & 13 \\ 0 & 0 & 1 & -13 & \vdots & -35 \end{bmatrix}$$

$$\begin{matrix} \\ \\ R_4 \\ R_3 \end{matrix} \begin{bmatrix} 1 & 1 & 0 & -3 & \vdots & -8 \\ 0 & 1 & 0 & -19 & \vdots & -57 \\ 0 & 0 & 1 & -13 & \vdots & -35 \\ 0 & 0 & -2 & 7 & \vdots & 13 \end{bmatrix}$$

— CONTINUED —

23. — CONTINUED —

$$2R_3+R_4\rightarrow \begin{bmatrix} 1 & 1 & 0 & -3 & \vdots & -8 \\ 0 & 1 & 0 & -19 & \vdots & -57 \\ 0 & 0 & 1 & -13 & \vdots & -35 \\ 0 & 0 & 0 & -19 & \vdots & -57 \end{bmatrix}$$

$$\tfrac{1}{19}R_4\rightarrow \begin{bmatrix} 1 & 1 & 0 & -3 & \vdots & -8 \\ 0 & 1 & 0 & -19 & \vdots & -57 \\ 0 & 0 & 1 & -13 & \vdots & -35 \\ 0 & 0 & 0 & 1 & \vdots & 3 \end{bmatrix}$$

$w = 3$

$z - 13(3) = -35 \Rightarrow z = 4$

$y - 19(3) = -57 \Rightarrow y = 0$

$x + 0 - 3(3) = -8 \Rightarrow x = 1$

Solution: $(1, 0, 4, 3)$

25. $x + 9 = A(x + 2)^2 + B(x + 1)(x + 2) + C(x + 1)$

$x + 9 = A(x^2 + 4x + 4) + B(x^2 + 3x + 2) + Cx + C$

$x + 9 = Ax^2 + 4Ax + 4A + Bx^2 + 3Bx + 2B + Cx + C$

$x + 9 = (A + B)x^2 + (4A + 3B + C)x + 4A + 2B + C$

Equating coefficients of corresponding terms:

$$\begin{cases} 0 = A + B \\ 1 = 4A + 3B + C \\ 9 = 4A + 2B + C \end{cases}$$

$$\begin{bmatrix} 1 & 1 & 0 & \vdots & 0 \\ 4 & 3 & 1 & \vdots & 1 \\ 4 & 2 & 1 & \vdots & 9 \end{bmatrix}$$

$$\begin{matrix} -4R_1 + R_2\rightarrow \\ -4R_1 + R_3\rightarrow \end{matrix} \begin{bmatrix} 1 & 1 & 0 & \vdots & 0 \\ 0 & -1 & 1 & \vdots & 1 \\ 0 & -2 & 1 & \vdots & 9 \end{bmatrix}$$

$$\begin{matrix} -R_2\rightarrow \\ -2R_2 + R_3\rightarrow \end{matrix} \begin{bmatrix} 1 & 1 & 0 & \vdots & 0 \\ 0 & 1 & -1 & \vdots & -1 \\ 0 & 0 & -1 & \vdots & 7 \end{bmatrix}$$

$$-R_3\rightarrow \begin{bmatrix} 1 & 1 & 0 & \vdots & 0 \\ 0 & 1 & -1 & \vdots & -1 \\ 0 & 0 & 1 & \vdots & -7 \end{bmatrix}$$

$C = 7$

$B - (-7) = -1 \Rightarrow B = -8$

$A - 8 = 0 \Rightarrow A = 8$

$$\frac{x + 9}{(x + 1)(x + 2)^2} = \frac{8}{x + 1} - \frac{8}{x + 2} - \frac{7}{(x + 2)^2}$$

27.
$$\begin{bmatrix} -1 & 1 & 2 & \vdots & 1 \\ 2 & 3 & 1 & \vdots & -2 \\ 5 & 4 & 2 & \vdots & 4 \end{bmatrix}$$

$$-R_1\rightarrow \begin{bmatrix} 1 & -1 & -2 & \vdots & -1 \\ 2 & 3 & 1 & \vdots & -2 \\ 5 & 4 & 2 & \vdots & 4 \end{bmatrix}$$

$$\begin{matrix} -2R_1 + R_2\rightarrow \\ -5R_1 + R_3\rightarrow \end{matrix} \begin{bmatrix} 1 & -1 & -2 & \vdots & -1 \\ 0 & 5 & 5 & \vdots & 0 \\ 0 & 9 & 12 & \vdots & 9 \end{bmatrix}$$

$$\tfrac{1}{5}R_2\rightarrow \begin{bmatrix} 1 & -1 & 2 & \vdots & -1 \\ 0 & 1 & 1 & \vdots & 0 \\ 0 & 9 & 12 & \vdots & 9 \end{bmatrix}$$

$$\begin{matrix} R_2 + R_1\rightarrow \\ \\ -9R_2 + R_3\rightarrow \end{matrix} \begin{bmatrix} 1 & 0 & -1 & \vdots & -1 \\ 0 & 1 & 1 & \vdots & 0 \\ 0 & 0 & 3 & \vdots & 9 \end{bmatrix}$$

$$\tfrac{1}{3}R_3\rightarrow \begin{bmatrix} 1 & 0 & -1 & \vdots & -1 \\ 0 & 1 & 1 & \vdots & 0 \\ 0 & 0 & 1 & \vdots & 3 \end{bmatrix}$$

$$\begin{matrix} R_3 + R_1\rightarrow \\ -R_3 + R_2\rightarrow \end{matrix} \begin{bmatrix} 1 & 0 & 0 & \vdots & 2 \\ 0 & 1 & 0 & \vdots & -3 \\ 0 & 0 & 1 & \vdots & 3 \end{bmatrix}$$

$x = 2, y = -3, z = 3$

Solution: $(2, -3, 3)$

29.
$$\begin{bmatrix} 2 & -1 & 9 & \vdots & -8 \\ -1 & -3 & 4 & \vdots & -15 \\ 5 & 2 & -1 & \vdots & 17 \end{bmatrix}$$

$$R_2 + R_1 \rightarrow \begin{bmatrix} 1 & -4 & 13 & \vdots & -23 \\ -1 & -3 & 4 & \vdots & -15 \\ 5 & 2 & -1 & \vdots & 17 \end{bmatrix}$$

$$\begin{matrix} R_1 + R_2 \rightarrow \\ -5R_1 + R_3 \rightarrow \end{matrix} \begin{bmatrix} 1 & -4 & 13 & \vdots & -23 \\ 0 & -7 & 17 & \vdots & -38 \\ 0 & 22 & -66 & \vdots & 132 \end{bmatrix}$$

$$\begin{matrix} R_3 \\ R_2 \end{matrix} \begin{bmatrix} 1 & -4 & 13 & \vdots & -23 \\ 0 & 22 & -66 & \vdots & 132 \\ 0 & -7 & 17 & \vdots & 38 \end{bmatrix}$$

$$\tfrac{1}{22}R_2 \rightarrow \begin{bmatrix} 1 & -4 & 13 & \vdots & -23 \\ 0 & 1 & -3 & \vdots & 6 \\ 0 & -7 & 17 & \vdots & -38 \end{bmatrix}$$

$$7R_2 + R_3 \rightarrow \begin{bmatrix} 1 & -4 & 13 & \vdots & -23 \\ 0 & 1 & -3 & \vdots & 6 \\ 0 & 0 & -4 & \vdots & 4 \end{bmatrix}$$

$$-\tfrac{1}{4}R_3 \begin{bmatrix} 1 & -4 & 13 & \vdots & -23 \\ 0 & 1 & -3 & \vdots & 6 \\ 0 & 0 & 1 & \vdots & -1 \end{bmatrix}$$

$$4R_2 + R_1 \rightarrow \begin{bmatrix} 1 & 0 & 1 & \vdots & 1 \\ 0 & 1 & -3 & \vdots & 6 \\ 0 & 0 & 1 & \vdots & -1 \end{bmatrix}$$

$$\begin{matrix} -R_3 + R_1 \rightarrow \\ 3R_3 + R_2 \rightarrow \end{matrix} \begin{bmatrix} 1 & 0 & 0 & \vdots & 2 \\ 0 & 1 & 0 & \vdots & 3 \\ 0 & 0 & 1 & \vdots & -1 \end{bmatrix}$$

$x = 2, y = 3, z = -1$

Solution: $(2, 3, -1)$

31. Use the reduced row–echelon form feature of a graphing utility.

$$\begin{bmatrix} 3 & -1 & 5 & -2 & \vdots & -44 \\ 1 & 6 & 4 & -1 & \vdots & 1 \\ 5 & -1 & 1 & 3 & \vdots & -15 \\ 0 & 4 & -1 & -8 & \vdots & 58 \end{bmatrix} \Rightarrow \begin{bmatrix} 1 & 0 & 0 & 0 & \vdots & 2 \\ 0 & 1 & 0 & 0 & \vdots & 6 \\ 0 & 0 & 1 & 0 & \vdots & -10 \\ 0 & 0 & 0 & 1 & \vdots & -3 \end{bmatrix}$$

$x = 2, y = 6, z = -10, w = -3$

Solution: $(2, 6, -10, -3)$

33. $\begin{bmatrix} -1 & x \\ y & 9 \end{bmatrix} = \begin{bmatrix} -1 & 12 \\ -7 & 9 \end{bmatrix} \Rightarrow x = 12$ and $y = -7$

35. $\begin{bmatrix} x+3 & 4 & -4y \\ 0 & -3 & 2 \\ -2 & y+5 & 6x \end{bmatrix} = \begin{bmatrix} 5x-1 & 4 & -44 \\ 0 & -3 & 2 \\ -2 & 16 & 6 \end{bmatrix}$

$\left.\begin{matrix} x+3 = 5x-1 \\ -4y = -44 \\ y+5 = 16 \\ 6x = 6 \end{matrix}\right\} x = 1$ and $y = 11$

37. Since A and B are both of order 2×2, $A + 3B$ can be performed.

39. Since A and B are not of the same order, $A + 3B$ cannot be performed.

41. $\begin{bmatrix} 7 & 3 \\ -1 & 5 \end{bmatrix} + \begin{bmatrix} 10 & -20 \\ 14 & -3 \end{bmatrix} = \begin{bmatrix} 7+10 & 3-20 \\ -1+14 & 5-3 \end{bmatrix} = \begin{bmatrix} 17 & -17 \\ 13 & 2 \end{bmatrix}$

43. $-2\begin{bmatrix} 1 & 2 \\ 5 & -4 \\ 6 & 0 \end{bmatrix} + 8\begin{bmatrix} 7 & 1 \\ 1 & 2 \\ 1 & 4 \end{bmatrix} = \begin{bmatrix} -2 & -4 \\ -10 & 8 \\ -12 & 0 \end{bmatrix} + \begin{bmatrix} 56 & 8 \\ 8 & 16 \\ 8 & 32 \end{bmatrix} = \begin{bmatrix} 54 & 4 \\ -2 & 24 \\ -4 & 32 \end{bmatrix}$

45. $3\begin{bmatrix} 8 & -2 & 5 \\ 1 & 3 & -1 \end{bmatrix} + 6\begin{bmatrix} 4 & -2 & -3 \\ 2 & 7 & 6 \end{bmatrix} = \begin{bmatrix} 24 & -6 & 15 \\ 3 & 9 & -3 \end{bmatrix} + \begin{bmatrix} 24 & -12 & -18 \\ 12 & 42 & 36 \end{bmatrix} = \begin{bmatrix} 48 & -18 & -3 \\ 15 & 51 & 33 \end{bmatrix}$

47. $X = 3A - 2B = 3\begin{bmatrix} -4 & 0 \\ 1 & -5 \\ -3 & 2 \end{bmatrix} - 2\begin{bmatrix} 1 & 2 \\ -2 & 1 \\ 4 & 4 \end{bmatrix}$

$= \begin{bmatrix} -14 & -4 \\ 7 & -17 \\ -17 & -2 \end{bmatrix}$

49. $X = \dfrac{1}{3}[B - 2A] = \dfrac{1}{3}\left(\begin{bmatrix} 1 & 2 \\ -2 & 1 \\ 4 & 4 \end{bmatrix} - 2\begin{bmatrix} -4 & 0 \\ 1 & -5 \\ -3 & 2 \end{bmatrix} \right)$

$= \dfrac{1}{3}\begin{bmatrix} 9 & 2 \\ -4 & 11 \\ 10 & 0 \end{bmatrix}$

51. Since A and B are both 2×2, AB can be performed.

53. Since A is 3×2 and B is 2×2, AB can be performed.

55. $\begin{bmatrix} 1 & 2 \\ 5 & -4 \\ 6 & 0 \end{bmatrix}\begin{bmatrix} 6 & -2 & 8 \\ 4 & 0 & 0 \end{bmatrix} = \begin{bmatrix} 1(6)+2(4) & 1(-2)+2(0) & 1(8)+2(0) \\ 5(6)+(-4)(4) & 5(-2)+(-4)(0) & 5(8)+(-4)(0) \\ 6(6)+(0)(4) & 6(-2)+(0)(0) & 6(8)+(0)(0) \end{bmatrix}$

$= \begin{bmatrix} 14 & -2 & 8 \\ 14 & -10 & 40 \\ 36 & -12 & 48 \end{bmatrix}$

57. $\begin{bmatrix} 1 & 5 & 6 \\ 2 & -4 & 0 \end{bmatrix}\begin{bmatrix} 6 & 4 \\ -2 & 0 \\ 8 & 0 \end{bmatrix} = \begin{bmatrix} 1(6)+5(-2)+6(8) & 1(4)+5(0)+6(0) \\ 2(6)-4(-2)+0(8) & 2(4)-4(0)+0(0) \end{bmatrix}$

$= \begin{bmatrix} 44 & 4 \\ 20 & 8 \end{bmatrix}$

59. $\begin{bmatrix} 4 \\ 6 \end{bmatrix}\begin{bmatrix} 6 & -2 \end{bmatrix} = \begin{bmatrix} 4(6) & 4(-2) \\ 6(6) & 6(-2) \end{bmatrix} = \begin{bmatrix} 24 & -8 \\ 36 & -12 \end{bmatrix}$

61. $\begin{bmatrix} 2 & 1 \\ 6 & 0 \end{bmatrix}\left(\begin{bmatrix} 4 & 2 \\ -3 & 1 \end{bmatrix} + \begin{bmatrix} -2 & 4 \\ 0 & 4 \end{bmatrix} \right) = \begin{bmatrix} 2 & 1 \\ 6 & 0 \end{bmatrix}\begin{bmatrix} 2 & 6 \\ -3 & 5 \end{bmatrix}$

$= \begin{bmatrix} 2(2)+1(-3) & 2(6)+1(5) \\ 6(2)+0 & 6(6)+0 \end{bmatrix}$

$= \begin{bmatrix} 1 & 17 \\ 12 & 36 \end{bmatrix}$

63. $\begin{bmatrix} 4 & 1 \\ 11 & -7 \\ 12 & 3 \end{bmatrix}\begin{bmatrix} 3 & -5 & 6 \\ 2 & -2 & -2 \end{bmatrix} = \begin{bmatrix} 14 & -22 & 22 \\ 19 & -41 & 80 \\ 42 & -66 & 66 \end{bmatrix}$

65. $\begin{bmatrix} 5 & 4 \\ -1 & 1 \end{bmatrix}\begin{bmatrix} x \\ y \end{bmatrix} = \begin{bmatrix} 2 \\ -22 \end{bmatrix}$

$\begin{bmatrix} 5x+4y \\ -x+y \end{bmatrix} = \begin{bmatrix} 2 \\ -22 \end{bmatrix}$

$\begin{cases} 5x+4y = 2 \\ -x+y = -22 \end{cases}$

67. (a) $BA = \begin{bmatrix} 10.25 & 14.50 & 17.75 \end{bmatrix} \begin{bmatrix} 8200 & 7400 \\ 6500 & 9800 \\ 5400 & 4800 \end{bmatrix} = \begin{bmatrix} \$274,150 & \$303,150 \end{bmatrix}$

The merchandise shipped to warehouse 1 is worth \$274,150, and the merchandise shipped to warehouse 2 is worth \$303,150.

(b) $A_n = 1.25A = \begin{bmatrix} 10,250 & 9250 \\ 8125 & 12,250 \\ 6750 & 6000 \end{bmatrix}$

$BA_n = \begin{bmatrix} \$342,687.50 & \$378,937.50 \end{bmatrix}$

69. $AB = \begin{bmatrix} 5 & -1 \\ 11 & -2 \end{bmatrix} \begin{bmatrix} -2 & 1 \\ -11 & 5 \end{bmatrix} = \begin{bmatrix} 1 & 0 \\ 0 & 1 \end{bmatrix} = I$

$BA = \begin{bmatrix} -2 & 1 \\ -11 & 5 \end{bmatrix} \begin{bmatrix} 5 & -1 \\ 11 & -2 \end{bmatrix} = \begin{bmatrix} 1 & 0 \\ 0 & 1 \end{bmatrix} = I$

71. $AB = \begin{bmatrix} 1 & -1 & 0 \\ -1 & 0 & -1 \\ 8 & -4 & 2 \end{bmatrix} = \begin{bmatrix} -2 & 1 & \frac{1}{2} \\ -3 & 1 & \frac{1}{2} \\ 2 & -2 & -\frac{1}{2} \end{bmatrix} = \begin{bmatrix} 1 & 0 & 0 \\ 0 & 1 & 0 \\ 0 & 0 & 1 \end{bmatrix} = I$

$BA = \begin{bmatrix} -2 & 1 & \frac{1}{2} \\ -3 & 1 & \frac{1}{2} \\ 2 & -2 & -\frac{1}{2} \end{bmatrix} \begin{bmatrix} 1 & -1 & 0 \\ -1 & 0 & -1 \\ 8 & -4 & 2 \end{bmatrix} = \begin{bmatrix} 1 & 0 & 0 \\ 0 & 1 & 0 \\ 0 & 0 & 1 \end{bmatrix} = I$

73. $[A \vdots I] = \begin{bmatrix} -3 & -5 & \vdots & 1 & 0 \\ 2 & 3 & \vdots & 0 & 1 \end{bmatrix}$

$2R_2 + R_1 \rightarrow \begin{bmatrix} 1 & 1 & \vdots & 1 & 2 \\ 2 & 3 & \vdots & 0 & 1 \end{bmatrix}$

$-2R_1 + R_2 \rightarrow \begin{bmatrix} 1 & 1 & \vdots & 1 & 2 \\ 0 & 1 & \vdots & -2 & -3 \end{bmatrix}$

$-R_2 + R_1 \rightarrow \begin{bmatrix} 1 & 0 & \vdots & 3 & 5 \\ 0 & 1 & \vdots & -2 & -3 \end{bmatrix} = [I \vdots A^{-1}]$

$A^{-1} = \begin{bmatrix} 3 & 5 \\ -2 & -3 \end{bmatrix}$

75. $[A \vdots I] = \begin{bmatrix} 0 & -2 & 1 & \vdots & 1 & 0 & 0 \\ -5 & -2 & -3 & \vdots & 0 & 1 & 0 \\ 7 & 3 & 4 & \vdots & 0 & 0 & 1 \end{bmatrix}$

$\begin{matrix} R_3 \\ \\ R_1 \end{matrix} \begin{bmatrix} 7 & 3 & 4 & \vdots & 0 & 0 & 1 \\ -5 & -2 & -3 & \vdots & 0 & 1 & 0 \\ 0 & -2 & 1 & \vdots & 1 & 0 & 0 \end{bmatrix}$

$\begin{matrix} R_2 + R_1 \rightarrow \\ 5R_1 + 2R_2 \rightarrow \\ {} \end{matrix} \begin{bmatrix} 2 & 1 & 1 & \vdots & 0 & 1 & 1 \\ 0 & 1 & -1 & \vdots & 0 & 7 & 5 \\ 0 & -2 & 1 & \vdots & 1 & 0 & 0 \end{bmatrix}$

$\begin{matrix} -R_2 + R_1 \rightarrow \\ {} \\ 2R_2 + R_3 \rightarrow \end{matrix} \begin{bmatrix} 2 & 0 & 2 & \vdots & 0 & -6 & -4 \\ 0 & 1 & -1 & \vdots & 0 & 7 & 5 \\ 0 & 0 & -1 & \vdots & 1 & 14 & 10 \end{bmatrix}$

— CONTINUED —

75. — CONTINUED —

$$\begin{matrix} \tfrac{1}{2}R_1 \rightarrow \\ \\ -R_3 \rightarrow \end{matrix} \begin{bmatrix} 1 & 0 & 1 & \vdots & 0 & -3 & -2 \\ 0 & 1 & -1 & \vdots & 0 & 7 & 5 \\ 0 & 0 & 1 & \vdots & -1 & -14 & -10 \end{bmatrix}$$

$$\begin{matrix} -R_3 + R_1 \rightarrow \\ R_3 + R_2 \rightarrow \\ \\ \end{matrix} \begin{bmatrix} 1 & 0 & 0 & \vdots & 1 & 11 & 8 \\ 0 & 1 & 0 & \vdots & -1 & -7 & -5 \\ 0 & 0 & 1 & \vdots & -1 & -14 & -10 \end{bmatrix} = [I \; \vdots \; A^{-1}]$$

$$A^{-1} = \begin{bmatrix} 1 & 11 & 8 \\ -1 & -7 & -5 \\ -1 & -14 & -10 \end{bmatrix}$$

77. $\begin{bmatrix} 3 & -10 \\ 4 & 2 \end{bmatrix}^{-1} = \dfrac{1}{46}\begin{bmatrix} 2 & 10 \\ -4 & 3 \end{bmatrix}$

79. $A = \begin{bmatrix} 1 & 4 & 6 \\ 2 & -3 & 1 \\ -1 & 18 & 16 \end{bmatrix}$

A^{-1} does not exist.

81. $A = \begin{bmatrix} 10 & 4 \\ 7 & 3 \end{bmatrix}$

$ad - bc = (10)(3) - (4)(7) = 2$

$$A^{-1} = \frac{1}{10(3) - 4(7)}\begin{bmatrix} 3 & -4 \\ -7 & 10 \end{bmatrix} = \frac{1}{2}\begin{bmatrix} 3 & -4 \\ -7 & 10 \end{bmatrix} = \begin{bmatrix} \tfrac{3}{2} & -2 \\ -\tfrac{7}{2} & 5 \end{bmatrix}$$

83. $A = \begin{bmatrix} -\tfrac{3}{4} & \tfrac{5}{2} \\ -\tfrac{4}{5} & -\tfrac{8}{3} \end{bmatrix}$

$ad - bc = \left(-\tfrac{3}{4}\right)\left(-\tfrac{8}{3}\right) - \left(\tfrac{5}{2}\right)\left(-\tfrac{4}{5}\right) = 2 + 2 = 4$

$$A^{-1} = \frac{1}{4}\begin{bmatrix} -\tfrac{8}{3} & -\tfrac{5}{2} \\ \tfrac{4}{5} & -\tfrac{3}{4} \end{bmatrix} = \begin{bmatrix} -\tfrac{2}{3} & -\tfrac{5}{8} \\ \tfrac{1}{5} & -\tfrac{3}{16} \end{bmatrix}$$

85. $\begin{cases} 5x - y = 13 \\ -9x + 2y = -24 \end{cases}$

$$\begin{bmatrix} x \\ y \end{bmatrix} = \begin{bmatrix} 5 & -1 \\ -9 & 2 \end{bmatrix}^{-1}\begin{bmatrix} 13 \\ -24 \end{bmatrix} = \begin{bmatrix} 2 & 1 \\ 9 & 5 \end{bmatrix}\begin{bmatrix} 13 \\ -24 \end{bmatrix} = \begin{bmatrix} 2 \\ -3 \end{bmatrix}$$

Solution: $(2, -3)$

87. $\begin{cases} 4x - 2y = -10 \\ -19x + 9y = 47 \end{cases}$

$$\begin{bmatrix} x \\ y \end{bmatrix} = \begin{bmatrix} 4 & -2 \\ -19 & 9 \end{bmatrix}^{-1}\begin{bmatrix} -10 \\ 47 \end{bmatrix} = \begin{bmatrix} -\tfrac{9}{2} & -1 \\ -\tfrac{19}{2} & -2 \end{bmatrix}\begin{bmatrix} -10 \\ 47 \end{bmatrix} = \begin{bmatrix} -2 \\ 1 \end{bmatrix}$$

Solution: $(-2, 1)$

89. $\begin{cases} -x + 4y - 2z = 12 \\ 2x - 9y + 5z = -25 \\ -x + 5y - 4z = 10 \end{cases}$

$$\begin{bmatrix} x \\ y \\ z \end{bmatrix} = \begin{bmatrix} -1 & 4 & -2 \\ 2 & -9 & 5 \\ -1 & 5 & -4 \end{bmatrix}^{-1} \begin{bmatrix} 12 \\ -25 \\ 10 \end{bmatrix} = \begin{bmatrix} -11 & -6 & -2 \\ -3 & -2 & -1 \\ -1 & -1 & -1 \end{bmatrix} \begin{bmatrix} 12 \\ -25 \\ 10 \end{bmatrix} = \begin{bmatrix} -2 \\ 4 \\ 3 \end{bmatrix}$$

Solution: $(-2, 4, 3)$

91. $\begin{cases} 3x - y + 5z = -14 \\ -x + y + 6z = 8 \\ -8x + 4y - z = 44 \end{cases}$

$$\begin{bmatrix} x \\ y \\ z \end{bmatrix} = \begin{bmatrix} 3 & -1 & 5 \\ -1 & 1 & 6 \\ -8 & 4 & -1 \end{bmatrix}^{-1} \begin{bmatrix} -14 \\ 8 \\ 44 \end{bmatrix} = \begin{bmatrix} \frac{25}{6} & -\frac{19}{6} & \frac{11}{6} \\ \frac{49}{6} & -\frac{37}{6} & \frac{23}{6} \\ -\frac{2}{3} & \frac{2}{3} & -\frac{1}{3} \end{bmatrix} \begin{bmatrix} -14 \\ 8 \\ 44 \end{bmatrix} = \begin{bmatrix} -3 \\ 5 \\ 0 \end{bmatrix}$$

Solution: $(-3, 5, 0)$

93. $\begin{cases} x + 3y = 23 \\ -6x + 2y = -18 \end{cases}$

$$\begin{bmatrix} x \\ y \end{bmatrix} = \begin{bmatrix} 1 & 3 \\ -6 & 2 \end{bmatrix}^{-1} \begin{bmatrix} 23 \\ -18 \end{bmatrix} = \begin{bmatrix} 0.1 & -0.15 \\ 0.3 & 0.05 \end{bmatrix} \begin{bmatrix} 23 \\ -18 \end{bmatrix} = \begin{bmatrix} 5 \\ 6 \end{bmatrix}$$

$x = 5, y = 6$

Solution: $(5, 6)$

95. $\begin{cases} x - 3y - 2z = 8 \\ -2x + 7y + 3z = -19 \\ x - y - 3z = 3 \end{cases}$

$$\begin{bmatrix} x \\ y \\ z \end{bmatrix} = \begin{bmatrix} 1 & -3 & -2 \\ -2 & 7 & 3 \\ 1 & -1 & -3 \end{bmatrix}^{-1} \begin{bmatrix} 8 \\ -19 \\ 3 \end{bmatrix} = \begin{bmatrix} -18 & -7 & 5 \\ -3 & -1 & 1 \\ -5 & -2 & 1 \end{bmatrix} \begin{bmatrix} 8 \\ -19 \\ 3 \end{bmatrix} = \begin{bmatrix} 4 \\ -2 \\ 1 \end{bmatrix}$$

$x = 4, y = -2, z = 1$

Solution: $(4, -2, 1)$

97. $\begin{vmatrix} -9 & 11 \\ 7 & -4 \end{vmatrix} = (-9)(-4) - (11)(7) = -41$

99. $\begin{vmatrix} 14 & -24 \\ 12 & -15 \end{vmatrix} = (14)(-15) - (-24)(12) = 78$

101. $\begin{bmatrix} 3 & 6 \\ 5 & -4 \end{bmatrix}$

(a) $M_{11} = -4$ (b) $C_{11} = M_{11} = -4$

     $M_{12} = 5$ $C_{12} = -M_{12} = -5$

     $M_{21} = 6$ $C_{21} = -M_{21} = -6$

     $M_{22} = 3$ $C_{22} = M_{22} = 3$

103. $\begin{bmatrix} 8 & 3 & 4 \\ 6 & 5 & -9 \\ -4 & 1 & 2 \end{bmatrix}$

(a) $M_{11} = \begin{vmatrix} 5 & -9 \\ 1 & 2 \end{vmatrix} = 19$

$M_{12} = \begin{vmatrix} 6 & -9 \\ -4 & 2 \end{vmatrix} = -24$

$M_{13} = \begin{vmatrix} 6 & 5 \\ -4 & 1 \end{vmatrix} = 26$

$M_{21} = \begin{vmatrix} 3 & 4 \\ 1 & 2 \end{vmatrix} = 2$

$M_{22} = \begin{vmatrix} 8 & 4 \\ -4 & 2 \end{vmatrix} = 32$

$M_{23} = \begin{vmatrix} 8 & 3 \\ -4 & 1 \end{vmatrix} = 20$

$M_{31} = \begin{vmatrix} 3 & 4 \\ 5 & -9 \end{vmatrix} = -47$

$M_{32} = \begin{vmatrix} 8 & 4 \\ 6 & -9 \end{vmatrix} = -96$

$M_{33} = \begin{vmatrix} 8 & 3 \\ 6 & 5 \end{vmatrix} = 22$

(b) $C_{11} = M_{11} = 19$

$C_{12} = -M_{12} = 24$

$C_{13} = M_{13} = 26$

$C_{21} = -M_{21} = -2$

$C_{22} = M_{22} = 32$

$C_{23} = -M_{23} = -20$

$C_{31} = M_{31} = -47$

$C_{32} = -M_{32} = 96$

$C_{33} = M_{33} = 22$

105. Expand using Row 3.

$$\begin{vmatrix} 4 & 7 & -1 \\ 2 & -3 & 4 \\ -5 & 1 & -1 \end{vmatrix} = -5\begin{vmatrix} 7 & -1 \\ -3 & 4 \end{vmatrix} - 1\begin{vmatrix} 4 & -1 \\ 2 & 4 \end{vmatrix} - 1\begin{vmatrix} 4 & 7 \\ 2 & -3 \end{vmatrix}$$

$$= -5(25) - (18) - (-26) = -117$$

107. Expand using Row 1, then use Row 3 of each 3×3 matrix.

$$\begin{vmatrix} -5 & 6 & 0 & 0 \\ 0 & 1 & -1 & 2 \\ -3 & 4 & -5 & 1 \\ 1 & 6 & 0 & 3 \end{vmatrix} = -5\begin{vmatrix} 1 & -1 & 2 \\ 4 & -5 & 1 \\ 6 & 0 & 3 \end{vmatrix} - 6\begin{vmatrix} 0 & -1 & 2 \\ -3 & -5 & 1 \\ 1 & 0 & 3 \end{vmatrix}$$

$$= -5[6(-1 + 10) + 3(-5 + 4)] - 6[(-1 + 10) + 3(0 - 3)]$$

$$= -5(54 - 3) - 6(9 - 9)$$

$$= -255$$

109. $\begin{cases} 3x + 8y = -7 \\ 9x - 5y = 37 \end{cases}$

$$x = \frac{\begin{vmatrix} -7 & 8 \\ 37 & -5 \end{vmatrix}}{\begin{vmatrix} 3 & 8 \\ 9 & -5 \end{vmatrix}} = \frac{-261}{-87} = 3 \qquad y = \frac{\begin{vmatrix} 3 & -7 \\ 9 & 37 \end{vmatrix}}{\begin{vmatrix} 3 & 8 \\ 9 & -5 \end{vmatrix}} = \frac{174}{-87} = -2$$

Solution: $(3, -2)$

111. $\begin{cases} 5x - 2y + z = 15 \\ 3x - 3y - z = -7 \\ 2x - y - 7z = -3 \end{cases}$ $\qquad D = \begin{vmatrix} 5 & -2 & 1 \\ 3 & -3 & -1 \\ 2 & -1 & -7 \end{vmatrix} = 65$

$$x = \frac{\begin{vmatrix} 15 & -2 & 1 \\ -7 & -3 & -1 \\ -3 & -1 & -7 \end{vmatrix}}{65} = \frac{390}{65} = 6$$

$$y = \frac{\begin{vmatrix} 5 & 15 & 1 \\ 3 & -7 & -1 \\ 2 & -3 & -7 \end{vmatrix}}{65} = \frac{520}{65} = 8$$

$$z = \frac{\begin{vmatrix} 5 & -2 & 15 \\ 3 & -3 & -7 \\ 2 & -1 & -3 \end{vmatrix}}{65} = \frac{65}{65} = 1$$

Solution: $(6, 8, 1)$

113. x = number of liters of 75% solution

y = number of liters of 50% solution

$\begin{cases} x + y = 100 \\ 0.75x + 0.50y = 60 \end{cases}$

$$\begin{bmatrix} 1 & 1 \\ 0.75 & 0.50 \end{bmatrix} \begin{bmatrix} x \\ y \end{bmatrix} = \begin{bmatrix} 100 \\ 60 \end{bmatrix}$$

$$D = \begin{vmatrix} 1 & 1 \\ 0.75 & 0.50 \end{vmatrix} = -0.25$$

$$x = \frac{\begin{vmatrix} 100 & 1 \\ 60 & 0.50 \end{vmatrix}}{-0.25} = \frac{-10}{-0.25} = 40$$

$$y = \frac{\begin{vmatrix} 1 & 100 \\ 0.75 & 60 \end{vmatrix}}{-0.25} = \frac{-15}{-0.25} = 60$$

Answer: 40 liters of 75% solution;
60 liters of 50% solution

115. x = number of units produced

y = number of units sold

$\begin{cases} x = y \\ 5.25y = 3.75x + 25{,}000 \end{cases}$

$\begin{cases} x - y = 0 \\ -3.75x + 5.25y = 25{,}000 \end{cases}$

$$\begin{bmatrix} 1 & -1 \\ -3.75 & 5.25 \end{bmatrix} \begin{bmatrix} x \\ y \end{bmatrix} = \begin{bmatrix} 0 \\ 25{,}000 \end{bmatrix}$$

$$D = \begin{vmatrix} 1 & -1 \\ -3.75 & 5.25 \end{vmatrix} = 1.5$$

$$y = \frac{\begin{vmatrix} 1 & 0 \\ -3.75 & 25{,}000 \end{vmatrix}}{1.5} = \frac{25{,}000}{1.5} \approx 16{,}667 \text{ units must be produced and sold.}$$

117. $(-4, 0), (4, 0), (0, 6)$

$$\text{Area} = \frac{1}{2}\begin{vmatrix} -4 & 0 & 1 \\ 4 & 0 & 1 \\ 0 & 6 & 1 \end{vmatrix} = \frac{1}{2}(48) = 24 \text{ square units}$$

119. $\left(\frac{3}{2}, 1\right), \left(4, -\frac{1}{2}\right), (4, 2)$

$$\text{Area} = \frac{1}{2}\begin{vmatrix} \frac{3}{2} & 1 & 1 \\ 4 & -\frac{1}{2} & 1 \\ 4 & 2 & 1 \end{vmatrix} = \frac{1}{2}\left(\frac{25}{4}\right) = \frac{25}{8} \text{ square units}$$

121. $(2, 5), (6, -1)$

$$\begin{vmatrix} x & y & 1 \\ 2 & 5 & 1 \\ 6 & -1 & 1 \end{vmatrix} = 0$$

$$6x + 4y - 32 = 0$$

$$3x + 2y - 16 = 0$$

123. $(-0.8, 0.2), (0.7, 3.2)$

$$\begin{vmatrix} x & y & 1 \\ -0.8 & 0.2 & 1 \\ 0.7 & 3.2 & 1 \end{vmatrix} = 0$$

$$-3x + 1.5y - 2.7 = 0 \quad \text{Multiply both sides by } -\frac{10}{3}.$$

$$10x - 5y + 9 = 0$$

125. R E T U R N _ T O _ B A S E _

$[18 \quad 5 \quad 20][21 \quad 18 \quad 14][0 \quad 20 \quad 15][0 \quad 2 \quad 1][19 \quad 5 \quad 0]$

$$A = \begin{bmatrix} 2 & 1 & 0 \\ -6 & -6 & -2 \\ 3 & 2 & 1 \end{bmatrix}$$

$[18 \quad 5 \quad 20]A = [66 \quad 28 \quad 10]$

$[21 \quad 18 \quad 14]A = [-24 \quad -59 \quad -22]$

$[0 \quad 20 \quad 15]A = [-75 \quad -90 \quad -25]$

$[0 \quad 2 \quad 1]A = [-9 \quad -10 \quad -3]$

$[19 \quad 5 \quad 0]A = [8 \quad -11 \quad -10]$

Cryptogram: 66 28 10 −24 −59 −22 −75 −90 −25 −9 −10 −3 8 −11 −10

127. $A^{-1} = \begin{bmatrix} -5 & 4 & -3 \\ 10 & -7 & 6 \\ 8 & -6 & 5 \end{bmatrix}$

$$\begin{bmatrix} 89 & -23 & 86 \\ 72 & 4 & 40 \\ 19 & -2 & 15 \\ 33 & 42 & -30 \\ 3 & 6 & -5 \\ 87 & -36 & 100 \\ 63 & 22 & 13 \\ 110 & -5 & 75 \\ -21 & 42 & -63 \end{bmatrix} \begin{bmatrix} -5 & 4 & -3 \\ 10 & -7 & 6 \\ 8 & -6 & 5 \end{bmatrix} = \begin{bmatrix} 13 & 1 & 25 \\ 0 & 20 & 8 \\ 5 & 0 & 6 \\ 15 & 18 & 3 \\ 5 & 0 & 2 \\ 5 & 0 & 23 \\ 9 & 20 & 8 \\ 0 & 25 & 15 \\ 21 & 0 & 0 \end{bmatrix} \begin{matrix} \text{M A Y} \\ \text{\_ T H} \\ \text{E \_ F} \\ \text{O R C} \\ \text{E \_ B} \\ \text{E \_ W} \\ \text{I T H} \\ \text{\_ Y O} \\ \text{U \_ \_} \end{matrix}$$

Message: MAY THE FORCE BE WITH YOU

129. Expand along Row 3.

$$\begin{vmatrix} a_{11} & a_{12} & a_{13} \\ a_{21} & a_{22} & a_{23} \\ a_{31} + c_1 & a_{32} + c_2 & a_{33} + c_3 \end{vmatrix} = (a_{31} + c_1)\begin{vmatrix} a_{12} & a_{13} \\ a_{22} & a_{23} \end{vmatrix} - (a_{32} + c_2)\begin{vmatrix} a_{11} & a_{13} \\ a_{21} & a_{23} \end{vmatrix} + (a_{33} + c_3)\begin{vmatrix} a_{11} & a_{12} \\ a_{21} & a_{22} \end{vmatrix}$$

$$= a_{31}\begin{vmatrix} a_{12} & a_{13} \\ a_{22} & a_{23} \end{vmatrix} - a_{32}\begin{vmatrix} a_{11} & a_{13} \\ a_{21} & a_{23} \end{vmatrix} + a_{33}\begin{vmatrix} a_{11} & a_{12} \\ a_{21} & a_{22} \end{vmatrix}$$

$$+ c_1\begin{vmatrix} a_{12} & a_{13} \\ a_{22} & a_{23} \end{vmatrix} - c_2\begin{vmatrix} a_{11} & a_{13} \\ a_{21} & a_{23} \end{vmatrix} + c_3\begin{vmatrix} a_{11} & a_{12} \\ a_{21} & a_{22} \end{vmatrix}$$

$$= \begin{vmatrix} a_{11} & a_{12} & a_{13} \\ a_{21} & a_{22} & a_{23} \\ a_{31} & a_{32} & a_{33} \end{vmatrix} + \begin{vmatrix} a_{11} & a_{12} & a_{13} \\ a_{21} & a_{22} & a_{23} \\ c_1 & c_2 & c_3 \end{vmatrix}$$

Note: Expand each of these matrices along Row 3 to see the previous step.

131. If A is a square matrix, the cofactor C_{ij} of the entry a_{ij} is $(-1)^{i+j}M_{ij}$, where M_{ij} is the determinant obtained by deleting the ith row and jth column of A. The determinant of A is the sum of the entries of any row or column of A multiplied by their respective cofactors.

133. The part of the matrix corresponding to the coefficients of the system reduces to a matrix in which the number of rows with nonzero entries is the same as the number of variables.

Chapter 8   Practice Test

1. Put the matrix in reduced row echelon form.

$$\begin{bmatrix} 1 & -2 & 4 \\ 3 & -5 & 9 \end{bmatrix}$$

For Exercises 2–4, use matrices to solve the system of equations.

2. $\begin{cases} 3x + 5y = 3 \\ 2x - y = -11 \end{cases}$

3. $\begin{cases} 2x + 3y = -3 \\ 3x + 2y = 8 \\ x + y = 1 \end{cases}$

4. $\begin{cases} x + 3z = -5 \\ 2x + y = 0 \\ 3x + y - z = 3 \end{cases}$

5. Multiply $\begin{bmatrix} 1 & 4 & 5 \\ 2 & 0 & -3 \end{bmatrix} \begin{bmatrix} 1 & 6 \\ 0 & -7 \\ -1 & 2 \end{bmatrix}$.

6. Given $A = \begin{bmatrix} 9 & 1 \\ -4 & 8 \end{bmatrix}$ and $B = \begin{bmatrix} 6 & -2 \\ 3 & 5 \end{bmatrix}$, find $3A - 5B$.

7. Find $f(A)$:

$$f(x) = x^2 - 7x + 8, \quad A = \begin{bmatrix} 3 & 0 \\ 7 & 1 \end{bmatrix}.$$

8. True or false:

$(A + B)(A + 3B) = A^2 + 4AB + 3B^2$ where A and B are matrices.

(Assume that A^2, AB, and B^2 exist.)

For Exercises 9–10, find the inverse of the matrix, if it exists.

9. $\begin{bmatrix} 1 & 2 \\ 3 & 5 \end{bmatrix}$

10. $\begin{bmatrix} 1 & 1 & 1 \\ 3 & 6 & 5 \\ 6 & 10 & 8 \end{bmatrix}$

11. Use an inverse matrix to solve the systems.

(a) $x + 2y = 4$

   $3x + 5y = 1$

(b) $x + 2y = 3$

   $3x + 5y = -2$

For Exercises 12–14, find the determinant of the matrix.

12. $\begin{bmatrix} 6 & -1 \\ 3 & 4 \end{bmatrix}$

13. $\begin{bmatrix} 1 & 3 & -1 \\ 5 & 9 & 0 \\ 6 & 2 & -5 \end{bmatrix}$

14. $\begin{bmatrix} 1 & 4 & 2 & 3 \\ 0 & 1 & -2 & 0 \\ 3 & 5 & -1 & 1 \\ 2 & 0 & 6 & 1 \end{bmatrix}$

15. Evaluate $\begin{vmatrix} 6 & 4 & 3 & 0 & 6 \\ 0 & 5 & 1 & 4 & 8 \\ 0 & 0 & 2 & 7 & 3 \\ 0 & 0 & 0 & 9 & 2 \\ 0 & 0 & 0 & 0 & 1 \end{vmatrix}$.

16. Use a determinant to find the area of the triangle with vertices $(0, 7)$, $(5, 0)$, and $(3, 9)$.

17. Find the equation of the line through $(2, 7)$ and $(-1, 4)$.

For Exercises 18–20, use Cramer's Rule to find the indicated value.

18. Find x.

$$\begin{cases} 6x - 7y = 4 \\ 2x + 5y = 11 \end{cases}$$

19. Find z.

$$\begin{cases} 3x \quad\;\; + \;z = 1 \\ \quad\;\; y + 4z = 3 \\ x - y \quad\;\; = 2 \end{cases}$$

20. Find y.

$$\begin{cases} 721.4x - 29.1y = 33.77 \\ 45.9x + 105.6y = 19.85 \end{cases}$$

CHAPTER 9
Sequences, Series, and Probability

C H A P T E R 9
Sequences, Series, and Probability

Section 9.1　　Sequences and Series

- Given the general nth term in a sequence, you should be able to find, or list, some of the terms.
- You should be able to find an expression for the apparent nth term of a sequence.
- You should be able to use and evaluate factorials.
- You should be able to use summation notation for a sum.
- You should know that the sum of the terms of a sequence is a series.

Solutions to Odd-Numbered Exercises

1. $a_n = 3n + 1$

$a_1 = 3(1) + 1 = 4$

$a_2 = 3(2) + 1 = 7$

$a_3 = 3(3) + 1 = 10$

$a_4 = 3(4) + 1 = 13$

$a_5 = 3(5) + 1 = 16$

3. $a_n = 2^n$

$a_1 = 2^1 = 2$

$a_2 = 2^2 = 4$

$a_3 = 2^3 = 8$

$a_4 = 2^4 = 16$

$a_5 = 2^5 = 32$

5. $a_n = (-2)^n$

$a_1 = (-2)^1 = -2$

$a_2 = (-2)^2 = 4$

$a_3 = (-2)^3 = -8$

$a_4 = (-2)^4 = 16$

$a_5 = (-2)^5 = -32$

7. $a_n = \dfrac{n + 2}{n}$

$a_1 = \dfrac{1 + 2}{1} = 3$

$a_2 = \dfrac{4}{2} = 2$

$a_3 = \dfrac{5}{3}$

$a_4 = \dfrac{6}{4} = \dfrac{3}{2}$

$a_5 = \dfrac{7}{5}$

9. $a_n = \dfrac{6n}{3n^2 - 1}$

$a_1 = \dfrac{6(1)}{3(1)^2 - 1} = 3$

$a_2 = \dfrac{6(2)}{3(2)^2 - 1} = \dfrac{12}{11}$

$a_3 = \dfrac{6(3)}{3(3)^2 - 1} = \dfrac{9}{13}$

$a_4 = \dfrac{6(4)}{3(4)^2 - 1} = \dfrac{24}{47}$

$a_5 = \dfrac{6(5)}{3(5)^2 - 1} = \dfrac{15}{37}$

11. $a_n = \dfrac{1 + (-1)^n}{n}$

$a_1 = 0$

$a_2 = \dfrac{2}{2} = 1$

$a_3 = 0$

$a_4 = \dfrac{2}{4} = \dfrac{1}{2}$

$a_5 = 0$

13. $a_n = 2 - \dfrac{1}{3^n}$

$a_1 = 2 - \dfrac{1}{3} = \dfrac{5}{3}$

$a_2 = 2 - \dfrac{1}{9} = \dfrac{17}{9}$

$a_3 = 2 - \dfrac{1}{27} = \dfrac{53}{27}$

$a_4 = 2 - \dfrac{1}{81} = \dfrac{161}{81}$

$a_5 = 2 - \dfrac{1}{243} = \dfrac{485}{243}$

15. $a_n = \dfrac{1}{n^{3/2}}$

$a_1 = \dfrac{1}{1} = 1$

$a_2 = \dfrac{1}{2^{3/2}}$

$a_3 = \dfrac{1}{3^{3/2}}$

$a_4 = \dfrac{1}{4^{3/2}} = \dfrac{1}{8}$

$a_5 = \dfrac{1}{5^{3/2}}$

17. $a_n = \dfrac{3^n}{n!}$

$a_1 = \dfrac{3^1}{1!} = \dfrac{3}{1} = 3$

$a_2 = \dfrac{3^2}{2!} = \dfrac{9}{2}$

$a_3 = \dfrac{3^3}{3!} = \dfrac{27}{6} = \dfrac{9}{2}$

$a_4 = \dfrac{3^4}{4!} = \dfrac{81}{24} = \dfrac{27}{8}$

$a_5 = \dfrac{3^5}{5!} = \dfrac{243}{120} = \dfrac{81}{40}$

19. $a_n = \dfrac{(-1)^n}{n^2}$

$a_1 = -\dfrac{1}{1} = -1$

$a_2 = \dfrac{1}{4}$

$a_3 = -\dfrac{1}{9}$

$a_4 = \dfrac{1}{16}$

$a_5 = -\dfrac{1}{25}$

21. $a_n = \dfrac{2}{3}$

$a_1 = \dfrac{2}{3}$

$a_2 = \dfrac{2}{3}$

$a_3 = \dfrac{2}{3}$

$a_4 = \dfrac{2}{3}$

$a_5 = \dfrac{2}{3}$

23. $a_n = n(n-1)(n-2)$

$a_1 = (1)(0)(-1) = 0$

$a_2 = (2)(1)(0) = 0$

$a_3 = (3)(2)(1) = 6$

$a_4 = (4)(3)(2) = 24$

$a_5 = (5)(4)(3) = 60$

25. $a_{25} = (-1)^{25}(3(25) - 2) = -73$

27. $a_{10} = \dfrac{2^{10}}{10!} = \dfrac{1024}{3,628,800} = \dfrac{4}{14,175} \approx 0.000282$

29. $a_{11} = \dfrac{4(11)}{2(11)^2 - 3} = \dfrac{44}{239}$

31. $a_n = \ln \dfrac{3}{4} n$

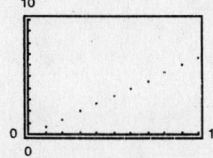

33. $a_n = 16(-0.5)^{n-1}$

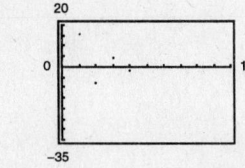

35. $a_n = \dfrac{2n}{n+1}$

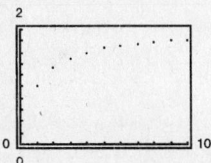

37. $a_n = \dfrac{8}{n+1}$

$a_1 = 4, \; a_{10} = \dfrac{8}{11}$

The sequence decreases

Matches graph (c)

39. $a_n = 4(0.5)^{n-1}$

$a_1 = 4, \; a_{10} = \dfrac{1}{128}$

The sequence decreases

Matches graph (d)

41. $1, 4, 7, 10, 13, \ldots$

$a_n = 1 + (n - 1)3 = 3n - 2$

43. $0, 3, 8, 15, 24, \ldots$

$a_n = n^2 - 1$

45. $-\dfrac{2}{3}, \dfrac{3}{4}, -\dfrac{4}{5}, \dfrac{5}{6}, -\dfrac{6}{7}, \ldots$

$a_n = (-1)^n \left(\dfrac{n + 1}{n + 2} \right)$

47. $\dfrac{2}{1}, \dfrac{3}{3}, \dfrac{4}{5}, \dfrac{5}{7}, \dfrac{6}{9}, \ldots$

$a_n = \dfrac{n + 1}{2n - 1}$

49. $1, \dfrac{1}{4}, \dfrac{1}{9}, \dfrac{1}{16}, \dfrac{1}{25}, \ldots$

$a_n = \dfrac{1}{n^2}$

51. $1, -1, 1, -1, 1, \ldots$

$a_n = (-1)^{n+1}$

53. $1 + \dfrac{1}{1}, 1 + \dfrac{1}{2}, 1 + \dfrac{1}{3}, 1 + \dfrac{1}{4}, 1 + \dfrac{1}{5}, \ldots$

$a_n = 1 + \dfrac{1}{n}$

55. $a_1 = 28$ and $a_{k+1} = a_k - 4$

$a_1 = 28$

$a_2 = a_1 - 4 = 28 - 4 = 24$

$a_3 = a_2 - 4 = 24 - 4 = 20$

$a_4 = a_3 - 4 = 20 - 4 = 16$

$a_5 = a_4 - 4 = 16 - 4 = 12$

57. $a_1 = 3$ and $a_{k+1} = 2(a_k - 1)$

$a_1 = 3$

$a_2 = 2(a_1 - 1) = 2(3 - 1) = 4$

$a_3 = 2(a_2 - 1) = 2(4 - 1) = 6$

$a_4 = 2(a_3 - 1) = 2(6 - 1) = 10$

$a_5 = 2(a_4 - 1) = 2(10 - 1) = 18$

59. $a_1 = 6$ and $a_{k+1} = a_k + 2$

$a_1 = 6$

$a_2 = a_1 + 2 = 6 + 2 = 8$

$a_3 = a_2 + 2 = 8 + 2 = 10$

$a_4 = a_3 + 2 = 10 + 2 = 12$

$a_5 = a_4 + 2 = 12 + 2 = 14$

In general, $a_n = 2n + 4$.

61. $a_1 = 81$ and $a_{k+1} = \dfrac{1}{3}a_k$

$a_1 = 81$

$a_2 = \dfrac{1}{3}a_1 = \dfrac{1}{3}(81) = 27$

$a_3 = \dfrac{1}{3}a_2 = \dfrac{1}{3}(27) = 9$

$a_4 = \dfrac{1}{3}a_3 = \dfrac{1}{3}(9) = 3$

$a_5 = \dfrac{1}{3}a_4 = \dfrac{1}{3}(3) = 1$

In general, $a_n = 81\left(\dfrac{1}{3}\right)^{n-1} = 81(3)\left(\dfrac{1}{3}\right)^n = \dfrac{243}{3^n}$.

63. $\dfrac{4!}{6!} = \dfrac{\cancel{1 \cdot 2 \cdot 3 \cdot 4}}{\cancel{1 \cdot 2 \cdot 3 \cdot 4} \cdot 5 \cdot 6} = \dfrac{1}{5 \cdot 6} = 30$

65. $\dfrac{10!}{8!} = \dfrac{\cancel{1 \cdot 2 \cdot 3 \cdot 4 \cdot 5 \cdot 6 \cdot 7 \cdot 8} \cdot 9 \cdot 10}{\cancel{1 \cdot 2 \cdot 3 \cdot 4 \cdot 5 \cdot 6 \cdot 7 \cdot 8}} = \dfrac{9 \cdot 10}{1} = 90$

67. $\dfrac{(n+1)!}{n!} = \dfrac{1 \cdot 2 \cdot 3 \cdots\cdots n \cdot (n+1)}{1 \cdot 2 \cdot 3 \cdots\cdots n} = \dfrac{n+1}{1} = n + 1$

69. $\dfrac{(2n-1)!}{(2n+1)!} = \dfrac{1 \cdot 2 \cdot 3 \cdots\cdots (2n-1)}{1 \cdot 2 \cdot 3 \cdots\cdots (2n-1) \cdot (2n) \cdot (2n+1)} = \dfrac{1}{2n(2n+1)}$

71. $\displaystyle\sum_{i=1}^{5} (2i+1) = (2+1) + (4+1) + (6+1) + (8+1) + (10+1) = 35$

73. $\displaystyle\sum_{k=1}^{4} 10 = 10 + 10 + 10 + 10 = 40$

75. $\displaystyle\sum_{i=0}^{4} i^2 = 0^2 + 1^2 + 2^2 + 3^2 + 4^2 = 30$

77. $\displaystyle\sum_{k=0}^{3} \dfrac{1}{k^2+1} = \dfrac{1}{1} + \dfrac{1}{1+1} + \dfrac{1}{4+1} + \dfrac{1}{9+1} = \dfrac{9}{5}$

79. $\displaystyle\sum_{k=2}^{5} (k+1)^2(k-3) = (3)^2(-1) + (4)^2(0) + (5)^2(1) + (6)^2(2) = 88$

81. $\displaystyle\sum_{i=1}^{4} 2^i = 2^1 + 2^2 + 2^3 + 2^4 = 30$

83. $\displaystyle\sum_{j=1}^{6} (24 - 3j) = 81$

85. $\displaystyle\sum_{k=0}^{4} \dfrac{(-1)^k}{k+1} = \dfrac{47}{60}$

87. $\dfrac{1}{3(1)} + \dfrac{1}{3(2)} + \dfrac{1}{3(3)} + \cdots + \dfrac{1}{3(9)} = \displaystyle\sum_{i=1}^{9} \dfrac{1}{3i}$

89. $\left[2\left(\dfrac{1}{8}\right) + 3\right] + \left[2\left(\dfrac{2}{8}\right) + 3\right] + \left[2\left(\dfrac{3}{8}\right) + 3\right] + \cdots + \left[2\left(\dfrac{8}{8}\right) + 3\right] = \displaystyle\sum_{i=1}^{8} \left[2\left(\dfrac{i}{8}\right) + 3\right]$

91. $3 - 9 + 27 - 81 + 243 - 729 = \displaystyle\sum_{i=1}^{6} (-1)^{i+1} 3^i$

93. $\dfrac{1}{1^2} - \dfrac{1}{2^2} + \dfrac{1}{3^2} - \dfrac{1}{4^2} + \cdots - \dfrac{1}{20^2} = \displaystyle\sum_{i=1}^{20} \dfrac{(-1)^{i+1}}{i^2}$

95. $\dfrac{1}{4} + \dfrac{3}{8} + \dfrac{7}{16} + \dfrac{15}{32} + \dfrac{31}{64} = \displaystyle\sum_{i=1}^{5} \dfrac{2^i-1}{2^{i+1}}$

97. $\displaystyle\sum_{i=1}^{4} 5\left(\dfrac{1}{2}\right)^i = 5\left(\dfrac{1}{2}\right) + 5\left(\dfrac{1}{2}\right)^2 + 5\left(\dfrac{1}{2}\right)^3 + 5\left(\dfrac{1}{2}\right)^4 = \dfrac{75}{16}$

99. $\displaystyle\sum_{n=1}^{3} 4\left(-\dfrac{1}{2}\right)^n = 4\left(-\dfrac{1}{2}\right) + 4\left(-\dfrac{1}{2}\right)^2 + 4\left(-\dfrac{1}{2}\right)^3 = -\dfrac{3}{2}$

101. $\displaystyle\sum_{i=1}^{\infty} 6\left(\dfrac{1}{10}\right)^i = 0.6 + 0.06 + 0.006 + 0.0006 + \cdots = \dfrac{2}{3}$

103. By using a calculator, we have

$\displaystyle\sum_{k=1}^{10} 7\left(\dfrac{1}{10}\right)^k \approx 0.7777777777$

$\displaystyle\sum_{k=1}^{50} 7\left(\dfrac{1}{10}\right)^k \approx 0.7777777778$

$\displaystyle\sum_{k=1}^{100} 7\left(\dfrac{1}{10}\right)^k \approx \dfrac{7}{9}$

The terms approach zero as $n \to \infty$.

Thus, we conclude that $\displaystyle\sum_{k=1}^{\infty} 7\left(\dfrac{1}{10}\right)^k = \dfrac{7}{9}$.

105. $A_n = 5000\left(1 + \dfrac{0.08}{4}\right)^n$, $n = 1, 2, 3, \ldots$

(a) $A_1 = \$5100.00$

$A_2 = \$5202.00$

$A_3 = \$5306.04$

$A_4 = \$5412.16$

$A_5 = \$5520.40$

$A_6 = \$5630.81$

$A_7 = \$5743.43$

$A_8 = \$5858.30$

(b) $A_{40} = \$11{,}040.20$

107. $a_n = 696 + 66.4n - 2.37n^2$, $n = -1, 0, 1, \ldots, 6$

$a_{-1} = \$627.23$

$a_0 = \$696.00$

$a_1 = \$760.03$

$a_2 = \$819.32$

$a_3 = \$873.87$

$a_4 = \$923.68$

$a_5 = \$968.75$

$a_6 = \$1009.08$

109. $\sum_{n=0}^{8} (1215 + 608.2n - 114.83n^2 + 11.00n^3)$

$\approx \$23,660.88$ million

Compare to the sum of the incomes shown in the figure:

$1250 + 1600 + 2000 + 2350 + 2700 + 2700$
$+ 3050 + 3500 + 4450 = \$23,600$ million

111. $a_1 = 1$, $a_2 = 1$, $a_{k+2} = a_{k+1} + a_k$, $k \geq 2$

$a_1 = 1$	$b_1 = \frac{1}{1} = 1$
$a_2 = 1$	$b_2 = \frac{2}{1} = 2$
$a_3 = 1 + 1 = 2$	$b_3 = \frac{3}{2}$
$a_4 = 2 + 1 = 3$	$b_4 = \frac{5}{3}$
$a_5 = 3 + 2 = 5$	$b_5 = \frac{8}{5}$
$a_6 = 5 + 3 = 8$	$b_6 = \frac{13}{8}$
$a_7 = 8 + 5 = 13$	$b_7 = \frac{21}{13}$
$a_8 = 13 + 8 = 21$	$b_8 = \frac{34}{21}$
$a_9 = 21 + 13 = 34$	$b_9 = \frac{55}{34}$
$a_{10} = 34 + 21 = 55$	$b_{10} = \frac{89}{55}$
$a_{11} = 55 + 34 = 89$	
$a_{12} = 89 + 55 = 144$	

113. $\dfrac{327.15 + 785.69 + 433.04 + 265.38 + 604.12 + 590.30}{6} \approx \$500.95$

115. $\displaystyle\sum_{i=1}^{n} (x_i - \bar{x}) = \sum_{i=1}^{n} x_i - \sum_{i=1}^{n} \bar{x}$

$\displaystyle = \left(\sum_{i=1}^{n} x_i \right) - n\bar{x}$

$\displaystyle = \left(\sum_{i=1}^{n} x_i \right) - n\left(\frac{1}{n} \sum_{i=1}^{n} x_i \right)$

$= 0$

117. True, $\displaystyle\sum_{i=1}^{4} (i^2 + 2i) = \sum_{i=1}^{4} i^2 + 2\sum_{i=1}^{4} i$

by the properties of sums.

119. (a) $A - B = \begin{bmatrix} 6 & 5 \\ 3 & 4 \end{bmatrix} - \begin{bmatrix} -2 & 4 \\ 6 & -3 \end{bmatrix} = \begin{bmatrix} 6 - (-2) & 5 - 4 \\ 3 - 6 & 4 - (-3) \end{bmatrix} = \begin{bmatrix} 8 & 1 \\ -3 & 7 \end{bmatrix}$

(b) $4B - 3A = 4\begin{bmatrix} -2 & 4 \\ 6 & -3 \end{bmatrix} - 3\begin{bmatrix} 6 & 5 \\ 3 & 4 \end{bmatrix} = \begin{bmatrix} -8 - 18 & 16 - 15 \\ 24 - 9 & -12 - 12 \end{bmatrix} = \begin{bmatrix} -26 & 1 \\ -15 & -24 \end{bmatrix}$

(c) $AB = \begin{bmatrix} 6 & 5 \\ 3 & 4 \end{bmatrix}\begin{bmatrix} -2 & 4 \\ 6 & -3 \end{bmatrix} = \begin{bmatrix} -12 + 30 & 24 - 15 \\ -6 + 24 & 12 - 12 \end{bmatrix} = \begin{bmatrix} 18 & 9 \\ 18 & 0 \end{bmatrix}$

(d) $BA = \begin{bmatrix} -2 & 4 \\ 6 & -3 \end{bmatrix}\begin{bmatrix} 6 & 5 \\ 3 & 4 \end{bmatrix} = \begin{bmatrix} -12 + 12 & -10 + 16 \\ 36 - 9 & 30 - 12 \end{bmatrix} = \begin{bmatrix} 0 & 6 \\ 27 & 18 \end{bmatrix}$

121. (a) $A - B = \begin{bmatrix} -2 & -3 & 6 \\ 4 & 5 & 7 \\ 1 & 7 & 4 \end{bmatrix} - \begin{bmatrix} 1 & 4 & 2 \\ 0 & 1 & 6 \\ 0 & 3 & 1 \end{bmatrix} = \begin{bmatrix} -2 - 1 & -3 - 4 & 6 - 2 \\ 4 - 0 & 5 - 1 & 7 - 6 \\ 1 - 0 & 7 - 3 & 4 - 1 \end{bmatrix} = \begin{bmatrix} -3 & -7 & 4 \\ 4 & 4 & 1 \\ 1 & 4 & 3 \end{bmatrix}$

(b) $4B - 3A = 4\begin{bmatrix} 1 & 4 & 2 \\ 0 & 1 & 6 \\ 0 & 3 & 1 \end{bmatrix} - 3\begin{bmatrix} -2 & -3 & 6 \\ 4 & 5 & 7 \\ 1 & 7 & 4 \end{bmatrix} = \begin{bmatrix} 4 - (-6) & 16 - (-9) & 8 - 18 \\ 0 - 12 & 4 - 15 & 24 - 21 \\ 0 - 3 & 12 - 21 & 4 - 12 \end{bmatrix} = \begin{bmatrix} 10 & 25 & -10 \\ -12 & -11 & 3 \\ -3 & -9 & -8 \end{bmatrix}$

(c) $AB = \begin{bmatrix} -2 & -3 & 6 \\ 4 & 5 & 7 \\ 1 & 7 & 4 \end{bmatrix}\begin{bmatrix} 1 & 4 & 2 \\ 0 & 1 & 6 \\ 0 & 3 & 1 \end{bmatrix} = \begin{bmatrix} -2 + 0 + 0 & -8 - 3 + 18 & -4 - 18 + 6 \\ 4 + 0 + 0 & 16 + 5 + 21 & 8 + 30 + 7 \\ 1 + 0 + 0 & 4 + 7 + 12 & 2 + 42 + 4 \end{bmatrix} = \begin{bmatrix} -2 & 7 & -16 \\ 4 & 42 & 45 \\ 1 & 23 & 48 \end{bmatrix}$

(d) $BA = \begin{bmatrix} 1 & 4 & 2 \\ 0 & 1 & 6 \\ 0 & 3 & 1 \end{bmatrix}\begin{bmatrix} -2 & -3 & 6 \\ 4 & 5 & 7 \\ 1 & 7 & 4 \end{bmatrix} = \begin{bmatrix} -2 + 16 + 2 & -3 + 20 + 14 & 6 + 28 + 8 \\ 0 + 4 + 6 & 0 + 5 + 42 & 0 + 7 + 24 \\ 0 + 12 + 1 & 0 + 15 + 7 & 0 + 21 + 4 \end{bmatrix} = \begin{bmatrix} 16 & 31 & 42 \\ 10 & 47 & 31 \\ 13 & 22 & 25 \end{bmatrix}$

123. $|A| = \begin{vmatrix} 3 & 5 \\ -1 & 7 \end{vmatrix} = 3(7) - 5(-1) = 26$

125. $|A| = \begin{vmatrix} 3 & 4 & 5 \\ 0 & 7 & 3 \\ 4 & 9 & -1 \end{vmatrix}$

$= 3\begin{vmatrix} 7 & 3 \\ 9 & -1 \end{vmatrix} + 4\begin{vmatrix} 4 & 5 \\ 7 & 3 \end{vmatrix}$

$= 3[7(-1) - 3(9)] + 4[4(3) - 5(7)]$

$= -194$

Section 9.2   Arithmetic Sequences and Partial Sums

- ■ You should be able to recognize an arithmetic sequence, find its common difference, and find its nth term.
- ■ You should be able to find the nth partial sum of an arithmetic sequence by using the formula

    $$S_n = \frac{n}{2}(a_1 + a_n).$$

Solutions to Odd-Numbered Exercises

1. $10, 8, 6, 4, 2, \ldots$

Arithmetic sequence, $d = -2$

3. $1, 2, 4, 8, 16, \ldots$

Not an arithmetic sequence

5. $\frac{9}{4}, 2, \frac{7}{4}, \frac{3}{2}, \frac{5}{4}, \ldots$

Arithmetic sequence, $d = -\frac{1}{4}$

7. $\frac{1}{3}, \frac{2}{3}, 1, \frac{4}{3}, \frac{5}{6}, \ldots$

Not and arithmetic sequence

9. $\ln 1, \ln 2, \ln 3, \ln 4, \ln 5, \ldots$

Not an arithmetic sequence

11. $a_n = 5 + 3n$

$8, 11, 14, 17, 20$

Arithmetic sequence, $d = 3$

13. $a_n = 3 - 4(n - 2)$

$7, 3, -1, -5, -9$

Arithmetic sequence, $d = -4$

15. $a_n = (-1)^n$

$-1, 1, -1, 1, -1$

Not an arithmetic sequence

17. $a_n = \dfrac{(-1)^n 3}{n}$

$-3, \dfrac{3}{2}, -1, \dfrac{3}{4}, -\dfrac{3}{5}$

Not an arithmetic sequence.

19. $a_1 = 15, \ a_{k+1} = a_k + 4$

$a_2 = 15 + 4 = 19$

$a_3 = 19 + 4 = 23$

$a_4 = 23 + 4 = 27$

$a_5 = 27 + 4 = 31$

$d = 4$

$c = a_1 - d = 15 - 4 = 11$

$a_n = 4n + 11$

21. $a_1 = 200, \ a_{k+1} = a_k - 10$

$a_2 = 200 - 10 = 190$

$a_3 = 190 - 10 = 180$

$a_4 = 180 - 10 = 170$

$a_5 = 170 - 10 = 160$

$d = -10$

$c = a_1 - d = 200 - (-10) = 210$

$a_n = -10n + 210$

23. $a_1 = \frac{5}{8}, \ a_{k+1} = a_k - \frac{1}{8}$

$a_1 = \frac{5}{8}$

$a_2 = \frac{5}{8} - \frac{1}{8} = \frac{1}{2}$

$a_3 = \frac{1}{2} - \frac{1}{8} = \frac{3}{8}$

$a_4 = \frac{3}{8} - \frac{1}{8} = \frac{1}{4}$

$a_5 = \frac{1}{4} - \frac{1}{8} = \frac{1}{8}$

$d = -\frac{1}{8}$

$c = a_1 - d = \frac{5}{8} - \left(-\frac{1}{8}\right) = \frac{3}{4}$

$a_n = -\frac{1}{8}n + \frac{3}{4}$

25. $a_1 = 5, \ d = 6$

$a_1 = 5$

$a_2 = 5 + 6 = 11$

$a_3 = 11 + 6 = 17$

$a_4 = 17 + 6 = 23$

$a_5 = 23 + 6 = 29$

27. $a_1 = -2.6, \ d = -0.4$

$a_1 = -2.6$

$a_2 = -2.6 + (-0.4) = -3.0$

$a_3 = -3.0 + (-0.4) = -3.4$

$a_4 = -3.4 + (-0.4) = -3.8$

$a_5 = -3.8 + (-0.4) = -4.2$

29. $a_1 = 2, \ a_{12} = 46$

$46 = 2 + (12 - 1)d$

$44 = 11d$

$4 = d$

$a_1 = 2$

$a_2 = 2 + 4 = 6$

$a_3 = 6 + 4 = 10$

$a_4 = 10 + 4 = 14$

$a_5 = 14 + 4 = 18$

31. $a_8 = 26, \ a_{12} = 42$

$a_{12} = a_8 + 4d$

$42 = 26 + 4d \Rightarrow d = 4$

$a_8 = a_1 + 7d$

$26 = a_1 + 28 \Rightarrow a_1 = -2$

$a_1 = -2$

$a_2 = -2 + 4 = 2$

$a_3 = 2 + 4 = 6$

$a_4 = 6 + 4 = 10$

$a_5 = 10 + 4 = 14$

33. $a_1 = 1, \ d = 3$

$a_n = a_1 + (n - 1)d = 1 + (n - 1)(3) = 3n - 2$

35. $a_1 = 100, \ d = -8$

$a_n = a_1 + (n - 1)d = 100 + (n - 1)(-8)$

$= -8n + 108$

37. $a_1 = x, \ d = 2x$

$a_n = a_1 + (n - 1)d = x + (n - 1)(2x) = 2xn - x$

39. $4, \frac{3}{2}, -1, -\frac{7}{2}, \ldots$

$d = -\frac{5}{2}$

$a_n = a_1 + (n - 1)d = 4 + (n - 1)\left(-\frac{5}{2}\right) = -\frac{5}{2}n + \frac{13}{2}$

41. $a_1 = 5, \ a_4 = 15$

$a_4 = a_1 + 3d \implies 15 = 5 + 3d \implies d = \frac{10}{3}$

$a_n = a_1 + (n-1)d = 5 + (n-1)\left(\frac{10}{3}\right) = \frac{10}{3}n + \frac{5}{3}$

43. $a_3 = 94, \ a_6 = 85$

$a_6 = a_3 + 3d \implies 85 = 94 + 3d \implies d = -3$

$a_1 = a_3 - 2d \implies a_1 = 94 - 2(-3) = 100$

$a_n = a_1 + (n-1)d = 100 + (n-1)(-3)$

$\qquad\qquad\qquad = -3n + 103$

45. $a_n = -\frac{3}{4}n + 8$

$d = -\frac{3}{4}$ so the sequence is decreasing,

and $a_1 = 7\frac{1}{4}$. Matches (b).

47. $a_n = 2 + \frac{3}{4}n$

$d = \frac{3}{4}$ so the sequence is increasing,

and $a_1 = 2\frac{3}{4}$. Matches (c).

49. $a_n = 15 - \frac{3}{2}n$

51. $a_n = 0.2n + 3$

53. $8, 20, 32, 44, \ldots$

$a_1 = 8, \ d = 12, \ n = 10$

$a_{10} = 8 + 9(12) = 116$

$S_{10} = \frac{10}{2}(8 + 116) = 620$

55. $4.2, 3.7, 3.2, 2.7, \ldots$

$a_1 = 4.2, d = -0.5, n = 12$

$a_{12} = 4.2 + 11(-0.5) = -1.3$

$S_{12} = \frac{12}{2}[4.2 + (-1.3)] = 17.4$

57. $40, 37, 34, 31, \ldots$

$a_1 = 40, d = -3, n = 10$

$a_{10} = 40 + 9(-3) = 13$

$S_{10} = \frac{10}{2}(40 + 13) = 265$

59. $a_1 = 100, \ a_{25} = 220, \ n = 25$

$S_n = \frac{n}{2}[a_1 + a_n]$

$S_{25} = \frac{25}{2}(100 + 220) = 4000$

61. $a_1 = 1, \ a_{50} = 50, \ n = 50$

$\sum_{n=1}^{50} n = \frac{50}{2}(1 + 50) = 1275$

63. $a_{10} = 60, a_{100} = 600, n = 91$

$\sum_{n=10}^{100} 6n = \frac{91}{2}(60 + 600) = 30{,}030$

65. $\sum_{n=11}^{30} n - \sum_{n=1}^{10} n = \frac{20}{2}(11 + 30) - \frac{10}{2}(1 + 10) = 355$

67. $a_1 = 1, a_{400} = 799, n = 400$

$\sum_{n=1}^{400}(2n - 1) = \frac{400}{2}(1 + 799) = 160{,}000$

69. $\sum_{n=1}^{20}(2n + 5) = 520$

71. $\sum_{n=1}^{100}\frac{n+4}{2} = 2725$

73. $\sum_{i=1}^{60}\left(250 - \frac{8}{3}i\right) = 10{,}120$

75. (a) $a_1 = 32{,}500, \ d = 1500$

$a_6 = a_1 + 5d = 32{,}500 + 5(1500) = \$40{,}000$

(b) $S_6 = \frac{6}{2}[32{,}500 + 40{,}000] = \$217{,}500$

77. $a_1 = 20, \ d = 4, \ n = 30$

$a_{30} = 20 + 29(4) = 136$

$S_{30} = \frac{30}{2}(20 + 136) = 2340$ seats

79. $a_1 = 14, a_{18} = 31$

$S_{18} = \frac{18}{2}(14 + 31) = 405$ bricks

81. 4.9, 14.7, 24.5, 34.3, . . .

$d = 9.8$

$a_{10} = 4.9 + 9(9.8) = 93.1$ meters

$S_{10} = \frac{10}{2}(4.9 + 93.1) = 490$ meters

83. True; given a_1 and a_2 then $d = a_2 - a_1$ and
$a_n = a_1 + (n - 1)d$

85. Since $a_n = d_n + c$, its geometric pattern is linear.

87. $a_n = 2n - 1$

$a_1 = 1, a_{100} = 199$

$\sum_{n=1}^{100} (2n - 1) = \frac{100}{2}(1 + 199) = 10,000$

89. (a) $1 + 3 = 4$

$1 + 3 + 5 = 9$

$1 + 3 + 5 + 7 = 16$

$1 + 3 + 5 + 7 + 9 = 25$

$1 + 3 + 5 + 7 + 9 + 11 = 36$

(b) $S_n = n^2$

$S_7 = 1 + 3 + 5 + 7 + 9 + 11 + 13 = 49 = 7^2$

(c) $S_n = \frac{n}{2}[1 + (2n - 1)] = \frac{n}{2}(2n) = n^2$

91. $S_{20} = \frac{20}{2}\{a_1 + [a_1 + (20 - 1)(3)]\} = 650$

$10(2a_1 + 57) = 650$

$2a_1 + 57 = 65$

$2a_1 = 8$

$a_1 = 4$

93.
$$\begin{cases} -2x - 3y - 3z = 0 \\ 4x - 2y - 6z = 0 \\ 8x + 2y - 3z = 0 \end{cases} \quad \text{Interchange equations.}$$

$$\begin{cases} -2x - 3y - 3z = 0 \\ -8y - 12z = 0 \quad 2\text{Eq.1} + \text{Eq.2} \\ -10y - 15z = 0 \quad 4\text{Eq.1} + \text{Eq.3} \end{cases}$$

$$\begin{cases} x + \frac{3}{2}y + \frac{3}{2}z = 0 \quad -\frac{1}{2}\text{Eq.1} \\ y + \frac{3}{2}z = 0 \quad -\frac{1}{8}\text{Eq.2} \\ y + \frac{3}{2}z = 0 \quad -\frac{1}{10}\text{Eq.3} \end{cases}$$

$$\begin{cases} x + \frac{3}{2}y + \frac{3}{2}z = 0 \\ y + \frac{3}{2}z = 0 \\ 0 = 0 \quad -\text{Eq.2} + \text{Eq.3} \end{cases}$$

Let $z = a$, then $y + \frac{3}{2}a = 0 \implies y = -\frac{3}{2}a$, and

$x + \frac{3}{2}\left(-\frac{3}{2}a\right) + \frac{3}{2}a = 0 \implies x = \frac{3}{4}a.$

Solution: $\left(\frac{3}{4}a, -\frac{3}{2}a, a\right)$ where a is any real number.

95.
$$\begin{cases} x - 3y + 2z = 0 \\ 9x + 2z = 0 \\ 7y - z = 0 \end{cases} \quad \text{Interchange equations.}$$

$$\begin{cases} x - 3y + 2z = 0 \\ 27y - 16z = 0 \quad -9\text{Eq.1} + \text{Eq.2} \\ 7y - z = 0 \end{cases}$$

$$\begin{cases} x - 3y + 2z = 0 \\ -y - 12z = 0 \quad -4\text{Eq.3} + \text{Eq.2} \\ 7y - z = 0 \end{cases}$$

$$\begin{cases} x - 3y + 2z = 0 \\ -y - 12z = 0 \\ -85z = 0 \quad 7\text{Eq.2} + \text{Eq.3} \end{cases}$$

$$\begin{cases} x - 3y + 2z = 0 \\ y + 12z = 0 \quad -\text{Eq.2} \\ z = 0 \quad -\frac{1}{85}\text{Eq.3} \end{cases}$$

$z = 0$

$y + 12(0) = 0 \implies y = 0$

$x - 3(0) + 2(0) = 0 \implies x = 0$

Solution: $(0, 0, 0)$

97. $\begin{cases} 2x - 6y = 2 \\ \quad\quad y = 1 \end{cases}$

$$\begin{bmatrix} 2 & -6 & \vdots & 2 \\ 0 & 1 & \vdots & 1 \end{bmatrix}$$

$6R_2 + R_1 \rightarrow \begin{bmatrix} 2 & 0 & \vdots & 8 \\ 0 & 1 & \vdots & 1 \end{bmatrix}$

$\frac{1}{2}R_1 \rightarrow \begin{bmatrix} 1 & 0 & \vdots & 4 \\ 0 & 1 & \vdots & 1 \end{bmatrix} \begin{array}{l} \Rightarrow x = 4 \\ \Rightarrow y = 1 \end{array}$

Solution: $(4, 1)$

99. $\begin{cases} 3x + y + z = 4 \\ x + 7y + 5z = 2 \\ 9x - 7y - 5z = 8 \end{cases}$

$$\begin{bmatrix} 3 & 1 & 1 & \vdots & 4 \\ 1 & 7 & 5 & \vdots & 2 \\ 9 & -7 & -5 & \vdots & 8 \end{bmatrix}$$

$R_2 + R_3 \rightarrow \begin{bmatrix} 3 & 1 & 1 & \vdots & 4 \\ 1 & 7 & 5 & \vdots & 2 \\ 10 & 0 & 0 & \vdots & 10 \end{bmatrix}$

$\frac{1}{10}R_3 \rightarrow \begin{bmatrix} 3 & 1 & 1 & \vdots & 4 \\ 1 & 7 & 5 & \vdots & 2 \\ 1 & 0 & 0 & \vdots & 1 \end{bmatrix}$

$\begin{array}{c} R_1 \\ \\ R_3 \end{array} \begin{bmatrix} 1 & 0 & 0 & \vdots & 1 \\ 1 & 7 & 5 & \vdots & 2 \\ 3 & 1 & 1 & \vdots & 4 \end{bmatrix}$

$\begin{array}{l} -R_1 + R_2 \rightarrow \\ -3R_1 + R_3 \rightarrow \end{array} \begin{bmatrix} 1 & 0 & 0 & \vdots & 1 \\ 0 & 7 & 5 & \vdots & 1 \\ 0 & 1 & 1 & \vdots & 1 \end{bmatrix}$

$\begin{array}{c} R_2 \\ R_3 \end{array} \begin{bmatrix} 1 & 0 & 0 & \vdots & 1 \\ 0 & 1 & 1 & \vdots & 1 \\ 0 & 7 & 5 & \vdots & 1 \end{bmatrix}$

$-7R_2 + R_3 \rightarrow \begin{bmatrix} 1 & 0 & 0 & \vdots & 1 \\ 0 & 1 & 1 & \vdots & 1 \\ 0 & 0 & -2 & \vdots & -6 \end{bmatrix}$

$-\frac{1}{2}R_3 \rightarrow \begin{bmatrix} 1 & 0 & 0 & \vdots & 1 \\ 0 & 1 & 1 & \vdots & 1 \\ 0 & 0 & 1 & \vdots & 3 \end{bmatrix}$

$-R_3 + R_2 \rightarrow \begin{bmatrix} 1 & 0 & 0 & \vdots & 1 \\ 0 & 1 & 0 & \vdots & -2 \\ 0 & 0 & 1 & \vdots & 3 \end{bmatrix} \begin{array}{l} \Rightarrow x = 1 \\ \Rightarrow y = -2 \\ \Rightarrow z = 3 \end{array}$

Solution: $(1, -2, 3)$

Section 9.3   Geometric Sequences and Series

■ You should be able to identify a geometric sequence, find its common ratio, and find the *n*th term.

■ You should know that the *n*th term of a geometric sequence with common ratio *r* is given by $a_n = a_1 r^{n-1}$.

■ You should know that the *n*th partial sum of a geometric sequence with common ratio $r \neq 1$ is given by

$$S_n = a_1 \left(\frac{1 - r^n}{1 - r} \right)$$

■ You should know that if $|r| < 1$, then

$$\sum_{n=1}^{\infty} a_1 r^{n-1} = \frac{a_1}{1 - r}.$$

Solutions to Odd-Numbered Exercises

1. 5, 15, 45, 135, . . .

Geometric sequence, $r = 3$

3. 3, 12, 21, 30, . . .

Not a geometric sequence

Note: It is an arithmetic sequence with $d = 9$.

5. $1, -\frac{1}{2}, \frac{1}{4}, -\frac{1}{8}, \ldots$

Geometric sequence, $r = -\frac{1}{2}$

7. $\frac{1}{8}, \frac{1}{4}, \frac{1}{2}, 1, \ldots$

Geometric sequence, $r = 2$

9. $1, \frac{1}{2}, \frac{1}{3}, \frac{1}{4}, \ldots$

Not a geometric sequence

11. $a_1 = 2, \ r = 3$

$a_1 = 2$

$a_2 = 2(3) = 6$

$a_3 = 6(3) = 18$

$a_4 = 18(3) = 54$

$a_5 = 54(3) = 162$

13. $a_1 = 1, \ r = \frac{1}{2}$

$a_1 = 1$

$a_2 = 1\left(\frac{1}{2}\right) = \frac{1}{2}$

$a_3 = \frac{1}{2}\left(\frac{1}{2}\right) = \frac{1}{4}$

$a_4 = \frac{1}{4}\left(\frac{1}{2}\right) = \frac{1}{8}$

$a_5 = \frac{1}{8}\left(\frac{1}{2}\right) = \frac{1}{16}$

15. $a_1 = 5, \ r = -\frac{1}{10}$

$a_1 = 5$

$a_2 = 5\left(-\frac{1}{10}\right) = -\frac{1}{2}$

$a_3 = \left(-\frac{1}{2}\right)\left(-\frac{1}{10}\right) = \frac{1}{20}$

$a_4 = \frac{1}{20}\left(-\frac{1}{10}\right) = -\frac{1}{200}$

$a_5 = \left(-\frac{1}{200}\right)\left(-\frac{1}{10}\right) = \frac{1}{2000}$

17. $a_1 = 1, \ r = e$

$a_1 = 1$

$a_2 = 1(e) = e$

$a_3 = (e)(e) = e^2$

$a_4 = (e^2)(e) = e^3$

$a_5 = (e^3)(e) = e^4$

19. $a_1 = 2, r = \frac{x}{4}$

$a_1 = 2$

$a_2 = 2\left(\frac{x}{4}\right) = \frac{x}{2}$

$a_3 = \left(\frac{x}{2}\right)\left(\frac{x}{4}\right) = \frac{x^2}{8}$

$a_4 = \left(\frac{x^2}{8}\right)\left(\frac{x}{4}\right) = \frac{x^3}{32}$

$a_5 = \left(\frac{x^3}{32}\right)\left(\frac{x}{4}\right) = \frac{x^4}{128}$

21. $a_1 = 64, \ a_{k+1} = \frac{1}{2}a_k$

$a_1 = 64$

$a_2 = \frac{1}{2}(64) = 32$

$a_3 = \frac{1}{2}(32) = 16$

$a_4 = \frac{1}{2}(16) = 8$

$a_5 = \frac{1}{2}(8) = 4$

$a_n = 64\left(\frac{1}{2}\right)^{n-1} = 128\left(\frac{1}{2}\right)^n$

23. $a_1 = 7, a_{k+1} = 2a_k$

$a_1 = 7$

$a_2 = 2(7) = 14$

$a_3 = 2(14) = 28$

$a_4 = 2(28) = 56$

$a_5 = 2(56) = 112$

$a_n = 7(2)^{n-1} = \frac{7}{2}(2)^n$

25. $a_1 = 6, a_{k+1} = -\frac{3}{2}a_k$

$a_1 = 6$

$a_2 = -\frac{3}{2}(6) = -9$

$a_3 = -\frac{3}{2}(-9) = \frac{27}{2}$

$a_4 = -\frac{3}{2}\left(\frac{27}{2}\right) = -\frac{81}{4}$

$a_5 = -\frac{3}{2}\left(-\frac{81}{4}\right) = \frac{243}{8}$

$a_n = 6\left(-\frac{3}{2}\right)^{n-1}$ or $a_n = -4\left(-\frac{3}{2}\right)^n$

27. $a_1 = 4, r = \frac{1}{2}, n = 10$

$a_n = a_1 r^{n-1}$

$a_{10} = 4\left(\frac{1}{2}\right)^9 = \left(\frac{1}{2}\right)^7 = \frac{1}{128}$

29. $a_1 = 6, r = -\frac{1}{3}, n = 12$

$a_n = a_1 r^{n-1}$

$a_{12} = 6\left(-\frac{1}{3}\right)^{11} = -\frac{2}{3^{10}}$

31. $a_1 = 100, r = e^x, n = 9$

$a_n = a_1 r^{n-1}$

$a_9 = 100(e^x)^8 = 100e^{8x}$

33. $a_1 = 500, r = 1.02, n = 40$

$a_n = a_1 r^{n-1}$

$a_{40} = 500(1.02)^{39} \approx 1082.372$

35. $a_1 = 16, a_4 = \frac{27}{4}, n = 3$

$\frac{27}{4} = 16r^3 \Rightarrow \frac{27}{64} = r^3 \Rightarrow r = \frac{3}{4}$

$a_n = a_1 r^{n-1}$

$a_3 = 16\left(\frac{3}{4}\right)^2 = 9$

37. $a_4 = -18, a_7 = \frac{2}{3}, n = 6$

$a_7 = a_4 r^3$

$\frac{2}{3} = -18r^3$

$-\frac{1}{27} = r^3$

$-\frac{1}{3} = r$

$a_6 = a_4 r^2 = -18\left(-\frac{1}{3}\right)^2 = -2$

39. $a_n = 18\left(\frac{2}{3}\right)^{n-1}$

$a_1 = 18$ and $r = \frac{2}{3}$

Since $0 < r < 1$, the sequence is decreasing.

Matches (a).

41. $a_n = 18\left(\frac{3}{2}\right)^{n-1}$

$a_1 = 18$ and $r = \frac{3}{2} > 1$, so the sequence is increasing.

Matches (b).

43. $a_n = 12(-0.75)^{n-1}$

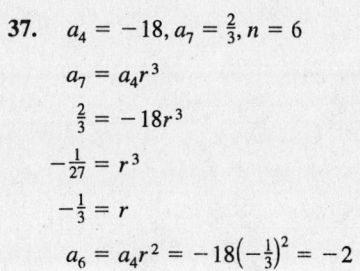

45. $a_n = 2(1.3)^{n-1}$

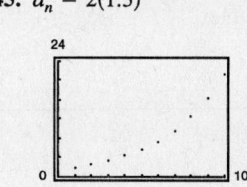

47. $\sum_{n=1}^{9} 2^{n-1} = 1 + 2^1 + 2^2 + \cdots + 2^8 \Rightarrow a_1 = 1, r = 2$

$S_9 = \frac{1(1 - 2^9)}{1 - 2} = 511$

49. $\sum_{i=1}^{7} 64\left(-\frac{1}{2}\right)^{i-1} = 64 + 64\left(-\frac{1}{2}\right)^1 + 64\left(-\frac{1}{2}\right)^2 + \cdots + 64\left(-\frac{1}{2}\right)^6 \Rightarrow a_1 = 64, r = -\frac{1}{2}$

$S_7 = 64\left[\frac{1 - \left(-\frac{1}{2}\right)^7}{1 - \left(-\frac{1}{2}\right)}\right] = \frac{128}{3}\left[1 - \left(-\frac{1}{2}\right)^7\right] = 43$

51. $\sum_{n=0}^{20} 3\left(\frac{3}{2}\right)^n = \sum_{n=1}^{21} 3\left(\frac{3}{2}\right)^{n-1} = 3 + 3\left(\frac{3}{2}\right)^1 + 3\left(\frac{3}{2}\right)^2 + \cdots + 3\left(\frac{3}{2}\right)^{20} \implies a_1 = 3,\ r = \frac{3}{2}$

$S_{21} = 3\left[\dfrac{1 - \left(\frac{3}{2}\right)^{21}}{1 - \frac{3}{2}}\right] = -6\left[1 - \left(\frac{3}{2}\right)^{21}\right] \approx 29{,}921.311$

53. $\sum_{n=0}^{5} 300(1.06)^n = \sum_{n=1}^{6} 300(1.06)^{n-1}$

$= 300 + 300(1.06)^1 + 300(1.06)^2 + 300(1.06)^3 + 300(1.06)^4 + 300(1.06)^5 \implies a_1 = 300,\ r = 1.06$

$S_6 = 300\left[\dfrac{1 - (1.06)^6}{1 - 1.06}\right] \approx 2092.596$

55. $\sum_{i=1}^{10} 8\left(-\frac{1}{4}\right)^{i-1} = 8 + 8\left(-\frac{1}{4}\right)^1 + 8\left(-\frac{1}{4}\right)^2 + \cdots + 8\left(-\frac{1}{4}\right)^9 \implies a_1 = 8,\ r = -\frac{1}{4}$

$S_{10} = 8\left[\dfrac{1 - \left(-\frac{1}{4}\right)^{10}}{1 - \left(-\frac{1}{4}\right)}\right] = \frac{32}{5}\left[1 - \left(-\frac{1}{4}\right)^{10}\right] \approx 6.400$

57. $5 + 15 + 45 + \cdots + 3645$

$r = 3$ and $3645 = 5(3)^{n-1}$

$729 = 3^{n-1} \implies 6 = n - 1 \implies n = 7$

Thus, the sum can be written as $\sum_{n=1}^{7} 5(3)^{n-1}$.

59. $2 - \frac{1}{2} + \frac{1}{8} - \cdots + \frac{1}{2048}$

$r = -\frac{1}{4}$ and $\frac{1}{2048} = 2\left(-\frac{1}{4}\right)^{n-1}$

By trial and error, we find that $n = 7$.

Thus, the sum can be written as $\sum_{n=1}^{7} 2\left(-\frac{1}{4}\right)^{n-1}$.

61. $0.1 + 0.4 + 1.6 + \cdots + 102.4$

$r = 4$ and $102.4 = 0.1(4)^{n-1}$

$1024 = 4^{n-1} \implies 5 = n - 1 \implies n = 6$

Thus, the sum can be written as $\sum_{n=1}^{6} = 0.1(4)^{n-1}$.

63. $\sum_{n=0}^{\infty} \left(\frac{1}{2}\right)^n = 1 + \left(\frac{1}{2}\right)^1 + \left(\frac{1}{2}\right)^2 + \cdots$

$a_1 = 1,\ r = \frac{1}{2}$

$\sum_{n=0}^{\infty} \left(\frac{1}{2}\right)^n = \frac{a_1}{1 - r} = \dfrac{1}{1 - \left(\frac{1}{2}\right)} = 2$

65. $\sum_{n=0}^{\infty} \left(-\frac{1}{2}\right)^n = 1 + \left(-\frac{1}{2}\right)^1 + \left(-\frac{1}{2}\right)^2 + \cdots \quad a_1 = 1,\ r = -\frac{1}{2}$

$\sum_{n=0}^{\infty} \left(-\frac{1}{2}\right)^n = \frac{a_1}{1 - r} = \dfrac{1}{1 - \left(-\frac{1}{2}\right)} = \frac{2}{3}$

67. $\sum_{n=0}^{\infty} 4\left(\frac{1}{4}\right)^n = 4 + 4\left(\frac{1}{4}\right)^1 + 4\left(\frac{1}{4}\right)^2 + \cdots \quad a_1 = 4,\ r = \frac{1}{4}$

$\sum_{n=0}^{\infty} 4\left(\frac{1}{4}\right)^n = \frac{a_1}{1 - r} = \dfrac{4}{1 - \left(\frac{1}{4}\right)} = \frac{16}{3}$

69. $\sum_{n=0}^{\infty} (0.4)^n = 1 + (0.4)^1 + (0.4)^2 + \cdots \quad a_1 = 1,\ r = 0.4$

$\sum_{n=0}^{\infty} (0.4)^n = \dfrac{1}{1 - 0.4} = \frac{5}{3}$

71. $\sum_{n=0}^{\infty} -3(0.9)^n = -3 - 3(0.9)^1 - 3(0.9)^2 - \cdots \quad a_1 = -3,\ r = 0.9$

$\sum_{n=0}^{\infty} -3(0.9)^n = \dfrac{-3}{1 - 0.9} = -30$

73. $8 + 6 + \dfrac{9}{2} + \dfrac{27}{8} + \cdots = \displaystyle\sum_{n=0}^{\infty} 8\left(\dfrac{3}{4}\right)^n = \dfrac{8}{1 - \frac{3}{4}} = 32$

75. $\dfrac{1}{9} - \dfrac{1}{3} + 1 - 3 + \ldots = \displaystyle\sum_{n=0}^{\infty} \dfrac{1}{9}(-3)^n$

The sum is undefined because

$|r| = |-3| = 3 > 1.$

77. $0.\overline{36} = \displaystyle\sum_{n=0}^{\infty} 0.36(0.01)^n = \dfrac{0.36}{1 - 0.01} = \dfrac{0.36}{0.99} = \dfrac{36}{99} = \dfrac{4}{11}$

79. $0.3\overline{18} = 0.3 + \displaystyle\sum_{n=0}^{\infty} 0.018(0.01)^n = \dfrac{3}{10} + \dfrac{0.018}{1 - 0.01}$

$= \dfrac{3}{10} + \dfrac{0.018}{0.99} = \dfrac{3}{10} + \dfrac{18}{990} = \dfrac{3}{10} + \dfrac{2}{110}$

$= \dfrac{35}{110} = \dfrac{7}{22}$

81. $f(x) = 6\left[\dfrac{1 - (0.5)^x}{1 - (0.5)}\right], \displaystyle\sum_{n=0}^{\infty} 6\left(\dfrac{1}{2}\right)^n = \dfrac{6}{1 - \frac{1}{2}} = 12$

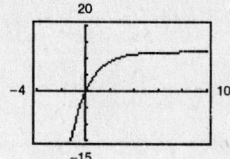

The horizontal asymptote of $f(x)$ is $y = 12$.
This corresponds to the sum of the series.

83. $A = P\left(1 + \dfrac{r}{n}\right)^{nt} = 1000\left(1 + \dfrac{0.06}{n}\right)^{n(10)}$

(a) $n = 1,\ A = 1000(1 + 0.06)^{10} \approx \$1790.85$

(b) $n = 2,\ A = 1000\left(1 + \dfrac{0.06}{2}\right)^{2(10)} \approx \$1806.11$

(c) $n = 4,\ A = 1000\left(1 + \dfrac{0.06}{4}\right)^{4(10)} \approx \$1814.02$

(d) $n = 12,\ A = 1000\left(1 + \dfrac{0.06}{12}\right)^{12(10)} \approx \$1819.40$

(e) $n = 365,\ A = 1000\left(1 + \dfrac{0.06}{365}\right)^{365(10)} \approx \$1822.03$

85. $V_5 = 135,000(0.70)^5 = \$22,689.45$

87. $A = \displaystyle\sum_{n=1}^{60} 100\left(1 + \dfrac{0.06}{12}\right)^n = \displaystyle\sum_{n=1}^{60} 100(1.005)^n = 100(1.005) \cdot \dfrac{[1 - 1.005^{60}]}{[1 - 1.005]} \approx \$7011.89$

89. Let $N = 12t$ be the total number of deposits.

$A = P\left(1 + \dfrac{r}{12}\right) + P\left(1 + \dfrac{r}{12}\right)^2 + \cdots + P\left(1 + \dfrac{r}{12}\right)^N$

$= \left(1 + \dfrac{r}{12}\right)\left[P + P\left(r + \dfrac{r}{12}\right) + \cdots + P\left(1 + \dfrac{r}{12}\right)^{N-1}\right]$

$= P\left(1 + \dfrac{r}{12}\right)\displaystyle\sum_{n=1}^{N}\left(1 + \dfrac{r}{12}\right)^{n-1}$

$= P\left(1 + \dfrac{r}{12}\right)\dfrac{1 - \left(1 + \dfrac{r}{12}\right)^N}{1 - \left(1 + \dfrac{r}{12}\right)}$

$= P\left(1 + \dfrac{r}{12}\right)\left(-\dfrac{12}{r}\right)\left[1 - \left(1 + \dfrac{r}{12}\right)^N\right]$

$= P\left(\dfrac{12}{r} + 1\right)\left[-1 + \left(1 + \dfrac{r}{12}\right)^N\right]$

$= P\left[\left(1 + \dfrac{r}{12}\right)^N - 1\right]\left(1 + \dfrac{12}{r}\right)$

$= P\left[\left(1 + \dfrac{r}{12}\right)^{12t} - 1\right]\left(1 + \dfrac{12}{r}\right)$

91. $P = \$50,\ r = 7\%,\ t = 20$ years

(a) Compounded monthly:

$A = 50\left[\left(1 + \dfrac{0.07}{12}\right)^{12(20)} - 1\right]\left(1 + \dfrac{12}{0.07}\right)$

$\approx \$26,198.27$

(b) Compounded continuously:

$A = \dfrac{50e^{0.07/12}(e^{0.07(20)} - 1)}{e^{0.07/12} - 1} \approx \$26,263.88$

93. $P = \$100$, $r = 10\%$, $t = 40$ years

(a) Compounded monthly: $A = 100\left[\left(1 + \dfrac{0.10}{12}\right)^{12(40)} - 1\right]\left(1 + \dfrac{12}{0.10}\right) \approx \$637,678.02$

(b) Compounded continuously: $A = \dfrac{100e^{0.10/12}\left(e^{(0.10)(40)} - 1\right)}{e^{0.10/12} - 1} \approx \$645,861.43$

95. $P = W\displaystyle\sum_{n=1}^{12t}\left[\left(1 + \dfrac{r}{12}\right)^{-1}\right]^{n}$

$= W\left(1 + \dfrac{r}{12}\right)^{-1}\left[\dfrac{1 - \left(1 + \dfrac{r}{12}\right)^{-12t}}{1 - \left(1 + \dfrac{r}{12}\right)^{-1}}\right]$

$= W\left(\dfrac{1}{1 + \dfrac{r}{12}}\right)\dfrac{\left[1 - \left(1 + \dfrac{r}{12}\right)^{-12t}\right]}{1 - \dfrac{1}{\left(1 + \dfrac{r}{12}\right)}}$

$= W\dfrac{\left[1 - \left(1 + \dfrac{r}{12}\right)^{-12t}\right]}{\left(1 + \dfrac{r}{12}\right) - 1}$

$= W\left(\dfrac{12}{r}\right)\left[1 - \left(1 + \dfrac{r}{12}\right)^{-12t}\right]$

97. $64 + 32 + 16 + 8 + 4 + 2 = 126$

Total area of shaded region is approximately 126 square inches.

99. $S_n = \displaystyle\sum_{i=1}^{n} 0.01(2)^{i-1} = 0.01\left(\dfrac{1 - 2^n}{1 - 2}\right) = 0.01(2^n - 1)$

(a) $S_{29} = \$5,368,709.11$

(b) $S_{30} = \$10,737,418.23$

(c) $S_{31} = \$21,474,836.47$

101. (a) Total distance $= \left[\displaystyle\sum_{n=0}^{\infty} 32(0.81)^n\right] - 16 = \dfrac{32}{1 - 0.81} - 16 \approx 152.42$ feet

(b) $t = 1 + 2\displaystyle\sum_{n=1}^{\infty} (0.9)^n = 1 + 2\left[\dfrac{0.9}{1 - 0.9}\right] = 19$ seconds

103. False. $a_n = a_1 r^{n-1}$, *NOT* ra_1^{n-1}

The nth term of a geometric sequence can be found by multiplying its first term by its common ratio raised to the $(n - 1)$th power.

105. Given a_1 and a_2, $r = \dfrac{a_2}{a_1}$ and $a_n = a_1 r^{n-1}$

Divide the second term by the first to obtain the common ratio. The nth term is the first term times the common ratio raised to the $n - 1$ power.

107. $f(x) = 3x + 1$

$f(x + 1) = 3(x + 1) + 1 = 3x + 4$

109. $g(x) = x^2 - 1$

$g(f(x + 1)) = g(3x + 4)$ From Exercise 107

$= (3x + 4)^2 - 1$

$= 9x^2 + 24x + 15$

111. $x^2 + 4x - 63$ Does not factor

113. $16x^2 - 4x^4 = 4x^2(4 - x^2)$

$$= 4x^2(2 + x)(2 - x)$$

115. $\dfrac{\cancel{x-2}}{\cancel{x+7}} \cdot \dfrac{\overset{1}{\cancel{2}}\cancel{(x+7)}}{\underset{3}{\cancel{6}}\cancel{(x-2)}} = \dfrac{1}{3}, \; x \neq -7, 2$

117. $\dfrac{x - 5}{x - 3} \div \dfrac{10 - 2x}{2(3 - x)} = \dfrac{\cancel{x-5}}{\cancel{x-3}} \cdot \dfrac{\cancel{-2(x-3)}}{\cancel{-2(x-5)}} = 1, \; x \neq 3, 5$

119. $8 - \dfrac{x - 1}{x + 4} - \dfrac{4}{x - 1} - \dfrac{x + 4}{(x - 1)(x + 4)} = \dfrac{8(x - 1)(x + 4) - (x - 1)^2 - 4(x + 4) - (x + 4)}{(x - 1)(x + 4)}$

$$= \dfrac{8(x^2 + 3x - 4) - (x^2 - 2x + 1) - 4x - 16 - x - 4}{(x - 1)(x + 4)}$$

$$= \dfrac{8x^2 + 24x - 32 - x^2 + 2x - 1 - 4x - 16 - x - 4}{(x - 1)(x + 4)}$$

$$= \dfrac{7x^2 + 21x - 53}{(x - 1)(x + 4)}$$

Section 9.4   Mathematical Induction

- You should be sure that you understand the principle of mathematical induction. If P_n is a statement involving the positive integer n, where P_1 is true and the truth of P_k implies the truth of P_{k+1}, then P_n is true for all positive integers n.

- You should be able to verify (by induction) the formulas for the sums of powers of integers and be able to use these formulas.

- You should be able to calculate the first and second differences of a sequence.

- You should be able to find the quadratic model for a sequence, when it exists.

Solutions to Odd-Numbered Exercises

1. $P_k = \dfrac{5}{k(k + 1)}$

$P_{k+1} = \dfrac{5}{(k + 1)[(k + 1) + 1]} = \dfrac{5}{(k + 1)(k + 2)}$

3. $P_k = \dfrac{k^2(k + 1)^2}{4}$

$P_{k+1} = \dfrac{(k + 1)^2[(k + 1) + 1]^2}{4} = \dfrac{(k + 1)^2(k + 2)^2}{4}$

5. 1   When $n = 1$, $S_1 = 2 = 1(1 + 1)$.

    2. Assume that

$$S_k = 2 + 4 + 6 + 8 + \cdots + 2k = k(k + 1).$$

Then,

$$S_{k+1} = 2 + 4 + 6 + 8 + \cdots + 2k + 2(k + 1)$$

$$= S_k + 2(k + 1) = k(k + 1) + 2(k + 1) = (k + 1)(k + 2).$$

Therefore, we conclude that the formula is valid for all positive integer values of n.

7. 1. When $n = 1$, $S_1 = 2 = \frac{1}{2}(5(1) - 1)$.

  2. Assume that

$$S_k = 2 + 7 + 12 + 17 + \cdots + (5k - 3) = \frac{k}{2}(5k - 1).$$

Then,

$$S_{k+1} = 2 + 7 + 12 + 17 + \cdots + (5k - 3) + [5(k + 1) - 3]$$

$$= S_k + (5k + 5 - 3) = \frac{k}{2}(5k - 1) + 5k + 2$$

$$= \frac{5k^2 - k + 10k + 4}{2} = \frac{5k^2 + 9k + 4}{2}$$

$$= \frac{(k + 1)(5k + 4)}{2} = \frac{(k + 1)}{2}[5(k + 1) - 1].$$

Therefore, we conclude that this formula is valid for all positive integer values of n.

9. 1. When $n = 1$, $S_1 = 1 = 2^1 - 1$.

  2. Assume that

$$S_k = 1 + 2 + 2^2 + 2^3 + \cdots + 2^{k-1} = 2^k - 1.$$

Then,

$$S_{k+1} = 1 + 2 + 2^2 + 2^3 + \cdots + 2^{k-1} + 2^k$$

$$= S_k + 2^k = 2^k - 1 + 2^k = 2(2^k) - 1 = 2^{k+1} - 1.$$

Therefore, we conclude that this formula is valid for all positive integer values of n.

11. 1. When $n = 1$, $S_1 = 1 = \frac{1(1 + 1)}{2}$.

  2. Assume that

$$S_k = 1 + 2 + 3 + 4 + \cdots + k = \frac{k(k + 1)}{2}.$$

Then,

$$S_{k+1} = 1 + 2 + 3 + 4 + \cdots + k + (k + 1)$$

$$= S_k + (k + 1) = \frac{k(k + 1)}{2} + \frac{2(k + 1)}{2} = \frac{(k + 1)(k + 2)}{2}.$$

Therefore, we conclude that this formula is valid for all positive integer values of n.

13. 1. When $n = 1$, $S_1 = 1^3 = 1 = \frac{1^2(1 + 1)^2}{4}$.

  2. Assume that

$$S_k = 1^3 + 2^3 + 3^3 + 4^3 + \cdots + k^3 = \frac{k^2(k + 1)^2}{4}.$$

— CONTINUED —

13. — CONTINUED —

Then,

$$S_{k+1} = 1^3 + 2^3 + 3^3 + 4^3 + \cdots + k^3 + (k + 1)^3$$

$$= S_k + (k + 1)^3 = \frac{k^2(k + 1)^2}{4} + (k + 1)^3 = \frac{k^2(k + 1)^2 + 4(k + 1)^3}{4}$$

$$= \frac{(k + 1)^2[k^2 + 4(k + 1)]}{4} = \frac{(k + 1)^2(k^2 + 4k + 4)}{4} = \frac{(k + 1)^2(k + 2)^2}{4}.$$

Therefore, we conclude that this formula is valid for all positive integer values of *n*.

15. 1. When $n = 1, S_1 = 1 = \dfrac{(1)^2(1 + 1)^2(2(1)^2 + 2(1) - 1)}{12}.$

2. Assume that

$$S_k = \sum_{i=1}^{k} i^5 = \frac{k^2(k + 1)^2(2k^2 + 2k - 1)}{12}.$$

Then,

$$S_{k+1} = \sum_{i=1}^{k+1} i^5 = \left(\sum_{i=1}^{k} i^5 \right) + (k + 1)^5$$

$$= \frac{k^2(k + 1)^2(2k^2 + 2k - 1)}{12} + \frac{12(k + 1)^5}{12}$$

$$= \frac{(k + 1)^2[k^2(2k^2 + 2k - 1) + 12(k + 1)^3]}{12}$$

$$= \frac{(k + 1)^2[2k^4 + 2k^3 - k^2 + 12(k^3 + 3k^2 + 3k + 1)]}{12}$$

$$= \frac{(k + 1)^2[2k^4 + 14k^3 + 35k^2 + 36k + 12]}{12}$$

$$= \frac{(k + 1)^2(k^2 + 4k + 4)(2k^2 + 6k + 3)}{12}$$

$$= \frac{(k + 1)^2(k + 2)^2[2(k + 1)^2 + 2(k + 1) - 1]}{12}.$$

Therefore, we conclude that this formula is valid for all positive integer values of *n*.

Note: The easiest way to complete the last two steps is to "work backwards." Start with the desired expression for S_{k+1} and multiply out to show that it is equal to the expression you found for $S_k + (k + 1)^5$.

17. 1. When $n = 1, S_1 = 2 = \dfrac{1(2)(3)}{3}.$

2. Assume that

$$S_k = 1(2) + 2(3) + 3(4) + \cdots + k(k + 1) = \frac{k(k + 1)(k + 2)}{3}.$$

— CONTINUED —

17. — CONTINUED —

Then,

$$S_{k+1} = 1(2) + 2(3) + 3(4) + \cdots + k(k + 1) + (k + 1)(k + 2)$$

$$= S_k + (k + 1)(k + 2) = \frac{k(k + 1)(k + 2)}{3} + \frac{3(k + 1)(k + 2)}{3}$$

$$= \frac{(k + 1)(k + 2)(k + 3)}{3}.$$

Therefore, we conclude that this formula is valid for all positive integer values of n.

19. $\displaystyle\sum_{n=1}^{15} n = \frac{15(15 + 1)}{2} = 120$

21. $\displaystyle\sum_{n=1}^{6} n^2 = \frac{6(6 + 1)[2(6) + 1]}{6} = 91$

23. $\displaystyle\sum_{n=1}^{5} n^4 = \frac{5(5 + 1)[2(5) + 1][3(5)^2 + 3(5) - 1]}{30} = 979$

25. $\displaystyle\sum_{n=1}^{6} (n^2 - n) = \sum_{n=1}^{6} n^2 - \sum_{n=1}^{6} n = \frac{6(6 + 1)[2(6) + 1]}{6} - \frac{6(6 + 1)}{2} = 91 - 21 = 70$

27. $\displaystyle\sum_{i=1}^{6} (6i - 8i^3) = 6\sum_{i=1}^{6} i - 8\sum_{i=1}^{6} i^3 = 6\left[\frac{6(6 + 1)}{2}\right] - 8\left[\frac{(6)^2(6 + 1)^2}{4}\right] = 6(21) - 8(441) = -3402$

29. $S_n = 1 + 5 + 9 + 13 + \cdots + (4n - 3)$

$S_1 = 1 = 1 \cdot 1$

$S_2 = 1 + 5 = 6 = 2 \cdot 3$

$S_3 = 1 + 5 + 9 = 15 = 3 \cdot 5$

$S_4 = 1 + 5 + 9 + 13 = 28 = 4 \cdot 7$

From this sequence, it appears that $S_n = n(2n - 1)$.

This can be verified by mathematical induction. The formula has already been verified for $n = 1$. Assume that the formula is valid for $n = k$.

Then,

$$S_{k+1} = [1 + 5 + 9 + 13 + \cdots + (4k - 3)] + [4(k + 1) - 3]$$

$$= k(2k - 1) + (4k + 1)$$

$$= 2k^2 + 3k + 1$$

$$= (k + 1)(2k + 1)$$

$$= (k + 1)[2(k + 1) - 1]$$

Thus, the formula is valid.

31. $S_n = 1 + \dfrac{9}{10} + \dfrac{81}{100} + \dfrac{729}{1000} + \cdots + \left(\dfrac{9}{10}\right)^{n-1}$

Since this series is geometric, we have

$$S_n = \sum_{i=1}^{n} \left(\frac{9}{10}\right)^{i-1} = \frac{1 - \left(\dfrac{9}{10}\right)^n}{1 - \dfrac{9}{10}} = 10\left[1 - \left(\frac{9}{10}\right)^n\right]$$

$$= 10 - 10\left(\frac{9}{10}\right)^n$$

33. $S_n = \dfrac{1}{4} + \dfrac{1}{12} + \dfrac{1}{24} + \dfrac{1}{40} + \cdots + \dfrac{1}{2n(n+1)}$

$S_1 = \dfrac{1}{4} = \dfrac{1}{2(2)}$

$S_2 = \dfrac{1}{4} + \dfrac{1}{12} = \dfrac{4}{12} = \dfrac{2}{6} = \dfrac{2}{2(3)}$

$S_3 = \dfrac{1}{4} + \dfrac{1}{12} + \dfrac{1}{24} = \dfrac{9}{24} = \dfrac{3}{8} = \dfrac{3}{2(4)}$

$S_4 = \dfrac{1}{4} + \dfrac{1}{12} + \dfrac{1}{24} + \dfrac{1}{40} = \dfrac{16}{40} = \dfrac{4}{10} = \dfrac{4}{2(5)}$

From this sequence, it appears that $S_n = \dfrac{n}{2(n+1)}$.

This can be verified by mathematical induction. The formula has already been verified for $n = 1$. Assume that the formula is valid for $n = k$.

Then,

$S_{k+1} = \left[\dfrac{1}{4} + \dfrac{1}{12} + \dfrac{1}{40} + \cdots + \dfrac{1}{2k(k+1)}\right] + \dfrac{1}{2(k+1)(k+2)}$

$= \dfrac{k}{2(k+1)} + \dfrac{1}{2(k+1)(k+2)}$

$= \dfrac{k(k+2) + 1}{2(k+1)(k+2)}$

$= \dfrac{k^2 + 2k + 1}{2(k+1)(k+2)}$

$= \dfrac{(k+1)^2}{2(k+1)(k+2)}$

$= \dfrac{k+1}{2(k+2)}$

Thus, the formula is valid.

35. 1. When $n = 4$, $4! = 24$ and $2^4 = 16$, thus $4! > 2^4$.

2. Assume

$k! > 2^k$, $k > 4$.

Then,

$(k+1)! = k!(k+1) > 2^k(2)$ since $k! > 2^k$ and $k+1 > 2$.

Thus, $(k+1)! > 2^{k+1}$.

Therefore, by extended mathematical induction, the inequality is valid for all integers n such that $n \geq 4$.

37. 1. When $n = 2$, $\dfrac{1}{\sqrt{1}} + \dfrac{1}{\sqrt{2}} \approx 1.707$ and $\sqrt{2} \approx 1.414$, thus $\dfrac{1}{\sqrt{1}} + \dfrac{1}{\sqrt{2}} > \sqrt{2}$.

2. Assume that

$\dfrac{1}{\sqrt{1}} + \dfrac{1}{\sqrt{2}} + \dfrac{1}{\sqrt{3}} + \cdots + \dfrac{1}{\sqrt{k}} > \sqrt{k}, k > 2.$

— CONTINUED —

37. — CONTINUED —

Then,

$$\frac{1}{\sqrt{1}} + \frac{1}{\sqrt{2}} + \frac{1}{\sqrt{3}} + \cdots + \frac{1}{\sqrt{k}} + \frac{1}{\sqrt{k+1}} > \sqrt{k} + \frac{1}{\sqrt{k+1}}.$$

Now it is sufficient to show that

$$\sqrt{k} + \frac{1}{\sqrt{k+1}} > \sqrt{k+1}, \ k > 2,$$

or equivalently (multiplying by $\sqrt{k+1}$.),

$$\sqrt{k}\sqrt{k+1} + 1 > k + 1.$$

This is true because

$$\sqrt{k}\sqrt{k+1} + 1 > \sqrt{k}\sqrt{k} + 1 = k + 1.$$

Therefore,

$$\frac{1}{\sqrt{1}} + \frac{1}{\sqrt{2}} + \frac{1}{\sqrt{3}} + \cdots + \frac{1}{\sqrt{k}} + \frac{1}{\sqrt{k+1}} > \sqrt{k+1}.$$

Therefore, by extended mathematical induction, the inequality is valid for all integers n such that $n \geq 2$.

39. $(1 + a)^n \geq na, n \geq 1$ and $a > 0$

Since a is positive, then all of the terms in the binomial expansion are positive.

$$(1 + a)^n = 1 + na + \cdots + na^{n-1} + a^n > na$$

41. 1. When $n = 1$, $(ab)^1 = a^1 b^1 = ab$.

2. Assume that $(ab)^k = a^k b^k$.

Then, $(ab)^{k+1} = (ab)^k (ab)$

$$= a^k b^k ab$$

$$= a^{k+1} b^{k+1}.$$

Thus, $(ab)^n = a^n b^n$.

43. 1. When $n = 1$, $(x_1)^{-1} = x_1^{-1}$.

2. Assume that

$$(x_1 x_2 x_3 \cdots x_k)^{-1} = x_1^{-1} x_2^{-1} x_3^{-1} \cdots x_k^{-1}.$$

Then,

$$(x_1 x_2 x_3 \cdots x_k x_{k+1})^{-1} = [(x_1 x_2 x_3 \cdots x_k) x_{k+1}]^{-1}$$

$$= (x_1 x_2 x_3 \cdots x_k)^{-1} x_{k+1}^{-1}$$

$$= x_1^{-1} x_2^{-1} x_3^{-1} \cdots x_k^{-1} x_{k+1}^{-1}.$$

Thus, the formula is valid.

45. 1. When $n = 1$, $x(y_1) = xy_1$.

2. Assume that

$$x(y_1 + y_2 + \cdots + y_k) = xy_1 + xy_2 + \cdots + xy_k.$$

Then,

$$xy_1 + xy_2 + \cdots + xy_k + xy_{k+1} = x(y_1 + y_2 + \cdots + y_k) + xy_{k+1}$$

$$= x[(y_1 + y_2 + \cdots + y_k) + y_{k+1}]$$

$$= x(y_1 + y_2 + \cdots + y_k + y_{k+1}).$$

Hence, the formula holds.

47. 1. When $n = 1$, $[1^3 + 3(1)^2 + 2(1)] = 6$ and 3 is a factor.

2. Assume that 3 is a factor of $k^3 + 3k^2 + 2k$.

Then,

$$(k + 1)^3 + 3(k + 1)^2 + 2(k + 1) = k^3 + 3k^2 + 3k + 1 + 3k^2 + 6k + 3 + 2k + 2$$
$$= (k^3 + 3k^2 + 2k) + (3k^2 + 9k + 6)$$
$$= (k^3 + 3k^2 + 2k) + 3(k^2 + 3k + 2).$$

Since 3 is a factor of $(k^3 + 3k^2 + 2k)$, our assumption, and 3 is a factor of $3(k^2 + 3k + 2)$, we conclude that 3 is a factor of the whole sum.

Thus, 3 is a factor of $(n^3 + 3n^2 + 2n)$ for every positive integer n.

49. 1. When $n = 2$, $(9^2 - 8(2) - 1) = 64$ and 64 is a factor.

2. Assume that 64 is a factor of $(9^k - 8k - 1)$.

Then,

$$9^{k+1} - 8(k + 1) - 1$$

$$= 9^{k+1} - 8k - 9$$

$$= (9^{k+1} - 72k - 9) + 64k$$

$$= 9(9^k - 8k - 1) + 64k$$

Since 64 is a factor of $(9^k - 8k - 1)$ and 64 is a factor of $64k$, we conclude that 64 is a factor of the whole sum.

Thus, 64 is a factor of $(9^n - 8n - 1)$ for all $n \geq 2$.

51. $a_0 = 10$, $a_n = 4a_{n-1}$

$a_0 = 10$

$a_1 = 4(10) = 40$

$a_2 = 4(40) = 160$

$a_3 = 4(160) = 640$

$a_4 = 4(640) = 2560$

53. $a_0 = 0$, $a_1 = 2$, $a_n = a_{n-1} + 2a_{n-2}$

$a_0 = 0$

$a_1 = 2$

$a_2 = 2 + 2(0) = 2$

$a_3 = 2 + 2(2) = 6$

$a_4 = 6 + 2(2) = 10$

55. $f(1) = 2$, $a_n = n - a_{n-1}$

$a_1 = f(1) = 2$

$a_2 = n - a_1 = 2 - 2 = 0$

$a_3 = n - a_2 = 3 - 0 = 3$

$a_4 = n - a_3 = 4 - 3 = 1$

$a_5 = n - a_5 = 5 - 1 = 4$

a_n: 2 0 3 1 4

First differences: -2 3 -2 3

Second differences: 5 -5 5

Since neither the first differences nor the second differences are equal, the sequence does not have a linear or quadratic model.

57. $f(2) = -3$, $a_n = -2a_{n-1}$

$a_2 = f(2) = -3 \Longrightarrow -3 = -2a_1$

$a_1 = \frac{3}{2}$

$a_3 = -2a_2 = -2(-3) = 6$

$a_4 = -2a_3 = -2(6) = -12$

$a_5 = -2a_4 = -2(-12) = 24$

a_n: $\frac{3}{2}$ -3 6 -12 24

First differences: $-\frac{9}{2}$ 9 -18 36

Second differences: $\frac{27}{2}$ -27 54

Since neither the first differences nor the second differences are equal, the sequence does not have a linear or quadratic model.

59. $a_0 = 2, \quad a_n = (a_{n-1})^2$

$a_0 = 2$

$a_1 = a_0{}^2 = 2^2 = 4$

$a_2 = a_1{}^2 = 4^2 = 16$

$a_3 = a_2{}^2 = 16^2 = 256$

$a_4 = a_3{}^2 = 256^2 = 65{,}536$

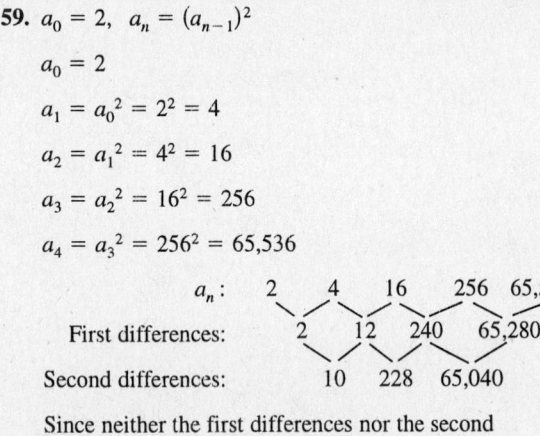

Since neither the first differences nor the second differences are equal, the sequence does not have a linear or quadratic model.

61. $f(1) = 0, \quad a_n = a_{n-1} + 2n$

$a_1 = 0$

$a_2 = a_1 + 2(2) = 0 + 4 = 4$

$a_3 = a_2 + 2(3) = 4 + 6 = 10$

$a_4 = a_3 + 2(4) = 10 + 8 = 18$

$a_5 = a_4 + 2(5) = 18 + 10 = 28$

a_n:	0	4	10	18	28
First differences:		4	6	8	10
Second differences:			2	2	2

Since the second differences are equal, the sequence has a quadratic model.

63. $a_0 = 0, \quad a_n = a_{n-1} - 1$

$a_0 = 0$

$a_1 = a_0 - 1 = 0 - 1 = -1$

$a_2 = a_1 - 1 = -1 - 1 = -2$

$a_3 = a_2 - 1 = -2 - 1 = -3$

$a_4 = a_3 - 1 = -3 - 1 = -4$

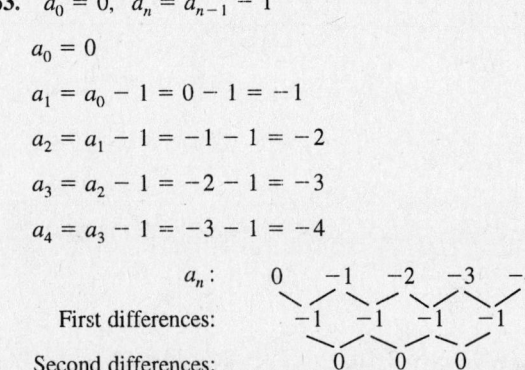

Since the first differences are equal, the sequence has a linear model.

65. $a_0 = 7, \quad a_1 = 6, \quad a_3 = 10$

Let $a_n = an^2 + bn + c$. Then,

$a_0 = a(0)^2 + b(0) + c = 7 \implies \qquad\qquad c = 7$
$a_1 = a(1)^2 + b(1) + c = 6 \implies a + b + c = 6$
$\qquad\qquad\qquad\qquad\qquad\qquad a + b \quad = -1$

$a_3 = a(3)^2 + b(3) + c = 10 \implies 9a + 3b + c = 10$
$\qquad\qquad\qquad\qquad\qquad\qquad\qquad 9a + 3b \quad = 3$
$\qquad\qquad\qquad\qquad\qquad\qquad\qquad 3a + b \quad = 1$

By elimination: $\quad -a - b = 1$
$\qquad\qquad\qquad\quad \underline{3a + b = 1}$
$\qquad\qquad\qquad\qquad\quad 2a = 2$
$\qquad\qquad\qquad\qquad\quad a = 1 \implies b = -2$

Thus, $a_n = n^2 - 2n + 7$.

67. $a_0 = 3, \quad a_2 = 0, \quad a_6 = 36$

Let $a_n = an^2 + bn + c$. Then,

$a_0 = a(0)^2 + b(0) + c = 3 \implies \qquad\qquad c = 3$
$a_2 = a(2)^2 + b(2) + c = 0 \implies 4a + 2b + c = 0$
$\qquad\qquad\qquad\qquad\qquad\qquad 4a + 2b \quad = -3$

$a_6 = a(6)^2 + b(6) + c = 36 \implies 36a + 6b + c = 36$
$\qquad\qquad\qquad\qquad\qquad\qquad\qquad 36a + 6b \quad = 33$
$\qquad\qquad\qquad\qquad\qquad\qquad\qquad 12a + 2b \quad = 11$

By elimination: $\quad -4a - 2b = 3$
$\qquad\qquad\qquad\quad \underline{12a + 2b = 11}$
$\qquad\qquad\qquad\qquad\quad 8a \qquad = 14$
$\qquad\qquad\qquad\qquad\quad a = \tfrac{7}{4} \implies b = -5$

Thus, $a_n = \tfrac{7}{4}n^2 - 5n + 3$.

69. False. For example, the statement in Exercise #35 is not true for $n = 1$.

71. False. It has $n - 2$ second differences.

73. (a) If P_3 is true and P_k implies P_{k+1}, then P_n is true for integers $n \geq 3$.

  (b) If $P_1, P_2, P_3, \ldots, P_{50}$ are all true, then P_n is true for integers $1 \leq n \leq 50$.

  (c) If $P_1, P_2,$ and P_3 are all true, but the truth of P_k does not imply that P_{k+1} is true, then you may only conclude that $P_1, P_2,$ and P_3 are true.

  (d) If P_2 is true and P_{2k} implies P_{2k+2}, then P_{2n} is true for any positive integer n.

75. $x - y^3 = 0 \Longrightarrow x = y^3$

$x - 2y^2 = 0$

$y^3 - 2y^2 = 0$

$y^2(y - 2) = 0 \Longrightarrow y = 0, 2$

When $y = 0$: $x = 0^3 = 0$.

When $y = 2$: $x = 2^3 = 8$.

Solution: $(0, 0)$ and $(8, 2)$

77. $2x + y - 2z = 1$

$x \quad\quad - z = 1$

$3x + 3y + z = 12$

$$A = \begin{bmatrix} 2 & 1 & -2 \\ 1 & 0 & -1 \\ 3 & 3 & 1 \end{bmatrix}, \quad A^{-1} = \tfrac{1}{4} \begin{bmatrix} -3 & 7 & 1 \\ 4 & -8 & 0 \\ -3 & 3 & 1 \end{bmatrix}$$

$$\begin{bmatrix} x \\ y \\ z \end{bmatrix} = \tfrac{1}{4} \begin{bmatrix} -3 & 7 & 1 \\ 4 & -8 & 0 \\ -3 & 3 & 1 \end{bmatrix} \begin{bmatrix} 1 \\ 1 \\ 12 \end{bmatrix} = \begin{bmatrix} 4 \\ -1 \\ 3 \end{bmatrix}$$

Thus, $x = 4, y = -1, z = 3$.

Solution: $(4, -1, 3)$

79. $(2x - y)^2 = 4x^2 - 4xy + y^2$

81. $(2x - 4y)^3 = 8x^3 - 48x^2y + 96xy^2 - 64y^3$

Section 9.5   The Binomial Theorem

■ You should be able to use the formula

$$(x + y)^n = x^n + nx^{n-1}y + \frac{n(n-1)}{2!}x^{n-2}y^2 + \cdots + {}_nC_r x^{n-r}y^r + \cdots + y^n$$

where ${}_nC_r = \dfrac{n!}{(n-r)!r!}$, to expand $(x + y)^n$.

■ You should be able to use Pascal's Triangle in binomial expansion.

Solutions to Odd-Numbered Exercises

1. ${}_5C_3 = \dfrac{5!}{3!2!} = \dfrac{5 \cdot 4}{2 \cdot 1} = 10$

3. ${}_{12}C_0 = \dfrac{12!}{0!12!} = 1$

5. ${}_{20}C_{15} = \dfrac{20!}{15!5!} = \dfrac{20 \cdot 19 \cdot 18 \cdot 17 \cdot 16}{5 \cdot 4 \cdot 3 \cdot 2 \cdot 1} = 15{,}504$

7. $\dbinom{10}{4} = \dfrac{10!}{6!4!} = \dfrac{10 \cdot 9 \cdot 8 \cdot 7 \cdot 6!}{6!(24)} = 210$

9. $\dbinom{100}{98} = \dfrac{100!}{2!98!} = \dfrac{100 \cdot 99}{2 \cdot 1} = 4950$

11.

```
            1
          1   1
        1   2   1
      1   3   3   1
    1   4   6   4   1
  1   5  10  10   5   1
1   6  15  20  15   6   1
1  7  21  35  35  21  7  1
1  8 28 56  70 (56) 28  8  1
```

$\dbinom{8}{5} = 56$, the 6th entry in the 9th row.

13.

```
            1
          1   1
        1   2   1
      1   3   3   1
    1   4   6   4   1
  1   5  10  10   5   1
1   6  15  20  15   6   1
1  7  21  35 (35) 21  7  1
```

$_7C_4 = 35$, the 5th entry in the 8th row.

15. $(x + 1)^4 = {}_4C_0x^4 + {}_4C_1x^3(1) + {}_4C_2x^2(1)^2 + {}_4C_3x(1)^3 + {}_4C_4(1)^4$

$\quad = x^4 + 4x^3 + 6x^2 + 4x + 1$

17. $(a + 6)^4 = {}_4C_0a^4 + {}_4C_1a^3(6) + {}_4C_2a^2(6)^2 + {}_4C_3a(6)^3 + {}_4C_4(6)^4$

$\quad\quad = 1a^4 + 4a^3(6) + 6a^2(6)^2 + 4a(6)^3 + 1(6)^4$

$\quad\quad = a^4 + 24a^3 + 216a^2 + 864a + 1296$

19. $(y - 4)^3 = {}_3C_0y^3 - {}_3C_1y^2(4) + {}_3C_2y(4)^2 - {}_3C_3(4)^3$

$\quad\quad = 1y^3 - 3y^2(4) + 3y(4)^2 - 1(4)^3$

$\quad\quad = y^3 - 12y^2 + 48y - 64$

21. $(x + y)^5 = {}_5C_0x^5 + {}_5C_1x^4y + {}_5C_2x^3y^2 + {}_5C_3x^2y^3 + {}_5C_4xy^4 + {}_5C_5y^5$

$\quad\quad = x^5 + 5x^4y + 10x^3y^2 + 10x^2y^3 + 5xy^4 + y^5$

23. $(r + 3s)^6 = {}_6C_0r^6 + {}_6C_1r^5(3s) + {}_6C_2r^4(3s)^2 + {}_6C_3r^3(3s)^3 + {}_6C_4r^2(3s)^4 + {}_6C_5r(3s)^5 + {}_6C_6(3s)^6$

$\quad\quad = 1r^6 + 6r^5(3s) + 15r^4(3s)^2 + 20r^3(3s)^3 + 15r^2(3s)^4 + 6r(3s)^5 + 1(3s)^6$

$\quad\quad = r^6 + 18r^5s + 135r^4s^2 + 540r^3s^3 + 1215r^2s^4 + 1458rs^5 + 729s^6$

25. $(3a - b)^5 = {}_5C_0(3a)^5 - {}_5C_1(3a)^4b + {}_5C_2(3a)^3b^2 - {}_5C_3(3a)^2b^3 + {}_5C_4(3a)b^4 - {}_5C_5b^5$

$\quad\quad = (1)(3a)^5 - (5)(3a)^4b + 10(3a)^3b^2 - (10)(3a)^2b^3 + (5)(3a)b^4 - (1)b^5$

$\quad\quad = 243a^5 - 405a^4b + 270a^3b^2 - 90a^2b^3 + 15ab^4 - b^5$

27. $(1 - 2x)^3 = {}_3C_01^3 - {}_3C_11^2(2x) + {}_3C_21(2x)^2 - {}_3C_3(2x)^3$

$\quad\quad = 1 - 3(2x) + 3(2x)^2 - (2x)^3$

$\quad\quad = 1 - 6x + 12x^2 - 8x^3$

29. $(x^2 + 5)^4 = {}_4C_0(x^2)^4 + {}_4C_1(x^2)^3(5) + {}_4C_2(x^2)^2(5)^2 + {}_4C_3(x^2)(5)^3 + {}_4C_4(5)^4$

$\quad\quad = x^8 + 4x^6(5) + 6x^4(25) + 4x^2(125) + 625$

$\quad\quad = x^8 + 20x^6 + 150x^4 + 500x^2 + 625$

31. $\left(\dfrac{1}{x} + y\right)^5 = {}_5C_0\left(\dfrac{1}{x}\right)^5 + {}_5C_1\left(\dfrac{1}{x}\right)^4y + {}_5C_2\left(\dfrac{1}{x}\right)^3y^2 + {}_5C_3\left(\dfrac{1}{x}\right)^2y^3 + {}_5C_4\left(\dfrac{1}{x}\right)y^4 + {}_5C_5y^5$

$\quad\quad = \dfrac{1}{x^5} + \dfrac{5y}{x^4} + \dfrac{10y^2}{x^3} + \dfrac{10y^3}{x^2} + \dfrac{5y^4}{x} + y^5$

33. $2(x-3)^4 + 5(x-3)^2 = 2[x^4 - 4(x^3)(3) + 6(x^2)(3^2) - 4(x)(3^3) + 3^4] + 5[x^2 - 2(x)(3) + 3^2]$

$$= 2(x^4 - 12x^3 + 54x^2 - 108x + 81) + 5(x^2 - 6x + 9)$$

$$= 2x^4 - 24x^3 + 113x^2 - 246x + 207$$

35. 5th Row of Pascal's Triangle: 1   5   10   10   5   1

$(2t - s)^5 = 1(2t)^5 - 5(2t)^4(s) + 10(2t)^3(s)^2 - 10(2t)^2(s)^3 + 5(2t)(s)^4 - 1(s)^5$

$$= 32t^5 - 80t^4s + 80t^3s^2 - 40t^2s^3 + 10ts^4 - s^5$$

37. 5th Row of Pascal's Triangle: 1   5   10   10   5   1

$(x + 2y)^5 = 1x^5 + 5x^4(2y) + 10x^3(2y)^2 + 10x^2(2y)^3 + 5x(2y)^4 + 1(2y)^5$

$$= x^5 + 10x^4y + 40x^3y^2 + 80x^2y^3 + 80xy^4 + 32y^5$$

39. The term involving x^5 in the expansion of $(x + 3)^{12}$ is

$${}_{12}C_7 x^5(3)^7 = \frac{12!}{7!5!} \cdot 3^7 x^5 = 1{,}732{,}104x^5.$$ The coefficient is $1{,}732{,}104$.

41. The term involving x^8y^2 in the expansion of $(x - 2y)^{10}$ is

$${}_{10}C_2 x^8(-2y)^2 = \frac{10!}{2!8!} \cdot 4x^8y^2 = 180x^8y^2.$$ The coefficient is 180.

43. The term involving x^4y^5 in the expansion of $(3x - 2y)^9$ is

$${}_9C_5 (3x)^4(-2y)^5 = \frac{9!}{5!4!}(81x^4)(-32y^5) = -326{,}592x^4y^5.$$ The coefficient is $-326{,}592$.

45. The term involving $x^8y^6 = (x^2)^4y^6$ in the expansion of $(x^2 + y)^{10}$ is ${}_{10}C_6 (x^2)^4y^6 = \frac{10!}{4!6!}(x^2)^4y^6 = 210x^8y^6$.

The coefficient is 210.

47. $\left(\sqrt{x} + 3\right)^4 = \left(\sqrt{x}\right)^4 + 4\left(\sqrt{x}\right)^3(3) + 6\left(\sqrt{x}\right)^2(3)^2 + 4\left(\sqrt{x}\right)(3)^3 + (3)^4$

$$= x^2 + 12x\sqrt{x} + 54x + 108\sqrt{x} + 81$$

$$= x^2 + 12x^{3/2} + 54x + 108x^{1/2} + 81$$

49. $(x^{2/3} - y^{1/3})^3 = (x^{2/3})^3 - 3(x^{2/3})^2 (y^{1/3}) + 3(x^{2/3}) (y^{1/3})^2 - (y^{1/3})^3$

$$= x^2 - 3x^{4/3}y^{1/3} + 3x^{2/3}y^{2/3} - y$$

51. $\dfrac{f(x + h) - f(x)}{h} = \dfrac{(x + h)^3 - x^3}{h}$

$$= \frac{x^3 + 3x^2h + 3xh^2 + h^3 - x^3}{h}$$

$$= \frac{h(3x^2 + 3xh + h^2)}{h}$$

$$= 3x^2 + 3xh + h^2, h \neq 0$$

53. $\dfrac{f(x + h) - f(x)}{h} = \dfrac{\sqrt{x + h} - \sqrt{x}}{h}$

$$= \frac{\sqrt{x + h} - \sqrt{x}}{h} \cdot \frac{\sqrt{x + h} + \sqrt{x}}{\sqrt{x + h} + \sqrt{x}}$$

$$= \frac{(x + h) - x}{h\left(\sqrt{x + h} + \sqrt{x}\right)}$$

$$= \frac{1}{\sqrt{x + h} + \sqrt{x}}, h \neq 0$$

55. $(1 + i)^4 = {}_4C_0(1)_4 + {}_4C_1(1)^3i + {}_4C_2(1)^2i^2 + {}_4C_3(1)i^3 + {}_4C_4i^4$

$\qquad = 1 + 4i - 6 - 4i + 1$

$\qquad = -4$

57. $(2 - 3i)^6 = {}_6C_02^6 - {}_6C_12^5(3i) + {}_6C_22^4(3i)^2 - {}_6C_32^3(3i)^3 + {}_6C_42^2(3i)^4 - {}_6C_52(3i)^5 + {}_6C_6(3i)^6$

$\qquad = (1)(64) - (6)(32)(3i) + 15(16)(-9) - 20(8)(-27i) + 15(4)(81) - 6(2)(243i) + (1)(-729)$

$\qquad = 64 - 576i - 2160 + 4320i + 4860 - 2916i - 729$

$\qquad = 2035 + 828i$

59. $\left(-\dfrac{1}{2} + \dfrac{\sqrt{3}}{2}i\right)^3 = \dfrac{1}{8}\left(-1 + \sqrt{3}i\right)^3$

$\qquad\qquad = \dfrac{1}{8}\left[(-1)^3 + 3(-1)^2\left(\sqrt{3}i\right) + 3(-1)\left(\sqrt{3}i\right)^2 + \left(\sqrt{3}i\right)^3\right]$

$\qquad\qquad = \dfrac{1}{8}\left[-1 + 3\sqrt{3}i + 9 - 3\sqrt{3}i\right]$

$\qquad\qquad = 1$

61. $(1.02)^8 = (1 + 0.02)^8 = 1 + 8(0.02) + 28(0.02)^2 + 56(0.02)^3 + 70(0.02)^4 + 56(0.02)^5$

$\qquad\qquad\qquad\qquad\quad + 28(0.02)^6 + 8(0.02)^7 + (0.02)^8$

$\qquad\qquad\qquad = 1 + 0.16 + 0.0112 + 0.000448 + \cdots \approx 1.172$

63. $(2.99)^{12} = (3 - 0.01)^{12}$

$\qquad = 3^{12} - 12(3)^{11}(0.01) + 66(3)^{10}(0.01)^2 - 220(3)^9(0.01)^3 + 495(3)^8(0.01)^4$

$\qquad\quad - 792(3)^7(0.01)^5 + 924(3)^6(0.01)^6 - 792(3)^5(0.01)^7 + 495(3)^4(0.01)^8$

$\qquad\quad - 220(3)^3(0.01)^9 + 66(3)^2(0.01)^{10} - 12(3)(0.01)^{11} + (0.01)^{12}$

$\qquad \approx 531{,}441 - 21{,}257.64 + 389.7234 - 4.3303 + 0.0325 - 0.0002 + \cdots \approx 510{,}568{,}785$

65. $f(x) = x^3 - 4x$

$\quad g(x) = f(x + 4)$

$\qquad\quad = (x + 4)^3 - 4(x + 4)$

$\qquad\quad = x^3 + 3x^2(4) + 3x(4)^2 + (4)^3 - 4x - 16$

$\qquad\quad = x^3 + 12x^2 + 48x + 64 - 4x - 16$

$\qquad\quad = x^3 + 12x^2 + 44x + 48$

The graph of g is the same as the graph of f shifted 4 units to the left.

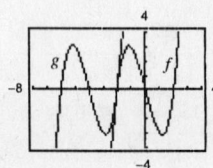

67. $f(x) = (1 - x)^3$

$\quad g(x) = 1 - 3x$

$\quad h(x) = 1 - 3x + 3x^2$

$\quad p(x) = 1 - 3x + 3x^2 - x^3$

Since $p(x)$ is the expansion of $f(x)$, they have the same graph.

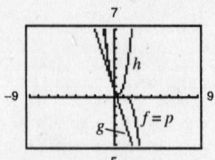

69. $_{10}C_3\left(\frac{1}{4}\right)^3\left(\frac{3}{4}\right)^7 = 120\left(\frac{1}{64}\right)\left(\frac{2187}{16,384}\right) \approx 0.2503$

71. $_8C_4\left(\frac{1}{2}\right)^4\left(\frac{1}{2}\right)^4 = 70\left(\frac{1}{16}\right)\left(\frac{1}{16}\right) \approx 0.273$

73. $f(t) = 0.0834t^2 + 0.07657t + 5.3680, 0 \le t \le 21$

(a) $g(t) = f(t + 4)$

$= 0.0834(t + 4)^2 + 0.07657(t + 4) + 5.3680$

$= 0.0834(t^2 + 8t + 16) + 0.07657t + 0.30628 + 5.3680$

$= 0.0834t^2 + 0.6672t + 1.3344 + 0.0765t + 0.30628 + 5.3680$

$= 0.0834t^2 + 0.74377t + 7.00868$

(b)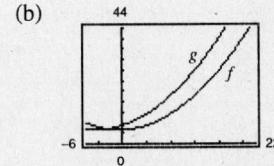

75. False. Expanding binomials that represent differences is just as accurate as expanding binomials that represent sums, but for differences the coefficient signs are alternating.

77.
```
              1
           1     1
        1     2     1
     1     3     3     1
   1     4     6     4     1
  1    5   10    10    5    1
 1   6   15   20   15   6   1
1  7  21  35  35  21  7  1
1  8  28 56  70  56 28  8  1
```

79. The signs of the terms in the expansion of $(x - y)^n$ alternate from positive to negative.

81. $0 = (1 - 1)^n = {_nC_0} - {_nC_1} + {_nC_2} - {_nC_3} + \cdots \pm {_nC_n}$

83. $_nC_0 + {_nC_1} + {_nC_2} + {_nC_3} + \cdots + {_nC_n} = (1 + 1)^n = 2^n$

85. $g(x) = f(x - 3)$

$g(x)$ is shifted 3 units to the right of $f(x)$.

87. $g(x) = -f(x)$

$g(x)$ is the reflection of $f(x)$ in the x-axis.

89. The graph of $f(x) = x^2$ has been reflected in the x-axis, shifted two units to the left, and shifted 3 units upward.

Thus, $g(x) = -(x + 2)^2 + 3$

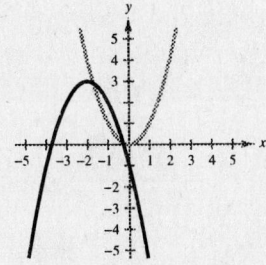

91. The graph of $f(x) = \sqrt{x}$ has been reflected in the x-axis, shifted two units to the left, and shifted 2 units downward.

Thus, $g(x) = -\sqrt{x + 1} - 2$

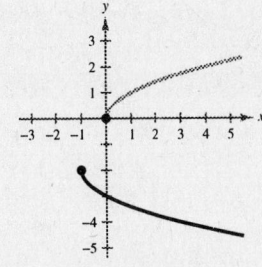

Section 9.6   Counting Principles

■ You should know The Fundamental Counting Principle.

■ $_nP_r = \dfrac{n!}{(n-r)!}$ is the number of permutations of n elements taken r at a time.

■ Given a set of n objects that has n_1 of one kind, n_2 of a second kind, and so on, the number of distinguishable permutations is

$$\frac{n!}{n_1!n_2!\ldots n_k!}.$$

■ $_nC_r = \dfrac{n!}{(n-r)!r!}$ is the number of combinations of n elements taken r at a time.

Solutions to Odd–Numbered Exercises

1. Odd integers: 1, 3, 5, 7, 9, 11

   6 ways

3. Prime integers: 2, 3, 5, 7, 11

   5 ways

5. Divisible by 4: 4, 8, 12

   3 ways

7. Sum is 8: $1 + 7,\ 2 + 6,\ 3 + 5,\ 4 + 4$

   4 ways

9. Amplifiers: 3 choices

   Compact disc players: 2 choices

   Speakers: 5 choices

   Total: $3 \cdot 2 \cdot 5 = 30$ ways

11. Chemist: 5 choices

   Statistician: 3 choices

   Total: $5 \cdot 3 = 15$ ways

13. $2^6 = 64$

15. 1st Position: 2 choices

   2nd Position: 2 choices

   3rd Position: 1 choice

   Total: $2 \cdot 2 \cdot 1 = 4$ ways

17. $26 \cdot 26 \cdot 26 \cdot 10 \cdot 10 \cdot 10 \cdot 10 = 175{,}760{,}000$ distinct license plate numbers.

19. (a) $9 \cdot 10 \cdot 10 = 900$

   (b) $9 \cdot 9 \cdot 8 = 648$

   (c) $9 \cdot 10 \cdot 2 = 180$

   (d) $6 \cdot 10 \cdot 10 = 600$

21. $40^3 = 64{,}000$

23. (a) $8 \cdot 7 \cdot 6 \cdot 5 \cdot 4 \cdot 3 \cdot 2 \cdot 1 = 40{,}320$

   (b) $8 \cdot 1 \cdot 6 \cdot 1 \cdot 4 \cdot 1 \cdot 2 \cdot 1 = 384$

25. $_nP_r = \dfrac{n!}{(n-r)!}$

So, $_4P_4 = \dfrac{4!}{0!} = 4! = 24$.

27. $_8P_3 = \dfrac{8!}{5!} = 8 \cdot 7 \cdot 6 = 336$

29. $_5P_4 = \dfrac{5!}{1!} = 120$

31. $14 \cdot {}_nP_3 = {}_{n+2}P_4$ Note: $n \geq 3$ for this to be defined.

$14\left(\dfrac{n!}{(n-3)!}\right) = \dfrac{(n+2)!}{(n-2)!}$

$14n(n-1)(n-2) = (n+2)(n+1)n(n-1)$ (We can divide here by $n(n-1)$ since $n \neq 0$, $n \neq 1$.)

$14(n-2) = (n+2)(n+1)$

$14n - 28 = n^2 + 3n + 2$

$0 = n^2 - 11n + 30$

$0 = (n-5)(n-6)$

$n = 5$ or $n = 6$

33. $_{20}P_5 = 1,860,480$

35. $_{100}P_3 = 970,200$

37. $_{20}C_5 = 15,504$

39. $\dfrac{7!}{2!1!3!1!} = \dfrac{7!}{2!3!} = 420$

41. $\dfrac{7!}{2!1!1!1!1!1!1!} = \dfrac{7!}{2!} = 7 \cdot 6 \cdot 5 \cdot 4 \cdot 3 = 2520$

43.

ABCD	BACD	CABD	DABC
ABDC	BADC	CADB	DACB
ACBD	BCAD	CBAD	DBAC
ACDB	BCDA	CBDA	DBCA
ADBC	BDAC	CDAB	DCAB
ADCB	BDCA	CDBA	DCBA

45. $_6C_2 = 15$

The 15 ways are listed below.

AB, AC, AD, AE, AF,

BC, BD, BE, BF, CD,

CE, CF, DE, DF, EF

47. $5! = 120$ ways

49. $_{12}P_4 = \dfrac{12!}{8!} = 12 \cdot 11 \cdot 10 \cdot 9 = 11,880$ ways

51. $_{20}C_4 = 4845$ groups

53. $_{40}C_6 = 3,838,380$ ways

55. $_{100}C_4 = 3,921,225$ subsets

57. $_7C_2 = 21$ lines

59. (a) $_8C_4 = \dfrac{8!}{(8-4)!4!} = \dfrac{8!}{4!4!} = \dfrac{8 \cdot 7 \cdot 6 \cdot 5}{4 \cdot 3 \cdot 2} = 70$ ways

(b) $_3C_2 \cdot {}_5C_2 = \dfrac{3!}{(3-2)!2!} \cdot \dfrac{5!}{(5-2)!2!} = 3 \cdot 10 = 30$ ways

61. (a) $_8C_4 = \dfrac{8!}{4!4!} = 70$ ways

(b) There are 16 ways that a group of four can be formed without any couples in the group. In this situation, this occurs if and only if each couple is represented in the group, since there would be exactly one individual from each couple. See part (c). Therefore, there are $70 - 16 = 54$ ways that a group of four can be selected including at least one couple.

(c) $2 \cdot 2 \cdot 2 \cdot 2 = 16$ ways

63. $_5C_2 - 5 = 10 - 5 = 5$ diagonals

65. $_8C_2 - 8 = 28 - 8 = 20$ diagonals

67. False. It is an example of a combination.

69. $_nC_r = {_n}C_{n-r}$ They are the same.

71. $_nP_{n-1} = \dfrac{n!}{(n-(n-1))!} = \dfrac{n!}{1!} = \dfrac{n!}{0!} = {_n}P_n$

73. $_nC_{n-1} = \dfrac{n!}{(n-(n-1))!(n-1)!} = \dfrac{n!}{(1)!(n-1)!} = \dfrac{n!}{(n-1)!1!} = {_n}C_1$

75. $_{100}P_{80} \approx 3.836 \times 10^{139}$

This number is too large for some calculators to evaluate.

77. $f(x) = 3x^2 + 8$

(a) $f(3) = 3(3)^2 + 8 = 35$

(b) $f(0) = 3(0)^2 + 8 = 8$

(c) $f(-5) = 3(-5)^2 + 8 = 83$

79. $f(x) = -|x - 5| + 6$

(a) $f(-5) = -|-5 - 5| + 6 = -10 + 6 = -4$

(b) $f(-1) = -|-1 - 5| + 6 = -6 + 6 = 0$

(c) $f(11) = -|11 - 5| + 6 = -6 + 6 = 0$

81. $(x + 1)^5 = x^5 + 5x^4 + 10x^3 + 10x^2 + 5x + 1$

83. $(x^2 + 2y)^5 = (x^2)^5 + 5(x^2)^4(2y) + 10(x^2)^3(2y)^2 + 10(x^2)^2(2y)^3 + 5(x^2)(2y)^4 + (2y)^5$

$= x^{10} + 10x^8y + 40x^6y^2 + 80x^4y^3 + 80x^2y^4 + 32y^5$

Section 9.7   Probability

You should know the following basic principles of probability.

■ If an event E has $n(E)$ equally likely outcomes and its sample space has $n(S)$ equally likely outcomes, then the probability of event E is

$$P(E) = \frac{n(E)}{n(S)}, \text{ where } 0 \leq P(E) \leq 1.$$

■ If A and B are mutually exclusive events, then $P(A \cup B) = P(A) + P(B)$.

If A and B are not mutually exclusive events, then $P(A \cup B) = P(A) + P(B) - P(A \cap B)$.

■ If A and B are independent events, then the probability that both A and B will occur is $P(A)P(B)$.

■ The complement of an event A is denoted by A' and its probability is $P(A') = 1 - P(A)$.

Solutions to Odd-Numbered Exercises

1. $\{(H, 1), (H, 2), (H, 3), (H, 4), (H, 5), (H, 6),$
$(T, 1), (T, 2), (T, 3), (T, 4), (T, 5), (T, 6)\}$

3. $\{ABC, ACB, BAC, BCA, CAB, CBA\}$

5. $\{(A, B), (A, C), (A, D), (A, E), (B, C), (B, D), (B, E), (C, D), (C, E), (D, E)\}$

7. $E = \{HHT, HTH, THH\}$

$$P(E) = \frac{n(E)}{n(S)} = \frac{3}{8}$$

9. $E = \{HHH, HHT, HTH, HTT, THH, THT, TTH\}$

$$P(E) = \frac{n(E)}{n(S)} = \frac{7}{8}$$

11. $E = \{K\clubsuit, K\blacklozenge, K\heartsuit, K\spadesuit, Q\clubsuit, Q\blacklozenge, Q\heartsuit, Q\spadesuit, J\clubsuit, J\blacklozenge, J\heartsuit, J\spadesuit\}$

$$P(E) = \frac{n(E)}{n(S)} = \frac{12}{52} = \frac{3}{13}$$

13. $E = \{K\blacklozenge, K\heartsuit, Q\blacklozenge, Q\heartsuit, J\blacklozenge, J\heartsuit\}$

$$P(E) = \frac{n(E)}{n(S)} = \frac{6}{52} = \frac{3}{26}$$

15. $E = \{(1, 3), (2, 2), (3, 1)\}$

$$P(E) = \frac{n(E)}{n(S)} = \frac{3}{36} = \frac{1}{12}$$

17. Use the complement.

$$E' = \{(5, 6), (6, 5), (6, 6)\}$$

$$P(E') = \frac{n(E')}{n(S)} = \frac{3}{36} = \frac{1}{12}$$

$$P(E) = 1 - P(E') = 1 - \frac{1}{12} = \frac{11}{12}$$

19. $E_3 = \{(1, 2), (2, 1)\}$, $n(E_3) = 2$

$E_5 = \{(1, 4), (2, 3), (3, 2), (4, 1)\}$, $n(E_5) = 4$

$E_7 = \{(1, 6), (2, 5), (3, 4), (4, 3), (5, 2), (6, 1)\}$, $n(E_7) = 6$

$E = E_3 \cup E_5 \cup E_7$

$n(E) = 2 + 4 + 6 = 12$

$$P(E) = \frac{n(E)}{n(S)} = \frac{12}{36} = \frac{1}{3}$$

21. $P(E) = \dfrac{_3C_2}{_6C_2} = \dfrac{3}{15} = \dfrac{1}{5}$

23. $P(E) = \dfrac{_4C_2}{_6C_2} = \dfrac{6}{15} = \dfrac{2}{5}$

25. $P(E') = 1 - P(E) = 1 - p = 1 - 0.7 = 0.3$

27. $P(E') = 1 - P(E) = 1 - p = 1 - \frac{1}{3} = \frac{2}{3}$

29. $P(E) = 1 - P(E') = 1 - p = 1 - 0.15 = 0.85$

31. $P(E) = 1 - P(E') = 1 - p = 1 - \frac{13}{20} = \frac{7}{20}$

33. (a) $0.06(1.3 \text{ million}) = 0.078 \text{ million} = 78{,}000$

(b) 30%

(c) 21% + 16% = 37%

35. (a) $\frac{290}{500} = 0.58 = 58\%$

(b) $\frac{478}{500} = 0.956 = 95.6\%$

(c) $\frac{2}{500} = 0.004 = 0.4\%$

37. (a) $\dfrac{672}{1254}$

(b) $\dfrac{582}{1254}$

(c) $\dfrac{672 - 124}{1254} = \dfrac{548}{1254}$

39. $p + p + 2p = 1$

$$p = 0.25$$

Taylor: $0.50 = \dfrac{1}{2}$

Moore: $0.25 = \dfrac{1}{4}$

Jenkins: $0.25 = \dfrac{1}{4}$

41. (a) $\dfrac{_{15}C_{10}}{_{20}C_{10}} = \dfrac{3003}{184{,}756} = \dfrac{21}{1292} \approx 0.016$

(b) $\dfrac{_{15}C_8 \cdot {}_5C_2}{_{20}C_{10}} = \dfrac{64{,}350}{184{,}756} = \dfrac{225}{646} \approx 0.348$

(c) $\dfrac{_{15}C_9 \cdot {}_5C_1}{_{20}C_{10}} + \dfrac{_{15}C_{10}}{_{20}C_{10}} = \dfrac{25{,}025 + 3003}{184{,}756} = \dfrac{28{,}028}{184{,}756} = \dfrac{49}{323} \approx 0.152$

43. Total ways to insert letters: $4! = 24$ ways

4 correct: 1 way

3 correct: not possible

2 correct: $_4C_2 = 6$ ways (because once you choose the two envelopes that will contain the correct letters, there is only one way to insert the letters)

1 correct: $4 \cdot 2 \cdot 1 = 8$ ways (4 ways to choose which envelope is paired with the correct letter, 2 ways to fill the next envelope incorrectly, and only 1 way to fill the remaining envelopes such that both are incorrect)

0 correct: $3 \cdot 3 \cdot 1 = 9$ ways (3 ways to fill the first envelope incorrectly, then 3 ways to fill the envelope whose correct letter was placed in the first envelope, and only 1 way to fill the remaining envelopes such that both are incorrect)

(a) $\dfrac{8}{24} = \dfrac{1}{3}$

(b) $\dfrac{8 + 6 + 1}{24} = \dfrac{15}{24} = \dfrac{5}{8}$

45. (a) $\dfrac{1}{_5P_5} = \dfrac{1}{120}$

(b) $\dfrac{1}{_4P_4} = \dfrac{1}{24}$

47. (a) $\dfrac{4}{52} \cdot \dfrac{4}{52} = \dfrac{1}{169}$

(b) $\dfrac{4}{52} \cdot \dfrac{3}{51} = \dfrac{1}{221}$

49. (a) $\dfrac{_9C_4}{_{12}C_4} = \dfrac{126}{495} = \dfrac{14}{55}$ (4 good units)

(b) $\dfrac{_9C_2 \cdot {}_3C_2}{_{12}C_4} = \dfrac{108}{495} = \dfrac{12}{55}$ (2 good units)

(c) $\dfrac{_9C_3 \cdot {}_3C_1}{_{12}C_4} = \dfrac{252}{495} = \dfrac{28}{55}$ (3 good units)

At least 2 good units: $\dfrac{12}{55} + \dfrac{28}{55} + \dfrac{14}{55} = \dfrac{54}{55}$

51. (a) $P(EE) = \dfrac{15}{30} \cdot \dfrac{15}{30} = \dfrac{1}{4}$

(b) $P(EO \text{ or } OE) = 2\left(\dfrac{15}{30}\right)\left(\dfrac{15}{30}\right) = \dfrac{1}{2}$

(c) $P(N_1 < 10, N_2 < 10) = \dfrac{9}{30} \cdot \dfrac{9}{30} = \dfrac{9}{100}$

(d) $P(N_1 N_1) = \dfrac{30}{30} \cdot \dfrac{1}{30} = \dfrac{1}{30}$

53. (a) $P(SS) = (0.985)^2 \approx 0.9702$

(b) $P(S) = 1 - P(FF) = 1 - (0.015)^2 \approx 0.9998$

(c) $P(FF) = (0.015)^2 \approx 0.0002$

55. (a) $\left(\dfrac{1}{4}\right)^5 = \dfrac{1}{1024}$

(b) $\left(\dfrac{3}{4}\right)^5 = \dfrac{243}{1024}$

(c) $1 - \dfrac{243}{1024} = \dfrac{781}{1024}$

57. $(0.78)^3 \approx 0.4746$

59. $1 - \dfrac{(45)^2}{(60)^2} = 1 - \left(\dfrac{45}{60}\right)^2 = 1 - \left(\dfrac{3}{4}\right)^2 = 1 - \dfrac{9}{16} = \dfrac{7}{16}$

61. True. Two events are independent if the occurance of one has no effect on the occurance of the other.

63. (a) As you consider successive people with distinct birthdays, the probabilities must decrease to take into account the birth dates already used. Because the birth dates of people are independent events, multiply the respective probabilities of distinct birthdays.

(b) $\dfrac{365}{365} \cdot \dfrac{364}{365} \cdot \dfrac{363}{365} \cdot \dfrac{362}{365}$

(c) $P_1 = \dfrac{365}{365} = 1$

$P_2 = \dfrac{365}{365} \cdot \dfrac{364}{365} = \dfrac{364}{365} P_1 = \dfrac{365 - (2-1)}{365} P_1$

$P_3 = \dfrac{365}{365} \cdot \dfrac{364}{365} \cdot \dfrac{363}{365} = \dfrac{363}{365} P_2 = \dfrac{365 - (3-1)}{365} P_2$

$P_n = \dfrac{365}{365} \cdot \dfrac{364}{365} \cdot \dfrac{363}{365} \cdot \cdots \cdot \dfrac{365 - (n-1)}{365} = \dfrac{365 - (n-1)}{365} P_{n-1}$

(d) Q_n is the probability that the birthdays are not distinct which is equivalent to at least two people having the same birthday.

(e)

n	10	15	20	23	30	40	50
P_n	0.88	0.75	0.59	0.49	0.29	0.11	0.03
Q_n	0.12	0.25	0.41	(0.51)	0.71	0.89	0.97

(f) 23,   See the chart above.

65. $6x^2 + 8 = 0$

$6x^2 = -8$

$x^2 = -\dfrac{4}{3}$

No real solution.

67. $x^3 - x^2 - 3x = 0$

$x(x^2 - x - 3) = 0$

$x = 0$ or $x^2 - x - 3 = 0$

$x = \dfrac{1 \pm \sqrt{1 - 4(1)(-3)}}{2(1)} = \dfrac{1 \pm \sqrt{13}}{2}$

69. $\dfrac{12}{x} = -3$

$12 = -3x$

$-4 = x$

71. $\dfrac{2}{x - 5} = 4$

$2 = 4(x - 5)$

$2 = 4x - 20$

$22 = 4x$

$\dfrac{11}{2} = x$

73. $\dfrac{3}{x - 2} + \dfrac{x}{x + 2} = 1$

$3(x + 2) + x(x - 2) = 1(x - 2)(x + 2)$

$3x + 6 + x^2 - 2x = x^2 - 4$

$x^2 + x + 6 = x^2 - 4$

$x + 6 = -4$

$x = -10$

75. $e^x = 27$

$\ln e^x = \ln 27$

$x = \ln 27 \approx 3.296$

77. $e^{2x} - 4e^x + 3 = 0$

$(e^x - 1)(e^x - 3) = 0$

$e^x = 1 \qquad \text{or} \qquad e^x = 3$

$x = \ln 1 \qquad \qquad x = \ln 3$

$x = 0 \qquad \qquad x \approx 1.099$

79. $200e^{-x} = 75$

$e^{-x} = \frac{75}{200}$

$-x = \ln \frac{3}{8}$

$x = -\ln \frac{3}{8} = \ln \frac{8}{3} \approx 0.981$

81. $\ln x = 8$

$x = e^8 \approx 2980.958$

83. $4 \ln 6x = 16$

$\ln 6x = 4$

$6x = e^4$

$x = \frac{e^4}{6} \approx 9.100$

Review Exercises for Chapter 9

Solutions to Odd-Numbered Exercises

1. $a_n = 2 + \dfrac{6}{n}$

$a_1 = 2 + \dfrac{6}{1} = 8$

$a_2 = 2 + \dfrac{6}{2} = 5$

$a_3 = 2 + \dfrac{6}{3} = 4$

$a_4 = 2 + \dfrac{6}{4} = \dfrac{7}{2}$

$a_5 = 2 + \dfrac{6}{5} = \dfrac{16}{5}$

3. $a_n = \dfrac{72}{n!}$

$a_1 = \dfrac{72}{1!} = 72$

$a_2 = \dfrac{72}{2!} = 36$

$a_3 = \dfrac{72}{3!} = 12$

$a_4 = \dfrac{72}{4!} = 3$

$a_5 = \dfrac{72}{5!} = \dfrac{3}{5}$

5. $5! = 5 \cdot 4 \cdot 3 \cdot 2 \cdot 1 = 120$

7. $\dfrac{3! \, 5!}{6!} = \dfrac{(3 \cdot 2 \cdot 1)5!}{6 \cdot 5!} = 1$

9. $\displaystyle\sum_{i=1}^{6} 5 = 6(5) = 30$

11. $\displaystyle\sum_{j=1}^{4} \dfrac{6}{j^2} = \dfrac{6}{1^2} + \dfrac{6}{2^2} + \dfrac{6}{3^2} + \dfrac{6}{4^2} = 6 + \dfrac{3}{2} + \dfrac{2}{3} + \dfrac{3}{8} = \dfrac{205}{24}$

13. $\displaystyle\sum_{k=1}^{10} 2k^3 = 2(1)^3 + 2(2)^3 + 2(3)^3 + \cdots + 2(10)^3 = 6050$

15. $\dfrac{1}{2(1)} + \dfrac{1}{2(2)} + \dfrac{1}{2(3)} + \cdots + \dfrac{1}{2(20)} = \displaystyle\sum_{k=1}^{20} \dfrac{1}{2k}$

17. $\displaystyle\sum_{i=1}^{\infty} \dfrac{5}{10^i} = 0.5 + 0.05 + 0.005 + 0.005 + \cdots = 0.5555 \cdots = \dfrac{5}{9}$

19. $\displaystyle\sum_{k=1}^{\infty} \dfrac{2}{100^k} = 0.02 + 0.0002 + 0.000002 + \cdots = 0.020202 \cdots = \dfrac{2}{99}$

21. $a_n = 34{,}000 + (n - 1)(2250)$

(a) $a_5 = 34{,}000 + 4(2250) = \$43{,}000$

(b) $S_5 = \frac{5}{2}(34{,}000 + 43{,}000) = \$192{,}500$

23. $5, 3, 1, -1, -3, \ldots$

Arithmetic sequence, $d = -2$

25. $\frac{1}{2}, 1, \frac{3}{2}, 2, \frac{5}{2}, \ldots$

Arithmetic sequence, $d = \frac{1}{2}$

27. $a_1 = 7, d = 12$

$a_n = 7 + (n - 1)12$

$\quad = 7 + 12n - 12$

$\quad = 12n - 5$

29. $a_1 = y, d = 3y$

$a_n = y + (n - 1)3y$

$\quad = y + 3ny - 3y$

$\quad = 3ny - 2y$

31. $\displaystyle\sum_{j=1}^{10} (2j - 3)$ is arithmetic. Therefore, $a_1 = -1, a_{10} = 17, S_{10} = \frac{10}{2}[-1 + 17] = 80$.

33. $\displaystyle\sum_{k=1}^{11} \left(\frac{2}{3}k + 4\right)$ is arithmetic. Therefore, $a_1 = \frac{14}{3}, a_{11} = \frac{34}{3}, S_{11} = \frac{11}{2}\left[\frac{14}{3} + \frac{34}{3}\right] = 88$.

35. $\displaystyle\sum_{k=1}^{100} 5k$ is arithmetic. Therefore, $a_1 = 5, a_{100} = 500, S_{500} = \frac{100}{2}(5 + 500) = 25{,}250$.

37. $a_n = 49 + n\left(-\frac{1}{2}\right)$

$a_{12} = 49 + 12\left(-\frac{1}{2}\right) = 43$ minutes

39. $a_1 = 4, r = -\frac{1}{4}$

$a_1 = 4$

$a_2 = 4\left(-\frac{1}{4}\right) = -1$

$a_3 = -1\left(-\frac{1}{4}\right) = \frac{1}{4}$

$a_4 = \frac{1}{4}\left(-\frac{1}{4}\right) = -\frac{1}{16}$

$a_5 = -\frac{1}{16}\left(-\frac{1}{4}\right) = \frac{1}{64}$

41. $a_1 = 9, a_3 = 4$

$a_3 = a_1 r^2$

$4 = 9r^2$

$\frac{4}{9} = r^2 \implies r = \pm\frac{2}{3}$

$a_1 = 9 \qquad\qquad a_1 = 9$

$a_2 = 9\left(\frac{2}{3}\right) = 6 \qquad a_2 = 9\left(-\frac{2}{3}\right) = -6$

$a_3 = 6\left(\frac{2}{3}\right) = 4 \quad$ OR $\quad a_3 = -6\left(-\frac{2}{3}\right) = 4$

$a_4 = 4\left(\frac{2}{3}\right) = \frac{8}{3} \qquad a_4 = 4\left(-\frac{2}{3}\right) = -\frac{8}{3}$

$a_5 = \frac{8}{3}\left(\frac{2}{3}\right) = \frac{16}{9} \qquad a_5 = -\frac{8}{3}\left(-\frac{2}{3}\right) = \frac{16}{9}$

43. $a_2 = a_1 r$

$-8 = 16r$

$-\frac{1}{2} = r$

$a_n = 16\left(-\frac{1}{2}\right)^{n-1}$

$\displaystyle\sum_{n=1}^{20} 16\left(-\frac{1}{2}\right)^{n-1} = 16\left[\frac{1 - \left(-\frac{1}{2}\right)^{20}}{1 - \left(-\frac{1}{2}\right)}\right] \approx 10.67$

45. $a_1 = 100, r = 1.05$

$a_n = 100(1.05)^{n-1}$

$$\sum_{n=1}^{20} 100(1.05)^{n-1} = 100\left[\frac{1 - 1.05^{20}}{1 - 1.05}\right] \approx 3306.60$$

47. $\displaystyle\sum_{i=1}^{7} 2^{i-1} = \frac{1 - 2^7}{1 - 2} = 127$

49. $\displaystyle\sum_{i=1}^{4}\left(\frac{1}{2}\right)^i = \frac{1}{2} + \frac{1}{4} + \frac{1}{8} + \frac{1}{16} = \frac{15}{16}$

51. $\displaystyle\sum_{i=1}^{5} (2)^{i-1} = 1 + 2 + 4 + 8 + 16 = 31$

53. $\displaystyle\sum_{i=1}^{10} 10\left(\frac{3}{5}\right)^{i-1} \approx 24.849$

55. $\displaystyle\sum_{i=1}^{25} 100(1.06)^{i-1} \approx 5486.45$

57. $\displaystyle\sum_{i=1}^{\infty}\left(\frac{7}{8}\right)^{i-1} = \frac{1}{1 - \frac{7}{8}} = 8$

59. $\displaystyle\sum_{i=1}^{\infty} (0.1)^{i-1} = \frac{1}{1 - 0.1} = \frac{10}{9}$

61. $\displaystyle\sum_{k=1}^{\infty} 4\left(\frac{2}{3}\right)^{k-1} = \frac{4}{1 - \frac{2}{3}} = 12$

63. (a) $a_t = 120{,}000(0.7)^t$

(b) $a_5 = 120{,}000(0.7)^5 = \$20{,}168.40$

65. 1. When $n = 1$, $1 = \frac{1}{2}(3(1) - 1)$.

2. Assume that

$$S_k = 1 + 4 + \cdots + (3k - 2) = \frac{k}{2}(3k - 1).$$

Then,

$$S_{k+1} = 1 + 4 + \cdots + (3k - 2) + [3(k + 1) - 2] = S_k + (3k + 1)$$

$$= \frac{k}{2}(3k - 1) + (3k + 1) = \frac{k(3k - 1) + 2(3k + 1)}{2}$$

$$= \frac{3k^2 + 5k + 2}{2} = \frac{(k + 1)(3k + 2)}{2} = \frac{(k + 1)}{2}[3(k + 1) - 1].$$

Therefore, by mathematical induction, the formula is valid for all positive integer values of n.

67. 1. When $n = 1$, $a = a\left(\frac{1 - r}{1 - r}\right)$.

2. Assume that

$$S_k = \sum_{i=0}^{k-1} ar^i = \frac{a(1 - r^k)}{1 - r}.$$

Then,

$$S_{k+1} = \sum_{i=0}^{k} ar^i = \left(\sum_{i=0}^{k-1} ar^i\right) + ar^k = \frac{a(1 - r^k)}{1 - r} + ar^k$$

$$= \frac{a(1 - r^k + r^k - r^{k+1})}{1 - r} = \frac{a(1 - r^{k+1})}{1 - r}.$$

Therefore, by mathematical induction, the formula is valid for all positive integer values of n.

69. $\displaystyle\sum_{n=1}^{30} n = \frac{30(31)}{2} = 465$

71. $\displaystyle\sum_{n=1}^{7} n^4 = \frac{7(8)(15)(167)}{30} = 4676$

73. $S_1 = 9 = 1(9) = 1[2(1) + 7]$

$S_2 = 9 + 13 = 22 = 2(11) = 2[2(2) + 7]$

$S_3 = 9 + 13 + 17 = 39 = 3(13) = 3[2(3) + 7]$

$S_4 = 9 + 13 + 17 + 21 = 60 = 4(15) = 4[2(4) + 7]$

$S_n = n(2n + 7)$

75. $S_1 = 1$

$S_2 = 1 + \dfrac{3}{5} = \dfrac{8}{5}$

$S_3 = 1 + \dfrac{3}{5} + \dfrac{9}{25} = \dfrac{49}{25}$

$S_4 = 1 + \dfrac{3}{5} + \dfrac{9}{25} + \dfrac{27}{125} = \dfrac{272}{125}$

Since the series is geometric,

$S_n = \dfrac{1 - \left(\frac{3}{5}\right)^n}{1 - \frac{3}{5}} = \dfrac{5}{2}\left[1 - \left(\dfrac{3}{5}\right)^n\right]$

77. $a_1 = f(1) = 5, \quad a_n = a_{n-1} + 5$

$a_1 = 5$

$a_2 = 5 + 5 = 10$

$a_3 = 10 + 5 = 15$

$a_4 = 15 + 5 = 20$

$a_5 = 20 + 5 = 25$

n:	1	2	3	4	5
a_n:	5	10	15	20	25

First differences: 5 5 5 5

Second differences: 0 0 0

The sequence has a linear model.

79. $a_1 = f(1) = 16, \quad a_n = a_{n-1} - 1$

$a_1 = 16$

$a_2 = 16 - 1 = 15$

$a_3 = 15 - 1 = 14$

$a_4 = 14 - 1 = 13$

$a_5 = 13 - 1 = 12$

n:	1	2	3	4	5
a_n:	16	15	14	13	12

First differences: -1 -1 -1 -1

Second differences: 0 0 0

The sequence has a linear model.

81. $_6C_4 = \dfrac{6!}{2!\,4!} = 15$

83. $_8C_5 = \dfrac{8!}{3!\,5!} = 56$

85. $\dbinom{7}{3} = 35$

87. $\dbinom{8}{6} = 28$

89. $\left(\dfrac{x}{2} + y\right)^4 = \left(\dfrac{x}{2}\right)^4 + 4\left(\dfrac{x}{2}\right)^3 y + 6\left(\dfrac{x}{2}\right)^2 y^2 + 4\left(\dfrac{x}{2}\right)y^3 + y^4$

$= \dfrac{x^4}{16} + \dfrac{x^3 y}{2} + \dfrac{3x^2 y^2}{2} + 2xy^3 + y^4$

91. $(a - 3b)^5 = a^5 - 5a^4(3b) + 10a^3(3b)^2 - 10a^2(3b)^3 + 5a(3b)^4 - (3b)^5$

$$= a^5 - 15a^4b + 90a^3b^2 - 270a^2b^3 + 405ab^4 - 243b^5$$

93. $(5 + 2i)^4 = (5)^4 + 4(5)^3(2i) + 6(5)^2(2i)^2 + 4(5)(2i)^3 + (2i)^4$

$$= 625 + 1000i + 600i^2 + 160i^3 + 16i^4$$

$$= 625 + 1000i - 600 - 160i + 16 = 41 + 840i$$

95. $E = \{(4, 6), (5, 5), (6, 4)\}$

A total of 10 can be obtained three different ways.

97. $(10)(10)(10)(10) = 10{,}000$ different telephone numbers

99. $10! = 3{,}628{,}800$

101. $_8C_3 = \dfrac{8!}{5!\,3!} = 56$

103. $(1)\left(\dfrac{1}{9}\right) = \dfrac{1}{9}$

105. (a) $25\% + 18\% = 43\%$

(b) $100\% - 18\% = 82\%$

107. $\left(\frac{1}{6}\right)\left(\frac{1}{6}\right)\left(\frac{1}{6}\right) = \frac{1}{216}$

109. $1 - \frac{13}{52} = 1 - \frac{1}{4} = \frac{3}{4}$

111. True. $\dfrac{(n + 2)!}{n!} = \dfrac{(n + 2)(n + 1)n!}{n!} = (n + 2)(n + 1)$

113. True. $\displaystyle\sum_{k=1}^{8} 3k = 3 \sum_{k=1}^{8} k$ by the properties of sums

115. The domain of an infinite sequence is the set of natural numbers.

117. (a) Each term is obtained by adding the same constant (common difference) to the previous term.

(b) Each term is obtained by multiplying the same constant (common ratio) by the previous term.

119. Each term of the sequence is defined in terms of the previous term.

121. $a_n = 4\left(\frac{1}{2}\right)^{n-1}$

$a_1 = 4, a_2 = 2, a_{10} = \frac{1}{128}$

The sequence is geometric and is decreasing.

Matches graph (d)

123. $a_n = \displaystyle\sum_{k=1}^{n} 4\left(\frac{1}{2}\right)^{k-1}$

$a_1 = 4$ and $a_n \rightarrow 8$ as $n \rightarrow \infty$

Matches graph (b)

125. The terms in the expansion of $(x + y)^n$ are posititve; the signs of the terms in the expansion of $(x - y)^n$ alternate.

127. $1 - P(E) = 1 - \frac{2}{3} = \frac{1}{3}$

The probability that an event does not occur is 1 minus the probability the it does occur.

Chapter 9   Practice Test

1. Write out the first five terms of the sequence $a_n = \dfrac{2n}{(n+2)!}$.

2. Write an expression for the nth term of the sequence $\frac{4}{3}, \frac{5}{9}, \frac{6}{27}, \frac{7}{81}, \frac{8}{243}, \cdots$.

3. Find the sum $\displaystyle\sum_{i=1}^{6} (2i - 1)$.

4. Write out the first five terms of the arithmetic sequence where $a_1 = 23$ and $d = -2$.

5. Find a_n for the arithmetic sequence with $a_1 = 12$, $d = 3$, and $n = 50$.

6. Find the sum of the first 200 positive integers.

7. Write out the first five terms of the geometric sequence with $a_1 = 7$ and $r = 2$.

8. Evaluate $\displaystyle\sum_{n=1}^{10} 6\left(\frac{2}{3}\right)^{n-1}$.

9. Evaluate $\displaystyle\sum_{n=0}^{\infty} (0.03)^n$.

10. Use mathematical induction to prove that $1 + 2 + 3 + 4 + \cdots + n = \dfrac{n(n+1)}{2}$.

11. Use mathematical induction to prove that $n! > 2^n, n \geq 4$.

12. Evaluate $_{13}C_4$.

13. Expand $(x + 3)^5$.

14. Find the term involving x^7 in $(x - 2)^{12}$.

15. Evaluate $_{30}P_4$.

16. How many ways can six people sit at a table with six chairs?

17. Twelve cars run in a race. How many different ways can they come in first, second, and third place? (Assume that there are no ties.)

18. Two six-sided dice are tossed. Find the probability that the total of the two dice is less than 5.

19. Two cards are selected at random form a deck of 52 playing cards without replacement. Find the probability that the first card is a King and the second card is a black ten.

20. A manufacturer has determined that for every 1000 units it produces, 3 will be faulty. What is the probability that an order of 50 units will have one or more faulty units?

C H A P T E R   1 0
Topics in Analytic Geometry

CHAPTER 10
Topics in Analytic Geometry

Section 10.1   Lines

Solutions to Odd-Numbered Exercises

- The **inclination** of a nonhorizontal line is the positive angle θ $(\theta < 180°)$ measured counterclockwise from the x-axis to the line. A horizontal line has an inclination of zero.
- If a nonvertical line has inclination of θ and slope m, then $m = \tan\theta$.
- If two nonperpendicular lines have slopes m_1 and m_2, then the angle between the lines is given by

$$\tan\theta = \left| \frac{m_2 - m_1}{1 + m_1 m_2} \right|.$$

- The distance between a point (x_1, y_1) and a line $Ax + By + C = 0$ is given by

$$d = \frac{|Ax_1 + By_1 + C|}{\sqrt{A^2 + B^2}}.$$

---

1. $m = \tan\dfrac{\pi}{6} = \dfrac{\sqrt{3}}{3}$

3. $m = \tan\dfrac{3\pi}{4} = -1$

5. $m = \tan\dfrac{\pi}{3} = \sqrt{3}$

7. $m = \tan 1.27 \approx 3.2236$

9. $m = -1$

$-1 = \tan\theta$

$\theta = 180° + \arctan(-1) = \dfrac{3\pi}{4}$ radians $= 135°$

11. $m = 1$

$1 = \tan\theta$

$\theta = \dfrac{\pi}{4}$ radians $= 45°$

13. $m = \dfrac{3}{4}$

$\dfrac{3}{4} = \tan\theta$

$\theta = \arctan\left(\dfrac{3}{4}\right) \approx 0.6435$ radian $\approx 36.9°$

15. $(6, 1), (10, 8)$

$m = \dfrac{8 - 1}{10 - 6} = \dfrac{7}{4}$

$\dfrac{7}{4} = \tan\theta$

$\theta = \arctan\left(\dfrac{7}{4}\right) \approx 1.0517$ radians $\approx 60.3°$

17. $(-2, 20), (10, 0)$

$m = \dfrac{0 - 20}{10 - (-2)} = -\dfrac{20}{12} = -\dfrac{5}{3}$

$-\dfrac{5}{3} = \tan\theta$

$\theta = \pi + \arctan\left(-\dfrac{5}{3}\right) \approx 2.1112$ radians $\approx 121.0°$

19. $6x - 2y + 8 = 0$

$y = 3x + 4 \Rightarrow m = 3$

$3 = \tan\theta$

$\theta = \arctan 3 \approx 1.2490$ radians $\approx 71.6°$

21. $5x + 3y = 0$

$$y = -\frac{5}{3}x \Rightarrow m = -\frac{5}{3}$$

$$-\frac{5}{3} = \tan\theta$$

$$\theta = \pi + \arctan\left(-\frac{5}{3}\right) \approx 2.1112 \text{ radians} \approx 121.0°$$

23. $3x + y = 3 \Rightarrow y = -3x + 3 \Rightarrow m_1 = -3$

 $x - y = 2 \Rightarrow y = x - 2 \quad \Rightarrow m_2 = 1$

$$\tan\theta = \left|\frac{1 - (-3)}{1 + (-3)(1)}\right| = 2$$

$$\theta = \arctan 2 \approx 1.1071 \text{ radians} \approx 63.4°$$

25. $x - y = 0 \quad \Rightarrow y = x \quad\quad \Rightarrow m_1 = 1$

 $3x - 2y = -1 \Rightarrow y = \frac{3}{2}x + \frac{1}{2} \Rightarrow m_2 = \frac{3}{2}$

$$\tan\theta = \left|\frac{\frac{3}{2} - 1}{1 + \left(\frac{3}{2}\right)(1)}\right| = \frac{1}{5}$$

$$\theta = \arctan\frac{1}{5} \approx 0.1974 \text{ radian} \approx 11.3°$$

27. $x - 2y = 7 \Rightarrow y = \frac{1}{2}x - \frac{7}{2} \quad \Rightarrow m_1 = \frac{1}{2}$

 $6x + 2y = 5 \Rightarrow y = -3x + \frac{5}{2} \Rightarrow m_2 = -3$

$$\tan\theta = \left|\frac{-3 - \frac{1}{2}}{1 + \left(\frac{1}{2}\right)(-3)}\right| = 7$$

$$\theta = \arctan 7 \approx 1.4289 \text{ radians} \approx 81.9°$$

29. $x + 2y = 8 \Rightarrow y = -\frac{1}{2}x + 4 \Rightarrow m_1 = -\frac{1}{2}$

 $x - 2y = 2 \Rightarrow y = \frac{1}{2}x - 1 \quad \Rightarrow m_2 = \frac{1}{2}$

$$\tan\theta = \left|\frac{\frac{1}{2} - \left(-\frac{1}{2}\right)}{1 + \left(-\frac{1}{2}\right)\left(\frac{1}{2}\right)}\right| = \frac{4}{3}$$

$$\theta = \arctan\left(\frac{4}{3}\right) \approx 0.9273 \text{ radian} \approx 53.1°$$

31. $0.05x - 0.03y = 0.21 \Rightarrow y = \frac{5}{3}x - 7 \quad \Rightarrow m_1 = \frac{5}{3}$

 $0.07x + 0.02y = 0.16 \Rightarrow y = -\frac{7}{2}x + 8 \Rightarrow m_2 = -\frac{7}{2}$

$$\tan\theta = \left|\frac{\left(-\frac{7}{2}\right) - \left(\frac{5}{3}\right)}{1 + \left(\frac{5}{3}\right)\left(-\frac{7}{2}\right)}\right| = \frac{31}{29}$$

$$\theta = \arctan\left(\frac{31}{29}\right) \approx 0.8187 \text{ radian} \approx 46.9°$$

33. Let $A = (2, 1)$, $B = (4, 4)$, and $C = (6, 2)$.

Slope of AB: $\quad m_1 = \dfrac{1 - 4}{2 - 4} = \dfrac{3}{2}$

Slope of BC: $\quad m_2 = \dfrac{4 - 2}{4 - 6} = -1$

Slope of AC: $\quad m_3 = \dfrac{1 - 2}{2 - 6} = \dfrac{1}{4}$

$$\tan A = \left|\frac{\frac{1}{4} - \frac{3}{2}}{1 + \left(\frac{3}{2}\right)\left(\frac{1}{4}\right)}\right| = \frac{\frac{5}{4}}{\frac{11}{8}} = \frac{10}{11}$$

$$A = \arctan\left(\frac{10}{11}\right) \approx 42.3°$$

$$\tan B = \left|\frac{\frac{3}{2} - (-1)}{1 + (-1)\left(\frac{3}{2}\right)}\right| = \frac{\frac{5}{2}}{\frac{1}{2}} = 5$$

$$B = \arctan 5 \approx 78.7°$$

$$\tan C = \left|\frac{-1 - \frac{1}{4}}{1 + \left(\frac{1}{4}\right)(-1)}\right| = \frac{\frac{5}{4}}{\frac{3}{4}} = \frac{5}{3}$$

$$C = \arctan\left(\frac{5}{3}\right) \approx 59.0°$$

35. Let $A = (-4, -1)$, $B - (3, 2)$, and $C = (1, 0)$.

Slope of AB: $\quad m_1 = \dfrac{-1 - 2}{-4 - 3} = \dfrac{3}{7}$

Slope of BC: $\quad m_2 = \dfrac{2 - 0}{3 - 1} = 1$

Slope of AC: $\quad m_3 = \dfrac{-1 - 0}{-4 - 1} = \dfrac{1}{5}$

$$\tan A = \left|\frac{\frac{1}{5} - \frac{3}{7}}{1 + \left(\frac{3}{7}\right)\left(\frac{1}{5}\right)}\right| = \frac{\frac{8}{35}}{\frac{38}{35}} = \frac{4}{19}$$

$$A = \arctan\left(\frac{4}{19}\right) \approx 11.9°$$

$$\tan B = \left|\frac{1 - \frac{3}{7}}{1 + \left(\frac{3}{7}\right)(1)}\right| = \frac{\frac{4}{7}}{\frac{10}{7}} = \frac{2}{5}$$

$$B = \arctan\left(\frac{2}{5}\right) \approx 21.8°$$

$$C = 180° - A - B$$

$$\approx 180° - 11.9° - 21.8° = 146.3°$$

37. $(0, 0) \Rightarrow x_1 = 0$ and $y_1 = 0$

$4x + 3y = 0 \Rightarrow A = 4, B = 3,$ and $C = 0$

$$d = \frac{|4(0) + 3(0) + 0|}{\sqrt{4^2 + 3^2}} = \frac{0}{5} = 0$$

Note: The point is *on* the line.

39. $(2, 3) \Rightarrow x_1 = 2$ and $y_1 = 3$

$4x + 3y - 10 = 0 \Rightarrow A = 4, B = 3,$ and $C = -10$

$$d = \frac{|4(2) + 3(3) + (-10)|}{\sqrt{4^2 + 3^2}} = \frac{7}{5}$$

41. $(6, 2) \Rightarrow x_1 = 6$ and $y_1 = 2$

$x + 1 = 0 \Rightarrow A = 1, B = 0,$ and $C = 1$

$$d = \frac{|1(6) + 0(2) + 1|}{\sqrt{1^2 + 0^2}} = 7$$

43. $(0, 8) \Rightarrow x_1 = 0$ and $y_1 = 8$

$6x - y = 0 \Rightarrow A = 6, B = -1,$ and $C = 0$

$$d = \frac{|6(0) + (-1)(8) + 0|}{\sqrt{6^2 + (-1)^2}}$$

$$= \frac{8}{\sqrt{37}} = \frac{8\sqrt{37}}{37} \approx 1.3152$$

45. $A = (0, 0), B = (1, 4), C = (4, 0)$

(a) The slope the line through AC is $m = \dfrac{0 - 0}{4 - 0} = 0.$

The equation of the line through AC is $y = 0.$

The distance between the line and $B = (1, 4)$ is $d = \dfrac{|0(1) + (1)(4) + 0|}{\sqrt{0^2 + 1^2}} = 4.$

(b) The distance between A and C is 4.

$$A = \frac{1}{2}(4)(4) = 8 \text{ square units.}$$

47. $A = \left(-\dfrac{1}{2}, \dfrac{1}{2}\right), B = (2, 3), C = \left(\dfrac{5}{2}, 0\right)$

(a) The slope of the line through AC is $m = \dfrac{\frac{1}{2} - 0}{\left(-\frac{1}{2}\right) - \frac{5}{2}} = -\dfrac{1}{6}.$

The equation of the line through AC is $y - 0 = -\dfrac{1}{6}\left(x - \dfrac{5}{2}\right) \Rightarrow 2x + 12y - 5 = 0.$

The distance between the line and $B = (2, 3)$ is $d = \dfrac{|2(2) + 12(3) + (-5)|}{\sqrt{2^2 + 12^2}} = \dfrac{35}{\sqrt{148}} = \dfrac{35\sqrt{37}}{74}.$

(b) The distance between A and C is $d = \sqrt{\left[\left(-\dfrac{1}{2}\right) - \left(\dfrac{5}{2}\right)\right]^2 + \left[\left(\dfrac{1}{2}\right) - 0\right]^2} = \dfrac{\sqrt{37}}{2}.$

$$A = \frac{1}{2}\left(\frac{\sqrt{37}}{2}\right)\left(\frac{35\sqrt{37}}{74}\right) = \frac{35}{8} \text{ square units}$$

49. $x + y = 1 \Rightarrow (0, 1)$ is a point on the line $\Rightarrow x_1 = 0$ and $y_1 = 1$

$x + y = 5 \Rightarrow A = 1, B = 1,$ and $C = -5$

$$d = \frac{|1(0) + 1(1) + (-5)|}{\sqrt{1^2 + 1^2}} = \frac{4}{\sqrt{2}} = 2\sqrt{2}$$

51. Slope: $m = \tan 0.1 \approx 0.1003$

Change in elevation: $\tan 0.1 = \dfrac{x}{2(5280)}$

$$x \approx 1059 \text{ feet}$$

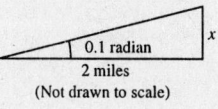

0.1 radian

2 miles

(Not drawn to scale)

53. (a) $\tan \theta = \dfrac{1}{3}$

$$\theta = \arctan\left(\dfrac{1}{3}\right) \approx 18.4°$$

(b) $\dfrac{5}{x} = \sin 18.4°$

$$x = \dfrac{5}{\sin 18.4°}$$

$$x \approx 15.8 \text{ meters}$$

55. $\tan \gamma = \dfrac{6}{9}$

$$\gamma = \arctan\left(\dfrac{2}{3}\right) \approx 33.69°$$

$$\beta = 90 - \gamma \approx 56.31°$$

Also, since the right triangles containing α and β are equal, $\alpha = \gamma \approx 33.69°$

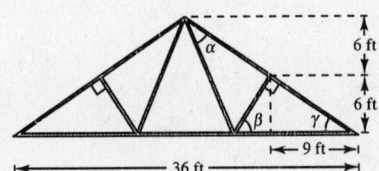

57. True. The inclination of a line is related to its slope by $m = \tan \theta$.

If the angle is greater than $\dfrac{\pi}{2}$ but less than π, then the angle is in the second quadrant where the tangent function is negative.

59. (a) $(0, 0) \Rightarrow x_1 = 0$ and $y_1 = 0$

$$y = mx + 4 \Rightarrow 0 = mx - y + 4$$

$$d = \dfrac{|m(0) + (-1)(0) + 4|}{\sqrt{m^2 + (-1)^2}} = \dfrac{4}{\sqrt{m^2 + 1}}$$

(c) The maximum distance of 4 occurs when the slope m is 0 and the line through $(0, 4)$ is horizontal.

(d) The graph has a horizontal asymptote at $d = 0$. As the slope becomes larger, the distance between the origin and the line, $y = mx + 4$, becomes smaller and approaches 0.

(b)

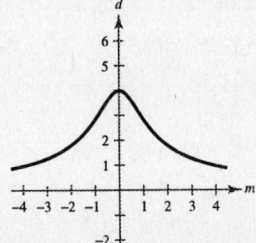

61. $f(x) = (x - 7)^2$

x-intercept: $0 = (x - 7)^2 \Rightarrow x = 7$

$$(7, 0)$$

y-intercept: $y = (0 - 7)^2 = 49$

$$(0, 49)$$

63. $f(x) = (x - 5)^2 - 5$

x-intercepts: $0 = (x - 5)^2 - 5$

$$5 = (x - 5)^2$$

$$\pm\sqrt{5} = x - 5$$

$$5 \pm \sqrt{5} = x$$

$$\left(5 \pm \sqrt{5}, 0\right)$$

y-intercept: $y = (0 - 5)^2 - 5 = 20$

$$(0, 20)$$

65. $f(x) = x^2 - 7x - 1$

x-intercepts: $0 = x^2 - 7x - 1$

$$x = \frac{7 \pm \sqrt{53}}{2} \text{ by the Quadratic Formula}$$

$$\left(\frac{7 \pm \sqrt{53}}{2}, 0 \right)$$

y-intercept: $y = 0^2 - 7(0) - 1 = -1$

$$(0, -1)$$

67. $f(x) = 3x^2 + 2x - 16$

$$= 3\left(x^2 + \frac{2}{3}x \right) - 16$$

$$= 3\left(x^2 + \frac{2}{3}x + \frac{1}{9} \right) - \frac{1}{3} - 16$$

$$= 3\left(x + \frac{1}{3} \right)^2 - \frac{49}{3}$$

Vertex: $\left(-\frac{1}{3}, -\frac{49}{3} \right)$

69. $f(x) = 5x^2 + 34x - 7$

$$= 5\left(x^2 + \frac{34}{5}x \right) - 7$$

$$= 5\left(x^2 + \frac{34}{5}x + \frac{289}{25} \right) - \frac{289}{5} - 7$$

$$= 5\left(x + \frac{17}{5} \right)^2 - \frac{324}{5}$$

Vertex: $\left(-\frac{17}{5}, -\frac{324}{5} \right)$

71. $f(x) = 6x^2 - x - 12$

$$= 6\left(x^2 - \frac{1}{6}x \right) - 12$$

$$= 6\left(x^2 - \frac{1}{6}x + \frac{1}{144} \right) - \frac{1}{24} - 12$$

$$= 6\left(x - \frac{1}{12} \right)^2 - \frac{289}{24}$$

Vertex: $\left(\frac{1}{12}, -\frac{289}{24} \right)$

Section 10.2   Introduction to Conics: Parabolas

- A **parabola** is the set of all points (x, y) that are equidistant from a fixed line (**directrix**) and a fixed point (**focus**) not on the line.

- The standard equation of a parabola with vertex (h, k) and:
  - (a) Vertical axis $x = h$ and directrix $y = k - p$ is:
    $(x - h)^2 = 4p(y - k), p \neq 0$
  - (b) Horizontal axis $y = k$ and directrix $x = h - p$ is:
    $(y - k)^2 = 4p(x - h), p \neq 0$

- The tangent line to a parabola at a point P makes **equal angles** with:
  - (a) the line through P and the focus.
  - (b) the axis of the parabola.

Solutions to Odd-Numbered Exercises

1. A circle is formed when a plane intersects the top or bottom half of a double-napped cone and is parallel to the vertex.

3. A parabola is formed when a plane intersects the top or bottom half of a double-napped cone, is parallel to the side of the cone, and does not intersect the vertex.

5. $y^2 = -4x$

Vertex: $(0, 0)$

Opens to the left since p is negative.

Matches graph (e).

7. $x^2 = -8y$

Vertex: $(0, 0)$

Opens downward since p is negative.

Matches graph (d).

9. $(y - 1)^2 = 4(x - 3)$

Vertex: $(3, 1)$

Opens to the right since p is positive.

Matches graph (a).

11. $y = \frac{1}{2}x^2$

$x^2 = 2y$

$x^2 = 4\left(\frac{1}{2}\right)y \Rightarrow h = 0, k = 0, p = \frac{1}{2}$

Vertex: $(0, 0)$

Focus: $\left(\frac{1}{2}, 0\right)$

Directrix: $y = -\frac{1}{2}$

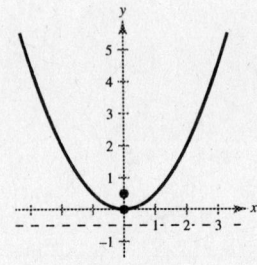

13. $y^2 = -6x$

$y^2 = 4\left(-\frac{3}{2}\right)x \Rightarrow h = 0, k = 0, p = -\frac{3}{2}$

Vertex: $(0, 0)$

Focus: $\left(-\frac{3}{2}, 0\right)$

Directrix: $x = \frac{3}{2}$

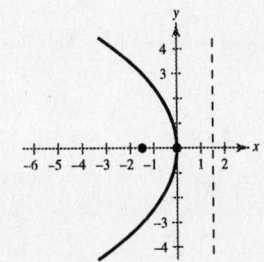

15. $x^2 + 6y = 0$

$x^2 = -6y = 4\left(-\frac{3}{2}\right)y \Rightarrow h = 0, k = 0, p = -\frac{3}{2}$

Vertex: $(0, 0)$

Focus: $\left(0, -\frac{3}{2}\right)$

Directrix: $y = \frac{3}{2}$

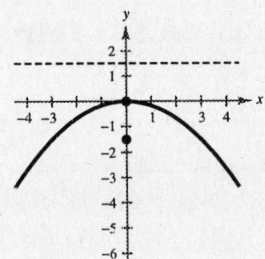

17. $(x - 1)^2 + 8(y + 2) = 0$

$\qquad (x - 1)^2 = 4(-2)(y + 2)$

$h = 1, k = -2, p = -2$

Vertex: $(1, -2)$

Focus: $(1, -4)$

Directrix: $y = 0$

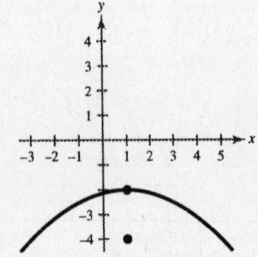

19. $\left(x + \frac{3}{2}\right)^2 = 4(y - 2)$

$\left(x + \frac{3}{2}\right)^2 = 4(1)(y - 2)$

$h = -\frac{3}{2}, k = 2, p = 1$

Vertex: $\left(-\frac{3}{2}, 2\right)$

Focus: $\left(-\frac{3}{2}, 3\right)$

Directrix: $y = 1$

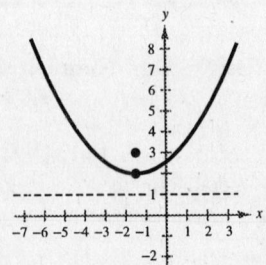

21.
$$y = \tfrac{1}{4}(x^2 - 2x + 5)$$
$$4y = x^2 - 2x + 5$$
$$4y - 5 + 1 = x^2 - 2x + 1$$
$$4y - 4 = (x - 1)^2$$
$$(x - 1)^2 = 4(1)(y - 1)$$
$$h = 1, k = 1, p = 1$$
Vertex: $(1, 1)$
Focus: $(1, 2)$
Directrix: $y = 0$

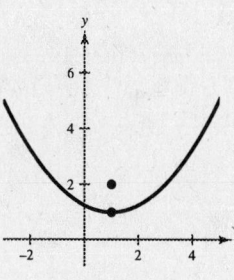

23. $y^2 + 6y + 8x + 25 = 0$
$$y^2 + 6y + 9 = -8x - 25 + 9$$
$$(y + 3)^2 = 4(-2)(x + 2)$$
$$h = -2, k = -3, p = -2$$
Vertex: $(-2, -3)$
Focus: $(-4, -3)$
Directrix: $x = 0$

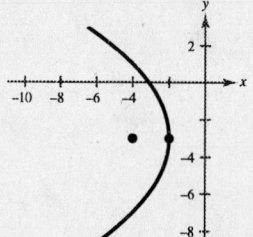

25. $x^2 + 4x + 6y - 2 = 0$
$$x^2 + 4x = -6y + 2$$
$$x^2 + 4x + 4 = -6y + 2 + 4$$
$$(x + 2)^2 = -6(y - 1)$$
$$(x + 2)^2 = 4\left(-\tfrac{3}{2}\right)(y - 1)$$
$$h = -2, k = 1, p = -\tfrac{3}{2}$$
Vertex: $(-2, 1)$
Focus: $\left(-2, -\tfrac{1}{2}\right)$
Directrix: $y = \tfrac{5}{2}$

On the graphing calculator, enter:
$$y_1 = \tfrac{1}{6}(x^2 + 4x - 2)$$

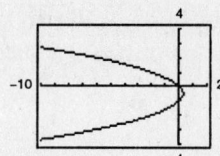

27. $y^2 + x + y = 0$
$$y^2 + y + \tfrac{1}{4} = -x + \tfrac{1}{4}$$
$$\left(y + \tfrac{1}{2}\right)^2 = 4\left(-\tfrac{1}{4}\right)\left(x - \tfrac{1}{4}\right)$$
$$h = \tfrac{1}{4}, k = -\tfrac{1}{2}, p = -\tfrac{1}{4}$$
Vertex: $\left(\tfrac{1}{4}, -\tfrac{1}{2}\right)$
Focus: $\left(0, -\tfrac{1}{2}\right)$
Directrix: $x = \tfrac{1}{2}$

To use a graphing calculator, enter:
$$y_1 = -\tfrac{1}{2} + \sqrt{\tfrac{1}{4} - x}$$
$$y_2 = -\tfrac{1}{2} - \sqrt{\tfrac{1}{4} - x}$$

29. $y^2 - 8x = 0 \Rightarrow y = \pm\sqrt{8x}$
$$x - y + 2 = 0 \Rightarrow y = x + 2$$
The point of tangency is $(2, 4)$.

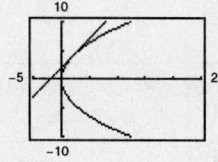

31. Vertex: $(0, 0) \Rightarrow h = 0, k = 0$

Graph opens upward.

$x^2 = 4py$

Point on graph: $(3, 6)$

$3^2 = 4p(6)$

$9 = 24p$

$\frac{3}{8} = p$

Thus, $x^2 = 4\left(\frac{3}{8}\right)y \Rightarrow x^2 = \frac{3}{2}y$

33. Vertex: $(0, 0) \Rightarrow h = 0, k = 0$

Focus: $\left(0, -\frac{3}{2}\right) \Rightarrow p = -\frac{3}{2}$

$x^2 = 4py$

$x^2 = 4\left(-\frac{3}{2}\right)y$

$x^2 = -6y$

35. Vertex: $(0, 0) \Rightarrow h = 0, k = 0$

Focus: $(-2, 0) \Rightarrow p = -2$

$y^2 = 4px$

$y^2 = 4(-2)x$

$y^2 = -8x$

37. Vertex: $(0, 0) \Rightarrow h = 0, k = 0$

Directrix: $y = -1 \Rightarrow p = 1$

$x^2 = 4py$

$x^2 = 4(1)y$

$x^2 = 4y$

39. Vertex: $(0, 0) \Rightarrow h = 0, k = 0$

Directrix: $y = 2 \Rightarrow p = -2$

$x^2 = 4py$

$x^2 = 4(-2)y$

$x^2 = -8y$

41. Vertex: $(0, 0) \Rightarrow h = 0, k = 0$

Horizontal axis and passes through the point $(4, 6)$

$y^2 = 4px$

$6^2 = 4p(4)$

$36 = 16p \Rightarrow p = \frac{9}{4}$

$y^2 = 4\left(\frac{9}{4}\right)x$

$y^2 = 9x$

43. Vertex: $(3, 1)$ and opens downward. Passes through $(2, 0)$ and $(4, 0)$.

$y = -(x - 2)(x - 4)$

$\quad = -x^2 + 6x - 8$

$\quad = -(x - 3)^2 + 1$

$(x - 3)^2 = -(y - 1)$

45. Vertex: $(-4, 0)$ and opens to the right. Passes through $(0, 4)$.

$(y - 0)^2 = 4p(x + 4)$

$4^2 = 4p(0 + 4)$

$16 = 16p$

$1 = p$

$y^2 = 4(x + 4)$

47. Vertex: $(5, 2)$

Focus: $(3, 2)$

Horizontal axis

$p = 3 - 5 = -2$

$(y - 2)^2 = 4(-2)(x - 5)$

$(y - 2)^2 = -8(x - 5)$

49. Vertex: $(0, 4)$

Directrix: $y = 2$

Vertical axis

$p = 4 - 2 = 2$

$(x - 0)^2 = 4(2)(y - 4)$

$\quad x^2 = 8(y - 4)$

51. Focus: $(2, 2)$

Directrix: $x = -2$

Horizontal axis

Vertex: $(0, 2)$

$p = 2 - 0 = 2$

$(y - 2)^2 = 4(2)(x - 0)$

$(y - 2)^2 = 8x$

53. $(y - 3)^2 = 6(x + 1)$

For the upper half of the parabola:

$y - 3 = +\sqrt{6(x + 1)}$

$y = \sqrt{6(x + 1)} + 3$

55. $x^2 = 2y \Rightarrow p = \dfrac{1}{2}$

Point: $(x_1, y_1) = (4, 8)$

Use: $y - y_1 = \dfrac{x_1}{2p}(x - x_1)$

$y - 8 = \dfrac{4}{2(1/2)}(x - 4)$

$y - 8 = 4x - 16$

$y = 4x - 8 \Rightarrow 0 = 4x - y - 8$

x-intercept: $(2, 0)$

57. $y = -2x^2 \Rightarrow x^2 = -\dfrac{1}{2}y \Rightarrow p = -\dfrac{1}{8}$

Point: $(x_1, y_1) = (-1, -2)$

Use: $y - y_1 = \dfrac{x_1}{2p}(x - x_1)$

$y + 2 = \dfrac{-1}{2(-1/8)}(x + 1)$

$y + 2 = 4(x + 1)$

$y = 4x + 2 \Rightarrow 0 = 4x - y + 2$

x-intercept: $\left(-\dfrac{1}{2}, 0\right)$

59. $R = 265x - \dfrac{5}{4}x^2$

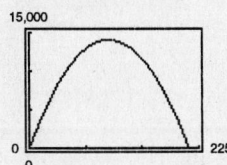

The revenue is maximum when $x = 106$ units.

61. Vertex: $(0, 0) \Rightarrow h = 0, k = 0$

Focus: $(0, 4.5) \Rightarrow p = 4.5$

$(x - h)^2 = 4p(y - k)$

$(x - 0)^2 = 4(4.5)(y - 0)$

$x^2 = 18y$ or $y = \dfrac{1}{18}x^2$

63. (a) Vertex: $(0, 0) \Rightarrow h = 0, k = 0$

Points on the parabola: $(\pm 16, -0.4)$

$x^2 = 4py$

$(\pm 16)^2 = 4p(-0.4)$

$256 = -1.6p$

$-160 = p$

$x^2 = 4(-160y)$

$x^2 = -640y$

$y = -\dfrac{1}{640}x^2$

(b) When $y = 0.1$ we have, $0.1 = -\dfrac{1}{640}x^2$

$64 = x^2$

$\pm 8 = x$

Thus, 8 feet away from the center of the road, the road surface is 0.1 foot lower than in the middle.

65. (a) $V = 17,500\sqrt{2}$ mi/hr

$\approx 24,750$ mi/hr

(b) $p = -4100, (h, k) = (0, 4100)$

$(x - 0)^2 = 4(-4100)(y - 4100)$

$x^2 = -16,400(y - 4100)$

67. The position of the target is on the x-axis, so first, let $y = 0$.

$$0 = 30,000 - \frac{x^2}{39,204}$$

$$\frac{x^2}{39,204} = 30,000$$

$$x^2 = 30,000(39,204)$$

$$x = \sqrt{30,000(39,204)}$$

$$x \approx 34,294.606 \text{ feet}$$

Since the bomber is flying at 792 feet per second,

$$\frac{34,294.606 \text{ feet}}{792 \text{ feet per second}} \approx 43.3 \text{ seconds}$$

The bomb should be released 43.3 seconds prior to being over the target.

69. True. If the axis (line connecting the vertex and focus) is horizontal, then the directrix must be vertical.

71. (a) $A = \frac{4}{3}(2)(4)^{3/2} = \frac{4}{3}(2)(8) = \frac{64}{3}$ square units

   (b) As p approaches zero, the parabola becomes narrower and narrower, thus the area becomes smaller and smaller.

73. $f(x) = 2x^3 + 3x^2 - 2$ One variation in sign.

  $f(-x) = -2x^3 + 3x^2 - 2$ Two variations in sign.

  The polynomial has one positive real zero and two or no negative real zeros.

75. $f(x) = 5x^5 - 2x^2 + 3$ Two variations in sign.

  $f(-x) = -5x^5 - 2x^2 + 3$ One variation in sign.

  The polynomial has two or no positive real zeros and one negative real zero.

77. $f(x) = x^3 - 2x^2 + 2x - 4$

  Possible rational zeros: $\pm 1, \pm 2, \pm 4$

79. $f(x) = 2x^5 + x^2 + 16$

  Possible rational zeros: $\pm 1, \pm 2, \pm 4, \pm 8, \pm 16, \pm \frac{1}{2}$

81. $f(x) = (x - 3)[x - (2 + i)][x - (2 - i)]$

  $ = (x - 3)[(x - 2) - i][(x - 2) + i]$

  $ = (x - 3)(x^2 - 4x + 5)$

  $ = x^3 - 7x^2 + 17x - 15$

83. $g(x) = 6x^4 + 7x^3 - 29x^2 - 28x + 20$

  Possible rational roots: $\pm 1, \pm 2, \pm 4, \pm 5, \pm 10, \pm 20,$

  $\pm \frac{1}{2}, \pm \frac{5}{2}, \pm \frac{1}{3}, \pm \frac{2}{3}, \pm \frac{4}{3}, \pm \frac{5}{3}, \pm \frac{10}{3}, \pm \frac{20}{3}, \pm \frac{1}{6}, \pm \frac{5}{6}$

  $x = \pm 2$ are both solutions.

$$
\begin{array}{r|rrrrr}
2 & 6 & 7 & -29 & -28 & 20 \\
  &   & 12 & 38 & 18 & -20 \\
\hline
  & 6 & 19 & 9 & -10 & 0 \\
-2 & 6 & 19 & 9 & -10 & \\
   &   & -12 & -14 & 10 & \\
\hline
   & 6 & 7 & -5 & 0 &
\end{array}
$$

$g(x) = (x - 2)(x + 2)(6x^2 + 7x - 5)$

$ = (x - 2)(x + 2)(2x - 1)(3x + 5)$

The zeros of $g(x)$ are $x = \pm 2$, $x = \frac{1}{2}$, $x = -\frac{5}{3}$.

Section 10.3   Ellipses

- An **ellipse** is the set of all points *(x, y)* the sum of whose distances from two distinct fixed points (**foci**) is constant.
- The standard equation of an ellipse with center *(h, k)* and major and minor axes of lengths 2*a* and 2*b* is:

  (a) $\dfrac{(x-h)^2}{a^2} + \dfrac{(y-k)^2}{b^2} = 1$ if the major axis is horizontal.

  (b) $\dfrac{(x-h)^2}{b^2} + \dfrac{(y-k)^2}{a^2} = 1$ if the major axis is vertical.

- $c^2 = a^2 - b^2$ where *c* is the distance from the center to a focus.

- The eccentricity of an ellipse is $e = \dfrac{c}{a}$.

Solutions to Odd-Numbered Exercises

1. $\dfrac{x^2}{4} + \dfrac{y^2}{9} = 1$

Center: $(0, 0)$

$a = 3, b = 2$

Vertical major axis

Matches graph (b).

3. $\dfrac{x^2}{4} + \dfrac{y^2}{25} = 1$

Center: $(0, 0)$

$a = 5, b = 2$

Vertical major axis

Matches graph (d).

5. $\dfrac{(x-2)^2}{16} + (y+1)^2 = 1$

Center: $(2, -1)$

$a = 4, b = 1$

Horizontal major axis

Matches graph (a).

7. $\dfrac{x^2}{25} + \dfrac{y^2}{16} = 1$

Center: $(0, 0)$

$a = 5, b = 4, c = 3$

Foci: $(\pm 3, 0)$

Vertices: $(\pm 5, 0)$

$e = \dfrac{3}{5}$

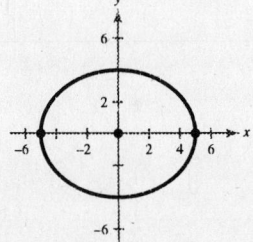

9. $\dfrac{x^2}{5} + \dfrac{y^2}{9} = 1$

$a = 3, b = \sqrt{5}, c = 2$

Center: $(0, 0)$

Foci: $(0, \pm 2)$

Vertices: $(0, \pm 3)$

$e = \dfrac{\sqrt{5}}{3}$

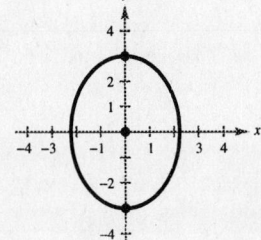

11. $\dfrac{(x+3)^2}{16} + \dfrac{(y-5)^2}{25} = 1$

Center: $(-3, 5)$

$a = 5, b = 4, c = 3$

Foci: $(-3, 8)(-3, 2)$

Vertices: $(-3, 10)(-3, 0)$

$e = \dfrac{3}{5}$

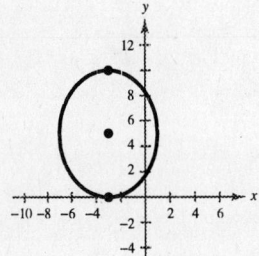

13. $\dfrac{(x+5)^2}{\frac{9}{4}} + (y-1)^2 = 1$

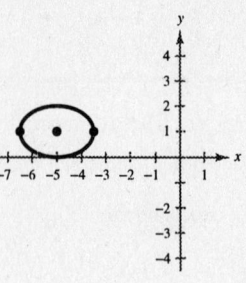

Center: $(-5, 1)$

$a = \dfrac{3}{2}, b = 1, c = \dfrac{\sqrt{5}}{2}$

Foci: $\left(-5 + \dfrac{\sqrt{5}}{2}, 1\right)\left(-5 - \dfrac{\sqrt{5}}{2}, 1\right)$

Vertices: $\left(-\dfrac{7}{2}, 1\right)\left(-\dfrac{13}{2}, 1\right)$

15. $9x^2 + 4y^2 + 36x - 24y + 36 = 0$

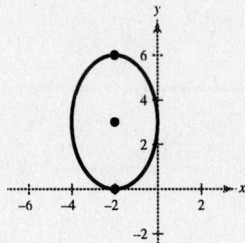

$9(x^2 + 4x + 4) + 4(y^2 - 6y + 9) = -36 + 36 + 36$

$9(x+2)^2 + 4(y-3) = 36$

$\dfrac{(x+2)^2}{4} + \dfrac{(y-3)^2}{9} = 1$

$a = 3, b = 2, c = \sqrt{5}$

Center: $(-2, 3)$

Foci: $\left(-2, 3 \pm \sqrt{5}\right)$

Vertices: $(-2, 6), (-2, 0)$

$e = \dfrac{\sqrt{5}}{3}$

17. $x^2 + 5y^2 - 8x - 30y - 39 = 0$

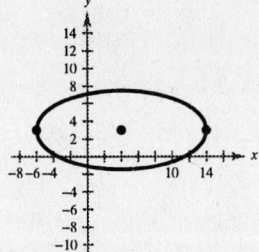

$(x^2 - 8x + 16) + 5(y^2 - 6y + 9) = 39 + 16 + 45$

$(x-4)^2 + 5(y-3)^2 = 100$

$\dfrac{(x-4)^2}{100} + \dfrac{(y-3)^2}{20} = 1$

Center: $(4, 3)$

$a = 10, b = 2\sqrt{5}, c = 4\sqrt{5}$

Foci: $\left(4 \pm 4\sqrt{5}, 3\right)$

Vertices: $(14, 3)(-6, 3)$

$e = \dfrac{4\sqrt{5}}{10} = \dfrac{2\sqrt{5}}{5}$

19.
$$6x^2 + 2y^2 + 18x - 10y + 2 = 0$$

$$6\left(x^2 + 3x + \frac{9}{4}\right) + 2\left(y^2 - 5y + \frac{25}{4}\right) = -2 + \frac{27}{2} + \frac{25}{2}$$

$$6\left(x + \frac{3}{2}\right)^2 + 2\left(y - \frac{5}{2}\right)^2 = 24$$

$$\frac{\left(x + \frac{3}{2}\right)^2}{4} + \frac{\left(y - \frac{5}{2}\right)^2}{12} = 1$$

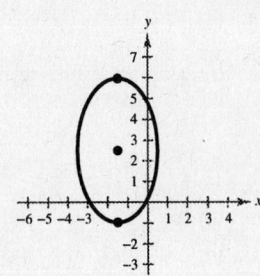

Center: $\left(-\frac{3}{2}, \frac{5}{2}\right)$

$a = 2\sqrt{3}, b = 2, c = 2\sqrt{2}$

Foci: $\left(-\frac{3}{2}, \frac{5}{2} \pm 2\sqrt{2}\right)$

Vertices: $\left(-\frac{3}{2}, \frac{5}{2} \pm 2\sqrt{3}\right)$

$e = \frac{2\sqrt{2}}{2\sqrt{3}} = \frac{\sqrt{6}}{3}$

21.
$$16x^2 + 25y^2 - 32x + 50y + 16 = 0$$

$$16(x^2 - 2x + 1) + 25(y^2 + 2y + 1) = -16 + 16 + 25$$

$$16(x - 1)^2 + 25(y + 1)^2 = 25$$

$$\frac{(x - 1)^2}{\frac{25}{16}} + (y + 1)^2 = 1$$

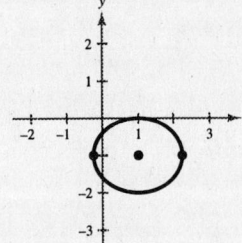

$a = \frac{5}{4}, b = 1, c = \frac{3}{4}$

Center: $(1, -1)$

Foci: $\left(\frac{7}{4}, -1\right), \left(\frac{1}{4}, -1\right)$

Vertices: $\left(\frac{9}{4}, -1\right), \left(-\frac{1}{4}, -1\right)$

$e = \frac{3}{5}$

23. $5x^2 + 3y^2 = 15$

$$\frac{x^2}{3} + \frac{y^2}{5} = 1$$

Center: $(0, 0)$

$a = \sqrt{5}, b = \sqrt{3}, c = \sqrt{2}$

Foci: $\left(0, \pm\sqrt{2}\right)$

Vertices: $\left(0, \pm\sqrt{5}\right)$

To graph, solve for y.

$$y^2 = \frac{15 - 5x^2}{3}$$

$$y_1 = \sqrt{\frac{15 - 5x^2}{3}}$$

$$y_2 = -\sqrt{\frac{15 - 5x^2}{3}}$$

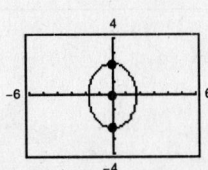

25. $12x^2 + 20y^2 - 12x + 40y - 37 = 0$

$$12\left(x^2 - x + \frac{1}{4}\right) + 20(y^2 + 2y + 1) = 37 + 3 + 20$$

$$12\left(x - \frac{1}{2}\right)^2 + 20(y + 1)^2 = 60$$

$$\frac{\left(x - \frac{1}{2}\right)^2}{5} + \frac{(y + 1)^2}{3} = 1$$

$a = \sqrt{5}, b = \sqrt{3}, c = \sqrt{2}$

Center: $\left(\frac{1}{2}, -1\right)$

Foci: $\left(\frac{1}{2} \pm \sqrt{2}, -1\right)$

Vertices: $\left(\frac{1}{2} \pm \sqrt{5}, -1\right)$

$e = \dfrac{\sqrt{10}}{5}$

To graph, solve for y.

$$(y + 1)^2 = 3\left[1 - \frac{(x - 0.5)^2}{5}\right]$$

$$y_1 = -1 + \sqrt{3\left[1 - \frac{(x - 0.5)^2}{5}\right]}$$

$$y_2 = -1 - \sqrt{3\left[1 - \frac{(x - 0.5)^2}{5}\right]}$$

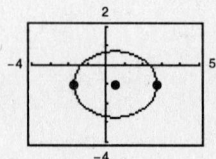

27. Center: $(0, 0)$

$a = 4, b = 2$

Vertical major axis

$$\frac{(x - h)^2}{b^2} + \frac{(y - k)^2}{a^2} = 1$$

$$\frac{x^2}{4} + \frac{y^2}{16} = 1$$

29. Vertices: $(\pm 6, 0)$

$a = 6, c = 2 \Rightarrow b = \sqrt{32} = 4\sqrt{2}$

Foci: $(\pm 2, 0)$

Horizontal major axis

Center: $(0, 0)$

$$\frac{(x - h)^2}{a^2} + \frac{(y - k)^2}{b^2} = 1$$

$$\frac{x^2}{36} + \frac{y^2}{32} = 1$$

31. Foci: $(\pm 5, 0) \Rightarrow c = 5$

Center: $(0, 0)$

Horizontal major axis

Major axis of length $12 \Rightarrow 2a = 12$

$$a = 6$$

$6^2 - b^2 = 5^2 \Rightarrow b^2 = 11$

$$\frac{(x - h)^2}{a^2} + \frac{(y - k)^2}{b^2} = 1$$

$$\frac{x^2}{36} + \frac{y^2}{11} = 1$$

33. Vertices: $(0, \pm 5) \Rightarrow a = 5$

Center: $(0, 0)$

Vertical major axis

$$\frac{(x - h)^2}{b^2} + \frac{(y - k)^2}{a^2} = 1$$

$$\frac{x^2}{b^2} + \frac{y^2}{25} = 1$$

Point: $(4, 2)$

$$\frac{4^2}{b^2} + \frac{2^2}{25} = 1$$

$$\frac{16}{b^2} = 1 - \frac{4}{25} = \frac{21}{25}$$

$$400 = 21b^2$$

$$\frac{400}{21} = b^2$$

$$\frac{x^2}{\frac{400}{21}} + \frac{y^2}{25} = 1$$

$$\frac{21x^2}{400} + \frac{y^2}{25} = 1$$

35. Center: $(2, 3)$

$a = 3, \quad b = 1$

Vertical major axis

$$\frac{(x - h)^2}{b^2} + \frac{(y - k)^2}{a^2} = 1$$

$$\frac{(x - 2)^2}{1} + \frac{(y - 3)^2}{9} = 1$$

37. Center: $(-2, 3)$

$a = 4, \quad b = 3$

Horizontal major axis

$$\frac{(x - h)^2}{a^2} + \frac{(y - k)^2}{b^2} = 1$$

$$\frac{(x + 2)^2}{16} + \frac{(y - 3)^2}{9} = 1$$

39. Vertices: $(0, 4), (4, 4) \Rightarrow a = 2$

Minor axis of length $2 \Rightarrow b = 1$

Center: $(2, 4) = (h, k)$

$$\frac{(x - h)^2}{a^2} + \frac{(y - k)^2}{b^2} = 1$$

$$\frac{(x - 2)^2}{4} + \frac{(y - 4)^2}{1} = 1$$

41. Foci: $(0, 0), (0, 8) \Rightarrow c = 4$

Major axis of length $16 \Rightarrow a = 8$

$b^2 = a^2 - c^2 = 64 - 16 = 48$

Center: $(0, 4) = (h, k)$

$$\frac{(x - h)^2}{b^2} + \frac{(y - k)^2}{a^2} = 1$$

$$\frac{x^2}{48} + \frac{(y - 4)^2}{64} = 1$$

43. Vertices: $(3, 1), (3, 9) \Rightarrow a = 4$

Center: $(3, 5)$

Minor axis of length $6 \Rightarrow b = 3$

Vertical major axis

$$\frac{(x - h)^2}{b^2} + \frac{(y - k)^2}{a^2} = 1$$

$$\frac{(x - 3)^2}{9} + \frac{(y - 5)^2}{16} = 1$$

45. Center: $(0, 4)$

Vertices: $(-4, 4), (4, 4) \Rightarrow a = 4$

$a = 2c \Rightarrow 4 = 2c \Rightarrow c = 2$

$2^2 = 4^2 - b^2 \Rightarrow b^2 = 12$

Horizontal major axis

$$\frac{(x - h)^2}{a^2} + \frac{(y - k)^2}{b^2} = 1$$

$$\frac{x^2}{16} + \frac{(y - 4)^2}{12} = 1$$

47. Vertices: $(\pm 5, 0) \Rightarrow a = 5$

Eccentricity: $\dfrac{3}{5} \Rightarrow c = \dfrac{3}{5} a = 3$

$b^2 = a^2 - c^2 = 25 - 9 = 16$

Center: $(0, 0) = (h, k)$

$$\dfrac{(x - h)^2}{a^2} + \dfrac{(y - k)^2}{b^2} = 1$$

$$\dfrac{x^2}{25} + \dfrac{y^2}{16} = 1$$

49. The tacks should be placed at the foci and the length of the string is the length of the major axis, $2a$.

Center: $(0, 0)$

$a = 3, b = 2, c = \sqrt{5}$

Foci (Positions of the tacks): $\left(\pm \sqrt{5}, 0\right)$

Length of string: 6 feet

51. Area of circle: $\pi r^2 = 100\pi$

Area of ellipse: $\pi(a)(10)$

$10a\pi = 2(100\pi)$

$10a\pi = 200\pi$

$a = 20$

Length of major axis: $2a = 40$

53. $a - c = 0.34$

$a + c = 4.08$

$\quad 2a = 4.42 \Rightarrow a = 2.21$

$\quad c = 4.08 - a \Rightarrow c = 1.87$

$b^2 = a^2 - c^2 = 2.21^2 - 1.87^2 = 1.3872 \Rightarrow b \approx 1.18$

$$\dfrac{x^2}{a^2} + \dfrac{y^2}{b^2} = 1$$

$$\dfrac{x^2}{4.88} + \dfrac{y^2}{1.39} = 1$$

55. For $\dfrac{x^2}{a^2} + \dfrac{y^2}{b^2} = 1$, we have $c^2 = a^2 - b^2$

When $x = c$: $\dfrac{c^2}{a^2} + \dfrac{y^2}{b^2} = 1$

$$y^2 = b^2\left(1 - \dfrac{a^2 - b^2}{a^2}\right) = \dfrac{b^4}{a^2}$$

$$y = \dfrac{b^2}{a}$$

Length of latus rectum: $2y = \dfrac{2b^2}{a}$

57. $\dfrac{x^2}{9} + \dfrac{y^2}{16} = 1$

$a = 4, b = 3, c = \sqrt{7}$

Points on the ellipse: $(\pm 3, 0), (0, \pm 4)$

Length of latus recta: $\dfrac{2b^2}{a} = \dfrac{2(3)^2}{4} = \dfrac{9}{2}$

Additional points: $\left(\pm \dfrac{9}{4}, -\sqrt{7}\right), \left(\pm \dfrac{9}{4}, \sqrt{7}\right)$

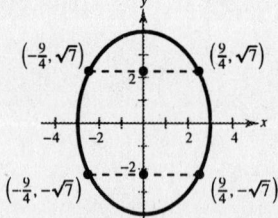

59. $5x^2 + 3y^2 = 15$

$$\frac{x^2}{3} + \frac{y^2}{5} = 1$$

$a = \sqrt{5}, b = \sqrt{3}, c = \sqrt{2}$

Points on the ellipse: $\left(\pm\sqrt{3}, 0\right), \left(0, \pm\sqrt{5}\right)$

Length of latus recta: $\dfrac{2b^2}{a} = \dfrac{2 \cdot 3}{\sqrt{5}} = \dfrac{6\sqrt{5}}{5}$

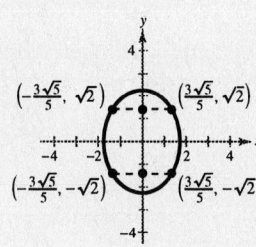

61. True. If e is close to 1, the ellipse is elongated and the foci are close to the vertices.

63. False. The foci of an ellipse cannot occur outside the ellipse because $0 < c < a$ and both the foci and vertices are on the major axis.

65. $\dfrac{x^2}{a^2} + \dfrac{y^2}{b^2} = 1$

(a) $a + b = 20 \Rightarrow b = 20 - a$

$A = \pi ab = \pi a(20 - a)$

(b) $264 = \pi a(20 - a)$

$0 = -\pi a^2 + 20\pi a - 264$

$0 = \pi a^2 - 20\pi a + 264$

By the Quadratic Formula: $a \approx 14$ or $a \approx 6$.

Choosing the larger value of a, we have $a \approx 14$ and $b \approx 6$.

The equation of an ellipse with an area of 264 is $\dfrac{x^2}{196} + \dfrac{y^2}{36} = 1$.

(c)

a	8	9	10	11	12	13
A	301.6	311.0	314.2	311.0	301.6	285.9

The area is maximum when $a = 10$ and the ellipse is a circle.

(d)

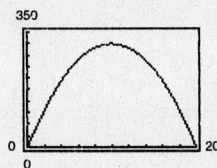

The area is maximum (314.16) when $a = b = 10$ and the ellipse is a circle.

67. $80, 40, 20, 10, 5, \ldots$

Geometric, $r = \frac{1}{2}$

69. $-\frac{1}{2}, \frac{1}{2}, \frac{3}{2}, \frac{5}{2}, \frac{7}{2}, \ldots$

Arithmetic, $d = 1$

71. $a_1 = 0, d = -\frac{1}{4}$

$\quad a_n = a_1 + (n - 1)d$

$\qquad = 0 + (n - 1)\left(-\frac{1}{4}\right)$

$\qquad = -\frac{1}{4}n + \frac{1}{4}$

73. $a_3 = 27, a_8 = 72$

$\quad a_8 = a_3 + 5d$

$\quad 72 = 27 + 5d$

$\quad 45 = 5d$

$\quad 9 = d$

$\quad a_3 = a_1 + 2d$

$\quad 27 = a_1 + 2(9)$

$\quad 9 = a_1$

$\quad a_n = a_1 + (n - 1)d$

$\qquad = 9 + (n - 1)9$

$\qquad = 9 + 9n - 9$

$\qquad = 9n$

75. $\displaystyle\sum_{n=0}^{6} (-3)^n = 1 - 3 + 9 - 27 + 81 - 243 + 729$

$\qquad\qquad\qquad = 547$

77. $\displaystyle\sum_{n=0}^{10} 5\left(\frac{4}{3}\right)^n = 5\frac{\left(1 - \left(\frac{4}{3}\right)^{11}\right)}{1 - \frac{4}{3}}$

$\qquad\qquad\qquad \approx 340.15$

Section 10.4   Hyperbolas

- A **hyperbola** is the set of all points (x, y) the difference of whose distances from two distinct fixed points (**foci**) is constant.

- The standard equation of a hyperbola with center (h, k) and transverse and conjugate axes of lengths $2a$ and $2b$ is:

  (a) $\dfrac{(x - h)^2}{a^2} - \dfrac{(y - k)^2}{b^2} = 1$ if the traverse axis is horizontal.

  (b) $\dfrac{(y - k)^2}{a^2} - \dfrac{(x - h)^2}{b^2} = 1$ if the traverse axis is vertical.

- $c^2 = a^2 + b^2$ where c is the distance from the center to a focus.

- The asymptotes of a hyperbola are:

  (a) $y = k \pm \dfrac{b}{a}(x - h)$ if the transverse axis is horizontal.

  (b) $y = k \pm \dfrac{a}{b}(x - h)$ if the transverse axis is vertical.

- The eccentricity of a hyperbola is $e = \dfrac{c}{a}$.

- To classify a nondegenerate conic from its general equation $Ax^2 + Cy^2 + Dx + Ey + F = 0$:
  (a) If $A = C$ ($A \neq 0, C \neq 0$), then it is a circle.
  (b) If $AC = 0$ ($A = 0$ or $C = 0$, but not both), then it is a parabola.
  (c) If $AC > 0$, then it is an ellipse.
  (d) If $AC < 0$, then it is a hyperbola.

Solutions to Odd-Numbered Exercises

1. $\dfrac{y^2}{9} - \dfrac{x^2}{25} = 1$

Center: $(0, 0)$

$a = 3, b = 5$

Vertical transverse axis

Matches graph (b).

3. $\dfrac{(x - 1)^2}{16} - \dfrac{y^2}{4} = 1$

Center: $(1, 0)$

$a = 4, b = 2$

Horizontal transverse axis

Matches graph (a).

5. $x^2 - y^2 = 1$

$a = 1, b = 1, c = \sqrt{2}$

Center: $(0, 0)$

Vertices: $(\pm 1, 0)$

Foci: $\left(\pm \sqrt{2}, 0\right)$

Asymptotes: $y = \pm x$

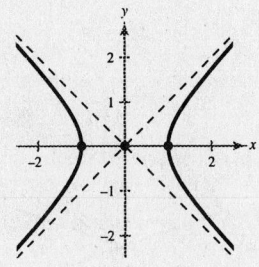

7. $\dfrac{y^2}{25} - \dfrac{x^2}{81} = 1$

$a = 5, b = 9, c = \sqrt{106}$

Center: $(0, 0)$

Vertices: $(0, \pm 5)$

Foci: $\left(0, \pm \sqrt{106}\right)$

Asymptotes: $y = \pm \dfrac{5}{9}x$

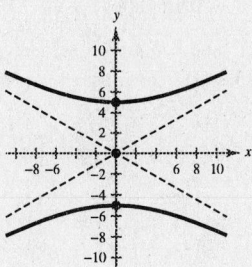

9. $\dfrac{(x - 1)^2}{4} - \dfrac{(y + 2)^2}{1} = 1$

$a = 2, b = 1, c = \sqrt{5}$

Center: $(1, -2)$

Vertices: $(-1, -2), (3, -2)$

Foci: $\left(1 \pm \sqrt{5}, -2\right)$

Asymptotes: $y = -2 \pm \dfrac{1}{2}(x - 1)$

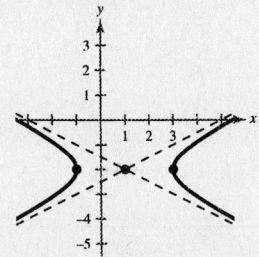

11. $\dfrac{(y + 6)^2}{\frac{1}{9}} - \dfrac{(x - 2)^2}{\frac{1}{4}} = 1$

$a = \dfrac{1}{3}, b = \dfrac{1}{2}, c = \dfrac{\sqrt{13}}{6}$

Center: $(2, -6)$

Vertices: $\left(2, -\dfrac{17}{3}\right), \left(2, -\dfrac{19}{3}\right)$

Foci: $\left(2, -6 \pm \dfrac{\sqrt{13}}{6}\right)$

Asymptotes: $y = -6 \pm \dfrac{2}{3}(x - 2)$

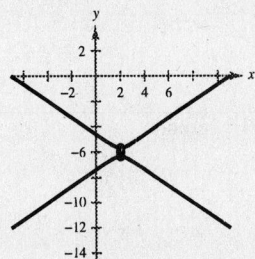

13.
$$9x^2 - y^2 - 36x - 6y + 18 = 0$$
$$9(x^2 - 4x + 4) - (y^2 + 6y + 9) = -18 + 36 - 9$$
$$9(x - 2)^2 - (y + 3)^2 = 9$$
$$\frac{(x - 2)^2}{1} - \frac{(y + 3)^2}{9} = 1$$

$a = 1, b = 3, c = \sqrt{10}$

Center: $(2, -3)$

Vertices: $(1, -3), (3, -3)$

Foci: $\left(2 \pm \sqrt{10}, -3\right)$

Asymptotes: $y = -3 \pm 3(x - 2)$

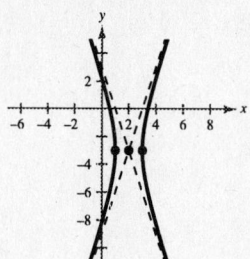

15.
$$x^2 - 9y^2 + 2x - 54y - 80 = 0$$
$$(x^2 + 2x + 1) - 9(y^2 + 6y + 9) = 80 + 1 - 81$$
$$(x + 1)^2 - 9(y + 3)^2 = 0$$
$$y + 3 = \pm\frac{1}{3}(x + 1)$$

Degenerate hyperbola is two lines intersecting at $(-1, -3)$.

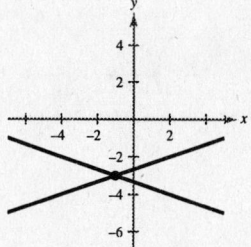

17. $2x^2 - 3y^2 = 6$

$$\frac{x^2}{3} - \frac{y^2}{2} = 1$$

$a = \sqrt{3}, b = \sqrt{2}, c = \sqrt{5}$

Center: $(0, 0)$

Vertices: $\left(\pm\sqrt{3}, 0\right)$

Foci: $\left(\pm\sqrt{5}, 0\right)$

Asymptotes: $y = \pm\sqrt{\frac{2}{3}}x = \pm\frac{\sqrt{6}}{3}x$

To use a graphing calculator, solve first for y.

$$y^2 = \frac{2x^2 - 6}{3}$$

$$\left.\begin{array}{l} y_1 = \sqrt{\dfrac{2x^2 - 6}{3}} \\[2em] y_2 = -\sqrt{\dfrac{2x^2 - 6}{3}} \end{array}\right\} \text{Hyperbola}$$

$$\left.\begin{array}{l} y_3 = \dfrac{\sqrt{6}}{3}x \\[2em] y_4 = -\dfrac{\sqrt{6}}{3}x \end{array}\right\} \text{Asymptotes}$$

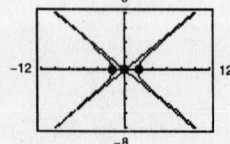

19.
$$9y^2 - x^2 + 2x + 54y + 62 = 0$$
$$9(y^2 + 6y + 9) - (x^2 - 2x + 1) = -62 - 1 + 81$$
$$9(y + 3)^2 - (x - 1)^2 = 18$$
$$\frac{(y + 3)^2}{2} - \frac{(x - 1)^2}{18} = 1$$

$a = \sqrt{2}, b = 3\sqrt{2}, c = 2\sqrt{5}$

Center: $(1, -3)$

Vertices: $\left(1, -3 \pm \sqrt{2}\right)$

Foci: $\left(1, -3 \pm 2\sqrt{5}\right)$

Asymptotes: $y = -3 \pm \frac{1}{3}(x - 1)$

To use a graphing calculator, solve for y first.

$$9(y + 3)^2 = 18 + (x - 1)^2$$

$$y = -3 \pm \sqrt{\frac{18 + (x - 1)^2}{9}}$$

$$\left.\begin{array}{l} y_1 = -3 + \dfrac{1}{3}\sqrt{18 + (x - 1)^2} \\[2em] y_2 = -3 - \dfrac{1}{3}\sqrt{18 + (x - 1)^2} \end{array}\right\} \text{Hyperbola}$$

$$\left.\begin{array}{l} y_3 = -3 + \dfrac{1}{3}(x - 1) \\[2em] y_4 = -3 - \dfrac{1}{3}(x - 1) \end{array}\right\} \text{Asymptotes}$$

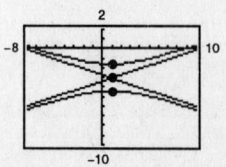

21. Vertices: $(0, \pm 2) \Rightarrow a = 2$

Foci: $(0, \pm 4) \Rightarrow c = 4$

$b^2 = c^2 - a^2 = 16 - 4 = 12$

Center: $(0, 0) = (h, k)$

$$\frac{(y - k)^2}{a^2} - \frac{(x - h)^2}{b^2} = 1$$

$$\frac{y^2}{4} - \frac{x^2}{12} = 1$$

23. Vertices: $(\pm 1, 0) \Rightarrow a = 1$

Asymptotes: $y = \pm 5x \Rightarrow \frac{b}{a} = 5, b = 5$

Center: $(0, 0) = (h, k)$

$$\frac{(x - h)^2}{a^2} - \frac{(y - k)^2}{b^2} = 1$$

$$\frac{x^2}{1} - \frac{y^2}{25} = 1$$

25. Foci: $(0, \pm 8) \Rightarrow c = 8$

Asymptotes: $y = \pm 4x \Rightarrow \frac{a}{b} = 4 \Rightarrow a = 4b$

Center: $(0, 0) = (h, k)$

$c^2 = a^2 + b^2 \Rightarrow 64 = 16b^2 + b^2$

$$\frac{64}{17} = b^2 \Rightarrow a^2 = \frac{1024}{17}$$

$$\frac{(y - k)^2}{a^2} - \frac{(x - h)^2}{b^2} = 1$$

$$\frac{y^2}{\frac{1024}{17}} - \frac{x^2}{\frac{64}{17}} = 1$$

$$\frac{17y^2}{1024} - \frac{17x^2}{64} = 1$$

27. Vertices: $(2, 0), (6, 0) \Rightarrow a = 2$

Foci: $(0, 0), (8, 0) \Rightarrow c = 4$

$b^2 = c^2 - a^2 = 16 - 4 = 12$

Center: $(4, 0) = (h, k)$

$$\frac{(x - h)^2}{a^2} - \frac{(y - k)^2}{b^2} = 1$$

$$\frac{(x - 4)^2}{4} - \frac{y^2}{12} = 1$$

29. Vertices: $(4, 1), (4, 9) \Rightarrow a = 4$

Foci: $(4, 0), (4, 10) \Rightarrow c = 5$

$b^2 = c^2 - a^2 = 25 - 16 = 9$

Center: $(4, 5) = (h, k)$

$$\frac{(y - k)^2}{a^2} - \frac{(x - h)^2}{b^2} = 1$$

$$\frac{(y - 5)^2}{16} - \frac{(x - 4)^2}{9} = 1$$

31. Vertices: $(2, 3), (2, -3) \Rightarrow a = 3$

Passes through the point: $(0, 5)$

Center: $(2, 0) = (h, k)$

$$\frac{(y - k)^2}{a^2} - \frac{(x - h)^2}{b^2} = 1$$

$$\frac{y^2}{9} - \frac{(x - 2)^2}{b^2} = 1 \Rightarrow \frac{(x - 2)^2}{b^2} = \frac{y^2}{9} - 1 = \frac{y^2 - 9}{9} \Rightarrow b^2 = \frac{9(x - 2)^2}{y^2 - 9} = \frac{9(-2)^2}{25 - 9} = \frac{36}{16} = \frac{9}{4}$$

$$\frac{y^2}{9} - \frac{(x - 2)^2}{9/4} = 1$$

$$\frac{y^2}{9} - \frac{4(x - 2)^2}{9} = 1$$

33. Vertices: $(0, 4), (0, 0) \Rightarrow a = 2$

Passes through the point $\left(\sqrt{5}, -1\right)$

Center: $(0, 2) = (h, k)$

$$\frac{(y - k)^2}{a^2} - \frac{(x - h)^2}{b^2} = 1$$

$$\frac{(y - 2)^2}{4} - \frac{x^2}{b^2} = 1 \Rightarrow \frac{x^2}{b^2} = \frac{(y - 2)^2}{4} - 1 = \frac{(y - 2)^2 - 4}{4}$$

$$\Rightarrow b^2 = \frac{4x^2}{(y - 2)^2 - 4} = \frac{4\left(\sqrt{5}\right)^2}{(-1 - 2)^2 - 4} = \frac{20}{5} = 4$$

$$\frac{(y - 2)^2}{4} - \frac{x^2}{4} = 1$$

35. Vertices: $(1, 2), (3, 2) \Rightarrow a = 1$

Asymptotes: $y = x, y = 4 - x$

$$\frac{b}{a} = 1 \Rightarrow \frac{b}{1} = 1 \Rightarrow b = 1$$

Center: $(2, 2) = (h, k)$

$$\frac{(x - h)^2}{a^2} - \frac{(y - k)^2}{b^2} = 1$$

$$\frac{(x - 2)^2}{1} - \frac{(y - 2)^2}{1} = 1$$

37. Vertices: $(0, 2), (6, 2) \Rightarrow a = 3$

Asymptotes: $y = \frac{2}{3}x, y = 4 - \frac{2}{3}x$

$$\frac{b}{a} = \frac{2}{3} \Rightarrow b = 2$$

Center: $(3, 2) = (h, k)$

$$\frac{(x - h)^2}{a^2} - \frac{(y - k)^2}{b^2} = 1$$

$$\frac{(x - 3)^2}{9} - \frac{(y - 2)^2}{4} = 1$$

39. Since $\overline{AB} = 1100$ feet and the sound takes one second longer
to reach B than A, the explosion must occur on the vertical line
through A and B below A.

Foci: $(\pm 3300, 0) \Rightarrow c = 3300$

Center: $(0, 0) = (h, k)$

$$\frac{\overline{CE}}{1100} - \frac{\overline{AE}}{1100} = 4 \Rightarrow 2a = 4400, a = \frac{4400}{2} = 2200$$

$$b^2 = c^2 - a^2 = (3300)^2 - (2200)^2 = 6{,}050{,}000$$

$$\frac{x^2}{(2200)^2} - \frac{y^2}{6{,}050{,}000} = 1$$

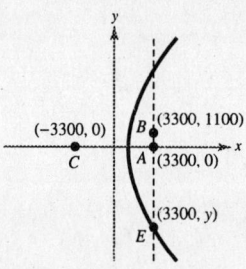

$$y^2 = 6{,}050{,}000\left(\frac{x^2}{(2200)^2} - 1\right)$$

$$y^2 = 6{,}050{,}000\left(\frac{(3300)^2}{(2200)^2} - 1\right) = 7{,}562{,}500$$

$$y = -2750$$

The explosion occurs at $(3300, -2750)$.

41. Center: $(0, 0) = (h, k)$

Focus: $(24, 0) \Rightarrow c = 24$

Solution point: $(24, 24)$

$24^2 = a^2 + b^2 \Rightarrow b^2 = 24^2 - a^2$

$$\frac{(x - h)^2}{a^2} - \frac{(y - k)^2}{b^2} = 1$$

$$\frac{x^2}{a^2} - \frac{y^2}{24^2 - a^2} = 1 \Rightarrow \frac{24^2}{a^2} - \frac{24^2}{24^2 - a^2} = 1$$

Solving yields $a^2 = \dfrac{(3 - \sqrt{5})24^2}{2} \approx 220.0124$ and $b^2 \approx 355.9876$.

Thus, we have $\dfrac{x^2}{220.0124} - \dfrac{y^2}{355.9876} = 1$.

The right vertex is at $(a, 0) \approx (14.83, 0)$.

43. $x^2 + 4y^2 - 6x + 16y + 21 = 0$

$AC = (1)(4) > 0$ and $A \neq C$

The graph is an ellipse.

45. $y^2 - 6y - 4x + 21 = 0$

$AC = (0)(1) = 0$

The graph is a parabola.

47. $4y^2 - 2x^2 - 4y - 8x - 15 = 0$

$AC = (-2)(4) < 0$

The graph is a hyperbola.

49. $4y^2 + 4x^2 - 24x + 35 = 0$

$A = C$

the graph is a circle.

51. False. For the trivial solution of two intersecting lines to occur, the standard form of the equation of the hyperbola would be equal to zero.

$$\frac{(x - h)^2}{a^2} - \frac{(y - k)^2}{b^2} = 0 \quad \text{or} \quad \frac{(y - k)^2}{a^2} - \frac{(x - h)^2}{b^2} = 0$$

53. The extended diagonals of the central rectangle are the asymptotes of the hyperbola.

55. $\left(3x - \frac{1}{2}\right)(x + 4) = 3x^2 + 12x - \frac{1}{2}x - 2$

$$= 3x^2 + \tfrac{23}{2}x - 2$$

57. $[(x + y) + 3]^2 = (x + y)^2 + 6(x + y) + 9$

$$= x^2 + 2xy + y^2 + 6x + 6y + 9$$

59. $x^2 + 14x + 49 = x^2 + 2(7)x + 7^2 = (x + 7)^2$

61. $6x^3 - 11x^2 - 10x = x(6x^2 - 11x - 10)$

$$= x(6x^2 - 15x + 4x - 10)$$

$$= x[3x(2x - 5) + 2(2x - 5)]$$

$$= x(3x + 2)(2x - 5)$$

63. $4 - x + 4x^2 - x^3 = 1(4 - x) + x^2(4 - x)$

$$= (1 + x^2)(4 - x)$$

$$= (x^2 + 1)(4 - x)$$

Section 10.5   Rotation of Conics

- The general second-degree equation $Ax^2 + Bxy + Cy^2 + Dx + Ey + F = 0$ can be rewritten as $A'(x')^2 + C'(y')^2 + D'x' + E'y' + F' = 0$ by rotating the coordinate axes through the angle θ, where $\cot 2\theta = (A - C)/B$.

- $x = x' \cos\theta - y' \sin\theta$
  $y = x' \sin\theta + y' \cos\theta$

- The graph of the nondegenerate equation $Ax^2 + Bxy + Cy^2 + Dx + Ey + F = 0$ is:

  (a)   An ellipse or circle if $B^2 - 4AC < 0$.

  (b)   A parabola if $B^2 - 4AC = 0$.

  (c)   A hyperbola if $B^2 - 4AC > 0$.

Solutions to Odd-Numbered Exercises

1. $\theta = 90°$; Point: $(0, 3)$

$x' = x \cos\theta - y \sin\theta = 0(\cos 90°) - 3(\sin 90°) = -3$

$y' = x \sin\theta + y \cos\theta = 0(\sin 90°) + 3(\cos 90°) = 0$

Thus, $(x', y') = (-3, 0)$.

3. $\theta = 30°$; Point: $(1, 3)$

$x' = x \cos\theta - y \sin\theta = 1(\cos 30°) - 3(\sin 30°) = \dfrac{\sqrt{3}}{2} - \dfrac{3}{2} = \dfrac{1}{2}\left(\sqrt{3} - 3\right)$

$y' = x \sin\theta + y \cos\theta = 1(\sin 30°) + 3(\cos 30°) = \dfrac{1}{2} + \dfrac{3\sqrt{3}}{2} = \dfrac{1}{2}\left(1 + 3\sqrt{3}\right)$

Thus, $(x', y') = \left(\dfrac{1}{2}\left(\sqrt{3} - 3\right), \dfrac{1}{2}\left(1 + 3\sqrt{3}\right)\right)$.

5. $\theta = 45°$; Point $(2, 1)$

$x' = x \cos\theta - y \sin\theta = 2(\cos 45°) - 1(\sin 45°) = \dfrac{2\sqrt{2}}{2} - \dfrac{\sqrt{2}}{2} = \dfrac{\sqrt{2}}{2}$

$y' = x \sin\theta + y \cos\theta = 2(\sin 45°) + 1(\cos 45°) = \dfrac{2\sqrt{2}}{2} + \dfrac{\sqrt{2}}{2} = \dfrac{3\sqrt{2}}{2}$

Thus, $(x', y') = \left(\dfrac{\sqrt{2}}{2}, \dfrac{3\sqrt{2}}{2}\right)$

7. $xy + 1 = 0$

$A = 0, B = 1, C = 0$

$$\cot 2\theta = \frac{A - C}{B} = 0 \Rightarrow 2\theta = \frac{\pi}{2} \Rightarrow \theta = \frac{\pi}{4}$$

$x = x' \cos \dfrac{\pi}{4} - y' \sin \dfrac{\pi}{4}$ $y = x' \sin \dfrac{\pi}{4} + y' \cos \dfrac{\pi}{4}$

$\quad = x' \left(\dfrac{\sqrt{2}}{2} \right) - y' \left(\dfrac{\sqrt{2}}{2} \right)$ $\quad = x' \left(\dfrac{\sqrt{2}}{2} \right) + y' \left(\dfrac{\sqrt{2}}{2} \right)$

$\quad = \dfrac{x' - y'}{\sqrt{2}}$ $\quad = \dfrac{x' + y'}{\sqrt{2}}$

$$xy + 1 = 0$$

$$\left(\frac{x' - y'}{\sqrt{2}} \right)\left(\frac{x' + y'}{\sqrt{2}} \right) + 1 = 0$$

$$\frac{(y')^2}{2} - \frac{(x')^2}{2} = 1$$

9. $x^2 - 2xy + y^2 - 1 = 0$

$A = 1, B = -2, C = 1$

$$\cot 2\theta = \frac{A - C}{B} = 0 \Rightarrow 2\theta = \frac{\pi}{2} \Rightarrow \theta = \frac{\pi}{4}$$

$x = x' \cos \dfrac{\pi}{4} - y' \sin \dfrac{\pi}{4}$ $y = x' \sin \dfrac{\pi}{4} + y' \cos \dfrac{\pi}{4}$

$\quad = x' \left(\dfrac{\sqrt{2}}{2} \right) - y' \left(\dfrac{\sqrt{2}}{2} \right)$ $\quad = x' \left(\dfrac{\sqrt{2}}{2} \right) + y' \left(\dfrac{\sqrt{2}}{2} \right)$

$\quad = \dfrac{x' - y'}{\sqrt{2}}$ $\quad = \dfrac{x' + y'}{\sqrt{2}}$

$$x^2 - 2xy + y^2 - 1 = 0$$

$$\left(\frac{x' - y'}{\sqrt{2}} \right)^2 - 2\left(\frac{x' - y'}{\sqrt{2}} \right)\left(\frac{x' + y'}{\sqrt{2}} \right) + \left(\frac{x' + y'}{\sqrt{2}} \right) - 1 = 0$$

$$\frac{(x')^2 - 2(x')(y') + (y')^2}{2} - \frac{2((x')^2 - (y')^2)}{2} + \frac{(x')^2 + 2(x')(y') + (y')^2}{2} - 1 = 0$$

$$2(y')^2 - 1 = 0$$

$$(y')^2 = \frac{1}{2}$$

$$y' = \pm \sqrt{\frac{1}{2}} = \pm \frac{\sqrt{2}}{2}$$

The graph is two parallel lines. Alternate solution.

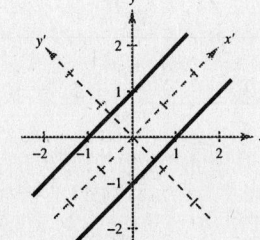

$$x^2 - 2xy + y^2 - 1 = 0$$

$$(x - y)^2 = 1$$

$$x - y = \pm 1$$

$$y = x \pm 1$$

11 $xy - 2y - 4x = 0$

$A = 0, B = 1, C = 0$

$\cot 2\theta = \dfrac{A - C}{B} = 0 \Rightarrow 2\theta = \dfrac{\pi}{2} \Rightarrow \theta = \dfrac{\pi}{4}$

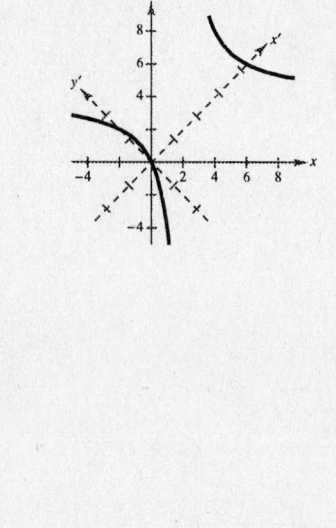

$x = x' \cos \dfrac{\pi}{4} - y' \sin \dfrac{\pi}{4}$ $\qquad$ $y = x' \sin \dfrac{\pi}{4} + y' \cos \dfrac{\pi}{4}$

$\quad = x'\left(\dfrac{\sqrt{2}}{2}\right) - y'\left(\dfrac{\sqrt{2}}{2}\right)$ $\qquad$ $= x'\left(\dfrac{\sqrt{2}}{2}\right) + y'\left(\dfrac{\sqrt{2}}{2}\right)$

$\quad = \dfrac{x' - y'}{\sqrt{2}}$ $\qquad\qquad\qquad$ $= \dfrac{x' + y'}{\sqrt{2}}$

$xy - 2y - 4x = 0$

$\left(\dfrac{x' - y'}{\sqrt{2}}\right)\left(\dfrac{x' + y'}{\sqrt{2}}\right) - 2\left(\dfrac{x' + y'}{\sqrt{2}}\right) - 4\left(\dfrac{x' - y'}{\sqrt{2}}\right) = 0$

$\dfrac{(x')^2}{2} - \dfrac{(y')^2}{2} - \sqrt{2}x' - \sqrt{2}y' - 2\sqrt{2}x' + 2\sqrt{2}y' = 0$

$\left[(x')^2 - 6\sqrt{2}x' + (3\sqrt{2})^2\right] - \left[(y')^2 - 2\sqrt{2}y' + (\sqrt{2})^2\right] = 0 + (3\sqrt{2})^2 - (\sqrt{2})^2$

$(x' - 3\sqrt{2})^2 - (y' - \sqrt{2})^2 = 16$

$\dfrac{(x' - 3\sqrt{2})^2}{16} - \dfrac{(y' - \sqrt{2})^2}{16} = 1$

13. $5x^2 - 6xy + 5y^2 - 12 = 0$

$A = 5, B = -6, C = 5$

$\cot 2\theta = \dfrac{A - C}{B} = 0 \Rightarrow 2\theta = \dfrac{\pi}{2} \Rightarrow \theta = \dfrac{\pi}{4}$

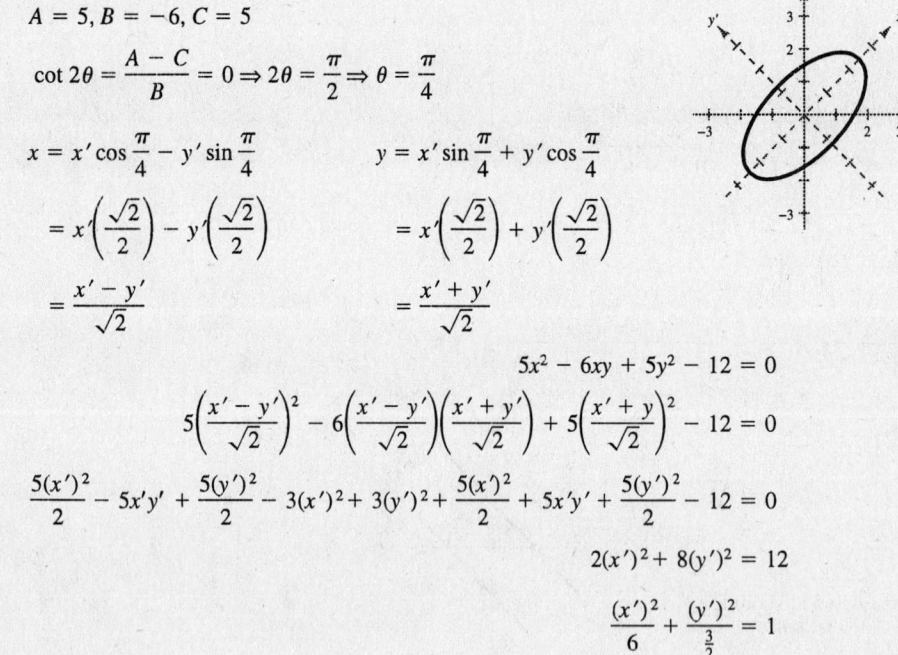

$x = x' \cos \dfrac{\pi}{4} - y' \sin \dfrac{\pi}{4}$ $\qquad$ $y = x' \sin \dfrac{\pi}{4} + y' \cos \dfrac{\pi}{4}$

$\quad = x'\left(\dfrac{\sqrt{2}}{2}\right) - y'\left(\dfrac{\sqrt{2}}{2}\right)$ $\qquad$ $= x'\left(\dfrac{\sqrt{2}}{2}\right) + y'\left(\dfrac{\sqrt{2}}{2}\right)$

$\quad = \dfrac{x' - y'}{\sqrt{2}}$ $\qquad\qquad\qquad$ $= \dfrac{x' + y'}{\sqrt{2}}$

$5x^2 - 6xy + 5y^2 - 12 = 0$

$5\left(\dfrac{x' - y'}{\sqrt{2}}\right)^2 - 6\left(\dfrac{x' - y'}{\sqrt{2}}\right)\left(\dfrac{x' + y'}{\sqrt{2}}\right) + 5\left(\dfrac{x' + y}{\sqrt{2}}\right)^2 - 12 = 0$

$\dfrac{5(x')^2}{2} - 5x'y' + \dfrac{5(y')^2}{2} - 3(x')^2 + 3(y')^2 + \dfrac{5(x')^2}{2} + 5x'y' + \dfrac{5(y')^2}{2} - 12 = 0$

$2(x')^2 + 8(y')^2 = 12$

$\dfrac{(x')^2}{6} + \dfrac{(y')^2}{\frac{3}{2}} = 1$

15. $3x^2 - 2\sqrt{3}xy + y^2 + 2x + 2\sqrt{3}y = 0$

$A = 3, B = -2\sqrt{3}, C = 1$

$\cot 2\theta = \dfrac{A - C}{B} = -\dfrac{1}{\sqrt{3}} \Rightarrow \theta = 60°$

$x = x'\cos 60° - y'\sin 60°$ $\qquad\qquad y = x'\sin 60° + y'\cos 60°$

$\quad = x'\left(\dfrac{1}{2}\right) - y'\left(\dfrac{\sqrt{3}}{2}\right) = \dfrac{x' - \sqrt{3}y'}{2}$ $\qquad = x'\left(\dfrac{\sqrt{3}}{2}\right) + y'\left(\dfrac{1}{2}\right) = \dfrac{\sqrt{3}x' + y'}{2}$

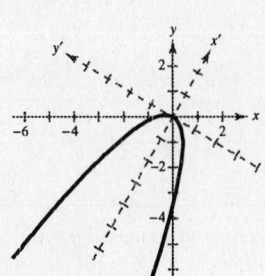

$3x^2 - 2\sqrt{3}xy + y^2 + 2x + 2\sqrt{3}y = 0$

$3\left(\dfrac{x' - \sqrt{3}y'}{2}\right)^2 - 2\sqrt{3}\left(\dfrac{x' - \sqrt{3}y'}{2}\right)\left(\dfrac{\sqrt{3}x' + y'}{2}\right) + \left(\dfrac{\sqrt{3}x' + y'}{2}\right)^2 + 2\left(\dfrac{x' - \sqrt{3}y'}{2}\right) + 2\sqrt{3}\left(\dfrac{\sqrt{3}x' + y'}{2}\right) = 0$

$\dfrac{3(x')^2}{4} - \dfrac{6\sqrt{3}x'y'}{4} + \dfrac{9(y')^2}{4} - \dfrac{6(x')^2}{4} + \dfrac{4\sqrt{3}x'y'}{4} + \dfrac{6(y')^2}{4} + \dfrac{3(x')^2}{4} + \dfrac{2\sqrt{3}x'y'}{4} + \dfrac{(y')^2}{4}$

$\qquad\qquad\qquad\qquad + x' - \sqrt{3}y' + 3x' + \sqrt{3}y' = 0$

$\qquad\qquad\qquad\qquad\qquad 4(y')^2 + 4x' = 0$

$\qquad\qquad\qquad\qquad\qquad\qquad x' = -(y')^2$

17. $9x^2 + 24xy + 16y^2 + 90x - 130y = 0$

$A = 9, B = 24, C = 16$

$\cot 2\theta = \dfrac{A - C}{B} = -\dfrac{7}{24} \Rightarrow \theta \approx 53.13°$

$\cos 2\theta = -\dfrac{7}{25}$

$\sin \theta = \sqrt{\dfrac{1 - \cos \theta}{2}} = \sqrt{\dfrac{1 - \left(-\frac{7}{25}\right)}{2}} = \dfrac{4}{5}$

$\cos \theta = \sqrt{\dfrac{1 + \cos 2\theta}{2}} = \sqrt{\dfrac{1 + \left(-\frac{7}{25}\right)}{2}} = \dfrac{3}{5}$

$x = x'\cos \theta - y'\sin \theta$ $\qquad\qquad y = x'\sin \theta + y'\cos \theta$

$\quad = x'\left(\dfrac{3}{5}\right) - y'\left(\dfrac{4}{5}\right) = \dfrac{3x' - 4y'}{5}$ $\qquad = x'\left(\dfrac{4}{5}\right) + y'\left(\dfrac{3}{5}\right)$

$\qquad\qquad\qquad\qquad\qquad\qquad = \dfrac{4x' + 3y'}{5}$

$9x^2 + 24xy + 16y^2 + 90x - 130y = 0$

$9\left(\dfrac{3x' - 4y'}{5}\right)^2 + 24\left(\dfrac{3x' - 4y'}{5}\right)\left(\dfrac{4x' + 3y'}{5}\right) + 16\left(\dfrac{4x' + 3y'}{5}\right)^2 + 90\left(\dfrac{3x' - 4y'}{5}\right) - 130\left(\dfrac{4x' + 3y'}{5}\right) = 0$

$\dfrac{81(x')^2}{25} - \dfrac{216x'y'}{25} + \dfrac{144(y')^2}{25} + \dfrac{288(x')^2}{25} - \dfrac{168x'y'}{25} - \dfrac{288(y')^2}{25} + \dfrac{256(x')^2}{25} + \dfrac{384x'y'}{25}$

$\qquad\qquad\qquad + \dfrac{144(y')^2}{25} + 54x' - 72y' - 104x' - 78y' = 0$

$\qquad\qquad\qquad\qquad 25(x')^2 - 50x' - 150y' = 0$

$\qquad\qquad\qquad\qquad (x')^2 - 2x' + 1 = 6y' + 1$

$\qquad\qquad\qquad\qquad\qquad y' = \dfrac{(x')^2}{6} - \dfrac{x'}{3}$

19. $x^2 + 2xy + y^2 = 20$

$A = 1, B = 2, C = 1$

$\cot 2\theta = \dfrac{A - C}{B} = \dfrac{1 - 1}{2} = 0 \Rightarrow \theta = \dfrac{\pi}{4}$ or $45°$

To graph the conic using a graphing calculator, we need to solve for y in terms of x.

$(x + y)^2 = 20$

$x + y = \pm\sqrt{20}$

$y = -x \pm \sqrt{20}$

Use $y_1 = -x + \sqrt{20}$

and $y_2 = -x - \sqrt{20}$

21. $17x^2 + 32xy - 7y^2 = 75$

$\cot 2\theta = \dfrac{A - C}{B} = \dfrac{17 + 7}{32} = \dfrac{24}{32} = \dfrac{3}{4} \Rightarrow \theta \approx 26.57°$

Solve for y in terms of x by completing the square.

$-7y^2 + 32xy = -17x^2 + 75$

$y^2 - \dfrac{32}{7}xy = \dfrac{17}{7}x^2 - \dfrac{75}{7}$

$y^2 - \dfrac{32}{7}xy + \dfrac{256}{49}x^2 = \dfrac{119}{49}x^2 - \dfrac{525}{49} + \dfrac{256}{49}x^2$

$\left(y - \dfrac{16}{7}x\right)^2 = \dfrac{375x^2 - 525}{49}$

$y = \dfrac{16}{7}x \pm \sqrt{\dfrac{375x^2 - 525}{49}}$

$y = \dfrac{16x \pm 5\sqrt{15x^2 - 21}}{7}$

Use $y_1 = \dfrac{16x + 5\sqrt{15x^2 - 21}}{7}$

and $y_2 = \dfrac{16x - 5\sqrt{15x^2 - 21}}{7}$.

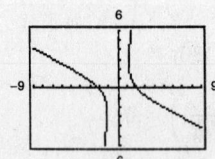

23. $32x^2 + 48xy + 8y^2 = 50$

$\cot 2\theta = \dfrac{A - C}{B} = \dfrac{24}{48} = \dfrac{1}{2} \Rightarrow \theta \approx 31.72°$

Solve for y in terms of x by completing the square.

$8y^2 + 48xy = -32x^2 + 50$

$y^2 + 6xy = -4x^2 + \dfrac{25}{4}$

$y^2 + 6xy + 9x^2 = -4x^2 + \dfrac{25}{4} + 9x^2$

$(y + 3x)^2 = 5x^2 + \dfrac{25}{4}$

$y + 3x = \pm\sqrt{5x^2 + \dfrac{25}{4}}$

$y = -3x \pm \sqrt{5x^2 + \dfrac{25}{4}}$

Use $y_1 = -3x + \sqrt{5x^2 + \dfrac{25}{4}}$

and $y_2 = -3x - \sqrt{5x^2 + \dfrac{25}{4}}$

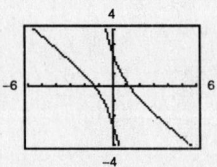

25. $4x^2 - 12xy + 9y^2 + (4\sqrt{13} - 12)x - (6\sqrt{13} + 8)y = 91$

$A = 4, B = -12, C = 9$

$\cot 2\theta = \dfrac{A - C}{B} = \dfrac{4 - 9}{-12} = \dfrac{5}{12}$

$\dfrac{1}{\tan 2\theta} = \dfrac{5}{12}$

$\tan 2\theta = \dfrac{12}{5}$

$2\theta \approx 67.38°$

$\theta \approx 33.69°$

Solve for y in terms of x with the quadratic formula:

$4x^2 - 12xy + 9y^2 + (4\sqrt{13} - 12)x - (6\sqrt{13} + 8)y = 91$

$9y^2 - (12x + 6\sqrt{13} + 8)y + (4x^2 + 4\sqrt{13}x - 12x - 91) = 0$

$a = 9, b = -(12x + 6\sqrt{13} + 8), c = 4x^2 + 4\sqrt{13}x - 12x - 91$

$y = \dfrac{-b \pm \sqrt{b^2 - 4ac}}{2a}$

$y = \dfrac{(12x + 6\sqrt{13} + 8) \pm \sqrt{(12x + 6\sqrt{13} + 8)^2 - 4(9)(4x^2 + 4\sqrt{13}x - 12x - 91)}}{18}$

$= \dfrac{(12x + 6\sqrt{13} + 8) \pm \sqrt{624x + 3808 + 96\sqrt{13}}}{18}$

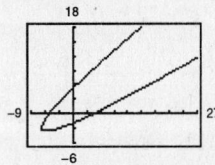

Enter $y_1 = \dfrac{12x + 6\sqrt{13} + 8 + \sqrt{624x + 3808 + 96\sqrt{13}}}{18}$

and $y_2 = \dfrac{12x + 6\sqrt{13} + 8 - \sqrt{624x + 3808 + 96\sqrt{13}}}{18}$.

27. $xy + 2 = 0$

$B^2 - 4AC = 1 \implies$ The graph is a hyperbola.

$\cot 2\theta = \dfrac{A - C}{B} = 0 \implies \theta = 45°$

Matches graph (e).

29. $-2x^2 + 3xy + 2y^2 + 3 = 0$

$B^2 - 4AC = (3)^2 - 4(-2)(2) = 25 \implies$ The graph is a hyperbola.

$\cot 2\theta = \dfrac{A - C}{B} = -\dfrac{4}{3} \implies \theta \approx -18.43°$

Matches graph (b).

31. $3x^2 + 2xy + y^2 - 10 = 0$

$B^2 - 4AC = (2)^2 - 4(3)(1) = -8 \implies$ The graph is an ellipse or circle.

$\cot 2\theta = \dfrac{A - C}{B} = 1 \implies \theta = 22.5°$

Matches graph (d).

33. $16x^2 - 8xy + y^2 - 10x + 5y = 0$

$B^2 - 4AC = (-8)^2 - 4(16)(1) = 0$

The graph is a parabola.

$y^2 + (-8x + 5)y + (16x^2 - 10x) = 0$

$$y = \frac{-(-8x + 5) \pm \sqrt{(-8x + 5)^2 - 4(1)(16x^2 - 10x)}}{2(1)}$$

$$= \frac{8x - 5 \pm \sqrt{(8x - 5)^2 - 4(16x^2 - 10x)}}{2}$$

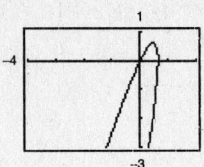

35. $12x^2 - 6xy + 7y^2 - 45 = 0$

$B^2 - 4AC = (-6)^2 - 4(12)(7) = -300 < 0$

The graph is an ellipse.

$7y^2 + (-6x)y + (12x^2 - 45) = 0$

$$y = \frac{-(-6x) \pm \sqrt{(-6x)^2 - 4(7)(12x^2 - 45)}}{2(7)}$$

$$= \frac{6x \pm \sqrt{36x^2 - 28(12x^2 - 45)}}{14}$$

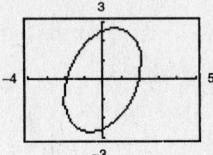

37. $x^2 - 6xy - 5y^2 + 4x - 22 = 0$

$B^2 - 4AC = (-6)^2 - 4(1)(-5) = 56 > 0$

The graph is a hyperbola.

$-5y^2 + (-6x)y + (x^2 + 4x - 22) = 0$

$$y = \frac{-(-6x) \pm \sqrt{(-6x)^2 - 4(-5)(x^2 + 4x - 22)}}{2(-5)}$$

$$= \frac{6x \pm \sqrt{36x^2 + 20(x^2 + 4x - 22)}}{-10}$$

$$= \frac{-6x \pm \sqrt{36x^2 + 20(x^2 + 4x - 22)}}{10}$$

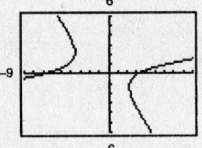

39. $x^2 + 4xy + 4y^2 - 5x - y - 3 = 0$

$B^2 - 4AC = (4)^2 - 4(1)(4) = 0$

The graph is a parabola.

$4y^2 + (4x - 1)y + (x^2 - 5x - 3) = 0$

$$y = \frac{-(4x - 1) \pm \sqrt{(4x - 1)^2 - 4(4)(x^2 - 5x - 3)}}{2(4)}$$

$$= \frac{-(4x - 1) \pm \sqrt{(4x - 1)^2 - 16(x^2 - 5x - 3)}}{8}$$

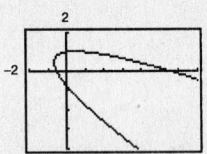

41. $y^2 - 9x^2 = 0$

$\qquad y^2 = 9x^2$

$\qquad y = \pm 3x$

Two intersecting lines

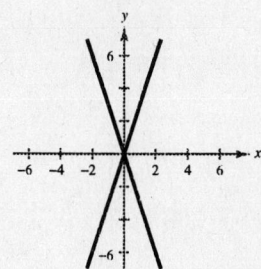

43. $x^2 + 2xy + y^2 - 1 = 0$

$\qquad (x + y)^2 - 1 = 0$

$\qquad (x + y)^2 = 1$

$\qquad x + y = \pm 1$

$\qquad y = -x \pm 1$

Two parallel lines

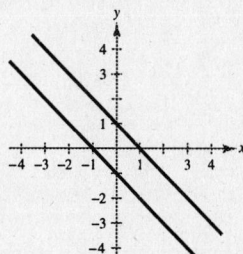

45.

$-x^2 + y^2 + 4x - 6y + 4 = 0 \Rightarrow (y - 3)^2 - (x - 2)^2 = 1$

$\underline{x^2 + y^2 - 4x - 6y + 12 = 0 \Rightarrow (x - 2)^2 + (y - 3)^2 = 1}$

$\qquad\qquad 2y^2 - 12y + 16 = 0$

$\qquad\qquad 2(y - 2)(y - 4) = 0$

$\qquad\qquad y = 2 \text{ or } y = 4$

For $y = 2$: $x^2 + 2^2 - 4x - 6(2) + 12 = 0$

$\qquad\qquad x^2 - 4x + 4 = 0$

$\qquad\qquad (x - 2)^2 = 0$

$\qquad\qquad x = 2$

For $y = 4$: $x^2 + 4^2 - 4x - 6(4) + 12 = 0$

$\qquad\qquad x^2 - 4x + 4 = 0$

$\qquad\qquad (x - 2)^2 = 0$

$\qquad\qquad x = 2$

The points of intersection are $(2, 2)$ and $(2, 4)$.

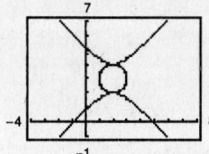

47. $-4x^2 - y^2 - 16x + 24y - 16 = 0$

$\underline{4x^2 + y^2 + 40x - 24y + 208 = 0}$

$ 24x + 192 = 0$

$ x = -8$

When $x = -8$: $4(-8)^2 + y^2 + 40(-8) - 24y + 208 = 0$

$y^2 - 24y + 144 = 0$

$(y - 12)^2 = 0$

$y = 12$

The point of intersection is $(-8, 12)$.

In standard form the equations are:

$\dfrac{(x + 2)^2}{36} + \dfrac{(y - 12)^2}{144} = 1$

$\dfrac{(x + 5)^2}{9} + \dfrac{(y - 12)^2}{36} = 1$

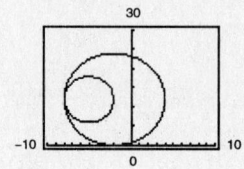

49. $x^2 - y^2 - 12x + 16y - 64 = 0$

$\underline{x^2 + y^2 - 12x - 16y + 64 = 0}$

$2x^2 - 24x = 0$

$2x(x - 12) = 0$

$x = 0 \quad \text{or} \quad x = 12$

When $x = 0$: $0^2 + y^2 - 12(0) - 16y + 64 = 0$

$y^2 - 16y + 64 = 0$

$(y - 8)^2 = 0$

$y = 8$

When $x = 12$: $12^2 + y^2 - 12(12) - 16y + 64 = 0$

$y^2 - 16y + 64 = 0$

$(y - 8)^2 = 0$

$y = 8$

The points of intersection are $(0, 8)$ and $(12, 8)$.

The standard forms of the equations are:

$\dfrac{(x - 6)^2}{36} - \dfrac{(y - 8)^2}{36} = 1$

$(x - 6)^2 + (y - 8)^2 = 36$

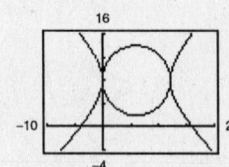

51. $-16x^2 - y^2 + 24y - 80 = 0$

$\underline{16x^2 + 25y^2 \qquad - 400 = 0}$

$\qquad 24y^2 + 24y - 480 = 0$

$\qquad 24(y + 5)(y - 4) = 0$

$\qquad y = -5 \text{ or } y = 4$

When $y = -5$: $16x^2 + 25(-5)^2 - 400 = 0$

$\qquad\qquad\qquad 16x^2 = -225$

$\qquad\qquad\qquad$ No real solution

When $y = 4$: $16x^2 + 25(4)^2 - 400 = 0$

$\qquad\qquad\qquad 16x^2 = 0$

$\qquad\qquad\qquad x = 0$

The point of intersection is $(0, 4)$.

In standard form the equations are:

$$\frac{x^2}{4} + \frac{(y - 12)^2}{64} = 1$$

$$\frac{x^2}{25} + \frac{y^2}{16} = 1$$

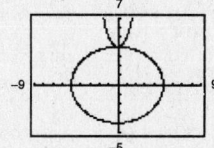

53. $x^2 \qquad + y^2 - 4 = 0$

$\underline{\qquad 3x - y^2 \qquad = 0}$

$x^2 + 3x \qquad - 4 = 0$

$\qquad (x + 4)(x - 1) = 0$

$\qquad x = -4 \quad \text{or} \quad x = 1$

When $x = -4$: $3(-4) - y^2 = 0$

$\qquad\qquad\qquad y^2 = -12$ No real solution

When $x = 1$: $3(1) - y^2 = 0$

$\qquad\qquad\qquad y^2 = 3$

$\qquad\qquad\qquad y = \pm\sqrt{3}$

The points of intersection are $\left(1, \sqrt{3}\right)$ and $\left(1, -\sqrt{3}\right)$.

The standard forms of the equations are:

$x^2 + y^2 = 4$

$\quad y^2 = 3x$

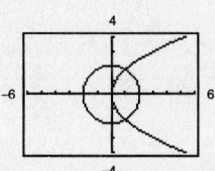

55. $x^2 + 2y^2 - 4x + 6y - 5 = 0$

$-x + y - 4 = 0 \Rightarrow y = x + 4$

$\qquad x^2 + 2(x + 4)^2 - 4x + 6(x + 4) - 5 = 0$

$x^2 + 2(x^2 + 8x + 16) - 4x + 6x + 24 - 5 = 0$

$\qquad\qquad\qquad 3x^2 + 18x + 51 = 0$

$\qquad\qquad\qquad 3(x^2 + 6x + 17) = 0$

$\qquad\qquad\qquad x^2 + 6x + 17 = 0$

$\qquad\qquad\qquad x^2 + 6x + 9 = -17 + 9$

$\qquad\qquad\qquad (x + 3)^2 = -8$

No real solution

No points of intersection

The standard forms of the equations are:

$$\frac{(x - 2)^2}{\frac{27}{2}} + \frac{\left(y + \frac{3}{2}\right)^2}{\frac{27}{4}} = 1$$

$x - y = -4$

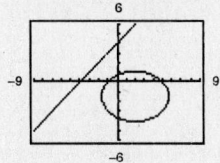

57.

$$xy + x - 2y + 3 = 0 \Rightarrow y = \frac{-x - 3}{x - 2}$$

The points of intersection are $\left(0, \frac{3}{2}\right)$, $(-3, 0)$.

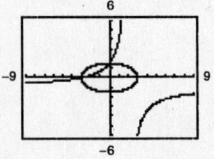

$$x^2 + 4y^2 - 9 = 0$$

$$x^2 + 4\left(\frac{-x - 3}{x - 2}\right)^2 = 9$$

$$x^2(x - 2)^2 + 4(-x - 3)^2 = 9(x - 2)^2$$

$$x^2(x^2 - 4x + 4) + 4(x^2 + 6x + 9) = 9(x^2 - 4x + 4)$$

$$x^4 - 4x^3 + 4x^2 + 4x^2 + 24x + 36 = 9x^2 - 36x + 36$$

$$x^4 - 4x^3 - x^2 + 60x = 0$$

$$x(x + 3)(x^2 - 7x + 20) = 0$$

$$x = 0 \text{ or } x = -3$$

Note: $x^2 - 7x + 20 = 0$ has no real solution.

When $x = 0$: $y = \dfrac{-0 - 3}{0 - 2} = \dfrac{3}{2}$

When $x = -3$: $y = \dfrac{-(-3) - 3}{-3 - 2} = 0$

59. $x^2 + xy + ky^2 + 6x + 10 = 0$

$B^2 - 4AC = 1^2 - 4(1)(k) = 1 - 4k > 0 \Rightarrow -4k > -1 \Rightarrow k < \frac{1}{4}$

True. For the graph to be a hyperbola, the discriminant must be greater than zero.

61. $(x')^2 + (y')^2 = (x \cos \theta - y \sin \theta)^2 + (y \cos \theta + x \sin \theta)^2$

$$= x^2 \cos^2 \theta - 2xy \cos \theta \sin \theta + y^2 \sin^2 \theta + y^2 \cos^2 \theta + 2xy \cos \theta \sin \theta + x^2 \sin^2 \theta$$

$$= x^2(\cos^2 \theta + \sin^2 \theta) + y^2(\sin^2 \theta + \cos^2 \theta) = x^2 + y^2 = r^2$$

63. $f(x) = \dfrac{x^2 - 9}{x + 1}$

$$\frac{x^2 - 9}{x + 1} = 0$$

$$x^2 - 9 = 0$$

$$x^2 = 9$$

$$x = \pm 3$$

65. $f(x) = 4 - \dfrac{8}{x^2 - 2}$

$$4 - \frac{8}{x^2 - 2} = 0$$

$$4 = \frac{8}{x^2 - 2}$$

$$4(x^2 - 2) = 8$$

$$x^2 - 2 = 2$$

$$x^2 = 4$$

$$x = \pm 2$$

67. $f(x) = \dfrac{x^2 + 4x + 4}{x^2 + 3}$

$$\dfrac{x^2 + 4x + 4}{x^2 + 3} = 0$$

$$x^2 + 4x + 4 = 0$$

$$(x + 2)^2 = 0$$

$$x + 2 = 0$$

$$x = -2$$

69. $g(x) = \dfrac{2}{2 - x}$

y-intercept: $(0, 1)$

Vertical asymptote: $x = 2$

Horizontal asymptote: $y = 0$

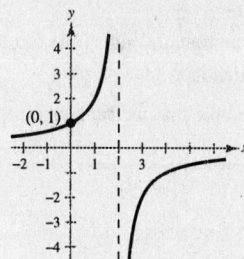

71. $g(t) = \dfrac{2}{1 + t}$

Intercept: $(0, 2)$

Vertical asymptote: $t = -1$

Horizontal asymptote: $y = 0$

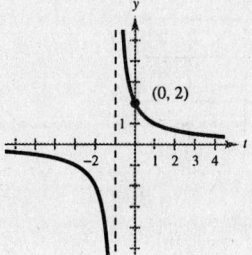

73. $g(x) = \dfrac{x^2 - 2x - 3}{x - 2} = \dfrac{(x - 3)(x + 1)}{x - 2}$

$$= x - \dfrac{3}{x - 2}$$

Intercepts: $(3, 0), (-1, 0), \left(0, \dfrac{3}{2}\right)$

Vertical asymptote: $x = 2$

Slant asymptote: $y = x$

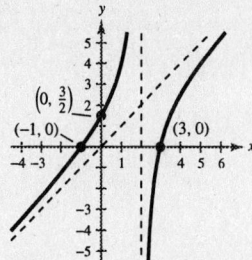

75. $g(s) = \dfrac{2}{4 - s^2}$

Intercept: $\left(0, \dfrac{1}{2}\right)$

Vertical asymptotes: $s = 2, s = -2$

Horizontal asymptote: $y = 0$

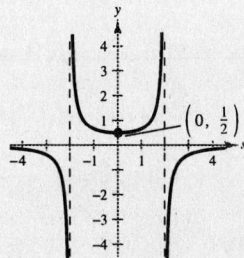

Section 10.6   Parametric Equations

■ If f and g are continuous functions of t on an interval I, then the set of ordered pairs $(f(t), g(t))$ is a *plane curve C*. The equations $x = f(t)$ and $y = g(t)$ are *parametric equations* for C and t is the *parameter*.

■ To eliminate the parameter:
   (a) Solve for t in one equation and substitute into the second equation.
   (b) Use trigonometric identities.

■ You should be able to find the parametric equations for a graph.

Solutions to Odd-Numbered Exercises

1. $x = \sqrt{t}, y = 3 - t$

(a)

t	0	1	2	3	4
x	0	1	$\sqrt{2}$	$\sqrt{3}$	2
y	3	2	1	0	-1

(b)

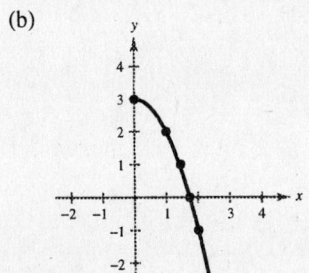

(c) $\quad x = \sqrt{t} \quad \Rightarrow x^2 = t$
$\quad\quad y = 3 - t \quad \Rightarrow \ y = 3 - x^2$

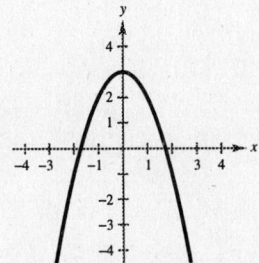

The graph of the parametric equations only shows the right half of the parabola, whereas the rectangular equation yields the entire parabola.

3. $x = 3t - 3 \Rightarrow t = \dfrac{x + 3}{3}$

$y = 2t + 1 \Rightarrow y = \dfrac{2}{3}(x + 3) + 1 = \dfrac{2}{3}x + 3$

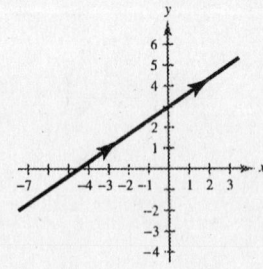

5. $x = \dfrac{1}{4}t \Rightarrow t = 4x$

$y = t^2 \Rightarrow y = 16x^2$

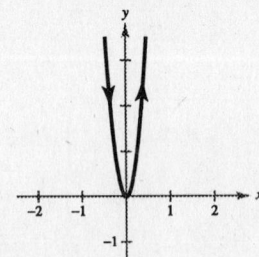

7. $x = t + 2 \Rightarrow t = x - 2$

$y = t^2 \quad \Rightarrow y = (x - 2)^2$

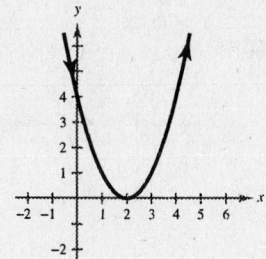

9. $x = t + 1 \Rightarrow t = x - 1$

$y = \dfrac{t}{t + 1} \Rightarrow y = \dfrac{x - 1}{x} = 1 - \dfrac{1}{x}$

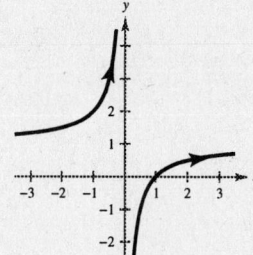

11. $x = 2(t + 1) \Rightarrow \dfrac{x}{2} - 1 = t \quad \text{or} \quad t = \dfrac{x - 2}{2}$

$y = |t - 2| \quad \Rightarrow \quad y = \left|\dfrac{x}{2} - 1 - 2\right| = \left|\dfrac{x}{2} - 3\right| = \left|\dfrac{x - 6}{2}\right|$

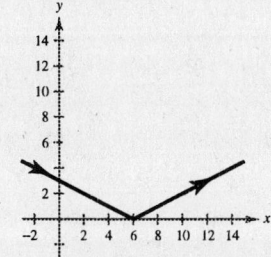

13. $x = 3 \cos \theta \Rightarrow \left(\dfrac{x}{3}\right)^2 = \cos^2 \theta$

$y = 3 \sin \theta \Rightarrow \left(\dfrac{y}{3}\right)^2 = \sin^2 \theta$

$\left(\dfrac{x}{3}\right)^2 + \left(\dfrac{y}{3}\right)^2 = 1$

$\quad x^2 + y^2 = 9$

15. $x = 4 \sin 2\theta \Rightarrow \left(\dfrac{x}{4}\right)^2 = \sin^2 2\theta$

$y = 2 \cos 2\theta \Rightarrow \left(\dfrac{y}{2}\right)^2 = \cos^2 2\theta$

$\left(\dfrac{x}{4}\right)^2 + \left(\dfrac{y}{2}\right)^2 = 1$

$\quad \dfrac{x^2}{16} + \dfrac{y^2}{4} = 1$

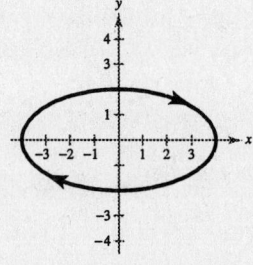

17. $x = 4 + 2\cos\theta \Rightarrow \left(\dfrac{x-4}{2}\right)^2 = \cos^2\theta$

$y = -1 + \sin\theta \Rightarrow (y+1)^2 = \sin^2\theta$

$\dfrac{(x-4)^2}{4} + \dfrac{(y+1)^2}{1} = 1$

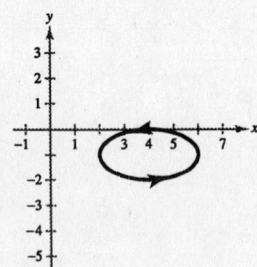

19. $x = e^{-t} \Rightarrow \dfrac{1}{x} = e^t$

$y = e^{3t} \Rightarrow y = (e^t)^3$

$y = \left(\dfrac{1}{x}\right)^3$

$y = \dfrac{1}{x^3},\ x > 0, y > 0$

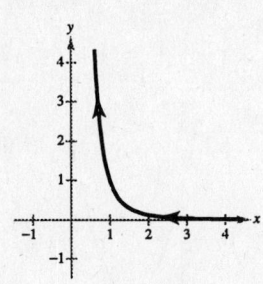

21. $x = t^3 \quad \Rightarrow x^{1/3} = t$

$y = 3\ln t \Rightarrow y = \ln t^3$

$y = \ln(x^{1/3})^3$

$y = \ln x$

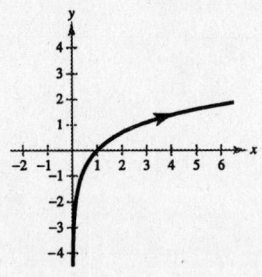

23. By eliminating the parameter, each curve becomes
$y = 2x + 1.$

(a) $x = t$

$y = 2t + 1$

There are no restrictions on x and y.

Domain: $(-\infty, \infty)$

Orientation: Left to right

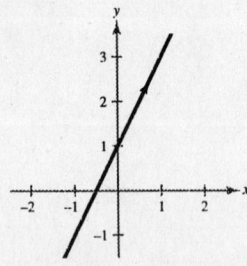

(b) $x = \cos\theta \qquad \Rightarrow -1 \le x \le 1$

$y = 2\cos\theta + 1 \Rightarrow -1 \le y \le 3$

The graph oscillates.

Domain: $[-1, 1]$

Orientation: Depends on θ

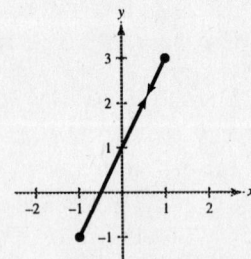

— CONTINUED —

23. — CONTINUED —

(c) $x = e^{-t} \qquad \Rightarrow x > 0$

$y = 2e^{-t} + 1 \Rightarrow y > 1$

Domain: $(0, \infty)$

Orientation: Downward or right to left

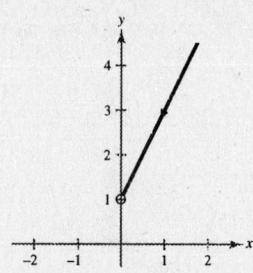

(d) $x = e^{t} \qquad \Rightarrow x > 0$

$y = 2e^{t} + 1 \Rightarrow y > 1$

Domain: $(0, \infty)$

Orientation: Upward or left to right

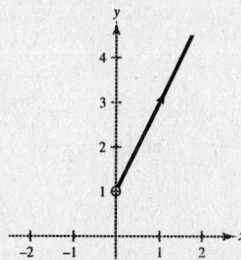

25. $x = x_1 + t(x_2 - x_1), y = y_1 + t(y_2 - y_1)$

$$\frac{x - x_1}{x_2 - x_1} = t$$

$$y = y_1 + \left(\frac{x - x_1}{x_2 - x_1}\right)(y_2 - y_1)$$

$$y - y_1 = \frac{y_2 - y_1}{x_2 - x_1}(x - x_1) = m(x - x_1)$$

27. $x = h + a \cos \theta, y = k + b \sin \theta$

$$\frac{x - h}{a} = \cos \theta, \frac{y - k}{b} = \sin \theta$$

$$\frac{(x - h)^2}{a^2} + \frac{(y - k)^2}{b^2} = 1$$

29. From Exercise 25 we have:

$x = 0 + t(6 - 0) = 6t$

$y = 0 + t(-3 - 0) = -3t$

31. From Exercise 26 we have:

$x = 3 + 4 \cos \theta$

$y = 2 + 4 \sin \theta$

33. Vertices: $(\pm 4, 0) \Rightarrow (h, k) = (0, 0)$ and $a = 4$

Foci: $(\pm 3, 0) \Rightarrow c = 3$

$c^2 = a^2 - b^2 \Rightarrow 9 = 16 - b^2 \Rightarrow b = \sqrt{7}$

From Exercise 27 we have:

$x = 4 \cos \theta$

$y = \sqrt{7} \sin \theta$

35. Vertices: $(\pm 4, 0) \Rightarrow (h, k) = (0, 0)$ and $a = 4$

Foci: $(\pm 5, 0) \Rightarrow c = 5$

$c^2 = a^2 + b^2 \Rightarrow 25 = 16 + b^2 \Rightarrow b = 3$

From Exercise 28 we have:

$x = 4 \sec \theta$

$y = 3 \tan \theta$

37. $y = 3x - 2$

(a) $t = x \Rightarrow x = t$ and $y = 3t - 2$

(b) $t = 2 - x \Rightarrow x = -t + 2$ and $y = 3(-t + 2) - 2 = -3t + 4$

39. $y = x^2$

(a) $t = x \Rightarrow x = t$ and $y = t^2$

(b) $t = 2 - x \Rightarrow x = -t + 2$ and $y = (-t + 2)^2 = t^2 - 4t + 4$

41. $y = x^2 + 1$

(a) $t = x \Rightarrow x = t$ and $y = t^2 + 1$

(b) $t = 2 - x \Rightarrow x = -t + 2$ and $y = (-t + 2)^2 + 1 = t^2 - 4t + 5$

43. $y = \dfrac{1}{x}$

(a) $t = x \Rightarrow x = t$ and $y = \dfrac{1}{t}$

(b) $t = 2 - x \Rightarrow x = -t + 2$ and $y = \dfrac{1}{-t + 2} = \dfrac{-1}{t - 2}$

45. $x = 4(\theta - \sin \theta)$
  $y = 4(1 - \cos \theta)$

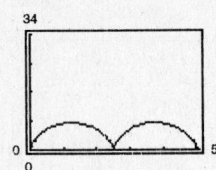

47. $x = \theta - \dfrac{3}{2} \sin \theta$

  $y = 1 - \dfrac{3}{2} \cos \theta$

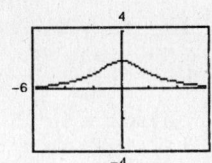

49. $x = 3 \cos^3 \theta$
  $y = 3 \sin^3 \theta$

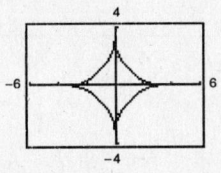

51. $x = 2 \cot \theta$
  $y = 2 \sin^2 \theta$

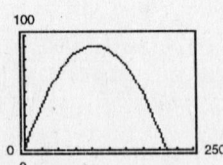

53. $x = 2 \cos \theta \Rightarrow -2 \le x \le 2$
  $y = \sin 2\theta \Rightarrow -1 \le y \le 1$
  Matches graph (b).
  Domain: $[-2, 2]$
  Range: $[-1, 1]$

55. $x = \dfrac{1}{2}(\cos \theta + \theta \sin \theta)$

  $y = \dfrac{1}{2}(\sin \theta - \theta \cos \theta)$

  Matches graph (d).
  Domain: $(-\infty, \infty)$
  Range: $(-\infty, \infty)$

57. $x = (v_0 \cos \theta)t$ and $y = h + (v_0 \sin \theta)t - 16t^2$

(a) $\theta = 60°, \; v_0 = 88$ ft/sec

  $x = (88 \cos 60°)t$ and $y = (88 \sin 60°)t - 16t^2$

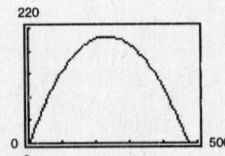

  Maximum height: 90.7 feet

  Range: 209.6 feet

(b) $\theta = 60°, \; v_0 = 132$ ft/sec

  $x = (132 \cos 60°)t$ and $y = (132 \sin 60°)t - 16t^2$

  Maximum height: 204.2 feet

  Range: 471.6 feet

— CONTINUED —

57. — CONTINUED —

(c) $\theta = 45°$, $v_0 = 88$ ft/sec

$x = (88 \cos 45°)t$ and $y = (88 \sin 45°)t - 16t^2$

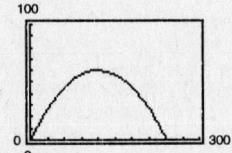

Maximum height: 60.5 ft

Range: 242.0 ft

(d) $\theta = 45°$, $v_0 = 132$ ft/sec

$x = (132 \cos 45°)t$ and $y = (132 \sin 45°)t - 16t^2$

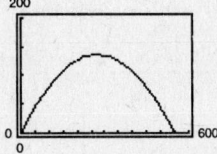

Maximum height: 136.1 ft

Range: 544.5 ft

59. (a) 100 miles per hour $= 100\left(\dfrac{5280}{3600}\right)$ ft/sec $= \dfrac{440}{3}$ ft/sec

$$x = \left(\frac{440}{3}\cos\theta\right)t \approx (146.67\cos\theta)t$$

$$y = 3 + \left(\frac{440}{3}\sin\theta\right)t - 16t^2 \approx 3 + (146.67\sin\theta)t - 16t^2$$

(b) For $\theta = 15°$, we have:

$$x = \left(\frac{440}{3}\cos 15°\right)t \approx 141.7t$$

$$y = 3 + \left(\frac{440}{3}\sin 15°\right)t - 16t^2 \approx 3 + 38.0t - 16t^2$$

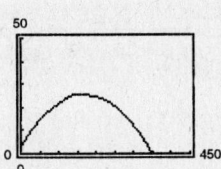

The ball hits the ground inside the ballpark, so it is not a home run.

(c) For $\theta = 23°$, we have:

$$x = \left(\frac{440}{3}\cos 23°\right)t \approx 135.0t$$

$$y = 3 + \left(\frac{440}{3}\sin 23°\right)t - 16t^2 \approx 3 + 57.3t - 16t^2$$

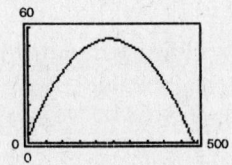

The ball easily clears the 10-foot fence at 400 feet so it is a home run.

(d) Find θ so that $y = 10$ when $x = 400$ by graphing the parametric equations for θ values between $15°$ and $23°$. This occurs when $\theta \approx 19.4°$.

61. $x = (v_0 \cos \theta)t \Rightarrow t = \dfrac{x}{v_0 \cos \theta}$

$y = h + (v_0 \sin \theta)t - 16t^2$

$\quad = h + (v_0 \sin \theta)\left(\dfrac{x}{v_0 \cos \theta}\right) - 16\left(\dfrac{x}{v_0 \cos \theta}\right)^2$

$\quad = h + (\tan \theta)x - \dfrac{16x^2}{v_0{}^2 \cos^2 \theta}$

$\quad = -\dfrac{16 \sec^2 \theta}{v_0{}^2}x^2 + (\tan \theta)x + h$

63. When the circle has rolled θ radians, the center is at $(a\theta, a)$.

$\sin \theta = \sin(180° - \theta)$

$\quad = \dfrac{|AC|}{b} = \dfrac{|BD|}{b} \Rightarrow |BD| = b \sin \theta$

$\cos \theta = -\cos(180° - \theta)$

$\quad = \dfrac{|AP|}{-b} \Rightarrow |AP| = -b \cos \theta$

Therefore, $x = a\theta - b \sin \theta$ and $y = a - b \cos \theta$.

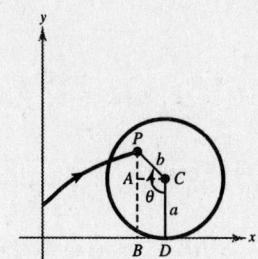

65. True

$x = t$

$y = t^2 + 1 \Rightarrow y = x^2 + 1$

$x = 3t$

$y = 9t^2 + 1 \Rightarrow y = x^2 + 1$

67. $\begin{aligned} 5x - 7y &= 11 \Rightarrow & 5x - 7y &= 11 \\ -3x + y &= -13 \Rightarrow & -21x + 7y &= -91 \\ \hline & & -16x &= -80 \\ & & x &= 5 \end{aligned}$

$5(5) - 7y = 11 \Rightarrow y = 2$

Solution: $(5, 2)$

69. $\begin{aligned} 3a - 2b + c &= 8 \Rightarrow & 9a - 6b + 3c &= 24 \\ 2a + b - 3c &= -3 \Rightarrow & 2a + b - 3c &= -3 \\ \hline & & 11a - 5b &= 21 \end{aligned}$

$\begin{aligned} 2a + b - 3c &= -3 \Rightarrow & 6a + 3b - 9c &= -9 \\ a - 3b + 9c &= 16 \Rightarrow & a - 3b + 9c &= 16 \\ \hline & & 7a &= 7 \\ & & a &= 1 \end{aligned}$

$a = 1 \quad 11(1) - 5b = 21 \Rightarrow b = -2$

$3(1) - 2(-2) + c = 8 \Rightarrow c = 1$

Solution: $(1, -2, 1)$

71. $y = ax^2 + bx + c$

$(0, 0): \quad 0 = a(0)^2 + b(0) + c \Rightarrow c = 0$

$(3, -3): -3 = a(3)^2 + b(3) \quad \Rightarrow -3 = 9a + 3b \Rightarrow -1 = 3a + b$

$(6, 0): \quad 0 = a(6)^2 + b(6) \quad \Rightarrow \quad 0 = 36a + 6b \Rightarrow b = -6a$

$\qquad\qquad b = -6a$

$\qquad -1 = 3a + b \Rightarrow -1 = 3a - 6a$

$\qquad\qquad -1 = -3a$

$\qquad\qquad \tfrac{1}{3} = a$

$\qquad\qquad b = -6\left(\tfrac{1}{3}\right) = -2$

Thus, $y = \tfrac{1}{3}x^2 - 2x$

73. $y = ax^2 + bx + c$

$(4, 12)$: $12 = a(4)^2 + b(4) + c \Rightarrow 16a + 4b + c = 12$

$(8, -2)$: $-2 = a(8)^2 + b(8) + c \Rightarrow 64a + 8b + c = -2$

$(12, 12)$: $12 = a(12)^2 + b(12) + c \Rightarrow 144a + 12b + c = 12$

$$\begin{array}{r} 64a + 8b + c = -2 \\ -16a - 4b - c = -12 \\ \hline 48a + 4b = -14 \end{array}$$

$$\begin{array}{r} 144a + 12b + c = 12 \\ -64a - 8b - c = 2 \\ \hline 80a + 4b = 14 \end{array}$$

$$\begin{array}{r} 80a + 4b = 14 \\ -48a - 4b = 14 \\ \hline 32a = 28 \end{array}$$

$$a = \tfrac{28}{32} = \tfrac{7}{8}$$

$$80\left(\tfrac{7}{8}\right) + 4b = 14 \Rightarrow 4b = -56 \Rightarrow b = -14$$

$$16\left(\tfrac{7}{8}\right) + 4(-14) + c = 12 \Rightarrow c = 54$$

Thus, $y = \tfrac{7}{8}x^2 - 14x + 54$

Section 10.7   Polar Coordinates

- In polar coordinates you do not have unique representation of points. The point (r, θ) can be represented by $(r, \theta \pm 2n\pi)$ or by $(-r, \theta \pm (2n + 1)\pi)$ where n is any integer. The pole is represented by $(0, \theta)$ where θ is any angle.

- To convert from polar coordinates to rectangular coordinates, use the following relationships.

  $x = r \cos \theta$
  $y = r \sin \theta$

- To convert from rectangular coordinates to polar coordinates, use the following relationships.

  $r = \pm\sqrt{x^2 + y^2}$
  $\tan \theta = y/x$

  If θ is in the same quadrant as the point (x, y), then r is positive. If θ is in the opposite quadrant as the point (x, y), then r is negative.

- You should be able to convert rectangular equations to polar form and vice versa.

Solutions to Odd-Numbered Exercises

1. Polar Coordinates: $\left(4, -\dfrac{\pi}{3}\right)$

Additional representations

$$\left(4, -\dfrac{\pi}{3} + 2\pi\right) = \left(4, \dfrac{5\pi}{3}\right)$$

$$\left(-4, -\dfrac{\pi}{3} - \pi\right) = \left(-4, -\dfrac{4\pi}{3}\right)$$

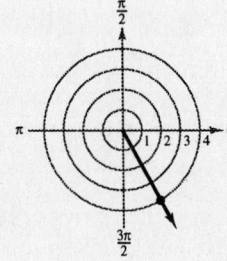

3. Polar Coordinates: $\left(0, -\dfrac{\pi}{6}\right)$

Additional representations

$\left(0, -\dfrac{7\pi}{6} + 2\pi\right) = \left(0, \dfrac{5\pi}{6}\right)$

$\left(0, -\dfrac{7\pi}{6} + \pi\right) = \left(0, -\dfrac{\pi}{6}\right)$

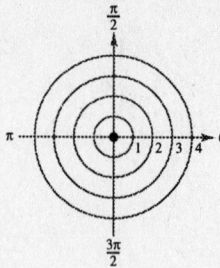

5. Polar Coordinates: $\left(\sqrt{2}, 2.36\right)$

Additional representations

$\left(\sqrt{2}, 2.36 + 2\pi\right) \approx \left(\sqrt{2}, 8.64\right)$

$\left(-\sqrt{2}, 2.36 - \pi\right) \approx \left(-\sqrt{2}, -0.78\right)$

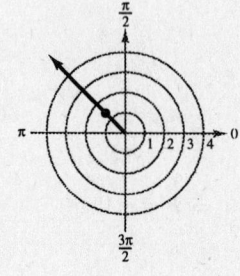

7. Polar Coordinates: $\left(2\sqrt{2}, 4.71\right)$

Additional representations

$\left(2\sqrt{2}, 4.71 + 2\pi\right) \approx \left(2\sqrt{2}, 10.99\right)$

$\left(-2\sqrt{2}, 4.71 - \pi\right) \approx \left(-2\sqrt{2}, 1.57\right)$

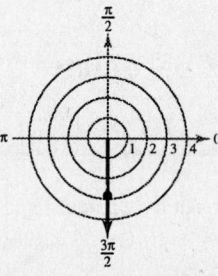

9. Polar Coordinates: $\left(3, \dfrac{\pi}{2}\right)$

$x = 3 \cos \dfrac{\pi}{2} = 0$

$y = 3 \sin \dfrac{\pi}{2} = 3$

Rectangular Coordinates: $(0, 3)$

11. Polar Coordinates: $\left(-1, \dfrac{5\pi}{4}\right)$

$x = -1 \cos\left(\dfrac{5\pi}{4}\right) = \dfrac{\sqrt{2}}{2},\ y = -1 \sin\left(\dfrac{5\pi}{4}\right) = \dfrac{\sqrt{2}}{2}$

Rectangular Coordinates: $\left(\dfrac{\sqrt{2}}{2}, \dfrac{\sqrt{2}}{2}\right)$

13. Polar Coordinates: $\left(2, \dfrac{3\pi}{4}\right)$

$x = 2 \cos \dfrac{3\pi}{4} = -\sqrt{2}$

$y = 2 \sin \dfrac{3\pi}{4} = \sqrt{2}$

Rectangular Coordinates: $\left(-\sqrt{2}, \sqrt{2}\right)$

15. Polar Coordinates: $(-2.5, 1.1)$

$x = -2.5 \cos 1.1 \approx -1.134$

$y = -2.5 \sin 1.1 \approx -2.228$

Rectangular Coordinates: $(-1.134, -2.228)$

17. Rectangular Coordinates: $(1, 1)$

$r = \pm\sqrt{2},\ \tan \theta = 1,\ \theta = \dfrac{\pi}{4} \text{ or } \dfrac{5\pi}{4}$

Polar Coordinates: $\left(\sqrt{2}, \dfrac{\pi}{4}\right), \left(-\sqrt{2}, \dfrac{5\pi}{4}\right)$

19. Rectangular Coordinates: $(-6, 0)$

$r = \pm 6,\ \tan \theta = 0,\ \theta = 0 \text{ or } \pi$

Polar Coordinates: $(6, \pi), (-6, 0)$

21. Rectangular Coordinates: $(-3, 4)$

$r = \pm\sqrt{9 + 16} = \pm 5$, $\tan\theta = -\dfrac{4}{3}$, $\theta \approx 2.2143, 5.3559$

Polar Coordinates: $(5, 2.2143), (-5, 5.3559)$

23. Rectangular Coordinates: $\left(-\sqrt{3}, -\sqrt{3}\right)$

$r = \pm\sqrt{3 + 3} = \pm\sqrt{6}$, $\tan\theta = 1$, $\theta = \dfrac{\pi}{4}$ or $\dfrac{5\pi}{4}$

Polar Coordinates: $\left(\sqrt{6}, \dfrac{5\pi}{4}\right), \left(-\sqrt{6}, \dfrac{\pi}{4}\right)$

25. Rectangular Coordinates: $(6, 9)$

$r = \pm\sqrt{6^2 + 9^2} = \pm\sqrt{117} = \pm 3\sqrt{13}$

$\tan\theta = \frac{9}{6}$, $\theta \approx 0.9828, 4.1244$

Polar Coordinates: $\left(3\sqrt{13}, 0.9828\right), \left(-3\sqrt{13}, 4.1244\right)$

27. Rectangular: $(3, -2)$

$(3, -2) \blacktriangleright$ Pol

$\approx (3.606, -0.5880)$

or $\left(\sqrt{13}, -0.5880\right)$

29. Rectangular: $\left(\sqrt{3}, 2\right)$

$\left(\sqrt{3}, 2\right) \blacktriangleright$ Pol

$\approx (2.646, 0.8571)$

or $\left(\sqrt{7}, 0.8571\right)$

31. Rectangular: $\left(\frac{5}{2}, \frac{4}{3}\right)$

$\left(\frac{5}{2}, \frac{4}{3}\right) \blacktriangleright$ Pol

$\approx (2.833, 0.4900)$

or $\left(\frac{17}{6}, 0.4900\right)$

33. $x^2 + y^2 = 9$

$r = 3$

35. $y = 4$

$r\sin\theta = 4$

$r = 4\csc\theta$

37. $3x - y + 2 = 0$

$3r\cos\theta - r\sin\theta + 2 = 0$

$r(3\cos\theta - \sin\theta) = -2$

$$r = \frac{-2}{3\cos\theta - \sin\theta}$$

39. $xy = 16$

$(r\cos\theta)(r\sin\theta) = 16$

$r^2 = 16\sec\theta\csc\theta = 32\csc 2\theta$

41. $y^2 - 8x - 16 = 0$

$r^2\sin^2\theta - 8r\cos\theta - 16 = 0$

By the Quadratic Formula, we have:

$$r = \frac{-(-8\cos\theta) \pm \sqrt{(-8\cos\theta)^2 - 4(\sin^2\theta)(-16)}}{2\sin^2\theta}$$

$$= \frac{8\cos\theta \pm \sqrt{64\cos^2\theta + 64\sin^2\theta}}{2\sin^2\theta}$$

$$= \frac{8\cos\theta \pm \sqrt{64(\cos^2\theta + \sin^2\theta)}}{2\sin^2\theta}$$

$$= \frac{8\cos\theta \pm 8}{2\sin^2\theta}$$

$$= \frac{4(\cos\theta \pm 1)}{1 - \cos^2\theta}$$

$$r = \frac{4(\cos\theta + 1)}{(1 + \cos\theta)(1 - \cos\theta)} = \frac{4}{1 - \cos\theta}$$

or

$$r = \frac{4(\cos\theta - 1)}{(1 + \cos\theta)(1 - \cos\theta)} = \frac{-4}{1 + \cos\theta}$$

43. $x^2 + y^2 = a^2$

$r^2 = a^2$

$r = a$

45.
$$y = b$$
$$r \sin \theta = b$$
$$r = b \csc \theta$$

47.
$$x^2 + y^2 - 2ax = 0$$
$$r^2 - 2a\, r \cos \theta = 0$$
$$r(r - 2a \cos \theta) = 0$$
$$r - 2a \cos \theta = 0$$
$$r = 2a \cos \theta$$

49.
$$r = 4 \sin \theta$$
$$r^2 = 4r \sin \theta$$
$$x^2 + y^2 = 4y$$
$$x^2 + y^2 - 4y = 0$$

51.
$$\theta = \frac{2\pi}{3}$$
$$\tan \theta = \tan \frac{2\pi}{3}$$
$$\frac{y}{x} = -\sqrt{3}$$
$$y = -\sqrt{3}x$$
$$\sqrt{3}x + y = 0$$

53.
$$r = 2 \csc \theta$$
$$r \sin \theta = 2$$
$$y = 2$$

55.
$$r = 2 \sin 3\theta$$
$$r = 2 \sin(\theta + 2\theta)$$
$$r = 2[\sin \theta \cos 2\theta + \cos \theta \sin 2\theta]$$
$$r = 2[\sin \theta(1 - 2\sin^2 \theta) + \cos \theta(2 \sin \theta \cos \theta)]$$
$$r = 2[\sin \theta - 2\sin^3 \theta + 2 \sin \theta \cos^2 \theta]$$
$$r = 2[\sin \theta - 2\sin^3 \theta + 2 \sin \theta(1 - \sin^2 \theta)]$$
$$r = 2(3 \sin \theta - 4 \sin^3 \theta)$$
$$r^4 = 6r^3 \sin \theta - 8r^3 \sin^3 \theta$$
$$(x^2 + y^2)^2 = 6(x^2 + y^2)y - 8y^3$$
$$(x^2 + y^2)^2 = 6x^2y - 2y^3$$

57.
$$r = \frac{6}{2 - \sin \theta}$$
$$r(2 - \sin \theta) = 6$$
$$2r = 6 + r \sin \theta$$
$$2\left(\pm\sqrt{x^2 + y^2}\right) = 6 + 3y$$
$$4\left(x^2 + y^2\right) = (6 + 3y)^2$$
$$4x^2 + 4y^2 = 36 + 36y + 9y^2$$
$$4x^2 - 5y^2 - 36y - 36 = 0$$

59.
$$r = 6$$
$$r^2 = 36$$
$$x^2 + y^2 = 36$$

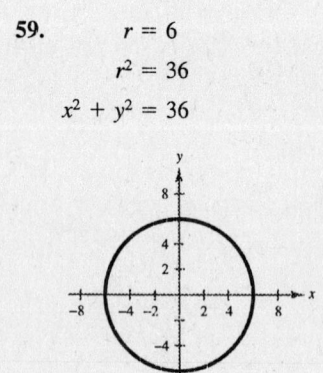

61.
$$\theta = \frac{\pi}{6}$$
$$\tan \theta = \tan \frac{\pi}{6}$$
$$\frac{y}{x} = \frac{\sqrt{3}}{3}$$
$$y = \frac{\sqrt{3}}{3}x$$
$$3y = \sqrt{3}x$$
$$-\sqrt{3}x + 3y = 0$$

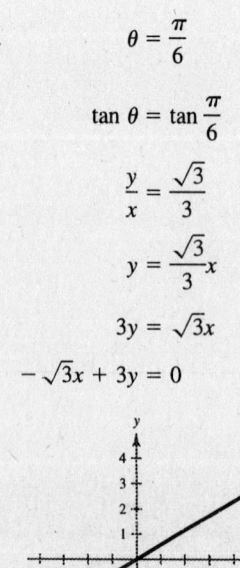

63.
$$r = 3 \sec \theta$$
$$r \cos \theta = 3$$
$$x = 3$$
$$x - 3 = 0$$

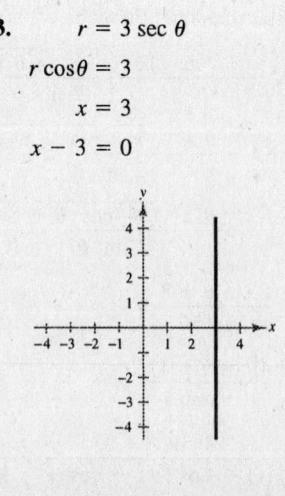

65. True. Because r is a directed distance, then the point (r, θ) can be represented as $(r, \theta + 2n\pi)$.

67.
$$r = 2(h \cos \theta + k \sin \theta)$$
$$r = 2\left(h\left(\frac{x}{r}\right) + k\left(\frac{y}{r}\right)\right)$$
$$r = \frac{2hx + 2ky}{r}$$
$$r^2 = 2hx + 2ky$$
$$x^2 + y^2 = 2hx + 2ky$$
$$x^2 - 2hx + y^2 - 2ky = 0$$
$$\left(x^2 - 2hx + h^2\right) + \left(y^2 - 2ky + k^2\right) = h^2 + k^2$$
$$(x - h)^2 + (y - k)^2 = h^2 + k^2$$

Center: (h, k)

Radius: $\sqrt{h^2 + k^2}$

69. (a) $(r_1, \theta_1) = (x_1, y_1)$ where $x_1 = r_1 \cos \theta_1$ and $y_1 = r_1 \sin \theta_1$.

$(r_2, \theta_2) = (x_2, y_2)$ where $x_2 = r_2 \cos \theta_2$ and $y_2 = r_2 \sin \theta_2$.

$$\begin{aligned} d &= \sqrt{(x_1 - x_2)^2 + (y_1 - y_2)^2} \\ &= \sqrt{x_1^2 - 2x_1x_2 + x_2^2 + y_1^2 - 2y_1y_2 + y_2^2} \\ &= \sqrt{(x_1^2 + y_1^2) + (x_2^2 + y_2 + y_2^2) - 2(x_1x_2 + y_1y_2)} \\ &= \sqrt{r_1^2 + r_2^2 - 2\left(r_1r_2 \cos \theta_1 \cos \theta_2 + r_1r_2 \sin \theta_1 \sin \theta_2\right)} \\ &= \sqrt{r_1^2 + r_2^2 - 2r_1r_2 \cos(\theta_1 - \theta_2)} \end{aligned}$$

(b) If $\theta_1 = \theta_2$, then
$$\begin{aligned} d &= \sqrt{r_1^2 + r_2^2 - 2r_1r_2} \\ &= \sqrt{(r_1 - r_2)^2} \\ &= |r_1 - r_2|. \end{aligned}$$
This represents the distance between two points on the line $\theta = \theta_1 = \theta_2$.

(c) If $\theta_1 - \theta_2 = 90°$, then
$$d = \sqrt{r_1^2 + r_2^2}.$$
This is the result of the Pythagorean Theorem.

(d) The results should be the same. For example, use the points
$$\left(3, \frac{\pi}{6}\right) \text{ and } \left(4, \frac{\pi}{3}\right).$$

The distance is $d \approx 2.053$.
Now use the representations
$$\left(-3, \frac{7\pi}{6}\right) \text{ and } \left(-4, \frac{4\pi}{3}\right).$$

The distance is still $d \approx 2.053$.

71. $5x - 7y = -11$

$-3x + y = -3$

By Cramer's Rule we have:

$$x = \frac{\begin{vmatrix} -11 & -7 \\ -3 & 1 \end{vmatrix}}{\begin{vmatrix} 5 & -7 \\ -3 & 1 \end{vmatrix}} = \frac{-32}{-16} = 2$$

$$y = \frac{\begin{vmatrix} 5 & -11 \\ -3 & -3 \end{vmatrix}}{\begin{vmatrix} 5 & -7 \\ -3 & 1 \end{vmatrix}} = \frac{-48}{-16} = 3$$

Solution: $(2, 3)$

73. $3a - 2b + c = 0$

$2a + b - 3c = 0$

$a - 3b + 9c = 8$

$$\begin{vmatrix} 3 & -2 & 1 \\ 2 & 1 & -3 \\ 1 & -3 & 9 \end{vmatrix} = 35$$

By Cramer's Rule we have:

$$x = \frac{\begin{vmatrix} 0 & -2 & 1 \\ 0 & 1 & -3 \\ 8 & -3 & 9 \end{vmatrix}}{35} = \frac{40}{35} = \frac{8}{7}$$

$$y = \frac{\begin{vmatrix} 3 & 0 & 1 \\ 2 & 0 & -3 \\ 1 & 8 & 9 \end{vmatrix}}{35} = \frac{88}{35}$$

$$z = \frac{\begin{vmatrix} 3 & -2 & 0 \\ 2 & 1 & 0 \\ 1 & -3 & 8 \end{vmatrix}}{35} = \frac{56}{35} = \frac{8}{5}$$

Solution: $\left(\dfrac{8}{7}, \dfrac{88}{35}, \dfrac{8}{5} \right)$

75. $x + y + 3w = -8$

$3x - y - w = 7$

$-x + y - 2w = -2$

$2y + w = -6$

$$\begin{vmatrix} 1 & 1 & 1 & -3 \\ 3 & -1 & -2 & 1 \\ -1 & 1 & -1 & 2 \\ 0 & 2 & 0 & 1 \end{vmatrix} = 20$$

By Cramer's Rule we have:

$$x = \frac{\begin{vmatrix} -8 & 1 & 1 & -3 \\ 7 & -1 & -2 & 1 \\ -2 & 1 & -1 & 2 \\ -6 & 2 & 0 & 1 \end{vmatrix}}{20} = \frac{20}{20} = 1$$

$$y = \frac{\begin{vmatrix} 1 & -8 & 1 & -3 \\ 3 & 7 & -2 & 1 \\ -1 & -2 & -1 & 2 \\ 0 & -6 & 0 & 1 \end{vmatrix}}{20} = \frac{-80}{20} = -4$$

$$z = \frac{\begin{vmatrix} 1 & 1 & -8 & -3 \\ 3 & -1 & 7 & 1 \\ -1 & 1 & -2 & 2 \\ 0 & 2 & -6 & 1 \end{vmatrix}}{20} = \frac{20}{20} = 1$$

$$w = \frac{\begin{vmatrix} 1 & 1 & 1 & -8 \\ 3 & -1 & -2 & 7 \\ -1 & 1 & -1 & -2 \\ 0 & 2 & 0 & -6 \end{vmatrix}}{20} = \frac{40}{20} = 2$$

Solution: $(1, -4, 1, 2)$

77. Points: $(4, -3), (6, -7), (-2, -1)$

$$\begin{vmatrix} 4 & -3 & 1 \\ 6 & -7 & 1 \\ -2 & -1 & 1 \end{vmatrix} = -20 \neq 0$$

The points are not collinear.

79. Points: $(-6, -4), (-1, -3), (1.5, -2.5)$

$$\begin{vmatrix} -6 & -4 & 1 \\ -1 & -3 & 1 \\ 1.5 & -2.5 & 1 \end{vmatrix} = 0$$

The points are collinear.

Section 10.8   Graphs of Polar Equations

■   When graphing polar equations:

1. Test for symmetry.
   (a) $\theta = \pi/2$: Replace (r, θ) by $(r, \pi - \theta)$ or $(-r, -\theta)$.
   (b) Polar axis: Replace (r, θ) by $(r, -\theta)$ or $(-r, \pi - \theta)$.
   (c) Pole: Replace (r, θ) by $(r, \pi + \theta)$ or $(-r, \theta)$.
   (d) $r = f(\sin \theta)$ is symmetric with respect to the line $\theta = \pi/2$.
   (e) $r = f(\cos \theta)$ is symmetric with respect to the polar axis.

2. Find the θ values for which $|r|$ is maximum.

3. Find the θ values for which $r = 0$.

4. Know the different types of polar graphs.
   (a) Limaçons $(0 < a, 0 < b)$
   $$r = a \pm b \cos \theta$$
   $$r = a \pm b \sin \theta$$

   (b) Rose Curves, $n \geq 2$
   $$r = a \cos n\theta$$
   $$r = a \sin n\theta$$

   (c) Circles
   $$r = a \cos \theta$$
   $$r = a \sin \theta$$
   $$r = a$$

   (d) Lemniscates
   $$r^2 = a^2 \cos 2\theta$$
   $$r^2 = a^2 \sin 2\theta$$

5. Plot additional points.

Solutions to Odd-Numbered Exercises

1. $r = 3 \cos 2\theta$

Rose curve with 4 petals

3. $r = 3(1 - 2 \cos \theta)$

Limaçon with inner loop

5. $r = 6 \sin 2\theta$

Rose curve with 4 petals

7. $r = 5 + 4 \cos \theta$

$\theta = \dfrac{\pi}{2}$: $-r = 5 + 4 \cos(-\theta)$

$-r = 5 + 4 \cos \theta$

Not an equivalent equation

Polar axis: $r = 5 + 4 \cos(-\theta)$

$r = 5 + 4 \cos \theta$

Equivalent equation

Pole: $-r = 5 + 4 \cos \theta$

Not an equivalent equation

Answer: Symmetric with respect to polar axis

9. $r = \dfrac{2}{1 + \sin \theta}$

$\theta = \dfrac{\pi}{2}:\quad r = \dfrac{2}{1 + \sin(\pi - \theta)}$

$\qquad r = \dfrac{2}{1 + \sin \pi \cos \theta - \cos \pi \sin \theta}$

$\qquad r = \dfrac{2}{1 + \sin \theta}$

Equivalent equation

Polar axis:
$\qquad r = \dfrac{2}{1 + \sin(-\theta)}$

$\qquad r = \dfrac{2}{1 - \sin \theta}$

Not an equivalent equation

Pole: $\qquad -r = \dfrac{2}{1 + \sin \theta}$

Answer: Symmetric with respect to $\theta = \pi/2$

11. $r^2 = 16 \cos 2\theta$

$\theta = \dfrac{\pi}{2}:\quad (-r)^2 = 16 \cos 2(-\theta)$

$\qquad\qquad r^2 = 16 \cos 2\theta$

Equivalent equation

Polar axis: $r^2 = 16 \cos 2(-\theta)$

$\qquad\qquad r^2 = 16 \cos 2\theta$

Equivalent equation

Pole: $\qquad (-r)^2 = 16 \cos 2\theta$

$\qquad\qquad r^2 = 16 \cos 2\theta$

Equivalent equation

Answer: Symmetric with respect to $\theta = \dfrac{\pi}{2}$, the polar axis, and the pole

13. $|r| = |10(1 - \sin \theta)| = 10|1 - \sin \theta| \le 10(2) = 20$

$|1 - \sin \theta| = 2$

$1 - \sin \theta = 2 \qquad$ or $\quad 1 - \sin \theta = -2$

$\qquad \sin \theta = -1 \qquad\qquad\qquad \sin \theta = 3$

$\qquad\qquad \theta = \dfrac{3\pi}{2} \qquad\qquad\qquad$ Not possible

Maximum: $|r| = 20$ when $\theta = \dfrac{3\pi}{2}$.

$0 = 10(1 - \sin \theta)$

$\sin \theta = 1$

$\qquad \theta = \dfrac{\pi}{2}$

Zero: $r = 0$ when $\theta = \dfrac{\pi}{2}$.

15. $|r| = |4 \cos 3\theta| = 4|\cos 3\theta| \le 4$

$|\cos 3\theta| = 1$

$\cos 3\theta = \pm 1$

$\qquad \theta = 0, \dfrac{\pi}{3}, \dfrac{2\pi}{3}$

Maximum: $|r| = 4$ when $\theta = 0, \dfrac{\pi}{3}, \dfrac{2\pi}{3}$.

$0 = 4 \cos 3\theta$

$\cos 3\theta = 0$

$\qquad \theta = \dfrac{\pi}{6}, \dfrac{\pi}{2}, \dfrac{5\pi}{6}$

Zero: $r = 0$ when $\theta = \dfrac{\pi}{6}, \dfrac{\pi}{2}, \dfrac{5\pi}{6}$.

17. Circle: $r = 5$

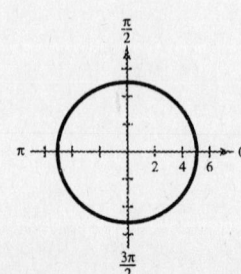

19. Circle: $r = \dfrac{\pi}{6}$

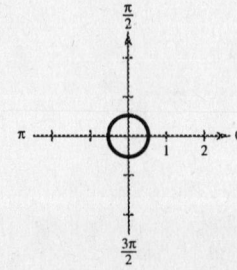

21. $r = 3 \sin \theta$

Symmetric with respect to $\theta = \dfrac{\pi}{2}$

Circle with a radius of $\dfrac{3}{2}$

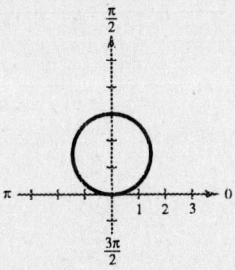

23. $r = 3(1 - \cos \theta)$

Symmetric with respect to the polar axis

$\dfrac{a}{b} = \dfrac{3}{3} = 1 \Rightarrow$ Cardioid

$|r| = 6$ when $\theta = \pi$.

$r = 0$ when $\pi = 0$.

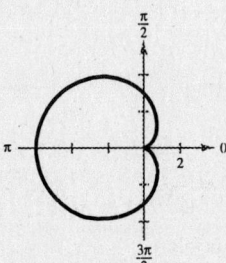

25. $r = 4(1 + \sin \theta)$

Symmetric with respect to $\theta = \dfrac{\pi}{2}$

$\dfrac{a}{b} = \dfrac{4}{4} = 1 \Rightarrow$ Cardioid

$|r| = 8$ when $\theta = \dfrac{\pi}{2}$.

$r = 0$ when $\theta = \dfrac{3\pi}{2}$.

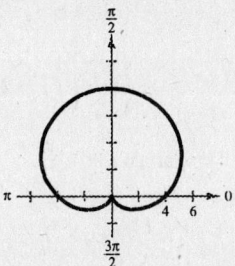

27. $r = 3 + 6 \sin \theta$

Symmetric with respect to $\theta = \dfrac{\pi}{2}$

$\dfrac{a}{b} = \dfrac{3}{6} < 1 \Rightarrow$ Limaçon with inner loop

$|r| = 9$ when $\theta = \dfrac{\pi}{2}$

$r = 0$ when $\theta = \dfrac{7\pi}{6}, \dfrac{11\pi}{6}$

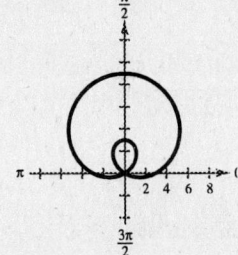

29. $r = 1 - 2 \sin \theta$

Symmetric with respect to $\theta = \dfrac{\pi}{2}$

$\dfrac{a}{b} = \dfrac{1}{2} < 1 \Rightarrow$ Limaçon with inner loop

$|r| = 3$ when $\theta = \dfrac{3\pi}{2}$

$r = 0$ when $\theta = \dfrac{\pi}{6}, \dfrac{5\pi}{6}$

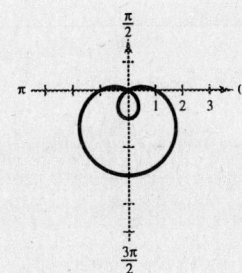

31. $r = 3 - 4 \cos \theta$

Symmetric with respect to the polar axis

$\dfrac{a}{b} = \dfrac{2}{4} < 1 \implies$ Limaçon with inner loop

$|r| = 7$ when $\theta = \pi$.

$r = 0$ when $\cos \theta = \dfrac{3}{4}$ or

$\theta \approx 0.723, 5.560$

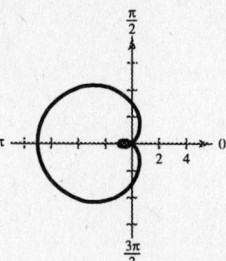

33. $r = 5 \sin 2\theta$

Symmetric with respect to $\theta = \dfrac{\pi}{2}$

Rose curve $(n = 2)$ with 4 petals

$|r| = 5$ when $\theta = \dfrac{\pi}{4}, \dfrac{3\pi}{4}, \dfrac{5\pi}{4}, \dfrac{7\pi}{4}$.

$r = 0$ when $\theta = 0, \dfrac{\pi}{2}, \pi$.

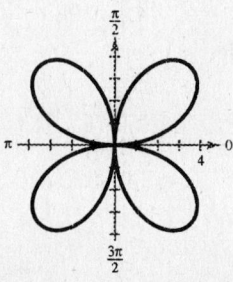

35. $r = 2 \sec \theta$

$r = \dfrac{2}{\cos \theta}$

$r \cos \theta = 2$

$x = 2 \implies$ Line

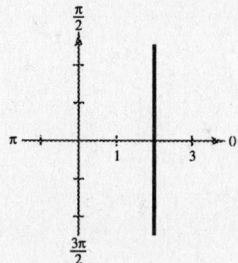

37. $r = \dfrac{3}{\sin \theta - 2 \cos \theta}$

$r(\sin \theta - 2 \cos \theta) = 3$

$y - 2x = 3$

$y = 2x + 3 \implies$ Line

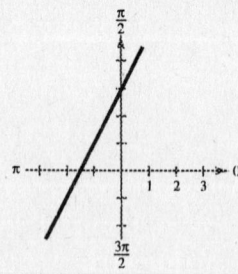

39. $r^2 = 9 \cos 2\theta$

Symmetric with respect to the polar axis, $\theta = \dfrac{\pi}{2}$,

and the pole

Lemniscate

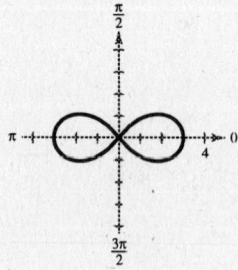

41. $r = 8 \cos \theta$

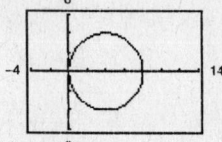

43. $r = 3(2 - \sin \theta)$

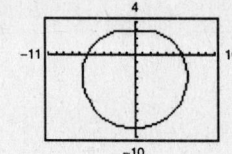

45. $r = 8 \sin \theta \cos^2 \theta$

47. $r = 3 - 4 \cos \theta$

$0 \le \theta < 2\pi$

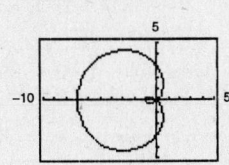

49. $r = 2 \cos\left(\dfrac{3\theta}{2}\right)$

$0 \le \theta < 4\pi$

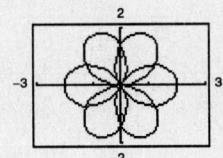

51. $r^2 = 9 \sin 2\theta$

$0 \le \theta < \pi$

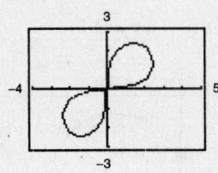

53.
$$r = 2 - \sec \theta = 2 - \frac{1}{\cos \theta}$$

$$r \cos \theta = 2 \cos \theta - 1$$

$$r(r \cos \theta) = 2r \cos \theta - r$$

$$\left(\pm \sqrt{x^2 + y^2}\right)x = 2x - \left(\pm \sqrt{x^2 + y^2}\right)$$

$$\left(\pm \sqrt{x^2 + y^2}\right)(x + 1) = 2x$$

$$\left(\pm \sqrt{x^2 + y^2}\right) = \frac{2x}{x + 1}$$

$$x^2 + y^2 = \frac{4x^2}{(x + 1)^2}$$

$$y^2 = \frac{4x^2}{(x + 1)^2} - x^2$$

$$= \frac{4x^2 - x^2(x + 1)^2}{(x + 1)^2} = \frac{4x^2 - x^2(x^2 + 2x + 1)}{(x + 1)^2}$$

$$= \frac{-x^4 - 2x^3 + 3x^2}{(x + 1)^2} = \frac{-x^2(x^2 + 2x - 3)}{(x + 1)^2}$$

$$y = \pm \sqrt{\frac{x^2(3 - 2x - x^2)}{(x + 1)^2}} = \pm \left| \frac{x}{x + 1} \right| \sqrt{3 - 2x - x^2}$$

The graph has an asymptote at $x = -1$.

55. $r = \dfrac{3}{\theta}$

$$\theta = \frac{3}{r} = \frac{3 \sin \theta}{r \sin \theta} = \frac{3 \sin \theta}{y}$$

$$y = \frac{3 \sin \theta}{\theta}$$

As $\theta \to 0$, $y \to 3$

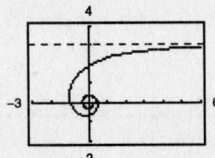

57. True. For a graph to have polar axis symmetry, replace (r, θ) by $(r, -\theta)$ or $(-r, \pi - \theta)$.

59. $r = 6\cos\theta$

(a) $0 \le \theta \le \dfrac{\pi}{2}$

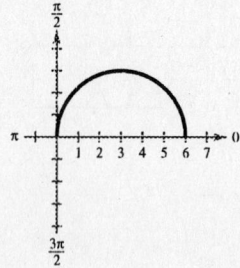

(b) $\dfrac{\pi}{2} \le \theta \le \pi$

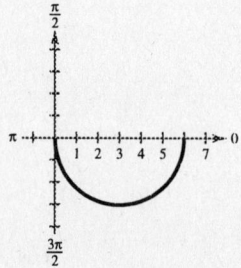

(c) $-\dfrac{\pi}{2} \le \theta \le \dfrac{\pi}{2}$

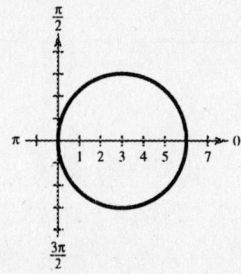

(d) $\dfrac{\pi}{4} \le \theta \le \dfrac{3\pi}{4}$

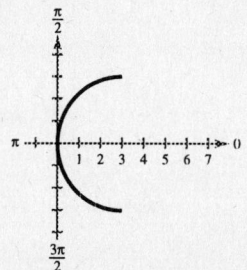

61. Let the curve $r = f(\theta)$ be rotated by ϕ to form the curve $r = g(\theta)$. If (r_1, θ_1) is a point on $r = f(\theta)$, then $(r_1, \theta_1 + \phi)$ is on $r = g(\theta)$. That is, $g(\theta_1 + \phi) = r_1 = f(\theta_1)$. Letting $\theta = \theta_1 + \phi$, or $\theta_1 = \theta - \phi$, we see that $g(\theta) = g(\theta_1 + \phi) = f(\theta_1) = f(\theta - \phi)$.

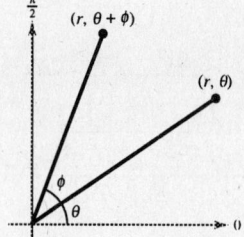

63. (a) $r = 2 - \sin\left(\theta - \dfrac{\pi}{4}\right)$

$= 2 - \left[\sin\theta\cos\dfrac{\pi}{4} - \cos\theta\sin\dfrac{\pi}{4}\right]$

$= 2 - \dfrac{\sqrt{2}}{2}(\sin\theta - \cos\theta)$

(c) $r = 2 - \sin(\theta - \pi)$

$= 2 - [\sin\theta\cos\pi - \cos\theta\sin\pi]$

$= 2 + \sin\theta$

(b) $r = 2 - \sin\left(\theta - \dfrac{\pi}{2}\right)$

$= 2 - \left[\sin\theta\cos\dfrac{\pi}{2} - \cos\theta\sin\dfrac{\pi}{2}\right]$

$= 2 + \cos\theta$

(d) $r = 2 - \sin\left(\theta - \dfrac{3\pi}{2}\right)$

$= 2 - \left[\sin\theta\cos\dfrac{3\pi}{2} - \cos\theta\sin\dfrac{3\pi}{2}\right]$

$= 2 - \cos\theta$

65. (a) $r = 1 - \sin\theta$

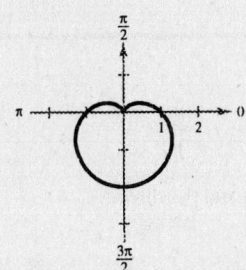

(b) $r = 1 - \sin\left(\theta - \dfrac{\pi}{4}\right)$

Rotate the graph in part (a) through the angle $\dfrac{\pi}{4}$.

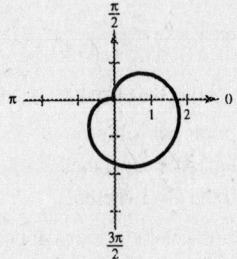

67. $r = 2 + k\sin\theta$

   $k = 0$: $r = 2$

       Circle

   $k = 1$: $r = 2 + \sin\theta$

       Convex limaçon

   $k = 2$: $r = 2 + 2\sin\theta$

       Cardioid

   $k = 3$: $r = 2 + 3\sin\theta$

       Limaçon with inner loop

69. $e^x = 19$

   $x = \ln 19 \approx 2.944$

71. $10^x = 84$

   $x = \log_{10} 84 \approx 1.924$

73. $\ln x = 4$

   $x = e^4 \approx 54.598$

75. $\quad y = \dfrac{x^2 - 9}{x + 1}$

   $\dfrac{x^2 - 9}{x + 1} = 0$

   $x^2 - 9 = 0$

   $x^2 = 9$

   $x = \pm 3$

77. $\quad y = 5 - \dfrac{3}{x - 2}$

   $5 - \dfrac{3}{x - 2} = 0$

   $5 = \dfrac{3}{x - 2}$

   $5(x - 2) = 3$

   $5x - 10 = 3$

   $5x = 13$

   $x = \dfrac{13}{5}$

Section 10.9   Polar Equations of Conics

■ The graph of a polar equation of the form

$$r = \frac{ep}{1 \pm e \cos \theta} \text{ or } r = \frac{ep}{1 \pm e \sin \theta}$$

is a conic, where $e > 0$ is the eccentricity and $|p|$ is the distance between the focus (pole) and the directrix.

(a) If $e < 1$, the graph is an ellipse.
(b) If $e = 1$, the graph is a parabola.
(c) If $e > 1$, the graph is a hyperbola.

■ Guidelines for finding polar equations of conics:

(a) Horizontal directrix above the pole: $r = \dfrac{ep}{1 + e \sin \theta}$

(b) Horizontal directrix below the pole: $r = \dfrac{ep}{1 - e \sin \theta}$

(c) Vertical directrix to the right of the pole: $r = \dfrac{ep}{1 + e \cos \theta}$

(d) Vertical directrix to the left of the pole: $r = \dfrac{ep}{1 - e \cos \theta}$

Solutions to Odd-Numbered Exercises

1. $r = \dfrac{4e}{1 + e \cos \theta}$

(a) $e = 1, r = \dfrac{4}{1 + \cos \theta}$, parabola

(b) $e = 0.5, r = \dfrac{2}{1 + 0.5 \cos \theta} = \dfrac{4}{2 + \cos \theta}$, ellipse

(c) $e = 1.5, r = \dfrac{6}{1 + 1.5 \cos \theta} = \dfrac{12}{2 + 3 \cos \theta}$, hyperbola

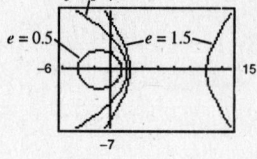

3. $r = \dfrac{4e}{1 - e \sin \theta}$

(a) $e = 1, r = \dfrac{4}{1 - \sin \theta}$, parabola

(b) $e = 0.5, r = \dfrac{2}{1 - 0.5 \sin \theta} = \dfrac{4}{2 - \sin \theta}$, ellipse

(c) $e = 1.5, r = \dfrac{6}{1 - 1.5 \sin \theta} = \dfrac{12}{2 - 3 \sin \theta}$, hyperbola

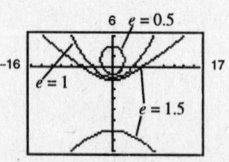

5. $r = \dfrac{2}{1 + \cos \theta}$

$e = 1 \Rightarrow$ Parabola

Vertical directrix to the right
of the pole
Matches graph (f).

7. $r = \dfrac{3}{1 + 2 \sin \theta}$

$e = 2 \Rightarrow$ Hyperbola

Matches graph (d).

9. $r = \dfrac{4}{2 + \cos \theta}$

$= \dfrac{2}{1 + 0.5 \cos \theta}$

$e = 0.5 \Rightarrow$ Ellipse

Matches graph (a).

11. $r = \dfrac{2}{1 - \cos \theta}$

$e = 1$, the graph is a parabola.

Vertex: $(1, \pi)$

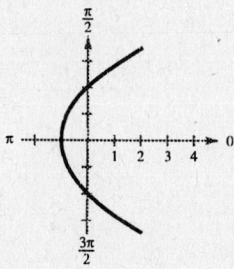

13. $r = \dfrac{5}{1 + \sin \theta}$

$e = 1$, the graph is a parabola.

Vertex: $\left(\dfrac{5}{2}, \dfrac{\pi}{2}\right)$

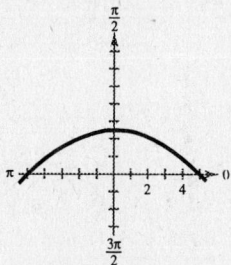

15. $r = \dfrac{2}{2 - \cos \theta} = \dfrac{1}{1 - \frac{1}{2} \cos \theta}$

$e = \dfrac{1}{2} < 1$, the graph is an ellipse.

Vertices: $(2, 0), \left(\dfrac{2}{3}, \pi\right)$

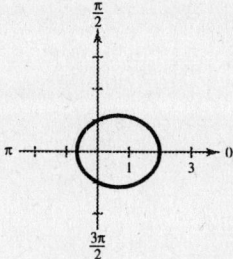

17. $r = \dfrac{6}{2 + \sin \theta} = \dfrac{3}{1 + \frac{1}{2} \sin \theta}$

$e = \dfrac{1}{2} < 1$, the graph is an ellipse.

Vertices: $\left(2, \dfrac{\pi}{2}\right), \left(6, \dfrac{3\pi}{2}\right)$

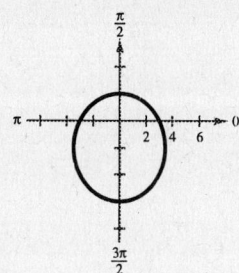

19. $r = \dfrac{3}{2 + 4 \sin \theta} = \dfrac{\frac{3}{2}}{1 + 2 \sin \theta}$

$e = 2 > 1$, the graph is a hyperbola.

Vertices: $\left(\dfrac{1}{2}, \dfrac{\pi}{2}\right), \left(-\dfrac{3}{2}, \dfrac{3\pi}{2}\right)$

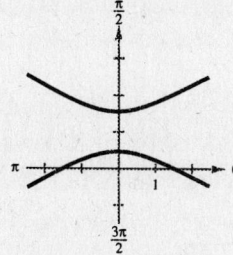

21. $r = \dfrac{3}{2 - 6 \cos \theta} = \dfrac{\frac{3}{2}}{1 - 3 \cos \theta}$

$e = 3 > 1$, the graph is a hyperbola.

Vertices: $\left(-\dfrac{3}{4}, 0\right), \left(\dfrac{3}{8}, \pi\right)$

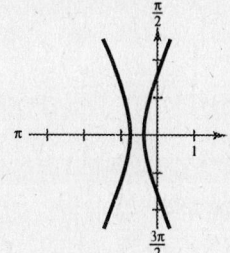

23. $r = \dfrac{4}{2 - \cos \theta} = \dfrac{2}{1 - \frac{1}{2} \cos \theta}$

$e = \dfrac{1}{2} < 1,$ the graph is an ellipse.

Vertices: $(4, 0), \left(\dfrac{4}{3}, \pi\right)$

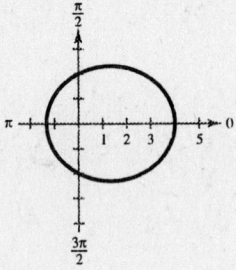

25. $r = \dfrac{-1}{1 - \sin \theta}$

$e = 1 \Rightarrow$ Parabola

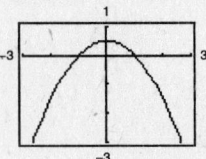

27. $r = \dfrac{3}{-4 + 2 \cos \theta}$

$e = \dfrac{1}{2} \Rightarrow$ Ellipse

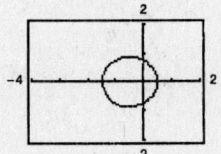

29. $r = \dfrac{2}{1 - \cos\left(\theta - \dfrac{\pi}{4}\right)}$

Rotate the graph in Exercise 11 through the angle $\dfrac{\pi}{4}$.

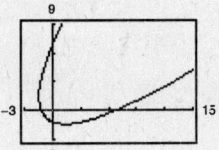

31. $r = \dfrac{6}{2 + \sin\left(\theta + \dfrac{\pi}{6}\right)}$

Rotate the graph in Exercise 17 through the angle $-\dfrac{\pi}{6}$.

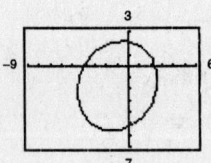

33. Parabola: $e = 1$

Directrix: $x = -1$

Vertical directrix to the left of the pole

$r = \dfrac{1(1)}{1 - 1 \cos \theta} = \dfrac{1}{1 - \cos \theta}$

35. Ellipse: $e = \dfrac{1}{2}$

Directrix: $y = 1$

$p = 1$

Horizontal directrix above the pole

$r = \dfrac{\frac{1}{2}(1)}{1 + \frac{1}{2} \sin \theta} = \dfrac{1}{2 + \sin \theta}$

37. Hyperbola: $e = 2$

Directrix: $x = 1$

$p = 1$

Vertical directrix to the right of the pole

$r = \dfrac{2(1)}{1 + 2 \cos \theta} = \dfrac{2}{1 + 2 \cos \theta}$

39. Parabola

Vertex: $\left(1, -\dfrac{\pi}{2}\right) \Rightarrow e = 1, p = 2$

Horizontal directrix below the pole

$r = \dfrac{1(2)}{1 - 1\sin\theta} = \dfrac{2}{1 - \sin\theta}$

41. Parabola

Vertex: $(5, \pi) \Rightarrow e = 1, p = 10$

Vertical directrix to the left of the pole

$r = \dfrac{1(10)}{1 - 1\cos\theta} = \dfrac{10}{1 - \cos\theta}$

43. Ellipse: Vertices $(2, 0), (10, \pi)$

Center: $(4, \pi)$; $c = 4, a = 6, e = \dfrac{2}{3}$

Vertical directrix to the right of the pole

$r = \dfrac{\frac{2}{3}p}{1 + \frac{2}{3}\cos\theta} = \dfrac{2p}{3 + 2\cos\theta}$

$2 = \dfrac{2p}{3 + 2\cos 0}$

$p = 5$

$r = \dfrac{2(5)}{3 + 2\cos\theta} = \dfrac{10}{3 + 2\cos\theta}$

45. Ellipse: Vertices $(20, 0), (4, \pi)$

Center: $(8, 0)$; $c = 8, a = 12, e = \dfrac{2}{3}$

Vertical directrix to the left of the pole

$r = \dfrac{\frac{2}{3}p}{1 - \frac{2}{3}\cos\theta} = \dfrac{2p}{3 - 2\cos\theta}$

$20 = \dfrac{2p}{3 - 2\cos 0}$

$p = 10$

$r = \dfrac{2(10)}{3 - 2\cos\theta} = \dfrac{20}{3 - 2\cos\theta}$

47. Hyperbola: Vertices $\left(1, \dfrac{3\pi}{2}\right), \left(9, \dfrac{3\pi}{2}\right)$

Center: $\left(5, \dfrac{3\pi}{2}\right)$; $c = 5, a = 4, e = \dfrac{5}{4}$

Horizontal directrix below the pole

$r = \dfrac{\frac{5}{4}p}{1 - \frac{5}{4}\sin\theta} = \dfrac{5p}{4 - 5\sin\theta}$

$1 = \dfrac{5p}{4 - 5\sin\dfrac{3\pi}{2}}$

$p = \dfrac{9}{5}$

$r = \dfrac{5\left(\frac{9}{5}\right)}{4 - 5\sin\theta} = \dfrac{9}{4 - 5\sin\theta}$

49. When $\theta = 0, r = c + a = ea + a = a(1 + e)$.

Therefore,

$$a(1 + e) = \dfrac{ep}{1 - e\cos 0}$$

$a(1 + e)(1 - e) = ep$

$a(1 - e^2) = ep.$

Thus, $r = \dfrac{ep}{1 - e\cos\theta} = \dfrac{(1 - e^2)a}{1 - e\cos\theta}$.

51. $r = \dfrac{[1 - (0.0167)^2](92.960 \times 10^6)}{1 - 0.0167\cos\theta}$

$\approx \dfrac{9.2934 \times 10^7}{1 - 0.0167\cos\theta}$

Perihelion distance:

$r = 92.960 \times 10^6(1 - 0.0167) \approx 9.1408 \times 10^7$

Aphelion distance:

$r = 92.960 \times 10^6(1 + 0.0167) \approx 9.4512 \times 10^7$

53. $r = \dfrac{[1 - (0.2481)^2](5.9 \times 10^9)}{1 - 0.2481\cos\theta}$

$\approx \dfrac{5.5368 \times 10^9}{1 - 0.2481\cos\theta}$

Perihelion distance:

$r = 5.9 \times 10^9(1 - 0.2481) \approx 4.4362 \times 10^9$

Aphelion distance:

$r = 5.9 \times 10^9(1 + 0.2481) \approx 7.3638 \times 10^9$

55. $r = \dfrac{[1 - (0.0934)^2](141 \times 10^6)}{1 - 0.0934 \cos \theta}$

$\approx \dfrac{1.3977 \times 10^8}{1 - 0.0934 \cos \theta}$

Perihelion distance:

$r = 141 \times 10^6(1 - 0.0934) \approx 1.2783 \times 10^8$

Aphelion distance:

$r = 141 \times 10^6(1 + 0.0934) \approx 1.5417 \times 10^8$

57. Vertex: $\left(4100, \dfrac{\pi}{2}\right)$

Focus: $(0, 0)$

$e = 1, p = 8200$

$r = \dfrac{ep}{1 + e \sin \theta} = \dfrac{8200}{1 + \sin \theta}$

When $\theta = 30°, r = 8200/1.5 \approx 5466.67$.
Distance between the surface of the earth
and the satellite is $r - 4000 \approx 1467$ miles.

59. False. If e remains fixed, and p changes, then the lengths of the major axis and minor axis change.

For example, graph $r = \dfrac{5}{1 - \frac{2}{3} \cos \theta}$, with $e = \dfrac{2}{3}$

and $p = \dfrac{15}{2}$ and $r = \dfrac{6}{1 - \frac{2}{3} \cos \theta}$, with $e = \dfrac{2}{3}$

and $p = 9$, on the same set of coordinate axes.

61.

$$\frac{x^2}{a^2} + \frac{y^2}{b^2} = 1$$

$$\frac{r^2 \cos^2 \theta}{a^2} + \frac{r^2 \sin^2 \theta}{b^2} = 1$$

$$\frac{r^2 \cos^2 \theta}{a^2} + \frac{r^2(1 - \cos^2 \theta)}{b^2} = 1$$

$$r^2 b^2 \cos^2 \theta + r^2 a^2 - r^2 a^2 \cos^2 \theta = a^2 b^2$$

$$r^2(b^2 - a^2)\cos^2 \theta + r^2 a^2 = a^2 b^2$$

Since $b^2 - a^2 = -c^2$, we have

$$-r^2 c^2 \cos^2 \theta + r^2 a^2 = a^2 b^2$$

$$-r^2\left(\frac{c}{a}\right)^2 \cos^2 \theta + r^2 = b^2, e = \frac{c}{a}$$

$$-r^2 e^2 \cos^2 \theta + r^2 = b^2$$

$$r^2(1 - e^2 \cos^2 \theta) = b^2$$

$$r^2 = \frac{b^2}{1 - e^2 \cos^2 \theta}$$

63. $\dfrac{x^2}{169} + \dfrac{y^2}{144} = 1$

$a = 13, b = 12, c = 5, e = \dfrac{5}{13}$

$r^2 = \dfrac{144}{1 - \left(\frac{25}{169}\right) \cos^2 \theta} = \dfrac{24{,}336}{169 - 25 \cos^2 \theta}$

65. $\dfrac{x^2}{9} - \dfrac{y^2}{16} = 1$

$a = 3, b = 4, c = 5, e = \dfrac{5}{3}$

$r^2 = \dfrac{-16}{1 - \left(\frac{25}{9}\right) \cos^2 \theta} = \dfrac{144}{25 \cos^2 \theta - 9}$

67. One focus: $\left(5, \dfrac{\pi}{2}\right)$

Vertices: $\left(4, \dfrac{\pi}{2}\right), \left(4, -\dfrac{\pi}{2}\right)$

$a = 4, c = 5 \Rightarrow b = 3$ and $e = \dfrac{5}{4}$

$$\frac{y^2}{16} - \frac{x^2}{9} = 1$$

$$\frac{r^2 \sin^2 \theta}{16} - \frac{r^2 \cos^2 \theta}{9} = 1$$

$$9r^2 \sin^2 \theta - 16r^2(1 - \sin^2 \theta) = 144$$

$$25r^2 \sin^2 \theta - 16r^2 = 144$$

$$r^2 = \frac{144}{25 \sin^2 \theta - 16}$$

69. $4\sqrt{3} \tan \theta - 3 = 1$

$4\sqrt{3} \tan \theta = 4$

$\tan \theta = \dfrac{1}{\sqrt{3}}$

$\theta = \dfrac{\pi}{6} + n\pi$

71. $12 \sin^2 \theta = 9$

$\sin^2 \theta = \dfrac{3}{4}$

$\sin \theta = \pm\dfrac{\sqrt{3}}{2}$

$\theta = \dfrac{\pi}{3} + 2n\pi, \dfrac{2\pi}{3} + 2n\pi, \dfrac{4\pi}{3} + 2n\pi, \dfrac{5\pi}{3} + 2n\pi$

73. $2 \cot x = 5 \cos \dfrac{\pi}{2}$

$2 \cot x = 0$

$\cot x = 0$

$x = \dfrac{\pi}{2} + n\pi$

For 75 and 77 use the following:

u and v are in Quadrant IV

$\sin u = -\dfrac{3}{5} \Rightarrow \cos u = \dfrac{4}{5}$

$\cos v = \dfrac{1}{\sqrt{2}} \Rightarrow \sin v = -\dfrac{1}{\sqrt{2}}$

75. $\cos(u + v) = \cos u \cos v - \sin u \sin v$

$= \left(\dfrac{4}{5}\right)\left(\dfrac{1}{\sqrt{2}}\right) - \left(-\dfrac{3}{5}\right)\left(-\dfrac{1}{\sqrt{2}}\right)$

$= \dfrac{4}{5\sqrt{2}} - \dfrac{3}{5\sqrt{2}}$

$= \dfrac{1}{5\sqrt{2}}$

$= \dfrac{\sqrt{2}}{10}$

77. $\cos(u - v) = \cos u \cos v + \sin u \sin v$

$= \left(\dfrac{4}{5}\right)\left(\dfrac{1}{\sqrt{2}}\right) + \left(-\dfrac{3}{5}\right)\left(-\dfrac{1}{\sqrt{2}}\right)$

$= \dfrac{4}{5\sqrt{2}} + \dfrac{3}{5\sqrt{2}}$

$= \dfrac{7}{5\sqrt{2}}$

$= \dfrac{7\sqrt{2}}{10}$

79. $\sin u = \dfrac{4}{5}, \dfrac{\pi}{2} < u < \pi \Rightarrow \cos u = -\dfrac{3}{5}$

$\sin 2u = 2 \sin u \cos u$

$= 2\left(\dfrac{4}{5}\right)\left(-\dfrac{3}{5}\right)$

$= -\dfrac{24}{25}$

$\cos 2u = \cos^2 u - \sin^2 u$

$= \left(-\dfrac{3}{5}\right)^2 - \left(\dfrac{4}{5}\right)^2$

$= \dfrac{9}{25} - \dfrac{16}{25}$

$= -\dfrac{7}{25}$

$\tan 2u = \dfrac{\sin 2u}{\cos 2u}$

$= \dfrac{-\frac{24}{25}}{-\frac{7}{25}}$

$= \dfrac{24}{7}$

Review Exercises for Chapter 10

Solutions to Odd-Numbered Exercises

1. Slope $m = \frac{3}{5}$

$\tan \theta = \frac{3}{5} \Rightarrow \theta = \arctan \frac{3}{5} \approx 30.96°$

3. $y = 2x + 4 \Rightarrow m = 2$

$\tan \theta = 2 \Rightarrow \theta = \arctan 2 \approx 63.43°$

5. $4x + y = 2 \Rightarrow y = -4x + 2 \Rightarrow m_1 = -4$

$-5x + y = -1 \Rightarrow y = 5x - 1 \Rightarrow m_2 = 5$

$\tan \theta = \left| \dfrac{5 - (-4)}{1 + (-4)(5)} \right| = \dfrac{9}{19}$

$\theta = \arctan \dfrac{9}{19} \approx 25.35°$

7. $2x - 7y = 8 \Rightarrow y = \dfrac{2}{7}x - \dfrac{8}{7} \Rightarrow m_1 = \dfrac{2}{7}$

$0.4x + y = 0 \Rightarrow y = -0.4x \Rightarrow m_2 = -0.4$

$\tan \theta = \left| \dfrac{-0.4 - \frac{2}{7}}{1 + \left(\frac{2}{7}\right)(-0.4)} \right| = \dfrac{24}{31}$

$\theta = \arctan \left(\dfrac{24}{31} \right) \approx 37.75°$

9. $(1, 2) \Rightarrow x_1 = 1, y_1 = 2$

$x - y - 3 = 0 \Rightarrow A = 1, B = -1, C = -3$

$d = \dfrac{|1(1) + (-1)(2) + (-3)|}{\sqrt{1^2 + (-1)^2}} = \dfrac{4}{\sqrt{2}} = 2\sqrt{2}$

11. Hyperbola

13. Vertex: $(4, 2) = (h, k)$

Focus: $(4, 0) \Rightarrow p = -2$

$(x - h)^2 = 4p(y - k)$

$(x - 4)^2 = -8(y - 2)$

15. Vertex: $(0, 2) = (h, k)$

Directrix: $x = -3 \Rightarrow p = 3$

$(y - k)^2 = 4p(x - h)$

$(y - 2)^2 = 12x$

17. $x^2 = -2y \Rightarrow p = -\dfrac{1}{2}$

Focus: $\left(0, -\dfrac{1}{2}\right)$

$d_1 = b + \dfrac{1}{2}$

$d_2 = \sqrt{(2 - 0)^2 + \left(-2 + \dfrac{1}{2}\right)^2}$

$\quad = \sqrt{4 + \dfrac{9}{4}} = \dfrac{5}{2}$

$d_1 = d_2$

$b + \dfrac{1}{2} = \dfrac{5}{2}$

$b = 2$

The slope of the line is $m = \dfrac{-2 - 2}{2 - 0} = -2$

Tangent line: $y = -2x + 2$

x-intercept: $(1, 0)$

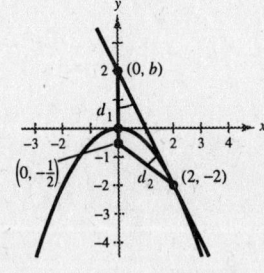

19. Parabola

Opens downward

Vertex: $(0, 12)$

$(x - h)^2 = 4p(y - k)$

$x^2 = 4p(y - 12)$

Solution points: $(\pm 4, 10)$

$16 = 4p(10 - 12)$

$16 = -8p$

$-2 = p$

$x^2 = -8(y - 12)$

To find the x-intercepts, let $y = 0$.

$x^2 = 96$

$x = \pm\sqrt{96} = \pm 4\sqrt{6}$

At the base z, the archway is $2(4\sqrt{6}) = 8\sqrt{6}$ meters wide.

21. Vertices: $(-3, 0), (7, 0) \Rightarrow a = 5$

$(h, k) = (2, 0)$

Foci: $(0, 0), (4, 0) \Rightarrow c = 2$

$b^2 = a^2 - c^2 = 25 - 4 = 21$

$\dfrac{(x - h)^2}{a^2} + \dfrac{(y - k)^2}{b^2} = 1$

$\dfrac{(x - 2)^2}{25} + \dfrac{y^2}{21} = 1$

23. Vertices: $(0, \pm 6) \Rightarrow a = 6, (h, k) = (0, 0)$

Passes through $(2, 2)$

$\dfrac{(x - h)^2}{b^2} + \dfrac{(y - k)^2}{a^2} = 1$

$\dfrac{x^2}{b^2} + \dfrac{y^2}{36} = 1 \Rightarrow b^2 = \dfrac{36x^2}{36 - y^2} = \dfrac{36(4)}{36 - 4} = \dfrac{9}{2}$

$\dfrac{x^2}{9/2} + \dfrac{y^2}{36} = 1$

$\dfrac{2x^2}{9} + \dfrac{y^2}{36} = 1$

25. $2a = 10 \Rightarrow a = 5$

$b = 4$

$c^2 = a^2 - b^2 = 25 - 16 = 9 \Rightarrow c = 3$

The foci occur 3 feet from the center of the arch on a line connecting the tops of the pillars.

27. $16x^2 + 9y^2 - 32x + 72y + 16 = 0$

$16(x^2 - 2x + 1) + 9(y^2 + 8y + 16) = -16 + 16 + 144$

$16(x - 1)^2 + 9(y + 4)^2 = 144$

$\dfrac{(x - 1)^2}{9} + \dfrac{(y + 4)^2}{16} = 1$

$a = 4, b = 3, c = \sqrt{7}$

Center: $(1, -4)$

Vertices: $(1, 0)$ and $(1, -8)$

Foci: $\left(1, -4 \pm \sqrt{7}\right)$

Eccentricity: $e = \dfrac{\sqrt{7}}{4}$

29. $\dfrac{(x+2)^2}{81} + \dfrac{(y-1)^2}{100} = 1$

$a = 10, b = 9, c = \sqrt{19}$

Center: $(-2, 1)$

Vertices: $(-2, 11)$ and $(-2, -9)$

Foci: $\left(-2, 1 \pm \sqrt{19}\right)$

Eccentricity: $e = \dfrac{\sqrt{19}}{10}$

31. Vertices: $(0, \pm 1) \Rightarrow a = 1, (h, k) = (0, 0)$

Foci: $(0, \pm 3) \Rightarrow c = 3$

$b^2 = c^2 - a^2 = 9 - 1 = 8$

$\dfrac{(y-k)^2}{a^2} - \dfrac{(x-h)^2}{b^2} = 1$

$y^2 - \dfrac{x^2}{8} = 1$

33. Foci: $(0, 0), (8, 0) \Rightarrow c = 4, (h, k) = (4, 0)$

Asymptotes: $y = \pm 2(x - 4) \Rightarrow \dfrac{b}{a} = 2, b = 2a$

$b^2 = c^2 - a^2 \Rightarrow 4a^2 = 16 - a^2 \Rightarrow a^2 = \dfrac{16}{5}$,

$b^2 = \dfrac{64}{5}$

$\dfrac{(x-h)^2}{a^2} - \dfrac{(y-k)^2}{b^2} = 1$

$\dfrac{(x-4)^2}{\frac{16}{5}} - \dfrac{y^2}{\frac{64}{5}} = 1$

$\dfrac{5(x-4)^2}{16} - \dfrac{5y^2}{64} = 1$

35. $9x^2 - 16y^2 - 18x - 32y - 151 = 0$

$9(x^2 - 2x + 1) - 16(y^2 + 2y + 1) = 151 + 9 - 16$

$9(x-1)^2 - 16(y+1)^2 = 144$

$\dfrac{(x-1)^2}{16} - \dfrac{(y+1)^2}{9} = 1$

$a = 4, b = 3, c = 5$

Center: $(1, -1)$

Vertices: $(5, -1)$ and $(-3, -1)$

Foci: $(6, -1)$ and $(-4, -1)$

Asymptotes: $y = -1 \pm \dfrac{3}{4}(x - 1)$

$y = \dfrac{3}{4}x - \dfrac{7}{4}$ or $y = -\dfrac{3}{4}x - \dfrac{1}{4}$

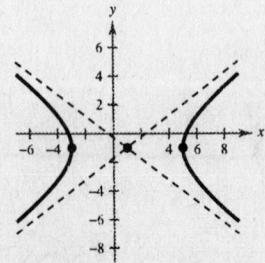

37. $\dfrac{(x-3)^2}{16} - \dfrac{(y+5)^2}{4} = 1$

$a = 4, b = 2, c = \sqrt{20} = 2\sqrt{5}$

Center: $(3, -5)$

Vertices: $(7, -5)$ and $(-1, -5)$

Foci: $\left(3 \pm 2\sqrt{5}, -5\right)$

Asymptotes: $y = -5 \pm \dfrac{1}{2}(x - 3)$

$y = \dfrac{1}{2}x - \dfrac{13}{2}$ or $y = -\dfrac{1}{2}x - \dfrac{7}{2}$

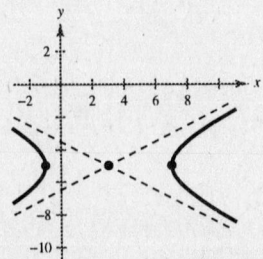

39. Foci: $(\pm 100, 0) \Rightarrow c = 100$

Center: $(0, 0)$

$$\frac{d_2}{186,000} - \frac{d_1}{186,000} = 0.0005 \Rightarrow d_2 - d_1 = 93 = 2a \Rightarrow a = 46.5$$

$$b^2 = c^2 - a^2 = 100^2 - 46.5^2 = 7837.75$$

$$\frac{x^2}{2162.25} - \frac{y^2}{7837.75} = 1$$

$$y^2 = 7837.75\left(\frac{60^2}{2162.25} - 1\right) \approx 5211.5736$$

$y \approx 72$ miles

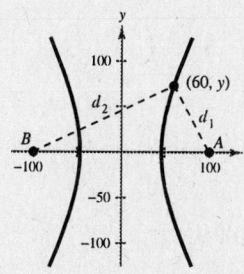

41. $5x^2 - 2y^2 + 10x - 4y + 17 = 0$

$AC = 5(-2) = -10 < 0$

The graph is a hyperbola.

43. $xy - 4 = 0$

$A = C = 0, B = 1$

$B^2 - 4AC = 1^2 - 4(0)(0) = 1 > 0$

The graph is a hyperbola.

$$\cot 2\theta = 0 \Rightarrow 2\theta = \frac{\pi}{2} \Rightarrow \theta = \frac{\pi}{4}$$

$$x = x'\cos\frac{\pi}{4} - y'\sin\frac{\pi}{4} = \frac{x' - y'}{\sqrt{2}}$$

$$y = x'\sin\frac{\pi}{4} + y'\cos\frac{\pi}{4} = \frac{x' + y'}{\sqrt{2}}$$

$$\left(\frac{x' - y'}{\sqrt{2}}\right)\left(\frac{x' + y'}{\sqrt{2}}\right) - 4 = 0$$

$$\frac{(x')^2 - (y')^2}{2} = 4$$

$$\frac{(x')^2}{8} - \frac{(y')^2}{8} = 1$$

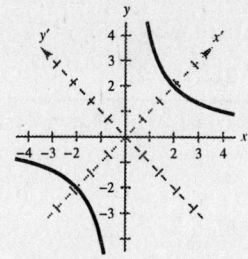

45. $5x^2 - 2xy + 5y^2 - 12 = 0$

$A = C = 5, B = -2$

$B^2 + 4AC = (-2)^2 - 4(5)(5) = -96 < 0$

The graph is an ellipse.

$$\cot 2\theta = 0 \Rightarrow 2\theta = \frac{\pi}{2} \Rightarrow \theta = \frac{\pi}{4}$$

$$x = x'\cos\frac{\pi}{4} - y'\sin\frac{\pi}{4} = \frac{x' - y'}{\sqrt{2}}$$

$$y = x'\sin\frac{\pi}{4} + y'\cos\frac{\pi}{4} = \frac{x' + y'}{\sqrt{2}}$$

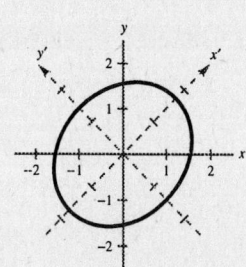

— CONTINUED —

45. **— CONTINUED —**

$$5\left(\frac{x'-y'}{\sqrt{2}}\right)^2 - 2\left(\frac{x'-y'}{\sqrt{2}}\right)\left(\frac{x'+y'}{\sqrt{2}}\right) + 5\left(\frac{x'+y'}{\sqrt{2}}\right)^2 - 12 = 0$$

$$\frac{5}{2}[(x')^2 - 2(x'y') + (y')^2] - [(x')^2 - (y')^2] + \frac{5}{2}[(x')^2 + 2(x'y') + (y')^2] = 12$$

$$4(x')^2 + 6(y')^2 = 12$$

$$\frac{(x')^2}{3} + \frac{(y')^2}{2} = 1$$

47. $16x^2 - 24xy + 9y^2 - 30x - 40y = 0$

$B^2 - 4AC = (-24)^2 - 4(16)(9) = 0$

The graph is a parabola.

To use a graphing utility, we need to solve for y in terms of x.

$9y^2 + (-24x - 40)y + (16x^2 - 30x) = 0$

$$y = \frac{-(-24x - 40) \pm \sqrt{(-24x - 40)^2 - 4(9)(16x^2 - 30x)}}{2(9)}$$

$$= \frac{(24x + 40) \pm \sqrt{(24x + 40)^2 - 36(16x^2 - 30x)}}{18}$$

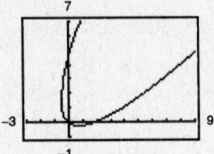

49. $x^2 + y^2 + 2xy + 2\sqrt{2}x - 2\sqrt{2}y + 2 = 0$

$B^2 - 4AC = 2^2 - 4(1)(1) = 0$

The graph is a parabola.

To use a graphing utility, we need to solve for y in terms of x.

$y^2 + \left(2x - 2\sqrt{2}\right)y + \left(x^2 + 2\sqrt{2}x + 2\right)$

$$y = \frac{-\left(2x - 2\sqrt{2}\right) \pm \sqrt{\left(2x - 2\sqrt{2}\right)^2 - 4\left(x^2 + 2\sqrt{2}x + 2\right)}}{2}$$

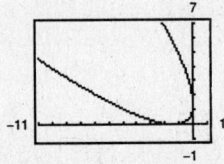

51. $x = 3\cos 0 = 3$

$y = 2\sin^2 0 = 0$

53. $x = 3\cos\frac{\pi}{6} = \frac{3\sqrt{3}}{2}$

$y = 2\sin^2\frac{\pi}{6} = \frac{1}{2}$

55. $x = 2t \Rightarrow \frac{x}{2} = t$

$y = 4t \Rightarrow y = 4\left(\frac{x}{2}\right) = 2x$

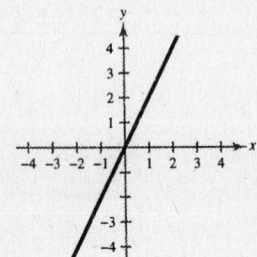

57. $x = t^2, \; x \geq 0$

$y = \sqrt{t} \Rightarrow y^2 = t$

$x = (y^2)^2 \Rightarrow x = y^4 \Rightarrow y = \sqrt[4]{x}$

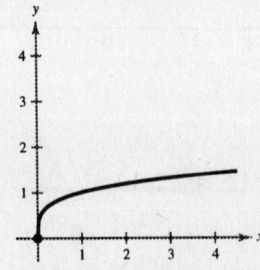

59. $x = 6 \cos \theta, y = 6 \sin \theta$

$\cos \theta = \dfrac{x}{6}, \sin \theta = \dfrac{y}{6}$

$\dfrac{x^2}{36} + \dfrac{y^2}{36} = 1$

$x^2 + y^2 = 36$

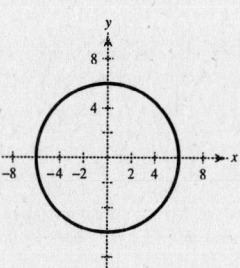

61. $(h, k) = (-3, 4)$

$2a = 8 \implies a = 4$

$2b = 6 \implies b = 3$

$\dfrac{(x + 3)^2}{16} + \dfrac{(y - 4)^2}{9} = 1$

$x = -3 + 4 \cos \theta$

$y = 4 + 3 \sin \theta$

This solution is not unique.

63. $x = \cos 3\theta + 5 \cos \theta$

$y = \sin 3\theta + 5 \sin \theta$

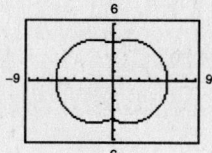

65. Polar coordinates: $\left(2, \dfrac{\pi}{4}\right)$

$x = 2 \cos \dfrac{\pi}{4} = \sqrt{2}$

$y = 2 \sin \dfrac{\pi}{4} = \sqrt{2}$

Rectangular coordinates: $\left(\sqrt{2}, \sqrt{2}\right)$

67. Polar coordinates: $(-7, 4.19)$

$x = -7 \cos 4.19 \approx 3.4927$

$y = -7 \sin 4.19 \approx 6.0664$

Rectangular coordinates: $(3.4927, 6.0664)$

69. Rectangular coordinates: $(0, 2)$

$r = \pm \sqrt{0^2 + 2^2} = \pm 2$

$\tan \theta$ is undefined $\implies \theta = \dfrac{\pi}{2}, \dfrac{3\pi}{2}$

Polar coordinates: $\left(2, \dfrac{\pi}{2}\right), \left(-2, \dfrac{3\pi}{2}\right), \left(2, \dfrac{5\pi}{2}\right)$

71. Rectangular coordinates: $(4, 6)$

$r = \pm \sqrt{4^2 + 6^2} = \pm \sqrt{52} \approx \pm 7.2111$

$\tan \theta = \dfrac{6}{4} \implies \theta \approx 0.9828, 4.1244$

Polar coordinates: $(7.2111, 0.9828), (-7.2111, 4.1244), (7.2111, 7.2660)$

73.
$\quad r = 3 \cos \theta$

$\quad\quad r^2 = 3r \cos \theta$

$\quad x^2 + y^2 = 3x$

75. $r = \dfrac{2}{1 + \sin \theta}$

$$r(1 + \sin \theta) = 2$$

$$r + r \sin \theta = 2$$

$$\pm \sqrt{x^2 + y^2} + y = 2$$

$$\pm \sqrt{x^2 + y^2} = 2 - y$$

$$x^2 + y^2 = (2 - y)^2$$

$$x^2 + y^2 = 4 - 4y + y^2$$

$$x^2 + 4y - 4 = 0$$

77. $(x^2 + y^2)^2 = ax^2 y$

$$(r^2)^2 = ar^2 \cos^2 \theta \, r \sin \theta$$

$$r = a \cos^2 \theta \sin \theta$$

79. $r = 4$

Circle of radius 4 centered at the pole

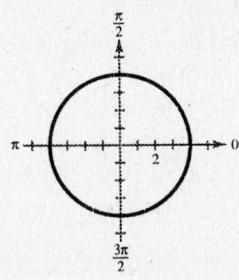

81. $r = 4 \sin 2\theta$

Symmetric with respect to $\theta = \pi/2$, the polar axis, and the pole.

Rose curve $(n = 2)$ with 4 petals

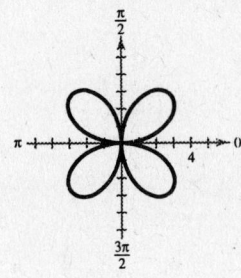

83. $r = -2(1 + \cos \theta)$

Symmetric with respect to the polar axis

$$\frac{a}{b} = \frac{2}{2} = 1 \implies \text{Cardioid}$$

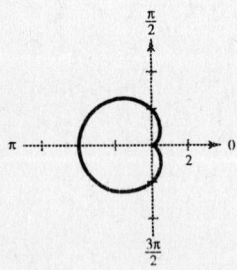

85. $r = 2 + 6 \sin \theta$

Limaçon with inner loop

$r = f(\sin \theta) \implies \theta = \dfrac{\pi}{2}$ symmetry

Maximum value: $|r| = 8$ when $\theta = \dfrac{\pi}{2}$

Zeros: $2 + 6 \sin \theta = 0 \implies \sin \theta = -\dfrac{1}{3} \implies \theta \approx 3.4814,\ 5.9433$

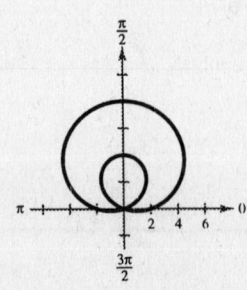

87. $r = -3 \cos 2\theta$

Rose curve with 4 petals

$r = f(\cos \theta) \Rightarrow$ polar axis symmetry

$\theta = \dfrac{\pi}{2}$: $r = -3 \cos 2(\pi - \theta) = -3 \cos(2\pi - 2\theta) = -3 \cos 2\theta$

Equivalent equation $\Rightarrow \theta = \dfrac{\pi}{2}$ symmetry

Pole: $r = -3 \cos 2(\pi + \theta) = -3 \cos(2\pi + 2\theta) = -3 \cos 2\theta$

Equivalent equation $\Rightarrow$ pole symmetry

Maximum value: $|r| = 3$ when $\theta = 0, \dfrac{\pi}{2}, \pi, \dfrac{3\pi}{2}$

Zeros: $-3 \cos 2\theta = 0$ when $\cos 2\theta = 0 \Rightarrow \theta = \dfrac{\pi}{4}, \dfrac{3\pi}{4}, \dfrac{5\pi}{4}, \dfrac{7\pi}{4}$

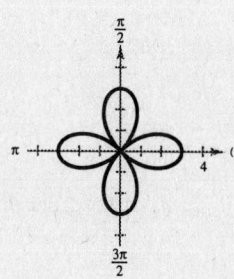

89. $r = 3(2 - \cos \theta)$

$\quad = 6 - 3 \cos \theta$

$\dfrac{a}{b} = \dfrac{6}{3} = 2$

The graph is a convex limaçon.

91. $r = 4 \cos 3\theta$

The graph is a rose curve with 3 petals.

93. $r = \dfrac{1}{1 + 2 \sin \theta}$, $e = 2$

Hyperbola symmetric with respect to $\theta = \dfrac{\pi}{2}$ and having

vertices at $\left(\dfrac{1}{3}, \dfrac{\pi}{2}\right)$ and $\left(-1, \dfrac{3\pi}{2}\right)$.

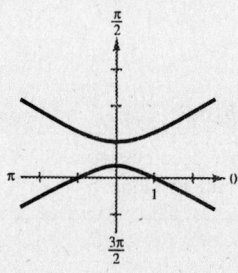

95. $r = \dfrac{4}{5 - 3 \cos \theta}$

$r = \dfrac{\frac{4}{5}}{1 - \left(\frac{3}{5}\right) \cos \theta}$, $e = \dfrac{3}{5}$

Ellipse symmetric with respect to the polar axis and

having vertices at $(2, 0)$ and $\left(\dfrac{1}{2}, \pi\right)$.

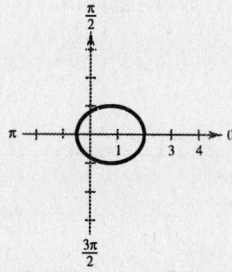

97. Parabola: $r = \dfrac{ep}{1 - e \cos \theta}$, $e = 1$

Vertex: $(2, \pi)$

Focus: $(0, 0) \Rightarrow p = 4$

$r = \dfrac{4}{1 - \cos \theta}$

99. Ellipse: $r = \dfrac{ep}{1 - e \cos \theta}$; Vertices: $(5, 0), (1, \pi) \Rightarrow a = 3$; One focus: $(0, 0) \Rightarrow c = 2$

$e = \dfrac{c}{a} = \dfrac{2}{3}, p = \dfrac{5}{2}$

$r = \dfrac{\left(\frac{2}{3}\right)\left(\frac{5}{2}\right)}{1 - \left(\frac{2}{3}\right) \cos \theta} = \dfrac{\frac{5}{3}}{1 - \left(\frac{2}{3}\right) \cos \theta} = \dfrac{5}{3 - 2 \cos \theta}$

101.
$$a + c = 122{,}000 + 4000 \Rightarrow a + c = 126{,}000$$
$$a - c = 119 + 4000 \quad \Rightarrow \underline{\quad a - c = \quad 4{,}119}$$
$$2a \quad\quad = 130{,}119$$
$$a \quad\quad = 65{,}029.5$$
$$c \quad\quad = 60{,}940.5$$

$e = \dfrac{c}{a} = \dfrac{60{,}940.5}{65{,}059.5} \approx 0.937$

$r = \dfrac{ep}{1 - e \cos \theta} \approx \dfrac{0.937p}{1 - 0.937 \cos \theta}$

$r = 126{,}000$ when $\theta = 0$

$126{,}000 = \dfrac{ep}{1 - e \cos 0}$

$ep = 126{,}000\left(1 - \dfrac{60{,}940.5}{65{,}059.5}\right) \approx 7977.2$

Thus, $r \approx \dfrac{7977.2}{1 - 0.937 \cos \theta}$

When $\theta = \dfrac{\pi}{3}, r \approx \dfrac{7977.2}{1 - 0.937 \cos \dfrac{\pi}{3}} \approx 15{,}008.8$ miles

The distance from the surface of Earth and the satellite is $15{,}008.8 - 4000 \approx 11{,}008.8$ miles.

103. False. When classifying equations of the form $Ax^2 + Bxy + Cy^2 + Dx + Ey + F = 0$, its graph can be determined by its discriminant. For a graph to be a parabola, its discriminant, $B^2 - 4AC$, must equal zero. So, if $B = 0$, then A **or** C equals 0.

105. False. The following are **two** sets of parametric equations for the line.

$x = t, y = 3 - 2t$

$x = 3t, y = 3 - 6t$

107. $2a = 10 \Rightarrow a = 5$

b must be less than 5; $0 < b < 5$

As b approaches 5, the ellipse becomes more circular and approaches a circle of radius 5.

109. $x = 4 \cos t$ and $y = 3 \sin t$

(a) $x = 4 \cos 2t$ and $y = 3 \sin 2t$

The speed would double.

(b) $x = 5 \cos t$ and $y = 3 \sin t$

The elliptical orbit would be flatter. The length of the major axis is greater.

111. (a) $x^2 + y^2 = 25$

$r = 5$

The graphs are the same.

They are both circles centered at $(0, 0)$ with a radius of 5.

(b) $x - y = 0 \Rightarrow y = x$

$\theta = \dfrac{\pi}{4}$

The graphs are the same.

They are both lines with slope 1 and intercept $(0, 0)$.

Chapter 10   Practice Test

1. Find the angle, θ, between the lines $3x + 4y = 12$ and $4x - 3y = 12$.

2. Find the distance between the point $(5, -9)$ and the line $3x - 7y = 21$.

3. Find the vertex, focus and directrix of the parabola $x^2 - 6x - 4y + 1 = 0$.

4. Find an equation of the parabola with its vertex at $(2, -5)$ and focus at $(2, -6)$.

5. Find the center, foci, vertices, and eccentricity of the ellipse $x^2 + 4y^2 - 2x + 32y + 61 = 0$.

6. Find an equation of the ellipse with vertices $(0, \pm 6)$ and eccentricity $e = \frac{1}{2}$.

7. Find the center, vertices, foci, and asymptotes of the hyperbola $16y^2 - x^2 - 6x - 128y + 231 = 0$.

8. Find an equation of the hyperbola with vertices at $(\pm 3, 2)$ and foci at $(\pm 5, 2)$.

9. Rotate the axes to eliminate the xy-term. Sketch the graph of the resulting equation, showing both sets of axes.

   $5x^2 + 2xy + 5y^2 - 10 = 0$

10. Use the discriminant to determine whether the graph of the equation is a parabola, ellipse, or hyperbola.

    (a) $6x^2 - 2xy + y^2 = 0$ (b) $x^2 + 4xy + 4y^2 - x - y + 17 = 0$

11. Convert the polar point $\left(\sqrt{2}, \dfrac{3\pi}{4} \right)$ to rectangular coordinates.

12. Convert the rectangular point $\left(\sqrt{3}, -1 \right)$ to polar coordinates.

13. Convert the rectangular equation $4x - 3y = 12$ to polar form.

14. Convert the polar equation $r = 5 \cos \theta$ to rectangular form.

15. Sketch the graph of $r = 1 - \cos \theta$.

16. Sketch the graph of $r = 5 \sin 2\theta$.

17. Sketch the graph of $r = \dfrac{3}{6 - \cos \theta}$.

18. Find a polar equation of the parabola with its vertex at $\left(6, \dfrac{\pi}{2} \right)$ and focus at $(0, 0)$.

For Exercises 19 and 20, eliminate the parameter and write the corresponding rectangular equation.

19. $x = 3 - 2 \sin \theta, y = 1 + 5 \cos \theta$ 20. $x = e^{2t}, y = e^{4t}$

Chapter P   Practice Test Solutions

1. $\dfrac{|-42| - 20}{15 - |-4|} = \dfrac{42 - 20}{15 - 4} = \dfrac{22}{11} = 2$

2. $\dfrac{x}{z} - \dfrac{z}{y} = \dfrac{x}{z} \cdot \dfrac{y}{y} - \dfrac{z}{y} \cdot \dfrac{z}{z} = \dfrac{xy - z^2}{yz}$

3. $|x - 7| \le 4$

4. $10(-5)^3 = 10(-125) = -1250$

5. $(-4x^3)(-2x^{-5})\left(\dfrac{1}{16}x\right) = (-4)(-2)\left(\dfrac{1}{16}\right)x^{3+(-5)+1} = \dfrac{8}{16}x^{-1} = \dfrac{1}{2x}$

6. $0.0000412 = 4.12 \times 10^{-5}$

7. $125^{2/3} = \left(\sqrt[3]{125}\right)^2 = (5)^2 = 25$

8. $\sqrt[4]{64x^7y^9} = \sqrt[4]{16 \cdot 4x^4x^3y^8y} = 2xy^2\sqrt[4]{4x^3y}$

9. $\dfrac{6}{\sqrt{12}} = \dfrac{6}{2\sqrt{3}} \cdot \dfrac{\sqrt{3}}{\sqrt{3}} = \dfrac{6\sqrt{3}}{6} = \sqrt{3}$

10. $3\sqrt{80} - 7\sqrt{500} = 3\left(4\sqrt{5}\right) - 7\left(10\sqrt{5}\right) = 12\sqrt{5} - 70\sqrt{5} = -58\sqrt{5}$

11. $(8x^4 - 9x^2 + 2x - 1) - (3x^3 + 5x + 4) = 8x^4 - 3x^3 - 9x^2 - 3x - 5$

12. $(x - 3)(x^2 + x - 7) = x^3 + x^2 - 7x - 3x^2 - 3x + 21 = x^3 - 2x^2 - 10x + 21$

13. $[(x - 2) - y]^2 = (x - 2)^2 - 2y(x - 2) + y^2$
$$= x^2 - 4x + 4 - 2xy + 4y + y^2 = x^2 + y^2 - 2xy - 4x + 4y + 4$$

14. $16x^4 - 1 = (4x^2 + 1)(4x^2 - 1) = (4x^2 + 1)(2x + 1)(2x - 1)$

15. $6x^2 + 5x - 4 = (2x - 1)(3x + 4)$

16. $x^3 - 64 = x^3 - 4^3 = (x - 4)(x^2 + 4x + 16)$

17. $-\dfrac{3}{x} + \dfrac{x}{x^2 + 2} = \dfrac{-3(x^2 + 2) + x^2}{x(x^2 + 2)} = \dfrac{-2x^2 - 6}{x(x^2 + 2)} = \dfrac{-2(x^2 + 3)}{x(x^2 + 2)}$

18. $\dfrac{x - 3}{4x} \div \dfrac{x^2 - 9}{x^2} = \dfrac{x - 3}{4x} \cdot \dfrac{x^2}{(x + 3)(x - 3)} = \dfrac{x}{4(x + 3)}$

19. $\dfrac{1 - \dfrac{1}{x}}{1 - \dfrac{1}{1 - (1/x)}} = \dfrac{\dfrac{x - 1}{x}}{1 - \dfrac{1}{(x - 1)/x}} = \dfrac{\dfrac{x - 1}{x}}{1 - \dfrac{x}{x - 1}} = \dfrac{\dfrac{x - 1}{x}}{\dfrac{-1}{x - 1}} = \dfrac{x - 1}{x} \cdot \dfrac{x - 1}{-1} = \dfrac{-(x - 1)^2}{x}$

20. (a)

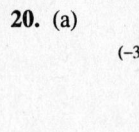

(b) $d = \sqrt{[5 - (-3)]^2 + (-1 - 7)^2}$

$= \sqrt{(8)^2 + (-8)^2}$

$= \sqrt{64 + 64}$

$= \sqrt{128}$

$= 8\sqrt{2}$

(c) $\left(\dfrac{-3 + 5}{2}, \dfrac{7 + (-1)}{2}\right)$

$= (1, 3)$

21. (a) $x^2 - 2x - 35 = 0$

$(x - 7)(x + 5) = 0$

$x - 7 = 0$ or $x + 5 = 0$

$x = 7$ or $\quad x = -5$

(b) $x^2 - 2x - 35 = 0$

$x^2 - 2x = 35$

$x^2 - 2x + 1 = 35 + 1$

$(x - 1)^2 = 36$

$x - 1 = \pm\sqrt{36}$

$x = 1 \pm 6$

$x = 7$ or $x = -5$

(c) $x^2 - 2x - 35 = 0$

$x = \dfrac{-(-2) \pm \sqrt{(-2)^2 - 4(1)(-35)}}{2(1)}$

$= \dfrac{2 \pm \sqrt{4 + 140}}{2}$

$= \dfrac{2 \pm 12}{2}$

$= 1 \pm 6$

Thus, $x = 7$ or $x = -5$.

22.

$x^5 - 5x^3 + 4x = 0$

$x(x^4 - 5x^2 + 4) = 0$

$x(x^2 - 1)(x^2 - 4) = 0$

$x(x + 1)(x - 1)(x + 2)(x - 2) = 0$

$x = 0, x = \pm 1, x = \pm 2$

23. $x = 2\sqrt{x + 3}$

$x^2 = 4(x + 3)$

$x^2 = 4x + 12$

$x^2 - 4x - 12 = 0$

$(x - 6)(x + 2) = 0$

$x - 6 = 0 \Rightarrow x = 6$

$x + 2 = 0 \Rightarrow x = -2, \quad$ extraneous

24. $\quad x^2 - 16 \le 0$

$(x + 4)(x - 4) \le 0$

Critical numbers: $x = \pm 4$

Test intervals: $(-\infty, -4), (-4, 4), (4, \infty)$

Test: Is $(x + 4)(x - 4) \le 0$?

Solution set: $[-4, 4]$

25. $\left|\dfrac{4 - x}{3}\right| > 2$

$\dfrac{4 - x}{3} < -2 \quad$ or $\quad \dfrac{4 - x}{3} > 2$

$4 - x < -6 \qquad\qquad 4 - x > 6$

$-x < -10 \qquad\qquad -x > 2$

$x > 10 \qquad\qquad\quad x < -2$

Chapter 1   Practice Test Solutions

1. $y = \sqrt{7 - x}$

x	7	6	3	-2
y	0	1	2	3

2. $y = \sqrt{25 - x^2}$

Domain: $25 - x^2 \geq 0$

$(5 - x)(5 + x) \geq 0$

Critical numbers: $x = \pm 5$

Test intervals: $(-\infty, -5), (-5, 5), (5, \infty)$

Solution set: $[-5, 5]$

3. $[x - (-3)]^2 + (y - 5)^2 = 6^2$

$(x + 3)^2 + (y - 5)^2 = 36$

4. $\quad m = \dfrac{-1 - 4}{3 - 2} = -5$

$y - 4 = -5(x - 2)$

$y - 4 = -5x + 10$

$y = -5x + 14$

5. $y = \dfrac{4}{3}x - 3$

6. $2x + 3y = 0$

$y = -\dfrac{2}{3}x$

$m_1 = -\dfrac{2}{3}$

$\perp m_2 = \dfrac{3}{2}$ through $(4, 1)$

$y - 1 = \dfrac{3}{2}(x - 4)$

$y - 1 = \dfrac{3}{2}x - 6$

$y = \dfrac{3}{2}x - 5$

7. $(5, 32)$ and $(9, 44)$

$m = \dfrac{44 - 32}{9 - 5} = \dfrac{12}{4} = 3$

$y - 32 = 3(x - 5)$

$y - 32 = 3x - 15$

$y = 3x + 17$

When $x = 20$, $y = 3(20) + 17$

$y = \$77.$

8. $f(x - 3) = (x - 3)^2 - 2(x - 3) + 1$

$= x^2 - 6x + 9 - 2x + 6 + 1$

$= x^2 - 8x + 16$

9. $\quad f(3) = 12 - 11 = 1$

$\dfrac{f(x) - f(3)}{x - 3} = \dfrac{(4x - 11) - 1}{x - 3}$

$= \dfrac{4x - 12}{x - 3}$

$= \dfrac{4(x - 3)}{x - 3} = 4, x \neq 3$

10. $f(x) = \sqrt{36 - x^2} = \sqrt{(6 + x)(6 - x)}$

Domain: $[-6, 6]$

Range: $[0, 6]$, because

$0 \le (6 + x)(6 - x) \le 36$ on this interval

11. (a) $6x - 5y + 4 = 0$

$$y = \frac{6x + 4}{5} \text{ is a function of } x.$$

(b) $x^2 + y^2 = 9$

$$y = \pm\sqrt{9 - x^2} \text{ is not a function of } x.$$

(c) $y^3 = x^2 + 6$

$$y = \sqrt[3]{x^2 + 6} \text{ is a function of } x.$$

12. Parabola

Vertex: $(0, -5)$

Intercepts: $(0, -5)$, $\left(\pm\sqrt{5}, 0\right)$

y-axis symmetry

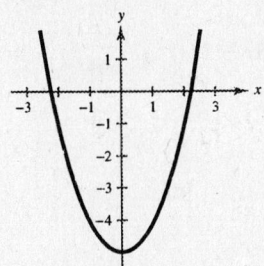

13. Intercepts: $(0, 3)$, $(-3, 0)$

x	0	1	-1	2	-2	-3	-4
y	3	4	2	5	1	0	1

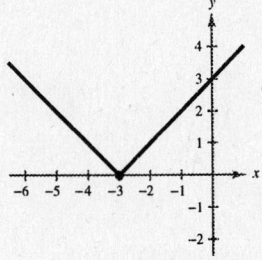

14.

x	0	1	2	3	-1	-2	-3
y	1	3	5	7	2	6	12

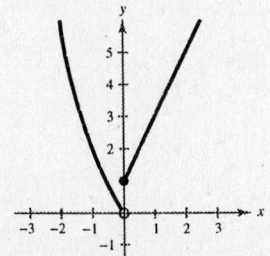

15. (a) $f(x + 2)$

Horizontal shift two units to the left

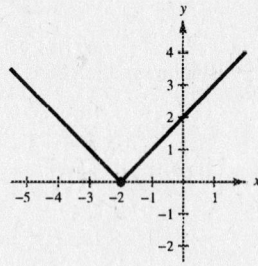

(b) $-f(x) + 2$

Reflection in the x-axis and a vertical shift two units upward

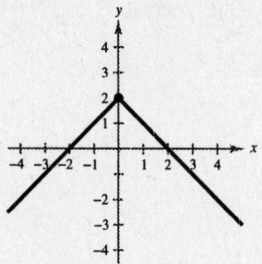

16. (a) $(g - f)(x) = g(x) - f(x)$

$$= (2x^2 - 5) - (3x + 7)$$

$$= 2x^2 - 3x - 12$$

(b) $(fg)(x) = f(x)g(x)$

$$= (3x + 7)(2x^2 - 5)$$

$$= 6x^3 + 14x^2 - 15x - 35$$

17. $f(g(x)) = f(2x + 3)$

$$= (2x + 3)^2 - 2(2x + 3) + 16$$

$$= 4x^2 + 12x + 9 - 4x - 6 + 16$$

$$= 4x^2 + 8x + 19$$

18. $f(x) = x^3 + 7$

$$y = x^3 + 7$$

$$x = y^3 + 7$$

$$x - 7 = y^3$$

$$\sqrt[3]{x - 7} = y$$

$$f^{-1}(x) = \sqrt[3]{x - 7}$$

19. (a) $f(x) = |x - 6|$ does not have an inverse.
Its graph does not pass the horizontal line test.

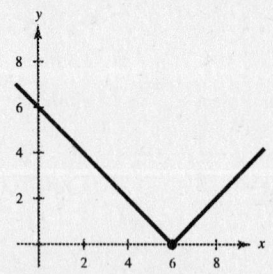

(b) $f(x) = ax + b, a \neq 0$ does have an inverse.

$$y = ax + b$$

$$x = ay + b$$

$$\frac{x - b}{a} = y$$

$$f^{-1}(x) = \frac{x - b}{a}$$

(c) $f(x) = x^3 - 19$ does have an inverse.

$$y = x^3 - 19$$

$$x = y^3 - 19$$

$$x + 19 = y^3$$

$$\sqrt[3]{x + 19} = y$$

$$f^{-1}(x) = \sqrt[3]{x + 19}$$

20.

$$f(x) = \sqrt{\frac{3-x}{x}}, \quad 0 < x \le 3, y \ge 0$$

$$y = \sqrt{\frac{3-x}{x}}$$

$$x = \sqrt{\frac{3-y}{y}}$$

$$x^2 = \frac{3-y}{y}$$

$$x^2 y = 3 - y$$

$$x^2 y + y = 3$$

$$y(x^2 + 1) = 3$$

$$y = \frac{3}{x^2 + 1}$$

$$f^{-1}(x) = \frac{3}{x^2 + 1}, \quad x \ge 0$$

21. False. The slopes of 3 and $\frac{1}{3}$ are not **negative** reciprocals.

22. True. Let $y = (f \circ g)(x)$.   Then $x = (f \circ g)^{-1}(y)$.

Also,

$$(f \circ g)(x) = y$$

$$f(g(x)) = y$$

$$g(x) = f^{-1}(y)$$

$$x = g^{-1}(f^{-1}(y))$$

$$x = (g^{-1} \circ f^{-1})(y)$$

Since $x = x$, we have $(f \circ g)^{-1}(y) = (g^{-1} \circ f^{-1})(y)$.

23. True. It must pass the vertical line test to be a function and it must pass the horizontal line test to have an inverse.

24.

$$z = \frac{cx^3}{\sqrt{y}}$$

$$-1 = \frac{c(-1)^3}{\sqrt{25}}$$

$$-1 = \frac{-c}{5}$$

$$5 = c$$

$$z = \frac{5x^3}{\sqrt{y}}$$

25. $y \approx 0.669x + 2.669$

Chapter 2   Practice Test Solutions

1. x-intercepts: $(1, 0)$, $(5, 0)$

   y-intercepts: $(0, 5)$

   Vertex: $(3, -4)$

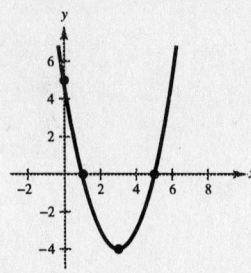

2. $a = 0.01, b = -90$

   $$\frac{-b}{2a} = \frac{90}{2(.01)} = 4500 \text{ units}$$

3. Vertex $(1, 7)$ opening downward through $(2, 5)$

   $y = a(x - 1)^2 + 7$ Standard form

   $5 = a(2 - 1)^2 + 7$

   $5 = a + 7$

   $a = -2$

   $y = -2(x - 1)^2 + 7$

   $\quad = -2(x^2 - 2x + 1) + 7$

   $\quad = -2x^2 + 4x + 5$

4. $y = \pm a(x - 2)(3x - 4)$ where a is any real number

   $y = \pm(3x^2 - 10x + 8)$

5. Leading coefficient: -3

   Degree: 5

   Moves down to the right and up to the left

6. $0 = x^5 - 5x^3 + 4x$

   $\quad = x(x^4 - 5x^2 + 4)$

   $\quad = x(x^2 - 1)(x^2 - 4)$

   $\quad = x(x + 1)(x - 1)(x + 2)(x - 2)$

   $x = 0, x = \pm 1, x = \pm 2$

7. $f(x) = x(x - 3)(x + 2)$

   $\quad = x(x^2 - x - 6)$

   $\quad = x^3 - x^2 - 6x$

8. Intercepts: $(0, 0)$, $\left(\pm 2\sqrt{3}, 0\right)$

   Moves up to the right.

   Moves down to the left.

   Origin Symmetry

x	-2	-1	0	1	2
y	16	11	0	-11	-16

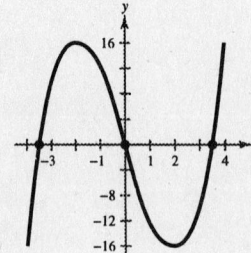

9.

$$
x - 3 \overline{\smash{\big)}\ 3x^4 + 0x^3 - 7x^2 + 2x - 10}
$$

$$
3x^3 + 9x^2 + 20x + 62 + \frac{176}{x - 3}
$$

$$
\underline{3x^4 - 9x^3}
$$
$$
9x^3 - 7x^2
$$
$$
\underline{9x^3 - 27x^2}
$$
$$
20x^2 + 2x
$$
$$
\underline{20x^2 - 60x}
$$
$$
62x - 10
$$
$$
\underline{62x - 186}
$$
$$
176
$$

10.

$$
x^2 + 2x - 1 \overline{\smash{\big)}\ x^3 + 0x^2 + 0x - 11}
$$

$$
x - 2 + \frac{5x - 13}{x^2 + 2x - 1}
$$

$$
\underline{x^3 + 2x^2 - x}
$$
$$
-2x^2 + x - 11
$$
$$
\underline{-2x^2 - 4x + 2}
$$
$$
5x - 13
$$

11.

$$
\begin{array}{r|rrrrrr}
-5 & 3 & 13 & 0 & 0 & 12 & -1 \\
   &   & -15 & 10 & -50 & 250 & -1310 \\
\hline
   & 3 & -2 & 10 & -50 & 262 & -1311
\end{array}
$$

$$
\frac{3x^5 + 13x^4 + 12x - 1}{x + 5} = 3x^4 - 2x^3 + 10x^2 - 50x + 262 - \frac{1311}{x + 5}
$$

12.

$$
\begin{array}{r|rrrr}
-6 & 7 & 40 & -12 & 15 \\
   &   & -42 & 12 & 0 \\
\hline
   & 7 & -2 & 0 & 15
\end{array}
$$

$$
f(-6) = 15
$$

13. $0 = x^3 - 19x - 30$

Possible rational roots:
$\pm 1, \pm 2, \pm 3, \pm 5, \pm 6, \pm 10, \pm 15, \pm 30$

$$
\begin{array}{r|rrrr}
-2 & 1 & 0 & -19 & -30 \\
   &   & -2 & 4 & 30 \\
\hline
   & 1 & -2 & -15 & 0
\end{array}
$$
$x = -2$ is a zero.

$0 = (x + 2)(x^2 - 2x - 15)$

$0 = (x + 2)(x + 3)(x - 5)$

Zeros: $x = -2, x = -3, x = 5$

14. $0 = x^4 + x^3 - 8x^2 - 9x - 9$

Possible rational roots: $\pm 1, \pm 3, \pm 9$

$$
\begin{array}{r|rrrrr}
3 & 1 & 1 & -8 & -9 & -9 \\
  &   & 3 & 12 & 12 & 9 \\
\hline
  & 1 & 4 & 4 & 3 & 0
\end{array}
$$
$x = 3$ is a zero.

$0 = (x - 3)(x^3 + 4x^2 + 4x + 3)$

Possible rational roots of $x^3 + 4x^2 + 4x + 3$: $\pm 1, \pm 3$

$$
\begin{array}{r|rrrr}
-3 & 1 & 4 & 4 & 3 \\
   &   & -3 & -3 & -3 \\
\hline
   & 1 & 1 & 1 & 0
\end{array}
$$
$x = -3$ is a zero.

$0 = (x - 3)(x + 3)(x^2 + x + 1)$

The zeros of $x^2 + x + 1$ are $x = \dfrac{-1 \pm \sqrt{3}\,i}{2}$ (by the Quadratic Formula).

Zeros: $x = 3, x = -3, x = -\dfrac{1}{2} + \dfrac{\sqrt{3}}{2}i, x = -\dfrac{1}{2} - \dfrac{\sqrt{3}}{2}i$

15. $0 = 6x^3 - 5x^2 + 4x - 15$

Possible rational roots: $\pm 1, \pm 3, \pm 5, \pm 15, \pm\frac{1}{2}, \pm\frac{3}{2}, \pm\frac{5}{2}, \pm\frac{15}{2}, \pm\frac{1}{3}, \pm\frac{5}{3}, \pm\frac{1}{6}, \pm\frac{5}{6}$

16. $0 = x^3 - \frac{20}{3}x^2 + 9x - \frac{10}{3}$

$0 = 3x^3 - 20x^2 + 27x - 10$

Possible rational roots: $\pm 1, \pm 2, \pm 5, \pm 10, \pm\frac{1}{3}, \pm\frac{2}{3}, \pm\frac{5}{3}, \pm\frac{10}{3}$

$$
\begin{array}{r|rrrr}
1 & 3 & -20 & 27 & -10 \\
  &   & 3 & -17 & 10 \\
\hline
  & 3 & -17 & 10 & 0
\end{array}
$$

$0 = (x - 1)(3x^2 - 17x + 10)$

$0 = (x - 1)(3x - 2)(x - 5)$

Zeros: $x = 1, x = \frac{2}{3}, x = 5$

17. Possible rational roots: $\pm 1, \pm 2, \pm 5, \pm 10$

$$
\begin{array}{r|rrrrr}
1 & 1 & 1 & 3 & 5 & -10 \\
  &   & 1 & 2 & 5 & 10 \\
\hline
  & 1 & 2 & 5 & 10 & 0
\end{array}
$$
$x = 1$ is a zero.

$$
\begin{array}{r|rrrr}
-2 & 1 & 2 & 5 & 10 \\
   &   & -2 & 0 & -10 \\
\hline
   & 1 & 0 & 5 & 0
\end{array}
$$
$x = -2$ is a zero.

$f(x) = (x - 1)(x + 2)(x^2 + 5)$

$ = (x - 1)(x + 2)(x + \sqrt{5}i)(x - \sqrt{5}i)$

18. $f(x) = (x - 2)[x - (3 + i)][x - (3 - i)]$

$ = (x - 2)[(x - 3) - i][(x - 3) + i]$

$ = (x - 2)[(x - 3)^2 - i^2]$

$ = (x - 2)[x^2 - 6x + 10]$

$ = x^3 - 8x^2 + 22x - 20$

19.
$$
\begin{array}{r|rrrr}
3i & 1 & 4 & 9 & 36 \\
   &   & 3i & 12i - 9 & -36 \\
\hline
   & 1 & 4 + 3i & 12i & 0
\end{array}
$$

20. Vertical asymptote: $x = 0$

Horizontal asymptote: $y = \frac{1}{2}$

x-intercept: $(1, 0)$

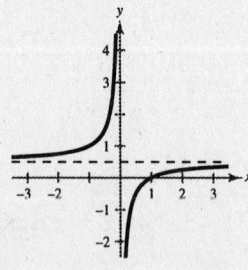

21. $y = 8$ is a horizontal asymptote since the degree on the numerator equals the degree of the denominator. There are no vertical asymptotes.

22. $x = 1$ is a vertical asymptote.

$$\frac{4x^2 - 2x + 7}{x - 1} = 4x + 2 + \frac{9}{x - 1}$$

thus, $y = 4x + 2$ is a slant asymptote.

23. (a) $(4 - 3i) - (-2 + i) = 4 - 3i + 2 - i = 6 - 4i$

(b) $(4 - 3i)(-2 + i) = -8 + 4i + 6i - 3i^2 = -8 + 10i + 3 = -5 + 10i$

(c) $\dfrac{4 - 3i}{-2 + i} = \dfrac{4 - 3i}{-2 + i} \cdot \dfrac{-2 - i}{-2 - i} = \dfrac{-8 - 4i + 6i + 3i^2}{4 + 1}$

$$= \dfrac{-11 + 2i}{5} = -\dfrac{11}{5} + \dfrac{2}{5}i$$

24. $\dfrac{1 - 2x}{x^2 + x} = \dfrac{1 - 2x}{x(x + 1)} = \dfrac{A}{x} + \dfrac{B}{x + 1}$

$1 - 2x = A(x + 1) + Bx$

When $x = 0, 1 = A.$

When $x = -1, 3 = -B \implies B = -3.$

$\dfrac{1 - 2x}{x^2 + x} = \dfrac{1}{x} - \dfrac{3}{x + 1}$

25. $\dfrac{6x - 17}{(x - 3)^2} = \dfrac{A}{x - 3} + \dfrac{B}{(x - 3)^2}$

$6x - 17 = A(x - 3) + B$

When $x = 3, 1 = B.$

When $x = 0, -17 = -3A + B \implies A = 6.$

$\dfrac{6x - 17}{(x - 3)^2} = \dfrac{6}{x - 3} + \dfrac{1}{(x - 3)^2}$

Chapter 3   Practice Test Solutions

1. $x^{3/5} = 8$

$x = 8^{5/3} = \left(\sqrt[3]{8}\right)^5 = 2^5 = 32$

2. $3^{x-1} = \frac{1}{81}$

$3^{x-1} = 3^{-4}$

$x - 1 = -4$

$x = -3$

3. $f(x) = 2^{-x} = \left(\frac{1}{2}\right)^x$

x	-2	-1	0	1	2
$f(x)$	4	2	1	$\frac{1}{2}$	$\frac{1}{4}$

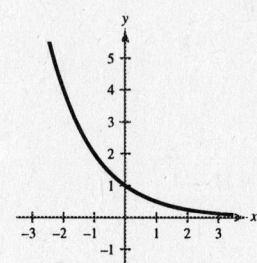

4. $g(x) = e^x + 1$

x	-2	-1	0	1	2
$g(x)$	1.14	1.37	2	3.72	8.39

5. (a) $A = P\left(1 + \dfrac{r}{n}\right)^{nt}$

$A = 5000\left(1 + \dfrac{0.09}{12}\right)^{12(3)} \approx \$6543.23$

(b) $A = P\left(1 + \dfrac{r}{n}\right)^{nt}$

$A = 5000\left(1 + \dfrac{0.09}{4}\right)^{4(3)} \approx \$6530.25$

(c) $A = Pe^{rt}$

$A = 5000e^{(0.09)(3)} \approx \$6549.82$

6. $7^{-2} = \dfrac{1}{49}$

$\log_7 \dfrac{1}{49} = -2$

7. $x - 4 = \log_2 \frac{1}{64}$

$2^{x-4} = \frac{1}{64}$

$2^{x-4} = 2^{-6}$

$x - 4 = -6$

$x = -2$

8. $\log_b \sqrt[4]{\frac{8}{25}} = \frac{1}{4} \log_b \frac{8}{25}$

$= \frac{1}{4}[\log_b 8 - \log_b 25]$

$= \frac{1}{4}[\log_b 2^3 - \log_b 5^2]$

$= \frac{1}{4}[3 \log_b 2 - 2 \log_b 5]$

$= \frac{1}{4}[3(0.3562) - 2(0.8271)]$

$= -0.1464$

9. $5 \ln x - \dfrac{1}{2} \ln y + 6 \ln z = \ln x^5 - \ln \sqrt{y} + \ln z^6 = \ln\!\left(\dfrac{x^5 z^6}{\sqrt{y}}\right)$, $z > 0$

10. $\log_9 28 = \dfrac{\log 28}{\log 9} \approx 1.5166$

11. $\log N = 0.6646$

$N = 10^{0.6646} \approx 4.62$

12.

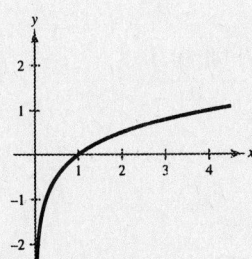

13. Domain:

$$x^2 - 9 > 0$$

$$(x + 3)(x - 3) > 0$$

$$x < -3 \text{ or } x > 3$$

14.

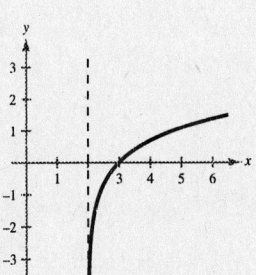

15. False. $\dfrac{\ln x}{\ln y} \neq \ln(x - y)$ since $\dfrac{\ln x}{\ln y} = \log_y x$.

16. $5^3 = 41$

$x = \log_5 41 = \dfrac{\ln 41}{\ln 5} \approx 2.3074$

17. $x - x^2 = \log_5 \dfrac{1}{25}$

$5^{x - x^2} = \dfrac{1}{25}$

$5^{x - x^2} = 5^{-2}$

$x - x^2 = -2$

$0 = x^2 - x - 2$

$0 = (x + 1)(x - 2)$

$x = -1$ or $x = 2$

18. $\log_2 x + \log_2(x - 3) = 2$

$\log_2[x(x - 3)] = 2$

$x(x - 3) = 2^2$

$x^2 - 3x = 4$

$x^2 - 3x - 4 = 0$

$(x + 1)(x - 4) = 0$

$x = 4$

$x = -1$ (extraneous)

$x = 4$ is the only solution.

19. $\dfrac{e^x + e^{-x}}{3} = 4$

$e^x(e^x + e^{-x}) = 12e^x$

$e^{2x} + 1 = 12e^x$

$e^{2x} - 12e^x + 1 = 0$

$e^x = \dfrac{12 \pm \sqrt{144 - 4}}{2}$

$e^x \approx 11.9161$ or $e^x \approx 0.0839$

$x = \ln 11.9161$ $x = \ln 0.0839$

$x \approx 2.478$ $x \approx -2.478$

20. $A = Pe^{et}$

$12{,}000 = 6000e^{0.13t}$

$2 = e^{0.13t}$

$0.13t = \ln 2$

$t = \dfrac{\ln 2}{0.13}$

$t \approx 5.3319$ years or 5 years 4 months

Chapter 4   Practice Test Solutions

1. $350° = 350\left(\dfrac{\pi}{180}\right) = \dfrac{35\pi}{18}$

2. $\dfrac{5\pi}{9} = \dfrac{5\pi}{9} \cdot \dfrac{180}{\pi} = 100°$

3. $135°14'12'' = \left(135 + \frac{14}{60} + \frac{12}{3600}\right)°$

$\approx 135.2367°$

4. $-22.569° = -(22° + 0.569(60)')$

$= -22°34.14'$

$= -(22°34' + 0.14(60)'')$

$\approx -22°34'8''$

5. $\cos\theta = \dfrac{2}{3}$

$x = 2, r = 3, y = \pm\sqrt{9-4} = \pm\sqrt{5}$

$\tan\theta = \dfrac{y}{x} = \pm\dfrac{\sqrt{5}}{2}$

6. $\sin\theta = 0.9063$

$\theta = \arcsin(0.9063)$

$\theta = 65° = \dfrac{13\pi}{36}$ or $\theta = 180° - 65° = 115° = \dfrac{23\pi}{36}$

7. $\tan 20° = \dfrac{35}{x}$

$x = \dfrac{35}{\tan 20°} \approx 96.1617$

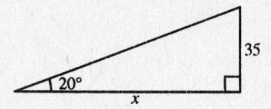

8. $\theta = \dfrac{6\pi}{5}$, θ is in Quadrant III.

Reference angle: $\dfrac{6\pi}{5} - \pi = \dfrac{\pi}{5}$ or $36°$

9. $\csc 3.92 = \dfrac{1}{\sin 3.92} \approx -1.4242$

10. $\tan\theta = 6 = \dfrac{6}{1}$, θ lies in Quandrant III.

$y = -6, x = -1, r = \sqrt{36+1} = \sqrt{37}$,

so $\sec\theta = \dfrac{\sqrt{37}}{-1} \approx -6.0828.$

11. Period: 4π

Amplitude: 3

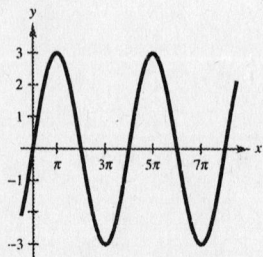

12. Period: 2π

Amplitude: 2

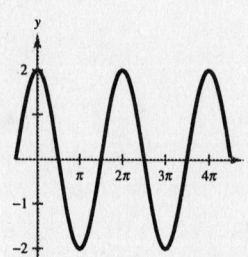

13. Period: $\dfrac{\pi}{2}$

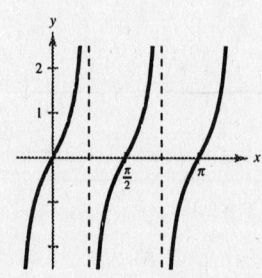

14. Period: 2π

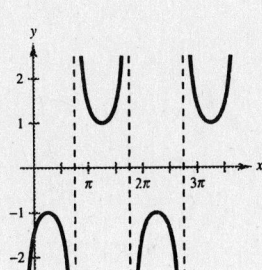

15.

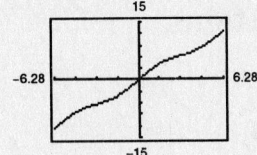

16.

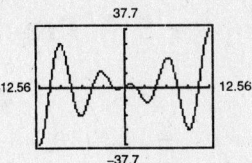

17. $\theta = \arcsin 1$

$\sin \theta = 1$

$\theta = \dfrac{\pi}{2} = 90°$

18. $\theta = \arctan(-3)$

$\tan \theta = -3$

$\theta \approx -1.249 \approx -71.565°$

19. $\sin\left(\arccos \dfrac{4}{\sqrt{35}}\right)$

$\sin \theta = \dfrac{\sqrt{19}}{\sqrt{35}} \approx 0.7368$

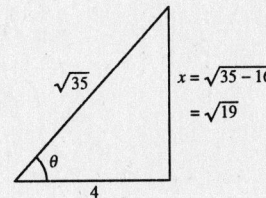

$x = \sqrt{35 - 16}$
$= \sqrt{19}$

20. $\cos\left(\arcsin \dfrac{x}{4}\right)$

$\cos \theta = \dfrac{\sqrt{16 - x^2}}{4}$

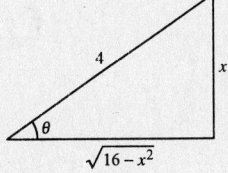

21. Given $A = 40°$, $c = 12$

$B = 90° - 40° = 50°$

$\sin 40° = \dfrac{a}{12}$

$a = 12 \sin 40° \approx 7.713$

$\cos 40° = \dfrac{b}{12}$

$b = 12 \cos 40° \approx 9.193$

22. Given $B = 6.84°$, $a = 21.3$

$A = 90° - 6.84° = 83.16°$

$\sin 83.16° = \dfrac{21.3}{c}$

$c = \dfrac{21.3}{\sin 83.16°} \approx 21.453$

$\tan 83.16° = \dfrac{21.3}{b}$

$b = \dfrac{21.3}{\tan 83.16°} \approx 2.555$

23. Given $a = 5$, $b = 9$

$c = \sqrt{25 + 81} = \sqrt{106} \approx 10.296$

$\tan A = \dfrac{5}{9}$

$A = \arctan \dfrac{5}{9} \approx 29.055°$

$B \approx 90° - 29.055° = 60.945°$

24. $\sin 67° = \dfrac{x}{20}$

$x = 20 \sin 67° \approx 18.41$ feet

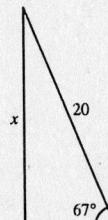

25. $\tan 5° = \dfrac{250}{x}$

$x = \dfrac{250}{\tan 5°}$

≈ 2857.513 feet

≈ 0.541 mi

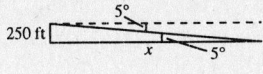

Chapter 5   Practice Test Solutions

1. $\tan x = \dfrac{4}{11}$, $\sec x < 0 \implies x$ is in Quadrant III.

   $y = -4$, $x = -11$, $r = \sqrt{16 + 121} = \sqrt{137}$

   $$\sin x = -\frac{4}{\sqrt{137}} = -\frac{4\sqrt{137}}{137} \qquad\qquad \csc x = -\frac{\sqrt{137}}{4}$$

   $$\cos x = -\frac{11}{\sqrt{137}} = -\frac{11\sqrt{137}}{137} \qquad\qquad \sec x = -\frac{\sqrt{137}}{11}$$

   $$\tan x = \frac{4}{11} \qquad\qquad\qquad\qquad \cot x = \frac{11}{4}$$

2. $\dfrac{\sec^2 x + \csc^2 x}{\csc^2 x(1 + \tan^2 x)} = \dfrac{\sec^2 x + \csc^2 x}{\csc^2 x + (\csc^2 x)\tan^2 x} = \dfrac{\sec^2 x + \csc^2 x}{\csc^2 x + \dfrac{1}{\sin^2 x} \cdot \dfrac{\sin^2 x}{\cos^2 x}}$

   $$= \frac{\sec^2 x + \csc^2 x}{\csc^2 x + \dfrac{1}{\cos^2 x}} = \frac{\sec^2 x + \csc^2 x}{\csc^2 x + \sec^2 x} = 1$$

3. $\ln|\tan \theta| - \ln|\cot \theta| = \ln\left|\dfrac{\tan \theta}{\cot \theta}\right| = \ln\left|\dfrac{\sin \theta/\cos\theta}{\cos \theta/\sin\theta}\right| = \ln\left|\dfrac{\sin^2 \theta}{\cos^2 \theta}\right| = \ln|\tan^2 \theta| = 2\ln|\tan \theta|$

4. $\cos\left(\dfrac{\pi}{2} - x\right) = \dfrac{1}{\csc x}$ is true since $\cos\left(\dfrac{\pi}{2} - x\right) = \sin x = \dfrac{1}{\csc x}$.

5. $\sin^4 x + (\sin^2 x)\cos^2 x = \sin^2 x(\sin^2 x + \cos^2 x) = \sin^2 x(1) = \sin^2 x$

6. $(\csc x + 1)(\csc x - 1) = \csc^2 x - 1 = \cot^2 x$

7. $\dfrac{\cos^2 x}{1 - \sin x} \cdot \dfrac{1 + \sin x}{1 + \sin x} = \dfrac{\cos^2 x(1 + \sin x)}{1 - \sin^2 x} = \dfrac{\cos^2 x(1 + \sin x)}{\cos^2 x} = 1 + \sin x$

8. $\dfrac{1 + \cos \theta}{\sin \theta} + \dfrac{\sin \theta}{1 + \cos \theta} = \dfrac{(1 + \cos \theta)^2 + \sin^2 \theta}{\sin \theta(1 + \cos \theta)}$

   $$= \frac{1 + 2\cos \theta + \cos^2 \theta + \sin^2 \theta}{\sin \theta(1 + \cos \theta)} = \frac{2 + 2\cos \theta}{\sin \theta(1 + \cos \theta)} = \frac{2}{\sin \theta} = 2\csc \theta$$

9. $\tan^4 x + 2\tan^2 x + 1 = (\tan^2 x + 1)^2 = (\sec^2 x)^2 = \sec^4 x$

10. (a) $\sin 105° = \sin(60° + 45°) = \sin 60° \cos 45° + \cos 60° \sin 45°$

$$= \frac{\sqrt{3}}{2} \cdot \frac{\sqrt{2}}{2} + \frac{1}{2} \cdot \frac{\sqrt{2}}{2} = \frac{\sqrt{2}}{4}(\sqrt{3} + 1)$$

(b) $\tan 15° = \tan(60° - 45°) = \dfrac{\tan 60° - \tan 45°}{1 + \tan 60° \tan 45°}$

$$= \frac{\sqrt{3} - 1}{1 + \sqrt{3}} \cdot \frac{1 - \sqrt{3}}{1 - \sqrt{3}} = \frac{2\sqrt{3} - 1 - 3}{1 - 3} = \frac{2\sqrt{3} - 4}{-2} = 2 - \sqrt{3}$$

11. $(\sin 42°) \cos 38° - (\cos 42°) \sin 38° = \sin(42° - 38°) = \sin 4°$

12. $\tan\left(\theta + \dfrac{\pi}{4}\right) = \dfrac{\tan \theta + \tan\left(\dfrac{\pi}{4}\right)}{1 - (\tan \theta) \tan\left(\dfrac{\pi}{4}\right)} = \dfrac{\tan \theta + 1}{1 - \tan \theta(1)} = \dfrac{1 + \tan \theta}{1 - \tan \theta}$

13. $\sin(\arcsin x - \arccos x) = \sin(\arcsin x) \cos(\arccos x) - \cos(\arcsin x) \sin(\arccos x)$

$$= (x)(x) - \left(\sqrt{1 - x^2}\right)\left(\sqrt{1 - x^2}\right) = x^2 - (1 - x^2) = 2x^2 - 1$$

14. (a) $\cos(120°) = \cos[2(60°)] = 2\cos^2 60° - 1 = 2\left(\dfrac{1}{2}\right)^2 - 1 = -\dfrac{1}{2}$

(b) $\tan(300°) = \tan[2(150°)] = \dfrac{2 \tan 150°}{1 - \tan^2 150°} = \dfrac{-\dfrac{2\sqrt{3}}{3}}{1 - \left(\dfrac{1}{3}\right)} = -\sqrt{3}$

15. (a) $\sin 22.5° = \sin \dfrac{45°}{2} = \sqrt{\dfrac{1 - \cos 45°}{2}} = \sqrt{\dfrac{1 - \dfrac{\sqrt{2}}{2}}{2}} = \dfrac{\sqrt{2 - \sqrt{2}}}{2}$

(b) $\tan \dfrac{\pi}{12} = \tan \dfrac{\dfrac{\pi}{6}}{2} = \dfrac{\sin \dfrac{\pi}{6}}{1 + \cos\left(\dfrac{\pi}{6}\right)} = \dfrac{\dfrac{1}{2}}{1 + \dfrac{\sqrt{3}}{2}} = \dfrac{1}{2 + \sqrt{3}} = 2 - \sqrt{3}$

16. $\sin \theta = \dfrac{4}{5}$, θ lies in Quadrant II $\Rightarrow \cos \theta = -\dfrac{3}{5}$.

$$\cos \frac{\theta}{2} = \sqrt{\frac{1 + \cos \theta}{2}} = \sqrt{\frac{1 - \frac{3}{5}}{2}} = \sqrt{\frac{2}{10}} = \frac{1}{\sqrt{5}} = \frac{\sqrt{5}}{5}$$

17. $(\sin^2 x) \cos^2 x = \dfrac{1 - \cos 2x}{2} \cdot \dfrac{1 + \cos 2x}{2} = \dfrac{1}{4}[1 - \cos^2 2x] = \dfrac{1}{4}\left[1 - \dfrac{1 + \cos 4x}{2}\right]$

$$= \frac{1}{8}[2 - (1 + \cos 4x)] = \frac{1}{8}[1 - \cos 4x]$$

18. $6(\sin 5\theta) \cos 2\theta = 6\left\{\dfrac{1}{2}[\sin(5\theta + 2\theta) + \sin(5\theta - 2\theta)]\right\} = 3[\sin 7\theta + \sin 3\theta]$

19. $\sin(x + \pi) + \sin(x - \pi) = 2\left(\sin\dfrac{[(x + \pi) + (x - \pi)]}{2}\right)\cos\dfrac{[(x + \pi) - (x - \pi)]}{2}$

$$= 2 \sin x \cos \pi = -2 \sin x$$

20. $\dfrac{\sin 9x + \sin 5x}{\cos 9x - \cos 5x} = \dfrac{2 \sin 7x \cos 2x}{-2 \sin 7x \sin 2x} = -\dfrac{\cos 2x}{\sin 2x} = -\cot 2x$

21. $\frac{1}{2}[\sin(u + v) - \sin(u - v)] = \frac{1}{2}\{(\sin u)\cos v + (\cos u)\sin v - [(\sin u)\cos v - (\cos u)\sin v]\}$

$$= \frac{1}{2}[2(\cos u)\sin v] = (\cos u)\sin v$$

22. $4 \sin^2 x = 1$

$\sin^2 x = \dfrac{1}{4}$

$\sin x = \pm\dfrac{1}{2}$

$\sin x = \dfrac{1}{2}$ or $\sin x = -\dfrac{1}{2}$

$x = \dfrac{\pi}{6}$ or $\dfrac{5\pi}{6}$ $x = \dfrac{7\pi}{6}$ or $\dfrac{11\pi}{6}$

23. $\tan^2 \theta + \left(\sqrt{3} - 1\right) \tan \theta - \sqrt{3} = 0$

$(\tan\theta - 1)(\tan\theta + \sqrt{3}) = 0$

$\tan \theta = 1$ or $\tan \theta = -\sqrt{3}$

$\theta = \dfrac{\pi}{4}$ or $\dfrac{5\pi}{4}$ $\theta = \dfrac{2\pi}{3}$ or $\dfrac{5\pi}{3}$

24. $\sin 2x = \cos x$

$2(\sin x)\cos x - \cos x = 0$

$\cos x(2 \sin x - 1) = 0$

$\cos x = 0$ or $\sin x = \dfrac{1}{2}$

$x = \dfrac{\pi}{2}$ or $\dfrac{3\pi}{2}$ $x = \dfrac{\pi}{6}$ or $\dfrac{5\pi}{6}$

25. $\tan^2 x - 6 \tan x + 4 = 0$

$$\tan x = \frac{-(-6) \pm \sqrt{(-6)^2 - 4(1)(4)}}{2(1)}$$

$$\tan x = \frac{6 \pm \sqrt{20}}{2} = 3 \pm \sqrt{5}$$

$\tan x = 3 + \sqrt{5}$ or $\tan x = 3 - \sqrt{5}$

$x \approx 1.3821$ or 4.5237 $x = 0.6524$ or 3.7940

Chapter 6   Practice Test Solutions

1. $C = 180° - (40° + 12°) = 128°$

$a = \sin 40°\left(\dfrac{100}{\sin 12°}\right) \approx 309.164$

$c = \sin 128°\left(\dfrac{100}{\sin 12°}\right) \approx 379.012$

2. $\sin A = 5\left(\dfrac{\sin 150°}{20}\right) = 0.125$

$A \approx 7.181°$

$B \approx 180° - (150° + 7.181°) = 22.819°$

$b = \sin 22.819°\left(\dfrac{20}{\sin 150°}\right) \approx 15.513$

3. Area $= \frac{1}{2}ab \sin C$

$= \frac{1}{2}(3)(6)\sin 130°$

≈ 6.894 square units

4. $h = b \sin A$

$= 35 \sin 22.5°$

≈ 13.394

$a = 10$

Since $a < h$ and A is acute, the triangle has no solution.

5. $\cos A = \dfrac{(53)^2 + (38)^2 - (49)^2}{2(53)(38)} \approx 0.4598$

$A \approx 62.627°$

$\cos B = \dfrac{(49)^2 + (38)^2 - (53)^2}{2(49)(38)} \approx 0.2782$

$B \approx 73.847°$

$C \approx 180° - (62.627° + 73.847°)$

$= 43.526°$

6. $c^2 = (100)^2 + (300)^2 - 2(100)(300)\cos 29°$

≈ 47522.8176

$c \approx 218$

$\cos A = \dfrac{(300)^2 + (218)^2 - (100)^2}{2(300)(218)} \approx 0.97495$

$A \approx 12.85°$

$B \approx 180° - (12.85° + 29°) = 138.15°$

7. $s = \dfrac{a + b + c}{2} = \dfrac{4.1 + 6.8 + 5.5}{2} = 8.2$

Area $= \sqrt{s(s - a)(s - b)(s - c)}$

$= \sqrt{8.2(8.2 - 4.1)(8.2 - 6.8)(8.2 - 5.5)}$

≈ 11.273 square units

8. $x^2 = (40)^2 + (70)^2 - 2(40)(70)\cos 168°$

≈ 11977.6266

$x \approx 190.442$ miles

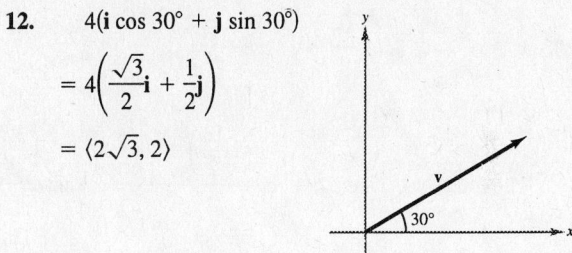

9. $\mathbf{w} = 4(3\mathbf{i} + \mathbf{j}) - 7(-\mathbf{i} + 2\mathbf{j})$

$= 19\mathbf{i} - 10\mathbf{j}$

10. $\dfrac{\mathbf{v}}{\|\mathbf{v}\|} = \dfrac{5\mathbf{i} - 3\mathbf{j}}{\sqrt{25 + 9}} = \dfrac{5}{\sqrt{34}}\mathbf{i} - \dfrac{3}{\sqrt{34}}\mathbf{j}$

$= \dfrac{5\sqrt{34}}{34}\mathbf{i} - \dfrac{3\sqrt{34}}{34}\mathbf{j}$

11. $\mathbf{u} = 6\mathbf{i} + 5\mathbf{j} \qquad \mathbf{v} = 2\mathbf{i} - 3\mathbf{j}$

$\mathbf{u} \cdot \mathbf{v} = 6(2) + 5(-3) = -3$

$\|\mathbf{u}\| = \sqrt{61} \qquad \|\mathbf{v}\| = \sqrt{13}$

$\cos \theta = \dfrac{-3}{\sqrt{61}\sqrt{13}}$

$\theta \approx 96.116°$

12. $4(\mathbf{i} \cos 30° + \mathbf{j} \sin 30°)$

$= 4\left(\dfrac{\sqrt{3}}{2}\mathbf{i} + \dfrac{1}{2}\mathbf{j}\right)$

$= \langle 2\sqrt{3}, 2 \rangle$

13. $\text{proj}_{\mathbf{v}}\mathbf{u} = \left(\dfrac{\mathbf{u} \cdot \mathbf{v}}{\|\mathbf{v}\|^2}\right)\mathbf{v} = \dfrac{-10}{20}\langle -2, 4 \rangle = \langle 1, -2 \rangle$

14. $r = \sqrt{25 + 25} = \sqrt{50} = 5\sqrt{2}$

$\tan \theta = \dfrac{-5}{5} = -1$

Since z is in Quadrant IV,

$\theta = 315°$

$z = 5\sqrt{2}(\cos 315° + i \sin 315°).$

15. $\cos 225° = -\dfrac{\sqrt{2}}{2}, \quad \sin 225° = -\dfrac{\sqrt{2}}{2}$

$z = 6\left(-\dfrac{\sqrt{2}}{2} - i\dfrac{\sqrt{2}}{2}\right)$

$= -3\sqrt{2} - 3\sqrt{2}i$

16. $[7(\cos 23° + i \sin 23°)][4(\cos 7° + i \sin 7°)] = 7(4)[\cos(23° + 7°) + i \sin(23° + 7°)]$

$= 28(\cos 30° + i \sin 30°)$

17. $\dfrac{9\left(\cos\frac{5\pi}{4}+i\sin\frac{5\pi}{4}\right)}{3(\cos\pi+i\sin\pi)}=\dfrac{9}{3}\left[\cos\left(\frac{5\pi}{4}-\pi\right)+i\sin\left(\frac{5\pi}{4}-\pi\right)\right]=3\left(\cos\frac{\pi}{4}+i\sin\frac{\pi}{4}\right)$

18. $(2+2i)^8=[2\sqrt{2}(\cos45°+i\sin45°)]^8=\left(2\sqrt{2}\right)^8[\cos(8)(45°)+i\sin(8)(45°)]$

$=4096[\cos360°+i\sin360°]=4096$

19. $z=8\left(\cos\frac{\pi}{3}+i\sin\frac{\pi}{3}\right),\ n=3$

The cube roots of z are: $\sqrt[3]{8}\left[\cos\dfrac{\frac{\pi}{3}+2\pi k}{3}+i\sin\dfrac{\frac{\pi}{3}+2\pi k}{3}\right],\ k=0,1,2$

For $k=0$, $\sqrt[3]{8}\left[\cos\dfrac{\frac{\pi}{3}}{3}+i\sin\dfrac{\frac{\pi}{3}}{3}\right]=2\left(\cos\frac{\pi}{9}+i\sin\frac{\pi}{9}\right)$

For $k=1$, $\sqrt[3]{8}\left[\cos\dfrac{\left(\frac{\pi}{3}\right)+2\pi}{3}+i\sin\dfrac{\left(\frac{\pi}{3}\right)+2\pi}{3}\right]=2\left(\cos\frac{7\pi}{9}+i\sin\frac{7\pi}{9}\right)$

For $k=2$, $\sqrt[3]{8}\left[\cos\dfrac{\frac{\pi}{3}+4\pi}{3}+i\sin\dfrac{\frac{\pi}{3}+4\pi}{3}\right]=2\left(\cos\frac{13\pi}{9}+i\sin\frac{13\pi}{9}\right)$

20. $x^4=-i=1\left(\cos\frac{3\pi}{2}+i\sin\frac{3\pi}{2}\right)$

The fourth roots are: $\sqrt[4]{1}\left[\cos\dfrac{\left(\frac{3\pi}{2}\right)+2\pi k}{4}+i\sin\dfrac{\left(\frac{3\pi}{2}\right)+2\pi k}{4}\right],\ k=0,1,2,3$

For $k=0$, $\cos\dfrac{\frac{3\pi}{2}}{4}+i\sin\dfrac{\frac{3\pi}{2}}{4}=\cos\frac{3\pi}{8}+i\sin\frac{3\pi}{8}$

For $k=1$, $\cos\dfrac{\frac{3\pi}{2}+2\pi}{4}+i\sin\dfrac{\frac{3\pi}{2}+2\pi}{4}=\cos\frac{7\pi}{8}+i\sin\frac{7\pi}{8}$

For $k=2$, $\cos\dfrac{\frac{3\pi}{2}+4\pi}{4}+i\sin\dfrac{\frac{3\pi}{2}+4\pi}{4}=\cos\frac{11\pi}{8}+i\sin\frac{11\pi}{8}$

For $k=3$, $\cos\dfrac{\frac{3\pi}{2}+6\pi}{4}+i\sin\dfrac{\frac{3\pi}{2}+6\pi}{4}=\cos\frac{15\pi}{8}+i\sin\frac{15\pi}{8}$

Chapter 7   Practice Test Solutions

1. $\begin{cases} x + y = 1 \\ 3x - y = 15 \implies y = 3x - 15 \end{cases}$

$x + (3x - 15) = 1$

$\qquad 4x = 16$

$\qquad\ x = 4$

$\qquad\ y = -3$

Solution: $(4, -3)$

2. $\begin{cases} x - 3y = -3 \implies x = 3y - 3 \\ x^2 + 6y = 5 \end{cases}$

$\qquad (3y - 3)^2 + 6y = 5$

$\qquad 9y^2 - 18y + 9 + 6y = 5$

$\qquad 9y^2 - 12y + 4 = 0$

$\qquad (3y - 2)^2 = 0$

$\qquad y = \frac{2}{3}$

$\qquad x = -1$

Solution: $\left(-1, \frac{2}{3}\right)$

3. $\begin{cases} x + y + z = 6 \implies z = 6 - x - y \\ 2x - y + 3z = 0 \implies 2x - y + 3(6 - x - y) = 0 \implies -x - 4y = -18 \implies x = 18 - 4y \\ 5x + 2y - z = -3 \implies 5x + 2y - (6 - x - y) = -3 \implies 6x + 3y = 3 \end{cases}$

$6(18 - 4y) + 3y = 3$

$\qquad -21y = -105$

$\qquad\quad y = 5$

$\qquad\quad x = 18 - 4y = -2$

$\qquad\quad z = 6 - x - y = 3$

Solution: $(-2, 5, 3)$

4. $x + y = 110 \implies y = 110 - x$

$\qquad xy = 2800$

$x(110 - x) = 2800$

$\qquad 0 = x^2 - 110x + 2800$

$\qquad 0 = (x - 40)(x - 70)$

$x = 40$ or $x = 70$

$y = 70 \qquad y = 40$

Solution: The two numbers are 40 and 70.

5. $2x + 2y = 170 \implies y = \dfrac{170 - 2x}{2} = 85 - x$

$\qquad xy = 1500$

$\qquad x(85 - x) = 1500$

$\qquad 0 = x^2 - 85x + 1500$

$\qquad 0 = (x - 25)(x - 60)$

$x = 25$ or $x = 60$

$y = 60 \qquad y = 25$

Dimensions: $60 \text{ ft} \times 25 \text{ ft}$

6. $\begin{cases} 2x + 15y = 4 \implies 2x + 15y = 4 \\ x - 3y = 23 \implies \underline{5x - 15y = 115} \end{cases}$

$\qquad\qquad\qquad 7x \quad\ = 119$

$\qquad\qquad\qquad\ x \ = 17$

$\qquad\qquad\qquad\ y = \dfrac{x - 23}{3}$

$\qquad\qquad\qquad\quad = -2$

Solution: $(17, -2)$

7. $\begin{cases} x + y = 2 \implies 19x + 19y = 38 \\ 38x - 19y = 7 \implies \underline{38x - 19y = 7} \end{cases}$

$\qquad\qquad\qquad 57x \quad\ = 45$

$x = \dfrac{45}{57} = \dfrac{15}{19}$

$y = 2 - x = \dfrac{38}{19} - \dfrac{15}{19} = \dfrac{23}{19}$

Solution: $\left(\dfrac{15}{19}, \dfrac{23}{19}\right)$

8. $\begin{cases} 0.4x + 0.5y = 0.112 \\ 0.3x - 0.7y = -0.131 \end{cases} \Rightarrow \begin{array}{l} 0.28x + 0.35y = 0.0784 \\ \underline{0.15x - 0.35y = -0.0655} \\ 0.43x = 0.0129 \end{array}$

$$x = \frac{0.0129}{0.43} = 0.03$$

$$y = \frac{0.112 - 0.4x}{0.5} = 0.20$$

Solution: $(0.03, 0.20)$

9. Let x = amount in 11% fund and y = amount in 13% fund.

$$x + y = 17000 \Rightarrow y = 17000 - x$$

$$0.11x + 0.13y = 2080$$

$$0.11x + 0.13(17000 - x) = 2080$$

$$-0.02x = -130$$

$$x = \$6500 \quad \text{at } 11\%$$

$$y = \$10{,}500 \text{ at } 13\%$$

10. $(4, 3), (1, 1), (-1, -2), (-2, -1)$

Use a calculator.

$$y = ax + b = \tfrac{11}{14}x - \tfrac{1}{7}$$

11. $\begin{cases} x + y = -2 \\ 2x - y + z = 11 \\ 4y - 3z = -20 \end{cases}$

$\begin{cases} x + y = -2 \\ -3y + z = 15 \\ 4y - 3z = -20 \end{cases}$ $\quad$ -2Eq.1 + Eq.2

$\begin{cases} x + y = -2 \\ y - 2z = -5 \\ 4y - 3z = -20 \end{cases}$ $\quad$ Eq.3 + Eq.2

$\begin{cases} x + y = -2 \\ y - 2z = -5 \\ 5z = 0 \end{cases}$ $\quad$ -4Eq.2 + Eq.3

$\begin{cases} x + y = -2 \\ y - 2z = -5 \\ z = 0 \end{cases}$

$$y - 2(0) = -5 \Rightarrow y = -5$$
$$x + (-5) = -2 \Rightarrow x = 3$$

Solution: $(3, -5, 0)$

12. $\begin{cases} 4x - y + 5z = 4 \\ 2x + y - z = 0 \\ 2x + 4y + 8z = 0 \end{cases}$

$\begin{cases} 2x + 4y + 8z = 0 \\ 2x + y - z = 0 \\ 4x - y + 5z = 4 \end{cases}$ $\quad$ Interchange equations.

$\begin{cases} 2x + 4y + 8z = 0 \\ -3y - 9z = 0 \\ -9y - 11z = 4 \end{cases}$ $\quad$ $\begin{array}{l} -\text{Eq.1 + Eq.2} \\ -2\text{Eq.1 + Eq.3} \end{array}$

$\begin{cases} 2x + 4y + 8z = 0 \\ -3y - 9z = 0 \\ 16z = 4 \end{cases}$ $\quad$ -3Eq.2 + Eq.3

$\begin{cases} x + 2y + 4z = 0 \\ y + 3z = 0 \\ z = \tfrac{1}{4} \end{cases}$ $\quad$ $\begin{array}{l} \tfrac{1}{2}\text{Eq.1} \\ -\tfrac{1}{3}\text{Eq.2} \\ \tfrac{1}{16}\text{Eq.3} \end{array}$

$$y + 3\left(\tfrac{1}{4}\right) = 0 \Rightarrow y = -\tfrac{3}{4}$$
$$x + 2\left(-\tfrac{3}{4}\right) + 4\left(\tfrac{1}{4}\right) = 0 \Rightarrow x = \tfrac{1}{2}$$

Solution: $\left(-\tfrac{1}{2}, -\tfrac{3}{4}, \tfrac{1}{4}\right)$

13. $\begin{cases} 3x + 2y - z = 5 \\ 6x - y + 5z = 2 \end{cases}$

$\begin{cases} 3x + 2y - z = 5 \\ -5y + 7z = -8 \end{cases}$ $\quad$ -2Eq.1 + Eq.2

$\begin{cases} x + \tfrac{2}{3}y - \tfrac{1}{3}z = \tfrac{5}{3} \\ y - \tfrac{7}{5}z = \tfrac{8}{5} \end{cases}$ $\quad$ $\begin{array}{l} \tfrac{1}{3}\text{Eq.1} \\ -\tfrac{1}{5}\text{Eq.2} \end{array}$

Let $a = z$.

Then $y = \tfrac{7}{5}a + \tfrac{8}{5}$, and

$$x + \tfrac{2}{3}\left(\tfrac{7}{5}a + \tfrac{8}{5}\right) - \tfrac{1}{3}a = \tfrac{5}{3}$$

$$x + \tfrac{2}{5}a = \tfrac{3}{5}$$

$$x = -\tfrac{3}{5}a + \tfrac{3}{5}$$

Solution: $\left(-\tfrac{3}{5}a + \tfrac{3}{5}, \tfrac{7}{5}a + \tfrac{8}{5}, a\right)$, where a is any real number.

14. $y = ax^2 + bx + c$ passes through $(0, -1)$, $(1, 4)$, and $(2, 13)$.

At $(0, -1)$: $-1 = a(0)^2 + b(0) + c \implies c = -1$

At $(1, 4)$: $4 = a(1)^2 + b(1) - 1 \implies 5 = a + b \implies 5 = a + b$

At $(2, 13)$: $13 = a(2)^2 + b(2) - 1 \implies 14 = 4a + 2b \implies \underline{-7 = -2a - b}$

$$-2 = -a$$
$$a = 2$$
$$b = 3$$

Thus, the equation of the parabola is $y = 2x^2 + 3x - 1$.

15. $s = \frac{1}{2}at^2 + v_0t + s_0$ passes through $(1, 12)$, $(2, 5)$, and $(3, 4)$.

At $(1, 12)$: $12 = \frac{1}{2}a + v_0 + s_0$

At $(2, 5)$: $5 = 2a + 2v_0 + s_0$

At $(3, 4)$: $4 = \frac{9}{2}a + 3v_0 + s_0$

$$\begin{cases} a + 2v_0 + 2s_0 = 24 \\ 2a + 2v_0 + s_0 = 5 \\ 9a + 6v_0 + 2s_0 = 8 \end{cases}$$

$$\begin{cases} a + 2v_0 + 2s_0 = 24 \\ -2v_0 - 3s_0 = -43 \quad -2\text{Eq.1} + \text{Eq.2} \\ -12v_0 - 16s_0 = -208 \quad -9\text{Eq.1} + \text{Eq.3} \end{cases}$$

$$\begin{cases} a + 2v_0 + 2s_0 = 24 \\ -2v_0 - 3s_0 = -43 \\ 2s_0 = 50 \quad -6\text{Eq.2} + \text{Eq.3} \end{cases}$$

$$\begin{cases} a + 2v_0 + 2s_0 = 24 \\ v_0 + \frac{3}{2}s_0 = \frac{43}{2} \quad -\frac{1}{2}\text{Eq.2} \\ s_0 = 25 \quad \frac{1}{2}\text{Eq.3} \end{cases}$$

$$v_0 + \frac{3}{2}(25) = \frac{43}{2} \implies v_0 = -16$$
$$a + 2(-16) + 2(25) = 24 \implies a = 6$$

Thus, $s = \frac{1}{2}(6)t^2 - 16t + 25 = 3t^2 - 16t + 25$.

16. $x^2 + y^2 \geq 9$

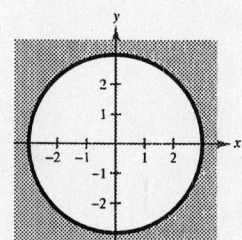

17. $\begin{cases} x + y \leq 6 \\ x \geq 2 \\ y \geq 0 \end{cases}$

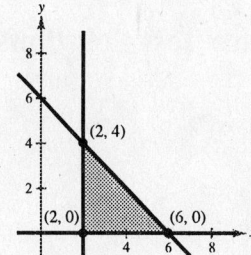

18. Line through $(0, 0)$ and $(0, 7)$:

$$x = 0$$

Line through $(0, 0)$ and $(2, 3)$:

$$y = \tfrac{3}{2}x \text{ or } 3x - 2y = 0$$

Line through $(0, 7)$ and $(2, 3)$:

$$y = -2x + 7 \text{ or } 2x + y = 7$$

Inequalities: $\begin{cases} x \geq 0 \\ 3x - 2y \leq 0 \\ 2x + y \leq 7 \end{cases}$

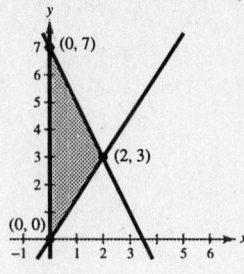

19. Vertices: $(0, 0), (0, 7), (6, 0), (3, 5)$

$$z = 30x + 26y$$

At $(0, 0)$: $z = 0$

At $(0, 7)$: $z = 182$

At $(6, 0)$: $z = 180$

At $(3, 5)$: $z = 220$

The maximum value of z occurs at $(3, 5)$ and is 220.

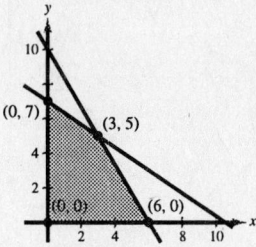

20. $x^2 + y^2 \leq 4$

$(x - 2)^2 + y^2 \geq 4$

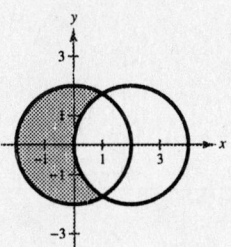

Chapter 8   Practice Test Solutions

1. $\begin{bmatrix} 1 & -2 & 4 \\ 3 & -5 & 9 \end{bmatrix}$

$-3R_1 + R_2 \rightarrow \begin{bmatrix} 1 & -2 & 4 \\ 0 & 1 & -3 \end{bmatrix}$

$2R_2 + R_1 \rightarrow \begin{bmatrix} 1 & 0 & -2 \\ 0 & 1 & -3 \end{bmatrix}$

2. $\begin{cases} 3x + 5y = 3 \\ 2x - y = -11 \end{cases}$

$\begin{bmatrix} 3 & 5 & \vdots & 3 \\ 2 & -1 & \vdots & -11 \end{bmatrix}$

$-R_2 + R_1 \rightarrow \begin{bmatrix} 1 & 6 & \vdots & 14 \\ 2 & -1 & \vdots & -11 \end{bmatrix}$

$-2R_1 + R_2 \rightarrow \begin{bmatrix} 1 & 6 & \vdots & 14 \\ 0 & -13 & \vdots & -39 \end{bmatrix}$

$-\tfrac{1}{13}R_2 \rightarrow \begin{bmatrix} 1 & 6 & \vdots & 14 \\ 0 & 1 & \vdots & 3 \end{bmatrix}$

$-6R_2 + R_1 \rightarrow \begin{bmatrix} 1 & 0 & \vdots & -4 \\ 0 & 1 & \vdots & 3 \end{bmatrix}$

$x = -4, y = 3$

Solution: $(-4, 3)$

3. $\begin{cases} 2x + 3y = -3 \\ 3x - 2y = 8 \\ x + y = 1 \end{cases}$

$$\begin{bmatrix} 2 & 3 & \vdots & -3 \\ 3 & 2 & \vdots & 8 \\ 1 & 1 & \vdots & 1 \end{bmatrix}$$

$$\begin{matrix} R_3 \to \\ \\ R_1 \to \end{matrix} \begin{bmatrix} 1 & 1 & \vdots & 1 \\ 3 & 2 & \vdots & 8 \\ 2 & 3 & \vdots & -3 \end{bmatrix}$$

$$\begin{matrix} \\ -3R_1 + R_2 \to \\ -2R_1 + R_3 \to \end{matrix} \begin{bmatrix} 1 & 1 & \vdots & 1 \\ 0 & -1 & \vdots & 5 \\ 0 & 1 & \vdots & -5 \end{bmatrix}$$

$$-R_2 \to \begin{bmatrix} 1 & 1 & \vdots & 1 \\ 0 & 1 & \vdots & -5 \\ 0 & 1 & \vdots & -5 \end{bmatrix}$$

$$\begin{matrix} -R_2 + R_1 \to \\ \\ -R_2 + R_3 \to \end{matrix} \begin{bmatrix} 1 & 0 & \vdots & 6 \\ 0 & 1 & \vdots & -5 \\ 0 & 0 & \vdots & 0 \end{bmatrix}$$

$x = 6, y = -5$

Solution: $(6, -5)$

4. $\begin{cases} x + 3z = -5 \\ 2x + y = 0 \\ 3x + y - z = -3 \end{cases}$

$$\begin{bmatrix} 1 & 0 & 3 & \vdots & -5 \\ 2 & 1 & 0 & \vdots & 0 \\ 3 & 1 & -1 & \vdots & 3 \end{bmatrix}$$

$$\begin{matrix} \\ -2R_1 + R_2 \to \\ -3R_1 + R_3 \to \end{matrix} \begin{bmatrix} 1 & 0 & 3 & \vdots & -5 \\ 0 & 1 & -6 & \vdots & 10 \\ 0 & 1 & -10 & \vdots & 18 \end{bmatrix}$$

$$\begin{matrix} \\ \\ -R_2 + R_3 \to \end{matrix} \begin{bmatrix} 1 & 0 & 3 & \vdots & -5 \\ 0 & 1 & -6 & \vdots & 10 \\ 0 & 0 & -4 & \vdots & 8 \end{bmatrix}$$

$$-\tfrac{1}{4}R_3 \to \begin{bmatrix} 1 & 0 & 3 & \vdots & -5 \\ 0 & 1 & -6 & \vdots & 10 \\ 0 & 0 & 1 & \vdots & -2 \end{bmatrix}$$

$$\begin{matrix} -3R_3 + R_1 \to \\ 6R_3 + R_2 \to \\ \\ \end{matrix} \begin{bmatrix} 1 & 0 & 0 & \vdots & 1 \\ 0 & 1 & 0 & \vdots & -2 \\ 0 & 0 & 1 & \vdots & -2 \end{bmatrix}$$

$x = 1, y = -2, z = -2$

Solution: $(1, -2, -2)$

5. $\begin{bmatrix} 1 & 4 & 5 \\ 2 & 0 & -3 \end{bmatrix} \begin{bmatrix} 1 & 6 \\ 0 & -7 \\ -1 & 2 \end{bmatrix} = \begin{bmatrix} (1)(1) + (4)(0) + (5)(-1) & (1)(6) + (4)(-7) + (5)(2) \\ (2)(1) + (0)(0) + (-3)(-1) & (2)(6) + (0)(-7) + (-3)(2) \end{bmatrix} = \begin{bmatrix} -4 & -12 \\ 5 & 6 \end{bmatrix}$

6. $3A - 5B = 3\begin{bmatrix} 9 & 1 \\ -4 & 8 \end{bmatrix} - 5\begin{bmatrix} 6 & -2 \\ 3 & 5 \end{bmatrix}$

$= \begin{bmatrix} 27 & 3 \\ -12 & 24 \end{bmatrix} - \begin{bmatrix} 30 & -10 \\ 15 & 25 \end{bmatrix}$

$= \begin{bmatrix} -3 & 13 \\ -27 & -1 \end{bmatrix}$

7. $f(A) = \begin{bmatrix} 3 & 0 \\ 7 & 1 \end{bmatrix}^2 - 7\begin{bmatrix} 3 & 0 \\ 7 & 1 \end{bmatrix} + 8\begin{bmatrix} 1 & 0 \\ 0 & 1 \end{bmatrix}$

$= \begin{bmatrix} 3 & 0 \\ 7 & 1 \end{bmatrix}\begin{bmatrix} 3 & 0 \\ 7 & 1 \end{bmatrix} - \begin{bmatrix} 21 & 0 \\ 49 & 7 \end{bmatrix} + \begin{bmatrix} 8 & 0 \\ 0 & 8 \end{bmatrix}$

$= \begin{bmatrix} 9 & 0 \\ 28 & 1 \end{bmatrix} - \begin{bmatrix} 21 & 0 \\ 49 & 7 \end{bmatrix} + \begin{bmatrix} 8 & 0 \\ 0 & 8 \end{bmatrix}$

$= \begin{bmatrix} -4 & 0 \\ -21 & 2 \end{bmatrix}$

8. False since

$(A + B)(A + 3B) = A(A + 3B) + B(A + 3B)$

$= A^2 + 3AB + BA + 3B^2$ and, in general, $AB \neq BA$.

9.
$$\begin{bmatrix} 1 & 2 & \vdots & 1 & 0 \\ 3 & 5 & \vdots & 0 & 1 \end{bmatrix}$$

$-3R_1 + R_2 \rightarrow \begin{bmatrix} 1 & 2 & \vdots & 1 & 0 \\ 0 & -1 & \vdots & -3 & 1 \end{bmatrix}$

$2R_2 + R_1 \rightarrow \begin{bmatrix} 1 & 0 & \vdots & -5 & 2 \\ 0 & -1 & \vdots & -3 & 1 \end{bmatrix}$

$-R_2 \rightarrow \begin{bmatrix} 1 & 0 & \vdots & -5 & 2 \\ 0 & 1 & \vdots & 3 & -1 \end{bmatrix}$

$A^{-1} = \begin{bmatrix} -5 & 2 \\ 3 & -1 \end{bmatrix}$

10.
$$\begin{bmatrix} 1 & 1 & 1 & \vdots & 1 & 0 & 0 \\ 3 & 6 & 5 & \vdots & 0 & 1 & 0 \\ 6 & 10 & 8 & \vdots & 0 & 0 & 1 \end{bmatrix}$$

$\begin{matrix} -3R_1 + R_2 \rightarrow \\ -6R_1 + R_3 \rightarrow \end{matrix} \begin{bmatrix} 1 & 1 & 1 & \vdots & 1 & 0 & 0 \\ 0 & 3 & 2 & \vdots & -3 & 1 & 0 \\ 0 & 4 & 2 & \vdots & -6 & 0 & 1 \end{bmatrix}$

$-R_3 + R_2 \rightarrow \begin{bmatrix} 1 & 1 & 1 & \vdots & 1 & 0 & 0 \\ 0 & -1 & 0 & \vdots & 3 & 1 & -1 \\ 0 & 4 & 2 & \vdots & -6 & 0 & 1 \end{bmatrix}$

$\begin{matrix} R_2 + R_1 \rightarrow \\ \\ 4R_2 + R_3 \rightarrow \end{matrix} \begin{bmatrix} 1 & 0 & 1 & \vdots & 4 & 1 & -1 \\ 0 & -1 & 0 & \vdots & 3 & 1 & -1 \\ 0 & 0 & 2 & \vdots & 6 & 4 & -3 \end{bmatrix}$

$\begin{matrix} -R_2 \rightarrow \\ \frac{1}{2}R_3 \rightarrow \end{matrix} \begin{bmatrix} 1 & 0 & 1 & \vdots & 4 & 1 & -1 \\ 0 & 1 & 0 & \vdots & -3 & -1 & 1 \\ 0 & 0 & 1 & \vdots & 3 & 2 & -\frac{3}{2} \end{bmatrix}$

$-R_3 + R_1 \rightarrow \begin{bmatrix} 1 & 0 & 0 & \vdots & 1 & -1 & \frac{1}{2} \\ 0 & 1 & 0 & \vdots & -3 & -1 & 1 \\ 0 & 0 & 1 & \vdots & 3 & 2 & -\frac{3}{2} \end{bmatrix}$

$A^{-1} = \begin{bmatrix} 1 & -1 & \frac{1}{2} \\ -3 & -1 & 1 \\ 3 & 2 & -\frac{3}{2} \end{bmatrix}$

11. (a) $\begin{cases} x + 2y = 4 \\ 3x + 5y = 1 \end{cases}$

$A = \begin{bmatrix} 1 & 2 \\ 3 & 5 \end{bmatrix}$

$A^{-1} = \dfrac{1}{5-6}\begin{bmatrix} 5 & -2 \\ -3 & 1 \end{bmatrix} = \begin{bmatrix} -5 & 2 \\ 3 & -1 \end{bmatrix}$

$\begin{bmatrix} x \\ y \end{bmatrix} = A^{-1}B = \begin{bmatrix} -5 & 2 \\ 3 & -1 \end{bmatrix}\begin{bmatrix} 4 \\ 1 \end{bmatrix} = \begin{bmatrix} -18 \\ 11 \end{bmatrix}$

$x = -18, y = 11$

Solution: $(-18, 11)$

(b) $\begin{cases} x + 2y = 3 \\ 3x + 5y = -2 \end{cases}$

Again, $A^{-1} = \begin{bmatrix} -5 & 2 \\ 3 & -1 \end{bmatrix}$.

$\begin{bmatrix} x \\ y \end{bmatrix} = A^{-1}B = \begin{bmatrix} -5 & 2 \\ 3 & -1 \end{bmatrix}\begin{bmatrix} 3 \\ -2 \end{bmatrix} = \begin{bmatrix} -19 \\ 11 \end{bmatrix}$

$x = -19, y = 11$

Solution: $(-19, 11)$

12. $\begin{vmatrix} 6 & -1 \\ 3 & 4 \end{vmatrix} = 24 - (-3) = 27$

13. $\begin{vmatrix} 1 & 3 & -1 \\ 5 & 9 & 0 \\ 6 & 2 & -5 \end{vmatrix} = -1\begin{vmatrix} 5 & 9 \\ 6 & 2 \end{vmatrix} - 5\begin{vmatrix} 1 & 3 \\ 5 & 9 \end{vmatrix} = -(-44) - 5(-6) = 74$

14. Expand along Row 2.

$\begin{vmatrix} 1 & 4 & 2 & 3 \\ 0 & 1 & -2 & 0 \\ 3 & 5 & -1 & 1 \\ 2 & 0 & 6 & 1 \end{vmatrix} = \begin{vmatrix} 1 & 2 & 3 \\ 3 & -1 & 1 \\ 2 & 6 & 1 \end{vmatrix} + 2\begin{vmatrix} 1 & 4 & 3 \\ 3 & 5 & 1 \\ 2 & 0 & 1 \end{vmatrix}$

$= 51 + 2(-29) = -7$

15.
$$\begin{vmatrix} 6 & 4 & 3 & 0 & 6 \\ 0 & 5 & 1 & 4 & 8 \\ 0 & 0 & 2 & 7 & 3 \\ 0 & 0 & 0 & 9 & 2 \\ 0 & 0 & 0 & 0 & 1 \end{vmatrix} = 6 \begin{vmatrix} 5 & 1 & 4 & 8 \\ 0 & 2 & 7 & 3 \\ 0 & 0 & 9 & 2 \\ 0 & 0 & 0 & 1 \end{vmatrix} = 6(5) \begin{vmatrix} 2 & 7 & 3 \\ 0 & 9 & 2 \\ 0 & 0 & 1 \end{vmatrix} = 6(5)(2) \begin{vmatrix} 9 & 2 \\ 0 & 1 \end{vmatrix} = 6(5)(2)(9) = 540$$

16. Area $= \dfrac{1}{2} \begin{vmatrix} 0 & 7 & 1 \\ 5 & 0 & 1 \\ 3 & 9 & 1 \end{vmatrix} = \dfrac{1}{2}(31) = \dfrac{31}{2}$

17. $\begin{vmatrix} x & y & 1 \\ 2 & 7 & 1 \\ -1 & 4 & 1 \end{vmatrix} = 3x - 3y + 15 = 0$ or, equivalently, $x - y + 5 = 0$

18. $x = \dfrac{\begin{vmatrix} 4 & -7 \\ 11 & 5 \end{vmatrix}}{\begin{vmatrix} 6 & -7 \\ 2 & 5 \end{vmatrix}} = \dfrac{97}{44}$

19. $z = \dfrac{\begin{vmatrix} 3 & 0 & 1 \\ 0 & 1 & 3 \\ 1 & -1 & 2 \end{vmatrix}}{\begin{vmatrix} 3 & 0 & 1 \\ 0 & 1 & 4 \\ 1 & -1 & 0 \end{vmatrix}} = \dfrac{14}{11}$

20. $y = \dfrac{\begin{vmatrix} 721.4 & 33.77 \\ 45.9 & 19.85 \end{vmatrix}}{\begin{vmatrix} 721.4 & -29.1 \\ 45.9 & 105.6 \end{vmatrix}} = \dfrac{12,769.747}{77,515.530} \approx 0.1647$

Chapter 9   Practice Test Solutions

1. $a_n = \dfrac{2n}{(n+2)!}$

$a_1 = \dfrac{2(1)}{3!} = \dfrac{2}{6} = \dfrac{1}{3}$

$a_2 = \dfrac{2(2)}{4!} = \dfrac{4}{24} = \dfrac{1}{6}$

$a_3 = \dfrac{2(3)}{5!} = \dfrac{6}{120} = \dfrac{1}{20}$

$a_4 = \dfrac{2(4)}{6!} = \dfrac{8}{720} = \dfrac{1}{90}$

$a_5 = \dfrac{2(5)}{7!} = \dfrac{10}{5040} = \dfrac{1}{504}$

Terms: $\dfrac{1}{3}, \dfrac{1}{6}, \dfrac{1}{20}, \dfrac{1}{90}, \dfrac{1}{504}$

2. $a_n = \dfrac{n+3}{3^n}$

3. $\displaystyle\sum_{i=1}^{6} (2i - 1) = 1 + 3 + 5 + 7 + 9 + 11 = 36$

4. $a_1 = 23, \ d = -2$

$a_2 = 23 + (-2) = 21$

$a_3 = 21 + (-2) = 19$

$a_4 = 19 + (-2) = 17$

$a_5 = 17 + (-2) = 15$

Terms: 23, 21, 19, 17, 15

5. $a_1 = 12, d = 3, n = 50$

$a_n = a_1 + (n-1)d$

$a_{50} = 12 + (50-1)3 = 159$

6. $a_1 = 1$

$a_{200} = 200$

$S_n = \dfrac{n}{2}(a_1 + a_n)$

$S_{200} = \dfrac{200}{2}(1 + 200) = 20{,}100$

7. $a_1 = 7, \ r = 2$

$a_2 = 7(2) = 14$

$a_3 = 7(2)^2 = 28$

$a_4 = 7(2)^3 = 56$

$a_5 = 7(2)^4 = 112$

Terms: 7, 14, 28, 56, 112

8. $\displaystyle\sum_{n=1}^{10} 6\left(\frac{2}{3}\right)^{n-1}, a_1 = 6, r = \frac{2}{3}, n = 10$

$$S_n = \frac{a_1(1 - r^n)}{1 - r} = \frac{6\left[1 - \left(\frac{2}{3}\right)^{10}\right]}{1 - \frac{2}{3}} = 18\left(1 - \frac{1024}{59{,}049}\right) = \frac{116{,}050}{6561} \approx 17.6879$$

9. $\displaystyle\sum_{n=0}^{\infty} (0.03)^n = \sum_{n=1}^{\infty} (0.03)^{n-1}, a_1 = 1, r = 0.03$

$$S = \frac{a_1}{1 - r} = \frac{1}{1 - 0.03} = \frac{1}{0.97} = \frac{100}{97} \approx 1.0309$$

10. For $n = 1, 1 = \dfrac{1(1 + 1)}{2}$.

Assume that $S_k = 1 + 2 + 3 + 4 + \cdots + k = \dfrac{k(k + 1)}{2}$.

Then $S_{k+1} = 1 + 2 + 3 + 4 + \cdots + k + (k + 1) = \dfrac{k(k + 1)}{2} + k + 1$

$$= \frac{k(k + 1)}{2} + \frac{2(k + 1)}{2}$$

$$= \frac{(k + 1)(k + 2)}{2}.$$

Thus, by the principle of mathematical induction, $1 + 2 + 3 + 4 + \cdots + n = \dfrac{n(n + 1)}{2}$ for all integers $n \geq 1$.

11. For $n = 4, 4! > 2^4$. Assume that $k! > 2^k$.

Then $(k + 1)! = (k + 1)(k!) > (k + 1)2^k > 2 \cdot 2^k = 2^{k+1}$.

Thus, by the extended principle of mathematical induction, $n! > 2^n$ for all integers $n \geq 4$.

12. $_{13}C_4 = \dfrac{13!}{(13-4)!4!} = 715$

13. $(x+3)^5 = x^5 + 5x^4(3) + 10x^3(3)^2 + 10x^2(3)^3 + 5x(3)^4 + (3)^5$

$\qquad\quad = x^5 + 15x^4 + 90x^3 + 270x^2 + 405x + 243$

14. $-_{12}C_5 x^7(2)^5 = -25{,}344x^7$

15. $_{30}P_4 = \dfrac{30!}{(30-4)!} = 657{,}720$

16. $6! = 720$ ways

17. $_{12}P_3 = 1320$

18. $P(2) + P(3) + P(4) = \dfrac{1}{36} + \dfrac{2}{36} + \dfrac{3}{36}$

$\qquad\qquad\qquad\qquad\;\; = \dfrac{6}{36} = \dfrac{1}{6}$

19. $P(K, B10) = \dfrac{4}{52} \cdot \dfrac{2}{51} = \dfrac{2}{663}$

20. Let A = probability of no faulty units.

$\quad P(A) = \left(\dfrac{997}{1000}\right)^{50} \approx 0.8605$

$\quad P(A') = 1 - P(A) \approx 0.1395$

Chapter 10   Practice Test Solutions

1. $3x + 4y = 12 \Rightarrow y = -\dfrac{3}{4}x + 3 \Rightarrow m_1 = -\dfrac{3}{4}$

$4x - 3y = 12 \Rightarrow y = \dfrac{4}{3}x - 4 \Rightarrow m_2 = \dfrac{4}{3}$

$\tan\theta = \left| \dfrac{\frac{4}{3} - \left(-\frac{3}{4}\right)}{1 + \left(\frac{4}{3}\right)\left(-\frac{3}{4}\right)} \right| = \left| \dfrac{\frac{25}{12}}{0} \right|$

Since $\tan\theta$ is undefined, the lines are perpendicular
(note that $m_2 = -1/m_1$)   and $\theta = 90°$.

2. $x_1 = 5, x_2 = -9, A = 3, B = -7, C = -21$

$d = \dfrac{|3(5) + (-7)(-9) + (-21)|}{\sqrt{3^2 + (-7)^2}} = \dfrac{57}{\sqrt{58}} \approx 7.484$

3. $x^2 - 6x - 4y + 1 = 0$

$\qquad x^2 - 6x + 9 = 4y - 1 + 9$

$\qquad\qquad (x - 3)^2 = 4y + 8$

$\qquad\qquad (x - 3)^2 = 4(1)(y + 2) \Rightarrow p = 1$

Vertex: $(3, -2)$

Focus: $(3, -1)$

Directrix: $y = -3$

4. Vertex: $(2, -5)$

Focus: $(2, -6)$

Vertical axis; opens downward with $p = -1$

$\qquad\qquad (x - h)^2 = 4p(y - k)$

$\qquad\qquad (x - 2)^2 = 4(-1)(y + 5)$

$\qquad\quad x^2 - 4x + 4 = -4y - 20$

$x^2 - 4x + 4y + 24 = 0$

5. $\qquad x^2 + 4y^2 - 2x + 32y + 61 = 0$

$(x^2 - 2x + 1) + 4(y^2 + 8y + 16) = -61 + 1 + 64$

$\qquad\quad (x - 1)^2 + 4(y + 4)^2 = 4$

$\qquad\quad \dfrac{(x - 1)^2}{4} + \dfrac{(y + 4)^2}{1} = 1$

$a = 2, b = 1, c = \sqrt{3}$

Horizontal major axis

Center: $(1, -4)$

Foci: $\left(1 \pm \sqrt{3}, -4\right)$

Vertices: $(3, -4), (-1, -4)$

Eccentricity: $e = \dfrac{\sqrt{3}}{2}$

6. Vertices: $(0, \pm 6)$

Eccentricity: $e = \dfrac{1}{2}$

Center: $(0, 0)$

Vertical major axis

$a = 6, e = \dfrac{c}{a} = \dfrac{c}{6} = \dfrac{1}{2} \Rightarrow c = 3$

$b^2 = (6)^2 - (3)^2 = 27$

$\dfrac{x^2}{27} + \dfrac{y^2}{36} = 1$

7. $\qquad 16y^2 - x^2 - 6x - 128y + 231 = 0$

$16(y^2 - 8y + 16) - (x^2 + 6x + 9) = -231 + 256 - 9$

$\qquad\quad 16(y - 4)^2 - (x + 3)^2 = 16$

$\qquad\quad \dfrac{(y - 4)^2}{1} - \dfrac{(x + 3)^2}{16} = 1$

$a = 1, b = 4, c = \sqrt{17}$

Center: $(-3, 4)$

Vertical transverse axis

Vertices: $(-3, 5), (-3, 3)$

Foci: $\left(-3, 4 \pm \sqrt{17}\right)$

Asymptotes: $y = 4 \pm \dfrac{1}{4}(x + 3)$

8. Vertices: $(\pm 3, 2)$

Foci: $(\pm 5, 2)$

Center: $(0, 2)$

Horizontal transverse axis

$a = 3, c = 5, b = 4$

$\dfrac{(x - 0)^2}{9} - \dfrac{(y - 2)^2}{16} = 1$

$\dfrac{x^2}{9} - \dfrac{(y - 2)^2}{16} = 1$

9. $5x^2 + 2xy + 5y^2 - 10 = 0$

$A = 5, B = 2, C = 5$

$\cot 2\theta = \dfrac{5 - 5}{2} = 0$

$2\theta = \dfrac{\pi}{2} \implies \theta = \dfrac{\pi}{4}$

$x = x' \cos \dfrac{\pi}{4} - y' \sin \dfrac{\pi}{4}$ $\qquad\qquad$ $x = x' \cos \dfrac{\pi}{4} + y' \sin \dfrac{\pi}{4}$

$= \dfrac{x' - y'}{\sqrt{2}}$ $\qquad\qquad\qquad\qquad$ $= \dfrac{x' + y'}{\sqrt{2}}$

$$5\left(\dfrac{x' - y'}{\sqrt{2}}\right)^2 + 2\left(\dfrac{x' - y'}{\sqrt{2}}\right)\left(\dfrac{x' + y'}{\sqrt{2}}\right) + 5\left(\dfrac{x' + y'}{\sqrt{2}}\right)^2 - 10 = 0$$

$$\dfrac{5(x')^2}{2} - \dfrac{10x'y'}{2} + \dfrac{5(y')^2}{2} + (x')^2 - (y')^2 + \dfrac{5(x')^2}{2} + \dfrac{10x'y'}{2} + \dfrac{5(y')^2}{2} - 10 = 0$$

$$6(x')^2 + 4(y')^2 - 10 = 0$$

$$\dfrac{3(x')^2}{5} + \dfrac{2(y')^2}{5} = 1$$

$$\dfrac{(x')^2}{5/3} + \dfrac{(y')^2}{5/2} = 1$$

Ellipse centered at the origin

10. (a) $6x^2 - 2xy + y^2 = 0$

$A = 6, B = -2, C = 1$

$B^2 - 4AC = (-2)^2 - 4(6)(1) = -20 < 0$

Ellipse

(b) $x^2 + 4xy + 4y^2 - x - y + 17 = 0$

$A = 1, B = 4, C = 4$

$B^2 - 4AC = (4)^2 - 4(1)(4) = 0$

Parabola

11. Polar: $\left(\sqrt{2}, \dfrac{3\pi}{4}\right)$

$x = \sqrt{2} \cos \dfrac{3\pi}{4} = \sqrt{2}\left(-\dfrac{1}{\sqrt{2}}\right) = -1$

$y = \sqrt{2} \sin \dfrac{3\pi}{4} = \sqrt{2}\left(\dfrac{1}{\sqrt{2}}\right) = 1$

Rectangular: $(-1, 1)$

12. Rectangular: $\left(\sqrt{3}, -1\right)$

$r = \pm\sqrt{\left(\sqrt{3}\right)^2 + (-1)^2} = \pm 2$

$\tan \theta = \dfrac{\sqrt{3}}{-1} = -\sqrt{3}$

$\theta = \dfrac{2\pi}{3}$ or $\theta = \dfrac{5\pi}{3}$

Polar: $\left(-2, \dfrac{2\pi}{3}\right)$ or $\left(2, \dfrac{5\pi}{3}\right)$

13. Rectangular: $4x - 3y = 12$

Polar: $4r \cos \theta - 3r \sin \theta = 12$

$r(4 \cos \theta - 3 \sin \theta) = 12$

$$r = \dfrac{12}{4 \cos \theta - 3 \sin \theta}$$

14. Polar: $r = 5 \cos \theta$

$\qquad r^2 = 5r \cos \theta$

Rectangular: $\qquad x^2 + y^2 = 5x$

$\qquad\qquad x^2 + y^2 - 5x = 0$

15. $r = 1 - \cos \theta$

Cardioid

Symmetry: Polar axis

Maximum value of $|r|$: $r = 2$ when $\theta = \pi$.

Zero of r: $r = 0$ when $\theta = 0$

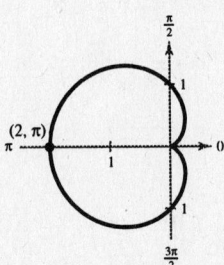

θ	0	$\dfrac{\pi}{2}$	π	$\dfrac{3\pi}{2}$
r	0	1	2	1

16. $r = 5 \sin 2\theta$

Rose curve with four petals

Symmetry: Polar axis, $\theta = \dfrac{\pi}{2}$, and pole

Maximum value of $|r|$: $|r| = 5$ when $\theta = \dfrac{\pi}{4}, \dfrac{3\pi}{4}, \dfrac{5\pi}{4}, \dfrac{7\pi}{4}$

Zeros of r: $r = 0$ when $\theta = 0, \dfrac{\pi}{2}, \pi, \dfrac{3\pi}{2}$

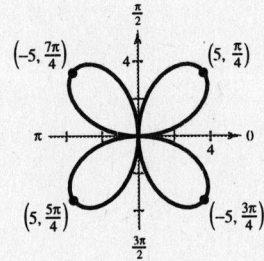

17. $r = \dfrac{3}{6 - \cos \theta}$

$r = \dfrac{\frac{1}{2}}{1 - \frac{1}{6} \cos \theta}$

$e = \dfrac{1}{6} < 1$, so the graph is an ellipse.

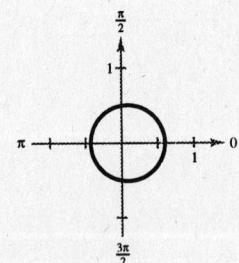

θ	0	$\dfrac{\pi}{2}$	π	$\dfrac{3\pi}{2}$
r	$\dfrac{3}{5}$	$\dfrac{1}{2}$	$\dfrac{3}{7}$	$\dfrac{1}{2}$

18. Parabola

Vertex: $\left(6, \dfrac{\pi}{2}\right)$

Focus: $(0, 0)$

$e = 1$

$r = \dfrac{ep}{1 + e\sin\theta}$

$r = \dfrac{p}{1 + \sin\theta}$

$6 = \dfrac{p}{1 + \sin(\pi/2)}$

$6 = \dfrac{p}{2}$

$12 = p$

$r = \dfrac{12}{1 + \sin\theta}$

19. $x = 3 - 2\sin\theta,\ y = 1 + 5\cos\theta$

$\dfrac{x - 3}{-2} = \sin\theta,\ \dfrac{y - 1}{5} = \cos\theta$

$\left(\dfrac{x - 3}{-2}\right)^2 + \left(\dfrac{y - 1}{5}\right)^2 = 1$

$\dfrac{(x - 3)^2}{4} + \dfrac{(y - 1)^2}{25} = 1$

20. $x = e^{2t},\ y = e^{4t}$

$x > 0,\ y > 0$

$y = (e^{2t})^2 = (x)^2 = x^2,\ x > 0,\ y > 0$

PART II

Chapter P   Chapter Test

1. $-\frac{10}{3} = -3\frac{1}{3}$

$-|-4| = -4$

$-\frac{10}{3} > -|-4|$

2. $\left|-5.4 - 3\frac{3}{4}\right| = 9.15$

3. (a) $27\left(-\frac{2}{3}\right) = -18$

(b) $\dfrac{5}{18} \div \dfrac{15}{8} = \dfrac{5}{18} \cdot \dfrac{8}{15} = \dfrac{4}{27}$

4. (a) $\left(-\dfrac{3}{5}\right)^3 = -\dfrac{27}{125}$

(b) $\left(\dfrac{3^2}{2}\right)^{-3} = \left(\dfrac{2}{9}\right)^3 = \dfrac{8}{729}$

5. (a) $\sqrt{5} \cdot \sqrt{125} = \sqrt{625} = 25$

(b) $\dfrac{\sqrt{72}}{\sqrt{2}} = \sqrt{36} = 6$

6. (a) $\dfrac{5.4 \times 10^8}{3 \times 10^3} = \dfrac{5.4}{3} \times 10^{8-3} = 1.8 \times 10^5$

(b) $(3 \times 10^4)^3 = 27 \times 10^{12} = 2.7 \times 10^{13}$

7. (a) $3z^2(2z^3)^2 = 3z^2(4z^6) = 12z^8$

(b) $(u - 2)^{-4}(u - 2)^{-3} = (u - 2)^{-7} = \dfrac{1}{(u-2)^7}$

(c) $\left(\dfrac{x^{-2}y^2}{3}\right)^{-1} = \dfrac{x^2y^{-2}}{3^{-1}} = \dfrac{3x^2}{y^2}$

8. (a) $9z\sqrt{8z} - 3\sqrt{2z^3} = 18z\sqrt{2z} - 3z\sqrt{2z} = 15z\sqrt{2z}$

(b) $-5\sqrt{16y} + 10\sqrt{y} = -20\sqrt{y} + 10\sqrt{y} = -10\sqrt{y}$

(c) $\sqrt[3]{\dfrac{16}{v^5}} = \dfrac{2\sqrt[3]{2}}{v\sqrt[3]{v^2}} = \dfrac{2}{v}\sqrt[3]{\dfrac{2}{v^2}}$

9. $(x^2 + 3) - [3x + (8 - x^2)] = x^2 + 3 - 3x - 8 + x^2$

$= 2x^2 - 3x - 5$

10. $\left(x + \sqrt{5}\right)\left(x - \sqrt{5}\right) = x^2 - \left(\sqrt{5}\right)^2 = x^2 - 5$

11. (a) $2x^4 - 3x^3 - 2x^2 = x^2(2x^2 - 3x - 2)$

$= x^2(2x + 1)(x - 2)$

(b) $x^3 + 2x^2 - 4x - 8 = x^2(x + 2) - 4(x + 2)$

$= (x + 2)(x^2 - 4)$

$= (x + 2)(x + 2)(x - 2)$

$= (x + 2)^2(x - 2)$

12. (a) $\dfrac{16}{\sqrt[3]{16}} = \dfrac{16}{\sqrt[3]{16}} \cdot \dfrac{\sqrt[3]{4}}{\sqrt[3]{4}} = \dfrac{16\sqrt[3]{4}}{\sqrt[3]{64}} = \dfrac{16\sqrt[3]{4}}{4} = 4\sqrt[3]{4}$

(b) $\dfrac{6}{1 - \sqrt{3}} = \dfrac{6}{1 - \sqrt{3}} \cdot \dfrac{1 + \sqrt{3}}{1 + \sqrt{3}} = \dfrac{6\left(1 + \sqrt{3}\right)}{1 - 3} = -3\left(1 + \sqrt{3}\right)$

13. $\frac{2}{3}(x - 1) + \frac{1}{4}x = 10$

$12\left[\frac{2}{3}(x - 1) + \frac{1}{4}x\right] = 12(10)$

$8(x - 1) + 3x = 120$

$8x - 8 + 3x = 120$

$11x = 128$

$x = \frac{128}{11}$

14. $(x - 3)(x + 2) = 14$

$x^2 - x - 6 = 14$

$x^2 - x - 20 = 0$

$(x + 4)(x - 5) = 0$

$x = -4 \quad \text{or} \quad x = 5$

15. $\dfrac{x - 2}{x + 2} + \dfrac{4}{x + 2} + 4 = 0$

$\dfrac{x + 2}{x + 2} = -4$

$1 \neq -4 \Rightarrow \text{No solution}$

16. $x^4 + x^2 - 6 = 0$

$(x^2 - 2)(x^2 + 3) = 0$

$x^2 = 2 \quad \Rightarrow x = \pm\sqrt{2}$

$x^2 = -3 \Rightarrow x = \pm\sqrt{3}i$

17. $2\sqrt{x} - \sqrt{2x + 1} = 1$

$-\sqrt{2x + 1} = 1 - 2\sqrt{x}$

$\left(-\sqrt{2x + 1}\right)^2 = \left(1 - 2\sqrt{x}\right)^2$

$2x + 1 = 1 - 4\sqrt{x} + 4x$

$-2x = -4\sqrt{x}$

$x = 2\sqrt{x}$

$x^2 = 4x$

$x^2 - 4x = 0$

$x(x - 4) = 0$

$x = 0 \quad \text{or} \quad x = 4$

Only $x = 4$ is a solution to the original equation.
$x = 0$ is extraneous.

18. $|3x - 1| = 7$

$3x - 1 = 7 \quad \text{or} \quad 3x - 1 = -7$

$3x = 8 \qquad\qquad 3x = -6$

$x = \frac{8}{3} \qquad\qquad x = -2$

19. $-3 \leq 2(x + 4) < 14$

$-3 \leq 2x + 8 < 14$

$-11 \leq 2x < 6$

$-\frac{11}{2} \leq x < 3$

20. $\dfrac{2}{x} > \dfrac{5}{x + 6}$

$\dfrac{2}{x} - \dfrac{5}{x + 6} > 0$

$\dfrac{2(x + 6) - 5x}{x(x + 6)} > 0$

$\dfrac{-3x + 12}{x(x + 6)} > 0$

$\dfrac{-3(x - 4)}{x(x + 6)} > 0$

Critical numbers: $x = 4, x = 0, x = -6$

Test intervals: $(-\infty, -6), (-6, 0), (0, 4), (4, \infty)$

Test: Is $\dfrac{-3(x - 4)}{x(x + 6)} > 0$?

Solution set: $(-\infty, -6) \cup (0, 4)$

In inequality notation: $x < -6 \quad \text{or} \quad 0 < x < 4$

21.
$$2x^2 + 5x > 12$$
$$2x^2 + 5x - 12 > 0$$
$$(2x - 3)(x + 4) > 0$$

Critical numbers: $x = \frac{3}{2}, x = -4$

Test intervals: $(-\infty, -4), \left(-4, \frac{3}{2}\right), \left(\frac{3}{2}, \infty\right)$

Test: Is $(2x - 3)(x + 4) > 0$?

Solution set: $(-\infty, -4) \cup \left(\frac{3}{2}, \infty\right)$

In inequality notation: $x < -4$ or $x > 3/2$

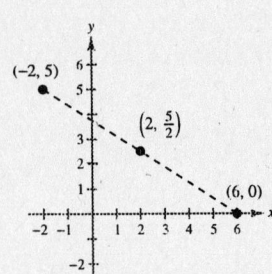

22. $|x - 15| \geq 5$

$$x - 15 \leq -5 \quad \text{or} \quad x - 15 \geq 5$$
$$x \leq 10 \qquad\qquad x \geq 20$$

23. $\dfrac{3x^2 + 5x - 2}{2x^2 + x - 6} = \dfrac{(3x - 1)(x + 2)}{(2x - 3)(x + 2)}$

$$= \frac{3x - 1}{2x - 3}, \quad x \neq -2$$

24. Part completed by both workers:

$$\frac{x}{4} + \frac{2x}{7} = \frac{7x + 8x}{28}$$
$$= \frac{15x}{28} = \frac{15}{28}x$$

Part completed by the first worker: $\dfrac{x}{4} = \dfrac{1}{4}x$

25.

Distance: $d = \sqrt{(-2 - 6)^2 + (5 - 0)^2}$

$$= \sqrt{64 + 25}$$
$$= \sqrt{89} \text{ miles}$$

Midpoint: $\left(\dfrac{-2 + 6}{2}, \dfrac{5 + 0}{2}\right) = \left(2, \dfrac{5}{2}\right)$

Chapter 1   Chapter Test

1. $y = 4 - \frac{3}{4}x$

No axis or origin symmetry

x-intercept: $\left(\frac{16}{3}, 0\right)$

y-intercept: $(0, 4)$

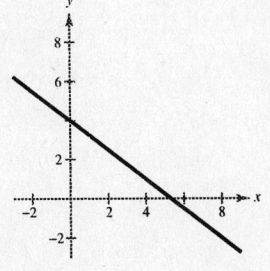

2. $y = 4 - \frac{3}{4}|x|$

y-axis symmetry

x-intercepts: $\left(\pm \frac{16}{3}, 0\right)$

y-intercept: $(0, 4)$

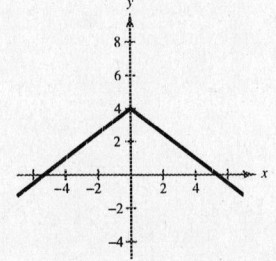

3. $y = 4 - (x - 2)^2$

Parabola; vertex: $(2, 4)$

No axis or origin symmetry

x-intercepts: $(0, 0)$ and $(4, 0)$

$$0 = 4 - (x - 2)^2$$
$$(x - 2)^2 = 4$$
$$x - 2 = \pm 2$$
$$x = 2 \pm 2$$
$$x = 4 \quad \text{or} \quad x = 0$$

y-intercept: $(0, 0)$

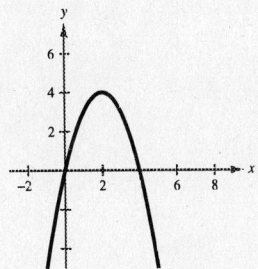

4. $m = \dfrac{9 - (-3)}{-4 - 2} = -2$

$$y - (-3) = -2(x - 2)$$
$$y + 3 = -2x + 4$$
$$y = -2x + 1$$
$$2x + y - 1 = 0$$

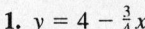

5. $m = \dfrac{-6 - 0.8}{7 - 3} = -1.7$

$$y - (-6) = -1.7(x - 7)$$
$$y + 6 = -1.7x + 11.9$$
$$y = -1.7x + 5.9$$
$$10y = -17x + 59$$
$$17x + 10y - 59 = 0$$

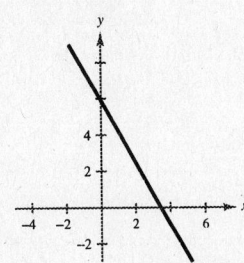

6. $-4x + 7y = -5$

$$7y = 4x - 5$$

$$y = \tfrac{4}{7}x - \tfrac{5}{7} \Rightarrow m_1 = \tfrac{4}{7}$$

(a) Parallel line: $m_2 = \tfrac{4}{7}$

$$y - 8 = \tfrac{4}{7}(x - 3)$$

$$7y - 56 = 4x - 12$$

$$-4x + 7y = 44$$

$$4x - 7y + 44 = 0$$

(b) Perpendicular line: $m_2 = -\tfrac{7}{4}$

$$y - 8 = -\tfrac{7}{4}(x - 3)$$

$$4y - 32 = -7x + 21$$

$$7x + 4y - 53 = 0$$

7. $f(x) = \dfrac{\sqrt{x + 9}}{x^2 - 81}$

(a) $f(7) = \dfrac{4}{-32} = -\dfrac{1}{8}$

(b) $f(-5) = \dfrac{2}{-56} = -\dfrac{1}{28}$

(c) $f(x - 9) = \dfrac{\sqrt{x}}{(x - 9)^2 - 81} = \dfrac{\sqrt{x}}{x^2 - 18x}$

8. $f(x) = \sqrt{100 - x^2}$

Domain:

$100 - x^2 \geq 0 \Rightarrow -10 \leq x \leq 10 \quad \text{or} \quad [-10, 10]$

9. $f(x) = |-x + 6| + 2$

Domain: All real numbers   or $(-\infty, \infty)$

10. $f(x) = 2x^6 + 5x^4 - x^2$

(a) $2x^6 + 5x^4 - x^2 = 0$

$x^2(2x^4 + 5x^2 - 1) = 0$

From the graph we have the following zeros:

$x = 0, x \approx \pm 0.431$

(b)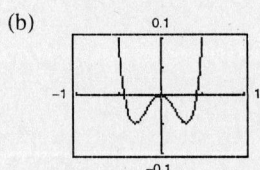

(c) decreasing on $(-\infty, -0.31), (0, 0.31)$

increasing on $(-0.31, 0), (0.31, \infty)$

(d) $f(-x) = f(x)$ so f is even.

11. $f(x) = 4x\sqrt{3 - x}$

(a) $4x\sqrt{3 - x} = 0$

$x = 0 \quad \text{or} \quad x = 3$

(b)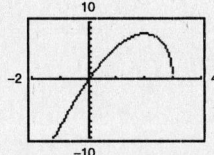

(c) decreasing on $(2, 3)$

increasing on $(-\infty, 2)$

(d) The function is neither odd nor even.

12. $f(x) = |x + 5|$

(a) $|x + 5| = 0$

$x + 5 = 0$

$x = -5$

(b)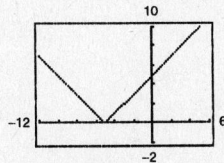

(c) decreasing on $(-\infty, -5)$

increasing on $(-5, \infty)$

(d) The function is neither odd nor even.

13. $f(x) = \begin{cases} 3x + 7, x \le -3 \\ 4x^2 - 1, x > -3 \end{cases}$

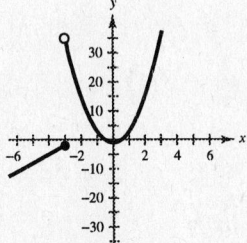

14. $h(x) = -x^3 - 7$

Common function: $f(x) = x^3$

Transformation: Reflection in the x-axis and a vertical shift 7 units downward.

15. $h(x) = -\sqrt{x + 5} + 8$

Common function: $f(x) = \sqrt{x}$

Transformation: Reflection in the x-axis, a horizontal shift 5 units to the left, and a vertical shift 8 units upward.

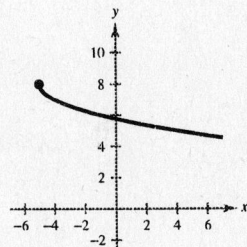

16. $h(x) = \frac{1}{4}|x + 1| - 3$

Common function: $f(x) = |x|$

Transformation: Vertical shrink, horizontal shift 1 unit to the left, vertical shift 3 units down.

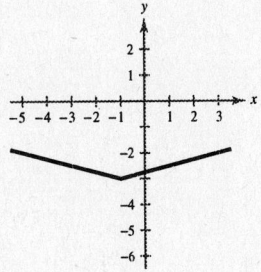

17. $(f + g)(2) = f(2) + g(2) = [3(2)^2 - 7] + [-(2)^2 - 4(2) + 5]$

$= 5 + (-7) = -2$

18. $(f - g)(-3) = f(-3) - g(-3)$

$= [3(-3)^2 - 7] - [-(-3)^2 - 4(-3) + 5]$

$= 20 - 8$

$= 12$

19. $(fg)(0) = f(0)g(0)$

$= [3(0)^2 - 7][-(0)^2 - 4(0) + 5]$

$= (-7)(5)$

$= -35$

20. $(g \circ f)(-1) = g(f(-1)) = g(3(-1)^2 - 7) = g(-4)$

$\qquad\qquad = -(-4)^2 - 4(-4) + 5$

$\qquad\qquad = 5$

21. $f(x) = x^3 + 8$

Since f is one-to-one, f has an inverse.

$$y = x^3 + 8$$

$$x = y^3 + 8$$

$$x - 8 = y^3$$

$$\sqrt[3]{x - 8} = y$$

$$f^{-1}(x) = \sqrt[3]{x - 8}$$

22. $f(x) = |x^2 - 3| + 6$

Since f is not on-to-one, f does not have an inverse.

23. $f(x) = \dfrac{3x\sqrt{x}}{8} = \dfrac{3}{8}x^{3/2}$

Since f is one-to-one, f has an inverse.

$$y = \frac{3}{8}x^{3/2}$$

$$x = \frac{3}{8}y^{3/2}$$

$$\frac{8}{3}x = y^{3/2}$$

$$\left(\frac{8}{3}x\right)^{2/3} = y, x \geq 0$$

$$f^{-1}(x) = \left(\frac{8}{3}x\right)^{2/3}, x \geq 0$$

24. $v = k\sqrt{s}$

$\qquad 24 = k\sqrt{16}$

$\qquad 24 = k(4)$

$\qquad\ \ 6 = k$

$\qquad\ \ v = 6\sqrt{s}$

25. $\quad A = kxy$

$\quad 500 = k(15)(8)$

$\quad 500 = k(120)$

$\quad \frac{25}{6} = k$

$\quad\ \ A = \frac{25}{6}xy$

26. $b = \dfrac{k}{a}$

$\quad 32 = \dfrac{k}{1.5}$

$\quad 48 = k$

$\quad\ \ b = \dfrac{48}{a}$

27. $(6, 58), (10, 78)$

$$m = \frac{78 - 58}{10 - 6} = \frac{20}{4} = 5$$

$$C - 58 = 5(x - 6)$$

$$C = 5x - 30 + 58$$

$$C = 5x + 28$$

When $x = 25$: $C = \$153$

Chapter 2   Chapter Test

1. $f(x) = x^2$

    (a) $g(x) = 2 - x^2$

       Reflection in the x-axis followed by a vertical shift two units upward

    (b) $g(x) = \left(x - \frac{3}{2}\right)^2$

       Horizontal shift $\frac{3}{2}$ units to the right

2. Vertex: $(3, -6)$

    $y = a(x - 3)^2 - 6$

    Point on the graph: $(0, 3)$

    $3 = a(0 - 3)^2 - 6$

    $9 = 9a \Longrightarrow a = 1$

    Thus, $y = (x - 3)^2 - 6$.

3. (a) $y = -\frac{1}{20}x^2 + 3x + 5$

$$= -\frac{1}{20}(x^2 - 60x + 900 - 900) + 5$$

$$= -\frac{1}{20}[(x - 30)^2 - 900] + 5$$

$$= -\frac{1}{20}(x - 30)^2 + 50$$

Vertex: $(30, 50)$

The maximum height is 50 feet.

    (b) $-\frac{1}{20}(x - 30)^2 + 50 = 0$

$$-\frac{1}{20}(x - 30)^2 = -50$$

$$(x - 30)^2 = 1000$$

$$x - 30 = \pm\sqrt{1000}$$

$$x = 30 \pm \sqrt{1000}$$

Choosing the positive value for x, the ball travels $x = 30 + \sqrt{1000} \approx 61.62$ feet.

4. $h(t) = -\frac{3}{4}t^5 + 2t^2$

The degree is odd and the leading coefficient is negative. The graph rises to the left and falls to the right.

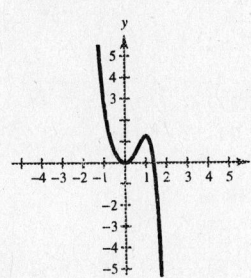

5.

$$
\begin{array}{r}
3x + \dfrac{x - 1}{x^2 + 1} \\[4pt]
x^2 + 0x + 1\ \overline{)\ 3x^3 + 0x^2 + 4x - 1} \\
\underline{3x^3 + 0x^2 + 3x} \\
x - 1
\end{array}
$$

Thus, $\dfrac{3x^3 + 4x - 1}{x^2 + 1} = 3x + \dfrac{x - 1}{x^2 + 1}$.

6.
$$
\begin{array}{r|rrrrr}
2 & 2 & 0 & -5 & 0 & -3 \\
  &   & 4 & 8 & 6 & 12 \\
\hline
  & 2 & 4 & 3 & 6 & 9
\end{array}
$$

Thus, $\dfrac{2x^4 - 5x^2 - 3}{x - 2} = 2x^3 + 4x^2 + 3x + 6 + \dfrac{9}{x - 2}$.

7.
$$
\begin{array}{r|rrrr}
\sqrt{3} & 4 & -1 & -12 & 3 \\
         &   & 4\sqrt{3} & 12 - \sqrt{3} & -3 \\
\hline
         & 4 & 4\sqrt{3} - 1 & -\sqrt{3} & 0
\end{array}
$$

$$
\begin{array}{r|rrr}
-\sqrt{3} & 4 & 4\sqrt{3} - 1 & -\sqrt{3} & 0 \\
          &   & -4\sqrt{3} & \sqrt{3} & \\
\hline
          & 4 & -1 & 0 &
\end{array}
$$

$4x^3 - x^2 - 12x + 3 = \left(x - \sqrt{3}\right)\left(x + \sqrt{3}\right)(4x - 1)$

The real solutions are $x = \pm\sqrt{3}$ and $x = \frac{1}{4}$.

8. (a) $10i - \left(3 + \sqrt{-25}\right) = 10i - (3 + 5i)$

$$= -3 + 5i$$

(b) $\left(2 + \sqrt{3}i\right)\left(2 - \sqrt{3}i\right) = 4 - 3i^2 = 7$

(c) $\dfrac{5}{2 + i} = \dfrac{5}{2 + i} \cdot \dfrac{2 - i}{2 - i}$

$$= \dfrac{5(2 - i)}{5}$$

$$= 2 - i$$

9. $g(t) = 2t^4 - 3t^3 + 16t - 24$

Possible rational zeros:
$\pm 1, \pm 2, \pm 3, \pm 4, \pm 6, \pm 8, \pm 12, \pm 24, \pm\frac{1}{2}, \pm\frac{3}{2}$

From the graph, we have $x = -2$ and $x = \frac{3}{2}$.

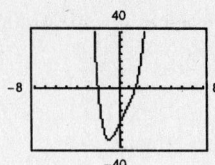

10. $h(x) = 3x^5 + 2x^4 - 3x - 2$

Possible rational zeros: $\pm 1, \pm 2, \pm\frac{1}{3}, \pm\frac{2}{3}$

From the graph, we have $x = \pm 1$ and $x = -\frac{2}{3}$.

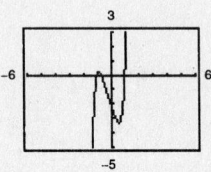

11. $f(x) = x^4 - x^3 + 2x^2 - 4x - 8$

Since $x = 2i$ is a zero, so is $x = -2i$.

$$
\begin{array}{r|rrrrr}
2i & 1 & -1 & 2 & -4 & -8 \\
   &   & 2i & -4 - 2i & 4 - 4i & 8 \\
\hline
   & 1 & -1 + 2i & -2 - 2i & -4i & 0 \\
\end{array}
$$

$$
\begin{array}{r|rrrr}
-2i & 1 & -1 + 2i & -2 - 2i & -4i \\
    &   & -2i & 2i & 4i \\
\hline
    & 1 & -1 & -2 & 0 \\
\end{array}
$$

$f(x) = (x - 2i)(x + 2i)(x^2 - x - 2)$

$\quad = (x - 2i)(x + 2i)(x + 1)(x - 2)$

The zeros of $f(x)$ are: $x = \pm 2i, -1, 2$.

12. $f(x) = x(x - 3)[x - (3 + i)][x - (3 - i)]$

$\quad = (x^2 - 3x)[(x - 3) - i][(x - 3) + i]$

$\quad = (x^2 - 3x)[(x - 3)^2 - i^2]$

$\quad = (x^2 - 3x)(x^2 - 6x + 10)$

$\quad = x^4 - 9x^3 + 28x^2 - 30x$

13. $f(x) = \left[x - \left(1 + \sqrt{3}i\right)\right]\left[x - \left(1 - \sqrt{3}i\right)\right](x - 2)(x - 2)$

$\quad = \left[(x - 1) - \sqrt{3}i\right]\left[(x - 1) + \sqrt{3}i\right](x^2 - 4x + 4)$

$\quad = \left[(x - 1)^2 - 3i^2\right](x^2 - 4x + 4)$

$\quad = (x^2 - 2x + 4)(x^2 - 4x + 4)$

$\quad = x^4 - 6x^3 + 16x^2 - 24x + 16$

14. $y = \dfrac{2}{4 - x}$

Domain: all real numbers except $x = 4$

Vertical asymptote: $x = 4$

Horizontal asymptote: $y = 0$

15. $f(x) = \dfrac{3 - x^2}{3 + x^2} = \dfrac{-x^2 + 3}{x^2 + 3}$

Domain: all real numbers

Vertical asymptote: None

Horizontal asymptote: $y = \dfrac{-1}{1} = -1$

16. $g(x) = \dfrac{x^2 + 2x - 3}{x - 2} = x + 4 + \dfrac{5}{x - 2}$

Domain: all real numbers except $x = 2$

Vertical asymptote: $x = 2$

Slant asymptote: $y = x + 4$

17. $h(x) = \dfrac{4}{x^2} - 1$

Vertical asymptote: $x = 0$

Horizontal asymptote: $y = -1$

x-intercepts: $(\pm 2, 0)$

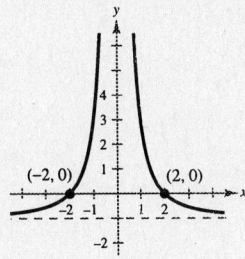

18. $g(x) = \dfrac{x^2 + 2}{x - 1} = x + 1 + \dfrac{3}{x - 1}$

Vertical asymptote: $x = 1$

Slant asymptote: $y = x + 1$

y-intercept: $(0, -2)$

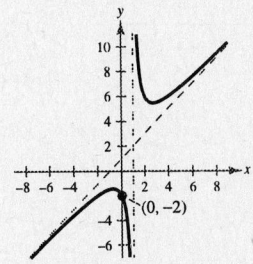

19. $\dfrac{2x + 5}{(x - 2)(x + 1)} = \dfrac{A}{x - 2} + \dfrac{B}{x + 1}$

$\quad\quad 2x + 5 = A(x + 1) + B(x - 2)$

Let $x = 2$: $\;9 = 3A \Longrightarrow A = 3$

Let $x = -1$: $\;3 = -3B \Longrightarrow B = -1$

Thus, $\dfrac{2x + 5}{x^2 - x - 2} = \dfrac{3}{x - 2} - \dfrac{1}{x + 1}$.

20. $\dfrac{3x^2 - 2x + 4}{x^2(2 - x)} = \dfrac{A}{x} + \dfrac{B}{x^2} + \dfrac{C}{2 - x}$

$3x^2 - 2x + 4 = Ax(2 - x) + B(2 - x) + Cx^2$

Let $x = 0$: $4 = 2B \Longrightarrow B = 2$

Let $x = 2$: $12 = 4C \Longrightarrow C = 3$

Let $x = 1$: $5 = A + B + C \Longrightarrow A = 0$

Thus, $\dfrac{3x^2 - 2x + 4}{x^2(2 - x)} = \dfrac{2}{x^2} + \dfrac{3}{2 - x} = \dfrac{2}{x^2} - \dfrac{3}{x - 2}$.

21. $\dfrac{x^2 + 5}{x(x - 1)(x + 1)} = \dfrac{A}{x} + \dfrac{B}{x - 1} + \dfrac{C}{x + 1}$

$\quad\quad x^2 + 5 = A(x - 1)(x + 1) + Bx(x + 1) + Cx(x - 1)$

Let $x = \;\;\;0$: $5 = -A \;\Longrightarrow\; A = -5$

Let $x = \;\;\;1$: $6 = 2B \;\Longrightarrow\; B = \;\;\;3$

Let $x = -1$: $6 = 2C \;\Longrightarrow\; C = \;\;\;3$

$\dfrac{x^2 + 5}{x^3 - x} = -\dfrac{5}{x} + \dfrac{3}{x - 1} + \dfrac{3}{x + 1}$

22. $\dfrac{x^2 - 4}{x(x^2 + 2)} = \dfrac{A}{x} + \dfrac{Bx + C}{x^2 + 2}$

$\quad\quad x^2 - 4 = A(x^2 + 2) + (Bx + C)x$

$\quad\quad\quad\quad = (A + B)x^2 + Cx + 2A$

By equating coefficients we have:

$\quad 1 = A + B$

$\quad 0 = C$

$\quad -4 = 2A \;\Longrightarrow\; A = -2 \;\Longrightarrow\; B = 3$

$\dfrac{x^2 - 4}{x^3 + 2x} = -\dfrac{2}{x} + \dfrac{3x}{x^2 + 2}$

Chapter 3   Chapter Test

1. $12.4^{2.79} \approx 1123.690$

2. $4^{3\pi/2} \approx 687.291$

3. $e^{-7/10} \approx 0.497$

4. $e^{3.1} \approx 22.198$

5. $f(x) = 10^{-x}$

x	-1	$-\frac{1}{2}$	0	$\frac{1}{2}$	1
$f(x)$	10	3.162	1	0.316	0.1

Asymptote: $y = 0$

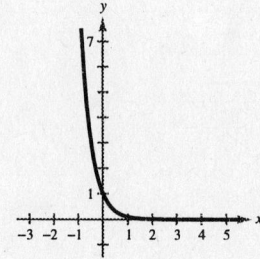

6. $f(x) = -6^{x-2}$

x	-1	0	1	2	3
$f(x)$	-0.005	-0.028	-0.167	-1	-6

Asymptote: $y = 0$

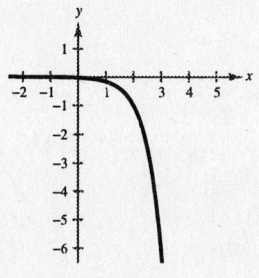

7. $f(x) = 1 - e^{2x}$

x	-1	$-\frac{1}{2}$	0	$\frac{1}{2}$	1
$f(x)$	0.865	0.632	0	-1.718	-6.389

Asymptote: $y = 1$

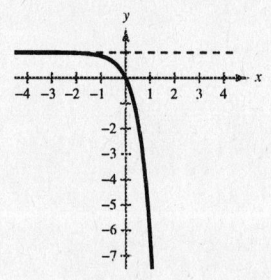

8. (a) $\log_7 7^{-0.89} = -0.89$

    (b) $4.6 \ln e^2 = 4.6(2) = 9.2$

9. $f(x) = -\log_{10} x - 6$

x	$\frac{1}{2}$	1	$\frac{3}{2}$	2	4
$f(x)$	-5.699	-6	-6.176	-6.301	-6.602

Asymptote: $x = 0$

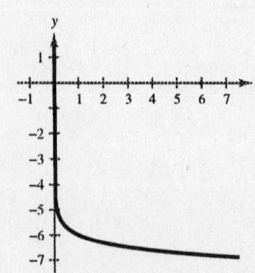

10. $f(x) = \ln(x - 4)$

x	5	7	9	11	13
$f(x)$	0	1.099	1.609	1.946	2.197

Asymptote: $x = 4$

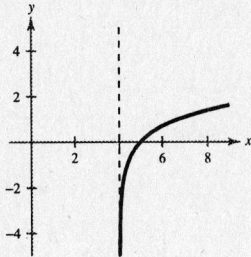

11. $f(x) = 1 + \ln(x + 6)$

x	-5	-3	-1	0	1
$f(x)$	1	2.099	2.609	2.792	2.946

Asymptote: $x = -6$

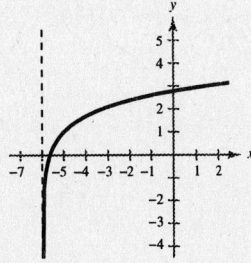

12. $\log_7 44 = \dfrac{\ln 44}{\ln 7} = \dfrac{\log_{10} 44}{\log_{10} 7} \approx 1.945$

13. $\log_{2/5} 0.9 = \dfrac{\ln 0.9}{\ln (2/5)} = \dfrac{\log_{10} 0.9}{\log_{10}(2/5)} \approx 0.115$

14. $\log_{24} 68 = \dfrac{\ln 68}{\ln 24} = \dfrac{\log_{10} 68}{\log_{10} 24} \approx 1.328$

15. $\log_2 3a^4 = \log_2 3 + \log_2 a^4 = \log_2 3 + 4 \log_2 |a|$

16. $\ln \dfrac{5\sqrt{x}}{6} = \ln(5\sqrt{x}) - \ln 6 = \ln 5 + \ln \sqrt{x} - \ln 6$

$\qquad\qquad = \ln 5 + \tfrac{1}{2} \ln x - \ln 6$

17. $\log_3 13 + \log_3 y = \log_3 13y$

18. $4 \ln x - 4 \ln y = \ln x^4 - \ln y^4 = \ln\!\left(\dfrac{x^4}{y^4}\right), x > 0, y > 0$

19. $\dfrac{1025}{8 + e^{4x}} = 5$

$\qquad 1025 = 5(8 + e^{4x})$

$\qquad\ \ 205 = 8 + e^{4x}$

$\qquad\ \ 197 = e^{4x}$

$\qquad \ln 197 = 4x$

$\qquad \dfrac{\ln 197}{4} = x$

$\qquad\qquad x \approx 1.321$

20. $\log_{10} x - \log_{10}(8 - 5x) = 2$

$\qquad\quad \log_{10} \dfrac{x}{8 - 5x} = 2$

$\qquad\qquad \dfrac{x}{8 - 5x} = 10^2$

$\qquad\qquad\quad x = 100(8 - 5x)$

$\qquad\qquad\quad x = 800 - 500x$

$\qquad\quad\ \ 510x = 800$

$\qquad\qquad\quad x = \dfrac{800}{501} \approx 1.597$

21. $y = Ce^{kt}$

$(0, 2745)$: $2745 = Ce^{k(0)} \Rightarrow C = 2745$

$$y = 2745e^{kt}$$

$(9, 11,277)$: $11,277 = 2745e^{k(9)}$

$$\frac{11,277}{2745} = e^{9k}$$

$$\ln\left(\frac{11277}{2745}\right) = 9k$$

$$\frac{1}{9}\ln\left(\frac{11277}{2745}\right) = k \Rightarrow k \approx 0.1570$$

Thus, $y = 2745e^{0.1570t}$

22. $y = Ce^{kt}$

$$\frac{1}{2}C = Ce^{k(22)}$$

$$\frac{1}{2} = e^{22k}$$

$$\ln\left(\frac{1}{2}\right) = 22k$$

$$\frac{\ln(1/2)}{22} = k \Rightarrow k \approx -0.0315$$

$$y = Ce^{-0.0315t}$$

When $t = 19$: $y = Ce^{-0.0315(19)} \approx 0.55C$

Thus, 55% will remain after 19 years.

23. $H = 70.228 + 5.104x + 9.222 \ln x, \frac{1}{4} \le x \le 6$

(a)

x	H(cm)
$\frac{1}{4}$	58.720
$\frac{1}{2}$	66.388
1	75.332
2	86.828
3	95.671
4	103.43
5	110.59
6	117.38

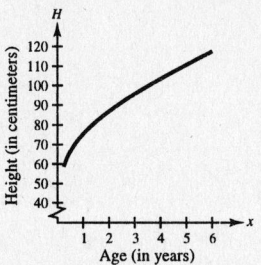

(b) When $x = 4$, $H \approx 103.43$ cm.

Chapters 1–3   Cumulative Test

1. $y = \sqrt{x - 5}$

Domain: $[5, \infty)$

x-intercept: $(5, 0)$

No axis or origin symmetry

x	5	6	9	14
y	0	1	2	3

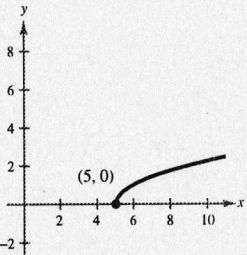

2. $y = |x - 5|$

Domain: All real numbers

x-intercept: $(5, 0)$

y-intercept: $(0, 5)$

No axis or origin symmetry

x	0	1	2	3	4	5	6	7	8
y	5	4	3	2	1	0	1	2	3

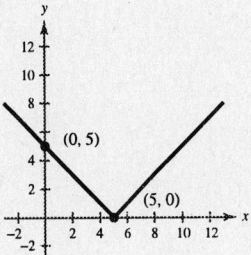

3. $y = x^3 - 4$

Domain: All real numbers

x-intercept: $\left(\sqrt[3]{4}, 0\right)$

y-intercept: $(0, -4)$

x	-1	0	1	2
y	-5	-4	-3	4

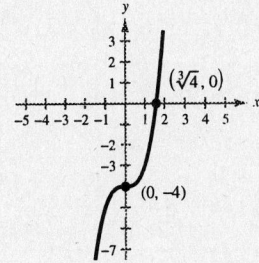

4. $m = \dfrac{8 - 1}{3 - \left(-\frac{1}{2}\right)} = \dfrac{7}{\frac{7}{2}} = 2$

$y - 8 = 2(x - 3)$

$y - 8 = 2x - 6$

$0 = 2x - y + 2$

5. It fails the vertical line test. For some values of x there correspond two values of y.

6. $f(x) = \dfrac{x}{x - 2}$

(a) $f(6) = \dfrac{6}{4} = \dfrac{3}{2}$

(b) $f(2)$ is undefined.

(c) $f(s + 2) = \dfrac{s + 2}{(s + 2) - 2} = \dfrac{s + 2}{s}$

7. $y = \sqrt[3]{x}$

(a) $r(x) = \dfrac{1}{2}\sqrt[3]{x}$ is a vertical shrink by $\dfrac{1}{2}$.

(b) $h(x) = \sqrt[3]{x} + 2$ is a vertical shift two units upward.

(c) $g(x) = \sqrt[3]{x + 2}$ is a horizontal shift two units to the left.

8. $f(x) = x - 3$, $g(x) = 4x + 1$

(a) $(f + g)(x) = f(x) + g(x)$

$$= (x - 3) + (4x + 1)$$

$$= 5x - 2$$

(b) $(f - g)(x) = f(x) - g(x)$

$$= (x - 3) - (4x + 1)$$

$$= -3x - 4$$

(c) $(fg)(x) = f(x)g(x)$

$$= (x - 3)(4x + 1)$$

$$= 4x^2 - 11x - 3$$

(d) $\left(\dfrac{f}{g}\right)(x) = \dfrac{f(x)}{g(x)}$

$$= \dfrac{x - 3}{4x + 1}, x \neq -\dfrac{1}{4}$$

9. $f(x) = \sqrt{x - 1}$, $g(x) = x^2 + 1$

(a) $(f + g)(x) = f(x) + g(x)$

$$= \sqrt{x - 1} + x^2 + 1$$

(b) $(f - g)(x) = f(x) - g(x)$

$$= \sqrt{x - 1} - x^2 - 1$$

(c) $(fg)(x) = f(x)g(x)$

$$= \sqrt{x - 1}(x^2 + 1) = x^2\sqrt{x - 1} + \sqrt{x - 1}$$

(d) $\left(\dfrac{f}{g}\right)(x) = \dfrac{f(x)}{g(x)}$

$$= \dfrac{\sqrt{x - 1}}{x^2 + 1}, x \geq 1$$

10. $f(x) = 2x^2$, $g(x) = \sqrt{x + 6}$

(a) $(f \circ g)(x) = f(g(x))$

$$= f\left(\sqrt{x + 6}\right)$$

$$= 2\left(\sqrt{x + 6}\right)^2$$

$$= 2(x + 6)$$

$$= 2x + 12$$

(b) $(g \circ f)(x) = g(f(x))$

$$= g(2x^2)$$

$$= \sqrt{2x^2 + 6}$$

11. $f(x) = x - 2$, $g(x) = |x|$

(a) $(f \circ g)(x) = f(g(x))$

$$= f(|x|)$$

$$= |x| - 2$$

(b) $(g \circ f)(x) = g(f(x))$

$$= g(x - 2)$$

$$= |x - 2|$$

12. $h(x)$ passes the Vertical Line Test, so it has an inverse.

$$h(x) = 5x - 2$$

$$y = 5x - 2$$

$$x = 5y - 2$$

$$x + 2 = 5y$$

$$\dfrac{1}{5}(x + 2) = y$$

$$h^{-1}(x) = \dfrac{1}{5}(x + 2)$$

13. Cost per person: $\dfrac{36{,}000}{n}$

If three additional people join the group, the cost per person is $\dfrac{36{,}000}{n + 3}$.

$$\dfrac{36{,}000}{n} = \dfrac{36{,}000}{n + 3} + 1000$$

$$36{,}000\,(n + 3) = 36{,}000n + 1000n(n + 3)$$

$$36(n + 3) = 36n + n(n + 3)$$

$$36n + 108 = 36n + n^2 + 3n$$

$$0 = n^2 + 3n - 108$$

$$0 = (n + 12)(n - 9)$$

Choosing the positive value, we have $n = 9$ people.

14. Vertex $(-8, 5)$

Point $(-4, -7)$

$$y = a(x - h)^2 + k$$

$$y = a(x + 8)^2 + 5$$

$$-7 = a(-4 + 8)^2 + 5$$

$$-12 = 16a$$

$$-\tfrac{3}{4} = a$$

$$y = -\tfrac{3}{4}(x + 8)^2 + 5$$

15. $h(x) = -(x^2 + 4x)$

$$= -(x^2 + 4x + 4 - 4)$$

$$= -(x + 2)^2 + 4$$

Parabola

Vertex: $(-2, 4)$

Intercepts: $(-4, 0), (0, 0)$

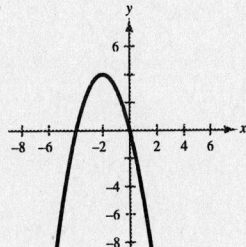

16. $f(t) = \tfrac{1}{4}t(t - 2)^2$

Cubic

Falls to the left

Rises to the right

Intercepts: $(0, 0), (2, 0)$

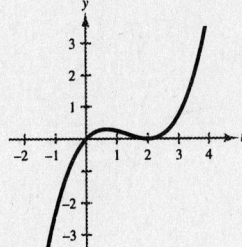

17. $g(s) = s^2 + 4s + 10$

$$= (s^2 + 4s + 4) - 4 + 10$$

$$= (s + 2)^2 + 6$$

Parabola

Vertex: $(-2, 6)$

Intercept: $(0, 10)$

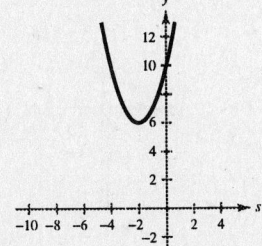

18. $f(x) = x^3 + 2x^2 + 4x + 8$

$$= x^2(x + 2) + 4(x + 2)$$

$$= (x + 2)(x^2 + 4)$$

$x + 2 = 0 \Longrightarrow x = -2$

$x^2 + 4 = 0 \Longrightarrow x = \pm 2i$

The zeros of $f(x)$ are -2 and $\pm 2i$.

19. $f(x) = x^4 + 4x^3 - 21x^2$

$$= x^2(x^2 + 4x - 21)$$

$$= x^2(x + 7)(x - 3)$$

The zeros of $f(x)$ are 0, -7, and 3.

20.

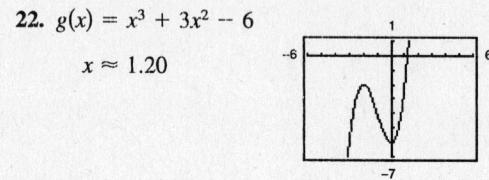

$$2x^2 + 0x + 1 \overline{\smash{\big)}\ 6x^3 - 4x^2 + 0x + 0} \qquad 3x - 2 + \frac{-3x + 2}{2x^2 + 1}$$

$$\underline{6x^3 + 0x^2 + 3x}$$
$$-4x^2 - 3x + 0$$
$$\underline{-4x^2 + 0x - 2}$$
$$-3x + 2$$

Thus, $\dfrac{6x^3 - 4x^2}{2x^2 + 1} = 3x - 2 - \dfrac{3x - 2}{2x^2 + 1}$.

21.

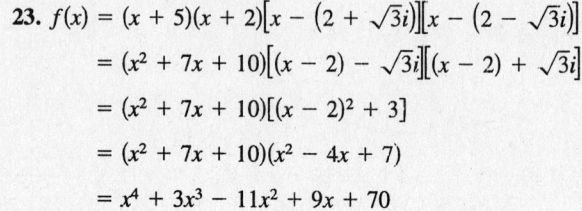

$$-2 \ \big|\begin{array}{rrrrr} 2 & 3 & 0 & -6 & 5 \\ & -4 & 2 & -4 & 20 \\ \hline 2 & -1 & 2 & -10 & 25 \end{array}$$

Thus,

$$\frac{2x^4 + 3x^3 - 6x + 5}{x + 2} = 2x^3 - x^2 + 2x - 10 + \frac{25}{x - 2}$$

22. $g(x) = x^3 + 3x^2 - 6$

$\quad\ x \approx 1.20$

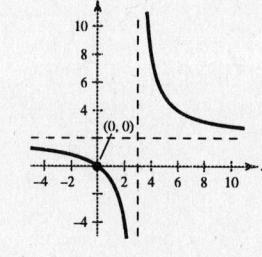

23. $f(x) = (x + 5)(x + 2)\big[x - \big(2 + \sqrt{3}i\big)\big]\big[x - \big(2 - \sqrt{3}i\big)\big]$

$\quad = (x^2 + 7x + 10)\big[(x - 2) - \sqrt{3}i\big]\big[(x - 2) + \sqrt{3}i\big]$

$\quad = (x^2 + 7x + 10)[(x - 2)^2 + 3]$

$\quad = (x^2 + 7x + 10)(x^2 - 4x + 7)$

$\quad = x^4 + 3x^3 - 11x^2 + 9x + 70$

24. $g(s) = \dfrac{2x}{x - 3}$

Vertical asymptote: $x = 3$

Horizontal asymptote: $y = 2$

Intercept: $(0, 0)$

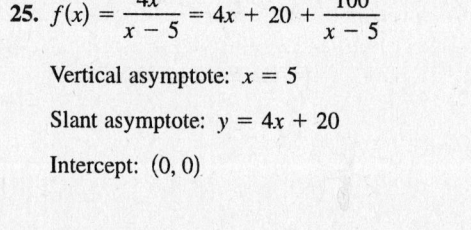

25. $f(x) = \dfrac{4x^2}{x - 5} = 4x + 20 + \dfrac{100}{x - 5}$

Vertical asymptote: $x = 5$

Slant asymptote: $y = 4x + 20$

Intercept: $(0, 0)$

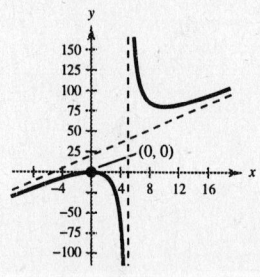

26. $f(x) = \dfrac{2x}{x^2 - 9}$

Vertical asymptotes: $x = \pm 3$

Horizontal asymptote: $y = 0$

Intercept: $(0, 0)$

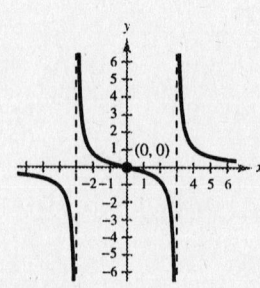

27. $\dfrac{8}{(x-7)(x+3)} = \dfrac{A}{x-7} + \dfrac{B}{x+3}$

$$8 = A(x+3) + B(x-7)$$

Let $x = 7$: $8 = 10A \implies A = \dfrac{4}{5}$

Let $x = -3$: $8 = -10B \implies B = -\dfrac{4}{5}$

$$\dfrac{8}{(x-7)(x+3)} = \dfrac{\frac{4}{5}}{x-7} - \dfrac{\frac{4}{5}}{x+3} = \dfrac{1}{5}\left[\dfrac{4}{x-7} - \dfrac{4}{x+3}\right]$$

28. $\dfrac{5x}{(x-4)^2} = \dfrac{A}{x-4} + \dfrac{B}{(x-4)^2}$

$$5x = A(x-4) + B$$

$$5x = Ax + (-4A + B)$$

By equating coefficients, we have:

$$5 = A$$

$$0 = -4A + B \implies B = 20$$

$$\dfrac{5x}{(x-4)^2} = \dfrac{5}{x-4} + \dfrac{20}{(x+4)^2}$$

29. $f(x) = \left(\frac{2}{5}\right)^x$

$g(x) = -\left(\frac{2}{5}\right)^{-x+3}$

g is a reflection in the x-axis, a reflection in the y-axis, and a horizontal shift 3 units to the right of the graph of f.

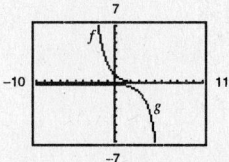

30. $f(x) = 2.2^x$

$g(x) = -2.2^x + 4$

g is a reflection in the x-axis, and a vertical shift 4 units upward of the graph of f.

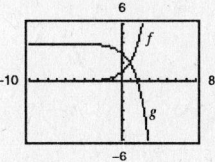

31. $\log_{10} 98 \approx 1.991$

32. $\log_{10}\left(\frac{6}{7}\right) \approx -0.067$

33. $\ln \sqrt{31} \approx 1.717$

34. $\ln\left(\sqrt{40} - 5\right) \approx 0.281$

35. $\log_7 1.8 = \dfrac{\log 1.8}{\log 7} = \dfrac{\ln 1.8}{\ln 7} \approx 0.302$

36. $\log_3 0.149 = \dfrac{\log 0.149}{\log 3} = \dfrac{\ln 0.149}{\ln 3} \approx -1.733$

37. $\log_{\frac{1}{2}} 17 = \dfrac{\log 17}{\log \left(\frac{1}{2}\right)} = \dfrac{\ln 17}{\ln \left(\frac{1}{2}\right)} \approx -4.087$

38. $\ln\left(\dfrac{x^2 - 16}{x^4}\right) = \ln(x^2 - 16) - \ln x^4$

$$= \ln(x+4)(x-4) - 4\ln x$$

$$= \ln(x+4) + \ln(x-4) - 4\ln x, \; x > 4$$

39. $2\ln x - \dfrac{1}{2}\ln(x+5) = \ln x^2 - \ln\sqrt{x+5}$

$$= \ln \dfrac{x^2}{\sqrt{x+5}}, \; x > 0$$

40. $6e^{2x} = 72$

$$e^{2x} = 12$$

$$2x = \ln 12$$

$$x = \dfrac{\ln 12}{2} \approx 1.242$$

41. $\log_2 x + \log_2 5 = 6$

$$\log_2 5x = 6$$

$$5x = 2^6$$

$$x = \dfrac{64}{5}$$

42. $f(x) = \dfrac{1000}{1 + 4e^{-0.2x}}$

Horizontal asymptotes: $y = 0$ and $y = 1000$

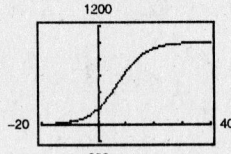

43. (a) and (b)

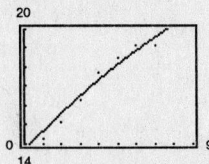

(c) The model appears to be a good fit to the data and looks like it could be used to predict the number of used cars sold in the "**near**" future, but eventually the parabola will decrease and even become negative and will cease to fit the data.

Chapter 4   Chapter Test

1. $\theta = \dfrac{5\pi}{4}$ (a)

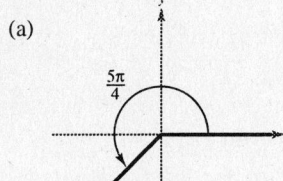

(b) $\dfrac{5\pi}{4} + 2\pi = \dfrac{13\pi}{4}$

$\dfrac{5\pi}{4} - 2\pi = -\dfrac{3\pi}{4}$

(c) $\dfrac{5\pi}{4}\left(\dfrac{180°}{\pi}\right) = 225°$

2. $90\dfrac{\text{km}}{\text{hr}} \times \dfrac{1 \text{ hr}}{60 \text{ min}} \times \dfrac{1000 \text{ m}}{1 \text{ km}} = 1500$ meters per minute

$\dfrac{\text{Revolutions}}{\text{minute}} = \dfrac{1500}{\pi}$

Circumference $= 2\pi\left(\dfrac{1}{2}\right) = \pi = \pi$ meters

Angular speed $= \dfrac{1500}{\pi} \cdot \pi = 1500$ radians per minute

3. $x = -2, \ y = 6$

$r = \sqrt{(-2)^2 + (6)^2} = 2\sqrt{10}$

$\sin\theta = \dfrac{y}{r} = \dfrac{6}{2\sqrt{10}} = \dfrac{3}{\sqrt{10}} = \dfrac{3\sqrt{10}}{10}$

$\cos\theta = \dfrac{x}{r} = \dfrac{-2}{2\sqrt{10}} = -\dfrac{1}{\sqrt{10}} = -\dfrac{\sqrt{10}}{10}$

$\tan\theta = \dfrac{y}{x} = \dfrac{6}{-2} = -3$

$\csc\theta = \dfrac{r}{y} = \dfrac{2\sqrt{10}}{6} = \dfrac{\sqrt{10}}{3}$

$\sec\theta = \dfrac{r}{x} = \dfrac{2\sqrt{10}}{-2} = -\sqrt{10}$

$\cot\theta = \dfrac{x}{y} = \dfrac{-2}{6} = -\dfrac{1}{3}$

4.

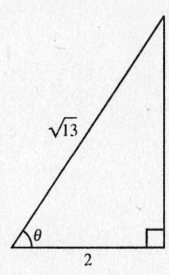

For $0 \le \theta < \dfrac{\pi}{2}$, we have

$\sin\theta = \dfrac{\text{opp}}{\text{hyp}} = \dfrac{3}{\sqrt{13}} = \dfrac{3\sqrt{13}}{13}$

$\cos\theta = \dfrac{\text{adj}}{\text{hyp}} = \dfrac{2}{\sqrt{13}} = \dfrac{2\sqrt{13}}{13}$

$\csc\theta = \dfrac{\text{hyp}}{\text{opp}} = \dfrac{\sqrt{13}}{3}$

$\sec\theta = \dfrac{\text{hyp}}{\text{adj}} = \dfrac{\sqrt{13}}{2}$

$\cot\theta = \dfrac{\text{adj}}{\text{opp}} = \dfrac{2}{3}$

For $\pi \le \theta < \dfrac{3\pi}{2}$, we have

$\sin\theta = -\dfrac{3\sqrt{13}}{13}$

$\cos\theta = -\dfrac{2\sqrt{13}}{13}$

$\csc\theta = -\dfrac{\sqrt{13}}{3}$

$\sec\theta = -\dfrac{\sqrt{13}}{2}$

$\cot\theta = \dfrac{2}{3}$

5. $\theta = 290°$

$\theta' = 360° - 290° = 70°$

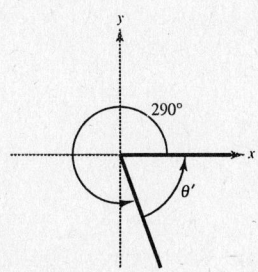

6. $\sec\theta < 0$ and $\tan\theta > 0$

$\dfrac{r}{x} < 0$ and $\dfrac{y}{x} > 0$

Quandrant III

7. $\cos \theta = -\dfrac{\sqrt{3}}{2}$

Reference angle is 30° and θ is in Quandrant II or III.

$\theta = 150°$ or $210°$

8. $\csc \theta = 1.030$

$\dfrac{1}{\sin \theta} = 1.030$

$\sin \theta = \dfrac{1}{1.030}$

$\theta = \arcsin \dfrac{1}{1.030}$

$\theta \approx 1.33$ and $\pi - 1.33 \approx 1.81$

9. $\cos \theta = \frac{3}{5}$, $\tan \theta < 0 \Longrightarrow \theta$ lies in Quadrant IV

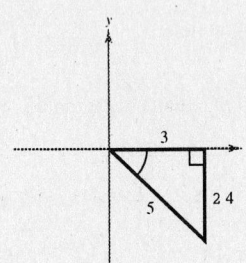

Let $x = 3$, $r = 5 \Longrightarrow y = -4$

$\sin \theta = -\frac{4}{5}$ $\csc \theta = -\frac{5}{4}$

$\cos \theta = \frac{3}{5}$ $\sec \theta = \frac{5}{3}$

$\tan \theta = -\frac{4}{3}$ $\cot \theta = -\frac{3}{4}$

10. $\sec \theta = -\frac{17}{8}$, $\sin \theta > 0 \Longrightarrow \theta$ lies in Quadrant II

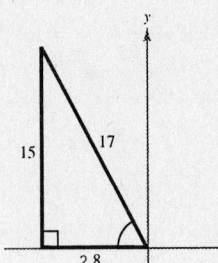

Let $r = 17$, $x = -8 \Longrightarrow y = 15$

$\sin \theta = \frac{15}{17}$ $\csc \theta = \frac{17}{15}$

$\cos \theta = -\frac{8}{17}$ $\sec \theta = -\frac{17}{8}$

$\tan \theta = -\frac{15}{8}$ $\cot \theta = -\frac{8}{15}$

11. $g(x) = -2 \sin\left(x - \dfrac{\pi}{4}\right)$

Period: 2π

Amplitude: $|-2| = 2$

Shifted to the right by $\dfrac{\pi}{4}$ units and reflected in the x-axis.

x	0	$\dfrac{\pi}{4}$	$\dfrac{\pi}{2}$	$\dfrac{3\pi}{4}$	π
y	$\sqrt{2}$	0	$-\sqrt{2}$	-2	$-\sqrt{2}$

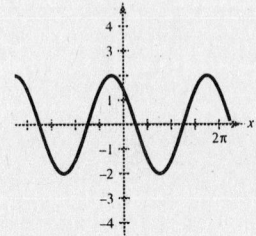

12. $f(\alpha) = \dfrac{1}{2} \tan 2\alpha$

Period: $\dfrac{\pi}{2}$

Asymptotes: $x = -\dfrac{\pi}{4}$, $x = \dfrac{\pi}{4}$

α	$-\dfrac{\pi}{8}$	0	$\dfrac{\pi}{8}$
$f(\alpha)$	$-\dfrac{1}{2}$	0	$\dfrac{1}{2}$

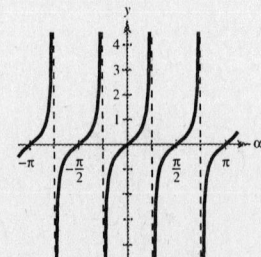

13. $y = \sin 2\pi x + 2 \cos \pi x$

Periodic: period = 2

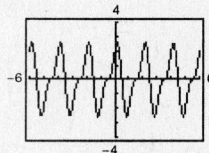

14. $y = 6e^{-0.12t} \cos(0.25t),\ 0 \le t \le 32$

Not periodic

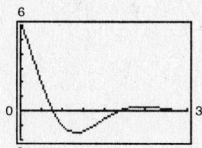

15. $f(x) = a \sin(bx + c)$

Amplitude: $2 \implies |a| = 2$

Reflected in the x-axis: $a = -2$

Period: $4\pi = \dfrac{2\pi}{b} \implies b = \dfrac{1}{2}$

Phase shift: $\dfrac{c}{b} = -\dfrac{\pi}{2} \implies c = -\dfrac{\pi}{4}$

$f(x) = -2 \sin\left(\dfrac{x}{2} - \dfrac{\pi}{4}\right)$

16. Let $u = \arccos \dfrac{2}{3}$,

$\cos u = \dfrac{2}{3}$.

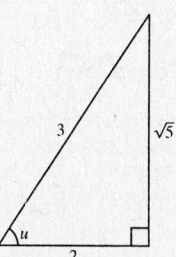

$\tan\left(\arccos \dfrac{2}{3}\right) = \tan u = \dfrac{\sqrt{5}}{2}$

17. $f(x) = 2 \arcsin\left(\dfrac{1}{2}x\right)$

Domain: $[-2, 2]$

Range: $[-\pi, \pi]$

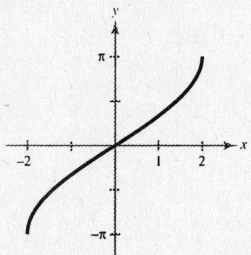

18.

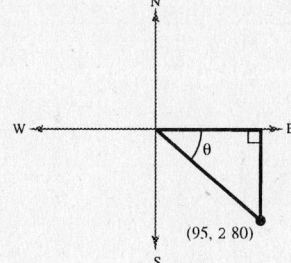

$\tan \theta = -\dfrac{80}{95} \implies \theta \approx -40.1°$

Bearing: $90° - 40.1° = 49.9°$

The plane is heading N 49.9°W.

19. $d = a \sin bt$

$a = -6$

$\dfrac{2\pi}{b} = 2 \implies b = \pi$

$d = -6 \sin \pi t$

Chapter 5   Chapter Test

1. $\tan \theta = \dfrac{3}{2}$ and $\cos \theta < 0$

θ is in Quadrant III.

$$\sec \theta = -\sqrt{1 + \tan^2 \theta} = -\sqrt{1 + \left(\dfrac{3}{2}\right)^2} = -\dfrac{\sqrt{13}}{2}$$

$$\cos \theta = \dfrac{1}{\sec \theta} = -\dfrac{2}{\sqrt{13}} = -\dfrac{2\sqrt{13}}{13}$$

$$\sin \theta = \tan \theta \cos \theta = \left(\dfrac{3}{2}\right)\left(-\dfrac{2}{\sqrt{13}}\right) = -\dfrac{3}{\sqrt{13}} = -\dfrac{3\sqrt{13}}{13}$$

$$\csc \theta = \dfrac{1}{\sin \theta} = -\dfrac{\sqrt{13}}{3}$$

$$\cot \theta = \dfrac{1}{\tan \theta} = \dfrac{2}{3}$$

2. $\csc^2 \beta \,(1 - \cos^2 \beta) = \dfrac{1}{\sin^2 \beta}\,(\sin^2 \beta) = 1$

3. $\dfrac{\sec^4 x - \tan^4 x}{\sec^2 x + \tan^2 x} = \dfrac{(\sec^2 x + \tan^2 x)(\sec^2 x - \tan^2 x)}{\sec^2 x + \tan^2 x}$

$$= \sec^2 x - \tan^2 x = 1$$

4. $\dfrac{\cos \theta}{\sin \theta} + \dfrac{\sin \theta}{\cos \theta} = \dfrac{\cos^2 \theta + \sin^2 \theta}{\sin \theta \cos \theta} = \dfrac{1}{\sin \theta \cos \theta}$

$$= \csc \theta \sec \theta$$

5. $y = \tan \theta,\ y = -\sqrt{\sec^2 \theta - 1}$

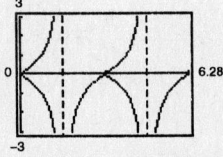

$\tan \theta = -\sqrt{\sec^2 \theta - 1}$ on

$\theta = 0, \dfrac{\pi}{2} < \theta \le \pi, \dfrac{3\pi}{2} < \theta < 2\pi.$

6. $y_1 = \cos x + \sin x \tan x,\ y_2 = \sec x$

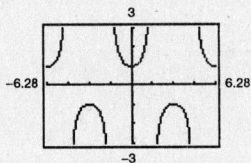

It appears that $y_1 = y_2$.

$\cos x + \sin x \tan x = \cos\ + \sin x \dfrac{\sin x}{\cos x}$

$$= \cos\ + \dfrac{\sin^2 x}{\cos x}$$

$$= \dfrac{\cos^2 x + \sin^2 x}{\cos x}$$

$$= \dfrac{1}{\cos x} = \sec x$$

7. $\sin\theta\sec\theta = \sin\theta\,\dfrac{1}{\cos\theta} = \dfrac{\sin\theta}{\cos\theta} = \tan\theta$

8. $\sec^2 x\tan^2 x + \sec^2 x = \sec^2 x\,(\sec^2 x - 1) + \sec^2 x$

$$= \sec^4 x - \sec^2 x + \sec^2 x$$

$$= \sec^4 x$$

9. $\dfrac{\csc\alpha + \sec\alpha}{\sin\alpha + \cos\alpha} = \dfrac{\dfrac{1}{\sin\alpha} + \dfrac{1}{\cos\alpha}}{\sin\alpha + \cos\alpha} = \dfrac{\dfrac{\cos\alpha + \sin\alpha}{\sin\alpha\cos\alpha}}{\sin\alpha + \cos\alpha} = \dfrac{1}{\sin\alpha\cos\alpha}$

$$= \dfrac{\cos^2\alpha + \sin^2\alpha}{\sin\alpha\cos\alpha} = \dfrac{\cos^2\alpha}{\sin\alpha\cos\alpha} + \dfrac{\sin^2\alpha}{\sin\alpha\cos\alpha}$$

$$= \dfrac{\cos\alpha}{\sin\alpha} + \dfrac{\sin\alpha}{\cos\alpha} = \cot\alpha + \tan\alpha$$

10. $\cos\left(x + \dfrac{\pi}{2}\right) = \cos\left(\dfrac{\pi}{2} - (-x)\right) = \sin(-x) = -\sin x$

11. $\sin(n\pi + \theta) = (-1)^n\sin\theta,\ n$ is an integer.

For n odd: $\sin(n\pi + \theta) = \sin n\pi\cos\theta + \cos n\pi\sin\theta$

$$= (0)\cos\theta + (-1)\sin\theta = -\sin\theta$$

For n even: $\sin(n\pi + \theta) = \sin n\pi\cos\theta + \cos n\pi\sin\theta$

$$= (0)\cos\theta + (1)\sin\theta = \sin\theta$$

When n is odd, $(-1)^n = -1$. When n is even $(-1)^n = 1$.

Thus, $\sin(n\pi + \theta) = (-1)^n\sin\theta$ for any integer n.

12. $(\sin x + \cos x)^2 = \sin^2 x + 2\sin x\cos x + \cos^2 x$

$$= 1 + 2\sin x\cos x$$

$$= 1 + \sin 2x$$

13. $\sin^4 x\tan^2 x = \sin^4 x\left(\dfrac{\sin^2 x}{\cos^2 x}\right) = \dfrac{\sin^6 x}{\cos^2 x} = \dfrac{(\sin^2 x)^3}{\cos^2 x}$

$$= \dfrac{\left(\dfrac{1 - \cos 2x}{2}\right)^3}{\dfrac{1 + \cos 2x}{2}}$$

$$= \dfrac{\dfrac{1 - 3\cos 2x + 3\cos^2 2x - \cos^3 2x}{8}}{\dfrac{1 + \cos 2x}{2}}$$

$$= \dfrac{\dfrac{1}{4}\left[1 - 3\cos 2x + 3\left(\dfrac{1 + \cos 4x}{2}\right) - \cos 2x\left(\dfrac{1 + \cos 4x}{2}\right)\right]}{1 + \cos 2x}$$

$$= \dfrac{\dfrac{1}{8}[2 - 6\cos 2x + 3 + 3\cos 4x - \cos 2x - \cos 2x\cos 4x]}{1 + \cos 2x}$$

$$= \dfrac{1}{8}\left[\dfrac{5 - 7\cos 2x + 3\cos 4x - \dfrac{1}{2}(\cos(-2x) + \cos(6x))}{1 + \cos 2x}\right]$$

$$= \dfrac{1}{16}\left[\dfrac{10 - 14\cos 2x + 6\cos 4x - \cos 2x - \cos 6x}{1 + \cos 2x}\right]$$

$$= \dfrac{1}{16}\left[\dfrac{10 - 15\cos 2x + 6\cos 4x - \cos 6x}{1 + \cos 2x}\right]$$

14. $\dfrac{\sin 4\theta}{1 + \cos 4\theta} = \tan \dfrac{4\theta}{2} = \tan 2\theta$

15. $4 \cos 2\theta \sin 4\theta = 4\left(\dfrac{1}{2}\right)[\sin(2\theta + 4\theta) - \sin(2\theta - 4\theta)]$

$$= 2[\sin 6\theta - \sin(-2\theta)]$$

$$= 2(\sin 6\theta + \sin 2\theta)$$

16. $\sin 3\theta - \sin 4\theta = 2 \cos\left(\dfrac{3\theta + 4\theta}{2}\right) \sin\left(\dfrac{3\theta - 4\theta}{2}\right)$

$$= 2 \cos \dfrac{7\theta}{2} \sin\left(\dfrac{-\theta}{2}\right)$$

$$= -2 \cos \dfrac{7\theta}{2} \sin \dfrac{\theta}{2}$$

17.

$$\tan^2 x + \tan x = 0$$

$$\tan x (\tan x + 1) = 0$$

$$\tan x = 0 \quad \text{or} \quad \tan x + 1 = 0$$

$$\tan x = -1$$

$$x = 0, \pi \qquad x = \dfrac{3\pi}{4}, \dfrac{7\pi}{4}$$

18.

$$\sin 2\alpha - \cos \alpha = 0$$

$$2 \sin\alpha \cos \alpha - \cos \alpha = 0$$

$$\cos\alpha(2 \sin\alpha - 1) = 0$$

$$\cos \alpha = 0 \quad \text{or} \quad 2 \sin \alpha - 1 = 0$$

$$\alpha = \dfrac{\pi}{2}, \dfrac{3\pi}{2} \qquad \sin \alpha = \dfrac{1}{2}$$

$$\alpha = \dfrac{\pi}{6}, \dfrac{5\pi}{6}$$

19.

$$4 \cos^2 x - 3 = 0$$

$$\cos^2 x = \dfrac{3}{4}$$

$$\cos x = \pm\sqrt{\dfrac{3}{4}} = \pm\dfrac{\sqrt{3}}{2}$$

$$x = \dfrac{\pi}{6}, \dfrac{5\pi}{6}, \dfrac{7\pi}{6}, \dfrac{11\pi}{6}$$

20.

$$\csc^2 x - \csc x - 2 = 0$$

$$(\csc x - 2)(\csc x + 1) = 0$$

$$\csc x - 2 = 0 \quad \text{or} \quad \csc x + 1 = 0$$

$$\csc x = 2 \qquad\qquad \csc = -1$$

$$\dfrac{1}{\sin x} = 2 \qquad\qquad \dfrac{1}{\sin x} = -1$$

$$\sin x = \dfrac{1}{2} \qquad\qquad \sin x = -1$$

$$x = \dfrac{\pi}{6}, \dfrac{5\pi}{6} \qquad\qquad x = \dfrac{3\pi}{2}$$

21. $3 \cos x - x = 0$

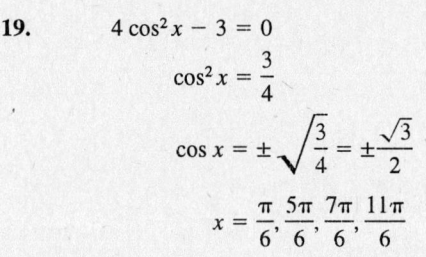

$x \approx -2.938, -2.663, 1.170$

22. $\cos^2 x + \cos x - 6 = 0$

$$\cos^2 x + \cos x = 6$$

The maximum value of $\cos^2 x$ is 1 and the maximum value of $\cos x$ is 1. Thus, $|\cos^2 x + \cos x| \le 2$ for all x and $\cos^2 x + \cos x$ can never equal 6.

23. $105° = 135° - 30°$

$\cos 105° = \cos(135° - 30°)$

$\qquad = \cos 135° \cos 30° + \sin 135° \sin 30°$

$\qquad = -\cos 45° \cos 30° + \sin 45° \sin 30°$

$\qquad = \left(-\dfrac{\sqrt{2}}{2}\right)\left(\dfrac{\sqrt{3}}{2}\right) + \left(\dfrac{\sqrt{2}}{2}\right)\left(\dfrac{1}{2}\right)$

$\qquad = \dfrac{-\sqrt{6} + \sqrt{2}}{4} = \dfrac{\sqrt{2} - \sqrt{6}}{4}$

24. $\sin 2u = 2 \sin u \cos u$

$\qquad = 2\left(\dfrac{2}{\sqrt{5}}\right)\left(\dfrac{1}{\sqrt{5}}\right) = \dfrac{4}{5}$

$\tan 2u = \dfrac{2 \tan u}{1 - \tan^2 u} = \dfrac{2(2)}{1 - (2)^2} = \dfrac{4}{-3} = -\dfrac{4}{3}$

25. $\qquad 1.5 = \dfrac{\sin\left(\dfrac{\theta}{2} + \dfrac{60°}{2}\right)}{\sin\left(\dfrac{\theta}{2}\right)}$

$1.5 \sin \dfrac{\theta}{2} = \sin \dfrac{\theta}{2} \cos 30° + \cos \dfrac{\theta}{2} \sin 30°$

$1.5 \sin \dfrac{\theta}{2} = \dfrac{\sqrt{3}}{2} \sin \dfrac{\theta}{2} + \dfrac{1}{2} \cos \dfrac{\theta}{2}$

$\left(1.5 - \dfrac{\sqrt{3}}{2}\right)\sin \dfrac{\theta}{2} = \dfrac{1}{2} \cos \dfrac{\theta}{2}$

$2\left(1.5 - \dfrac{\sqrt{3}}{2}\right) = \cot \dfrac{\theta}{2}$

$3 - \sqrt{3} = \dfrac{1}{\tan \dfrac{\theta}{2}}$

$\tan \dfrac{\theta}{2} = \dfrac{1}{3 - \sqrt{3}}$

$\dfrac{\theta}{2} = \arctan\left(\dfrac{1}{3 - \sqrt{3}}\right) \approx 38.26°$

$\theta \approx 76.5°$

Chapter 6   Chapter Test

1. $A = 24°, B = 68°, a = 12.2$

$C = 180° - 24° - 68° = 88°$

$b = \dfrac{a \sin B}{\sin A} = \dfrac{12.2 \sin 68°}{\sin 24°} \approx 27.81$

$c = \dfrac{a \sin C}{\sin A} = \dfrac{12.2 \sin 88°}{\sin 24°} \approx 29.98$

2. $B = 104°, C = 33°, a = 18.1$

$A = 180° - 104° - 33° = 43°$

$b = \dfrac{a \sin B}{\sin A} = \dfrac{18.1 \sin 104°}{\sin 43°} \approx 25.75$

$c = \dfrac{a \sin C}{\sin A} = \dfrac{18.1 \sin 33°}{\sin 43°} \approx 14.45$

3. $A = 24°, a = 11.2, b = 13.4$

$$\sin B = \frac{b \sin A}{a} = \frac{13.4 \sin 24°}{11.2} \approx 0.4866$$

Two Solutions

$B \approx 29.12°$ or $B \approx 150.88°$

$C \approx 126.88°$ $C \approx 5.12°$

$c = \dfrac{a \sin C}{\sin A} = \dfrac{11.2 \sin 126.88°}{\sin 24°}$ $c = \dfrac{11.2 \sin 5.12°}{\sin 24°}$

$c \approx 22.03$ $c \approx 2.46$

4. $a = 4.0, b = 7.3, c = 12.4$

$$\cos C = \frac{a^2 + b^2 - c^2}{2ab} = \frac{4^2 + 7.3^2 - 12.4^2}{2(4)(7.3)} \approx -1.4464 < -1$$

No solution

5. $B = 100°, a = 15, b = 23$

$$\sin A = \frac{a \sin B}{b} = \frac{15 \sin 100°}{23} \Longrightarrow A \approx 39.96°$$

$$C \approx 180° - 100° - 39.96° = 40.04°$$

$$c \approx \frac{b \sin C}{\sin B} = \frac{23 \sin 40.04°}{\sin 100°} \approx 15.02$$

6. $C = 123°, a = 41, b = 57$

$$c^2 = 41^2 + 57^2 - 2(41)(57)\cos 123° \Longrightarrow c \approx 86.46$$

$$\sin A = \frac{a \sin C}{c} = \frac{41 \sin 123°}{86.46} \Longrightarrow A \approx 23.43°$$

$$B \approx 180° - 23.43° - 123° = 33.57°$$

7. $a = 60, b = 70, c = 82$

$$s = \frac{60 + 70 + 82}{2} = 106$$

$$\text{Area} = \sqrt{106(46)(36)(24)} \approx 2052.5 \text{ square meters}$$

8.

240 mi C

37°

13°

B 167°

370 mi

24°

A (Not drawn to scale)

$$b^2 = 370^2 + 240^2 - 2(370)(240)\cos 167°$$

$$b \approx 606.3 \text{ miles}$$

$$\sin A = \frac{a \sin B}{b} = \frac{240 \sin 167°}{606.3}$$

$$A \approx 5°$$

Bearing: N 24° + 5° E = N 29° E

9. Initial Point: $(-3, 7)$

Terminal Point: $(11, -16)$

$$\mathbf{v} = \langle 11 - (-3), -16 - 7 \rangle = \langle 14, -23 \rangle$$

10. $\mathbf{v} = 12\left(\dfrac{\mathbf{u}}{\|\mathbf{u}\|}\right) = 12\left(\dfrac{\langle 3, -5 \rangle}{\sqrt{3^2 + (-5)^2}}\right) = \dfrac{12}{\sqrt{34}}\langle 3, -5 \rangle$

$\qquad = \dfrac{6\sqrt{34}}{17}\langle 3, -5 \rangle = \left\langle \dfrac{18\sqrt{34}}{17}, -\dfrac{30\sqrt{34}}{17} \right\rangle$

11. $\mathbf{u} + \mathbf{v} = \langle 3, 5 \rangle + \langle -7, 1 \rangle = \langle -4, 6 \rangle$

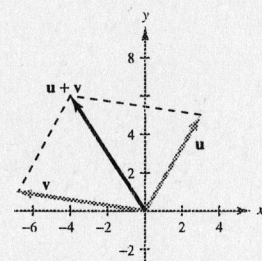

12. $\mathbf{u} - \mathbf{v} = \langle 3, 5 \rangle - \langle -7, 1 \rangle = \langle 10, 4 \rangle$

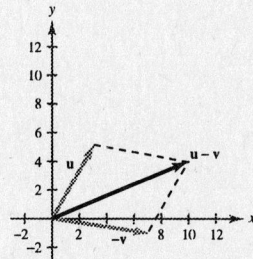

13. $5\mathbf{u} - 3\mathbf{v} = 5\langle 3, 5 \rangle - 3\langle -7, 1 \rangle = \langle 15, 25 \rangle + \langle 21, -3 \rangle$
$$= \langle 36, 22 \rangle$$

14. $\dfrac{\mathbf{u}}{\|\mathbf{u}\|} = \dfrac{\langle 4, -3 \rangle}{\sqrt{4^2 + (-3)^2}} = \dfrac{1}{5}\langle 4, -3 \rangle = \left\langle \dfrac{4}{5}, -\dfrac{3}{5} \right\rangle$

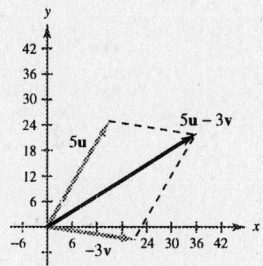

15. $\mathbf{u} = 250(\cos 45° \, \mathbf{i} + \sin 45° \, \mathbf{j})$

$\mathbf{v} = 130(\cos -60° \, \mathbf{i} + \sin -60° \, \mathbf{j})$

$\mathbf{R} = \mathbf{u} + \mathbf{v} \approx 241.7767 \, \mathbf{i} + 64.1934 \, \mathbf{j}$

$\|\mathbf{R}\| \approx \sqrt{241.7767^2 + 64.1934^2} \approx 250.15$ pounds

$\tan \theta \approx \dfrac{64.1934}{241.7767} \implies \theta \approx 14.9°$

16. $\mathbf{u} = \langle -1, 5 \rangle, \mathbf{v} = \langle 3, -2 \rangle$

$\cos \theta = \dfrac{\mathbf{u} \cdot \mathbf{v}}{\|\mathbf{u}\|\|\mathbf{v}\|} = \dfrac{-13}{\sqrt{26}\sqrt{13}} \implies \theta = 135°$

17. $\mathbf{u} = \langle 6, 10 \rangle, \mathbf{v} = \langle 2, 3 \rangle$

$\mathbf{u} \cdot \mathbf{v} = 42 \neq 0 \implies \mathbf{u}$ and $\mathbf{v}$ are not orthogonal.

18. $\mathbf{u} = \langle 6, 7 \rangle, \mathbf{v} = \langle -5, -1 \rangle$

$\mathbf{w}_1 = \text{proj}_\mathbf{v} \, \mathbf{u} = \left(\dfrac{\mathbf{u} \cdot \mathbf{v}}{\|\mathbf{v}\|^2} \right)\mathbf{v} = -\dfrac{37}{26}\langle -5, -1 \rangle = \dfrac{37}{26}\langle 5, 1 \rangle$

$\mathbf{w}_2 = \mathbf{u} - \mathbf{w}_1 = \langle 6, 7 \rangle - \dfrac{37}{26}\langle 5, 1 \rangle$

$= \left\langle -\dfrac{29}{26}, \dfrac{145}{26} \right\rangle$

$= \dfrac{29}{26}\langle -1, 5 \rangle$

19. $z = 5 - 5i$

$|z| = \sqrt{5^2 + (-5)^2} = \sqrt{50} = 5\sqrt{2}$

$\tan \theta = \dfrac{-5}{5} = -1$ and θ is in Quadrant IV $\implies \theta = \dfrac{7\pi}{4}$

$z = 5\sqrt{2}\left(\cos \dfrac{7\pi}{4} + i \sin \dfrac{7\pi}{4} \right)$

20. $z = 6(\cos 120° + i \sin 120°) = 6\left(-\dfrac{1}{2} + \dfrac{\sqrt{3}}{2}i\right) = -3 + 3\sqrt{3}i$

21. $\left[3\left(\cos\dfrac{7\pi}{6} + i \sin\dfrac{7\pi}{6}\right)\right]^8 = 3^8\left(\cos\dfrac{28\pi}{3} + i \sin\dfrac{28\pi}{3}\right)$

$$= 6561\left(-\dfrac{1}{2} - \dfrac{\sqrt{3}}{2}i\right) = -\dfrac{6561}{2} - \dfrac{6561\sqrt{3}}{2}i$$

22. $(3 - 3i)^6 = \left[3\sqrt{2}\left(\cos\dfrac{7\pi}{4} + i \sin\dfrac{7\pi}{4}\right)\right]^6$

$$= \left(3\sqrt{2}\right)^6\left(\cos\dfrac{21\pi}{2} + i \sin\dfrac{21\pi}{2}\right)$$

$$= 5832(0 + i)$$

$$= 5832i$$

23. $z = 256\left(1 + \sqrt{3}i\right)$

$|z| = 256\sqrt{1^2 + \left(\sqrt{3}\right)^2} = 256\sqrt{4} = 512$

$\tan\theta = \dfrac{\sqrt{3}}{1} \implies \theta = \dfrac{\pi}{3}$

$z = 512\left(\cos\dfrac{\pi}{3} + i \sin\dfrac{\pi}{3}\right)$

Fourth roots of $z = \sqrt[4]{512}\left[\cos\dfrac{\dfrac{\pi}{3} + 2\pi k}{4} + i \sin\dfrac{\dfrac{\pi}{3} + 2\pi k}{4}\right], k = 0, 1, 2, 3$

$k = 0:\ 4\sqrt[4]{2}\left(\cos\dfrac{\pi}{12} + i \sin\dfrac{\pi}{12}\right)$

$k = 1:\ 4\sqrt[4]{2}\left(\cos\dfrac{7\pi}{12} + i \sin\dfrac{7\pi}{12}\right)$

$k = 2:\ 4\sqrt[4]{2}\left(\cos\dfrac{13\pi}{12} + i \sin\dfrac{13\pi}{12}\right)$

$k = 3:\ 4\sqrt[4]{2}\left(\cos\dfrac{19\pi}{12} + i \sin\dfrac{19\pi}{12}\right)$

24. $x^3 - 27i = 0 \implies x = 27i$

The solutions to the equation are the cube roots of $27i = 27\left(\cos\dfrac{\pi}{2} + i \sin\dfrac{\pi}{2}\right)$.

Cube roots: $\sqrt[3]{27}\left[\cos\dfrac{\dfrac{\pi}{2} + 2\pi k}{3} + i \sin\dfrac{\dfrac{\pi}{2} + 2\pi k}{3}\right], k = 0, 1, 2$

$k = 0:\ 3\left(\cos\dfrac{\pi}{6} + i \sin\dfrac{\pi}{6}\right) = 3\left(\dfrac{\sqrt{3}}{2} + \dfrac{1}{2}i\right) = \dfrac{3\sqrt{3}}{2} + \dfrac{3}{2}i$

$k = 1:\ 3\left(\cos\dfrac{5\pi}{6} + i \sin\dfrac{5\pi}{6}\right) = 3\left(-\dfrac{\sqrt{3}}{2} + \dfrac{1}{2}i\right) = -\dfrac{3\sqrt{3}}{2} + \dfrac{3}{2}i$

$k = 2:\ 3\left(\cos\dfrac{3\pi}{2} + i \sin\dfrac{3\pi}{2}\right) = 3(0 - i) = -3i$

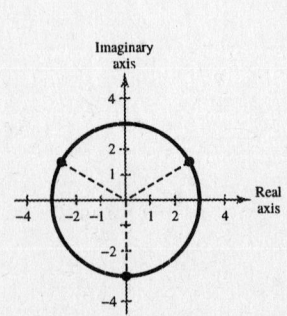

Chapters 4–6 Cumulative Test

1. (a)

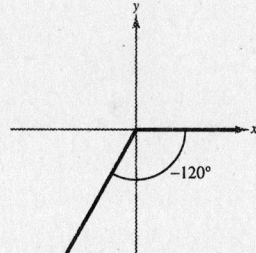

(b) $-120° + 360° = 240°$

(c) $-120\left(\dfrac{\pi}{180°}\right) = -\dfrac{2\pi}{3}$

(d) $-120°$ is located in Quadrant III.

$240° - 180° = 60°$

(e) $\sin(-120°) = -\sin 60° = -\dfrac{\sqrt{3}}{2}$

$\cos(-120°) = -\cos 60° = -\dfrac{1}{2}$

$\tan(-120°) = \tan 60° = \sqrt{3}$

$\csc(-120°) = \dfrac{1}{-\sin 60°} = -\dfrac{2\sqrt{3}}{3}$

$\sec(-120°) = \dfrac{1}{-\cos 60°} = -2$

$\cot(-120°) = \dfrac{1}{\tan 60°} = \dfrac{\sqrt{3}}{3}$

2. $2.35\left(\dfrac{180°}{\pi}\right) \approx 134.6°$

3. $\tan \theta = \dfrac{y}{x} = -\dfrac{4}{3} \implies r = 5$

Since $\sin \theta < 0$ θ is in Quadrant IV, $\implies x = 3$.

$\cos \theta = \dfrac{x}{r} = \dfrac{3}{5}$

4. $f(x) = 3 - 2 \sin \pi x$

Period: $\dfrac{2\pi}{\pi} = 2$

Amplitude: $|a| = |-2| = 2$

Upward shift of 3 units (reflected in x-axis prior to shift)

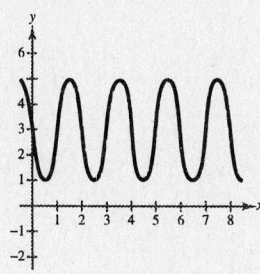

5. $g(x) = \dfrac{1}{2} \tan\left(x - \dfrac{\pi}{2}\right)$

Period: π

Asymptotes: $x = 0, x = \pi$

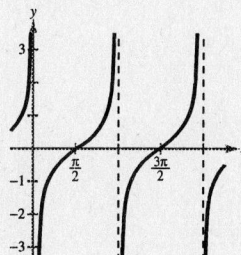

6. $h(x) = a \cos(bx + c)$

Graph is reflected in x-axis.

Amplitude: $a = -3$

Period: $2 = \dfrac{2\pi}{\pi} \implies b = \pi$

No phase shift: $c = 0$

$h(x) = -3 \cos(\pi x)$

7. $f(x) = \dfrac{x}{2} \sin x, \ -3\pi \le x \le 3\pi$

$-\dfrac{x}{2} \le f(x) \le \dfrac{x}{2}$

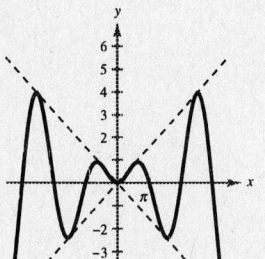

8. $\tan(\arctan 6.7) = 6.7$

9. $\tan\left(\arcsin \dfrac{3}{5}\right) = \dfrac{3}{4}$

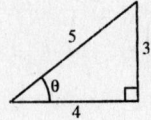

10. $y = \arccos(2x)$

$\sin y = \sin(\arccos(2x)) = \sqrt{1 - 4x^2}$

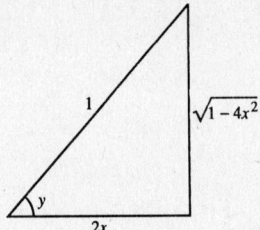

11. $\cos\left(\dfrac{\pi}{2} - x\right)\csc x = \sin x\left(\dfrac{1}{\sin x}\right) = 1$

12. $\dfrac{\sin\theta - 1}{\cos\theta} - \dfrac{\cos\theta}{\sin\theta - 1} = \dfrac{\sin\theta - 1}{\cos\theta} - \dfrac{\cos\theta(\sin\theta + 1)}{\sin^2\theta - 1}$

$\qquad = \dfrac{\sin\theta - 1}{\cos\theta} + \dfrac{\cos\theta(\sin\theta + 1)}{\cos^2\theta} = \dfrac{\sin\theta - 1}{\cos\theta} + \dfrac{\sin\theta + 1}{\cos\theta} = \dfrac{2\sin\theta}{\cos\theta} = 2\tan\theta$

13. $\cot^2\alpha(\sec^2\alpha - 1) = \cot^2\alpha\tan^2\alpha = 1$

14. $\sin(x + y)\sin(x - y) = \dfrac{1}{2}[\cos(x + y - (x - y)) - \cos(x + y + x - y)]$

$\qquad = \dfrac{1}{2}[\cos 2y - \cos 2x] = \dfrac{1}{2}[1 - 2\sin^2 y - (1 - 2\sin^2 x)] = \sin^2 x - \sin^2 y$

15. $\sin^2 x\cos^2 x = \left(\dfrac{1 - \cos 2x}{2}\right)\left(\dfrac{1 + \cos 2x}{2}\right)$

$\qquad = \dfrac{1}{4}(1 - \cos 2x)(1 + \cos 2x)$

$\qquad = \dfrac{1}{4}(1 - \cos^2 2x)$

$\qquad = \dfrac{1}{4}\left(1 - \dfrac{1 + \cos 4x}{2}\right)$

$\qquad = \dfrac{1}{8}(2 - (1 + \cos 4x))$

$\qquad = \dfrac{1}{8}(1 - \cos 4x)$

16. $2\cos^2\beta - \cos\beta = 0$

$\cos\beta(2\cos\beta - 1) = 0$

$\cos\beta = 0 \qquad 2\cos\beta - 1 = 0$

$\beta = \dfrac{\pi}{2}, \dfrac{3\pi}{2} \qquad \cos\beta = \dfrac{1}{2}$

$\qquad\qquad\qquad \beta = \dfrac{\pi}{3}, \dfrac{5\pi}{3}$

Answer: $\dfrac{\pi}{3}, \dfrac{\pi}{2}, \dfrac{3\pi}{2}, \dfrac{5\pi}{3}$

17. $3 \tan \theta - \cot \theta = 0$

$$3 \tan \theta - \frac{1}{\tan \theta} = 0$$

$$\frac{3 \tan^2 \theta - 1}{\tan \theta} = 0$$

$$3 \tan^2 \theta - 1 = 0$$

$$\tan^2 \theta = \frac{1}{3}$$

$$\tan \theta = \pm \frac{\sqrt{3}}{3}$$

$$\theta = \frac{\pi}{6}, \frac{5\pi}{6}, \frac{7\pi}{6}, \frac{11\pi}{6}$$

18. $\sin^2 x + 2 \sin x + 1 = 0$

$$(\sin x + 1)(\sin x + 1) = 0$$

$$\sin x + 1 = 0$$

$$\sin x = -1$$

$$x = \frac{3\pi}{2}$$

19. $\sin u = \frac{12}{13} \implies \cos u = \frac{5}{13}$ and $\tan u = \frac{12}{5}$ since u is in Quadrant I.

$\cos v = \frac{3}{5} \implies \sin v = \frac{4}{5}$ and $\tan v = \frac{4}{3}$ since v is in Quadrant I.

$$\tan(u - v) = \frac{\tan u - \tan v}{1 + \tan u \tan v} = \frac{\dfrac{12}{5} - \dfrac{4}{3}}{1 + \left(\dfrac{12}{5}\right)\left(\dfrac{4}{3}\right)} = \frac{16}{63}$$

20. $\tan \theta = \frac{1}{2}$

$$\tan 2\theta = \frac{2 \tan \theta}{1 - \tan^2 \theta} = \frac{2\left(\dfrac{1}{2}\right)}{1 - \left(\dfrac{1}{2}\right)^2} = \frac{4}{3}$$

21. $\tan \theta = \frac{4}{3} \implies \cos \theta = \pm \frac{3}{5}$

$$\sin \frac{\theta}{2} = \pm \sqrt{\frac{1 - \cos \theta}{2}} = \pm \sqrt{\frac{1 - \frac{3}{5}}{2}} = \pm \frac{\sqrt{5}}{5}$$

$$\text{or} = \pm \sqrt{\frac{1 + \frac{3}{5}}{2}} = \pm \frac{2\sqrt{5}}{5}$$

22. $5 \sin \dfrac{3\pi}{4} \cos \dfrac{7\pi}{4} = \dfrac{5}{2}\left[\sin\left(\dfrac{3\pi}{4} + \dfrac{7\pi}{4}\right) + \sin\left(\dfrac{3\pi}{4} - \dfrac{7\pi}{4}\right) \right]$

$$= \frac{5}{2}\left[\sin \frac{5\pi}{2} + \sin(-\pi) \right]$$

$$= \frac{5}{2}\left(\sin \frac{5\pi}{2} - \sin \pi \right)$$

23. Given: $A = 30°, a = 9, b = 8$

$$\frac{\sin B}{8} = \frac{\sin 30°}{9}$$

$$\sin B = \frac{8}{9}\left(\frac{1}{2}\right)$$

$$B = \arcsin\left(\frac{4}{9}\right)$$

$$B \approx 26.4°$$

$$C = 180° - A - B \approx 123.6°$$

$$\frac{c}{\sin 123.6°} = \frac{9}{\sin 30°}$$

$$x \approx 15.0$$

24. Given: $A = 30°, b = 8, c = 10$

$$a^2 = 8^2 + 10^2 - 2(8)(10)\cos 30°$$

$$a^2 \approx 25.4$$

$$a \approx 5.0$$

$$\cos B = \frac{5.0^2 + 10^2 - 8^2}{2(5.0)(10)}$$

$$\cos B = 0.61$$

$$B \approx 52.4°$$

$$C = 180° - A - B \approx 97.6°$$

25. Given: $A = 30°, c = 90°, b = 10$

$$B = 180° - 30° - 90° = 60°$$

$$\tan 30° = \frac{a}{10} \implies a = 10 \tan 30° \approx 5.8$$

$$\cos 30° = \frac{10}{c} \implies c = \frac{10}{\cos 30°} \approx 11.5$$

26. $a = 4, b = 8, c = 9$

$$\cos C = \frac{4^2 + 8^2 - 9^2}{2(4)(8)} = \frac{-1}{64} \implies C \approx 90.9°$$

$$\sin A \approx \frac{4 \sin 90.9°}{9} \implies A \approx 26.4°$$

$$B \approx 180° - 26.4° - 90.9° = 62.7°$$

27. Area $= \frac{1}{2}(7)(12) \sin 60° \approx 36.4$ square inches

28. $s = \dfrac{11 + 16 + 17}{2} = 22$

Area $= \sqrt{22(11)(6)(5)} \approx 85.2$ square inches

29. $\mathbf{u} = \langle 3, 5 \rangle = 3\mathbf{i} + 5\mathbf{j}$

30. $\mathbf{u} = 3\mathbf{i} + 4\mathbf{j}, \mathbf{v} = \mathbf{i} - 2\mathbf{j}$

$$\mathbf{u} \cdot \mathbf{v} = 3(1) + 4(-2) = -5$$

31. $\mathbf{u} = \langle 8, -2 \rangle, \mathbf{v} = \langle 1, 5 \rangle$

$$\mathbf{w}_1 = \text{proj}_\mathbf{v} \mathbf{u} = \left(\frac{\mathbf{u} \cdot \mathbf{v}}{\|\mathbf{v}\|^2} \right) \mathbf{v} = \frac{-2}{26} \langle 1, 5 \rangle = -\frac{1}{13} \langle 1, 5 \rangle$$

$$\mathbf{w}_2 = \mathbf{u} - \mathbf{w}_1 = \langle 8, -2 \rangle - \left\langle -\frac{1}{13}, -\frac{5}{13} \right\rangle = \left\langle \frac{105}{13}, -\frac{21}{13} \right\rangle$$

$$= \frac{21}{13} \langle 5, -1 \rangle$$

32. $r = |-2 + 2i| = \sqrt{(-2)^2 + (2)^2} = 2\sqrt{2}$

$$\tan \theta = \frac{2}{-2} = -1$$

Since $\tan \dfrac{3\pi}{4} = -1$ and $-2 + 2i$ lies in Quadrant II,

$\theta = \dfrac{3\pi}{4}$. Thus, $-2 + 2i = 2\sqrt{2}\left(\cos \dfrac{3\pi}{4} + i \sin \dfrac{3\pi}{4} \right)$.

33. $[4(\cos 30° + i \sin 30°)][6(\cos 120° + i \sin 120°)] = (4)(6)[\cos(30° + 120°) + i \sin(30° + 120°)]$

$$= 24(\cos 150° + i \sin 150°)$$

$$= 24\left(-\frac{\sqrt{3}}{2} + \frac{1}{2}i \right)$$

$$= -12\sqrt{3} + 12i$$

34. $1 = 1(\cos 0 + i \sin 0)$

$$\sqrt[3]{1} = \sqrt[3]{1}\left[\cos\left(\frac{0 + 2\pi k}{3} \right) + i \sin\left(\frac{0 + 2\pi k}{3} \right) \right], k = 0, 1, 2$$

$$k = 0: \sqrt[3]{1}\left[\left(\cos\left(\frac{0 + 2\pi(0)}{3} \right) + i \sin\left(\frac{0 + 2\pi(0)}{3} \right) \right) \right] = 1$$

$$k = 1: \sqrt[3]{1}\left[\left(\cos\left(\frac{0 + 2\pi(1)}{3} \right) + i \sin\left(\frac{0 + 2\pi(1)}{3} \right) \right) \right] = \cos \frac{2\pi}{3} + i \sin \frac{2\pi}{3} = -\frac{1}{2} + \frac{\sqrt{3}}{2}i$$

$$k = 2: \sqrt[3]{1}\left[\left(\cos\left(\frac{0 + 2\pi(2)}{3} \right) + i \sin\left(\frac{0 + 2\pi(2)}{3} \right) \right) \right] = \cos \frac{4\pi}{3} + i \sin \frac{4\pi}{3} = -\frac{1}{2} - \frac{\sqrt{3}}{2}i$$

35. $x^4 - 256i = 0 \implies x^4 = 256i$

The solutions to the equation are the fourth roots of $z = 256i = 256\left(\cos\dfrac{\pi}{2} + i \sin\dfrac{\pi}{2}\right)$, which are:

$$\sqrt[4]{256}\left[\cos\dfrac{\dfrac{\pi}{2} + 2\pi k}{4} + i \sin\dfrac{\dfrac{\pi}{2} + 2\pi k}{4}\right], k = 0, 1, 2, 3$$

$k = 0$: $\quad 4\left(\cos\dfrac{\pi}{8} + i \sin\dfrac{\pi}{8}\right)$

$k = 1$: $\quad 4\left(\cos\dfrac{5\pi}{8} + i \sin\dfrac{5\pi}{8}\right)$

$k = 2$: $\quad 4\left(\cos\dfrac{9\pi}{8} + i \sin\dfrac{9\pi}{8}\right)$

$k = 3$: $\quad 4\left(\cos\dfrac{13\pi}{8} + i \sin\dfrac{13\pi}{8}\right)$

36. Height of smaller triangle:

$\tan 16° 45' = \dfrac{h_1}{200}$

$\qquad h_1 = 200 \tan 16.75° \approx 60.2$ feet

Height of larger triangle:

$\tan 18° = \dfrac{h_2}{200}$

$\qquad h_2 = 200 \tan 18° \approx 65.0$ feet

Height of flag:

$h_2 - h_1 = 65.0 - 60.2 \approx 5$ feet

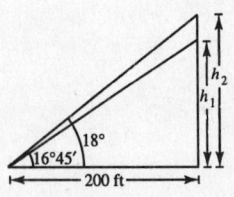

(Not drawn to scale)

37. Angular speed $= (2\pi)(45) = 90\pi$ radians per minute

Speed $= 3(90\pi) = 270\pi \approx 848.23$ inches per minute

38. $\tan \theta = \dfrac{5}{12} \implies \theta \approx 22.6°$

39. $\quad d = a \cos bt$

$|a| = 4 \implies a = 4$

$\dfrac{2\pi}{b} = 8 \implies b = \dfrac{\pi}{4}$

$d = 4 \cos\dfrac{\pi}{4}t$

40. $\quad \mathbf{v}_1 = 500\langle\cos 60°, \sin 60°\rangle = \langle 250, 250\sqrt{3}\rangle$

$\mathbf{v}_2 = 50\langle\cos 30°, \sin 30°\rangle = \langle 25\sqrt{3}, 25\rangle$

$\mathbf{v} = \mathbf{v}_1 + \mathbf{v}_2 = \langle 250 + 25\sqrt{3}, 250\sqrt{3} + 25\rangle$

$\qquad \approx \langle 293.3, 458.0\rangle$

$\|\mathbf{v}\| = \sqrt{(293.3)^2 + (458.0)^2} \approx 543.9$

$\tan \theta = \dfrac{458.0}{293.3} \approx 1.56 \implies \theta \approx 57.4°$

The plane is traveling N 32.6° E at 543.9 kilometers per hour.

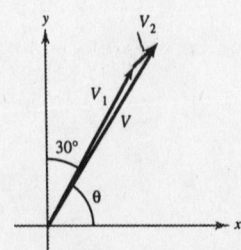

Chapter 7   Chapter Test

1. $\begin{cases} x - y = -7 \implies y = x + 7 \\ 4x + 5y = 8 \implies 4x + 5(x + 7) = 8 \end{cases}$

$$9x + 35 = 8$$
$$9x = -27$$
$$x = -3 \implies y = 4$$

Solution: $(-3, 4)$

2. $\begin{cases} y = x - 1 \\ y = (x - 1)^3 \end{cases}$

$$x - 1 = (x - 1)^3$$
$$x - 1 = x^3 - 3x^2 + 3x - 1$$
$$0 = x^3 - 3x^2 + 2x$$
$$0 = x(x - 1)(x - 2)$$
$$x = 0, \quad x = 1, \quad x = 2$$
$$y = -1, \quad y = 0, \quad y = 1$$

Solutions: $(0, -1), (1, 0), (2, 1)$

3. $\begin{cases} x - y = 4 \implies x = y + 4 \\ 2x - y^2 = 0 \implies 2(y + 4) - y^2 = 0 \end{cases}$

$$0 = y^2 - 2y - 8$$
$$0 = (y + 2)(y - 4)$$
$$y = -2 \quad \text{or} \quad y = 4$$
$$x = 2 \qquad x = 8$$

Solutions: $(2, -2), (8, 4)$

4. $\begin{cases} 2x - 3y = 0 \\ 2x + 3y = 12 \end{cases}$

Solution: $(3, 2)$

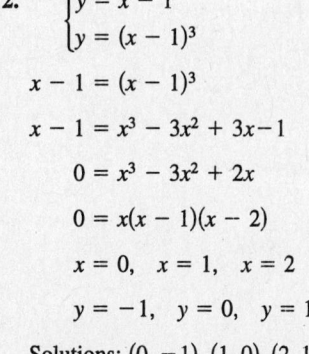

5. $\begin{cases} y = 9 - x^2 \\ y = x + 3 \end{cases}$

Solutions: $(-3, 0), (2, 5)$

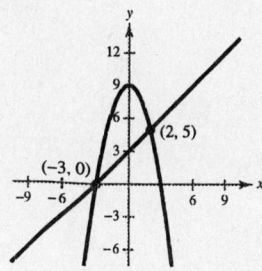

6. $\begin{cases} y - \ln x = 12 \implies y = 12 + \ln x \\ 7x - 2y + 11 = -6 \implies y = \frac{7}{2}x + \frac{17}{2} \end{cases}$

Solutions: $(1, 12), (0.034, 8.619)$

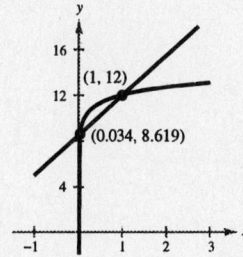

7. $\begin{cases} 2x + 3y = 17 \implies 8x + 12y = 68 \\ 5x - 4y = -15 \implies \underline{15x - 12y = -45} \end{cases}$

$$23x = 23$$
$$x = 1 \implies y = 5$$

Solution: $(1, 5)$

8. $\begin{cases} x - 2y + 3z = 11 \\ 2x \quad\quad - z = 3 \\ \quad\quad 3y + z = -8 \end{cases}$

$\begin{cases} x - 2y + 3z = 11 \\ \quad\quad 4y - 7z = -19 \quad -2\text{Eq.1} + \text{Eq.2} \\ \quad\quad 3y + z = -8 \end{cases}$

$\begin{cases} x - 2y + 3z = 11 \\ \quad\quad y - 8z = -11 \quad -\text{Eq.3} + \text{Eq.2} \\ \quad\quad 3y + z = -8 \end{cases}$

$\begin{cases} x - 2y + 3z = 11 \\ \quad\quad y - 8z = -11 \\ \quad\quad\quad 25z = 25 \quad -3\text{Eq.2} + \text{Eq.3} \end{cases}$

$\begin{cases} x - 2y + 3z = 11 \\ \quad\quad y - 8z = -11 \\ \quad\quad\quad z = 1 \quad \frac{1}{25}\text{Eq.3} \end{cases}$

$y - 8(1) = -11 \implies y = -3$

$x - 2(-3) + 3(1) = 11 \implies x = 2$

Solution: $(2, -3, 1)$

9. There are infinitely many systems with the solution $\left(\frac{4}{3}, -5\right)$.

Since $3\left(\frac{4}{3}\right) - (-5) = 9$

and $6\left(\frac{4}{3}\right) + (-5) - 3$

One possibility is:

$\begin{cases} 3x - y = 9 \\ 6x + y = 3 \end{cases}$

(Answer is not unique.)

10. $y = ax^2 + bx + c$

$(0, 6): \quad 6 = c$

$(-2, 2): \quad 2 = 4a - 2b + c$

$\left(3, \frac{9}{2}\right): \quad \frac{9}{2} = 9a + 3b + c$

Solving this system yields: $a = -\frac{1}{2}, b = 1,$ and $c = 6$.

Thus, $y = -\frac{1}{2}x^2 + x + 6$.

11. There are infinitely many systems with the solution $\left(-\frac{1}{2}, 6, -\frac{5}{4}\right)$.

Since $2\left(-\frac{1}{2}\right) - 6 - 4\left(-\frac{5}{4}\right) = -2$,

$4\left(-\frac{1}{2}\right) + 3(6) + 8\left(-\frac{5}{4}\right) = 6$,

and $-6\left(-\frac{1}{2}\right) + 6 - 12\left(-\frac{5}{4}\right) = 24$,

One possibility is:

$\begin{cases} 2x - y - 4z = -2 \\ 4x + 3y + 8z = 6 \\ -6x + y - 12z = 24 \end{cases}$

(Answer is not unique.)

12. $2x + y \leq 4$

$2x - y \geq 0$

$x \geq 0$

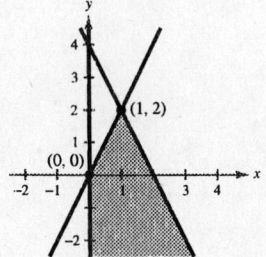

13. $y < -x^2 + x + 4$

$y > 4x$

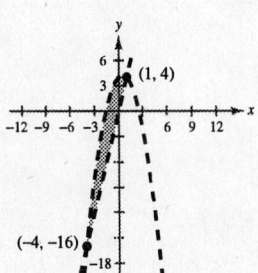

14. $x^2 + y^2 \leq 16$

$\quad\quad x \geq 1$

$\quad\quad y \geq -3$

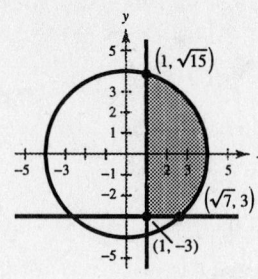

15. Maximize $z = 20x + 12y$ subject to:

$$\begin{cases} x \geq 0, y \geq 0 \\ x + 4y \leq 32 \\ 3x + 2y \leq 36 \end{cases}$$

At $(0, 0)$ we have $z = 0$.

At $(0, 8)$ we have $z = 96$.

At $(8, 6)$ we have $z = 232$.

At $(12, 0)$ we have $z = 240$.

The maximum value, $z = 240$, occurs at $(12, 0)$.

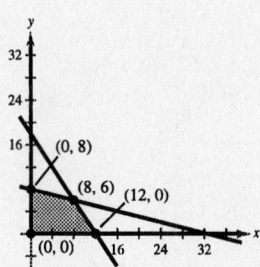

16. Maximize $P = 55x + 75y$ subject to:

$$\begin{cases} x \geq 0, \ y \geq 0 \\ x + y \leq 300 \\ 275x + 400y \leq 100{,}000 \end{cases}$$

At $(0, 0)$ we have $z = 0$.

At $(0, 250)$ we have $z = 18{,}750$.

At $(160, 140)$ we have $z = 19{,}300$.

At $(300, 0)$ we have $z = 16{,}500$.

The merchant should stock 160 units of the $275 model and 140 units of the $400 model to realize a maximum profit of $19,300.

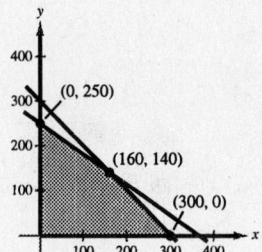

17. Maximize $P = 30x + 40y$ subject to:

$$\begin{cases} x \geq 0, \ y \geq 0 \\ 0.5x + 0.75y \leq 4000 \\ 2.0x + 1.5y \leq 8950 \\ 0.5x + 0.5y \leq 2650 \end{cases}$$

At $(0, 0)$: $P = 0$

At $(0, 5300)$: $P = 212{,}000$

At $(2000, 3300)$: $P = 192{,}000$

At $(4475, 0)$: $P = 134{,}250$

The manufacturer should produce 5300 units of Model II and not produce any of Model I to realize a maximum profit of $212,000.

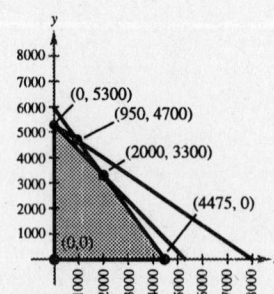

Chapter 8   Chapter Test

1.
$$\begin{bmatrix} 1 & -1 & 5 \\ 6 & 2 & 3 \\ 5 & 3 & -3 \end{bmatrix}$$

$$\begin{matrix} -6R_1 + R_2 \rightarrow \\ -5R_1 + R_3 \rightarrow \end{matrix} \begin{bmatrix} 1 & -1 & 5 \\ 0 & 8 & -27 \\ 0 & 8 & -28 \end{bmatrix}$$

$$-R_2 + R_3 \rightarrow \begin{bmatrix} 1 & -1 & 5 \\ 0 & 8 & -27 \\ 0 & 0 & -1 \end{bmatrix}$$

$$\begin{matrix} \frac{1}{8}R_2 \rightarrow \\ -R_3 \rightarrow \end{matrix} \begin{bmatrix} 1 & -1 & 5 \\ 0 & 1 & -\frac{27}{8} \\ 0 & 0 & 1 \end{bmatrix}$$

$$R_2 + R_1 \rightarrow \begin{bmatrix} 1 & 0 & \frac{13}{8} \\ 0 & 1 & -\frac{27}{8} \\ 0 & 0 & 1 \end{bmatrix}$$

$$\begin{matrix} -\frac{13}{8}R_3 + R_1 \rightarrow \\ \frac{27}{8}R_3 + R_2 \rightarrow \end{matrix} \begin{bmatrix} 1 & 0 & 0 \\ 0 & 1 & 0 \\ 0 & 0 & 1 \end{bmatrix}$$

2.
$$\begin{bmatrix} 1 & 0 & -1 & 2 \\ -1 & 1 & 1 & -3 \\ 1 & 1 & -1 & 1 \\ 3 & 2 & -3 & 4 \end{bmatrix}$$

$$\begin{matrix} R_1 + R_2 \rightarrow \\ -R_1 + R_3 \rightarrow \\ -3R_1 + R_4 \rightarrow \end{matrix} \begin{bmatrix} 1 & 0 & -1 & 2 \\ 0 & 1 & 0 & -1 \\ 0 & 1 & 0 & -1 \\ 0 & 2 & 0 & -2 \end{bmatrix}$$

$$\begin{matrix} -R_2 + R_3 \rightarrow \\ -2R_2 + R_4 \rightarrow \end{matrix} \begin{bmatrix} 1 & 0 & -1 & 2 \\ 0 & 1 & 0 & -1 \\ 0 & 0 & 0 & 0 \\ 0 & 0 & 0 & 0 \end{bmatrix}$$

3.
$$\begin{bmatrix} 4 & 3 & -2 & \vdots & 14 \\ -1 & -1 & 2 & \vdots & -5 \\ 3 & 1 & -4 & \vdots & 8 \end{bmatrix}$$

$$3R_2 + R_1 \rightarrow \begin{bmatrix} 1 & 0 & 4 & \vdots & -1 \\ -1 & -1 & 2 & \vdots & -5 \\ 3 & 1 & -4 & \vdots & 8 \end{bmatrix}$$

$$\begin{matrix} R_1 + R_2 \rightarrow \\ -3R_1 + R_3 \rightarrow \end{matrix} \begin{bmatrix} 1 & 0 & 4 & \vdots & -1 \\ 0 & -1 & 6 & \vdots & -6 \\ 0 & 1 & -16 & \vdots & 11 \end{bmatrix}$$

$$R_2 + R_3 \rightarrow \begin{bmatrix} 1 & 0 & 4 & \vdots & -1 \\ 0 & -1 & 6 & \vdots & -6 \\ 0 & 0 & -10 & \vdots & 5 \end{bmatrix}$$

$$\begin{matrix} -R_2 \rightarrow \\ -\frac{1}{10}R_3 \rightarrow \end{matrix} \begin{bmatrix} 1 & 0 & 4 & \vdots & -1 \\ 0 & 1 & -6 & \vdots & 6 \\ 0 & 0 & 1 & \vdots & -\frac{1}{2} \end{bmatrix}$$

$$\begin{matrix} -4R_3 + R_1 \rightarrow \\ 6R_3 + R_2 \rightarrow \end{matrix} \begin{bmatrix} 1 & 0 & 0 & \vdots & 1 \\ 0 & 1 & 0 & \vdots & 3 \\ 0 & 0 & 1 & \vdots & -\frac{1}{2} \end{bmatrix}$$

Solution: $\left(1, 3, -\frac{1}{2}\right)$

4. $y = ax^2 + bx + c$

$(-2, -2)$: $-2 = 4a - 2b + c$

$(2, 2)$: $2 = 4a + 2b + c$

$(4, -2)$: $-2 = 16a + 4b + c$

$$\begin{bmatrix} 4 & -2 & 1 & \vdots & -2 \\ 4 & 2 & 1 & \vdots & 2 \\ 16 & 4 & 1 & \vdots & -2 \end{bmatrix}$$

$$\begin{matrix} -R_1 + R_2 \rightarrow \\ -4R_1 + R_3 \rightarrow \end{matrix} \begin{bmatrix} 4 & -2 & 1 & \vdots & -2 \\ 0 & 4 & 0 & \vdots & 4 \\ 0 & 12 & -3 & \vdots & 6 \end{bmatrix}$$

$$\begin{matrix} \frac{1}{2}R_2 + R_1 \rightarrow \\ -3R_2 + R_3 \rightarrow \end{matrix} \begin{bmatrix} 4 & 0 & 1 & \vdots & 0 \\ 0 & 4 & 0 & \vdots & 4 \\ 0 & 0 & -3 & \vdots & -6 \end{bmatrix}$$

$$\begin{matrix} \frac{1}{4}R_1 \rightarrow \\ \frac{1}{4}R_2 \rightarrow \\ -\frac{1}{3}R_3 \rightarrow \end{matrix} \begin{bmatrix} 1 & 0 & \frac{1}{4} & \vdots & 0 \\ 0 & 1 & 0 & \vdots & 1 \\ 0 & 0 & 1 & \vdots & 2 \end{bmatrix}$$

$$-\frac{1}{4}R_3 + R_1 \rightarrow \begin{bmatrix} 1 & 0 & 0 & \vdots & -\frac{1}{2} \\ 0 & 1 & 0 & \vdots & 1 \\ 0 & 0 & 1 & \vdots & 2 \end{bmatrix}$$

Therefore, $a = -\frac{1}{2}$, $b = 1$, and $c = 2$.

The equation of the parabola is $y = -\frac{1}{2}x^2 + x + 2$.

5. (a) $A - B = \begin{bmatrix} 5 & 4 \\ -4 & -4 \end{bmatrix} - \begin{bmatrix} 4 & -1 \\ -4 & 0 \end{bmatrix}$

$= \begin{bmatrix} 1 & 5 \\ 0 & -4 \end{bmatrix}$

(b) $3A = 3\begin{bmatrix} 5 & 4 \\ -4 & -4 \end{bmatrix} = \begin{bmatrix} 15 & 12 \\ -12 & -12 \end{bmatrix}$

(c) $3A - 2B = 3\begin{bmatrix} 5 & 4 \\ -4 & -4 \end{bmatrix} - 2\begin{bmatrix} 4 & -1 \\ -4 & 0 \end{bmatrix}$

$= \begin{bmatrix} 15 & 12 \\ -12 & -12 \end{bmatrix} - \begin{bmatrix} 8 & -2 \\ -8 & 0 \end{bmatrix}$

$= \begin{bmatrix} 7 & 14 \\ -4 & -12 \end{bmatrix}$

(d) $AB = \begin{bmatrix} 5 & 4 \\ -4 & -4 \end{bmatrix}\begin{bmatrix} 4 & -1 \\ -4 & 0 \end{bmatrix}$

$= \begin{bmatrix} (5)(4) + (4)(-4) & (5)(-1) + (4)(0) \\ (-4)(4) + (-4)(-4) & (-4)(-1) + (-4)(0) \end{bmatrix}$

$= \begin{bmatrix} 4 & -5 \\ 0 & 4 \end{bmatrix}$

6. $\begin{bmatrix} -6 & 4 \\ 10 & -5 \end{bmatrix}^{-1} = \dfrac{1}{(-6)(-5) - (4)(10)}\begin{bmatrix} -5 & -4 \\ -10 & -6 \end{bmatrix} = \begin{bmatrix} \frac{1}{2} & \frac{2}{5} \\ 1 & \frac{3}{5} \end{bmatrix}$

7.
$$\begin{bmatrix} -2 & 4 & -6 & \vdots & 1 & 0 & 0 \\ 2 & 1 & 0 & \vdots & 0 & 1 & 0 \\ 4 & -2 & 5 & \vdots & 0 & 0 & 1 \end{bmatrix}$$

$\begin{matrix} \\ R_1 + R_2 \rightarrow \\ 2R_1 + R_3 \rightarrow \end{matrix}\begin{bmatrix} -2 & 4 & -6 & \vdots & 1 & 0 & 0 \\ 0 & 5 & -6 & \vdots & 1 & 1 & 0 \\ 0 & 6 & -7 & \vdots & 2 & 0 & 1 \end{bmatrix}$

$\begin{matrix} -\frac{1}{2}R_1 \rightarrow \\ -R_3 + R_2 \rightarrow \\ \\ \end{matrix}\begin{bmatrix} 1 & -2 & 3 & \vdots & -\frac{1}{2} & 0 & 0 \\ 0 & -1 & 1 & \vdots & -1 & 1 & -1 \\ 0 & 6 & -7 & \vdots & 2 & 0 & 1 \end{bmatrix}$

$\begin{matrix} -2R_2 + R_1 \rightarrow \\ \\ 6R_2 + R_3 \rightarrow \end{matrix}\begin{bmatrix} 1 & 0 & 1 & \vdots & \frac{3}{2} & -2 & 2 \\ 0 & -1 & 1 & \vdots & -1 & 1 & -1 \\ 0 & 0 & -1 & \vdots & -4 & 6 & -5 \end{bmatrix}$

$\begin{matrix} \\ -R_2 \rightarrow \\ -R_3 \rightarrow \end{matrix}\begin{bmatrix} 1 & 0 & 1 & \vdots & \frac{3}{2} & -2 & 2 \\ 0 & 1 & -1 & \vdots & 1 & -1 & 1 \\ 0 & 0 & 1 & \vdots & 4 & -6 & 5 \end{bmatrix}$

$\begin{matrix} -R_3 + R_1 \rightarrow \\ R_3 + R_2 \rightarrow \\ \\ \end{matrix}\begin{bmatrix} 1 & 0 & 0 & \vdots & -\frac{5}{2} & 4 & -3 \\ 0 & 1 & 0 & \vdots & 5 & -7 & 6 \\ 0 & 0 & 1 & \vdots & 4 & -6 & 5 \end{bmatrix}$

$A^{-1} = \begin{bmatrix} -\frac{5}{2} & 4 & -3 \\ 5 & -7 & 6 \\ 4 & -6 & 5 \end{bmatrix}$

8. $\begin{cases} -6x + 4y = 10 \\ 10x - 5y = 20 \end{cases}$

$\begin{bmatrix} x \\ y \end{bmatrix} = \begin{bmatrix} \frac{1}{2} & \frac{2}{5} \\ 1 & \frac{3}{5} \end{bmatrix}\begin{bmatrix} 10 \\ 20 \end{bmatrix} = \begin{bmatrix} \frac{1}{2}(10) + \frac{2}{5}(20) \\ 1(10) + \frac{3}{5}(20) \end{bmatrix} = \begin{bmatrix} 13 \\ 22 \end{bmatrix}$

Solution: $(13, 22)$

9. $\begin{vmatrix} -9 & 4 \\ 13 & 16 \end{vmatrix} = (-9)(16) - (4)(13) = -196$

10. $\begin{vmatrix} \frac{5}{2} & \frac{13}{4} \\ -8 & \frac{6}{5} \end{vmatrix} = \left(\frac{5}{2}\right)\left(\frac{6}{5}\right) - \left(\frac{13}{4}\right)(-8) = 29$

11. $\begin{cases} 7x + 6y = 9 \\ -2x - 11y = -49 \end{cases}$ $D = \begin{vmatrix} 7 & 6 \\ -2 & -11 \end{vmatrix} = -65$

$$x = \frac{\begin{vmatrix} 9 & 6 \\ -49 & -11 \end{vmatrix}}{-65} = \frac{195}{-65} = -3$$

$$y = \frac{\begin{vmatrix} 7 & 9 \\ -2 & -49 \end{vmatrix}}{-65} = \frac{-325}{-65} = 5$$

Solution: $(-3, 5)$

12. $\begin{cases} 6x - y + 2z = -4 \\ -2x + 3y - z = 10 \\ 4x - 4y + z = -18 \end{cases}$ $D = \begin{vmatrix} 6 & -1 & 2 \\ -2 & 3 & -1 \\ 4 & -4 & 1 \end{vmatrix} = -12$

$$x = \frac{\begin{vmatrix} -4 & -1 & 2 \\ 10 & 3 & -1 \\ -18 & -4 & 1 \end{vmatrix}}{-12} = \frac{24}{-12} = -2$$

$$y = \frac{\begin{vmatrix} 6 & -4 & 2 \\ -2 & 10 & -1 \\ 4 & -18 & 1 \end{vmatrix}}{-12} = \frac{-48}{-12} = 4$$

$$z = \frac{\begin{vmatrix} 6 & -1 & -4 \\ -2 & 3 & 10 \\ 4 & -4 & -18 \end{vmatrix}}{-12} = \frac{-72}{-12} = 6$$

Solution: $(-2, 4, 6)$

13. $A = -\frac{1}{2} \begin{vmatrix} -5 & 0 & 1 \\ 4 & 4 & 1 \\ 3 & 2 & 1 \end{vmatrix} = -\frac{1}{2}(-14) = 7$

14. $\begin{matrix} K & N & O \\ C & K & - \\ O & N & - \\ W & O & O \\ D & - & - \end{matrix} \begin{bmatrix} 11 & 14 & 15 \\ 3 & 11 & 0 \\ 15 & 14 & 0 \\ 23 & 15 & 15 \\ 4 & 0 & 0 \end{bmatrix} \begin{bmatrix} 1 & -1 & 0 \\ 1 & 0 & -1 \\ 6 & -2 & -3 \end{bmatrix} = \begin{bmatrix} 115 & -41 & -59 \\ 14 & -3 & -11 \\ 29 & -15 & -14 \\ 128 & -53 & -60 \\ 4 & -4 & 0 \end{bmatrix}$

Message: $[11 \ 14 \ 15], [3 \ 11 \ 0], [15 \ 14 \ 0], [23 \ 15 \ 15], [4 \ 0 \ 0]$

Encoded Message: $115 \ -41 \ -59 \ 14 \ -3 \ -11 \ 29 \ -15 \ -14 \ 128 \ -53 \ -60 \ 4 \ -4 \ 0$

15. Let $x = $ amount of 60% solution and $y = $ amount of 20% solution.

$$\begin{cases} x + y = 100 \implies y = 100 - x \\ 0.60x + 0.20y = 0.50(100) \implies 6x + 2y = 500 \end{cases}$$

By substitution, we have

$$6x + 2(100 - x) = 500$$

$$6x + 200 - 2x = 500$$

$$4x = 300$$

$$x = 75$$

$$y = 100 - x = 25$$

Answer: 75 liters of 60% solution and 25 liters of 20% solution.

Chapter 9   Chapter Test

1. $a_n = \dfrac{(-1)^n}{3n + 2}$

$a_1 = -\dfrac{1}{5}$

$a_2 = \dfrac{1}{8}$

$a_3 = -\dfrac{1}{11}$

$a_4 = \dfrac{1}{14}$

$a_5 = -\dfrac{1}{17}$

2. $\dfrac{3}{1!}, \dfrac{4}{2!}, \dfrac{5}{3!}, \dfrac{6}{4!}, \dfrac{7}{5!}, \cdots$

$a_n = \dfrac{n + 2}{n!}$

3. $6 + 17 + 28 + 39 + \cdots$

$a_n = 11n - 5$

$a_5 = 50$

$S_5 = 6 + 17 + 28 + 39 + 50$

$\quad = 140$

4. $a_5 = 5.4, a_{12} = 11.0$

$a_{12} = a_5 + 7d$

$11.0 = 5.4 + 7d$

$5.6 = 7d$

$0.8 = d$

$a_{30} = a_{12} + 18d$

$\quad = 11.0 + 18(0.8)$

$\quad = 25.4$

5. $a_n = 5(2)^{n-1}$

$a_1 = 5$

$a_2 = 10$

$a_3 = 20$

$a_4 = 40$

$a_5 = 80$

6. $\displaystyle\sum_{i=1}^{50} (2i^2 + 5) = 2\sum_{i=1}^{50} i^2 + \sum_{i=1}^{50} 5$

$\quad = 2\left[\dfrac{50(51)(101)}{6}\right] + 50(5)$

$\quad = 86{,}100$

7. $\displaystyle\sum_{i=1}^{\infty} 4\left(\dfrac{1}{2}\right)^i = \dfrac{2}{1 - \dfrac{1}{2}} = 4$

8. $5 + 10 + 15 + \cdots + 5n = \dfrac{5n(n + 1)}{2}$

When $n = 1$, $S_1 = 5 = \dfrac{5(1)(2)}{2}$, so the formula is valid.

Assume that $S_k = 5 + 10 + 15 + \cdots + 5k = \dfrac{5k(k + 1)}{2}$, then $S_{k+1} = S_k + a_{k+1}$

$$= \dfrac{5k(k + 1)}{2} + 5(k + 1)$$

$$= \dfrac{5k(k + 1)}{2} + \dfrac{10(k + 1)}{2}$$

$$= \dfrac{5k(k + 1) + 10(k + 1)}{2}$$

$$= \dfrac{5(k + 1)(k + 2)}{2}$$

$$= \dfrac{5(k + 1)[(k + 1) + 1]}{2}$$

Thus, the formula is valid for all integers $n \geq 1$.

9. $(x + 2y)^4 = x^4 + 4x^3(2y) + 6x^2(2y)^2 + 4x(2y)^3 + (2y)^4$
$= x^4 + 8x^3y + 24x^2y^2 + 32xy^3 + 16y^4$

10. $(6)(10)(3) = 180$ outfits

11. (a) $_9P_2 = \dfrac{9!}{7!} = 72$

(b) $_{70}P_3 = \dfrac{70!}{67!} = 328{,}440$

12. (a) $_{11}C_4 = \dfrac{11!}{7!4!} = 330$

(b) $_{66}C_4 = \dfrac{66!}{62!4!} = 720{,}720$

13. $\underbrace{(1)}_{\substack{\text{owner}}} \cdot \underbrace{(3)(2)}_{\substack{\text{bow} \\ \text{seats}}} \cdot \underbrace{(5)(4)(3)(2)(1)}_{\substack{\text{remaining} \\ \text{seats}}} = 720$ seating arrangements

14. $\dfrac{20}{300} = \dfrac{1}{15} \approx 0.0667$

15. $\dfrac{1}{_{60}C_8} \approx 3.908 \times 10^{-10}$

16. $P(A') = 1 - 0.75 = 0.25 = 25\%$

Chapters 7–9   Cumulative Test

1. $\begin{cases} y = 3 - x^2 \\ 2(y - 2) = x - 1 \end{cases} \Longrightarrow 2(3 - x^2 - 2) = x - 1$

$$2(1 - x^2) = x - 1$$

$$2 - 2x^2 = x - 1$$

$$0 = 2x^2 + x - 3$$

$$0 = (2x + 3)(x - 1)$$

$$x = -\tfrac{3}{2} \quad \text{or} \quad x = 1$$

$$y = \tfrac{3}{4} \qquad \quad y = 2$$

Solutions: $\left(-\tfrac{3}{2}, \tfrac{3}{4}\right)$, $(1, 2)$

2. $\begin{cases} x + 3y = -1 \\ 2x + 4y = 0 \end{cases}$ $\begin{aligned} \Rightarrow \quad & 4x + 12y = -4 \\ \Rightarrow \quad & \underline{-6x - 12y = 0} \\ & \quad -2x \qquad = -4 \\ & \qquad x = 2 \Rightarrow y = -1 \end{aligned}$

Solution: $(2, -1)$

3. $\begin{cases} -2x + 4y - z = 3 \\ x - 2y + 2z = -6 \\ x - 3y - z = 1 \end{cases}$

Interchange equations.

$\begin{cases} x - 2y + 2z = -6 \qquad \text{Eq.1} \\ -2x + 4y - z = 3 \qquad \text{Eq.2} \\ x - 3y - z = 1 \qquad \text{Eq.3} \end{cases}$

$\begin{cases} x - 2y + 2z = -6 \\ \qquad\qquad 3z = -9 \qquad 2\text{Eq.1} + \text{Eq.2} \\ \qquad -y - 3z = 7 \qquad -\text{Eq.1} + \text{Eq.3} \end{cases}$

From Equation 2 we have $z = -3$. Substituting this into Equation 3 yields $y = 2$. Using these in Equation 1 yields $x = 4$.

Solution: $(4, 2, -3)$

4. $\begin{cases} x + 3y - 2z = -7 \\ -2x + y - z = -5 \\ 4x + y + z = 3 \end{cases}$

$\begin{cases} x + 3y - 2z = -7 \\ \qquad 7y - 5z = -19 \qquad 2\text{Eq.1} + \text{Eq.2} \\ \qquad -11y + 9z = 31 \qquad -4\text{Eq.1} + \text{Eq.3} \end{cases}$

$\begin{cases} x + 3y - 2z = -7 \\ \qquad y - \frac{5}{7}z = -\frac{19}{7} \qquad \frac{1}{7}\text{Eq.2} \\ \qquad -11y + 9z = 31 \end{cases}$

$\begin{cases} x \qquad + \frac{1}{7}z = \frac{8}{7} \qquad -3\text{Eq.2} + \text{Eq.1} \\ \qquad y - \frac{5}{7}z = -\frac{19}{7} \\ \qquad\qquad \frac{8}{7}z = \frac{8}{7} \qquad 11\text{Eq.2} + \text{Eq.3} \end{cases}$

$\begin{cases} x \qquad + \frac{1}{7}z = \frac{8}{7} \\ \qquad y - \frac{5}{7}z = -\frac{19}{7} \\ \qquad\qquad z = 1 \qquad \frac{7}{8}\text{Eq.3} \end{cases}$

$\begin{cases} x \qquad = 1 \qquad -\frac{1}{7}\text{Eq.3} + \text{Eq.1} \\ \qquad y \qquad = -2 \qquad \frac{5}{7}\text{Eq.3} + \text{Eq.2} \\ \qquad\qquad z = 1 \end{cases}$

Solution: $(1, -2, 1)$

5. $\begin{cases} 2x + y \geq -3 \\ x - 3y \leq 2 \end{cases}$

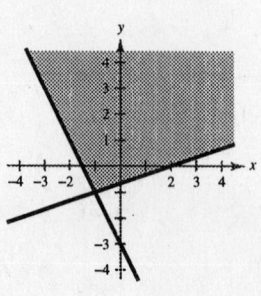

6. $\begin{cases} x - y > 6 \\ 5x + 2y < 10 \end{cases}$

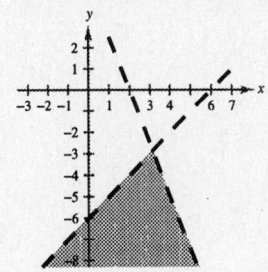

7. Maximize $z = 3x + 2y$.

Subject to: $x + 4y \le 20$

$\qquad\qquad 2x + y \le 12$

$\qquad\qquad x \ge 0, y \ge 0$

At $(0, 0)$: $z = 0$

At $(0, 5)$: $z = 10$

At $(4, 4)$: $z = 20$

At $(6, 0)$: $z = 18$

Maximum of $z = 20$ at $(4, 4)$

8. $\begin{cases} x + y = 200 \implies y = 200 - x \\ 0.75x + 1.25y = 0.95(200) \end{cases}$

$0.75x + 1.25y(200 - x) = 190$

$0.75x + 250 - 1.25x = 190$

$\qquad\qquad\quad -0.50x = -60$

$\qquad\qquad\qquad\quad x = 120$

$\qquad\qquad y = 200 - x = 80$

Answer: 120 pounds of $0.75 seed and 80 pounds of $1.25 seed

9. $y = ax^2 + bx + c$

$(0, 4)$: $4 = a(0)^2 + b(0) + c \implies c = 4$

$(3, 1)$: $1 = a(3)^2 + b(3) + 4 \implies 9a + 3b = -3$

$\qquad\qquad\qquad\qquad\qquad\qquad 3a + b = -1$

$(6, 4)$: $4 = a(6)^2 + b(6) + 4 \implies 36a + 6b = 0$

$\qquad\qquad\qquad\qquad\qquad\qquad 6a + b = 0$

Solving the system: $\begin{cases} 3a + b = -1 \\ 6a + b = 0 \end{cases}$

yields $a = \frac{1}{3}$ and $b = -2$.

Thus, the equation of the parabola is $y = \frac{1}{3}x^2 - 2x + 4$.

10. $\begin{cases} -x + 2y - z = 9 \\ 2x - y + 2z = -9 \\ 3x + 3y - 4z = 7 \end{cases}$ $\qquad \begin{bmatrix} -1 & 2 & -1 & \vdots & 9 \\ 2 & -1 & 2 & \vdots & -9 \\ 3 & 3 & -4 & \vdots & 7 \end{bmatrix}$

11. $\begin{bmatrix} -1 & 2 & -1 & \vdots & 9 \\ 2 & -1 & 2 & \vdots & -9 \\ 3 & 3 & -4 & \vdots & 7 \end{bmatrix}$

$\begin{matrix} \\ 2R_1 + R_2 \to \\ 3R_1 + R_3 \to \end{matrix} \begin{bmatrix} -1 & 2 & -1 & \vdots & 9 \\ 0 & 3 & 0 & \vdots & 9 \\ 0 & 9 & -7 & \vdots & 34 \end{bmatrix}$

$\begin{matrix} -R_1 \\ \\ -3R_2 + R_3 \to \end{matrix} \begin{bmatrix} 1 & -2 & 1 & \vdots & -9 \\ 0 & 3 & 0 & \vdots & 3 \\ 0 & 0 & -7 & \vdots & 7 \end{bmatrix}$

— **CONTINUED** —

11. — CONTINUED —

$$\begin{array}{c} \\ \frac{1}{3}R_2 \rightarrow \\ -\frac{1}{7}R_3 \rightarrow \end{array} \begin{bmatrix} 1 & -2 & 1 & : & -9 \\ 0 & 1 & 0 & : & 3 \\ 0 & 0 & 1 & : & -1 \end{bmatrix}$$

$$\begin{array}{c} 2R_2 + R_1 \rightarrow \\ \\ \\ \end{array} \begin{bmatrix} 1 & 0 & 1 & : & -3 \\ 0 & 1 & 0 & : & 3 \\ 0 & 0 & 1 & : & -1 \end{bmatrix}$$

$$\begin{array}{c} -R_3 + R_1 \rightarrow \\ \\ \\ \end{array} \begin{bmatrix} 1 & 0 & 0 & : & -2 \\ 0 & 1 & 0 & : & 3 \\ 0 & 0 & 1 & : & -1 \end{bmatrix}$$

Solution: $(-2, 3, -1)$

12. $A - B = \begin{bmatrix} 4 & 0 \\ -1 & 2 \end{bmatrix} - \begin{bmatrix} -1 & 3 \\ 1 & 0 \end{bmatrix} = \begin{bmatrix} 5 & -3 \\ -2 & 2 \end{bmatrix}$ **13.** $-2B = -2\begin{bmatrix} -1 & 3 \\ 1 & 0 \end{bmatrix} = \begin{bmatrix} 2 & -6 \\ -2 & 0 \end{bmatrix}$

14. Use the result of Exercise 13.

$$A - 2B = A + (-2B) = \begin{bmatrix} 4 & 0 \\ -1 & 2 \end{bmatrix} + \begin{bmatrix} 2 & -6 \\ -2 & 0 \end{bmatrix} = \begin{bmatrix} 6 & -6 \\ -3 & 2 \end{bmatrix}$$

15. $AB = \begin{bmatrix} 4 & 0 \\ -1 & 2 \end{bmatrix}\begin{bmatrix} -1 & 3 \\ 1 & 0 \end{bmatrix} = \begin{bmatrix} (4)(-1) + (0)(1) & (4)(3) + (0)(0) \\ (-1)(-1) + 2(1) & (-1)(3) + (2)(0) \end{bmatrix}\begin{bmatrix} -4 & 12 \\ 3 & -3 \end{bmatrix}$

16.

$$\begin{bmatrix} 1 & 2 & -1 & : & 1 & 0 & 0 \\ 3 & 7 & -10 & : & 0 & 1 & 0 \\ -5 & -7 & -15 & : & 0 & 0 & 1 \end{bmatrix}$$

$$\begin{array}{c} -3R_1 + R_2 \rightarrow \\ 5R_1 + R_3 \rightarrow \end{array} \begin{bmatrix} 1 & 2 & -1 & : & 1 & 0 & 0 \\ 0 & 1 & -7 & : & -3 & 1 & 0 \\ 0 & 3 & -20 & : & 5 & 0 & 1 \end{bmatrix}$$

$$\begin{array}{c} -2R_2 + R_1 \rightarrow \\ \\ -3R_2 + R_3 \rightarrow \end{array} \begin{bmatrix} 1 & 0 & 13 & : & 7 & -2 & 0 \\ 0 & 1 & -7 & : & -3 & 1 & 0 \\ 0 & 0 & 1 & : & 14 & -3 & 1 \end{bmatrix}$$

$$\begin{array}{c} -13R_3 + R_1 \rightarrow \\ 7R_3 + R_2 \rightarrow \end{array} \begin{bmatrix} 1 & 0 & 0 & : & -175 & 37 & -13 \\ 0 & 1 & 0 & : & 95 & -20 & 7 \\ 0 & 0 & 1 & : & 14 & -3 & 1 \end{bmatrix}$$

$$\begin{bmatrix} 1 & 2 & -1 \\ 3 & 7 & -10 \\ -5 & -7 & -15 \end{bmatrix}^{-1} = \begin{bmatrix} -175 & 37 & -13 \\ 95 & -20 & 7 \\ 14 & -3 & 1 \end{bmatrix}$$

17. Let x = total sales of gym shoes ($ millions)

y = total sales of jogging shoes ($ millions)

z = total sales of walking shoes ($ millions)

$$\begin{bmatrix} 0.14 & 0.13 & 0.03 \\ 0.05 & 0.10 & 0.04 \\ 0.10 & 0.19 & 0.11 \end{bmatrix} \begin{bmatrix} x \\ y \\ z \end{bmatrix} = \begin{bmatrix} 518.97 \\ 336.16 \\ 753.37 \end{bmatrix}$$

$$\begin{bmatrix} 0.14 & 0.13 & 0.03 & \vdots & 518.97 \\ 0.05 & 0.10 & 0.04 & \vdots & 336.16 \\ 0.10 & 0.19 & 0.11 & \vdots & 753.37 \end{bmatrix}$$

$$\begin{matrix} 100R_1 \to \\ 20R_2 \to \\ 100R_3 \to \end{matrix} \begin{bmatrix} 14 & 13 & 3 & \vdots & 51,897 \\ 1 & 2 & 0.8 & \vdots & 6723.2 \\ 10 & 19 & 11 & \vdots & 75,337 \end{bmatrix}$$

$$\begin{matrix} R_1 \\ R_2 \end{matrix} \begin{bmatrix} 1 & 2 & 0.8 & \vdots & 6723.2 \\ 14 & 13 & 3 & \vdots & 51,897 \\ 10 & 19 & 11 & \vdots & 75,337 \end{bmatrix}$$

$$\begin{matrix} \\ -14R_1 + R_2 \to \\ -10R_1 + R_3 \to \end{matrix} \begin{bmatrix} 1 & 2 & 0.8 & \vdots & 6723.2 \\ 0 & -15 & -8.2 & \vdots & -42,227.8 \\ 0 & -1 & 3 & \vdots & 8105 \end{bmatrix}$$

$$\begin{matrix} \\ R_2 \\ R_3 \end{matrix} \begin{bmatrix} 1 & 2 & 0.8 & \vdots & 6723.2 \\ 0 & -1 & 3 & \vdots & 8105 \\ 0 & -15 & -8.2 & \vdots & -42,227.8 \end{bmatrix}$$

$$\begin{matrix} 2R_2 + R_1 \to \\ \\ -15R_2 + R_3 \to \end{matrix} \begin{bmatrix} 1 & 0 & 6.8 & \vdots & 22,933.2 \\ 0 & -1 & 3 & \vdots & 8105 \\ 0 & 0 & -53.2 & \vdots & -163,802.8 \end{bmatrix}$$

$$\begin{matrix} \\ -R_2 \to \\ -\frac{1}{53.2}R_3 \to \end{matrix} \begin{bmatrix} 1 & 0 & 6.8 & \vdots & 22,933.2 \\ 0 & 1 & -3 & \vdots & -8105 \\ 0 & 0 & 1 & \vdots & 3079 \end{bmatrix}$$

$$\begin{matrix} -6.8R_3 + R_1 \to \\ 3R_3 + R_2 \to \\ \end{matrix} \begin{bmatrix} 1 & 0 & 0 & \vdots & 1996 \\ 0 & 1 & 0 & \vdots & 1132 \\ 0 & 0 & 1 & \vdots & 3079 \end{bmatrix}$$

Therefore, $x = 1996$, $y = 1132$, and $z = 3079$.

In 1996, sales amounted to $1.996 billion of gym shoes, $1.132 billion of jogging shoes, and $3.079 billion of walking shoes.

18. $\begin{cases} 8x - 3y = -52 \\ 3x + 5y = 5 \end{cases}$ $D = \begin{vmatrix} 8 & -3 \\ 3 & 5 \end{vmatrix} = 49$

$$x = \frac{\begin{vmatrix} -52 & -3 \\ 5 & 5 \end{vmatrix}}{49} = \frac{-245}{49} = -5$$

$$y = \frac{\begin{vmatrix} 8 & -52 \\ 3 & 5 \end{vmatrix}}{49} = \frac{196}{49} = 4$$

Solution: $(-5, 4)$

19. $\begin{cases} 5x + 4y + 3z = 7 \\ -3x - 8y + 7z = -9 \\ 7x - 5y - 6z = -53 \end{cases}$ $D = \begin{vmatrix} 5 & 4 & 3 \\ -3 & -8 & 7 \\ 7 & -5 & -6 \end{vmatrix} = 752$

$x = \dfrac{\begin{vmatrix} 7 & 4 & 3 \\ -9 & -8 & 7 \\ -53 & -5 & -6 \end{vmatrix}}{752} = \dfrac{-2256}{752} = -3$

$y = \dfrac{\begin{vmatrix} 5 & 7 & 3 \\ -3 & -9 & 7 \\ 7 & -53 & -6 \end{vmatrix}}{752} = \dfrac{3008}{752} = 4$

$z = \dfrac{\begin{vmatrix} 5 & 4 & 7 \\ -3 & -8 & -9 \\ 7 & -5 & -53 \end{vmatrix}}{752} = \dfrac{1504}{752} = 2$

Solution: $(-3, 4, 2)$

20. $A = \pm\dfrac{1}{2}\begin{vmatrix} -2 & 3 & 1 \\ 1 & 5 & 1 \\ 4 & 1 & 1 \end{vmatrix} = -\dfrac{1}{2}(-18) = 9$

21. $a_n = \dfrac{(-1)^{n+1}}{2n + 3}$

$a_1 = \dfrac{1}{5}$

$a_2 = -\dfrac{1}{7}$

$a_3 = \dfrac{1}{9}$

$a_4 = -\dfrac{1}{11}$

$a_5 = \dfrac{1}{13}$

22. $\dfrac{2!}{4}, \dfrac{3!}{5}, \dfrac{4!}{6}, \dfrac{5!}{7}, \dfrac{6!}{8}, \cdots$

$a_n = \dfrac{(n + 1)!}{n + 3}$

23. $8, 12, 16, 20, \ldots$

$a_n = 4n + 4$

$a_1 = 8, \; a_{20} = 84$

$S_{20} = \dfrac{20}{2}(8 + 84) = 920$

24. $a_6 = 20.6$

$a_9 = 30.2$

$a_9 = a_6 + 3d$

$30.2 = 20.6 + 3d$

$9.6 = 3d$

$3.2 = d$

$a_{20} = a_9 + 11d$

$\quad = 30.2 + 11(3.2)$

$\quad = 65.4$

25. $a_n = 3(2)^{n-1}$

$a_1 = 3$

$a_2 = 6$

$a_3 = 12$

$a_4 = 24$

$a_5 = 48$

26. $\displaystyle\sum_{i=0}^{\infty} 3\left(\frac{1}{2}\right)^i = \frac{3}{1 - (1/2)} = 6$

27. $S_1 = 3 = 1[2(1) + 1]$

Assume that $S_k = 3 + 7 + 11 + 15 + \cdots + (4k - 1) = k(2k + 1)$.

Then, $S_{k+1} = 3 + 7 + 11 + 15 + \cdots + (4k - 1) + [4(k + 1) - 1]$

$$= S_k + (4k + 3)$$

$$= k(2k + 1) + (4k + 3)$$

$$= 2k^2 + 5k + 3$$

$$= (k + 1)(2k + 3)$$

$$= (k + 1)[2(k + 1) + 1].$$

Therefore, the formula is valid for all integers $n \geq 1$.

28. $(z - 3)^4 = z^4 - 4z^3(3) + 6z^2(3)^2 - 4z(3)^3 + (3)^4$

$$= z^4 - 12z^3 + 54z^2 - 108z + 81$$

29. $_7P_3 = \dfrac{7!}{(7 - 3)!} = \dfrac{7!}{4!} = 210$

30. $_{25}P_2 = \dfrac{25!}{(25 - 2)!} = \dfrac{25!}{23!} = 600$

31. $\dbinom{8}{4} = {}_8C_4 = \dfrac{8!}{(8 - 4)!4!} = \dfrac{8!}{4!4!} = 70$

32. $_{10}C_3 = \dfrac{10!}{(10 - 3)!3!} = \dfrac{10!}{7!3!} = 120$

33. $_{10}P_3 = \dfrac{10!}{(10 - 3)!} = \dfrac{10!}{7!} = 720$

34. The first digit is 4 or 5, so the probability of picking it correctly is $\frac{1}{2}$. Then there are two numbers left for the second digit so its probability is also $\frac{1}{2}$. If these two are correct, then the third digit must be the remaining number. The probability of winning is:

$$\left(\tfrac{1}{2}\right)\left(\tfrac{1}{2}\right)(1) = \tfrac{1}{4}$$

Chapter 10   Chapter Test

1. $2x - 7y + 3 = 0$

$$y = \frac{2}{7}x + \frac{3}{7}$$

$$\tan \theta = \frac{2}{7}$$

$$\theta \approx 15.9°$$

2. $3x + 2y - 4 = 0 \Rightarrow y = -\frac{3}{2}x + 2 \Rightarrow m_1 = -\frac{3}{2}$

$4x - y + 6 = 0 \Rightarrow y = 4x + 6 \Rightarrow m_2 = 4$

$$\tan \theta = \left| \frac{4 - \left(-\frac{3}{2}\right)}{1 + 4\left(-\frac{3}{2}\right)} \right| = \frac{11}{10}$$

$$\theta \approx 47.7°$$

3. $y = 5 - x \Rightarrow x + y - 5 = 0 \Rightarrow A = 1, B = 1, C = -5$

$(x_1, y_1) = (7, 5)$

$$d = \frac{|(1)(7) + (1)(5) + (-5)|}{\sqrt{1^2 + 1^2}} = \frac{7}{\sqrt{2}} = \frac{7\sqrt{2}}{2}$$

4. $y^2 - 4x + 4 = 0$

$$y^2 = 4(x - 1)$$

Parabola

Vertex: $(1, 0)$

Focus: $(2, 0)$

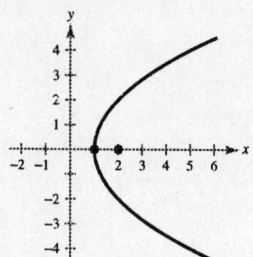

5. $x^2 - 4y^2 - 4x = 0$

$(x - 2)^2 - 4y^2 = 4$

$$\frac{(x - 2)^2}{4} - \frac{y^2}{1} = 1$$

Hyperbola

Center: $(2, 0)$

Horizontal transverse axis

$a = 2, b = 1, c^2 = 1 + 4 = 5 \Rightarrow c = \sqrt{5}$

Vertices: $(0, 0), (4, 0)$

Foci: $\left(2 \pm \sqrt{5}, 0\right)$

Asymptotes: $y = \pm\frac{1}{2}(x - 2)$

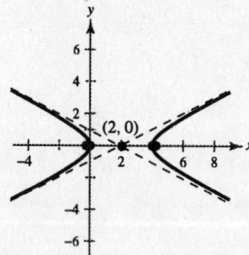

6. $9x^2 + 16y^2 + 54x - 32y - 47 = 0$

$9(x^2 + 6x + 9) + 16(y^2 - 2y + 1) = 47 + 81 + 16$

$9(x + 3)^2 + 16(y - 1)^2 = 144$

$$\frac{(x + 3)^2}{16} + \frac{(y - 1)^2}{9} = 1$$

Ellipse

Center: $(-3, 1)$

$a = 4, b = 3, c = \sqrt{7}$

Foci: $\left(-3 \pm \sqrt{7}, 1\right)$

Vertices: $(1, 1), (-7, 1)$

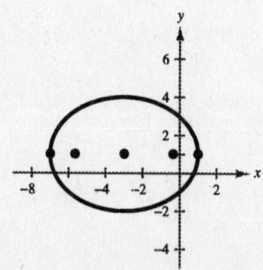

7.

$$2x^2 + 2y^2 - 8x - 4y + 9 = 0$$

$$2(x^2 - 4x + 4) + 2(y^2 - 2y + 1) = -9 + 8 + 2$$

$$2(x - 2)^2 + 2(y - 1)^2 = 1$$

$$(x - 2)^2 + (y - 1)^2 = \frac{1}{2}$$

Circle

Center: $(2, 1)$

Radius: $\sqrt{\dfrac{1}{2}} = \dfrac{\sqrt{2}}{2} \approx 0.707$

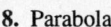

8. Parabola

Vertex: $(3, -2)$

Vertical axis

Point: $(0, 4)$

$$(x - h)^2 = 4p(y - k)$$

$$(x - 3)^2 = 4p(y + 2)$$

$$(0 - 3)^2 = 4p(4 + 2)$$

$$9 = 24p$$

$$p = \frac{9}{24} = \frac{3}{8}$$

Equation: $(x - 3)^2 = 4\left(\dfrac{3}{8}\right)(y + 2)$

$$(x - 3)^2 = \frac{3}{2}(y + 2)$$

9. Hyperbola

Foci: $(0, 0)$ and $(0, 4) \Rightarrow c = 2$

Asymptotes: $y = \pm\dfrac{1}{2}x + 2$

Vertical transverse axis

Center: $(0, 2) = (h, k)$

$$\frac{a}{b} = \frac{1}{2} \Rightarrow 2a = b$$

$$c^2 = a^2 + b^2$$

$$4 = a^2 + (2a)^2$$

$$4 = 5a^2$$

$$\frac{4}{5} = a^2$$

$$b^2 = (2a)^2 = 4a^2 = \frac{16}{5}$$

$$\frac{(y - k)^2}{a^2} - \frac{(x - h)^2}{b^2} = 1$$

$$\frac{(y - 2)^2}{\frac{4}{5}} - \frac{x^2}{\frac{16}{5}} = 1$$

$$\frac{5(y - 2)^2}{4} - \frac{5x^2}{16} = 1$$

10. (a) $x^2 + 6xy + y^2 - 6 = 0$

$A = 1, B = 6, C = 1$

$$\cot 2\theta = \frac{1 - 1}{6} = 0$$

$$2\theta = 90°$$

$$\theta = 45°$$

(b) $x = x'\cos 45° - y'\sin 45°$

$$= \frac{x' - y'}{\sqrt{2}}$$

$y = x'\sin 45° + y'\cos 45°$

$$= \frac{x' + y'}{\sqrt{2}}$$

— CONTINUED —

10. — CONTINUED —

$$\left(\frac{x' - y'}{\sqrt{2}}\right)^2 + 6\left(\frac{x' - y'}{\sqrt{2}}\right)\left(\frac{x' + y'}{\sqrt{2}}\right) + \left(\frac{x' + y'}{\sqrt{2}}\right)^2 - 6 = 0$$

$$\frac{1}{2}((x')^2 - 2(x')(y') + (y')^2) + 3((x')^2 - (y')^2) + \frac{1}{2}((x')^2 + 2(x')(y') + (y')^2) - 6 = 0$$

$$4(x')^2 - 2(y')^2 = 6$$

$$\frac{2(x')^2}{3} - \frac{(y')^2}{3} = 1$$

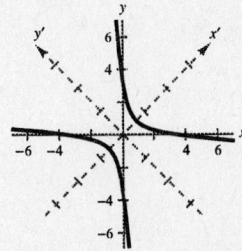

For the graphing utility, we need to solve for y in terms of x.

$$y^2 + 6xy + 9x^2 = 6 - x^2 + 9x^2$$

$$(y + 3x)^2 = 6 + 8x^2$$

$$y + 3x = \pm\sqrt{6 + 8x^2}$$

$$y = -3x \pm \sqrt{6 + 8x}$$

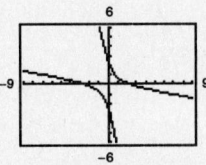

11. $x = 2 + 3\cos\theta$

$y = 2\sin\theta$

θ	0	$\pi/2$	π	$3\pi/2$
x	5	2	-1	2
y	0	2	0	-2

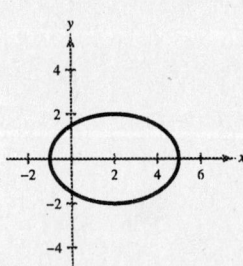

$x = 2 + 3\cos\theta \implies \dfrac{x - 2}{3} = \cos\theta$

$y = 2\sin\theta \implies \dfrac{y}{2} = \sin\theta$

$\cos^2\theta + \sin^2\theta = 1$

$\dfrac{(x - 2)^2}{9} + \dfrac{y^2}{4} = 1$

12. $(6, 4), (2, -3)$

$x = x_1 + t(x_2 - x_1) = 6 + t(2 - 6) = 6 - 4t$

$y = y_1 + t(y_2 - y_1) = 4 + t(-3 - 4) = 4 - 7t$

Answers are not unique. Another possible set:

$x = 6 + 4t$

$y = 4 + 7t$

13. Polar Coordinates: $\left(-2, \dfrac{5\pi}{6}\right)$

$x = -2\cos\dfrac{5\pi}{6} = -2\left(-\dfrac{\sqrt{3}}{2}\right) = \sqrt{3}$

$y = -2\sin\dfrac{5\pi}{6} = -2\left(\dfrac{1}{2}\right) = -1$

Rectangular Coordinates: $\left(\sqrt{3}, -1\right)$

14. Rectangular Coordinates: $(2, -2)$

$r = \pm\sqrt{2^2 + (-2)^2} = \pm\sqrt{8} = \pm2\sqrt{2}$

$\tan \theta = -1 \implies \theta = \dfrac{3\pi}{4}, \dfrac{7\pi}{4}$

Polar Coordinates:

$\left(2\sqrt{2}, \dfrac{7\pi}{4}\right), \left(-2\sqrt{2}, \dfrac{3\pi}{4}\right), \left(2\sqrt{2}, -\dfrac{\pi}{4}\right)$

15. $x^2 + y^2 - 4y = 0$

$r^2 - 4r\sin \theta = 0$

$r^2 = 4r\sin \theta$

$r = 4\sin \theta$

16. $r = \dfrac{4}{1 + \cos \theta}$

$e = 1 \implies$ Parabola

Vertex: $(2, 0)$

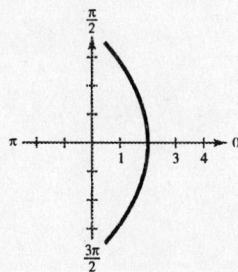

17. $r = \dfrac{4}{2 + \cos \theta} = \dfrac{2}{1 + \frac{1}{2}\cos \theta}$

$e = \dfrac{1}{2} \implies$ Ellipse

Vertex: $\left(\dfrac{4}{3}, 0\right), (4, \pi)$

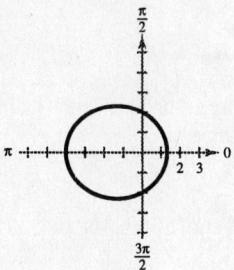

18. $r = 2 + 3\sin \theta$

$\dfrac{a}{b} = \dfrac{2}{3} < 1$ Limaçon with inner loop

θ	0	$\dfrac{\pi}{2}$	π	$\dfrac{3\pi}{2}$
r	2	5	2	-1

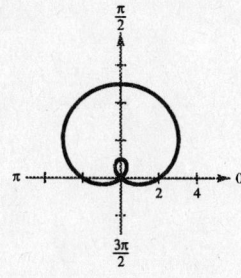

19. $r = 3\sin 2\theta$

Rose curve ($n = 2$) with four petals

$|r| = 3$ when $\theta = \dfrac{\pi}{4}, \dfrac{3\pi}{4}, \dfrac{5\pi}{4}, \dfrac{7\pi}{4}$

$r = 0$ when $\theta = 0, \dfrac{\pi}{2}, \pi, \dfrac{3\pi}{2}$

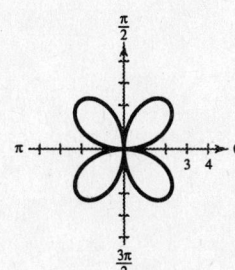

20.

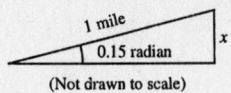

(Not drawn to scale)

Slope: $m = \tan 0.15 \approx 0.1511$

$$\sin 0.15 = \frac{x}{5280 \text{ feet}}$$

$$x = 5280 \sin 0.15 \approx 789 \text{ feet}$$

21. $x = (115 \cos \theta)t$ and $y = 3 + (115 \sin \theta)t - 16t^2$

When $\theta = 30°$: $x = (115 \cos 30°)t$

$y = 3 + (115 \sin 30°)t - 16t^2$

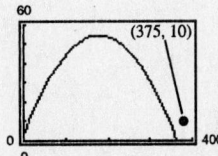

The ball hits the ground inside the ballpark, so it is not a home run.

When $\theta = 35°$: $x = (115 \cos 35°)t$

$y = 3 + (115 \sin 35°)t - 16t^2$

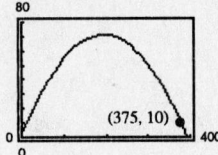

The ball clears the 10 foot fence at 375 feet, so it is a home run.

PART III

C H A P T E R P
Prerequisites

CHAPTER P
Prerequisites

Section P.1   Real Numbers
Solutions to Even-Numbered Exercises

2. $\sqrt{5}, -7, -\frac{7}{3}, 0, 3.12, \frac{5}{4}, -3, 12, 5$

  (a) Natural numbers: $12, 5$

  (b) Integers: $-7, 0, -3, 12, 5$

  (c) Rational numbers: $-7, -\frac{7}{3}, 0, 3.12, \frac{5}{4}, -3, 12, 5$

  (d) Irrational numbers: $\sqrt{5}$

4. $2.3030030003\ldots, 0.7575, -4.63, \sqrt{10}, -75, 15, 31$

  (a) Natural numbers: $15, 31$

  (b) Integers: $-75, 15, 31$

  (c) Rational numbers: $0.7575, -4.63, \sqrt{10}, -75, 15, 31$

  (d) Irrational numbers: $2.3030030003\ldots, \sqrt{10}$

6. $25, -17, -\frac{12}{5}, \sqrt{9}, 3.12, \frac{1}{2}\pi, 7, -11.1, 13$

  (a) Natural numbers: $25, \sqrt{9}, 7, 13$

  (b) Integers: $25, -17, \sqrt{9}, 7, 13$

  (c) Rational numbers: $25, -17, -\frac{12}{5}, \sqrt{9}, 3.12, 7, -11.1, 13$

  (d) Irrational numbers: $\frac{1}{2}\pi$

8. $\frac{1}{3} = 0.\overline{3}$

10. $\frac{6}{11} = 0.\overline{54}$

12. $8.5 = \frac{17}{2}$

14. $5.\overline{45} = \frac{60}{11}$

16. $-1.6\overline{5} = \dfrac{-149}{90}$

18. $-6 < -2.5$

20. $-3.5 < 1$

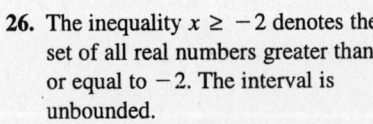

22. $1 < \frac{16}{3}$

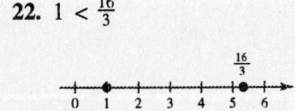

24. $-\frac{8}{7} < -\frac{3}{7}$

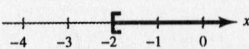

26. The inequality $x \geq -2$ denotes the set of all real numbers greater than or equal to -2. The interval is unbounded.

28. The inequality $x > 3$ denotes the set of all real numbers greater than 3. The interval is unbounded.

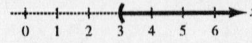

30. The inequality $x < 2$ denotes the set of all real numbers less than 2. The interval is unbounded.

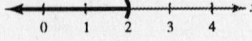

32. The inequality $0 \leq x \leq 5$ denotes the set of all real numbers greater than or equal to zero and less than or equal to 5. The interval is bounded.

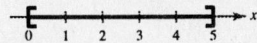

34. The inequality $0 < x \leq 6$ denotes the set of all real numbers greater than zero and less than or equal to 6. The interval is bounded.

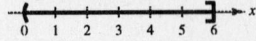

36. $\frac{381}{220} \approx 1.73\overline{18}$, 1.7320, $\sqrt{3} \approx 1.7321$, $\frac{2103}{1214} \approx 1.7331$, $\frac{26}{15} \approx 1.73\overline{3}$

38. $-6 \leq y < 0$ **40.** $y \leq 25$ **42.** $-3 \leq k < 5$ **44.** $2.5\% \leq r \leq 5\%$

46. This interval consists of all real numbers greater than or equal to -5 and less than or equal to 7.

48. This interval consists of all real numbers less than or equal to 4.

50. $|0| = 0$

52. If $x \leq 4$, then $|4 - x| = 4 - x$.

If $x > 4$, then $|4 - x| = -(4 - x) = -4 + x = x - 4$.

54. $-3 - |-3| = -3 - (3) = -6$

56. $-3|-3| = -3(3) = -9$

58. If $x > 1$, then $x - 1$ is positive.

Thus, $\dfrac{|x - 1|}{x - 1} = \dfrac{x - 1}{x - 1} = 1$.

60. $|-4| = |4|$ since $|-4| = 4$ and $|4| = 4$.

62. $-|-6| < |-6|$ since $|-6| = 6$ and

$-|-6| = -(6) = -6$.

64. $-(-2) > -2$ since $-(-2) = 2$.

66. $d\left(-4, -\frac{3}{2}\right) = \left|-4 - \left(-\frac{3}{2}\right)\right| = \left|-4 + \frac{3}{2}\right| = \frac{5}{2}$

68. $d(-126, -75) = |-126 - (-75)| = 51$

70. $d\left(\frac{1}{4}, \frac{11}{4}\right) = \left|\frac{1}{4} - \frac{11}{4}\right| = \frac{5}{2}$

72. $d(9.34, -5.65) = |9.34 - (-5.65)| = 14.99$

74. (a) Since $C < 0$, $-C > 0$. The expression is positive.

(b) Since $A > C$, $A - C > 0$. The expression is positive.

76. $d(103, 86) = |103 - 86| = 17$ miles

78. $d(48°, 82°) = |82° - 48°| = 34°$

80. $d(x, -10) = |x + 10|$, and $d(x, -10) \geq 6$, thus, $|x + 10| \geq 6$.

82. $d(y, a) = |y - a|$ and $d(y, a) \leq 2$, thus $|y - a| \leq 2$.

84.

Budgeted Expense, b	Actual Expense, a	$|a - b|$	$0.05b$
$9400	$9772	$372	$0.05(9400) = $470

The actual expense difference is less than $500 (but is less than 5% of the budget) so the actual expense does pass the test.

86.

Budgeted Expense, b	Actual Expense, a	$|a - b|$	$0.05b$
$2575	$2613	$38	$0.05(2575) = $128.75

Since $38 < $500, and $38 < $128.75, the actual expense passes the "budget variance test."

88. Receipts = $517.1 billion; |Receipts − Outlay| = |517.1 − 590.9| = $73.8 billion deficit

90. Receipts = $1657.9 billion; |Receipts − Outlay| = |1657.9 − 1667.8| = $9.9 billion deficit

92. $6x^3 - 5x$

Terms: $6x^3, -5x$

Coefficients: $6, -5$

94. $3\sqrt{3}\,x^2 + 1$

Terms: $3\sqrt{3}\,x^2, 1$

Coefficients: $3\sqrt{3}$

96. $3x^4 - \dfrac{x^2}{4}$

Terms: $3x^4, -\dfrac{x^2}{4}$

Coefficients: $3, -\dfrac{1}{4}$

98. $9 - 7x$

(a) $9 - 7(-3) = 9 + 21 = 30$

(b) $9 - 7(3) = 9 - 21 = -12$

100. $-x^2 + 5x = 4$

(a) $-(-1)^2 + 5(-1) - 4 = -1 - 5 - 4 = -10$

(b) $-(1)^2 + 5(1) - 4 = -1 + 5 - 4 = 0$

102. $\dfrac{x}{x+2}$

(a) $\dfrac{2}{2+2} = \dfrac{2}{4} = \dfrac{1}{2}$

(b) $\dfrac{-2}{-2+2} = \dfrac{2}{0}$

Division by 0 is undefined.

104. $2\left(\dfrac{1}{2}\right) = 1$

Multiplicative Inverse Property

106. $(x + 3) - (x + 3) = 0$

Additive Inverse Property

108. $(z - 2) + 0 = z - 2$

Additive Identity Property

110. $x + (y + 10) = (x + y) + 10$

Associative Property of Addition

112. $\dfrac{1}{7}(7 \cdot 12) = \left(\dfrac{1}{7} \cdot 7\right)12$ Associative Property of Multiplication

$= 1 \cdot 12$ Multiplicative Inverse Property

$= 12$ Multiplicative Identity Property

114. $\dfrac{6}{7} - \dfrac{4}{7} = \dfrac{6 - 4}{7} = \dfrac{2}{7}$

116. $\dfrac{10}{11} + \dfrac{6}{33} - \dfrac{13}{66} = \dfrac{60}{66} + \dfrac{12}{66} - \dfrac{13}{66} = \dfrac{59}{66}$

118. $-\left(6 \cdot \dfrac{4}{8}\right) = -6 \cdot \dfrac{1}{2} = -3$

120. $\dfrac{5x}{6} \cdot \dfrac{2}{9} = \dfrac{5x}{3} \cdot \dfrac{1}{9} = \dfrac{5x}{27}$

122. $3\left(-\dfrac{5}{12} + \dfrac{3}{8}\right) \approx -0.13$

124. $\dfrac{\frac{1}{5}(-8 - 9)}{-\frac{1}{3}} = 10.20$

126. (a)

n	1	10	100	10,000	100,000
$5/n$	5	0.5	0.05	0.0005	0.00005

(b) The value of $5/n$ approaches 0 as n increases without bound.

128. Yes. y is nonnegative if $y \geq 0$. y is positive if $y > 0$.

130. False. If $a < b$, then $\dfrac{1}{a} > \dfrac{1}{b}$, where $a \neq b \neq 0$.

132.

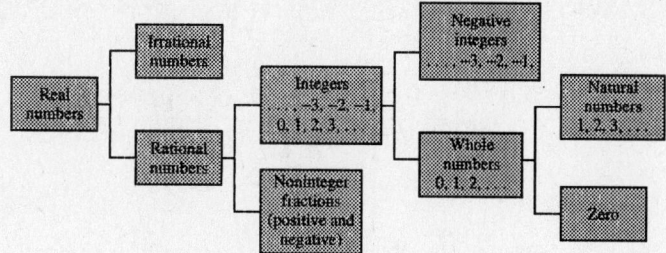

Section P.2   Exponents and Radicals

Solutions to Even-Numbered Exercises

2. $(-2)^7 = (-2) \times (-2) \times (-2) \times (-2) \times (-2) \times (-2) \times (-2)$

4. $11.3^4 = (11.3) \times (11.3) \times (11.3) \times (11.3)$

6. $\left(2\sqrt{5}\right)\left(2\sqrt{5}\right)\left(2\sqrt{5}\right)\left(2\sqrt{5}\right) = \left(2\sqrt{5}\right)^4$

8. $-\left(\frac{3}{2} \times \frac{3}{2} \times \frac{3}{2} \times \frac{3}{2}\right) = -\left(\frac{3}{2}\right)^4$

10. (a) $\dfrac{5^5}{5^2} = 5^3 = 125$

    (b) $\dfrac{3^2}{3^4} = 3^{-2} = \dfrac{1}{3^2} = \dfrac{1}{9}$

12. (a) $(2^3 \cdot 3^2)^2 = 2^{3\cdot2} \cdot 3^{2\cdot2}$

$$= 2^6 \cdot 3^4$$

$$= 64 \cdot 81 = 5184$$

    (b) $\left(-\dfrac{3}{5}\right)^3\left(\dfrac{5}{3}\right)^2 = (-1)^3\dfrac{3^3}{5^3} \cdot \dfrac{5^2}{3^2}$

$$= -1 \cdot 3^{3-2} \cdot 5^{2-3}$$

$$= -3 \cdot 5^{-1} = -\dfrac{3}{5}$$

14. (a) $\dfrac{4 \cdot 3^{-2}}{2^{-2} \cdot 3^{-1}} = 4 \cdot 2^2 \cdot 3^{-2-(-1)}$

$$= 4 \cdot 4 \cdot 3^{-1} = \dfrac{16}{3}$$

    (b) $(-2)^0 = 1$

16. (a) $3^{-1} + 2^{-2} = \dfrac{1}{3} + \dfrac{1}{4} = \dfrac{4}{12} + \dfrac{3}{12} = \dfrac{7}{12}$

    (b) $(3^{-2})^2 = 3^{-4} = \dfrac{1}{3^4} = \dfrac{1}{81}$

18. $(8^{-4})(10^3) \approx 0.244$

20. $\dfrac{4^3}{3^{-4}} = 5184$

22. When $x = 4$,

$$7x^{-2} = 7(4)^{-2} = \dfrac{7}{4^2} = \dfrac{7}{16}.$$

24. When $x = 3$,

$5(-x)^3 = 5(-3)^3 = 5(-27) = -135.$

26. When $x = -2$,

$-3x^4 = -3(-2)^4 = -3(16) = -48.$

28. When $x = \frac{1}{3}$,

$5(-x)^3 = 5\left(-\frac{1}{3}\right)^3 = 5\left(-\frac{1}{27}\right) = -\frac{5}{27}.$

30. (a) $(3x)^2 = 3^2x^2 = 9x^2$

    (b) $(4x^3)^2 = 4^2x^{3\cdot2} = 16x^6$

32. (a) $(-z)^3(3z^4) = (-1)^3(z^3)3z^4$

$= -1 \cdot 3 \cdot z^{3+4} = -3z^7$

(b) $\dfrac{25y^8}{10y^4} = \dfrac{5}{2}y^{8-4} = \dfrac{5}{2}y^4$

34. (a) $\dfrac{r^4}{r^6} = r^{4-6} = r^{-2} = \dfrac{1}{r^2}$

(b) $\left(\dfrac{4}{y}\right)^3\left(\dfrac{3}{y}\right)^4 = \dfrac{4^3}{y^3} \cdot \dfrac{3^4}{y^4} = \dfrac{64 \cdot 81}{y^{3+4}} = \dfrac{5184}{y^7}$

36. (a) $(2x^5)^0 = 1, x \neq 0$

(b) $(z+2)^{-3}(z+2)^{-1} = (z+2)^{-4} = \dfrac{1}{(z+2)^4}$

38. (a) $(4y^{-2})(8y^4) = (4)(8)(y^{4-2}) = 32y^2$

(b) $\left(\dfrac{x^{-3}y^4}{5}\right)^{-3} = \left(\dfrac{5x^3}{y^4}\right)^3 = \dfrac{125x^9}{y^{12}}$

40. (a) $[(x^2y^{-2})^{-1}]^{-1} = [x^{-2}y^2]^{-1} = x^2y^{-2} = \dfrac{x^2}{y^2}$

(b) $(5x^2z^6)^3(5x^2z^6)^{-3} = (5x^2z^6)^0 = 1$

42. (a) $\dfrac{x^2 \cdot x^n}{x^3 \cdot x^n} = \dfrac{x^{2+n}}{x^{3+n}} = x^{2+n \cdot 3-n} = x^{-1} = \dfrac{1}{x}$

(b) $\left(\dfrac{a^{-3}}{b^{-3}}\right)\left(\dfrac{a}{b}\right)^3 = \dfrac{a^{-3}}{b^{-3}} \cdot \dfrac{a^3}{b^3} = \dfrac{a^{-3+3}}{b^{-3+3}} = \dfrac{a^0}{b^0} = 1$

Radical Form	*Rational Exponent Form*
44. $\sqrt[3]{64} = 4$, Given	$64^{1/3} = 4$, Answer
46. $-\sqrt{144} = -12$, Answer	$-(144^{1/2}) = -12$, Given
48. $\sqrt[3]{614.125} = 8.5$, Given	$(614.125)^{1/3} = 8.5$, Answer
50. $\sqrt[5]{-243} = -3$, Answer	$(-243)^{1/5} = -3$, Given
52. $\left(\sqrt[4]{81}\right)^3 = 27$, Given	$81^{3/4} = 27$, Answer
54. $\sqrt[4]{16^5}$, Answer	$16^{5/4} = 3/2$, Given

56. (a) $\sqrt{49} = 7$

(b) $\sqrt[3]{\dfrac{27}{8}} = \dfrac{3}{2}$

58. (a) $\sqrt[3]{0} = 0$

(b) $\dfrac{\sqrt[4]{81}}{3} = \dfrac{3}{3} = 1$

60. (a) $\sqrt[4]{562^4} = 562$

(b) $36^{3/2} = 216$

62. (a) $100^{-3/2} = \left(\sqrt{100}\right)^{-3} = 10^{-3} = \dfrac{1}{1000}$

(b) $\left(\dfrac{9}{4}\right)^{-1/2} = \left(\dfrac{4}{9}\right)^{1/2} = \dfrac{4^{1/2}}{9^{1/2}} = \dfrac{2}{3}$

64. (a) $\left(-\dfrac{125}{27}\right)^{-1/3} = \left(-\dfrac{27}{125}\right)^{1/3} = \dfrac{(-27)^{1/3}}{(125)^{1/3}} = \dfrac{-3}{5} = -\dfrac{3}{5}$

(b) $-\left(\dfrac{1}{125}\right)^{-4/3} = -(125)^{4/3}$

$= -(125^{1/3})^4 = -(5)^4 = -625$

66. (a) $\sqrt[3]{45^2} \approx 12.651$

(b) $\sqrt[5]{125} \approx 2.236$

68. (a) $(15.25)^{-1.4} \approx 0.022$

(b) $(3.4)^{2.5} \approx 21.316$

70. (a) $\dfrac{7 - (4.1)^{-3.2}}{2} \approx 3.495$

(b) $\left(\dfrac{13}{3}\right)^{-3/2} - \left(-\dfrac{3}{2}\right)^{13/3} \approx 5.906$

72. (a) $\sqrt[3]{\dfrac{16}{27}} = \dfrac{\sqrt[3]{2^3 \cdot 2}}{\sqrt[3]{3^3}} = \dfrac{2\sqrt[3]{2}}{3}$

(b) $\sqrt{\dfrac{75}{4}} = \dfrac{\sqrt{5^2 \cdot 3}}{\sqrt{2^2}} = \dfrac{5\sqrt{3}}{2}$

74. (a) $\sqrt{54xy^4} = \sqrt{6 \cdot 3^2 \cdot x \cdot (y^2)^2} = 3y^2\sqrt{6x}$

(b) $\sqrt{\dfrac{32a^4}{b^2}} = \dfrac{\sqrt{(2^2)^2 \cdot 2 \cdot (a^2)^2}}{\sqrt{b^2}} = \dfrac{4a^2\sqrt{2}}{|b|}$

76. (a) $\sqrt[4]{(3x^2)^4} = 3x^2$

(b) $\sqrt[5]{96x^5} = \sqrt[5]{3 \cdot 2^5 \cdot x^5} = 2x\sqrt[5]{3}$

78. $\dfrac{8^{12/5}}{8^{2/5}} = 8^{(12/5)-(2/5)} = 8^{10/5} = 8^2 = 64$

80. $\dfrac{x^{4/3}y^{2/3}}{(xy)^{1/3}} = \dfrac{x^{4/3}y^{2/3}}{x^{1/3}y^{1/3}} = x^{3/3}y^{1/3} = xy^{1/3}$

82. $\dfrac{5^{-1/2} \cdot 5x^{5/2}}{(5x)^{3/2}} = \dfrac{5^{-1/2} \cdot 5x^{5/2}}{5^{3/2}x^{3/2}} = 5^{-1}x = \dfrac{x}{5}, \; x > 0$

84. (a) $\dfrac{5}{\sqrt{10}} = \dfrac{5}{\sqrt{10}} \cdot \dfrac{\sqrt{10}}{\sqrt{10}} = \dfrac{5\sqrt{10}}{10} = \dfrac{\sqrt{10}}{2}$

(b) $\dfrac{5}{\sqrt[3]{(5x)^2}} = \dfrac{5}{\sqrt[3]{(5x)^2}} \cdot \dfrac{\sqrt[3]{5x}}{\sqrt[3]{5x}} = \dfrac{5\sqrt[3]{5x}}{5x} = \dfrac{\sqrt[3]{5x}}{x}$

86. (a) $\dfrac{5}{\sqrt{14}-2} = \dfrac{5}{\sqrt{14}-2} \cdot \dfrac{\sqrt{14}+2}{\sqrt{14}+2} = \dfrac{5\sqrt{14}+10}{14-4} = \dfrac{5\sqrt{14}+10}{10} = \dfrac{\sqrt{14}+2}{2}$

(b) $\dfrac{5}{\sqrt{10}-5} = \dfrac{5}{\sqrt{10}-5} \cdot \dfrac{\sqrt{10}+5}{\sqrt{10}+5} = \dfrac{5\sqrt{10}+25}{10-25} = \dfrac{5\sqrt{10}+25}{-15} = \dfrac{\sqrt{10}+5}{-3}$

88. (a) $\dfrac{\sqrt{2}}{3} = \dfrac{\sqrt{2}}{3} \cdot \dfrac{\sqrt{2}}{\sqrt{2}} = \dfrac{2}{3\sqrt{2}}$

(b) $\sqrt[4]{\dfrac{5}{4}} = \dfrac{\sqrt[4]{5}}{\sqrt[4]{4}} \cdot \dfrac{\sqrt[4]{5^3}}{\sqrt[4]{5^3}} = \dfrac{5}{\sqrt[4]{4 \cdot 125}} = \dfrac{5}{\sqrt[4]{500}}$

90. (a) $\dfrac{\sqrt{3}-\sqrt{2}}{2} = \dfrac{\sqrt{3}-\sqrt{2}}{2} \cdot \dfrac{\sqrt{3}+\sqrt{2}}{\sqrt{3}+\sqrt{2}}$

$= \dfrac{3-2}{2(\sqrt{3}+\sqrt{2})} = \dfrac{1}{2(\sqrt{3}+\sqrt{2})}$

(b) $\dfrac{2\sqrt{3}+\sqrt{3}}{3} = \dfrac{3\sqrt{3}}{3} \cdot \dfrac{\sqrt{3}}{\sqrt{3}} = \dfrac{9}{3\sqrt{3}} = \dfrac{3}{\sqrt{3}}$

92. (a) $\sqrt[6]{x^3} = x^{3/6} = x^{1/2} = \sqrt{x}$

(b) $\sqrt[4]{(3x^2)^4} = 3x^2$

94. (a) $\sqrt{\sqrt{243(x+1)}} = [(243(x+1))^{1/2}]^{1/2}$

$= (243(x+1))^{1/4}$

$= \sqrt[4]{243(x+1)}$

$= \sqrt[4]{3 \cdot 3^4(x+1)}$

$= 3\sqrt[4]{3(x+1)}$

(b) $\sqrt{\sqrt[3]{10a^7b}} = ((10a^7b)^{1/3})^{1/2}$

$= (10a^7b)^{1/6}$

$= \sqrt[6]{10a \cdot a^6 \cdot b}$

$= a\sqrt[6]{10ab}$

96. (a) $4\sqrt{27} - \sqrt{75} = 4\sqrt{3^2 \cdot 3} - \sqrt{5^2 \cdot 3}$

$= 4 \cdot 3\sqrt{3} - 5\sqrt{3}$

$= 12\sqrt{3} - 5\sqrt{3}$

$= 7\sqrt{3}$

(b) $\sqrt[3]{16} + 3\sqrt[3]{54} = \sqrt[3]{2 \cdot 2^3} + 3\sqrt[3]{2 \cdot 3^3}$

$= 2\sqrt[3]{2} + 3 \cdot 3\sqrt[3]{2}$

$= 2\sqrt[3]{2} + 9\sqrt[3]{2}$

$= 11\sqrt[3]{2}$

98. (a) $8\sqrt{49x} - 14\sqrt{100x} = 8\sqrt{7^2 \cdot x} - 14\sqrt{10^2 \cdot x}$

$= 8 \cdot 7\sqrt{x} - 14 \cdot 10\sqrt{x} = 56\sqrt{x} - 140\sqrt{x}$

$= -84\sqrt{x}$

(b) $-3\sqrt{48x^2} + 7\sqrt{75x^2} = -3\sqrt{3 \cdot 4^2 \cdot x^2} + 7\sqrt{3 \cdot 5^2 \cdot x^2}$

$= -3 \cdot 4x\sqrt{3} + 7 \cdot 5x\sqrt{3}$

$= -12x\sqrt{3} + 35x\sqrt{3} = 23x\sqrt{3}$

100. (a) $-\sqrt{x^3 - 7} + 5\sqrt{x^3 - 7} = 4\sqrt{x^3 - 7}$

   (b) $11\sqrt{245x^3} - 9\sqrt{45x^3} = 11\sqrt{5 \cdot 7^2 \cdot x \cdot x^2} - 9\sqrt{5 \cdot 3^2 \cdot x \cdot x^2}$

   $= 11 \cdot 7x\sqrt{5x} - 9 \cdot 3x\sqrt{5x}$

   $= 77x\sqrt{5x} - 27x\sqrt{5x}$

   $= 50x\sqrt{5x}$

102. $\sqrt{\dfrac{3}{11}} = \dfrac{\sqrt{3}}{\sqrt{11}}$

104. $\sqrt{3^2 + 4^2} = \sqrt{9 + 16} = \sqrt{25} = 5$

   Thus, $5 = \sqrt{3^2 + 4^2}$.

106. $9{,}461{,}000{,}000{,}000{,}000 = 9.460 \times 10^{15}$ kilometers

108. $0.00003937 = 3.937 \times 10^{-5}$ inch

110. $1.5 \times 10^7 = 15{,}000{,}000$ degrees

112. $9.0 \times 10^{-5} = 0.00009$ meter

114. (a) $(1.2 \times 10^7)(5 \times 10^{-3}) = 6.0 \times 10^4 = 60{,}000$

   (b) $\dfrac{(6.0 \times 10^8)}{(3.0 \times 10^{-3})} = 2.0 \times 10^{11}$

116. (a) $(9.3 \times 10^6)^3 (6.1 \times 10^{-4}) \approx 4.907 \times 10^{17}$

   (b) $\dfrac{(2.414 \times 10^4)^6}{(1.68 \times 10^5)^5} \approx 1.479$

118. (a) $(2.65 \times 10^{-4})^{1/3} \approx 0.064$

   (b) $\sqrt{9 \times 10^{-4}} = 0.030$

120. $\left(\dfrac{2}{\sqrt{5}}\right)^2 = \dfrac{2^2}{(\sqrt{5})^2} = \dfrac{4}{5}$

   This is not equivalent to rationalizing the denominator because rationalizing the denominator produces a number equivalent to the original fraction but squaring does not.

122. Size $= 0.03\sqrt{v}$; For $v = \dfrac{3}{4}$:

   Size $= 0.03\sqrt{\dfrac{3}{4}}$

   $= 0.03 \cdot \dfrac{\sqrt{3}}{\sqrt{4}}$

   $= 0.03\dfrac{\sqrt{3}}{2}$

   ≈ 0.026 inch

124. Time $= \dfrac{\text{Distance}}{\text{Rate}} = \dfrac{93{,}000{,}000 \text{ miles}}{11{,}160{,}000 \text{ miles per minute}}$

   $= \dfrac{25}{3}$ minutes

126. Paper: $0.381(2.097 \times 10^8) = 7.99 \times 10^7$ tons

   Metals: $0.077(2.097 \times 10^8) = 1.61 \times 10^7$ tons

   Glass: $0.059(2.097 \times 10^8) = 1.24 \times 10^7$ tons

   Plastics: $0.094(2.097 \times 10^8) = 1.97 \times 10^7$ tons

   Yard waste: $0.134(2.097 \times 10^8) = 2.81 \times 10^7$ tons

   Other: $0.255(2.097 \times 10^8) = 5.35 \times 10^7$ tons

128. False. When a power is raised to a power, you multiply the exponents: $(a^n)^k = a^{nk}$.

130. (a) 3 is also raised to the negative one power so, $(3x)^{-1} = \dfrac{1}{3x}$.

(b) When two powers have the same base, the exponents are added, $y^3 \cdot y^2 = y^5$.

(c) When a power is raised to a power, exponents are multiplied, $(a^2 b^3)^4 \cdot a^8 b^{12}$.

(d) The square of a binomial contains a cross product term, $(a + b)^2 = a^2 + 2ab + b^2$.

(e) If $x < 0$, then $\sqrt{4x^2} > 0$ but $2x < 0$, $\sqrt{4x^2} = 2|x|$.

(f) Radicals can only be added together if they have the same radicand and index: $\sqrt{z} + \sqrt{z} = 2\sqrt{z}$.

132.

Planet	Mercury	Venus	Earth	Mars	Jupiter
x	0.387	0.723	1.0	1.523	5.203
$\sqrt{x}$	0.622	0.850	1.0	1.234	2.281
y	0.241	0.615	1.0	1.881	11.861
$\sqrt[3]{y}$	0.622	0.850	1.0	1.234	2.281

$y^{3/2}$, the time is takes for a planet to orbit the sun is equal to the average distance of a planet from the sun raised to the 3/2 power.

Section P.3   Polynomials and Factoring

2. (e) $-3x^5 + 2x^3 + x$ is a trinomial of degree five.

4. (a) $3x^2$ is a monomial with positive degree.

6. (c) $x^3 + 3x^2 + 3x + 1$ is a third-degree polynomial with leading coefficient 1.

8. $6x^5 + 3x + 1$
(Answers will vary.)

10. $20x^3 + 5$
(Answers will vary.)

12. Standard form: $-3x^4 + 2x^2 - 5$

Degree: 4

Leading coefficient: -3

14. Standard form: 3

Degree: 0

Leading coefficient: 3

16. Standard form:
$-x^5y + 2x^2y^2 + xy^4$

Degree: 6

Leading coefficient: -1

18. $2x^3 + x - 3x^{-1}$ is *not* a polynomial because it includes a term with a negative exponent.

20. $\dfrac{x^2 + 2x - 3}{2}$ *is* a polynomial.

Standard form: $\dfrac{1}{2}x^2 + x - \dfrac{3}{2}$

22. $\sqrt{y^2 - y^4}$ is *not* a polynomial because of the square root.

24. $-(5x^2 - 1) - (-3x^2 + 5) = -5x^2 + 1 + 3x^2 - 5$
$$= (-5x^2 + 3x^2) + (1 - 5)$$
$$= -2x^2 - 4$$

26. $(15.2x^4 - 18x - 19.1) - (13.9x^4 - 9.6x + 15) = 15.2x^4 - 18x - 19.1 - 13.9x^4 + 9.6x - 15$
$$= (15.2x^4 - 13.9x^4) + (-18x + 9.6x) + (-19.1 - 15)$$
$$= 1.3x^4 - 8.4x - 34.1$$

28. $(y^3 + 1) - [(y^2 + 1) + (3y - 7)] = y^3 + 1 - (y^2 + 1) - (3y - 7)$
$$= y^3 + 1 - y^2 - 1 - 3y + 7$$
$$= y^3 - y^2 - 3y + (1 - 1 + 7)$$
$$= y^3 - y^2 - 3y + 7$$

30. $y^2(4y^2 + 2y - 3) = y^2(4y^2) + y^2(2y) + y^2(-3)$
$$= 4y^4 + 2y^3 - 3y^2$$

32. $(-3x)(5x + 2) = -3x(5x) + (-3x)(2) = -15x^2 - 6x$

34. $-4x(3 - x^3) = -4x(3) + (-4x)(-x^3)$
$$= -12x + 4x^4$$
$$= 4x^4 - 12x$$

36. $(2 - 3.5y)(2y^3) = 2(2y^3) + (-3.5y)(2y^3) = 4y^3 - 7y^4$
$$= -7y^4 + 4y^3$$

38. $2y\left(4 - \dfrac{7}{8}y\right) = 2y(4) + 2y\left(-\dfrac{7}{8}y\right) = 8y - \dfrac{7}{4}y^2 = -\dfrac{7}{4}y^2 + 8y$

40. $(x - 5)(x + 10) = x^2 + 10x - 5x - 50$ FOIL
$$= x^2 + 5x - 50$$

42. $(7x - 2)(4x - 3) = 28x^2 - 21x - 8x + 6$ FOIL
$$= 28x^2 - 29x + 6$$

44. $(4x + 5)^2 = (4x)^2 + 2(4x)(5) + 5^2$
$$= 16x^2 + 40x + 25$$

46. $(5 - 8x)^2 = 5^2 + (2)(5)(-8x) + (-8x)^2$
$$= 25 - 80x + 64x^2$$

48. $(2x + 3)(2x - 3) = (2x)^2 - 3^2 = 4x^2 - 9$

50. $(2x + 3y)(2x - 3y) = (2x)^2 - (3y)^2 = 4x^2 - 9y^2$

52. $[(x + y) + 1][(x + y) - 1] = (x + y)^2 - 1^2 = x^2 + 2xy + y^2 - 1$

54. $[(x + 1) - y]^2 = (x + 1)^2 + 2(x + 1)(-y) + (-y)^2$
$$= x^2 + 2x + 1 - 2xy - 2y + y^2$$
$$= x^2 - 2xy + y^2 + 2x - 2y + 1$$

56. $(3a^3 - 4b^2)(3a^3 + 4b^2) = (3a^3)^2 - (4b^2)^2$
$$= 9a^6 - 16b^4$$

58. $(x - 2)^3 = x^3 - 3x^2(2) + 3x(2)^2 - 2^3$
$$= x^3 - 6x^2 + 12x - 8$$

60. $(4x^3 - 3)^2 = (4x^3)^2 + (2)(4x^3)(-3) + (-3)^2$
$$= 16x^6 - 24x^3 + 9$$

62. $\left(\frac{2}{3}t + 5\right)^2 = \left(\frac{2}{3}t\right)^2 + 2\left(\frac{2}{3}t\right)(5) + (5)^2$
$$= \frac{4}{9}t^2 + \frac{20}{3}t + 25$$

64. $\left(2x + \frac{1}{5}\right)\left(2x - \frac{1}{5}\right) = (2x)^2 - \left(\frac{1}{5}\right)^2 = 4x^2 - \frac{1}{25}$

66. $(1.5y - 3)^2 = (1.5y)^2 + 2(1.5y)(-3) + (-3)^2$
$$= 2.25y^2 - 9y + 9$$

68. $(2.5y + 3)(2.5y - 3) = (2.5y)^2 - (3)^2 = 6.25y^2 - 9$

70. $(2x - 1)(x + 3) + 3(x + 3) = (2x + 2)(x + 3) = 2x^2 + 6x + 2x + 6$ FOIL
$$= 2x^2 + 8x + 6$$

72. $(x + y)(x - y)(x^2 + y^2) = (x^2 - y^2)(x^2 + y^2)$
$$= (x^2)^2 - (y^2)^2 = x^4 - y^4$$

74. $\left(5 + \sqrt{x}\right)\left(5 - \sqrt{x}\right) = (5)^2 - \left(\sqrt{x}\right)^2 = 25 - x$

76. $\left(x + \sqrt{3}\right)^2 = x^2 + 2x\sqrt{3} + \left(\sqrt{3}\right)^2$
$$= x^2 + 2\sqrt{3}x + 3$$

78. Not completely factored:
$$x^3 + 3x^2 - 9x - 27 = (x + 3)(x^2 - 9)$$
$$= (x + 3)(x + 3)(x - 3)$$

80. Not completely factored:
$$4x^4 + 12x^3 - x^2 - 3x = (x^2 + 3x)(4x^2 - 1)$$
$$= x(x + 3)(2x + 1)(2x - 1)$$

82. $5y - 30 = 5(y - 6)$

84. $4x^3 - 6x^2 + 12x = 2x(2x^2 - 3x + 6)$

86. $3x(x + 2) - 4(x + 2) = (x + 2)(3x - 4)$

88. $(3x - 1)^2 + (3x - 1) = (3x - 1 + 1)(3x - 1) = 3x(3x - 1)$

90. $\frac{1}{3}y^4 - 5y^2 + 2y = \frac{1}{3}y^4 - \frac{15}{3}y^2 + \frac{6}{3}y = \frac{1}{3}y(y^3 - 15y + 6)$

92. $\frac{4}{5}y(y + 1) - 2(y + 1) = \frac{4}{5}y(y + 1) - \frac{10}{5}(y + 1) = \frac{2}{5}(y + 1)(2y - 5)$

94. $49 - 9y^2 = 7^2 - (3y)^2 = (7 + 3y)(7 - 3y)$

96. $\frac{4}{25}y^2 - 64 = \left(\frac{2}{5}y\right)^2 - 8^2 = \left(\frac{2}{5}y + 8\right)\left(\frac{2}{5}y - 8\right)$

98. $25 - (z + 5)^2 = 5^2 - (z + 5)^2$
$$= (5 - (z + 5))(5 + (z + 5))$$
$$= (5 - z - 5)(5 + z + 5)$$
$$= -z(z + 10)$$

100. $25x^2 - 16y^2 = (5x)^2 - (4y)^2 = (5x + 4y)(5x - 4y)$

102. $x^2 + 10x + 25 = x^2 + 2(5)(x) + 5^2 = (x + 5)^2$

104. $9x^2 - 12x + 4 = (3x)^2 - 2(3x)(2) + 2^2$
$$= (3x - 2)^2$$

106. $4x^2 - 4xy + y^2 = (2x)^2 - 2(2x)y + y^2$
$$= (2x - y)^2$$

108. $z^2 + z + \frac{1}{4} = z^2 + 2(z)(\frac{1}{2}) + (\frac{1}{2})^2$
$$= (z + \frac{1}{2})^2$$

110. $x^2 + 5x + 6 = x^2 + 2x + 3x + 6$
$$= (x + 2)(x + 3)$$

112. $t^2 - t - 6 = t^2 + 2t - 3t - 6$
$$= (t + 2)(t - 3)$$

114. $24 + 5z - z^2 = 24 + 8z - 3z - z^2$
$$= (8 - z)(3 + z)$$

116. $2x^2 - x - 1 = 2x^2 - 2x + x - 1$
$$= (2x + 1)(x - 1)$$

118. $12x^2 + 7x + 1 = 12x^2 + 3x + 4x + 1$
$$= (3x + 1)(4x + 1)$$

120. $-5u^2 - 13u + 6 = -5u^2 - 15u + 2u + 6$
$$= (-5u + 2)(u + 3)$$

122. $x^3 - 27 = x^3 - 3^3 = (x - 3)(x^2 + 3x + 9)$

124. $z^3 + 125 = z^3 + 5^3 = (z + 5)(z^2 - 5z + 25)$

126. $27x^3 + 8 = (3x)^3 + 2^3 = (3x + 2)(9x^2 - 6x + 4)$

128. $64x^3 - y^3 = (4x)^3 - y^3 = (4x - y)(16x^2 + 4xy + y^2)$

130. $x^3 + 5x^2 - 5x - 25 = x^2(x + 5) - 5(x + 5)$
$$= (x + 5)(x^2 - 5)$$

132. $6 + 2x - 3x^3 - x^4 = 2(3 + x) - x^3(3 + x)$
$$= (2 - x^3)(3 + x)$$

134. $8x^5 - 6x^2 + 12x^3 - 9 = 2x^2(4x^3 - 3) + 3(4x^3 - 3)$
$$= (2x^2 + 3)(4x^3 - 3)$$

136. $a \cdot c = (2)(9) = 18$. Rewrite the middle term, $9x = 6x + 3x$, since $(6)(3) = 18$ and $6 + 3 = 9$.
$$2x^2 + 9x + 9 = 2x^2 + 6x + 3x + 9$$
$$= 2x(x + 3) + 3(x + 3)$$
$$= (x + 3)(2x + 3)$$

138. $a \cdot c = (12)(1) = 12$. Rewrite the middle term, $-13x = -12x - x$, since $(-12)(-1) = 12$ and $-12 - 1 = -13$.

$$12x^2 - 13x + 1 = 12x^2 - 12x - x + 1$$
$$= 12x(x - 1) - 1(x - 1)$$
$$= (x - 1)(12x - 1)$$

140. $12x^2 - 48 = 12(x^2 - 4) = 12(x + 2)(x - 2)$

142. $x^3 - 9x = x(x^2 - 9) = x(x + 3)(x - 3)$

144. $2y^3 - 7y^2 - 15y = y(2y^2 - 7y - 15)$
$$= y(2y^2 - 10y + 3y - 15)$$
$$= y(2y + 3)(y - 5)$$

146. $13x + 6 + 5x^2 = 5x^2 + 13x + 6$
$$= 5x^2 + 10x + 3x + 6$$
$$= (5x + 3)(x + 2)$$

148. $\frac{1}{8}x^2 - \frac{1}{96}x - \frac{1}{16} = \frac{1}{8}\left(x^2 - \frac{1}{12}x - \frac{1}{2}\right)$

150. $3u - 2u^2 + 6 - u^3 = -u^3 - 2u^2 + 3u + 6$
$$= -u^2(u + 2) + 3(u + 2)$$
$$= (u + 2)(-u^2 + 3)$$
$$= (u + 2)(3 - u^2)$$

152. $(x^2 + 8)^2 - 36x^2 = (x^2 + 8 + 6x)(x^2 + 8 - 6x)$
$$= (x^2 + 6x + 8)(x^2 - 6x + 8)$$
$$= (x + 4)(x + 2)(x - 4)(x - 2)$$

154. $5x^3 + 40 = 5(x^3 + 8)$
$$= 5(x + 2)(x^2 - 2x + 4)$$

156. $5(3 - 4x)^2 - 8(3 - 4x)(5x - 1) = (3 - 4x)[5(3 - 4x) - 8(5x - 1)]$
$$= (3 - 4x)[15 - 20x - 40x + 8]$$
$$= (3 - 4x)(-60x + 23)$$
$$= (3 - 4x)(23 - 60x)$$

158. $7x(2)(x^2 + 1)(2x) - (x^2 + 1)^2(7) = 7(x^2 + 1)[4x^2 - (x^2 + 1)]$
$$= 7(x^2 + 1)(3x^2 - 1)$$

160. $5(x^6 + 1)^4(6x^5)(3x + 2)^3 + 3(3x + 2)^2(3)(x^6 + 1)^5 = 3(3x + 2)^2(x^6 + 1)^4[10x^5(3x + 2) + 3(x^6 + 1)]$
$$= 3(3x + 2)^2(x^6 + 1)^4[30x^6 + 20x^5 + 3x^6 + 3]$$
$$= 3(3x + 2)^2(x^6 + 1)^4(33x^6 + 20x^5 + 3)$$

162. For $x^2 + bx + 50$ to be factorable, b must equal $m + n$ where $mn = 50$.

Factors of 50	Sum of factors
$(50)(1)$	$50 + 1 = 51$
$(-50)(-1)$	$(-50) + (-1) = -51$
$(25)(2)$	$25 + 2 = 27$
$(-25)(-2)$	$(-25) + (-2) = -27$
$(10)(5)$	$10 + 5 = 15$
$(-10)(-5)$	$(-10) + (-5) = -15$

The possible b values are
$51, -51, 27, -27, 15, -15.$

164. For $x^2 + bx + 24$ to be factorable, b must equal $m + n$ where $mn = 24$.

Factors of 24	Sum of factors
$(24)(1)$	$24 + 1 = 25$
$(-24)(-1)$	$(-24) + (-1) = -25$
$(12)(2)$	$12 + 2 = 14$
$(-12)(-2)$	$(-12) + (-2) = -14$
$(8)(3)$	$8 + 3 = 11$
$(-8)(-3)$	$(-8) + (-3) = -11$
$(6)(4)$	$6 + 4 = 10$
$(-6)(-4)$	$(-6) + (-4) = -10$

The possible b values are
$25, -25, 14, -14, 11, -11, 10, -10.$

166. For $3x^2 - 10x + c$ to be factorable, the factors of $3c$ must add up to -10.

Possible c values	$3c$	Factors of $3c$ that add up to -10
3	9	$(-9)(-1) = 9$ and $(-9) + (-1) = -10$
-8	-24	$(-12)(2) = -24$ and $(-12) + 2 = -10$
8	24	$(-6)(-4) = 24$ and $(-6) + (-4) = -10$

These are a few possible c values. There are many correct answers.

If $c = 3$: $3x^2 - 10x + 3 = (3x - 1)(x - 3)$

If $c = -8$: $3x^2 - 10x - 8 = (3x + 2)(x - 4)$

If $c = 8$: $3x^2 - 10x + 8 = (3x - 4)(x - 2)$

168. For $2x^2 + 9x + c$ to be factorable, the factors of $2c$ must add up to 9.

Possible c values	$2c$	Factors of $2c$ that add up to 9
4	8	$(8)(1) = 8$ and $8 + 1 = 9$
-5	-10	$(10)(-1) = -10$ and $10 + (-1) = 9$
7	14	$(7)(2) = 14$ and $7 + 2 = 9$
9	18	$(3)(6) = 18$ and $3 + 6 = 9$

These are a few possible c values. There are many correct answers.

If $c = 4$: $2x^2 + 9x + 4 = (2x + 1)(x + 4)$

If $c = -5$: $2x^2 + 9x - 5 = (2x - 1)(x + 5)$

If $c = 7$: $2x^2 + 9x + 7 = (2x + 7)(x + 1)$

If $c = 9$: $2x^2 + 9x + 9 = (2x + 3)(x + 3)$

170. Profit = Revenue − Cost

Profit = $36x - (460 + 12x) = 36x - 460 - 12x$

$\qquad = 24x - 460$

For $x = 42$: Profit $= 24(42) - 460 = 1008 - 460 = 548$ dollars per month

172. (a) $1200(1 + r)^3 = 1200(1 + 3r + 3r^2 + r^3)$

$\qquad\qquad = 1200r^3 + 3600r^2 + 3600r + 1200$

(b)

r	$2\frac{1}{2}\%$	3%	4%	$4\frac{1}{2}\%$	5%
$1200(1 + r)^3$	\$1292.27	\$1311.27	\$1349.84	\$1369.40	\$1389.15

(c) As r increases, the amount increases.

174. (a) Area of shaded region = Area of outer rectangle − Area of inner rectangle

$A = 2x(2x + 6) - x(x + 4)$

$\quad = 4x^2 + 12x - x^2 - 4x$

$\quad = 3x^2 + 8x$

(b) Area of shaded region = Area of outer triangle − Area of inner triangle

$A = \frac{1}{2}(9x)(12x) - \frac{1}{2}(6x)(8x)$

$\quad = 54x^2 - 24x^2$

$\quad = 30x^2$

176. Area = length × width = $(2x + 14)(22) = (2x)(22) + (14)(22) = 44x + 308$

178. (a) $T = R + B = 1.1x + (0.14x^2 - 4.43x + 58.40)$

$\qquad\qquad = 0.14x^2 - 3.33x + 58.40$

(b)

x mi/hr	30	40	55
T feet	84.50	149.20	298.75

(c) Stopping distance required increases as speed increases.

180. $2x^2 + 7x + 3 = (2x + 1)(x + 3)$

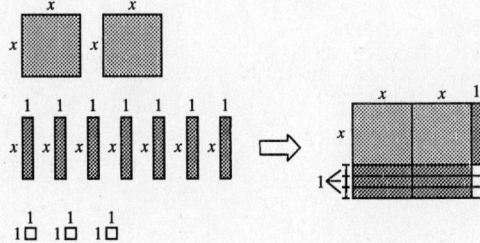

182. $A = (2r)^2 - \pi r^2$

$\quad = 4r^2 - \pi r^2$

$\quad = (4 - \pi)r^2$

184. $A = \frac{1}{2}\left[\frac{5}{4}(x + 3)\right](x + 3) - \frac{1}{2}(5)(4)$

$\quad = \frac{5}{8}(x + 3)^2 - 10 = \frac{5}{8}(x^2 + 6x + 9) - 10$

$\quad = \frac{5}{8}(x^2 + 6x - 7) = \frac{5}{8}(x + 7)(x - 1)$

186. $kQx - kx^2 = kx(Q - x)$

188. False. $(x + 3) + (-x + 4) = 7$

190. False. $x^2 + y^2$ cannot be factored.

$\quad (x + y)^2 = x^2 + 2xy + y^2 \neq x^2 + y^2$

192. The degree of the sum of two polynomials of degrees m and n, $m < n$, is n.

194. (a) $(x - 1)(x + 1) = x^2 - 1$

(b) $(x - 1)(x^2 + x + 1) = x^3 + x^2 + x - x^2 - x - 1$

$$= x^3 - 1$$

(c) $(x - 1)(x^3 + x^2 + x + 1) = x^4 + x^3 + x^2 + x - x^3 - x^2 - x - 1$

$$= x^4 - 1$$

From the pattern in the products above, $(x - 1)(x^4 + x^3 + x^2 + x + 1) = x^5 - 1$

196. $x^{3n} + y^{3n} = (x^n)^3 + (y^n)^3$

$$= (x^n + y^n)(x^{2n} - x^n y^n + y^{2n})$$

Section P.4   Rational Expressions

Solutions to Even-Numbered Exercises

2. The domain of the polynomial $2x^2 + 5x - 2$ is the set of all real numbers.

4. The domain of the polynomial $6x^2 - 9, x > 0$ is the set of all positive real numbers because the polynomial is restricted to that set.

6. The domain of $\dfrac{x + 1}{2x + 1}$ is the set of all real numbers such that $x \neq -\dfrac{1}{2}$.

8. The domain of $\sqrt{6 - x}$ is the set of all real numbers x such that $x \leq 6$.

10. $\dfrac{3}{4} = \dfrac{3(x + 1)}{4(x + 1)}$

The missing factor is $(x + 1)$, where $x \neq -1$.

12. $\dfrac{3y - 4}{y + 1} = \dfrac{(3y - 4)(y - 1)}{(y + 1)(y - 1)} = \dfrac{(3y - 4)(y - 1)}{y^2 - 1}$

The missing factor is $(y - 1)$, where $y \neq 1$.

14. $\dfrac{1 - z}{z^2} = \dfrac{(1 - z)(z + 1)}{z^2(z + 1)} = \dfrac{(1 - z)(z + 1)}{z^3 + z^2}$

The missing factor is $(z + 1)$, where $z \neq -1$.

16. $\dfrac{18y^2}{60y^5} = \dfrac{6y^2(3)}{6y^2(10y^3)} = \dfrac{3}{10y^3}$

18. $\dfrac{2x^2y}{xy - y} = \dfrac{2x^2y}{y(x - 1)} = \dfrac{2x^2}{x - 1}$

20. $\dfrac{9x^2 + 9x}{2x + 2} = \dfrac{9x(x + 1)}{2(x + 1)} = \dfrac{9x}{2}, \quad x \neq -1$

22. $\dfrac{12 - 4x}{x - 3} = \dfrac{4(3 - x)}{x - 3} = -4, x \neq 3$

24. $\dfrac{x^2 - 25}{5 - x} = \dfrac{(x + 5)(x - 5)}{-1(x - 5)} = -(x + 5), \quad x \neq 5$

26. $\dfrac{x^2 + 8x - 20}{x^2 + 11x + 10} = \dfrac{(x + 10)(x - 2)}{(x + 10)(x + 1)} = \dfrac{x - 2}{x - 1}, \quad x \neq -10$

28. $\dfrac{x^2 - 7x + 6}{x^2 + 11x + 10} = \dfrac{(x - 6)(x - 1)}{(x + 10(x + 1)}$

30. $\dfrac{x^2 - 9}{x^3 + x^2 - 9x - 9} = \dfrac{x^2 - 9}{(x^2 - 9)(x + 1)} = \dfrac{1}{x + 1}, \quad x \neq \pm 3$

32. $\dfrac{y^3 - 2y^2 - 3y}{y^3 + 1} = \dfrac{y(y-3)(y+1)}{(y+1)(y^2 - y + 1)} = \dfrac{y(y-3)}{y^2 - y + 1}, \quad y \neq -1$

34.

x	0	1	2	3	4	5	6
$\dfrac{x-3}{x^2 - x - 6}$	$\dfrac{1}{2}$	$\dfrac{1}{3}$	$\dfrac{1}{4}$	Undef.	$\dfrac{1}{6}$	$\dfrac{1}{7}$	$\dfrac{1}{8}$
$\dfrac{1}{x+2}$	$\dfrac{1}{2}$	$\dfrac{1}{3}$	$\dfrac{1}{4}$	$\dfrac{1}{5}$	$\dfrac{1}{6}$	$\dfrac{1}{7}$	$\dfrac{1}{8}$

The expressions are equivalent except at $x = 3$.

36. $\dfrac{x^3 + 25x}{x^2 - 2x - 15} = \dfrac{x(x^2 + 25)}{(x-5)(x+3)}$

The expression cannot be simplified.

38. Area of shaded portion: $\left(\dfrac{x+5}{2}\right)^2 = \dfrac{(x+5)^2}{4}$

Area of total figure: $(2x+3)(x+5)$

Ratio: $\dfrac{\dfrac{(x+5)^2}{4}}{(2x+3)(x+5)} = \dfrac{\dfrac{(x+5)}{4}}{(2x+3)} = \dfrac{x+5}{4(2x+3)}$

40. $\dfrac{x+13}{x^3(3-x)} \cdot \dfrac{x(x-3)}{5} = \dfrac{x+13}{x^3(x-3)(-1)} \cdot \dfrac{x(x-3)}{5}$

$= \dfrac{x+13}{-5x^2} = -\dfrac{x+13}{5x^2}, \quad x \neq 3$

42. $\dfrac{(x-9)(x+7)}{x+1} \cdot \dfrac{x}{9-x} = \dfrac{(x-9)(x+7)}{x+1} \cdot \dfrac{x}{(-1)(x-9)}$

$= \dfrac{x(x+7)}{(-1)(x+1)}$

$= -\dfrac{x(x+7)}{x+1}, x \neq 9$

44. $\dfrac{4y-16}{5y+15} \cdot \dfrac{2y+6}{4-y} = \dfrac{4(y-4)}{5(y+3)} \cdot \dfrac{2(y+3)}{(-1)(y-4)}$

$= \dfrac{8}{-5} = -\dfrac{8}{5}, \ y \neq -3, 4$

46. $\dfrac{y^3 - 8}{2y^3} \cdot \dfrac{4y}{y^2 - 5y + 6} = \dfrac{(y-2)(y^2 + 2y + 4)}{2y^3} \cdot \dfrac{4y}{(y-2)(y-3)}$

$= \dfrac{2(y^2 + 2y + 4)}{y^2(y-3)}, \ y \neq 2$

48. $\dfrac{x^3 - 1}{x+1} \cdot \dfrac{x^2 + 1}{x^2 - 1} = \dfrac{(x-1)(x^2 + x + 1)}{x+1} \cdot \dfrac{x^2 + 1}{(x+1)(x-1)}$

$= \dfrac{(x^2 + x + 1)(x^2 + 1)}{(x+1)^2}, \ x \neq 1$

50. $\dfrac{x+2}{5(x-3)} \div \dfrac{x-2}{5(x-3)} = \dfrac{x+2}{5(x-3)} \cdot \dfrac{5(x-3)}{x-2}$

$= \dfrac{x+2}{x-2}, \ x \neq 3$

52. $\dfrac{3x+18}{x^4} \div \dfrac{x+6}{x^2} = \dfrac{3(x+6)}{x^4} \cdot \dfrac{x^2}{x+6} = \dfrac{3}{x^2}, \ x \neq -6$

54. $\dfrac{x^2 - 14x + 49}{x^2 - 49} \div \dfrac{3x - 21}{x+7} = \dfrac{(x-7)(x-7)}{(x+7)(x-7)} \cdot \dfrac{x+7}{3(x-7)}$

$= \dfrac{1}{3}, \ x \neq \pm 7$

56. $\dfrac{2x-1}{x+3} + \dfrac{1-x}{x+3} = \dfrac{2x - 1 + 1 - x}{x+3} = \dfrac{x}{x+3}$

58. $\dfrac{3}{x-1} - 5 = \dfrac{3}{x-1} - \dfrac{5(x-1)}{x-1} = \dfrac{3 - 5(x-1)}{x-1} = \dfrac{3 - 5x + 5}{x-1} = \dfrac{8 - 5x}{x-1}$

60. $\dfrac{2x}{x-5} - \dfrac{5}{5-x} = \dfrac{2x}{x-5} - \dfrac{5(-1)}{(-1)(5-x)} = \dfrac{2x}{x-5} - \dfrac{-5}{x-5} = \dfrac{2x+5}{x-5}$

62. $\dfrac{x}{x^2+x-2} - \dfrac{1}{x+2} = \dfrac{x}{(x+2)(x-1)} - \dfrac{1(x-1)}{(x+2)(x-1)}$

$$= \dfrac{x-(x-1)}{(x+2)(x-1)} = \dfrac{x-x+1}{(x+2)(x-1)} = \dfrac{1}{(x+2)(x-1)}$$

64. $\dfrac{2}{x^2-x-2} + \dfrac{10}{x^2+2x-8} = \dfrac{2}{(x-2)(x+1)} + \dfrac{10}{(x+4)(x-2)}$

$$= \dfrac{2(x+4)}{(x-2)(x+1)(x+4)} + \dfrac{10(x+1)}{(x-2)(x+1)(x+4)}$$

$$= \dfrac{2x+8+10x+10}{(x-2)(x+1)(x+4)} = \dfrac{12x+19}{(x-2)(x+1)(x+4)} = \dfrac{6(2x+3)}{(x-2)(x+1)(x+4)}$$

66. $\dfrac{2}{x+1} + \dfrac{2}{x-1} + \dfrac{1}{x^2-1} = \dfrac{2}{x+1} + \dfrac{2}{x-1} + \dfrac{1}{(x+1)(x-1)}$

$$= \dfrac{2(x-1)}{(x+1)(x-1)} + \dfrac{2(x+1)}{(x+1)(x-1)} + \dfrac{1}{(x+1)(x-1)}$$

$$= \dfrac{2x-2+2x+2+1}{(x+1)(x-1)} = \dfrac{4x+1}{(x+1)(x-1)}$$

68. $x^5 - 5x^{-3} = x^{-3}(x^8 - 5) = \dfrac{x^8 - 5}{x^3}$

70. $5x^5 - 3x^{-3/2} = x^{-3/2}(5x^{13/2} - 3) = \dfrac{5x^{13/2} - 3}{x^{3/2}}$

72. $2x(x-5)^{-3} - 4x^2(x-5)^{-4} = -2x(x-5)^{-4}[-(x-5) + 2x]$

$$= -2x(x-5)^{-4}(-x + 5 + 2x)$$

$$= \dfrac{-2x(x+5)}{(x-5)^4}$$

74. $4x^3(2x-1)^{3/2} - 2x(2x-1)^{-1/2} = (2x-1)^{-1/2}[4x^3(2x-1)^2 - 2x]$

$$= \dfrac{4x^3(2x-1)^2 - 2x}{(2x-1)^{1/2}}$$

76. $\dfrac{6-x}{x(x+2)} + \dfrac{x+2}{x^2} + \dfrac{8}{x^2(x+2)} = \dfrac{x(6-x)}{x^2(x+2)} + \dfrac{(x+2)^2}{x^2(x+2)} + \dfrac{8}{x^2(x+2)}$

$$= \dfrac{6x - x^2 + x^2 + 4x + 4 + 8}{x^2(x+2)} = \dfrac{10x+12}{x^2(x+2)} = \dfrac{2(5x+6)}{x^2(x+2)}$$

The error was an incorrect expansion of $(x+2)^2$ in the numerator.

78. $\dfrac{(x-4)}{\left(\dfrac{x}{4} - \dfrac{4}{x}\right)} = \dfrac{\left(\dfrac{x-4}{1}\right)}{\left(\dfrac{x^2}{4x} - \dfrac{16}{4x}\right)} = \dfrac{\left(\dfrac{x-4}{1}\right)}{\left(\dfrac{x^2-16}{4x}\right)} = \dfrac{x-4}{1} \cdot \dfrac{4x}{x^2-16} = \dfrac{x-4}{1} \cdot \dfrac{4x}{(x+4)(x-4)} = \dfrac{4x}{x+4}, \ x \neq 0, 4$

80. $\dfrac{\left(\dfrac{x^2-1}{x}\right)}{\left[\dfrac{(x-1)^2}{x}\right]} = \dfrac{x^2-1}{x} \cdot \dfrac{x}{(x-1)^2} = \dfrac{(x+1)(x-1)}{x} \cdot \dfrac{x}{(x-1)(x-1)} = \dfrac{x+1}{x-1}, \ x \neq 0$

82. $\dfrac{\left(\dfrac{5}{y} - \dfrac{6}{2y+1}\right)}{\left(\dfrac{5}{y} + 4\right)} = \dfrac{\left(\dfrac{5(2y+1)}{y(2y+1)} - \dfrac{6y}{y(2y+1)}\right)}{\left(\dfrac{5}{y} + \dfrac{4y}{y}\right)} = \dfrac{\left(\dfrac{10y+5-6y}{y(2y+1)}\right)}{\left(\dfrac{5+4y}{y}\right)} = \dfrac{4y+5}{y(2y+1)} \cdot \dfrac{y}{5+4y} = \dfrac{1}{2y+1}, \ y \neq 0, -\dfrac{5}{4}$

84. $\dfrac{\left(\dfrac{x+4}{x+5} - \dfrac{x}{x+1}\right)}{4} = \dfrac{\left(\dfrac{(x+4)(x+1)}{(x+5)(x+1)} - \dfrac{x(x+5)}{(x+5)(x+1)}\right)}{\dfrac{4}{1}} = \left(\dfrac{(x+4)(x+1)}{(x+5)(x+1)} - \dfrac{x(x+5)}{(x+5)(x+1)}\right) \cdot \dfrac{1}{4}$

$= \left(\dfrac{x^2+5x+4-x^2-5x}{(x+5)(x+1)}\right) \cdot \dfrac{1}{4} = \dfrac{4}{(x+5)(x+1)} \cdot \dfrac{1}{4} = \dfrac{1}{(x+5)(x+1)}$

86. $\dfrac{\left(\dfrac{x+h}{x+h+1} - \dfrac{x}{x+1}\right)}{h} = \dfrac{\left(\dfrac{(x+h)(x+1)}{(x+h+1)(x+1)} - \dfrac{x(x+h+1)}{(x+h+1)(x+1)}\right)}{\dfrac{h}{1}}$

$= \left(\dfrac{(x+h)(x+1)}{(x+h+1)(x+1)} - \dfrac{x(x+h+1)}{(x+h+1)(x+1)}\right) \cdot \dfrac{1}{h}$

$= \left(\dfrac{x^2+x+hx+h-x^2-xh-x}{(x+h+1)(x+1)}\right) \cdot \dfrac{1}{h}$

$= \dfrac{h}{(x+h+1)(x+1)} \cdot \dfrac{1}{h} = \dfrac{1}{(x+h+1)(x+1)}, \ h \neq 0$

88. $\dfrac{\dfrac{t^2}{\sqrt{t^2+1}} - \sqrt{t^2+1}}{t^2} = \dfrac{\left[\dfrac{t^2}{\sqrt{t^2+1}} - \sqrt{t^2+1}\right]}{t^2} \cdot \dfrac{\sqrt{t^2+1}}{\sqrt{t^2+1}}$

$= \dfrac{t^2 - (t^2+1)}{t^2\sqrt{t^2+1}} = -\dfrac{1}{t^2\sqrt{t^2+1}}$

90. $\dfrac{-x^3(1-x^2)^{-1/2} - 2x(1-x^2)^{1/2}}{x^4} = \dfrac{\dfrac{-x^3}{(1-x^2)^{1/2}} - 2x(1-x^2)^{1/2}}{x^4}$

$= \dfrac{\dfrac{-x^3}{(1-x^2)^{1/2}} - \dfrac{2x(1-x^2)^{1/2}(1-x^2)^{1/2}}{(1-x^2)^{1/2}}}{x^4} = \dfrac{\dfrac{-x^3 - 2x(1-x^2)}{(1-x^2)^{1/2}}}{x^4}$

$= \dfrac{-x^3 - 2x + 2x^3}{(1-x^2)^{1/2}} \cdot \dfrac{1}{x^4} = \dfrac{x^3 - 2x}{(1-x^2)^{1/2}} \cdot \dfrac{1}{x^4}$

$= \dfrac{x(x^2-2)}{x^4(1-x^2)^{1/2}} = \dfrac{x^2-2}{x^3(1-x^2)^{1/2}}$

92. $\dfrac{(2x+1)^{1/3} - \dfrac{4x}{3(2x+1)^{2/3}}}{(2x+1)^{2/3}} = \dfrac{\dfrac{3(2x+1)^{1/3}(2x-1)^{2/3}}{3(2x+1)^{2/3}} - \dfrac{4x}{3(2x+1)^{2/3}}}{(2x+1)^{2/3}} = \dfrac{\dfrac{3(2x+1)-4x}{3(2x+1)^{2/3}}}{(2x+1)^{2/3}}$

$$= \frac{3(2x+1)-4x}{3(2x+1)^{2/3}} \cdot \frac{1}{(2x+1)^{2/3}} = \frac{6x+3-4x}{3(2x+1)^{2/3}} \cdot \frac{1}{(2x+1)^{2/3}} = \frac{2x+3}{3(2x+1)^{4/3}}$$

94. $\dfrac{\sqrt{z-3} - \sqrt{z}}{3} = \dfrac{\sqrt{z-3} - \sqrt{z}}{3} \cdot \dfrac{\sqrt{z-3} + \sqrt{z}}{\sqrt{z-3} + \sqrt{z}}$

$$= \frac{(z-3)-z}{3\left(\sqrt{z-3} + \sqrt{z}\right)} = \frac{-3}{3\left(\sqrt{z-3} + \sqrt{z}\right)} = \frac{-1}{\sqrt{z-3} + \sqrt{z}}$$

96. $\dfrac{t}{3} + \dfrac{t}{5} = \dfrac{5(t)}{5(3)} + \dfrac{3(t)}{3(5)} = \dfrac{5t}{15} + \dfrac{3t}{15} = \dfrac{8t}{15} = \dfrac{8}{15}t$

98. Space in each part: $\dfrac{\dfrac{3x}{4} - \dfrac{x}{3}}{4} = \dfrac{\dfrac{3(3x)}{3(4)} - \dfrac{4(x)}{4(3)}}{4} = \dfrac{\dfrac{9x}{12} - \dfrac{4x}{12}}{4} = \dfrac{\dfrac{5x}{12}}{4} = \dfrac{5x}{12} \cdot \dfrac{1}{4} = \dfrac{5x}{48}$

First number: $\dfrac{x}{3} + \dfrac{5x}{48} = \dfrac{16(x)}{16(3)} + \dfrac{5x}{48} = \dfrac{16x}{48} + \dfrac{5x}{48} = \dfrac{21x}{48} = \dfrac{7x}{16}$

Second number: $\dfrac{7x}{16} + \dfrac{5x}{48} = \dfrac{21x}{48} + \dfrac{5x}{48} = \dfrac{26x}{48} = \dfrac{13x}{24}$

Third number: $\dfrac{13x}{24} + \dfrac{5x}{48} = \dfrac{26x}{48} + \dfrac{5x}{48} = \dfrac{31x}{48}$

The three numbers are $\dfrac{7x}{16}, \dfrac{13x}{24},$ and $\dfrac{31x}{48}$.

100. (a) $N = 5 \times 12 = 60$ payments, $M = \$400, P = \$20,000$

$$r = \frac{\left[\dfrac{24(NM-P)}{N}\right]}{\left(P + \dfrac{NM}{12}\right)} = \frac{\left[\dfrac{24(60 \cdot 400 - 20,000)}{60}\right]}{\left(20,000 + \dfrac{60 \cdot 400}{12}\right)} = 0.0727 \text{ or } 7.27\%$$

(b) $r = \dfrac{\left[\dfrac{24(NM-P)}{N}\right]}{\left(P + \dfrac{NM}{12}\right)} = \dfrac{\left[\dfrac{24(NM-P)}{N}\right]}{\left(\dfrac{12P + NM}{12}\right)} = \dfrac{24(NM-P)}{N} \cdot \dfrac{12}{12P + NM} = \dfrac{288(NM-P)}{N(NM+12P)}$

$$r = \frac{288(60 \cdot 400 - 20,000)}{60(12 \cdot 20,000 + 60 \cdot 400)} = 0.0727 \text{ or } 7.27\%$$

102. (a)

Year	1992	1993	1994	1995	1996	1997
Gold	\$345	\$364	\$383	\$399	\$404	\$366
Silver	\$3.91	\$4.01	\$4.71	\$5.13	\$4.97	\$4.81

The estimates are fairly close to the actual values.

—CONTINUED—

102. —CONTINUED—

(b) $\dfrac{\dfrac{-38.5t + 310.1}{0.007t^2 - 0.176t + 1}}{\dfrac{0.242t^2 - 1.86t + 4.02}{0.056t^2 - 0.45t + 1}} = \dfrac{-38.5t + 310.1}{0.007t^2 - 0.176t + 1} \cdot \dfrac{0.056t^2 - 0.45t + 1}{0.242t^2 - 1.86t + 4.02}$

$$= \frac{-2.156t^3 + 34.691t^2 - 178.045t + 310.1}{0.0017t^4 - 0.056t^3 + 0.598t^2 - 2.568t + 4.02}$$

Year	1992	1993	1994	1995	1996	1997
Ratio	88.31	92.59	89.67	91.69	101.17	109.86

Increase

104. $\dfrac{x\left(\dfrac{x}{2}\right)}{x(2x + 1)} = \dfrac{\dfrac{x}{2}}{2x + 1} \cdot \dfrac{2}{2} = \dfrac{x}{2(2x + 1)}$

106. Probability $= \dfrac{\text{Shaded area}}{\text{(area of triangle)}} = \dfrac{\dfrac{1}{2} \cdot \dfrac{4}{x}(x + 2)(x + x + 4)}{\dfrac{1}{2}(x + 4)\left[(x + 2) + \dfrac{4}{x}(x + 2)\right]}$

$= \dfrac{\dfrac{4(x + 2)(2x + 4)}{x}}{(x + 4)(x + 2)\left(1 + \dfrac{4}{x}\right)} = \dfrac{\dfrac{4 \cdot 2(x + 2)^2}{x}}{(x + 4)(x + 2)\left(1 + \dfrac{4}{x}\right)}$

$= \dfrac{8(x + 2)^2}{x} \cdot \dfrac{1}{(x + 4)(x + 2)\left(1 + \dfrac{4}{x}\right)}$

$= \dfrac{8(x + 2)^2}{(x + 4)(x + 2)(x + 4)} = \dfrac{8(x + 2)}{(x + 4)^2}$

108. False. The two expressions are equivalent for all values of x such that $x \neq 1$.

110. Factor the numerator and the denominator and cancel all common factors.

Section P.5   Solving Equations

2. $3(x + 2) = 5x + 4$ is *conditional*. There are real values of x for which the equation is not true (for example, $x = 0$).

4. $3(x + 2) - 5 = 3x + 1$ is an *identity* by simplification. It is true for all real values of x.
$$3(x + 2) - 5 = 3x + 6 - 5 = 3x + 1$$

6. $-7(x - 3) + 4x = 3(7 - x)$ is an *identity* by simplification. It is true for all real values of x.
$$-7(x - 3) + 4x = -7x + 21 + 4x = 21 - 3x = 3(7 - x)$$

8. $x^2 + 2(3x - 2) = x^2 + 6x - 4$ is an *identity* by simplification. It is true for all real values of x.

10. $\dfrac{5}{x} + \dfrac{3}{x} = 24$ is *conditional*. There are real values of x for which the equation is not true (for example, $x = 1$).

12.
$$7 - x = 19$$
$$7 - x + x = 19 + x$$
$$7 = 19 + x$$
$$7 - 19 = 19 + x - 19$$
$$-12 = x$$

14.
$$7x + 2 = 23$$
$$7x + 2 - 2 = 23 - 2$$
$$7x = 21$$
$$\frac{7x}{7} = \frac{21}{7}$$
$$x = 3$$

16.
$$7x + 3 = 3x - 17$$
$$7x + 3 - 3 - 3x = 3x - 17 - 3 - 3x$$
$$4x = -20$$
$$x = -5$$

18. $3(x + 3) = 5(1 - x) - 1$
$$3x + 9 = 5 - 5x - 1$$
$$3x + 9 = 4 - 5x$$
$$8x = -5$$
$$x = -\frac{5}{8}$$

20. $9x - 10 = 5x + 2(2x - 5)$
$$9x - 10 = 5x + 4x - 10$$
$$9x - 10 = 9x - 10$$
The solution is the set of all real numbers.

22.
$$\frac{x}{5} - \frac{x}{2} = 3 + \frac{3x}{10}$$
$$10\left(\frac{x}{5} - \frac{x}{2}\right) = 10\left(3 + \frac{3x}{10}\right)$$
$$2x - 5x = 30 + 3x$$
$$-6x = 30$$
$$x = -5$$

24.
$$\frac{3x}{2} + \frac{1}{4}(x - 2) = 10$$
$$(4)\left(\frac{3x}{2}\right) + (4)\frac{1}{4}(x - 2) = (4)10$$
$$6x + (x - 2) = 40$$
$$7x - 2 = 40$$
$$7x = 42$$
$$x = 6$$

26. $0.60x + 0.40(100 - x) = 50$
$$0.60x + 40 - 0.40x = 50$$
$$0.20x = 10$$
$$x = 50$$

28. $8(x + 2) - 3(2x + 1) = 2(x + 5)$

$$8x + 16 - 6x - 3 = 2x + 10$$

$$2x + 13 = 2x + 10$$

$$13 = 10$$

False equation $\Rightarrow$ no solution

30.

$$\frac{17 + y}{y} + \frac{32 + y}{y} = 100$$

$$(y)\frac{17 + y}{y} + (y)\frac{32 + y}{y} = 100(y)$$

$$17 + y + 32 + y = 100y$$

$$49 + 2y = 100y$$

$$49 = 98y$$

$$\frac{1}{2} = y$$

32. $\dfrac{10x + 3}{5x + 6} = \dfrac{1}{2}$

$$2(10x + 3) = 1(5x + 6)$$

$$20x + 6 = 5x + 6$$

$$15x = 0$$

$$x = 0$$

34. $\dfrac{15}{x} - 4 = \dfrac{6}{x} + 3$

$$\frac{15}{x} - \frac{6}{x} = 7$$

$$\frac{9}{x} = 7$$

$$9 = 7x$$

$$\frac{9}{7} = x$$

36. $3 = 2 + \dfrac{2}{z + 2}$

$$3(z + 2) = \left(2 + \frac{2}{z + 2}\right)(z + 2)$$

$$3z + 6 = 2z + 4 + 2$$

$$z = 0$$

38.

$$\frac{7}{2x + 1} - \frac{8x}{2x - 1} = -4$$

$$(2x + 1)(2x - 1)\frac{7}{2x + 1} - (2x + 1)(2x - 1)\frac{8x}{2x - 1} = -4(2x + 1)(2x - 1)$$

$$7(2x - 1) - 8x(2x + 1) = -4(2x + 1)(2x - 1)$$

$$14x - 7 - 16x^2 - 8x = -16x^2 + 4$$

$$6x = 11$$

$$x = \frac{11}{6}$$

40.

$$\frac{4}{x - 1} + \frac{6}{3x + 1} = \frac{15}{3x + 1}$$

$$(x - 1)(3x + 1)\frac{4}{x - 1} + (x - 1)(3x + 1)\frac{6}{3x + 1} = (x - 1)(3x + 1)\frac{15}{3x + 1}$$

$$4(3x + 1) + 6(x - 1) = 15(x - 1)$$

$$12x + 4 + 6x - 6 = 15x - 15$$

$$18x - 2 = 15x - 15$$

$$3x = -13$$

$$x = -\frac{13}{3}$$

42.
$$\frac{1}{x - 2} + \frac{3}{x + 3} = \frac{4}{x^2 + x - 6}$$

$$(x^2 + x - 6)\frac{1}{x - 2} + (x^2 + x - 6)\frac{3}{x + 3} = (x^2 + x - 6)\frac{4}{x^2 + x - 6}$$

$$(x + 3) + 3(x - 2) = 4$$

$$x + 3 + 3x - 6 = 4$$

$$4x - 3 = 4$$

$$4x = 7$$

$$x = \frac{7}{4}$$

44.
$$\frac{6}{x} - \frac{2}{x + 3} = \frac{3(x + 5)}{x^2 + 3x}$$

$$x^2 + 3x\frac{6}{x} - x^2 + 3x\frac{2}{x + 3} = x^2 + 3x\frac{3(x + 5)}{x^2 + 3x}$$

$$6(x + 3) - 2x = 3(x + 5)$$

$$6x + 18 - 2x = 3x + 15$$

$$4x + 18 = 3x + 15$$

$$x = -3$$

Check: $\dfrac{6}{-3} - \dfrac{2}{-3 + 3} = \dfrac{3(-3 + 5)}{[(-3)^2 + 3(-3)]}$

$$-2 - \frac{2}{0} = \frac{-6}{0}$$

Division by zero is undefined. Thus, $x = -3$ is not a solution, and the original equation has no solution.

46. $(x + 1)^2 + 2(x - 2) = (x + 1)(x - 2)$

$$x^2 + 2x + 1 + 2x - 4 = x^2 - x - 2$$

$$5x = 1$$

$$x = \frac{1}{5}$$

48. $(2x + 1)^2 = 4(x^2 + x + 1)$

$$4x^2 + 4x + 1 = 4x^2 + 4x + 4$$

$$1 = 4$$

This is a false equation. Thus, the equation has no solution.

50. $x^2 = 16x$

General form: $x^2 - 16x = 0$

52.
$$13 - 3(x + 7)^2 = 0$$

$$13 - 3(x^2 + 14x + 49) = 0$$

$$13 - 3x^2 - 42x - 147 = 0$$

General form: $-3x^2 - 42x - 134 = 0$

54.
$$x(x + 2) = 5x^2 + 1$$

$$x^2 + 2x = 5x^2 + 1$$

$$-4x^2 + 2x - 1 = 0$$

$$(-1)(-4x^2 + 2x - 1) = -1(0)$$

General form: $4x^2 - 2x + 1 = 0$

56.
$$9x^2 - 1 = 0$$

$$(3x + 1)(3x - 1) = 0$$

$$3x + 1 = 0 \Rightarrow x = -\frac{1}{3}$$

$$3x - 1 = 0 \Rightarrow x = \frac{1}{3}$$

58. $x^2 - 10x + 9 = 0$

$$(x - 9)(x - 1) = 0$$

$$x - 9 = 0 \Rightarrow x = 9$$

$$x - 1 = 0 \Rightarrow x = 1$$

60. $4x^2 + 12x + 9 = 0$

$(2x + 3)(2x + 3) = 0$

$2x + 3 = 0 \Rightarrow x = -\frac{3}{2}$

62. $2x^2 = 19x + 33$

$2x^2 - 19x - 33 = 0$

$(2x + 3)(x - 11) = 0$

$2x + 3 = 0 \Rightarrow x = -\frac{3}{2}$

$x - 11 = 0 \Rightarrow x = 11$

64. $-x^2 + 8x = 12$

$-x^2 + 8x - 12 = 0$

$(-1)(-x^2 + 8x - 12) = (-1)(0)$

$x^2 - 8x + 12 = 0$

$(x - 6)(x - 2) = 0$

$x - 6 = 0 \Rightarrow x = 6$

$x - 2 = 0 \Rightarrow x = 2$

66. $\frac{1}{8}x^2 - x - 16 = 0$

$x^2 - 8x - 128 = 0$

$(x - 16)(x + 8) = 0$

$x - 16 = 0 \Rightarrow x = 16$

$x + 8 = 0 \Rightarrow x = -8$

68. $(x + a)^2 - b^2 = 0$

$x^2 + 2ax + a^2 - b^2 = 0$

$[x + (a + b)][x + (a - b)] = 0$

$x + (a + b) = 0 \Rightarrow x = -a - b$

$x + (a - b) = 0 \Rightarrow x = -a + b$

70. $x^2 = 169$

$x = \pm\sqrt{169} = \pm 13 = \pm 13.00$

72. $x^2 = 32$

$x = \pm\sqrt{32} = \pm 4\sqrt{2} = \pm 5.66$

74. $9x^2 = 36$

$x^2 = 4$

$x = \pm\sqrt{4} = \pm 2 = \pm 2.00$

76. $(x + 13)^2 = 25$

$x + 13 = \pm\sqrt{25}$

$x + 13 = \pm 5$

$x = 13 \pm 5 = 8, 18 = 8.00, 18.00$

78. $(x - 5)^2 = 30$

$x - 5 = \pm\sqrt{30}$

$x = 5 \pm \sqrt{30} = -0.48, 10.48$

80. $(4x + 7)^2 = 44$

$4x + 7 = \pm\sqrt{44}$

$4x = -7 \pm 2\sqrt{11}$

$x = \dfrac{-7 \pm 2\sqrt{11}}{4} = \dfrac{7}{4} \pm \dfrac{\sqrt{11}}{2} = -3.41, -0.09$

82. $(x + 5)^2 = (x + 4)^2$

$x + 5 = \pm(x + 4)$

$x + 5 = +(x + 4)$

$5 = 4$

No solution

$x + 5 = -(x + 4)$

$x + 5 = -x - 4$

$2x = -9$

$x = -\frac{9}{2} = -4.50$

84. $x^2 + 4x = 0$

$x^2 + 4x + 2^2 = 2^2$

$(x + 2)^2 = 4$

$x + 2 = \pm\sqrt{4}$

$x = -2 \pm 2 = 0, -4$

86.
$$x^2 - 2x - 3 = 0$$
$$x^2 - 2x = 3$$
$$x^2 - 2x + (-1)^2 = 3 + 1$$
$$(x - 1)^2 = 4$$
$$x - 1 = \pm\sqrt{4}$$
$$x = 1 \pm 2 = 3, -1$$

88. $x^2 + 8x + 14 = 0$
$$x^2 + 8x = -14$$
$$x^2 + 8x + 4^2 = -14 + 16$$
$$(x + 4)^2 = 2$$
$$x + 4 = \pm\sqrt{2}$$
$$x = -4 \pm \sqrt{2}$$

90.
$$9x^2 - 12x = 14$$
$$x^2 - \tfrac{4}{3}x = \tfrac{14}{9}$$
$$x^2 - \tfrac{4}{3}x + \left(\tfrac{2}{3}\right)^2 = \tfrac{14}{9} + \tfrac{4}{9}$$
$$\left(x - \tfrac{2}{3}\right)^2 = \tfrac{18}{9}$$
$$\left(x - \tfrac{2}{3}\right)^2 = 2$$
$$x - \tfrac{2}{3} = \pm\sqrt{2}$$
$$x = \tfrac{2}{3} \pm \sqrt{2}$$

92. $4x^2 - 4x - 99 = 0$
$$x^2 - x = \tfrac{99}{4}$$
$$x^2 - x + \left(\tfrac{1}{2}\right)^2 = \tfrac{99}{4} + \tfrac{1}{4}$$
$$\left(x - \tfrac{1}{2}\right)^2 = \tfrac{100}{4}$$
$$\left(x - \tfrac{1}{2}\right)^2 = 25$$
$$x - \tfrac{1}{2} = \pm\sqrt{25}$$
$$x = \tfrac{1}{2} \pm 5 = \tfrac{11}{2}, -\tfrac{9}{2}$$

94. $2x^2 - x - 1 = 0$
$$x = \frac{-b \pm \sqrt{b^2 - 4ac}}{2a}$$
$$= \frac{-(-1) \pm \sqrt{(-1)^2 - 4(2)(-1)}}{2(2)}$$
$$= \frac{1 \pm \sqrt{1 + 8}}{4}$$
$$= \frac{1 \pm 3}{4} = 1, -\frac{1}{2}$$

96. $25x^2 - 20x + 3 = 0$
$$x = \frac{-b \pm \sqrt{b^2 - 4ac}}{2a}$$
$$= \frac{-(-20) \pm \sqrt{(-20)^2 - 4(25)(3)}}{2(25)}$$
$$= \frac{20 \pm \sqrt{400 - 300}}{50}$$
$$= \frac{20 \pm 10}{50} = \frac{3}{5}, \frac{1}{5}$$

98. $x^2 - 10x + 22 = 0$
$$x = \frac{-b \pm \sqrt{b^2 - 4ac}}{2a}$$
$$= \frac{-(-10) \pm \sqrt{(-10)^2 - 4(1)(22)}}{2(1)}$$
$$= \frac{10 \pm \sqrt{100 - 88}}{2}$$
$$= \frac{10 \pm 2\sqrt{3}}{2} = 5 \pm \sqrt{3}$$

100.
$$6x = 4 - x^2$$
$$x^2 + 6x - 4 = 0$$
$$x = \frac{-b \pm \sqrt{b^2 - 4ac}}{2a}$$
$$= \frac{-6 \pm \sqrt{6^2 - 4(1)(-4)}}{2(1)}$$
$$= \frac{-6 \pm \sqrt{36 + 16}}{2}$$
$$= \frac{-6 \pm 2\sqrt{13}}{2}$$
$$= -3 \pm \sqrt{13}$$

102. $4x^2 - 4x - 4 = 0$

$$x^2 - x - 1 = 0$$

$$x = \frac{-b \pm \sqrt{b^2 - 4ac}}{2a}$$

$$= \frac{-(-1) \pm \sqrt{(-1)^2 - 4(1)(-1)}}{2(1)}$$

$$= \frac{1 \pm \sqrt{1 + 4}}{2}$$

$$= \frac{1}{2} \pm \frac{\sqrt{5}}{2}$$

104. $16x^2 + 22 = 40x$

$$8x^2 - 20x + 11 = 0$$

$$x = \frac{-b \pm \sqrt{b^2 - 4ac}}{2a}$$

$$= \frac{-(-20) \pm \sqrt{(-20)^2 - 4(8)(11)}}{2(8)}$$

$$= \frac{20 \pm \sqrt{400 - 352}}{16} = \frac{20 \pm 4\sqrt{3}}{16}$$

$$= \frac{5}{4} \pm \frac{\sqrt{3}}{4}$$

106. $36x^2 + 24x - 7 = 0$

$$x = \frac{-b \pm \sqrt{b^2 - 4ac}}{2a}$$

$$= \frac{-24 \pm \sqrt{24^2 - 4(36)(-7)}}{2(36)}$$

$$= \frac{-24 \pm \sqrt{576 + 1008}}{72}$$

$$= \frac{-24 \pm 12\sqrt{11}}{72}$$

$$= -\frac{1}{3} \pm \frac{\sqrt{11}}{6}$$

108. $16x^2 - 40x + 5 = 0$

$$x = \frac{-b \pm \sqrt{b^2 - 4ac}}{2a}$$

$$= \frac{-(-40) \pm \sqrt{(-40)^2 - 4(16)(5)}}{2(16)}$$

$$= \frac{40 \pm \sqrt{1600 - 320}}{32}$$

$$= \frac{40 \pm 16\sqrt{5}}{32}$$

$$= \frac{5}{4} \pm \frac{\sqrt{5}}{2}$$

110. $3x + x^2 - 1 = 0$

$$x^2 + 3x - 1 = 0$$

$$x = \frac{-b \pm \sqrt{b^2 - 4ac}}{2a}$$

$$= \frac{-3 \pm \sqrt{3^2 - 4(1)(-1)}}{2(1)}$$

$$= \frac{-3 \pm \sqrt{13}}{2}$$

$$= -\frac{3}{2} \pm \frac{\sqrt{13}}{2}$$

112. $25h^2 + 80h + 61 = 0$

$$h = \frac{-b \pm \sqrt{b^2 - 4ac}}{2a}$$

$$= \frac{-80 \pm \sqrt{80^2 - 4(25)(61)}}{2(25)}$$

$$= \frac{-80 \pm \sqrt{6400 - 6100}}{50}$$

$$= -\frac{8}{5} \pm \frac{10\sqrt{3}}{50}$$

$$= -\frac{8}{5} \pm \frac{\sqrt{3}}{5}$$

114. $(z + 6)^2 = -2z$

$$z^2 + 12z + 36 = -2z$$

$$z^2 + 14z + 36 = 0$$

$$z = \frac{-b \pm \sqrt{b^2 - 4ac}}{2a}$$

$$= \frac{-14 \pm \sqrt{14^2 - 4(1)(36)}}{2(1)}$$

$$= \frac{-14 \pm \sqrt{52}}{2}$$

$$= -7 \pm \sqrt{13}$$

116. $\left(\frac{5}{7}x - 14\right)^2 = 8x$

$$\frac{25}{49}x^2 - 20x + 196 = 8x$$

$$\frac{25}{49}x^2 - 28x + 196 = 0$$

$$25x^2 - 1372x + 9604 = 0$$

$$x = \frac{-b \pm \sqrt{b^2 - 4ac}}{2a} = \frac{-(-1372) \pm \sqrt{(-1372)^2 - 4(25)(9604)}}{2(25)}$$

$$= \frac{1372 \pm \sqrt{921,984}}{50} = \frac{686 \pm 196\sqrt{6}}{25} = \frac{686}{25} \pm \frac{196\sqrt{6}}{25}$$

118. $2x^2 - 2.50x - 0.42 = 0$

$$x = \frac{-b \pm \sqrt{b^2 - 4ac}}{2a}$$

$$= \frac{-(-2.50) \pm \sqrt{(-2.50)^2 - 4(2)(-0.42)}}{2(2)}$$

$$= 1.400, \ -0.150$$

120. $-0.005x^2 + 0.101x - 0.193 = 0$

$$x = \frac{-b \pm \sqrt{b^2 - 4ac}}{2a}$$

$$= \frac{-0.101 \pm \sqrt{(0.101)^2 - 4(-0.005)(-0.193)}}{2(-0.005)}$$

$$\approx 2.137, \ 18.063$$

122. $1100x^2 + 326x - 715 = 0$

$$x = \frac{-b \pm \sqrt{b^2 - 4ac}}{2a} = \frac{-326 \pm \sqrt{(326)^2 - 4(1100)(-715)}}{2(1100)}$$

$$\approx 0.672, \ -0.968$$

124. $-3.22x^2 - 0.08x + 28.651 = 0$

$$x = \frac{-b \pm \sqrt{b^2 - 4ac}}{2a} = \frac{-(-0.08) \pm \sqrt{(-0.08)^2 - 4(-3.22)(28.651)}}{2(-3.22)}$$

$$\approx -2.995, \ 2.971$$

126. $11x^2 + 33x = 0$

$11x(x + 3) = 0$

$11x = 0 \implies x = 0$

$x + 3 = 0 \implies x = -3$

128. $x^2 - 14x + 49 = 0$

$(x - 7)^2 = 0$

$x - 7 = 0 \implies x = 7$

130. $x^2 + 3x - \frac{3}{4} = 0$

$x^2 + 3x + \left(\frac{3}{2}\right)^2 = \frac{3}{4} + \frac{9}{4}$

$\left(x + \frac{3}{2}\right)^2 = 3$

$x + \frac{3}{2} = \pm\sqrt{3}$

$x = -\frac{3}{2} \pm \sqrt{3}$

132. $a^2x^2 - b^2 = 0$

$(ax + b)(ax - b) = 0$

$ax + b = 0 \implies x = -\dfrac{b}{a}$

$ax - b = 0 \implies x = \dfrac{b}{a}$

134. $4x^2 + 2x + 4 = 2x + 8$

$4x^2 - 4 = 0$

$4(x^2 - 1) = 0$

$4(x + 1)(x - 1) = 0$

$x + 1 = 0 \implies x = -1$

$x - 1 = 0 \implies x = 1$

136. $20x^3 - 125x = 0$

$5x(4x^2 - 25) = 0$

$5x(2x + 5)(2x - 5) = 0$

$5x = 0 \implies x = 0$

$2x + 5 = 0 \implies x = -\frac{5}{2}$

$2x - 5 = 0 \implies x = \frac{5}{2}$

138.
$$x^6 - 64 = 0$$
$$(x^3 - 8)(x^3 + 8) = 0$$
$$(x - 2)(x^2 + 2x + 4)(x + 2)(x^2 - 2x + 4) = 0$$
$$x - 2 = 0 \Longrightarrow x = 2$$
$$x^2 + 2x + 4 = 0 \Longrightarrow \text{No real solutions}$$
$$x + 2 = 0 \Longrightarrow x = -2$$
$$x^2 - 2x + 4 = 0 \Longrightarrow \text{No real solutions}$$

Real solutions: $x = 2, -2$

140.
$$27x^3 - 512 = 0$$
$$(3x - 8)(9x^2 + 24x + 64) = 0$$
$$3x - 8 = 0 \Longrightarrow x = \frac{8}{3}$$
$$9x^2 + 24x + 64 = 0 \Longrightarrow \text{No real solutions}$$

Real solution: $x = \frac{8}{3}$

142. $9x^4 - 24x^3 + 16x^2 = 0$
$$x^2(9x^2 - 24x + 16) = 0$$
$$x^2(3x - 4)^2 = 0$$
$$x^2 = 0 \Longrightarrow x = 0$$
$$3x - 4 = 0 \Longrightarrow x = \tfrac{4}{3}$$

144. $x^3 + 2x^2 + 3x + 6 = 0$
$$x^2(x + 2) + 3(x + 2) = 0$$
$$(x + 2)(x^2 + 3) = 0$$
$$x + 2 = 0 \Longrightarrow x = -2$$
$$x^2 + 3 = 0 \Longrightarrow \text{No real solutions}$$

Real solution: $x = -2$

146.
$$x^4 + 2x^3 - 8x - 16 = 0$$
$$x^3(x + 2) - 8(x + 2) = 0$$
$$(x^3 - 8)(x + 2) = 0$$
$$(x - 2)(x^2 + 2x + 4)(x + 2) = 0$$
$$x - 2 = 0 \Longrightarrow x = 2$$
$$x^2 + 2x + 4 = 0 \Longrightarrow \text{No real solutions}$$
$$x + 2 = 0 \Longrightarrow x = -2$$

Real solutions: $x = 2, -2$

148.
$$x^4 + 5x^2 - 36 = 0$$
$$(x^2 + 9)(x^2 - 4) = 0$$
$$(x^2 + 9)(x + 2)(x - 2) = 0$$
$$x^2 + 9 = 0 \Longrightarrow \text{No real solutions}$$
$$x + 2 = 0 \Longrightarrow x = -2$$
$$x - 2 = 0 \Longrightarrow x = 2$$

Real solutions: $x = 2, -2$

150.
$$36t^4 + 29t^2 - 7 = 0$$
$$(36t^2 - 7)(t^2 + 1) = 0$$
$$\left(6t + \sqrt{7}\right)\left(6t - \sqrt{7}\right)(t^2 + 1) = 0$$
$$6t + \sqrt{7} = 0 \Rightarrow t = -\frac{\sqrt{7}}{6}$$
$$6t - \sqrt{7} = 0 \Rightarrow t = \frac{\sqrt{7}}{6}$$
$$t^2 + 1 = 0 \Rightarrow \text{No real solutions}$$

Real solutions: $t = \pm\dfrac{\sqrt{7}}{6}$

152.
$$x^6 + 3x^3 + 2 = 0$$
$$(x^3 + 2)(x^3 + 1) = 0$$
$$\left(x + \sqrt[3]{2}\right)\left[x^2 - \sqrt[3]{2}x + \left(\sqrt[3]{2}\right)^2\right](x + 1)(x^2 - x + 1) = 0$$
$$x + \sqrt[3]{2} = 0 \Rightarrow x = -\sqrt[3]{2}$$
$$x^2 - \sqrt[3]{2}x + \left(\sqrt[3]{2}\right)^2 = 0 \Rightarrow \text{No real solutions}$$
$$x + 1 = 0 \Rightarrow x = -1$$
$$x^2 - x + 1 = 0 \Rightarrow \text{No real solutions}$$

Real solutions: $x = -\sqrt[3]{2}, -1$

154.
$$4\sqrt{x} - 3 = 0$$
$$4\sqrt{x} = 3$$
$$16x = 9$$
$$x = \tfrac{9}{16}$$

156.
$$\sqrt{5 - x} - 3 = 0$$
$$\sqrt{5 - x} = 3$$
$$5 - x = 9$$
$$x = -4$$

158.
$$\sqrt[3]{3x + 1} - 5 = 0$$
$$\sqrt[3]{3x + 1} = 5$$
$$3x + 1 = 125$$
$$3x = 124$$
$$x = \tfrac{124}{3}$$

160.
$$x + \sqrt{31 - 9x} = 5$$
$$\sqrt{31 - 9x} = 5 - x$$
$$31 - 9x = 25 - 10x + x^2$$
$$0 = x^2 - x - 6$$
$$0 = (x - 3)(x - 2)$$
$$0 = x - 3 \Rightarrow x = 3$$
$$0 = x - 2 \Rightarrow x = 2$$

162.
$$\sqrt{x + 5} = \sqrt{x - 5}$$
$$x + 5 = x - 5$$
$$5 = -5$$

No solution

164.
$$(x + 3)^{3/2} = 8$$
$$(x + 3)^3 = 8^2$$
$$(x + 3)^3 = 64$$
$$x + 3 = \sqrt[3]{64}$$
$$x = -3 + 4 = 1$$

166.
$$(x + 2)^{2/3} = 9$$
$$(x + 2)^2 = 9^3$$
$$x + 2 = \pm\sqrt{729}$$
$$x = -2 \pm 27 = -29, 25$$

168. $(x^2 - x - 22)^{3/2} = 27$

$\qquad x^2 - x - 22 = 27^{2/3}$

$\qquad x^2 - x - 22 = 9$

$\qquad x^2 - x - 31 = 0$

$$x = \frac{-(-1) \pm \sqrt{(-1)^2 - 4(1)(-31)}}{2(1)}$$

$$= \frac{1 \pm 5\sqrt{5}}{2} = \frac{1}{2} \pm \frac{5\sqrt{5}}{2}$$

170. $\quad 4x^2(x - 1)^{1/3} + 6x(x - 1)^{4/3} = 0$

$\qquad 2x[2x(x - 1)^{1/3} + 3(x - 1)^{4/3}] = 0$

$\qquad 2x(x - 1)^{1/3}[2x + 3(x - 1)] = 0$

$\qquad 2x(x - 1)^{1/3}(5x - 3) = 0$

$\qquad\qquad 2x = 0 \Rightarrow x = 0$

$\qquad\qquad x - 1 = 0 \Rightarrow x = 1$

$\qquad\qquad 5x - 3 = 0 \Rightarrow x = \frac{3}{5}$

172. $\qquad \dfrac{4}{x} - \dfrac{5}{3} = \dfrac{x}{6}$

$$(6x)\frac{4}{x} - (6x)\frac{5}{3} = (6x)\frac{x}{6}$$

$\qquad 24 - 10x = x^2$

$\qquad x^2 + 10x - 24 = 0$

$\qquad (x + 12)(x - 2) = 0$

$\qquad\qquad x + 12 = 0 \Rightarrow x = -12$

$\qquad\qquad x - 2 = 0 \Rightarrow x = 2$

174. $$\frac{x}{x^2 - 4} + \frac{1}{x + 2} = 3$$

$$(x + 2)(x - 2)\frac{x}{x^2 - 4} + (x + 2)(x - 2)\frac{1}{x + 2} = 3(x + 2)(x - 2)$$

$$x + x - 2 = 3x^2 - 12$$

$$3x^2 - 2x - 10 = 0$$

$a = 3, b = -2, c = -10$

$$x = \frac{-(-2) \pm \sqrt{(-2)^2 - 4(3)(-10)}}{2(3)} = \frac{2 \pm \sqrt{124}}{6} = \frac{2 \pm 2\sqrt{31}}{6} = \frac{1 \pm \sqrt{31}}{3} = \frac{1}{3} \pm \frac{\sqrt{31}}{3}$$

176. $\qquad 4x + 1 = \dfrac{3}{x}$

$$(x)4x + (x)1 = (x)\frac{3}{x}$$

$\qquad 4x^2 + x = 3$

$\qquad 4x^2 + x - 3 = 0$

$\qquad (4x - 3)(x + 1) = 0$

$\qquad\qquad 4x - 3 = 0 \Rightarrow x = \frac{3}{4}$

$\qquad\qquad x + 1 = 0 \Rightarrow x = -1$

178. $\qquad \dfrac{x + 1}{3} - \dfrac{x + 1}{x + 2} = 0$

$$3(x + 2)\frac{x + 1}{3} - 3(x + 2)\frac{x + 1}{x + 2} = 0$$

$\qquad (x + 2)(x + 1) - 3(x + 1) = 0$

$\qquad x^2 + 3x + 2 - 3x - 3 = 0$

$\qquad\qquad x^2 - 1 = 0$

$\qquad\qquad (x + 1)(x - 1) = 0$

$\qquad\qquad x + 1 = 0 \Rightarrow x = -1$

$\qquad\qquad x - 1 = 0 \Rightarrow x = 1$

180. $|3x + 2| = 7$

$3x + 2 = 7 \Rightarrow x = \frac{5}{3}$

$-(3x + 2) = 7$

$-3x - 2 = 7 \Rightarrow x = -3$

182. $|x^2 + 6x| = 3x + 18$

First equation:

$x^2 + 6x = 3x + 18$

$x^2 + 3x - 18 = 0$

$(x - 3)(x + 6) = 0$

$x - 3 = 0 \Rightarrow x = 3$

$x + 6 = 0 \Rightarrow x = -6$

Second equation:

$-(x^2 + 6x) = 3x + 18$

$0 = x^2 + 9x + 18$

$0 = (x + 3)(x + 6)$

$0 = x + 3 \Rightarrow x = -3$

$0 = x + 6 \Rightarrow x = -6$

184. $|x - 10| = x^2 - 10x$

First equation:

$x - 10 = x^2 - 10x$

$0 = x^2 - 11x + 10$

$0 = (x - 1)(x - 10)$

$0 = x - 1 \Rightarrow x = 1$, not a solution

$0 = x - 10 \Rightarrow x = 10$

Second equation:

$-(x - 10) = x^2 - 10x$

$0 = x^2 - 9x - 10$

$0 = (x - 10)(x + 1)$

$0 = x - 10 \Rightarrow x = 10$

$0 = x + 1 \Rightarrow x = -1$

186. $y = 0.449x - 12.15 = 19$

$x = \dfrac{19 + 12.15}{0.449} \approx 69.4$ inches, which is approximately

69 inches, so it is likely that both the foot bones and the thigh bone came from the same person.

188.   Let h be the number of feet above flood level after t hours.

$h = -\dfrac{1}{4}t + 8$

$1 = -\dfrac{1}{4}t + 8 \Rightarrow t = 28$ hours

190. $S = x^2 + 4xh$

$84 = x^2 + 4x(2)$

$0 = x^2 + 8x - 84$

$0 = (x + 14)(x - 6)$

$x = -14$ or $x = 6$

Since x must be positive, we have $x = 6$ inches.
The dimensions of the base are 6 inches $\times$ 6 inches.

192. $x^2 = 10^2 + \left(\dfrac{1}{2}x\right)^2$

$x^2 = 100 + \dfrac{1}{4}x^2$

$\dfrac{3}{4}x^2 = 100$

$x^2 = \dfrac{400}{3}$

$x = \pm\sqrt{\dfrac{400}{3}} = \pm\dfrac{20}{\sqrt{3}} = \pm\dfrac{20\sqrt{3}}{3}$

Choose the positive value for x. So, the length of each side is $\dfrac{20\sqrt{3}}{3}$ inches.

194. $C = \sqrt{0.2x + 1} = 2.5$

$0.2x + 1 = (2.5)^2$

$0.2x = 6.25 - 1$

$x = 26.25$

26,250 passengers

196.

$p = 40 - \sqrt{0.01x + 1}$

$37.55 = 40 - \sqrt{0.01x + 1}$

$40 - 37.55 = \sqrt{0.01x + 1}$

$(2.45)^2 = 0.01x + 1$

$x = 500.25$

The demand is approximately 500 units per day.

198. False. $x(3 - x) = 10$ is a quadratic equation.

200. False. An absolute value equation may have only one solution or no solutions in some cases. For example, $|x| = -7$ has no solution.

202. Answers will vary. For example:

Two equations are equivalent if they differ only by algebraic simplification steps and have the same solutions.

$x^2 + 3x + 4 = x + 1$ is equivalent to $x^2 + 2x + 3 = 0$.

204. (a) $3(x + 4)^2 + (x + 4) - 2 = 0$

Let $u = x + 4$.

$3u^2 + u - 2 = 0$

$(3u - 2)(u + 1) = 0$

$u = \frac{2}{3}, -1$

$x = u - 4 = -\frac{10}{3}, -5$

(b) $3(x^2 + 8x + 16) + x + 4 - 2 = 0$

$3x^2 + 24x + 48 + x + 4 - 2 = 0$

$3x^2 + 25x + 50 = 0$

$(3x + 10)(x + 5) = 0$

$x = -\frac{10}{3}, -5$

(c) Answers will vary. Method (a) is slightly easier since there are less algebraic steps.

206. $x + |x - a| = b$

Solving for x we have:

First equation:

$x + x - a = b$

$x = \frac{a + b}{2}$

Second equation:

$x - x + a = b$

$a = b$

Thus, $x = 9$ will be the only solution if $9 = \frac{a + b}{2}$ and $a \neq b$.

For example,

$a = 0, b = 18$

$a = 2, b = 16$, etc.

Answers will vary.

Section P.6   Solving Inequalities

2. Interval: $(2, 10]$

Inequality: $2 < x \le 10$

The interval is bounded.

4. Interval: $[-5, \infty)$

Inequality:
$-5 \le x < \infty$ or $x \ge -5$

The interval is unbounded.

6. Interval: $(-\infty, 7]$

Inequality:
$-\infty < x \le 7$ or $x \le -7$

The interval is unbounded.

8. $x \ge 5$

Matches (f).

10. $0 \le x \le \frac{9}{2}$

Matches (c).

12. $|x| > 4 \Rightarrow x > 4$ or $x < -4$

Matches (a).

14. $2x + 1 < -3$

(a) $x = 0$

$$2(0) + 1 \overset{?}{<} -3$$

$$1 \not< -3$$

No, $x = 0$ is not a solution.

(b) $x = -\frac{1}{4}$

$$2\left(-\frac{1}{4}\right) + 1 \overset{?}{<} -3$$

$$\tfrac{1}{2} \not< -3$$

No, $x = -\frac{1}{4}$ is not a solution.

(c) $x = -4$

$$2(-4) + 1 \overset{?}{<} -3$$

$$-7 < -3$$

Yes, $x = -4$ is a solution.

(d) $x = -\frac{3}{2}$

$$2\left(-\frac{3}{2}\right) + 1 \overset{?}{<} -3$$

$$-2 \not< -3$$

No, $x = -\frac{3}{2}$ is not a solution.

16. $-1 < \dfrac{3 - x}{2} \le 1$

(a) $x = 0$

$$-1 \overset{?}{<} \frac{3 - 0}{2} \overset{?}{\le} 1$$

$$-1 < \frac{3}{2} \not\le 1$$

No, $x = 0$ is not a solution.

(b) $x = -5$

$$-1 \overset{?}{<} \frac{3 + 5}{2} \overset{?}{\le} 1$$

$$-1 < 4 \not\le 1$$

No, $x = -5$ is not a solution.

(c) $x = 1$

$$-1 \overset{?}{<} \frac{3 - 1}{2} \overset{?}{\le} 1$$

$$-1 < 1 \le 1$$

Yes, $x = 1$ is a solution.

(d) $x = 5$

$$-1 \overset{?}{<} \frac{3 - 5}{2} \overset{?}{\le} 1$$

$$-1 \not< -1 \le 1$$

No, $x = 5$ is not a solution.

18. $|2x - 3| < 15$

(a) $x = -6$

$$|2(-6) - 3| \overset{?}{<} 15$$

$$15 \not< 15$$

No, $x = -6$ is not a solution.

(b) $x = 0$

$$|2(0) - 3| \overset{?}{<} 15$$

$$1 < 15$$

Yes, $x = 0$ is a solution.

(c) $x = 12$

$$|2(12) - 3| \overset{?}{<} 15$$

$$21 \not< 15$$

No, $x = 12$ is not a solution.

(d) $x = 7$

$$|2(7) - 3| \overset{?}{<} 15$$

$$11 < 15$$

Yes, $x = 7$ is a solution.

20. $-10x < 40$

$$x > -4$$

22. $-6x > 15$

$$x < -\frac{15}{6}$$

$$x < -\frac{5}{2}$$

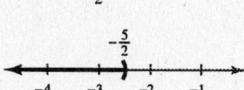

24. $x + 7 \le 12$

$$x \le 5$$

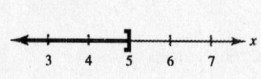

26. $3x + 1 \geq 2 + x$

$2x \geq 1$

$x \geq \frac{1}{2}$

28. $6x - 4 \leq 2 + 8x$

$-2x \leq 6$

$x \geq -3$

30. $4(x + 1) < 2x + 3$

$4x + 4 < 2x + 3$

$2x < -1$

$x < -\frac{1}{2}$

32. $3 + \frac{2}{7}x > x - 2$

$21 + 2x > 7x - 14$

$-5x > -35$

$x < 7$

34. $9x - 1 < \frac{3}{4}(16x - 2)$

$36x - 4 < 48x - 6$

$-12x < -2$

$x > \frac{1}{6}$

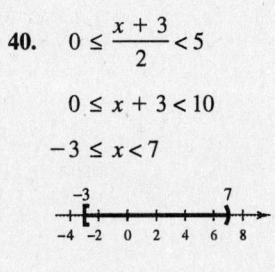

36. $15.6 - 1.3x < -5.2$

$-1.3x < -20.8$

$x > 16$

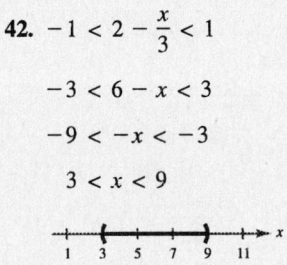

38. $-8 \leq -(3x + 5) < 13$

$-8 \leq -3x - 5 < 13$

$-3 \leq -3x < 18$

$-6 < x \leq 1$

40. $0 \leq \frac{x + 3}{2} < 5$

$0 \leq x + 3 < 10$

$-3 \leq x < 7$

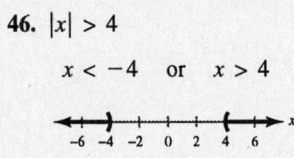

42. $-1 < 2 - \frac{x}{3} < 1$

$-3 < 6 - x < 3$

$-9 < -x < -3$

$3 < x < 9$

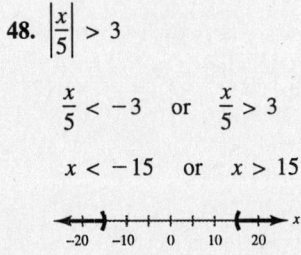

44. $4.5 > \frac{1.5x + 6}{2} > 10.5$

$9 > 1.5x + 6 > 21$

$3 > 1.5x > 15$

$2 > x > 10$

There is no solution.

46. $|x| > 4$

$x < -4 \quad \text{or} \quad x > 4$

48. $\left|\frac{x}{5}\right| > 3$

$\frac{x}{5} < -3 \quad \text{or} \quad \frac{x}{5} > 3$

$x < -15 \quad \text{or} \quad x > 15$

50. $|x - 5| \geq 0$

$x - 5 \geq 0 \quad \text{or} \quad -(x - 5) \geq 0$

$x \geq 5 \quad \text{or} \quad -x + 5 \geq 0$

$-x \geq -5$

$x \leq 5$

All real numbers x

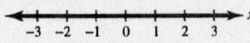

52. $|x - 7| < -5$

No solution.

54. $|1 - 2x| < 5$

$-5 < 1 - 2x < 5$

$-6 < -2x < 4$

$3 > x > -2$

$-2 < x < 3$

56. $\left|1 - \dfrac{2x}{3}\right| < 1$

$\quad -1 < 1 - \dfrac{2x}{3} < 1$

$\quad -2 < -\dfrac{2x}{3} < 0$

$\quad\quad 3 > x > 0$

$\quad\quad 0 < x < 3$

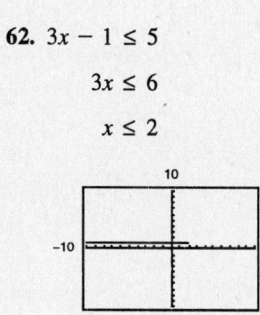

58. $|x + 14| + 3 > 17$

$\quad\quad |x + 14| > 14$

$\quad x + 14 < -14 \quad$ or $\quad x + 14 > 14$

$\quad\quad x < -28 \quad$ or $\quad\quad x > 0$

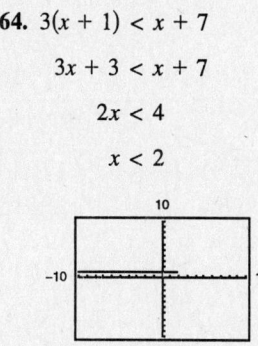

60. $3|4 - 5x| \le 9$

$\quad |4 - 5x| \le 3$

$\quad -3 \le 4 - 5x \le 3$

$\quad -7 \le -5x \le -1$

$\quad \dfrac{7}{5} \ge x \ge \dfrac{1}{5}$

$\quad \dfrac{1}{5} \le x \le \dfrac{7}{5}$

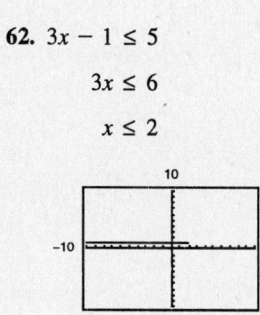

62. $3x - 1 \le 5$

$\quad\quad 3x \le 6$

$\quad\quad x \le 2$

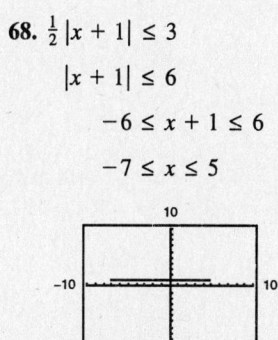

64. $3(x + 1) < x + 7$

$\quad 3x + 3 < x + 7$

$\quad\quad 2x < 4$

$\quad\quad x < 2$

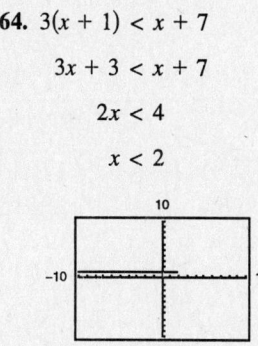

66. $|2x + 9| > 13$

$\quad 2x + 9 < -13 \quad$ or $\quad 2x + 9 > 13$

$\quad\quad 2x < -22 \quad$ or $\quad\quad 2x > 4$

$\quad\quad x < -11 \quad$ or $\quad\quad x > 2$

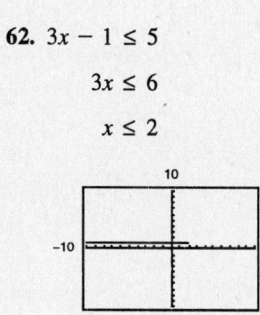

68. $\dfrac{1}{2}|x + 1| \le 3$

$\quad |x + 1| \le 6$

$\quad -6 \le x + 1 \le 6$

$\quad -7 \le x \le 5$

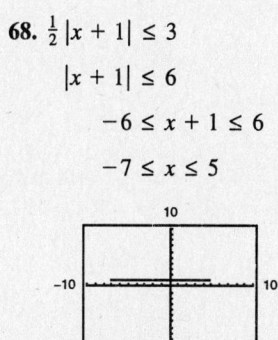

70. $\sqrt{x - 10}$

$\quad x - 10 \ge 0$

$\quad\quad x \ge 10$

$\quad [10, \infty)$

72. $\sqrt{3 - x}$

$\quad 3 - x \ge 0$

$\quad\quad 3 \ge x$

$\quad (-\infty, 3]$

74. $\sqrt[4]{6x + 15}$

$\quad 6x + 15 \ge 0$

$\quad\quad 6x \ge -15$

$\quad\quad x \ge -\dfrac{5}{2}$

$\quad \left[-\dfrac{5}{2}, \infty\right)$

76. $|x - 8| > 4$

All real numbers more than 4 units from 8

78. The graph shows all real numbers more than 3 units from 0.

$|x - 0| > 3$

$\quad |x| > 3$

80. The graph shows all real numbers no more than 4 units from -1.

$|x + 1| \le 4$

82. All real numbers at least 5 units from 8

$|x - 8| \ge 5$

84. All real numbers no more than 7 units from -6

$|x + 6| \le 7$

86. $x^2 - x - 12 \geq 0$

(a) $x = 5$

$$(5)^2 - (5) - 12 \overset{?}{\geq} 0$$

$$8 \geq 0$$

Yes, $x = 5$ is a solution.

(c) $x = -4$

$$(-4)^2 - (-4) - 12 \overset{?}{\geq} 0$$

$$16 + 4 - 12 \overset{?}{\geq} 0$$

$$8 \geq 0$$

Yes, $x = -4$ is a solution.

(b) $x = 0$

$$(0)^2 - 0 - 12 \overset{?}{\geq} 0$$

$$-12 \ngeq 0$$

No, $x = 0$ is not a solution.

(d) $x = -3$

$$(-3)^2 - (-3) - 12 \overset{?}{\geq} 0$$

$$9 + 3 - 12 \overset{?}{\geq} 0$$

$$0 \geq 0$$

Yes, $x = -3$ is a solution.

88. $\dfrac{3x^2}{x^2 + 4} < 1$

(a) $x = -2$

$$\frac{3(-2)^2}{(-2)^2 + 4} \overset{?}{<} 1$$

$$\frac{12}{8} \nless 1$$

No, $x = -2$ is not a solution.

(c) $x = 0$

$$\frac{3(0)^2}{(0)^2 + 4} \overset{?}{<} 1$$

$$0 < 1$$

Yes, $x = 0$ is a solution.

(b) $x = -1$

$$\frac{3(-1)^2}{(-1)^2 + 4} \overset{?}{<} 1$$

$$\frac{3}{5} < 1$$

Yes, $x = -1$ is a solution.

(d) $x = 3$

$$\frac{3(3)^2}{(3)^2 + 4} \overset{?}{<} 1$$

$$\frac{27}{13} \nless 1$$

No, $x = 3$ is not a solution.

90. $9x^3 - 25x^2 = 0$

$$x^2(9x - 25) = 0$$

$$x^2 = 0 \Rightarrow x = 0$$

$$9x - 25 = 0 \Rightarrow x = \frac{25}{9}$$

The critical numbers are 0 and $\frac{25}{9}$.

92. $\dfrac{x}{x + 2} - \dfrac{2}{x - 1} = \dfrac{x(x - 1) - 2(x + 2)}{(x + 2)(x - 1)}$

$$= \frac{x^2 - x - 2x - 4}{(x + 2)(x - 1)}$$

$$= \frac{(x - 4)(x + 1)}{(x + 2)(x - 1)}$$

$$(x - 4)(x + 1) = 0$$

$$x - 4 = 0 \Rightarrow x = 4$$

$$x + 1 = 0 \Rightarrow x = -1$$

$$(x + 2)(x - 1) = 0$$

$$x + 2 = 0 \Rightarrow x = -2$$

$$x - 1 = 0 \Rightarrow x = 1$$

The critical numbers are $-2, -1, 1, 4$.

94.
$$x^2 < 5$$
$$x^2 - 5 < 0$$
$$\left(x + \sqrt{5}\right)\left(x - \sqrt{5}\right) = 0$$

Critical numbers: $x = \pm\sqrt{5}$

Test intervals: $\left(-\infty, -\sqrt{5}\right) \Rightarrow \left(x + \sqrt{5}\right)\left(x - \sqrt{5}\right) > 0$

$\left(-\sqrt{5}, \sqrt{5}\right) \Rightarrow \left(x + \sqrt{5}\right)\left(x - \sqrt{5}\right) < 0$

$\left(\sqrt{5}, \infty\right) \Rightarrow \left(x + \sqrt{5}\right)\left(x - \sqrt{5}\right) > 0$

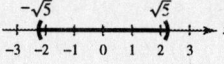

Solution interval: $\left(-\sqrt{5}, \sqrt{5}\right)$

96.
$$(x - 3)^2 \geq 1$$
$$x^2 - 6x + 8 \geq 0$$
$$(x - 2)(x - 4) \geq 0$$

Critical numbers: $x = 2, x = 4$

Test intervals: $(-\infty, 2) \Rightarrow (x - 2)(x - 4) > 0$

$(2, 4) \Rightarrow (x - 2)(x - 4) < 0$

$(4, \infty) \Rightarrow (x - 2)(x - 4) > 0$

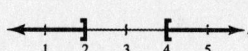

Solution intervals: $(-\infty, 2] \cup [4, \infty)$

98.
$$x^2 - 6x + 9 < 16$$
$$x^2 - 6x - 7 < 0$$
$$(x + 1)(x - 7) < 0$$

Critical numbers: $x = -1, x = 7$

Test intervals: $(-\infty, -1) \Rightarrow (x + 1)(x - 7) > 0$

$(-1, 7) \Rightarrow (x + 1)(x - 7) < 0$

$(7, \infty) \Rightarrow (x + 1)(x - 7) > 0$

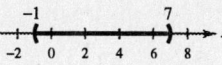

Solution interval: $(-1, 7)$

100.
$$x^2 + 2x > 3$$
$$x^2 + 2x - 3 > 0$$
$$(x + 3)(x - 1) > 0$$

Critical numbers: $x = -3, x = 1$

Test intervals: $(-\infty, -3) \Rightarrow (x + 3)(x - 1) > 0$

$(-3, 1) \Rightarrow (x + 3)(x - 1) < 0$

$(1, \infty) \Rightarrow (x + 3)(x - 1) > 0$

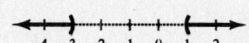

Solution intervals: $(-\infty, -3) \cup (1, \infty)$

102. $x^2 - 4x - 1 > 0$

$$x = \frac{4 \pm \sqrt{16 + 4}}{2} = 2 \pm \sqrt{5}$$

Critical numbers: $x = 2 - \sqrt{5}, x = 2 + \sqrt{5}$

Test intervals: $(-\infty, 2 - \sqrt{5}) \Rightarrow x^2 - 4x - 1 > 0$

$(2 - \sqrt{5}, 2 + \sqrt{5}) \Rightarrow x^2 - 4x - 1 < 0$

$(2 + \sqrt{5}, \infty) \Rightarrow x^2 - 4x - 1 > 0$

Solution intervals: $(-\infty, 2 - \sqrt{5}) \cup (2 + \sqrt{5}, \infty)$

104. $-2x^2 + 6x + 15 \le 0$

$2x^2 - 6x - 15 \ge 0$

$$x = \frac{-(-6) \pm \sqrt{(-6)^2 - 4(2)(-15)}}{2(2)} = \frac{6 \pm \sqrt{156}}{4}$$

$$= \frac{6 \pm 2\sqrt{39}}{4} = \frac{3}{2} \pm \frac{\sqrt{39}}{2}$$

Critical numbers: $x = \frac{3}{2} - \frac{\sqrt{39}}{2}, x = \frac{3}{2} + \frac{\sqrt{39}}{2}$

Test intervals: $\left(-\infty, \frac{3}{2} - \frac{\sqrt{39}}{2}\right) \Rightarrow -2x^2 + 6x + 15 < 0$

$\left(\frac{3}{2} - \frac{\sqrt{39}}{2}, \frac{3}{2} + \frac{\sqrt{39}}{2}\right) \Rightarrow -2x^2 + 6x + 15 > 0$

$\left(\frac{3}{2} + \frac{\sqrt{39}}{2}, \infty\right) \Rightarrow -2x^2 + 6x + 15 < 0$

Solution intervals: $\left(-\infty, \frac{3}{2} - \frac{\sqrt{39}}{2}\right] \cup \left[\frac{3}{2} + \frac{\sqrt{39}}{2}, \infty\right)$

106. $x^3 + 2x^2 - 4x - 8 \le 0$

$x^2(x + 2) - 4(x + 2) \le 0$

$(x + 2)(x^2 - 4) \le 0$

Critical numbers: $x = -2, x = 2$

Test intervals: $(-\infty, -2) \Rightarrow x^3 + 2x^2 - 4x - 8 < 0$

$(-2, 2) \Rightarrow x^3 + 2x^2 - 4x - 8 < 0$

$(2, \infty) \Rightarrow x^3 + 2x^2 - 4x - 8 > 0$

Solution interval: $(-\infty, 2]$

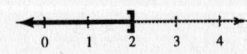

108. $2x^3 + 13x^2 - 8x - 46 \geq 6$

$2x^3 + 13x^2 - 8x - 52 \geq 0$

$2x(x^2 - 4) + 13(x^2 - 4) \geq 0$

$(2x + 13)(x + 2)(x - 2) \geq 0$

Critical numbers: $x = -\frac{13}{2}, x = -2, x = 2$

Test intervals: $\left(-\infty, -\frac{13}{2}\right) \Rightarrow (2x + 13)(x + 2)(x - 2) < 0$

$\left(-\frac{13}{2}, -2\right) \Rightarrow (2x + 13)(x + 2)(x - 2) > 0$

$(-2, 2) \Rightarrow (2x + 13)(x + 2)(x - 2) < 0$

$(2, \infty) \Rightarrow (2x + 13)(x + 2)(x - 2) > 0$

Solution intervals: $\left[-\frac{13}{2}, -2\right] \cup [2, \infty)$

110. $4x^3 - 12x^2 > 0$

$4x^2(x - 3) > 0$

Critical numbers: $x = 0, x = 3$

Test intervals: $(-\infty, 0) \Rightarrow 4x^2(x - 3) < 0$

$(0, 3) \Rightarrow 4x^2(x - 3) < 0$

$(3, \infty) \Rightarrow 4x^2(x - 3) > 0$

Solution interval: $(3, \infty)$

112. $2x^3 - x^4 \leq 0$

$x^3(2 - x) \leq 0$

Critical numbers: $x = 0, x = 2$

Test intervals: $(-\infty, 0) \Rightarrow x^3(2 - x) < 0$

$(0, 2) \Rightarrow x^3(2 - x) > 0$

$(2, \infty) \Rightarrow x^3(2 - x) < 0$

Solution intervals: $(-\infty, 0] \cup [2, \infty)$

114. $x^4(x - 3) \leq 0$

Critical numbers: $x = 0, x = 3$

Test intervals: $(-\infty, 0) \Rightarrow x^4(x - 3) < 0$

$(0, 3) \Rightarrow x^4(x - 3) < 0$

$(3, \infty) \Rightarrow x^4(x - 3) > 0$

Solution intervals: $(-\infty, 0] \cup [0, 3]$ or $(-\infty, 3]$

116. $\dfrac{1}{x} - 4 < 0$

$\dfrac{1 - 4x}{x} < 0$

Critical numbers: $x = 0, x = \dfrac{1}{4}$

Test intervals: $(-\infty, 0) \Rightarrow \dfrac{1 - 4x}{x} < 0$

$\left(0, \dfrac{1}{4}\right) \Rightarrow \dfrac{1 - 4x}{x} > 0$

$\left(\dfrac{1}{4}, \infty\right) \Rightarrow \dfrac{1 - 4x}{x} < 0$

Solution interval: $(-\infty, 0) \cup \left(\dfrac{1}{4}, \infty\right)$

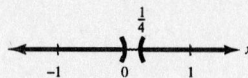

118.

$$\frac{x + 12}{x + 2} - 3 \geq 0$$

$$\frac{x + 12 - 3(x + 2)}{x + 2} \geq 0$$

$$\frac{6 - 2x}{x + 2} \geq 0$$

Critical numbers: $x = -2, x = 3$

Test intervals: $(-\infty, -2) \Rightarrow \dfrac{6 - 2x}{x + 2} < 0$

$(-2, 3) \Rightarrow \dfrac{6 - 2x}{x + 2} > 0$

$(3, \infty) \Rightarrow \dfrac{6 - 2x}{x + 2} < 0$

Solution interval: $(-2, 3]$

120.

$$\frac{5 + 7x}{1 + 2x} < 4$$

$$\frac{5 + 7x - 4(1 + 2x)}{1 + 2x} < 0$$

$$\frac{1 - x}{1 + 2x} < 0$$

Critical numbers: $x = -\dfrac{1}{2}, x = 1$

Test intervals: $\left(-\infty, -\dfrac{1}{2}\right) \Rightarrow \dfrac{1 - x}{1 + 2x} < 0$

$\left(-\dfrac{1}{2}, 1\right) \Rightarrow \dfrac{1 - x}{1 + 2x} > 0$

$(1, \infty) \Rightarrow \dfrac{1 - x}{1 + 2x} < 0$

Solution intervals: $\left(-\infty, -\dfrac{1}{2}\right) \cup (1, \infty)$

122.

$$\frac{5}{x - 6} > \frac{3}{x + 2}$$

$$\frac{5(x + 2) - 3(x - 6)}{(x - 6)(x + 2)} > 0$$

$$\frac{2x + 28}{(x - 6)(x + 2)} > 0$$

Critical numbers: $x = -14, x = -2, x = 6$

Test intervals: $(-\infty, -14) \Rightarrow \dfrac{2x + 28}{(x - 6)(x + 2)} < 0$

$(-14, -2) \Rightarrow \dfrac{2x + 28}{(x - 6)(x + 2)} > 0$

$(-2, 6) \Rightarrow \dfrac{2x + 28}{(x - 6)(x + 2)} < 0$

$(6, \infty) \Rightarrow \dfrac{2x + 28}{(x - 6)(x + 2)} > 0$

Solution intervals: $(-14, -2) \cup (6, \infty)$

124.

$$\frac{1}{x} \geq \frac{1}{x + 3}$$

$$\frac{1(x + 3) - 1(x)}{x(x + 3)} \geq 0$$

$$\frac{3}{x(x + 3)} \geq 0$$

Critical numbers: $x = -3, x = 0$

Test intervals: $(-\infty, -3) \Rightarrow \dfrac{3}{x(x + 3)} > 0$

$(-3, 0) \Rightarrow \dfrac{3}{x(x + 3)} < 0$

$(0, \infty) \Rightarrow \dfrac{3}{x(x + 3)} > 0$

Solution intervals: $(-\infty, -3) \cup (0, \infty)$

126. $\dfrac{x^2 + x - 6}{x} \geq 0$

$\dfrac{(x + 3)(x - 2)}{x} \geq 0$

Critical numbers: $x = -3, x = 0, x = 2$

Test intervals: $(-\infty, -3) \Rightarrow \dfrac{(x + 3)(x - 2)}{x} < 0$

$(-3, 0) \Rightarrow \dfrac{(x + 3)(x - 2)}{x} > 0$

$(0, 2) \Rightarrow \dfrac{(x + 3)(x - 2)}{x} < 0$

$(2, \infty) \Rightarrow \dfrac{(x + 3)(x - 2)}{x} > 0$

Solution intervals: $[-3, 0) \cup [2, \infty)$

128. $\dfrac{3x}{x - 1} \leq \dfrac{x}{x + 4} + 3$

$\dfrac{3x(x + 4) - x(x - 1) - 3(x + 4)(x - 1)}{(x - 1)(x + 4)} \leq 0$

$\dfrac{-x^2 + 4x + 12}{(x - 1)(x + 4)} \leq 0$

$\dfrac{-(x - 6)(x + 2)}{(x - 1)(x + 4)} \leq 0$

Critical numbers: $x = -4, x = -2, x = 1, x = 6$

Test intervals: $(-\infty, -4) \Rightarrow \dfrac{-(x - 6)(x + 2)}{(x - 1)(x + 4)} < 0$

$(-4, -2) \Rightarrow \dfrac{-(x - 6)(x + 2)}{(x - 1)(x + 4)} > 0$

$(-2, 1) \Rightarrow \dfrac{-(x - 6)(x + 2)}{(x - 1)(x + 4)} < 0$

$(1, 6) \Rightarrow \dfrac{-(x - 6)(x + 2)}{(x - 1)(x + 4)} > 0$

$(6, \infty) \Rightarrow \dfrac{-(x - 6)(x + 2)}{(x - 1)(x + 4)} < 0$

Solution intervals: $(-\infty, -4), [-2, 1), [6, \infty)$

130. $x^2 - 4 \geq 0$

$(x + 2)(x - 2) \geq 0$

Critical numbers: $x = -2, x = 2$

Test intervals: $(-\infty, -2) \Rightarrow (x + 2)(x - 2) > 0$

$(-2, 2) \Rightarrow (x + 2)(x - 2) < 0$

$(2, \infty) \Rightarrow (x + 2)(x - 2) > 0$

Domain: $(-\infty, -2] \cup [2, \infty)$

132. $144 - 9x^2 \geq 0$

$9(4 - x)(4 + x) \geq 0$

Critical numbers: $x = -4, x = 4$

Test intervals: $(-\infty, -4) \Rightarrow 9(4 - x)(4 + x) < 0$

$(-4, 4) \Rightarrow 9(4 - x)(4 + x) > 0$

$(4, \infty) \Rightarrow 9(4 - x)(4 + x) < 0$

Domain: $[-4, 4]$

134. $\dfrac{x}{x^2 - 9} \geq 0$

$\dfrac{x}{(x + 3)(x - 3)} \geq 0$

Critical numbers: $x = -3, x = 0, x = 3$

Test intervals: $(-\infty, -3) \Rightarrow \dfrac{x}{(x + 3)(x - 3)} < 0$

$(-3, 0) \Rightarrow \dfrac{x}{(x + 3)(x - 3)} > 0$

$(0, 3) \Rightarrow \dfrac{x}{(x + 3)(x - 3)} < 0$

$(3, \infty) \Rightarrow \dfrac{x}{(x + 3)(x - 3)} > 0$

Domain: $(-3, 0] \cup (3, \infty)$

136. $-1.3x^2 + 3.78 > 2.12$

$-1.3x^2 + 1.66 > 0$

Critical numbers: $x \approx \pm 1.13$

Test intervals: $(-\infty, -1.13) \Rightarrow -1.3x^2 + 1.66 < 0$

$(-1.13, 1.13) \Rightarrow -1.3x^2 + 1.66 > 0$

$(1.13, \infty) \Rightarrow -1.3x^2 + 1.66 < 0$

Solution set: $(-1.13, 1.13)$

138. $1.2x^2 + 4.8x + 3.1 < 5.3$

$1.2x^2 + 4.8x - 2.2 < 0$

Critical numbers: $x \approx -4.42, x \approx 0.42$

Test intervals:

$(-\infty, -4.42) \implies 1.2x^2 + 4.8x - 2.2 > 0$

$(-4.42, 0.42) \implies 1.2x^2 + 4.8x - 2.2 < 0$

$(0.42, \infty) \implies 1.2x^2 + 4.8x - 2.2 > 0$

Solution set: $(-4.42, 0.42)$

140.
$$\frac{2}{3.1x - 3.7} > 5.8$$

$$\frac{2 - 5.8(3.1x - 3.7)}{3.1x - 3.7} > 0$$

$$\frac{23.46 - 17.98x}{3.1x - 3.7} > 0$$

Critical numbers: $x \approx 1.19, x \approx 1.30$

Test intervals: $(-\infty, 1.19) \implies \dfrac{23.46 - 17.98x}{3.1x - 3.7} < 0$

$(1.19, 1.30) \implies \dfrac{23.46 - 17.98x}{3.1x - 3.7} > 0$

$(1.30, \infty) \implies \dfrac{23.46 - 17.98x}{3.1x - 3.7} < 0$

Solution interval: $(1.19, 1.30)$

142. Let x be the number of copies.

$3000 + 0.03x < 0.10x$

$3000 < 0.07x$

$42,857.1 < x$

You must make at least 42,858 copies.

144. $1.266x - 35.766 > 200$

$1.266x > 235.766$

$x > 186.2$ pounds

146. $|h - 50| \le 30$

$-30 \le h - 50 \le 30$

$20 \le h \le 80$

148. $2L + 2W = 440 \implies W = 220 - L$

$LW \ge 8000$

$L(220 - L) \ge 8000$

$-L^2 + 220L - 8000 \ge 0$

By the Quadratic Formula we have:

Critical numbers: $L = 110 \pm 10\sqrt{41}$

Test intervals: $\left(-\infty, 110 - 10\sqrt{41}\right) \implies -L^2 + 220L - 8000 < 0$

$\left(110 - 10\sqrt{41}, 110 + \sqrt{41}\right) \implies -L^2 + 220L - 8000 > 0$

$\left(110 + 10\sqrt{41}, \infty\right) \implies -L^2 + 220L - 8000 < 0$

Solution set: $110 - 10\sqrt{41} \le L \le 110 + 10\sqrt{41}$

45.97 feet $\le L \le 174.03$ feet

150.

$$P = R - C$$

$$1{,}650{,}000 \le R - C$$

$$1{,}650{,}000 \le x(50 - 0.0002x) - (12x + 150{,}000)$$

$$1{,}650{,}000 \le -0.0002x^2 + 38x - 150{,}000$$

$$0.0002x^2 - 38x + 1{,}800{,}000 \le 0$$

$$x^2 - 190{,}000x + 9{,}000{,}000{,}000 \le 0$$

$$(x - 100{,}000)(x - 90{,}000) \le 0$$

Critical numbers: $x = 90{,}000$ and $x = 100{,}000$

Test intervals: $(-\infty, 90{,}000) \Rightarrow (x - 100{,}000)(x - 90{,}000) > 0$

$$(90{,}000, 100{,}000) \Rightarrow (x - 100{,}000)(x - 90{,}000) < 0$$

$$(100{,}000, \infty) \Rightarrow (x - 100{,}000)(x - 90{,}000) > 0$$

Solution interval: $[90{,}000, 100{,}000]$ or $90{,}000$ units $\le x \le 100{,}000$ units

152. (a)

d	4	6	8	10	12
Load	2223.9	5593.9	10,312	16,378	23,792

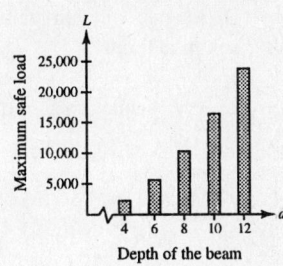

(b)

$$2000 \le 168.5d^2 - 472.1$$

$$2472.1 \le 168.5d^2$$

$$14.67 \le d^2$$

$$3.83 \le d$$

154. False. If $-10 \le x \le 8$, then $10 \ge -x$ and $-x \ge -8$.

156. True.

$$\tfrac{3}{2}x^2 + 3x + 6 = \tfrac{3}{2}(x^2 + 2x + 4)$$

$$= \tfrac{3}{2}(x^2 + 2x + 1 + 4 - 1)$$

$$= \tfrac{3}{2}(x + 1)^2 + \tfrac{9}{5}$$

For any real number x, $\tfrac{3}{2}(x + 1)^2 + \tfrac{9}{5} \ge 0$

158. $|ax - b| \le c \Rightarrow c$ must be greater than or equal to zero.

$$-c \le ax - b \le c$$

$$b - c \le ax \le b + c$$

Let $a = 1$, then $b - c = 0$ and $b + c = 10$.
This is true when $b = c = 5$. One set of values is:
$a = 1, b = 5, c = 5$.

(Note: This solution is not unique. Any positive multiple
of these values will also work, such as:

$$a = 2, b = c = 10$$

$$a = 3, b = c = 15.)$$

160. $x^2 + bx - 4 = 0$

To have at least one real solution,

$$b^2 - 4(1)(-4) \ge 0$$

$$b^2 + 16 \ge 0.$$

This is true for all values of b:

$$-\infty < b < \infty$$

162. $2x^2 + bx + 5 = 0$

To have at least one real solution,

$$b^2 - 4(2)(5) \geq 0$$

$$b^2 - 40 \geq 0$$

This is true for $b \leq -2\sqrt{10}$ or $b \geq 2\sqrt{10}$,

$$\left(-\infty, -2\sqrt{10}\right] \cup \left[2\sqrt{10}, \infty\right)$$

164. Since the intervals for b are symmetric about $b = 0$, the center of the interval is $b = 0$.

Section P.7   Errors and the Algebra of Calculus

Solutions to Even-Numbered Exercises

2. $5z + 3(x - 2) = 5z + 3x - 2$

The 3 is distributed to both terms.

4. $\dfrac{1 - x}{(5 - x)(-x)} = \dfrac{x - 1}{x(x - 5)}$

The expression on the right should be negative.

6. $x(yz) = (xy)(xz)$

yz is one term, not two.

8. $(4x^2) = 4x^2$

The exponent applies to the coefficient also.

$$(4x)^2 = 16x^2$$

10. $\sqrt{25 - x^2} = 5 - x$

Do not apply radicals term-by-term.

$$\sqrt{25 - x^2} = \sqrt{(5 + x)(5 - x)}$$

12. $\dfrac{2x^2 + 1}{5x} = \dfrac{2x + 1}{5}$

Divide out common factors not common terms.

$\dfrac{2x^2 + 1}{5x}$ cannot be simplified.

14. $\dfrac{1}{a^{-1} + b^{-1}} = \left(\dfrac{1}{a + b}\right)^{-1}$

To get rid of negative exponents:

$$\dfrac{1}{a^{-1} + b^{-1}} = \dfrac{1}{a^{-1} + b^{-1}} \cdot \dfrac{ab}{ab} = \dfrac{ab}{b + a}$$

16. $(x^2 + 5x)^{1/2} = x(x + 5)^{1/2}$

Factor within grouping symbols before applying the exponent to each factor.

$$(x^2 + 5x)^{1/2} = [x(x + 5)]^{1/2} = x^{1/2}(x + 5)^{1/2}$$

18. $(3x^2 - 6x)^3 = 3x(x - 2)^3$

Factor within grouping symbols before applying the exponent to each factor.

$$(3x^2 - 6x)^3 = [3x(x - 2)]^3 = 27x^3(x - 2)^3$$

20. $\dfrac{7 + 5(x + 3)}{x + 3} = 12$

The 5 needs to be distributed before the addition can take place.

$$\dfrac{7 + 5(x + 3)}{x + 3} = \dfrac{7 + 5x + 15}{x + 3} = \dfrac{5x + 22}{x + 3}$$

22. $\dfrac{1}{2y} = \left(\dfrac{1}{2}\right)y$

Be careful when using a slash to denote division.

$$\left(\dfrac{1}{2}\right)y = \dfrac{1}{2} \cdot y = \dfrac{y}{2}$$

24. $\dfrac{7x^2}{10} = \dfrac{7}{10}(x^2)$

The required factor is x^2.

26. $\dfrac{3}{4}x + \dfrac{1}{2} = \dfrac{3}{4}x + \dfrac{2}{4} = \dfrac{1}{4}(3x + 2)$

The required factor is $3x + 2$.

28. $x^2(x^3 - 1)^4 = \dfrac{1}{3}(x^3 - 1)^4(3x^2)$

The required factor is $\dfrac{1}{3}$.

30. $\dfrac{4x + 6}{(x^2 + 3x + 7)^3} = \dfrac{2(2x + 3)}{(x^2 + 3x + 7)^3} = \dfrac{2}{1} \cdot \dfrac{(2x + 3)}{1} \cdot \dfrac{1}{(x^2 + 3x + 7)^3} = (2)\dfrac{1}{(x^2 + 3x + 7)^3}(2x + 3)$

The required factor is 2.

32. $\dfrac{1}{(x - 1)\sqrt{(x - 1)^4 - 4}} = \dfrac{(x - 1)}{(x - 1)(x - 1)\sqrt{(x - 1)^4 - 4}} = \dfrac{(x - 1)}{(x - 1)^2\sqrt{(x - 1)^4 - 4}}$

The required factor is $(x - 1)$.

34. $\dfrac{(x - 1)^2}{169} + (y + 5)^2 = \dfrac{(x - 1)(x - 1)^2}{(x - 1)(169)} + (y + 5)^2 = \dfrac{(x - 1)^3}{169(x - 1)} + (y + 5)^2$

The required factor is $(x - 1)$.

36. $\dfrac{3x^2}{4} - \dfrac{9y^2}{16} = \dfrac{\left(\frac{1}{3}\right)3x^2}{\left(\frac{1}{3}\right)4} - \dfrac{\left(\frac{1}{9}\right)9y^2}{\left(\frac{1}{9}\right)16} = \dfrac{x^2}{\frac{4}{3}} - \dfrac{y^2}{\frac{16}{9}}$

The required factors are $\dfrac{4}{3}$ and $\dfrac{16}{9}$.

38. $\dfrac{x^2}{4/9} + \dfrac{y^2}{7/8} = x^2\left(\dfrac{9}{4}\right) + y^2\left(\dfrac{8}{7}\right) = \dfrac{9x^2}{4} + \dfrac{8y^2}{7}$

The required factors are 4 and 7.

40. $3(2x + 1)x^{1/2} + 4x^{3/2} = x^{1/2}[3(2x + 1) + 4x]$

$$= x^{1/2}(6x + 3 + 4x)$$

$$= x^{1/2}(10x + 3)$$

The required factor is $10x + 3$.

42. $\dfrac{1}{2\sqrt{x}} + 5x^{3/2} - 10x^{5/2} = \dfrac{1}{2\sqrt{x}} + \dfrac{5x^{3/2}\left(2\sqrt{x}\right)}{2\sqrt{x}} - \dfrac{10x^{5/2}\left(2\sqrt{x}\right)}{2\sqrt{x}}$

$$= \dfrac{1}{2\sqrt{x}}\left(1 + 5x^{3/2}\sqrt{x} - 10x^{5/2}\sqrt{x}\right)$$

$$= \dfrac{1}{2\sqrt{x}}\left(1 + 10x^2 - 20x^3\right)$$

The required factor is $(1 + 10x^2 - 20x^3)$.

44. $\dfrac{3}{7}(t + 1)^{7/3} - \dfrac{3}{4}(t + 1)^{4/3} = \dfrac{12}{28}(t + 1)^{4/3}(t + 1)^{3/3} - \dfrac{21}{28}(t + 1)^{4/3}$

$$= \dfrac{3(t + 1)^{4/3}}{28}[4(t + 1) - 7]$$

$$= \dfrac{3(t + 1)^{4/3}}{28}(4t - 3)$$

The required factor is $(4t - 3)$.

46. $\dfrac{x^3 - 5x^2 + 4}{x^2} = \dfrac{x^3}{x^2} - \dfrac{5x^2}{x^2} + \dfrac{4}{x^2} = x - 5 + \dfrac{4}{x^2}$

48. $\dfrac{2x^5 - 3x^3 + 5x - 1}{x^{3/2}} = \dfrac{2x^5}{x^{3/2}} - \dfrac{3x^3}{x^{3/2}} + \dfrac{5x}{x^{3/2}} - \dfrac{1}{x^{3/2}}$

$$= 2x^{5 - 3/2} - 3x^{3 - 3/2} + 5x^{1 - 3/2} - x^{-3/2}$$

$$= 2x^{7/2} - 3x^{3/2} + 5x^{-1/2} - \dfrac{1}{x^{3/2}}$$

50. $\dfrac{x^3 - 5x^4}{3x^2} = \dfrac{x^3}{3x^2} - \dfrac{5x^4}{3x^2} = \dfrac{x}{3} = \dfrac{5x^2}{3}$

52. $\dfrac{x^5(-3)(x^2 + 1)^{-4}(2x) - (x^2 + 1)^{-3}(5)x^4}{(x^5)^2} = \dfrac{x^4(x^2 + 1)^{-3}[-6x^2(x^2 + 1)^{-1} - 5]}{x^{10}}$

$$= \dfrac{-6x^2(x^2 + 1)^{-1} - 5}{(x^2 + 1)^3 x^6} = \dfrac{\dfrac{-6x^2}{x^2 + 1} - 5}{x^6(x^2 + 1)^3} = \dfrac{\dfrac{-6x^2}{x^2 + 1} - \dfrac{5(x^2 + 1)}{x^2 + 1}}{x^6(x^2 + 1)^3}$$

$$= \dfrac{(x^2 + 1)^{-1}(-6x^2 - 5x^2 - 5)}{x^6(x^2 + 1)^3} = \dfrac{-11x^2 - 5}{x^6(x^2 + 1)^4}$$

54. $\dfrac{(4x^2 + 9)^{1/2} - (2x + 3)\left(\frac{1}{2}\right)(4x^2 + 9)^{-1/2}(8x)}{[(4x^2 + 9)^{1/2}]^2} = \dfrac{2(4x^2 + 9)^{-1/2}[(4x^2 + 9) - 2x(2x + 3)]}{(4x^2 + 9)}$

$$= \dfrac{2(4x^2 + 9 - 4x^2 - 6x)}{(4x^2 + 9)^{3/2}} = \dfrac{2(9 - 6x)}{(4x^2 + 9)^{3/2}} = \dfrac{-6(2x - 3)}{(4x^2 + 9)^{3/2}}$$

56. $(2x - 1)^{1/2} - (x + 2)(2x - 1)^{-1/2} = (2x - 1)^{1/2} - \dfrac{(x + 2)}{(2x - 1)^{1/2}}$

$$= \dfrac{2x - 1}{(2x - 1)^{1/2}} - \dfrac{(x + 2)}{(2x - 1)^{1/2}} = \dfrac{2x - 1 - x - 2}{(2x - 1)^{1/2}} = \dfrac{x - 3}{(2x - 1)^{1/2}}$$

58. $\dfrac{(x+1)(\frac{1}{2})(2x-3x^2)^{-1/2}(2-6x)-(2x-3x^2)^{1/2}}{(x+1)^2} = \dfrac{(x+1)(2x-3x^2)^{-1/2}(1-3x)-(2x-3x^2)^{1/2}}{(x+1)^2}$

$$= \dfrac{(2x-3x^2)^{-1/2}[(x+1)(1-3x)-(2x-3x^2)]}{(x+1)^2}$$

$$= \dfrac{x-3x^2+1-3x-2x+3x^2}{(2x-3x^2)^{1/2}(x+1)^2}$$

$$= \dfrac{-6(2x-3)}{(4x^2+9)^{3/2}}$$

60. $\dfrac{1}{x^2-6}(2x) + \dfrac{1}{2x+5}(2) = \dfrac{2x(2x+5)+2(x^2-6)}{(x^2-6)(2x+5)}$

$$= \dfrac{4x^2+10x+2x^2-12}{(x^2-6)(2x+5)} = \dfrac{6x^2+10x-12}{(x^2-6)(2x+5)}$$

$$= \dfrac{2(3x^2+5x-6)}{(x^2-6)(2x+5)}$$

62. $(3x+2)^{-1/2}(3)(x-6)^{1/2}(1) + (x-6)^3\left(-\dfrac{1}{2}\right)(3x+2)^{-3/2}(3) = 3(3x+2)^{-1/2}(x-6)^{1/2} + \left(\dfrac{-3}{2}\right)(x-6)^3(3x+2)^{-3/2}$

$$= \dfrac{3}{2}(x-6)^{1/2}(3x+2)^{-3/2}[2(3x+2)-(x-6)^{5/2}]$$

$$= \dfrac{3(x-6)^{1/2}[6x+4-(x-6)^{5/2}]}{2(3x+2)^{3/2}}$$

64. (a) $y_1 = \dfrac{-\sqrt{9-x^2}}{x^2} - \dfrac{1}{\sqrt{9-x^2}} = \dfrac{-\sqrt{9-x^2}\left(\sqrt{9-x^2}\right)}{x^2\sqrt{9-x^2}} - \dfrac{x^2}{x^2\sqrt{9-x^2}}$

$$= \dfrac{-(9-x^2)-x^2}{x^2\sqrt{9-x^2}} = \dfrac{-9+x^2-x^2}{x^2\sqrt{9-x^2}} = \dfrac{-9}{x^2\sqrt{9-x^2}} = y_2$$

(b)

x	-2	-1	$-\frac{1}{2}$	$\frac{1}{4}$	1	2	$\frac{5}{2}$
y_1	-1.01	-3.18	-12.17	-48.17	-3.18	-1.01	-0.87
y_2	-1.01	-3.18	-12.17	-48.17	-3.18	-1.01	-0.87

66. True. $x^{-1} + y^{-2} = \dfrac{1}{x} + \dfrac{1}{y^2} = \dfrac{y^2+x}{xy^2}$

68. True. $\dfrac{1}{\sqrt{x}+4} = \dfrac{1}{\sqrt{x}+4} \cdot \dfrac{\sqrt{x}-4}{\sqrt{x}-4} = \dfrac{\sqrt{x}-4}{\sqrt{x}-16}$

70. $x^n \cdot x^{3n} = x^{3n^2}$

Add exponents when multiplying powers with like bases.

$x^n \cdot x^{3n} = x^{4n} \neq x^{3n^2}$

72. $x^{2n} + y^{2n} = (x^n + y^n)^2$

When squaring binomials, there is also a middle term.

$(x^n + y^n)^2 = x^{2n} + 2x^n y^n + y^{2n} \neq x^{2n} + y^{2n}$

74. The two answers are equivalent and can be obtained by factoring.

$\frac{1}{10}(2x-1)^{5/2} + \frac{1}{6}(2x-1)^{3/2} = \frac{1}{60}(2x-1)^{3/2}[6(2x-1)+10]$

$$= \frac{1}{60}(2x-1)^{3/2}(12x+4)$$

$$= \frac{4}{60}(2x-1)^{3/2}(3x+1)$$

$$= \frac{1}{15}(2x-1)^{3/2}(3x+1)$$

Section P.8   Graphical Representation of Data

Solutions to Even-Numbered Exercises

2.

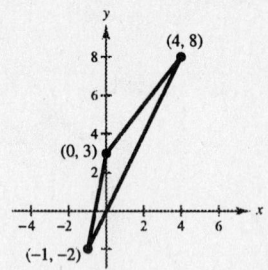

4.

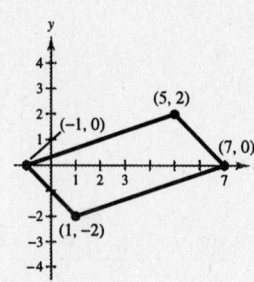

6. $A: \left(\frac{3}{2}, -4\right)$; $B: (0, -2)$;

$C: \left(-3, \frac{5}{2}\right)$, $D: (-6, 0)$

8. $(4, -8)$

10. $(-12, 0)$

12. $x < 0$ and $y < 0$ in Quadrant III.

14. $x > 2$ and $y = 3$ in Quadrant I.

16. $x > 4$ in Quadrants I and IV.

18. If $(-x, y)$ is in Quadrant IV, then (x, y) must be in Quadrant III.

20. If $xy < 0$, then x and y have opposite signs. This happens in Quadrants II and IV.

22. $(-3 + 6, 6 - 3) = (3, 3)$

$(-5 + 6, 3 - 3) = (1, 0)$

$(-3 + 6, 0 - 3) = (3, -3)$

$(-1 + 6, 3 - 3) = (5, 0)$

24. $(5 - 10, 8 - 6) = (-5, 2)$

$(3 - 10, 6 - 6) = (-7, 0)$

$(7 - 10, 6 - 6) = (-3, 0)$

$(5 - 10, 2 - 6) = (-5, -4)$

26.

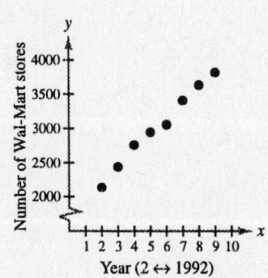

28. Price of milk in 1992 = \$1.39

Highest price of milk = \$1.65

Percent change $= \dfrac{\$1.65 - \$1.39}{\$1.39} = 0.19$ or 19%

30. (a) Cost during Super Bowl XXVII (1993) = \$850,000

Cost during Super Bowl XXI (1987) = \$600,000

Increase = \$850,000 − \$600,000 = \$250,000

(b) Cost during Super Bowl XXXIII (1999) = \$1,600,000

Increase = \$1,600,000 − \$850,000 = \$750,000

32. (a) Minimum wage in 1990 = \$3.80

Minimum wage in 1995 = \$4.25

Percent Increase $= \dfrac{\$4.25 - \$3.80}{\$3.80} = 0.12$ or 12%

(b) Minimum wage in 1955 = \$0.75

Percent increase $= \dfrac{\$4.25 - \$0.75}{\$0.75} = 4.67$ or 467%

34. No. There are many variables that will affect the final exam score.

36. $d = |1 - 8| = |-7| = 7$

38. $d = |-4 - 6| = |-10| = 10$

40. (a) $(1, 0), (13, 5)$

Distance $= \sqrt{(13 - 1)^2 + (5 - 0)^2}$

$= \sqrt{12^2 + 5^2} = \sqrt{169} = 13$

$(13, 5), (13, 0)$

Distance $= |5 - 0| = |5| = 5$

$(1, 0), (13, 0)$

Distance $= |1 - 13| = |-12| = 12$

(b) $5^2 + 12^2 = 25 + 144 = 169 = 13^2$

42. (a) $(1, 5), (5, -2)$

Distance $= \sqrt{(1 - 5)^2 + (5 - (-2))^2}$

$= \sqrt{(-4)^2 + (7)^2} = \sqrt{16 + 49} = \sqrt{65}$

$(1, 5), (1, -2)$

Distance $= |5 - (-2)| = |5 + 2| = |7| = 7$

$(1, -2), (5, -2)$

Distance $= |1 - 5| = |-4| = 4$

(b) $4^2 + 7^2 = 16 + 49 = 65 = \left(\sqrt{65}\right)^2$

44.

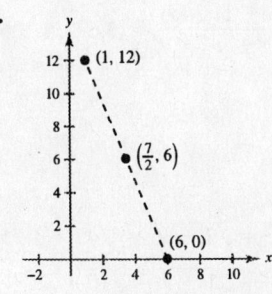

(b) $d = \sqrt{(1 - 6)^2 + (12 - 0)^2}$

$= \sqrt{25 + 144} = 13$

(c) $\left(\dfrac{1 + 6}{2}, \dfrac{12 + 0}{2}\right) = \left(\dfrac{7}{2}, 6\right)$

46. (a)

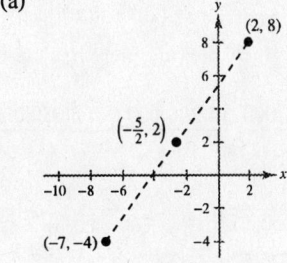

(b) $d = \sqrt{(-7 - 2)^2 + (-4 - 8)^2}$

$= \sqrt{81 + 144} = 15$

(c) $\left(\dfrac{-7 + 2}{2}, \dfrac{-4 + 8}{2}\right) = \left(-\dfrac{5}{2}, 2\right)$

48. (a)

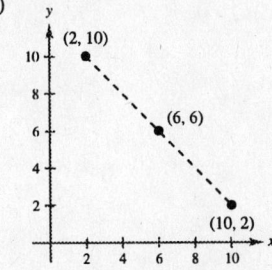

(b) $d = \sqrt{(2 - 10)^2 + (10 - 2)^2}$

$= \sqrt{64 + 64} = 8\sqrt{2}$

(c) $\left(\dfrac{2 + 10}{2}, \dfrac{10 + 2}{2}\right) = (6, 6)$

50. (a)

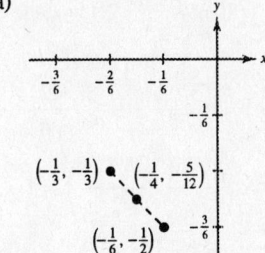

(b) $d = \sqrt{\left(-\dfrac{1}{3} + \dfrac{1}{6}\right)^2 + \left(-\dfrac{1}{3} + \dfrac{1}{2}\right)^2}$

$= \sqrt{\dfrac{1}{36} + \dfrac{1}{36}} = \dfrac{\sqrt{2}}{6}$

(c) $\left(\dfrac{-\dfrac{1}{3} + \left(-\dfrac{1}{6}\right)}{2}, \dfrac{-\dfrac{1}{3} + \left(-\dfrac{1}{2}\right)}{2}\right) = \left(-\dfrac{1}{4}, -\dfrac{5}{12}\right)$

52. (a)

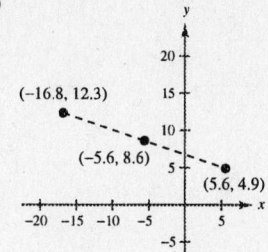

(b) $d = \sqrt{(-16.8 - 5.6)^2 + (12.3 - 4.9)^2}$

$= \sqrt{501.76 + 54.76} = \sqrt{556.52}$

(c) $\left(\dfrac{-16.8 + 5.6}{2}, \dfrac{12.3 + 4.9}{2}\right) = (-5.6, 8.6)$

54. (a)

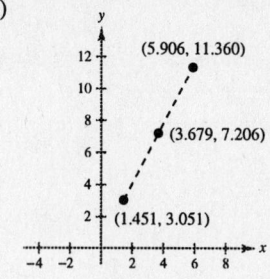

(b) $d = \sqrt{(1.451 - 5.906)^2 + (3.051 - 11.360)^2}$

$\approx \sqrt{88.887}$

(c) $\left(\dfrac{1.451 + 5.906}{2}, \dfrac{3.051 + 11.360}{2}\right) \approx (3.679, 7.206)$

56. Midpoint $= \left(\dfrac{1996 + 2000}{2}, \dfrac{\$4,200,000 + \$5,650,000}{2}\right) = (1998, \$4,925,000)$

58. $d_1 = \sqrt{(1 - 3)^2 + (-3 - 2)^2} = \sqrt{4 + 25} = \sqrt{29}$

$d_2 = \sqrt{(3 + 2)^2 + (2 - 4)^2} = \sqrt{25 + 4} = \sqrt{29}$

$d_3 = \sqrt{(1 + 2)^2 + (-3 - 4)^2} = \sqrt{9 + 49} = \sqrt{58}$

$d_1 = d_2$

60. $d_1 = \sqrt{(0 - 3)^2 + (1 - 7)^2} = \sqrt{9 + 36} = \sqrt{45} = 3\sqrt{5}$

$d_2 = \sqrt{(3 - 4)^2 + (7 - 4)^2} = \sqrt{1 + 9} = \sqrt{10}$

$d_3 = \sqrt{(4 - 1)^2 + (4 + 2)^2} = \sqrt{9 + 36} = \sqrt{45} = 3\sqrt{5}$

$d_4 = \sqrt{(0 - 1)^2 + (1 + 2)^2} = \sqrt{1 + 9} = \sqrt{10}$

Opposite sides have equal lengths of $3\sqrt{5}$ and $\sqrt{10}$.

62. (a) $(x_2, y_2) = (2x_m - x_1, 2y_m - y_1)$

$= (2 \cdot 4 - 1, 2(-1) - (-2)) = (7, 0)$

(b) $(x_2, y_2) = (2x_m - x_1, 2y_m - y_1)$

$= (2 \cdot 2 - (-5), 2 \cdot 4 - 11) = (9, -3)$

64. (a) $\left(\dfrac{3x_1 + x_2}{4}, \dfrac{3y_1 + y_2}{4}\right) = \left(\dfrac{3 \cdot 1 + 4}{4}, \dfrac{3(-2) - 1}{4}\right) = \left(\dfrac{7}{4}, -\dfrac{7}{4}\right)$

$\left(\dfrac{x_1 + x_2}{2}, \dfrac{y_1 + y_2}{2}\right) = \left(\dfrac{1 + 4}{2}, \dfrac{-2 - 1}{2}\right) = \left(\dfrac{5}{2}, -\dfrac{3}{2}\right)$

$\left(\dfrac{x_1 + 3x_2}{4}, \dfrac{y_1 + 3y_2}{4}\right) = \left(\dfrac{1 + 3 \cdot 4}{4}, \dfrac{-2 + 3(-1)}{4}\right) = \left(\dfrac{13}{4}, -\dfrac{5}{4}\right)$

(b) $\left(\dfrac{3x_1 + x_2}{4}, \dfrac{3y_1 + y_2}{4}\right) = \left(\dfrac{3(-2) + 0}{4}, \dfrac{3(-3) + 0}{4}\right) = \left(-\dfrac{3}{2}, -\dfrac{9}{4}\right)$

$\left(\dfrac{x_1 + x_2}{2}, \dfrac{y_1 + y_2}{2}\right) = \left(\dfrac{-2 + 0}{2}, \dfrac{-3 + 0}{2}\right) = \left(-1, -\dfrac{3}{2}\right)$

$\left(\dfrac{x_1 + 3x_2}{4}, \dfrac{y_1 + 3y_2}{4}\right) = \left(\dfrac{-2 + 0}{4}, \dfrac{-3 + 0}{4}\right) = \left(-\dfrac{1}{2}, -\dfrac{3}{4}\right)$

66. Let $(0, 0)$ represent the coordinates of the point of departure and let $(100, 150)$ represent the coordinates of the destination.

Distance $= \sqrt{(0 - 100)^2 + (0 - 150)^2}$

$= \sqrt{10,000 + 22,500}$

$= \sqrt{325,000}$

$= 50\sqrt{13} \approx 180.28$ miles

68. (a) The number of artists elected each year seems to be nearly steady except for the first few years. Between 6 and 8 artists will be elected in 2001.

    (b) Elections for inclusion in the Rock and Roll Hall of Fame began in 1986.

70. $\dfrac{\$1118.7 + \$1371.4}{2} = \$1245.05$ million

72. True. Two sides of the triangle have lengths $\sqrt{149}$ and the third side has a length of $\sqrt{18}$.

74. No. It depends on the magnitude of the quantities measured.

76. Since (x_0, y_0) lies in Quadrant II, $(x_0, -y_0)$ must lie in Quadrant III. Matches (b).

78. Since (x_0, y_0) lies in Quadrant II, $\left(x_0, \frac{1}{2}y_0\right)$ must lie in Quadrant II. Matches (d).

Review Exercises for Chapter P

2. $\left\{ \sqrt{15}, -22, -\frac{10}{3}, 0, 5.2, \frac{3}{7} \right\}$

(a) Natural numbers: none

(b) Integers: $\{-22, 0\}$

(c) Rational numbers: $\left\{ -22, -\frac{10}{3}, 0, 5.2, \frac{3}{7} \right\}$

(d) Irrational numbers: $\left\{ \sqrt{15} \right\}$

4. (a) $\frac{9}{25} = 0.36$

(b) $\frac{5}{7} = 0.\overline{714285}$

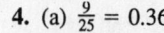

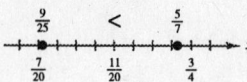

6. $x > 1$

All real numbers greater than 1.

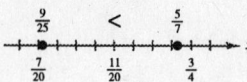

8. $|a - b| = |-12.4 - (-27.13)| = 14.73$

10. $|-37.234| = 37.234$

12. $|34 + (-6.8)| = 27.2$

14. $-x^2 + x - 1$

(a) $-(1)^2 + (1) - 1 = -1$

(b) $-(-1)^2 + (-1) - 1 = -3$

16. $|-3| + 4(-2) - 6 = -11$

18. $\frac{5}{18} \div \frac{10}{3} = \frac{5}{18} \cdot \frac{3}{10} = \frac{1}{12}$

20. $6[4 - 2(6 + 8)] = 6[4 - 2(14)] = 6[-24] = -144$

22. (a) $\frac{6^2 u^3 v^{-3}}{12 u^{-2} v} = \frac{36 u^3 u^2}{12 v^3 v} = \frac{3 u^5}{v^4}$

(b) $\frac{3^{-4} m^{-1} n^{-3}}{9^{-2} m n^{-3}} = \frac{9^2}{3^4 m^2} = \frac{1}{m^2}$

24. $\$33,674,000 = \$3.3674 \times 10^7$

26. $\left(\sqrt[3]{216} \right)^3 = 216$

28. $\sqrt{18u}\sqrt{2u} = \sqrt{36u^2} = 6u$

30. (a) $\sqrt{50} - \sqrt{18} = 5\sqrt{2} - 3\sqrt{2} = 2\sqrt{2}$

(b) $2\sqrt{32} + 3\sqrt{72} = 8\sqrt{2} + 18\sqrt{2} = 26\sqrt{2}$

32. $\frac{1}{2 - \sqrt{3}} \cdot \frac{2 + \sqrt{3}}{2 + \sqrt{3}} = \frac{2 + \sqrt{3}}{4 - 3} = 2 + \sqrt{3}$

34. $(16)^{3/2} = (16^{1/2})^3 = 4^3 = 64$

36. $(3x^{2/5})(2x^{1/2}) = 6x^{(2/5 + 1/2)} = 6x^{9/10}$

38. $\sqrt{16} = 4, \ 16^{1/2} = 4$

40. $3 - 11x^2$

Standard form: $-11x^2 + 3$

42. $-4 - 12x^2$

Standard form: $-12x^2 - 4$

44. $-(3x^2 + 2x) + (1 - 5x) = -3x^2 - 2x + 1 - 5x$

$= -3x^2 - 7x + 1$

46. $(3x - 6)(5x + 1) = 15x^2 + 3x - 30x - 6 = 15x^2 - 27x - 6$

48. $(2x - 3)^2 = (2x)^2 + 2(2x)(-3) + (-3)^2$

$= 4x^2 - 12x + 9$

50. $\left(3\sqrt{5} + 2 \right)\left(3\sqrt{5} - 2 \right) = \left(3\sqrt{5} \right)^2 - (2)^2$

$= 45 - 4 = 41$

52. (a) $R = 1600(3000) - 0.50(3000)^2 = \$300{,}000$

(b) $R = 1600(2000) - 0.50(2000)^2 = 1{,}200{,}000$

$1{,}200{,}000 = 2000p \Rightarrow p = \$600$

54. $x(x - 3) + 4(x - 3) = (x + 4)(x - 3)$

56. $x^2 - 12x + 36 = (x - 6)^2$

58. $8x^3 + 27 = (2x)^3 + 3^3 = (2x + 3)(4x^2 - 6x + 9)$

60. $3x^2 + 14x + 8 = (3x + 2)(x + 4)$

62. $x^3 - 4x^2 + 2x - 8 = x^2(x - 4) + 2(x - 4)$

$= (x^2 + 2)(x - 4)$

64. $\sqrt{x + 4}$

Domain: $x + 4 \geq 0$

$x \geq -4$

66. $\dfrac{x^3 + 27}{x^2 + x - 6} = \dfrac{(x + 3)(x^2 - 3x + 9)}{(x + 3)(x - 2)}$

$= \dfrac{x^2 - 3x + 9}{x - 2}, x \neq -3$

68. $\dfrac{4x - 6}{(x - 1)^2} \div \dfrac{2x^2 - 3x}{x^2 + 2x - 3} = \dfrac{2(2x - 3)}{(x - 1)^2} \cdot \dfrac{(x + 3)(x - 1)}{x(2x - 3)}$

$= \dfrac{2(x + 3)}{x(x - 1)}, x \neq -3, \dfrac{3}{2}$

70. $\dfrac{1}{x} - \dfrac{x - 1}{x^2 + 1} = \dfrac{x^2 + 1 - x(x - 1)}{x(x^2 + 1)} = \dfrac{x + 1}{x(x^2 + 1)}$

72. $\dfrac{3x}{x + 2} - \dfrac{4x^2 - 5}{2x^2 + 3x - 2} = \dfrac{3x(2x - 1) - (4x^2 - 5)}{(x + 2)(2x - 1)}$

$= \dfrac{2x^2 - 3x + 5}{(x + 2)(2x - 1)}$

74. $\dfrac{\left(\dfrac{1}{2x - 3} - \dfrac{1}{2x + 3}\right)}{\left(\dfrac{1}{2x} - \dfrac{1}{2x + 3}\right)} = \dfrac{\left(\dfrac{6}{(2x - 3)(2x + 3)}\right)}{\left(\dfrac{3}{2x(2x + 3)}\right)}$

$= \dfrac{6}{(2x - 3)(2x + 3)} \cdot \dfrac{2x(2x + 3)}{3}$

$= \dfrac{4x}{2x - 3}, x \neq -\dfrac{3}{2}, 0$

76. $3(x - 2) + 2x = 2(x + 3)$

$3x - 6 + 2x = 2x + 6$

$3x = 12$

Conditional equation

78. $3(x^2 - 4x + 8) = -10(x + 2) - 3x^2 + 6$

$3x^2 - 12x + 24 = -10x - 20 - 3x^2 + 6$

$6x^2 - 2x + 38 = 0$

Conditional equation

80. $4x + 2(7 - x) = 5$

$4x + 14 - 2x = 5$

$2x = -9$

$x = -\dfrac{9}{2}$

82. $\dfrac{1}{2}(x - 3) - 2(x + 1) = 5$

$x - 3 - 4x - 4 = 10$

$-3x = 17$

$x = -\dfrac{17}{3}$

84. $15 + x - 2x^2 = 0$

$2x^2 - x - 15 = 0$

$(2x + 5)(x - 3) = 0$

$x = -\dfrac{5}{2}, 3$

86. $6 = 3x^2$

$x^2 = 2$

$x = \pm\sqrt{2}$

88. $(x + 4)^2 = 18$

$x + 4 = \pm 3\sqrt{2}$

$x = -4 \pm 3\sqrt{2}$

90. $x^2 - 12x + 30 = 0$

$$x = \frac{-(-12) \pm \sqrt{(-12)^2 - 4(1)(30)}}{2(1)}$$

$$= 6 \pm \sqrt{6}$$

92. $-2x^2 - 5x + 27 = 0$

$$x = \frac{-(-5) \pm \sqrt{(-5)^2 - 4(-2)(27)}}{2(-2)}$$

$$= \frac{-5 \pm \sqrt{241}}{4}$$

94. $5x^4 - 12x^3 = 0$

$x^3(5x - 12) = 0$

$x = 0, \frac{12}{5}$

96. $x^4 - 5x^2 + 6 = 0$

Let $u = x^2$

$u^2 - 5u + 6 = 0$

$(u - 2)(u - 3) = 0$

$u = 2, 3$

$x^2 = 2, 3$

$x = \pm\sqrt{2}, \pm\sqrt{3}$

98. $\sqrt{x + 4} = 3$

$x + 4 = 9$

$x = 5$

100. $2\sqrt{x} - 5 = x$

$2\sqrt{x} = x + 5$

$4x = x^2 + 10x + 25$

$x^2 + 6x + 25 = 0$

$b^2 - 4ac = 6^2 - 4(1)(25) = -64 < 0$
$\Rightarrow$ no real solutions.

Original equation has no real solutions.

102. $(x - 1)^{2/3} - 25 = 0$

$x - 1 = 25^{3/2}$

$x - 1 = \pm 125$

$x = 126, -124$

104. $(x + 4)^{1/2} + 5x(x + 4)^{3/2} = 0$

$(x + 4)^{1/2}[1 + 5x(x + 4)] = 0$

$(x + 4)^{1/2}[5x^2 + 20x + 1] = 0$

$(x + 4)^{1/2} = 0$

$x = -4$

$5x^2 + 20x + 1 = 0$

$$x = \frac{-20 \pm \sqrt{20^2 - 4(5)(1)}}{2(5)} = \frac{-10 \pm \sqrt{95}}{5}$$

$$x = -4, \frac{-10 \pm \sqrt{95}}{5}$$

106. $|x - 5| = 10$

First Equation	*Second Equation*
$x - 5 = 10$	$x - 5 = -10$
$x = 15$	$x = -5$

108. $|x^2 - 3| = 2x$

First Equation

$x^2 - 3 = 2x$

$x^2 - 2x - 3 = 0$

$(x - 3)(x + 1) = 0$

$x - 3 = 0 \Rightarrow x = 3$

$x + 1 = 0 \Rightarrow x = -1$, not a solution

Second equation

$-(x^2 - 3) = 2x$

$x^2 + 2x - 3 = 0$

$(x + 3)(x - 1) = 0$

$x + 3 = 0 \Rightarrow x = -3$, not a solution

$x - 1 = 0 \Rightarrow x = 1$

110. $42 - \sqrt{0.001x + 2} = 29.95$

$42 - 29.95 = \sqrt{0.001x + 2}$

$(12.05)^2 = 0.001x + 2$

$x = 143{,}202.5$

Number of units demanded per day: 143,203

112. $-3 \le \dfrac{x - 3}{5} < 2$

(a) $x = 3$

$-3 \overset{?}{\le} \dfrac{3 - 3}{5} \overset{?}{<} 2$

$-3 \le 0 < 2$

Yes, $x = 3$ is a solution.

(b) $x = -12$

$-3 \overset{?}{\le} \dfrac{-12 - 3}{5} \overset{?}{<} 2$

$-3 \le -3 < 2$

Yes, $x = -12$ is a solution.

(c) $x = 13$

$-3 \overset{?}{\le} \dfrac{13 - 3}{5} \overset{?}{<} 2$

$-3 \le 2 \not< 2$

No, $x = 13$ is not a solution.

(d) $x = -18$

$-3 \overset{?}{\le} \dfrac{-18 - 3}{5} < 2$

$-3 \not\le -\dfrac{21}{5} < 2$

No, $x = -18$ is not a solution.

114. $\dfrac{15}{2}x + 4 > 3x - 5$

$15x + 8 > 6x - 10$

$9x > -18$

$x > -2$

$(-2, \infty)$

116. $\dfrac{1}{2}(3 - x) > \dfrac{1}{3}(2 - 3x)$

$3(3 - x) > 2(2 - 3x)$

$9 - 3x > 4 - 6x$

$3x > -5$

$x > -\dfrac{5}{3}$

$\left(-\dfrac{5}{3}, \infty\right)$

118. $-3 \le \dfrac{2x - 5}{3} < 5$

$-9 \le 2x - 5 < 15$

$-4 \le 2x < 20$

$-2 \le x < 10$

$[-2, 10)$

120. $|x - 2| < 1$

$-1 < x - 2 < 1$

$1 < x < 3$

$(1, 3)$

122. $\left|x - \dfrac{3}{2}\right| \ge \dfrac{3}{2}$

$x - \dfrac{3}{2} \le -\dfrac{3}{2} \qquad x - \dfrac{3}{2} \ge \dfrac{3}{2}$

$x \le 0 \qquad\qquad x \ge 3$

$(-\infty, 0], [3, \infty)$

124. $A = s^2$

$s = 19.3 \pm 0.5$ cm

$A = (19.3)^2 \approx 372$ cm^2

Smallest area: $A = (18.8)^2 \approx 353$ cm^2

Largest area: $A = (19.8)^2 \approx 392$ cm^2

Interval containing area of square:
353 cm$^2 < A < 392$ cm^2

126. $x^2 - 2x \ge 3$

$x^2 - 2x - 3 \ge 0$

$(x - 3)(x + 1) \ge 0$

Critical numbers: $-1, 3$

Test intervals: $(-\infty, -1) \Rightarrow (x - 3)(x + 1) > 0$

$(-1, 3) \Rightarrow (x - 3)(x + 1) < 0$

$(3, \infty) \Rightarrow (x - 3)(x + 1) > 0$

Solution intervals: $(-\infty, -1] \cup [3, \infty)$

128.
$$2x^2 + x \geq 15$$
$$2x^2 + x - 15 \geq 0$$
$$(2x - 5)(x + 3) \geq 0$$

Critical numbers: $-3, \dfrac{5}{2}$

Test intervals: $(-\infty, -3) \Rightarrow (2x - 5)(x + 3) > 0$

$$\left(-3, \frac{5}{2}\right) \Rightarrow (2x - 5)(x + 3) < 0$$

$$\left(\frac{5}{2}, \infty\right) \Rightarrow (2x - 5)(x + 3) > 0$$

Solution intervals: $(-\infty, -3] \cup \left[\dfrac{5}{2}, \infty\right)$

130. $\dfrac{x - 5}{3 - x} < 0$

Critical numbers: 3, 5

Test intervals: $(-\infty, 3) \Rightarrow \dfrac{x - 5}{3 - x} < 0$

$$(3, 5) \Rightarrow \frac{x - 5}{3 - x} > 0$$

$$(5, \infty) \Rightarrow \frac{x - 5}{3 - x} < 0$$

Solution intervals: $(-\infty, 3) \cup (5, \infty)$

132.
$$\frac{1}{x - 2} > \frac{1}{x}$$

$$\frac{1}{x - 2} - \frac{1}{x} > 0$$

$$\frac{2}{x(x - 2)} > 0$$

Critical numbers: 0, 2

Test intervals: $(-\infty, 0) \Rightarrow \dfrac{2}{x(x - 2)} > 0$

$$(0, 2) \Rightarrow \frac{2}{x(x - 2)} < 0$$

$$(2, \infty) \Rightarrow \frac{2}{x(x - 2)} > 0$$

Solution intervals: $(-\infty, 0) \cup (2, \infty)$

134. $P = \dfrac{1000(1 + 3t)}{5 + t} \geq 2000$

$$\frac{1000(1 + 3t)}{5 + t} - 2000 \geq 0$$

$$\frac{1000t - 9000}{t + 5} \geq 0$$

t must be greater than zero, since the critical value to check is $t = 9$.

$$(0, 9) \Rightarrow \frac{1000t - 9000}{t + 5} < 0$$

$$(9, \infty) \Rightarrow \frac{1000t - 9000}{t + 5} > 0$$

$$t \geq 9$$

So, the required time is at least 9 days.

136. $\left(\dfrac{1}{3}x\right)\left(\dfrac{1}{3}y\right) = \dfrac{1}{3}xy$ ✗

$\dfrac{1}{3}$ occurs twice as a factor.

$$\left(\frac{1}{3}x\right)\left(\frac{1}{3}y\right) = \frac{1}{3} \cdot \frac{1}{3} \cdot x \cdot y$$

$$= \frac{1}{9}xy$$

138. $(-x)^6 = -x^6$ ✗

The negative sign is also raised to the 6th power.

$$(-x)^6 = (-1 \cdot x)^6$$
$$= (-1)^6 x^6$$
$$= x^6$$

140. $\sqrt{3^2 + 4^2} = 3 + 4$ ✗

Do not apply radicals term-by-term.

$$\sqrt{3^2 + 4^2} = \sqrt{9 + 16}$$
$$= \sqrt{25}$$
$$= 5$$

142. $(9x + 12)^2 = 3(3x + 4)^2$ ✗

When factoring, apply exponent to all factors.

$$(9x + 12)^2 = [3(3x + 4)]^2$$
$$= 3^2(3x + 4)^2$$
$$= 9(3x + 4)^2$$

144. $\dfrac{t}{\sqrt{t + 1}} - \sqrt{t + 1} = \dfrac{1}{\sqrt{t + 1}}\left(\right)$

$$\frac{t}{\sqrt{t + 1}} - \sqrt{t + 1} = \frac{t - (t + 1)}{\sqrt{t + 1}} = \frac{-1}{\sqrt{t + 1}}$$

The missing factor is -1.

146. $y(y - 1)^{5/4} - y^2(y - 1)^{1/4} = y(y - 1)^{1/4} \left(\right)$

$\quad y(y - 1)^{5/4} - y^2(y - 1)^{1/4} = y(y - 1)^{1/4}(y - 1 - y)$

$\qquad\qquad\qquad\qquad\qquad = y(y - 1)^{1/4}(-1)$

The missing factor is -1.

148. $\dfrac{2}{3}x(4 + x)^{-1/2} - \dfrac{2}{15}(4 + x)^{3/2} = -\dfrac{2}{15}(4 + x)^{-1/2}[-5x + (4 + x)^2]$

$\qquad\qquad\qquad\qquad\qquad\qquad = -\dfrac{2}{15}(4 + x)^{-1/2}[-5x + (16 + 8x + x^2)]$

$\qquad\qquad\qquad\qquad\qquad\qquad = -\dfrac{12}{5}\left[\dfrac{x^2 + 8x + 16}{(4 + x)^{1/2}}\right]$

150. $\dfrac{3x^3 + 4x^2 + x - 5}{x^2} = \dfrac{3x^3}{x^2} + \dfrac{4x^2}{x^2} + \dfrac{x}{x^2} - \dfrac{5}{x^2}$

$\qquad\qquad\qquad\qquad = 3x + 4 + \dfrac{1}{x} - \dfrac{5}{x^2}$

$\qquad\qquad\qquad\qquad = 3x + 4 + x^{-1} - 5x^{-2}$

152. $\dfrac{8x^4 + 5x^3 - 10x + 5}{5x^2} = \dfrac{8x^4}{5x^2} + \dfrac{5x^3}{5x^2} - \dfrac{10x}{5x^2} + \dfrac{5}{5x^2}$

$\qquad\qquad\qquad\qquad\qquad = \dfrac{8}{5}x^2 + x - \dfrac{2}{x} + \dfrac{1}{x^2}$

$\qquad\qquad\qquad\qquad\qquad = \dfrac{8}{5}x^2 + x - 2x^{-1} + x^{-2}$

154. Parallelogram: $(1, 2), (8, 3), (9, 6), (2, 5)$

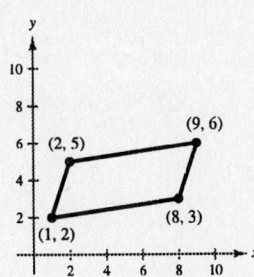

$(1, 2)$ and $(2, 5)$

$d = \sqrt{(2 - 1)^2 + (5 - 2)^2}$

$\quad = \sqrt{1^2 + 3^2} = \sqrt{10}$

$(2, 5)$ and $(9, 6)$

$d = \sqrt{(9 - 2)^2 + (6 - 5)^2}$

$\quad = \sqrt{7^2 + 1^2}$

$\quad = \sqrt{50} = 5\sqrt{2}$

$(9, 6)$ and $(8, 3)$

$d = \sqrt{(8 - 9)^2 + (3 - 6)^2}$

$\quad = \sqrt{(-1)^2 + (-3)^2} = \sqrt{10}$

$(8, 3)$ and $(1, 2)$

$d = \sqrt{(1 - 8)^2 + (2 - 3)^2}$

$\quad = \sqrt{(-7)^2 + (-1)^2}$

$\quad = \sqrt{50} = 5\sqrt{2}$

Opposite sides have equal lengths of $\sqrt{10}$ and $5\sqrt{2}$.

156. $y > 0$

(x, y) lies in quadrants I and II.

158. $xy = 4$

x and y are both positive or both negative.
(x, y) lies in quadrants I and III.

160. (a)

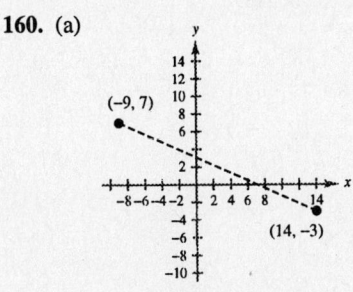

(b) $d = \sqrt{(-9 - 14)^2 + (7 - (-3))^2}$

$\quad = \sqrt{629}$

162. (a)

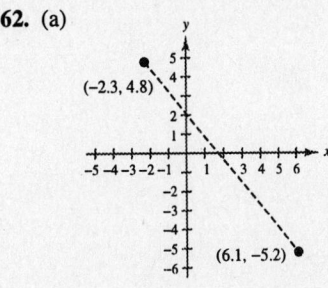

(b) $d = \sqrt{(-2.3 - 6.1)^2 + (4.8 - (-5.2))^2}$

$\quad = \sqrt{170.56} \approx 13.06$

164. (a)

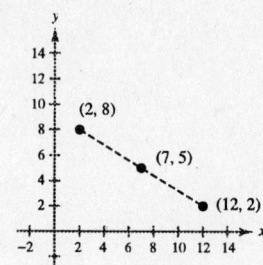

(b) Midpoint: $\left(\dfrac{2+12}{2}, \dfrac{8+2}{2}\right) = (7, 5)$

166. (a)

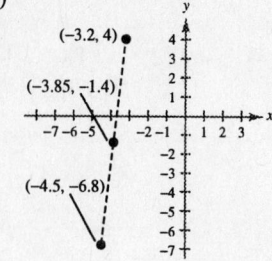

(b) Midpoint: $\left(\dfrac{-3.2 + (-4.5)}{2}, \dfrac{4 + (-6.8)}{2}\right)$

$= (-3.85, -1.4)$

168. False.

$\dfrac{x^3 - 1}{x - 1} = x^2 + x + 1$ for all $x, x \neq 1$.

170. False.

$x^n - y^n = (x - y)(x^{n-1} + x^{n-2}y + \ldots y^{n-1})$, for odd values of n.

172. True. Since $b^2 - 4ac = (-717)^2 - 4(325)(398) < 0$, the equation has no real solutions.

174. (a)

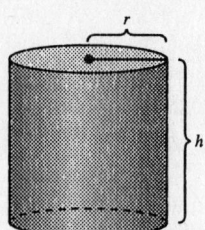

Area of top and bottom: area of circle $= \pi r^2$

Area of side: area of rectangle of sides $2\pi r$
and $h = 2\pi rh$

Total area $= 2\pi r^2 + 2\pi rh$

(b) $r = 6$ inches

$h = 8$ inches

$S = 2\pi r^2 + 2\pi rh$

$\quad = 2\pi(6)^2 + 2\pi(6)(8) = 168\pi$ square inches

$\quad \approx 527.79$ square inches

176. Certain algebraic steps, such as squaring an equation, may introduce extraneous solutions. Some solutions may not be in the domain of the original equation.

178. $|11x - 4| = -26$

There is no solution since the absolute value of an expression is always non negative.

C H A P T E R 1
Functions and Their Graphs

CHAPTER 1
Equations and Inequalities

Section 1.1   Graphs of Equations

Solutions to Even-Numbered Exercises

2. $y = x^2 - 3x + 2$

(a) $(2, 0)$: $(2)^2 - 3(2) + 2 \overset{?}{=} 0$

$$4 - 6 + 2 \overset{?}{=} 0$$

$$0 = 0$$

Yes, the point *is* on the graph.

(b) $(-2, 8)$: $(-2)^2 - 3(-2) + 2 \overset{?}{=} 8$

$$4 + 6 + 2 \overset{?}{=} 8$$

$$12 \neq 8$$

No, the point *is not* on the graph.

4. $y = \frac{1}{3}x^3 - 2x^2$

(a) $\left(2, -\frac{16}{3}\right)$: $\frac{1}{3}(2)^3 - 2(2)^2 \overset{?}{=} -\frac{16}{3}$

$$\frac{1}{3} \cdot 8 - 2 \cdot 4 \overset{?}{=} -\frac{16}{3}$$

$$\frac{8}{3} - 8 \overset{?}{=} -\frac{16}{3}$$

$$\frac{8}{3} - \frac{24}{3} \overset{?}{=} -\frac{16}{3}$$

$$-\frac{16}{3} = -\frac{16}{3}$$

Yes, the point *is* on the graph.

(b) $(-3, 9)$: $\frac{1}{3}(-3)^3 - 2(-3)^2 \overset{?}{=} 9$

$$\frac{1}{3}(-27) - 2(9) \overset{?}{=} 9$$

$$-9 - 18 \overset{?}{=} 9$$

$$-27 \neq 9$$

No, the point *is not* on the graph.

6. $y = \frac{3}{4}x - 1$

-2	0	1	$\frac{4}{3}$	2
$-\frac{5}{2}$	-1	$-\frac{1}{4}$	0	$\frac{1}{2}$

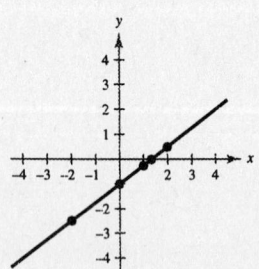

8. $5 - x^2$

-2	-1	0	1	2
1	4	5	4	1

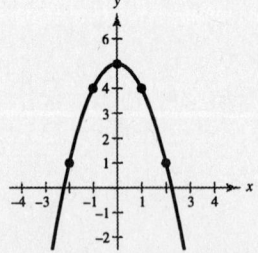

10. $x - (-y)^2 = 0 \Longrightarrow x - y^2 = 0$

x-axis symmetry

12. $y = x^4 - x^2 + 3$

$y = (-x)^4 - (-x)^2 + 3$

$y = x^4 - x^2 + 3$

y-axis symmetry

14. $y = \sqrt{9 - x^2}$

$y = \sqrt{9 - (-x)^2}$

$y = \sqrt{9 - x^2}$

y-axis symmetry

16. $xy = 4$

$(-x)(-y) = 4$

$xy = 4$

Origin symmetry

18.
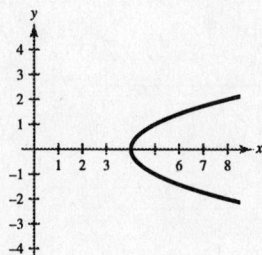

20.
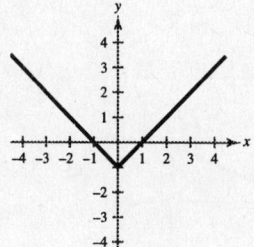

22. $y = x^2 - 2x$ is a parabola. Matches (a).

24. $y = |x| - 3$ involves an absolute value. Matches (d).

26. $y = (x + 2)^2$

x-intercept: $0 = (x + 2)^2$

$0 = x + 2$

$x = -2$

$(-2, 0)$

y-intercept: $y = (0 + 2)^2$

$y = 2^2$

$y = 4$

$(0, 4)$

28. $y^2 = x + 1$

x-intercept: $0 = x + 1$

$x = -1$

$(-1, 0)$

y-intercepts: $y^2 = 0 + 1$

$y = \pm 1$

$(0, 1), (0, -1)$

30. $y = 2x - 3$

x-intercept: $\left(\frac{3}{2}, 0\right)$

y-intercept: $(0, -3)$

No symmetry

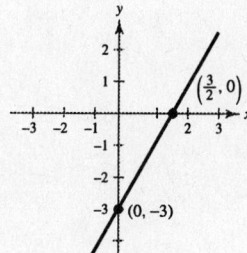

32. $y = -x^2 - 2x$

x-intercept: $(-2, 0), (0, 0)$

y-intercept: $(0, 0)$

No symmetry

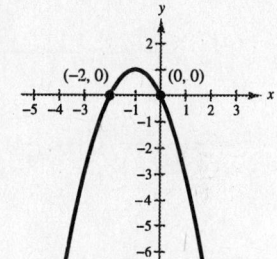

34. $y = x^3 - 1$

x-intercept: $(1, 0)$

y-intercept: $(0, -1)$

No symmetry

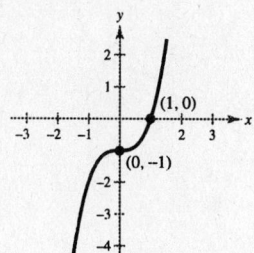

36. $y = \sqrt{1 - x}$

Domain: $(-\infty, 1]$

y-intercept: $(0, 1)$

No symmetry

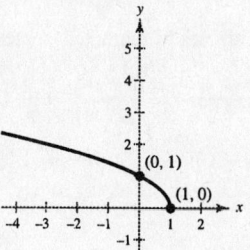

38. $y = 1 - |x|$

x-intercepts: $(\pm 1, 0)$

y-intercept: $(0, 1)$

y-axis symmetry

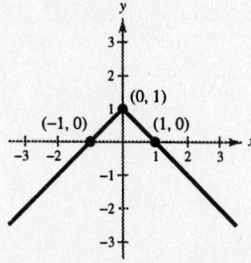

40. $x = y^2 - 5$

x-intercept: $(-5, 0)$

y-intercept: $\left(0, \pm\sqrt{5}\right)$

x-axis symmetry

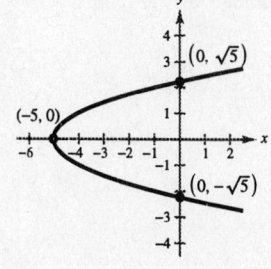

42. $y = \frac{2}{3}x - 1$

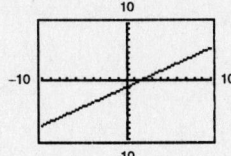

Intercepts: $(0, -1), \left(\frac{3}{2}, 0\right)$

44. $y = x^2 + x - 2$

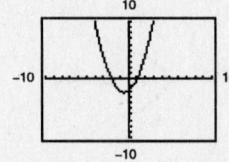

Intercepts: $(-2, 0), (1, 0), (0, -2)$

46. $y = \frac{4}{x^2 + 1}$

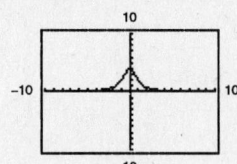

Intercept: $(0, 4)$

48. $y = \sqrt[3]{x + 1}$

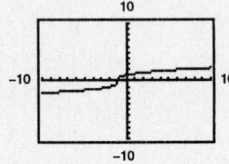

Intercepts: $(-1, 0), (0, 1)$

50. $y = (6 - x)\sqrt{x}$

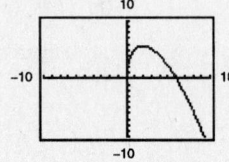

Intercepts: $(0, 0), (6, 0)$

52. $y = 2 - |x|$

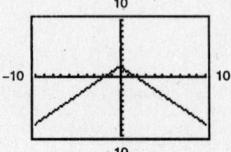

Intercepts: $(\pm 2, 0), (0, 2)$

54. $(x - 0)^2 + (y - 0)^2 = 5^2$

$\qquad x^2 + y^2 = 25$

56. $(x - (-7))^2 + (y - (-4))^2 = 7^2$

$\qquad (x + 7)^2 + (y + 4)^2 = 49$

58. $r = \sqrt{(3 - (-1))^2 + (-2 - 1)^2}$

$\quad = \sqrt{4^2 + (-3)^2} = \sqrt{25} = 5$

$(x - 3)^2 + (y - (-2))^2 = 5^2$

$\qquad (x - 3)^2 + (y + 2)^2 = 25$

60. $r = \frac{1}{2}\sqrt{(-4 - 4)^2 + (-1 - 1)^2}$

$\quad = \frac{1}{2}\sqrt{(-8)^2 + (-2)^2}$

$\quad = \frac{1}{2}\sqrt{64 + 4}$

$\quad = \frac{1}{2}\sqrt{68} = \left(\frac{1}{2}\right)(2)\sqrt{17} = \sqrt{17}$

Midpoint of diameter (center of circle):

$\left(\frac{-4 + 4}{2}, \frac{-1 + 1}{2}\right) = (0, 0)$

$(x - 0)^2 + (y - 0)^2 = \left(\sqrt{17}\right)^2$

$\qquad x^2 + y^2 = 17$

62. $x^2 + y^2 = 16$

Center: $(0, 0)$, radius: 4

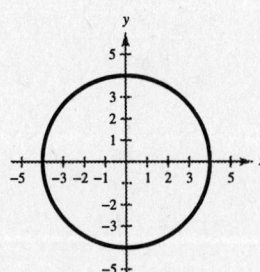

64. $x^2 + (y - 1)^2 = 1$

Center: $(0, 1)$, radius: 1

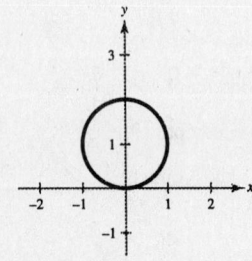

66. $(x - 2)^2 + (y + 1)^2 = 3$

Center: $(2, -1)$; radius: $\sqrt{3}$

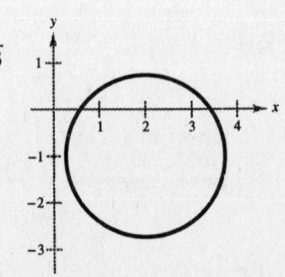

68. $y_1 = 2 + \sqrt{16 - (x - 1)^2}$

$y_2 = 2 - \sqrt{16 - (x - 1)^2}$

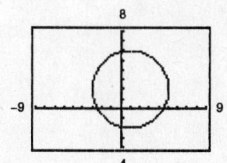

A circle is bounded by their graphs.

70. $y = 8100 - 929t, 0 \le t \le 6$

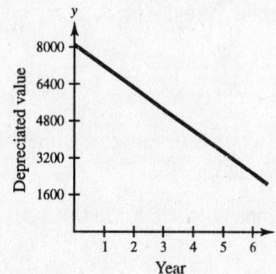

72. (a)

(b) $2x + 2w = 22$

$x + w = 11 \Longrightarrow w = 11 - x$

$A = x \cdot w = x(11 - x)$

(c)

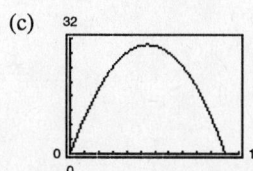

(d) The area is maximized when $x = 5.5$ and $w = 11 - 5.5 = 5.5$.

$x = 5.5$ yards

$w = 5.5$ yards

74. (a) and (b)

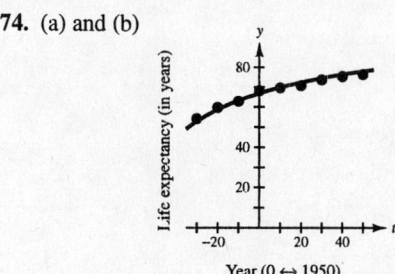

(b) The curve seems to be a good fit for the data.

(c) For the year 2002, $t = 52$ and $y = 78.2$ years.
For the year 2004, $t = 54$ and $y = 78.5$ years.

76. False. To find y-intercepts, let x be zero and solve the equation for y.

78. The viewing rectangle is incorrect. Change the viewing rectangle. Answers will vary.

80. Assuming that the graph does not go beyond the vertical limits of the display, you will see the graph for the larger values of x.

82. $(3 + 4)^2 = (7)^2 = 49$

$3^2 + 4^2 = 9 + 16 = 25$

$49 \neq 25$

False

84. $-(7 \times 7 \times 7 \times 7) = -(7)^4 = -7^4$

86. $\sqrt[4]{x^5} = \sqrt[4]{x \cdot x^4} = |x|\sqrt[4]{x}$

88. $\dfrac{55}{\sqrt{20} - 3} = \dfrac{55}{\sqrt{20} - 3} \cdot \dfrac{\sqrt{20} + 3}{\sqrt{20} + 3}$

$= \dfrac{55(\sqrt{20} + 3)}{20 - 9} = \dfrac{55(\sqrt{20} + 3)}{11}$

$= 5(\sqrt{20} + 3) = 5(2\sqrt{5} + 3)$

90. $\sqrt[3]{\sqrt{y}} = (y^{1/2})^{1/3} = y^{1/6} = \sqrt[6]{y}$

Section 1.2   Linear Equations in Two Variables

Solutions to Even-Numbered Exercises

2. (a) $m = 0$. The line is horizontal. Matches L_2.

   (b) $m = -\frac{3}{4}$. Because the slope is negative, the line falls. Matches L_1.

   (c) $m = 1$. Because the slope is positive, the line rises. Matches L_3.

4.

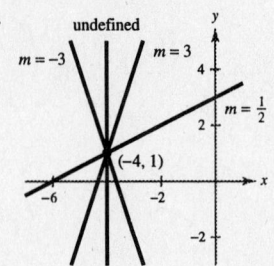

6. The line appears to go through $(1, 0)$ and $(4, 8)$.

$$\text{Slope} = \frac{y_2 - y_1}{x_2 - x_1} = \frac{8 - 0}{4 - 1} = \frac{8}{3}$$

8. The line appears to go through $(0, 7)$ and $(7, 0)$.

$$\text{Slope} = \frac{y_2 - y_1}{x_2 - x_1} = \frac{0 - 7}{7 - 0} = -1$$

10. The line appears to go through $(0, 1)$ and $(6, 5)$.

$$\text{Slope} = \frac{y_2 - y_1}{x_2 - x_1} = \frac{5 - 1}{6 - 0} = \frac{4}{6} = \frac{2}{3}$$

12. $\text{Slope} = \dfrac{-4 - 4}{4 - 2} = -4$

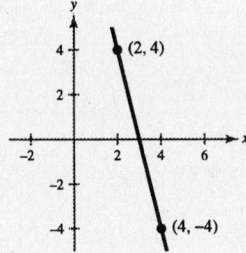

14. $\text{Slope} = \dfrac{0 - (-10)}{-4 - 0} = -\dfrac{5}{2}$

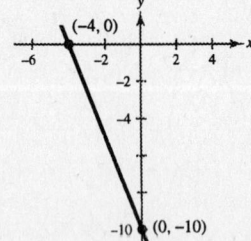

16. $\text{Slope} = \dfrac{-\frac{1}{4} - \frac{3}{4}}{\frac{5}{4} - \frac{7}{8}} = \dfrac{-1}{\frac{3}{8}} = -\dfrac{8}{3}$

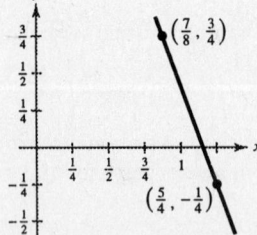

18. Slope $= \dfrac{-2.6 - (-8.3)}{2.25 - (-1.75)} = 1.425$

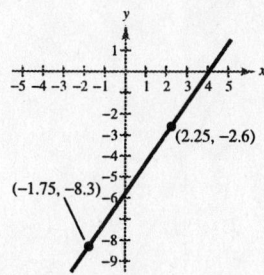

20. Because m is undefined, x does not change. Three other points are: $(-4, 0), (-4, 3), (-4, 5)$.

22. Because $m = -1$, y decreases by 1 for every one unit increase in x. Three other points are: $(0, 4), (9, -5),$ $(11, -7)$.

24. Because $m = 0$, y does not change. Three other points are: $(-4, -1), (-2, -1), (0, -1)$.

26. Because $m = -2$, y decreases by 2 for every one unit increase in x. Three other points are: $(-2, -5), (1, -11),$ $(3, -15)$.

28. Because $m = -\frac{1}{2}$, y decreases by 1 for every 2 unit increase in x. Three other points are: $(-3, -5), (1, -7),$ $(5, -9)$.

30. L_1: $(-2, -1), (1, 5)$

$m_1 = \dfrac{5 - (-1)}{1 - (-2)} = \dfrac{6}{3} = 2$

L_2: $(1, 3), (5, -5)$

$m_2 = \dfrac{-5 - 3}{5 - 1} = \dfrac{-8}{4} = -2$

The lines are neither parallel nor perpendicular.

32. L_1: $(4, 8), (-4, 2)$

$m_1 = \dfrac{2 - 8}{-4 - 4} = \dfrac{-6}{-8} = \dfrac{3}{4}$

L_2: $(3, -5), \left(-1, \dfrac{1}{3}\right)$

$m_2 = \dfrac{\frac{1}{3} - (-5)}{-1 - 3} = \dfrac{\frac{16}{3}}{-4} = -\dfrac{4}{3}$

The lines are perpendicular.

34. (a) $m = 400$. The revenues are increasing \$400 per day.

    (b) $m = 100$. The revenues are increasing \$100 per day.

    (c) $m = 0$. There is no change in revenue. (Revenue remains constant.)

36. (a) The steepest portion of the graph is between 1996 and 1997 (greatest increase). The most level portion of the graph is between 1988 and 1989 (smallest increase).

    (b) Slope $= \dfrac{1.10 - 0.37}{11 - 1} = 0.073$

    (c) Each year the dividends per share increase by \$0.073.

38. $y = \frac{6}{100}x$

$y = \frac{6}{100}(200) = 12$ feet

40. $y = 5x + 3$

Slope: $m = 5$

y-intercept: $(0, 3)$

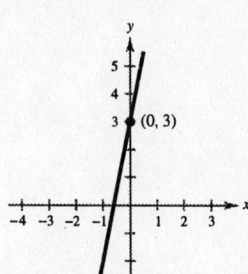

42. $5x - 2 = 0$

$x = \frac{2}{5}$

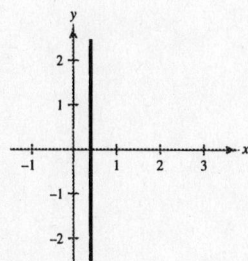

Slope: undefined

No y-intercept

44. $7x + 6y = 30$

$$y = -\frac{7}{6}x + 5$$

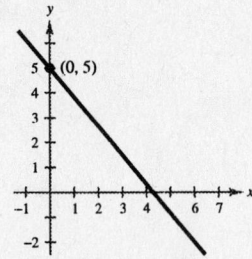

Slope: $m = -\frac{7}{6}$

y-intercept: $(0, 5)$

46. $y + 2 = 3(x - 0)$

$$y = 3x - 2$$

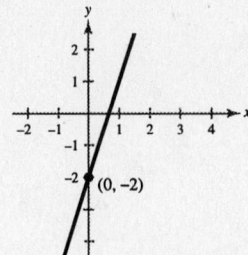

48. $y - 6 = -2(x + 3)$

$$y = -2x$$

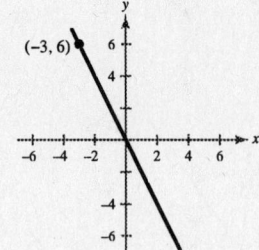

50. $y - 0 = -\frac{1}{3}(x - 4)$

$$y = -\frac{1}{3}x + \frac{4}{3}$$

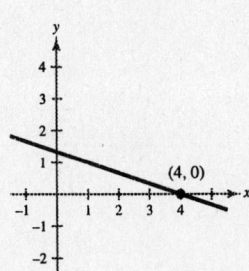

52. $x = 6$

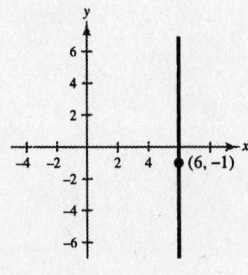

54. $y - \frac{5}{2} = \frac{4}{3}(x - 4)$

$$y = \frac{4}{3}x - \frac{17}{6}$$

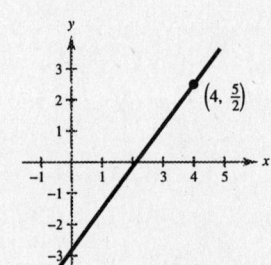

56. $y - 1.8 = 5(x - (-5.1))$

$$y = 5x + 27.3$$

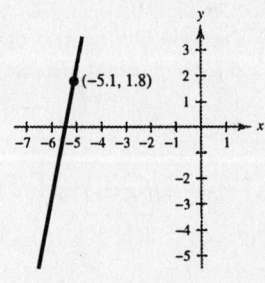

58. $y + 1 = \dfrac{5 + 1}{-5 - 5}(x - 5)$

$$y = -\frac{3}{5}(x - 5) - 1$$

$$y = -\frac{3}{5}x + 2$$

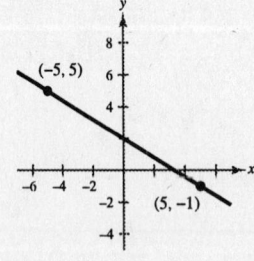

60. Since both points have $x = -8$, the slope is undefined.

$$x = -8$$

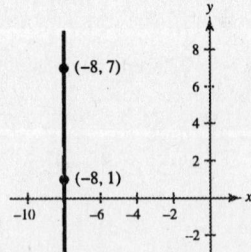

62. $y - \dfrac{1}{2} = \dfrac{\frac{5}{4} - \frac{1}{2}}{\frac{1}{2} - 2}(x - 2)$

$y = -\dfrac{1}{2}(x - 2) + \dfrac{1}{2}$

$y = -\dfrac{1}{2}x + \dfrac{3}{2}$

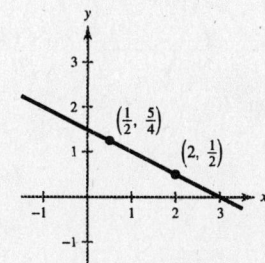

64. $y - \left(-\dfrac{3}{5}\right) = \dfrac{-\frac{9}{5} - \left(-\frac{3}{5}\right)}{\frac{9}{10} - \left(-\frac{1}{10}\right)}\left(x - \left(-\dfrac{1}{10}\right)\right)$

$y = -\dfrac{6}{5}\left(x + \dfrac{1}{10}\right) - \dfrac{3}{5}$

$y = -\dfrac{6}{5}x - \dfrac{18}{25}$

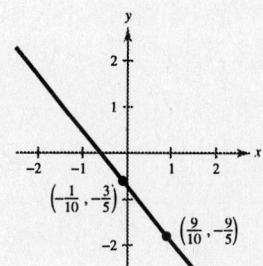

66. $y - 0.6 = \dfrac{-0.6 - 0.6}{-2 - 1}(x - 1)$

$y = 0.4(x - 1) + 0.6$

$y = 0.4x + 0.2$

68. $\dfrac{x}{2} + \dfrac{y}{3} = 1$

$3x + 2y - 6 = 0$

70. $\dfrac{x}{-\frac{1}{6}} + \dfrac{y}{-\frac{2}{3}} = 1$

$6x + \dfrac{3}{2}y = -1$

$12x + 3y + 2 = 0$

72. $\dfrac{x}{c} + \dfrac{y}{c} = 1, \ c \neq 0$

$x + y = c$

$1 + 2 = c$

$3 = c$

$x + y = 3$

$x + y - 3 = 0$

74. $4x - 2y = 3$

$y = 2x - \dfrac{3}{2}$

Slope: $m = 2$

(a) $y - 1 = 2(x - 2)$

$y = 2x - 3$

(b) $y - 1 = -\dfrac{1}{2}(x - 2)$

$y = -\dfrac{1}{2}x + 2$

76. $3x + 4y = 7$

$y = -\dfrac{3}{4}x + \dfrac{7}{4}$

Slope: $m = -\dfrac{3}{4}$

(a) $y - \dfrac{7}{8} = -\dfrac{3}{4}\left(x - \left(-\dfrac{2}{3}\right)\right)$

$y = -\dfrac{3}{4}x + \dfrac{3}{8}$

(b) $y - \dfrac{7}{8} = \dfrac{4}{3}\left(x - \left(-\dfrac{2}{3}\right)\right)$

$y = \dfrac{4}{3}x + \dfrac{127}{72}$

78. $y = -3$

Slope: $m = 0$

(a) $y = 0$

(b) $x = -1 \Longrightarrow x + 1 = 0$

80. $x - y = 4$

$y = x - 4$

Slope: $m = 1$

(a) $y - 6.8 = 1(x - 2.5)$

$y = x + 4.3$

(b) $y - 6.8 = (-1)(x - 2.5)$

$y = -x + 9.3$

82. (a) $y = 2x$

(b) $y = -2x$

(c) $y = \frac{1}{2}x$

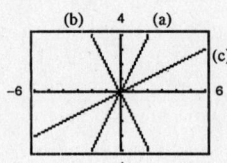

(b) and (c) are perpendicular.

84. (a) $y = -\frac{1}{2}x$

(b) $y = -\frac{1}{2}x + 3$

(c) $y = 2x - 4$

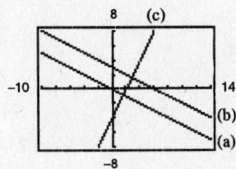

(a) and (b) are parallel.

(c) is perpendicular to (a) and (b).

86. $(1, 2540), m = 125$

$V - 2540 = 125(t - 1)$

$V - 2540 = 125t - 125$

$V = 125t + 2415$

88. The slope is $m = -20$. This represents the decrease in the amount of the loan each week. Matches graph (b).

90. The slope is $m = 0.32$. This represents the increase in travel cost for each mile driven. Matches graph (a).

92. Set the distance between $(4, -1)$ and (x, y) equal to the distance between $(-2, 3)$ and (x, y).

$$\sqrt{(x - 4)^2 + [y - (-1)]^2} = \sqrt{[x - (-2)]^2 + (y - 3)^2}$$

$$(x - 4)^2 + (y + 1)^2 = (x + 2)^2 + (y - 3)^2$$

$$x^2 - 8x + 16 + y^2 + 2y + 1 = x^2 + 4x + 4 + y^2 - 6y + 9$$

$$-8x + 2y + 17 = 4x - 6y + 13$$

$$0 = 12x - 8y - 4$$

$$0 = 4(3x - 2y - 1)$$

$$0 = 3x - 2y - 1$$

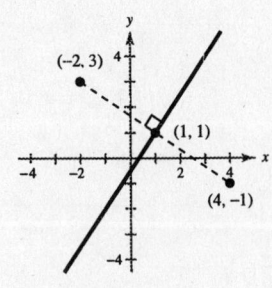

This line is the perpendicular bisector of the line segment connecting $(4, -1)$ and $(-2, 3)$.

94. Set the distance between $\left(3, \frac{5}{2}\right)$ and (x, y) equal to the distance between $(-7, 1)$ and (x, y).

$$\sqrt{(x-3)^2 + \left(y - \tfrac{5}{2}\right)^2} = \sqrt{[x - (-7)]^2 + (y-1)^2}$$

$$(x-3)^2 + \left(y - \tfrac{5}{2}\right)^2 = (x+7)^2 + (y-1)^2$$

$$x^2 - 6x + 9 + y^2 - 5y + \tfrac{25}{4} = x^2 + 14x + 49 + y^2 - 2y + 1$$

$$-6x - 5y + \tfrac{61}{4} = 14x - 2y + 50$$

$$-24x - 20y + 61 = 56x - 8y + 200$$

$$80x + 12y + 139 = 0$$

This line is the perpendicular bisector of the line segment connecting $\left(3, \frac{5}{2}\right)$ and $(-7, 1)$.

96. $(0, 0.26), (1, 0.70)$

$$y - 0.26 = \frac{0.70 - 0.26}{1 - 0}(x - 0)$$

$$y = 0.44x + 0.26$$

For year 2000, $x = 2$; $y = 0.44(2) + 0.26 = \$1.14$

For year 2001, $x = 3$; $y = 0.44(3) + 0.26 = \$1.58$

98. Using the points $(0, 32)$ and $(100, 212)$, we have

$$m = \frac{212 - 32}{100 - 0} = \frac{180}{100} = \frac{9}{5}$$

$$F - 32 = \frac{9}{5}(C - 0)$$

$$F = \frac{9}{5}C + 32.$$

100. Using the points $(1998, 28{,}500)$ and $(2000, 32{,}900)$, we have

$$m = \frac{32{,}900 - 28{,}500}{2000 - 1998} = \frac{4400}{2} = 2200$$

$$S - 28{,}500 = 2200(t - 1998)$$

$$S = 2200t - 4{,}367{,}100$$

When $t = 2003$, we have $S = 2200(2003) - 4{,}367{,}100$, or $\$39{,}500$.

102. Using the points $(0, 875)$ and $(5, 0)$, where the first coordinate represents the year t and the second coordinate represents the value V, we have

$$m = \frac{0 - 875}{5 - 0} = -175$$

$$V = -175t + 875, \ 0 \le t \le 5.$$

104. Sale price = List price $-$ 15% of the list price

$$S = L - 0.15L$$

$$S = 0.85L$$

106. (a) $C = 36{,}500 + 5.25t + 11.50t$

$$= 16.75t + 36{,}500$$

(c) $P = R - C$

$$= 27t - (16.75t + 36{,}500)$$

$$= 10.25t - 36{,}500$$

(b) $R = 27t$

(d)

$$0 = 10.25t - 36{,}500$$

$$36{,}500 = 10.25t$$

$$t \approx 3561 \text{ hours}$$

108. (a)

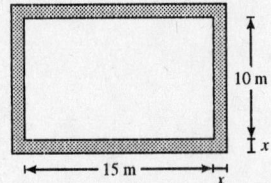

(b) $y = 2(15 + 2x) + 2(10 + 2x)$

$= 8x + 50$

(c)

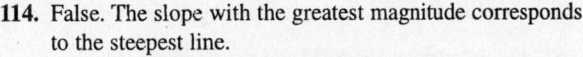

(d) Since $m = 8$, each 1 meter increase in x will increase y by 8 meters.

110. $C = 120 + 0.31x$

112. Two approximate points on this line are $(2, 600)$ and $(4, 1000)$.

$$m = \frac{1000 - 600}{4 - 2} \approx 200$$

$$y - 1000 = 200(t - 4)$$

$$y = 200t + 200$$

This answer may vary depending on the points used.

114. False. The slope with the greatest magnitude corresponds to the steepest line.

116. By finding the distance between each pair of points and using the Pythagorean Theorem.

118. No. The slope cannot be determined without knowing the scale on the y-axis. The slopes could be the same.

120. The V-intercept measures the initial cost and the slope measures annual depreciation.

122. No, the slopes of two perpendicular lines have opposite signs. (Assume that neither line is vertical or horizontal.)

124. $y = 8 - \sqrt{x}$

Intercepts: $(64, 0)$, $(0, 8)$

Matching graph is (c).

126. $y = |x + 2| - 1$

Intercepts: $(-1, 0)$, $(-3, 0)$, $(0, 1)$

Matching graph is (b).

128. $\dfrac{8}{2x - 7} = \dfrac{4}{9 - 4x}$

$8(9 - 4x) = 4(2x - 7)$

$72 - 32x = 8x - 28$

$-40x = -100$

$x = \dfrac{5}{2}$

130. $x^2 - 8x + 3 = 0$

$$x = \frac{-b \pm \sqrt{b^2 - 4ac}}{2a} = \frac{-(-8) \pm \sqrt{(-8)^2 - 4(1)(3)}}{2(1)}$$

$$= \frac{8 \pm \sqrt{52}}{2} = 4 \pm \sqrt{13}$$

132. $3x - 16\sqrt{x} + 5 = 0$

$\left(3\sqrt{x} - 1\right)\left(\sqrt{x} - 5\right) = 0$

$3\sqrt{x} - 1 = 0 \Rightarrow x = \dfrac{1}{9}$

$\sqrt{x} - 5 = 0 \Rightarrow x = 25$

Section 1.3   Functions

Solutions to Even-Numbered Exercises

2. No, it is not a function. The domain value of -1 is matched with two output values.

4. Yes, it is a function. Each domain value is matched with only one range value.

6. No, the table does not represent a function. The input values of 0 and 1 are each matched with two different output values.

8. Yes, the table does represent a function. Each input value is matched with only one output value.

10. (a) The element c in A is matched with two elements, 2 and 3 of B, so it is not a function.

(b) Each element of A is matched with exactly one element of B, so it does represent a function.

(c) This is not a function from A to B (it represents a function from B to A instead).

(d) Each element of A is matched with exactly one element of B, so it does represent a function.

12. Reading from the graph, $f(1994)$ is approximately 16 million.

14. $x = y^2 \Longrightarrow y = \pm\sqrt{x}$

Thus, y is *not* a function of x.

18. $(x - 2)^2 + y^2 = 4 \Longrightarrow y = \pm\sqrt{4 - (x - 2)^2}$

Thus, y is *not* a function of x.

16. $x + y^2 = 4 \Longrightarrow y = \pm\sqrt{4 - x}$

Thus, y is *not* a function of x.

20. $y = \sqrt{x + 5}$

This is a function of x.

22. $|y| = 4 - x \Longrightarrow y = 4 - x$ or $y = -(4 - x)$

Thus, y is *not* a function of x.

24. $g(x) = x^2 - 2x$

(a) $g(2) = (2)^2 - 2(2)$

(b) $g(-3) = (-3)^2 - 2(-3)$

(c) $g(t + 1) = (t + 1)^2 - 2(t + 1)$

(d) $g(x + c) = (x + c)^2 - 2(x + c)$

26. $g(y) = 7 - 3y$

(a) $g(0) = 7 - 3(0) = 7$

(b) $g\left(\frac{7}{3}\right) = 7 - 3\left(\frac{7}{3}\right) = 0$

(c) $g(s + 2) = 7 - 3(s + 2)$

$\qquad\qquad = 7 - 3s - 6 = 1 - 3s$

28. $h(t) = t^2 - 2t$

(a) $h(2) = 2^2 - 2(2) = 0$

(b) $h(1.5) = (1.5)^2 - 2(1.5) = -0.75$

(c) $h(x + 2) = (x + 2)^2 - 2(x + 2) = x^2 + 2x$

30. $f(x) = \sqrt{x + 8} + 2$

(a) $f(-8) = \sqrt{(-8) + 8} + 2 = 2$

(b) $f(1) = \sqrt{(1) + 8} + 2 = 5$

(c) $f(x - 8) = \sqrt{(x - 8) + 8} + 2 = \sqrt{x} + 2$

32. $q(t) = \dfrac{2t^2 + 3}{t^2}$

(a) $q(2) = \dfrac{2(2)^2 + 3}{(2)^2} = \dfrac{8 + 3}{4} = \dfrac{11}{4}$

(b) $q(0) = \dfrac{2(0)^2 + 3}{(0)^2}$

Division by zero is undefined.

(c) $q(-x) = \dfrac{2(-x)^2 + 3}{(-x)^2} = \dfrac{2x^2 + 3}{x^2}$

34. $f(x) = |x| + 4$

(a) $f(2) = |2| + 4 = 6$

(b) $f(-2) = |-2| + 4 = 6$

(c) $f(x^2) = |x^2| + 4 = x^2 + 4$

36. $f(x) = \begin{cases} x^2 + 2, & x \le 1 \\ 2x^2 + 2, & x > 1 \end{cases}$

(a) $f(-2) = (-2)^2 + 2 = 6$

(b) $f(1) = (1)^2 + 2 = 3$

(c) $f(2) = 2(2)^2 + 2 = 10$

38. $g(x) = \sqrt{x - 3}$

$g(3) = \sqrt{3 - 3} = 0$

$g(4) = \sqrt{4 - 3} = 1$

$g(5) = \sqrt{5 - 3} = \sqrt{2}$

$g(6) = \sqrt{6 - 3} = \sqrt{3}$

$g(7) = \sqrt{7 - 3} = 2$

x	3	4	5	6	7
$g(x)$	0	1	$\sqrt{2}$	$\sqrt{3}$	2

40. $f(s) = \dfrac{|s - 2|}{s - 2}$

$f(0) = \dfrac{|0 - 2|}{0 - 2} = \dfrac{2}{-2} = -1$

$f(1) = \dfrac{|1 - 2|}{1 - 2} = \dfrac{1}{-1} = -1$

$f\left(\dfrac{3}{2}\right) = \dfrac{\left|\frac{3}{2} - 2\right|}{\frac{3}{2} - 2} = \dfrac{\frac{1}{2}}{-\frac{1}{2}} = -1$

$f\left(\dfrac{5}{2}\right) = \dfrac{\left|\frac{5}{2} - 2\right|}{\frac{5}{2} - 2} = \dfrac{\frac{1}{2}}{\frac{1}{2}} = 1$

$f(4) = \dfrac{|4 - 2|}{4 - 2} = \dfrac{2}{2} = 1$

s	0	1	$\frac{3}{2}$	$\frac{5}{2}$	4
$f(s)$	-1	-1	-1	1	1

42. $h(x) = \begin{cases} 9 - x^2, & x < 3 \\ x - 3, & x \ge 3 \end{cases}$

$h(1) = 9 - (1)^2 = 8$

$h(2) = 9 - (2)^2 = 5$

$h(3) = (3) - 3 = 0$

$h(4) = (4) - 3 = 1$

$h(5) = (5) - 3 = 2$

s	1	2	3	4	5
$h(x)$	8	5	0	1	2

44. $f(x) = 5x + 1$

$5x + 1 = 0$

$x = -\dfrac{1}{5}$

46. $f(x) = \dfrac{12 - x^2}{5}$

$\dfrac{12 - x^2}{5} = 0$

$x^2 = 12$

$x = \pm\sqrt{12} = \pm 2\sqrt{3}$

48. $f(x) = x^2 - 8x + 15$

$x^2 - 8x + 15 = 0$

$(x - 5)(x - 3) = 0$

$x - 5 = 0 \Rightarrow x = 5$

$x - 3 = 0 \Rightarrow x = 3$

50. $f(x) = x^3 - x^2 - 4x + 4$

$x^3 - x^2 - 4x + 4 = 0$

$x^2(x - 1) - 4(x - 1) = 0$

$(x - 1)(x^2 - 4) = 0$

$x - 1 = 0 \Rightarrow x = 1$

$x^2 - 4 = 0 \Rightarrow x = \pm 2$

52. $f(x) = g(x)$

$x^2 + 2x + 1 = 3x + 3$

$x^2 - x - 2 = 0$

$(x - 2)(x + 1) = 0$

$x - 2 = 0 \Rightarrow x = 2$

$x + 1 = 0 \Rightarrow x = -1$

54.
$$f(x) = g(x)$$
$$x^4 - 2x^2 = 2x^2$$
$$x^4 - 4x^2 = 0$$
$$x^2(x^2 - 4) = 0$$
$$x^2(x + 2)(x - 2) = 0$$
$$x^2 = 0 \Rightarrow x = 0$$
$$x + 2 = 0 \Rightarrow x = -2$$
$$x - 2 = 0 \Rightarrow x = 2$$

56. $f(x) = 1 - 2x^2$

Because $f(x)$ is a polynomial, the domain is all real numbers x.

58. $s(y) = \dfrac{3y}{y + 5}$

$$y + 5 \neq 0$$
$$y \neq -5$$

The domain is all real numbers $y \neq 5$.

60. $f(t) = \sqrt[3]{t + 4}$

Because $f(t)$ is a cube root, the domain is all real numbers t.

62. $f(x) = \sqrt[4]{x^2 + 3x}$

$$x^2 + 3x \geq 0$$
$$x(x + 3) \geq 0$$

Test intervals:
$(-\infty, -3), (-3, 0), (0, \infty)$

The domain is all real numbers $x \leq -3, x \geq 0$

64. $h(x) = \dfrac{10}{x^2 - 2x}$

$$x^2 - 2x \neq 0$$
$$x(x - 2) \neq 0$$

The domain is all real numbers $x \neq 0$ and $x \neq 2$.

66. $f(x) = \dfrac{\sqrt{x + 6}}{6 + x}$

$$6 + x \neq 0$$
$$x \neq -6$$

The domain is all real numbers $x \neq -6$.

68. $f(x) = \dfrac{x - 5}{x^2 - 9}$

$$x^2 - 9 \neq 0$$
$$x^2 \neq 9$$
$$x \neq \pm 3$$

The domain is all real numbers $x \neq \pm 3$.

70. $f(x) = \dfrac{2x}{x^2 + 1}$

$$\left\{ \left(-2, -\frac{4}{5}\right), (-1, -1), (0, 0), (1, 1), \left(2, \frac{4}{5}\right) \right\}$$

72. $f(x) = |x + 1|$

$$\{(-2, 1), (-1, 0), (0, 1), (1, 2), (2, 3)\}$$

74. By plotting the data, you can see that they represent a line, or $f(x) = cx$. Because $(0, 0)$ and $\left(1, \frac{1}{4}\right)$ are on the line, the slope is $\frac{1}{4}$. Thus, $f(x) = \frac{1}{4}x$.

76. By plotting the data, you can see that they represent $h(x) = c\sqrt{|x|}$. Because $\sqrt{|-4|} = 2$ and $\sqrt{|-1|} = 1$ but the corresponding y values are 6 and 3. Thus, $c = 3$ and $h(x) = 3\sqrt{|x|}$.

78.
$$f(x) = 5x - x^2$$
$$f(5 + h) = 5(5 + h) - (5 + h)^2$$
$$= 25 + 5h - (25 + 10h + h^2)$$
$$= 25 + 5h - 25 - 10h - h^2$$
$$= -h^2 - 5h$$
$$f(5) = 5(5) - (5)^2$$
$$= 25 - 25 = 0$$
$$\frac{f(5 + h) - f(5)}{h} = \frac{-h^2 - 5h}{h}$$
$$= \frac{-h(h + 5)}{h} = -(h + 5)$$

80.
$$f(x) = 2x$$
$$f(x + c) = 2(x + c) = 2x + 2c$$
$$f(x) = 2x$$
$$\frac{f(x + c) - f(x)}{c} = \frac{2x + 2c - 2x}{c} = 2$$

82.
$$f(t) = \frac{1}{t}$$

$$f(1) = \frac{1}{1} = 1$$

$$\frac{f(t) - f(1)}{t - 1} = \frac{\frac{1}{t} - 1}{t - 1} = \frac{\frac{1}{t} - \frac{t}{t}}{t - 1} = \frac{\frac{1 - t}{t}}{t - 1} = \frac{\left(-\frac{1}{t}\right)(t - 1)}{t - 1} = -\frac{1}{t}$$

84.
$$f(x) = x^{2/3} + 1$$
$$f(8) = 8^{2/3} + 1 = 5$$
$$\frac{f(x) - f(8)}{x - 8} = \frac{x^{2/3} + 1 - 5}{x - 8} = \frac{x^{2/3} - 4}{x - 8}$$

86. $A = \pi r^2, \quad C = 2\pi r$

$$r = \frac{C}{2\pi}$$

$$A = \pi \left(\frac{C}{2\pi}\right)^2 = \frac{C^2}{4\pi}$$

88. $A = \frac{1}{2}bh$, in an equilateral triangle $b = s$ and

$$s^2 = h^2 + \left(\frac{s}{2}\right)^2$$

$$h = \sqrt{s^2 - \left(\frac{s}{2}\right)^2}$$

$$h = \sqrt{\frac{4s^2}{4} - \frac{s^2}{4}} = \frac{\sqrt{3}s}{2}$$

$$A = \frac{1}{2}s \cdot \frac{\sqrt{3}s}{2} = \frac{\sqrt{3}s^2}{4}$$

90. (a)

Units x	Price p	Profit P
110	$90 - 10(0.15)$	$110[90 - 10(0.15)] - 110(60) = 3135$
120	$90 - 20(0.15)$	$120[90 - 20(0.15)] - 120(60) = 3240$
130	$90 - 30(0.15)$	$130[90 - 30(0.15)] - 130(60) = 3315$
140	$90 - 40(0.15)$	$140[90 - 40(0.15)] - 140(60) = 3360$
150	$90 - 50(0.15)$	$150[90 - 50(0.15)] - 150(60) = 3375$
160	$90 - 60(0.15)$	$160[90 - 60(0.15)] - 160(60) = 3360$

The maximum profit is $3375.

(b)

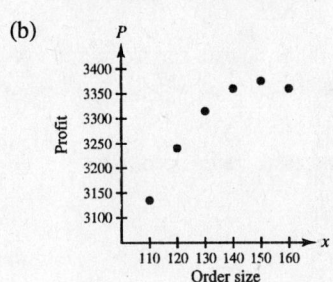

Yes

(c) Profit = Revenue − Cost

= (price per unit)(number of units) − (cost)(number of units)

$= [90 - (x - 100)(0.15)]x - 60x, \ x > 100$

$= (90 - 0.15x + 15)x - 60x$

$= (105 - 0.15x)x - 60x$

$= 105x - 0.15x^2 - 60x$

$= 45x - 0.15x^2, \ x > 100$

92. $A = l \cdot w = (2x)y = 2xy$

But $y = \sqrt{36 - x^2}$, so $A = 2x\sqrt{36 - x^2}, \ 0 < x < 6$.

94. (a) $V = l \cdot w \cdot h = x \cdot y \cdot x = x^2y$ where $4x + y = 108$.

Thus, $y = 108 - 4x$ and $V = x^2(108 - 4x) = 108x^2 - 4x^3$

(b) Domain: $0 < x < 27$

(c)

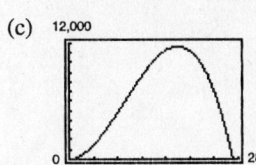

(d) The dimensions that will maximize the volume of the package are $18 \times 18 \times 36$. From the graph, the maximum volume occurs when $x = 18$. To find the dimension for y, use the equation $y = 108 - 4x$.

$y = 108 - 4x = 108 - 4(18) = 108 - 72 = 36$.

96. (a) *Model:* (Total cost) = (Fixed costs) + (Variable costs)

Labels: Total cost $= C$

Fixed cost $= 6000$

Variable costs $= 0.95x$

Equation: $C = 6000 + 0.95x$

(b) $\overline{C} = \dfrac{C}{x} = \dfrac{6000 + 0.95x}{x}$

98. $F(y) = 149.76\sqrt{10}\,y^{5/2}$

(a)

y	5	10	20	30	40
F(y)	26,474.08	149,760.00	847,170.49	2,334,527.36	4,792,320

The force, in tons, of the water against the dam increases with the depth of the water.

(b) It appears that approximately 21 feet of water would produce 1,000,000 tons of force. You can find a better estimate by creating a new table with y at smaller intervals between 20 and 25.

100. (a) $\dfrac{f(1994) - f(1991)}{1994 - 1991} = \dfrac{9 - 60}{3} = -17$

Over the years 1991 through 1994, there was an average decrease in the lynx population of 17 lynx per year.

(b)

x	-2	-1	0	1	2	3	4	5
N	9.0	19.8	43.9	53.6	30.9	16.7	10.2	6.9
Actual data	10	16	50	60	28	15	9	8

The model yields values that are similar to the actual data.

102. False. The range is $(-1, \infty)$.

104. No. The element 3 in the domain corresponds to two elements in the range.

106. An advantage to function notation is that it gives a name to the relationship so it can be easily referenced. When evaluating a function, you see both the input and output values.

108. $\dfrac{3}{t} + \dfrac{5}{t} = 1$

$\dfrac{8}{t} = 1$

$8 = t$

110. $\dfrac{12}{x} - 3 = \dfrac{4}{x} + 9$

$\dfrac{12}{x} - \dfrac{4}{x} = 9 + 3$

$\dfrac{8}{x} = 12$

$\dfrac{8}{12} = x$

$x = \dfrac{2}{3}$

112.   Slope $= \dfrac{9 - 0}{1 - 10} = \dfrac{9}{-9} = -1$

$m = -1$

$y - 0 = (-1)(x - 10)$

$y = -x + 10$

$x + y - 10 = 0$

114.   Slope $= \dfrac{-\dfrac{1}{3} - 3}{\dfrac{11}{2} - \left(-\dfrac{1}{2}\right)} = \dfrac{-\dfrac{10}{3}}{\dfrac{12}{2}} = -\dfrac{10}{3} \cdot \dfrac{1}{6} = -\dfrac{5}{9}$

$m = -\dfrac{5}{9}$

$y - 3 = -\dfrac{5}{9}\left(x - \left(-\dfrac{1}{2}\right)\right)$

$y - 3 = -\dfrac{5}{9}x - \dfrac{5}{18}$

$18y - 54 = -10x - 5$

$10x + 18y - 49 = 0$

Section 1.4 Analyzing Graphs of Functions

Solutions to Even-Numbered Exercises

2. $f(x) = x^3 - 3x + 2$

Domain: all real numbers
$$(-\infty, \infty)$$

Range: all real numbers $(-\infty, \infty)$

4. $f(x) = \sqrt{x - 1}$

Domain: $x - 1 \geq 0$
$$x \geq 1$$
$$[1, \infty)$$

Range: $[0, \infty)$

6. $f(x) = \frac{1}{2}|x - 2|$

Domain: $(-\infty, \infty)$

Range: $[0, \infty)$

8. $g(x) = \dfrac{|x - 1|}{x - 1}$

Domain: $x - 1 \neq 0$
$$x \neq 1$$
$$(-\infty, 1), (1, \infty)$$

Range: $-1, 1$

10. $y = \dfrac{1}{4}x^3$

A vertical line intersects the graph no more than once, so y is a function of x.

12. $x^2 + y^2 = 25$

A vertical line intersects the graph more than once, so y is not a function of x.

14. $x = |y + 2|$

A vertical line intersects the graph more than once, so y is not a function of x.

16. $f(x) = 3x^2 + 22x - 16$
$$0 = (3x - 2)(x + 8)$$
$$3x - 2 = 0 \Rightarrow x = \tfrac{2}{3}$$
$$x + 8 = 0 \Rightarrow x = -8$$

18. $f(x) = \dfrac{x^2 - 9x + 14}{4x}$
$$0 = \dfrac{x^2 - 9x + 14}{4x}$$
$$0 = (x - 7)(x - 2)$$
$$x - 7 = 0 \Rightarrow x = 7$$
$$x - 2 = 0 \Rightarrow x = 2$$

20. $f(x) = x^3 - 4x^2 - 9x + 36$
$$0 = x^3 - 4x^2 - 9x + 36$$
$$0 = x^2(x - 4) - 9(x - 4)$$
$$0 = (x - 4)(x^2 - 9)$$
$$x - 4 = 0 \Rightarrow x = 4$$
$$x^2 - 9 = 0 \Rightarrow x = \pm 3$$

22. $f(x) = 9x^4 - 25x^2$
$$0 = 9x^4 - 25x^2$$
$$0 = x^2(9x^2 - 25)$$
$$x^2 = 0 \Rightarrow x = 0$$
$$9x^2 - 25 = 0 \Rightarrow x = \pm\tfrac{5}{3}$$

24. $f(x) = x(x - 7)$
$$0 = x(x - 7)$$
$$x = 0$$
$$x - 7 = 0 \Rightarrow x = 7$$

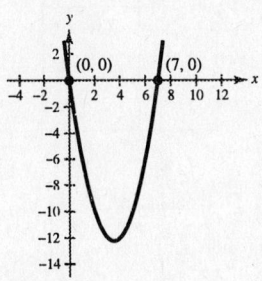

26. $f(x) = \sqrt{3x - 14} - 8$
$$0 = \sqrt{3x - 14} - 8$$
$$8 = \sqrt{3x - 14}$$
$$64 = 3x - 14$$
$$x = 26$$

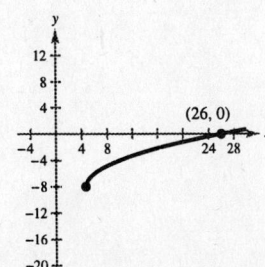

28. $f(x) = \dfrac{2x^2 - 9}{3 - x}$

$0 = \dfrac{2x^2 - 9}{3 - x}$

$2x^2 - 9 = 0 \Rightarrow x = \pm\dfrac{3\sqrt{2}}{2}$

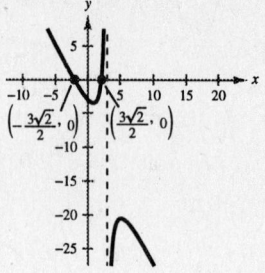

30. $f(x) = x^2 - 4x$

(a) The graph is decreasing on $(-\infty, 2)$ and increasing on $(2, \infty)$.

(b) $f(-x) = (-x)^2 - 4(-x) = x^2 + 4x$

$x^2 + 4x \neq f(x)$

$x^2 + 4x \neq -f(x)$

The function is neither odd nor even.

32. $f(x) = \sqrt{x^2 - 1}$

(a) The graph is decreasing on $(-\infty, -1)$ and increasing on $(1, \infty)$.

(b) $f(-x) = \sqrt{(-x)^2 - 1} = \sqrt{x^2 - 1} = f(x)$

The function is even.

34. $g(x) = x$

(a)

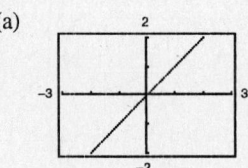

Increasing on $(-\infty, \infty)$

(b)

x	-2	-1	0	1	2
$g(x)$	-2	-1	0	1	2

36. $f(x) = -x - 10$

(a)

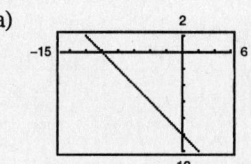

Decreasing on $(-\infty, \infty)$

(b)

x	-12	-8	-4	0	4
$f(x)$	2	-2	-6	-10	-14

38. $h(x) = x^2 - 4$

(a)

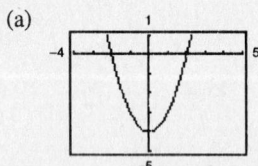

Decreasing on $(-\infty, 0)$

Increasing on $(0, \infty)$

(b)

x	-2	-1	0	1	2
$h(x)$	0	-3	-4	-3	0

40. $f(x) = 3x^4 - 6x^2$

(a)

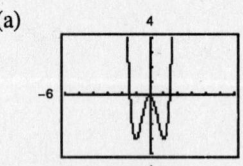

Increasing on $(-1, 0), (1, \infty)$

Decreasing on $(-\infty, -1), (0, 1)$

(b)

x	-2	-1	0	1	2
$f(x)$	24	-3	0	-3	24

42. $f(x) = x\sqrt{x + 3}$

(a)

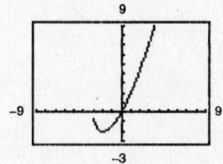

Increasing on $(-2, \infty)$

Decreasing on $(-3, -2)$

(b)

x	-3	-2	-1	0	1
$f(x)$	0	-2	-1.414	0	2

44. $f(x) = x^{3/2}$

(a)

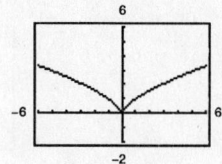

Decreasing on $(-\infty, 0)$

Increasing on $(0, \infty)$

(b)

x	-2	-1	0	1	2
$f(x)$	1.59	1	0	1	1.59

46. $f(x) = \sqrt[4]{x + 5}$

(a)

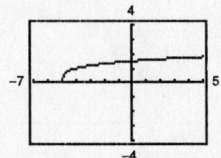

Increasing on $(-5, \infty)$

(b)

x	-5	-3	-1	1	3
$f(x)$	0	1.19	1.41	1.57	1.68

48. $f(x) = |x + 1| + |x - 1|$

(a)

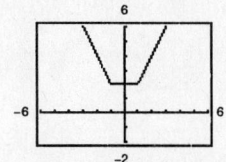

Decreasing on $(-\infty, -1)$

Constant on $(-1, 1)$

Increasing on $(1, \infty)$

(b)

x	-3	-2	-1	0	1	2	3
$f(x)$	6	4	2	2	2	4	6

50. $f(x) = \begin{cases} 2x + 1, & x \le -1 \\ x^2 - 2, & x > -1 \end{cases}$

(a)

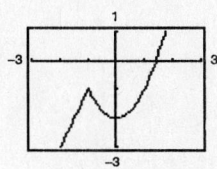

Increasing on $(-\infty, -1)$ and $(0, \infty)$

Decreasing on $(-1, 0)$

(b)

x	-2	-1	$-\frac{1}{2}$	0	1	2
$f(x)$	-3	-1	-1.75	-2	-1	2

52. $f(x) = 3x^2 - 2x - 5$

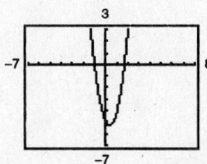

Relative minimum: $\left(\frac{1}{3}, -\frac{16}{3}\right)$

54. $f(x) = x^3 - 3x^2 - x + 1$

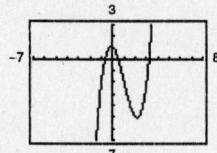

Relative maximum: $(-0.15, 1.08)$

Relative minimum: $(2.15, -5.08)$

56. $f(x) = 8x^4 - 3x - 1$

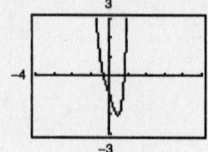

Relative minimum: $(-0.45, -2.02)$

58. $f(x) = 11 - 3x$

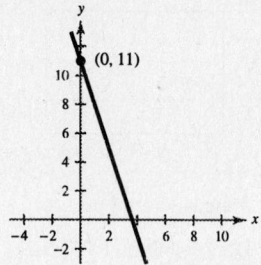

60. $f(x) = 3x - \frac{5}{2}$

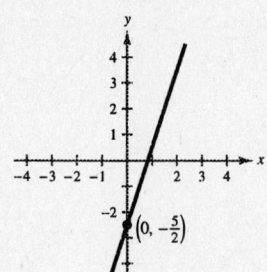

62. $f(x) = \frac{5}{6} - \frac{2}{3}x$

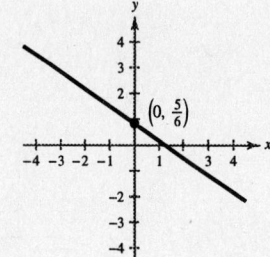

64. $f(x) = 10.2 + 3.1x$

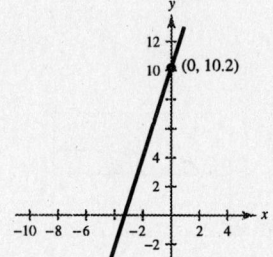

66. $f(-3) = -8, f(1) = 2$

$(-3, -8), (1, 2)$

$$m = \frac{2 - (-8)}{1 - (-3)} = \frac{10}{4} = \frac{5}{2}$$

$$f(x) - 2 = \frac{5}{2}(x - 1)$$

$$f(x) = \frac{5}{2}x - \frac{1}{2}$$

68. $f(3) = 9, f(-1) = -11$

$(3, 9), (-1, -11)$

$$m = \frac{-11 - 9}{-1 - 3} = \frac{-20}{-4} = 5$$

$$f(x) - 9 = 5(x - 3)$$

$$f(x) = 5x - 6$$

70. $f(-10) = 12, f(16) = -1$

$(-10, 12), (16, -1)$

$$m = \frac{-1 - 12}{16 - (-10)} = \frac{-13}{26} = -\frac{1}{2}$$

$$f(x) - (-1) = -\frac{1}{2}(x - 16)$$

$$f(x) = -\frac{1}{2}x + 7$$

72. $f\left(\dfrac{2}{3}\right) = -\dfrac{15}{2}, f(-4) = -11$

$\left(\dfrac{2}{3}, -\dfrac{15}{2}\right), (-4, -11)$

$$m = \dfrac{-11 - \left(-\dfrac{15}{2}\right)}{-4 - \dfrac{2}{3}} = \dfrac{-\dfrac{7}{2}}{-\dfrac{14}{3}} = \left(-\dfrac{7}{2}\right) \cdot \left(-\dfrac{3}{14}\right) = \dfrac{3}{4}$$

$f(x) - (-11) = \dfrac{3}{4}(x - (-4))$

$f(x) = \dfrac{3}{4}x - 8$

74.

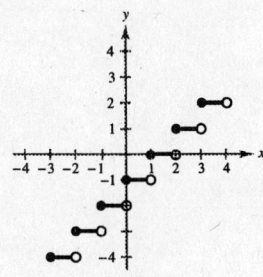

Shift 1 unit right

76. $f(x) = \begin{cases} \sqrt{4 + x}, & x < 0 \\ \sqrt{4 - x}, & x \geq 0 \end{cases}$

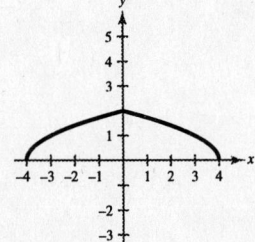

78. $f(x) = \begin{cases} 1 - (x - 1)^2, & x \leq 2 \\ \sqrt{x - 2}, & x > 2 \end{cases}$

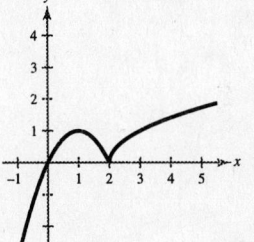

80. $f(x) = 4x + 2$

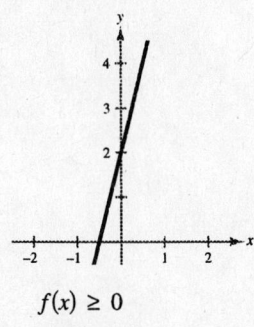

$f(x) \geq 0$

$4x + 2 \geq 0$

$4x \geq -2$

$x \geq -\dfrac{1}{2}$

$\left[-\dfrac{1}{2}, \infty\right)$

82. $f(x) = x^2 - 4x$

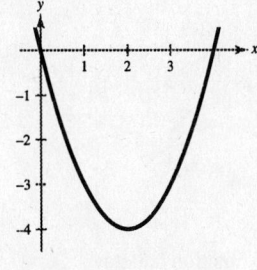

$f(x) \geq 0$

$x^2 - 4x \geq 0$

$x(x - 4) \geq 0$

$(-\infty, 0], [4, \infty)$

84. $f(x) = \sqrt{x + 2}$

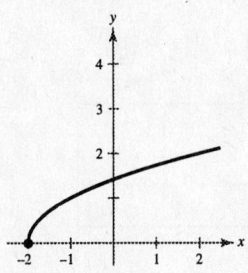

$f(x) \geq 0$

$\sqrt{x + 2} \geq 0$

$x + 2 \geq 0$

$x \geq -2$

$[-2, \infty)$

86. $f(x) = -(1 + |x|)$

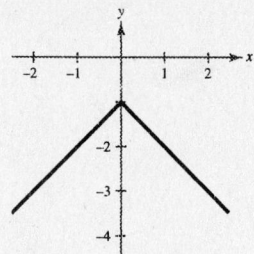

$f(x)$ is never greater than 0.
($f(x) < 0$ for all x.)

88. $f(x) = \frac{1}{2}(2 + |x|)$

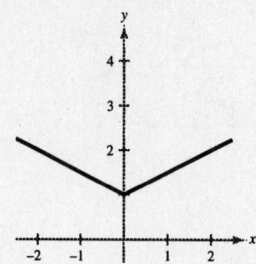

$f(x)$ is always greater than 0.
$(-\infty, \infty)$

90. $f(x) = \begin{cases} \sqrt{x-5}, & x > 5 \\ x^2 + x - 1, & x \le 5 \end{cases}$

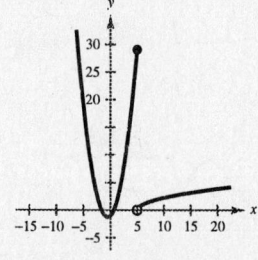

$$f(x) \ge 0$$
$$\sqrt{x - 5} \ge 0$$
$$x - 5 \ge 0$$
$$x \ge 5$$
$$x^2 + x - 1 \ge 0$$
$$x = \frac{-1 \pm \sqrt{1^2 - 4(1)(-1)}}{2(1)}$$
$$= \frac{-1 \pm \sqrt{5}}{2}$$
$$\left(-\infty, \frac{-1 - \sqrt{5}}{2}\right], \left[\frac{-1 + \sqrt{5}}{2}, \infty\right)$$

92. $g(x) = 2\left(\frac{1}{4}x - \left[\!\left[\frac{1}{4}x\right]\!\right]\right)^2$

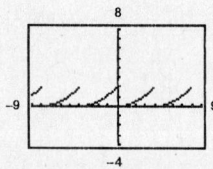

Domain: $(-\infty, \infty)$

Range: $(0, 2)$

Pattern: sawtooth

94. $h(x) = x^3 - 5$

$h(-x) = (-x)^3 - 5$

$\quad = -x^3 - 5$

$\quad \ne h(x)$

$\quad \ne -h(x)$

The function is neither odd nor even.

96. $f(x) = x\sqrt{1 - x^2}$

$f(-x) = -x\sqrt{1 - (-x)^2}$

$\quad = -x\sqrt{1 - x^2}$

$\quad = -f(x)$

The function is odd.

98. $g(s) = 4s^{2/3}$

$g(-s) = 4(-s)^{2/3}$

$\quad = 4s^{2/3}$

$\quad = g(s)$

The function is even.

100. $\left(-\frac{5}{3}, -7\right)$

(a) If f is even, another point is $\left(\frac{5}{3}, -7\right)$.

(b) If f is odd, another point is $\left(\frac{5}{3}, 7\right)$.

102. $(5, -1)$

(a) If f is even, another point is $(-5, -1)$.

(b) If f is odd, another point is $(-5, 1)$.

104. Model: (Total cost) = (Flat rate) + (Rate per pound)

Labels: Total cost = C

Flat rate = 9.80

Rate per pound = $2.50[\![x]\!]$, $x > 0$

Equation: $C = 9.80 + 2.50[\![x]\!]$, $x > 0$

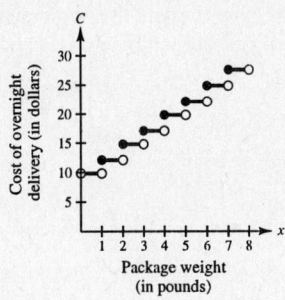

106. $h = \text{top} - \text{bottom}$

$= (-x^2 + 4x - 1) - 2$

$= -x^2 + 4x - 3$

108. $h = \text{top} - \text{bottom}$

$= (4x - x^2) - 2x$

$= 2x - x^2$

110. $L = \text{right} - \text{left}$

$= \frac{1}{2}y^2 - 0$

$= \frac{1}{2}y^2$

112. $L = \text{right} - \text{left}$

$= 4 - y^2$

114. (a) $1.47x^3 - 16.41x^2 + 31.24x - 95.20$

(b) Domain: $0 \le x \le 7$

(c)
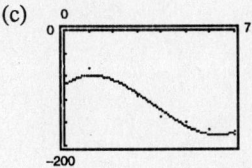

(d) Most accurate in 1992

Least accurate in 1991

116. (a) For the average salaries of college professors, a scale of $10,000 would be appropriate.

(b) For the population of the United States, use a scale of 50,000,000.

(c) For the percent of the civilian workforce that is unemployed, use a scale of 1%.

118. False. The function $f(x) = \sqrt{x^2 + 1}$ has a domain of all real numbers.

120. $f(x) = a_{2n+1}x^{2n+1} + a_{2n-1}x^{2n-1} + \cdots + a_3x^3 + a_1x$

$f(-x) = a_{2n+1}(-x)^{2n+1} + a_{2n-1}(-x)^{2n-1} + \cdots + a_3(-x)^3 + a_1(-x)$

$= -a_{2n+1}x^{2n+1} - a_{2n-1}x^{2n-1} - \cdots - a_3x^3 - a_1x = -f(x)$

Therefore, $f(x)$ is odd.

122. (a) Even. The graph is a reflection in the x-axis.

(b) Even. The graph is a reflection in the y-axis.

(c) Even. The graph is a vertical translation of f.

(d) Neither. The graph is a horizontal translation of f.

124. No, the graph in Exercise 12 does not represent x as a function of y because for some values of y there correspond more than one value of x.

126. The graph of $y = x^7$ will pass through the origin and will be symmetric with the origin.

The graph of $y = x^8$ will pass through the origin and will be symmetric with respect to the y-axis.

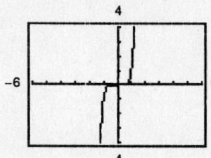   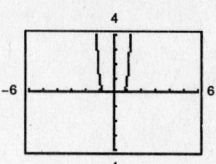

128. $100 - (x - 5)^2 = 0$

$(x - 5)^2 = 100$

$x - 5 = \pm 10$

$x - 5 = -10 \Rightarrow x = -5$

$x - 5 = 10 \Rightarrow x = 15$

130. $16x^2 - 40x + 25 = 0$

$(4x - 5)(4x - 5) = 0$

$4x - 5 = 0 \Rightarrow x = \frac{5}{4}$

132. $f(x) = x^2 - 10x$

(a) $f(4) = (4)^2 - 10(4) = 16 - 40 = -24$

(b) $f(-8) = (-8)^2 - 10(-8) = 64 + 80 = 144$

(c) $f(x - 4) = (x - 4)^2 - 10(x - 4) = x^2 - 8x + 16 - 10x + 40$

$\qquad = x^2 - 18x + 56$

134. $f(x) = x^4 - x - 5$

(a) $f(-1) = (-1)^4 - (-1) - 5 = 1 + 1 - 5 = -3$

(b) $f\left(\dfrac{1}{2}\right) = \left(\dfrac{1}{2}\right)^4 - \dfrac{1}{2} - 5 = -\dfrac{87}{16}$

(c) $f\left(2\sqrt{3}\right) = \left(2\sqrt{3}\right)^4 - 2\sqrt{3} - 5 = 16(9) - 2\sqrt{3} - 5 = 139 - 2\sqrt{3}$

136. $f(x) = 5 + 6x - x^2, \quad \dfrac{f(6 + h) - f(6)}{h}, h \neq 0$

$$\dfrac{f(6 + h) - f(6)}{h} = \dfrac{5 + 6(6 + h) - (6 + h)^2 - 5 - 6(6) + 6^2}{h}$$

$$= \dfrac{5 + 36 + 6h - 36 - 12h - h^2 - 5 - 36 + 36}{h}$$

$$= \dfrac{-h^2 - 6h}{h} = -h - 6, h \neq 0$$

Section 1.5   Shifting, Reflecting, and Stretching Graphs

Solutions to Even-Numbered Exercises

2. (a) $f(x) = |x| + c$

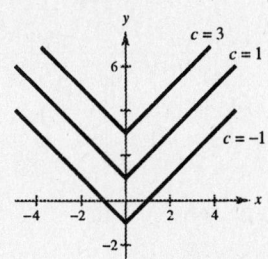

(b) $f(x) = |x - c|$

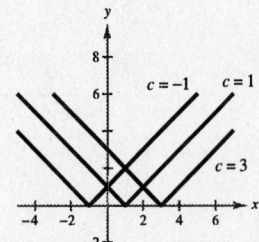

(c) $f(x) = |x + 4| + c$

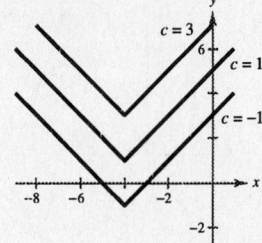

4. (a) $f(x) = \begin{cases} x^2 + c, & x < 0 \\ -x^2 + c, & x \geq 0 \end{cases}$

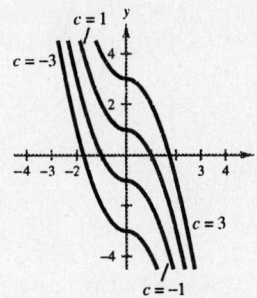

(b) $f(x) = \begin{cases} (x + c)^2, & x < 0 \\ -(x + c)^2, & x \geq 0 \end{cases}$

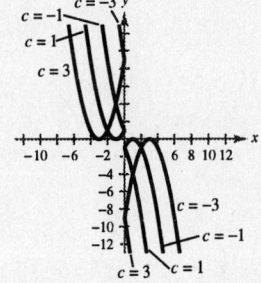

6. (a) $y = f(-x)$

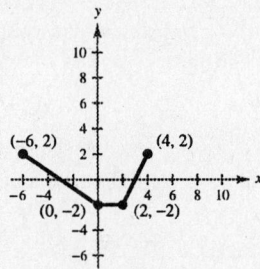

(b) $y = f(x) + 4$

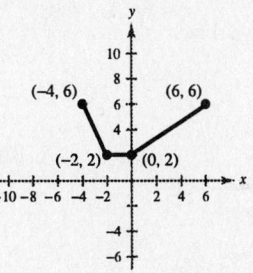

(c) $y = 2f(x)$

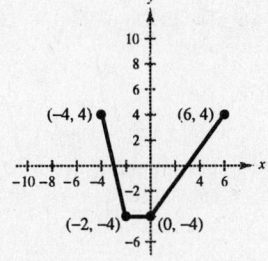

(d) $y = -f(x - 4)$

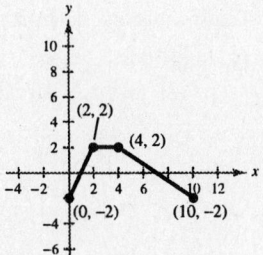

(e) $y = f(x) - 3$

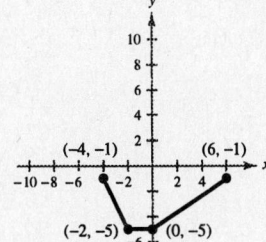

(f) $y = -f(x) - 1$

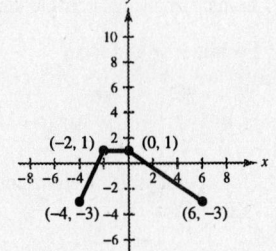

8. (a) $y = f(x - 5)$

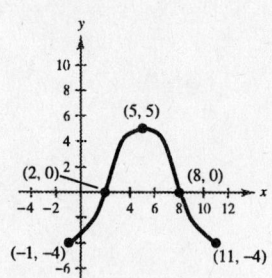

(b) $y = -f(x) + 3$

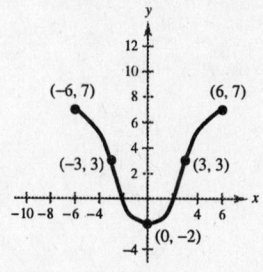

(c) $y = \frac{1}{3}f(x)$

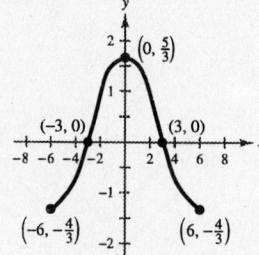

(d) $y = -f(x + 1)$

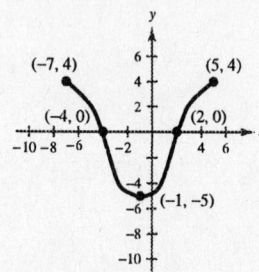

(e) $y = f(-x)$

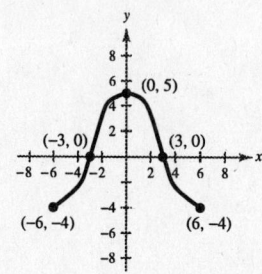

(f) $y = f(x) - 10$

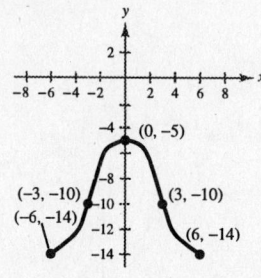

10. (a) The graph of $f(x) = x^3$ was reflected in the x-axis and shifted upward one unit.

$$y = -x^3 + 1 = 1 - x^3$$

(b) The graph of $f(x) = x^3$ was shifted to the right one unit and upward one unit.

$$y = (x - 1)^3 + 1$$

(c) The graph of $f(x) = x^3$ was reflected in the x-axis and shifted to the left three units and downward one unit.

$$y = -(x + 3)^3 - 1$$

(d) The graph of $f(x) = x^3$ was shifted to the right ten units and downward four units.

$$y = (x - 10)^3 - 4$$

12. (a) The graph of $f(x) = \sqrt{x}$ was shifted down three units.

$$y = \sqrt{x} - 3$$

(b) The graph of $f(x) = \sqrt{x}$ was shifted downward seven units and to the left one unit.

$$y = \sqrt{x + 1} - 7$$

(c) The graph of $f(x) = \sqrt{x}$ was reflected in the x-axis and shifted to the right five units and upward five units.

(d) The graph of $f(x) = \sqrt{x}$ was reflected about the x- and y-axis and shifted to the right three units and downward four units.

$$y = -\sqrt{-x + 3} - 4 = -\sqrt{-(x - 3)} - 4$$

14. Common function: $y = x$

Transformation: vertical shrink

Formula: $y = \frac{1}{2}x$

16. Common function: constant function

Formula: $y = 7$

18. Common function: $y = |x|$

Transformation: horizontal shift

Formula: $y = |x + 2|$

20. $f(x) = (x - 8)^2$

Horizontal shift of eight units to the right.

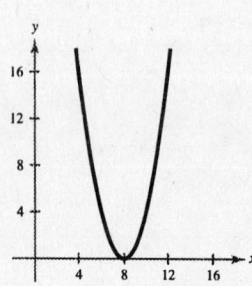

22. $f(x) = -x^3 - 1$

Reflection in the x-axis; vertical shift of one unit downward.

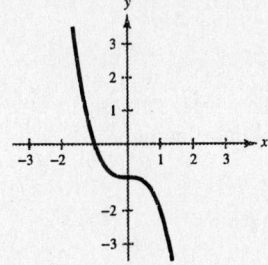

24. $f(x) = -(x + 10)^2 + 5$

Reflection in the x-axis; horizontal shift of 10 units to the left; vertical shift of 5 units upward.

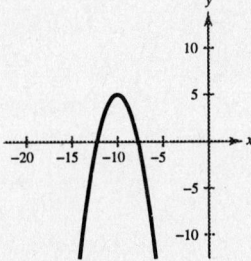

26. $f(x) = -(x + 3)^3 - 10$

Reflection in the x-axis; horizontal shift of 3 units to the left; vertical shift of 10 units downward.

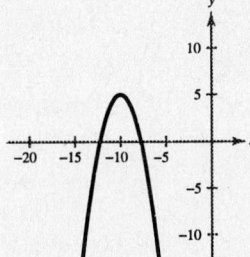

28. $f(x) = 6 - |x + 5|$

Reflection in the x-axis; horizontal shift of 5 units to the left; vertical shift of 6 units upward.

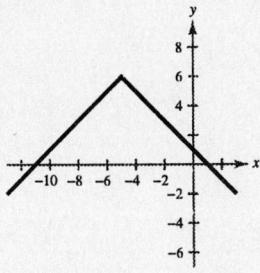

30. $f(x) = |-x + 3| + 9$

Reflection in the y-axis; horizontal shift of 3 units to the left; vertical shift of 9 units upward.

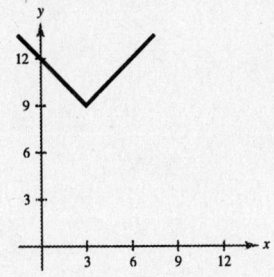

32. $f(x) = \sqrt{x + 4} + 8$

Horizontal shift of 4 units to the left; vertical shift of 8 units upward.

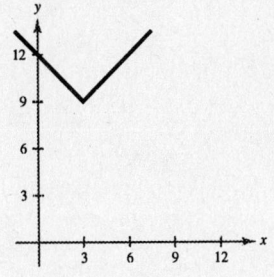

34. $f(x) = -\sqrt{x + 1} - 6$

Reflection in the x-axis; horizontal shift of 1 unit to the left; vertical shift of 6 units downward.

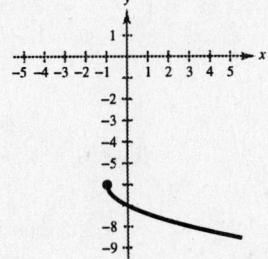

36. $f(x) = -(x + 3)^2 + 7$

38. $f(x) = (-x + 6)^3 - 6$

40. $f(x) = |x + 1| - 7$

42. $f(x) = -\sqrt{-x} - 9$

44. $f(x) = x^3$

  (a) Vertical shrink by a factor of $\frac{1}{4}$.

  $y = \frac{1}{4}x^3$

  (b) Reflection in the x-axis and a vertical stretch by a factor of 2.

  $y = -2x^3$

46. $f(x) = \sqrt{x}$

  (a) Vertical stretch by a factor of 8.

  $y = 8\sqrt{x}$

  (b) Reflection in the x-axis and a vertical shrink by a factor of $\frac{1}{4}$.

  $y = -\frac{1}{4}\sqrt{x}$

48. Common function: $f(x) = |x|$

Vertical stretch by a factor of 6.

$y = 6|x|$

50. Common function: $f(x) = \sqrt{x}$

Vertical stretch by a factor of 3.

$y = 3\sqrt{x}$

52. Common function: $f(x) = |x|$

Reflection in the x-axis; vertical shift of 2 units downward; vertical stretch by a factor of 2.

$y = -2|x| - 2$

54. The graph of $y = |x|$ has a horizontal shift of 4 units to the left and a vertical shift of 2 units downward.

$y = |x + 4| - 2$

56. The graph of $y = x^2$ has a horizontal shift of 2 units to the right and a vertical shift of 4 units upward.

$y = (x - 2)^2 + 4$

58. (a) $g(x) = f(x) - 5$

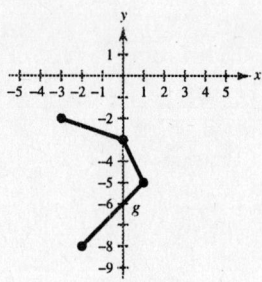

(b) $g(x) = f(x) + \frac{1}{2}$

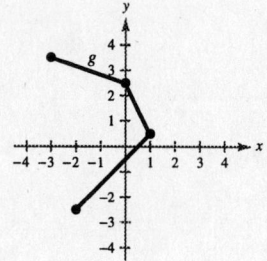

(c) $g(x) = f(-x)$

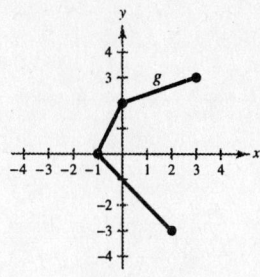

(d) $g(x) = -4f(x)$

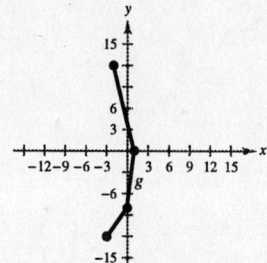

60. (a) The graph of $f(t) = \sqrt{t}$ has a vertical stretch by a factor of 1.5 and a vertical shift of 1.25 units downward.

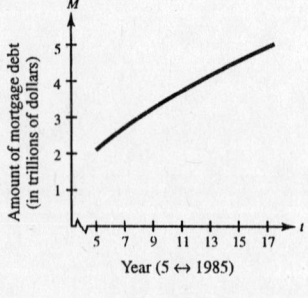

(b) $f(t) = 1.5\sqrt{t + 10} - 1.25$

By shifting the graph 10 units to the left, you obtain $t = 5$ representing 1995.

62. False. The point $(-2, -61)$ lies on the transformation.

64. If you consider the x-axis to be a mirror, the graph of $y = -f(x)$ is the mirror image of the graph of $y = f(x)$.

66. Answers will vary.

68. $\dfrac{2}{x+5} - \dfrac{2}{x-5}$

$$\frac{2}{x+5} - \frac{2}{x-5} = \frac{2(x-5) - 2(x+5)}{(x+5)(x-5)} = \frac{2x - 10 - 2x - 10}{(x+5)(x-5)} = \frac{-20}{(x+5)(x-5)}$$

70. $\dfrac{x}{x-5} + \dfrac{1}{2}$

$$\frac{x}{x-5} + \frac{1}{2} = \frac{2x + x - 5}{2(x-5)} = \frac{3x - 5}{2(x-5)}$$

72. $\left(\dfrac{x}{x^2-4}\right)\left(\dfrac{x^2 - x - 2}{x^2}\right)$

$$\left(\frac{x}{x^2-4}\right)\left(\frac{x^2 - x - 2}{x^2}\right) = \frac{x(x-2)(x+1)}{x^2(x-2)(x+2)} = \frac{x+1}{x(x+2)}, x \neq 2$$

74. $\left(\dfrac{x}{x^2 - 3x - 28}\right) \div \left(\dfrac{x^2 + 3x}{x^2 + 5x + 4}\right)$

$$\left(\frac{x}{x^2 - 3x - 28}\right) \div \left(\frac{x^2 + 3x}{x^2 + 5x + 4}\right) = \left(\frac{x}{x^2 - 3x - 28}\right) \cdot \left(\frac{x^2 + 5x + 4}{x^2 + 3x}\right)$$

$$= \frac{x(x+4)(x+1)}{(x-7)(x+4)x(x+3)} = \frac{x+1}{(x-7)(x+3)}, x \neq -4, -1, 0$$

76. $f(x) = \sqrt{x + 10} - 3$

(a) $f(-10) = \sqrt{-10 + 10} - 3 = -3$

(b) $f(26) = \sqrt{26 + 10} - 3 = \sqrt{36} - 3 = 3$

(c) $f(x - 10) = \sqrt{x - 10 + 10} - 3 = \sqrt{x} - 3$

78. $f(x) = \dfrac{\sqrt{x-3}}{x-8}$

Domain: $x \geq 3, x \neq 8$

80. $f(x) = \sqrt[3]{4 - x^2}$

Domain: All real numbers

Section 1.6   Combinations of Functions

Solutions to Even-Numbered Exercises

2.

x	-2	-1	0	1	2
$f(x)$	-2	0	-1	-1	1
$g(x)$	1	1	0	2	2
$h(x) = (f + g)(x)$	-1	1	-1	1	3

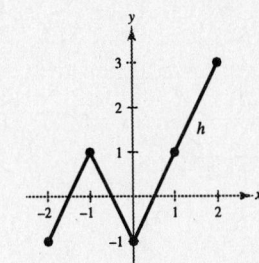

4.

x	0	1	2	3	4
$f(x)$	2	2	2	2	2
$g(x)$	0	1	$\sqrt{2}$	$\sqrt{3}$	2
$h(x) = (f+g)(x)$	2	3	$2+\sqrt{2}$	$2+\sqrt{3}$	4

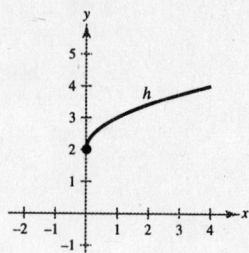

6. $f(x) = 2x - 5, \; g(x) = 2 - x$

(a) $(f+g)(x) = 2x - 5 + 2 - x$

$\qquad = x - 3$

(b) $(f-g)(x) = 2x - 5 - (2-x)$

$\qquad = 2x - 5 - 2 + x$

$\qquad = 3x - 7$

(c) $(fg)(x) = (2x-5)(2-x)$

$\qquad = 4x - 2x^2 - 10 + 5x$

$\qquad = -2x^2 + 9x - 10$

(d) $\left(\dfrac{f}{g}\right)(x) = \dfrac{2x-5}{2-x}$

Domain: $2 - x \neq 0$

$\qquad\qquad x \neq 2$

8. $f(x) = 2x - 5, \; g(x) = 4$

(a) $(f+g)(x) = 2x - 5 + 4 = 2x - 1$

(b) $(f-g)(x) = 2x - 5 - 4 = 2x - 9$

(c) $(fg)(x) = (2x-5)(4) = 8x - 20$

(d) $\left(\dfrac{f}{g}\right)(x) = \dfrac{2x-5}{4} = \dfrac{1}{2}x - \dfrac{5}{4}$

Domain: $-\infty < x < \infty$

10. $f(x) = \sqrt{x^2 - 4}, \; g(x) = \dfrac{x^2}{x^2 + 1}$

(a) $(f+g)(x) = \sqrt{x^2 - 4} + \dfrac{x^2}{x^2 + 1}$

(b) $(f-g)(x) = \sqrt{x^2 - 4} - \dfrac{x^2}{x^2 + 1}$

(c) $(fg)(x) = \sqrt{x^2 - 4}\left(\dfrac{x^2}{x^2 + 1}\right)$

$\qquad = \dfrac{x^2\sqrt{x^2 - 4}}{x^2 + 1}$

(d) $\left(\dfrac{f}{g}\right)(x) = \sqrt{x^2 - 4} \div \dfrac{x^2}{x^2 + 1}$

$\qquad = \dfrac{(x^2 + 1)\sqrt{x^2 - 4}}{x^2}$

Domain: $x^2 - 4 \geq 0$

$\qquad\qquad x^2 \geq 4 \Rightarrow x \geq 2 \text{ or } x \leq -2$

Domain: $|x| \geq 2$

12. $f(x) = \dfrac{x}{x+1}, \; g(x) = x^3$

(a) $(f+g)(x) = \dfrac{x}{x+1} + x^3 = \dfrac{x + x^4 + x^3}{x + 1}$

(b) $(f-g)(x) = \dfrac{x}{x+1} - x^3 = \dfrac{x - x^4 - x^3}{x + 1}$

(c) $(fg)(x) = \dfrac{x}{x+1} \cdot x^3 = \dfrac{x^4}{x+1}$

(d) $\left(\dfrac{f}{g}\right)(x) = \dfrac{x}{x+1} \div x^3$

$\qquad = \dfrac{x}{x+1} \cdot \dfrac{1}{x^3} = \dfrac{1}{x^2(x+1)}$

Domain: $x \neq 0, -1$

14. $(f - g)(-1) = f(-1) - g(-1)$

$$= (-1)^2 + 1 - (-1 - 4)$$

$$= 1 + 1 - (-5)$$

$$= 7$$

16. $(f + g)(1) = f(1) + g(1)$

$$= (1)^2 + 1 + (1) - 4$$

$$= -1$$

18. $(f + g)(t - 2) = f(t - 2) + g(t - 2)$

$$= (t - 2)^2 + 1 + (t - 2) - 4$$

$$= t^2 - 4t + 4 + 1 + t - 2 - 4$$

$$= t^2 - 3t - 1$$

20. $(fg)(-6) = f(-6) \cdot g(-6)$

$$= [(-6)^2 + 1][(-6) - 4]$$

$$= (37)(-10)$$

$$= -370$$

22. $\left(\dfrac{f}{g}\right)(0) = \dfrac{f(0)}{g(0)} = \dfrac{0^2 + 1}{0 - 4} = -\dfrac{1}{4}$

24. $(2f)(5) = 2 \cdot f(5) = 2(5^2 + 1) = 52$

26. $f(x) = \frac{1}{3}x$, $g(x) = -x + 4$

$(f + g)(x) = \frac{1}{3}x - x + 4 = -\frac{2}{3}x + 4$

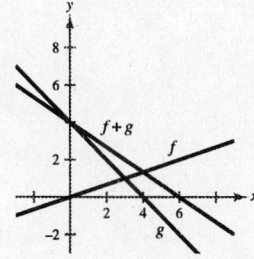

28. $f(x) = 4 - x^2$, $g(x) = x$

$(f + g)(x) = 4 - x^2 + x = 4 + x - x^2$

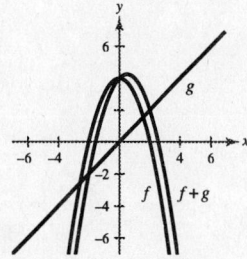

30. $f(x) = \dfrac{x}{2}$, $g(x) = \sqrt{x}$

$(f + g)(x) = \dfrac{x}{2} + \sqrt{x}$

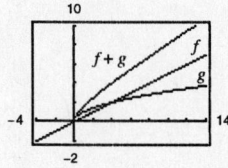

$g(x)$ contributes most to the magnitude of the sum for $0 \le x \le 2$. $f(x)$ contributes most to the magnitude of the sum for $x > 6$.

32. Total sales $= R_1 + R_2$

$$= 480 - 8t - 0.8t^2 + 254 + 0.78t$$

$$= 734 - 7.22t - 0.8t^2$$

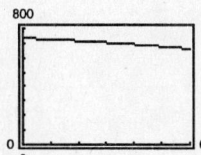

34. $y_1 = -0.59x^2 + 7.66x + 144.90$

$y_2 = 16.58x + 245.06$

$y_3 = 1.85x + 21.88$

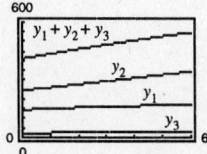

The total amount spent on health services and supplies in 2000 was \$613.74 billion.

36. From 0 to 6, $T(t) = 60$.
From 6 to 6.5, $T(t)$ goes from 60 to 72.

$$T(t) - 60 = \frac{72 - 60}{6.5 - 6}(t - 6)$$

$$T(t) - 60 = 24t - 144$$

$$T(t) = 24t - 84$$

From 6.5 to 20.5, $T(t) = 72$.
From 20.5 to 21, $T(t)$ goes from 72 to 60.

$$T(t) - 60 = \frac{72 - 60}{20.5 - 21}(t - 21)$$

$$T(t) - 60 = -24(t - 21)$$

$$T(t) = -24t + 564$$

From 21 to 24, $T(t) = 60$.

$$T(t) = \begin{cases} 60, & 0 \le t \le 6 \\ 24t - 84, & 6 < t < 6.5 \\ 72, & 6.5 \le t \le 20.5 \\ -24t + 564, & 20.5 < t < 21 \\ 60, & 21 \le t \le 24 \end{cases}$$

38. $f(x) = \sqrt[3]{x - 1}$, $g(x) = x^3 + 1$

(a) $(f \circ g)(x) = f(g(x))$

$$= f(x^3 + 1)$$

$$= \sqrt[3]{(x^3 + 1) - 1}$$

$$= \sqrt[3]{x^3} = x$$

(b) $(g \circ f)(x) = g(f(x))$

$$= g(\sqrt[3]{x - 1})$$

$$= (\sqrt[3]{x - 1})^3 + 1$$

$$= (x - 1) + 1 = x$$

(c) $(f \circ f)(x) = f(f(x))$

$$= f(\sqrt[3]{x - 1})$$

$$= \sqrt[3]{\sqrt[3]{x - 1} - 1}$$

40. $f(x) = x^3$, $g(x) = \dfrac{1}{x}$

(a) $(f \circ g)(x) = f(g(x))$

$$= f\left(\frac{1}{x}\right)$$

$$= \left(\frac{1}{x}\right)^3 = \frac{1}{x^3}$$

(b) $(g \circ f)(x) = g(f(x))$

$$= g(x^3)$$

$$= \frac{1}{x^3}$$

(c) $(f \circ f)(x) = f(f(x))$

$$= f(x^3)$$

$$= (x^3)^3 = x^9$$

42. $f(x) = \sqrt[3]{x - 5}$, $g(x) = x^3 + 1$

(a) $(f \circ g)(x) = f(g(x))$

$$= f(x^3 + 1)$$

$$= \sqrt[3]{x^3 + 1 - 5}$$

$$= \sqrt[3]{x^3 - 4}$$

(b) $(g \circ f)(x) = g(f(x))$

$$= g(\sqrt[3]{x - 5})$$

$$= (\sqrt[3]{x - 5})^3 + 1$$

$$= x - 5 + 1 = x - 4$$

Domain of $f, g, f \circ g, g \circ f$: all real numbers

44. $f(x) = x^2 + 1$, $g(x) = \sqrt{x}$

(a) $(f \circ g)(x) = f(g(x))$

$$= f(\sqrt{x})$$

$$= (\sqrt{x})^2 + 1$$

$$= x + 1$$

(b) $(g \circ f)(x) = g(f(x))$

$$= g(x^2 + 1)$$

$$= \sqrt{x^2 + 1}$$

Domain of $f, g \circ f$: all real numbers

Domain of $g, f \circ g$: $x \ge 0$

46. $f(x) = \sqrt{x}, g(x) = 2x - 3$

(a) $(f \circ g)(x) = f(g(x))$

$\qquad = f(2x - 3)$

$\qquad = \sqrt{2x - 3}$

Domain of $f, g \circ f$: $x \geq 0$

Domain of g: all real numbers

Domain of $f \circ g$: $x \geq \frac{3}{2}$

(b) $(g \circ f)(x) = g(f(x))$

$\qquad = g(\sqrt{x})$

$\qquad = 2\sqrt{x} - 3$

48. $f(x) = x^{2/3}, \; g(x) = x^6$

(a) $(f \circ g)(x) = f(g(x))$

$\qquad = f(x^6)$

$\qquad = (x^6)^{2/3} = x^4$

Domain of $f, g, f \circ g, g \circ f$: all real numbers

(b) $(g \circ f)(x) = g(f(x))$

$\qquad = g(x^{2/3})$

$\qquad = (x^{2/3})^6 = x^4$

50. $f(x) = \dfrac{3}{x^2 - 1}, g(x) = x + 1$

(a) $(f \circ g)(x) = f(g(x))$

$\qquad = f(x + 1)$

$\qquad = \dfrac{3}{(x + 1)^2 - 1}$

$\qquad = \dfrac{3}{x^2 + 2x + 1 - 1}$

$\qquad = \dfrac{3}{x^2 + 2x}$

Domain of $f, g \circ f$: all real numbers $x \neq \pm 1$

Domain of g: all real numbers

Domain of $f \circ g$: all real numbers $x \neq 0, -2$

(b) $(g \circ f)(x) = g(f(x))$

$\qquad = g\left(\dfrac{3}{x^2 - 1}\right)$

$\qquad = \dfrac{3}{x^2 - 1} + 1$

$\qquad = \dfrac{3 + x^2 - 1}{x^2 - 1}$

$\qquad = \dfrac{x^2 + 2}{x^2 - 1}$

52. (a) $(f - g)(1) = f(1) - g(1)$

$\qquad = 2 - 3 = -1$

(b) $(fg)(4) = f(4) \cdot g(4) = 0$

$\qquad = 4 \cdot 0 = 0$

54. (a) $(f \circ g)(1) = f(g(1))$

$\qquad = f(3) = 2$

(b) $(g \circ f)(3) = g(f(3))$

$\qquad = g(2) = 2$

56. $h(x) = (1 - x)^3$

One possibility: Let $g(x) = 1 - x$ and $f(x) = x^3$.

$(f \circ g)(x) = f(1 - x) = (1 - x)^3 = h(x)$

58. $h(x) = \sqrt{9 - x}$

One possibility: Let $g(x) = 9 - x$ and $f(x) = \sqrt{x}$.

$(f \circ g)(x) = f(9 - x) = \sqrt{9 - x} = h(x)$

60. $h(x) = \dfrac{4}{(5x + 2)^2}$

One possibility: Let $g(x) = 5x + 2$ and $f(x) = \dfrac{4}{x^2}$.

$(f \circ g)(x) = f(5x + 2) = \dfrac{4}{(5x + 2)^2} = h(x)$

62. $h(x) = \dfrac{27x^3 + 6x}{10 - 27x^3}$

One possibility: Let $g(x) = x^3$ and $f(x) = \dfrac{27x + 6\sqrt[3]{x}}{10 - 27x}$.

$(f \circ g)(x) = f(x^3) = \dfrac{27x^3 + 6\sqrt[3]{x^3}}{10 - 27x^3} = h(x)$

64. $(A \circ r)(t) = A(r(t)) = A(0.6t) = \pi(0.6t)^2 = 0.36\pi t^2$

$A \circ r$ represents the area of the circle at time t.

66. False. $(f \circ g)(x) = 6x + 1$ and $(g \circ f)(x) = 6x + 6$.

68. (a) $f(g(x)) = f(0.03x) = 0.03x - 500{,}000$

(b) $g(f(x)) = g(x - 500{,}000) = 0.03(x - 500{,}000)$

$g(f(x))$ represents 3% of an amount over \$500,000.

70. Let $f(x)$ be an odd function, $g(x)$ be an even function and define $h(x) = f(x)g(x)$. Then

$h(-x) = f(-x)g(-x)$

$\quad = [-f(x)]g(x) \qquad$ Since f is odd and g is even.

$\quad = -f(x)g(x)$

$\quad = -h(x)$

Thus, h is odd.

72.
$$f(x) = 1 - x^2$$
$$f(x + h) = 1 - (x + h)^2$$
$$= 1 - (x^2 + 2hx + h^2)$$
$$= 1 - x^2 - 2hx - h^2$$
$$\frac{f(x + h) - f(x)}{h} = \frac{1 - x^2 - 2hx - h^2 - (1 - x^2)}{h}$$
$$= \frac{-2hx - h^2}{h} = -2x - h$$

74.
$$f(x) = \sqrt{2x + 1}$$
$$f(x + h) = \sqrt{2(x + h) + 1}$$
$$\frac{f(x + h) - f(x)}{h} = \frac{\sqrt{2(x + h) + 1} - \sqrt{2x + 1}}{h}$$
$$= \frac{\sqrt{2(x + h) + 1} - \sqrt{2x + 1}}{h} \cdot \frac{\sqrt{2(x + h) + 1} + \sqrt{2x + 1}}{\sqrt{2(x + h) + 1} + \sqrt{2x + 1}}$$
$$= \frac{[2(x + h) + 1] - (2x + 1)}{h(\sqrt{2(x + h) + 1} + \sqrt{2x + 1})}$$
$$= \frac{2x + 2h + 1 - 2x - 1}{h(\sqrt{2(x + h) + 1} + \sqrt{2x + 1})}$$
$$= \frac{2}{(\sqrt{2(x + h) + 1} + \sqrt{2x + 1})}$$

76. $(-6, 3), m = -1$

$\qquad y - 3 = (-1)(x - (-6))$

$\qquad y - 3 = -x - 6$

$\qquad x + y + 3 = 0$

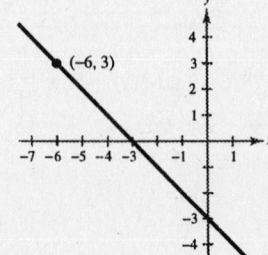

78. $(7, 0), m = \frac{5}{7}$

$\qquad y - 0 = \frac{5}{7}(x - 7)$

$\qquad 7y = 5x - 35$

$\qquad 5x - 7y - 35 = 0$

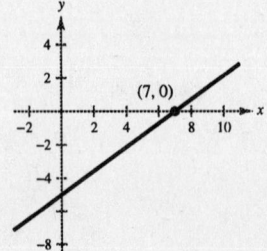

Section 1.7   Inverse Functions

Solutions to Even-Numbered Exercises

2. The inverse is a line through $(0, 6)$ and $(6, 0)$. Matches graph (b).

4. The inverse is a third-degree equation through $(0, 0)$. Matches graph (d).

6.
$$f(x) = \tfrac{1}{3}x$$
$$f^{-1}(x) = 3x$$
$$f(f^{-1}(x)) = f(3x) = \tfrac{1}{3}(3x) = x$$
$$f^{-1}(f(x)) = f^{-1}(\tfrac{1}{3}x) = 3(\tfrac{1}{3}x) = x$$

8.
$$f(x) = x - 4$$
$$f^{-1}(x) = x + 4$$
$$f(f^{-1}(x)) = f(x + 4) = x + 4 - 4 = x$$
$$f^{-1}(f(x)) = f^{-1}(x - 4) = x - 4 + 4 = x$$

10.
$$f(x) = \frac{x - 1}{5}$$
$$f^{-1}(x) = 5x + 1$$
$$f(f^{-1}(x)) = f(5x + 1) = \frac{5x + 1 - 1}{5} = \frac{5x}{5} = x$$
$$f^{-1}(f(x)) = f^{-1}\left(\frac{x - 1}{5}\right) = 5\left(\frac{x - 1}{5}\right) + 1 = x - 1 + 1 = x$$

12.
$$f(x) = x^5$$
$$f^{-1}(x) = \sqrt[5]{x}$$
$$f(f^{-1}(x)) = f(\sqrt[5]{x}) = (\sqrt[5]{x})^5 = x$$
$$f^{-1}(f(x)) = f^{-1}(x^5) = \sqrt[5]{x^5} = x$$

14. (a) $f(x) = x - 5, \; g(x) = x + 5$
$$f(g(x)) = f(x + 5) = (x + 5) - 5 = x$$
$$g(f(x)) = g(x - 5) = (x - 5) + 5 = x$$

(b)

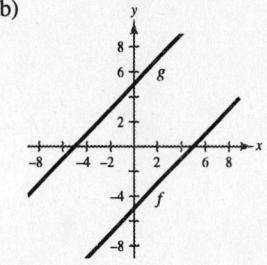

16. (a) $f(x) = 3 - 4x, \; g(x) = \dfrac{3 - x}{4}$
$$f(g(x)) = f\left(\frac{3 - x}{4}\right) = 3 - 4\left(\frac{3 - x}{4}\right) = 3 - (3 - x) = x$$
$$g(f(x)) = g(3 - 4x) = \frac{3 - (3 - 4x)}{4} = \frac{4x}{4} = x$$

(b)

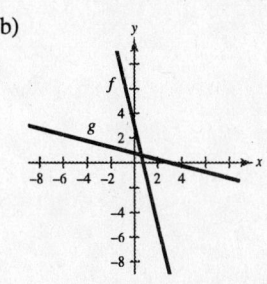

18. (a) $f(x) = \dfrac{1}{x}, \; g(x) = \dfrac{1}{x}$

(b)

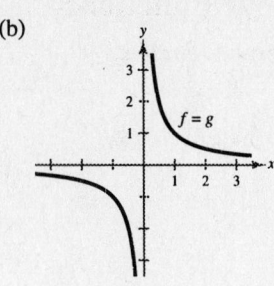

$$f(g(x)) = f\left(\frac{1}{x}\right) = \frac{1}{\dfrac{1}{x}} = 1 \div \frac{1}{x} = 1 \cdot \frac{x}{1} = x$$

$$g(f(x)) = g\left(\frac{1}{x}\right) = \frac{1}{\dfrac{1}{x}} = 1 \div \frac{1}{x} = 1 \cdot \frac{x}{1} = x$$

20. (a) $f(x) = 1 - x^3, \; g(x) = \sqrt[3]{1 - x}$

(b)

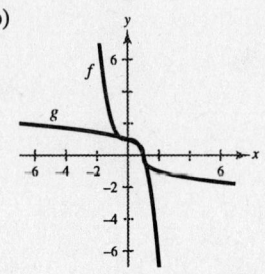

$$f(g(x)) = f\left(\sqrt[3]{1-x}\right) = 1 - \left(\sqrt[3]{1-x}\right)^3 = 1 - (1 - x) = x$$

$$g(f(x)) = g(1 - x^3) = \sqrt[3]{1 - (1 - x^3)} = \sqrt[3]{x^3} = x$$

22. (a) $f(x) = \dfrac{1}{1 + x}, \; x \ge 0; \; g(x) = \dfrac{1 - x}{x}, \; 0 < x \le 1$

$$f(g(x)) = f\left(\frac{1-x}{x}\right) = \frac{1}{1 + \left(\dfrac{1-x}{x}\right)} = \frac{1}{\dfrac{x}{x} + \dfrac{1-x}{x}} = \frac{1}{\dfrac{1}{x}} = x$$

$$g(f(x)) = g\left(\frac{1}{1+x}\right) = \frac{1 - \left(\dfrac{1}{1+x}\right)}{\left(\dfrac{1}{1+x}\right)} = \frac{\dfrac{1+x}{1+x} - \dfrac{1}{1+x}}{\dfrac{1}{1+x}} = \frac{\dfrac{x}{1+x}}{\dfrac{1}{1+x}} = \frac{x}{1+x} \cdot \frac{x+1}{1} = x$$

(b)

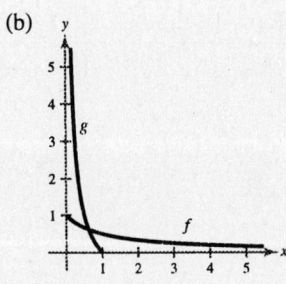

24. (a) $f(x) = \dfrac{x+3}{x-2}, g(x) = \dfrac{2x+3}{x-1}$

$$f(g(x)) = f\left(\frac{2x+3}{x-1}\right) = \frac{\dfrac{2x+3}{x-1} + 3}{\dfrac{2x+3}{x-1} - 2} = \frac{\dfrac{2x+3+3x-3}{x-1}}{\dfrac{2x+3-2x+2}{x-1}}$$

$$= \frac{5x}{5} = x$$

$$g(f(x)) = g\left(\frac{x+3}{x-2}\right) = \frac{2\left(\dfrac{x+3}{x-2}\right) + 3}{\dfrac{x+3}{x-2} - 1}$$

$$= \frac{\dfrac{2x+6+3x-6}{x-2}}{\dfrac{x+3-x+2}{x-2}} = \frac{5x}{5} = x$$

(b)

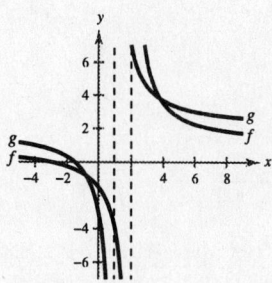

26. Yes, $\{(-3, 10), (-2, 6), (-1, 4), (0, 1), (2, -3),$
$(2, -10)\}$ does represent a function.

28.

x	-10	-7	-4	-1	2	5
$f^{-1}(x)$	-3	-2	-1	0	1	2

30. No, because some horizontal lines intersect the graph twice, f does not have an inverse.

32. Yes, because no horizontal lines intersect the graph at more than one point, f has an inverse.

34. $f(x) = 10$

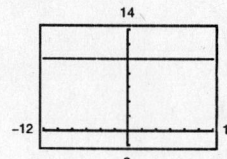

f does not pass the horizontal line test, so f has no inverse.

36. $g(x) = (x + 5)^3$

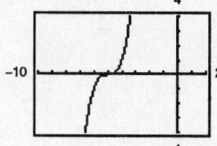

g passes the horizontal line test, so g has an inverse.

38. $f(x) = \frac{1}{8}(x + 2)^2 - 1$

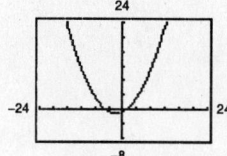

f does not pass the horizontal line test, so f has no inverse.

40. $f(x) = 3x + 1$
$$y = 3x + 1$$
$$x = 3y + 1$$
$$\frac{x-1}{3} = y$$
$$f^{-1}(x) = \frac{x-1}{3}$$

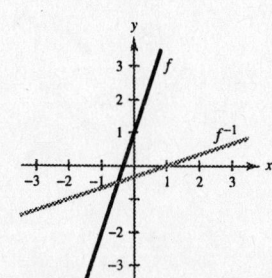

42. $f(x) = x^3 + 1$
$$y = x^3 + 1$$
$$x = y^3 + 1$$
$$x - 1 = y^3$$
$$\sqrt[3]{x-1} = y$$
$$f^{-1}(x) = \sqrt[3]{x-1}$$

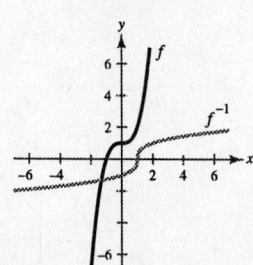

44. $f(x) = x^2,\ x \geq 0$
$$y = x^2$$
$$x = y^2$$
$$\sqrt{x} = y$$
$$f^{-1}(x) = \sqrt{x}$$

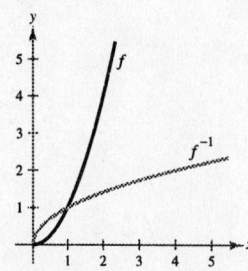

46.
$$f(x) = x^2 - 2, x \le 0$$
$$y = x^2 - 2$$
$$x = y^2 - 2$$
$$\pm\sqrt{x + 2} = y$$
$$f^{-1}(x) = -\sqrt{x + 2}$$

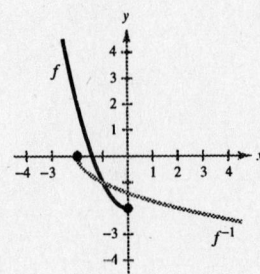

48. $f(x) = -\dfrac{2}{x}$

$$y = -\dfrac{2}{x}$$
$$x = -\dfrac{2}{y}$$
$$y = -\dfrac{2}{x}$$
$$f^{-1}(x) = -\dfrac{2}{x}$$

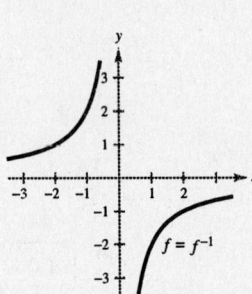

50.
$$f(x) = \dfrac{x - 3}{x + 2}$$
$$y = \dfrac{x - 3}{x + 2}$$
$$x = \dfrac{y - 3}{y + 2}$$
$$xy + 2x - y + 3 = 0$$
$$y(x - 1) = -2x - 3$$
$$y = \dfrac{-2x - 3}{x - 1}$$
$$f^{-1}(x) = \dfrac{-2x - 3}{x - 1}$$

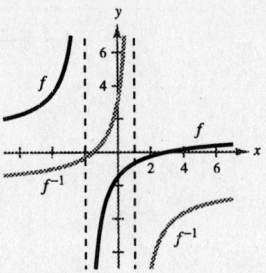

52. $f(x) = x^{3/5}$
$$y = x^{3/5}$$
$$x = y^{3/5}$$
$$x^{5/3} = (y^{3/5})^{5/3}$$
$$x^{5/3} = y$$
$$f^{-1}(x) = x^{5/3}$$

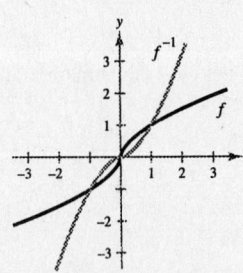

54.
$$f(x) = \dfrac{8x - 4}{2x + 6}$$
$$y = \dfrac{8x - 4}{2x + 6}$$
$$x = \dfrac{8y - 4}{2y + 6}$$
$$2xy + 6x = 8y - 4$$
$$y(2x - 8) = -6x - 4$$
$$y = \dfrac{-6x - 4}{2x - 8}$$

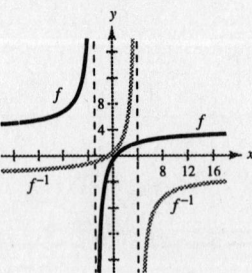

56. $f(x) = \dfrac{1}{x^2}$

$$y = \dfrac{1}{x^2}$$
$$x = \dfrac{1}{y^2}$$
$$y^2 = \dfrac{1}{x}$$
$$y = \pm\sqrt{\dfrac{1}{x}}$$

This does not represent y as a function of x. f does not have an inverse.

58. $f(x) = 3x + 5$

$y = 3x + 5$

$x = 3y + 5$

$x - 5 = 3y$

$\dfrac{x - 5}{3} = y$

This is a function of x, so f has an inverse.

$f^{-1}(x) = \dfrac{x - 5}{3}$

60. $f(x) = \dfrac{3x + 4}{5}$

$y = \dfrac{3x + 4}{5}$

$x = \dfrac{3y + 4}{5}$

$5x = 3y + 4$

$5x - 4 = 3y$

$\dfrac{5x - 4}{3} = y$

This is a function of x, so f has an inverse.

$f^{-1}(x) = \dfrac{5x - 4}{3}$

62. $q(x) = (x - 5)^2$

$y = (x - 5)^2$

$x = (y - 5)^2$

$\pm\sqrt{x} = y - 5$

$5 \pm \sqrt{x} = y$

This does not represent y as a function of x, so q does not have an inverse.

64. $f(x) = \begin{cases} -x, & x \le 0 \\ x^2 - 3x, & x > 0 \end{cases}$

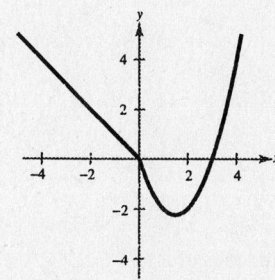

The graph fails the horizontal line test, so f does not have an inverse.

66. $f(x) = |x - 2|, \ x \le 2 \Rightarrow y \ge 0$

$y = |x - 2|, \ x \le 2, \ y \ge 0$

$x = |y - 2|, \ y \le 2, \ x \ge 0$

$x = y - 2 \quad \text{or} \quad -x = y - 2$

$2 + x = y \quad \text{or} \quad 2 - x = y$

The portion that satisfies the conditions $y \le 2$ and $x \ge 0$ is $2 - x = y$. This is a function of x, so f has an inverse.

$f^{-1}(x) = 2 - x, \ x \ge 0$

68. $f(x) = \sqrt{x - 2} \Rightarrow x \ge 2, \ y \ge 0$

$y = \sqrt{x - 2}, \ x \ge 2, \ y \ge 0$

$x = \sqrt{y - 2}, \ y \ge 2, \ x \ge 0$

$x^2 = y - 2, \ x \ge 0, \ y \ge 2$

$x^2 + 2 = y, \ x \ge 0, \ y \ge 2$

This is a function of x, so f has an inverse.

$f^{-1}(x) = x^2 + 2, \ x \ge 0$

70. $(g^{-1} \circ f^{-1})(-3) = g^{-1}(f^{-1}(-3))$

$= g^{-1}(8(-3 + 3))$

$= g^{-1}(0) = \sqrt[3]{0} = 0$

72. $(g^{-1} \circ g^{-1})(-4) = g^{-1}(g^{-1}(-4))$

$= g^{-1}\left(\sqrt[3]{-4}\right) = \sqrt[3]{\sqrt[3]{-4}} = \sqrt[9]{-4}$

74. $g^{-1} \circ f^{-1} = g^{-1}(f^{-1}(x))$

$= g^{-1}(8(x + 3))$

$= \sqrt[3]{8(x + 3)}$

$= 2\sqrt[3]{x + 3}$

76. $f^{-1} \circ g^{-1}(x) = f^{-1}(g^{-1}(x))$

$$= f^{-1}\left(\frac{x+5}{2}\right)$$

$$= \frac{x+5}{2} - 4$$

$$= \frac{x+5-8}{2}$$

$$= \frac{x-3}{2}$$

78. $(g \circ f)(x) = g(f(x))$

$$= g(x+4)$$

$$= 2(x+4) - 5$$

$$= 2x + 8 - 5$$

$$= 2x + 3$$

$$y = 2x + 3$$

$$x = 2y + 3$$

$$x - 3 = 2y$$

$$\frac{x-3}{2} = y$$

$$(g \circ f)^{-1}(x) = \frac{x-3}{2}$$

80. (a) $(\text{Total cost}) = \left(\begin{array}{c}\text{Cost of}\\\text{first commodity}\end{array}\right) + \left(\begin{array}{c}\text{Cost of}\\\text{second commodity}\end{array}\right)$

Labels: Total cost $= y$

Amount of first commodity $= x$

Amount of second commodity $= 50 - x$

Cost of first commodity $= 1.25x$

Cost of second commodity $= 1.60(50 - x)$

Equation: $y = 1.25x + 1.60(50 - x)$

(b) $x = 1.25y + 1.60(50 - y)$

$$x = 1.25y + 80 - 1.60y$$

$$x - 80 = -0.35y$$

$$\frac{x - 80}{-0.35} = y$$

$$y = \frac{80 - x}{0.35}$$

$x =$ total cost

$y =$ number of pounds of less expensive commodity

(c) $0 \le y \le 50$

$$0 \le \frac{80 - x}{0.35} \le 50$$

$$0 \le 80 - x \le 17.5$$

$$-80 \le -x \le -62.5$$

$$62.5 \le x \le 80$$

(d) $\dfrac{80 - 73}{0.35} = y = 20$ pounds

82. (a) Yes, since no y-value is paired with two different x-values, f^{-1} does exist.

(b) f^{-1} yields the year for a given total value of new car sales (in billions of dollars).

(c) $f^{-1}(456.2) = 5$

84. (a) $f^{-1}(51) = 5$

(b) f^{-1} yields the year for a given average local bill (in dollars) for cellular phones in the United States.

(c) $f(t) = -5.36t + 78.95$

(d) $f(t) = -5.36t + 78.95$

$$y = -5.36t + 78.95$$

$$t = -5.36y + 78.95$$

$$\frac{t - 78.95}{-5.36} = y$$

$$f^{-1}(t) = \frac{t - 78.95}{-5.36}$$

(e) $f^{-1}(11) = \dfrac{11 - 78.95}{-5.36} = 12.677$

86. False. $f(x) = x^2$ is even and does not have an inverse.

88. True. If $f(x) = x^3$, then $f^{-1}(x) = \sqrt[3]{x}$.

90.

x	1	3	4	6
f	1	2	6	7

x	1	2	6	7
$f^{-1}(x)$	1	3	4	6

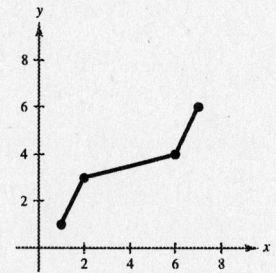

92.

x	-2	-1	3	4
f	6	0	-2	-3

x	-3	-2	0	6
$f^{-1}(x)$	4	3	-1	-2

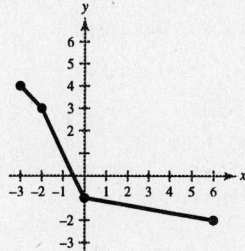

94. If $f(x) = k(2 - x - x^3)$ has an inverse and $f^{-1}(3) = -2$, then $f(-2) = 3$. Thus,

$$f(-2) = k(2 - (-2) - (-2)^3) = 3$$

$$k(2 + 2 + 8) = 3$$

$$12k = 3$$

$$k = \tfrac{3}{12} = \tfrac{1}{4}$$

Thus, $k = \tfrac{1}{4}$.

96. $(x - 5)^2 = 8$

$$x - 5 = \pm\sqrt{8}$$

$$x = 5 \pm 2\sqrt{2}$$

98. $9x^2 + 12x + 3 = 0$

$$(9x + 3)(x + 1) = 0$$

$$9x + 3 = 0 \Longrightarrow x = -\tfrac{1}{3}$$

$$x + 1 = 0 \Longrightarrow x = -1$$

100. $2x^2 - 4x - 6 = 0$

$$2(x^2 - 2x - 3) = 0$$

$$2(x + 1)(x - 3) = 0$$

$$x + 1 = 0 \Longrightarrow x = -1$$

$$x - 3 = 0 \Longrightarrow x = 3$$

102. $2x^2 + 4x - 9 = 2(x - 1)^2$

$$2x^2 + 4x - 9 = 2(x^2 - 2x + 1)$$

$$2x^2 + 4x - 9 = 2x^2 - 4x + 2$$

$$8x - 11 = 0$$

$$8x = 11$$

$$x = \tfrac{11}{8}$$

104. $f(x) = \sqrt{x + 6}$

$$x + 6 \geq 0$$

$$x \geq -6$$

Domain: $x \geq -6$

106. $h(x) = \dfrac{x}{5x + 7}$

$$5x + 7 \neq 0$$

$$5x \neq -7$$

$$x \neq -\frac{7}{5}$$

Domain: All real numbers, $x \neq -\frac{7}{5}$

108. $(200 - 2x)(100 - 2x) = \frac{1}{4}(100)(200)$

$20,000 - 600x + 4x^2 = 5000$

$4x^2 - 600x + 15,000 = 0$

$4(x^2 - 150x + 3750) = 0$

Thus, $a = 1$, $b = -150$, and $c = 3750$.

$x = \dfrac{-(-150) \pm \sqrt{(-150)^2 - 4(1)(3750)}}{2(1)}$

$x \approx \dfrac{150 + 86.6025}{2} \approx 118.301$ ft. (not possible since lot is only 100 ft. wide)

$x \approx \dfrac{150 - 86.6025}{2} \approx 31.669$ ft.

The first person must mow an approximately 31.7-foot wide strip along each side. The person must go around the lot approximately

$\dfrac{31.7}{24 \text{ inches}} = \dfrac{31.7}{2 \text{ feet}} \approx 16$ times.

110. Given $h = 2b$ and $A = 10$

$A = \frac{1}{2}bh$

$10 = \frac{1}{2}b(2b)$

$10 = b^2$

$\sqrt{10} = b$ and $h = 2b = 2\sqrt{10}$

The base is $\sqrt{10}$ feet and the height is $2\sqrt{10}$ feet.

Section 1.8   Mathematical Modeling

Solutions to Even-Numbered Exercises

2.

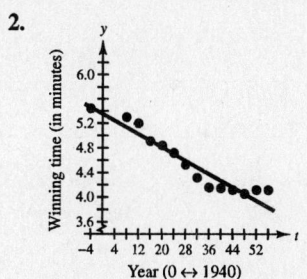

The model is a "good fit" for the actual data.

4. The graph appears to represent $y = \frac{3}{2}x$ which is a direct variation.

6.

x	2	4	6	8	10
$y = kx^2$	8	32	72	128	200

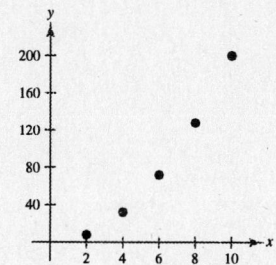

8.

x	2	4	6	8	10
$y = kx^2$	1	4	9	16	25

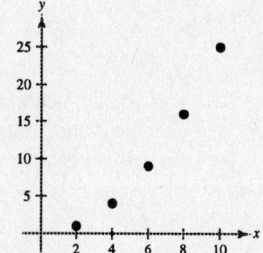

10.

x	2	4	6	8	10
$y = \dfrac{k}{x^2}$	$\dfrac{5}{4}$	$\dfrac{5}{16}$	$\dfrac{5}{36}$	$\dfrac{5}{64}$	$\dfrac{1}{20}$

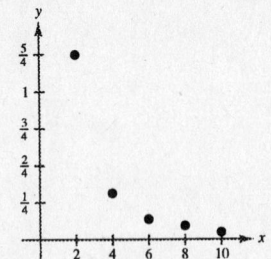

12.

x	2	4	6	8	10
$y = \dfrac{k}{x^2}$	5	$\dfrac{5}{4}$	$\dfrac{5}{9}$	$\dfrac{5}{16}$	$\dfrac{1}{5}$

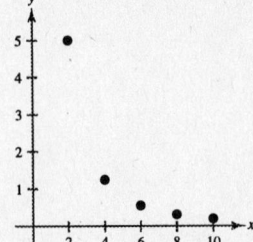

14. The table represents the equation $y = \frac{2}{5}x$.

16.
$$y = \frac{k}{x}$$
$$24 = \frac{k}{5}$$
$$120 = k$$
Thus, $y = \dfrac{120}{x}$.

This equation checks with the other points given in the table.

18.
$$y = kx$$
$$14 = k(2)$$
$$7 = k$$
$$y = 7x$$

20.
$$y = kx$$
$$580 = k(6)$$
$$\frac{290}{3} = k$$
$$y = \frac{290}{3}x$$

22.
$$I = kP$$
$$187.50 = k(5000)$$
$$0.0375 = k$$
$$I = 0.0375P$$

24.
$$y = kx$$
$$53 = k(14)$$
$$\frac{53}{14} = k$$
$$y = \frac{53}{14}x$$

Gallons	5	10	20	25	30
Liters	18.9	37.9	75.7	94.6	113.6

26.
$$y = kx$$
$$10.22 = k(145.99)$$
$$0.07 \approx k$$
$$y = 0.07x$$
$$y = 0.07(540.50)$$
$$y \approx 37.84$$
The sales tax is \$37.84.

28.
$$d = kF$$
$$0.12 = k(220)$$
$$\frac{3}{5500} = k$$
$$d = \frac{3}{5500}F$$
$$0.16 = \frac{3}{5500}F$$
$$\frac{880}{3} = F$$
The required force is $293\frac{1}{3}$ newtons.

30. $d = kF$
$$1 = k(15)$$
$$k = \frac{1}{15}$$
$$d = \frac{1}{15}F$$
$$\frac{8}{2} = \frac{1}{15}F$$
$$F = 60 \text{ lb per spring}$$
Combined lifting force $= 2F = 120$ lbs.

32. $V = ke^3$

34. $h = \dfrac{k}{\sqrt{s}}$

36. $z = kx^2y^3$

38. $R = k(T - T_e)$

40. $R = kS(S - L)$

42. $S = 4\pi r^2$

The surface area of a sphere varies directly as the square of the radius r.

44. $V = \pi r^2 h$

The volume of a right circular cylinder is jointly proportional to the height and the square of the radius.

46. $\omega = \sqrt{\dfrac{kg}{W}}$

ω varies directly as the square root of g and inversely as the square root of W.
(Note: The constant of proportionality is $\sqrt{k}$.)

48.

$$y = \frac{k}{x}$$

$$3 = \frac{k}{25}$$

$$75 = k$$

$$y = \frac{75}{x}$$

50.

$$z = kxy$$

$$64 = k(4)(8)$$

$$2 = k$$

$$z = 2xy$$

52.

$$P = \frac{kx}{y^2}$$

$$\frac{28}{3} = \frac{k(42)}{9^2}$$

$$\frac{28}{3} \cdot \frac{81}{42} = k$$

$$\frac{2 \cdot 27}{3} = k$$

$$18 = k$$

$$P = \frac{18x}{y^2}$$

54.

$$v = \frac{kpq}{s^2}$$

$$1.5 = \frac{k(4.1)(6.3)}{(1.2)^2}$$

$$\frac{(1.5)(1.44)}{(4.1)(6.3)} = k$$

$$\frac{2.16}{25.83} = k$$

$$k = \frac{24}{287}$$

$$v = \frac{24pq}{287s^2}$$

56. $d = kv^2$

If the velocity is doubled:

$$d = k(2v)^2$$

$$d = k \cdot 4v^2$$

$$\frac{4kv^2}{kv^2} = 4$$

58. From Exercise 57,
$k \approx 5.73 \times 10^{-8}$.

$$r = \frac{4(5.73 \times 10^{-8})l}{\pi d^2}$$

$$d = \sqrt{\frac{4(5.73 \times 10^{-8})l}{\pi r}}$$

$$d = \sqrt{\frac{4(5.73 \times 10^{-8})(14)}{\pi(0.05)}}$$

$d \approx 0.0045$ feet $= 0.054$ inch

60. $d = ks^2$

$$75 = k(30)^2$$

$$\frac{1}{12} = k$$

$$d = \frac{1}{12}s^2$$

$$d = \frac{1}{12}(50)^2$$

$$d = 208\frac{1}{3} \text{ feet}$$

62.

$$d = \frac{k}{p}$$

$$500 = \frac{k}{3.75}$$

$$1875 = k$$

$$d = \frac{1875}{p}$$

$$d = \frac{1875}{4.25} \approx 441 \text{ units}$$

64. Load $= \dfrac{kwd^2}{l}$

(a) load $= \dfrac{k(2w)d^2}{2l} = \dfrac{kwd^2}{l}$

The safe load is unchanged.

(b) load $= \dfrac{k(2w)(2d)^2}{l} = \dfrac{8kwd^2}{l}$

The safe load is 8 times as great.

(c) load $= \dfrac{k(2w)(2d)^2}{2l} = \dfrac{4kwd^2}{l}$

The safe load is 4 times as great.

(d) load $= \dfrac{kw\left(\dfrac{d}{2}\right)^2}{l} = \dfrac{\frac{1}{4}kwd^2}{l}$

The safe load is one-fourth as great

66. (a)

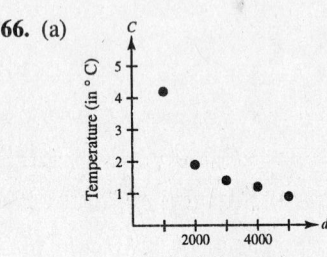

Depth (in meters)

(b) Yes, the data appears to be modeled (approximately) by the inverse proportion model.

$$4.2 = \dfrac{k}{1000}$$

$$k = 4200$$

(c)

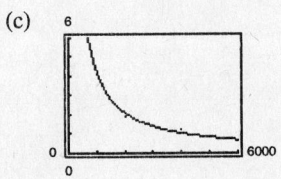

(d) $3 = \dfrac{4200}{d}$

$d = 1400$ meters

68. $I = \dfrac{k}{d^2}$

When the distance is doubled:

$$I = \dfrac{k}{(2d)^2} = \dfrac{k}{4d^2}$$

The illumination is one-fourth as great.

The model given in Exercise 67 is very close to

$I = \dfrac{k}{d^2}$. The difference is probably due to

measurement error.

70. (a) $y = 1.10t + 126.9$

(b)

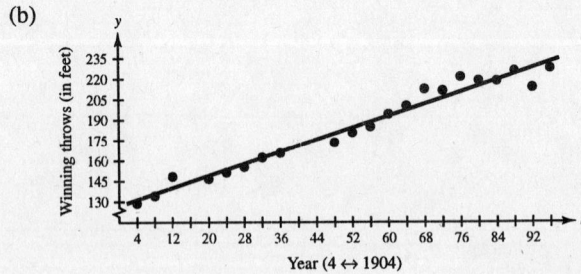

Year (4 ↔ 1904)

(c) $y(100) = 1.10(100) + 126.9 = 236.9$ feet

(d) Answers will vary.

72. (a) $y = -3.24x + 12,368$

(b)

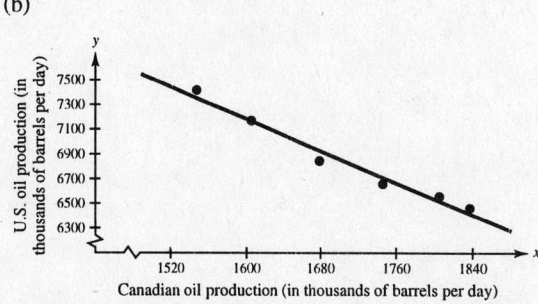

Canadian oil production (in thousands of barrels per day)

(c) $y(2000) = -3.24(2000) + 12,368$

≈ 5888 thousand barrels per day

(d) For each one thousand barrel increase in Canadian oil production, the U.S. oil production decreases by 3.24 thousand barrels.

74. False. y will increase if k is positive and y will decrease if k is negative.

76. The data shown could be represented by a linear model which would be a good approximation.

78. The points do not follow a linear pattern. A linear model would not be a good approximation.

80.

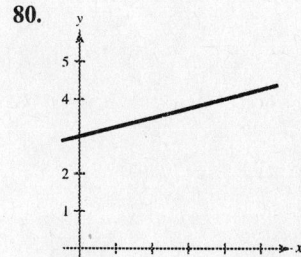

Using the points $(0, 3)$ and $(4, 4)$, we have $y = \frac{1}{4}x + 3$.

82.

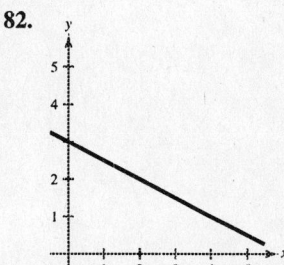

Using the points $(2, 2)$ and $(4, 1)$, we have $y = -\frac{1}{2}x + 3$.

84. The accuracy of the model in predicting prize winnings is questionable because the model is based on limited data.

86. $3(x + 1)(x - 3) < 0$

Critical numbers: $x = -1, x = 3$

Test intervals: $(-\infty, -1), (-1, 3), (3, \infty)$

Test: Is $3(x + 1)(x - 3) < 0$?

Solution: $-1 < x < 3$

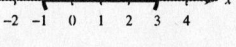

88. $x^4(x - 8) \geq 0$

Critical numbers: $x = 0, x = 8$

Test intervals: $(-\infty, 0), (0, 8), (8, \infty)$

Test: Is $x^4(x - 8) \geq 0$?

Solution: $x = 0, x \geq 8$

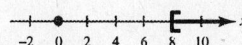

90. $f(x) = \begin{cases} -x^2 + 10, & x \geq -2 \\ 6x^2 - 1, & x < -2 \end{cases}$

(a) $f(-2) = -(-2)^2 + 10 = -4 + 10 = 6$

(b) $f(1) = -(1)^2 + 10 = -1 + 10 = 9$

(c) $f(-8) = 6(-8)^2 - 1 = 384 - 1 = 383$

94. $f(x) = \dfrac{\sqrt{x - 3}}{x - 6}$

$x - 3 \geq 0 \implies x \geq 3$ Domain: $x \geq 3, x \neq 6$

$x - 6 \neq 0 \implies x \neq 6$

92. $f(x) = \sqrt[3]{x - 2}$

Domain: All real numbers

Review Exercises for Chapter 1

2. $y = -\frac{1}{2}x + 2$

x	-2	0	2
y	3	2	1

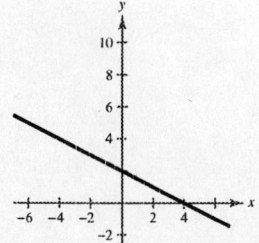

4. $y = 2x^2 - x - 9$

x	-2	-1	0	1	2
y	1	-6	-9	-8	-3

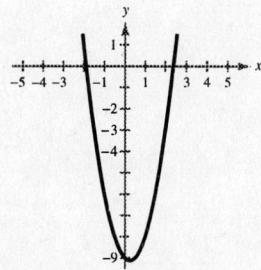

6. $y = |x - 4| - 4$

    y-intercept: $y = |0 - 4| - 4 = 0$

          $(0, 0)$

    x-intercepts: $y = |x - 4| - 4 = 0$

    $-x + 4 - 4 = 0$ $x - 4 - 4 = 0$

          $x = 0$ $x = 8$

    $(0, 0), (8, 0)$

8. $y = x\sqrt{9 - x^2}$

    y-intercept: $y = 0\sqrt{9 - 0^2} = 0$

          $(0, 0)$

    x-intercepts: $y = x\sqrt{9 - x^2} = 0$

    $x = 0$ $\sqrt{9 - x^2} = 0$

                    $x = \pm 3$

    $(0, 0), (\pm 3, 0)$

10. $y = x^3 + 3$

    Intercepts: $(0, 3), \left(-\sqrt[3]{3}, 0\right) \approx (-1.44, 0)$

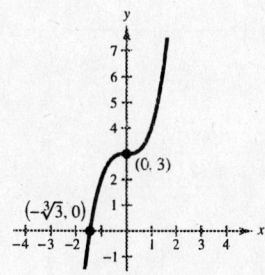

12. $y = 1 - |x|$

    Intercepts: $(0, 1), (\pm 1, 0)$

    Symmetry: y-axis

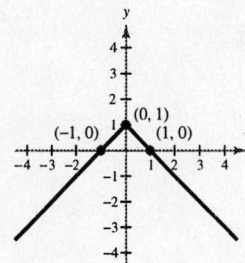

14. $x^2 + y^2 = 4$

Center: $(0, 0)$ Radius: $\sqrt{4} = 2$

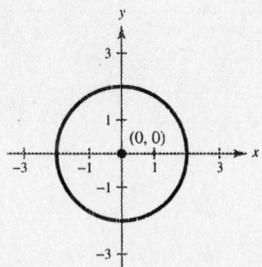

16. $x^2 + (y - 8)^2 = 81$

Center: $(0, 8)$ Radius: $\sqrt{81} = 9$

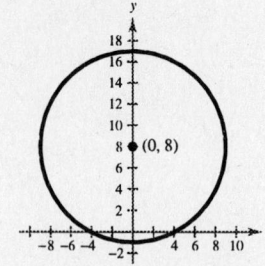

18. Endpoints of diameter: $A(-2, -3), B(4, -10)$

Center: Midpoint of $\overline{AB} = \left(\dfrac{-2 + 4}{2}, \dfrac{-3 + -10}{2} \right) = \left(1, -\dfrac{13}{2} \right)$

Radius $= \sqrt{(1 - (-2))^2 + \left(-\dfrac{13}{2} - (-3) \right)^2} = \sqrt{\dfrac{85}{4}}$

$$(x - 1)^2 + \left(y + \dfrac{13}{2} \right)^2 = \dfrac{85}{4}$$

20. $A = -2x^2 + 100x$

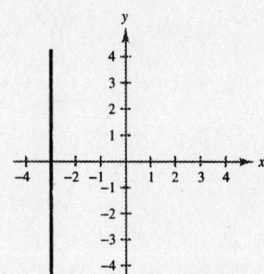

Maximum area: 1250 square feet

Length: 50 feet; Width: 25 feet

22. $x = -3$

Slope: undefined

y-intercept: none

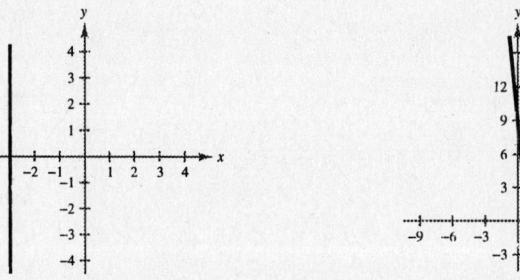

24. $y = -10x + 9$

Slope: -10

y-intercept: $(0, 9)$

26.

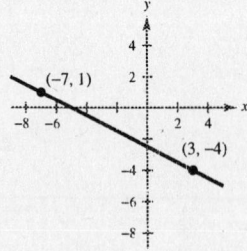

Slope: $m = \dfrac{1 - (-4)}{-7 - 3} = \dfrac{5}{-10} = -\dfrac{1}{2}$

28.

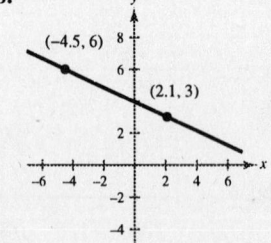

Slope: $m = \dfrac{6 - 3}{-4.5 - 2.1} = \dfrac{3}{-6.6} = -\dfrac{5}{11}$

30. $(0, 0)$, $(0, 10)$

Slope: $m = \dfrac{10 - 0}{0 - 0} \implies$ undefined

Vertical line passing through $(0, 0)$: $x = 0$

32. $(-1, 4)$, $(2, 0)$

Slope: $m = \dfrac{4 - 0}{-1 - 2} = -\dfrac{4}{3}$

$$y - 0 = -\dfrac{4}{3}(x - 2)$$
$$3y = -4x + 8$$
$$4x + 3y - 8 = 0$$

34. Point: $(0, -5)$ Slope: $m = \dfrac{3}{2}$

$$y - (-5) = \dfrac{3}{2}(x - 0)$$
$$2y + 10 = 3x$$
$$3x - 2y - 10 = 0$$

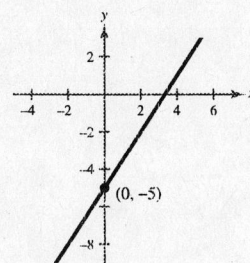

36. Point: $(10, -3)$ Slope: $m = -\dfrac{1}{2}$

$$y - (-3) = -\dfrac{1}{2}(x - 10)$$
$$2y + 6 = -x + 10$$
$$x + 2y - 4 = 0$$

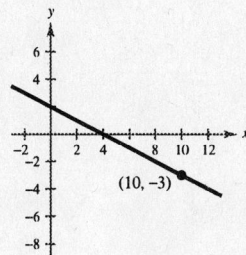

38. Point: $(3, -2)$, Line: $5x - 4y = 8$

(a) Parallel line: $m = \dfrac{5}{4}$

$$y - (-2) = \dfrac{5}{4}(x - 3)$$
$$4y + 8 = 5x - 15$$
$$5x - 4y - 23 = 0$$

(b) Perpendicular line: $m = -\dfrac{4}{5}$

$$y - (-2) = -\dfrac{4}{5}(x - 3)$$
$$5y + 10 = -4x + 12$$
$$4x + 5y - 2 = 0$$

40. 2000 *Value*: $12,500

Slope: $850 increase per year

$V = 850t + 12,500$

42. $16x - y^4 = 0$

No. This determines x as a function of y.

44. $y = \sqrt{1 - x}$

Yes. This determines y as a function of x.

46. $f(x) = x^2 + 1$

(a) $f(2) = 2^2 + 1 = 5$

(c) $f(t^2) = (t^2)^2 + 1 = t^4 + 1$

(b) $f(-4) = (-4)^2 + 1 = 17$

(d) $-f(x) = -(x^2 + 1)$

$\qquad = -x^2 - 1$

48. $f(x) = \sqrt{25 - x^2}$

Domain: $25 - x^2 \geq 0$

$\qquad -5 \leq x \leq 5$

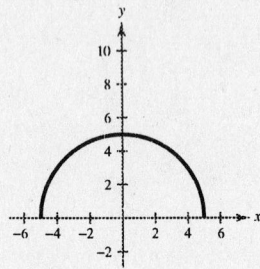

50. $h(x) = \dfrac{x}{x^2 - x - 6}$

$x^2 - x - 6 = 0$

$(x - 3)(x + 2) = 0$

$x \neq -2, 3$

Domain: All real numbers

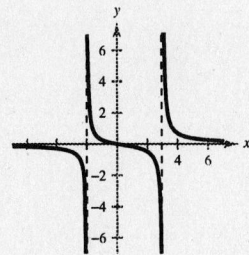

52. $v(t) = -32t + 48$

(a) $v(1) = -32(1) + 48 = 16$ feet per second

(c) $v(2) = -32t + 48 = -32(2) + 48$

$\qquad = -16$ feet per second

(b) $v(t) = 0$

$-32t + 48 = 0$

$t = \dfrac{48}{32} = 1.5$ seconds

54. $y = (x - 3)^2$

All vertical lines intersect graph exactly once
$\Longrightarrow y$ is a function of x.

56. $x - 4 = y^2$

Some vertical lines intersect graph more than once
$\Longrightarrow y$ is not a function of x.

58. $f(x) = 3x^2 - 16x + 21$

$3x^2 - 16x + 21 = 0$

$(3x - 7)(x - 3) = 0$

Zeros: $x = \dfrac{7}{3}, 3$

60. $f(x) = \dfrac{8x + 3}{11 - x}$

$\dfrac{8x + 3}{11 - x} = 0$

$8x + 3 = 0$

Zero: $x = -\dfrac{3}{8}$

62. $g(x) = |x + 2| - |x - 2|$

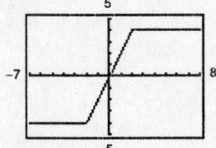

Increasing: $(-2, 2)$

Constant: $(-\infty, -2), (2, \infty)$

64. $h(x) = 4x^3 - x^4$

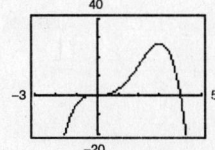

Increasing: $(-\infty, 3)$

Decreasing: $(3, \infty)$

66. $f(2) = -6, f(-1) = 3$

Two points: $(2, -6), (-1, 3)$

Slope: $m = \dfrac{-6 - 3}{2 - (-1)} = \dfrac{-9}{3} = -3$

$f(x) - 3 = -3(x + 1)$

$f(x) = -3x$

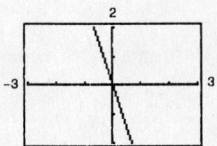

68. $f\left(-\dfrac{4}{5}\right) = 2, f\left(\dfrac{11}{5}\right) = 7$

Two points: $\left(-\dfrac{4}{5}, 2\right), \left(\dfrac{11}{5}, 7\right)$

Slope: $m = \dfrac{2 - 7}{-\frac{4}{5} - \frac{11}{5}} = \dfrac{-5}{-\frac{15}{5}} = \dfrac{5}{3}$

$f(x) - 7 = \dfrac{5}{3}\left(x - \dfrac{11}{5}\right)$

$f(x) = \dfrac{5}{3}x + \dfrac{10}{3}$

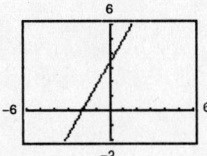

70. $f(x) = \begin{cases} 5x - 3, & x \ge -1 \\ -4x + 5, & x < -1 \end{cases}$

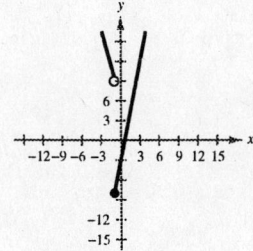

72. $f(x) = x^5 + 4x - 7$

$f(-x) = -x^5 - 4x - 7$

$f(-x) \ne f(x)$

$f(-x) \ne -f(x)$

Neither.

74. $f(x) = 2x\sqrt{x^2 + 3}$

$f(-x) = -2x\sqrt{x^2 + 3}$

Odd.

76. The function is $y = x^3$ shifted to the left by 4 units and upward by 4 units.

78. $h(x) = x^2 - 9$ Vertical shift 9 units downward.

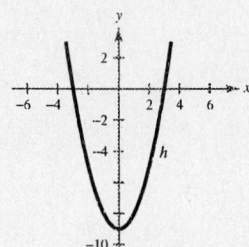

80. $h(x) = |x + 3| - 5$ Horizontal shift 3 units to the left and a vertical shift 5 units downward.

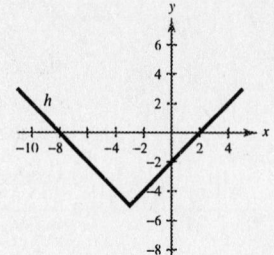

82. $h(x) = -\sqrt{x + 1} + 9$ Reflection in the x-axis, horizontal shift 1 unit to the left, and a vertical shift 9 units upward.

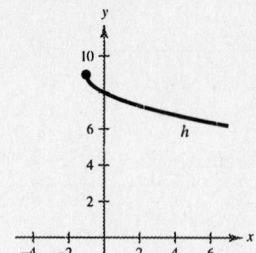

84. $f(x) = 3 - 2x, g(x) = \sqrt{x}$

$$(f - g)(4) = f(4) - g(4)$$
$$= 3 - 2(4) - \sqrt{4}$$
$$= -7$$

86. $g(x) = \sqrt{x}, h(x) = 3x^2 + 2$

$$(h \circ g)(7) = 3(g(7))^2 + 2$$
$$= 3(\sqrt{7})^2 + 2$$
$$= 23$$

88. $(2, 35.2), (3, 39.9), (4, 49.5), (5, 62.1),$
$(6, 74.3), (7, 85.9)$

$y_1 = 0.80t^2 + 3.34t + 24.23$

$(2, 98.6), (3, 111.2), (4, 128.4), (5, 144.4),$
$(6, 155.9), (7, 168.2)$

$y_2 = -0.43t^2 + 18.14t + 62.89$

90.
$$f(x) = 6x$$
$$y = 6x$$
$$x = 6y$$
$$\frac{x}{6} = y$$
$$f^{-1}(x) = \frac{x}{6}$$
$$f(f^{-1}(x)) = 6\left(\frac{x}{6}\right) = x$$
$$f^{-1}(f(x)) = \frac{6x}{6} = x$$

92.
$$f(x) = x - 7$$
$$y = x - 7$$
$$x = y - 7$$
$$x + 7 = y$$
$$f^{-1}(x) = x + 7$$
$$f(f^{-1}(x)) = (x + 7) - 7 = x$$
$$f^{-1}(f(x)) = (x - 7) + 7 = x$$

94. $f(x) = 3x^3 - 5$

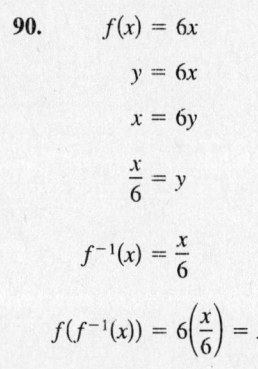

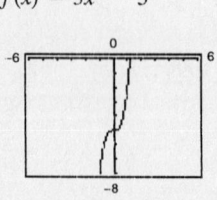

$f(x)$ passes Horizontal Line Test $\Rightarrow$ it has an inverse.

96. $f(x) = -\sqrt{4 - x}$

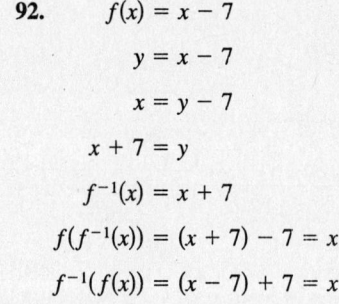

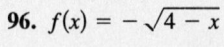

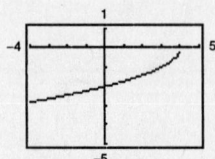

$f(x)$ passes Horizontal Line Test $\Rightarrow$ it has an inverse.

98. $f(x) = \frac{1}{2}x - 3$

    (a) $\quad y = \frac{1}{2}x - 3$

          $x = \frac{1}{2}y - 3$

       $2x + 6 = y$

       $f^{-1}(x) = 2x + 6$

    (c) $f^{-1}(f(x)) = 2\left[\frac{1}{2}x - 3\right] + 6 = x$

       $f(f^{-1}(x)) = \frac{1}{2}[2x + 6] - 3 = x$

(b)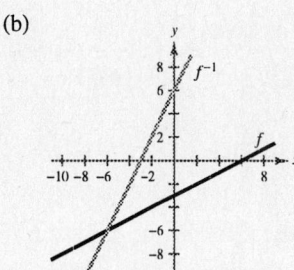

100. $f(x) = \sqrt{x + 1}$

    (a) $\quad y = \sqrt{x + 1}$

          $x = \sqrt{y + 1}$

      $x^2 - 1 = y$

      $f^{-1}(x) = x^2 - 1$

    (c) $f^{-1}(f(x)) = \left[\sqrt{x + 1}\right]^2 - 1 = x$

       $f(f^{-1}(x)) = \sqrt{[x^2 - 1] + 1} = x$

(b)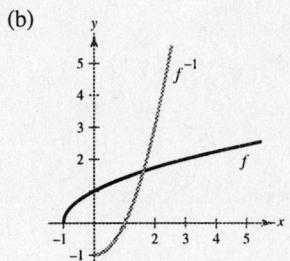

102. $f(x) = 2(x - 4)^2$

    $f(x)$ is increasing on the interval $(4, \infty)$.

       $y = 2(x - 4)^2$

       $x = 2(y - 4)^2$

   $\pm\sqrt{\dfrac{x}{2}} = y - 4$

    Choose positive root, corresponding to $(4, \infty)$ as the domain of $f(x)$.

   $4 + \sqrt{\dfrac{x}{2}} = y$

       $f^{-1}(x) = \sqrt{\dfrac{x}{2}} + 4$

104. (a)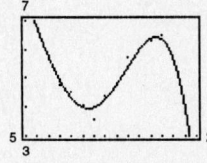

       The model and the data agree well for $8 \le t \le 17$, 1988 through 1997, the entire range of the data.

    (c) The model shows a decrease of approximately 0.30 billion dollars from 1989-1991, whereas the data shows a decrease of 0.9 billion dollars.

(b) Explanations for the downturn from 1989 through 1991 will vary, e.g., reduced manufacturing, decrease in demand, economic recession. The model shows this downturn also.

(d) 2001 corresponds to $t = 21$.

    $S(21) \approx -3.47$ billion dollars.

    The model is not accurate in predicting future sales because the sales become negative.

106. $P = kS^3$

$750 = k(27)^3 \Longrightarrow k \approx 0.038104$

$P = k(40)^3 \approx (0.038104)(40)^3 \approx 2438.7$ kilowatts

108. y is inversely proportional to x: $y = \dfrac{k}{x}$

$y = 9$ when $x = 5.5$

$9 = \dfrac{k}{5.5} \Longrightarrow k = (9)(5.5) = 49.5$

So, $y = \dfrac{49.5}{x}$

110. (a) Mining wages versus time:

$(4, 14.89), (5, 15.30), (6, 15.60), (7, 16.17)$

$y_1 = 0.414x + 13.213$

Construction wages versus time:

$(4, 14.69), (5, 15.08), (6, 15.43), (7, 16.03)$

$y_2 = 0.437x + 12.904$

(b)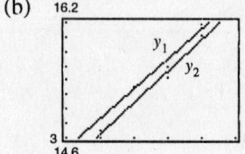

(c) Mining hourly wages increase at a rate of $0.41 per year.

Construction hourly rates increase at a rate of $0.44 per year.

(d) Year 2002 corresponds to $t = 12$.

Mining: $0.414(12) + 13.213 \approx \$18.18$ per hour.

Construction: $0.437(12) + 12.904 \approx \$18.14$ per hour.

112. True. If $f(x) = x^3$ and $g(x) = \sqrt[3]{x}$, then the domain of g is all real numbers, which is equal to the domain of f, and vice versa.

114. The Vertical Line Test is used to determine if a graph of y is a function of x. The Horizontal Line Test is used to determine if a function has an inverse.

C H A P T E R 2
Polynomial and Rational Functions

CHAPTER 2
Polynomial and Rational Functions

Section 2.1   Quadratic Functions

Solutions to Even-Numbered Exercises

2. $f(x) = (x + 4)^2$ opens upward and has vertex $(-4, 0)$. Matches graph (c).

4. $f(x) = 3 - x^2$ opens downward and has vertex $(0, 3)$. Matches graph (h).

6. $f(x) = (x + 1)^2 - 2$ opens upward and has vertex $(-1, -2)$. Matches graph (a).

8. $f(x) = -(x - 4)^2$ opens downward and has vertex $(4, 0)$. Matches graph (d).

10. (a) $y = x^2 + 1$

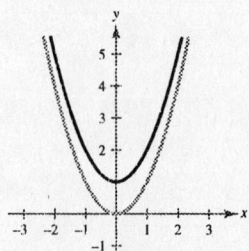

Vertical translation 1 unit upward.

(b) $y = x^2 - 1$

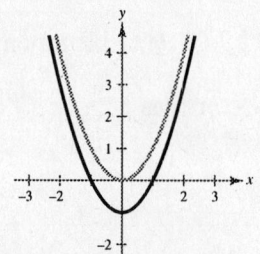

Vertical translation 1 unit downward.

(c) $y = x^2 + 3$

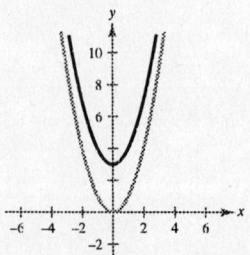

Vertical translation 3 units upward.

(d) $y = x^2 - 3$

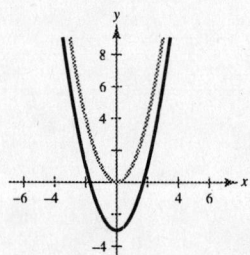

Vertical translation 3 units downward.

12. (a) $y = -\frac{1}{2}(x - 2)^2 + 1$

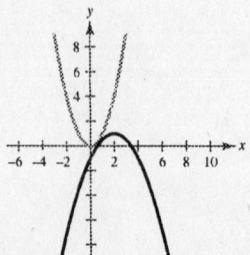

Horizontal translation 2 units to right, vertical shrink by $\frac{1}{2}$, reflection in the x-axis, and vertical translation 1 unit upward.

(b) $y = \frac{1}{2}(x - 2)^2 + 1$

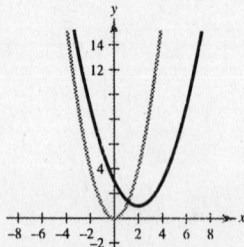

Horizontal translation 2 units to right, vertical shrink by $\frac{1}{2}$, and vertical translation 1 unit upward.

—CONTINUED—

840

12. —CONTINUED—

(c) $y = -\frac{1}{2}(x + 2)^2 - 1$

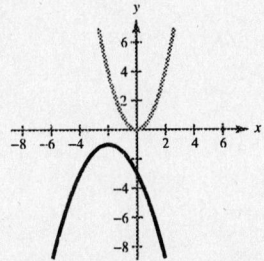

Horizontal translation 2 units to left, vertical shrink by $\frac{1}{2}$, reflection in x-axis, and vertical translation 1 unit downward.

(d) $y = \frac{1}{2}(x + 2)^2 - 1$

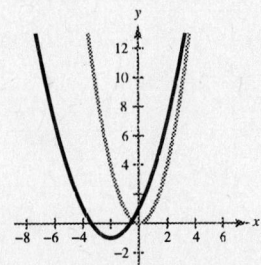

Horizontal translation 2 units to left, vertical shrink by $\frac{1}{2}$, and vertical translation 1 unit downward.

14. $h(x) = 25 - x^2$

Vertex: $(0, 25)$

Find x-intercepts: $25 - x^2 = 0$

$$x^2 = 25$$

$$x = \pm 5$$

x-intercepts: $(\pm 5, 0)$

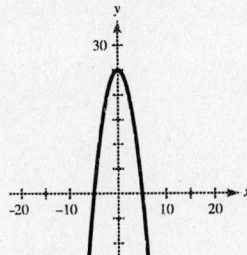

16. $f(x) = 16 = \frac{1}{4}x^2 = -\frac{1}{4}x^2 + 16$

Vertex: $(0, 16)$

Find x-intercepts: $16 - \frac{1}{4}x^2 = 0$

$$x^2 = 64$$

$$x = \pm 8$$

x-intercepts: $(\pm 8, 0)$

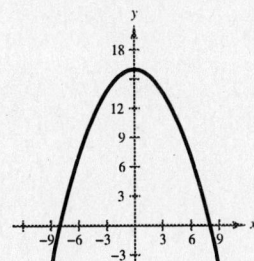

18. $f(x) = (x - 6)^2 + 3$

Vertex: $(6, 3)$

Find x-intercepts: $(x - 6)^2 + 3 = 0$

$$(x - 6)^2 = -3$$

Not possible for real x.

No x-intercepts

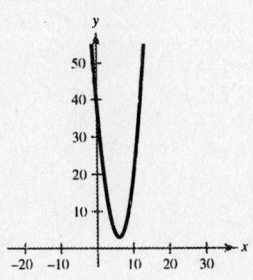

20. $g(x) = x^2 + 2x + 1 = (x + 1)^2$

Vertex: $(-1, 0)$

x-intercept: $(-1, 0)$

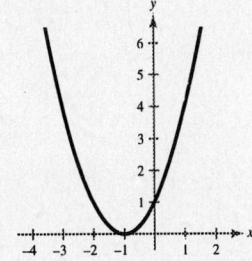

22. $f(x) = x^2 + 3x + \dfrac{1}{4} = \left(x^2 + 3x + \dfrac{9}{4}\right) - \dfrac{9}{4} + \dfrac{1}{4} = \left(x + \dfrac{3}{2}\right)^2 - 2$

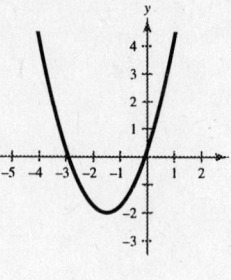

Vertex: $\left(-\dfrac{3}{2}, -2\right)$

Find x-intercepts: $x^2 + 3x + \dfrac{1}{4} = 0$

$$x = \dfrac{-3 \pm \sqrt{9 - 1}}{2} = -\dfrac{3}{2} \pm \sqrt{2}$$

x-intercepts: $\left(-\dfrac{3}{2} \pm \sqrt{2}, 0\right)$

24. $f(x) = -x^2 - 4x + 1 = -(x^2 + 4x) + 1$

$\qquad\qquad = -(x^2 + 4x + 4) - (-4) + 1$

$\qquad\qquad = -(x + 2)^2 + 5$

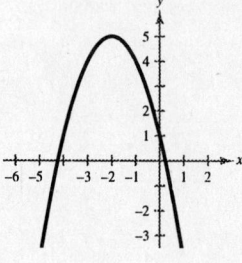

Vertex: $(-2, 5)$

Find x-intercepts: $-x^2 - 4x + 1 = 0$

$\qquad\qquad\quad x^2 + 4x - 1 = 0$

$$x = \dfrac{-4 \pm \sqrt{16 + 4}}{2}$$

$$= -2 \pm \sqrt{5}$$

x-intercepts: $\left(-2 \pm \sqrt{5}, 0\right)$

26. $f(x) = 2x^2 - x + 1$

$\qquad = 2\left(x^2 - \dfrac{1}{2}x\right) + 1$

$\qquad = 2\left(x - \dfrac{1}{4}\right)^2 - 2\left(\dfrac{1}{16}\right) + 1$

$\qquad = 2\left(x - \dfrac{1}{4}\right)^2 + \dfrac{7}{8}$

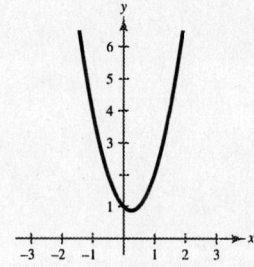

Vertex: $\left(\dfrac{1}{4}, \dfrac{7}{8}\right)$

Find x-intercepts: $2x^2 - x + 1 = 0$

$$x = \dfrac{1 \pm \sqrt{1 - 8}}{2(2)}$$

Not a real number

No x-intercepts

28. $f(x) = -\dfrac{1}{3}x^2 + 3x - 6$

$\qquad = -\dfrac{1}{3}(x^2 - 9x) - 6$

$\qquad = -\dfrac{1}{3}\left(x^2 - 9x + \dfrac{81}{4}\right) + \dfrac{1}{3}\left(\dfrac{81}{4}\right) - 6$

$\qquad = -\dfrac{1}{3}\left(x - \dfrac{9}{2}\right)^2 + \dfrac{3}{4}$

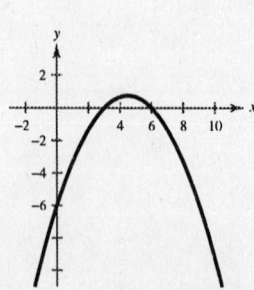

Vertex: $\left(\dfrac{9}{2}, \dfrac{3}{4}\right)$

Find x-intercepts: $-\dfrac{1}{3}x^2 + 3x - 6 = 0$

$\qquad\qquad\quad x^2 - 9x + 18 = 0$

$\qquad\qquad\quad (x - 3)(x - 6) = 0$

x-intercepts: $(3, 0), (6, 0)$

30. $f(x) = -(x^2 + x - 30)$

$\qquad = -(x^2 + x) + 30$

$\qquad = -\left(x^2 + x + \frac{1}{4}\right) + \frac{1}{4} + 30$

$\qquad = -\left(x + \frac{1}{2}\right)^2 + \frac{121}{4}$

Vertex: $\left(-\frac{1}{2}, \frac{121}{4}\right)$

x-intercepts: $(-6, 0), (5, 0)$

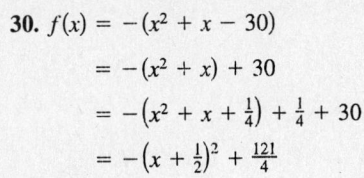

32. $f(x) = x^2 + 10x + 14$

$\qquad = (x^2 + 10x + 25) - 25 + 14$

$\qquad = (x + 5)^2 - 11$

Vertex: $(-5, -11)$

x-intercepts: $\left(-5 \pm \sqrt{11}, 0\right)$

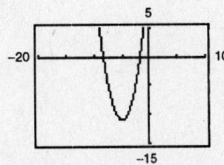

34. $f(x) = -4x^2 + 24x - 41$

$\qquad = -4(x^2 - 6x) - 41$

$\qquad = -4(x^2 - 6x + 9) + 36 - 41$

$\qquad = -4(x - 3)^2 - 5$

Vertex: $(3, -5)$

No x-intercepts

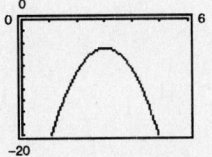

36. $f(x) = \frac{3}{5}(x^2 + 6x - 5)$

$\qquad = \frac{3}{5}(x^2 + 6x + 9) - \frac{27}{5} - 3$

$\qquad = \frac{3}{5}(x + 3)^2 - \frac{42}{5}$

Vertex: $\left(-3, -\frac{42}{5}\right)$

x-intercepts: $\left(-3 \pm \sqrt{14}, 0\right)$

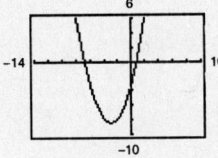

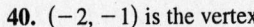

38. $(0, 1)$ is the vertex.

$\quad f(x) = a(x - 0)^2 + 1 = ax^2 + 1$

Since the graph passes through $(1, 0)$,

$\quad 0 = a(1)^2 + 1$

$\quad -1 = a.$

Thus, $y = -x^2 + 1$.

40. $(-2, -1)$ is the vertex.

$\quad f(x) = a(x + 2)^2 - 1$

Since the graph passes through $(0, 3)$,

$\quad 3 = a(0 + 2)^2 - 1$

$\quad 3 = 4a - 1$

$\quad 4 = 4a$

$\quad 1 = a.$

Thus, $y = (x + 2)^2 - 1$.

42. $(2, 0)$ is the vertex.

$f(x) = a(x - 2)^2 + 0 = a(x - 2)^2$

Since the graph passes through $(3, 2)$,

$2 = a(3 - 2)^2$

$2 = a$.

Thus, $y = 2(x - 2)^2$.

44. $(4, -1)$ is the vertex.

$f(x) = a(x - 4)^2 - 1$

Since the graph passes through $(2, 3)$,

$3 = a(2 - 4)^2 - 1$

$3 = 4a - 1$

$4 = 4a$

$1 = a$.

Thus, $f(x) = (x - 4)^2 - 1$.

46. $(2, 3)$ is the vertex.

$f(x) = a(x - 2)^2 + 3$

Since the graph passes through $(0, 2)$,

$2 = a(0 - 2)^2 + 3$

$2 = 4a + 3$

$-1 = 4a$

$-\frac{1}{4} = a$.

Thus, $f(x) = -\frac{1}{4}(x - 2)^2 + 3$.

48. $(-2, -2)$ is the vertex.

$f(x) = a(x + 2)^2 - 2$

Since the graph passes through $(-1, 0)$,

$0 = a(-1 + 2)^2 - 2$

$0 = a - 2$

$2 = a$.

Thus, $f(x) = 2(x + 2)^2 - 2$.

50. $\left(\frac{5}{2}, -\frac{3}{4}\right)$ is the vertex.

$f(x) = a\left(x - \frac{5}{2}\right)^2 - \frac{3}{4}$

Since the graph passes through $(-2, 4)$,

$4 = a\left(-2 - \frac{5}{2}\right)^2 - \frac{3}{4}$

$4 = \frac{81}{4}a - \frac{3}{4}$

$\frac{19}{4} = \frac{81}{4}a$

$\frac{19}{81} = a$

Thus, $f(x) = \frac{19}{81}\left(x - \frac{5}{2}\right)^2 - \frac{3}{4}$.

52. $(6, 6)$ is the vertex.

$f(x) = a(x - 6)^2 + 6$

Since the graph passes through $\left(\frac{61}{10}, \frac{3}{2}\right)$,

$\frac{3}{2} = a\left(\frac{61}{10} - 6\right)^2 + 6$

$\frac{3}{2} = \frac{1}{100}a + 6$

$-\frac{9}{2} = \frac{1}{100}a$

$-450 = a$

Thus, $f(x) = -450(x - 6)^2 + 6$.

54. $y = x^2 - 6x + 9$

x-intercept: $(3, 0)$

$0 = x^2 - 6x + 9$

$0 = (x - 3)^2$

$x = 3$

The x-intercept and solution of the equation are the same.

56. $y = 2x^2 + 5x - 3$

x-intercepts: $\left(\frac{1}{2}, 0\right)$, $(-3, 0)$

$0 = 2x^2 + 5x - 3$

$0 = (2x - 1)(x + 3)$

$x = \frac{1}{2}, -3$

The x-intercepts and solutions of the equation are the same.

58. $f(x) = -2x^2 + 10x$

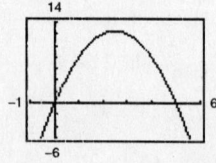

x-intercepts: $(0, 0)$, $(5, 0)$

$0 = -2x^2 + 10x$

$0 = -2x(x - 5)$

$-2x = 0 \Rightarrow x = 0$

$x - 5 = 0 \Rightarrow x = 5$

60. $f(x) = x^2 - 8x - 20$

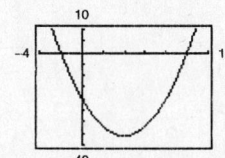

x-intercepts: $(-2, 0), (10, 0)$

$$0 = x^2 - 8x - 20$$

$$0 = (x + 2)(x - 10)$$

$$x + 2 = 0 \Rightarrow x = -2$$

$$x - 10 = 0 \Rightarrow x = 10$$

62. $f(x) = 4x^2 + 25x - 21$

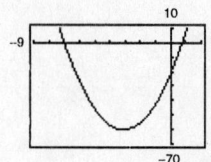

x-intercepts: $(-7, 0), \left(\frac{3}{4}, 0\right)$

$$0 = 4x^2 + 25x - 21$$

$$0 = (x + 7)(4x - 3)$$

$$x + 7 = 0 \Rightarrow x = -7$$

$$4x - 3 = 0 \Rightarrow x = \frac{3}{4}$$

64. $f(x) = \frac{7}{10}(x^2 + 12x - 45)$

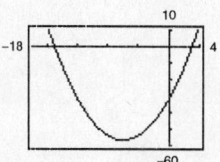

x-intercepts: $(-15, 0), (3, 0)$

$$0 = \frac{7}{10}(x^2 + 12x - 45)$$

$$0 = (x + 15)(x - 3)$$

$$x + 15 = 0 \Rightarrow x = -15$$

$$x - 3 = 0 \Rightarrow x = 3$$

66. $f(x) = [x - (-5)](x - 5)$

$$= (x + 5)(x - 5)$$

$$= x^2 - 25, \text{ opens upward}$$

$$g(x) = -f(x), \text{ opens downward}$$

$$g(x) = -x^2 + 25$$

Note: $f(x) = a(x^2 - 25)$ has x-intercepts
$(-5, 0)$ and $(5, 0)$ for all real numbers $a \neq 0$.

68. $f(x) = (x - 4)(x - 8)$

$$= x^2 - 12x + 32, \text{ opens upward}$$

$$g(x) = -f(x), \text{ opens downward}$$

$$g(x) = -x^2 + 12x - 32$$

Note: $f(x) = a(x - 4)(x - 8)$ has x-intercepts
$(4, 0)$ and $(8, 0)$ for all real numbers $a \neq 0$.

70. $f(x) = 2\left[x - \left(-\frac{5}{2}\right)\right](x - 2)$

$$= 2\left(x + \frac{5}{2}\right)(x - 2)$$

$$= 2\left(x^2 + \frac{1}{2}x - 5\right)$$

$$= 2x^2 + x - 10, \text{ opens upward}$$

$$g(x) = -f(x), \text{ opens downward}$$

$$g(x) = -2x^2 - x + 10$$

Note: $f(x) = a\left(x + \frac{5}{2}\right)(x - 2)$ has x-intercepts $\left(-\frac{5}{2}, 0\right)$
and $(2, 0)$ for all real numbers $a \neq 0$.

72. Let x = first number and y = second number.

Then, $x + y = S, y = S - x$. The product is

$$P(x) = xy = x(S - x).$$

$$P(x) = Sx - x^2$$

$$= -x^2 + Sx$$

$$= -\left(x^2 - Sx + \frac{S^2}{4} - \frac{S^2}{4}\right)$$

$$= -\left(x - \frac{S}{2}\right)^2 + \frac{S^2}{4}$$

The maximum value of the product occurs at the vertex of
$P(x)$ and is $S^2/4$. This happens when $x = y = S/2$.

74. Let x = the first number and y = the second number.

Then the sum is $x + 3y = 42 \Rightarrow y = \dfrac{42 - x}{3}$.

The product is $P(x) = xy = x\left(\dfrac{42 - x}{3}\right)$.

$$P(x) = \frac{1}{3}(-x^2 + 42x)$$

$$= -\frac{1}{3}(x^2 - 42x + 441 - 441)$$

$$= -\frac{1}{3}[(x - 21)^2 - 441] = -\frac{1}{3}(x - 21)^2 + 147$$

The maximum value of the product occurs at the vertex of
$P(x)$ and is 147. This happens when $x = 21$ and
$y = \dfrac{42 - 21}{3} = 7$. Thus, the numbers are 21 and 7.

76. Let x = length of rectangle and y = width of rectangle.

$$2x + 2y = 36$$

$$y = 18 - x$$

(a) $A(x) = xy = x(18 - x)$

Domain: $0 < x < 18$

(c) The area is maximum (81 square meters) when $x = y = 9$ meters. The rectangle has dimensions 9 meters $\times$ 9 meters.

(b)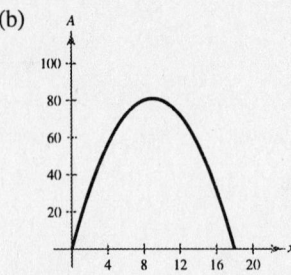

78. (a) Radius of semicircular ends of track: $r = \frac{1}{2}y$
distance around two semicircular parts of track:

$$d = 2\pi r = 2\pi\left(\frac{1}{2}y\right) = \pi y$$

(c) Area of rectangular region:

$$A = xy = x\left(\frac{200 - 2x}{\pi}\right)$$

$$= \frac{1}{\pi}(200x - 2x^2)$$

$$= -\frac{2}{\pi}(x^2 - 100x)$$

$$= -\frac{2}{\pi}(x^2 - 100x + 2500 - 2500)$$

$$= -\frac{2}{\pi}(x - 50)^2 + \frac{5000}{\pi}$$

The area is maximum when $x = 50$ and

$$y = \frac{200 - 2(50)}{\pi} = \frac{100}{\pi}.$$

(b) Distance traveled around track in one lap:

$$d = \pi y + 2x = 200$$

$$\pi y = 200 - 2x$$

$$y = \frac{200 - 2x}{\pi}$$

80. $R = 100x - 0.0002x^2 = -0.0002x^2 + 100x$

The vertex occurs at

$$x = -\frac{b}{2a} = -\frac{100}{2(-0.0002)} = 250,000.$$

The revenue is maximum when $x = 250,000$ units.

82. $C = 10,000 - 110x + 0.045x^2$

The vertex occurs at

$$x = -\frac{-110}{2(0.045)} \approx 1222.$$

The cost is minimum when $x \approx 1222$ units.

84. $P = 230 + 20x - 0.5x^2$

The vertex occurs at

$$x = -\frac{b}{2a} = -\frac{20}{2(-0.5)} = 20.$$

Because x is in hundreds of dollars, $20 \times 100 = 2000$ dollars is the amount spent on advertising that gives maximum profit.

86. $V = 0.77x^2 - 1.32x - 9.31, 5 \le x \le 40$

(a)

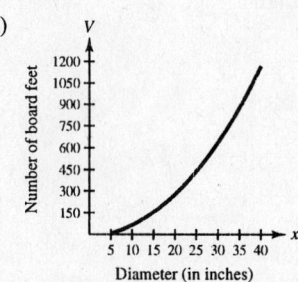

Diameter (in inches)

(b) $V(16) = 166.69$ board feet

(c) $500 = 0.77x^2 - 1.32x - 9.31$

$0 = 0.77x^2 - 1.32x - 509.31$

Using the Quadratic Formula and selecting the positive value for x, we have $x \approx 26.6$ inches in diameter.

88. (a)

(b) $0.002s^2 + 0.005s - 0.029 = 10$

$2s^2 + 5s - 29 = 10,000$

$2s^2 + 5s - 10,029 = 0$

$a = 2, b = 5, c = -10,029$

$$s = \frac{-5 \pm \sqrt{5^2 - 4(2)(-10,029)}}{2(2)}$$

$$s = \frac{-5 \pm \sqrt{80,257}}{4}$$

$s \approx -72.1, 69.6$

The maximum speed if power is not to exceed 10 horsepower is 69.6 miles per hour.

90. (a)

$y = -0.0082x^2 + 0.746x + 13.47$

(b) The maximum occurs at

$$x = -\frac{b}{2a} = -\frac{0.746}{2(-0.0082)} \approx 45.5.$$

The mileage is greatest at a speed of about 45.5 miles per hour.

92. True. The equation has no real solution, so the graph has no x-intercepts.

94. $f(x) = ax^2 + bx + c$

$$= a\left(x^2 + \frac{b}{a}x\right) + c$$

$$= a\left(x^2 + \frac{b}{a}x + \frac{b^2}{4a^2} - \frac{b^2}{4a^2}\right) + c$$

$$= a\left(x + \frac{b}{2a}\right)^2 - \frac{b^2}{4a} + c$$

$$= a\left(x - \left(-\frac{b}{2a}\right)\right)^2 + \frac{4ac - b^2}{4a}$$

$$f\left(-\frac{b}{2a}\right) = a\left(\frac{b^2}{4a^2}\right) + b\left(-\frac{b}{2a}\right) + c$$

$$= \frac{b^2}{4a} - \frac{b^2}{2a} + c$$

$$= \frac{b^2 - 2b^2 + 4ac}{4a} = \frac{4ac - b^2}{4a}$$

So, the vertex occurs at

$$\left(-\frac{b}{2a}, \frac{4ac - b^2}{4a}\right) = \left(-\frac{b}{2a}, f\left(-\frac{b}{2a}\right)\right)$$

96. Yes. A graph of a quadratic equation whose vertex is $(0, 0)$ has only one x-intercept.

98. (a)

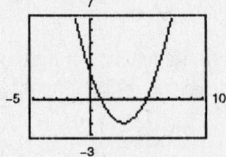

The x-coordinate of the vertex is 3, which is the average of the zeros 1 and 5.

(b)

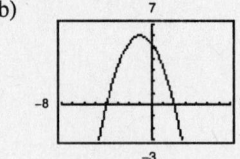

The x-coordinate of the vertex is -1, which is the average of the zeros -4 and 2.

100. $\left(\frac{7}{2}, 2\right), m = \frac{3}{2}$

$$y - 2 = \frac{3}{2}\left(x - \frac{7}{2}\right)$$

$$y - 2 = \frac{3}{2}x - \frac{21}{4}$$

$$y = \frac{3}{2}x - \frac{13}{4}$$

102. $y = -3x + 2$

$m = -3$

For a parallel line, $m = -3$.

So, for $(-8, 4)$, the line is

$$y - 4 = -3(x - (-8))$$

$$y - 4 = -3x - 24$$

$$y = -3x - 20$$

104. $(g - f)(2) = 8(2)^2 - 14(2) + 3 = 32 - 28 + 3 = 7$

106. $\left(\dfrac{f}{g}\right)(-1.5) = \dfrac{14(-1.5) - 3}{8(-1.5)^2} = \dfrac{-24}{18} = -\dfrac{4}{3}$

108. $(g \circ f)(0) = g(f(0)) = g(14(0) - 3) = g(-3)$

$$= 8(-3)^2 = 72$$

Section 2.2 Polynomial Functions of Higher Degree

Solutions to Even-Numbered Exercises

2. $f(x) = x^2 - 4x$ is a parabola with intercepts $(0, 0)$ and $(4, 0)$ and opens upward. Matches graph (g).

4. $f(x) = 2x^3 - 3x + 1$ has intercepts $(0, 1)$, $(1, 0)$, $\left(-\frac{1}{2} - \frac{1}{2}\sqrt{3}, 0\right)$ and $\left(-\frac{1}{2} + \frac{1}{2}\sqrt{3}, 0\right)$. Matches graph (f).

6. $f(x) = -\frac{1}{3}x^3 + x^2 - \frac{4}{3}$ has y-intercept $\left(0, -\frac{4}{3}\right)$. Matches graph (e).

8. $f(x) = \frac{1}{5}x^5 - 2x^3 + \frac{9}{5}x$ has intercepts $(0, 0)$, $(1, 0)$, $(-1, 0)$, $(3, 0)$, $(-3, 0)$. Matches (b).

10. $y = x^5$

(a) $f(x) = (x + 1)^5$

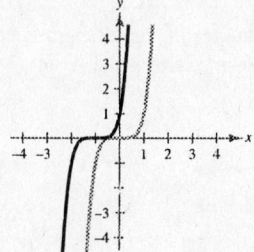

Horizontal shift 1 unit to the left

(b) $f(x) = x^5 + 1$

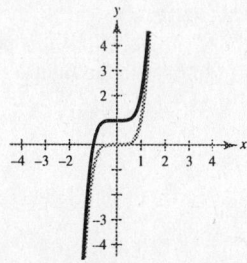

Vertical shift 1 unit upward

(c) $f(x) = 1 - \frac{1}{2}x^5$

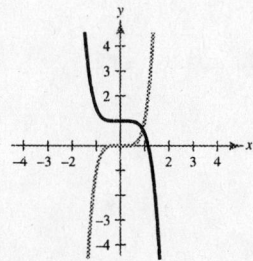

Reflection in the x-axis, vertical shrink by a factor of $\frac{1}{2}$, and vertical shift 1 unit upward

(d) $f(x) = -\frac{1}{2}(x + 1)^5$

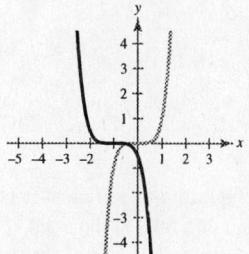

Reflection in the x-axis, vertical shrink by a factor of $\frac{1}{2}$, and horizontal shift 1 unit to the left

12. $y = x^6$

(a) $f(x) = -\frac{1}{8}x^6$

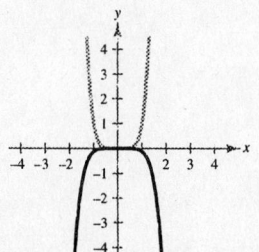

Vertical shrink by a factor of $\frac{1}{8}$ and reflection in the x-axis

(b) $f(x) = (x + 2)^6 - 4$

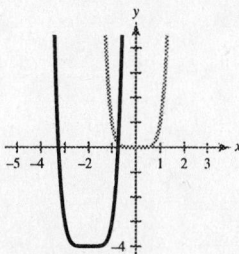

Horizontal shift 2 units to the left and vertical shift 4 units downward

(c) $f(x) = x^6 - 4$

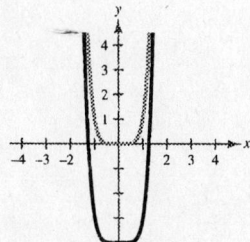

Vertical shift 4 units downward

(d) $f(x) = -\frac{1}{4}x^6 + 1$

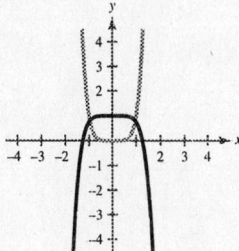

Reflection in the x-axis, vertical shrink by a factor of $\frac{1}{4}$, and vertical shift 1 unit upward

14. $f(x) = 2x^2 - 3x + 1$

Degree: 2

Leading coefficient: 2

The degree is even and the leading coefficient is positive. The graph rises to the left and rises to the right.

16. $h(x) = 1 - x^6$

Degree: 6

Leading coefficient: -1

The degree is even and the leading coefficient is negative. The graph falls to the left and falls to the right.

18. $f(x) = 2x^5 - 5x + 7.5$

Degree: 5

Leading coefficient: 2

The degree is odd and the leading coefficient is positive. The graph falls to the left and rises to the right.

20. $f(x) = \dfrac{3x^4 - 2x + 5}{4}$

Degree: 4

Leading coefficient: $\frac{3}{4}$

The degree is even and the leading coefficient is positive. The graph rises to the left and rises to the right.

22. $f(s) = -\frac{7}{8}(s^3 + 5s^2 - 7s + 1)$

Degree: 3

Leading coefficient: $-\frac{7}{8}$

The degree is odd and the leading coefficient is negative. The graph rises to the left and falls to the right.

24. $f(x) = -\frac{1}{3}(x^3 - 3x + 2),\ g(x) = -\frac{1}{3}x^3$

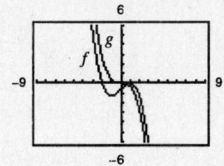

26. $f(x) = 3x^4 - 6x^2,\ g(x) = 3x^4$

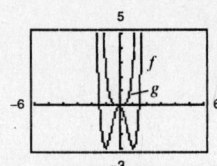

28. $f(x) = 49 - x^2$

$= (7 - x)(7 + x)$

$x = \pm 7$

30. $f(x) = x^2 + 10x + 25$

$= (x + 5)^2$

$x = -5$

32. $f(x) = \frac{1}{2}x^2 + \frac{5}{2}x - \frac{3}{2}$

$a = \frac{1}{2},\ b = \frac{5}{2},\ c = -\frac{3}{2}$

$x = \dfrac{-\frac{5}{2} \pm \sqrt{\left(\frac{5}{2}\right)^2 - 4\left(\frac{1}{2}\right)\left(-\frac{3}{2}\right)}}{1} = -\frac{5}{2} \pm \sqrt{\dfrac{37}{4}} = \dfrac{-5 \pm \sqrt{37}}{2}$

34. $g(x) = 5(x^2 - 2x - 1)$

$a = 1,\ b = -2,\ c = -1$

$x = \dfrac{-(-2) \pm \sqrt{(-2)^2 - 4(1)(-1)}}{2}$

$x = 1 \pm \sqrt{2}$

36. $f(x) = x^4 - x^3 - 20x^2$

$= x^2(x^2 - x - 20)$

$= x^2(x + 4)(x - 5)$

$x = 0,\ -4,\ 5$

38. $f(x) = x^5 + x^3 - 6x$

$= x(x^4 + x^2 - 6)$

$= x(x^2 + 3)(x^2 - 2)$

$x = 0,\ \pm\sqrt{2}$

40. $f(x) = 2x^4 - 2x^2 - 40$

$0 = 2(x^2 + 4)\left(x + \sqrt{5}\right)\left(x - \sqrt{5}\right)$

$x = \pm\sqrt{5}$

42. $f(x) = x^3 - 4x^2 - 25x + 100$

$\quad = x^2(x - 4) - 25(x - 4)$

$\quad = (x^2 - 25)(x - 4)$

$\quad = (x + 5)(x - 5)(x - 4)$

$x = \pm 5, 4$

44. $y = 4x^3 + 4x^2 - 7x + 2$

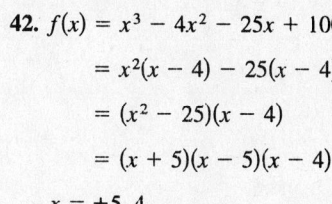

$0 = 4x^3 + 4x^2 - 7x + 2$

$\quad = (2x - 1)(2x^2 + 3x - 2)$

$\quad = (2x - 1)(2x - 1)(x + 2)$

$x = -2, \frac{1}{2}$

x-intercepts: $(-2, 0), \left(\frac{1}{2}, 0\right)$

46. $y = \frac{1}{4}x^3(x^2 - 9)$

$0 = \frac{1}{4}x^3(x^2 - 9)$

$x = 0, \pm 3$

x-intercepts: $(0, 0), (\pm 3, 0)$

48. $f(x) = (x - 0)(x - (-3))$

$\quad = x(x + 3)$

$\quad = x^2 + 3x$

Note: $f(x) = ax(x + 3)$ has zeros 0 and -3 for all real numbers a.

50. $f(x) = (x - (-4))(x - 5)$

$\quad = (x + 4)(x - 5)$

$\quad = x^2 - x - 20$

Note: $f(x) = a(x + 4)(x - 5)$ has zeros -4 and 5 for all real numbers a.

52. $f(x) = (x - 0)(x - 2)(x - 5)$

$\quad = x(x - 2)(x - 5)$

$\quad = x(x^2 - 7x + 10)$

$\quad = x^3 - 7x^2 + 10x$

Note: $f(x) = ax(x - 2)(x - 5)$ has zeros 0, 2, 5 for all real numbers a.

54. $f(x) = \big(x - (-2)\big)\big(x - (-1)\big)(x - 0)(x - 1)(x - 2)$

$\quad = x(x + 2)(x + 1)(x - 1)(x - 2)$

$\quad = x(x^2 - 4)(x^2 - 1)$

$\quad = x(x^4 - 5x^2 + 4)$

$\quad = x^5 - 5x^3 + 4x$

Note: $f(x) = ax(x + 2)(x + 1)(x - 1)(x - 2)$ has zeros $-2, -1, 0, 1, 2$ for all real numbers a.

56. $f(x) = (x - 2)\big[x - \big(4 + \sqrt{5}\big)\big]\big[x - \big(4 - \sqrt{5}\big)\big]$

$\quad = (x - 2)\big[(x - 4) + \sqrt{5}\big]\big[(x - 4) - \sqrt{5}\big]$

$\quad = (x - 2)\big[(x - 4)^2 - 5\big]$

$\quad = x(x - 4)^2 - 5x - 2(x - 4)^2 + 10$

$\quad = x^3 - 8x^2 + 16x - 5x - 2x^2 + 16x - 32 + 10$

$\quad = x^3 - 10x^2 + 27x - 22$

Note: $f(x) = a(x^3 - 10x^2 + 27x - 22)$ has these zeros for all real numbers a.

58. $f(x) = [x - (-8)][x - (-4)] = (x + 8)(x + 4) = x^2 + 12x + 32$

Note: $f(x) = a(x^2 + 12x + 32)$, $a \neq 0$, has degree 2 and zeros $x = -8$ and -4.

60. $f(x) = (x + 2)(x - 4)(x - 7) = (x + 2)(x^2 - 11x + 28) = x^3 - 9x^2 + 6x + 56$

Note: $f(x) = a(x^3 - 9x^2 + 6x + 56)$, $a \neq 0$, has degree 3 and zeros $x = -2, 4$, and 7.

62. $f(x) = (x - 9)^3 = x^3 - 27x^2 + 243x - 729$

Note: $f(x) = a(x^3 - 27x^2 + 243x - 729)$, $a \neq 0$, has degree 3 and zero $x = 9$.

64. $f(x) = (x + 4)(x + 1)(x - 3)(x - 6) = x^4 - 4x^3 - 23x^2 + 54x + 72$

Note: $f(x) = a(x^4 - 4x^3 - 23x^2 + 54x + 72)$, $a \neq 0$, has degree 4 and zeros $x = -4, -1, 3$, and 6.

66. $f(x) = (x + 3)^2(x - 1)(x - 5)(x - 6) = x^5 - 6x^4 - 22x^3 + 108x^2 + 189x - 270$

or $f(x) = (x + 3)(x - 1)^2(x - 5)(x - 6) = x^5 - 10x^4 + 14x^3 + 88x^2 - 183x + 90$

or $f(x) = (x - 3)(x - 1)(x - 5)^2(x - 6) = x^5 - 14x^4 + 50x^3 + 68x^2 - 555x + 450$

or $f(x) = (x - 3)(x - 1)(x - 5)(x - 6)^2 = x^5 - 15x^4 + 59x^3 + 63x^2 - 648x + 540$

Note: Any nonzero multiple of these functions would also have degree 5 and zeros $x = -3, 1, 5$, and 6.

68. $g(x) = x^4 - 4x^2 = x^2(x + 2)(x - 2)$

(a) Rises to the left
     Rises to the right

(b) Zeros: $-2, 0, 2$

(c)

x	± 0.5	± 1	± 1.5	± 2.5
$g(x)$	-0.94	-3	-3.94	14.1

(d)

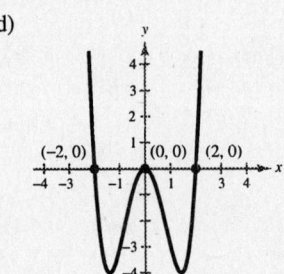

70. $g(x) = -x^2 + 10x - 16 = -(x - 2)(x - 8)$

(a) Falls to the left
     Falls to the right

(b) Zeros: 2, 8

(c)

x	1	3	5	7	9
$g(x)$	-7	5	9	5	-7

(d)

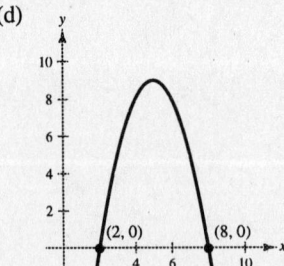

72. $f(x) = 1 - x^3$

(a) Rises to the left
     Falls to the right

(b) Zero: 1

(c)

x	-2	-1	0	1	2
$f(x)$	9	2	1	0	-7

(d)

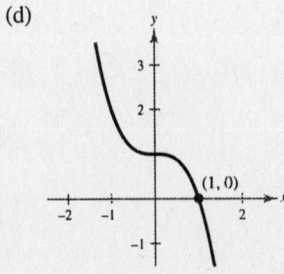

74. $f(x) = -4x^3 + 4x^2 + 15x$

$= -x(4x^2 - 4x - 15)$

$= -x(2x - 5)(2x + 3)$

(a) Rises to the left
Falls to the right

(b) Zeros: $-\frac{3}{2}, 0, \frac{5}{2}$

(c)

x	-3	-2	-1	0	1	2	3
$f(x)$	99	18	-7	0	15	14	-27

(d)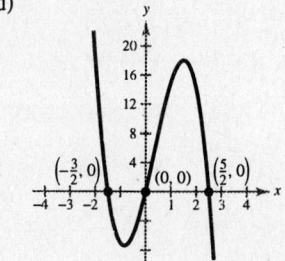

76. $f(x) = -48x^2 + 3x^4$

$= 3x^2(x^2 - 16)$

(a) Rises to the left
Rises to the right

(b) Zeros: $0, \pm 4$

(c)

x	-5	-4	-3	-2	-1	0	1	2	3	4	5
$f(x)$	675	0	-189	-144	-45	0	-45	-144	-189	0	675

(d)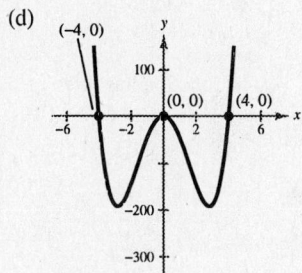

78. $h(x) = \frac{1}{3}x^3(x - 4)^2$

(a) Falls to the left
Rises to the right

(b) Zeros: 0 and 4

(c)

x	-1	0	1	2	3	4	5
$h(x)$	$-\frac{25}{3}$	0	3	$\frac{32}{3}$	9	0	$\frac{125}{3}$

(d)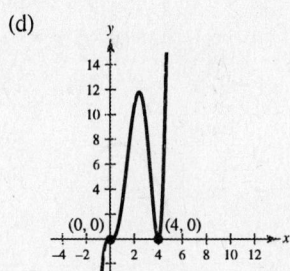

80. $g(x) = \frac{1}{10}(x + 1)^2(x - 3)^3$

(a) Falls to the left
Rises to the right

(b) Zeros: $-1, 3$

(c)

x	-2	-1	0	1	2
$f(x)$	-12.5	0	-2.7	-3.2	-0.9

(d)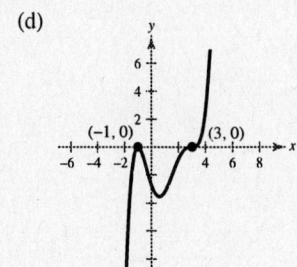

82. $f(x) = \frac{1}{4}x^4 - 2x^2$

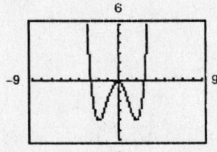

Zeros: -2.828 and 2.828 odd multiplicity; 0, even multiplicity

84. $h(x) = \frac{1}{5}(x + 2)^2(3x - 5)^2$

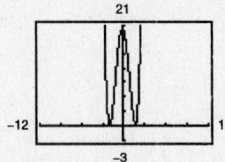

Zeros: $-2, \frac{5}{3}$, even multiplicity

86. $f(x) = 0.11x^3 - 2.07x^2 + 9.81x - 6.88$

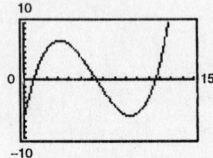

The function has three zeros. They are in the intervals $[0, 1], [6, 7],$ and $[11, 12]$.

88. $h(x) = x^4 - 10x^2 + 3$

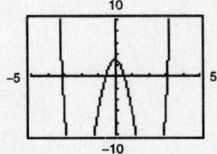

The function has four zeros. They are in the intervals $[-4, -3], [-1, 0], [0, 1],$ and $[3, 4]$.

90. (a) Volume $= l \cdot w \cdot h = (24 - 2x)(24 - 4x)x$
$$= 2(12 - x) \cdot 4(6 - x)x$$
$$= 8x(12 - x)(6 - x)$$

(b) $x > 0, \qquad 12 - x > 0, \qquad 6 - x > 0$
$$x < 12 \qquad\quad x < 6$$

Domain: $0 < x < 6$

(c)

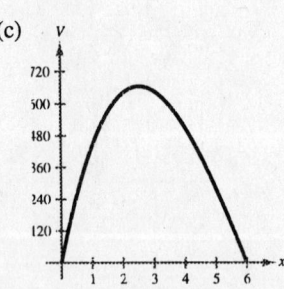

$x \approx 2.55$ when $V(x)$ is maximum.

92. $G = -0.003t^3 + 0.137t^2 + 0.458t - 0.839$

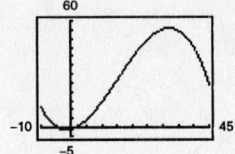

The tree is growing most rapidly at $t \approx 15$.

94. True. $f(x) = (x - 1)^6$ has one repeated solution.

96. $f(x) = x^4$; $f(x)$ is even.

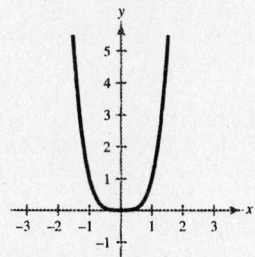

(a) $g(x) = f(x) + 2$

Vertical shift two units upward

$g(-x) = f(-x) + 2$

$\qquad = f(x) + 2$

$\qquad = g(x)$

Even

(b) $g(x) = f(x + 2)$

Horizontal shift two units to the left
Neither odd nor even

(c) $g(x) = f(-x) = (-x)^4 = x^4$

Reflection in the y-axis. The graph looks the same.
Even

(d) $g(x) = -f(x) = -x^4$

Reflection in the x-axis
Even

(e) $g(x) = f(\frac{1}{2}x) = \frac{1}{16}x^4$

Horizontal stretch
Even

(f) $g(x) = \frac{1}{2}f(x) = \frac{1}{2}x^4$

Vertical shrink
Even

(g) $g(x) = f(x^{3/4}) = (x^{3/4})^4 = x^3$

Odd

(h) $g(x) = (f \circ f)(x) = f(f(x)) = f(x^4) = (x^4)^4 = x^{16}$

Even

98. $2x^2 - x - 28 = 0$

$(2x + 7)(x - 4) = 0$

$\qquad 2x + 7 = 0 \Rightarrow x = -\frac{7}{2}$

$\qquad x - 4 = 0 \Rightarrow x = 4$

100. $12x^2 + 11x - 5 = 0$

$(3x - 1)(4x + 5) = 0$

$\qquad 3x - 1 = 0 \Rightarrow x = \frac{1}{3}$

$\qquad 4x + 5 = 0 \Rightarrow x = -\frac{5}{4}$

102. $\qquad x^2 - 2x - 21 = 0$

$(x^2 - 2x + (-1)^2) - 21 - 1 = 0$

$\qquad (x - 1)^2 - 22 = 0$

$\qquad (x - 1)^2 = 22$

$\qquad x - 1 = \pm\sqrt{22}$

$\qquad x = 1 \pm \sqrt{22}$

104. $\qquad 2x^2 + 5x - 20 = 0$

$\qquad 2\left(x^2 + \frac{5}{2}x\right) - 20 = 0$

$2\left(x^2 + \frac{5}{2}x + \left(\frac{5}{4}\right)^2\right) - 20 - \frac{25}{8} = 0$

$\qquad 2\left(x + \frac{5}{4}\right)^2 - \frac{185}{8} = 0$

$\qquad \left(x + \frac{5}{4}\right)^2 = \frac{185}{16}$

$\qquad x + \frac{5}{4} = \pm\frac{\sqrt{185}}{4}$

$\qquad x = \frac{-5 \pm \sqrt{185}}{4}$

106. $5x^2 + 7x - 24 = (5x - 8)(x + 3)$

108. $4x^4 - 7x^3 - 15x^2 = x^2(4x^2 - 7x - 15)$
$$= x^2(4x + 5)(x - 3)$$

110. (a) The graph does not pass the horizontal line test.

(b) Since $(3, 1)$ is on the graph, $g(3) = 1$. Therefore, $g^{-1}(1) = 3$.

Section 2.3   Polynomial and Synthetic Division

Solutions to Even-Numbered Exercises

2. $y_1 = \dfrac{3x - 5}{x - 3}$ and $y_2 = 3 + \dfrac{4}{x - 3}$

$$\begin{array}{r} 3 \\ x - 3 \overline{)\ 3x - 5} \\ \underline{3x - 9} \\ 4 \end{array}$$

So, $y_1 = \dfrac{3x - 5}{x - 3} = 3 + \dfrac{4}{x - 3} = y_2$.

4. $y_1 = \dfrac{x^2}{x + 2}$ and $y_2 = x - 2 + \dfrac{4}{x + 2}$

$$\begin{array}{r} x - 2 \\ x + 2 \overline{)\ x^2 + 0x + 0} \\ \underline{x^2 + 2x} \\ -2x + 0 \\ \underline{-2x - 4} \\ 4 \end{array}$$

So, $y_1 = \dfrac{x^2}{x + 2} = x - 2 + \dfrac{4}{x + 2} = y_2$.

6.

$y_1 = \dfrac{x^3 - 2x^2 + 5}{x^2 + x + 1}$ and $y_2 = x - 3 + \dfrac{2(x + 4)}{x^2 + x + 1}$

$$\begin{array}{r} x - 3 \\ x^2 + x + 1 \overline{)\ x^3 - 2x^2 + 0x + 5} \\ \underline{x^3 + x^2 + x} \\ -3x^2 - x + 5 \\ \underline{-3x^2 - 3x - 3} \\ 2x + 8 \end{array}$$

So, $y_1 = \dfrac{x^3 - 2x^2 + 5}{x^2 + x + 1} = x - 3 + \dfrac{2(x + 4)}{x^2 + x + 1} = y_2$.

8.

$$\begin{array}{r} 5x + 3 \\ x - 4 \overline{)\ 5x^2 - 17x - 12} \\ \underline{5x^2 - 20x} \\ 3x - 12 \\ \underline{3x - 12} \\ 0 \end{array}$$

$\dfrac{5x^2 - 17x - 12}{x - 4} = 5x + 3$

10.

$$\begin{array}{r} 2x^2 - 4x + 3 \\ 3x - 2 \overline{)\ 6x^3 - 16x^2 + 17x - 6} \\ \underline{6x^3 - 4x^2} \\ -12x^2 + 17x \\ \underline{-12x^2 + 8x} \\ 9x - 6 \\ \underline{9x - 6} \\ 0 \end{array}$$

$\dfrac{6x^3 - 16x^2 + 17x - 6}{3x - 2} = 2x^2 - 4x + 3$

12.

$$
\begin{array}{r}
x^2 + 7x + 18 \\
x - 3 \overline{\smash{\big)}\ x^3 + 4x^2 - 3x - 12} \\
\underline{x^3 - 3x^2} \\
7x^2 - 3x \\
\underline{7x^2 - 21x} \\
18x - 12 \\
\underline{18x - 54} \\
42
\end{array}
$$

$$\frac{x^3 + 4x^2 - 3x - 12}{x - 3} = x^2 + 7x + 18 + \frac{42}{x - 3}$$

14.

$$
\begin{array}{r}
4 \\
2x + 1 \overline{\smash{\big)}\ 8x - 5} \\
\underline{8x + 4} \\
-9
\end{array}
$$

$$\frac{8x - 5}{2x + 1} = 4 - \frac{9}{2x + 1}$$

16.

$$
\begin{array}{r}
x \\
x^2 + 0x + 1 \overline{\smash{\big)}\ x^3 + 0x^2 + 0x - 9} \\
\underline{x^3 + 0x^2 + x} \\
-x - 9
\end{array}
$$

$$\frac{x^3 - 9}{x^2 + 1} = x - \frac{x + 9}{x^2 + 1}$$

18.

$$
\begin{array}{r}
x^2 \\
x^3 + 0x^2 + 0x - 1 \overline{\smash{\big)}\ x^5 + 0x^4 + 0x^3 + 0x^2 + 0x + 7} \\
\underline{x^5 + 0x^4 + 0x^3 - x^2} \\
x^2 + 7
\end{array}
$$

$$\frac{x^5 + 7}{x^3 - 1} = x^2 + \frac{x^2 + 7}{x^3 - 1}$$

20.

$$
\begin{array}{r}
2x \\
x^2 - 2x + 1 \overline{\smash{\big)}\ 2x^3 - 4x^2 - 15x + 5} \\
\underline{2x^3 - 4x^2 + 2x} \\
-17x + 5
\end{array}
$$

$$\frac{2x^3 - 4x^2 - 15x + 5}{(x - 1)^2} = 2x - \frac{17x - 5}{x^2 - 2x + 1}$$

22.

$$
\begin{array}{r|rrrr}
-3 & 5 & 18 & 7 & -6 \\
   &   & -15 & -9 & 6 \\
\hline
   & 5 & 3 & -2 & 0
\end{array}
$$

$$\frac{5x^3 + 18x^2 + 7x - 6}{x + 3} = 5x^2 + 3x - 2$$

24.

$$
\begin{array}{r|rrrr}
2 & 9 & -18 & -16 & 32 \\
  &   & 18 & 0 & -32 \\
\hline
  & 9 & 0 & -16 & 0
\end{array}
$$

$$\frac{9x^3 - 18x^2 - 16x + 32}{x - 2} = 9x^2 - 16$$

26.

$$
\begin{array}{r|rrrr}
6 & 3 & -16 & 0 & -72 \\
  &   & 18 & 12 & 72 \\
\hline
  & 3 & 2 & 12 & 0
\end{array}
$$

$$\frac{3x^3 - 16x^2 - 72}{x - 6} = 3x^2 + 2x + 12$$

28.

$$
\begin{array}{r|rrrr}
-2 & 5 & 0 & 6 & 8 \\
   &   & -10 & 20 & -52 \\
\hline
   & 5 & -10 & 26 & -44
\end{array}
$$

$$\frac{5x^3 + 6x + 8}{x + 2} = 5x^2 - 10x + 26 - \frac{44}{x + 2}$$

30.

$$
\begin{array}{r|rrrrrr}
-3 & 1 & -13 & 0 & 0 & -120 & 80 \\
   &   & -3 & 48 & -144 & 432 & -936 \\
\hline
   & 1 & -16 & 48 & -144 & 312 & -856
\end{array}
$$

$$\frac{x^5 - 13x^4 - 120x + 80}{x + 3} = x^4 - 16x^3 + 48x^2 - 144x + 312 - \frac{856}{x + 3}$$

32. 9 | 1   0   0   −729

         9 81   729

     1 9 81   0

$$\frac{x^3 - 729}{x - 9} = x^2 + 9x + 81$$

34. −2 | −3 0   0   0   0

          6 −12 24 −48

    −3 6 −12 24 −48

$$\frac{-3x^4}{x + 2} = -3x^3 + 6x^2 - 12x + 24 - \frac{48}{x + 2}$$

36. −1 | −1   2 −3   5

         1 −3   6

    −1 3 −6 11

$$\frac{5 - 3x + 2x^2 - x^3}{x + 1} = -x^2 + 3x - 6 + \frac{11}{x + 1}$$

38. $\frac{3}{2}$ | 3 −4   0   5

         $\frac{9}{2}$ $\frac{3}{4}$ $\frac{9}{8}$

    3 $\frac{1}{2}$ $\frac{3}{4}$ $\frac{49}{8}$

$$\frac{3x^3 - 4x^2 + 5}{x - \frac{3}{2}} = 3x^2 + \frac{1}{2}x + \frac{3}{4} + \frac{49}{8x - 12}$$

40. $f(x) = x^3 - 5x^2 - 11x + 8, k = -2$

  −2 | 1 −5 −11   8

           −2   14 −6

     1 −7   3   2

$f(x) = (x + 2)(x^2 - 7x + 3) + 2$

$f(-2) = (-2)^3 - 5(-2)^2 - 11(-2) + 8$

$\quad\quad = -8 - 20 + 22 + 8 = 2$

42. $f(x) = 10x^3 - 22x^2 - 3x + 4, k = \frac{1}{5}$

  $\frac{1}{5}$ | 10 −22 −3   4

             2 −4 −$\frac{7}{5}$

     10 −20 −7 $\frac{13}{5}$

$f(x) = \left(x - \frac{1}{5}\right)(10x^2 - 20x - 7) + \frac{13}{5}$

$f\left(\frac{1}{5}\right) = 10\left(\frac{1}{5}\right)^3 - 22\left(\frac{1}{5}\right)^2 - 3\left(\frac{1}{5}\right) + 4$

$\quad\quad = \frac{2}{25} - \frac{22}{25} - \frac{3}{5} + 4 = \frac{65}{25} = \frac{13}{5}$

44. $f(x) = x^3 + 2x^2 - 5x - 4, k = -\sqrt{5}$

  $-\sqrt{5}$ | 1   2   −5   −4

            $-\sqrt{5}$ $-2\sqrt{5} + 5$ 10

      1 $2 - \sqrt{5}$ $-2\sqrt{5}$ 6

$f(x) = \left(x + \sqrt{5}\right)\left[x^2 + \left(2 - \sqrt{5}\right)x - 2\sqrt{5}\right] + 6$

$f\left(-\sqrt{5}\right) = \left(-\sqrt{5}\right)^3 + 2\left(-\sqrt{5}\right)^2 - 5\left(-\sqrt{5}\right) - 4$

$\quad\quad = -5\sqrt{5} + 10 + 5\sqrt{5} - 4 = 6$

46. $f(x) = -3x^3 + 8x^2 + 10x - 8, k = 2 + \sqrt{2}$

  $2 + \sqrt{2}$ | −3   8   10   −8

              $-6 - 3\sqrt{2}$ $-2 - 4\sqrt{2}$ 8

       −3 $2 - 3\sqrt{2}$ $8 - 4\sqrt{2}$ 0

$f(x) = \left(x - 2 - \sqrt{2}\right)\left[-3x^2 + \left(2 - 3\sqrt{2}\right)x + 8 - 4\sqrt{2}\right]$

$f\left(2 + \sqrt{2}\right) = -3\left(2 + \sqrt{2}\right)^3 + 8\left(2 + \sqrt{2}\right)^2 + 10\left(2 + \sqrt{2}\right) - 8$

$\quad\quad = -3\left(20 + 14\sqrt{2}\right) + 8\left(6 + 4\sqrt{2}\right) + 10\left(2 + \sqrt{2}\right) - 8$

$\quad\quad = -60 - 42\sqrt{2} + 48 + 32\sqrt{2} + 20 + 10\sqrt{2} - 8$

$\quad\quad = 0$

48. $g(x) = x^6 - 4x^4 + 3x^2 + 2$

(a)

$$\begin{array}{r|rrrrrrr} 2 & 1 & 0 & -4 & 0 & 3 & 0 & 2 \\ & & 2 & 4 & 0 & 0 & 6 & 12 \\ \hline & 1 & 2 & 0 & 0 & 3 & 6 & 14 \end{array}$$

$g(2) = 14$

(b)

$$\begin{array}{r|rrrrrrr} -4 & 1 & 0 & -4 & 0 & 3 & 0 & 2 \\ & & -4 & 16 & -48 & 192 & -780 & 3120 \\ \hline & 1 & -4 & 12 & -48 & 195 & -780 & 3122 \end{array}$$

$g(-4) = 3122$

(c)

$$\begin{array}{r|rrrrrrr} 3 & 1 & 0 & -4 & 0 & 3 & 0 & 2 \\ & & 3 & 9 & 15 & 45 & 144 & 432 \\ \hline & 1 & 3 & 5 & 15 & 48 & 144 & 434 \end{array}$$

$g(3) = 434$

(d)

$$\begin{array}{r|rrrrrrr} -1 & 1 & 0 & -4 & 0 & 3 & 0 & 2 \\ & & -1 & 1 & 3 & -3 & 0 & 0 \\ \hline & 1 & -1 & -3 & 3 & 0 & 0 & 2 \end{array}$$

$g(-1) = 2$

50. $f(x) = 0.4x^4 - 1.6x^3 + 0.7x^2 - 2$

(a)

$$\begin{array}{r|rrrrr} 1 & 0.4 & -1.6 & 0.7 & 0 & -2 \\ & & 0.4 & -1.2 & -0.5 & -0.5 \\ \hline & 0.4 & -1.2 & -0.5 & -0.5 & -2.5 \end{array}$$

$f(1) = -2.5$

(b)

$$\begin{array}{r|rrrrr} -2 & 0.4 & -1.6 & 0.7 & 0 & -2 \\ & & -0.8 & 4.8 & -11 & 22 \\ \hline & 0.4 & -2.4 & 5.5 & -11 & 20 \end{array}$$

$f(-2) = 20$

(c)

$$\begin{array}{r|rrrrr} 5 & 0.4 & -1.6 & 0.7 & 0 & -2 \\ & & 2.0 & 2.0 & 13.5 & 67.5 \\ \hline & 0.4 & 0.4 & 2.7 & 13.5 & 65.5 \end{array}$$

$f(5) = 65.5$

(d)

$$\begin{array}{r|rrrrr} -10 & 0.4 & -1.6 & 0.7 & 0 & -2 \\ & & -4.0 & 56.0 & -567 & 5670 \\ \hline & 0.4 & -5.6 & 56.7 & -567 & 5668 \end{array}$$

$f(-10) = 5668$

52.

$$\begin{array}{r|rrrr} -4 & 1 & 0 & -28 & -48 \\ & & -4 & 16 & 48 \\ \hline & 1 & -4 & -12 & 0 \end{array}$$

$x^3 - 28x - 48 = (x + 4)(x^2 - 4x - 12)$
$$= (x + 4)(x - 6)(x + 2)$$

Zeros: $-4, -2, 6$

54.

$$\begin{array}{r|rrrr} \frac{2}{3} & 48 & -80 & 41 & -6 \\ & & 32 & -32 & 6 \\ \hline & 48 & -48 & 9 & 0 \end{array}$$

$48x^3 - 80x^2 + 41x - 6 = \left(x - \frac{2}{3}\right)(48x^2 - 48x + 9)$
$$= \left(x - \frac{2}{3}\right)(4x - 3)(12x - 3)$$
$$= (3x - 2)(4x - 3)(4x - 1)$$

Zeros: $\frac{2}{3}, \frac{3}{4}, \frac{1}{4}$

56.

$$\begin{array}{r|rrrr} \sqrt{2} & 1 & 2 & -2 & -4 \\ & & \sqrt{2} & 2\sqrt{2} + 2 & 4 \\ \hline & 1 & 2 + \sqrt{2} & 2\sqrt{2} & 0 \end{array}$$

$x^3 + 2x^2 - 2x - 4 = (x - \sqrt{2})\left[x^2 + (2 + \sqrt{2})x + 2\sqrt{2}\right]$
$$= (x - \sqrt{2})(x + 2)(x + \sqrt{2})$$

Zeros: $-2, -\sqrt{2}, \sqrt{2}$

58.

$$\begin{array}{r|rrrr} 2 - \sqrt{5} & 1 & -1 & -13 & -3 \\ & & 2 - \sqrt{5} & 7 - 3\sqrt{5} & 3 \\ \hline & 1 & 1 - \sqrt{5} & -6 - 3\sqrt{5} & 0 \end{array}$$

$x^3 - x^2 - 13x - 3 = \left[x - \left(2 - \sqrt{5}\right)\right]\left[x^2 + \left(1 - \sqrt{5}\right)x - \left(6 + 3\sqrt{5}\right)\right]$
$$= \left(x - 2 + \sqrt{5}\right)\left(x - 2 - \sqrt{5}\right)(x + 3)$$

Zeros: $2 - \sqrt{5}, 2 + \sqrt{5}, -3$

60. $f(x) = 3x^3 + 2x^2 - 19x + 6$; Factors: $(x + 3)$, $(x - 2)$

(a)
$$
\begin{array}{r|rrrr}
-3 & 3 & 2 & -19 & 6 \\
   &   & -9 & 21 & -6 \\
\hline
   & 3 & -7 & 2 & 0
\end{array}
$$

$$
\begin{array}{r|rrr}
2 & 3 & -7 & 2 \\
  &   & 6 & -2 \\
\hline
  & 3 & -1 & 0
\end{array}
$$

(b) The remaining factor is $(3x - 1)$.

(c) $f(x) = 3x^3 + 2x^2 - 19x + 6$

$\qquad = (3x - 1)(x + 3)(x - 2)$

(d) Zeros: $\frac{1}{3}, -3, 2$

(e)
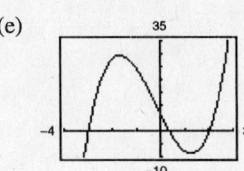

62. $f(x) = 8x^4 - 14x^3 - 71x^2 - 10x + 24$;
Factors: $(x + 2)$. $(x - 4)$

(a)
$$
\begin{array}{r|rrrrr}
-2 & 8 & -14 & -71 & -10 & 24 \\
   &   & -16 & 60 & 22 & -24 \\
\hline
   & 8 & -30 & -11 & 12 & 0
\end{array}
$$

$$
\begin{array}{r|rrrr}
4 & 8 & -30 & -11 & 12 \\
  &   & 32 & 8 & -12 \\
\hline
  & 8 & 2 & -3 & 0
\end{array}
$$

(b) $8x^2 + 2x - 3 = (4x + 3)(2x - 1)$

The remaining factors are $(4x + 3)$ and $(2x - 1)$.

(c) $f(x) = (4x + 3)(2x - 1)(x + 2)(x - 4)$

(d) Zeros: $-\frac{3}{4}, \frac{1}{2}, -2, 4$

(e)
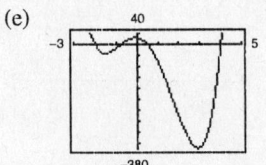

64. $f(x) = 10x^3 - 11x^2 - 72x + 45$;
Factors: $(2x + 5)$, $(5x - 3)$

(a)
$$
\begin{array}{r|rrrr}
-\frac{5}{2} & 10 & -11 & -72 & 45 \\
   &   & -25 & 90 & -45 \\
\hline
   & 10 & -36 & 18 & 0
\end{array}
$$

$$
\begin{array}{r|rrr}
\frac{3}{5} & 10 & -36 & 18 \\
  &   & 6 & -18 \\
\hline
  & 10 & -30 & 0
\end{array}
$$

(b) $10x - 30 = 10(x - 3)$

This shows that $\dfrac{f(x)}{\left(x + \frac{5}{2}\right)\left(x - \frac{3}{5}\right)} = 10(x - 3)$,

so $\dfrac{f(x)}{(2x + 5)(5x - 3)} = x - 3$.

The remaining factor is $(x - 3)$.

(c) $f(x) = (x - 3)(2x + 5)(5x - 3)$

(d) Zeros: $3, -\frac{5}{2}, \frac{3}{5}$

(e)
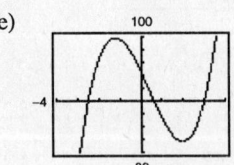

66. $f(x) = x^3 + 3x^2 - 48x - 144$;
Factors: $\left(x + 4\sqrt{3}\right)$, $(x + 3)$

(a)
$$
\begin{array}{r|rrrr}
-3 & 1 & 3 & -48 & -144 \\
   &   & -3 & 0 & 144 \\
\hline
   & 1 & 0 & -48 & 0
\end{array}
$$

$$
\begin{array}{r|rrr}
-4\sqrt{3} & 1 & 0 & -48 \\
  &   & -4\sqrt{3} & 48 \\
\hline
  & 1 & -4\sqrt{3} & 0
\end{array}
$$

(b) The remaining factor is $\left(x - 4\sqrt{3}\right)$.

(c) $f(x) = \left(x - 4\sqrt{3}\right)\left(x + 4\sqrt{3}\right)(x + 3)$

(d) Zeros: $\pm 4\sqrt{3}, -3$

(e)
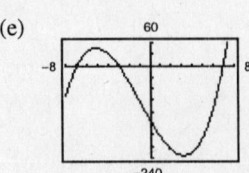

68. $g(x) = x^3 - 4x^2 - 2x + 8$

(a) The zeros of g are $x = 4$, $x \approx -1.414$, $x \approx 1.414$.

(b)
$$
\begin{array}{r|rrrr}
4 & 1 & -4 & -2 & 8 \\
  &   & 4 & 0 & -8 \\
\hline
  & 1 & 0 & -2 & 0
\end{array}
$$

$f(x) = (x - 4)(x^2 - 2)$

$\qquad = (x - 4)(x - \sqrt{2})(x + \sqrt{2})$

70. $f(s) = s^3 - 12s^2 + 40s - 24$

(a) The zeros of f are $s = 6$, $s \approx 0.764$, $s \approx 5.236$

(b)
$$
\begin{array}{r|rrrr}
6 & 1 & -12 & 40 & -24 \\
  &   & 6 & -36 & 24 \\
\hline
  & 1 & -6 & 4 & 0
\end{array}
$$

$f(s) = (s - 6)(s^2 - 6s + 4)$

$\qquad = (s - 6)\big[s - (3 + \sqrt{5})\big]\big[s - (3 - \sqrt{5})\big]$

72. $\dfrac{x^3 + x^2 - 64x - 64}{x + 8}$

$$
\begin{array}{r|rrrr}
-8 & 1 & 1 & -64 & -64 \\
   &   & -8 & 56 & 64 \\
\hline
   & 1 & -7 & -8 & 0
\end{array}
$$

$\dfrac{x^3 + x^2 - 64x - 64}{x + 8} = x^2 - 7x - 8$

74. $\dfrac{2x^3 + 3x^2 - 3x - 2}{x - 1}$

$$
\begin{array}{r|rrrr}
1 & 2 & 3 & -3 & -2 \\
  &   & 2 & 5 & 2 \\
\hline
  & 2 & 5 & 2 & 0
\end{array}
$$

$\dfrac{2x^3 + 3x^2 - 3x - 2}{x - 1} = 2x^2 + 5x + 2$

76. $\dfrac{x^4 + 9x^3 - 5x^2 - 36x + 4}{(x + 2)(x - 2)}$

$$
\begin{array}{r|rrrrr}
2 & 1 & 9 & -5 & -36 & 4 \\
  &   & 2 & 22 & 34 & -4 \\
\hline
  & 1 & 11 & 17 & -2 & 0
\end{array}
$$

$$
\begin{array}{r|rrrr}
-2 & 1 & 11 & 17 & -2 \\
   &   & -2 & -18 & 2 \\
\hline
   & 1 & 9 & -1 & 0
\end{array}
$$

$\dfrac{x^4 + 9x^3 - 5x^2 - 36x + 4}{x^2 - 4} = x^2 + 9x - 1$

78. (a) and (b)

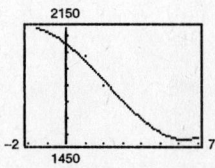

$M = 2.412t^3 - 15.557t^2 - 90.488t + 2056.617$

(c)

t	-1	0	1	2	3	4	5	6
M	2129	2057	1953	1833	1710	1600	1517	1475

(d)
$$
\begin{array}{r|rrrr}
11 & 2.412 & -15.557 & -90.488 & 2056.617 \\
   &   & 26.532 & 120.725 & 332.607 \\
\hline
   & 2.412 & 10.975 & 30.237 & 2389.224
\end{array}
$$

$M(11) \approx 2389$ thousand

No, this model would not be used to predict the number of military personnel in the future because the model will approach infinity quickly.

80. True.

$$\frac{1}{2} \begin{array}{|ccccccc} 6 & 1 & -92 & 45 & 184 & 4 & -48 \\ & 3 & 2 & -45 & 0 & 92 & 48 \\ \hline 6 & 4 & -90 & 0 & 184 & 96 & 0 \end{array}$$

$f(x) = (2x - 1)(x + 1)(x - 2)(x - 3)(3x + 2)(x + 4)$

82.

$$\begin{array}{r} x^{2n} - x^n + 3 \\ x^n - 2 \overline{\smash{\big)}\ x^{3n} - 3x^{2n} + 5x^n - 6} \\ \underline{x^{3n} - 2x^{2n}} \\ -x^{2n} + 5x^n \\ \underline{-x^{2n} + 2x^n} \\ 3x^n - 6 \\ \underline{3x^n - 6} \\ 0 \end{array}$$

$\dfrac{x^{3n} - 3x^{2n} + 5x^n - 6}{x^n - 2} = x^{2n} - x^n + 3$

84. You can check polynomial division by multiplying the quotient by the divisor. This should yield the original dividend if the multiplication was performed correctly.

86.

$$-2 \begin{array}{|cccccc} 1 & 0 & 0 & -2 & 1 & c \\ & -2 & 4 & -8 & 20 & -42 \\ \hline 1 & -2 & 4 & -10 & 21 & c - 42 \end{array}$$

To divide evenly, $c - 42$ must equal zero. Thus, c must equal 42.

88. In this case it is easier to evaluate $f(2)$ directly because $f(x)$ is in factored form. To evaluate using synthetic division you would have to expand each factor and then multiply it all out.

90.
$$9x^2 - 25 = 0$$
$$(3x - 5)(3x + 5) = 0$$
$$3x - 5 = 0 \Rightarrow x = \tfrac{5}{3}$$
$$3x + 5 = 0 \Rightarrow x = -\tfrac{5}{3}$$

92. $5x^2 - 3x - 14 = 0$

$(5x + 7)(x - 2) = 0$

$5x + 7 = 0 \Rightarrow x = -\tfrac{7}{5}$

$x - 2 = 0 \Rightarrow x = 2$

94. $2x^2 + 6x + 3 = 0$

$$x = \frac{-b \pm \sqrt{b^2 - 4ac}}{2a} = \frac{-6 \pm \sqrt{6^2 - 4(2)(3)}}{2(2)} = \frac{-6 \pm \sqrt{12}}{4}$$

$$= \frac{-3 \pm \sqrt{3}}{2}$$

96. $f(x) = (x - 0)(x - 3)(x - 4) = x(x - 3)(x - 4) = x(x^2 - 7x + 12)$

$= x^3 - 7x^2 + 12x$

Note: Any nonzero scalar multiple of $f(x)$ would also have these zeros.

98. $f(x) = [x - (-3)][x - (1 + \sqrt{2})][x - (1 - \sqrt{2})]$

$= (x + 3)[(x - 1) - \sqrt{2}][(x - 1) + \sqrt{2}]$

$= (x + 3)[(x - 1)^2 - (\sqrt{2})^2]$

$= (x + 3)(x^2 - 2x - 1)$

$= x^3 + x^2 - 7x - 3$

Note: Any nonzero scalar multiple of $f(x)$ would also have these zeros.

Section 2.4 Complex Numbers

Solutions to Even-Numbered Exercises

2. $a + bi = 13 + 4i$

$a = 13$

$b = 4$

4. $(a + 6) + 2bi = 6 - 5i$

$2b = -5$

$b = -\frac{5}{2}$

$a + 6 = 6$

$a = 0$

6. $3 + \sqrt{-16} = 3 + 4i$

8. $1 + \sqrt{-8} = 1 + 2\sqrt{2}i$

10. $\sqrt{-4} = 2i$

12. 45

14. $-4i^2 + 2i = -4(-1) + 2i$

$= 4 + 2i$

16. $\sqrt{-0.0004} = 0.02i$

18. $(13 - 2i) + (-5 + 6i) = 8 + 4i$

20. $(3 + 2i) - (6 + 13i) = 3 + 2i - 6 - 13i$

$= -3 - 11i$

22. $\left(8 + \sqrt{-18}\right) - \left(4 + 3\sqrt{2}i\right) = 8 + 3\sqrt{2}i - 4 - 3\sqrt{2}i$

$= 4$

24. $22 + (-5 + 8i) + 10i = 17 + 18i$

26. $(1.6 + 3.2i) + (-5.8 + 4.3i) = -4.2 + 7.5i$

28. $\sqrt{-5} \cdot \sqrt{-10} = \left(\sqrt{5}i\right)\left(\sqrt{10}i\right)$

$= \sqrt{50}i^2 = 5\sqrt{2}(-1) = -5\sqrt{2}$

30. $\left(\sqrt{-75}\right)^2 = \left(\sqrt{75}i\right)^2 = 75i^2 = -75$

32. $(6 - 2i)(2 - 3i) = 12 - 18i - 4i + 6i^2$

$= 12 - 22i - 6 = 6 - 22i$

34. $-8i(9 + 4i) = -72i - 32i^2$

$= 32 - 72i$

36. $\left(3 + \sqrt{-5}\right)\left(7 - \sqrt{-10}\right) = \left(3 + \sqrt{5}\,i\right)\left(7 - \sqrt{10}\,i\right)$

$$= 21 - 3\sqrt{10}\,i + 7\sqrt{5}\,i - \sqrt{50}\,i^2$$

$$= 21 + \sqrt{50} + 7\sqrt{5}\,i - 3\sqrt{10}\,i$$

$$= \left(21 + 5\sqrt{2}\right) + \left(7\sqrt{5} - 3\sqrt{10}\right)i$$

38. $(2 - 3i)^2 = 4 - 12i + 9i^2$

$$= 4 - 9 - 12i$$

$$= -5 - 12i$$

40. $(1 - 2i)^2 - (1 + 2i)^2 = 1 - 4i + 4i^2 - (1 + 4i + 4i^2)$

$$= 1 - 4i + 4i^2 - 1 - 4i - 4i^2$$

$$= -8i$$

42. The complex conjugate of $7 - 12i$ is $7 + 12i$.

$$(7 - 12i)(7 + 12i) = 49 - 144i^2$$

$$= 49 - (-144)$$

$$= 193$$

44. The complex conjugate of $-3 + \sqrt{2}\,i$ is $-3 - \sqrt{2}\,i$.

$$\left(-3 + \sqrt{2}\,i\right)\left(-3 - \sqrt{2}\,i\right) = 9 - 2i^2$$

$$= 9 - (-2)$$

$$= 11$$

46. The complex conjugate of $\sqrt{-15} = \sqrt{15}\,i$ is $-\sqrt{15}\,i$.

$$\left(\sqrt{15}\,i\right)\left(-\sqrt{15}\,i\right) = -15i^2 = -(-15) = 15$$

48. The complex conjugate of $1 + \sqrt{8}$ is $1 + \sqrt{8}$.

$$\left(1 + \sqrt{8}\right)\left(1 + \sqrt{8}\right) = 1 + 2\sqrt{8} + 8$$

$$= 9 + 4\sqrt{2}$$

50. $-\dfrac{14}{2i} \cdot \dfrac{-2i}{-2i} = \dfrac{28i}{-4i^2} = \dfrac{28i}{4} = 7i$

52. $\dfrac{5}{1 - i} \cdot \dfrac{1 + i}{1 + i} = \dfrac{5 + 5i}{1 - i^2} = \dfrac{5 + 5i}{2} = \dfrac{5}{2} + \dfrac{5}{2}i$

54. $\dfrac{6 - 7i}{1 - 2i} \cdot \dfrac{1 + 2i}{1 + 2i} = \dfrac{6 + 12i - 7i - 14i^2}{1 - 4i^2}$

$$= \dfrac{20 + 5i}{5} = \dfrac{20}{5} + \dfrac{5}{5}i = 4 + i$$

56. $\dfrac{8 + 16i}{2i} \cdot \dfrac{-2i}{-2i} = \dfrac{-16i - 32i^2}{-4i^2} = 8 - 4i$

58. $\dfrac{5i}{(2 + 3i)^2} = \dfrac{5i}{4 + 12i + 9i^2} = \dfrac{5i}{-5 + 12i} \cdot \dfrac{-5 - 12i}{-5 - 12i}$

$$= \dfrac{-25i - 60i^2}{25 - 144i^2} = \dfrac{60 - 25i}{169} = \dfrac{60}{169} - \dfrac{25}{169}i$$

60. $\dfrac{2i}{2 + i} + \dfrac{5}{2 - i} = \dfrac{2i(2 - i)}{(2 + i)(2 - i)} + \dfrac{5(2 + i)}{(2 + i)(2 - i)}$

$$= \dfrac{4i - 2i^2 + 10 + 5i}{4 - i^2}$$

$$= \dfrac{12 + 9i}{5}$$

$$= \dfrac{12}{5} + \dfrac{9}{5}i$$

62. $\dfrac{1 + i}{i} - \dfrac{3}{4 - i} = \dfrac{(1 + i)(4 - i) - 3i}{i(4 - i)}$

$$= \dfrac{4 - i + 4i - i^2 - 3i}{4i - i^2}$$

$$= \dfrac{5}{1 + 4i} \cdot \dfrac{1 - 4i}{1 - 4i}$$

$$= \dfrac{5 - 20i}{1 - 16i^2}$$

$$= \dfrac{5}{17} - \dfrac{20}{17}i$$

64. $x^2 + 6x + 10 = 0; \quad a = 1, b = 6, c = 10$

$$x = \frac{-6 \pm \sqrt{6^2 - 4(1)(10)}}{2(1)}$$

$$= \frac{-6 \pm \sqrt{-4}}{2}$$

$$= -3 \pm i$$

66. $9x^2 - 6x + 37 = 0; a = 9, b = -6, c = 37$

$$x = \frac{-(-6) \pm \sqrt{(-6)^2 - 4(9)(37)}}{2(9)}$$

$$= \frac{6 \pm \sqrt{-1296}}{18}$$

$$= \frac{1}{3} \pm \frac{36i}{18}$$

$$= \frac{1}{3} \pm 2i$$

68. $16t^2 - 4t + 3 = 0; \quad a = 16, \quad b = -4, \quad c = 3$

$$t = \frac{-(-4) \pm \sqrt{(-4)^2 - 4(16)(3)}}{2(16)}$$

$$= \frac{4 \pm \sqrt{-176}}{32}$$

$$= \frac{4 \pm 4\sqrt{11}i}{32}$$

$$= \frac{1}{8} \pm \frac{\sqrt{11}}{8}i$$

70. $\frac{7}{8}x^2 - \frac{3}{4}x + \frac{5}{16} = 0$

$14x^2 - 12x + 5 = 0; a = 14, b = -12, c = 5$

$$x = \frac{-(-12) \pm \sqrt{(-12)^2 - 4(14)(5)}}{2(14)}$$

$$= \frac{12 \pm \sqrt{-136}}{28}$$

$$= \frac{12 \pm 2i\sqrt{34}}{28}$$

$$= \frac{3}{7} \pm \frac{\sqrt{34}}{14}i$$

72. $4.5x^2 - 3x + 12 = 0; a = 4.5, b = -3, c = 12$

$$x = \frac{-(-3) \pm \sqrt{(-3)^2 - 4(4.5)(12)}}{2(4.5)}$$

$$= \frac{3 \pm \sqrt{-207}}{9} = \frac{3 \pm 3i\sqrt{23}}{9} = \frac{1}{3} \pm \frac{\sqrt{23}}{3}i$$

74. $-6i^3 + i^2 = -6i^2i + i^2$

$$= -6(-1)i + (-1)$$

$$= 6i - 1$$

$$= -1 + 6i$$

76. $-5i^5 = -5i^2i^2i$

$$= -5(-1)(-1)i$$

$$= -5i$$

78. $\left(\sqrt{-75}\right)^3 = \left(5\sqrt{3}i\right)^3$

$$= 5^3\left(\sqrt{3}\right)^3 i^3$$

$$= 125\left(3\sqrt{3}\right)(-1)i$$

$$= -375\sqrt{3}i$$

80. $\dfrac{1}{i^3} = \dfrac{1}{-i} = \dfrac{1}{-i} \cdot \dfrac{i}{i} = \dfrac{i}{-i^2} = \dfrac{i}{1} = i$

82. $(2)^3 = 8$

$$(-1 + \sqrt{3}i)^3 = (-1)^3 + 3(-1)^2(\sqrt{3}i) + 3(-1)(\sqrt{3}i)^2 + (\sqrt{3}i)^3$$

$$= -1 + 3\sqrt{3}i - 9i^2 + 3\sqrt{3}i^3$$

$$= -1 + 3\sqrt{3}i + 9 - 3\sqrt{3}i$$

$$= 8$$

$$(-1 - \sqrt{3}i)^3 = (-1)^3 + 3(-1)^2\left(-\sqrt{3}i\right) + 3(-1)\left(-\sqrt{3}i\right)^2 + \left(-\sqrt{3}i\right)^3$$

$$= -1 - 3\sqrt{3}i - 9i^2 - 3\sqrt{3}i^3$$

$$= -1 - 3\sqrt{3}i + 9 + 3\sqrt{3}i$$

$$= 8$$

84. (a) $z_1 = 5 + 2i, z_2 = 3 - 4i$

$$\frac{1}{z} = \frac{1}{z_1} + \frac{1}{z_2}$$

$$= \frac{1}{5 + 2i} + \frac{1}{3 - 4i}$$

$$= \frac{3 - 4i + 5 + 2i}{(5 + 2i)(3 - 4i)}$$

$$= \frac{8 - 2i}{23 - 14i}$$

$$z = \left(\frac{23 - 14i}{8 - 2i}\right)\left(\frac{8 + 2i}{8 + 2i}\right)$$

$$= \frac{212 - 66i}{68} = \frac{53}{17} - \frac{33}{34}i$$

(b) $z_1 = 9 + 16i, z_2 = 20 - 10i$

$$\frac{1}{z} = \frac{1}{z_1} + \frac{1}{z_2}$$

$$= \frac{1}{9 + 16i} + \frac{1}{20 - 10i}$$

$$= \frac{20 - 10i + 9 + 16i}{(9 + 16i)(20 - 10i)}$$

$$= \frac{29 + 6i}{340 + 230i}$$

$$z = \left(\frac{340 + 230i}{29 + 6i}\right)\left(\frac{29 - 6i}{29 - 6i}\right)$$

$$= \frac{11{,}240 + 4630i}{877} = \frac{11{,}240}{877} + \frac{4630}{877}i$$

86. True. $x^4 - x^2 + 14 = 56$

$$\left(-i\sqrt{6}\right)^4 - \left(-i\sqrt{6}\right)^2 + 14 \overset{?}{=} 56$$

$$36 + 6 + 14 \overset{?}{=} 56$$

$$56 = 56$$

88. $\sqrt{-6}\sqrt{-6} = \sqrt{6}i\sqrt{6}i = 6i^2 = -6$

90. Answers will vary.

92. $(x^3 - 3x^2) - (6 - 2x - 4x^2) = x^3 - 3x^2 - 6 + 2x + 4x^2$

$$= x^3 + x^2 + 2x - 6$$

94. $(2x - 5)^2 = (2x)^2 - 2(2x)(5) + (5)^2$

$$= 4x^2 - 20x + 25$$

96. $8 - 3x = -34$

$$-3x = -42$$

$$x = 14$$

98. $5[x - (3x + 11)] = 20x - 15$

$$5x - 15x - 55 = 20x - 15$$

$$-30x = 40$$

$$x = \frac{40}{-30} = -\frac{4}{3}$$

100. $F = \alpha \dfrac{m_1 m_2}{r^2}$

$$r^2 = \alpha \frac{m_1 m_2}{F}$$

$$r = \sqrt{\frac{\alpha m_1 m_2}{F}} = \frac{\sqrt{\alpha m_1 m_2}}{\sqrt{F}} \cdot \frac{\sqrt{F}}{\sqrt{F}} = \frac{\sqrt{\alpha m_1 m_2 F}}{F}$$

102. $r \times t = d$

Model: $(\text{Average speed}) = \dfrac{(\text{distance on first leg}) + (\text{distance on second leg})}{(\text{time for first leg}) + (\text{time for second leg})}$

Labels: Average speed $= S$, distance on first leg $= 200$ kilometers, distance on second leg $= 200$ kilometers,

time for first leg $= \dfrac{d}{r} = \dfrac{200}{100} = 2$ hours, time for second leg $= \dfrac{d}{r} = \dfrac{200}{80} = \dfrac{5}{2}$ hours

Expression: $S = \dfrac{200 + 200}{2 + 2.5} \approx 88.89$ kilometers per hour

Section 2.5 Zeros of Polynomial Functions

Solutions to Even-Numbered Exercises

2. $f(x) = x^2(x + 3)(x^2 - 1) = x^2(x + 3)(x + 1)(x - 1)$

The five zeros are: $0, 0, -3, \pm 1$.

4. $f(x) = (x + 5)(x - 8)^2$

The three zeros are: $-5, 8, 8$.

6. $h(t) = (t - 3)(t - 2)(t - 3i)(t + 3i)$

The four zeros are: $3, 2, \pm 3i$.

8. $f(x) = x^3 - 4x^2 - 4x + 16$

$p = $ factor of 16

$q = $ factor of 1

Possible rational zeros: $\pm 1, \pm 2, \pm 4, \pm 8, \pm 16$

Zeros shown on graph: $-2, 2, 4$

10. $f(x) = 4x^5 - 8x^4 - 5x^3 + 10x^2 + x - 2$

$p = $ factor of -2

$q = $ factor of 4

Possible rational zeros: $\pm 1, \pm 2, \pm \frac{1}{2}, \pm \frac{1}{4}$

Zeros shown on graph: $-1, -\frac{1}{2}, \frac{1}{2}, 1, 2$

12. $f(x) = x^3 - 7x - 6$

Possible rational zeros: $\pm 1, \pm 2, \pm 3, \pm 6$

$$
3 \begin{array}{|rrrr}
1 & 0 & -7 & -6 \\
 & 3 & 9 & 6 \\
\hline
1 & 3 & 2 & 0
\end{array}
$$

$f(x) = (x - 3)(x^2 + 3x + 2) = (x - 3)(x + 2)(x + 1)$

Thus, the real zeros are $-2, -1, 3$.

14. $h(x) = x^3 - 9x^2 + 20x - 12$

Possible rational zeros: $\pm 1, \pm 2, \pm 3, \pm 4, \pm 6, \pm 12$

$$
1 \begin{array}{|rrrr}
1 & -9 & 20 & -12 \\
 & 1 & -8 & 12 \\
\hline
1 & -8 & 12 & 0
\end{array}
$$

$h(x) = (x - 1)(x^2 - 8x + 12)$

$\quad\ = (x - 1)(x - 2)(x - 6)$

Thus, the real zeros are $1, 2, 6$.

16. $p(x) = x^3 - 9x^2 + 27x - 27$

Possible rational zeros: $\pm 1, \pm 3, \pm 9, \pm 27$

$$
3 \begin{array}{|rrrr}
1 & -9 & 27 & -27 \\
 & 3 & -18 & 27 \\
\hline
1 & -6 & 9 & 0
\end{array}
$$

$f(x) = (x - 3)(x^2 - 6x + 9)$

$\quad\ = (x - 3)(x - 3)(x - 3)$

Thus, the real zero is 3.

18. $f(x) = 3x^3 - 19x^2 + 33x - 9$

Possible rational zeros: $\pm 1, \pm 3, \pm 9, \pm \frac{1}{3}$

$$
3 \begin{array}{|rrrr}
3 & -19 & 33 & -9 \\
 & 9 & -30 & 9 \\
\hline
3 & -10 & 3 & 0
\end{array}
$$

$f(x) = (x - 3)(3x^2 - 10x + 3)$

$\quad\ = (x - 3)(3x - 1)(x - 3)$

Thus, the real zeros are $3, \frac{1}{3}$.

20. $f(x) = 2x^4 - 15x^3 + 23x^2 + 15x - 25$

Possible rational zeros: $\pm 1, \pm 5, \pm 25, \pm \frac{1}{2}, \pm \frac{5}{2}, \pm \frac{25}{2}$

$$
5 \begin{array}{|rrrrr}
2 & -15 & 23 & 15 & -25 \\
 & 10 & -25 & -10 & 25 \\
\hline
2 & -5 & -2 & 5 & 0
\end{array}
$$

$$
1 \begin{array}{|rrrr}
2 & -5 & -2 & 5 \\
 & 2 & -3 & -5 \\
\hline
2 & -3 & -5 & 0
\end{array}
$$

$$
-1 \begin{array}{|rrr}
2 & -3 & -5 \\
 & -2 & 5 \\
\hline
2 & -5 & 0
\end{array}
$$

$f(x) = (x - 5)(x - 1)(x + 1)(2x - 5)$

Thus, the real zeros are $5, 1, -1, \frac{5}{2}$.

22. $x^4 - 13x^2 - 12x = 0$

$x(x^3 - 13x - 12) = 0$

$$\begin{array}{r|rrrr} -1 & 1 & 0 & -13 & -12 \\ & & -1 & 1 & 12 \\ \hline & 1 & -1 & -12 & 0 \end{array}$$

$x(x + 1)(x^2 - x - 12) = 0$

$x(x + 1)(x - 4)(x + 3) = 0$

The real zeros are $0, -1, 4, -3$.

24. $x^5 - x^4 - 3x^3 + 5x^2 - 2x = 0$

$x(x^4 - x^3 - 3x^2 + 5x - 2) = 0$

$$\begin{array}{r|rrrrr} 1 & 1 & -1 & -3 & 5 & -2 \\ & & 1 & 0 & -3 & 2 \\ \hline & 1 & 0 & -3 & 2 & 0 \end{array}$$

$$\begin{array}{r|rrrr} -2 & 1 & 0 & -3 & 2 \\ & & -2 & 4 & -2 \\ \hline & 1 & -2 & 1 & 0 \end{array}$$

$x(x - 1)(x + 2)(x^2 - 2x + 1) = 0$

$x(x - 1)(x + 2)(x - 1)(x - 1) = 0$

The real zeros are $-2, 0, 1$.

26. $f(x) = -3x^3 + 20x^2 - 36x + 16$

(a) Possible rational zeros: $\pm 1, \pm 2, \pm 4, \pm 8, \pm 16, \pm \frac{1}{3},$ $\pm \frac{2}{3}, \pm \frac{4}{3}, \pm \frac{8}{3}, \pm \frac{16}{3}$

(b)

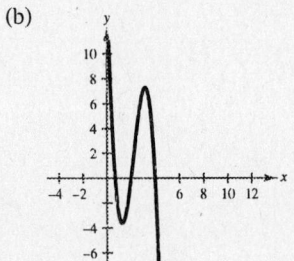

(c) Real zeros: $\frac{2}{3}, 2, 4$

28. $f(x) = 4x^3 - 12x^2 - x + 15$

(a) Possible rational zeros: $\pm 1, \pm 3, \pm 5, \pm 15, \pm \frac{1}{2}, \pm \frac{3}{2},$ $\pm \frac{5}{2}, \pm \frac{15}{2}, \pm \frac{1}{4}, \pm \frac{3}{4}, \pm \frac{5}{4}, \pm \frac{15}{4}$

(b)

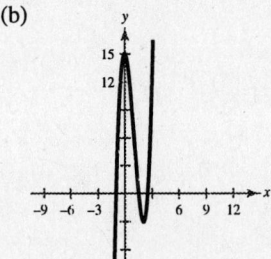

(c) Real zeros: $-1, \frac{3}{2}, \frac{5}{2}$

30. $f(x) = 4x^4 - 17x^2 + 4$

(a) Possible rational zeros: $\pm 1, \pm 2, \pm 4, \pm \frac{1}{2}, \pm \frac{1}{4}$

(b)

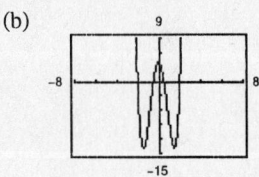

(c) Real zeros: $\pm 2, \pm \frac{1}{2}$

32. $f(x) = 4x^3 + 7x^2 - 11x - 18$

(a) Possible rational zeros: $\pm 1, \pm 2, \pm 3, \pm 6, \pm 9, \pm 18,$ $\pm \frac{1}{2}, \pm \frac{3}{2}, \pm \frac{9}{2}, \pm \frac{1}{4}, \pm \frac{3}{4}, \pm \frac{9}{4}$

(b)

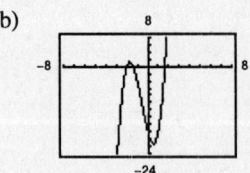

(c) Real zeros: $-2, \dfrac{1}{8} \pm \dfrac{\sqrt{145}}{8}$

34. $P(t) = t^4 - 7t^2 + 12$

(a) $t = \pm 2, \pm 1.732$

(b) $$\begin{array}{r|rrrrr} 2 & 1 & 0 & -7 & 0 & 12 \\ & & 2 & 4 & -6 & -12 \\ \hline & 1 & 2 & -3 & -6 & 0 \end{array}$$

$$\begin{array}{r|rrrr} -2 & 1 & 2 & -3 & -6 \\ & & -2 & 0 & 6 \\ \hline & 1 & 0 & -3 & 0 \end{array}$$

$P(t) = (t - 2)(t + 2)(t^2 - 3)$

$= (t - 2)(t + 2)(t - \sqrt{3})(t + \sqrt{3})$

36. $g(x) = 6x^4 - 11x^3 - 51x^2 + 99x - 27$

(a) $x = \pm 3, 1.5, 0.333$

(b)
$$
\begin{array}{r|rrrrr}
3 & 6 & -11 & -51 & 99 & -27 \\
  &   & 18 & 21 & -90 & 27 \\
\hline
  & 6 & 7 & -30 & 9 & 0
\end{array}
$$

$$
\begin{array}{r|rrrr}
-3 & 6 & 7 & -30 & 9 \\
   &   & -18 & 33 & -9 \\
\hline
   & 6 & -11 & 3 & 0
\end{array}
$$

$g(x) = (x - 3)(x + 3)(6x^2 - 11x + 3)$

$ = (x - 3)(x + 3)(3x - 1)(2x - 3)$

38. $f(x) = (x - 4)(x - 3i)(x + 3i)$

$ = (x - 4)(x^2 + 9)$

$ = x^3 - 4x^2 + 9x - 36$

Note: $f(x) = a(x^3 - 4x^2 + 9x - 36)$, where a is any real number, has the zeros $4, 3i$ and $-3i$.

40. $f(x) = (x - 2)(x - 4 - i)(x - 4 + i)$

$ = (x - 2)(x^2 - 8x + 17)$

$ = x^3 - 10x^2 + 33x - 34$

Note: $f(x) = a(x^3 - 10x^2 + 33x - 34)$ where a is any real number, has the zeros $2, 4 \pm i$.

42. $f(x) = (x + 5)^2(x - 1 - \sqrt{3}i)(x - 1 + \sqrt{3}i)$

$ = (x^2 + 10x + 25)(x^2 - 2x + 4)$

$ = x^4 + 8x^3 + 9x^2 - 10x + 100$

Note: $f(x) = a(x^4 + 8x^3 + 9x^2 - 10x + 100)$, where a is any real number, has the zeros $-5, -5, 1 \pm \sqrt{3}i$.

44. $f(x) = x^4 - 2x^3 - 3x^2 + 12x - 18$

(a) $f(x) = (x^2 - 6)(x^2 - 2x + 3)$

(b) $f(x) = (x + \sqrt{6})(x - \sqrt{6})(x^2 - 2x + 3)$

(c) $f(x) = (x + \sqrt{6})(x - \sqrt{6})(x - 1 - \sqrt{2}i)(x - 1 + \sqrt{2}i)$

46. $f(x) = x^4 - 3x^3 - x^2 - 12x - 20$

(a) $f(x) = (x^2 + 4)(x^2 - 3x - 5)$

(b) $f(x) = (x^2 + 4)\left(x - \dfrac{3 + \sqrt{29}}{2}\right)\left(x - \dfrac{3 - \sqrt{29}}{2}\right)$

(c) $f(x) = (x + 2i)(x - 2i)\left(x - \dfrac{3 + \sqrt{29}}{2}\right)\left(x - \dfrac{3 - \sqrt{29}}{2}\right)$

48. $f(x) = x^3 + x^2 + 9x + 9$

Since $3i$ is a zero, so is $-3i$.

$$
\begin{array}{r|rrrr}
3i & 1 & 1 & 9 & 9 \\
   &   & 3i & -9 + 3i & -9 \\
\hline
   & 1 & 1 + 3i & 3i & 0
\end{array}
$$

$$
\begin{array}{r|rrr}
-3i & 1 & 1 + 3i & 3i \\
    &   & -3i & -3i \\
\hline
    & 1 & 1 & 0
\end{array}
$$

The zero of $x + 1$ is $x = -1$.

The zeros of f are $x = -1, \pm 3i$.

50. $g(x) = x^3 - 7x^2 - x + 87$

Since $5 + 2i$ is a zero, so is $5 - 2i$.

$$
\begin{array}{r|rrrr}
5 + 2i & 1 & -7 & -1 & 87 \\
       &   & 5 + 2i & -14 + 6i & -87 \\
\hline
       & 1 & -2 + 2i & -15 + 6i & 0
\end{array}
$$

$$
\begin{array}{r|rrr}
5 - 2i & 1 & -2 + 2i & -15 + 6i \\
       &   & 5 - 2i & 15 - 6i \\
\hline
       & 1 & 3 & 0
\end{array}
$$

The zero of $x + 3$ is $x = -3$.

The zeros of f are $x = -3, 5 \pm 2i$.

52. $h(x) = 3x^3 - 4x^2 + 8x + 8$

Since $1 - \sqrt{3}i$ is a zero, so is $1 + \sqrt{3}i$.

$$
\begin{array}{r|rrrr}
1 - \sqrt{3}i & 3 & -4 & 8 & 8 \\
 & & 3 - 3\sqrt{3}i & -10 - 2\sqrt{3}i & -8 \\
\hline
 & 3 & -1 - 3\sqrt{3}i & -2 - 2\sqrt{3}i & 0 \\
1 + \sqrt{3}i & 3 & -1 - 3\sqrt{3}i & -2 - 2\sqrt{3}i & \\
 & & 3 + 3\sqrt{3}i & 2 + 2\sqrt{3}i & \\
\hline
 & 3 & 2 & 0 &
\end{array}
$$

The zero of $3x + 2$ is $x = -\frac{2}{3}$.

The zeros of f are $x = -\frac{2}{3}, 1 \pm \sqrt{3}i$.

54. $f(x) = x^3 + 4x^2 + 14x + 20$

Since $-1 - 3i$ is a zero, so is $-1 + 3i$.

$$
\begin{array}{r|rrrr}
-1 - 3i & 1 & 4 & 14 & 20 \\
 & & -1 - 3i & -12 - 6i & -20 \\
\hline
 & 1 & 3 - 3i & 2 - 6i & 0 \\
-1 + 3i & 1 & 3 - 3i & 2 - 6i & \\
 & & -1 + 3i & -2 + 6i & \\
\hline
 & 1 & 2 & 0 &
\end{array}
$$

The zero of $x + 2$ is $x = -2$.

The zeros of f are $x = -2, -1 \pm 3i$.

56. $f(x) = x^2 - x + 56$

By the Quadratic Formula, the zeros of $f(x)$ are

$$x = \frac{1 \pm \sqrt{1 - 224}}{2} = \frac{1 \pm \sqrt{223}i}{2}.$$

$$f(x) = \left(x - \frac{1 - \sqrt{223}i}{2}\right)\left(x - \frac{1 + \sqrt{223}i}{2}\right)$$

58. $g(x) = x^2 + 10x + 23$

By the Quadratic Formula, the zeros of $f(x)$ are

$$x = \frac{-10 \pm \sqrt{100 - 92}}{2} = \frac{-10 \pm \sqrt{8}}{2} = -5 \pm \sqrt{2}.$$

$$g(x) = \left(x + 5 + \sqrt{2}\right)\left(x + 5 - \sqrt{2}\right)$$

60. $f(y) = y^4 - 625$

$$= (y^2 + 25)(y^2 - 25)$$

Zeros: $y = \pm 5, \pm 5i$

$$f(y) = (y + 5)(y - 5)(y + 5i)(y - 5i)$$

62. $h(x) = x^3 - 3x^2 + 4x - 2$

$$
\begin{array}{r|rrrr}
1 & 1 & -3 & 4 & -2 \\
 & & 1 & -2 & 2 \\
\hline
 & 1 & -2 & 2 & 0
\end{array}
$$

By the Quadratic Formula, the zeros of $x^2 - 2x + 2$

are $x = \dfrac{2 \pm \sqrt{4 - 8}}{2} = 1 \pm i$.

Zeros: $x = 1, 1 \pm i$

$$h(x) = (x - 1)(x - 1 - i)(x - 1 + i)$$

64. $f(x) = x^3 - 2x^2 - 11x + 52$

$$
\begin{array}{r|rrrr}
-4 & 1 & -2 & -11 & 52 \\
 & & -4 & 24 & -52 \\
\hline
 & 1 & -6 & 13 & 0
\end{array}
$$

By the Quadratic Formula, the zeros of $x^2 - 6x + 13$

are $x = \dfrac{6 \pm \sqrt{36 - 52}}{2} = 3 \pm 2i$.

Zeros: $x = -4, 3 \pm 2i$

$$f(x) = (x + 4)(x - 3 - 2i)(x - 3 + 2i)$$

66. $h(x) = x^3 + 9x^2 + 27x + 35$

$$
\begin{array}{r|rrrr}
-5 & 1 & 9 & 27 & 35 \\
 & & -5 & -20 & -35 \\
\hline
 & 1 & 4 & 7 & 0
\end{array}
$$

By the Quadratic Formula, the zeros of $x^2 + 4x + 7$

are $x = \dfrac{-4 \pm \sqrt{16 - 28}}{2} = -2 \pm \sqrt{3}i$.

Zeros: $-5, -2 \pm \sqrt{3}i$

$$h(x) = (x + 5)\left(x + 2 + \sqrt{3}i\right)\left(x + 2 - \sqrt{3}i\right)$$

68. $g(x) = 3x^3 - 4x^2 + 8x + 8$

$$
\begin{array}{r|rrrr}
-\frac{2}{3} & 3 & -4 & 8 & 8 \\
 & & -2 & 4 & -8 \\
\hline
 & 3 & -6 & 12 & 0
\end{array}
$$

By the Quadratic Formula, the zeros of
$3x^2 - 6x + 12 = 3(x^2 - 2x + 4)$ are

$$x = \frac{2 \pm \sqrt{4 - 16}}{2} = 1 \pm \sqrt{3}i$$

Zeros: $x = -\frac{2}{3}, 1 \pm \sqrt{3}i$

$g(x) = (3x + 2)(x - 1 + \sqrt{3}i)(x - 1 - \sqrt{3}i)$

70. $h(x) = x^4 + 6x^3 + 10x^2 + 6x + 9$

$$
\begin{array}{r|rrrrr}
-3 & 1 & 6 & 10 & 6 & 9 \\
 & & -3 & -9 & -3 & -9 \\
\hline
 & 1 & 3 & 1 & 3 & 0 \\
-3 & 1 & 3 & 1 & 3 & \\
 & & -3 & 0 & -3 & \\
\hline
 & 1 & 0 & 1 & 0 &
\end{array}
$$

The zeros of $x^2 + 1$ are $x = \pm i$

Zeros: $x = -3, \pm i$

$h(x) = (x + 3)^2(x + i)(x - i)$

72. $f(x) = x^4 + 29x^2 + 100$

$\quad = (x^2 + 25)(x^2 + 4)$

Zeros: $x = \pm 2i, \pm 5i$

$\quad f(x) = (x + 2i)(x - 2i)(x + 5i)(x - 5i)$

74. $f(s) = 2s^3 - 5s^2 + 12s - 5$

Possible rational zeros: $\pm 1, \pm 5, \pm \frac{1}{2}, \pm \frac{5}{2}$

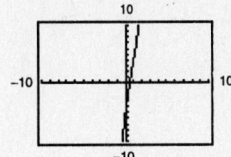

Based on the graph, try $x = \frac{1}{2}$.

$$
\begin{array}{r|rrrr}
\frac{1}{2} & 2 & -5 & 12 & -5 \\
 & & 1 & -2 & 5 \\
\hline
 & 2 & -4 & 10 & 0
\end{array}
$$

Zeros: $s = \frac{1}{2}, \dfrac{4 \pm \sqrt{64}i}{4} = 1 \pm 2i$

76. $f(x) = 9x^3 - 15x^2 + 11x - 5$

Possible rational zeros: $\pm 1, \pm 5, \pm \frac{1}{3}, \pm \frac{5}{3}, \pm \frac{1}{9}, \pm \frac{5}{9}$

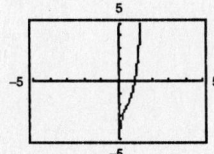

Based on the graph, try $x = 1$.

$$
\begin{array}{r|rrrr}
1 & 9 & -15 & 11 & -5 \\
 & & 9 & -6 & 5 \\
\hline
 & 9 & -6 & 5 & 0
\end{array}
$$

Zeros: $x = 1, \dfrac{6 \pm \sqrt{144}i}{18} = \frac{1}{3} \pm \frac{2}{3}i$

78. $g(x) = x^5 - 8x^4 + 28x^3 - 56x^2 + 64x - 32$

Possible rational zeros: $\pm 1, \pm 2, \pm 4, \pm 8, \pm 16, \pm 32$

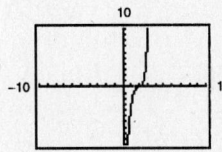

Based on the graph, try $x = 2$.

$$
\begin{array}{r|rrrrrr}
2 & 1 & -8 & 28 & -56 & 64 & -32 \\
 & & 2 & -12 & 32 & -48 & 32 \\
\hline
 & 1 & -6 & 16 & -24 & 16 & 0 \\
2 & 1 & -6 & 16 & -24 & 16 & \\
 & & 2 & -8 & 16 & -16 & \\
\hline
 & 1 & -4 & 8 & -8 & 0 & \\
2 & 1 & -4 & 8 & -8 & & \\
 & & 2 & -4 & 8 & & \\
\hline
 & 1 & -2 & 4 & 0 & &
\end{array}
$$

Zeros: $x = 2, \dfrac{2 \pm \sqrt{12}i}{2} = 1 \pm \sqrt{3}i$

80. $h(x) = 4x^2 - 8x + 3$

Sign variations: 2, positive zeros: 2 or 0

$h(-x) = 4x^2 + 8x + 3$

Sign variations: 0, negative zeros: 0

82. $h(x) = 2x^4 - 3x + 2$

Sign variations: 2, positive zeros: 2 or 0

$h(-x) = 2x^4 + 3x + 2$

Sign variations: 0, negative zeros: 0

84. $f(x) = 4x^3 - 3x^2 + 2x - 1$

Sign variations: 3, positive zeros: 3 or 1

$f(-x) = -4x^3 - 3x^2 - 2x - 1$

Sign variations: 0, negative zeros: 0

86. $f(x) = 3x^3 + 2x^2 + x + 3$

Sign variations: 0, positive zeros: 0

$f(-x) = -3x^3 + 2x^2 - x + 3$

Sign variations: 3, negative zeros: 3 or 1

88. $f(x) = 2x^3 - 3x^2 - 12x + 8$

(a)

4	2	−3	−12	8
		8	20	32
	2	5	8	40

4 is an upper bound.

(b)

−3	2	−3	−12	8
		−6	27	−45
	2	−9	15	−37

−3 is a lower bound.

90. $f(x) = 2x^4 - 8x + 3$

(a)

3	2	0	0	−8	3
		6	18	54	138
	2	6	18	46	141

3 is an upper bound.

(b)

−4	2	0	0	−8	3
		−8	32	−128	544
	2	−8	32	−136	547

−4 is a lower bound.

92. $f(z) = 12z^3 - 4z^2 - 27z + 9$

Possible rational zeros: $\pm 1, \pm 3, \pm 9, \pm\frac{1}{2}, \pm\frac{3}{2}, \pm\frac{9}{2}, \pm\frac{1}{3},$ $\pm\frac{1}{4}, \pm\frac{3}{4}, \pm\frac{9}{4}, \pm\frac{1}{6}, \pm\frac{1}{12}$

$\frac{3}{2}$	12	−4	−27	9
		18	21	−9
	12	14	−6	0

$f(z) = 2\left(z - \frac{3}{2}\right)(6z^2 + 7z - 3)$

$= (2z - 3)(3z - 1)(2z + 3)$

Real zeros: $-\frac{3}{2}, \frac{1}{3}, \frac{3}{2}$

94. $g(x) = 3x^3 - 2x^2 + 15x - 10$

Possible rational zeros: $\pm 1, \pm 2, \pm 5, \pm 10, \pm\frac{1}{3}, \pm\frac{2}{3}, \pm\frac{5}{3}, \pm\frac{10}{3}$

$\frac{2}{3}$	3	−2	15	−10
		2	0	10
	3	0	15	0

$g(x) = \left(x - \frac{2}{3}\right)(3x^2 + 15) = (3x - 2)(x^2 + 5)$

Real zeros: $\frac{2}{3}$

96. $f(x) = \frac{1}{2}(2x^3 - 3x^2 - 23x + 12)$

Possible rational zeros: $\pm 1, \pm 2, \pm 3, \pm 4, \pm 6, \pm 12, \pm\frac{1}{2}, \pm\frac{3}{2}$

4	2	−3	−23	12
		8	20	−12
	2	5	−3	0

$f(x) = \frac{1}{2}(x - 4)(2x^2 + 5x - 3)$

$= \frac{1}{2}(x - 4)(2x - 1)(x + 3)$

Rational zeros: $-3, \frac{1}{2}, 4$

98. $f(z) = \frac{1}{6}(6z^3 + 11z^2 - 3z - 2)$

Possible rational zeros: $\pm 1, \pm 2, \pm\frac{1}{2}, \pm\frac{1}{3}, \pm\frac{2}{3}, \pm\frac{1}{6}$

−2	6	11	−3	−2
		−12	2	2
	6	−1	−1	0

$f(x) = \frac{1}{6}(x + 2)(6x^2 - x - 1)$

$= \frac{1}{6}(x + 2)(3x + 1)(2x - 1)$

Rational zeros: $-2, -\frac{1}{3}, \frac{1}{2}$

100. $f(x) = x^3 - 2$

$\quad = \left(x - \sqrt[3]{2}\right)\left(x^2 + \sqrt[3]{2}x + \sqrt[3]{4}\right)$

Rational zeros: 0

Irrational zeros: 1 $\left(x = \sqrt[3]{2}\right)$

Matches (a).

102. $f(x) = x^3 - 2x$

$\quad = x(x^2 - 2)$

$\quad = x\left(x + \sqrt{2}\right)\left(x - \sqrt{2}\right)$

Rational zeros: 1 $\ (x = 0)$

Irrational zeros: 2 $\left(x = \pm\sqrt{2}\right)$

Matches (c).

104.

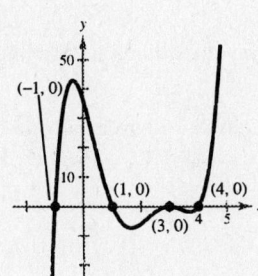

106. (a) $-2, 0, 2$

(b) The graph touches the x-axis at $x = 0$.

(c) The least possible degree of f is 4 because there are at least 4 real zeros (0 is repeated) and a function can have at most the number of real zeros equal to the degree of the function. The degree cannot be odd by the definition of multiplicity.

(d) The leading coefficient of f is negative. From the information in the table, you can conclude that the graph will eventually fall to the left and fall to the right.

(e) $f(x) = -(x - 0)^2[x - (-2)](x - 2)$

$\quad = -x^2(x + 2)(x - 2) = -x^2(x^2 - 4) = -x^4 + 4x^2$

(f)

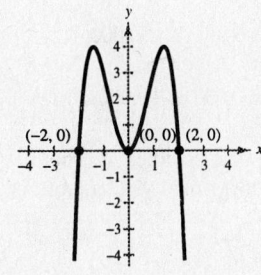

108. (a) Combined length and width:

$4x + y = 120 \Rightarrow y = 120 - 4x$

Volume $= l \cdot w \cdot h = x^2 y$

$\quad\quad\quad\quad = x^2(120 - 4x)$

$\quad\quad\quad\quad = 4x^2(30 - x)$

(b)

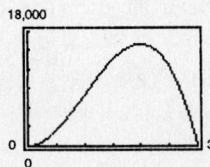

Dimensions with maximum volume:

20 in. × 20 in. × 40 in.

(c) $\quad\quad\quad 13{,}500 = 4x^2(30 - x)$

$4x^3 - 120x^2 + 13{,}500 = 0$

$\quad x^3 - 30x^2 + 3375 = 0$

$$
\begin{array}{r|rrrr}
15 & 1 & -30 & 0 & 3375 \\
   &   & 15 & -225 & -3375 \\
\hline
   & 1 & -15 & -225 & 0
\end{array}
$$

$(x - 15)(x^2 - 15x - 225) = 0$

Using the Quadratic Formula,

$x = 15, \dfrac{15 \pm 15\sqrt{5}}{2}.$

The value of $\dfrac{15 - 15\sqrt{5}}{2}$ is not possible because it is negative.

110.
$$P = -45x^3 + 2500x^2 - 275,000$$
$$800,000 = -45x^3 + 2500x^2 - 275,000$$
$$0 = 45x^3 - 2500x^2 + 1,075,000$$
$$0 = 9x^3 - 500x^2 + 215,000$$

The zeros of this equation are $x \approx -18.0$, $x \approx 31.5$, and $x \approx 42.0$. Because $0 \le x \le 50$, disregard $x \approx -18.02$. The smaller remaining solution is $x \approx 31.5$, or $315,000.

112. (a)

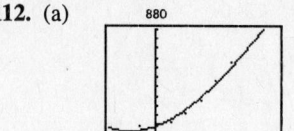

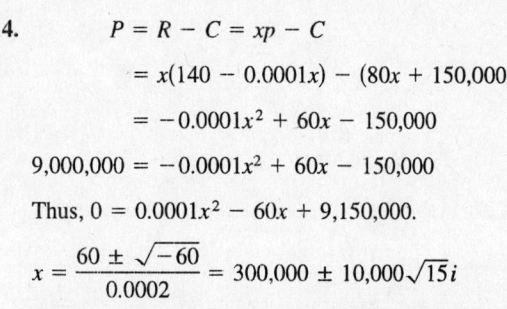

(b) $750 = -0.222t^3 + 6.432t^2 + 23.328t + 473.991$

$0 = -0.222t^3 + 6.432t^2 + 23.328t - 276.009$

$t \approx 5$

The annual value of imports will reach 750 billion dollars in 1995.

(c) No. The right-hand behavior will eventually decrease.

114.
$$P = R - C = xp - C$$
$$= x(140 - 0.0001x) - (80x + 150,000)$$
$$= -0.0001x^2 + 60x - 150,000$$
$$9,000,000 = -0.0001x^2 + 60x - 150,000$$

Thus, $0 = 0.0001x^2 - 60x + 9,150,000$.

$$x = \frac{60 \pm \sqrt{-60}}{0.0002} = 300,000 \pm 10,000\sqrt{15}\,i$$

Since the solutions are both complex, it is not possible to determine a price p that would yield a profit of 9 million dollars.

116. False. f does not have real coefficients.

118. $g(x) = 3f(x)$. This function has the same zeros as f because it is a vertical stretch of f. The zeros of g are r_1, r_2, and r_3.

120. $g(x) = f(2x)$. Note that x is a zero of g if and only if $2x$ is a zero of f. The zeros of g are $\dfrac{r_1}{2}$, $\dfrac{r_2}{2}$, and $\dfrac{r_3}{2}$.

122. $g(x) = f(-x)$. Note that x is a zero of g if and only if $-x$ is a zero of f. The zeros of g are $-r_1$, $-r_2$, and $-r_3$.

124. (a) $g(x) = f(x - 2)$
No. This function is a horizontal shift of $f(x)$. Note that x is a zero of g if and only if $x - 2$ is a zero of f; the number of real and complex zeros is not affected by a horizontal shift.

(b) $g(x) = f(2x)$
No. Since x is a zero of g if and only if $2x$ is a zero of f, the number of real and complex zeros of g is the same as the number of real and complex zeros of f.

126. (a) No. The graph is not of $f(x) = x^2(x + 2)(x - 3.5)$ because this function has a $(0, 0)$ as an intercept and the given graph does not go through $(0, 0)$.

(b) No. The graph is not of $f(x) = (x + 2)(x - 3.5)$ because this function's graph is a parabola and the graph given is not. The function shown in the graph must be at least a fourth-degree polynomial.

(c) Yes. The function shown in the graph is $h(x) = (x + 2)(x - 3.5)(x^2 + 1)$.

(d) The graph is not of $k(x) = (x + 1)(x + 2)(x - 3.5)$ because this function has $(-1, 0)$ as an intercept and the given graph does not.

128. $(12 - 5i) + 16i = 12 + 11i$

130. $(9 - 5i)(9 + 5i) = 81 - 25i^2 = 81 + 25 = 106$

132. $(3 + i)^3 = 3^3 + 3(i)(3)^2 + 3(i)^2(3) + (i)^3$

$= 27 + 27i + 9i^2 + i^3$

$= 27 + 27i - 9 - i$

$= 18 + 26i$

134. $g(x) = f(x) - 2$

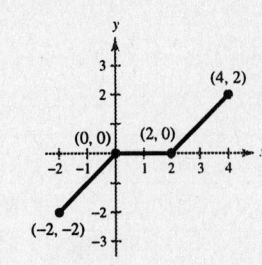

136. $g(x) = f(-x)$

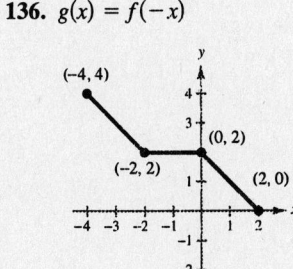

138. $g(x) = f\left(\frac{1}{2}x\right)$

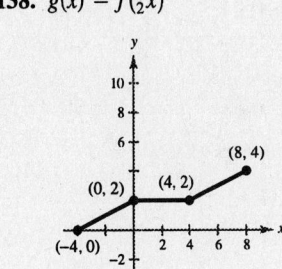

Section 2.6   Rational Functions

2. $f(x) = \dfrac{5x}{x-1}$

(a)

x	$f(x)$	x	$f(x)$	x	$f(x)$
0.5	-5	1.5	15	5	6.25
0.9	-45	1.1	55	10	$5.\overline{55}$
0.99	-495	1.01	505	100	$5.\overline{05}$
0.999	-4995	1.001	5005	1000	$5.\overline{005}$

(b) The zero of the denominator is $x = 1$, so $x = 1$ is a vertical asymptote. The degree of the numerator is equal to the degree of the denominator, so the line $y = \frac{5}{1} = 5$ is a horizontal asymptote.

(c) The domain is all real numbers except $x = 1$.

4. $f(x) = \dfrac{2}{|x-1|}$

(a)

x	$f(x)$	x	$f(x)$	x	$f(x)$
0.5	4	1.5	4	5	0.50
0.9	20	1.1	20	10	$0.\overline{22}$
0.99	200	1.01	200	100	$0.\overline{02}$
0.999	2000	1.001	2000	1000	$0.\overline{002}$

(b) The zero of the denominator is $x = 1$, so $x = 1$ is a vertical asymptote. Because the degree of the numerator is less than the degree of the denominator, the x-axis or $y = 0$ is a horizontal asymptote.

(c) The domain is all real numbers except $x = 1$.

6. $f(x) = \dfrac{4x}{x^2 - 1}$

(a)

x	$f(x)$	x	$f(x)$	x	$f(x)$
0.5	$-2.\overline{66}$	1.5	4.8	5	$0.8\overline{33}$
0.9	-18.95	1.1	20.95	10	$0.\overline{40}$
0.99	-199	1.01	201	100	0.04
0.999	-1999	1.001	2001	1000	0.004

(b) The zeros of the denominator are $x = \pm 1$ so both $x = 1$ and $x = -1$ are vertical asymptotes. Because the degree of the numerator is less than the degree of the denominator, the x-axis or $y = 0$ is a horizontal asymptote.

(c) The domain is all real numbers except $x = \pm 1$.

8. $f(x) = \dfrac{4}{(x-2)^3}$

Domain: all real numbers except $x = 2$

Vertical asymptote: $x = 2$

Horizontal asymptote: $y = 0$

[Degree of $N(x)$ < degree of $D(x)$]

10. $f(x) = \dfrac{1 - 5x}{1 + 2x} = \dfrac{-5x + 1}{2x + 1}$

Domain: all real numbers except $x = -\frac{1}{2}$

Vertical asymptote: $x = -\frac{1}{2}$

Horizontal asymptote: $y = -\frac{5}{2}$

[Degree of $N(x)$ = degree of $D(x)$]

12. $f(x) = \dfrac{2x^2}{x+1}$

Domain: all real numbers except $x = -1$

Vertical asymptote: $x = -1$

Horizontal asymptote: None

[Degree of $N(x)$ > degree of $D(x)$]

14. $f(x) = \dfrac{3x^2 + x - 5}{x^2 + 1}$

Domain: all real numbers. (The denominator has no real zeros.)

Vertical asymptote: None

Horizontal asymptote: $y = 3$

[Degree of $N(x)$ = degree of $D(x)$]

16. $f(x) = \dfrac{1}{x-5}$

Vertical asymptote: $x = 5$

Horizontal asymptote: $y = 0$

Matches graph (a).

18. $f(x) = \dfrac{1-x}{x}$

Vertical asymptote: $x = 0$

Horizontal asymptote: $y = -1$

Matches graph (c).

20. $f(x) = -\dfrac{x+2}{x+4}$

Vertical asymptote: $x = -4$

Horizontal asymptote: $y = -1$

Matches graph (b).

22. $h(x) = 2 + \dfrac{5}{x^2 + 2}$

There are no real zeros.

24. $g(x) = \dfrac{x^3 - 8}{x^2 + 1}$

The zero of g corresponds to the zero of the numerator and is $x = 2$.

26. $f(x) = \dfrac{1}{x-3}$

(a) Intercept: $\left(0, -\dfrac{1}{3}\right)$

(b) Vertical asymptote: $x = 3$
   Horizontal asymptote: $y = 0$

(c) No axis or origin symmetry

(d)

x	0	1	2	4	5	6
y	$-\frac{1}{3}$	$-\frac{1}{2}$	-1	1	$\frac{1}{2}$	$\frac{1}{3}$

(e)

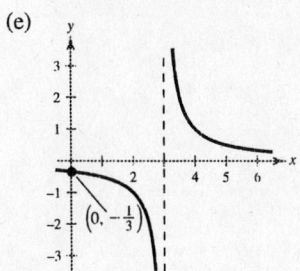

28. $g(x) = \dfrac{1}{3-x} = -\dfrac{1}{x-3}$

(a) Intercept: $\left(0, \dfrac{1}{3}\right)$

(b) Vertical asymptote: $x = 3$
   Horizontal asymptote: $y = 0$

(c) No axis or origin symmetry

(d)

x	0	1	2	4	5	6
y	$\frac{1}{3}$	$\frac{1}{2}$	1	-1	$-\frac{1}{2}$	$-\frac{1}{3}$

(e)

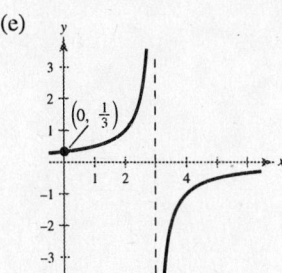

Note: This is the graph of $f(x) = \dfrac{1}{x-3}$

(Exercise 26) reflected about the x-axis.

30. $P(x) = \dfrac{1 - 3x}{1 - x} = \dfrac{3x - 1}{x - 1}$

   (a) Intercepts: $\left(\dfrac{1}{3}, 0\right)$, $(0, 1)$

   (b) Vertical asymptote: $x = 1$
       Horizontal asymptote: $y = 3$

   (c) No axis or origin symmetry

   (d)

x	-1	0	2	3
y	2	1	5	4

   (e)

   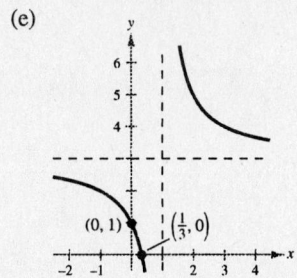

32. $f(x) = 2 - \dfrac{3}{x^2}$

   (a) Intercepts: $\left(-\dfrac{\sqrt{6}}{2}, 0\right)$, $\left(\dfrac{\sqrt{6}}{2}, 0\right)$

   (b) Vertical asymptote: $x = 0$
       Horizontal asymptote: $y = 2$

   (c) y-axis symmetry

   (d)

x	-2	-1	$-\frac{1}{2}$	$\frac{1}{2}$	1	2
y	$\frac{5}{4}$	-1	-10	-10	-1	$\frac{5}{4}$

   (e)

   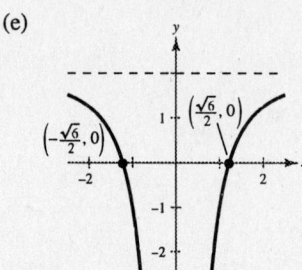

34. $f(t) = \dfrac{1 - 2t}{t} = -\dfrac{2t - 1}{t}$

   (a) Intercept: $\left(\dfrac{1}{2}, 0\right)$

   (b) Vertical asymptote: $t = 0$
       Horizontal asymptote: $y = -2$

   (c) No axis or origin symmetry

   (d)

t	-2	-1	$\frac{1}{2}$	1	2
y	$-\frac{5}{2}$	-3	0	-1	$-\frac{3}{2}$

   (e)

   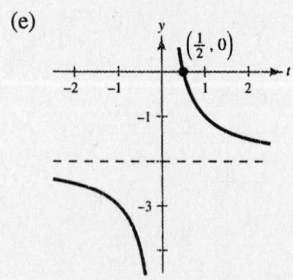

36. $g(x) = \dfrac{x}{x^2 - 9}$

   (a) Intercept: $(0, 0)$

   (b) Vertical asymptotes: $x = \pm 3$
       Horizontal asymptote: $y = 0$

   (c) Origin symmetry

   (d)

x	-5	-4	-2	0	2	4	5
y	$-\frac{5}{16}$	$-\frac{4}{7}$	$\frac{2}{5}$	0	$-\frac{2}{5}$	$\frac{4}{7}$	$\frac{5}{16}$

   (e)

   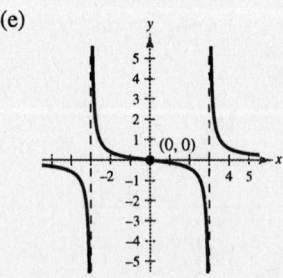

38. $f(x) = -\dfrac{1}{(x-2)^2}$

(a) Intercept: $\left(0, -\dfrac{1}{4}\right)$

(b) Vertical asymptote: $x = 2$
Horizontal asymptote: $y = 0$

(c) No axis or origin symmetry

(d)

x	0	$\frac{1}{2}$	1	$\frac{3}{2}$	$\frac{5}{2}$	3	$\frac{7}{2}$	4
y	$-\frac{1}{4}$	$-\frac{4}{9}$	-1	-4	-4	-1	$-\frac{4}{9}$	$-\frac{1}{4}$

(e)

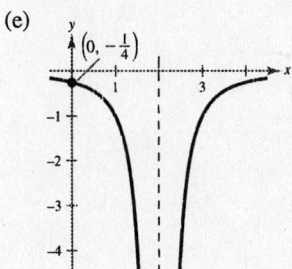

40. $h(x) = \dfrac{2}{x^2(x-2)}$

(a) No intercepts

(b) Vertical asymptotes: $x = 0, x = 2$
Horizontal asymptote: $y = 0$

(c) No axis or origin symmetry

(d)

x	-2	-1	$\frac{1}{2}$	1	$\frac{3}{2}$	$\frac{5}{2}$	3
y	$-\frac{1}{8}$	$-\frac{2}{3}$	$-\frac{16}{5}$	-2	$-\frac{16}{9}$	$\frac{16}{25}$	$\frac{2}{9}$

(e)

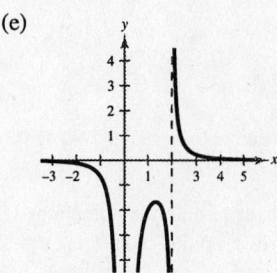

42. $f(x) = \dfrac{2x}{x^2+x-2} = \dfrac{2x}{(x+2)(x-1)}$

(a) Intercept: $(0, 0)$

(b) Vertical asymptotes: $x = -2, x = 1$
Horizontal asymptote: $y = 0$

(c) No axis or origin symmetry

(d)

x	-4	-3	-1	0	$\frac{1}{2}$	2	3
y	$-\frac{4}{5}$	$-\frac{3}{2}$	1	0	$-\frac{4}{5}$	1	$\frac{3}{5}$

(e)

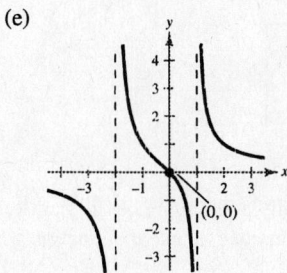

44. $f(x) = \dfrac{3(x^2 + 1)}{x^2 + 2x - 15} = \dfrac{3(x^2 + 1)}{(x - 3)(x + 5)}$

(a) Intercept: $\left(0, -\frac{1}{5}\right)$

(b) Vertical asymptotes: $x = -5, x = 3$
    Horizontal asymptote: $y = 3$

(c) No axis or origin symmetry

(d)

x	-15	-12	-9	-6	-3	0	6	9	12	15
y	$\frac{113}{30}$	$\frac{29}{7}$	$\frac{41}{8}$	$\frac{37}{3}$	$-\frac{5}{2}$	$-\frac{1}{5}$	$\frac{37}{11}$	$\frac{41}{14}$	$\frac{145}{51}$	$\frac{113}{40}$

(e)

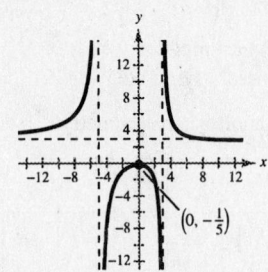

46. $f(x) = \dfrac{x^2(x - 2)}{x^2 - 2x}, \; g(x) = x$

(a) Domain of f: all real numbers except $x = 0$ and $x = 2$
    Domain of g: all real numbers

(b) Since $x^2 - 2x$ is a factor of both the numerator and the denominator of f, neither $x = 0$ nor $x = 2$ is a vertical asymptote of f. Thus, f has no vertical asymptotes.

(c)

x	-1	0	1	1.5	2	2.5	3
$f(x)$	-1	Undef.	1	1.5	Undef.	2.5	3
$g(x)$	-1	0	1	1.5	2	2.5	3

(d)

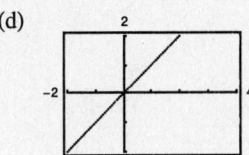

(e) Because there are only a finite number of pixels, the utility may not attempt to evaluate the function where it does not exist.

48. $f(x) = \dfrac{2x - 6}{x^2 - 7x + 12}, \; g(x) = \dfrac{2}{x - 4}$

(a) Domain of f: all real numbers except $x = 3$ and $x = 4$
    Domain of g: all real numbers except $x = 4$

(b) Since $x - 3$ is a factor of both the numerator and the denominator of f, $x = 3$ is not a vertical asymptote of f. Thus, f has $x = 4$ as its only vertical asymptote.

(c)

x	0	1	2	3	4	5	6
$f(x)$	$-\frac{1}{2}$	$-\frac{2}{3}$	-1	Undef.	Undef.	2	1
$g(x)$	$-\frac{1}{2}$	$-\frac{2}{3}$	-1	-2	Undef.	2	1

(d)

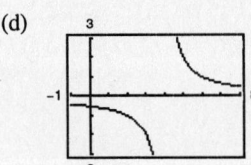

(e) Because there are only a finite number of pixels, the utility may not attempt to evaluate the function where it does not exist.

50. $g(x) = -\dfrac{x}{(x - 2)^2}$

Domain: all real numbers except $x = 2$

Vertical asymptote: $x = 2$

Horizontal asymptote: $y = 0$

x	-1	0	1	$\frac{3}{2}$	$\frac{5}{2}$	3	4
y	$\frac{1}{9}$	0	-1	-6	-10	-3	-1

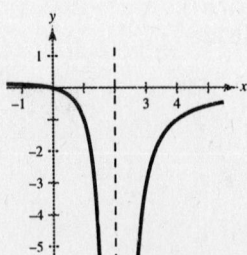

52. $f(x) = \dfrac{x + 4}{x^2 + x - 6}$

Domain: all real numbers except $x = -3$ and $x = 2$

Vertical asymptotes: $x = -3, x = 2$

Horizontal asymptote: $y = 0$

x	-6	-4	-2	-1	0	1	3	4
y	$-\frac{1}{12}$	0	$-\frac{1}{2}$	$-\frac{1}{2}$	$-\frac{2}{3}$	$-\frac{5}{4}$	$\frac{7}{6}$	$\frac{4}{7}$

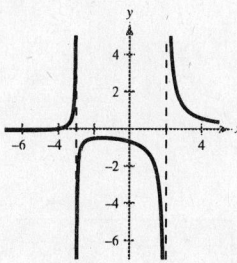

54. $f(x) = 5\left(\dfrac{1}{x - 4} - \dfrac{1}{x + 2}\right) = \dfrac{30}{(x - 4)(x + 2)}$

Domain: all real numbers except $x = -2$ and $x = 4$

Vertical asymptotes: $x = -2, x = 4$

Horizontal asymptote: $y = 0$

x	-4	-3	-1	0	1	2	3	5	6	7
y	$\frac{15}{8}$	$\frac{30}{7}$	-6	$-\frac{15}{4}$	$-\frac{10}{3}$	$-\frac{15}{4}$	-6	$\frac{30}{7}$	$\frac{15}{8}$	$\frac{10}{9}$

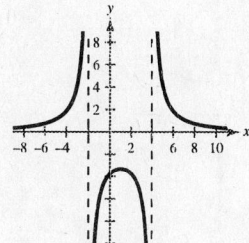

56. $f(x) = \dfrac{1 - x^2}{x} = -x + \dfrac{1}{x}$

(a) Intercepts: $(-1, 0), (1, 0)$

(b) Vertical asymptote: $x = 0$

Slant asymptote: $y = -x$

(c) Origin symmetry

(d)

-6	-4	-2	2	4	6
$\frac{35}{6}$	$\frac{15}{4}$	$\frac{3}{2}$	$-\frac{3}{2}$	$-\frac{15}{4}$	$-\frac{35}{6}$

(e)

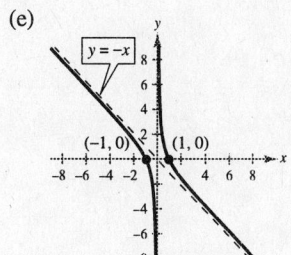

58. $h(x) = \dfrac{x^2}{x - 1} = x + 1 + \dfrac{1}{x - 1}$

(a) Intercept: $(0, 0)$

(b) Vertical asymptote: $x = 1$
Slant asymptote: $y = x + 1$

(c) No axis or origin symmetry

(d)

-4	-2	2	4	6
$-\frac{16}{5}$	$-\frac{4}{3}$	4	$-\frac{16}{3}$	$\frac{36}{5}$

(e)

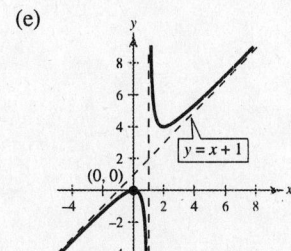

60. $g(x) = \dfrac{x^3}{2x^2 - 8} = \dfrac{1}{2}x + \dfrac{4x}{2x^2 - 8}$

(a) Intercept: $(0, 0)$

(b) Vertical asymptotes: $x = \pm 2$

Slant asymptote: $y = \dfrac{1}{2}x$

(c) Origin symmetry

(d)

-6	-4	-1	1	4	6
$-\dfrac{27}{8}$	$-\dfrac{8}{3}$	$\dfrac{1}{6}$	$-\dfrac{1}{6}$	$\dfrac{8}{3}$	$\dfrac{27}{8}$

(e)

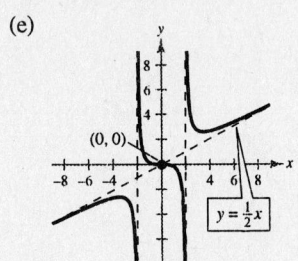

62. $f(x) = \dfrac{2x^2 - 5x + 5}{x - 2} = 2x - 1 + \dfrac{3}{x - 2}$

(a) Intercept: $\left(0, -\dfrac{5}{2}\right)$

(b) Vertical asymptote: $x = 2$
   Slant asymptote: $y = 2x - 1$

(c) No axis or origin symmetry

(d)

-6	-4	1	3	6	7
$-\dfrac{107}{8}$	$-\dfrac{38}{5}$	-2	8	$\dfrac{47}{4}$	$\dfrac{122}{7}$

(e)

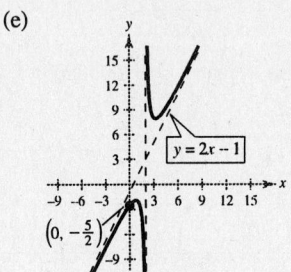

64. $f(x) = \dfrac{2x^2 + x}{x + 1} = 2x - 1 + \dfrac{1}{x + 1}$

Domain: all real numbers except $x = -1$

Intercepts: $\left(-\dfrac{1}{2}, 0\right), (0, 0), (0, 0)$

Vertical asymptote: $x = -1$

Slant asymptote: $y = 2x - 1$

Line: $y = 2x - 1$

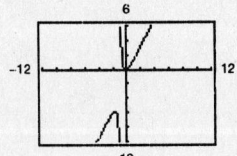

66. $h(x) = \dfrac{12 - 2x - x^2}{2(4 + x)} = -\dfrac{1}{2}x + 1 + \dfrac{2}{4 + x}$

Domain: all real numbers except $x = -4$

Intercepts: $(-4.61, 0), (2.61, 0), \left(0, \dfrac{3}{2}\right)$

Vertical asymptote: $x = -4$

Slant asymptote: $y = -\dfrac{1}{2}x + 1$

Line: $y = -\dfrac{1}{2}x + 1$

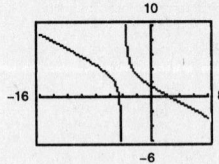

68. (a) x-intercept: $(0, 0)$

(b) $0 = \dfrac{2x}{x - 3}$

$0 = 2x$

$0 = x$

70. (a) x-intercepts: $(1, 0), (2, 0)$

(b) $0 = x - 3 + \dfrac{2}{x}$

$0 = x^2 - 3x + 2$

$0 = (x - 1)(x - 2)$

$x = 1, 2$

72. $C = \dfrac{25,000p}{100 - p}, 0 \le p < 100$

(a) $C = \dfrac{25,000(15)}{100 - 15} = \$4,411.776$

(b) $C = \dfrac{25,000(50)}{100 - 50} = \$25,000$

(c) $C = \dfrac{25,000(90)}{100 - 90} = \$225,000$

(d) No. The function is undefined at $p = 100$ and the cost effectively grows without bound as 100% is approached.

74. (a) Let C be the fractional concentration of brine in final solution.

$$C = \frac{(\text{brine in 25\% solution}) + (\text{brine in 75\% solution})}{\text{total amount of solution}}$$

$$= \frac{50 \cdot 0.25 + x \cdot 0.75}{50 + x} = \frac{12.5 + 0.75x}{x + 50} = \frac{3x + 50}{4(x + 50)}$$

(b) The amount x of added 75% solution can be any number of liters greater than or equal to zero that will fit in the 1000-liter tank:

$0 \le x \le 950$ or $[0, 950]$

(c)

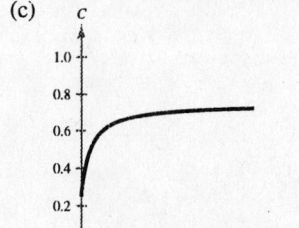

The concentration of brine increases at a slower rate.
The concentration of brine appears to be approaching 0.75 or 75%.

76. Let w be the width of the page and h be the height. The total of the horizontal margins is 3 inches and the total of the vertical margins is 2 inches. Thus,

64 square inches $= (w - 3)(h - 2)$

Solving $64 = (w - 3)(h - 2)$ for h gives

$h = 2 + \dfrac{64}{w - 3}$.

The total area of the paper is

$A = w \cdot h = w\left(2 + \dfrac{64}{w - 3}\right) = \dfrac{2w^2 + 58w}{w - 3}$.

Plotting A versus w using a graphing utility, the graph has a minimum, for $w > 3$, at $w \approx 12.80$ inches.

$h \approx 2 + \dfrac{64}{12.80 - 3} \approx 8.53$ inches

Width: 12.80 inches

Height: 8.53 inches

78. (a) Average speed $= \dfrac{\text{total distance}}{\text{total time}}$

$50 = \dfrac{200}{\dfrac{100}{x} + \dfrac{100}{y}}$

$50 = \dfrac{2xy}{x + y}$

$50x + 50y = 2xy$

$y = \dfrac{25x}{x - 25}$

(b) Vertical asymptote: $x = 25$

Horizontal asymptote: $y = 25$

80. False. A rational function with the x-axis as a horizontal asymptote may cross the x-axis. For example, the graph of $f(x) = \dfrac{x}{x^2 + 1}$ crosses $y = 0$, which is a horizontal asymptote.

82. Answers may vary. For example, $f(x) = \dfrac{1}{x^2 + 1}$ has no vertical asymptote and has $y = 0$ as its horizontal asymptote.

84. Answers will vary. For example, $f(x) = \dfrac{-6x^2 + 15x + 1}{x(2x - 5)}$

86. An asymptote is a line to which a graph gets arbitrarily close to, but does not reach, as $|x|$ or $|y|$ increases without bound.

88. $h(x) = \dfrac{6 - 2x}{3 - x}$

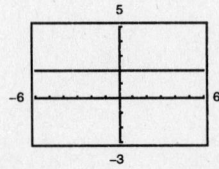

Although $x = 3$ is not in the domain of $h(x)$,

$$h(x) = \frac{2(3 - x)}{3 - x} = 2 \text{ for all real numbers except 3.}$$

90. $x^2 - 15x + 56 = (x - 7)(x - 8)$

92. $x^3 - 5x^2 + 4x - 20 = x^2(x - 5) + 4(x - 5)$
$$= (x^2 + 4)(x - 5)$$

94. $10 - 3x \le 0$
$$3x \ge 10$$
$$x \ge \tfrac{10}{3}$$

96. $|4(x - 2)| < 20$
$$-20 < 4x - 8 < 20$$
$$-12 < 4x < 28$$
$$-3 < x < 7$$

Section 2.7   Partial Fractions

Solutions to Even-Numbered Exercises

2. $\dfrac{3x-1}{x^2(x-4)} = \dfrac{A}{x} + \dfrac{B}{x^2} + \dfrac{C}{x-4}$

Matches (c).

4. $\dfrac{3x-1}{x(x^2-4)} = \dfrac{3x-1}{x(x-2)(x+2)} = \dfrac{A}{x} + \dfrac{B}{x-2} + \dfrac{C}{x+2}$

Matches (a).

6. $\dfrac{x-2}{x^2+4x+3} = \dfrac{x-2}{(x+3)(x+1)} = \dfrac{A}{x+3} + \dfrac{B}{x+1}$

8. $\dfrac{x^2-3x+2}{4x^3+11x^2} = \dfrac{x^2-3x+2}{x^2(4x+11)} = \dfrac{A}{x} + \dfrac{B}{x^2} + \dfrac{C}{4x+11}$

10. $\dfrac{6x+5}{(x+2)^4} = \dfrac{6x+5}{(x+2)(x+2)(x+2)(x+2)} = \dfrac{A}{x+2} + \dfrac{B}{(x+2)^2} + \dfrac{C}{(x+2)^3} + \dfrac{D}{(x+2)^4}$

12. $\dfrac{x-6}{2x^3+8x} = \dfrac{x-6}{2x(x^2+4)} = \dfrac{A}{2x} + \dfrac{B}{x^2+4}$

14. $\dfrac{x+4}{x^2(3x-1)^2} = \dfrac{A}{x} + \dfrac{B}{x^2} + \dfrac{C}{3x-1} + \dfrac{D}{(3x-1)^2}$

16. $\dfrac{1}{4x^2-9} = \dfrac{A}{2x+3} + \dfrac{B}{2x-3}$

$\qquad 1 = A(2x-3) + B(2x+3)$

Let $x = -\dfrac{3}{2}$: $1 = -6A \implies A = -\dfrac{1}{6}$

Let $x = \dfrac{3}{2}$: $1 = 6B \implies B = \dfrac{1}{6}$

$\dfrac{1}{4x^2-9} = \dfrac{1}{6}\left(\dfrac{1}{2x-3} - \dfrac{1}{2x+3}\right)$

18. $\dfrac{3}{x^2-3x} = \dfrac{A}{x-3} + \dfrac{B}{x}$

$\qquad 3 = Ax + B(x-3)$

Let $x = 3$: $3 = 3A \implies A = 1$

Let $x = 0$: $3 = -3B \implies B = -1$

$\dfrac{3}{x^2-3x} = \dfrac{1}{x-3} - \dfrac{1}{x}$

20. $\dfrac{5}{x^2+x-6} = \dfrac{A}{x+3} + \dfrac{B}{x-2}$

$\qquad 5 = A(x-2) + B(x+3)$

Let $x = -3$: $5 = -5A \implies A = -1$

Let $x = 2$: $5 = 5B \implies B = 1$

$\dfrac{5}{x^2+x-6} = \dfrac{1}{x-2} - \dfrac{1}{x+3}$

22. $\dfrac{x+1}{x^2+4x+3} = \dfrac{x+1}{(x+3)(x+1)}$

$\qquad\qquad = \dfrac{1}{x+3}, x \neq -1$

24. $\dfrac{x+2}{x(x-4)} = \dfrac{A}{x} + \dfrac{B}{x-4}$

$x + 2 = A(x-4) + Bx$

Let $x = 0$: $2 = -4A \implies A = -\dfrac{1}{2}$

Let $x = 4$: $6 = 4B \implies B = \dfrac{3}{2}$

$\dfrac{x+2}{x(x-4)} = \dfrac{1}{2}\left(\dfrac{3}{x-4} - \dfrac{1}{x}\right)$

26. $\dfrac{2x-3}{(x-1)^2} = \dfrac{A}{x-1} + \dfrac{B}{(x-1)^2}$

$2x - 3 = A(x-1) + B$

Let $x = 1$: $-1 = B$

Let $x = 0$: $-3 = -A + B$

$\qquad\qquad -3 = -A - 1$

$\qquad\qquad\quad 2 = A$

$\dfrac{2x-3}{(x-1)^2} = \dfrac{2}{x-1} - \dfrac{1}{(x-1)^2}$

28. $\dfrac{6x^2 + 1}{x^2(x - 1)^2} = \dfrac{A}{x} + \dfrac{B}{x^2} + \dfrac{C}{x - 1} + \dfrac{D}{(x - 1)^2}$

$6x^2 + 1 = Ax(x - 1)^2 + B(x - 1)^2 + Cx^2(x - 1) + Dx^2$

Let $x = 0 : 1 = B$

Let $x = 1 : 7 = D$

Substitute B and D into the equation, expand the binomials, collect like terms, and equate the coefficients of like terms.

$-2x^2 + 2x = Ax^3 + (-2A - C)x^2 + Ax$

$\qquad A = 2$

$-2A - C = -2 \Rightarrow C = -2$

$\dfrac{6x^2 + 1}{x^2(x - 1)^2} = \dfrac{2}{x} + \dfrac{1}{x^2} - \dfrac{2}{x - 1} + \dfrac{7}{(x - 1)^2}$

30. $\dfrac{x}{(x - 1)(x^2 + x + 1)} = \dfrac{A}{x - 1} + \dfrac{Bx + C}{x^2 + x + 1}$

$x = A(x^2 + x + 1) + (Bx + C)(x - 1)$

$\quad = Ax^2 + Ax + A + Bx^2 - Bx + Cx - C$

$\quad = (A + B)x^2 + (A - B + C)x + (A - C)$

Equating coefficients of like powers gives $0 = A + B$, $1 = A - B + C$, and $0 = A - C$.
Substituting $-A$ for B and A for C in the second equation gives $1 = 3A$, so $A = \frac{1}{3}$, $B = -\frac{1}{3}$, and $C = \frac{1}{3}$.

$\dfrac{x}{(x - 1)(x^2 + x + 1)} = \dfrac{1}{3}\left(\dfrac{1}{x - 1} - \dfrac{x - 1}{x^2 + x + 1}\right)$

32. $\dfrac{x + 6}{x^3 - 3x^2 - 4x + 12} = \dfrac{x + 6}{(x + 2)(x - 2)(x - 3)} = \dfrac{A}{x + 2} + \dfrac{B}{x - 2} + \dfrac{C}{x - 3}$

$x + 6 = A(x - 2)(x - 3) + B(x + 2)(x - 3) + C(x + 2)(x - 2)$

Let $x = 3 : \quad 9 = 5C \implies \frac{9}{5} = C$

Let $x = -2 : 4 = 20A \implies \frac{1}{5} = A$

Let $x = 2 : \quad 8 = -4B \implies -2 = B$

$\dfrac{x + 6}{x^3 - 3x^2 - 4x + 12} = \dfrac{\frac{1}{5}}{x + 2} + \dfrac{-2}{x - 2} + \dfrac{\frac{9}{5}}{x - 3} = \dfrac{1}{5}\left(\dfrac{1}{x + 2} - \dfrac{10}{x - 2} + \dfrac{9}{x - 3}\right)$

34. $\dfrac{2x^2 + x + 8}{(x^2 + 4)^2} = \dfrac{Ax + B}{x^2 + 4} + \dfrac{Cx + D}{(x^2 + 4)^2}$

$2x^2 + x + 8 = (Ax + B)(x^2 + 4) + Cx + D$

$2x^2 + x + 8 = Ax^3 + Bx^2 + (4A + C)x + (4B + D)$

Equating coefficients of like powers:

$0 = A$

$2 = B$

$1 = 4A + C \Rightarrow C = 1$

$8 = 4B + D \Rightarrow D = 0$

$\dfrac{2x^2 + x + 8}{(x^2 + 4)^2} = \dfrac{2}{x^2 + 4} + \dfrac{x}{(x^2 + 4)^2}$

36. $\dfrac{x + 1}{x^3 + x} = \dfrac{A}{x} + \dfrac{Bx + C}{x^2 + 1}$

$\quad = (A + B)x^2 + Cx + A$

Equating coefficients of like powers gives
$0 = A + B$, $1 = C$, and $1 = A$.
Therefore, $A = 1$, $B = -1$, and $C = 1$.

$\dfrac{x + 1}{x^3 + x} = \dfrac{1}{x} - \dfrac{x - 1}{x^2 + 1}$

38. $\dfrac{x^2 - 4x + 7}{(x + 1)(x^2 - 2x + 3)} = \dfrac{A}{x + 1} + \dfrac{Bx + C}{x^2 - 2x + 3}$

$$x^2 - 4x + 7 = A(x^2 - 2x + 3) + (Bx + C)(x + 1)$$

$$= Ax^2 - 2Ax + 3A + Bx^2 + Bx + Cx + C$$

$$= (A + B)x^2 + (-2A + B + C)x + (3A + C)$$

Equating coefficients of like terms gives $1 = A + B$, $-4 = -2A + B + C$, and $7 = 3A + C$. Adding the second and third equations, and subtracting the first, gives $2 = 2C$, so $C = 1$. Therefore, $A = 2$, $B = -1$, and $C = 1$.

$$\dfrac{x^2 - 4x + 7}{(x + 1)(x^2 - 2x + 3)} = \dfrac{2}{x + 1} - \dfrac{x - 1}{x^2 - 2x + 3}$$

40. $\dfrac{x^2 - 4x}{x^2 + x + 6}$

Using long division gives

$$\dfrac{x^2 - 4x}{x^2 + x + 6} = 1 - \dfrac{5x + 6}{x^2 + x + 6}$$

42. $\dfrac{x^3 + 2x^2 - x + 1}{x^2 + 3x - 4}$

Using long division gives

$$\dfrac{x^3 + 2x^2 - x + 1}{x^2 + 3x - 4} = x - 1 - \dfrac{3}{x^2 + 3x - 4}$$

$$\dfrac{x^3 + 2x^2 - x + 1}{x^2 + 3x - 4} - x + 1 = -\dfrac{3}{x^2 + 3x - 4} = \dfrac{-3}{(x + 4)(x - 1)}$$

$$= -\left(\dfrac{A}{x + 4} + \dfrac{B}{x - 1}\right)$$

$$\dfrac{6x - 3}{(x + 4)(x - 1)} = -\left(\dfrac{A}{x + 4} + \dfrac{B}{x - 1}\right)$$

$$6x - 3 = -A(x - 1) - B(x + 4)$$

$$6x - 3 = (-A - B)x + (A - 4B)$$

$$-A - B = 6 \Rightarrow \qquad A = -6 - B$$

$$-A - 4B = -3 \Rightarrow -6 - B - 4B = -3$$

$$-6 - 5B = -3$$

$$-5B = 3$$

$$B = -\dfrac{3}{5}$$

$$A = -6 + \dfrac{3}{5} = \dfrac{-30 + 3}{5} = \dfrac{-27}{5}$$

$$\dfrac{x^3 + 2x^2 - x + 1}{x^2 + 3x - 4} = x - 1 - \left(\dfrac{-\dfrac{27}{5}}{x + 4} + \dfrac{-\dfrac{3}{5}}{x - 1}\right)$$

$$= x - 1 + \dfrac{1}{5}\left(\dfrac{27}{x + 4} + \dfrac{3}{x - 1}\right)$$

44. $\dfrac{16x^4}{(2x - 1)^3} = \dfrac{16x^4}{8x^3 - 12x^2 + 6x - 1} = 2x + 3 + \dfrac{24x^2 - 16x + 3}{(2x - 1)^3}$

$\dfrac{24x^2 - 16x + 3}{(2x - 1)^2} = \dfrac{A}{2x - 1} + \dfrac{B}{(2x - 1)^2} + \dfrac{C}{(2x - 1)^3}$

$24x^2 - 16x + 3 = A(2x - 1)^2 + B(2x - 1) + C$

Let $x = \dfrac{1}{2}: 1 = C$

$24x^2 - 16x + 3 = 4Ax^2 - 2Ax + A + 2Bx - B + 1$

$24x^2 - 16x + 3 = 4Ax^2 + (-2A + 2B)x + (A - B + 1)$

Equating coefficients of like powers:

$6 = A, 3 = A - B + 1$

$\qquad 3 = 6 - B + 1$

$\qquad 4 = B$

$\dfrac{16x^4}{(2x - 1)^3} = 2x + 3 + \dfrac{6}{2x - 1} + \dfrac{4}{(2x - 1)^2} + \dfrac{1}{(2x - 1)^3}$

46. $\dfrac{3x^2 - 7x - 2}{x^3 - x} = \dfrac{A}{x} + \dfrac{B}{x + 1} + \dfrac{C}{x - 1}$

$3x^2 - 7x - 2 = A(x^2 - 1) + Bx(x - 1) + Cx(x + 1)$

Let $x = 0: -2 = -A \implies A = 2$

Let $x = -1: 8 = 2B \implies B = 4$

Let $x = 1: -6 = 2C \implies C = -3$

$\dfrac{3x^2 - 7x - 2}{x^3 - x} = \dfrac{2}{x} + \dfrac{4}{x + 1} - \dfrac{3}{x - 1}$

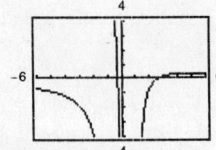

48. $\dfrac{4x^2 - 1}{2x(x + 1)^2} = \dfrac{A}{2x} + \dfrac{B}{x + 1} + \dfrac{C}{(x + 1)^2}$

$4x^2 - 1 = A(x + 1)^2 + 2Bx(x + 1) + 2Cx$

Let $x = 0: -1 = A$

Let $x = -1: 3 = -2C \implies C = -\dfrac{3}{2}$

Let $x = 1: 3 = 4A + 4B + 2C$

$\qquad 3 = -4 + 4B - 3$

$\qquad \dfrac{5}{2} = B$

$\dfrac{4x^2 - 1}{2x(x + 1)^2} = \dfrac{1}{2}\left[-\dfrac{1}{x} + \dfrac{5}{x + 1} - \dfrac{3}{(x + 1)^2} \right]$

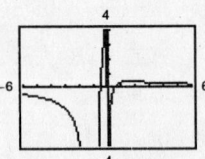

50. $\dfrac{x^3}{(x + 2)^2(x - 2)^2} = \dfrac{A}{x + 2} + \dfrac{B}{(x + 2)^2} + \dfrac{C}{x - 2} + \dfrac{D}{(x - 2)^2}$

$\qquad x^3 = A(x + 2)(x - 2)^2 + B(x - 2)^2 + C(x + 2)^2(x - 2) + D(x + 2)^2$

Let $x = -2: -8 = 16B \implies B = -\dfrac{1}{2}$

Let $x = 2: 8 = 16D \implies D = \dfrac{1}{2}$

—CONTINUED—

50. **—CONTINUED—**

$x^3 = A(x + 2)(x - 2)^2 - \frac{1}{2}(x - 2)^2 + C(x + 2)^2(x - 2) + \frac{1}{2}(x + 2)^2$

$x^3 - 4 = (A + C)x^3 + (-2A + 2C)x^2 + (-4A - 4C)x + (8A - 8C)$

Equating coefficients of like powers:

$0 = -2A + 2C \implies A = C$

$1 = A + C$

$1 = 2A \implies A = \frac{1}{2} \implies C = \frac{1}{2}$

$\dfrac{x^3}{(x + 2)^2(x - 2)^2} = \dfrac{1}{2}\left[\dfrac{1}{x + 2} - \dfrac{1}{(x + 2)^2} + \dfrac{1}{x - 2} + \dfrac{1}{(x - 2)^2}\right]$

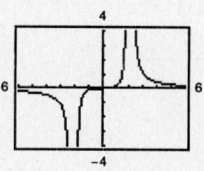

52. $\dfrac{x^3 - x + 3}{x^2 + x - 2} = x - 1 + \dfrac{2x + 1}{(x + 2)(x - 1)}$

$\dfrac{2x + 1}{(x + 2)(x - 1)} = \dfrac{A}{x + 2} + \dfrac{B}{x - 1}$

$2x + 1 = A(x - 1) + B(x + 2)$

Let $x = -2$: $-3 = -3A \implies A = 1$

Let $x = 1$: $3 = 3B \implies B = 1$

$\dfrac{x^3 - x + 3}{x^2 + x - 2} = x - 1 + \dfrac{1}{x + 2} + \dfrac{1}{x - 1}$

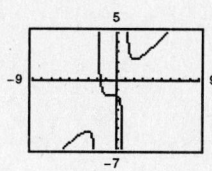

54. $y = \dfrac{2(x + 1)^2}{x(x^2 + 1)} = \dfrac{A}{x} + \dfrac{Bx + C}{x^2 + 1}$

$2(x + 1)^2 = A(x^2 + 1) + Bx^2 + Cx$

$2x^2 + 4x + 2 = (A + B)x^2 + Cx + A$

Equating coefficients of like powers gives
$2 = A + B$, $4 = C$, and $2 = A$.

Therefore, $A = 2$, $B = 0$, and $C = 4$.

$\dfrac{2(x + 1)^2}{x(x^2 + 1)} = \dfrac{2}{x} + \dfrac{4}{x^2 + 1}$

The vertical asymptote of $y = \dfrac{2}{x}$ is the same as the vertical asymptote of the rational function.

$\dfrac{2(x + 1)^2}{x(x^2 + 1)}$

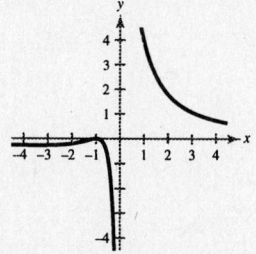

Vertical asymptote at $x = 0$

$y = \dfrac{2}{x}$ and $y = \dfrac{4}{x^2 + 1}$

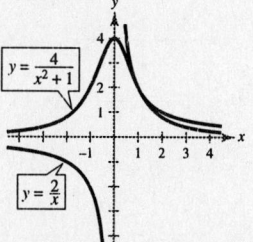

$y = \dfrac{2}{x}$ has vertical asymptote $x = 0$.

56. $y = \dfrac{2(4x^2 - 15x + 39)}{x^2(x^2 - 10x + 26)} = \dfrac{A}{x} + \dfrac{Bx}{x^2} + \dfrac{Cx + D}{x^2 - 10x + 26}$

$2(4x^2 - 15x + 39) = Ax(x^2 - 10x + 26) + B(x^2 - 10x + 26) + Cx^3 + Dx^2$

$8x^2 - 30x + 78 = Ax^3 - 10Ax^2 + 26Ax + Bx^2 - 10Bx + 26B + Cx^3 + Dx^2$

$\qquad\qquad\qquad = (A + C)x^3 + (-10A + B + D)x^2 + (26A - 10B)x + 26B$

Equating coefficients of like powers gives $0 = A + C$, $8 = -10A + B + D$, $-30 = 26A - 10B$, and $78 = 26B$. Since $78 = 26B$, $B = 3$. Therefore, $A = 0$, $B = 3$, $C = 0$, and $D = 5$.

$\dfrac{2(4x^2 - 15x + 39)}{x^2(x^2 - 10x + 26)} = \dfrac{3}{x^2} + \dfrac{5}{x^2 - 10x + 26}$

$\dfrac{2(4x^2 - 15x + 39)}{x^2(x^2 - 10x + 26)}$
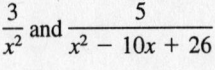
$\dfrac{3}{x^2}$ and $\dfrac{5}{x^2 - 10x + 26}$

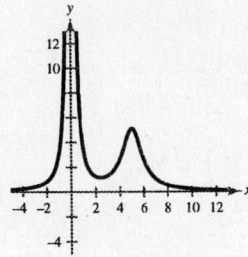

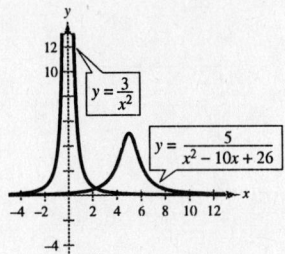

Vertical asymptote is $x = 0$.

$y = \dfrac{3}{x^2}$ has vertical asymptote $x = 0$.

The vertical asymptote of $y = \dfrac{3}{x^2}$ is the same as the vertical asymptote of the rational function.

58. False. The partial fraction decomposition is $\dfrac{A}{x + 10} + \dfrac{B}{x - 10} + \dfrac{C}{(x - 10)^2}$.

60. $\dfrac{1}{a^2 - x^2} = \dfrac{A}{a + x} + \dfrac{B}{a - x}$, a is a constant.

$\qquad 1 = A(a - x) + B(a + x)$

Let $x = -a$: $1 = 2aA \implies A = \dfrac{1}{2a}$

Let $x = a$: $1 = 2aB \implies B = \dfrac{1}{2a}$

$\dfrac{1}{a^2 - x^2} = \dfrac{1}{2a}\!\left(\dfrac{1}{a + x} + \dfrac{1}{a - x}\right)$

62. $\dfrac{1}{y(a - y)} = \dfrac{A}{y} + \dfrac{B}{a - y}$

$\qquad 1 = A(a - y) + By$

Let $y = 0$: $1 = aA \implies A = \dfrac{1}{a}$

Let $y = a$: $1 = aB \implies B = \dfrac{1}{a}$

$\dfrac{1}{y(a - y)} = \dfrac{1}{a}\!\left(\dfrac{1}{y} + \dfrac{1}{a - y}\right)$

64. $f(x) = -3x + 7$

x-intercepts: $\left(\frac{7}{3}, 0\right)$

y-intercepts: $(0, 7)$

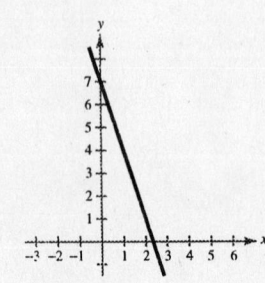

66. $f(x) = -2x^2$

Intercepts: $(0, 0)$

Graph falls to the left and falls to the right.

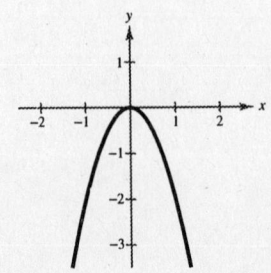

68. $f(x) = x^2 - 9x + 18 = (x - 6)(x - 3)$

Intercepts: $(0, 18), (3, 0), (6, 0)$

Graph rises to the left and rises to the right.

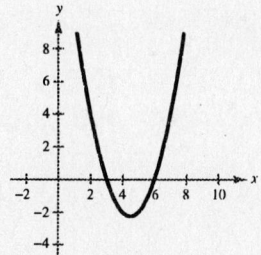

70. $f(x) = -x^2(x - 3)$

Intercepts: $(0, 0), (3, 0)$

Graph rises to the left and falls to the right.

72. $f(x) = \dfrac{6}{x - 1}$

y-intercept: $(0, -6)$

Vertical asymptote: $x = 1$

Horizontal asymptote: $y = 0$

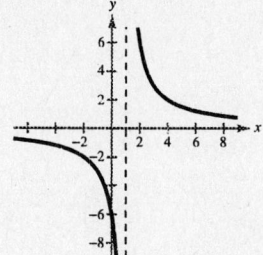
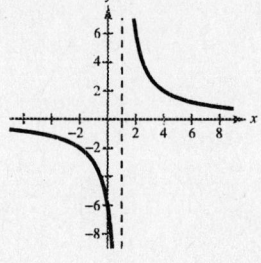

74. $f(x) = \dfrac{x^2 + x - 6}{x + 5}$

x-intercept: $(-3, 0), (2, 0)$

y-intercept: $\left(0, -\dfrac{6}{5}\right)$

Vertical asymptote: $x = -5$

Slant asymptote: $y = x - 4$

No horizontal asymptote.

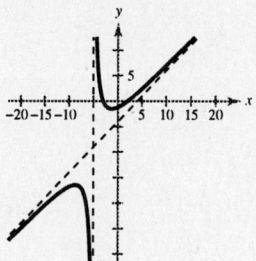

76. $f(x) = \dfrac{3(x^2 - 1)}{x^2 + 4x - 5} = \dfrac{3(x + 1)(x - 1)}{(x + 5)(x - 1)} = \dfrac{3(x + 1)}{x + 5}, x \neq 1$

x-intercept: $(-1, 0)$

y-intercept: $\left(0, \dfrac{3}{5}\right)$

Vertical asymptote: $x = -5$

Horizontal asymptote: $y = 3$

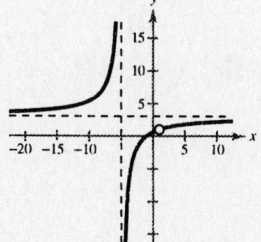

Review Exercises for Chapter 2

2. (a) $y = x^2 - 4$

Vertical shift downward 4 units

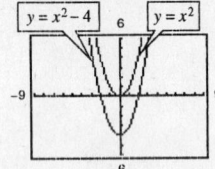

(b) $y = 4 - x^2$

Reflected in x-axis and vertical shift upward 4 units

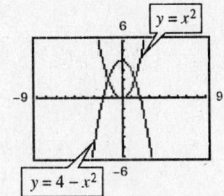

(c) $y = (x - 3)^2$

Horizontal shift to the right 3 units

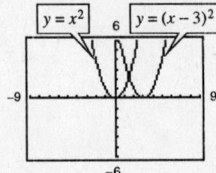

(d) $y = \frac{1}{2}x^2 - 1$

Vertical shrink by factor of $\frac{1}{2}$ and vertical shift downward 1 unit.

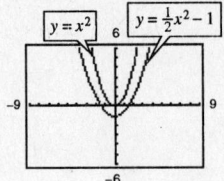

4. Vertex: $(2, 2) \Longrightarrow f(x) = a(x - 2)^2 + 2$

Point: $(0, 3) \Longrightarrow 3 = a(0 - 2)^2 + 2$

$$3 = 4a + 2$$
$$1 = 4a$$
$$\tfrac{1}{4} = a$$
$$f(x) = \tfrac{1}{4}(x - 2)^2 + 2$$

6. Vertex: $(2, 3) \Longrightarrow f(x) = a(x - 2)^2 + 3$

Point: $(-1, 6) \Longrightarrow 6 = a(-1 - 2)^2 + 3$

$$6 = 9a + 3$$
$$3 = 9a$$
$$\tfrac{1}{3} = a$$
$$f(x) = \tfrac{1}{3}(x - 2)^2 + 3$$

8. $f(x) = 6x - x^2$

$$= -(x^2 - 6x + 9 - 9)$$
$$= -(x - 3)^2 + 9$$

Vertex $(3, 9)$

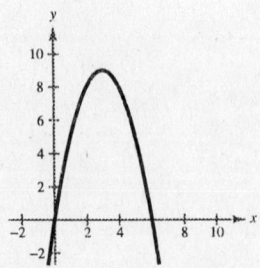

10. $h(x) = 3 + 4x - x^2$

$$= -(x^2 - 4x - 3)$$
$$= -(x^2 - 4x + 4 - 4 - 3)$$
$$= -[(x - 2)^2 - 7]$$
$$= -(x - 2)^2 + 7$$

Vertex $(2, 7)$

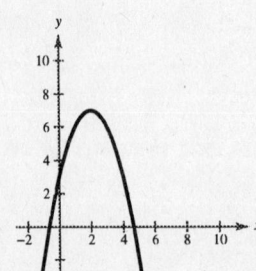

12. $f(x) = x^2 - 8x + 12$

$$= x^2 - 8x + 16 - 16 + 12$$
$$= (x - 4)^2 - 4$$

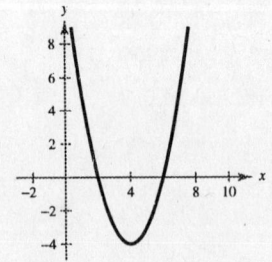

14. $f(x) = x^2 - 6x + 1$

$= x^2 - 6x + 9 - 9 + 1$

$= (x - 3)^2 - 8$

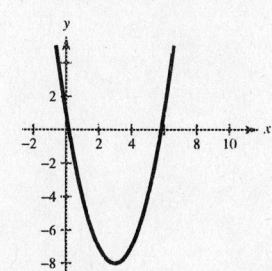

16. $f(x) = 4x^2 + 4x + 5$

$= 4\left(x^2 + x + \frac{1}{4} - \frac{1}{4} + \frac{5}{4}\right)$

$= 4\left[\left(x + \frac{1}{2}\right)^2 + 1\right]$

$= 4\left(x + \frac{1}{2}\right)^2 + 4$

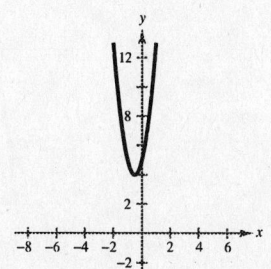

18. $f(x) = \frac{1}{2}(6x^2 - 24x + 22)$

$= 3x^2 - 12x + 11$

$= 3(x^2 - 4x + 4 - 4) + 11$

$= 3(x - 2)^2 + 3(-4) + 11$

$= 3(x - 2)^2 - 1$

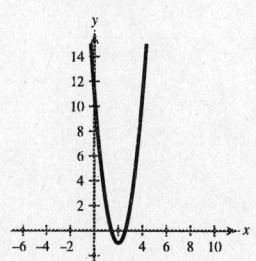

20. Let x = the number of $30 increases in rent. Then,

Rent $= 540 + 30x$

Number of occupied units $= 50 - x$

Revenue $=$ (Number of occupied units)(rent)

$R = (50 - x)(540 + 30x)$

Cost $=$ (Number of occupied units)($18)

$C = (50 - x)(18)$

Profit $=$ Revenue $-$ Cost

$P = (50 - x)(540 + 30x) - (50 - x)(18)$

$= 27,000 + 960x - 30x^2 - 900 + 18x$

$= -30x^2 + 978x + 26,100$

The maximum profit occurs at the vertex.

$-\dfrac{b}{2a} = \dfrac{-978}{2(-30)} = 16.3 \approx 16$ increases

The corresponding rent is $540 + 30(16) = \$1020$.

22. $y = -0.00428x^2 + 1.442x - 3.136, 20 \le x \le 55$

$y = 30 \Longrightarrow -0.00428x^2 + 1.442x - 33.136 = 0$

$x = \dfrac{-1.442 \pm \sqrt{(1.442)^2 - 4(-0.00428)(-33.136)}}{2(-0.00428)}$

$\approx 24.8, 312$

Average age of bride: 25

24. $y = x^3, f(x) = -4x^3$

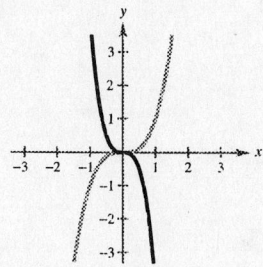

26. $y = x^4, f(x) = 2(x - 2)^4$

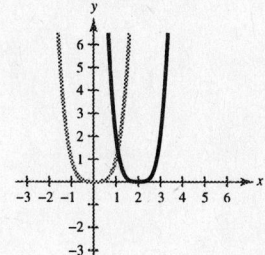

28. $y = x^5, f(x) = \frac{1}{2}x^5 + 3$

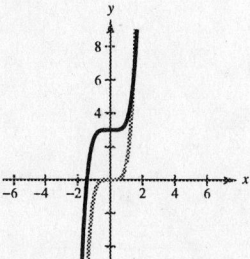

30. $f(x) = \frac{1}{2}x^3 + 2x$

The degree is odd and the leading coefficient is positive. The graph falls to the left and rises to the right.

32. $h(x) = -x^5 - 7x^2 + 10x$

The degree is odd and the leading coefficient is negative. The graph rises to the left and falls to the right.

34. $f(x) = x(x + 3)^2$

$x(x + 3)^2 = 0$

Zeros: $x = -3, 0$

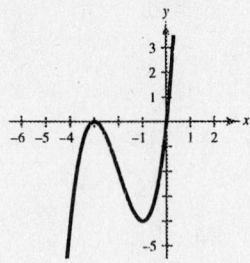

36. $f(x) = x^3 - 8x^2$

$x^3 - 8x^2 = x^2(x - 8) = 0$

Zeros: $x = 0, 8$

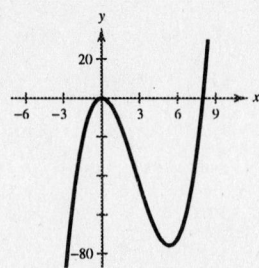

38. $g(x) = x^4 - x^3 - 2x^2$

$x^4 - x^3 - 2x^2 = x^2(x^2 - x - 2)$

$\qquad\qquad\qquad = x^2(x - 2)(x + 1)$

Zeros: $x = -1, 0, 2$

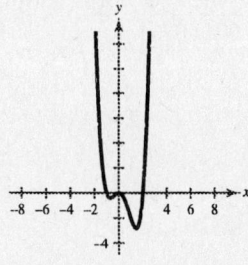

40. $f(x) = 0.25x^3 - 3.65x + 6.12$

By the Intermediate Value Theorem, the following interval is guaranteed to have a zero: $(-5, -4)$.

42. $f(x) = 7x^4 + 3x^3 - 10x^2 + 2$

By the Intermediate Value Theorem, the following intervals are guaranteed to have a zero:
$(-2, -1), (-1, 0), (0, 1)$

44.

$$
\begin{array}{r}
\dfrac{4}{3} \\
3x - 2 \overline{)\, 4x + 7} \\
4x - \dfrac{8}{3} \\
\hline
\dfrac{29}{3}
\end{array}
$$

$$\frac{4x + 7}{3x - 2} = \frac{4}{3} + \frac{29}{3(3x - 2)}$$

46.

$$
\begin{array}{r}
3x^2 + 3 \\
x^2 - 1 \overline{)\, 3x^4 + 0x^3 + 0x^2 + 0x + 0} \\
3x^4 - 3x^2 \\
\hline
3x^2 \\
3x^2 - 3 \\
\hline
3
\end{array}
$$

$$\frac{3x^4}{x^2 - 1} = 3x^2 + 3 + \frac{3}{x^2 - 1}$$

48.

$$
\begin{array}{r}
3x^2 + 5x + 8 \\
2x^2 - 1 \overline{)\, 6x^4 + 10x^3 + 13x^2 - 5x + 2} \\
6x^4 - 3x^2 \\
\hline
10x^3 + 16x^2 \\
10x^3 - 5x \\
\hline
16x^2 \\
16x^2 - 8 \\
\hline
10
\end{array}
$$

$$\frac{6x^4 + 10x^3 + 13x^2 - 5x + 2}{2x^2 - 1} = 3x^2 + 5x + 8 + \frac{10}{2x^2 - 1}$$

50.

$$
5 \,\big|\,
\begin{array}{rrrr}
0.1 & 0.3 & 0 & -0.5 \\
 & 0.5 & 4 & 20 \\
\hline
0.1 & 0.8 & 4 & 19.5
\end{array}
$$

$$\frac{0.1x^3 + 0.3x^2 - 0.5}{x - 5} = 0.1x^2 + 0.8x + 4 + \frac{19.5}{x - 5}$$

52.

$$
-3 \,\big|\,
\begin{array}{rrrr}
3 & 20 & 29 & -12 \\
 & -9 & -33 & 12 \\
\hline
3 & 11 & -4 & 0
\end{array}
$$

$$\frac{3x^3 + 20x^2 + 29x - 12}{x + 3} = 3x^2 + 11x - 4$$

54. $f(x) = 3x^3 - 8x^2 - 20x + 16$

(a)
$$
4 \,\big|\,
\begin{array}{rrrr}
3 & -8 & -20 & 16 \\
 & 12 & 16 & -16 \\
\hline
3 & 4 & -4 & 0 = f(4)
\end{array}
$$

$x = 4$ is a zero of f.

(b)
$$
-4 \,\big|\,
\begin{array}{rrrr}
3 & -8 & -20 & 16 \\
 & -12 & 80 & -240 \\
\hline
3 & -20 & 60 & -224 = f(-4)
\end{array}
$$

$x = -4$ is not a zero of f.

(c)
$$
\tfrac{2}{3} \,\big|\,
\begin{array}{rrrr}
3 & -8 & -20 & 16 \\
 & 2 & -4 & -16 \\
\hline
3 & -6 & -24 & 0 = f\!\left(\tfrac{2}{3}\right)
\end{array}
$$

$x = \tfrac{2}{3}$ is a zero of f.

(d)
$$
-1 \,\big|\,
\begin{array}{rrrr}
3 & -8 & -20 & 16 \\
 & -3 & 11 & 9 \\
\hline
3 & -11 & -9 & 25 = f(-1)
\end{array}
$$

$x = -1$ is not a zero of f.

56. $g(t) = 2t^5 - 5t^4 - 8t + 20$

(a)
$$
-4 \,\big|\,
\begin{array}{rrrrrr}
2 & -5 & 0 & 0 & -8 & 20 \\
 & -8 & 52 & -208 & 832 & -3296 \\
\hline
2 & -13 & 52 & -208 & 824 & -3276 = g(-4)
\end{array}
$$

(b)
$$
\sqrt{2} \,\big|\,
\begin{array}{rrrrrr}
2 & -5 & 0 & 0 & -8 & 20 \\
 & 2\sqrt{2} & -5\sqrt{2}+4 & -10+4\sqrt{2} & -10\sqrt{2}+8 & -20 \\
\hline
2 & -5+2\sqrt{2} & -5\sqrt{2}+4 & -10+4\sqrt{2} & -10\sqrt{2} & 0 = g\!\left(\sqrt{2}\right)
\end{array}
$$

58. $f(x) = 2x^3 + 11x^2 - 21x - 90$; Factor: $(x + 6)$

(a)
$$
-6 \,\big|\,
\begin{array}{rrrr}
2 & 11 & -21 & -90 \\
 & -12 & 6 & 90 \\
\hline
2 & -1 & -15 & 0
\end{array}
$$

(b) $2x^2 - x - 15 = (2x + 5)(x - 3)$

(c) $f(x) = (x + 6)(2x + 5)(x - 3)$

(d) Zeros: $-6, -\tfrac{5}{2}, 3$

(e)

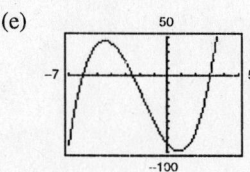

60. $f(x) = x^4 - 11x^3 + 41x^2 - 61x + 30$;
Factors: $(x - 2)(x - 5)$

(a)
$$
2 \,\big|\,
\begin{array}{rrrrr}
1 & -11 & 41 & -61 & 30 \\
 & 2 & -18 & 46 & -30 \\
\hline
1 & -9 & 23 & -15 & 0
\end{array}
$$

$$
5 \,\big|\,
\begin{array}{rrrr}
1 & -9 & 23 & -15 \\
 & 5 & -20 & 15 \\
\hline
1 & -4 & 3 & 0
\end{array}
$$

(b) $x^2 - 4x + 3 = (x - 3)(x - 1)$

(c) $f(x) = (x - 1)(x - 2)(x - 3)(x - 5)$

(d) Zeros: $1, 2, 3, 5$

(e)

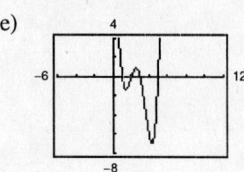

62. $6 + \sqrt{-4} = 6 + 2i$

64. $i^2 + 3i = -1 + 3i$

66. $(7 + 5i) + (-4 + 2i) = 3 + 7i$

68. $5i(13 - 8i) = 40 + 65i$

70. $(10 - 8i)(2 - 3i) = 20 - 30i - 16i + 24i^2$
$$= -4 - 46i$$

72. $\dfrac{6 + i}{4 - i} = \dfrac{6 + i}{4 - i} \cdot \dfrac{4 + i}{4 + i} = \dfrac{23 + 10i}{17} = \dfrac{23}{17} + \dfrac{10}{17}i$

74. $\dfrac{4}{2 - 3i} + \dfrac{2}{1 + i} = \dfrac{4}{2 - 3i} \cdot \dfrac{2 + 3i}{2 + 3i} + \dfrac{2}{1 + i} \cdot \dfrac{1 - i}{1 - i}$
$$= \dfrac{8 + 12i}{13} + \dfrac{2 - 2i}{2} = \dfrac{21 - i}{13}$$
$$= \dfrac{21}{13} - \dfrac{1}{13}i$$

76. $3x^2 + 1 = 0$
$$x^2 = -\dfrac{1}{3}$$
$$x = \pm\dfrac{\sqrt{3}}{3}i$$

78. $x^2 - 2x + 10 = 0$
$$x = \dfrac{-(-2) \pm \sqrt{(-2)^2 - 4(1)(10)}}{2(1)}$$
$$= \dfrac{2 \pm \sqrt{-36}}{2} = \dfrac{2 \pm 6i}{2}$$
$$= 1 \pm 3i$$

80. $f(x) = 3x(x - 2)^2$

3 zeros

Zeros: $0, 2, 2$

82. $f(x) = x^2 - 9x + 8$

2 zeros

$x^2 - 9x + 8 = (x - 1)(x - 8)$

Zeros: $1, 8$

84. $f(x) = (x + 4)(x - 6)(x - 2i)(x + 2i)$

4 zeros

Zeros: $-4, 6, 2i, -2i$

86. $f(x) = -4x^3 + 8x^2 - 3x + 15$

Possible rational zeros:
$\pm 1, \pm 3, \pm 5, \pm 15, \pm\frac{1}{2}, \pm\frac{3}{2}, \pm\frac{5}{2}, \pm\frac{15}{2}, \pm\frac{1}{4}, \pm\frac{3}{4}, \pm\frac{5}{4}, \pm\frac{15}{4}$

88. $f(x) = x^3 - 2x^2 - 21x - 18$

$$
\begin{array}{r|rrrr}
-1 & 1 & -2 & -21 & -18 \\
   &   & -1 & 3 & 18 \\
\hline
   & 1 & -3 & -18 & 0
\end{array}
$$

$x^2 - 3x - 18 = (x + 3)(x - 6)$

$f(x) = (x + 1)(x + 3)(x - 6)$

Real zeros: $6, -1, -3$

90. $f(x) = x^3 - 10x^2 + 17x - 8$

$$
\begin{array}{r|rrrr}
1 & 1 & -10 & 17 & -8 \\
  &   & 1 & -9 & 8 \\
\hline
  & 1 & -9 & 8 & 0
\end{array}
$$

$x^2 - 9x + 8 = (x - 1)(x - 8)$

$f(x) = (x - 1)^2(x - 8)$

Real zeros: $1, 8$

92. $f(x) = x^4 + x^3 - 11x^2 + x - 12$

$$
\begin{array}{r|rrrrr}
3 & 1 & 1 & -11 & 1 & -12 \\
  &   & 3 & 12 & 3 & 12 \\
\hline
  & 1 & 4 & 1 & 4 & 0
\end{array}
$$

$$
\begin{array}{r|rrrr}
-4 & 1 & 4 & 1 & 4 \\
   &   & -4 & 0 & -4 \\
\hline
   & 1 & 0 & 1 & 0
\end{array}
$$

$x^2 + 1$ has no real zeros.

Real zeros: $-4, 3$

94. Zeros: $\frac{2}{3}, 4, \sqrt{3}i$

$$\left(x - \tfrac{2}{3}\right)(x - 4)(x - \sqrt{3}i)(x + \sqrt{3}i) = (3x - 2)(x - 4)(x^2 + 3)$$
$$= 3x^4 - 14x^3 + 17x^2 - 42x + 24$$

96. $f(x) = x^4 - 2x^3 + 4x^2 + 2x - 5$

$$
\begin{array}{r}
x^2 - 2x + 5 \\
x^2 - 1 \overline{\smash{)}\ x^4 - 2x^3 + 4x^2 + 2x - 5} \\
\underline{x^4 \qquad\quad - x^2} \\
-2x^3 + 5x^2 + 2x \\
\underline{-2x^3 \qquad\quad + 2x} \\
5x^2 \qquad\quad -5 \\
\underline{5x^2 \qquad\quad -5} \\
0
\end{array}
$$

(a) $f(x) = (x + 1)(x - 1)(x^2 - 2x + 5)$

(b) $f(x) = (x + 1)(x - 1)(x^2 - 2x + 5)$

(c) By the Quadratic Formula, the zeros of $x^2 - 2x + 5$ are

$$
x = \frac{-(-2) \pm \sqrt{(-2)^2 - 4(1)(5)}}{2(1)}
$$

$$
= \frac{2 \pm \sqrt{-16}}{2} = 1 \pm 2i
$$

So, $f(x) = (x + 1)(x - 1)(x - 1 - 2i)(x - 1 + 2i)$

98. $f(x) = x^3 - 12x^2 + x - 12$; zero: i

Since i is a zero, so is $-i$.

$(x - i)(x + i) = x^2 + 1$

$$
\begin{array}{r}
x - 12 \\
x^2 + 1 \overline{\smash{)}\ x^3 - 12x^2 + x - 12} \\
\underline{x^3 \qquad\quad + x} \\
-12x^2 \\
\underline{-12x^2 \qquad\quad -12} \\
0
\end{array}
$$

The zero of $x - 12$ is 12.

The zeros of f are 12, $\pm i$.

100. $g(x) = 5x^3 + 3x^2 - 6x + 9$

Sign variations: 2, positive zeros: 2 or 0

$g(-x) = -5x^3 + 3x^2 + 6x + 9$

Sign variations: 1, negative zeros: 1

102. $f(x) = \dfrac{5x}{x + 12}$

$x + 12 = 0$

$x = -12$

Domain: all real numbers $x \neq -12$

104. $f(x) = \dfrac{8}{x^2 - 10x + 24}$

$x^2 - 10x + 24 = (x - 6)(x - 4)$

Domain: all real numbers $x \neq 4, 6$

106. $f(x) = \dfrac{4}{x + 3}$

Horizontal asymptote: $y = 0$

Vertical asymptote: $x = -3$

108. $g(x) = \dfrac{x^2}{x^2 - 4}$

Horizontal asymptote: $y = 1$

Vertical asymptotes: $x = \pm 2$

110. $f(x) = \dfrac{-5}{x^2}$

Intercepts: none

Symmetry: y-axis

Vertical asymptote: $x = 0$

Horizontal asymptote: $y = 0$

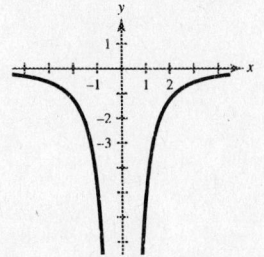

112. $g(x) = \dfrac{2 + x}{1 - x}$

Intercepts: $(0, 2)$, $(-2, 0)$

Symmetry: none

Vertical asymptote: $x = 1$

Horizontal asymptote: $y = -1$

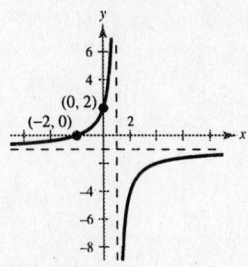

114. $p(x) = \dfrac{x^2}{x^2 + 1}$

Intercept: $(0, 0)$

Symmetry: y-axis

Vertical asymptote: none

Horizontal asymptote:
$y = 1$

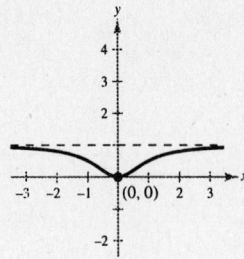

116. $f(x) = \dfrac{x}{x^2 + 1}$

Intercept: $(0, 0)$

Symmetry: origin

Vertical asymptote: none

Horizontal asymptote:
$y = 0$

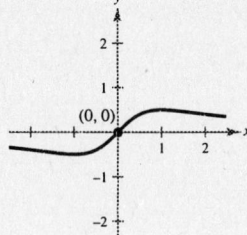

118. $f(x) = \dfrac{-6x^2}{x^2 + 1}$

Intercept: $(0, 0)$

Symmetry: y-axis

Vertical asymptote: none

Horizontal asymptote: $y = -6$

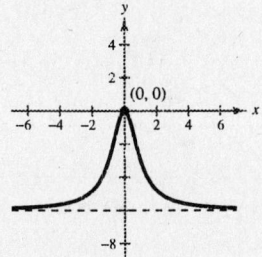

120. $y = \dfrac{x}{x^2 - 1}$

Intercept: $(0, 0)$

Symmetry: origin

Vertical asymptotes: $x = \pm 1$

Horizontal asymptote: $y = 0$

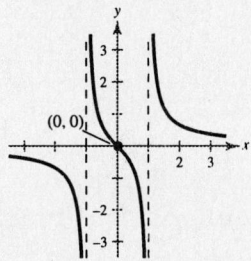

122. $f(x) = \dfrac{2x^3}{x^2 + 1} = 2x + \dfrac{-2x}{x^2 + 1}$

Slant asymptote: $y = 2x$

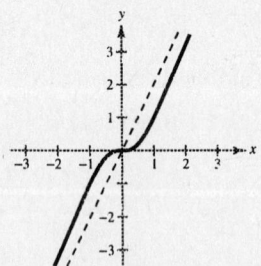

124. $f(x) = \dfrac{x^2 + 3x - 10}{x + 2} = x + 1 + \dfrac{-12}{x + 2}$

Slant asymptote: $y = x + 1$

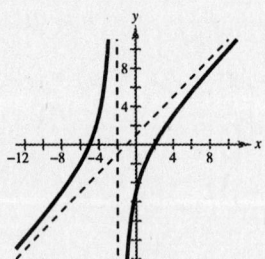

126. $\overline{C} = \dfrac{C}{x} = \dfrac{0.5x + 500}{x}, \, x > 0$

Horizontal asymptote: $y = 0.5$

Average cost per unit as the number of units increases without bound is 0.5.

128. $y = \left(\dfrac{0.80 - 0.54x}{1 + 2.72x}\right)^2,\ x > 0$

$y = 0.1$ inch

$$0.1 = \left(\frac{0.80 - 0.54x}{1 + 2.72x}\right)^2$$

$$0.1(1 + 2.72x)^2 = (0.80 - 0.54x)^2$$

$$0.73984x^2 + 0.544x + 0.1 = 0.2916x^2 - 0.864x + 0.64$$

$$0.44824x^2 + 1.408x - 0.54 = 0$$

Using the Quadratic Formula, $x \approx -3.49, 0.346$.

Diameter of tube: 0.346 inches

130. $\dfrac{3}{x^2 + 20x} = \dfrac{3}{x(x + 20)} = \dfrac{A}{x} + \dfrac{B}{x + 20}$

132. $\dfrac{3x - 4}{x^3 - 5x^2} = \dfrac{3x - 4}{x^2(x - 5)} = \dfrac{A}{x} + \dfrac{B}{x^2} + \dfrac{C}{x - 5}$

134. $\dfrac{4 - x}{x^2 + 6x + 8} = \dfrac{4 - x}{(x + 2)(x + 4)} = \dfrac{A}{x + 2} + \dfrac{B}{x + 4}$

$4 - x = A(x + 4) + B(x + 2)$

Let $x = -2$: $A = 3$

Let $x = -4$: $B = -4$

$\dfrac{4 - x}{x^2 + 6x + 8} = \dfrac{3}{x + 2} - \dfrac{4}{x + 4}$

136. Using long division,

$$\frac{x^2}{x^2 + 2x - 15} = 1 + \frac{-2x + 15}{x^2 + 2x - 15}$$

$$\frac{-2x + 15}{x^2 + 2x - 15} = \frac{-2x + 15}{(x + 5)(x - 3)} = \frac{A}{x + 5} + \frac{B}{x - 3}$$

$$-2x + 15 = A(x - 3) + B(x + 5)$$

Let $x = -5$: $A = -\dfrac{25}{8}$

Let $x = 3$: $\quad B = \dfrac{9}{8}$

$$\frac{x^2}{x^2 + 2x - 15} = 1 - \frac{25}{8(x + 5)} + \frac{9}{8(x - 3)}$$

138. $\dfrac{x^2 + 2x}{x^3 - x^2 + x - 1} = \dfrac{x^2 + 2x}{(x - 1)(x^2 + 1)} = \dfrac{A}{x - 1} + \dfrac{Bx + C}{x^2 + 1}$

$x^2 + 2x = A(x^2 + 1) + (Bx + C)(x - 1)$

Let $x = 1$: $A = \dfrac{3}{2}$

$x^2 + 2x = \left(\dfrac{3}{2} + B\right)x^2 + (C - B)x + \left(\dfrac{3}{2} - C\right)$

Equating coefficients of x gives:

$1 = \dfrac{3}{2} + B$: $B = -\dfrac{1}{2}$

$0 = \dfrac{3}{2} - C$: $C = \dfrac{3}{2}$

$\dfrac{x^2 + 2x}{x^3 - x^2 + x - 1} = \dfrac{3}{\left(\frac{1}{2}\right)(x - 1)} - \dfrac{x - 3}{(x^2 + 1)\left(\frac{1}{2}\right)}$

140. $\dfrac{3x^3 + 4x}{(x^2 + 1)^2} = \dfrac{Ax + B}{x^2 + 1} + \dfrac{Cx + D}{(x^2 + 1)^2}$

$3x^3 + 4x = (Ax + B)(x^2 + 1) + Cx + D$

$\qquad\qquad = Ax^3 + Bx^2 + (A + C)x + (B + D)$

Equating coefficients of x gives:

$A = 3$

$B = 0$

$3 + C = 4$: $C = 1$

$D = 0$

$\dfrac{3x^3 + 4x}{(x^2 + 1)^2} = \dfrac{3x}{x^2 + 1} + \dfrac{x}{(x^2 + 1)^2}$

142. False. If $-8i$ is a zero, then $8i$ must also be a zero. If $4i$ is a zero, then $-4i$ must also be a zero. A fourth degree polynomial can have at most four zeros.

144. Answers will vary.

$ax^2 + bx + c = 0$

(a) $b^2 - 4ac > 0$

$x^2 - 3x + 2 = 0$

$x = 1, 2$

(b) $b^2 - 4ac < 0$

$x^2 + 2x + 4 = 0$

$x = -1 \pm \sqrt{3}i$

(c) $b^2 - 4ac < 0$

$x^2 + 1 = 0$

$x = \pm i$

146. Exactly 2 real zeros and 2 complex zeros $\Rightarrow$ 4 total zeros $\Rightarrow$ function is of degree 4.

CHAPTER 3
Exponential and Logarithmic Functions

C H A P T E R 3
Exponential and Logarithmic Functions

Section 3.1   Exponential Functions and Their Graphs

Solutions to Even-Numbered Exercises

2. $5000(2^{-1.5}) \approx 1767.767$ **4.** $8^{2\pi} \approx 472,369.379$ **6.** $\sqrt[3]{4395} \approx 16.380$

8. $e^{1/2} \approx 1.649$ **10.** $e^{3.2} \approx 24.533$

12. $f(x) = 2^x + 1$ rises to the right.

Asymptote: $y = 1$

Intercept: $(0, 2)$

Matches graph (c)

14. $f(x) = 2^{x-2}$ rises to the right.

Asymptote: $y = 0$

Intercept: $\left(0, \frac{1}{4}\right)$

Matches graph (b)

16. $f(x) = 4^x$, $g(x) = 4^x + 1$

Because $g(x) = f(x) + 1$, the graph of g can be obtained by shifting the graph of f one unit upward.

18. $f(x) = 10^x$, $g(x) = 10^{-x+3}$

Because $g(x) = f(-x + 3)$, the graph of g can be obtained by reflecting the graph of f in the y-axis and shifting f three units to the right. (Note: This is equivalent to shifting f three units to the left and then reflecting the graph in the y-axis.)

20. $f(x) = \left(\frac{7}{2}\right)^x$, $g(x) = -\left(\frac{7}{2}\right)^{-x+6}$

Because $g(x) = -f(-x + 6)$, the graph of g can be obtained by reflecting the graph of f in the x-axis and y-axis and shifting f six units to the right. (Note: This is equivalent to shifting f six units to the left and then reflecting the graph in the x-axis and y-axis.)

22. $f(x) = 3.6^x$, $g(x) = -3.6^{-x} + 8$

Because $g(x) = -f(-x) + 8$, the graph of g can be obtained by reflecting the graph of f in the x-axis and y-axis and shifting f eight units upward.

24. $f(x) = 6^x$

x	-2	-1	0	1	2
$f(x)$	0.028	0.167	1	6	36

Asymptote: $y = 0$

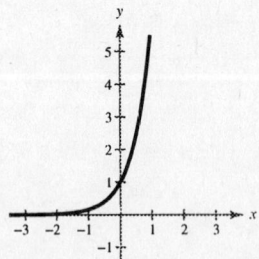

26. $f(x) = 6^{-x}$

x	-2	-1	0	1	2
$f(x)$	36	6	1	0.167	0.028

Asymptote: $y = 0$

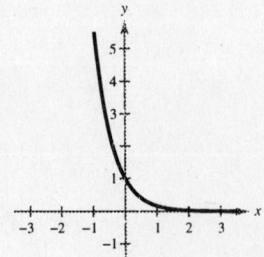

902

28. $f(x) = 3^{x+2}$

x	-4	-3	-2	-1	0
$f(x)$	0.111	0.333	1	3	9

Asymptote: $y = 0$

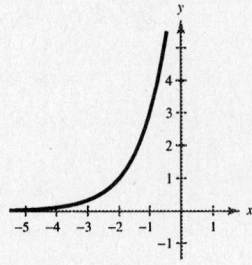

30. $f(x) = e^{-x}$

x	-2	-1	0	1	2
$f(x)$	7.389	2.718	1	0.368	0.135

Asymptote: $y = 0$

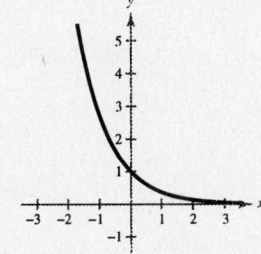

32. $f(x) = 2e^{-0.5x}$

x	-2	-1	0	1	2
$f(x)$	5.437	3.297	2	1.213	0.736

Asymptote: $y = 0$

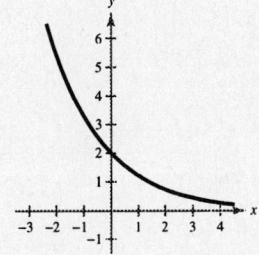

34. $f(x) = 2 + e^{x-5}$

x	0	2	4	5	6
$f(x)$	2.007	2.050	2.368	3	4.718

Asymptote: $y = 2$

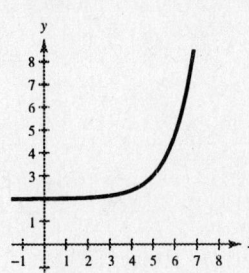

36. $f(x) = -4^{x-3} - 3$

x	-1	0	1	3	4
$f(x)$	-3.004	-3.016	-3.063	-4	-7

Asymptote: $y = -3$

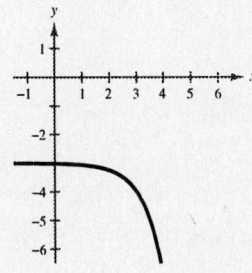

38. $f(x) = \left(\frac{3}{2}\right)^x$

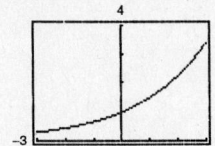

40. $h(x) = \left(\frac{3}{2}\right)^{-x}$

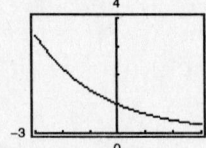

42. $g(x) = \left(\frac{3}{2}\right)^{x+2}$

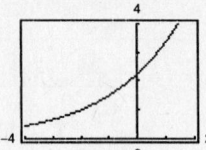

44. $f(x) = \left(\frac{3}{2}\right)^{-x} + 2$

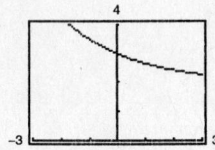

46. $y = 3^{-|x|}$

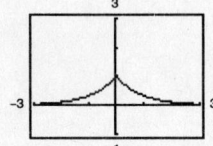

48. $y = 4^{x+1} - 2$

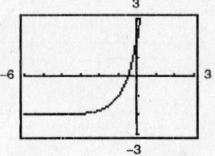

50. $y = 1.08^{5x}$

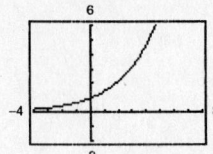

52. $s(t) = 3e^{-0.2t}$

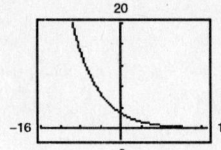

54. $h(x) = e^{x-2}$

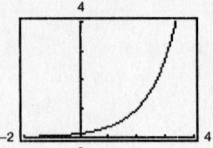

56. $P = \$1000, r = 6\%, t = 10$ years

Compounded n times per year: $A = 1000\left(1 + \frac{0.06}{n}\right)^{10n}$

Compounded continuously: $A = 1000e^{0.06(10)}$

n	1	2	4	12	365	Continuous
A	\$1790.85	\$1806.11	\$1814.02	\$1819.40	\$1822.03	\$1822.12

58. $P = \$1000, r = 6\%, t = 40$ years

Compounded n times per year: $A = 1000\left(1 + \frac{0.06}{n}\right)^{40n}$

Compounded continuously: $A = 1000e^{0.06(40)}$

n	1	2	4	12	365	Continuous
A	\$10,285.72	\$10,640.89	\$10,828.46	\$10,957.45	\$11,021.00	\$11,023.18

60. $A = Pe^{rt}$

$A = 12,000e^{0.06t}$

t	1	10	20	30	40	50
A	\$12,742.04	\$21,865.43	\$39,841.40	\$72,595.77	\$132,278.12	\$241,026.44

62. $A = Pe^{rt}$

$A = 12,000e^{0.075t}$

t	1	10	20	30	40	50
A	\$12,934.61	\$25,404.00	\$53,780.27	\$113,852.83	\$241,026.44	\$510,252.98

64. $A = 5000e^{(0.075)(50)} \approx \$212,605.41$

66. $V(t) = 20,000\left(\dfrac{3}{4}\right)^t$

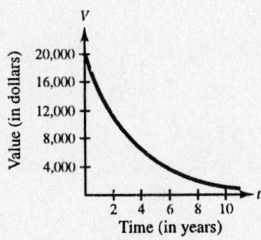

$V(2) = 20,000\left(\dfrac{3}{4}\right)^2 = \$11,250$

68. $p = 5000\left(1 - \dfrac{4}{4 + e^{-0.002x}}\right)$

(a)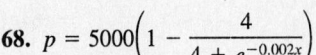

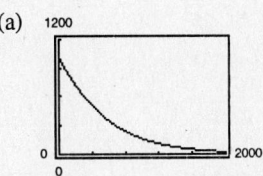

(b) When $x = 500$:

$$p = 5000\left(1 - \frac{4}{4 + e^{-0.002(500)}}\right) \approx \$421.12$$

(c) Since $(600, 350.13)$ is on the graph in part (a), it appears that the greatest price that will still yield a demand of at least 600 units is about \$350.

70. $P(t) = 2500e^{0.0293t}$

(a) $P(10) = 2500e^{0.0293(10)} \approx 3351$

(b) $P(20) = 2500e^{0.0293(20)} \approx 4492$

72. $Q = 10\left(\frac{1}{2}\right)^{t/5730}$

(a) When $t = 0$: $Q = 10\left(\frac{1}{2}\right)^{0/5730}$

$= 10(1) = 10$ grams

(b) When $t = 2000$: $Q = 10\left(\frac{1}{2}\right)^{2000/5730}$

≈ 7.85 grams

(c)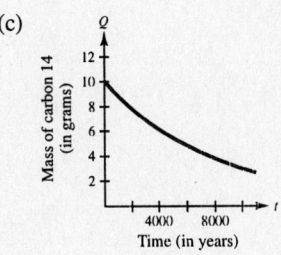

74. $y = \dfrac{300}{3 + 17e^{-0.065x}}$

(a)

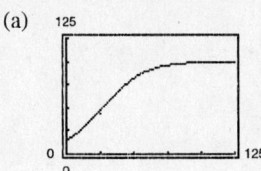

(b)

x	0	25	50	75	100
y	15	47	82	96	99

The model is a "good fit."

(c) When $x = 36$: $y = \dfrac{300}{3 + 17e^{-0.065(36)}} \approx 64.7\%$

(d) $\dfrac{2}{3} = \dfrac{300}{3 + 17e^{-0.065x}}$ when $x \approx 37$.

76. False, $e \neq \dfrac{271{,}801}{99{,}990}$.

e is an irrational number.

78. $g(x) = 2^{2x+6}$
$= 2^{2x} \cdot 2^{6}$
$= 64(2^{2x})$
$= 64(2^{2})^{x}$
$= 64(4^{x})$
$= h(x)$

Thus, $g(x) = h(x)$ but $g(x) \neq f(x)$.

80. $f(x) = 5^{-x} + 3$
$g(x) = 5^{3-x} = 5^{3} \cdot 5^{-x}$
$h(x) = -5^{x-3} = -(5^{x} \cdot 5^{-3})$

Thus, none are equal.

82. $y = \left(\frac{1}{2}\right)^{x}$ and $y = \left(\frac{1}{4}\right)^{x}$

x	-2	-1	0	1	2
$\left(\frac{1}{2}\right)^{x}$	4	2	1	$\frac{1}{2}$	$\frac{1}{4}$
$\left(\frac{1}{4}\right)^{x}$	16	4	1	$\frac{1}{4}$	$\frac{1}{16}$

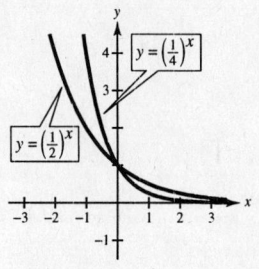

(a) $\left(\frac{1}{4}\right)^{x} < \left(\frac{1}{2}\right)^{x}$ when $x > 0$.

(b) $\left(\frac{1}{4}\right)^{x} > \left(\frac{1}{2}\right)^{x}$ when $x < 0$.

84. (a) $f(x) = x^{2}e^{-x}$

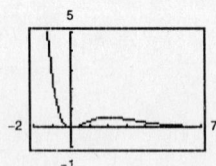

Decreasing: $(-\infty, 0)$, $(2, \infty)$

Increasing: $(0, 2)$

Relative maximum: $(2, 4e^{-2})$

Relative minimum: $(0, 0)$

(b) $g(x) = x2^{3-x}$

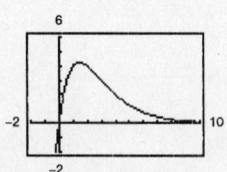

Decreasing: $(1.44, \infty)$

Increasing: $(-\infty, 1.44)$

Relative maximum: $(1.44, 4.25)$

86. The exponential function, $y = e^{x}$, increases at a faster rate than the polynomial function, $y = x^{n}$.

88. $f(x) = \left(1 + \dfrac{0.5}{x}\right)^x$ and $g(x) = e^{0.5}$

(Horizontal line)

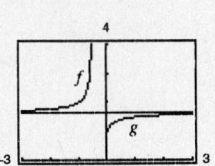

As $x \to \infty$, $f(x) \to g(x)$.

As $x \to -\infty$, $f(x) \to g(x)$.

90. The functions (c) 3^x and (d) 2^{-x} are exponential.

92.

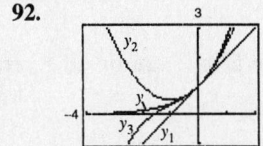

94. (a) $f(u + v) = a^{u+v}$

$\qquad\qquad = a^u \cdot a^v$

$\qquad\qquad = f(u) \cdot f(v)$

(b) $f(2x) = a^{2x}$

$\qquad\qquad = (a^x)^2$

$\qquad\qquad = [f(x)]^2$

96. $x^2 + 3y = 4$

$\qquad 3y = 4 - x^2$

$\qquad y = \tfrac{1}{3}(4 - x^2)$

98. $x - |y| = 2$

$\qquad x - 2 = |y|$

$\qquad y = \begin{cases} x - 2, & x \geq 2 \\ -(x - 2), & x < 2 \end{cases}$

100. $f(x) = \dfrac{4x - 3}{x}$

Vertical asymptote: $x = 0$

Horizontal asymptote: $y = 4$

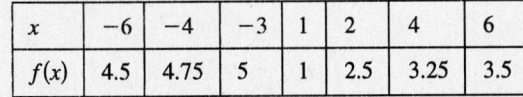

x	-6	-4	-3	1	2	4	6
$f(x)$	4.5	4.75	5	1	2.5	3.25	3.5

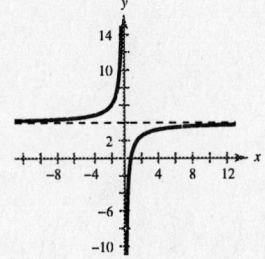

102. $f(x) = \dfrac{x^2 - 7x + 12}{x + 2}$

Vertical asymptote: $x = -2$

x	-20	-15	-10	-5	0	5	10	15	20
$f(x)$	-30.7	-26.3	-22.8	-24	6	0.3	3.5	7.8	12.4

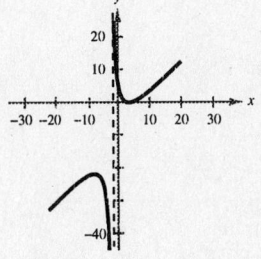

Section 3.2   Logarithmic Functions and Their Graphs

Solutions to Even-Numbered Exercises

2. $\log_3 81 = 4 \implies 3^4 = 81$

4. $\log_{10} \frac{1}{1000} = -3 \implies 10^{-3} = \frac{1}{1000}$

6. $\log_{16} 8 = \frac{3}{4} \implies 16^{3/4} = 8$

8. $\ln 4 = 1.386\ldots \implies e^{1.386\ldots} = 4$

10. $8^2 = 64 \implies \log_8 64 = 2$

12. $9^{3/2} = 27 \implies \log_9 27 = \frac{3}{2}$

14. $10^{-3} = 0.001 \implies \log_{10} 0.001 = -3$

16. $e^x = 4 \implies \ln 4 = x$

18. $u^v = w \implies \log_u w = v$

20. $\log_2 \frac{1}{8} = \log_2 2^{-3} = -3$

22. $\log_{27} 9 = \log_{27} 27^{2/3} = \frac{2}{3}$

24. $\log_{10} 1000 = \log_{10} 10^3 = 3$

26. $\log_{10} 10 = \log_{10} 10^1 = 1$

28. $\log_9 243 = \log_9 9^{5/2} = \frac{5}{2}$

30. $\ln e^{-2} = -2$

32. $\log_b b^{-3} = -3$

34. $\log_{10} 145 \approx 2.161$

36. $\log_{10} 12.5 \approx 1.097$

38. $\ln \sqrt{42} \approx 1.869$

40. $2 \ln 0.75 = -0.575$

42. $\ln\left(\sqrt{5} - 2\right) \approx -1.444$

44. $\ln\left(\frac{1}{2}\right) = -0.693$

46. $f(x) = -\log_3 x$

Asymptote: $x = 0$

Point on graph: $(1, 0)$

Matches graph (f)

48. $f(x) = \log_3(x - 1)$

Asymptote: $x = 1$

Point on graph: $(2, 0)$

Matches graph (e)

50. $f(x) = -\log_3(-x)$

Asymptote: $x = 0$

Point on graph: $(-1, 0)$

Matches graph (a)

52. $g(x) = \log_6 x$

Domain: $(0, \infty)$

x-intercept: $(1, 0)$

Vertical asymptote: $x = 0$

$y = \log_6 x \implies 6^y = x$

x	$\frac{1}{6}$	1	$\sqrt{6}$	6
y	-1	0	$\frac{1}{2}$	2

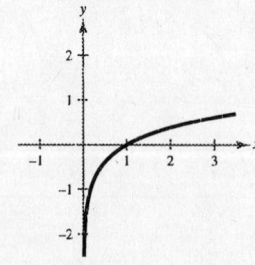

54. $h(x) = \log_4(x - 3)$

Domain: $x - 3 > 0 \Rightarrow x > 3$

The domain is $(3, \infty)$.

x-intercept: $\log_4(x - 3) = 0$

$$4^0 = x - 3$$
$$1 = x - 3$$
$$4 = x$$

The x-intercept is $(4, 0)$.

Vertical asymptote: $x - 3 = 0 \Rightarrow x = 3$

$y = \log_4(x - 3) \Rightarrow 4^y + 3 = x$

x	$3\frac{1}{4}$	4	7	19
y	-1	0	1	2

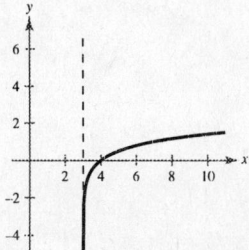

56. $y = \log_5(x - 1) + 4$

Domain: $x - 1 > 0 \Rightarrow x > 1$

The domain is $(1, \infty)$.

x-intercept: $\log_5(x - 1) + 4 = 0$

$$\log_5(x - 1) = -4$$
$$5^{-4} = x - 1$$
$$\frac{1}{625} = x - 1$$
$$\frac{626}{625} = x$$

The x-intercept is $\left(\frac{626}{625}, 0\right)$.

Vertical asymptote: $x - 1 = 0 \Rightarrow x = 1$

$y = \log_5(x - 1) + 4 \Rightarrow 5^{y-4} + 1 = x$

x	1.00032	1.0016	1.008	1.04	1.2
y	-1	0	1	2	3

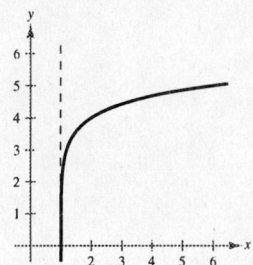

58. $y = \log_{10}(-x)$

Domain: $-x > 0 \Rightarrow x < 0$

The domain is $(-\infty, 0)$.

x-intercept: $\log_{10}(-x) = 0$

$$10^0 = -x$$
$$-1 = x$$

The x-intercept is $(-1, 0)$.

Vertical asymptote: $x = 0$

$y = \log_{10}(-x) \Rightarrow -10^y = x$

x	$-\frac{1}{100}$	$-\frac{1}{10}$	-1	-10
y	-2	-1	0	1

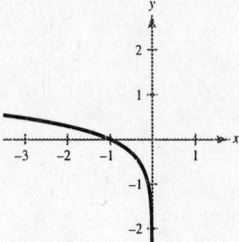

60. $h(x) = \ln(x + 1)$

Domain: $x + 1 > 0 \Rightarrow x > -1$

The domain is $(-1, \infty)$.

x-intercept: $\ln(x + 1) = 0$

$$e^0 = x + 1$$
$$1 = x + 1$$
$$0 = x$$

The x-intercept is $(0, 0)$.

Vertical asymptote: $x + 1 = 0 \Rightarrow x = -1$

$y = \ln(x + 1) \Rightarrow e^y - 1 = x$

x	-0.39	0	1.72	6.39	19.09
y	$-\frac{1}{2}$	0	1	2	3

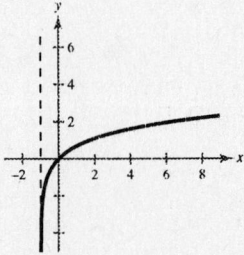

62. $f(x) = \ln(3 - x)$

Domain: $3 - x > 0 \Rightarrow x < 3$

The domain is $(-\infty, 3)$.

x-intercept: $\ln(3 - x) = 0$

$$e^0 = 3 - x$$
$$1 = 3 - x$$
$$2 = x$$

The x-intercept is $(2, 0)$.

Vertical asymptote: $3 - x = 0 \Rightarrow x = 3$

$y = \ln(3 - x) \Rightarrow 3 - e^y = x$

x	2.95	2.86	2.63	2	0.28
y	-3	-2	-1	0	1

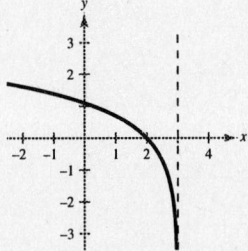

64. $f(x) = \log_{10}(x - 1)$

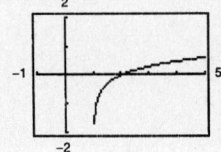

66. $f(x) = \ln(x + 2)$

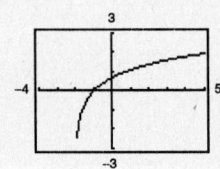

68. $f(x) = 3\ln x - 1$

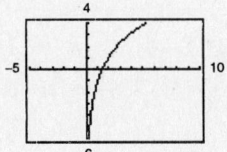

70. $t = \dfrac{10 \ln 2}{\ln 67 - \ln 50} \approx 23.68$ years

72. $t = \dfrac{\ln K}{0.095}$

(a)

K	1	2	4	6	8	10	12
t	0	7.3	14.6	18.9	21.9	24.2	26.2

(b)

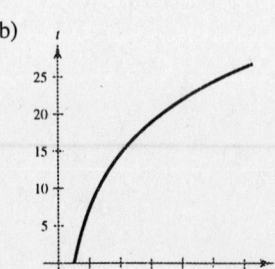

The number of years required to multiply the original investment by K increases with K. However, the larger the value of K, the fewer the years required to increase the value of the investment by an additional multiple of the original investment.

74. (a) $\dfrac{450}{30} = 15$ cubic feet per minute

(b) 380 cubic feet of air space per child

(c) Total air space required $= 380(30)$

$$= 11,400 \text{ cubic feet}$$

Let $x =$ square feet of floor space and $h = 30$ feet.

$$V = xh$$

$$11,400 = x(30)$$

$$380 = x$$

If the ceiling height is 30 feet, the minimum number of square feet of floor space required is 380 square feet.

76. $\beta = 10 \log_{10}\left(\dfrac{I}{10^{-12}}\right)$

(a) $\beta = 10 \log_{10}\left(\dfrac{1}{10^{-12}}\right) = 10 \log_{10}(10^{12}) = 120$ decibels

(b) $\beta = 10 \log_{10}\left(\dfrac{10^{-2}}{10^{-12}}\right) = 10 \log_{10}(10^{10}) = 100$ decibels

(c) No, the difference is due to the logarithmic relationship between intensity and number of decibels.

78. $t = 12.542 \ln\left(\dfrac{1254.68}{1254.68 - 1000}\right) \approx 20$ years

80. Total amount $= (1254.68)(12)(20) \approx \$301,123.20$

Interest $= \$301,123.20 - 150,000 = \$151,123.20$

82. False. Reflecting $g(x)$ about the line $y = x$ will determine the graph of $f(x)$.

84. $f(x) = 3^x$, $g(x) = \log_3 x$

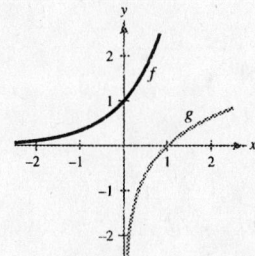

f and g are inverses. Their graphs are reflected about the line $y = x$.

86. $f(x) = e^x$, $g(x) = \ln x$

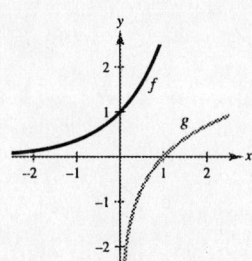

f and g are inverses. Their graphs are reflected about the line $y = x$.

88. (a) $f(x) = \ln x$

$g(x) = \sqrt{x}$

The natural log function grows at a slower rate than the square root function.

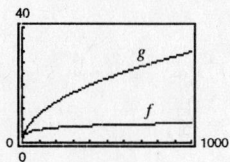

(b) $f(x) = \ln x$

$g(x) = \sqrt[4]{x}$

The natural log function grows at a slower rate than the fourth root function.

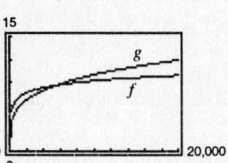

90. $y = \ln x$

$y_1 = x - 1$

$y_2 = (x - 1) - \frac{1}{2}(x - 1)^2$

$y_3 = (x - 1) - \frac{1}{2}(x - 1)^2 + \frac{1}{3}(x - 1)^3$

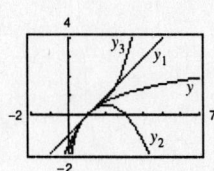

92. $f(x) = \log_{10} x$

   (a) Domain: $(0, \infty)$

   (b) $y = \log_{10} x$

            $x = \log_{10} y$

           $10^x = y$

        $f^{-1}(x) = 10^x$

   (c) Since $\log_{10} 1000 = 3$ and $\log_{10} 10{,}000 = 4$, the interval in which $f(x)$ will be found is $(3, 4)$.

   (d) When $f(x)$ is negative, x is in the interval $(0, 1)$.

   (e) $0 = \log_{10} 1$

       $1 = \log_{10} 10$

       $2 = \log_{10} 100$

       $3 = \log_{10} 1000$

   When $f(x)$ is increased by one unit, x is increased by a factor of 10.

   (f) $f(x_1) = 3n$ $f(x_2) = n$

        $\log_{10} x_1 = 3n$ $\log_{10} x_2 = n$

            $x_1 = 10^{3n}$ $x_2 = 10^n$

      $x_1 : x_2 = 10^{3n} : 10^n = 10^{2n} : 1$

94. (a) $h(x) = \ln(x^2 + 1)$

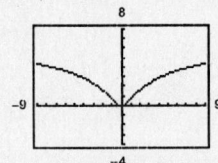

   (b) Increasing on $(0, \infty)$.

        Decreasing on $(-\infty, 0)$.

   (c) Relative minimum: $(0, 0)$

96. $g(x) = \dfrac{12 \ln x}{x}$

   (a)

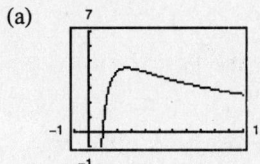

   (b) Increasing on $(0, 2.72)$.

        Decreasing on $(2.72, \infty)$.

   (c) Relative maximum: $(2.72, 4.41)$

98. $9.25 + 0.75q$

100. $A = l \cdot w$

      $= (10 + w)w$

      $= 10w + w^2$

102. $f(x) = \dfrac{2x^3 - 3}{x^2}$

   Vertical asymptote: $x = 0$

   Slant asymptote: $y = 2x$

104. $f(x) = \dfrac{2x^2(x - 5)}{x - 7}$

   Vertical asymptote: $x = 7$

106. $e^{3/2} = 4.482$

108. $4e^{-6} = 0.010$

Section 3.3   Properties of Logarithms

Solutions to Even-Numbered Exercises

2. $\log_7 4 = \dfrac{\log_{10} 4}{\log_{10} 7} = \dfrac{\ln 4}{\ln 7} \approx 0.712$

4. $\log_{1/4} 5 = \dfrac{\log_{10} 5}{\log_{10} \frac{1}{4}} = \dfrac{\ln 5}{\ln \frac{1}{4}} \approx -1.161$

6. $\log_{20} 0.125 = \dfrac{\log_{10} 0.125}{\log_{10} 20} = \dfrac{\ln 0.125}{\ln 20} \approx -0.694$

8. $\log_3 0.015 = \dfrac{\log_{10} 0.015}{\log_{10} 3} = \dfrac{\ln 0.015}{\ln 3} \approx -3.823$

10. (a) $\log_3 x = \dfrac{\log_{10} x}{\log_{10} 3}$

   (b) $\log_3 x = \dfrac{\ln x}{\ln 3}$

12. (a) $\log_{1/3} x = \dfrac{\log_{10} x}{\log_{10} \frac{1}{3}}$

(b) $\log_{1/3} x = \dfrac{\ln x}{\ln \frac{1}{3}}$

14. (a) $\log_x \dfrac{3}{4} = \dfrac{\log_{10} \frac{3}{4}}{\log_{10} x}$

(b) $\log_x \dfrac{3}{4} = \dfrac{\ln \frac{3}{4}}{\ln x}$

16. (a) $\log_{7.1} x = \dfrac{\log_{10} x}{\log_{10} 7.1}$

(b) $\log_{7.1} x = \dfrac{\ln x}{\ln 7.1}$

18. $f(x) = \log_4 x = \dfrac{\log_{10} x}{\log_{10} 4} = \dfrac{\ln x}{\ln 4}$

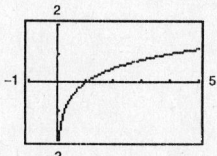

20. $f(x) = \log_{1/4} x = \dfrac{\log_{10} x}{\log_{10} \frac{1}{4}} = \dfrac{\ln x}{\ln \frac{1}{4}}$

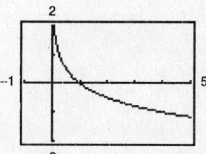

22. $f(x) = \log_{12.4} x = \dfrac{\log_{10} x}{\log_{10} 12.4} = \dfrac{\ln x}{\ln 12.4}$

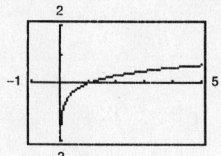

24. $\log_{10} 10z = \log_{10} 10 + \log_{10} z$

(Note: This is equivalent to $1 + \log_{10} z$.)

26. $\log_{10} \dfrac{y}{2} = \log_{10} y - \log_{10} 2$

28. $\log_6 z^{-3} = -3 \log_6 z$

30. $\ln \sqrt[3]{t} = \ln t^{1/3} = \dfrac{1}{3} \ln t$

32. $\ln \dfrac{xy}{z} = \ln x + \ln y - \ln z$

34. $\ln\!\left(\dfrac{x^2 - 1}{x^3}\right) = \ln(x^2 - 1) - \ln x^3$

$= \ln[(x + 1)(x - 1)] - \ln x^3$

$= \ln(x + 1) + \ln(x - 1) - 3 \ln x$

36. $\ln \dfrac{x}{\sqrt{x^2 + 1}} = \ln x - \ln \sqrt{x^2 + 1}$

$= \ln x - \ln(x^2 + 1)^{1/2}$

$= \ln x - \dfrac{1}{2} \ln(x^2 + 1)$

38. $\ln \sqrt{\dfrac{x^2}{y^3}} = \ln\!\left(\dfrac{x^2}{y^3}\right)^{1/2} = \dfrac{1}{2} \ln\!\left(\dfrac{x^2}{y^3}\right)$

$= \dfrac{1}{2}(\ln x^2 - \ln y^3)$

$= \dfrac{1}{2}(2 \ln x - 3 \ln y)$

40. $\ln\sqrt{x^2(x+2)} = \ln[x^2(x+2)]^{1/2}$

$\qquad = \ln[x(x+2)^{1/2}]$

$\qquad = \ln x + \ln(x+2)^{1/2}$

$\qquad = \ln x + \dfrac{1}{2}\ln(x+2)$

42. $\log_b \dfrac{\sqrt{x}\,y^4}{z^4} = \log_b \sqrt{x}\,y^4 - \log_b z^4$

$\qquad = \log_b x^{1/2} + \log_b y^4 - \log_b z^4$

$\qquad = \dfrac{1}{2}\log_b x + 4\log_b y - 4\log_b z$

44. $\ln y + \ln t = \ln yt = \ln ty$

46. $\log_5 8 - \log_5 t = \log_5 \dfrac{8}{t}$

48. $-4\log_6 2x = \log_6(2x)^{-4} = \log_6 \dfrac{1}{16x^4}$

50. $\dfrac{2}{3}\log_7(z-2) = \log_7(z-2)^{2/3}$

52. $2\ln 8 + 5\ln z = \ln 8^2 + \ln z^5$

$\qquad = \ln 64z^5$

54. $3\ln x + 4\ln y - 4\ln z = \ln x^3 + \ln y^4 - \ln z^4$

$\qquad = \ln x^3 y^4 - \ln z^4$

$\qquad = \ln \dfrac{x^3 y^4}{z^4}$

56. $4[\ln z + \ln(z+5)] - 2\ln(z-5) = 4[\ln z(z+5)] - \ln(z-5)^2$

$\qquad = \ln[z(z+5)]^4 - \ln(z-5)^2$

$\qquad = \ln \dfrac{z^4(z+5)^4}{(z-5)^2}$

58. $2[\ln x - \ln(x+1) - \ln(x-1)] = 2\left[\ln \dfrac{x}{x+1} - \ln(x-1)\right]$

$\qquad = 2\left[\ln \dfrac{x}{(x+1)(x-1)}\right]$

$\qquad = 2\left[\ln \dfrac{x}{x^2-1}\right]$

$\qquad = \ln\left(\dfrac{x}{x^2-1}\right)^2$

60. $\dfrac{1}{2}[\ln(x+1) + 2\ln(x-1)] + 6\ln x = \dfrac{1}{2}[\ln(x+1) + \ln(x-1)^2] + \ln x^6$

$\qquad = \dfrac{1}{2}[\ln(x+1)(x-1)^2] + \ln x^6$

$\qquad = \ln[(x+1)(x-1)^2]^{1/2} + \ln x^6$

$\qquad = \ln[(x+1)^{1/2}(x-1)] + \ln x^6$

$\qquad = \ln[x^6(x-1)\sqrt{x+1}]$

62. $\dfrac{3}{2}\ln 5t^6 - \dfrac{3}{4}\ln t^4 = \ln(5t^6)^{3/2} - \ln(t^4)^{3/4}$

$\qquad = \ln 5^{3/2} t^9 - \ln t^3$

$\qquad = \ln \dfrac{5\sqrt{5}\,t^9}{t^3}$

$\qquad = \ln 5\sqrt{5}\,t^6$

64. $\log_7 \sqrt{70} = \frac{1}{2} \log_7 70 = \frac{1}{2}[\log_7 7 + \log_7 10]$

$\qquad = \frac{1}{2}[1 + \log_7 10]$

$\qquad = \frac{1}{2} + \frac{1}{2} \log_7 10$

$\qquad = \frac{1}{2} + \log_7 \sqrt{10}$ by Property 1 and Property 3

66. $\log_6 \sqrt[3]{6} = \log_6 6^{1/3} = \frac{1}{3} \log_6 6 = \frac{1}{3}(1) = \frac{1}{3}$

68. $\log_5 \frac{1}{125} = \log_5 5^{-3} = -3 \log_5 5 = -3(1) = -3$

70. $\log_2(-16)$ is undefined because -16 is not in the domain of $\log_2 x$.

72. $\log_4 2 + \log_4 32 = \log_4 4^{1/2} + \log_4 4^{5/2}$

$\qquad = \frac{1}{2} \log_4 4 + \frac{5}{2} \log_4 4$

$\qquad = \frac{1}{2}(1) + \frac{5}{2}(1)$

$\qquad = 3$

74. $3 \ln e^4 = (3)(4) \ln e$

$\qquad = 12(1)$

$\qquad = 12$

76. $\ln 1 = 0$

78. $\ln \sqrt[4]{e^3} = \ln e^{3/4}$

$\qquad = \frac{3}{4} \ln e$

$\qquad = \frac{3}{4}(1)$

$\qquad = \frac{3}{4}$

80. $\log_2(4^2 \cdot 3^4) = \log_2 4^2 + \log_2 3^4$

$\qquad = 2 \log_2 4 + 4 \log_2 3$

$\qquad = 2 \log_2 2^2 + 4 \log_2 3$

$\qquad = 4 \log_2 2 + 4 \log_2 3$

$\qquad = 4 + 4 \log_2 3$

82. $\log_{10} \frac{9}{300} = \log_{10} \frac{3}{100}$

$\qquad = \log_{10} 3 - \log_{10} 100$

$\qquad = \log_{10} 3 - \log_{10} 10^2$

$\qquad = \log_{10} 3 - 2 \log_{10} 10$

$\qquad = \log_{10} 3 - 2$

84. $\ln \frac{6}{e^2} = \ln 6 - \ln e^2$

$\qquad = \ln 6 - 2 \ln e$

$\qquad = \ln 6 - 2$

86. $\beta = 10 \log_{10}\left(\frac{I}{10^{-12}}\right)$

$\qquad = 10[\log_{10} I - \log_{10} 10^{-12}]$

$\qquad = 10[\log_{10} I - (-12)\log_{10} 10]$

$\qquad = 10[\log_{10} I + 12]$

For $I = 10^{-6}$, $\beta = 10[\log_{10} 10^{-6} + 12] = 60$ decibels

88. $f(ax) = f(a) + f(x), a > 0, x > 0$

True, because

$f(ax) = \ln ax = \ln a + \ln x$

$\qquad = f(a) + f(x)$.

90. $\sqrt{f(x)} = \frac{1}{2}f(x)$; False.

$\sqrt{f(x)} = \sqrt{\ln x}$ can't be simplified further.

$f(\sqrt{x}) = \ln \sqrt{x} = \ln x^{1/2} = \frac{1}{2} \ln x = \frac{1}{2}f(x)$

92. If $f(x) < 0$, then $0 < x < 1$.

True.

94. Let $x = \log_b u$, then $u = b^x$ and $u^n = b^{nx}$.

$\log_b u^n = \log_b b^{nx} = nx = n \log_b u$

96. $f(x) = \ln x$

$g(x) = \dfrac{\log_{10} x}{\log_{10} e}$

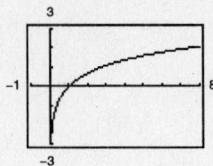

$f(x) = g(x)$

98. $\ln 2 \approx 0.6931, \ln 3 \approx 1.0986, \ln 5 \approx 1.6094$

$\ln 2 \approx 0.6931$

$\ln 3 \approx 1.0986$

$\ln 4 = \ln(2 \cdot 2) = \ln 2 + \ln 2 \approx 0.6931 + 0.6931 = 1.3862$

$\ln 5 \approx 1.6094$

$\ln 6 = \ln(2 \cdot 3) = \ln 2 + \ln 3 \approx 0.6931 + 1.0986 = 1.7917$

$\ln 8 = \ln 2^3 = 3 \ln 2 \approx 3(0.6931) = 2.0793$

$\ln 9 = \ln 3^2 = 2 \ln 3 \approx 2(1.0986) = 2.1972$

$\ln 10 = \ln(5 \cdot 2) = \ln 5 + \ln 2 \approx 1.6094 + 0.6931 = 2.3025$

$\ln 12 = \ln(2^2 \cdot 3) = \ln 2^2 + \ln 3 = 2 \ln 2 + \ln 3 \approx 2(0.6931) + 1.0986 = 2.4848$

$\ln 15 = \ln(5 \cdot 3) = \ln 5 + \ln 3 \approx 1.6094 + 1.0986 = 2.7080$

$\ln 16 = \ln 2^4 = 4 \ln 2 \approx 4(0.6931) = 2.7724$

$\ln 18 = \ln(3^2 \cdot 2) = \ln 3^2 + \ln 2 = 2 \ln 3 + \ln 2 \approx 2(1.0986) + 0.6931 = 2.8903$

$\ln 20 = \ln(5 \cdot 2^2) = \ln 5 + \ln 2^2 = \ln 5 + 2 \ln 2 \approx 1.6094 + 2(0.6931) = 2.9956$

100. $\left(\dfrac{2x^2}{3y}\right)^{-3} = \left(\dfrac{3y}{2x^2}\right)^3$

$= \dfrac{(3y)^3}{(2x^2)^3}$

$= \dfrac{27y^3}{8x^6}$

102. $xy(x^{-1} + y^{-1})^{-1} = \dfrac{xy}{x^{-1} + y^{-1}}$

$= \dfrac{xy}{\dfrac{1}{x} + \dfrac{1}{y}}$

$= \dfrac{xy}{\dfrac{y + x}{xy}}$

$= \dfrac{(xy)^2}{x + y}$

104. $40(6^{-3.2}) \approx 0.129$

106. $1.4^{3\pi} \approx 23.836$

108. $96^{\sqrt{3}} \approx 2712.655$

110. $\log_{10} \frac{5}{8} \approx -0.204$

112. $\ln\left(\sqrt{7} + 1\right) \approx 1.294$

Section 3.4   Exponential and Logarithmic Equations

Solutions to Even-Numbered Exercises

2. $2^{3x+1} = 32$

(a) $x = -1$

$2^{3(-1)+1} = 2^{-2} = \frac{1}{4}$

No, $x = -1$ is not a solution.

(b) $x = 2$

$2^{3(2)+1} = 2^7 = 128$

No, $x = 2$ is not a solution.

4. $5^{2x+3} = 812$

(a) $x = -1.5 + \log_5 \sqrt{812}$

$5^{2(-1.5+\log_5\sqrt{812})+3} = 5^{-3+2\log_5\sqrt{812}+3}$

$= 5^{2\log_5 812^{1/2}}$

$= 5^{\log_5(812^{1/2})^2}$

$= 5^{\log_5 812} = 812$

Yes, $x = -1.5 + \log_5\sqrt{812}$ is a solution.

(c) $x = \frac{1}{2}\left(-3 + \frac{\ln 812}{\ln 5}\right)$

$5^{2[1/2(-3+(\ln 812/\ln 5))]+3} = 5^{-3+(\ln 812/\ln 5)+3}$

$= 5^{\ln 812/\ln 5}$

$= 5^{\log_5 812}$

$= 812$

Yes, $x = \frac{1}{2}\left(-3 + \frac{\ln 812}{\ln 5}\right)$ is a solution.

(b) $x \approx 0.581$

$5^{2(0.581)+3} = 5^{4.162} \approx 812$

No, $x \approx 0.581$ is not a solution.

6. $\ln(x - 1) = 3.8$

(a) $x = 1 + e^{3.8}$

$\ln(1 + e^{3.8} - 1) = \ln e^{3.8} = 3.8$

Yes, $x = 1 + e^{3.8}$ is a solution.

(c) $x = 1 + \ln 3.8$

$\ln(1 + \ln 3.8 - 1) = \ln(\ln 3.8) \approx 0.289$

No, $x = 1 + \ln 3.8$ is not a solution.

(b) $x \approx 45.701$

$\ln(45.701 - 1) = \ln(44.701) \approx 3.8$

Yes, $x \approx 45.701$ is a solution.

8. $3^x = 243$

$3^x = 3^5$

$x = 5$

10. $3^x = 729$

$3^x = 3^6$

$x = 6$

12. $8^x = 4$

$8^x = 8^{2/3}$

$x = \frac{2}{3}$

14. $\left(\frac{1}{4}\right)^x = 64$

$4^{-x} = 4^3$

$-x = 3$

$x = -3$

16. $\left(\frac{2}{3}\right)^x = \frac{4}{9}$

$\left(\frac{2}{3}\right)^x = \left(\frac{2}{3}\right)^2$

$x = 2$

18. $2^{x-3} = 32$

$2^{x-3} = 2^5$

$x - 3 = 5$

$x = 8$

20. $\ln x - \ln 5 = 0$

$\ln x = \ln 5$

$x = 5$

22. $e^x = 4$

$\ln e^x = \ln 4$

$x = \ln 4$

$x \approx 1.386$

24. $\ln x = -7$

$e^{\ln x} = e^{-7}$

$x = e^{-7}$

$x \approx 0.000912$

26. $\log_x 625 = 4$

$x^{\log_x 625} = x^4$

$625 = x^4$

$\sqrt[4]{625} = x$

$5 = x$

28. $\log_{10} x + 3 = 0$

$\log_{10} x = -3$

$10^{\log_{10} x} = 10^{-3}$

$x = 10^{-3}$

$x = 0.001$

30. $\ln(2x - 1) = 0$

$e^{\ln(2x-1)} = e^0$

$2x - 1 = 1$

$2x = 2$

$x = 1$

32. $f(x) = g(x)$

$27^x = 9$

$27^x = 27^{2/3}$

$x = \frac{2}{3}$

Point of intersection: $\left(\frac{2}{3}, 9\right)$

34. $f(x) = g(x)$

$\ln(x - 4) = 0$

$e^{\ln(x-4)} = e^0$

$x - 4 = 1$

$x = 5$

Point of intersection: $(5, 0)$

36. $\log_6 6^{2x-1} = 2x - 1$

38. $4^{\log_4 x^3} = x^3$

40. $\ln e^{x^4} = x^4$

42. $e^{\ln x^2} = x^2$

44. $-8 + e^{\ln x^3} = -8 + x^3 = x^3 - 8$

46. $4e^x = 91$

$e^x = \frac{91}{4}$

$\ln e^x = \ln \frac{91}{4}$

$x = \ln \frac{91}{4} \approx 3.125$

48. $-14 + 3e^x = 11$

$3e^x = 25$

$e^x = \frac{25}{3}$

$\ln e^x = \ln \frac{25}{3}$

$x = \ln \frac{25}{3} \approx 2.120$

50. $e^{2x} = 50$

$\ln e^{2x} = \ln 50$

$2x = \ln 50$

$x = \frac{\ln 50}{2} \approx 1.956$

52. $1000e^{-4x} = 75$

$e^{-4x} = \frac{3}{40}$

$\ln e^{-4x} = \ln \frac{3}{40}$

$-4x = \ln \frac{3}{40}$

$x = -\frac{1}{4} \ln \frac{3}{40} \approx 0.648$

54. $e^{2x} - 5e^x + 6 = 0$

$(e^x - 2)(e^x - 3) = 0$

$e^x = 2 \text{ or } e^x = 3$

$x = \ln 2 \approx 0.693 \text{ or } x = \ln 3 \approx 1.099$

56. $\dfrac{400}{1 + e^{-x}} = 350$

$400 = 350(1 + e^{-x})$

$\dfrac{8}{7} = 1 + e^{-x}$

$\dfrac{8}{7} - 1 = e^{-x}$

$\dfrac{1}{7} = e^{-x}$

$\ln \dfrac{1}{7} = \ln e^{-x}$

$-x = \ln \dfrac{1}{7}$

$-x = \ln 7^{-1}$

$-x = -\ln 7$

$x = \ln 7 \approx 1.946$

58. $10^x = 570$

$\log_{10} 10^x = \log_{10} 570$

$x = \log_{10} 570$

≈ 2.756

60. $6^{5x} = 3000$

$\ln 6^{5x} = \ln 3000$

$(5x) \ln 6 = \ln 3000$

$5x = \dfrac{\ln 3000}{\ln 6}$

$x = \dfrac{\ln 3000}{5 \ln 6}$

≈ 0.894

62. $4^{-3t} = 0.10$

$\ln 4^{-3t} = \ln 0.10$

$(-3t) \ln 4 = \ln 0.10$

$-3t = \dfrac{\ln 0.10}{\ln 4}$

$t = -\dfrac{\ln 0.10}{3 \ln 4} \approx 0.554$

64. $8^{-2-x} = 431$

$\ln 8^{-2-x} = \ln 431$

$(-2 - x)\ln 8 = \ln 431$

$-2 \ln 8 - x \ln 8 = \ln 431$

$-x \ln 8 = \ln 431 + \ln 8^2$

$x \ln 8 = -\ln 431 - \ln 64$

$x = \dfrac{-\ln 431 - \ln 64}{\ln 8} \approx -4.917$

66. $f(x) = -4e^{-x-1} + 15$

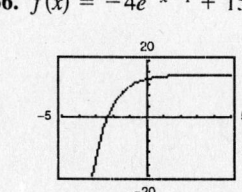

The zero is -2.322.

68. $g(x) = 8e^{-2x/3} - 11$

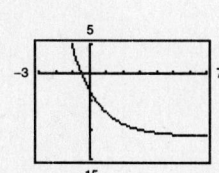

The zero is -0.478.

70. $f(x) = -e^{1.8x} + 7$

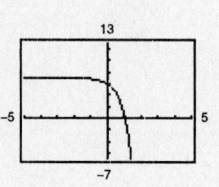

The zero is 1.081.

72. $f(x) = e^{2.724x} - 29$

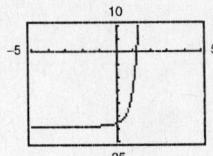

The zero is 1.236.

74.
$$5(10^{x-6}) = 7$$
$$10^{x-6} = \frac{7}{5}$$
$$\log_{10} 10^{x-6} = \log_{10} \frac{7}{5}$$
$$x - 6 = \log_{10} \frac{7}{5}$$
$$x = 6 + \log_{10} \frac{7}{5} \approx 6.146$$

76.
$$8(3^{6-x}) = 40$$
$$3^{6-x} = 5$$
$$\ln 3^{6-x} = \ln 5$$
$$(6-x)\ln 3 = \ln 5$$
$$6 - x = \frac{\ln 5}{\ln 3}$$
$$-x = \frac{\ln 5}{\ln 3} - 6$$
$$x = 6 - \frac{\ln 5}{\ln 3}$$
$$\approx 4.535$$

78.
$$\left(4 - \frac{2.471}{40}\right)^{9t} = 21$$
$$3.938225^{9t} = 21$$
$$\ln 3.938225^{9t} = \ln 21$$
$$9t \ln 3.938225 = \ln 21$$
$$t = \frac{\ln 21}{9 \ln 3.938225}$$
$$\approx 0.247$$

80.
$$\left(16 - \frac{0.878}{26}\right)^{3t} = 30$$
$$\ln\left(16 - \frac{0.878}{26}\right)^{3t} = \ln 30$$
$$3t \ln\left(16 - \frac{0.878}{26}\right) = \ln 30$$
$$t = \frac{\ln 30}{3 \ln\left(16 - \frac{0.878}{26}\right)} \approx 0.409$$

82.
$$\frac{119}{e^{6x} - 14} = 7$$
$$119 = 7(e^{6x} - 14)$$
$$17 = e^{6x} - 14$$
$$31 = e^{6x}$$
$$\ln 31 = \ln e^{6x}$$
$$\ln 31 = 6x$$
$$x = \frac{\ln 31}{6} \approx 0.572$$

84. $\ln x = 2$
$$e^{\ln x} = e^2$$
$$x = e^2 \approx 7.389$$

86. $\ln 4x = 1$
$$e^{\ln 4x} = e^1$$
$$4x = e$$
$$x = \frac{e}{4} \approx 0.680$$

88. $2 \ln x = 7$
$$\ln x = \frac{7}{2}$$
$$e^{\ln x} = e^{7/2}$$
$$x = e^{7/2} \approx 33.115$$

90. $\ln\sqrt{x-8} = 5$

$\quad e^{\ln\sqrt{x-8}} = e^5$

$\quad\quad \sqrt{x-8} = e^5$

$\quad\quad\quad x-8 = e^{10}$

$\quad\quad\quad\quad x = e^{10} + 8 \approx 22{,}034.466$

92. $\ln x + \ln(x+1) = 1$

$\quad\quad \ln[x(x+1)] = 1$

$\quad\quad\quad e^{\ln[x(x+1)]} = e^1$

$\quad\quad\quad x(x+1) = e^1$

$\quad\quad\quad x^2 + x - e = 0$

$$x = \frac{-1 \pm \sqrt{1+4e}}{2}$$

The only solution is $x = \dfrac{-1 \pm \sqrt{1+4e}}{2} \approx 1.223$.

94. $\ln x + \ln(x+3) = 1$

$\quad\quad \ln[x(x+3)] = 1$

$\quad\quad\quad e^{\ln[x(x+3)]} = e^1$

$\quad\quad\quad x(x+3) = e^1$

$\quad x^2 + 3x - e = 0$

$$x = \frac{-3 \pm \sqrt{9+4e}}{2}$$

The only solution is $x = \dfrac{-3 + \sqrt{9+4e}}{2} \approx 0.729$.

96. $\ln(x+1) - \ln(x-2) = \ln x^2$

$$\ln\!\left(\frac{x+1}{x-2}\right) = \ln x^2$$

$$\frac{x+1}{x-2} = x^2$$

$$x+1 = x^3 - 2x^2$$

$$0 = x^3 - 2x^2 - x - 1$$

From the graph, we have $x \approx 2.547$.

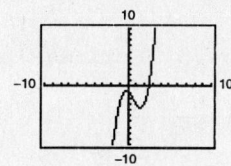

98. $\log_{10} x^2 = 6$

$\quad 10^{\log_{10} x^2} = 10^6$

$\quad\quad x^2 = 10^6$

$\quad\quad x = \pm 10^3 = \pm 1000$

100. $5\log_{10}(x-2) = 11$

$\quad\quad \log_{10}(x-2) = \frac{11}{5}$

$\quad\quad\quad 10^{\log_{10}(x-2)} = 10^{11/5}$

$\quad\quad\quad x-2 = 10^{11/5}$

$\quad\quad\quad x = 10^{11/5} + 2 \approx 160.489$

102. $\log_2 x + \log_2(x+2) = \log_2(x+6)$

$\quad\quad \log_2[x(x+2)] = \log_2(x+6)$

$\quad\quad\quad x(x+2) = x+6$

$\quad\quad\quad x^2 + x - 6 = 0$

$\quad\quad\quad (x+3)(x-2) = 0$

$x = -3 \text{ or } x = 2$

The value $x = -3$ is extraneous.

The only solution is $x = 2$.

104. $\log_3 x + \log_3(x-8) = 2$

$\quad\quad \log_3[x(x-8)] = 2$

$\quad\quad\quad 3^{\log_3(x^2-8x)} = 3^2$

$\quad\quad\quad x^2 - 8x = 9$

$\quad\quad\quad x^2 - 8x - 9 = 0$

$\quad\quad\quad (x-9)(x+1) = 0$

$x = 9 \text{ or } x = -1$

The value $x = -1$ is extraneous.

The only solution is $x = 9$.

106. $\log_{10} 4x - \log_{10}(12 + \sqrt{x}) = 2$

$$\log_{10}\left(\frac{4x}{12 + \sqrt{x}}\right) = 2$$

$$10^{\log_{10}(4x/(12 + \sqrt{x}))} = 10^2$$

$$\frac{4x}{12 + \sqrt{x}} = 100$$

$$4x = 100(12 + \sqrt{x})$$

$$4x = 1200 + 100\sqrt{x}$$

$$4x - 1200 = 100\sqrt{x}$$

$$x - 300 = 25\sqrt{x}$$

$$(x - 300)^2 = \left(25\sqrt{x}\right)^2$$

$$x^2 - 600x + 90{,}000 = 625x$$

$$x^2 - 1225x + 90{,}000 = 0$$

$$x = \frac{1225 \pm \sqrt{(-1225)^2 - 4(1)(90{,}000)}}{2}$$

$$x = \frac{1225 \pm \sqrt{1{,}140{,}625}}{2}$$

$$x = \frac{1225 \pm 125\sqrt{73}}{2}$$

$$x \approx 78.500 \text{ (extraneous) or } x \approx 1146.500$$

The only solution is $x = \dfrac{1225 + 125\sqrt{73}}{2} \approx 1146.500$.

108. $y_1 = 500$

$y_2 = 1500e^{-x/2}$

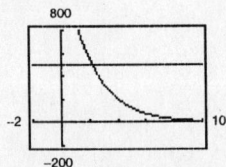

From the graph, we have $x \approx 2.197$.

The point of intersection is approximately $(2.197, 500)$.

110. $y_1 = 10$

$y_2 = 4\ln(x - 2)$

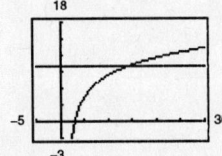

From the graph, we have $x \approx 14.182$.

The point of intersection is approximately $(14.182, 10)$.

112. $r = 0.12$

$A = Pe^{rt}$

$2000 = 1000e^{0.12t}$

$2 = e^{0.12t}$

$\ln 2 = \ln e^{0.12t}$

$\ln 2 = 0.12t$

$\dfrac{\ln 2}{0.12} = t$

$t \approx 5.8$ years

114. $r = 0.12$

$A = Pe^{rt}$

$3000 = 1000e^{0.12t}$

$3 = e^{0.12t}$

$\ln 3 = \ln e^{0.12t}$

$\ln 3 = 0.12t$

$\dfrac{\ln 3}{0.12} = t$

$t = 9.2$ years

116. $p = 5000\left(1 - \dfrac{4}{4 + e^{-0.002x}}\right)$

(a) When $p = \$600$:

$$600 = 5000\left(1 - \frac{4}{4 + e^{-0.002x}}\right)$$

$$0.12 = 1 - \frac{4}{4 + e^{-0.002x}}$$

$$\frac{4}{4 + e^{-0.002x}} = 0.88$$

$$4 = 3.52 + 0.88e^{-0.002x}$$

$$0.48 = 0.88e^{-0.002x}$$

$$\frac{6}{11} = e^{-0.002x}$$

$$\ln\frac{6}{11} = \ln e^{-0.002x}$$

$$\ln\frac{6}{11} = -0.002x$$

$$x = -\frac{\ln(6/11)}{0.002} \approx 303 \text{ units}$$

(b) When $p = \$400$:

$$400 = 5000\left(1 - \frac{4}{4 + e^{-0.002x}}\right)$$

$$0.08 = 1 - \frac{4}{4 + e^{-0.002x}}$$

$$\frac{4}{4 + e^{-0.002x}} = 0.92$$

$$4 = 3.68 + 0.92e^{-0.002x}$$

$$0.32 = 0.92e^{-0.002x}$$

$$\frac{8}{23} = e^{-0.002x}$$

$$\ln\frac{8}{23} = \ln e^{-0.002x}$$

$$\ln\frac{8}{23} = -0.002x$$

$$x = -\frac{\ln(8/23)}{0.002} \approx 528 \text{ units}$$

118. $N = 68(10^{-0.04x})$

When $N = 21$:

$$21 = 68(10^{-0.04x})$$

$$\frac{21}{68} = 10^{-0.04x}$$

$$\log_{10}\frac{21}{68} = -0.04x$$

$$x = -\frac{\log_{10}(21/68)}{0.04} \approx 12.76 \text{ inches}$$

120. $P = \dfrac{0.83}{1 + e^{-0.2n}}$

(a)
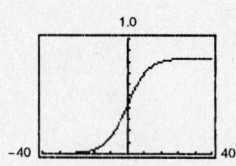

(b) Horizontal asymptotes: $P = 0$, $P = 0.83$
The upper asymptote, $P = 0.83$, indicates that the proportion of correct responses will approach 0.83 as the number of trials increases.

—CONTINUED—

120. —CONTINUED—

(c) When $P = 60\%$ or $P = 0.60$:

$$0.60 = \frac{0.83}{1 + e^{-0.2n}}$$

$$1 + e^{-0.2n} = \frac{0.83}{0.60}$$

$$e^{-0.2n} = \frac{0.83}{0.60} - 1$$

$$\ln e^{-0.2n} = \ln\left(\frac{0.83}{0.60} - 1\right)$$

$$-0.2n = \ln\left(\frac{0.83}{0.60} - 1\right)$$

$$n = -\frac{\ln\left(\dfrac{0.83}{0.60} - 1\right)}{0.2} \approx 5 \text{ trials}$$

122. $y = -3.00 + 11.88 \ln x + \dfrac{36.94}{x}$

(a)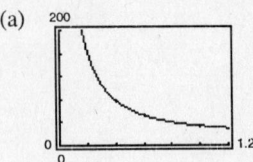

The model seems to fit the data well.

(b) When $y = 30$:

$$30 = -3.00 + 11.88 \ln x + \frac{36.94}{x}$$

Add the graph of $y = 30$ to the graph in part (a) and estimate the point of intersection of the two graphs. We find that $x \approx 1.20$ meters.

(c) No, it is probably not practical to lower the number of g's experienced during impact to less than 23 because the required distance traveled at $y = 23$ is $x \approx 2.27$ meters. It is probably not practical to design a car allowing a passenger to move forward 2.27 meters (or 7.45 feet) during an impact.

124. $\log_a(u + v) = \left(\log_a u\right)(\log_a v)$

False. $2.04 \approx \log_{10}(10 + 100) \neq (\log_{10} 10)(\log_{10} 100) = 2$

126. $\log_a\left(\dfrac{u}{v}\right) = \log_a u - \log_a v$

True by Property 2 in Section 5.3.

128.

Doubling Time	Quadrupling Time
$2P = Pe^{rt}$	$4P = Pe^{rt}$
$2 = e^{rt}$	$4 = e^{rt}$
$\ln 2 = rt$	$\ln 4 = rt$
$\dfrac{\ln 2}{r} = t$	$\dfrac{\ln 4}{r} = t$
	$\dfrac{\ln 2^2}{r} = t$
	$\dfrac{2\ln 2}{r} = t$
	$2\left(\dfrac{\ln 2}{r}\right) = t$

Yes, it takes twice as long to quadruple.

130. $\sqrt{48x^2y^5} = \sqrt{16x^2y^4 3y} = 4|x|y^2\sqrt{3y}$

132. $\sqrt[3]{25}\sqrt[3]{15} = \sqrt[3]{375} = \sqrt[3]{125 \cdot 3} = 5\sqrt[3]{3}$

134. $M = kp^3$

136. $d = kab$

138. $C = \dfrac{k}{\sqrt{w}}$

140. $\log_3 4 = \dfrac{\log_{10} 4}{\log_{10} 3} = \dfrac{\ln 4}{\ln 3} \approx 1.262$

142. $\log_8 22 = \dfrac{\log_{10} 22}{\log_{10} 8} = \dfrac{\ln 22}{\ln 8} \approx 1.486$

Section 3.5   Exponential and Logarithmic Models

Solutions to Even-Numbered Exercises

2. $y = 6e^{-x/4}$

This is an exponential decay model. Matches graph (e).

4. $y = 3e^{-(x-2)^2/5}$

This is a Gaussian model. Matches graph (a).

6. $y = \dfrac{4}{1 + e^{-2x}}$

This is a logistic growth model. Matches graph (f).

8. Since $A = 20{,}000e^{0.105t}$, the time to double is given by $40{,}000 = 20{,}000e^{0.105t}$, and we have

$$40{,}000 = 20{,}000e^{0.105t}$$

$$2 = e^{0.105t}$$

$$\ln 2 = \ln e^{0.105t}$$

$$\ln 2 = 0.105t$$

$$t = \frac{\ln 2}{0.105} \approx 6.60 \text{ years.}$$

Amount after 10 years: $A = 20{,}000e^{0.105(10)} \approx \$57{,}153.02$

10. Since $A = 10{,}000e^{rt}$ and $A = 20{,}000$ when $t = 12$, we have

$$20{,}000 = 10{,}000e^{12r}$$

$$2 = e^{12r}$$

$$\ln 2 = \ln e^{12r}$$

$$\ln 2 = 12r$$

$$r = \frac{\ln 2}{12} \approx 0.057762 = 5.7762\%$$

Amount after 10 years:

$$A = 10{,}000e^{0.057762(10)} \approx \$17{,}817.97$$

12. Since $A = 600e^{rt}$ and $A = 19{,}205$ when $t = 10$, we have

$$19{,}205 = 600e^{10r}$$

$$\frac{19{,}205}{600} = e^{10r}$$

$$\ln\left(\frac{19{,}205}{600}\right) = \ln e^{10r}$$

$$\ln\left(\frac{19{,}205}{600}\right) = 10r$$

$$r = \frac{\ln(19{,}205/600)}{10} \approx 0.3466 \text{ or } 34.66\%.$$

The time to double is given by

$$1200 = 600e^{0.3466t}$$

$$t = \frac{\ln 2}{0.3466} \approx 2 \text{ years.}$$

14. Since $A = Pe^{0.08t}$ and $A = 20{,}000$ when $t = 10$, we have

$$20{,}000 = Pe^{0.08(10)}$$

$$P = \frac{20{,}000}{e^{0.08(10)}} \approx \$8986.58.$$

The time to double is given by

$$t = \frac{\ln 2}{0.08} \approx 8.66 \text{ years.}$$

16.
$$A = P\left(1 + \frac{r}{n}\right)^{nt}$$

$$500{,}000 = P\left(1 + \frac{0.12}{12}\right)^{12(40)}$$

$$P = \$4214.16$$

18. $P = 1000, \ r = 10.5\% = 0.105$

(a) $n = 1$

$$t = \frac{\ln 2}{\ln(1 + 0.105)} \approx 6.94 \text{ years}$$

(b) $n = 12$

$$t = \frac{\ln 2}{12\ln\left(1 + \dfrac{0.105}{12}\right)} \approx 6.63 \text{ years}$$

—CONTINUED—

18. —CONTINUED—

(c) $n = 365$

$$t = \frac{\ln 2}{365 \ln\left(1 + \dfrac{0.105}{365}\right)} \approx 6.602 \text{ years}$$

(d) Compounded continuously

$$t = \frac{\ln 2}{0.105} \approx 6.601 \text{ years}$$

20.

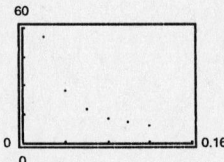

Using the power regression feature of a graphing utility,

$t = 1.099 r^{-1}$.

22.

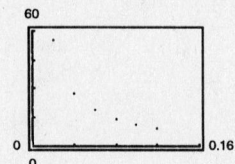

Using the power regression feature of a graphing utility,

$t = 1.222 r^{-1}$.

24.

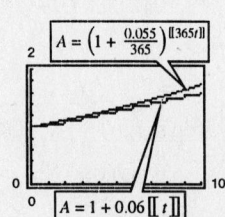

From the graph, $5\frac{1}{2}\%$ compounded daily grows faster than 6% simple interest.

26. $\dfrac{1}{2}C = Ce^{k(1620)}$

$\dfrac{1}{2} = e^{k(1620)}$

$\ln\dfrac{1}{2} = \ln e^{k(1620)}$

$\ln\dfrac{1}{2} = k(1620)$

$k = \dfrac{\ln\frac{1}{2}}{1620}$

Given $y = 1.5$ grams after 1000 years, we have

$1.5 = Ce^{[\ln(1/2)/1620](1000)}$

$C \approx 2.30$ grams.

28. $\dfrac{1}{2}C = Ce^{k(5730)}$

$\dfrac{1}{2} = e^{k(5730)}$

$\ln\dfrac{1}{2} = \ln e^{k(5730)}$

$\ln\dfrac{1}{2} = k(5730)$

$k = \dfrac{\ln\frac{1}{2}}{5730}$

Given $C = 3$ grams, after 1000 years we have

$y = 3e^{[(\ln 1/2)/5730](1000)}$

$y \approx 2.66$ grams.

30. $\dfrac{1}{2}C = Ce^{k(24,360)}$

$\dfrac{1}{2} = e^{k(24,360)}$

$\ln\dfrac{1}{2} = \ln e^{k(24,360)}$

$\ln\dfrac{1}{2} = k(24,360)$

$k = \dfrac{\ln\frac{1}{2}}{24,360}$

Given $y = 0.4$ grams after 1000 years, we have

$0.4 = Ce^{[(\ln 1/2)/24,360](1000)}$

$C \approx 0.41$ grams.

32. $y = ae^{bx}$

$\dfrac{1}{2} = ae^{b(0)} \implies a = \dfrac{1}{2}$

$5 = \dfrac{1}{2}e^{b(4)}$

$10 = e^{4b}$

$\ln 10 = \ln e^{4b}$

$\ln 10 = 4b$

$\dfrac{\ln 10}{4} = b \implies b \approx 0.5756$

Thus, $y = \frac{1}{2}e^{0.5756x}$.

34. $y = ae^{bx}$

$1 = ae^{b(0)} \implies 1 = a$

$\dfrac{1}{4} = e^{b(3)}$

$\ln\left(\dfrac{1}{4}\right) = \ln e^{3b}$

$\ln\left(\dfrac{1}{4}\right) = 3b$

$\dfrac{\ln\left(\frac{1}{4}\right)}{3} = b \implies b \approx -0.4621$

Thus, $y = e^{-0.4621x}$.

36. $P = 240{,}360e^{0.012t}$

$$275{,}000 = 240{,}360e^{0.012t}$$

$$\frac{275{,}000}{240{,}360} = e^{0.012t}$$

$$\frac{27{,}500}{24{,}036} = e^{0.012t}$$

$$\ln\!\left(\frac{27{,}500}{24{,}036}\right) = \ln e^{0.012t}$$

$$\ln\!\left(\frac{27{,}500}{24{,}036}\right) = 0.012t$$

$$t = \frac{\ln(27{,}500/24{,}036)}{0.012} \approx 11$$

The population will reach 275,000 in 2011.

38. For 1960, we use $t = -40$.

$$100{,}250 = 140{,}500e^{k(-40)}$$

$$\frac{100{,}250}{140{,}500} = e^{k(-40)}$$

$$\frac{10{,}025}{14{,}050} = e^{k(-40)}$$

$$\ln\!\left(\frac{10{,}025}{14{,}050}\right) = \ln e^{k(-40)}$$

$$\ln\!\left(\frac{10{,}025}{14{,}050}\right) = k(-40)$$

$$k = \frac{\ln(10{,}025/14{,}050)}{-40} \approx 0.0084$$

For 2020, we use $t = 20$.

$$P = 140{,}500e^{0.0084(20)} \approx 166{,}203$$

40. $N = 100e^{kt}$

$$300 = 100e^{5k}$$

$$3 = e^{5k}$$

$$\ln 3 = \ln e^{5k}$$

$$\ln 3 = 5k$$

$$k = \frac{\ln 3}{5} \approx 0.2197$$

$$N = 100e^{0.2197t}$$

$$200 = 100e^{0.2197t}$$

$$t = \frac{\ln 2}{0.2197} \approx 3.15 \text{ hours}$$

42. $y = Ce^{kt}$

$$\frac{1}{2}C = Ce^{(1620)k}$$

$$\frac{1}{2} = e^{(1620)k}$$

$$\ln\frac{1}{2} = \ln e^{(1620)k}$$

$$\ln\frac{1}{2} = 1620k$$

$$k = \frac{\ln(1/2)}{1620}$$

When $t = 100$, we have

$$y = Ce^{[\ln(1/2)/1620](100)} \approx 0.958C = 95.8\%C.$$

After 100 years, approximately 95.8% of the radioactive radium will remain.

44. $(0,\ 22{,}000)$, $(2,\ 13{,}000)$

(a) $m = \dfrac{13{,}000 - 22{,}000}{2 - 0} = -4500$

$b = 22{,}000$

Thus, $V = -4500t + 22{,}000$.

(b) $a = 22{,}000$

$$13{,}000 = 22{,}000e^{k(2)}$$

$$\frac{13}{22} = e^{2k}$$

$$\ln\!\left(\frac{13}{22}\right) = \ln e^{2k}$$

$$\ln\!\left(\frac{13}{22}\right) = 2k \Longrightarrow k \approx -0.263$$

Thus, $V = 22{,}000e^{-0.263t}$.

(c) The exponential model depreciates faster in the first two years.

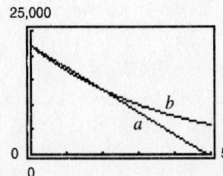

(d)

t	1	3
$V = -4500t + 22{,}000$	$17,500	$8500
$V = 22{,}000e^{-0.263t}$	$16,912	$9995

(e) The slope of the linear model means that the car depreciates $4500 per year.

46. $S(t) = 100(1 - e^{kt})$

(a)　　$15 = 100(1 - e^{k(1)})$

　　　$-85 = -100e^k$

　　　$\dfrac{85}{100} = e^k$

　　　$0.85 = e^k$

　　$\ln 0.85 = \ln e^k$

　　　　$k = \ln 0.85$

　　　　$k \approx -0.1625$

　　$S(t) = 100(1 - e^{-0.1625t})$

(c)　$S(5) = 100(1 - e^{-0.1625(5)})$

　　　　　$\approx 55.625 = 55,625$ units

(b)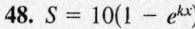

48. $S = 10(1 - e^{kx})$

$x = 5$ (in hundreds), $S = 2.5$ (in thousands)

(a)　$2.5 = 10(1 - e^{k(5)})$

　　$0.25 = 1 - e^{5k}$

　　$e^{5k} = 0.75$

　$\ln e^{5k} = \ln 0.75$

　　$5k = \ln 0.75$

　　$k \approx -0.0575$

　　$S = 10(1 - e^{-0.0575x})$

(b) When $x = 7$,

$S = 10(1 - e^{-0.0575(7)}) \approx 3.314$

which corresponds to 3314 units.

50. $N = 30(1 - e^{kt})$

(a)　　$N = 19,\ t = 20$

　　　$19 = 30(1 - e^{20k})$

　　$30e^{20k} = 11$

　　　$e^{20k} = \dfrac{11}{30}$

　$\ln e^{20k} = \ln\left(\dfrac{11}{30}\right)$

　　$20k = \ln\dfrac{11}{30}$

　　　$k \approx -0.050$

　　　$N = 30(1 - e^{-0.050t})$

(c) No. It is not a linear function.

(b)　　$N = 25$

　　$25 = 30(1 - e^{-0.050t})$

　　$\dfrac{5}{30} = e^{-0.050t}$

　$\ln\left(\dfrac{5}{30}\right) = \ln e^{-0.050t}$

　$\ln\left(\dfrac{5}{30}\right) = -0.050t$

　　$t = -\dfrac{\ln(5/30)}{-0.050} \approx 36$ days

52. $R = \log_{10}\dfrac{I}{I_0} = \log_{10} I$ since $I_0 = 1$.

(a) $R = \log_{10} 80,500,000 \approx 7.91$　　(b) $R = \log_{10} 48,275,000 \approx 7.68$　　(c) $R = \log_{10} 251,200 \approx 5.40$

54. $\beta = 10 \log_{10} \dfrac{I}{I_0}$ where $I_0 = 10^{-12}$ watt/m²

(a) $\beta = 10 \log_{10} \dfrac{10^{-10}}{10^{-12}} = 10 \log_{10} 10^2 = 20$ decibels

(b) $\beta = 10 \log_{10} \dfrac{10^{-5}}{10^{-12}} = 10 \log_{10} 10^7 = 70$ decibels

(c) $\beta = 10 \log_{10} \dfrac{10^{-2.5}}{10^{-12}} = 10 \log_{10} 10^{9.5} = 95$ decibels

(d) $\beta = 10 \log_{10} \dfrac{1}{10^{-12}} = 10 \log_{10} 10^{12} = 120$ decibels

56. $\beta = 10 \log_{10} \dfrac{I}{I_0}$

$\dfrac{\beta}{10} = \log_{10} \dfrac{I}{I_0}$

$10^{\beta/10} = 10^{\log_{10} I/I_0}$

$10^{\beta/10} = \dfrac{I}{I_0}$

$I = I_0 10^{\beta/10}$

% decrease $= \dfrac{I_0 10^{9.3} - I_0 10^{8.0}}{I_0 10^{9.3}} \times 100 \approx 95\%$

58. $pH = -\log_{10}[H^+] = -\log_{10}(2.3 \times 10^{-5}) \approx 4.64$

60. $5.8 = -\log_{10}[H^+]$

$-5.8 = \log_{10}[H^+]$

$10^{-5.8} = 10^{\log_{10}[H^+]}$

$10^{-5.8} = [H^+]$

$[H^+] \approx 1.58 \times 10^{-6}$ moles per liter

62. $2.5 = -\log_{10}[H^+]$

$-2.5 = \log_{10}[H^+]$

$10^{-2.5} = 10^{\log_{10}[H^+]}$

$10^{-2.5} = [H^+]$ for the fruit.

$9.5 = -\log_{10}[H^+]$

$10^{-9.5} = [H^+]$ for the antacid tablet

$\dfrac{10^{-2.5}}{10^{-9.5}} = 10^7$

64. Interest: $u = M - \left(M - \dfrac{Pr}{12}\right)\left(1 + \dfrac{r}{12}\right)^{12t}$

Principal: $v = \left(M - \dfrac{Pr}{12}\right)\left(1 + \dfrac{r}{12}\right)^{12t}$

(a) $P = 120{,}000$, $t = 35$, $r = 0.075$, $M = 809.39$

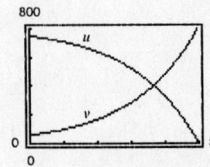

(c) $P = 120{,}000$, $t = 20$, $r = 0.075$, $M = 966.71$

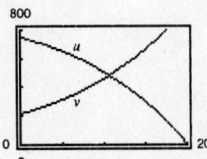

(b) In the early years of the mortgage, the majority of the monthly payment goes toward interest. The principal and interest are nearly equal when $t \approx 26$ years.

The interest is still the majority of the monthly payment in the early years. Now the principal and interest are nearly equal when $t \approx 10.729 \approx 11$ years.

66. $t_1 = 40.757 + 0.556s - 15.817 \ln s$

$t_2 = 1.2259 + 0.0023s^2$

(a) Linear model: $t_3 = 0.2729s - 6.0143$

Exponential model: $t_4 = 1.5385e^{0.02913s}$ or $t_4 = 1.5385(1.0296)^s$

(b)

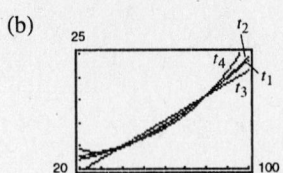

(c)

s	30	40	50	60	70	80	90
t_1	3.6	4.6	6.7	9.4	12.5	15.9	19.6
t_2	3.3	4.9	7.0	9.5	12.5	15.9	19.9
t_3	2.2	4.9	7.6	10.4	13.1	15.8	18.5
t_4	3.7	4.9	6.6	8.8	11.8	15.8	21.2

(d) Model t_1: $S_1 = |3.4 - 3.6| + |5 - 4.6| + |7 - 6.7| + |9.3 - 9.4| + |12 - 12.5| + |15.8 - 15.9| + |20 - 19.6| = 2.0$

Model t_2: $S_2 = |3.4 - 3.3| + |5 - 4.9| + |7 - 7| + |9.3 - 9.5| + |12 - 12.5| + |15.8 - 15.9| + |20 - 19.9| = 1.1$

Model t_3: $S_3 = |3.4 - 2.2| + |5 - 4.9| + |7 - 7.6| + |9.3 - 10.4| + |12 - 13.1| + |15.8 - 15.8| + |20 - 18.5| = 5.6$

Model t_4: $S_4 = |3.4 - 3.7| + |5 - 4.9| + |7 - 6.6| + |9.3 - 8.8| + |12 - 11.8| + |15.8 - 15.8| + |20 - 21.2| = 2.7$

The quadratic model, t_2, best fits the data.

68. False. The domain can be the set of real numbers for a logistics growth function.

70. False. The graph of $f(x)$ is the graph of $g(x)$ shifted upward five units.

72. Answers will vary.

74.
$$-4 \begin{array}{|rrrr} 4 & 4 & -39 & 36 \\ & -16 & 48 & -36 \\ \hline 4 & -12 & 9 & 0 \end{array}$$

Thus, $\dfrac{4x^3 + 4x^2 - 39x + 36}{x + 4} = 4x^2 - 12x + 9.$

76.
$$4 \begin{array}{|rrrr} 2 & -8 & 3 & -9 \\ & 8 & 0 & 12 \\ \hline 2 & 0 & 3 & 3 \end{array}$$

Thus, $\dfrac{2x^3 - 8x^2 + 3x - 9}{x - 4} = 2x^2 + 3 + \dfrac{3}{x - 4}.$

78. $y = 10 - 3x$

Line

Slope: $m = -3$

y-intercept: $(0, 10)$

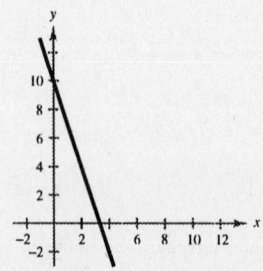

80. $y = -2x^2 - 3$

$y = -2(x - 0)^2 - 3$

Parabola

Vertex: $(0, -3)$

82. $3x^2 - 4y = 0$

$3x^2 = 4y$

$x^2 = \frac{4}{3}y$

Parabola

Vertex: $(0, 0)$

Focus: $\left(0, \frac{1}{3}\right)$

Directrix: $y = -\frac{1}{3}$

84. $y = \dfrac{4}{1 - 3x}$

Vertical Asymptote: $x = \dfrac{1}{3}$

Horizontal Asymptote: $y = 0$

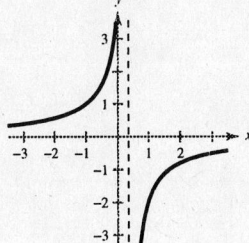

86. $x^2 + (y - 8)^2 = 25$

Circle

Center: $(0, 8)$

Radius: 5

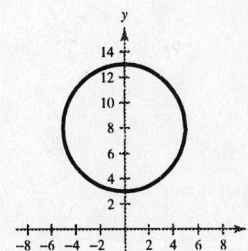

88. $f(x) = 2^{x-1} + 5$

Horizontal Asymptote: $y = 5$

x	-5	-3	-1	0	1	3	5
$f(x)$	5.02	5.06	5.3	5.5	6	9	21

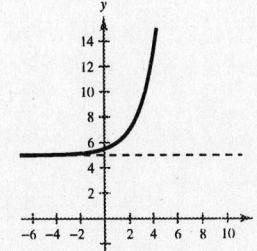

90. $f(x) = 3^x - 4$

Horizontal Asymptote: $y = -4$

x	-4	-2	-1	0	1	2
$f(x)$	-3.98	-3.89	-3.67	-3	-1	5

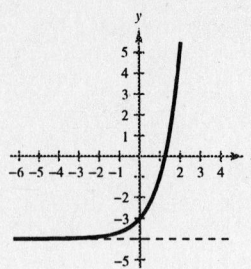

Review Exercises for Chapter 3

Solutions to Even-Numbered Exercises

2. $-14(5^{-0.8}) \approx -3.863$

4. $\sqrt[5]{1278} \approx 4.181$

6. $7^{-\sqrt{11}} \approx 0.002$

8. $f(x) = 4^{-x}$

Intercept: $(0,1)$
Horizontal asymptote: $y = 0$
Decreasing on: $(-\infty, \infty)$
Matches graph (d)

10. $f(x) = 4^x + 1$

Intercept: $(0, 2)$
Horizontal asymptote: $y = 1$
Increasing on: $(-\infty, \infty)$
Matches graph (b)

12. $f(x) = -4^x - 3$

Horizontal Asymptote: $y = -3$

x	-2	-1	0	1	2
$f(x)$	-3.063	-3.25	-4	-7	-19

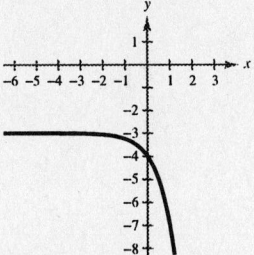

14. $f(x) = 2.65^{x-1}$

Horizontal Asymptote: $y = 0$

x	-3	-1	0	1	3
$f(x)$	0.020	0.142	0.377	1	7.023

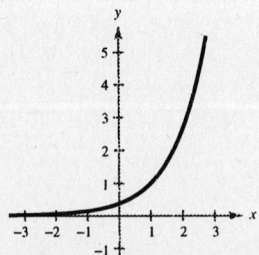

16. $f(x) = 2^{x-6} - 5$

Horizontal Asymptote: $y = -5$

x	0	5	6	7	8	9
$f(x)$	-4.984	-4.5	-4	-3	-1	3

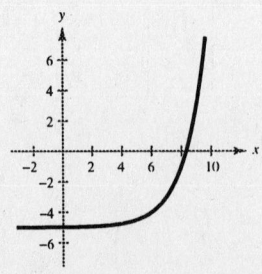

18. $f(x) = \left(\frac{1}{8}\right)^{x+2} - 5$

Horizontal Asymptote: $y = -5$

x	-3	-2	-1	0	2
$f(x)$	3	-4	-4.875	-4.984	-5

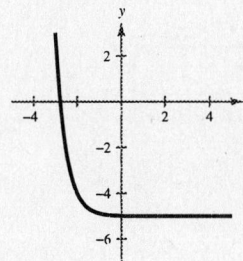

20. $e^{5/8} \approx 1.868$

22. $e^{0.278} = 1.320$

24. $h(x) = 2 - e^{-x/2}$

x	-2	-1	0	1	2
y	-0.72	0.35	1	1.39	1.63

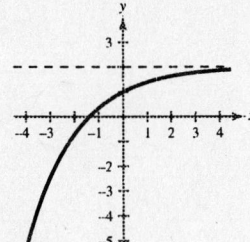

26. $s(t) = 4e^{-2/t}, t > 0$

t	$\frac{1}{2}$	1	2	3	4
y	0.07	0.54	1.47	2.05	2.43

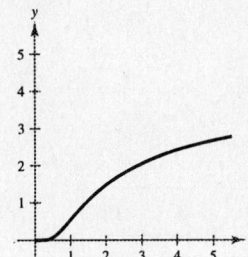

28. $A = 2000\left(1 + \dfrac{0.05}{n}\right)^{30n}$ or $A = 2000e^{(0.05)(30)}$

n	1	2	4	12	365	Continuous
A	$8643.88	$8799.58	$8880.43	$8935.49	$8962.46	$8963.38

30. $200{,}000 = P\left(1 + \dfrac{0.06}{12}\right)^{12t} = P(1.005)^{12t}$

$P = \dfrac{200{,}000}{(1.005)^{12t}}$

t	1	10	20	30	40	50
P	$188,381.07	$109,926.55	$60,419.23	$33,208.39	$18,252.42	$10,032.13

32. $V(t) = 14{,}000\left(\frac{3}{4}\right)^t$

(a)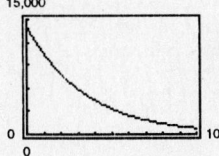

(b) $V(2) = 14{,}000\left(\frac{3}{4}\right)^2 = \$7875$

(c) According to the model, the car depreciates most rapidly at the beginning. Yes, this is realistic.

34. $y = 28e^{0.6 - 0.012s}$, $s \geq 50$

s	50	55	60	65	70
y	28	26.4	24.8	23.4	22.0

36. $25^{3/2} = 125$

$\log_{25} 125 = \frac{3}{2}$

38. $\log_9 3 = \log_9 9^{1/2} = \dfrac{1}{2}$

40. $\log_a \dfrac{1}{a} = \log_a a^{-1} = -1$

42. $g(x) = \log_5 x \implies 5^y = x$

Domain: $(0, \infty)$

Vertical asymptote: $x = 0$

x	$\frac{1}{25}$	$\frac{1}{5}$	1	5	25
$g(x)$	-2	-1	0	1	2

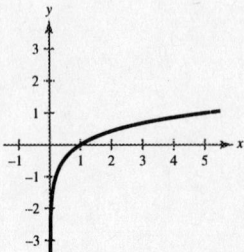

44. $f(x) = 6 + \log_{10} x$

Domain: $(0, \infty)$

Vertical asymptote: $x = 0$

x	1	2	4	6	8	10
$f(x)$	6	6.3	6.6	6.8	6.9	7

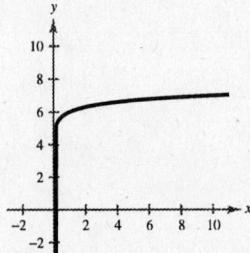

46. $f(x) = \log_{10}(x - 3) + 1$

Domain: $(3, \infty)$

Vertical asymptote: $x = 3$

x	4	5	6	7	8
$f(x)$	1	1.3	1.5	1.6	1.7

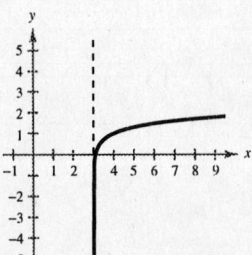

48. $\ln 0.98 \approx -0.020$

50. $\ln e^7 = 7$

52. $\ln\left(\dfrac{\sqrt{3}}{8}\right) \approx -1.530$

54. $f(x) = \ln(x - 3)$

Domain: $(3, \infty)$

Vertical asymptote: $x = 3$

x	3.5	4	4.5	5	5.5
y	-0.69	0	0.41	0.69	0.92

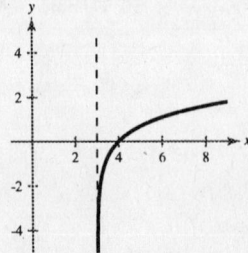

56. $f(x) = \frac{1}{4} \ln x$

Domain: $(0, \infty)$

Vertical asymptote: $x = 0$

x	$\frac{1}{2}$	1	$\frac{3}{2}$	2	$\frac{5}{2}$	3
y	-0.17	0	0.10	0.17	0.23	0.27

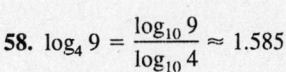

58. $\log_4 9 = \dfrac{\log_{10} 9}{\log_{10} 4} \approx 1.585$

$\log_4 9 = \dfrac{\ln 9}{\ln 4} \approx 1.585$

60. $\log_{1/2} 5 = \dfrac{\log_{10} 5}{\log_{10}(1/2)} \approx -2.322$

$\log_{1/2} 5 = \dfrac{\ln 5}{\ln(1/2)} \approx -2.322$

62. $\ln 8 + \ln 5 = \ln[(8)(5)] = \ln 40$

64. $\ln \sqrt[4]{\dfrac{x}{y}} = \ln\left(\dfrac{x}{y}\right)^{1/4} = \ln\left(\dfrac{x^{1/4}}{y^{1/4}}\right)$

$= \ln x^{1/4} - \ln y^{1/4} = \dfrac{1}{4} \ln x - \dfrac{1}{4} \ln y$

66. $\log_{10}\left(\dfrac{p^2 q^3}{r}\right) = \log_{10}(p^2 q^3) - \log_{10} r$

$= \log_{10} p^2 + \log_{10} q^3 - \log_{10} r$

$= 2 \log_{10} p + 3 \log_{10} q - \log_{10} r$

68. $\log_7 \dfrac{\sqrt{x}}{4} = \log_7 \sqrt{x} - \log_7 4$

$= \log_7 x^{1/2} - \log_7 4$

$= \dfrac{1}{2} \log_7 x - \log_7 4$

70. $\ln\left|\dfrac{x-1}{x+1}\right| = \ln|x-1| - \ln|x+1|$

72. $\log_6 y - 2 \log_6 z = \log_6 y - \log_6 z^2$

$= \log_6 \dfrac{y}{z^2}$

74. $5 \ln|x-2| - \ln|x+2| - 3\ln|x| = \ln|x-2|^5 - \ln|x+2| - \ln|x|^3$

$= \ln\left|\dfrac{(x-2)^5}{(x+2)x^3}\right|$

76. $8^x = 512$

$8^x = 8^3$

$x = 3$

78. $6^x = \frac{1}{216}$

$6^x = 6^{-3}$

$x = -3$

80. $\log_7 x = 4$

$7^{\log_7 x} = 7^4$

$x = 7^4$

$x = 2401$

82. $e^x = 12$

$\ln e^x = \ln 12$

$x = \ln 12 \approx 2.485$

84. $3e^{-5x} = 132$

$e^{-5x} = 44$

$\ln e^{-5x} = \ln 44$

$-5x = \ln 44$

$x = \dfrac{\ln 44}{-5} \approx -0.757$

86. $e^x + 13 = 35$

$e^x = 22$

$\ln e^x = \ln 22$

$x = \ln 22 \approx 3.091$

88. $-4(5^x) = -68$

$5^x = 17$

$\ln 5^x = \ln 17$

$x \ln 5 = \ln 17$

$x = \dfrac{\ln 17}{\ln 5} \approx 1.760$

90. $e^{2x} - 7e^x + 10 = 0$

$(e^x - 2)(e^x - 5) = 0$

$e^x = 2 \qquad\qquad e^x = 5$

$\ln e^x = \ln 2 \qquad \ln e^x = \ln 5$

$x = \ln 2 \approx 0.693 \qquad x = \ln 5 \approx 1.609$

92. $2^{0.6x} - 3x = 0$

Graph $y_1 = 2^{0.6x} - 3x$.

The x-intercepts are at
$x \approx 0.39$ and at $x \approx 7.48$.

94. $25e^{-0.3x} = 12$

Graph $y_1 = 25e^{-0.3x}$ and $y_2 = 12$.

The graphs intersect at $x \approx 2.45$.

96. $\ln 3x = 8.2$

$e^{\ln 3x} = e^{8.2}$

$3x = e^{8.2}$

$x = \dfrac{e^{8.2}}{3} \approx 1213.650$

98. $2 \ln 4x = 15$

$\ln 4x = \frac{15}{2}$

$e^{\ln 4x} = e^{7.5}$

$4x = e^{7.5}$

$x = \frac{1}{4}e^{7.5} \approx 452.011$

100. $\ln x - \ln 3 = 2$

$\ln \dfrac{x}{3} = 2$

$e^{\ln \frac{x}{3}} = e^2$

$\dfrac{x}{3} = e^2$

$x = 3e^2 \approx 22.167$

102. $\ln\sqrt{x + 1} = 2$

$\frac{1}{2}\ln(x + 1) = 2$

$\ln(x + 1) = 4$

$e^{\ln(x+1)} = e^4$

$x + 1 = e^4$

$x = e^4 - 1 \approx 53.598$

104. $\log_{10}(x - 1) = \log_{10}(x - 2) - \log_{10}(x + 2)$

$\log_{10}(x - 1) = \log_{10}\left(\dfrac{x - 2}{x + 2}\right)$

$10^{\log_{10}(x-1)} = 10^{\log_{10}(x - 2/x + 2)}$

$x - 1 = \dfrac{x - 2}{x + 2}$

$(x - 1)(x + 2) = x - 2$

$x^2 + x - 2 = x - 2$

$x^2 = 0$

$x = 0$

Since $x = 0$ is not in the domain of $\ln(x - 1)$ or of
$\ln(x - 2)$, it is an extraneous solution. The equation
has no solution.

106. $\log_{10}(1 - x) = -1$

$10^{\log_{10}(1 - x)} = 10^{-1}$

$1 - x = 10^{-1}$

$1 - \frac{1}{10} = x$

$x = 0.900$

108. $2 \ln(x + 3) + 3x = 8$

Graph $y_1 = 2 \ln(x + 3) + 3x$ and $y_2 = 8$.

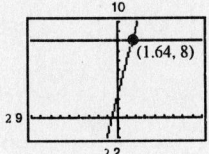

The graphs intersect at approximately $(1.64, 8)$.
The solution of the equation is $x \approx 1.64$.

110. $4 \ln(x + 5) - x = 10$

Graph $y_1 = 4 \ln(x + 5) - x$ and $y_2 = 10$.

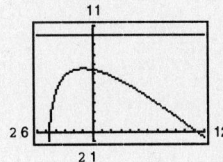

The graphs do not intersect.
The equation has no solution.

112. $3(7550) = 7550e^{0.0725t}$

$$3 = e^{0.0725t}$$

$$\ln 3 = \ln e^{0.0725t}$$

$$\ln 3 = 0.0725t$$

$$t = \frac{\ln 3}{0.0725} \approx 15.2 \text{ years}$$

114. $p = 500 - 0.5e^{0.004x}$

(a) $p = 450$

$$450 = 500 - 0.5e^{0.004x}$$

$$0.5e^{0.004x} = 50$$

$$e^{0.004x} = 100$$

$$0.004x = \ln 100$$

$$x \approx 1151 \text{ units}$$

(b) $p = 400$

$$400 = 500 - 0.5e^{0.004x}$$

$$0.5e^{0.004x} = 100$$

$$e^{0.004x} = 200$$

$$0.004x = \ln 200$$

$$x \approx 1325 \text{ units}$$

116. $y = 4e^{2x/3}$

Exponential growth model

Matches graph (b)

118. $y = 7 - \log_{10}(x + 3)$

Logarithmic model

Vertical asymptote: $x = -3$

Matches graph (d)

120. $y = \dfrac{6}{1 + 2e^{-2x}}$

Logistics growth model

Matches graph (c)

122. $y = Ce^{kt}$

$$\frac{1}{2}C = Ce^{(250,000)k}$$

$$\ln \frac{1}{2} = \ln e^{(250,000)k}$$

$$\ln \frac{1}{2} = 250,000k$$

$$k = \frac{\ln(1/2)}{250,000}$$

When $t = 5000$, we have
$y = Ce^{[\ln(1/2)/250,000](5000)} \approx 0.986C = 98.6\%C$.

After 5000 years, approximately 98.6% of the
radioactive uranium II will remain.

124. $y = ae^{bx}$

$$2 = ae^{b(0)} \implies a = 2$$

$$3 = 2e^{b(4)}$$

$$1.5 = e^{4b}$$

$$\ln 1.5 = 4b \implies b \approx 0.1014$$

Thus, $y \approx 2e^{0.1014x}$

126. $y = 0.0499e^{-(x-71)^2/128}$

(a) Graph $y_1 = 0.0499e^{-(x-71)^2/128}$

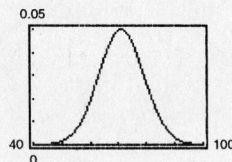

(b) The average test score is 71.

128.
$$\beta = 10 \log_{10}\left(\frac{I}{10^{-16}}\right)$$

$$125 = 10 \log_{10}\left(\frac{I}{10^{-16}}\right)$$

$$12.5 = \log_{10}\left(\frac{I}{10^{-16}}\right)$$

$$10^{12.5} = \frac{I}{10^{-16}}$$

$$I = 10^{-3.5} \text{ watt/cm}^2$$

130. True. By the inverse properties, $\log_b b^{2x} = 2x$.

132. False. $\ln x + \ln y = \ln(xy) \neq \ln(x + y)$

134. True. $\log_{10}\left(\dfrac{10}{x}\right) = \log_{10} 10 - \log_{10} x = 1 - \log_{10} x$

136. Order: $b < d < a < c$

Since graphs (b) and (d) represent exponential decay, b and d are negative.

Since graph (a) and (c) represent exponential growth, a and c are positive.

C H A P T E R 4
Trigonometry

Section 4.1   Radian and Degree Measure

2. 5.5 radians

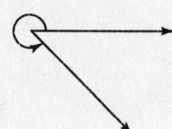

4. -4 radians

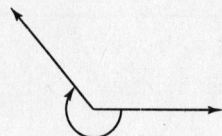

6. 6 radians

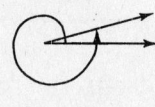

8. (a) Since $\pi < \dfrac{11\pi}{8} < \dfrac{3\pi}{2}$; $\dfrac{11\pi}{8}$ lies in Quadrant III.

(b) Since $\pi < \dfrac{9\pi}{8} < \dfrac{3\pi}{2}$; $\dfrac{9\pi}{8}$ lies in Quadrant III.

10. (a) Since $-\dfrac{\pi}{2} < -1 < 0$; -1 lies in Quadrant IV.

(b) Since $-\pi < -2 < -\dfrac{\pi}{2}$; -2 lies in Quadrant III.

12. (a) Since $\dfrac{3\pi}{2} < 6.02 < 2\pi$; 6.02 lies in Quadrant IV.

(b) Since $-\dfrac{3\pi}{2} < -4.25 < -\pi$; 4.25 lies in Quadrant II.

14. (a) $-\dfrac{7\pi}{4}$

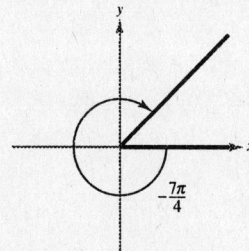

(b) $-\dfrac{5\pi}{2}$

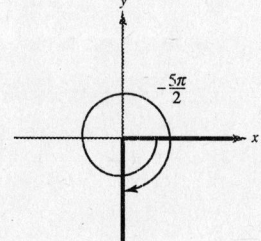

16. (a) 4

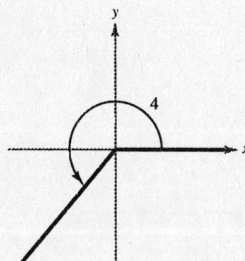

(b) -3

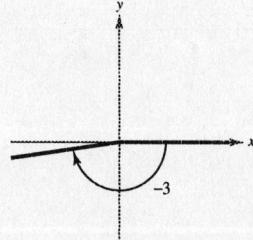

18. (a) $\dfrac{7\pi}{6} + 2\pi = \dfrac{19\pi}{6}$

$\dfrac{7\pi}{6} - 2\pi = -\dfrac{5\pi}{6}$

(b) $-\dfrac{11\pi}{6} + 2\pi = \dfrac{\pi}{6}$

$-\dfrac{11\pi}{6} - 2\pi = -\dfrac{23\pi}{6}$

20. (a) $-\dfrac{9\pi}{4} + 2\pi = -\dfrac{\pi}{4}$

$-\dfrac{9\pi}{4} + 4\pi = \dfrac{7\pi}{4}$

(b) $-\dfrac{2\pi}{15} + 2\pi = \dfrac{28\pi}{15}$

$-\dfrac{2\pi}{15} - 2\pi = -\dfrac{32\pi}{15}$

22. (a) Complement: $\dfrac{\pi}{2} - \dfrac{\pi}{12} = \dfrac{5\pi}{12}$

Supplement: $\pi - \dfrac{\pi}{12} = \dfrac{11\pi}{12}$

(b) Complement: none $\left(\dfrac{11\pi}{12} > \dfrac{\pi}{2}\right)$

Supplement: $\pi - \dfrac{11\pi}{12} = \dfrac{\pi}{12}$

24. (a) Complement: none $\left(3 > \dfrac{\pi}{2}\right)$

Supplement: $\pi - 3 \approx 0.14$

(b) Complement: $\dfrac{\pi}{2} - 1.5 \approx 0.07$

Supplement: $\pi - 1.5 \approx 1.64$

26. (a) $315° = 315°\left(\dfrac{\pi}{180°}\right) = \dfrac{7\pi}{4}$

(b) $120° = 120°\left(\dfrac{\pi}{180°}\right) = \dfrac{2\pi}{3}$

28. (a) $-270° = -270°\left(\dfrac{\pi}{180°}\right) = -\dfrac{3\pi}{2}$

(b) $144° = 144°\left(\dfrac{\pi}{180°}\right) = \dfrac{4\pi}{5}$

30. $87.4° = 87.4°\left(\dfrac{\pi}{180°}\right) \approx 1.525$ radians

32. $-48.27° = -48.27°\left(\dfrac{\pi}{180°}\right) \approx -0.842$ radians

34. $345° = 345°\left(\dfrac{\pi}{180°}\right) \approx 6.021$ radians

36. $0.54° = 0.54°\left(\dfrac{\pi}{180°}\right) \approx 0.009$ radians

38. (a) $-\dfrac{7\pi}{12} = -\dfrac{7\pi}{12}\left(\dfrac{180°}{\pi}\right) = -105°$

(b) $\dfrac{\pi}{9} = \dfrac{\pi}{9}\left(\dfrac{180°}{\pi}\right) = 20°$

40. (a) $\dfrac{11\pi}{6} = \dfrac{11\pi}{6}\left(\dfrac{180°}{\pi}\right) = 330°$

(b) $\dfrac{34\pi}{15} = \dfrac{34\pi}{15}\left(\dfrac{180°}{\pi}\right) = 408°$

42. $\dfrac{5\pi}{11} = \dfrac{5\pi}{11}\left(\dfrac{180°}{\pi}\right) \approx 81.818°$

44. $\dfrac{13\pi}{2} = \dfrac{13\pi}{2}\left(\dfrac{180°}{\pi}\right) = 1170°$

46. $4.8\pi = 4.8\pi\left(\dfrac{180°}{\pi}\right) = 864°$

48. $-0.57 = -0.57\left(\dfrac{180°}{\pi}\right) \approx -32.659°$

50. $120°$

52. $-330°$

54. $10°$

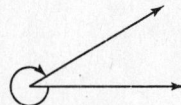

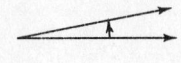

56. (a) Since $0° < 8.3° < 90°$; $8.3°$ lies in Quadrant I.

(b) Since $180° < 257°\,30' < 270°$; $257°\,30'$ lies in Quadrant III.

58. (a) Since $-270° < -260° < -180°$; $-260°$ lies in Quadrant II.

(b) Since $-90° < -3.4° < 0°$; $-3.4°$ lies in Quadrant IV.

60. (a) $-270°$

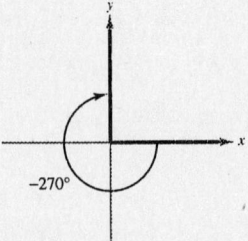

(b) $-120°$

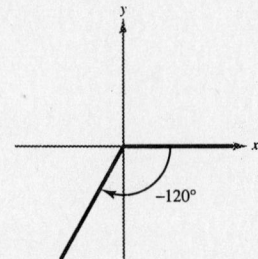

62. (a) $-750°$

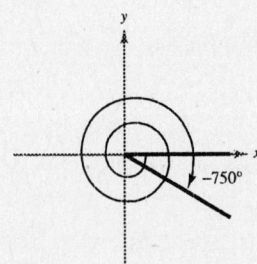

(b) $-600°$

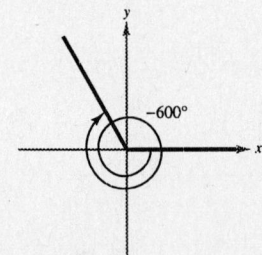

64. (a) $120° + 360° = 480°$

$120° - 360° = -240°$

(b) $-420° + 720° = 300°$

$-420° + 360° = -60°$

66. (a) $-420° + 720° = 300°$

$-420° + 360° = -60°$

(b) $230° + 360° = 590°$

$230° - 360° = -130°$

68. (a) Complement: $90° - 3° = 87°$

Supplement: $180° - 3° = 177°$

(b) Complement: $90° - 64° = 26°$

Supplement: $180° - 64° = 116°$

70. (a) Complement: none $(130° > 90°)$

Supplement: $180° - 130° = 50°$

(b) Complement: none $(170° > 90°)$

Supplement: $180° - 170° = 10°$

72. (a) $245°10' = 245° + \left(\frac{10}{60}\right)°$

$\approx 245° + 0.167°$

$= 245.167°$

(b) $2°12' = 2° + \left(\frac{12}{60}\right)°$

$= 2° + 0.2° = 2.2°$

74. (a) $-135°36'' = -135° - \left(\frac{36}{3600}\right)°$

$= -135° - 0.01° = -135.01°$

(b) $-408°16'20'' = -\left(408° + \left(\frac{16}{60}\right)° + \left(\frac{20}{3600}\right)°\right)$

$\approx -(408° + 0.2667° + 0.0056°)$

$= 408.272°$

76. (a) $-345.12° = -(345° + (0.12)(60'))$

$$= -(345° + 7' + 0.2(60''))$$

$$= -345° 7' 12''$$

(b) $0.45° = 0° + (0.45)(60')$

$$= 0° + 27'$$

$$= 0°27'$$

78. (a) $-0.355° = -(0° + (0.355)(60'))$

$$= -(0° + 21' + (0.3)(60''))$$

$$= -(0° + 21' + 18'')$$

$$= -0°21'18''$$

(b) $0.7865 = 0° + (0.7865)(60')$

$$= 0° + 47' + (0.19)(60'')$$

$$= 0° + 47' + 11.4''$$

$$= 0°47'11.4''$$

80. $s = r\theta$

$29 = 10\,\theta$

$\theta = \frac{29}{10}$ radians

82. $s = r\theta$

$60 = 75\theta$

$\theta = \frac{60}{75} = \frac{4}{5}$ radians

Because the angle represented is clockwise, this angle is $-\frac{4}{5}$ radians.

84. $r = 14$ feet, $s = 8$ feet

$\theta = \dfrac{s}{r} = \dfrac{8}{14} = \dfrac{4}{7}$ radians

86. $r = 80$ kilometers, $s = 160$ kilometers

$\theta = \dfrac{s}{r} = \dfrac{160}{80} = 2$ radians

88. $r = 9$ feet, $\theta = 60° = \dfrac{\pi}{3}$

$s = r\theta = 9\left(\dfrac{\pi}{3}\right) = 3\pi$ feet

90. $r = 20$ centimeters, $\theta = \dfrac{\pi}{4}$

$s = r\theta = 20\left(\dfrac{\pi}{4}\right) = 5\pi$ centimeters

92. $r = 4000$ miles

$\theta = 47° 36' 32'' - 37° 46' 39'' = 9° 49' 53''$

$$\approx 0.1716 \text{ radian}$$

$s = r\theta \approx (4000)(0.1716) \approx 686.36$ miles

94. $r = 4000$ miles

$\theta = 31° 47' + 26° 10' = 57° 57'$

$$\approx 1.0114 \text{ radians}$$

$s = r\theta \approx (4000)(1.0114) \approx 4045.67$ miles

96. $r = 6378$ kilometers, $s = 500$ kilometers

$\theta = \dfrac{s}{r} = \dfrac{500}{6378} \approx 0.0784$ radians $= 0.0784\left(\dfrac{180°}{\pi}\right) \approx 4.49°$

98. $\theta = \dfrac{s}{r} = \dfrac{24}{5} = 4.8$ radians $= 4.8\left(\dfrac{180°}{\pi}\right) \approx 275°$

100. Linear velocity for either pulley: $1700(2\pi) = 3400\pi$ in/min

(a) Angular speed of motor pulley: $\omega = \dfrac{v}{r} = \dfrac{3400\pi}{1} = 3400\pi$ rad/min

Angular speed of the saw arbor: $\omega = \dfrac{v}{r} = \dfrac{3400\pi}{2} = 1700\pi$ rad/min

(b) Revolutions per minute of the saw arbor: $\dfrac{1700\pi}{2\pi} = 850$ rev/min

102. (a) Arc length of larger sprocket in feet:

$$s = r\theta$$

$$s = \frac{1}{3}(2\pi) = \frac{2\pi}{3} \text{ feet}$$

Therefore, the chain moves $\dfrac{2\pi}{3}$ feet as does the smaller rear sprocket.

Thus, the angle θ of the smaller sprocket is $\left(r = 2 \text{ inches} = \dfrac{2}{12} \text{ feet}\right)$.

$$\theta = \frac{s}{r} = \frac{\dfrac{2\pi}{3} \text{ ft}}{\dfrac{2}{12} \text{ ft}} = 4\pi$$

and the arc length of the tire in feet is:

$$s = \theta r$$

$$s = (4\pi)\left(\frac{14}{12}\right) = \frac{14\pi}{3} \text{ feet}$$

$$\text{Speed} = \frac{s}{t} = \frac{\dfrac{14\pi}{3}}{1 \text{ sec}} = \frac{14\pi}{3} \text{ feet per second}$$

(b) $\dfrac{14\pi \text{ feet}}{3 \text{ seconds}} \times \dfrac{3600 \text{ seconds}}{1 \text{ hour}} \times \dfrac{1 \text{ mile}}{5280 \text{ feet}} \approx 10$ miles per hour

104. True. If α and β are coterminal angles,

then

$$\alpha = \beta + n(360°)$$

where n is an integer.

The difference between α and β

is $\alpha - \beta = n(360°)$

$$= 2\pi n$$

106. Increases, since the linear speed is proportional to the radius.

108. The arc length is increasing. In order for the angle θ to remain constant as the radius r increases, the arc length s must increase in proportion to r, as can be seen from the formula $s = r\theta$.

110. $f(x) = (x - 2)^5$

Graph of $y = x^5$ shifted to the right by 2 units.

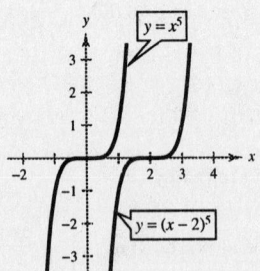

112. $f(x) = 2 - x^5$

Graph of $y = x^5$ reflected in x-axis and shifted upward by 2 units.

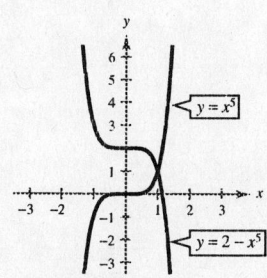

114. Horizontal asymptote: $y = 0$

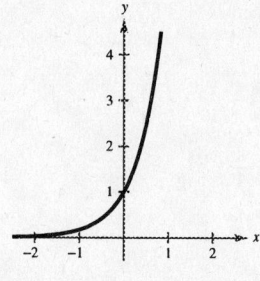

116. Reflection in the y-axis of the graph of $y = 6^x$.

Horizontal asymptote: $y = 0$

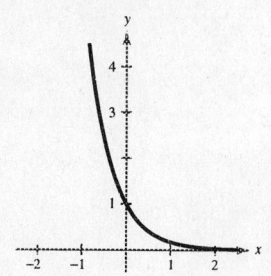

118. Vertical asymptote: $x = 0$

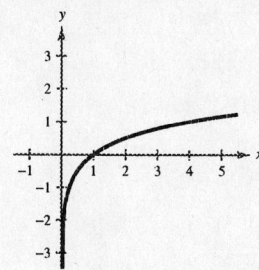

120. Reflection in the x-axis of the graph of $y = \log_4 x$.

Vertical asymptote: $x = 0$

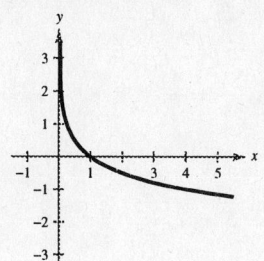

122. Reflection in the y-axis of the graph of $y = \log_4(x)$

Vertical asymptote: $x = 0$

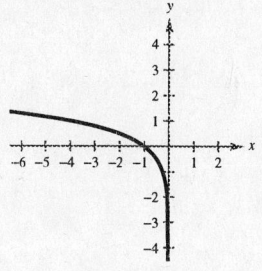

124. $\dfrac{4}{4\sqrt{2}} = \dfrac{4}{4\sqrt{2}} \cdot \dfrac{\sqrt{2}}{\sqrt{2}} = \dfrac{4\sqrt{2}}{8} = \dfrac{\sqrt{2}}{2}$

126. $\dfrac{2\sqrt{3}}{\sqrt{6}} = 2\sqrt{\dfrac{3}{6}} = 2\sqrt{\dfrac{1}{2}} = \dfrac{2}{\sqrt{2}} \cdot \dfrac{\sqrt{2}}{\sqrt{2}} = \sqrt{2}$

128. $\sqrt{2^2 + 6^2} = \sqrt{4 + 36} = \sqrt{40} = \sqrt{4 \cdot 10} = 2\sqrt{10}$

130. $\sqrt{18^2 - 6^2} = \sqrt{324 - 36} = \sqrt{288} = \sqrt{144 \cdot 2} = 12\sqrt{2}$

Section 4.2   Trigonometric Functions: The Unit Circle

2. $x = 12, y = 5$

$r = \sqrt{12^2 + 5^2} = 13$

$\sin \theta = \dfrac{y}{r} = \dfrac{5}{13}$ $\csc \theta = \dfrac{r}{y} = \dfrac{13}{5}$

$\cos \theta = \dfrac{x}{r} = \dfrac{12}{13}$ $\sec \theta = \dfrac{r}{x} = \dfrac{13}{12}$

$\tan \theta = \dfrac{y}{x} = \dfrac{5}{12}$ $\cot \theta = \dfrac{x}{y} = \dfrac{12}{5}$

4. $x = -4, y = -3$

$r = \sqrt{(-4)^2 + (-3)^2} = 5$

$\sin \theta = \dfrac{y}{r} = -\dfrac{3}{5}$ $\csc \theta = \dfrac{r}{y} = -\dfrac{5}{3}$

$\cos \theta = \dfrac{x}{r} = -\dfrac{4}{5}$ $\sec \theta = \dfrac{r}{x} = -\dfrac{5}{4}$

$\tan \theta = \dfrac{y}{x} = \dfrac{3}{4}$ $\cot \theta = \dfrac{x}{y} = \dfrac{4}{3}$

6. $t = \dfrac{\pi}{3}, (x\,y) = \left(\dfrac{1}{2}, \dfrac{\sqrt{3}}{2}\right)$

8. $t = \dfrac{5\pi}{4}, (x, y) = \left(-\dfrac{\sqrt{2}}{2}, -\dfrac{\sqrt{2}}{2}\right)$

10. $t = \dfrac{5\pi}{3}, (x, y) = \left(\dfrac{1}{2}, -\dfrac{\sqrt{3}}{2}\right)$

12. $t = \pi, (x, y) = (-1, 0)$

14. $t = \dfrac{\pi}{3}, (x, y) = \left(\dfrac{1}{2}, \dfrac{\sqrt{3}}{2}\right)$

$\sin \dfrac{\pi}{3} = \dfrac{\sqrt{3}}{2}$

$\cos \dfrac{\pi}{3} = \dfrac{1}{2}$

$\tan \dfrac{\pi}{3} = \dfrac{\frac{\sqrt{3}}{2}}{\frac{1}{2}} = \sqrt{3}$

16. $t = -\dfrac{\pi}{4}, (x, y) = \left(\dfrac{\sqrt{2}}{2}, -\dfrac{\sqrt{2}}{2}\right)$

$\sin\left(-\dfrac{\pi}{4}\right) = -\dfrac{\sqrt{2}}{2}$

$\cos\left(-\dfrac{\pi}{4}\right) = \dfrac{\sqrt{2}}{2}$

$\tan\left(-\dfrac{\pi}{4}\right) = \dfrac{-\frac{\sqrt{2}}{2}}{\frac{\sqrt{2}}{2}} = -1$

18. $t = -\dfrac{4\pi}{3}, (x, y) = \left(-\dfrac{1}{2}, \dfrac{\sqrt{3}}{2}\right)$

$\sin\left(-\dfrac{4\pi}{3}\right) = \dfrac{\sqrt{3}}{2}$

$\cos\left(-\dfrac{4\pi}{3}\right) = -\dfrac{1}{2}$

$\tan\left(-\dfrac{4\pi}{3}\right) = \dfrac{\frac{\sqrt{3}}{2}}{-\frac{1}{2}} = -\sqrt{3}$

20. $t = \dfrac{5\pi}{3}, (x, y) = \left(\dfrac{1}{2}, -\dfrac{\sqrt{3}}{2}\right)$

$\sin \dfrac{5\pi}{3} = -\dfrac{\sqrt{3}}{2}$

$\cos \dfrac{5\pi}{3} = \dfrac{1}{2}$

$\tan \dfrac{5\pi}{3} = \dfrac{-\frac{\sqrt{3}}{2}}{\frac{1}{2}} = -\sqrt{3}$

22. $t = -2\pi, (x, y) = (1, 0)$

$\sin(-2\pi) = 0$

$\cos(-2\pi) = 1$

$\tan(-2\pi) = \dfrac{0}{1} = 0$

24. $t = \dfrac{5\pi}{6}, (x, y) = \left(-\dfrac{\sqrt{3}}{2}, \dfrac{1}{2}\right)$

$\sin \dfrac{5\pi}{6} = \dfrac{1}{2}$

$\cos \dfrac{5\pi}{6} = -\dfrac{\sqrt{3}}{2}$

$\tan \dfrac{5\pi}{6} = \dfrac{\frac{1}{2}}{-\frac{\sqrt{3}}{2}} = -\dfrac{\sqrt{3}}{3}$

$\csc \dfrac{5\pi}{6} = \dfrac{1}{\sin t} = 2$

$\sec \dfrac{5\pi}{6} = \dfrac{1}{\cos t} = -\dfrac{2\sqrt{3}}{3}$

$\cot \dfrac{5\pi}{6} = \dfrac{1}{\tan t} = -\sqrt{3}$

26. $t = \dfrac{3\pi}{2}, (x, y) = (0, -1)$

$\sin \dfrac{3\pi}{2} = -1$

$\cos \dfrac{3\pi}{2} = 0$

$\tan \dfrac{3\pi}{2}$ is undefined.

$\csc \dfrac{3\pi}{2} = \dfrac{1}{\sin t} = -1$

$\sec \dfrac{3\pi}{2}$ is undefined.

$\cot \dfrac{3\pi}{2} = \dfrac{0}{-1} = 0$

28. $t = -\dfrac{3\pi}{2}, (x, y) = (0, 1)$

$\sin\left(-\dfrac{3\pi}{2}\right) = 1$

$\cos\left(-\dfrac{3\pi}{2}\right) = 0$

$\tan\left(-\dfrac{3\pi}{2}\right)$ is undefined.

$\csc\left(-\dfrac{3\pi}{2}\right) = \dfrac{1}{\sin t} = 1$

$\sec\left(-\dfrac{3\pi}{2}\right)$ is undefined.

$\cot\left(-\dfrac{3\pi}{2}\right) = \dfrac{0}{1} = 0$

30. $\cos 5\pi = \cos \pi = -1$

32. $\sin \dfrac{9\pi}{4} = \sin \dfrac{\pi}{4} = \dfrac{\sqrt{2}}{2}$

34. $\sin -3\pi = \sin(-\pi) = 0$

36. $\cos\left(-\dfrac{8\pi}{3}\right) = \cos\dfrac{4\pi}{3} = -\dfrac{1}{2}$

38. $\sin(-t) = \dfrac{3}{8}$

    (a) $\sin t = -\sin(-t) = -\dfrac{3}{8}$

    (b) $\csc t = \dfrac{1}{\sin t} = -\dfrac{8}{3}$

40. $\cos t = -\dfrac{3}{4}$

    (a) $\cos(-t) = \cos t = -\dfrac{3}{4}$

    (b) $\sec(-t) = \sec t = \dfrac{1}{\cos t} = -\dfrac{4}{3}$

42. $\cos t = \dfrac{4}{5}$

    (a) $\cos(\pi - t) = -\cos t = -\dfrac{4}{5}$

    (b) $\cos(t + \pi) = -\cos t = -\dfrac{4}{5}$

44. $\tan\dfrac{\pi}{3} \approx 1.7321$

46. $\cot 1 \approx 0.6421$

48. $\cos(-2.5) \approx -0.8011$

50. $\sec 1.8 \approx -4.4014$

52. $\sin(-0.9) \approx -0.7833$

54. (a) $\sin 0.75 = y \approx 0.7$

    (b) $\cos 2.5 = x \approx -0.8$

56. (a) $\sin t = -0.75$

       $t \approx 4.0$ or $t \approx 5.4$

    (b) $\cos t = 0.75$

       $t \approx 0.7$ or $t \approx 5.6$

58. $\sin 1 = \sin(0.25 + 0.75) \approx 0.8415$

    $\sin 0.25 + \sin 0.75 \approx 0.2474 + 0.6816$

                  ≈ 0.9290

60. $y(t) = \dfrac{1}{4}e^{-t}\cos 6t$

    (a) $t = 0$ $y(0) = \dfrac{1}{4}e^{-0}\cos 0 = \dfrac{1}{4} = 0.2500$ foot

    (b) $t = \dfrac{1}{4}$ $y\left(\dfrac{1}{4}\right) = \dfrac{1}{4}e^{-1/4}\cos\left(6 \cdot \dfrac{1}{4}\right) \approx 0.0138$ foot

    (c) $t = \dfrac{1}{2}$ $y\left(\dfrac{1}{2}\right) = \dfrac{1}{4}e^{-1/2}\cos\left(6 \cdot \dfrac{1}{2}\right) \approx -0.1501$ foot

62. True. $\tan a = \tan(a - 6\pi)$ since the period of tan is π.

64. (a) (x_1, y_1) and (x_2, y_2) are symmetric about the origin.

    (b) Since $(x_2, y_2) = (-x_1, -y_1)$, $\sin(t_1 + \pi) = -\sin t_1$.

    (c) Since $(x_2, y_2) = (-x_1, -y_1)$, $\cos(t_1 + \pi) = -\cos t_1$.

66. $h(t) = f(t)g(t)$ is an odd function, since

    $h(-t) = f(-t)g(-t)$

        $= -f(t)g(t)$

        $= -h(t)$

68. $f(x) = \dfrac{1}{2}(3x - 2)$

    $y = \dfrac{1}{2}(3x - 2)$

    $x = \dfrac{1}{2}(3y - 2)$

    $2x = 3y - 2$

    $\dfrac{2}{3}x + \dfrac{2}{3} = y$

    $f^{-1}(x) = \dfrac{2}{3}x + \dfrac{2}{3}$

70. $f(x) = \sqrt{x^2 - 4},\ x \geq 2$

    $y = \sqrt{x^2 - 4}$

    $x = \sqrt{y^2 - 4}$

    $x^2 = y^2 - 4$

    $\pm\sqrt{x^2 + 4} = y$

    $f^{-1}(x) = \sqrt{x^2 + 4}$

Section 4.3   Right Triangle Trigonometry

2.

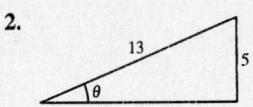

$$\text{adj} = \sqrt{13^2 - 5^2} = \sqrt{169 - 25} = 12$$

$$\sin \theta = \frac{\text{opp}}{\text{hyp}} = \frac{5}{13} \qquad \csc \theta = \frac{\text{hyp}}{\text{opp}} = \frac{13}{5}$$

$$\cos \theta = \frac{\text{adj}}{\text{hyp}} = \frac{12}{13} \qquad \sec \theta = \frac{\text{hyp}}{\text{adj}} = \frac{13}{12}$$

$$\tan \theta = \frac{\text{opp}}{\text{adj}} = \frac{5}{12} \qquad \cot \theta = \frac{\text{adj}}{\text{opp}} = \frac{12}{5}$$

4.

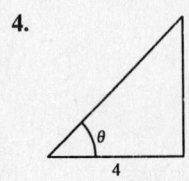

$$\text{hyp} = \sqrt{4^2 + 4^2} = \sqrt{32} = 4\sqrt{2}$$

$$\sin \theta = \frac{\text{opp}}{\text{hyp}} = \frac{4}{4\sqrt{2}} = \frac{1}{\sqrt{2}} = \frac{\sqrt{2}}{2} \qquad \csc \theta = \frac{\text{hyp}}{\text{opp}} = \frac{4\sqrt{2}}{4} = \sqrt{2}$$

$$\cos \theta = \frac{\text{adj}}{\text{hyp}} = \frac{4}{4\sqrt{2}} = \frac{1}{\sqrt{2}} = \frac{\sqrt{2}}{2} \qquad \sec \theta = \frac{\text{hyp}}{\text{adj}} = \frac{4\sqrt{2}}{4} = \sqrt{2}$$

$$\tan \theta = \frac{\text{opp}}{\text{adj}} = \frac{4}{4} = 1 \qquad \cot \theta = \frac{\text{adj}}{\text{opp}} = \frac{4}{4} = 1$$

6.

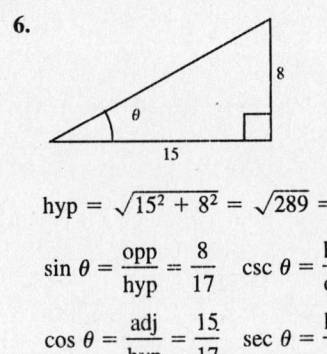

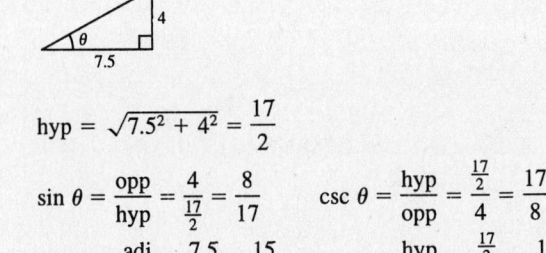

$$\text{hyp} = \sqrt{15^2 + 8^2} = \sqrt{289} = 17$$

$$\sin \theta = \frac{\text{opp}}{\text{hyp}} = \frac{8}{17} \qquad \csc \theta = \frac{\text{hyp}}{\text{opp}} = \frac{17}{8}$$

$$\cos \theta = \frac{\text{adj}}{\text{hyp}} = \frac{15}{17} \qquad \sec \theta = \frac{\text{hyp}}{\text{adj}} = \frac{17}{15}$$

$$\tan \theta = \frac{\text{opp}}{\text{adj}} = \frac{8}{15} \qquad \cot \theta = \frac{\text{adj}}{\text{opp}} = \frac{15}{8}$$

$$\text{hyp} = \sqrt{7.5^2 + 4^2} = \frac{17}{2}$$

$$\sin \theta = \frac{\text{opp}}{\text{hyp}} = \frac{4}{\frac{17}{2}} = \frac{8}{17} \qquad \csc \theta = \frac{\text{hyp}}{\text{opp}} = \frac{\frac{17}{2}}{4} = \frac{17}{8}$$

$$\cos \theta = \frac{\text{adj}}{\text{hyp}} = \frac{7.5}{\frac{17}{2}} = \frac{15}{17} \qquad \sec \theta = \frac{\text{hyp}}{\text{adj}} = \frac{\frac{17}{2}}{7.5} = \frac{17}{15}$$

$$\tan \theta = \frac{\text{opp}}{\text{adj}} = \frac{4}{7.5} = \frac{8}{15} \qquad \cot \theta = \frac{\text{adj}}{\text{opp}} = \frac{7.5}{4} = \frac{15}{8}$$

The function values are the same because the triangles are similar, and corresponding sides are proportional.

8.

$$\text{hyp} = \sqrt{1^2 + 2^2} = \sqrt{5}$$

$$\sin \theta = \frac{\text{opp}}{\text{hyp}} = \frac{1}{\sqrt{5}} = \frac{\sqrt{5}}{5} \qquad \csc \theta = \frac{\text{hyp}}{\text{opp}} = \frac{\sqrt{5}}{1} = \sqrt{5}$$

$$\cos \theta = \frac{\text{adj}}{\text{hyp}} = \frac{2}{\sqrt{5}} = \frac{2\sqrt{5}}{5} \qquad \sec \theta = \frac{\text{hyp}}{\text{adj}} = \frac{\sqrt{5}}{2}$$

$$\tan \theta = \frac{\text{opp}}{\text{adj}} = \frac{1}{2} \qquad \cot \theta = \frac{\text{adj}}{\text{opp}} = \frac{2}{1} = 2$$

$$\text{hyp} = \sqrt{3^2 + 6^2} = 3\sqrt{5}$$

$$\sin \theta = \frac{3}{3\sqrt{5}} = \frac{1}{\sqrt{5}} = \frac{\sqrt{5}}{5} \qquad \csc \theta = \frac{3\sqrt{5}}{3} = \sqrt{5}$$

$$\cos \theta = \frac{6}{3\sqrt{5}} = \frac{2}{\sqrt{5}} = \frac{2\sqrt{5}}{5} \qquad \sec \theta = \frac{3\sqrt{5}}{6} = \frac{\sqrt{5}}{2}$$

$$\tan \theta = \frac{3}{6} = \frac{1}{2} \qquad \cot \theta = \frac{6}{3} = 2$$

The function values are the same because the triangles are similar, and corresponding sides are proportional.

10.

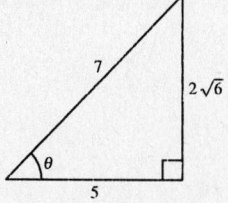

$$\text{hyp} = \sqrt{7^2 - 5^2} = \sqrt{24} = 2\sqrt{6}$$

$$\sin \theta = \frac{\text{opp}}{\text{hyp}} = \frac{2\sqrt{6}}{7}$$

$$\tan \theta = \frac{\text{opp}}{\text{adj}} = \frac{2\sqrt{6}}{5}$$

$$\csc \theta = \frac{1}{\sin \theta} = \frac{7}{2\sqrt{6}} = \frac{7\sqrt{6}}{12}$$

$$\sec \theta = \frac{1}{\cos \theta} = \frac{7}{5}$$

$$\cot \theta = \frac{1}{\tan \theta} = \frac{5}{2\sqrt{6}} = \frac{5\sqrt{6}}{12}$$

12.

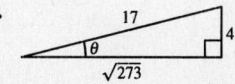

$$\text{hyp} = \sqrt{5^2 + 1^2} = \sqrt{26}$$

$$\sin \theta = \frac{\text{opp}}{\text{hyp}} = \frac{1}{\sqrt{26}} = \frac{\sqrt{26}}{26}$$

$$\cos \theta = \frac{\text{adj}}{\text{hyp}} = \frac{5}{\sqrt{26}} = \frac{5\sqrt{26}}{26}$$

$$\tan \theta = \frac{\text{opp}}{\text{adj}} = \frac{1}{5}$$

$$\csc \theta = \frac{\text{hyp}}{\text{opp}} = \frac{\sqrt{26}}{1} = \sqrt{26}$$

$$\sec \theta = \frac{\text{hyp}}{\text{adj}} = \frac{\sqrt{26}}{5}$$

14.

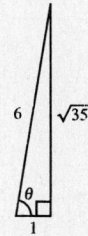

$$\text{opp} = \sqrt{6^2 - 1^2} = \sqrt{35}$$

$$\sin \theta = \frac{\text{opp}}{\text{hyp}} = \frac{\sqrt{35}}{6}$$

$$\cos \theta = \frac{\text{adj}}{\text{hyp}} = \frac{1}{6}$$

$$\tan \theta = \frac{\text{opp}}{\text{adj}} = \frac{\sqrt{35}}{1} = \sqrt{35}$$

$$\csc \theta = \frac{\text{hyp}}{\text{opp}} = \frac{6}{\sqrt{35}} = \frac{6\sqrt{35}}{35}$$

$$\cot \theta = \frac{\text{adj}}{\text{opp}} = \frac{1}{\sqrt{35}} = \frac{\sqrt{35}}{35}$$

16.

$$\text{adj} = \sqrt{17^2 - 4^2} = \sqrt{273}$$

$$\sin \theta = \frac{\text{opp}}{\text{hyp}} = \frac{4}{17}$$

$$\cos \theta = \frac{\text{adj}}{\text{hyp}} = \frac{\sqrt{273}}{17}$$

$$\tan \theta = \frac{\text{opp}}{\text{adj}} = \frac{4}{\sqrt{273}} = \frac{4\sqrt{273}}{273}$$

$$\sec \theta = \frac{1}{\cos \theta} = \frac{17}{\sqrt{273}} = \frac{17\sqrt{273}}{273}$$

$$\cot \theta = \frac{1}{\tan \theta} = \frac{\sqrt{273}}{4}$$

18. $\sin 30° = \dfrac{1}{2}$, $\tan 30° = \dfrac{\sqrt{3}}{3}$

   (a) $\csc 30° = \dfrac{1}{\sin 30°} = 2$

   (b) $\cot 60° = \tan(90° - 60°) = \tan 30° = \dfrac{\sqrt{3}}{3}$

   (c) $\cos 30° = \dfrac{\sin 30°}{\tan 30°} = \dfrac{\frac{1}{2}}{\frac{\sqrt{3}}{3}} = \dfrac{3}{2\sqrt{3}} = \dfrac{\sqrt{3}}{2}$

   (d) $\cot 30° = \dfrac{1}{\tan 30°} = \dfrac{3}{\sqrt{3}} = \dfrac{3\sqrt{3}}{3} = \sqrt{3}$

20. $\sec \theta = 5$, $\tan \theta = 2\sqrt{6}$

   (a) $\cos \theta = \dfrac{1}{\sec \theta} = \dfrac{1}{5}$

   (b) $\cot \theta = \dfrac{1}{\tan \theta} = \dfrac{1}{2\sqrt{6}} = \dfrac{\sqrt{6}}{12}$

   (c) $\cot(90° - \theta) = \tan \theta = 2\sqrt{6}$

   (d) $\sin \theta = \tan \theta \cos \theta = \left(2\sqrt{6}\right)\left(\dfrac{1}{5}\right) = \dfrac{2\sqrt{6}}{5}$

22. $\tan \beta = 5$

   (a) $\cot \beta = \dfrac{1}{\tan \beta} = \dfrac{1}{5}$

   (b) $\cos \beta = \dfrac{1}{\sqrt{1 + \tan^2 \beta}} = \dfrac{1}{\sqrt{1 + 5^2}}$

          $= \dfrac{1}{\sqrt{26}} = \dfrac{\sqrt{26}}{26}$

   (c) $\tan(90° - \beta) = \cot \beta = \dfrac{1}{\tan \beta} = \dfrac{1}{5}$

   (d) $\csc \beta = \sqrt{1 + \cot^2 \beta}$

          $= \sqrt{1 + \left(\dfrac{1}{5}\right)^2}$

          $= \sqrt{1 + \dfrac{1}{25}} = \sqrt{\dfrac{26}{25}} = \dfrac{\sqrt{26}}{5}$

24. (a) $\cot 45° = \dfrac{1}{1} = 1$

   (b) $\cos 45° = \dfrac{1}{\sqrt{2}} = \dfrac{\sqrt{2}}{2}$

   (c) $\csc 45° = \dfrac{\sqrt{2}}{1} = \sqrt{2}$

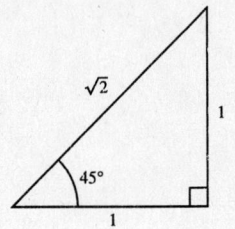

26. (a) $\sin 60° = \dfrac{\sqrt{3}}{2}$

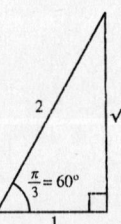

   (b) $\tan 45° = \dfrac{1}{1} = 1$

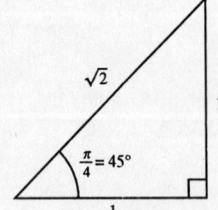

   (c) $\sec 30° = \dfrac{2}{\sqrt{3}} = \dfrac{2\sqrt{3}}{3}$

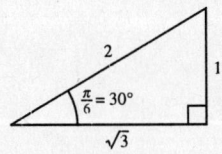

28. (a) $\tan 23.5° \approx 0.4348$

   (b) $\cot 66.5° = \dfrac{1}{\tan 66.5°} \approx 0.4348$

30. (a) $\cos 16° \, 18' = \cos\left(16 + \dfrac{18}{60}\right)° \approx 0.9598$

   (b) $\sin 73° \, 56' = \sin\left(73 + \dfrac{56}{60}\right)° \approx 0.9609$

32. (a) $\cos 4° \, 50' \, 15'' = \cos\left(4 + \dfrac{50}{60} + \dfrac{15}{3600}\right)°$

≈ 0.9964

(b) $\sec 4° \, 50' \, 15'' = \dfrac{1}{\cos 4° \, 50' \, 15''}$

≈ 1.0036

34. (a) $\sec 56° \, 8' \, 10'' = \sec\left(56 + \dfrac{8}{60} = \dfrac{10}{3600}\right)° \approx 1.7946$

(b) $\cos 56° \, 8' \, 10'' = \cos\left(56 + \dfrac{8}{60} + \dfrac{10}{3600}\right)° \approx 0.5572$

36. (a) $\sec\left(\dfrac{9}{5} \cdot 20 + 32\right)° \approx 2.6695$

(b) $\cot\left(\dfrac{9}{5} \cdot 30 + 32\right)° \approx 0.0699$

38. (a) $\cos \theta = \dfrac{\sqrt{2}}{2} \Longrightarrow \theta = 45° = \dfrac{\pi}{4}$

(b) $\tan \theta = 1 \Longrightarrow \theta = 45° = \dfrac{\pi}{4}$

40. (a) $\tan \theta = \sqrt{3} \Longrightarrow \theta = 60° = \dfrac{\pi}{3}$

(b) $\cos \theta = \dfrac{1}{2} \Longrightarrow \theta = 60° = \dfrac{\pi}{3}$

42. (a) $\cot \theta = \dfrac{\sqrt{3}}{3}$

$\tan \theta = \dfrac{3}{\sqrt{3}} = \sqrt{3} \Longrightarrow \theta = 60° = \dfrac{\pi}{3}$

(b) $\sec \theta = \sqrt{2}$

$\cos \theta = \dfrac{1}{\sqrt{2}} = \dfrac{\sqrt{2}}{2} \Longrightarrow \theta = 45° = \dfrac{\pi}{4}$

44. (a) $\cos \theta = 0.9848 \Longrightarrow \theta \approx 10° \approx 0.175$

(b) $\cos \theta = 0.8746 \Longrightarrow \theta \approx 29° \approx 0.506$

46. (a) $\sin \theta = 0.3746 \Longrightarrow \theta \approx 22° \approx 0.384$

(b) $\cos \theta = 0.3746 \Longrightarrow \theta \approx 68° \approx 1.187$

48. $\sin 60° = \dfrac{y}{18}$

$y = 18 \sin 60° = 18 \dfrac{\sqrt{3}}{2}$

$= 9\sqrt{3}$

50. $\sin 45° = \dfrac{20}{r}$

$r = \dfrac{20}{\sin 45°} = \dfrac{20}{\dfrac{\sqrt{2}}{2}} = 20\sqrt{2}$

52. $\cos \theta \sec \theta = \cos \theta \dfrac{1}{\cos \theta} = 1$

54. $\cot \alpha \sin \alpha = \dfrac{\cos \alpha}{\sin \alpha} \sin \alpha = \cos \alpha$

56. $(1 + \sin \theta)(1 - \sin \theta) = 1 - \sin^2 \theta = \cos^2 \theta$

58. $\sin^2 \theta - \cos^2 \theta = \sin^2 \theta - (1 - \sin^2 \theta)$

$= \sin^2 \theta - 1 + \sin^2 \theta$

$= 2 \sin^2 \theta - 1$

60. $\dfrac{\tan \beta + \cot \beta}{\tan \beta} = \dfrac{\tan \beta}{\tan \beta} + \dfrac{\cot \beta}{\tan \beta}$

$= 1 + \dfrac{\cot \beta}{\left(\dfrac{1}{\cot \beta}\right)}$

$= 1 + \cot^2 \beta = \csc^2 \beta$

62. $\dfrac{h}{30} = \dfrac{6}{10}$

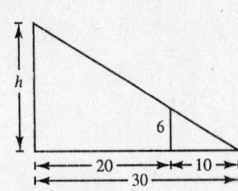

$h = 30\dfrac{6}{10} = 18$ feet

64. $\tan\theta = \dfrac{\text{opp}}{\text{adj}}$

$\tan 54° = \dfrac{w}{100}$

$w = 100\tan 54° \approx 137.6$ feet

66. (a)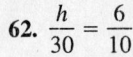

(b) $\sin\theta = \dfrac{\text{opp}}{\text{hyp}}$

$\sin\theta = \dfrac{3\frac{1}{3}}{20}$

(c) $\sin\theta = \dfrac{1}{6} \Longrightarrow \theta = 9.59°$

68. $\tan 3° = \dfrac{x}{15}$

$x = 15\tan 3°$

$d = 5 + 2x = 5 + 2(15\tan 3°) \approx 6.57$ centimeters

70. $x \approx 2.588,\ y \approx 9.659$

$\sin 75° = \dfrac{y}{10} \approx 0.97 \qquad \csc 75° = \dfrac{10}{y} \approx 1.04$

$\cos 75° = \dfrac{x}{10} \approx 0.26 \qquad \sec 75° = \dfrac{10}{x} \approx 3.86$

$\tan 75° = \dfrac{y}{x} \approx 3.73 \qquad \cot 75° = \dfrac{x}{y} \approx 0.27$

72. $\sec 30° = \csc 60°$

True, because $\sec(90° - \theta) = \csc\theta$.

74. $\cot^2 10° - \csc^2 10° = -1$

True, because

$1 + \cot^2\theta = \csc^2\theta$

$\cot^2\theta = \csc^2\theta - 1$

$\cot^2\theta - \csc^2\theta = -1.$

76. $\tan[(5°)^2] = \tan^2(5°)$

False.

$\tan[(5°)^2] = \tan 25° \approx 0.4663$

$\tan^2(5°) = (\tan 5°)(\tan 5°)$

≈ 0.0077

78. Yes. Given $\tan\theta$, $\sec\theta$ can be found from the identity $1 + \tan^2\theta = \sec^2\theta$.

80. (a)

θ	0°	18°	36°	54°	72°	90°
$\sin\theta$	0	0.3090	0.5878	0.8090	0.9511	1
$\cos\theta$	1	0.9511	0.8090	0.5878	0.3090	0

(b) $\sin\theta$ increases from 0 to 1.

(c) $\cos\theta$ decreases from 1 to 0.

(d) As the angle increases the length of the side opposite the angle increases relative to the length of the hypotenuse and the length of the side adjacent to the angle decreases relative to the length of the hypotenuse. Thus the sine increases and the cosine decreases.

82. $\dfrac{2t^2 + 5t - 12}{9 - 4t^2} \div \dfrac{t^2 - 16}{4t^2 + 12t + 9} = \dfrac{2t^2 + 5t - 12}{9 - 4t^2} \cdot \dfrac{4t^2 + 12t + 9}{t^2 - 16}$

$$= \dfrac{(2t - 3)(t + 4)}{(3 + 2t)(3 - 2t)} \cdot \dfrac{(2t + 3)(2t + 3)}{(t + 4)(t - 4)} = -\dfrac{(2t + 3)}{(t - 4)}$$

$$= \dfrac{2t + 3}{4 - t}, t \neq \pm\dfrac{3}{2}, -4$$

84. $\dfrac{\left(\dfrac{3}{x} - \dfrac{1}{4}\right)}{\left(\dfrac{12}{x} - 1\right)} = \dfrac{\dfrac{12 - x}{4x}}{\dfrac{12 - x}{x}} = \dfrac{12 - x}{4x} \cdot \dfrac{x}{12 - x} = \dfrac{1}{4}, x \neq 0, 12$

86. $\dfrac{6}{x} = \dfrac{72}{9x^2 - 6x}$

$6(9x^2 - 6x) = x(72)$

$54x^2 - 36x = 72x$

$54x^2 - 108x = 0$

$54x(x - 2) = 0$

$x = 0, 2$

$x = 2$ is the only solution of the original equation.

88. $\dfrac{3x + 2}{x^2 + x - 2} = \dfrac{4}{x + 2} - \dfrac{2}{1 - x}$

$\dfrac{3x + 2}{(x + 2)(x - 1)} = \dfrac{4}{x + 2} + \dfrac{2}{x - 1}$

$\dfrac{3x + 2}{(x + 2)(x - 1)} = \dfrac{4(x - 1) + 2(x + 2)}{(x + 2)(x - 1)}$

$3x + 2 = 4x - 4 + 2x + 4$

$-3x + 2 = 0$

$x = \dfrac{2}{3}$

Section 4.4   Trigonometric Functions of Any Angle

2. (a) $x = -12, y = -5$

$r = \sqrt{(-12)^2 + (-5)^2} = 13$

$\sin \theta = \dfrac{y}{r} = -\dfrac{5}{13}$

$\cos \theta = \dfrac{x}{r} = -\dfrac{12}{13}$

$\tan \theta = \dfrac{y}{x} = \dfrac{-5}{-12} = \dfrac{5}{12}$

$\csc \theta = \dfrac{r}{y} = \dfrac{13}{-5} = \dfrac{13}{-5}$

$\sec \theta = \dfrac{r}{x} = \dfrac{13}{-12} = -\dfrac{13}{12}$

$\cot \theta = \dfrac{x}{y} = \dfrac{-12}{-5} = \dfrac{12}{5}$

(b) $x = -1, y = 1$

$r = \sqrt{(-1)^2 + 1^2} = \sqrt{2}$

$\sin \theta = \dfrac{y}{r} = \dfrac{1}{\sqrt{2}} = \dfrac{\sqrt{2}}{2}$

$\cos \theta = \dfrac{x}{r} = \dfrac{-1}{\sqrt{2}} = -\dfrac{\sqrt{2}}{2}$

$\tan \theta = \dfrac{y}{x} = \dfrac{1}{-1} = -1$

$\csc \theta = \dfrac{r}{y} = \dfrac{\sqrt{2}}{1} = \sqrt{2}$

$\sec \theta = \dfrac{r}{x} = \dfrac{\sqrt{2}}{-1} = -\sqrt{2}$

$\cot \theta = \dfrac{x}{y} = \dfrac{-1}{1} = -1$

4. (a) $x = 3, y = 1$

$$r = \sqrt{3^2 + 1^2} = \sqrt{10}$$

$$\sin \theta = \frac{y}{r} = \frac{1}{\sqrt{10}} = \frac{\sqrt{10}}{10}$$

$$\cos \theta = \frac{x}{r} = \frac{3}{\sqrt{10}} = \frac{3\sqrt{10}}{10}$$

$$\tan \theta = \frac{y}{x} = \frac{1}{3}$$

$$\csc \theta = \frac{r}{y} = \frac{\sqrt{10}}{1} = \sqrt{10}$$

$$\sec \theta = \frac{r}{x} = \frac{\sqrt{10}}{3}$$

$$\cot \theta = \frac{x}{y} = \frac{3}{1} = 3$$

(b) $x = 4, y = -4$

$$r = \sqrt{4^2 + (-4)^2} = 4\sqrt{2}$$

$$\sin \theta = \frac{y}{r} = \frac{-4}{4\sqrt{2}} = -\frac{\sqrt{2}}{2}$$

$$\cos \theta = \frac{x}{r} = \frac{4}{4\sqrt{2}} = \frac{\sqrt{2}}{2}$$

$$\tan \theta = \frac{y}{x} = \frac{-4}{4} = -1$$

$$\csc \theta = \frac{r}{y} = \frac{4\sqrt{2}}{-4} = -\sqrt{2}$$

$$\sec \theta = \frac{r}{x} = \frac{4\sqrt{2}}{4} = \sqrt{2}$$

$$\cot \theta = \frac{x}{y} = \frac{4}{-4} = -1$$

6. $x = 8, y = 15$

$$r = \sqrt{8^2 + 15^2} = 17$$

$$\sin \theta = \frac{y}{r} = \frac{15}{17}$$

$$\cos \theta = \frac{x}{r} = \frac{8}{17}$$

$$\tan \theta = \frac{y}{x} = \frac{15}{8}$$

$$\csc \theta = \frac{r}{y} = \frac{17}{15}$$

$$\sec \theta = \frac{r}{x} = \frac{17}{8}$$

$$\cot \theta = \frac{x}{y} = \frac{8}{15}$$

8. $x = -5, y = -2$

$$r = \sqrt{(-5)^2 + (-2)^2} = \sqrt{29}$$

$$\sin \theta = \frac{y}{r} = \frac{-2}{\sqrt{29}} = -\frac{2\sqrt{29}}{29}$$

$$\cos \theta = \frac{x}{r} = \frac{-5}{\sqrt{29}} = -\frac{5\sqrt{29}}{29}$$

$$\tan \theta = \frac{y}{x} = \frac{-2}{-5} = \frac{2}{5}$$

$$\csc \theta = \frac{r}{y} = \frac{\sqrt{29}}{-2} = -\frac{\sqrt{29}}{2}$$

$$\sec \theta = \frac{r}{x} = \frac{\sqrt{29}}{-5} = -\frac{\sqrt{29}}{5}$$

$$\cot \theta = \frac{x}{y} = \frac{-5}{-2} = \frac{5}{2}$$

10. $x = 3\frac{1}{2} = \frac{7}{2}, y = -7\frac{3}{4} = -\frac{31}{4}$

$$r = \sqrt{\left(\frac{7}{2}\right)^2 + \left(-\frac{31}{4}\right)^2} = \frac{\sqrt{1157}}{4}$$

$$\sin \theta = \frac{x}{r} = \frac{-\dfrac{31}{4}}{\dfrac{\sqrt{1157}}{4}} = -\frac{31\sqrt{1157}}{1157}$$

$$\csc \theta = \frac{r}{y} = \frac{\dfrac{\sqrt{1157}}{4}}{-\dfrac{31}{4}} = -\frac{\sqrt{1157}}{31}$$

$$\cos \theta = \frac{x}{r} = \frac{\dfrac{7}{2}}{\dfrac{\sqrt{1157}}{4}} = \frac{14\sqrt{1157}}{1157}$$

$$\sec \theta = \frac{r}{x} = \frac{\dfrac{\sqrt{1157}}{4}}{\dfrac{7}{2}} = \frac{\sqrt{1157}}{14}$$

$$\tan \theta = \frac{y}{x} = \frac{-\dfrac{31}{4}}{\dfrac{7}{2}} = -\frac{31}{14}$$

$$\cot \theta = \frac{x}{y} = \frac{\dfrac{7}{2}}{-\dfrac{31}{4}} = -\frac{14}{31}$$

12. $\sin \theta > 0$ and $\cos \theta > 0$

$\dfrac{y}{r} > 0$ and $\dfrac{x}{r} > 0$

Quadrant I

14. $\sec \theta > 0$ and $\cot \theta < 0$

$\dfrac{r}{x} > 0$ and $\dfrac{x}{y} < 0$

Quadrant IV

16. $\cos \theta = \dfrac{x}{r} = \dfrac{-4}{5} \Longrightarrow y = |3|$

θ in Quadrant III $\Longrightarrow y = -3$

$\sin \theta = \dfrac{y}{r} = -\dfrac{3}{5}$ $\qquad \csc \theta = -\dfrac{5}{3}$

$\cos \theta = \dfrac{x}{r} = -\dfrac{4}{5}$ $\qquad \sec \theta = -\dfrac{5}{4}$

$\tan \theta = \dfrac{y}{x} = \dfrac{3}{4}$ $\qquad \cot \theta = \dfrac{4}{3}$

18. $\cos \theta = \dfrac{x}{r} = \dfrac{8}{17} \Longrightarrow y = |15|$

$\tan \theta < 0 \Longrightarrow y = -15$

$\sin \theta = \dfrac{y}{r} = \dfrac{-15}{17} = -\dfrac{15}{17}$ $\quad \csc \theta = -\dfrac{17}{15}$

$\cos \theta = \dfrac{x}{r} = \dfrac{8}{17}$ $\qquad \sec \theta = \dfrac{17}{8}$

$\tan \theta = \dfrac{y}{x} = \dfrac{-15}{8} = -\dfrac{15}{8}$ $\quad \cot \theta = -\dfrac{8}{15}$

20. $\csc \theta = \dfrac{r}{y} = \dfrac{4}{1} \Longrightarrow x = |\sqrt{15}|$

$\cot \theta < 0 \Longrightarrow x = -\sqrt{15}$

$\sin \theta = \dfrac{y}{r} = \dfrac{1}{4}$ $\qquad \csc \theta = 4$

$\cos \theta = \dfrac{x}{r} = -\dfrac{\sqrt{15}}{4}$ $\qquad \sec \theta = -\dfrac{4\sqrt{15}}{15}$

$\tan \theta = \dfrac{y}{x} = -\dfrac{\sqrt{15}}{15}$ $\qquad \cot \theta = -\sqrt{15}$

22. $\sin \theta = 0 \Longrightarrow \theta = 0 + \pi n$

$\sec \theta = -1 \Longrightarrow \theta = \pi + 2\pi n$

$y = 0, x = -r$

$\sin \theta = 0$

$\cos \theta = \dfrac{x}{r} = \dfrac{-r}{r} = -1$

$\tan \theta = \dfrac{y}{x} = 0$

$\csc \theta = \dfrac{r}{y}$ is undefined

$\sec \theta = \dfrac{r}{x} = -1$

$\cot \theta = \dfrac{x}{y}$ is undefined

24. $\tan \theta$ is undefined $\Longrightarrow \theta = n\pi + \dfrac{\pi}{2}$

$\pi \le \theta \le 2\pi \Longrightarrow \theta = \dfrac{3\pi}{2}, x = 0, y = -r$

$\sin \theta = \dfrac{y}{r} = \dfrac{-r}{r} = -1$ $\qquad \csc \theta = \dfrac{r}{y} = -1$

$\cos \theta = \dfrac{x}{r} = \dfrac{0}{r} = 0$ $\qquad \sec \theta = \dfrac{r}{x}$ is undefined.

$\tan \theta = \dfrac{y}{x}$ is undefined. $\qquad \cot \theta = \dfrac{x}{y} = \dfrac{0}{y} = 0$

26. Let $x > 0$.

$\left(-x, -\dfrac{1}{3}x\right)$ Quadrant III

$r = \sqrt{x^2 + \dfrac{1}{9}x^2} = \dfrac{\sqrt{10}\,x}{3}$

$\sin \theta = \dfrac{y}{r} = \dfrac{\left(-\dfrac{1}{3}\right)x}{\dfrac{\sqrt{10}\,x}{3}} = -\dfrac{\sqrt{10}}{10}$

$\cos \theta = \dfrac{x}{r} = \dfrac{-x}{\dfrac{\sqrt{10}\,x}{3}} = -\dfrac{3\sqrt{10}}{10}$

$\tan \theta = \dfrac{y}{x} = \dfrac{\left(-\dfrac{1}{3}\right)x}{-x} = \dfrac{1}{3}$

$\csc \theta = \dfrac{r}{y} = \dfrac{\dfrac{\sqrt{10}\,x}{3}}{\left(-\dfrac{1}{3}\right)x} = -\sqrt{10}$

$\sec \theta = \dfrac{r}{x} = \dfrac{\dfrac{\sqrt{10}\,x}{3}}{-x} = -\dfrac{\sqrt{10}}{3}$

$\cot \theta = \dfrac{x}{y} = \dfrac{-x}{\left(-\dfrac{1}{3}\right)x} = 3$

28. Let $x > 0$.

$4x + 3y = 0 \implies y = -\dfrac{4}{3}x$

$\left(x, -\dfrac{4}{3}x\right)$ Quadrant IV

$r = \sqrt{x^2 + \dfrac{16}{9}x^2} = \dfrac{5}{3}x$

$\sin \theta = \dfrac{y}{r} = \dfrac{\left(-\dfrac{4}{3}\right)x}{\dfrac{5}{3}x} = -\dfrac{4}{5}$ $\qquad \csc \theta = -\dfrac{5}{4}$

$\cos \theta = \dfrac{x}{r} = \dfrac{x}{\dfrac{5}{3}x} = \dfrac{3}{5}$ $\qquad \sec \theta = \dfrac{5}{3}$

$\tan \theta = \dfrac{y}{x} = \dfrac{\left(-\dfrac{4}{3}\right)x}{x} = -\dfrac{4}{3}$ $\qquad \tan \theta = -\dfrac{3}{4}$

30. $\cos \dfrac{3\pi}{2} = \dfrac{x}{r} = \dfrac{0}{1} = 0$

since $\dfrac{3\pi}{2}$ corresponds to $(0, -1)$.

32. $\sec \dfrac{3\pi}{2} = \dfrac{r}{x} = \dfrac{1}{0} \implies$ undefined

since $\dfrac{3\pi}{2}$ corresponds to $(0, -1)$.

34. $\tan \pi = \dfrac{y}{x} = \dfrac{0}{-1} = 0$

since π corresponds to $(-1, 0)$.

36. $\csc \pi = \dfrac{r}{y} = \dfrac{1}{0} \implies$ undefined

since π corresponds to $(-1, 0)$.

38. $\theta = 309°$

$\theta' = 360° - 309° = 51°$

40. $\theta = -145°$ is coterminal with $215°$.

$\theta' = 215° - 180° = 35°$

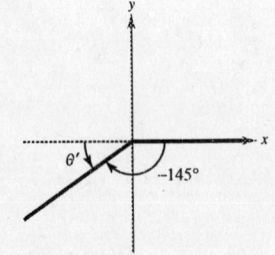

42. $\theta = \dfrac{7\pi}{4}$

$\theta' = 2\pi - \dfrac{7\pi}{4} = \dfrac{\pi}{4}$

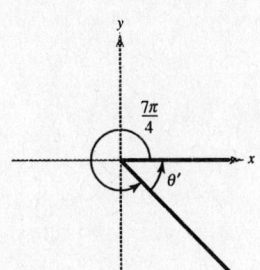

44. $\theta = \dfrac{11\pi}{3}$ is coterminal

with $\dfrac{5\pi}{3}$.

$\theta' = 2\pi - \dfrac{5\pi}{3} = \dfrac{\pi}{3}$

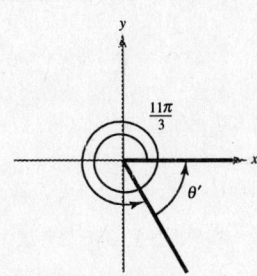

46. $\theta = 300°$, $\theta' = 360° - 300° = 60°$, Quadrant IV

$\sin 300° = -\sin 60° = -\dfrac{\sqrt{3}}{2}$

$\cos 300° = \cos 60° = \dfrac{1}{2}$

$\tan 300° = -\tan 60° = -\sqrt{3}$

48. $\theta = -405°$ is coterminal with $315°$.

$\theta' = 360° - 315° = 45°$ in Quadrant IV

$\sin(-405°) = -\sin 45° = -\dfrac{\sqrt{2}}{2}$

$\cos(-405°) = \cos 45° = \dfrac{\sqrt{2}}{2}$

$\tan(-405°) = -\tan 45° = -1$

50. $\theta = -840°$ is coterminal with $240°$.

$\theta' = 240° - 180° = 60°$ in Quadrant III.

$\sin(-840°) = -\sin 60° = -\dfrac{\sqrt{3}}{2}$

$\cos(-840°) = -\cos 60° = -\dfrac{1}{2}$

$\tan(-840°) = \tan 60° = \sqrt{3}$

52. $\theta = \dfrac{\pi}{4}$, $\theta' = \dfrac{\pi}{4}$ in Quadrant I

$\sin \dfrac{\pi}{4} = \dfrac{\sqrt{2}}{2}$

$\cos \dfrac{\pi}{4} = \dfrac{\sqrt{2}}{2}$

$\tan \dfrac{\pi}{4} = 1$

54. $\theta = -\dfrac{\pi}{2}$ is coterminal with $\dfrac{3\pi}{2}$.

$\sin\left(-\dfrac{\pi}{2}\right) = \sin \dfrac{3\pi}{2} = -1$

$\cos\left(-\dfrac{\pi}{2}\right) = \cos \dfrac{3\pi}{2} = 0$

$\tan\left(-\dfrac{\pi}{2}\right) = \tan \dfrac{3\pi}{2}$ is undefined.

56. $\theta = \dfrac{10\pi}{3}$ is coterminal with $\dfrac{4\pi}{3}$.

$\theta' = \dfrac{4\pi}{3} - \pi = \dfrac{\pi}{3}$ in Quadrant III.

$\sin \dfrac{10\pi}{3} = -\sin \dfrac{\pi}{3} = -\dfrac{\sqrt{3}}{2}$

$\cos \dfrac{10\pi}{3} = -\cos \dfrac{\pi}{3} = -\dfrac{1}{2}$

$\tan \dfrac{10\pi}{3} = \tan \dfrac{\pi}{3} = \sqrt{3}$

58. $\theta = -\dfrac{25\pi}{4}$ is coterminal with $\dfrac{7\pi}{4}$.

$\theta' = 2\pi - \dfrac{7\pi}{4} = \dfrac{\pi}{4}$ in Quadrant IV.

$\sin\left(-\dfrac{25\pi}{4}\right) = -\sin\left(\dfrac{\pi}{4}\right) = -\dfrac{\sqrt{2}}{2}$

$\cos\left(-\dfrac{25\pi}{4}\right) = \cos\left(\dfrac{\pi}{4}\right) = \dfrac{\sqrt{2}}{2}$

$\tan\left(-\dfrac{25\pi}{4}\right) = -\tan\left(\dfrac{\pi}{4}\right) = -1$

60. $\sec 225° = \dfrac{1}{\cos 225°} \approx -1.4142$

62. $\csc(-330°) = \dfrac{1}{\sin(-330°)} = 2.0000$

64. $\cot 1.35 = \dfrac{1}{\tan 1.35} \approx 0.2245$

66. $\tan\left(-\dfrac{\pi}{9}\right) \approx -0.3640$

68. $\sin 0.65 \approx 0.6052$

70. (a) $\cos \theta = \dfrac{\sqrt{2}}{2} \Longrightarrow$ reference angle is 45° or $\dfrac{\pi}{4}$ and θ is in Quadrant I or IV.

Values in degrees: 45°, 315°

Values in radians: $\dfrac{\pi}{4}, \dfrac{7\pi}{4}$

(b) $\cos \theta = -\dfrac{\sqrt{2}}{2} \Longrightarrow$ reference angle is 45° or $\dfrac{\pi}{4}$ and θ is in Quadrant II or III.

Values in degrees: 135°, 225°

Values in radians: $\dfrac{3\pi}{4}, \dfrac{5\pi}{4}$

72. (a) $\sec \theta = 2 \Longrightarrow$ reference angle is 60° or $\dfrac{\pi}{3}$ and θ is in Quadrant I or IV.

Values in degrees: 60°, 300°

Values in radians: $\dfrac{\pi}{3}, \dfrac{5\pi}{3}$

(b) $\sec \theta = -2 \Longrightarrow$ reference angle is 60° or $\dfrac{\pi}{3}$ and θ is in Quadrant II or III.

Values in degrees: 120°, 240°

Values in radians: $\dfrac{2\pi}{3}, \dfrac{4\pi}{3}$

74. (a) $\sin \theta = \dfrac{\sqrt{3}}{2} \Longrightarrow$ reference angle is 60° or $\dfrac{\pi}{3}$ and θ is in Quadrant I or II.

Values in degrees: 60°, 120°

Values in radians: $\dfrac{\pi}{3}, \dfrac{2\pi}{3}$

(b) $\sin \theta = -\dfrac{\sqrt{3}}{2} \Longrightarrow$ reference angle is 60° or $\dfrac{\pi}{3}$ and θ is in Quadrant III or IV.

Values in degrees: 240°, 300°

Values in radians: $\dfrac{4\pi}{3}, \dfrac{5\pi}{3}$

76. $\cos \theta = 0.8746$

Quadrant I: $\theta = \cos^{-1} 0.8746 \approx 29.00°$

Quadrant IV: $\theta = 360° - 29.00° = 331.00°$

78. $\sin \theta = -0.6514$

$\sin^{-1}(-0.6514) \approx -40.65°$

Quadrant III: $\theta = 180° + 40.65° = 220.65°$

Quadrant IV: $\theta = 360° - 40.65° = 319.35°$

80. $\sin \theta = 0.0175$

Quadrant I: $\theta = \sin^{-1} 0.0175 \approx 0.018$

Quadrant II: $\theta = \pi - 0.018 = 3.124$

82. $\cot \theta = 5.671 \Longrightarrow \dfrac{1}{\tan \theta} = 5.671$

Quadrant I: $\theta = \tan^{-1}\left(\dfrac{1}{5.671}\right) \approx 0.175$

Quadrant III: $\theta = \pi + 0.1745 \approx 3.317$

84. $\cos \theta = -0.3214$

Quadrant II: $\theta = \cos^{-1}(-0.3214) \approx 1.898$

Quadrant III: $\theta = 2\pi - 1.898 \approx 4.385$

86. $\cot \theta = -3$

$1 + \cot^2 \theta = \csc^2 \theta$

$1 + (-3)^2 = \csc^2 \theta$

$\qquad 10 = \csc^2 \theta$

$\csc \theta > 0$ in Quadrant II.

$\sqrt{10} = \csc \theta$

$\csc \theta = \dfrac{1}{\sin \theta}$

$\sin \theta = \dfrac{1}{\csc \theta} = \dfrac{1}{\sqrt{10}} = \dfrac{\sqrt{10}}{10}$

88. $\csc \theta = -2$

$1 + \cot^2 \theta = \csc^2 \theta$

$\qquad \cot^2 \theta = \csc^2 \theta - 1$

$\qquad \cot^2 \theta = (-2)^2 - 1$

$\qquad \cot^2 \theta = 3$

$\cot \theta < 0$ in Quadrant IV.

$\cot \theta = -\sqrt{3}$

90. $\sec \theta = -\dfrac{9}{4}$

$1 + \tan^2 \theta = \sec^2 \theta$

$\qquad \tan^2 \theta = \sec^2 \theta - 1$

$\qquad \tan^2 \theta = \left(-\dfrac{9}{4}\right)^2 - 1$

$\qquad \tan^2 \theta = \dfrac{65}{16}$

$\tan \theta > 0$ in Quadrant III.

$\tan \theta = \dfrac{\sqrt{65}}{4}$

92. $S = 23.1 + 0.442t + 4.3 \sin \dfrac{\pi t}{6}$

(a) February 2001 $\Longrightarrow t = 2$

$S = 23.1 + 0.442(2) + 4.3 \sin \dfrac{2\pi}{6}$

≈ 27.7 thousand or 27,700 units

(b) February 2002 $\Longrightarrow t = 14$

$S = 23.1 + 0.442(14) + 4.3 \sin \dfrac{14\pi}{6}$

≈ 33.0 thousand or 33,000 units

(c) September 2001 $\Longrightarrow t = 9$

$S = 23.1 + 0.442(9) + 4.3 \sin \dfrac{9\pi}{6} \approx 22.8$ thousand

or 22,800 units

(d) September 2002 $\Longrightarrow t = 21$

$S = 23.1 + 0.442(21) + 4.3 \sin \dfrac{21\pi}{6}$

≈ 28.1 thousand or 28,100 units

94. $y(t) = 2e^{-t} \cos 6t$

(a) $t = 0$

$y(0) = 2e^{-0} \cos 0 = 2$ centimeters

(b) $t = \dfrac{1}{4}$

$y\left(\dfrac{1}{4}\right) = 2e^{-1/4} \cos\left(6 \cdot \dfrac{1}{4}\right) \approx 0.11$ centimeters

(c) $t = \dfrac{1}{2}$

$y\left(\dfrac{1}{2}\right) = 2e^{-1/2} \cos\left(6 \cdot \dfrac{1}{2}\right) \approx -1.2$ centimeters

96. $\sin \theta = \dfrac{6}{d} \Longrightarrow d = \dfrac{6}{\sin \theta}$

(a) $\theta = 30°$

$d = \dfrac{6}{\sin 30°} = \dfrac{6}{\frac{1}{2}} = 12$ miles

(b) $\theta = 90°$

$d = \dfrac{6}{\sin 90°} = \dfrac{6}{1} = 6$ miles

(c) $\theta = 120°$

$d = \dfrac{6}{\sin 120°} \approx 6.9$ miles

98. False. Let $n = 1$ and $\theta = 225°$. $0 \leq 135 \leq 360$, but $360n - \theta = 135$ is not the reference angle. The reference angle would be $45°$.

100. Determine the trigonometric function of the reference angle and prefix the appropriate sign.

102. $y = 2^{x-1}$

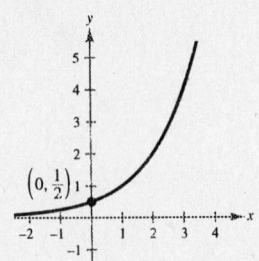

Intercept: $\left(0, \frac{1}{2}\right)$

Horizontal asymptote: $y = 0$

Domain: all real numbers

Range: $y > 0$

104. $y = 3^{-x/2}$

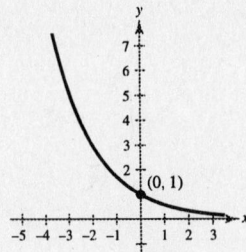

Intercept: $(0, 1)$

Vertical asymptote: $y = 0$

Domain: all real numbers

Range: $y > 0$

106. $y = \ln(x - 1)$

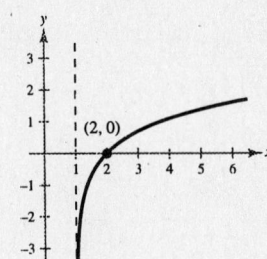

Intercept: $(2, 0)$

Vertical asymptote: $x = 1$

Domain: $x > 1$

Range: all real numbers

108. $y = \log_{10}(x + 2)$

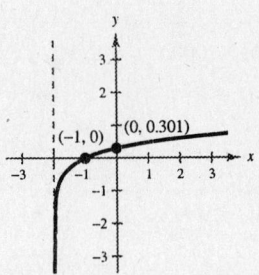

Intercept: $(-1, 0), (0, 0.301)$

Vertical asymptote: $x = -2$

Domain: $x > -2$

Range: all real numbers

Section 4.5   Graphs of Sine and Cosine Functions

Solutions to Even-Numbered Exercises

2. $y = 2 \cos 3x$

$\text{Period} = \dfrac{2\pi}{b} = \dfrac{2\pi}{3}$

$\text{Amplitude} = |a| = 2$

4. $y = -3 \sin \dfrac{x}{3}$

$\text{Period} = \dfrac{2\pi}{b} = \dfrac{2\pi}{\frac{1}{3}} = 6\pi$

$\text{Amplitude} = |a| = |-3| = 3$

6. $y = \dfrac{3}{2} \cos \dfrac{\pi x}{2}$

$\text{Period} = \dfrac{2\pi}{b} = \dfrac{2\pi}{\frac{\pi}{2}} = 4$

$\text{Amplitude} = |a| = \dfrac{3}{2}$

8. $y = -\cos \dfrac{2x}{3}$

$\text{Period} = \dfrac{2\pi}{b} = \dfrac{2\pi}{\frac{2}{3}} = 3\pi$

$\text{Amplitude} = |a| = |-1| = 1$

10. $y = \dfrac{1}{3} \sin 8x$

$\text{Period} = \dfrac{2\pi}{b} = \dfrac{2\pi}{8} = \dfrac{\pi}{4}$

$\text{Amplitude} = |a| = \dfrac{1}{3}$

12. $y = \dfrac{5}{2} \cos \dfrac{x}{4}$

$\text{Period} = \dfrac{2\pi}{b} = \dfrac{2\pi}{\frac{1}{4}} = 8\pi$

$\text{Amplitude} = |a| = \dfrac{5}{2}$

14. $y = \dfrac{2}{3} \cos \dfrac{\pi x}{10}$

$\text{Period} = \dfrac{2\pi}{b} = \dfrac{2\pi}{\frac{\pi}{10}} = 20$

$\text{Amplitude} = |a| = \dfrac{2}{3}$

16. $f(x) = \cos x, \ g(x) = \cos(x + \pi)$

g is a horizontal shift of f π units to the left.

18. $f(x) = \sin 3x, \ g(x) = \sin(-3x)$

g is a reflection of f about the y-axis.

20. $f(x) = \sin x, \ g(x) = \sin 3x$

The period of g is one-third the period of f.

22. $f(x) = \cos 4x, \ g(x) = -2 + \cos 4x$

g is a vertical shift of f two units downward.

24. The period of g is one-third the period of f.

26. Shift the graph of *f* two units upward to obtain the graph of *g*.

28. $f(x) = \sin x$, $g(x) = \sin \dfrac{x}{3}$

x	0	$\dfrac{\pi}{2}$	π	$\dfrac{3\pi}{2}$	2π
$\sin x$	0	1	0	-1	0
$\sin \dfrac{x}{3}$	0	$\dfrac{1}{2}$	$\dfrac{\sqrt{3}}{2}$	1	$\dfrac{\sqrt{3}}{2}$

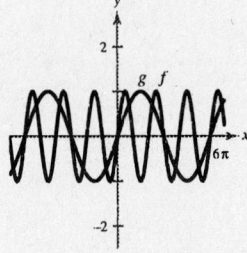

30. $f(x) = 2\cos 2x$, $g(x) = -\cos 4x$

x	0	$\dfrac{\pi}{4}$	$\dfrac{\pi}{2}$	$\dfrac{3\pi}{4}$	π
$2\cos 2x$	2	0	-2	0	2
$-\cos 4x$	-1	1	-1	1	-1

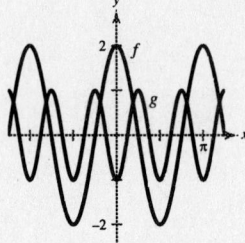

32. $f(x) = 4\sin \pi x$, $g(x) = 4\sin \pi x - 3$

x	0	$\dfrac{1}{2}$	1	$\dfrac{3}{2}$	2
$f(x)$	0	4	0	-4	0
$g(x)$	-3	1	-3	-7	-3

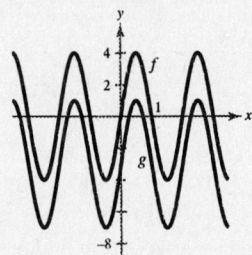

34. $f(x) = -\cos x$

$g(x) = -\cos(x - \pi)$

x	0	$\dfrac{\pi}{2}$	π	$\dfrac{3\pi}{2}$	2π
$-\cos x$	-1	0	1	0	-1
$-\cos(x - \pi)$	1	0	-1	0	1

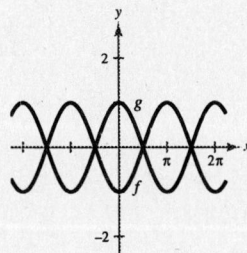

36. $y = -3\cos 4x$

Period $= \dfrac{2\pi}{4} = \dfrac{\pi}{2}$

Amplitude $= 3$

x	0	$\dfrac{\pi}{8}$	$\dfrac{\pi}{4}$	$\dfrac{3\pi}{8}$	$\dfrac{\pi}{2}$
y	-3	0	3	0	-3

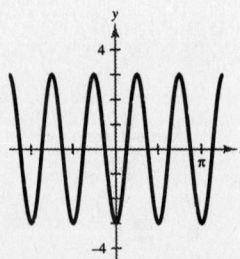

38. $y = \sin\dfrac{\pi x}{4}$

x	0	2	4	6	8
y	0	1	0	−1	0

Period $= \dfrac{2\pi}{\dfrac{\pi}{4}} = 8$

Amplitude $= 1$

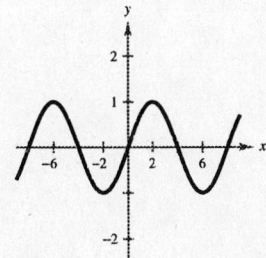

40. $y = -10\cos\dfrac{\pi x}{6}$

x	0	3	6	9	12
y	−10	0	10	0	−10

Period $= \dfrac{2\pi}{\dfrac{\pi}{6}} = 12$

Amplitude $= 10$

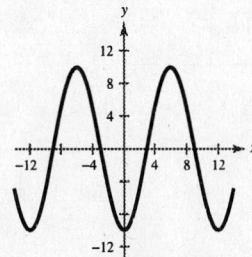

42. $y = \sin(x - \pi)$

x	0	$\dfrac{\pi}{2}$	π	$\dfrac{3\pi}{2}$	2π
y	0	−1	0	1	0

Period $= 2\pi$

Amplitude $= 1$

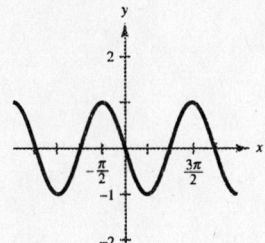

44. $y = 4\cos\left(x + \dfrac{\pi}{4}\right)$

Period $= 2\pi$

Amplitude $= 4$

x	0	$\dfrac{\pi}{2}$	π	$\dfrac{3\pi}{2}$	2π
y	$2\sqrt{2}$	$-2\sqrt{2}$	$-2\sqrt{2}$	$2\sqrt{2}$	$2\sqrt{2}$

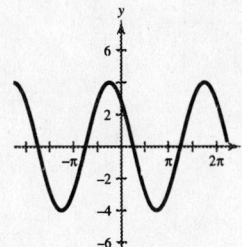

46. $y = -3 + 5\cos\dfrac{\pi t}{12}$

Period $= \dfrac{2\pi}{\dfrac{\pi}{12}} = 24$

Amplitude $= 5$

x	0	6	12	18	24
y	2	−3	−8	−3	2

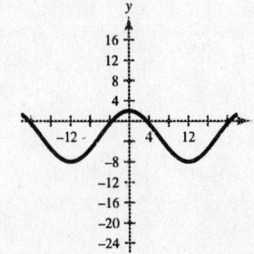

48. $y = 2\cos x - 3$

Period $= 2\pi$

Amplitude $= 2$

x	0	$\dfrac{\pi}{2}$	π	$\dfrac{3\pi}{2}$	2π
y	-1	-3	-5	-3	-1

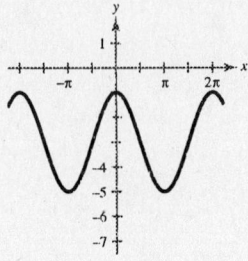

50. $y = 4\cos\left(x + \dfrac{\pi}{4}\right) + 4$

Period $= 2\pi$

Amplitude $= 4$

x	$-\dfrac{\pi}{4}$	$\dfrac{\pi}{4}$	$\dfrac{3\pi}{4}$	$\dfrac{5\pi}{4}$	$\dfrac{7\pi}{4}$
y	8	4	0	4	8

52. $y = -3\cos(6x + \pi)$

Period $= \dfrac{2\pi}{6} = \dfrac{\pi}{3}$

Amplitude $= 3$

x	0	$\dfrac{\pi}{12}$	$\dfrac{\pi}{6}$	$\dfrac{3\pi}{12}$	$\dfrac{\pi}{3}$
y	3	0	-3	0	3

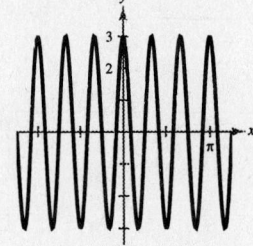

54. $y = -4\sin\left(\dfrac{2}{3}x - \dfrac{\pi}{3}\right)$

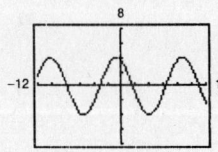

56. $y = 3\cos\left(\dfrac{\pi x}{2} + \dfrac{\pi}{2}\right) - 2$

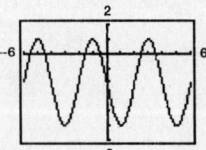

58. $y = 5\cos(\pi - 2x) + 2$

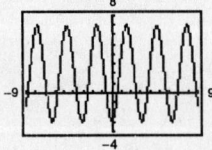

60. $y = \dfrac{1}{100}\sin 120\,\pi t$

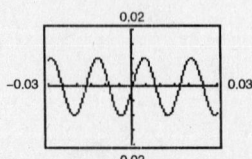

62. $f(x) = a\cos x + d$

Amplitude $= \dfrac{1 - (-3)}{2} = 2$

$1 = 2\cos 0 + d$

$d = 1 - 2 = -1$

$a = 2, d = -1$

64. $f(x) = a\cos x + d$

Amplitude $= \dfrac{-2 - (-4)}{2} = 1$

Reflected in the x-axis: $a = -1$

$-4 = -1\cos 0 + d$

$d = -3$

$a = -1, d = -3$

66. $y = a \sin(bx - c)$

Amplitude $= 2 \Longrightarrow a = 2$

Period $= 4\pi$

$\dfrac{2\pi}{b} = 4\pi \Longrightarrow b = \dfrac{1}{2}$

Phase shift: $c = 0$

$a = 2, b = \dfrac{1}{2}, c = 0$

68. $y = a \sin(bx - c)$

Amplitude $= 2 \Longrightarrow a = 2$

Period $= 4$

$\dfrac{2\pi}{b} = 4 \Longrightarrow b = \dfrac{\pi}{2}$

Phase shift: $\dfrac{c}{b} = -1 \Longrightarrow c = -\dfrac{\pi}{2}$

$a = 2, b = \dfrac{\pi}{2}, c = -\dfrac{\pi}{2}$

70. $y_1 = \cos x$

$y_2 = -1$

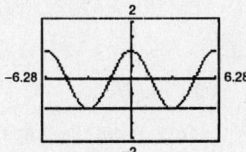

$y_1 = y_2$ when $x = \pi, -\pi$

72. $y_1 = \sin x$

$y_2 = \dfrac{\sqrt{3}}{2}$

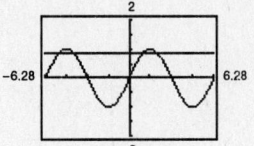

$y_1 = y_2$ when $x = \dfrac{\pi}{3}, \dfrac{2\pi}{3}, -\dfrac{4\pi}{3}, -\dfrac{5\pi}{3}$.

74. $v = 1.75 \sin \dfrac{\pi t}{2}$

(a) Period $= \dfrac{2\pi}{\dfrac{\pi}{2}} = 4$ seconds

(b) $\dfrac{1 \text{ cycle}}{4 \text{ seconds}} \cdot \dfrac{60 \text{ seconds}}{1 \text{ minute}} = 15$ cycles per minute

(c)

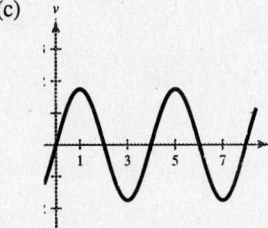

76. $P = 100 - 20 \cos \dfrac{5\pi t}{3}$

(a) Period $= \dfrac{2\pi}{\dfrac{5\pi}{3}} = \dfrac{6}{5}$ seconds

(b) $\dfrac{1 \text{ heartbeat}}{\dfrac{6}{5} \text{ seconds}} \cdot \dfrac{60 \text{ seconds}}{1 \text{ minute}} = 50$ heartbeats per minute

78.

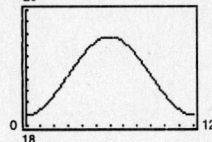

80. $C = 30.3 + 21.6 \sin\left(\dfrac{2\pi t}{365} + 10.9\right)$

(a)   Period $= \dfrac{2\pi}{\dfrac{2\pi}{365}} = 365$

Yes, this is what is expected because there are 365 days in a year.

(b)   The average daily fuel consumption is given by the amount of the vertical shift (from 0) which is given by the constant 30.3.

(c)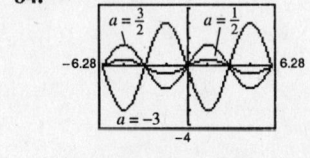

The consumption exceeds 40 gallons per day when $124 < x < 252$.

82. False. The graph of $\sin(x + 2\pi)$ is the graph of $\sin(x)$ translated to the *left* by one period, and the graphs are indeed identical.

84.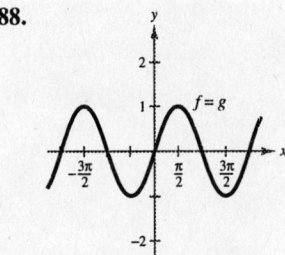

As a changes from $\dfrac{1}{2}$ to $\dfrac{3}{2}$, the amplitude increases. When $a = -3$, the amplitude again increases but the graph is reflected in the x-axis also.

86.   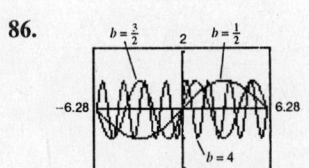   As b increases the period decreases.

88.   Since the graphs are the same, the conjecture is that $\sin(x) = \cos\left(x - \dfrac{\pi}{2}\right)$.

90.   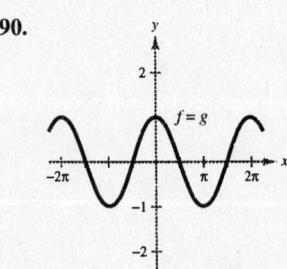   Since the graphs are the same, the conjecture is that $\cos x = -\sin\left(x - \dfrac{\pi}{2}\right)$

92. (a)

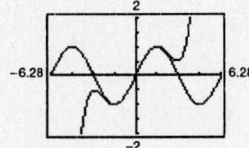

The graphs nearly the same for $-\dfrac{\pi}{2} < x < \dfrac{\pi}{2}$

(b)

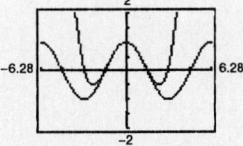

The graphs are nearly the same for $-\dfrac{\pi}{2} < x < \dfrac{\pi}{2}$

(c) $\sin x \approx x - \dfrac{x^3}{3!} + \dfrac{x^5}{5!} - \dfrac{x^7}{7!}$

$\cos x \approx 1 - \dfrac{x^2}{2!} + \dfrac{x^4}{4!} - \dfrac{x^6}{6!}$

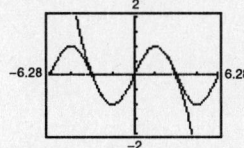

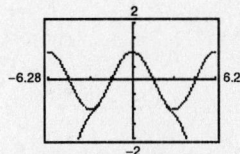

The graphs now agree over a wider range,

$-\dfrac{3\pi}{4} < x < \dfrac{3\pi}{4}$

94. (a)

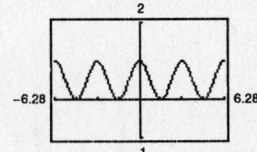

h is even

(b)

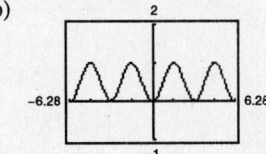

h is even

96. $\log_{10}\sqrt{x-2} = \log_{10}(x-2)^{1/2} = \dfrac{1}{2}\log_{10}(x-2) = \dfrac{1}{2}\log(x-2)$

98. $\ln\dfrac{t^3}{t-1} = \ln t^3 - \ln(t-1) = 3\ln t - \ln(t-1)$

100. $\dfrac{1}{2}(\log_{10}x + \log_{10}y) = \dfrac{1}{2}\log_{10}(xy)$

$= \log_{10}\sqrt{xy}$

102. $\ln 3x - 4\ln y = \ln 3x - \ln y^4$

$= \ln\left(\dfrac{3x}{y^4}\right)$

Section 4.6   Graphs of Other Trigonometric Functions

Solutions to Even-Numbered Exercises

2. $y = \tan\dfrac{x}{2}$

Period $= \dfrac{\pi}{b} = \dfrac{\pi}{\dfrac{1}{2}} = 2\pi$

Asymptotes: $x = -\pi, x = \pi$

Matches graph (c).

4. $y = \dfrac{1}{2}\sec\dfrac{\pi x}{2}$

Period $= \dfrac{2\pi}{b} = \dfrac{2\pi}{\dfrac{\pi}{2}} = 4$

Asymptotes: $x = -1, x = 1$

Matches graph (f).

6. $y = -2 \sec \dfrac{\pi x}{2}$

Period $= \dfrac{2\pi}{b} = \dfrac{2\pi}{\dfrac{\pi}{2}} = 4$

Asymptotes: $x = -1, x = 1$

Reflected in x-axis

Matches graph (b).

8. $y = \dfrac{1}{4} \tan x$

Period $= \pi$

Asymptotes: $x = -\dfrac{\pi}{2}, x = \dfrac{\pi}{2}$

x	$-\dfrac{\pi}{4}$	0	$\dfrac{\pi}{4}$
y	$-\dfrac{1}{4}$	0	$\dfrac{1}{4}$

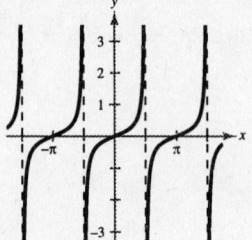

10. $y = -3 \tan \pi x$

Period $= \dfrac{\pi}{\pi} = 1$

Asymptotes: $x = -\dfrac{1}{2}, x = \dfrac{1}{2}$

x	$-\dfrac{1}{4}$	0	$\dfrac{1}{4}$
y	3	0	-3

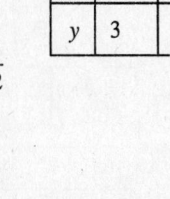

12. $y = \dfrac{1}{4} \sec x$

Period $= 2\pi$

Asymptotes: $x = -\dfrac{\pi}{2}, x = \dfrac{\pi}{2}$

x	$-\dfrac{\pi}{4}$	0	$\dfrac{\pi}{4}$
y	0.354	$\dfrac{1}{4}$	0.354

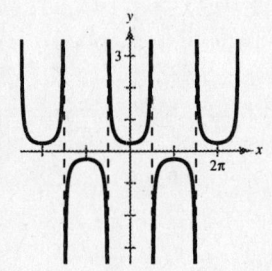

14. $y = 3 \csc 4x$

Period $= \dfrac{2\pi}{4} = \dfrac{\pi}{2}$

Asymptotes: $x = 0, x = \dfrac{\pi}{4}$

x	$\dfrac{\pi}{16}$	$\dfrac{\pi}{8}$	$\dfrac{3\pi}{16}$
y	4.243	3	4.243

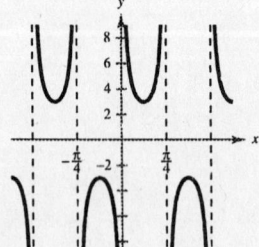

16. $y = -2 \sec 4x + 2$

Period $= \dfrac{2\pi}{4} = \dfrac{\pi}{2}$

Asymptotes: $x = -\dfrac{\pi}{8}, x = \dfrac{\pi}{8}$

x	$-\dfrac{\pi}{16}$	0	$\dfrac{\pi}{16}$
y	-0.828	0	-0.828

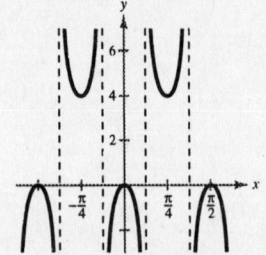

18. $y = \csc \dfrac{x}{3}$

x	π	2π	4π
y	1.155	1.155	-1.155

Period $= \dfrac{2\pi}{\frac{1}{3}} = 6\pi$

Asymptotes: $x = 0, x = 3\pi$

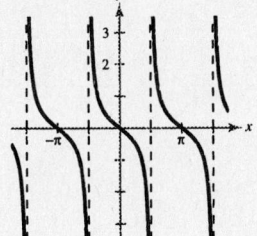

20. $y = 3 \cot \dfrac{\pi x}{2}$

x	$\dfrac{1}{4}$	1	$\dfrac{3}{2}$
y	7.243	0	-3

Period $= \dfrac{\pi}{\frac{\pi}{2}} = 2$

Asymptotes: $x = 0, x = 2$

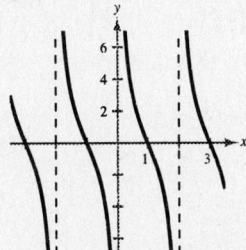

22. $y = -\dfrac{1}{2} \tan x$

Period $= \pi$

Asymptotes: $x = -\dfrac{\pi}{2}, x = \dfrac{\pi}{2}$

x	$-\dfrac{\pi}{4}$	0	$\dfrac{\pi}{4}$
y	$\dfrac{1}{2}$	0	$-\dfrac{1}{2}$

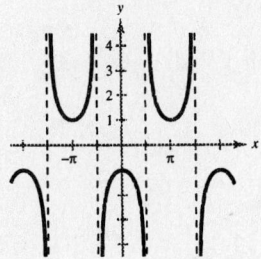

24. $y = \tan(x + \pi)$

Period $= \pi$

Asymptotes: $x = -\dfrac{\pi}{2}, x = \dfrac{\pi}{2}$

x	$-\dfrac{\pi}{4}$	0	$\dfrac{\pi}{4}$
y	-1	0	1

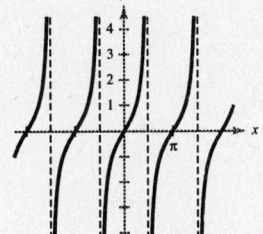

26. $y = \sec(\pi - x)$

Period $= 2\pi$

Asymptotes: $x = -\dfrac{\pi}{2}, x = \dfrac{\pi}{2}$

x	$-\dfrac{\pi}{4}$	0	$\dfrac{\pi}{4}$
y	-1.414	-1	-1.414

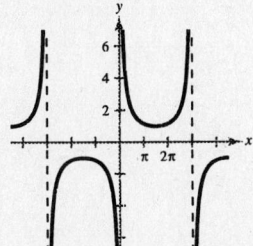

28. $y = 2 \cot\left(x + \dfrac{\pi}{2}\right)$

Period $= \pi$

Asymptotes: $x = -\dfrac{\pi}{2}, x = \dfrac{\pi}{2}$

x	$-\dfrac{\pi}{4}$	0	$\dfrac{\pi}{4}$
y	2	0	-2

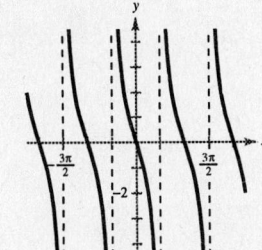

30. $y = -\tan 2x$

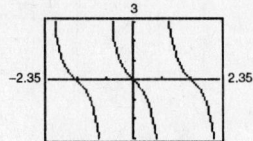

32. $y = \sec \pi x \Longrightarrow y = \dfrac{1}{\cos(\pi x)}$

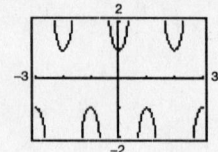

34. $y = -\csc(4x - \pi)$

$$y = \dfrac{-1}{\sin(4x - \pi)}$$

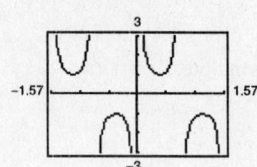

36. $y = 2\sec(2x - \pi) \Longrightarrow y = \dfrac{2}{\cos(2x - \pi)}$

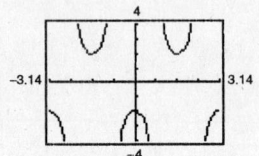

38. $y = \dfrac{1}{3}\sec\left(\dfrac{\pi x}{2} + \dfrac{\pi}{2}\right) \Longrightarrow y = \dfrac{1}{3\cos\left(\dfrac{\pi x}{2} + \dfrac{\pi}{2}\right)}$

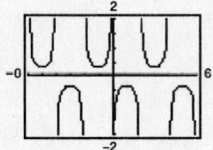

40. $\tan x = \sqrt{3}$

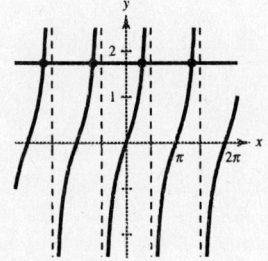

$$x = -\dfrac{5\pi}{3}, -\dfrac{2\pi}{3}, \dfrac{\pi}{3}, \dfrac{4\pi}{3}$$

42. $\cot x = 1$

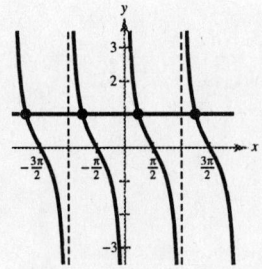

$$x = -\dfrac{7\pi}{4}, -\dfrac{3\pi}{4}, \dfrac{\pi}{4}, \dfrac{5\pi}{4}$$

44. $\sec x = 2$

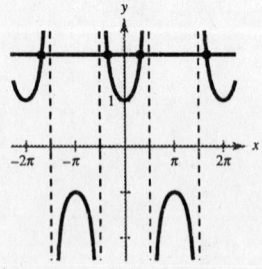

$$x = -\dfrac{5\pi}{3}, -\dfrac{\pi}{3}, \dfrac{\pi}{3}, \dfrac{5\pi}{3}$$

46. $\csc x = -\dfrac{2\sqrt{3}}{3}$

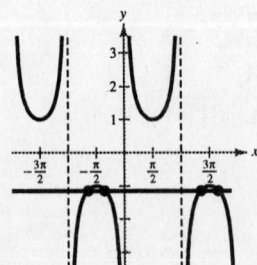

$$x = -\dfrac{2\pi}{3}, -\dfrac{\pi}{3}, \dfrac{4\pi}{3}, \dfrac{5\pi}{3}$$

48. $f(x) = \tan x$

$\tan(-x) = -\tan x$

Thus, the function is odd and the graph of $y = \tan x$ is symmetric with the origin.

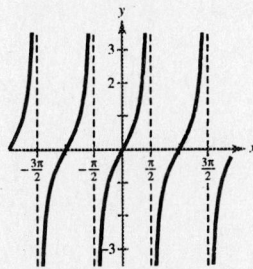

52. $y_1 = \sin x \sec x, y_2 = \tan x$

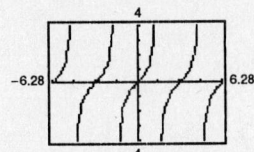

It appears that $y_1 = y_2$.

$$\sin x \sec x = \sin x \frac{1}{\cos x} = \frac{\sin x}{\cos x} = \tan x$$

56. $f(x) = x \sin x$

Matches graph (a) as $x \longrightarrow 0, f(x) \longrightarrow 0$.

60. $f(x) = \sin x - \cos\left(x + \dfrac{\pi}{2}\right)$

$g(x) = 2 \sin x$

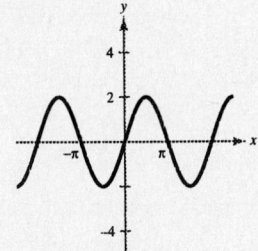

It appears that $f(x) = g(x)$. That is, that

$$\sin x - \cos\left(x + \frac{\pi}{2}\right) = 2 \sin x.$$

50. $f(x) = \tan \dfrac{\pi x}{2}, g(x) = \dfrac{1}{2} \sec \dfrac{\pi x}{2}$

(a)

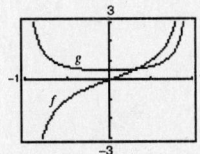

(b)   The interval in which $f < g$ is $\left(-1, \frac{1}{3}\right)$.

(c)   The interval in which $2f < 2g$ is $\left(-1, \frac{1}{3}\right)$, which is the same interval as part (b).

54. $y_1 = \sec^2 x - 1, y_2 = \tan^2 x$

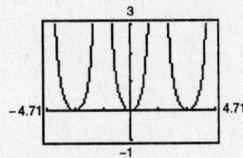

It appears that $y_1 = y_2$.

$1 + \tan^2 x = \sec^2 x$

$\tan^2 x = \sec^2 x - 1$

58. $g(x) = |x| \cos x$

Matches graph (c) as $x \longrightarrow 0, g(x) \longrightarrow 0$.

62. $f(x) = \cos^2 \dfrac{\pi x}{2}$

$g(x) = \dfrac{1}{2}(1 + \cos \pi x)$

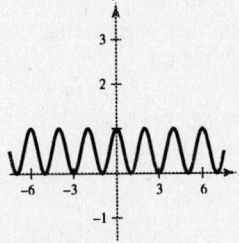

It appears that $f(x) = g(x)$. That is, that

$$\cos^2 \frac{\pi x}{2} = \frac{1}{2}(1 + \cos \pi x).$$

64. $f(x) = e^{-x} \cos x$

Damping factor: e^{-x}

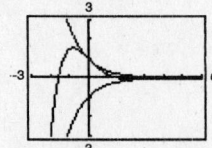

As $x \longrightarrow \infty, f(x) \longrightarrow 0$.

66. $h(x) = 2^{-x^2/4} \sin x$

Damping factor: $2^{-x^2/4}$

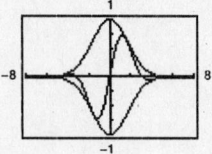

As $x \longrightarrow \infty, h(x) \longrightarrow 0$.

68. $y = \dfrac{4}{x} + \sin 2x, \, x > 0$

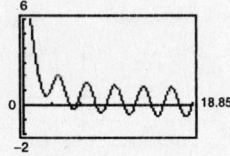

As $x \longrightarrow 0, y \longrightarrow \infty$

70. $f(x) = \dfrac{1 - \cos x}{x}$

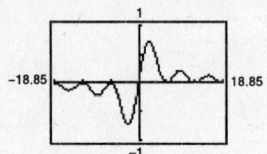

As $x \longrightarrow 0, f(x) \longrightarrow 0$.

72. $h(x) = x \sin \dfrac{1}{x}$

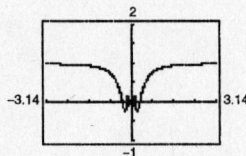

As $x \longrightarrow 0, h(x)$ oscillates.

74. $\cos x = \dfrac{27}{d}$

$d = \dfrac{27}{\cos x} = 27 \sec x, \, -\dfrac{\pi}{2} < x < \dfrac{\pi}{2}$

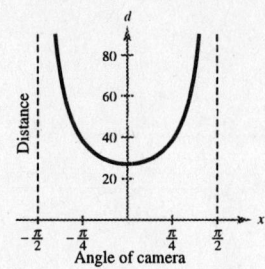
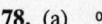

76. When the prey population is highest, the predator population is increasing most rapidly.
When the prey population is lowest, the predator population is decreasing most rapidly.
When the predator population is lowest, the prey population is increasing most rapidly.
When the predator population is highest, the prey population is decreasing most rapidly.

78. (a)

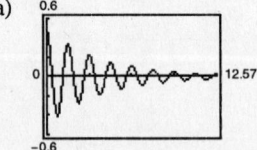

$y = \frac{1}{2} e^{-t/4} \cos 4t$

(b) The displacement is a damped sine wave.
$y \longrightarrow 0$ as t increases.

80. True. The graph of $y = \sec x$ can be obtained by

translating the graph of $y = \csc x$ to the left by $\dfrac{\pi}{2}$ units.

Thus, $y = \sec x = \csc\left(x + \dfrac{\pi}{2}\right) = \dfrac{1}{\sin\left(x + \dfrac{\pi}{2}\right)}$

82. As $x \longrightarrow \pi$ from the left, $f(x) = \csc x \longrightarrow \infty$.

As $x \longrightarrow \pi$ from the right, $f(x) = \csc x \longrightarrow -\infty$.

84.

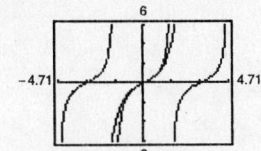

$y = \tan x$

$$y = x + \frac{2x^3}{3!} + \frac{16x^5}{5!}$$

The graphs are nearly the same for $-1.1 < x < 1.1$

86. (a) $y_1 = \dfrac{4}{\pi}\left(\sin \pi x + \dfrac{1}{3}\sin 3\pi x\right)$

(b) $y_3 = \dfrac{4}{\pi}\left(\sin \pi x + \dfrac{1}{3}\sin 3\pi x + \dfrac{1}{5}\sin 5\pi x + \dfrac{1}{7}\sin 7\pi x\right)$

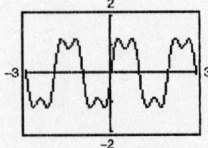

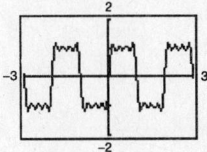

$y_2 = \dfrac{4}{\pi}\left(\sin \pi x + \dfrac{1}{3}\sin 3\pi x + \dfrac{1}{5}\sin 5\pi x\right)$

(c) $y_4 = \dfrac{4}{\pi}\left(\sin \pi x + \dfrac{1}{3}\sin 3\pi x + \dfrac{1}{5}\sin 5\pi x + \dfrac{1}{7}\sin 7\pi x + \dfrac{1}{9}\sin 9\pi x\right)$

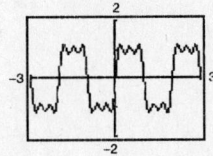

88. $8^{3x} = 98$

$3x = \log_8 98$

$x = \dfrac{\ln 98}{3 \ln 8} \approx 0.735$

90. $\left(1 + \dfrac{0.15}{365}\right)^{365t} = 5$

$1 + \dfrac{0.15}{365} \approx 1.00041096$

$1.00041096^{365t} = 5$

$365t = \log_{1.00041096} 5$

$t = \dfrac{1}{365}\left(\dfrac{\log_{10} 5}{\log_{10} 1.00041096}\right) \approx 10.732$

92. $\ln(14 - 2x) = 68$

$14 - 2x = e^{68}$

$14 - e^{68} = 2x$

$x = \dfrac{14 - e^{68}}{2} \approx -1.702 \times 10^{29}$

94. $\ln\sqrt{x + 4} = 5$

$\dfrac{1}{2}\ln(x + 4) = 5$

$\ln(x + 4) = 10$

$x + 4 = e^{10}$

$x = e^{10} - 4 \approx 22{,}022.466$

96. $\log_6 x + \log_6(x^2 - 1) = \log_6(64x)$

$\log_6(x(x^2 - 1)) = \log_6(64x)$

$x(x^2 - 1) = 64x$

$x^2 - 1 = 64$

$x = \pm\sqrt{65}$

Since $-\sqrt{65}$ is not in the domain of $\log_6 x$, the only solution is
$x = \sqrt{65} \approx 8.062$

Section 4.7   Inverse Trigonometric Functions

Solutions to Even-Numbered Exercises

2. $y = \arcsin 0 \Longrightarrow \sin y = 0$ for $-\dfrac{\pi}{2} \le y \le \dfrac{\pi}{2} \Longrightarrow y = 0$

4. $y = \arccos 0 \Longrightarrow \cos y = 0$ for $0 \le y \le \pi \Longrightarrow y = \dfrac{\pi}{2}$

6. $y = \arctan(-1) \Longrightarrow \tan y = -1$ for $-\dfrac{\pi}{2} < y < \dfrac{\pi}{2} \Longrightarrow y = -\dfrac{\pi}{4}$

8. $y = \arcsin\left(-\dfrac{\sqrt{2}}{2}\right) \Longrightarrow \sin y = -\dfrac{\sqrt{2}}{2}$ for $-\dfrac{\pi}{2} \le y \le \dfrac{\pi}{2} \Longrightarrow y = -\dfrac{\pi}{4}$

10. $y = \arctan\left(\sqrt{3}\right) \Longrightarrow \tan y = \sqrt{3}$ for $-\dfrac{\pi}{2} < y < \dfrac{\pi}{2} \Longrightarrow y = \dfrac{\pi}{3}$

12. $y = \arcsin \dfrac{\sqrt{2}}{2} \Longrightarrow \sin y = \dfrac{\sqrt{2}}{2}$ for $-\dfrac{\pi}{2} \le y \le \dfrac{\pi}{2} \Longrightarrow y = \dfrac{\pi}{4}$

14. $y = \arctan\left(-\dfrac{\sqrt{3}}{3}\right) \Longrightarrow \tan y = -\dfrac{\sqrt{3}}{3}$ for $-\dfrac{\pi}{2} < y < \dfrac{\pi}{2} \Longrightarrow y = -\dfrac{\pi}{6}$

16. $y = \arccos 1 \Longrightarrow \cos y = 1$ for $0 \le y \le \pi \Longrightarrow y = 0$

18. $\arcsin 0.45 \approx 0.47$

20. $\arccos(-0.7) \approx 2.35$

22. $\arctan 15 \approx 1.50$

24. $\arccos 0.26 \approx 1.31$

26. $\arcsin(-0.125) \approx -0.13$

28. $\arctan 2.8 \approx 1.23$

30. $\arccos\left(-\dfrac{1}{3}\right) \approx 1.91$

32. $\arctan\left(-\dfrac{95}{7}\right) \approx -1.50$

34. $\arccos(-1) = \pi$

$\arccos\left(-\dfrac{1}{2}\right) = \dfrac{2\pi}{3}$

$\cos\left(\dfrac{\pi}{6}\right) = \dfrac{\sqrt{3}}{2}$

36. $f(x) = \sin x$

$g(x) = \arcsin x$

$y = x$

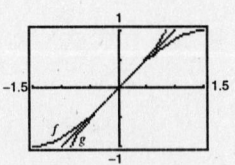

38. $\cos \theta = \dfrac{4}{x}$

$\theta = \arccos \dfrac{4}{x}$

40. $\tan \theta = \dfrac{x+1}{10}$

$\theta = \arctan\left(\dfrac{x+1}{10}\right)$

42. $\tan \theta = \dfrac{x-1}{x^2-1} = \dfrac{1}{x+1}$

$$\theta = \arctan \dfrac{1}{x+1}$$

$$x \neq 1$$

44. $\tan(\arctan 25) = 25$

46. $\sin[\arcsin(-0.2)] = -0.2$

48. $\arccos\left(\cos \dfrac{7\pi}{2}\right) = \arccos 0 = \dfrac{\pi}{2}$

Note: $\dfrac{7\pi}{2}$ is not in the range of the arccosine function.

50. Let $u = \arcsin \dfrac{4}{5}$,

$\sin u = \dfrac{4}{5}, 0 < u < \dfrac{\pi}{2}.$

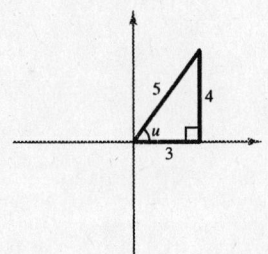

$\sec\left(\arcsin \dfrac{4}{5}\right) = \sec u = \dfrac{\text{hyp}}{\text{adj}} = \dfrac{5}{3}$

52. Let $u = \arccos \dfrac{\sqrt{5}}{5}$,

$\cos u = \dfrac{\sqrt{5}}{5}, 0 < u < \dfrac{\pi}{2}.$

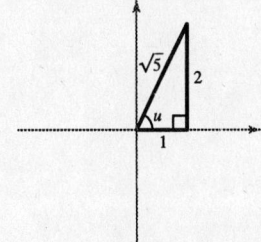

$\sin\left(\arccos \dfrac{\sqrt{5}}{5}\right) = \sin u = \dfrac{2}{\sqrt{5}} = \dfrac{2\sqrt{5}}{5}$

54. Let $u = \arctan\left(-\dfrac{5}{12}\right)$,

$\tan u = -\dfrac{5}{12}, -\dfrac{\pi}{2} < u < 0.$

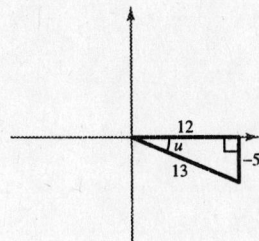

$\csc\left[\arctan\left(-\dfrac{5}{12}\right)\right] = \csc u = \dfrac{\text{hyp}}{\text{opp}} = -\dfrac{13}{5}$

56. Let $u = \arcsin\left(-\dfrac{3}{4}\right)$,

$\sin u = -\dfrac{3}{4}, -\dfrac{\pi}{2} < u < 0.$

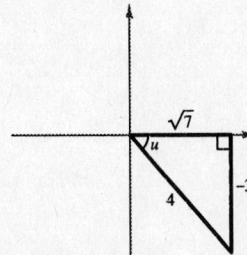

$\tan\left[\arcsin\left(-\dfrac{3}{4}\right)\right] = \tan u = -\dfrac{3}{\sqrt{7}} = -\dfrac{3\sqrt{7}}{7}$

58. Let $u = \arctan \dfrac{5}{8}$,

$\tan u = \dfrac{5}{8}, 0 < u < \dfrac{\pi}{2}.$

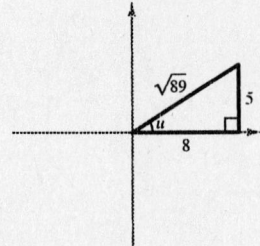

$\cot\left(\arctan \dfrac{5}{8}\right) = \cot u = \dfrac{\text{adj}}{\text{opp}} = \dfrac{8}{5}$

60. Let $u = \arctan x$,

$\tan u = x = \dfrac{x}{1}.$

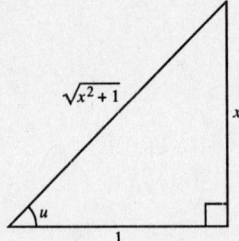

$\sin(\arctan x) = \sin u = \dfrac{\text{opp}}{\text{hyp}} = \dfrac{x}{\sqrt{x^2 + 1}}$

62. Let $u = \arctan 3x$,

$\tan u = 3x = \dfrac{3x}{1}.$

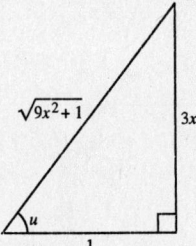

$\sec(\arctan 3x) = \sec u = \dfrac{\text{hyp}}{\text{adj}} = \sqrt{9x^2 + 1}$

64. Let $u = \arcsin(x - 1)$,

$\sin u = x - 1 = \dfrac{x - 1}{1}.$

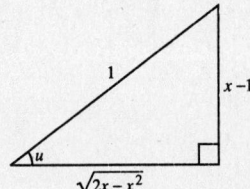

$\sec[\arcsin(x - 1)] = \sec u = \dfrac{\text{hyp}}{\text{adj}} = \dfrac{1}{\sqrt{2x - x^2}}$

66. Let $u = \arctan \dfrac{1}{x}$,

$\tan u = \dfrac{1}{x}.$

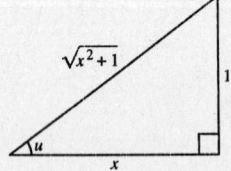

$\cot\left(\arctan \dfrac{1}{x}\right) = \cot u = \dfrac{\text{adj}}{\text{opp}} = x$

68. Let $u = \arcsin \dfrac{x - h}{r}$,

$\sin u = \dfrac{x - h}{r}.$

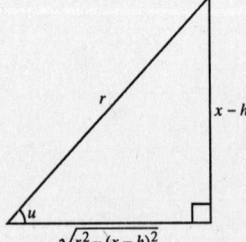

$\cos\left(\arcsin \dfrac{x - h}{r}\right) = \cos u = \dfrac{\sqrt{r^2 - (x - h)^2}}{r}$

70. $f(x) = \tan\left(\arccos \dfrac{x}{2}\right)$

$g(x) = \dfrac{\sqrt{4 - x^2}}{x}$

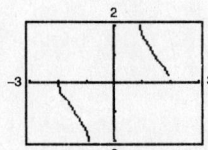

Asymptote: $x = 0$

These are equal because:

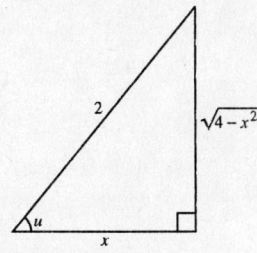

Let $u = \arccos \dfrac{x}{2}$.

$\tan\left(\arccos \dfrac{x}{2}\right) = \tan u = \dfrac{\sqrt{4 - x^2}}{x}$

74. If $\arccos \dfrac{x - 2}{2} = u$,

then $\cos u = \dfrac{x - 2}{2}$.

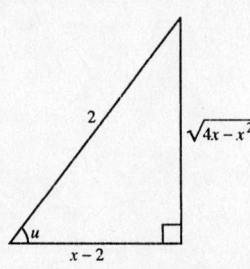

$\arccos \dfrac{x - 2}{2} = \arctan \dfrac{\sqrt{4x - x^2}}{x - 2}$

78. $g(t) = \arccos(t + 2)$

Domain: $[-3, -1]$,
Range: $[0, \pi]$

This is the graph of $y = \arccos t$ shifted two units to the left.

72. If $\arcsin \dfrac{\sqrt{36 - x^2}}{6} = u$,

then $\sin u = \dfrac{\sqrt{36 - x^2}}{6}$.

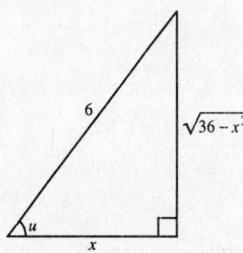

$\arcsin \dfrac{\sqrt{36 - x^2}}{6} = \arccos \dfrac{x}{6}$

76. $y = \arcsin \dfrac{x}{2}$

Domain: $[-2, 2]$

Range: $\left[-\dfrac{\pi}{2}, \dfrac{\pi}{2}\right]$

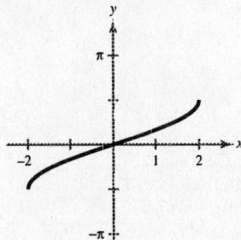

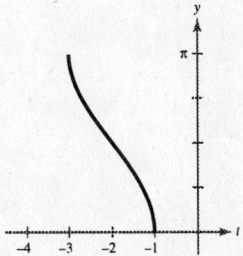

80. $f(x) = \dfrac{\pi}{2} + \arctan x$

Domain: $(-\infty, \infty)$

Range: $(0, \pi)$

This is the graph of $y = \arctan x$ shifted

upward $\dfrac{\pi}{2}$ units.

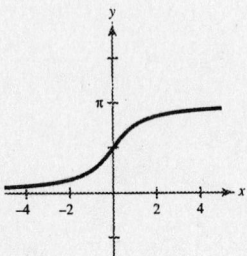

82. $f(x) = \arccos \dfrac{x}{4}$

Domain: $[-4, 4]$

Range: $[0, \pi]$

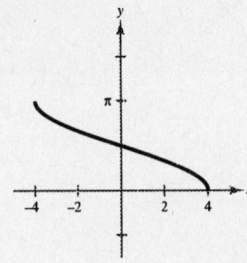

84. $f(x) = \pi \arcsin (4x)$

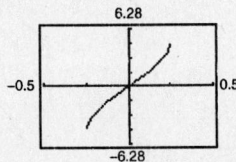

86. $f(x) = -3 + \arctan (\pi x)$

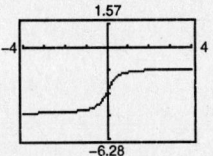

88. $f(x) = \dfrac{\pi}{2} + \arccos \left(\dfrac{1}{\pi}\right) \approx 2.82$

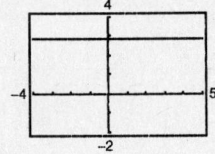

90. $f(t) = 4 \cos \pi t + 3 \sin \pi t$

$$= \sqrt{4^2 + 3^2} \sin\left(\pi t + \arctan \dfrac{4}{3}\right)$$

$$= 5 \sin\left(\pi t + \arctan \dfrac{4}{3}\right)$$

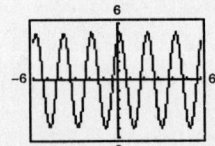

The graph implies that

$$A \cos \omega t + B \sin \omega t = \sqrt{A^2 + B^2} \sin\left(\omega t + \arctan \dfrac{A}{B}\right)$$

is true.

92. (a) $\tan \theta = \dfrac{s}{750}$

$\theta = \arctan \dfrac{s}{750}$

(b) When $s = 300$,

$\theta = \arctan \dfrac{300}{750} \approx 0.38 \approx 21.8°.$

When $s = 1200$,

$\theta = \arctan \dfrac{1200}{750} \approx 1.01 \approx 58.0°.$

94. (a) $\tan \theta = \dfrac{6}{x}$

$\theta = \arctan \dfrac{6}{x}$

(b) $x = 7$ miles

$\theta = \arctan \dfrac{6}{7} \approx 0.71 \approx 40.6°$

$x = 1$ mile

$\theta = \arctan \dfrac{6}{1} \approx 1.41 \approx 89.5°$

96. False.

$\dfrac{5\pi}{6}$ is not in the range of arcsin (x).

$\arcsin \dfrac{1}{2} = \dfrac{\pi}{6}$

98. Area $= \arctan b - \arctan a$

(a) $a = 0, b = 1$

Area $= \arctan 1 - \arctan 0 = \dfrac{\pi}{4} - 0 = \dfrac{\pi}{4}$

(c) $a = 0, b = 3$

Area $= \arctan 3 - \arctan 0$

$\approx 1.25 - 0 = 1.25$

$= 1.25$

(b) $a = -1, b = 1$

Area $= \arctan 1 - \arctan(-1)$

$= \dfrac{\pi}{4} - \left(-\dfrac{\pi}{4}\right) = \dfrac{\pi}{2}$

(d) $a = -1, b = 3$

Area $= \arctan 3 - \arctan(-1)$

$\approx 1.25 - \left(-\dfrac{\pi}{4}\right) \approx 2.03$

100. $y = \operatorname{arcsec} x$ if and only if $\sec y = x$ where

$x \le -1 \cup x \ge 1$ and $0 \le y \le \dfrac{\pi}{2}$ and $\dfrac{\pi}{2} < y \le \pi$. The domain of $y \operatorname{arcsec} x$ is $(-\infty, -1] \cup [1, \infty)$ and the range is $\left[0, \dfrac{\pi}{2}\right) \cup \left(\dfrac{\pi}{2}, \pi\right]$.

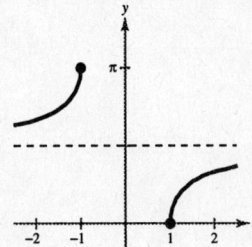

102. (a) $y = \operatorname{arcsec} \sqrt{2} \Longrightarrow \sec y = \sqrt{2}$ and $0 \le y < \dfrac{\pi}{2} \cup \dfrac{\pi}{2} < y \le \pi \Longrightarrow y = \dfrac{\pi}{4}$

(b) $y = \operatorname{arcsec} 1 \Longrightarrow \sec y = 1$ and $0 \le y < \dfrac{\pi}{2} \cup \dfrac{\pi}{2} < y \le \pi \Longrightarrow y = 0$

(c) $y = \operatorname{arccot}\left(-\sqrt{3}\right) \Longrightarrow \cot y = -\sqrt{3}$ and $0 < y < \pi \Longrightarrow y = \dfrac{5\pi}{6}$

(d) $y = \operatorname{arccsc} 2 \Longrightarrow \csc y = 2$ and $-\dfrac{\pi}{2} \le y < 0 \cup 0 < y \le \dfrac{\pi}{2} \Longrightarrow y = \dfrac{\pi}{6}$

104. (a) $f \cdot f^{-1} = \sin(\arcsin x)$

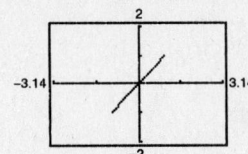

$f^{-1} \cdot f = \arcsin(\sin x)$

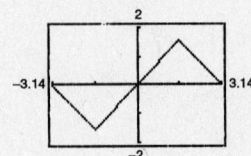

(b) The graphs coincide with the graph of $y = x$ only for certain values of x.

$f \cdot f^{-1} = x$ over its entire domain, $-1 \le x \le 1$.

$f^{-1} \cdot f = x$ over the region $-\dfrac{\pi}{2} \le x \le \dfrac{\pi}{2}$,

corresponding to the region where $\sin x$ is one-to-one and thus has an inverse.

106.
$$y = \arctan(-x)$$
$$\tan y = -x, \quad -\frac{\pi}{2} < y < \frac{\pi}{2}$$
$$-\tan y = x$$
$$\tan(-y) = x, \quad -\frac{\pi}{2} < -y < \frac{\pi}{2}$$
$$\arctan(\tan(-y)) = \arctan x$$
$$-y = \arctan x$$
$$y = -\arctan x$$

108. $y_2 = \dfrac{\pi}{2} - y_1$

$$\arctan x + \arctan \frac{1}{x} = y_1 + y_2$$
$$= y_1 + \left(\frac{\pi}{2} - y_1\right) = \frac{\pi}{2}$$

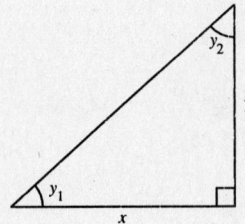

110. $\arcsin x = \arcsin \dfrac{x}{1} = \arctan \dfrac{x}{\sqrt{1-x^2}}$

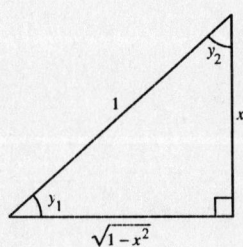

112. $\tan \theta = 2$

$\text{hyp} = \sqrt{1^2 + 2^2} = \sqrt{5}$

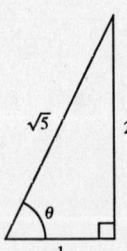

114. $\sec \theta = 3$

$\text{opp} = \sqrt{3^2 - 1^2} = 2\sqrt{2}$

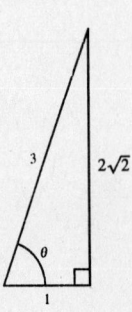

116. $10(14)^{-2} = \dfrac{10}{14^2} = \dfrac{10}{196} \approx 0.051$

118. $16^{-2\pi} = \dfrac{1}{16^{2\pi}} \approx 2.718 \times 10^{-8}$

120. Rate downstream: $18 + x$

Rate upstream: $18 - x$

rate $\times$ time = distance $\Longrightarrow t = \dfrac{d}{r}$

(Time to go upstream) + (Time to go downstream) = 4

$$\frac{35}{18 - x} + \frac{35}{18 + x} = 4$$

$$35(18 + x) + 35(18 - x) = 4(18 - x)(18 + x)$$

$$630 + 35x + 630 - 35x = 4(324 - x^2)$$

$$1260 = 4(324 - x^2)$$

$$315 = 324 - x^2$$

$$x^2 = 9$$

$$x = \pm 3$$

The speed of the current is 3 miles per hour.

Section 4.8   Applications and Models

Solutions to Even-Numbered Exercises

2. $B = 54°, c = 15$

$A = 90° - B = 90° - 54° = 36°$

$\sin B = \dfrac{b}{c} \Longrightarrow b = c \sin B$

$\qquad = 15 \sin 54° \approx 12.14$

$\cos B = \dfrac{a}{c} \Longrightarrow a = c \cos B$

$\qquad = 15 \cos 54° \approx 8.82$

4. $A = 8.4°, a = 40.5$

$B = 90° - A = 90° - 8.4° = 81.6°$

$\tan A = \dfrac{a}{b} \Longrightarrow b = \dfrac{a}{\tan A}$

$\qquad = \dfrac{40.5}{\tan 8.4°} \approx 274.27$

$\sin A = \dfrac{a}{c} \Longrightarrow c = \dfrac{a}{\sin A}$

$\qquad = \dfrac{40.5}{\sin 8.4°} \approx 277.24$

6. $a = 25, c = 35$

$b = \sqrt{c^2 - a^2} = \sqrt{35^2 - 25^2} = \sqrt{600} \approx 24.49$

$\sin A = \dfrac{a}{c} \Longrightarrow A = \arcsin \dfrac{a}{c}$

$\qquad = \arcsin \dfrac{25}{35} \approx 45.58°$

$\cos B = \dfrac{a}{c} \Longrightarrow B = \arccos \dfrac{a}{c}$

$\qquad = \arccos \dfrac{25}{35} \approx 44.42°$

8. $b = 1.32, c = 9.45$

$a = \sqrt{c^2 - b^2} = \sqrt{87.5601} \approx 9.36$

$\cos A = \dfrac{b}{c} \Longrightarrow A = \arccos \dfrac{b}{c}$

$\qquad = \arccos \dfrac{1.32}{9.45} \approx 81.97°$

$\sin B = \dfrac{b}{c} \Longrightarrow B = \arcsin \dfrac{b}{c}$

$\qquad = \arcsin \dfrac{1.32}{9.45} \approx 8.03°$

10. $B = 65° \, 12'$, $a = 14.2$

$A = 90° - B = 90° - 65° \, 12' = 24° \, 48'$

$\cos B = \dfrac{a}{c} \Longrightarrow c = \dfrac{a}{\cos B}$

$\qquad = \dfrac{14.2}{\cos 65° \, 12'} \approx 33.85$

$\tan B = \dfrac{b}{a} \Longrightarrow b = a \tan B$

$\qquad = 14.2 \tan 65° \, 12'$

$\qquad \approx 30.73$

12. $\theta = 18°$, $b = 10$ meters

$\tan \theta = \dfrac{\text{altitude}}{\dfrac{b}{2}}$

$\text{altitude} = \dfrac{b}{2} \tan \theta$

$\qquad = \dfrac{10}{2} \tan 18° \approx 1.62$ meters

14. $\theta = 27°$, $b = 11$ feet

$\tan \theta = \dfrac{\text{altitude}}{\dfrac{b}{2}}$

$\text{altitude} = \dfrac{b}{2} \tan \theta$

$\qquad = \dfrac{11}{2} \tan 27° \approx 2.80$ feet

16. $\tan 20° = \dfrac{600}{x}$

$x - \dfrac{600}{\tan 20°} \approx 1648.5$ feet

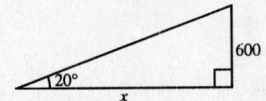

18. $\tan 33° = \dfrac{h}{125}$

$\quad h = 125 \tan 33° \approx 81.2$ feet

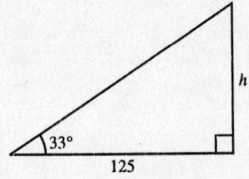

20. $\tan 51° = \dfrac{h}{100}$

$\quad h = 100 \tan 51° \approx 123.5$ feet

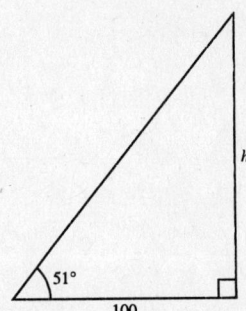

22. $\sin 60° = \dfrac{h}{75}$

$\quad h = 75 \sin 60 \approx 65$ feet

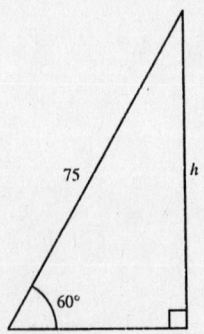

24. (a)

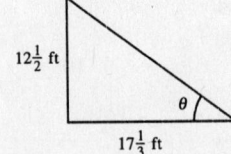

(b) $\tan \theta = \dfrac{12\frac{1}{2}}{17\frac{1}{3}}$

(c) $\theta = \arctan \dfrac{12\frac{1}{2}}{17\frac{1}{3}} \approx 35.8°$

26. (Not drawn to scale)

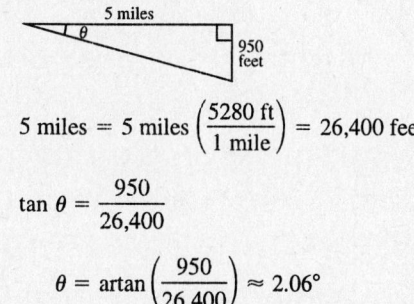

$$5 \text{ miles} = 5 \text{ miles} \left(\frac{5280 \text{ ft}}{1 \text{ mile}}\right) = 26,400 \text{ feet}$$

$$\tan \theta = \frac{950}{26,400}$$

$$\theta = \text{artan}\left(\frac{950}{26,400}\right) \approx 2.06°$$

28.

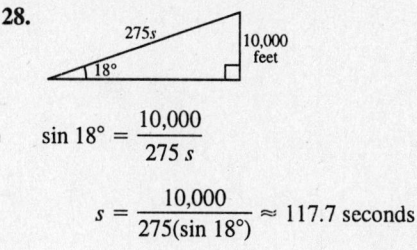

$$\sin 18° = \frac{10,000}{275 \, s}$$

$$s = \frac{10,000}{275(\sin 18°)} \approx 117.7 \text{ seconds}$$

30.

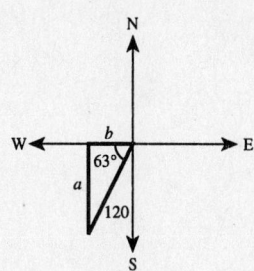

Angle of grade: $\tan \theta = \dfrac{12x}{100x}$

$\theta = \arctan 0.12 \approx 6.8°$

Change in elevation:

$$\sin \theta = \frac{y}{21,120}$$

$$y = 21,120 \sin \theta$$

$$= 21,120 \sin(\arctan 0.12)$$

$$\approx 2516.3 \text{ feet}$$

32. $\sin 63° = \dfrac{a}{120} \Longrightarrow a \approx 107$ nautical miles south

$\cos 63° = \dfrac{b}{120} \Longrightarrow b \approx 54.5$ nautical miles west

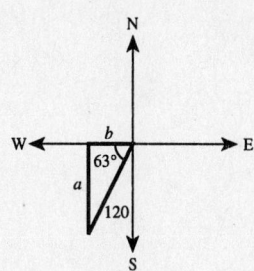

34. $\tan 14° = \dfrac{d}{x} \Longrightarrow x = d \cot 14°$

$\tan 34° = \dfrac{d}{y} \Longrightarrow \dfrac{d}{30 - x} = \dfrac{d}{30 - d \cot 14°}$

$$\cot 34° = \frac{30 - d \cot 14°}{d}$$

$$d \cot 34° = 30 - d \cot 14°$$

$$d = \frac{30}{\cot 34° + \cot 14°}$$

$$\approx 5.46 \text{ kilometers}$$

36. $\tan \theta = \dfrac{85}{120} \Longrightarrow \theta = 35.3°$

Bearing: S 35.3° W

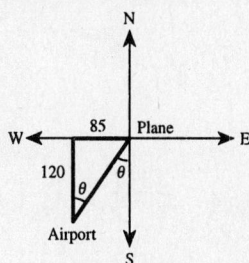

38.

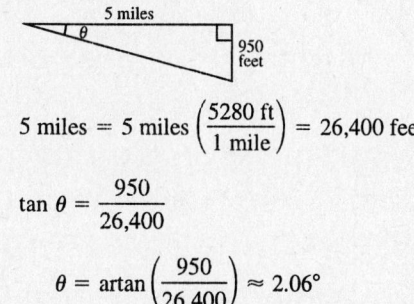

$\cot 55° = \dfrac{d}{10} \Longrightarrow d \approx 7$ kilometers

$\cot 28° = \dfrac{D}{10} \Longrightarrow D \approx 18.8$ kilometers

Distance between towns:

$$D - d = 18.8 - 7 = 11.8 \text{ kilometers}$$

40. $\tan 2.5° = \dfrac{h}{x}$

$$x = \frac{h}{\tan 2.5°}$$

$$\tan 9° = \frac{h}{x - 17}$$

$$x = \frac{h}{\tan 9°} + 17$$

$$\frac{h}{\tan 2.5°} = \frac{h}{\tan 9°} + 17$$

$$h = \frac{17}{\left(\dfrac{1}{\tan 2.5°} - \dfrac{1}{\tan 9°}\right)} \approx 1.025 \text{ miles}$$

$$\approx 5410 \text{ feet}$$

(Not drawn to scale)

42. $L_1 = 2x - y = 8 \Longrightarrow m_1 = 2$

$L_2 = x - 5y = -4 \Longrightarrow m_2 = \dfrac{1}{5}$

$\tan \alpha = \left| \dfrac{m_2 - m_1}{1 + m_2 m_1} \right|$

$\alpha = \arctan \left| \dfrac{m_2 - m_1}{1 + m_2 m_1} \right|$

$\quad = \arctan \left| \dfrac{\frac{1}{5} - 2}{1 + \frac{1}{5}(2)} \right|$

$\quad = \arctan \left(\dfrac{9}{7} \right) \approx 52.1°$

44.

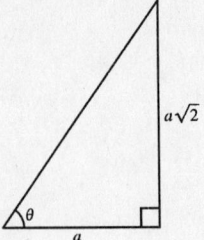

$\tan \theta = \dfrac{a\sqrt{2}}{a} = \sqrt{2}$

$\theta = \arctan \sqrt{2} \approx 54.7°$

46.

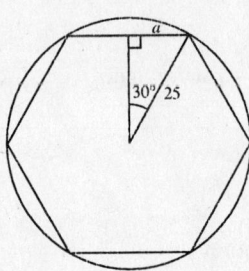

$\sin 30° = \dfrac{a}{25}$

$a = 25 \sin 30° = 12.5$

Length of side $= 2a = 2(12.5) = 25$ inches

48.

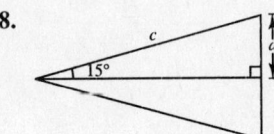

$c = \dfrac{35}{2} = 17.5$

$\sin 15° = \dfrac{a}{c}$

$a = c \sin 15° = 17.5 \sin 15° \approx 4.53$

Distance $= 2a \approx 9.06$ centimeters

50.

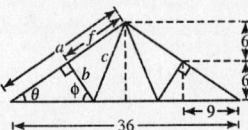

$\tan \theta = \dfrac{12}{18}$

$\theta = \arctan \dfrac{2}{3} = 0.588 \text{ rad} \approx 33.7°$

$\cos \theta = \dfrac{18}{a}$

$a = \dfrac{18}{\cos \theta} \approx 21.6$ feet

$f \approx \dfrac{21.6}{2} = 10.8$

$\phi \approx 90 - 33.7 = 56.3°$

$\sin \phi = \dfrac{6}{b}$

$b = \dfrac{6}{\sin \phi} \approx 7.2$ feet

$c = \sqrt{10.8^2 + 7.2^2} \approx 12$ feet

52. $d = \dfrac{1}{2} \cos 20 \, \pi t$

(a) Maximum displacement: $|a| = \left| \dfrac{1}{2} \right| = \dfrac{1}{2}$

(b) Frequency

$\dfrac{\omega}{2\pi} = \dfrac{20\pi}{2\pi} = 10$

(c) Least positive value for t for which $d = 0$

$\dfrac{1}{2} \cos 20 \, \pi t = 0$

$\cos 20\pi t = 0$

$20\pi t = \arccos 0$

$20\pi t = \dfrac{\pi}{2}$

$t = \dfrac{\pi}{2} \cdot \dfrac{1}{20\pi} = \dfrac{1}{40}$

54. $d = \dfrac{1}{64} \sin 792 \, \pi t$

(a) Maximum displacement:

$$|a| = \left| \frac{1}{64} \right| = \frac{1}{64}$$

(b) Frequency

$$\frac{\omega}{2\pi} = \frac{792\pi}{2\pi} = 396$$

(c) Least positive value for t for which $d = 0$

$$\frac{1}{64} \sin 792 \, \pi t = 0$$

$$\sin 792 \, \pi t = 0$$

$$792 \, \pi t = \arcsin 0$$

$$792 \, \pi t = \pi$$

$$t = \frac{\pi}{792 \, \pi} = \frac{1}{792}$$

56. Displacement at $t = 0$ is $0 \Longrightarrow d = a \sin \omega t$

Amplitude: $|a| = 3$

Period: $\dfrac{2\pi}{\omega} = 6 \Longrightarrow \omega = \dfrac{\pi}{3}$

$$d = 3 \sin \left(\frac{\pi t}{3} \right)$$

58. Displacement at $t = 0$ is $2 \Longrightarrow d = a \cos \omega t$

Amplitude: $|a| = 2$

Period: $\dfrac{2\pi}{\omega} = 10 \Longrightarrow \omega = \dfrac{\pi}{5}$

$$d = 2 \cos \left(\frac{\pi t}{5} \right)$$

60. At $t = 0$, buoy is at its high point $\Longrightarrow d = a \cos \omega t$.

Distance from high to low $= 2|a| = 3.5$

$$|a| = \frac{7}{4}$$

Returns to high point every 10 seconds:

$$\text{Period} = \frac{2\pi}{\omega} = 10 \Longrightarrow \omega = \frac{\pi}{5}$$

$$d = \frac{7}{4} \cos \frac{\pi t}{5}$$

62. False. Since the tower is not exactly vertical, a right triangle with sides 191 ft and d is not formed.

64. (a)

θ	L_1	L_2	$L_1 + L_2$
0.1	$\dfrac{2}{\sin 0.1}$	$\dfrac{3}{\cos 0.1}$	23.0
0.2	$\dfrac{2}{\sin 0.2}$	$\dfrac{3}{\cos 0.2}$	13.1
0.3	$\dfrac{2}{\sin 0.3}$	$\dfrac{3}{\cos 0.3}$	9.9
0.4	$\dfrac{2}{\sin 0.4}$	$\dfrac{3}{\cos 0.4}$	8.4

(b)

θ	L_1	L_2	$L_1 + L_2$
0.5	$\dfrac{2}{\sin 0.5}$	$\dfrac{3}{\cos 0.5}$	7.6
0.6	$\dfrac{2}{\sin 0.6}$	$\dfrac{3}{\cos 0.6}$	7.2
0.7	$\dfrac{2}{\sin 0.7}$	$\dfrac{3}{\cos 0.7}$	7.0
0.8	$\dfrac{2}{\sin 0.8}$	$\dfrac{3}{\cos 0.8}$	7.1

The minimum length of the elevator is 7.0 meters.

(c) $L = L_1 + L_2 = \dfrac{2}{\sin \theta} + \dfrac{3}{\cos \theta}$

(d)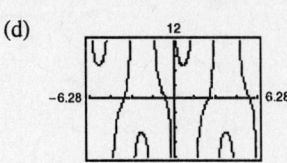

From the graph, it appears that the minimum length is 7.0 meters, which agrees with the estimate of part (b).

66. (a)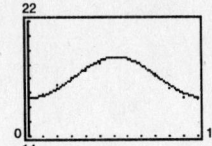

(b) Period $= \dfrac{2\pi}{b} = \dfrac{2\pi}{\dfrac{\pi}{6}} = 12$

Yes, this is what is expected there are 12 months in one year.

(c) Amplitude: $|a| = |1.41| = 1.41$, which represents the maximum change in time of sunset from the average time ($d = 18.09$) of sunset.

68. $3x - 2y = 4$

Line

Intercepts: $(0, -2)$ and $\left(\dfrac{4}{3}, 0\right)$

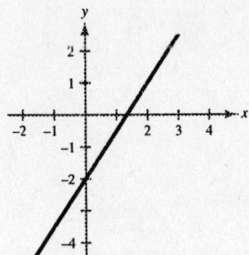

70. $(y - 2)^2 = 8(x + 2)$

Parabola opening to the right

Vertex: $(-2, 2)$

Intercepts: $(0, -2)$ and $(0, 6)$

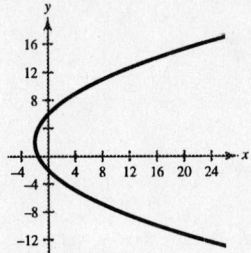

72. $\dfrac{x^2}{4} + y^2 = 1$

Ellipse with center $(0, 0)$

Horizontal major axis

Vertices: $(\pm 2, 0)$

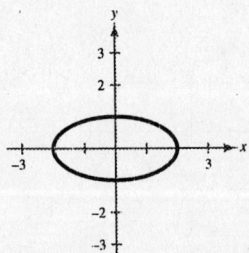

74. $\dfrac{x^2}{4} - y^2 = 1$

Hyperbola with center $(0, 0)$

Horizontal transverse axis

Asymptotes: $y = \pm \dfrac{1}{2}x$

Vertices: $(\pm 2, 0)$

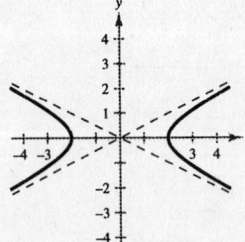

76. $\dfrac{x^2}{4} + \dfrac{y^2}{4} = 1$

Circle

Center: $(0, 0)$

Radius: 2

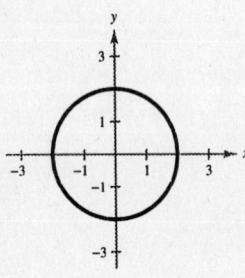

Review Exercises for Chapter 4

2.

2 radians

4.

−3.5 radians

6.

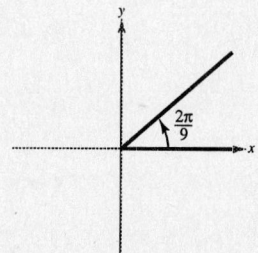

$$\frac{2\pi}{9} + 2\pi = \frac{20\pi}{9}$$

$$\frac{2\pi}{9} - 2\pi = -\frac{16\pi}{9}$$

8.

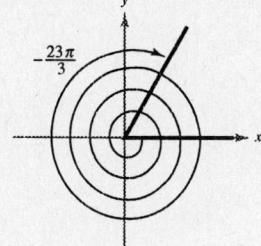

$$-\frac{23\pi}{3} + 8\pi = \frac{\pi}{3}$$

$$-\frac{23\pi}{3} + 2\pi = -\frac{17\pi}{3}$$

10.

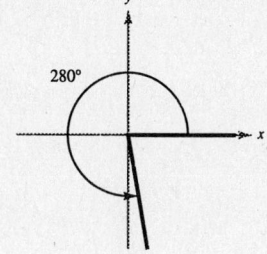

$$280° + 360° = 640°$$

$$280° - 360° = -80°$$

12.

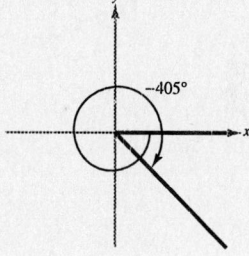

$$-405° + 720° = 315°$$

$$-405° + 360° = -45°$$

14. $-\dfrac{11\pi}{6} \cdot \dfrac{180°}{\pi} = -330.00°$

16. $5.7 \cdot \dfrac{180°}{\pi} \approx 326.59°$

18. $-127.5° \cdot \dfrac{\pi}{180°} \approx -2.2253$

20. $196° \, 77' = \left(196 + \dfrac{77}{60}\right)° \cdot \dfrac{\pi}{180°} \approx 3.4432$

22. (linear speed) = (angular speed) · (radius)

= $(5\pi \, \text{rad}/s) \cdot (13.5 \text{ inches})$

= 67.5π inches per second

≈ 212.1 inches per second

≈ 12.06 miles per hour

24. $t = \dfrac{3\pi}{4}, \, (x, y) = \left(-\dfrac{\sqrt{2}}{2}, \dfrac{\sqrt{2}}{2}\right)$

26. $t = -\dfrac{4\pi}{3}, \, (x, y) = \left(-\dfrac{1}{2}, \dfrac{\sqrt{3}}{2}\right)$

28. $t = \dfrac{\pi}{4}$

$\sin \dfrac{\pi}{4} = \dfrac{\sqrt{2}}{2}$ $\csc \dfrac{\pi}{4} = \sqrt{2}$

$\cos \dfrac{\pi}{4} = \dfrac{\sqrt{2}}{2}$ $\sec \dfrac{\pi}{4} = \sqrt{2}$

$\tan \dfrac{\pi}{4} = 1$ $\cot \dfrac{\pi}{4} = 1$

30. $t = 2\pi$

$\sin 2\pi = 0$ $\csc 2\pi$ is undefined.

$\cos 2\pi = 1$ $\sec 2\pi = 1$

$\tan 2\pi = 0$ $\cot 2\pi$ is undefined.

32. $\cos 4\pi = \cos 0 = 1$

34. $\cos\left(-\dfrac{13\pi}{3}\right) = \cos\left(\dfrac{5\pi}{3}\right) = \dfrac{1}{2}$

36. $\csc 10.5 \approx -1.14$

38. $\sin\left(-\dfrac{\pi}{9}\right) \approx -0.34$

40. adj $= 6$, opp $= 6$

hyp $= \sqrt{6^2 + 6^2} = 6\sqrt{2}$

$\sin \theta = \dfrac{6}{6\sqrt{2}} = \dfrac{\sqrt{2}}{2}$ $\csc \theta = \dfrac{6\sqrt{2}}{6} = \sqrt{2}$

$\cos \theta = \dfrac{6}{6\sqrt{2}} = \dfrac{\sqrt{2}}{2}$ $\sec \theta = \dfrac{6\sqrt{2}}{6} = \sqrt{2}$

$\tan \theta = \dfrac{6}{6} = 1$ $\cot \theta = \dfrac{6}{6} = 1$

42. opp $= 5$, hyp $= 9$

adj $= \sqrt{9^2 - 5^2} = 2\sqrt{14}$

$\sin \theta = \dfrac{5}{9}$ $\csc \theta = \dfrac{9}{5}$

$\cos \theta = \dfrac{2\sqrt{14}}{9}$ $\sec \theta = \dfrac{9}{2\sqrt{14}} = \dfrac{9\sqrt{14}}{28}$

$\tan \theta = \dfrac{5}{2\sqrt{14}} = \dfrac{5\sqrt{14}}{28}$ $\cot = \dfrac{2\sqrt{14}}{5}$

44. $\tan \theta = 4$

(a) $\cot \theta = \dfrac{1}{\tan \theta} = \dfrac{1}{4}$

(b) $\sec \theta = \sqrt{1 + \tan^2 \theta} = \sqrt{1 + 16} = \sqrt{17}$

(c) $\cos \theta = \dfrac{1}{\sec \theta} = \dfrac{1}{\sqrt{17}} = \dfrac{\sqrt{17}}{17}$

(d) $\csc \theta = \sqrt{1 + \cot^2 \theta} = \sqrt{1 + \dfrac{1}{16}} = \dfrac{\sqrt{17}}{4}$

46. $\csc \theta = 5$

(a) $\sin \theta = \dfrac{1}{\csc \theta} = \dfrac{1}{5}$

(b) $\cot \theta = \sqrt{\csc^2 \theta - 1} = \sqrt{25 - 1} = 2\sqrt{6}$

(c) $\tan \theta = \dfrac{1}{\cot \theta} = \dfrac{1}{2\sqrt{6}} = \dfrac{\sqrt{6}}{12}$

(d) $\sec(90° - \theta) = \csc \theta = 5$

48. $\csc 11° \approx 5.24$

50. $\sec 79.3° \approx 5.39$

52. $\cos 78° \, 11' \, 58'' = \cos\left(78 + \dfrac{11}{60} + \dfrac{58}{3600}\right)° \approx 0.20$

54.

$\tan 52° = \dfrac{25}{x}$

$x = \dfrac{25}{\tan 52°} \approx 19.5$ feet

56. $(x, y) = (3, -4)$

$r = \sqrt{3^2 + (-4)^2} = 5$

$\sin \theta = \dfrac{y}{r} = -\dfrac{4}{5}$ $\csc \theta = \dfrac{r}{y} = -\dfrac{5}{4}$

$\cos \theta = \dfrac{x}{r} = \dfrac{3}{5}$ $\sec \theta = \dfrac{r}{x} = \dfrac{5}{3}$

$\tan \theta = \dfrac{y}{x} = -\dfrac{4}{3}$ $\cot \theta = \dfrac{x}{y} = -\dfrac{3}{4}$

58. $(x, y) = \left(-\dfrac{10}{3}, -\dfrac{2}{3}\right)$

$$r = \sqrt{\left(-\dfrac{10}{3}\right)^2 + \left(-\dfrac{2}{3}\right)^2} = \dfrac{2\sqrt{26}}{3}$$

$\sin \theta = \dfrac{y}{r} = \dfrac{-\dfrac{2}{3}}{\dfrac{2\sqrt{26}}{3}} = -\dfrac{\sqrt{26}}{26}$ $\csc \theta = \dfrac{r}{y} = \dfrac{\dfrac{2\sqrt{26}}{3}}{-\dfrac{2}{3}} = -\sqrt{26}$

$\cos \theta = \dfrac{x}{r} = \dfrac{-\dfrac{10}{3}}{\dfrac{2\sqrt{26}}{3}} = -\dfrac{5\sqrt{26}}{26}$ $\sec \theta = \dfrac{r}{x} = \dfrac{\dfrac{2\sqrt{26}}{3}}{-\dfrac{10}{3}} = -\dfrac{\sqrt{26}}{5}$

$\tan \theta = \dfrac{y}{x} = \dfrac{-\dfrac{2}{3}}{-\dfrac{10}{3}} = \dfrac{1}{5}$ $\cot \theta = \dfrac{x}{y} = \dfrac{-\dfrac{10}{3}}{-\dfrac{2}{3}} = 5$

60. $(x, y) = (0.3, 0.4)$

$r = \sqrt{(0.3)^2 + (0.4)^2} = 0.5$

$\sin \theta = \dfrac{y}{r} = \dfrac{0.4}{0.5} = \dfrac{4}{5} = 0.8$

$\cos \theta = \dfrac{x}{r} = \dfrac{0.3}{0.5} = \dfrac{3}{5} = 0.6$

$\tan \theta = \dfrac{y}{x} = \dfrac{0.4}{0.3} = \dfrac{4}{3} \approx 1.33$

$\csc \theta = \dfrac{r}{y} = \dfrac{0.5}{0.4} = \dfrac{5}{4} = 1.25$

$\sec \theta = \dfrac{r}{x} = \dfrac{0.5}{0.3} = \dfrac{5}{3} \approx 1.67$

$\cot \theta = \dfrac{x}{y} = \dfrac{0.3}{0.4} = \dfrac{3}{4} = 0.75$

62. $(x', y') = (-2x, -3x), x > 0$

$r = \sqrt{(-2x)^2 + (-3x)^2} = \sqrt{13}x$

$\sin \theta = \dfrac{y'}{r} = \dfrac{-3x}{\sqrt{13}x} = -\dfrac{3\sqrt{13}}{13}$

$\cos \theta = \dfrac{x'}{r} = \dfrac{-2x}{\sqrt{13}x} = -\dfrac{2\sqrt{13}}{13}$

$\tan \theta = \dfrac{y'}{x'} = \dfrac{-3x}{-2x} = \dfrac{3}{2}$

$\csc \theta = \dfrac{r}{y'} = \dfrac{\sqrt{13}x}{-3x} = -\dfrac{\sqrt{13}}{3}$

$\sec \theta = \dfrac{r}{x'} = \dfrac{\sqrt{13}x}{-2x} = -\dfrac{\sqrt{13}}{2}$

$\cot \theta = \dfrac{x'}{y'} = \dfrac{-2x}{-3x} = \dfrac{2}{3}$

64. $\csc \theta = \dfrac{3}{2}, \cos \theta < 0$

θ is in Quadrant II.

$\sin \theta = \dfrac{1}{\csc \theta} = \dfrac{2}{3}$

$\cos \theta = -\sqrt{1 - \sin^2 \theta} = -\dfrac{\sqrt{5}}{3}$

$\tan \theta = \dfrac{\sin \theta}{\cos \theta} = -\dfrac{2\sqrt{5}}{5}$

$\sec \theta = \dfrac{1}{\cos \theta} = -\dfrac{3\sqrt{5}}{5}$

$\cot \theta = \dfrac{1}{\tan \theta} = -\dfrac{\sqrt{5}}{2}$

66. $\tan \theta = \dfrac{5}{4}, \cos \theta < 0$

θ is in Quadrant III.

$\sec \theta = -\sqrt{1 + \tan^2 \theta} = -\sqrt{1 + \left(\dfrac{25}{16}\right)} = -\dfrac{\sqrt{41}}{4}$

$\cos \theta = \dfrac{1}{\sec \theta} = -\dfrac{4\sqrt{41}}{41}$

$\sin \theta = -\sqrt{1 - \cos^2 \theta} = -\sqrt{1 - \dfrac{16}{41}} = -\dfrac{5\sqrt{41}}{41}$

$\csc \theta = \dfrac{1}{\sin \theta} = -\dfrac{\sqrt{41}}{5}$

$\cot \theta = \dfrac{1}{\tan \theta} = \dfrac{4}{5}$

68. $\sin \theta = -\dfrac{2}{4} = -\dfrac{1}{2}$, $\cos \theta > 0$

θ is in Quadrant IV.

$\csc \theta = \dfrac{1}{\sin \theta} = -2$

$\cos \theta = \sqrt{1 - \sin^2 \theta} = \sqrt{1 - \left(\dfrac{1}{4}\right)} = \dfrac{\sqrt{3}}{2}$ $\qquad$ $\sec \theta = \dfrac{1}{\cos \theta} = \dfrac{2\sqrt{3}}{3}$

$\tan \theta = \dfrac{\sin \theta}{\cos \theta} = -\dfrac{\sqrt{3}}{3}$ $\qquad$ $\cot \theta = \dfrac{1}{\tan \theta} = -\sqrt{3}$

70. $\sec \dfrac{\pi}{4} = \dfrac{1}{\cos \dfrac{\pi}{4}} = \dfrac{1}{\dfrac{1}{\sqrt{2}}} = \sqrt{2}$ $\qquad$ **72.** $\cot\left(-\dfrac{5\pi}{4}\right) = \cot\left(\dfrac{3\pi}{4}\right) = \dfrac{\cos\left(\dfrac{3\pi}{4}\right)}{\sin\left(\dfrac{3\pi}{4}\right)} = -1$

74. $\sin(-150°) = \sin(210°) = -\dfrac{1}{2}$ $\qquad\qquad$ **76.** $\tan 3 \approx -0.14$

78. $\cot(-4.8) \approx 0.09$ $\qquad$ **80.** $\cot(1.5\pi) = 0$ $\qquad$ **82.** $\tan\left(\dfrac{-25\pi}{7}\right) \approx 4.38$

84. $y = \cos x$ $\qquad\qquad$ **86.** $f(x) = 8\cos\left(-\dfrac{x}{4}\right)$ $\qquad\qquad$ **88.** $y = -4 - \cos \pi x$

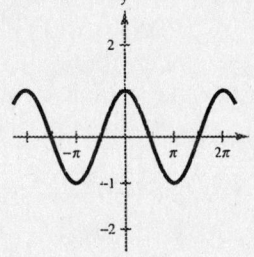 $\qquad$ 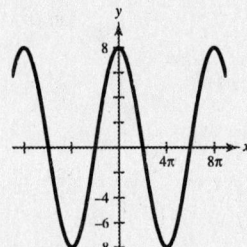 $\qquad$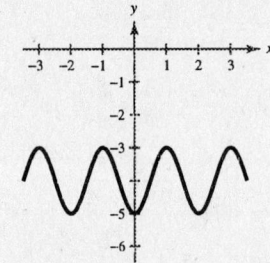

90. $g(t) = 3\cos(t + \pi)$ $\qquad\qquad$ **92.** $y = a\cos bx$

Amplitude: $2 \Rightarrow a = 2$

Period: $\dfrac{1}{264}$ second $\Rightarrow b = \dfrac{2\pi}{\dfrac{1}{264}} = 582\pi$

$y = 2\cos(528\pi x)$

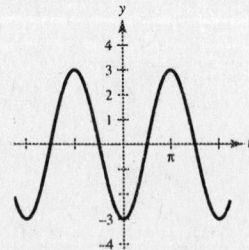

94. $f(t) = \tan\left(t - \dfrac{\pi}{4}\right)$

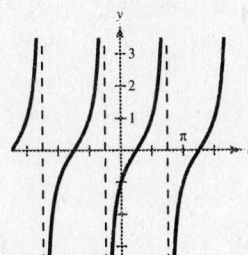

96. $g(t) = 2 \cot 2t$

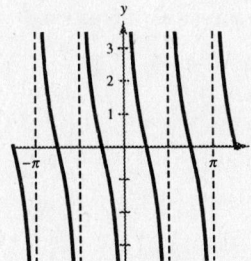

98. $h(t) = \sec\left(t - \dfrac{\pi}{4}\right)$

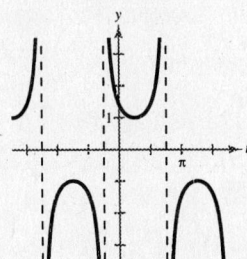

100. $f(t) = 3 \csc\left(2t + \dfrac{\pi}{4}\right)$

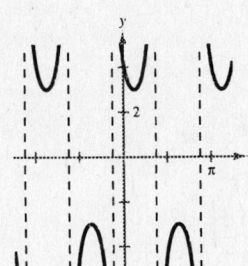

102. $g(x) = e^x \cos x$

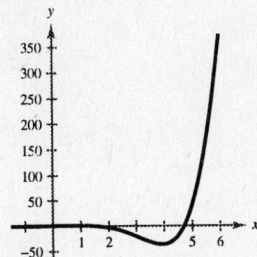

104. $\arcsin(-1) = -\dfrac{\pi}{2}$

106. $\arcsin(0.213) \approx 0.21$

108. $\sin^{-1}(0.89) \approx 1.10$

110. $\arccos\left(\dfrac{\sqrt{2}}{2}\right) = \dfrac{\pi}{4}$

112. $\cos^{-1}\left(\dfrac{\sqrt{3}}{2}\right) = \dfrac{\pi}{6}$

114. $\arccos(-0.888) \approx 2.66$

116. $\arctan(2.34) \approx 1.17$

118. $\arctan(99.1) \approx 1.56$

120. $\tan^{-1}(8.2) \approx 1.45$

122. $\cos(\arccos 0.25) = 0.25$

124. $\arccos[\cos(-5\pi)] = \arccos(-1) = \pi$

126. Let $u = \arccos \dfrac{3}{5}$

$\tan\left(\arccos \dfrac{3}{5}\right) = \tan u = \dfrac{4}{3}$

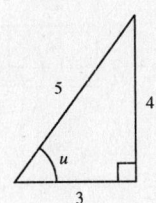

128. Let $u = \arcsin\left(-\dfrac{12}{13}\right)$

$\cot\left[\arcsin\left(-\dfrac{12}{13}\right)\right] = \cot u$

$= -\dfrac{5}{12}$

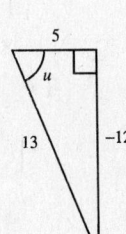

130. $\tan 21° = \dfrac{h}{25}$

$h = 25 \tan 21° \approx 9.6 \text{ feet}$

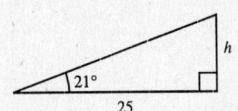

132. Amplitude: $\dfrac{1.5}{2} = 0.75$ inches

Period: 3 seconds

$d = a \cos bt$

$a = 0.75$

$b = \dfrac{2\pi}{3}$

$d = 0.75 \cos\left(\dfrac{2\pi t}{3}\right)$

134. False. An interval of length π for y must be chosen so that $y = \arcsin x$ is a function.

136. False. The range of arctan is $\left(-\dfrac{\pi}{2}, \dfrac{\pi}{2}\right)$, so $\arctan(-1) = -\dfrac{\pi}{4}$.

138. $y = -3\sin x$ matches graph (a).

Period: 2π

Amplitude: 3

140. $y = 2\sin\dfrac{x}{2}$ matches graph (c).

Period: 4π

Amplitude: 2

142. (a) $f(t - 2c) = f(t)$
t and $t - 2c$ differ by an integer multiple of the period.

(b) $f\left(t + \tfrac{1}{2}c\right) \neq f\left(\tfrac{1}{2}t\right)$
$\left(t + \tfrac{1}{2}c\right) - \left(\tfrac{1}{2}t\right) = \tfrac{1}{2}t + \tfrac{1}{2}c$ which is not an integer multiple of the period.

(c) $f\left(\tfrac{1}{2}[t + c]\right) \neq f\left(\tfrac{1}{2}t\right)$
$\left(\tfrac{1}{2}[t + c]\right) - \left(\tfrac{1}{2}t\right) = \tfrac{1}{2}c$ which is not an integer multiple of the period.

144. $y = Ae^{-kt}\cos bt = \tfrac{1}{5}e^{-t/10}\cos 6t$

(a) A is changed from $\tfrac{1}{5}$ to $\tfrac{1}{3}$:
The displacement is increased.

(b) k is changed from $\tfrac{1}{10}$ to $\tfrac{1}{3}$:
The friction damps the oscillations more rapidly.

(c) b is changed from 6 to 9:
The frequency of oscillation is increased.

146. (a) $\arcsin x \approx x + \dfrac{x^3}{6} + \dfrac{3x^5}{40} + \dfrac{5x^7}{112}$

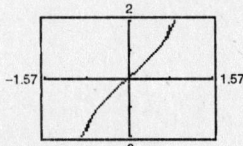

The approximation appears to be accurate over most of the domain of $\arcsin(x)$, $-1 \leq x \leq 1$.

(c) $\arctan x \approx x + \dfrac{x^3}{3} + \dfrac{x^5}{5} + \dfrac{x^7}{7} + \dfrac{x^9}{9}$

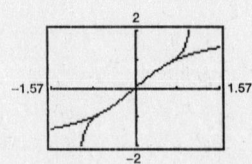

The accuracy improved.

(b) $\arctan x \approx x + \dfrac{x^3}{3} + \dfrac{x^5}{5} + \dfrac{x^7}{7}$

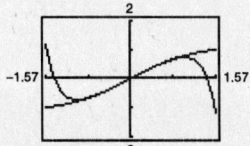

The approximation appears to be accurate over the interval $-0.5 < x < 0.5$.

CHAPTER 5
Analytic Trigonometry

CHAPTER 5
Analytic Trigonometry

Section 5.1   Using Fundamental Identities

Solutions to Even-Numbered Exercises

2. $\tan x = \dfrac{\sqrt{3}}{3}$, $\cos x = -\dfrac{\sqrt{3}}{2}$

x is in Quadrant III.

$\sin x = -\sqrt{1 - \left(-\dfrac{\sqrt{3}}{2}\right)^2} = -\sqrt{\dfrac{1}{4}} = -\dfrac{1}{2}$

$\csc x = \dfrac{1}{\sin x} = -2$

$\sec x = \dfrac{1}{\cos x} = -\dfrac{2}{\sqrt{3}} = -\dfrac{2\sqrt{3}}{3}$

$\cot x = \dfrac{1}{\tan x} = \dfrac{3}{\sqrt{3}} = \sqrt{3}$

4. $\csc \theta = \dfrac{5}{3}$, $\tan \theta = \dfrac{3}{4}$

θ is in Quadrant I.

$\sin \theta = \dfrac{1}{\csc \theta} = \dfrac{3}{5}$

$\cos \theta = \dfrac{\sin \theta}{\tan \theta} = \dfrac{3}{5} \cdot \dfrac{4}{3} = \dfrac{4}{5}$

$\sec \theta = \dfrac{1}{\cos \theta} = \dfrac{5}{4}$

$\cot \theta = \dfrac{1}{\tan \theta} = \dfrac{4}{3}$

6. $\cot \phi = -3$, $\sin \phi = \dfrac{\sqrt{10}}{10}$

ϕ is in Quadrant II.

$\cos \phi = \cot \phi \sin \phi = -\dfrac{3\sqrt{10}}{10}$

$\tan \phi = \dfrac{1}{\cot \phi} = -\dfrac{1}{3}$

$\csc \phi = \dfrac{1}{\sin \phi} = \sqrt{10}$

$\sec \phi = \dfrac{1}{\cos \phi} = -\dfrac{10}{3\sqrt{10}} = -\dfrac{\sqrt{10}}{3}$

8. $\cos \left(\dfrac{\pi}{2} - x\right) = \dfrac{3}{5}$, $\cos x = \dfrac{4}{5}$

x is in Quadrant I.

$\sin x = \sqrt{1 - \left(\dfrac{4}{5}\right)^2} = \dfrac{3}{5}$

$\tan x = \dfrac{\sin x}{\cos x} = \dfrac{3}{5} \cdot \dfrac{5}{4} = \dfrac{3}{4}$

$\csc x = \dfrac{1}{\sin x} = \dfrac{5}{3}$

$\sec x = \dfrac{1}{\cos x} = \dfrac{5}{4}$

$\cot x = \dfrac{1}{\tan x} = \dfrac{4}{3}$

10. $\sec x = 4, \sin x > 0$

x is in Quadrant I.

$\cos x = \dfrac{1}{\sec x} = \dfrac{1}{4}$

$\sin x = \sqrt{1 - \left(\dfrac{1}{4}\right)^2} = \dfrac{\sqrt{15}}{4}$

$\tan x = \dfrac{\sin x}{\cos x} = \dfrac{\sqrt{15}}{4} \cdot \dfrac{4}{1} = \sqrt{15}$

$\csc x = \dfrac{1}{\sin x} = \dfrac{4}{\sqrt{15}} = \dfrac{4\sqrt{15}}{15}$

$\cot x = \dfrac{1}{\tan x} = \dfrac{1}{\sqrt{15}} = \dfrac{\sqrt{15}}{15}$

12. $\csc \theta = -5, \cos \theta < 0$

θ is in Quadrant III.

$\sin \theta = \dfrac{1}{\csc \theta} = -\dfrac{1}{5}$

$\cos \theta = -\sqrt{1 - \left(-\dfrac{1}{5}\right)^2} = \dfrac{-2\sqrt{6}}{5}$

$\tan \theta = \dfrac{\sin \theta}{\cos \theta} = -\dfrac{1}{5} \cdot -\dfrac{5}{2\sqrt{6}} = \dfrac{\sqrt{6}}{12}$

$\sec \theta = \dfrac{1}{\cos \theta} = -\dfrac{5}{2\sqrt{6}} = -\dfrac{5\sqrt{6}}{12}$

$\cot \theta = \dfrac{1}{\tan \theta} = \dfrac{12}{\sqrt{6}} = 2\sqrt{6}$

14. $\tan \theta$ is undefined, $\sin \theta > 0$.

$\theta = \dfrac{\pi}{2}$

$\tan \theta = \dfrac{\sin \theta}{\cos \theta}$ is undefined $\Rightarrow \cos \theta = 0$

$\sin \theta = \sqrt{1 - 0^2} = 1$

$\csc \theta = \dfrac{1}{\sin \theta} = 1$

$\sec \theta = \dfrac{1}{\cos \theta}$ is undefined.

$\cot \theta = \dfrac{\cos \theta}{\sin \theta} = \dfrac{0}{1} = 0$

16. $\tan x \csc x = \dfrac{\sin x}{\cos x} \cdot \dfrac{1}{\sin x} = \dfrac{1}{\cos x} = \sec x$

Matches (a).

18. $(1 - \cos^2 x)(\csc x) = (\sin^2 x)\dfrac{1}{\sin x} = \sin x$

Matches (f).

20. $\dfrac{\sin\left[\left(\dfrac{\pi}{2}\right) - x\right]}{\cos\left[\left(\dfrac{\pi}{2}\right) - x\right]} = \dfrac{\cos x}{\sin x} = \cot x$

Matches (c).

22. $\cos^2 x(\sec^2 x - 1) = \cos^2 x(\tan^2 x)$

$\qquad = \cos^2 x\left(\dfrac{\sin^2 x}{\cos^2 x}\right)$

$\qquad = \sin^2 x$

Matches (c).

24. $\cot x \sec x = \dfrac{\cos x}{\sin x} \cdot \dfrac{1}{\cos x} = \dfrac{1}{\sin x} = \csc x$

Matches (a).

26. $\dfrac{\cos^2\left[\left(\dfrac{\pi}{2}\right) - x\right]}{\cos x} = \dfrac{\sin^2 x}{\cos x} = \dfrac{\sin x}{\cos x}\sin x$

$\qquad = \tan x \sin x$

Matches (d).

28. $\cos \beta \tan \beta = \cos \beta \dfrac{\sin \beta}{\cos \beta} = \sin \beta$

30. $\sec^2 x(1 - \sin^2 x) = \sec^2 x - \sec^2 x \sin^2 x$

$\qquad\qquad\qquad\quad = \sec^2 x - \dfrac{1}{\cos^2 x} \cdot \sin^2 x$

$\qquad\qquad\qquad\quad = \sec^2 x - \dfrac{\sin^2 x}{\cos^2 x}$

$\qquad\qquad\qquad\quad = \sec^2 x - \tan^2 x$

$\qquad\qquad\qquad\quad = 1$

32. $\dfrac{\csc \theta}{\sec \theta} = \dfrac{\dfrac{1}{\sin \theta}}{\dfrac{1}{\cos \theta}} = \dfrac{\cos \theta}{\sin \theta} = \cot \theta$

34. $\dfrac{1}{\tan^2 x + 1} = \dfrac{1}{\sec^2 x} = \dfrac{1}{\dfrac{1}{\cos^2 x}} = \cos^2 x$

36. $\dfrac{\tan^2 \theta}{\sec^2 \theta} = \dfrac{\sin^2 \theta}{\cos^2 \theta} \cdot \dfrac{1}{\sec^2 \theta} = \dfrac{\sin^2 \theta}{\cos^2 \theta} \cdot \dfrac{1}{\dfrac{1}{\cos^2 \theta}} = \dfrac{\sin^2 \theta \cos^2 \theta}{\cos^2 \theta} = \sin^2 \theta$

38. $\cot\left(\dfrac{\pi}{2} - x\right) \cos x = \tan x \cos x = \dfrac{\sin x}{\cos x} \cdot \cos x = \sin x$

40. $(\cos t)(1 + \tan^2 t) = (\cos t)(\sec^2 t) = \dfrac{\cos t}{\cos^2 t} = \dfrac{1}{\cos t} = \sec t$

42. $\csc \phi \tan \phi + \sec \phi = \dfrac{1}{\sin \phi} \cdot \dfrac{\sin \phi}{\cos \phi} + \sec \phi$

$\qquad\qquad\qquad\qquad\quad = \dfrac{1}{\cos \phi} + \sec \phi = 2 \sec \phi$

44. $\sin \theta \sec \theta + \cos \theta \csc \theta = \dfrac{\sin \theta}{\cos \theta} + \dfrac{\cos \theta}{\sin \theta}$

$\qquad\qquad\qquad\qquad\qquad = \dfrac{\sin^2 \theta + \cos^2 \theta}{\cos \theta \sin \theta}$

$\qquad\qquad\qquad\qquad\qquad = \dfrac{1}{\cos \theta \sin \theta}$

$\qquad\qquad\qquad\qquad\qquad = \sec \theta \csc \theta$

46. $\sin^2 x \csc^2 x - \sin^2 x = \sin^2 x(\csc^2 x - 1)$

$\qquad\qquad\qquad\qquad\quad = \sin^2 x \cot^2 x$

$\qquad\qquad\qquad\qquad\quad = \sin^2 x \cdot \dfrac{\cos^2 x}{\sin^2 x}$

$\qquad\qquad\qquad\qquad\quad = \cos^2 x$

48. $\cos^2 x + \cos^2 x \tan^2 x = \cos^2 x(1 + \tan^2 x)$

$\qquad\qquad\qquad\qquad\qquad = \cos^2 x + (\sec^2 x)$

$\qquad\qquad\qquad\qquad\qquad = \cos^2 x\left(\dfrac{1}{\cos^2 x}\right)$

$\qquad\qquad\qquad\qquad\qquad = 1$

50. $\dfrac{\cos^2 x - 4}{\cos x - 2} = \dfrac{(\cos x + 2)(\cos x - 2)}{\cos x - 2}$

$\qquad\qquad\qquad\quad = \cos x + 2$

52. $1 - 2\cos^2 x + \cos^4 x = (1 - \cos^2 x)^2$

$\qquad\qquad\qquad\qquad\quad = (\sin^2 x)^2$

$\qquad\qquad\qquad\qquad\quad = \sin^4 x$

54. $\sec^4 x - \tan^4 x = (\sec^2 x + \tan^2 x)(\sec^2 x - \tan^2 x)$

$\qquad\qquad = (\sec^2 x + \tan^2 x)(1)$

$\qquad\qquad = \sec^2 x + \tan^2 x$

56. $\sec^3 x - \sec^2 x - \sec x + 1 = \sec^2 x(\sec x - 1) - (\sec x - 1)$

$\qquad\qquad\qquad\qquad = (\sec^2 x - 1)(\sec x - 1)$

$\qquad\qquad\qquad\qquad = \tan^2 x(\sec x - 1)$

58. $(\cot x + \csc x)(\cot x - \csc x) = \cot^2 x - \csc^2 x$

$\qquad\qquad\qquad\qquad\qquad = -1$

60. $(3 - 3 \sin x)(3 + 3 \sin x) = 9 - 9 \sin^2 x$

$\qquad\qquad\qquad\qquad\qquad = 9(1 - \sin^2 x)$

$\qquad\qquad\qquad\qquad\qquad = 9 \cos^2 x$

62. $\dfrac{1}{\sec x + 1} - \dfrac{1}{\sec x - 1} = \dfrac{\sec x - 1 - (\sec x + 1)}{(\sec x + 1)(\sec x - 1)}$

$\qquad\qquad\qquad\qquad = \dfrac{\sec x - 1 - \sec x - 1}{\sec^2 x - 1}$

$\qquad\qquad\qquad\qquad = \dfrac{-2}{\tan^2 x}$

$\qquad\qquad\qquad\qquad = -2\left(\dfrac{1}{\tan^2 x}\right) = -2 \cot^2 x$

64. $\tan x - \dfrac{\sec^2 x}{\tan x} = \dfrac{\tan^2 x - \sec^2 x}{\tan x}$

$\qquad\qquad\qquad = \dfrac{-1}{\tan x} = -\cot x$

66. $\dfrac{5}{\tan x + \sec x} \cdot \dfrac{\tan x - \sec x}{\tan x - \sec x} = \dfrac{5(\tan x - \sec x)}{\tan^2 x - \sec^2 x}$

$\qquad\qquad\qquad\qquad\qquad = \dfrac{5(\tan x - \sec x)}{-1}$

$\qquad\qquad\qquad\qquad\qquad = 5(\sec x - \tan x)$

68. $\dfrac{\tan^2 x}{\csc x + 1} \cdot \dfrac{\csc x - 1}{\csc x - 1} = \dfrac{\tan^2 x(\csc x - 1)}{\csc^2 x - 1}$

$\qquad\qquad\qquad\qquad = \dfrac{\tan^2 x(\csc x - 1)}{\cot^2 x}$

$\qquad\qquad\qquad\qquad = \tan^2 x(\csc x - 1)\tan^2 x$

$\qquad\qquad\qquad\qquad = \tan^4 x(\csc x - 1)$

70. $y_1 = \sec x - \cos x,\ y_2 = \sin x \tan x$

x	0.2	0.4	0.6	0.8	1.0	1.2	1.4
y_1	0.0403	0.1646	0.3863	0.7386	1.3105	2.3973	5.7135
y_2	0.0403	0.1646	0.3863	0.7386	1.3105	2.3973	5.7135

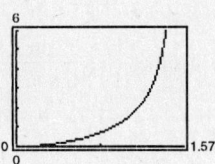

It appears that $y_1 = y_2$.

72. $y_1 = \sec^4 x - \sec^2 x,\ y_2 = \tan^2 x + \tan^4 x$

x	0.2	0.4	0.6	0.8	1.0	1.2	1.4
y_1	0.0428	0.2107	0.6871	2.1841	8.3087	50.3869	1163.6143
y_2	0.0428	0.2107	0.6871	2.1841	8.3087	50.3869	1163.6143

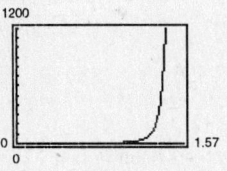

It appears that $y_1 = y_2$.

74. $y_1 = \sec x \csc x - \tan x$

y_1 and $y_2 = \sin x$

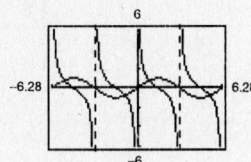

y_1 and $y_2 = \cos x$

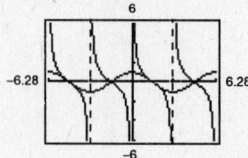

y_1 and $y_2 = \tan x$

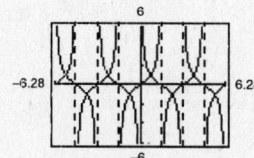

y_1 and $y_2 = \csc x$

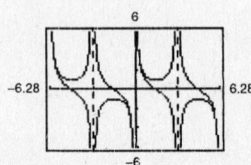

y_1 and $y_2 = \sec x$

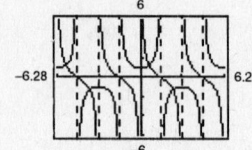

y_1 and $y_2 = \cot x$

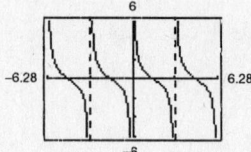

It appears that $\sec x \csc x - \tan x = \cot x$.

76. $y_1 = \dfrac{1}{2}\left(\dfrac{1 + \sin \theta}{\cos \theta} + \dfrac{\cos \theta}{1 + \sin \theta}\right)$

y_1 and $y_2 = \sin \theta$

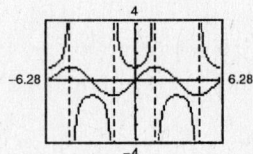

y_1 and $y_2 = \cos \theta$

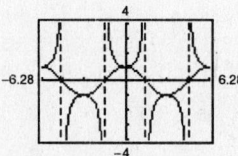

y_1 and $y_2 = \tan \theta$

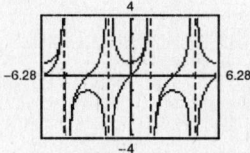

y_1 and $y_2 = \dfrac{1}{\sin \theta} = \csc \theta$

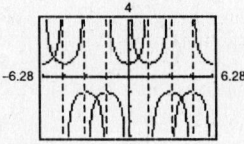

y_1 and $y_2 = \dfrac{1}{\cos \theta} = \sec \theta$

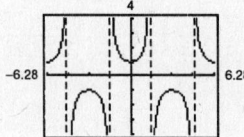

y_1 and $y_2 = \dfrac{1}{\tan \theta} = \cot \theta$

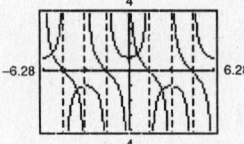

It appears that $\dfrac{1}{2}\left(\dfrac{1 + \sin \theta}{\cos \theta} + \dfrac{\cos \theta}{1 + \sin \theta}\right) = \sec \theta$.

78. Let $x = 2 \cos \theta$

$$\sqrt{64 - 16x^2} = \sqrt{64 - 16(2 \cos \theta)^2}$$
$$= \sqrt{64(1 - \cos^2 \theta)}$$
$$= \sqrt{64 \sin^2 \theta}$$
$$= 8 \sin \theta$$

80. Let $x = 2 \sec \theta$.

$$\sqrt{x^2 - 4} = \sqrt{(2 \sec \theta)^2 - 4}$$
$$= \sqrt{4(\sec^2 \theta - 1)}$$
$$= \sqrt{4 \tan^2 \theta}$$
$$= 2 \tan \theta$$

82. Let $x = 10 \tan \theta$.

$$\sqrt{x^2 + 100} = \sqrt{(10 \tan \theta)^2 + 100}$$
$$= \sqrt{100(\tan^2 \theta + 1)}$$
$$= \sqrt{100 \sec^2 \theta}$$
$$= 10 \sec \theta$$

84. $x = 6 \sin \theta$

$3 = \sqrt{36 - x^2}$

$\quad = \sqrt{36 - (6 \sin \theta)^2}$

$\quad = \sqrt{36(1 - \sin^2\theta)}$

$\quad = \sqrt{36 \cos^2 \theta}$

$\quad = 6 \cos \theta$

$\cos \theta = \dfrac{3}{6} = \dfrac{1}{2}$

$\sin \theta = \pm\sqrt{1 - \cos^2 \theta}$

$\quad = \pm\sqrt{1 - \left(\dfrac{1}{2}\right)^2}$

$\quad = \pm\sqrt{\dfrac{3}{4}}$

$\quad = \pm\dfrac{\sqrt{3}}{2}$

86. $x = 10 \cos \theta$

$-5\sqrt{3} = \sqrt{100 - x^2}$

$\quad = \sqrt{100 - (10 \cos \theta)^2}$

$\quad = \sqrt{100(1 - \cos^2 \theta)}$

$\quad = \sqrt{100 \sin^2 \theta}$

$\quad = 10 \sin \theta$

$\sin \theta = -\dfrac{5\sqrt{3}}{10}$

$\quad = -\dfrac{\sqrt{3}}{2}$

$\cos \theta = \sqrt{1 - \sin^2 \theta}$

$\quad = \sqrt{1 - \left(-\dfrac{\sqrt{3}}{2}\right)^2}$

$\quad = \dfrac{1}{2}$

88. $\cos \theta = -\sqrt{1 - \sin^2 \theta}$

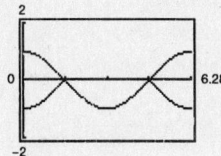

$\dfrac{\pi}{2} < \theta < \dfrac{3\pi}{2}$

90. $\csc \theta = \sqrt{1 + \cot^2 \theta}$

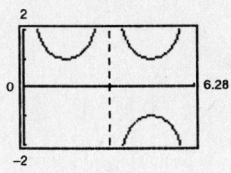

$0 < \theta < \pi$

92. $\ln|\sec x| + \ln|\sin x| = \ln|\sec x \sin x|$

$\quad = \ln\left|\dfrac{1}{\cos x} \cdot \sin x\right|$

$\quad = \ln|\tan x|$

94. $\ln(\cos^2 t) + \ln(1 + \tan^2 t) = \ln[\cos^2 t(1 + \tan^2 t)]$

$\quad = \ln[\cos^2 t \sec^2 t]$

$\quad = \ln\left(\cos^2 t \cdot \dfrac{1}{\cos^2 t}\right)$

$\quad = \ln(1)$

$\quad = 0$

96. $\tan^2 \theta + 1 = \sec^2 \theta$

(a) $\theta = 346°$

$(\tan 346°)^2 + 1 \approx 1.0622$

$(\sec 346°)^2 = \left(\dfrac{1}{\cos 346°}\right)^2 \approx 1.0622$

(b) $\theta = 3.1$

$(\tan 3.1)^2 + 1 \approx 1.00173$

$(\sec 3.1)^2 = \left(\dfrac{1}{\cos 3.1}\right)^2 \approx 1.00173$

98. $\sin(-\theta) = -\sin \theta$

(a) $\theta = 250°$

$\sin(-250°) \approx 0.9397$

$-(\sin 250°) \approx 0.9397$

(b) $\theta = \frac{1}{2}$

$\sin\left(-\frac{1}{2}\right) \approx -0.4794$

$-\left(\sin \frac{1}{2}\right) \approx -0.4794$

100. True.

For example, $\sin(-x) = -\sin(x)$ means the graph of $\sin(x)$ is symmetric about the origin.

102. As $x \to \dfrac{\pi^-}{2}$, $\sin x \to 1$

and $\csc x \to 1$

104. As $x \to \dfrac{\pi^-}{2}$, $\tan x \to \infty$

and $\cot x \to 0$.

106. $\cos \theta = \sqrt{1 - \sin^2 \theta}$ is not an identity.

$\cos^2 \theta + \sin^2 \theta = 1 \Rightarrow \cos \theta = \pm \sqrt{1 - \sin^2 \theta}$

108. $\dfrac{\sin k\theta}{\cos k\theta} = \tan \theta$ is not an identity.

$\dfrac{\sin k\theta}{\cos k\theta} = \tan k\theta$

110. $\sin \theta \csc \theta = 1$ is an identity.

$\sin \theta \cdot \dfrac{1}{\sin \theta} = 1$, provided $\sin \theta \neq 0$.

112. Since $\sin^2 \theta + \cos^2 \theta = 1$ and $\cos^2 \theta = 1 - \sin^2 \theta$:

$\cos \theta = \pm \sqrt{1 - \sin^2 \theta}$

$\tan \theta = \dfrac{\sin \theta}{\cos \theta} = \pm \dfrac{\sin \theta}{\sqrt{1 - \sin^2 \theta}}$

$\cot \theta = \dfrac{1}{\tan \theta} = \pm \dfrac{\sqrt{1 - \sin^2 \theta}}{\sin \theta}$

$\sec \theta = \dfrac{1}{\cos \theta} = \pm \dfrac{1}{\sqrt{1 - \sin^2 \theta}}$

$\csc \theta = \dfrac{1}{\sin \theta}$

114. $\left(\sqrt{x} + 5\right)\left(\sqrt{x} - 5\right) = \left(\sqrt{x}\right)^2 - (5)^2 = x - 25$

116. $\left(2\sqrt{z} + 3\right)^2 = \left(2\sqrt{z}\right)^2 + 2\left(2\sqrt{z}\right)(3) + (3)^2$

$= 4z + 12\sqrt{z} + 9$

118. $y = -4 \sin(2x - 2\pi)$

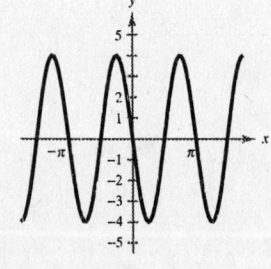

120. $y = 2 - \frac{1}{2} \tan 2x$

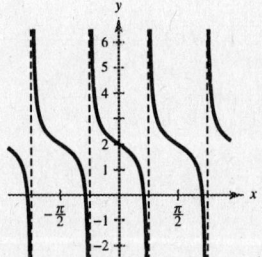

Section 5.2   Verifying Trigonometric Identities

Solutions to Even-Numbered Exercises

2. $\sec y \cos y = \left(\dfrac{1}{\cos y}\right)\cos y = 1$

4. $\cot^2 y(\sec^2 y - 1) = \cot^2 y \tan^2 y = 1$

6. $\cos^2 \beta - \sin^2 \beta = \cos^2 \beta - (1 - \cos^2 \beta)$

$= 2\cos^2 \beta - 1$

8. $2 - \sec^2 z = 2 - (1 + \tan^2 z)$

$= 1 - \tan^2 z$

10. $\cos x + \sin x \tan x = \cos x + \sin x\left(\dfrac{\sin x}{\cos x}\right)$

$$= \frac{\cos^2 x + \sin^2 x}{\cos x}$$

$$= \frac{1}{\cos x}$$

$$= \sec x$$

12. $\cos t(\csc^2 t - 1) = \cos t \cot^2 t$

$$= \sin t\left(\frac{\cos t}{\sin t}\right)\cot^2 t$$

$$= \frac{1}{\csc t}\cot^3 t$$

$$= \frac{\cot^3 t}{\csc t}$$

14. $\dfrac{1}{\tan \beta} + \tan \beta = \dfrac{1 + \tan^2 \beta}{\tan \beta}$

$$= \frac{\sec^2 \beta}{\tan \beta}$$

16. $\sec^6 x(\sec x \tan x) - \sec^4 x(\sec x \tan x) = \sec^4 x(\sec x \tan x)(\sec^2 x - 1)$

$$= \sec^4 x(\sec x \tan x)\tan^2 x$$

$$= \sec^5 x \tan^3 x$$

18. $\dfrac{\sec \theta - 1}{1 - \cos \theta} = \dfrac{\sec \theta - 1}{1 - (1/\sec \theta)} \cdot \dfrac{\sec \theta}{\sec \theta}$

$$= \frac{\sec \theta(\sec \theta - 1)}{\sec \theta - 1}$$

$$= \sec \theta$$

20. $\sec x - \cos x = \dfrac{1}{\cos x} - \cos x$

$$= \frac{1 - \cos^2 x}{\cos x}$$

$$= \frac{\sin^2 x}{\cos x}$$

$$= \sin x \cdot \frac{\sin x}{\cos x}$$

$$= \sin x \tan x$$

22. $\dfrac{\sec x + \tan x}{\sec x - \tan x} = \dfrac{\sec x + \tan x}{\sec x - \tan x} \cdot \dfrac{\sec x + \tan x}{\sec x + \tan x}$

$$= \frac{(\sec x + \tan x)^2}{\sec^2 x - \tan^2 x}$$

$$= \frac{(\sec x + \tan x)^2}{1}$$

$$= (\sec x + \tan x)^2$$

24. $\dfrac{1}{\sin x} - \dfrac{1}{\csc x} = \dfrac{\csc x - \sin x}{\sin x \csc x} = \dfrac{\csc x - \sin x}{1} = \csc x - \sin x$

26. $\dfrac{1 + \sin \theta}{\cos \theta} + \dfrac{\cos \theta}{1 + \sin \theta} = \dfrac{(1 + \sin \theta)^2 + \cos^2 \theta}{\cos \theta(1 + \sin \theta)}$

$$= \frac{1 + 2\sin \theta + \sin^2 \theta + \cos^2 \theta}{\cos \theta(1 + \sin \theta)} = \frac{2 + 2\sin \theta}{\cos \theta(1 + \sin \theta)}$$

$$= \frac{2(1 + \sin \theta)}{\cos \theta(1 + \sin \theta)} = \frac{2}{\cos \theta}$$

$$= 2\sec \theta$$

28. $\cos x - \dfrac{\cos x}{1 - \tan x} = \dfrac{\cos x(1 - \tan x) - \cos x}{1 - \tan x}$

$$= \frac{-\cos x \tan x}{1 - \tan x}$$

$$= \frac{-\cos x(\sin x/\cos x)}{1 - (\sin x/\cos x)} \cdot \frac{\cos x}{\cos x}$$

$$= \frac{-\sin x \cos x}{\cos x - \sin x}$$

$$= \frac{\sin x \cos x}{\sin x - \cos x}$$

30. $\dfrac{\cos[(\pi/2) - x]}{\sin[(\pi/2) - x]} = \dfrac{\sin x}{\cos x} = \tan x$

32. $(1 + \sin y)[1 + \sin(-y) = (1 + \sin y)(1 - \sin y)$

$$= 1 - \sin^2 y$$

$$= \cos^2 y$$

34. $\dfrac{\csc(-\theta) + 1}{\cos(-\theta) + \cot(-\theta)} = \dfrac{-\csc\theta + 1}{\cos\theta - \cot\theta}$

$$= \frac{-\csc\theta + 1}{\cos\theta\left[1 - \dfrac{1}{\sin\theta}\right]}$$

$$= \frac{1 - \csc\theta}{\cos\theta(1 - \csc\theta)}$$

$$= \frac{1}{\cos\theta}$$

$$= \sec\theta$$

36. $\dfrac{\tan x + \tan y}{1 - \tan x \tan y} = \dfrac{\dfrac{1}{\cot x} + \dfrac{1}{\cot y}}{1 - \dfrac{1}{\cot x} \cdot \dfrac{1}{\cot y}} \cdot \dfrac{\cot x \cot y}{\cot x \cot y}$

$$= \frac{\cot y + \cot x}{\cot x \cot y - 1}$$

38. $\dfrac{\cos x - \cos y}{\sin x + \sin y} + \dfrac{\sin x - \sin y}{\cos x + \cos y} = \dfrac{(\cos x - \cos y)(\cos x + \cos y) + (\sin x - \sin y)(\sin x + \sin y)}{(\sin x + \sin y)(\cos x + \cos y)}$

$$= \frac{\cos^2 x - \cos^2 y + \sin^2 x - \sin^2 y}{(\sin x + \sin y)(\cos x + \cos y)}$$

$$= \frac{(\cos^2 x + \sin^2 x) - (\cos^2 y + \sin^2 y)}{(\sin x + \sin y)(\cos x + \cos y)}$$

$$= 0$$

40. $\sqrt{\dfrac{1 - \cos\theta}{1 + \cos\theta}} = \sqrt{\dfrac{1 - \cos\theta}{1 + \cos\theta} \cdot \dfrac{1 - \cos\theta}{1 - \cos\theta}}$

$$= \sqrt{\frac{(1 - \cos\theta)^2}{1 - \cos^2\theta}}$$

$$= \sqrt{\frac{(1 - \cos\theta)^2}{\sin^2\theta}}$$

$$= \frac{1 - \cos\theta}{|\sin\theta|}$$

42. $\sec^2 y - \cot^2\left(\dfrac{\pi}{2} - y\right) = \sec^2 y - \tan^2 y = 1$

44. $\sec^2\left(\dfrac{\pi}{2} - x\right) - 1 = \csc^2 x - 1 = \cot^2 x$

46. $\csc x(\csc x - \sin x) + \dfrac{\sin x - \cos x}{\sin x} + \cot x = \csc^2 x - \csc x \sin x + 1 - \dfrac{\cos x}{\sin x} + \cot x$

$$= \csc^2 x - 1 + 1 - \cot x + \cot x$$

$$= \csc^2 x$$

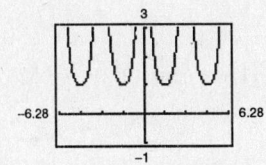

48. $4\tan^4 x + \tan^2 x - 3 = (\tan^2 x + 1)(4\tan^2 x - 3)$

$$= \sec^2 x(4\tan^2 x - 3)$$

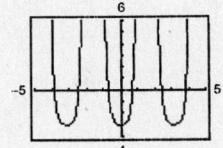

50. $(\sin^4 \beta - 2\sin^2 \beta + 1)\cos \beta = (\sin^2 \beta - 1)^2 \cos \beta$

$$= (-\cos^2 \beta)^2 \cos \beta$$

$$= \cos^5 \beta$$

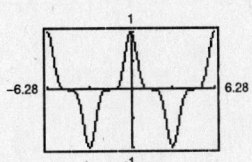

52. $\csc^4 \theta - \cot^4 \theta = (\csc^2 \theta - \cot^2 \theta)(\csc^2 \theta + \cot^2 \theta)$

$$= \csc^2 \theta + \cot^2 \theta$$

$$= \csc^2 \theta + (\csc^2 \theta - 1)$$

$$= 2\csc^2 \theta - 1$$

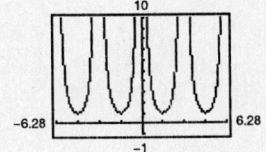

54. $\dfrac{\cot \alpha}{\csc \alpha - 1} \cdot \dfrac{\csc \alpha + 1}{\csc \alpha + 1} = \dfrac{\cot \alpha(\csc \alpha + 1)}{\csc^2 \alpha - 1}$

$$= \dfrac{\cot \alpha(\csc \alpha + 1)}{\cot^2 \alpha}$$

$$= \dfrac{\csc \alpha + 1}{\cot \alpha}$$

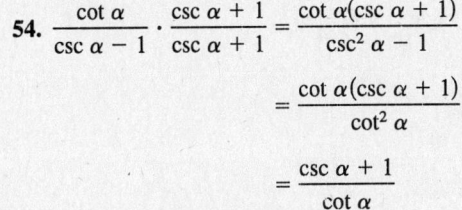

56. $\dfrac{\sin^3 \beta + \cos^3 \beta}{\sin \beta + \cos \beta} = \dfrac{(\sin \beta + \cos \beta)(\sin^2 \beta - \sin \beta \cos \beta + \cos^2 \beta)}{\sin \beta + \cos \beta}$

$$= \sin^2 \beta + \cos^2 \beta - \sin \beta \cos \beta$$

$$= 1 - \sin \beta \cos \beta$$

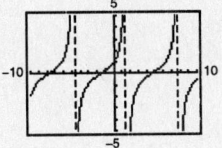

58. $\ln|\sec \theta| = \ln\left|\dfrac{1}{\cos \theta}\right| = \ln|\cos \theta| = -\ln|\cos \theta|$

60. $-\ln|\sec \theta + \tan \theta| = -\ln\left|\dfrac{1}{\cos \theta} + \dfrac{\sin \theta}{\cos \theta}\right|$

$$= \ln\left|\dfrac{1 + \sin \theta}{\cos \theta}\right|^{-1}$$

$$= \ln\left|\dfrac{\cos \theta}{1 + \sin \theta} \cdot \dfrac{1 - \sin \theta}{1 - \sin \theta}\right|$$

$$= \ln\left|\dfrac{\cos \theta - \cos \theta \sin \theta}{1 - \sin^2 \theta}\right|$$

$$= \ln\left|\dfrac{\cos \theta - \cos \theta \sin \theta}{\cos^2 \theta}\right|$$

62. $\cos^2 55° + \cos^2 35° = \cos^2 55° + \sin^2(90° - 35°)$

$$= \cos^2 55° + \sin^2 55°$$

$$= 1$$

64. $\sin^2 12° + \sin^2 40° + \sin^2 50° + \sin^2 78° = \sin^2 12° + \sin^2 78° + \sin^2 40° + \sin^2 50°$

$$= \cos^2(90° - 12°) + \sin^2 78° + \cos^2(90° - 40°) + \sin^2 50°$$

$$= \cos^2 78° + \sin^2 78° + \cos^2 50° + \sin^2 50°$$

$$= 1 + 1 = 2$$

66. False. For the equation to be an identity, it must be true for all values of θ in the domain.

68. Since $\sin^2 \theta = 1 - \cos^2 \theta$, then $\sin \theta = \pm \sqrt{1 - \cos^2 \theta}$; $\sin \theta \neq \sqrt{1 - \cos \theta}$ if θ lies in Quadrant III or IV.

One such angle is $\theta = \dfrac{7\pi}{4}$.

70. $\sqrt{\tan^2 \theta} = |\tan \theta|$

$\sqrt{\tan^2 \theta} \neq \tan \theta$ if θ lies in Quadrant II or IV.

One such angle is $\theta = \dfrac{3\pi}{4}$.

72. When n is even,

$$\cos\left[\frac{(2n + 1)\pi}{2}\right] = \cos \frac{\pi}{2} = 0.$$

When n is odd,

$$\cos\left[\frac{(2n + 1)\pi}{2}\right] = \cos \frac{3\pi}{2} = 0.$$

Thus, $\cos\left[\dfrac{(2n + 1)\pi}{2}\right] = 0$ for all integers n.

74. $(2 + 3i) - \sqrt{-26} = 2 + 3i - \sqrt{26}i = 2 + \left(3 - \sqrt{26}\right)i$

76. $\sqrt{-16}\left(1 + \sqrt{-4}\right) = 4i(1 + 2i) = 4i + 8i^2 = 4i - 8$

78. $x^2 - 6x + 12 = 0$

$$x = \frac{6 \pm \sqrt{(-6)^2 - 4(1)(12)}}{2(1)}$$

$$= \frac{6 \pm \sqrt{-12}}{2}$$

$$= \frac{6 \pm 2\sqrt{3}i}{2}$$

$$= 3 \pm \sqrt{3}i$$

80. $3x^2 + 6x + 12 = 0$

$$x^2 + 2x + 4 = 0$$

$$x = \frac{-2 \pm \sqrt{2^2 - 4(1)(4)}}{2(1)}$$

$$= \frac{-2 \pm \sqrt{-12}}{2}$$

$$= \frac{-2 \pm 2\sqrt{3}i}{2}$$

$$= -1 \pm \sqrt{3}i$$

82. $-4x^2 + 3x - 12 = 0$

$$x = \frac{-3 \pm \sqrt{3^2 - 4(-4)(-12)}}{2(-4)}$$

$$= \frac{-3 \pm \sqrt{-183}}{-8}$$

$$= \frac{3 \pm \sqrt{183}i}{8}$$

84. $11x^2 - x + 22 = 0$

$$x = \frac{1 \pm \sqrt{(-1)^2 - 4(11)(22)}}{2(11)}$$

$$= \frac{1 \pm \sqrt{-967}}{22}$$

$$= \frac{1 \pm \sqrt{967}i}{22}$$

Section 5.3   Solving Trigonometric Equations

Solutions to Even-Numbered Exercises

2. $\sec x - 2 = 0$

(a) $x = \dfrac{\pi}{3}$

$$\sec \frac{\pi}{3} - 2 = \frac{1}{\cos \dfrac{\pi}{3}} - 2$$

$$= \frac{1}{\dfrac{1}{2}} - 2$$

$$= 2 - 2 = 0$$

(b) $x = \dfrac{5\pi}{3}$

$$\sec \frac{5\pi}{3} - 2 = \frac{1}{\cos \dfrac{5\pi}{3}} - 2$$

$$= \frac{1}{\dfrac{1}{2}} - 2$$

$$= 2 - 2 = 0$$

4. $2\cos^2 4x - 1 = 0$

(a) $x = \dfrac{\pi}{16}$

$$2\cos^2\left[4\left(\frac{\pi}{16}\right)\right] - 1 = 2\cos^2 \frac{\pi}{4} - 1$$

$$= 2\left(\frac{\sqrt{2}}{2}\right)^2 - 1$$

$$= 2\left(\frac{1}{2}\right) - 1 = 1 - 1 = 0$$

(b) $x = \dfrac{3\pi}{16}$

$$2\cos^2\left[4\left(\frac{3\pi}{16}\right)\right] - 1 = 2\cos^2 \frac{3\pi}{4} - 1$$

$$= 2\left(-\frac{\sqrt{2}}{2}\right)^2 - 1$$

$$= 2\left(\frac{1}{2}\right) - 1 = 0$$

6. $\csc^4 x - 4\csc^2 x = 0$

(a) $x = \dfrac{\pi}{6}$

$$\csc^4 \frac{\pi}{6} - 4\csc^2 \frac{\pi}{6} = \frac{1}{\sin^4 \dfrac{\pi}{6}} - \frac{4}{\sin^2 \dfrac{\pi}{6}}$$

$$= \frac{1}{\left(\dfrac{1}{2}\right)^4} - \frac{4}{\left(\dfrac{1}{2}\right)^2}$$

$$= 16 - 16 = 0$$

(b) $x = \dfrac{5\pi}{6}$

$$\csc^4 \frac{5\pi}{6} - 4\csc \frac{5\pi}{6} = \frac{1}{\sin^4 \dfrac{5\pi}{6}} - \frac{4}{\sin^2 \dfrac{5\pi}{6}}$$

$$= \frac{1}{\left(\dfrac{1}{2}\right)^4} - \frac{4}{\left(\dfrac{1}{2}\right)^2}$$

$$= 16 - 16 = 0$$

8. $2\sin x - 1 = 0$

$$2\sin x = 1$$

$$\sin x = \frac{1}{2}$$

$$x = \frac{\pi}{6} + 2n\pi$$

or

$$x = \frac{5\pi}{6} + 2n\pi$$

10. $\tan x + \sqrt{3} = 0$

$$\tan x = -\sqrt{3}$$

$$x = \frac{2\pi}{3} + n\pi$$

12. $3\cot^2 x - 1 = 0$

$$\cot^2 x = \frac{1}{3}$$

$$\cot x = \pm\frac{1}{\sqrt{3}}$$

$$x = \frac{\pi}{3} + n\pi$$

or

$$x = \frac{2\pi}{3} + n\pi$$

14. $(3\tan^2 x - 1)(\tan^2 x - 3) = 0$

$3\tan^2 x - 1 = 0$ or $\tan^2 x - 3 = 0$

$\tan x = \pm\dfrac{1}{\sqrt{3}}$ $\tan x = \pm\sqrt{3}$

$x = \dfrac{\pi}{6} + n\pi$ $x = \dfrac{\pi}{3} + n\pi$

or   or

$x = \dfrac{5\pi}{6} + n\pi$ $x = \dfrac{2\pi}{3} + n\pi$

16. $\sin^2 x = 3\cos^2 x$

$\sin^2 x - 3(1 - \sin^2 x) = 0$

$4\sin^2 x = 3$

$\sin x = \pm\dfrac{\sqrt{3}}{2}$

$x = \dfrac{\pi}{3} + n\pi$

or

$x = \dfrac{2\pi}{3} + n\pi$

18. $\tan^2 3x = 3$

$\tan 3x = \pm\sqrt{3}$

$3x = \dfrac{\pi}{3} + n\pi \Rightarrow x = \dfrac{\pi}{9} + \dfrac{n\pi}{3}$

or

$3x = \dfrac{2\pi}{3} + n\pi \Rightarrow x = \dfrac{2\pi}{9} + \dfrac{n\pi}{3}$

20. $\cos 2x(2\cos x + 1) = 0$

$\cos 2x = 0$ or $2\cos x + 1 = 0$

$2x = \dfrac{\pi}{2} + n\pi$ $\cos x = -\dfrac{1}{2}$

$x = \dfrac{\pi}{4} + \dfrac{n\pi}{2}$ $x = \dfrac{2\pi}{3} + 2n\pi$

or

$x = \dfrac{4\pi}{3} + 2n\pi$

22. $\sec^2 x - 1 = 0$

$\sec^2 x = 1$

$\sec x = \pm 1$

$x = 0$ or $x = \pi$

24. $2\sin^2 x = 2 + \cos x$

$2 - 2\cos^2 x = 2 + \cos x$

$2\cos^2 x + \cos x = 0$

$\cos x(2\cos x + 1) = 0$

$\cos x = 0$ or $2\cos x + 1 = 0$

$x = \dfrac{\pi}{2}, \dfrac{3\pi}{2}$ $2\cos x = -1$

$\cos x = -\dfrac{1}{2}$

$x = \dfrac{2\pi}{3}, \dfrac{4\pi}{3}$

26.
$$\sec x \csc x = 2 \csc x$$
$$\sec x \csc x - 2 \csc x = 0$$
$$\csc x(\sec x - 2) = 0$$
$$\csc x = 0 \quad \text{or} \quad \sec x - 2 = 0$$
No solution $\qquad\qquad \sec x = 2$
$$x = \frac{\pi}{3}, \frac{5\pi}{3}$$

28.
$$\sec x + \tan x = 1$$
$$\frac{1}{\cos x} + \frac{\sin x}{\cos x} = 1$$
$$1 + \sin x = \cos x$$
$$(1 + \sin x)^2 = \cos^2 x$$
$$1 + 2\sin x + \sin^2 x = \cos^2 x$$
$$1 + 2\sin x + \sin^2 x = 1 - \sin^2 x$$
$$2\sin^2 x + 2\sin x = 0$$
$$2\sin x(\sin x + 1) = 0$$
$$\sin x = 0 \quad \text{or} \quad \sin x + 1 = 0$$
$$x = 0, \pi \qquad\qquad \sin x = -1$$
$$x = \frac{3\pi}{2}$$
$(\pi \text{ is extraneous}) \qquad \left(\dfrac{3\pi}{2} \text{ is extraneous}\right)$

$x = 0$ is the only solution.

30.
$$2\sin^2 x + 3\sin x + 1 = 0$$
$$(2\sin x + 1)(\sin x + 1) = 0$$
$$2\sin x + 1 = 0 \quad \text{or} \quad \sin x + 1 = 0$$
$$\sin x = -\frac{1}{2} \qquad\qquad \sin x = -1$$
$$x = \frac{7\pi}{6}, \frac{11\pi}{6} \qquad\qquad x = \frac{3\pi}{2}$$

32.
$$\cos x + \sin x \tan x = 2$$
$$\cos x + \sin x\left(\frac{\sin x}{\cos x}\right) = 2$$
$$\frac{\cos^2 x + \sin^2 x}{\cos x} = 2$$
$$\frac{1}{\cos x} = 2$$
$$\cos x = \frac{1}{2}$$
$$x = \frac{\pi}{3}, \frac{5\pi}{3}$$

34. $\sin 2x = -\dfrac{\sqrt{3}}{2}$
$$2x = \frac{4\pi}{3} + 2n\pi \quad \text{or} \quad 2x = \frac{5\pi}{3} + 2n\pi$$
$$x = \frac{2\pi}{3} + n\pi \qquad\qquad x = \frac{5\pi}{6} + n\pi$$

36. $\sec 4x = 2$
$$4x = \frac{\pi}{3} + 2n\pi \quad \text{or} \quad 4x = \frac{5\pi}{3} + 2n\pi$$
$$x = \frac{\pi}{12} + \frac{n\pi}{2} \qquad\qquad x = \frac{5\pi}{12} + \frac{n\pi}{2}$$

38. $\sin \dfrac{x}{2} = -\dfrac{\sqrt{3}}{2}$
$$\frac{x}{2} = \frac{4\pi}{3} + 2\pi \quad \text{or} \quad \frac{x}{2} = \frac{5\pi}{3} + 2\pi$$
$$x = \frac{8\pi}{3} + 4\pi \qquad\qquad x = \frac{10\pi}{3} + 4\pi$$

40. $y = \sin \pi x + \cos \pi x$

$$\sin \pi x + \cos \pi x = 0$$

$$\sin \pi x = -\cos \pi x$$

$$\pi x = -\frac{\pi}{4} + n\pi$$

$$x = -\frac{1}{4} + n$$

For $-1 < x < 3$ the intercepts are $-\frac{1}{4}, \frac{3}{4}, \frac{7}{4}, \frac{11}{4}$

42. $y = \sec^4\left(\frac{\pi x}{8}\right) - 4$

$$\sec^4\left(\frac{\pi x}{8}\right) - 4 = 0$$

$$\sec^4\left(\frac{\pi x}{8}\right) = 4$$

$$\sec\left(\frac{\pi x}{8}\right) = \pm\sqrt{2}$$

$$\frac{\pi x}{8} = \frac{\pi}{4} + \frac{\pi}{2}n$$

$$x = 2 + 4n$$

For $-3 < x < 3$ the intercepts are -2 and 2.

44. $y^2 + y - 20 = 0$

$$(y + 5)(y - 4) = 0$$

$$y + 5 = 0 \quad \text{or} \quad y - 4 = 0$$

$$y = -5 \qquad\quad y = 4$$

$$\sin^2 x + \sin x - 20 = 0$$

$$(\sin x + 5)(\sin x - 4) = 0$$

$$\sin x = -5 \quad \text{or} \quad \sin x = 4$$

No solution   No solution

46. $4 \sin^3 x + 2 \sin^2 x - 2 \sin x - 1 = 0$

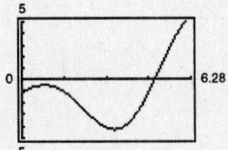

$x \approx 0.7854, 2.3562, 3.6652, 3.9270, 5.4978, 5.7596$

48. $\dfrac{\cos x \cot x}{1 - \sin x} = 3$

$$y_1 = \left(\frac{\dfrac{\cos x}{\tan x}}{1 - \sin x}\right) - 3$$

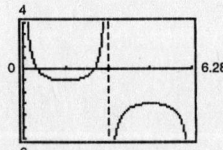

$x \approx 0.5236, 2.6180$

50. $x \cos x - 1 = 0$

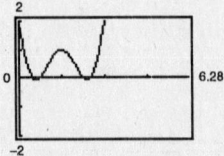

$x \approx 4.9172$

52. $\csc^2 x + 0.5 \cot x - 5 = 0$

$$y_1 = \left(\frac{1}{\sin x}\right)^2 + \frac{1}{2 \tan x} - 5$$

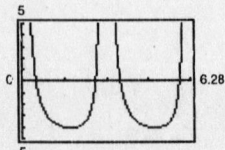

$x \approx 0.5153, 2.7259, 3.6569, 5.8675$

54. $6 \sin^2 x - 7 \sin x + 2 = 0$

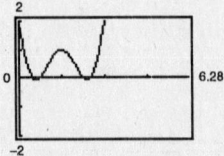

$x \approx 0.5236, 0.7297, 2.4119, 2.6180$

56. $3 \tan^2 x + 4 \tan x - 4 = 0$

$\tan x = \dfrac{-4 \pm \sqrt{4^2 - 4(3)(-4)}}{2(3)} = \dfrac{-4 \pm \sqrt{64}}{6} = -2, \dfrac{2}{3}$

$\tan x = -2 \qquad\qquad \tan x = \dfrac{2}{3}$

$x = \arctan(-2) + n\pi \qquad x = \arctan\left(\dfrac{2}{3}\right) + n\pi$

$\approx -1.1071 + n\pi \qquad\quad \approx 0.5880 + n\pi$

The values of x in $[0, 2\pi)$ are
0.5880, 3.7296, 2.0344, 5.1760.

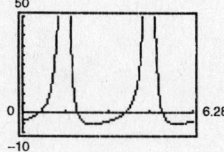

58. $4 \cos^2 x - 4 \cos x - 1 = 0$

$\cos x = \dfrac{4 \pm \sqrt{(-4)^2 - 4(4)(-1)}}{2(4)}$

$= \dfrac{4 \pm \sqrt{32}}{8} = \dfrac{1 \pm \sqrt{2}}{2}$

$\cos x = \dfrac{1\sqrt{2}}{2} \qquad\qquad \cos x = \dfrac{1 + \sqrt{2}}{2}$

$x = \arccos\left(\dfrac{1 - \sqrt{2}}{2}\right) \qquad$ No solution

$\approx 1.7794 \qquad\qquad \left(\dfrac{1 + \sqrt{2}}{2} > 1\right)$

Solutions in $[0, 2\pi)$ are $\arccos\left(\dfrac{1 - \sqrt{2}}{2}\right)$ and

$2\pi - \arccos\left(\dfrac{1 - \sqrt{2}}{2}\right)$: 1.7794, 4.5038.

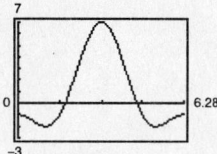

60. $\sec^2 x + \tan x - 3 = 0$

$1 + \tan^2 x + \tan x - 3 = 0$

$\tan^2 x + \tan x - 2 = 0$

$(\tan x + 2)(\tan x - 1) = 0$

$\tan x + 2 = 0 \qquad\qquad \tan x - 1 = 0$

$\tan x = -2 \qquad\qquad\quad \tan x = 1$

$x = \arctan(-2) + n\pi \qquad x = \arctan(1) + n\pi$

$\approx -1.1071 + n\pi \qquad\quad = \dfrac{\pi}{4} + n\pi$

Solutions in $[0, 2\pi)$ are $\arctan(-2) + \pi$, $\arctan(-2) + 2\pi$, $\dfrac{\pi}{4}, \dfrac{5\pi}{4}$.

62. $2 \sin^2 x - 7 \sin x + 3 = 0$

$(\sin x - 3)(2 \sin x - 1) = 0$

$\sin x - 3 = 0 \qquad 2 \sin x - 1 = 0$

No solution $\qquad\quad \sin x = \dfrac{1}{2}$

$\qquad\qquad\qquad\quad x = \dfrac{\pi}{6}, \dfrac{5\pi}{6}$

Solutions in $[0, 2\pi)$ are $\dfrac{\pi}{6}, \dfrac{5\pi}{6}$.

64. (a) $f(x) = 2 \sin x + \cos 2x$

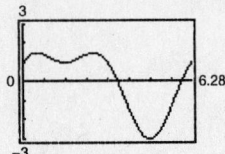

max: $(0.5240, 1.5)$ min: $(1.5708, 1.0)$

max: $(2.6180, 1.5)$ min: $(4.7124, -3.0)$

(b) $2 \cos x - 4 \sin x \cos x = 0$

$2 \cos x(1 - 2 \sin x) = 0$

$2 \cos x = 0$ $\qquad\qquad\qquad$ $1 - 2 \sin x = 0$

$x = \dfrac{\pi}{2}, \dfrac{3\pi}{2}$ $\qquad\qquad$ $x = \dfrac{\pi}{2}, \dfrac{3\pi}{2}$

$\approx 1.5708, 4.7124$

$\sin x = \dfrac{1}{2}$

$x = \dfrac{\pi}{6}, \dfrac{5\pi}{6}$

$\approx 0.5240, 2.6180$

66. Graph $y = \cos x$ and $y = x$ on the same set of axes. Their point of intersection gives the value of c such that $f(c) = c \implies \cos c = c$.

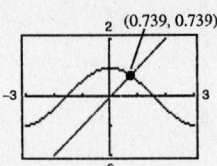

$c \approx 0.739$

68. $f(x) = \dfrac{\sin x}{x}$

(a) Domain: all real numbers except $x = 0$.

(b) The graph has y-axis symmetry.

(c) As $x \to 0, f(x) \to 1$.

(d) $\dfrac{\sin x}{x} = 0$ has four solutions in the interval $[-8, 8]$.

$(\sin x)\left(\dfrac{1}{x}\right) = 0$

$\sin x = 0$

$x = -2\pi, -\pi, \pi, 2\pi$

70. $y_1 = 1.56e^{-0.22t} \cos 4.9t$

$y_2 = \dfrac{1}{12}$ (1 inch since displacement is given in feet.)

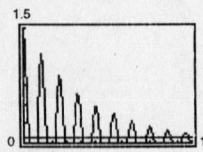

Right most point of intersection: $\left(12.91, \dfrac{1}{12}\right)$

The displacement does not exceed one inch from equilibrium after $t = 12.91$ seconds.

72. $\qquad\qquad$ range $= 300$ feet

$v_0 = 100$ feet per second

$r = \dfrac{1}{32}v_0{}^2 \sin 2\theta$

$\dfrac{1}{32}(100)^2 \sin 2\theta = 300$

$\sin 2\theta = 0.96$

$2\theta = \arcsin(0.96) \approx 73.74°$

$\theta \approx 36.9°$

or

$2\theta = 180° - \arcsin(0.96) \approx 106.26°$

$\theta \approx 53.1°$

74. $A = 2x \cos x$, $0 < x < \dfrac{\pi}{2}$

(a)

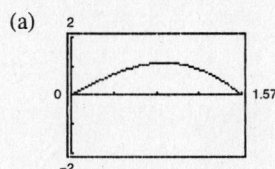

The maximum area of $A \approx 1.12$
occurs when $x \approx 0.86$.

(b) $A \geq 1$ for $0.6 < x < 1.1$

76. (a)

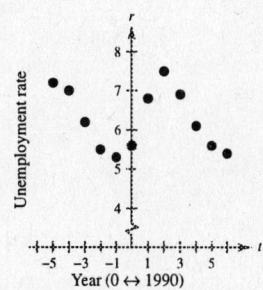

(b) By checking the graphs we see that
$(3)r = \sin[0.91(t + 6.44)] + 6.26$ best fits the data.

(c) The constant term gives the rate of 6.26%.

(d) Period: $\dfrac{2\pi}{0.91} \approx 7$ years

(e) $r \approx 6$ when $t \approx 11$ which corresponds to 2001.

78. False.
$\sin x = 3.4$ has no solution since 3.4 is outside the
range of sin. Also, 3.4 is outside the domain of arcsin,
so $x = \arcsin(3.4)$ is an invalid equation.

80. By inspecting the graphs of y_1 and y_2, it appears they
intersect at three points.

82.

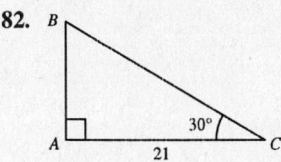

Given: $A = 90°$, $C = 30°$, $b = 21$

$B = 90° - 30° = 60°$

$\cos 30° = \dfrac{21}{a}$

$a = \dfrac{21}{\cos 30°} = \dfrac{21}{\dfrac{\sqrt{3}}{2}} = \dfrac{42\sqrt{3}}{3} \approx 24.25$

$\tan 30° = \dfrac{c}{21}$

$c = 21 \tan 30° = \dfrac{21\sqrt{3}}{3} = 7\sqrt{3} \approx 12.12$

84.

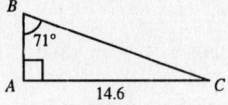

Given: $A = 90°$, $B = 71°$, $b = 14.6$

$C = 90° - 71° = 19°$

$\sin 71° = \dfrac{14.6}{a}$

$a = \dfrac{14.6}{\sin 71} \approx 15.4$

$\tan 71° = \dfrac{14.6}{c}$

$c = \dfrac{14.6}{\tan 71°} \approx 5.0$

86. 570°

$570° - 360° = 210°$ \quad Quadrant III

Reference angle: 30°

$\sin 570° = -\sin 30° = -\dfrac{1}{2}$

$\cos 570° = -\cos 30° = -\dfrac{\sqrt{3}}{2}$

$\tan 570° = \tan 30° = \dfrac{\sqrt{3}}{3}$

88. 855°

$855° - 2(360°) = 135°$ \quad Quadrant II

Reference angle: 45°

$\sin 855° = \sin 45° = \dfrac{\sqrt{2}}{2}$

$\cos 855° = -\cos 45° = -\dfrac{\sqrt{2}}{2}$

$\tan 855° = -\tan 45° = -1$

90. $-1410°$

$-1410° + 4(360°) = 30°$ Quadrant I

$\sin(-1410°) = \sin 30° = \dfrac{1}{2}$

$\cos(-1410°) = \cos 30° = \dfrac{\sqrt{3}}{2}$

$\tan(-1410°) = \tan 30° = \dfrac{\sqrt{3}}{3}$

92.

(Not drawn to scale)

$\tan\theta = \dfrac{250 \text{ feet}}{2 \text{ miles}} \times \dfrac{1 \text{ mile}}{5280 \text{ feet}} \approx 0.02367$

$\theta \approx 1.36°$

Section 5.4   Sum and Difference Formulas

Solutions to Even-Numbered Exercises

2. (a) $\sin\left(\dfrac{3\pi}{4} + \dfrac{5\pi}{6}\right) = \sin\dfrac{3\pi}{4}\cos\dfrac{5\pi}{6} + \cos\dfrac{3\pi}{4}\sin\dfrac{5\pi}{6}$

$\qquad\qquad = \left(\dfrac{\sqrt{2}}{2}\right)\left(-\dfrac{\sqrt{3}}{2}\right) + \left(-\dfrac{\sqrt{2}}{2}\right)\left(\dfrac{1}{2}\right)$

$\qquad\qquad = -\dfrac{\sqrt{6} + \sqrt{2}}{4}$

(b) $\sin\dfrac{3\pi}{4} + \sin\dfrac{5\pi}{6} = \dfrac{\sqrt{2}}{2} + \dfrac{1}{2} = \dfrac{\sqrt{2} + 1}{2}$

4. (a) $\cos\left(\dfrac{2\pi}{3} - \dfrac{\pi}{6}\right) = \cos\dfrac{2\pi}{3}\cos\dfrac{\pi}{6} + \sin\dfrac{2\pi}{3}\sin\dfrac{\pi}{6}$

$\qquad\qquad = \left(-\dfrac{1}{2}\right)\left(\dfrac{\sqrt{3}}{2}\right) + \left(\dfrac{\sqrt{3}}{2}\right)\left(\dfrac{1}{2}\right) = 0$

(b) $\cos\dfrac{2\pi}{3} + \cos\dfrac{\pi}{6} = -\dfrac{1}{2} + \dfrac{\sqrt{3}}{2} = \dfrac{\sqrt{3} - 1}{2}$

6. (a) $\sin(135° - 30°) = \sin 135° \cos 30° - \cos 135° \sin 30°$

$\qquad\qquad = \left(\dfrac{\sqrt{2}}{2}\right)\left(\dfrac{\sqrt{3}}{2}\right) - \left(-\dfrac{\sqrt{2}}{2}\right)\left(\dfrac{1}{2}\right)$

$\qquad\qquad = \dfrac{\sqrt{6} + \sqrt{2}}{4}$

(b) $\sin 135° - \cos 30° = \dfrac{\sqrt{2}}{2} - \dfrac{\sqrt{3}}{2}$

$\qquad\qquad = \dfrac{\sqrt{2} - \sqrt{3}}{2}$

8. $165° = 135° + 30°$

$\sin 165° = \sin(135° + 30°)$

$\qquad = \sin 135° \cos 30° + \sin 30° \cos 135°$

$\qquad = \sin 45° \cos 30° - \sin 30° \cos 45°$

$\qquad = \dfrac{\sqrt{2}}{2} \cdot \dfrac{\sqrt{3}}{2} - \dfrac{1}{2} \cdot \dfrac{\sqrt{2}}{2}$

$\qquad = \dfrac{\sqrt{2}}{4}\left(\sqrt{3} - 1\right)$

$\cos 165° = \cos(135° + 30°)$

$\qquad = \cos 135° \cos 30° - \sin 135° \sin 30°$

$\qquad = -\cos 45° \cos 30° - \sin 45° \sin 30°$

$\qquad = -\dfrac{\sqrt{2}}{2} \cdot \dfrac{\sqrt{3}}{2} - \dfrac{\sqrt{2}}{2} \cdot \dfrac{1}{2}$

$\qquad = -\dfrac{\sqrt{2}}{4}\left(\sqrt{3} + 1\right)$

$\tan 165° = \tan(135° + 30°)$

$\qquad = \dfrac{\tan 135° + \tan 30°}{1 - \tan 135° \tan 30°}$

$\qquad = \dfrac{-\tan 45° + \tan 30°}{1 + \tan 45° \tan 30°}$

$\qquad = \dfrac{-1 + \dfrac{\sqrt{3}}{3}}{1 + \dfrac{\sqrt{3}}{3}}$

$\qquad = -2 + \sqrt{3}$

10. $255° = 300° - 45°$

$\sin 255° = \sin(300° - 45°)$

$\qquad = \sin 300° \cos 45° - \sin 45° \cos 300°$

$\qquad = -\sin 60° \cos 45° - \sin 45° \cos 60°$

$\qquad = -\dfrac{\sqrt{3}}{2} \cdot \dfrac{\sqrt{2}}{2} - \dfrac{\sqrt{2}}{2} \cdot \dfrac{1}{2}$

$\qquad = -\dfrac{\sqrt{2}}{4}\left(\sqrt{3} + 1\right)$

$\cos 255° = \cos(300° - 45°)$

$\qquad = \cos 300° \cos 45° + \sin 300° \sin 45°$

$\qquad = \cos 60° \cos 45° - \sin 60° \sin 45°$

$\qquad = \dfrac{1}{2} \cdot \dfrac{\sqrt{2}}{2} - \dfrac{\sqrt{3}}{2} \cdot \dfrac{\sqrt{2}}{2}$

$\qquad = \dfrac{\sqrt{2}}{4}\left(1 - \sqrt{3}\right)$

$\tan 255° = \tan(300° - 45°)$

$\qquad = \dfrac{\tan 300° - \tan 45°}{1 + \tan 300° \tan 45°}$

$\qquad = \dfrac{-\tan 60° - \tan 45°}{1 - \tan 60° \tan 45°}$

$\qquad = \dfrac{-\sqrt{3} - 1}{1 - \sqrt{3}} = 2 + \sqrt{3}$

12. $\dfrac{7\pi}{12} = \dfrac{\pi}{3} + \dfrac{\pi}{4}$

$\sin \dfrac{7\pi}{12} = \sin\left(\dfrac{\pi}{3} + \dfrac{\pi}{4}\right)$

$\qquad = \sin \dfrac{\pi}{3} \cos \dfrac{\pi}{4} + \sin \dfrac{\pi}{4} \cos \dfrac{\pi}{3}$

$\qquad = \dfrac{\sqrt{3}}{2} \cdot \dfrac{\sqrt{2}}{2} + \dfrac{\sqrt{2}}{2} \cdot \dfrac{1}{2}$

$\qquad = \dfrac{\sqrt{2}}{4}\left(\sqrt{3} + 1\right)$

$\cos \dfrac{7\pi}{12} = \cos\left(\dfrac{\pi}{3} + \dfrac{\pi}{4}\right)$

$\qquad = \cos \dfrac{\pi}{3} \cos \dfrac{\pi}{4} - \sin \dfrac{\pi}{3} \sin \dfrac{\pi}{4}$

$\qquad = \dfrac{1}{2} \cdot \dfrac{\sqrt{2}}{2} - \dfrac{\sqrt{3}}{2} \cdot \dfrac{\sqrt{2}}{2}$

$\qquad = \dfrac{\sqrt{2}}{4}\left(1 - \sqrt{3}\right)$

$\tan \dfrac{7\pi}{12} = \tan\left(\dfrac{\pi}{3} + \dfrac{\pi}{4}\right)$

$\qquad = \dfrac{\tan \dfrac{\pi}{3} + \tan \dfrac{\pi}{4}}{1 - \tan \dfrac{\pi}{3} \tan \dfrac{\pi}{4}}$

$\qquad = \dfrac{\sqrt{3} + 1}{1 - \sqrt{3}}$

$\qquad = -2 - \sqrt{3}$

14. $-\dfrac{\pi}{12} = \dfrac{\pi}{6} - \dfrac{\pi}{4}$

$\sin\left(-\dfrac{\pi}{12}\right) = \sin\left(\dfrac{\pi}{6} - \dfrac{\pi}{4}\right)$

$\qquad = \sin \dfrac{\pi}{6} \cos \dfrac{\pi}{4} - \sin \dfrac{\pi}{4} \cos \dfrac{\pi}{6}$

$\qquad = \dfrac{1}{2} \cdot \dfrac{\sqrt{2}}{2} - \dfrac{\sqrt{2}}{2} \cdot \dfrac{\sqrt{3}}{2}$

$\qquad = \dfrac{\sqrt{2}}{4}\left(1 - \sqrt{3}\right)$

$\cos\left(-\dfrac{\pi}{12}\right) = \cos\left(\dfrac{\pi}{6} - \dfrac{\pi}{4}\right)$

$\qquad = \cos \dfrac{\pi}{6} \cos \dfrac{\pi}{4} + \sin \dfrac{\pi}{6} \sin \dfrac{\pi}{4}$

$\qquad = \dfrac{\sqrt{3}}{2} \cdot \dfrac{\sqrt{2}}{2} + \dfrac{1}{2} \cdot \dfrac{\sqrt{2}}{2}$

$\qquad = \dfrac{\sqrt{2}}{4}\left(\sqrt{3} + 1\right)$

$\tan\left(-\dfrac{\pi}{12}\right) = \tan\left(\dfrac{\pi}{6} - \dfrac{\pi}{4}\right)$

$\qquad = \dfrac{\tan \dfrac{\pi}{6} - \tan \dfrac{\pi}{4}}{1 + \tan \dfrac{\pi}{6} \tan \dfrac{\pi}{4}}$

$\qquad = \dfrac{\dfrac{\sqrt{3}}{3} - 1}{1 + \dfrac{\sqrt{3}}{3}}$

$\qquad = -2 + \sqrt{3}$

16. $-105 = 30° - 135°$

$\sin(30° - 135°) = \sin 30° \cos 135° - \cos 30° \sin 135°$

$$= \sin 30°(-\cos 45°) - \cos 30° \sin 45°$$

$$= \left(\frac{1}{2}\right)\left(-\frac{\sqrt{2}}{2}\right) - \left(\frac{\sqrt{3}}{2}\right)\left(\frac{\sqrt{2}}{2}\right)$$

$$= -\frac{\sqrt{2}}{4}\left(1 + \sqrt{3}\right)$$

$\cos(30° - 135°) = \cos 30° \cos 135° + \sin 30° \sin 135°$

$$= \cos 30°(-\cos 45°) + \sin 30° \sin 45°$$

$$= \left(\frac{\sqrt{3}}{2}\right)\left(-\frac{\sqrt{2}}{2}\right) + \left(\frac{1}{2}\right)\left(\frac{\sqrt{2}}{2}\right)$$

$$= \frac{\sqrt{2}}{4}\left(1 - \sqrt{3}\right)$$

$\tan(30° - 135°) = \dfrac{\tan 30° - \tan 135°}{1 + \tan 30° \tan 135°}$

$$= \frac{\tan 30° - (-\tan 45°)}{1 + \tan 30°(-\tan 45°)}$$

$$= \frac{\dfrac{\sqrt{3}}{3} - (-1)}{1 + \left(\dfrac{\sqrt{3}}{3}\right)(-1)} = 2 + \sqrt{3}$$

18. $15° = 45° - 30°$

$\sin 15° = \sin(45° - 30°) = \sin 45° \cos 30° - \cos 45° \sin 30°$

$$= \left(\frac{\sqrt{2}}{2}\right)\left(\frac{\sqrt{3}}{2}\right) - \left(\frac{\sqrt{2}}{2}\right)\left(\frac{1}{2}\right) = \frac{\sqrt{2}(\sqrt{3} - 1)}{4} = \frac{\sqrt{2}}{4}\left(\sqrt{3} - 1\right)$$

$\cos 15° = \cos(45° - 30°) = \cos 45° \cos 30° + \sin 45° \sin 30°$

$$= \left(\frac{\sqrt{2}}{2}\right)\left(\frac{\sqrt{3}}{2}\right) + \left(\frac{\sqrt{2}}{2}\right)\left(\frac{1}{2}\right) = \frac{\sqrt{2}(\sqrt{3} + 1)}{4} = \frac{\sqrt{2}}{4}\left(\sqrt{3} + 1\right)$$

$\tan 15° = \tan(45° - 30°) = \dfrac{\tan 45° - \tan 30°}{1 + \tan 45° \tan 30°}$

$$= \frac{1 - \dfrac{\sqrt{3}}{3}}{1 + (1)\left(\dfrac{\sqrt{3}}{3}\right)} = \frac{\dfrac{3 - \sqrt{3}}{3}}{\dfrac{3 + \sqrt{3}}{3}} = \frac{3 - \sqrt{3}}{3 + \sqrt{3}} \cdot \frac{3 - \sqrt{3}}{3 - \sqrt{3}} = \frac{12 - 6\sqrt{3}}{6} = 2 - \sqrt{3}$$

20. $-\dfrac{7\pi}{12} = -\dfrac{\pi}{3} - \dfrac{\pi}{4}$

$$\sin\left(-\frac{7\pi}{12}\right) = \sin\left(-\frac{\pi}{3} - \frac{\pi}{4}\right) = \sin\left(-\frac{\pi}{3}\right)\cos\left(\frac{\pi}{4}\right) - \cos\left(-\frac{\pi}{3}\right)\sin\left(\frac{\pi}{4}\right)$$

$$= \left(-\frac{\sqrt{3}}{2}\right)\left(\frac{\sqrt{2}}{2}\right) - \left(\frac{1}{2}\right)\left(\frac{\sqrt{2}}{2}\right) = -\frac{\sqrt{2}}{4}\left(\sqrt{3} + 1\right)$$

$$\cos\left(-\frac{7\pi}{12}\right) = \cos\left(-\frac{\pi}{3} - \frac{\pi}{4}\right) = \cos\left(-\frac{\pi}{3}\right)\cos\left(\frac{\pi}{4}\right) + \sin\left(-\frac{\pi}{3}\right)\sin\left(\frac{\pi}{4}\right)$$

$$= \left(\frac{1}{2}\right)\left(\frac{\sqrt{2}}{2}\right) + \left(-\frac{\sqrt{3}}{2}\right)\left(\frac{\sqrt{2}}{2}\right) = \frac{\sqrt{2}}{4}\left(1 - \sqrt{3}\right)$$

$$\tan\left(-\frac{7\pi}{12}\right) = \tan\left(-\frac{\pi}{3} - \frac{\pi}{4}\right) = \frac{\tan\left(-\frac{\pi}{3}\right) - \tan\left(\frac{\pi}{4}\right)}{1 + \tan\left(-\frac{\pi}{3}\right)\tan\left(\frac{\pi}{4}\right)}$$

$$= \frac{-\sqrt{3} - 1}{1 + (-\sqrt{3})(1)} = 2 + \sqrt{3}$$

22. $\dfrac{5\pi}{12} = \dfrac{\pi}{4} + \dfrac{\pi}{6}$

$$\sin\left(\frac{\pi}{4} + \frac{\pi}{6}\right) = \sin\frac{\pi}{4}\cos\frac{\pi}{6} + \cos\frac{\pi}{4}\sin\frac{\pi}{6}$$

$$= \left(\frac{\sqrt{2}}{2}\right)\left(\frac{\sqrt{3}}{2}\right) + \left(\frac{\sqrt{2}}{2}\right)\left(\frac{1}{2}\right) = \frac{\sqrt{2}}{4}\left(\sqrt{3} + 1\right)$$

$$\cos\left(\frac{\pi}{4} + \frac{\pi}{6}\right) = \cos\frac{\pi}{4}\cos\frac{\pi}{6} - \sin\frac{\pi}{4}\sin\frac{\pi}{6}$$

$$= \left(\frac{\sqrt{2}}{2}\right)\left(\frac{\sqrt{3}}{2}\right) - \left(\frac{\sqrt{2}}{2}\right)\left(\frac{1}{2}\right) = \frac{\sqrt{2}}{2}\left(\sqrt{3} - 1\right)$$

$$\tan\left(\frac{\pi}{4} + \frac{\pi}{6}\right) = \frac{\tan\frac{\pi}{4} + \tan\frac{\pi}{6}}{1 - \tan\frac{\pi}{4}\tan\frac{\pi}{6}} = \frac{1 + \frac{\sqrt{3}}{3}}{1 - (1)\left(\frac{\sqrt{3}}{3}\right)} = \sqrt{3} + 2$$

24. $\sin 140° \cos 50° + \cos 140° \sin 50° = \sin(140° + 50°) = \sin 190°$

26. $\dfrac{\tan 140° - \tan 60°}{1 + \tan 140° \tan 60°} = \tan(140° - 60°) = \tan 80°$

28. $\cos\dfrac{\pi}{7}\cos\dfrac{\pi}{5} - \sin\dfrac{\pi}{7}\sin\dfrac{\pi}{5} = \cos\left(\dfrac{\pi}{7} + \dfrac{\pi}{5}\right)$

$$= \cos\frac{12\pi}{35}$$

30. $\cos 3x \cos 2y + \sin 3x \sin 2y = \cos(3x - 2y)$

32. $\cos 15° \cos 60° + \sin 15° \sin 60° = \cos(15° - 60°)$

$$= \cos(-45°) = \frac{\sqrt{2}}{2}$$

34. $\cos\dfrac{\pi}{16}\cos\dfrac{3\pi}{16} - \sin\dfrac{\pi}{16}\sin\dfrac{3\pi}{16} = \cos\left(\dfrac{\pi}{16} + \dfrac{3\pi}{16}\right)$

$\qquad\qquad\qquad\qquad\qquad = \cos\dfrac{\pi}{4} - \dfrac{\sqrt{2}}{2}$

36. $\dfrac{\tan\left(\dfrac{5\pi}{4}\right) - \tan\left(\dfrac{\pi}{12}\right)}{1 + \tan\left(\dfrac{5\pi}{4}\right)\tan\left(\dfrac{\pi}{12}\right)} = \tan\left(\dfrac{5\pi}{4} - \dfrac{\pi}{12}\right)$

$\qquad\qquad\qquad\qquad = \tan\left(\dfrac{7\pi}{6}\right)$

$\qquad\qquad\qquad\qquad = \tan\left(\dfrac{\pi}{6}\right) = \dfrac{\sqrt{3}}{3}$

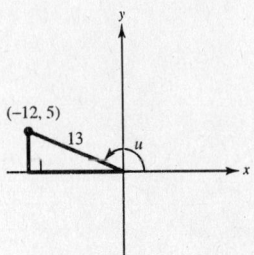
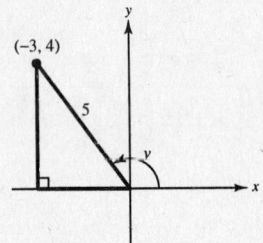

Figures for Exercises 38–44

38. $\cos(u - v) = \cos u \cos v + \sin u \sin v$

$\qquad = \left(-\dfrac{12}{13}\right)\left(-\dfrac{3}{5}\right) + \left(\dfrac{5}{13}\right)\left(\dfrac{4}{5}\right)$

$\qquad = \dfrac{36}{65} + \dfrac{20}{65} = \dfrac{56}{65}$

40. $\sin(v - u) = \sin v \cos u - \cos v \sin u$

$\qquad = \left(\dfrac{4}{5}\right)\left(-\dfrac{12}{13}\right) - \left(-\dfrac{3}{5}\right)\left(\dfrac{5}{13}\right)$

$\qquad = -\dfrac{48}{65} + \dfrac{15}{65} = -\dfrac{33}{65}$

42. $\csc(u - v) = \dfrac{1}{\sin(u - v)} = \dfrac{1}{-\sin(v - u)}$

$\qquad = \dfrac{1}{-\left(-\dfrac{33}{65}\right)} = \dfrac{65}{33}$

44. $\cot(u + v) = \dfrac{1}{\tan(u + v)} = \dfrac{1}{-\dfrac{63}{16}} = -\dfrac{16}{63}$

$\tan(u + v) = \dfrac{\tan u + \tan v}{1 - \tan u \tan v} = \dfrac{\left(-\dfrac{5}{12}\right) + \left(-\dfrac{4}{3}\right)}{1 - \left(-\dfrac{5}{12}\right)\left(-\dfrac{4}{3}\right)}$

$\qquad\qquad = \dfrac{-\dfrac{7}{4}}{\dfrac{4}{9}} = -\dfrac{63}{16}$

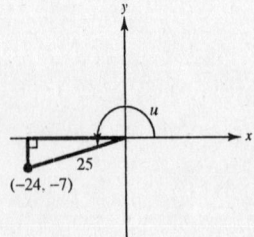
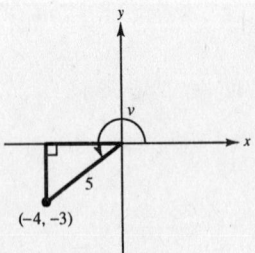

Figures for Exercises 46–50

46. $\sin(u + v) = \sin u \cos v + \cos u \sin v$

$\qquad = \left(-\dfrac{7}{25}\right)\left(-\dfrac{4}{5}\right) + \left(-\dfrac{24}{25}\right)\left(-\dfrac{3}{5}\right)$

$\qquad = \dfrac{28}{125} + \dfrac{72}{125} = \dfrac{100}{125} = \dfrac{4}{5}$

48. $\cot(v - u) = \dfrac{1}{\tan(v - u)} = \dfrac{1}{\dfrac{44}{117}} = \dfrac{117}{44}$

$\tan(v - u) = \dfrac{\tan v - \tan u}{1 + \tan v \tan u} = \dfrac{\left(\dfrac{3}{4}\right) - \left(\dfrac{7}{24}\right)}{1 + \left(\dfrac{3}{4}\right)\left(\dfrac{7}{24}\right)}$

$\qquad\qquad = \dfrac{\dfrac{11}{24}}{\dfrac{39}{32}} = \dfrac{44}{117}$

50. $\csc(u - v) = \dfrac{1}{\sin(u - v)} = \dfrac{1}{-\frac{44}{125}} = -\dfrac{125}{44}$

$\sin(u - v) = \sin u \cos v - \cos u \sin v = \left(-\dfrac{7}{25}\right)\left(-\dfrac{4}{5}\right) - \left(-\dfrac{24}{25}\right)\left(-\dfrac{3}{5}\right)$

$\qquad = \dfrac{28}{125} - \dfrac{72}{125} = -\dfrac{44}{125}$

52. Let:

$\qquad u = \arctan 2x$ and $v = \arccos x$

$\tan u = 2x \qquad \cos v = x$

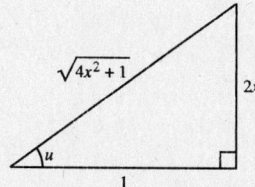 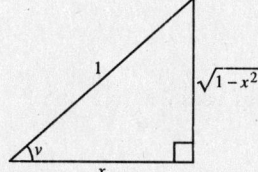

$\sin(\arctan 2x - \arccos x) = \sin(u - v)$

$\qquad\qquad = \sin u \cos v - \cos u \sin v$

$\qquad\qquad = \dfrac{2x}{\sqrt{4x^2 + 1}}(x) - \dfrac{1}{\sqrt{4x^2 + 1}}\left(\sqrt{1 - x^2}\right)$

$\qquad\qquad = \dfrac{2x^2 - \sqrt{1 - x^2}}{\sqrt{4x^2 + 1}}$

54. Let:

$\qquad u = \arccos x$ and $v = \arctan x$

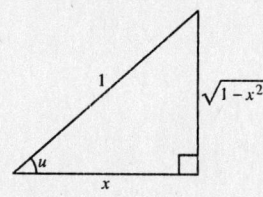 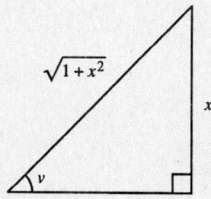

$\cos(\arccos x - \arctan x) = \cos(u - v)$

$\qquad\qquad = \cos u \cos v + \sin u \sin v$

$\qquad\qquad = (x)\left(\dfrac{1}{\sqrt{1 + x^2}}\right)\left(\sqrt{1 - x^2}\right)\left(\dfrac{x}{\sqrt{1 + x^2}}\right)$

$\qquad\qquad = \dfrac{x + x\sqrt{1 - x^2}}{\sqrt{1 + x^2}}$

56. $\sin\left(\dfrac{\pi}{2} + x\right) = \sin\dfrac{\pi}{2}\cos x + \sin x \cos\dfrac{\pi}{2}$

$\qquad\qquad = (1)(\cos x) + (\sin x)(0)$

$\qquad\qquad = \cos x$

58. $\cos\left(\dfrac{5\pi}{4} - x\right) = \cos\dfrac{5\pi}{4}\cos x + \sin\dfrac{5\pi}{4}\sin x$

$\qquad\qquad = -\dfrac{\sqrt{2}}{2}(\cos x + \sin x)$

60. $\tan\left(\dfrac{\pi}{4} - \theta\right) = \dfrac{\tan\dfrac{\pi}{4} - \tan\theta}{1 + \tan\dfrac{\pi}{4}\tan\theta} = \dfrac{1 - \tan\theta}{1 + \tan\theta}$

62. $\sin(x + y)\sin(x - y) = (\sin x \cos y + \sin y \cos x)(\sin x \cos y - \sin y \cos x)$

$= \sin^2 x \cos^2 y - \sin^2 y \cos^2 x$

$= \sin^2 x(1 - \sin^2 y) - \sin^2 y \cos^2 x$

$= \sin^2 x - \sin^2 x \sin^2 y - \sin^2 y \cos^2 x$

$= \sin^2 x - \sin^2 y(\sin^2 x + \cos^2 x)$

$= \sin^2 x - \sin^2 y$

64. $\cos(x + y) + \cos(x - y) = \cos x \cos y - \sin x \sin y + \cos x \cos y + \sin x \sin y$

$= 2 \cos x \cos y$

66. $\cos(\pi + x) = \cos \pi \cos x - \sin \pi \sin x$

$= (-1) \cos x - (0) \sin x$

$= -\cos x$

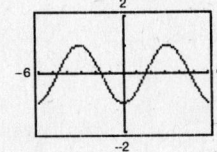

68. $\tan(\pi + \theta) = \dfrac{\tan \pi + \tan \theta}{1 - \tan \pi \tan \theta}$

$= \dfrac{0 + \tan \theta}{1 - (0) \tan \theta}$

$= \tan \theta$

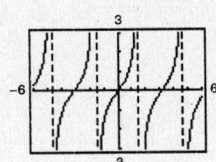

70.
$$\sin\left(x + \frac{\pi}{6}\right) - \sin\left(x - \frac{\pi}{6}\right) = \frac{1}{2}$$

$$\sin x \cos \frac{\pi}{6} + \cos x \sin \frac{\pi}{6} - \left(\sin x \cos \frac{\pi}{6} - \cos x \sin \frac{\pi}{6}\right) = \frac{1}{2}$$

$$2 \cos x(0.5) = \frac{1}{2}$$

$$\cos x = \frac{1}{2}$$

$$x = \frac{\pi}{3}, \frac{5\pi}{3}$$

72.
$$\tan(x + \pi) + 2\sin(x + \pi) = 0$$

$$\frac{\tan x + \tan \pi}{1 - \tan x \tan \pi} + 2(\sin x \cos \pi + \cos x \sin \pi) = 0$$

$$\frac{\tan x + 0}{1 - \tan x(0)} + 2[\sin x(-1) + \cos x(0)] = 0$$

$$\frac{\tan x}{1} - 2\sin x = 0$$

$$\frac{\sin x}{\cos x} = 2\sin x$$

$$\sin x = 2\sin x \cos x$$

$$\sin x(1 - 2\cos x) = 0$$

$$\sin x = 0 \quad \text{or} \quad \cos x = \frac{1}{2}$$

$$x = 0, \pi \qquad x = \frac{\pi}{3}, \frac{5\pi}{3}$$

74. $\tan(x + \pi) - \cos\left(x + \dfrac{\pi}{2}\right) = 0$

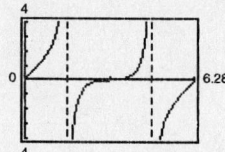

Answers: $(0, 0), (3.14, 0) \implies x = 0, \pi$

76.
$$y_1 = A \cos 2\pi\left(\frac{t}{T} - \frac{x}{\lambda}\right)$$

$$y_2 = A \cos 2\pi\left(\frac{t}{T} + \frac{x}{\lambda}\right)$$

$$y_1 + y_2 = A \cos 2\pi\left(\frac{t}{T} - \frac{x}{\lambda}\right) + A \cos 2\pi\left(\frac{t}{T} + \frac{x}{\lambda}\right)$$

$$y_1 + y_2 = A\left[\cos 2\pi\frac{t}{T}\cos 2\pi\frac{x}{\lambda} + \sin 2\pi\frac{t}{T}\sin 2\pi\frac{x}{\lambda}\right] + A\left[\cos 2\pi\frac{t}{T}\cos 2\pi\frac{x}{\lambda} - \sin 2\pi\frac{t}{T}\sin 2\pi\frac{x}{\lambda}\right]$$

$$= 2A \cos 2\pi\frac{t}{T}\cos 2\pi\frac{x}{\lambda}$$

78. False.

$$\cos(u \pm v) = \cos u \cos v \pm \sin u \sin v$$

80. True.

$$\sin\left(x - \frac{\pi}{2}\right) = -\sin\left(\frac{\pi}{2} - x\right) = -\cos x$$

82. $\sin(n\pi + \theta) = \sin n\pi \cos \theta + \sin \theta \cos n\pi$

$$= (0)(\cos \theta) + (\sin \theta)(-1)^n$$

$$= (-1)^n(\sin \theta), \text{ where } n \text{ is an integer.}$$

84. $C = \arctan \dfrac{a}{b} \implies \sin C = \dfrac{a}{\sqrt{a^2 + b^2}}, \cos C = \dfrac{b}{\sqrt{a^2 + b^2}}$

$$\sqrt{a^2 + b^2}\cos(B\theta - C) = \sqrt{a^2 + b^2}\left(\cos B\theta \cdot \dfrac{b}{\sqrt{a^2 + b^2}} + \sin B\theta \cdot \dfrac{a}{\sqrt{a^2 + b^2}}\right)$$

$$= b\cos B\theta + a\sin B\theta$$

$$= a\sin B\theta + b\cos B\theta$$

86. $3\sin 2\theta + 4\cos 2\theta$

$a = 3, b = 4, B = 2$

(a) $C = \arctan \dfrac{b}{a} = \arctan \dfrac{4}{3} \approx 0.9273$

$3\sin 2\theta + 4\cos 2\theta = \sqrt{a^2 + b^2}\,\sin(B\theta + C)$

$\approx 5\sin(2\theta + 0.9273)$

(b) $C = \arctan \dfrac{a}{b} = \arctan \dfrac{3}{4} \approx 0.6435$

$3\sin 2\theta + 4\cos 2\theta = \sqrt{a^2 + b^2}\,\cos(B\theta - C)$

$\approx 5\cos(2\theta - 0.6435)$

88. $\sin 2\theta - \cos 2\theta$

$a = 1, b = -1, B = 2$

(a) $C = \arctan \dfrac{b}{a} = \arctan(-1) = -\dfrac{\pi}{4}$

$\sin 2\theta - \cos 2\theta = \sqrt{a^2 + b^2}\,\sin(B\theta + C)$

$= \sqrt{2}\,\sin\!\left(2\theta - \dfrac{\pi}{4}\right)$

(b) $C = \arctan \dfrac{a}{b} = \arctan(-1) = -\dfrac{\pi}{4}$

$\sin 2\theta - \cos 2\theta = \sqrt{a^2 + b^2}\,\cos(B\theta - C)$

$= \sqrt{2}\,\cos\!\left(2\theta + \dfrac{\pi}{4}\right)$

90. $C = \arctan \dfrac{a}{b} = -\dfrac{3\pi}{4} \implies a = b, a < 0, b < 0$

$\sqrt{a^2 + b^2} = 5 \implies a = b = \dfrac{-5\sqrt{2}}{2}$

$B = 1$

$5\cos\!\left(\theta + \dfrac{3\pi}{4}\right) = -\dfrac{5\sqrt{2}}{2}\sin\theta - \dfrac{5\sqrt{2}}{2}\cos\theta$

92. For $m_2 > m_1 > 0$, the angle θ between the lines is

$\theta = \arctan\!\left(\dfrac{m_2 - m_1}{1 + m_1 m_2}\right).$

$m_2 = 1$

$m_1 = \dfrac{1}{\sqrt{3}}$

$\theta = \arctan\!\left(\dfrac{1 - \dfrac{1}{\sqrt{3}}}{1 + \dfrac{1}{\sqrt{3}}}\right) = \arctan\!\left(2 - \sqrt{3}\right) = 15°$

94. From the figure, it appears that $u + v = w$. Assume that u, v, and w are all in Quadrant I. From the figure:

$\tan u = \dfrac{s}{3s} = \dfrac{1}{3}$

$\tan v = \dfrac{s}{2s} = \dfrac{1}{2}$

$\tan w = \dfrac{s}{s} = 1$

$\tan(u + v) = \dfrac{\tan u + \tan v}{1 - \tan u \tan v} = \dfrac{1/3 + 1/2}{1 - (1/3)(1/2)} = \dfrac{5/6}{1 - (1/6)} = 1 = \tan w.$

Thus, $\tan(u + v) = \tan w$. Because u, v, and w are all in Quadrant I, we have

$\arctan[\tan(u + v)] = \arctan[\tan w]$

$u + v = w.$

96. First, prove $\cos(u - v) = \cos u \cos v + \sin u \sin v$
using the figure containing points

$A(1, 0)$

$B(\cos(u - v), \sin(u - v))$

$C(\cos v, \sin v)$

$D(\cos u, \sin u)$

on the unit circle.

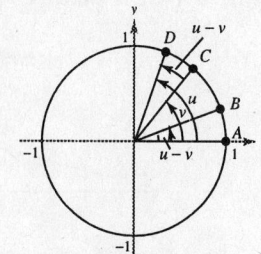

Since chords AB and CD are each subtended by angle $u - v$, their lengths are equal.
Equating $[d(A, B)]^2 = [d(C, D)]^2$ we have $(\cos(u - v) - 1)^2 + \sin^2(u - v) = (\cos u - \cos v)^2 + (\sin u - \sin v)^2$.
Simplifying and solving for $\cos(u - v)$, we have $\cos(u - v) = \cos u \cos v + \sin u \sin v$.

Using $\sin \theta = \cos\left(\dfrac{\pi}{2} - \theta\right)$ we have

$$\sin(u - v) = \cos\left[\frac{\pi}{2} - (u - v)\right] = \cos\left[\left(\frac{\pi}{2} - u\right) - (-v)\right]$$

$$= \cos\left(\frac{\pi}{2} - u\right)\cos(-v) + \sin\left(\frac{\pi}{2} - u\right)\sin(-v)$$

$$= \sin u \cos v - \cos u \sin v.$$

98.
$$f(x) = \frac{7 - x}{8}$$

$$y = \frac{7 - x}{8}$$

$$8y = 7 - x$$

$$x = 7 - 8y \Longrightarrow f^{-1}(x) = -8x + 7$$

$$f(f^{-1}(x)) = \frac{7 - f^{-1}(x)}{8}$$

$$= \frac{7 - (-8x + 7)}{8}$$

$$= x$$

$$f^{-1}(f(x)) = -8\left(\frac{7 - x}{8}\right) + 7$$

$$= x$$

100.
$$f(x) = \sqrt{x - 16}$$

$$y = \sqrt{x - 16}$$

$$y^2 = x - 16$$

$$x = y^2 + 16 \Longrightarrow f^{-1}(x) = x^2 + 16$$

$$f(f^{-1}(x)) = \sqrt{(x^2 + 16) - 16} = x$$

$$f^{-1}(f(x)) = \left(\sqrt{x - 16}\right)^2 + 16 = x$$

102. $\log_8 8^{3x^2} = 3x^2$

104. $12x + e^{\ln x(x - 2)} = 12x + x(x - 2)$

$$= 12x + x^2 - 2x$$

$$= x^2 + 10x$$

Section 5.5   Multiple–Angle and Product–to–Sum Formulas

Solutions to Even-Numbered Exercises

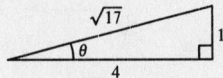

Figure for Exercises 2–8

2. $\tan \theta = \dfrac{1}{4}$

4. $\sin 2\theta = 2 \sin \theta \cos \theta = 2\left(\dfrac{1}{\sqrt{17}}\right)\left(\dfrac{4}{\sqrt{17}}\right) = \dfrac{8}{17}$

6. $\sec 2\theta = \dfrac{1}{\cos 2\theta}$

$= \dfrac{1}{\cos^2 \theta - \sin^2 \theta}$

$= \dfrac{1}{\left(\dfrac{4}{\sqrt{17}}\right)^2 - \left(\dfrac{1}{\sqrt{17}}\right)^2} = \dfrac{1}{\dfrac{16}{17} - \dfrac{1}{17}} = \dfrac{17}{15}$

8. $\cot 2\theta = \dfrac{1}{\tan 2\theta} = \dfrac{1 - \tan^2 \theta}{2 \tan \theta} = \dfrac{1 - \left(\dfrac{1}{4}\right)^2}{2\left(\dfrac{1}{4}\right)}$

$= \dfrac{15}{8}$

10.
$$\sin 2x + \cos x = 0$$
$$2 \sin x \cos x + \cos x = 0$$
$$\cos x(2 \sin x + 1) = 0$$

$\cos x = 0 \qquad$ or $\quad 2 \sin x + 1 = 0$

$x = \dfrac{\pi}{2}, \dfrac{3\pi}{2} \qquad\qquad \sin x = -\dfrac{1}{2}$

$x = \dfrac{7\pi}{6}, \dfrac{11\pi}{6}$

12.
$$\sin 2x \sin x = \cos x$$
$$2 \sin x \cos x \sin x - \cos x = 0$$
$$\cos x(2 \sin^2 x - 1) = 0$$

$\cos x = 0 \qquad$ or $\quad 2 \sin^2 x - 1 = 0$

$x = \dfrac{\pi}{2}, \dfrac{3\pi}{2} \qquad\qquad \sin^2 x = \dfrac{1}{2}$

$\sin x = \pm \dfrac{\sqrt{2}}{2}$

$x = \dfrac{\pi}{4}, \dfrac{3\pi}{4}, \dfrac{5\pi}{4}, \dfrac{7\pi}{4}$

14.
$$\cos 2x + \sin x = 0$$
$$1 - 2 \sin^2 x + \sin x = 0$$
$$2 \sin^2 x - \sin x - 1 = 0$$
$$(2 \sin x + 1)(\sin x - 1) = 0$$

$2 \sin x + 1 = 0 \qquad$ or $\quad \sin x - 1 = 0$

$\sin x = -\dfrac{1}{2} \qquad\qquad \sin x = 1$

$x = \dfrac{7\pi}{6}, \dfrac{11\pi}{6} \qquad\qquad x = \dfrac{\pi}{2}$

16.
$$\tan 2x - 2\cos x = 0$$

$$\frac{2\tan x}{1 - \tan^2 x} = 2\cos x$$

$$2\tan x = 2\cos x(1 - \tan^2 x)$$

$$2\tan x = 2\cos x - 2\cos x \tan^2 x$$

$$2\tan x = 2\cos x - 2\cos x \frac{\sin^2 x}{\cos^2 x}$$

$$2\tan x = 2\cos x - 2\frac{\sin^2 x}{\cos x}$$

$$\tan x = \cos x - \frac{\sin^2 x}{\cos x}$$

$$\frac{\sin x}{\cos x} = \cos x - \frac{\sin^2 x}{\cos x}$$

$$\frac{\sin x}{\cos x} + \frac{\sin^2 x}{\cos x} - \cos x = 0$$

$$\frac{\sin x + \sin^2 x - \cos^2 x}{\cos x} = 0$$

$$\frac{1}{\cos x}[\sin x + \sin^2 x - (1 - \sin^2 x)] = 0$$

$$\sec x[2\sin^2 x + \sin x - 1] = 0$$

$$\sec x(2\sin x - 1)(\sin x + 1) = 0$$

$\sec x = 0$ or $2\sin x - 1 = 0$ or $\sin x + 1 = 0$

No solution

$$\sin x = \frac{1}{2}$$

$$\sin x = -1$$

$$x = \frac{3\pi}{2}$$

$$x = \frac{\pi}{6}, \frac{5\pi}{6}$$

Also, values for which $\cos x = 0$ need to be checked.

$\dfrac{\pi}{2}, \dfrac{3\pi}{2}$ are solutions.

$$x = \frac{\pi}{6}, \frac{\pi}{2}, \frac{5\pi}{6}, \frac{3\pi}{2}$$

18.
$$(\sin 2x + \cos 2x)^2 = 1$$

$$\sin^2 2x + 2\sin 2x \cos 2x + \cos^2 2x = 1$$

$$2\sin 2x \cos 2x = 0$$

$$\sin 4x = 0$$

$$4x = n\pi$$

$$x = \frac{n\pi}{4}$$

$$x = 0, \frac{\pi}{4}, \frac{\pi}{2}, \frac{3\pi}{4}, \pi, \frac{5\pi}{4}, \frac{3\pi}{2}, \frac{7\pi}{4}$$

20. $6 \cos^2 x - 3 = 3(2\cos^2 x - 1)$

$\qquad = 3 \cos 2x$

22. $(\cos x + \sin x)(\cos x - \sin x) = \cos^2 x - \sin^2 x$

$\qquad = \cos 2x$

24. $\cos u = -\dfrac{2}{3}, \dfrac{\pi}{2} < u < \pi$

$\sin 2u = 2 \sin u \cos u = 2 \cdot \dfrac{\sqrt{5}}{3}\left(-\dfrac{2}{3}\right) = -\dfrac{4\sqrt{5}}{9}$

$\cos 2u = \cos^2 u - \sin^2 u = \dfrac{4}{9} - \dfrac{5}{9} = -\dfrac{1}{9}$

$\tan 2u = \dfrac{2 \tan u}{1 - \tan^2 u} = \dfrac{2\left(-\dfrac{\sqrt{5}}{2}\right)}{1 - \dfrac{5}{4}} = 4\sqrt{5}$

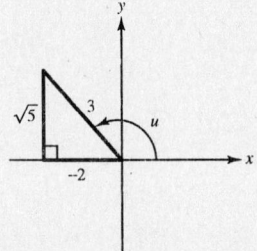

$\csc u = 3, \dfrac{\pi}{2} < u < \pi$

26. $\cot u = -4, \dfrac{3\pi}{2} < u < 2\pi$

$\sin 2u = 2 \sin u \cos u = 2\left(-\dfrac{1}{\sqrt{17}}\right)\left(\dfrac{4}{\sqrt{17}}\right) = -\dfrac{8}{17}$

$\cos 2u = \cos^2 u - \sin^2 u$

$\qquad = \left(\dfrac{4}{\sqrt{17}}\right)^2 - \left(-\dfrac{1}{\sqrt{17}}\right)^2 = \dfrac{15}{17}$

$\tan 2u = \dfrac{2 \tan u}{1 - \tan^2 u} = \dfrac{2\left(-\dfrac{1}{4}\right)}{1 - \left(-\dfrac{1}{4}\right)^2} = -\dfrac{8}{15}$

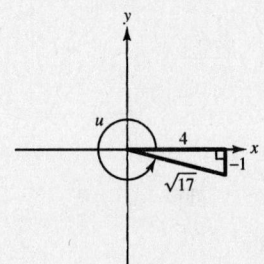

28. $\sin 2u = 2 \sin u \cos u = 2 \cdot \dfrac{1}{3}\left(-\dfrac{2\sqrt{2}}{3}\right) = -\dfrac{4\sqrt{2}}{9}$

$\cos 2u = \cos^2 u - \sin^2 u = \left(-\dfrac{2\sqrt{2}}{3}\right)^2 - \left(\dfrac{1}{3}\right)^2 = \dfrac{7}{9}$

$\tan 2u = \dfrac{2 \tan u}{1 - \tan^2 u} = \dfrac{2\left(-\dfrac{\sqrt{2}}{4}\right)}{1 - \left(-\dfrac{\sqrt{2}}{4}\right)^2} = -\dfrac{4\sqrt{2}}{7}$

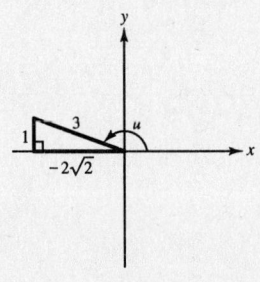

30. $\sin^8 x = \sin^4 x \sin^4 x = (\sin^2 x \sin^2 x)(\sin^2 x \sin^2 x)$

$\sin^2 x = \dfrac{1 - \cos 2x}{2}$

$\sin^4 x = \left(\dfrac{1 - \cos 2x}{2}\right)\left(\dfrac{1 - \cos 2x}{2}\right)$

$\qquad = \dfrac{1}{4}(1 - 2 \cos 2x + \cos^2 2x)$

$\qquad = \dfrac{1}{4}\left(1 - 2 \cos 2x + \left(\dfrac{1 + \cos 4x}{2}\right)\right)$

$\qquad = \dfrac{1}{8}(3 - 4 \cos 2x + \cos 4x)$

—CONTINUED—

30. **—CONTINUED—**

$\sin^8 x = \sin^4 x \sin^4 x$

$$= \frac{1}{64}(3 - 4\cos 2x + \cos 4x)(3 - 4\cos 2x + \cos 4x)$$

$$= \frac{1}{64}(9 - 24\cos 2x + 16\cos^2 2x + 6\cos 4x - 8\cos 2x \cos 4x + \cos^2 4x)$$

$$= \frac{1}{64}\left[9 - 24\cos 2x + 16\left(\frac{1 + \cos 4x}{2}\right) + 6\cos 4x - 8\frac{1}{2}(\cos 6x + \cos 2x) + \left(\frac{1 + \cos 8x}{2}\right)\right]$$

$$= \frac{1}{64}\left[\frac{35}{2} - 28\cos 2x + 14\cos 4x - 4\cos 6x + \frac{1}{2}\cos 8x\right]$$

$$= \frac{1}{128}[35 - 56\cos 2x + 28\cos 4x - 8\cos 6x + \cos 8x]$$

In the above, we used $\cos 2x \cos 4x = \frac{1}{2}(\cos 6x + \cos 2x)$ which follows from $\cos x(4x \pm 2x) = \cos 4x \cos 2x \pm \sin 4x \sin 2x$.

32. $\sin^4 x \cos^4 x = \sin^2 x \sin^2 x \cos^2 x \cos^2 x$

$$= (\sin^2 x \cos^2 x)(\sin^2 x \cos^2 x)$$

$$= \left(\frac{1}{4}\sin^2 2x\right)\left(\frac{1}{4}\sin^2 2x\right)$$

$$= \left[\frac{1}{4}\left(\frac{1 - \cos 4x}{2}\right)\right]\left[\frac{1}{4}\left(\frac{1 - \cos 4x}{2}\right)\right]$$

$$= \frac{1}{64}[1 - 2\cos 4x + \cos^2 4x]$$

$$= \frac{1}{64}\left[1 - 2\cos 4x + \left(\frac{1 + \cos 8x}{2}\right)\right]$$

$$= \frac{1}{64}\left[\frac{3}{2} - 2\cos 4x + \frac{1}{2}\cos 8x\right]$$

$$= \frac{1}{128}(3 - 4\cos 4x + \cos 8x)$$

34. $\sin^4 x \cos^2 x = \sin^2 x \sin^2 x \cos^2 x$

$$= \left(\frac{1 - \cos 2x}{2}\right)\left(\frac{1 - \cos 2x}{2}\right)\left(\frac{1 + \cos 2x}{2}\right)$$

$$= \frac{1}{8}(1 - \cos 2x)(1 - \cos^2 2x)$$

$$= \frac{1}{8}(1 - \cos 2x - \cos^2 2x + \cos^3 2x)$$

$$= \frac{1}{8}\left[1 - \cos 2x - \left(\frac{1 + \cos 4x}{2}\right) + \cos 2x\left(\frac{1 + \cos 4x}{2}\right)\right]$$

$$= \frac{1}{16}[2 - 2\cos 2x - 1 - \cos 4x + \cos 2x + \cos 2x \cos 4x]$$

$$= \frac{1}{16}\left[1 - \cos 2x - \cos 4x + \frac{1}{2}\cos 2x + \frac{1}{2}\cos 6x\right]$$

$$= \frac{1}{32}[2 - 2\cos 2x - 2\cos 4x + \cos 2x + \cos 6x]$$

$$= \frac{1}{32}[2 - \cos 2x - 2\cos 4x + \cos 6x]$$

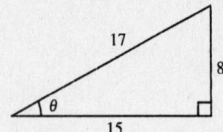

Figure for Exercises 36–40

36. $\sin\dfrac{\theta}{2} = \sqrt{\dfrac{1-\cos\theta}{2}} = \sqrt{\dfrac{1-\dfrac{15}{17}}{2}}$

$\qquad = \sqrt{\dfrac{\dfrac{2}{17}}{2}} = \dfrac{1}{\sqrt{17}} = \dfrac{\sqrt{17}}{17}$

38. $\sec\dfrac{\theta}{2} = \dfrac{1}{\cos\dfrac{\theta}{2}} = \dfrac{1}{\sqrt{\dfrac{1+\cos\theta}{2}}}$

$\qquad = \dfrac{1}{\sqrt{\dfrac{1+\dfrac{15}{17}}{2}}} = \dfrac{1}{\sqrt{\dfrac{16}{17}}}$

$\qquad = \dfrac{\sqrt{17}}{4}$

40. $\cot\dfrac{\theta}{2} = \dfrac{1}{\tan\dfrac{\theta}{2}} = \dfrac{\sin\theta}{1-\cos\theta} = \dfrac{\dfrac{8}{17}}{1-\dfrac{15}{17}}$

$\qquad = \dfrac{\dfrac{8}{17}}{\dfrac{2}{17}} = 4$

42. $\sin 165° = \sin\left(\dfrac{1}{2}\cdot 330°\right) = \sqrt{\dfrac{1-\cos 330°}{2}} = \sqrt{\dfrac{1-\dfrac{\sqrt{3}}{2}}{2}} = \dfrac{1}{2}\sqrt{2-\sqrt{3}}$

$\cos 165° = \cos\left(\dfrac{1}{2}\cdot 330°\right) = -\sqrt{\dfrac{1+\cos 330°}{2}} = -\sqrt{\dfrac{1+\dfrac{\sqrt{3}}{2}}{2}} = -\dfrac{1}{2}\sqrt{2+\sqrt{3}}$

$\tan 165° = \tan\left(\dfrac{1}{2}\cdot 330°\right) = \dfrac{\sin 330°}{1+\cos 330°} = \dfrac{-\dfrac{1}{2}}{1+\dfrac{\sqrt{3}}{2}} = \dfrac{-1}{2+\sqrt{3}} = \sqrt{3}-2$

44. $\sin 67° 30' = \sin\left(\dfrac{1}{2}\cdot 135°\right) = \sqrt{\dfrac{1-\cos 135°}{2}} = \sqrt{\dfrac{1+\dfrac{\sqrt{2}}{2}}{2}} = \dfrac{1}{2}\sqrt{2+\sqrt{2}}$

$\cos 67° 30' = \cos\left(\dfrac{1}{2}\cdot 135°\right) = \sqrt{\dfrac{1+\cos 135°}{2}} = \sqrt{\dfrac{1-\dfrac{\sqrt{2}}{2}}{2}} = \dfrac{1}{2}\sqrt{2-\sqrt{2}}$

$\tan 67° 30' = \tan\left(\dfrac{1}{2}\cdot 135°\right) = \dfrac{\sin 135°}{1+\cos 135°} = \dfrac{\dfrac{\sqrt{2}}{2}}{1-\dfrac{\sqrt{2}}{2}} = 1+\sqrt{2}$

46. $\sin\dfrac{\pi}{12} = \sin\left[\dfrac{1}{2}\left(\dfrac{\pi}{6}\right)\right] = \sqrt{\dfrac{1 - \cos\dfrac{\pi}{6}}{2}} = \sqrt{\dfrac{1 - \dfrac{\sqrt{3}}{2}}{2}} = \dfrac{1}{2}\sqrt{2 - \sqrt{3}}$

$\cos\dfrac{\pi}{12} = \cos\left[\dfrac{1}{2}\left(\dfrac{\pi}{6}\right)\right] = \sqrt{\dfrac{1 + \cos\dfrac{\pi}{6}}{2}} = \dfrac{1}{2}\sqrt{2 + \sqrt{3}}$

$\tan\dfrac{\pi}{12} = \tan\left[\dfrac{1}{2}\left(\dfrac{\pi}{6}\right)\right]\dfrac{\sin\dfrac{\pi}{6}}{1 + \cos\dfrac{\pi}{6}} = \dfrac{\dfrac{1}{2}}{1 + \dfrac{\sqrt{3}}{2}} = 2 - \sqrt{3}$

48. $\sin\dfrac{7\pi}{12} = \sin\left[\dfrac{1}{2}\left(\dfrac{7\pi}{6}\right)\right] = \sqrt{\dfrac{1 - \cos(7\pi(6))}{2}} = \sqrt{\dfrac{1 + \dfrac{\sqrt{3}}{2}}{2}} = \dfrac{1}{2}\sqrt{2 + \sqrt{3}}$

$\cos\dfrac{7\pi}{12} = \cos\left[\dfrac{1}{2}\left(\dfrac{7\pi}{6}\right)\right] = -\sqrt{\dfrac{1 + \cos\dfrac{7\pi}{6}}{2}} = \sqrt{\dfrac{1 - \dfrac{\sqrt{3}}{2}}{2}} = \dfrac{1}{2}\sqrt{2 - \sqrt{3}}$

$\tan\dfrac{7\pi}{12} = \tan\left[\dfrac{1}{2}\left(\dfrac{7\pi}{6}\right)\right] = \dfrac{\sin\dfrac{7\pi}{6}}{1 + \cos\dfrac{7\pi}{6}} = \dfrac{-\dfrac{1}{2}}{1 - \dfrac{\sqrt{3}}{2}} = -2 - \sqrt{3}$

50. $\cos u = \dfrac{3}{5}, 0 < u < \dfrac{\pi}{2}$

$\sin\left(\dfrac{u}{2}\right) = \sqrt{\dfrac{1 - \cos u}{2}} = \sqrt{\dfrac{1 - \dfrac{3}{5}}{2}} = \dfrac{\sqrt{5}}{5}$

$\cos\left(\dfrac{u}{2}\right) = \sqrt{\dfrac{1 + \cos u}{2}} = \sqrt{\dfrac{1 + \dfrac{3}{5}}{2}} = \dfrac{2\sqrt{5}}{5}$

$\tan\left(\dfrac{u}{2}\right) = \dfrac{\sin u}{1 + \cos u} = \dfrac{\dfrac{4}{5}}{1 + \dfrac{3}{5}} = \dfrac{1}{2}$

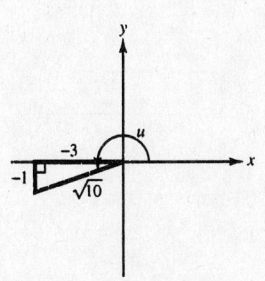

52. $\cot u = 3, \pi < u < \dfrac{3\pi}{2}$

$\sin\left(\dfrac{u}{2}\right) = \sqrt{\dfrac{1 - \cos u}{2}} = \sqrt{\dfrac{1 + \dfrac{3}{\sqrt{10}}}{2}} = \sqrt{\dfrac{10 + 3\sqrt{10}}{20}} = \dfrac{1}{2}\sqrt{\dfrac{10 + 3\sqrt{10}}{5}}$

$\cos\left(\dfrac{u}{2}\right) = -\sqrt{\dfrac{1 + \cos u}{2}} = -\sqrt{\dfrac{1 - \dfrac{3}{\sqrt{10}}}{2}} = -\sqrt{\dfrac{10 - 3\sqrt{10}}{20}} = -\dfrac{1}{2}\sqrt{\dfrac{10 - 3\sqrt{10}}{5}}$

$\tan\left(\dfrac{u}{2}\right) = \dfrac{1 - \cos u}{\sin u} = \dfrac{1 + \dfrac{3}{\sqrt{10}} - \dfrac{1}{\sqrt{10}}}{-\dfrac{1}{\sqrt{10}}} = -3 - \sqrt{10}$

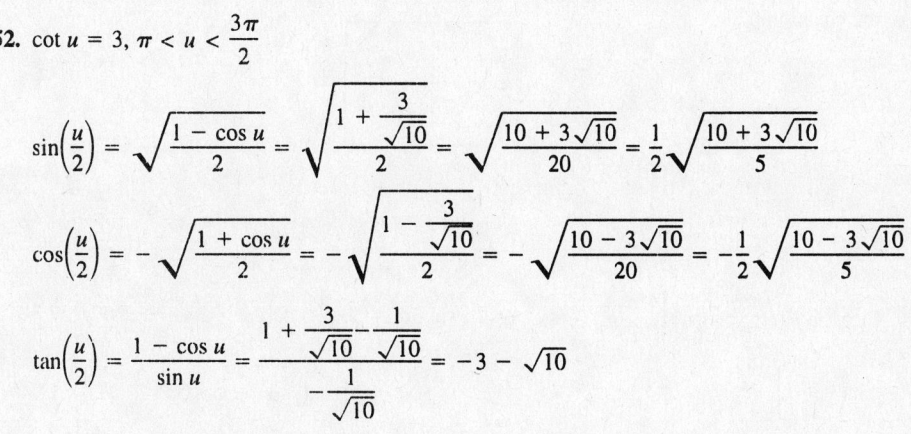

54. $\sec u = -\dfrac{7}{2}, \dfrac{\pi}{2} < u < \pi$

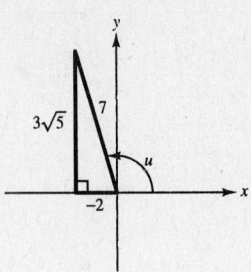

$$\sin\left(\frac{u}{2}\right) = \sqrt{\frac{1 - \cos u}{2}} = \sqrt{\frac{1 + \frac{2}{7}}{2}} = \frac{3\sqrt{14}}{14}$$

$$\cos\left(\frac{u}{2}\right) = \sqrt{\frac{1 + \cos u}{2}} = \sqrt{\frac{1 - \frac{2}{7}}{2}} = \frac{\sqrt{70}}{14}$$

$$\tan\left(\frac{u}{2}\right) = \frac{1 - \cos u}{\sin u} = \frac{1 + \frac{2}{7}}{3\frac{\sqrt{5}}{7}} = \frac{3\sqrt{5}}{5}$$

56. $\sqrt{\dfrac{1 + \cos 4x}{2}} = \left|\cos\dfrac{4x}{2}\right| = |\cos 2x|$

58. $-\sqrt{\dfrac{1 - \cos(x - 1)}{2}} = -\left|\sin\left(\dfrac{x - 1}{2}\right)\right|$

60. $h(x) = \sin\dfrac{x}{2} + \cos x - 1$

$$\sin\frac{x}{2} + \cos x - 1 = 0$$

$$\pm\sqrt{\frac{1 - \cos x}{2}} = 1 - \cos x$$

$$\frac{1 - \cos x}{2} = 1 - 2\cos x + \cos^2 x$$

$$1 - \cos x = 2 - 4\cos x + 2\cos^2 x$$

$$2\cos^2 x - 3\cos x + 1 = 0$$

$$(2\cos x - 1)(\cos x - 1) = 0$$

$$2\cos x - 1 = 0 \quad \text{or} \quad \cos x - 1 = 0$$

$$\cos x = \frac{1}{2} \qquad\qquad \cos x = 1$$

$$x = \frac{\pi}{3}, \frac{5\pi}{3} \qquad\qquad x = 0$$

$0, \dfrac{\pi}{3}$, and $\dfrac{5\pi}{3}$ are all solutions to the equation.

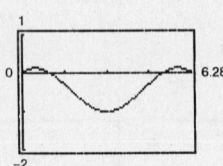

62. $g(x) = \tan\dfrac{x}{2} - \sin x$

$$\tan\frac{x}{2} - \sin x = 0$$

$$\frac{1 - \cos x}{\sin x} = \sin x$$

$$1 - \cos x = \sin^2 x$$

$$1 - \cos x = 1 - \cos^2 x$$

$$\cos^2 x - \cos x = 0$$

$$\cos x(\cos x - 1) = 0$$

$$\cos x = 0 \quad \text{or} \quad \cos x - 1 = 0$$

$$x = \frac{\pi}{2}, \frac{3\pi}{2} \qquad\qquad \cos x = 1$$

$$x = 0$$

$0, \dfrac{\pi}{2}$, and $\dfrac{3\pi}{2}$ are all solutions to the equation.

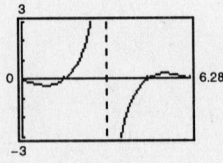

64. $4\cos\dfrac{\pi}{3}\sin\dfrac{5\pi}{6} = 4 \cdot \dfrac{1}{2}\left[\sin\left(\dfrac{\pi}{3} + \dfrac{5\pi}{6}\right) - \sin\left(\dfrac{\pi}{3} - \dfrac{5\pi}{6}\right)\right]$

$$= 2\left[\sin\left(\frac{7\pi}{6}\right) - \sin\left(-\frac{\pi}{2}\right)\right]$$

$$= 2\left[\sin\left(\frac{7\pi}{6}\right) + \sin\left(\frac{\pi}{2}\right)\right]$$

66. $3\sin 2\alpha \sin 3\alpha = 3 \cdot \dfrac{1}{2}[\cos(2\alpha - 3\alpha) - \cos(2\alpha + 3\alpha)]$

$$= \frac{3}{2}[\cos(-\alpha) - \cos 5\alpha]$$

$$= \frac{3}{2}(\cos\alpha - \cos 5\alpha)$$

68. $\cos 2\theta \cos 4\theta = \frac{1}{2}[\cos(2\theta - 4\theta) + \cos(2\theta + 4\theta)]$
$= \frac{1}{2}[\cos(-2\theta) + \cos 6\theta]$
$= \frac{1}{2}(\cos 2\theta + \cos 6\theta)$

70. $\sin(x + y)\cos(x - y) = \frac{1}{2}(\sin 2x + \sin 2y)$

72. $\sin(\theta + \pi)\sin(\theta - \pi) = \frac{1}{2}(\cos 2\pi - \cos 2\theta)$

74. $6\sin 45° \cos 15° = 6\frac{1}{2}(\sin 60° + \sin 30°)$
$= 3(\sin 60° + \sin 30°)$

76. $\cos 120° + \cos 30° = 2\cos\left(\dfrac{120° + 30°}{2}\right)\cos\left(\dfrac{120° - 30°}{2}\right)$
$= 2\cos 75° \cos 45°$

78. $\sin\dfrac{5\pi}{4} - \sin\dfrac{3\pi}{4} = 2\cos\left(\dfrac{\dfrac{5\pi}{4} + \dfrac{3\pi}{4}}{2}\right)\sin\left(\dfrac{\dfrac{5\pi}{4} - \dfrac{3\pi}{4}}{2}\right)$
$= 2\cos \pi \sin\dfrac{\pi}{4}$

80. $\sin 3\theta + \sin \theta = 2\sin\left(\dfrac{3\theta + \theta}{2}\right)\cos\left(\dfrac{3\theta - \theta}{2}\right)$
$= 2\sin 2\theta \cos \theta$

82. $\sin x + \sin 5x = 2\sin\left(\dfrac{x + 5x}{2}\right)\cos\left(\dfrac{x - 5x}{2}\right)$
$= 2\sin 3x \cos(-2x)$
$= 2\sin 3x \cos 2x$

84. $\cos(\phi + 2\pi) + \cos \phi = 2\cos\left(\dfrac{\phi + 2\pi + \phi}{2}\right)\cos\left(\dfrac{\phi + 2\pi - \phi}{2}\right)$
$= 2\cos(\phi + \pi)\cos(\pi)$

86. $\sin\left(x + \dfrac{\pi}{2}\right) + \sin\left(x - \dfrac{\pi}{2}\right) = 2\sin\left(\dfrac{x + \dfrac{\pi}{2} + x - \dfrac{\pi}{2}}{2}\right)\cos\left(\dfrac{x + \dfrac{\pi}{2} - \left(x - \dfrac{\pi}{2}\right)}{2}\right)$
$= 2\sin x \cos\dfrac{\pi}{2}$

88. $h(x) = \cos 2x - \cos 6x$
$\cos 2x - \cos 6x = 0$
$-2\sin 4x \sin(-2x) = 0$
$2\sin 4x \sin 2x = 0$

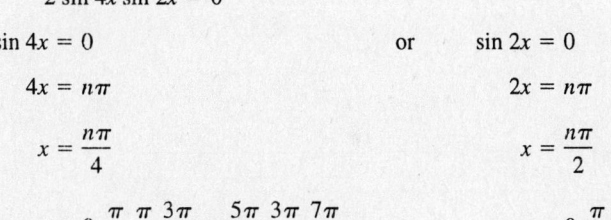

$\sin 4x = 0 \qquad\qquad$ or $\qquad \sin 2x = 0$
$4x = n\pi \qquad\qquad\qquad\qquad 2x = n\pi$
$x = \dfrac{n\pi}{4} \qquad\qquad\qquad\qquad x = \dfrac{n\pi}{2}$
$x = 0, \dfrac{\pi}{4}, \dfrac{\pi}{2}, \dfrac{3\pi}{4}, \pi, \dfrac{5\pi}{4}, \dfrac{3\pi}{2}, \dfrac{7\pi}{4} \qquad\qquad x = 0, \dfrac{\pi}{2}, \pi, \dfrac{3\pi}{2}$

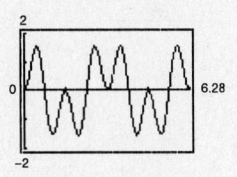

90. $f(x) = \sin^2 3x - \sin^2 x$

$$\sin^2 3x - \sin^2 x = 0$$

$$(\sin 3x + \sin x)(\sin 3x - \sin x) = 0$$

$$(2 \sin 2x \cos x)(2 \cos 2x \sin x) = 0$$

$$\sin 2x = 0 \implies x = 0, \frac{\pi}{2}, \pi, \frac{3\pi}{2} \quad \text{or}$$

$$\cos x = 0 \implies x = \frac{\pi}{2}, \frac{3\pi}{2} \quad \text{or}$$

$$\cos 2x = 0 \implies x = \frac{\pi}{4}, \frac{3\pi}{4}, \frac{5\pi}{4}, \frac{7\pi}{4} \quad \text{or}$$

$$\sin x = 0 \implies x = 0, \pi$$

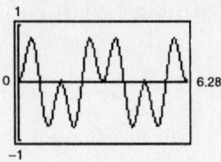

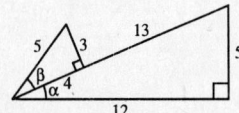

Figure for Exercises 92 and 94

92. $\cos^2 \alpha = (\cos \alpha)^2 = \left(\frac{12}{13}\right)^2 = \frac{144}{169}$

$\cos^2 \alpha = 1 - \sin^2 \alpha$

$= 1 - \left(\frac{5}{13}\right)^2$

$= 1 - \frac{25}{169} = \frac{144}{169}$

94. $\cos \alpha \sin \beta = \left(\frac{12}{13}\right)\left(\frac{3}{5}\right) = \frac{36}{65}$

$\cos \alpha \sin \beta = \sin\left(\frac{\pi}{2} - \alpha\right)\cos\left(\frac{\pi}{2} - \beta\right)$

$= \left(\frac{12}{13}\right)\left(\frac{3}{5}\right) = \frac{36}{65}$

96. $\sec 2\theta = \dfrac{1}{\cos 2\theta} = \dfrac{1}{\cos^2 \theta - \sin^2 \theta}$

$= \dfrac{\dfrac{1}{\cos^2 \theta}}{1 - \dfrac{\sin^2 \theta}{\cos^2 \theta}}$

$= \dfrac{\sec^2 \theta}{1 - \tan^2 \theta}$

$= \dfrac{\sec^2 \theta}{1 - (\sec^2 \theta - 1)}$

$= \dfrac{\sec^2 \theta}{2 - \sec^2 \theta}$

98. $\cos^4 x - \sin^4 x = (\cos^2 x - \sin^2 x)(\cos^2 x + \sin^2 x)$

$= (\cos 2x)(1)$

$= \cos 2x$

100. $\sin\left(\frac{\alpha}{3}\right)\cos\left(\frac{\alpha}{3}\right) = \frac{1}{2}\left[2\left(\sin\left(\frac{\alpha}{3}\right)\cos\left(\frac{\alpha}{3}\right)\right)\right]$

$= \frac{1}{2}\sin\frac{2\alpha}{3}$

102. $\dfrac{\cos 3\beta}{\cos \beta} = \dfrac{\cos^3 \beta - 3 \sin^2 \beta \cos \beta}{\cos \beta}$

$= \cos^2 \beta - 3\sin^2 \beta$

$= 1 - \sin^2 \beta - 3 \sin^2 \beta$

$= 1 - 4 \sin^2 \beta$

104. $\tan\dfrac{u}{2} = \dfrac{1 - \cos u}{\sin u}$

$\qquad = \dfrac{1}{\sin u} - \dfrac{\cos u}{\sin u}$

$\qquad = \csc u - \cot u$

106. $\dfrac{\sin x \pm \sin y}{\cos x + \cos y} = \dfrac{2 \sin\left(\dfrac{x \pm y}{2}\right) \cos\left(\dfrac{x \mp y}{2}\right)}{2 \cos\left(\dfrac{x + y}{2}\right) \cos\left(\dfrac{x - y}{2}\right)}$

$\qquad\qquad\qquad = \tan\left(\dfrac{x \pm y}{2}\right)$

108. $\dfrac{\cos t + \cos 3t}{\sin 3t - \sin t} = \dfrac{2 \cos\left(\dfrac{4t}{2}\right) \cos\left(-\dfrac{2t}{2}\right)}{2 \cos\left(\dfrac{4t}{2}\right) \sin\left(\dfrac{2t}{2}\right)}$

$\qquad\qquad\qquad = \dfrac{\cos(-t)}{\sin(t)}$

$\qquad\qquad\qquad = \dfrac{\cos(t)}{\sin(t)}$

$\qquad\qquad\qquad = \cot t$

110. $\cos\left(\dfrac{\pi}{3} + x\right) + \cos\left(\dfrac{\pi}{3} - x\right) = 2 \cos\left(\dfrac{\dfrac{\pi}{3} + x + \dfrac{\pi}{3} - x}{2}\right) \cos\left(\dfrac{\dfrac{\pi}{3} + x - \left(\dfrac{\pi}{3} - x\right)}{2}\right)$

$\qquad\qquad\qquad\qquad\qquad = 2 \cos\left(\dfrac{\pi}{3}\right) \cos(x)$

$\qquad\qquad\qquad\qquad\qquad = 2\left(\dfrac{1}{2}\right) \cos x = \cos x$

112. $\sin 4\beta = 2 \sin x\, 2\beta \cos 2\beta$

$\qquad = 2(2 \sin \beta \cos \beta)(1 - 2 \sin^2 \beta)$

$\qquad = 4 \sin \beta \cos \beta (1 - 2 \sin^2 \beta)$

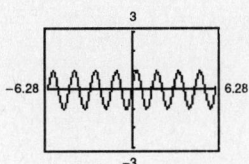

114. $\dfrac{\cos 3x - \cos x}{\sin 3x - \sin x} = \dfrac{-2 \sin\left(\dfrac{3x + x}{2}\right) \sin\left(\dfrac{3x - x}{2}\right)}{2 \cos\left(\dfrac{3x + x}{2}\right) \sin\left(\dfrac{3x - x}{2}\right)}$

$\qquad\qquad\qquad = \dfrac{-2 \sin 2x \sin x}{2 \cos 2x \sin x}$

$\qquad\qquad\qquad = -\tan 2x$

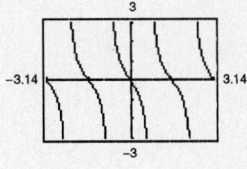

116. $f(x) = \cos^2 x = \dfrac{1 + \cos 2x}{2} = \dfrac{1}{2} + \dfrac{\cos 2x}{2}$

Shifted upward by $\dfrac{1}{2}$ unit.

Amplitude: $|a| = \dfrac{1}{2}$

Period: $\dfrac{2\pi}{2} = \pi$

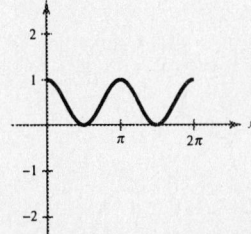

118. $\cos(2 \arccos x) = \cos^2(\arccos x) - \sin^2(\arccos x)$

$\qquad\qquad\qquad = x^2 - (1 - x^2) = 2x^2 - 1$

120. $r = \frac{1}{32} v_0^2 \sin 2\theta$

$\qquad = \frac{1}{32} v_0^2 (\sin \theta \cos \theta)$

$\qquad = \frac{1}{16} v_0^2 \sin \theta \cos \theta$

122. $\dfrac{x}{2} = 2r \sin^2 \dfrac{\theta}{2} = 2r \left(\dfrac{1 - \cos \theta}{2} \right)$

$\qquad = r(1 - \cos \theta)$

124. False.

$\sin \dfrac{u}{2} = \sqrt{\dfrac{1 - \cos u}{2}}$

when u is in the second quadrant.

126. $f(x) = \cos 2x - 2 \sin x$

(a)

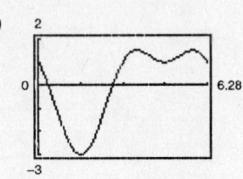

Maximum points: $(3.6652, 1.5), (5.7596, 1.5)$

Minimum points: $(1.5708, -3), (4.7124, 1)$

(b) $-2 \cos x (2 \sin x + 1) = 0$

$\quad -2 \cos x = 0 \qquad$ or $\qquad 2 \sin x + 1 = 0$

$\qquad \cos x = 0 \qquad\qquad\qquad \sin x = -\dfrac{1}{2}$

$\qquad\qquad x = \dfrac{\pi}{2}, \dfrac{3\pi}{2} \qquad\qquad\qquad x = \dfrac{7\pi}{6}, \dfrac{11\pi}{6}$

$\quad \dfrac{\pi}{2} \approx 1.5708 \qquad\qquad \dfrac{7\pi}{6} \approx 3.6652$

$\quad \dfrac{3\pi}{2} \approx 4.7124 \qquad\qquad \dfrac{11\pi}{2} \approx 5.7596$

128. (a)

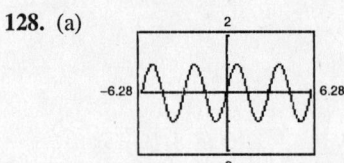

(b) The graph appears to be that of $\sin 2x$.

(c) $2 \sin x \left[2 \cos^2 \left(\dfrac{x}{2} \right) - 1 \right] = 2 \sin x \cos x$

$\qquad\qquad\qquad\qquad\qquad = \sin 2x$

130. $d_1 = 48t \qquad d_2 = 56t$

$\quad d_2 - d_1 = 8t = 12 \Longrightarrow t = \dfrac{12}{8} = 1.5$ hours

132. $d = 90\sqrt{2}$ feet ≈ 127.3 feet

Review Exercises for Chapter 5

Solutions to Even-Numbered Exercises

2. $\dfrac{1}{\sin x} = \csc x$

4. $\dfrac{1}{\tan x} = \cot x$

6. $\sqrt{1 + \tan^2 x} = \sqrt{\sec^2 x} = |\sec x|$

8. $\tan \theta = \dfrac{2}{3}$, $\sec \theta = \dfrac{\sqrt{13}}{3}$

θ is in Quadrant I.

$\cos \theta = \dfrac{1}{\sec \theta} = \dfrac{3}{\sqrt{13}} = \dfrac{3\sqrt{13}}{13}$

$\sin \theta = \sqrt{1 = \cos^2 \theta} = \sqrt{1 - \dfrac{9}{13}} = \sqrt{\dfrac{4}{13}} = \dfrac{2\sqrt{13}}{13}$

$\csc \theta = \dfrac{1}{\sin \theta} = \dfrac{\sqrt{13}}{2}$

$\cot \theta = \dfrac{1}{\tan \theta} = \dfrac{3}{2}$

10. $\csc\left(\dfrac{\pi}{2} - \theta\right) = \sec \theta = 9$, $\sin \theta = \dfrac{4\sqrt{5}}{9}$

θ is in Quadrant I.

$\cos \theta = \dfrac{1}{\sec \theta} = \dfrac{1}{9}$

$\tan \theta = \dfrac{\sin \theta}{\cos \theta} = \dfrac{\frac{4\sqrt{5}}{9}}{\frac{1}{9}} = 4\sqrt{5}$

$\csc \theta = \dfrac{1}{\sin \theta} = \dfrac{9}{4\sqrt{5}} = \dfrac{9\sqrt{5}}{20}$

$\cot \theta = \dfrac{1}{\tan \theta} = \dfrac{1}{4\sqrt{5}} = \dfrac{\sqrt{5}}{20}$

12. $\dfrac{\tan \theta}{1 - \cos^2 \theta} = \dfrac{\frac{\sin \theta}{\cos \theta}}{\sin^2 \theta} = \dfrac{1}{\sin \theta \cos \theta}$

$\qquad = \csc \theta \sec \theta$

14. $\cot^2 x(\sin^2 x) = \dfrac{\cos^2 x}{\sin^2 x} \sin^2 x = \cos^2 x$

16. $\dfrac{\cot\left(\frac{\pi}{2} - u\right)}{\cos u} = \dfrac{\tan u}{\cos u} = \tan u \sec u$

18. $\tan^2 \theta \csc^2 \theta - \tan^2 \theta = \tan^2 \theta(\csc^2 \theta - 1)$

$\qquad\qquad\qquad\qquad = \tan^2 \theta \cot^2 \theta = 1$

20. $(\sec x - \tan x)^2 = \sec^2 x - 2 \sec x \tan x + \tan^2 x$

$\qquad\qquad = 1 + \tan^2 x - 2 \sec x \tan x + \tan^2 x$

$\qquad\qquad = 1 - 2 \sec x \tan x + 2 \tan^2 x$

22. $\dfrac{\cos^2 x}{1 - \sin x} = \dfrac{\cos^2 x}{(1 - \sin x)} \cdot \dfrac{(1 + \sin x)}{(1 + \sin x)}$

$\qquad = \dfrac{\cos^2 x(1 + \sin x)}{1 - \sin^2 x}$

$\qquad = 1 + \sin x$

24. $\cos x(\tan^2 x + 1) = \cos x \sec^2 x$

$\qquad = \dfrac{1}{\sec x} \sec^2 x$

$\qquad = \sec x$

26. $\cos\left(x + \dfrac{\pi}{2}\right) = \cos x \cos \dfrac{\pi}{2} - \sin x \sin \dfrac{\pi}{2}$

$\qquad = (\cos x)(0) - (\sin x)(1)$

$\qquad = -\sin x$

28. $\dfrac{1}{\tan\theta\csc\theta} = \dfrac{1}{\dfrac{\sin\theta}{\cos\theta}\cdot\dfrac{1}{\sin\theta}} = \cos\theta$

30. $\sin^5 x\cos^2 x = \sin^4 x\cos^2 x\sin x$

$\qquad\qquad = (1 - \cos^2 x)^2\cos^2 x\sin x$

$\qquad\qquad = (1 - 2\cos^2 x + \cos^4 x)\cos^2 x\sin x$

$\qquad\qquad = (\cos^2 x - 2\cos^4 x + \cos^6 x)\sin x$

32. $\sin x = \sqrt{3} - \sin x$

$\qquad \sin x = \dfrac{\sqrt{3}}{2}$

$\qquad x = \dfrac{\pi}{3} + 2\pi n, \dfrac{2\pi}{3} + 2\pi n$

34. $3\sqrt{3}\tan u = 3$

$\qquad \tan u = \dfrac{1}{\sqrt{3}}$

$\qquad u = \dfrac{\pi}{6} + n\pi$

36. $3\csc^2 x = 4$

$\qquad \csc^2 x = \dfrac{4}{3}$

$\qquad \sin x = \pm\dfrac{\sqrt{3}}{2}$

$\qquad x = \dfrac{\pi}{3} + 2\pi n, \dfrac{2\pi}{3} + 2\pi n, \dfrac{4\pi}{3} + 2\pi n, \dfrac{5\pi}{3} + 2\pi n$

38. $2\cos^2 x - \cos x = 1$

$\qquad 2\cos^2 x - \cos x - 1 = 0$

$\qquad (2\cos x + 1)(\cos x - 1) = 0$

$2\cos x + 1 = 0 \qquad\qquad \cos x - 1 = 0$

$\qquad \cos x = -\dfrac{1}{2} \qquad\qquad \cos x = 1$

$\qquad x = \dfrac{2\pi}{3}, \dfrac{4\pi}{3} \qquad\qquad x = 0$

40. $\cos^2 x + \sin x = 1$

$1 - \sin^2 x + \sin x - 1 = 0$

$\qquad -\sin x(\sin x - 1) = 0$

$\sin x = 0 \qquad \sin x - 1 = 0$

$\quad x = 0, \pi \qquad\quad \sin x = 1$

$\qquad\qquad\qquad\quad x = \dfrac{\pi}{2}$

42. $2\sin 2x - \sqrt{2} = 0$

$\qquad \sin 2x = \dfrac{\sqrt{2}}{2}$

$2x = \dfrac{\pi}{4} + 2\pi n, \dfrac{3\pi}{4} + 2\pi n$

$\quad x = \dfrac{\pi}{8} + \pi n, \dfrac{3\pi}{8} + \pi n$

$\quad x = \dfrac{\pi}{8}, \dfrac{3\pi}{8}, \dfrac{9\pi}{8}, \dfrac{11\pi}{8}$

44. $\cos 4x(\cos x - 1) = 0$

$\cos 4x = 0 \qquad\qquad\qquad \cos x - 1 = 0$

$\quad 4x = \dfrac{\pi}{2} + 2\pi n, \dfrac{3\pi}{2} + 2\pi n \qquad \cos x = 1$

$\quad\; x = \dfrac{\pi}{8} + \dfrac{\pi}{2}n, \dfrac{3\pi}{8} + \dfrac{\pi}{2}n \qquad\qquad x = 0$

$x = 0, \dfrac{\pi}{8}, \dfrac{3\pi}{8}, \dfrac{5\pi}{8}, \dfrac{7\pi}{8}, \dfrac{9\pi}{8}, \dfrac{11\pi}{8}, \dfrac{13\pi}{8}, \dfrac{15\pi}{8}$

46. $\sin^2 x - 2\sin x = 0$

$\sin x(\sin x - 2) = 0$

$\sin x = 0 \qquad \sin x - 2 = 0$

$\; x = 0, \pi \qquad\quad$ No solution

48. $\tan^2 \theta + \tan \theta - 12 = 0$

$(\tan \theta + 4)(\tan \theta - 3) = 0$

$\tan \theta + 4 = 0$ $\tan \theta - 3 = 0$

$\theta = \arctan(-4) + n\pi$ $\theta = \arctan 3 + n\pi$

$\theta = \arctan(-4) + \pi, \arctan(-4) + 2\pi, \arctan 3, \arctan 3 + \pi$

50. $\sin 285° = \sin(315° - 30°)$

$= \sin 315° \cos 30° - \cos 315° \sin 30°$

$= \left(-\dfrac{\sqrt{2}}{2}\right)\left(\dfrac{\sqrt{3}}{2}\right) - \left(\dfrac{\sqrt{2}}{2}\right)\left(\dfrac{1}{2}\right)$

$= -\dfrac{\sqrt{2}}{4}(\sqrt{3} + 1)$

$\cos 285° = \cos(315° - 30°)$

$= \cos 315° \cos 30° + \sin 315° \sin 30°$

$= \left(-\dfrac{\sqrt{2}}{2}\right)\left(\dfrac{\sqrt{3}}{2}\right) + \left(-\dfrac{\sqrt{2}}{2}\right)\left(\dfrac{1}{2}\right)$

$= -\dfrac{\sqrt{2}}{4}(\sqrt{3} - 1)$

$\tan 285° = \tan(315° - 30°) = \dfrac{\tan 315° - \tan 30°}{1 + \tan 315° \tan 30°}$

$= \dfrac{(-1) - \left(\dfrac{\sqrt{3}}{3}\right)}{1 + (-1)\left(\dfrac{\sqrt{3}}{3}\right)} = -2 - \sqrt{3}$

52. $\sin \dfrac{25\pi}{12} = \sin\left(\dfrac{11\pi}{6} + \dfrac{\pi}{4}\right) = \sin \dfrac{11\pi}{6} \cos \dfrac{\pi}{4} + \cos \dfrac{11\pi}{6} \sin \dfrac{\pi}{4}$

$= \left(-\dfrac{1}{2}\right)\left(\dfrac{\sqrt{2}}{2}\right) + \left(\dfrac{\sqrt{3}}{2}\right)\left(\dfrac{\sqrt{2}}{2}\right) = \dfrac{\sqrt{2}}{4}(\sqrt{3} - 1)$

$\cos \dfrac{25\pi}{12} = \cos\left(\dfrac{11\pi}{6} + \dfrac{\pi}{4}\right) = \cos \dfrac{11\pi}{6} \cos \dfrac{\pi}{4} - \sin \dfrac{11\pi}{6} \sin \dfrac{\pi}{4}$

$= \left(\dfrac{\sqrt{3}}{2}\right)\left(\dfrac{\sqrt{2}}{2}\right) - \left(-\dfrac{1}{2}\right)\left(\dfrac{\sqrt{2}}{2}\right) = \dfrac{\sqrt{2}}{4}(\sqrt{3} + 1)$

$\tan \dfrac{25\pi}{12} = \tan\left(\dfrac{11\pi}{6} + \dfrac{\pi}{4}\right) = \dfrac{\tan \dfrac{11\pi}{6} + \tan \dfrac{\pi}{4}}{1 - \tan \dfrac{11\pi}{6} \tan \dfrac{\pi}{4}}$

$= \dfrac{\left(-\dfrac{\sqrt{3}}{3}\right) + 1}{1 - \left(-\dfrac{\sqrt{3}}{3}\right)(1)} = 2 - \sqrt{3}$

54. $\sin 60° \cos 45° - \cos 60° \sin 45° = \sin(60° - 45°) = \sin 15°$

56. $\dfrac{\tan 25° + \tan 10°}{1 - \tan 25° \tan 10°} = \tan(25° + 10°)$

$\qquad\qquad\qquad\quad = \tan 35°$

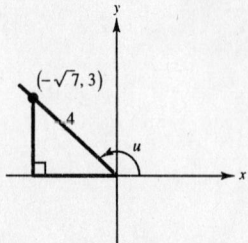 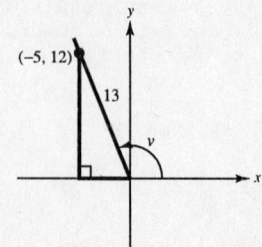

Figures for Exercises 58–62

58. $\sin(u + v) = \sin u \cos v + \cos u \sin v$

$\qquad\qquad = \left(\dfrac{3}{4}\right)\left(-\dfrac{5}{13}\right) + \left(-\dfrac{\sqrt{7}}{4}\right)\left(\dfrac{12}{13}\right)$

$\qquad\qquad = -\dfrac{3}{52}\left(5 + 4\sqrt{7}\right)$

60. $\cos(u - v) = \cos u \cos v + \sin u \sin v$

$\qquad\qquad = \left(-\dfrac{\sqrt{7}}{4}\right)\left(-\dfrac{5}{13}\right) + \left(\dfrac{3}{4}\right)\left(\dfrac{12}{13}\right)$

$\qquad\qquad = \dfrac{1}{52}\left(5\sqrt{7} + 36\right)$

62. $\cos(u + v) = \cos u \cos v - \sin u \sin v$

$\qquad\qquad = \left(-\dfrac{\sqrt{7}}{4}\right)\left(-\dfrac{5}{13}\right) - \left(\dfrac{3}{4}\right)\left(\dfrac{12}{13}\right)$

$\qquad\qquad = \dfrac{1}{52}\left(5\sqrt{7} - 36\right)$

64. $\sin\left(x + \dfrac{\pi}{4}\right) - \sin\left(x - \dfrac{\pi}{4}\right) = 1$

$\qquad\qquad 2 \cos x \sin \dfrac{\pi}{4} = 1$

$\qquad\qquad\qquad\quad \cos x = \dfrac{\sqrt{2}}{2}$

$\qquad\qquad\qquad\qquad x = \dfrac{\pi}{4}, \dfrac{7\pi}{4}$

66. $\sin\left(x + \dfrac{\pi}{2}\right) - \sin\left(x - \dfrac{\pi}{2}\right) = \sqrt{3}$

$\qquad\qquad 2 \cos x \sin \dfrac{\pi}{2} = \sqrt{3}$

$\qquad\qquad\qquad \cos x = \dfrac{\sqrt{3}}{2}$

$\quad x = \dfrac{\pi}{6}, \dfrac{11\pi}{6}$

68. $\sin 4x = 2 \sin 2x \cos 2x$

$\qquad\quad = 2[2 \sin x \cos x(\cos^2 x - \sin^2 x)]$

$\qquad\quad = 4 \sin x \cos x(2 \cos^2 x - 1)$

$\qquad\quad = 8 \cos^3 x \sin x - 4 \cos x \sin x$

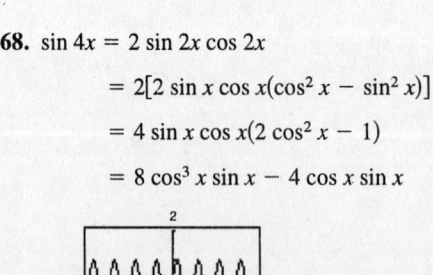

70. $\sin u = -\dfrac{4}{5}, \ \pi < u < \dfrac{3\pi}{2}$

$\cos u = \sqrt{1 - \sin^2 u} = \dfrac{3}{5}$

$\tan u = \dfrac{\sin u}{\cos u} = -\dfrac{4}{3}$

$\sin 2u = 2 \sin u \cos u = 2\left(-\dfrac{4}{5}\right)\left(\dfrac{3}{5}\right) = -\dfrac{24}{25}$

$\cos 2u = \cos^2 u - \sin^2 u = \left(\dfrac{3}{5}\right)^2 - \left(-\dfrac{4}{5}\right)^2 = -\dfrac{7}{25}$

$\tan 2u = \dfrac{2 \tan u}{1 - \tan^2 u} = \dfrac{2\left(-\dfrac{4}{3}\right)}{1 + \left(-\dfrac{4}{3}\right)^2} = \dfrac{24}{7}$

72. $r = \dfrac{1}{32} v_0{}^2 \sin 2\theta$

range $= 100$ feet

$v_0 = 80$ feet per second

$r = \dfrac{1}{32}(80)^2 \sin 2\theta = 100$

$\sin 2\theta = 0.5$

$2\theta = 30°, 150°$

$\theta = 15°$ or $75°$

74. $\cos^2 3x = \dfrac{1 + \cos 6x}{2}$

76. $\cos^2 x + \tan^2 x = \sin^2 x = \dfrac{1 - \cos 2x}{2}$

78. $\sin 15° = \sin\left(\dfrac{30°}{2}\right) = \sqrt{\dfrac{1 - \cos 30°}{2}} = \sqrt{\dfrac{1 - \dfrac{\sqrt{3}}{2}}{2}}$

$\qquad = \dfrac{1}{2}\sqrt{2 - \sqrt{3}}$

$\cos 15° = \cos\left(\dfrac{30°}{2}\right) = \sqrt{\dfrac{1 + \cos 30°}{2}} = \sqrt{\dfrac{1 + \dfrac{\sqrt{3}}{2}}{2}}$

$\qquad = \dfrac{1}{2}\sqrt{2\sqrt{3}}$

$\tan 15° = \tan\left(\dfrac{30°}{2}\right) = \dfrac{1 - \cos 30°}{\sin 30°} = \dfrac{1 - \dfrac{\sqrt{3}}{2}}{\dfrac{1}{2}}$

$2 = \sqrt{3}$

80. $\sin\left(-\dfrac{17\pi}{12}\right) = \sin\left(-\dfrac{\dfrac{17\pi}{6}}{2}\right) = \sqrt{\dfrac{1 + \cos\left(-\dfrac{17\pi}{6}\right)}{2}} = \sqrt{\dfrac{1 + \left(-\dfrac{\sqrt{3}}{2}\right)}{2}}$

$\qquad = \dfrac{1}{2}\sqrt{2\sqrt{3}}$

$\cos\left(-\dfrac{17\pi}{12}\right) = \cos\left(-\dfrac{\dfrac{17\pi}{6}}{2}\right) = -\sqrt{\dfrac{1 + \cos\left(-\dfrac{17\pi}{6}\right)}{2}} = -\sqrt{\dfrac{1 + \left(-\dfrac{\sqrt{3}}{2}\right)}{2}}$

$\qquad = -\dfrac{1}{2}\sqrt{2 - \sqrt{3}}$

$\tan\left(-\dfrac{17\pi}{12}\right) = \tan\left(\dfrac{-\left(\dfrac{17\pi}{6}\right)}{2}\right) = \dfrac{1 - \cos\left(-\dfrac{17\pi}{6}\right)}{\sin\left(-\dfrac{17\pi}{6}\right)} = \dfrac{1 - \left(-\dfrac{\sqrt{3}}{2}\right)}{-\dfrac{1}{2}} = -2 - \sqrt{3}$

82. $\dfrac{\sin 6x}{1 + \cos 6x} = \tan 3x$

84. $\cos \dfrac{\pi}{6} \sin \dfrac{\pi}{6} = \dfrac{1}{2}\left[\sin \dfrac{\pi}{3} - \sin 0\right]$

86. $\cos 5\theta \cos 3\theta = \frac{1}{2}[\cos 2\theta + \cos 8\theta]$

88. $\sin 60° + \sin 90° = 2 \sin 75° \cos 15°$

90. $\cos\left(x + \dfrac{\pi}{6}\right) - \cos\left(x - \dfrac{\pi}{6}\right) = -2 \sin(x) \sin\left(\dfrac{\pi}{6}\right)$

92. (a) $y = 1.5 \sin 8t - 0.5 \cos 8t = \dfrac{1}{2}(3 \sin 8t - 1 \cos 8t)$

Using the identity

$a \sin B\theta + b \cos B\theta = \sqrt{a^2 + b^2} \sin(B\theta + C)$,

$C = \arctan \dfrac{b}{a}, a > 0$

(Exercise 83, Section 7.4), we have

$y = \dfrac{1}{2}\sqrt{(3)^2 + (-1)^2} \sin\left(8t + \arctan\left(-\dfrac{1}{3}\right)\right)$

$= \dfrac{\sqrt{10}}{2} \sin\left(8t - \arctan\left(\dfrac{1}{3}\right)\right)$

(b) Amplitude $= \dfrac{\sqrt{10}}{2}$ feet

(c) Frequency $= \dfrac{1}{\dfrac{2\pi}{8}} = \dfrac{4}{\pi}$ cycles per second

94. False. The correct identity is

$\sin(x + y) = \sin x \cos y + \cos x \sin y$.

96. True. It can be verified using a product-to-sum identity.

$4 \sin 45° \cos 15° = 4 \cdot \dfrac{1}{2}[\sin 60° + \sin 30°]$

$= 2\left[\dfrac{\sqrt{3}}{2} + \dfrac{1}{2}\right] = \sqrt{3} + 1$

98. $\sin(-x) = -\sin x, \cos(-x) = \cos x, \tan(-x) = -\tan x$.

Thus, the odd functions are $\sin x, \tan x, \csc x, \cot x$.

100. $a \sin x - b = 0$

$\sin x = \dfrac{b}{a}$

If $|b| > |a|$, then $\left|\dfrac{b}{a}\right| > 1$ and there is no solution

since $|\sin x| \le 1$ for all x.

102. $y_1 = \dfrac{\cos 3x}{\cos x} \qquad y_2 = (2 \sin x)^2$

If the graph of y_2 is reflected in the x-axis and then shifted upward by one unit, it coincides with the graph of y_1. Therefore,

$\dfrac{\cos 3x}{\cos x} = -(2 \sin x)^2 + 1$.

104. $y = 2 = \dfrac{1}{2}x^2 + 3 \sin \dfrac{\pi x}{2}$

Approximate roots:
$-3.1395, -2.0000, -0.4378, 2.0000$

$y = 2 = \dfrac{1}{2}x^2 + 3 \sin \dfrac{\pi x}{2}$

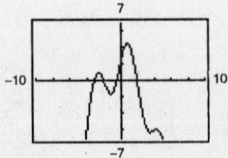

C H A P T E R 6
Additional Topics in Trigonometry

C H A P T E R 6
Additional Topics in Trigonometry

Section 6.1   Law of Sines

Solutions to Even-Numbered Exercises

2.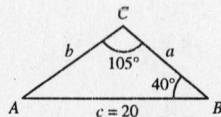

Given: $B = 40°, C = 105°, c = 20$

$A = 180° - B - C = 35°$

$a = \dfrac{c}{\sin C}(\sin A) = \dfrac{20 \sin 35°}{\sin 105°} \approx 11.88$

$b = \dfrac{c}{\sin C}(\sin B) = \dfrac{20 \sin 40°}{\sin 105°} \approx 13.31$

4.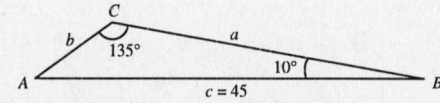

Given: $B = 10°, C = 135°, c = 45$

$A = 180° - B - C = 35°$

$a = \dfrac{c}{\sin C}(\sin A) = \dfrac{45 \sin 35°}{\sin 135°} \approx 36.50$

$b = \dfrac{c}{\sin C}(\sin B) = \dfrac{45 \sin 10°}{\sin 135°} \approx 11.05$

6. Given: $A = 60°, a = 9, c = 10$

$\sin C = \dfrac{c \sin A}{a} = \dfrac{10 \sin 60°}{9} \approx 0.9623 \implies C \approx 74.21°$ or $C \approx 105.79°$

Case 1

$C \approx 74.21°$

$B = 180° - A - C \approx 45.79°$

$b = \dfrac{a}{\sin A}(\sin B) \approx \dfrac{9 \sin 45.79°}{\sin 60°} \approx 7.45$

Case 2

$C \approx 105.79°$

$B = 180° - A - C \approx 14.21°$

$b = \dfrac{a}{\sin A}(\sin B) \approx \dfrac{9 \sin 14.21°}{\sin 60°} \approx 2.55$

8. Given: $A = 24.3°, C = 54.6°, c = 2.68$

$B = 180° - A - C = 101.1°$

$a = \dfrac{c}{\sin C}(\sin A) = \dfrac{2.68 \sin 24.3°}{\sin 54.6°} \approx 1.35$

$b = \dfrac{c}{\sin C}(\sin B) = \dfrac{2.68 \sin 101.1°}{\sin 54.6°} \approx 3.23$

10. Given: $A = 5° \, 40', B = 8° \, 15', b = 4.8$

$C = 180° - A - B = 166° \, 5'$

$a = \dfrac{b}{\sin B}(\sin A) = \dfrac{4.8 \sin 5° \, 40'}{\sin 8° \, 15'} \approx 3.30$

$c = \dfrac{b}{\sin B}(\sin C) = \dfrac{4.8 \sin 166° \, 5'}{\sin 8° \, 15'} \approx 8.05$

12. Given: $B = 2° \, 45', b = 6.2, c = 5.8$

$\sin C = \dfrac{c \sin B}{b} = \dfrac{5.8 \sin 2° \, 45'}{6.2} \approx 0.04488 \implies C \approx 2.57°$

$A = 180° - B - C \approx 174.68°$

$a = \dfrac{b}{\sin B}(\sin A) \approx \dfrac{6.2 \sin 174.68°}{\sin 2° \, 45'} \approx 11.99$

14. Given: $A = 100°, a = 125, c = 10$

$$\sin C = \frac{c \sin A}{a} = \frac{10 \sin 100°}{125} \approx 0.07878 \implies C \approx 4.52°$$

$$B = 180° - A - C \approx 75.48°$$

$$b = \frac{a}{\sin A}(\sin B) \approx \frac{125 \sin 75.48°}{\sin 100°} \approx 122.87$$

16. Given: $C = 85° \, 20', a = 35, c = 50$

$$\sin A = \frac{a \sin C}{c} = \frac{35 \sin 85° \, 20'}{50} \approx 0.6977 \implies A \approx 44.24°$$

$$B = 180° - A - C \approx 50.43°$$

$$b = \frac{C \sin B}{\sin C} \approx \frac{50 \sin 50.43°}{\sin 85° \, 20'} \approx 38.67$$

18. Given: $B = 28°, C = 104°, a = 3\frac{5}{8}$

$$A = 180° - B - C = 48°$$

$$b = \frac{a \sin B}{\sin A} = \frac{3\frac{5}{8} \sin 28°}{\sin 48°} \approx 2.29$$

$$c = \frac{a \sin C}{\sin A} = \frac{3\frac{5}{8} \sin 104°}{\sin 48°} \approx 4.73$$

20. Given: $A = 58°, a = 11.4, c = 12.8$

$$\sin B = \frac{b \sin A}{a} = \frac{12.8 \sin 58°}{11.4} \approx 0.9522 \implies B \approx 72.2° \text{ or } B \approx 107.8°$$

Case 1

$B \approx 72.2°$

$C = 180° - A - B \approx 49.8°$

$c = \dfrac{a}{\sin A}(\sin C) \approx \dfrac{11.4 \sin 49.8°}{\sin 58°} \approx 10.27$

Case 2

$B \approx 107.8°$

$C = 180° - A - B \approx 14.2°$

$c = \dfrac{a}{\sin A}(\sin C) \approx \dfrac{11.4 \sin 14.2°}{\sin 58°} \approx 3.30$

22. Given: $A = 76°, a = 34, b = 21$

$\sin B = \dfrac{b \sin A}{a} = \dfrac{21 \sin 76°}{34} \approx 0.5993 \implies B \approx 36.82°$

$C = 180° - A - B \approx 67.18°$

$c = \dfrac{a \sin C}{\sin A} \approx \dfrac{34 \sin 67.18°}{\sin 76°} \approx 32.30$

24. Given: $A = 110°, a = 125, b = 100$

$\sin B = \dfrac{b \sin A}{a} = \dfrac{100 \sin 110°}{125} \approx 0.75175 \implies B \approx 48.74°$

$C = 180° - A - B \approx 21.26°$

$c = \dfrac{a \sin C}{\sin A} \approx \dfrac{125 \sin 21.26°}{\sin 110°} \approx 48.23$

26. Given: $A = 22°, a = \dfrac{5}{7}, b = \dfrac{5}{7}$

$\sin B = \dfrac{b \sin A}{a} = \dfrac{\frac{5}{7} \sin 22°}{\frac{5}{7}} = \sin 22° \implies B = 22°$

$C = 180° - A - B = 136°$

$c = \dfrac{a \sin C}{\sin A} = \dfrac{\frac{5}{7} \sin 136°}{\sin 22°} \approx 1.32$

28. Given: $A = 60°, a = 10$

(a) One solution if $b \leq 10$ or $b = \dfrac{10}{\sin 60°}$.

(b) Two solutions if $10 < b < \dfrac{10}{\sin 60°}$.

(c) No solutions if $b > \dfrac{10}{\sin 60°}$.

30. Given: $A = 88°$, $a = 315.6$

   (a) One solution if $b \leq 315.6$ or $b = \dfrac{315.6}{\sin 88°}$

   (b) Two solutions if $315.6 < b < \dfrac{315.6}{\sin 88°}$

   (c) No solutions if $b > \dfrac{315.6}{\sin 88°}$

32. Area $= \dfrac{1}{2}ac \sin B = \dfrac{1}{2}(62)(20) \sin 130° \approx 474.9$

34. $A = 5° \, 15'$, $b = 4.5$, $c = 22$

   Area $= \frac{1}{2}bc \sin A$

   $= \left(\frac{1}{2}\right)(4.5)(22) \sin 5.25° \approx 4.529$

36. $C = 84° \, 30'$, $a = 16$, $b = 20$

   Area $= \frac{1}{2}ab \sin C$

   $= \left(\frac{1}{2}\right)(16)(20) \sin 84.5° \approx 159.3$

38. (a)
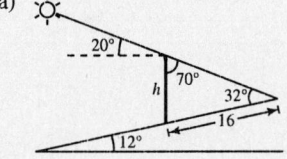

   (b) $\dfrac{h}{\sin 32°} = \dfrac{16}{\sin 70°}$

   (c) $h = \dfrac{16 \sin 32°}{\sin 70°} \approx 9.0$ meters

40.
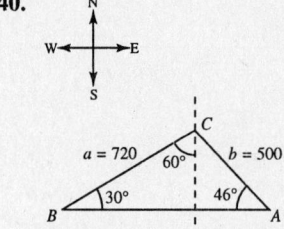

   Given: $A = 46°$, $a = 720$, $b = 500$

   $\sin B = \dfrac{b \sin A}{a} = \dfrac{500 \sin 46°}{720} \approx 0.50 \Rightarrow B \approx 30°$

   The bearing from C to B is $S \, 60° \, W$.

42.
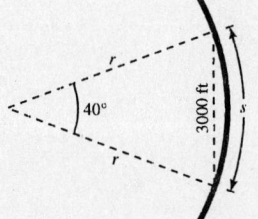

   (b) $r = \dfrac{3000 \sin\left[\frac{1}{2}(180° - 40°)\right]}{\sin 40°} \approx 4385.71$ feet

   (c) $s \approx 40°\left(\dfrac{\pi}{180°}\right)4385.71 \approx 8061.80$ feet

44.
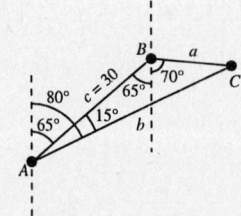

   Given: $A = 15°$, $B = 135°$, $c = 30$

   $C = 180° - A - B = 30°$

   From Pine Knob:

   $b = \dfrac{c \sin B}{\sin C} = \dfrac{30 \sin 135°}{\sin 30°} \approx 42.4$ kilometers

   From Colt Station:

   $a = \dfrac{c \sin A}{\sin C} = \dfrac{30 \sin 15°}{\sin 30°} \approx 15.5$ kilometers

46. $A = 90° - 62° = 28°$

$B = 90° + 38° = 128°$, $c = 5$

$C = 180° - 128° - 28° = 24°$

$a = \dfrac{c}{\sin C}(\sin A) = \dfrac{5}{\sin 24°}(\sin 28°) \approx 5.77$

$d = a\sin(90° - 38°) \approx 5.77 \sin 52° \approx 4.55$ miles

48. True. The longest side of a triangle is always opposite the largest angle.

50. (a) $\dfrac{\sin \alpha}{9} = \dfrac{\sin \beta}{18}$

$\sin \alpha = 0.5 \sin \beta$

$\alpha = \arcsin(0.5 \sin \beta)$

(b)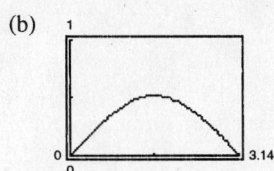

Domain: $0 < \beta < \pi$

Range: $0 < \alpha \le \dfrac{\pi}{6}$

(c) $\gamma = \pi - \alpha - \beta = \pi - \beta - \arcsin(0.5 \sin \beta)$

$\dfrac{c}{\sin \gamma} = \dfrac{18}{\sin \beta}$

$c = \dfrac{18 \sin \gamma}{\sin \beta} = \dfrac{18 \sin[\pi - \beta - \arcsin(0.5 \sin \beta)]}{\sin \beta}$

(d)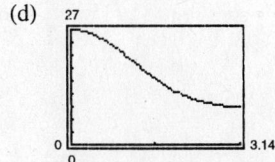

Domain: $0 < \beta < \pi$

Range: $9 < \alpha < 27$

(e)

β	0.4	0.8	1.2	1.6	2.0	2.4	2.8
α	0.1960	0.3669	0.4848	0.5234	0.4720	0.3445	0.1683
c	25.95	27.07	19.19	15.33	12.29	10.31	9.27

As $\beta \to 0$, $c \to 27$

As $\beta \to \pi$, $c \to 9$

52. $\sin x = \frac{2}{5}, \frac{\pi}{2} < x < \pi$

$$\cos x = -\sqrt{1 - \sin^2 x} = -\sqrt{1 - \left(\frac{2}{5}\right)^2} = -\frac{\sqrt{21}}{5}$$

$$\tan x = \frac{\sin x}{\cos x} = \frac{\frac{2}{5}}{-\frac{\sqrt{21}}{5}} = -\frac{2\sqrt{21}}{21}$$

$$\csc x = \frac{1}{\sin x} - \frac{1}{\frac{2}{5}} - \frac{5}{2}$$

$$\sec x = \frac{1}{\cos x} = \frac{1}{-\frac{\sqrt{21}}{5}} = -\frac{5\sqrt{21}}{21}$$

$$\cot x = \frac{1}{\tan x} = \frac{1}{-\frac{2\sqrt{21}}{21}} = -\frac{\sqrt{21}}{2}$$

54. $\sec x = -4, \pi < x < \frac{3\pi}{2}$

$$\cos x = \frac{1}{\sec x} = -\frac{1}{4}$$

$$\sin x = -\sqrt{1 - \cos^2 x} = -\sqrt{1 - \left(-\frac{1}{4}\right)^2} = -\frac{\sqrt{15}}{4}$$

$$\tan x = \frac{\sin x}{\cos x} = \frac{-\frac{\sqrt{15}}{4}}{-\frac{1}{4}} = \sqrt{15}$$

$$\csc x = \frac{1}{\sin x} = \frac{1}{-\frac{\sqrt{15}}{4}} = -\frac{4\sqrt{15}}{15}$$

$$\cot x = \frac{1}{\tan x} = \frac{1}{\sqrt{15}} = \frac{\sqrt{15}}{15}$$

56. $\sin x \cot x = \sin x \dfrac{\cos x}{\sin x} = \cos x$

58. $1 - \sin^2\left(\dfrac{\pi}{2} - x\right) = 1 - \cos^2 x = \sin^2 x$

Section 6.2   Law of Cosines

Solutions to Even-Numbered Exercises

2. Given: $a = 8, b = 3, c = 9$

$$\cos A = \frac{b^2 + c^2 - a^2}{2bc} = \frac{3^2 + 9^2 - 8^2}{2(3)(9)} \approx 0.4815 \implies A \approx 61.2°$$

$$\cos c = \frac{a^2 + b^2 - c^2}{2ab} = \frac{8^2 + 3^2 - 9^2}{2(8)(3)} \approx -0.1667 \implies C \approx 99.6°$$

$$B \approx 180° - 61.2° - 99.6° \approx 19.2°$$

4. Given: $C = 105°, a = 10, b = 4.5$

$$c^2 = a^2 + b^2 - 2ab \cos C = 10^2 + 4.5^2 - 2(10)(4.5) \cos 105° \approx 143.5437 \implies c \approx 12.0$$

$$\cos B = \frac{a^2 + c^2 - b^2}{2ac} \approx \frac{10^2 + (12.0)^2 - (4.5)^2}{2(10)(12.0)} \approx 0.93187 \implies B \approx 21.3°$$

$$A = 180° - 105° - 21.3° \approx 53.7°$$

6. Given: $a = 55, b = 25, c = 72$

$$\cos C = \frac{a^2 + b^2 - c^2}{2ab} = \frac{55^2 + 25^2 - 72^2}{2(55)(25)} \approx -0.5578 \implies C \approx 123.91°$$

$$\cos A = \frac{b^2 + c^2 - a^2}{2bc} = \frac{25^2 + 72^2 - 55^2}{2(25)(72)} \approx 0.7733 \implies A \approx 39.35°$$

$$B = 180° - 123.91° - 39.35° \approx 16.75°$$

8. Given: $a = 1.42, b = 0.75, c = 1.25$

$$\cos A = \frac{b^2 + c^2 - a^2}{2bc} = \frac{(0.75)^2 + (1.25)^2 - (1.42)^2}{2(0.75)(1.25)} = 0.05792 \implies A \approx 86.7°$$

$$\cos B = \frac{a^2 + c^2 - b^2}{2ac} = \frac{(1.42)^2 + (1.25)^2 - (0.75)^2}{2(1.42)(1.25)} \approx 0.8497 \implies B \approx 31.8°$$

$$C = 180° - 86.7° - 31.8° \approx 61.5°$$

10. Given: $A = 55°, b = 3, c = 10$

$$a^2 = b^2 + c^2 - 2bc \cos A = 3^2 + 10^2 - 2(3)(10) \cos 55° \approx 74.585 \implies a \approx 8.64$$

$$\sin B = \frac{b \sin A}{a} \approx \frac{3 \sin 55°}{8.64} \approx 0.2846 \implies A \approx 16.5°$$

$$C \approx 180° - 16.5° - 55° \approx 108.5°$$

12. Given: $B = 75° \, 20', a = 6.2, c = 9.5$

$$b^2 = a^2 + c^2 - 2ac \cos B = (6.2)^2 + (9.5)^2 - 2(6.2)(9.5) \cos 75° \, 20' \approx 98.8636 \implies b \approx 9.94$$

$$\sin A = \frac{a \sin B}{b} \approx \frac{6.2 \sin 75° \, 20'}{9.94} \approx 0.6032 \implies A \approx 37.1°$$

$$C \approx 180° - 75° \, 20' - 37.1° \approx 67.6°$$

14. Given: $C = 15° \, 15', a = 6.25, b = 2.15$

$$c^2 = a^2 + b^2 - 2ab \cos C = (6.25)^2 + (2.15)^2 - 2(6.25)(2.15) \cos 15° \, 15' \approx 17.7563 \implies c \approx 4.21$$

$$\cos A = \frac{b^2 + c^2 - a^2}{2bc} \approx \frac{(2.15)^2 + (4.21)^2 - (6.25)^2}{2(2.15)(4.21)} \approx -0.92076 \implies A \approx 157.0°$$

$$B \approx 180° - 15° \, 15' - 157.4° \approx 7.7°$$

16. Given: $C = 103°, a = \dfrac{3}{8}, b = \dfrac{3}{4}$

$$c^2 = a^2 + b^2 - 2ab \cos C = \left(\frac{3}{8}\right)^2 + \left(\frac{3}{4}\right)^2 - 2\left(\frac{3}{8}\right)\left(\frac{3}{4}\right) \cos 103° \approx 0.8297 \implies c \approx 0.41$$

$$\cos A = \frac{b^2 + c^2 - a^2}{2bc} \approx \frac{\left(\frac{3}{4}\right)^2 + (0.91)^2 - \left(\frac{3}{8}\right)^2}{2\left(\frac{3}{4}\right)(0.91)} \approx 0.9160 \implies A \approx 23.6°$$

$$B \approx 180° - 23.6° - 103° \approx 53.4°$$

18.

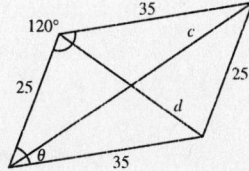

$$c^2 = 25^2 + 35^2 - 2(25)(35) \cos 120°$$

$$= 2725 \implies c \approx 52.20$$

$$\theta = \frac{1}{2}[360° - 2(120°)] = 60°$$

$$d^2 = 25^2 + 35^2 - 2(25)(35) \cos 60°$$

$$= 975 \implies d \approx 31.22$$

20.

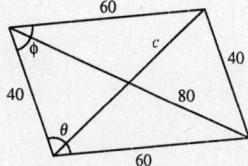

$$\cos \theta = \frac{40^2 + 60^2 - 80^2}{2(40)(60)} = -\frac{1}{4} \implies \theta \approx 104.5°$$

$$\phi \approx \frac{1}{2}[360° - 2(104.5°)] \approx 75.5°$$

$$c^2 \approx 40^2 + 60^2 - 2(40)(60) \cos 75.5° = 4000$$

$$c \approx 63.25$$

22. $\cos \alpha = \dfrac{25^2 + 17.5^2 - 25^2}{2(25)(17.5)}$

$\alpha \approx 69.512°$

$\beta \approx 180 - \alpha \approx 110.488°$

$a^2 = 17.5^2 + 25^2 - 2(17.5)(25) \cos 110.488°$

$a \approx 35.18$

$z = 180 - 2\alpha \approx 40.975$

$\cos \mu = \dfrac{25^2 + 35.18^2 - 17.5^2}{2(25)(35.18)}$

$\mu \approx 27.775°$

$\theta = \mu + z \approx 68.7°$

$\omega = 180° - \mu - \beta \approx 41.738°$

$\phi = \omega + \alpha \approx 111.3°$

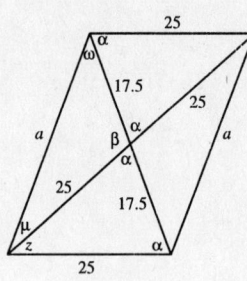

24. $a = 12,\ b = 15,\ c = 9 \implies s = \dfrac{12 + 15 + 9}{2} = 18$

$\text{Area} = \sqrt{18(6)(3)(9)} = 54$

26. Given: $a = 75.4, b = 52, c = 52$

$s = \dfrac{75.4 + 52 + 52}{2} = 89.7$

$\text{Area} = \sqrt{s(s - a)(s - b)(s - c)}$

$\quad\ = \sqrt{89.7(14.3)(37.7)(37.7)} \approx 1350$

28. Given: $a = 3.05, b = 0.75, c = 2.45$

$s = \dfrac{3.05 + 0.75 + 2.45}{2} = 3.125$

$\text{Area} = \sqrt{s(s - a)(s - b)(s - c)}$

$\quad\ = \sqrt{3.125(0.075)(2.375)(0.675)}$

$\quad\ \approx 0.61$

30.

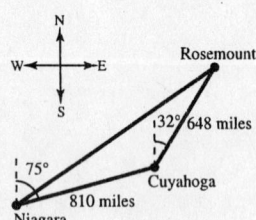

Distance from Niagara to Rosemount:

$d = \sqrt{810^2 + 648^2 - 2(810)(648) \cos(137°)}$

$\quad \approx 1357.8 \text{ miles}$

Bearing from Niagara to Rosemount:

$\text{N} (75° - \theta)\, \text{E}$

$\cos \theta \approx \dfrac{(1357.8)^2 + 810^2 - 648^2}{2(1357.8)(810)}$

$\qquad \approx 0.9456$

$\theta \approx 19.0°$

$\text{N } 56.0° \text{ E}$

32. $\cos A = \dfrac{115^2 + 76^2 - 92^2}{2(115)(76)} \approx 0.6028 \implies A \approx 52.9°$

$\cos C = \dfrac{115^2 + 92^2 - 76^2}{2(115)(92)} \approx 0.75203 \implies c \approx 41.2°$

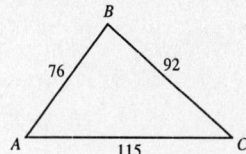

34. $\cos \theta = \dfrac{2^2 + 3^2 - (4.5)^2}{2(2)(3)} \approx -0.60417$

$\theta \approx 127.2°$

36. The angles at the base of the tower are 96° and 84°. The longer guy wire g_1 is given by:

$g_1^2 = 75^2 + 100^2 - 2(75)(100) \cos 96° \approx 17,192.9 \implies g_1 \approx 131.1$ feet

The shorter guy wire g_2 is given by:

$g_2^2 = 75^2 + 100^2 - 2(75)(100) \cos 84° \approx 14,057.1 \implies g_2 \approx 118.6$ feet

38.

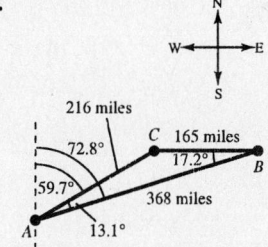

$a = 165, b = 216, c = 368$

$\cos B = \dfrac{165^2 + 368^2 - 216^2}{2(165)(368)} \approx 0.9551$

$B \approx 17.2°$

$\cos A = \dfrac{216^2 + 368^2 - 165^2}{2(216)(368)} \approx 0.9741$

$A \approx 13.1°$

(a) Bearing of Minneapolis (C) from Phoenix (A)

   N $(90° - 17.2° - 13.1°)$ E

   N 59.7 E

(b) Bearing of Albany (B) from Phoenix (A)

   N $(90° - 17.2°)$ E

   N 72.8° E

40. $d = \sqrt{330^2 + 420^2 - 2(330)(420) \cos 8°}$

   ≈ 103.9 feet

42. $a = \sqrt{20^2 + 20^2 - 2(20)(20) \cos 11°}$

   ≈ 3.8 miles

44. (a) $7^2 = 1.5^2 + x^2 - 2(1.5) x \cos \theta$

   $49 = 2.25 + x^2 - 3x \cos \theta$

   $x^2 - 3x \cos \theta - 46.75 = 0$

(b) $x = \dfrac{3 \cos \theta \pm \sqrt{(-3 \cos \theta)^2 - 4(1)(-46.75)}}{2(1)}$

   $x = \dfrac{1}{2}\left(3 \cos \theta + \sqrt{9 \cos^2 \theta + 187}\right)$

(c)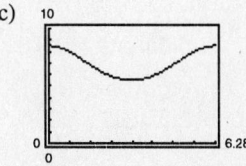

(d) Maximum: 8.5 inches

46.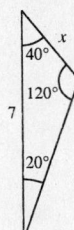

$$\frac{x}{\sin 20°} = \frac{7}{\sin 120°}$$

$$x = \frac{7 \sin 20°}{\sin 120°} \approx 2.76 \text{ feet}$$

48. area $= 2\left[\frac{1}{2}(70)(100) \sin 70°\right]$

$\qquad \approx 6577.8$

(The area of the parallelogram is the sum of the areas of two triangles.)

50. False. To solve an SSA triangle, the Law of Sines is needed.

52. $a = 25, b = 55, c = 72$

(a) area of triangle: $s = \frac{1}{2}(25 + 55 + 72) = 76$

$\qquad$ area $= \sqrt{76(51)(21)(4)} \approx 570.60$

(b) area of circumscribed circle:

$$\cos C = \frac{25^2 + 55^2 - 72^2}{2(25)(55)} \approx -0.5578 \Rightarrow C \approx 123.9°$$

$$R = \frac{1}{2}\left(\frac{c}{\sin C}\right) \approx 43.38$$

$\qquad$ area $= \pi R^2 \approx 5910.68$

(c) area of inscribed circle:

$$r = \sqrt{\frac{(s-a)(s-b)(s-c)}{s}} = \sqrt{\frac{(51)(21)(4)}{76}} \approx 7.51$$

$\qquad$ area $= \pi r^2 \approx 177.09$

54. $\frac{1}{2}bc(1 + \cos A) = \frac{1}{2}bc\left[1 + \frac{b^2 + c^2 - a^2}{2bc}\right]$

$\qquad = \frac{1}{2}bc\left[\frac{2bc + b^2 + c^2 - a^2}{2bc}\right]$

$\qquad = \frac{1}{4}[(b + c)^2 - a^2]$

$\qquad = \frac{1}{4}[(b + c) + a][(b + c) - a]$

$\qquad = \frac{b + c + a}{2} \cdot \frac{b + c - a}{2}$

$\qquad = \frac{a + b + c}{2} \cdot \frac{-a + b + c}{2}$

56. $\arcsin(-1) = -\frac{\pi}{2}$

58. $\arctan\sqrt{3} = \frac{\pi}{3}$

60. $\arcsin\left(-\frac{\sqrt{3}}{2}\right) = -\frac{\pi}{3}$

62. Let $\theta = \arcsin 2x$, then

$$\sin \theta = 2x = \frac{2x}{1} \text{ and } \sec \theta = \frac{1}{\sqrt{1 - 4x^2}}.$$

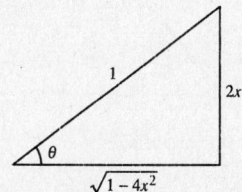

64. Let $\theta = \arctan(x - 2)$, then

$$\tan \theta = x - 2 = \frac{x - 2}{1} \text{ and } \cot \theta = \frac{1}{x - 2}.$$

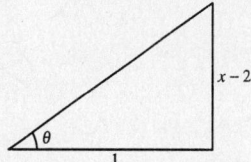

66. $5 = \sqrt{25 - x^2}, x = 5 \sin \theta$

$5 = \sqrt{25 - (5 \sin \theta)^2}$

$5 = \sqrt{25(1 - \sin^2 \theta)}$

$5 = 5 \cos \theta$

$\cos \theta = 1$

$\sec \theta = \dfrac{1}{\cos \theta} = 1$

$\csc \theta$ is undefined.

68. $-\sqrt{3} = \sqrt{x^2 - 9}, x = 3 \sec \theta$

$-\sqrt{3} = \sqrt{(3 \sec \theta)^2 - 9}$

$-\sqrt{3} = \sqrt{9(\sec^2 \theta - 1)}$

$-\sqrt{3} = 3 \tan \theta$

$\tan \theta = -\dfrac{\sqrt{3}}{3}$

$\sec \theta = \sqrt{1 + \tan^2 \theta} = \sqrt{1 + \left(-\dfrac{\sqrt{3}}{3}\right)^2} = \dfrac{2\sqrt{3}}{3}$

$\cot \theta = \dfrac{1}{\tan \theta} = -\sqrt{3}$

$\csc \theta = -\sqrt{1 + \cot^2 \theta} = -\sqrt{1 + \left(-\sqrt{3}\right)^2} = -2$

Section 6.3   Vectors in the Plane

Solutions to Even-Numbered Exercises

2. Initial point: $(0, 0)$

Terminal point: $(-4, -2)$

$\mathbf{v} = \langle -4 - 0, -2 - 0 \rangle = \langle -4, -2 \rangle$

$\|\mathbf{v}\| = \sqrt{(-4)^2 + (-2)^2} = \sqrt{20} = 2\sqrt{5}$

4. Initial point: $(-1, -1)$

Terminal point: $(3, 5)$

$\mathbf{v} = \langle 3 - (-1), 5 - (-1) \rangle = \langle 4, 6 \rangle$

$\|\mathbf{v}\| = \sqrt{4^2 + 6^2} = \sqrt{52} = 2\sqrt{13}$

6. Initial point: $(-4, -1)$

Terminal point: $(3, -1)$

$\mathbf{v} = \langle 3 - (-4), -1 - (-1) \rangle = \langle 7, 0 \rangle$

$\|\mathbf{v}\| = \sqrt{7^2 + 0^2} = 7$

8. Initial point: $(1, 11)$

Terminal point: $(9, 3)$

$\mathbf{v} = \langle 9 - 1, 3 - 11 \rangle = \langle 8, -8 \rangle$

$\|\mathbf{v}\| = \sqrt{8^2 + (-8)^2} = 8\sqrt{2}$

10. Initial point: $(-3, 11)$

Terminal point: $(9, 40)$

$\mathbf{v} = \langle 9 - (-3), 40 - 11 \rangle = \langle 12, 29 \rangle$

$\|\mathbf{v}\| = \sqrt{12^2 + 29^2} = \sqrt{985}$

12. Initial point: $(-2, 7)$

Terminal point: $(5, -17)$

$\mathbf{v} = \langle 5 - (-2), -17 - 7 \rangle = \langle 7, -24 \rangle$

$\|\mathbf{v}\| = \sqrt{7^2 + (-24)^2} = 25$

14. 5**v**

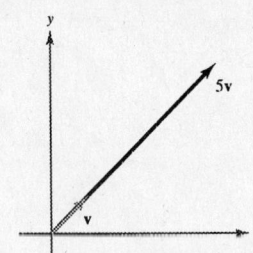

16. **u** − **v**

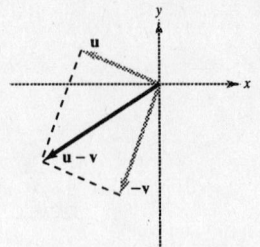

18. **v** − $\frac{1}{2}$**u**

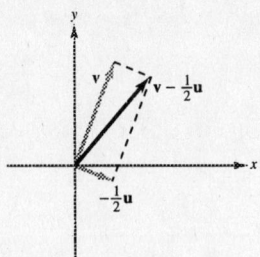

20. **u** = ⟨2, 3⟩, **v** = ⟨4, 0⟩

  (a) **u** + **v** = ⟨6, 3⟩

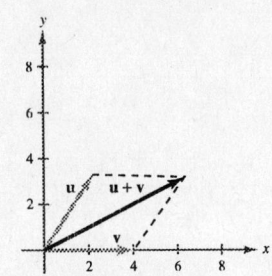

  (b) **u** − **v** = ⟨−2, 3⟩

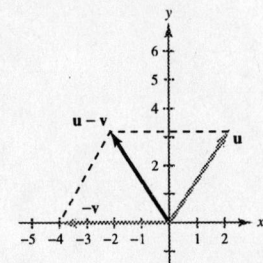

  (c) 2**u** − 3**v** = ⟨4, 6⟩ − ⟨12, 0⟩

            = ⟨−8, 6⟩

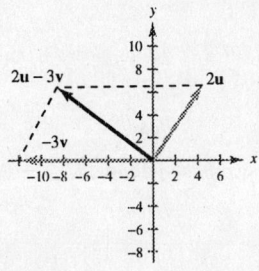

22. **u** = ⟨0, 0⟩, **v** = ⟨2, 1⟩

  (a) **u** + **v** = ⟨2, 1⟩

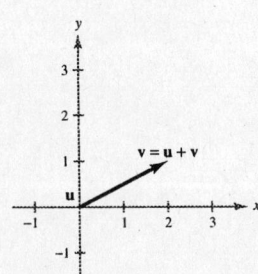

  (b) **u** − **v** = ⟨−2, −1⟩

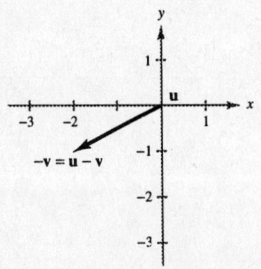

  (c) 2**u** − 3**v** = ⟨0, 0⟩ − ⟨6, 3⟩

            = ⟨−6, −3⟩

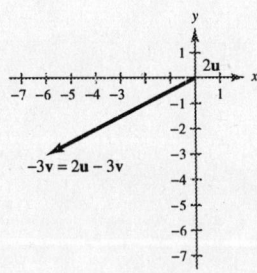

24. **u** = −2**i** + **j**, **v** = −**i** + 2**j**

  (a) **u** + **v** = −3**i** + 3**j**

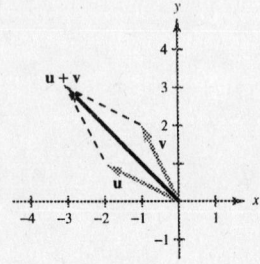

  (b) **u** − **v** = −**i** − **j**

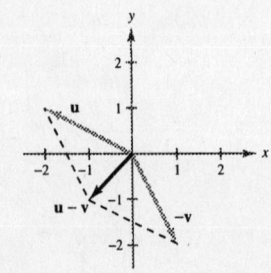

— CONTINUED —

24. — CONTINUED —

(c) $2\mathbf{u} - 3\mathbf{v} = (-4\mathbf{i} + 2\mathbf{j}) - (-3\mathbf{i} + 6\mathbf{j}) = -\mathbf{i} - 4\mathbf{j}$

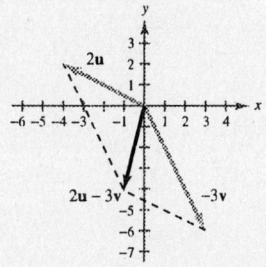

26. $\mathbf{u} = 3\mathbf{j}, \mathbf{v} = 2\mathbf{i}$

(a) $\mathbf{u} + \mathbf{v} = 2\mathbf{i} + 3\mathbf{j}$ 　(b) $\mathbf{u} - \mathbf{v} = -2\mathbf{i} + 3\mathbf{j}$ 　(c) $2\mathbf{u} - 3\mathbf{v} = 6\mathbf{j} - 6\mathbf{i}$

$$= -6\mathbf{i} + 6\mathbf{j}$$

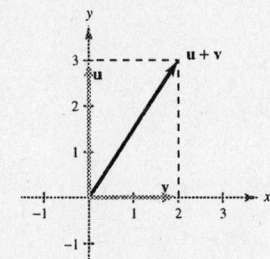 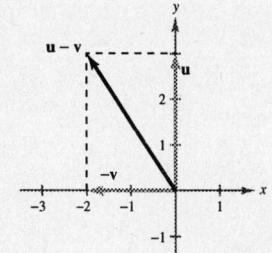 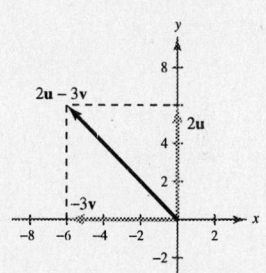

28. $\mathbf{u} = \langle 0, -2 \rangle$

$$\mathbf{v} = \frac{1}{\|\mathbf{u}\|}\mathbf{u} = \frac{1}{\sqrt{0^2 + (-2)^2}} \langle 0, -2 \rangle$$

$$= \frac{1}{2}\langle 0, -2 \rangle = \langle 0, -1 \rangle$$

30. $\mathbf{v} = \langle 5, -12 \rangle$

$$\mathbf{u} = \frac{1}{\|\mathbf{v}\|}\mathbf{v} = \frac{1}{\sqrt{5^2 + (-12)^2}} \langle 5, -12 \rangle$$

$$= \frac{1}{13}\langle 5, -12 \rangle$$

$$= \left\langle \frac{5}{13}, -\frac{12}{13} \right\rangle$$

32. $\mathbf{v} = \mathbf{i} + \mathbf{j}$

$$\mathbf{u} = \frac{1}{\|\mathbf{v}\|}\mathbf{v}$$

$$= \frac{1}{\sqrt{1^2 + 1^2}}(\mathbf{i} + \mathbf{j})$$

$$= \frac{1}{\sqrt{2}}(\mathbf{i} + \mathbf{j})$$

$$= \frac{\sqrt{2}}{2}\mathbf{i} + \frac{\sqrt{2}}{2}\mathbf{j}$$

34. $\mathbf{w} = -6\mathbf{i}$

$$\mathbf{v} = \frac{1}{\|\mathbf{w}\|}\mathbf{w} = \frac{1}{\sqrt{(-6)^2 + 0^2}}(-6\mathbf{i})$$

$$= \frac{1}{6}(-6\mathbf{i}) = -\mathbf{i}$$

36. $\mathbf{w} = 7\mathbf{j} - 3\mathbf{i}$

$\mathbf{v} = \dfrac{1}{\|\mathbf{w}\|}\mathbf{w} = \dfrac{1}{\sqrt{(-3)^2 + 7^2}}(-3\mathbf{i} + 7\mathbf{j})$

$= -\dfrac{3}{\sqrt{58}}\mathbf{i} + \dfrac{7}{\sqrt{58}}\mathbf{j}$

38. $\mathbf{v} = 6\left(\dfrac{1}{\|\mathbf{u}\|}\mathbf{u}\right) = 6\left(\dfrac{1}{\sqrt{(-3)^2 + 3^2}}\langle -3, 3 \rangle\right)$

$= 6\left(\dfrac{1}{3\sqrt{2}}\langle -3, 3 \rangle\right) = \left\langle -\dfrac{6}{\sqrt{2}}, \dfrac{6}{\sqrt{2}} \right\rangle$

40. $\mathbf{v} = 10\left(\dfrac{1}{\|\mathbf{u}\|}\mathbf{u}\right)$

$= 10\left(\dfrac{1}{\sqrt{0^2 + (-10)^2}}\langle -10, 0 \rangle\right)$

$= 10\left(\dfrac{1}{10}\langle -10, 0 \rangle\right)$

$= \langle -10, 0 \rangle$

42. $\mathbf{v} = \dfrac{3}{4}\mathbf{w} = \dfrac{3}{4}(\mathbf{i} + 2\mathbf{j})$

$= \dfrac{3}{4}\mathbf{i} + \dfrac{3}{2}\mathbf{j} = \left\langle \dfrac{3}{4}, \dfrac{3}{2} \right\rangle$

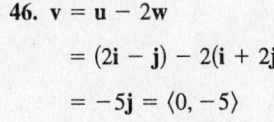

44. $\mathbf{v} = -\mathbf{u} + \mathbf{w}$

$= -(2\mathbf{i} - \mathbf{j}) + (\mathbf{i} + 2\mathbf{j})$

$= -\mathbf{i} + 3\mathbf{j} = \langle -1, 3 \rangle$

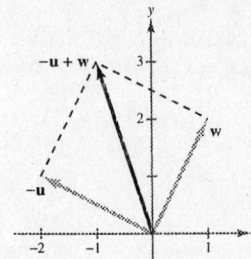

46. $\mathbf{v} = \mathbf{u} - 2\mathbf{w}$

$= (2\mathbf{i} - \mathbf{j}) - 2(\mathbf{i} + 2\mathbf{j})$

$= -5\mathbf{j} = \langle 0, -5 \rangle$

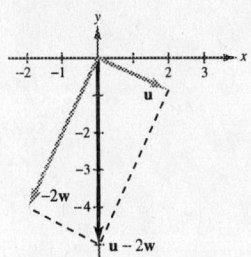

48. $\mathbf{v} = 8(\cos 135° \, \mathbf{i} + \sin 135° \, \mathbf{j})$

$\|\mathbf{v}\| = 8, \ \theta = 135°$

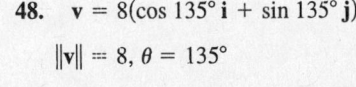

50. $\mathbf{v} = -5\mathbf{i} + 4\mathbf{j}$

$\|\mathbf{v}\| = \sqrt{(-5)^2 + 4^2} = \sqrt{41}$

$\tan \theta = -\dfrac{4}{5}$

Since $\mathbf{v}$ lies in Quadrant II,

$\theta = 141.3°.$

52. $\mathbf{v} = \langle \cos 45°, \sin 45° \rangle$

$= \left\langle \dfrac{\sqrt{2}}{2}, \dfrac{\sqrt{2}}{2} \right\rangle$

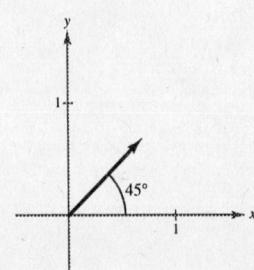

54. $\mathbf{v} = \left\langle \dfrac{5}{2}\cos 45°, \dfrac{5}{2}\sin 45° \right\rangle$

$= \left\langle \dfrac{5\sqrt{2}}{4}, \dfrac{5\sqrt{2}}{4} \right\rangle$

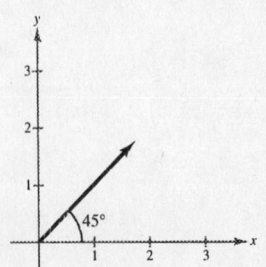

56. $\mathbf{v} = \left\langle 4\sqrt{3}\cos 90°, 4\sqrt{3}\sin 90° \right\rangle$

$\quad = \left\langle 0, 4\sqrt{3} \right\rangle$

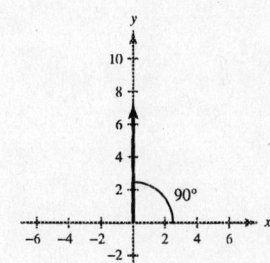

58. $\mathbf{v} = 3\left(\dfrac{1}{\sqrt{3^2 + 4^2}} \right)(3\mathbf{i} + 4\mathbf{j})$

$\quad = \dfrac{3}{5}(3\mathbf{i} + 4\mathbf{j})$

$\quad = \dfrac{9}{5}\mathbf{i} + \dfrac{12}{5}\mathbf{j} = \left\langle \dfrac{9}{5}, \dfrac{12}{5} \right\rangle$

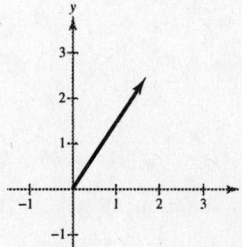

60. $\mathbf{u} = \langle 4\cos 60°, 4\sin 60° \rangle = \langle 2, 2\sqrt{3} \rangle$

$\quad \mathbf{v} = \langle 4\cos 90°, 4\sin 90° \rangle = \langle 0, 4 \rangle$

$\quad \mathbf{u} + \mathbf{v} = \langle 2, 4 + 2\sqrt{3} \rangle$

62. $\mathbf{u} = \langle 50\cos 30°, 50\sin 30° \rangle = \langle 25\sqrt{3}, 25 \rangle$

$\quad \approx \langle 43.301, 25 \rangle$

$\quad \mathbf{v} = \langle 30\cos 110°, 30\sin 110° \rangle \approx \langle -10.261, 28.191 \rangle$

$\quad \mathbf{u} + \mathbf{v} \approx \langle 33.04, 53.19 \rangle$

64. $\mathbf{v} = 3\mathbf{i} - 2\mathbf{j}$

$\quad \mathbf{w} = 2\mathbf{i} + 2\mathbf{j}$

$\quad \mathbf{u} = \mathbf{v} - \mathbf{w} = \mathbf{i} - 4\mathbf{j}$

$\quad \cos\theta = \dfrac{\|\mathbf{v}\|^2 + \|\mathbf{w}\|^2 - \|\mathbf{v} - \mathbf{w}\|^2}{2\|\mathbf{v}\|\,\|\mathbf{w}\|} = \dfrac{13 + 8 - 17}{2\sqrt{13}\sqrt{8}}$

$\quad\quad = \dfrac{1}{\sqrt{13}\sqrt{2}}$

$\quad \theta \approx 78.7°$

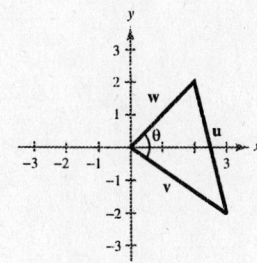

66. $\mathbf{v} = \mathbf{i} + 2\mathbf{j}$

$\quad \mathbf{w} = 2\mathbf{i} - \mathbf{j}$

$\quad \mathbf{u} = \mathbf{v} - \mathbf{w} = -\mathbf{i} + 3\mathbf{j}$

$\quad \cos\theta = \dfrac{\|\mathbf{v}\|^2 + \|\mathbf{w}\|^2 - \|\mathbf{v} - \mathbf{w}\|^2}{2\|\mathbf{v}\|\,\|\mathbf{w}\|} = \dfrac{5 + 5 - 10}{2\sqrt{5}\sqrt{5}} = 0$

$\quad \theta = 90°$

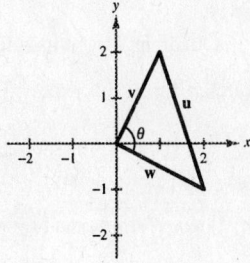

68. Force One: $\mathbf{u} = 3000\mathbf{i}$

Force Two: $\mathbf{v} = 1000\cos\theta\mathbf{i} + 1000\sin\theta\mathbf{j}$

Resultant Force: $\mathbf{u} + \mathbf{v} = (3000 + 1000\cos\theta)\mathbf{i} + 1000\sin\theta\mathbf{j}$

$\|\mathbf{u} + \mathbf{v}\| = \sqrt{(3000 + 1000\cos\theta)^2 + (1000\sin\theta)^2} = 3750$

$\quad\quad 9,000,000 + 6,000,000\cos\theta + 1,000,000 = 14,062,500$

$\quad\quad\quad 6,000,000\cos\theta = 4,062,500$

$\quad\quad\quad\quad \cos\theta = \dfrac{4,062,500}{6,000,000} \approx 0.6771$

$\quad\quad\quad\quad\quad \theta \approx 47.4°$

70.
$$\mathbf{u} = (2000 \cos 30°)\mathbf{i} + (2000 \sin 30°\mathbf{j})$$

$$\approx 1732.05\mathbf{i} + 1000\mathbf{j}$$

$$\mathbf{v} = (900 \cos(-45°))\mathbf{i} + (900 \sin(-45°)\mathbf{j})$$

$$\approx 636.4\mathbf{i} + -636.4\mathbf{j}$$

$$\mathbf{u} + \mathbf{v} \approx 2368.4\mathbf{i} + 363.6\mathbf{j}$$

$$\|\mathbf{u} + \mathbf{v}\| \approx \sqrt{(2368.4)^2 + (363.6)^2} \approx 2396.19$$

$$\tan \theta = \frac{363.6}{2368.4} \approx 0.1535 \Rightarrow \theta \approx 8.7°$$

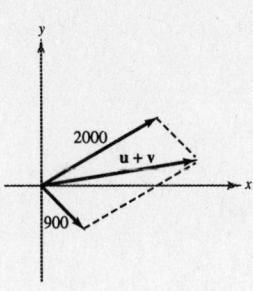

72.
$$\mathbf{u} = (70 \cos 30°)\mathbf{i} - (70 \sin 30°)\mathbf{j} \approx 60.62\mathbf{i} - 35\mathbf{j}$$

$$\mathbf{v} = (40 \cos 45°)\mathbf{i} + (40 \sin 45°)\mathbf{j} \approx 28.28\mathbf{i} + 28.28\mathbf{j}$$

$$\mathbf{w} = (60 \cos 135°)\mathbf{i} + (60 \sin 135°)\mathbf{j} \approx -42.43\mathbf{i} + 42.43\mathbf{j}$$

$$\mathbf{u} + \mathbf{v} + \mathbf{w} = 46.48\mathbf{i} + 35.71\mathbf{j}$$

$$\|\mathbf{u} + \mathbf{v} + \mathbf{w}\| \approx 58.61 \text{ pounds}$$

$$\tan \theta \approx \frac{35.71}{46.47} \approx 0.7683$$

$$\theta \approx 37.5°$$

74. Horizontal component of velocity: $1200 \cos 6° \approx 1193.4$ ft/sec

Vertical component of velocity: $1200 \sin 6° \approx 125.4$ ft/sec

76. Rope $\overrightarrow{AC}$: $\mathbf{u} = 10\mathbf{i} - 24\mathbf{j}$

The vector lies in Quadrant IV and its reference angle is $\arctan\left(\frac{12}{5}\right)$.

$$\mathbf{u} = \|\mathbf{u}\|\left[\cos\left(\arctan \tfrac{12}{5}\right)\mathbf{i} - \sin\left(\arctan \tfrac{12}{5}\right)\mathbf{j}\right]$$

Rope $\overrightarrow{BC}$: $\mathbf{v} = -20\mathbf{i} - 24\mathbf{j}$

The vector lies in Quadrant III and its reference angle is $\arctan\left(\frac{6}{5}\right)$.

$$\mathbf{v} = \|\mathbf{v}\|\left[-\cos\left(\arctan \tfrac{6}{5}\right)\mathbf{i} - \sin\left(\arctan \tfrac{6}{5}\right)\mathbf{j}\right]$$

Resultant: $\mathbf{u} + \mathbf{v} = -5000\mathbf{j}$

$$\|\mathbf{u}\| \cos\left(\arctan \tfrac{12}{5}\right) - \|\mathbf{v}\| \cos\left(\arctan \tfrac{6}{5}\right) = 0$$

$$-\|\mathbf{u}\| \sin\left(\arctan \tfrac{12}{5}\right) - \|\mathbf{v}\| \sin\left(\arctan \tfrac{6}{5}\right) = -5000$$

Solving this system of equations yields: $T_{AC} = \|\mathbf{u}\| \approx 3611.1$ pounds

$$T_{BC} = \|\mathbf{v}\| \approx 2169.5 \text{ pounds}$$

78. Rope 1: $\mathbf{u} = \|\mathbf{u}\| (\cos 70°\mathbf{i} - \sin 70°\mathbf{j})$

Rope 2: $\mathbf{v} = \|\mathbf{u}\| (-\cos 70°\mathbf{i} - \sin 70°\mathbf{j})$

Resultant: $\mathbf{u} + \mathbf{v} = -100\mathbf{j}$

$$-\|\mathbf{u}\| \sin 70° - \|\mathbf{u}\| \sin 70° = -100$$

$$\|\mathbf{u}\| \approx 53.2$$

Therefore, the tension of each rope is $\|\mathbf{u}\| \approx 53.2$ pounds.

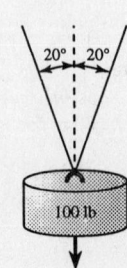

80. Plane: $\mathbf{u} = (580 \cos 150°)\mathbf{i} + (580 \sin 150°)\mathbf{j} \approx -502.3\mathbf{i} + 290\mathbf{j}$

Wind: $\mathbf{v} = (60 \cos 45°)\mathbf{i} + (60 \sin 45°)\mathbf{j} \approx 42.4\mathbf{i} + 42.4\mathbf{j}$

$\mathbf{u} + \mathbf{v} \approx -459.9\mathbf{i} + 332.4\mathbf{j}$

$\|\mathbf{u} + \mathbf{v}\| \approx \sqrt{(-459.9)^2 + (332.4)^2} \approx 567.4$

$\tan \theta \approx -\dfrac{332.4}{459.9} \approx -0.7229 \implies \theta \approx 144.1°$

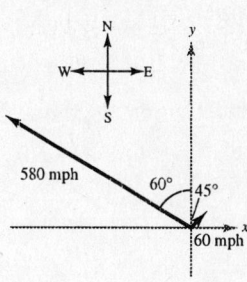

The ground speed is 567.4 miles per hour and the heading is N 54.1° W.

82. Horizontal force: $\mathbf{u} = \|\mathbf{u}\|\mathbf{i}$

Weight: $\mathbf{w} = -\mathbf{j}$

Rope: $\mathbf{t} = \|\mathbf{t}\| (\cos 135°\mathbf{i} + \sin 135°\mathbf{j})$

$\mathbf{u} + \mathbf{w} + \mathbf{t} = \mathbf{0} \implies \|\mathbf{u}\| + \|\mathbf{t}\| \cos 135° = 0$

$-1 + \|\mathbf{t}\| \sin 135° = 0$

$\|\mathbf{t}\| \approx \sqrt{2}$ pounds

$\|\mathbf{u}\| \approx 1$ pound

84. True, by the definition of a unit vector.

$\mathbf{u} = \dfrac{\mathbf{v}}{\|\mathbf{v}\|} \implies \mathbf{v} = \|\mathbf{v}\|\mathbf{u}$

86. True.

$\|\mathbf{u}\| = \sqrt{a^2 + b^2} = 1 \implies a^2 + b^2 = 1$

88. $\mathbf{F}_1 = \langle 10, 0 \rangle, \mathbf{F}_2 = 5\langle \cos \theta, \sin \theta \rangle$

(a) $\mathbf{F}_1 + \mathbf{F}_2 = \langle 10 + 5 \cos \theta, 5 \sin \theta \rangle$

$\|\mathbf{F}_1 + \mathbf{F}_2\| = \sqrt{(10 + 5 \cos \theta)^2 + (5 \sin \theta)^2}$

$= \sqrt{100 + 100 \cos \theta + 25 \cos^2 \theta + 25 \sin^2 \theta}$

$= 5\sqrt{4 + 4 \cos \theta + \cos^2 \theta + \sin^2 \theta}$

$= 5\sqrt{4 + 4 \cos \theta + 1}$

$= 5\sqrt{5 + 4 \cos \theta}$

(b)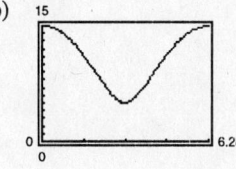

(c) Range: $[5, 15]$

Maximum is 15 when $\theta = 0$.

Minimum is 5 when $\theta = \pi$.

(d) The magnitude of the resultant is never 0 because the magnitudes of $\mathbf{F}_1$ and $\mathbf{F}_2$ are not the same.

90. The following program is written for a *TI-82* or *TI-83* or *TI-83 Plus* graphing calculator. The program sketches two vectors $\mathbf{u} = a\mathbf{i} + b\mathbf{j}$ and $\mathbf{v} = c\mathbf{i} + d\mathbf{j}$ in standard position, and then sketches the vector difference $\mathbf{u} - \mathbf{v}$ using the parallelogram law.

```
PROGRAM:  SUBVECT
:Input "ENTER A", A
:Input "ENTER B", B
:Input "ENTER C", C
:Input "ENTER D", D
:Line (0, 0, A, B)
:Line (0, 0, C, D)
:Pause
:A-C→E
:B-D→F
:Line (A, B, C, D)
:Line (A, B, E, F)
:Line (0, 0, E, F)
:Pause
:ClrDraw
:Stop
```

92. $\quad \mathbf{u} = \langle 80 - 10, 80 - 60 \rangle = \langle 70, 20 \rangle$

$\quad \mathbf{v} = \langle -20 - (-100), 70 - 0 \rangle = \langle 80, 70 \rangle$

$\mathbf{u} - \mathbf{v} = \langle 70 - 80, 20 - 70 \rangle = \langle -10, -50 \rangle$

$\mathbf{v} - \mathbf{u} = \langle 80 - 70, 70 - 20 \rangle = \langle 10, 50 \rangle$

94. $x = 8 \sin \theta$

$$\sqrt{64 - x^2} = \sqrt{64 - (8 \sin^2 \theta)}$$
$$= \sqrt{64 - 64 \sin^2 \theta}$$
$$= 8\sqrt{1 - \sin^2 \theta}$$
$$= 8\sqrt{\cos^2 \theta}$$
$$= 8 \cos \theta$$

96. $x = 5 \sec \theta$

$$\sqrt{(x^2 - 25)^3} = \sqrt{[(5 \sec \theta)^2 - 25]^3}$$
$$= \sqrt{(25 \sec^2 \theta - 25)^3}$$
$$= \sqrt{[25(\sec^2 \theta - 1)]^3}$$
$$= \sqrt{(25 \tan^2 \theta)^3}$$
$$= \sqrt{15,625 \tan^6 \theta}$$
$$= 125 \tan^3 \theta$$

98. $\sin x(2 \sin x + \sqrt{2}) = 0$

$\sin x = 0 \qquad\qquad 2 \sin x + \sqrt{2} = 0$

$\quad x = 0 + n\pi \qquad\qquad\qquad \sin x = -\dfrac{\sqrt{2}}{2}$

$$x = \frac{5\pi}{4} + 2\pi n, \frac{7\pi}{4} + 2\pi n$$

$$x = n\pi, \frac{5\pi}{4} + 2\pi n, \frac{7\pi}{4} + 2\pi n$$

100. $\cos x \csc x + \cos x \sqrt{2} = 0$

$\quad \cos x(\csc x + \sqrt{2}) = 0$

$\cos x = 0 \qquad\qquad \csc x + \sqrt{2} = 0$

$\quad x = \dfrac{\pi}{2} + n\pi \qquad\qquad \csc x = -\sqrt{2}$

$$x = \frac{5\pi}{4} + 2\pi n, \frac{7\pi}{4} + 2\pi n$$

$$x = \frac{\pi}{2} + n\pi, \frac{5\pi}{4} + 2\pi n, \frac{7\pi}{4} + 2\pi n$$

102. $(2 \cos^2 x - 3)(\cos^2 x - 1) = 0$

$2 \cos^2 x - 3 = 0 \qquad \cos^2 x - 1 = 0$

$\quad \cos^2 x = \frac{3}{2} \qquad\qquad \cos^2 x = 1$

No solution $\qquad\qquad \cos x = \pm 1$

$$x = 0 + \pi n$$

$x = \pi n$

Section 6.4   Vectors and Dot Products

Solutions to Even-Numbered Exercises

2. $\mathbf{u} = \langle 5, 12 \rangle, \mathbf{v} = \langle -3, 2 \rangle$

$\mathbf{u} \cdot \mathbf{v} = 5(-3) + 12(2) = 9$

4. $\quad \mathbf{u} = 3\mathbf{i} + 4\mathbf{j}, \mathbf{v} = 7\mathbf{i} - 2\mathbf{j}$

$\mathbf{u} \cdot \mathbf{v} = 3(7) + 4(-2) = 13$

6. $\mathbf{v} = \langle -3, 4 \rangle$

$\|\mathbf{v}\| + 3 = \sqrt{\mathbf{v} \cdot \mathbf{v}} + 3$

$\qquad\qquad = \sqrt{(-3)(-3) + 4(4)} + 3 = 8$

The result is a scalar.

8. $\mathbf{u} = \langle 2, 2 \rangle, \mathbf{v} = \langle -3, 4 \rangle$

$3\mathbf{u} \cdot \mathbf{v} = 3[(2)(-3) + (2)(4)] = 3(2) = 6$

The result is a scalar.

10. $\mathbf{u} = \langle 2, -4 \rangle$

$\|\mathbf{u}\| = \sqrt{\mathbf{u} \cdot \mathbf{u}}$

$\quad = \sqrt{2(2) + (-4)(-4)}$

$\quad = \sqrt{20} = 2\sqrt{5}$

12. $\mathbf{u} = 12\mathbf{i} - 16\mathbf{j}$

$\|\mathbf{u}\| = \sqrt{\mathbf{u} \cdot \mathbf{u}} = \sqrt{12(12) + (-16)(-16)}$

$\quad = \sqrt{400} = 20$

14. $\mathbf{u} = -21\mathbf{i}$

$\|\mathbf{u}\| = \sqrt{\mathbf{u} \cdot \mathbf{u}} = \sqrt{(-21)(-21) + 0(0)}$

$\quad = \sqrt{21^2} = 21$

16. $\mathbf{u} = \langle 3, 2 \rangle, \mathbf{v} = \langle 4, 0 \rangle$

$\cos \theta = \dfrac{\mathbf{u} \cdot \mathbf{v}}{\|\mathbf{u}\| \, \|\mathbf{v}\|} = \dfrac{3(4) + 2(0)}{\sqrt{13} \, (4)}$

$\quad = \dfrac{3}{\sqrt{13}} \approx 0.8321$

$\theta \approx 33.7°$

18. $\mathbf{u} = 2\mathbf{i} - 3\mathbf{j}, \mathbf{v} = \mathbf{i} - 2\mathbf{j}$

$\cos \theta = \dfrac{\mathbf{u} \cdot \mathbf{v}}{\|\mathbf{u}\| \, \|\mathbf{v}\|}$

$\quad = \dfrac{2(1) + (-3)(-2)}{\sqrt{2^2 + 3^2}\sqrt{1^2 + 2^2}}$

$\quad = \dfrac{8}{\sqrt{65}} \approx 0.992278$

$\theta \approx 7.13°$

20. $\mathbf{u} = -6\mathbf{i} - 3\mathbf{j}, \mathbf{v} = -8\mathbf{i} + 4\mathbf{j}$

$\cos \mathbf{u} = \dfrac{\mathbf{u} \cdot \mathbf{v}}{\|\mathbf{u}\| \, \|\mathbf{v}\|} = \dfrac{-6(-8) + (-3)(4)}{\sqrt{45}\sqrt{80}}$

$\quad = \dfrac{36}{60} = 0.6$

$\theta \approx 53.13°$

22. $\mathbf{u} = 2\mathbf{i} - 3\mathbf{j}, \mathbf{v} = 4\mathbf{i} + 3\mathbf{j}$

$\cos \theta = \dfrac{\mathbf{u} \cdot \mathbf{v}}{\|\mathbf{u}\| \, \|\mathbf{v}\|} = \dfrac{2(4) + (-3)(3)}{\sqrt{13}\sqrt{25}} \approx -0.0555$

$\theta \approx 93.18°$

24. $\mathbf{u} = \cos\left(\dfrac{\pi}{4}\right)\mathbf{i} + \sin\left(\dfrac{\pi}{4}\right)\mathbf{j} = \dfrac{\sqrt{2}}{2}\mathbf{i} + \dfrac{\sqrt{2}}{2}\mathbf{j}$

$\mathbf{v} = \cos\left(\dfrac{\pi}{2}\right)\mathbf{i} + \sin\left(\dfrac{\pi}{2}\right)\mathbf{j} = \mathbf{j}$

$\cos \theta = \dfrac{\mathbf{u} \cdot \mathbf{v}}{\|\mathbf{u}\| \, \|\mathbf{v}\|} = \dfrac{\dfrac{\sqrt{2}}{2}(0) + \dfrac{\sqrt{2}}{2}(1)}{1 \cdot 1} = \dfrac{\sqrt{2}}{2}$

$\theta = \dfrac{\pi}{4}$

26. $P = (-3, -4), Q = (1, 7), R = (8, 2)$

$\overrightarrow{PQ} = \langle 4, 11 \rangle, \overrightarrow{QR} = \langle 7, -5 \rangle,$

$\overrightarrow{PR} = \langle 11, 6 \rangle, \overrightarrow{QP} = \langle -4, -11 \rangle$

$\cos \alpha = \dfrac{\overrightarrow{PQ} \cdot \overrightarrow{PR}}{\|\overrightarrow{PQ}\| \, \|\overrightarrow{PR}\|} = \dfrac{110}{\left(\sqrt{137}\right)\left(\sqrt{157}\right)}$

$\Rightarrow \alpha \approx 41.4°$

$\cos \beta = \dfrac{\overrightarrow{QR} \cdot \overrightarrow{QP}}{\|\overrightarrow{QR}\| \, \|\overrightarrow{QP}\|} = \dfrac{27}{\left(\sqrt{74}\right)\left(\sqrt{137}\right)}$

$\Rightarrow \beta \approx 74.4°$

$\alpha \approx 180° - 41.4° - 74.4° = 64.2°$

28. $P = (-3, 5), Q = (-1, 9), R = (7, 9)$

$\overrightarrow{PQ} = \langle 2, 4 \rangle, \overrightarrow{QR} = \langle 8, 0 \rangle,$

$\overrightarrow{PR} = \langle 10, 4 \rangle, \overrightarrow{QP} = \langle -2, -4 \rangle$

$\cos \alpha = \dfrac{\overrightarrow{PQ} \cdot \overrightarrow{PR}}{\|\overrightarrow{PQ}\| \, \|\overrightarrow{PR}\|} = \dfrac{36}{\left(\sqrt{20}\right)\left(\sqrt{116}\right)}$

$\Rightarrow \alpha \approx 41.6°$

$\cos \beta = \dfrac{\overrightarrow{QR} \cdot \overrightarrow{QP}}{\|\overrightarrow{QR}\| \, \|\overrightarrow{QP}\|} = \dfrac{-16}{8\left(\sqrt{20}\right)}$

$\Rightarrow \beta \approx 116.6°$

$y \approx 180° - 41.6° - 116.6° = 21.8°$

30. $\|\mathbf{u}\| = 100, \|\mathbf{v}\| = 250, \theta = \dfrac{\pi}{6}$

$\mathbf{u} \cdot \mathbf{v} = \|\mathbf{u}\| \|\mathbf{v}\| \cos \theta$

$\quad = (100)(250) \cos \dfrac{\pi}{6}$

$\quad = 25{,}000 \cdot \dfrac{\sqrt{3}}{2}$

$\quad = 12{,}500\sqrt{3}$

32. $\|\mathbf{u}\| = 9, \|\mathbf{v}\| = 144, \theta = \dfrac{\pi}{2}$

$\mathbf{u} \cdot \mathbf{v} = \|\mathbf{u}\| \|\mathbf{v}\| \cos \theta$

$\quad = (9)(144) \cos \dfrac{\pi}{2}$

$\quad = 0$

34. $\mathbf{u} = \langle 3, 15 \rangle, \mathbf{v} = \langle -1, 5 \rangle$

$\mathbf{u} \neq k\mathbf{v} \Rightarrow$ Not parallel

$\mathbf{u} \cdot \mathbf{v} \neq 0 \Rightarrow$ Not orthogonal

Neither

36. $\mathbf{u} = 1, \mathbf{v} = -2\mathbf{i} + 2\mathbf{j}$

$\mathbf{u} \neq k\mathbf{v} \Rightarrow$ Not parallel

$\mathbf{u} \cdot \mathbf{v} \neq 0 \Rightarrow$ Not orthogonal

Neither

38. $\mathbf{u} = \langle \cos \theta, \sin \theta \rangle$

$\mathbf{v} = \langle \sin \theta, -\cos \theta \rangle$

$\mathbf{u} \cdot \mathbf{v} = 0 \Rightarrow \mathbf{u}$ and $\mathbf{v}$ are orthogonal.

40. $\mathbf{u} = \langle 4, 2 \rangle, \mathbf{v} = \langle 1, -2 \rangle$

$\mathbf{w}_1 = \text{proj}_{\mathbf{v}}\mathbf{u} = \left(\dfrac{\mathbf{u} \cdot \mathbf{v}}{\|\mathbf{v}\|^2}\right)\mathbf{v} = 0\langle 1, -2 \rangle = \langle 0, 0 \rangle$

$\mathbf{w}_2 = \mathbf{u} - \mathbf{w}_1 = \langle 4, 2 \rangle - \langle 0, 0 \rangle = \langle 4, 2 \rangle$

42. $\mathbf{u} = \langle -3, -2 \rangle, \mathbf{v} = \langle -4, -1 \rangle$

$\mathbf{w}_1 = \text{proj}_{\mathbf{v}}\mathbf{u} = \left(\dfrac{\mathbf{u} \cdot \mathbf{v}}{\|\mathbf{v}\|^2}\right)\mathbf{v} = \left(\dfrac{14}{17}\right)\langle -4, -1 \rangle$

$\mathbf{w}_2 = \mathbf{u} - \mathbf{w}_1 = \langle -3, -2 \rangle - \dfrac{14}{17}\langle -4, -1 \rangle$

$\quad = \dfrac{5}{17}\langle 1, -4 \rangle$

44. $\mathbf{u} = \langle -8, 3 \rangle$

For $\mathbf{v}$ to be orthogonal to $\mathbf{u}$, $\mathbf{u} \cdot \mathbf{v}$ must be equal to 0.

Two possibilities: $\langle 3, 8 \rangle, \langle -3, -8 \rangle$

46. $\mathbf{u} = -\frac{5}{2}\mathbf{i} - 3\mathbf{j}$

For $\mathbf{v}$ to be orthogonal to $\mathbf{u}$, $\mathbf{u} \cdot \mathbf{v}$ must be equal to 0.

Two possibilities: $\mathbf{v} = 3\mathbf{i} - \frac{5}{2}\mathbf{j}$

$\quad\quad \mathbf{v} = -3\mathbf{i} + \frac{5}{2}\mathbf{j}$

48. $P = (1, 3), Q = (-3, 5), \mathbf{v} = -2\mathbf{i} + 3\mathbf{j}$

work $= \mathbf{v} \cdot \overrightarrow{PQ}$

$\quad = (-2\mathbf{i} + 3\mathbf{j}) \cdot (-4\mathbf{i} + 2\mathbf{j})$

$\quad = (-2)(-4) + 3(2) = 14$

50. $\mathbf{u} = \langle 1650, 3200 \rangle$

$\mathbf{v} = \langle 15.25, 10.50 \rangle$

Increase prices by 5%: $1.05\mathbf{v}$

$\mathbf{u} \cdot 1.05\mathbf{v} = 1.05\mathbf{u} \cdot \mathbf{v}$

$\quad = 1.05[1650(15.25) + 3200(10.50)]$

$\quad = 1.05(58{,}762.50)$

$\quad = 61{,}700.63$

52. (a) $\mathbf{F} = -30,000\mathbf{j}$ Gravitational force

$$\mathbf{v} = (\cos 8°)\mathbf{i} + (\sin 8°)\mathbf{j}$$

$$\mathbf{w}_1 = \text{proj}_{\mathbf{v}}\mathbf{F} = \left(\frac{\mathbf{F} \cdot \mathbf{v}}{\|\mathbf{v}\|^2}\right)\mathbf{v}$$

$$= (\mathbf{F} \cdot \mathbf{v})\mathbf{v} \approx -4175.2\mathbf{v}$$

The magnitude of this force is 4175.2; therefore, a force of 4175.2 pounds is needed to keep the truck from rolling down the hill.

(b) $\mathbf{w}_2 = \mathbf{F} - \mathbf{w}_1 = -30,000\mathbf{j} + 4175.2[(\cos 8°)\mathbf{i} + (\sin 8°)\mathbf{j}]$

$$= (4175.2 \cos 8°)\mathbf{i} + (-30,000 + 4175.2 \sin 8°)\mathbf{j}$$

$$\|\mathbf{w}_2\| \approx 29,708.0 \text{ pounds}$$

54. work $= (2400)(5) = 12,000$ foot-pounds

56. work $= (\cos 35°)(15, 691)(800)$

$$\approx 10,282,651 \text{ newton} - \text{meters}$$

58. True.

$W = \mathbf{F} \cdot \overrightarrow{PQ} = 0$ if $\mathbf{F}$ and $\overrightarrow{PQ}$ are orthogonal.

60. (a) $\text{proj}_{\mathbf{v}}\mathbf{u} = \mathbf{u} \Rightarrow \mathbf{u}$ and $\mathbf{v}$ are parallel.

(b) $\text{proj}_{\mathbf{v}}\mathbf{u} = 0 \Rightarrow \mathbf{u}$ and $\mathbf{v}$ are orthogonal.

62. Let $\mathbf{u} = \langle u_1, u_2 \rangle$ and $\mathbf{v} = \langle v_1, v_2 \rangle$.

$\mathbf{u} - \mathbf{v} = \langle u_1 - v_1, u_2 - v_2 \rangle$

$\|\mathbf{u} - \mathbf{v}\|^2 = (u_1 - v_1)^2 + (u_2 - v_2)^2$

$$= u_1^2 - 2u_1v_1 + v_1^2 + u_2^2 - 2u_2v_2 + v_2^2$$

$$= u_1^2 + u_2^2 + v_1^2 + v_2^2 - 2u_1v_1 - 2u_2v_2$$

$$= \|\mathbf{u}\|^2 + \|\mathbf{v}\|^2 - 2(u_1v_1 + u_2v_2)$$

$$= \|\mathbf{u}\|^2 + \|\mathbf{v}\|^2 - 2\mathbf{u} \cdot \mathbf{v}$$

64. Let $\mathbf{u} \cdot \mathbf{v} = 0$ and $\mathbf{u} \cdot \mathbf{w} = 0$.

Then, $\mathbf{u} \cdot (c\mathbf{v} + d\mathbf{w}) = \mathbf{u} \cdot c\mathbf{v} + \mathbf{u} \cdot d\mathbf{w}$

$$= c\mathbf{u} \cdot \mathbf{v} + d\mathbf{u} \cdot \mathbf{w}$$

$$= c(0) + d(0)$$

$$= 0.$$

Thus for all scalars c and d, $\mathbf{u}$ is orthogonal to $c\mathbf{v} + d\mathbf{w}$.

66. $\sin 2x + \sqrt{2} \cos x = 0$

$2 \sin x \cos x + \sqrt{2} \cos x = 0$

$\cos x(2 \sin x + \sqrt{2}) = 0$

$\cos x = 0$ $2 \sin x + \sqrt{2} = 0$

$$x = \frac{\pi}{2}, \frac{3\pi}{2} \qquad \sin x = -\frac{\sqrt{2}}{2}$$

$$x = \frac{5\pi}{4}, \frac{7\pi}{4}$$

$$x = \frac{\pi}{2}, \frac{5\pi}{4}, \frac{3\pi}{2}, \frac{7\pi}{4}$$

68. $\cos 2x - 3 \sin x = 2$

$1 - 2\sin^2 x - 3 \sin x - 2 = 0$

$2 \sin^2 x + 3 \sin x + 1 = 0$

$(2 \sin x + 1)(\sin x + 1) = 0$

$2 \sin x + 1 = 0$ $\sin x + 1 = 0$

$$\sin x = -\frac{1}{2} \qquad\qquad \sin x = -1$$

$$x = \frac{7\pi}{6}, \frac{11\pi}{6} \qquad\qquad x = \frac{3\pi}{2}$$

$$x = \frac{7\pi}{6}, \frac{3\pi}{2}, \frac{11\pi}{6}$$

70. $\sin u = -\dfrac{12}{13},\ \cos u = \sqrt{1 - \left(-\dfrac{12}{13}\right)^2} = \dfrac{5}{13}$

$\cos v = \dfrac{24}{25},\ \sin v = -\sqrt{1 - \left(\dfrac{24}{25}\right)^2} = -\dfrac{7}{25}$

$\sin(u + v) = \sin u \cos v + \cos u \sin v$

$\qquad = \left(-\dfrac{12}{13}\right)\left(\dfrac{24}{25}\right) + \left(\dfrac{5}{13}\right)\left(-\dfrac{7}{25}\right)$

$\qquad = -\dfrac{323}{325}$

72. $\sin u = -\dfrac{12}{13},\ \cos u = \dfrac{5}{13},\ \tan u = -\dfrac{12}{5}$

$\cos v = \dfrac{24}{25},\ \sin v = -\dfrac{7}{25},\ \tan v = -\dfrac{7}{24}$

$\tan(u - v) = \dfrac{\tan u - \tan v}{1 + \tan u \tan v}$

$\qquad = \dfrac{\left(-\dfrac{12}{5}\right) - \left(-\dfrac{7}{24}\right)}{1 + \left(-\dfrac{12}{5}\right)\left(-\dfrac{7}{24}\right)} = \dfrac{-\dfrac{253}{120}}{\dfrac{17}{10}}$

$\qquad = -\dfrac{253}{204}$

Section 6.5   Trigonometric Form of a Complex Number

Solutions to Even-Numbered Exercises

2. $|-7| = \sqrt{(-7)^2 + 0^2} = \sqrt{49} = 7$

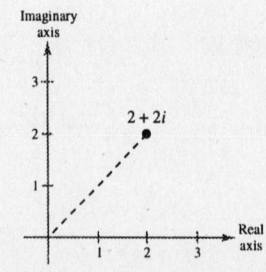

4. $|5 - 12i| = \sqrt{5^2 + (-12)^2}$

$\qquad = \sqrt{169} = 13$

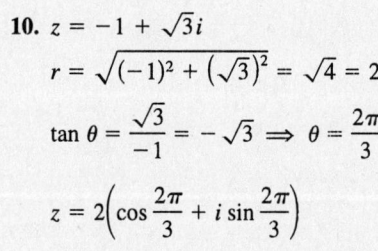

6. $|-8 + 3i| = \sqrt{(-8)^2 + (3)^2}$

$\qquad = \sqrt{73}$

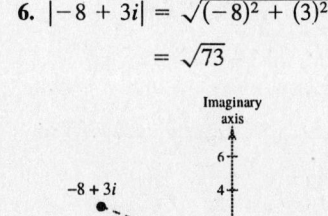

8. $z = -2$

$r = \sqrt{(-2)^2 + 0^2} = \sqrt{4} = 2$

$\tan \theta = \dfrac{0}{-2} \Rightarrow \theta = \pi$

$z = 2(\cos \pi + i \sin \pi)$

10. $z = -1 + \sqrt{3}i$

$r = \sqrt{(-1)^2 + \left(\sqrt{3}\right)^2} = \sqrt{4} = 2$

$\tan \theta = \dfrac{\sqrt{3}}{-1} = -\sqrt{3} \Rightarrow \theta = \dfrac{2\pi}{3}$

$z = 2\left(\cos \dfrac{2\pi}{3} + i \sin \dfrac{2\pi}{3}\right)$

12. $z = 2 + 2i$

$r = \sqrt{2^2 + 2^2} = \sqrt{8} = 2\sqrt{2}$

$\tan \theta = \dfrac{2}{2} = 1 \Rightarrow \theta = \dfrac{\pi}{4}$

$z = 2\sqrt{2}\left(\cos \dfrac{\pi}{4} + i \sin \dfrac{\pi}{4}\right)$

14. $z = 4 - 4\sqrt{3}i$

$r = \sqrt{4^2 + \left(-4\sqrt{3}\right)^2} = 8$

$\tan \theta = \dfrac{-4\sqrt{3}}{4} = -\sqrt{3} \Longrightarrow \theta = \dfrac{5\pi}{3}$

$z = 8\left(\cos \dfrac{5\pi}{3} + i \sin \dfrac{5\pi}{3}\right)$

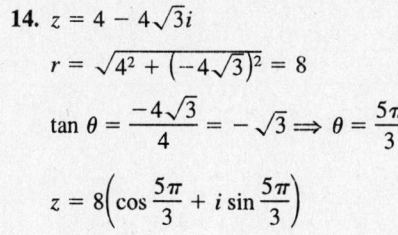
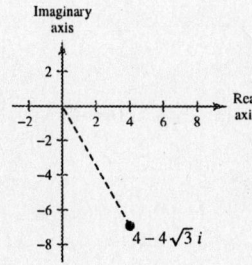

16. $z = \dfrac{5}{2}\left(\sqrt{3} - i\right)$

$r = \sqrt{\left(\dfrac{5}{2}\sqrt{3}\right)^2 + \left(\dfrac{5}{2}(-1)\right)^2} = \sqrt{\dfrac{100}{4}} = \sqrt{25} = 5$

$\tan \theta = \dfrac{-1}{\sqrt{3}} = \dfrac{-\sqrt{3}}{3} \Longrightarrow \theta = \dfrac{11\pi}{6}$

$z = 5\left(\cos \dfrac{11\pi}{6} + i \sin \dfrac{11\pi}{6}\right)$

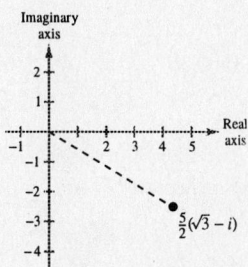

18. $z = 4i$

$r = \sqrt{0^2 + 4^2} = \sqrt{16^2} = 4$

$\tan \theta = \dfrac{4}{0}, \text{ undefined} \Longrightarrow \theta = \dfrac{\pi}{2}$

$z = 4\left(\cos \dfrac{\pi}{2} + i \sin \dfrac{\pi}{2}\right)$

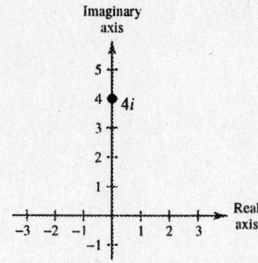

20. $z = 3 - i$

$r = \sqrt{(3)^2 + (-1)^2} = \sqrt{10}$

$\tan \theta = \dfrac{-1}{3} = \theta \approx -18.4°$

$z = \sqrt{10}(\cos(-18.4°) + i \sin(-18.4°))$

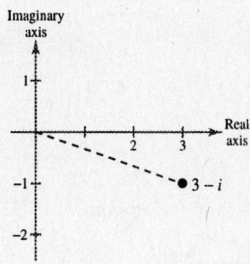

22. $z = 4$

$r = \sqrt{4^2 + 0^2} = \sqrt{16^2} = 4$

$\tan \theta = \dfrac{0}{4} = 0 \Longrightarrow \theta = 0$

$z = 4(\cos 0 + i \sin 0)$

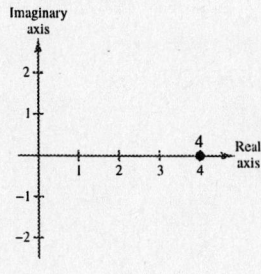

24. $z = 2\sqrt{2} - i$

$r = \sqrt{\left(2\sqrt{2}\right)^2 + (-1)^2} = \sqrt{9} = 3$

$\tan \theta = \dfrac{-1}{2\sqrt{2}} = -\dfrac{\sqrt{2}}{4} \Longrightarrow \theta \approx (-19.5°)$

$z = 3(\cos(-19.5°) + i \sin(-19.5°))$

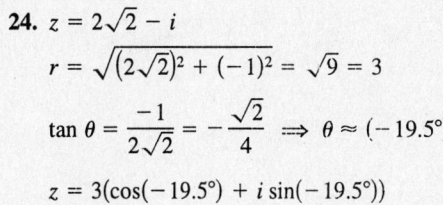
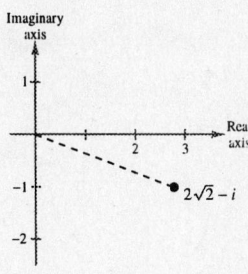

26. $z = 1 + 3i$

$r = \sqrt{1^2 + 3^2} = \sqrt{10}$

$\tan \theta = \frac{3}{1} = 3 \implies \theta \approx 71.6°$

$z \approx \sqrt{10}(\cos 71.6° + i \sin 71.6°)$

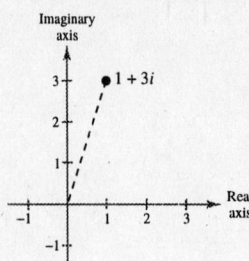

28. $8 + 3i \approx 8.54 \angle 0.36$

$= 8.54(\cos 0.36 + i \sin 0.36)$

30. $-5 - i \approx 5.10 \angle 3.34$

$= 5.10(\cos 3.34 + i \sin 3.34)$

32. $4\sqrt{5} - 4i \approx 9.80 \angle 5.86$

$= 9.80(\cos 5.86 + i \sin 5.86)$

34. $-9 - 2\sqrt{10}i \approx 11.0 \angle 3.75$

$= 11.0(\cos 3.75 + i \sin 3.75)$

36. $5(\cos 135° + i \sin 135°) = 5\left[-\frac{\sqrt{2}}{2} + i\left(\frac{\sqrt{2}}{2}\right) \right]$

$= -\frac{5\sqrt{2}}{2} + \frac{5\sqrt{2}}{2}i$

38. $\frac{1}{4}(\cos 225° + i \sin 225°) = \frac{1}{4}\left(-\frac{\sqrt{2}}{2} + i\left(-\frac{\sqrt{2}}{2}\right) \right)$

$= -\frac{\sqrt{2}}{8} - i\frac{\sqrt{2}}{8}$

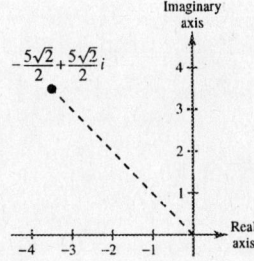

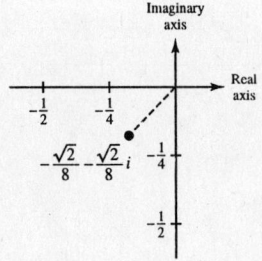

40. $6\left(\cos \frac{5\pi}{12} + i \sin \frac{5\pi}{12} \right) \approx 1.5529 + i\,5.7956$

42. $7(\cos 0° + i \sin 0°) = 7$

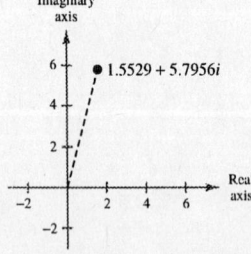

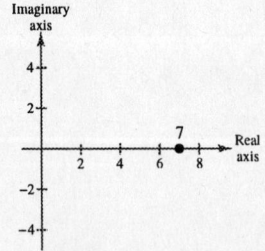

44. $6[\cos(230° \, 30') + i \sin(230° \, 30')] \approx -3.816 - 4.630i$

$\approx -3.8165 - 4.6297i$

46. $10\left(\cos \frac{2\pi}{5} + i \sin \frac{2\pi}{5} \right) \approx 3.09 + 9.51i$

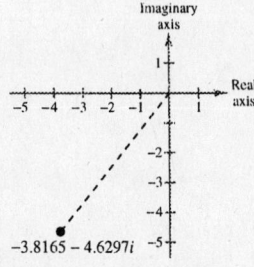

48. $9(\cos 58° + i \sin 58°) \approx 4.77 + 7.63i$

50. $\left[\dfrac{3}{4}\left(\cos\dfrac{\pi}{3} + i\sin\dfrac{\pi}{3}\right)\right]\left[4\left(\cos\dfrac{3\pi}{4} + i\sin\dfrac{3\pi}{4}\right)\right] = \left(\dfrac{3}{4}\right)(4)\left[\cos\left(\dfrac{\pi}{3} + \dfrac{3\pi}{4}\right) + i\sin\left(\dfrac{\pi}{3} + \dfrac{3\pi}{4}\right)\right]$

$$= 3\left(\cos\dfrac{13\pi}{12} + i\sin\dfrac{13\pi}{12}\right)$$

52. $[0.5(\cos 100° + i \sin 100°)][0.8(\cos 300° + i \sin 300°)] = (0.5)(0.8)[\cos(100° + 300°) + i \sin(100° + 300°)]$

$$= 0.4(\cos 400° + i \sin 400°)$$

$$= 0.4(\cos 40° + i \sin 40°)$$

54. $(\cos 5° + i \sin 5°)(\cos 20° + i \sin 20°) = \cos(5° + 20°) + i \sin(5° + 20°)$

$$= \cos 25° + i \sin 25°$$

56. $\dfrac{2(\cos 120° + i \sin 120°)}{4(\cos 40° + i \sin 40°)} = \dfrac{2}{4}[\cos(120° - 40°) + i \sin(120° - 40°)]$

$$= \dfrac{1}{2}(\cos 80° + i \sin 80°)$$

58. $\dfrac{5[\cos(4.3) + i\sin(4.3)]}{4[\cos(2.1) + i\sin(2.1)]} = \dfrac{5}{4}[\cos(4.3 - 2.1) + i\sin(4.3 - 2.1)]$

$$= \dfrac{5}{4}[\cos(2.2) + i\sin(2.2)]$$

60. $\dfrac{6[\cos 40° + i\sin 40°]}{7[\cos 100° + i\sin 100°]} = \dfrac{6}{7}[\cos(40° - 100°) + i\sin(40° - 100°)]$

$$= \dfrac{6}{7}[\cos 300° + i\sin 300°]$$

62. (a) $\sqrt{3} + i = 2(\cos 30° + i \sin 30°)$

$\quad\quad 1 + i = \sqrt{2}(\cos 45° + i \sin 45°)$

(b) $\left(\sqrt{3} + i\right)(1 + i) = [2(\cos 30° + i \sin 30°)]\left[\sqrt{2}(\cos 45° + i \sin 45°)\right]$

$$= 2\sqrt{2}(\cos 75° + i \sin 75°)$$

$$= 2\sqrt{2}\left[\left(\dfrac{\sqrt{6} - \sqrt{2}}{4}\right) + \left(\dfrac{\sqrt{6} + \sqrt{2}}{4}\right)i\right]$$

$$= \left(\sqrt{3} - 1\right) + \left(\sqrt{3} + 1\right)i$$

(c) $\left(\sqrt{3} + i\right)(1 + i) = \sqrt{3} + \left(\sqrt{3} + 1\right)i + i^2 = \left(\sqrt{3} - 1\right) + \left(\sqrt{3} + 1\right)i$

64. (a) $4 = 4(\cos 0 + i \sin 0)$

$$1 - \sqrt{3}i = 2\left(\cos\left(-\frac{\pi}{3}\right) + i \sin\left(\frac{-\pi}{3}\right)\right)$$

(b) $4\left(1 - \sqrt{3}i\right) = 8\left(\cos\left(-\frac{\pi}{3}\right) + i \sin\left(-\frac{\pi}{3}\right)\right)$

$$= 8\left(\frac{1}{2} + i\left(-\frac{\sqrt{3}}{2}\right)\right)$$

$$= 4 - 4\sqrt{3}i$$

(c) $4\left(1 - \sqrt{3}i\right) = 4 - 4\sqrt{3}i$

66. (a) $1 + \sqrt{3}i = 2\left(\cos\frac{\pi}{3} + i \sin\frac{\pi}{3}\right)$

$$6 - 3i \approx 3\sqrt{5}[\cos(-0.464) + i \sin(-0.464)]$$

(b) $\dfrac{1 + \sqrt{3}i}{6 - 3i} \approx \dfrac{2}{3\sqrt{5}}\left[\cos\left(\frac{\pi}{3} + 0.464\right) + i \sin\left(\frac{\pi}{3} + 0.464\right)\right]$

$$\approx \frac{2\sqrt{5}}{15}[\cos 1.51 + i \sin 1.51]$$

$$\approx 0.018 + 0.298i$$

(c) $\dfrac{1 + \sqrt{3}i}{6 - 3i} \cdot \dfrac{6 + 3i}{6 + 3i} = \dfrac{\left(6 - 3\sqrt{3}\right) + i\left(3 + 6\sqrt{3}\right)}{45}$

$$= \frac{2 - \sqrt{3}}{15} + i\frac{1 + 2\sqrt{3}}{15}$$

$$\approx 0.018 + 0.298i$$

68. (a) $4i = 4(\cos 90° + i \sin 90°)$

$$-4 + 2i = 2\sqrt{5}(\cos 153.4° + i \sin 153.4°)$$

(b) $\dfrac{4i}{-4 + 2i} = \dfrac{4(\cos 90° + i \sin 90°)}{2\sqrt{5}(\cos 153.4° + i \sin 153.4°)}$

$$= \frac{2\sqrt{5}}{5}(\cos 296.6° + i \sin 296.6°)$$

$$\approx 0.400 - 0.800i$$

(c) $\dfrac{4i}{-4 + 2i} = \dfrac{4i}{-4 + 2i} \cdot \dfrac{-4 - i}{-4 - 2i}$

$$= \frac{8 - 16i}{20}$$

$$= \frac{2}{5} - \frac{4}{5}i$$

$$= 0.400 - 0.800i$$

70. $|z| = 3$

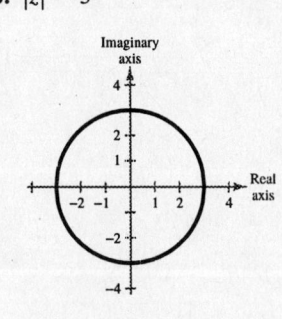

72. $\theta = \dfrac{5\pi}{4}$

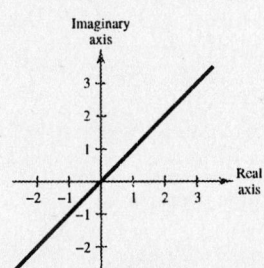

74. $(2 + 2i)^6 = \left[2\sqrt{2}\left(\cos \dfrac{\pi}{4} + i \sin \dfrac{\pi}{4} \right) \right]^6$

$\qquad = \left(2\sqrt{2} \right)^6 \left(\cos \dfrac{6\pi}{4} + i \sin \dfrac{6\pi}{4} \right)$

$\qquad = 512 \left(\cos \dfrac{3\pi}{2} + i \sin \dfrac{3\pi}{2} \right)$

$\qquad = -512i$

76. $(3 - 2i)^8 = \left[\sqrt{13}\left(\cos\left(-\arctan\left(\tfrac{2}{3}\right)\right) + i \sin\left(-\arctan\left(\tfrac{2}{3}\right)\right) \right) \right]^8$

$\qquad = \left(\sqrt{13} \right)^8 \left[\cos\left(-8\arctan\left(\tfrac{2}{3}\right)\right) + i \sin\left(-8\arctan\left(\tfrac{2}{3}\right)\right) \right]$

$\qquad = -239 + 28{,}560i$

78. $4\left(1 - \sqrt{3}i\right)^3 = 4\left[2\left(\cos \dfrac{5\pi}{3} + i \sin \dfrac{5\pi}{3} \right) \right]^3$

$\qquad = 4\left[2^3\left(\cos 5\pi + i \sin 5\pi \right) \right]$

$\qquad = 32(-1)$

$\qquad = -32$

80. $[3(\cos 150° + i \sin 150°)]^4 = 3^4(\cos 600° + i \sin 600°)$

$\qquad = 81(\cos 240° + i \sin 240°)$

$\qquad = 81(-\cos 60° - i \sin 60°)$

$\qquad = -\dfrac{81}{2} - \dfrac{81\sqrt{3}}{2}i$

82. $\left[2\left(\cos \dfrac{\pi}{2} + i \sin \dfrac{\pi}{2} \right) \right]^8 = 2^8(\cos 4\pi + i \sin 4\pi)$

$\qquad = 256(\cos 0 + i \sin 0)$

$\qquad = 256$

84. $(\cos 0 + i \sin 0)^{20} = \cos 0 + i \sin 0$

$\qquad = 1$

86. $\left(\sqrt{5} - 4i \right)^3 = -43\sqrt{5} + 4i$

88. $[2(\cos 10° + i \sin 10°)]^8 = 256(\cos 80° + i \sin 80°)$

$\qquad \approx 44.4539 + 252.1108i$

90. $\left[2\left(\cos \dfrac{\pi}{8} + i \sin \dfrac{\pi}{8} \right) \right]^6 = 64\left(\cos \dfrac{3\pi}{4} + i \sin \dfrac{3\pi}{4} \right)$

$\qquad = -32\sqrt{2} + 32\sqrt{2}i$

92. (a) Square roots of $16(\cos 60° + i \sin 60°)$:

$\qquad \sqrt{16}\left[\cos\left(\dfrac{60° + k\,360°}{2} \right) + i \sin\left(\dfrac{60° + k\,360°}{2} \right) \right]$

$\qquad k = 0, 1$

$\qquad k = 0: \ 4(\cos 30° + i \sin 30°)$

$\qquad k = 1: \ 2(\cos 210° + i \sin 210°)$

(b)

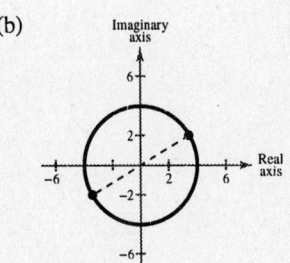

(c) $2\sqrt{3} + 2i, \ -2\sqrt{3} - 2i$

94. (a) Fifth roots of $32\left(\cos\dfrac{5\pi}{6} + i\sin\dfrac{5\pi}{6}\right)$:

$$\sqrt[5]{32}\left[\cos\left(\dfrac{\dfrac{5\pi}{6} + 2k\pi}{5}\right) + i\sin\left(\dfrac{\dfrac{5\pi}{6} + 2k\pi}{5}\right)\right]$$

$k = 0, 1, 2, 3, 4$

$k = 0$: $2\left(\cos\dfrac{\pi}{6} + i\sin\dfrac{\pi}{6}\right)$

$k = 1$: $2\left(\cos\dfrac{17\pi}{30} + i\sin\dfrac{17\pi}{30}\right)$

$k = 2$: $2\left(\cos\dfrac{29\pi}{30} + i\sin\dfrac{29\pi}{30}\right)$

$k = 3$: $2\left(\cos\dfrac{41\pi}{30} + i\sin\dfrac{41\pi}{30}\right)$

$k = 4$: $2\left(\cos\dfrac{53\pi}{30} + i\sin\dfrac{53\pi}{30}\right)$

(b)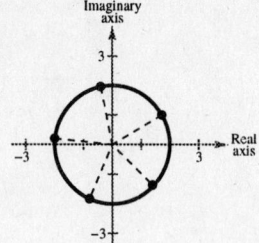

(c) $\sqrt{3} + i$, $-0.4158 + 1.9563i$, $-1.9890 + 0.2091i$, $-0.8135 - 1.8271i$, $1.4863 - 1.3383i$

96. (a) Fourth roots of $625i = 625\left(\cos\dfrac{\pi}{2} + i\sin\dfrac{\pi}{2}\right)$:

$$\sqrt[4]{625}\left[\cos\left(\dfrac{\dfrac{\pi}{2} + 2k\pi}{4}\right) + i\sin\left(\dfrac{\dfrac{\pi}{2} + 2k\pi}{2}\right)\right]$$

$k = 0, 1, 2, 3$

$k = 0$: $5\left(\cos\dfrac{\pi}{8} + i\sin\dfrac{\pi}{8}\right)$

$k = 1$: $5\left(\cos\dfrac{5\pi}{8} + i\sin\dfrac{5\pi}{8}\right)$

$k = 2$: $5\left(\cos\dfrac{9\pi}{8} + i\sin\dfrac{9\pi}{8}\right)$

$k = 3$: $5\left(\cos\dfrac{13\pi}{8} + i\sin\dfrac{13\pi}{8}\right)$

(b)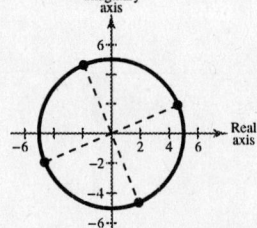

(c) $4.6194 + 1.9134i$, $-1.9134 + 4.6194i$, $-4.6194 - 1.9134i$, $1.9134 - 4.6194i$

98. (a) Cube roots of $-4\sqrt{2}(1-i) = 8\left(\cos\dfrac{3\pi}{4} + i\sin\dfrac{3\pi}{4}\right)$:

$$\sqrt[3]{8}\left[\cos\left(\dfrac{\dfrac{3\pi}{4} + 2k\pi}{3}\right) + i\sin\left(\dfrac{\dfrac{3\pi}{4} + 2k\pi}{3}\right)\right]$$

$k = 0, 1, 2$

$k = 0: \ 2\left(\cos\dfrac{\pi}{4} + i\sin\dfrac{\pi}{4}\right)$

$k = 1: \ 2\left(\cos\dfrac{11\pi}{12} + i\sin\dfrac{11\pi}{12}\right)$

$k = 2: \ 2\left(\cos\dfrac{19\pi}{12} + i\sin\dfrac{19\pi}{12}\right)$

(c) $1.414 + 1.414i, \ -1.932 + 0.5176i, \ 0.5176 - 1.9319i$

(b)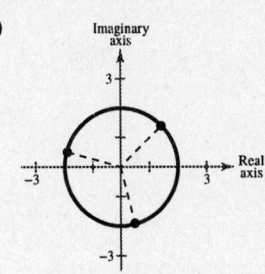

100. (a) Fourth roots of $i = \cos\dfrac{\pi}{2} + i\sin\dfrac{\pi}{2}$:

$$\sqrt[4]{1}\left[\cos\left(\dfrac{\dfrac{\pi}{2} + 2k\pi}{4}\right) + i\sin\left(\dfrac{\dfrac{\pi}{2} + 2k\pi}{4}\right)\right]$$

$k = 0, 1, 2, 3$

$k = 0: \ \cos\dfrac{\pi}{8} + i\sin\dfrac{\pi}{8}$

$k = 1: \ \cos\dfrac{5\pi}{8} + i\sin\dfrac{5\pi}{8}$

$k = 2: \ \cos\dfrac{9\pi}{8} + i\sin\dfrac{9\pi}{8}$

$k = 3: \ \cos\dfrac{13\pi}{8} + i\sin\dfrac{13\pi}{8}$

(c) $0.9239 + 0.3827i, \ -0.3827 + 0.9239i,$
$-0.9239 - 0.3827i, \ 0.3827 - 0.9239i$

(b)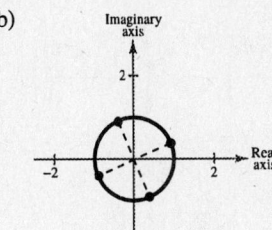

102. (a) Cube roots of $1000 = 1000(\cos 0 + i\sin 0)$:

$$\sqrt[3]{1000}\left(\cos\dfrac{2k\pi}{3} + i\sin\dfrac{2k\pi}{3}\right)$$

$k = 0, 1, 2$

$k = 0: \ 10(\cos 0 + i\sin 0)$

$k = 1: \ 10\left(\cos\dfrac{2\pi}{3} + i\sin\dfrac{2\pi}{3}\right)$

$k = 2: \ 10\left(\cos\dfrac{4\pi}{3} + i\sin\dfrac{4\pi}{3}\right)$

(c) $10, \ -5 + 5\sqrt{3}i, \ -5 - 5\sqrt{3}i$

(b)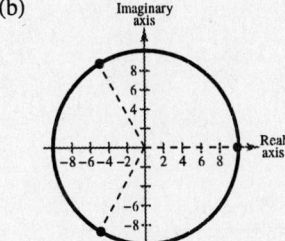

104. (a) Fourth roots of $-4 = 4(\cos \pi + i \sin \pi)$:

$$\sqrt[4]{4}\left[\cos\left(\frac{\pi + 2k\pi}{4}\right) + i \sin\left(\frac{\pi + 2k\pi}{4}\right)\right]$$

$k = 0, 1, 2, 3$

$k = 0$: $\sqrt{2}\left(\cos \frac{\pi}{4} + i \sin \frac{\pi}{4}\right)$

$k = 1$: $\sqrt{2}\left(\cos \frac{3\pi}{4} + i \sin \frac{3\pi}{4}\right)$

$k = 2$: $\sqrt{2}\left(\cos \frac{5\pi}{4} + i \sin \frac{5\pi}{4}\right)$

$k = 3$: $\sqrt{2}\left(\cos \frac{7\pi}{4} + i \sin \frac{7\pi}{4}\right)$

(b)

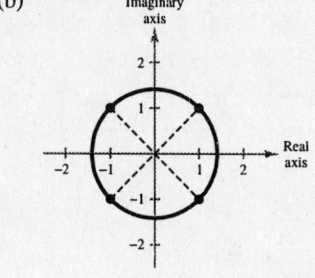

(c) $1 + i, -1 + i, -1 - i, 1 - i$

106. (a) Sixth roots of $64i = 64\left(\cos \frac{\pi}{2} + i \sin \frac{\pi}{2}\right)$:

$$\sqrt[6]{64}\left[\cos\left(\frac{\frac{\pi}{2} + 2k\pi}{6}\right) + i \sin\left(\frac{\frac{\pi}{2} + 2k\pi}{6}\right)\right]$$

$k = 0, 1, 2, 3, 4, 5$

$k = 0$: $2\left(\cos \frac{\pi}{12} + i \sin \frac{\pi}{12}\right)$

$k = 1$: $2\left(\cos \frac{5\pi}{12} + i \sin \frac{5\pi}{12}\right)$

$k = 2$: $2\left(\cos \frac{3\pi}{4} + i \sin \frac{3\pi}{4}\right)$

$k = 3$: $2\left(\cos \frac{13\pi}{12} + i \sin \frac{13\pi}{12}\right)$

$k = 4$: $2\left(\cos \frac{17\pi}{12} + i \sin \frac{17\pi}{12}\right)$

$k = 5$: $2\left(\cos \frac{7\pi}{4} + i \sin \frac{7\pi}{4}\right)$

(b)

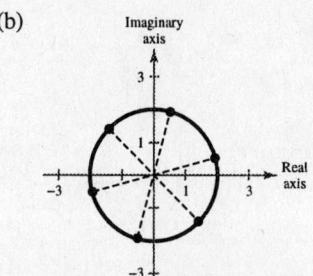

(c) $1.9319 + 0.5176i, 0.5176 + 1.9319i, -\sqrt{2} + \sqrt{2}i,$
$-1.9319 - 0.5176i, -0.5176 - 1.9319i, \sqrt{2} - \sqrt{2}i$

108. $x^3 + 1 = 0$

$x^3 = -1$

The solutions are the cube roots of
$-1 = \cos \pi + i \sin \pi$.

$$\cos\left(\frac{\pi + 2k\pi}{3}\right) + i \sin\left(\frac{\pi + 2k\pi}{3}\right)$$

$k = 0, 1, 2$

$k = 0$: $\cos \frac{\pi}{3} + i \sin \frac{\pi}{3} = \frac{1}{2} + \frac{\sqrt{3}}{2}i$

$k = 1$: $\cos \pi + i \sin \pi = -1$

$k = 2$: $\cos \frac{5\pi}{3} + i \sin \frac{5\pi}{3} = \frac{1}{2} - \frac{\sqrt{3}}{2}i$

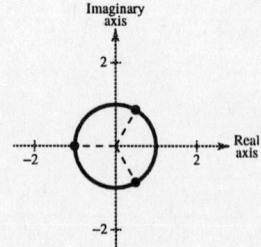

110. $x^3 - 27 = 0$

$$x^3 = 27$$

The solutions are the cube roots of
$27 = 27(\cos 0 + i \sin 0)$:

$$\sqrt[3]{27}\left[\cos\left(\frac{2k\pi}{3}\right) + i\sin\left(\frac{2k\pi}{3}\right)\right]$$

$k = 0, 1, 2$

$k = 0$: $3(\cos 0 + i \sin 0) = 3$

$k = 1$: $3\left(\cos\frac{2\pi}{3} + i\sin\frac{2\pi}{3}\right) = -\frac{3}{2} + \frac{3\sqrt{3}}{2}$

$k = 2$: $3\left(\cos\frac{4\pi}{3} + i\sin\frac{4\pi}{3}\right) = -\frac{3}{2} - \frac{3\sqrt{3}}{2}$

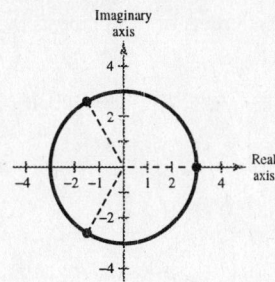

112. $x^6 - 64i = 0$

$$x^6 = 64i$$

The solutions are the sixth roots of $64i$:

$$\sqrt[6]{64}\left[\cos\left(\frac{\frac{\pi}{2} + 2k\pi}{6}\right) + i\sin\left(\frac{\frac{\pi}{2} + 2k\pi}{6}\right)\right]$$

$k = 0, 1, 2, 3, 4, 5$

$k = 0$: $2\left(\cos\frac{\pi}{12} + i\sin\frac{\pi}{12}\right) \approx 1.932 + 0.5176i$

$k = 1$: $2\left(\cos\frac{5\pi}{12} + i\sin\frac{5\pi}{12}\right) \approx 0.5176 + 1.932i$

$k = 2$: $2\left(\cos\frac{3\pi}{4} + i\sin\frac{3\pi}{4}\right) \approx -1.414 + 1.414i$

$k = 3$: $2\left(\cos\frac{13\pi}{12} + i\sin\frac{13\pi}{12}\right) \approx -1.932 - 0.5176i$

$k = 4$: $2\left(\cos\frac{17\pi}{12} + i\sin\frac{17\pi}{12}\right) \approx -0.5176 - 1.932i$

$k = 5$: $2\left(\cos\frac{7\pi}{4} + i\sin\frac{7\pi}{4}\right) \approx 1.414 - 1.414i$

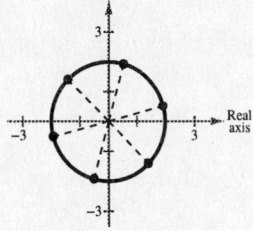

114. $x^4 + (1 + i) = 0$

$$x^4 = -1 - i = \sqrt{2}(\cos 225° + i \sin 225°)$$

The solutions are the fourth roots of $-1 - i$:

$$\sqrt[4]{\sqrt{2}}\left[\cos\left(\frac{225° + 360°k}{4}\right) + i\sin\left(\frac{225° + 360°k}{4}\right)\right]$$

$k = 0, 1, 2, 3$

$k = 0$: $\sqrt[8]{2}(\cos 56.25° + i \sin 56.25°) \approx 0.6059 + 0.9067i$

$k = 1$: $\sqrt[8]{2}(\cos 146.25° + i \sin 146.25°) \approx -0.9067 + 0.6059i$

$k = 2$: $\sqrt[8]{2}(\cos 236.25° + i \sin 236.25°) \approx -0.6059 - 0.9067i$

$k = 3$: $\sqrt[8]{2}(\cos 326.25° + i \sin 326.25°) \approx 0.9067 - 0.6059i$

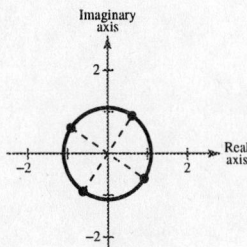

116. True, because successive nth roots have arguments that differ by $2\pi/n$.

118. False. The complex number must be converted to trigonometric form before applying DeMoivre's Theorem.

$$\left(4 + \sqrt{6}i\right)^8 = \left[\sqrt{22}\left(\cos\left(\arctan\frac{\sqrt{6}}{4}\right) + i\sin\left(\arctan\frac{\sqrt{6}}{4}\right)\right)\right]^8$$

120. $\bar{z} = r[\cos(-\theta) + i\sin(-\theta)]$

$\quad = r[\cos\theta + -i\sin\theta]$

$\quad = r\cos\theta - ir\sin\theta$

which is the complex conjugate of
$r(\cos\theta + i\sin\theta) = r\cos\theta + ir\sin\theta.$

122. $\quad z = r(\cos\theta + i\sin\theta)$

$\quad -z = -r(\cos\theta + i\sin\theta)$

$\quad = r(-\cos\theta + -i\sin\theta)$

$\quad = r(\cos(\theta + \pi) + i\sin(\theta + \pi))$

124.
$$2^{-1/4}(1 - i) = 2^{-1/4}\left[\sqrt{2}\left(\cos\frac{7\pi}{4} + i\sin\frac{7\pi}{4}\right)\right]$$

$$= 2^{1/4}\left(\cos\frac{7\pi}{4} + i\sin\frac{7\pi}{4}\right)$$

$$\left[2^{1/4}\left(\cos\frac{7\pi}{4} + i\sin\frac{7\pi}{4}\right)\right]^4 = (2^{1/4})^4(\cos 7\pi + i\sin 7\pi)$$

$$= 2(\cos\pi + i\sin\pi)$$

$$= -2$$

126. (a) $3(\cos 45° + i\sin 45°)$

$\quad 3(\cos 135° + i\sin 135°)$

$\quad 3(\cos 225° + i\sin 225°)$

$\quad 3(\cos 315° + i\sin 315°)$

(b) These are the fourth roots of -81.

(c) The fourth roots of -81:

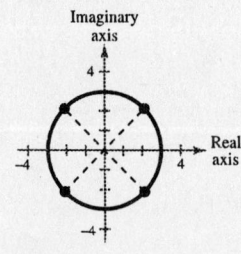

128. $B = 66°, a = 33.5$

$\quad A = 90° - 66° = 24°$

$\quad b = \dfrac{a\sin B}{\sin A} = \dfrac{(33.5)\sin 66°}{\sin 24°} \approx 75.24$

$\quad c = \dfrac{a\sin C}{\sin A} = \dfrac{(33.5)\sin 90°}{\sin 24°} \approx 82.36$

130. $B = 6°, b = 211.2$

$\quad A = 90° - 6° = 84°$

$\quad a = \dfrac{b\sin A}{\sin B} = \dfrac{(211.2)\sin 84°}{\sin 6°} \approx 2009.43$

$\quad c = \dfrac{b\sin C}{\sin B} = \dfrac{(211.2)\sin 90°}{\sin 6°} \approx 2020.50$

132. $B = 81° 30', c = 6.8$

$\quad A = 90° - 81° 30' = 8° 30'$

$\quad a = \dfrac{c\sin A}{\sin C} = \dfrac{(6.8)\sin 8° 30'}{1} \approx 1.01$

$\quad b = \dfrac{c\sin B}{\sin C} = \dfrac{(6.8)\sin 81° 30'}{1} \approx 6.73$

134. $d = \dfrac{1}{8} \cos 12\pi t$

Maximum displacement: $\dfrac{1}{8}$

$d = 0$ when $12\pi t = \dfrac{\pi}{2}$, or $t = \dfrac{1}{24}$

136. $d = \dfrac{1}{12} \sin 60\pi t$

Maximum displacement: $\dfrac{1}{12}$

$d = 0$ when $60\pi t = 0$, or $t = 0$

Review Exercises for Chapter 6

Solutions to Even-Numbered Exercises

2. Given: $A = 22°, B = 121°, a = 17$

$C = 180 - A - B = 37°$

$b = \dfrac{a \sin B}{\sin A} = \dfrac{17 \sin 121°}{\sin 22°} \approx 38.90$

$c = \dfrac{a \sin C}{\sin A} = \dfrac{17 \sin 37°}{\sin 22°} \approx 27.31$

4. Given: $B = 10°, C - = 20°, c = 33$

$A = 180° - B - C = 150°$

$a = \dfrac{c \sin A}{\sin C} = \dfrac{33 \sin 150°}{\sin 20°} \approx 48.24$

$b = \dfrac{c \sin B}{\sin C} = \dfrac{33 \sin 10°}{\sin 20°} \approx 16.75$

6. Given: $A = 95°, B = 45°, c = 104.8$

$C = 180° - A - B = 40°$

$a = \dfrac{c \sin A}{\sin C} = \dfrac{104.8 \sin 95°}{\sin 40°} \approx 162.42$

$b = \dfrac{c \sin B}{\sin C} = \dfrac{104.8 \sin 45°}{\sin 40°} \approx 115.29$

8. Given: $B = 64°, C = 36°, a = 367$

$A = 180° - B - C = 80°$

$b = \dfrac{a \sin B}{\sin A} = \dfrac{367 \sin 64°}{\sin 80°} \approx 334.95$

$c = \dfrac{a \sin C}{\sin A} = \dfrac{367 \sin 36°}{\sin 80°} \approx 219.04$

10. Given: $B = 150°, a = 10, b = 3$

$\sin A = \dfrac{a \sin B}{b} = \dfrac{10 \sin 150°}{3} \approx 1.67 > 1$

No solution

12. Given: $B = 25°, \ a = 6.2, \ b = 4$

$\sin A = \dfrac{a \sin B}{b} \approx 0.6551 \implies A \approx 40.9°$ or $139.1°$

Case 1: $A \approx 40.9°$

$C \approx 180° - 25° - 40.9° = 114.1°$

$c \approx 8.6$

Case 2: $A \approx 139.1°$

$C \approx 180° - 25° - 139.1° = 15.9°$

$c \approx 2.6$

14. $B = 80°, a = 4, c = 8$

Area $= \frac{1}{2}ac \sin B = \frac{1}{2}(4)(8)(0.9848) = 15.76$

16. $A = 11°, b = 22, c = 21$

Area $= \frac{1}{2}bc \sin A \approx \frac{1}{2}(22)(21)(0.1908)$

$= 44.08$

18. $16^2 = w^2 + 12^2 - 2w(12) \cos 140°$

$w^2 - (24 \cos 140°)w - 112 = 0 \implies w \approx 4.83$

20. Given: $a = 5, b = 8, c = 10$

$\cos C = \dfrac{a^2 + b^2 - c^2}{2ab} = 0.1375 \implies C \approx 97.90°$

$\cos B = \dfrac{a^2 + c^2 - b^2}{2ac} = 0.61 \implies B \approx 52.41°$

$A = 180° - B - C \approx 29.69°$

22. Given: $a = 2.5, b = 5.0, c = 4.5$

$$\cos B = \frac{a^2 + c^2 - b^2}{2ac} = 0.0667 \Rightarrow B \approx 86.18°$$

$$\cos C = \frac{a^2 + b^2 - c^2}{2ab} = 0.44 \Rightarrow C \approx 63.90°$$

$$A = 180° - B - C \approx 29.93°$$

24. Given: $B = 110°, a = 4, c = 4$

$$b = \sqrt{a^2 + c^2 - 2ac \cos B} \approx 6.55$$

$$A = C = \tfrac{1}{2}(180° - 110°) = 35°$$

26. Given: $C = 43°, a = 22.5, b = 31.4$

$$c = \sqrt{a^2 + b^2 - 2ab \cos C} \approx 21.42$$

$$\cos B = \frac{a^2 + c^2 - b^2}{2ac} \approx -0.02169 \Rightarrow B \approx 91.24°$$

$$A = 180 - B - C \approx 45.76°$$

28. Length of AC = $\sqrt{300^2 + 425^2 - 2(300)(425) \cos 115°}$

$$\approx 615.1 \text{ meters}$$

30. $a = 4, \; b = 5, \; c = 7$

$$s = \frac{a + b + c}{2} = \frac{4 + 5 + 7}{2} = 8$$

$$\text{Area} = \sqrt{s(s - a)(s - b)(s - c)}$$

$$= \sqrt{8(4)(3)(1)} \approx 9.798$$

32. $a = 12.3, b = 15.8, c = 3.7$

$$s = \frac{a + b + c}{2} = \frac{12.3 + 15.8 + 3.7}{2} = 15.9$$

$$\text{Area} = \sqrt{s(s - a)(s - b)(s - c)}$$

$$= \sqrt{15.9(3.6)(0.01)(12.2)}$$

$$= 8.3$$

34.

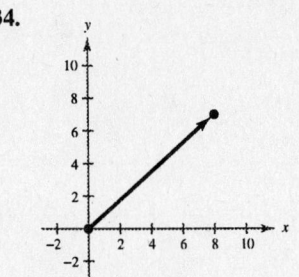

36.

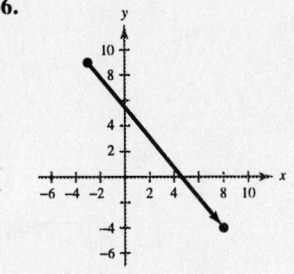

38. Initial point: $(-5, 4)$

Terminal point: $(2, -1)$

$$\mathbf{v} = \langle 2 - (-5), -1 - 4 \rangle = \langle 7, -5 \rangle$$

40. Initial point: $(0, 10)$

Terminal point: $(7, 3)$

$$\mathbf{v} = \langle 7 - 0, 3 - 10 \rangle = \langle 7, -7 \rangle$$

42. $\langle 8 \cos 120°, 8 \sin 120° \rangle = \left(-4, 4\sqrt{3} \right)$

44. $\mathbf{u} = 6\mathbf{i} - 5\mathbf{j}, \mathbf{v} = 10\mathbf{i} + 3\mathbf{j}$

$$2\mathbf{u} + \mathbf{v} = 2(6\mathbf{i} - 5\mathbf{j}) + (10\mathbf{i} + 3\mathbf{j})$$

$$= 22\mathbf{i} - 7\mathbf{j}$$

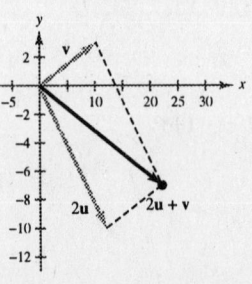

46. $\mathbf{v} = 10\mathbf{i} + 3\mathbf{j}$

$3\mathbf{v} = 3(10\mathbf{i} + 3\mathbf{j}) = 30\mathbf{i} + 9\mathbf{j}$

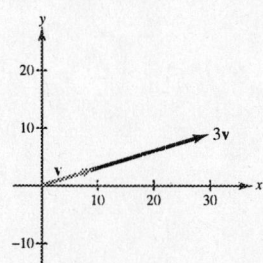

48. $\mathbf{u} = \langle -3, 4 \rangle = -3\mathbf{i} + 4\mathbf{j}$

50. Initial point: $(3, 4)$

Terminal point: $(9, 8)$

$\mathbf{u} = (9 - 3)\mathbf{i} + (8 - 4)\mathbf{j} = 6\mathbf{i} + 4\mathbf{j}$

52. $\mathbf{v} = -10\mathbf{i} + 10\mathbf{j}$

$\|\mathbf{v}\| = \sqrt{(-10)^2 + (10)^2} = \sqrt{200} = 10\sqrt{2}$

$\tan \theta = \dfrac{10}{-10} = -1 \implies \theta = 135°$ since

v is in Quadrant II.

$\mathbf{v} = 10\sqrt{2}(\mathbf{i} \cos 135° + \mathbf{j} \sin 135°)$

54. $\mathbf{v} = 7(\cos 60° \, \mathbf{i} + \sin 60° \, \mathbf{j})$

$\|\mathbf{v}\| = 7$

$\theta = 60°$

56. $\mathbf{v} = 5\mathbf{i} + 4\mathbf{j}$

$\|\mathbf{v}\| = \sqrt{5^2 + 4^2} = \sqrt{41}$

$\tan \theta = \dfrac{4}{5} \implies \theta \approx 38.7°$

58. $\mathbf{v} = -3\mathbf{i} - 3\mathbf{j}$

$\|\mathbf{v}\| = \sqrt{(-3)^2 + (-3)^2} = 3\sqrt{2}$

$\tan \theta = \dfrac{-3}{-3} = 1 \implies \theta = 225°$

60. Magnitude of resultant:

$c = \sqrt{85^2 + 50^2 - 2(85)(50) \cos 165°}$

≈ 133.92 pounds

Let θ be the angle between the resultant and the 85-pound force

$\cos \theta \approx \dfrac{(133.92)^2 + 85^2 - 50^2}{2(133.92)(85)}$

≈ 0.9953

$\implies \theta \approx 5.5°$

62. Airspeed: $\mathbf{u} = 724(\cos 60°\mathbf{i} + \sin 60°\mathbf{j})$

$= 362\left(\mathbf{i} + \sqrt{3}\mathbf{j}\right)$

Wind: $\mathbf{w} = 32\mathbf{i}$

Groundspeed $= \mathbf{u} + \mathbf{w} = \left(394\mathbf{i} + 362\sqrt{3}\mathbf{j}\right)$

$\|\mathbf{u} + \mathbf{w}\| = \sqrt{(394)^2 + (362\sqrt{3})^2} \approx 740.5$ km/hr

$\tan \theta = \dfrac{362\sqrt{3}}{394} \implies \theta \approx 57.9°$

Bearing: N 32.1° E

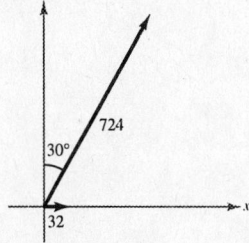

64. $\mathbf{u} = \langle -7, 12 \rangle, \mathbf{v} = \langle -4, -14 \rangle$

$\mathbf{u} \cdot \mathbf{v} = -7(-4) + 12(-14) = -140$

66. $\mathbf{u} = -7\mathbf{i} + 2\mathbf{j}, \mathbf{v} = 16\mathbf{i} - 12\mathbf{j}$

$\mathbf{u} \cdot \mathbf{v} = -7(16) + 2(-12) = -136$

68. $\mathbf{v} = \langle 2, 1 \rangle$

$\|\mathbf{v}\|^2 = \mathbf{v} \cdot \mathbf{v} = 2^2 + 1^2 = 5;$ scalar

70. $\mathbf{u} = \langle -3, 4 \rangle, \mathbf{v} = \langle 2, 1 \rangle$

$3\mathbf{u} \cdot \mathbf{v} = 3(-3(2) + 4(1)) = 3(-2) = -6;$ scalar

72. $\mathbf{u} = \cos 45° \, \mathbf{i} + \sin 45° \, \mathbf{j}$

$\mathbf{v} = \cos 300° \, \mathbf{i} + \sin 300° \, \mathbf{j}$

Angle between $\mathbf{u}$ and $\mathbf{v}$: $60° + 45° = 105°$

74. $\mathbf{u} = \langle 3, \sqrt{3} \rangle$, $\mathbf{v} = \langle 4, 3\sqrt{3} \rangle$

$\cos \theta = \dfrac{\mathbf{u} \cdot \mathbf{v}}{\|\mathbf{u}\| \, \|\mathbf{v}\|} = \dfrac{21}{\sqrt{12}\sqrt{43}}$

$\Rightarrow \theta \approx 22.4°$

76. $\mathbf{u} = \left\langle \frac{1}{4}, -\frac{1}{2} \right\rangle$, $\mathbf{v} = \langle -2, 4 \rangle$

$\mathbf{v} = -8\mathbf{u} \Rightarrow$ Parallel

78. $\mathbf{u} = -2\mathbf{i} + \mathbf{j}$, $\mathbf{v} = 3\mathbf{i} + 6\mathbf{j}$

$\mathbf{u} \cdot \mathbf{v} = 0 \Rightarrow$ Orthogonal

80. $\mathbf{u} = \langle 5, 6 \rangle$, $\mathbf{v} = \langle 10, 0 \rangle$

$\text{proj}_{\mathbf{v}}\mathbf{u} = \left(\dfrac{\mathbf{u} \cdot \mathbf{v}}{\|\mathbf{v}\|^2} \right)\mathbf{v} = \dfrac{50}{100}\langle 10, 0 \rangle = \langle 5, 0 \rangle$

$\mathbf{u} - \text{proj}_{\mathbf{v}}\mathbf{u} = \langle 0, 6 \rangle$

82. $\mathbf{u} = \langle -3, 5 \rangle$, $\mathbf{v} = \langle -5, 2 \rangle$

$\text{proj}_{\mathbf{v}}\mathbf{u} = \left(\dfrac{\mathbf{u} \cdot \mathbf{v}}{\|\mathbf{v}\|^2} \right)\mathbf{v} = \dfrac{25}{29}\langle -5, 2 \rangle$

$\mathbf{u} - \text{proj}_{\mathbf{v}}\mathbf{u} = \langle -3, 5 \rangle - \dfrac{25}{29}\langle -5, 2 \rangle$

$= \dfrac{19}{29}\langle 2, 5 \rangle$

84. $\text{work} = \mathbf{v} \cdot \overrightarrow{PQ}$

$= (3\mathbf{i} - 6\mathbf{j}) \cdot (-10\mathbf{i} + 17\mathbf{j})$

$= -30 - 102$

$= -132$

86. $|-6i| = 6$

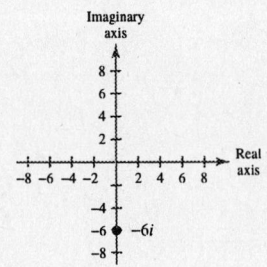

88. $|-10 - 4i| = \sqrt{(-10)^2 + (-4)^2}$

$= 2\sqrt{29}$

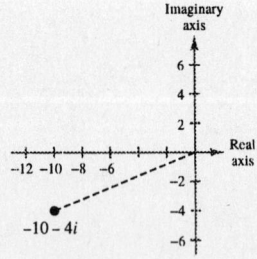

90. $z = 5 + 12i$

$|z| = \sqrt{5^2 + 12^2} = 13$

$\tan \theta = \dfrac{12}{5} \Rightarrow \theta \approx 1.176$

$z \approx 13(\cos 1.176 + i \sin 1.176)$

92. $z = -7$

$|z| = 7$

$\tan \theta = \dfrac{0}{-7} = 0 \Rightarrow \theta = \pi$

$z = 7(\cos \pi + i \sin \pi)$

94. (a) $z_1 = -3(1 + i) = 3\sqrt{2}\left(\cos\frac{5\pi}{4} + i\sin\frac{5\pi}{4}\right)$

$z_2 = 2(\sqrt{3} + i) = 4\left(\cos\frac{\pi}{6} + i\sin\frac{\pi}{6}\right)$

(b) $z_1 z_2 = \left[3\sqrt{2}\left(\cos\frac{5\pi}{4} + i\sin\frac{5\pi}{4}\right)\right]\left[4\left(\cos\frac{\pi}{6} + i\sin\frac{\pi}{6}\right)\right]$

$= 12\sqrt{2}\left(\cos\frac{17\pi}{12} + i\sin\frac{17\pi}{12}\right)$

$\dfrac{z_1}{z_2} = \dfrac{3\sqrt{2}\left[\cos\frac{5\pi}{4} + i\sin\frac{5\pi}{4}\right]}{4\left[\cos\frac{\pi}{6} + i\sin\frac{\pi}{6}\right]}$

$= \dfrac{3\sqrt{2}}{4}\left(\cos\frac{13\pi}{12} + i\sin\frac{13\pi}{12}\right)$

96. $\left[2\left(\cos\frac{4\pi}{15} + i\sin\frac{4\pi}{15}\right)\right]^5 = 2^5\left(\cos\frac{4\pi}{3} + i\sin\frac{4\pi}{3}\right)$

$= 32\left(-\frac{1}{2} - \frac{\sqrt{3}}{2}i\right)$

$= -16 - 16\sqrt{3}i$

98. $(1 - i)^8 = \left[\sqrt{2}(\cos 315° + i\sin 315°)\right]^8$

$= 16(\cos 2520° + i\sin 2520°)$

$= 16(\cos 0° + i\sin 0°)$

$= 16$

100. (a) The trigonometric forms of the four roots shown are:

$4(\cos 60° + i\sin 60°)$

$4(\cos 150° + i\sin 150°)$

$4(\cos 240° + i\sin 240°)$

$4(\cos 330° + i\sin 330°)$

(b) Since there are four evenly spaced roots on the circle of radius 4, they are fourth roots of a complex number of modulus 4^4. In this case, raising them to the fourth power yields $-128 - 128\sqrt{3}i$.

102. Fourth roots of $256 = 256(\cos 0 + i\sin 0)$:

$\sqrt[4]{256}\left(\cos\frac{2\pi k}{4} + i\sin\frac{2\pi k}{4}\right)$

$k = 0, 1, 2, 3$

$k = 0$: $4(\cos 0 + i\sin 0) = 4$

$k = 1$: $4\left(\cos\frac{\pi}{2} + i\sin\frac{\pi}{2}\right) = 4i$

$k = 2$: $4(\cos \pi + i\sin \pi) = -4$

$k = 3$: $4\left(\cos\frac{3\pi}{2} + i\sin\frac{3\pi}{2}\right) = -4i$

104. $x^5 - 32 = 0$

$$x^5 = 32$$

$$32 = 32(\cos 0 + i \sin 0)$$

$$\sqrt[5]{32} = \sqrt[5]{32}\left[\cos\left(0 + \frac{2\pi k}{5}\right) + i \sin\left(0 + \frac{2\pi k}{5}\right)\right]$$

$k = 0, 1, 2, 3, 4$

$k = 0$: $2(\cos 0 + i \sin 0) = 2$

$k = 1$: $2\left(\cos\dfrac{2\pi}{5} + i \sin\dfrac{2\pi}{5}\right) = 0.6180 + 1.9021i$

$k = 2$: $2\left(\cos\dfrac{4\pi}{5} + i \sin\dfrac{4\pi}{5}\right) = -1.6180 + 1.1756i$

$k = 3$: $2\left(\cos\dfrac{6\pi}{5} + i \sin\dfrac{6\pi}{5}\right) = -1.6180 - 1.1756i$

$k = 4$: $2\left(\cos\dfrac{8\pi}{5} + i \sin\dfrac{8\pi}{5}\right) = 0.6180 - 1.9021i$

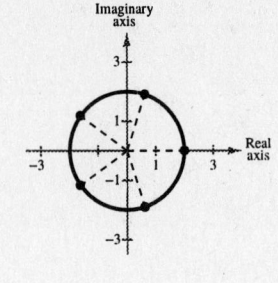

106. $(x^3 - 1)(x^2 + 1) = 0$

$$x^3 - 1 = 0$$

$$x^2 + 1 = 0$$

$$x^3 = 1$$

$$1 = 1(\cos 0 + i \sin 0)$$

$$\sqrt[3]{1} = \sqrt[3]{1}\left[\cos\left(\frac{0 + 2\pi k}{3}\right) + i \sin\left(\frac{0 + 2\pi k}{3}\right)\right], \; k = 0, 1, 2$$

$1(\cos 0 + i \sin 0) = 1$

$1\left(\cos\dfrac{2\pi}{3} + i \sin\dfrac{2\pi}{3}\right) = -\dfrac{1}{2} + \dfrac{\sqrt{3}}{2}i$

$1\left(\cos\dfrac{4\pi}{3} + i \sin\dfrac{4\pi}{3}\right) = -\dfrac{1}{2} - \dfrac{\sqrt{3}}{2}i$

$$x^2 + 1 = 0$$

$$x^2 = -1$$

$$-1 = 1(\cos \pi + i \sin \pi)$$

$$\sqrt{-1} = \sqrt{1}\left[\cos\left(\frac{\pi + 2\pi k}{2}\right) + i \sin\left(\frac{\pi + 2\pi k}{2}\right), \; k = 0, 1\right.$$

$k = 0, 1$

$1\left(\cos\dfrac{\pi}{2} + i \sin\dfrac{\pi}{2}\right) = i$

$1\left(\cos\dfrac{3\pi}{2} + i \sin\dfrac{3\pi}{2}\right) = -i$

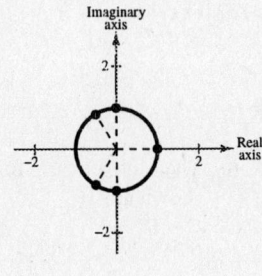

108. False. There may be no solution, one solution, or two solutions.

110. $a^2 = b^2 + c^2 - 2bc \cos A$

$b^2 = a^2 + c^2 - 2ac \cos B$

$c^2 = a^2 + b^2 - 2ab \cos C$

112. A vector in the plane has both a magnitude and a direction.

114. $\|\mathbf{u} + \mathbf{v}\|$ is larger in figure (a) since the angle between $\mathbf{u}$ and $\mathbf{v}$ is acute rather than obtuse.

116. The sum of $\mathbf{u}$ and $\mathbf{v}$ lies on the diagonal of the parallelogram with $\mathbf{u}$ and $\mathbf{v}$ as its adjacent sides.

118. (a) z has 4 fourth roots. Three are not shown.

(b) The roots are located on the circle at $\theta = 30° + 90°k$, $k = 0, 1, 2, 3$. The three roots not shown are located at $120°, 210°, 300°$.

C H A P T E R 7
Systems of Equations and Inequalities

CHAPTER 7
Systems of Equations and Inequalities

Section 7.1   Solving Systems of Equations

Solutions to Even-Numbered Exercises

2. $\begin{cases} 4x^2 + y = 3 \\ -x - y = 11 \end{cases}$

(a) $4(2)^2 + (-13) \overset{?}{=} 3$

$16 - 13 = 3$

$-2 - (-13) \overset{?}{=} 11$

$-2 + 13 = 11$

$(2, -13)$ is a solution.

(b) $4(2)^2 + (-9) \overset{?}{=} 3$

$16 - 9 \neq 3$

$(2, -9)$ is not a solution.

(c) $4\left(-\dfrac{3}{2}\right)^2 + \left(-\dfrac{31}{3}\right) \overset{?}{=} 3$

$\dfrac{36}{4} - \dfrac{31}{3} \neq 3$

$\left(-\dfrac{3}{2}, -\dfrac{31}{3}\right)$ is not a solution.

(d) $4\left(-\dfrac{7}{4}\right)^2 + \left(-\dfrac{37}{4}\right) \overset{?}{=} 3$

$\dfrac{49}{4} - \dfrac{37}{4} = 3$

$-\left(-\dfrac{7}{4}\right) - \left(-\dfrac{37}{4}\right) \overset{?}{=} 11$

$\dfrac{7}{4} + \dfrac{37}{4} = 11$

$\left(-\dfrac{7}{4}, -\dfrac{37}{4}\right)$ is a solution.

4. $\begin{cases} -\log x + 3 = y \\ \frac{1}{9}x + y = \frac{28}{9} \end{cases}$

(a) $-\log 9 + 3 \neq \dfrac{37}{9}$

$\left(9, \dfrac{37}{9}\right)$ is not a solution.

(b) $-\log 10 + 3 = 2$

$\dfrac{1}{9}(10) + 2 = \dfrac{28}{9}$

$(10, 2)$ is a solution.

(c) $-\log(1) + 3 = 3$

$\dfrac{1}{9}(1) + 3 = \dfrac{28}{9}$

$(1, 3)$ is a solution.

(d) $-\log 2 + 3 \neq 4$

$(2, 4)$ is not a solution.

6. $\begin{cases} x - y = -4 & \text{Equation 1} \\ x + 2y = 5 & \text{Equation 2} \end{cases}$

Solve for x in Equation 1: $x = y - 4$

Substitute for x in Equation 2: $(y - 4) + 2y = 5$

Solve for y: $3y - 4 = 5 \Longrightarrow y = 3$

Back-substitute $y = 3$: $x = 3 - 4 = -1$

Solution: $(-1, 3)$

8. $\begin{cases} 3x \quad\; + y = 2 & \text{Equation 1} \\ x^3 - 2 + y = 0 & \text{Equation 2} \end{cases}$

Solve for y in Equation 1: $y = 2 - 3x$

Substitute for y in Equation 2: $x^3 - (2 + 2 - 3x) = 0$

$$x^3 - 3x = 0$$

Solve for x: $x^3 - 3x = 0 \Rightarrow x(x^2 - 3) = 0 \Rightarrow x = 0, \pm\sqrt{3}$

Back-substitute $x = 0$: $y = 2 - 3(0) = 2$

Back-substitute $x = \sqrt{3}$: $y = 2 - 3\sqrt{3}$

Back-substitute $x = -\sqrt{3}$: $y = 2 - 3\left(-\sqrt{3}\right) = 2 + 3\sqrt{3}$

Solutions: $(0, 2), \left(\sqrt{3}, 2 - 3\sqrt{3}\right), \left(-\sqrt{3}, 2 + 3\sqrt{3}\right)$

10. $\begin{cases} \quad\; x + y = 0 & \text{Equation 1} \\ x^3 - 5x - y = 0 & \text{Equation 2} \end{cases}$

Solve for y in Equation 1: $y = -x$

Substitute for y in Equation 2: $x^3 - 5x - (-x) = 0$

Solve for x: $x^3 - 4x = 0 \Rightarrow x(x^2 - 4) = 0 \Rightarrow x = 0, \pm 2$

Back-substitute $x = 0$: $y = -0 = 0$

Back-substitute $x = 2$: $y = -2$

Back-substitute $x = -2$: $y = -(-2) = 2$

Solutions: $(0, 0), (2, -2), (-2, 2)$

12. $\begin{cases} y = -2x^2 + 2 & \text{Equation 1} \\ y = 2(x^4 - 2x^2 + 1) & \text{Equation 2} \end{cases}$

Substitute for y in Equation 1:
$$2(x^4 - 2x^2 + 1) = -2x^2 + 2$$

Solve for x: $x^4 - 2x^2 + 1 + x^2 - 1 = 0$

$$x^4 - x^2 = 0$$

$$x^2(x^2 - 1) = 0 \Rightarrow x = 0, \pm 1$$

Back-substitute $x = 0$: $y = -2(0)^2 + 2 = 2$

Back-substitute $x = 1$: $y = -2(1)^2 + 2 = 0$

Back-substitute $x = -1$: $y = -2(-1)^2 + 2 = 0$

Solutions: $(0, 2), (1, 0), (-1, 0)$

14. $\begin{cases} y = x^3 - 3x^2 + 4 & \text{Equation 1} \\ y = -2x + 4 & \text{Equation 2} \end{cases}$

Substitute for y in Equation 1: $-2x + 4 = x^3 - 3x^2 + 4$

Solve for x: $0 = x^3 - 3x^2 + 2x$

$$0 = x(x^2 - 3x + 2)$$

$$0 = x(x - 2)(x - 1) \Rightarrow x = 0, 1, 2$$

Back-substitute $x = 0$: $y = -2(0) + 4 = 4$

Back-substitute $x = 1$: $y = -2(1) + 4 = 2$

Back-substitute $x = 2$: $y = -2(2) + 4 = 0$

Solutions: $(0, 4), (1, 2), (2, 0)$

16. $\begin{cases} x + 2y = \quad\; 1 & \text{Equation 1} \\ 5x - 4y = -23 & \text{Equation 2} \end{cases}$

Solve for x in Equation 1: $x = 1 - 2y$

Substitute for x in Equation 2: $5(1 - 2y) - 4y = -23$

Solve for y: $-14y = -28 \Rightarrow y = 2$

Back-substitute $y = 2$: $x = 1 - 2y = 1 - 2(2) = -3$

Solution: $(-3, 2)$

18. $\begin{cases} 6x - 3y - 4 = 0 & \text{Equation 1} \\ x + 2y - 4 = 0 & \text{Equation 2} \end{cases}$

Solve for x in Equation 2: $x = 4 - 2y$

Substitute for x in Equation 1: $6(4 - 2y) - 3y - 4 = 0$

Solve for y: $24 - 12y - 3y - 4 = 0 \Rightarrow -15y = -20 \Rightarrow y = \frac{4}{3}$

Back-substitute $y = \frac{4}{3}$: $x = 4 - 2y = 4 - 2\left(\frac{4}{3}\right) = \frac{4}{3}$

Solution: $\left(\frac{4}{3}, \frac{4}{3}\right)$

20. $\begin{cases} 0.5x + 3.2y = 9.0 & \text{Equation 1} \\ 0.2x - 1.6y = -3.6 & \text{Equation 2} \end{cases}$

Multiply the equations by 10.

$5x + 32y = 90$ Revised Equation 1

$2x - 16y = -36$ Revised Equation 2

Solve for x in revised Equation 2: $x = 8y - 18$

Substitute for x in revised Equation 1: $5(8y - 18) + 32y = 90$

Solve for y: $40y - 90 + 32y = 90 \implies 72y = 180$

$$\implies y = \tfrac{5}{2}$$

Back-substitute $y = \tfrac{5}{2}$: $x = 8\left(\tfrac{5}{2}\right) - 18 = 2$

Solution: $\left(2, \tfrac{5}{2}\right)$

22. $\begin{cases} \tfrac{1}{2}x + \tfrac{3}{4}y = 10 & \text{Equation 1} \\ \tfrac{3}{4}x - y = 4 & \text{Equation 2} \end{cases}$

Solve for y in Equation 2: $y = \tfrac{3}{4}x - 4$

Substitute for y in Equation 1: $\tfrac{1}{2}x + \tfrac{3}{4}\left(\tfrac{3}{4}x - 4\right) = 10$

Solve for x: $\tfrac{1}{2}x + \tfrac{9}{16}x - 3 = 10 \implies \tfrac{17}{16}x = 13 \implies x = \tfrac{208}{17}$

Back-substitute $x = \tfrac{208}{17}$: $y = \tfrac{3}{4}\left(\tfrac{208}{17}\right) - 4 = \tfrac{88}{17}$

Solution: $\left(\tfrac{208}{17}, \tfrac{88}{17}\right)$

24. $\begin{cases} -\tfrac{2}{3}x + y = 2 & \text{Equation 1} \\ 2x - 3y = 6 & \text{Equation 2} \end{cases}$

Solve for y in Equation 1: $y = \tfrac{2}{3}x + 2$

Substitute for y in Equation 2: $2x - 3\left(\tfrac{2}{3}x + 2\right) = 6$

Solve for x: $2x - 2x - 6 = 6 \implies 0 = 12$ Inconsistent

No solution

26. $\begin{cases} x - 2y = 0 & \text{Equation 1} \\ 3x - y^2 = 0 & \text{Equaiton 2} \end{cases}$

Solve for x in Equation 1: $x = 2y$

Substitute for x in Equation 2: $3(2y) - y^2 = 0$

Solve for y:
$6y - y^2 = 0 \implies y(6 - y) = 0 \implies y = 0, 6$

Back-substitute $y = 0$: $x = 2(0) = 0$

Back-substitute $y = 6$: $x = 2(6) = 12$

Solutions: $(0, 0), (12, 6)$

28. $\begin{cases} y = -x & \text{Equation 1} \\ y = x^3 + 3x^2 + 2x & \text{Equation 2} \end{cases}$

Substitute for y in Equation 2: $-x = x^3 + 3x^2 + 2x$

Solve for x: $x^3 + 3x^2 + 3x = 0 \implies x(x^2 + 3x + 3) = 0$

$$\implies x = 0, \frac{-3 \pm i\sqrt{3}}{2}$$

Back-substitute $x = 0$: $y = 0$

The only real solution is $(0, 0)$.

30. $\begin{cases} x + y = 0 \\ 3x - 2y = 10 \end{cases}$

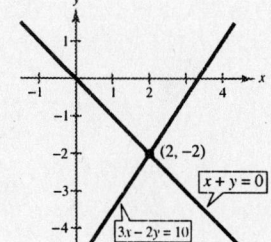

Point of intersection: $(2, -2)$

32. $\begin{cases} -x + 2y = 1 \\ x - y = 2 \end{cases}$

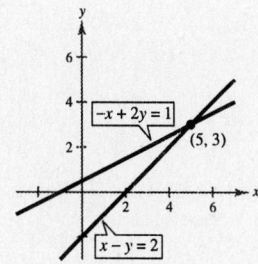

Point of intersection: $(5, 3)$

34. $\begin{cases} -x + y = 3 \\ x^2 - 6x - 27 + y^2 = 0 \end{cases}$

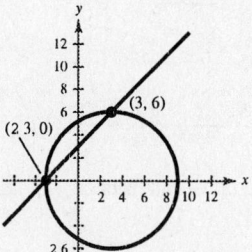

Points of intersection:
$(-3, 0), (3, 6)$

36. $\begin{cases} y^2 - 4x + 11 = 0 \\ -\frac{1}{2}x + y = -\frac{1}{2} \end{cases}$

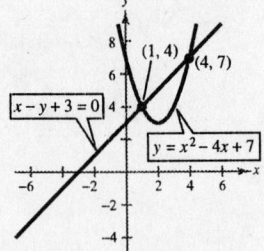

Points of intersection: $(3, 1), (15, 7)$

38. $\begin{cases} x - y = 0 \\ 5x - 2y = 6 \end{cases}$

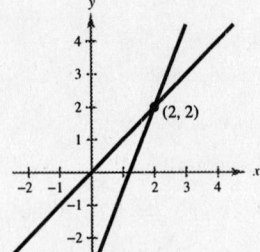

Point of intersection: $(2, 2)$

40. $\begin{cases} 2x - y + 3 = 0 \\ x^2 + y^2 - 4x = 0 \end{cases}$

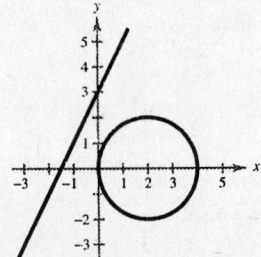

No points of intersection

42. $\begin{cases} x^2 + y^2 = 25 \\ (x - 8)^2 + y^2 = 41 \end{cases}$

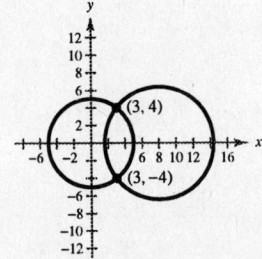

Points of intersection: $(3, 4), (3, -4)$

44. $\begin{cases} y = -4e^{-x} \\ y + 3x + 8 = 0 \end{cases}$

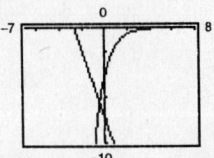

Point of intersection: $(-0.49, -6.53)$

46. $\begin{cases} y = -2 + \ln(x - 1) \\ 3y + 2x = 9 \end{cases}$

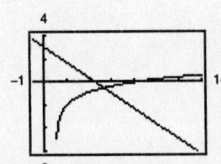

Point of intersection: $(5.31, -0.54)$

48. $\begin{cases} x - y = 3 \Longrightarrow y_1 = x - 3 \\ x - y^2 = 1 \Longrightarrow y_2 = \sqrt{x - 1}, y_3 = -\sqrt{x - 1} \end{cases}$

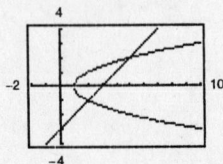

Points of intersection: $(5, 2), (2, -1)$

50. $\begin{cases} x^2 + y^2 = 4 \Longrightarrow y_1 = \sqrt{4 - x^2}, y_2 = -\sqrt{4 - x^2} \\ 2x^2 - y = 2 \Longrightarrow y_3 = 2x^2 - 2 \end{cases}$

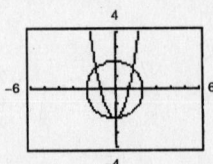

Points of intersection: $(0, -2), \left(\frac{1}{2}\sqrt{7}, \frac{3}{2}\right), \left(-\frac{1}{2}\sqrt{7}, \frac{3}{2}\right)$

52. $\begin{cases} x + y = 4 & \text{Equation 1} \\ x^2 + y = 2 & \text{Equation 2} \end{cases}$

Solve for y in Equation 1: $y = 4 - x$

Substitute for y in Equation 2: $x^2 + (4 - x) = 2$

Solve for x: $x^2 - x + 2 = 0$

No real solutions because the discriminant in the Quadratic Formula is negative.

Inconsistent. No solution

54. $\begin{cases} x^2 + y^2 = 25 & \text{Equation 1} \\ 2x + y = 10 & \text{Equation 2} \end{cases}$

Solve for y in Equation 2: $y = 10 - 2x$

Substitute for y in Equation 1: $x^2 + (10 - 2x)^2 = 25$

Solve for x: $x^2 + 100 - 40x + 4x^2 = 25 \Rightarrow x^2 - 8x + 15 = 0$

$$\Rightarrow (x - 5)(x - 3) = 0 \Rightarrow x = 3, 5$$

Back-substitute $x = 3$: $y = 10 - 2(3) = 4$

Back-substitute $x = 5$: $y = 10 - 2(5) = 0$

Solutions: $(3, 4), (5, 0)$

56. $\begin{cases} y = (x + 1)^3 \\ y = \sqrt{x - 1} \end{cases}$

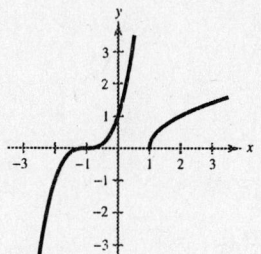

No points of intersection

58. $\begin{cases} x^2 + y = 4 \Rightarrow y = 4 - x^2 \\ e^x - y = 0 \Rightarrow y = e^x \end{cases}$

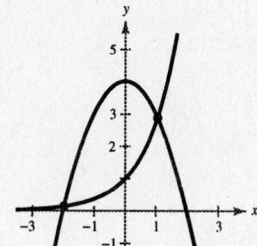

Points of intersection:
Approximately $(-1.96, 0.14), (1.06, 2.88)$

60. $\begin{cases} y = x^3 - 2x^2 + x - 1 & \text{Equation 1} \\ y = -x^2 + 3x - 1 & \text{Equation 2} \end{cases}$

Substitute for y in Equation 1:

$$-x^2 + 3x - 1 = x^3 - 2x^2 + x - 1$$

Solve for x: $0 = x^3 - x^2 - 2x$

$$0 = x(x^2 - x - 2)$$

$$0 = x(x - 2)(x + 1) \Rightarrow x = 0, 2, -1$$

Back-substitute $x = 0$ in Equation 2:

$$y = -0^2 + 3(0) - 1 = -1$$

Back-substitute $x = 2$ in Equation 2:

$$y = -2^2 + 3(2) - 1 = 1$$

Back-substitute $x = -1$ in Equation 2:

$$y = -(-1)^2 + 3(-1) - 1 = -5$$

Solutions: $(0, -1), (2, 1), (-1, -5)$

62. $\begin{cases} x - 2y = 1 & \text{Equation 1} \\ \quad y = \sqrt{x-1} & \text{Equation 2} \end{cases}$

Substitute for y in Equation 1: $x - 2\sqrt{x-1} = 1$

Solve for x: $\qquad\qquad x - 1 = 2\sqrt{x-1}$

$$(x-1)^2 = 4(x-1)$$

$$x^2 - 2x + 1 = 4x - 4$$

$$x^2 - 6x + 5 = 0$$

$$(x-1)(x-5) = 0 \Rightarrow x = 1, 5$$

Back-substitute $x = 1$: $y = \sqrt{1-1} = 0$

Back-substitute $x = 5$: $y = \sqrt{5-1} = 2$

Solutions: $(1, 0), (5, 2)$

64. $\qquad C = 2.65x + 350,000, \ R = 4.15x$

$$R = C$$

$$4.15x = 2.65x + 350,000$$

$$1.50x = 350,000$$

$$x \approx 233,333 \text{ units}$$

66. $\qquad\qquad C = 7.8\sqrt{x} + 18,500, R = 12.84x$

$$R = C$$

$$12.84x = 7.8\sqrt{x} + 18,500$$

$$12.84x - 7.8\sqrt{x} - 18,500 = 0$$

Let $u = \sqrt{x}$

$$12.84u^2 - 7.8u - 18,500 = 0$$

$$u = \frac{7.8 \pm \sqrt{(-7.8)^2 - 4(12.84)(-18,500)}}{2(12.84)} = \frac{7.8 \pm \sqrt{950,220.84}}{25.68}$$

$$u \approx -37.655, 38.263$$

Choosing the positive value for u, we have $\Rightarrow x = (38.263)^2 \approx 1464$ units.

68. $C = 21.60x + 5000, \ R = 34.10x$

(a) $\qquad R = C$

$$34.10x = 21.60x + 5000$$

$$12.5x = 5000$$

$$x = 400 \text{ units}$$

(b) $P = R - C$

$$8500 = 34.10x - (21.60x + 5000)$$

$$8500 = 12.5x - 5000$$

$$13,500 = 12.5x$$

$$x = 1080 \text{ units}$$

70. (a) $\begin{cases} \qquad x + y = 20,000 \\ 0.065x + 0.085y = 1600 \end{cases}$

(b) $y_1 = 20,000 - x$

$$y_2 = \frac{1600 - 0.065x}{0.085}$$

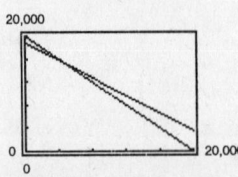

As the amount invested at 6.5% increases, the amount invested at 8.5% decreases and the interest is fixed at $1600.

(c) The point of intersection occurs when $x = 5000$, so in order to meet the requirement of $1600 per year in interest, $5000 must be invested at 6.5%.

72. $25{,}000 + 0.02x = 20{,}000 + 0.03x$

$\qquad\qquad 5000 = 0.01x$

$\qquad\quad 500{,}000 = x$

For the second offer to be better, you would have to sell more than \$500,000 per year.

74. $p = 1.45 + 0.00014x^2$

$p = (2.388 - 0.007x)^2$

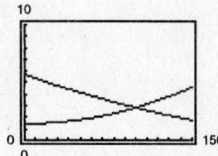

The market equilibrium (point of intersection) is approximately $(99.99, 2.85)$.

76. $2l + 2w = 280 \Rightarrow l + w = 140$

$w = l - 20 \Rightarrow l + (l - 20) = 140$

$\qquad\qquad\qquad\qquad 2l = 160$

$\qquad\qquad\qquad\qquad l = 80$

$w = l - 20 = 80 - 20 = 60$

Dimensions: 60×80 centimeters

78. $2l + 2w = 210 \Rightarrow l + w = 105$

$\qquad l = \frac{3}{2}w \Rightarrow \frac{3}{2}w + w = 105$

$\qquad\qquad\qquad\qquad \frac{5}{2}w = 105$

$\qquad\qquad\qquad\qquad w = 42$

$l = \frac{3}{2}(42) = 63$

Dimensions: 42×63 feet

80. $A = \frac{1}{2}bh$

$1 = \frac{1}{2}a^2$

$a^2 = 2$

$a = \sqrt{2}$

The dimensions are $\sqrt{2} \times \sqrt{2}$ inches.

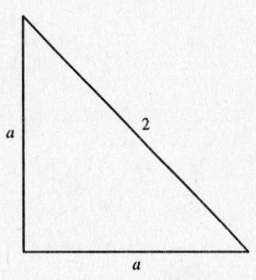

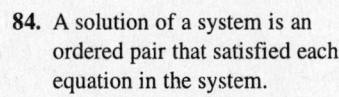

82. False. To solve a system of equations by substitution, you can solve for either variable in one of the two equations and then back-substitute.

84. A solution of a system is an ordered pair that satisfied each equation in the system.

86. The advantage of the method of substitution over the graphical method is that substitution gives exact solutions but graphical solutions may only be approximate.

88. (a)

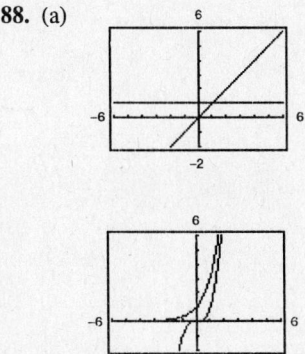

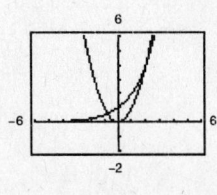

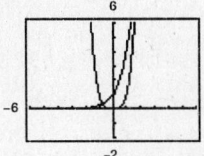

(b) Three

90. $(3.5, 4), (10, 6)$

$$m = \frac{6 - 4}{10 - 3.5} = \frac{2}{6.5}$$

$$y - 6 = \frac{2}{6.5}(x - 10)$$

$$6.5y - 39 = 2x - 20$$

$$2x - 6.5y + 19 = 0$$

92. $(4, -2), (4, 5)$

$$x = 4$$

$$x - 4 = 0$$

94. $\left(-\frac{7}{3}, 8\right), \left(\frac{5}{2}, \frac{1}{2}\right)$

$$m = \frac{8 - (1/2)}{-(7/3) - (5/2)} = \frac{15/2}{-29/6} = -\frac{45}{29}$$

$$y - \frac{1}{2} = -\frac{45}{29}\left(x - \frac{5}{2}\right)$$

$$29y - \frac{29}{2} = -45x + \frac{225}{2}$$

$$45x + 29y - 127 = 0$$

96. $f(x) = \frac{2x - 7}{3x + 2}$

Domain: All real numbers except $x = -\frac{2}{3}$

Horizontal asymptote: $y = \frac{2}{3}$

Vertical asymptote: $x = -\frac{2}{3}$

98. $f(x) = 3 - \frac{2}{x^2}$

Domain: All real numbers except $x = 0$

Horizontal asymptote: $y = 3$

Vertical asymptote: $x = 0$

100. $y = 2^{-0.5x}$

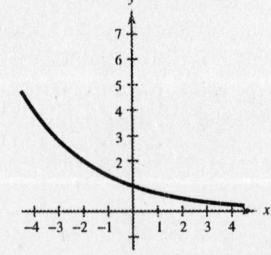

102. $y = \frac{2 + e^{-x}}{5}$

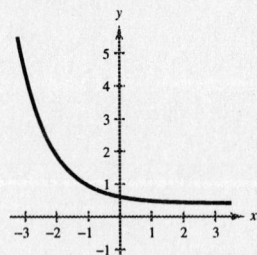

Section 7.2   Two-Variable Linear Systems

Solutions to Even-Numbered Exercises

2. $\begin{cases} x + 3y = 1 & \text{Equation 1} \\ -x + 2y = 4 & \text{Equation 2} \end{cases}$

Add to eliminate x: $x + 3y = 1$

$$\underline{-x + 2y = 4}$$

$$5y = 5 \Rightarrow y = 1$$

Substitute $y = 1$ in Equation 1: $x + 3(1) = 1 \Rightarrow x = -2$

Solution: $(-2, 1)$

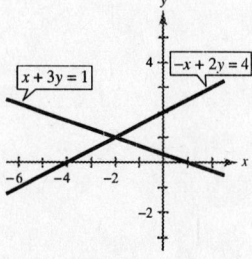

4. $\begin{cases} 2x - y = 3 & \text{Equation 1} \\ 4x + 3y = 21 & \text{Equation 2} \end{cases}$

Multiply Equation 1 by 3: $6x - 3y = 9$

Add this to Equation 2 to eliminate y: $6x - 3y = 9$

$$\underline{4x + 3y = 21}$$

$$10x \qquad = 30$$

$$\Rightarrow x = 3$$

Substitute $x = 3$ in Equation 1: $2(3) - y = 3 \Rightarrow y = 3$

Solution: $(3, 3)$

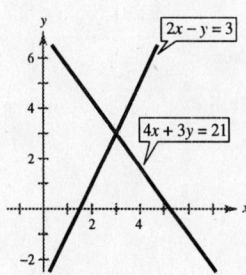

6. $\begin{cases} 3x + 2y = 3 & \text{Equation 1} \\ 6x + 4y = 14 & \text{Equation 2} \end{cases}$

Multiply Equation 1 by -2: $-6x - 4y = -6$

Add this to Equation 2: $-6x - 4y = -6$

$$\underline{6x + 4y = 14}$$

$$0 = 8$$

There are no solutions.

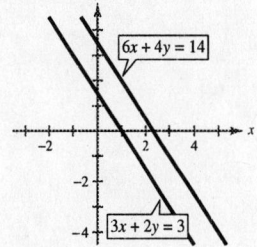

8. $\begin{cases} 9x - 3y = -15 & \text{Equation 1} \\ -3x + y = 5 & \text{Equation 2} \end{cases}$

Multiply Equation 2 by 3: $-9x + 3y = 15$

Add this to Equation 1: $9x - 3y = -15$

$$\underline{-9x + 3y = 15}$$

$$0 = 0$$

There are infinitely many solutions. Let $x = a$

$-3a + y = 5 \Rightarrow y = 3a + 5$

Solution: $(a, 3a + 5)$, where a is any real number.

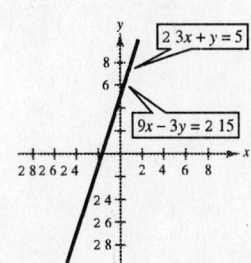

10. $\begin{cases} 5x + 3y = -18 & \text{Equation 1} \\ 2x - 6y = 1 & \text{Equation 2} \end{cases}$

Multiply Equation 1 by 2: $10x + 6y = -36$

Add this to Equation 2 to eliminate y:

$$10x + 6y = -36$$
$$\underline{ 2x - 6y = 1}$$
$$12x = -35 \Longrightarrow x = \frac{-35}{12}$$

Substitute $x = -\frac{35}{12}$ in Equation 2:

$$2\left(-\tfrac{35}{12}\right) - 6y = 1 \Longrightarrow y = -\tfrac{41}{36}$$

Solution: $\left(-\frac{35}{12}, -\frac{41}{36}\right)$

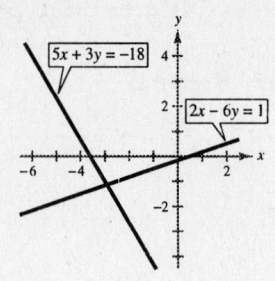

12. $\begin{cases} 3x - 5y = 2 & \text{Equation 1} \\ 2x + 5y = 13 & \text{Equation 2} \end{cases}$

Add to eliminate y: $3x - 5y = 2$

$$\underline{ 2x + 5y = 13}$$
$$5x = 15 \Longrightarrow x = 3$$

Substitute $x = 3$ in Equation 1: $3(3) - 5y = 2 \Longrightarrow y = \frac{7}{5}$

Solution: $\left(3, \frac{7}{5}\right)$

14. $\begin{cases} x + 7y = 12 & \text{Equation 1} \\ 3x - 5y = 10 & \text{Equation 2} \end{cases}$

Multiply Equation 1 by -3: $-3x - 21y = -36$

Add this to Equation 2 to eliminate x:

$$-3x - 21y = -36$$
$$\underline{ 3x - 5y = 10}$$
$$-26y = -26$$
$$\Longrightarrow y = 1$$

Substitute $y = 1$ in Equation 1: $x + 7 = 12 \Longrightarrow x = 5$

Solution: $(5, 1)$

16. $\begin{cases} 2r + 4s = 5 & \text{Equation 1} \\ 16r + 50s = 55 & \text{Equation 2} \end{cases}$

Multiply Equation 1 by (-8): $-16r - 32s = -40$

Add this to Equation 2 to eliminate r:

$$-16r - 32s = -40$$
$$\underline{ 16r + 50s = 55}$$
$$18s = 15$$
$$\Longrightarrow s = \tfrac{5}{6}$$

Substitute $s = \frac{5}{6}$ in Equation 1:

$$2r + 4\left(\tfrac{5}{6}\right) = 5 \Longrightarrow r = \tfrac{5}{6}$$

Solution: $\left(\frac{5}{6}, \frac{5}{6}\right)$

18. $\begin{cases} 3x + 11y = 4 & \text{Equation 1} \\ -2x - 5y = 9 & \text{Equation 2} \end{cases}$

Multiply Equation 1 by 2 and Equation 2 by 3:

$$\begin{cases} 6x + 22y = 8 \\ -6x - 15y = 27 \end{cases}$$

Add to eliminate x: $6x + 22y = 8$

$$\underline{ -6x - 15y = 27}$$
$$7y = 35 \Longrightarrow y = 5$$

Substitute $y = 5$ in Equation 1: $3x + 11(5) = 4$

$$\Longrightarrow x = -17$$

Solution: $(-17, 5)$

20. $\begin{cases} 3.1x - 2.9y = -10.2 & \text{Equation 1} \\ 15.5x - 14.5y = 21 & \text{Equation 2} \end{cases}$

Multiply Equation 1 by 10 and Equation 2 by (-2):

$\begin{cases} 31x - 29y = -102 \\ -31x + 29y = -42 \end{cases}$

Add to eliminate x:

$\begin{array}{r} 31x - 29y = -102 \\ -31x + 29y = -42 \\ \hline 0 = -144 \end{array}$

There are no solutions.

24. $\begin{cases} 6.3x + 7.2y = 5.4 & \text{Equation 1} \\ 5.6x + 6.4y = 4.8 & \text{Equation 2} \end{cases}$

Multiply Equation 1 by 56 and Equation 2 by -63:

$\begin{cases} 352.8x + 403.2y = 302.4 \\ -352.8x - 403.2y = -302.4 \end{cases}$

Add to eliminate x and y:

$\begin{array}{r} 352.8x + 403.2y = 302.4 \\ -352.8x - 403.2y = -302.4 \\ \hline 0 = 0 \end{array}$

There are infinitely many solutions. Let $x = a$

$5.6a + 6.4y = 4.8 \implies y = 0.875a + 0.75$

Solution: $(a, -0.875a + 0.75)$, where a is any real number

28. $\begin{cases} 2x + 5y = 8 & \text{Equation 1} \\ 5x + 8y = 10 & \text{Equation 2} \end{cases}$

Multiply Equation 1 by 5 and Equation 2 by (-2):

$\begin{cases} 10x + 25y = 40 \\ -10x - 16y = -20 \end{cases}$

Add to eliminate x:

$\begin{array}{r} 10x + 25y = 40 \\ -10x - 16y = -20 \\ \hline 9y = 20 \implies y = \dfrac{20}{9} \end{array}$

Substitute $y = \dfrac{20}{9}$ in Equation 1: $2x + 5\left(\dfrac{20}{9}\right) = 8$

$$\implies x = -\frac{14}{9}$$

Solution: $\left(-\dfrac{14}{9}, \dfrac{20}{9}\right)$

22. $\begin{cases} \frac{2}{3}x + \frac{1}{6}y = \frac{2}{3} & \text{Equation 1} \\ 4x + y = 4 & \text{Equation 2} \end{cases}$

Multiply Equation 1 by (-6): $-4x - y = -4$

Add this to Equation 2: $\begin{array}{r} -4x - y = -4 \\ 4x + y = 4 \\ \hline 0 = 0 \end{array}$

There are infinitely many solutions. Let $x = a$

$4a + y = 4 \implies y = 4 - 4a$

Solution: $(a_1, 4 - 4a)$ where a is any real number

26. $\begin{cases} 0.2x - 0.5y = -27.8 & \text{Equation 1} \\ 0.3x + 0.4y = 68.7 & \text{Equation 2} \end{cases}$

Multiply Equation 1 by 4 and Equation 2 by 5:

$\begin{cases} 0.8x - 2y = -111.2 \\ 1.5x + 2y = 343.5 \end{cases}$

Add these to eliminate y:

$\begin{array}{r} 0.8x - 2y = -111.2 \\ 1.5x + 2y = 343.5 \\ \hline 2.3x = 232.3 \\ \implies x = 101 \end{array}$

Substitute $x = 101$ in Equation 1:

$0.2(101) - 0.5y = -27.8 \implies y = 96$

Solution: $(101, 96)$

30. $\begin{cases} \dfrac{x-1}{2} + \dfrac{y+2}{3} = 4 & \text{Equation 1} \\ x - 2y = 5 & \text{Equation 2} \end{cases}$

Multiply Equation 1 by 6:

$3(x - 1) + 2(y + 2) = 24 \implies 3x + 2y = 23$

Add this to Equation 2 to eliminate y:

$\begin{array}{r} 3x + 2y = 23 \\ x - 2y = 5 \\ \hline 4x = 28 \\ \implies x = 7 \end{array}$

Substitute $x = 7$ in Equation 2: $7 - 2y = 5 \implies y = 1$

Solution: $(7, 1)$

32. $\begin{cases} 2x + y = 5 \\ x - 2y = -1 \end{cases}$

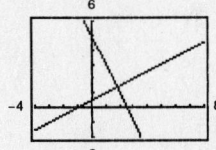

The system is consistent. There is one solution.

34. $\begin{cases} 4x - 6y = 9 \\ \frac{16}{3}x - 8y = 12 \end{cases}$

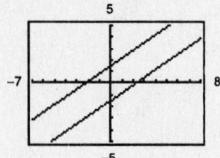

The lines are parallel. The system is inconsistent. There are no solutions.

36. $\begin{cases} 8x - 14y = 5 \\ 2x - 3.5y = 1.25 \end{cases}$

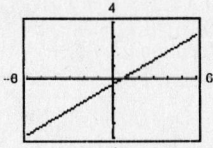

The system is consistent.
There are infinitely many solutions.

38. $\begin{cases} -7x + 6y = -4 \\ y + \frac{7}{6}x = -1 \end{cases}$

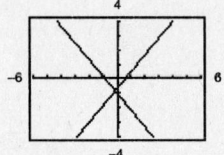

The system is consistent.
There is one solution.

40. $\begin{cases} 4y = -8 \\ 7x - 2y = 25 \end{cases}$

Solution: $(3, -2)$

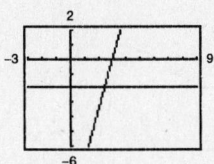

42. $\begin{cases} \frac{3}{4}x - \frac{5}{2}y = -9 \\ -x + 6y = 28 \end{cases}$

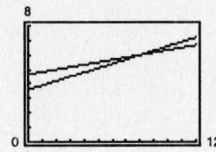

Solution: $(8, 6)$

44. $\begin{cases} 2.4x + 3.8y = -17.6 \\ 4x - 0.2y = -3.2 \end{cases}$

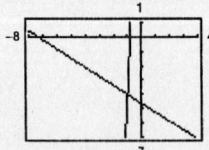

Solution: $(-1, -4)$

46. $\begin{cases} 10x - 13y = -20 \\ 8x + 11y = -16 \end{cases}$

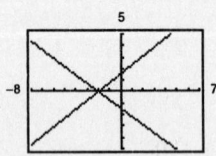

Solution: $(-2, 0)$

48. $\begin{cases} -x + 3y = 17 & \text{Equation 1} \\ 4x + 3y = 7 & \text{Equation 2} \end{cases}$

Subtract Equation 2 from Equation 1 to eliminate y:

$$\begin{array}{r} -x + 3y = 17 \\ \underline{-4x - 3y = -7} \\ -5x \quad\quad = 10 \Longrightarrow x = -2 \end{array}$$

Substitute $x = -2$ in Equation 1:
$$-(-2) + 3y = 17 \Longrightarrow y = 5$$

Solution: $(-2, 5)$

50. $\begin{cases} 7x + 3y = 16 & \text{Equation 1} \\ y = x + 2 & \text{Equation 2} \end{cases}$

Substitute for y in Equation 1:

$$7x + 3(x + 2) = 16$$
$$7x + 3x + 6 = 16$$
$$10x = 10 \Longrightarrow x = 1$$

Substitute $x = 1$ in Equation 2: $y = 1 + 2 = 3$

Solution: $(1, 3)$

52. $\begin{cases} y = -3x - 8 & \text{Equation 1} \\ y = 15 - 2x & \text{Equation 2} \end{cases}$

Since both equations are solved for y, set them equal to one another and solve for x:

$$-3x - 8 = 15 - 2x$$
$$-x = 23$$
$$x = -23$$

Back-substitute $x = -23$ into Equation 1:

$$y = -3(-23) - 8 = 61$$

Solution: $(-23, 61)$

54. $\begin{cases} 4x - 3y = 6 & \text{Equation 1} \\ -5x + 7y = -1 & \text{Equation 2} \end{cases}$

Multiply Equation 1 by 5 and Equation 2 by 4:

$$\begin{cases} 20x - 15y = 30 \\ -20x + 28y = -4 \end{cases}$$

Add to eliminate x:

$$\begin{array}{r} 20x - 15y = 30 \\ \underline{-20x + 28y = -4} \\ 13y = 26 \Longrightarrow y = 2 \end{array}$$

Back-substitute $y = 2$ into Equation 1:

$$4x - 3(2) = 6 \Longrightarrow x = 3$$

Solution: $(3, 2)$

56. Supply = Demand

$$25 + 0.1x = 100 - 0.05x$$
$$0.15x = 75$$
$$x = 500$$
$$p = 75$$

Equilibrium point: $(500, 75)$

58. Supply = Demand

$$225 + 0.0005x = 400 - 0.0002x$$
$$0.0007x = 175$$
$$x = 250,000$$
$$p = 350$$

Equilibrium point: $(250,000, 350)$

60. Let x = the speed of the plane that leaves first and y = the speed of the plane that leaves second.

$$\begin{cases} y - x = 80 & \text{Equation 1} \\ 2x + \frac{3}{2}y = 3200 & \text{Equation 2} \end{cases}$$

$$\begin{array}{r} -2x + 2y = 160 \\ \underline{2x + \frac{3}{2}y = 3200} \\ \frac{7}{2}y = 3360 \\ y = 960 \end{array}$$

$$960 - x = 80$$
$$x = 880$$

Solution: First plane:
880 kilometers per hour;
Second plane:
960 kilometers per hour

62. Let x = the number of gallons of 87 octane gasoline; y = the number of gallons of 92 octane gasoline

(a) $\begin{cases} x + y = 500 & \text{Equation 1} \\ 87x + 92y = 44{,}500 & \text{Equation 2} \end{cases}$

(b)

As the amount of 87 octane gasoline increases, the amount of 92 octane gasoline decreases.

(c) (-87) Equation 1 $\quad -87x - 87y = -43{,}500$

Equation 2 $\quad \underline{87x + 92y = 44{,}500}$

$5y = 1000$

$y = 200$

$x + 200 = 500$

$x = 300$

Solution: 87 octane: 300 gallons; 92 octane: 200 gallons

64. Let x = the amount invested at 5.75%; y = the amount invested at 6.25%

$\begin{cases} x + y = 32{,}000 & \text{Equation 1} \Rightarrow (-5.75) \text{ Equation 1} \\ 0.0575x + 0.0625y = 1900 & \text{Equation 2} \Rightarrow (100) \text{ Equation 2} \end{cases}$

$-5.75x - 5.75y = -184{,}000$

$\underline{5.75x + 6.25y = 190{,}000}$

$0.5y = 6000$

$y = 12{,}000$

$x + 12{,}000 = 32{,}000$

$x = 20{,}000$

The amount that should be invested in the bond that pays 5.75% interest is \$20,000.

66. Let x = the number of jackets sold before noon; y = the number of jackets sold after noon

$\begin{cases} x + y = 214 & \text{Equation 1} \Rightarrow (-31.95) \text{ Equation 1} \\ 31.95x + 18.95y = 5108.30 & \text{Equation 2} \Rightarrow \end{cases}$

$-31.95x - 31.95y = -6837.30$

Equation 2 $\quad \underline{31.95x + 18.95y = 5108.30}$

$-13y = -1729$

$y = 133$

$x + 133 = 214$

$x = 81$

So, 81 jackets were sold before noon and 133 jackets were sold afternoon.

68. Let x = the number of balloons inflated by the child; y = the number of balloons inflated by the father

$\begin{cases} x + y = 80 & \text{Equation 1} \Rightarrow (-2) \text{ Equation 1} \\ 2x = 3y & \text{Equation 2} \Rightarrow \end{cases}$

$-2x - 2y = -160$

Equation 2 $\quad \underline{2x - 3y = 0}$

$-5y = -160$

$y = 32$

$x + 32 = 80$

$x = 48$

The child inflated 48 balloons and the father inflated 32 balloons.

70. $\begin{cases} 5b + 10a = 11.7 \Rightarrow & -10b - 20a = -23.4 \\ 10b + 30a = 25.6 \Rightarrow & \underline{10b + 30a = 25.6} \end{cases}$

$$10a = 2.2$$
$$a = 0.22$$
$$5b + 10(0.22) = 11.7$$
$$b = 1.9$$

Least squares regression line: $y = 0.22x + 1.9$

72. $\begin{cases} 6b + 15a = 23.6 \Rightarrow & -15b - 37.5a = -59 \\ 15b + 55a = 48.8 \Rightarrow & \underline{15b + 55a = 48.8} \end{cases}$

$$17.5a = -10.2$$
$$a \approx -0.583$$
$$b \approx 5.390$$

Least squares regression line: $y = -0.583x + 5.390$

74. $\begin{cases} 8b + 28a = 8 \Rightarrow & -224b - 784a = -224 \\ 28b + 116a = 37 \Rightarrow & \underline{224b + 928a = 296} \end{cases}$

$$144a = 72$$
$$a = \tfrac{1}{2}$$
$$8b + 28\left(\tfrac{1}{2}\right) = 8$$
$$b = -\tfrac{3}{4}$$

Least squares regression line: $y = \tfrac{1}{2}x - \tfrac{3}{4}$

76. (a) $(1.0, 32)$, $(1.5, 41)$, $(2.0, 48)$, $(2.5, 53)$

$\begin{cases} 4b + 7a = 174 \Rightarrow & -7b - 12.25a = -304.5 \\ 7b + 13.5a = 322 \Rightarrow & \underline{7b + 13.5a = 322} \end{cases}$

$$1.25a = 17.5$$
$$a = 14$$
$$4b + 98 = 174$$
$$b = 19$$

Least squares regression line: $y = 14x + 19$

(b) $y = 14x + 19$

(c)

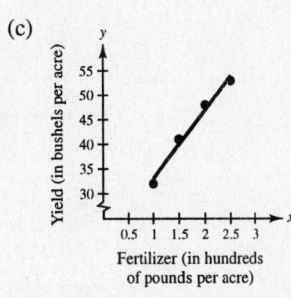

(d) When $x = 1.6$: $y = 14(1.6) + 19 = 41.4$ bushels per acre.

78. False. Solving a system of equations algebraically will always give an exact solution.

80. There are infinitely many systems that have the solution $(6, 3)$. One possible system is:

$$\begin{cases} x + y = 9 \\ 3x - 2y = 12 \end{cases}$$

82. There are infinitely many systems that have the solution $\left(3, \tfrac{5}{2}\right)$. One possible system is:

$$\begin{cases} 2x + 2y = 11 \\ x - 4y = -7 \end{cases}$$

84. $\begin{cases} 100y - x = 200 & \text{Equation 1} \\ 99y - x = -198 & \text{Equation 2} \end{cases}$

Subtract Equation 2 from
Equation 1 to eliminate x: $\quad 100y - x = 200$

$$\underline{-99y + x = 198}$$
$$y = 398$$

Substitute $y = 398$ into Equation 1:
$$100(398) - x = 200 \implies x = 39{,}600$$

Solution: $(39{,}600, \ 398)$

The lines are not parallel. The scale on the axes must be changed to see the point of intersection.

86. No, it is not possible for a consistent system of linear equations to have exactly two solutions. Either the lines will intersect once or they will coincide and then the system would have infinite solutions.

88. $\begin{cases} 4x - 8y = -3 & \text{Equation 1} \\ 2x + ky = 16 & \text{Equation 2} \end{cases}$

Multiply Equation 2 by -2: $-4x - 2ky = -32$

Add this to Equation 1:

$$\begin{array}{r} 4x - 8y = -3 \\ -4x - 2ky = -32 \\ \hline -8y - 2ky = -35 \end{array}$$

The system in inconsistent if $-8y - 2ky = 0$.
This occurs when $k = -4$.

90. $-11 - 6x \geq 33$

$ -6x \geq 44$

$ x \leq -\frac{22}{3}$

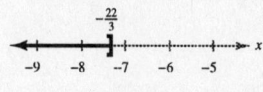

92. $8x - 15 \leq -4(2x - 1)$

$8x - 15 \leq -8x + 4$

$ 16x \leq 19$

$ x \leq \frac{19}{16}$

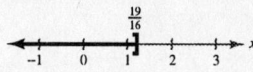

94. $|x - 8| < 10$

$-10 < x - 8 < 10$

$ -2 < x < 18$

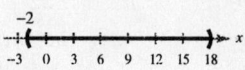

96. $2x^2 + 3x - 35 < 0$

$(2x - 7)(x + 5) < 0$

Critical numbers: $x = -5, \frac{7}{2}$

Test intervals: $(-\infty, -5), \left(-5, \frac{7}{2}\right), \left(\frac{7}{2}, \infty\right)$

Test: Is $(2x - 7)(x + 5) < 0$?

Solution: $-5 < x < \frac{7}{2}$

98. $\dfrac{x - 1}{x^2 + 11x + 30} = \dfrac{x - 1}{(x + 5)(x + 6)} = \dfrac{A}{x + 5} + \dfrac{B}{x + 6}$

$x - 1 = A(x + 6) + B(x + 5)$

Let $x = -6$: $-7 = -B \Rightarrow B = 7$

Let $x = -5$: $-6 = A$

$\dfrac{x - 1}{x^2 + 11x + 30} = \dfrac{-6}{x + 5} + \dfrac{7}{x + 6}$

100. $\ln x + \ln 6 = \ln(6x)$

102. $\log_9 12 - \log_9 x = \log_9\left(\dfrac{12}{x}\right)$

104. $\begin{cases} 2x - y = 4 \Rightarrow y = 2x - 4 \\ -4x + 2y = -12 \end{cases}$

$$-4x + 2(2x - 4) = -12$$
$$-4x + 4x - 8 = 12$$
$$-8 = 12$$

There are no solutions.

Section 7.3   Multivariable Linear Systems

Solutions to Even-Numbered Exercises

2. $\begin{cases} 3x + 4y - z = 17 \\ 5x - y + 2z = -2 \\ 2x - 3y + 7z = -21 \end{cases}$

(a) $3(3) + 4(-1) - 2 \neq 17$

    $(3, -1, 2)$ is *not* a solution.

(b) $3(1) + 4(3) - (-2) = 17$

    $5(1) - 3 + 2(-2) = -2$

    $2(1) - 3(3) + 7(-2) = -21$

    $(1, 3, -2)$ is a solution.

(c) $3(4) + 4(1) - (-3) \neq 17$

    $(4, 1, -3)$ is *not* a solution.

(d) $3(1) + 4(-2) - 2 \neq 17$

    $(1, -2, 2)$ is *not* a solution.

4. $\begin{cases} -4x - y - 8z = -6 \\ y + z = 0 \\ 4x - 7y = 6 \end{cases}$

(a) $-4(-2) - (-2) - 8(2) = -6$

           $-2 + 2 = 0$

      $4(-2) - 7(-2) = 6$

    $(-2, -2, 2)$ is a solution.

(b) $-4\left(-\frac{33}{2}\right) - (-10) - 8(10) \neq -6$

    $\left(-\frac{33}{2}, -10, 10\right)$ is *not* a solution.

(c) $-4\left(\frac{1}{8}\right) - \left(-\frac{1}{2}\right) - 8\left(\frac{1}{2}\right) \neq -6$

    $\left(\frac{1}{8}, -\frac{1}{2}, \frac{1}{2}\right)$ is *not* a solution.

(d) $-4\left(-\frac{11}{2}\right) - (-4) - 8(4) = -6$

           $-4 + 4 = 0$

      $4\left(-\frac{11}{2}\right) - 7(-4) = 6$

    $\left(-\frac{11}{2}, -4, 4\right)$ is a solution.

6. $\begin{cases} 4x - 3y - 2z = 21 & \text{Equation 1} \\ 6y - 5z = -8 & \text{Equation 2} \\ z = -2 & \text{Equation 3} \end{cases}$

Back-substitute $z = -2$ in Equation 2:

$6y - 5(-2) = -8$

         $y = -3$

Back-substitute $z = -2$ and $y = -3$ in Equation 1:

$4x - 3(-3) - 2(-2) = 21$

         $4x + 13 = 21$

            $x = 2$

Solution: $(2, -3, -2)$

8. $\begin{cases} x = 8 & \text{Equation 1} \\ 2x + 3y = 10 & \text{Equation 2} \\ x - y + 2z = 22 & \text{Equation 3} \end{cases}$

Back-substitute $x = 8$ in Equation 2:

$2(8) + 3y = 10$

         $y = -2$

Back-substitute $x = 8$ and $y = -2$ in Equation 3:

$8 - (-2) + 2z = 22$

         $z = 6$

Solution: $(8, -2, 6)$

10. $\begin{cases} 5x \quad - 8z = 22 \\ 3y - 5z = 10 \\ \qquad z = -4 \end{cases}$

Back-substitute $z = -4$ in Equation 2:

$3y - 5(-4) = 10 \implies y = -\frac{10}{3}$

Back-substitute $z = -4$ in Equation 1:

$5x - 8(-4) = 22 \implies x = -2$

Solution: $\left(-2, -\frac{10}{3}, -4\right)$

12. $\begin{cases} x - 2y + 3z = 5 \\ -x + 3y - 5z = 4 \\ 2x \qquad - 3z = 0 \end{cases}$ Equation 1   Equation 2   Equation 3

Add -2 times Equation 1 to Equation 3.

$\begin{cases} x - 2y + 3z = \quad 5 \\ -x + 3y - 5z = \quad 4 \\ \qquad 4y - 9z = -10 \end{cases}$

This is the first step in putting the system in row-echelon form.

14. $\begin{cases} x + \quad y + z = \quad 3 \\ x - 2y + 4z = \quad 5 \\ \qquad 3y + 4z = \quad 5 \end{cases}$ Equation 1   Equation 2   Equation 3

$\begin{cases} x + \quad y + z = 3 \\ \quad -3y + 3z = 2 \\ \qquad 3y + 4z = 5 \end{cases}$ (-1)Eq.1 + Eq.2

$\begin{cases} x + \quad y + z = 3 \\ \quad -3y + 3z = 2 \\ \qquad\qquad 7z = 7 \end{cases}$ Eq.2 + Eq.3

$\begin{cases} x + \quad y + z = \quad 3 \\ \qquad y - z = -\frac{2}{3} \\ \qquad\qquad z = \quad 1 \end{cases}$ $\left(-\frac{1}{3}\right)$Eq.2 $\left(\frac{1}{7}\right)$Eq.3

$y - 1 = -\frac{2}{3} \implies y = \frac{1}{3}$

$x + \frac{1}{3} + 1 = \quad 3 \implies x = \frac{5}{3}$

Solution: $\left(\frac{5}{3}, \frac{1}{3}, 1\right)$

16. $\begin{cases} x + \quad y - z = -1 \\ 2x + 4y + z = \quad 1 \\ x - 2y - 3z = \quad 2 \end{cases}$ Interchange equations

$\begin{cases} x + \quad y - z = -1 \\ \qquad 2y + 3z = \quad 3 \\ \qquad -3y - 2z = \quad 3 \end{cases}$ (-2)Eq.1 + Eq.2 (-1)Eq.1 + Eq.3

$\begin{cases} x + \quad y - z = -1 \\ \qquad 2y + 3z = \quad 3 \\ \qquad -6y - 4z = \quad 6 \end{cases}$ 2 Eq.3

$\begin{cases} x + \quad y - z = -1 \\ \qquad 2y + 3z = \quad 3 \\ \qquad\qquad 5z = 15 \end{cases}$ 3Eq.2 + Eq.3

$\begin{cases} x + \quad y - z = -1 \\ \qquad y + \frac{3}{2}z = \frac{3}{2} \\ \qquad\qquad z = 3 \end{cases}$ $\left(\frac{1}{2}\right)$Eq.2 $\left(\frac{1}{5}\right)$Eq.3

$y + \frac{3}{2}(3) = \frac{3}{2} \implies y = -3$

$x - 3 - 3 = -1 \implies x = \quad 5$

Solution: $(5, -3, 3)$

18. $\begin{cases} x + 4y + \quad z = \quad 0 \\ 2x + 4y - \quad z = \quad 7 \\ 2x - 4y + 2z = -6 \end{cases}$ Interchange equations

$\begin{cases} x + 4y + \quad z = \quad 0 \\ \quad -4y - 3z = \quad 7 \\ \quad -12y \qquad = -6 \end{cases}$ (-2)Eq.1 + Eq.2 (-2)Eq.1 + Eq.3

$\begin{cases} x + 4y + \quad z = \quad 0 \\ \quad -4y - 3z = \quad 7 \\ \qquad\qquad 9z = -27 \end{cases}$ (-3)Eq.2 + Eq.3

$\begin{cases} x + 4y + \quad z = \quad 0 \\ \qquad y + \frac{3}{4}z = -\frac{7}{4} \\ \qquad\qquad z = -3 \end{cases}$ $\left(-\frac{1}{4}\right)$Eq.2 $\left(\frac{1}{9}\right)$Eq.3

$y + \frac{3}{4}(-3) = -\frac{7}{4} \implies y = \frac{1}{2}$

$x + 4\left(\frac{1}{2}\right) + (-3) = \quad 0 \implies x = 1$

Solution: $\left(1, \frac{1}{2}, -3\right)$

20. $\begin{cases} x - 11y + 4z = 3 \\ 5x - 3y + 2z = 3 \\ 2x + 4y - z = 7 \end{cases}$ Interchange equations

$\begin{cases} x - 11y + 4z = \quad 3 \\ \qquad 52y - 18z = -12 \\ \qquad 26y - 9z = \quad 1 \end{cases}$ (-5)Eq.1 + Eq.2 (-2)Eq.1 + Eq.3

$\begin{cases} x - 11y + 4z = \quad 3 \\ \qquad 52y - 18z = -12 \\ \qquad\qquad 0 = \quad 7 \end{cases}$ $\left(-\frac{1}{2}\right)$Eq.2 + Eq.3

Inconsistent; no solution

22. $\begin{cases} 2x + y + 3z = 1 & \text{Equation 1} \\ 2x + 6y + 8z = 3 & \text{Equation 2} \\ 6x + 8y + 18z = 5 & \text{Equation 3} \end{cases}$

$\begin{cases} 2x + y + 3z = 1 \\ 5y + 5z = 2 & (-1)\text{Eq.1 + Eq.2} \\ 5y + 9z = 2 & (-3)\text{Eq.1 + Eq.3} \end{cases}$

$\begin{cases} 2x + y + 3z = 1 \\ 5y + 5z = 2 \\ 4z = 0 & (-1)\text{Eq.2 + Eq.3} \end{cases}$

$\begin{cases} x + \frac{1}{2}y + \frac{3}{2}z = \frac{1}{2} & \left(\frac{1}{2}\right)\text{Eq.1} \\ y + z = \frac{2}{5} & \left(\frac{1}{5}\right)\text{Eq.2} \\ z = 0 & \left(\frac{1}{4}\right)\text{Eq.3} \end{cases}$

$y + 0 = \frac{2}{5} \Longrightarrow y = \frac{2}{5}$

$x + \frac{1}{2}\left(\frac{2}{5}\right) + \frac{3}{2}(0) = \frac{1}{2} \Longrightarrow x = \frac{3}{10}$

Solution: $\left(\frac{3}{10}, \frac{2}{5}, 0\right)$

24. $\begin{cases} 2x + y - 3z = 4 & \text{Equation 1} \\ 4x + 2z = 10 & \text{Equation 2} \\ -2x + 3y - 13z = -8 & \text{Equation 3} \end{cases}$

$\begin{cases} 2x + y - 3z = 4 & (-2)\text{Eq.1 + Eq.2} \\ -2y + 8z = 2 & \text{Eq.1 + Eq.3} \\ 4y - 16z = -4 \end{cases}$

$\begin{cases} 2x + y - 3z = 4 \\ -2y + 8z = 2 \\ 0 = 0 & 2\text{Eq.2 + Eq.3} \end{cases}$

$\begin{cases} 2x + z = 5 & \left(\frac{1}{2}\right)\text{Eq.2 + Eq.1} \\ -2y - 8z = 2 \end{cases}$

$\begin{cases} x + z/2 = \frac{5}{2} & \left(\frac{1}{2}\right)\text{Eq.1} \\ y - 4z = -1 & \left(-\frac{1}{2}\right)\text{Eq. 2} \end{cases}$

$z = a$

$y - 4a = -1 \Longrightarrow y = 4a - 1$

$x + \frac{1}{2}a = \frac{5}{2} \Longrightarrow x = -\frac{1}{2}a + \frac{5}{2}$

Solution: $\left(-\frac{1}{2}a + \frac{5}{2}, 4a - 1, a\right)$

26. $\begin{cases} x + 4z = 13 & \text{Equation 1} \\ 4x - 2y + z = 7 & \text{Equation 2} \\ 2x - 2y - 7z = -19 & \text{Equation 3} \end{cases}$

$\begin{cases} x + 4z = 13 \\ -2y - 15z = -45 & (-4)\text{Eq.1 + Eq.2} \\ -2y - 15z = -45 & (-2)\text{Eq.1 + Eq.3} \end{cases}$

$\begin{cases} x + 4z = 13 \\ -2y - 15z = -45 \\ 0 = 0 & (-1)\text{Eq.2 + Eq.3} \end{cases}$

$\begin{cases} x + 4z = 13 \\ y + \frac{15}{2}z = \frac{45}{2} & \left(-\frac{1}{2}\right)\text{Eq.2} \end{cases}$

$z = a$

$y + \frac{15}{2}a = \frac{45}{2} \Longrightarrow y = -\frac{15}{2}a + \frac{45}{2}$

$x + 4a = 13 \Longrightarrow x = -4a + 13$

Solution: $\left(-4a + 13, -\frac{15}{2}a + \frac{45}{2}, a\right)$

28. $\begin{cases} x - 3y + 2z = 18 & \text{Equation 1} \\ 5x - 13y + 12z = 80 & \text{Equation 2} \end{cases}$

$\begin{cases} x - 3y + 2z = 18 \\ 2y + 2z = -10 & (-5)\text{Eq.1 + Eq.2} \end{cases}$

$\begin{cases} x - 3y + 2z = 18 \\ y + z = -5 & \left(\frac{1}{2}\right)\text{Eq.2} \end{cases}$

$\begin{cases} x + 5z = 3 & 3\text{Eq.2 + Eq.1} \\ y + z = -5 \end{cases}$

Let $z = a$, then: $y + a = -5 \Longrightarrow y = -a - 5$

$x + 5a = 3 \Longrightarrow x = -5a + 3$

Solution: $(-5a + 3, -a - 5, a)$

30. $\begin{cases} 2x + 3y + 3z = 7 & \text{Equation 1} \\ 4x + 18y + 15z = 44 & \text{Equation 2} \end{cases}$

$\begin{cases} 2x + 3y + 3z = 7 \\ 12y + 9z = 30 \end{cases}$ (-2)Eq.1 + Eq.2

$\begin{cases} 2x + \frac{3}{4}z = -\frac{1}{2} & (-\frac{1}{4})\text{Eq.2 + Eq.1} \\ 12y + 9z = 30 \end{cases}$

$\begin{cases} x + \frac{3}{8}z = -\frac{1}{4} & (\frac{1}{2})\text{Eq.1} \\ y + \frac{3}{4}z = \frac{5}{2} & (\frac{1}{12})\text{Eq.2} \end{cases}$

Let $z = a$, then:

$y + \frac{3}{4}a = \frac{5}{2} \Longrightarrow y = -\frac{3}{4}a + \frac{5}{2}$

$x + \frac{3}{8}a = -\frac{1}{4} \Longrightarrow x = -\frac{3}{8}a - \frac{1}{4}$

Solution: $\left(-\frac{3}{8}a - \frac{1}{4}, -\frac{3}{4}a + \frac{5}{2}, a\right)$

32. $\begin{cases} x + y + z + w = 6 & \text{Equation 1} \\ 2x + 3y - w = 0 & \text{Equation 2} \\ -3x + 4y + z + 2w = 4 & \text{Equation 3} \\ x + 2y - z + w = 0 & \text{Equation 4} \end{cases}$

$\begin{cases} x + y + z + w = 6 \\ y - 2z - 3w = -12 & (-2)\text{Eq.1 + Eq.2} \\ 7y + 4z + 5w = 22 & 3\text{Eq.1 + Eq.3} \\ y - 2z = -6 & (-1)\text{Eq.1 + Eq.4} \end{cases}$

$\begin{cases} x + y + z + w = 6 \\ y - 2z - 3w = -12 \\ 18z + 26w = 106 & (-7)\text{Eq.2 + Eq.3} \\ 3w = 6 & (-1)\text{Eq.2 + Eq.4} \end{cases}$

$\begin{cases} x + y + z + w = 6 \\ y - 2z - 3w = -12 \\ z + \frac{13}{9}w = \frac{53}{9} & (\frac{1}{18})\text{Eq.3} \\ w = 2 & (\frac{1}{3})\text{Eq.4} \end{cases}$

$z + \frac{13}{9}(2) = \frac{53}{9} \Longrightarrow z = 3$

$y - 2(3) - 3(2) = -12 \Longrightarrow y = 0$

$x + 0 + 3 + 2 = 6 \Longrightarrow x = 1$

Solution: $(1, 0, 3, 2)$

34. $\begin{cases} 2x - 2y - 6z = -4 & \text{Equation 1} \\ -3x + 2y + 6z = 1 & \text{Equation 2} \\ x - y - 5z = -3 & \text{Equation 3} \end{cases}$

$\begin{cases} x - y - 5z = -3 \\ -3x + 2y + 6z = 1 & \text{Interchange equations} \\ 2x - 2y - 6z = -4 \end{cases}$

$\begin{cases} x - y - 5z = -3 \\ -y - 9z = -8 & 3\text{Eq.1 + Eq.2} \\ 4z = 2 & (-2)\text{Eq.1 + Eq.3} \end{cases}$

$\begin{cases} x - y - 5z = -3 \\ y + 9z = 8 & (-1)\text{Eq.2} \\ z = \frac{1}{2} & (\frac{1}{4})\text{Eq.3} \end{cases}$

$y + 9\left(\frac{1}{2}\right) = 8 \Longrightarrow y = \frac{7}{2}$

$x - \frac{7}{2} - 5\left(\frac{1}{2}\right) = -3 \Longrightarrow x = 3$

Solution: $\left(3, \frac{7}{2}, \frac{1}{2}\right)$

36. $\begin{cases} 4x + 3y + 17z = 0 \\ 5x + 4y + 22z = 0 \\ 4x + 2y + 19z = 0 \end{cases}$

$\begin{cases} 5x + 4y + 22z = 0 \\ 4x + 3y + 17z = 0 & \text{Interchange} \\ 4x + 2y + 19z = 0 & \text{equations} \end{cases}$

$\begin{cases} x + y + 5z = 0 & (-1)\text{Eq.2 + Eq.1} \\ 4x + 3y + 17z = 0 \\ 4x + 2y + 19z = 0 \end{cases}$

$\begin{cases} x + y + 5z = 0 \\ -y - 3z = 0 & (-4)\text{Eq.1 + Eq.2} \\ -2y - z = 0 & (-4)\text{Eq.1 + Eq.3} \end{cases}$

$\begin{cases} x + y + 5z = 0 \\ y + 3z = 0 & (-1)\text{Eq.2} \\ 5z = 0 & (-2)\text{Eq.2 + Eq.3} \end{cases}$

$\begin{cases} x + y + 5z = 0 \\ y + 3z = 0 \\ z = 0 & (\frac{1}{5})\text{Eq.3} \end{cases}$

$y + 3(0) = 0 \Longrightarrow y = 0$

$x + 0 + 5(0) = 0 \Longrightarrow x = 0$

Solution: $(0, 0, 0)$

38. $\begin{cases} 2x - y - z = 0 & \text{Equation 1} \\ -2x + 6y + 4z = 2 & \text{Equation 2} \end{cases}$

$\begin{cases} 2x - y - z = 0 \\ \quad\quad 5y + 3z = 2 & \text{Eq.1 + Eq.2} \end{cases}$

$\begin{cases} x - \frac{1}{2}y - \frac{1}{2}z = 0 & \left(\frac{1}{2}\right)\text{Eq.1} \\ \quad\quad y + \frac{3}{5}z = \frac{2}{5} & \left(\frac{1}{5}\right)\text{Eq.2} \end{cases}$

Let $z = a$, then:

$$y + \frac{3}{5}a = \frac{2}{5} \Rightarrow y = -\frac{3}{5}a + \frac{2}{5}$$

$$x - \frac{1}{2}\left(-\frac{3}{5}a + \frac{2}{5}\right) - \frac{1}{2}a = 0 \Rightarrow x = \frac{1}{5}a + \frac{1}{5}$$

Solution: $\left(\frac{1}{5}a + \frac{1}{5}, \; -\frac{3}{5}a + \frac{2}{5}, \; a\right)$

40. $y = ax^2 + bx + c$ passing through

$(0, 3), (1, 4), (2, 3)$

$(0, 3)$: $\quad 3 = \quad\quad\quad\quad c$

$(1, 4)$: $\quad 4 = a + b + c \Rightarrow 1 = a + b$

$(2, 3)$: $\quad 3 = 4a + 2b + c \Rightarrow 0 = 2a + b$

Solution: $a = -1, b = 2, c = 3$

The equation of the parabola is $y = -x^2 + 2x + 3$.

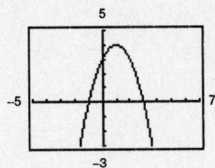

42. $y = ax^2 + bx + c$ passing through

$(1, 3), (2, 2), (3, -3)$

$(1, 3)$: $\quad 3 = a + b + c$

$(2, 2)$: $\quad 2 = 4a + 2b + c$

$(3, -3)$: $-3 = 9a + 3b + c$

$\begin{cases} a + b + c = 3 \\ 3a + b = -1 & (-1)\text{Eq.1 + Eq.2} \\ 8a + 2b = -6 & (-1)\text{Eq.1 + Eq.3} \end{cases}$

$\begin{cases} a + b + c = 3 \\ 3a + b = -1 \\ 2a = -4 & (-2)\text{Eq.2 + Eq.3} \end{cases}$

Solution: $a = -2, b = 5, c = 0$

The equation of the parabola is $y = -2x^2 + 5x$.

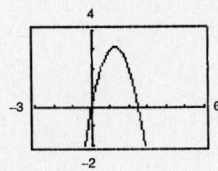

44. $x^2 + y^2 + Dx + Ey + F = 0$

passing through $(0, 0), (0, 6), (3, 3)$

$(0, 0)$: $\quad\quad\quad\quad F = 0$

$(0, 6)$: $\quad\quad 36 + 6E + F = 0 \Rightarrow E = -6$

$(3, 3)$: $18 + 3D + 3E + F = 0 \Rightarrow D = 0$

The equation of the circle is $x^2 + y^2 - 6y = 0$.

To graph, complete the square first, then solve for y.

$$x^2 + (y^2 - 6y + 9) = 9$$

$$x^2 + (y - 3)^2 = 9$$

$$(y - 3)^2 = 9 - x^2$$

$$y - 3 = \pm\sqrt{9 - x^2}$$

$$y = 3 \pm \sqrt{9 - x^2}$$

Let $y_1 = 3 + \sqrt{9 - x^2}$ and $y_2 = 3 - \sqrt{9 - x^2}$.

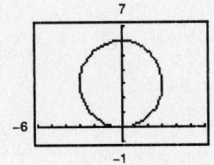

46. $x^2 + y^2 + Dx + Ey + F = 0$ passing through $(0, 0), (0, -2), (3, 0)$

$(0, 0)$: $\quad\quad\quad\quad F = 0$

$(0, -2)$: $4 \quad -2E + F = 0 \Rightarrow E = 2$

$(3, 0)$: $\quad 9 + 3D \quad + F = 0 \Rightarrow D = -3$

The equation of the circle is $x^2 + y^2 - 3x + 2y = 0$.

—CONTINUED—

46. —CONTINUED—

To graph, complete the squares first, then solve for y.

$$\left(x^2 - 3x + \tfrac{9}{4}\right) + (y^2 + 2y + 1) = \tfrac{9}{4} + 1$$

$$\left(x - \tfrac{3}{2}\right)^2 + (y + 1)^2 = \tfrac{13}{4}$$

$$(y + 1)^2 = \tfrac{13}{4} - \left(x - \tfrac{3}{2}\right)^2$$

$$y + 1 = \pm\sqrt{\tfrac{13}{4} - \left(x - \tfrac{3}{2}\right)^2}$$

$$y = -1 \pm \sqrt{\tfrac{13}{4} - \left(x - \tfrac{3}{2}\right)^2}$$

Let $y_1 = -1 + \sqrt{\tfrac{13}{4} - \left(x - \tfrac{3}{2}\right)^2}$ and $y_2 = -1 - \sqrt{\tfrac{13}{4} - \left(x - \tfrac{3}{2}\right)^2}$.

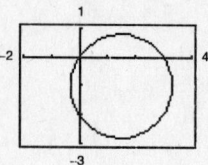

48. $s = \tfrac{1}{2}at^2 + v_0 t + s_0$

$(1, 48), (2, 64), (3, 48)$

$$\begin{cases} 48 = \tfrac{1}{2}a + v_0 + s_0 \\ 64 = 2a + 2v_0 + s_0 \\ 48 = \tfrac{9}{2}a + 3v_0 + s_0 \end{cases}$$

$$\begin{cases} a + 2v_0 + 2s_0 = 96 & \text{2Eq. 1} \\ 2a + 2v_0 + s_0 = 64 \\ 9a + 6v_0 + 2s_0 = 96 & \text{2Eq. 3} \end{cases}$$

$$\begin{cases} a + 2v_0 + 2s_0 = 96 \\ -2v_0 - 3s_0 = -128 & (-2)\text{Eq.1 + Eq.2} \\ -12v_0 - 16s_0 = -768 & (-9)\text{Eq.1 + Eq.3} \end{cases}$$

$$\begin{cases} a + 2v_0 + 2s_0 = 96 \\ -2v_0 - 3s_0 = -128 \\ 2s_0 = 0 & (-6)\text{Eq.2 + Eq.3} \end{cases}$$

$$\begin{cases} a + 2v_0 + 2s_0 = 96 \\ v_0 + 1.5s_0 = 64 & (-0.5)\text{Eq.2} \\ s_0 = 0 & (0.5)\text{Eq.3} \end{cases}$$

$$v_0 + 1.5(0) = 64 \Longrightarrow v_0 = 64$$
$$a + 2(64) + 2(0) = 96 \Longrightarrow a = -32$$

Thus, $s = \tfrac{1}{2}(-32)t^2 + 64t + 0$

$$= -16t^2 + 64t.$$

50. $s = \tfrac{1}{2}at^2 + v_0 t + s_0$

$(1, 132), (2, 100), (3, 36)$

$$\begin{cases} 132 = \tfrac{1}{2}a + v_0 + s_0 \\ 100 = 2a + 2v_0 + s_0 \\ 36 = \tfrac{9}{2}a + 3v_0 + s_0 \end{cases}$$

$$\begin{cases} a + 2v_0 + 2s_0 = 264 & \text{2Eq. 1} \\ 2a + 2v_0 + s_0 = 100 \\ 9a + 6v_0 + 2s_0 = 72 & \text{2Eq. 3} \end{cases}$$

$$\begin{cases} a + 2v_0 + 2s_0 = 264 \\ -2v_0 - 3s_0 = -428 & (-2)\text{Eq.1 + Eq.2} \\ -12v_0 - 16s_0 = -2304 & (-9)\text{Eq.1 + Eq.3} \end{cases}$$

$$\begin{cases} a + 2v_0 + 2s_0 = 264 \\ -2v_0 - 3s_0 = -428 \\ 2s_0 = 264 & (-6)\text{Eq.2 + Eq.3} \end{cases}$$

$$\begin{cases} a + 2v_0 + 2s_0 = 264 \\ v_0 + 1.5s_0 = 214 & (-0.5)\text{Eq.2} \\ s_0 = 132 & (0.5)\text{Eq.3} \end{cases}$$

$$v_0 + 1.5(132) = 214 \Longrightarrow v_0 = 16$$
$$a + 2(16) + 2(132) = 264 \Longrightarrow a = -32$$

Thus, $s = \tfrac{1}{2}(-32)t^2 + 16t + 132$

$$= -16t^2 + 16t + 132.$$

52. Let $x =$ number of 3-point baskets.
Let $y =$ number of 2-point baskets.
Let $z =$ number of free-throws.

$$\begin{cases} 3x + 2y + z = 104 \\ y = 2z \\ z = 2x \end{cases}$$

$$y = 2(2x) = 4x$$

$$3x + 2(4x) + 2x = 104 \Longrightarrow x = 8$$

$$y = 4(8) = 32$$

$$z = 2(8) = 16$$

Solution: 8 3-point baskets
32 2-point baskets
16 free-throws

54. Let $x =$ amount at 8%
Let $y =$ amount at 9%
Let $z =$ amount at 10%

$$\begin{cases} x + y + z = 800{,}000 \\ 0.08x + 0.09y + 0.10z = 67{,}000 \\ x = 5z \end{cases}$$

$$\begin{cases} y + 6z = 800{,}000 \\ 0.09y + 0.5z = 67{,}000 \end{cases}$$

$$z = 125{,}000$$

$$y = 800{,}000 - 6(125{,}000) = 50{,}000$$

$$x = 5(125{,}000) = 625{,}000$$

Solution: $x = \$625{,}000$ at 8%
$y = \$50{,}000$ at 9%
$z = \$125{,}000$ at 10%

56. Let C = amount in certificates of deposit

Let M = amount in municipal bonds

Let B = amount in blue-chip stocks

Let G = amount in growth or speculative stocks

$$\begin{cases} C + M + B + G = 500{,}000 \\ 0.09C + 0.05M + 0.12B + 0.14G = 0.10(500{,}000) \\ B + G = \tfrac{1}{4}(500{,}000) \end{cases}$$

This system has infinitely many solutions.

Let $G = s$, then $B = 125{,}000 - s$

$$M = \tfrac{1}{2}s - 31{,}250$$

$$C = 406{,}250 - \tfrac{1}{2}s.$$

Solution:

$406{,}250 - \tfrac{1}{2}s$ in certificates of deposit,

$-31{,}250 + \tfrac{1}{2}s$ in municipal bonds,

$125{,}000 - s$ in blue-chip stocks,

s in growth stocks

One possible solution is to let $s = \$100{,}000$.

Certificates of deposit: $356{,}250

Municipal bonds: $18{,}750

Blue-chip stocks: $25{,}000

Growth or speculative stocks: $100{,}000

58. (a) To use as little of the 50% solution as possible, the chemist should use no 10% solution.

$$x(0.20) + (10 - x)(0.50) = 10(0.25)$$

$$x(0.20) + 5 - 0.50x = 2.5$$

$$-0.30x = -2.5$$

$$x = 8\tfrac{1}{3} \text{ liters of 20\% solution}$$

$$10 - x = 1\tfrac{2}{3} \text{ liters of 50\% solution}$$

(b) To use as much 50% solution as possible, the chemist should use no 20% solution.

$$x(0.10) + (10 - x)0.50 = 10(0.25)$$

$$0.10x + 5 - 0.50x = 2.5$$

$$-0.40x = -2.5$$

$$x = 6\tfrac{1}{4} \text{ liters of 10\% solution}$$

$$10 - x = 3\tfrac{3}{4} \text{ liters of 50\% solution}$$

(c) To use 2 liters of 50% solution we let x = the number of liters at 10% and y = the number of liters at 20%.

$$0.10x + 0.20y + 2(0.50) = 10(0.25) \qquad \text{Equation 1}$$

$$x + y = 8 \qquad \text{Equation 2}$$

Solution: $y = 7$ liters of 20% solution;

$x = 1$ liter of 10% solution

60.
$$\begin{cases} I_1 - I_2 + I_3 = 0 & \text{Equation 1} \\ 3I_1 + 2I_2 = 7 & \text{Equation 2} \\ 2I_2 + 4I_3 = 8 & \text{Equation 3} \end{cases}$$

$$\begin{cases} I_1 - I_2 + I_3 = 0 \\ 5I_2 - 3I_3 = 7 \qquad (-3)\text{Eq.1} + \text{Eq.2} \\ 2I_2 + 4I_3 = 8 \end{cases}$$

$$\begin{cases} I_1 - I_2 + I_3 = 0 \\ 10I_2 - 6I_3 = 14 \qquad 2\text{Eq.2} \\ 10I_2 + 20I_3 = 40 \qquad 5\text{Eq.3} \end{cases}$$

$$\begin{cases} I_1 - I_2 + I_3 = 0 \\ 10I_2 - 6I_3 = 14 \\ 26I_3 = 26 \qquad (-1)\text{Eq.2} + \text{Eq.3} \end{cases}$$

$$26I_3 = 26 \Longrightarrow I_3 = 1$$

$$10I_2 - 6(1) = 14 \Longrightarrow I_2 = 2$$

$$I_1 - 2 + 1 = 0 \Longrightarrow I_1 = 1$$

Solution: $I_1 = 1, I_2 = 2, I_3 = 1$

62.
$$\begin{cases} t_1 - 2t_2 = 0 & \text{Equation 1} \\ t_1 - 2a = 128 & \text{Equation 2} \\ t_2 + 2a = 64 & \text{Equation 3} \end{cases}$$

$$\begin{cases} t_1 - 2t_2 = 0 \\ 2t_2 - 2a = 128 \qquad (-1)\text{Eq.1} + \text{Eq.2} \\ t_2 + 2a = 64 \end{cases}$$

$$\begin{cases} t_1 - 2t_2 = 0 \\ 2t_2 - 2a = 128 \\ 3a = 0 \qquad \left(-\tfrac{1}{2}\right)\text{Eq.2} + \text{Eq.3} \end{cases}$$

$$3a = 0 \Longrightarrow a = 0$$

$$2t_2 - 2(0) = 128 \Longrightarrow t_2 = 64$$

$$t_1 - 2(64) = 0 \Longrightarrow t_1 = 128$$

Solution: $a = 0$ ft/sec^2

$$t_1 = 128 \text{ lb}$$

$$t_2 = 64 \text{ lb}$$

64. $\dfrac{3}{x^2 + x - 2} = \dfrac{A}{x - 1} + \dfrac{B}{x + 2}$

$$3 = A(x + 2) + B(x - 1)$$

$$3 = Ax + 2A + Bx - B$$

$$3 = (A + B)x + (2A - B)$$

By equating coefficients, we have: $0 = A + B \implies A = -B$

$$3 = 2A - B \implies 3 = 2(-B) - B \implies B = -1$$

$$A = -(-1) = 1$$

$$\frac{3}{x^2 + x - 2} = \frac{1}{x - 1} - \frac{1}{x + 2}$$

66. $\dfrac{12}{x(x - 2)(x + 3)} = \dfrac{A}{x} + \dfrac{B}{x - 2} + \dfrac{C}{x + 3}$

$$12 = A(x - 2)(x + 3) + Bx(x + 3) + Cx(x - 2)$$

$$12 = Ax^2 + Ax - 6A + Bx^2 + 3Bx + Cx^2 - 2Cx$$

$$12 = (A + B + C)x^2 + (A + 3B - 2C)x - 6A$$

By equating coefficients, we have

$0 = A + B + C$

$0 = A + 3B - 2C$

$12 = -6A \qquad \implies A = -2$

$$2 = B + C \implies 4 = 2B + 2C$$

$$2 = 3B - 2C \implies \underline{2 = 3B - 2C}$$

$$6 = 5B$$

$$B = \frac{6}{5}$$

$$C = \frac{4}{5}$$

$$\frac{12}{x(x - 2)(x + 3)} = -\frac{2}{x} + \frac{6}{5(x - 2)} + \frac{4}{5(x + 3)}$$

68. $\begin{cases} 5c & + 10a = 8 \\ 10b & = 12 \\ 10c & + 34a = 22 \end{cases}$

$\begin{cases} 5c & + 10a = 8 \\ 10b & = 12 \\ & 14a = 6 \qquad (-2)\text{Eq.1} + \text{Eq.3} \end{cases}$

$14a = 6 \implies a = \frac{3}{7}$

$10b = 12 \implies b = \frac{6}{5}$

$5c + 10\left(\frac{3}{7}\right) = 8 \implies c = \frac{26}{35}$

Least squares regression parabola: $y = \frac{3}{7}x^2 + \frac{6}{5}x + \frac{26}{35}$

70. $\begin{cases} 4c + & 6b + & 14a = 25 \\ 6c + & 14b + & 36a = 21 \\ 14c + & 36b + & 98a = 33 \end{cases}$

$\begin{cases} 4c + & 6b + & 14a = 25 \\ & -10b - & 30a = 33 \qquad 3\text{Eq.1} - 2\text{Eq.2} \\ & -60b - & 196a = 218 \qquad 14\text{Eq.1} - 4\text{Eq.3} \end{cases}$

$\begin{cases} 4c + & 6b + & 14a = 25 \\ & -10b - & 30a = 33 \\ & & -16a = 20 \qquad (-6)\text{Eq.2} + \text{Eq.3} \end{cases}$

$-16a = 20 \implies a = -\frac{5}{4}$

$-10b - 30\left(-\frac{5}{4}\right) = 33 \implies b = \frac{9}{20}$

$4c + 6\left(\frac{9}{20}\right) + 14\left(-\frac{5}{4}\right) = 25 \implies c = \frac{199}{20}$

Least squares regression parabola: $y = -\frac{5}{4}x^2 + \frac{9}{20}x + \frac{199}{20}$

72. (a) (100, 75), (120, 68), (140, 55)

$$\begin{cases} c + 100b + 10{,}000a = 75 & \text{Equation 1} \\ c + 120b + 14{,}400a = 68 & \text{Equation 2} \\ c + 140b + 19{,}600a = 55 & \text{Equation 3} \end{cases}$$

$$\begin{cases} c + 100b + 10{,}000a = 75 \\ 20b + 4400a = -7 & (-1)\text{Eq.1} + \text{Eq.2} \\ 40b + 9600a = -20 & (-1)\text{Eq.1} + \text{Eq.3} \end{cases}$$

$$\begin{cases} c + 100b + 10{,}000a = 75 \\ 20b + 4400a = -7 \\ 800a = -6 & (-2)\text{Eq.2} + \text{Eq.3} \end{cases}$$

$$\begin{cases} c + 100b + 10{,}000a = 75 \\ b + \phantom{10{,}0}220a = -\frac{7}{20} & \left(\frac{1}{20}\right)\text{Eq.2} \\ \phantom{c + b + 10{,}00} a = -\frac{6}{800} & \left(\frac{1}{800}\right)\text{Eq.2} \end{cases}$$

$$a = -\frac{6}{800} = -0.0075$$

$$b + 220(-0.0075) = -\frac{7}{20} \implies b = \frac{26}{20} = 1.3$$

$$c + 100(1.3) + 10{,}000(-0.0075) = 75 \implies c = 20$$

So, $y = -0.0075x^2 + 1.3x + 20$

(b)

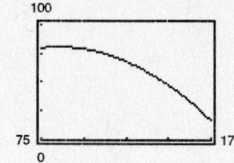

(c) For $x = 170$:

$$y = -0.0075(170)^2 + 1.3(170) + 20$$

$$= 24.25\%$$

74. $\begin{cases} 2x + \lambda = 0 \\ 2y + \lambda = 0 \\ x + y - 4 = 0 \end{cases}$ $\left.\begin{matrix}\\\\\end{matrix}\right\}$ $x = y = -\dfrac{\lambda}{2}$

$\implies 2x - 4 = 0$

$$2x = 4$$

$$x = 2$$

$$y = 2$$

$$\lambda = -4$$

76. $\begin{cases} 2 + 2y + 2\lambda = 0 \\ 2x + 2 + \lambda = 0 \\ 2x + y - 100 = 0 \end{cases} \implies \lambda = -2x - 1$

$$2 + 2y + 2(-2x - 1) = 0 \implies -4x + 2y = 0 \implies -4x + 2y = 0$$

$$2x + y - 100 = 0 \implies 2x + y = 100 \implies \underline{4x + 2y = 200}$$

$$4y = 200$$

$$y = 50$$

$$x = 25$$

$$\lambda = -2(25) - 1 = -51$$

78. True. If a system of three linear equations is inconsistent, then it has no points in common to all three equations.

80. The first system is inconsistent because 4 times Equation 1 added to Equation 2 yields $0 = 20$.

82. There are an infinite number of linear systems that have $(4, -1, 2)$ as their solution. One such system is as follows:

$$\begin{cases} 3x + y - z = 9 \\ x + 2y - z = 0 \\ -x + y + 3z = 1 \end{cases}$$

84. There are an infinite number of linear systems that have $\left(3, -\frac{1}{2}, \frac{7}{4}\right)$ as their solution. One such system is as follows:

$$\begin{cases} x + 2y - 4z = -5 \\ -x - 4y + 8z = 13 \\ x + 6y + 4z = 7 \end{cases}$$

86. $(0.075)(85) = 6.375$

88. $(0.005)n = 400$

$n = 80,000$

90. $f(x) = x^3 + x^2 - 12x$

(a) $x^3 + x^2 - 12x = 0$

$x(x^2 + x - 12) = 0$

$x(x + 4)(x - 3) = 0$

Zeros: $x = -4, 0, 3$

(b)
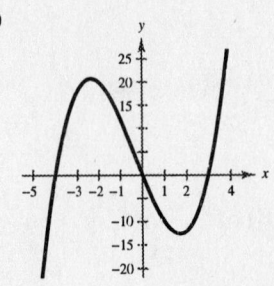

92. $f(x) = 2x^3 + 5x^2 - 21x - 36$

(a) $2x^3 + 5x^2 - 21x - 36 = 0$

$$\begin{array}{r|rrr} 3 & 2 & 5 & -21 & -36 \\ & & 6 & 33 & 36 \\ \hline & 2 & 11 & 12 & 0 \end{array}$$

$f(x) = (x - 3)(2x^2 + 11x + 12)$

$= (x - 3)(x + 4)(2x + 3)$

Zeros: $x = -4, -\frac{3}{2}, 3$

(b)
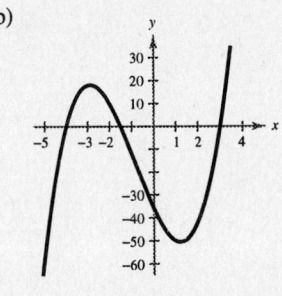

94. $y = 4^{x-4} - 5$

x	-2	0	2	4	5
y	-5	-4.996	-4.938	-4	-1

Horizontal asymptote: $y = -5$

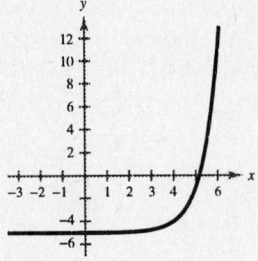

96. $y = 1.9^{-0.8x} + 3$

x	-2	-1	0	1	2
y	5.793	4.671	4	3.598	3.358

Horizontal asymptote: $y = 3$

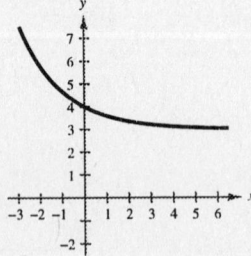

98. $\begin{cases} 2x + y = 120 & \text{Equation 1} \\ x + 2y = 120 & \text{Equation 2} \end{cases}$

$$\begin{array}{rl} 2x + y = & 120 \\ -2x - 4y = & -240 \qquad (-2)\text{Eq.2} \\ \hline -3y = & -120 \\ y = & 40 \end{array}$$

$x + 2(40) = 120 \Longrightarrow x = 40$

Solution: $(40, 40)$

Section 7.4   Systems of Inequalities

Solutions to Even-Numbered Exercises

2. $x \leq 4$

Using a solid line, graph the vertical line $x = 4$, and shade to the left of this line.

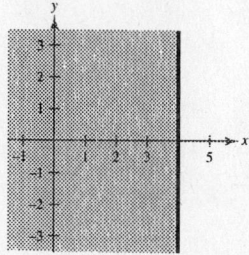

4. $y \leq 3$

Using a solid line, graph the horizontal line $y = 3$, and shade below this line.

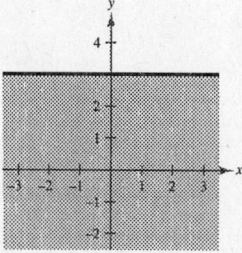

6. $y > 2x - 4$

Using a dashed line, graph $y = 2x - 4$, and shade above the line. (Use $(0, 0)$ as a test point.)

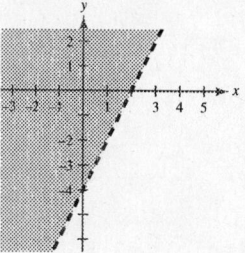

8. $5x + 3y \geq -15$

Using a solid line, graph $5x + 3y = -15$, and shade above the line. (Use $(0, 0)$ as a test point.)

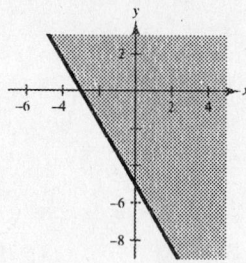

10. $y^2 - x < 0$

Using a dashed line, graph the parabola $y^2 - x = 0$, and shade the region inside this parabola.
(Use $(1, 0)$ as a test point.)

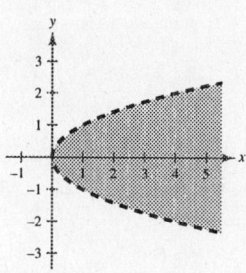

12. $y > \dfrac{-15}{x^2 + x + 4}$

Using a dashed line, graph
$$y = \frac{-15}{x^2 + x + 4}$$
and then shade above the curve. (Use $(0, 0)$ as a test point.)

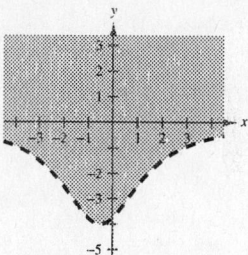

14. $y \geq 6 - \ln(x + 5)$

Using a solid line, graph $y = 6 - \ln(x + 5)$ and shade above the curve.
(Use $(0, 6)$ as a test point.)

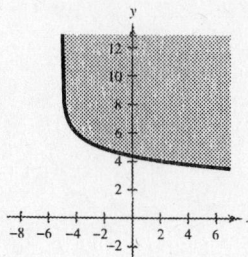

16. $y \leq 2^{2x - 0.5} - 7$

Using a solid line, graph $y = 2^{2x - 0.5} - 7$ and shade below the curve.
(Use $(0, 0)$ as a test point.)

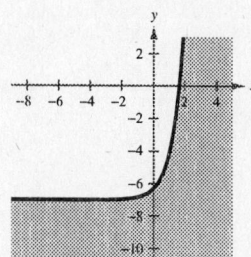

18. $y \leq 6 - \frac{3}{2}x$

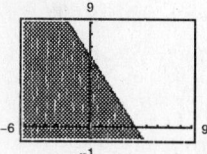

20. $y \geq -20.74 + 2.66x$

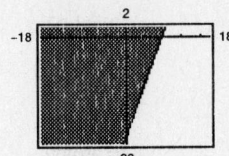

22. $2x^2 - y - 3 > 0$

$$y < 2x^2 - 3$$

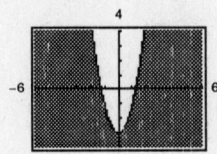

24. $-\frac{1}{10}x^2 - \frac{3}{8}y < -\frac{1}{4}$

$$y > \frac{2}{3} - \frac{4}{15}x^2$$

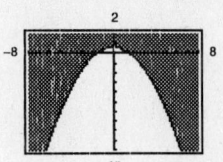

26. The parabola through $(-2, 0)$, $(0, -4)$, $(2, 0)$ is $y = x^2 - 4$. For the shaded region inside the parabola, we have $y \geq x^2 - 4$.

28. The circle shown is $x^2 + y^2 = 9$. For the shaded region inside the circle, we have $x^2 + y^2 \leq 9$.

30. $\begin{cases} -2x + 5y \geq 3 \\ \qquad\quad y < 4 \\ -4x + 2y < 7 \end{cases}$

(a) $-2(0) + 5(2) \geq 3$, True

$2 < 4$, True

$-4(0) + 2(2) < 7$, True

$(0, 2)$ is a solution

(c) $-2(-8) + 5(-2) \geq 3$, True

$-2 < 4$, True

$-4(-8) + 2(-2) < 7$, False

$(-8, -2)$ is *not* a solution.

(b) $-2(-6) + 5(4) \geq 3$, True

$4 < 4$, False

$(-6, 4)$ is *not* a solution.

(d) $-2(-3) + 5(2) \geq 3$, True

$2 < 4$, True

$-4(-3) + 2(2) < 7$, False

$(-3, 2)$ is *not* a solution.

32. $\begin{cases} \quad x^2 + y^2 \geq 36 \\ -3x + y \leq 10 \\ \frac{2}{3}x - y \geq 5 \end{cases}$

(a) $(-1)^2 + 7^2 \geq 36$, True

$-3(-1) + 7 \leq 10$, True

$\frac{2}{3}(-1) - 7 \geq 5$, False

$(-1, 7)$ is *not* a solution.

(c) $6^2 + 0^2 \geq 36$, True

$-3(6) + 0 \leq 0$, True

$\frac{2}{3}(6) - 0 \geq 5$, False

$(6, 0)$ is *not* a solution.

(b) $(-5)^2 + 1^2 \geq 36$, False

$(-5, 1)$ is *not* a solution.

(d) $4^2 + (-8)^2 \geq 36$, True

$-3(4) - 8 \leq 10$, True

$\frac{2}{3}(4) - (-8) \geq 5$, True

$(4, -8)$ is a solution.

34. $\begin{cases} 3x + 2y < 6 \\ x > 0 \\ y > 0 \end{cases}$

First, find the points of intersection
of each pair of equations.

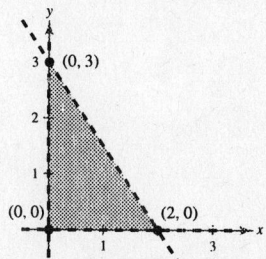

Vertex A	Vertex B	Vertex C
$3x + 2y = 6$	$x = 0$	$3x + 2y = 6$
$x = 0$	$y = 0$	$y = 0$
$(0, 3)$	$(0, 0)$	$(2, 0)$

36. $\begin{cases} 2x^2 + y \geq 2 \\ x \leq 2 \\ y \leq 1 \end{cases}$

First, find the points of intersection
of each pair of equations.

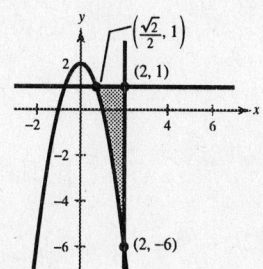

Need new art

3506331

Vertex A	Vertex B	Vertex C
$2x + y = 2$	$x = 2$	$2x^2 + y = 2$
$x = 2$	$y = 1$	$y = 1$
$(2, -6)$	$(2, 1)$	$\left(\dfrac{\sqrt{2}}{2}, 1\right)$

38. $\begin{cases} x - 7y > -36 \\ 5x + 2y > 5 \\ 6x - 5y > 6 \end{cases}$

First, find the points of intersection
of each pair of equations.

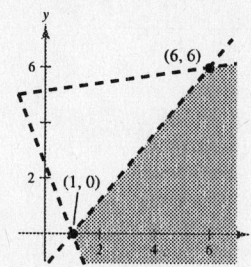

Vertex A	Vertex B	Vertex C
$x - 7y = -36$	$5x + 2y = 5$	$x - 7y = -36$
$5x + 2y = 5$	$6x - 5y = 6$	$6x - 5y = 6$
$(-1, 5)$	$(1, 0)$	$(6, 6)$

40. $\begin{cases} x - 2y < -6 \\ 5x - 3y > -9 \end{cases}$

Point of intersection: $(0, 3)$

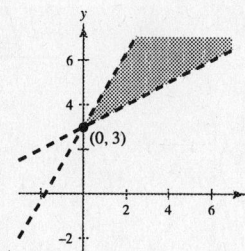

42. $\begin{cases} x - y^2 > 0 \\ x - y > 2 \end{cases}$

Points of intersection:

$$y^2 = y + 2$$
$$y^2 - y - 2 = 0$$
$$(y + 1)(y - 2) = 0$$
$$y = -1, 2$$

$(1, -1), (4, 2)$

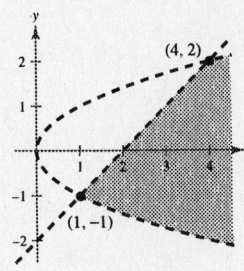

44. $\begin{cases} x^2 + y^2 \le 25 \\ 4x - 3y \le 0 \end{cases}$

Points of intersection:

$$x^2 + \left(\tfrac{4}{3}x\right)^2 = 25$$
$$\tfrac{25}{9}x^2 = 25$$
$$x = \pm 3$$

$(-3, -4), (3, 4)$

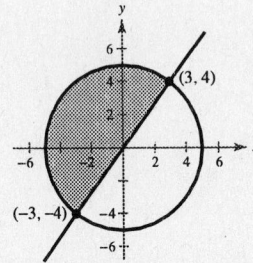

46. $\begin{cases} x < 2y - y^2 \\ 0 < x + y \end{cases}$

Points of intersection:

$$-y = 2y - y^2$$
$$y^2 - 3y = 0$$
$$y(y - 3) = 0$$
$$y = 0, 3$$

$(0, 0), (-3, 3)$

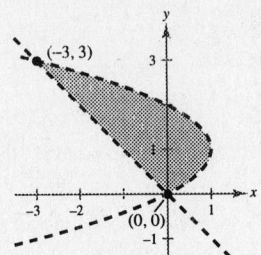

48. $\begin{cases} y < -x^2 + 2x + 3 \\ y > x^2 - 4x + 3 \end{cases}$

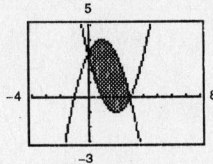

50. $\begin{cases} y \ge x^4 - 2x^2 + 1 \\ y \le 1 - x^2 \end{cases}$

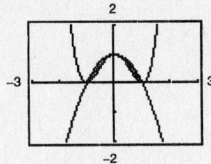

52. $\begin{cases} y \le e^{-x^2/2} \\ y \ge 0 \\ -2 \le x \le 2 \end{cases}$

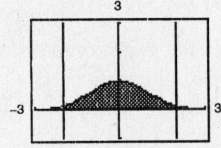

54. $(0, 6), (3, 0), (0, -3)$

$$\begin{cases} y < 6 - 2x \\ y \ge x - 3 \\ x \ge 1 \end{cases}$$

56. Circle: $x^2 + y^2 > 4$

58. $(0, 0), (0, 4), \left(\sqrt{8}, \sqrt{8}\right)$

$$\begin{cases} x^2 + y^2 \le 16 \\ x \le y \\ x \ge 0 \end{cases}$$

60. Parallelogram with vertices at $(0, 0), (4, 0), (1, 4), (5, 4)$

$(0, 0), (4, 0)$: $y \ge 0$

$(4, 0), (5, 4)$: $4x - y \le 16$

$(1, 4), (5, 4)$: $y \le 4$

$(0, 0), (1, 4)$: $4x - y \ge 0$

$$\begin{cases} 4x - y \ge 0 \\ 4x - y \le 16 \\ 0 \le y \le 4 \end{cases}$$

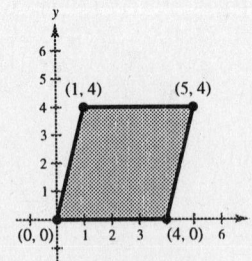

62. Triangle with vertices at $(-1, 0), (1, 0), (0, 1)$

$(-1, 0), (1, 0)$: $y \geq 0$

$(-1, 0), (0, 1)$: $y \leq x + 1$

$(0, 1), (1, 0)$: $y \leq -x + 1$

$$\begin{cases} y \leq \ \ x + 1 \\ y \leq -x + 1 \\ y \geq \ \ 0 \end{cases}$$

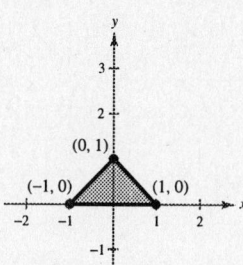

64.   Demand $=$ Supply

$100 - 0.05x = 25 + 0.1x$

$75 = 0.15x$

$500 = x$

$75 = p$

Point of equilibrium: $(500, 75)$

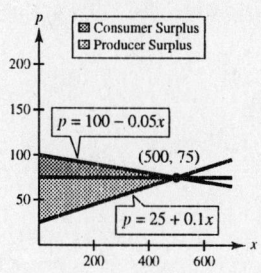

The consumer surplus is the area of the triangular region defined by

$$\begin{cases} p \leq 100 - 0.05x \\ p \geq 75 \\ x \geq 0. \end{cases}$$

Consumer surplus $= \frac{1}{2}$(base)(height) $= \frac{1}{2}(500)(25) = 6250$

The producer surplus is the area of the triangular region defined by

$$\begin{cases} p \geq 25 + 0.1x \\ y \leq 75 \\ x \geq 0. \end{cases}$$

Producer surplus $= \frac{1}{2}$(base)(height) $= \frac{1}{2}(500)(50) = 12{,}500$

66.   Demand $=$ Supply

$400 - 0.0002x = 225 + 0.0005x$

$175 = 0.0007x$

$250{,}000 = x$

$350 = p$

Point of equilibrium: $(250{,}000, 350)$

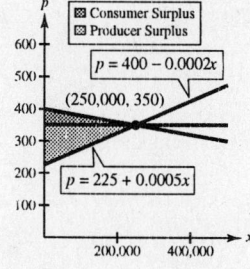

The consumer surplus is the area of the triangular region defined by

$$\begin{cases} p \leq 400 - 0.0002x \\ p \geq 350 \\ x \geq 0. \end{cases}$$

Consumer surplus
$= \frac{1}{2}$(base)(height) $= \frac{1}{2}(250{,}000)(50) = 6{,}250{,}000$

The producer surplus is the area of the triangular region defined by

$$\begin{cases} p \geq 225 + 0.0005x \\ p \leq 350 \\ x \geq 0. \end{cases}$$

Producer surplus
$= \frac{1}{2}$(base)(height) $= \frac{1}{2}(250{,}000)(125) = 15{,}625{,}000$

68. x = number of model A

y = number of model B

$$\begin{cases} x \ge 2y \\ 8x + 12y \le 200 \\ x \ge 4 \\ y \ge 2 \end{cases}$$

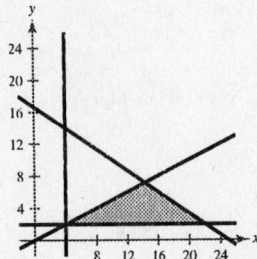

70. x = number of \$30 tickets

y = number of \$20 tickets

$$\begin{cases} x + y \le 3000 \\ 30x + 20y \ge 75{,}000 \\ x \le 2000 \\ x \ge 0 \\ y \ge 0 \end{cases}$$

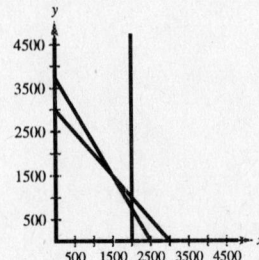

72. x = number of ounces of food X

y = number of ounces of food Y

$$\begin{cases} 20x + 10y \ge 300 \quad \text{(calcium)} \\ 15x + 10y \ge 150 \quad \text{(iron)} \\ 10x + 20y \ge 200 \quad \text{(vitamin B)} \\ x \ge 0 \\ y \ge 0 \end{cases}$$

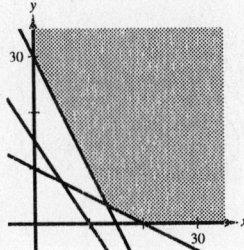

74. True. The figure is a rectangle with length of 9 units and width of 11 units.

76. $\begin{cases} x^2 + y^2 \le 16 \Longrightarrow \text{region inside the circle} \\ x + y \ge 4 \Longrightarrow \text{region above the line} \end{cases}$

Matches graph (d).

78. $\begin{cases} x^2 + y^2 \ge 16 \Longrightarrow \text{region outside the circle} \\ x + y \ge 4 \Longrightarrow \text{region above the line} \end{cases}$

Matches graph (c).

80. (a) The boundary would be included in the solution.

(b) The solution would be the half-plane on the opposite side of the boundary.

82. Test a point on either side of the boundary.

84. $(-2, 6), (4, -4)$

$$m = \frac{-4 - 6}{4 - (-2)} = \frac{-10}{6} = -\frac{5}{3}$$

$$y - (-4) = -\frac{5}{3}(x - 4)$$

$$3y + 12 = -5x + 20$$

$$5x + 3y - 8 = 0$$

86. $\left(\frac{3}{4}, -2\right), \left(-\frac{7}{2}, 5\right)$

$$m = \frac{5 - (-2)}{-\frac{7}{2} - \frac{3}{4}} = \frac{7}{-\frac{17}{4}} = -\frac{28}{17}$$

$$y - (-2) = -\frac{28}{17}\left(x - \frac{3}{4}\right)$$

$$17y + 34 = -28x + 21$$

$$28x + 17y + 13 = 0$$

88. $(3.4, -5.2), (-2.6, 0.8)$

$$m = \frac{0.8 - (-5.2)}{-2.6 - 3.4} = \frac{6}{-6} = -1$$

$$y - 0.8 = -1(x - (-2.6))$$

$$y - 0.8 = -x - 2.6$$

$$x + y + 1.8 = 0$$

90. $M = 1.686t + 40.081$

$M = -0.243t^2 + 3.871t + 35.871$

The quadratic model represents the data more closely than the linear model.

92. $150(4^{-2.6}) \approx 4.081$

94. $(3.815)^6 \approx 3082.955$

96. $e^{-\sqrt{13}} \approx 0.027$

98.
$$\begin{cases} 4x + 4z = -16 \\ 7x - 3y + 5z = -28 \\ 7x + 2y - z = 0 \end{cases}$$ Interchange Equations

$$\begin{cases} x + z = -4 \\ 7x - 3y + 5z = -28 \\ 7x + 2y - z = 0 \end{cases}$$ $\left(\frac{1}{4}\right)$Eq.1

$$\begin{cases} x + z = -4 \\ -3y - 2z = 0 \\ 2y - 8z = 28 \end{cases}$$ (-7)Eq.1 + Eq.2
(-7)Eq.1 + Eq.3

$$\begin{cases} x + z = -4 \\ 2y - 8z = 28 \\ -3y - 2z = 0 \end{cases}$$ Interchange equations

$$\begin{cases} x + z = -4 \\ 2y - 8z = 28 \\ -14z = 42 \end{cases}$$ $\left(\frac{3}{2}\right)$Eq.2 + Eq.3

$$\begin{cases} x + z = -4 \\ y - 4z = 14 \\ z = -3 \end{cases}$$ $\left(-\frac{1}{2}\right)$Eq.2
$\left(-\frac{1}{14}\right)$Eq.3

$y - 4(-3) = 14 \Longrightarrow y = 2$

$x + (-3) = -4 \Longrightarrow x = -1$

Solution: $(-1, 2, -3)$

Section 7.5   Linear Programming

Solutions to Even-Numbered Exercises

2. $z = 2x + 8y$

At $(0, 4)$: $z = 2(0) + 8(4) = 32$
At $(0, 0)$: $z = 2(0) + 8(0) = 0$
At $(2, 0)$: $z = 2(2) + 8(0) = 4$

The minimum value is 0 at $(0, 0)$.
The maximum value is 32 at $(0, 4)$.

4. $z = 7x + 3y$

At $(0, 4)$: $z = 7(0) + 3(4) = 12$
At $(0, 0)$: $z = 7(0) + 3(0) = 0$
At $(2, 0)$: $z = 7(2) + 3(0) = 14$

The minimum value is 0 at $(0, 0)$.
The maximum value is 14 at $(2, 0)$.

6. $z = 4x + 5y$

At $(0, 2)$: $z = 4(0) + 5(2) = 10$
At $(0, 4)$: $z = 4(0) + 5(4) = 20$
At $(3, 0)$: $z = 4(3) + 5(0) = 12$
At $(4, 3)$: $z = 4(4) + 5(3) = 31$

The minimum value is 10 at $(0, 2)$.
The maximum value is 31 at $(4, 3)$.

8. $z = 2x + y$

At $(0, 2)$: $z = 2(0) + 2 = 2$
At $(0, 4)$: $z = 2(0) + 4 = 4$
At $(3, 0)$: $z = 2(3) + 0 = 6$
At $(4, 3)$: $z = 2(4) + 3 = 11$

The minimum value is 2 at $(0, 2)$.
The maximum value is 11 at $(4, 3)$.

10. $z = 25x + 35y$

At $(0, 400)$: $z = 25(0) + 35(400) = 14,000$
At $(0, 800)$: $z = 25(0) + 35(800) = 28,000$
At $(450, 0)$: $z = 25(450) + 35(0) = 11,250$
At $(900, 0)$: $z = 25(900) + 35(0) = 22,500$

The minimum value is 11,250 at $(450, 0)$.
The maximum value is 28,000 at $(0, 800)$.

12. $z = 15x + 20y$

At $(0, 400)$: $z = 15(0) + 20(400) = 8000$
At $(0, 800)$: $z = 15(0) + 20(800) = 16,000$
At $(450, 0)$: $z = 15(450) + 20(0) = 6750$
At $(900, 0)$: $z = 15(900) + 20(0) = 13,500$

The minimum value is 6750 at $(450, 0)$.
The maximum value is 16,000 at $(0, 800)$.

14. $z = 7x + 8y$

At $(0, 8)$: $z = 7(0) + 8(8) = 64$
At $(4, 0)$: $z = 7(4) + 8(0) = 28$
At $(0, 0)$: $z = 7(0) + 8(0) = 0$

The minimum value is 0 at $(0, 0)$.
The maximum value is 64 at $(0, 8)$.

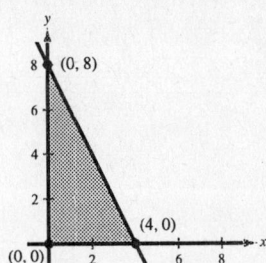

16. $z = 7x + 2y$

At $(0, 8)$: $z = 7(0) + 2(8) = 16$
At $(4, 0)$: $z = 7(4) + 2(0) = 28$
At $(0, 0)$: $z = 7(0) + 2(0) = 0$

The minimum value is 0 at $(0, 0)$.
The maximum value is 28 at $(4, 0)$.

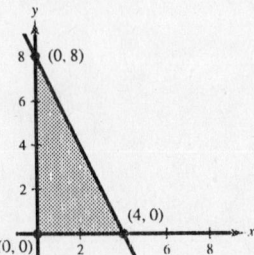

18. $z = 4x + 5y$

At $(0, 0)$: $z = 4(0) + 5(0) = 0$
At $(5, 0)$: $z = 4(5) + 5(0) = 20$
At $(4, 1)$: $z = 4(4) + 5(1) = 21$
At $(0, 3)$: $z = 4(0) + 5(3) = 15$

The minimum value is 0 at $(0, 0)$.
The maximum value is 21 at $(4, 1)$.

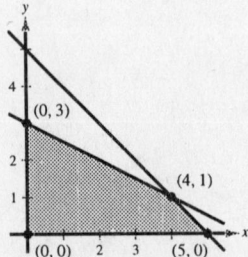

20. $z = 2x - y$

At $(0, 0)$: $z = 2(0) - 0 = 0$
At $(5, 0)$: $z = 2(5) - 0 = 10$
At $(4, 1)$: $z = 2(4) - 1 = 7$
At $(0, 3)$: $z = 2(0) - 3 = -3$

The minimum value is -3 at $(0, 3)$.
The maximum value is 10 at $(5, 0)$.

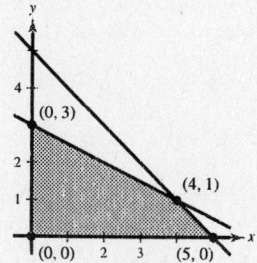

22. $z = x$

At $(0, 0)$: $z = 0$
At $(12, 0)$: $z = 12$
At $(10, 8)$: $z = 10$
At $(6, 16)$: $z = 6$
At $(0, 20)$: $z = 0$

The minimum value is 0 at any point along the line segment connecting $(0, 0)$ and $(0, 20)$. The maximum value is 12 at $(12, 0)$.

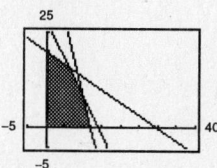

24. $z = y$

At $(0, 0)$: $z = 0$
At $(12, 0)$: $z = 0$
At $(10, 8)$: $z = 8$
At $(6, 16)$: $z = 16$
At $(0, 20)$: $z = 20$

The minimum value is 0 at any point along the line segment connecting $(0, 0)$ and $(12, 0)$. The maximum value is 20 at $(0, 20)$.

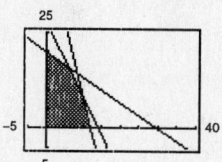

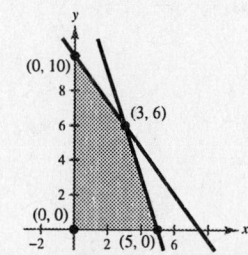

Figure for Exercises 26 and 28

26. $z = 5x + y$

At $(0, 10)$: $z = 5(0) + 10 = 10$
At $(3, 6)$: $z = 5(3) + 6 = 21$
At $(5, 0)$: $z = 5(5) + 0 = 25$
At $(0, 0)$: $z = 5(0) + 0 = 0$

The maximum value is 25 at $(5, 0)$.

28. $z = 3x + y$

At $(0, 10)$: $z = 3(0) + 10 = 10$
At $(3, 6)$: $z = 3(3) + 6 = 15$
At $(5, 0)$: $z = 3(5) + 0 = 15$
At $(0, 0)$: $z = 3(0) + 0 = 0$

The maximum value is 15 at any point along the line segment connecting $(3, 6)$ and $(5, 0)$.

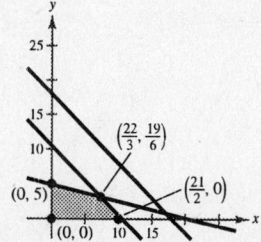

Figure for Exercises 30 and 32

30. $z = 2x + 4y$

At $(0, 5)$: $z = 2(0) + 4(5) = 20$
At $\left(\frac{22}{3}, \frac{19}{6}\right)$: $z = 2\left(\frac{22}{3}\right) + 4\left(\frac{19}{6}\right) = \frac{82}{3}$
At $\left(\frac{21}{2}, 0\right)$: $z = 2\left(\frac{21}{2}\right) + 4(0) = 21$
At $(0, 0)$: $z = 2(0) + 4(0) = 0$
The maximum value is $\frac{82}{3}$ at $\left(\frac{22}{3}, \frac{19}{6}\right)$.

32. $z = 4x + y$

At $(0, 5)$: $z = 4(0) + 5 = 5$
At $\left(\frac{22}{3}, \frac{19}{6}\right)$: $z = 4\left(\frac{22}{3}\right) + \frac{19}{6} = \frac{65}{2}$
At $\left(\frac{21}{2}, 0\right)$: $z = 4\left(\frac{21}{2}\right) + 0 = 42$
At $(0, 0)$: $z = 4(0) + 0 = 0$
The maximum value is 42 at $\left(\frac{21}{2}, 0\right)$.

34. x = number of Model A; y = number of Model B

Constraints: $2.5x + 3y \le 4000$

$2x + y \le 2500$

$0.75x + 1.25y \le 1500$

$x \ge 0$

$y \ge 0$

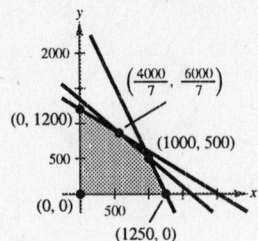

Objective function: $P = 50x + 52y$

Vertices: $(0, 0)$, $(0, 1200)$, $\left(\frac{4000}{7}, \frac{6000}{7}\right)$, $(1000, 500)$, $(1250, 0)$

At $(0, 0)$: $P = 50(0) + 52(0) = 0$
At $(0, 1200)$: $P = 50(0) + 52(1200) = 62,400$

At $\left(\frac{4000}{7}, \frac{6000}{7}\right)$: $P = 50\left(\frac{4000}{7}\right) + 52\left(\frac{6000}{7}\right) \approx 73,142.86$
At $(1000, 500)$: $P = 50(1000) + 52(500) = 76,000$
At $(1250, 0)$: $P = 50(1250) + 52(0) = 62,500$

The maximum profit of $76,000 occurs when 1000 units of Model A and 500 units of Model B are produced.

36. x = number of acres for crop A; y = number of acres for crop B

Constraints: $x + y \le 150$

$x + 2y \le 240$

$0.3x + 0.1y \le 30$

$x \ge 0$

$y \ge 0$

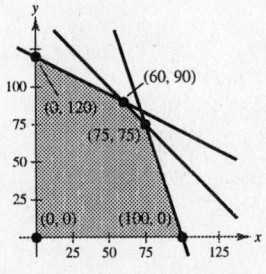

Objective function: $P = 140x + 235y$

Vertices: $(0, 0)$, $(100, 0)$, $(0, 120)$, $(60, 90)$, $(75, 75)$

At $(0, 0)$: $P = 140(0) + 235(0) = 0$
At $(100, 0)$: $P = 140(100) + 235(0) = 14,000$
At $(0, 120)$: $P = 140(0) + 235(120) = 28,200$
At $(60, 90)$: $P = 140(60) + 235(90) = 29,550$
At $(75, 75)$: $P = 140(75) + 235(75) = 28,125$

To maximize the profit, the fruit grower should plant 60 acres of crop A and 90 acres of crop B. The maximum profit is $29,550.

38. x = fraction of gallon of 80 octane

y = fraction of gallon of 92 octane

Constraints: $x + y = 1$

$80x + 92y \ge 90$

$x \ge 0$

$y \ge 0$

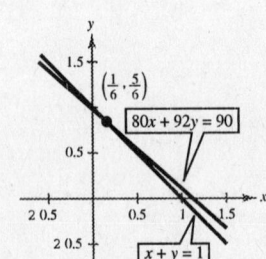

Objective function: $C = 1.13x + 1.28y$

At $\left(\frac{1}{6}, \frac{5}{6}\right)$: $C = 1.13\left(\frac{1}{6}\right) + 1.28\left(\frac{5}{6}\right) = 1.255$

To minimize cost, use $\frac{1}{6}$ gallon of 80 octane and $\frac{5}{6}$ gallon of 92 octane. The minimum cost per gallon is $1.255.

40. New objective function: $R = 1000x + 300y$

At $(0, 0)$: $R = 1000(0) + 300(0) = 0$
At $(0, 48)$: $R = 1000(0) + 300(48) = 14{,}400$
At $(4, 32)$: $R = 1000(4) + 300(32) = 13{,}600$
At $(8, 0)$: $R = 1000(8) + 300(0) = 8000$

The revenue will be maximum if the firm does no audits and 48 tax returns. The maximum revenue is \$14,400.

42. Objective function: $z = x + y$

Constraints: $x \geq 0, y \geq 0, -x + y \leq 1, -x + 2y \leq 4$

At $(0, 0)$: $z = 0 + 0 = 0$
At $(0, 1)$: $z = 0 + 1 = 1$
At $(2, 3)$: $z = 2 + 3 = 5$

The constraints do not form a closed set of points. Therefore, $z = x + y$ is unbounded.

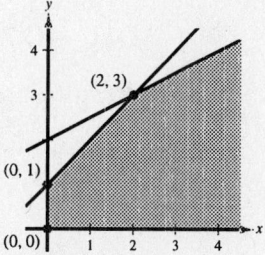

44. Objective function: $z = x + y$

Constraints: $x \geq 0, y \geq 0, -x + y \leq 0, -3x + y \geq 3$

The feasible set is empty.

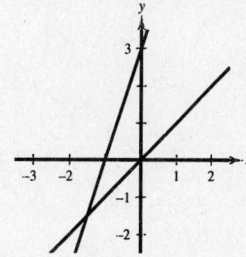

46. Objective function: $z = x + 2y$

Constraints: $x \geq 0, y \geq 0, x + 2y \leq 4, 2x + y \leq 4$

At $(0, 0)$: $z = 0 + 2(0) = 0$

At $(0, 2)$: $z = 0 + 2(2) = 4$

At $\left(\frac{4}{3}, \frac{4}{3}\right)$: $z = \frac{4}{3} + 2\left(\frac{4}{3}\right) = 4$

At $(2, 0)$: $z = 2 + 2(0) = 2$

The maximum value is 4 at any point along the line segment connecting $(0, 2)$ and $\left(\frac{4}{3}, \frac{4}{3}\right)$.

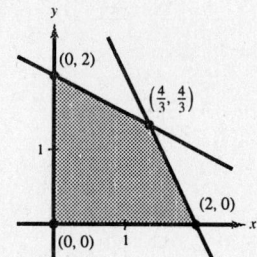

48. True. If an objective function has a maximum value at more than one vertex, then any point on the line segment connecting the points will produce the maximum value.

50. Constraints:
$$x \geq 0, y \geq 0, x + 2y \geq 4, x - y \leq 1$$

$$z = 3x + ty$$

At $(0, 0)$: $z = 3(0) + t(0) = 0$
At $(1, 0)$: $z = 3(1) + t(0) = 3$
At $(2, 1)$: $z = 3(2) + t(1) = 6 + t$
At $(0, 2)$: $z = 3(0) + t(2) = 2t$

(a) For the maximum value to be at $(2, 1)$, $z = 6 + t$ must be greater than $z = 2t$ and $z = 3$.

$$6 + t > 2t \quad \text{and} \quad 6 + t > 3$$
$$6 > t \qquad\qquad t > -3$$

Thus, $-3 < t < 6$.

(b) For maximum value to be at $(0, 2)$, $z = 2t$ must be greater than $z = 6 + t$ and $z = 3$.

$$2t > 6 + t \quad \text{and} \quad 2t > 3$$
$$t > 6 \qquad\qquad t > \tfrac{3}{2}$$

Thus, $t > 6$.

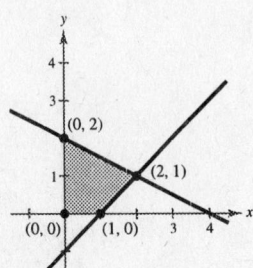

52. There are an infinite number of objective functions that would have a maximum at $(4, 3)$. One such objective function is $z = x + y$.

54. There are an infinite number of objective functions that would have a minimum at $(5, 0)$. One such objective function is $z = -10x + y$.

56. $\dfrac{\left(1 + \dfrac{2}{x}\right)}{x - \dfrac{4}{x}} = \dfrac{\dfrac{x + 2}{x}}{\dfrac{x^2 - 4}{x}} = \dfrac{x + 2}{x} \cdot \dfrac{x}{x^2 - 4} = \dfrac{x + 2}{x} \cdot \dfrac{x}{(x + 2)(x - 2)} = \dfrac{1}{x - 2}, \; x \neq 0, -2$

58. $\dfrac{\left(\dfrac{1}{x + 1} + \dfrac{1}{2}\right)}{\left(\dfrac{3}{2x^2 + 4x + 2}\right)} = \dfrac{\dfrac{x + 3}{2(x + 1)}}{\dfrac{3}{2(x + 1)^2}} = \dfrac{x + 3}{2(x + 1)} \cdot \dfrac{2(x + 1)^2}{3} = \dfrac{(x + 3)(x + 1)}{3}$

60. $e^{2x} - 10e^x + 24 = 0$

$(e^x - 4)(e^x - 6) = 0$

$e^x = 4 \quad \text{or} \quad e^x = 6$

$x = \ln 4 \qquad x = \ln 6$

$x \approx 1.386 \qquad x \approx 1.792$

62. $\dfrac{150}{e^{-x} - 4} = 75$

$150 = 75e^{-x} - 300$

$75e^{-x} = 450$

$e^{-x} = 6$

$-x = \ln 6$

$x = -\ln 6$

$x \approx -1.792$

64. $\ln(x + 9)^2 = 2$

$2 \ln(x + 9) = 2$

$\ln(x + 9) = 1$

$x + 9 = e$

$x = e - 9$

$x \approx -6.282$

Review Exercises for Chapter 7

Solutions to Even-Numbered Exercises

2. $\begin{cases} x^2 + y^2 = 169 \\ 3x + 2y = 39 \Rightarrow x = \dfrac{1}{3}(39 - 2y) \end{cases}$

$$\left[\frac{1}{3}(39 - 2y)\right]^2 + y^2 = 169$$

$$\frac{1}{9}(1521 - 156y + 4y^2) + y^2 = 169$$

$$1521 - 156y + 4y^2 + 9y^2 = 1521$$

$$13y^2 - 156y = 0$$

$$13y(y - 12) = 0 \Rightarrow y = 0, 12$$

$y = 0: \quad x = \dfrac{1}{3}(39 - 2(0)) = 13$

$y = 12: \quad x = \dfrac{1}{3}(30 - 2(12)) = 5$

Solution: $(13, 0), (5, 12)$

4. $\begin{cases} x = y + 3 \\ x = y^2 + 1 \end{cases}$

$y + 3 = y^2 + 1$

$\quad 0 = y^2 - y - 2$

$\quad 0 = (y - 2)(y + 1) \Rightarrow y = 2, -1$

$y = 2: \quad x = \quad 2 + 3 = 5$

$y = -1: \quad x = -1 + 3 = 2$

Solution: $(5, 2), (2, -1)$

6. $y^2 - 2y + x = 0 \implies (y - 1)^2 = 1 - x \implies y = 1 \pm \sqrt{1 - x}$

$\quad x + y = 0 \implies y = -x$

Points of intersection: $(0, 0)$ and $(-3, 3)$

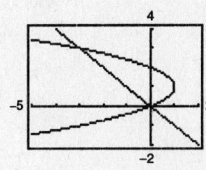

8. $y = 2(6 - x)$

$y = 2^{x-2}$

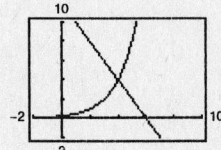

Point of intersection: $(4, 4)$

10. $y = \ln(x - 1) - 3$

$y = 4 - \frac{1}{2}x$

Point of intersection: $(9.68, -0.84)$

12. $\begin{cases} y = 22,500 + 0.015x \\ y = 20,000 + 0.02x \end{cases}$

$22,500 + 0.015x = 20,000 + 0.02x$

$2500 = 0.005x$

$\$500,000 = x$

For the second offer to be better, you would have to sell more than $500,000 per year.

14. $\begin{cases} 2x - y = 2 \implies 16x - 8y = 16 \\ 6x + 8y = 39 \implies \underline{6x + 8y = 39} \end{cases}$

$22x = 55$

$ x = \frac{55}{22} = \frac{5}{2}$

Back-substitute $x = \frac{5}{2}$ into Equation 1

$2\left(\frac{5}{2}\right) - y = 2$

$ y = 3$

Solution: $\left(\frac{5}{2}, 3\right)$

16. $\begin{cases} 0.2x + 0.3y = 0.14 \implies 20x + 30y = 14 \implies 20x + 30y = 14 \\ 0.4x + 0.5y = 0.20 \implies 4x + 5y = 2 \implies \underline{-20x - 25y = -10} \end{cases}$

$ 5y = 4$

$ y = \frac{4}{5}$

Back-substitute $y = \frac{4}{5}$ into Equation 2.

$ 4x + 5\left(\frac{4}{5}\right) = 2$

$ 4x = -2$

$ x = -\frac{1}{2}$

Solution: $\left(-\frac{1}{2}, \frac{4}{5}\right) = (-0.5, 0.8)$

18. $\begin{cases} 3x - 2y = 0 \implies 3x - 2y = 0 \\ 3x + 2(y + 5) = 10 \implies \underline{3x + 2y = 0} \end{cases}$

$ 6x = 0$

$ x = 0$

Back-substitute $x = 0$ into Equation 1.

$3(0) - 2y = 0$

$ 2y = 0$

$ y = 0$

Solution: $(0, 0)$

20. $\begin{cases} 1.25x - 2y = 3.5 \implies 5x - 8y = 14 \\ 5x - 8y = 14 \implies -5x + 8y = -14 \end{cases}$

$ 0 = 0$

There are infinitely many solutions

Let $y = a$, then $5x - 8a = 14 \implies x = \frac{8}{5}a + \frac{14}{5}a$.

Solution: $\left(\frac{8}{5}a + \frac{14}{5}, a\right)$

22. $\begin{cases} -3x - 5y = -1 \\ 6x + y = 4 \end{cases}$

The system is consistent. The lines intersect at one point so there is one solution.

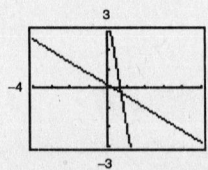

24. $\begin{cases} 6x - 14.4y = 1.8 \\ 1.2x - 2.88y = 0.36 \end{cases}$

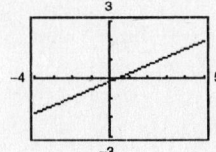

The system is consistent. The lines are identical.
There are infinitely many solutions.

26. Let x = the amount of 90% solution

y = the amount of 50% solution

$\begin{cases} x + y = 200 \implies y = 200 - x \\ 0.90x + 0.50y = 0.075(200) \end{cases}$

$0.90x + 0.50(200 - x) = 150$

$0.90x + 100 - 0.50x = 150$

$0.40x = 50$

$x = 125$

$y = 200 - 125 = 75$

Solution: 125 liters of 90% solution,
75 liters of 50% solution

28. Let x = speed of the slower plane

Let y = speed of the faster plane

Then, distance of first plane + distance of second plane = 275 miles

(rate of first plane)(time) + (rate of second plane)(time) = 275 miles

$\begin{cases} x\left(\frac{40}{60}\right) + y\left(\frac{40}{60}\right) = 275 \\ y = x + 25 \end{cases}$

$\frac{2}{3}x + \frac{2}{3}(x + 25) = 275$

$4x + 50 = 825$

$4x = 775$

$x = 193.75$ mph

$y = x + 25 = 218.75$ mph

30. $45 + 0.0002x = 120 - 0.0001x$

$0.0003x = 75$

$x = 250,000$ units

$p = \$95.00$

Point of equilibrium: (250,000, 95)

32. $\begin{cases} x - 7y + 8z = 85 \\ y - 9z = -35 \\ z = 3 \end{cases}$

$y - 9(3) = -35 \implies y = -8$

$x - 7(-8) + 8(3) = 85 \implies x = 5$

Solution: $(5, -8, 3)$

34.
$$\begin{cases} x + 3y - z = 13 & \text{Equation 1} \\ 2x - 5z = 23 & \text{Equation 2} \\ 4x - y - 2z = 14 & \text{Equation 3} \end{cases}$$

$$\begin{cases} x + 3y - z = 13 & \\ -6y - 3z = -3 & (-2)\text{Eq.1} + \text{Eq.2} \\ -13y + 2z = -38 & (-4)\text{Eq.1} + \text{Eq.3} \end{cases}$$

$$\begin{cases} x + 3y - z = 13 & \\ -6y - 3z = -3 & \\ \frac{17}{2}z = -\frac{63}{2} & (-\frac{13}{6})\text{Eq.2} + \text{Eq.3} \end{cases}$$

$$\begin{cases} x + 3y - z = 13 & \\ y + \frac{1}{2}z = \frac{1}{2} & (-\frac{1}{6})\text{Eq.2} \\ z = -\frac{63}{17} & (\frac{2}{17})\text{Eq.3} \end{cases}$$

$$y + \frac{1}{2}\left(-\frac{63}{17}\right) = \frac{1}{2} \Longrightarrow y = \frac{40}{17}$$

$$x + 3\left(\frac{40}{17}\right) - \left(-\frac{63}{17}\right) = 13 \Longrightarrow x = \frac{38}{17}$$

Solution: $\left(\frac{38}{17}, \frac{40}{17}, -\frac{63}{17}\right)$

36.
$$\begin{cases} 2x + 6z = -9 & \text{Equation 1} \\ 3x - 2y + 11z = -16 & \text{Equation 2} \\ 3x - y + 7z = -11 & \text{Equation 3} \end{cases}$$

$$\begin{cases} -x + 2y - 5z = 7 & (-1)\text{Eq.2} + \text{Eq.1} \\ 3x - 2y + 11z = -16 & \\ 3x - y + 7z = -11 & \end{cases}$$

$$\begin{cases} -x + 2y - 5z = 7 & \\ 4y - 4z = 5 & 3\text{Eq.1} + \text{Eq.2} \\ 5y - 8z = 10 & 3\text{Eq.1} + \text{Eq.3} \end{cases}$$

$$\begin{cases} -x + 2y - 5z = 7 & \\ 4y - 4z = 5 & \\ -3y = 0 & (-2)\text{Eq.2} + \text{Eq.3} \end{cases}$$

$$\begin{cases} -x + 2y - 5z = 7 & \\ y - z = \frac{5}{4} & (\frac{1}{4})\text{Eq.2} \\ y = 0 & (-\frac{1}{3})\text{Eq.3} \end{cases}$$

$$(0) - z = \frac{5}{4} \Longrightarrow z = -\frac{5}{4}$$

$$-x + 2(0) - 5\left(-\frac{5}{4}\right) = 7 \Longrightarrow x = -\frac{3}{4}$$

Solution: $\left(-\frac{3}{4}, 0, -\frac{5}{4}\right)$

38. $y = ax^2 + bx + c$ through $(-5, 6)$, $(1, 0)$, $(2, 20)$.

$(-5, 6)$: $6 = 25a - 5b + c$

$(1, 0)$: $0 = a + b + c \Longrightarrow c = -a - b$

$(2, 20)$: $20 = 4a + 2b + c$

$$\begin{cases} 24a - 6b = 6 \Longrightarrow 24a - 6b = 6 \\ 3a + b = 20 \Longrightarrow -24a - 8b = -120 \end{cases}$$

$$-14b = -154$$

$$b = 11$$

$$3a + 11 = 20 \Longrightarrow a = 3$$

$$c = -3 - 11 \Longrightarrow c = -14$$

The equation of the parabola is $y = 3x^2 + 11x - 14$.

40. $x^2 + y^2 + Dx + Ey + F = 0$ through $(1, 4)$, $(4, 3)$, $(-2, -5)$.

$(1, 4)$: $17 + D + 4E + F = 0$

$(4, 3)$: $25 + 4D + 3E + F = 0$

$(-2, -5)$: $29 - 2D - 5E + F = 0$

$$\begin{cases} D + 4E + F = -17 & \text{Equation 1} \\ 4D + 3E + F = -25 & \text{Equation 2} \\ 2D + 5E - F = 29 & \text{Equation 3} \end{cases}$$

$$\begin{cases} D + 4E + F = -17 & \\ -13E - 3F = 43 & (-4)\text{Eq.1} + \text{Eq.2} \\ -3E - 3F = 63 & (-2)\text{Eq.1} + \text{Eq.3} \end{cases}$$

$$\begin{cases} D + 4E + F = -17 & \\ -3E - 3F = 63 & \text{Interchange equations} \\ -13E - 3F = 43 & \end{cases}$$

$$\begin{cases} D + 4e + F = -17 & \\ -3E - 3F = 63 & \\ 10F = -230 & (-\frac{13}{3})\text{Eq.2} + \text{Eq.3} \end{cases}$$

$$F = -23, E = 2, D = -2$$

The equation of the circle is $x^2 + y^2 - 2x + 2y - 23 = 0$.

42. $\begin{cases} 6b + 141.5a = 152.5 \\ 141.5b + 3337.75a = 3597.27 \end{cases}$

$\begin{cases} b + \frac{283}{12}a = \frac{305}{12} \qquad \left(\frac{1}{6}\right)\text{Eq.1} \\ 141.5b + 3337.75a = 3597.27 \end{cases}$

$\begin{cases} b + \frac{283}{12}a = \frac{305}{12} \\ \qquad\quad \frac{17}{24}a = \frac{487}{600} \end{cases}$

$\qquad\qquad\qquad\qquad (-141.5)\text{Eq.1} + \text{Eq.2}$

$\begin{cases} b + \frac{283}{12}a = \frac{305}{12} \\ \qquad\quad a = \frac{487}{425} \qquad \left(\frac{24}{17}\right)\text{Eq.2} \end{cases}$

$b + \frac{283}{12}\left(\frac{487}{425}\right) = \frac{305}{12} \Longrightarrow b \approx -1.607$

$a = \frac{487}{425} \Longrightarrow a \approx 1.146$

Least squares regression line: $y = 1.146x - 1.607$

(b)
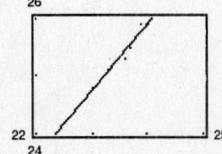

(c) The line seems to be a good fit to the data.

(d) A 1-year change in x results in a 1.146-year change in y.

44. $\begin{cases} 2x + 5y - 19z = 34 \Longrightarrow \quad 6x + 15y - 57z = 102 \\ 3x + 8y - 31z = 54 \Longrightarrow \underline{-6x - 16y + 62z = -108} \\ \qquad\qquad\qquad\qquad\qquad\quad -y + 5z = -6 \end{cases}$

Let $z = a$. Then:

$\qquad\qquad -y + 5a = -6 \Longrightarrow y = 5a + 6$

$2x + 5(5a + 6) - 19a = 34 \Longrightarrow x = -3a + 2$

Solution: $(-3a + 2, 5a + 6, a)$ where a is any real number.

46. Let $x =$ amount invested at 7%

$\quad y =$ amount invested at 9%

$\quad z =$ amount invested at 11%.

$y = x - 3000$ and $z = x - 5000 \Longrightarrow y + z = 2x - 8000$

$\begin{cases} x + y + z = 40,000 \\ 0.07x + 0.09y + 0.11z = 3500 \\ y + z = 2x - 8000 \end{cases}$

$x + (2x - 8000) = 40,000 \Longrightarrow x = 16,000$

$\qquad\qquad\qquad y = 16,000 - 3000 \Longrightarrow y = 13,000$

$\qquad\qquad\qquad z = 16,000 - 5000 \Longrightarrow z = 11,000$

Thus, \$16,000 was invested at 7%, \$13,000 at 9% and \$11,000 at 11%.

48. $y \le 5 - \frac{1}{2}x$

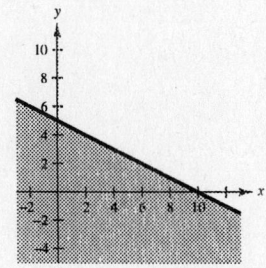

50. $y - 4x^2 > -1$

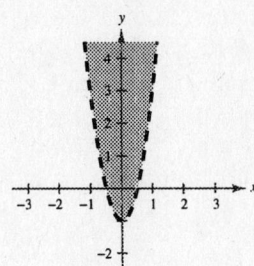

52. $\begin{cases} x + 2y \le 160 \\ 3x + y \le 180 \\ \quad x \ge 0 \\ \quad y \ge 0 \end{cases}$

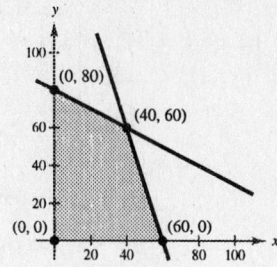

Vertex A	Vertex B	Vertex C	Vertex D
$x + 2y = 160$	$x + 2y = 160$	$3x + y = 180$	$x = 0$
$3x + y = 180$	$x = 0$	$y = 0$	$y = 0$
$(40, 60)$	$(0, 80)$	$(60, 0)$	$(0, 0)$

54. $\begin{cases} 3x + 2y \ge 24 \\ x + 2y \ge 12 \\ 2 \le x \le 15 \\ \quad y \le 15 \end{cases}$

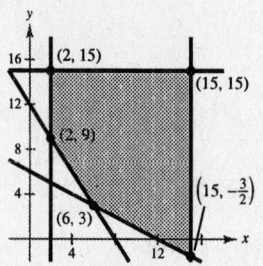

Vertex A	Vertex B	Vertex C	Vertex D	Vertex E
$3x + 2y = 24$	$3x + 2y = 24$	$x = 2$	$x = 15$	$x + 2y = 12$
$x + 2y = 12$	$x = 2$	$y = 15$	$y = 15$	$x = 15$
$(6, 3)$	$(2, 9)$	$(2, 15)$	$(15, 15)$	$\left(15, -\frac{3}{2}\right)$

56. $\begin{cases} y < x + 1 \\ y > x^2 - 1 \end{cases}$

Vertices:

$x + 1 = x^2 - 1$

$\quad 0 = x^2 - x - 2 = (x + 1)(x - 2)$

$x = -1$ or $x = 2$

$y = 0 \qquad y = 3$

$(-1, 0) \qquad (2, 3)$

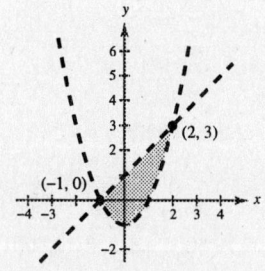

58. $\begin{cases} 2x - 3y \ge 0 \\ 2x - y \le 8 \\ \quad y \ge 0 \end{cases}$

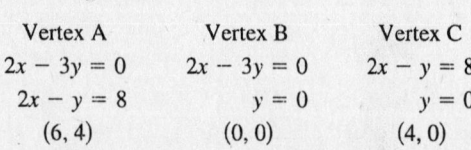

Vertex A	Vertex B	Vertex C
$2x - 3y = 0$	$2x - 3y = 0$	$2x - y = 8$
$2x - y = 8$	$y = 0$	$y = 0$
$(6, 4)$	$(0, 0)$	$(4, 0)$

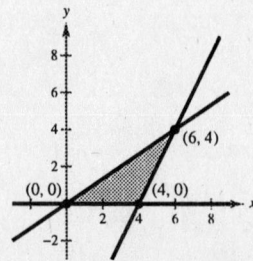

60. Let x = the number of bushels for Harrisburg, and
y = the number of bushels for Philadelphia.

$$\begin{cases} x \geq 400 \\ y \geq 600 \\ x + y \leq 1500 \end{cases}$$

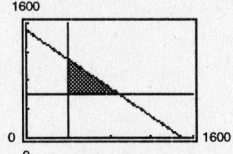

62. $160 - 0.0001x = 70 + 0.0002x$

$$90 = 0.0003x$$

$$x = 300{,}000 \text{ units}$$

$$p = \$130$$

Point of equilibrium: $(300{,}000, 130)$

Consumer surplus: $\frac{1}{2}(300{,}000)(30) = \$4{,}500{,}000$

Producer surplus: $\frac{1}{2}(300{,}000)(60) = \$9{,}000{,}000$

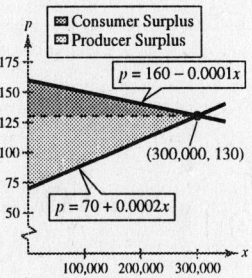

64. Maximize $z = 3x + 4y$ subject to the
following constraints.

$$\begin{cases} x \geq 0 \\ y \geq 0 \\ 2x + 5y \leq 50 \\ 4x + y \leq 28 \end{cases}$$

At $(0, 0)$: $z = 0$

At $(0, 10)$: $z = 40$

At $(5, 8)$: $z = 47$

At $(7, 0)$: $z = 21$

The maximum value is 47 at $(5, 8)$.

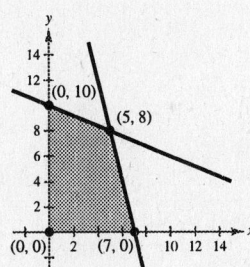

66. Minimize $z = 1.75x + 2.25y$ subject to the
following constraints.

$$\begin{cases} 2x + y \geq 25 \\ 3x + 2y \geq 45 \\ x \geq 0 \\ y \geq 0 \end{cases}$$

At $(0, 25)$: $z = 56.25$

At $(5, 15)$: $z = 42.5$

At $(15, 0)$: $z = 26.25$

The minimum value is 26.25 at $(15, 0)$.

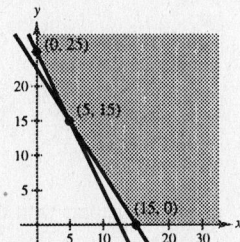

68. Let x = number of haircuts

y = number of permanents

Maximize $R = 25x + 70y$ subject
to the following constraints:

$$\begin{cases} x \geq 0 \\ y \geq 0 \\ \left(\tfrac{20}{60}\right)x + \left(\tfrac{70}{60}\right)y \leq 24 \Longrightarrow 2x + 7y \leq 144 \end{cases}$$

At $(0, 0)$: $R = 0$

At $(72, 0)$: $R = 1800$

At $\left(0, \tfrac{144}{7}\right)$: $R = 1440$

The revenue is maximum if the student does haircuts and no permanents. The maximum revenue is \$1800.

70. Let x = the number of bags of Brand X, and
y = the number of bags of Brand Y.

Objective function: Minimize $C = 15x + 30y$

Constraints: $\begin{cases} 8x + 2y \geq 16 \\ x + y \geq 5 \\ 2x + 7y \geq 20 \\ x \quad\quad \geq 0 \\ y \geq 0 \end{cases}$

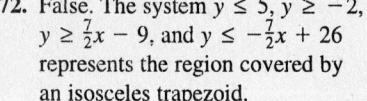

At $(0, 8)$: $C = 15(0) + 30(8) = 240$

At $(1, 4)$: $C = 15(1) + 30(4) = 135$

At $(3, 2)$: $C = 15(3) + 30(2) = 105$

At $(10, 0)$: $C = 15(10) + 30(0) = 150$

To minimize cost, use three bags of Brand X and two bags of Brand Y. The minimum cost is \$105.

72. False. The system $y \leq 5$, $y \geq -2$,
$y \geq \tfrac{7}{2}x - 9$, and $y \leq -\tfrac{7}{2}x + 26$
represents the region covered by
an isosceles trapezoid.

74. There are an infinite number of
linear systems with the solution
$(-6, 8)$. One possible solution is:

$$\begin{cases} x + y = 2 \\ x + y = -14 \end{cases}$$

76. There are infinite linear systems
with the solution $\left(\tfrac{4}{3}, 3\right)$.
One possible solution is:

$$\begin{cases} 3x + y = 7 \\ -6x + 3y = 1 \end{cases}$$

78. There are an infinite number of linear systems with the
solution $(4, -1, 3)$. One possible system is as follows:

$$\begin{cases} x + y + z = 6 \\ x + y - z = 0 \\ x - y - z = 2 \end{cases}$$

80. There are an infinite number of linear systems with the
solution $\left(5, \tfrac{3}{2}, 2\right)$. One possible solution is:

$$\begin{cases} 2x + 2y - 3z = 7 \\ x - 2y + z = 4 \\ -x + 4y - z = -1 \end{cases}$$

82.
$$\begin{cases} 3x - 5y = 8 \\ 2x + k_1y = k_2 \end{cases}$$

$$6x - 10y = 16$$
$$\underline{-6x - 3k_1y = -3k_2}$$
$$(-10 - 3k_1)y = 16 - 3k_2$$

For this system to have an infinite number of solutions, this last equation should be $0 = 0$.
Thus,

$$-10 - 3k_1 = 0 \quad \text{and} \quad 16 - 3k_2 = 0$$
$$-10 = 3k_1 \qquad\qquad 16 = 3k_2$$
$$-\tfrac{10}{3} = k_1 \qquad\qquad \tfrac{16}{3} = k_2$$

84. There will be a contradicting equation of the form $0 = N$, where N is a nonzero real number.

86. The lines are distinct and parallel.
$$\begin{cases} x + 2y = 3 \\ 2x + 4y = 9 \end{cases}$$

CHAPTER 8
Matrices and Determinants

C H A P T E R 8
Matrices and Determinants

Section 8.1 Matrices and Systems of Equations

Solutions to Even-Numbered Exercises

2. Since the matrix has one row and four columns, its order is 1×4.

4. Since the matrix has three rows and four columns, its order is 3×4.

6. Since the matrix has two rows and three columns, its order is 2×3.

8. $\begin{cases} 7x + 4y = 22 \\ 5x - 9y = 15 \end{cases}$

$\begin{bmatrix} 7 & 4 & \vdots & 22 \\ 5 & -9 & \vdots & 15 \end{bmatrix}$

10. $\begin{cases} -x - 8y + 5z = 8 \\ -7x \quad\quad - 15z = -38 \\ 3x - y + 8z = 20 \end{cases}$

$\begin{bmatrix} -1 & -8 & 5 & \vdots & 8 \\ -7 & 0 & -15 & \vdots & -38 \\ 3 & -1 & 8 & \vdots & 20 \end{bmatrix}$

12. $\begin{cases} 9x + 2y - 3z = 20 \\ -25y + 11z = -5 \end{cases}$

$\begin{bmatrix} 9 & 2 & -3 & \vdots & 20 \\ 0 & -25 & 11 & \vdots & -5 \end{bmatrix}$

14. $\begin{bmatrix} 7 & -5 & \vdots & 0 \\ 8 & 3 & \vdots & -2 \end{bmatrix}$

$\begin{cases} 7x - 5y = 0 \\ 8x + 3y = -2 \end{cases}$

16. $\begin{bmatrix} 4 & -5 & -1 & \vdots & 18 \\ -11 & 0 & 6 & \vdots & 25 \\ 3 & 8 & 0 & \vdots & -29 \end{bmatrix}$

$\begin{cases} 4x - 5y - z = 18 \\ -11x \quad\quad + 6z = 25 \\ 3x + 8y \quad\quad = -29 \end{cases}$

18. $\begin{bmatrix} 6 & 2 & -1 & -5 & \vdots & -25 \\ -1 & 0 & 7 & 3 & \vdots & 7 \\ 4 & -1 & -10 & 6 & \vdots & 23 \\ 0 & 8 & 1 & -11 & \vdots & -21 \end{bmatrix}$

$\begin{cases} 6x + 2y - z - 5w = -25 \\ -x \quad\quad + 7z + 3w = 7 \\ 4x - y - 10z + 6w = 23 \\ 8y + z - 11w = -21 \end{cases}$

20. $\begin{bmatrix} 1 & 3 & 0 & 0 \\ 0 & 0 & 1 & 8 \\ 0 & 0 & 0 & 0 \end{bmatrix}$

This matrix is in reduced row-echelon form.

22. $\begin{bmatrix} 1 & 0 & 2 & 1 \\ 0 & 1 & -3 & 10 \\ 0 & 0 & 1 & 0 \end{bmatrix}$

This matrix is in row-echelon form.

24. $\begin{bmatrix} 3 & 6 & 8 \\ 4 & -3 & 6 \end{bmatrix}$

$\tfrac{1}{3}R_1 \rightarrow \begin{bmatrix} 1 & \boxed{2} & \tfrac{8}{3} \\ 4 & -3 & 6 \end{bmatrix}$

26. $\begin{bmatrix} 2 & 4 & 8 & 3 \\ 1 & -1 & -3 & 2 \\ 2 & 6 & 4 & 9 \end{bmatrix}$

$\tfrac{1}{2}R_1 \rightarrow \begin{bmatrix} 1 & \boxed{2} & \boxed{4} & \boxed{\tfrac{3}{2}} \\ 1 & -1 & -3 & 2 \\ 2 & 6 & 4 & 9 \end{bmatrix}$

$\begin{matrix} \\ -R_1 + R_2 \rightarrow \\ -2R_1 + R_2 \rightarrow \end{matrix} \begin{bmatrix} 1 & 2 & 4 & \tfrac{3}{2} \\ 0 & \boxed{-3} & -7 & \tfrac{1}{2} \\ 0 & 2 & \boxed{-4} & \boxed{6} \end{bmatrix}$

28. $\begin{bmatrix} 3 & -1 & -4 \\ -4 & 3 & 7 \end{bmatrix} \rightarrow \begin{bmatrix} 3 & -1 & -4 \\ 5 & 0 & -5 \end{bmatrix}$

Add 3 times Row 1 to Row 2.

30. $\begin{bmatrix} -1 & -2 & 3 & -2 \\ 2 & -5 & 1 & -7 \\ 5 & 4 & -7 & 6 \end{bmatrix} \rightarrow \begin{bmatrix} -1 & -2 & 3 & -2 \\ 0 & -9 & 7 & -11 \\ 0 & -6 & 8 & -4 \end{bmatrix}$

Add 2 times Row 1 to Row 2.
Add 5 times Row 1 to Row 3.

32. $\begin{bmatrix} 7 & 1 \\ 0 & 2 \\ -3 & 4 \\ 4 & 1 \end{bmatrix}$

(a) $\begin{bmatrix} 7 & 1 \\ 0 & 2 \\ -3 & 4 \\ 1 & 5 \end{bmatrix}$
(b) $\begin{bmatrix} 1 & 5 \\ 0 & 2 \\ -3 & 4 \\ 7 & 1 \end{bmatrix}$
(c) $\begin{bmatrix} 1 & 5 \\ 0 & 2 \\ 0 & 19 \\ 7 & 1 \end{bmatrix}$

(d) $\begin{bmatrix} 1 & 5 \\ 0 & 2 \\ 0 & 19 \\ 0 & -34 \end{bmatrix}$
(e) $\begin{bmatrix} 1 & 5 \\ 0 & 1 \\ 0 & 19 \\ 0 & -34 \end{bmatrix}$
(f) $\begin{bmatrix} 1 & 0 \\ 0 & 1 \\ 0 & 0 \\ 0 & 0 \end{bmatrix}$ This matrix is in reduced row-echelon form.

34. $\begin{bmatrix} 1 & 2 & -1 & 3 \\ 3 & 7 & -5 & 14 \\ -2 & -1 & -3 & 8 \end{bmatrix}$

$\begin{matrix} -3R_1 + R_2 \rightarrow \\ 2R_1 + R_3 \rightarrow \end{matrix} \begin{bmatrix} 1 & 2 & -1 & 3 \\ 0 & 1 & -2 & 5 \\ 0 & 3 & -5 & 14 \end{bmatrix}$

$\begin{matrix} \\ -3R_2 + R_3 \rightarrow \end{matrix} \begin{bmatrix} 1 & 2 & -1 & 3 \\ 0 & 1 & -2 & 5 \\ 0 & 0 & 1 & -1 \end{bmatrix}$

36. $\begin{bmatrix} 1 & -3 & 0 & -7 \\ -3 & 10 & 1 & 23 \\ 4 & -10 & 2 & -24 \end{bmatrix}$

$\begin{matrix} 3R_1 + R_2 \rightarrow \\ -4R_1 + R_3 \rightarrow \end{matrix} \begin{bmatrix} 1 & -3 & 0 & -7 \\ 0 & 1 & 1 & 2 \\ 0 & 2 & 2 & 4 \end{bmatrix}$

$\begin{matrix} \\ -2R_2 + R_3 \rightarrow \end{matrix} \begin{bmatrix} 1 & -3 & 0 & -7 \\ 0 & 1 & 1 & 2 \\ 0 & 0 & 0 & 0 \end{bmatrix}$

38. Use the reduced row-echelon form feature of a graphing utility.

$\begin{bmatrix} 1 & 3 & 2 \\ 5 & 15 & 9 \\ 2 & 6 & 10 \end{bmatrix} \Rightarrow \begin{bmatrix} 1 & 3 & 0 \\ 0 & 0 & 1 \\ 0 & 0 & 0 \end{bmatrix}$

40. Use the reduced row-echelon form feature of a graphing utility.

$\begin{bmatrix} -2 & 3 & -1 & -2 \\ 4 & -2 & 5 & 8 \\ 1 & 5 & -2 & 0 \\ 3 & 8 & -10 & -30 \end{bmatrix} \Rightarrow \begin{bmatrix} 1 & 0 & 0 & 0 \\ 0 & 1 & 0 & 0 \\ 0 & 0 & 1 & 0 \\ 0 & 0 & 0 & 1 \end{bmatrix}$

42. Use the reduced row-echelon form feature of a graphing utility.

$\begin{bmatrix} 5 & 1 & 2 & 4 \\ -1 & 5 & 10 & -32 \end{bmatrix} \Rightarrow \begin{bmatrix} 1 & 0 & 0 & 2 \\ 0 & 1 & 2 & -6 \end{bmatrix}$

44. $\begin{cases} x + 5y = 0 \\ \quad\quad y = -1 \end{cases}$

$x + 5(-1) = 0$

$x = 5$

Solution: $(5, -1)$

46.
$$\begin{cases} x + 2y & - 2z = -1 \\ & y + & z = 9 \\ & & z = -3 \end{cases}$$

$$y + (-3) = 9$$
$$y = 12$$
$$x + 2(12) - 2(-3) = -1$$
$$x = -31$$

Solution: $(-31, 12, -3)$

48. $\begin{bmatrix} 1 & 0 & \vdots & -6 \\ 0 & 1 & \vdots & 10 \end{bmatrix}$

$x = -6$
$y = 10$

Solution: $(-6, 10)$

50. $\begin{bmatrix} 1 & 0 & 0 & \vdots & 5 \\ 0 & 1 & 0 & \vdots & -3 \\ 0 & 0 & 1 & \vdots & 0 \end{bmatrix}$

$x = 5$
$y = -3$
$z = 0$

Solution: $(5, -3, 0)$

52.
$$\begin{cases} 2x + 6y = 16 \\ 2x + 3y = 7 \end{cases}$$

$$\begin{bmatrix} 2 & 6 & \vdots & 16 \\ 2 & 3 & \vdots & 7 \end{bmatrix}$$

$$-R_1 + R_2 \rightarrow \begin{bmatrix} 2 & 6 & \vdots & 16 \\ 0 & -3 & \vdots & -9 \end{bmatrix}$$

$$\begin{matrix} \frac{1}{2}R_1 \rightarrow \\ -\frac{1}{3}R_2 \rightarrow \end{matrix} \begin{bmatrix} 1 & 3 & \vdots & 8 \\ 0 & 1 & \vdots & 3 \end{bmatrix}$$

$$\begin{cases} x + 3y = 8 \\ y = 3 \end{cases}$$

$$y = 3$$
$$x + 3(3) = 8 \Longrightarrow x = -1$$

Solution: $(-1, 3)$

54.
$$\begin{cases} -x + y = 4 \\ 2x - 4y = -34 \end{cases}$$

$$\begin{bmatrix} -1 & 1 & \vdots & 4 \\ 2 & -4 & \vdots & -34 \end{bmatrix}$$

$$\begin{matrix} (-1)R_1 \rightarrow \\ (\frac{1}{2})R_2 \rightarrow \end{matrix} \begin{bmatrix} 1 & -1 & \vdots & -4 \\ 1 & -2 & \vdots & -17 \end{bmatrix}$$

$$-R_1 + R_2 \rightarrow \begin{bmatrix} 1 & -1 & \vdots & -4 \\ 0 & -1 & \vdots & -13 \end{bmatrix}$$

$$(-1)R_2 \rightarrow \begin{bmatrix} 1 & -1 & \vdots & -4 \\ 0 & 1 & \vdots & 13 \end{bmatrix}$$

$$\begin{cases} x - y = -4 \\ y = 13 \end{cases}$$

$$y = 13$$
$$x - 13 = -4 \Longrightarrow x = 9$$

Solution: $(9, 13)$

56.
$$\begin{cases} 5x - 5y = -5 \\ -2x - 3y = 7 \end{cases}$$

$$\begin{bmatrix} 5 & -5 & \vdots & -5 \\ -2 & -3 & \vdots & 7 \end{bmatrix}$$

$$\frac{1}{5}R_1 \rightarrow \begin{bmatrix} 1 & -1 & \vdots & -1 \\ -2 & -3 & \vdots & 7 \end{bmatrix}$$

$$2R_1 + R_2 \rightarrow \begin{bmatrix} 1 & -1 & \vdots & -1 \\ 0 & -5 & \vdots & 5 \end{bmatrix}$$

$$-\frac{1}{5}R_2 \rightarrow \begin{bmatrix} 1 & -1 & \vdots & -1 \\ 0 & 1 & \vdots & -1 \end{bmatrix}$$

$$\begin{cases} x - y = -1 \\ y = -1 \end{cases}$$

$$y = -1$$
$$x - (-1) = -1 \Longrightarrow x = -2$$

Solution: $(-2, -1)$

58.
$$\begin{cases} x - 3y = 5 \\ -2x + 6y = -10 \end{cases}$$

$$\begin{bmatrix} 1 & -3 & \vdots & 5 \\ -2 & 6 & \vdots & -10 \end{bmatrix}$$

$$2R_1 + R_2 \rightarrow \begin{bmatrix} 1 & -3 & \vdots & 5 \\ 0 & 0 & \vdots & 0 \end{bmatrix}$$

$$x - 3y = 5$$
$$y = a$$
$$x = 3a + 5$$

Solution: $(3a + 5, a)$, where a is a real number

60. $\begin{cases} 2x - y + 3z = 24 \\ \quad\quad 2y - z = 14 \\ 7x - 5y \quad\quad = 6 \end{cases}$

$$\begin{bmatrix} 2 & -1 & 3 & \vdots & 24 \\ 0 & 2 & -1 & \vdots & 14 \\ 7 & -5 & 0 & \vdots & 6 \end{bmatrix}$$

$R_3 + (-3)R_1 \rightarrow \begin{bmatrix} 1 & -2 & -9 & \vdots & -66 \\ 0 & 2 & -1 & \vdots & 14 \\ 7 & -5 & 0 & \vdots & 6 \end{bmatrix}$

$-7R_1 + R_3 \rightarrow \begin{bmatrix} 1 & -2 & -9 & \vdots & -66 \\ 0 & 2 & -1 & \vdots & 14 \\ 0 & 9 & 63 & \vdots & 468 \end{bmatrix}$

$4R_2 \rightarrow \begin{bmatrix} 1 & -2 & -9 & \vdots & -66 \\ 0 & 8 & -4 & \vdots & 56 \\ 0 & 9 & 63 & \vdots & 468 \end{bmatrix}$

$-R_3 + R_2 \rightarrow \begin{bmatrix} 1 & -2 & -9 & \vdots & -66 \\ 0 & -1 & -67 & \vdots & -412 \\ 0 & 9 & 63 & \vdots & 468 \end{bmatrix}$

$9R_2 + R_3 \rightarrow \begin{bmatrix} 1 & -2 & -9 & \vdots & -66 \\ 0 & -1 & -67 & \vdots & -412 \\ 0 & 0 & -540 & \vdots & -3240 \end{bmatrix}$

$\begin{array}{c} -R_2 \rightarrow \\ -\frac{1}{540}R_3 \rightarrow \end{array} \begin{bmatrix} 1 & -2 & -9 & \vdots & -66 \\ 0 & 1 & 67 & \vdots & 412 \\ 0 & 0 & 1 & \vdots & 6 \end{bmatrix}$

$\begin{cases} x - 2y - 9z = -66 \\ \quad\quad y + 67z = 412 \\ \quad\quad\quad\quad z = 6 \end{cases}$

$z = 6$

$y + 67(6) = 412 \implies y = 10$

$x - 2(10) - 9(6) = -66 \implies x = 8$

Solution: $(8, 10, 6)$

62. $\begin{cases} 2x + 2y - z = 2 \\ x - 3y + z = -28 \\ -x + y \quad\quad = 14 \end{cases}$

$$\begin{bmatrix} 2 & 2 & -1 & \vdots & 2 \\ 1 & -3 & 1 & \vdots & -28 \\ -1 & 1 & 0 & \vdots & 14 \end{bmatrix}$$

$\begin{array}{c} R_2 \\ R_1 \end{array} \begin{bmatrix} 1 & -3 & 1 & \vdots & -28 \\ 2 & 2 & -1 & \vdots & 2 \\ -1 & 1 & 0 & \vdots & 14 \end{bmatrix}$

$\begin{array}{c} R_3 \\ R_2 \end{array} \begin{bmatrix} 1 & -3 & 1 & \vdots & -28 \\ -1 & 1 & 0 & \vdots & 14 \\ 2 & 2 & -1 & \vdots & 2 \end{bmatrix}$

$\begin{array}{c} R_1 + R_2 \rightarrow \\ -2R_1 + R_3 \rightarrow \end{array} \begin{bmatrix} 1 & -3 & 1 & \vdots & -28 \\ 0 & -2 & 1 & \vdots & -14 \\ 0 & 8 & -3 & \vdots & 58 \end{bmatrix}$

$4R_2 + R_3 \rightarrow \begin{bmatrix} 1 & -3 & 1 & \vdots & -28 \\ 0 & -2 & 1 & \vdots & -14 \\ 0 & 0 & 1 & \vdots & 2 \end{bmatrix}$

$-\frac{1}{2}R_2 \rightarrow \begin{bmatrix} 1 & -3 & 1 & -28 \\ 0 & 1 & -\frac{1}{2} & 7 \\ 0 & 0 & 1 & 2 \end{bmatrix}$

$\begin{cases} x - 3y + z = -28 \\ \quad\quad y - \frac{1}{2}z = 7 \\ \quad\quad\quad\quad z = 2 \end{cases}$

$z = 2$

$y - \frac{1}{2}(2) = 7 \implies y = 8$

$x - 3(8) + 2 = -28 \implies x = -6$

Solution: $(-6, 8, 2)$

64. $\begin{cases} 3x - 2y + z = 15 \\ -x + y + 2z = -10 \\ x - y - 4z = 14 \end{cases}$

$$\begin{bmatrix} 3 & -2 & 1 & \vdots & 15 \\ -1 & 1 & 2 & \vdots & -10 \\ 1 & -1 & -4 & \vdots & 14 \end{bmatrix}$$

$\begin{matrix} R_3 \\ \\ R_1 \end{matrix} \begin{bmatrix} 1 & -1 & -4 & \vdots & 14 \\ -1 & 1 & 2 & \vdots & -10 \\ 3 & -2 & 1 & \vdots & 15 \end{bmatrix}$

$\begin{matrix} R_1 + R_2 \rightarrow \\ -3R_1 + R_3 \rightarrow \end{matrix} \begin{bmatrix} 1 & -1 & -4 & \vdots & 14 \\ 0 & 0 & -2 & \vdots & 4 \\ 0 & 1 & 13 & \vdots & -27 \end{bmatrix}$

$\begin{matrix} R_3 \\ R_2 \end{matrix} \begin{bmatrix} 1 & -1 & -4 & 14 \\ 0 & 1 & 13 & -27 \\ 0 & 0 & -2 & 4 \end{bmatrix}$

$\begin{matrix} \\ \\ -\frac{1}{2}R_3 \rightarrow \end{matrix} \begin{bmatrix} 1 & -1 & -4 & \vdots & 14 \\ 0 & 1 & 13 & \vdots & -27 \\ 0 & 0 & 1 & \vdots & -2 \end{bmatrix}$

$\begin{cases} x - y - 4z = 14 \\ y + 13z = -27 \\ z = -2 \end{cases}$

$z = -2$

$y + 13(-2) = -27 \Rightarrow y = -1$

$x - (-1) - 4(-2) = 14 \Rightarrow x = 5$

Solution: $(5, -1, -2)$

66. $\begin{cases} 2x + 3z = 3 \\ 4x - 3y + 7z = 5 \\ 8x - 9y + 15z = 9 \end{cases}$

$$\begin{bmatrix} 2 & 0 & 3 & \vdots & 3 \\ 4 & -3 & 7 & \vdots & 5 \\ 8 & -9 & 15 & \vdots & 9 \end{bmatrix}$$

$\begin{matrix} -2R_1 + R_2 \rightarrow \\ -4R_1 + R_3 \rightarrow \end{matrix} \begin{bmatrix} 2 & 0 & 3 & \vdots & 3 \\ 0 & -3 & 1 & \vdots & -1 \\ 0 & -9 & 3 & \vdots & -3 \end{bmatrix}$

$\begin{matrix} \\ -3R_2 + R_3 \rightarrow \end{matrix} \begin{bmatrix} 2 & 0 & 3 & \vdots & 3 \\ 0 & -3 & 1 & \vdots & -1 \\ 0 & 0 & 0 & \vdots & 0 \end{bmatrix}$

$\begin{matrix} \frac{1}{2}R_1 \rightarrow \\ -\frac{1}{3}R_2 \rightarrow \end{matrix} \begin{bmatrix} 1 & 0 & \frac{3}{2} & \vdots & \frac{3}{2} \\ 0 & 1 & -\frac{1}{3} & \vdots & \frac{1}{3} \\ 0 & 0 & 0 & \vdots & 0 \end{bmatrix}$

$z = a$

$y = \frac{1}{3}a + \frac{1}{3}$

$x = -\frac{3}{2}a + \frac{3}{2}$

Solution: $\left(-\frac{3}{2}a + \frac{3}{2}, \frac{1}{3}a + \frac{1}{3}, a\right)$, where a is a real number.

68. $\begin{cases} 4x + 12y - 7z - 20w = 22 \\ 3x + 9y - 5z - 28w = 30 \end{cases}$

$$\begin{bmatrix} 4 & 12 & -7 & -20 & \vdots & 22 \\ 3 & 9 & -5 & -28 & \vdots & 30 \end{bmatrix}$$

$-R_2 + R_1 \rightarrow \begin{bmatrix} 1 & 3 & -2 & 8 & \vdots & -8 \\ 3 & 9 & -5 & -28 & \vdots & 30 \end{bmatrix}$

$-3R_1 + R_2 \rightarrow \begin{bmatrix} 1 & 3 & -2 & 8 & \vdots & -8 \\ 0 & 0 & 1 & -52 & \vdots & 54 \end{bmatrix}$

$2R_2 + R_1 \rightarrow \begin{bmatrix} 1 & 3 & 0 & -96 & \vdots & 100 \\ 0 & 0 & 1 & -52 & \vdots & 54 \end{bmatrix}$

$w = a$

$z = 52a + 54$

$y = b$

$x = -3b + 96a + 100$

Solution: $(-3b + 96a + 100, b, 52a + 54, a)$
where a and b are real numbers.

70. $\begin{cases} x + 2y = 0 \\ x + y = 6 \\ 3x - 2y = 8 \end{cases}$

$$\begin{bmatrix} 1 & 2 & \vdots & 0 \\ 1 & 1 & \vdots & 6 \\ 3 & -2 & \vdots & 8 \end{bmatrix}$$

$\begin{matrix} -R_1 + R_2 \rightarrow \\ -3R_1 + R_3 \rightarrow \end{matrix} \begin{bmatrix} 1 & 2 & \vdots & 0 \\ 0 & -1 & \vdots & 6 \\ 0 & -8 & \vdots & 8 \end{bmatrix}$

$\begin{matrix} \\ -8R_2 + R_3 \rightarrow \end{matrix} \begin{bmatrix} 1 & 2 & \vdots & 0 \\ 0 & -1 & \vdots & 6 \\ 0 & 0 & \vdots & -40 \end{bmatrix}$

The system in inconsistent and there is no solution.

72. Use the reduced row-echelon form feature of a graphing utility.

$$\begin{cases} 2x + 10y + 2z = 6 \\ x + 5y + 2z = 6 \\ x + 5y + z = 3 \\ -3x - 15y - 3z = -9 \end{cases}$$

$$\begin{bmatrix} 2 & 10 & 2 & \vdots & 6 \\ 1 & 5 & 2 & \vdots & 6 \\ 1 & 5 & 1 & \vdots & 3 \\ -3 & -15 & -3 & \vdots & -9 \end{bmatrix} \Rightarrow \begin{bmatrix} 1 & 5 & 0 & \vdots & 0 \\ 0 & 0 & 1 & \vdots & 3 \\ 0 & 0 & 0 & \vdots & 0 \\ 0 & 0 & 0 & \vdots & 0 \end{bmatrix}$$

$$\begin{cases} z = 3 \\ x + 5y = 0 \end{cases}$$

$z = 3$

$y = a$

$x + 5a = 0 \Rightarrow x = -5a$

Solution: $(-5a, a, 3)$, where a is a real number.

74. Use the reduced row-echelon form feature of a graphing utility.

$$\begin{cases} x + 2y + 2z + 4w = 11 \\ 3x + 6y + 5z + 12w = 30 \\ x + 3y - 3z + 2w = -5 \\ 6x - y - z + w = -9 \end{cases}$$

$$\begin{bmatrix} 1 & 2 & 2 & 4 & \vdots & 11 \\ 3 & 6 & 5 & 12 & \vdots & 30 \\ 1 & 3 & -3 & 2 & \vdots & -5 \\ 6 & -1 & -1 & 1 & \vdots & -9 \end{bmatrix} \Rightarrow \begin{bmatrix} 1 & 0 & 0 & 0 & \vdots & -1 \\ 0 & 1 & 0 & 0 & \vdots & 1 \\ 0 & 0 & 1 & 0 & \vdots & 3 \\ 0 & 0 & 0 & 1 & \vdots & 1 \end{bmatrix}$$

$$\begin{cases} x = -1 \\ y = 1 \\ z = 3 \\ w = 1 \end{cases}$$

$w = 1$

$z = 3$

$y = 1$

$x = -1$

Solution: $(-1, 1, 3, 1)$

76. $\begin{cases} x + 2y + z + 3w = 0 \\ x - y + w = 0 \\ y - z + 2w = 0 \end{cases}$

$$\begin{bmatrix} 1 & 2 & 1 & 3 & \vdots & 0 \\ 1 & -1 & 0 & 1 & \vdots & 0 \\ 0 & 1 & -1 & 2 & \vdots & 0 \end{bmatrix} \Rightarrow \begin{bmatrix} 1 & 0 & 0 & 2 & \vdots & 0 \\ 0 & 1 & 0 & 1 & \vdots & 0 \\ 0 & 0 & 1 & -1 & \vdots & 0 \end{bmatrix}$$

$$\begin{cases} x + 2w = 0 \\ y + w = 0 \\ z - w = 0 \end{cases}$$

$w = a, z = a, y = -a, x = -2a$

Solution: $(-2a, -a, a, a)$, where a is a real number.

78. (a) $\begin{cases} x - 3y + 4z = -11 \\ \quad\quad y - z = -4 \\ \quad\quad\quad\quad z = 2 \end{cases}$

$$y - 2 = -4$$
$$y = -2$$
$$x - 3(-2) + 4(2) = -11$$
$$x = -25$$

(b) $\begin{cases} x + 4y \quad\quad = -11 \\ \quad\quad y + 3z = 4 \\ \quad\quad\quad\quad z = 2 \end{cases}$

$$y + 3(2) = 4$$
$$y = -2$$
$$x + 4(-2) = -11$$
$$x = -3$$

The systems do *not* yield the same solution.

80. (a) $\begin{cases} x + 3y - z = 19 \\ \quad\quad y + 6z = -18 \\ \quad\quad\quad\quad z = -4 \end{cases}$

$$y + 6(-4) = -18$$
$$y = 6$$
$$x + 3(6) - (-4) = 19$$
$$x = -3$$

(b) $\begin{cases} x - y + 3z = -15 \\ \quad\quad y - 2z = 14 \\ \quad\quad\quad\quad z = -4 \end{cases}$

$$y - 2(-4) = 14$$
$$y = 6$$
$$x - 6 + 3(-4) = -15$$
$$x = 3$$

The systems do *not* yield the same solution.

82. $\begin{cases} I_1 - I_2 + I_3 = 0 \\ 3I_1 + 4I_2 \quad\quad = 18 \\ \quad\quad I_2 + 3I_3 = 6 \end{cases}$

$$\begin{bmatrix} 1 & -1 & 1 & \vdots & 0 \\ 3 & 4 & 0 & \vdots & 18 \\ 0 & 1 & 3 & \vdots & 6 \end{bmatrix}$$

$-3R_1 + R_2 \rightarrow \begin{bmatrix} 1 & -1 & 1 & \vdots & 0 \\ 0 & 7 & -3 & \vdots & 18 \\ 0 & 1 & 3 & \vdots & 6 \end{bmatrix}$

$\begin{matrix} \\ R_3 \\ R_2 \end{matrix} \begin{bmatrix} 1 & -1 & 1 & \vdots & 0 \\ 0 & 1 & 3 & \vdots & 6 \\ 0 & 7 & -3 & \vdots & 18 \end{bmatrix}$

$-7R_2 + R_3 \rightarrow \begin{bmatrix} 1 & -1 & 1 & \vdots & 0 \\ 0 & 1 & 3 & \vdots & 6 \\ 0 & 0 & -24 & \vdots & -24 \end{bmatrix}$

$-\frac{1}{24}R_3 \rightarrow \begin{bmatrix} 1 & -1 & 1 & \vdots & 0 \\ 0 & 1 & 3 & \vdots & 6 \\ 0 & 0 & 1 & \vdots & 1 \end{bmatrix}$

$\begin{cases} I_1 - I_2 + I_3 = 0 \\ \quad\quad I_2 + 3I_3 = 6 \\ \quad\quad\quad\quad I_3 = 1 \end{cases}$

$I_3 = 1$

$I_2 + 3(1) = 6 \Rightarrow I_2 = 3$

$I_1 - 3 + 1 = 0 \Rightarrow I_1 = 2$

84. x = amount at 7%,
y = amount at 8%,
z = amount at 10%.
$z = 4x \implies -4x + z = 0$

$\begin{cases} x + \quad y + \quad z = 1{,}500{,}000 \\ 0.07x + 0.08y + 0.10z = 130{,}500 \\ -4x + \quad\quad\quad z = 0 \end{cases}$

$$\begin{bmatrix} 1 & 1 & 1 & \vdots & 1{,}500{,}000 \\ 0.07 & 0.08 & 0.10 & \vdots & 130{,}500 \\ -4 & 0 & 1 & \vdots & 0 \end{bmatrix}$$

$\begin{matrix} -0.07R_1 + R_2 \rightarrow \\ 4R_1 + R_3 \rightarrow \end{matrix} \begin{bmatrix} 1 & 1 & 1 & \vdots & 1{,}500{,}000 \\ 0 & 0.01 & 0.03 & \vdots & 25{,}500 \\ 0 & 4 & 5 & \vdots & 6{,}000{,}000 \end{bmatrix}$

$100R_2 \rightarrow \begin{bmatrix} 1 & 1 & 1 & \vdots & 1{,}500{,}000 \\ 0 & 1 & 3 & \vdots & 2{,}550{,}000 \\ 0 & 4 & 5 & \vdots & 6{,}000{,}000 \end{bmatrix}$

$-4R_2 + R_3 \rightarrow \begin{bmatrix} 1 & 1 & 1 & \vdots & 1{,}500{,}000 \\ 0 & 1 & 3 & \vdots & 2{,}550{,}000 \\ 0 & 0 & -7 & \vdots & -4{,}200{,}000 \end{bmatrix}$

$-\frac{1}{7}R_3 \rightarrow \begin{bmatrix} 1 & 1 & 1 & \vdots & 1{,}500{,}000 \\ 0 & 1 & 3 & \vdots & 2{,}550{,}000 \\ 0 & 0 & 1 & \vdots & 600{,}000 \end{bmatrix}$

$\begin{cases} x + y + z = 1{,}500{,}000 \\ \quad\quad y + 3z = 2{,}550{,}000 \\ \quad\quad\quad\quad z = 600{,}000 \end{cases}$

$y + 3(600{,}000) = 2{,}550{,}000 \implies y = 750{,}000$

$x + 750{,}000 + 600{,}000 = 1{,}500{,}000 \implies x = 150{,}000$

Solution: \$150,000 at 7%, \$750,000 at 8%,
and \$600,000 at 10%

86. $y = ax^2 + bx + c$

$$\begin{cases} a + b + c = 8 \\ 4a + 2b + c = 13 \\ 9a + 3b + c = 20 \end{cases}$$

$$\begin{bmatrix} 1 & 1 & 1 & \vdots & 8 \\ 4 & 2 & 1 & \vdots & 13 \\ 9 & 3 & 1 & \vdots & 20 \end{bmatrix}$$

$$\begin{matrix} \\ -4R_1 + R_2 \rightarrow \\ -9R_1 + R_3 \rightarrow \end{matrix} \begin{bmatrix} 1 & 1 & 1 & \vdots & 8 \\ 0 & -2 & -3 & \vdots & -19 \\ 0 & -6 & -8 & \vdots & -52 \end{bmatrix}$$

$$\begin{matrix} \\ -\frac{1}{2}R_2 \rightarrow \\ -3R_2 + R_3 \rightarrow \end{matrix} \begin{bmatrix} 1 & 1 & 1 & \vdots & 8 \\ 0 & 1 & \frac{3}{2} & \vdots & \frac{19}{2} \\ 0 & 0 & 1 & \vdots & 5 \end{bmatrix}$$

$$\begin{cases} a + b + c = 8 \\ b + \frac{3}{2}c = \frac{19}{2} \\ c = 5 \end{cases}$$

$c = 5$

$b + \frac{3}{2}(5) = \frac{19}{2} \implies b = 2$

$a + 2 + 5 = 8 \implies a = 1$

Equation of parabola: $y = x^2 + 2x + 5$

88. (a) $(0, 5.0)$, $(15, 9.6)$, $(30, 12.4)$

$y = ax^2 + bx + c$

$$\begin{cases} c = 5 \\ 225a + 15b + c = 9.6 \implies 225a + 15b = 4.6 \\ 900a + 30b + c = 12.4 \implies 900a + 30b = 7.4 \end{cases}$$

$$\begin{bmatrix} 225 & 15 & \vdots & 4.6 \\ 900 & 30 & \vdots & 7.4 \end{bmatrix}$$

$$-4R_1 + R_2 \rightarrow \begin{bmatrix} 225 & 15 & \vdots & 4.6 \\ 0 & -30 & \vdots & -11 \end{bmatrix}$$

$$\begin{matrix} \frac{1}{225}R_1 \rightarrow \\ \left(-\frac{1}{30}\right)R_2 \rightarrow \end{matrix} \begin{bmatrix} 1 & \frac{1}{15} & \vdots & \frac{23}{1125} \\ 0 & 1 & \vdots & \frac{11}{30} \end{bmatrix}$$

$$\begin{cases} a + \frac{1}{15}b = \frac{23}{1125} \\ b = \frac{11}{30} \end{cases}$$

$a + \frac{1}{15}\left(\frac{11}{30}\right) = \frac{23}{1125} \implies a = -\frac{1}{250} = -0.004$

Equation of parabola: $y = -0.004x^2 + 0.367x + 5$.

(b)

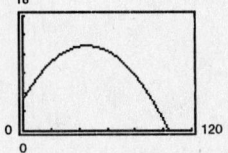

The maximum height is approximately 13 feet and the ball strikes the ground at approximately 104 feet.

(c) The maximum occurs at the vertex.

$$x = -\frac{b}{2a} = \frac{-0.367}{2(-0.004)} = 45.875$$

$$y = -0.004(45.875)^2 + 0.367(45.875) + 5 = 13.418 \text{ feet}$$

The ball strikes the ground when $y = 0$.

$$-0.004x^2 + 0.367x + 5 = 0$$

By the Quadratic Formula and using the positive value for x we have $x \approx 103.793$ feet.

90. (a) $x_1 + x_3 = 600$

$x_1 = x_2 + x_4 \implies x_1 - x_2 - x_4 = 0$

$x_2 + x_5 = 500$

$x_3 + x_6 = 600$

$x_4 + x_7 = x_6 \implies x_4 - x_6 + x_7 = 0$

$x_5 + x_7 = 500$

$$\begin{bmatrix} 1 & 0 & 1 & 0 & 0 & 0 & 0 & : & 600 \\ 1 & -1 & 0 & -1 & 0 & 0 & 0 & : & 0 \\ 0 & 1 & 0 & 0 & 1 & 0 & 0 & : & 500 \\ 0 & 0 & 1 & 0 & 0 & 1 & 0 & : & 600 \\ 0 & 0 & 0 & 1 & 0 & -1 & 1 & : & 0 \\ 0 & 0 & 0 & 0 & 1 & 0 & 1 & : & 500 \end{bmatrix}$$

$$\begin{matrix} \\ -R_1 + R_2 \rightarrow \\ R_2 + R_3 \rightarrow \\ R_3 + R_4 \rightarrow \\ R_4 + R_5 \rightarrow \\ -R_5 + R_6 \rightarrow \end{matrix} \begin{bmatrix} 1 & 0 & 1 & 0 & 0 & 0 & 0 & : & 600 \\ 0 & -1 & -1 & -1 & 0 & 0 & 0 & : & -600 \\ 0 & 0 & -1 & -1 & 1 & 0 & 0 & : & -100 \\ 0 & 0 & 0 & -1 & 1 & 1 & 0 & : & 500 \\ 0 & 0 & 0 & 0 & 1 & 0 & 1 & : & 500 \\ 0 & 0 & 0 & 0 & 0 & 0 & 0 & : & 0 \end{bmatrix}$$

$$\begin{matrix} \\ -R_3 + R_2 \rightarrow \\ -R_4 + R_3 \rightarrow \\ -R_4 \rightarrow \\ \\ \end{matrix} \begin{bmatrix} 1 & 0 & 1 & 0 & 0 & 0 & 0 & : & 600 \\ 0 & -1 & 0 & 0 & -1 & 0 & 0 & : & -500 \\ 0 & 0 & -1 & 0 & 0 & -1 & 0 & : & -600 \\ 0 & 0 & 0 & 1 & -1 & -1 & 0 & : & -500 \\ 0 & 0 & 0 & 0 & 1 & 0 & 1 & : & 500 \\ 0 & 0 & 0 & 0 & 0 & 0 & 0 & : & 0 \end{bmatrix}$$

$$\begin{matrix} \\ -R_2 \rightarrow \\ -R_3 \rightarrow \\ \\ \\ \end{matrix} \begin{bmatrix} 1 & 0 & 1 & 0 & 0 & 0 & 0 & : & 600 \\ 0 & 1 & 0 & 0 & 1 & 0 & 0 & : & 500 \\ 0 & 0 & 1 & 0 & 0 & 1 & 0 & : & 600 \\ 0 & 0 & 0 & 1 & -1 & -1 & 0 & : & -500 \\ 0 & 0 & 0 & 0 & 1 & 0 & 1 & : & 500 \\ 0 & 0 & 0 & 0 & 0 & 0 & 0 & : & 0 \end{bmatrix}$$

$$\begin{cases} x_1 + x_3 = 600 \\ x_2 + x_5 = 500 \\ x_3 + x_6 = 600 \\ x_4 - x_5 - x_6 = -500 \\ x_5 + x_7 = 500 \end{cases}$$

Let $x_7 = t$ and $x_6 = s$, then $x_5 = 500 - t$,

$\qquad x_4 = -500 + s + (500 - t) = s - t$,

$\qquad x_3 = 600 - s, x_2 = 500 - (500 - t) = t$,

$\qquad x_1 = 600 - (600 - s) = s$.

Solution: $(s, t, 600 - s, s - t, 500 - t, s, t)$

(b) $s = 0, t = 0$: $x_1 = 0, x_2 = 0, x_3 = 600, x_4 = 0, x_5 = 500, x_6 = 0, x_7 = 0$

(c) $s = 0, t = -500$: $x_1 = 0, x_2 = -500, x_3 = 600, x_4 = 500, x_5 = 1000, x_6 = 0, x_7 = -500$

92. False. It is a 2×4 matrix.

94. False. Gaussian elimination reduces a matrix until a row-echelon form is obtained and Gauss-Jordan elimination reduces a matrix until a reduced row-echelon form is obtained.

96. (a) In the row-echelon form of an augmented matrix that corresponds to an inconsistent system of linear equations, there exists a row consisting of all zeros except for the entry in the last column.

(b) In the row-echelon form of an augmented matrix that corresponds to a system with an infinite number of solutions, there are fewer rows with nonzero entries than there are variables.

98. They are the same.

100. $f(x) = \dfrac{7}{-x - 1}$

Vertical asymptote: $x = -1$

Horizontal asymptote: $y = 0$

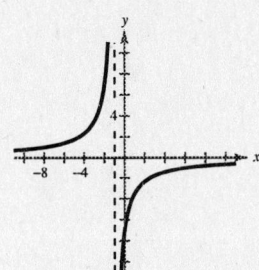

102. $f(x) = 2^{x-1}$

x	-1	0	1	2	3
$f(x)$	$-\frac{1}{4}$	$\frac{1}{2}$	1	2	4

Horizontal asymptote: $y = 0$

Intercept: $\left(0, \frac{1}{2}\right)$

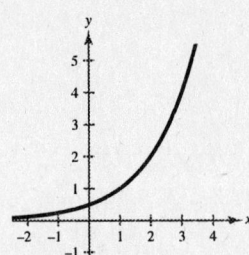

104. $h(x) = \ln(x - 1)$

x	1.5	2	3	4	5
$h(x)$	-0.693	0	0.693	1.099	1.386

Vertical asymptote: $x = 1$

Intercept: $(2, 0)$

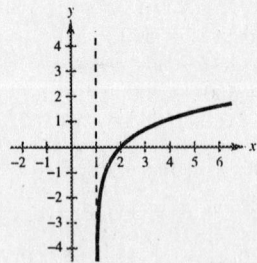

82. $2000e^{-x/5} = 400$

$$e^{-x/5} = \frac{1}{5}$$

$$\ln e^{-x/5} = \ln \frac{1}{5}$$

$$-\frac{x}{5} = \ln \frac{1}{5}$$

$$x = -5 \ln \frac{1}{5} \approx 8.05$$

84. $\ln x + \ln(x - 1) = 0$

$$\ln[x(x - 1)] = 0$$

$$e^{\ln[x(x-1)]} = e^0$$

$$x(x - 1) = 1$$

$$x^2 - x - 1 = 0$$

$$x = \frac{1 \pm \sqrt{1 - 4(-1)}}{2}$$

$$x = \frac{1 \pm \sqrt{5}}{2}$$

Choose the positive value only:

$$x = \frac{1 + \sqrt{5}}{2} \approx 1.62$$

86. $\dfrac{1}{8} \begin{bmatrix} -6 & 2 & 0 \\ -4 & -24 & 18 \end{bmatrix} = \begin{bmatrix} -\frac{6}{8} & \frac{2}{8} & \frac{0}{8} \\ -\frac{4}{8} & -\frac{24}{8} & \frac{18}{8} \end{bmatrix}$

$$= \begin{bmatrix} -\frac{3}{4} & \frac{1}{4} & 0 \\ -\frac{1}{2} & -3 & \frac{9}{4} \end{bmatrix}$$

88. $8\begin{bmatrix} 2 & -3 \\ 1 & 0 \end{bmatrix} + \begin{bmatrix} 12 & 17 \\ -7 & 9 \end{bmatrix}$

$$= \begin{bmatrix} 16 & -24 \\ 8 & 0 \end{bmatrix} + \begin{bmatrix} 12 & 17 \\ -7 & 9 \end{bmatrix}$$

$$= \begin{bmatrix} 16 + 12 & -24 + 17 \\ 8 - 7 & 0 + 9 \end{bmatrix} = \begin{bmatrix} 28 & -7 \\ 1 & 9 \end{bmatrix}$$

Section 8.2 Operations with Matrices

Solutions to Even-Numbered Exercises

2. $x = 13, y = 12$

4. $x + 2 = 2x + 6, \quad y + 2 = 11$
$$-4 = x \qquad\qquad y = 9$$

6. (a) $A + B = \begin{bmatrix} 1 & 2 \\ 2 & 1 \end{bmatrix} + \begin{bmatrix} -3 & -2 \\ 4 & 2 \end{bmatrix} = \begin{bmatrix} 1-3 & 2-2 \\ 2+4 & 1+2 \end{bmatrix} = \begin{bmatrix} -2 & 0 \\ 6 & 3 \end{bmatrix}$

(b) $A - B = \begin{bmatrix} 1 & 2 \\ 2 & 1 \end{bmatrix} - \begin{bmatrix} -3 & -2 \\ 4 & 2 \end{bmatrix} = \begin{bmatrix} 1+3 & 2+2 \\ 2-4 & 1-2 \end{bmatrix} = \begin{bmatrix} 4 & 4 \\ -2 & -1 \end{bmatrix}$

(c) $3A = 3\begin{bmatrix} 1 & 2 \\ 2 & 1 \end{bmatrix} = \begin{bmatrix} 3(1) & 3(2) \\ 3(2) & 3(1) \end{bmatrix} = \begin{bmatrix} 3 & 6 \\ 6 & 3 \end{bmatrix}$

(d) $3A - 2B = \begin{bmatrix} 3 & 6 \\ 6 & 3 \end{bmatrix} - 2\begin{bmatrix} -3 & -2 \\ 4 & 2 \end{bmatrix} = \begin{bmatrix} 3+6 & 6+4 \\ 6-8 & 3-4 \end{bmatrix} = \begin{bmatrix} 9 & 10 \\ -2 & -1 \end{bmatrix}$

8. (a) $A + B = \begin{bmatrix} 2 & 1 & 1 \\ -1 & -1 & 4 \end{bmatrix} + \begin{bmatrix} 2 & -3 & 4 \\ -3 & 1 & -2 \end{bmatrix} = \begin{bmatrix} 2+2 & 1-3 & 1+4 \\ -1-3 & -1+1 & 4-2 \end{bmatrix} = \begin{bmatrix} 4 & -2 & 5 \\ -4 & 0 & 2 \end{bmatrix}$

(b) $A - B = \begin{bmatrix} 2 & 1 & 1 \\ -1 & -1 & 4 \end{bmatrix} - \begin{bmatrix} 2 & -3 & 4 \\ -3 & 1 & -2 \end{bmatrix} = \begin{bmatrix} 2-2 & 1-(-3) & 1-4 \\ -1-(-3) & -1-1 & 4-(-2) \end{bmatrix} = \begin{bmatrix} 0 & 4 & -3 \\ 2 & -2 & 6 \end{bmatrix}$

(c) $3A = 3\begin{bmatrix} 2 & 1 & 1 \\ -1 & -1 & 4 \end{bmatrix} = \begin{bmatrix} 3(2) & 3(1) & 3(1) \\ 3(-1) & 3(-1) & 3(4) \end{bmatrix} = \begin{bmatrix} 6 & 3 & 3 \\ -3 & -3 & 12 \end{bmatrix}$

(d) $3A - 2B = \begin{bmatrix} 6 & 3 & 3 \\ -3 & -3 & 12 \end{bmatrix} - 2\begin{bmatrix} 2 & -3 & 4 \\ -3 & 1 & -2 \end{bmatrix} = \begin{bmatrix} 6 & 3 & 3 \\ -3 & -3 & 12 \end{bmatrix} + \begin{bmatrix} -4 & 6 & -8 \\ 6 & -2 & 4 \end{bmatrix}$

$$= \begin{bmatrix} 2 & 9 & -5 \\ 3 & -5 & 16 \end{bmatrix}$$

10. (a) $A + B = \begin{bmatrix} -1 & 4 & 0 \\ 3 & -2 & 2 \\ 5 & 4 & -1 \\ 0 & 8 & -6 \\ -4 & -1 & 0 \end{bmatrix} + \begin{bmatrix} -3 & 5 & 1 \\ 2 & -4 & -7 \\ 10 & -9 & -1 \\ 3 & 2 & -4 \\ 0 & 1 & -2 \end{bmatrix}$

$$= \begin{bmatrix} -1-3 & 4+5 & 0+1 \\ 3+2 & -2-4 & 2-7 \\ 5+10 & 4-9 & -1-1 \\ 0+3 & 8+2 & -6-4 \\ -4+0 & -1+1 & 0-2 \end{bmatrix} = \begin{bmatrix} -4 & 9 & 1 \\ 5 & -6 & -5 \\ 15 & -5 & -2 \\ 3 & 10 & -10 \\ -4 & 0 & -2 \end{bmatrix}$$

—CONTINUED—

10. **—CONTINUED—**

(b) $A - B = \begin{bmatrix} -1 & 4 & 0 \\ 3 & -2 & 2 \\ 5 & 4 & -1 \\ 0 & 8 & -6 \\ -4 & -1 & 0 \end{bmatrix} - \begin{bmatrix} -3 & 5 & 1 \\ 2 & -4 & -7 \\ 10 & -9 & -1 \\ 3 & 2 & -4 \\ 0 & 1 & -2 \end{bmatrix}$

$= \begin{bmatrix} -1+3 & 4-5 & 0-1 \\ 3-2 & -2+4 & 2+7 \\ 5-10 & 4+9 & -1+1 \\ 0-3 & 8-2 & -6+4 \\ -4-0 & -1-1 & 0+2 \end{bmatrix} = \begin{bmatrix} 2 & -1 & -1 \\ 1 & 2 & 9 \\ -5 & 13 & 0 \\ -3 & 6 & -2 \\ -4 & -2 & 2 \end{bmatrix}$

(c) $3A = 3\begin{bmatrix} -1 & 4 & 0 \\ 3 & -2 & 2 \\ 5 & 4 & -1 \\ 0 & 8 & -6 \\ -4 & -1 & 0 \end{bmatrix} = \begin{bmatrix} -3 & 12 & 0 \\ 9 & -6 & 6 \\ 15 & 12 & -3 \\ 0 & 24 & -18 \\ -12 & -3 & 0 \end{bmatrix}$

(d) $3A - 2B = \begin{bmatrix} -3 & 12 & 0 \\ 9 & -6 & 6 \\ 15 & 12 & -3 \\ 0 & 24 & -18 \\ -12 & -3 & 0 \end{bmatrix} - 2\begin{bmatrix} -3 & 5 & 1 \\ 2 & -4 & -7 \\ 10 & -9 & -1 \\ 3 & 2 & -4 \\ 0 & 1 & -2 \end{bmatrix}$

$= \begin{bmatrix} -3 & 12 & 0 \\ 9 & -6 & 6 \\ 15 & 12 & -3 \\ 0 & 24 & -18 \\ -12 & -3 & 0 \end{bmatrix} + \begin{bmatrix} 6 & -10 & -2 \\ -4 & 8 & 14 \\ -20 & 18 & 2 \\ -6 & -4 & 8 \\ 0 & -2 & 4 \end{bmatrix}$

$= \begin{bmatrix} 3 & 2 & -2 \\ 5 & 2 & 20 \\ -5 & 30 & -1 \\ -6 & 20 & -10 \\ -12 & -5 & 4 \end{bmatrix}$

12. (a) $A + B$ is not possible. A and B do not have the same order.

(b) $A - B$ is not possible. A and B do not have the same order.

(c) $3A = 3\begin{bmatrix} 3 \\ 2 \\ -1 \end{bmatrix} = \begin{bmatrix} 9 \\ 6 \\ -3 \end{bmatrix}$

(d) $3A - 2B$ is not possible. A and B do not have the same order.

14. $\begin{bmatrix} 6 & 8 \\ -1 & 0 \end{bmatrix} + \begin{bmatrix} 0 & 5 \\ -3 & -1 \end{bmatrix} + \begin{bmatrix} -11 & -7 \\ 2 & -1 \end{bmatrix} = \begin{bmatrix} 6+0+(-11) & 8+5+(-7) \\ -1+(-3)+2 & 0+(-1)+(-1) \end{bmatrix} = \begin{bmatrix} -5 & 6 \\ -2 & -2 \end{bmatrix}$

16. $\frac{1}{2}([5 \quad -2 \quad 4 \quad 0] + [14 \quad 6 \quad -18 \quad 9]) = \frac{1}{2}[5 + 14 \quad -2 + 6 \quad 4 + (-18) \quad 0 + 9]$

$$= \frac{1}{2}[19 \quad 4 \quad -14 \quad 9]$$

$$= \left[\frac{19}{2} \quad 2 \quad -7 \quad \frac{9}{2}\right]$$

18. $-1\begin{bmatrix} 4 & 11 \\ -2 & -1 \\ 9 & 3 \end{bmatrix} + \frac{1}{6}\left(\begin{bmatrix} -5 & -1 \\ 3 & 4 \\ 0 & 13 \end{bmatrix} + \begin{bmatrix} 7 & 5 \\ -9 & -1 \\ 6 & -1 \end{bmatrix}\right) = \begin{bmatrix} -4 & -11 \\ 2 & 1 \\ -9 & -3 \end{bmatrix} + \frac{1}{6}\begin{bmatrix} -5 + 7 & -1 + 5 \\ 3 + (-9) & 4 + (-1) \\ 0 + 6 & 13 + (-1) \end{bmatrix}$

$$= \begin{bmatrix} -4 & -11 \\ 2 & 1 \\ -9 & -3 \end{bmatrix} + \frac{1}{6}\begin{bmatrix} 2 & 4 \\ -6 & 3 \\ 6 & 12 \end{bmatrix}$$

$$= \begin{bmatrix} -4 & -11 \\ 2 & 1 \\ -9 & -3 \end{bmatrix} + \begin{bmatrix} \frac{1}{3} & \frac{2}{3} \\ -1 & \frac{1}{2} \\ 1 & 2 \end{bmatrix}$$

$$= \begin{bmatrix} -4 + \frac{1}{3} & -11 + \frac{2}{3} \\ 2 + (-1) & 1 + \frac{1}{2} \\ -9 + 1 & -3 + 2 \end{bmatrix} = \begin{bmatrix} -\frac{11}{3} & -\frac{31}{3} \\ 1 & \frac{3}{2} \\ -8 & -1 \end{bmatrix}$$

20. $55\left(\begin{bmatrix} 14 & -11 \\ -22 & 19 \end{bmatrix} + \begin{bmatrix} -22 & 20 \\ 13 & 6 \end{bmatrix}\right) = 55\begin{bmatrix} 14 + (-22) & -11 + 20 \\ -22 + 13 & 19 + 6 \end{bmatrix}$

$$= 55\begin{bmatrix} -8 & 9 \\ -9 & 25 \end{bmatrix} = \begin{bmatrix} -440 & 495 \\ -495 & 1375 \end{bmatrix}$$

22. $-12\left(\begin{bmatrix} 6 & 20 \\ 1 & -9 \\ -2 & 5 \end{bmatrix} + \begin{bmatrix} 14 & -15 \\ -8 & -6 \\ 7 & 0 \end{bmatrix} + \begin{bmatrix} -31 & -19 \\ 16 & 10 \\ 24 & -10 \end{bmatrix}\right) = -12\begin{bmatrix} 6 + 14 + (-31) & 20 + (-15) + (-19) \\ 1 + (-8) + 16 & -9 + (-6) + 10 \\ -2 + 7 + 24 & 5 + 0 + (-10) \end{bmatrix}$

$$= -12\begin{bmatrix} -11 & -14 \\ 9 & -5 \\ 29 & -5 \end{bmatrix} = \begin{bmatrix} 132 & 168 \\ -108 & 60 \\ -348 & 60 \end{bmatrix}$$

24. $2X = 2A - B$

$$X = A - \frac{1}{2}B = \begin{bmatrix} -2 & -1 \\ 1 & 0 \\ 3 & -4 \end{bmatrix} - \frac{1}{2}\begin{bmatrix} 0 & 3 \\ 2 & 0 \\ -4 & -1 \end{bmatrix} = \begin{bmatrix} -2 & -1 \\ 1 & 0 \\ 3 & -4 \end{bmatrix} - \begin{bmatrix} 0 & \frac{3}{2} \\ 1 & 0 \\ -2 & -\frac{1}{2} \end{bmatrix} = \begin{bmatrix} -2 & -\frac{5}{2} \\ 0 & 0 \\ 5 & -\frac{7}{2} \end{bmatrix}$$

26. $2A + 4B = -2X$

$$X = -A - 2B = -1\begin{bmatrix} -2 & -1 \\ 1 & 0 \\ 3 & -4 \end{bmatrix} - 2\begin{bmatrix} 0 & 3 \\ 2 & 0 \\ -4 & -1 \end{bmatrix} = \begin{bmatrix} 2 & 1 \\ -1 & 0 \\ -3 & 4 \end{bmatrix} + \begin{bmatrix} 0 & -6 \\ -4 & 0 \\ 8 & 2 \end{bmatrix} = \begin{bmatrix} 2 & -5 \\ -5 & 0 \\ 5 & 6 \end{bmatrix}$$

28. (a) $AB = \begin{bmatrix} 2 & -1 \\ 1 & 4 \end{bmatrix}\begin{bmatrix} 0 & 0 \\ 3 & -3 \end{bmatrix} = \begin{bmatrix} 2(0) + (-1)3 & 2(0) + (-1)(-3) \\ 1(0) + 4(3) & 1(0) + 4(-3) \end{bmatrix} = \begin{bmatrix} -3 & 3 \\ 12 & -12 \end{bmatrix}$

(b) $BA = \begin{bmatrix} 0 & 0 \\ 3 & -3 \end{bmatrix}\begin{bmatrix} 2 & -1 \\ 1 & 4 \end{bmatrix} = \begin{bmatrix} 0(2) + (0)1 & 0(-1) + (0)(4) \\ 3(2) + (-3)(1) & 3(-1) + (-3)4 \end{bmatrix} = \begin{bmatrix} 0 & 0 \\ 3 & -15 \end{bmatrix}$

(c) $A^2 = \begin{bmatrix} 2 & -1 \\ 1 & 4 \end{bmatrix}\begin{bmatrix} 2 & -1 \\ 1 & 4 \end{bmatrix} = \begin{bmatrix} 2(2) + (-1)(1) & 2(-1) + (-1)4 \\ 1(2) + 4(1) & 1(-1) + 4(4) \end{bmatrix} = \begin{bmatrix} 3 & -6 \\ 6 & 15 \end{bmatrix}$

30. (a) $AB = \begin{bmatrix} 1 & -1 \\ 1 & 1 \end{bmatrix}\begin{bmatrix} 1 & 3 \\ -3 & 1 \end{bmatrix} = \begin{bmatrix} 1(1) + (-1)(-3) & 1(3) + (-1)(1) \\ 1(1) + 1(-3) & 1(3) + 1(1) \end{bmatrix} = \begin{bmatrix} 4 & 2 \\ -2 & 4 \end{bmatrix}$

   (b) $BA = \begin{bmatrix} 1 & 3 \\ -3 & 1 \end{bmatrix}\begin{bmatrix} 1 & -1 \\ 1 & 1 \end{bmatrix} = \begin{bmatrix} 1(1) + (3)1 & 1(-1) + 3(1) \\ -3(1) + (1)(1) & -3(-1) + 1(1) \end{bmatrix} = \begin{bmatrix} 4 & 2 \\ -2 & 4 \end{bmatrix}$

   (c) $A^2 = \begin{bmatrix} 1 & -1 \\ 1 & 1 \end{bmatrix}\begin{bmatrix} 1 & -1 \\ 1 & 1 \end{bmatrix} = \begin{bmatrix} 1(1) + (-1)(1) & 1(-1) + (-1)(1) \\ 1(1) + (1)(1) & 1(-1) + 1(1) \end{bmatrix} = \begin{bmatrix} 0 & -2 \\ 2 & 0 \end{bmatrix}$

32. (a) $AB = \begin{bmatrix} 3 & 2 & 1 \end{bmatrix}\begin{bmatrix} 2 \\ 3 \\ 0 \end{bmatrix} = [3(2) + 2(3) + 1(0)] = [12]$

   (b) $BA = \begin{bmatrix} 2 \\ 3 \\ 0 \end{bmatrix}\begin{bmatrix} 3 & 2 & 1 \end{bmatrix} = \begin{bmatrix} 2(3) & 2(2) & 2(1) \\ 3(3) & 3(2) & 3(1) \\ 0(3) & 0(2) & 0(1) \end{bmatrix} = \begin{bmatrix} 6 & 4 & 2 \\ 9 & 6 & 3 \\ 0 & 0 & 0 \end{bmatrix}$

   (c) The number of columns of A does not equal the number of rows of A; the multiplication is not possible.

34. A is 2×4, B is 2×2. AB is not possible.

36. A is 3×2, B is 2×2 $\Rightarrow$ AB is 3×2.

$$AB = \begin{bmatrix} -1 & 3 \\ 4 & -5 \\ 0 & 2 \end{bmatrix}\begin{bmatrix} 1 & 2 \\ 0 & 7 \end{bmatrix} = \begin{bmatrix} -1 & 19 \\ 4 & -27 \\ 0 & 14 \end{bmatrix}$$

38. A is 3×3, B is 3×3 $\Rightarrow$ AB is 3×3.

$$AB = \begin{bmatrix} 5 & 0 & 0 \\ 0 & -8 & 0 \\ 0 & 0 & 7 \end{bmatrix}\begin{bmatrix} \frac{1}{5} & 0 & 0 \\ 0 & -\frac{1}{8} & 0 \\ 0 & 0 & \frac{1}{2} \end{bmatrix} = \begin{bmatrix} 1 & 0 & 0 \\ 0 & 1 & 0 \\ 0 & 0 & \frac{7}{2} \end{bmatrix}$$

40. A is 2×1, B is 1×4 $\Rightarrow$ AB is 2×4.

$$\begin{bmatrix} 10 \\ 12 \end{bmatrix}\begin{bmatrix} 6 & -2 & 1 & 6 \end{bmatrix} = \begin{bmatrix} 60 & -20 & 10 & 60 \\ 72 & -24 & 12 & 72 \end{bmatrix}$$

42. $\begin{bmatrix} 11 & -12 & 4 \\ 14 & 10 & 12 \\ 6 & -2 & 9 \end{bmatrix}\begin{bmatrix} 12 & 10 \\ -5 & 12 \\ 15 & 16 \end{bmatrix} = \begin{bmatrix} 252 & 30 \\ 298 & 452 \\ 217 & 180 \end{bmatrix}$

44. A is 3×3, B is 4×2. AB is not possible.

46. $\begin{bmatrix} 15 & -18 \\ -4 & 12 \\ -8 & 22 \end{bmatrix}\begin{bmatrix} -7 & 22 & 1 \\ 8 & 16 & 24 \end{bmatrix} = \begin{bmatrix} -249 & 42 & -417 \\ 124 & 104 & 284 \\ 232 & 176 & 520 \end{bmatrix}$

48. $-3\left(\begin{bmatrix} 6 & 5 & -1 \\ 1 & -2 & 0 \end{bmatrix}\begin{bmatrix} 0 & 3 \\ -1 & -3 \\ 4 & 1 \end{bmatrix}\right) = \begin{bmatrix} 27 & -6 \\ -6 & -27 \end{bmatrix}$

50. $\begin{bmatrix} 3 \\ -1 \\ 5 \\ 7 \end{bmatrix}([5 \quad -6] + [7 \quad -1] + [-8 \quad 9]) = \begin{bmatrix} 12 & 6 \\ -4 & -2 \\ 20 & 10 \\ 28 & 14 \end{bmatrix}$

52. (a) $\begin{bmatrix} 2 & 3 \\ 1 & 4 \end{bmatrix}\begin{bmatrix} x_1 \\ x_2 \end{bmatrix} = \begin{bmatrix} 5 \\ 10 \end{bmatrix}$

   (b) $\begin{array}{c} R_2 \\ R_1 \end{array} \begin{bmatrix} 1 & 4 & \vdots & 10 \\ 2 & 3 & \vdots & 5 \end{bmatrix}$

$$-2R_1 + R_2 \rightarrow \begin{bmatrix} 1 & 4 & \vdots & 10 \\ 0 & -5 & \vdots & -15 \end{bmatrix}$$

$$\begin{array}{c} -4R_2 + R_1 \rightarrow \\ -\frac{1}{5}R_2 \rightarrow \end{array} \begin{bmatrix} 1 & 0 & \vdots & -2 \\ 0 & 1 & \vdots & 3 \end{bmatrix}$$

$$X = \begin{bmatrix} -2 \\ 3 \end{bmatrix}$$

54. (a) $\begin{bmatrix} -4 & 9 \\ 1 & -3 \end{bmatrix}\begin{bmatrix} x_1 \\ x_2 \end{bmatrix} = \begin{bmatrix} -13 \\ 12 \end{bmatrix}$

(b) $\begin{matrix} R_1 \\ R_2 \end{matrix} \begin{bmatrix} 1 & -3 & \vdots & 12 \\ -4 & 9 & \vdots & -13 \end{bmatrix}$

$4R_1 + R_2 \to \begin{bmatrix} 1 & -3 & \vdots & 12 \\ 0 & -3 & \vdots & 35 \end{bmatrix}$

$-\frac{1}{3}R_2 \to \begin{bmatrix} 1 & -3 & \vdots & 12 \\ 0 & 1 & \vdots & -\frac{35}{3} \end{bmatrix}$

$3R_2 + R_1 \to \begin{bmatrix} 1 & 0 & \vdots & -23 \\ 0 & 1 & \vdots & -\frac{35}{3} \end{bmatrix}$

$X = \begin{bmatrix} -23 \\ -\frac{35}{3} \end{bmatrix}$

56. (a) $\begin{bmatrix} 1 & 1 & -3 \\ -1 & 2 & 0 \\ 1 & -1 & 1 \end{bmatrix}\begin{bmatrix} x_1 \\ x_2 \\ x_3 \end{bmatrix} = \begin{bmatrix} 9 \\ 6 \\ -5 \end{bmatrix}$

(b) $\begin{bmatrix} 1 & 1 & -3 & \vdots & 9 \\ -1 & 2 & 0 & \vdots & 6 \\ 1 & -1 & 1 & \vdots & -5 \end{bmatrix}$

$\begin{matrix} R_1 + R_2 \to \\ -R_1 + R_3 \to \end{matrix} \begin{bmatrix} 1 & 1 & -3 & \vdots & 9 \\ 0 & 3 & -3 & \vdots & 15 \\ 0 & -2 & 4 & \vdots & -14 \end{bmatrix}$

$\frac{1}{3}R_2 \to \begin{bmatrix} 1 & 1 & -3 & \vdots & 9 \\ 0 & 1 & -1 & \vdots & 5 \\ 0 & -2 & 4 & \vdots & -14 \end{bmatrix}$

$\begin{matrix} -R_2 + R_1 \to \\ \\ 2R_2 + R_3 \to \end{matrix} \begin{bmatrix} 1 & 0 & -2 & \vdots & 4 \\ 0 & 1 & -1 & \vdots & 5 \\ 0 & 0 & 2 & \vdots & -4 \end{bmatrix}$

$\frac{1}{2}R_3 \to \begin{bmatrix} 1 & 0 & -2 & \vdots & 4 \\ 0 & 1 & -1 & \vdots & 5 \\ 0 & 0 & 1 & \vdots & -2 \end{bmatrix}$

$\begin{matrix} 2R_3 + R_1 \to \\ R_3 + R_2 \to \end{matrix} \begin{bmatrix} 1 & 0 & 0 & \vdots & 0 \\ 0 & 1 & 0 & \vdots & 3 \\ 0 & 0 & 1 & \vdots & -2 \end{bmatrix}$

$X = \begin{bmatrix} 0 \\ 3 \\ -2 \end{bmatrix}$

58. (a) $\begin{bmatrix} 1 & -1 & 4 \\ 1 & 3 & 0 \\ 0 & -6 & 5 \end{bmatrix}\begin{bmatrix} x_1 \\ x_2 \\ x_3 \end{bmatrix} = \begin{bmatrix} 17 \\ -11 \\ 40 \end{bmatrix}$

(b) $\begin{bmatrix} 1 & -1 & 4 & \vdots & 17 \\ 1 & 3 & 0 & \vdots & -11 \\ 0 & -6 & 5 & \vdots & 40 \end{bmatrix}$

$-R_1 + R_2 \to \begin{bmatrix} 1 & -1 & 4 & \vdots & 17 \\ 0 & 4 & -4 & \vdots & -28 \\ 0 & -6 & 5 & \vdots & 40 \end{bmatrix}$

$\frac{1}{4}R_2 \to \begin{bmatrix} 1 & -1 & 4 & \vdots & 17 \\ 0 & 1 & -1 & \vdots & -7 \\ 0 & -6 & 5 & \vdots & 40 \end{bmatrix}$

$6R_2 + R_3 \to \begin{bmatrix} 1 & -1 & 4 & \vdots & 17 \\ 0 & 1 & -1 & \vdots & -7 \\ 0 & 0 & -1 & \vdots & -2 \end{bmatrix}$

$\begin{matrix} R_2 + R_1 \to \\ \\ -R_3 \to \end{matrix} \begin{bmatrix} 1 & 0 & 3 & \vdots & 10 \\ 0 & 1 & -1 & \vdots & -7 \\ 0 & 0 & 1 & \vdots & 2 \end{bmatrix}$

$\begin{matrix} -3R_3 + R_1 \to \\ R_3 + R_2 \to \end{matrix} \begin{bmatrix} 1 & 0 & 0 & \vdots & 4 \\ 0 & 1 & 0 & \vdots & -5 \\ 0 & 0 & 1 & \vdots & 2 \end{bmatrix}$

$X = \begin{bmatrix} 4 \\ -5 \\ 2 \end{bmatrix}$

For 60–68, A **is of order** 2×3, B **is of order** 2×3, C **is of order** 3×2, **and** D **is of order** 2×2.

60. $B - 3C$ is not possible. B and C are not of the same order.

62. BC is possible. The resulting order is 2×2.

64. $CB - D$ is not possible. The order of CB is 3×3, but the order of D is 2×2.

66. $(BC)D$ is possible. The resulting order is 2×2.

68. $(BC - D)A$ is possible. The resulting order is 2×3.

70. $1.10 \begin{bmatrix} 100 & 90 & 70 & 30 \\ 40 & 20 & 60 & 60 \end{bmatrix} = \begin{bmatrix} 110 & 99 & 77 & 33 \\ 44 & 22 & 66 & 66 \end{bmatrix}$

72. $BA = \begin{bmatrix} \$20.50 & \$26.50 & \$29.50 \end{bmatrix} \begin{bmatrix} 5{,}000 & 4{,}000 \\ 6{,}000 & 10{,}000 \\ 8{,}000 & 5{,}000 \end{bmatrix} = \begin{bmatrix} \$497{,}500 & \$494{,}500 \end{bmatrix}$

The entries represent the costs of the three models of the product at the two warehouses.

74. $P^2 = \begin{bmatrix} 0.6 & 0.1 & 0.1 \\ 0.2 & 0.7 & 0.1 \\ 0.2 & 0.2 & 0.8 \end{bmatrix} \begin{bmatrix} 0.6 & 0.1 & 0.1 \\ 0.2 & 0.7 & 0.1 \\ 0.2 & 0.2 & 0.8 \end{bmatrix} = \begin{bmatrix} 0.40 & 0.15 & 0.15 \\ 0.28 & 0.53 & 0.17 \\ 0.32 & 0.32 & 0.68 \end{bmatrix}$

The P^2 matrix gives the proportion of the voting population that changed parties or remained loyal to their party from the first election to the third.

76. $P^3 = P^2 P = \begin{bmatrix} 0.40 & 0.15 & 0.15 \\ 0.28 & 0.53 & 0.17 \\ 0.32 & 0.32 & 0.68 \end{bmatrix} \begin{bmatrix} 0.6 & 0.1 & 0.1 \\ 0.2 & 0.7 & 0.1 \\ 0.2 & 0.2 & 0.8 \end{bmatrix} = \begin{bmatrix} 0.300 & 0.175 & 0.175 \\ 0.308 & 0.433 & 0.217 \\ 0.392 & 0.392 & 0.608 \end{bmatrix}$

$P^4 = P^3 P = \begin{bmatrix} 0.300 & 0.175 & 0.175 \\ 0.308 & 0.433 & 0.217 \\ 0.392 & 0.392 & 0.608 \end{bmatrix} \begin{bmatrix} 0.6 & 0.1 & 0.1 \\ 0.2 & 0.7 & 0.1 \\ 0.2 & 0.2 & 0.8 \end{bmatrix} = \begin{bmatrix} 0.250 & 0.188 & 0.188 \\ 0.315 & 0.377 & 0.248 \\ 0.435 & 0.435 & 0.565 \end{bmatrix}$

$P^5 = P^4 P = \begin{bmatrix} 0.250 & 0.188 & 0.188 \\ 0.315 & 0.377 & 0.248 \\ 0.435 & 0.435 & 0.565 \end{bmatrix} \begin{bmatrix} 0.6 & 0.1 & 0.1 \\ 0.2 & 0.7 & 0.1 \\ 0.2 & 0.2 & 0.8 \end{bmatrix} = \begin{bmatrix} 0.225 & 0.194 & 0.194 \\ 0.314 & 0.345 & 0.267 \\ 0.461 & 0.461 & 0.539 \end{bmatrix}$

$P^6 = \begin{bmatrix} 0.213 & 0.197 & 0.197 \\ 0.311 & 0.326 & 0.280 \\ 0.477 & 0.477 & 0.523 \end{bmatrix}$

$P^7 = \begin{bmatrix} 0.206 & 0.198 & 0.198 \\ 0.308 & 0.316 & 0.288 \\ 0.486 & 0.486 & 0.514 \end{bmatrix}$

$P^8 = \begin{bmatrix} 0.203 & 0.199 & 0.199 \\ 0.305 & 0.309 & 0.292 \\ 0.492 & 0.492 & 0.508 \end{bmatrix}$

As P is raised to higher and higher powers, the resulting matrices appear to be approaching the matrix

$\begin{bmatrix} 0.2 & 0.2 & 0.2 \\ 0.3 & 0.3 & 0.3 \\ 0.5 & 0.5 & 0.5 \end{bmatrix}$.

78. False. For most matrices, $AB \neq BA$.

80. $AC = \begin{bmatrix} 0 & 1 \\ 0 & 1 \end{bmatrix}\begin{bmatrix} 2 & 3 \\ 2 & 3 \end{bmatrix} = \begin{bmatrix} 2 & 3 \\ 2 & 3 \end{bmatrix}$

$BC = \begin{bmatrix} 1 & 0 \\ 1 & 0 \end{bmatrix}\begin{bmatrix} 2 & 3 \\ 2 & 3 \end{bmatrix} = \begin{bmatrix} 2 & 3 \\ 2 & 3 \end{bmatrix}$

Thus, $AC = BC$ even though $A \neq B$.

82. $A^2 = \begin{bmatrix} i & 0 \\ 0 & i \end{bmatrix}\begin{bmatrix} i & 0 \\ 0 & i \end{bmatrix} = \begin{bmatrix} (i)(i) + (0)(0) & (i)(0) + (0)(i) \\ (0)(i) + (i)(0) & (0)(0) + (i)(i) \end{bmatrix} = \begin{bmatrix} -1 & 0 \\ 0 & -1 \end{bmatrix}$ and $i^2 = -1$

$A^3 = A^2A = \begin{bmatrix} -1 & 0 \\ 0 & -1 \end{bmatrix}\begin{bmatrix} i & 0 \\ 0 & i \end{bmatrix} = \begin{bmatrix} (-1)(i) + (0)(0) & (-1)(0) + (0)(i) \\ (0)(i) + (-1)(0) & (0)(0) + (-1)(i) \end{bmatrix} = \begin{bmatrix} -i & 0 \\ 0 & -i \end{bmatrix}$ and $i^3 = -i$

$A^4 = A^3A = \begin{bmatrix} -i & 0 \\ 0 & -i \end{bmatrix}\begin{bmatrix} i & 0 \\ 0 & i \end{bmatrix} = \begin{bmatrix} (-i)(i) + (0)(0) & (i)(0) + (0)(i) \\ (0)(i) + (-i)(0) & (0)(0) + (-i)(i) \end{bmatrix} = \begin{bmatrix} 1 & 0 \\ 0 & 1 \end{bmatrix}$ and $i^4 = 1$

84. The product of two diagonal matrices of the same order is a diagonal matrix whose entries are the products of the corresponding diagonal entries of A and B.

86. $8x^2 - 10x - 3 = 0$

$(2x - 3)(4x + 1) = 0$

$2x - 3 = 0 \implies x = \frac{3}{2}$

$4x + 1 = 0 \implies x = -\frac{1}{4}$

Solutions: $-\frac{1}{4}, \frac{3}{2}$

88. $3x^3 + 22x^2 - 45x = 0$

$x(3x^2 + 22x - 45) = 0$

$x(x + 9)(3x - 5) = 0$

$x = 0$

$x + 9 = 0 \implies x = -9$

$3x - 5 = 0 \implies x = \frac{5}{3}$

Solutions: $0, -9, \frac{5}{3}$

90. $2x^3 - 5x^2 - 12x + 30 = 0$

$x^2(2x - 5) - 6(2x - 5) = 0$

$(2x - 5)(x^2 - 6) = 0$

$2x - 5 = 0 \implies x = \frac{5}{2}$

$x^2 - 6 = 0 \implies x^2 = 6 \implies x = \pm\sqrt{6}$

$x = \pm\sqrt{6}$

Solutions: $\frac{5}{2}, \pm\sqrt{6}$

92. $\begin{cases} 8x - 3y = -17 \\ -6x + 7y = 27 \end{cases}$ Equation 1 / Equation 2

$\begin{array}{rl} 48x - 18y = -102 & \text{6 Eq. 1} \\ -48x + 56y = 216 & \text{8 Eq. 2} \\ \hline 38y = 114 & \text{Add equations.} \\ y = 3 \end{array}$

$8x - 3(3) = -17 \implies x = -1$

Solution: $(-1, 3)$

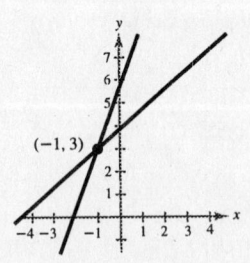

94. $\begin{cases} 6x - 13y = 11 \\ 9x + 5y = 41 \end{cases}$ Equation 1 / Equation 2

$\begin{array}{rl} 18x - 39y = 33 & \text{3 Eq. 1} \\ -18x - 10y = -82 & \text{-2 Eq. 2} \\ \hline -49y = -49 & \text{Add equations.} \\ y = 1 \end{array}$

$6x - 13(1) = 11 \implies x = 4$

Solution: $(4, 1)$

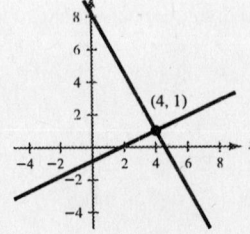

Section 8.3   The Inverse of a Square Matrix

Solutions to Even-Numbered Exercises

2. $AB = \begin{bmatrix} 1 & -1 \\ -1 & 2 \end{bmatrix}\begin{bmatrix} 2 & 1 \\ 1 & 1 \end{bmatrix} = \begin{bmatrix} 2-1 & 1-1 \\ -2+2 & -1+2 \end{bmatrix} = \begin{bmatrix} 1 & 0 \\ 0 & 1 \end{bmatrix}$

$BA = \begin{bmatrix} 2 & 1 \\ 1 & 1 \end{bmatrix}\begin{bmatrix} 1 & -1 \\ -1 & 2 \end{bmatrix} = \begin{bmatrix} 2-1 & -2+2 \\ 1-1 & -1+2 \end{bmatrix} = \begin{bmatrix} 1 & 0 \\ 0 & 1 \end{bmatrix}$

4. $AB = \begin{bmatrix} 1 & -1 \\ 2 & 3 \end{bmatrix}\begin{bmatrix} \frac{3}{5} & \frac{1}{5} \\ -\frac{2}{5} & \frac{1}{5} \end{bmatrix} = \begin{bmatrix} \frac{3}{5}+\frac{2}{5} & \frac{1}{5}-\frac{1}{5} \\ \frac{6}{5}-\frac{6}{5} & \frac{2}{5}+\frac{3}{5} \end{bmatrix} = \begin{bmatrix} 1 & 0 \\ 0 & 1 \end{bmatrix}$

$AB = \begin{bmatrix} \frac{3}{5} & \frac{1}{5} \\ -\frac{2}{5} & \frac{1}{5} \end{bmatrix}\begin{bmatrix} 1 & -1 \\ 2 & 3 \end{bmatrix} = \begin{bmatrix} \frac{3}{5}+\frac{2}{5} & -\frac{3}{5}+\frac{3}{5} \\ -\frac{2}{5}+\frac{2}{5} & \frac{2}{5}+\frac{3}{5} \end{bmatrix} = \begin{bmatrix} 1 & 0 \\ 0 & 1 \end{bmatrix}$

6. $AB = \begin{bmatrix} -4 & 1 & 5 \\ -1 & 2 & 4 \\ 0 & -1 & -1 \end{bmatrix}\begin{bmatrix} -\frac{1}{2} & 1 & \frac{3}{2} \\ \frac{1}{4} & -1 & -\frac{11}{4} \\ -\frac{1}{4} & 1 & \frac{7}{4} \end{bmatrix}$

$= \begin{bmatrix} 2+\frac{1}{4}-\frac{5}{4} & -4-1+5 & -6-\frac{11}{4}+\frac{35}{4} \\ \frac{1}{2}+\frac{1}{2}-1 & -1-2+4 & -\frac{3}{2}-\frac{11}{2}+7 \\ -\frac{1}{4}+\frac{1}{4} & 1-1 & \frac{11}{4}-\frac{7}{4} \end{bmatrix}$

$= \begin{bmatrix} 1 & 0 & 0 \\ 0 & 1 & 0 \\ 0 & 0 & 1 \end{bmatrix}$

$BA = \begin{bmatrix} -\frac{1}{2} & 1 & \frac{3}{2} \\ \frac{1}{4} & -1 & -\frac{11}{4} \\ -\frac{1}{4} & 1 & \frac{7}{4} \end{bmatrix}\begin{bmatrix} -4 & 1 & 5 \\ -1 & 2 & 4 \\ 0 & -1 & -1 \end{bmatrix}$

$= \begin{bmatrix} 2-1 & -\frac{1}{2}+2-\frac{3}{2} & -\frac{5}{2}+4-\frac{3}{2} \\ -1+1 & \frac{1}{4}-2+\frac{11}{4} & \frac{5}{4}-4+\frac{11}{4} \\ 1-1 & -\frac{1}{2}+2-\frac{3}{2} & -\frac{5}{4}+4-\frac{7}{4} \end{bmatrix}$

$= \begin{bmatrix} 1 & 0 & 0 \\ 0 & 1 & 0 \\ 0 & 0 & 1 \end{bmatrix}$

8. $AB = \begin{bmatrix} -2 & 0 & 1 & 0 \\ 1 & -1 & -3 & 0 \\ -2 & -1 & 0 & -2 \\ 0 & 1 & 3 & -1 \end{bmatrix}\begin{bmatrix} -3 & -3 & 1 & -2 \\ 12 & 14 & -5 & 10 \\ -5 & -6 & 2 & -4 \\ -3 & -4 & 1 & -3 \end{bmatrix}$

$= \begin{bmatrix} 6-5 & 6-6 & -2+2 & 4-4 \\ -3-12+15 & -3-14+18 & 1+5-6 & -2-10+12 \\ 6-12+6 & 6-14+8 & -2+5-2 & 4-10+6 \\ 12-15+3 & 14-18+4 & -5+6-1 & 10-12+3 \end{bmatrix}$

$= \begin{bmatrix} 1 & 0 & 0 & 0 \\ 0 & 1 & 0 & 0 \\ 0 & 0 & 1 & 0 \\ 0 & 0 & 0 & 1 \end{bmatrix}$

—CONTINUED—

8. —CONTINUED—

$$BA = \begin{bmatrix} -3 & -3 & 1 & -2 \\ 12 & 14 & -5 & 10 \\ -5 & -6 & 2 & -4 \\ -3 & -4 & 1 & -3 \end{bmatrix} \begin{bmatrix} -2 & 0 & 1 & 0 \\ 1 & -1 & -3 & 0 \\ -2 & -1 & 0 & -2 \\ 0 & 1 & 3 & -1 \end{bmatrix}$$

$$= \begin{bmatrix} 6-3-2 & 3-1-2 & -3+9-6 & -2+2 \\ -24+14+10 & -14+5+10 & 12-42+30 & 10-10 \\ 10-6-4 & 6-2-4 & -5+18-12 & -4+4 \\ 6-4-2 & 4-1-3 & -3+12-9 & -2+3 \end{bmatrix}$$

$$= \begin{bmatrix} 1 & 0 & 0 & 0 \\ 0 & 1 & 0 & 0 \\ 0 & 0 & 1 & 0 \\ 0 & 0 & 0 & 1 \end{bmatrix}$$

10. $AB = \frac{1}{3} \begin{bmatrix} -1 & 1 & 0 & -1 \\ 1 & -1 & 1 & 0 \\ -1 & 1 & 2 & 0 \\ 0 & -1 & 1 & 1 \end{bmatrix} \begin{bmatrix} -3 & 1 & 1 & -3 \\ -3 & -1 & 2 & -3 \\ 0 & 1 & 1 & 0 \\ -3 & -2 & 1 & 0 \end{bmatrix}$

$$= \frac{1}{3} \begin{bmatrix} 3-3+3 & -1-1+2 & -1+2-1 & 3-3 \\ -3+3 & 1+1+1 & 1-2+1 & -3+3 \\ 3-3 & -1-1+2 & -1+2+2 & 3-3 \\ 3-3 & 1+1-2 & -2+1+1 & 3 \end{bmatrix}$$

$$= \begin{bmatrix} 1 & 0 & 0 & 0 \\ 0 & 1 & 0 & 0 \\ 0 & 0 & 1 & 0 \\ 0 & 0 & 0 & 1 \end{bmatrix}$$

$$BA = \frac{1}{3} \begin{bmatrix} -3 & 1 & 1 & -3 \\ -3 & -1 & 2 & -3 \\ 0 & 1 & 1 & 0 \\ -3 & -2 & 1 & 0 \end{bmatrix} \begin{bmatrix} -1 & 1 & 0 & -1 \\ 1 & -1 & 1 & 0 \\ -1 & 1 & 2 & 0 \\ 0 & -1 & 1 & 1 \end{bmatrix}$$

$$= \frac{1}{3} \begin{bmatrix} 3+1-1 & -3-1+1+3 & 1+2-3 & 3-3 \\ 3-1-2 & -3+1+2+3 & -1+4-3 & 3-3 \\ 1-1 & -1+1 & 1+2 & 0 \\ 3-2-1 & -3+2+1 & -2+2 & 3 \end{bmatrix}$$

$$= \begin{bmatrix} 1 & 0 & 0 & 0 \\ 0 & 1 & 0 & 0 \\ 0 & 0 & 1 & 0 \\ 0 & 0 & 0 & 1 \end{bmatrix}$$

12. $[A \vdots I] = \begin{bmatrix} 1 & 2 & \vdots & 1 & 0 \\ 3 & 7 & \vdots & 0 & 1 \end{bmatrix}$

$-3R_1 + R_2 \rightarrow \begin{bmatrix} 1 & 2 & \vdots & 1 & 0 \\ 0 & 1 & \vdots & -3 & 1 \end{bmatrix}$

$-2R_2 + R_1 \rightarrow \begin{bmatrix} 1 & 0 & \vdots & 7 & -2 \\ 0 & 1 & \vdots & -3 & 1 \end{bmatrix} = [I \vdots A^{-1}]$

$A^{-1} = \begin{bmatrix} 7 & -2 \\ -3 & 1 \end{bmatrix}$

14. $[A \vdots I] = \begin{bmatrix} -7 & 33 & \vdots & 1 & 0 \\ 4 & -19 & \vdots & 0 & 1 \end{bmatrix}$

$2R_2 + R_1 \rightarrow \begin{bmatrix} 1 & -5 & \vdots & 1 & 2 \\ 4 & -19 & \vdots & 0 & 1 \end{bmatrix}$

$-4R_1 + R_2 \rightarrow \begin{bmatrix} 1 & -5 & \vdots & 1 & 2 \\ 0 & 1 & \vdots & -4 & -7 \end{bmatrix}$

$5R_2 + R_1 \rightarrow \begin{bmatrix} 1 & 0 & \vdots & -19 & -33 \\ 0 & 1 & \vdots & -4 & -7 \end{bmatrix} = [I \vdots A^{-1}]$

$A^{-1} = \begin{bmatrix} -19 & -33 \\ -4 & -7 \end{bmatrix}$

16. $[A \ \vdots \ I] = \begin{bmatrix} 11 & 1 & \vdots & 1 & 0 \\ -1 & 0 & \vdots & 0 & 1 \end{bmatrix}$

$10R_2 + R_1 \rightarrow \begin{bmatrix} 1 & 1 & \vdots & 1 & 10 \\ -1 & 0 & \vdots & 0 & 1 \end{bmatrix}$

$R_1 + R_2 \rightarrow \begin{bmatrix} 1 & 1 & \vdots & 1 & 10 \\ 0 & 1 & \vdots & 1 & 11 \end{bmatrix}$

$-R_2 + R_1 \rightarrow \begin{bmatrix} 1 & 0 & \vdots & 0 & -1 \\ 0 & 1 & \vdots & 1 & 11 \end{bmatrix} = [I \ \vdots \ A^{-1}]$

$A^{-1} = \begin{bmatrix} 0 & -1 \\ 1 & 11 \end{bmatrix}$

18. $[A \ \vdots \ I] = \begin{bmatrix} 2 & 3 & \vdots & 1 & 0 \\ 1 & 4 & \vdots & 0 & 1 \end{bmatrix}$

$\begin{matrix} R_2 \\ R_1 \end{matrix} \begin{bmatrix} 1 & 4 & \vdots & 0 & 1 \\ 2 & 3 & \vdots & 1 & 0 \end{bmatrix}$

$-2R_1 + R_2 \rightarrow \begin{bmatrix} 1 & 4 & \vdots & 0 & 1 \\ 0 & -5 & \vdots & 1 & -2 \end{bmatrix}$

$-\frac{1}{5}R_2 \rightarrow \begin{bmatrix} 1 & 4 & \vdots & 0 & 1 \\ 0 & 1 & \vdots & -\frac{1}{5} & \frac{2}{5} \end{bmatrix}$

$-4R_2 + R_1 \rightarrow \begin{bmatrix} 1 & 0 & \vdots & \frac{4}{5} & -\frac{3}{5} \\ 0 & 1 & \vdots & -\frac{1}{5} & \frac{2}{5} \end{bmatrix} = [I \ \vdots \ A^{-1}]$

$A^{-1} = \frac{1}{5}\begin{bmatrix} 4 & -3 \\ -1 & 2 \end{bmatrix}$

20. $A = \begin{bmatrix} -2 & 5 \\ 6 & -15 \\ 0 & 1 \end{bmatrix}$ A has no inverse because it is not square.

22. $[A \ \vdots \ I] = \begin{bmatrix} 1 & 2 & 2 & \vdots & 1 & 0 & 0 \\ 3 & 7 & 9 & \vdots & 0 & 1 & 0 \\ -1 & -4 & -7 & \vdots & 0 & 0 & 1 \end{bmatrix}$

$\begin{matrix} -3R_1 + R_2 \rightarrow \\ R_1 + R_3 \rightarrow \end{matrix} \begin{bmatrix} 1 & 2 & 2 & \vdots & 1 & 0 & 0 \\ 0 & 1 & 3 & \vdots & -3 & 1 & 0 \\ 0 & -2 & -5 & \vdots & 1 & 0 & 1 \end{bmatrix}$

$\begin{matrix} -2R_2 + R_1 \rightarrow \\ \\ 2R_2 + R_3 \rightarrow \end{matrix} \begin{bmatrix} 1 & 0 & -4 & \vdots & 7 & -2 & 0 \\ 0 & 1 & 3 & \vdots & -3 & 1 & 0 \\ 0 & 0 & 1 & \vdots & -5 & 2 & 1 \end{bmatrix}$

$\begin{matrix} 4R_3 + R_1 \rightarrow \\ -3R_3 + R_2 \rightarrow \end{matrix} \begin{bmatrix} 1 & 0 & 0 & \vdots & -13 & 6 & 4 \\ 0 & 1 & 0 & \vdots & 12 & -5 & -3 \\ 0 & 0 & 1 & \vdots & -5 & 2 & 1 \end{bmatrix} = [I \ \vdots \ A^{-1}]$

$A^{-1} = \begin{bmatrix} -13 & 6 & 4 \\ 12 & -5 & -3 \\ -5 & 2 & 1 \end{bmatrix}$

24. $[A \ \vdots \ I] = \begin{bmatrix} 1 & 0 & 0 & \vdots & 1 & 0 & 0 \\ 3 & 0 & 0 & \vdots & 0 & 1 & 0 \\ 2 & 5 & 5 & \vdots & 0 & 0 & 1 \end{bmatrix} \begin{matrix} -3R_1 + R_2 \rightarrow \\ -2R_1 + R_3 \rightarrow \end{matrix} \begin{bmatrix} 1 & 0 & 0 & \vdots & 1 & 0 & 0 \\ 0 & 0 & 0 & \vdots & -3 & 1 & 0 \\ 0 & 5 & 5 & \vdots & -2 & 0 & 1 \end{bmatrix}$

Since the first three entries of row 2 are all zeros, the inverse of A does not exist.

26.
$$[A \; \vdots \; I] = \begin{bmatrix} 1 & 3 & -2 & 0 & \vdots & 1 & 0 & 0 & 0 \\ 0 & 2 & 4 & 6 & \vdots & 0 & 1 & 0 & 0 \\ 0 & 0 & -2 & 1 & \vdots & 0 & 0 & 1 & 0 \\ 0 & 0 & 0 & 5 & \vdots & 0 & 0 & 0 & 1 \end{bmatrix}$$

$$\begin{matrix} \\ \frac{1}{2}R_2 \rightarrow \\ \\ \frac{1}{5}R_4 \rightarrow \end{matrix} \begin{bmatrix} 1 & 3 & -2 & 0 & \vdots & 1 & 0 & 0 & 0 \\ 0 & 1 & 2 & 3 & \vdots & 0 & \frac{1}{2} & 0 & 0 \\ 0 & 0 & -2 & 1 & \vdots & 0 & 0 & 1 & 0 \\ 0 & 0 & 0 & 1 & \vdots & 0 & 0 & 0 & \frac{1}{5} \end{bmatrix}$$

$$\begin{matrix} -3R_2 + R_1 \rightarrow \\ R_3 + R_2 \rightarrow \\ -R_4 + R_3 \rightarrow \\ \\ \end{matrix} \begin{bmatrix} 1 & 0 & -8 & -9 & \vdots & 1 & -\frac{3}{2} & 0 & 0 \\ 0 & 1 & 0 & 4 & \vdots & 0 & \frac{1}{2} & 1 & 0 \\ 0 & 0 & -2 & 0 & \vdots & 0 & 0 & 1 & -\frac{1}{5} \\ 0 & 0 & 0 & 1 & \vdots & 0 & 0 & 0 & \frac{1}{5} \end{bmatrix}$$

$$\begin{matrix} -4R_3 + R_1 \rightarrow \\ -4R_4 + R_2 \rightarrow \\ -\frac{1}{2}R_3 \rightarrow \\ \\ \end{matrix} \begin{bmatrix} 1 & 0 & 0 & -9 & \vdots & 1 & -\frac{3}{2} & -4 & \frac{4}{5} \\ 0 & 1 & 0 & 0 & \vdots & 0 & \frac{1}{2} & 1 & -\frac{4}{5} \\ 0 & 0 & 1 & 0 & \vdots & 0 & 0 & -\frac{1}{2} & \frac{1}{10} \\ 0 & 0 & 0 & 1 & \vdots & 0 & 0 & 0 & \frac{1}{5} \end{bmatrix}$$

$$9R_4 + R_1 \rightarrow \begin{bmatrix} 1 & 0 & 0 & 0 & \vdots & 1 & -\frac{3}{2} & -4 & \frac{13}{5} \\ 0 & 1 & 0 & 0 & \vdots & 0 & \frac{1}{2} & 1 & -\frac{4}{5} \\ 0 & 0 & 1 & 0 & \vdots & 0 & 0 & -\frac{1}{2} & \frac{1}{10} \\ 0 & 0 & 0 & 1 & \vdots & 0 & 0 & 0 & \frac{1}{5} \end{bmatrix} = [I \; \vdots \; A^{-1}]$$

$$A^{-1} = \frac{1}{10} \begin{bmatrix} 10 & -15 & -40 & 26 \\ 0 & 5 & 10 & -8 \\ 0 & 0 & -5 & 1 \\ 0 & 0 & 0 & 2 \end{bmatrix}$$

28. $A = \begin{bmatrix} 10 & 5 & -7 \\ -5 & 1 & 4 \\ 3 & 2 & -2 \end{bmatrix}$

$A^{-1} = \begin{bmatrix} -10 & -4 & 27 \\ 2 & 1 & -5 \\ -13 & -5 & 35 \end{bmatrix}$

30. $A = \begin{bmatrix} 3 & 2 & 2 \\ 2 & 2 & 2 \\ -4 & 4 & 3 \end{bmatrix}$

$A^{-1} = \begin{bmatrix} 1 & -1 & 0 \\ 7 & -8.5 & 1 \\ -8 & 10 & -1 \end{bmatrix}$

32. $\begin{bmatrix} -\frac{5}{6} & \frac{1}{3} & \frac{11}{6} \\ 0 & \frac{2}{3} & 2 \\ 1 & -\frac{1}{2} & -\frac{5}{2} \end{bmatrix}$

A^{-1} does not exist.

34. $A = \begin{bmatrix} 0.6 & 0 & -0.3 \\ 0.7 & -1 & 0.2 \\ 1 & 0 & -0.9 \end{bmatrix}$

$A^{-1} = \begin{bmatrix} 3.75 & 0 & -1.25 \\ 3.458\overline{3} & -1 & -1.375 \\ 4.1\overline{6} & 0 & -2.5 \end{bmatrix}$

36. $A = \begin{bmatrix} 4 & 8 & -7 & 14 \\ 2 & 5 & -4 & 6 \\ 0 & 2 & 1 & -7 \\ 3 & 6 & -5 & 10 \end{bmatrix}$

$A^{-1} = \begin{bmatrix} 27 & -10 & 4 & -29 \\ -16 & 5 & -2 & 18 \\ -17 & 4 & -2 & 20 \\ -7 & 2 & -1 & 8 \end{bmatrix}$

38. $A = \begin{bmatrix} 1 & -2 & -1 & -2 \\ 3 & -5 & -2 & -3 \\ 2 & -5 & -2 & -5 \\ -1 & 4 & 4 & 11 \end{bmatrix}$, $A^{-1} = \begin{bmatrix} -24 & 7 & 1 & -2 \\ -10 & 3 & 0 & -1 \\ -29 & 7 & 3 & -2 \\ 12 & -3 & -1 & 1 \end{bmatrix}$

40. $A = \begin{bmatrix} 7 & 12 \\ -8 & -5 \end{bmatrix}$

$ad - bc = 7(-5) - 12(-8) = -35 + 96 = 61$

$A^{-1} = \dfrac{1}{61}\begin{bmatrix} -5 & -12 \\ 8 & 7 \end{bmatrix} = \begin{bmatrix} -\frac{5}{61} & -\frac{12}{61} \\ \frac{8}{61} & \frac{7}{61} \end{bmatrix}$

42. $A = \begin{bmatrix} -12 & 3 \\ 5 & -2 \end{bmatrix}$

$ad - bc = (-12)(-2) - 3(5) = 24 - 15 = 9$

$A^{-1} = \dfrac{1}{9}\begin{bmatrix} -2 & -3 \\ -5 & -12 \end{bmatrix} = \begin{bmatrix} -\frac{2}{9} & -\frac{1}{3} \\ -\frac{5}{9} & -\frac{4}{3} \end{bmatrix}$

44. $A = \begin{bmatrix} -\frac{1}{4} & \frac{9}{4} \\ \frac{5}{3} & \frac{8}{9} \end{bmatrix}$

$ad - bc = \left(-\frac{1}{4}\right)\left(\frac{8}{9}\right) - \left(\frac{9}{4}\right)\left(\frac{5}{3}\right) = -\frac{143}{36}$

$A^{-1} = -\dfrac{36}{143}\begin{bmatrix} \frac{8}{9} & -\frac{9}{4} \\ -\frac{5}{3} & -\frac{1}{4} \end{bmatrix} = \begin{bmatrix} -\frac{32}{143} & \frac{81}{143} \\ \frac{60}{143} & \frac{9}{143} \end{bmatrix}$

46. $\begin{bmatrix} x \\ y \end{bmatrix} = \begin{bmatrix} -3 & 2 \\ -2 & 1 \end{bmatrix}\begin{bmatrix} 0 \\ 3 \end{bmatrix} = \begin{bmatrix} 6 \\ 3 \end{bmatrix}$

Solution: $(6, 3)$

48. $\begin{bmatrix} x \\ y \end{bmatrix} = \begin{bmatrix} -3 & 2 \\ -2 & 1 \end{bmatrix}\begin{bmatrix} 1 \\ -2 \end{bmatrix} = \begin{bmatrix} -7 \\ -4 \end{bmatrix}$

Solution: $(-7, -4)$

50. $\begin{bmatrix} x \\ y \\ z \end{bmatrix} = \begin{bmatrix} 1 & 1 & -1 \\ -3 & 2 & -1 \\ 3 & -3 & 2 \end{bmatrix}\begin{bmatrix} -1 \\ 2 \\ 0 \end{bmatrix} = \begin{bmatrix} 1 \\ 7 \\ -9 \end{bmatrix}$

Solution: $(1, 7, -9)$

52. $\begin{bmatrix} x \\ y \\ z \\ w \end{bmatrix} = \begin{bmatrix} -24 & 7 & 1 & -2 \\ -10 & 3 & 0 & -1 \\ -29 & 7 & 3 & -2 \\ 12 & -3 & -1 & 1 \end{bmatrix}\begin{bmatrix} 1 \\ -2 \\ 0 \\ -3 \end{bmatrix} = \begin{bmatrix} -32 \\ -13 \\ -37 \\ 15 \end{bmatrix}$

Solution: $(-32, -13, -37, 15)$

54. $A = \begin{bmatrix} 18 & 12 \\ 30 & 24 \end{bmatrix}$

$A^{-1} = \dfrac{1}{432 - 360}\begin{bmatrix} 24 & -12 \\ -30 & 18 \end{bmatrix}$

$\begin{bmatrix} x \\ y \end{bmatrix} = \dfrac{1}{72}\begin{bmatrix} 24 & -12 \\ -30 & 18 \end{bmatrix}\begin{bmatrix} 13 \\ 23 \end{bmatrix}$

$= \dfrac{1}{72}\begin{bmatrix} 36 \\ 24 \end{bmatrix} = \begin{bmatrix} \frac{1}{2} \\ \frac{1}{3} \end{bmatrix}$

Solution: $\left(\frac{1}{2}, \frac{1}{3}\right)$

56. $A = \begin{bmatrix} 0.2 & -0.6 \\ -1 & 1.4 \end{bmatrix}$

$A^{-1} = \dfrac{1}{0.28 - 0.6}\begin{bmatrix} 1.4 & 0.6 \\ 1 & 0.2 \end{bmatrix}$

$\begin{bmatrix} x \\ y \end{bmatrix} = -\dfrac{1}{0.32}\begin{bmatrix} 1.4 & 0.6 \\ 1 & 0.2 \end{bmatrix}\begin{bmatrix} 2.4 \\ -8.8 \end{bmatrix}$

$= -\dfrac{1}{0.32}\begin{bmatrix} -1.92 \\ 0.64 \end{bmatrix} = \begin{bmatrix} 6 \\ -2 \end{bmatrix}$

Solution: $(6, -2)$

58. $A = \begin{bmatrix} 3 & 2 \\ 2 & 10 \end{bmatrix}$

$A^{-1} = \dfrac{1}{30 - 4}\begin{bmatrix} 10 & -2 \\ -2 & 3 \end{bmatrix}$

$\begin{bmatrix} x \\ y \end{bmatrix} = \dfrac{1}{26}\begin{bmatrix} 10 & -2 \\ -2 & 3 \end{bmatrix}\begin{bmatrix} 1 \\ 6 \end{bmatrix} = \dfrac{1}{26}\begin{bmatrix} -2 \\ 16 \end{bmatrix} = \begin{bmatrix} -\frac{1}{13} \\ \frac{8}{13} \end{bmatrix}$

Solution: $\left(-\frac{1}{13}, \frac{8}{13}\right)$

60. $A = \begin{bmatrix} \frac{5}{6} & -1 \\ \frac{4}{3} & -\frac{7}{2} \end{bmatrix}$

$A^{-1} = \dfrac{1}{-\frac{35}{12} + \frac{4}{3}} \begin{bmatrix} -\frac{7}{2} & 1 \\ \frac{4}{3} & \frac{5}{6} \end{bmatrix}$

$\begin{bmatrix} x \\ y \end{bmatrix} = -\dfrac{12}{19} \begin{bmatrix} -\frac{7}{2} & 1 \\ -\frac{4}{3} & \frac{5}{6} \end{bmatrix} \begin{bmatrix} -20 \\ -51 \end{bmatrix}$

$\qquad = -\dfrac{12}{19} \begin{bmatrix} 19 \\ -\frac{95}{6} \end{bmatrix} = \begin{bmatrix} -12 \\ 10 \end{bmatrix}$

Solution: $(-12, 10)$

62. $A = \begin{bmatrix} 4 & -2 & 3 \\ 2 & 2 & 5 \\ 8 & -5 & -2 \end{bmatrix}$

$A^{-1} = \dfrac{1}{82} \begin{bmatrix} -21 & 19 & 16 \\ -44 & 32 & 14 \\ 26 & -4 & -12 \end{bmatrix}$

$\begin{bmatrix} x \\ y \\ z \end{bmatrix} = \dfrac{1}{82} \begin{bmatrix} -21 & 19 & 16 \\ -44 & 32 & 14 \\ 26 & -4 & -12 \end{bmatrix} \begin{bmatrix} -2 \\ 16 \\ 4 \end{bmatrix} = \dfrac{1}{82} \begin{bmatrix} 410 \\ 656 \\ -164 \end{bmatrix} = \begin{bmatrix} 5 \\ 8 \\ -2 \end{bmatrix}$

Solution: $(5, 8, -2)$

64. $A = \begin{bmatrix} 3 & -2 & 1 \\ -4 & 1 & -3 \\ 1 & -5 & 1 \end{bmatrix}$

$A^{-1} = \begin{bmatrix} 0.56 & 0.12 & -0.2 \\ -0.04 & -0.08 & -0.2 \\ -0.76 & -0.52 & 0.2 \end{bmatrix}$

$\begin{bmatrix} x \\ y \\ z \end{bmatrix} = \begin{bmatrix} 0.56 & 0.12 & -0.2 \\ -0.04 & -0.08 & -0.2 \\ -0.76 & -0.52 & 0.2 \end{bmatrix} \begin{bmatrix} -29 \\ 37 \\ -24 \end{bmatrix} = \begin{bmatrix} -7 \\ 3 \\ -2 \end{bmatrix}$

Solution: $(-7, 3, -2)$

66. $A = \begin{bmatrix} -8 & 7 & -10 \\ 12 & 3 & -5 \\ 15 & -9 & 2 \end{bmatrix}$

$A^{-1} \approx \begin{bmatrix} -0.034 & 0.066 & -0.004 \\ -0.086 & 0.117 & -0.139 \\ -0.133 & 0.029 & -0.094 \end{bmatrix}$

$\begin{bmatrix} x \\ y \\ z \end{bmatrix} \approx \begin{bmatrix} -0.034 & 0.066 & -0.004 \\ -0.086 & 0.117 & -0.139 \\ -0.133 & 0.029 & -0.094 \end{bmatrix} \begin{bmatrix} -151 \\ 86 \\ 187 \end{bmatrix} \approx \begin{bmatrix} 10 \\ -3 \\ 5 \end{bmatrix}$

Solution: $(10, -3, 5)$

68. $A = \begin{bmatrix} 2 & 5 & 0 & 1 \\ 1 & 4 & 2 & -2 \\ 2 & -2 & 5 & 1 \\ 1 & 0 & 0 & -3 \end{bmatrix}$

$A^{-1} \approx \begin{bmatrix} 0.338 & -0.352 & 0.141 & 0.394 \\ 0.042 & 0.164 & -0.066 & -0.117 \\ -0.141 & 0.230 & 0.108 & -0.164 \\ 0.113 & -0.117 & 0.047 & -0.202 \end{bmatrix}$

$\begin{bmatrix} x \\ y \\ z \\ w \end{bmatrix} \approx \begin{bmatrix} 0.338 & -0.352 & 0.141 & 0.394 \\ 0.042 & 0.164 & -0.066 & -0.117 \\ -0.141 & 0.230 & 0.108 & -0.164 \\ 0.113 & -0.117 & 0.047 & -0.202 \end{bmatrix} \begin{bmatrix} 11 \\ -7 \\ 3 \\ -1 \end{bmatrix} \approx \begin{bmatrix} 6.21 \\ -0.77 \\ -2.67 \\ 2.40 \end{bmatrix}$

Solution: $(6.21, -0.77, -2.67, 2.40)$

70. $A = \begin{bmatrix} 1 & 1 & 1 \\ 0.065 & 0.07 & 0.09 \\ 0 & 2 & -1 \end{bmatrix}$

$[A \ : \ I] = \begin{bmatrix} 1 & 1 & 1 & : & 1 & 0 & 0 \\ 0.065 & 0.07 & 0.09 & : & 0 & 1 & 0 \\ 0 & 2 & -1 & : & 0 & 0 & 1 \end{bmatrix}$

$200R_2 \rightarrow \begin{bmatrix} 1 & 1 & 1 & : & 1 & 0 & 0 \\ 13 & 14 & 18 & : & 0 & 200 & 0 \\ 0 & 2 & -1 & : & 0 & 0 & 1 \end{bmatrix}$

—CONTINUED—

70. —CONTINUED—

$$-13R_1 + R_2 \to \begin{bmatrix} 1 & 1 & 1 & \vdots & 1 & 0 & 0 \\ 0 & 1 & 5 & \vdots & -13 & 200 & 0 \\ 0 & 2 & -1 & \vdots & 0 & 0 & 1 \end{bmatrix}$$

$$\begin{matrix} -R_2 + R_1 \to \\ \\ -2R_2 + R_3 \to \end{matrix} \begin{bmatrix} 1 & 0 & -4 & \vdots & 14 & -200 & 0 \\ 0 & 1 & 5 & \vdots & -13 & 200 & 0 \\ 0 & 0 & -11 & \vdots & 26 & -400 & 1 \end{bmatrix}$$

$$-\tfrac{1}{11}R_3 \to \begin{bmatrix} 1 & 0 & -4 & \vdots & 14 & -200 & 0 \\ 0 & 1 & 5 & \vdots & -13 & 200 & 0 \\ 0 & 0 & 1 & \vdots & -\tfrac{26}{11} & \tfrac{400}{11} & -\tfrac{1}{11} \end{bmatrix}$$

$$\begin{matrix} 4R_3 + R_1 \to \\ -5R_3 + R_2 \to \\ \\ \end{matrix} \begin{bmatrix} 1 & 0 & 0 & \vdots & \tfrac{50}{11} & -\tfrac{600}{11} & -\tfrac{4}{11} \\ 0 & 1 & 0 & \vdots & -\tfrac{13}{11} & \tfrac{200}{11} & \tfrac{5}{11} \\ 0 & 0 & 1 & \vdots & -\tfrac{26}{11} & \tfrac{400}{11} & -\tfrac{1}{11} \end{bmatrix} = \begin{bmatrix} I & \vdots & A^{-1} \end{bmatrix}$$

$$X = A^{-1}B = \frac{1}{11} \begin{bmatrix} 50 & -600 & -4 \\ -13 & 200 & 5 \\ -26 & 400 & -1 \end{bmatrix} \begin{bmatrix} 10,000 \\ 760 \\ 0 \end{bmatrix} = \begin{bmatrix} 4000 \\ 2000 \\ 4000 \end{bmatrix}$$

Solution: $4000 in AAA-rated bonds, $2000 in A-rated bonds, $4000 in B-rated bonds.

72. Use the inverse matrix A^{-1} from Exercise 70.

$$X = A^{-1}B = \frac{1}{11} \begin{bmatrix} 50 & -600 & -4 \\ -13 & 200 & 5 \\ -26 & 400 & -1 \end{bmatrix} \begin{bmatrix} 500,000 \\ 38,000 \\ 0 \end{bmatrix} = \begin{bmatrix} 200,000 \\ 100,000 \\ 200,000 \end{bmatrix}$$

Solution: $200,000 in AAA-rated bonds, $100,000 in A-rated bonds, and $200,000 in B-rated bonds.

74.

$$A = \begin{bmatrix} 2 & 0 & 4 \\ 0 & 1 & 4 \\ 1 & 1 & -1 \end{bmatrix}$$

$$\begin{bmatrix} A & \vdots & I \end{bmatrix} = \begin{bmatrix} 2 & 0 & 4 & \vdots & 1 & 0 & 0 \\ 0 & 1 & 4 & \vdots & 0 & 1 & 0 \\ 1 & 1 & -1 & \vdots & 0 & 0 & 1 \end{bmatrix}$$

$$\begin{matrix} R_3 \\ \\ R_1 \end{matrix} \begin{bmatrix} 1 & 1 & -1 & \vdots & 0 & 0 & 1 \\ 0 & 1 & 4 & \vdots & 0 & 1 & 0 \\ 2 & 0 & 4 & \vdots & 1 & 0 & 0 \end{bmatrix}$$

$$-2R_1 + R_3 \to \begin{bmatrix} 1 & 1 & -1 & \vdots & 0 & 0 & 1 \\ 0 & 1 & 4 & \vdots & 0 & 1 & 0 \\ 0 & -2 & 6 & \vdots & 1 & 0 & -2 \end{bmatrix}$$

$$\begin{matrix} -R_2 + R_1 \to \\ \\ 2R_2 + R_3 \to \end{matrix} \begin{bmatrix} 1 & 0 & -5 & \vdots & 0 & -1 & 1 \\ 0 & 1 & 4 & \vdots & 0 & 1 & 0 \\ 0 & 0 & 14 & \vdots & 1 & 2 & -2 \end{bmatrix}$$

$$\tfrac{1}{14}R_3 \to \begin{bmatrix} 1 & 0 & -5 & \vdots & 0 & -1 & 1 \\ 0 & 1 & 4 & \vdots & 0 & 1 & 0 \\ 0 & 0 & 1 & \vdots & \tfrac{1}{14} & \tfrac{1}{7} & -\tfrac{1}{7} \end{bmatrix}$$

$$\begin{matrix} 5R_3 + R_1 \to \\ -4R_3 + R_2 \to \\ \\ \end{matrix} \begin{bmatrix} 1 & 0 & 0 & \vdots & \tfrac{5}{14} & -\tfrac{2}{7} & \tfrac{2}{7} \\ 0 & 1 & 0 & \vdots & -\tfrac{2}{7} & \tfrac{3}{7} & \tfrac{4}{7} \\ 0 & 0 & 1 & \vdots & \tfrac{1}{14} & \tfrac{1}{7} & -\tfrac{1}{7} \end{bmatrix} = \begin{bmatrix} I & \vdots & A^{-1} \end{bmatrix}$$

—CONTINUED—

74. —CONTINUED—

$$A^{-1} = \tfrac{1}{14} \begin{bmatrix} 5 & -4 & 4 \\ -4 & 6 & 8 \\ 1 & 2 & -2 \end{bmatrix}$$

$$\begin{bmatrix} I_1 \\ I_2 \\ I_3 \end{bmatrix} = \tfrac{1}{14} \begin{bmatrix} 5 & -4 & 4 \\ -4 & 6 & 8 \\ 1 & 2 & -2 \end{bmatrix} \begin{bmatrix} 24 \\ 23 \\ 0 \end{bmatrix} = \begin{bmatrix} 2 \\ 3 \\ 5 \end{bmatrix}$$

Solution: $I_1 = 2$ amperes, $I_2 = 3$ amperes, $I_3 = 5$ amperes

76. True. If A and B are both square matrices and $AB = I_N$, it can be shown that $BA = I_N$.

78. $AA^{-1} = \begin{bmatrix} a & b \\ c & d \end{bmatrix} \left(\dfrac{1}{ad - bc} \right) \begin{bmatrix} d & -b \\ -c & a \end{bmatrix} = \dfrac{1}{ad - bc} \begin{bmatrix} a & b \\ c & d \end{bmatrix} \begin{bmatrix} d & -b \\ -c & a \end{bmatrix}$

$\qquad = \dfrac{1}{ad - bc} \begin{bmatrix} ad - bc & 0 \\ 0 & ad - bc \end{bmatrix} = \begin{bmatrix} 1 & 0 \\ 0 & 1 \end{bmatrix}$

$A^{-1}A = \dfrac{1}{ad - bc} \begin{bmatrix} d & -b \\ -c & a \end{bmatrix} \begin{bmatrix} a & b \\ c & d \end{bmatrix} = \dfrac{1}{ad - bc} \begin{bmatrix} ad - bc & 0 \\ 0 & ad - bc \end{bmatrix} = \begin{bmatrix} 1 & 0 \\ 0 & 1 \end{bmatrix}$

80. (a) Given $A = \begin{bmatrix} a_{11} & 0 \\ 0 & a_{22} \end{bmatrix}$, $A^{-1} = \begin{bmatrix} \dfrac{1}{a_{11}} & 0 \\ 0 & \dfrac{1}{a_{22}} \end{bmatrix}$.

$\qquad$ Given $A = \begin{bmatrix} a_{11} & 0 & 0 \\ 0 & a_{22} & 0 \\ 0 & 0 & a_{33} \end{bmatrix}$, $A^{-1} = \begin{bmatrix} \dfrac{1}{a_{11}} & 0 & 0 \\ 0 & \dfrac{1}{a_{22}} & 0 \\ 0 & 0 & \dfrac{1}{a_{33}} \end{bmatrix}$.

(b) In general, the inverse of a matrix in the form of A is

$$\begin{bmatrix} \dfrac{1}{a_{11}} & 0 & 0 & \cdots & 0 \\ 0 & \dfrac{1}{a_{22}} & 0 & \cdots & 0 \\ 0 & 0 & \dfrac{1}{a_{33}} & \cdots & 0 \\ \vdots & \vdots & \vdots & \cdots & \vdots \\ 0 & 0 & 0 & \cdots & \dfrac{1}{a_{NN}} \end{bmatrix}.$$

Section 8.4   The Determinant of a Square Matrix

Solutions to Even-Numbered Exercises

2. -8

4. $\begin{vmatrix} -3 & 1 \\ 5 & 2 \end{vmatrix} = (-3)(2) - (5)(1) = -11$

6. $\begin{vmatrix} 2 & -2 \\ 4 & 3 \end{vmatrix} = (2)(3) - (4)(-2) = 14$

8. $\begin{vmatrix} 4 & -3 \\ 0 & 0 \end{vmatrix} = (4)(0) - (0)(-3) = 0$

10. $\begin{vmatrix} 2 & -3 \\ -6 & 9 \end{vmatrix} = (2)(9) - (-6)(-3) = 0$

12. $\begin{vmatrix} 4 & 7 \\ -2 & 5 \end{vmatrix} = (4)(5) - (-2)(7) = 34$

14. $\begin{vmatrix} 0 & 6 \\ -3 & 2 \end{vmatrix} = (0)(2) - (-3)(6) = 18$

16. $\begin{vmatrix} \frac{2}{3} & \frac{4}{3} \\ -1 & -\frac{1}{3} \end{vmatrix} = \left(\frac{2}{3}\right)\left(-\frac{1}{3}\right) - (-1)\left(\frac{4}{3}\right) = \frac{10}{9}$

18. $\begin{vmatrix} 0.1 & 0.2 & 0.3 \\ -0.3 & 0.2 & 0.2 \\ 0.5 & 0.4 & 0.4 \end{vmatrix} = -0.022$

20. $\begin{vmatrix} 0.1 & 0.1 & -4.3 \\ 7.5 & 6.2 & 0.7 \\ 0.3 & 0.6 & -1.2 \end{vmatrix} = -11.217$

22. $\begin{vmatrix} 2 & 3 & 1 \\ 0 & 5 & -2 \\ 0 & 0 & -2 \end{vmatrix} = -20$

24. $\begin{bmatrix} 11 & 0 \\ -3 & 2 \end{bmatrix}$

(a) $M_{11} = 2$

$M_{12} = -3$

$M_{21} = 0$

$M_{22} = 11$

(b) $C_{11} = M_{11} = 2$

$C_{12} = M_{12} = 3$

$C_{21} = M_{21} = 0$

$C_{22} = M_{22} = 11$

26. $\begin{bmatrix} -6 & 5 \\ 7 & -2 \end{bmatrix}$

(a) $M_{11} = -2$

$M_{12} = 7$

$M_{21} = 5$

$M_{22} = -6$

(b) $C_{11} = M_{11} = -2$

$C_{12} = -M_{12} = -7$

$C_{21} = -M_{21} = -5$

$C_{22} = M_{22} = -6$

28. $\begin{bmatrix} 1 & -1 & 0 \\ 3 & 2 & 5 \\ 4 & -6 & 4 \end{bmatrix}$

(a) $M_{11} = \begin{vmatrix} 2 & 5 \\ -6 & 4 \end{vmatrix} = 8 - (-30) = 38$

$M_{12} = \begin{vmatrix} 3 & 5 \\ 4 & 4 \end{vmatrix} = 12 - 20 = -8$

$M_{13} = \begin{vmatrix} 3 & 2 \\ 4 & -6 \end{vmatrix} = -18 - 8 = -26$

$M_{21} = \begin{vmatrix} -1 & 0 \\ -6 & 4 \end{vmatrix} = -4 - 0 = -4$

$M_{22} = \begin{vmatrix} 1 & 0 \\ 4 & 4 \end{vmatrix} = 4 - 0 = 4$

$M_{23} = \begin{vmatrix} 1 & -1 \\ 4 & -6 \end{vmatrix} = -6 - (-4) = -2$

$M_{31} = \begin{vmatrix} -1 & 0 \\ 2 & 5 \end{vmatrix} = -5 - 0 = -5$

$M_{32} = \begin{vmatrix} 1 & 0 \\ 3 & 5 \end{vmatrix} = 5 - 0 = 5$

$M_{33} = \begin{vmatrix} 1 & -1 \\ 3 & 2 \end{vmatrix} = 2 - (-3) = 5$

(b) $C_{11} = (-1)^2 M_{11} = 38$

$C_{12} = (-1)^3 M_{12} = 8$

$C_{13} = (-1)^4 M_{13} = -26$

$C_{21} = (-1)^3 M_{21} = 4$

$C_{22} = (-1)^4 M_{22} = 4$

$C_{23} = (-1)^5 M_{23} = 2$

$C_{31} = (-1)^4 M_{31} = -5$

$C_{32} = (-1)^5 M_{32} = -5$

$C_{33} = (-1)^6 M_{33} = 5$

30. $\begin{bmatrix} -2 & 9 & 4 \\ 7 & -6 & 0 \\ 6 & 7 & -6 \end{bmatrix}$

(a) $M_{11} = \begin{vmatrix} -6 & 0 \\ 7 & -6 \end{vmatrix} = 36$

$M_{12} = \begin{vmatrix} 7 & 0 \\ 6 & -6 \end{vmatrix} = -42$

$M_{13} = \begin{vmatrix} 7 & -6 \\ 6 & 7 \end{vmatrix} = 85$

$M_{21} = \begin{vmatrix} 9 & 4 \\ 7 & -6 \end{vmatrix} = -82$

$M_{22} = \begin{vmatrix} -2 & 4 \\ 6 & -6 \end{vmatrix} = -12$

$M_{23} = \begin{vmatrix} -2 & 9 \\ 6 & 7 \end{vmatrix} = -68$

$M_{31} = \begin{vmatrix} 9 & 4 \\ -6 & 0 \end{vmatrix} = 24$

$M_{32} = \begin{vmatrix} -2 & 4 \\ 7 & 0 \end{vmatrix} = -28$

$M_{33} = \begin{vmatrix} -2 & 9 \\ 7 & -6 \end{vmatrix} = -51$

(b) $C_{11} = (-1)^2 M_{11} = 36$

$C_{12} = (-1)^3 M_{12} = 42$

$C_{13} = (-1)^4 M_{13} = 85$

$C_{21} = (-1)^3 M_{21} = 82$

$C_{22} = (-1)^4 M_{22} = -12$

$C_{23} = (-1)^5 M_{23} = 68$

$C_{31} = (-1)^4 M_{31} = 24$

$C_{32} = (-1)^5 M_{32} = 28$

$C_{33} = (-1)^6 M_{33} = -51$

32. (a) $\begin{vmatrix} -3 & 4 & 2 \\ 6 & 3 & 1 \\ 4 & -7 & -8 \end{vmatrix} = -6\begin{vmatrix} 4 & 2 \\ -7 & -8 \end{vmatrix} + 3\begin{vmatrix} -3 & 2 \\ 4 & -8 \end{vmatrix} - 1\begin{vmatrix} -3 & 4 \\ 4 & -7 \end{vmatrix} = -6(-18) + 3(16) - (5) = 151$

(b) $\begin{vmatrix} -3 & 4 & 2 \\ 6 & 3 & 1 \\ 4 & -7 & -8 \end{vmatrix} = 2\begin{vmatrix} 6 & 3 \\ 4 & -7 \end{vmatrix} - \begin{vmatrix} -3 & 4 \\ 4 & -7 \end{vmatrix} - 8\begin{vmatrix} -3 & 4 \\ 6 & 3 \end{vmatrix} = 2(-54) - (5) - 8(-33) = 151$

34. (a) $\begin{vmatrix} 10 & -5 & 5 \\ 30 & 0 & 10 \\ 0 & 10 & 1 \end{vmatrix} = 0\begin{vmatrix} -5 & 5 \\ 0 & 10 \end{vmatrix} - 10\begin{vmatrix} 10 & 5 \\ 30 & 10 \end{vmatrix} + \begin{vmatrix} 10 & -5 \\ 30 & 0 \end{vmatrix} = 0(-50) - 10(-50) + 150 = 650$

(b) $\begin{vmatrix} 10 & -5 & 5 \\ 30 & 0 & 10 \\ 0 & 10 & 1 \end{vmatrix} = 10\begin{vmatrix} 0 & 10 \\ 10 & 1 \end{vmatrix} - 30\begin{vmatrix} -5 & 5 \\ 10 & 1 \end{vmatrix} + 0\begin{vmatrix} -5 & 5 \\ 0 & 10 \end{vmatrix} = 10(-100) - 30(-55) + 0(-50) = 650$

36. (a) $\begin{vmatrix} 10 & 8 & 3 & -7 \\ 4 & 0 & 5 & -6 \\ 0 & 3 & 2 & 7 \\ 1 & 0 & -3 & 2 \end{vmatrix} = 0\begin{vmatrix} 8 & 3 & -7 \\ 0 & 5 & -6 \\ 0 & -3 & 2 \end{vmatrix} - 3\begin{vmatrix} 10 & 3 & -7 \\ 4 & 5 & -6 \\ 1 & -3 & 2 \end{vmatrix} + 2\begin{vmatrix} 10 & 8 & -7 \\ 4 & 0 & -6 \\ 1 & 0 & 2 \end{vmatrix} - 7\begin{vmatrix} 10 & 8 & 3 \\ 4 & 0 & 5 \\ 1 & 0 & -3 \end{vmatrix}$

$= 0(-64) - 3(-3) + 2(-112) - 7(136) = -1167$

(b) $\begin{vmatrix} 10 & 8 & 3 & -7 \\ 4 & 0 & 5 & -6 \\ 0 & 3 & 2 & 7 \\ 1 & 0 & -3 & 2 \end{vmatrix} = 10\begin{vmatrix} 0 & 5 & -6 \\ 3 & 2 & 7 \\ 0 & -3 & 2 \end{vmatrix} - 4\begin{vmatrix} 8 & 3 & -7 \\ 3 & 2 & 7 \\ 0 & -3 & 2 \end{vmatrix} + 0\begin{vmatrix} 8 & 3 & -7 \\ 0 & 5 & -6 \\ 0 & -3 & 2 \end{vmatrix} - 1\begin{vmatrix} 8 & 3 & -7 \\ 0 & 5 & -6 \\ 3 & 2 & 7 \end{vmatrix}$

$= 10(24) - 4(245) + 0(-64) - 1(427) = -1167$

38. Expand along Row 3.

$\begin{vmatrix} -2 & 2 & 3 \\ 1 & -1 & 0 \\ 0 & 1 & 4 \end{vmatrix} = 0\begin{vmatrix} 2 & 3 \\ -1 & 0 \end{vmatrix} - 1\begin{vmatrix} -2 & 3 \\ 1 & 0 \end{vmatrix} + 4\begin{vmatrix} -2 & 2 \\ 1 & -1 \end{vmatrix}$

$= 0(3) - 1(-3) + 4(0) = 3$

40. Expand along Column 3.

$\begin{vmatrix} 1 & 1 & 2 \\ 3 & 1 & 0 \\ -2 & 0 & 3 \end{vmatrix} = 2\begin{vmatrix} 3 & 1 \\ -2 & 0 \end{vmatrix} - 0\begin{vmatrix} 1 & 1 \\ -2 & 0 \end{vmatrix} + 3\begin{vmatrix} 1 & 1 \\ 3 & 1 \end{vmatrix}$

$= 2(2) - 0(2) + 3(-2) = -2$

42. Expand along Row 1.

$\begin{vmatrix} 1 & 0 & 0 \\ -4 & -1 & 0 \\ 5 & 1 & 5 \end{vmatrix} = 1\begin{vmatrix} -1 & 0 \\ 1 & 5 \end{vmatrix} - 0\begin{vmatrix} -4 & 0 \\ 5 & 5 \end{vmatrix} + 0\begin{vmatrix} -4 & -1 \\ 5 & 1 \end{vmatrix}$

$= 1(-5) - 0(-20) + 0(1) = -5$

44. Expand along Row 3.

$\begin{vmatrix} 2 & -1 & 3 \\ 1 & 4 & 4 \\ 1 & 0 & 2 \end{vmatrix} = 1\begin{vmatrix} -1 & 3 \\ 4 & 4 \end{vmatrix} - 0\begin{vmatrix} 1 & 4 \\ 1 & 2 \end{vmatrix} + 2\begin{vmatrix} 2 & -1 \\ 1 & 4 \end{vmatrix} = 1(-16) - 0(-2) + 2(9) = 2$

46. Expand along Row 1.

$\begin{vmatrix} -3 & 0 & 0 \\ 7 & 11 & 0 \\ 1 & 2 & 2 \end{vmatrix} = -3\begin{vmatrix} 11 & 0 \\ 2 & 2 \end{vmatrix} - 0\begin{vmatrix} 7 & 4 \\ 2 & 1 \end{vmatrix} + 0\begin{vmatrix} 7 & 11 \\ 1 & 2 \end{vmatrix}$

$= -3(22) - 0(-1) + 0(3) = -66$

48. Expand along Row 2.

$$\begin{vmatrix} 3 & 6 & -5 & 4 \\ -2 & 0 & 6 & 0 \\ 1 & 1 & 2 & 2 \\ 0 & 3 & -1 & -1 \end{vmatrix} = -(-2)\begin{vmatrix} 6 & -5 & 4 \\ 1 & 2 & 2 \\ 3 & -1 & -1 \end{vmatrix} - 6\begin{vmatrix} 3 & 6 & 4 \\ 1 & 1 & 2 \\ 0 & 3 & -1 \end{vmatrix} = 2(-63) - 6(-3) = -108$$

50. Expand along Row 3.

$$\begin{vmatrix} 1 & 4 & 3 & 2 \\ -5 & 6 & 2 & 1 \\ 0 & 0 & 0 & 0 \\ 3 & -2 & 1 & 5 \end{vmatrix} = 0$$

52. Expand along Column 1.

$$\begin{vmatrix} 5 & 2 & 0 & 0 & -2 \\ 0 & 1 & 4 & 3 & 2 \\ 0 & 0 & 2 & 6 & 3 \\ 0 & 0 & 3 & 4 & 1 \\ 0 & 0 & 0 & 0 & 2 \end{vmatrix} = 5\begin{vmatrix} 1 & 4 & 3 & 2 \\ 0 & 2 & 6 & 3 \\ 0 & 3 & 4 & 1 \\ 0 & 0 & 0 & 2 \end{vmatrix} = 5 \cdot 1\begin{vmatrix} 2 & 6 & 3 \\ 3 & 4 & 1 \\ 0 & 0 & 2 \end{vmatrix} = 5(-20) = -100$$

54. $\begin{vmatrix} 5 & -8 & 0 \\ 9 & 7 & 4 \\ -8 & 7 & 1 \end{vmatrix} = 223$

56. $\begin{vmatrix} 3 & 0 & 0 \\ -2 & 5 & 0 \\ 12 & 5 & 7 \end{vmatrix} = 105$

58. $\begin{vmatrix} 0 & -3 & 8 & 2 \\ 8 & 1 & -1 & 6 \\ -4 & 6 & 0 & 9 \\ -7 & 0 & 0 & 14 \end{vmatrix} = 7441$

60. $\begin{vmatrix} -2 & 0 & 0 & 0 & 0 \\ 0 & 3 & 0 & 0 & 0 \\ 0 & 0 & -1 & 0 & 0 \\ 0 & 0 & 0 & 2 & 0 \\ 0 & 0 & 0 & 0 & -4 \end{vmatrix} = -48$

62. (a) $|A| = \begin{vmatrix} -2 & 1 \\ 4 & -2 \end{vmatrix} = 0$

(b) $|B| = \begin{vmatrix} 1 & 2 \\ 0 & -1 \end{vmatrix} = -1$

(c) $AB = \begin{bmatrix} -2 & 1 \\ 4 & -2 \end{bmatrix}\begin{bmatrix} 1 & 2 \\ 0 & -1 \end{bmatrix} = \begin{bmatrix} -2 & -5 \\ 4 & 10 \end{bmatrix}$

(d) $|AB| = \begin{vmatrix} -2 & -5 \\ 4 & 10 \end{vmatrix} = 0$

64. (a) $|A| = \begin{vmatrix} 5 & 4 \\ 3 & -1 \end{vmatrix} = -17$

(b) $|B| = \begin{vmatrix} 0 & 6 \\ 1 & -2 \end{vmatrix} = -6$

(c) $AB = \begin{bmatrix} 5 & 4 \\ 3 & -1 \end{bmatrix}\begin{bmatrix} 0 & 6 \\ 1 & -2 \end{bmatrix} = \begin{bmatrix} 4 & 22 \\ -1 & 20 \end{bmatrix}$

(d) $|AB| = \begin{vmatrix} 4 & 22 \\ -1 & 20 \end{vmatrix} = 102$

66. (a) $|A| = \begin{vmatrix} 3 & 2 & 0 \\ -1 & -3 & 4 \\ -2 & 0 & 1 \end{vmatrix} = -23$

(b) $|B| = \begin{vmatrix} -3 & 0 & 1 \\ 0 & 2 & -1 \\ -2 & -1 & 1 \end{vmatrix} = 1$

(c) $AB = \begin{bmatrix} 3 & 2 & 0 \\ -1 & -3 & 4 \\ -2 & 0 & 1 \end{bmatrix}\begin{bmatrix} -3 & 0 & 1 \\ 0 & 2 & -1 \\ -2 & -1 & 1 \end{bmatrix} = \begin{bmatrix} -9 & 4 & 1 \\ -5 & -10 & 6 \\ 4 & -1 & -1 \end{bmatrix}$

(d) $|AB| = \begin{vmatrix} -9 & 4 & 1 \\ -5 & -10 & 6 \\ 4 & -1 & -1 \end{vmatrix} = -23$

68. (a) $|A| = \begin{vmatrix} 2 & 0 & 1 \\ 1 & -1 & 2 \\ 3 & 1 & 0 \end{vmatrix} = 0$

(b) $|B| = \begin{vmatrix} 2 & -1 & 4 \\ 0 & 1 & 3 \\ 3 & -2 & 1 \end{vmatrix} = -7$

(c) $AB = \begin{bmatrix} 2 & 0 & 1 \\ 1 & -1 & 2 \\ 3 & 1 & 0 \end{bmatrix}\begin{bmatrix} 2 & -1 & 4 \\ 0 & 1 & 3 \\ 3 & -2 & 1 \end{bmatrix} = \begin{bmatrix} 7 & -4 & 9 \\ 8 & -6 & 3 \\ 6 & -2 & 15 \end{bmatrix}$

(d) $|AB| = \begin{vmatrix} 7 & -4 & 9 \\ 8 & -6 & 3 \\ 6 & -2 & 15 \end{vmatrix} = 0$

70. $\begin{vmatrix} w & cx \\ y & cz \end{vmatrix} = cwz - cxy = c(wz - xy)$

$c\begin{vmatrix} w & x \\ y & z \end{vmatrix} = c(wz - xy)$

Thus, $\begin{vmatrix} w & cx \\ y & cz \end{vmatrix} = c\begin{vmatrix} w & x \\ y & z \end{vmatrix}$.

72. $\begin{vmatrix} w & x \\ cw & cx \end{vmatrix} = cxw - cxw = 0$

Thus, $\begin{vmatrix} w & x \\ cw & cx \end{vmatrix} = 0$.

74. $\begin{vmatrix} a+b & a & a \\ a & a+b & a \\ a & a & a+b \end{vmatrix} = (a+b)\begin{vmatrix} a+b & a \\ a & a+b \end{vmatrix} - a\begin{vmatrix} a & a \\ a & a+b \end{vmatrix} + a\begin{vmatrix} a & a \\ a+b & a \end{vmatrix}$

$= (a+b)[(a+b)^2 - a^2] - a[a(a+b) - a^2] + a[a^2 - a(a+b)]$

$= (a+b)^3 - a^2(a+b) - a^2(a+b) + a^3 + a^3 - a^2(a+b)$

$= (a+b)^3 - 3a^2(a+b) + 2a^3$

$= a^3 + 3a^2b + 3ab^2 + b^3 - 3a^3 - 3a^2b + 2a^3$

$= 3ab^2 + b^3 = b^2(3a + b)$

76. $\begin{vmatrix} x-2 & -1 \\ -3 & x \end{vmatrix} = 0$

$x(x-2) - (-3)(-1) = 0$

$x^2 - 2x - 3 = 0$

$(x+1)(x-3) = 0$

$x = -1 \text{ or } x = 3$

78. $\begin{vmatrix} x+4 & -2 \\ 7 & x-5 \end{vmatrix} = 0$

$(x+4)(x-5) - 7(-2) = 0$

$x^2 - x - 6 = 0$

$(x+2)(x-3) = 0$

$x = -2 \text{ or } x = 3$

80. $\begin{vmatrix} 3x^2 & -3y^2 \\ 1 & 1 \end{vmatrix} = 3x^2 - (-3y^2) = 3x^2 + 3y^2$

82. $\begin{vmatrix} e^{-x} & xe^{-x} \\ -e^{-x} & (1-x)e^{-x} \end{vmatrix} = (1-x)e^{-2x} - (-xe^{-2x}) = e^{-2x} - xe^{-2x} + xe^{-2x} = e^{-2x}$

84. $\begin{vmatrix} x & x\ln x \\ 1 & 1 + \ln x \end{vmatrix} = x(1 + \ln x) - x\ln x = x + x\ln x - x\ln x = x$

86. True. If a square matrix has two columns that are equal, then elementary column operations can be used to create a column with all zeros.

88. (a) $\begin{vmatrix} 4 & 5 & 6 \\ 7 & 8 & 9 \\ 10 & 11 & 12 \end{vmatrix} = 0$

$\begin{vmatrix} 33 & 34 & 35 \\ 36 & 37 & 38 \\ 39 & 40 & 41 \end{vmatrix} = 0 \qquad \begin{vmatrix} -5 & -4 & -3 \\ -2 & -1 & 0 \\ 1 & 2 & 3 \end{vmatrix} = 0$

$\begin{vmatrix} 19 & 20 & 21 & 22 \\ 23 & 24 & 25 & 26 \\ 27 & 28 & 29 & 30 \\ 31 & 32 & 33 & 34 \end{vmatrix} = 0 \qquad \begin{vmatrix} 57 & 58 & 59 & 60 \\ 61 & 62 & 63 & 64 \\ 65 & 66 & 67 & 68 \\ 69 & 70 & 71 & 72 \end{vmatrix} = 0$

For an $n \times n$ matrix $(n > 2)$ with consecutive integer entries, the determinant appears to be 0.

(b) $\begin{vmatrix} x & x+1 & x+2 \\ x+3 & x+4 & x+5 \\ x+6 & x+7 & x+8 \end{vmatrix} = x\begin{vmatrix} x+4 & x+5 \\ x+7 & x+8 \end{vmatrix} - (x+1)\begin{vmatrix} x+3 & x+5 \\ x+6 & x+8 \end{vmatrix} + (x+2)\begin{vmatrix} x+3 & x+4 \\ x+6 & x+7 \end{vmatrix}$

$= x[(x+4)(x+8) - (x+7)(x+5)] - (x+1)[(x+3)(x+8)$

$\qquad - (x+6)(x+5)] + (x+2)[(x+3)(x+7) - (x+6)(x+4)]$

$= x[(x^2 + 12x + 32) - (x^2 + 12x + 35)] - (x+1)[(x^2 + 11x + 24)$

$\qquad - (x^2 + 11x + 30)] + (x+2)[(x^2 + 10x + 21) - (x^2 + 10x + 24)]$

$= -3x - (x+1)(-6) + (x+2)(-3)$

$= -3x + 6x + 6 - 3x - 6 = 0$

90. Let $A = \begin{bmatrix} x_{11} & x_{12} & x_{13} \\ x_{21} & x_{22} & x_{23} \\ x_{31} & x_{32} & x_{33} \end{bmatrix}$ and $|A| = 5$.

$2A = \begin{bmatrix} 2x_{11} & 2x_{12} & 2x_{13} \\ 2x_{21} & 2x_{22} & 2x_{23} \\ 2x_{31} & 2x_{32} & 2x_{33} \end{bmatrix}$

$|2A| = 2x_{11} \begin{vmatrix} 2x_{22} & 2x_{23} \\ 2x_{32} & 2x_{33} \end{vmatrix} - 2x_{12} \begin{vmatrix} 2x_{21} & 2x_{23} \\ 2x_{31} & 2x_{33} \end{vmatrix} + 2x_{13} \begin{vmatrix} 2x_{21} & 2x_{22} \\ 2x_{31} & 2x_{32} \end{vmatrix}$

$= 2[x_{11}(4x_{22}x_{33} - 4x_{32}x_{23}) - x_{12}(4x_{21}x_{33} - 4x_{31}x_{23}) + x_{13}(4x_{21}x_{32} - 4x_{31}x_{22})]$

$= 8[x_{11}(x_{22}x_{33} - x_{32}x_{23}) - x_{12}(x_{21}x_{33} - x_{31}x_{23}) + x_{13}(x_{21}x_{32} - x_{31}x_{22})]$

$= 8|A|$

Thus, $|2A| = 8|A| = 8(5) = 40$.

92.

94. $[A \quad \vdots \quad I] = \begin{bmatrix} -5 & -8 & \vdots & 1 & 0 \\ 3 & 6 & \vdots & 0 & 1 \end{bmatrix}$

$\underset{R_1}{\overset{R_2}{\curvearrowleft}} \begin{bmatrix} 3 & 6 & \vdots & 0 & 1 \\ -5 & -8 & \vdots & 1 & 0 \end{bmatrix}$

$\tfrac{1}{3}R_1 \rightarrow \begin{bmatrix} 1 & 2 & \vdots & 0 & \tfrac{1}{3} \\ -5 & -8 & \vdots & 1 & 0 \end{bmatrix}$

$5R_1 + R_2 \rightarrow \begin{bmatrix} 1 & 2 & \vdots & 0 & \tfrac{1}{3} \\ 0 & 2 & \vdots & 1 & \tfrac{5}{3} \end{bmatrix}$

$\tfrac{1}{2}R_2 \rightarrow \begin{bmatrix} 1 & 2 & \vdots & 0 & \tfrac{1}{3} \\ 0 & 1 & \vdots & \tfrac{1}{2} & \tfrac{5}{6} \end{bmatrix}$

$-2R_2 + R_1 \rightarrow \begin{bmatrix} 1 & 0 & \vdots & -1 & -\tfrac{4}{3} \\ 0 & 1 & \vdots & \tfrac{1}{2} & \tfrac{5}{6} \end{bmatrix} = [I \quad \vdots \quad A^{-1}]$

$A^{-1} = \begin{bmatrix} -1 & -\tfrac{4}{3} \\ \tfrac{1}{2} & \tfrac{5}{6} \end{bmatrix}$

96. $[A \quad \vdots \quad I] = \begin{bmatrix} -6 & 2 & 0 & \vdots & 1 & 0 & 0 \\ 1 & 3 & -2 & \vdots & 0 & 1 & 0 \\ -2 & 0 & 1 & \vdots & 0 & 0 & 1 \end{bmatrix}$

$\begin{matrix} R_2 \\ R_1 \end{matrix} \begin{bmatrix} 1 & 3 & -2 & \vdots & 0 & 1 & 0 \\ -6 & 2 & 0 & \vdots & 1 & 0 & 0 \\ -2 & 0 & 1 & \vdots & 0 & 0 & 1 \end{bmatrix}$

$\begin{matrix} R_3 \\ R_2 \end{matrix} \begin{bmatrix} 1 & 3 & -2 & \vdots & 0 & 1 & 0 \\ -2 & 0 & 1 & \vdots & 0 & 0 & 1 \\ -6 & 2 & 0 & \vdots & 1 & 0 & 0 \end{bmatrix}$

$\begin{matrix} \\ 2R_1 + R_2 \rightarrow \\ 6R_1 + R_3 \rightarrow \end{matrix} \begin{bmatrix} 1 & 3 & -2 & \vdots & 0 & 1 & 0 \\ 0 & 6 & -3 & \vdots & 0 & 2 & 1 \\ 0 & 20 & -12 & \vdots & 1 & 6 & 0 \end{bmatrix}$

$\begin{matrix} \\ \frac{1}{6}R_2 \rightarrow \\ \\ \end{matrix} \begin{bmatrix} 1 & 3 & -2 & \vdots & 0 & 1 & 0 \\ 0 & 1 & -\frac{1}{2} & \vdots & 0 & \frac{1}{3} & \frac{1}{6} \\ 0 & 20 & -12 & \vdots & 1 & 6 & 0 \end{bmatrix}$

$\begin{matrix} \\ \\ -20R_2 + R_3 \rightarrow \end{matrix} \begin{bmatrix} 1 & 3 & -2 & \vdots & 0 & 1 & 0 \\ 0 & 1 & -\frac{1}{2} & \vdots & 0 & \frac{1}{3} & \frac{1}{6} \\ 0 & 0 & -2 & \vdots & 1 & -\frac{2}{3} & -\frac{10}{3} \end{bmatrix}$

$\begin{matrix} \\ \\ -\frac{1}{2}R_3 \rightarrow \end{matrix} \begin{bmatrix} 1 & 3 & -2 & \vdots & 0 & 1 & 0 \\ 0 & 1 & -\frac{1}{2} & \vdots & 0 & \frac{1}{3} & \frac{1}{6} \\ 0 & 0 & 1 & \vdots & -\frac{1}{2} & \frac{1}{3} & \frac{5}{3} \end{bmatrix}$

$\begin{matrix} -3R_2 + R_1 \rightarrow \\ \\ \end{matrix} \begin{bmatrix} 1 & 0 & -\frac{1}{2} & \vdots & 0 & 0 & -\frac{1}{2} \\ 0 & 1 & -\frac{1}{2} & \vdots & 0 & \frac{1}{3} & \frac{1}{6} \\ 0 & 0 & 1 & \vdots & -\frac{1}{2} & \frac{1}{3} & \frac{5}{3} \end{bmatrix}$

$\begin{matrix} \frac{1}{2}R_3 + R_1 \rightarrow \\ \frac{1}{2}R_3 + R_2 \rightarrow \\ \\ \end{matrix} \begin{bmatrix} 1 & 0 & 0 & \vdots & -\frac{1}{4} & \frac{1}{6} & \frac{1}{3} \\ 0 & 1 & 0 & \vdots & -\frac{1}{4} & \frac{1}{2} & 1 \\ 0 & 0 & 1 & \vdots & -\frac{1}{2} & \frac{1}{3} & \frac{5}{3} \end{bmatrix} = [I \quad \vdots \quad A^{-1}]$

$A^{-1} = \begin{bmatrix} -\frac{1}{4} & \frac{1}{6} & \frac{1}{3} \\ -\frac{1}{4} & \frac{1}{2} & 1 \\ -\frac{1}{2} & \frac{1}{3} & \frac{5}{3} \end{bmatrix}$

Section 8.5   Applications of Matrices and Determinants

Solutions to Even-Numbered Exercises

2. $\begin{cases} -4x - 7y = 47 \\ -x + 6y = -27 \end{cases}$

$$x = \frac{\begin{vmatrix} 47 & -7 \\ -27 & 6 \end{vmatrix}}{\begin{vmatrix} -4 & -7 \\ -1 & 6 \end{vmatrix}} = \frac{93}{-31} = -3$$

$$y = \frac{\begin{vmatrix} -4 & 47 \\ -1 & -27 \end{vmatrix}}{\begin{vmatrix} -4 & -7 \\ -1 & 6 \end{vmatrix}} = \frac{155}{-31} = -5$$

Solution: $(-3, 5)$

4. $\begin{cases} 2.4x - 1.3y = 14.63 \\ -4.6x + 0.5y = -11.51 \end{cases}$

$$x = \frac{\begin{vmatrix} 14.63 & -1.3 \\ -11.51 & 0.5 \end{vmatrix}}{\begin{vmatrix} 2.4 & -1.3 \\ -4.6 & 0.5 \end{vmatrix}} = \frac{-7.648}{-4.78} = \frac{8}{5}$$

$$y = \frac{\begin{vmatrix} 2.4 & 14.63 \\ -4.6 & -11.51 \end{vmatrix}}{\begin{vmatrix} 2.4 & -1.3 \\ -4.6 & 0.5 \end{vmatrix}} = \frac{39.674}{-4.78} = \frac{-83}{10}$$

Solution: $\left(\dfrac{8}{5}, -\dfrac{83}{10} \right)$

6. $\begin{cases} 4x - 2y + 3z = -2 \\ 2x + 2y + 5z = 16 \\ 8x - 5y - 2z = 4 \end{cases}$

$$D = \begin{vmatrix} 4 & -2 & 3 \\ 2 & 2 & 5 \\ 8 & -5 & -2 \end{vmatrix} = -82$$

$$x = \frac{\begin{vmatrix} -2 & -2 & 3 \\ 16 & 2 & 5 \\ 4 & -5 & -2 \end{vmatrix}}{-82} = \frac{-401}{-82} = 5$$

$$y = \frac{\begin{vmatrix} 4 & -2 & 3 \\ 2 & 16 & 5 \\ 8 & 4 & -2 \end{vmatrix}}{-82} = \frac{-656}{-82} = 8$$

$$z = \frac{\begin{vmatrix} 4 & -2 & -2 \\ 2 & 2 & 16 \\ 8 & -5 & 4 \end{vmatrix}}{-82} = \frac{164}{-82} = -2$$

Solution: $(5, 8, -2)$

8. $\begin{cases} 5x - 4y + z = -14 \\ -x + 2y - 2z = 10 \\ 3x + y + z = 1 \end{cases}$

$$D = \begin{vmatrix} 5 & -4 & 1 \\ -1 & 2 & -2 \\ 3 & 1 & 1 \end{vmatrix} = 33$$

$$x = \frac{\begin{vmatrix} -14 & -4 & 1 \\ 10 & 2 & -2 \\ 1 & 1 & 1 \end{vmatrix}}{33} = \frac{0}{33} = 0$$

$$y = \frac{\begin{vmatrix} 5 & -14 & 1 \\ -1 & 10 & -2 \\ 3 & 1 & 1 \end{vmatrix}}{33} = \frac{99}{33} = 3$$

$$z = \frac{\begin{vmatrix} 5 & -4 & -14 \\ -1 & 2 & 10 \\ 3 & 1 & 1 \end{vmatrix}}{33} = -\frac{66}{33} = -2$$

Solution: $(0, 3, -2)$

10. $\begin{cases} x + 2y - z = -7 \\ 2x - 2y - 2z = -8 \\ -x + 3y + 4z = 8 \end{cases}$

$$D = \begin{vmatrix} 1 & 2 & -1 \\ 2 & -2 & -2 \\ -1 & 3 & 4 \end{vmatrix} = -18$$

$$x = \frac{\begin{vmatrix} -7 & 2 & -1 \\ -8 & -2 & -2 \\ 8 & 3 & 4 \end{vmatrix}}{-18} = -3$$

$$y = \frac{\begin{vmatrix} 1 & -7 & -1 \\ 2 & -8 & -2 \\ -1 & 8 & 4 \end{vmatrix}}{-18} = -1$$

$$z = \frac{\begin{vmatrix} 1 & 2 & -7 \\ 2 & -2 & -8 \\ -1 & 3 & 8 \end{vmatrix}}{-18} = 2$$

Solution: $(-3, -1, 2)$

12. $\begin{cases} 2x + 3y + 5z = 4 \\ 3x + 5y + 9z = 7 \\ 5x + 9y + 17z = 13 \end{cases}$

$$D = \begin{vmatrix} 2 & 3 & 5 \\ 3 & 5 & 9 \\ 5 & 9 & 17 \end{vmatrix} = 0$$

Cramer's Rule does not apply.

14. Vertices: $(0, 0), (4, 5), (5, -2)$

$$\text{Area} = -\frac{1}{2}\begin{vmatrix} 0 & 0 & 1 \\ 4 & 5 & 1 \\ 5 & -2 & 1 \end{vmatrix} = -\frac{1}{2}\begin{vmatrix} 4 & 5 \\ 5 & -2 \end{vmatrix} = \frac{33}{2} \text{ square units}$$

16. Vertices: $(-2, 1), (1, 6), (3, -1)$

$$\text{Area} = -\frac{1}{2}\begin{vmatrix} -2 & 1 & 1 \\ 1 & 6 & 1 \\ 3 & -1 & 1 \end{vmatrix} = -\frac{1}{2}\left(-2\begin{vmatrix} 6 & 1 \\ -1 & 1 \end{vmatrix} - \begin{vmatrix} 1 & 1 \\ 3 & 1 \end{vmatrix} + \begin{vmatrix} 1 & 6 \\ 3 & -1 \end{vmatrix}\right) = -\frac{1}{2}(-14 + 2 - 19) = \frac{31}{2} \text{ square units}$$

18. Vertices: $(-4, -5), (6, 10), (6, -1)$

$$\text{Area} = -\frac{1}{2}\begin{vmatrix} -4 & -5 & 1 \\ 6 & 10 & 1 \\ 6 & -1 & 1 \end{vmatrix} = -\frac{1}{2}\left(6\begin{vmatrix} -5 & 1 \\ 10 & 1 \end{vmatrix} - (-1)\begin{vmatrix} -4 & 1 \\ 6 & 1 \end{vmatrix} + \begin{vmatrix} -4 & -5 \\ 6 & 10 \end{vmatrix}\right) = 55 \text{ square units}$$

20. Vertices: $(0, -2), (-1, 4), (3, 5)$

$$\text{Area} = -\frac{1}{2}\begin{vmatrix} 0 & -2 & 1 \\ -1 & 4 & 1 \\ 3 & 5 & 1 \end{vmatrix} = -\frac{1}{2}\left(2\begin{vmatrix} -1 & 1 \\ 3 & 1 \end{vmatrix} + \begin{vmatrix} -1 & 4 \\ 3 & 5 \end{vmatrix}\right) = -\frac{1}{2}(-8 - 17) = \frac{25}{2} \text{ square units}$$

22. Vertices: $(-2, 4), (1, 5), (3, -2)$

$$\text{Area} = -\frac{1}{2}\begin{vmatrix} -2 & 4 & 1 \\ 1 & 5 & 1 \\ 3 & -2 & 1 \end{vmatrix} = -\frac{1}{2}\left(-2\begin{vmatrix} 5 & 1 \\ -2 & 1 \end{vmatrix} - \begin{vmatrix} 4 & 1 \\ -2 & 1 \end{vmatrix} + 3\begin{vmatrix} 4 & 1 \\ 5 & 1 \end{vmatrix}\right) = -\frac{1}{2}(-14 - 6 - 3) = \frac{23}{2} \text{ square units}$$

24. $4 = \pm\dfrac{1}{2}\begin{vmatrix} -4 & 2 & 1 \\ -3 & 5 & 1 \\ -1 & x & 1 \end{vmatrix}$

$\pm 8 = \begin{vmatrix} -3 & 5 \\ -1 & x \end{vmatrix} - \begin{vmatrix} -4 & 2 \\ -1 & x \end{vmatrix} + \begin{vmatrix} -4 & 2 \\ -3 & 5 \end{vmatrix}$

$\pm 8 = -3x + 5 - (-4x + 2) - 20 + 6$

$\pm 8 = -3x + 5 + 4x - 2 - 20 + 6$

$\pm 8 = x - 11$

$x = 11 \pm 8$

$x = 19$ or $x = 3$

26. $6 = \pm\dfrac{1}{2}\begin{vmatrix} 1 & 0 & 1 \\ 5 & -3 & 1 \\ -3 & x & 1 \end{vmatrix}$

$\pm 12 = \begin{vmatrix} -3 & 1 \\ x & 1 \end{vmatrix} + \begin{vmatrix} 5 & -3 \\ -3 & x \end{vmatrix}$

$\pm 12 = -3 - x + 5x - 9$

$\pm 12 = 4x - 12$

$x = \dfrac{12 \pm 12}{4} = 3 \pm 3$

$x = 6$ or $x = 0$

28. Vertices: $(0, 30), (85, 0), (20, -50)$

$\text{Area} = -\dfrac{1}{2}\begin{vmatrix} 0 & 30 & 1 \\ 85 & 0 & 1 \\ 20 & -50 & 1 \end{vmatrix} = 3100$ square feet

30. Points: $(-3, -5), (6, 1), (10, 2)$

$\begin{vmatrix} -3 & -5 & 1 \\ 6 & 1 & 1 \\ 10 & 2 & 1 \end{vmatrix} = \begin{vmatrix} 6 & 1 \\ 10 & 2 \end{vmatrix} - \begin{vmatrix} -3 & -5 \\ 10 & 2 \end{vmatrix} + \begin{vmatrix} -3 & -5 \\ 6 & 1 \end{vmatrix} = 2 - 44 + 27 = -15 \neq 0$

The points are not collinear.

32. Points: $(0, 1), (4, -2), \left(-2, \frac{5}{2}\right)$

$\begin{vmatrix} 0 & 1 & 1 \\ 4 & -2 & 1 \\ -2 & \frac{5}{2} & 1 \end{vmatrix} = -\begin{vmatrix} 4 & 1 \\ -2 & 1 \end{vmatrix} + \begin{vmatrix} 4 & -2 \\ -2 & \frac{5}{2} \end{vmatrix} = -6 + 6 = 0$

The points are collinear.

34. Points: $(2, 3), (3, 3.5), (-1, 2)$

$\begin{vmatrix} 2 & 3 & 1 \\ 3 & 3.5 & 1 \\ -1 & 2 & 1 \end{vmatrix} = \begin{vmatrix} 3 & 3.5 \\ -1 & 2 \end{vmatrix} - \begin{vmatrix} 2 & 3 \\ -1 & 2 \end{vmatrix} + \begin{vmatrix} 2 & 3 \\ 3 & 3.5 \end{vmatrix} = 9.5 - 7 + (-2) = \dfrac{1}{2} \neq 0$

The points are not collinear.

36. $\begin{vmatrix} -6 & 2 & 1 \\ -5 & x & 1 \\ -3 & 5 & 1 \end{vmatrix} = 0$

$\begin{vmatrix} -5 & x \\ -3 & 5 \end{vmatrix} - \begin{vmatrix} -6 & 2 \\ -3 & 5 \end{vmatrix} + \begin{vmatrix} -6 & 2 \\ -5 & x \end{vmatrix} = 0$

$-25 + 3x + 24 - 6x + 10 = 0$

$-3x = -9$

$x = 3$

38. Points: $(0, 0), (-2, 2)$

Equation: $\begin{vmatrix} x & y & 1 \\ 0 & 0 & 1 \\ -2 & 2 & 1 \end{vmatrix} = \begin{vmatrix} x & y \\ -2 & 2 \end{vmatrix} = (2x + 2y) = 0$ or $x + y = 0$

40. Points: $(10, 7), (-2, -7)$

Equation:

$\begin{vmatrix} x & y & 1 \\ 10 & 7 & 1 \\ -2 & -7 & 1 \end{vmatrix} = \begin{vmatrix} 10 & 7 \\ -2 & -7 \end{vmatrix} - \begin{vmatrix} x & y \\ -2 & -7 \end{vmatrix} + \begin{vmatrix} x & y \\ 10 & 7 \end{vmatrix} = -70 + 14 - (-7x + 2y) + 7x - 10y = 0$ or $7x - 6y - 28 = 0$

42. Points: $\left(\frac{2}{3}, 4\right), (6, 12)$

Equation: $\begin{vmatrix} x & y & 1 \\ \frac{2}{3} & 4 & 1 \\ 6 & 12 & 1 \end{vmatrix} = \begin{vmatrix} \frac{2}{3} & 4 \\ 6 & 12 \end{vmatrix} - \begin{vmatrix} x & y \\ 6 & 12 \end{vmatrix} + \begin{vmatrix} x & y \\ \frac{2}{3} & 4 \end{vmatrix} = -16 - (12x - 6y) + 4x - \frac{2}{3}y = 0$ or $3x - 2y + 6 = 0$

44. $\begin{bmatrix} 16 & 12 & 5 \end{bmatrix} \begin{bmatrix} 4 & 2 & 1 \\ -3 & -3 & -1 \\ 3 & 2 & 1 \end{bmatrix} = \begin{bmatrix} 43 & 6 & 9 \end{bmatrix}$

$\begin{bmatrix} 1 & 19 & 5 \end{bmatrix} \begin{bmatrix} 4 & 2 & 1 \\ -3 & -3 & -1 \\ 3 & 2 & 1 \end{bmatrix} = \begin{bmatrix} -38 & -45 & -13 \end{bmatrix}$

$\begin{bmatrix} 0 & 19 & 5 \end{bmatrix} \begin{bmatrix} 4 & 2 & 1 \\ -3 & -3 & -1 \\ 3 & 3 & 1 \end{bmatrix} = \begin{bmatrix} -42 & -47 & -14 \end{bmatrix}$

$\begin{bmatrix} 14 & 4 & 0 \end{bmatrix} \begin{bmatrix} 4 & 2 & 1 \\ -3 & -3 & -1 \\ 3 & 1 & 1 \end{bmatrix} = \begin{bmatrix} 44 & 16 & 10 \end{bmatrix}$

$\begin{bmatrix} 13 & 15 & 14 \end{bmatrix} \begin{bmatrix} 4 & 2 & 1 \\ -3 & -3 & -1 \\ 3 & 2 & 1 \end{bmatrix} = \begin{bmatrix} 49 & 9 & 12 \end{bmatrix}$

$\begin{bmatrix} 5 & 25 & 0 \end{bmatrix} \begin{bmatrix} 4 & 2 & 1 \\ -3 & -3 & -1 \\ 3 & 2 & 1 \end{bmatrix} = \begin{bmatrix} -55 & -65 & -20 \end{bmatrix}$

Solution: Uncoded: $\begin{bmatrix} 16 & 12 & 5 \end{bmatrix}, \begin{bmatrix} 1 & 19 & 5 \end{bmatrix}, \begin{bmatrix} 0 & 19 & 5 \end{bmatrix}, \begin{bmatrix} 14 & 4 & 0 \end{bmatrix}, \begin{bmatrix} 13 & 15 & 14 \end{bmatrix}, \begin{bmatrix} 5 & 25 & 0 \end{bmatrix}$
Encoded: $\begin{bmatrix} 43 & 6 & 9 \end{bmatrix}, \begin{bmatrix} -38 & -45 & -13 \end{bmatrix}, \begin{bmatrix} -42 & -47 & -14 \end{bmatrix},$
$\begin{bmatrix} 44 & 16 & 10 \end{bmatrix}, \begin{bmatrix} 49 & 9 & 12 \end{bmatrix}, \begin{bmatrix} -55 & -65 & -20 \end{bmatrix}$

46. I C E B E R G __ D E A D __ A H E A D

[9 3 5] [2 5 18] [7 0 4] [5 1 4] [0 1 8] [5 1 4]

$$[9 \quad 3 \quad 5]\begin{bmatrix} 1 & 2 & 2 \\ 3 & 7 & 9 \\ -1 & -4 & -7 \end{bmatrix} = [13 \quad 19 \quad 10]$$

$$[2 \quad 5 \quad 18]\begin{bmatrix} 1 & 2 & 2 \\ 3 & 7 & 9 \\ -1 & -4 & -7 \end{bmatrix} = [-1 \quad -33 \quad -77]$$

$$[7 \quad 0 \quad 4]\begin{bmatrix} 1 & 2 & 2 \\ 3 & 7 & 9 \\ -1 & -4 & -7 \end{bmatrix} = [3 \quad -2 \quad -14]$$

$$[5 \quad 1 \quad 4]\begin{bmatrix} 1 & 2 & 2 \\ 3 & 7 & 9 \\ -1 & -4 & -7 \end{bmatrix} = [4 \quad 1 \quad -9]$$

$$[0 \quad 1 \quad 8]\begin{bmatrix} 1 & 2 & 2 \\ 3 & 7 & 9 \\ -1 & -4 & -7 \end{bmatrix} = [-5 \quad -25 \quad -47]$$

$$[5 \quad 1 \quad 4]\begin{bmatrix} 1 & 2 & 2 \\ 3 & 7 & 9 \\ -1 & -4 & -7 \end{bmatrix} = [4 \quad 1 \quad -9]$$

Cryptogram: 13 19 10 −1 −33 −77 3 −2 −14
4 1 −9 −5 −25 −47 4 1 −9

48. O P E R A T I O N __ O V E R L O A D

[15 16 5] [18 1 20] [9 15 14] [0 15 22] [5 18 12] [15 1 4]

$$[15 \quad 16 \quad 5]\begin{bmatrix} 1 & 2 & 2 \\ 3 & 7 & 9 \\ -1 & -4 & -7 \end{bmatrix} = [58 \quad 122 \quad 139]$$

$$[18 \quad 1 \quad 20]\begin{bmatrix} 1 & 2 & 2 \\ 3 & 7 & 9 \\ -1 & -4 & -7 \end{bmatrix} = [1 \quad -37 \quad -95]$$

$$[9 \quad 15 \quad 14]\begin{bmatrix} 1 & 2 & 2 \\ 3 & 7 & 9 \\ -1 & -4 & -7 \end{bmatrix} = [40 \quad 67 \quad 55]$$

$$[0 \quad 15 \quad 22]\begin{bmatrix} 1 & 2 & 2 \\ 3 & 7 & 9 \\ -1 & -4 & -7 \end{bmatrix} = [23 \quad 17 \quad -19]$$

$$[5 \quad 18 \quad 12]\begin{bmatrix} 1 & 2 & 2 \\ 3 & 7 & 9 \\ -1 & -4 & -7 \end{bmatrix} = [47 \quad 88 \quad 88]$$

$$[15 \quad 1 \quad 4]\begin{bmatrix} 1 & 2 & 2 \\ 3 & 7 & 9 \\ -1 & -4 & -7 \end{bmatrix} = [14 \quad 21 \quad 11]$$

Cryptogram: 58 122 139 1 −37 −95 40 67 55 23 17 −19 47 88 88 14 21 11

50.
$$A^{-1} = \begin{bmatrix} -3 & 2 \\ -7 & 5 \end{bmatrix}$$

$$\begin{bmatrix} -136 & 58 \end{bmatrix} \begin{bmatrix} -3 & 2 \\ -7 & 5 \end{bmatrix} = \begin{bmatrix} 2 & 18 \end{bmatrix} \quad \text{B} \quad \text{R}$$

$$\begin{bmatrix} -173 & 72 \end{bmatrix} \begin{bmatrix} -3 & 2 \\ -7 & 5 \end{bmatrix} = \begin{bmatrix} 15 & 14 \end{bmatrix} \quad \text{O} \quad \text{N}$$

$$\begin{bmatrix} -120 & 51 \end{bmatrix} \begin{bmatrix} -3 & 2 \\ -7 & 5 \end{bmatrix} = \begin{bmatrix} 3 & 15 \end{bmatrix} \quad \text{C} \quad \text{O}$$

$$\begin{bmatrix} -95 & 38 \end{bmatrix} \begin{bmatrix} -3 & 2 \\ -7 & 5 \end{bmatrix} = \begin{bmatrix} 19 & 0 \end{bmatrix} \quad \text{S}$$

$$\begin{bmatrix} -178 & 73 \end{bmatrix} \begin{bmatrix} -3 & 2 \\ -7 & 5 \end{bmatrix} = \begin{bmatrix} 23 & 9 \end{bmatrix} \quad \text{W} \quad \text{I}$$

$$\begin{bmatrix} -70 & 28 \end{bmatrix} \begin{bmatrix} -3 & 2 \\ -7 & 5 \end{bmatrix} = \begin{bmatrix} 14 & 0 \end{bmatrix} \quad \text{N}$$

$$\begin{bmatrix} -242 & 101 \end{bmatrix} \begin{bmatrix} -3 & 2 \\ -7 & 5 \end{bmatrix} = \begin{bmatrix} 19 & 21 \end{bmatrix} \quad \text{S} \quad \text{U}$$

$$\begin{bmatrix} -115 & 47 \end{bmatrix} \begin{bmatrix} -3 & 2 \\ -7 & 5 \end{bmatrix} = \begin{bmatrix} 16 & 5 \end{bmatrix} \quad \text{P} \quad \text{E}$$

$$\begin{bmatrix} -90 & 36 \end{bmatrix} \begin{bmatrix} -3 & 2 \\ -7 & 5 \end{bmatrix} = \begin{bmatrix} 18 & 0 \end{bmatrix} \quad \text{R}$$

$$\begin{bmatrix} -115 & 49 \end{bmatrix} \begin{bmatrix} -3 & 2 \\ -7 & 5 \end{bmatrix} = \begin{bmatrix} 2 & 15 \end{bmatrix} \quad \text{B} \quad \text{O}$$

$$\begin{bmatrix} -199 & 82 \end{bmatrix} \begin{bmatrix} -3 & 2 \\ -7 & 5 \end{bmatrix} = \begin{bmatrix} 23 & 12 \end{bmatrix} \quad \text{W} \quad \text{L}$$

Message: BRONCOS WIN SUPER BOWL

52.
$$A^{-1} = \begin{bmatrix} 11 & 2 & -8 \\ 4 & 1 & -3 \\ -8 & -1 & 6 \end{bmatrix}$$

$$[112 \quad -140 \quad 83] \begin{bmatrix} 11 & 2 & -8 \\ 4 & 1 & -3 \\ -8 & -1 & 6 \end{bmatrix} = [8 \quad 1 \quad 22] \quad \text{H} \quad \text{A} \quad \text{V}$$

$$[19 \quad -25 \quad 13] \begin{bmatrix} 11 & 2 & -8 \\ 4 & 1 & -3 \\ -8 & -1 & 6 \end{bmatrix} = [5 \quad 0 \quad 1] \quad \text{E} \qquad \text{A}$$

$$[72 \quad -76 \quad 61] \begin{bmatrix} 11 & 2 & -8 \\ 4 & 1 & -3 \\ -8 & -1 & 6 \end{bmatrix} = [0 \quad 7 \quad 18] \qquad \text{G} \quad \text{R}$$

$$[95 \quad -118 \quad 71] \begin{bmatrix} 11 & 2 & -8 \\ 4 & 1 & -3 \\ -8 & -1 & 6 \end{bmatrix} = [5 \quad 1 \quad 20] \quad \text{E} \quad \text{A} \quad \text{T}$$

$$[20 \quad 21 \quad 38] \begin{bmatrix} 11 & 2 & -8 \\ 4 & 1 & -3 \\ -8 & -1 & 6 \end{bmatrix} = [0 \quad 23 \quad 5] \qquad \text{W} \quad \text{E}$$

$$[35 \quad -23 \quad 36] \begin{bmatrix} 11 & 2 & -8 \\ 4 & 1 & -3 \\ -8 & -1 & 6 \end{bmatrix} = [5 \quad 11 \quad 5] \quad \text{E} \quad \text{K} \quad \text{E}$$

$$[42 \quad -48 \quad 32] \begin{bmatrix} 11 & 2 & -8 \\ 4 & 1 & -3 \\ -8 & -1 & 6 \end{bmatrix} = [14 \quad 4 \quad 0] \quad \text{N} \quad \text{D}$$

Message: HAVE A GREAT WEEKEND

54.
$$[13 \quad -19 \quad -59] \begin{bmatrix} -13 & 6 & 4 \\ 12 & -5 & -3 \\ -5 & 2 & 1 \end{bmatrix} = [18 \quad 5 \quad 20] \quad \text{R} \quad \text{E} \quad \text{T}$$

$$[61 \quad 112 \quad 106] \begin{bmatrix} -13 & 6 & 4 \\ 12 & -5 & -3 \\ -5 & 2 & 1 \end{bmatrix} = [21 \quad 18 \quad 14] \quad \text{U} \quad \text{R} \quad \text{N}$$

$$[-17 \quad -73 \quad -131] \begin{bmatrix} -13 & 6 & 4 \\ 12 & -5 & -3 \\ -5 & 2 & 1 \end{bmatrix} = [0 \quad 1 \quad 20] \qquad \_\_ \quad \text{A} \quad \text{T}$$

$$[11 \quad 24 \quad 29] \begin{bmatrix} -13 & 6 & 4 \\ 12 & -5 & -3 \\ -5 & 2 & 1 \end{bmatrix} = [0 \quad 4 \quad 1] \qquad \_\_ \quad \text{D} \quad \text{A}$$

$$[65 \quad 144 \quad 172] \begin{bmatrix} -13 & 6 & 4 \\ 12 & -5 & -3 \\ -5 & 2 & 1 \end{bmatrix} = [23 \quad 14 \quad 0] \quad \text{W} \quad \text{N} \quad \_\_$$

Message: RETURN AT DAWN

56.
$$[5 \quad 2]\begin{bmatrix} 1 & 1 \\ -1 & -2 \end{bmatrix} = [3 \quad 1] \qquad C \quad A$$

$$[25 \quad 11]\begin{bmatrix} 1 & 1 \\ -1 & -2 \end{bmatrix} = [14 \quad 3] \qquad N \quad C$$

$$[-2 \quad -7]\begin{bmatrix} 1 & 1 \\ -1 & -2 \end{bmatrix} = [5 \quad 12] \qquad E \quad L$$

$$[-15 \quad -15]\begin{bmatrix} 1 & 1 \\ -1 & -2 \end{bmatrix} = [0 \quad 15] \qquad \_ \quad O$$

$$[32 \quad 14]\begin{bmatrix} 1 & 1 \\ -1 & -2 \end{bmatrix} = [18 \quad 4] \qquad R \quad D$$

$$[-8 \quad -13]\begin{bmatrix} 1 & 1 \\ -1 & -2 \end{bmatrix} = [5 \quad 18] \qquad E \quad R$$

$$[38 \quad 19]\begin{bmatrix} 1 & 1 \\ -1 & -2 \end{bmatrix} = [19 \quad 0] \qquad S \quad \_$$

$$[-19 \quad -19]\begin{bmatrix} 1 & 1 \\ -1 & -2 \end{bmatrix} = [0 \quad 19] \qquad \_ \quad S$$

$$[37 \quad 16]\begin{bmatrix} 1 & 1 \\ -1 & -2 \end{bmatrix} = [21 \quad 5] \qquad U \quad E$$

58. False. If the determinant of the coefficient matrix is zero, the system has either no solution or infinitely many solutions.

60.
$$\begin{cases} -x - 7y = -22 \\ 5x + y = -26 \end{cases} \qquad \text{Equation 1} \\ \qquad\qquad\qquad\qquad \text{Equation 2}$$

$$\begin{array}{ll} -5x - 35y = -110 & 5 \text{ Eq.1} \\ \underline{5x + y = -26} & \\ -34y = -136 & \text{Add equations.} \\ y = 4 & \\ -x - 7(4) = -22 & \\ x = -6 & \end{array}$$

Solution: $(-6, 4)$

62.
$$\begin{cases} -x - 3y + 5z = -14 \\ 4x + 2y - z = -1 \\ 5x - 3y + 2z = -11 \end{cases}$$

$$A^{-1} = \begin{bmatrix} -1 & -3 & 5 \\ 4 & 2 & -1 \\ 5 & -3 & 2 \end{bmatrix}^{-1}$$

$$= \frac{1}{72}\begin{bmatrix} -1 & 9 & 7 \\ 13 & 27 & -19 \\ 22 & 18 & -10 \end{bmatrix}$$

$$\begin{bmatrix} x \\ y \\ z \end{bmatrix} = A^{-1}\begin{bmatrix} -14 \\ -1 \\ -11 \end{bmatrix} = \begin{bmatrix} -1 \\ 0 \\ -3 \end{bmatrix}$$

Solution: $(-1, 0, -3)$

64. Objective function: $z = 6x + 4y$

Constraints:
$$\begin{aligned} x &\geq 0 \\ y &\geq 0 \\ x + 6y &\leq 30 \\ 6x + y &\leq 40 \end{aligned}$$

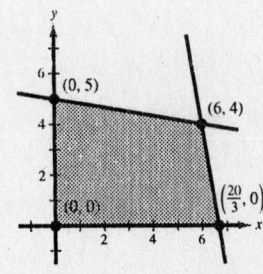

At $(0, 0)$: $z = 6(0) + 4(0) = 0$

At $(0, 5)$: $z = 6(0) + 4(5) = 20$

At $(6, 4)$: $z = 6(6) + 4(4) = 52$

At $\left(\frac{20}{3}, 0\right)$: $z = 6\left(\frac{20}{3}\right) + 4(0) = 40$

The minimum value of 0 occurs at $(0, 0)$.

The maximum value of 52 occurs at $(6, 4)$.

66. $\begin{vmatrix} -8 & 5 \\ 7 & -9 \end{vmatrix} = (-8)(-9) - (7)(5) = 37$

68. $\begin{vmatrix} -6 & -1 & 5 \\ -3 & 0 & 4 \\ -2 & 4 & -5 \end{vmatrix} = -(-1)\begin{vmatrix} -3 & 4 \\ -2 & -5 \end{vmatrix} - 4\begin{vmatrix} -6 & 5 \\ -3 & 4 \end{vmatrix}$

$$= -(-1)(15 + 8) - 4(-24 + 15)$$

$$= 59$$

Review Exercises for Chapter 8

Solutions to Even-Numbered Exercises

2. $\begin{bmatrix} 3 & -1 & 0 & 6 \\ -2 & 7 & 1 & 4 \end{bmatrix}$

Since the matrix has two rows and four columns, its order is 2×4.

4. $[6 \quad 2 \quad -5 \quad 8 \quad 0]$

Since the matrix has one row and five columns, its order is 1×5.

6. $\begin{cases} 8x - 7y + 4z = 12 \\ 3x - 5y + 2z = 20 \\ 5x + 3y - 3z = 26 \end{cases}$

$\begin{bmatrix} 8 & -7 & 4 & \vdots & 12 \\ 3 & -5 & 2 & \vdots & 20 \\ 5 & 3 & -3 & \vdots & 26 \end{bmatrix}$

8. $\begin{bmatrix} 13 & 16 & 7 & 3 & \vdots & 2 \\ 1 & 21 & 8 & 5 & \vdots & 12 \\ 4 & 10 & -4 & 3 & \vdots & -1 \end{bmatrix}$

$\begin{cases} 13x + 16y + 7z + 3w = 2 \\ x + 21y + 8z + 5w = 12 \\ 4x + 10y - 4z + 3w = -1 \end{cases}$

10.

$\begin{bmatrix} 1 & 1 & 1 & 0 \\ 1 & 1 & 0 & 1 \\ 1 & 0 & 1 & 1 \\ 0 & 1 & 1 & 1 \end{bmatrix}$

$\begin{matrix} \\ -R_1 + R_2 \rightarrow \\ -R_1 + R_3 \rightarrow \\ \\ \end{matrix} \begin{bmatrix} 1 & 1 & 1 & 0 \\ 0 & 0 & -1 & 1 \\ 0 & -1 & 0 & 1 \\ 0 & 1 & 1 & 1 \end{bmatrix}$

$\begin{matrix} R_3 + R_1 \rightarrow \\ \\ \\ R_3 + R_4 \rightarrow \end{matrix} \begin{bmatrix} 1 & 0 & 1 & 1 \\ 0 & 0 & -1 & 1 \\ 0 & -1 & 0 & 1 \\ 0 & 0 & 1 & 2 \end{bmatrix}$

$\begin{matrix} \\ -R_2 \rightarrow \\ -R_3 \rightarrow \\ R_2 + R_4 \rightarrow \end{matrix} \begin{bmatrix} 1 & 0 & 1 & 1 \\ 0 & 0 & 1 & -1 \\ 0 & 1 & 0 & -1 \\ 0 & 0 & 0 & 3 \end{bmatrix}$

$\begin{matrix} \begin{cases} R_3 \\ R_2 \end{cases} \\ \frac{1}{3}R_4 \rightarrow \end{matrix} \begin{bmatrix} 1 & 0 & 1 & 1 \\ 0 & 1 & 0 & -1 \\ 0 & 0 & 1 & -1 \\ 0 & 0 & 0 & 1 \end{bmatrix}$

$\begin{matrix} -R_4 + R_1 \rightarrow \\ R_4 + R_2 \rightarrow \\ R_4 + R_3 \rightarrow \\ \\ \end{matrix} \begin{bmatrix} 1 & 0 & 1 & 0 \\ 0 & 1 & 0 & 0 \\ 0 & 0 & 1 & 0 \\ 0 & 0 & 0 & 1 \end{bmatrix}$

$\begin{matrix} -R_3 + R_1 \rightarrow \\ \\ \\ \\ \end{matrix} \begin{bmatrix} 1 & 0 & 0 & 0 \\ 0 & 1 & 0 & 0 \\ 0 & 0 & 1 & 0 \\ 0 & 0 & 0 & 1 \end{bmatrix}$

12. $\begin{bmatrix} 1 & 2 & 3 & \vdots & 9 \\ 0 & 1 & -2 & \vdots & 2 \\ 0 & 0 & 0 & \vdots & 8 \end{bmatrix}$

Inconsistent

14. $\begin{bmatrix} 1 & 2 & 3 & 10 & 6 & : & 0 \\ 0 & 1 & -5 & -2 & 0 & : & 5 \\ 0 & 0 & 1 & 12 & 0 & : & -2 \\ 0 & 0 & 0 & 1 & 1 & : & 0 \end{bmatrix}$

Consistent
Infinitely many solutions.

16. $\begin{bmatrix} 2 & -5 & : & 2 \\ 3 & -7 & : & 1 \end{bmatrix}$

$\frac{1}{2}R_1 \rightarrow \begin{bmatrix} 1 & -\frac{5}{2} & : & 1 \\ 3 & -7 & : & 1 \end{bmatrix}$

$-3R_1 + R_2 \rightarrow \begin{bmatrix} 1 & -\frac{5}{2} & : & 1 \\ 0 & \frac{1}{2} & : & -2 \end{bmatrix}$

$2R_3 \rightarrow \begin{bmatrix} 1 & -\frac{5}{2} & : & 1 \\ 0 & 1 & : & -4 \end{bmatrix}$

$\begin{cases} x - \frac{5}{2}y = 1 \\ y = -4 \end{cases}$

$y = -4$

$x - \frac{5}{2}(-4) = 1 \Rightarrow x = -9$

Solution: $(-9, -4)$

18. $\begin{bmatrix} 0.2 & -0.1 & : & 0.07 \\ 0.4 & -0.5 & : & -0.01 \end{bmatrix}$

$\begin{matrix} 5R_1 \rightarrow \\ -2R_1 + R_2 \rightarrow \end{matrix} \begin{bmatrix} 1 & -0.5 & : & 0.35 \\ 0 & -0.3 & : & -0.15 \end{bmatrix}$

$-\frac{1}{0.3}R_2 \rightarrow \begin{bmatrix} 1 & -0.5 & : & 0.35 \\ 0 & 1 & : & 0.5 \end{bmatrix}$

$\begin{cases} x - 0.5y = 0.35 \\ y = 0.5 \end{cases}$

$y = 0.5$

$x - 0.5(0.5) = 0.35 \Rightarrow x = 0.6$

20. $\begin{bmatrix} 2 & 3 & 3 & : & 3 \\ 6 & 6 & 12 & : & 13 \\ 12 & 9 & -1 & : & 2 \end{bmatrix}$

$\begin{matrix} -3R_1 + R_2 \rightarrow \\ -6R_1 + R_3 \rightarrow \end{matrix} \begin{bmatrix} 2 & 3 & 3 & : & 3 \\ 0 & -3 & 3 & : & 4 \\ 0 & -9 & -19 & : & -16 \end{bmatrix}$

$\begin{matrix} R_2 + R_1 \rightarrow \\ \\ -3R_2 + R_3 \rightarrow \end{matrix} \begin{bmatrix} 2 & 0 & 6 & : & 7 \\ 0 & -3 & 3 & : & 4 \\ 0 & 0 & -28 & : & -28 \end{bmatrix}$

$\begin{matrix} \frac{1}{2}R_1 \rightarrow \\ -\frac{1}{3}R_2 \rightarrow \\ -\frac{1}{28}R_3 \rightarrow \end{matrix} \begin{bmatrix} 1 & 0 & 3 & : & \frac{7}{2} \\ 0 & 1 & -1 & : & -\frac{4}{3} \\ 0 & 0 & 1 & : & 1 \end{bmatrix}$

$\begin{cases} x + 3z = \frac{7}{2} \\ y - z = -\frac{4}{3} \\ z = 1 \end{cases}$

$z = 1$

$y - 1 = -\frac{4}{3} \Rightarrow y = -\frac{1}{3}$

$x + 3(1) = \frac{7}{2} \Rightarrow x = \frac{1}{2}$

Solution: $\left(\frac{1}{2}, -\frac{1}{3}, 1\right)$

22. $\begin{bmatrix} 1 & 2 & 6 & : & 1 \\ 2 & 5 & 15 & : & 4 \\ 3 & 1 & 3 & : & -6 \end{bmatrix}$

$\begin{matrix} -2R_1 + R_2 \rightarrow \\ -3R_1 + R_3 \rightarrow \end{matrix} \begin{bmatrix} 1 & 2 & 6 & : & 1 \\ 0 & 1 & 3 & : & 2 \\ 0 & -5 & -15 & : & -9 \end{bmatrix}$

$5R_2 + R_3 \rightarrow \begin{bmatrix} 1 & 2 & 6 & : & 1 \\ 0 & 1 & 3 & : & 2 \\ 0 & 0 & 0 & : & 1 \end{bmatrix}$

Because the last row consists of all zeros except for the last entry, the system is inconsistent and there is no solution.

24.

$$\begin{bmatrix} 1 & 2 & 0 & 1 & \vdots & 3 \\ 0 & -3 & 3 & 0 & \vdots & 0 \\ 4 & 4 & 1 & 2 & \vdots & 0 \\ 2 & 0 & 1 & 0 & \vdots & 3 \end{bmatrix}$$

$$\begin{matrix} \\ -\frac{1}{3}R_2 \rightarrow \\ -4R_1 + R_3 \rightarrow \\ -2R_1 + R_3 \rightarrow \end{matrix} \begin{bmatrix} 1 & 2 & 0 & 1 & \vdots & 3 \\ 0 & 1 & -1 & 0 & \vdots & 0 \\ 0 & -4 & 1 & -2 & \vdots & -12 \\ 0 & -4 & 1 & -2 & \vdots & -3 \end{bmatrix}$$

$$\begin{matrix} \\ \\ \\ -R_3 + R_4 \rightarrow \end{matrix} \begin{bmatrix} 1 & 2 & 0 & 1 & \vdots & 3 \\ 0 & 1 & -1 & 0 & \vdots & 0 \\ 0 & -4 & 1 & -2 & \vdots & -12 \\ 0 & 0 & 0 & 0 & \vdots & 9 \end{bmatrix}$$

Because the last row consists of all zeros except for the last entry, the system is inconsistent and there is no solution.

26. $3x - 2 = A(x - 3)^2 + B(x - 4)(x - 3) + C(x - 4)$

$3x - 2 = A(x^2 - 6x + 9) + B(x^2 - 7x + 12) + Cx - 4C$

$3x - 2 = Ax^2 - 6Ax + 9A + Bx^2 - 7Bx + 12B + Cx - 4C$

$3x - 2 = (A + B)x^2 + (-6A - 7B + C)x + (9A + 12B - 4C)$

Equating coefficients of corresponding terms:

$$\begin{cases} 0 = & A + & B \\ 3 = & -6A - & 7B + & C \\ -2 = & 9A + & 12B - 4C \end{cases}$$

$$\begin{bmatrix} 1 & 1 & 0 & \vdots & 0 \\ -6 & -7 & 1 & \vdots & 3 \\ 9 & 12 & -4 & \vdots & -2 \end{bmatrix}$$

$$\begin{matrix} 6R_1 + R_2 \rightarrow \\ -9R_1 + R_3 \rightarrow \end{matrix} \begin{bmatrix} 1 & 1 & 0 & \vdots & 0 \\ 0 & -1 & 1 & \vdots & 3 \\ 0 & 3 & -4 & \vdots & -2 \end{bmatrix}$$

$$\begin{matrix} \\ -R_2 \rightarrow \\ \end{matrix} \begin{bmatrix} 1 & 1 & 0 & \vdots & 0 \\ 0 & 1 & -1 & \vdots & -3 \\ 0 & 3 & -4 & \vdots & -2 \end{bmatrix}$$

$$\begin{matrix} \\ \\ -3R_2 + R_3 \rightarrow \end{matrix} \begin{bmatrix} 1 & 1 & 0 & \vdots & 0 \\ 0 & 1 & -1 & \vdots & -3 \\ 0 & 0 & -1 & \vdots & 7 \end{bmatrix}$$

$$\begin{matrix} \\ \\ -R_3 \rightarrow \end{matrix} \begin{bmatrix} 1 & 1 & 0 & \vdots & 0 \\ 0 & 1 & -1 & \vdots & -3 \\ 0 & 0 & 1 & \vdots & -7 \end{bmatrix}$$

$$\begin{cases} A + B & = 0 \\ B - C & = -3 \\ C & = -7 \end{cases}$$

$B - (-7) = -3 \Rightarrow B = -10$

$A + (-10) = 0 \Rightarrow A = 10$

$$\frac{3x - 2}{(x - 4)(x - 3)^2} = \frac{10}{x - 4} - \frac{10}{x - 3} - \frac{7}{(x - 3)^2}$$

28. $\begin{cases} 4x + 4y + 4z = 5 \\ 4x - 2y - 8z = 1 \\ 5x + 3y + 8z = 6 \end{cases}$

$$\begin{bmatrix} 4 & 4 & 4 & \vdots & 5 \\ 4 & -2 & -8 & \vdots & 1 \\ 5 & 3 & 8 & \vdots & 6 \end{bmatrix}$$

$\frac{1}{4}R_1 \rightarrow \begin{bmatrix} 1 & 1 & 1 & \vdots & \frac{5}{4} \\ 4 & -2 & -8 & \vdots & 1 \\ 5 & 3 & 8 & \vdots & 6 \end{bmatrix}$

$\begin{matrix} \\ -4R_1 + R_2 \rightarrow \\ -5R_1 + R_3 \rightarrow \end{matrix} \begin{bmatrix} 1 & 1 & 1 & \vdots & \frac{5}{4} \\ 0 & -6 & -12 & \vdots & -4 \\ 0 & -2 & 3 & \vdots & -\frac{1}{4} \end{bmatrix}$

$-\frac{1}{6}R_2 \rightarrow \begin{bmatrix} 1 & 1 & 1 & \vdots & \frac{5}{4} \\ 0 & 1 & 2 & \vdots & \frac{2}{3} \\ 0 & -2 & 3 & \vdots & -\frac{1}{4} \end{bmatrix}$

$\begin{matrix} -R_2 + R_1 \rightarrow \\ \\ 2R_2 + R_3 \rightarrow \end{matrix} \begin{bmatrix} 1 & 0 & -1 & \vdots & \frac{7}{12} \\ 0 & 1 & 2 & \vdots & \frac{2}{3} \\ 0 & 0 & 7 & \vdots & \frac{13}{12} \end{bmatrix}$

$\frac{1}{7}R_3 \rightarrow \begin{bmatrix} 1 & 0 & -1 & \vdots & \frac{7}{12} \\ 0 & 1 & 2 & \vdots & \frac{2}{3} \\ 0 & 0 & 1 & \vdots & \frac{13}{84} \end{bmatrix}$

$\begin{matrix} R_3 + R_1 \rightarrow \\ -2R_3 + R_2 \rightarrow \\ \end{matrix} \begin{bmatrix} 1 & 0 & 0 & \vdots & \frac{31}{42} \\ 0 & 1 & 0 & \vdots & \frac{5}{14} \\ 0 & 0 & 1 & \vdots & \frac{13}{84} \end{bmatrix}$

$x = \frac{31}{42}$

$y = \frac{5}{14}$

$z = \frac{13}{84}$

Solution: $\left(\frac{31}{42}, \frac{5}{14}, \frac{13}{84}\right)$

30. $\begin{cases} -3x + y + 7z = -20 \\ 5x - 2y - z = 34 \\ -x + y + 4z = -8 \end{cases}$

$$\begin{bmatrix} -3 & 1 & 7 & \vdots & -20 \\ 5 & -2 & -1 & \vdots & 34 \\ -1 & 1 & 4 & \vdots & -8 \end{bmatrix}$$

$\begin{matrix} R_3 \\ \\ R_1 \end{matrix} \begin{bmatrix} -1 & 1 & 4 & \vdots & -8 \\ 5 & -2 & -1 & \vdots & 34 \\ -3 & 1 & 7 & \vdots & -20 \end{bmatrix}$

$-1R_1 \begin{bmatrix} 1 & -1 & -4 & \vdots & 8 \\ 5 & -2 & -1 & \vdots & 34 \\ -3 & 1 & 7 & \vdots & -20 \end{bmatrix}$

$\begin{matrix} -5R_1 + R_2 \rightarrow \\ 3R_1 + R_3 \rightarrow \end{matrix} \begin{bmatrix} 1 & -1 & -4 & \vdots & 8 \\ 0 & 3 & 19 & \vdots & -6 \\ 0 & -2 & -5 & \vdots & 4 \end{bmatrix}$

$\frac{1}{3}R_2 \rightarrow \begin{bmatrix} 1 & -1 & -4 & \vdots & 8 \\ 0 & 1 & \frac{19}{3} & \vdots & -2 \\ 0 & -2 & -5 & \vdots & 4 \end{bmatrix}$

$\begin{matrix} R_2 + R_1 \rightarrow \\ \\ 2R_2 + R_3 \rightarrow \end{matrix} \begin{bmatrix} 1 & 0 & \frac{7}{3} & \vdots & 6 \\ 0 & 1 & \frac{19}{3} & \vdots & -2 \\ 0 & 0 & \frac{23}{3} & \vdots & 0 \end{bmatrix}$

$\frac{3}{23}R_3 \rightarrow \begin{bmatrix} 1 & 0 & \frac{7}{3} & \vdots & 6 \\ 0 & 1 & \frac{19}{3} & \vdots & -2 \\ 0 & 0 & 1 & \vdots & 0 \end{bmatrix}$

$\begin{matrix} -\frac{7}{3}R_3 + R_1 \rightarrow \\ \\ -\frac{19}{3}R_3 + R_2 \rightarrow \end{matrix} \begin{bmatrix} 1 & 0 & 0 & \vdots & 6 \\ 0 & 1 & 0 & \vdots & -2 \\ 0 & 0 & 1 & \vdots & 0 \end{bmatrix}$

$x = 6, y = -2, z = 0$

Solution: $(6, -2, 0)$

32. Use the reduced row-echelon form feature of the graphing utility.

$$\begin{bmatrix} 4 & 12 & 2 & \vdots & 20 \\ 1 & 6 & 4 & \vdots & 12 \\ 1 & 6 & 1 & \vdots & 8 \\ -2 & -10 & -2 & \vdots & -10 \end{bmatrix} \Longrightarrow \begin{bmatrix} 1 & 0 & 0 & \vdots & 0 \\ 0 & 1 & 0 & \vdots & 0 \\ 0 & 0 & 1 & \vdots & 0 \\ 0 & 0 & 0 & \vdots & 1 \end{bmatrix}$$

The system is inconsistent and there is no solution.

34. $\begin{bmatrix} -1 & 0 \\ x & 5 \\ -4 & y \end{bmatrix} = \begin{bmatrix} -1 & 0 \\ 8 & 5 \\ -4 & 0 \end{bmatrix} \Longrightarrow x = 8, y = 0$

36. $\begin{bmatrix} -9 & 4 & 2 & -5 \\ 0 & -3 & 7 & -4 \\ 6 & -1 & 1 & 0 \end{bmatrix} = \begin{bmatrix} -9 & 4 & x-10 & -5 \\ 0 & -3 & 7 & 2y \\ \frac{1}{2}x & -1 & 1 & 0 \end{bmatrix}$

$\left. \begin{matrix} 6 = \frac{1}{2}x \\ 2 = x - 10 \\ -4 = 2y \end{matrix} \right\} x = 12, y = -2$

38. Since A and B are both of order 3×2, $A + 3B$ can be performed.

40. Since A and B are not of the same order, $A + 3B$ cannot be performed.

42. Since the matrices are not of the same order, the operation cannot be performed.

44. $-\begin{bmatrix} 8 & -1 & 8 \\ -2 & 4 & 12 \\ 0 & -6 & 0 \end{bmatrix} - 5\begin{bmatrix} -2 & 0 & -4 \\ 3 & -1 & 1 \\ 6 & 12 & -8 \end{bmatrix}$

$= \begin{bmatrix} -8 & 1 & -8 \\ 2 & -4 & -12 \\ 0 & 6 & 0 \end{bmatrix} + \begin{bmatrix} 10 & 0 & 20 \\ -15 & 5 & -5 \\ -30 & -60 & 40 \end{bmatrix}$

$= \begin{bmatrix} -8 + 10 & 1 + 0 & -8 + 20 \\ 2 - 15 & -4 + 5 & -12 - 5 \\ 0 - 30 & 6 - 60 & 0 + 40 \end{bmatrix} = \begin{bmatrix} 2 & 1 & 12 \\ -13 & 1 & -17 \\ -30 & -54 & 40 \end{bmatrix}$

46. $-5\begin{bmatrix} 2 & 0 \\ 7 & -2 \\ 8 & 2 \end{bmatrix} + 4\begin{bmatrix} 4 & -2 \\ 6 & 11 \\ -1 & 3 \end{bmatrix} = \begin{bmatrix} 6 & -8 \\ -11 & 54 \\ -44 & 2 \end{bmatrix}$

48. $X = \frac{1}{6}(4A + 3B) = \frac{1}{6}\left(4\begin{bmatrix} -4 & 0 \\ 1 & -5 \\ -3 & 2 \end{bmatrix} + 3\begin{bmatrix} 1 & 2 \\ -2 & 1 \\ 4 & 4 \end{bmatrix} \right) = \frac{1}{6}\left(\begin{bmatrix} -16 & 0 \\ 4 & -20 \\ -12 & 8 \end{bmatrix} + \begin{bmatrix} 3 & 6 \\ -6 & 3 \\ 12 & 12 \end{bmatrix} \right) = \frac{1}{6}\begin{bmatrix} -16 + 3 & 0 + 6 \\ 4 - 6 & -20 + 3 \\ -12 + 12 & 8 + 12 \end{bmatrix}$

$= \frac{1}{6}\begin{bmatrix} -13 & 6 \\ -2 & -17 \\ 0 & 20 \end{bmatrix} = \begin{bmatrix} -\frac{13}{6} & 1 \\ -\frac{1}{3} & -\frac{17}{6} \\ 0 & \frac{10}{3} \end{bmatrix}$

50. $X = \frac{1}{3}(2A - 5B) = \frac{1}{3}\left(2\begin{bmatrix} -4 & 0 \\ 1 & -5 \\ -3 & 2 \end{bmatrix} - 5\begin{bmatrix} 1 & 2 \\ -2 & 1 \\ 4 & 4 \end{bmatrix} \right) = \frac{1}{3}\left(\begin{bmatrix} -8 & 0 \\ 2 & -10 \\ -6 & 4 \end{bmatrix} + \begin{bmatrix} -5 & -10 \\ 10 & -5 \\ -20 & -20 \end{bmatrix} \right) = \frac{1}{3}\begin{bmatrix} -8 - 5 & 0 - 10 \\ 2 + 10 & -10 - 5 \\ -6 - 20 & 4 - 20 \end{bmatrix}$

$= \frac{1}{3}\begin{bmatrix} -13 & -10 \\ 12 & -15 \\ -26 & -16 \end{bmatrix} = \begin{bmatrix} -\frac{13}{3} & -\frac{10}{3} \\ 4 & -5 \\ -\frac{26}{3} & -\frac{16}{3} \end{bmatrix}$

52. Not possible because the number and columns of A does not equal the number of rows of B.

54. Yes, AB exists because the number of columns of A equals the number of rows of B.

56. Not possible because the number of columns of the first matrix does not equal the number of rows of the second matrix.

58. $\begin{bmatrix} 1 & 3 & 2 \\ 0 & 2 & -4 \\ 0 & 0 & 3 \end{bmatrix}\begin{bmatrix} 4 & -3 & 2 \\ 0 & 3 & -1 \\ 0 & 0 & 2 \end{bmatrix} = \begin{bmatrix} 1(4) & 1(-3) + 3(3) & 1(2) + 3(-1) + 2(2) \\ 0 & 2(3) & 2(-1) + (-4)(2) \\ 0 & 0 & 3(2) \end{bmatrix}$

$= \begin{bmatrix} 4 & 6 & 3 \\ 0 & 6 & -10 \\ 0 & 0 & 6 \end{bmatrix}$

60. $\begin{bmatrix} 4 & -2 & 6 \end{bmatrix}\begin{bmatrix} -2 & 1 \\ 0 & -3 \\ 2 & 0 \end{bmatrix} = \begin{bmatrix} 4(-2) - 2(0) + 6(2) & 4(1) - 2(-3) + 6(0) \end{bmatrix}$

$= \begin{bmatrix} 4 & 10 \end{bmatrix}$

62. $-3\begin{bmatrix} 1 & -1 \\ 4 & 2 \end{bmatrix}\left(\begin{bmatrix} 0 & 3 \\ 1 & 2 \end{bmatrix}\begin{bmatrix} 1 & 0 \\ 5 & -3 \end{bmatrix}\right) = \begin{bmatrix} -3 & 3 \\ -12 & -6 \end{bmatrix}\begin{bmatrix} 0(1) + 3(5) & 0(0) + 3(-3) \\ 1(1) + 2(5) & 1(0) + 2(-3) \end{bmatrix}$

$= \begin{bmatrix} -3 & 3 \\ -12 & -6 \end{bmatrix}\begin{bmatrix} 15 & -9 \\ 11 & -6 \end{bmatrix}$

$= \begin{bmatrix} -3(15) + 3(11) & -3(-9) + 3(-6) \\ -12(15) - 6(11) & -12(-9) - 6(-6) \end{bmatrix}$

$= \begin{bmatrix} -12 & 9 \\ -246 & 144 \end{bmatrix}$

64. $\begin{bmatrix} -2 & 3 & 10 \\ 4 & -2 & 2 \end{bmatrix}\begin{bmatrix} 1 & 1 \\ -5 & 2 \\ 3 & 2 \end{bmatrix} = \begin{bmatrix} 13 & 24 \\ 20 & 4 \end{bmatrix}$

66. $\begin{cases} 2x + 3y + z = 10 \\ 2x - 3y - 3z = 22 \\ 4x - 2y + 3z = -2 \end{cases}$

$\begin{bmatrix} 2 & 3 & 1 \\ 2 & -3 & -3 \\ 4 & -2 & 3 \end{bmatrix}\begin{bmatrix} x \\ y \\ z \end{bmatrix} = \begin{bmatrix} 10 \\ 22 \\ -2 \end{bmatrix}$

68. $AB = \begin{bmatrix} -4 & -1 \\ 7 & 2 \end{bmatrix}\begin{bmatrix} -2 & -1 \\ 7 & 4 \end{bmatrix} = \begin{bmatrix} -4(-2) + (-1)(7) & -4(-1) + (-1)(4) \\ 7(-2) + 2(7) & 7(-1) + 2(4) \end{bmatrix}$

$= \begin{bmatrix} 1 & 0 \\ 0 & 1 \end{bmatrix} = I$

$BA = \begin{bmatrix} -2 & -1 \\ 7 & 4 \end{bmatrix}\begin{bmatrix} -4 & -1 \\ 7 & 2 \end{bmatrix} = \begin{bmatrix} -2(-4) + (-1)(7) & -2(-1) + (-1)(2) \\ 7(-4) + 4(7) & 7(-1) + 4(2) \end{bmatrix}$

$= \begin{bmatrix} 1 & 0 \\ 0 & 1 \end{bmatrix} = I$

70. $AB = \begin{bmatrix} 1 & 1 & 0 \\ 1 & 0 & 1 \\ 6 & 2 & 3 \end{bmatrix}\begin{bmatrix} -2 & -3 & 1 \\ 3 & 3 & -1 \\ 2 & 4 & -1 \end{bmatrix}$

$= \begin{bmatrix} 1(-2) + 1(3) + 0(2) & 1(-3) + 1(3) + 0(4) & 1(1) + 1(-1) + 0(-1) \\ 1(-2) + 0(3) + 1(2) & 1(-3) + 0(3) + 1(4) & 1(1) + 0(-1) + 1(-1) \\ 6(-2) + 2(3) + 3(2) & 6(-3) + 2(3) + 3(4) & 6(1) + 2(-1) + 3(-1) \end{bmatrix}$

$= \begin{bmatrix} 1 & 0 & 0 \\ 0 & 1 & 0 \\ 0 & 0 & 1 \end{bmatrix} = I$

$BA = \begin{bmatrix} -2 & -3 & 1 \\ 3 & 3 & -1 \\ 2 & 4 & -1 \end{bmatrix}\begin{bmatrix} 1 & 1 & 0 \\ 1 & 0 & 1 \\ 6 & 2 & 3 \end{bmatrix}$

$= \begin{bmatrix} -2(1) + (-3)(1) + 1(6) & -2(1) + (-3)(0) + 1(2) & -2(0) + (-3)(1) + 1(3) \\ 3(1) + 3(1) + (-1)(6) & 3(1) + 3(0) + (-1)(2) & 3(0) + 3(1) + (-1)(3) \\ 2(1) + 4(1) + (-1)(6) & 2(1) + 4(0) + (-1)(2) & 2(0) + 4(1) + (-1)(3) \end{bmatrix}$

$= \begin{bmatrix} 1 & 0 & 0 \\ 0 & 1 & 0 \\ 0 & 0 & 1 \end{bmatrix} = I$

72. $[A \; : \; I] = \begin{bmatrix} -6 & 5 & : & 1 & 0 \\ -5 & 4 & : & 0 & 1 \end{bmatrix}$

$-\frac{1}{6}R_1 \rightarrow \begin{bmatrix} 1 & -\frac{5}{6} & : & -\frac{1}{6} & 0 \\ -5 & 4 & : & 0 & 1 \end{bmatrix}$

$5R_1 + R_2 \rightarrow \begin{bmatrix} 1 & -\frac{5}{6} & : & -\frac{1}{6} & 0 \\ 0 & -\frac{1}{6} & : & -\frac{5}{6} & 1 \end{bmatrix}$

$-6R_2 \rightarrow \begin{bmatrix} 1 & -\frac{5}{6} & : & -\frac{1}{6} & 0 \\ 0 & 1 & : & 5 & -6 \end{bmatrix}$

$\frac{5}{6}R_2 + R_1 \rightarrow \begin{bmatrix} 1 & 0 & : & 4 & -5 \\ 0 & 1 & : & 5 & -6 \end{bmatrix} = [I \; : \; A^{-1}]$

$A^{-1} = \begin{bmatrix} 4 & -5 \\ 5 & -6 \end{bmatrix}$

74. $[A \; : \; I] = \begin{bmatrix} -1 & -2 & -2 & : & 1 & 0 & 0 \\ 3 & 7 & 9 & : & 0 & 1 & 0 \\ 1 & 4 & 7 & : & 0 & 0 & 1 \end{bmatrix}$

$-R_1 \rightarrow \begin{bmatrix} 1 & 2 & 2 & : & -1 & 0 & 0 \\ 3 & 7 & 9 & : & 0 & 1 & 0 \\ 1 & 4 & 7 & : & 0 & 0 & 1 \end{bmatrix}$

$\begin{matrix} \\ -3R_1 + R_2 \rightarrow \\ -R_1 + R_3 \rightarrow \end{matrix} \begin{bmatrix} 1 & 2 & 2 & : & -1 & 0 & 0 \\ 0 & 1 & 3 & : & 3 & 1 & 0 \\ 0 & 2 & 5 & : & 1 & 0 & 1 \end{bmatrix}$

$\begin{matrix} -2R_2 + R_1 \rightarrow \\ \\ -2R_2 + R_3 \rightarrow \end{matrix} \begin{bmatrix} 1 & 0 & -4 & : & -7 & -2 & 0 \\ 0 & 1 & 3 & : & 3 & 1 & 0 \\ 0 & 0 & -1 & : & -5 & -2 & 1 \end{bmatrix}$

$\begin{matrix} -4R_3 + R_1 \rightarrow \\ 3R_3 + R_2 \rightarrow \\ -R_3 \rightarrow \end{matrix} \begin{bmatrix} 1 & 0 & 0 & : & 13 & 6 & -4 \\ 0 & 1 & 0 & : & -12 & -5 & 3 \\ 0 & 0 & 1 & : & 5 & 2 & -1 \end{bmatrix} = [I \; : \; A^{-1}]$

$A^{-1} = \begin{bmatrix} 13 & 6 & -4 \\ -12 & -5 & 3 \\ 5 & 2 & -1 \end{bmatrix}$

76. $\begin{bmatrix} 2 & 6 \\ 3 & -6 \end{bmatrix}^{-1} = \begin{bmatrix} \frac{1}{5} & \frac{1}{5} \\ \frac{1}{10} & -\frac{1}{15} \end{bmatrix}$

78. $\begin{bmatrix} 2 & 0 & 3 \\ -1 & 1 & 1 \\ 2 & -2 & 1 \end{bmatrix}^{-1} = \begin{bmatrix} \frac{1}{2} & -1 & -\frac{1}{2} \\ \frac{1}{2} & -\frac{2}{3} & -\frac{5}{6} \\ 0 & \frac{2}{3} & \frac{1}{3} \end{bmatrix}$

80. $A = \begin{bmatrix} -7 & 2 \\ -8 & 2 \end{bmatrix}$

$A^{-1} = \frac{1}{-7(2) - 2(-8)} \begin{bmatrix} 2 & -2 \\ 8 & -7 \end{bmatrix} = \frac{1}{2} \begin{bmatrix} 2 & -2 \\ 8 & -7 \end{bmatrix} = \begin{bmatrix} 1 & -1 \\ 4 & -\frac{7}{2} \end{bmatrix}$

82. $A = \begin{bmatrix} -\frac{1}{2} & 20 \\ \frac{3}{10} & -6 \end{bmatrix}$

$A^{-1} = \dfrac{1}{-\frac{1}{2}(-6) - 20\left(\frac{3}{10}\right)} \begin{bmatrix} -6 & -20 \\ -\frac{3}{10} & -\frac{1}{2} \end{bmatrix} = -\dfrac{1}{3} \begin{bmatrix} -6 & -20 \\ -\frac{3}{10} & -\frac{1}{2} \end{bmatrix}$

$\qquad = \begin{bmatrix} 2 & \frac{20}{3} \\ \frac{1}{10} & \frac{1}{6} \end{bmatrix}$

84. $\begin{cases} -x + 4y = 8 \\ 2x - 7y = -5 \end{cases}$

$\begin{bmatrix} x \\ y \end{bmatrix} = \begin{bmatrix} -1 & 4 \\ 2 & -7 \end{bmatrix}^{-1} \begin{bmatrix} 8 \\ -5 \end{bmatrix} = \begin{bmatrix} 7 & 4 \\ 2 & 1 \end{bmatrix} \begin{bmatrix} 8 \\ -5 \end{bmatrix}$

$\qquad = \begin{bmatrix} 7(8) + 4(-5) \\ 2(8) + 1(-5) \end{bmatrix} = \begin{bmatrix} 36 \\ 11 \end{bmatrix}$

Solution: $(36, 11)$

86. $\begin{cases} -3x + 10y = 8 \\ 5x - 17y = -13 \end{cases}$

$\begin{bmatrix} x \\ y \end{bmatrix} = \begin{bmatrix} -3 & 10 \\ 5 & -17 \end{bmatrix}^{-1} \begin{bmatrix} 8 \\ -13 \end{bmatrix} = \begin{bmatrix} -17 & -10 \\ -5 & -3 \end{bmatrix} \begin{bmatrix} 8 \\ -13 \end{bmatrix}$

$\qquad = \begin{bmatrix} -17(8) + (-10)(-13) \\ -5(8) + (-3)(-13) \end{bmatrix} = \begin{bmatrix} -6 \\ -1 \end{bmatrix}$

Solution: $(-6, -1)$

88. $\begin{cases} 3x + 2y - z = 6 \\ x - y + 2z = -1 \\ 5x + y + z = 7 \end{cases}$

$\begin{bmatrix} x \\ y \\ z \end{bmatrix} = \begin{bmatrix} 3 & 2 & -1 \\ 1 & -1 & 2 \\ 5 & 1 & 1 \end{bmatrix}^{-1} \begin{bmatrix} 6 \\ -1 \\ 7 \end{bmatrix} = \begin{bmatrix} -1 & -1 & 1 \\ 3 & \frac{8}{3} & -\frac{7}{3} \\ 2 & \frac{7}{3} & -\frac{5}{3} \end{bmatrix} \begin{bmatrix} 6 \\ -1 \\ 7 \end{bmatrix}$

$\qquad = \begin{bmatrix} -1(6) - 1(-1) + 1(7) \\ 3(6) + \frac{8}{3}(-1) - \frac{7}{3}(7) \\ 2(6) + \frac{7}{3}(-1) - \frac{5}{3}(7) \end{bmatrix} = \begin{bmatrix} 2 \\ -1 \\ -2 \end{bmatrix}$

Solution: $(2, -1, -2)$

90. $\begin{cases} -2x + y + 2z = -13 \\ -x - 4y + z = -11 \\ -y - z = 0 \end{cases}$

$\begin{bmatrix} x \\ y \\ z \end{bmatrix} = \begin{bmatrix} -2 & 1 & 2 \\ -1 & -4 & 1 \\ 0 & -1 & -1 \end{bmatrix}^{-1} \begin{bmatrix} -13 \\ -11 \\ 0 \end{bmatrix} = \begin{bmatrix} -\frac{5}{9} & \frac{1}{9} & -1 \\ \frac{1}{9} & -\frac{2}{9} & 0 \\ -\frac{1}{9} & \frac{2}{9} & -1 \end{bmatrix} \begin{bmatrix} -13 \\ -11 \\ 0 \end{bmatrix}$

$\qquad = \begin{bmatrix} -\frac{5}{9}(-13) + \frac{1}{9}(-11) - 1(0) \\ \frac{1}{9}(-13) - \frac{2}{9}(-11) + 0(0) \\ -\frac{1}{9}(-13) + \frac{2}{9}(-11) - 1(0) \end{bmatrix} = \begin{bmatrix} 6 \\ 1 \\ -1 \end{bmatrix}$

Solution: $(6, 1, -1)$

92. $\begin{cases} x + 2y = -1 \\ 3x + 4y = -5 \end{cases}$

$\begin{bmatrix} x \\ y \end{bmatrix} = \begin{bmatrix} 1 & 2 \\ 3 & 4 \end{bmatrix}^{-1} \begin{bmatrix} -1 \\ -5 \end{bmatrix} = \begin{bmatrix} -2 & 1 \\ \frac{3}{2} & -\frac{1}{2} \end{bmatrix} \begin{bmatrix} -1 \\ -5 \end{bmatrix} = \begin{bmatrix} -3 \\ 1 \end{bmatrix}$

Solution: $(-3, 1)$

94. $\begin{cases} -3x - 3y - 4z = 2 \\ y + z = -1 \\ 4x + 3y + 4z = -1 \end{cases}$

$$\begin{bmatrix} x \\ y \\ z \end{bmatrix} = \begin{bmatrix} -3 & -3 & -4 \\ 0 & 1 & 1 \\ 4 & 3 & 4 \end{bmatrix}^{-1} \begin{bmatrix} 2 \\ -1 \\ -1 \end{bmatrix} = \begin{bmatrix} 1 & 0 & 1 \\ 4 & 4 & 3 \\ -4 & -3 & -3 \end{bmatrix} \begin{bmatrix} 2 \\ -1 \\ -1 \end{bmatrix} = \begin{bmatrix} 1 \\ 1 \\ -2 \end{bmatrix}$$

Solution: $(1, 1, -2)$

96. $\begin{vmatrix} 8 & 5 \\ 2 & -4 \end{vmatrix} = 8(-4) - 5(2) = -42$

98. $\begin{vmatrix} 50 & -30 \\ 10 & 5 \end{vmatrix} = 50(5) - (-30)(10) = 550$

100. $\begin{bmatrix} 2 & -1 \\ 7 & 4 \end{bmatrix}$

(a) $M_{11} = 4$

$M_{12} = 7$

$M_{21} = -1$

$M_{22} = 2$

(b) $C_{11} = M_{11} = 4$

$C_{12} = -M_{12} = -7$

$C_{21} = -M_{21} = 1$

$C_{22} = M_{22} = 2$

102. $\begin{bmatrix} 3 & 2 & -1 \\ -2 & 5 & 0 \\ 1 & 8 & 6 \end{bmatrix}$

(a) $M_{11} = \begin{vmatrix} 5 & 0 \\ 8 & 6 \end{vmatrix} = 30$

$M_{12} = \begin{vmatrix} -2 & 0 \\ 1 & 6 \end{vmatrix} = -12$

$M_{13} = \begin{vmatrix} -2 & 5 \\ 1 & 8 \end{vmatrix} = -21$

$M_{21} = \begin{vmatrix} 2 & -1 \\ 8 & 6 \end{vmatrix} = 20$

$M_{22} = \begin{vmatrix} 3 & -1 \\ 1 & 6 \end{vmatrix} = 19$

$M_{23} = \begin{vmatrix} 3 & 2 \\ 1 & 8 \end{vmatrix} = 22$

$M_{31} = \begin{vmatrix} 2 & -1 \\ 5 & 0 \end{vmatrix} = 5$

$M_{32} = \begin{vmatrix} 3 & -1 \\ -2 & 0 \end{vmatrix} = -2$

$M_{33} = \begin{vmatrix} 3 & 2 \\ -2 & 5 \end{vmatrix} = 19$

(b) $C_{11} = M_{11} = 30$

$C_{12} = -M_{12} = 12$

$C_{13} = M_{13} = -21$

$C_{21} = -M_{21} = -20$

$C_{22} = M_{22} = 19$

$C_{23} = -M_{23} = -22$

$C_{31} = M_{31} = 5$

$C_{32} = -M_{32} = 2$

$C_{33} = M_{33} = 19$

104. Expand using Column 2.

$$\begin{vmatrix} -2 & 4 & 1 \\ -6 & 0 & 2 \\ 5 & 3 & 4 \end{vmatrix} = -4\begin{vmatrix} -6 & 2 \\ 5 & 4 \end{vmatrix} - 3\begin{vmatrix} -2 & 1 \\ -6 & 2 \end{vmatrix}$$

$$= -4(-34) - 3(2) = 130$$

106. Expand along Row 1.

$$\begin{vmatrix} 3 & 0 & -4 & 0 \\ 0 & 8 & 1 & 2 \\ 6 & 1 & 8 & 2 \\ 0 & 3 & -4 & 1 \end{vmatrix} = 3\begin{vmatrix} 8 & 1 & 2 \\ 1 & 8 & 2 \\ 3 & -4 & 1 \end{vmatrix} + (-4)\begin{vmatrix} 0 & 8 & 2 \\ 6 & 1 & 2 \\ 0 & 3 & 1 \end{vmatrix}$$

$$= 3[8(8 - (-8)) - 1(1 - 6) + 2(-4 - 24)] - 4[0 - 6(8 - 6) + 0]$$

$$= 3[128 + 5 - 56] - 4[-12]$$

$$= 279$$

108. $\begin{cases} 5x - 2y = 6 \\ -11x + 3y = -23 \end{cases}$

$$x = \frac{\begin{vmatrix} 6 & -2 \\ -23 & 3 \end{vmatrix}}{\begin{vmatrix} 5 & -2 \\ -11 & 3 \end{vmatrix}} = \frac{-28}{-7} = 4$$

$$y = \frac{\begin{vmatrix} 5 & 6 \\ -11 & -23 \end{vmatrix}}{\begin{vmatrix} 5 & -2 \\ -11 & 3 \end{vmatrix}} = \frac{-49}{-7} = 7$$

Solution: $(4, 7)$

110. $\begin{cases} -2x + 3y - 5z = -11 \\ 4x - y + z = -3 \\ -x - 4y + 6z = 15 \end{cases}$

$$D = \begin{vmatrix} -2 & 3 & -5 \\ 4 & -1 & 1 \\ -1 & -4 & 6 \end{vmatrix} = -2(-1)^2\begin{vmatrix} -1 & 1 \\ -4 & 6 \end{vmatrix} + 4(-1)^3\begin{vmatrix} 3 & -5 \\ -4 & 6 \end{vmatrix} - 1(-1)^4\begin{vmatrix} 3 & -5 \\ -1 & 1 \end{vmatrix}$$

$$= -2(-2) - 4(-2) - (-2) = 14$$

$$x = \frac{\begin{vmatrix} -11 & 3 & -5 \\ -3 & -1 & 1 \\ 15 & -4 & 6 \end{vmatrix}}{14} = \frac{-11(-1)^2\begin{vmatrix} -1 & 1 \\ -4 & 6 \end{vmatrix} - 3(-1)^3\begin{vmatrix} 3 & -5 \\ -4 & 6 \end{vmatrix} + 15(-1)^4\begin{vmatrix} 3 & -5 \\ -1 & 1 \end{vmatrix}}{14}$$

$$= \frac{-11(-2) + 3(-2) + 15(-2)}{14} = \frac{-14}{14} = -1$$

$$y = \frac{\begin{vmatrix} -2 & -11 & -5 \\ 4 & -3 & 1 \\ -1 & 15 & 6 \end{vmatrix}}{14} = \frac{-2(-1)^2\begin{vmatrix} -3 & 1 \\ 15 & 6 \end{vmatrix} + 4(-1)^3\begin{vmatrix} -11 & -5 \\ 15 & 6 \end{vmatrix} - 1(-1)^4\begin{vmatrix} -11 & -5 \\ -3 & 1 \end{vmatrix}}{14}$$

$$= \frac{-2(-33) - 4(9) - 1(-26)}{14} = \frac{56}{14} = 4$$

—CONTINUED—

110. —CONTINUED—

$$z = \frac{\begin{vmatrix} -2 & 3 & -11 \\ 4 & -1 & -3 \\ -1 & -4 & 15 \end{vmatrix}}{14} = \frac{-2(-1)^2 \begin{vmatrix} -1 & -3 \\ -4 & 15 \end{vmatrix} + 4(-1)^3 \begin{vmatrix} 3 & -11 \\ -4 & 15 \end{vmatrix} - 1(-1)^4 \begin{vmatrix} 3 & -11 \\ -1 & -3 \end{vmatrix}}{14}$$

$$= \frac{-2(-27) - 4(1) - 1(-20)}{14} = \frac{70}{14} = 5$$

Solution: $(-1, 4, 5)$

112. x = number of carnations,

y = number of roses

$$\begin{cases} x + y = 12 \\ 1.50x + 3.50y = 30.00 \end{cases}$$

$$x = \frac{\begin{vmatrix} 12 & 1 \\ 30 & 3.50 \end{vmatrix}}{\begin{vmatrix} 1 & 1 \\ 1.50 & 3.50 \end{vmatrix}} = \frac{12}{2} = 6$$

$$y = \frac{\begin{vmatrix} 1 & 12 \\ 1.50 & 30 \end{vmatrix}}{\begin{vmatrix} 1 & 1 \\ 1.50 & 3.50 \end{vmatrix}} = \frac{12}{2} = 6$$

Solution: 6 carnations, 6 roses

114. $(-1, 2)$, $(0, 3)$, $(1, 6)$

$y = ax^2 + bx + c$

$$\begin{cases} a - b + c = 2 \\ c = 3 \\ a + b + c = 6 \end{cases}$$

$$D = \begin{vmatrix} 1 & -1 & 1 \\ 0 & 0 & 1 \\ 1 & 1 & 1 \end{vmatrix} = -2$$

$$a = \frac{\begin{vmatrix} 2 & -1 & 1 \\ 3 & 0 & 1 \\ 6 & 1 & 1 \end{vmatrix}}{-2} = \frac{-2}{-2} = 1$$

$$b = \frac{\begin{vmatrix} 1 & 2 & 1 \\ 0 & 3 & 1 \\ 1 & 6 & 1 \end{vmatrix}}{-2} = \frac{-4}{-2} = 2; \; c = 3$$

Thus, $y = x^2 + 2x + 3$.

116. $(1, 0)$, $(5, 0)$, $(5, 8)$

$$\text{Area} = \frac{1}{2} \begin{vmatrix} 1 & 0 & 1 \\ 5 & 0 & 1 \\ 5 & 8 & 1 \end{vmatrix} \frac{1}{2} \left(1 \begin{vmatrix} 0 & 1 \\ 8 & 1 \end{vmatrix} + 1 \begin{vmatrix} 5 & 0 \\ 5 & 8 \end{vmatrix} \right) = \frac{1}{2}(-8 + 40) = \frac{1}{2}(32)$$

$$= 16 \text{ square units}$$

118. $\left(\frac{1}{2}, 1\right)$, $\left(2, -\frac{5}{2}\right)$, $\left(\frac{3}{2}, 1\right)$

$$\text{Area} = \frac{1}{2} \begin{vmatrix} \frac{1}{2} & 1 & 1 \\ 2 & -\frac{5}{2} & 1 \\ \frac{3}{2} & 1 & 1 \end{vmatrix} = \frac{1}{2} \left(1 \begin{vmatrix} 2 & -\frac{5}{2} \\ \frac{3}{2} & 1 \end{vmatrix} - 1 \begin{vmatrix} \frac{1}{2} & 1 \\ \frac{3}{2} & 1 \end{vmatrix} + 1 \begin{vmatrix} \frac{1}{2} & 1 \\ 2 & -\frac{5}{2} \end{vmatrix} \right)$$

$$= \frac{1}{2} \left(\frac{23}{4} - (-1) + \left(-\frac{13}{4} \right) \right) = \frac{1}{2} \left(\frac{14}{4} \right) = \frac{7}{4} \text{ square units}$$

120. $(-4, 0), (4, 4)$

$$\begin{vmatrix} x & y & 1 \\ -4 & 0 & 1 \\ 4 & 4 & 1 \end{vmatrix} = 0$$

$$1\begin{vmatrix} -4 & 0 \\ 4 & 4 \end{vmatrix} - 1\begin{vmatrix} x & y \\ 4 & 4 \end{vmatrix} + 1\begin{vmatrix} x & y \\ -4 & 0 \end{vmatrix} = 0$$

$$-16 - (4x - 4y) + 4y = 0$$

$$-4x + 8y - 16 = 0$$

$$x - 2y + 4 = 0$$

122. $\left(-\frac{5}{2}, 3\right), \left(\frac{7}{2}, 1\right)$

$$\begin{vmatrix} x & y & 1 \\ -\frac{5}{2} & 3 & 1 \\ \frac{7}{2} & 1 & 1 \end{vmatrix} = 0$$

$$1\begin{vmatrix} -\frac{5}{2} & 3 \\ \frac{7}{2} & 1 \end{vmatrix} - 1\begin{vmatrix} x & y \\ \frac{7}{2} & 1 \end{vmatrix} + 1\begin{vmatrix} x & y \\ -\frac{5}{2} & 3 \end{vmatrix} = 0$$

$$-13 - \left(x - \frac{7}{2}y\right) + \left(3x + \frac{5}{2}y\right) = 0$$

$$2x + 6y - 13 = 0$$

124. L O O K   O U T   B E L O W

$$\begin{bmatrix} 12 & 15 & 15 \end{bmatrix} \begin{bmatrix} 11 & 0 & 15 \end{bmatrix} \begin{bmatrix} 21 & 20 & 0 \end{bmatrix} \begin{bmatrix} 2 & 5 & 12 \end{bmatrix} \begin{bmatrix} 15 & 23 & 0 \end{bmatrix}$$

$$A = \begin{bmatrix} 2 & -2 & 0 \\ 3 & 0 & -3 \\ -6 & 2 & 3 \end{bmatrix}$$

$$\begin{bmatrix} 12 & 15 & 15 \end{bmatrix} \begin{bmatrix} 2 & -2 & 0 \\ 3 & 0 & -3 \\ -6 & 2 & 3 \end{bmatrix} = \begin{bmatrix} -21 & 6 & 0 \end{bmatrix}$$

$$\begin{bmatrix} 11 & 0 & 15 \end{bmatrix} \begin{bmatrix} 2 & -2 & 0 \\ 3 & 0 & -3 \\ -6 & 2 & 3 \end{bmatrix} = \begin{bmatrix} -68 & 8 & 45 \end{bmatrix}$$

$$\begin{bmatrix} 21 & 20 & 0 \end{bmatrix} \begin{bmatrix} 2 & -2 & 0 \\ 3 & 0 & -3 \\ -6 & 2 & 3 \end{bmatrix} = \begin{bmatrix} 102 & -42 & -60 \end{bmatrix}$$

$$\begin{bmatrix} 2 & 5 & 12 \end{bmatrix} \begin{bmatrix} 2 & -2 & 0 \\ 3 & 0 & -3 \\ -6 & 2 & 3 \end{bmatrix} = \begin{bmatrix} -53 & 20 & 21 \end{bmatrix}$$

$$\begin{bmatrix} 15 & 23 & 0 \end{bmatrix} \begin{bmatrix} 2 & -2 & 0 \\ 3 & 0 & -3 \\ -6 & 2 & 3 \end{bmatrix} = \begin{bmatrix} 99 & -30 & -69 \end{bmatrix}$$

Cryptogram: -21 6   0 -68 8   45   102
          -42 -60 -53 20   21   99 -30 -69

126. $A^{-1} = \begin{bmatrix} -1 & 2 & -3 \\ 2 & 1 & 0 \\ 4 & -2 & 5 \end{bmatrix}$

$[-5 \quad 11 \quad -2] \begin{bmatrix} -1 & 2 & -3 \\ 2 & 1 & 0 \\ 4 & -2 & 5 \end{bmatrix} = [19 \quad 5 \quad 5] \quad \text{S} \quad \text{E} \quad \text{E}$

$[370 \quad -265 \quad 225] \begin{bmatrix} -1 & 2 & -3 \\ 2 & 1 & 0 \\ 4 & -2 & 5 \end{bmatrix} = [0 \quad 25 \quad 15] \quad \_ \quad \text{Y} \quad \text{O}$

$[-57 \quad 48 \quad -33] \begin{bmatrix} -1 & 2 & -3 \\ 2 & 1 & 0 \\ 4 & -2 & 5 \end{bmatrix} = [21 \quad 0 \quad 6] \quad \text{U} \quad \_ \quad \text{F}$

$[32 \quad -15 \quad 20] \begin{bmatrix} -1 & 2 & -3 \\ 2 & 1 & 0 \\ 4 & -2 & 5 \end{bmatrix} = [18 \quad 9 \quad 4] \quad \text{R} \quad \text{I} \quad \text{D}$

$[245 \quad -171 \quad 147] \begin{bmatrix} -1 & 2 & -3 \\ 2 & 1 & 0 \\ 4 & -2 & 5 \end{bmatrix} = [1 \quad 25 \quad 0] \quad \text{A} \quad \text{Y} \quad \_$

Message: SEE YOU FRIDAY

128. False. The matrix must be square.

130. The matrix must be square and its determinant nonzero.

132. No. Each matrix is in row-echelon form, but the third matrix cannot be achieved from the first or second matrix with elementary row operations.

134. $\begin{vmatrix} 2 - \lambda & 5 \\ 3 & -8 - \lambda \end{vmatrix} = 0$

$(2 - \lambda)(-8 - \lambda) - 15 = 0$

$-16 + 6\lambda + \lambda^2 - 15 = 0$

$\lambda^2 + 6\lambda - 31 = 0$

$\lambda = \dfrac{-6 \pm \sqrt{36 - 4(-31)}}{2}$

$\lambda = -3 \pm 2\sqrt{10}$

CHAPTER 9
Sequences, Series, and Probability

C H A P T E R 9
Sequences, Series, and Probability

Section 9.1   Sequences and Series
Solutions to Even-Numbered Exercises

2. $a_n = 5n - 3$

$a_1 = 5(1) - 3 = 2$

$a_2 = 5(2) - 3 = 7$

$a_3 = 5(3) - 3 = 12$

$a_4 = 5(4) - 3 = 17$

$a_5 = 5(5) - 3 = 22$

4. $a_n = \left(\frac{1}{2}\right)^n$

$a_1 = \left(\frac{1}{2}\right)^1 = \frac{1}{2}$

$a_2 = \left(\frac{1}{2}\right)^2 = \frac{1}{4}$

$a_3 = \left(\frac{1}{2}\right)^3 = \frac{1}{8}$

$a_4 = \left(\frac{1}{2}\right)^4 = \frac{1}{16}$

$a_5 = \left(\frac{1}{2}\right)^5 = \frac{1}{32}$

6. $a_n = \left(-\frac{1}{2}\right)^n$

$a_1 = \left(-\frac{1}{2}\right)^1 = -\frac{1}{2}$

$a_2 = \left(-\frac{1}{2}\right)^2 = \frac{1}{4}$

$a_3 = \left(-\frac{1}{2}\right)^3 = -\frac{1}{8}$

$a_4 = \left(-\frac{1}{2}\right)^4 = \frac{1}{16}$

$a_5 = \left(-\frac{1}{2}\right)^5 = -\frac{1}{32}$

8. $a_n = \dfrac{n}{n + 2}$

$a_1 = \dfrac{1}{1 + 2} = \dfrac{1}{3}$

$a_2 = \dfrac{2}{2 + 2} = \dfrac{1}{2}$

$a_3 = \dfrac{3}{3 + 2} = \dfrac{3}{5}$

$a_4 = \dfrac{4}{4 + 2} = \dfrac{2}{3}$

$a_5 = \dfrac{5}{5 + 2} = \dfrac{5}{7}$

10. $a_n = \dfrac{3n^2 - n + 4}{2n^2 + 1}$

$a_1 = \dfrac{3(1)^2 - 1 + 4}{2(1)^2 + 1} = 2$

$a_2 = \dfrac{3(2)^2 - 2 + 4}{2(2)^2 + 1} = \dfrac{14}{9}$

$a_3 = \dfrac{3(3) - 3 + 4}{2(3)^2 + 1} = \dfrac{28}{19}$

$a_4 = \dfrac{3(4) - 4 + 4}{2(4)^2 + 1} = \dfrac{16}{11}$

$a_5 = \dfrac{3(5)^2 - 5 + 4}{2(5)^2 + 1} = \dfrac{74}{51}$

12. $a_n = 1 + (-1)^n$

$a_1 = 1 + (-1)^1 = 0$

$a_2 = 1 + (-1)^2 = 2$

$a_3 = 1 + (-1)^3 = 0$

$a_4 = 1 + (-1)^4 = 2$

$a_5 = 1 + (-1)^5 = 0$

14. $a_n = \dfrac{2^n}{3^n}$

$a_1 = \dfrac{2^1}{3^1} = \dfrac{2}{3}$

$a_2 = \dfrac{2^2}{3^2} = \dfrac{4}{9}$

$a_3 = \dfrac{2^3}{3^3} = \dfrac{8}{27}$

$a_4 = \dfrac{2^4}{3^4} = \dfrac{16}{81}$

$a_5 = \dfrac{2^5}{3^5} = \dfrac{32}{243}$

16. $a_n = \dfrac{10}{n^{2/3}} = \dfrac{10}{\sqrt[3]{n^2}}$

$a_1 = \dfrac{10}{1} = 10$

$a_2 = \dfrac{10}{\sqrt[3]{2^2}} = \dfrac{10}{\sqrt[3]{4}}$

$a_3 = \dfrac{10}{\sqrt[3]{3^2}} = \dfrac{10}{\sqrt[3]{9}}$

$a_4 = \dfrac{10}{\sqrt[3]{4^2}} = \dfrac{10}{\sqrt[3]{16}}$

$a_5 = \dfrac{10}{\sqrt[3]{5^2}} = \dfrac{10}{\sqrt[3]{25}}$

18. $a_n = \dfrac{n!}{n}$

$a_1 = \dfrac{1!}{1} = 1$

$a_2 = \dfrac{2!}{2} = 1$

$a_3 = \dfrac{3!}{3} = 2$

$a_4 = \dfrac{4!}{4} = 6$

$a_5 = \dfrac{5!}{5} = 24$

20. $a_n = (-1)^n \left(\dfrac{n}{n+1} \right)$

$a_1 = (-1)^1 \dfrac{1}{1+1} = -\dfrac{1}{2}$

$a_2 = (-1)^2 \dfrac{2}{2 \div 1} = \dfrac{2}{3}$

$a_3 = (-1)^3 \dfrac{3}{3+1} = -\dfrac{3}{4}$

$a_4 = (-1)^4 \dfrac{4}{4+1} = \dfrac{4}{5}$

$a_5 = (-1)^5 \dfrac{5}{5+1} = -\dfrac{5}{6}$

22. $a_n = 0.3$

$a_1 = 0.3$

$a_2 = 0.3$

$a_3 = 0.3$

$a_4 = 0.3$

$a_5 = 0.3$

24. $a_n = n(n^2 - 6)$

$a_1 = 1(1^2 - 6) = -5$

$a_2 = 2(2^2 - 6) = -4$

$a_3 = 3(3^2 - 6) = 9$

$a_4 = 4(4^2 - 6) = 40$

$a_5 = 5(5^2 - 6) = 95$

26. $a_n = (-1)^{n-1}[n(n-1)]$

$a_{16} = (-1)^{16-1}[16(16-1)] = -240$

28. $a_n = \dfrac{n!}{2n}$

$a_8 = \dfrac{8!}{2(8)} = 2520$

30. $a_n = \dfrac{4n^2 - n + 3}{n(n-1)(n+2)}$

$a_{13} = \dfrac{4(13)^2 - 13 + 3}{13(13-1)(13+2)} = \dfrac{37}{130}$

32. $a_n = 2 - \dfrac{4}{n}$

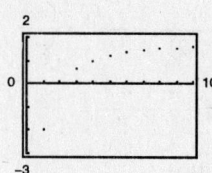

34. $a_n = 8(0.75)^{n-1}$

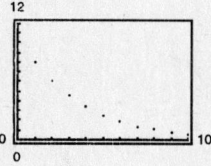

36. $a_n = \dfrac{n^2}{n^2 + 2}$

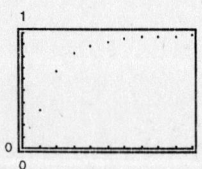

38. $a_n = \dfrac{8n}{n+1}$

$a_n \to 8$ as $n \to \infty$

$a_1 = 4, \quad a_3 = \dfrac{24}{4} = 6$

Matches graph (b).

40. $a_n = \dfrac{4^n}{n!}$

$a_n \to 0$ as $n \to \infty$

$a_1 = 4, a_4 = \dfrac{4^4}{4!} = \dfrac{256}{24} = 10\dfrac{2}{3}$

Matches graph (a).

42. 3, 7, 11, 15, 19, . . .

n: 1 2 3 4 5 . . . n

Terms: 3 7 11 15 19 . . . a_n

Apparent pattern: Each term is one less than four times n, which implies that $a_n = 4n - 1$.

44. 2, -4, 6, -8, 10 . . .

n: 1 2 3 4 5 . . . n

Terms: 2 -4 6 -8 10 . . . a_n

Apparent pattern: Each term is the product of $(-1)^{n+1}$ and twice n, which implies that $a_n = (-1)^{n+1}(2n)$.

46. $\dfrac{1}{2}, \dfrac{-1}{4}, \dfrac{1}{8}, \dfrac{-1}{16}, \cdots$

n: 1   2   3   4 $\cdots$ n

Terms: $\dfrac{1}{2}$ $\dfrac{-1}{4}$ $\dfrac{1}{8}$ $\dfrac{-1}{16}$ $\cdots$ a_n

Apparent pattern: Each term is $(-1)^{n-1}$ divided by 2 raised to the n, which implies that

$$a_n = \frac{(-1)^{n+1}}{2^n}.$$

48. $\dfrac{1}{3}, \dfrac{2}{9}, \dfrac{4}{27}, \dfrac{8}{81}, \cdots$

n: 1   2   3   4 $\cdots$ n

Terms: $\dfrac{1}{3}$ $\dfrac{2}{9}$ $\dfrac{4}{27}$ $\dfrac{8}{81}$ $\cdots$ a_n

Apparent pattern: Each term is 2^{n-1} divided by 3 raised to the n, which implies that

$$a_n = \frac{2^{n-1}}{3^n}.$$

50. $1, \dfrac{1}{2}, \dfrac{1}{6}, \dfrac{1}{24}, \dfrac{1}{120}, \cdots$

n: 1   2   3   4   5 $\cdots$ n

Terms: 1 $\dfrac{1}{2}$ $\dfrac{1}{6}$ $\dfrac{1}{24}$ $\dfrac{1}{120}$ $\cdots$ a_n

Apparent pattern: Each term is the reciprocal of $n!$, which implies that

$$a_n = \frac{1}{n!}.$$

52. $1, 2, \dfrac{2^2}{2}, \dfrac{2^3}{6}, \dfrac{2^4}{24}, \dfrac{2^5}{120}, \cdots$

n: 1   2   3   4   5   6 $\cdots$ n

Terms: 1   2 $\dfrac{2^2}{2}$ $\dfrac{2^3}{6}$ $\dfrac{2^4}{24}$ $\dfrac{2^5}{120}$ $\cdots$ a_n

Apparent pattern: Each term is 2^{n-1} divided by $(n-1)!$, which implies that

$$a_n = \frac{2^{n-1}}{(n-1)!}.$$

54. $1 + \dfrac{1}{2}, 1 + \dfrac{3}{4}, 1 + \dfrac{7}{8}, 1 + \dfrac{15}{16}, 1 + \dfrac{31}{32}, \cdots$

n: 1   2   3   4   5 $\cdots$ n

Terms: $1 + \dfrac{1}{2}$ $1 + \dfrac{3}{4}$ $1 + \dfrac{7}{8}$ $1 + \dfrac{15}{16}$ $1 + \dfrac{31}{32}$ $\cdots$ a_n

Apparent pattern: Each term is the sum of 1 and the quantity 1 less than 2^n divided by 2^n, which implies that

$$a_n = 1 + \frac{2^n - 1}{2^n}.$$

56. $a_1 = 15, \quad a_{k+1} = a_k + 3$

$a_1 = 15$

$a_2 = a_1 + 3 = 15 + 3 = 18$

$a_3 = a_2 + 3 = 18 + 3 = 21$

$a_4 = a_3 + 3 = 21 + 3 = 24$

$a_5 = a_4 + 3 = 24 + 3 = 27$

58. $a_1 = 32, \quad a_{k+1} = \dfrac{1}{2}a_k$

$a_1 = 32$

$a_2 = \dfrac{1}{2}a_1 = \dfrac{1}{2}(32) = 16$

$a_3 = \dfrac{1}{2}a_2 = \dfrac{1}{2}(16) = 8$

$a_4 = \dfrac{1}{2}a_3 = \dfrac{1}{2}(8) = 4$

$a_5 = \dfrac{1}{2}a_4 = \dfrac{1}{2}(4) = 2$

60. $a_1 = 25, \quad a_{k+1} = a_k - 5$

$a_1 = 25$

$a_2 = a_1 - 5 = 25 - 5 = 20$

$a_3 = a_2 - 5 = 20 - 5 = 15$

$a_4 = a_3 - 5 = 15 - 5 = 10$

$a_5 = a_4 - 5 = 10 - 5 = 5$

In general, $a_n = 30 - 5n$.

62. $a_1 = 14, \quad a_{k+1} = (-2)a_k$

$a_1 = 14$

$a_2 = (-2)a_1 = (-2)(14) = -28$

$a_3 = (-2)a_2 = (-2)(-28) = 56$

$a_4 = (-2)a_3 = (-2)(56) = -112$

$a_5 = (-2)(a_4) = (-2)(-112) = 224$

In general, $a_n = 14(-2)^{n-1}$.

64. $\dfrac{5!}{8!} = \dfrac{\cancel{1 \cdot 2 \cdot 3 \cdot 4 \cdot 5}}{\cancel{1 \cdot 2 \cdot 3 \cdot 4 \cdot 5} \cdot 6 \cdot 7 \cdot 8} = \dfrac{1}{6 \cdot 7 \cdot 8} = \dfrac{1}{336}$

66. $\dfrac{25!}{23!} = \dfrac{\cancel{1 \cdot 2 \cdot 3 \cdots\cdots 23} \cdot 24 \cdot 25}{\cancel{1 \cdot 2 \cdot 3 \cdots\cdots 23}}$

$= \dfrac{24 \cdot 25}{1} = 600$

68. $\dfrac{(n+2)!}{n!} = \dfrac{\cancel{1 \cdot 2 \cdot 3 \cdots\cdots n} \cdot (n+1) \cdot (n+2)}{\cancel{1 \cdot 2 \cdot 3 \cdots\cdots n}}$

$= (n+1)(n+2)$

70. $\dfrac{(3n+1)!}{(3n)!} = \dfrac{\cancel{1 \cdot 2 \cdot 3 \cdots\cdots (3n)} \cdot (3n+1)}{\cancel{1 \cdot 2 \cdot 3 \cdots\cdots (3n)}}$

$= \dfrac{3n+1}{1} = 3n+1$

72. $\displaystyle\sum_{i=1}^{6} (3i-1) = (3 \cdot 1 - 1) + (3 \cdot 2 - 1) + (3 \cdot 3 - 1) + (3 \cdot 4 - 1) + (3 \cdot 5 - 1) + (3 \cdot 6 - 1) = 57$

74. $\displaystyle\sum_{k=1}^{5} 5 = 5 + 5 + 5 + 5 + 5 = 25$

76. $\displaystyle\sum_{i=0}^{5} 2i^2 = 2(0^2) + 2(1^2) + 2(2^2) + 2(3^2) + 2(4^2) + 2(5^2)$

$= 110$

78. $\displaystyle\sum_{j=3}^{5} \dfrac{1}{j^2 - 3} = \dfrac{1}{3^2 - 3} + \dfrac{1}{4^2 - 3} + \dfrac{1}{5^2 - 3} = \dfrac{124}{429}$

80. $\displaystyle\sum_{i=1}^{4} [(i-1)^2 + (i+1)^3] = [(0)^2 + (2)^3] + [(1)^2 + (3)^3] + [(2)^2 + (4)^3] + [(3)^2 + (5)^3] = 238$

82. $\displaystyle\sum_{j=0}^{4} (-2)^j = (-2)^0 + (-2)^1 + (-2)^2 + (-2)^3 + (-2)^4 = 11$

84. $\displaystyle\sum_{j=1}^{10} \dfrac{3}{j+1} \approx 6.06$

86. $\displaystyle\sum_{k=0}^{4} \dfrac{(-1)^k}{k!} = \dfrac{3}{8}$

88. $\dfrac{5}{1+1} + \dfrac{5}{1+2} + \dfrac{5}{1+3} + \cdots + \dfrac{5}{1+15} = \displaystyle\sum_{i=1}^{15} \dfrac{5}{1+i}$

90. $\left[1 - \left(\dfrac{1}{6}\right)^2\right] + \left[1 - \left(\dfrac{2}{6}\right)^2\right] + \cdots + \left[1 - \left(\dfrac{6}{6}\right)^2\right] = \displaystyle\sum_{k=1}^{6} \left[1 - \left(\dfrac{k}{6}\right)^2\right]$

92. $1 - \dfrac{1}{2} + \dfrac{1}{4} - \dfrac{1}{8} + \cdots - \dfrac{1}{128} = \dfrac{1}{2^0} - \dfrac{1}{2^1} + \dfrac{1}{2^2} - \dfrac{1}{2^3} + \cdots - \dfrac{1}{2^7} = \sum\limits_{n=0}^{7} \left(-\dfrac{1}{2}\right)^n$

94. $\dfrac{1}{1 \cdot 3} + \dfrac{1}{2 \cdot 4} + \dfrac{1}{3 \cdot 5} + \cdots + \dfrac{1}{10 \cdot 12} = \sum\limits_{k=1}^{10} \dfrac{1}{k(k+2)}$ **96.** $\dfrac{1}{2} + \dfrac{2}{4} + \dfrac{6}{8} + \dfrac{24}{16} + \dfrac{120}{32} + \dfrac{720}{64} = \sum\limits_{k=1}^{6} \dfrac{k!}{2^k}$

98. $\sum\limits_{i=1}^{5} 2\left(\dfrac{1}{3}\right)^i = 2\left(\dfrac{1}{3}\right)^1 + 2\left(\dfrac{1}{3}\right)^2 + 2\left(\dfrac{1}{3}\right)^3 + 2\left(\dfrac{1}{3}\right)^4 + 2\left(\dfrac{1}{3}\right)^5$

$\qquad = \dfrac{242}{243}$

100. $\sum\limits_{n=1}^{4} 8\left(-\dfrac{1}{4}\right)^n = 8\left(-\dfrac{1}{4}\right)^1 + 8\left(-\dfrac{1}{4}\right)^2 + 8\left(-\dfrac{1}{4}\right)^3 + 8\left(-\dfrac{1}{4}\right)^4$

$\qquad = -\dfrac{51}{32}$

102. $\sum\limits_{k=1}^{\infty} \left(\dfrac{1}{10}\right)^k = \dfrac{1}{10} + \dfrac{1}{10^2} + \dfrac{1}{10^3} + \dfrac{1}{10^4} + \dfrac{1}{10^5} + \cdots$

$\qquad = 0.1 + 0.01 + 0.001 + 0.0001 + 0.00001 + \ldots$

$\qquad = 0.11111\ldots$

$\qquad = \dfrac{1}{9}$

104. $\sum\limits_{i=1}^{\infty} 2\left(\dfrac{1}{10}\right)^i = 2\left(\dfrac{1}{10} + \dfrac{1}{10^2} + \dfrac{1}{10^3} + \dfrac{1}{10^4} + \cdots\right)$

$\qquad = 2(0.1 + 0.01 + 0.001 + 0.0001 + \ldots)$

$\qquad = 2(0.111 \ldots)$

$\qquad = 0.222$

$\qquad = \dfrac{2}{9}$

106. (a) $A_1 = 100(101)[(1.01)^1 - 1] = \$101.00$

$\qquad A_2 = 100(101)[(1.01)^2 - 1] = \$203.01$

$\qquad A_3 = 100(101)[(1.01)^3 - 1] \approx \$306.04$

$\qquad A_4 = 100(101)[(1.01)^4 - 1] \approx \$410.10$

$\qquad A_5 = 100(101)[(1.01)^5 - 1] \approx \$515.20$

$\qquad A_6 = 100(101)[(1.01)^6 - 1] \approx \$621.35$

(b) $A_{60} = 100(101)[(1.01)^{60} - 1] \approx \$8248.64$

(c) $A_{240} = 100(101)[(1.01)^{240} - 1] \approx \$99{,}914.79$

108. $a_n = \sqrt{10.9 + 2.8n},\ n = -1, 0, 1, \ldots, 6$

$\qquad a_{-1} = \sqrt{10.9 + 2.8(-1)} \approx \$2.85$

$\qquad a_0 = \sqrt{10.9 + 2.8(0)} \approx \$3.30$

$\qquad a_1 = \sqrt{10.9 + 2.8(1)} \approx \$3.70$

$\qquad a_2 = \sqrt{10.9 + 2.8(2)} \approx \$4.06$

$\qquad a_3 = \sqrt{10.9 + 2.8(3)} \approx \$4.39$

$\qquad a_4 = \sqrt{10.9 + 2.8(4)} \approx \$4.70$

$\qquad a_5 = \sqrt{10.9 + 2.8(5)} \approx \$4.99$

$\qquad a_6 = \sqrt{10.9 + 2.8(6)} \approx \$5.26$

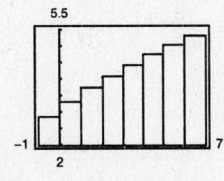

110. $a_n = (4.27 + 0.294n - 2.934 \ln n)$, $n = 10, \ldots, 18$

$a_{10} = (4.27 + 0.294(10) - 2.934 \ln(10)) \approx 0.45$

$a_{11} = (4.27 + 0.294(11) - 2.934 \ln(11)) \approx 0.47$

$a_{12} = (4.27 + 0.294(12) - 2.934 \ln(12)) \approx 0.51$

$a_{13} = (4.27 + 0.294(13) - 2.934 \ln(13)) \approx 0.57$

$a_{14} = (4.27 + 0.294(14) - 2.934 \ln(14)) \approx 0.64$

$a_{15} = (4.27 + 0.294(15) - 2.934 \ln(15)) \approx 0.73$

$a_{16} = (4.27 + 0.294(16) - 2.934 \ln(16)) \approx 0.84$

$a_{17} = (4.27 + 0.294(17) - 2.934 \ln(17)) \approx 0.96$

$a_{18} = (4.27 + 0.294(18) - 2.934 \ln(18)) \approx 1.08$

$$\sum_{n=10}^{18} (4.27 + 0.249n - 2.934 \ln n) \approx 6.25$$

112. $b_n = \dfrac{a_{n+1}}{a_n}$; $b_1 = 1$, $b_2 = 2$, $b_3 = \dfrac{3}{2}$, $b_4 = \dfrac{5}{3}, \ldots$

$b_2 = 1 + \dfrac{1}{b_1} = 1 + \dfrac{1}{1} = 2$

$b_3 = 1 + \dfrac{1}{b_2} = 1 + \dfrac{1}{2} = \dfrac{3}{2}$

$b_4 = 1 + \dfrac{1}{b_3} = 1 + \dfrac{2}{3} = \dfrac{5}{3}$

$b_5 = 1 + \dfrac{1}{b_4} = 1 + \dfrac{3}{5} = \dfrac{8}{5}$

$b_n = 1 + \dfrac{1}{b_{n-1}}$

114. $\bar{x} = \dfrac{1}{n} \sum\limits_{i=1}^{n} x_i = \dfrac{1.279 + 1.259 + 1.289 + 1.329 + 1.349}{5} = \$1.301$

116. $\sum\limits_{i=1}^{n} (x_i - \bar{x})^2 = \sum\limits_{i=1}^{n} (x_i^2 - 2x_i\bar{x} + \bar{x}^2) = \sum\limits_{i=1}^{n} x_i^2 - 2\bar{x}\sum\limits_{i=1}^{n} x_i + n\bar{x}^2$

$\qquad = \sum\limits_{i=1}^{n} x_i^2 - 2 \cdot \dfrac{1}{n}\sum\limits_{i=1}^{n} x_i \sum\limits_{i=1}^{n} x_i + n \cdot \dfrac{1}{n}\sum\limits_{i=1}^{n} x_i \cdot \dfrac{1}{n}\sum\limits_{i=1}^{n} x_i$

$\qquad = \sum\limits_{i=1}^{n} x_i^2 + \sum\limits_{i=1}^{n} x_i \sum\limits_{i=1}^{n} x_i \left(-\dfrac{2}{n} + \dfrac{1}{n}\right) = \sum\limits_{i=1}^{n} x_i^2 - \dfrac{1}{n}\left(\sum\limits_{i=1}^{n} x_i\right)^2$

118. $\sum\limits_{j=1}^{4} 2^j = \sum\limits_{j=3}^{6} 2^{j-2}$

True, because $2^1 + 2^2 + 2^3 + 2^4 = 2^{3-2} + 2^{4-2} + 2^{5-2} + 2^{6-2}$.

120. (a) $A - B = \begin{bmatrix} 10 & 7 \\ -4 & 6 \end{bmatrix} - \begin{bmatrix} 0 & -12 \\ 8 & 11 \end{bmatrix} = \begin{bmatrix} 10 - 0 & 7 - (-12) \\ -4 - 8 & 6 - 11 \end{bmatrix}$

$\qquad = \begin{bmatrix} 10 & 19 \\ -12 & -5 \end{bmatrix}$

(b) $4B - 3A = 4\begin{bmatrix} 0 & -12 \\ 8 & 11 \end{bmatrix} - 3\begin{bmatrix} 10 & 7 \\ -4 & 6 \end{bmatrix} = \begin{bmatrix} 0 - 30 & -48 - 21 \\ 32 + 12 & 44 - 18 \end{bmatrix}$

$\qquad = \begin{bmatrix} -30 & -69 \\ 44 & 26 \end{bmatrix}$

(c) $AB = \begin{bmatrix} 10 & 7 \\ -4 & 6 \end{bmatrix}\begin{bmatrix} 0 & -12 \\ 8 & 11 \end{bmatrix} = \begin{bmatrix} 0 + 56 & -120 + 77 \\ 0 + 48 & 48 + 66 \end{bmatrix}$

$\qquad = \begin{bmatrix} 56 & -43 \\ 48 & 114 \end{bmatrix}$

(d) $BA = \begin{bmatrix} 0 & -12 \\ 8 & 11 \end{bmatrix}\begin{bmatrix} 10 & 7 \\ -4 & 6 \end{bmatrix} = \begin{bmatrix} 0 + 48 & 0 - 72 \\ 80 - 44 & 56 + 66 \end{bmatrix}$

$\qquad = \begin{bmatrix} 48 & -72 \\ 36 & 122 \end{bmatrix}$

122. (a) $A - B = \begin{bmatrix} -1 & 4 & 0 \\ 5 & 1 & 2 \\ 0 & -1 & 3 \end{bmatrix} - \begin{bmatrix} 0 & 4 & 0 \\ 3 & 1 & -2 \\ -1 & 0 & 2 \end{bmatrix}$

$= \begin{bmatrix} -1-0 & 4-4 & 0-0 \\ 5-3 & 1-1 & 2-(-2) \\ 0-(-1) & -1-0 & 3-2 \end{bmatrix} = \begin{bmatrix} -1 & 0 & 0 \\ 2 & 0 & 4 \\ 1 & -1 & 1 \end{bmatrix}$

(b) $4B - 3A = 4\begin{bmatrix} 0 & 4 & 0 \\ 3 & 1 & -2 \\ -1 & 0 & 2 \end{bmatrix} - 3\begin{bmatrix} -1 & 4 & 0 \\ 5 & 1 & 2 \\ 0 & -1 & 3 \end{bmatrix}$

$= \begin{bmatrix} 0-(-3) & 16-12 & 0-0 \\ 12-15 & 4-3 & -8-6 \\ -4-0 & 0-(-3) & 8-9 \end{bmatrix} = \begin{bmatrix} 3 & 4 & 0 \\ -3 & 1 & -14 \\ -4 & 3 & -1 \end{bmatrix}$

(c) $AB = \begin{bmatrix} -1 & 4 & 0 \\ 5 & 1 & 2 \\ 0 & -1 & 3 \end{bmatrix}\begin{bmatrix} 0 & 4 & 0 \\ 3 & 1 & -2 \\ -1 & 0 & 2 \end{bmatrix}$

$= \begin{bmatrix} 0+12+0 & -4+4+0 & 0-8+0 \\ 0+3-2 & 20+1+0 & 0-2+4 \\ 0-3-3 & 0-1+0 & 0+2+6 \end{bmatrix}$

$= \begin{bmatrix} 12 & 0 & -8 \\ 1 & 21 & 2 \\ -6 & -1 & 8 \end{bmatrix}$

(d) $BA = \begin{bmatrix} 0 & 4 & 0 \\ 3 & 1 & -2 \\ -1 & 0 & 2 \end{bmatrix}\begin{bmatrix} -1 & 4 & 0 \\ 5 & 1 & 2 \\ 0 & -1 & 3 \end{bmatrix}$

$= \begin{bmatrix} 0+20+0 & 0+4+0 & 0+8+0 \\ -3+5+0 & 12+1+2 & 0+2-6 \\ 1+0+0 & -4+0-2 & 0+0+6 \end{bmatrix}$

$= \begin{bmatrix} 20 & 4 & 8 \\ 2 & 15 & -4 \\ 1 & -6 & 6 \end{bmatrix}$

124. $\begin{vmatrix} -2 & 8 \\ 12 & 15 \end{vmatrix} = -2(15) - 8(12) = -126$

126. $|A| = 16(C_{11}) + 9(C_{21}) - 2(C_{31}) - 4(C_{41})$

$C_{11} = (-1)^{1+1}\begin{vmatrix} 8 & 3 & 7 \\ -1 & 12 & 3 \\ 6 & 2 & 1 \end{vmatrix} = \begin{vmatrix} 8 & 3 & 7 \\ -1 & 12 & 3 \\ 6 & 2 & 1 \end{vmatrix}$

$= 8\begin{vmatrix} 12 & 3 \\ 2 & 1 \end{vmatrix} - 3\begin{vmatrix} -1 & 3 \\ 6 & 1 \end{vmatrix} + 7\begin{vmatrix} -1 & 12 \\ 6 & 2 \end{vmatrix}$

$= 8(12 - 6) - 3(-1 - 18) + 7(-2 - 72) = -413$

$C_{21} = (-1)^{2+1}\begin{vmatrix} 11 & 10 & 2 \\ -1 & 12 & 3 \\ 6 & 2 & 1 \end{vmatrix} = \begin{vmatrix} -11 & -10 & -2 \\ 1 & -12 & -3 \\ -6 & -2 & -1 \end{vmatrix}$

$= -11\begin{vmatrix} -12 & -3 \\ -2 & -1 \end{vmatrix} - 1\begin{vmatrix} -10 & -2 \\ -2 & -1 \end{vmatrix} - 6\begin{vmatrix} -10 & -2 \\ -12 & -3 \end{vmatrix}$

$= -11(12 - 6) - 1(10 - 4) - 6(30 - 24) = -108$

—CONTINUED—

126. —CONTINUED—

$$C_{31} = (-1)^{3+1} \begin{vmatrix} 11 & 10 & 2 \\ 8 & 3 & 7 \\ 6 & 2 & 1 \end{vmatrix} = \begin{vmatrix} 11 & 10 & 2 \\ 8 & 3 & 7 \\ 6 & 2 & 1 \end{vmatrix}$$

$$= 11\begin{vmatrix} 3 & 7 \\ 2 & 1 \end{vmatrix} - 8\begin{vmatrix} 10 & 2 \\ 2 & 1 \end{vmatrix} + 6\begin{vmatrix} 10 & 2 \\ 3 & 7 \end{vmatrix}$$

$$= 11(3 - 14) - 8(10 - 4) + 6(70 - 6) = 215$$

$$C_{41} = (-1)^{4+1} \begin{vmatrix} 11 & 10 & 2 \\ 8 & 3 & 7 \\ -1 & 12 & 3 \end{vmatrix} = \begin{vmatrix} -11 & -10 & -2 \\ -8 & -3 & -7 \\ 1 & -12 & -3 \end{vmatrix}$$

$$= -11\begin{vmatrix} -3 & -7 \\ -12 & -3 \end{vmatrix} - (-8)\begin{vmatrix} -10 & -2 \\ -12 & -3 \end{vmatrix} + 1\begin{vmatrix} -10 & -2 \\ -3 & -7 \end{vmatrix}$$

$$= -11(9 - 84) + 8(30 - 24) + 1(70 - 6) = 937$$

So, $|A| = 16(-413) + 9(-108) - 2(215) - 4(937)$

$$= -11{,}758$$

Section 9.2   Arithmetic Sequences and Partial Sums

Solutions to Even-Numbered Exercises

2. 4, 7, 10, 13, 16, . . .

Arithmetic sequence, $d = 3$

4. 80, 40, 20, 10, 5, . . .

Not an arithmetic sequence

6. $3, \frac{5}{2}, 2, \frac{3}{2}, 1, \ldots$

Arithmetic sequence, $d = -\frac{1}{2}$

8. 5.3, 5.7, 6.1, 6.5, 6.9, . . .

Arithmetic sequence, $d = 0.4$

10. $1^2, 2^2, 3^2, 4^2, 5^2, \ldots$

Not an arithmetic sequence

12. $a_n = 100 - 3n$

97, 94, 91, 88, 85

Arithmetic sequence, $d = -3$

14. $a_n = 1 + (n - 1)4$

1, 5, 9, 13, 17

Arithmetic sequence, $d = 4$

16. $a_n = 2^{n-1}$

1, 2, 4, 8, 16

Not an arithmetic sequence

18. $a_n = (2^n)n$

2, 8, 24, 64, 160

Not an arithmetic sequence

20. $a_1 = 6, a_{k+1} = a_k + 5$

$a_2 = 6 + 5 = 11$

$a_3 = 11 + 5 = 16$

$a_4 = 16 + 5 = 21$

$a_5 = 21 + 5 = 26$

$d = 5$

$a_n = dn + c$

$a_n = 5n + c$

$c = a_1 - d$

$\quad = 6 - 5$

$\quad = 1$

So, $a_n = 5n + 1$

22. $a_1 = 72, a_{k+1} = a_k - 6$

$a_2 = 72 - 6 = 66$

$a_3 = 66 - 6 = 60$

$a_4 = 60 - 6 = 54$

$a_5 = 54 - 6 = 48$

$d = -6$

$a_n = dn + c$

$a_n = -6n + c$

$c = a_1 - d$

$\quad = 72 - (-6)$

$\quad = 78$

So, $a_n = -6n + 78$

24. $a_1 = 0.375, a_{k+1} = a_k + 0.25$

$a_2 = 0.375 + 0.25 = 0.625$

$a_3 = 0.625 + 0.25 = 0.875$

$a_4 = 0.875 + 0.25 = 1.125$

$a_5 = 1.125 + 0.25 = 1.375$

$d = 0.25$

$a_n = dn + c$

$a_n = 0.25n + c$

$c = a_1 - d$

$\quad = 0.375 - 0.25$

$\quad = 0.125$

So, $a_n = 0.25n + 0.125$

26. $a_1 = 5, d = -\frac{3}{4}$

$a_1 = 5$

$a_2 = 5 - \frac{3}{4} = \frac{17}{4}$

$a_3 = \frac{17}{4} - \frac{3}{4} = \frac{14}{4} = \frac{7}{2}$

$a_4 = \frac{7}{2} - \frac{3}{4} = \frac{11}{4}$

$a_5 = \frac{11}{4} - \frac{3}{4} = \frac{8}{4} = 2$

28. $a_1 = 16.5, d = 0.25$

$a_1 = 16.5$

$a_2 = 16.5 + 0.25 = 16.75$

$a_3 = 16.75 + 0.25 = 17$

$a_4 = 17 + 0.25 = 17.25$

$a_5 = 17.25 + 0.25 = 17.5$

30. $a_4 = 16, a_{10} = 46$

$16 = a_4 = a_1 + (n-1)d = a_1 + 3d$

$46 = a_{10} = a_1 + (n-1)d = a_1 + 9d$

Answer: $a_1 = 1, d = 5$

$a_1 = 1$

$a_2 = 1 + 5 = 6$

$a_3 = 6 + 5 = 11$

$a_4 = 11 + 5 = 16$

$a_5 = 16 + 5 = 21$

32. $a_3 = 19, a_{15} = -1.7$

$19 = a_3 = a_1 + (n-1)d = a_1 + 2d$

$-1.7 = a_{15} = a_1 + (n-1)d = a_1 + 14d$

Answer: $a_1 = 22.45, d = -1.725$

$a_1 = 22.45$

$a_2 = 22.45 - 1.725 = 20.725$

$a_3 = 20.725 - 1.725 = 19$

$a_4 = 19 - 1.725 = 17.275$

$a_5 = 17.275 - 1.725 = 15.55$

34. $a_1 = 15, d = 4$

$a_n = a_1 + (n-1)d = 15 + (n-1)4$
$\qquad = 4n + 11$

36. $a_1 = 0, d = -\frac{2}{3}$

$a_n = a_1 + (n-1)d = (n-1)\left(-\frac{2}{3}\right)$
$\qquad = -\frac{2}{3}n + \frac{2}{3}$

38. $a_1 = -y, d = 5y$

$a_n = a_1 + (n-1)d = -y + (n-1)(5y)$
$\qquad = 5yn - 6y$

40. $10, 5, 0, -5, -10, \ldots$

$d = -5$

$a_n = a_1 + (n-1)d = 10 + (n-1)(-5) = -5n + 15$

42. $a_1 = -4, a_5 = 16$

$a_n = a_1 + (n-1)d$

$16 = -4 + 4d$

$d = 5$

$a_n = a_1 + (n-1)d = -4 + (n-1)5$
$\qquad = 5n - 9$

44. $a_5 = 190, a_{10} = 115$

$a_{10} = a_5 + 5d \Rightarrow 115 = 190 + 5d \Rightarrow d = -15$

$a_1 = a_5 - 4d \Rightarrow a_1 = 190 - 4(-15) = 250$

$a_n = a_1 + (n-1)d = 250 + (n-1)(-15)$
$\qquad = -15n + 265$

46. $a_n = 3n - 5$

$d = 3$ so the sequence is increasing

and $a_1 = -2$.

Matches (d).

48. $a_n = 25 - 3n$

$d = -3$ so the sequence is decreasing

and $a_1 = 22$.

Matches (a).

50. $a_n = -5 + 2n$

52. $a_n = -0.3n + 8$

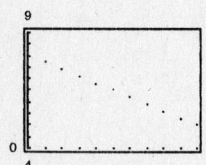

54. $2, 8, 14, 20, \ldots, n = 25$

$d = 6, c = 2 - 6 = -4$

$a_n = 6n - 4$

$a_1 = 2$ and $a_{25} = 146$

$S_{25} = \frac{25}{2}(2 + 146) = 1850$

56. $0.5, 0.9, 1.3, 1.7, \ldots, n = 10$

$d = 0.4, c = 0.1$

$a_n = 0.4n + 0.1$

$a_1 = 0.5$ and $a_{10} = 4.1$

$S_{10} = \frac{10}{2}(0.5 + 4.1) = 23$

58. $75, 70, 65, 60, \ldots, n = 25$

$d = -5, c = 80$

$a_n = -5n + 80$

$a_1 = 75$ and $a_{25} = -45$

$S_{25} = \frac{25}{2}(75 - 45) = 375$

60. $a_1 = 15, a_{100} = 307, n = 100$

$S_{100} = \frac{100}{2}(15 + 307) = 16,100$

62. $a_n = 2n$

$a_1 = 2, a_{100} = 200, n = 100$

$\sum_{n=1}^{100} 2n = \frac{100}{2}(2 + 200) = 10,100$

64. $a_n = 7n$

$a_{51} = 357, a_{100} = 700$

$\sum_{n=51}^{100} 7n = \frac{50}{2}(357 + 700) = 26,425$

66. $\sum_{n=51}^{100} n - \sum_{n=1}^{50} n = \frac{50}{2}(51 + 100) - \frac{50}{2}(1 + 50) = 3775 - 1275 = 2500$

68. $a_n = 1000 - n$

$a_1 = 999, a_{250} = 750, n = 250$

$\sum_{n=1}^{250} (1000 - n) = \frac{250}{2}(999 + 750) = 218,625$

70. $a_0 = 1000, a_{50} = 750, n = 51$

$\sum_{n=0}^{50} (100 - 5n) = \frac{51}{2}(1000 + 750) = 44,625$

72. $a_0 = \frac{1}{2}, a_{100} = \frac{-73}{4}, n = 101$

$\sum_{n=0}^{100} \frac{8 - 3n}{16} = \frac{101}{2}\left(\frac{1}{2} - \frac{73}{4}\right) = -896.375$

74. $a_1 = 4.525, a_{200} = 9.5, n = 200$

$\sum_{j=1}^{200} (4.5 + 0.025j) = \frac{200}{2}(4.525 + 9.5) = 1402.5$

76. (a) $a_1 = 36,800, d = 1750$

$a_6 = a_1 + 5d = 36,800 + 5(1750) = \$45,550$

(b) $S_6 = \frac{6}{2}[36,800 + 45,550] = \$247,050$

78. $a_1 = 15, d = 3, n = 36$

$a_{36} = 15 + 35(3) = 120$

$S_{36} = \frac{36}{2}(15 + 120) = 2430$ seats

80. $a_1 = 14, a_{28} = 0.5, n = 28$

$S_{28} = \frac{28}{2}(14 + 0.5) = 203$ bricks

82. $a_1 = 4.9, a_2 = 14.7, a_3 = 24.5, a_4 = 34.3$

$d = 9.8$

$c = a_1 - d = 4.9 - 9.8 = -4.9$

$a_n = 9.8n - 4.9$

$a_{17} = 9.8(17) - 4.9 = 161.7$ meters

84. True, by the formula for the sum of a finite arithmetic sequence,

$$S_n = \frac{n}{2}(a_1 + a_n)$$

86. First term plus $(n - 1)$ times the common difference.

88. $a_0 = -10, a_{61} = 50, n = 61$

$$\sum_{i=0}^{61} (i - 10) = \frac{61}{2}(-10 + 50) = 1220$$

90. If an arithmetic sequence is defined by $a_1, a_2, a_3, a_4, \ldots$ and the common difference is $a_2 - a_1 = d$.

(a) A constant C is added to each term: $a_1 + C, a_2 + C, a_3 + C, a_4 + C, \ldots$

The resulting sequence is arithmetic, and the common difference is the original common difference:

$$a_2 + C - (a_1 + C) = a_2 + C - a_1 - C$$
$$= a_2 - a_1 = d.$$

(b) Each term is multiplied by a nonzero constant C: $Ca_1, Ca_2, Ca_3, Ca_4, \ldots$

The resulting sequence is arithmetic, and the common difference is C times the original common difference:

$$Ca_2 - Ca_1 = C(a_2 - a_1) = Cd.$$

(c) If each term is squared, the sequence is not arithmetic.

92. Let $S_n = \frac{n}{2}(a_1 + a_n)$ be the sum of the first n terms of the original sequence.

$$S_n' = \frac{n}{2}(a_1 + 5 + a_n + 5)$$

$$= \frac{n}{2}(a_1 + a_n + 10)$$

$$= \frac{n}{2}(a_1 + a_n) + \frac{n}{2}(10)$$

$$= \frac{n}{2}(a_1 + a_n) + 5n$$

$$= S_n + 5n$$

94.
$$\begin{cases} -x - y + 2z = 0 \\ 2x + y - 3z = 0 \\ 4x - 3y - z = 0 \end{cases} \quad \text{Interchange equations}$$

$$\begin{cases} -x - y + 2z = 0 \\ -y + z = 0 \quad 2\text{Eq.1} + \text{Eq.2} \\ -7y + 7z = 0 \quad 4\text{Eq.1} + \text{Eq.3} \end{cases}$$

$$\begin{cases} -x - y + 2z = 0 \\ y - z = 0 \quad -\text{Eq.2} \\ y - z = 0 \quad -\frac{1}{7}\text{Eq.3} \end{cases}$$

$$\begin{cases} -x - y + 2z = 0 \\ y - z = 0 \\ 0 = 0 \quad -\text{Eq.2} + \text{Eq.3} \end{cases}$$

$$\begin{cases} -x - y + 2z = 0 \\ y - z = 0 \end{cases}$$

Let $z = a$. Then

$$y - a = 0 \Longrightarrow y = a$$
$$-x - a + 2(a) = 0 \Longrightarrow x = a$$

Solution: (a, a, a)

96. $\begin{cases} -x + 6y + 4z = 0 \\ 5x - 3y + 7z = 0 \\ 6x + 3y + 4z = 0 \end{cases}$ Interchange equations

$\begin{cases} -x + 6y + 4z = 0 \\ \quad\;\; 27y + 27z = 0 \\ \quad\;\; 39y + 28z = 0 \end{cases}$ 5Eq.1 + Eq.2
6Eq.1 + Eq.3

$\begin{cases} -x - 6y - 4z = 0 \\ \quad\;\; y + z = 0 \\ \quad\;\; 39y + 28z = 0 \end{cases}$ $\frac{1}{27}$Eq.2

$\begin{cases} x - 6y - 4z = 0 \\ \quad\;\; y + z = 0 \\ \quad\quad\; -11z = 0 \end{cases}$ -39Eq.2 + Eq.3

$\begin{cases} x - 6y - 4z = 0 \\ \quad\;\; y + z = 0 \\ \quad\quad\;\;\; z = 0 \end{cases}$ $-\frac{1}{11}$Eq.3

$z = 0$
$y + 0 = 0 \Longrightarrow y = 0$
$x - 6(0) - 4(0) = 0 \Longrightarrow x = 0$

Solution: $(0, 0, 0)$

100. $\begin{cases} 3x + y \quad\;\; = 0 \\ x \quad\;\; - 2z = 0 \\ 2x - 3y + z = 0 \end{cases}$

$\begin{bmatrix} 3 & 1 & 0 & \vdots & 0 \\ 1 & 0 & -2 & \vdots & 0 \\ 2 & -3 & 1 & \vdots & 0 \end{bmatrix}$

$\begin{matrix} R_2 \\ R_1 \end{matrix} \begin{bmatrix} 1 & 0 & -2 & \vdots & 0 \\ 3 & 1 & 0 & \vdots & 0 \\ 2 & -3 & 1 & \vdots & 0 \end{bmatrix}$

$\begin{matrix} -3R_1 + R_2 \to \\ -2R_1 + R_3 \to \end{matrix} \begin{bmatrix} 1 & 0 & -2 & \vdots & 0 \\ 0 & 1 & 6 & \vdots & 0 \\ 0 & -3 & 5 & \vdots & 0 \end{bmatrix}$

$3R_2 + R_3 \to \begin{bmatrix} 1 & 0 & -2 & \vdots & 0 \\ 0 & 1 & 6 & \vdots & 0 \\ 0 & 0 & 23 & \vdots & 0 \end{bmatrix}$

$\frac{1}{23}R_3 \to \begin{bmatrix} 1 & 0 & -2 & \vdots & 0 \\ 0 & 1 & 6 & \vdots & 0 \\ 0 & 0 & 1 & \vdots & 0 \end{bmatrix}$

$\begin{cases} x \quad\;\; - 2z = 0 \\ y + 6z = 0 \\ \quad\quad\;\; z = 0 \end{cases}$

$y + 6(0) = 0 \Longrightarrow y = 0$
$x - 2(0) = 0 \Longrightarrow x = 0$

Solution: $(0, 0, 0)$

98. $\begin{cases} 7x + 3y = 0 \\ x + y = 4 \end{cases}$

$\begin{bmatrix} 7 & 3 & \vdots & 0 \\ 1 & 1 & \vdots & 4 \end{bmatrix}$

$\begin{matrix} R_2 \\ R_1 \end{matrix} \begin{bmatrix} 1 & 1 & \vdots & 4 \\ 7 & 3 & \vdots & 0 \end{bmatrix}$

$-7R_1 + R_2 \to \begin{bmatrix} 1 & 1 & \vdots & 4 \\ 0 & -4 & \vdots & -28 \end{bmatrix}$

$-\frac{1}{4}R_2 \to \begin{bmatrix} 1 & 1 & \vdots & 4 \\ 0 & 1 & \vdots & 7 \end{bmatrix}$

$\begin{cases} x + y = 4 \\ y = 7 \end{cases}$

$x + 7 = 4 \Longrightarrow x = -3$

Solution: $(-3, 7)$

Section 9.3   Geometric Sequences and Series

Solutions to Even-Numbered Exercises

2. 3, 12, 48, 192, . . .

Geometric sequence, $r = 4$

4. 36, 27, 18, 9, . . .

Not a geometric sequence

6. 5, 1, 0.2, 0.04, . . .

Geometric sequence, $r = \frac{1}{5} = 0.2$

8. $9, -6, 4, -\frac{8}{3}, \ldots$

Geometric sequence, $r = -\frac{2}{3}$

10. $\frac{1}{5}, \frac{2}{7}, \frac{3}{9}, \frac{4}{11}, \ldots$

Not a geometric sequence

12. $a_1 = 6, r = 2$

$a_1 = 6$

$a_2 = 6(2)^1 = 12$

$a_3 = 6(2)^2 = 24$

$a_4 = 6(2)^3 = 48$

$a_5 = 6(2)^4 = 96$

14. $a_1 = 1, r = \frac{1}{3}$

$a_1 = 1$

$a_2 = 1\left(\frac{1}{3}\right)^1 = \frac{1}{3}$

$a_3 = 1\left(\frac{1}{3}\right)^2 = \frac{1}{9}$

$a_4 = 1\left(\frac{1}{3}\right)^3 = \frac{1}{27}$

$a_5 = 1\left(\frac{1}{3}\right)^4 = \frac{1}{81}$

16. $a_1 = 6, r = -\frac{1}{4}$

$a_1 = 6$

$a_2 = 6\left(-\frac{1}{4}\right)^1 = -\frac{3}{2}$

$a_3 = 6\left(-\frac{1}{4}\right)^2 = \frac{3}{8}$

$a_4 = 6\left(-\frac{1}{4}\right)^3 = -\frac{3}{32}$

$a_5 = 6\left(-\frac{1}{4}\right)^4 = \frac{3}{128}$

18. $a_1 = 3, r = \sqrt{5}$

$a_1 = 3$

$a_2 = 3\left(\sqrt{5}\right)^1 = 3\sqrt{5}$

$a_3 = 3\left(\sqrt{5}\right)^2 = 15$

$a_4 = 3\left(\sqrt{5}\right)^3 = 15\sqrt{5}$

$a_5 = 3\left(\sqrt{5}\right)^4 = 75$

20. $a_1 = 5, r = 2x$

$a_1 = 5$

$a_2 = 5(2x)^1 = 10x$

$a_3 = 5(2x)^2 = 20x^2$

$a_4 = 5(2x)^3 = 40x^3$

$a_5 = 5(2x)^4 = 80x^4$

22. $a_1 = 81, a_{k+1} = \frac{1}{3}a_k$

$a_1 = 81$

$a_2 = \frac{1}{3}(81) = 27$

$a_3 = \frac{1}{3}(27) = 9$

$a_4 = \frac{1}{3}(9) = 3$

$a_5 = \frac{1}{3}(3) = 1$

$a_n = 81\left(\frac{1}{3}\right)^{n-1} = 243\left(\frac{1}{3}\right)^n$

24. $a_1 = 5, a_{k+1} = -2a_k$

$a_1 = 5$

$a_2 = -2(5) = -10$

$a_3 = -2(-10) = 20$

$a_4 = -2(20) = -40$

$a_5 = -2(-40) = 80$

$a_n = 5(-2)^{n-1} = -\frac{5}{2}(-2)^n$

26. $a_1 = 48, a_{k+1} = -\frac{1}{2}a_k$

$a_1 = 48$

$a_2 = -\frac{1}{2}(48) = -24$

$a_3 = -\frac{1}{2}(-24) = 12$

$a_4 = -\frac{1}{2}(12) = -6$

$a_5 = -\frac{1}{2}(-6) = 3$

$a_n = 48\left(-\frac{1}{2}\right)^{n-1} = -96\left(-\frac{1}{2}\right)$

28. $a_1 = 5,\ \ r = \frac{3}{2},\ \ n = 8$

$a_n = a_1 r^{n-1}$

$a_8 = 5\left(\frac{3}{2}\right)^7 = \frac{10,935}{128}$

30. $a_1 = 64, r = -\frac{1}{4}, n = 10$

$a_n = a_1 r^{n-1}$

$a_{10} = 64\left(-\frac{1}{4}\right)^9 = -\frac{64}{262,144} = -\frac{1}{4096}$

32. $a_1 = 1, r = \sqrt{3}, n = 8$

$a_n = a_1 r^{n-1}$

$a_n = 1\left(\sqrt{3}\right)^7 = 27\sqrt{3}$

34. $a_1 = 1000, \ r = 1.005, \ n = 60$

$a_n = a_1 r^{n-1}$

$a_6 = 1000(1.005)^{59} \approx 1342.139$

36. $a_2 = 3, \ a_5 = \frac{3}{64}, \ n = 1$

$a_2 r^3 = a_5$

$3r^3 = \frac{3}{64}$

$r^3 = \frac{1}{64}$

$r = \frac{1}{4}$

$a_2 = a_1 r$

$3 = a_1 \frac{1}{4}$

$a_1 = 12$

38. $a_3 = \frac{16}{3}, \ a_5 = \frac{64}{27}, \ n = 7$

$a_3 r^2 = a_5$

$\frac{16}{3} r^2 = \frac{64}{27}$

$r^2 = \frac{4}{9}$

$r = \pm\frac{2}{3}$

$a_7 = a_5 r^2 = \frac{64}{27}\left(\pm\frac{2}{3}\right)^2 = \frac{256}{243}$

40. $a_n = 18\left(-\frac{2}{3}\right)^{n-1}$

$r = \left(-\frac{2}{3}\right) > -1$, so that the sequence alternates as it approaches 0. Matches (c).

42. $a_n = 18\left(-\frac{3}{2}\right)^{n-1}$

$r = \left(-\frac{3}{2}\right) < -1$, so the sequence alternates as it approaches ∞. Matches (d).

44. $a_n = 12(-0.4)^{n-1}$

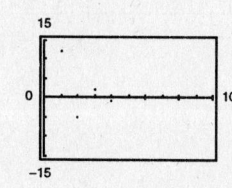

46. $a_n = 2(-1.4)^{n-1}$

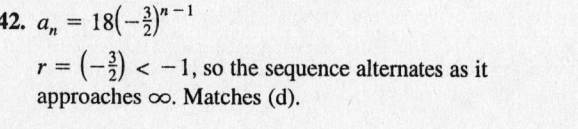

48. $\displaystyle\sum_{n=1}^{9} (-2)^{n-1} \Longrightarrow a_1 = 1, r = -2, n = 9$

$S_9 = 1\left(\dfrac{1 - (-2)^9}{1 - (-2)}\right) = 171$

50. $\displaystyle\sum_{i=1}^{6} 32\left(\frac{1}{4}\right)^{i-1} = 32 + 32\left(\frac{1}{4}\right)^1 + 32\left(\frac{1}{4}\right)^2 + 32\left(\frac{1}{4}\right)^3 + 32\left(\frac{1}{4}\right)^4 + 32\left(\frac{1}{4}\right)^5 \Longrightarrow a_1 = 32, r = \frac{1}{4}, n = 6$

$S_6 = 32\left(\dfrac{1 - \left(\frac{1}{4}\right)^6}{1 - \frac{1}{4}}\right) = \dfrac{1365}{32}$

52. $\displaystyle\sum_{n=0}^{15} 2\left(\frac{4}{3}\right)^n = \sum_{n=1}^{16} 2\left(\frac{4}{3}\right)^{n-1} = 2 + 2\left(\frac{4}{3}\right)^1 + 2\left(\frac{4}{3}\right)^2 + \cdots + 2\left(\frac{4}{3}\right)^{15} \Rightarrow a_1 = 2, r = \frac{4}{3}, n = 16$

$S_{16} = 2\left(\dfrac{1 - \left(\frac{4}{3}\right)^{16}}{1 - \frac{4}{3}}\right) \approx 592.647$

54. $\displaystyle\sum_{n=0}^{6} 500(1.04)^n = \sum_{n=1}^{7} 500(1.04)^{n-1} = 500 + 500(1.04)^1 + 500(1.04)^2 + \cdots + 500(1.04)^6 \Rightarrow a_1 = 500, r = 1.04, n = 7$

$S_7 = 500\left(\dfrac{1 - (1.04)^7}{1 - 1.04}\right) \approx 3949.47$

56. $\displaystyle\sum_{i=1}^{10} 5\left(-\frac{1}{3}\right)^{i-1} = 5 + 5\left(-\frac{1}{3}\right)^1 + 5\left(-\frac{1}{3}\right)^2 + \cdots + 5\left(-\frac{1}{3}\right)^9 \Rightarrow a_1 = 5, r = -\frac{1}{3}, n = 10$

$S_{10} = 5\left(\dfrac{1 - \left(-\frac{1}{3}\right)^{10}}{1 - \left(-\frac{1}{3}\right)}\right) \approx 3.750$

58. $7 + 14 + 28 + \cdots + 896$

$a_1 = 7 \qquad r = 2$

$7(2)^{n-1} = 896$

$2^{n-1} = 128$

$2^{n-1} = 2^7$

$n - 1 = 7$

$n = 8$

Thus, the sum can be written as $\displaystyle\sum_{n=1}^{8} 7(2)^{n-1}$.

60. $15 - 3 + \dfrac{3}{5} - \cdots - \dfrac{3}{625}$

$a_1 = 15, r = -\dfrac{1}{5}$

$15\left(-\dfrac{1}{5}\right)^{n-1} = -\dfrac{3}{625}$

$\left(-\dfrac{1}{5}\right)^{n-1} = -\dfrac{1}{3125}$

$\left(-\dfrac{1}{5}\right)^{n} = \dfrac{1}{15,625}$

By trial and error, we find that $n = 6$.
Thus, the sum can be written as

$\displaystyle\sum_{n=1}^{6} 15\left(-\frac{1}{5}\right)^{n-1}.$

62. $32 + 24 + 18 + \cdots + 10.125$

$a_1 = 32, r = \dfrac{3}{4}$

$32\left(\dfrac{3}{4}\right)^{n-1} = 10.125 = \dfrac{81}{8}$

$\left(\dfrac{3}{4}\right)^{n-1} = \dfrac{81}{256}$

$\left(\dfrac{3}{4}\right)^{n-1} = \left(\dfrac{3}{4}\right)^4$

$n - 1 = 4$

$n = 5$

Thus, the sum can be written as

$\displaystyle\sum_{n=1}^{5} 32\left(\frac{3}{4}\right)^{n-1}.$

64. $\displaystyle\sum_{n=0}^{\infty} 2\left(\frac{2}{3}\right)^n = 2 + 2\left(\frac{2}{3}\right)^1 + 2\left(\frac{2}{3}\right)^2 + \cdots$

$a_1 = 2, r = \dfrac{2}{3}$

$\displaystyle\sum_{n=0}^{\infty} 2\left(\frac{2}{3}\right)^n = \dfrac{a_1}{1 - r} = \dfrac{2}{1 - \frac{2}{3}} = 6$

66. $\displaystyle\sum_{n=0}^{\infty} 2\left(-\frac{2}{3}\right)^n = 2 + 2\left(-\frac{2}{3}\right)^1 + 2\left(-\frac{2}{3}\right)^2 + \cdots$

$a_1 = 2, r = -\frac{2}{3}$

$\displaystyle\sum_{n=0}^{\infty} 2\left(-\frac{2}{3}\right)^n = \frac{a_1}{1-r} = \frac{2}{1-\left(-\frac{2}{3}\right)} = \frac{6}{5}$

68. $\displaystyle\sum_{n=0}^{\infty}\left(\frac{1}{10}\right)^n = 1 + \left(\frac{1}{10}\right)^1 + \left(\frac{1}{10}\right)^2 + \cdots$

$a_1 = 1, r = \frac{1}{10}$

$\displaystyle\sum_{n=0}^{\infty}\left(\frac{1}{10}\right)^n = \frac{a_1}{1-r} = \frac{1}{1-\frac{1}{10}} = \frac{10}{9}$

70. $\displaystyle\sum_{n=0}^{\infty} 4(0.2)^n = 4 + 4(0.2)^1 + 4(0.2)^2 + \cdots$

$a_1 = 4, r = 0.2$

$\displaystyle\sum_{n=0}^{\infty} 4(0.2)^n = \frac{4}{1-0.2} = 5$

72. $\displaystyle\sum_{n=0}^{\infty}\left[-10(0.2)^n\right] = -10 - 10(0.2)^1 - 10(0.2)^2 - \cdots$

$a_1 = -10, r = 0.2$

$\displaystyle\sum_{n=0}^{\infty} -10(0.2)^n = \frac{-10}{1-0.2} = -12.5$

74. $9 + 6 + 4 + \frac{8}{3} + \cdots$

$a_1 = 9, r = \frac{2}{3}$

$\displaystyle\sum_{n=0}^{\infty} 9\left(\frac{2}{3}\right)^n = \frac{9}{1-\frac{2}{3}} = 27$

76. $\dfrac{-125}{36} + \dfrac{25}{6} - 5 + 6 - \ldots = \displaystyle\sum_{n=0}^{\infty} -\frac{125}{36}\left(-\frac{6}{5}\right)^n$

The sum is undefined because

$|r| = \left|-\frac{6}{5}\right| = \frac{6}{5} > 1.$

78. $0.\overline{297} = \displaystyle\sum_{n=0}^{\infty} 0.297(0.001)^n = \frac{0.297}{1-0.001} = \frac{0.297}{0.999} = \frac{297}{999} = \frac{11}{37}$

80. $1.3\overline{8} = 1.3 + \displaystyle\sum_{n=0}^{\infty} 0.08(0.1)^n = 1.3 + \frac{0.08}{1-0.1} = 1.3 + \frac{0.08}{0.9} = 1\frac{3}{10} + \frac{4}{45} = 1\frac{7}{18} = \frac{25}{18}$

82. $f(x) = 2\left[\dfrac{1-(0.8)^x}{1-(0.8)}\right], \displaystyle\sum_{n=0}^{\infty} 2\left(\frac{4}{5}\right)^n = \frac{2}{1-\frac{4}{5}} = 10$

The horizontal asymptote of $f(x)$ is $y = 10$.
This corresponds to the sum of the series.

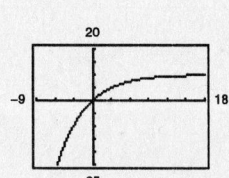

84. $A = P\left(1 + \dfrac{r}{n}\right)^{nt} = 2500\left(1 + \dfrac{0.08}{n}\right)^{n(20)}$

   (a) $n = 1, A = 2500\left(1 + \dfrac{0.08}{1}\right)^{1(20)} \approx \$11,652.39$

   (b) $n = 2, A = 2500\left(1 + \dfrac{0.08}{2}\right)^{2(20)} \approx \$12,002.55$

   (c) $n = 4, A = 2500\left(1 + \dfrac{0.08}{4}\right)^{4(20)} \approx \$12,188.60$

   (d) $n = 12, A = 2500\left(1 + \dfrac{0.08}{12}\right)^{12(20)} \approx \$12,317.01$

   (e) $n = 365, A = 2500\left(1 + \dfrac{0.08}{365}\right)^{365(20)} \approx \$12,380.41$

86. P = population after n years

P_0 = initial population = 250,000

  r = rate of increase = 1.3%

  n = number of years = 30

$P = P_0(1 + r)^n = 250,000(1.013)^{30} \approx 368,318$

88. $A = \sum_{n=1}^{60} 50 \left(1 + \dfrac{0.08}{12}\right)^n$

$= 50(1.006666667)\left(\dfrac{1 - (1.006666667)^{60}}{1 - 1.006666667}\right)$

$\approx \$3698.34$

90. Let $N = 12t$ be the total number of deposits.

$A = Pe^{r/12} + Pe^{2r/12} + \cdots + Pe^{Nr/12}$

$= \sum_{n=1}^{N} Pe^{r/12 \cdot n}$

$= Pe^{r/12} \dfrac{(1 - (e^{r/12})^N)}{(1 - e^{r/12})}$

$= Pe^{r/12} \dfrac{(1 - (e^{r/12})^{12t})}{1 - e^{r/12}}$

$= \dfrac{Pe^{r/12}(e^{rt} - 1)}{(e^{r/12} - 1)}$

92. $P = \$75, r = 9\%, t = 25$ years

(a) Compounded monthly: $A = 75\left[\left(1 + \dfrac{0.09}{12}\right)^{12(25)} - 1\right]\left(1 + \dfrac{12}{0.09}\right) \approx \$84,714.78$

(b) Compounded continuously: $A = \dfrac{75e^{0.09/12}(e^{0.09(25)} - 1)}{e^{0.09/12} - 1} \approx \$85,196.05$

94. $P = \$20, r = 6\%, t = 50$ years

(a) Compounded monthly: $A = 20\left[\left(1 + \dfrac{0.06}{12}\right)^{12(50)} - 1\right]\left(1 + \dfrac{12}{0.06}\right) \approx \$76,122.54$

(b) Compounded continuously: $A = \dfrac{20e^{0.06/12}(e^{0.06(50)} - 1)}{e^{0.06/12} - 1} \approx \$76,533.16$

96. $W = \$2000, t = 20, r = 9\%$

$P = W\left(\dfrac{12}{r}\right)\left[1 - \left(1 + \dfrac{r}{12}\right)^{-12t}\right]$

$P = 2000\left(\dfrac{12}{0.09}\right)\left[1 - \left(1 + \dfrac{0.09}{12}\right)^{-12(20)}\right] \approx \$222,289.91$

98. $\sum_{n=0}^{6} 3.978e^{0.11n} = \sum_{n=1}^{7} 3.978(e^{0.11})^{n-1}$

$= 3.978\left(\dfrac{1 - (e^{0.11})^7}{1 - e^{0.11}}\right) = \$39.7$ billion

100. $a_n = 30,000(1.05)^{n-1}$

$T = \sum_{n=1}^{40} 30,000(1.05)^{n-1} = 30,000\dfrac{(1 - 1.05^{40})}{(1 - 1.05)} \approx \$3,623,993.23$

102. False. A sequence is geometric if the ratios of consecutive terms are the same.

104. Given a real number r between -1 and 1, as the exponent n increases, r^n approaches zero.

106. $g(x) = x^2 - 1$

$g(x + 1) = (x + 1)^2 - 1$

$= x^2 + 2x + 1 - 1 = x^2 + 2x$

108. $f(x) = 3x + 1, g(x) = x^2 - 1$

$f(g(x + 1)) = f(x^2 + 2x)$

$= 3(x^2 + 2x) + 1$

$= 3x^2 + 6x + 1$

110. $9x^3 - 64x = x(9x^2 - 64) = x(3x + 8)(3x - 8)$

112. $6x^2 - 13x - 5 = (3x + 1)(2x - 5)$

114. $\dfrac{3}{x+3} \cdot \dfrac{x(x+3)}{x-3} = \dfrac{3x}{x-3}, x \neq -3$

116. $\dfrac{x}{3} \div \dfrac{3x}{6x+3} = \dfrac{x}{3} \cdot \dfrac{3(2x+1)}{3x} = \dfrac{2x+1}{3}, x \neq 0$

118. $5 + \dfrac{7}{x+2} + \dfrac{2}{x-2} = \dfrac{5(x+2)(x-2) + 7(x-2) + 2(x+2)}{(x+2)(x-2)}$

$$= \dfrac{5(x^2-4) + 7(x-2) + 2(x+2)}{(x+2)(x-2)}$$

$$= \dfrac{5x^2 - 20 + 7x - 14 + 2x + 4}{(x+2)(x-2)} = \dfrac{5x^2 + 9x - 30}{(x+2)(x-2)}$$

Section 9.4   Mathematical Induction

Solutions to Even-Numbered Exercises

2. $P_k = \dfrac{1}{2(k+2)}$

$P_{k+1} = \dfrac{1}{2(k+1+2)} = \dfrac{1}{2(k+3)}$

4. $P_k = \dfrac{k}{3}(2k+1)$

$P_{k+1} = \dfrac{k+1}{3}[2(k+1)+1] = \dfrac{k+1}{3}(2k+3)$

6. 1. When $n = 1$, $S_1 = 3 = 1(2 \cdot 1 + 1)$.

2. Assume that

$S_k = 3 + 7 + 11 + 15 + \cdots + (4k - 1) = k(2k + 1)$.

Then,

$S_{k+1} = S_k + a_{k+1} = (3 + 7 + 11 + 15 + \cdots + (4k-1)) + [4(k+1) - 1]$

$= k(2k+1) + (4k+3)$

$= 2k^2 + 5k + 3$

$= (k+1)(2k+3)$

$= (k+1)[2(k+1)+1]$.

Therefore, we conclude that this formula is valid.

8. 1. When $n = 1$,

$S_1 = 1 = \dfrac{1}{2}(3 \cdot 1 - 1)$.

2. Assume that

$S_k = 1 + 4 + 7 + 10 + \cdots + (3k - 2) = \dfrac{k}{2}(3k - 1)$.

—CONTINUED—

8. —CONTINUED—

Then,

$$S_{k+1} = S_k + a_{k+1} = (1 + 4 + 7 + 10 + \cdots + (3k - 2)) + (3(k + 1) - 2)$$

$$= \frac{k}{2}(3k - 1) + (3k + 1)$$

$$= \frac{3k^2 - k + 6k + 2}{2}$$

$$= \frac{3k^2 + 5k + 2}{2}$$

$$= \frac{(k + 1)(3k + 2)}{2}$$

$$= \frac{k + 1}{2}[3(k + 1) - 1].$$

Therefore, we conclude that this formula is valid for all positive integer values of n.

10. 1. When $n = 1, s_1 = 2 = 3^1 - 1$

2. Assume that

$$S_k = 2(1 + 3 + 3^2 + 3^3 + \cdots + 3^{k-1}) = 3^k - 1.$$

Then,

$$S_{k+1} = S_k + a_{k+1}$$

$$= [2(1 + 3 + 3^2 + 3^3 + \cdots + 3^{k-1})] + 2 \cdot 3^{k+1-1}$$

$$= 3^k - 1 + 2 \cdot 3^k$$

$$= 3 \cdot 3^k - 1$$

$$= 3^{k+1} - 1.$$

Therefore, we conclude that this formula is valid for all positive integer values of n.

12. 1. When $n = 1$,

$$S_1 = 1 = \frac{1(1 + 1)(2 \cdot 1 + 1)}{6}.$$

2. Assume that

$$S_k = 1^2 + 2^2 + 3^2 + 4^2 + \cdots + k^2 = \frac{k(k + 1)(2k + 1)}{6}.$$

Then,

$$S_{k+1} = S_k + a_{k+1} = (1^2 + 2^2 + 3^2 + 4^2 + \cdots + k^2) + (k + 1)^2$$

$$= \frac{k(k + 1)(2k + 1)}{6} + (k + 1)^2$$

$$= \frac{k(k + 1)(2k + 1) + 6(k + 1)^2}{6}$$

$$= \frac{(k + 1)[2k^2 + k + 6k + 6]}{6}$$

$$= \frac{(k + 1)(k + 2)(2k + 3)}{6}.$$

Therefore, we conclude that this formula is valid for all positive integer values of n.

14. 1. When $n = 1$, $S_1 = 2 = 1 + 1$.

2. Assume that

$$S_k = \left(1 + \frac{1}{1}\right)\left(1 + \frac{1}{2}\right)\left(1 + \frac{1}{3}\right)\cdots\left(1 + \frac{1}{k}\right) = k + 1.$$

Then,

$$S_{k+1} = S_k + a_{k+1} = \left(1 + \frac{1}{1}\right)\left(1 + \frac{1}{2}\right)\left(1 + \frac{1}{3}\right)\cdots\left(1 + \frac{1}{k}\right)\left(1 + \frac{1}{k+1}\right)$$

$$= (k + 1)\left(1 + \frac{1}{k+1}\right)$$

$$= k + 1 + 1$$

$$= k + 2.$$

Therefore, we conclude that this formula is valid for all positive integer values of n.

16. 1. When $n = 1$,

$$S_1 = 1^4 = \frac{1(1 + 1)(2 \cdot 1 + 1)(3 \cdot 1^2 + 3 \cdot 1 - 1)}{30}.$$

2. Assume that

$$S_k = \sum_{i=1}^{k} i^4 = \frac{k(k + 1)(2k + 1)(3k^2 + 3k - 1)}{30}.$$

Then,

$$S_{k+1} = S_k + a_{k+1} = S_k + (k + 1)^4$$

$$= \frac{k(k + 1)(2k + 1)(3k^2 + 3k - 1)}{30} + (k + 1)^4$$

$$= \frac{k(k + 1)(2k + 1)(3k^2 + 3k - 1) + 30(k + 1)^4}{30}$$

$$= \frac{(k + 1)[k(2k + 1)(3k^2 + 3k - 1) + 30(k + 1)^3]}{30}$$

$$= \frac{(k + 1)(6k^4 + 39k^3 + 91k^2 + 89k + 30)}{30}$$

$$= \frac{(k + 1)(k + 2)(2k + 3)(3k^2 + 9k + 5)}{30}$$

$$= \frac{(k + 1)(k + 2)(2(k + 1) + 1)(3(k + 1)^2 + 3(k + 1) - 1)}{30}.$$

Therefore, we conclude that this formula is valid for all positive integer values of n.

18. 1. When $n = 1$,

$$S_1 = \frac{1}{2} = \frac{1}{2 \cdot 1 + 1}.$$

2. Assume that

$$S_k = \sum_{i=0}^{k} \frac{1}{(2i - 1)(2i + 1)} = \frac{k}{2k + 1}.$$

Then,

$$S_{k+1} = S_k + a_{k+1} = S_k + \frac{1}{(2(k + 1) - 1)(2(k + 1) + 1)}$$

$$= \frac{k}{2k + 1} + \frac{1}{(2k + 1)(2k + 3)}$$

$$= \frac{k(2k + 3) + 1}{(2k + 1)(2k + 3)}$$

$$= \frac{2k^2 + 3k + 1}{(2k + 1)(2k + 3)}$$

$$= \frac{(2k + 1)(k + 1)}{(2k + 1)(2k + 3)}$$

$$= \frac{k + 1}{2(k + 1) + 1}.$$

Therefore, we conclude that this formula is valid for all positive integer values of n.

20. $\displaystyle\sum_{n=1}^{30} n = \frac{30(30 + 1)}{2} = 465$

22. $\displaystyle\sum_{n=1}^{10} n^3 = \frac{10^2(10 + 1)^2}{4} = 3025$

24. $\displaystyle\sum_{n=1}^{8} n^5 = \frac{8^2(8 + 1)^2(2(8)^2 + 2(8) - 1)}{12} = 61{,}776$

26. $\displaystyle\sum_{n=1}^{20} (n^3 - n) = \sum_{n=1}^{20} n^3 - \sum_{n=1}^{20} n$

$$= \frac{(20)^2(20 + 1)^2}{4} - \frac{20(20 + 1)}{2}$$

$$= \frac{(20)^2(21)^2 - 2(20)(21)}{4} = 43{,}890$$

28. $\displaystyle\sum_{j=1}^{10} \left(3 - \frac{1}{2}j + \frac{1}{2}j^2\right) = \sum_{j=1}^{10} 3 - \frac{1}{2}\sum_{j=1}^{10} j + \frac{1}{2}\sum_{j=1}^{10} j^2$

$$= 3(10) - \frac{1}{2} \cdot \frac{10(10 + 1)}{2} + \frac{1}{2} \cdot \frac{10(10 + 1)(2 \cdot 10 + 1)}{6}$$

$$= \frac{3(10)(12) - 3(10)(11) + 10(11)(21)}{12}$$

$$= 195$$

30. $S_n = 25 + 22 + 19 + 16 + \cdots + (-3n + 28)$

$$S_1 = 25 = \frac{1}{2}(50)$$

$$S_2 = 25 + 22 = 47 = \frac{2}{2}(47)$$

$$S_3 = 25 + 22 + 19 = 66 = \frac{3}{2}(44)$$

$$S_4 = 25 + 22 + 19 + 16 = 82 = \frac{4}{2}(41)$$

From the sequence, it appears that $S_n = \frac{n}{2}(-3n + 53)$.

This can be verified by mathematical induction.
The formula has already been verified for $n = 1$.
Assume that the formula is valid for $n = k$.

Then, $S_{k+1} = [25 + 22 + 19 + 16 + \cdots + (-3k + 28)] + [-3(k + 1) + 28]$

$$= \frac{k}{2}(-3k + 53) + (-3k + 25)$$

$$= \frac{1}{2}(-3k^2 + 47k + 50)$$

$$= -\frac{1}{2}(3k^2 - 47k - 50)$$

$$= -\frac{1}{2}(k + 1)(3k - 50)$$

$$= \frac{k}{2}[-3(k + 1) + 53]$$

Thus, the formula is valid.

32. $S_n = 3 - \frac{9}{2} + \frac{27}{4} - \frac{81}{8} + \cdots + 3\left(-\frac{3}{2}\right)^{n-1}$

Since the series is geometric, we have

$$S_r = \sum_{i=1}^{\infty} 3\left(-\frac{3}{2}\right)^{n-1} = 3\left[\frac{1 - \left(-\frac{3}{2}\right)^n}{1 - \left(-\frac{3}{2}\right)}\right] = \frac{6}{5}\left[1 - \left(-\frac{3}{2}\right)^n\right]$$

34. $S_n = \frac{1}{2 \cdot 3} + \frac{1}{3 \cdot 4} + \frac{1}{4 \cdot 5} + \frac{1}{5 \cdot 6} + \cdots + \frac{1}{(n + 1)(n + 2)}$

$$S_1 = \frac{1}{6} = \frac{1}{2 \cdot 3}$$

$$S_2 = \frac{1}{6} + \frac{1}{12} = \frac{1}{4} = \frac{2}{2 \cdot 4}$$

$$S_3 = \frac{1}{6} + \frac{1}{12} + \frac{1}{20} = \frac{3}{10} = \frac{3}{2 \cdot 5}$$

$$S_4 = \frac{1}{6} + \frac{1}{12} + \frac{1}{20} + \frac{1}{30} = \frac{1}{3} = \frac{4}{2 \cdot 6}$$

— CONTINUED —

34. — CONTINUED —

From this sequence, it appears that $S_n = \dfrac{n}{2(n + 2)}$.

This can be verified by mathematical induction.
The formula has already been verified for $n = 1$.
Assume that the formula is valid for $n = k$.

Then, $S_{k+1} = \left[\dfrac{1}{6} + \dfrac{1}{12} + \dfrac{1}{20} + \dfrac{1}{30} + \ldots + \dfrac{1}{(k + 1)(k + 2)} \right] + \dfrac{1}{(k + 2)(k + 3)}$

$$= \frac{k}{2(k + 2)} + \frac{1}{(k + 2)(k + 3)}$$

$$= \frac{k(k + 3) + 2}{2(k + 2)(k + 3)}$$

$$= \frac{k^2 + k + 2}{2(k + 2)(k + 3)}$$

$$= \frac{(k + 1)(k + 2)}{2(k + 2)(k + 3)}$$

$$= \frac{k + 1}{2[(k + 1) + 2]}$$

Thus, the formula is valid.

36. 1. When $n = 7$, $\left(\dfrac{4}{3}\right)^7 \approx 7.4915 > 7$.

2. Assume that $\left(\dfrac{4}{3}\right)^k > k, k > 7$.

Then, $\left(\dfrac{4}{3}\right)^{k+1} = \left(\dfrac{4}{3}\right)^k \left(\dfrac{4}{3}\right) > k\left(\dfrac{4}{3}\right) = k + \dfrac{k}{3} > k + 1$ for $k > 7$.

Thus, $\left(\dfrac{4}{3}\right)^{k+1} > k + 1$.

Therefore, the inequality $\left(\dfrac{4}{3}\right)^n > n$ is valid for all integers n such that $n \geq 7$.

38. 1. When $n = 1$, $\left(\dfrac{x}{y}\right)^2 < \left(\dfrac{x}{y}\right)$ and $(0 < x < y)$.

2. Assume that

$$\left(\frac{x}{y}\right)^{k+1} < \left(\frac{x}{y}\right)^k$$

$\left(\dfrac{x}{y}\right)^{k+1} < \left(\dfrac{x}{y}\right)^k \Rightarrow \left(\dfrac{x}{y}\right)\left(\dfrac{x}{y}\right)^{k+1} < \left(\dfrac{x}{y}\right)\left(\dfrac{x}{y}\right)^k \Rightarrow \left(\dfrac{x}{y}\right)^{k+2} < \left(\dfrac{x}{y}\right)^{k+1}$.

Therefore, $\left(\dfrac{x}{y}\right)^{n+1} < \left(\dfrac{x}{y}\right)^n$ for all integers $n \geq 1$.

40. $2n^2 > (n + 1)^2, n \geq 3$

  1. For $n = 3$, the statement is true, because
$2(3)^2 = 18 > (3 + 1)^2 = 16$.

  2. Assuming that $2k^2 > (k + 1)^2$
you need to show that $2(k + 1)^2 > (k + 2)^2$. For
$n = k$, you have

$$(k + 2)^2 = k^2 + 4k + 4$$
$$= k^2 + 2k + 1 + 2k + 3$$
$$= (k + 1)^2 + 2k + 3.$$

By the assumption $(k + 1)^2 < 2k^2$, you have

$$(k + 1)^2 + 2k + 3 < 2k^2 + 2k + 3.$$

Because $2k + 3 < 4k + 2$, or $1 < 2k$ for all $k > 3$,
you can say that

$$2k^2 + 2k + 3 < 2k^2 + 4k + 2 = 2(k + 1)^2.$$

It follows that $(k + 2)^2 < 2k^2 + 2k + 3 < 2(k + 1)^2$

or $2(k + 1)^2 > (k + 2)^2$.

Therefore, $2n^2 > (n + 1)^2$, for all $n \geq 3$.

44. 1. When $n = 1$, $\ln x_1 = \ln x_1$.

  2. Assume that

$$\ln(x_1 x_2 x_3 \ldots x_k) = \ln x_1 + \ln x_2 + \ln x_3 + \cdots + \ln x_k.$$

Then, $\ln(x_1 x_2 x_3 \ldots x_k x_{k+1}) = \ln[(x_1 x_2 x_3 \ldots x_k)x_{k+1}]$

$$= \ln(x_1 x_2 x_3 \ldots x_k) + \ln x_{k+1}$$
$$= \ln x_1 + \ln x_2 + \ln x_3 + \cdots + \ln x_k + \ln x_{k+1}.$$

Thus, $\ln(x_1 x_2 x_3 \ldots x_n) = \ln x_1 + \ln x_2 + \ln x_3 + \cdots \ln x_n.$

46. 1. When $n = 1$, $a + bi$ and $a - bi$ are complex conjugates by definition.

  2. Assume that $(a + bi)^k$ and $(a - bi)^k$ are complex conjugates.

That is, if $(a + bi)^k = c + di$, then $(a - bi)^k = c - di$.

Then,

$$(a + bi)^{k+1} = (a + bi)^k(a + bi) = (c + di)(a + bi)$$
$$= (ac - bd) + i(bc + ad)$$

and $(a - bi)^{k+1} = (a - bi)^k (a - bi) = (c - di)(a - bi)$

$$= (ac - bd) - i(bc + ad).$$

This implies that $(a + bi)^{k+1}$ and $(a - bi)^{k+1}$ are complex conjugates.
Therefore, $(a + bi)^n$ and $(a - bi)^n$ are complex conjugates for $n \geq 1$.

42. 1. When $n = 1$, $\left(\dfrac{a}{b}\right)^1 = \dfrac{a^1}{b^1}$.

  2. Assume that $\left(\dfrac{a}{b}\right)^k = \dfrac{a^k}{b^k}$.

Then, $\left(\dfrac{a}{b}\right)^{k+1} = \left(\dfrac{a}{b}\right)^k\left(\dfrac{a}{b}\right) = \dfrac{a^k}{b^k} \cdot \dfrac{a}{b} = \dfrac{a^{k+1}}{b^{k+1}}$.

Thus, $\left(\dfrac{a}{b}\right)^n = \dfrac{a^n}{b^n}$.

48. 1. When $n = 1$, $(2^{2(1)-1} + 3^{2(1)-1}) = 2 + 3 = 5$ and 5 is a factor.

    2. Assume that 5 is a factor of $(2^{2k-1} + 3^{2k-1})$.

       Then, $2^{2(k+1)-1} + 3^{2(k+1)-1} = 2^{2k+2-1} + 3^{2k+2-1}$

$$= 2^{2k-1}2^2 + 3^{2k-1}3^2$$

$$= 4 \cdot 2^{2k-1} + 9 \cdot 3^{2k-1}$$

$$= (2^{2k-1} + 3^{2k-1}) + (2^{2k-1} + 3^{2k-1})$$

$$+ (2^{2k-1} + 3^{2k-1}) + (2^{2k-1} + 3^{2k-1}) + 5 \cdot 3^{2k-1}.$$

Since 5 is a factor of each set of parenthesis and 5 is a factor of $5 \cdot 3^{2k-1}$, then 5 is a factor of the whole sum. Thus, 5 is a factor of $(2^{2n-1} + 3^{2n-1})$ for every positive integer n.

50. $a_0 = 1, a_n = a_{n-1} + 2$

$a_0 = 1$

$a_1 = a_0 + 2 = 1 + 2 = 3$

$a_2 = a_1 + 2 = 3 + 2 = 5$

$a_3 = a_2 + 2 = 5 + 2 = 7$

$a_4 = a_3 + 2 = 7 + 2 = 9$

52. $a_0 = 4, a_1 = 2, a_n = a_{n-1} - a_{n-2}$

$a_0 = 4$

$a_1 = 2$

$a_2 = a_1 - a_0 = 2 - 4 = -2$

$a_3 = a_2 - a_1 = -2 - 2 = -4$

$a_4 = a_3 - a_2 = -4 - (-2) = -2$

54. $a_1 = 0, a_n = a_{n-1} + 3$

$a_1 = a_1 = 0$

$a_2 = a_1 + 3 = 0 + 3 = 3$

$a_3 = a_2 + 3 = 3 + 3 = 6$

$a_4 = a_3 + 3 = 6 + 3 = 9$

$a_5 = a_4 + 3 = 9 + 3 = 12$

a_n: 0   3   6   9   12

First differences: 3 3 3 3

Second differences: 0 0 0

Since the first differences are equal, the sequence has a linear model.

56. $a_1 = 3, a_n = a_{n-1} - n$

$a_1 = a_1 = 3$

$a_2 = a_1 - 2 = 3 - 2 = 1$

$a_3 = a_2 - 3 = 1 - 3 = -2$

$a_4 = a_3 - 4 = -2 - 4 = -6$

$a_5 = a_4 - 5 = -6 - 5 = -11$

a_n: 3   1   -2   -6   -11

First differences: -2 -3 -4 -5

Second differences: -1 -1 -1

Since the second differences are all the same, the sequence has a quadratic model.

58. $a_0 = 0, a_n = a_{n-1} + n$

$a_0 = 0$

$a_1 = a_0 + 1 = 0 + 1 = 1$

$a_2 = a_1 + 2 = 1 + 2 = 3$

$a_3 = a_2 + 3 = 3 + 3 = 6$

$a_4 = a_3 + 4 = 6 + 4 = 10$

a_n: 0   1   3   6   10

First differences: 1 2 3 4

Second differences: 1 1 1

Since the second differences are equal, the sequence has a quadratic model.

60. $a_1 = 2, a_n = a_{n-1} + 2$

$a_1 = a_1 = 2$

$a_2 = a_1 + 2 = 2 + 2 = 4$

$a_3 = a_2 + 2 = 4 + 2 = 6$

$a_4 = a_3 + 2 = 6 + 2 = 8$

$a_5 = a_4 + 2 = 8 + 2 = 10$

a_n: 2   4   6   8   10

First differences: 2 2 2 2

Second differences: 0 0 0

Since the second differences are equal, the sequence has a linear model.

62. $a_0 = 1, a_n = a_{n-1} + n^2$

$a_0 = 1$

$a_1 = 1 + 1^2 = 2$

$a_2 = 2 + 2^2 = 6$

$a_3 = 6 + 3^2 = 15$

$a_4 = 15 + 4^2 = 31$

a_n: 1   2   6   15   31

First differences: 1   4   9   16

Second differences: 3   5   7

Since neither the first differences nor the second differences are equal, the sequence does not have a linear or a quadratic model.

64. $a_0 = 3, a_1 = 3, a_4 = 15$

Let $a_n = an^2 + bn + c$.

Thus: $a_0 = a(0)^2 + b(0) + c = 3 \implies c = 3$

$a_1 = a(1)^2 + b(1) + c = 3 \implies a + b + c = 3$

$a + b = 0$

$a_4 = a(4)^2 + b(4) + c = 15 \implies 16a + 4b + c = 15$

$16a + 4b = 12$

$4a + b = 3$

By elimination: $-a - b = 0$

$\underline{4a + b = 3}$

$3a \quad = 3$

$a = 1 \implies b = -1$

Thus, $a_n = n^2 - n + 3$.

66. $a_0 = -3, a_2 = 1, a_4 = 9$

Let $a_n = an^2 + bn + c$.

Then: $a_0 = a(0)^2 + b(0) + c = -3 \implies c = -3$

$a_2 = a(2)^2 + b(2) + c = 1 \implies 4a + 2b + c = 1$

$4a + 2b = 4$

$2a + b = 2$

$a_4 = a(4)^2 + b(4) + c = 9 \implies 16a + 4b + c = 9$

$16a + 4b = 12$

$4a + b = 3$

By elimination: $-2a - b = -2$

$\underline{4a + b = 3}$

$2a \quad = 1$

$a = \tfrac{1}{2} \implies b = 1$

Thus, $a_n = \tfrac{1}{2}n^2 + n - 3$.

68. True. P_7 may be false.

70. True. If the second differences are all zero, then the first differences are all the same, so the sequence is arithmetic.

72. See page 609.

74. $\begin{cases} y = x^2 \\ -3x + 2y = 2 \end{cases} \implies -3x + 2x^2 = 2$

$$2x^2 - 3x - 2 = 0$$

$$(2x + 1)(x - 2) = 0$$

$$x = -\tfrac{1}{2} \text{ or } x = 2$$

$$y = \tfrac{1}{4} \qquad y = 4$$

Points of intersection: $\left(-\tfrac{1}{2}, \tfrac{1}{4}\right), (2, 4)$

76. $\begin{cases} x - y = -1 \\ x + 2y - 2z = 3 \\ 3x - y + 2z = 3 \end{cases}$

Using an augmented matrix, we have:

$$\begin{bmatrix} 1 & -1 & 0 & \vdots & -1 \\ 1 & 2 & -2 & \vdots & 3 \\ 3 & -1 & 2 & \vdots & 3 \end{bmatrix}$$

$$\begin{matrix} \\ -R_1 + R_2 \rightarrow \\ -3R_1 + R_3 \rightarrow \end{matrix} \begin{bmatrix} 1 & -1 & 0 & \vdots & -1 \\ 0 & 3 & -2 & \vdots & 4 \\ 0 & 2 & 2 & \vdots & 6 \end{bmatrix}$$

$$\begin{matrix} \\ -R_3 + R_2 \rightarrow \\ \tfrac{1}{2}R_3 \rightarrow \end{matrix} \begin{bmatrix} 1 & -1 & 0 & \vdots & -1 \\ 0 & 1 & -4 & \vdots & -2 \\ 0 & 1 & 1 & \vdots & 3 \end{bmatrix}$$

$$\begin{matrix} R_2 + R_1 \rightarrow \\ \\ -R_2 + R_3 \rightarrow \end{matrix} \begin{bmatrix} 1 & 0 & -4 & \vdots & -3 \\ 0 & 1 & -4 & \vdots & -2 \\ 0 & 0 & 5 & \vdots & 5 \end{bmatrix}$$

$$\begin{matrix} 4R_3 + R_1 \rightarrow \\ 4R_3 + R_2 \rightarrow \\ \tfrac{1}{5}R_3 \rightarrow \end{matrix} \begin{bmatrix} 1 & 0 & 0 & \vdots & 1 \\ 0 & 1 & 0 & \vdots & 2 \\ 0 & 0 & 1 & \vdots & 1 \end{bmatrix}$$

Thus, $x = 1, y = 2, z = 1$.

Solution: $(1, 2, 1)$

78. $(2x^2 - 1)^2 = (2x^2 - 1)(2x^2 - 1) = 4x^4 - 4x^2 + 1$

80. $(5 - 4x)^3 = -64x^4 + 240x^2 - 300x + 125$

Section 9.5   The Binomial Theorem

Solutions to Even-Numbered Exercises

2. $_8C_6 = \dfrac{8!}{6! \cdot 2!} = \dfrac{8 \cdot 7}{2 \cdot 1} = 28$

4. $_{20}C_{20} = \dfrac{20!}{20! \cdot 0!} = 1$

6. $_{12}C_5 = \dfrac{12!}{5! \cdot 7!} = \dfrac{(12 \cdot 11 \cdot 10 \cdot 9 \cdot 8) \cdot 7\!\!\!/}{5! 7\!\!\!/} = \dfrac{12 \cdot 11 \cdot 10 \cdot 9 \cdot 8}{5 \cdot 4 \cdot 3 \cdot 2 \cdot 1} = 792$

8. $\dbinom{10}{6} = \dfrac{10!}{6! \cdot 4!} = \dfrac{(10 \cdot 9 \cdot 8 \cdot 7) \cdot 6\!\!\!/}{6\!\!\!/ \cdot 4!} = \dfrac{10 \cdot 9 \cdot 8 \cdot 7}{4 \cdot 3 \cdot 2 \cdot 1} = 210$

10. $\dbinom{100}{2} = \dfrac{100!}{98! \cdot 2!} = \dfrac{(100 \cdot 99) \cdot 98\!\!\!/}{98\!\!\!/ \cdot 2!} = \dfrac{100 \cdot 99}{2 \cdot 1}$

$$= 4950$$

12.

```
            1
          1   1
        1   2   1
      1   3   3   1
    1   4   6   4   1
  1   5  10  10   5   1
1   6  15  20  15   6   1
1   7  21  35  35  21   7   1
1   8  28  56  70  56  28  ⑧   1
```

$\binom{8}{7} = 8$, the 7th entry in the 8th row.

14.

```
            1
          1   1
        1   2   1
      1   3   3   1
    1   4   6   4   1
  1   5  10  10   5   1
1   6  15  ⑳  15   6   1
```

$_6C_3 = 20$, the 3rd entry in the 6th row.

16. $(x + 1)^6 = {}_6C_0x^6 + {}_6C_1x^5(1) + {}_6C_2x^4(1)^2 + {}_6C_3x^3(1)^3 + {}_6C_4x^2(1)^4 + {}_6C_5x(1)^5 + {}_6C_6(1)^6$

$\qquad = x^6 + 6x^5 + 15x^4 + 20x^3 + 15x^2 + 6x + 1$

18. $(a + 5)^5 = {}_5C_0a^5 + {}_5C_1a^4(5) + {}_5C_2a^3(5)^2 + {}_5C_3a^2(5)^3 + {}_5C_4a(5)^4 + {}_5C_5(5)^5$

$\qquad = a^5 + 25a^4 + 250a^3 + 1250a^2 + 3125a + 3125$

20. $(y - 2)^5 = {}_5C_0y^5 - {}_5C_1y^4(2) + {}_5C_2\,y^3(2)^2 - {}_5C_3y^2(2)^3 + {}_5C_4y(2)^4 - {}_5C_5(2)^5$

$\qquad = y^5 - 10y^4 + 40y^3 - 80y^2 + 80y - 32$

22. $(c + d)^3 = {}_3C_0c^3 + {}_3C_1c^2d + {}_3C_2cd^2 + {}_3C_3d^3$

$\qquad = c^3 + 3c^2d + 3cd^2 + d^3$

24. $(x + 2y)^4 = {}_4C_0\,x^4 + {}_4C_1x^3(2y) + {}_4C_2x^2(2y)^2 + {}_4C_3x(2y)^3 + {}_4C_4(2y)^4$

$\qquad = x^4 + 4x^3(2y) + 6x^2(4y^2) + 4x(8y^3) + 16y^4$

$\qquad = x^4 + 8x^3y + 24x^2y^2 + 32xy^3 + 16y^4$

26. $(2x - y)^5 = {}_5C_0(2x)^5 - {}_5C_1(2x)^4y + {}_5C_2(2x)^3y^2 - {}_5C_3(2x)^2y^3 + {}_5C_4(2x)y^4 - {}_5C_5(2x)y^5$

$\qquad = 32x^5 - 5(16x^4)y + 10(8x^3)y^2 - 10(4x^2)y^3 + 5(2x)y^4 - y^5$

$\qquad = 32x^5 - 80x^4y + 80x^3y^2 - 40x^2y^3 + 10xy^4 - y^5$

28. $(5 - 3y)^3 = 5^3 - 3(5)^2 3y + 3(5)(3y)^2 - (3y)^3$

$\qquad = 125 - 225y + 135y^2 - 27y^3$

30. $(x^2 + y^2)^6 = {}_6C_0(x^2)^6 + {}_6C_1(x^2)^5(y^2) + {}_6C_2(x^2)^4(y^2)^2 + {}_6C_3(x^2)^3(y^2)^3 + {}_6C_4(x^2)^2(y^2)^4 + {}_6C_5(x^2)(y^2)^5 + {}_6C_6(y^2)^6$

$\qquad = x^{12} + 6x^{10}y^2 + 15x^8y^4 + 20x^6y^6 + 15x^4y^8 + 6x^2y^{10} + y^{12}$

32. $\left(\dfrac{1}{x} + 2y\right)^6 = {}_6C_0\left(\dfrac{1}{x}\right)^6 + {}_6C_1\left(\dfrac{1}{x}\right)^5(2y) + {}_6C_2\left(\dfrac{1}{x}\right)^4(2y)^2 + {}_6C_3\left(\dfrac{1}{x}\right)^3(2y)^3 + {}_6C_4\left(\dfrac{1}{x}\right)^2(2y)^4 + {}_6C_5\left(\dfrac{1}{x}\right)(2y)^5 + {}_6C_6(2y)^6$

$\qquad = 1\left(\dfrac{1}{x}\right)^6 + 6(2)\left(\dfrac{1}{x}\right)^5y + 15(4)\left(\dfrac{1}{x}\right)^4y^2 + 20(8)\left(\dfrac{1}{x}\right)^3y^3 + 15(16)\left(\dfrac{1}{x}\right)^2y^4 + 6(32)\left(\dfrac{1}{x}\right)y^5 + 1(64)y^6$

$\qquad = \dfrac{1}{x^6} + \dfrac{12y}{x^5} + \dfrac{60y^2}{x^4} + \dfrac{160y^3}{x^3} + \dfrac{240y^4}{x^2} + \dfrac{192y^5}{x} + 64y^6$

34. $3(x + 1)^5 - 4(x + 1)^3 = 3[_5C_0x^5 + _5C_1x^4(1) + _5C_2x^3(1)^2 + _5C_3x^2(1)^3 + _5C_4x(1)^4 + _5C_5(1)^5]$

$$- 4[_3C_0x^3 + _3C_1x^2(1) + _3C_2x(1)^2 + _3C_3(1)^3]$$

$$= 3[(1)x^5 + 5x^4 + 10x^3 + 10x^2 + 5x + 1] - 4[(1)x^3 + 3x^2 + 3x + 1]$$

$$= 3x^5 + 15x^4 + 26x^3 + 18x^2 + 3x - 1$$

36. 4th Row of Pascal's Triangle: 1   4   6   4   1

$$(3 - 2z)^4 = 3^4 - 4(3)^3(2z) + 6(3)^2(2z)^2 - 4(3)(2z)^3 + (2z)^4$$

$$= 81 - 216z + 216z^2 - 96z^3 + 16z^4$$

38. 6th Row of Pascal's Triangle: 1   6   15   20   15   6   1

$$(2v + 3)^6 = (2v)^6 + 6(2v)^5(3) + 15(2v)^4(3)^2 + 20(2v)^3(3)^3 + 15(2v)^2(3)^4 + 6(2v)(3)^5 + (3)^6$$

$$= 64v^6 + 576v^5 + 2160v^4 + 4320v^3 + 4860v^2 + 2916v + 729$$

40. The term involving x^8 in the expansion of $(x^2 + 3)^{12}$ is $_{12}C_8(x^2)^4(3)^8 = \dfrac{12!}{(12 - 8)!8!} \cdot 3^8x^8 = 3{,}247{,}695x^8$.
The coefficient is 3,247,695.

42. The term involving x^2y^8 in the expansion of $(4x - y)^{10}$ is $_{10}C_8(4x)^2(-y)^8 = \dfrac{10!}{(10 - 8)!8!} \cdot 16x^2y^8 = 720x^2y^8$.
The coefficient is 720.

44. The term involving x^6y^2 in the expansion of $(2x - 3y)^8$ is $_8C_2(2x)^6(-3y)^2 = \dfrac{8!}{(8 - 2)!2!}(64x^6)(9y^2) = 16{,}128x^6y^2$.

The coefficient is 16,128.

46. The term involving z^4t^8 in the expansion of $(z^2 - t)^{10}$ is $_{10}C_8(z^2)^2(-t)^8 = \dfrac{10!}{(10 - 8)!8!}z^4t^8 = 45z^4t^8$.

The coefficient is 45.

48. $\left(2\sqrt{t} - 1\right)^3 = \left(2\sqrt{t}\right)^3 + 3\left(2\sqrt{t}\right)^2(-1) + 3\left(2\sqrt{t}\right)(-1)^2 + (-1)^3$

$$= 8t^{3/2} - 12t + 6t^{1/2} - 1$$

50. $(u^{3/5} + 2)^5 = (u^{3/5})^5 + 5(u^{3/5})^4(2) + 10(u^{3/5})^3(2)^2 + 10(u^{3/5})^2(2)^3 + 5(u^{3/5})(2)^4 + 2^5$

$$= u^3 + 10u^{12/5} + 40u^{9/5} + 80u^{6/5} + 80u^{3/5} + 32$$

52. $\dfrac{f(x + h) - f(x)}{h} = \dfrac{(x + h)^4 - x^4}{h}$

$$= \dfrac{x^4 + 4x^3h + 6x^2h^2 + 4xh^3 + h^4 - x^4}{h}$$

$$= \dfrac{h(4x^3 + 6x^2h + 4xh^2 + h^3)}{h}$$

$$= 4x^3 + 6x^2h + 4xh^2 + h^3$$

54. $\dfrac{f(x+h)-f(x)}{h} = \dfrac{\dfrac{1}{x+h}-\dfrac{1}{x}}{h}$

$$= \dfrac{\dfrac{x-(x+h)}{x(x+h)}}{h}$$

$$= \dfrac{\dfrac{-h}{x(x+h)}}{h}$$

$$= -\dfrac{1}{x(x+h)}$$

56. $(2-i)^5 = {}_5C_0 2^5 - {}_5C_1 2^4 i + {}_5C_2 2^3 i^2 - {}_5C_3 2^2 i^3 + {}_5C_4 2 i^4 - {}_5C_5 i^5$

$$= 32 - 80i - 80 + 40i + 10 - i$$

$$= -38 - 41i$$

58. $\left(5+\sqrt{-9}\right)^3 = (5+3i)^3$

$$= 5^3 + 3 \cdot 5^2 (3i) + 3 \cdot 5(3i)^2 + (3i)^3$$

$$= 125 + 225i - 135 - 27i$$

$$= -10 + 198i$$

60. $\left(5-\sqrt{3}i\right)^4 = 5^4 - 4 \cdot 5^3\left(\sqrt{3}i\right) + 6 \cdot 5^2\left(\sqrt{3}i\right)^2 - 4 \cdot 5\left(\sqrt{3}i\right)^3 + \left(\sqrt{3}i\right)^4$

$$= 625 - 500\sqrt{3}i - 450 + 60\sqrt{3}i + 9$$

$$= 184 - 440\sqrt{3}i$$

62. $(2.005)^{10} = (2+0.005)^{10} = 2^{10} + 10(2)^9(0.005) + 45(2)^8(0.005)^2 + 120(2)^7(0.005)^3 + 210(2)^6(0.005)^4$

$$+ 252(2)^5(0.005)^5 + 210(2)^4(0.005)^6 + 120(2)^3(0.005)^7 + 45(2)^2(0.005)^8$$

$$+ 10(2)(0.005)^9 + (0.005)^{10}$$

$$= 1024 + 25.6 + 0.288 + 0.00192 + 0.0000084 + \cdots$$

$$\approx 1049.890$$

64. $(1.98)^9 = (2-0.02)^9 = 2^9 - 9(2)^8(0.02) + 36(2)^7(0.02)^2 - 84(2)^6(0.02)^3 + 126(2)^5(0.02)^4$

$$- 126(2)^4(0.02)^5 + 84(2)^3(0.02)^6 - 36(2)^2(0.02)^7 + 9(2)(0.02)^8 - (0.02)^9$$

$$= 512 - 46.08 + 1.8432 - 0.043008 + 0.00064512$$

$$\approx 467.721$$

66. $f(x) = -x^4 + 4x^2 - 1, g(x) = f(x - 3)$

$g(x) = f(x - 3)$

$\quad = -(x - 3)^4 + 4(x - 3)^2 - 1$

$\quad = -(x^4 + 4x^3(-3) + 6x^2(-3)^2 + 4x(-3)^3 + (-3)^4) + 4(x^2 - 6x + 9) - 1$

$\quad = -x^4 + 12x^3 - 54x^2 + 108x - 81 + 4x^2 - 24x + 36 - 1$

$\quad = -x^4 + 12x^3 - 50x^2 + 84x - 46$

The graph of g is the same as the graph of f shifted 3 units to the right.

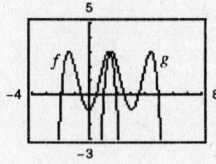

68. $_7C_4\left(\frac{1}{2}\right)^4\left(\frac{1}{2}\right)^3 = \frac{7!}{3!4!}\left(\frac{1}{16}\right)\left(\frac{1}{8}\right) = 35\left(\frac{1}{16}\right)\left(\frac{1}{8}\right) \approx 0.273$

70. $_8C_4\left(\frac{1}{3}\right)^4\left(\frac{2}{3}\right)^4 = \frac{8!}{4!4!}\left(\frac{1}{81}\right)\left(\frac{16}{81}\right) = 70\left(\frac{1}{81}\right)\left(\frac{16}{81}\right) \approx 0.171$

72. $f(t) = 0.0348t^2 + 5.1083t + 41.0250, \ 0 \le t \le 16$

(a) $g(t) = f(t + 10)$

$\quad = 0.0348(t + 10)^2 + 5.1083(t + 10) + 41.0250$

$\quad = 0.0348(t^2 + 20t + 100) + 5.1083t + 51.083 + 41.0250$

$\quad = 0.0348t^2 + 5.8043t + 95.588$

(b)

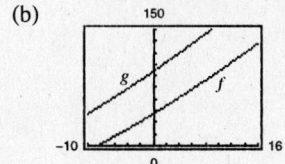

74. False. Each row of Pascal's Triangle could be used to find the coefficients of the Binomial Theorem.

76. The first and last numbers in each row are 1. Every other number in each row is formed by adding the two numbers immediately above the number.

78. $(n + 1)$ terms

80. $_nC_{n-r} = \dfrac{n!}{(n - (n - r))!(n - r)!}$

$= \dfrac{n!}{r!(n - r)!}$

$= \dfrac{n!}{(n - r)!r!}$

$= {_nC_r}$

82. $_nC_r + {_nC_{r-1}} = \dfrac{n!}{(n - r)!r!} + \dfrac{n!}{(n - r + 1)!(r - 1)!}$

$= \dfrac{n!(n - r + 1)!(r - 1)! + n!(n - r)!r!}{(n - r)!r!(n - r + 1)!(r - 1)!}$

$= \dfrac{n![(n - r + 1)!(r - 1)! + r!(n - r)!]}{(n - r)!r!(n - r + 1)!(r - 1)!}$

$= \dfrac{n!(r - 1)![(n - r + 1)! + r(n - r)!]}{(n - r)!r!(n - r + 1)!(r - 1)!}$

$= \dfrac{n!(n - r)![(n - r + 1) + r]}{(n - r)!r!(n - r + 1)!}$

$= \dfrac{n![n + 1]}{r!(n - r + 1)!}$

$= \dfrac{(n + 1)!}{[(n + 1) - r]!r!}$

$= {_{n+1}C_r}$

84. $g(x) = f(x) + 8$

$g(x)$ is shifted upward 8 units from $f(x)$.

86. $g(x) = f(-x)$

$g(x)$ is the reflection of $f(x)$ in the y-axis.

88. The graph of $f(x) = x^2$ is shifted three units to the right. Thus, $g(x) = (x - 3)^2$.

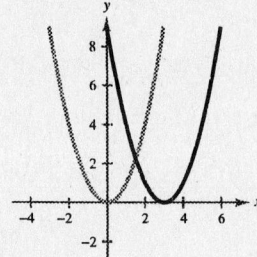

90. The graph of $f(x) = \sqrt{x}$ is shifted two units to the left and shifted one unit upward. Thus, $g(x) = \sqrt{x + 2} + 1$.

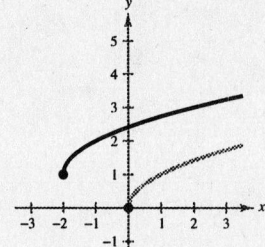

Section 9.6   Counting Principles

Solutions to Even-Numbered Exercises

2. Even integers: 2, 4, 6, 8, 10, 12

6 ways

4. Greater than 9: 10, 11, 12

3 ways

6. Divisible by 3: 3, 6, 9, 12

4 ways

8. Two *distinct* integers whose sum is 8:

$1 + 7, 2 + 6, 3 + 5$

3 ways

10. Monitors: 4

Keyboards: 3

Computers: 5

Total: $4 \cdot 3 \cdot 5 = 60$ ways

12. Math courses: 2

Science courses: 3

Social sciences and humanities courses: 5

Total: $2 \cdot 3 \cdot 5 = 30$ ways

14. $2^{12} = 4096$ ways

16. 1st position: 2

2nd position: 1

3rd position: 6

4th position: 5

5th position: 4

6th position: 3

7th position: 2

8th position: 1

Total: 2!6! = 1440 ways

18. $24 \cdot 24 \cdot 10 \cdot 10 \cdot 10 \cdot 10 = 5,760,000$ distinct license plates.

20. (a) $9 \cdot 10 \cdot 10 \cdot 10 = 9000$ numbers

(b) $9 \cdot 9 \cdot 8 \cdot 7 = 4536$ numbers

(c) $4 \cdot 10 \cdot 10 \cdot 10 = 4000$ numbers

(d) $9 \cdot 10 \cdot 10 \cdot 5 = 4500$ numbers

22. $50^3 = 125,000$ combinations

24. (a) $8! = 40,320$ orders

(b) $4!4! = 576$ orders

26. $_nP_r = \dfrac{n!}{(n-r)!}$

$_5P_5 = \dfrac{5!}{(5-5)!} = \dfrac{5!}{0!} = 120$

28. $_{20}P_2 = \dfrac{20!}{18!} = 20 \cdot 19 = 380$

30. $_7P_4 = \dfrac{7!}{3!} = 7 \cdot 6 \cdot 5 \cdot 4 = 840$

32. $_nP_5 = 18 \cdot {}_{n-2}P_4$ Note: $n \geq 6$ for this to be defined.

$$\frac{n!}{(n-5)!} = 18\left(\frac{(n-2)!}{(n-6)!}\right)$$

$$n(n-1)(n-2)(n-3)(n-4) = 18(n-2)(n-3)(n-4)(n-5) \quad \left(\begin{array}{l}\text{We can divide by } (n-2), (n-3), \\ (n-4) \text{ since } n \neq 2, n \neq 3, \text{ and } n \neq 4.\end{array}\right)$$

$$n^2 - n = 18n - 90$$

$$n^2 - 19n + 90 = 0$$

$$(n-1)(n-10) = 0$$

$$n = 9 \text{ or } n = 10$$

34. $_{100}P_5 = 9,034,502,400$

36. $_{10}P_8 = 1,814,400$

38. $_{10}C_7 = 120$

40. $\dfrac{8!}{3!5!} = 56$

42. $\dfrac{11!}{1!4!4!2!} = \dfrac{11!}{4!4!2!} = 34,650$

44. A B C D

A C B D

D B C A

D C B A

46. $_6C_3 = \dfrac{6!}{3!3!} = 20$

ABC, ABD, ABE, ABF, ACD,
ACE, ACF, ADE, ADF, AEF,
BCD, BCE, BCF, BDE, BDF,
BEF, CDE, CDF, CEF, DEF

48. $6! = 720$ ways

50. $4! = 24$ ways

52. $_{12}C_{10} = \dfrac{12!}{2!10!} = 66$ ways

54. $_{50}C_6 = \dfrac{50!}{44!6!} = 15{,}890{,}700$ ways

56. $_{80}C_5 = \dfrac{80!}{75!5!} = 24{,}040{,}016$ subsets

58. There are 7 good units and 3 defective units.

(a) $_7C_4 = \dfrac{7!}{3!4!} = 35$ ways

(b) $_7C_2 \cdot {}_3C_2 = \dfrac{7!}{5!2!} \cdot \dfrac{3!}{1!2!} = 21 \cdot 3 = 63$ ways

(c) $_7C_4 + {}_7C_3 \cdot {}_3C_1 + {}_7C_2 {}_3C_2 = \dfrac{7!}{3!4!} + \dfrac{7!}{4!3!} \cdot \dfrac{3!}{2!1!} + \dfrac{7!}{5!2!} \cdot \dfrac{3!}{1!2!}$

$= 35 + 35 \cdot 3 + 21 \cdot 3$

$= 203$ ways

60. Select type of card for three of a kind: $_{13}C_1$

Select three of four cards for three of a kind: $_4C_3$

Select type of card for pair: $_{12}C_1$

Select two of four cards for pair: $_4C_2$

$_{13}C_1 \cdot {}_4C_3 \cdot {}_{12}C_1 \cdot {}_4C_2 = 13 \cdot 4 \cdot 12 \cdot 6 = 3744$ ways
to get a full house

62. (a) $_3C_2 = \dfrac{3!}{2!1!} = 3$ relationships

(b) $_8C_2 = \dfrac{8!}{2!6!} = \dfrac{8 \cdot 7}{2} = 28$ relationships

(c) $_{12}C_2 = \dfrac{12!}{2!10!} = \dfrac{12 \cdot 11}{2} = 66$ relationships

(d) $_{20}C_2 = \dfrac{20!}{2!18!} = \dfrac{20 \cdot 19}{2} = 190$ relationships

64. $_6C_2 - 6 = 15 - 6 = 9$ diagonals

66. $_{10}C_2 - 10 = 45 - 10 = 35$ diagonals

68. True

70. $_{10}P_6 > {}_{10}C_6$
Changing the order of any of the six elements selected
results in a different permutation but the same combination.

72. $_nC_n = \dfrac{n!}{(n - n)!n!} = \dfrac{n!}{0!n!} = \dfrac{n!}{n!0!} = \dfrac{n!}{(n - 0)!0!} = {}_nC_0$

74. $_nC_r = \dfrac{n!}{(n - r)!r!}$

$= \dfrac{n(n - 1)(n - 2) \cdots (n - r + 1)(n - r)!}{(n - r)!r!}$

$= \dfrac{n(n - 1)(n - 2) \cdots (n - r + 1)}{r!}$

$= \dfrac{_nP_r}{r!}$

76. The symbol $_nP_r$ denotes the number of ways to choose
and order r elements out of a collection of n elements.

78. $g(x) = \sqrt{x - 3} + 2$

(a) $g(3) = \sqrt{3 - 3} + 2 = 2$

(b) $g(7) = \sqrt{7 - 3} + 2 = 4$

(c) $g(x + 3) = \sqrt{x + 3 - 3} + 2 = \sqrt{x} + 2$

80. $f(x) = \begin{cases} x^2 - 2x + 5, & x \le -4 \\ -x^2 - 2, & x > -4 \end{cases}$

(a) $f(-4) = (-4)^2 - 2(-4) + 5 = 29$

(b) $f(-1) = -(-1)^2 - 2 = -3$

(c) $f(-20) = (-20)^2 - 2(-20) + 5 = 445$

82. $(y - 2)^6 = y^6 + 6y^5(-2) + 15y^4(-2)^2 + 20y^3(-2)^3 + 15y^2(-2)^4 + 6y(-2)^5 + (-2)^6$

$\qquad = y^6 - 12y^5 + 60y^4 - 160y^3 + 240y^2 - 192y + 64$

84. $(x^2 - y^2)^4 = (x^2)^4 + 4(x^2)^3(-y^2) + 6(x^2)^2(-y^2)^2 + 4(x^2)(-y^2)^3 + (-y^2)^4$

$\qquad = x^8 - 4x^6y^2 + 6x^4y^4 - 4x^2y^6 + y^8$

Section 9.7   Probability

Solutions to Even-Numbered Exercises

2. $\{2, 3, 4, 5, 6, 7, 8, 9, 10, 11, 12\}$

4. $\{(\text{red, red}), (\text{red, blue}), (\text{red, black}), (\text{blue, blue}), (\text{blue, black})\}$

6. $\{SSS, SSF, SFS, FSS, SFF, FFS, FSF, FFF\}$

8. $E = \{HHH, HHT, HTH, HTT\}$

$P(E) = \dfrac{n(E)}{n(s)} = \dfrac{4}{8} = \dfrac{1}{2}$

10. $E = \{HHH, HHT, HTH, THH\}$

$P(E) = \dfrac{n(E)}{n(s)} = \dfrac{4}{8} = \dfrac{1}{2}$

12. The probability that the card is *not* a face card is the complement of getting a face card. (See Exercise 11.)

$P(E') = 1 - P(E) = 1 - \dfrac{3}{13} = \dfrac{10}{13}$

14. There are six possible cards in each of 4 suits:

$6 \cdot 4 = 24$

$P(E) = \dfrac{n(E)}{n(s)} = \dfrac{24}{52} = \dfrac{6}{13}$

16. $E = \{(1, 6), (2, 5), (2, 6), (3, 4), (3, 5), (3, 6), (4, 3),$
$(4, 4), (4, 5), (4, 6), (5, 2), (5, 3), (5, 4), (5, 5), (5, 6),$
$(6, 1), (6, 2), (6, 3), (6, 4), (6, 5), (6, 6)\}$

$P(E) = \dfrac{n(E)}{n(s)} = \dfrac{21}{36} = \dfrac{7}{12}$

18. $E = \{(1, 1), (1, 2), (2, 1), (6, 6)\}$

$P(E) = \dfrac{n(E)}{n(s)} = \dfrac{4}{36} = \dfrac{1}{9}$

20. $E = \{(1, 1), (1, 2), (1, 4), (1, 6), (2, 1), (2, 3), (2, 5),$
$(3, 2), (3, 4), (3, 6), (4, 1), (4, 3), (4, 5), (5, 2), (5, 4),$
$(5, 6), (6, 1), (6, 3), (6, 5)\}$

$P(E) = \dfrac{n(E)}{n(s)} = \dfrac{19}{36}$

22. $P(E) = \dfrac{{}_2C_2}{{}_6C_2} = \dfrac{1}{15}$

24. $P(E) = \dfrac{{}_1C_1 \cdot {}_2C_1 + {}_1C_1 \cdot {}_3C_1 + {}_2C_1 \cdot {}_3C_1}{{}_6C_2}$

$\qquad = \dfrac{2 + 3 + 6}{15} = \dfrac{11}{15}$

26. $1 - p = 1 - 0.36 = 0.64$

28. $1 - p = 1 - \frac{5}{6} = \frac{1}{6}$

30. $1 - p = 1 - 0.84 = 0.16$

32. $1 - p = 1 - \frac{87}{100} = \frac{13}{100}$

34. (a) $(0.33)(111,000,000) = 36,630,000$

 (b) 27%

 (c) $27\% + 29\% = 56\%$

36. (a) $\frac{34}{100} = 0.34 = 34\%$

 (b) $\frac{45}{100} = 0.45 = 45\%$

 (c) $\frac{23}{100} = 0.23 = 23\%$

38. (a) $\frac{18 + 12}{72} = \frac{30}{72} = \frac{5}{12}$

 (b) $1 - \frac{5}{12} = \frac{7}{12}$

 (c) $\frac{10}{72} = \frac{5}{36}$

40. $1 - 0.37 - 0.44 = 0.19 = 19\%$

42. (a) $\frac{_6C_5}{_8C_5} = \frac{6}{56} = \frac{3}{28}$

 (b) $\frac{_6C_4 \cdot {_2C_1}}{_8C_5} = \frac{15 \cdot 2}{56} = \frac{15}{28}$

 (c) $\frac{3}{28} + \frac{15}{28} = \frac{18}{28} = \frac{9}{14}$

44. Total ways to insert paychecks: $5! = 120$ ways

 5 correct: 1 way

 4 correct: not possible

 3 correct: $_5C_3 = 10$ ways (because once you choose the three envelopes that will contain the correct paychecks, there is only one way to insert the paychecks so that the other two are wrong)

 2 correct: $_5C_3 \cdot 2 = 20$ ways (because once you choose the two envelopes that will contain the correct paychecks, there are two ways to fill the next envelope incorrectly, then only one incorrect way to insert the remaining paychecks)

 1 correct: $5 \cdot 3 \cdot 3 = 45$ ways (five ways to choose which envelope is paired with the correct paycheck, three ways to fill the next envelope incorrectly, then three ways to fill the envelope whose correct paycheck was placed in the second envelope, and only one way to fill the remaining two envelopes such that both are incorrect)

 0 correct: $120 - 10 - 20 - 34 = 44$ ways

 (a) $\frac{45}{120} = \frac{3}{8}$

 (b) $\frac{45 + 20 + 10 + 1}{120} = \frac{19}{30}$

46. (a) $\frac{1}{_4P_4} = \frac{1}{24}$

 (b) $\frac{1}{_3P_3} = \frac{1}{6}$

48. $\frac{_{13}C_1 \cdot {_4C_3} \cdot {_{12}C_1} \cdot {_4C_2}}{_{52}C_5} = \frac{13 \cdot 4 \cdot 12 \cdot 6}{2,598,960}$

$= \frac{3744}{2,598,960}$

$= \frac{6}{4165}$

50. (a) $\frac{_{16}C_5}{_{20}C_5} = \frac{4368}{15,504} = \frac{91}{323}$ (5 good units)

 (b) $\frac{_{16}C_4 \cdot {_4C_1}}{_{20}C_5} = \frac{1820 \cdot 4}{15,504} = \frac{455}{969}$ (4 good units)

 (c) Probability of at least one defective unit $= 1 -$ (Probability of no defective units.)
 Probability of no defective units $=$ Probability of 5 good units

 P (at least one defective unit) $= 1 - \frac{91}{323} = \frac{232}{323}$

52. (a) $P(EE) = \frac{20}{40} \cdot \frac{20}{40} = \frac{1}{4}$

(b) $P(EO \text{ or } OE) = 2\left(\frac{20}{40}\right)\left(\frac{20}{40}\right) = \frac{1}{2}$

(c) $P(N_1 < 30, N_2 < 30) = \frac{29}{40} \cdot \frac{29}{40} = \frac{841}{1600}$

(d) $P(N_1 N_1) = \frac{40}{40} \cdot \frac{1}{40} = \frac{1}{40}$

54. (a) $P(AA) = (0.90)^2 = 0.81$

(b) $P(NN) = (0.10)^2 = 0.01$

(c) $P(A) = 1 - P(NN) = 1 - 0.01 = 0.99$

56. (a) $P(BBBB) = \left(\frac{1}{2}\right)^4 = \frac{1}{16}$

(b) $P(BBBB) + P(GGGG) = \left(\frac{1}{2}\right)^4 + \left(\frac{1}{2}\right)^4 = \frac{1}{8}$

(c) $P(\text{at least one boy}) = 1 - P(\text{no boys})$

$= 1 - P(GGGG) = 1 - \frac{1}{16} = \frac{15}{16}$

58. $(0.32)^2 = 0.124$

60. (a) If the *center* of the coin falls within the circle of radius $d/2$ around a vertex, the coin will cover the vertex.

$$P(\text{coin covers a vertex}) = \frac{\text{Area in which coin may fall}}{\text{so that it covers a vertex}}$$
$$\frac{}{\text{Total area}}$$

$$= \frac{n\left[\pi\left(\frac{d}{2}\right)^2\right]}{nd^2} = \frac{\pi}{4}$$

(b) Experimental results will vary.

62. False. The complement of the event is to roll a number greater than or equal to 3 and its probability is 2/3.

64. If a weather forecast indicates that the probability of rain is 40%, this means the meteorological records indicate that over an extended period of time with similar weather conditions it will rain 40% of the time.

66. $4x^2 + 6x - 12 = 0$

$2x^2 + 3x - 6 = 0$

$x = \frac{-b \pm \sqrt{b^2 - 4ac}}{2a} = \frac{-3 \pm \sqrt{3^2 - 4(2)(-6)}}{2(2)}$

$= \frac{-3 \pm \sqrt{57}}{4}$

68. $x^5 + x^3 - 2x = 0$

$x(x^4 + x^2 - 2) = 0$

$x(x^2 + 2)(x^2 - 1) = 0$

$x = 0$

$x^2 - 1 = 0 \Rightarrow x = \pm 1$

$x = 0, \pm 1$

70. $\frac{32}{x} = 2x$

$32 = 2x^2$

$16 = x^2$

$\pm 4 = x$

72. $\frac{3}{2x + 3} - 4 = \frac{-1}{2x + 3}$

$\frac{3}{2x + 3} + \frac{1}{2x + 3} = 4$

$\frac{4}{2x + 3} = 4$

$4 = 4(2x + 3)$

$4 = 8x + 12$

$8x = -8$

$x = -1$

74. $\frac{2}{x} - \frac{5}{x - 2} = \frac{-13}{x^2 - 2x}$

$\frac{2(x - 2) - 5x}{x^2 - 2x} = \frac{-13}{x^2 - 2x}$

$2x - 4 - 5x = -13$

$-4 - 3x = -13$

$3x = 9$

$x = 3$

76. $e^x + 7 = 35$

$\quad e^x = 28$

$\quad x \ln e = \ln 28$

$\quad\quad x = \ln 28 \approx 3.332$

78. $e^{2x} - 7e^x + 12 = 0$

$\quad (e^x - 4)(e^x - 3) = 0$

$\quad e^x - 4 = 0 \quad\quad\quad e^x - 3 = 0$

$\quad\quad e^x = 4 \quad\quad\quad\quad e^x = 3$

$\quad x \ln e = \ln 4 \quad\quad x \ln 3 = \ln 3$

$\quad\quad x = \ln 4 \approx 1.386 \quad\quad x = \ln 3 \approx 1.099$

80. $800e^{-x} = 250$

$\quad e^{-x} = 0.3125$

$\quad e^x = 3.2$

$\quad x \ln e = \ln 3.2$

$\quad\quad x = \ln 3.2 \approx 1.163$

82. $3 - 4 \ln x = 6$

$\quad -4 \ln x = 3$

$\quad \ln x = -\dfrac{3}{4}$

$\quad e^{\ln x} = e^{-3/4}$

$\quad\quad x = 0.472$

84. $5 \ln 2x - 4 = 11$

$\quad 5 \ln 2x = 15$

$\quad \ln 2x = 3$

$\quad e^{\ln 2x} = e^3$

$\quad 2x = e^3$

$\quad x = \dfrac{e^3}{2} \approx 10.043$

Review Exercises for Chapter 9

Solutions to Even-Numbered Exercises

2. $a_n = \dfrac{5n}{2n - 1}$

$a_1 = \dfrac{5(1)}{2(1) - 1} = 5$

$a_2 = \dfrac{5(2)}{2(2) - 1} = \dfrac{10}{3}$

$a_3 = \dfrac{5(3)}{2(3) - 1} = 3$

$a_4 = \dfrac{5(4)}{2(4) - 1} = \dfrac{20}{7}$

$a_5 = \dfrac{5(5)}{2(5) - 1} = \dfrac{25}{9}$

4. $a_n = n(n - 1)$

$a_1 = 1(1 - 1) = 0$

$a_2 = 2(2 - 1) = 2$

$a_3 = 3(3 - 1) = 6$

$a_4 = 4(4 - 1) = 12$

$a_5 = 5(5 - 1) = 20$

6. $3! \cdot 2! = (3 \cdot 2 \cdot 1) \cdot (2 \cdot 1) = 12$

8. $\dfrac{7! \cdot 6!}{6! \cdot 8!} = \dfrac{7! \cdot 6!}{6!(8 \cdot 7!)} = \dfrac{1}{8}$

10. $\displaystyle\sum_{k=2}^{5} 4k = 4(2) + 4(3) + 4(4) + 4(5)$

$\quad = 8 + 12 + 16 + 20 = 56$

12. $\displaystyle\sum_{i=1}^{8} \dfrac{i}{i + 1} = \dfrac{1}{1 + 1} + \dfrac{2}{2 + 1} + \dfrac{3}{3 + 1} + \dfrac{4}{4 + 1} + \dfrac{5}{5 + 1} + \dfrac{6}{6 + 1} + \dfrac{7}{7 + 1} + \dfrac{8}{8 + 1}$

$\quad = \dfrac{1}{2} + \dfrac{2}{3} + \dfrac{3}{4} + \dfrac{4}{5} + \dfrac{5}{6} + \dfrac{6}{7} + \dfrac{7}{8} + \dfrac{8}{9} \approx 6.17$

14. $\sum_{j=0}^{4}(j^2+1)=(0^2+1)+(1^2+1)+(2^2+1)+(3^2+1)+(4^2+1)$

$$=1+2+5+10+17=35$$

16. $\dfrac{1}{2}+\dfrac{2}{3}+\dfrac{3}{4}+\cdots+\dfrac{9}{10}=\sum_{k=1}^{9}\dfrac{k}{k+1}$

18. $\sum_{i=1}^{\infty}\dfrac{3}{10^i}=\sum_{i=1}^{\infty}3\left(\dfrac{1}{10^i}\right)=\dfrac{\frac{3}{10}}{1-\frac{1}{10}}=\dfrac{1}{3}$

20. $\sum_{k=2}^{\infty}\dfrac{9}{10^k}=\sum_{k=2}^{\infty}9\left(\dfrac{1}{10^k}\right)=\dfrac{\frac{9}{100}}{1-\frac{1}{10}}=\dfrac{1}{10}$

22. $a_1=123, d=112-123=-11$

$n=8$

$a_8=213+7(-11)=46$

$S_8=\dfrac{8}{2}(123+46)=676$

24. $0, 1, 3, 6, 10, \ldots$

Not an arithmetic sequence

26. $\dfrac{9}{9}, \dfrac{8}{9}, \dfrac{7}{9}, \dfrac{6}{9}, \dfrac{5}{9}, \ldots$

Arithmetic sequence, $d=-\dfrac{1}{9}$

28. $a_1=25, d=-3$

$a_n=dn+c$

$a_n=-3n+c$

$c=a_1-d=25-(-3)=28$

So, $a_n=-3n+28$

30. $a_1=-2x, d=x$

$a_n=dn+c$

$a_n=xn+c$

$c=a_1-d=-2x-x=-3x$

So, $a_n=xn-3x$

32. $\sum_{j=1}^{8}(20-3j)=\sum_{j=1}^{8}20-3\sum_{j=1}^{8}j=8(20)-3\left[\dfrac{(8)(9)}{2}\right]=52$

34. $\sum_{k=1}^{25}\left(\dfrac{3k+1}{4}\right)=\dfrac{3}{4}\sum_{k=1}^{25}k+\sum_{k=1}^{25}\dfrac{1}{4}=\dfrac{3}{4}\left[\dfrac{(25)(26)}{2}\right]+25\left(\dfrac{1}{4}\right)=250$

36. $\sum_{n=20}^{80}n=\sum_{n=1}^{80}n-\sum_{n=1}^{19}n=\dfrac{(80)(81)}{2}-\dfrac{(19)(20)}{2}=3050$

38. $a_1=2, d=0.5, n=14$

$a_{14}=2+13(0.5)=8.5$ miles

40. $a_1=2, r=2$

$a_1=2$

$a_2=2(2)=4$

$a_3=4(2)=8$

$a_4=8(2)=16$

$a_5=16(2)=32$

42. $a_1 = 2, a_3 = 12$

$$a_3 = a_1 r^2$$
$$12 = 2r^2$$
$$6 = r^2$$
$$\pm\sqrt{6} = r$$

$a_1 = 2$		$a_1 = 2$
$a_2 = 2(\sqrt{6}) = 2\sqrt{6}$		$a_2 = 2(-\sqrt{6}) = -2\sqrt{6}$
$a_3 = 2\sqrt{6}(\sqrt{6}) = 12$	or	$a_3 = -2\sqrt{6}(-\sqrt{6}) = 12$
$a_4 = 12(\sqrt{6}) = 12\sqrt{6}$		$a_4 = 12(-\sqrt{6}) = -12\sqrt{6}$
$a_5 = 12\sqrt{6}(\sqrt{6}) = 72$		$a_5 = -12\sqrt{6}(-\sqrt{6}) = 72$

44. $a_3 = 6, a_4 = 1$

$$a_3 r = a_4$$
$$6r = 1$$
$$r = \frac{1}{6}$$
$$a_3 = a_1 r^2$$
$$6 = a_1\left(\frac{1}{6}\right)^2$$
$$6 = a_1\left(\frac{1}{36}\right)$$
$$a_1 = 216$$
$$a_n = 216\left(\frac{1}{6}\right)^{n-1}$$
$$S_{20} = 216\left(\frac{1 - \left(\frac{1}{6}\right)^{20}}{1 - \frac{1}{6}}\right) = 259.2$$

46. $a_1 = 5, r = 0.2$

$$a_n = 5(0.2)^{n-1}$$
$$S_{20} = 5\left(\frac{1 - (0.2)^{20}}{1 - 0.2}\right) = 6.25$$

48. $\displaystyle\sum_{i=1}^{5} 3^{i-1} = 1\left(\frac{1 - 3^5}{1 - 3}\right) = 121$

50. $\displaystyle\sum_{i=1}^{6}\left(\frac{1}{3}\right)^{i-1} = \left(\frac{1 - \left(\frac{1}{3}\right)^6}{1 - \frac{1}{3}}\right)$

$$= \frac{1 - \frac{1}{729}}{1 - \frac{1}{3}} = \frac{364}{243}$$

52. $\displaystyle\sum_{i=1}^{4} 6(3)^i = 6(3)\left(\frac{1 - 3^4}{1 - 3}\right) = 720$

54. $\displaystyle\sum_{i=1}^{15} 20(0.2)^{i-1} = 25$

56. $\displaystyle\sum_{i=1}^{20} 8\left(\frac{6}{5}\right)^{i-1} = 1493.50$

58. $\displaystyle\sum_{i=1}^{\infty}\left(\frac{1}{3}\right)^{i-1} = \frac{1}{1 - \frac{1}{3}} = \frac{3}{2}$

60. $\displaystyle\sum_{i=1}^{\infty}(0.5)^{i-1} = \frac{1}{1 - 0.5} = 2$

62. $\displaystyle\sum_{k=1}^{\infty} 1.3\left(\frac{1}{10}\right)^{k-1} = \frac{1.3}{1 - \frac{1}{10}} = \frac{13}{9}$

64. $a_1 = 32,000, r = 1.055$

$$\sum_{i=1}^{40} 32,000(1.055)^{i-1} = 32,000\left[\frac{1 - (1.055)^{40}}{1 - 1.055}\right]$$
$$= \$4,371,379.65$$

66. 1. When $n = 1, S_1 = 1 = \dfrac{1}{4}(1 + 3) = 1$.

2. Assume that $S_k = 1 + \dfrac{3}{2} + 2 + \dfrac{5}{2} + \cdots + \dfrac{1}{2}(k + 1) = \dfrac{k}{4}(k + 3)$. Then,

$$S_{k+1} = S_k + a_{k+1} = \left(1 + \frac{3}{2} + 2 + \frac{5}{2} + \cdots + \frac{1}{2}(k + 1)\right) + \frac{1}{2}(k + 2)$$

$$= \frac{k}{4}(k + 3) + \frac{1}{2}(k + 2)$$

$$= \frac{k(k + 3) + 2(k + 2)}{4}$$

$$= \frac{k^2 + 5k + 4}{4}$$

$$= \frac{(k + 1)(k + 4)}{4}$$

$$= \frac{k + 1}{4}[(k + 1) + 3].$$

Thus, the formula holds for all positive integers n.

68. 1. When $n = 1, S_1 = a + 0 \cdot d = a = \dfrac{1}{2}[2a + (1 - 1)d] = a$.

2. Assume that $S_k = \displaystyle\sum_{k=0}^{i-1}(a + kd) = \dfrac{i}{2}[2a + (i - 1)d]$. Then,

$$S_{k+1} = S_k + a_{k+1}$$

$$\sum_{k=0}^{i+1-1}(a + kd) = \frac{i}{2}[2a + (i - 1)d] + [a + id]$$

$$= \frac{2ia + i(i - 1)d + 2a + 2id}{2} = \frac{2a(i + 1) + id(i + 1)}{2} = \left(\frac{i + 1}{2}\right)[2a + id].$$

Thus, the formula holds for all positive integers n.

70. $\displaystyle\sum_{n=1}^{10} n^2 = \dfrac{10(10 + 1)(2 \cdot 10 + 1)}{6}$

$$= \frac{10(11)(21)}{6} = 385$$

72. $\displaystyle\sum_{n=1}^{6} n^5 = \dfrac{6^2(6 + 1)^2(2 \cdot 6^2 + 2 \cdot 6 - 1)}{12} = \dfrac{36(49)(83)}{12}$

$$= 12,201$$

74. $S_1 = 68 = 4 \cdot 17$

$S_2 = 68 + 60 = 128 = 8 \cdot 16$

$S_3 = 68 + 60 + 52 = 180 = 12 \cdot 15$

$S_4 = 68 + 60 + 52 + 44 = 224 = 16 \cdot 14$

$S_n = 4n(18 - n)$

76. $S_1 = 12$

$S_2 = 12 - 1 = 11$

$S_3 = 12 - 1 + \dfrac{1}{12} = \dfrac{133}{12}$

$S_4 = 12 - 1 + \dfrac{1}{12} - \dfrac{1}{144} = \dfrac{1595}{144}$

Since the series is geometric,

$$S_n = 12\frac{1 - \left(-\frac{1}{12}\right)^n}{\left[1 - \left(-\frac{1}{12}\right)\right]} = \frac{144}{13}\left[1 - \left(-\frac{1}{12}\right)^n\right]$$

78. $a_1 = -3$

$a_n = a_{n-1} - 2n$

$a_1 = -3$

$a_2 = a_1 - 2(2) = -3 - 4 = -7$

$a_3 = a_2 - 2(3) = -7 - 6 = -13$

$a_4 = a_3 - 2(4) = -13 - 8 = -21$

$a_5 = a_4 - 2(5) = -21 - 10 = -31$

a_n: -3 -7 -13 -21 -31

First differences: -4 -6 -8 -10

Second differences: -2 -2 -2

Since the second differences are all the same, the sequence has a quadratic model.

80. $a_0 = 0, a_n = n - a_{n-1}$

$a_0 = 0$

$a_1 = 1 - a_0 = 1 - 0 = 1$

$a_2 = 2 - a_1 = 2 - 1 = 1$

$a_3 = 3 - a_2 = 3 - 1 = 2$

$a_4 = 4 - a_3 = 4 - 2 = 2$

a_n: 0 1 1 2 2

First differences: 1 0 1 0

Second differences: -1 1 -1

Since neither the first differences nor the second differences are equal, the sequence does not have a linear or a quadratic model.

82. $_{10}C_7 = \dfrac{10!}{7!3!} = \dfrac{10 \cdot 9 \cdot 8 \cdot 7!}{7!3!}$

$= \dfrac{10 \cdot 9 \cdot 8}{3 \cdot 2 \cdot 1} = 120$

84. $_{12}C_3 = \dfrac{12!}{3!9!} = \dfrac{12 \cdot 11 \cdot 10 \cdot 9!}{3! \cdot 9!} = \dfrac{12 \cdot 11 \cdot 10}{3 \cdot 2 \cdot 1} = 220$

86.

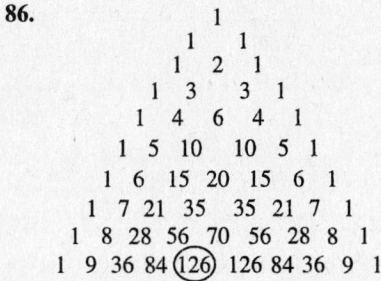

$$
\begin{array}{ccccccccccccc}
 & & & & & & 1 & & & & & & \\
 & & & & & 1 & & 1 & & & & & \\
 & & & & 1 & & 2 & & 1 & & & & \\
 & & & 1 & & 3 & & 3 & & 1 & & & \\
 & & 1 & & 4 & & 6 & & 4 & & 1 & & \\
 & 1 & & 5 & & 10 & & 10 & & 5 & & 1 & \\
1 & & 6 & & 15 & & 20 & & 15 & & 6 & & 1
\end{array}
$$

1 7 21 35   35 21 7 1

1 8 28 56 70 56 28 8 1

1 9 36 84 $\boxed{126}$ 126 84 36 9 1

$\dbinom{9}{4} = 126$, the 4th entry in the 9th row.

88.

$$
\begin{array}{ccccccccc}
 & & & & 1 & & & & \\
 & & & 1 & & 1 & & & \\
 & & 1 & & 2 & & 1 & & \\
 & 1 & & 3 & & 3 & & 1 & \\
1 & & 4 & & 6 & & 4 & & 1
\end{array}
$$

1 5 10 $\boxed{10}$ 5 1

$\dbinom{5}{3} = 10$, the 3rd entry in the 5th row.

90. $\left(\dfrac{2}{x} - 3x\right)^6 = {}_6C_0\left(\dfrac{2}{x}\right)^6 + {}_6C_1\left(\dfrac{2}{x}\right)^5(-3x) + {}_6C_2\left(\dfrac{2}{x}\right)^4(-3x)^2 + {}_6C_3\left(\dfrac{2}{x}\right)^3(-3x)^3 + {}_6C_4\left(\dfrac{2}{x}\right)^2(-3x)^4 + {}_6C_5\left(\dfrac{2}{x}\right)(-3x)^5 + {}_6C_6(-3x)^6$

$= \left(\dfrac{2}{x}\right)^6 + 6\left(\dfrac{2}{x}\right)^5(-3x) + 15\left(\dfrac{2}{x}\right)^4(-3x)^2 + 20\left(\dfrac{2}{x}\right)^3(-3x)^3 + 15\left(\dfrac{2}{x}\right)^2(-3x)^4 + 6\left(\dfrac{2}{x}\right)(-3x)^5 + (-3x)^6$

$= \dfrac{64}{x^6} - \dfrac{576}{x^4} + \dfrac{2160}{x^2} - 4320 + 4860x^2 - 2916x^4 + 729x^6$

92. $(3x + y^2)^7 = {}_7C_0(3x)^7 + {}_7C_1(3x)^6(y^2) + {}_7C_2(3x)^5(y^2)^2 + {}_7C_3(3x)^4(y^2)^3 + {}_7C_4(3x)^3(y^2)^4 + {}_7C_5(3x)^2(y^2)^5$

$+ {}_7C_6(3x)(y^2)^6 + {}_7C_7(y^2)^7$

$= (3x)^7 + 7(3x)^6y^2 + 21(3x)^5(y^2)^2 + 35(3x)^4(y^2)^3 + 35(3x)^3(y^2)^4 + 21(3x)^2(y^2)^5 + 7(3x)(y^2)^6 + (y^2)^7$

$= 2187x^7 + 5103x^6y^2 + 5103x^5y^4 + 2835x^4y^6 + 945x^3y^8 + 189x^2y^{10} + 21xy^{12} + y^{14}$

94. $(4 - 5i)^3 = {_3}C_0(4^3) + {_3}C_1(4^2)(-5i) + {_3}C_2(4)(-5i)^2 + {_3}C_3(-5i)^3$

$= 4^3 - 3(4)^2(5i) + 3(4)(5i)^2 - (5i)^3$

$= 64 - 240i - 300 + 125i$

$= -236 - 115i$

96.

First Number:	1	2	3	4	5	6	7	8	9	10	11
Second Number:	11	10	9	8	7	6	5	4	3	2	1

From this list, you can see that a total of 12 occurs 11 different ways.

98. $5 \cdot 10 \cdot 10 \cdot 10 \cdot 10 = 50{,}000$ different telephone numbers

100. ${_{10}}P_3 = \dfrac{10!}{7!} = \dfrac{10 \cdot 9 \cdot 8 \cdot 7!}{7!} = 10 \cdot 9 \cdot 8 = 720$ different ways

102. ${_{20}}C_3 = \dfrac{20!}{3!17!} = \dfrac{20 \cdot 19 \cdot 18 \cdot 17!}{3!17!} = \dfrac{20 \cdot 19 \cdot 18}{3 \cdot 2 \cdot 1}$

$= 1140$ combinations

104. $P(E) = \dfrac{n(E)}{n(S)} = \dfrac{1}{5!} = \dfrac{1}{120}$

106. (a) $\dfrac{208}{500} = 0.416$ or 41.6%

(b) $\dfrac{400}{500} = 0.8$ or 80%

(c) $\dfrac{37}{500} = 0.074$ or 7.4%

108. $\left(\dfrac{6}{6}\right)\left(\dfrac{5}{6}\right)\left(\dfrac{4}{6}\right)\left(\dfrac{3}{6}\right)\left(\dfrac{2}{6}\right)\left(\dfrac{1}{6}\right) = \dfrac{6!}{6^6} = \dfrac{720}{46{,}656} = \dfrac{5}{324}$

110. $1 - P(HHHHH) = 1 - \left(\dfrac{1}{2}\right)^5 = \dfrac{31}{32}$

112. True by properties of sums

114. True because $2^1 + 2^2 + 2^3 + 2^4 + 2^5 + 2^6 = 2^{3-2} + 2^{4-2} + 2^{5-2} + 2^{6-2} + 2^{7-2} + 2^{8-2}$

116. (a) Odd-numbered terms are negative.

(b) Even-numbered terms are negative.

118. (a) Arithmetic. There is a constant difference between consecutive terms.

(b) Geometric. Each term is a constant multiple of the previous term. In this case the common ratio is greater than 1.

120. Increased powers of real numbers between 0 and 1 approach zero.

122. $a_n = 4\left(-\dfrac{1}{2}\right)^{n-1}$

$a_1 = 4$ and a_n fluctuates from positive to negative. Matches graph (a).

124. $a_n = \displaystyle\sum_{k=1}^{n} 4\left(-\dfrac{1}{2}\right)^{k-1}$

$a_1 = 4$ and $a_n \to \dfrac{8}{3}$ as $n \to \infty$.

Matches graph (c).

126. $0 \le p \le 1$, closed interval

128. Meteorological records indicate that over an extended period of time with similar weather conditions, it will rain 60% of the time.

CHAPTER 10
Topics in Analytic Geometry

CHAPTER 10
Topics in Analytic Geometry

Section 10.1   Lines

Solutions to Even-Numbered Exercises

2. $m = \tan\dfrac{\pi}{4} = 1$

4. $m = \tan\dfrac{2\pi}{3} = -\sqrt{3}$

6. $m = \tan\dfrac{5\pi}{6} = -\dfrac{\sqrt{3}}{3}$

8. $m = \tan 2.88 \approx -0.2677$

10. $-2 = \tan\theta$

$\theta = \tan^{-1}(-2) + \pi \approx 2.034 \text{ radians} \approx 116.6°$

12. $2 = \tan\theta$

$\theta = \tan^{-1} 2 \approx 1.107 \text{ radians} \approx 63.4°$

14. $-\dfrac{5}{2} = \tan\theta$

$\theta = \tan^{-1}\left(-\dfrac{5}{2}\right) + \pi \approx 1.9513 \text{ radians} \approx 111.8°$

16. $m = \dfrac{8 - (-3)}{12 - (-4)} = \dfrac{11}{16}$

$\dfrac{11}{16} = \tan\theta$

$\theta = \tan^{-1}\dfrac{11}{16} \approx 0.6023 \text{ radians} \approx 34.5°$

18. $m = \dfrac{100 - 0}{0 - 50} = -2$

$-2 = \tan\theta$

$\theta = \tan^{-1}(-2) + \pi \approx 2.0344 \text{ radians} \approx 116.6°$

20. $4x + 5y - 9 = 0$

$y = -\dfrac{4}{5}x + \dfrac{9}{5} \Rightarrow m = -\dfrac{4}{5}$

$-\dfrac{4}{5} = \tan\theta$

$\theta = \tan^{-1}\left(-\dfrac{4}{5}\right) + \pi$

$\approx 2.4669 \text{ radians} \approx 141.3°$

22. $x - y - 10 = 0$

$y = x - 10 \Rightarrow m = 1$

$1 = \tan\theta$

$\theta = \tan^{-1} 1 = 45° = \dfrac{\pi}{4} \text{ radian}$

24. $x + 3y = 2 \implies y = -\dfrac{1}{3}x + \dfrac{2}{3} \implies m_1 = -\dfrac{1}{3}$

$x - 2y = -3 \implies y = \dfrac{1}{2}x + \dfrac{3}{2} \implies m_2 = \dfrac{1}{2}$

$\tan\theta = \left|\dfrac{(1/2) - (-1/3)}{1 + (-1/3)(1/2)}\right| = 1$

$\theta = \tan^{-1} 1 = 45° = \dfrac{\pi}{4} \text{ radian}$

26. $2x - y = 2 \implies y = 2x - 2 \implies m_1 = 2$

$4x + 3y = 24 \implies y = -\dfrac{4}{3}x + 8 \implies m_2 = -\dfrac{4}{3}$

$\tan\theta = \left|\dfrac{(-4/3) - 2}{1 + (2)(-4/3)}\right| = 2$

$\theta = \tan^{-1} 2 \approx 63.4° \approx 1.1071 \text{ radians}$

28. $5x + 2y = 16 \implies y = -\frac{5}{2}x + 8 \implies m_1 = -\frac{5}{2}$

$3x - 5y = -1 \implies y = \frac{3}{5}x + \frac{1}{5} \implies m_2 = \frac{3}{5}$

$\tan \theta = \left| \dfrac{(-5/2) - (3/5)}{1 + (-5/2)(3/5)} \right| = \dfrac{31}{5}$

$\theta = \tan^{-1} \dfrac{31}{5} \approx 80.8° \approx 1.4109$ radians

30. $3x - 5y = 3 \implies y = \frac{3}{5}x - \frac{3}{5} \implies m_1 = \frac{3}{5}$

$3x + 5y = 12 \implies y = -\frac{3}{5}x + \frac{12}{5} \implies m_2 = -\frac{3}{5}$

$\tan \theta = \left| \dfrac{(3/5) - (-3/5)}{1 + (3/5)(-3/5)} \right| = \dfrac{15}{8}$

$\theta = \tan^{-1} \dfrac{15}{8} \approx 61.9° \approx 1.0808$ radians

32. $0.02x - 0.05y = -0.19 \implies y = \frac{2}{5}x + \frac{19}{5} \implies m_1 = \frac{2}{5}$

$0.03x + 0.04y = 0.52 \implies y = -\frac{3}{4}x + 13 \implies m_2 = -\frac{3}{4}$

$\tan \theta = \left| \dfrac{(-3/4) - (2/5)}{1 + (2/5)(-3/4)} \right| \approx \dfrac{23}{14}$

$\theta = \tan^{-1}\left(\dfrac{23}{14} \right) \approx 58.7° \approx 1.0240$ radians

34. Let $A = (-3, 2)$, $B = (1, 3)$, and $C = (2, 0)$.

Slope of AB: $m_1 = \dfrac{2 - 3}{-3 - 1} = \dfrac{1}{4}$

Slope of BC: $m_2 = \dfrac{3 - 0}{1 - 2} = -3$

Slope of AC: $m_3 = \dfrac{2 - 0}{-3 - 2} = -\dfrac{2}{5}$

$\tan A = \left| \dfrac{(1/4) - (-2/5)}{1 + (-2/5)(1/4)} \right| = \dfrac{13/20}{18/20} = \dfrac{13}{18}$

$A = \tan^{-1}\left(\dfrac{13}{18} \right) \approx 35.8°$

$\tan C = \left| \dfrac{-3 - (-2/5)}{1 + (-3)(-2/5)} \right| \approx \dfrac{13/5}{11/5} = \dfrac{13}{11}$

$C = \tan^{-1}\left(\dfrac{13}{11} \right) \approx 49.8°$

$B = 180° - A - C \approx 180° - 35.8° - 49.8°$

$= 94.4°$

36. Let $A = (-3, 4)$, $B = (2, 1)$, and $C = (-2, 2)$.

Slope of AB: $m_1 = \dfrac{4 - 1}{-3 - 2} = -\dfrac{3}{5}$

Slope of BC: $m_2 = \dfrac{1 - 2}{2 - (-2)} = -\dfrac{1}{4}$

Slope of AC: $m_3 = \dfrac{4 - 2}{-3 - (-2)} = -2$

$\tan A = \left| \dfrac{(-3/5) - (-2)}{1 + (-3/5)(-2)} \right| = \dfrac{7}{11}$

$A = \tan^{-1}\left(\dfrac{7}{11} \right) \approx 32.5°$

$\tan B = \left| \dfrac{(-3/5) - (-1/4)}{1 + (-3/5)(-1/4)} \right| = \dfrac{7}{23}$

$B = \tan^{-1}\left(\dfrac{7}{23} \right) \approx 16.9°$

$C = 180° - A - B \approx 180° - 32.5° - 16.9°$

$= 130.6°$

38. $(0, 0) \implies x_1 = 0$ and $y_1 = 0$

$2x - y - 4 = 0 \implies A = 2, B = -1,$ and $C = -4$

$d = \dfrac{|2(0) + (-1)(0) + (-4)|}{\sqrt{2^2 + (-1)^2}}$

$= \dfrac{4}{\sqrt{5}} = \dfrac{4\sqrt{5}}{5} \approx 1.7889$

40. $(-2, 1) \implies x_1 = -2$ and $y_1 = 1$

$x - y - 2 = 0 \implies A = 1, B = -1,$ and $C = -2$

$d = \dfrac{|1(-2) + (-1)(1) + (-2)|}{\sqrt{1^2 + (-1)^2}}$

$= \dfrac{5}{\sqrt{2}} = \dfrac{5\sqrt{2}}{2} \approx 3.5355$

42. $(10, 8) \implies x_1 = 10$ and $y_1 = 8$

$y - 4 = 0 \implies A = 0, B = 1,$ and $C = -4$

$d = \dfrac{|0(10) + 1(8) + (-4)|}{\sqrt{0^2 + 1^2}} = \dfrac{4}{1} = 4$

44. $(4, 2) \implies x_1 = 4$ and $y_1 = 2$

$x - y - 20 = 0 \implies A = 1, B = -1,$ and $C = -20$

$d = \dfrac{|1(4) + (-1)(2) + (-20)|}{\sqrt{1^2 + (-1)^2}}$

$\quad = \dfrac{18}{\sqrt{2}} = 9\sqrt{2} \approx 12.7279$

46. (a) The slope of the line through AC is $m = \dfrac{0 + 2}{0 - 5} = -\dfrac{2}{5}$.

The equation of the line is $y - 0 = -\dfrac{2}{5}(x - 0) \implies 2x + 5y = 0$.

The altitude from vertex B to side AC is the distance between the line through AC and

$B = (4, 5) \implies d = \dfrac{|2(4) + 5(5) + 0|}{\sqrt{2^2 + 5^2}} = \dfrac{33}{\sqrt{29}} = \dfrac{33\sqrt{29}}{29}$.

(b) The distance between A and C is $d = \sqrt{(0 - 5)^2 + (0 + 2)^2} = \sqrt{29}$, which is the length of the base of the triangle.

So, $A = \dfrac{1}{2}\sqrt{29}\left(\dfrac{33\sqrt{29}}{29}\right) = \dfrac{33}{2}$ square units

48. (a) The slope of the line through AC is $m = \dfrac{12 - (-5)}{6 - (-4)} = \dfrac{17}{10}$.

The equation of the line through AC is $y - 12 = \dfrac{17}{10}(x - 6) \implies 17x - 10y + 18 = 0$.

The altitude from vertex B to side AC is the distance between the line through AC and

$B = (3, 10) \implies d = \dfrac{|17(3) + (-10)(10) + 18|}{\sqrt{17^2 + (-10)^2}} = \dfrac{31}{\sqrt{389}} = \dfrac{31\sqrt{389}}{389}$.

(b) The distance between A and C is $d = \sqrt{(6 + 4)^2 + (12 + 5)^2} = \sqrt{389}$, which is the length of the base of the triangle.

$A = \dfrac{1}{2}\left(\sqrt{389}\right)\left(\dfrac{31\sqrt{389}}{389}\right) = \dfrac{31}{2}$

50. $3x - 4y = 1$

$3x - 4y = 10$

A point on $3x - 4y = 10$ is $\left(0, -\dfrac{5}{2}\right)$. The distance between $\left(0, -\dfrac{5}{2}\right)$ and $3x - 4y = 1$ is:

$A = 3, B = -4, C = -1, x_1 = 0, y_1 = -\dfrac{5}{2}$

$d = \dfrac{|3(0) + (-4)(-5/2) - 1|}{\sqrt{3^2 + (-4)^2}} = \dfrac{9}{5}$

52. Slope: $m = \tan 0.2 \approx 0.2027$

Change in elevation:

$\sin 0.20 = \dfrac{x}{5280} \implies x = 5280 \sin 0.20 \approx 1049$ feet

54. Slope $= \dfrac{3}{5}$

Inclination $= \tan^{-1}\dfrac{3}{5} \approx 31.0°$

56. (a) $m_1 = \tan(\pi - 1.10) \approx -1.965$

$m_2 = \tan 0.84 \approx 1.116$

$\tan \theta = \left| \dfrac{m_2 - m_1}{1 + m_1 m_2} \right| \approx \left| \dfrac{(1.116) - (-1.965)}{1 + (1.116)(-1.965)} \right|$

$\approx 2.5843 \implies \theta \approx 1.2016$

(b) Vertical climb:

$(6700)\sin 1.10 \approx 5971$ feet

$(3250)\sin 0.84 \approx 2420$ feet

58. False. Substitute $m_1 = \tan \theta_1$ and $m_2 = \tan \theta_2$ into the formula for the angle between two lines.

60. Slope m and y-intercept $(0, 4)$

(a) $(x_1, y_1) = (3, 1)$ and line: $y = mx + 4$

$A = -m, B = 1, C = -4$

$d = \dfrac{|(-m)(3) + (1)(1) + (-4)|}{\sqrt{(-m)^2 + 1^2}} = \dfrac{3|m + 1|}{\sqrt{m^2 + 1}}$

(b)

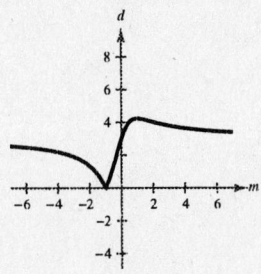

(c) From the graph it appears that the maximum distance is obtained when $m = 1$.

(d) From the graph it appears that the distance is 0 when $m = -1$.

(e) The asymptote of the graph in part (b) is $d = 3$. As the line approaches the vertical, the distance approaches 3.

62. $f(x) = (x + 9)^2$

$f(x) = (x + 9)^2 = 0 \implies x = -9$

x-intercept: $(-9, 0)$

$f(0) = (0 + 9)^2 = 81$

y-intercept: $(0, 81)$

64. $f(x) = (x + 11)^2 + 12$

$f(x) = (x + 11)^2 + 12 = 0$

$(x + 11)^2 = -12$

No solution

x-intercept: none

$f(0) = (0 + 11)^2 + 12 = 133$

y-intercept: $(0, 133)$

66. $f(x) = x^2 + 9x - 22$

$f(x) = x^2 + 9x - 22 = 0$

$(x + 11)(x - 2) = 0$

$\qquad\qquad x = -11, 2$

x-intercepts: $(-11, 0), (2, 0)$

$f(0) = -22$

y-intercept: $(0, -22)$

68. $f(x) = 2x^2 - x - 21$

$= 2\left[x^2 - \tfrac{1}{2}x - \tfrac{21}{2}\right] = 2\left[x^2 - \tfrac{1}{2}x + \tfrac{1}{16} - \tfrac{1}{16} - \tfrac{21}{2}\right]$

$= 2\left[\left(x - \tfrac{1}{4}\right)^2 - \tfrac{169}{16}\right]$

$= 2\left(x - \tfrac{1}{4}\right)^2 - \tfrac{169}{8}$

Vertex: $\left(\tfrac{1}{4}, -\tfrac{169}{8}\right)$

70. $f(x) = -x^2 - 8x - 15$

$= -[x^2 + 8x + 15] = -[x^2 + 8x + 16 - 16 + 15]$

$= -[(x + 4)^2 - 1] = -(x + 4)^2 + 1$

Vertex: $(-4, 1)$

72. $f(x) = -8x^2 - 34x - 21$

$= -8\left[x^2 + \frac{17}{4}x + \frac{21}{8}\right]$

$= -8\left[x^2 + \frac{17}{4}x + \frac{289}{64} - \frac{289}{64} + \frac{21}{8}\right]$

$= -8\left[\left(x + \frac{17}{8}\right)^2 - \frac{121}{64}\right]$

$= -8\left(x + \frac{17}{8}\right)^2 + \frac{121}{8}$

Vertex: $\left(-\frac{17}{8}, \frac{121}{8}\right)$

Section 10.2   Introduction to Conics: Parabolas

Solutions to Even-Numbered Exercises

2. An ellipse is formed when a plane intersects only the top or bottom half of a double–napped cone but is not perpendicular to the axis of the cone, not parallel to the side of the cone, and does not intersect the vertex.

4. A hyperbola is formed when a plane intersects both halves of a double–napped cone, is parallel to the axis of the cone, and does not intersect the vertex.

6. $x^2 = 2y$

Vertex: $(0, 0)$

$p = \frac{1}{2} > 0$

Opens upward.

Matches graph (b).

8. $y^2 = -12x$

Vertex: $(0, 0)$

$p = -3 < 0$

Opens to the left.

Matches graph (f).

10. $(x + 3)^2 = -2(y - 1)$

Vertex: $(-3, 1)$

$p = -\frac{1}{2} < 0$

Opens downward.

Matches graph (c).

12. $y = -2x^2 \implies x^2 = 4\left(-\frac{1}{8}\right)y$

Vertex: $(0, 0)$

Focus: $\left(0, -\frac{1}{8}\right)$

Directrix: $y = \frac{1}{8}$

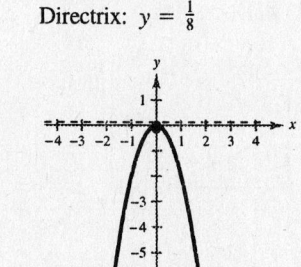

14. $y^2 = 3x \implies 4\left(\frac{3}{4}\right)x$

Vertex: $(0, 0)$

Focus: $\left(\frac{3}{4}, 0\right)$

Directrix: $x = -\frac{3}{4}$

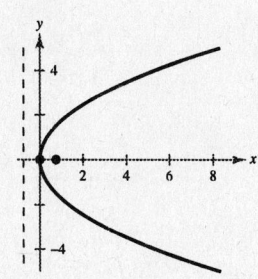

16. $x + y^2 = 0$

$y^2 = -x = 4\left(-\frac{1}{4}\right)x$

Vertex: $(0, 0)$

Focus: $\left(-\frac{1}{4}, 0\right)$

Directrix: $x = \frac{1}{4}$

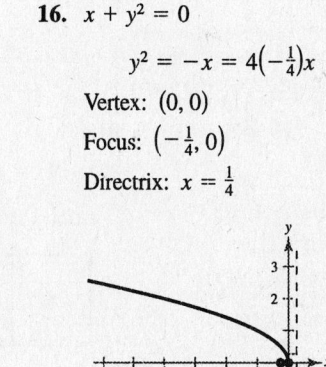

18. $(x + 5) + (y - 1)^2 = 0$

$(y - 1)^2 = 4\left(-\frac{1}{4}\right)(x + 5)$

Vertex: $(-5, 1)$

Focus: $\left(-5 + \left(-\frac{1}{4}\right), 1\right) \Rightarrow \left(-\frac{21}{4}, 1\right)$

Directrix: $x = -5 - \left(-\frac{1}{4}\right) = -\frac{19}{4}$

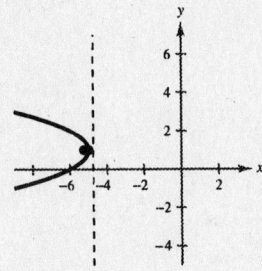

20. $\left(x + \frac{1}{2}\right)^2 = 4(y - 1) = 4(1)(y - 1)$

Vertex: $\left(-\frac{1}{2}, 1\right)$

Focus: $\left(-\frac{1}{2}, 1 + 1\right) \Rightarrow \left(-\frac{1}{2}, 2\right)$

Directrix: $y = 1 - 1 = 0$

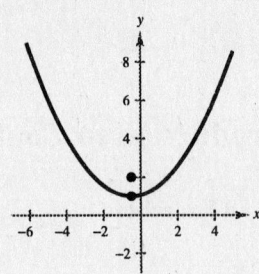

22. $\quad x = \frac{1}{4}(y^2 + 2y + 33)$

$\quad 4x = y^2 + 2y + 1 - 1 + 33 = (y + 1)^2 + 32$

$(y + 1)^2 = 4(1)(x - 8)$

Vertex: $(8, -1)$

Focus: $(9, -1)$

Directrix: $x = 7$

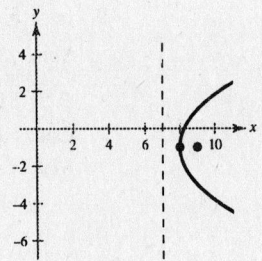

24. $y^2 - 4y - 4x = 0$

$\quad y^2 - 4y + 4 = 4x + 4$

$\quad (y - 2)^2 = 4(1)(x + 1)$

Vertex: $(-1, 2)$

Focus: $(0, 2)$

Directrix: $x = -2$

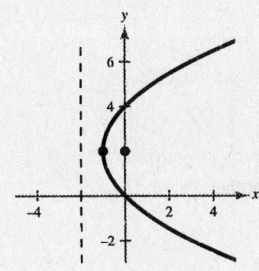

26. $x^2 - 2x + 8y + 9 = 0$

$\quad x^2 - 2x + 1 = -8y - 9 + 1$

$\quad\quad (x - 1)^2 = -8(y + 1) = 4(-2)(y + 1)$

Vertex: $(1, -1)$

Focus: $(1, -3)$

Directrix: $y = 1$

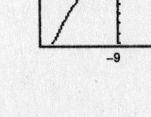

28. $y^2 - 4x - 4 = 0$

$\quad\quad y^2 = 4x + 4 = 4(1)(x + 1)$

Vertex: $(-1, 0)$

Focus: $(0, 0)$

Directrix: $x = -2$

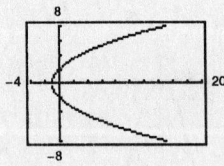

30. $x^2 + 12y = 0 \Rightarrow y_1 = -\frac{1}{12}x^2$

$\quad x + y - 3 = 0 \Rightarrow y_2 = 3 - x$

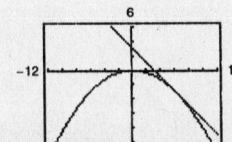

Using the trace or intersect feature,
the point of tangency is $(6, -3)$.

32. Point: $(-2, 6)$

$\quad x = ay^2$

$\quad -2 = a(6)^2$

$\quad -\frac{1}{18} = a$

$\quad x = -\frac{1}{18}y^2$

$\quad y^2 = -18x$

34. Focus: $(2, 0) \Rightarrow p = 2$

$\quad y^2 = 4px$

$\quad y^2 = 8x$

36. Focus: $(0, -2) \implies p = -2$

$x^2 = 4py$

$x^2 = -8y$

38. Directrix: $y = 3 \implies p = -3$

$x^2 = 4py$

$x^2 = -12y$

40. Directrix: $x = -3 \implies p = 3$

$y^2 = 4px$

$y^2 = 12x$

42. Vertical axis

Passes through: $(-3, -3)$

$x^2 = 4py$

$(-3)^2 = 4p(-3)$

$9 = -12p$

$p = -\frac{3}{4}$

$x^2 = -3y$

44. Vertex: $(5, 3) \implies h = 5,$
$\qquad k = 3$

Passes through: $(4.5, 4)$

$(y - k)^2 = 4p(x - h)$

$(y - 3)^2 = 4p(x - 5)$

$1 = 4p(4.5 - 5)$

$p = -\frac{1}{2}$

$(y - 3)^2 = -2(x - 5)$

46. Vertex: $(3, -3) \implies h = 3,$
$\qquad k = -3$

Passes through: $(0, 0)$

$(x - h)^2 = 4p(y - k)$

$(x - 3)^2 = 4p(y + 3)$

$9 = 12p$

$p = \frac{3}{4}$

$(x - 3)^2 = 3(y + 3)$

48. Vertex: $(-1, 2) \implies h = -1, \quad k = 2$

Focus: $(-1, 0) \implies p = -2$

$(x - h)^2 = 4p(y - k)$

$(x + 1)^2 = 4(-2)(y - 2)$

$(x + 1)^2 = -8(y - 2)$

50. Vertex: $(-2, 1) \implies h = -2, \quad k = 1$

Directrix: $x = 1 \implies p = -3$

$(y - k)^2 = 4p(x - h)$

$(y - 1)^2 = 4(-3)(x + 2)$

$(y - 1)^2 = -12(x + 2)$

52. Focus: $(0, 0)$

Directrix: $y = 8 \implies p = -4 \implies h = 0, k = 4$

$(x - h)^2 = 4p(y - k)$

$x^2 = 4(-4)(y - 4)$

$x^2 = -16(y - 4)$

54. $(y + 1)^2 = 2(x - 4)$

$y + 1 = \pm\sqrt{2(x - 4)}$

$y = -1 \pm \sqrt{2(x - 4)}$

Lower half of parabola: $y = -1 - \sqrt{2(x - 4)}$

56. $x^2 = 2y$

$x^2 = 4\left(\frac{1}{2}\right)y$

$4\left(\frac{1}{2}\right)y = x^2$

$p = \frac{1}{2}$

Focus: $\left(0, \frac{1}{2}\right)$

$d_1 = \frac{1}{2} - b$

$d_2 = \sqrt{(-3 - 0)^2 + \left(\frac{9}{2} - \frac{1}{2}\right)^2} = 5$

$\frac{1}{2} - b = 5$

$b = -\frac{9}{2}$

$m = \frac{-(9/2) - (9/2)}{0 + 3} = -3$

Tangent line: $y = -3x - \frac{9}{2} \implies 6x + 2y + 9 = 0$

x-intercept: $\left(-\frac{3}{2}, 0\right)$

58. $y = -2x^2$

$-\frac{1}{2}y = x^2$

$4\left(-\frac{1}{8}\right)y = x^2$

$p = -\frac{1}{8}$

Focus: $\left(0, -\frac{1}{8}\right)$

$d_1 = \frac{1}{8} + b$

$d^2 = \sqrt{(2 - 0)^2 + \left(-8 - \left(-\frac{1}{8}\right)\right)^2} = \frac{65}{8}$

$\frac{1}{8} + b = \frac{65}{8}$

$b = \frac{64}{8} = 8$

$m = \frac{-8 - 8}{2 - 0} = -8$

Tangent line: $y = -8x + 8 \implies 8x + y - 8 = 0$

x-intercept: $(1, 0)$

60. Maximum revenue occurs at $x = 135$

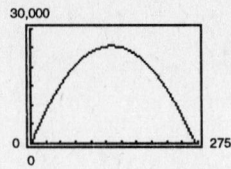

62. (a)

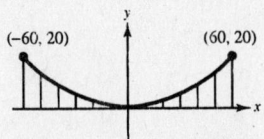

(c)

x	0	20	40	60
y	0	$2\frac{2}{9}$	$8\frac{8}{9}$	20

(b) $(x - 0)^2 = 4p(y - 0)$

$$x^2 = 4py$$

At $(60, 20)$: $60^2 = 4p(20) \implies p = 45$

$$x^2 = 4(45)y$$

$$y = \frac{x^2}{180}$$

64. Vertex: $(0, 0)$

$$(y - 0)^2 = 4p(x - 0)$$

$$y^2 = 4px$$

At $(1000, 800)$: $800^2 = 4p(1000) \implies p = 160$

$$y^2 = 4(160)x$$

$$y^2 = 640x$$

66. (a)

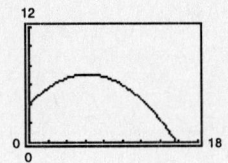

(b) Highest point: $(6.25, 7.125)$

Range: 15.69 feet

68. False. It is not possible for a parabola to intersect its directrix. If the graph crossed the directrix there would exist points nearer the directrix than the focus.

70. (a)

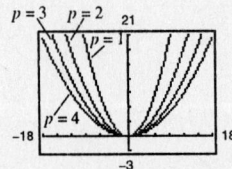

As p increases, the graph becomes wider.

(b) $(0, 1), (0, 2), (0, 3), (0, 4)$

(c) 4, 8, 12, 16. The chord passing through the focus and parallel to the directrix has length $|4p|$.

(d) This provides an easy way to determine two additional

72. $y - y_1 = \dfrac{x_1}{2p}(x - x_1)$

Slope: $m = \dfrac{x_1}{2p}$

74. $f(x) = 3x^4 - 2x^3 + 6x - 3$

3 variations in sign $\implies$ 1 or 3 positive real zeros

$f(-x) = 3x^4 + 2x^3 - 6x - 3$

1 variation in sign $\implies$ 1 negative real zero

76. $f(x) = x^5 - 2x^4 + x^3 + x^2 - 3x + 1$

4 variations in sign $\implies$ 4, 2 or 0 positive real zeros

$f(-x) = -x^5 - 2x^4 - x^3 + x^2 + 3x + 1$

1 variation in sign $\implies$ 1 negative real zero

78. $f(x) = 2x^3 + 4x^2 - 3x + 10$

Rational zeros $\frac{p}{q}$: p = factor or 10, q = factor of 2

Possible rational zeros: $\pm\frac{1}{2}, \pm 1, \pm 2, \pm\frac{5}{2}, \pm 5, \pm 10$

80. $f(x) = 3x^3 - 12x + 22$

Rational zeros $\frac{p}{q}$: p = factor of 22, q = factor of 3

Possible rational zeros: $\pm\frac{1}{3}, \pm\frac{2}{3}, \pm 1, \pm 2, \pm\frac{11}{3}, \pm\frac{22}{3},$
$\pm 11, \pm 22$

82. $f(x) = 2x^3 - 3x^2 + 50x - 75$

$$
\begin{array}{r|rrrr}
\frac{3}{2} & 2 & -3 & 50 & -75 \\
 & & 3 & 0 & 75 \\
\hline
 & 2 & 0 & 50 & 0
\end{array}
$$

$2x^2 + 50 = 0 \implies x^2 = -25 \implies x = \pm 5i$

Zeros: $x = \frac{3}{2}, \pm 5i$

84. $h(x) = 2x^4 + x^3 - 19x^2 - 9x + 9$

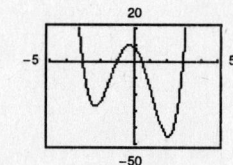

Zeros: $x = \pm 3, -1, \frac{1}{2}$

Section 10.3   Ellipses

Solutions to Even-Numbered Exercises

2. $\dfrac{x^2}{9} + \dfrac{y^2}{4} = 1$

Center: $(0, 0)$

$a = 3, b = 2$

Horizontal major axis
Matches graph (c).

4. $\dfrac{y^2}{4} + \dfrac{x^2}{4} = 1$

Center: $(0, 0)$
Circle of radius: 2
Matches graph (f).

6. $\dfrac{(x + 2)^2}{9} + \dfrac{(y + 2)^2}{4} = 1$

Center: $(-2, -2)$

$a = 3, b = 2$

Horizontal major axis
Matches graph (e).

8. $\dfrac{x^2}{81} + \dfrac{y^2}{144} = 1$

$a^2 = 144, b^2 = 81, c^2 = 63$

Center: $(0, 0)$

Vertices: $(0, \pm 12)$

Foci: $\left(0, \pm 3\sqrt{7}\right)$

Eccentricity: $e = \dfrac{c}{a} = \dfrac{\sqrt{7}}{4}$

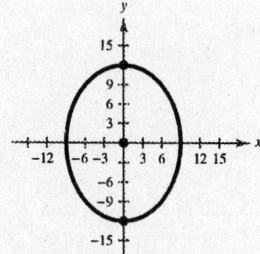

10. $\dfrac{x^2}{64} + \dfrac{y^2}{28} = 1$

$a^2 = 64, b^2 = 28, c^2 = 36$

Center: $(0, 0)$

Vertices: $(\pm 8, 0)$

Foci: $(\pm 6, 0)$

Eccentricity: $e = \dfrac{c}{a} = \dfrac{3}{4}$

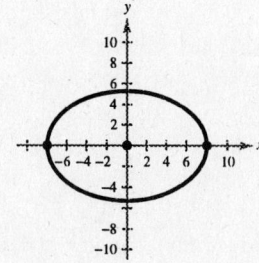

12. $\dfrac{(x-4)^2}{12} + \dfrac{(y+3)^2}{16} = 1$

$a^2 = 16, b^2 = 12, c^2 = 4$

Center: $(4, -3)$

Vertices: $(4, 1), (4, -7)$

Foci: $(4, -1), (4, -5)$

Eccentricity: $e = \dfrac{c}{a} = \dfrac{1}{2}$

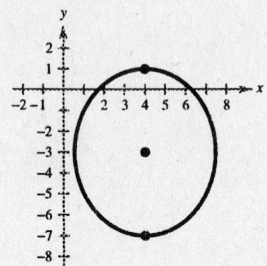

14. $\dfrac{(x+2)^2}{1} + \dfrac{(y+4)^2}{\frac{1}{4}} = 1$

$a^2 = 1, b^2 = \dfrac{1}{4}, c^2 = \dfrac{3}{4}$

Center: $(-2, -4)$

Vertices: $(-1, -4), (-3, -4)$

Foci: $\left(-2 \pm \dfrac{\sqrt{3}}{2}, -4\right) \Rightarrow \left(\dfrac{-4 \pm \sqrt{3}}{2}, -4\right)$

$e = \dfrac{\sqrt{3}}{2}$

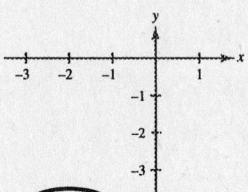

16. $9x^2 + 4y^2 - 54x + 40y + 37 = 0$

$9(x^2 - 6x + 9) + 4(y^2 + 10y + 25) = -37 + 81 + 100$

$\dfrac{(x-3)^2}{16} + \dfrac{(y+5)^2}{36} = 1$

$a^2 = 36, b^2 = 16, c^2 = 20$

Center: $(3, -5)$

Vertices: $(3, 1), (3, -11)$

Foci: $\left(3, -5 \pm 2\sqrt{5}\right)$

Eccentricity: $e = \dfrac{c}{a} = \dfrac{\sqrt{5}}{3}$

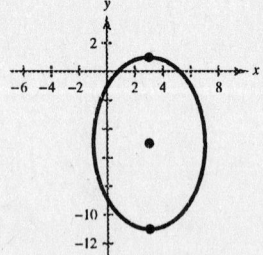

18. $3x^2 + y^2 + 18x - 2y - 8 = 0$

$3(x^2 + 6x + 9) + (y^2 - 2y + 1) = 8 + 27 + 1$

$\dfrac{(x+3)^2}{12} + \dfrac{(y-1)^2}{36} = 1$

$a^2 = 36, b^2 = 12, c^2 = 24$

Center: $(-3, 1)$

Vertices: $(-3, 7), (-3, -5)$

Foci: $\left(-3, 1 \pm 2\sqrt{6}\right)$

Eccentricity: $e = \dfrac{c}{a} = \dfrac{\sqrt{6}}{3}$

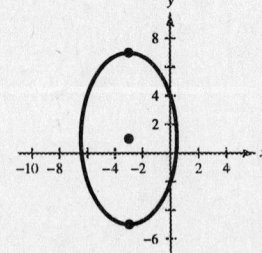

20.
$$x^2 + 4y^2 - 6x + 20y - 2 = 0$$

$$(x^2 - 6x + 9) + 4\left(y^2 + 5y + \frac{25}{4}\right) = 2 + 9 + 25$$

$$\frac{(x - 3)^2}{36} + \frac{\left(y + \frac{5}{2}\right)^2}{9} = 1$$

$$a^2 = 36, b^2 = 9, c^2 = 27$$

Center: $\left(3, -\frac{5}{2}\right)$

Vertices: $\left(9, -\frac{5}{2}\right), \left(-3, -\frac{5}{2}\right)$

Foci: $\left(3 \pm 3\sqrt{3}, -\frac{5}{2}\right)$

Eccentricity: $e = \frac{c}{a} = \frac{\sqrt{3}}{2}$

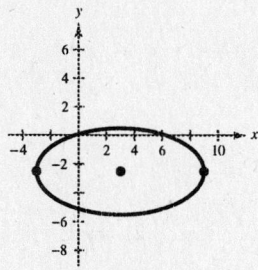

22.
$$9x^2 + 25y^2 - 36x - 50y + 60 = 0$$

$$9(x^2 - 4x + 4) + 25(y^2 - 2y + 1) = -60 + 36 + 25$$

$$\frac{(x - 2)^2}{\frac{1}{9}} + \frac{(y - 1)^2}{\frac{1}{25}} = 1$$

$$a^2 = \frac{1}{9}, b^2 = \frac{1}{25}, c^2 = \frac{16}{225}$$

Center: $(2, 1)$

Vertices: $\left(\frac{5}{3}, 1\right), \left(\frac{7}{3}, 1\right)$

Foci: $\left(\frac{34}{15}, 1\right), \left(\frac{26}{15}, 1\right)$

Eccentricity: $e = \frac{c}{a} = \frac{4}{5}$

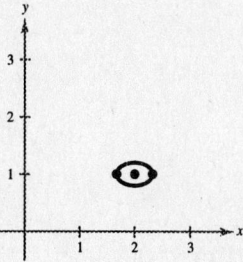

24. $3x^2 + 4y^2 = 12$

$$\frac{x^2}{4} + \frac{y^2}{3} = 1$$

$$a^2 = 4, b^2 = 3, c^2 = 1$$

Center: $(0, 0)$

Vertices: $(\pm 2, 0)$

Foci: $(\pm 1, 0)$

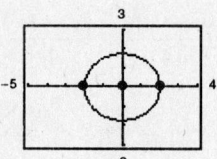

26.
$$36x^2 + 9y^2 + 48x - 36y - 72 = 0$$

$$36\left(x^2 + \frac{4}{3}x + \frac{4}{9}\right) + 9(y^2 - 4y + 4) = 72 + 16 + 36$$

$$\frac{\left(x + \frac{2}{3}\right)^2}{\frac{31}{9}} + \frac{(y - 2)^2}{\frac{124}{9}} = 1$$

$$a^2 = \frac{124}{9}, 6^2 = \frac{31}{9}, c^2 = \frac{31}{3}$$

Center: $\left(-\frac{2}{3}, 2\right)$

Vertices: $\left(-\frac{2}{3}, 2 \pm \frac{2\sqrt{31}}{3}\right)$

Foci: $\left(-\frac{2}{3}, 2 \pm \frac{\sqrt{93}}{3}\right)$

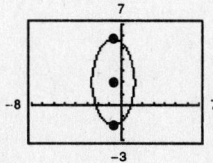

28. Vertices: $(\pm 2, 0) \implies a = 2$

Endpoints of minor axis: $\left(0, \pm\dfrac{3}{2}\right) \implies b = \dfrac{3}{2}$

$$\frac{x^2}{a^2} + \frac{y^2}{b^2} = 1$$

$$\frac{x^2}{2^2} + \frac{y^2}{\left(\frac{3}{2}\right)^2} = 1$$

$$\frac{x^2}{4} + \frac{4y^2}{9} = 1$$

30. Vertices: $(0, \pm 8) \implies a = 8$

Foci: $(0, \pm 4) \implies c = 4$

$b^2 = a^2 - c^2 = 64 - 16 = 48$

$$\frac{x^2}{b^2} + \frac{y^2}{a^2} = 1$$

$$\frac{x^2}{48} + \frac{y^2}{64} = 1$$

32. Foci: $(\pm 2, 0) \implies c = 2$

Major axis length: $8 \implies a = 4$

$b^2 = a^2 - c^2 = 16 - 4 = 12$

$$\frac{x^2}{a^2} + \frac{y^2}{b^2} = 1$$

$$\frac{x^2}{16} + \frac{y^2}{12} = 1$$

34. Major axis vertical

Passes through: $(0, 4)$ and $(2, 0)$

$a = 4, b = 2$

$$\frac{x^2}{b^2} + \frac{y^2}{a^2} = 1$$

$$\frac{x^2}{4} + \frac{y^2}{16} = 1$$

36. Vertices: $(4, \pm 4) \implies a = 4$

Center: $(4, 0) \implies h = 4, k = 0$

Endpoints of minor axis: $(1, 0), (7, 0) \implies b = 3$

$$\frac{(x-h)^2}{b^2} + \frac{(y-k)^2}{a^2} = 1$$

$$\frac{(x-4)^2}{9} + \frac{y^2}{16} = 1$$

38. Vertices: $(0, -1), (4, -1) \implies a = 2$

Center: $(2, -1) \implies h = 2, k = -1$

Endpoints of minor axis: $(2, 0), (2, -2) \implies b = 1$

$$\frac{(x-h)^2}{a^2} + \frac{(y-k)^2}{b^2} = 1$$

$$\frac{(x-2)^2}{4} + \frac{(y+1)^2}{1} = 1$$

40. Foci: $(0, 0), (4, 0) \implies c = 2, h = 2, k = 0$

Major axis length: $8 \implies a = 4$

$b^2 = a^2 - c^2 = 16 - 4 = 12$

$$\frac{(x-h)^2}{a^2} + \frac{(y-k)^2}{b^2} = 1$$

$$\frac{(x-2)^2}{16} + \frac{y^2}{12} = 1$$

42. Center: $(2, -1) \implies h = 2, k = -1$

Vertex: $\left(2, \dfrac{1}{2}\right) \implies a = \dfrac{3}{2}$

Minor axis length: $2 \implies b = 1$

$$\frac{(x-h)}{b^2} + \frac{(y-k)^2}{a^2} = 1$$

$$\frac{(x-2)^2}{1} + \frac{(y+1)^2}{\left(\frac{3}{2}\right)^2} = 1$$

$$(x-2)^2 + \frac{4(y+1)^2}{9} = 1$$

44. Center: $(3, 2) \implies h = 3, k = 2$

$a = 3c$

Foci: $(1, 2), (5, 2) \implies c = 2, a = 6$

$b^2 = a^2 - c^2 = 36 - 4 = 32$

$$\frac{(x-h)^2}{a^2} + \frac{(y-k)^2}{b^2} = 1$$

$$\frac{(x-3)^2}{36} + \frac{(y-2)^2}{32} = 1$$

46. Vertices: $(5, 0), (5, 12) \implies a = 6$

Endpoints of the minor axis:

$(1, 6), (9, 6) \implies b = 4$

Center: $(5, 6) \implies h = 5, k = 6$

$$\frac{(x-h)^2}{b^2} + \frac{(y-k)^2}{a^2} = 1$$

$$\frac{(x-5)^2}{16} + \frac{(y-6)^2}{36} = 1$$

48. Vertices: $(0, \pm 8) \implies a = 8$

$e = \dfrac{1}{2} \implies \dfrac{c}{a} = \dfrac{1}{2}, c = 4$

$b^2 = a^2 - c^2 = 64 - 16 = 48$

Center: $(0, 0)$

$\dfrac{x^2}{b^2} + \dfrac{y^2}{a^2} = 1$

$\dfrac{x^2}{48} + \dfrac{y^2}{64} = 1$

50. (a)

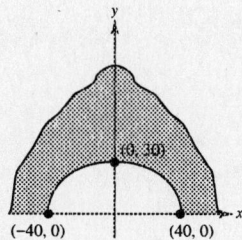

(b) $a = 40, b = 30$

$\dfrac{x^2}{a^2} + \dfrac{y^2}{b^2} = 1$

$\dfrac{x^2}{1600} + \dfrac{y^2}{900} = 1$

(c) When $x = \pm 35$, you are five feet from the edge of the tunnel.

$\dfrac{35^2}{1600} + \dfrac{y^2}{900} = 1$

$y^2 = 900 - 900\left(\dfrac{1225}{1600}\right) = \dfrac{3375}{16}$

$y = \pm\sqrt{\dfrac{3375}{16}} \approx \pm 14.5$

The height of the tunnel five feet from its edge is 14.5 feet.

52. $A = \dfrac{36.18}{2} = 18.09$

$e = \dfrac{c}{a} = 0.97$

$c = ea \approx 17.55$

$b^2 = a^2 - c^2 \approx 19.34$

$\dfrac{x^2}{a^2} + \dfrac{y^2}{b^2} = 1$

$\dfrac{x^2}{327.25} + \dfrac{y^2}{19.34} = 1$

54. $a + c = 6378 + 938 = 7316$

$a - c = 6378 + 212 = 6590$

Solving this system for a and c gives

$a = 6953, c = 363$

$e = \dfrac{c}{a} = \dfrac{363}{6953} \approx 0.052$

56. $\dfrac{x^2}{4} + \dfrac{y^2}{1} = 1$

$a = 2, b = 1, c = \sqrt{3}$

Points on the ellipse: $(\pm 2, 0), (0, \pm 1)$

Length of latera recta: $\dfrac{2b^2}{a} = \dfrac{2(1)^2}{2} = 1$

Additional points: $\left(-\sqrt{3}, \pm\dfrac{1}{2}\right), \left(\sqrt{3}, \pm\dfrac{1}{2}\right)$

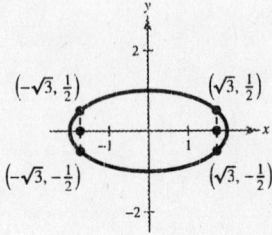

58. $9x^2 + 4y^2 = 36$

$\dfrac{x^2}{4} + \dfrac{y^2}{9} = 1$

$a = 3, b = 2, c = \sqrt{5}$

Points on the ellipse: $(\pm 2, 0), (0, \pm 3)$

Length of latera recta: $\dfrac{2b^2}{a} = \dfrac{2 \cdot 2^2}{3} = \dfrac{8}{3}$

Additional points: $\left(\pm\dfrac{4}{3}, -\sqrt{5}\right), \left(\pm\dfrac{4}{3}, \sqrt{5}\right)$

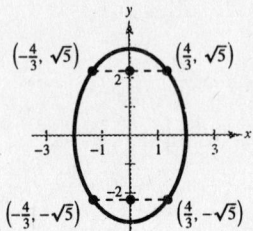

60. False. The graph of $\dfrac{x^2}{4} + y^4 = 1$ is not an ellipse.

The degree on y is 4, not 2.

62. True. The area of the circle is 16π. The area of the ellipse is $4\pi b$, where $b < 4$ since $2a = 8$ is the major axis length.

64. (a) Length of string $= 2a$

(b) By keeping the string taut, the sum of the distances from the two fixed points is constant (equal to the length of the string).

66. $66, 55, 44, 33, 22, \ldots$

arithmetic sequence

68. $\dfrac{1}{4}, \dfrac{1}{2}, 1, 2, 4$

geometric sequence

70. $a_1 = 13, d = 3$

$a_n = 10 + 3n$

72. $a_1 = 5, a_4 = 9.5$

$a_4 - a_1 = 3d \implies d = 1.5$

$a_n = 3.5 + 1.5n$

74. $\displaystyle\sum_{n=0}^{6} 3^n = \sum_{n=1}^{7} 3^{(n-1)} \implies a_1 = 1, r = 3$

$$S_7 = \dfrac{1(1 - 3^7)}{1 - 3} = 1093$$

76. $\displaystyle\sum_{n=1}^{10} 4\left(\dfrac{3}{4}\right)^{n-1} \implies a_1 = 4, r = \dfrac{3}{4}$

$$S_{10} = \dfrac{4\left(1 - \left(\dfrac{3}{4}\right)^{10}\right)}{1 - \dfrac{3}{4}} \approx 15.10$$

Section 10.4   Hyperbolas

Solutions to Even-Numbered Exercises

2. $\dfrac{y^2}{25} - \dfrac{x^2}{9} = 1$

Center: $(0, 0)$

$a = 5, b = 3$

Vertical transverse axis
Matches graph (c).

4. $\dfrac{(x + 1)^2}{16} - \dfrac{(y - 2)^2}{9} = 1$

Center: $(-1, 2)$

$a = 4, b = 3$

Horizontal transverse axis
Matches graph (d).

6. $\dfrac{x^2}{9} - \dfrac{y^2}{25} = 1$

$a = 3, b = 5$

$c = \sqrt{3^2 + 5^2} = \sqrt{34}$

Center: $(0, 0)$

Vertices: $(\pm 3, 0)$

Foci: $\left(\pm\sqrt{34}, 0\right)$

Asymptotes: $y = \pm\dfrac{5}{3}x$

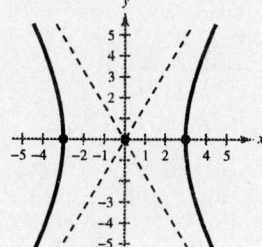

8. $\dfrac{x^2}{36} - \dfrac{y^2}{4} = 1$

$a = 6, b = 2,$

$c = \sqrt{36 + 4} = 2\sqrt{10}$

Center: $(0, 0)$

Vertices: $(\pm 6, 0)$

Foci: $\left(\pm 2\sqrt{10}, 0\right)$

Asymptotes: $y = \pm\dfrac{1}{3}x$

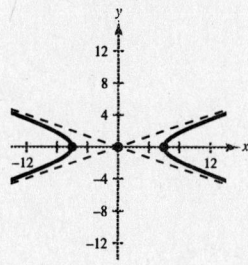

10. $\dfrac{(x + 3)^2}{144} - \dfrac{(y - 2)^2}{25} = 1$

$a = 12, b = 5$

$c = \sqrt{144 + 25} = 13$

Center: $(-3, 2)$

Vertices: $(9, 2), (-15, 2)$

Foci: $(10, 2), (-16, 2)$

Asymptotes: $y = 2 \pm \dfrac{5}{12}(x + 3)$

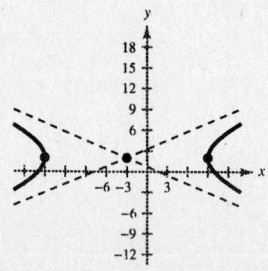

12. $\dfrac{(y - 1)^2}{\frac{1}{4}} - \dfrac{(x + 3)^2}{\frac{1}{16}} = 1$

$a = \dfrac{1}{2}, b = \dfrac{1}{4}$

$c = \sqrt{\dfrac{1}{4} + \dfrac{1}{16}} = \dfrac{\sqrt{5}}{4}$

Center: $(-3, 1)$

Vertices: $\left(-3, \dfrac{3}{2}\right), \left(-3, \dfrac{1}{2}\right)$

Foci: $\left(-3, 1 \pm \dfrac{\sqrt{5}}{4}\right)$

Asymptotes: $y = 1 \pm 2(x + 3)$

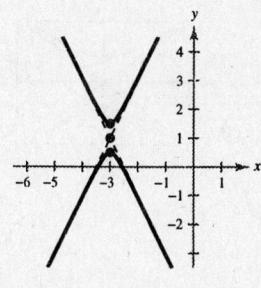

14. $x^2 - 9y^2 + 36y - 72 = 0$

$x^2 - 9(y^2 - 4y + 4) = 72 - 36$

$x^2 - 9(y - 2)^2 = 36$

$\dfrac{x^2}{36} - \dfrac{(y - 2)^2}{4} = 1$

$a = 6, b = 2, c = \sqrt{36 + 4} = 2\sqrt{10}$

Center: $(0, 2)$

Vertices: $(\pm 6, 2)$

Foci: $\left(\pm 2\sqrt{10}, 2\right)$

Asymptotes: $y = 2 \pm \dfrac{1}{3}x$

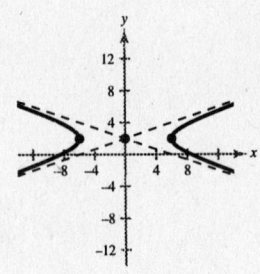

16. $16y^2 - x^2 + 2x + 64y + 63 = 0$

$16(y^2 + 4y + 4) - (x^2 - 2x + 1) = -63 + 64 - 1$

$16(y + 2)^2 - (x - 1)^2 = 0$

$y + 2 = \pm\tfrac{1}{4}(x - 1)$

Degenerate hyperbola: The graph is two lines intersecting at $(1, -2)$.

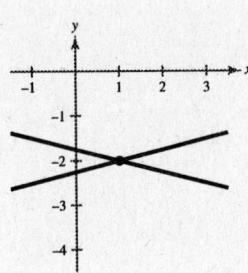

18. $6y^2 - 3x^2 = 18$

$\dfrac{y^2}{3} - \dfrac{x^2}{6} = 1$

$a = \sqrt{3}, b = \sqrt{6}, c = \sqrt{3 + 6} = 3$

Center: $(0, 0)$

Vertices: $\left(0, \pm\sqrt{3}\right)$

Foci: $(0, \pm 3)$

Asymptotes: $y = \pm\dfrac{\sqrt{2}}{2}x$

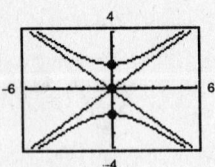

20. $9x^2 - y^2 + 54x + 10y + 55 = 0$

$9(x^2 + 6x + 9) - (y^2 - 10y + 25) = -55 + 81 - 25$

$\dfrac{(x + 3)^2}{\frac{1}{9}} - \dfrac{(y - 5)^2}{1} = 1$

$a = \dfrac{1}{3}, b = 1, c = \dfrac{\sqrt{10}}{3}$

Center: $(-3, 5)$

Vertices: $\left(-3 \pm \dfrac{1}{3}, 5\right) \Rightarrow \left(-\dfrac{10}{3}, 5\right), \left(-\dfrac{8}{3}, 5\right)$

Foci: $\left(-3 \pm \dfrac{\sqrt{10}}{3}, 5\right)$

Asymptotes: $y = 5 \pm 3(x + 3)$

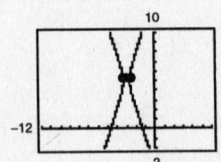

22. Vertices: $(\pm 4, 0) \Rightarrow a = 4$

Foci: $(\pm 6, 0) \Rightarrow c = 6$

$b^2 = c^2 - a^2 = 36 - 16 = 20 \Rightarrow b = 2\sqrt{5}$

$\dfrac{x^2}{a^2} - \dfrac{y^2}{b^2} = 1$

$\dfrac{x^2}{16} - \dfrac{y^2}{20} = 1$

24. Vertices: $(0, \pm 3) \Rightarrow a = 3$

Asymptotes: $y = \pm 3x \Rightarrow \dfrac{a}{b} = 3, b = 1$

$\dfrac{y^2}{a^2} - \dfrac{x^2}{b^2} = 1$

$\dfrac{y^2}{9} - x^2 = 1$

26. Foci: $(\pm 10, 0) \implies c = 10$

Asymptotes: $y = \pm \dfrac{3}{4}x \implies \dfrac{b}{a} = \dfrac{3m}{4m}$

$c^2 = a^2 + b^2 \implies 100 = (3m)^2 + (4m)^2$

$$100 = 25m^2$$
$$2 = m$$

$a = 4(2) = 8$

$b = 3(2) = 6$

$$\dfrac{x^2}{a^2} - \dfrac{y^2}{b^2} = 1$$

$$\dfrac{x^2}{64} - \dfrac{y^2}{36} = 1$$

28. Vertices: $(2, 3), (2, -3) \implies a = 3$

Center: $(2, 0)$

Foci: $(2, 6), (2, -6) \implies c = 6$

$b^2 = c^2 - a^2 = 36 - 9 = 27$

$$\dfrac{(y-k)^2}{a^2} - \dfrac{(x-h)^2}{b^2} = 1$$

$$\dfrac{y^2}{9} - \dfrac{(x-2)^2}{27} = 1$$

30. Vertices: $(-2, 1), (2, 1) \implies a = 2$

Center: $(0, 1)$

Foci: $(-3, 1), (3, 1) \implies c = 3$

$b^2 = c^2 - a^2 = 9 - 4 = 5$

$$\dfrac{(x-h)^2}{a^2} - \dfrac{(y-k)^2}{b^2} = 1$$

$$\dfrac{x^2}{4} - \dfrac{(y-1)^2}{5} = 1$$

32. Vertices: $(-2, 1), (2, 1) \implies a = 2$

Center: $(0, 1)$

Point on curve: $(5, 4)$

$$\dfrac{(x-h)^2}{a^2} - \dfrac{(y-k)^2}{b^2} = 1$$

$$\dfrac{x^2}{4} - \dfrac{(y-1)^2}{b^2} = 1$$

$$\dfrac{25}{4} - \dfrac{9}{b^2} = 1$$

$$b^2 = \dfrac{12}{7}$$

$$\dfrac{x^2}{4} - \dfrac{(y-1)^2}{\frac{12}{7}} = 1$$

$$\dfrac{x^2}{4} - \dfrac{7(y-1)^2}{12} = 1$$

34. Vertices: $(1, \pm 2) \implies a = 2$

Center: $(1, 0)$

Point on curve: $\left(0, \sqrt{5}\right)$

$$\dfrac{(y-k)^2}{a^2} - \dfrac{(x-h)^2}{b^2} = 1$$

$$\dfrac{y^2}{4} - \dfrac{(x-1)^2}{b^2} = 1$$

$$\dfrac{5}{4} - \dfrac{1}{b^2} = 1$$

$$b^2 = 4$$

$$\dfrac{y^2}{4} - \dfrac{(x-1)^2}{4} = 1$$

36. Vertices: $(3, 0), (3, 6) \implies a = 3$

Center: $(3, 3)$

Asymptotes: $y = 6 - x, y = x$

$$\dfrac{a}{b} = 1 \implies b = 3$$

$$\dfrac{(y-k)^2}{a^2} - \dfrac{(x-h)^2}{b^2} = 1$$

$$\dfrac{(y-3)^2}{9} - \dfrac{(x-3)^2}{9} = 1$$

38. Vertices: $(3, 0), (3, 4) \implies a = 2$

Asymptotes: $y = \dfrac{2}{3}x, y = 4 - \dfrac{2}{3}x$

$\dfrac{a}{b} = \dfrac{2}{3} \implies b = 3$

Center: $(3, 2) = (h, k)$

$\dfrac{(y - k)^2}{a^2} - \dfrac{(x - h)^2}{b^2} = 1$

$\dfrac{(y - 2)^2}{4} - \dfrac{(x - 3)^2}{9} = 1$

40. Foci: $(\pm 150, 0) \implies c = 150$

Center: $(0, 0) = (h, k)$

$\dfrac{d_2}{186{,}000} - \dfrac{d_1}{186{,}000} = 0.001 \implies 2a = 186, a = 93$

$b^2 = c^2 - a^2 = 150^2 - 93^2 = 13{,}851$

$\dfrac{x^2}{93^2} - \dfrac{y^2}{13{,}851} = 1$

$x^2 = 93^2\left(1 + \dfrac{75^2}{13{,}851}\right) \approx 12{,}161$

$x \approx 110.3$ miles

42. $x^2 + y^2 - 6x + 4y + 9 = 0$

$A = 1, C = 1$

$A = C \implies$ Circle

44. $4x^2 - y^2 - 4x - 3 = 0$

$A = 4, C = -1$

$AC = (4)(-1) = -4 < 0 \implies$ Hyperbola

46. $4x^2 + 3y^2 + 8x - 24y + 51 = 0$

$A = 4, C = 3$

$AC = 4(3) = 12 > 0 \implies$ Ellipse

48. $25x^2 - 10x - 200y - 119 = 0$

$A = 25, C = 0$

$AC = 25(0) = 0 \implies$ Parabola

50. True. For a hyperbola, $c^2 = a^2 + b^2$ or $e^2 = \dfrac{c^2}{a^2} = 1 + \dfrac{b^2}{a^2}$.

The larger the ratio of b to a, the larger the eccentricity $e = \dfrac{c}{a}$ of the hyperbola.

52. Let (x, y) be such that the difference of the distances from $(c, 0)$ and $(-c, 0)$ is $2a$ (again only deriving one of the forms).

$$2a = \left|\sqrt{(x + c)^2 + y^2} - \sqrt{(x - c)^2 + y^2}\right|$$

$$2a + \sqrt{(x - c)^2 + y^2} = \sqrt{(x + c)^2 + y^2}$$

$$4a^2 + 4a\sqrt{(x - c)^2 + y^2} + (x - c)^2 + y^2 = (x + c)^2 + y^2$$

$$4a\sqrt{(x - c)^2 + y^2} = 4cx - 4a^2$$

$$a\sqrt{(x - c)^2 + y^2} = cx - a^2$$

$$a^2(x^2 - 2cx + c^2 + y^2) = c^2x^2 - 2a^2cx + a^4$$

$$a^2(c^2 - a^2) = (c^2 - a^2)x^2 - a^2y^2$$

Let $b^2 = c^2 - a^2$. Then $a^2b^2 = b^2x^2 - a^2y^2 \implies 1 = \dfrac{x^2}{a^2} - \dfrac{y^2}{b^2}$.

54. $\left(x^3 - 3x^2\right) - \left(6 - 2x - 4x^2\right) = x^3 - 3x^2 - 6 + 2x + 4x^2$
$\qquad\qquad\qquad\qquad\qquad\qquad = x^3 + x^2 + 2x - 6$

56.
$$
\begin{array}{r}
x^2 - 2x + 1 + \dfrac{2}{x + 2} \\[4pt]
x + 2 \overline{\smash{\big)}\, x^3 + 0x^2 - 3x + 4} \\
\underline{x^3 + 2x^2} \\
-2x^2 - 3x \\
\underline{-2x^2 - 4x} \\
x + 4 \\
\underline{x + 2} \\
2
\end{array}
$$

Thus, $\dfrac{x^3 - 3x + 4}{x + 2} = x^2 - 2x + 1 + \dfrac{2}{x + 2}.$

58. $x^3 - 16x = x(x^2 - 16) = x(x + 4)(x - 4)$

60. $2x^3 - 24x^2 + 72x = 2x(x^2 - 12x + 36) = 2x(x - 6)^2$

62. $16x^3 + 54 = 2[(2x)^3 + 3^3]$
$\qquad\qquad\quad = 2(2x + 3)(4x^2 - 6x + 9)$

Section 10.5   Rotation of Conics

Solutions to Even-Numbered Exercises

2. $\theta = 45°$; Point: $(3, 3)$

$x' = x \cos \theta - y \sin \theta = 3 \cos 45° - 3 \sin 45° = 0$

$y' = x \sin \theta + y \cos \theta = 3 \sin 45° + 3 \cos 45° = 3\sqrt{2}$

Thus, $(x', y') = \left(0, 3\sqrt{2}\right)$.

4. $\theta = 60°$; Point: $(3, 1)$

$x' = x \cos \theta - y \sin \theta = 3 \cos 60° - 1 \sin 60° = \dfrac{3}{2} - \dfrac{\sqrt{3}}{2}$

$y' = x \sin \theta + y \cos \theta = 3 \sin 60° + 1 \cos 60° = \dfrac{3\sqrt{3}}{2} + \dfrac{1}{2}$

Thus, $(x', y') = \left(\dfrac{1}{2}(3 - \sqrt{3}), \dfrac{1}{2}(3\sqrt{3} + 1)\right)$.

6. $\theta = 30°$; Point: $(2, 4)$

$x' = x \cos \theta - y \sin \theta = 2 \cos 30° - 4 \sin 30° = \sqrt{3} - 2$

$y' = x \sin \theta + y \cos \theta = 2 \sin 30° + 4 \cos 30° = 1 + 2\sqrt{3}$

Thus, $(x', y') = \left(\sqrt{3} - 2, 1 + 2\sqrt{3}\right)$

8. $xy - 2 = 0$

$A = 0, B = 1, C = 0$

$$\cot 2\theta = \frac{A - C}{B} = 0 \implies 2\theta = \frac{\pi}{2} \implies \theta = \frac{\pi}{4}$$

$$x = x' \cos \frac{\pi}{4} - y' \sin \frac{\pi}{4} \qquad\qquad y = x' \sin \frac{\pi}{4} + y' \cos \frac{\pi}{4}$$

$$= \frac{x' - y'}{\sqrt{2}} \qquad\qquad\qquad\qquad = \frac{x' + y'}{\sqrt{2}}$$

$$xy - 2 = 0$$

$$\left(\frac{x' - y'}{\sqrt{2}}\right)\left(\frac{x' + y'}{\sqrt{2}}\right) - 2 = 0$$

$$\frac{(x')^2 - (y')^2}{2} = 2$$

$$\frac{(x')^2}{4} - \frac{(y')^2}{4} = 1$$

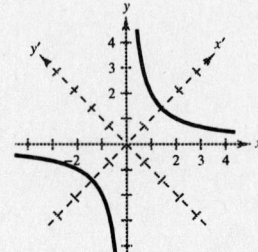

10. $xy + x - 2y + 3 = 0$

$A = 0, B = 1, C = 0$

$$\cot 2\theta = \frac{A - C}{B} = 0 \implies 2\theta = \frac{\pi}{2} \implies \theta = \frac{\pi}{4}$$

$$x = x' \cos \frac{\pi}{4} - y' \sin \frac{\pi}{4} \qquad\qquad y = x' \sin \frac{\pi}{4} + y' \cos \frac{\pi}{4}$$

$$= x'\left(\frac{\sqrt{2}}{2}\right) - y'\left(\frac{\sqrt{2}}{2}\right) \qquad\qquad = x'\left(\frac{\sqrt{2}}{2}\right) + y'\left(\frac{\sqrt{2}}{2}\right)$$

$$= \frac{x' - y'}{\sqrt{2}} \qquad\qquad\qquad\qquad = \frac{x' + y'}{\sqrt{2}}$$

$$xy + x - 2y + 3 = 0$$

$$\left(\frac{x' - y'}{\sqrt{2}}\right)\left(\frac{x' + y'}{\sqrt{2}}\right) + \left(\frac{x' - y'}{\sqrt{2}}\right) - 2\left(\frac{x' + y'}{\sqrt{2}}\right) + 3 = 0$$

$$\frac{(x')^2}{2} - \frac{(y')^2}{2} + \frac{x'}{\sqrt{2}} - \frac{y'}{\sqrt{2}} - \frac{2x'}{\sqrt{2}} - \frac{2y'}{\sqrt{2}} + 3 = 0$$

$$\left[(x')^2 - \sqrt{2}x' + \left(\frac{\sqrt{2}}{2}\right)^2\right] - \left[(y')^2 + 3\sqrt{2}y' + \left(\frac{3\sqrt{2}}{2}\right)^2\right] = -6 + \left(\frac{\sqrt{2}}{2}\right)^2 - \left(\frac{3\sqrt{2}}{2}\right)^2$$

$$\left(x' - \frac{\sqrt{2}}{2}\right)^2 - \left(y' + \frac{3\sqrt{2}}{2}\right)^2 = -10$$

$$\frac{\left(y' + \frac{3\sqrt{2}}{2}\right)^2}{10} - \frac{\left(x' - \frac{\sqrt{2}}{2}\right)^2}{10} = 1$$

12. $2x^2 - 3xy - 2y^2 + 10 = 0$

$A = 2, B = -3, C = -2$

$\cot 2\theta = \dfrac{A - C}{B} = -\dfrac{4}{3} \implies \theta \approx 71.57°$

$\cos 2\theta = -\dfrac{4}{5}$

$\sin \theta = \sqrt{\dfrac{1 - \cos 2\theta}{2}} = \sqrt{\dfrac{1 - (-4/5)}{2}} = \dfrac{3}{\sqrt{10}}$

$\cos \theta = \sqrt{\dfrac{1 + \cos 2\theta}{2}} = \sqrt{\dfrac{1 + (-4/5)}{2}} = \dfrac{1}{\sqrt{10}}$

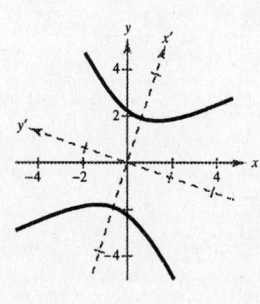

$x = x' \cos \theta - y' \sin \theta$

$= x'\left(\dfrac{1}{\sqrt{10}}\right) - y'\left(\dfrac{3}{\sqrt{10}}\right)$

$= \dfrac{x' - 3y'}{\sqrt{10}}$

$y = x' \sin \theta + y' \cos \theta$

$= x'\left(\dfrac{3}{\sqrt{10}}\right) + y'\left(\dfrac{1}{\sqrt{10}}\right)$

$= \dfrac{3x' + y'}{\sqrt{10}}$

$$2x^2 - 3xy - 2y^2 + 10 = 0$$

$$2\left(\dfrac{x' - 3y'}{\sqrt{10}}\right)^2 - 3\left(\dfrac{x' - 3y'}{\sqrt{10}}\right)\left(\dfrac{3x' + y'}{\sqrt{10}}\right) - 2\left(\dfrac{3x' + y'}{\sqrt{10}}\right)^2 + 10 = 0$$

$$\dfrac{(x')^2}{5} - \dfrac{6x'y'}{5} + \dfrac{9(y')^2}{5} - \dfrac{9(x')^2}{10} + \dfrac{24x'y'}{10} + \dfrac{9(y')^2}{10} - \dfrac{9(x')^2}{5} - \dfrac{6x'y'}{5} - \dfrac{(y')^2}{5} + 10 = 0$$

$$-\dfrac{5}{2}(x')^2 + \dfrac{5}{2}(y')^2 = -10$$

$$\dfrac{(x')^2}{4} - \dfrac{(y')^2}{4} = 1$$

14. $13x^2 + 6\sqrt{3}xy + 7y^2 - 16 = 0$

$A = 13, B = 6\sqrt{3}, C = 7$

$\cot 2\theta = \dfrac{A - C}{B} = \dfrac{1}{\sqrt{3}} \implies 2\theta = \dfrac{\pi}{3} \implies \theta = \dfrac{\pi}{6}$

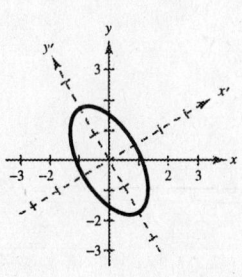

$x = x' \cos \dfrac{\pi}{6} - y' \sin \dfrac{\pi}{6}$

$= x'\left(\dfrac{\sqrt{3}}{2}\right) - y'\left(\dfrac{1}{2}\right)$

$= \dfrac{\sqrt{3}x' - y'}{2}$

$y = x' \sin \dfrac{\pi}{6} + y' \cos \dfrac{\pi}{6}$

$= x'\left(\dfrac{1}{2}\right) + y'\left(\dfrac{\sqrt{3}}{2}\right)$

$= \dfrac{x' + \sqrt{3}y'}{2}$

$$13x^2 + 6\sqrt{3}xy + 7y^2 - 16 = 0$$

$$13\left(\dfrac{\sqrt{3}x' - y'}{2}\right)^2 + 6\sqrt{3}\left(\dfrac{\sqrt{3}x' - y'}{2}\right)\left(\dfrac{x' + \sqrt{3}y'}{2}\right) + 7\left(\dfrac{x' + \sqrt{3}y'}{2}\right)^2 - 16 = 0$$

$$\dfrac{39(x')^2}{4} - \dfrac{13\sqrt{3}x'y'}{2} + \dfrac{13(y')^2}{4} + \dfrac{18(x')^2}{4} + \dfrac{18\sqrt{3}x'y'}{4} - \dfrac{6\sqrt{3}x'y'}{4}$$

$$-\dfrac{18(y')^2}{4} + \dfrac{7(x')^2}{4} + \dfrac{7\sqrt{3}x'y'}{2} + \dfrac{21(y')^2}{4} - 16 = 0$$

$$16(x')^2 + 4(y')^2 = 16$$

$$\dfrac{(x')^2}{1} + \dfrac{(y')^2}{4} = 1$$

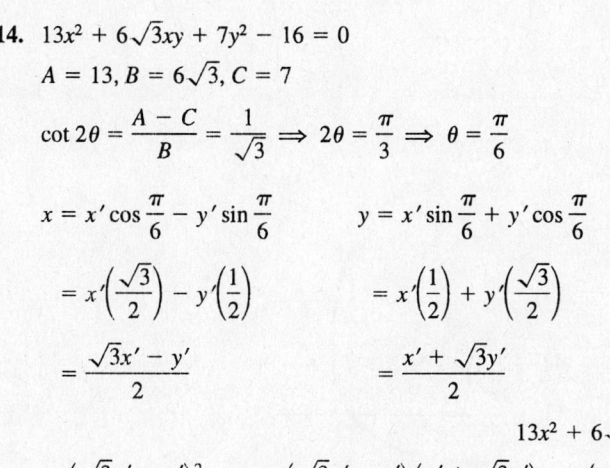

16. $16x^2 - 24xy + 9y^2 - 60x - 80y + 100 = 0$

$A = 16, B = -24, C = 9$

$\cot 2\theta = \dfrac{A - C}{B} = -\dfrac{7}{24} \implies \theta \approx 53.13°$

$\cos 2\theta = -\dfrac{7}{25}$

$\sin \theta = \sqrt{\dfrac{1 - \cos 2\theta}{2}} = \sqrt{\dfrac{1 - (-7/25)}{2}} = \dfrac{4}{5}$

$\cos \theta = \sqrt{\dfrac{1 + \cos 2\theta}{2}} = \sqrt{\dfrac{1 + (-7/25)}{2}} = \dfrac{3}{5}$

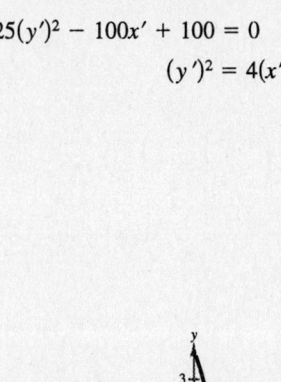

$x = x' \cos \theta - y' \sin \theta \qquad\qquad y = x' \sin \theta + y' \cos \theta$

$= x'\left(\dfrac{3}{5}\right) - y'\left(\dfrac{4}{5}\right) \qquad\qquad = x'\left(\dfrac{4}{3}\right) + y'\left(\dfrac{3}{5}\right) = \dfrac{4x' + 3y'}{5}$

$$16x^2 - 24xy + 9y^2 - 60x - 80y + 100 = 0$$

$$16\left(\dfrac{3x' - 4y'}{5}\right)^2 - 24\left(\dfrac{3x' - 4y'}{5}\right)\left(\dfrac{4x' + 3y'}{5}\right) + 9\left(\dfrac{4x' + 3y'}{5}\right)^2 - 60\left(\dfrac{3x' - 4y'}{5}\right)$$

$$- 80\left(\dfrac{4x' + 3y'}{5}\right) + 100 = 0$$

$$\dfrac{144(x')^2}{25} - \dfrac{384x'y'}{25} + \dfrac{256(y')^2}{25} - \dfrac{288(x')^2}{25} + \dfrac{168x'y'}{25} + \dfrac{288(y')^2}{25} + \dfrac{144(x')^2}{25} + \dfrac{216x'y'}{25}$$

$$+ \dfrac{81(y')^2}{25} - 36x' + 48y' - 64x' - 48y' + 100 = 0$$

$$25(y')^2 - 100x' + 100 = 0$$

$$(y')^2 = 4(x' - 1)$$

18. $9x^2 + 24xy + 16y^2 + 80x - 60y = 0$

$A = 9, B = 24, C = 16$

$\cot 2\theta = \dfrac{A - C}{B} = -\dfrac{7}{24} \implies \theta \approx 53.13°$

$\cos 2\theta = -\dfrac{7}{25}$

$\sin \theta = \sqrt{\dfrac{1 - \cos 2\theta}{2}} = \sqrt{\dfrac{1 - (-7/25)}{2}} = \dfrac{4}{5}$

$\cos \theta = \sqrt{\dfrac{1 + \cos 2\theta}{2}} = \sqrt{\dfrac{1 + (-7/25)}{2}} = \dfrac{3}{5}$

$x = x' \cos \theta - y' \sin \theta \qquad\qquad y = x' \sin \theta + y' \cos \theta$

$= x'\left(\dfrac{3}{5}\right) - y'\left(\dfrac{4}{5}\right) \qquad\qquad = x'\left(\dfrac{4}{5}\right) + y'\left(\dfrac{3}{5}\right)$

$= \dfrac{3x' - 4y'}{5} \qquad\qquad\qquad = \dfrac{4x' + 3y}{5}$

— CONTINUED —

18. — CONTINUED —

$$9x^2 + 24xy + 16y^2 + 80x - 60y = 0$$

$$9\left(\frac{3x' - 4y'}{5}\right)^2 + 24\left(\frac{3xy - 4y'}{5}\right)\left(\frac{4x' + 3y'}{5}\right) + 16\left(\frac{4x' + 3y'}{5}\right)^2 + 80\left(\frac{3x' - 4y'}{5}\right) - 60\left(\frac{4x' + 3y'}{5}\right) = 0$$

$$\frac{81(x')^2}{25} - \frac{216x'y'}{25} + \frac{144(y')^2}{25} + \frac{288(x')^2}{25} - \frac{168x'y'}{25} - \frac{288(y')^2}{25} + \frac{256(x')^2}{25} + \frac{384x'y'}{25}$$

$$+ \frac{144(y')^2}{25} + 48x' - 64x' - 48x' - 36x' = 0$$

$$25(x')^2 - 100y' = 0$$

$$(x')^2 = 4y'$$

$$\frac{1}{4}(x')^2 = y'$$

20. $x^2 - 4xy + 2y^2 = 6$

$A = 1, B = -4, C = 2$

$$\cot 2\theta = \frac{A - C}{B} = \frac{1 - 2}{-4} = \frac{1}{4}$$

$$\frac{1}{\tan 2\theta} = \frac{1}{4}$$

$$\tan 2\theta = 4$$

$$2\theta \approx 75.96$$

$$\theta \approx 37.98°$$

To graph conic with a graphing calculator, we need to solve for y in terms of x.

$$x^2 - 4xy + 2y^2 = 6$$

$$y^2 - 2xy + x^2 = 3 - \frac{x^2}{2} + x^2$$

$$(y - x)^2 = 3 + \frac{x^2}{2}$$

$$y - x = \pm\sqrt{3 + \frac{x^2}{2}}$$

$$y = x \pm \sqrt{3 + \frac{x^2}{2}}$$

Enter $y_1 = x + \sqrt{3 + \frac{x^2}{2}}$ and $y_2 = x - \sqrt{3 + \frac{x^2}{2}}$.

22. $40x^2 + 36xy + 25y^2 = 52$

$A = 40, B = 36, C = 25$

$$\cot 2\theta = \frac{A - C}{B} = \frac{40 - 25}{36} = \frac{5}{12}$$

$$\frac{1}{\tan 2\theta} = \frac{5}{12}$$

$$\tan 2\theta = \frac{12}{5}$$

$$2\theta \approx 67.38°$$

$$\theta \approx 33.69°$$

Solve for y in terms of x by completing the square:

$$25y^2 + 36xy = 52 - 40x^2$$

$$y^2 + \frac{36}{25}xy = \frac{52}{25} - \frac{40}{25}x^2$$

$$y^2 + \frac{36}{25}xy + \frac{324}{625}x^2 = \frac{52}{25} - \frac{40}{25}x^2 + \frac{324}{625}x^2$$

$$\left(y + \frac{18}{25}x\right)^2 = \frac{1300 - 676x^2}{625}$$

$$y + \frac{18}{25}x = \pm\sqrt{\frac{1300 - 676x^2}{625}}$$

$$y = \frac{-18x \pm \sqrt{1300 - 676x^2}}{25}$$

Enter $y_1 = \dfrac{-18x + \sqrt{1300 - 676x^2}}{25}$ and $y_2 = \dfrac{-18x - \sqrt{1300 - 676x^2}}{25}$.

24. $24x^2 + 18xy + 12y^2 = 34$

$A = 24, B = 18, C = 12$

$$\cot 2\theta = \frac{A - C}{B} = \frac{24 - 12}{18} = \frac{2}{3}$$

$$\tan 2\theta = \frac{3}{2}$$

$$2\theta \approx 56.31°$$

$$\theta \approx 28.15°$$

Solve for y in terms of x by completing the square:

$$12x^2 + 9xy + 6y^2 = 17$$

$$6\left(y^2 + \frac{3}{2}xy + \frac{9}{16}x^2\right) = 17 - 12x^2 + \frac{27}{8}x^2 = 17 - \frac{69}{8}x^2$$

$$\left(y + \frac{3}{4}x\right)^2 = \frac{136 - 69x^2}{48}$$

$$y = -\frac{3}{4}x \pm \sqrt{\frac{136 - 69x^2}{48}} = \frac{-9x \pm \sqrt{3(136 - 69x^2)}}{12}$$

Enter $y_1 = \dfrac{-9x + \sqrt{3(136 - 69x^2)}}{12}$ and $y_2 = \dfrac{-9x - \sqrt{3(136 - 69x^2)}}{12}$.

26. $6x^2 - 4xy + 8y^2 + (5\sqrt{5} - 10)x - (7\sqrt{5} + 5)y = 80$

$A = 6, B = -4, C = 8$

$$\cot 2\theta = \frac{A - C}{B} = \frac{6 - 8}{-4} = \frac{1}{2}$$

$\tan 2\theta = 2$

$2\theta \approx 63.43°$

$\theta \approx 31.72°$

Solve for y in terms of x using the quadratic formula:

$8y^2 - (4x + 7\sqrt{5} + 5)y + 6x^2 + (5\sqrt{5} - 10)x - 80 = 0$

$$y = \frac{1}{16}\left[4x + 7\sqrt{5} + 5 \pm \sqrt{(4x + 7\sqrt{5} + 5)^2 - 32(6x^2 + (5\sqrt{5} - 10)x - 80)}\right]$$

Enter y_1 and y_2 from the above expression.

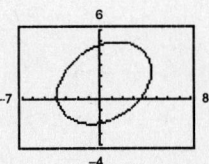

28. $x^2 + 2xy + y^2 = 0$

$\quad (x + y)^2 = 0$

$\quad\quad x + y = 0$

$\quad\quad\quad y = -x$

The graph is a line. Matches graph (f).

30. $x^2 - xy + 3y^2 - 5 = 0$

$A = 1, B = -1, C = 3$

$B^2 - 4AC = (-1)^2 - 4(1)(3) = -11$

The graph is an ellipse.

$$\cot 2\theta = \frac{A - C}{B} = \frac{1 - 3}{-1} = 2 \implies \theta \approx 13.28°$$

Matches graph (a).

32. $x^2 - 4xy + 4y^2 + 10x - 30 = 0$

$A = 1, B = -4, C = 4$

$B^2 - 4AC = (-4)^2 - 4(1)(4) = 0$

The graph is a parabola.

$$\cot 2\theta = \frac{A - C}{B} = \frac{1 - 4}{-4} = \frac{3}{4} \implies \theta \approx 26.57°$$

Matches graph (c).

34. $x^2 - 4xy - 2y^2 - 6 = 0$

$A = 1, B = -4, C = -2$

$B^2 - 4AC = (-4)^2 - 4(1)(-2) = 24 > 0$

Hyperbola

$-2y^2 - 4xy + x^2 - 6 = 0$

$$y = -\frac{1}{4}\left[4x \pm \sqrt{16x^2 + 8(x^2 - 6)}\right]$$

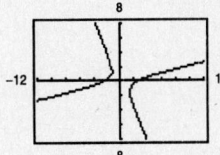

36. $2x^2 + 4xy + 5y^2 + 3x - 4y - 20 = 0$

$A = 2, B = 4, C = 5$

$B^2 - 4AC = 4^2 - 4(2)(5) = 16 - 40 = -24 < 0$

Ellipse

$5y^2 + (4x - 4)y + 2x^2 + 3x - 20 = 0$

$$y = \frac{1}{10}\left[-(4x - 4) \pm \sqrt{(4x - 4)^2 - 20(2x^2 + 3x - 20)}\right]$$

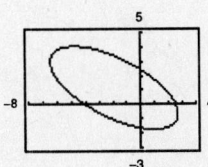

38. $36x^2 - 60xy + 25y^2 + 9y = 0$

$A = 36, B = -60, C = 25$

$B^2 - 4AC = (-60)^2 - 4(36)(25) = 0$

Parabola

$25y^2 - (60x - 9)y + 36x^2 = 0$

$y = \dfrac{1}{50}\left[60x - 9 \pm \sqrt{(60x - 9)^2 - 3600x^2}\right]$

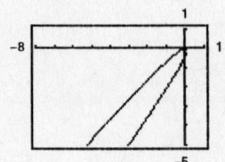

40. $x^2 + xy + 4y^2 + x + y - 4 = 0$

$A = 1, B = 1, C = 4$

$B^2 - 4AC = 1^2 - 4(1)(4) = -15$

Ellipse

$4y^2 + (x + 1)y + x^2 + x - 4 = 0$

$y = \dfrac{1}{8}\left[-(x + 1) \pm \sqrt{(x + 1)^2 - 16(x^2 + x - 4)}\right]$

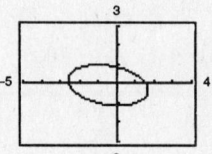

42. $\qquad x^2 + y^2 - 2x + 6y + 10 = 0$

$(x^2 - 2x + 1) + (y^2 + 6y + 9) = -10 + 1 + 9$

$\qquad (x - 1)^2 + (y + 3)^2 = 0$

Point at $(1, -3)$

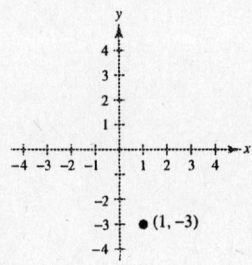

44. $\qquad x^2 - 10xy + y^2 = 0$

$\qquad y^2 - 10xy + 25x^2 = 25x^2 - x^2$

$\qquad\qquad (y - 5x)^2 = 24x^2$

$\qquad\qquad y - 5x = \pm\sqrt{24x^2}$

$\qquad\qquad\qquad y = 5x \pm 2\sqrt{6}x$

$\qquad\qquad\qquad y = \left(5 \pm 2\sqrt{6}\right)x$

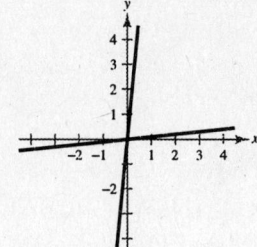

46. $-x^2 - y^2 - 8x + 20y - 7 = 0 \implies (x + 4)^2 + (y - 10)^2 = 109$

$\underline{x^2 + 9y^2 + 8x + 4y + 7 = 0} \implies (x + 4)^2 + 9\left(y + \dfrac{2}{9}\right)^2 = \dfrac{85}{9}$

$\qquad 8y^2 \qquad\quad + 24y \qquad = 0$

$\qquad\qquad 8y(y + 3) = 0$

$\qquad\qquad\qquad y = 0 \text{ or } y = -3$

When $y = 0$: $\quad x^2 + 9(0)^2 + 8x + 4(0) + 7 = 0$

$\qquad\qquad\qquad (x + 7)(x + 1) = 0$

$\qquad\qquad\qquad\qquad x = -7, -1$

When $y = -3$: $\quad x^2 + 9(-3)^2 + 8x + 4(-3) + 7 = 0$

$\qquad\qquad\qquad x^2 + 8x + 76 = 0$

$\qquad\qquad$ No real solution

Points of intersection: $(-7, 0), (-1, 0)$

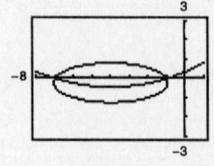

48. $x^2 - 4y^2 - 20x - 64y - 172 = 0 \implies (x - 10)^2 - 4(y + 8)^2 = 16$

$\dfrac{16x^2 + 4y^2 - 320x + 64y + 1600 = 0}{17x^2 \qquad -340x \qquad\quad 1428 = 0} \implies 16(x - 10)^2 + 4(y + 8)^2 = 256$

$$(17x - 238)(x - 6) = 0$$

$$x = 6 \text{ or } x = 14$$

When $x = 6$: $6^2 - 4y^2 - 20(6) - 64y - 172 = 0$

$$-4y^2 - 64y - 256 = 0$$

$$y^2 + 16y + 64 = 0$$

$$(y + 8)^2 = 0$$

$$y = -8$$

When $x = 14$: $14^2 - 4y^2 - 20(14) - 64y - 172 = 0$

$$-4y^2 - 64y - 256 = 0$$

$$y^2 + 16y + 64 = 0$$

$$(y + 8)^2 = 0$$

$$y = -8$$

Points of intersection: $(6, -8), (14, -8)$

50. $x^2 + 4y^2 - 2x - 8y + 1 = 0 \implies (x - 1)^2 + 4(y - 1)^2 = 4$

$\dfrac{-x^2 \qquad\quad + 2x - 4y - 1 = 0}{4y^2 \qquad -12y \qquad = 0} \implies y = -\frac{1}{4}(x - 1)^2$

$$4y(y - 3) = 0$$

$$y = 0 \text{ or } y = 3$$

When $y = 0$: $x^2 + 4(0)^2 - 2x - 8(0) + 1 = 0$

$$x^2 - 2x + 1 = 0$$

$$(x - 1)^2 = 0$$

$$x = 1$$

When $y = 3$: $-x^2 + 2x - 4(3) - 1 = 0$

$$x^2 - 2x + 13 = 0$$

No real solution

Point of intersection: $(1, 0)$

52. $16x^2 - y^2 \qquad + 16y - 128 = 0 \implies 16x^2 - (y - 8)^2 = 64$

$\dfrac{y^2 - 48x - 16y - 32 = 0}{16x^2 \qquad - 48x \qquad - 160 = 0} \implies (y - 8)^2 - 48x = 96$

$$16(x^2 - 3x - 10) = 0$$

$$(x - 5)(x + 2) = 0$$

$$x = 5 \text{ or } x = -2$$

When $x = 5$: $y^2 - 48(5) - 16y - 32 = 0$

$$y^2 - 16y - 272 = 0$$

$$y = 8 \pm 4\sqrt{21}$$

When $x = -2$: $y^2 - 48(-2) - 16y - 32 = 0$

$$y^2 - 16y + 64 = 0$$

$$(y - 8)^2 = 0$$

$$y = 8$$

Points of intersection: $\left(5, 8 + 4\sqrt{21}\right), \left(5, 8 - 4\sqrt{21}\right), (-2, 8)$

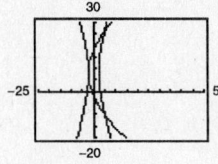

54. $4x^2 + 9y^2 - 36y = 0 \implies 4x^2 + 9(y - 2)^2 = 36$

$x^2 + 9y - 27 = 0 \implies y = -\dfrac{x^2}{9} + 3$

$4(27 - 9y) + 9y^2 - 36y = 0$

$\qquad 9y^2 - 72y + 108 = 0$

$\qquad 9(y - 6)(y - 2) = 0$

$\qquad\qquad\qquad y = 6 \text{ or } y = 2$

When $y = 6$: $\quad x^2 = 27 - 9(6) = -27$

$\qquad\qquad$ No real solution

When $y = 2$: $\quad x^2 = 27 - 9(2) = 9$

$\qquad\qquad\qquad x = \pm 3$

Points of intersection: $(3, 2), (-3, 2)$

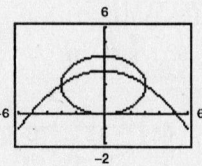

56. $x^2 + 2y^2 - 4x + 6y - 5 = 0 \implies 2(x - 2)^2 + 4\left(y + \dfrac{3}{2}\right)^2 = 27$

$x^2 - 4x - y + 4 = 0 \implies y = x^2 - 4x + 4$

$y - 4 + 2y^2 + 6y - 5 = 0$

$\qquad 2y^2 + 7y - 9 = 0$

$\qquad (2y + 9)(y - 1) = 0$

$\qquad\qquad\qquad y = -\dfrac{9}{2} \text{ or } y = 1$

When $y = 1$: $\quad x^2 - 4x - 1 + 4 = 0$

$\qquad\qquad (x - 3)(x - 1) = 0$

$\qquad\qquad\qquad x = 1 \text{ or } x = 3$

When $y = -\dfrac{9}{2}$: $\quad x^2 - 4x - \left(-\dfrac{9}{2}\right) + 4 = 0$

$\qquad\qquad\qquad x^2 - 4x + \dfrac{17}{2} = 0$

$\qquad\qquad$ No real solution

Points of intersection: $(1, 1), (3, 1)$

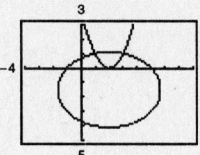

58. $5x^2 - 2xy + 5y^2 - 12 = 0$

$\qquad x + y - 1 = 0 \implies y = 1 - x$

$5x^2 - 2x(1 - x) + 5(1 - x)^2 - 12 = 0$

$5x^2 - 2x + 2x^2 + 5(1 - 2x + x^2) - 12 = 0$

$5x^2 - 2x + 2x^2 + 5 - 10x + 5x^2 - 12 = 0$

$\qquad\qquad 12x^2 - 12x - 7 = 0$

$\qquad\qquad\qquad x = \dfrac{3 \pm \sqrt{30}}{6}$

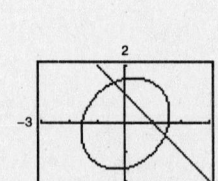

When $x = \dfrac{3 + \sqrt{30}}{6}$: $\; y = 1 - \dfrac{3 + \sqrt{30}}{6} = \dfrac{3 - \sqrt{30}}{6}$

When $x = \dfrac{3 - \sqrt{30}}{6}$: $\; y = 1 - \dfrac{3 - \sqrt{30}}{6} = \dfrac{3 + \sqrt{30}}{6}$

Points of intersection: $\left(\dfrac{1}{6}(3 + \sqrt{30}), \dfrac{1}{6}(3 - \sqrt{30})\right), \left(\dfrac{1}{6}(3 - \sqrt{30}), \dfrac{1}{6}(3 + \sqrt{30})\right)$

60. False. The coefficients of the new equation, after rotation of axes, are obtained by making the substitutions.

$$x = x' \cos \theta - y' \sin \theta,$$

$$y = x' \sin \theta + y' \cos \theta$$

62. In Exercise 14, the equation of the rotated ellipse is:

$$\frac{(x')^2}{1} + \frac{(y')^2}{4} = 1$$

$$a^2 = 4 \implies a = 2$$

$$b^2 = 1 \implies b = 1$$

Length of major axis is $2a = 2(2) = 4$.

Length of minor axis is $2b = 2(1) = 2$.

64. $f(x) = \dfrac{3}{x^2 + 1}$

No zeros

66. $f(x) = \dfrac{x^3 - 27}{x^2 - 1}$

Zeros: $x = 3$

68. $f(x) = \dfrac{x^2 - 1}{2x^2 + 3x - 2}$

Zeros: $x = \pm 1$

70. $f(x) = \dfrac{2x}{2 - x}$

Intercept: $(0, 0)$

Vertical asymptote: $x = 2$

Horizontal asymptote: $y = -2$

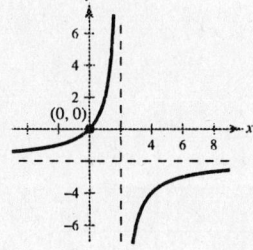

72. $h(t) = \dfrac{2t}{2 + t}$

Intercept: $(0, 0)$

Vertical asymptote: $t = -2$

Horizontal asymptote: $y = 2$

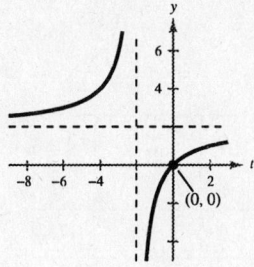

74. $f(x) = \dfrac{x^2}{2 - x} = -x - 2 + \dfrac{4}{2 - x}$

Intercept: $(0, 0)$

Vertical asymptote: $x = 2$

Slant asymptote: $y = -x - 2$

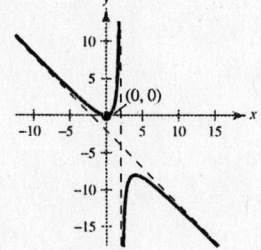

76. $f(t) = \dfrac{t}{t^2 - t - 6} = \dfrac{t}{(t - 3)(t + 2)}$

Intercept: $(0, 0)$

Vertical asymptotes: $t = -2, t = 3$

Horizontal asymptote: $y = 0$

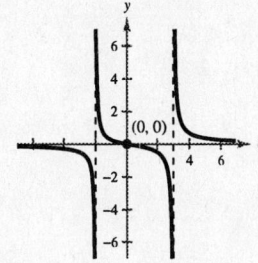

Section 10.6 Parametric Equations

Solutions to Even-Numbered Exercises

2. $x = 4\cos^2\theta, y = 2\sin\theta$

(a)

θ	$-\pi/2$	$-\pi/4$	0	$\pi/4$	$\pi/2$
x	0	2	4	2	0
y	-2	$-\sqrt{2}$	0	$\sqrt{2}$	2

(b)

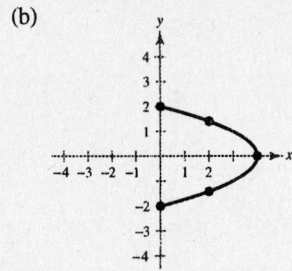

(c) $\dfrac{x}{4} = \cos^2\theta, \dfrac{y}{2} = \sin\theta$

$\cos^2\theta + \sin^2\theta = 1$

$\dfrac{x}{4} + \left(\dfrac{y}{2}\right)^2 = 1$

$\dfrac{x}{4} + \dfrac{y^2}{4} = 1$

$x = -y^2 + 4$

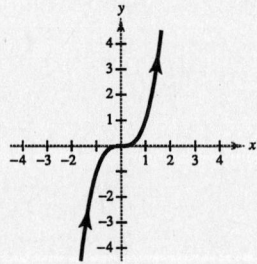

The rectangular version of the graph continues into the second and third quadrants.

4. $x = 3 - 2t \implies t = -\frac{1}{2}x + \frac{3}{2}$

$y = 2 + 3t$

t	-3	-2	-1	0	1	2	3
x	9	7	5	3	1	-1	-3
y	-7	-4	-1	2	5	8	11

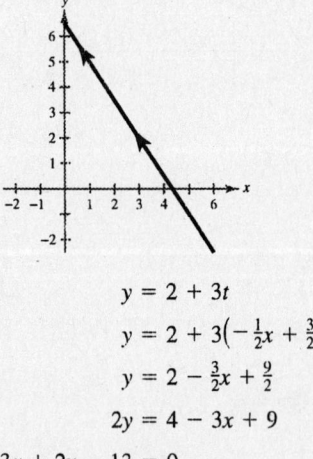

$y = 2 + 3t$

$y = 2 + 3\left(-\frac{1}{2}x + \frac{3}{2}\right)$

$y = 2 - \frac{3}{2}x + \frac{9}{2}$

$2y = 4 - 3x + 9$

$3x + 2y - 13 = 0$

6. $x = t$

$y = t^3$

t	-3	-2	-1	0	1	2	3
x	-3	-2	-1	0	1	2	3
y	-27	-8	-1	0	1	8	27

$y = t^3$

$y = x^3$

8. $x = \sqrt{t} \implies x^2 = t, t \geq 0$

$y = 1 - t$

t	0	1	2	3
x	0	1	$\sqrt{2}$	$\sqrt{3}$
y	1	0	-1	-2

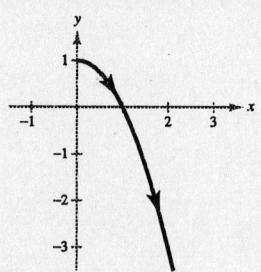

$y = 1 - t$

$y = 1 - x^2, x \geq 0$

10. $x = t - 1 \implies t = x + 1$

$y = \dfrac{t}{t-1}$

t	-3	-2	-1	0	2	3
x	-4	-3	-2	-1	1	2
y	$\frac{3}{4}$	$\frac{2}{3}$	$\frac{1}{2}$	0	2	$\frac{3}{2}$

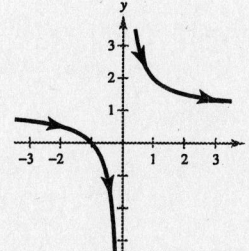

$y = \dfrac{t}{t-1}$

$y = \dfrac{x+1}{x+1-1} = \dfrac{x+1}{x}$

12. $x = |t - 1|$

$y = t + 2 \implies t = y - 2$

t	-3	-2	-1	0	1	2	3
x	4	3	2	1	0	1	2
y	-1	0	1	2	3	4	5

$x = |t - 1|$

$x = |y - 2 - 1| \implies x = |y - 3|$

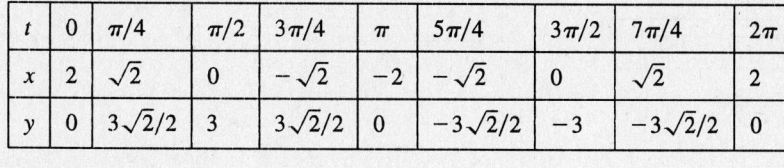
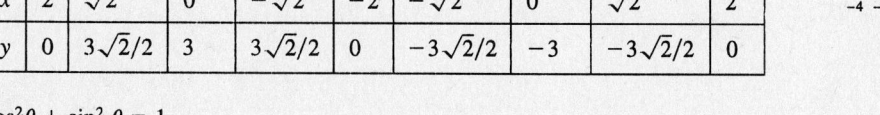

14. $x = 2 \cos \theta$

$y = 3 \sin \theta$

t	0	$\pi/4$	$\pi/2$	$3\pi/4$	π	$5\pi/4$	$3\pi/2$	$7\pi/4$	2π
x	2	$\sqrt{2}$	0	$-\sqrt{2}$	-2	$-\sqrt{2}$	0	$\sqrt{2}$	2
y	0	$3\sqrt{2}/2$	3	$3\sqrt{2}/2$	0	$-3\sqrt{2}/2$	-3	$-3\sqrt{2}/2$	0

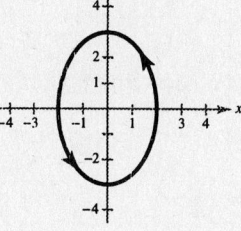

$\cos^2 \theta + \sin^2 \theta = 1$

$\left(\dfrac{x}{2}\right)^2 + \left(\dfrac{y}{3}\right)^2 = 1$

$\dfrac{x^2}{4} + \dfrac{y^2}{9} = 1$

16. $x = \cos\theta$

$y = 2\sin 2\theta$

t	0	$\pi/4$	$\pi/2$	$3\pi/4$	π	$5\pi/4$	$3\pi/2$	$7\pi/4$	2π
x	1	$\sqrt{2}/2$	0	$-\sqrt{2}/2$	-1	$-\sqrt{2}/2$	0	$\sqrt{2}/2$	1
y	0	2	0	-2	0	2	0	-2	0

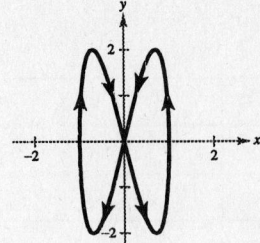

$y = 2\sin 2\theta$

$y = 2(2\sin\theta\cos\theta)$

$y^2 = 16\sin^2\theta\cos^2\theta$

$y^2 = 16(1 - x^2)x^2$

$y^2 = 16x^2(1 - x^2)$

18. $x = 4 + 2\cos\theta$

$y = 2 + 3\sin\theta$

t	0	$\pi/4$	$\pi/2$	$3\pi/4$	π	$5\pi/4$	$3\pi/2$	$7\pi/4$	2π
x	6	$4 + \sqrt{2}$	4	$4 - \sqrt{2}$	2	$4 - \sqrt{2}$	4	$4 + \sqrt{2}$	6
y	2	$2 + \left(3\sqrt{2}/2\right)$	5	$2 + \left(3\sqrt{2}/2\right)$	2	$2 - \left(3\sqrt{2}/2\right)$	-1	$2 - \left(3\sqrt{2}/2\right)$	2

$\cos^2\theta + \sin^2\theta = 1$

$\dfrac{(x - 4)^2}{4} + \dfrac{(y - 2)}{9} = 1$

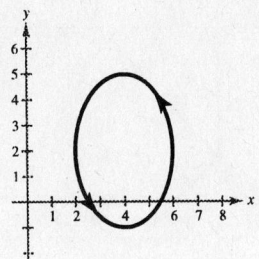

20. $x = e^{2t}$

$y = e^t \implies y^2 = e^{2t}$

t	-3	-2	-1	0	1	2
x	0.0025	0.0183	0.1353	1	7.3891	54.5982
y	0.0498	0.1353	0.3679	1	2.7183	7.3891

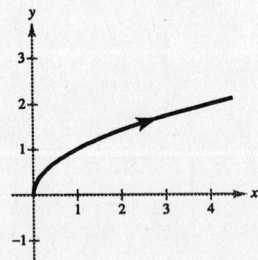

$x = e^{2t} = y^2$

$y^2 = x, y > 0$

22. $x = \ln 2t \implies t = \frac{1}{2}e^x$

$y = 2t^2$

t	1	2	3	4
x	0.6931	1.3863	1.7981	2.0794
y	2	8	18	32

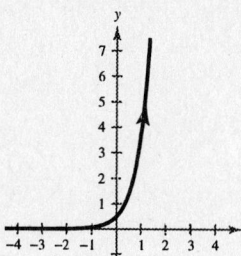

$y = 2t^2 = 2\left(\frac{1}{2}e^x\right)^2 = \frac{1}{2}e^{2x}$

24. By eliminating the parameter, each curve represents a portion of $y = x^2 - 1$.

(a) $x = t$

$y = t^2 - 1$

There are no restrictions on x.

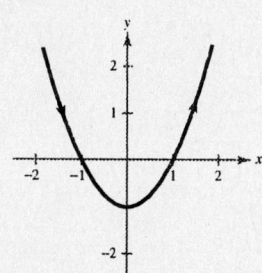

Domain: $(-\infty, \infty)$

Orientation: Left to right

(b) $x = t^2 \implies x \geq 0$

$y = t^4 - 1$

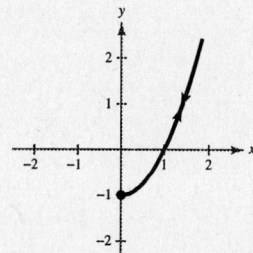

Domain: $[0, \infty)$

Orientation: Depends on t

(c) $x = \sin t \implies -1 \leq x \leq 1$

$y = \sin^2 t - 1$

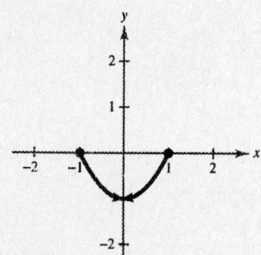

Domain: $[-1, 1]$

Orientation: Depends on t

(d) $x = e^t \implies x > 0$

$y = e^{2t} - 1$

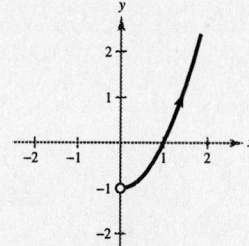

Domain: $(0, \infty)$

Orientation: Left to right

26. $x = h + r \cos \theta, y = k + r \sin \theta$

$\cos \theta = \dfrac{x - h}{r}, \sin \theta = \dfrac{y - k}{r}$

$\cos^2 \theta + \sin^2 \theta = \dfrac{(x - h)^2}{r^2} + \dfrac{(y - k)^2}{r^2} = 1$

$(x - h)^2 + (y - k)^2 = r^2$

28. $x = h + a \sec \theta, y = k + b \tan \theta$

$\dfrac{x - h}{a} = \sec \theta, \dfrac{y - k}{b} = \tan \theta$

$\dfrac{(x - h)^2}{a^2} - \dfrac{(y - k)^2}{b^2} = 1$

30. Line through $(2, 3)$ and $(6, -3)$

From Exercise 25 we have:

$x = x_1 + t(x_2 - x_1) = 2 + t(6 - 2) = 2 + 4t$

$y = y_1 + t(y_2 - y_1) = 3 + t(-3 - 3) = 3 - 6t$

32. Circle with center $(-3, 2)$; radius: 5

From Exercise 26 we have:

$x = h + r \cos \theta = -3 + 5 \cos \theta$

$y = k + r \sin \theta = 2 + 5 \sin \theta$

34. Ellipse

Vertices: $(4, 7), (4, -3) \implies (h, k) = (4, 2), a = 5$

Foci: $(4, 5), (4, -1) \implies c = 3$

$b^2 = a^2 - c^2 = 25 - 9 = 16 \implies b = 4$

From Exercise 27 we have:

$x = h + a \cos \theta = 4 + 5 \cos \theta$

$y = k + b \sin \theta = 2 + 4 \sin \theta$

36. Hyperbola

Vertices: $(0, \pm 2) \implies (h, k) = (0, 0), a = 2$

Foci: $(0, \pm 4) \implies c = 4$

$b^2 = c^2 - a^2 = 16 - 4 = 12 \implies b = 2\sqrt{3}$

From Exercise 28 we have:

$x = h + a \sec \theta, y = k + b \tan \theta$ for a hyperbola with horizontal transverse axis. For a vertical transverse axis we have:

$x = h + b \tan \theta = 2\sqrt{3} \tan \theta$

$y = k + a \sec \theta = 2 \sec \theta$

38. $x = 3y - 2$

(a) $t = x$

$x = t$

$y = \frac{1}{3}(t + 2)$

(b) $t = 2 - x$

$x = 2 - t$

$y = \frac{1}{3}(x + 2) = \frac{1}{3}(4 - t)$

40. $y = x^3$

(a) $t = x$

$x = t$

$y = t^3$

(b) $t = 2 - x$

$x = 2 - t$

$y = (2 - t)^3$

42. $y = 2 - x$

(a) $t = x$

$x = t$

$y = 2 - t$

(b) $t = 2 - x$

$x = 2 - t$

$y = 2 - (2 - t) = t$

44. $y = \dfrac{1}{2x}$

(a) $t = x$

$x = t$

$y = \dfrac{1}{2t}$

(b) $t = 2 - x$

$x = 2 - t$

$y = \dfrac{1}{2(2 - t)} = \dfrac{1}{4 - 2t}$

46. $x = \theta + \sin \theta$

$y = 1 - \cos \theta$

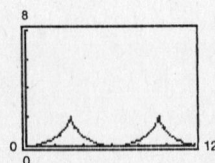

48. $x = 2\theta - 4 \sin \theta$

$y = 2 - 4 \cos \theta$

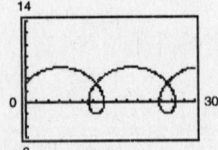

50. $x = 8\theta - 4\sin\theta$

$y = 8 - 4\cos\theta$

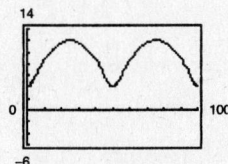

52. $x = \dfrac{3t}{1 + t^3}$

$y = \dfrac{3t^2}{1 + t^3}$

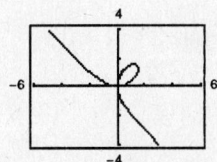

54. $x = 4\cos^3\theta \implies -4 \le x \le 4$

$y = 6\sin^3\theta \implies -6 \le y \le 6$

Matches graph (c).

Domain: $[-4, 4]$

Range: $[-6, 6]$

56. $x = \frac{1}{2}\cot\theta \implies -\infty < x < \infty$

$y = 4\sin\theta\cos\theta \implies -2 \le y \le 2$

Matches graph (a).

Domain: $(-\infty, \infty)$

Range: $[-2, 2]$

58. $x = (v_0\cos\theta)t$

$y = h + (v_0\sin\theta)t - 16t^2$

(a) $\theta = 15°, v_0 = 60$ ft/sec

Maximum height: 3.8 feet
Range: 56.3 feet

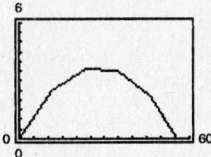

(b) $\theta = 15°, v_0 = 100$ ft/sec

Maximum height: 10.5 feet
Range: 156.3 feet

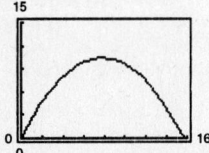

(c) $\theta = 30°, v_0 = 60$ ft/sec

Maximum height: 14.1 feet
Range: 97.4 feet

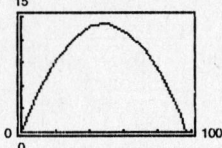

(d) $\theta = 30°, v_0 = 100$ ft/sec

Maximum height: 39.1 feet
Range: 270.6 feet

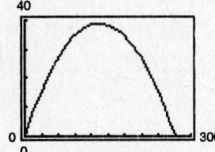

60. (a) $x = (v_0 \cos \theta)t$

$y = h + (v_0 \sin \theta)t - 16t^2$

$h = 5, v_0 = 240, \theta = 10°$

$x = (240 \cos 10°)t$

$y = 5 + (240 \sin 10°)t - 16t^2$

(c)

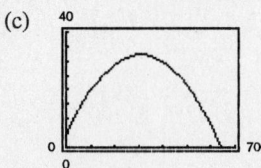

Maximum height: 32.1 feet

(b) $y = 5 + (240 \sin 10°)t - 16t^2 = 0$

$t = \dfrac{-240 \sin 10° \pm \sqrt{(240 \sin 10°)^2 - 4(-16)5}}{2(-16)}$

$t \approx -0.1149, 2.7196$

Distance traveled before arrow hits ground:

$(240 \cos 10°)(2.7196) \approx 643$ feet

(d) Time arrow is in the air: 2.72 seconds

(see part b)

62. $y = 7 + x - 0.02x^2$

(a) Exercise 61 result: $y = -\dfrac{16 \sec^2 \theta}{v_0^2}x^2 + (\tan \theta)x + h$

$h = 7$

$\tan \theta = 1 \implies \theta = 45°$

$\dfrac{16 \sec^2 45°}{v_0^2} = 0.02 \implies v_0 = 40$

$x = (v_0 \cos \theta)t = (40 \cos 45°)t$

$y = h + (v_0 \sin \theta)t - 16t^2 \approx 7 + (40 \cos 45°)t - 16t^2$

(b)

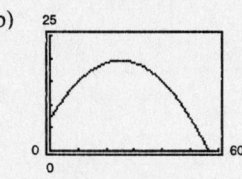

(c) Maximum height: 19.5 feet

Range: 56.2 feet

64. The coordinates of point (x, y) can be thought of as the sum of two vectors:

From origin to center of small circle:

$\langle 3 \cos \theta, 3 \sin \theta \rangle$

From center of small circle to point (x, y):

$\langle \cos \beta, \sin \beta \rangle$

Because the small circle rotates by 2θ when its center has rotated by θ, we have $\beta = \pi + 3\theta$.

$x = 3 \cos \theta + \cos(\pi + 3\theta) = 3 \cos \theta - \cos 3\theta$

$y = 3 \sin \theta + \sin(\pi + 3\theta) = 3 \sin \theta - \sin 3\theta$

66. False. Since $t^2 \geq 0$, the graph is that of $y = x$ for $x \geq 0$.

68. $\begin{cases} 3x + 5y = 9 \implies 6x + 10y = 18 \\ 4x - 2y = -14 \implies 20x - 10y = -70 \end{cases}$

$ 26x = -52$

$ x = -2$

$3(-2) + 5y = 9 \implies y = 3$

Solution: $(-2, 3)$

70. $\begin{cases} 5u + 7v + 9w = 4 & \text{Equation 1} \\ u - 2v - 3w = 7 & \text{Equation 2} \\ 8u - 2v + w = 20 & \text{Equation 3} \end{cases}$

$\begin{cases} u - 2v - 3w = 7 & \text{Interchange Eq.1 and Eq.2} \\ 5u + 7v + 9w = 4 \\ 8u - 2v + w = 20 \end{cases}$

$\begin{cases} u - 2v - 3w = 7 \\ \quad\quad 17v + 24w = -31 & (-5)\text{ Eq.1 + Eq.2} \\ \quad\quad 14v + 25w = -36 & (-8)\text{ Eq.1 + Eq.3} \end{cases}$

$\begin{cases} u - 2v - 3w = 7 \\ \quad\quad 17v + 24w = -31 \\ \quad\quad\quad\quad\quad 89w = -178 & (-14)\text{ Eq.1 + (17) Eq.3} \end{cases}$

$89w = -178 \Rightarrow w = -2$

$17v + 24(-2) = -31 \Rightarrow v = 1$

$u - 2(1) - 3(-2) = 7 \Rightarrow u = 3$

Solution: $(3, 1, -2)$

72. Parabola $y = ax^2 + bx + c$ passes through three points:

$(0, -6), (2, -2), (4, -6)$

$-6 = a(0)^2 + b(0) + c \Rightarrow c = -6$

$-2 = a(2)^2 + b(2) - 6 \Rightarrow 2a + b = 2$

$-6 = a(4)^2 + b(4) - 6 \Rightarrow 4a + b = 0$

Solving this system for a, b gives $a = -1, b = 4$.

Thus, the equation of the parabola is $y = -x^2 + 4x - 6$.

74. Parabola $y = ax^2 + bx + c$ passes through three points:

$(-8, -6), (-7, -8), (-6, -6)$

$-6 = a(-8)^2 + b(-8) + c \Rightarrow 64a - 8b + c = -6$

$-8 = a(-7)^2 + b(-7) + c \Rightarrow 49a - 7b + c = -8$

$-6 = a(-6)^2 + b(-6) + c \Rightarrow 36a - 6b + c = -6$

Solving this system for a, b, c gives
$a = 2, b = 28, c = 90$.

Thus, the equation of the parabola is
$y = 2x^2 + 28x + 90$.

Section 10.7   Polar Coordinates

Solutions to Even-Numbered Exercises

2. $\left(-1, -\dfrac{3\pi}{4}\right)$

$\left(1, \dfrac{\pi}{4}\right)$

$\left(-1, \dfrac{5\pi}{4}\right)$

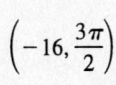

4. $\left(16, \dfrac{5\pi}{2}\right)$

$\left(16, \dfrac{\pi}{2}\right)$

$\left(-16, \dfrac{3\pi}{2}\right)$

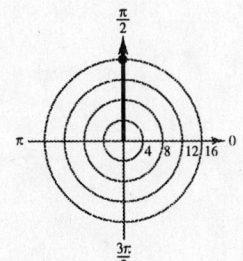

6. $(-3, -1.57)$

  $(3, 1.5716)$

  $(-3, 4.7132)$

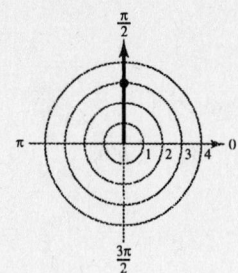

8. $(-5, -2.36)$

  $(5, 0.7816)$

  $(-5, 3.9232)$

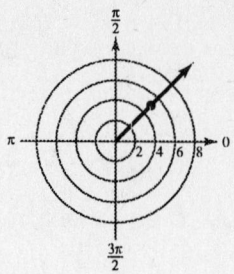

10. Polar coordinates: $\left(3, \dfrac{3\pi}{2}\right) = (r, \theta)$

  $x = r \cos \theta = 3 \cos \dfrac{3\pi}{2} = 0$

  $y = r \sin \theta = 3 \sin \dfrac{3\pi}{2} = -3$

  Rectangular coordinates: $(0, -3)$

12. Polar coordinates: $(0, -\pi) = (r, \theta)$

  $x = r \cos \theta = 0$

  $y = r \sin \theta = 0$

  Rectangular coordinates: $(0, 0)$

14. Polar coordinates: $\left(-2, \dfrac{7\pi}{6}\right) = (r, \theta)$

  $x = r \cos \theta = -2 \cos \dfrac{7\pi}{6} = \sqrt{3}$

  $y = r \sin \theta = -2 \sin \dfrac{7\pi}{6} = 1$

  Rectangular coordinates: $\left(\sqrt{3}, 1\right)$

16. Polar coordinates: $(8.25, 3.5) = (r, \theta)$

  $x = r \cos \theta = 8.25 \cos 3.5 \approx -7.7258$

  $y = r \sin \theta = 8.25 \sin 3.5 \approx -2.8940$

  Rectangular coordinates: $(-7.7258, -2.8940)$

18. Rectangular coordinates: $(-3, -3)$

  $r = \pm 3\sqrt{2}, \ \tan \theta = 1, \ \theta = \dfrac{\pi}{4} \ \text{or} \ \theta = \dfrac{5\pi}{4}$

  Polar coordinates: $\left(3\sqrt{2}, \dfrac{5\pi}{4}\right), \left(-3\sqrt{2}, \dfrac{\pi}{4}\right)$

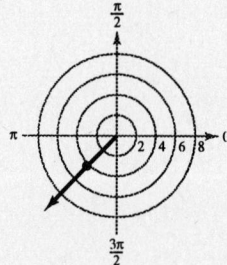

20. Rectangular coordinates: $(0, -5)$

  $r = \pm 5, \ \tan \theta \ \text{undefined}, \ \theta = \dfrac{\pi}{2} \ \text{or} \ \theta = \dfrac{3\pi}{2}$

  Polar coordinates: $\left(5, \dfrac{3\pi}{2}\right), \left(-5, \dfrac{\pi}{2}\right)$

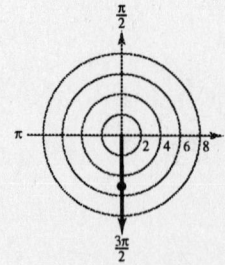

22. Rectangular coordinates: $(3, -1)$

$r = \sqrt{9 + 1} = \pm\sqrt{10}$, $\tan \theta = -\frac{1}{3}$, $\theta \approx -0.322 \approx 5.961$ or $\theta \approx 2.820$

Polar coordinates: $\left(-\sqrt{10}, 2.820\right), \left(\sqrt{10}, 5.961\right)$

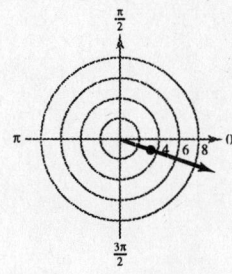

24. Rectangular coordinates: $\left(\sqrt{3}, -1\right)$

$r = \sqrt{3 + 1} = \pm 2$, $\tan \theta = -\frac{1}{\sqrt{3}}$, $\theta = \frac{11\pi}{6}$ or $\theta = \frac{5\pi}{6}$

Polar coordinates: $\left(2, \frac{11\pi}{6}\right), \left(-2, \frac{5\pi}{6}\right)$

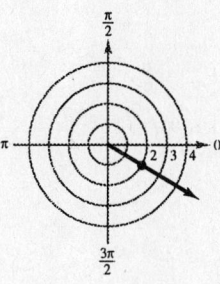

26. Rectangular coordinates: $(5, 12)$

$r = \sqrt{25 + 144} = \pm 13$, $\tan \theta = \frac{12}{5}$, $\theta \approx 1.176$ or $\theta \approx 4.318$

Polar coordinates: $(13, 1.176), (-13, 4.318)$

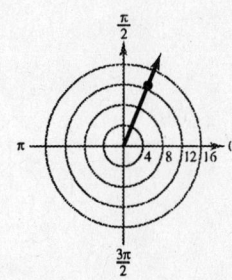

28. Rectangular coordinates: $(-5, 2)$

$R \blacktriangleright Pr(-5, 2) \approx 5.385$

$R \blacktriangleright P\theta(-5, 2) \approx 2.761$

$\approx (5.385, 2.761)$

30. Rectangular coordinates: $\left(3\sqrt{2}, 3\sqrt{2}\right)$

$R \blacktriangleright Pr\left(3\sqrt{2}, 3\sqrt{2}\right) = 6$

$R \blacktriangleright P\theta\left(3\sqrt{2}, 3\sqrt{2}\right) \approx 0.785$

$= \left(6, \frac{\pi}{4}\right)$

32. Rectangular coordinates: $\left(\frac{7}{4}, \frac{3}{2}\right)$

$R \blacktriangleright Pr\left(\frac{7}{4}, \frac{3}{2}\right) \approx 2.305$

$R \blacktriangleright P\theta\left(\frac{7}{4}, \frac{3}{2}\right) \approx 0.709$

$\approx (2.305, 0.709)$

34. $x^2 + y^2 = 16$

$r = 4$

36. $x = 10$

$r \cos \theta = 10$

$r = 10 \sec \theta$

38. $3x + 5y - 2 = 0$

$3r \cos \theta + 5r \sin \theta - 2 = 0$

$r(3 \cos \theta + 5 \sin \theta) = 2$

$$r = \frac{2}{3 \cos \theta + 5 \sin \theta}$$

40. $y = x$

$r \cos \theta = r \sin \theta$

$1 = \tan \theta$

$\theta = \dfrac{\pi}{4}$

42. $(x^2 + y^2)^2 = 9(x^2 - y^2)$

$(r^2)^2 = 9(r^2 \cos^2 \theta - r^2 \sin^2 \theta)$

$= 9r^2(\cos^2 \theta - \sin^2 \theta)$

$r^2 = 9 \cos 2\theta$

44. $x^2 + y^2 = 9a^2$

$r = 3a$

46. $x = 4a$

$r \cos \theta = 4a$

$r = 4a \sec \theta$

48. $x^2 + y^2 - 2ay = 0$

$r^2 - 2ar \sin \theta = 0$

$r = 2a \sin \theta$

50. $r = 3 \cos \theta$

$r^2 = 3r \cos \theta$

$x^2 + y^2 = 3x$

$x^2 + y^2 - 3x = 0$

52. $r = 4$

$r^2 = 16$

$x^2 + y^2 = 16$

54. $r^2 = \sin 2\theta = 2 \sin \theta \cos \theta$

$r^2 = 2\left(\dfrac{y}{r}\right)\left(\dfrac{x}{r}\right) = \dfrac{2xy}{r^2}$

$r^4 = 2xy$

$(x^2 + y^2)^2 = 2xy$

56. $r = \dfrac{1}{1 - \cos \theta}$

$r - r \cos \theta = 1$

$\sqrt{x^2 + y^2} - x = 1$

$x^2 + y^2 = 1 + 2x + x^2$

$y^2 = 2x + 1$

58. $r = \dfrac{6}{2 \cos \theta - 3 \sin \theta}$

$r = \dfrac{6}{2(x/r) - 3(y/r)}$

$r = \dfrac{6r}{2x - 3y}$

$1 = \dfrac{6}{2x - 3y}$

$2x - 3y = 6$

60. $r = 8$

$r^2 = 64$

$x^2 + y^2 = 64$

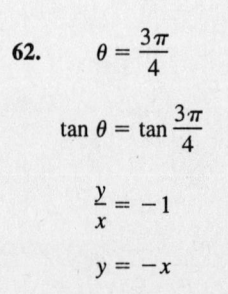

62. $\theta = \dfrac{3\pi}{4}$

$\tan \theta = \tan \dfrac{3\pi}{4}$

$\dfrac{y}{x} = -1$

$y = -x$

$x + y = 0$

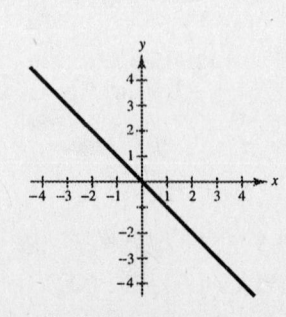

64. $r = 2 \csc \theta$

$r \sin \theta = 2$

$y = 2$

$y - 2 = 0$

66. False.

(r_1, θ) and (r_2, θ) represent the same point only if $r_1 = r_2$.

68. $r = \cos \theta + 3 \sin \theta$

$r = \dfrac{x}{r} + \dfrac{3y}{r}$

$r^2 = x + 3y$

$x^2 + y^2 = x + 3y$

$x^2 - x + y^2 - 3y = 0$

$\left(x - \dfrac{1}{2}\right)^2 + \left(y - \dfrac{3}{2}\right)^2 = \dfrac{5}{2}$

The graph is a circle.

70. (a) For horizontal moves, just the x-coordinate changes.
For vertical moves, just the y-coordinate changes.

(b) For horizontal moves, both r and θ change.
For vertical moves, both r and θ change.

(c) Unlike r and θ, x and y measure horizontal and vertical changes, respectively.

72. $\begin{cases} 3x + 5y = 10 \\ 4x - 2y = -5 \end{cases}$

By Cramer's Rule we have:

$$x = \frac{\begin{vmatrix} 10 & 5 \\ -5 & -2 \end{vmatrix}}{\begin{vmatrix} 3 & 5 \\ 4 & -2 \end{vmatrix}} = \frac{5}{-26} = -\frac{5}{26} \text{ and } y = \frac{\begin{vmatrix} 3 & 10 \\ 4 & -5 \end{vmatrix}}{\begin{vmatrix} 3 & 5 \\ 4 & -2 \end{vmatrix}} = \frac{-55}{-26} = \frac{55}{26}$$

Solution: $\left(-\dfrac{5}{25}, \dfrac{55}{26}\right)$

74. $\begin{cases} 5u + 7v + 9w = 15 \\ u - 2v - 3w = 7 \\ 8u - 2v + w = 0 \end{cases} \implies \begin{vmatrix} 5 & 7 & 9 \\ 1 & -2 & -3 \\ 8 & -2 & 1 \end{vmatrix} = -89$

$$u = \frac{\begin{vmatrix} 15 & 7 & 9 \\ 7 & -2 & -3 \\ 0 & -2 & 1 \end{vmatrix}}{-89} = \frac{-295}{-89} = \frac{295}{89}, \ v = \frac{\begin{vmatrix} 5 & 15 & 9 \\ 1 & 7 & -3 \\ 8 & 0 & 1 \end{vmatrix}}{-89} = \frac{-844}{-89} = \frac{844}{89}, \ w = \frac{\begin{vmatrix} 5 & 7 & 15 \\ 1 & -2 & 7 \\ 8 & -2 & 0 \end{vmatrix}}{-89} = \frac{672}{-89} = -\frac{672}{89}$$

Solution: $\left(\dfrac{295}{89}, \dfrac{844}{89}, -\dfrac{672}{89}\right)$

76. $\begin{cases} 2y + 5z + 6w = 32 \\ 2x + 4y - 5z - w = -7 \\ 3x - 6y + z + 5w = 6 \\ 4x - 2y - z = -12 \end{cases}$

$\begin{vmatrix} 0 & 2 & 5 & 6 \\ 2 & 4 & -5 & -1 \\ 3 & -6 & 1 & 5 \\ 4 & -2 & -1 & 0 \end{vmatrix} = 852$

$x = \dfrac{\begin{vmatrix} 32 & 2 & 5 & 6 \\ -7 & 4 & -5 & -1 \\ 6 & -6 & 1 & 5 \\ -12 & -2 & -1 & 0 \end{vmatrix}}{852} = \dfrac{-1704}{852} = -2$

$y = \dfrac{\begin{vmatrix} 0 & 32 & 5 & 6 \\ 2 & -7 & -5 & -1 \\ 3 & 6 & 1 & 5 \\ 4 & -12 & -1 & 0 \end{vmatrix}}{852} = \dfrac{1278}{852} = \dfrac{3}{2}$

$z = \dfrac{\begin{vmatrix} 0 & 2 & 32 & 6 \\ 2 & 4 & -7 & -1 \\ 3 & -6 & 6 & 5 \\ 4 & -2 & -12 & 0 \end{vmatrix}}{852} = \dfrac{852}{852} = 1$

$w = \dfrac{\begin{vmatrix} 0 & 2 & 5 & 32 \\ 2 & 4 & -5 & -7 \\ 3 & -6 & 1 & 6 \\ 4 & -2 & -1 & -12 \end{vmatrix}}{852} = \dfrac{3408}{852} = 4$

Solution: $\left(-2, \dfrac{3}{2}, 1, 4\right)$

78. Points: $(-2, 4), (0, 1), (4, -5)$

$\begin{vmatrix} -2 & 4 & 1 \\ 0 & 1 & 1 \\ 4 & -5 & 1 \end{vmatrix} = 0 \implies$ collinear

80. Points: $(-2.3, 5), (-0.5, 0), (1.5, -3)$

$\begin{vmatrix} -2.3 & 5 & 1 \\ -0.5 & 0 & 1 \\ 1.5 & -3 & 1 \end{vmatrix} = 4.6 \implies$ not collinear

Section 10.8   Graphs of Polar Equations

Solutions to Even-Numbered Exercises

2. $r = 5 - 5\sin\theta$
Cardioid

4. $r^2 = 16\cos 2\theta$
Lemniscate

6. $r = 3\cos\theta$
Circle

8. $r = 16 \cos 3\theta$

$\theta = \dfrac{\pi}{2}:$ $-r = 16 \cos(3(-\theta))$

$\quad\quad\quad -r = 16 \cos(-3\theta)$

$\quad\quad\quad -r = 16 \cos 3\theta$

Not an equivalent equation

Polar axis: $r = 16 \cos(3(-\theta))$

$\quad\quad\quad r = 16 \cos(-3\theta)$

$\quad\quad\quad r = 16 \cos 3\theta$

Equivalent equation

Pole: $-r = 16 \cos 3\theta$

Not an equivalent equation

Answer: Symmetric with respect to polar axis

10. $r = \dfrac{3}{2 + \cos \theta}$

$\theta = \dfrac{\pi}{2}:$ $-r = \dfrac{3}{2 + \cos(-\theta)}$

Not an equivalent equation

Polar axis: $r = \dfrac{3}{2 + \cos(-\theta)}$

Equivalent equation

Pole: $-r = \dfrac{3}{2 + \cos \theta}$

Not an equivalent equation

Answer: Symmetric with respect to polar axis

12. $r^2 = 36 \sin 2\theta$

$\theta = \dfrac{\pi}{2}:$ $(-r)^2 = 36 \sin(-2\theta)$

Not an equivalent equation

Polar axis: $r^2 = 36 \sin(-2\theta)$

Not an equivalent equation

Pole: $(-r)^2 = 36 \sin 2\theta$

Equivalent equation

Answer: Symmetric with respect to pole

14. $|r| = |6 + 12 \cos \theta| \le |6| + |12 \cos \theta|$

$\quad\quad = 6 + 12|\cos \theta| \le 18$

$\cos \theta = 1$

$\quad \theta = 0$

Maximum: $|r| = 18$ when $\theta = 0$

$\quad 0 = 6 + 12 \cos \theta$

$\cos \theta = -\dfrac{1}{2}$

$\quad\quad \theta = \dfrac{2\pi}{3}, \dfrac{4\pi}{3}$

Zero: $r = 0$ when $\theta = \dfrac{2\pi}{3}, \dfrac{4\pi}{3}$

16. $|r| = |3 \sin 2\theta| = 3|\sin 2\theta| \le 3$

$\quad\quad |\sin 2\theta| = 1$

$\quad\quad\quad \sin 2\theta = \pm 1$

$\quad\quad\quad\quad \theta = \dfrac{\pi}{4}, \dfrac{3\pi}{4}, \dfrac{5\pi}{4}, \dfrac{7\pi}{4}$

Maximum: $|r| = 3$ when $\theta = \dfrac{\pi}{4}, \dfrac{3\pi}{4}, \dfrac{5\pi}{4}, \dfrac{7\pi}{4}$

$\quad 0 = 3 \sin 2\theta$

$\sin 2\theta = 0$

$\quad \theta = 0, \dfrac{\pi}{2}, \pi, \dfrac{3\pi}{2}$

Zero: $r = 0$ when $\theta = 0, \dfrac{\pi}{2}, \pi, \dfrac{3\pi}{2}, 2\pi$

18. Circle: $r = 2$

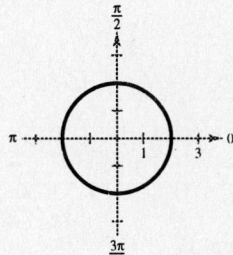

20. $r = -\dfrac{3\pi}{4}$

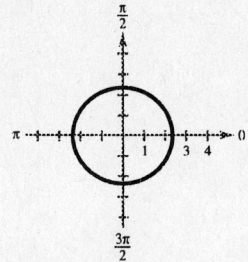

22. $r = 4\cos\theta$

Symmetric with respect to polar axis.

Circle with radius 2.

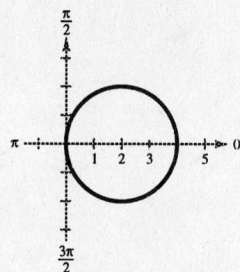

24. $r = 4(1 - \sin\theta)$

Symmetric with respect to $\pi/2$.

$\dfrac{a}{6} = \dfrac{4}{4} = 1 \implies$ Cardioid

$|r| = 8$ when $\theta = \dfrac{3\pi}{2}$.

$r = 0$ when $\theta = \dfrac{\pi}{2}$.

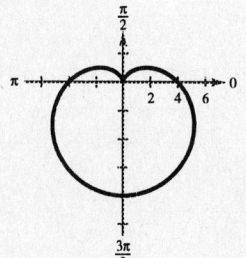

26. $r = 2(1 + \cos\theta)$

Symmetric with respect to polar axis.

$\dfrac{a}{6} = \dfrac{2}{2} = 1 \implies$ Cardioid

$|r| = 4$ when $\theta = 0$.

$r = 0$ when $\theta = \pi$.

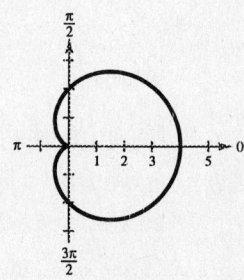

28. $r = 4 - 3\sin\theta$

Symmetric with respect to $\pi/2$.

$a = 4, b = 3$

$\dfrac{a}{b} = \dfrac{4}{3} \implies$ Dimpled limaçon

$|r| = 7$ when $\theta = \dfrac{3\pi}{2}$.

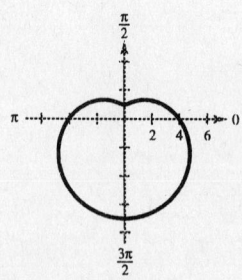

30. $r = 1 - 2\cos\theta$

Symmetric with respect to the polar axis.

$\dfrac{a}{b} = \dfrac{1}{2} \implies$ Limaçon with inner loop

$|r| = 3$ when $\theta = \pi$.

$r = 0$ when $\theta = \dfrac{\pi}{3}, \dfrac{5\pi}{3}$.

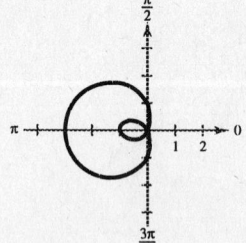

32. $r = 4 + 3\cos\theta$

Symmetric with respect to the polar axis.

$\dfrac{a}{b} = \dfrac{4}{3} > 1 \Rightarrow$ Dimpled limaçon

$|r| = 7$ when $\theta = 0$.

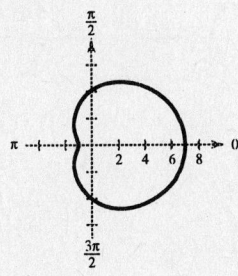

34. $r = 3\cos 2\theta$

Symmetric with respect to the polar axis.

Rose curve $(n = 2)$ with four petals

$|r| = 3$ when $\theta = 0, \dfrac{\pi}{2}, \pi, \dfrac{3\pi}{2}$.

$r = 0$ when $\theta = \dfrac{\pi}{4}, \dfrac{3\pi}{4}, \dfrac{5\pi}{4}, \dfrac{7\pi}{4}$.

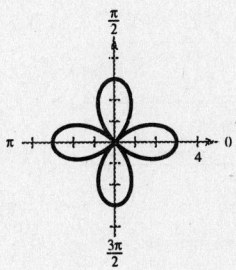

36. $r = 5\csc\theta$

$r\sin\theta = 5$

$\quad y = 5 \Rightarrow$ Line

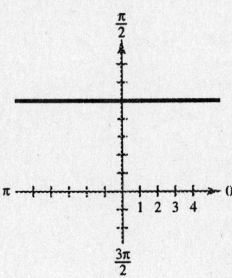

38. $r = \dfrac{6}{2\sin\theta - 3\cos\theta}$

$r(2\sin\theta - 3\cos\theta) = 6$

$\qquad 2y - 3x = 6$

$\qquad\quad y = \dfrac{3}{2}x + 3 \Rightarrow$ Line

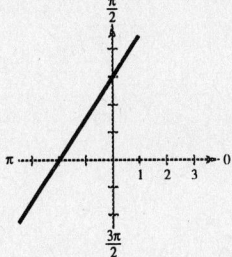

40. $r^2 = 4\sin\theta$

$r = 2\sqrt{\sin\theta}$

$r = -2\sqrt{\sin\theta}$

$0 \le \theta \le \pi$

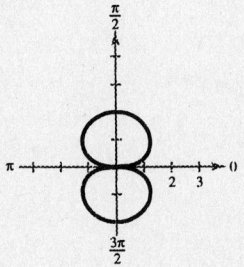

42. $r = \cos 2\theta$

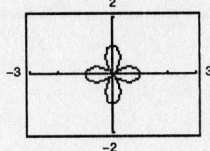

44. $r = 2\cos(3\theta - 2)$

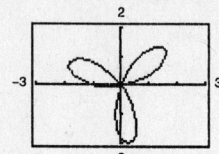

46. $r = 2\csc\theta + 5 = \dfrac{2}{\sin\theta} + 5$

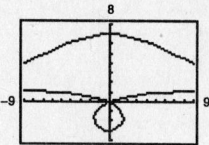

48. $r = 5 + 4\cos\theta$

$0 \le \theta < 2\pi$

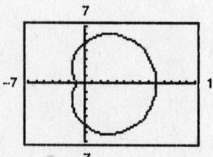

50. $r = 3\sin\left(\dfrac{5\theta}{2}\right)$

$0 \le \theta < 4\pi$

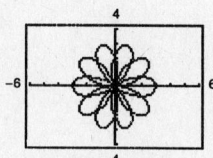

52. $r^2 = \dfrac{1}{\theta}$

$0 < \theta < \infty$

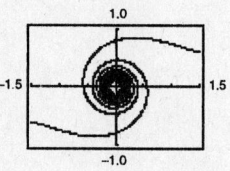

54.

$$r = 2 + \csc\theta = 2 + \frac{1}{\sin\theta}$$

$$r\sin\theta = 2\sin\theta + 1$$

$$r(r\sin\theta) = 2r\sin\theta + r$$

$$\left(\pm\sqrt{x^2 + y^2}\right)(y) = 2y + \left(\pm\sqrt{x^2 + y^2}\right)$$

$$\left(\pm\sqrt{x^2 + y^2}\right)(y - 1) = 2y$$

$$\left(\pm\sqrt{x^2 + y^2}\right) = \frac{2y}{y - 1}$$

$$x^2 + y^2 = \frac{4y^2}{(y - 1)^2}$$

$$x^2 = \frac{y^2(3 + 2y - y^2)}{(y - 1)^2}$$

$$x = \sqrt{\frac{y^2(3 + 2y - y^2)}{(y - 1)^2}} = \pm\left|\frac{y}{y - 1}\right|\sqrt{3 + 2y - y^2}$$

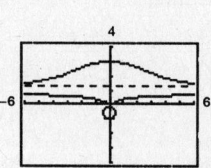

The graph has an asymptote at $y = 1$.

56. $\quad r = 2 \cos 2\theta \sec \theta = \dfrac{2 \cos 2\theta}{\cos \theta}$

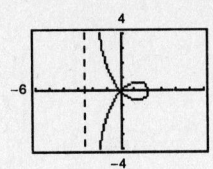

$$r = \frac{2(\cos^2 \theta - \sin^2 \theta)}{\cos \theta}$$

$$r \cos \theta = 2(\cos^2 \theta - \sin^2 \theta)$$

$$x = 2(\cos^2 \theta - \sin^2 \theta)$$

As $\theta \to \dfrac{\pi}{2}, x \to -2.$

58. False. For a graph to be symmetric about the pole, one portion of the graph coincides with the other portion when rotated π radians about the pole.

60. $r = 6[1 + \cos(\theta - \phi)]$

(a)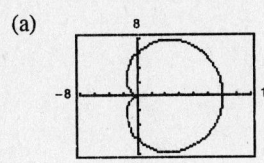

(b)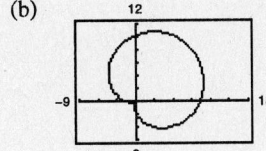

(c)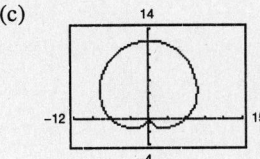

The angle ϕ has the effect of rotating the graph by the angle ϕ. For part (c),

$$r = 6\left[1 + \cos\left(\theta - \frac{\pi}{2}\right)\right]$$

$$= 6(1 + \sin \theta).$$

62. Use the result of Exercise 61.

(a) Rotation: $\phi = \dfrac{\pi}{2}$

Original graph: $r = f(\sin \theta)$

Rotated graph: $r = f\left(\sin\left(\theta - \dfrac{\pi}{2}\right)\right) = f(-\cos \theta)$

(b) Rotation: $\phi = \pi$

Original graph: $r = f(\sin \theta)$

Rotated graph: $r = f(\sin(\theta - \pi)) = f(-\sin \theta)$

(c) Rotation: $\phi = \dfrac{3\pi}{2}$

Original graph: $r = f(\sin \theta)$

Rotated graph: $r = f\left(\sin\left(\theta - \dfrac{3\pi}{2}\right)\right) = f(\cos \theta)$

64. $r = 2 \sin 2\theta$

(a) $r = 2 \sin\left[2\left(\theta - \dfrac{\pi}{6}\right)\right]$

$\quad = 2\left[2 \sin\left(\theta - \dfrac{\pi}{6}\right) \cos\left(\theta - \dfrac{\pi}{6}\right)\right]$

$\quad = 4 \sin\left(\theta - \dfrac{\pi}{6}\right) \cos\left(\theta - \dfrac{\pi}{6}\right)$

(b) $r = 2 \sin\left[2\left(\theta - \dfrac{\pi}{2}\right)\right]$

$\quad = 2 \sin(2\theta - \pi)$

$\quad = -2 \sin 2\theta$

$\quad = -2(2 \sin \theta \cos \theta)$

$\quad = -4 \sin \theta \cos \theta$

(c) $r = 2 \sin\left[2\left(\theta - \dfrac{2\pi}{3}\right)\right]$

$\quad = 2\left[2 \sin\left(\theta - \dfrac{2\pi}{3}\right) \cos\left(\theta - \dfrac{2\pi}{3}\right)\right]$

$\quad = 4 \sin\left(\theta - \dfrac{2\pi}{3}\right) \cos\left(\theta - \dfrac{2\pi}{3}\right)$

(d) $r = 2 \sin[2(\theta - \pi)]$

$\quad = 2 \sin(2\theta - 2\pi)$

$\quad = 2 \sin 2\theta$

$\quad = 2[2 \sin \theta \cos \theta]$

$\quad = 4 \sin \theta \cos \theta$

66. (a) $r = 3 \sec \theta$

$$r = \frac{3}{\cos \theta}$$

$$r \cos \theta = 3 \Longrightarrow x = 3$$

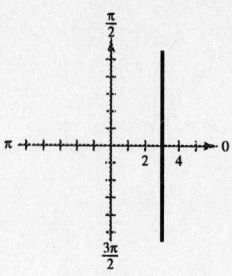

(b) $r = 3 \sec\left(\theta - \dfrac{\pi}{4}\right)$

$$r = \frac{3}{\cos(\theta - (\pi/4))}$$

$$r = \frac{3}{\cos \theta \cos(\pi/4) + \sin \theta \sin(\pi/4)}$$

$$\frac{\sqrt{2}}{2} r \cos \theta + \frac{\sqrt{2}}{2} r \sin \theta = 3$$

$$\frac{\sqrt{2}}{2} x + \frac{\sqrt{2}}{2} y = 3$$

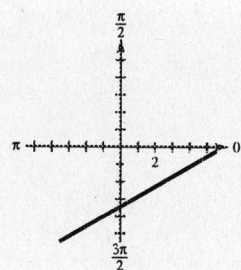

(c) $r = 3 \sec\left(\theta + \dfrac{\pi}{3}\right)$

$$r = \frac{3}{\cos(\theta + (\pi/3))}$$

$$r = \frac{3}{\cos \theta \cos(\pi/3) - \sin \theta \sin(\pi/3)}$$

$$\frac{1}{2} r \cos \theta - \frac{\sqrt{3}}{2} r \sin \theta = 3$$

$$\frac{1}{2} x - \frac{\sqrt{3}}{2} y = 3$$

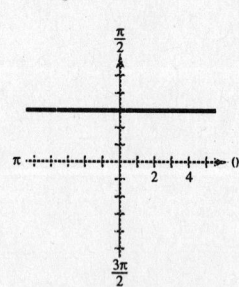

(d) $r = 3 \sec\left(\theta - \dfrac{\pi}{2}\right)$

$$r = \frac{3}{\cos(\theta - (\pi/2))}$$

$$r = \frac{3}{\cos \theta \cos(\pi/2) + \sin \theta \sin(\pi/2)}$$

$$r \sin \theta = 3 \Longrightarrow y = 3$$

68. $r = 3 \sin k\theta$

(a) $r = 3 \sin 1.5\theta$

   $0 \le \theta < 4\pi$

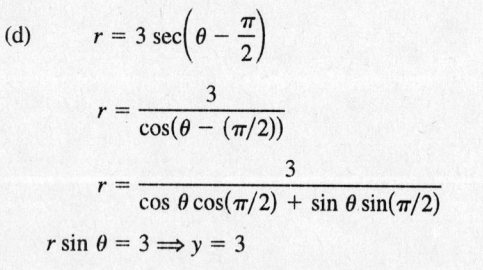

(b) $r = 3 \sin 2.5\theta$

   $0 \le \theta < 4\pi$

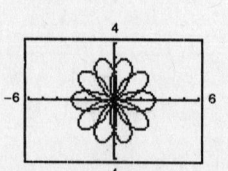

(c) Yes. $r = 3 \sin(k\theta)$.

Find the minimum value of $\theta (\theta > 0)$ that is a multiple of 2π that makes $k\theta$ a multiple of 2π.

70. $6e^x = 47$

$$x = \ln \frac{47}{6} \approx 2.058$$

72. $5^{2x} = 60$

$$2x = \log_5 60$$

$$x = \frac{1}{2}(\log_5 60) \approx 1.272$$

74. $4 \ln 4x = 18$

$$x = \frac{1}{4}e^{9/2} \approx 22.504$$

76. $y = 6 + \dfrac{4}{x^2 + 4}$

No zeros

78. $y = \dfrac{x^3 - 27}{x^2 + 4}$

Zero: $x = 3$

Section 10.9   Polar Equations of Conics

Solutions to Even-Numbered Exercises

2. $r = \dfrac{4e}{1 - e \cos \theta}$

   (a) $e = 1, r = \dfrac{4}{1 - \cos \theta}$, parabola

   (b) $e = 0.5, r = \dfrac{2}{1 - 0.5 \cos \theta}$, ellipse

   (c) $e = 1.5, r = \dfrac{6}{1 - 1.5 \cos \theta}$, hyperbola

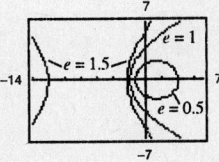

4. $r = \dfrac{4e}{1 + e \sin \theta}$

   (a) $e = 1, r = \dfrac{4}{1 + \sin \theta}$, parabola

   (b) $e = 0.5, r = \dfrac{2}{1 + 0.5 \sin \theta}$, ellipse

   (c) $e = 1.5, r = \dfrac{6}{1 + 1.5 \sin \theta}$, hyperbola

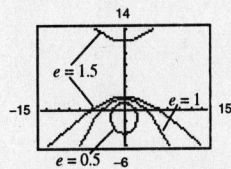

6. $r = \dfrac{3}{2 - \cos \theta}$

$e = \dfrac{1}{2} \implies$ Ellipse

Vertical directrix to the left of the pole
Matches graph (c).

8. $r = \dfrac{2}{1 - \sin \theta}$

$e = 1 \implies$ Parabola

Horizontal directrix below pole
Matches graph (e).

10. $r = \dfrac{4}{1 - 3 \sin \theta}$

$e = 3 \implies$ Hyperbola

Horizontal directrix below pole
Matches graph (b).

12. $r = \dfrac{3}{1 + \sin \theta}$

$e = 1 \implies$ Parabola

Vertex: $\left(\dfrac{3}{2}, \dfrac{\pi}{2} \right)$

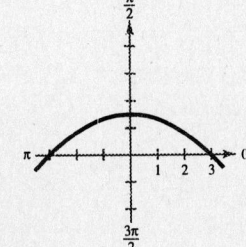

14. $r = \dfrac{6}{1 + \cos\theta}$

$e = 1 \implies$ Parabola

Vertex: $(3, 0)$

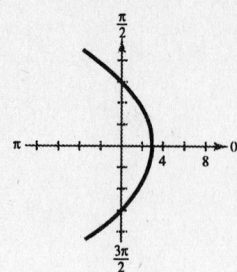

16. $r = \dfrac{3}{3 + \sin\theta} = \dfrac{1}{1 + (1/3)\sin\theta}$

$e = \dfrac{1}{3} < 1 \implies$ Ellipse

Vertices: $\left(\dfrac{3}{4}, \dfrac{\pi}{2}\right), \left(\dfrac{3}{2}, \dfrac{3\pi}{2}\right)$

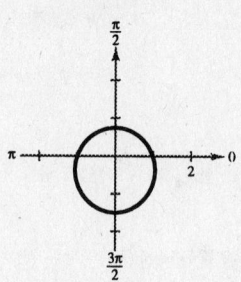

18. $r = \dfrac{9}{3 - 2\cos\theta} = \dfrac{3}{1 - (2/3)\cos\theta}$

$e = \dfrac{2}{3} < 1 \implies$ Ellipse

Vertices: $(9, 0), \left(\dfrac{9}{5}, \pi\right)$

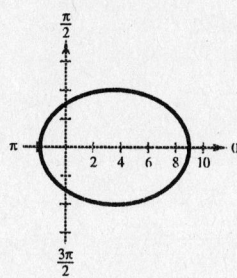

20. $r = \dfrac{5}{-1 + 2\cos\theta} = \dfrac{-5}{1 - 2\cos\theta}$

$e = 2 > 1 \implies$ Hyperbola

Vertices: $(5, 0), \left(-\dfrac{5}{3}, \pi\right)$

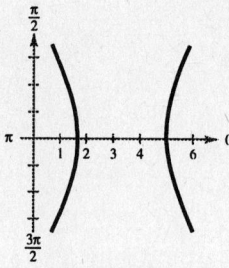

22. $r = \dfrac{3}{2 + 6\sin\theta} = \dfrac{3/2}{1 + 3\sin\theta}$

$e = 3 > 1 \implies$ Hyperbola

Vertices: $\left(\dfrac{3}{8}, \dfrac{\pi}{2}\right), \left(-\dfrac{3}{4}, \dfrac{3\pi}{2}\right)$

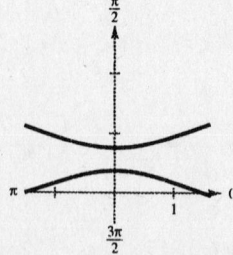

24. $r = \dfrac{2}{2 + 3\sin\theta} = \dfrac{1}{1 + (3/2)\sin\theta}$

$e = \dfrac{3}{2} > 1 \implies$ Hyperbola

Vertices: $\left(\dfrac{2}{5}, \dfrac{\pi}{2}\right), \left(-2, \dfrac{3\pi}{2}\right)$

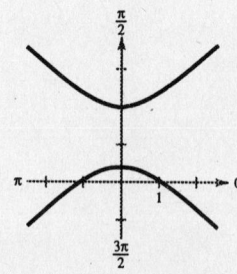

26. $r = \dfrac{-5}{2 + 4 \sin \theta} = \dfrac{-(5/2)}{1 + 2 \sin \theta}$

$e = 2 \implies$ Hyperbola

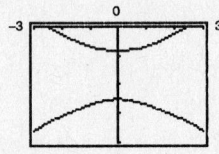

28. $r = \dfrac{4}{1 - 2 \cos \theta}$

$e = 2 \implies$ Hyperbola.

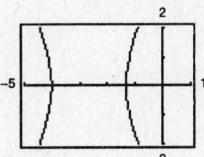

30. $r = \dfrac{3}{3 + \sin\left(\theta - \dfrac{\pi}{3}\right)}$

Rotate the graph in Exercise 16 through the angle $\pi/3$.

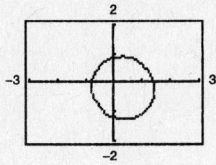

32. $r = \dfrac{5}{-1 + 2 \cos\left(\theta + \dfrac{2\pi}{3}\right)}$

Rotate the graph in Exercise 20 through the angle $-2\pi/3$.

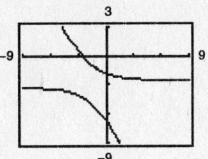

34. Parabola: $e = 1$

Directrix: $y = -2$

$p = 2$

Horizontal directrix below the pole

$r = \dfrac{1(2)}{1 - 1 \sin \theta} = \dfrac{2}{1 - \sin \theta}$

36. Ellipse: $e = \dfrac{3}{4}$

Directrix: $y = -3$

$p = 3$

Horizontal directrix below the pole

$r = \dfrac{(3/4)(3)}{1 - (3/4) \sin \theta} = \dfrac{9}{4 - 3 \sin \theta}$

38. Hyperbola: $e = \dfrac{3}{2}$

Directrix: $x = -1$

$p = 1$

Vertical directrix to the left of the pole

$r = \dfrac{(3/2)(1)}{1 - (3/2)\cos \theta} = \dfrac{3}{2 - 3 \cos \theta}$

40. Parabola

Vertex: $(6, 0) \implies e = 1, p = 12$

Vertical directrix to the right of the pole

$r = \dfrac{1(12)}{1 + 1 \cos \theta} = \dfrac{12}{1 + \cos \theta}$

42. Parabola

Vertex: $\left(10, \dfrac{\pi}{2}\right) \implies e = 1, p = 20$

Horizontal directrix above the pole

$$r = \frac{1(20)}{1 + 1 \sin \theta} = \frac{20}{1 + \sin \theta}$$

44. Ellipse

Vertices: $\left(2, \dfrac{\pi}{2}\right), \left(4, \dfrac{3\pi}{2}\right)$

Center: $\left(1, \dfrac{3\pi}{2}\right); c = 1, a = 3, e = \dfrac{1}{3}$

Horizontal directrix above the axis

$$r = \frac{1/3p}{1 + (1/3) \sin \theta} = \frac{p}{3 + \sin \theta}$$

$$2 = \frac{p}{3 + \sin(\pi/2)}$$

$$p = 8$$

$$r = \frac{8}{3 + \sin \theta}$$

46. Hyperbola

Vertices: $(2, 0), (8, 0)$

Center: $(5, 0); c = 5, a = 3, e = \dfrac{5}{3}$

Vertical directrix to the right of the pole

$$r = \frac{(5/3)p}{1 + (5/3)\cos \theta} = \frac{5p}{3 + 5 \cos \theta}$$

$$2 = \frac{5p}{3 + 5 \cos 0}$$

$$p = \frac{16}{5}$$

$$r = \frac{5(16/5)}{3 + 5 \cos \theta} = \frac{16}{3 + 5 \cos \theta}$$

48. Hyperbola

Vertices: $\left(4, \dfrac{\pi}{2}\right), \left(-1, \dfrac{3\pi}{2}\right)$

Center: $\left(\dfrac{5}{2}, \dfrac{\pi}{2}\right); c = \dfrac{5}{2}, a = \dfrac{3}{2}, e = \dfrac{5}{3}$

Horizontal directrix above the pole

$$r = \frac{5/3p}{1 + (5/3) \sin \theta} = \frac{5p}{3 + 5 \sin \theta}$$

$$1 = \frac{5p}{3 + 5 \sin(-3\pi/2)}$$

$$p = \frac{8}{5}$$

$$r = \frac{5(8/5)}{3 + 5 \sin \theta} = \frac{8}{3 + 5 \sin \theta}$$

50. Minimum distance occurs when $\theta = \pi$.

$$r = \frac{(1 - e^2)a}{1 - e \cos \pi} = \frac{(1 - e)(1 + e)a}{1 + e} = a(1 - e)$$

Maximum distance occurs when $\theta = 0$.

$$r = \frac{(1 - e^2)a}{1 - e \cos 0} = \frac{(1 - e)(1 + e)a}{1 - e} = a(1 + e)$$

52. $r = \dfrac{[1 - (0.0543)^2](1.429 \times 10^9)}{1 - 0.0543 \cos \theta} \approx \dfrac{1.4248 \times 10^9}{1 - 0.0543 \cos \theta}$

Perihelion distance: $r = 1.429 \times 10^9(1 - 0.0543) \approx 1.3514 \times 10^9$ kilometers

Aphelion distance: $r = 1.429 \times 10^9(1 + 0.0543) \approx 1.5066 \times 10^9$ kilometers

54. $r = \dfrac{[1 - (0.2056)^2](35.98 \times 10^6)}{1 - 0.2056 \cos \theta} \approx \dfrac{3.4459 \times 10^7}{1 - 0.2056 \cos \theta}$

Perihelion distance: $r = 35.98 \times 10^6(1 - 0.2056) \approx 2.8583 \times 10^7$ miles

Aphelion distance: $r = 35.98 \times 10^6(1 + 0.2056) \approx 4.3377 \times 10^7$ miles

56. $r = \dfrac{[1 - (0.0484)^2](778.40 \times 10^6)}{1 - 0.0484 \cos \theta} \approx \dfrac{7.7658 \times 10^8}{1 - 0.0484 \cos \theta}$

Perihelion distance: $r = 778.40 \times 10^6(1 - 0.0484) \approx 7.4073 \times 10^8$ kilometers

Aphelion distance: $r = 778.40 \times 10^6(1 + 0.0484) \approx 8.1607 \times 10^8$ kilometers

58. From Exercise 57, $r = \dfrac{8200}{1 + \sin \theta}$

$\theta = 60°$: $r = \dfrac{8200}{1 + \sin 60°} \approx 4394.4$

Distance between surface of Earth and satellite:

$\quad 4394.4 - 4000 = 394.4$ miles

60. True. The graphs are identical, although the graphs are not traced out in the same order as θ goes from 0 to 2π.

62.

$$\frac{x^2}{a^2} - \frac{y^2}{b^2} = 1$$

$$\frac{r^2 \cos^2 \theta}{a^2} - \frac{r^2 \sin^2 \theta}{b^2} = 1$$

$$\frac{r^2 \cos^2 \theta}{a^2} - \frac{r^2(1 - \cos^2 \theta)}{b^2} = 1$$

$$r^2 b^2 \cos^2 \theta - r^2 a^2 + r^2 a^2 \cos^2 \theta = a^2 b^2$$

$$r^2(b^2 + a^2) \cos^2 \theta - r^2 a^2 = a^2 b^2$$

$$a^2 + b^2 = c^2$$

$$r^2 c^2 \cos^2 \theta - r^2 a^2 = a^2 b^2$$

$$r^2 \left(\frac{c}{a}\right)^2 \cos^2 \theta - r^2 = b^2, e = \frac{c}{a}$$

$$r^2 e^2 \cos^2 \theta - r^2 = b^2$$

$$r^2(e^2 \cos^2 \theta - 1) = b^2$$

$$r^2 = \frac{b^2}{e^2 \cos^2 \theta - 1}$$

$$= \frac{-b^2}{1 - e^2 \cos^2 \theta}$$

64. $\dfrac{x^2}{25} + \dfrac{y^2}{16} = 1$

$a = 5, b = 4, c = 3, e = \dfrac{3}{5}$

$r^2 = \dfrac{400}{25 - 9 \cos^2 \theta}$

66. $\dfrac{x^2}{36} - \dfrac{y^2}{4} = 1$

$a = 6, b = 2, c = 2\sqrt{10}, e = \dfrac{\sqrt{10}}{3}$

$r^2 = \dfrac{-4}{1 - (10/9) \cos^2 \theta} = \dfrac{-36}{9 - 10 \cos^2 \theta}$

$\quad = \dfrac{36}{10 \cos^2 \theta - 9}$

68. Ellipse

One focus: $(4, 0)$

Vertices: $(5, 0), (5, \pi)$

$a = 5, c = 4, b = 3, e = \dfrac{4}{5}$

$r^2 = \dfrac{9}{1 - (16/25) \cos^2 \theta} = \dfrac{225}{25 - 16 \cos^2 \theta}$

70. $6 \cos x - 2 = 1$

$$\cos x = \frac{1}{2}$$

$$x = \frac{\pi}{3} + 2\pi m, \frac{5\pi}{3} + 2\pi m$$

72. $9 \csc^2 x - 10 = 2$

$$\csc^2 x = \frac{4}{3}$$

$$\sin x = \pm \frac{\sqrt{3}}{2}$$

$$x = \frac{\pi}{3} + \pi n, \frac{2\pi}{3} + \pi n$$

74. $\sqrt{2} \sec \theta = 2 \csc \frac{\pi}{4}$

$$\cos \theta = \frac{1}{2}$$

$$\theta = \frac{\pi}{3} + 2\pi m, \frac{5\pi}{3} + 2\pi m$$

76. $\sin u = -\frac{3}{5}, \cos u = \frac{4}{5}$

$$\cos v = \frac{1}{\sqrt{2}} = \frac{\sqrt{2}}{2}, \sin v = -\frac{\sqrt{2}}{2}$$

$$\sin(u + v) = \sin u \cos v + \cos u \sin v$$

$$= \left(-\frac{3}{5}\right)\left(\frac{\sqrt{2}}{2}\right) + \left(\frac{4}{5}\right)\left(-\frac{\sqrt{2}}{2}\right)$$

$$= \frac{-7\sqrt{2}}{10}$$

78. $\sin u = -\frac{3}{5}, \cos u = \frac{4}{5}$

$$\cos v = \frac{1}{\sqrt{2}} = \frac{\sqrt{2}}{2}, \sin v = -\frac{\sqrt{2}}{2}$$

$$\sin(u - v) = \sin u \cos v - \cos u \sin v$$

$$= \left(-\frac{3}{5}\right)\left(\frac{\sqrt{2}}{2}\right) - \left(\frac{4}{5}\right)\left(-\frac{\sqrt{2}}{2}\right)$$

$$= \frac{\sqrt{2}}{10}$$

80. $\tan u = -\sqrt{3}, \frac{3\pi}{2} < u < 2\pi$

$$\sin u = -\frac{\sqrt{3}}{2}, \cos u = \frac{1}{2}$$

$$\sin 2u = 2 \sin u \cos u = 2\left(-\frac{\sqrt{3}}{2}\right)\left(\frac{1}{2}\right) = -\frac{\sqrt{3}}{2}$$

$$\cos 2u = \cos^2 u - \sin^2 u = \left(\frac{1}{2}\right)^2 - \left(-\frac{\sqrt{3}}{2}\right)^2 = -\frac{1}{2}$$

$$\tan 2u = \frac{2 \tan u}{1 - \tan^2 u} = \frac{2\left(-\sqrt{3}\right)}{1 - \left(-\sqrt{3}\right)^2} = \sqrt{3}$$

Review Exercises for Chapter 10

Solutions to Even-Numbered Exercises

2. $m = \dfrac{4 - 7}{3 - (-2)} = -\dfrac{3}{5} = \tan \theta$

$\theta \approx 149°$

4. $6x - 7y - 5 = 0$

$m = \frac{6}{7} = \tan \theta$

$\theta \approx 40.6°$

6. $-5x + 3y = 3$

$-2x + 3y = 1$

$m_1 = \dfrac{5}{3}$

$m_2 = \dfrac{2}{3}$

$\tan \theta = \left| \dfrac{(5/3) - (2/3)}{1 + (5/3)(2/3)} \right| = \dfrac{9}{19}$

$\theta \approx 25.35°$

8. $0.02x + 0.07y = 0.18$

$0.09x - 0.04y = 0.17$

$m_1 = -\dfrac{2}{7}$

$m_2 = \dfrac{9}{4}$

$\tan \theta = \left| \dfrac{(9/4) - (-2/7)}{1 + (-2/7)(9/4)} \right| = \dfrac{71}{10}$

$\theta \approx 81.98°$

10. $(0, 4) \Longrightarrow x_1 = 0, y_1 = 4$

$x + 2y - 2 = 0 \Longrightarrow A = 1, B = 2, C = -2$

$d = \dfrac{|1(0) + (2)(4) + (-2)|}{\sqrt{1^2 + 2^2}} = \dfrac{6}{\sqrt{5}} = \dfrac{6\sqrt{5}}{5}$

12. A parabola is formed.

14. Vertex: $(2, 0) = (h, k)$

Focus: $(0, 0) \Longrightarrow p = -2$

$(y - k)^2 = 4p(x - h)$

$y^2 = -8(x - 2)$

16. Vertex: $(2, 2) = (h, k)$

Directrix: $y = 0 \Longrightarrow p = 2$

$(x - h)^2 = 4p(y - k)$

$(x - 2)^2 = 8(y - 2)$

18. $x^2 = -2y$

$p = -\dfrac{1}{2}$

Focus: $\left(0, -\dfrac{1}{2} \right)$

Tangent line through point $(-4, -8)$:

Slope: m

y-intercept: $(0, b)$

$d_1 = b + \dfrac{1}{2}$

$d_2 = \sqrt{(-4 - 0)^2 + \left(-8 + \dfrac{1}{2} \right)^2} = \dfrac{17}{2}$

$d_1 = d_2 \Longrightarrow b = 8$

$m = \dfrac{-8 - 8}{-4 - 0} = 4$

$y = 4x + 8$

x-intercept of tangent line: $(-2, 0)$

20. $y^2 = 4px$

$p = 1.5$

$y^2 = 6x$

22. Vertices: $(2, 0), (2, 4) \Longrightarrow a = 2, (h, k) = (2, 2)$

Foci: $(2, 1), (2, 3) \Longrightarrow c = 1$

$b^2 = a^2 - c^2 = 4 - 1 = 3$

$\dfrac{(x - h)^2}{b^2} + \dfrac{(y - k)^2}{a^2} = 1$

$\dfrac{(x - 2)^2}{3} + \dfrac{(y - 2)^2}{4} = 1$

24. Vertices: $(0, 1), (4, 1) \Longrightarrow a = 2, (h, k) = (2, 1)$

Endpoints of minor axis: $(2, 0), (2, 2) \Longrightarrow b = 1$

$\dfrac{(x - h)^2}{a^2} + \dfrac{(y - k)^2}{b^2} = 1$

$\dfrac{(x - 2)^2}{4} + (y - 1)^2 = 1$

26. $\dfrac{x^2}{324} + \dfrac{y^2}{196} = 1$

$a = \sqrt{324} = 18, b = \sqrt{196} = 14$

$c = \sqrt{a^2 - b^2} = \sqrt{128} = 8\sqrt{2}$

Longest distance: $2a = 36$ feet

Shortest distance: $2b = 28$ feet

Distance between foci: $2c = 16\sqrt{2}$ feet

28. $4x^2 + 25y^2 + 16x - 150y + 141 = 0$

$4(x^2 + 4x + 4) + 25(y^2 - 6y + 9) = -141 + 16 + 225$

$\dfrac{(x + 2)^2}{25} + \dfrac{(y - 3)^2}{4} = 1$

Center: $(-2, 3)$

$a = 5, b = 2, c = \sqrt{a^2 - b^2} = \sqrt{21}$

Vertices: $(3, 3), (-7, 3)$

Foci: $\left(-2 \pm \sqrt{21}, 3\right)$

Eccentricity: $e = \dfrac{c}{a} = \dfrac{\sqrt{21}}{5}$

30. $\dfrac{(x - 5)^2}{1} + \dfrac{(y + 3)^2}{36} = 1$

Center: $(5, -3)$

$a = 6, b = 1, c = \sqrt{a^2 - b^2} = \sqrt{35}$

Vertices: $(5, 3), (5, -9)$

Foci: $\left(5, -3 \pm \sqrt{35}\right)$

Eccentricity: $e = \dfrac{c}{a} = \dfrac{\sqrt{35}}{6}$

32. Vertices: $(2, 2), (-2, 2) \Rightarrow a = 2, (h, k) = (0, 2)$

Foci: $(4, 2), (-4, 2) \Rightarrow c = 4$

$b^2 = c^2 - a^2 = 16 - 4 = 12$

$\dfrac{(x - h)^2}{a^2} - \dfrac{(y - k)^2}{b^2} = 1$

$\dfrac{x^2}{4} - \dfrac{(y - 2)^2}{12} = 1$

34. Foci: $(3, \pm 2) \Rightarrow c = 2, (h, k) = (3, 0)$

Asymptotes: $y = \pm 2(x - 3) \Rightarrow \dfrac{a}{b} = 2, a = 2b$

$b^2 = c^2 - a^2 = 4 - 4b^2 \Rightarrow b^2 = \dfrac{4}{5}, a^2 = \dfrac{16}{5}$

$\dfrac{(y - k)^2}{a^2} - \dfrac{(x - h)^2}{b^2} = 1$

$\dfrac{y^2}{16/5} - \dfrac{(x - 3)^2}{4/5} = 1 \Rightarrow \dfrac{5y^2}{16} - \dfrac{5(x - 3)^2}{4} = 1$

36. $-4x^2 + 25y^2 - 8x + 150y + 121 = 0$

$-4(x^2 + 2x + 1) + 25(y^2 + 6y + 9) = -121 - 4 + 225$

$$\frac{(y + 3)^2}{4} - \frac{(x + 1)^2}{25} = 1$$

Center: $(-1, -3)$

$a = 2, b = 5, c = \sqrt{a^2 + b^2} = \sqrt{29}$

Vertices: $(-1, -1), (-1, -5)$

Foci: $\left(-1, -3 \pm \sqrt{29}\right)$

Asymptotes: $y = -3 \pm \dfrac{2}{5}(x + 1)$

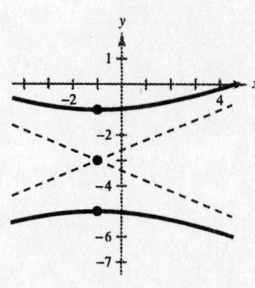

38. $\dfrac{(y - 1)^2}{4} - x^2 = 1$

Center: $(0, 1)$

$a = 2, b = 1, c = \sqrt{a^2 + b^2} = \sqrt{5}$

Vertices: $(0, 3), (0, -1)$

Foci: $\left(0, 1 \pm \sqrt{5}\right)$

Asymptotes: $y = 1 \pm 2x$

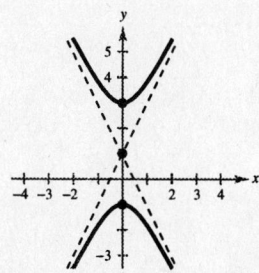

40. $BD = AD + 6\left(\dfrac{1100}{5280}\right)$

$CD = AD + 8\left(\dfrac{1100}{5280}\right)$

$2a = CD - BD = 2\left(\dfrac{1100}{5280}\right)$

$a = \dfrac{5}{24}, c = 2 \Rightarrow b^2 = \dfrac{2279}{576}$

Thus, we have $\dfrac{576x^2}{25} - \dfrac{576y^2}{2279} = 1$

OR:

$CD = AD + 8\left(\dfrac{1100}{5280}\right)$

$BD = AD + 6\left(\dfrac{1100}{5280}\right)$

$2a = BD - AD = 6\left(\dfrac{1100}{5280}\right)$

$a = 3\left(\dfrac{5}{24}\right) = \dfrac{5}{8}, c = 1 \Rightarrow b^2 = \dfrac{39}{64}$

Center: $(1, 0)$

$\dfrac{64(x - 1)^2}{25} - \dfrac{64y^2}{39} = 1$

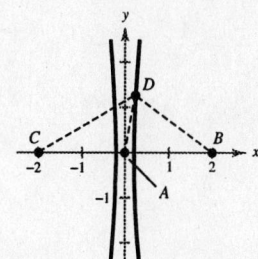

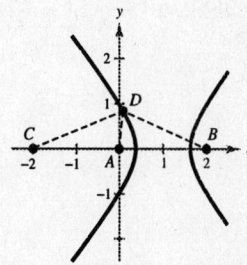

42. $-4y^2 + 5x + 3y + 7 = 0$

$AC = (0)(-4) = 0 \implies$ Parabola

44. $x^2 - 10xy + y^2 + 1 = 0$

$B^2 - 4AC = (-10)^2 - 4(1)(1) = 96 > 0 \implies$ Hyperbola

$\cot 2\theta = \dfrac{A - C}{B} = \dfrac{1 - 1}{-10} = 0 \implies 2\theta = \dfrac{\pi}{2} \implies \theta = \dfrac{\pi}{4}$

$x = x' \cos \dfrac{\pi}{4} - y' \sin \dfrac{\pi}{4} = \dfrac{1}{\sqrt{2}}(x' - y')$

$y = x' \sin \dfrac{\pi}{4} + y' \cos \dfrac{\pi}{4} = \dfrac{1}{\sqrt{2}}(x' + y')$

$\dfrac{1}{2}(x' - y')^2 - 5(x' - y')(x' + y') + \dfrac{1}{2}(x' + y')^2 + 1 = 0$

$6(y')^2 - 4(x')^2 + 1 = 0$

$\dfrac{(x')^2}{1/4} - \dfrac{(y')^2}{1/6} = 1$

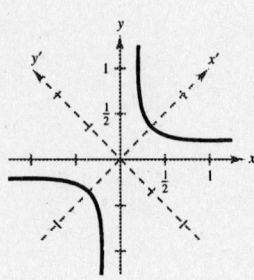

46. $4x^2 + 8xy + 4y^2 + 7\sqrt{2}x + 9\sqrt{2}y = 0$

$B^2 - 4AC = 8^2 - 4(4)(4) = 0 \implies$ Parabola

$\cot 2\theta = \dfrac{A - C}{B} = \dfrac{4 - 4}{8} = 0 \implies 2\theta = \dfrac{\pi}{2} \implies \theta = \dfrac{\pi}{4}$

$x = x' \cos \dfrac{\pi}{4} - y' \sin \dfrac{\pi}{4} = \dfrac{1}{\sqrt{2}}(x' - y')$

$y = x' \sin \dfrac{\pi}{4} + y' \cos \dfrac{\pi}{4} - \dfrac{1}{\sqrt{2}}(x' + y')$

$2(x' - y')^2 + 4(x' - y')(x' + y') + 2(x' + y')^2 + 7(x' - y') + 9(x' + y') = 0$

$8(x')^2 + 16x' + 2y' = 0$

$y' = -4(x')^2 - 8x'$

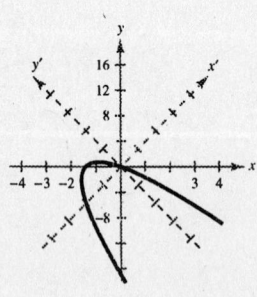

48. $13x^2 - 8xy + 7y^2 - 45 = 0$

$B^2 - 4AC = (-8)^2 - 4(13)(7) = -300 < 0 \implies$ Ellipse

Use the Quadratic Formula to solve for y in terms of x:

$7y^2 - 8xy + 13x^2 - 45 = 0$

$y = \dfrac{1}{14}\left[8x \pm \sqrt{64x^2 - 28(13x^2 - 45)}\right]$

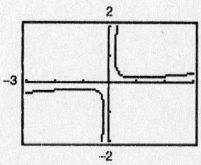

50. $x^2 - 10xy + y^2 + 1 = 0$

Since $B^2 - 4AC = (-10)^2 - 4(1)(1) > 0 \implies$ Hyperbola

Use the Quadratic Formula to solve for y in terms of x:

$y^2 - 10xy + x^2 + 1 = 0$

$y = \tfrac{1}{2}\left[10x \pm \sqrt{100x^2 - 4(x^2 + 1)}\right]$

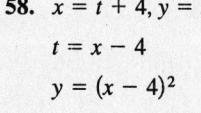

52. $x = 3 \cos \theta, y = 2 \sin^2 \theta$

$\theta = \dfrac{\pi}{3}$

$x = 3 \cos \dfrac{\pi}{3} = \dfrac{3}{2}, y = 2 \sin^2 \dfrac{\pi}{3} = \dfrac{3}{2}$

54. $x = 3 \cos \theta, y = 2 \sin^2 \theta$

$\theta = -\dfrac{\pi}{4}$

$x = 3 \cos\left(-\dfrac{\pi}{4}\right) = \dfrac{3\sqrt{2}}{2}, y = 2 \sin^2\left(-\dfrac{\pi}{4}\right) = 1$

56. $x = 1 + 4t, y = 2 - 3t$

$t = \dfrac{x - 1}{4}$

$y = 2 - 3\left(\dfrac{x - 1}{4}\right)$

$3x + 4y = 11$

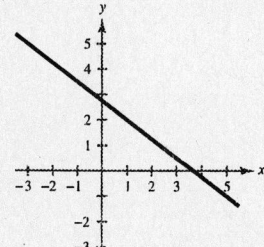

58. $x = t + 4, y = t^2$

$t = x - 4$

$y = (x - 4)^2$

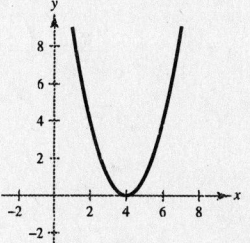

60. $x = 3 + 3 \cos \theta, y = 2 + 5 \sin \theta$

$\cos \theta = \dfrac{x - 3}{3}, \sin \theta = \dfrac{y - 2}{5}$

$\dfrac{(x - 3)^2}{9} + \dfrac{(y - 2)^2}{25} = 1$

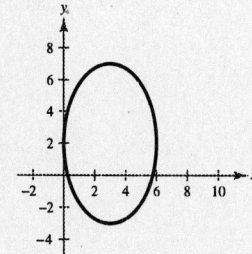

62. Hyperbola

Vertices: $(0, \pm 4)$

Foci: $(0, \pm 5)$

Center: $(0, 0)$

$a = 4, c = 5, b = \sqrt{c^2 - a^2} = 3$

$x = 3 \tan \theta, y = 4 \sec \theta$

64.
$$y = \overline{QB} - \overline{QA}$$
$$\overline{QP} = \text{arc } QC = r\theta$$
$$\overline{QA} = r\theta \sin(90° - \theta)$$
$$= r\theta \cos \theta$$
$$\overline{QB} = r \sin \theta$$

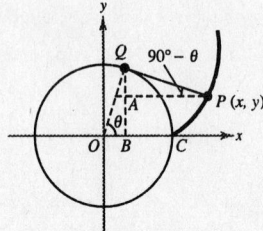

Therefore, $y = r \sin \theta - r\theta \cos \theta = r(\sin \theta - \theta \cos \theta)$.

Similarly, $x = \overline{OB} + \overline{AP}$. Therefore, $x = r \cos \theta + r\theta \sin \theta = r(\cos \theta + \theta \sin \theta)$.

66. Polar coordinates: $\left(-5, -\dfrac{\pi}{3}\right) = \left(5, \dfrac{2\pi}{3}\right)$

Rectangular coordinates:

$$\left(5 \cos \frac{2\pi}{3}, 5 \sin \frac{2\pi}{3}\right) = \left(-\frac{5}{2}, \frac{5\sqrt{3}}{2}\right)$$

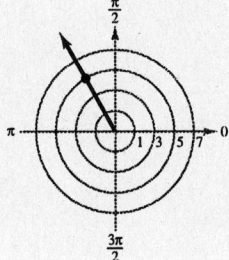

68. Polar coordinates: $\left(\sqrt{3}, 2.62\right)$

Rectangular coordinates: $\left(\sqrt{3} \cos 2.62, \sqrt{3} \sin 2.62\right)$

$$\approx (-1.5017, 0.8630)$$

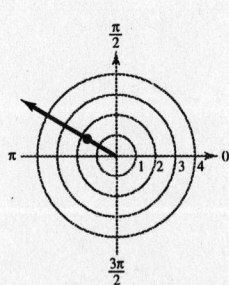

70. Rectangular coordinates: $\left(-\sqrt{5}, \sqrt{5}\right)$

Polar coordinates:

$$r = \sqrt{\left(-\sqrt{5}\right)^2 + \left(\sqrt{5}\right)^2} = \sqrt{10}$$

$$\tan \theta = -1, \theta = \frac{3\pi}{4}$$

$$\left(\sqrt{10}, \frac{3\pi}{4}\right), \left(-\sqrt{10}, \frac{7\pi}{4}\right)$$

72. Rectangular coordinates: $(3, -4)$

Polar coordinates:

$$r = \sqrt{3^2 + (-4)^2} = 5$$

$$\tan \theta = -\frac{4}{3}, \theta \approx -0.9273$$

$$(5, 5.356), (-5, 2.214)$$

74. $r = 10$
$r^2 = 100$
$x^2 + y^2 = 100$

76. $r^2 = \cos 2\theta$
$r^2 = \left(\dfrac{x}{r}\right)^2 - \left(\dfrac{y}{r}\right)^2$
$(x^2 + y^2)^2 = x^2 - y^2$

78. $x^2 + y^2 - 4x = 0$
$r^2 - 4r \cos \theta = 0$
$r = 4 \cos \theta$

80. $r = 2\theta$

Symmetric with respect to $\theta = \dfrac{\pi}{2}$

Spiral

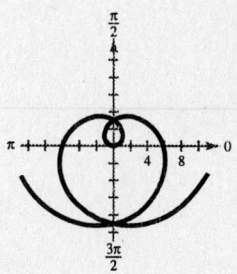

82. $r = \cos 5\theta$

Symmetric with respect to polar axis
Rose curve $(n = 5)$ with five petals

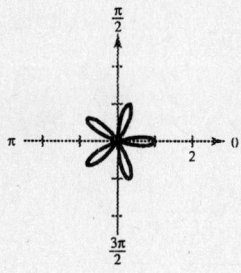

84. $r = 3 - 4 \cos \theta$

Symmetric with respect to polar axis

$\dfrac{a}{b} = \dfrac{3}{4} < 0 \Rightarrow$ Limaçon with inner loop

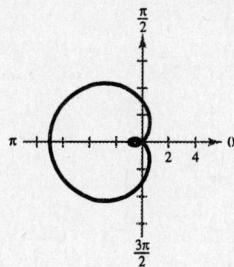

86. $r = 5 - 5 \cos \theta$

$r = 5(1 - \cos \theta)$

Symmetry: polar axis

Maximum values of $|r|$: $|r| = 10$ when $\theta = \pi$.

Zeros of r: $r = 0$ when $\theta = 0, 2\pi$.

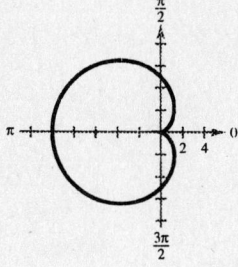

88. $r^2 = \cos 2\theta$

Symmetry: polar axis, $\theta = \dfrac{\pi}{2}$, pole

Maximum values of $|r|$: $|r| = 1$ when $\theta = 0, \pi$.

Zeros of r: $r = 0$ when $\theta = \dfrac{\pi}{4}, \dfrac{3\pi}{4}$

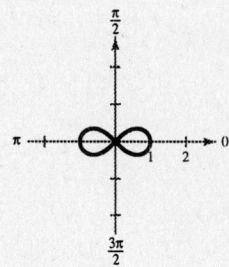

90. $r = 3(1 - 2\cos\theta)$

$r = 3 - 6\cos\theta$

Limaçon with inner loop.

92. $r^2 = 9\cos 2\theta$

Lemniscate

94. $r = \dfrac{2}{1 - \sin\theta}, e = 1$

Parabola symmetric with $\theta = \pi/2$ and the vertex at $(1, 3\pi/2)$

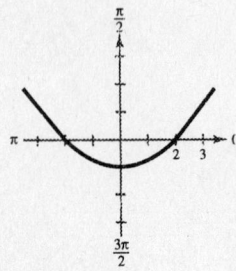

96. $r = \dfrac{16}{4 + 5\cos\theta}$

$r = \dfrac{4}{1 + (5/4)\cos\theta}$

$e = \dfrac{5}{4}$

Hyperbola

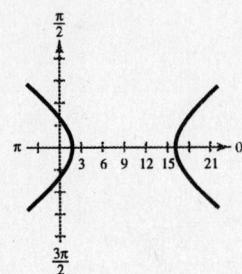

98. Parabola: $r = \dfrac{ep}{1 + e\sin\theta}, \quad e = 1$

Vertex: $\left(2, \dfrac{\pi}{2}\right)$

Focus: $(0, 0) \implies p = 4$

$r = \dfrac{4}{1 + \sin\theta}$

100. Hyperbola: $r = \dfrac{ep}{1 + e\cos\theta}$

Vertices: $(1, 0), (7, 0) \implies a = 3$

One focus: $(0, 0) \implies c = 4$

$e = \dfrac{c}{a} = \dfrac{4}{3}, p = \dfrac{7}{4}$

$r = \dfrac{(4/3)(7/4)}{1 + (4/3)\cos\theta} = \dfrac{7/3}{1 + (4/3)\cos\theta} = \dfrac{7}{3 + 4\cos\theta}$

102. Parabola: $r = \dfrac{ep}{1 + e\sin\theta}, e = 1$

Vertex: $\left((6{,}000{,}000), \dfrac{\pi}{2}\right)$

Focus: $(0, 0) \implies p = 12{,}000{,}000$

$r = \dfrac{12{,}000{,}000}{1 + \sin\theta}$

$\theta = -\dfrac{\pi}{3}$

$r \approx 89{,}600{,}000$ miles

104. False.

$\dfrac{x^2}{4} - y^4 = 1$ is a fourth-degree equation.

The equation of a hyperbola is a second degree equation.

106. False.

$(r, \theta), (r, \theta + 2\pi), (-r, \theta + \pi)$, etc.

All represent the same point.

108. Yes. The orientation would be reversed.

110. (a) $\left(-4, \dfrac{\pi}{6}\right), \left(4, \dfrac{\pi}{6}\right)$: symmetric about the pole

(b) $\left(4, -\dfrac{\pi}{6}\right), \left(4, \dfrac{\pi}{6}\right)$: symmetric about the polar axis

(c) $\left(-4, -\dfrac{\pi}{6}\right), \left(4, \dfrac{\pi}{6}\right)$: symmetric about the $\theta = \dfrac{\pi}{2}$ axis.